Mobil
Travel Guide®
2000

Mid-Atlantic

Delaware • District of Columbia • Maryland
New Jersey • North Carolina • Pennsylvania
South Carolina • Virginia • West Virginia

CONSUMERGUIDE™

Publications International, Ltd.

Acknowledgments

We gratefully acknowledge the help of our field representatives for their efficient and perceptive inspection of every lodging and dining establishment listed; the establishments' proprietors for their cooperation in showing their facilities and providing information about them; the many users of previous editions of the *Mobil Travel Guide* who have taken the time to share their experiences; and for their time and information, the thousands of chambers of commerce, convention and visitors bureaus, city, state, and provincial tourism offices, and government agencies who assisted in our research.

Mobil

Maps © Rand McNally & Co. 2000, www.randmcnally.com

917.3
m687mi
2000

Published by Publications International, Ltd.
7373 N. Cicero Avenue
Lincolnwood, IL 60712

travel@pubint.com

Cover photo: Peter Gridley/FPG International

Mid-Atlantic
ISBN 0-7853-4156-0
ISSN 1090-6975

Printed in the United States of America.
10 9 8 7 6 5 4 3 2 1

Contents

A Word to Our Readers xxv

Welcome xxvi

How to Use This Book.................................... xxvii

Making the Most of Your Trip xxxii

Important Toll-Free Numbers xxxv

Four-Star and Five-Star Establishments in the
     Mid-Atlantic xxxvii

Mid-Atlantic

Delaware 1

District of Columbia....................................... 13

Maryland 36

New Jersey 81

North Carolina... 130

Pennsylvania... 196

South Carolina 298

Virginia 334

West Virginia 427

Appendix A: Restaurant List............................... 454

Appendix B: Lodging List 465

City Index 478

Maps

Interstate Highways....................................... iv-v

Mid-Atlantic Region....................................... vi-vii

Distance/Driving Time .... viii-ix

Delaware/Maryland .... x-xi

Washington, D.C... xii

Downtown Washington xiii

Baltimore... xiii

New Jersey .... xiv-xv

North Carolina/South Carolina .... xvi-xvii

Pennsylvania .... xviii-xix

Philadelphia xx

Downtown Philadelphia xxi

Pittsburgh xxi

Virginia/West Virginia.................................... xxii-xxiii

Richmond.. xxiv

Tidewater xxiv

Larger, more detailed maps are available at many Mobil service stations

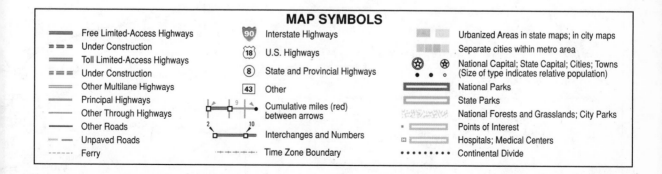

MAP SYMBOLS				
Free Limited-Access Highways	**90**	Interstate Highways		Urbanized Areas in state maps; in city maps
Under Construction	**18**	U.S. Highways		Separate cities within metro area
Toll Limited-Access Highways	**8**	State and Provincial Highways		National Capital; State Capital; Cities; Towns (Size of type indicates relative population)
Under Construction	**43**	Other		National Parks
Other Multilane Highways		Cumulative miles (red) between arrows		State Parks
Principal Highways				National Forests and Grasslands; City Parks
Other Through Highways				Points of Interest
Other Roads		Interchanges and Numbers		Hospitals; Medical Centers
Unpaved Roads		Time Zone Boundary		Continental Divide
Ferry				

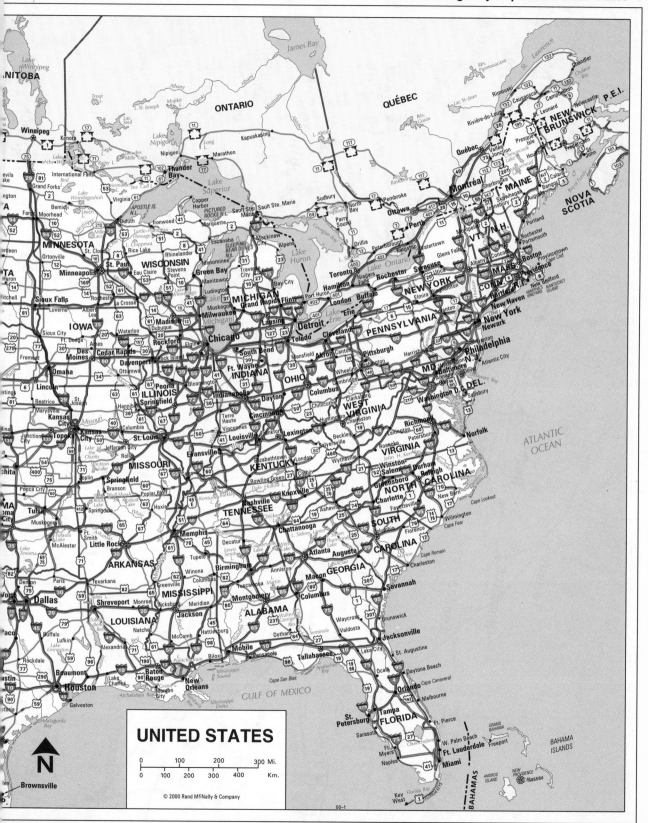

UNITED STATES

0   100   200   300 Mi.

0   100   200   300   400 Km.

© 2000 Rand McNally & Company

00-1

MID-ATLANTIC REGION

Concord

150
3:15

MASSACHUSETTS

CONNECTICUT

New York

Philadelphia

Atlantic City

DELAWARE

MARYLAND

Albany

159
2:51

NEW JERSEY

2:31
141
2:03

61
1:03

148
2:34

270
5:41

310
6:31

NEW YORK

147
2:31

184
3:10

141
2:33

109

127
2:13

198
3:30

114
1:58

150
2:04

Baltimore

35
0:43

106
1:50

Watertown

135
2:21

289
4:59

Scranton

122
2:06

416
6:56

87
1:31

125
2:17

Washington

236
4:49

Syracuse

154
2:43

217
2:43

Harrisburg

204
3:28

251
4:21

289
6:09

72
1:16

288
5:39

PENNSYLVANIA

269
4:35

368
6:20

369
6:09

347
5:47

Buffalo

220
4:00

217
3:41

Pittsburgh

229
3:49

WEST VIRGINIA

Toronto

105
1:45

162
3:06

191
3:11

Youngstown

80
1:24

181
3:13

420
7:12

250
4:16

132
2:12

132
2:12

London

76
1:20

175
2:59

141
2:26

167
3:27

Lake Ontario

Lake Erie

Detroit

Cleveland

119
1:59

144
2:45

Columbus

OHIO

Lake Huron

62
1:06

Toledo

ATLANTIC   OCEAN

Norfolk

NORTH CAROLINA

Richmond

VIRGINIA

Roanoke

Raleigh

Wilmington

Myrtle Beach

Charleston

Savannah

Greensboro

Charlotte

Florence

Columbia

Bluefield

Charleston

SOUTH CAROLINA

Asheville

Augusta

GEORGIA

Lexington

KENTUCKY

Knoxville

TENNESSEE

Atlanta

93   1:37
175   3:19
270   4:46
259   4:10
652
130   2:14
69   1:30
186   3:06
148   2:40
201   3:21
171   2:55
204   4:18
119   2:30
68   1:29
97   1:47
172   3:24
78   1:22
168   2:48
228   3:48
79   1:21
172   2:56
105   2:05
98   2:04
97   1:41
91   1:26
112   1:54
175   3:01
155   2:39
331   5:31
180   3:00
170   2:54
261   4:25
157   2:31
88   1:10
128   2:03
112   1:56
254   4:18
125   2:05
217   3:57
213   3:10
252   3:57
314   5:20
233   3:57
257   4:21
206   3:36
240   3:36
151   2:21
177   2:57
115   1:57
215   3:29
173   2:55

Cities and Towns

Delaware

Bethany Beach	D-10
Bridgeville	D-9
Claymont	A-9
Dover	C-9
Felton	C-9
Fenwick Island	E-10
Frederica	C-9
Georgetown	D-9
Harrington	C-9
Kenton	C-9
Laurel	D-9
Lewes	D-10
Middletown	B-9
Milford	C-9
Millsboro	D-10
Milton	D-10
New Castle	A-9
Newark	A-9
Odessa	B-9
Rehoboth Beach	D-10
Seaford	D-9
Smyrna	B-9
Wilmington	A-9

Maryland and District of Columbia

Aberdeen	B-8	Reisterstown	B-6
Annapolis	C-7	Frederick	B-5
Baltimore	B-7	Rock Hall	C-8
Bel Air	B-7	Rockville	C-6
Berlin	E-10	St. Mary's City	E-7
Bethesda	C-6	St. Michaels	D-8
Boonsboro	B-5	Salisbury	E-9
Bowie	C-7	Scotland	F-7
Cambridge	D-8	Silver Spring	C-6
Centreville	C-8	Snow Hill	E-9
Chesapeake City	B-8	Suitland	D-6
Chestertown	C-8	Taneytown	A-6
Clear Spring	A-4	Taylors Island	E-7
Cockeysville	B-7	Thurmont	B-5
College Park	C-6	Tilghman	D-7
Columbia	C-6	Towson	B-7
Crisfield	F-9	Upper Marlboro	D-7
Cumberland	A-2	Waldorf	D-6
Darlington	A-8	Washington, D.C.	C-6
Easton	D-8	Wenona	E-8
Edgewood	B-7	Westernport	B-2
Elkton	B-9	Westminster	B-6
Ellicott City	B-6		
Emmitsburg	A-5		
Frostburg	A-2		
Gaithersburg	C-6		
Germantown	C-5		
Grantsville	A-1		
Hagerstown	A-4		
Hampstead	B-6		
Hancock	A-3		
Havre De Grace	B-8		
La Plata	D-6		
Laurel	C-6		
Leonardtown	E-7		
Lexington Park	E-7		
Mount Airy	B-6		
Nanticoke	E-8		
Oakland	B-1		
Ocean City	E-10		
Olney	C-6		
Pikesville	B-7		
Pocomoke City	F-9		
Prince Frederick	D-7		
Princess Anne	E-9		

DELAWARE MARYLAND

© 2000 Rand McNally & Company

York
Gettysburg
Gettysburg Nat'l. Mil. Pk.
Hanover
Red Lion
Gap
Coatesville
West Chester
Philadelphia
Camden
Chester
Claymont
Wilmington
Brandywine Cr. S.P.
448 ft. Highest Pt. in Del.
Glassboro
Oxford
Newark
New Castle
Fair Hill
Conowingo
Susquehanna S.P.
Darlington
Level
Churchville
Shawsville
Rocks S.P.
Taneytown
Hampstead
Topiary Gardens
Bel Air
Havre de Grace
Elkton
Chesapeake City
Ft. Delaware S.P.
Glasgow
Salem
Vineland
Bridgeton
Millville
Westminster
Libertytown
Reisterstown
erick
Mount Airy
Cooksville
Cockeysville
Kingsville
J.F.K.
Aberdeen
Edgewood
Galena
Odessa
Middletown
Smyrna
Pikesville
Liberty Res.
Patapsco Valley S.P.
Towson
Baltimore
North Point S.P.
Sassafras
Chestertown
Church Hill
Bombay Hook N.W.R.
Kenton
Dover
Columbia
Olney
Gaithersburg
Ellicott City
Elkridge
Sudlersville
Dickinson Mansion
Silver Spring
Laurel
College Pk.
Bowie
Rock Hall
Centreville
Ingleside
Felton
Frederica
Delaware Bay
Bethesda
Washington
Falls Church
Arlington
U.S. Naval Academy
Annapolis
Grasonville
Queenstown
Tuckahoe S.P.
Harrington
Killens Pond S.P.
Milford
Suitland
Eastern Bay
Romancoke
Lothian
Wye Oak S.P.
Denton
Greenwood
Milton
Lewes
Cape Henlopen S.P.
Rehoboth Bch.
Alexandria
Upper Marlboro
Chesapeake Bay Maritime Museum
St. Michaels
Easton
Oxford
Bridgeville
Georgetown
Rehoboth Bay
Delaware Seashore S.P.
Woodbridge
White Plains
Waldorf
Tilghman
Fairbank
Sunderland
Cornersville
James
Seaford
Millsboro
Dagsboro
Smallwood S.P.
Thomas Stone Nat'l Hist. Site
La Plata
Bel Alton
Prince Frederick
Cambridge
Trap Pond S.P.
Laurel
Mason–Dixon Monument
Cypress Swamp
Bethany Beach
Fenwick I.
Riverside
Newburg
Taylors Island
Old Trinity Church (1670)
Delmar
Fenwick Island
Leonardtown
Solomons
St. Mary's River S.P.
Honga
Blackwater Nat'l. Wildlife Refuge
Salisbury
Berlin
Ocean City
Assateague S.P.
St. Mary's City
First Capital of Maryland
George Washington Birthplace Nat'l. Mon.
Lexington Park
Crocheron
Nanticoke
Princess Anne
Snow Hill
Chincoteague Bay
Assateague Is. Nat'l Seashore
Ridge
Scotland
Wenona
Pocomoke City
Janes Island S.P.
Assateague Island
Tappahannock
Point Lookout
Pt. Lookout S.P.
Smith Island
Glen Martin Nat'l. Wildlife Refuge
Crisfield
Virginia
Chincoteague
Atlantic Ocean
Reedville
Chesapeake Bay
Tangier I.
Pocomoke Sound

PENN.
MD.
DEL.
NEW JERSEY
VIRGINIA
N

WASHINGTON
AND VICINITY

0   1   2   3 Mi.
0 1 2 3 4 Km.

© 2000 Rand McNally

WASHINGTON DOWNTOWN

0   0.1   0.2   0.3 Mi.

0   0.25   Km.

© 2000 Rand McNally

The following places are identified only by a letter-number key:

A-1 American Pharmaceutical Inst.
A-2 American Red Cross-
     D.C. Chapter
A-3 American Red Cross-
     Nat'l. Hdqtrs.
A-4 Arts and Industries Bldg.
C-1 Chamber of Commerce (U.S.)
C-2 Commerce Department
C-3 Constitution Hall
C-4 Continental Hall
C-5 Corcoran Gallery of Art
C-6 Customs Service
D-1 Department of Agriculture
D-2 Department of the Interior South
F-1 Federal Office Bldg.
F-2 Freer Gallery of Art
G-1 General Services Admin. Bldg.
G-2 G.S.A. Regional Office Building
H-1 Hirshhorn Museum & Sculpture
     Garden
H-2 House Office Building

H-4 Housing & Urban Development
J-2 Judiciary Square
J-3 Justice Department
M   Metro Station Locations
N-1 National Academy of Sciences
N-2 National Building Museum
N-3 Nat'l. Collection of Fine Arts
     & Portrait Gallery
N-4 Nat'l. Museum of African Art
O-1 Office of Personnel Management
O-2 Old Post Office
R-1 Ripley Center
S-1 Securities & Exchange Comm.
S-4 Smithsonian Discovery Theater
S-5 Sackler Gallery of Asian Art
U-1 U.S. Holocaust Memorial Museum
U-2 U.S. Navy Memorial

BALTIMORE
AND VICINITY

0   1   2   3 Mi.

0   1   2   3   4 Km.

© 2000 Rand McNally

Cities and Towns

New Jersey

City/Town	Grid
Asbury Park	E-6
Atlantic City	J-4
Avalon	K-4
Batsto	H-4
Beach Haven	H-5
Beachwood	F-5
Berlin	G-3
Bernardsville	C-4
Blackwood	G-3
Boonton	B-4
Bordentown	E-4
Branchville	B-3
Bridgeton	H-2
Burlington	F-3
Butler	B-5
Caldwell	C-5
Camden	F-2
Cape May	K-3
Cape May Court House	K-3
Chatham	C-5
Cherry Hill	F-3
Clifton	C-5
Clinton	C-4
Cranford	C-5
Deepwater	G-1
Dover	B-4
East Brunswick	D-4
East Orange	C-5
Eatontown	E-5
Edison	D-4
Elizabeth	C-5
Englewood	B-6
Flemington	D-3
Forked River	G-5
Fort Lee	B-6
Freehold	E-5
Gibbstown	G-2
Glassboro	G-2
Hackensack	C-3
Haddonfield	F-3
Hammonton	H-3
Hightstown	E-4
Hillsdale	B-5
Hoboken	C-5
Ho-Ho-Kus	B-5
Hopatcong	B-4
Jackson	F-5
Jamesburg	D-4
Jersey City	C-5
Lakewood	F-5
Lambertville	D-3
Linden	C-5
Livingston	C-5
Long Branch	E-6
Matawan	E-5
Metuchen	D-5
Millburn	C-5
Millville	H-3
Montclair	C-5
Montvale	B-5
Moorestown	F-3
Morristown	C-4
Mount Holly	F-3
New Brunswick	D-4
Newark	C-5
Newfoundland	B-4
Newton	B-3
Oakland	B-5
Ocean City	J-4
Paramus	B-5
Parsippany	C-4
Passaic	C-5
Paterson	B-5
Paulsboro	G-2
Perth Amboy	D-5
Phillipsburg	D-4
Plainfield	C-5
Pleasantville	J-4
Point Pleasant	F-5
Princeton	D-3
Ramsey	B-5
Red Bank	E-5
Ridgewood	B-5
Rockaway	B-4
Rutherford	C-5
Saddle Brook	C-3
Salem	H-1
Sayreville	D-5
Scotch Plains	C-4
Seaside Heights	G-5
Seaside Park	G-5
Secaucus	C-6
Ship Bottom	G-5
Somers Point	J-4
Somerville	D-4
South River	D-5
Sparta	B-3
Spring Lake	E-5
Stanhope	B-4
Stone Harbor	K-3
Toms River	F-5
Trenton	E-3
Union	C-5
Vernon	A-4
Vineland	H-3
Washington	C-3
Wayne	B-5
West Milford	B-4
West Orange	C-5
Wildwood	L-3
Wildwood Crest	K-3
Williamstown	G-3
Willingboro	F-3
Woodbridge	D-4
Woodbury	G-2

NEW JERSEY

© 2000 Rand McNally & Company

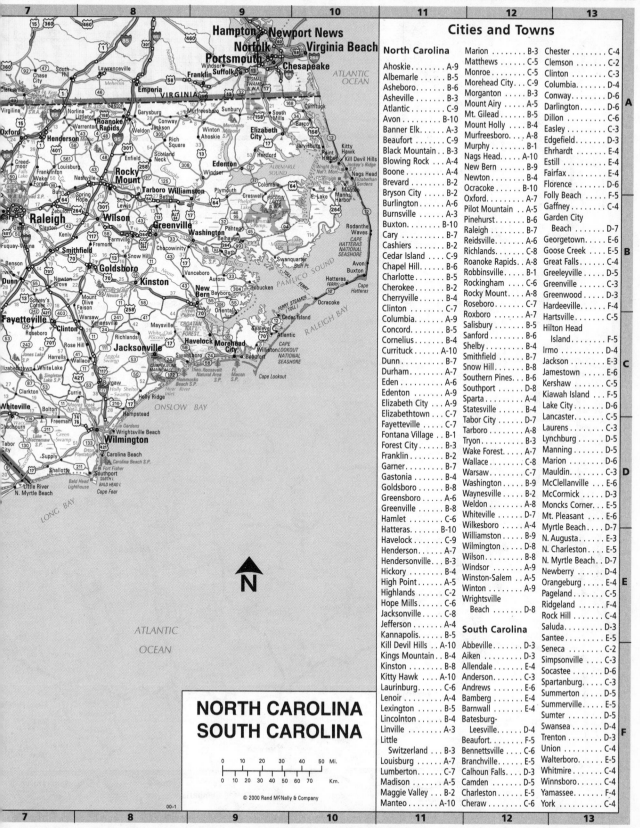

Cities and Towns

North Carolina

Ahoskie	A-9
Albemarle	B-5
Asheboro	B-6
Asheville	B-3
Atlantic	C-9
Avon	B-10
Banner Elk	A-3
Beaufort	C-9
Black Mountain	B-3
Blowing Rock	A-4
Boone	A-4
Brevard	B-2
Bryson City	B-2
Burlington	A-6
Burnsville	A-3
Buxton	B-10
Cary	B-7
Cashiers	B-2
Cedar Island	C-9
Chapel Hill	B-6
Charlotte	B-5
Cherokee	B-2
Cherryville	B-4
Clinton	C-7
Columbia	A-9
Concord	B-5
Cornelius	B-4
Currituck	A-10
Dunn	B-7
Durham	A-7
Eden	A-6
Edenton	A-9
Elizabeth City	A-9
Elizabethtown	C-7
Fayetteville	C-7
Fontana Village	B-1
Forest City	B-3
Franklin	B-2
Garner	B-7
Gastonia	B-4
Goldsboro	B-8
Greensboro	A-6
Greenville	B-8
Hamlet	C-6
Hatteras	B-10
Havelock	C-9
Henderson	A-7
Hendersonville	B-3
Hickory	B-4
High Point	A-5
Highlands	C-2
Hope Mills	C-6
Jacksonville	C-8
Jefferson	A-4
Kannapolis	B-5
Kill Devil Hills	A-10
Kings Mountain	B-4
Kinston	B-8
Kitty Hawk	A-10
Laurinburg	C-6
Lenoir	A-4
Lexington	B-5
Lincolnton	B-4
Linville	A-3
Little Switzerland	B-3
Louisburg	A-7
Lumberton	C-7
Madison	A-5
Maggie Valley	B-2
Manteo	A-10

Marion	B-3
Matthews	C-5
Monroe	C-5
Morehead City	C-9
Morganton	B-3
Mount Airy	A-5
Mt. Gilead	B-5
Mount Holly	B-4
Murfreesboro	A-8
Murphy	B-1
Nags Head	A-10
New Bern	B-9
Newton	B-4
Ocracoke	B-10
Oxford	A-7
Pilot Mountain	A-5
Pinehurst	B-6
Raleigh	B-7
Reidsville	A-6
Richlands	C-8
Roanoke Rapids	A-8
Robbinsville	B-1
Rockingham	C-6
Rocky Mount	A-8
Roseboro	C-7
Roxboro	A-7
Salisbury	B-5
Sanford	B-6
Shelby	B-4
Smithfield	B-7
Snow Hill	B-8
Southern Pines	B-6
Southport	D-8
Sparta	A-4
Statesville	B-4
Tabor City	D-7
Tarboro	A-8
Tryon	B-3
Wake Forest	A-7
Wallace	C-8
Warsaw	C-7
Washington	B-9
Waynesville	B-2
Weldon	A-8
Whiteville	D-7
Wilkesboro	A-4
Williamston	B-9
Wilmington	D-8
Wilson	B-8
Windsor	A-9
Winston-Salem	A-5
Winton	A-9
Wrightsville Beach	D-8

South Carolina

Abbeville	D-3
Aiken	D-3
Allendale	E-4
Anderson	C-3
Andrews	E-6
Bamberg	E-4
Barnwall	E-4
Batesburg-Leesville	D-4
Beaufort	F-5
Bennettsville	C-6
Branchville	E-5
Calhoun Falls	D-3
Camden	D-5
Charleston	E-5
Cheraw	C-6

Chester	C-4
Clemson	C-2
Clinton	C-3
Columbia	D-4
Conway	D-6
Darlington	D-6
Dillon	C-6
Easley	C-3
Edgefield	D-3
Ehrhardt	E-4
Estill	E-4
Fairfax	E-4
Florence	D-6
Folly Beach	F-5
Gaffney	C-4
Garden City Beach	D-7
Georgetown	E-6
Goose Creek	E-5
Great Falls	C-4
Greeleyville	D-5
Greenville	C-3
Greenwood	C-3
Hardeeville	F-4
Hartsville	C-5
Hilton Head Island	F-5
Irmo	D-4
Jackson	E-3
Jamestown	E-6
Kershaw	C-5
Kiawah Island	F-5
Lake City	D-6
Lancaster	C-5
Laurens	C-3
Lynchburg	D-5
Manning	D-5
Marion	D-6
Mauldin	C-3
McClellanville	E-6
McCormick	D-3
Moncks Corner	E-5
Mt. Pleasant	E-6
Myrtle Beach	D-7
N. Augusta	E-3
N. Charleston	E-5
N. Myrtle Beach	D-7
Newberry	D-4
Orangeburg	E-4
Pageland	C-5
Ridgeland	F-4
Rock Hill	C-4
Saluda	D-3
Santee	E-5
Seneca	C-2
Simpsonville	C-3
Socastee	D-6
Spartanburg	C-3
Summerton	D-5
Summerville	E-5
Sumter	D-5
Swansea	D-4
Trenton	D-3
Union	C-4
Walterboro	E-5
Whitmire	C-4
Winnsboro	C-4
Yamassee	F-4
York	C-4

NORTH CAROLINA SOUTH CAROLINA

0 10 20 30 40 50 Mi.

0 10 20 30 40 50 60 70 Km.

© 2000 Rand McNally & Company

00–1

Cities and Towns

Pennsylvania

Allentown D-9	Bethel Park E-2	Canadensis C-9	Denver E-8	Galeton B-6	Hollidaysburg . . . E-4
Altoona E-4	Bethlehem D-9	Carbondale C-9	Donegal E-3	Gettysburg F-6	Honesdale C-9
Ambridge D-1	Bird-in-Hand . . . F-8	Carlisle E-6	Downingtown . . . E-10	Gibsonia D-2	Huntingdon E-5
Ashland D-8	Bloomsburg D-7	Chambersburg . . F-5	Doylestown E-10	Greensburg E-2	Indiana D-3
Bangor D-9	Bradford B-4	Chester F-9	Du Bois C-4	Greenville C-1	Jenkintown F-10
Beaver Falls . . . D-1	Breezewood F-4	Clarion C-3	Easton D-9	Greenville C-1	Jim Thorpe D-9
Bedford F-4	Bristol E-10	Clearfield D-4	Ebensburg E-3	Hamburg E-8	Johnstown E-3
Bellefonte D-5	Brookville C-3	Conneaut Lake . . B-1	Edinboro B-2	Hanover F-7	Kane B-4
Berwick D-8	Bushkill C-10	Connellsville . . . F-2	Ephrata E-8	Harmony D-1	Kennett Square . . F-9
	Butler D-2	Cornwall E-8	Erie A-2	Harrisburg E-7	King of Prussia . . F-9
		Corry B-2	Fort Washington . E-9	Hawley C-9	Kulpsville E-9
		Danville D-7	Franklin C-2	Hazleton D-8	Kutztown E-9
				Hershey E-7	

PENNSYLVANIA

Lancaster F-8	Media F-9	Oil City C-2	Sayre B-7	Souderton E-9	Washington E-1
Latrobe E-3	Mercer C-1	Orbisonia E-5	Scranton C-9	State College . . D-5	Waynesboro . . . F-6
Lebanon E-7	Milford C-10	Philadelphia . . F-10	Selinsgrove . . . D-7	Stroudsburg . . . C-9	Wellsboro B-6
Lewisburg . . . D-7	Monroeville . . . E-2	Phoenixville . . . E-9	Shamokin D-7	Sunbury D-7	West Chester . . F-9
Lewistown . . . E-6	Mount Pocono . C-9	Pittsburgh E-2	Shamokin Dam . D-7	Tamaqua D-8	West Middlesex . C-1
Ligonier E-3	Nazareth D-9	Port Allegany . . B-4	Sharon C-1	Tannersville . . . C-9	White Haven . . . D-9
Limerick E-9	New Castle . . . D-1	Pottstown E-9	Shartlesville . . . E-8	Titusville B-2	Wilkes-Barre . . . C-8
Lock Haven . . C-6	New Hope E-10	Pottsville D-8	Shawnee on	Towanda B-7	Williamsport . . C-7
Manheim E-8	New Kensington E-2	Punxsutawney . . D-3	Delaware . . . D-10	Tyrone D-4	Willow Grove . . F-10
Mansfield . . . B-6	New Stanton . . E-2	Quakertown . . . E-9	Shenandoah . . . D-8	Uniontown F-2	Wrightsville . . . F-7
McKeesport . . E-2	Norristown . . . E-9	Reading E-8	Shippensburg . . F-6	Valley Forge . . . E-9	York F-7
Meadville . . . B-2	North East . . . A-2	St. Marys C-4	Somerset F-3	Warren B-3	

0   10   20   30   40 Mi.

0   10   20   30   40   50   60 Km.

© 2000 Rand McNally & Company

VIRGINIA
WEST VIRGINIA

0 10 20 30 40 50 Mi.

0 10 20 30 40 50 60 70 Km.

© 2000 Rand McNally & Company

Cities and Towns

VIRGINIA

Abingdon	F-3
Alexandria	C-8
Amherst	E-6
Appomattox	E-6
Arlington	C-8
Ashland	E-8
Basye	C-7
Bedford	E-6
Berryville	C-7
Big Stone Gap	F-2
Blacksburg	E-5
Bland	F-4
Bluefield	E-4
Bowling Green	D-8
Bristol	F-3
Brookneal	E-6
Buena Vista	E-6
Burkeville	E-7

Cape Charles	E-10
Charlottesville	D-7
Chase City	F-7
Chesapeake	F-10
Chincoteague	D-10
Christiansburg	E-5
Clarksville	F-7
Clifton Forge	E-5
Courtland	F-9
Covington	E-5
Culpeper	D-7
Cumberland	E-7
Danville	F-6
Dumfries	D-8
Elkton	D-7
Emporia	F-8
Fairfax	C-8
Falls Church	C-8
Farmville	E-7
Floyd	F-5

Fork Union	E-7
Franklin	F-9
Fredericksburg	D-8
Front Royal	C-7
Galax	F-4
Gate City	F-2
Gloucester	E-9
Gordonsville	D-7
Grottoes	D-7
Hampton	F-9
Hanover	E-8
Harrisonburg	D-6
Hillsville	F-4
Hollins	E-5
Hopewell	E-8
Hot Springs	D-5
Irvington	E-9
Jonesville	F-2
Kilmarnock	E-9
Kiptopeke	E-10
Lancaster	E-9
Leesburg	C-8

Lexington	E-6
Livingston	E-6
Lunenburg	F-7
Luray	C-7
Lynchburg	E-6
Manassas	C-8
Marion	F-3
Mathews	E-9
McKenney	F-8
McLean	C-8
Middletown	C-7
Monterey	D-6
Montross	D-9
New Market	D-7
Newport News	F-9
Norfolk	F-9
Onancock	D-10
Orange	D-7
Pearisburg	E-4
Petersburg	E-8
Port Royal	D-8

Portsmouth	F-9
Pound	E-2
Pulaski	F-4
Radford	F-4
Reedville	E-9
Reston	C-8
Richlands	E-3
Richmond	E-8
Roanoke	E-5
Salem	E-5
Saluda	E-9
Shenandoah	D-6
South Boston	F-6
South Hill	F-7
Sperryville	C-7
Springfield	C-8
Staunton	D-6
Strasburg	C-7
Suffolk	F-9
Surry	E-9
Tangier	E-10
Tappahannock	D-9

Tazewell	F-3
Triangle	D-8
Trout Dale	F-3
Tysons Corner	C-8
Vansant	E-3
Virginia Beach	F-10
Warm Springs	D-5
Warrenton	C-8
Washington	C-7
Waverly	F-8
Waynesboro	D-6
West Point	E-9
White Stone	E-9
Williamsburg	E-9
Winchester	C-7
Windsor	F-9
Wise	E-2
Woodbridge	C-8
Woodstock	C-7
Wytheville	F-4
Yorktown	E-9

WEST VIRGINIA

Aurora	C-6
Beckley	E-4
Berkeley Springs	B-7
Bethany	A-5
Bluefield	E-4
Buckhannon	C-5
Cedar Grove	D-4
Charles Town	D-3
Charleston	C-5
Clarksburg	C-5
Clay	D-4
Davis	C-6
Elkins	C-6
Fairmont	B-5
Frametown	C-4
Franklin	C-6
Gauley Bridge	D-4
Glenville	C-5
Grafton	C-5
Green Bank	D-5
Harpers Ferry	C-8

Hillsboro	D-5
Hinton	E-4
Huntington	D-2
Huttonsville	D-5
Keyser	B-6
Lewisburg	D-5
Madison	D-3
Man	D-3
Marlinton	D-5
Martinsburg	B-7
Middlebourne	B-4
Moorefield	C-6
Morgantown	B-5
Moundsville	B-4
Mount Storm	C-6
New Martinsville	B-4
Nitro	C-4
Oak Hill	D-4
Parkersburg	C-3
Parsons	C-6
Petersburg	C-6
Philippi	C-5

Pineville	E-3
Point Pleasant	C-3
Princeton	E-4
Rainelle	D-4
Richwood	D-5
Ripley	D-3
St. Albans	D-3
Shepherdstown	B-8
Spencer	C-4
Summersville	D-4
Sutton	C-4
Union	E-5
Wayne	D-2
Webster Springs	D-5
Weirton	A-5
Welch	E-3
West Union	C-4
Weston	C-4
Wheeling	A-4
White Sulphur Springs	E-5
Williamson	E-3

Would you like to spend less time buying gas?

With *Speedpass,* getting gas just got a little more exciting. All you have to do is wave it at the pump, gas up and go. Fast and easy. You can link it to a major credit card or check card that you *already* have. So call toll-free **1-877-MY MOBIL** or visit mobil.com/speedpass to enroll. Join the over 3 million people who already use *Speedpass.* It's safe, secure and best of all... it's free.

Mobil
Speedpass
The fastest way to get gas.

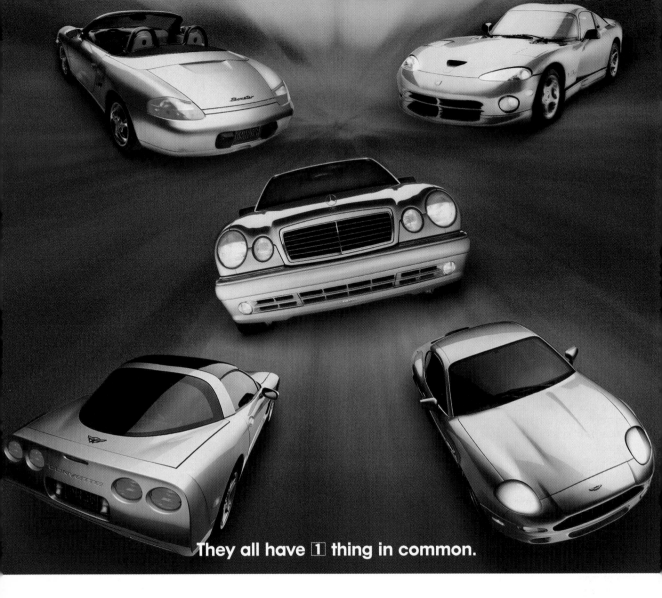

They all have 1 thing in common.

They all start out with Mobil 1® in their engines: all Aston Martin,® Corvette,® Porsche,® Viper® and Mercedes-Benz AMG models. And with their engines goes the recommendation that when you change oil, to keep on using Mobil 1. This advice is the car makers' way of helping you protect your investment. And to protect *their* reputations. Mobil 1 is the world's number one synthetic because it has

proven itself to be almost perfect. In one test, engine parts protected by Mobil 1 still met factory specs after 200,000 miles. What that proves is the value of a basic Mobil goal—to create products that aren't just as good as necessary, but as good as possible. We're honored that Mobil 1 is a first choice for dream cars. But also, for millions of reality cars using it every day. Visit us at www.mobil1.com.

Nothing outperforms

A Word to Our Readers

Some 50 years after the establishment of the U.S. interstate highway system, Americans continue to take to the roads in enormous numbers—for day trips, for extended family vacations, and for business. Airline travel, too, is ever-increasing. You, the traveler, deserve the best food and accommodations available in every city or town you visit. You could query local residents about quality places to stay and eat, but that time-consuming option is neither practical nor any guarantee of good advice.

Leave it to the *Mobil Travel Guide,* then, to direct you to satisfying places to eat and stay, as well as to events and attractions, in thousands of locations across America. Mobil Corporation has sponsored the *Mobil Travel Guide* since 1958. Now, in partnership with Consumer Guide, Mobil presents the latest edition of the annual Travel Guide series.

The information database that is the foundation of every title in the *Mobil Travel Guide* series is an astonishing resource: enormous, detailed, and continually updated to be as accurate and useful as it can be. Exhaustive, computerized inspection reports from highly trained field representatives spread out across the country are evaluated by senior staff, who also utilize the comments of *more than 100,000 readers* to arrive at fair, accurate, and useful assessments of hotels, motels, and restaurants. Valuable capsule descriptions of each site are highlighted by Mobil's respected and world-famous one- to five-star ratings system. All this, plus detailed information about thousands of attractions and things to do!

Space limitations make it impossible for us to include *every* hotel, motel, and restaurant in America. Instead, our database is comprised of a generous, representative sampling with information about places that are above-average of their type. In essence, you can patronize with confidence any of the restaurants, places of lodging, and attractions listed in the *Mobil Travel Guide* series.

You'll find that the *Mobil Travel Guide* books include information about a great variety of establishments. Perhaps you favor rustic lodgings and restaurants, or perhaps you're most comfortable with elegance and high style. Money may be no object or,

like most of us, you may be on a budget. It's possible that you place a high premium on 24-hour room service or vegetarian menu items. Whatever your needs and desires, they will be reflected in the *Mobil Travel Guide* series.

Allow us to emphasize that no establishment is charged for inclusion in our guides. We have no relationship with any of the businesses and attractions we list, and act only as a consumer advocate. In essence, we do the investigative legwork so you won't have to.

When you look over the "How to Use This Book" section that follows, you'll discover just how simple it is to quickly obtain all the information you need. And for terrific tips on saving money, travel safety, and other ways to enjoy your traveling to the utmost, be sure to read our special section, "Making the Most of Your Trip."

Keep in mind that the "hospitality" business is ever-changing. Restaurants and places of lodging—particularly small chains or stand-alone establishments—can change management or even go out of business with surprising quickness. Although every effort has been made to double-check information during our annual updates, we nevertheless recommend that you call ahead to be sure a place you have selected is open and still offers all the features you want.

We hope that all your travel experiences are easy, fun, and relaxing. If any aspects of your accommodations or dining move you to comment, please drop us a line. We depend a great deal on our readers' remarks, so you can be assured that your comments will be read and assimilated into our research. General comments about our books are also welcome. You can write us at *Mobil Travel Guide,* 7373 North Cicero Ave., Lincolnwood, IL 60712, or send e-mail to travel@pubint.com.

Take your *Mobil Travel Guide* books along on every trip. You'll be pleased by their convenience, ease of use, and breadth of dependable coverage.

Happy travels in the new millennium!

THE EDITORS

Welcome

For over 40 years the *Mobil Travel Guide* has provided travelers in North America with reliable advice on finding good value, quality service, and the distinctive attractions that give a destination its special character. During this time our teams of culinary and hospitality experts have worked hard to develop objective and exacting standards. In so doing, they seek to fully meet the desires and expectations of a broad range of customers.

It is our hope, whether your travels are for business or leisure, over a long distance or a short one, that this book will be your companion, dependably guiding you to quality and value in lodging and dining. By including local attractions (both seasonal and year round) we are striving to provide you with experiences that will make your trip more interesting, pleasant, and memorable.

Because we continually update our attractions and evaluate our listings, we invite you to help us enhance the guides. Whether you wish to provide us with your reactions to the places you have visited or to make suggestions to improve the guides, we would consider it a privilege to hear from you. Please take the time to fill out the customer feedback form at the back of this book or contact us on the Internet at www.mobil.com/travel.

Thank you, and travel safely.

Lucio A. Noto
Chairman and Chief Executive Officer
Mobil Corporation

How to Use This Book

The *Mobil Travel Guide* is easy to use. Each state chapter begins with a general introduction that both provides a general geographical and historical orientation to the state and covers basic statewide tourist information, from state recreation areas to seat-belt laws. The balance of each chapter is devoted to the travel destinations within the state—cities and towns, state and national parks, and tourist regions—which, like the states themselves, are arranged alphabetically.

What follows is an explanation of the wealth of information you'll find within those travel destinations—information on the area, on things to see and do there, and on where to stay and eat.

Maps and Map Coordinates

The first thing you'll notice is that next to each destination is a set of map coordinates. These refer to the appropriate state map in the front of this book. In addition, there are maps of selected larger cities in the front section as well as maps of key neighborhoods within the sections on the cities themselves.

Destination Information

Because many travel destinations are so close to other cities and towns where visitors might find additional attractions, accomodations, and restaurants, cross-references to those places are included whenever possible. Also listed are addresses and phone numbers for travel-information resources—usually the local chamber of commerce or office of tourism—as well as pertinent vital statistics and a brief introduction to the area.

What to See and Do

More than 11,000 museums, art galleries, amusement parks, universities, historic sites and houses, plantations, churches, state parks, ski areas, and other attractions are described in the *Mobil Travel Guide*. A white star on a black background ⭐ signals that the attraction is one of the best in the state.

Since municipal parks, public tennis courts, swimming pools, and small educational institutions are common to most towns, they are generally excluded.

Following the attraction's description are the months and days it's open, address/location and phone number, and admission costs (see the inside front cover for an explanation of the cost symbols). Note that directions are given from the center of the town under which the attraction is listed, which may not necessarily be the town in which the attraction is located. Zip codes are listed only if they differ from those given for the town.

Events

Events—categorized as annual, seasonal, or special—are highlighted. An annual event is one that's held every year for a period of usually no longer than a week to 10 days; festivals and fairs are typical entries. A seasonal event is one that may or may not be annual and that is held for a number of weeks or months in the year, such as horse racing, summer theater, concert or opera festivals, and professional sports. Special event listings occur infrequently and mark a certain date or event, such as a centennial or other commemorative celebration.

Major Cities

Additional information on airports and transportation, suburbs, and neighborhoods may be included for large cities.

Lodging and Restaurant Listings

ORGANIZATION

For both lodgings and restaurants, when a property is in a town that does not have its own heading, the listing appears under the town nearest its location with the address and town in parentheses immediately after the establishment name. In large cities, lodgings located within 5 miles of major commercial airports are listed under a separate "Airport" heading, following the city listings.

LODGING CLASSIFICATIONS

Each property is classified by type according to the characteristics below. Because the following features and services are found at most motels, lodges, motor hotels, and hotels, they are not shown in those listings:

- Year-round operation with a single rate structure unless otherwise quoted
- European plan (meals not included in room rate)
- Bathroom with tub and/or shower in each room
- Air-conditioned/heated, often with individual room control
- Cots
- Daily maid service
- Phones in rooms
- Elevators

Motels and Lodges. Accommodations are in low-rise structures with rooms easily accessible to parking (usually free). Properties have outdoor room entry and small, functional lobbies. Service is often limited, and dining may not be offered in lower-rated motels and lodges. Shops and businesses are found only in higher-rated properties, as are bellhops, room service, and restaurants serving three meals daily.

Lodges differ from motels primarily in their emphasis on outdoor recreational activities and in location. They are often found in resort and rural areas rather than in major cities or along highways.

Motor Hotels. Offering the convenience of motels along with many of the features of hotels, motor hotels range from low-rise structures offering limited services to multistory buildings with a wide range of services and facilities. Multiple building entrances, elevators, inside hallways, and parking areas (generally free) near access doors are some of the features of a motor hotel. Lobbies offer sitting areas and 24-hour desk and switchboard services. Often bellhop and valet services as well as restaurants serving three meals a day are found. Expanded recreational facilities and more than one restaurant are available in higher-rated properties.

The distinction between motor hotels and hotels in metropolitan areas is minor.

Hotels. To be categorized as a hotel, an establishment must have most of the following facilities and services: multiple floors, a restaurant and/or coffee shop, elevators, room service, bellhops, a spacious lobby, and recreational facilities. In addition, the following features and services not shown in listings are also found:

- Valet service (one-day laundry/cleaning service)
- Room service during hours restaurant is open
- Bellhops
- Some oversize beds

Resorts. These specialize in stays of three days or more and usually offer American plan and/or housekeeping accommodations. Their emphasis is on recreational facilities, and a social director is often available. Food services are of primary importance, and guests must be able to eat three meals a day on the premises, either in restaurants or by having access to an on-site grocery store and preparing their own meals.

Inns. Frequently thought of as a small hotel, an inn is a place of homelike comfort and warm hospitality. It is often a structure of historic significance, with an equally interesting setting. Meals are a special occasion, and refreshments are frequently served in late afternoon. Rooms are usually individually decorated, often with antiques or furnishings representative of the locale. Phones, bathrooms, and TVs may not be available in every room.

Guest Ranches. Like resorts, guest ranches specialize in stays of three days or more. Guest ranches also offer meal plans and extensive outdoor activities. Horseback riding is usually a feature; there are stables and trails on the ranch property, and trail rides and daily instruction are part of the program. Many guest ranches are working ranches, ranging from casual to rustic, and guests are encouraged to participate in ranch life. Eating is often family-style and may also include cookouts. Western saddles are assumed; phone ahead to inquire about English saddle availability.

Cottage Colonies. These are housekeeping cottages and cabins that are usually found in recreational areas. Any dining or recreational facilities are noted in our listing.

DINING CLASSIFICATIONS

Restaurants. Most dining establishments fall into this category. All have a full kitchen and offer table service and a complete menu. Parking on or near the premises, in a lot or garage, is assumed. When a property offers valet or other special parking features, or when only street parking is available, it is noted in the listing.

Unrated Dining Spots. These places, listed after Restaurants in many cities, are chosen for their unique atmosphere, specialized menu, or local flavor. They include delis, ice-cream parlors, cafeterias, tearooms, and pizzerias. Because they may not have a full kitchen or table service, they are not given a *Mobil Travel Guide* rating. Often they offer extraordinary value and quick service.

QUALITY RATINGS

The *Mobil Travel Guide* has been rating lodgings and restaurants on a national basis since the first edition was published in 1958. For years the guide was the only source of such ratings, and it remains among the few guidebooks to rate restaurants across the country.

All listed establishments were inspected by experienced field representatives or evaluated by a senior staff member. Ratings are based upon their detailed inspection reports of the individual properties, on written evaluations of staff members who stay and dine anonymously, and on an extensive review of comments from our readers.

You'll find a key to the rating categories, ★ through ★ ★ ★ ★ ★, on the inside front cover. All establishments in the book are recommended. Even a ★ place is above average, usually providing a basic, informal experience. Rating categories reflect both the features the property offers and its quality in relation to similar establishments.

For example, lodging ratings take into account the number and quality of facilities and services, the luxury of appointments, and the attitude and professionalism of staff and management. A ★ establishment provides a comfortable night's lodging. A ★ ★ property offers more than a facility that rates one star, and the decor is well planned and integrated. Establishments that rate ★ ★ ★ are professionally managed and staffed and often beautifully appointed; the lodging experience is truly excellent and the range of facilities is extensive. Properties that have been given ★ ★ ★ ★ not only offer many services but also have their own style and personality; they are luxurious, creatively decorated, and superbly maintained. The ★ ★ ★ ★ ★ properties are among the best in North America, superb in every respect and entirely memorable, year in and year out.

Restaurant evaluations reflect the quality of the food and the ingredients, preparation, and presentation as well as service levels and the property's decor and ambience. A restaurant that has fairly simple goals for menu and decor but that achieves those goals superbly might receive the same number of stars as a restaurant with somewhat loftier ambitions whose execution falls somewhat short of the mark. In general, ★ indicates a restaurant that's a good choice in its area, usually fairly simple and perhaps catering to a clientele of locals and families; ★ ★ denotes restaurants that are more highly recommended in their area; ★ ★ ★ restaurants are of national caliber, with professional and attentive service and a skilled chef in the kitchen; ★ ★ ★ ★ reflects superb dining choices, where remarkable food is served in equally remarkable surroundings; and ★ ★ ★ ★ ★ represents that rarefied group of the best restaurants in the country, where in addition to near perfection in every detail, there's that special something extra that makes for an unforgettable dining experience.

A list of the four-star and five-star establishments in each region is located just before the state listings.

Each rating is reviewed annually and each establishment must work to maintain its rating (or improve it). Every effort is made to assure that ratings are fair and accurate; the designated ratings are published purely as an aid to travelers.

In general, properties that are very new or have recently undergone major management changes are considered difficult to assess fairly and are often listed without ratings.

Good Value Check Mark. In all locales, you'll find a wide range of lodging and dining establishments with a ✔ in front of a star rating. This indicates an unusually good value at economical prices as follows:

In Major Cities and Resort Areas

Lodging: average $105-$125 per night for singles; average $115-$140 per night for doubles

Restaurants: average $25 for a complete lunch; average $40 for a complete dinner, exclusive of beverages and gratuities

Local Area Listings

Lodging: average $50-$60 per night for singles; average $60-$75 per night for doubles

Restaurants: average $12 for a complete lunch; average $20 for a complete dinner, exclusive of beverages and gratuities

LODGINGS

Each listing gives the name, address, directions (when there is no street address), neighborhood and/or directions from downtown (in major cities), phone number (local and 800), fax number, number and type of rooms available, room rates, and seasons open (if not year-round). Also included are details on recreational and dining facilities on property or nearby, the presence of a luxury level, and credit-card information. A key to the symbols at the end of each listing is on the inside front cover. (Note that Mobil Corporation credit cards cannot be used for payment of meals and room charges.)

All prices quoted in the *Mobil Travel Guide* publications are expected to be in effect at the time of publication and during the entire year; however, prices cannot be guaranteed. In some localities there may be short-term price variations because of special events or holidays. Whenever possible, these price charges are noted. Certain resorts have complicated rate structures that vary with the time of year; always confirm listed rates when you make your plans.

RESTAURANTS

Each listing gives the name, address, directions (when there is no street address), neighborhood and/or directions from downtown (in major cities), phone number, hours and days of operation (if not open daily year-round), reservation policy, cuisine (if other than American), price range for each meal served, children's meals (if offered), specialties, and credit-card information. Additionally, special features such as chef ownership, ambience, and entertainment are noted. By carefully reading the detailed restaurant information and comparing prices, you can easily determine whether the restaurant is formal and elegant or informal and comfortable for families.

TERMS AND ABBREVIATIONS IN LISTINGS

The following terms and abbreviations are used throughout the listings:

A la carte entrees With a price, refers to the cost of entrees/main dishes only that are not accompanied by side dishes.

AP American plan (lodging plus all meals).

Bar Liquor, wine, and beer are served in a bar or cocktail lounge and usually with meals unless otherwise indicated (e.g., "wine, beer").

Business center The property has a designated area accessible to all guests with business services.

Business serve avail The property can perform/arrange at least two of the following services for a guest: audiovisual equipment rental, binding, computer rental, faxing, messenger services, modem availability, notary service, obtaining office supplies, photocopying, shipping, and typing.

Cable Standard cable service; "premium" indicates that HBO, Disney, Showtime, or similar services are available.

Ck-in, ck-out Check-in time, check-out time.

Coin lndry Self-service laundry.

Complete meal Soup and/or salad, entree, and dessert, plus nonalcoholic beverage.

Continental bkfst Usually coffee and a roll or doughnut.

Cr cds: A, American Express; 0, Carte Blanche; D, Diners Club; DS, Discover; ER, enRoute; JCB, Japanese Credit Bureau; MC, MasterCard; V, Visa.

D Followed by a price, indicates room rate for a "double"— two people in one room in one or two beds (the charge may be higher for two double beds).

Downhill/x-country ski Downhill and/or cross-country skiing within 20 miles of property,

Each addl Extra charge for each additional person beyond the stated number of persons at a reduced price.

Early-bird dinner A meal served at specified hours, typically around 4:30-6:30 pm.

Exc Except.

Exercise equipt Two or more pieces of exercise equipment on the premises.

Exercise rm Both exercise equipment and room, with an instructor on the premises.

Fax Facsimile machines available to all guests.

Golf privileges Privileges at a course within 10 miles.

Hols Holidays.

In-rm modem link Every guest room has a connection for a modem that's separate from the phone line.

Kit. or kits. A kitchen or kitchenette that contains stove or microwave, sink, and refrigerator and that is either part of the room or a separate room. If the kitchen is not fully equipped, the listing will indicate "no equipt" or "some equipt."

Luxury level A special section of a lodging, covering at least an entire floor, that offers increased luxury accommodations. Management must provide no less than three of these four services: separate check-in and check-out, concierge, private lounge, and private elevator service (key access). Complimentary breakfast and snacks are commonly offered.

MAP Modified American plan (lodging plus two meals).

Movies Prerecorded videos are available for rental.

No cr cds accepted No credit cards are accepted.

No elvtr In hotels with more than two stories, it's assumed there are elevators; only their absence is noted.

No phones Phones, too, are assumed; only their absence is noted.

Parking There is a parking lot on the premises.

Private club A cocktail lounge or bar available to members and their guests. In motels and hotels where these clubs exist, registered guests can usually use the club as guests of the management; the same is frequently true of restaurants.

Prix fixe A full meal for a stated price; usually one price is quoted.

Res Reservations.

S Followed by a price, indicates room rate for a "single," i.e., one person.

Semi-a la carte Meals include vegetable, salad, soup, appetizer, or other accompaniments to the main dish.

Serv bar A service bar, where drinks are prepared for dining patrons only.

Serv charge Service charge is the amount added to the restaurant check in lieu of a tip.

Table d'hôte A full meal for a stated price, dependent upon entree selection; no a la carte options are available.

Tennis privileges Privileges at tennis courts within 5 miles.

TV Indicates color television.

Under certain age free Children under that age are not charged if staying in room with a parent.

Valet parking An attendant is available to park and retrieve a car.

VCR VCRs in all guest rooms.

VCR avail VCRs are available for hookup in guest rooms.

Special Information for Travelers with Disabilities

The *Mobil Travel Guide* symbol [D] shown in accommodation and restaurant listings indicates establishments that are at least partially accessible to people with mobility problems.

The *Mobil Travel Guide* criteria for accessibility are unique to our publication. Please do not confuse them with the universal symbol for wheelchair accessibility. When the [D] symbol appears following a listing, the establishment is equipped with facilities to accommodate people using wheelchairs or crutches or otherwise needing easy access to doorways and rest rooms. Travelers with severe mobility problems or with hearing or visual impairments may or may not find facilities they need. Always phone ahead to make sure that an establishment can meet your needs.

All lodgings bearing our [D] symbol have the following facilities:

- ISA-designated parking near access ramps
- Level or ramped entryways to building
- Swinging building entryway doors minimum 3′0″
- Public rest rooms on main level with space to operate a wheelchair; handrails at commode areas
- Elevators equipped with grab bars and lowered control buttons
- Restaurants with accessible doorways; rest rooms with space to operate wheelchair; handrails at commode areas
- Minimum 3′0″ width entryway to guest rooms
- Low-pile carpet in rooms
- Telephone at bedside and in bathroom
- Bed placed at wheelchair height
- Minimum 3′0″ width doorway to bathroom

• Bath with open sink—no cabinet; room to operate wheel-chair
• Handrails at commode areas; tub handrails
• Wheelchair accessible peephole in room entry door
• Wheelchair accessible closet rods and shelves

All restaurants bearing our D symbol offer the following facilities:

• ISA-designated parking beside access ramps
• Level or ramped front entryways to building
• Tables to accommodate wheelchairs
• Main-floor rest rooms; minimum 3'0" width entryway
• Rest rooms with space to operate wheelchair; handrails at commode areas

In general, the newest properties are apt to impose the fewest barriers.

To get the kind of service you need and have a right to expect, do not hesitate when making a reservation to question the management in detail about the availability of accessible rooms, parking, entrances, restaurants, lounges, or any other facilities that are important to you, and confirm what is meant by "accessible." Some guests with mobility impairments report that lodging establishments' housekeeping and maintenance departments are most helpful in describing barriers. Also inquire about any special equipment, transportation, or services you may need.

Making the Most of Your Trip

A few diehard souls might fondly remember the trip where the car broke down and they were stranded for a week, or the vacation that cost twice what it was supposed to. For most travelers, though, the best trips are those that are safe, smooth, and within their budget. To help you make your trip the best it can be, we've assembled a few tips and resources.

Saving Money

ON LODGING

After you've seen the published rates, it's time to look for discounts. Many hotels and motels offer them—for senior citizens, business travelers, families, you name it. It never hurts to ask—politely, that is. Sometimes, especially in late afternoon, desk clerks are instructed to fill beds, and you might be offered a lower rate, or a nicer room, to entice you to stay. Look for bargains on stays over multiple nights, in the off-season, and on weekdays or weekends (depending on location). Many hotels in major metropolitan areas, for example, have special weekend package plans, which offer considerable savings on rooms and may include breakfast, cocktails, and meal discounts. Prices change frequently throughout the year, so phone ahead.

Another way to save money is to choose accommodations that give you more than just a standard room. Rooms with kitchen facilities enable you to cook some meals for yourself, reducing restaurant costs. A suite might save money for two couples traveling together. Even hotel luxury levels can provide good value, as many include breakfast or cocktails in the price of the room.

State and city sales taxes as well as special room taxes can increase your room rates as much as 25% per day. We are unable to bring this specific information into the listings, but we strongly urge that you ask about these taxes when placing reservations in order to understand the total price to you.

Watch out for telephone-usage charges that hotels frequently impose on long-distance calls, credit-card calls, and other phone calls—even those that go unanswered. Before phoning from your room, read the information given to you at check-in, and then be sure to read your bill carefully before checking out. You won't be expected to pay for charges that weren't spelled out. (On the other hand, it's not unusual for a hotel to bill you for your calls after you return home.) Consider using public telephones in hotel lobbies; the savings may outweigh the inconvenience.

ON DINING

There are several ways to get a less-expensive meal at a more-expensive restaurant. Early-bird dinners are popular in many parts of the country and offer considerable savings. If you're interested in sampling a 4- or 5-star establishment, consider going at lunchtime. While the prices then are probably relatively high, they may be half of those at dinner and come with the same ambience, service, and cuisine.

PARK PASSES

While many national parks, monuments, seashores, historic sites, and recreation areas may be used free of charge, others charge an entrance fee (ranging from $1 to $6 per person to $5 to $15 per carload) and/or a "use fee" for special services and facilities. If you plan to make several visits to federal recreation areas, consider one of the following National Park Service money-saving programs:

Park Pass. This is an annual entrance permit to a specific unit in the National Park Service system that normally charges an entrance fee. The pass admits the permit holder and any accompanying passengers in a private noncommercial vehicle or, in the case of walk-in facilities, the holder's spouse, children, and parents. It is valid for entrance fees only. A Park Pass may be purchased in person or by mail from the National Park Service unit at which the pass will be honored. The cost is $15 to $20, depending upon the area.

Golden Eagle Passport. This pass, available to people who are between 17 and 61, entitles the purchaser and accompanying passengers in a private noncommercial vehicle to enter any outdoor NPS unit that charges an entrance fee and admits the purchaser and family to most walk-in fee-charging areas. Like the Park Pass, it is good for one year and does not cover use fees. It may be purchased from the National

Park Service, Office of Public Inquiries, Room 1013, US Department of the Interior, 18th and C Sts NW, Washington, DC 20240, phone 202/208-4747; at any of the 10 regional offices throughout the country; and at any NPS area that charges a fee. The cost is $50.

Golden Age Passport. Available to citizens and permanent residents of the United States 62 years or older, this is a life-time entrance permit to fee-charging recreation areas. The fee exemption extends to those accompanying the permit holder in a private noncommercial vehicle or, in the case of walk-in facilities, to the holder's spouse and children. The passport also entitles the holder to a 50% discount on use fees charged in park areas but not to fees charged by concessionaires. Golden Age Passports must be obtained in person. The applicant must show proof of age, i.e., a driver's license, birth certificate, or signed affidavit attesting to age (Medicare cards are not acceptable proof). Passports are available at most park service units where they're used, at National Park Service headquarters (see above), at park system regional offices, at National Forest Supervisors' offices, and at most Ranger Station offices. The cost is $10.

Golden Access Passport. Issued to citizens and permanent residents of the United States who are physically disabled or visually impaired, this passport is a free lifetime entrance permit to fee-charging recreation areas. The fee exemption extends to those accompanying the permit holder in a private noncommercial vehicle or, in the case of walk-in facilities, to the holder's spouse and children. The passport also entitles the holder to a 50% discount on use fees charged in park areas but not to fees charged by concessionaires. Golden Access Passports must be obtained in person. Proof of eligibility to receive federal benefits is required (under programs such as Disability Retirement, Compensation for Military Service-Connected Disability, Coal Mine Safety and Health Act, etc.), or an affidavit must be signed attesting to eligibility. These passports are available at the same outlets as Golden Age Passports.

FOR SENIOR CITIZENS
Look for the senior-citizen discount symbol in the lodging and restaurant listings. Always call ahead to confirm that the discount is being offered, and be sure to carry proof of age. At places not listed in the book, it never hurts to ask if a senior-citizen discount is offered. Additional information for mature travelers is available from the American Association of Retired Persons (AARP), 601 E St NW, Washington, DC 20049, phone 202/434-2277.

Tipping

Tipping is an expression of appreciation for good service, and often service workers rely on tips as a significant part of their income. However, you never need to tip if service is poor.

IN HOTELS
Doormen in major city hotels are usually given $1 for getting you a cab. Bellhops expect $1 per bag, usually $2 if you have only one bag. Concierges are tipped according to the service they perform. It's not mandatory to tip when you've asked for suggestions on sightseeing or restaurants or help in making reservations for dining. However, when a concierge books you a table at a restaurant known to be difficult to get into, a gratuity of $5 is appropriate. For obtaining theater or sporting event tickets, $5-$10 is expected. Maids, often overlooked by guests, may be tipped $1-$2 per day of stay.

AT RESTAURANTS
Coffee shop and counter service wait staff are usually given 8%–10% of the bill. In full-service restaurants, tip 15% of the bill, before sales tax. In fine restaurants, where the staff is large and shares the gratuity, 18%–20% for the waiter is appropriate. In most cases, tip the maitre d' only if service has been extraordinary and only on the way out; $20 is the minimum in upscale properties in major metropolitan areas. If there is a wine steward, tip him or her at least $6 a bottle, more if the wine was decanted or if the bottle was very expensive. If your busboy has been unusually attentive, $2 pressed into his hand on departure is a nice gesture. An increasing number of restaurants automatically add a service charge to the bill in lieu of a gratuity. Before tipping, carefully review your check.

AT AIRPORTS
Curbside luggage handlers expect $1 per bag. Car-rental shuttle drivers who help with your luggage appreciate a $1 or $2 tip.

Staying Safe

The best way to deal with emergencies is to be prepared enough to avoid them. However, unforeseen situations do happen, and you can prepare for them.

IN YOUR CAR
Before your trip, make sure your car has been serviced and is in good working order. Change the oil, check the battery and belts, and make sure tires are inflated properly (this can also improve gas mileage). Other inspections recommended by the car's manufacturer should be made, too.

Next, be sure you have the tools and equipment to deal with a routine breakdown: jack, spare tire, lug wrench, repair kit, emergency tools, jumper cables, spare fan belt, auto fuses, flares and/or reflectors, flashlights, first-aid kit, and, in winter, a windshield scraper and shovel.

Bring all appropriate and up-to-date documentation—licenses, registration, and insurance cards—and know what's covered by your insurance. Also bring an extra set of keys, just in case.

En route, always buckle up!

If your car does break down, get out of traffic as soon as possible—pull well off the road. Raise the hood and turn on your emergency flashers or tie a white cloth to the roadside door handle or antenna. Stay near your car. Use flares or reflectors to keep your car from being hit.

IN YOUR LODGING

Chances are slim that you will encounter a hotel or motel fire. The 🔥 in a listing indicates that there were smoke detectors and/or sprinkler systems in the rooms we inspected. Once you've checked in, make sure that any smoke detector in your room is working properly. Ascertain the locations of fire extinguishers and at least two fire exits. Never use an elevator in a fire.

For personal security, use the peephole in your room's door.

PROTECTING AGAINST THEFT

To guard against theft wherever you go, don't bring any more of value than you need. If you do bring valuables, leave them at your hotel rather than in your car, and if you have something very expensive, lock it in a safe. Many hotels have one in each room; others will store your valuables in the hotel's safe. And of course, don't carry more money than you need; use traveler's checks and credit cards, or visit cash machines.

For Travelers With Disabilities

A number of publications can provide assistance. The most complete listing of published material for travelers with disabilities is available from The Disability Bookshop, Twin Peaks Press, Box 129, Vancouver, WA 98666, phone 360/694-2462. A comprehensive guidebook to the national parks is *Easy Access to National Parks: The Sierra Club Guide for People with Disabilities* ($16), distributed by Random House.

The Reference Section of the National Library Service for the Blind and Physically Handicapped (Library of Congress, Washington, DC 20542, phone 202/707-9276 or 202/707-5100) provides information and resources for persons with mobility problems and hearing and vision impairments, as well as information about the NILS talking program (or visit your local library).

Important Toll-Free Numbers

and On-Line Information

HOTELS AND MOTELS

Adam's Mark 800/444–2326
www.adamsmark.com
Baymont Inns and Suites 800/428–3438
www.budgetel.com
Best Western.....................800/780–7234, TDD 800/528–2222
www.bestwestern.com
Budget Host 800/283–4678
www.budgethost.com
Clarion...800/252–7466
Comfort Inn 800/228–5150
www.choicehotels.com
Courtyard by Marriott 800/321–2211
www.courtyard.com
Days Inn 800/325–2525
www.daysinn.com
Doubletree 800/222–8733
www.doubletreehotels.com/
Drury Inns 800/325–8300
www.drury-inn.com
Econo Lodge 800/446–6900
www.econolodge.com
Embassy Suites 800/362–2779
www.embassy-suites.com
Exel Inns of America 800/356–8013
www.exlinns.com
Fairfield Inn by Marriott 800/228–2800
www.fairfieldinn.com
Fairmont Hotels 800/527–4727
www.fairmont.com
Forte 800/225–5843
www.forte-hotels.com
Four Seasons 800/819–5053
www.fourseasons.com
Friendship Inns 800/453–4511
www.hotelchoice.com
Hampton Inn 800/426–7866
www.hampton-inn.com
Hilton ....800/445–8667, TDD 800/368–1133
www.hilton.com
Holiday Inn ....800/465–4329, TDD 800/238–5544
www.holiday-inn.com
Howard Johnson ....800/446–4656, TDD 800/654–8442
www.hojo.com
Hyatt & Resorts 800/233–1234
www.hyatt.com
Inns of America 800/826–0778
www.innsamerica.com
Inter-Continental 800/327–0200
www.interconti.com
La Quinta ....800/531–5900, TDD 800/426–3101
www.laquinta.com

Loews 800/235–6397
www.loewshotels.com
Marriott 800/228–9290
www.marriott.com
Master Hosts Inns 800/251–1962
www.reservahost.com
Meridien 800/225–5843
www.forte-hotels.com
Motel 6 ....800/466–8356
Nikko International 800/645–5687
www.nikkohotels.com
Omni 800/843–6664
www.omnirosen.com
Quality Inn 800/228–5151
www.qualityinn.com
Radisson 800/333–3333
www.radisson.com
Ramada ....800/228–2828, TDD 800/228–3232
www.ramada.com
Red Carpet Inns 800/251–1962
www.reservahost.com
Red Lion 800/733–5466
www.redlion.com
Red Roof Inn.......................................800/843–7663
www.redroof.com
Renaissance 800/468–3571
www.renaissancehotels.com
Residence Inn by Marriott 800/331–3131
www.marriott.com
Ritz-Carlton 800/241–3333
www.ritzcarlton.com
Rodeway 800/228–2000
www.rodeway.com
Sheraton 800/325–3535
www.sheraton.com
Shilo Inn 800/222–2244
www.shiloinns.com
Signature Inns 800/822–5252
www.signature-inns.com
Sleep Inn 800/753–3746
www.sleepinn.com
Super 8 ....800/800–8000
www.super8motels.com
Susse Chalet 800/524–2538
www.sussechalet.com
Travelodge 800/578–7878
www.travelodge.com
Vagabond Inns......................................800/522–1555
www.vagabondinns.com
Westin Hotels & Resorts 800/937–8461
www.westin.com
Wyndham Hotels & Resorts 800/996–3426
www.travelweb.com

AIRLINES

Air Canada 800/776–3000
www.aircanada.ca
Alaska...800/252–7522
www.alaska-air.com
American 800/433–7300
www.americaair.com
America West 800/235–9292
www.americawest.com
British Airways 800/247–9297
www.british-airways.com
Canadian 800/426–7000
www.cdnair.ca
Continental 800/523–3273
www.flycontinental.com
Delta 800/221–1212
www.delta-air.com/
IslandAir 800/323–3345
Mesa 800/637–2247
www.mesa-air.com
Northwest 800/225–2525
www.nwa.com
SkyWest 800/453–9417
www.skywest.com
Southwest 800/435–9792
www.iflyswa.com
TWA 800/221–2000
www.twa.com
United 800/241–6522
www.ual.com
USAir 800/428–4322
www.usair.com

TRAINS

Amtrak 800/872–7245
www.amtrak.com

BUSES

Greyhound 800/231–2222
www.greyhound.com

CAR RENTALS

Advantage 800/777–5500
www.arac.com
Alamo 800/327–9633
www.goalamo.com
Allstate 800/634–6186
www.bnm.com/as.htm
Avis 800/831–2847
www.avis.com
Budget 800/527–0700
www.budgetrentacar.com
Dollar 800/800–3665
www.dollarcar.com
Enterprise 800/325–8007
www.pickenterprise.com
Hertz 800/654–3131
www.hertz.com
National 800/227–7368
www.nationalcar.com
Payless 800/729–5377
www.800-payless.com
Rent-A-Wreck 800/944–7501
www.rent-a-wreck.com
Sears 800/527–0770
Thrifty 800/847–4369
www.thrifty.com

Four-Star and Five-Star Establishments
in the Mid-Atlantic

DELAWARE

★★★★ Lodgings
Hotel Du Pont, *Wilmington*
Inn at Montchanin Village, *Wilmington*

★★★★ Restaurant
Krazy Kat's Restaurant, *Wilmington*

MARYLAND

★★★★ Lodgings
Inn at Perry Cabin, *St Michaels*
Lighthouse Club Hotel, *Ocean City*

★★★★ Restaurants
Hampton's, *Baltimore*
Oregon Grill, *Cockeysville*

NEW JERSEY

★★★★ Lodgings
Bally's Park Place Casino Hotel &
   Tower, *Atlantic City*
Bernards Inn, *Bernardsville*
Hilton, *Millburn*

★★★★ Restaurants
Restaurant Serenade, *Chatham*
Ryland Inn, *Somerville*

NORTH CAROLINA

★★★★★ Lodging
Fearrington House, *Chapel Hill*

★★★★ Lodgings
Eseeola Lodge, *Linville*
The Park Hotel, *Charlotte*
Pinehurst Resort/Country Club,
   Pinehurst
Richmond Hill Inn, *Asheville*
The Swag, *Waynesville*
Washington Duke Inn, *Durham*

★★★★ Restaurant
Fearrington House, *Chapel Hill*

PENNSYLVANIA

★★★★ Lodgings
Four Seasons Hotel, *Philadelphia*
The Hotel Hershey, *Hershey*
The Rittenhouse Hotel, *Philadelphia*

★★★★ Restaurants
Brasserie Perrier, *Philadelphia*
Fountain, *Philadelphia*
Jake's, *Philadelphia*
La Famiglia, *Philadelphia*
Le Bec-Fin, *Philadelphia*
Striped Bass, *Philadelphia*
Susanna Foo, *Philadelphia*

SOUTH CAROLINA

★★★★ Lodgings
Charleston Place, *Charleston*
Rhett House Inn & Fine Dining, *Beaufort*
Woodlands Resort & Inn, *Charleston*

★★★★ Restaurant
Charleston Grill, *Charleston*

VIRGINIA

★★★★★ Lodging
The Inn at Little Washington,
   Washington

★★★★★ Restaurant
The Inn at Little Washington,
   Washington

★★★★ Lodgings
The Homestead Resort, *Hot Springs*
The Jefferson, *Richmond*
Kingsmill Resort, *Williamsburg*
Martha Washington Inn, *Abingdon*
Morrison House, *Alexandria*
Ritz-Carlton Pentagon City, *Arlington
   County (National Airport Area)*
Ritz-Carlton Tysons Corner, *Tysons
   Corner*
Williamsburg Inn, *Williamsburg*

WASHINGTON, DC

★★★★ Lodgings
Four Seasons Washington, *Washington*
Park Hyatt Hotel Washington,
   Washington
The St. Regis Washington, *Washington*
Westin Fairfax Hotel, *Washington*
Willard Inter-Continental, *Washington*

★★★★ Restaurants
Gerard's Place, *Washington*
Kinkead's, *Washington*
Lespinasse, *Washington*
Nora, *Washington*
Red Sage Restaurant, *Washington*

WEST VIRGINIA

★★★★ Lodging
The Greenbrier Inn, *White Sulphur
   Springs*

Delaware

Population: 666,168
Land area: 1,982 square miles
Elevation: 0-442 feet
Highest point: Ebright Road (New Castle County)
Entered union: First state to ratify Constitution (December 7, 1787)
Capital: Dover
Motto: Liberty and independence
Nickname: First State, Small Wonder, Diamond State, Blue Hen State
State flower: Peach blossom
State bird: Blue hen chicken
State tree: American holly
State fair: July 20-29, 2000, in Harrington (see Dover)
Time zone: Eastern

Delaware ". . . is like a diamond, diminutive, but having within it inherent value," wrote John Lofland, the eccentric "Bard of Milford," in 1847. The state is 96 miles long and from nine to 35 miles wide. With more than half of its 1,982 square miles (excluding marshes) used for farming, Delaware produces a flood of agricultural products. Poultry contributes approximately half of the state's total farm income, with soybeans, corn, tomatoes, strawberries, asparagus, fruit and other crops bringing in about $170 million more each year. Booming industry in northern and central Delaware balances the agricultural sector of the economy. Consistent state corporate policies have persuaded more than 183,000 corporations to make their headquarters in the "corporate capital of the world." Forty major US banks alone have established lending and credit operations in the state.

Compact but diverse, Delaware has rolling, forested hills in the north, stretches of bare sand dunes in the south and mile upon mile of lonely marsh along the coast. Visitors can tour a modern agricultural or chemical research center in the morning and search for buried pirate treasure in the afternoon. The deBraak, which foundered off Lewes in 1798, was raised in 1986 because of the belief that it may have had a fortune in captured Spanish coin or bullion aboard. The coins that frequently come ashore at Coin Beach below Rehoboth are believed to come from the Faithful Steward, a passenger vessel lost in 1785.

Delaware's history started on a grim note. The first colonists, 28 men under Dutch auspices, landed in the spring of 1631 near what is now Lewes. A year later, following an argument with a Lenni-Lenape chief, the bones of all 28 were found mingled with those of their cattle and strewn over their burned fields. In 1638 a group of Swedes established the first permanent settlement, Fort Christina, at a spot now in Wilmington. This was also the first permanent settlement of Swedes in North America. Dutch, English, Scottish and Irish colonists soon followed, with German, Italian and Polish groups coming in the late 19th century.

Henry Hudson, in Dutch service, discovered Delaware Bay in 1609. A year later Thomas Argall reported it to English navigators, naming it for his superior, Lord De La Warr, Governor of Virginia. Ownership changed rapidly from Swedish to Dutch to English hands. Later the area was claimed by both Lord Baltimore and the Penn family. The Maryland-Delaware boundary was set by British court order in 1750 and surveyed as part of the Mason-Dixon Line in 1763-1767. The boundary with New Jersey, also long disputed, was confirmed by the Supreme Court in 1935.

The "First State" (first to adopt the Constitution—December 7, 1787) is proud of its history of sturdy independence, both military and political. During the Revolution, the "Delaware line" was a crack regiment of the Continental Army. After heavy casualties in 1780, the unit was reorganized. The men would "fight all day and dance all night," according to a dispatch by General Greene. How well they danced is open to question, but they fought with such gallantry that they were mentioned in nearly all of the General's dispatches.

Delaware statesman John Dickinson, "penman of the Revolution" and one of the state's five delegates to the Constitutional Convention, was instrumental in the decision to write a new document rather than simply patch up the Articles of Confederation. Later he effected the compromise on representation, a problem that had threatened to break up the convention completely.

In addition to Lofland and Dickinson, Delaware has produced many literary figures, including the 19th-century playwright and novelist Robert Montgomery Bird, writer and illustrator Howard Pyle, Henry Seidel Canby (founder of the Saturday Review) and novelist John P. Marquand.

A fine highway network tempts motorists to drive through diminutive Delaware without really seeing it. Those who take time to leave the major highways and explore the countryside will find much that is rewarding.

When to Go/Climate

Delaware's climate is generally mild; long Indian summers are not unusual, and there's seldom frost until late autumn. Temperatures at the shore can be 10°F higher in winter or lower in summer than inland temperatures.

AVERAGE HIGH/LOW TEMPERATURES (°F)

WILMINGTON

Jan 39/22	May 73/52	Sept 78/58
Feb 42/25	June 81/62	Oct 67/46
Mar 52/33	July 86/67	Nov 56/37
Apr 63/42	Aug 84/66	Dec 44/28

Parks and Recreation Finder

Directions to and information about the parks and recreation areas below are given under their respective town/city sections. Please refer to those sections for details.

STATE PARK AND RECREATION AREAS

Key to abbreviations. I.P. = Interstate Park; S.A.P. = State Archaeological Park; S.B. = State Beach; S.C. = State Conservation Area; S.C.P. = State Conservation Park; S.Cp. = State Campground; S.F. = State Forest; S.G. = State Garden; S.H.A. = State Historic Area; S.H.P. = State Historic Park; S.H.S. = State Historic Site; S.M.P. = State Marine Park; S.N.A. = State Natural Area; S.P. = State Park; S.P.C. = State Public Campground; S.R. = State Reserve; S.R.A. = State Recreation Area; S.Res. = State Reservoir; S.Res.P. = State Resort Park; S.R.P. = State Rustic Park.

Place Name	Listed Under
Bellevue S.P.	WILMINGTON
Brandywine Creek S.P.	WILMINGTON
Cape Henlopen S.P.	LEWES
Delaware Seashore S.P.	REHOBOTH BEACH
Fenwick Island S.P.	FENWICK ISLAND
Fort Delaware S.P.	same
Holts Landing S.P.	BETHANY BEACH
Killens Pond S.P.	DOVER
Lums Pond S.P.	ODESSA
White Clay Creek S.P.	NEWARK

Water-related activities, hiking, riding, various other sports, picnicking and visitor centers are available in many of these areas. Delaware state parks are open all year, 8 am-sunset, except Fort Delaware (late Apr-late Sept). Most areas have fishing, boat ramps and picnicking. There is a vehicle entrance fee from Memorial Day-Labor Day, daily; May & Sept-Oct, wkends & hols. Camping is available from mid-Mar-mid-Nov at Delaware Seashore; Apr-Oct at Lums Pond, Trap Pond and Cape Henlopen; year-round at Killens Pond. There is a two-week maximum stay at campgrounds; no reservations are accepted; campsites run from $12-$26/night/site. For further information contact Department of Natural Resources & Environmental Control, Division of Parks & Recreation, 89 Kings Highway, Dover 19901; 302/739-4702.

FISHING & HUNTING

Both fresh and saltwater fishing are excellent. The state owns, leases or licenses 33,000 acres of game and fish lands and waters. More than 50 well-stocked state and privately owned ponds are scattered throughout the state. Many miles of ocean shoreline between Rehoboth Beach and Indian River Inlet are ideal for surf fishing. Common saltwater fish include trout, bluefish, porgie, sea bass, flounder and croaker; freshwater fish include bass, bluegill, pickerel, crappie, perch and trout.

CALENDAR HIGHLIGHTS

MAY

Wilmington Garden Day (Wilmington). Tour of famous houses and gardens.

JUNE

Zwaanendael Heritage Garden Tour (Lewes). Tour of hidden gardens of Lewes. Vendors. Phone 302/645-8073.

JULY

Delaware State Fair (Dover). In Harrington. Arts & crafts, home & trade show, carnival rides, entertainment, homemaking, agricultural and livestock exhibits. Phone 302/398-3269.

OCTOBER

Sea Witch Halloween and Fiddlers' Festival (Rehoboth Beach).

An annual nonresident hunting license is $86; nonresident 3-day small game license $35; nonresident trapping license $25; additional single deer permit $10. An annual resident freshwater fishing license is $8.50; nonresident license $15; 7-day nonresident license $5.20. A license is not required for tidal saltwater fishing. For further information on fishing or hunting, contact the Department of Natural Resources & Environmental Control, Division of Fish & Wildlife, 89 Kings Highway, Dover 19901; 302/739-4431 or -5297.

Driving Information

Safety belts are mandatory for all persons in front seat of vehicle. Children under 4 years and 40 pounds in weight must be in an approved safety seat anywhere in vehicle; children ages 4-15 must use a regulation seat belt anywhere in vehicle. For further information phone 302/739-5938.

INTERSTATE HIGHWAY SYSTEM

The following alphabetical listing of Delaware towns in *Mobil Travel Guide* shows that these cities are within 10 miles of the indicated interstate highway. A highway map, however, should be checked for the nearest exit.

Highway Number	Cities/Towns within 10 miles
Interstate 95	Newark, New Castle, Wilmington.

Additional Visitor Information

Delaware Tourism Office, 99 Kings Highway, Dover 19901, will provide tourist information; phone 302/739-4271

Visitor centers also provide information and brochures on points of interest in the state. Their locations are as follows: Delaware Memorial Bridge Plaza, jct I-295 and the bridge at New Castle; I-95 rest area, Greater Wilmington Convention and Visitors Bureau, Wilmington; Delaware State Information Center, Duke of York & Federal Sts, Dover; Smyrna, 1 mi N on US 13; Bethany-Fenwick Area Chamber of Commerce, DE 1, north of Fenwick Island.

Bethany Beach (D-10)

(See also Fenwick Island, Lewes, Rehoboth Beach)

Founded 1901 **Pop** 326 **Elev** 8 ft **Area Code** 302 **Zip** 19930 **E-mail** info@bethany-fenwick.org **Web** www.bethany-fenwick.org
Information Bethany-Fenwick Area Chamber of Commerce, Coastal Hwy/DE 1, PO Box 1450; 302/539-2100 or 800/962-7873

A quiet beach town on the Atlantic Ocean, Bethany Beach was founded as a site for revival camp meetings; hence the biblical name. Surf fishing and bathing are excellent here.

What to See and Do

Holts Landing State Park. A 203-acre park located along the Indian River Bay. Fishing, crabbing, clamming; sailing, boating (launch ramp providing access to bay). Picnicking, playground, ball fields. Standard hrs, fees. 8 mi NW via DE 26 & DE 346, N of Millville. Phone 302/539-9060 or 302/539-1055 (summer).

Annual Event

Boardwalk Arts Festival. The Boardwalk, Garfield Pkwy. Juried, original handmade works; woodcarving, photography, jewelry, batik, watercolor paintings. Late Aug.

Motels

★ **BETHANY ARMS.** *99 Hollywood St (19930), at S Atlantic Ave.* 302/539-9603. Web www.beach-net.com/bethanyarms. 52 units, 2-3 story, 36 kit. units. No elvtr. July-Aug: S, D $105-$160; each addl $10; under 6 free; wkly rates; lower rates mid-Mar-June, Sept-mid-Oct. Closed mid-Oct-mid-Mar. Crib $5. TV; cable. Restaurant adj 7 am-9 pm. Ck-out 11 am. Many refrigerators. Balconies. On ocean; beach. Cr cds: C, MC, V.

[D] [symbols]

★ **HARBOR VIEW MOTEL.** *RR 1 (19930), 2 mi N on DE 1. 302/539-0500; FAX 302/539-5170.* 60 rms, 2 story, 8 kit. units. July-Aug: S, D $95-$139; each addl $10; kit. units $100-$139; lower rates rest of yr. Crib $10. TV; cable (premium). Pool. Complimentary continental bkfst. Restaurant 5-10 pm; closed Dec-Jan. Ck-out 11 am. Meeting rm. Refrigerators, microwaves. Balconies. Picnic tables, grills. On bay; swimming. Cr cds: A, C, D, DS, MC, V.

[D] [symbols]

Dover (C-9)

(See also Odessa, Smyrna)

Founded 1717 **Pop** 27,630 **Elev** 36 ft **Area Code** 302 **Zip** 19901 **E-mail** cdcc@dmv.com

Information Central Delaware Chamber of Commerce, PO Box 576, 19903; 302/678-0892

The capital of Delaware since 1777, Dover was laid out by William Penn around the city's lovely green. For almost 200 years there were coach houses and inns on King's Road between Philadelphia and Lewes. Circling the green north and south on State Street are fine 18th- and 19th-century houses.

Today, because of Delaware's favorable corporation laws, more than 60,000 US firms pay taxes in Dover. At Dover Air Force Base, south off US 113, the Military Airlift Command operates one of the biggest air cargo terminals in the world, utilizing the giant C5-A aircraft. Dover is also the home of Delaware State College, Wesley College and the Terry campus of Delaware Technical and Community College.

What to See and Do

Delaware Agricultural Museum and Village. Museum of farm life from early settlement to 1960. Main exhibition hall and historic structures representing a late-19th-century farming community; includes gristmill, blacksmith-wheelwright shop, farmhouse, outbuildings, one-room schoolhouse, store and train station. Gift shop. (Apr-Dec, daily exc Mon; rest of yr, Mon-Fri) 866 N du Pont Hwy (US 13). Phone 302/734-1618. ¢¢

Delaware State Museums. Complex of three buildings: **Meeting House Galleries I and II** (1790). Exhibit devoted to archaeology. **1880 Gallery.** Turn-of-the-century drugstore, blacksmith shop, general store, post office, shoemaker's shop and printer's shop; and Johnson building. (Tues-Sat; closed hols) 316 S Governors Ave. Phone 302/739-4266. **Free**

Delaware State Visitor Center. Administered by Division of Historical and Cultural Affairs, center offers information on attractions throughout state. Exhibit galleries; audiovisual show. (Daily; closed hols) 406 Federal St. Phone 302/739-4266. **Free**

Dover Heritage Trail. Guided walking tour of historic areas, buildings and other attractions. (By appt only) Departs from State Visitor Center. Phone 302/678-2040. ¢¢

Hall of Records. Delaware's historical public records; archive includes Royal Charter granted by King Charles II to James, Duke of York, for Delaware territory in 1682. (Mon-Fri; closed hols) Court St & Legislative Ave. Phone 302/739-5318. **Free**

John Dickinson Plantation (1740). Restored boyhood residence of Dickinson, the "penman of the Revolution." Reconstructed farm complex. (Mar-Dec, Tues-Sat, also Sun afternoons; rest of yr, Tues-Sat; closed hols) 6 mi SE, near jct US 113 & DE 9 on Kitts Hummock Rd. Phone 302/739-3277. **Free**

Johnson Victrola Museum. Tribute to Eldridge Reeves Johnson, founder of the Victor Talking Machine Company. Collection of talking machines, Victrolas, early recordings and equipment. (Tues-Sat; closed hols) Bank Lane & New St. Phone 302/739-4266. **Free**

Killens Pond State Park. A 1,083-acre park with a 66-acre pond. Swimming pool; fishing; boating (rentals). Hiking, fitness trails; game fields. Picnicking. Camping (hookups, dump station). Standard hrs, fees. 13 mi S via US 13. Phone 302/284-4526.

The Old State House (1792). Second-oldest seat of government in continuous use in the US, the State House, restored in 1976, contains a courtroom, ceremonial governor's office, legislative chambers and county offices, including Levy Courtroom. A larger-than-life portrait of George Washington in the Senate Chamber was commissioned in 1802 by the legislature as a memorial to the nation's first president. Although Delaware's General Assembly moved to nearby Legislative Hall in 1934, the State House remains the state's symbolic capitol. (Daily exc Mon; closed state hols) Federal St, The Green. For information phone 302/739-4266. **Free**

Annual Events

Old Dover Days. Tours of historic houses and gardens not usually open to the public. Crafts exhibits, many other activities. For information & tickets contact Kent County Tourism, 800/233-KENT. 1st wkend May.

Delaware State Fair. 17 mi S on US 13 in Harrington. Arts & crafts, home & trade show, carnival rides, shows; homemaking, agricultural and livestock exhibits. Phone 302/398-3269. July 20-29.

Seasonal Events

Harrington Raceway. 17 mi S on US 13, at fairgrounds in Harrington. Harness horse racing. Wagering most nights of the week. Phone 302/398-3269. Sept-Nov.

Dover Downs. 1131 N du Pont Hwy (US 13). Racing events include NASCAR Winston Cup auto racing (June, Sept); harness racing (mid-Nov-Mar). For fees and schedule, phone 302/674-4600.

Motels

★ **COMFORT INN.** *222 S Dupont Hwy (19904). 302/674-3300; FAX 302/674-3300; res: 800/228-5150.* 94 rms, 2 story. May-Sept: S $47-$51; D $51-$55; each addl $5; kit. units $65; family, wkly rates; higher rates NASCAR races; lower rates rest of yr. Crib free. TV; cable. Pool; lifeguard. Complimentary continental bkfst. Restaurant adj 11 am-10 pm. Ck-out noon. Sundries. Some refrigerators. Grill. Cr cds: A, C, D, DS, ER, JCB, MC, V.

[symbols] SC

✓ ★ **DOVER BUDGET INN.** *1426 N Dupont Hwy (19901). 302/734-4433; FAX 302/734-4433.* 68 rms, 2 story. May-Sept: S $42-$50; D $47-$55; each addl $5; lower rates rest of yr. Crib free. TV; cable. Pool; lifeguard. Complimentary coffee in lobby. Restaurant opp 8 am-9 pm. Ck-out 11 am. Coin lndry. Sundries. Cr cds: A, C, D, DS, MC, V.

[symbols] SC

Motor Hotel

★★★ **SHERATON INN.** *1570 N Dupont Hwy (19901). 302/678-8500; FAX 302/678-9073; res: 800/544-5064.* E-mail sherdov@dmv.com; web www.sheratondover.com. 152 rms, 7 story. S, D $95; each addl $10; under 18 free. TV; cable. Indoor pool; whirlpool. Restaurant 6:30 am-10 pm. Rm serv to 10:30 pm. Bars 4 pm-1 am; entertainment exc Sun. Ck-out noon. Meeting rms. Business servs avail. In-rm modem link. Bellhops. Sundries. Exercise equipt. Cr cds: A, C, D, DS, MC, V.

[D] [symbols] SC

Restaurants

★★★ **BLUE COAT INN.** *800 N State St (19901). 302/674-1776.* Hrs: 11:30 am-9 pm; Fri to 10 pm; Sat 11:30 am-3 pm, 4:30-10 pm; Sun noon-9 pm. Closed Mon; Dec 25. Res accepted. Bar. Semi-a la carte: lunch $4.95-$11.95, dinner $8.95-$32.95. Child's meals. Specializes in fresh seafood, steak. Own baking. Entertainment Fri, Sat. Early American decor. Lake setting. Cr cds: A, C, D, DS, MC, V.

★★ **VILLAGE INN.** *DE 9 (19901), E on DE 8 to DE 9.* *302/734-3245.* Hrs: 11 am-2 pm, 4:30-10 pm; Sat 11 am-10 pm; Sun noon-9 pm. Closed Dec 25. Res accepted. Bar. Semi-a la carte: lunch $4.95-$9.95, dinner $12.95-$19.95. Specialties: stuffed flounder, prime rib. Colonial decor; fireplace, antiques. Cr cds: C, DS, MC, V.

Fenwick Island (E-10)

(See also Bethany Beach, Lewes, Rehoboth Beach; also see Ocean City, MD)

Pop 186 **Elev** 4 ft **Area Code** 302 **Zip** 19944 **E-mail** info@bethany-fenwick.org **Web** www.bethany-fenwick.org
Information Bethany-Fenwick Area Chamber of Commerce, Coastal Hwy/DE 1, PO Box 1450, Bethany Beach 19930; 302/539-2100 or 800/962-7873

Fenwick Island, at the southeast corner of Delaware, was named for Thomas Fenwick, a wealthy Virginia landowner who purchased the land in 1686. For a time, a dispute raged over whether Fenwick Island was part of Maryland or Pennsylvania. It ended in 1751, when the Transpeninsular Line placed Fenwick Island in Delaware. In 1775, James and Jacob Brasure, residents of the island, began extracting salt from the ocean, and until 1825, "salt making" was big business. In the latter part of the 19th century, Fenwick Island grew as a religious-oriented summer campground. After World War I, Fenwick Island became fashionable as a summer resort.

What to See and Do

Discoveries from the Sea. Contains changing exhibits of shipwreck artifacts recovered on the Delmarva Peninsula. (Memorial Day-Labor Day, daily; rest of yr, Sat, Sun) 708 Ocean Hwy. Phone 302/539-9366 or 888/743-5524. **Free**

Fenwick Island Lighthouse. Historic 87-foot-tall lighthouse; light was first turned on Aug 1, 1859. (June-Aug, 2 Wed afternoons per month; also by appt) W of town via DE 54. Phone 410/250-1098.

Fenwick Island State Park. This 208-acre seashore park is located between the Atlantic Ocean and Little Assawoman Bay. Surfing, swimming, bathhouse; surf fishing; sailing (rentals). Standard hrs, fees. 1 mi N on DE 1. Phone 302/539-9060 or 302/539-1055 (summer).

Annual Event

Surf-Fishing Tournaments. Phone 302/539-2100. 1st Sat May & Columbus Day wkend.

Motel

★ **ATLANTIC BUDGET INN.** *Ocean Hwy & Route 54 (19945). 302/539-7673; FAX 302/539-7673; res: 800/432-8038.* Web www.beach-net.com/lodgeatbudget. 48 rms, 1-2 story, 3 kit. units. Memorial Day, July 4-Labor Day (3-day min): S, D $90-$105; each addl $8; kit. units $105; lower rates mid-Apr-June, after Labor Day-Oct. Closed rest of yr. Crib $5. TV; cable. Pool; lifeguard. Complimentary coffee in lobby. Restaurant nearby. Ck-out 11 am. Refrigerators, microwaves. Beach 1 blk. Cr cds: A, C, D, DS, MC, V.

Restaurants

✓★★ **HARPOON HANNA'S.** *DE 54 At The Bay (19944). 302/539-3095.* Hrs: 11-1 am; Sun from 10 am; Sun brunch 10 am-3 pm. Bar. A la carte entrees: lunch $3.95-$7.95, dinner $7.95-$29.95. Sun

brunch $3.95-$7.95. Child's meals. Specializes in fresh seafood. Entertainment Fri, Sat. Outdoor dining. Casual, contemporary decor; fireplace. On waterfront. Cr cds: A, C, DS, MC, V.

★★ **TOM & TERRY'S.** *DE 54 At The Bay (19944). 302/436-4161.* Hrs: 11:30 am-10 pm; early-bird dinner 5-6 pm. Closed Dec 25. Bar. Semi-a la carte: lunch $6.95-$10.50, dinner $16.95-$22.95. Specializes in fresh local seafood, prime rib. View of Ocean City & bay. Cr cds: C, DS, MC, V.

D

Fort Delaware State Park (B-9)

(See also Newark, New Castle, Odessa, Wilmington)

(On Pea Patch Island, opposite Delaware City)

This grim gray fort was built as a coastal defense in 1860. The fort was used as a prisoner of war depot for three years, housing up to 12,500 Confederate prisoners at a time. The damp, low-lying terrain and the poor conditions encouraged epidemics, leading to some 2,400 deaths. The fort was modernized in 1896 and remained in commission until 1943.

Restoration of the site is a continuing process. Available are overlook of heronry, picnicking; living history programs. Museum has scale model of fort, model Civil War relics, orientation video. Special events throughout summer. Boat trip to island from Delaware City (mid-June-Labor Day, Wed-Sun; last wkend Apr-mid-June & Sept, Sat, Sun & hols). No pets. For further information contact the Park Superintendent, 45 Clinton St, PO Box 170, Delaware City 19706; 302/834-7941. Round trip ¢¢¢

Lewes (D-10)

(See also Bethany Beach, Fenwick Island, Rehoboth Beach)

Settled 1631 **Pop** 2,295 **Elev** 10 ft **Area Code** 302 **Zip** 19958 **E-mail** inquiry@leweschamber.com **Web** www.leweschamber.com
Information Chamber of Commerce, Fisher-Martin House, 120 Kings Hwy, PO Box 1; 302/645-8073

Lewes (LOO-is) has been home base to Delaware Bay pilots for 300 years. Weather-beaten, cypress-shingled houses still line the streets where privateers plundered and Captain Kidd bargained away his loot. The treacherous sandbars outside the harbor have claimed their share of ships, and stories of sunken treasure have circulated for centuries. Some buildings show scars from cannonballs that hit their mark when the British bombarded Lewes in the War of 1812. Traces of the original stockade were discovered in 1964.

What to See and Do

Cape Henlopen State Park. More than 3,000 acres at confluence of Delaware Bay and Atlantic Ocean; site of decommissioned Fort Miles, part of coastal defense system during World War II. Supervised swimming; fishing. Nature center, programs and trails. Picnicking, concession. Camping (water hookups, dump station). Standard hrs, fees. 1 mi E of ferry terminal on Cape Henlopen Dr. Phone 302/645-8983.

Lewes-Cape May, NJ, Ferry. Sole connection between US 13 (Ocean Hwy) on the Delmarva Peninsula and southern terminus of Garden State Pkwy (NJ). Trip across Delaware Bay (16 mi) takes 70 min. (Daily; 22 crossings in summer, 10 in winter, 14-18 in spring and fall) Phone 302/645-6313 or 800/643-3779 (reservations). Per person, one way ¢¢¢¢-¢¢¢¢¢

Restored buildings. Maintained by the Lewes Historical Society. Cannon Ball House and US Lifesaving Station have marine exhibits and lightship *Overfalls*. Other buildings open are Thompson country store, Plank House, Rabbit's Ferry House, Burton-Ingram House, Ellegood House, Hiram R. Burton House and old doctor's office. (June-Labor Day, Tues-Sat) Tickets at Rabbit's Ferry House. Walking tours and varied events take place during summer season. Phone 302/645-7670. Tour ¢¢

Zwaanendael Museum. Adaptation of Hoorn, Holland Town Hall was built in 1931 as memorial to original Dutch founders of Lewes (1631). Highlights the town's maritime heritage with colonial, Native American and Dutch exhibits. (Daily exc Mon; closed hols) Savannah Rd & Kings Hwy. Phone 302/645-1148.   **Free**

Annual Events

Great Delaware Kite Festival. Cape Henlopen State Park (see). Festival heralding the beginning of spring. Fri before Easter.

Zwaanendael Heritage Garden Tour. Visit hidden gardens of Lewes. Vendors. Phone 302/645-8073. 3rd Sat June.

Coast Day. University of Delaware Marine Studies Complex. Facilities and research vessel open to public; marine exhibits, research demonstrations, nautical films. Phone 302/645-4346. 1st Sun Oct.

Motels

★ **ANGLER'S MOTEL.** *110 Anglers Rd (19958), ½ blk NE of Canal Bridge.* 302/645-2831. E-mail anchor@dca.net. 25 rms, 1-2 story, 2 kits. Mid-May-mid-Sept (3-day min wknds, hols): S, D $70-$105; each addl $5; kit. units $85-$105; lower rates rest of yr. Closed Dec-Feb. Crib free. TV; cable. Pool. Restaurant nearby. Picnic tables, grills. Sun deck. Overlooks canal, marina opp. Boat docking. Cr cds: A, C, MC, V.

★ **BEACON MOTEL.** *514 E Savannah Rd (19958).* 302/645-4888; FAX 302/645-8138; res: 800/735-4888. E-mail bconmotl@dmv.com; web www.dmv.com/rehoboth. 66 rms, 3 story. Aug: S, D $105-$155; each addl $5; under 12 free; hol rates; lower rates rest of yr. Closed mid-Nov-Mar. Crib $5. TV; cable (premium). Complimentary coffee in lobby. Restaurant adj 6 am-6 pm. Ck-out 11 am. Meeting rms. Business servs avail. Bellhops. Pool. Refrigerators. Balconies. Cr cds: A, C, DS, MC, V.

Hotel

★★★ **NEW DEVON INN.** *142 2nd St (19958).* 302/645-6466; FAX 302/645-7196; res: 800/824-8754. E-mail newdevon@dca.net; web www.beach-net.com/newdevoninn. 26 rms, 4 story. Mid-June-mid-Oct: S, D $65-$130; suites $110-$170; package plans; lower rates rest of yr. Restaurant 11 am-10 pm. Ck-out 11 am. Business servs avail. Shopping arcade. Built 1926. Cr cds: A, C, D, DS, MC, V.

Inn

★★★ **INN AT CANAL SQUARE.** *122 Market St (19958).* 302/644-3377; FAX 302/644-6565; res: 888/644-1911. E-mail innatcanalsquare@ce.net; web www.lewis-beach.com/canalsquare.html. 19 rms, 4 story. Late June-Sept: D $155-$175; each addl $15; 2-bedrm houseboat avail; wkly rates; wknds (2-day min); lower rates rest of yr. Crib $15. TV; cable (premium). Complimentary continental bkfst. Restaurant nearby. Ck-out 11 am. Concierge serv. Meeting rm. Refrigerators avail. Balconies. On canal. Cr cds: A, C, D, DS, MC, V.

Restaurants

★ **ASHBY'S OYSTER HOUSE.** *24 Peddlers Vlg (19958), at Peddler's Village.* 302/945-4070. Hrs: 11:30-1 am; Sun from 9 am. Closed Thanksgiving, Dec 25. Bar. Semi-a la carte: lunch $3.95-$6.95, dinner $11.95-$19.95. Sun bkfst buffet $6.95. Child's meals. Specializes in seafood, raw bar. Casual dining. Cr cds: A, C, DS, MC, V.

★★ **GILLIGAN'S.** *134 Market St (19958), at Front St.* 302/645-7866. Hrs: 11 am-11 pm. Closed Nov-Mar. Bar. A la carte entrees: lunch $6.50-$10, dinner $13-$20. Wine list. Specializes in seafood, crab cakes, vegetarian dishes. Outside dining deck, waterfront bar. Part of exterior resembles the "good ship Minnow." View of harbor. Cr cds: A, C, DS, MC, V.

★★★ **KUPCHICK'S RESTAURANT.** *3 East Bay Ave (19958).* 302/645-0420. E-mail kupchicks@dmv.com. Hrs: 4:30-10 pm. Closed Easter, Thanksgiving, Dec 25. Res accepted; required summer wknds. Continental menu. Bar. A la carte entrees: dinner $11.95-$23.95. Child's meals. Specializes in fresh seafood, Angus beef. Jazz Fri, Sat. Victorian atmosphere. Original art, antiques. Cr cds: A, C, D, DS, MC, V.

★ **LIGHTHOUSE.** *Savannah Rd At Anglers Rd (19958), just over the drawbridge.* 302/645-6271. Hrs: 6 am-10 pm; Sept-Mar 7 am-9 pm. Closed Thanksgiving, Dec 24, 25. Bar from 11 am. Semi-a la carte: bkfst $3.75-$6.95, lunch $3.25-$12.95, dinner $12.95-$17.95. Child's meals. Specializes in fresh seafood. Entertainment wknds. Outdoor dining. Overlooks Lewes Harbor. Cr cds: C, MC, V.

Newark (A-9)

(See also New Castle, Wilmington)

Settled 1685 **Pop** 25,098 **Elev** 124 ft **Area Code** 302
Information Greater Wilmington Convention & Visitors Bureau-Visitors Center, 100 W 10th St, Wilmington 19801; 302/652-4088

Newark grew up at the crossroads of two well-traveled Native American trails. The site of the only Revolutionary battle on Delaware soil is at nearby Cooch's Bridge, southeast of Newark. According to tradition, Betsy Ross's flag was first raised in battle at Cooch's Bridge on September 3, 1777.

What to See and Do

University of Delaware (1743). (18,000 students) Founded as a small private academy; stately elm trees, fine lawns and Georgian-style brick buildings adorn the central campus. Tours from Visitors Center, 196 S College Ave (Mon-Fri, also Sat mornings). Phone 302/831-8123. On campus is

University of Delaware Mineral Collection. Also fossil exhibit. Penny Hall, Academy St. (Mon-Fri, by appt only; closed hols) Phone 302/831-2569.   **Free**

White Clay Creek State Park. A 1,483-acre day park with farmlands, forest and streams. Fishing. Nature, fitness trails. Picnicking. Standard hrs, fees. 3 mi NW via DE 896. Phone 302/368-6900.

Motels

★★ **BEST WESTERN.** *260 Chapman Rd (19702), at I-95.* 302/738-3400; FAX 302/738-3414; res: 800/633-3203. 99 rms, 2 story. S $55-$65; D $60-$75; each addl $5; under 18 free; wkend rates. Crib free. TV; cable. Pool. Restaurant 5-9 pm. Rm serv. Bar 4 pm-1 am. Ck-out noon. Meeting rms. Business servs avail. Sundries. Cr cds: A, C, D, DS, MC, V.

✓★★ **COMFORT INN.** *1120 S College Ave (19713), Exit 1- I95 to DE 896 N. 302/368-8715; FAX 302/368-6454; res: 800/228-5150.* 102 rms, 2 story. S $50-$54; D $56-$60; each addl $6; under 18 free. Crib free. Pet accepted. TV; cable, VCR avail (movies). Pool; lifeguard. Complimentary continental bkfst. Ck-out 11 am. Meeting rm. Business servs avail. In-rm modem link. Some refrigerators. Cr cds: A, C, D, DS, JCB, MC, V.

⊡ 🐾 ⇌ ⋈ 🔥 SC

★★ **HOLIDAY INN.** *1203 Christiana Rd (19713). 302/737-2700; FAX 302/737-3214; res: 800/465-4329.* 144 rms, 2 story. S $71-$81; D $77-$87; each addl $6; under 18 free. Crib free. TV; cable. Pool; lifeguard. Restaurant 6:30 am-10 pm. Rm serv. Bar noon-1 am. Ck-out noon. Coin lndry. Meeting rms. Business servs avail. In-rm modem link. Valet serv. Sundries. Cr cds: A, C, D, DS, JCB, MC, V.

⊡ ⇌ ⋈ 🔥 SC

★★ **HOWARD JOHNSON HOTEL & SUITES.** *1119 S College Ave (19713). 302/368-8521; FAX 302/368-9868; res: 800/654-2000.* 142 rms, 2 story. S, D $55; each addl $10; under 18 free. Crib free. Pet accepted. TV; cable. Pool. Complimentary continental bkfst. Ck-out noon. Meeting rms. Business servs avail. In-rm modem link. Valet serv. Health club privileges. Private patios, balconies. Cr cds: A, C, D, DS, ER, JCB, MC, V.

⊡ 🐾 ⇌ ⋈ 🔥 SC

✓★ **MCINTOSH INN.** *100 McIntosh Plz (19713). 302/453-9100; FAX 302/453-9114; res: 800/444-2775.* 108 rms. S $41.95; D $46.95; each addl $5. Crib free. TV. Restaurant adj open 24 hrs. Ck-out 11 am. Some refrigerators. Cr cds: A, C, D, MC, V.

⊡ ⋈ 🔥 SC

Hotel

★★★ **BRANDYWINE VALLEY COUNTRY ESTATE.** *100 Continental Dr (19713), I-95 exit 4B (Stanton). 302/454-1500; FAX 302/454-0233; res: 800/348-3133.* 266 rms, 4 story. S, D $99-$199; each addl $10; suites $185-$325; family plans; higher rates univ graduation. Crib free. TV; cable. Heated pool; whirlpool, poolside serv, lifeguard. Restaurant 6:30 am-10 pm. Bar 11-1 am. Ck-out 11:30 am. Meeting rms. Business center. In-rm modem link. Concierge. RR station transportation. Tennis privileges. Golf privileges. Exercise equipt. Luxury level. Cr cds: A, C, D, DS, ER, JCB, MC, V.

⊡ 🁢 ⮌ ⇌ 🚶 🎿 ⋈ 🔥 SC 🏃

Restaurant

✓★ **KLONDIKE KATE'S.** *158 E Main St. 302/737-6100.* Hrs: 11-1 am; Sun from 10 am. Closed Thanksgiving, Dec 25. Southwestern menu. Bar. Semi-a la carte: lunch, dinner $4.95-$12.95. Child's meals. Specializes in fresh seafood, Tex-Mex dishes. Outdoor dining. In former courthouse/jail. Cr cds: A, C, DS, MC, V.

New Castle (A-9)

(See also Newark, Wilmington)

Settled 1651 **Pop** 4,837 **Elev** 19 ft **Area Code** 302 **Zip** 19720
Information Mayor and Council of New Castle, 220 Delaware St; 302/322-9801

New Castle—meeting place of the colonial assemblies, first capital of the state and an early center of culture and communication—was one of Delaware's first settlements. Its fine harbor made it a busy port in the 18th century until its commerce was taken over by Wilmington, which is closer to Philadelphia. Today, New Castle is a historian's and architect's delight—charming, mellow and relaxed. Three signers of the Declaration of Inde-

pendence made their homes here: George Read, Thomas McKean and George Ross, Jr (considered a Pennsylvanian by some). New Castle lies at the foot of the Delaware Memorial Bridge, which connects with the southern end of the New Jersey Turnpike.

What to See and Do

Amstel House Museum (1730). Restored brick mansion of seventh governor of Delaware; an earlier structure was incorporated into the service wing. Houses colonial furnishings and arts; complete colonial kitchen. (Mar-Dec, daily exc Mon; rest of yr, Sat & Sun; closed major hols) Combination ticket avail with Old Dutch House. 2 E 4th St at Delaware St. Phone 302/322-2794. ¢

George Read II House (1804). Federal-style house with elegant interiors: gilded fanlights; silver door hardware; carved woodwork; relief plasterwork. Furnished with period antiques; garden design dates from 1847. (Mar-Dec, daily exc Mon; rest of yr, Sat & Sun) 42 The Strand. Phone 302/322-8411. ¢¢

Old Dutch House (late 17th century). Thought to be Delaware's oldest dwelling in its original form; Dutch colonial furnishings; decorative arts. (Mar-Dec, daily exc Mon; rest of yr, Sat & Sun; closed major hols) Combination ticket avail with Amstel House Museum. 32 E 3rd St. Phone 302/322-2794. ¢

Old Library Museum (1892). Unusual semi-octagonal Victorian building houses temporary exhibits relating to area. (Sat-Sun) 40 E 3rd St. Phone 302/322-2794. **Free**

Old New Castle Court House (1732). Original colonial capitol and oldest surviving courthouse in the state; furnishings and exhibits on display; cupola is the center of a 12-mi circle that delineates Delaware-Pennsylvania border. (Daily exc Mon; closed hols) 211 Delaware St, on The Green. Phone 302/323-4453. **Free**

The Green. Laid out by direction of Peter Stuyvesant, this public square of the old town is surrounded by dozens of historically important buildings. Delaware & 3rd Sts.

Annual Event

Separation Day. Battery Park. Observance of Delaware's declaration of independence from Great Britain. Regatta, shows, bands, concerts, fireworks. June.

Seasonal Event

Band concerts. Battery Park. Wed evenings, June-early Aug.

Motels

★★ **RAMADA INN.** *I-295 & Rte 13 (19971), Manor Branch, 1 mi S of DE Memorial Bridge at jct US 13, I-295. 302/658-8511; FAX 302/658-3071.* 131 rms, 2 story. S $75-$81; D $78-$84; each addl $10; under 18 free. Crib free. TV; cable. Pool; poolside serv, lifeguard. Restaurant 7 am-10 pm. Rm serv. Bar 4:30 pm-midnight. Ck-out noon. Meeting rms. Business servs avail. In-rm modem link. Valet serv. Sundries. RR station, bus depot transportation. Cr cds: A, C, D, DS, MC, V.

⊡ ⇌ ⋈ 🔥 SC

✓★ **RODEWAY INN.** *111 S Dupont Hwy (19720). 302/328-6246; FAX 302/328-9493; res: 800/228-2000.* 40 rms. S $49-$59; D $55-$69; each addl $5; under 18 free. Crib $5. Pet accepted. TV; cable. Complimentary continental bkfst. Restaurant adj 11 am-10 pm. Ck-out noon. Business servs avail. Some refrigerators, microwaves. Cr cds: A, C, D, DS, MC, V.

🐾 ⋈ 🔥 SC

Restaurants

★★ **AIR TRANSPORT COMMAND.** *143 N Du Pont Hwy US 13 (19720). 302/328-3527.* Hrs: 11 am-4 pm, 5-11 pm; Fri to midnight; Sat 4:30-midnight; Sun 4-10 pm; Sun brunch 10 am-3 pm. Res accepted; required Sat. Bar to 1 am. Semi-a la carte: lunch $4.50-$8.95, dinner

$9.95-$23.95. Sun brunch $14.95. Child's meals. Specialty: prime rib. Outdoor dining. Replica of WWII-era Scottish farmhouse; war memorabilia. Overlooks airfield. Cr cds: A, C, D, DS, MC, V.

★★ **ARSENAL ON THE GREEN.** *30 Market St (19720), in historic district.* 302/328-1290. Hrs: 11:30 am-2:30 pm, 5-9 pm; Sun 1-8 pm. Closed Mon. Res accepted. Semi-a la carte: lunch $4.75-$13.95, dinner $11.95-$28.95. Specialties: Delaware crab cakes, crab imperial. Building constructed in 1809 by the Federal government; originally used as arsenal. Colonial decor. Cr cds: C, MC, V.

D

★★★ **LYNNHAVEN INN.** *154 N Du Pont Hwy US 13/40/30 (19720).* 302/328-2041. Hrs: 11:30 am-9:30 pm; Sat 4-10 pm; Sun 1-9 pm. Closed Dec 24-25. Res accepted. Bar. Semi-a la carte: lunch $4.95-$11.95, dinner $10.95-$25.95. Child's meals. Specialties: imperial crab, prime rib. Early American decor. Cr cds: A, C, D, DS, MC, V.

Odessa (B-9)

(See also New Castle, Smyrna, Wilmington)

Settled 1721 **Pop** 303 **Elev** 50 ft **Area Code** 302 **Zip** 19730

Once a prosperous grain-shipping center, Odessa tried to protect its shipping trade by haughtily telling the Delaware Railroad, in 1855, to lay its tracks elsewhere. To glorify itself that same year, the town changed its name from Cantwell's Bridge to that of the Russian grain port on the Black Sea. But the sloops and schooners that transported grain eventually found less shortsighted ports of call. Odessa was an important station on the Underground Railroad for many years before the Civil War. Now it is a crossroads town, at the junction of US 13 and DE 299. The town exhibits numerous fine examples of 18th- and 19th-century domestic architecture.

What to See and Do

Fort Delaware State Park (see). Approx 9 mi NE on Pea Patch Island, opposite Delaware City.

Historic Houses of Odessa. For full tour of houses, arrive by 2 pm. (Daily exc Mon; closed major hols; also Jan-Feb) Individual house tickets available. Main St. Phone 302/378-4069. Combination ticket ¢¢¢

Corbit-Sharp House (1774). Georgian house built by William Corbit, Odessa's leading citizen, was lived in by his family for 150 yrs. Restored and furnished with many family pieces, the interior reflects period from 1774-1818. Maintained by Winterthur Museum, Garden and Library (see WILMINGTON).

Wilson-Warner House (1769). Handsome red-brick Georgian house, with L-shape plan typical of early Delaware architecture, is accurately furnished to portray life in early 19th century. Maintained by Winterthur Museum, Garden and Library (see WILMINGTON).

Brick Hotel Gallery and Manney Collection of Belter Furniture. Federal-style, 19th-century building was a hotel and tavern for nearly a century. Gallery houses the largest private collection of Belter furniture in existence. Very high-styled Victorian furniture, Belter parlor and bedroom suites, made in New York in the mid-19th century, were famous for craftsmanship, particularly elaborate carvings. ¢¢

Lums Pond State Park. More than 1,800-acre park centered around 200-acre pond. Supervised swimming; fishing; boating (rentals). Hiking and fitness trails, game courts. Picnicking. Camping (showers, dump station; Apr-Oct). Standard hrs, fees. Approx 3 mi W on DE 299 to Middletown, then 8 mi N on US 301 & DE 71. Phone 302/368-6989. Per vehicle ¢¢

Rehoboth Beach (D-10)

(See also Bethany Beach, Fenwick Island, Lewes)

Settled 1872 **Pop** 1,234 **Elev** 16 ft **Area Code** 302 **Zip** 19971 **E-mail** rehoboth@beach-fun.com **Web** www.beach-fun.com

Information Rehoboth Beach-Dewey Beach Chamber of Commerce, 501 Rehoboth Ave, PO Box 216; 302/227-2233 or 800/441-1329

The "nation's summer capital" got its nickname by being a favorite with Washington diplomats and legislators. A two-and-one-half-hour drive from Washington, DC, the largest summer resort in Delaware began as a spot for camp meetings amid sweet-smelling pine groves. In the 1920s, real estate boomed, triggering Rehoboth Beach's rebirth as a resort town with a variety of accommodations, shopping areas and eateries. Deep-sea and freshwater fishing, sailing, swimming, biking and strolling along cherry tree-lined Rehoboth Avenue have kept it a favorite retreat from Washington's summer heat.

What to See and Do

Delaware Seashore State Park. Seven-mi strip of land separates Rehoboth and Indian River Bays from the Atlantic. Bay and ocean swimming, fishing, surfing and boating (marina, launch, rentals). Picnicking, concession. Primitive and improved campsites (hookups). Standard hrs, fees. 6 mi S on Rte 1. Phone 302/227-2800.

Annual Event

Sea Witch Halloween and Fiddlers' Festival. Phone 800/441-1329, ext 11. Late Oct.

Seasonal Event

Bandstand concerts. Bandstand, Rehoboth Ave. Open-air concerts. Sat and Sun evenings, Memorial Day-Labor Day.

Motels

★★ **ADAMS OCEANFRONT VILLAS.** *4 Read St (19720), 1 mi S on DE 1.* 302/227-3030; FAX 302/227-1034; res: 800/448-8080. 23 rms, 3 story, 12 villas. No elvtr. Late June-Aug: S, D $95-$115; each addl $6; villas (up to 7) $250-$295 (3-day min); lower rates mid-Mar-late June, Sept-Oct. Closed rest of yr. Crib $6. TV; cable (premium). Pool. Complimentary continental bkfst. Ck-out 11 am; villas 10 am. Refrigerators; microwaves avail. Picnic tables, grills; some balconies. On beachfront. Cr cds: C, MC, V.

★★ **ADMIRAL MOTEL.** *2 Baltimore Ave (19971).* 302/227-2103; FAX 302/227-3620; res: 888/882-4188. E-mail admiral@beach.net. 73 rms, 5 story. June-Labor Day: S, D $110-$199; each addl $10; suites $155-$245; wkend rates; 3-day min stay in season; lower rates rest of yr. TV; cable. Indoor pool; whirlpool. Complimentary coffee in lobby. Restaurant adj 7 am-9 pm. Gift shop. Refrigerators; some in-rm whirlpools. Cr cds: A, C, DS, MC, V.

✓★ **ATLANTIC VIEW MOTEL.** *2 Clayton St (19971), 1 mi S on DE 1.* 302/227-3878; FAX 302/226-2640; res: 800/777-4162. 35 rms, 4 story. No elvtr. Mid-June-Labor Day (2-4-day min): S, D $99-$169; each addl $7; lower rates Apr-mid-June, after Labor Day-mid-Oct. Closed rest of yr. Crib $5. TV; cable (premium). Pool. Complimentary coffee in lobby. Restaurant nearby. Ck-out 11 am. Coin lndry. Refrigerators. Balconies. Cr cds: A, C, DS, MC, V.

★ **BAY RESORT MOTEL.** *126 Bellevue St (19971).* *302/227-6400; FAX 302/227-5800; res: 800/922-9240.* Web www.dol.net/ bayresort. 68 kit. units, 3 story. July-Labor Day: D $119-$199; each addl $10; under 12 free; wkend, wkly rates; lower rates Apr-June & Sept-Oct. Closed rest of yr. Crib $10. TV; cable (premium). Pool. Complimentary continental bkfst. Ck-out 11 am. Coin lndry. Some private patios, balconies. Cr cds: C, DS, MC, V.

🐾 🏊 🏋 🔥

★★ **BEACH VIEW MOTEL.** *6 Wilmington Ave (19971).* *302/227-2999; FAX 302/226-2640; res: 800/288-5962.* 38 rms, 4 story. Mid-June-early Sept: D $80-$155; each addl $7; under 7 free; lower rates Apr-mid-June, early Sept-Nov. Closed rest of yr. Crib $5. TV; cable (premium). Pool. Complimentary continental bkfst. Restaurant adj 8 am-11 pm. Ck-out 11 am. Coin lndry. Refrigerators. Some balconies. Cr cds: A, C, DS, MC, V.

🏊 🏋 🔥

★★ **BEST WESTERN GOLDEN LEAF.** *1400 Hwy One (19971), 2 mi S on DE 1.* *302/226-1100; FAX 302/226-9785; res: 800/528-1234; res: 800/422-8566.* Web www.ravenet.com/goldleaf. 75 rms, 4 story. Mid-June-Aug: S, D $149-$189; each addl $10; under 12 free; lower rates rest of yr. Crib $10. TV; cable (premium). Pool. Complimentary continental bkfst. Restaurant opp 8 am-9 pm. Ck-out 11 am. Coin lndry. Meeting rms. Business servs avail. Covered parking. Refrigerators, microwaves. Balconies. Ocean ½ blk; swimming beach. Cr cds: A, C, D, DS, ER, JCB, MC, V.

D 🏊 🏋 🔥 SC

★★ **DINNER BELL INN.** *2 Christian St (19971), off Rehoboth Ave.* *302/227-2561; FAX 302/227-0323.* E-mail bell@ce.net; web www.dmv.com/dinnerbellinn. 28 rms, 2 story, 4 kit. units, 1 cottage. Late June-Aug: D $85-$175; each addl $15; kit. units $150-$210; cottage $250; under 12 free; lower rates Apr-mid-June & late Sept. Closed Jan-Feb. Crib $15. TV; cable (premium). Complimentary continental bkfst. Restaurant 4-10 pm. Bar. Ck-out 11 am. Meeting rm. Business servs avail. Individually decorated rms. Ocean 2 blks. Cr cds: A, C, MC, V.

🏋 🔥

✓ ★ **ECONO LODGE.** *4361 Hwy 1 (19971).* *302/227-0500; FAX 302/227-2170; res: 800/645-5690.* 79 rms, 3 story. June-Sept: S, D $85-$135; each addl $10; under 16 free; lower rates rest of yr. Crib free. TV; cable (premium). Pool; lifeguard. Complimentary coffee in lobby. Restaurant nearby. Ck-out 11 am. Coin lndry. Business servs avail. Some refrigerators. Microwaves avail. Lawn games. Balconies. Cr cds: A, C, D, DS, ER, JCB, MC, V.

D 🏊 🏋 🔥 MC SC

★★ **OCEANUS MOTEL.** *6 Second Street (19803).* *302/227-8200; res: 800/852-5011.* Web www.oceanusmotel.com. 38 rms, 3 story. No elvtr. July-Aug: D $129-$169; each addl $10; under 12 free; wkly rates; lower rates Apr-June, Sept-Oct. Closed rest of yr. Crib $7. TV; cable (premium). Pool; lifeguard. Complimentary continental bkfst. Restaurant opp 8-2 am. Ck-out noon. Coin lndry. Refrigerators. Microwaves avail. Cr cds: C, DS, MC, V.

🏊 🏋 🔥

★★ **SANDCASTLE MOTEL.** *123 2nd St (19971).* *302/227-0400; FAX 302/226-9288; res: 800/372-2112.* Web www.washingtonpost.com/ yp/sandcastle. 60 rms, 3 story. July-Labor Day: S, D $100-$130; each addl $10; under 12 free; lower rates Mar-July & Labor Day-Dec. Closed rest of yr. Crib $10. TV; cable. Indoor pool. Sauna. Complimentary coffee in lobby. Ck-out 11 am. Refrigerators. Microwaves avail; $5/day. Balconies. Cr cds: A, C, DS, MC, V.

D 🏊 🏋 🔥

★ **SEAESTA MOTEL III.** *1409 Hwy One (19971), 2 mi S on DE 1, at Rodney Ave.* *302/227-4343; FAX 302/227-3049; res: 800/436-6591.* Web www.seaesta.com. 33 kit. units, 3 story. July-Aug: S, D $100-$150; each addl $10; under 12 free; lower rates rest of yr. Pet accepted; $5/day. TV; cable (premium). Complimentary coffee in lobby. Restaurant

nearby. Ck-out 11 am. Covered parking. Balconies. Ocean 1 blk; swimming beach. Cr cds: A, C, D, DS, MC, V.

D 🐾 🏋 🔥 SC

★ **THE ATLANTIC BUDGET INN.** *154 Rehoboth Ave (19971).* *302/227-9446; FAX 302/227-9446; res: 800/245-2112.* 97 rms, 1-4 story, 10 kits. Mid-July-late Aug, hol wkends: D $69-$159; each addl $10; kits. $109-$179; under 11 free; lower rates rest of yr. Crib $6. TV; cable, VCR avail (movies). Pool. Complimentary coffee. Restaurant nearby. Ck-out 11 am. Coin lndry. Some refrigerators, microwaves. Cr cds: A, C, D, DS, MC, V.

🏊 🏋 🔥

Motor Hotels

★ **BRIGHTON SUITES HOTELS.** *34 Wilmington Ave (19971).* *302/227-5780; FAX 302/227-6815; res: 800/227-5788.* Web brighton.brightonsuites.com. 66 suites, 4 story. July-Aug: suites $189-$239; each addl $10; under 16 free; mid-wk rates; package plans; lower rates rest of yr. Crib $6. TV; cable (premium). Heated pool. Coffee in rms. Restaurant opp 11 am-9 pm. Ck-out 11 am. Meeting rms. Business servs avail. Bellhops in season. Garage parking. Exercise equipt. Refrigerators, wet bars; microwaves avail. Cr cds: A, C, D, DS, MC, V.

🏊 🏋 🏋 🔥 SC

★★ **HENLOPEN HOTEL INC.** *511 N Boardwalk (19971).* *302/227-2551; FAX 302/227-8147; res: 800/441-8450.* Web www.henlo penhotel.com. 93 rms, 8 story. July-Aug (2-day min wkends, hols): S, D $179-$279; each addl $10; under 16 free; varied lower rates Apr-May & Sept-Oct. Closed Jan-Mar 15. Crib free. TV; cable. Coffee in rms. Restaurant 8-11 am, 5-10 pm. Ck-out 11 am. Meeting rms. Business servs avail. Some refrigerators. Balconies. On beach; ocean views. Cr cds: A, C, D, DS, MC, V.

🏋 🔥

Hotel

★★★ **BOARDWALK PLAZA HOTEL.** *2 Olive Ave (19971).* *302/227-7169; FAX 302/227-0561; res: 800/332-3224.* Web www.board walkplazahotel.com. 84 units, 4 story, 45 suites, 6 kit. units. Memorial Day-Labor Day: S, D $135-$300; each addl $20; suites $245-$395; kit. units $1,800-$3,000/wk (Memorial Day-Labor Day 1-wk min); under 6 free; lower rates rest of yr. Crib free. TV; cable, VCR avail (movies). Indoor/outdoor pool; poolside serv. Complimentary coffee in rms. Restaurant 7 am-10 pm. Rm serv. Ck-out 11 am. Meeting rms. Business servs avail. In-rm modem link. Exercise equipt. Minibars; microwaves avail. Some balconies. On beach; ocean swimming. Victorian decor & architectural detail in modern structure; antiques, period furnishings; glass-encased oceanview elvtr; rooftop sun deck. Luxury level. Cr cds: A, C, D, DS, MC, V.

D 🏊 🏋 🏋 🔥 SC

Inn

★★★ **CHESAPEAKE LANDING.** *101 Chesapeake St (19971).* *302/227-2973; FAX 302/227-0301.* E-mail chesland4@aol.com; web www.atbeach.com/lodging/de/bnb/chesland. 4 rms, 3 with shower only, 3 story. No rm phones. May-Oct: S, D $95-$225; wkends, hols (2-3 day min); lower rates rest of yr. Children over 16 yrs only. TV in common rm; cable, VCR avail (movies). Complimentary full bkfst; afternoon refreshments. Ck-out noon, ck-in 2 pm. In-rm modem link. Luggage handling. Valet serv. Health club privileges. Heated pool. Antiques. Totally nonsmoking. Cr cds: C, MC, V.

🐾 🏊 🏋 🔥

Restaurants

★★ **BLUE MOON.** *35 Baltimore Ave (19971). 302/227-6515.* Hrs: 6-11 pm; Sun brunch noon-3 pm. Closed Jan. Res accepted. Bar 4 pm-1 am. Semi-a la carte: dinner $9-$26. Sun brunch $6.25-$9.50. Specializes in fresh seafood, vegetarian dishes. Outdoor dining. Cr cds: A, C, D, DS, MC, V.

★★★ **CHEZ LA MER.** *210 2nd St (19971). 302/227-6494.* E-mail chezlamer@aol.com. Hrs: 5:30-10 pm; Fri, Sat to 10:30 pm. Closed Mon-Wed off season; Thanksgiving; also Dec-Mar. Res accepted. Continental menu. Bar to 1 am. Semi-a la carte: dinner $16-$23. Child's meals. Specializes in fresh seafood, veal. Outdoor dining. Restored house with French provincial decor. Sun porch. Cr cds: A, C, D, DS, MC, V.

★★ **DINARDO'S BY THE SEA.** *330 Rehoboth Ave (19971), at State Rd. 302/227-7451.* Hrs: 11:30 am-10 pm; Fri-Sun to 11 pm. Res accepted. Bar. Semi-a la carte: lunch $4-$12, dinner $12-$22. Dinner buffet (Fri, Sat): $22.95. Child's meals. Specializes in seafood, prime rib, crabs. Parking. Cr cds: A, C, D, DS, MC, V.

★★★ **GARDEN GOURMET.** *4121 DE 1 (19971). 302/227-4747.* Hrs: 5 pm-1 am. Closed Jan, Feb. Res accepted. American-Contemporary menu. Bar. Wine list. Semi-a la carte: dinner $18-$25. Complete meals: dinner $38-$45. Specializes in fresh local seafood, veal, vegetarian specials. Parking. Renovated farm homestead (1898). Totally nonsmoking. Cr cds: C, DS, MC, V.

★ **IRISH EYES.** *15 Wilmington Ave (19971). 302/227-2888.* Hrs: 5 pm-1 am; Sat, Sun from noon. Closed Thanksgiving; also 3 wks Dec. Bar to 1 am. Semi-a la carte: lunch $4.75-$9.25, dinner $8.75-$19 (cover charge $5 during comedy club). Child's meals. Specializes in overstuffed sandwiches, steak, seafood. Irish music in season. Irish pub atmosphere. Cr cds: C, MC, V.

★★ **LA LA LAND.** *22 Wilmington Ave (19971). 302/227-3887.* Hrs: 6-11 pm. Closed Nov-mid-Apr. Res accepted. Bar 6 pm-1 am. A la carte entrees: dinner $19-$27. Specialty: rack of lamb. Outdoor dining. Artistic atmosphere; hand-painted walls & chairs; bamboo garden. Cr cds: A, C, DS, MC, V.

★★ **LAMP POST RESTAURANT.** *4534 Highway One (19971). 302/645-9132.* Hrs: 7 am-9:30 pm; Fri, Sat to 10 pm. Closed Thanksgiving, Dec 25. Bar. Semi-a la carte: bkfst $3.50-$9.50, lunch $3.50-$12, dinner $8.95-$25. Child's meals. Specializes in fresh seafood, steak. Parking. Cr cds: A, C, DS, MC, V.

★★ **RUSTY RUDDER.** *113 Dickinson St, Dewey Beach (19971), 2 mi S on DE 1. 302/227-3888.* E-mail rudder@dmv.com; web www.dmv.com/rustyrudder. Hrs: 11:30 am-9 pm, Fri, Sat to 10 pm; Memorial Day-Labor Day to 11 pm; Sun to 9 pm; Sun brunch 10 am-2 pm. Bar to 1 am. Semi-a la carte: lunch $5.95-$8.95, dinner $14.95-$25.95. Sun brunch $11.95. Child's meals. Specializes in prime rib, seafood. Salad bar. Entertainment. Parking. Outdoor dining. Nautical decor; on bay. Cr cds: A, C, D, DS, MC, V.

★★ **SYDNEY'S SIDE STREET.** *25 Christian St (19971). 302/227-1339.* E-mail syds-blues@aol.com. Hrs: 4 pm-1 am. Closed Thanksgiving, Dec 25; hrs vary Nov-Apr. Res accepted. Bar. Semi-a la carte: dinner $9.50-$19.50. Specializes in New Orleans cuisine. Own desserts. Blues, jazz evenings. Outdoor dining. Restored old schoolhouse. Cr cds: A, C, D, DS, MC, V.

✓★ **TIJUANA TAXI.** *207 Rehoboth Ave (19971). 302/227-1986.* Hrs: 5-11 pm; Fri, Sat noon-midnight; Sun noon-11 pm. Closed Super Bowl Sun, Dec 25. Mexican menu. Bar. Semi-a la carte: lunch, din-

ner $9-$12. Specializes in chili, nachos, vegetarian dishes. Street parking. Mexican cantina atmosphere. Cr cds: C, MC, V.

Smyrna (B-9)

(See also Dover, Odessa)

Founded 1768 **Pop** 5,231 **Elev** 36 ft **Area Code** 302 **Zip** 19977
Information Chamber of Commerce, PO Box 576, Dover 19903; phone; 302/653-9291; or visit the Smyrna Visitors Center, 5500 Du Pont Hwy; phone 302/653-8910

Named in 1806 for the chief seaport of Turkish Asia Minor, Smyrna in the 1850s was an active shipping center for produce grown in central Delaware.

What to See and Do

Bombay Hook National Wildlife Refuge. Annual fall and spring resting and feeding spot for migratory waterfowl, including a variety of ducks and tens of thousands of snow geese and Canada geese; also home for bald eagles, shorebirds, deer, fox and muskrat. Auto tour route (12 mi), wildlife foot trails, observation towers; visitor center offering interpretive and environmental education programs. (Spring and fall, daily, summer and winter, Mon-Fri) Golden Eagle, Golden Age and Golden Access passports accepted (see MAKING THE MOST OF YOUR TRIP). 5 mi E on DE 6, then 3 mi S on DE 9. Phone 302/653-6872. Per vehicle ¢¢

Smyrna Museum. Furnishings and memorabilia from early Federal to late Victorian periods; restored 18th-century plank house on premises; changing exhibits. (Sat, limited hrs; call for appt Sun-Fri) 11 S Main St. Phone 302/653-8844 or 302/653-9502. **Free**

Restaurants

★★ **THOMAS ENGLAND HOUSE.** *1165 S Du Pont Blvd. (US 13) (19977). 302/653-1420.* Hrs: 4-10 pm; wkends to 11 pm; early-bird dinner to 7 pm. Res accepted; required Sat. Continental menu. Bar. Semi-a la carte: dinner $9.95-$29.95. Child's meals. Specializes in fresh seafood, prime rib. Colonial building that housed troops during Revolutionary War and was a stop on Underground Railroad. Cr cds: C, MC, V.

SC

✓★ **WAYSIDE INN.** *130 N Dupont Blvd (19977), at Mt Vernon, 1 blk S of DE 300. 302/653-8047.* Hrs: 11 am-9 pm; Sun to 8 pm. Res accepted. Semi-a la carte: lunch $4.25-$8.50, dinner $10.95-$22.50. Child's meals. Specializes in seafood, prime rib. Cr cds: A, C, D, DS, MC, V.

Wilmington (A-9)

(In PA see also Chester, Kennett Square, Philadelphia)

Settled 1638 **Pop** 71,529 **Elev** 120 ft **Area Code** 302
Information Greater Wilmington Convention & Visitors Bureau, 100 W 10th St, 19801; 302/652-4088

Wilmington, the "chemical capital of the world," international hub of industry and shipping, is the largest city in Delaware. The Swedish, Dutch and British have all left their mark on the city. The first settlement was made by Swedes seeking their fortunes; they founded the colony of New Sweden. In 1655 the little colony was taken without bloodshed by Dutch soldiers under Peter Stuyvesant, governor of New Amsterdam. Nine years later the English became entrenched in the town, which grew under the influence of wealthy Quakers as a market and shipping center. Abundant water power in creeks of the Brandywine River Valley, plus accessibility to other eastern ports, stimulated early industrial growth. When Eleuthère du Pont built his powder mill on Brandywine Creek in 1802, the valley had already known a century of industry. From here come vulcanized fiber, glazed leathers, dyed cotton, rubber hose, autos and many other products.

What to See and Do

Amtrak Station. Victorian railroad station, which continues to function as such, designed by master architect Frank Furness. Restored. (Daily) Martin Luther King Blvd & French St.

Banning Park. Fishing. Tennis, playing fields. Picnicking; pavilions. (Daily) 2 mi S on DE 4. Middleboro Rd & Maryland Ave. Phone 302/571-4250. **Free**

Bellevue State Park. Fishing. Nature, fitness trails, bicycling, horseback riding trails; tennis, game courts. Picnicking (pavilions). Standard hrs, fees. 4 mi NE via I-95, Marsh Rd exit. Phone 302/577-3390.

Brandywine Creek State Park. A 1,000-acre day-use park. Fishing. Nature and fitness trails. Cross-country skiing. Picnicking. Nature center. Standard hrs, fees. 4 mi N on DE 100. Phone 302/577-3534.

Brandywine Springs Park. Site of a once-famous resort hotel (1827-1845) for southern planters and politicos. Here, Lafayette met Washington under the Council Oak before the Battle of Brandywine in 1777. Picnicking, fireplaces, pavilions, baseball fields. Pets on leash only. (Daily) 4 mi W on DE 41, 3300 Faulkland Rd. Phone 302/577-3534. **Free**

Brandywine Zoo and Park. Designed by Frederick Law Olmsted, the park includes Josephine Garden with fountain and roses; stands of Japanese cherry trees. The zoo, along North Park Dr, features animals from North and South America (daily). Picnicking; playgrounds. On both sides of Brandywine River, from Augustine to Market St bridges. Phone 302/571-7747. Zoo ¢¢; Nov-Mar **Free**

Delaware Art Museum. Expanded facility features Howard Pyle Collection of American illustrations, with works by Pyle, N. C. Wyeth and Maxfield Parrish; American painting collection, with works by West, Homer, Church, Glackens and Hopper; Bancroft Collection of English Pre-Raphaelite art, with works by Rossetti and Burne-Jones; and Phelps Collection of Andrew Wyeth works; also changing exhibits, children's participatory gallery; store. (Daily exc Mon; closed major hols) Guided tours by appt. 2301 Kentmere Pkwy. Phone 302/571-9590. ¢¢

Delaware History Museum. Changing exhibits on history and decorative arts. (Tues-Fri afternoons & Sat; closed major hols) 504 Market St. Phone 302/656-0637. **Donation**

Delaware Museum of Natural History. Exhibits of shells, birds, mammals; also largest bird egg and 500-pound clam. (Daily; closed major hols) 5 mi NW on DE 52 in Greenville. Phone 302/658-9111. ¢¢

Fort Christina Monument. Monument marks location where Swedes settled in 1638. Presented in 1938 to Wilmington by the people of Sweden, monument consists of black granite plinth surmounted by pioneers' flagship, the *Kalmar Nyckel*, sculpted by Carl Milles. Complex includes nearby log cabin, moved to this location as a reminder of Finnish and Swedish contributions to our nation. Foot of E 7th St.

Fort Delaware State Park (see). Approx 15 mi S on Pea Patch Island, opp Delaware City.

Grand Opera House (1871). Historic landmark built by Masons, this restored Victorian theater now serves as Delaware's Center for the Performing Arts, home of Opera Delaware (Nov-May) and Delaware Symphony (Sept-May). Facade is fine example of style of the Second Empire interpreted in cast iron. 818 Market St Mall. Phone 302/658-7898 or 302/652-5577 (ticket box office).

Hagley Museum. Old riverside stone mill buildings, one-room schoolhouse and millwright shop highlight 19th-century explosive manufacturing and community life; 240-acre historic site of E. I. du Pont's original black-powder mills, including exhibit building with working models and dioramas, operating water wheel, stationary steam engine and a fully operable 1875 machine shop. Admission includes bus ride along river for tour of 1803 Eleutherian Mills, residence with antiques reflecting five generations of du Ponts, a 19th-century garden and a barn with a collection of antique wagons. Museum store. (Mid-Mar-Dec, daily; rest of yr, Sat & Sun, limited hrs Mon-Fri; closed Thanksgiving, Dec 25 & 31) 3 mi NW off DE 141. Phone 302/658-2400. ¢¢¢

Holy Trinity (Old Swedes) Church and Hendrickson House. Founded by Swedish settlers in 1698, the church stands as originally built and still has regular services. The house, a Swedish farmhouse built in 1690, is now a museum containing 17th- and 18th-century artifacts. (Mon-Sat; closed major hols) 606 Church St. Phone 302/652-5629. **Free**

Nemours Mansion and Gardens. Country estate (300 acres) of Alfred I. du Pont. Mansion (1910) is modified Louis XVI, by Carrère and Hastings, with 102 rooms of rare antique furniture, Oriental rugs, tapestries and paintings dating from 15th century. Formal French gardens extend one-third of a mile along main vista from house with terraces, statuary and pools. Tours (May-Nov, daily exc Mon; res required) Over 16 yrs only. Rockland Rd between DE 141 & US 202. Phone 302/651-6912. ¢¢¢

Rockwood Museum. A 19th-century Gothic-revival estate with gardens in English-Romantic style. On grounds are manor house, conservatory, porter's lodge and other outbuildings. Museum furnished with English, European and American decorative arts of the 17th through 19th centuries. Guided tours (Mar-Dec, daily exc Mon; Jan & Feb, Tues-Sat). (See ANNUAL EVENTS) 610 Shipley Rd. Phone 302/761-4340. ¢¢

Willingtown Square. Historic square surrounded by four 18th-century houses moved to this location between 1973 and 1976. One houses museum gift shop for the Historical Society of Delaware; others serve as office and conference space. 500 block Market St Mall. Phone 302/655-7161.

Wilmington & Western Railroad. Round-trip steam-train ride (9 mi) to and from Mt Cuba picnic grove. (May-Oct, Sun; rest of yr, schedule varies) 4 mi SW, near jct DE 2 & DE 41 at Greenbank Station. Phone 302/998-1930. ¢¢¢

🟤 **Winterthur Museum, Garden and Library.** Museum houses decorative arts representing period from 1640 to 1860; collection of over 89,000 objects is displayed in two buildings. First-floor exhibition in the Galleries introduces 200 yrs of American antiques. The Period Rooms (seen on guided tours) were arranged by Henry Francis du Pont in his 9-story country house. Museum is surrounded by 60 acres of naturally landscaped garden, also arranged by du Pont, on a 980-acre estate. The Galleries at Winterthur offer self-guided tours. (Daily; closed hols) Admission varies with tour. 6 mi NW on DE 52. Phone 302/888-4600 or 800/448-3883. ¢¢¢

Annual Events

Wilmington Garden Day. Tour of famous gardens and houses. 1st Sat May.

Victorian Ice Cream Festival. Rockwood Museum. Victorian festival featuring high-wheeled bicycles, hot-air balloons, marionettes, old-fashioned medicine show, baby parade, crafts; homemade ice cream. Phone 302/761-4340. Mid-July.

Delaware Nature Society Harvest Moon Festival. 3 mi NW via US 41, at Ashland Nature Center in Hockessin. Cider-pressing demonstrations, hay rides, nature walks, farm animals, arts & crafts, musical entertainment, pony rides, games. Phone 302/239-2334. 1st wkend Oct.

Seasonal Event

Horse racing. Delaware Park. 7 mi S on I-95 exit 4B. Thoroughbred racing. Phone 302/994-2521. Mid-Mar-early Nov.

Motels

✓★★ **BEST WESTERN BRANDYWINE VALLEY INN.** *1807 Concord Pike* (19803), I-95 exit 8. 302/656-9436; FAX 302/656-8564; res: 800/528-1234; res: 800/537-7772. E-mail info@brandywineinn.com; web www.brandywineinn.com. 95 rms, 2 story, 12 kit. suites. S $77; D $97; each addl $5; kit. suites $110; under 18 free. Crib $5. Pet accepted. TV; cable (premium), VCR avail. Pool; wading pool, whirlpool, lifeguard. Complimentary coffee in rms. Restaurant adj 7 am-11 pm. Ck-out noon. Meeting rms. Business servs avail. In-rm modem link. Bellhops. Valet serv. Sundries. Gift shop. Exercise equipt. Microwaves avail. Cr cds: A, C, D, DS, MC, V.

★★ **HOLIDAY INN NORTH.** *4000 Concord Pike (19801), I-95 exit 8.* 302/478-2222; *FAX 302/479-0850; res: 800/465-4329.* Web www.holiday-inn.com. 138 rms, 2 story. S, D $99; each addl $6; under 18 free; wkend rates. Crib free. TV; cable (premium). Pool; lifeguard. Coffee in rms. Restaurant 7 am-10 pm. Rm serv. Bar 4 pm-midnight. Ck-out noon. Coin lndry. Meeting rms. Business servs avail. In-rm modem link. Bellhops. Sundries. Health club privileges. Cr cds: A, C, D, DS, JCB, MC, V.

D 🏊 🖼 🔥 SC

Hotels

★★★ **BRANDYWINE SUITES HOTEL.** *707 N King St (19801).* 302/656-9300; *FAX 302/656-2459; res: 800/756-0070.* 49 suites, 4 story. S, D $109-$225; under 12 free; wkend rates. Crib free. Parking $7.50. TV; cable (premium), VCR avail (movies). Complimentary continental bkfst. Complimentary coffee in rms. Restaurant 6:30-8:30 am, 11:30 am-2 pm, 5-10 pm; Sat, Sun 8-10 am, 5-10 pm. Bar 2-10 pm. Ck-out noon. Meeting rms. Business servs avail. In-rm modem link. Free airport, RR station, bus depot transportation. Bathrm phones; microwaves avail. Modern decor with European accents; atrium. Cr cds: A, C, D, MC, V.

D 🖼 🔥 SC

★★ **COURTYARD BY MARRIOTT.** *1102 W St (33431).* 302/429-7600; *FAX 302/429-9167; res: 800/321-2211.* 126 rms, 10 story. S $139-$170; D $149-$180; each addl $10; wkend rates. Crib free. Garage $8.50; free Fri, Sat. TV; cable (premium). Coffee in rms. Ck-out noon. Guest lndry. Business servs avail. In-rm modem link. Airport, RR station, bus depot transportation. Exercise equipt. Health club privileges. Refrigerators, wet bar; some in-rm whirlpools; microwaves avail. Cr cds: A, C, D, DS, MC, V.

D 🚶 🖼 🔥 SC

★★★ **DOUBLETREE HOTEL.** *4727 Concord Pike (19803).* 302/478-6000; *FAX 302/477-1492; res: 800/333-3333; res: 888/478-2923.* Web www.doubletreehotel.com. 154 rms, 7 story. S, D $129-$189; each addl $10; suites $189-$229; under 18 free. Crib $10. TV; cable (premium), VCR avail (movies). Pool. Restaurant 6:30 am-10 pm. Bar 5-11 pm. Ck-out noon. Meeting rms. Business servs avail. In-rm modem link. Exercise equipt. Health club privileges. Some refrigerators. Cr cds: A, C, D, DS, ER, JCB, MC, V.

D 🏊 🚶 🖼 🔥 SC

★★★ **HILTON WILMINGTON HOTEL NORTH.** *630 Naamans Rd; I-95 (19703), I-95N exit 11, or I-495S exit 6.* 302/792-2700; *FAX 302/798-6182.* 193 rms, 7 story. S, D $99-$136; each addl $15; suites $150-$275; under 12 free; wkend rates. Pet accepted; $60. TV; cable (premium). Pool. Playground. Coffee in rms. Restaurant 6:30 am-2 pm, 4:30-11 pm. Bar 3:30 pm-1 am. Ck-out noon. Meeting rms. Business servs avail. In-rm modem link. Valet serv. Free airport transportation. Exercise equipt. Some refrigerators; microwaves avail. Cr cds: A, C, D, DS, MC, V.

D 🐾🏊 🚶 🖼 🔥 SC

★★★★ **HOTEL DU PONT.** *11th & Market Sts (19801).* 302/594-3100; *FAX 302/594-3108; res: 800/441-9019.* Web www.preferredhotel.com/preferred.htm. The spacious guest rooms in this renovated landmark are furnished with reproductions of 18th-century antiques. 216 rms, 12 story. S, D $149-$269; suites $395-$495; under 12 free; wkend rates, special packages. Crib free. Valet parking $13. TV; cable (premium). Restaurants (see BRANDYWINE ROOM and GREEN ROOM). Rm serv 24 hrs. Bar; entertainment. Ck-out 1 pm. Meeting rms. Business center. In-rm modem link. Concierge. Shopping arcade. Barber, beauty shop. Airport, RR station transportation. Tennis privileges. 54-hole golf privileges, greens fee, pro, putting green, driving range. Exercise rm; sauna. Massage. Health club privileges. Pool privileges. Minibars; microwaves avail. Cr cds: A, C, D, DS, ER, JCB, MC, V.

D 🚶🖐 🚶 🖼 🔥 SC 🏃

★★★ **SHERATON SUITES.** *422 Delaware Ave (19801).* 302/654-8300; *FAX 302/654-6036; res: 800/544-5064.* E-mail mary_fitts@ittsheraton.com; web www.ittsheraton.com. 228 suites, 16 story. S, D $175-

$195; each addl $15; under 18 free; wkend rates. Crib free. Garage $9; Fri, Sat free. TV; cable (premium), VCR avail. Indoor pool. Complimentary coffee in rms. Restaurant 6:30-10 am, 11:30 am-10:30 pm; Sun 7 am-10:30 pm. Bar. Ck-out noon. Coin lndry. Meeting rms. Business center. In-rm modem link. Gift shop. Airport transportation. Exercise equipt; sauna. Health club privileges. Refrigerators; microwaves avail. Cr cds: A, C, D, DS, ER, JCB, MC, V.

D 🏊 🚶 🖼 🔥 SC 🏃

Inns

★★★ **DARLEY MANOR INN BED & BREAKFAST.** *3701 Philadelphia Pike (19703), 6 mi N on I-95, exit 10.* 302/792-2127; *FAX 302/798-6143; res: 800/824-4703.* E-mail darley@dca.net; web www.dca.net/darley. 6 rms, 3 story. No elvtr. S, D $95-$109; each addl $10; suites $99-$119. Children over 9 yrs only. TV; cable, VCR. Whirlpool. Complimentary full bkfst. Restaurant nearby. Ck-out noon, ck-in 4 pm. Business servs avail. Exercise equipt. Totally nonsmoking. Cr cds: A, C, D, DS, MC, V.

🚶 🖼 🔥

★★★★ **INN AT MONTCHANIN VILLAGE.** *Rte 100 & Kirk Rd (72342), 6 mi N on DE 52.* 302/888-2133; *FAX 302/888-0389; res: 800/269-2473.* E-mail montchan@gte.com; web www.montchanin.net. This authentically restored 19th-century hamlet, nestled in the heart of Brandywine Valley, was formerly a settlement for workers at the DuPont factories along the Brandywine River. Rooms are individually decorated in period and reproduction furniture, and the multi-structure village provides unique vistas and private baths and gardens. 26 rms, 2-3 story, 16 suites. S, D $170; suites $190-$400; package plans; wkends, hols (2-day min). Crib free. TV; cable, VCR avail. Complimentary full bkfst. Complimentary coffee in rms. Restaurant (see KRAZY KAT'S). Rm serv Sun-Thurs. Ck-out 11 am, ck-in 3 pm. Business center. In-rm modem link. Luggage handling. Valet serv. Concierge serv. Lighted tennis privileges. 48-hole golf privileges, greens fee $65-$99. Health club privileges. Refrigerators, microwaves, wet bars; some in-rm whirlpools, fireplaces. Balconies. Picnic tables. Totally nonsmoking. Cr cds: A, C, D, MC, V.

🔥 🚶🖐 🏃 🖼 🔥 🏃

✓ ★★★ **THE BOULEVARD BED & BREAKFAST.** *1909 Baynard Blvd (19802).* 302/656-9700; *FAX 302/656-9701.* E-mail blvdbb@wserv.com. 6 rms, 2 share bath, 3 story. S $65-$80; D $70-$85; each addl $10-$15; hol wkends (2-day min). TV; cable (premium), VCR (free movies). Complimentary full bkfst. Ck-out 11 am, ck-in 2 pm. Business servs avail. In-rm modem link. Brick house built 1913. Antiques. Cr cds: A, C, MC, V.

🖼 🔥

Restaurants

★★★ **BACK BURNER.** *425 Hockessin Corner (19707), DE 48 to DE 41, then N 9 mi.* 302/239-2314. Web www.backburner.com. Hrs: 11:15 am-2:15 pm, 5-9 pm; Fri, Sat 11:15 am-2:15 pm, 5:30-9:45 pm. Closed Sun; major hols; also wk before Labor Day. Res required. Bar. Wine cellar. Semi-a la carte: lunch $6-$12, dinner $13-$25. Specialties: black Angus beef, soft shell crabs, rack of lamb. Elegeant dining in country atmosphere; renovated barn with arched walls, display kitchen. Cr cds: A, C, D, DS, MC, V.

D ♥

★★★ **BLACK TRUMPET BISTRO.** *1717 Delaware Ave (19806).* 302/777-0454. Hrs: 11:30 am-2 pm, 5:30-10 pm; Sat from 5:30 pm. Closed Sun; Memorial Day, Dec 25. Res required. French menu. Bar. Wine cellar. A la carte entrees: lunch $6-$12, dinner $15-$24. Specialties: exotic wild mushrooms, grilled chicken breast with potato risotto. Own pastries, ice cream. Intimate atmosphere; original artwork adorns walls. Totally nonsmoking. Cr cds: A, C, MC, V.

D

★★★ **BRANDYWINE ROOM.** *(See Hotel du Pont) 302/594-3156.* Web www.preferredhotels.com/preferred.html. Hrs: 6-11 pm; Sun 5-10 pm. Closed Fri, Sat. Res accepted. Bar. Semi-a la carte: $18-$32. Specializes in steak, rack of lamb, seafood. Club atmosphere; Wyeth paintings. Cr cds: A, C, D, DS, ER, JCB, MC, V.

[D]

★★★ **COLUMBUS INN.** *2216 Pennsylvania Ave (19806), I-95 Delaware Ave exit, 3 mi W.* 302/571-1492. E-mail columbus@gim.net; web www.columbusinn.com. Hrs: 11 am-11 pm; Fri, Sat to midnight. Closed Memorial Day, Labor Day, Dec 25. Res accepted. Continental menu. Bar. Wine cellar. A la carte entrees: lunch $5.95-$11.95, dinner $12-$22. Child's meals. Specializes in fresh seafood, beef. Entertainment Fri, Sat. Valet parking. Early American decor in 200-yr-old house. Fireplaces. Outdoor dining. Family-owned since 1957. Cr cds: A, C, D, DS, MC, V.

[D] [≡]

★★★ **FOX POINT GRILL.** *321 E Lea Blvd (19802).* 302/762-5655. Hrs: 11:30 am-2:30 pm, 4:30-10 pm; Sat from 4:30 pm. Closed Sun; Dec 25. Res accepted. Regional Amer menu. Bar. Wine list. Semi-a la carte: lunch $5.75-$11.50, dinner $16.50-$24. Child's meals. Specialties: Chincoteague crab cakes, live lobster, grilled rack of lamb. Own baking. Elegant atmosphere. Cr cds: A, C, D, DS, MC, V.

[≡] [♥]

★★★ **GREEN ROOM.** *(See Hotel Du Pont)* 302/594-3154. Web www.preferredhotels.com/preferred.html. Hrs: 6:30 am-2 pm; Fri, Sat 7 am-2 pm, 6-10 pm; Sun brunch 10 am-2:15 pm. Res accepted; required Sun brunch. Continental menu. Bar. Wine list. Semi-a la carte: bkfst $8.50-$14. A la carte entrees: lunch $10-$20, dinner $25-$35. Sun brunch $31.50. Child's meals. Specializes in lobster, rack of lamb, filet mignon. Harpist Fri, Sat. Valet parking. Elegant dining rm in historic hotel; gold leaf ceiling, oak paneled. Cr cds: A, C, D, DS, ER, JCB, MC, V.

[D] [♥]

★★★ **HARRY'S SAVOY GRILL.** *2020 Naaman's Rd (19810), I-95 Naaman's Rd exit, 2 mi on DE 92W.* 302/475-3000. E-mail dmd@harrys-savoy.com; web www.harrys-savoy.com. Hrs: 11 am-10:30 pm; Fri to 11:30 pm; Sat 4:30-11:30 pm; Sun 4-10:30 pm; Sun brunch 10:30 am-3 pm; early-bird dinner Mon-Fri to 6 pm. Closed Dec 25. Res accepted. Bar to 1 am. Wine cellar. A la carte entrees: lunch $6.95-$14.95, dinner $11.95-$20.95. Sun brunch $7.95-$14.95. Child's meals. Specializes in prime rib, fresh seafood. Musicians Fri, Sat; magicians perform at tables Tues evenings. Parking. Outdoor dining. Fireplaces. Cr cds: A, C, D, DS, MC, V.

[D] [≡]

★ **INDIA PALACE.** *101 N Maryland Ave (19804).* 302/655-8772. Hrs: 11:30 am-2:30 pm, 5-10 pm; Fri, Sat to 10:30 pm. Closed Mon. Res accepted. Indian menu. Wine, beer. Semi-a la carte: lunch $5.95, dinner $6.95-$15.95. Specializes in vegetarian and tandoori meals. Native American art. Cooking observed behind glass wall. Cr cds: A, C, D, DS, MC, V.

[≡]

✓★ **KID SHELLEENS.** *1801 W 14th St (19810), I-95 Delaware Ave exit to PA Ave, rt on N Scott, left on W 14th St.* 302/658-4600. Hrs: 11 am-midnight; Sun brunch 10 am-2 pm. Closed Thanksgiving, Dec 25. Bar. A la carte entrees: lunch $4.95-$8.95, dinner $7.95-$13.95. Child's meals. Specializes in grilled dishes, fresh seafood. Parking. Outdoor dining. Casual atmosphere. Cr cds: A, C, D, DS, MC, V.

[D] [♥]

★★★★ **KRAZY KAT'S RESTAURANT.** *(See Inn at Montchanin Village)* 302/888-4200. E-mail montchan@gte.net; web www.montchanin.com. The fanciful cat-themed decor (check out the tiger-print chairs and the cat "portraits" lining the walls) may be incongruous considering the quaint surroundings, but it is the perfect backdrop for chef Fred Kellerman's eclectic fare. The menu, which changes every two weeks, borrows liberally from Korean, Chinese, Southwestern, and Mediterranean cuisines. Hrs: 7-9 am, 11 am-2 pm, 5:30-10 pm; Sat, Sun 8 am-noon, 5:30-10 pm.

Res accepted. Wine cellar. Complete meal: bkfst $14.50. Semi-a la carte: lunch $5-$14, dinner $19-$26. Specialties: crab cakes with shrimp mousseline, Krazy Kat's mixed grille. Restored 18th-century blacksmith shop; original fireplace and art. Totally nonsmoking. Cr cds: A, C, D, MC, V.

[D]

★★★ **PICCOLO MONDO.** *3604 Silverside Rd (19810), at Talleyville Towne Shoppes.* 302/478-9028. Hrs: 11:30 am-2 pm, 5-10 pm; Sat from 5 pm. Closed Sun; most major hols. Res accepted. Italian menu. Bar. Wine list. A la carte entrees: lunch $6-$9, dinner $10-$18. Specialties: risotto primavera, grilled shrimp on rosemary branch, cannelloni con frutti di mare. Own pastries. Italian decor with open hearth kitchen; wine bottles displayed. Cr cds: A, C, DS, MC, V.

[D] [≡]

★★★ **POSITANO.** *2401 Pennsylvania Ave (19806), in Devon Bldg.* 302/656-6788. Hrs: 11:30 am-2 pm, 5:30-10 pm. Closed Sun; major hols. Res required. Italian, French menu. Wine list. Semi-a la carte: lunch $8.50-$12.50, dinner $21.75-$32.50. Specializes in veal, fresh seafood. Parking. Elegant and intimate dining. Jacket. Totally nonsmoking. Cr cds: A, C, D, DS, MC, V.

[D]

★★★ **SIENNA.** *1616 Delaware Ave (19806).* 302/652-0653. Hrs: 11 am-10 pm; Fri, Sat to 11 pm; Sun 4-9 pm. Closed Dec 25. Res accepted. Bar. A la carte entrees: lunch $5-$10, dinner $12.50-$26. Specialties: rack of lamb provencale, shellfish paella, risotto funghi. Entertainment Mon-Sat. Old World atmosphere; antiques, stained-glass windows. Cr cds: A, C, D, DS, MC, V.

[D] [SC] [≡]

★★★ **SILK PURSE & SOW'S EAR.** *1307 N Scott St (19806).* 302/654-7666. E-mail eziosilkl@aol.com. Hrs: 5:30-9:30 pm. Closed Sun, Mon; major hols. Res accepted. Eclectic menu. Wine list. A la carte entrees: dinner $13.50-$18.50. Specializes in fresh seasonal ingredients, game, fish. Own baking. In converted town house. Cr cds: A, C, MC, V.

[D] [≡]

★★★ **TAVOLA TOSCANA.** *1412 N Dupont St (19806).* 302/654-8001. E-mail bigchefguy@aol.com. Hrs: 11:30 am-2 pm, 5:30-10 pm; Sun 5:30-9:30 pm. Closed major hols. Res accepted; required wkends. Italian menu. Bar. Wine list. A la carte entrees: lunch $10-$15, dinner $18-$24. Specializes in hand-rolled pasta, shared specialty appetizers. Parking. Atmosphere of European bistro. Cr cds: A, C, D, DS, MC, V.

[D] [≡]

★★★ **VINCENTE'S.** *1601 Concord Pike (19803), in Independence Mall.* 302/652-5142. Hrs: 11 am-10 pm; Sat from 4 pm. Closed Sun; most major hols. Res accepted. Italian menu. Bar. Extensive wine list. Semi-a la carte: lunch $6.50-$12.50, dinner $16.95-$28.95. Child's meals. Specializes in veal, steak, seafood. Own pasta, desserts. Contemporary decor; Caesar salad made tableside. Cr cds: A, C, D, DS, MC, V.

[D] [≡]

★★ **WATERWORKS CAFE.** *16th & French Sts (19801), 4 blks N of Rodney Square.* 302/652-6022. Hrs: 11 am-2:30 pm, 5:30-10 pm; Sat from 5:30 pm. Closed Sun, Mon; major hols. Res accepted. Bar to midnight. A la carte entrees: lunch $5.95-$14.95, dinner $13.95-$26.95. Specializes in fresh seafood. Parking. Outdoor dining. Old waterworks on Brandywine River. Cr cds: A, C, DS, MC, V.

[D] [≡]

District of Columbia

Population: 606,900
Land area: 63 square miles
Elevation: 1-410 feet
Highest point: Tenleytown
State flower: American Beauty rose
State bird: Wood thrush
Time zone: Eastern
Web: www.washington.org

Washington

(see C-8 VA-WV map; C-6 DE-MD map)

Area Code 202

Washington, designed by Major Pierre Charles L'Enfant in about 1791, was the first American city ever planned for a specific purpose. It is a beautiful city, with wide, tree-lined streets laid out according to a design that is breathtaking in its scope and imagination. For its purpose the broad plan still works well even though L'Enfant could not have foreseen the automobile or the fact that the United States would come to have a population of more than 250 million people. Nevertheless, L'Enfant's concept was ambitious, allowing for vast growth. Washington, named for the first US president, has been the nation's capital since 1800. The city's business is centered around government and tourism; there is little heavy industry.

The District of Columbia and Washington are one and the same. Originally the District was a 10-mile square crossing the Potomac River into Virginia, but the Virginia portion (31 square miles) was turned back to the state in 1846. Residences of federal workers spill into Virginia and Maryland; so do government offices. In 1800, there were 130 federal employees; at the end of the Civil War there were 7,000; now there are well over half a million. Although the city was a prime Confederate target in the Civil War, it was barely damaged. The assassination of Abraham Lincoln, however, struck a blow to the nation and drove home to Americans the fact that Washington was not merely a center of government. What happened here affected everyone.

This is a cosmopolitan city. Perhaps no city on earth has a populace with so many different origins. Representatives from all nations and men and women from every state work here—and vote in their home states by absentee ballot. It is a dignified, distinguished capital. Many who visit the city go first to the House of Representatives or Senate office buildings and chat with their representatives, who receive constituent visitors when they can. At these offices visitors obtain tickets to the Senate and House galleries. From the top of the Washington Monument there is a magnificent view of the capital. The Lincoln Memorial and the Jefferson Memorial cannot fail to capture the imagination.

When to Go/Climate

DC winters are relatively mild, while summers are hot and humid. The city is alive with color in spring and fall—cherry blossoms bloom in April and May and vibrant fall foliage begins around September.

AVERAGE HIGH/LOW TEMPERATURES (°F)

WASHINGTON NATL AIRPORT

Jan 42/27	**May** 76/57	**Sept** 80/63
Feb 46/29	**June** 85/67	**Oct** 69/50
Mar 57/38	**July** 89/71	**Nov** 58/41
Apr 67/46	**Aug** 87/70	**Dec** 47/32

Visitor Information

Washington DC Convention and Visitors Association, 1212 New York Ave NW, Suite 600, Washington, DC 20005, has brochures and schedules of events; phone 202/789-7000 (Mon-Fri, 9 am-5 pm).

The National Park Service maintains information kiosks at several key points in the city as well as a White House Visitors Center at 1450 Pennsylvania Ave NW which distributes free tickets to tour the White House.

Note: By writing to your representative or senator ahead of time, tickets can be obtained for two Congressional Tours: a guided White House tour that differs slightly from the normal tour and begins at 8:15, 8:30 or 8:45 am (Tues-Sat; specific times are assigned); or passes to the House and Senate visitors' galleries to watch Congressional sessions in progress. Without this ticket, the chambers can only be viewed when Congress is not in session.

WASHINGTON D.C.
NEIGHBORHOODS

© 2000, Rand McNally

0   0.25   0.5 km
0   0.25   0.5 mile

Write your senator at the United States Senate, Washington, DC 20510. Address your representative at the United States House of Representatives, Washington, DC 20515. All tickets are free, but in peak season, which starts in spring, White House tickets may be limited. In the letter, include the date you will be in Washington, first- and second-choice dates for the tours and the number of people in your party. Also include your home phone number, should your representative's or senator's aide need to contact you. You can also get tickets, if available, directly from the office of your senator or representative after you arrive in Washington.

Transportation

Airports. *Ronald Reagan Washington National,* 3 mi S in Virginia (see Arlington County (RONALD REAGAN WASHINGTON-NATIONAL AIRPORT AREA) under Virginia); *Dulles Intl,* 26 mi W in Virginia (see DULLES INTL AIRPORT AREA under Virginia), phone 703/419-8000; *Baltimore/Washington Intl,* 32 mi NE in Maryland (see BALTIMORE/WASHINGTON INTL AIRPORT AREA under Maryland), phone 410/859-7100.

Car Rental Agencies. See IMPORTANT TOLL-FREE NUMBERS.

Public Transportation. The Metrorail system is the least expensive means of getting around the capital. Metro (as it is called) provides a coordinated transportation system between buses and rail. The rapid rail system links the major commercial districts and neighborhoods, from the Capitol to the Pentagon and from the National Zoo to the National Airport and beyond. Trains operate every 6-12 minutes on the average: Monday-Friday, 5:30 am-midnight; Saturday & Sunday from 8 am. Phone 202/637-7000.

Rail Passenger Service. Amtrak 800/872-7245.

Driving in Washington

Since the city is divided into four quarters, or quadrants, emanating from the Capitol, driving may be confusing for the first-time visitor. The quadrants are northeast (NE), northwest (NW), southeast (SE) and southwest (SW). All Washington addresses have these designations listed after the street name. It is advisable to obtain a city map before attempting to drive through the city, especially during rush hours.

Safety belts are mandatory for all persons in front seat of vehicle. All children under 3 years must be in an approved safety seat anywhere in vehicle. Children 3-16 years must be properly restrained in either a safety belt or child safety seat anywhere in the vehicle. For further information phone 202/939-8018.

What to See and Do

American Red Cross. National headquarters includes three buildings bounded by 17th, 18th, D & E Sts NW. The 17th St building includes marble busts, *Faith, Hope* and *Charity,* by sculptor Hiram Powers and three original Tiffany stained-glass windows. (Mon-Fri) 430 17th St NW. Phone 202/737-8300   **Free**

Anacostia Museum. Smithsonian Institution. An exhibition and research center for black heritage in the historic Anacostia section of SE Washington. Changing exhibits. (Daily; closed Dec 25) 1901 Fort Place SE. Phone 202/357-2700.   **Free**

Art Museum of the Americas, OAS. Dedicated to Latin American and Caribbean contemporary art; paintings, graphics, sculpture. (Tues-Sat; closed major hols) 201 18th St NW. Phone 202/458-6016.   **Free**

B'nai B'rith Klutznick Museum. Permanent exhibition of Jewish ceremonial and folk art. Changing exhibits. (Daily exc Sat; closed major Jewish hols, some legal hols) B'nai B'rith International Center, 1640 Rhode Island Ave NW. Phone 202/857-6583.   **Free**

Basilica of the National Shrine of the Immaculate Conception. On Metro Red Line stop. Largest Roman Catholic church in US and one of largest in the world. Byzantine and Romanesque architecture; extensive and elaborate collection of mosaics and artwork. (Daily) Carillon concerts (Sun afternoons); organ recitals (June-Aug, Sun evenings). Guided tours (daily). Phone 202/526-8300.

Blair House (1824). Guest house for heads of government and state who are visiting the US as guests of the president. Not open to public. 1651 Pennsylvania Ave NW.

Bureau of Engraving and Printing. Headquarters for making US paper money; guided tours (every 10 min). (Mon-Fri; closed hols and Dec 24-Jan 3) 14th & C Sts SW, S of Mall; enter on 14th St. Phone 202/874-3019 or 202/874-3186.   **Free**

Capital Children's Museum. Hands-on museum where children of all ages can explore exhibits on computers, human development and Mexican culture. (Daily; closed some major hols) 800 3rd St NE. Phone 202/675-4120.   ¢¢¢

☒ **The Capitol.** The Capitol is the meeting place of Congress—the legislative branch of the government—as well as a symbol of the US government. George Washington laid the cornerstone in 1793, and part of the originally planned building opened in 1800. Construction continued on and off over a number of years (including rebuilding after the British burned the Capitol in 1814) until the original building, which was crowned with a low copper-covered dome, was completed in 1826. Expansion in the 1850s and 1860s included the new wings, today's House and Senate chambers, and the cast-iron dome seen today, which was completed during the Civil War. The Rotunda, in the center, is the main ceremonial room of the Capitol, where dignitaries have lain in state. National Statuary Hall, just to the south, houses part of the state statue collection (each state can contribute two), but was originally built for the House as its chamber. (Tour every 15 min; closed Jan 1, Thanksgiving, Dec 25) Public dining room on 1st floor of Senate wing (Mon-Fri). Summer band concerts (see SEASONAL EVENTS). Between Constitution & Independence Aves, at Pennsylvania Ave, E end of Mall. Phone 202/225-6827.   **Free**

Congress. Tickets to the House and Senate visitors' galleries can be obtained from the office of your congressman or senator. Foreign visitors can obtain passes to the Senate Gallery from the appointment desk, 1st floor, Senate Wing; and to the House of Representatives Gallery from the check stand, 3rd floor, House wing (identification required).

Old Senate Chamber. Original Senate chamber has been restored to its 1850s appearance. N of rotunda.

West Front. Along the Capitol's west front are terraces, gardens and lawns designed by Frederick Law Olmstead, who also planned New York City's Central Park. Halfway down the hill are the Peace Monument (on the north) and the Garfield Monument (on the south). At the foot of Capitol Hill is Union Square with a reflecting pool and Grant Monument.

The Catholic University of America (1887). (6,500 students) Open to all faiths. Hartke Theatre (year-round). 620 Michigan Ave NE. Phone 202/319-5000.

Chesapeake and Ohio Canal Boat Rides. Narrated round-trip canal tours (1½ hrs) by park rangers in period clothing aboard mule-drawn boats. Ticket office adj. (Mid-Apr-Oct, Wed-Sun) Departs from Level on Thomas Jefferson St, between 30th & 31st Sts. Phone 202/653-5190.   ¢¢ (Also see CHESAPEAKE AND OHIO CANAL NATIONAL HISTORIC PARK in Maryland)

Chinatown. Recognizable by the Chinatown Friendship Archway at 7th and H Sts. Archway is decorated in Chinese architectural styles of Qing and Ming dynasties and is topped with nearly 300 painted dragons. G & H Streets, between 6th & 8th Sts NW.

Clara Barton National Historic Site. Thirty-six-rm house (1891) of unusual architecture was both the national headquarters of the Red Cross and the home of Clara Barton for the last 15 yrs of her life. Contents include many items belonging to the founder of the American Red Cross. Period costumes worn during some special programs. Guided tours only. (Daily; closed major hols) 5801 Oxford Rd, 8 mi NW in Glen Echo, MD. Phone 301/492-6245.   **Free**

Constitution Gardens. This 45-acre park, with a man-made lake, is also the site of the Signers of the Declaration of Independence Memorial. Along Constitution Ave between 18th & 22nd Sts NW. Phone 202/426-6841.   **Free**

Corcoran Gallery of Art (1869). Oldest and largest private gallery in the city has world's most comprehensive collection of 18th-20th-century American art; Walker and Clark collections of European art; changing exhibitions (fee) of painting, sculpture and photography. (Daily exc Tues; closed major hols) 17th St between New York Ave & E St NW. For general information phone 202/639-1700.   **Free**

DAR Headquarters. Includes Memorial Continental Hall (1904) and Constitution Hall (1920); DAR Museum Gallery, located in administration building, has 33 state period rooms; outstanding genealogical research library (fee for nonmembers). Guided tours (daily exc Sat). 1776 D St NW. Phone 202/628-1776 or 202/879-3239.   **Free**

Department of Commerce Building. (1932). Pennsylvania Ave, between 14th & 15th Sts NW. In the building is the

    National Aquarium. The nation's oldest public aquarium was established in 1873. It now exhibits more than 1,700 specimens representing approx 260 species, both freshwater and saltwater. Touch tank; theater. Shark feeding (Mon, Wed, Sat); piranha feeding (Tues, Thurs, Sun). (Daily; closed Dec 25) Phone 202/482-2826.   **¢**

Department of Energy, Pennsylvania Ave between 12th & 13th Sts NW; **Interstate Commerce Commission** (1934), Constitution Ave, between 12th & 13th Sts NW; **Customs Department,** Constitution Ave, between 13th & 14th Sts NW; and the **District Building,** Pennsylvania Ave, between 13th & 14th Sts NW, Washington's ornate 1908 city hall.

Department of Justice Building (1934). Pennsylvania Ave, between 9th & 10th Sts NW. (Not open to the public) Across Pennsylvania Ave is

    FBI Headquarters. Tours of historical exhibits, including FBI laboratory; very large firearm collection; demonstration of firearms. J. Edgar Hoover Building, 935 Pennsylvania Ave, NW, between 9th & 10th Sts NW; tour entrance on 9th St NW. (Mon-Fri; closed major hols) Phone 202/324-3447.   **Free**

Department of the Interior (1938). Within is museum with exhibits and dioramas depicting history and activities of the department and its various bureaus. Photo ID required. (Mon-Fri; closed major hols) Reference library open to public. 1849 C St NW, between 18th & 19th Sts NW. Phone 202/208-4743.   **Free**

Department of State Building. The State Department's Diplomatic Reception Rooms, furnished with 18th-century American furniture and decorative art, are used by secretary of state and cabinet members for formal entertaining. Tours (Mon-Fri; closed federal hols & special events; 3-4 wks advance reservation; children over 12 yrs preferred). 21st, 22nd, C & D Sts NW. Phone 202/647-3241.   **Free**

Department of the Treasury. According to legend, this Greek-revival building, one of the oldest (1836-1869) in the city, was built in the middle of Pennsylvania Avenue because Andrew Jackson, tired of endless wrangling over the location, walked out of the White House, planted his cane in the mud and said, "Here." The building has been extensively restored. Tours (90 min) include office used by President Andrew Johnson after the Lincoln assassination, and the two-story marble Cash Room (Sat; by advance reservation). Pennsylvania Ave at 15th St NW, E of White House. Phone 202/622-0896.   **Free**

Dumbarton Oaks (1800). Famous gardens (16 acres) are both formal and Romantic in design. Mansion has antiques and European art, including El Greco's *The Visitation;* galleries of Byzantine art; library of rare books on gardening and horticulture. Museum of pre-Columbian artifacts housed in structure by Philip Johnson. Garden (daily; closed major hols); house and museum (Tues-Sun afternoons; closed major hols). 1703 32nd St NW; garden entrance 31st & R Sts. Phone 202/339-6400. Gard.   **¢¢** Museum **Donation**

Dupont-Kalorama Museum Walk. This is a joining of forces of seven museums to create an awareness of the area. Information and brochures are available at any of the museums concerned. The participating museums are

    Anderson House Museum. Museum of the American Revolution and national headquarters of the Society of the Cincinnati has portraits by early American artists; 18th-century paintings; 17th-century tapestries; decorative arts of Europe and Asia; displays of books, medals and swords, silver, glass and china. (Tues-Sat; closed legal hols) Free concert series. 2118 Massachusetts Ave NW. Phone 202/785-2040.   **Donation**

    Christian Heurich Mansion (1892). Four-story, 31-rm neo-Renaissance/late Victorian mansion has elaborate furnishings and garden; houses the Historical Society of Washington, DC, and the society's Library of Washington History; changing exhibits. House tours (Wed-Sat afternoons; closed major hols). Library (Wed, Fri, Sat; closed major hols). 1307 New Hampshire Ave NW, near Dupont Circle. Phone 202/785-2068.   **¢¢**

    Fondo del Sol. Dedicated to presenting, promoting and preserving cultures of the Americas, the museum presents exhibitions of contemporary artists and craftsmen; holds special events; hosts traveling exhibits

for museums and other institutions. (Wed-Sat afternoons; closed major hols) 2112 R St NW. Phone 202/483-2777.   **¢¢**

Meridian International Center. Housed in two historic mansions designed by John Russell Pope; hosts international exhibits, concerts, lectures and symposia promoting international understanding. Period furnishings, Mortlake tapestry; gardens with linden grove. (Daily, afternoons; closed major hols) 1630 Crescent Place NW. Phone 202/939-5544.   **Donation**

Phillips Collection. Oldest museum of modern art in the nation. Founded in 1918, the museum continues to emphasize the work of emerging as well as established international artists. Permanent collection of 19th- and 20th-century Impressionist, Post-Impressionist and modern painting and sculpture. (Daily exc Mon; closed some major hols) Introductory tours (Wed and Sat). Concerts (Sept-May, Sun). Wkday admission by donation. 1600 21st St NW. Phone 202/387-2151 or 202/387-0961. Wkend admission   **¢¢¢**

Textile Museum. Founded in 1925 with the collection of George Hewitt Myers, the museum features changing exhibits of non-Western textiles, Oriental rugs and other handmade textile art. Guided tours (Sept-May, Wed, Sat, Sun; by appt). (Daily) 2320 S St NW. Phone 202/667-0441.   **Free**

Woodrow Wilson House (1915). Red-brick Georgian-revival town house to which President Wilson retired after leaving office; family furnishings and gifts-of-state. A National Trust for Historic Preservation property. (Daily exc Mon; closed Jan 1, Thanksgiving, Dec 25) 2340 S St NW. Phone 202/387-4062.   **¢¢**

Eastern Market. Meat, fish and produce sold. Also crafts and farmers market on wkends. (Daily exc Mon) 225 7th St SE. Phone 202/546-2698.

Emancipation Statue. Bronze work of Thomas Ball paid for by voluntary subscriptions from emancipated slaves, depicting Lincoln presenting Emancipation Proclamation to black man, was dedicated Apr 14, 1876, the 11th anniversary of Lincoln's assassination, with Fredrick Douglass in attendance. Lincoln Park, E Capitol St NE between 11th & 13th Sts NE. Also here is

    Mary McLeod Bethune Memorial. Honors the noted educator and advisor to President Lincoln and founder of the National Council of Negro Women.

Embassy Row. This neighborhood, within the city's northwest quadrant, is centered around Sheridan Circle, at the intersection of Massachusetts Ave and 23rd St NW. Dozens of foreign legations can be found in the area and north along Massachusetts Ave.

Explorers Hall. National Geographic Society headquarters. Permanent science center shows the Society's explorations and exhibits on geography; Earth Station One; also a 1,100-pound, free-standing world globe 11 ft in diameter; changing exhibits. (Daily; closed Dec 25) 17th & M Sts NW. Phone 202/857-7588 (recording).   **Free**

Federal Reserve Building (1937). Primarily an office building, but noteworthy for its architecture; rotating art exhibits; film (20 min). Public tours (Thurs afternoons). C St between 20th & 21st Sts NW. Phone 202/452-3149.   **Free**

Federal Trade Commission Building (1938). (Mon-Fri; closed major hols) 600 Pennsylvania Ave NW, between 6th & 7th Sts. Phone 202/326-2222.   **Free**

Federal Triangle. The Triangle consists of a group of government buildings, of which nine were built for $78 million in the 1930s in modern classic design. The "crown jewel" of the triangle is the Ronald Reagan and International Trade Center, located on Pennsylvania Ave at 13th St NW.

★ **Ford's Theatre.** Where John Wilkes Booth shot Abraham Lincoln on Apr 14, 1865. Restored as a functioning theater with Broadway and original productions offered throughout the yr. Phone 202/347-4833 for tickets. Tours (daily; closed Dec 25). 511 10th St NW. Phone 202/426-6924. Tours **Free;** Performance tickets   **¢¢¢¢-¢¢¢¢¢**   In basement is

    Lincoln Museum. Exhibits and displays focus on Lincoln's life and assassination. (Daily; closed Dec 25)   **Free**   Across the street is

    Petersen House. (House where Lincoln died). The house to where President Lincoln was carried after the shooting at Ford's Theatre; he died here the following morning. The house has been restored to its appearance at that time. (Daily; closed Dec 25) 516 10th St NW. Phone 202/426-6830.   **Free**

Fort Dupont Park. Picnicking, hiking and bicycling in hilly terrain; cultural arts performances in summer (see SEASONAL EVENTS). Also films, slides and activities including natural science; environmental education programs; nature discovery room; Junior Ranger program; programs for sr citizens and disabled persons; garden workshops and programmed activities by reservation. Randle Circle & Minnesota Aves. Phone 202/426-7723 or 202/426-7745.   **Free**   Nearby is

Fort Dupont Sports Complex. Skating, ice hockey (fee); tennis courts; basketball courts; ball fields (daily; free), jogging. E on Pennsylvania Ave SE; N on Minnesota Ave; E on Ely Pl. Phone 202/584-5007   (ice rink).

Fort Stevens Park. General Jubal Early and his Confederate troops tried to invade Washington at this point on July 11 & 12, 1864. President Lincoln risked his life at the fort during the fighting. (Daily) Piney Branch Rd & Quackenbos St NW. Phone 202/282-1063.   **Free**

Fort Washington National Park. Earliest defense of the city (1809), the original fort was destroyed in 1814; reconstructed by 1824. View of Potomac River; picnicking; history exhibits. (Daily) 4 mi S on MD 210, 3½ mi on Fort Washington Rd in Fort Washington, MD. Phone 301/763-4600. Per vehicle   ¢¢; per person   ¢

Franciscan Monastery. Within the church and grounds is the "Holy Land of America"; replicas of sacred Holy Land shrines include the Manger at Bethlehem, Garden of Gethsemane and Holy Sepulchre. Also Grotto at Lourdes and Roman catacombs. Guided tours by the friars (daily). 1400 Quincy St NE. Phone 202/526-6800.   **Free**

Frederick Douglass National Historic Site, "Cedar Hill." This 21-rm house on 9 acres is where Douglass, a former slave who became Minister to Haiti and a leading black spokesman, lived from 1877 until his death in 1895; visitor center with film, memorabilia. (Daily; closed Jan 1, Thanksgiving, Dec 25) 1411 W St SE. Phone 202/426-5961 or 800/967-2283 (tour reservations).   ¢¢

General Services Administration Building (1917). Was originally Department of Interior. 18th, 19th, E & F Sts NW.

George Washington University (1821). (20,000 students) Theater; art exhibits in Dimock Gallery (Mon-Fri; closed hols) and University Library. 19th to 24th Sts NW, F St to Pennsylvania Ave. Phone 202/994-6460.

Georgetown. Georgetown, a neighborhood within the city's northwest quadrant, is actually older than Washington. In colonial days, it was a busy commercial center along the Potomac. Today, Georgetown is an area of fine 18th- and 19th-century residences and fashionable shops and restaurants; the commercial center radiates from the intersection of Pennsylvania Ave and M St, northwest of the White House.

Georgetown University (1789). (12,000 students) Oldest Catholic college in US, a Jesuit school. Campus tours (daily exc Sun, by res). Main entrance 37th & O Sts NW. Phone 202/687-3600.

Government Printing Office. Four buildings with 35 acres of floor space where most of the material issued by US Government, including production and distribution of the Congressional Record, Federal Register and US passports, is printed. (No public tours; to schedule private tours phone 202/512-1991.) Office includes the **Main Government Bookstore**, 710 N Capitol St NW. Nearly 20,000 publications available (Mon-Fri; closed hols). On N Capitol St, between G & H Sts. Phone 202/512-0132.

Great Falls of the Potomac. (See CHESAPEAKE AND OHIO CANAL NATIONAL HISTORICAL PARK in Maryland)

Harness racing. (Thurs-Sat) Rosecroft Raceway. 6336 Rosecroft Dr, 8 mi SE in Oxon Hill, MD. Phone 301/567-4000.   ¢

House Office Buildings. Pedestrian tunnel connects two of the oldest House Office Buildings with the Capitol. Along Independence Ave, S side of Capitol grounds at Independence & New Jersey Aves.

Howard University (1867). (12,000 students) Main campus: 2400 6th St NW between W & Harvard Sts NW. West Campus: 2900 Van Ness St NW. Three other campuses in area. Main campus has Gallery of Fine Art, with permanent Alain Locke African Collection; changing exhibits (Sept-July, Mon-Fri). Phone 202/806-6100.

Islamic Center. Leading mosque in the US has landscaped courtyard, intricate interior mosaics. (Daily; no tours during Fri prayer service) 2551 Massachusetts Ave NW. Phone 202/332-8343.

Iwo Jima Statue. Across Theodore Roosevelt Bridge on Arlington Blvd. (See ARLINGTON COUNTY in Virginia)

John F. Kennedy Center for the Performing Arts. Official memorial to President Kennedy. Single structure, designed by Edward Durell Stone, incorporates opera house, concert hall, AFI movie theater, Eisenhower Theatre, Terrace Theatre and Theatre Lab; two restaurants; library. Tours (daily, limited hrs). New Hampshire Ave at F St NW. Phone 202/416-8340 (tours) or 202/467-4600 (performance tickets).

Judiciary Square. Two square blocks of judiciary buildings, including five federal and district courts and the US District Court (1820) and US Court of Appeals (1910). At D St halfway between 4th & 5th Sts is the first completed statue of Abraham Lincoln (1868). D, E, & F Sts, between 4th & 5th Sts NW.

Kenilworth Aquatic Gardens. Water lilies, lotuses, other water plants bloom from mid-May until frost. Gardens (daily). Guided walks (Memorial Day-Labor Day, Sat, Sun & hols, also by appt). Anacostia Ave & Douglas St NE. Phone 202/426-6905.   **Free**

Labor Department. Lobby contains the Labor Hall of Fame, an exhibit depicting labor in United States; library on second floor is open to public. (Mon-Fri; closed major hols) Francis H. Perkins Building, 200 Constitution Ave NW. Phone 202/219-5000 or 202/219-6992 (library).   **Free**

Lafayette Square. Statue of Andrew Jackson on horseback in center was first equestrian figure in Washington (1853). One of park benches was known as Bernard Baruch's office in 1930s and is dedicated to him. On square is

Decatur House Museum (1818). Federal town house built for naval hero Commodore Stephen Decatur by Benjamin H. Latrobe, second architect of the Capitol. After Decatur's death in 1820, the house was occupied by a succession of American and foreign statesmen and was a center of political and social life in the city. The ground floor family rooms reflect Decatur's federal-period lifestyle; the second-floor rooms retain their Victorian character. Operated by National Trust for Historic Preservation. (Daily exc Mon; closed Jan 1, Thanksgiving, Dec 25) 748 Jackson Place NW. Phone 202/842-0920.   ¢¢

Library of Congress (1800). Treasures include a Gutenberg Bible, the first great book printed with movable metal type; the Giant Bible of Mainz, a 500-yr-old illuminated manuscript. Collection includes books, manuscripts, newspapers, maps, recordings, prints, photographs, posters and more than 30 million books and pamphlets in 60 languages. In the elaborate Jefferson Building is the Great Hall, decorated with murals, mosaics and marble carvings; exhibition halls (some sections closed for renovation). In the Madison Building, a 22-min audiovisual presentation, *America's Library*, provides a good introduction to the library and its facilities. (Daily exc Sun; closed federal hols) 10 1st St SE. For reading room schedule, calendar of events, phone 202/707-6400; for information on exhibitions & free guided tours, phone 202/707-8000.   **Free**   Library complex includes

Folger Shakespeare Library (1932). Houses the finest collection of Shakespeare materials in the world, including the 1623 First Folio edition and large holdings of rare books and manuscripts of the English and continental Renaissance. The Great Hall offers year-round exhibits from the Folger's extensive collection. The Elizabethan Theatre, which was designed to resemble an innyard theater of Shakespeare's day, is the site of the Folger Shakespeare Library's series of museum and performing arts programs, which includes literary readings, drama, lectures, and education and family programs. Guided tours (mornings). (Daily exc Sun; closed federal hols) 201 E Capitol St SE. Phone 202/544-4600.   **Free**   North on Ist St are the

☒ **Lincoln Memorial.** Dedicated in 1922, Daniel Chester French's Lincoln looks across a reflecting pool to the Washington Monument and Capitol. Lincoln's Gettysburg Address and Second Inaugural Address are inscribed on the walls of the temple-like structure, which is particularly impressive at night. Tours. *(Interior to remain open to the public during restoration study.)* (Daily, 24 hrs; closed Dec 25) 23rd St NW, at Daniel French & Henry Bacon Dr. Phone 202/426-6841.   **Free**

Martin Luther King Memorial Library (1972). Main branch of DC public library was designed by architect Mies van der Rohe. Martin Luther King mural. Books, periodicals, photographs, films, videocassettes, recordings, microfilms, Washingtoniana and the *Washington Star* collection. Library for the visually impaired; librarian for the hearing impaired; black studies division; AP wire service machine; community information service. Underground parking. (Mon-Sat, also Sun afternoons; closed hols) 901 G St NW. Phone 202/727-1111.   **Free**

MCI Center. Home of the NBA's Washington Wizards and the NHL's Washington Capitals, this 220,000-sq-ft venue also has the Discovery Channel Destination, a retail and interactive store with 3 themed floors: the earth's surface, a terrestrial level, and space and sky. An Insiders View, a behind-the-scenes look at Washington DC and its history, shown on high-definition screen (fee). Backstage tour of entire center (fee; includes film). Also 19,000-sq-ft sports restaurant overlooking the Wizards' practice court. (Daily) 601 F St NW. Phone 202/628-3200. Also here is

> **MCI National Sports Gallery.** 25,000-sq-ft museum commemorates and showcases the best of American sports history. Includes sports memorabilia collections; participatory and technology-driven exhibits with basketball, football, hockey and baseball themes. Rotating exhibits feature special-interest sports. Home of the American Sportscasters Association Hall of Fame and Museum, honoring the memorable voices that brought us our greatest sports moments. Gallery ¢¢¢

✪ **Mount Vernon.** 18 mi S via George Washington Memorial Pkwy. (See MOUNT VERNON in Virginia)

National Academy of Sciences (1924). Established in 1863 to stimulate research and communication among scientists and to advise the federal government in science and technology. A famous 21-ft bronze statue of Albert Einstein by Robert Berks is on the front lawn. Art exhibits, concerts. (Schedule varies) 2101 Constitution Ave, between 21st & 22nd Sts NW. Phone 202/334-2436. **Free**

The National Archives (1934). Original copies of the Declaration of Independence, Bill of Rights, Constitution; a 1297 version of the Magna Carta and other historic documents, maps and photographs. Guided tours by appt only; Pennsylvania Ave between 7th & 9th Sts NW; exhibition entrance on Constitution Ave, phone 202/501-5205. Archives also available to public for genealogical and historical research (daily exc Sun; closed federal hols). (Daily; closed Dec 25) Phone 202/501-5000 (recording) or 202/501-5400 (research library & exhibition hall). **Free**

National Building Museum. Deals with architecture, design, engineering and construction. Permanent exhibits include drawings, blueprints, models, photographs, artifacts; architectural evolution of Washington's buildings and monuments. The museum's enormous Great Hall is supported by eight of the world's largest Corinthian columns. Guided tours (afternoons: wkdays, 1 tour; wkends, 2 tours). Museum (Mon-Sat; also Sun afternoons). Housed in Old Pension Building, F St between 4th & 5th Sts NW. Phone 202/272-2448. **Free**

National Colonial Farm. Approx 150 acres in Piscataway National Park. A "living history" farm of mid-18th century; crops, herb garden, livestock, methods of the period are used; replicated farm buildings. (Daily exc Mon; closed Jan 1, Thanksgiving, Dec 25) I-95 exit 3A, then 10 mi S on MD 210, right on Bryan Point Rd, 3 mi in Accokeek, MD. Phone 301/283-2113. ¢

National Gallery of Art. The West Building (1941), designed by John Russell Pope, contains Western European and American art, spanning periods between the 13th and 20th centuries: highlights include the only Leonardo da Vinci painting in the western hemisphere, *Ginevra de' Benci,* a comprehensive collection of Italian paintings and sculpture; major French Impressionists; numerous Rembrandts and examples of the Dutch school; masterpieces from the Mellon, Widener, Kress, Dale and Rosenwald collections; special exhibitions. The East Building (1978), designed by architect I. M. Pei, houses the gallery's growing collection of 20th-century art, including Picasso's *Family of Saltimbanques* and Jackson Pollock's *Lavender Mist.* (Daily; closed Jan 1, Dec 25) Constitution Ave, between 3rd & 7th Sts. Phone 202/737-4215. **Free**

National Museum of American Art. American paintings, sculpture, prints and graphic art from the 18th century to the present. (Daily; closed Dec 25) 8th & G Sts NW, Gallery Place. Phone 202/357-2700. **Free**

National Museum of Health and Medicine. One of the most important medical collections in America. Interprets the link between history and technology; AIDS education exhibit; an interactive exhibit on human anatomy and lifestyle choices; collection of microscopes, medical teaching aids, tools and instruments (1862-1965) and famous historical icons exhibits. (Daily; closed Dec 25) Bldg #54, Walter Reed Army Medical Center. Phone 202/782-2200. **Free**

National Museum of Women in the Arts. Focus on women's contributions to history of art. More than 1,200 works by women artists from Renaissance to present. Paintings, drawings, sculpture, pottery, prints. Library, research center by appt. Guided tours (by appt). (Daily; closed Jan 1, Thanksgiving, Dec 25) 1250 New York Ave NW. Phone 202/783-5000. **Donation**

National Portrait Gallery. Portraits and statues of people who have made significant contributions to the history, development and culture of the US. (Daily; closed Dec 25) 8th & F Sts NW. Phone 202/357-2700. **Free**

National Presbyterian Church and Center. Chapel of the President contains memorabilia of past US presidents; faceted glass windows depict history of man and church. Self-guided tours (daily; no tours hols). Guided tours (Sun following service). 4101 Nebraska Ave NW. Phone 202/537-0800.

Navy Yard. Along the Anacostia River, at a location chosen by George Washington, the yard was founded in 1799 and was nearly destroyed during the War of 1812. Outside the yard, at 636 G St SE, is the John Phillip Sousa house, where the "march king" wrote many of his famous compositions; the house is private. M St between 1st & 11th Sts SE. One blk E is

> **Marine Barracks.** Parade ground, more than two centuries old, is surrounded by handsome and historic structures, including the Commandant's House, facing G St, which is said to be the oldest continuously occupied public building in the city. Spectacular parade is open to public Tues & Fri evenings in summer (see SEASONAL EVENTS). Entrance to Navy Yard is at end of 9th St at M St SE. Inside is G St between 8th & 9th Sts SE.

> **Marine Corps Museum.** Weapons, uniforms, maps, flags, and other artifacts describe the history of the US Marine Corps. Housed in restored 19th-century structure; also used as marine barracks from 1941 to 1975. (Daily exc Tues; closed Jan 1, Dec 25) 901 M St. Phone 202/433-3840. **Free**

> **Navy Museum.** History of US Navy from the American Revolution to the space age. Dioramas depict achievements of early naval heroes; displays development of naval weapons; fully rigged foremast fighting top and gun deck from frigate *Constitution* on display; World War II guns that can be trained and elevated; submarine room has operating periscopes. Approx 5,000 objects on display include paintings, ship models, flags, uniforms, naval decorations and the bathyscaphe *Trieste.* Two-acre outdoor park displays 19th- and 20th-century guns, cannon, other naval artifacts; US Navy destroyer *Barry* located on the waterfront. (Daily; closed Jan 1, Thanksgiving, Dec 24, 25) Tours (Mon-Fri). Bldg 76, Washington Navy Yard, 805 Kidder Breese SE. Phone 202/433-6897 or 202/433-4882. **Free**   Nearby is

New York Ave Presbyterian Church. The church where Lincoln worshiped; rebuilt 1950-1951 with Lincoln's pew. Dr. Peter Marshall was pastor 1939-1949. Mementos on display include first draft of Emancipation Proclamation. (Daily, services Sun morning; closed hols) 1313 New York Ave, at H St NW. Phone 202/393-3700.

Octagon House (1798-1800). Federal town house built for Colonel John Tayloe III, based on designs by Dr. William Thornton. Served as temporary quarters for President and Mrs James Madison after White House was burned in War of 1812; also site of ratification of the Treaty of Ghent. Restored with period furnishings (1800-1828). Changing exhibits on architecture and allied arts. (Daily exc Mon; closed major hols) 1799 New York Ave NW, at 18th & E Sts NW. Phone 202/638-3105. ¢¢

Old Executive Office Building (1875). Second Empire/Victorian architecture. Built as War Office; was also home to State Department; now offices for president's staff. Guided tours by appt (Sat morning only). Pennsylvania Ave & 17th St NW. Phone 202/395-5895. **Free**

Old Stone House (1765). Believed to be the oldest pre-Revolutionary building in Washington. Constructed on parcel No. 3 of the original tract of land that was then Georgetown, the house was used as both a residence and a place of business; five rooms are furnished with household items that reflect a middle-class residence of the late 18th century. The grounds are lush with fruit trees and seasonal blooms. (Wed-Sun; closed hols) 3051 M St NW. Phone 202/426-6851 (also TTY service). **Free**

Organization of American States (OAS). Headquarters of OAS, set up to maintain international peace and security and to promote integral development in the Americas. Tropical patio, Hall of Heroes and Flags, Hall of the Americas, Aztec Garden, Council Chamber. (Mon-Fri; closed hols) Constitution Ave & 17th St NW. Phone 202/458-3000. **Free**

Oxon Hill Farm. Living history farm circa 1898-1914 located on working farm with livestock; participation activities. (Daily; closed Jan 1, Thanksgiving, Dec 25) Entrance from Oxon Hill Rd, 300 yds W of jct MD 210 & I-95 in Oxon Hill, MD. Phone 301/839-1177.   **Free**

Pavilion at the Old Post Office (1899). Romanesque structure, which for years was headquarters of the US Postal Service, has been remodeled into a festival marketplace with 100 shops and restaurants, a miniature golf course and daily entertainment. In the 315-ft tower are replicas of the bells of Westminster Abbey, a Bicentennial gift from Great Britain; the tower, which is the second-highest point in DC, offers spectacular views from an open-air observation deck (free). Above the Pavilion shops is the headquarters for the National Endowment for the Arts. (Daily; closed Jan 1, Thanksgiving, Dec 25) Pennsylvania Ave, between 11th & 12th Sts NW. Phone 202/289-4224.   **Free**

Potomac Park (East and West). On the banks of the Potomac River, park recreational activities include fishing, pedalboating; golf, tennis; picnicking. Washington's famous cherry trees can be found around the Tidal Basin. Hundreds of **Yoshino and Akebono cherry trees**, a gift from Japan in 1912, come into full bloom in a celebration of spring (see ANNUAL EVENTS), an unforgettable floral display (late-Mar-early-Apr). West Potomac park is the site of the Franklin Delano Roosevelt Memorial. NW & SE of the Jefferson Memorial. For park information phone 202/619-7222.

⭐ **President Kennedy's Gravesite.** South Gate, Arlington National Cemetery. (See ARLINGTON COUNTY in Virginia)

Professional sports.

  NBA (Washington Wizards). MCI Center, 601 F St NW. Phone 202/628-3200.

  NFL (Washington Redskins). Jack Kent Cooke Stadium, Landover, MD. Phone 703/478-8900.

  NHL (Washington Capitals). MCI Center, 601 F St NW. Phone 202/628-3200.

Renwick Gallery. American crafts from 1900 to the present. A department of the National Museum of American Art. (Daily; closed Dec 25) Pennsylvania Ave NW at 17th St NW. Phone 202/357-2700.   **Free**

Rock Creek Park. More than 1,700 acres with working gristmill; 18-hole golf course, hiking, exercise course, historic sites, tennis courts, picnicking, self-guided nature trails, stables, bridle paths and biking trails, ball fields. Fee for some activities. NW on Beach Dr. Phone 202/282-1063. Also here are

  Art Barn. Historic carriage house (1831). Art exhibitions. (Thurs-Sun Noon-6:00 pm) 2401 Tilden St & Beach Dr NW. Phone 202/244-2482. **Free**

  Carter Barron Amphitheater. This 4,200-seat outdoor theater in wooded area is setting for summer performances of symphonic, folk, pop and jazz music (see SEASONAL EVENTS) and Shakespearean theater. Some fees. 16th St & Colorado Ave NW. Phone 202/426-6837 for tickets.

  National Zoological Park. A branch of the Smithsonian Institution, the zoo features approx 5,000 animals of 500 species, including a giant panda; lions, tigers and cheetahs; great apes; elephants and rhinos; small mammals; reptiles and invertebrates; birdhouse and wetlands; rain forest exhibit. Picnicking, refreshments. Guided tours (wkends). Metrorail (Red Line) stop. Limited parking (fee). (Daily; closed Dec 25) Main entrance at 3000 blk of Connecticut Ave NW; other entrances at Beach Dr (Rock Creek Pkwy) and jct Adams Mill Rd & Harvard St. Phone 202/673-4800.   **Free**

  Nature Center. Planetarium, films, exhibits, nature demonstrations. (Wed-Sun; closed hols) 5200 Glover Rd NW. Phone 202/426-6829. **Free**

Shops at National Place. Tri-level marketplace—at, above and below street grade—featuring more than 100 specialty shops and restaurants. (Daily) National Press Building, F St, between 13th & 14th Sts. Phone 202/662-1200.

Theaters. Shakespeare Theatre. Lansburgh Theater, 450 7th St NW, phone 202/393-2700. **The National,** E St, 1 blk N of 13th & Pennsylvania Ave, phone 202/628-6161. **Arena Stage,** 6th & Maine Ave SW, phone 202/488-3300. **The Warner,** 13th & E Sts NW, phone 202/628-1818. Also see Kennedy Center.

Theodore Roosevelt Memorial. N end of Theodore Roosevelt Island, accessible only by footbridge from George Washington Memorial Pkwy, northbound lane, in Arlington, VA. The island is an 88-acre wilderness

preserve; the 17-ft statue of Roosevelt was designed by Paul Manship. (Daily; closed Dec 25) Phone 703/285-2530.   **Free**

Senate Office Buildings. Constitution Ave on both sides of 1st St NE. Linked by private subway to Capitol.

Sewall-Belmont House (1680, 1800). The Sewall-Belmont House is a living monument to Alice Paul, the author of the Equal Rights Amendment. From this house she spearheaded the fight for the passage of the amendment. The house, now a national landmark, contains portraits and sculptures of women from the beginning of the suffrage movement; extensive collection of memorabilia of the suffrage and equal rights movements; headquarters of the National Woman's Party. (Tues-Fri, also Sat afternoons; closed Jan 1, Thanksgiving, Dec 25) 144 Constitution Ave NE. Phone 202/546-3989 or 202/546-1210.   **Free**

Sightseeing tours.

  Gray Line bus tours. Tours of city and area attractions depart from terminal in Union Station. For information contact 5500 Tuxedo Rd, Tuxedo, MD 20781; phone 301/386-8300 or 800/862-1400.

  Tourmobile Sightseeing. Narrated shuttle tours to 18 historic sites on the National Mall and in Arlington National Cemetery. Unlimited reboarding throughout day (daily; no tours Dec 25). Additional tours separately or in combinations: Arlington National Cemetery; Mount Vernon (Apr-Oct) and Frederick Douglass Home (mid-June-Labor Day). Phone 202/554-7950, -5100 or -7020. ¢¢¢¢

⭐ **Smithsonian Institution.** The majority of Smithsonian museums are located on the National Mall. Smithsonian headquarters are located in the Smithsonian Institution Building, the "Castle" (1855), located at 1000 Jefferson Dr SW, on the Mall. The headquarters contain administrative offices, Smithson's crypt and the Smithsonian Information Center, which has information on all Smithsonian museums. Many visitors begin their day here. (All buildings open daily; closed Dec 25; Anacostia Museum and National Zoo hrs vary) For general information and schedule phone 202/357-2700.   **Free**   Smithsonian museums on the Mall include

National Museum of Natural History. Gems (including Hope Diamond), minerals; botanical, zoological and geological materials; live insect "zoo"; Dinosaur Hall, Discovery Room, with hands-on activities for children; living coral reef; cultures of Africa, Asia, the Pacific and the Americas are explored; Western civilization is traced to its roots. Cafeteria. Special Exhibition Hall. Constitution Ave, between 9th & 12th Sts NW.   **Donation**   To the West is

National Museum of American History. Cultural and technological development of the US; Star-Spangled Banner; glass exhibit; numismatic exhibit; political history exhibits; gowns of First Ladies; interactive video stations; ship models; Railroad Hall. Cafeteria, snack bar, ice cream parlor. Constitution Ave, between 12th & 14th Sts NW.   **Donation**   Across the Mall is

Freer Gallery. Asian art with objects dating from Neolithic period to the early 20th century. Also works by late 19th- and early 20th-century American artists, including a major collection of James McNeill Whistler's work, highlighted by the famous Peacock Room. Jefferson Dr at 12th St SW. Phone 202/357-2700. Next to the Freer is the Smithsonian Institution Building, or "the Castle."   **Free**   Connected to the Freer is the

Arthur M. Sackler Gallery. Changing exhibitions of Asian art, both Near- and Far-Eastern, from major national and international collections. Permanent collection includes Chinese and South and Southeast Asian art objects presented by Arthur Sackler.   **Free**   Between the Freer Gallery and the Arts and Industries Building is the **Enid A. Haupt Garden,** four acres that comprise the "roof" of the Sackler Gallery, the International Gallery, an underground Smithsonian research and education complex and 1050 Independence Ave SW.

National Museum of African Art. Devoted to collection, study, research and exhibition of African art. The museum collection, numbering about 6,000 objects, is a primary source for the study of African art and culture; highlighted by traditional arts of sub-Saharan Africa, including collection of utilitarian objects. Guided tours by appt. 950 Independence Ave SW.   **Free**   To the east is

Arts and Industries Building. The south hall contains the Experimental Gallery, an exhibit space dedicated to innovative and creative exhibits from museums in the Smithsonian and from around the world. Discovery Theater (fee) hosts performances for children. 900 Jefferson Dr SW. **Free**   Directly to the east is

Hirshhorn Museum and Sculpture Garden. Modern, circular museum houses a collection of more than 6,000 works of art donated by Joseph H. Hirshhorn. Emphasis on contemporary art, as well as 19th- and 20th-century painting and sculpture. Sculpture garden is on the Mall, between 7th & 9th Sts SW. Independence Ave, between 7th & 9th Sts SW. **Free**   Directly east is

National Air and Space Museum. Museum presents exhibits on history of aviation and space age; artifacts include the original *Kitty Hawk Flyer, Spirit of St Louis* and *Friendship 7;* also touchable moon rocks. In honor of the 500th anniversary of Columbus' voyage to the Western Hemisphere, the exhibit *Where Next, Columbus?* looks ahead to the next 500 yrs with a study of the scientific, technological, economic, ethical and political issues of future space travel. Five-story theater shows IMAX films on air and space travel (fee; for schedule phone 202/357-1686). Museum also encompasses Albert Einstein Planetarium (fee). Independence Ave, between 7th & 4th Sts SW.

For a behind-the-scenes look at the restoration of the museum's reserve collection of approx 90 aircraft, spacecraft, engines, propellers and flight-related objects, visit the **Paul E. Garber Facility** in Suitland, MD (15 mi SE via Independence Ave to Pennsylvania Ave to Silver Hill Rd). Guided tours (daily; closed Dec 25; reservations must be made two wks in advance by contacting Tour Scheduler, Office of Volunteer Services, National Air and Space Museum, Smithsonian Institution, Washington, DC 20560; phone 202/357-1400).   **Free**

St John's Church. Oldest Episcopal congregation in Georgetown, established 1796; original design of church by William Thornton, architect of the Capitol. Many presidents since Madison have worshiped here. Francis Scott Key was a founding member. Tours (by appt). 3240 O St NW. Phone 202/338-1796.

Supreme Court of the United States. Designed by Cass Gilbert in neo-classical style. Court is in session Oct-Apr (Mon-Wed, at 2-wk intervals from first Mon in Oct) and on the first workday of each week in May & June; court sessions are open to the public (10 am & 1 pm), on a first-come basis; lectures are offered in the courtroom (Mon-Fri exc when court is in session; 20-min lectures hrly on half-hr); on ground floor are exhibits and film (23 min), cafeteria, snack bar, gift shop (Mon-Fri; closed hols). 1st St NE at Maryland Ave, E of Capitol. Phone 202/479-3211.   **Free**

⭐ **Thomas Jefferson Memorial** (1943). Memorial honors the 2nd President of the United States and author of both the Declaration of Independence and Bill of Rights. Tours. (Daily; closed Dec 25) *(Site to remain open to the public during restoration study.)* S edge of Tidal Basin. Phone 202/426-6841.   **Free**

Tudor Place (1805). Twelve-rm federal-style mansion was designed by Dr. William Thornton, architect of Capitol, for Martha Custis Peter, granddaughter of Martha Washington. Peter family lived in house for 180 yrs. All furnishings and objets d'art original. More than five acres of gardens (daily exc Sun). Guided tours (Tues-Sat, by reservation; closed hols). 1644 31st St NW. Phone 202/965-0400. Garden only   ¢; House and garden   ¢¢

Union Station. Restored beaux-arts train station, designed by Daniel Burnham and completed in 1907, features lavish interior spaces under 96-ft-high, coffered, gold-leafed ceiling. Located within original station and train shed are 130 shops, restaurants and movie theater complex. Original spaces, such as the presidential suite, have been turned into restaurants without extensive alteration. Also located within the station are the Amtrak depot and Gray Line and Tourmobile Sightseeing operators (see SIGHTSEEING TOURS). (Daily) On Massachusetts Ave between 1st & 2nd Sts.   **Free**   Also here is

United States Navy Memorial. Dedicated to those who have served in the Navy in war and in peacetime. A 100-ft diameter granite world map dominates the Plaza, where the *Lone Sailor,* a 7-ft bronze sculpture stands and the US Navy Band stages performances (Memorial Day-Labor Day, Tues evenings). Visitors Center features electronic kiosks with interactive video displays on naval history; also Navy Memorial Log Room and US Presidents Room. (Mon-Sat, also Sun afternoons) Pennsylvania Ave, at 7th & 9th Sts NW. Phone 202/737-2300.   **Free**

At Sea. Underwritten by Mobil Corp, this is an award-winning high-resolution 70mm film that conveys the experience of being at sea aboard a US Navy aircraft carrier. The 241-seat theater employs a 2-story, 52-ft-wide screen and 6-track digital audio to surround the audience with the sights and sounds of carrier operations. Showings (Mon-Sat, 4 times daily; Sun, 2 times). Arleigh and Roberta Burke Theater.   ¢¢

US Botanic Gardens. The Botanic Garden, one of the oldest in the country, was established by Congress in 1820 for public education and exhibition. It features plants collected by the famous Wilkes Expedition of the South Seas. Conservatory has tropical, subtropical and desert plants; seasonal displays. Exterior gardens are planted for seasonal blooming; also here is Bartholdi Fountain, designed by sculptor of the Statue of Liberty. (closed until late 2000) Maryland Ave & 1st St SW, at base of Capitol Hill. Phone 202/225-8333.   **Free**

⭐ **US Holocaust Memorial Museum.** Interprets the story of the Holocaust through modern exhibition techniques and authentic objects, including a railroad freight car used to transport Polish Jews from Warsaw, concentration camp uniforms, photographs, diaries. Visitors are taken from Hall of Witness directly to the fourth floor, and begin a chronological journey from the roots of the Holocaust to its aftermath. Changing exhibits include "Remember the Children," which interprets Holocaust events from a child's perspective. (Daily; closed Yom Kippur, Dec 25) Permanent exhibits recommended for ages 11 and over only. Entrances at Raoul Wallenberg Place (15th St SW) and at 14th St SW. Phone 202/488-0400. **Free**

US National Arboretum. Floral displays spring, summer, fall and winter on 444 acres; Japanese garden, National Bonsai and Penjing Museum (daily); National Herb Garden, major collections of azaleas (15,000), wildflowers, ferns, magnolias, crabapples, cherries, dogwoods; aquatic plantings; dwarf conifers (world's largest evergreen collection). (Daily; closed Dec 25) Under 16 yrs admitted only with adult. 3501 New York Ave NE. Phone 202/544-8733.   **Free**

⭐ **Vietnam Veterans Memorial.** Designed by Maya Ying Lyn, the memorial's polished black granite walls are inscribed with the names of the 58,175 US citizens who died in or remain missing from the Vietnam War (a large directory helps visitors locate names). Also Statue of Three Servicemen. Built with private contributions of American citizens. (Daily) Constitution Ave between Henry Bacon Dr & 21st St NW. Phone 202/634-1568. **Free**

Voice of America. Live radio broadcasts to foreign countries; 45-min guided tours (Mon-Fri, res required; closed major hols). 330 Independence Ave SW between 3rd & 4th Sts SW; enter on C St. Phone 202/619-3919. **Free**

Washington Dolls' House & Toy Museum. Splendid collection of antique doll houses, dolls, toys and games; museum shop. (Daily exc Mon; closed Jan 1, Thanksgiving, Dec 25) 5236 44th St NW. Phone 202/363-6400.   ¢¢

Washington Harbour. This is a dining and shopping complex that features lavish fountains, life-size statuary and a boardwalk with a view of the Potomac River. 30th & K Sts NW.

⭐ **Washington Monument.** Parking lot on N side, off Constitution Ave. The obelisk, tallest masonry structure in the world (555 ft), was dedicated in 1885 to the memory of the first US president. (Daily; extended hrs in summer; closed Dec 25) *(Site to remain open to the public during restoration.)* Elevator to observation room at 500-ft level. To take the 898 steps up or down, arrangements must be made in advance. Mall at 15th St NW. Phone 202/426-6839 or 202/426-6841 (Visitor Center).   **Free**

⭐ **Washington National Cathedral.** Cornerstone of the Gothic cathedral was laid in 1907; final stone was set in 1990; structure, built entirely in the manner and materials of medieval cathedrals, took 83 yrs, 5 architects and the terms of 7 bishops to complete. Details are intentionally irregular to avoid uniform features typical of machine-age building. Tombs of Woodrow Wilson, Helen Keller and others are within structure. Pilgrim Observation Gallery overlooks Washington from city's highest geographic point. Within the grounds are trees grown from a cutting of England's Glastonbury Thorne, which by legend grew from the staff of Joseph of Arimathea; museum shop; Bishop's Garden, a medieval, walled garden; Herb Cottage; greenhouse with potted herbs for sale. Shops (daily). Services (daily). Carillon recitals (Sat). Organ recitals (Sun). Tours (daily). Massachusetts & Wisconsin Aves NW. Phone 202/537-6200 (recording), 202/537-6247 or 202/537-6207 (tours).   **Donation**

⭐ **White House** (1800). Constructed under the supervision of George Washington, the house has been lived in by every president since John Adams. It was burned by the British during the War of 1812 and reconstructed under the guidance of James Monroe (1817-1825). The West Wing, which includes the oval office, was built during Theodore Roosevelt's administration (1901-1909); before its construction, executive offices shared the second floor with the president's private quarters. The interior of the White House was gutted and rebuilt, using modern construction techniques, during the Truman administration; President Truman and family resided at Blair House for four years during the reconstruction. The Library and the Vermeil Room (on Ground Floor), the East Room, Green, Blue and Red rooms and the State Dining Room (on State Floor) are accessible to public. Tours (mid-Mar-Oct, Tues-Sat mornings; tickets avail at the new White House Visitor Center, 1450 Pennsylvania Ave NW; closed Jan 1, Dec 25 and presidential functions). 1600 Pennsylvania Ave NW. Phone 202/456-7041 (recording).   **Free**

Wild World. Thrill rides, water attractions, children's rides; wave pool; Wild One Rollercoaster. Entertainment; game gallery. Parking fee. (Mid-May-Labor Day, schedule varies) E via Capital Beltway to exit 15A, then E on Central Ave (MD 214) in Mitchellville, MD, follow signs. Phone 301/249-1500. ¢¢¢¢

Yellow House (1733). One of Georgetown's oldest homes, typical of the area's mansions. (Private residence) 1430 33rd St NW.

Annual Events

Cherry Blossom Festival. Celebrates the blooming Japanese cherry trees. Also Japanese Lantern Lighting ceremony and marathon run; parade. Phone 202/619-7275. Late Mar-early Apr.

Easter Egg Roll. White House Lawn. First introduced to Washington by Dolley Madison. Phone 202/456-2200 (recording). Mon after Easter.

Georgetown House Tour. Held since 1927, participants view 12 well-known and less well-known houses in Georgetown. St John's Episcopal Church members serve as hosts, guides and serve tea in the Parish Hall in the afternoon. Phone 202/338-1796. Late Apr.

Georgetown Garden Tour. Fourteen or more different gardens open to the public. Proceeds go to Georgetown Children's House; includes "Evermay" garden, which features grand expanses, fountains and sculptures. Self-guided tours. Phone 202/333-4953. Late Apr or early May.

Goodwill Industries Embassy Tour. Six to eight embassies are open to the public; only time embassies are open to public; visitors can view artifacts and design peculiar to each government's legation. Complimentary refreshments and illustrated tour booklet. Walking tour with shuttle bus between embassies. Tickets limited. No children under age 10. Phone 202/636-4225. 2nd Sat May.

Memorial Day Ceremony. Arlington National Cemetery (See ARLINGTON COUNTY in Virginia). Wreaths placed at Tomb of the Unknown Soldier. The National Symphony Orchestra gives a concert later in the evening on the lawn of the Capitol.

Festival of American Folklife. The Mall. Festival of folklife traditions from America and abroad. Sponsored by the Smithsonian Institution and National Park Service. Phone 202/357-2700 or 202/619-7222. Late June-early July.

July 4 Celebration. Washington Monument and Capitol west steps. Music, celebrations.

Washington National Cathedral Open House. Washington National Cathedral. Special tours, entertainment, food; demonstrations of cathedral arts. Only day of the year when central tower is open to the public. Phone 202/537-6200. Sat nearest Sept 29.

Taste of DC. Pennsylvania Ave NW between 9th & 14th St. Selected DC restaurants offer sample-size specialities. Phone 202/724-4093. Mid-Oct.

Pageant of Peace. Ellipse, S of White House. Seasonal music, caroling, the giant Christmas tree near the White House is lit by the president. Dec.

Seasonal Events

Evening Parade. US Marine Barracks, I St between 8th & 9th Sts SE. Spectacular parade with Marine Band, US Marine Drum and Bugle Corps, Color Guard, Silent Drill Team and marching companies. Written request for reservations suggested at least 3 wks in advance. Phone 202/433-6060. Tues & Fri evenings, early-May-late Aug.

Concerts. Sylvan Theater, Washington Monument grounds, June-Aug, days vary, phone 202/619-7222. US Capitol, west terrace, June-late Aug, Mon-Wed, Fri, Sun, phone 202/619-7222. Natl Gallery of Art, west garden court, Oct-June, Sun evenings; first-come basis, phone 202/842-6941. Phillips Collection, a Dupont-Kalorama museum, Sept-May, Sun, phone 202/387-2151.

Wolf Trap Farm Park for the Performing Arts. In Vienna, VA, 14 mi NW via Washington Memorial Pkwy, VA 123, US 7, then S on Towlston Rd (Trap Rd), (VA 676), then follow signs. Phone 703/255-1900. (See FAIRFAX in Virginia) Late May-Sept (Filene Center) & mid-Oct-mid-May (Barnes Center).

Musical programs. In Carter Barron Amphitheater, Rock Creek Park. Phone 202/619-7222. Mid-June-Aug.

Fort Dupont Summer Theatre. Fort Dupont Park. Musicals, concerts, plays, dancing. Phone 202/426-7723. Fri evenings, late June-late Aug.

Washington Area Suburbs

The following suburbs and towns in the Washington, DC, area are included in the *Mobil Travel Guide*. For information on any one of them, see the individual alphabetical listing. In Virginia: Alexandria, Arlington County (Ronald Reagan Washington-National Airport Area), Fairfax, Falls Church, McLean, Springfield, Tysons Corner. In Maryland: Bethesda, Bowie, College Park, Laurel, Rockville, Silver Spring.

Airport Areas

For additional attractions and accommodations, see ARLINGTON COUNTY (RONALD REAGAN WASHINGTON-NATIONAL AIRPORT AREA) and DULLES INTL AIRPORT AREA in Virginia. Also see BALTIMORE/WASHINGTON INTL AIRPORT AREA in Maryland.

City Neighborhoods

Many of the restaurants, unrated dining establishments and some lodgings listed under Washington include neighborhoods as well as exact street addresses. Geographic descriptions of these areas are given.

Adams Morgan. North of Dupont Circle; along Columbia Rd between 18th Street NW and Kalorama, NW/Kalorama Park.

Capitol Hill. Both the Hill upon which the Capitol is built (south of Constitution Ave, west of 1st Street NE and SE, north of Independence Ave and east of 1st Street NW and SW) and the surrounding area south of F Street NW and NE, west of 14th Street NE and SE, north of the Southwest Frwy (I-395) and east of 3rd Street NW and SW.

Chinatown. Area of Downtown along G and H Streets NW between 6th and 8th Streets NW.

Downtown. South of Massachusetts Ave, west of N Capitol Street, north of Pennsylvania Ave and east of 19th Street. **North of Downtown:** North of Massachusetts Ave. **South of Downtown:** South of Independence Ave. **West of Downtown:** West of 19th St.

Dupont Circle. On and around the circle where Massachusetts, New Hampshire, Connecticut Aves and 19th and P Streets NW intersect.

Embassy Row. Area north of Dupont Circle; along Massachusetts Ave between Observatory Circle on the north and Sheridan Circle on the south.

Foggy Bottom. Area along the Potomac River south of K Street NW (US 29), west of 19th Street NW and north of Constitution Ave and I-66 interchange.

Georgetown. Northwest of Downtown; south of the Naval Observatory and W Street NW, west of Rock Creek Park and north and east of the Potomac River; area around intersection of Wisconsin Ave and M Street NW.

Kalorama. East and west of Connecticut Ave NW, south of Rock Creek Park and Calvert Street, west of Columbia Rd and north of R Street.

Motor Hotels

★★ CHANNEL INN HOTEL. *650 Water St SW (20024), on waterfront, south of downtown. 202/554-2400; FAX 202/863-1164; res: 800/368-5668.* Web www.channelinn.com. 100 rms, 3 story. S, D $115-$145; each addl $10; suites $145-$175; under 13 free; wkend rates. Crib free. TV; cable (premium). Pool; lifeguard. Restaurant 7 am-11 pm; Sun to 9 pm. Rm serv. Bar 11:30-1 am; Fri, Sat to 2 am; Sun to 10 pm; entertainment. Ck-out noon. Meeting rms. In-rm modem link. Bellhops. Garage parking. Health club privileges. Balconies. Near piers. Cr cds: A, C, D, DS, JCB, MC, V.

D ➤ ⚓ 🔥 SC

✓★★ **THE PREMIER HOTEL.** *2601 Virginia Ave NW (20037), in Foggy Bottom.* 202/965-2700; FAX 202/337-5417; res: 800/965-6869. 192 rms, 8 story. Mid-Mar-Oct: S, D $89-$159; each addl $10; under 18 free; lower rates rest of yr. Crib free. TV; cable (premium). Rooftop pool; lifeguard (Memorial Day-Labor Day). Restaurant 6 am-11 pm. Fri, Sat 24 hrs. Ck-out noon. Coin lndry. Meeting rm. Business servs avail. In-rm modem link. Gift shop. Exercise equipt. Refrigerators. Some balconies. Cr cds: A, C, D, DS, JCB, MC, V.

D ➤ ⚓ 🏃 ⚓ 🔥 SC

★ **WINDSOR PARK HOTEL.** *2116 Kalorama Rd NW (20008), off Connecticut Ave & 21st St, in Kalorama.* 202/483-7700; FAX 202/332-4547; res: 800/247-3064. 43 rms, 5 story, 6 suites. S $88-$98; D $98-$108; each addl $10; suites $125-$155; under 16 free; wkend rates (2-day min). TV; cable (premium). Complimentary continental bkfst. Restaurant nearby. Ck-out noon. Business servs avail. Refrigerators. Cr cds: A, C, D, DS, MC, V.

⚓ 🔥 SC

Hotels

★★★ **CAPITAL HILTON.** *1001 16th St NW (20036), downtown.* 202/393-1000; FAX 202/639-5784; res: 800/445-8667. Web www.hilton. com. 544 rms, 15 story. S $195-$275; D $220-$300; each addl $30; suites $495-$1,100; family, wkend rates; package plans. Crib free. TV; cable (premium). Restaurants 6:30 am-midnight (also see FRAN O'BRIEN'S). Rm serv 24 hrs. Bar 11-2 am; entertainment Tues-Fri. Ck-out noon. Convention facilities. Business center. In-rm modem link. Concierge. Shopping arcade. Barber, beauty shop. Valet parking 24 hrs. Exercise equipt; sauna. Minibars; many wet bars; some refrigerators. Luxury level. Cr cds: A, C, D, DS, JCB, MC, V.

D 🏃 ➤ ⚓ 🔥 SC 🏃

★ **CAPITOL HILL SUITES.** *200 C St SE (20003), on Capitol Hill.* 202/543-6000; FAX 202/547-2608; res: 800/424-9165. 152 kit rms, 5 story. Feb-June: S $139; D $149; each addl $20; suites $169; under 18 free; lower rates rest of yr. Crib free. Valet parking $12. TV; cable (premium), VCR avail. Complimentary continental bkfst. Coffee in rms. Restaurant nearby. Ck-out noon. Meeting rms. Business servs avail. Valet serv. Health club privileges. Refrigerators. Cr cds: A, C, D, DS, MC, V.

⚓ 🔥 SC

✓★ **CENTER CITY HOTEL.** *1201 13th St NW (20005), north of downtown.* 202/682-5300; FAX 202/371-9624; res: 800/458-2817. 100 rms, 8 story. Apr-Sept: S $85-$115; D $95-$125; each addl $10; under 16 free; wkend rates; lower rates rest of yr. Parking $10 in/out. TV; cable (premium). Complimentary continental bkfst. Coffee in rms. Restaurant. Ck-out 11 am. Coin lndry. Meeting rm. Business servs avail. Cr cds: A, C, D, DS, MC, V.

D ⚓ 🔥 SC

★★ **CLARION HAMPSHIRE.** *1310 New Hampshire Ave NW (20036), at N & 20th St, in Dupont Circle area.* 202/296-7600; FAX 202/293-2476; res: 800/368-5691. Web www.expedia.msn.com. 82 rms, 10 story. Mid-Mar-June, early Sept-mid-Nov: S $189; D $209; each addl $20; under 12 free; wkend, monthly rates; lower rates rest of yr. Crib free. Valet parking $12. TV; cable (premium). Complimentary coffee in rms. Restaurant 7 am-10 pm. Bar. Ck-out noon. Meeting rms. Business center. In-rm modem link. Health club privileges. Refrigerators, microwaves, minibars. Some balconies. Cr cds: A, C, D, DS, JCB, MC, V.

D ⚓ 🔥 SC 🏃

★★★ **COURTYARD BY MARRIOTT.** *1900 Connecticut Ave NW (20009), in Kalorama.* 202/332-9300; FAX 202/328-7039; res: 800/321-2311. E-mail dcctyard@erols.com; web www.marriott.com/courtyard/wasnw. 147 rms, 9 story. S $89-$170; D $89-$200; each addl $15; under 18 free; wkend rates (2-day min). Crib free. Garage parking, valet $10. TV; cable (premium), VCR avail. Pool; lifeguard. Coffee in rms. Restaurant 6:30-10:30 am, 5-10 pm. Bar 5-11 pm. Ck-out noon. Coin lndry. Meeting rms. Business servs avail. In-rm modem link. Exercise equipt. Health club privileges. Some minibars. Cr cds: A, C, D, DS, MC, V.

D ➤ 🏃 ⚓ 🔥 SC

★ **DOUBLETREE GUEST SUITES HOTEL.** *2500 Pennsylvania Ave NW (20037), in Foggy Bottom.* 202/333-8060; FAX 202/338-3818; res: 800/222-8733. Web www.doubletree.com. 123 kit. suites, 10 story. S $109-$169; D $109-$184; each addl $15; under 18 free. Crib free. Pet accepted; $12/day. Garage $15. TV; cable (premium). Coffee in rms. Restaurant adj 11 am-midnight. Ck-out noon. Business servs avail. In-rm modem link. Health club privileges. Microwaves. Cr cds: A, C, D, DS, MC, V.

🐾 ⚓ 🔥 SC

★★★ **DOUBLETREE PARK TERRACE.** *1515 Rhode Island Ave NW (20005), in Embassy Row area.* 202/232-7000; FAX 202/332-7152; res: 800/222-8733. Web www.doubletreehotels.com. 220 rms, 8 story, 40 suites. S $155-$175; D $175-$195; each addl $20; suites $185-$225; higher rates Apr-June, Sept-mid Nov; under 16 free. Crib free. Valet parking $12.50. TV; cable (premium). Pool privileges. Complimentary coffee in rms. Restaurant 6 am-11 pm. Rm serv 24 hrs. Bar from 4 pm. Ck-out noon. Coin lndry. Meeting rms. Business servs avail. In-rm modem link. Gift shop. Exercise equipt. Health club privileges. Minibars; microwaves avail. Cr cds: A, C, D, DS, JCB, MC, V.

D 🏃 ⚓ 🔥 SC

★★★ **EMBASSY SQUARE SUITES.** *2000 North St NW (20036), in Dupont Circle area.* 202/659-9000; FAX 202/429-9546; res: 800/424-2999. E-mail emsgreserv@staydc.com; web www.staydc.com. 278 suites, 10 story. Mar-mid-June, mid-Sept-mid-Nov: S $139-$250; D $159-$279; each addl $20; under 18 free; wkly, wkend rates; lower rates rest of yr. Crib free. Garage $12. TV; cable (premium). Pool; lifeguard. Complimentary continental bkfst. Ck-out noon. Coin lndry. Meeting rms. Business servs avail. In-rm modem link. Exercise equipt. Microwaves. Some balconies. Cr cds: A, C, D, DS, MC, V.

D ➤ 🏃 ⚓ 🔥 SC

★★ **EMBASSY SUITES.** *1250 22nd St NW (20037), west of downtown.* 202/857-3388; FAX 202/293-3173; res: 800/362-2779. Web www.embassy-dc.com. 318 suites, 9 story. S $159-$369; D $179-$389; each addl $20; 2-bedrm suites $600-$900; under 16 free; wkend rates. Crib free. TV; cable (premium). Indoor pool; whirlpool, lifeguard. Complimentary full bkfst. Complimentary coffee in rms. Restaurant 11 am-11 pm. Bar. Ck-out noon. Meeting rms. Business center. In-rm modem link. Concierge. Exercise equipt; sauna. Game rm. Refrigerators, microwaves, wet bars. Cr cds: A, C, D, DS, JCB, MC, V.

D ➤ 🏃 ⚓ 🔥 SC 🏃

★★ **EMBASSY SUITES HOTEL.** *4300 Military Rd NW (20015), north of downtown.* 202/362-9300; FAX 202/686-3405; res: 800/362-2779. Web www.embassy-suites.com. 198 suites, 8 story. Mar-Oct: S, D $160-$200; each addl $15; wkend rates; lower rates rest of yr. Crib avail. Garage $10. TV; cable (premium). Indoor pool. Complimentary full bkfst. Complimentary coffee in rms. Rm serv 11:30 am-10 pm. Ck-out noon. Coin lndry. Meeting rms. Business servs avail. Exercise rm. Refrigerators, microwaves, wet bars. Atrium. Connected to shopping center. Cr cds: A, C, D, DS, MC, V.

D ➤ 🏃 ⚓ 🔥 SC

★★★★ **FOUR SEASONS WASHINGTON.** *2800 Pennsylvania Ave NW (20007), in Georgetown.* 202/342-0444; FAX 202/944-2076. E-mail seasons@erols.com; web www.fshr.com. This highly efficient, midsize hotel on the edge of Georgetown has a strong dedication to guest service.

Rooms, some of which have park views, are comfortably furnished and well-lighted. 260 rms, 6 story. S $350-$365; D $350-$395; each addl $30; suites $750-$4,000; under 18 free; wkend rates. Crib free. Pet accepted. Valet parking $25. TV; cable (premium), VCR avail (movies). Indoor pool. Restaurant 7-2 am (also see SEASONS). Rm serv 24 hrs. Afternoon tea. Bar from 11 am. Ck-out noon. Meeting rms. Business center. In-rm modem link. Concierge. Exercise rm; steam rm. Spa. Bathrm phones, minibars; microwaves avail. Some balconies. Cr cds: A, C, D, ER, JCB, MC, V.

⊡ ⦿ ≈ ✕ ≱ ⚹ ⚘

★ **GEORGETOWN DUTCH INN.** *1075 Thomas Jefferson St NW (20007), in Georgetown.* 202/337-0900; FAX 202/333-6526; res: 800/388-2410. 47 kit. suites, 7 story. Feb-mid-June, Sept-mid-Nov: S $135-$165; D $145-$180; each addl $20; suites $250-$350; under 16 free; wkly, monthly rates; higher rates Cherry Blossom season; lower rates rest of yr. Crib free. TV; cable (premium). Complimentary continental bkfst. Ck-out noon. Business servs avail. In-rm modem link. Limited free covered parking. Health club privileges. Bathrm phones. Cr cds: A, C, D, MC, V.

≱ ⚹ SC

★★ **GEORGETOWN INN.** *1310 Wisconsin Ave NW (20007), in Georgetown.* 202/333-8900; FAX 202/333-8308; res: 800/424-2979. 96 rms, 6 story, 10 suites. S, D $195-$225; each addl $20; suites $275-$325; under 13 free; wkend, hol rates. Crib free. Valet parking $15. TV; cable (premium), VCR avail. Restaurant 6:30 am-2 pm, 5-11 pm. Bar 11-1 am. Ck-out noon. Meeting rms. Business servs avail. In-rm modem link. Exercise equipt. Refrigerators avail. Cr cds: A, C, D, DS, JCB, MC, V.

⊡ ✕ ≱ ⚹ SC

★ **GOVERNORS HOUSE HOTEL.** *1615 Rhode Island Ave NW (20036), at 17th Street NW & Scott Circle, downtown.* 202/296-2100; FAX 202/463-6614; res: 800/821-4367. 149 units, 9 story, 24 kits. Mar-June, Sept-Oct: S $125-$195; D $140-$210; each addl $15; suites $175-$225; kit. units $145-$155; under 16 free; wkend, monthly rates. Crib free. Valet parking $16. TV; cable (premium). Pool; lifeguard. Restaurant 7 am-midnight. Bar from 11:30 am. Ck-out noon. Meeting rms. Business servs avail. In-rm modem link. Exercise rm. Health club privileges. Microwaves avail. On original site of Governor of Pennsylvania's house. Cr cds: A, C, D, DS, JCB, MC, V.

⊡ ≈ ✕ ≱ ⚹ SC

★★★ **GRAND HYATT WASHINGTON.** *1000 H St NW (20001), opp Washington Convention Center, downtown.* 202/582-1234; FAX 202/637-4781; res: 800/233-1234. Web www.travelweb.com/hyatt.html. 888 rms, 12 story. S $235-$299; D $250-$299; each addl $25; suites $425-$1,500; under 18 free; wkend rates. Crib free. Garage in/out $12. TV; cable (premium), VCR avail. Indoor pool; whirlpool. Restaurant 6:30-1 am. Bar; entertainment. Ck-out noon. Convention facilities. Business center. In-rm modem link. Gift shop. Exercise rm; sauna. Health club privileges. Minibars. 12-story atrium lobby; 3-story cascading waterfall. Luxury level. Cr cds: A, C, D, DS, JCB, MC, V.

⊡ ≈ ✕ ≱ ⚹ SC ⚘

★★★ **HAY ADAMS HOTEL.** *800 16th St NW (20006), opp White House, downtown.* 202/638-6600; FAX 202/638-2716; res: 800/424-5054. 143 rms, 7 story. S, D $275-$500; each addl $30; suites $575-$2,250; under 13 free; wkend rates. Pet accepted, some restrictions. TV; cable (premium). Restaurant (see LAFAYETTE). Rm serv 24 hrs. Bar 4:30 pm-midnight; Fri, Sat to 1 am. Ck-out noon. Business servs avail. In-rm modem link. Meeting rms. Concierge. Valet parking $24. Health club privileges. Bathrm phones; some refrigerators, minibars, fireplaces. Some balconies. Cr cds: A, C, D, DS, JCB, MC, V.

⦿ ≱ ⚹

★★★ **HENLEY PARK HOTEL.** *926 Massachusetts Ave NW (20001), 1 blk from Washington Convention Center, downtown.* 202/638-5200; FAX 202/414-0513; res: 800/222-8474. 96 rms, 8 story. Mar-May, Oct-Nov: S $165-$235; D $185-$255; each addl $20; suites $295-$875; under 16 free; wkend rates; lower rates rest of yr. Crib free. Valet parking $16. TV; cable (premium). Restaurant 7-10:30 am, 11:30 am-2 pm, 6-10

pm. Rm serv 24 hrs. Bar 11-12:30 am; entertainment. Ck-out noon. Meeting rms. Business servs avail. In-rm modem link. Health club privileges. Bathrm phones, refrigerators, minibars. Wet bar in suites. Tudor detailing; 1918 structure. Cr cds: A, C, D, DS, MC, V.

≱ ⚹ SC

★★★ **HILTON & TOWERS.** *1919 Connecticut Ave NW (20009), in Kalorama.* 202/483-3000; FAX 202/232-0438; res: 800/445-8667. Web www.hilton.com. 1,118 rms, 10 story. S $169-$355; D $189-$355; each addl $25; suites $444-$1,400; wkend rates. Crib free. Pet accepted, some restrictions. Garage $12. TV; cable (premium), VCR avail (movies). Heated pool; poolside serv, lifeguard (in season). Supervised child's activities (May-Sept). Restaurants 6:30 am-11 pm. Bar 11:30-2 am; entertainment. Ck-out noon. Convention facilities. Business center. In-rm modem link. Gift shop. Lighted tennis, pro. Exercise rm. Minibars. Resort atmosphere; on 7 landscaped acres. Luxury level. Cr cds: A, C, D, DS, JCB, MC, V.

⊡ ⦿ ⚓ ≈ ✕ ≱ ⚹ SC ⚘

★★ **HILTON WASHINGTON EMBASSY ROW.** *2015 Massachusetts Ave NW (20036), in Embassy Row.* 202/265-1600; FAX 202/328-7526; res: 800/445-8667. Web www.hilton.com. 193 rms, 9 story. S, D $130-$200; each addl $20; under 17 free; family, wkend, wkly, hol rates; higher rates special events. Crib free. Valet parking $15. TV; cable (premium). Complimentary coffee in rms. Restaurant 6:30 am-10 pm. Rm serv 24 hrs. Bar 11:30-1 am; entertainment. Ck-out noon. Meeting rms. Business center. In-rm modem link. Concierge. Free guest lndry. Exercise equipt. Pool; poolside serv, lifeguard. Many bathrm phones; some refrigerators, microwaves, wet bars. Cr cds: A, C, D, DS, MC, V.

⊡ ≈ ✕ ≱ ⚹ SC ⚘

★★ **HOLIDAY INN CAPITOL.** *550 C St SW (20024), 2 blks from Mall museums, south of downtown.* 202/479-4000; FAX 202/479-4353; res: 800/465-4329. E-mail HICsales@aol.com. 529 rms, 9 story. S, D $179; suites $219-$299; under 18 free; wkend rates. Crib free. Garage $10. TV; cable (premium), Pool; lifeguard. Coffee in rms. Restaurant 6:30 am-10 pm. Bar 11-1 am. Ck-out noon. Coin lndry. Convention facilities. Business servs avail. In-rm modem link. Exercise equipt. Health club privileges. Microwaves avail. Cr cds: A, C, D, DS, JCB, MC, V.

⊡ ≈ ✕ ≱ ⚹ SC

✓★★ **HOLIDAY INN CENTRAL.** *1501 Rhode Island Ave NW (20005), north of downtown.* 202/483-2000; FAX 202/797-1078; res: 800/248-0016. E-mail holiday@inn-dc.com; web www.inn-dc.com. 212 rms, 10 story. Apr-May & Oct: S, D $89-$149; family, wkly, wkend rates; lower rates rest of yr. Crib free. Covered parking $10. TV; cable (premium). Pool; lifeguard. Coffee in lobby. Restaurant 6:30 am-10 pm. Bar. Ck-out noon. Free guest lndry. Meeting rms. Business servs avail. In-rm modem link. Gift shop. Exercise equipt. Game rm. Some refrigerators. Balconies. Cr cds: A, C, D, DS, JCB, MC, V.

⊡ ≈ ✕ ≱ ⚹ SC

★ **HOLIDAY INN GEORGETOWN WASHINGTON DC.** *2101 Wisconsin Ave NW (20007), in Georgetown.* 202/338-4600; FAX 202/333-6113; res: 800/465-4329. 296 rms, 7 story. S $110-$140; D $120-$149; each addl $10; suites $175; under 18 free. Crib free. Parking in/out $10. TV; cable (premium). Pool; lifeguard. Restaurant 6:30 am-2 pm; 5-10 pm. Bar 4-11 pm. Ck-out noon. Coin lndry. Meeting rms. Business servs avail. In-rm modem link. Gift shop. Exercise equipt. Refrigerators avail. Cr cds: A, C, D, DS, JCB, MC, V.

⊡ ≈ ✕ ≱ ⚹ SC

✓★★ **HOLIDAY INN ON THE HILL.** *415 New Jersey Ave NW (20001), on Capitol Hill.* 202/638-1616; FAX 202/638-0707; res: 800/465-4329. 342 rms, 10 story. Feb-May, Sept-Nov: S, D $99-$169; each addl $10; suites $198-$475; under 18 free; wkend rates; lower rates rest of yr. Crib free. Pet accepted, some restrictions. TV; cable (premium). Rooftop pool; poolside serv, lifeguard. Restaurant 6:30 am-midnight. Bar 11-2 am. Ck-out noon. Business servs avail. In-rm modem link. Sundries. Covered parking. Exercise equipt. Cr cds: A, C, D, DS, JCB, MC, V.

✓ ★ **HOTEL HARRINGTON.** *436 11th St NW (20004), downtown.* 202/628-8140; FAX 202/347-3924; res: 800/424-8532. E-mail reservations@hotel-harrington.com; web www.hotel-harrington.com. 260 rms, 11 story, 29 suites. Mar-Oct: S $75-$85; D $85-$95; each addl $5; suites $115; under 16 free; package plans; lower rates rest of yr. Crib avail. Pet accepted, some restrictions. Garage $6.50/day. TV; cable (premium). Restaurants 7 am-midnight. Bar from 11 am. Ck-out noon. Meeting rm. Gift shop. Coin lndry. Refrigerators avail. Cr cds: A, C, D, DS, JCB, MC, V.

★ ★ **HOTEL LOMBARDY.** *2019 I St NW (20006), Foggy Bottom, west of downtown.* 202/828-2600; FAX 202/872-0503; res: 800/424-5486. 125 units, 11 story. Mar-May, Sept-Oct: S $130-$150; D $150-$170; each addl $20; suites $170-$200; under 16 free; wkend rates; lower rates rest of yr. Crib free. TV; cable. Restaurant 7 am-2:30 pm, 5:30-9:30 pm; Sat, Sun 8 am-1 pm, 5-9:30 pm. Ck-out noon. Meeting rms. Business servs avail. In-rm modem link. Health club privileges. Refrigerators, minibars. Cr cds: A, C, D, DS, JCB, MC, V.

★ ★ ★ **HOTEL SOFITEL.** *1914 Connecticut Ave NW (20009), in Kalorama area.* 202/797-2000; FAX 202/462-0944; res: 800/424-2464. 144 units, 9 story, 36 suites. S $199-$229; D $209-$249; each addl $20; suites $249-$279; under 12 free; wkend rates. Crib free. Pet accepted; $50 deposit. Garage parking; valet $15. TV; cable (premium). Restaurant 6:30 am-10:30 pm. Rm serv 24 hrs. Bar noon-11:30 pm; Fri, Sat to 1 am; pianist. Meeting rms. Business servs avail. In-rm modem link. Concierge. Exercise equipt. Health club privileges. Bathrm phones, minibars; microwaves avail. Refurbished apartment building; built 1904. Cr cds: A, C, D, JCB, MC, V.

★ ★ **HOTEL WASHINGTON.** *515 15th & Pennsylvania Ave NW (20004), at Pennsylvania Ave, 1 blk from White House, downtown.* 202/638-5900; FAX 202/638-4275; res: 800/424-9540. E-mail sales@hotelwashington.com; web www.hotelwashington.com. 350 rms, 11 story. S $170-$235; D $185-$235; each addl $18; suites $430-$668; under 14 free; wkend rates. Crib free. Pet accepted, some restrictions. TV; cable (premium). Restaurant 7 am-10 pm. Bar 11-1 am. Ck-out 1 pm. Meeting rms. Business center. In-rm modem link. Gift shop. Exercise equipt; sauna. Bathrm phones. Original Jardin D'Armide tapestry (1854). One of the oldest continuously-operated hotels in the city. Cr cds: A, C, D, DS, JCB, MC, V.

★ ★ **HOWARD JOHNSON.** *1430 Rhode Island Ave NW (20005), downtown.* 202/462-7777; FAX 202/332-3519; res: 800/446-4656; res: 800/368-5690. E-mail info@hojodc.com; web www.hojodc.com. 184 units, 10 story, 158 kit. units. S $109-$129; D $119-$139; each addl $10; under 18 free; wkend rates. Crib free. Garage parking; valet $10. TV; cable (premium). Pool; lifeguard. Restaurant 7 am-2:30 pm, 5-10:30 pm. Bar 5-11 pm. Ck-out noon. Coin lndry. Business servs avail. In-rm modem link. Exercise equipt. Game rm. Microwaves avail. Cr cds: A, C, D, DS, ER, JCB, MC, V.

★ ★ ★ **HYATT REGENCY.** *400 New Jersey Ave NW (20001), 2 blks N of Capitol.* 202/737-1234; FAX 202/737-5773; res: 800/233-1234. E-mail pr@hyattdc.com; web www.hyatt.com. 834 rms, 11 story. S $235; D $260; each addl $25; under 18 free. Crib free. Garage $22. TV; cable (premium). Indoor pool. Restaurants 6:30 am-11 pm. Bar 11-2 am. Ck-out noon. Meeting rms. Business center. In-rm modem link. Concierge. Gift

shop. Barber, beauty shop. Exercise rm; sauna. Health club privileges. Minibars; some refrigerators; microwaves avail. Luxury level. Cr cds: A, C, D, DS, JCB, MC, V.

★ ★ ★ **J W MARRIOTT HOTEL.** *1331 Pennsylvania Ave NW (20004), at National Place, 2 blks E of White House, downtown.* 202/393-2000; FAX 202/626-6991; res: 800/228-9290. Web www.marriott.com/marriott/dc-042.htm. 772 rms, 12 story. S, D $214-$239; each addl $20; suites $275-$1,550; higher rates Mar-June, Sept-Nov; lower rates rest of yr; family, wkend rates. Crib free. Valet parking $20. TV; cable (premium). Indoor pool; whirlpool. Restaurant 7 am-11 pm. Rm serv 24 hrs. Bars; entertainment. Ck-out noon. Convention facilities. Business center. In-rm modem link. Concierge. Shopping arcade. Exercise rm; sauna. Massage. Game area. Bathrm phones, refrigerator in suites. Private patios on 7th, 12th floors. Luxurious hotel with elegant interior detail; extensive use of marble, mirrors; a large collection of artwork is displayed throughout the lobby. Luxury level. Cr cds: A, C, D, DS, JCB, MC, V.

★ ★ ★ **JEFFERSON HOTEL.** *1200 16th St NW (20036), downtown.* 202/347-2200; FAX 202/331-7982; res: 800/555-8000. E-mail jeffersonres@compuserve.com; web www.slh.com/slh/jefferson. 100 rms, 8 story, 32 suites. Jan-June, Sept-Nov: S $270-$310; D $285-$325; each addl $25; suites $360-$1,200; under 12 free; wkend rates; lower rates rest of yr. Crib free. Garage, valet parking $20. TV; cable (premium), VCR (movies). Pool privileges. Restaurant 6:30 am-10:30 pm (also see THE JEFFERSON). Rm serv 24 hrs. Afternoon tea 3-5 pm. Bar 11-1 am. Ck-out 1 pm. Business servs avail. In-rm modem link. Concierge. Health club privileges. Microwaves avail. Opened in 1923; individually decorated rms have four-poster beds, antiques. Cr cds: A, C, D, DS, JCB, MC, V.

★ **LINCOLN SUITES.** *1823 L St NW (20036), downtown.* 202/223-4320; FAX 202/223-8546; res: 800/424-2970. 99 rms, 10 story, 24 kit. units. S, D, kit. units $175; each addl $15; under 17 free. Crib free. Garage parking $16. TV; cable (premium). Complimentary coffee in rms. Restaurant 7-10 am, 11:30 am-1:30 pm, 5-10 pm. Bar. Ck-out noon. Meeting rms. Business servs avail. Health club privileges. Refrigerators, microwaves. Cr cds: A, C, D, DS, MC, V.

★ ★ ★ **LOEWS L'ENFANT PLAZA.** *480 L'enfant Plaza SW (20024), south of downtown.* 202/484-1000; FAX 202/646-4456. Web www.loewshotels.com/lenfanthome.html. 370 rms on floors 11-15. S, D $189-$279; each addl $20; suites $370-$1,200; under 18 free; wkend rates. Crib free. Pet accepted. Valet parking $16. TV; cable (premium), VCR (movies avail). Pool; poolside serv, lifeguard. Restaurant 6:30 am-midnight. Bar from 11:30 am. Ck-out 1 pm. Convention facilities. Business center. In-rm modem link. Concierge. Underground shopping arcade with Metro subway stop. Gift shop. Extensive exercise rm. Refrigerators, minibars; microwaves avail. Many balconies. Cr cds: A, C, D, DS, MC, V.

★ ★ **MARRIOTT.** *1221 22nd St NW (20037), at M St, west of downtown.* 202/872-1500; FAX 202/872-1424; res: 800/228-9290. 418 rms, 9 story. S, D $179-$199; suites $250-$500; under 18 free; wkend rates. Crib free. Garage $15. TV; cable (premium). Heated pool; whirlpool, poolside serv, lifeguard. Complimentary coffee in lobby. Restaurant 6:30 am-10 pm; Fri, Sat to 11 pm. Bars 11:30 am-midnight. Ck-out noon. Meeting rms. Business center. In-rm modem link. Concierge. Gift shop. Exercise equipt; sauna. Refrigerators avail. Luxury level. Cr cds: A, C, D, DS, JCB, MC, V.

★ ★ **MARRIOTT AT METRO CENTER.** *775 12th St NW (20005), downtown.* 202/737-2200; FAX 202/347-5886; res: 800/228-9290. 456 rms, 15 story. Late Feb-June, mid-Sept-mid-Nov: S, D $179-$219; wkend rates; higher rates Cherry Blossom Festival; lower rates rest of yr. Crib free. Valet parking $16. TV; cable (premium). Indoor pool; whirlpool.

Restaurant 6:30 am-2:30 pm; 5:30-10 pm; Sat, Sun 6:30 am-noon, 5:30-10 pm. Rm serv to midnight. Bar 11 am-midnight. Ck-out noon. Meeting rms. Business center. In-rm modem link. Concierge. Gift shop. Exercise equipt; sauna. Minibars; microwaves avail. Luxury level. Cr cds: A, C, D, DS, JCB, MC, V.

★★★ **MARRIOTT'S WARDMAN PARK HOTEL.** 2660 Woodley Rd NW (20008), north of downtown. 202/328-2000; FAX 202/234-0015; res: 800/544-5064. 1,350 rms, 10 story. Mar-June: S, D $149-$209; each addl $30; suites $250-$2,200; under 18 free; lower rates rest of yr. Crib free. Pet accepted. Valet parking $17; garage $15. TV; cable (premium), VCR avail. Heated pool. Complimentary coffee in rms. Restaurants 6:30 am-11 pm. Bar 11-2 am. Ck-out noon. Convention facilities. Business center. Concierge. Gift shop. Exercise equipt; sauna. Some refrigerators. Balconies. Cr cds: A, C, D, DS, JCB, MC, V.

✓★★ **NORMANDY INN.** 2118 Wyoming Ave NW (20008), in Kalorama. 202/483-1350; FAX 202/387-8241. 75 rms, 6 story. S $103-$133; D 113-$143; each addl $10; under 12 free. Crib free. Garage $10. TV; cable (premium). Complimentary coffee in rms. Restaurant nearby. Ck-out noon. Coin lndry. In-rm modem link. Health club privileges. Refrigerators. In residential neighborhood. Cr cds: A, C, D, DS, MC, V.

★★ **OMNI SHOREHAM HOTEL.** 2500 Calvert St NW (20008), north of downtown. 202/234-0700; FAX 202/265-7972; res: 800/843-6664. 836 rms, 8 story. S, D $109-$259; each addl $30; suites $400-$1,600; under 18 free; wkend, hol rates. Crib free. Pet accepted, some restrictions. Garage $14. TV; cable (premium), VCR avail. Pool; wading pool, poolside serv, lifeguard. Restaurant 6:30 am-11 pm. Bar 11-2 am; entertainment. Ck-out noon. Meeting rms. Business center. Shopping arcade. Lighted tennis, pro. Exercise equipt; sauna. Lawn games. Microwave avail in suites. Cr cds: A, C, D, DS, JCB, MC, V.

★★ **ONE WASHINGTON CIRCLE HOTEL.** 1 Washington Cir NW (20037), at New Hampshire Ave, in Foggy Bottom. 202/872-1680; FAX 202/887-4989; res: 800/424-9671. E-mail sales@onewashcirclehotel.com; web www.onewashcirclehotel.com. 151 kit. suites, 9 story. S, D $125-$275; each addl $15; under 18 free; wkend rates. Garage $16. TV; cable (premium), VCR avail. Pool. Coffee in rms. Restaurant 7 am-11:30 pm; Fri, Sat to midnight. Bar; entertainment. Ck-out noon. Meeting rms. Business servs avail. In-rm modem link. Concierge. Exercise equipt. Some bathrm phones; microwaves avail. Balconies. Elegant furnishings; landscaped grounds. Cr cds: A, C, D, MC, V.

★★★ **PARK HYATT HOTEL WASHINGTON.** 1201 24th St NW (20037), west of downtown. 202/789-1234; FAX 202/457-8823; res: 800/233-1234. Web www.hyatt.com. An impressive collection of modern art distinguishes the interiors of this hotel, softened by touches of bronze and chinoiserie. Guest rooms are furnished with a mix of contemporary and antique pieces as well as museum reproductions of Oriental antiques. 224 units, 10 story, 133 suites. S $244-$310; D $269-$325; each addl $25; suites $520-$1,975; under 18 free; wkend rates; lower rates July, Aug. Crib free. TV; cable (premium), VCR avail. Indoor pool; whirlpool, poolside serv. Restaurant (see MELROSE). Afternoon tea 3-5 pm, Thurs-Sun. Rm serv 24 hrs. Bar 11:30-1 am; Fri, Sat to 2 am; pianist. Ck-out noon. Meeting rms. Business servs avail. In-rm modem link. Concierge. Gift shop. Barber, beauty shop. Underground valet parking. Golf privileges. Exercise rm; steam rm, sauna. Massage. Bathrm phones, refrigerators; microwaves avail. Cr cds: A, C, D, DS, JCB, MC, V.

★★ **PHOENIX PARK HOTEL.** 520 N Capitol St NW (20001), opp Union Station, on Capitol Hill. 202/638-6900; FAX 202/393-3236; res: 800/824-5419. E-mail phoenixpark@worldnet.att.net. 148 rms, 9 story. S $179-$219; D $199-$239; each addl $20; suites $350-$750; under 16 free;

wkend plans. Crib free. Valet parking $19. TV; cable (premium). Coffee in rms. Restaurant 7-2 am. Bar from 11 am; Fri, Sat to 3 am; entertainment. Ck-out 1 pm. Meeting rms. Business center. In-rm modem link. Exercise equipt. Health club privileges. Minibars; some refrigerators. Near Capitol; traditional European decor. Cr cds: A, C, D, DS, MC, V.

★★ **QUALITY HOTEL DOWNTOWN.** 1315 16th St NW (20036), downtown. 202/232-8000; FAX 202/667-9827; res: 800/221-2222. E-mail tajhotels@gcol.com; web www.quality-suite.com/online/quality.html. 137 rms, 10 story. S $169; D $189; each addl $15; under 18 free. Crib free. Garage $10.50. TV; cable (premium). Pool privileges. Restaurant 6 am-12:30 pm, 6-10 pm. Bar 5-11 pm. Ck-out noon. Guest lndry. Meeting rms. Business center. Gift shop. Exercise equipt. Health club privileges. Microwaves avail. Cr cds: A, C, D, DS, JCB, MC, V.

★★ **RADISSON BARCELO HOTEL.** 2121 P St NW (20037), in Dupont Circle area. 202/293-3100; FAX 202/857-0134; res: 800/333-3333. 301 rms, 10 story. S, D $160-$180; each addl $20; suites $210-$550; under 17 free; wkend rates. Crib free. Valet parking $15. TV; cable (premium). Pool; lifeguard. Restaurant (see GABRIEL). Bar 11 am-midnight. Ck-out noon. Meeting rms. Business servs avail. In-rm modem link. Concierge. Gift shop. Exercise equipt; sauna. Bathrm phones, minibars. Cr cds: A, C, D, DS, JCB, MC, V.

★★★ **RENAISSANCE MAYFLOWER HOTEL.** 1127 Connecticut Ave NW (20036), 4 blks NW of White House, downtown. 202/347-3000; FAX 202/776-9182; res: 800/468-3571. Web www.renaissancehotels.com. 660 rms, 10 story, 78 suites. S, D $250-$360; each addl $30; suites $450-$3,500; under 19 free; wkend rates. Crib free. Valet parking $23. Garage adj $11.50. TV; cable (premium), VCR avail. Complimentary coffee. Restaurant 6:30 am-11:30 pm. Rm serv 24 hrs. Bar 11-1:30 am; entertainment. Ck-out 1 pm. Convention facilities. Business center. In-rm modem link. Concierge. Exercise equipt. Health club privileges. Bathrm phones; refrigerators, microwaves avail. Foreign currency exchange. Opened in 1925 for Calvin Coolidge's inauguration; ornate gilded interior, stained-glass skylights. Cr cds: A, C, D, DS, ER, JCB, MC, V.

★★★ **RENAISSANCE WASHINGTON HOTEL.** 999 9th St NW (20001), near Convention Center & MCI Arena, downtown. 202/898-9000; FAX 202/289-0947; res: 800/228-9290. E-mail sales@renhotels.com; web www.renaissance.com. 801 rms, 16 story. Apr-June, Sept-Nov: S, D $229-$270; each addl $25; suites $500-$2,000; under 18 free; wkend rates; lower rates rest of yr. Crib free. Pet accepted, some restrictions. Garage $15. TV; cable (premium), VCR avail. Indoor pool; whirlpool. Complimentary coffee in rms. Restaurant 6:30 am-11 pm. Rm serv 24 hrs. Bar 11-1 am. Ck-out 1 pm. Convention facilities. Business center. In-rm modem link. Concierge. Shopping arcade. Exercise rm; sauna. Minibars; some bathrm phones; microwaves avail. Luxury level. Cr cds: A, C, D, DS, ER, JCB, MC, V.

★★ **RIVER INN.** 924 25th St NW (20037), 2 blks from Kennedy Center, in Foggy Bottom. 202/337-7600; FAX 202/337-6520; res: 800/424-2741. E-mail Riverinn@erols.com. 126 kit. suites. S $125-$175; D $140-$190; each addl $15; under 18 free; higher rates Apr-May, Sept-Oct. Crib free. Pet accepted, some restrictions; $100. Parking $15. TV; cable (premium). Restaurant 7-10 am, 11:30 am-2 pm, 5-10 pm; Sat 8-10 am, 11 am-2 pm, 5:30-11:30 pm; Sun 8-10 am, 11 am-2 pm, 5-10 pm. Bar. Ck-out noon. Meeting rm. Business servs avail. In-rm modem link. Health club privileges. Microwaves. Cr cds: A, C, D, MC, V.

★★ **ST. JAMES SUITES.** 950 24th St NW (20037), in Foggy Bottom. 202/457-0500; FAX 202/659-4492; res: 800/852-8512. E-mail jhaddock@aol.com; web www.stjamessuites.com. 195 kit. suites, 12 story. Feb-June, Sept-Oct: suites $139-$169; under 16 free; wkend rates; higher rates Cherry Blossom Festival; lower rates rest of yr. Crib free. Garage parking $16; valet. TV; cable, VCR avail. Pool; lifeguard. Complimentary continental bkfst. Coffee in rms. Restaurant nearby. Ck-out noon. Coin lndry. Meeting rms. Business servs avail. In-rm modem link. Concierge. Exercise equipt. Cr cds: A, C, D, DS, MC, V.

[D] [symbols] SC

★★ **STATE PLAZA HOTEL.** 2117 East St NW (20037), in Foggy Bottom. 202/861-8200; FAX 202/659-8601; res: 800/424-2859. 223 kit. suites, 8 story. S $95-$145; D $115-$165; each addl $20; under 16 free; wkend rates; higher rates Mar-June, Sept-Nov. Crib free. Garage $12. TV; cable (premium). Complimentary continental bkfst. Restaurant 7 am-11 pm. Bar from 11 am. Ck-out noon. Coin lndry. Meeting rms. Business servs avail. In-rm modem link. Exercise equipt. Minibars, microwaves. Two rooftop sun decks. Cr cds: A, C, D, DS, JCB, MC, V.

[D] [symbols] SC

★★★ **SWISS HOTEL WATERGATE.** 2650 Virginia Ave NW (20037), adj Kennedy Center, in Foggy Bottom. 202/965-2300; FAX 202/337-7915; res: 800/424-2736. 232 rms, 13 story. S $295-$395; D $320-$420; each addl $25; suites $545-$1,600; under 18 free; wkend, hol rates. Crib free. Pet accepted, some restrictions. Valet parking $25. TV; cable (premium), VCR avail (movies). Indoor pool; whirlpool, lifeguard. Restaurant (see AQUARELLE). Rm serv 24 hrs. Bar 11:30-1 am; pianist. Ck-out noon. Meeting rms. Business center. In-rm modem link. Concierge. Shopping arcade. Barber, beauty shop. Exercise rm; sauna, steam rm. Massage. Bathrm phones, minibars; microwaves avail. Many balconies. Kennedy Center adj. Overlooks Potomac River. Cr cds: A, C, D, DS, JCB, MC, V.

[D] [symbols] SC

★★ **THE CANTERBURY.** 1733 North St. NW (20036), downtown, off Dupont Circle. 202/393-3000; FAX 202/785-9581; res: 800/424-2950. 99 kit. units, 10 story. S $140-$195; D $160-$215; each addl $20; under 12 free; wkend plans. Crib free. Garage $13. TV; cable (premium), VCR avail. Complimentary continental bkfst. Complimentary coffee in rms. Restaurant 7 am-2:30 pm, 5-10 pm. wkend hrs vary. Bar 5-10 pm. Ck-out noon. Meeting rms. Business servs avail. In-rm modem link. Health club privileges. Refrigerators, microwaves. On site of "Little White House,: where Theodore Roosevelt lived during his vice-presidency and first weeks of his presidency. Cr cds: A, C, D, DS, JCB, MC, V.

[symbols] SC

★★ **THE LATHAM HOTEL GEORGETOWN.** 3000 M St NW (20007), in Georgetown. 202/726-5000; FAX 202/337-4250; res: 800/368-5922. 143 rms, 10 story. S $135-$190; D $165-$210; each addl $20; suites $225-$390; under 18 free; wkend rates. Valet parking $14. TV; cable (premium). Pool. Restaurant (see CITRONELLE). Bar 11-1 am; Fri, Sat to 2 am. Ck-out noon. Meeting rms. Business servs avail. In-rm modem link. Concierge. Health club privileges. Some minibars. Refrigerators avail. Sun deck. Overlooks historic Chesapeake & Ohio Canal. Cr cds: A, C, D, DS, MC, V.

[D] [symbols] SC

★★★ **THE MADISON HOTEL.** 1177 15th St NW (20005), downtown. 202/862-1600; FAX 202/785-1255; res: 800/424-8577. 353 rms, 14 story. S, D $235-$405; each addl $20; suites $425-$3,000; wkend packages. Crib free. Valet, garage $15. TV; cable (premium). Restaurant 6:30 am-11 pm. Rm serv 24 hrs. Bar 11-2 am. Ck-out 1 pm. Meeting rms. Business center. In-rm modem link. Concierge. Exercise rm. Bathrm phones, refrigerators, minibars. Original paintings, antiques, Oriental rugs. Cr cds: A, C, D, JCB, MC, V.

[D] [symbols] [symbols]

✓★★★★ **THE ST. REGIS WASHINGTON.** 923 16th & K St NW (20006), downtown. 202/638-2626; FAX 202/638-4231; res: 800/562-5661. Web www.starwood.com. Located one block from the White House, this hotel is convenient for visitors to all of Washington, D.C.'s most famous attractions. Built in 1926 to replicate an Italian Renaissance palace, the property was designated as a Washington historical landmark in 1964. Calvin Coolidge cut the ceremonial ribbon, and every President since has visited the hotel. A terrific choice for an elegant trip to the nation's capital. 192 rms, 8 story. S, D $280-$360; each addl $25; suites $600-$2,500; under 18 free; wkend rates. Crib free. Pet accepted, some restrictions. Covered valet parking $22. TV; cable (premium), VCR avail. Pool privileges. Restaurant 7-10:30 am, noon-2 pm, 6-10 pm; Sat 7-11 am, 6-10 pm; Sun to 11 am. Rm serv 24 hrs. Bar. Ck-out 1 pm. Meeting rms. Business servs avail. In-rm modem link. Concierge. Gift shop. Tennis privileges. Exercise equipt. Health club privileges. Bathrm phones, refrigerators, minibars; microwaves avail. Italian Renaissance mansion with courtyard terrace. Cr cds: A, C, D, DS, ER, JCB, MC, V.

[D] [symbols] SC

★★★ **THE WESTIN GRAND.** 2350 M St NW (20037), east of Georgetown. 202/429-0100; FAX 202/429-9759; res: 800/937-8461. 262 rms, 4 story. Sept-June: S $229-$299; D $249-$325; each addl $30; suites $450-$3,000; under 18 free; wkend rates; lower rates rest of yr. Crib free. Covered valet parking $20/day. TV; cable (premium), VCR avail. Heated pool; poolside serv. Restaurant 6:30 am-10:30 pm. Rm serv 24 hrs. Bar. Ck-out 1 pm. Meeting rms. Business center. In-rm modem link. Concierge. Gift shop. Exercise equipt. Minibars. Bathrm phones; some fireplaces; whirlpool in suites. Some balconies. Many rms with view of landscaped interior courtyard. Luxury level. Cr cds: A, C, D, DS, JCB, MC, V.

[D] [symbols] SC [symbols]

★★★ **WASHINGTON COURT ON CAPITOL HILL.** 525 New Jersey Ave NW (20001), on Capitol Hill. 202/628-2100; FAX 202/879-7918; res: 800/321-3010. 264 rms, 15 story. S, D $195-$275; each addl $25; suites $250-$1,500; under 16 free; wkend rates. Crib free. Pet accepted, some restrictions. Valet parking $18. TV; cable (premium), VCR avail. Restaurant 6:30 am-11 pm. Bar; pianist. Ck-out noon. Meeting rms. Business servs avail. In-rm modem link. Concierge. Exercise equipt; sauna. Gift shop. Bathrm phones, refrigerators. Large atrium lobby. Cr cds: A, C, D, DS, MC, V.

[D] [symbols] SC

★★★ **WASHINGTON MONARCH HOTEL.** 2401 M St NW (20037), west of downtown. 202/429-2400; FAX 202/457-5010; res: 877/222-2266. 415 rms, 10 story. S, D $280-$310; each addl $30; suites $700-$1,700; under 18 free; wkend, summer rates. Crib free. Covered parking; valet $19. Pet accepted, some restrictions. TV; cable (premium), VCR avail. Indoor pool; whirlpool. Restaurant 6:30 am-11 pm. Rm serv 24 hrs. Bar 4 pm-midnight; entertainment. Ck-out 1 pm. Convention facilities. Business center. In-rm modem link. Concierge. Gift shop. Exercise rm; sauna, steam rm. Massage. Squash, racquetball courts. Bathrm phones, refrigerators, minibars. Some balconies. Luxury level. Cr cds: A, C, D, DS, JCB, MC, V.

[D] [symbols] SC [symbols]

✓★★★★ **WESTIN FAIRFAX HOTEL.** 2100 Massachusetts Ave NW (20008), 1 blk NW of Dupont Circle, in Embassy Row Area. 202/293-2100; FAX 202/293-0641; res: 800/241-3333. This intimate hotel has the air of an English hunt club with its classic 18th-century European furnishings and extensive collection of 18th and 19th century British oils of dogs and horses. 206 rms, 8 story. S, D $185-$500; suites $400-$3,000; under 18 free; wkend rates. Crib free. Valet parking $23. TV; cable (premium), VCR avail. Restaurant 6:30 am-10:30 pm (also see JOCKEY CLUB). Bar 3 pm-1 am; entertainment. Ck-out noon. Meeting rms. Business center. In-rm modem link. Concierge. Tennis privileges. Golf privileges. Exercise equipt; sauna. Massage. Health club privileges. Bathrm phones, minibars. Elegant ballroom. Within 10 min of Georgetown. Cr cds: A, C, D, DS, JCB, MC, V.

[D] [symbols] SC [symbols]

✓★★★★ **WILLARD INTER-CONTINENTAL.** 1401 Pennsylvania Ave NW (20004), 2 blks E of White House, downtown. 202/628-9100; FAX 202/637-7326. Web www.interconti.com. This opulent Beaux Arts hotel was host to every president from Franklin Pierce to Dwight D. Eisenhower on the eve of their inaugurations. A faithful renovation has returned elegance to the stately columns, mosaic floors and turn-of-the-century decor. Guest rooms are furnished with mahogany Queen Anne-style reproductions. 341 rooms, 12 story, 35 suites. S $335-$450; D $365-$480; each addl $30; suites $800-$3,600; under 14 free; wkend rates. Crib free. Pet accepted, some restrictions. Covered parking, valet $20. TV; cable (premium), VCR avail. Restaurant 6:30 am-11 pm (also see WILLARD ROOM). Rm serv 24 hrs. Bar 11-1 am; Sun 11:30 am-midnight; entertainment. Ck-out noon. Convention facilities. Business center. In-rm modem link. Concierge. Shopping arcade. Exercise equipt. Bathrm phones, minibars; some microwaves avail. Cr cds: A, C, D, DS, JCB, MC, V.

⬛️🐾🧍🖊️🔥 SC 🚶

★★★ **WYNDHAM BRISTOL HOTEL.** 2430 Pennsylvania Ave NW (20037), west of downtown. 202/955-6400; FAX 202/775-8489; res: 800/996-3426. 240 kit. units, 8 story, 37 suites. S $179-$219; D $199-$229; each addl $20; suites $285-$850; under 17 free; monthly rates; wkend plans. Crib free. Valet garage parking $16. TV; cable, VCR avail. Complimentary coffee in rms. Restaurant 6:30 am-11 pm. Rm serv 24 hrs. Bar 11-1 am. Ck-out noon. Meeting rms. Business servs avail. In-rm modem link. Concierge. Exercise equipt. Bathrm phones; microwaves avail. Classic English furnishings, art. Cr cds: A, C, D, DS, JCB, MC, V.

⬛️🧍🖊️🔥 SC

★★ **WYNDHAM CITY CENTER.** 1143 New Hampshire Ave NW (20037), at 21st & M Sts, west of downtown. 202/331-9491; res: 800/544-5064; res: 800/526-7495. 353 rms, 9 story. Mar-May, Aug-Oct: S $199-$220; D $219-$245; each addl $15; suites $250-$600; under 18 free; lower rates rest of yr. Crib free. Parking $16. TV; cable (premium). Coffee in rms. Restaurant 6 am-10 pm. Bar noon-1 am; entertainment Mon-Fri. Ck-out noon. Meeting rms. Business center. In-rm modem link. Concierge. Gift shop. Exercise equipt. Health club privileges. Some refrigerators. Luxury level. Cr cds: A, C, D, DS, JCB, MC, V.

⬛️🧍🖊️🔥 SC 🚶

Inns

✓★ **KALORAMA GUEST HOUSE.** 1854 Mintwood Pl NW (20009), in Kalorama Triangle. 202/667-6369; FAX 202/319-1262. 31 rms, some share bath, 3 story. S $45-$95; D $50-$105; each addl $5; suites $75-$125; wkly rates. TV in common rm. Complimentary continental bkfst; afternoon refreshments. Ck-out 11 am, ck-in noon. Limited parking avail. Business servs avail. Created from 4 Victorian town houses (1890s); rms individually decorated, antiques. Garden. Cr cds: A, C, D, DS, MC, V.

🖊️🔥 SC

✓★ **KALORAMA GUEST HOUSE.** 2700 Cathedral Ave NW (20008), north of downtown. 202/328-0860; FAX 202/328-8730. 19 rms, 7 share baths, 4 story, 2 suites. No rm phones. Mar-mid-June, Sept-Nov: S $45-$95; D $55-$105; each addl $5; wkly rates; lower rates rest of yr. Children over 5 yrs only. TV in sitting rm. Complimentary continental bkfst; afternoon refreshments. Restaurant nearby. Ck-out 11 am, ck-in noon. Free lndry facilities. Limited off-street parking. Sitting rm; antiques. Two early 20th-century townhouses (1910). Cr cds: A, C, D, DS, MC, V.

🖊️🔥 SC

★★★ **MORRISON-CLARK INN.** 1015 L St NW (20001), at Massachusetts Ave, downtown. 202/898-1200; FAX 202/289-8576; res: 800/332-7898. 54 units, 4 story, 14 suites. Mar-June, Sept-Nov: S $155-$240; D $175-$260; each addl $20; suites $180-$240; under 12 free; wkend rates; lower rates rest of yr. Crib free. TV; cable (premium), VCR avail. Complimentary continental bkfst. Dining rm (see MORRISON-CLARK). Rm serv. Ck-out noon, ck-in 3 pm. Luggage handling. Valet serv. Business servs avail. In-rm modem link. Exercise equipt. Health club privileges. Underground parking. Minibars; microwaves avail. Restored Victorian mansion (1864); period furnishings. Cr cds: A, C, D, DS, MC, V.

🧍🖊️🔥 SC

✓★ **TAFT BRIDGE INN.** 2007 Wyoming Ave NW (20009), in Kalorama. 202/387-2007; FAX 202/387-5019. Web www.quikpage.T/taft bridge. 12 rms, 7 share bath, 3 with shower only, 3 story. Mar-June, Sept-Nov: S $49-$99; D $69-$109; each addl $10; kit. unit $109-$119; wkly, hol

rates; lower rates rest of yr. TV in some rms; cable, VCR avail. Complimentary continental bkfst. Restaurant nearby. Ck-out 11 am, ck-in 2 pm. In-rm modem link. Valet serv. Guest lndry. Some balconies. Georgian-style house built in 1905; eclectic antique, art collection. Totally nonsmoking. Cr cds: C, MC, V.

🖊️🔥

✓★ **WINDSOR INN.** 1842 16th St NW (20009), north of downtown. 202/667-0300; FAX 202/667-4503; res: 800/423-9111. Web www.washpost.com/yp/embassyinn. 45 rms, 4 story, 9 suites. No elvtr. S $79-$110; D $89-$125; suites $105-$175; under 14 free; wkend rates. Crib free. TV; cable (premium). Complimentary continental bkfst; afternoon refreshments. Restaurant nearby. Ck-out noon, ck-in 2 pm. Business servs avail. Health club privileges. Refrigerator in suites. Originally a boarding house (1922); bed & breakfast atmosphere. Cr cds: A, C, D, MC, V.

🖊️🔥 SC

Restaurants

★★★ **1789 RESTAURANT.** 1226 36th St NW (20007), in Georgetown. 202/965-1789. Hrs: 6-10 pm; Fri, Sat to 11 pm. Closed Dec 25. Res accepted. Bar. Wine list. Semi-a la carte: dinner $18-$32. Prix fixe: pre-theater dinner $25. Specializes in seafood, rack of lamb. Own baking. Valet parking. In restored mansion; 5 dining rms on 3 levels. Federal-period decor. Fireplace. Jacket. Cr cds: A, C, D, DS, MC, V.

🖈

★★★ **701 PENNSYLVANIA AVE RESTAURANT.** 701 Pennsylvania Ave NW (20004), across from the National Archives, downtown. 202/393-0701. Hrs: 11:30 am-3 pm, 5:30-10:30 pm; Wed, Thurs to 11 pm; Fri to 11:30 pm; Sat 5:30-11:30 pm; Sun 5-9:30 pm. Closed major hols. Res accepted. Continental menu. Bar. Wine list. Semi-a la carte: lunch $8.50-$19.50, dinner $13.50-$23.50. Specializes in seafood, lamb chops, New York strip steak. Pianist Sun-Thurs; Jazz combo Fri, Sat. Free valet parking (dinner). Outdoor dining. Overlooks fountain at Navy Memorial. Cr cds: A, C, D, MC, V.

⬛️❤️

✓★★ **ADITI INDIAN CUISINE.** 3299 M St NW (20007), in Georgetown. 202/625-6825. Hrs: 11:30 am-2:30 pm, 5:30-10 pm; Fri, Sat to 10:30 pm. Closed Thanksgiving. Res accepted. Indian menu. Serv bar. Semi-a la carte: lunch $4.95-$9.95, dinner $4.95-$13.95. Specializes in tandoori charbroiled meats, vegetarian dishes, seafood. Cr cds: A, C, D, DS, MC, V.

★★ **ANNA MARIA'S.** 1737 Connecticut Ave (20009), on Dupont Circle. 202/667-1444. Hrs: 11-1 am; Fri to 3 am; Sat 5 pm-3 am; Sun 5 pm-1 am. Closed most major hols. Res accepted. Italian menu. Bar. Semi-a la carte: lunch $7.95-$10.95, dinner $12.95-$19.95. Specializes in homemade pasta, veal. Atrium rm; fireplace. Cr cds: A, C, D, MC, V.

★★★ **AQUARELLE.** (See The Swiss Hotel Watergate) 202/298-4455. Hrs: 7-10:30 am, 11:30 am-2:30 pm, 5-10:30 pm; Sun brunch 11:30 am-2:30 pm; early-bird dinner 5-7:30 pm. Res accepted. Continental menu. Bar 11:30-1 am. Wine cellar. A la carte entrees: bkfst $7-$16, lunch $12-$22, dinner $14-$25. Complete meal: dinner $35-$65. Sun brunch $38. Specialties: quail stuffed with wild game bird mousseline, filet of sea bass in pesto broth, warm plumb tart. Own pasta. Valet parking. Panoramic view of the Potomac River. Cr cds: A, C, D, DS, JCB, MC, V.

⬛️🖈

✓★★ **BACCHUS RESTAURANT.** 1827 Jefferson Place NW (20036), in Dupont Circle area. 202/785-0734. Hrs: noon-2:30 pm, 6-10 pm; Fri to 10:30 pm; Sat 6-10:30 pm. Closed Sun; most major hols. Res accepted. Lebanese menu. A la carte entrees: lunch $6.50-$10.75, dinner $11.75-$16.25. Specializes in authentic Lebanese cuisine. Valet parking (dinner). Cr cds: A, C, MC, V.

★★ **BEDUCI.** *2100 P St NW (20037), in Dupont Circle.* *202/223-3824.* Hrs: 11:30 am-2:30 pm, 5:30-10 pm; Fri to 10:30 pm; Sat 5:30-10:30 pm; Sun 5:30-9:30 pm. Closed late Aug; major hols. Res accepted. Mediterranean menu. Bar. Semi-a la carte: lunch $9.50-$23, dinner $10.50-$25. Specializes in game, seafood. Three dining areas. Contemporary decor. Cr cds: A, C, D, DS, MC, V.

★ **BILLY MARTIN'S TAVERN.** *1264 Wisconsin Ave NW (20007), in Georgetown.* *202/333-7370.* Hrs: 8-1 am; Fri, Sat to 2:30 am; Sat, Sun brunch to 5 pm. Closed Dec 25. Res accepted. Bar. Semi-a la carte: bkfst $3.95-$7.95, lunch $5.95-$8.95, dinner $6.50-$18.95. Sat, Sun brunch $5.95-$12.95. Specializes in steak, seafood, chops. Parking. Outdoor dining. Established 1933. Family-owned. Cr cds: A, C, D, DS, MC, V.

 ♥

★★ **BISTRO FRANCAIS.** *3128 M St NW (20007), in Georgetown.* *202/338-3830.* Hrs: 11-3 am; Fri, Sat to 4 am; early-bird dinner 5-7 pm, 10:30 pm-1 am; Sat, Sun brunch 11 am-4 pm. Closed Dec 24 eve, 25. Res accepted. Country French menu. Semi-a la carte: lunch $6.95-$11.95, dinner $12.95-$19.95. Wkday brunch: $11.95. Sat, Sun brunch $13.95. Specializes in rotisserie chicken, fresh seafood. Cr cds: A, C, D, JCB, MC, V.

✓★★ **BISTROT LEPIC.** *1736 Wisconsin Ave NW (20007), in upper Georgetown.* *202/333-0111.* Hrs: 11:30 am-2:30 pm, 5:30-10 pm; Fri, Sat to 10:30 pm; Sun to 9:30 pm. Closed Mon; major hols. Res accepted. French menu. Semi-a la carte: lunch $9.75-$12.95, dinner $13.95-17.95. Specialties: roasted rack of lamb, salmon in braro crust, soft shell crab. Storefront restaurant. Cr cds: A, C, DS, MC, V.

✓★ **BLUE PLATE.** *2002 P St NW (20036), in Dupont Circle.* *202/293-2248.* Hrs: 11:30 am-11 pm; Fri, Sat to midnight; Sun noon-10 pm. Closed most major hols. Serv bar. Semi-a la carte: lunch, dinner $8.25-$11.95. Specializes in grilled fish, steak. Own baking. Casual cafe atmosphere. Totally nonsmoking. Cr cds: C, MC, V.

★★★ **BOMBAY CLUB.** *815 Connecticut Ave NW (20006), across from White House, downtown.* *202/659-3727.* Hrs: 11:30 am-2:30 pm, 6-10:30 pm; Sat 6-11 pm; Sun 5:30-9 pm; Sun brunch 11:30 am-2:30 pm. Closed some major hols. Res accepted. Indian menu. Bar 11:30 am-3 pm, 5-11 pm. Semi-a la carte: lunch, dinner $7-$18.50. Sun brunch $16.50. Specialties: tandoori salmon, lamb Roganjosh, chicken Tikka Makhani. Pianist evenings, Sun brunch. Valet parking (dinner). Outdoor dining. Extensive vegetarian menu. Elegant club-like atmosphere reminiscent of British colonial India. Cr cds: A, C, D, MC, V.

D ▭

✓★★ **BOMBAY PALACE.** *2020 K St NW (20006), downtown.* *202/331-4200.* Hrs: 11:30 am-2:30 pm, 5:30-10 pm; Fri, Sat to 10:30 pm. Res accepted. Northern Indian menu. Bar. A la carte entrees: lunch, dinner $8.50-$19.95. Complete meals: lunch, dinner $16.95-$19.95. Specialties: butter chicken, gosht patiala, jumbo prawns tandoori. Indian decor and original art; 350-gallon fish tank. Totally nonsmoking. Cr cds: A, C, D, MC, V.

D

✓★ **BUA.** *1635 P St NW (20036), in Dupont Circle.* *202/265-0828.* Hrs: 11:30 am-2:30 pm, 5-10:30 pm; Fri to 11 pm; Sat noon-4 pm, 5-11 pm; Sun noon-4 pm. Closed Thanksgiving, Dec 25. Res accepted. Thai menu. Bar. A la carte entrees: lunch $5.85-$7.75, dinner $7.50-$12.95. Specializes in seafood. Outdoor dining on 2nd-floor balcony. In townhouse on side street; fireplace. Cr cds: A, C, D, DS, MC, V.

▭

★ **BURMA RESTAURANT.** *740 6th St NW (20001), in Chinatown.* *202/638-1280.* Hrs: 11 am-3 pm, 6-10 pm; Sat, Sun from 6 pm. Closed major hols. Res accepted. Burmese menu. Serv bar. Semi-a la carte: lunch, dinner $5.95-$7.95. Specialties: green tea leaf salad, tamarind fish, mohingar. Burmese decor. Cr cds: A, C, D, DS, MC, V.

▭

★★ **BUSARA RESTAURANT.** *2340 Wisconsin Ave NW (20007), near the Naval Observatory, in Upper Georgetown.* *202/337-2340.* Web www.washingtonpost.com/yp/busara. Hrs: 11:30 am-3 pm, 5-11 pm; Fri to midnight; Sat 5 pm-midnight; Sun 5-11 pm. Closed most major hols. Res required Fri, Sat. Thai menu. Bar. Semi-a la carte: lunch $5.95-$8.50, dinner $7.25-$15.95. Specialties: panang gai, crispy whole flounder, pad Thai. Outdoor dining in a Japanese garden. New wave decor. Cr cds: A, C, D, DS, MC, V.

D ▭

✓★★ **CAFE ATLANTICO.** *405 8th St NW (20004), in Penn Quarter, downtown.* *202/393-0812.* Hrs: 11:30 am-10 pm; Fri, Sat to 11 pm; Sun 5:30-10 pm. Closed most major hols. Res accepted. Latin Amer menu. Bar to midnight. Semi-a la carte: lunch $7.95-$13.95, dinner $13.95-$19.95. Complete meals (Sun-Wed): dinner $19.95-$21.95. Menu changes bi-weekly. Valet parking. Outdoor dining. Contemporary decor with modern artwork; central circular stairway leads to second dining level. Cr cds: A, C, D, MC, V.

D ▭

★★ **CAFE MILANO.** *3251 Prospect St NW (20007), in Georgetown.* *202/333-6183.* Hrs: 11-1 am; Sun noon-11 pm. Closed Thanksgiving, Dec 25. Res accepted. Italian menu. Bar. Semi-a la carte: lunch $9-$26, dinner $13-$28. Specialties: strozzapreti moschino, costoletta di vitello. Outdoor dining. Large tie/scarf collection hanging on walls. Cr cds: A, C, D, MC, V.

D ▭

★ **CAFE MOZART.** *1331 H St NW (20005), behind deli, downtown.* *202/347-5732.* Hrs: 7:30 am-10 pm; Sat from 9 am; Sun from 11 am. Closed Jan 1, Thanksgiving, Dec 25. Res accepted. German, Austrian menu. Bar. Semi-a la carte: bkfst $3.10-$6.95, lunch $4.85-$21.50, dinner $8.95-$22.50. Child's meals. Specialties: Wienerschnitzel, pork roast, Kasseler rippchen. Entertainment Thurs-Sat. German deli on premises. Cr cds: A, C, D, DS, JCB, MC, V.

D ▭

★★ **CASHION'S EAT PLACE.** *1819 Columbia Rd NW (20009), in Adams Morgan area.* *202/797-1819.* Hrs: 5:30-11 pm; Sun, Tues to 10 pm; Sun brunch 11:30 am-2:30 pm. Closed Mon; most major hols. Res accepted. Bar. Semi-a la carte: dinner $10.95-$17.95. Complete meal: dinner $25-$40. Sun brunch $3.95-$8.95. Specializes in lamb, duck, seafood. Own desserts. Valet parking. Outdoor dining. Contemporary decor; skylights. Cr cds: C, MC, V.

★★★ **CITRONELLE.** *(See The Latham Hotel)* *202/625-2150.* Hrs: 6:30-10:30 am, noon-2 pm, 5:30-10 pm; Fri, Sat 5:30-10:30 pm. Res accepted. French menu. Bar. Semi-a la carte: bkfst $7.50-$12.50, lunch $20-$30, dinner $35-$55. Specialties: foie gras, filet mignon, canard a l'orange. Multi-level dining rm. Contemporary decor with modern art. Cr cds: A, C, D, DS, MC, V.

D

✓★★ **CLYDE'S.** *3236 M St NW (20007), at Wisconsin Ave, in Georgetown.* *202/333-9180.* Web www.clydes.com. Hrs: 11:30-2 am; Fri to 3 am; Sat 10-3 am; Sun from 9 am. Closed Dec 25. Res accepted. Bars. Semi-a la carte: lunch $6.95-$10.95, dinner $9.95-$14.95. Sun brunch $4.25-$9.95. Child's meals. Specializes in seafood, crab cakes, ribs. Garage parking. Atrium dining. Classic saloon decor. Cr cds: A, C, D, DS, MC, V.

D ▭

★★ **COCO LOCO.** *810 7th St NW (20001), downtown.* 202/289-2626. Hrs: 11:30 am-2:30 pm, 5:30-10:30 pm; Sat 5:30-11 pm. Closed Sun. Res accepted. Spanish menu. Bar. A la carte entrees: lunch $4.50-$11, dinner $5-$12. Prix fixe: $29.95. Specialties: stuffed ravioles, grilled chicken, stuffed shrimp. Salad bar. Entertainment. Outdoor dining. Modern tropical decor. Cr cds: A, C, D, MC, V.

D

✓★★ **COPPI'S VIGORELLI.** *3421 Connecticut Ave NW (20008), in Cleveland Park area, north of downtown.* 202/244-6437. Hrs: noon-11 pm; Fri to midnight; Sat noon-3 pm, 5 pm-midnight; Sun 5-11 pm. Closed Thanksgiving, Dec 24, 25. Northern Italian menu. Bar. Semi-a la carte: lunch, dinner $7.95-$15.95. Child's meals. Specialties: wood-oven broiled fish, baked ligurian risotto. Own pasta. Decor celebrates Italian bicycle racing. Cr cds: A, C, D, DS, MC, V.

D

★★ **DISTRICT CHOPHOUSE.** *509 7th St NW (20004), downtown.* 202/347-3434. Hrs: 11 am-11 pm; Sat, Sun 4-11 pm. Closed Thanksgiving, Dec 25. Res accepted. Bar. Semi-a la carte: lunch $9-$13, dinner $18-$30. Child's meals. Specializes in steaks, chops, seafood. Street parking. Brewery. Cr cds: A, C, D, MC, V.

D

★★ **DOLCETTO TRATTORIA.** *3201 New Mexico Ave NW (20116), north of downtown.* 202/966-0500. Hrs: noon-3 pm, 5:30-10 pm; Fri, Sat to 11 pm; Sun brunch noon-3 pm. Closed July 4, Dec 25. Res accepted. Northern Italian menu. Bar. A la carte entrees: lunch $6-$13, dinner $8-$16. Sun brunch $12. Own baking. Piano Fri, Sat. Parking. Outdoor dining. Totally nonsmoking. Cr cds: A, C, MC, V.

D

★ **EL CARIBE.** *3288 M St (20007), in Georgetown.* 202/338-3121. E-mail cfearless@aol.com; web www.digitalcity.com/caribe. Hrs: 11:30 am-11 pm; Fri, Sat to 11:30 pm; Sun to 10 pm. Res accepted. South Amer, Spanish menu. Bar. Semi-a la carte: lunch $6.95-$12.95, dinner $9.95-$19.50. Specialties: fritadas con Llapingachos, paella. Spanish decor. Family-owned. Cr cds: A, C, D, DS, MC, V.

★★★ **EL CATALAN.** *1319 F St NW (20005), near Metro Center, downtown.* 202/628-2299. Hrs: 11:30 am-2:30 pm, 5:30-10 pm; Fri to 11 pm; Sat 5:30-11 pm. Closed Sun; also major hols. Res required (lunch). French, Catalonian menu. Bar. A la carte entrees: lunch $13.75-$19.50, dinner $14.74-$25. Specializes in seafood, chicken, lamb. Valet parking. Cr cds: A, C, D, MC, V.

D

★★ **FILOMENA.** *1063 Wisconsin Ave NW (20007), off M St on the canal, in Georgetown.* 202/338-8800. E-mail Filorest@erols.com; web www.erols.com/eire/filomena.html. Hrs: 11:30 am-11 pm; Sat, Sun brunch to 3 pm. Closed Jan 1, Thanksgiving, Dec 25. Res accepted. Italian menu. Bar. A la carte entrees: lunch $5.95-$12.95, dinner $11.95-$29.95. Lunch buffet $7.95. Sat, Sun brunch $9.95. Specializes in pasta, seafood, regional Italian dishes. Own baking, pasta. Italian garden-like atmosphere; antiques. Overlooks Chesapeake & Ohio Canal. Cr cds: A, C, D, DS, JCB, MC, V.

✓★ **FIO'S.** *3636 16th St (20010), in Woodner Apts, Mt Pleasant, north of downtown.* 202/667-3040. Hrs: 5-10:45 pm. Closed Mon; some major hols; last 2 wks Aug. Italian menu. Bar. Semi-a la carte: dinner $5.50-$12.50. Specializes in seafood, veal, pasta. Own bread, pasta. Free garage parking. Informal atmosphere; building overlooks Rock Creek Park. Cr cds: A, C, D, DS, MC, V.

D

★★★ **FRAN O'BRIEN'S STADIUM STEAK HOUSE.** *(See The Capital Hilton)* 202/783-2599. Hrs: 11:30 am-11 pm; Sat, Sun from 5 pm. Closed most major hols. Res accepted. Bar to midnight. Wine cellar. Semi-a la carte: lunch $8.25-$19.95, dinner $17.95-$29.95. Child's meals. Specialties: rib-eye steak, filet mignon, Maryland crab cakes with lobster cream sauce. Own desserts. Valet parking (dinner). Club-like atmosphere with sports themes; large collection of football memorabilia. Cr cds: A, C, D, MC, V.

D

★★ **GABRIEL.** *(See Radisson Barcelo Hotel)* 202/956-6690. Web www.gabrielrest.com. Hrs: 6:30 am-10 pm; Sat 7 am-10:30 pm; Sun to 9 pm; Sun brunch 11 am-3 pm. Closed Dec 25. Res accepted. Spanish/Latin Amer menu. Bar 11 am-midnight. Semi-a la carte: bkfst $3.50-$9.50, lunch $7.25-$15, dinner $8-$24. Sun brunch $19.75. Specialties: grilled sea scallops, grilled lamb chops, smoked black bean soup. Outdoor dining. Mediterranean decor. Cr cds: A, C, D, DS, JCB, MC, V.

D

★★★ **GALILEO RESTAURANT.** *1110 21st St NW (20036), in Foggy Bottom.* 202/293-7191. E-mail roberto@robertodonna.com; web www.robertodonna.com. Hrs: 7:30-9:30 am, 11:30 am-2 pm, 5:30-10 pm; Fri to 10:30 pm; Sat from 5:30 pm; Sun 5-10 pm. Closed some major hols. Res accepted. Northern Italian menu. Bar. Wine cellar. A la carte entrees: bkfst $3.95-$9.95, lunch $10.95-$17.95, dinner $16.95-$29.95. Specializes in game, seasonal dishes, pasta. Free valet parking (dinner) exc Sun. Outdoor dining. Mediterranean decor. Cr cds: A, C, D, DS, MC, V.

D

✓★ **GARRETT'S.** *3003 M St NW (20007), in Georgetown.* 202/333-1033. E-mail rhinorest@aol.com. Hrs: 11:30 am-10:30 pm; Fri, Sat to 11 pm. Res accepted. Bars 11:30-2 am; Fri, Sat to 3 am. Semi-a la carte: lunch $3.95-$8.50, dinner $4.75-$13.95. Specializes in steaks, pasta, seafood. 1794 landmark bldg; originally house of MD governor T.S. Lee. Cr cds: A, C, D, DS, MC, V.

★★★ **GEORGIA BROWN'S.** *950 15th St NW (20005), at McPherson Square, downtown.* 202/393-4499. Hrs: 11:30 am-10:30 pm; Fri to 11:30 pm; Sat 5:30-11:30 pm; Sun 11:30 am-3 pm (brunch), 5:30-10:30 pm. Closed Dec 25. Res accepted. South Carolina Low Country menu. Bar. Semi-a la carte: lunch, dinner $10.95-$19.95. Specialties: head-on Carolina shrimp with spicy sausage, frogmore stew, Southern fried chicken. Jazz & blues Sun afternoons. Valet parking (dinner). View of McPherson's Square. Cr cds: A, C, D, DS, MC, V.

D

★★★★ **GERARD'S PLACE.** *915 15th St NW (20005), at McPherson Square, downtown.* 202/737-4445. Hrs: 11:30 am-2:30 pm, 5:30-10 pm; Fri to 10:30 pm. Closed Sun; most major hols. Res accepted. French menu. Wine list. A la carte entrees: lunch $15.50-$19.50, dinner $16.50-$32.50. Prix fixe: dinner $58. Specializes in contemporary French cooking. Outdoor dining. Casual bistro atmosphere. Some modern art. Cr cds: A, C, D, MC, V.

★★ **GERMAINE'S.** *2400 Wisconsin Ave NW (20007), in Upper Georgetown.* 202/965-1185. Hrs: 11:30 am-2:30 pm, 5:30-10 pm; Fri to 11 pm; Sat 5:30-11 pm; Sun 5:30-10 pm. Closed Jan 1, Dec 25. Res accepted. Pan-Asian menu. Bar. A la carte entrees: lunch $7.25-$12.95, dinner $12.25-$28. Specializes in grilled Asian dishes, seafood. Skylighted atrium dining rm. Cr cds: A, C, D, MC, V.

★★★ **GOLDONI RESTAURANT.** *1120 20th St NW (20036), west of downtown.* 202/293-1511. Hrs: 11:30 am-3 pm; Fri 11:30 am-2 pm, 5-10:30 pm; Sat 5-10:30 pm; Sun 5-9:30 pm. Closed most major hols. Res accepted. Italian menu. Bar. Wine list. Semi-a la carte: lunch $8.95-$21.95, dinner $15.95-$28.95. Complete meal: dinner $39.95-

$59.95. Specialties: grilled wild rockfish with polenta, mushrooms and cherry tomatoes; cappellacci with lobster and foie gras with white truffles. Own pasta, desserts. Validated parking. Gallery setting has look and feel of Italian villa. Cr cds: A, C, D, DS, MC, V.

★★ **GREENWOOD.** *3529 Connecticut Ave NW (20008), at Cleveland Park, north of downtown.* 202/686-1640. Hrs: 6-11 pm; Tues, Sun to 10 pm. Closed Mon; also major hols. Res required. Contemporary Amer menu. Bar. A la carte entrees: dinner $13.95-$26. Specialties: seared rare tuna, smoked salmon stack with asparagus & goat cheese, grilled prime, dry-aged steak. Parking. Cr cds: A, C, MC, V.

★ **GRILL FROM IPANEMA.** *1858 Columbia Rd NW (20009), in Adams Morgan area.* 202/986-0757. Hrs: 5-11 pm; Fri to midnight; Sat noon-midnight; Sun noon to 11 pm; Sat, Sun brunch to 4 pm. Closed Jan 1, Dec 25. Res accepted. Brazilian menu. Bar. Semi-a la carte: dinner $8.95-$15.95. Sat, Sun brunch $11.95. Specialties: feijoada, moqueca, bobo de camarao. Cr cds: A, C, D, DS, MC, V.

✓ ★ **GUAPOS MEXICAN CUISINE.** *4515 Wisconsin Ave NW (20016), north of downtown.* 202/686-3588. Hrs: 11:30 am-11:30 pm; Fri, Sat to midnight. Res accepted. Latin Amer, Mexican menu. Bar. Semi-a la carte: lunch $3.95-$10.25, dinner $4.95-$13.95. Specializes in fajitas. Outdoor dining. Colorful dining rms with Mexican decor. Cr cds: A, C, DS, MC, V.

★ **GUARDS.** *2915 M St NW (20007), E end in Georgetown.* 202/965-2350. Hrs: 11:30 am-11 pm; Fri, Sat to midnight; Sun brunch 11:30 am-5 pm. Res accepted. Continental menu. Bar. Semi-a la carte: lunch $5.50-$12.95, dinner $13.95-$22.95. Sun brunch $5.95-$12.95. Specializes in veal, Angus beef, fresh seafood. Valet parking $4. Atrium dining rm; country-English decor. Cr cds: A, C, D, DS, MC, V.

✓ ★ **HAAD THAI.** *1100 New York Ave NW (20005), downtown.* 202/682-1111. Hrs: 11:30 am-2:30 pm, 5-10:30 pm; Sun from 5 pm. Closed most major hols. Res accepted. Thai menu. Bar. Semi-a la carte: lunch $5.95-$7.95, dinner $8.95-$13.95. Specialties: pad thai, pla yang, surf-n-turf. Tropical atmosphere. Cr cds: A, C, D, MC, V.

★★ **HOGATES SEAFOOD RESTAURANT.** *800 Water St SW (20024), on the waterfront, south of downtown.* 202/484-6300. Hrs: Mon-Thurs 11 am-10 pm; Fri to 11 pm, Sat noon-11 pm; Sun 10:30 am-10 pm; Sun brunch to 2:30 pm. Closed Dec 25. Res accepted. Bar. Semi-a la carte: lunch $6-$13, dinner $13-$35. Lunch buffet $12.95. Sun brunch $18.95. Child's meals. Specialties: mariner's platter, wood grilled fish, rum buns. Brunch entertainment. Indoor parking $1.50/hr. Outdoor dining. Overlooks Potomac River. Cr cds: A, C, D, DS, MC, V.

★★ **HUNAN CHINATOWN.** *624 H St NW (20001), in Chinatown.* 202/783-5858. Hrs: 11 am-10 pm; Fri, Sat to 11 pm. Hunan, Szechwan menu. Serv bar. Semi-a la carte: lunch $7.50-$15, dinner $10-$23. Specialties: General Tso's chicken, tea-smoked duck, crispy prawns with walnuts. Parking (dinner). Modern, bi-level dining room. Cr cds: A, C, D, DS, MC, V.

✓ ★★ **I MATTI TRATTORIA.** *2436 18th St NW (20009), in Adams Morgan area.* 202/462-8844. E-mail imatti@robertodonna.com; web www.robertodonna.com. Hrs: noon-2:30 pm, 5:30-10:30 pm; Fri to 11 pm; Sat noon-2:30 pm, 5:30-10:30 pm; Sun 5:30-10 pm. Closed Jan 1, Thanksgiving, Dec 25. Res accepted. Northern Italian menu. Bar to 11 pm

Fri, Sat. A la carte entrees: lunch, dinner $10-$17. Specializes in traditional Tuscan cooking. Valet parking Tues-Sat. Upscale dining; lower dining area less formal. Cr cds: A, C, D, MC, V.

★★★ **ISABELLA.** *809 15th St NW (20005), at McPherson Square, downtown.* 202/408-9500. Hrs: 11:30 am-10:30 pm; Fri to 11 pm; Sat 5:30-11 pm. Closed most major hols. Res accepted. Italian menu. Bar. Wine list. Semi-a la carte: lunch, dinner $7.95-$19.95. Specializes in seafood, pastas, grilled meats. Own baking. Free valet parking (dinner). Outdoor dining. Contemporary Mediterranean decor; fabric wall hangings; palm trees. Cr cds: A, C, DS, MC, V.

★ **J PAUL'S.** *3218 M St NW (20007), in Georgetown.* 202/333-3450. Web www.capitalrestaurants.com. Hrs: 11:30-1 am; Sun 10:30 am-11:30 pm; Sun brunch to 4 pm. Bar to 1:30 am. Semi-a la carte: lunch, dinner $5.25-$20.95. Sun brunch $7.95-$12.95. Child's meals. Specializes in ribs, crab cakes, burgers. Turn-of-the-century saloon decor; antique bar from Chicago's old Stockyard Inn. Cr cds: A, C, D, DS, MC, V.

★★ **JALEO.** *480 7th St NW (20004), downtown.* 202/628-7949. E-mail tapasymas@msn.com; web dc.diningweb.com/restaurants/jaleo. Hrs: 11:30 am-11:30 pm; Sun, Mon to 10 pm; Fri, Sat to midnight. Closed Thanksgiving, Dec 24, 25. Spanish menu. Bar. Semi-a la carte: lunch $7.75-$9.95, dinner $10.50-$18. Specializes in hot & cold tapas, Spanish-style fish. Sevillanas dancers Wed nights. Valet parking $5. Murals of flamenco dancers cover the walls of this lively restaurant. Cr cds: A, C, D, DS, MC, V.

★★★ **JOCKEY CLUB.** *(See The Westin Fairfax Hotel)* 202/659-8000. Hrs: 6:30-11 am, noon-2:30 pm, 6-10:30 pm; Sat, Sun 7-11:30 am, noon-2:30 pm, 6-10:30 pm. Res accepted. Classic French, international menu. Bar. A la carte entrees: bkfst $4.50-$18.50, lunch $12.50-$24.50, dinner $24.50-$34. Specializes in veal, fresh seafood, crab cakes. Own baking. Free valet parking. Tableside cooking. Club-like atmosphere in 1928 landmark building. Jacket. Cr cds: A, C, D, DS, JCB, MC, V.

★★★★ **KINKEAD'S.** *2000 Pennsylvania Ave NW (20006), at I St, in Foggy Bottom.* 202/296-7700. Chef Bob Kinkead has created two distinct but delicious dining options in this multichambered restaurant. Downstairs is a more informal and inexpensive pub-style eatery, while upstairs you can watch Kinkead and company turn out grilled dishes with an emphasis on seafood. Specialties: pepita-crusted salmon, pepper-seared tuna, grilled squid. Hrs: 11:30 am-10 pm; Fri, Sat to 10:30 pm; Sun brunch to 2:30 pm. Closed Jan 1, Thanksgiving, Dec 25. Res accepted. Bar to midnight. Semi-a la carte: lunch $12-$16, dinner $18-$24. Sun brunch $8-$12. Free valet parking (dinner). Outdoor dining. Jazz pianist. Seafood/raw bar. Cr cds: A, C, D, DS, MC, V.

✓ ★★ **KRUPIN'S RESTAURANT.** *4620 Wisconsin Ave NW (20016), north of downtown.* 202/686-1989. Hrs: 8 am-10 pm. Closed Dec 25. Semi-a la carte: bkfst $3.50-$15.95, lunch, dinner $5.25-$15.95. Child's meals. Specializes in smoked fish, meatloaf, beef stew. Old fashioned decor. Cr cds: A, C, D, MC, V.

★★ **LA CHAUMIERE.** *2813 M St NW (20007), E end in Georgetown.* 202/338-1784. Hrs: 11:30 am-2:30 pm, 5:30-10:30 pm; Sat from 5:30 pm. Closed Sun; major hols. Res accepted. Country French menu. Semi-a la carte: lunch $10.95-$15.95, dinner $14.95-$24.95. Specializes in seafood, veal, game. Intimate room with beamed ceiling, open-hearth fireplace. Family-owned. Cr cds: A, C, D, MC, V.

★★ **LA COLLINE.** *400 N Capitol St NW (20001), on Capitol Hill.* 202/737-0400. Hrs: 7-10 am, 11:30 am-3 pm, 6-10 pm; Sat from 6 pm. Closed Sun; major hols. Res accepted. French menu. Bar. Semi-a la carte: bkfst $3.50-$8.75, lunch $9-$17, dinner $15-$22. Prix fixe: dinner $22-$27. Specializes in seasonal foods, fowl, seafood. Outdoor dining. Across from Union Station. Cr cds: A, C, D, JCB, MC, V.

[D] [≡]

★★ **LA FOURCHETTE.** *2429 18th St NW (20009), in Adams Morgan area.* 202/332-3077. Hrs: 11:30 am-10:30 pm; Sat 4-11 pm; Sun 4-10 pm. Closed major hols. Res accepted. French menu. Semi-a la carte: lunch $8.95-$19.95, dinner $10.95-$21.95. Specialties: bouillabaisse, rack of lamb, poitrine de poulet farcie au crabe. Outdoor dining. Former townhouse; painted murals on walls. Cr cds: A, C, D, MC, V.

★★★ **LAFAYETTE.** *(See Hay-Adams Hotel)* 202/638-2570. Hrs: 6:30 am-2 pm, 5-10 pm; Sat, Sun from 7 am; Sun brunch 11:30 am-2 pm. Res accepted. Wine list. Semi-a la carte: bkfst $5.50-$15.25, lunch $14-$24, dinner $18-$34. Sun brunch $39.50. Specialties: grilled Dover sole in lobster pesto sauce, veal stuffed with asparagus and crab, sauteed big eye tuna in rice paper crust. Pianist. Overlooking Lafayette Park and the White House. Cr cds: A, C, D, DS, JCB, MC, V.

[≡] [♥]

★★ **LAURIOL PLAZA.** *1801 18th St NW (20009), in Dupont Circle.* 202/387-0035. Hrs: 11:30 am-11 pm; Fri, Sat to midnight; Sun brunch 11 am-3 pm. Res accepted wkdays. Latin Amer menu. Bar. A la carte entrees: lunch, dinner $5.95-$15. Sun brunch $5.95-$7.95. Specialties: paella, pollo asado, lomo saltado. Outdoor dining. Oil paintings and exotic flower arrangements. Cr cds: A, C, D, DS, MC, V.

[≡]

✓★★ **LAVANDOU.** *3321 Connecticut Ave NW (20008), north of downtown.* 202/966-3002. E-mail FD3321@aol.com; web www.dinenet.com. Hrs: 11:30 am-2:30 pm, 5-10 pm; Fri to 11 pm; Sat 5-11 pm; Sun 5-10 pm. Closed most major hols. Res accepted, required on wkends. Southern French menu. Serv bar. Semi-a la carte: lunch $9.95-$13.50, dinner $12.95-$17.95. Complete meals: dinner (to 6:30 pm) $14.95. Specialties: clam a l'ail, truite saumnonee, daube Provençale. French bistro atmosphere features country artifacts. Free parking. Cr cds: A, C, D, MC, V.

[≡]

✓★★ **LEBANESE TAVERNA.** *2641 Connecticut Ave NW (20008), north of downtown.* 202/265-8681. Hrs: 11:30 am-2:30 pm, 5:30-10:30 pm; Fri, Sat to 11 pm; Sun 5-10 pm. Closed major hols. Lebanese menu. Bar. Semi-a la carte: lunch $8-$12, dinner $10-$16. Specializes in falafel, shish kabob. Contemporary decor. Cr cds: A, C, D, DS, MC, V.

[D]

★★ **LEGAL SEAFOODS.** *2020 K St NW (20006), downtown.* 202/496-1111. Hrs: 11 am-10 pm; Fri to 10:30 pm; Sat 4-10:30 pm; Sun 4-9 pm. Closed Thanksgiving, Dec 25. Res accepted. Seafood menu. Bar. Semi-a la carte: lunch $6.95-$12.95, dinner $12.95-$19.95. Child's meals. Specializes in fresh fish. Valet parking. Family-owned since 1950. Cr cds: A, C, D, DS, JCB, MC, V.

[D] [≡] [♥]

★ **LES HALLES.** *1201 Pennsylvania Ave NW (20004), downtown.* 202/347-6848. Hrs: 11:30 am-midnight; Sun brunch to 4 pm. Res accepted. French, Amer menu. Bar. Semi-a la carte: lunch $12.50-$19.95, dinner $15-$22.50. Sun brunch $14.95. Child's meals. Specialties: onglet, cassoulet. Outdoor dining. Three-level dining area. Cr cds: A, C, D, DS, JCB, MC, V.

[≡]

★★★★ **LESPINASSE.** *923 16th St NW (20016), 1 blk from the Capitol.* 202/879-6900; FAX 202/347-6961. This formal, elegant dining room is more contemporary than its New York sister, but the food is every bit as sophisticated. The cooking blends flavors and techniques from France and the Far East, and the service is attentive and accommodating.

Hrs: 11:30 am-midnight; Sun brunch to 4 pm. Res accepted. French, Amer menu. Bar. Semi-a la carte: lunch $12.50-$19.95, dinner $15-$22.50. Sun brunch $14.95. Child's meals. Specialties: onglet, cassoulet. Outdoor dining. Three-level dining area. Cr cds: C.

★★ **LUIGINO.** *1100 New York Ave NW (20005), downtown.* 202/371-0595. E-mail luigino@erols.com; web www.erols.com/luigino. Hrs: 11:30 am-2:30 pm, 5:30-10:30 pm; Fri to 11:30 pm; Sat 5:30-11:30 pm; Sun 5-10 pm. Closed major hols. Res accepted. Italian menu. Bar. Semi-a la carte: lunch $8.25-$15.50, dinner $12.50-$22.50. Child's meals. Specializes in pasta, seafood, game. Outdoor dining. Trattoria with contemporary atmosphere. Cr cds: A, C, D, MC, V.

[D] [≡]

★ **MARKET INN.** *200 E St SW (20024), south of downtown.* 202/554-2100. E-mail seafrest@aol.com. Hrs: 11 am-11 pm; Fri to midnight; Sat 4:30 pm-midnight; major hols from 5 pm. Closed Thanksgiving, Dec 25. Res accepted. Bar. Semi-a la carte: lunch $6-$13.50, dinner $12.95-$24.95. Sun brunch $19.95. Child's meals. Specializes in Maine lobster, beef. Entertainment; jazz Sun brunch. Free valet parking. Outdoor dining. English pub ambience. Family-owned. Cr cds: A, C, D, DS, JCB, MC, V.

[≡]

✓★★ **MCCORMICK & SCHMICK'S.** *1652 K St NW (20006), downtown.* 202/861-2233. Hrs: 11 am-11 pm; Fri to midnight; Sat 5 pm-midnight; Sun 5-10 pm. Closed Dec 25. Res accepted. Seafood menu. Bar to midnight; Fri, Sat to 1 am; Sun to 11 pm. Semi-a la carte: lunch, dinner $5.95-$19.95. Child's meals. Specialties: Alaskan halibut stuffed with dungeness crab, bay shrimp and brie; cedar plank salmon with berry sauce; seared yellowfin tuna with wasabi and soy sauce. Own pastries. Valet parking (dinner). Old fashioned decor with large open grill. Cr cds: A, C, D, DS, JCB, MC, V.

[D]

★★★ **MELROSE.** *(See Park Hyatt Hotel)* 202/955-3899. Hrs: 6:30 am-2:30 pm, 5:30-10:30 pm; Fri, Sat to 11 pm; Sun brunch 10:30 am-2:30 pm. Res accepted. Contemporary Amer menu. Bar 11-1 am; Fri, Sat to 2 am. Wine cellar. Semi-a la carte: bkfst $8.50-$15, lunch $14-$22, dinner $19-$28. Sun brunch $33-$36. Child's meals. Specializes in fresh fish, seafood, veal. Own baking. Pianist. Valet parking. Outdoor dining. Sunlit atrium. Italian fountain. Cr cds: A, C, D, DS, JCB, MC, V.

[D] [≡]

✓★★ **MESKEREM.** *2434 18th St NW (20009), in Adams Morgan area.* 202/462-4100. Hrs: noon-midnight; Fri, Sat to 1 am. Closed Thanksgiving, Dec 25. Res accepted. Ethiopian menu. Bar. Semi-a la carte: lunch, dinner $8.50-$11.95. Specializes in lamb, beef, chicken. Own Ethiopian breads. Ethiopian band Fri-Sun. Tri-level dining rm; traditional Ethiopian decor, sunny and bright. Cr cds: A, C, D, MC, V.

[≡]

★★ **MONOCLE ON CAPITOL HILL.** *107 D St NE (20002), adj to US Senate Office Bldg, on Capitol Hill.* 202/546-4488. Hrs: 11:30 am-midnight. Closed Sat, Sun; major hols. Res accepted. Bar. A la carte entrees: lunch $7-$16, dinner $12-$25. Child's meals. Specializes in seafood, aged beef. Valet parking. Located in 1865 Jenkens Hill building; fireplace. Close to Capitol; frequented by members of Congress and other politicians. Family-owned. Cr cds: A, C, D, MC, V.

[≡]

★★ **MORRISON-CLARK RESTAURANT.** *(See Morrison-Clark Hotel)* 202/289-8580. Hrs: 11:30 am-2 pm, 6-9:30 pm; Fri to 10 pm; Sat 6-10 pm; Sun brunch 11 am-2 pm. Closed some hols. Res accepted. Bar. Wine cellar. Semi-a la carte: lunch $15-$20, dinner $20-$25. Sun brunch $27.50-$32. Specialties: sauteed chicken breast with country ham and sage, marinated wild rockfish in citrus with fava beans and fennel, grilled rabbit with rabbit sausage and shelled beans. Own desserts. Free valet parking. Outdoor dining. Elegant Victorian dining rm; antiques; elaborately dressed floor-to-ceiling windows. Cr cds: A, C, D, DS, MC, V.

★★★ **MORTON'S OF CHICAGO.** *3251 Prospect St NW (20007), in Georgetown.* 202/342-6258. Hrs: 5-11 pm; Sun 5-10 pm. Closed some major hols. Res accepted. Bar. Wine list. A la carte entrees: dinner $17.95-$29.95. Specializes in steak, lobster, seafood. Valet parking. Collection of Leroy Neiman paintings. Cr cds: A, C, D, JCB, MC, V.

D ⬛

✓★ **MR. SMITH'S.** *3104 M St NW (20007), in Georgetown.* 202/333-3104. E-mail mrsmithsgt@aol.com. Hrs: 11:30-2 am; Fri, Sat to 3 am; Sat, Sun brunch 11 am-4:30 pm. Bar. Semi-a la carte: lunch, dinner $4.95-$14.95. Sat, Sun brunch $4.50-$8. Specializes in seafood, pasta, hamburgers. Pianist 9 pm-1 am. Old tavern atmosphere. Outdoor dining. Family-owned. Cr cds: A, C, D, MC, V.

⬛

★ **MR. YUNG'S RESTAURANT.** *740 6th St NW (20001), in Chinatown.* 202/628-1098. Web www.menusonline.com/cities/wash_dc/desc/mryungs.shtml. Hrs: 11 am-10:30 pm. Chinese, Cantonese menu. Serv bar. Semi-a la carte: lunch $5.95-$7.95, dinner $6.95-$25.95. Specialties: sauteed shrimp with snow pea leaves, steamed lobster in garlic sauce. Enclosed outdoor dining. Modern Asian decor. Cr cds: A, C, D, DS, MC, V.

D ⬛

✓★ **MURPHY'S OF D.C.** *2609 24th St NW (20008), at Calvert St, north of downtown.* 202/462-7171. Hrs: 11-2 am. Irish, Amer menu. Beer. Semi-a la carte: lunch $5.95-$7.95, dinner $5.95-$11.95. Child's meals. Specializes in steaks, burgers, seafood. Traditional Irish music. Patio dining. Wood-burning fireplace. Cr cds: A, C, D, MC, V.

⬛

✓★ **MUSIC CITY ROADHOUSE.** *1050 30th St NW (20007), between M & K in the Foundry Building, in Georgetown.* 202/337-4444. E-mail mergm@aol.com. Hrs: 4:30 pm-2 am; Fri, Sat to 3 am; Sun 11 am-midnight; Sun brunch to 2 pm. Closed Mon; also most major hols. Res accepted. Bar. Semi-a la carte: dinner $10.95-$13.95. Sun brunch $12.95. Child's meals. Specialties: fried chicken, BBQ ribs, country fried steak. Old fashioned roadhouse with pictures of country singers. Cr cds: A, C, D, DS, MC, V.

D ⬛

★★ **NATHANS.** *3150 M St NW (20007), in Georgetown.* 202/338-2000. Hrs: 11 am-3 pm, 6-11 pm; Thurs-Sat to midnight; Sat, Sun brunch 10 am-3 pm. Res accepted. Northern Italian, Amer menu. Bar 11-2 am; Fri, Sat to 3 am. Semi-a la carte: lunch $5.25-$12.50, dinner $14.50-$30.50. Sat, Sun brunch $5.25-$12.50. Specializes in pasta, grilled fish. Entertainment Fri, Sat. Antiques. Family-owned. Cr cds: A, C, D, MC, V.

⬛

★★ **NEW HEIGHTS.** *2317 Calvert St NW (20008), north of downtown.* 202/234-4110. Hrs: 5:30-10 pm; Fri, Sat to 11 pm; Sun brunch 11 am-2:30 pm. Closed major hols. Res accepted. New Amer cuisine. Bar from 5 pm. Semi-a la carte: dinner $15-$25. Sun brunch $8-$15. Specializes in calamari fritti, grilled salmon, fresh trout. Menu changes seasonally; some entrees offered in half-portions. Outdoor dining. Main dining rm on 2nd floor overlooks Rock Creek Park. Cr cds: A, C, D, DS, MC, V.

★★★★ **NORA.** *2132 Florida Ave NW (20008), in Dupont Circle.* 202/462-5143. E-mail tthyme@erols.com; web www.noras.com. Certified in American organic cuisine with continental and Mediterranean influence. Hrs: 6-10 pm; Fri, Sat to 10:30 pm. Closed Sun; major hols; last wk of Aug, 1 wk of Sept. Res accepted. Bar. A la carte: entrees $19-$28. Menu changes daily. Own desserts. Atrium dining. In 1890 building with American folk art, Amish quilts on walls. Totally nonsmoking. Cr cds: C, MC, V.

♥

★★ **OBELISK.** *2029 P St NW (20036), in Dupont Circle.* 202/872-1180. Hrs: 6-10 pm. Closed Sun, Mon; major hols. Res accepted. Italian menu. Serv bar. Complete meals: dinner $42-$45. Specializes in seasonal dishes. Menu changes daily. Intimate dining rm on 2nd floor of town house. Totally nonsmoking. Cr cds: C, D, MC, V.

★★ **OCCIDENTAL GRILL.** *1475 Pennsylvania Ave NW (20004), downtown.* 202/783-1475. Hrs: 11:30 am-11 pm; Sun noon-9:30 pm. Closed Thanksgiving, Dec 25. Res accepted. Regional Amer menu. Bar. A la carte entrees: lunch $8-$20, dinner $13-$27. Specializes in grilled seafood, beef, lamb. Own desserts. Turn-of-the-century Victorian decor with autographed photos of celebrities; originally opened 1906. Cr cds: A, C, D, MC, V.

D ⬛

✓★★ **OLD EBBITT GRILL.** *675 15th St NW (20005), downtown.* 202/347-4800. Hrs: 7:30-1 am; Sat from 8 am; Sun from 9:30 am; Sun brunch to 4 pm. Res accepted. Bar to 2 am; Fri, Sat to 3 am. Semi-a la carte: bkfst $5.95-$9.95; lunch, dinner $7.95-$16.95. Sun brunch $6.95-$16.95. Specializes in fresh oysters, seafood, hamburgers. Own pasta. Valet parking (dinner, Sun brunch). In old vaudeville theater built in early 1900s. Victorian decor, gaslights; atrium dining. Cr cds: A, C, D, DS, MC, V.

D ⬛

★★ **OLD EUROPE RESTAURANT.** *2434 Wisconsin Ave NW (20007), north of downtown.* 202/333-7600. Hrs: 11:30 am-3 pm, 5-10 pm; Sun 4-9 pm. Closed July 4, Dec 24, 25. Res accepted. German menu. Serv bar. Semi-a la carte: lunch $5-$9, dinner $10-$20. Child's meals. Specialties: schnitzel Old Europe, Wienerschnitzel, sauerbraten. Pianist Thurs-Sun. Cr cds: A, C, D, MC, V.

⬛

★★ **OVAL ROOM.** *800 Connecticut Ave (20006), 1½ blocks from White House, downtown.* 202/463-8700. Hrs: 11:30 am-3:00 pm, 5:30-10:30 pm; Fri to 11 pm; Sat 5:30-11 pm. Closed Sun; some major hols. Res accepted. Bar. A la carte entrees: lunch $10.50-$22.50, dinner $13.50-$22.50. Specializes in New American cuisine. Menu changes seasonally. Pianist. Valet parking after 5:30 pm. Outdoor dining. Cr cds: A, C, D, MC, V.

D

★★ **PALM RESTAURANT.** *1225 19th St NW (20036), in Dupont Circle.* 202/293-9091. Hrs: 11:30 am-10:30 pm; Sat from 6 pm; Sun 5:30-9:30 pm. Closed major hols. Res accepted. Bar. A la carte entrees: lunch $8.50-$17, dinner $14-$30. Specializes in steak, lobster. Valet parking (dinner). 1920s New York-style steak house. Family-owned. Cr cds: A, C, D, MC, V.

D ⬛

★★ **PAOLO'S.** *1303 Wisconsin Ave NW (20007), in Georgetown.* 202/333-7353. Hrs: 11:30-2 am; Fri, Sat to 3 am; Sun 11 am-2 am; Sat, Sun brunch to 4 pm. Italian menu. Bar. Semi-a la carte: lunch, dinner $7.95-$18.95. Sun brunch $6.95. Specializes in pizza, pasta, seafood. Jazz combo Sun afternoons. Patio dining; wood-burning pizza oven. Cr cds: A, C, D, DS, MC, V.

⬛ ♥

★★ **PESCE.** *2016 P St NW (20036), in Dupont Circle.* 202/466-3474. Web www.robertodonna.com. Hrs: 11:30 am-2:30 pm, 5:30-10 pm; Fri, Sat to 10:30 pm; Sun 5-9:30 pm. Closed Labor Day, Dec 25. Semi-a la carte: lunch, dinner $13.50-$22.95. Specializes in seafood. Valet parking Thurs-Sat. Modern decor. Cr cds: A, C, D, MC, V.

SC

★★ **PETITTO'S.** *2653 Connecticut Ave NW (20008), north of downtown.* 202/667-5350. Hrs: 5:30-10:30 pm; Sun to 9:30 pm. Closed major hols. Res accepted. Italian menu. Bar. A la carte entrees: dinner $11-

$18. Specializes in pasta, fish, veal. Valet parking. Outdoor dining. Turn-of-the century Victorian townhouse overlooking Connecticut Ave; fireplaces. Dessert, cappuccino rm downstairs. Cr cds: A, C, D, DS, MC, V.

🖼️

✓★ **PIZZERIA PARADISO.** *2029 P St NW (20036), in Dupont Circle.* 202/223-1245. Hrs: 11 am-11 pm; Fri, Sat to midnight; Sun noon-10 pm. Closed some major hols. Italian menu. Wine, beer. A la carte entrees: lunch, dinner $5.50-$15.95. Specializes in pizza, salads, sandwiches. Lively, colorful atmosphere; pizza-makers visible from dining area. Totally nonsmoking. Cr cds: C, D, MC, V.

★★★ **PRIME RIB.** *2020 K St NW (20006), downtown.* 202/466-8811. Hrs: 11:30 am-3 pm, 5-11 pm; Fri to 11:30 pm; Sat 5-11:30 pm. Closed Sun; major hols. Res accepted. Bar. Semi-a la carte: lunch $10-$18. A la carte entrees: dinner $18-$29. Specializes in roast prime rib, Chesapeake seafood, aged thick-cut steak. Pianist. Free valet parking (dinner). Art deco decor; 1920s lithographs. 1940s New York supper club atmosphere. Jacket. Cr cds: A, C, D, MC, V.

🖼️ 🖼️

✓★★ **PRIMI PIATTI.** *2013 I St NW (20006), downtown.* 202/223-3600. Hrs: 11:30 am-2:30 pm, 5:30-10:30 pm; Fri, Sat 5:30-11:30 pm. Closed Sun; most major hols. Res accepted. Italian menu. Bar. Semi-a la carte: lunch $10-$15.50, dinner $11-$20. Specializes in grilled fish, meat. Own pasta. Outdoor dining. Cr cds: A, C, D, JCB, MC, V.

🖼️ 🖼️

★★★ **PROVENCE.** *2401 Pennsylvania Ave NW (20037), west of downtown.* 202/296-1166. Hrs: noon-2 pm, 6-10 pm; Fri, Sat 5:30-11 pm; Sun 5:30-9:30 pm. Res accepted. French menu. Bar. A la carte entrees: lunch $16-$25, dinner $22-$36. Specializes in French Provencal cooking. Mediterranean setting. Cr cds: A, C, D, MC, V.

🖼️

✓★ **RAKU-AN ASIAN DINER.** *1900 Q St NW (20009), in Dupont Circle.* 202/265-7258. Web www.dinersgrapevine.com/raku. Hrs: 11:30 am-midnight; Fri, Sat to 1 am; winter to 11 pm; Fri, Sat to midnight. Closed Thanksgiving, Dec 25. Pan-Asian menu. Bar. Semi-a la carte: lunch, dinner $4-$18. Specializes in noodle dishes, dumplings, satays. Street parking. Outdoor dining. Casual teahouse decor with varied Asian accents. Cr cds: C, MC, V.

🖼️ 🖼️

★★★★ **RED SAGE RESTAURANT.** *605 14th St NW (20005), in Westory Bldg, downtown.* 202/638-4444. Web www.dinersgrapevine.com/redsage. Hrs: 11:30 am-2 pm, 5:30-10 pm; Sun from 5 pm. Closed Dec 25. Res accepted. Eclectic menu. Bar. A la carte entrees: lunch $8.50-$15.50, dinner $18.50-$31. Specializes in Western dishes with Native American influences. Validated parking. Designed as a contemporary interpretation of the American West; each of dining level's four major areas exhibits a particular style and mood. Cr cds: A, C, D, DS, MC, V.

🖼️ 🖼️

★★ **ROOF TERRACE.** *2700 F St NW (20566), within Kennedy Center, in Foggy Bottom.* 202/416-8555. Hrs: 11:30 am-3 pm only on matinee days, 5:30-9 pm on performance eves. Sun brunch 11:30 am-2:30 pm. Res accepted. Semi-a la carte: lunch $12-$16, dinner $20-$29. Sun brunch $25.95. Child's meals. Specializes in regional American cuisine. Garage parking. Summer outdoor dining. Contemporary decor; floor-to-ceiling windows offer views of Lincoln Memorial, Washington Monument, Potomac River and Virginia. Totally nonsmoking. Cr cds: A, C, D, JCB, MC, V.

🖼️

★★ **SAIGON GOURMET.** *2635 Connecticut Ave NW (20008), north of downtown.* 202/265-1360. Hrs: 11 am-3 pm, 5-10:30 pm. Closed Thanksgiving. Res accepted. Vietnamese menu. Serv bar. Semi-a la carte:

lunch $5.95-$7.95, dinner $8.95-$13.95. Specialties: Saigon noodles, roasted quail, caramel chicken. Valet parking. Patio dining overlooking upper Connecticut Ave. Cr cds: A, C, D, DS, MC, V.

🖼️ 🖼️

✓★ **SAIGONNAIS.** *2307 18th St NW (20009), in Adams Morgan area.* 202/232-5300. Hrs: 11:30 am-3 pm, 5-11 pm; Sun 5-10:30 pm. Closed Jan 1, Thanksgiving, Dec 25. Res accepted. Vietnamese menu. Semi-a la carte: lunch, dinner $7.95-$14.50. Specialties: lemongrass beef, shrimp on sugar cane stick. Outdoor dining. Vietnamese artwork. Cr cds: A, C, MC, V.

🖼️

★★★ **SAM & HARRY'S.** *1200 19th St NW (20036), in Dupont Circle.* 202/296-4333. Hrs: 11:30 am-2:30 pm, 5:30-10:30 pm; Sat from 5:30 pm. Closed Sun; major hols. Res accepted. Bar. A la carte entrees: lunch $11.95-$22.95, dinner $17.95-$32.95. Specializes in prime-aged beef, Maine lobster, fresh seafood. Valet parking (dinner). Club-like atmosphere with mahogany paneling, paintings of jazz legends. Cr cds: A, C, D, DS, MC, V.

🖼️ 🖼️

★★ **SEA CATCH.** *1054 31st St NW (20007), at M St, in Georgetown.* 202/337-8855. Hrs: noon-3 pm, 5:30-10 pm. Closed Sun. Res accepted. Bar. Semi-a la carte: lunch $4.75-$12, dinner $14-$24. Specializes in fresh seafood, lobster, crab cakes. Own pastries. Valet parking. Outdoor dining on deck overlooking historic Chesapeake & Ohio Canal. Cr cds: A, C, D, DS, MC, V.

🖼️ 🖼️

★★★ **SEASONS.** *(See Four Seasons Hotel)* 202/342-0810. Hrs: 7-11 am, noon-2:30 pm, 6:30-10:30 pm; Sun brunch 10 am-2:30 pm. Res accepted. Bar 11-2 am. Wine list. Semi-a la carte: bkfst $9-$21, lunch $14-$23, dinner $25-$40. Child's meals. Specializes in regional and seasonal dishes. Own baking. Pianist. Valet parking. Overlooks Rock Creek Park. Cr cds: A, C, D, ER, JCB, MC, V.

🖼️ 🖼️ ❤️

★★ **SEQUOIA.** *3000 K St NW (20007), Washington Harbour complex, in Georgetown.* 202/944-4200. Hrs: 11:30 am-midnight; Fri, Sat to 1 am; Sat, Sun brunch 10:30 am-4 pm. Res accepted. Bar. Semi-a la carte: lunch, dinner $7.95-$28.95. Sun brunch $14.95. Specializes in beef, chicken. Outdoor dining. Terrace and multi-story dining rm windows overlook Kennedy Center, Potomac River and Roosevelt Bridge, Island. Cr cds: A, C, D, DS, MC, V.

🖼️ 🖼️

★★ **SOSTANZA.** *1606 20th St NW (20009), in Dupont Circle.* 202/667-0047. Hrs: 6-10 pm. Closed Sun; also some major hols. Res accepted. Italian menu. Bar. A la carte entrees: dinner $14.75-$27.75. Complete meal: 4-course dinner $29-$35. Specialty: Italian beef. Own pastas, breads. Valet parking. Outdoor dining. Totally nonsmoking. Cr cds: A, C, D, MC, V.

🖼️

★ **SUSHI KO.** *2309 Wisconsin Ave NW (20007), north of downtown.* 202/333-4187. E-mail sushiko@vni.net; web www.sushiko.com. Hrs: noon-2:30 pm, 6-10:30 pm; Mon from 6 pm; Sat 5-10:30 pm; Sun 5-10 pm. Closed July 4, Thanksgiving, Dec 25. Res accepted. Japanese menu. Semi-a la carte: lunch $6.50-$10.50, dinner $7.50-$18.50. Specializes in traditional and modern Japanese dishes. Casual decor. Cr cds: A, C, MC, V.

★★★ **TABERNA DEL ALABARDERO.** *1776 I St NW (20006), entrance on 18th St, downtown.* 202/429-2200. Hrs: 11:30 am-2:30 pm, 6-10:30 pm; Fri to 11 pm; Sat 6-11 pm. Closed Sun; major hols. Res accepted. Basque, Spanish menu. Bar. Semi-a la carte: lunch $14-$20, dinner $16-$28. Complete meals: lunch $17.50, dinner $35. Specializes in beef, fish, paella. Tapas bar. Own baking. Flamenco dancers Mar, Oct. Garage parking (dinner). Outdoor dining. Ornate, 19th-century Spanish decor. Jacket. Cr cds: A, C, D, DS, MC, V.

[icon]

✓★ **THAI KINGDOM.** *2021 K St NW (20006), downtown.* *202/835-1700.* Hrs: 11:30 am-2:30 pm, 5-10:30 pm; Sat noon-11 pm; Sun noon-10 pm. Closed some major hols. Res accepted. Thai menu. Bar. A la carte entrees: lunch $6.50-$8.95, dinner $7.25-$9.95. Specialties: crispy chili fish, scallops wrapped in minced chicken, Thai Kingdom grilled chicken. Bi-level dining rm with full windows overlooking K St; authentic Thai decor. Cr cds: A, C, D, MC, V.

[icon] [icon]

★★★ **THE CAPITOL GRILL.** *601 Pennsylvania Ave NW (20004), on Capitol Hill.* *202/737-6200.* Hrs: 11:30 am-3 pm, 5-10 pm; Fri to 11 pm; Sat 5-11 pm; Sun from 5 pm. Closed Thanksgiving, Dec 25. Res accepted. Bar. A la carte entrees: lunch $9.95-$19.95, dinner $15.95-$27.95. Specializes in steak. Free valet parking (dinner). Club atmosphere. Cr cds: A, C, D, DS, MC, V.

[icon] [icon]

★★★ **THE JEFFERSON.** *(See Jefferson Hotel)* *202/833-6206.* Hrs: 6:30-11 am, 11:30 am-2:30 pm. Sun brunch 10:30 am-2:30 pm. Res accepted. Bar 11-1 am. Wine list. Semi-a la carte: bkfst $5.50-$15.50, lunch $12-$22, dinner $20-$27. Sun brunch $17.50-$26. Specializes in natural American cuisine. Valet parking. Jeffersonian-era decor. Cr cds: A, C, D, DS, JCB, MC, V.

[icon] [icon]

✓★ **TOMBS.** *1226 36th St NW (20007), in Georgetown.* *202/337-6668.* Hrs: 11:30 am-midnight; Sat from 11 am; Sun brunch 9:30 am-3 pm. Closed Thanksgiving, Dec 24, 25. Bar. Semi-a la carte: lunch, dinner $4.95-$10.95. Sun brunch $5.25-$7.95. Specializes in chicken, pasta, burgers. Vintage crew gear and prints on walls. Cr cds: A, C, D, DS, MC, V.

★★ **TONY CHENG'S MONGOLIAN BARBECUE.** *619 H St NW (20001), in Chinatown.* *202/842-8669.* Hrs: 11 am-11 pm; Fri, Sat to midnight. Res accepted. Mongolian barbecue menu. Prix fixe: lunch $8.50, dinner $13.95 (serv charge 15%). Food bar encircles Mongolian grill. Diners may select own ingredients to be stir-fried, grilled or steeped tableside. Asian decor. Cr cds: A, C, MC, V.

[icon]

★★ **TONY & JOE'S SEAFOOD PLACE.** *3000 K St NW (20007), at Washington Harbour complex, in Georgetown.* *202/944-4545.* Web www.diningweb.com/restaurants/tonyandjoes. Hrs: 11 am-11 pm; Fri, Sat to midnight; Sun brunch to 3 pm. Closed Dec 25. Res accepted. Bar Fri, Sat to 2 am. Semi-a la carte: lunch $6.95-$22.95, dinner $14.95-$27.95. Sun brunch $18.95-$23.95. Specializes in seafood. Own desserts. Entertainment Tues-Sat. Outdoor dining. Overlooks Potomac River. Cr cds: A, C, D, DS, JCB, MC, V.

[icon] [icon]

★★ **TWO QUAIL.** *320 Massachusetts Ave NE (20002), on Capitol Hill.* *202/543-8030.* Hrs: 11:30 am-2:30 pm, 5-10:30 pm; Sat, Sun from 5 pm. Closed Dec 25. Res accepted. Semi-a la carte: lunch $7-$14, dinner $11-$19. Specializes in New American cuisine, pork chops, seafood. Country inn atmosphere in Victorian townhouse; eclectic furnishings. Cr cds: A, C, D, DS, MC, V.

★★★ **VIDALIA.** *1990 M St NW (20036), in Dupont Circle.* *202/659-1990.* Hrs: 11:30 am-2:30 pm, 5:30-10 pm; Fri to 10:30 pm; Sat 5:30-10:30 pm; Sun 5-9:30 pm. Closed Sun (Jul-Aug); also most major hols. Res accepted. Bar. Semi-a la carte: lunch $11-$19, dinner $18-$25. Specialties: sauteed shrimp with creamed grits, pan-roasted sweetbreads. Country manor house decor. Cr cds: A, C, D, DS, MC, V.

[icon]

★★ **VILLA FRANCO.** *601 Pennsylvania Ave NW (20004), downtown.* *202/638-2423.* Hrs: 11:30 am-3 pm, 5:30-11 pm; Fri to 11:30 pm; Sat 5:30-11:30 pm; Sun 5:30-10:30 pm. Closed Jan 1, Thanksgiving, Dec 25. Res accepted. Southern Italian menu. Bar. A la carte entrees: lunch $11-$17.50, dinner $13-$32. Child's meals. Specializes in fish, beef, chicken. Own pasta, desserts. Valet parking. Outdoor dining. Cr cds: A, C, D, DS, MC, V.

[icon] [icon]

★★ **VINTAGE WINE BISTRO.** *2809 M St NW (20007), in Georgetown.* *202/625-0077.* Hrs: 11:30 am-3 pm, 5:30-11 pm; Sat 5:30-11 pm. Closed Sun. Res accepted. French menu. Bar. A la carte entrees: lunch $10-$18, dinner $12-$22. Specializes in beef, chicken. Street parking. French bistro atmosphere & decor. Cr cds: A, C, DS, MC, V.

[icon] [icon]

★★★ **WILLARD ROOM.** *(See Willard Inter-Continental Hotel)* *202/637-7440.* Hrs: 7:30-10 am, 11:30 am-2 pm, 6-10 pm; Sat from 6 pm. Res accepted. Bar 11-1 am. Wine list. European, regional Amer menu. A la carte entrees: bkfst $8.50-$13.75, lunch $10.50-$17.50, dinner $18.50-$29.50. Complete meals: breakfast $12-$17.50, lunch $24-$28, dinner $36-$65. Specializes in regional seafood, lamb, beef. Seasonal specialties. Own pastries. Pianist. Valet parking (dinner). Cr cds: A, C, D, DS, JCB, MC, V.

[icon] [icon]

✓★ **ZED'S ETHIOPIAN.** *3318 M St NW (20007), in Georgetown.* *202/333-4710.* Hrs: 11 am-11 pm. Closed most major hols. Ethiopian menu. Serv bar. Semi-a la carte: lunch $6.95-$10.75, dinner $7.75-$12.95. Specializes in seafood, beef, vegetarian dishes. No silverware is used at the restaurant; communal dining from trays. Cr cds: A, C, D, DS, MC, V.

[icon]

✓★★ **ZUKI MOON.** *824 New Hampshire Ave NW (20037), 2 blks NE of Kennedy Center, in Foggy Bottom.* *202/333-3312.* Hrs: 7-10 am, 11:30-2:30 pm, 5-11 pm; Sat 8-11 am, 5-11 pm; Sun 8-11 am, 5-10 pm. Closed some major hols. Res accepted. Japanese menu. Bar. A la carte entrees: bkfst $2-$4.50. Semi-a la carte: lunch, dinner $7.95-$15.50. Specializes in meal-in-a-bowl noodle soups, grilled meats and fish. Valet parking (lunch & dinner). Outdoor dining. Modern Japanese garden decor. Totally nonsmoking. Cr cds: A, C, D, MC, V.

[icon]

Unrated Dining Spots

ARMAND'S CHICAGO PIZZERIA. *4231 Wisconsin Ave NW, north of downtown.* *202/686-9450.* Hrs: 11:30 am-11 pm; Fri, Sat to 1 am. Closed Thanksgiving, Dec 25. Bar. A la carte entrees: lunch, dinner $4-$7. Buffet: lunch (pizza & salad) $4.99. Specializes in Chicago-style deep-dish pizza, sandwiches, salads. Outdoor dining. Cr cds: A, C, DS, MC, V.

AUSTIN GRILL. *2404 Wisconsin Ave NW (20007), in Georgetown.* *202/337-8080.* Web www.austingrill.com. Hrs: 11:30 am-11 pm; Fri, Sat to midnight; Sat, Sun brunch 11 am-3 pm. Closed Thanksgiving, Dec 25. Tex-Mex menu. Bar. Semi-a la carte: lunch, dinner $4.95-$14.95. Sat, Sun brunch $4.95-$6.95. Specializes in enchiladas, fajitas. Southwestern decor. Cr cds: A, C, D, DS, MC, V.

[icon]

C.F. FOLKS. *1225 19th St NW (20036), in Dupont Circle.* *202/293-0162.* Hrs: 11:45 am-3 pm. Closed Sat, Sun; major hols. Semi-a la carte: lunch $4.95-$8.95. Complete meals: lunch $8.50-$12. Specializes in daily & seasonally changing cuisines. Outdoor dining. Old-fashioned lunch counter. Cr cds: C.

[icon]

KRAMERBOOKS & AFTERWORDS. *1517 Connecticut Ave (20036), in Dupont Circle.* *202/387-1462.* E-mail hp@kramers.com; web www.kramers.com. Hrs: 7:30-1 am; Fri, Sat open 24 hrs; Sun brunch 9:30 am-3 pm. Closed Thanksgiving, Dec 25. Bar. Semi-a la carte: bkfst $3.95-$7.50, lunch, dinner $6.75-$12.75. Sun brunch $8.25-$13.25. Specialties: Thai jambalaya, grilled portobello mushroom sandwich. Entertainment Wed-Sat. Outdoor dining. In 2-story greenhouse & terrace behind Kramerbooks bookshop. Cr cds: A, C, DS, MC, V.

D ⊡

PATISSERIE-CAFE DIDIER. *3206 Grace St NW (20007), in Georgetown.* *202/342-9083.* Hrs: 8 am-6:30 pm; Sun to 5 pm. Closed Mon; Jan 1, Dec 25. Semi-a la carte: bkfst $1.10-$7.95, lunch $5.99-$8.99. Specializes in European desserts, quiche, pizza. European-style cafe and pastry house. Cr cds: C, D, DS, MC, V.

⊡

PHILLIPS FLAGSHIP. *900 Water St SW, on waterfront, south of downtown.* *202/488-8515.* Hrs: 11 am-10 pm; Fri to 11 pm; Sat, Sun 11 am-11 pm. Closed Dec 25. Bar. Buffet: lunch $14.95, dinner $24.95; Sun $19.95. A la carte bar menu: $3.50-$9.95. Specializes in seafood. Sushi bar. Garage parking. Outdoor dining. Antiques; Tiffany lamps, stained glass. Cr cds: A, C, D, DS, MC, V.

D SC ⊡

THE BREAD LINE. *1751 Pennsylvania Ave NW (20006), west of downtown.* *202/822-8900.* Hrs: 7 am-6 pm. Closed Sat, Sun. Semi-a la carte: bkfst, lunch $2-$9. Child's meals. Specializes in traditional stuffed, grilled & filled breads. Street parking. Outdoor dining. Food inspired by international street foods. Cr cds: A, C, MC, V.

D

Maryland

Population: 4,917,269
Land area: 9,838 square miles
Elevation: 0-3,360 feet
Highest point: Backbone Mountain (Garrett County)
Entered union: Seventh of original 13 states (April 28, 1788)
Capital: Annapolis
Motto: Manly deeds, womanly words
Nickname: Old Line State, Free State
State flower: Black-eyed Susan
State bird: Baltimore oriole
State tree: Wye oak
State fair: August 26-September 4, 2000,
in Timonium (see Towson)
Time zone: Eastern
Web: www.mdisfun.org

Maryland prides itself on its varied terrain and diverse economy. Metropolitan life around the great cities of Baltimore and Washington, DC (the land was ceded from Maryland in 1791) is balanced by the rural atmosphere in central and southern Maryland and on the Eastern Shore, across Chesapeake Bay. Green mountains in the western counties contrast with white Atlantic beaches. A flourishing travel industry, agricultural and dairy wealth in central Maryland, the seafood industry of the Bay and its tidal rivers, manufacturing and commerce in the cities, plus federal government and defense contracts combine to make the state prosperous.

Maryland's three-and-one-half centuries of history began in March, 1634, when Lord Baltimore's brother, Leonard Calvert, solemnly knelt on tiny St Clements Island, near the wide mouth of the Potomac, and named his new province in honor of Henrietta Maria, wife of Charles I, King of England. Calvert's awkward little ships, the *Ark* and the *Dove,* then carried the 222 passengers, including religious refugees, to a Native American village a few miles away. They purchased the village and named it Saint Maries City (now St Mary's City). Religious tolerance was practiced from the colony's founding and was assured by law in 1649. The land was cleared, tobacco was planted, and over the years, profits built elegant mansions, many of which still stand.

Maryland was one of the 13 original colonies. Its first capital was St Mary's City. In 1694 the capital was transferred to Annapolis, where it remains today.

Every war waged on US soil has seen major action by Marylanders. In 1755, British General Edward Braddock, assisted by Lt Colonel George Washington, trained his army at Cumberland for the fight against the French and Indians. In the Revolution, General William Howe invaded Maryland at the head of Chesapeake Bay, and a battle was joined at Brandywine Creek in Pennsylvania before the British moved on to capture Philadelphia. Maryland troops in the Battle of Long Island made a heroic bayonet coverage of the retreat. The courageous action of the "Old Line" gave the state one of its nicknames. The War of 1812 saw Fort McHenry at Baltimore withstand attack by land and sea, with the action immortalized in the national anthem by Francis Scott Key, a Frederick lawyer. In the Civil War, Maryland was a major battleground at Antietam; troops moved back and forth through the state for the four bloody years of destruction.

A border state with commercial characteristics of both North and South, Maryland found its original dependence on tobacco relieved by the emerging Industrial Revolution. Modern factories, mills and ironworks around Baltimore became important to the state's economy. Educational institutions were established and the port of Baltimore, at the mouth of the Patapsco River, flourished. In the mid-19th century, with the Baltimore & Ohio Railroad and the Chesapeake & Ohio Canal carrying freight to the fast-developing western states, Maryland thrived.

Sports enthusiasts have always thought well of Maryland. The state's thousands of miles of tidal shoreline allows plenty of elbow room for aquatic diversion. Maryland's race tracks include Pimlico (see BALTIMORE), featuring the nationally known Preakness Stakes, and Laurel. The "Maryland Million" is held alternately at Laurel and Pimlico. Deer hunting is allowed in most counties and goose hunting on the Eastern Shore. Historical sites cover the landscape, and more are constantly being opened up to the public by the state and National Park Service. Highways are good; reaching places in the Baltimore-Washington, DC area is simplified by direct, high-speed, four-lane highways constructed around, between and radiating from these cities.

When to Go/Climate

Spring and autumn are the best times to visit Maryland. Winter weather is unpredictable and summers are hot and humid.

AVERAGE HIGH/LOW TEMPERATURES (°F)

BALTIMORE

Jan 40/23	May 74/53	Sept 79/58
Feb 44/26	June 83/62	Oct 67/46
Mar 54/34	July 87/67	Nov 57/37
Apr 64/43	Aug 85/66	Dec 45/28

Parks and Recreation Finder

Directions to and information about the parks and recreation areas below are given under their respective town/city sections. Please refer to those sections for details.

NATIONAL PARK AND RECREATION AREAS

Key to abbreviations. I.H.S. = International Historic Site; I.P.M. = International Peace Memorial; N.B. = National Battlefield; N.B.P. = National Battlefield Park; N.B.C. = National Battlefield & Cemetery; N.C. = National Conservation Area; N.E.M. = National Expansion Memorial; N.F. = National Forest; N.G. = National Grassland; N.H. = National Historical Park; N.H.C. = National Heritage Corridor; N.H.S. = National Historic Site; N.L. = National Lakeshore; N.M. = National Monument; N.M.P. = National Military Park; N.Mem. = National Memorial; N.P. = National Park; N.Pres. = National Preserve; N.R. = National Recreational Area; N.R.R. = National Recreational River; N.Riv. = National River; N.S. = National Seashore;

N.S.R. = National Scenic Riverway; N.S.T. = National Scenic Trail; N.Sc. = National Scientific Reserve; N.V.M. = National Volcanic Monument.

Place Name	Listed Under
Antietam National Battlefield	same
Assateague Island N.S.	OCEAN CITY
Catoctin Mountain N.P.	THURMONT
Chesapeake and Ohio Canal N.H.	same
Fort McHenry N.M. and Historic Shrine	BALTIMORE
Hampton N.H.S.	TOWSON

STATE PARK AND RECREATION AREAS

Key to abbreviations. I.P. = Interstate Park; S.A.P. = State Archaeological Park; S.B. = State Beach; S.C. = State Conservation Area; S.C.P. = State Conservation Park; S.Cp. = State Campground; S.F. = State Forest; S.G. = State Garden; S.H.A. = State Historic Area; S.H.P. = State Historic Park; S.H.S. = State Historic Site; S.M.P. = State Marine Park; S.N.A. = State Natural Area; S.P. = State Park; S.P.C. = State Public Campground; S.R. = State Reserve; S.R.A. = State Recreation Area; S.Res. = State Reservoir; S.Res.P. = State Resort Park; S.R.P. = State Rustic Park.

Place Name	Listed Under
Assateague S.P.	OCEAN CITY
Cedarville S.F.	WALDORF
Cunningham Falls S.P.	THURMONT
Dans Mountain S.P.	CUMBERLAND
Deep Creek Lake S.P.	OAKLAND
Elk Neck S.F.	ELKTON
Elk Neck S.P.	ELKTON
Fort Frederick S.P.	HAGERSTOWN
Gambrill S.P.	FREDERICK
Garrett S.F.	OAKLAND
Green Ridge S.F.	CUMBERLAND
Greenbrier S.P.	HAGERSTOWN
Gunpowder Falls S.P. (Hammerman Area)	BALTIMORE
Herrington Manor S.P.	OAKLAND
Janes Island S.P.	CRISFIELD
New Germany S.P.	GRANTSVILLE
Patapsco Valley S.P.	ELLICOTT CITY
Point Lookout S.P.	ST MARY'S CITY
Potomac S.F.	OAKLAND
Rocky Gap S.P.	CUMBERLAND
Sandy Point S.P.	ANNAPOLIS
Savage River S.F.	GRANTSVILLE
Seneca Creek S.P.	GAITHERSBURG
Smallwood S.P.	LA PLATA
Susquehanna S.P.	HAVRE DE GRACE
Swallow Falls S.P.	OAKLAND
Tuckahoe S.P.	EASTON

Water-related activities, hiking, riding, various other sports, picnicking and visitor centers, as well as camping, are available in many of these areas. Most state-maintained areas have small charges for parking and special services. Camping: $2-$22/site/night; stays limited to two wks; most areas are open late Mar-early Dec, but season varies from one park to the next; ck-out 3 pm; reservations for a stay of 1 wk are available at Assateague—they may be obtained by writing directly to the park (see OCEAN CITY). Pets allowed at the following parks (some special restrictions may apply; phone ahead): Green Ridge Forest, Elk Neck, Patapsco (Hollofield), Point Lookout, Rocky Gap, Savage River Forest, Susquehanna, Swallow Falls, Garrett Forest, Potomac Forest and Pocomoke River (Milburn Landing). Day use: 8 am-sunset; closed Dec 25; fee Mar-Oct. For complete information, including information on cabins, contact the Maryland Dept of Natural Resources, State Forest and Park Service, Tawes State Office Bldg E-3, 580 Taylor Ave, Annapolis 21401; 888/432-2267 or 800/830-3974. It is advisable to call parks before visiting, as some may be closed during the off season.

CALENDAR HIGHLIGHTS

FEBRUARY

National Outdoor Show (Cambridge). Goose and duck calling, log sawing, crab picking, trap setting contests; entertainment. Phone 800/522-TOUR.

APRIL

Point-to-point Steeplechase (Cockeysville). Three well-known meets on consecutive weekends—My Lady's Manor, Grand National, and Maryland Hunt Cup. Phone 410/666-7777 or 410/429-4231.

MAY

Maryland Preakness Celebration (Baltimore). Statewide festival; events include hot air balloon festival, parade, steeplechase, celebrity golf tournament, block parties and schooner race. Phone 410/837-3030.

Mid-Atlantic Maritime Festival (St Michaels). Chesapeake Bay Maritime Museum. Nautical celebration with fly-fishing demonstration, skipjack races, boat building contest, boat parade, seafood festival cooking contest. Phone 410/745-2916.

JULY

Drumfest (Cumberland). Greenway Ave Stadium. Drum and bugle corps championship. Phone 301/689-8739.

AUGUST

Montgomery County Agricultural Fair (Gaithersburg). One of the East Coast's leading county fairs; emphasis on agriculture, 4-H activities; animal exhibits, home arts; antique farm equipment; tractor pull, horse pull, demolition derby; rodeo; entertainment. Phone 301/926-3100.

State Fair (Towson). Timonium Fairgrounds. Ten-day festival of home arts; entertainment, midway; agricultural demonstrations, Thoroughbred horse racing, livestock presentations. Phone 410/252-0200.

SEPTEMBER

New Market Days (Frederick). New Market. Nostalgic revival of the atmosphere of a 19th-century village; costumed guides, period crafts and events held in the "Antiques Capital of Maryland" Phone 301/831-6755.

OCTOBER

St Mary's County Oyster Festival (Leonardtown). County Fairgrounds. National oyster shucking contests; oyster cook-off, seafood and crafts. Phone 301/863-5015.

Autumn Glory Festival (Oakland). Celebrates fall foliage. Features arts and crafts, five-string banjo contest, state fiddle contest, western Maryland tournament of bands, parades, antique show. Phone 301/387-4386.

NOVEMBER

Annapolis by Candlelight (Annapolis). For information, contact Historic Annapolis Foundation, 410/269-0432.

FISHING & HUNTING

Non-tidal, nonresident fishing license, $20; 5-day, $7; trout stamp, $5. Chesapeake Bay nonresident fishing license, $12; 5-day, $4.

Nonresident hunting licenses: consolidated, $83-$120.50, depending on state of residence; 3-day, $35; waterfowl stamp $6; regular deer stamp, $9.50; bow hunting deer stamp, $3.50; black powder deer stamp, $3.50; 2nd deer stamp, $10. For latest information, including *Maryland Sportfishing Guide* or the *Guide to Hunting, Trapping in Maryland,* contact Maryland Dept of Natural Resources, Licensing & Registration Service, 580 Taylor Ave B-1, Annapolis 21404-1869; 410/260-8200.

Driving Information

Safety belts are mandatory for driver and passengers in front seat of vehicle. Children 10 years and under must be in an approved passenger restraint anywhere in the vehicle. Children under 4 years or weighing 40 pounds or less must be in an approved safety seat. For further information phone 410/486-3101.

INTERSTATE HIGHWAY SYSTEM

The following alphabetical listing of Maryland towns in *Mobil Travel Guide* shows that these cities are within 10 miles of the indicated Interstate highways. A highway map should be checked, however, for the nearest exit.

Highway Number	Cities/Towns within 10 miles
Interstate 68	Cumberland.
Interstate 70	Baltimore, Columbia, Ellicott City, Frederick, Hagerstown.
Interstate 81	Hagerstown.
Interstate 83	Baltimore, Cockeysville, Towson.
Interstate 95	Aberdeen, Baltimore, College Park, Elkton, Havre de Grace, Laurel, Silver Spring, Towson.

Additional Visitor Information

The Maryland guide to travel, *Destination Maryland,* and a calendar of events can be obtained from the Maryland Office of Tourism Development, 217 E Redwood St, Baltimore 21202; 800/543-1036.

There are several visitor information centers in Maryland; visitors who stop by will find information and brochures helpful in planning stops at points of interest. Their locations are as follows: on I-95 (N & S) near Laurel; on I-70 (E & W) between Hagerstown and Frederick; on US 15S at Emmitsburg; on I-95S near North East; on US 48E near Friendsville; on US 13N near Maryland-Virginia line; in the State House, Annapolis; Crain memorial, on US 301 N, Newburg; and in Bay Country, on US 301N/S, Centreville. (Daily; closed some major hols)

Aberdeen (B-8)

Pop 13,087 Elev 83 ft Area Code 410 & 443 Zip 21001

This is the home of the 75,000-acre Aberdeen Proving Grounds, a federal reservation along Chesapeake Bay. Various types of army materiel, ranging from gunsights to tanks, are tested under simulated combat conditions.

What to See and Do

Peco Energy Company. Hydroelectric plant on the Susquehanna River. Limited area of plant is open for guided tours (Apr-Sept, Sat; rest of yr, by appt; closed hols). 7 mi NE on US 40 or I-95, then 11 mi NW on US 222 to Conowingo. Phone the Conowingo Information Center at 410/457-5011 for more information.   **Free**   Nearby is

Recreation area. with 14-mi-long man-made lake; picnicking; hiking; swimming pool (fee); boating (ramps, marinas); fishing; fishermen's gallery (over 12 yrs only). Phone 410/457-5011.   **Free**

US Army Ordnance Museum. Tanks, artillery, self-propelled artillery, extensive small arms and ammunition collection. (Daily; closed most major hols) At Aberdeen Proving Ground, off I-95 exit 85, 3 mi E on MD 22, follow signs. Phone 410/278-3602.   **Free**

Motels

✓ ★ **DAYS INN.** *783 W Bel Air Ave (21001), I-95 exit 85.* 410/272-8500; FAX 410/272-5782; res: 800/329-7466. 49 rms, 2 story. S $43; D $47; each addl $4; under 16 free. Crib free. Pet accepted; $5. TV; cable (premium). Pool. Complimentary continental bkfst. Restaurant nearby. Ck-out 11 am. Business servs avail. Refrigerators avail. Cr cds: A, C, D, DS, JCB, MC, V.

D 🐾 ⊠ ⊠ 🔥 SC

★ ★ **HOLIDAY INN CHESAPEAKE HOUSE.** *1007 Beards Hill Rd (21001).* 410/272-8100; FAX 410/272-1714; res: 800/465-4329. 122 rms, 5 story. S, D $95-$115; each addl $10; suites $150; kit. units $105-$120; under 18 free; wkend rates. Pet accepted. TV; cable (premium), VCR avail. Indoor pool. Restaurant 6 am-2 pm, 5-10 pm; Sat, Sun from 7 am. Bar. Ck-out noon. Meeting rms. Sundries. Exercise equipt. Health club privileges. Some refrigerators. Balconies. Cr cds: A, C, D, DS, JCB, MC, V.

D 🐾 ⊠ 🕴 ⊠ 🔥 SC

★ **QUALITY INN & SUITES.** *793 W Belair Ave (24382).* 410/272-6000; FAX 410/272-2287. 124 rms, 2 story. Feb-Oct: S, D $49.95-$59.95; each addl $5; under 19 free; wkly, wkend rates; lower rates rest of yr. Crib free. TV; cable (premium), VCR avail. Pool; wading pool. Complimentary continental bkfst. Restaurant adj 6 am-2 pm, 5-10 pm. Ck-out noon. Coin lndry. Meeting rms. Business servs avail. Cr cds: A, C, D, DS, JCB, MC, V.

D ⊠ ⊠ 🔥 SC

Annapolis (C-7)

(See also Baltimore, Baltimore/Washington Intl Airport Area)

Founded 1649 Pop 33,187 Elev 57 ft Area Code 410 & 443 Web www.visit-annapolis.org

Information Annapolis and Anne Arundel County Conference and Visitors Bureau, 26 West St, 21401; 410/268-TOUR. Information is also available at the Visitor Information Booth located at the city dock

The capital of Maryland, gracious and dignified in the colonial tradition, Annapolis has had a rich history for more than 300 years. Planned and laid out as the provincial capital in 1695, it was the first peacetime capital of the United States (Congress met here November 26, 1783-August 13, 1784). In 1845 the US Naval Academy was established here, at the Army's Fort Severn. Town life centers on sport and commercial water-oriented activities, state government and the academy. Every May, at commencement time, thousands of visitors throng the narrow brick streets.

What to See and Do

Boat trips. 40-min narrated tours of city harbor, USNA and Severn River aboard *Harbor Queen* (Memorial Day-Labor Day, daily); 90-min cruises to locations aboard *Providence* and *Rebecca,* cruises to St Michaels aboard the *Annapolitan II* (Memorial Day-Labor Day); 40-min cruises up Spa Creek, residential areas, city harbor and USNA aboard the *Miss Anne* and *Miss Anne II* (Memorial Day-Labor Day). Some cruises early spring and late fall, weather permitting. Fees vary. From city dock at foot of Main St. Phone 410/268-7600, 410/269-6776 (Baltimore) or 301/261-2719 (DC).

Chesapeake Bay Bridge. The 7¼-mi link of US 50 across the Bay. Toll (charged eastbound only)   ¢¢

Government House (1868). This Victorian structure was remodeled in 1935 into a Georgian country house; furnishings reflect Maryland's history and culture. Tours by appt (Jan-mid-Apr, Tues and Thurs; rest of yr, Tues-Thurs). Between State & Church Circles. Phone 410/974-3531.   **Free**

Hammond-Harwood House (1774). Georgian house designed by William Buckland; antique furnishings; garden. Matthias Hammond, a Revolutionary patriot, was its first owner. Guided tours. (Daily; closed Jan 1, Thanksgiving, Dec 25) 19 Maryland Ave, at King George St, 1 blk W of US Naval Academy. Phone 410/269-1714.   ¢¢

Historic Annapolis Foundation Welcome Center and Museum Store. This (ca 1815) building stands on the site of a storehouse for Revolutionary War troops that was burned in 1790. Audiocassette walking tours. Products reflecting Annapolis history. (Mon-Sat, also Sun afternoons; closed Easter, Thanksgiving, Dec 25) 18 Pinkney St. Phone 410/268-5576.

London Town (ca 1760). Once considered a site for Maryland's capital; the only surviving structure of the Lost Town is the William Brown House, a Georgian mansion on banks of South River. Has 8 acres of woodland gardens. Museum and garden shop; boat docking. Special events. Guided tours. (Mon-Sat, also Sun afternoon; closed major hols). 8 mi SE via MD 2S, (Mayo Rd) in Edgewater, at the end of Londontown Rd (#839). Phone 410/222-1919.   ¢¢

Sailing tours. Two-hr narrated trips through Chesapeake Bay aboard 74-ft sailing yacht *Woodwind*. (May-Sept, Tues-Sun 4 trips daily, Mon Sunset Sail only; Apr, Oct, Nov, schedule varies) Departs from Pusser's Landing next to City Dock. Phone 410/263-8619.   ¢¢¢¢¢

Sandy Point State Park. 786 acres. The park's location on the Atlantic Flyway makes it a fine area for bird watching; view of Bay Bridge and oceangoing vessels. Swimming in bay at 2 guarded beaches, 2 bathhouses; surf fishing, crabbing; boating (rentals, launches). Concession. Standard fees. (See ANNUAL EVENTS) 7 mi E on US 50, at W end of Chesapeake Bay Bridge. Phone 410/757-1841.

St John's College (1784). (400 students) Nonsectarian liberal arts college. This 36-acre campus, one of the oldest in the country, is a National Historic Landmark. The college succeeded King William's School, founded in 1696. George Washington's two nephews and step-grandson studied here; Francis Scott Key was an alumnus. College Ave. For information phone 410/626-2539. On campus are

    Charles Carroll, Barrister House (1722). Birthplace of the author of the Maryland Bill of Rights; moved in 1955 to the campus and restored; now an administration building. Not open to public.

    Elizabeth Myers Mitchell Art Gallery. Displays museum quality traveling exhibitions. (Academic yr, daily exc Mon) For schedule phone 410/626-2556.   **Free**

    Liberty Tree. Tulip poplar, thought to be more than 400 yrs old, under which the Sons of Liberty met during the Revolution.

    McDowell Hall (begun 1742, finished 1789). Named for St John's first president; the main classroom building was originally built as the Governor's Mansion. Lafayette was feted here in 1824. Not open to public.

State House (1772-1779). Oldest state house in continuous legislative use in US, this was the first peacetime capitol of the US. Here in 1784, a few weeks after receiving George Washington's resignation as commander-in-chief, Congress ratified the Treaty of Paris, which officially ended the American Revolution. Visitors Information Center. Guide service (closed Jan 1, Thanksgiving). (Daily; closed Dec 25) State Circle, center of town. Phone 410/974-3400.   **Free**

United States Naval Academy (1845). (4,000 students) World-renowned school for naval officers; Leftwich Visitor Center provides guided walking tours, film, exhibits, gift shop (daily; closed Jan 1, Thanksgiving, Dec 25). The remains of John Paul Jones, removed from their original burial place in France, lie here beneath the chapel in a crypt similar to Napoleon's in Paris. Naval Academy Museum exhibits 300 yrs of American naval history. Sites include Bancroft Hall, dormitory for all midshipmen, a bust of Tamanend, replica of figurehead of USS *Delaware*, renamed *Tecumseh*. Parades, concerts and other events are held annually and during "Commissioning Week" (late May), culminated by midshipmen's graduation. Enter through Gate 1, King George St. Phone 410/263-6933. Grounds **Free**; tours ¢¢¢

🛏 **Walking tours.**

    Historic Annapolis Foundation. Self-guided audiocassette walking tours. Includes Historic District, State House, Old Treasury, US Naval Academy and William Paca House. (Mar-Nov, daily) Tours leave from museum store, 77 Main St. Phone 410/267-7619 or 410/269-0432.   ¢¢

    Three Centuries Tours of Annapolis. Walking tours of US Naval Academy and Historic District conducted by guides in colonial attire. Tour includes historic Maryland State House, St John's College, William Paca Garden, Naval Academy Chapel, Crypt of John Paul Jones, Bancroft Hall Dormitory and Armel-Leftwich Visitor Center. Morning tour leaves from Visitor Center at 26 West St; afternoon tour leaves from Visitor Info Booth on City Dock. (Apr-Oct, daily) Phone 410/263-5401 to confirm departure points and schedule.   ¢¢¢

William Paca Garden. Restored two-acre pleasure garden originally developed in 1765 by William Paca, a signer of the Declaration of Independence and governor of Maryland during the Revolutionary War. Includes waterways, formal parterres and a garden wilderness. (Mon-Sat, also Sun afternoons; closed Thanksgiving, Dec 25) 186 Prince George St. Also here is

    William Paca House. Paca built this five-part Georgian mansion in 1765. (Mon-Sat, also Sun afternoons; closed Thanksgiving, Dec 25) Phone 410/263-5553. Combination ticket (includes house and garden) ¢¢¢

Annual Events

Maryland Renaissance Festival. Food, craftsmen, minstrels, dramatic productions. Phone 800/296-7304. Usually last wk Aug-3rd wkend Oct.

Maryland Seafood Festival. Sandy Point State Park. Food; entertainment. Phone 410/268-7682. Usually wkend after Labor Day.

US Sailboat Show. City dock & harbor. Features world's largest in-water display of sailboats; exhibits of related marine products. Phone 410/268-8828. Early-mid-Oct.

US Powerboat Show. City dock & harbor. Extensive in-water display of powerboats; exhibits of related marine products. Phone 410/268-8828. Mid-Oct.

Chesapeake Appreciation Days. Sandy Point State Park. Skipjack sailing festival honors state's oystermen. Usually last wkend Oct.

Annapolis by Candlelight. For information, reservations contact Historic Annapolis Foundation; for dates phone 410/267-0432. Usually early Nov.

Seasonal Event

Christmas in Annapolis. Features decorated 18th-century mansions, parade of yachts, private home tours, pub crawls, concerts, holiday meals, First Night celebration, caroling by candlelight at the State House and other events. For free events calendar phone 410/268-8687. Thanksgiving-Jan 1.

Motels

✓★ **COMFORT INN.** US 50 & Old Mill Bottom Rd (21401), US 50/301 exit 28 to Bay Dale Dr. 410/757-8500; FAX 410/757-4409. 60 rms, 2 story. Apr-Oct: S $65-$110; D $70-$120; each addl $5; under 18 free; lower rates rest of yr. Crib free. TV; cable (premium). Pool; lifeguard. Complimentary continental bkfst. Restaurant nearby. Ck-out 11 am. Coin lndry. Business servs avail. Cr cds: A, C, D, DS, ER, JCB, MC, V.

D ⛱ 🛬 🐾 SC

★★ **COURTYARD BY MARRIOTT.** 2559 Riva Rd (21401). 410/266-1555; FAX 410/266-6376; res: 800/321-2211. E-mail cy.bwian.gm@marriott.com; web www.courtyard.com. 149 units, 3 story. S, D $109-$119; suites $129-$149; under 12 free. Crib free. TV; cable (premium). Indoor pool; whirlpool, lifeguard. Complimentary coffee in rms. Restaurant 6:30 am-1:30 pm; Sat, Sun from 7 am. Bar 4-10 pm. Ck-out noon. Coin lndry. Meeting rms. Business servs avail. In-rm modem link. Valet serv. Sundries. Exercise equipt. Refrigerator in suites. Cr cds: A, C, D, DS, MC, V.

D ⛱ 🏋 🛬 🐾 SC

✓★★ **DAYS INN.** 2520 Riva Rd (21401). 410/224-2800; FAX 410/266-5539; res: 800/329-7466. 152 rms, 2 story. Mid-Mar-mid-Nov: S, D $59-$119; suites $119-$129; lower rates rest of yr. Crib free. TV; cable (premium). Pool. Complimentary continental bkfst. Restaurant adj 11 am-

10 pm. Bar. Ck-out 11 am. Meeting rms. Business servs avail. Coin lndry. Health club privileges. Game rm. Some refrigerators. Cr cds: A, C, D, DS, MC, V.

[D] [≈] [≍] [🔥] [SC]

Motor Hotels

★★★ **HOLIDAY INN.** *210 Holiday Ct (21401).* *410/224-3150; FAX 410/224-3413; res: 800/465-4329.* 220 rms, 6 story. S $79-$119; D $89-$129; suites $139; under 18 free. Crib free. Pet accepted. TV; cable (premium). Pool; lifeguard. Restaurant 6:30 am-2 pm, 5-10 pm. Rm serv. Bar 4 pm-midnight. Ck-out noon. Meeting rms. Business servs avail. In-rm modem link. Bellhops. Valet serv. Sundries. Health club privileges. Microwaves avail. Cr cds: A, C, D, DS, JCB, MC, V.

[D] [🐾] [≈] [≍] [🔥] [SC]

✓ ★★★ **WYNDHAM GARDEN HOTEL.** *173 Jennifer Rd (21401).* *410/266-3131; FAX 410/266-6247; res: 800/351-9209.* Web www.travel web.com. 197 rms, 6 story. S $89-$139; D $99-$149; each addl $10; suites $109-$209; under 18 free; hol rates; higher rates special events. Crib free. TV; cable. Indoor pool; whirlpool, lifeguard. Coffee in rms. Restaurant 6:30 am-2:30 pm, 5-10 pm. Rm serv 5-10 pm. Bar 4 pm-midnight. Ck-out noon. Meeting rms. Business servs avail. In-rm modem link. Exercise equipt; sauna. Health club privileges. Some refrigerators; microwaves avail. Cr cds: A, C, D, DS, MC, V.

[D] [≈] [🏋] [≍] [🔥] [SC]

Hotels

★★★ **LOEWS ANNAPOLIS HOTEL.** *126 West St (21401).* *410/263-7777; FAX 410/263-0084; res: 800/526-2593.* Web www.loewsan napolis.com. 217 rms, 6 story, 11 suites. S, D $119-$185; each addl $15; suites $185-$350; under 17 free. Crib free. Pet accepted. Valet parking $10. TV; cable (premium). Pool privileges. Restaurant (see CORINTHIAN). Bar 11-2 am. Ck-out noon. Meeting rms. Business center. In-rm modem link. Concierge. Gift shop. Barber, beauty shop. Exercise equipt. Health club privileges. Refrigerators, minibars. Private patios, balconies. Luxury level. Cr cds: A, C, D, DS, MC, V.

[D] [🐾] [🏋] [≍] [🔥] [SC] [🚶]

★★★ **MARRIOTT WATERFRONT.** *80 Compromise St (21401), opp Naval Academy.* *410/268-7555; FAX 410/269-5864; res: 800/336-0072.* Web www.marriott.com. 150 rms, 6 story. May-Sept: S, D $159-$269; varied rates rest of yr. Crib free. Garage $12. TV; cable (premium), VCR avail. Restaurant 6:30 am-11 pm. Bar 11-2 am. Ck-out 11 am. Meeting rms. Business servs avail. In-rm modem link. Exercise equipt. Some in-rm whirlpools; refrigerators, microwaves avail. Some balconies. On waterfront; 300 ft dockage. Cr cds: A, C, D, DS, MC, V.

[D] [🏋] [≍] [🔥] [SC]

Inns

★★ **CHESAPEAKE BAY LIGHTHOUSE.** *1423 Sharps Point Rd (21401).* *410/757-0248; FAX 410/757-0248.* E-mail baylight@toad.net; web 199.75.220.16/aabus/cbbb/chesbnb.htm. 5 rms, 2 story. No rm phones. S, D $110-$210; each addl $10. Children over 12 only. TV in sitting rm. Complimentary continental bkfst. Restaurant nearby. Ck-out 11 am, ck-in 3-7 pm. Working lighthouse in Chesapeake Bay. Totally nonsmoking. Cr cds: C, DS, MC, V.

[⛵] [≍] [🔥]

★★ **GIBSONS LODGINGS.** *110 Prince George St (21401).* *410/268-5555; FAX 410/268-2775.* Web www.avmcyber.com/gibson. 20 rms, 13 share bath in 3 bldgs, 3 story. Some rm phones. S $58-$110; D $68-$125; each addl $15. TV in some rms; cable, VCR avail. Complimen-

tary continental bkfst; afternoon refreshments. Restaurant nearby. Ck-out 11 am, ck-in 2 pm. Meeting rm. Business servs avail. Microwaves avail. Antiques; library. Totally nonsmoking. Cr cds: A, C, MC, V.

[D] [≍] [🔥]

★★★ **GOVERNOR CALVERT HOUSE.** *58 State Cir (21401).* *410/263-2641; FAX 410/268-3813; res: 800/847-8882.* 51 rms, 4 story. S, D $125-$175; each addl $10; suites $185-$285; under 18 free; higher rates special events. Crib free. Valet parking $12. TV; cable (premium). Restaurant nearby. Ck-out noon, ck-in 3 pm. Meeting rms. Business servs avail. In-rm modem link. Lighted tennis privileges. Golf privileges. Health club privileges. Refrigerators, microwaves avail. 18th-century state house with modern addition; colonial gardens, atrium. Cr cds: A, C, D, DS, JCB, MC, V.

[D] [🎿] [🎾] [≍] [🔥] [SC]

★★ **MARYLAND INN.** *58 State Cir (21401).* *410/263-2641; FAX 410/268-3813; res: 800/847-8882.* 44 rms, 4 story. S $105-$135; D $105-$165; each addl $10; suites $145-$260; under 18 free; higher rates special events. Crib free. Valet parking $12. TV; cable (premium). Restaurant (see TREATY OF PARIS). Bar; entertainment. Ck-out noon, ck-in 3 pm (at Governor Calvert House). Business servs avail. In-rm modem link. Bellhops. Lighted tennis, golf privileges. Health club privileges. Some refrigerators; microwaves avail. View of bay. Historic inn built 1772; many antique furnishings. Cr cds: A, C, D, DS, JCB, MC, V.

[🎿] [🎾] [≍] [🔥] [SC]

★★★ **PRINCE GEORGE INN.** *232 Prince George St (21401).* *410/263-6418; FAX 410/626-0009.* E-mail pginn@annap.infi.net; web www.princegeorgeinn.com. 4 rms, 2 share bath, 3 story. No rm phones. S $90-$100; D $110-$115; under 8 free; wkends (2-day min). Parking $4. TV; cable, VCR. Complimentary full bkfst. Restaurant nearby. Ck-out noon, ck-in 4-6 pm. Refrigerators. Victorian townhouse built in 1884. Totally nonsmoking. Cr cds: C, DS, MC, V.

[≍] [🔥]

★★ **ROBERT JOHNSON HOUSE.** *23 State Circle (21401).* *410/263-2641; FAX 410/268-3613; res: 800/847-8882.* 29 rms, 4 story. S $105-$135; D $105-$165; each addl $10; suites $260; under 18 free; higher rates special events. Crib free. Valet parking $12. TV; cable (premium). Restaurant nearby. Ck-out noon, ck-in 3 pm (at Governor Calvert House). Business servs avail. In-rm modem link. Lighted tennis privileges. Golf privileges. Health club privileges. Refrigerators, microwaves avail. Consists of 18th-century mansion plus 2 connecting townhouses of the same period. Cr cds: A, C, D, DS, JCB, MC, V.

[D] [🎿] [🎾] [≍] [🔥] [SC]

✓ ★★ **WILLIAM PAGE INN.** *8 Martin St (21401).* *410/626-1506; FAX 410/263-4841; res: 800/364-4160.* E-mail wmpageinn@aol.com; web www.williampageinn.com. 5 rms, 2 share bath, 3 story. S, D $95-$195; wkly rates. Complimentary full bkfst. Restaurant nearby. Ck-out noon, ck-in 4-6 pm. Business servs avail. Former clubhouse (1908). Totally nonsmoking. Cr cds: C, MC, V.

[≍] [🔥]

Restaurants

★★ **BUSCH'S CHESAPEAKE INN.** *321 Busch's Frontage Rd US 50 (21401).* *410/757-1717.* Hrs: 11:30 am-9 pm; Fri to 10 pm; Sat to 11 pm; Sun 11 am-9 pm; Sun brunch to 3 pm. Closed Dec 23-26. Res accepted. Bar. Semi-a la carte: lunch $5.25-$9.95, dinner $14.95-$24.95. Buffet: lunch $8.50. Sun brunch $16.95. Child's meals. Specializes in seafood. Nautical decor. Braille menu. Family-owned. Cr cds: A, C, D, DS, MC, V.

[D] [SC]

★★★ **CAFE BRETTON.** *849 Baltimore/Annapolis Blvd (21146), N on MD 2, N of College Pkwy.* *410/647-8222.* Hrs: 5-10 pm; early-bird dinner to 6 pm. Closed Sun, Mon; some major hols. Res required Fri, Sat.

French menu. Bar. Wine list. Semi-a la carte: dinner $10.95-$26.95. Specializes in lamb shank, seafood. Own baking. Country French atmosphere with original artwork. Totally nonsmoking. Cr cds: C, MC, V.

D

★★ **CAFE NORMANDIE.** 185 Main St (21401), in Historic District. 410/263-3382. Hrs: 8 am-10 pm; Fri, Sat to 10:30 pm. French menu. Serv bar. Semi-a la carte: bkfst $3-$6, lunch $5.50-$15, dinner $8.95-$21. Specializes in seafood, Maryland crab dishes. French-style cafe. Cr cds: A, C, D, DS, MC, V.

D

★★ **CARROL'S CREEK.** 410 Severn Ave (21403), ¼ mi across Eastport Bridge at City Marina. 410/263-8102. E-mail carrols cc@aol.com. Hrs: 11:30 am-4 pm, 5-10 pm; Sun brunch 10 am-2 pm. Res accepted Mon-Thurs; required hols. Bar. Semi-a la carte: lunch $4.95-$9.95, dinner $14-$22. Sun brunch $16.95. Specializes in local seafood. Own baking. Outdoor dining. On water. Cr cds: A, C, D, DS, MC, V.

D

★★★ **CORINTHIAN.** (See Loews Annapolis Hotel) 410/263-1299. Hrs: 6:30 am-2 pm, 5-10 pm; Sun brunch from 10 am. Res accepted Sat. Bar. Wine list. Semi-a la carte: bkfst $6.50-$14.95, lunch $6.95-$15.95, dinner $18.95-$28.95. Sun brunch $22. Child's meals. Specializes in fresh seafood, prime beef. Valet parking. Elegant atmosphere. Cr cds: A, C, D, DS, MC, V.

D SC

★★ **FRED'S.** 2348 Solomons Island Rd (21401), MD 2, 1 blk S of MD 450. 410/224-2386. Hrs: 11 am-10 pm; Fri, Sat to 11 pm; early-bird dinner Mon-Fri 4-6 pm, Sat & Sun noon-6 pm. Closed Thanksgiving, Dec 25. Res accepted. Continental menu. Bar. Semi-a la carte: lunch $4.50-$8.95, dinner $9.95-$33.95. Child's meals. Specializes in seafood, steak, Italian dishes. Victorian decor; antiques. Family-owned. Cr cds: A, C, D, MC, V.

D

✓★★ **GRIFFINS RESTAURANT.** 24 Market Space (21401). 410/268-2576. E-mail griffins@toad.net; web www.griffins-citydock.com. Hrs: 11 am-midnight; Fri, Sat to 1 am; Sun brunch 11 am-1 pm. Closed Dec 25. Res accepted Mon-Thurs. Bar to 1:30 am. Semi-a la carte: lunch $6.95-$8.95, dinner $8.95-$12.95. Sun brunch $6.95-$9.95. Child's meals. Specializes in seafood, steak, pasta. Own desserts. Cr cds: A, C, D, DS, MC, V.

D

★★★ **HARRY BROWNE'S.** 66 State Circle (21401). 410/263-4332. E-mail rusrom@aol.com. Hrs: 11 am-3 pm, 5:30-10 pm; wkends to 11 pm; Sun brunch 10 am-3 pm. Closed Jan 1, Dec 25. Res accepted. Continental menu. Bar. Wine cellar. Semi-a la carte: lunch $6.95-$12, dinner $17-$22. Specialties: crab cakes, rack of lamb. Entertainment Mon, Fri, Sat. Valet parking Fri, Sat. Decorated with mirrors and pressed gold tin ceiling. Cr cds: A, C, D, DS, MC, V.

D

★★ **LEWNES' STEAKHOUSE.** 401 4th St (21403), at Severn Ave. 410/263-1617. Hrs: 5-10 pm; Fri, Sat to 10:30 pm. Closed Thanksgiving, Dec 25. Res required. Bar. A la carte entrees: dinner $15-$27. Specializes in prime steak, seafood. Street parking. 1950s steakhouse atmosphere; casual fine dining. Cr cds: A, C, D, MC, V.

D

★★ **MIDDLETON TAVERN.** 2 Market Space (21401). 410/263-3323. Hrs: 11:30-2 am; Sat, Sun from 10 am. Bar. Semi-a la carte: lunch $5.95-$10.95, dinner $11.95-$23.95. Specializes in seafood, crab dishes. Oyster bar. Entertainment. Outdoor dining. Restored building (1750), traditional tavern decor. Overlooks harbor. Family-owned. Cr cds: A, C, DS, MC, V.

♥

★★★ **NORTHWOODS.** 609 Melvin Ave (21401). 410/268-2609. Hrs: 5:30-10 pm; Sun 5-9 pm. Closed most major hols. Res accepted. Continental menu. Wine list. Semi-a la carte: dinner $18.95-$23. Complete meals: dinner $26.95. Specializes in fresh seafood, Italian dishes. Outdoor dining. Casual elegance in romantic setting. Cr cds: A, C, D, DS, MC, V.

D

★★ **O'LEARY'S SEAFOOD RESTAURANT.** 310 3rd St (21403). 410/263-0884. Hrs: 5:30-10 pm; Fri, Sat 5-11 pm; Sun 5-10 pm. Closed Thanksgiving, Dec 24, 25. Res accepted. Bar. Semi-a la carte: dinner $10.95-$29.95. Child's meals. Specializes in seafood. Own desserts. Cr cds: A, C, D, MC, V.

D

★★★ **REYNOLD'S TAVERN.** 7 Church Circle (21401). 410/626-0380. Hrs: 6-9 pm; Fri, Sat to 10 pm; Sun 5-8 pm. Closed Jan 1, July 4, Dec 25. Res accepted. Bar. A la carte entrees: dinner $4.25-$24.95. Specializes in seafood. Entertainment. Outdoor dining. Colonial decor. Cr cds: A, C, MC, V.

D

★★★ **TREATY OF PARIS RESTAURANT.** (See Maryland Inn) 410/263-2641. Hrs: 7 am-2:30 pm, 5:30-10:30 pm; Fri, Sat to 11:30 pm; Sun to 9:30 pm; Sun brunch 10 am-2:30 pm. Closed Jan 1. Res accepted; required Fri, Sat. Continental menu. Bar 11-2 am; Sun to 1 am. Wine cellar. Semi-a la carte: bkfst $3.50-$9, lunch $6.95-$10, dinner $14-$22. Complete meals: dinner $20, $25. Sun brunch $18.95. Specializes in New American cuisine, fresh local seafood. Salad bar (lunch). Valet parking (dinner). Early American tavern atmosphere; fireplace. Cr cds: A, C, D, DS, JCB, MC, V.

D SC

★★★ **VESPUCCI'S.** 87 Prince George St (21401). 410/571-0100. Hrs: 11 am-11 pm; Sun from 10 am; Sun brunch to 4 pm. Closed Thanksgiving, Dec 25. Res accepted. Italian, Amer menu. Bar. Semi-a la carte: lunch $5-$18, dinner $8-$27. Sun brunch $12.95. Child's meals. Specializes in veal, seafood. Own baking, pasta. Valet parking Fri, Sat (dinner). Outdoor dining. Three distinct dining areas vary from casual bistro to formal setting; view of harbor. Totally nonsmoking. Cr cds: A, C, D, DS, MC, V.

D

Antietam National Battlefield (B-4)

(10 mi S of Hagerstown on MD 65)

On September 17, 1862, the bloodiest day in Civil War annals, more than 23,000 men were killed or wounded as Union forces blocked the first Confederate invasion of the North. A Union advantage was gained beforehand when a soldier accidentally found Lee's orders wrapped around some cigars. In spite of knowing Lee's tactical game plan, McClellan moved cautiously. The battle, critical because British aid to the Confederacy depended on the outcome, was a tactical draw but a strategic victory for the North. This victory allowed Lincoln to issue the Emancipation Proclamation, which expanded the war from simply reuniting the country to a crusade to end slavery. The rebels withdrew across the Potomac on the night of September 18, but for some reason McClellan, with twice the manpower, delayed his pursuit. Lincoln relieved him of command of the Army of the Potomac seven weeks later. Clara Barton, who was to found the Red Cross 19 years later, attended the wounded at a field hospital on the battlefield.

Approximately 350 iron tablets, monuments and battlefield maps, located on eight miles of paved avenues, describe the events of the battle. The Visitor Center houses a museum and offers information, literature and a 26-minute orientation movie (shown on the hour). Visitor Center (daily; closed Jan 1, Thanksgiving, Dec 25); battlefield (daily); ranger-conducted walks, talks and demonstrations (Memorial Day-Labor Day, daily). Golden Age Passport (see MAKING THE MOST OF YOUR TRIP). For information phone 301/432-5124. Entrance fee per person ¢, maximum per family ¢¢

Baltimore (B-7)

Settled 1661 **Pop** 736,014 **Elev** 32 ft **Area Code** 410 & 443 **Web** www.baltimore.org

Information Baltimore Area Convention & Visitors Assn, 100 Light St, 12th floor, 21202; 410/659-7300 or 800/343-3468

Suburbs Aberdeen, Cockeysville, Columbia, Ellicott City, Pikesville, Towson. (See individual alphabetical listings.)

Metropolis of Maryland and one of America's great cities, Baltimore is a city of neighborhoods built on strong ethnic foundations, a city of historic events that helped shape the nation and a city that has achieved an incredible downtown renaissance in the past 20 years. It is a major East Coast manufacturing center and, almost from its beginning, a world seaport. Several colleges and universities, foremost of which is Johns Hopkins, make their home here.

Lying midway between North and South and enjoying a rich cultural mixture of both, Baltimore is one of the nation's oldest cities. When British troops threatened Philadelphia during the Revolution, the Continental Congress fled to Baltimore, which served as the nation's capital for a little more than two months.

In October 1814, a British fleet attacked the city by land and sea. The defenders of Fort McHenry withstood the naval bombardment for 25 hours until the British gave up. Francis Scott Key saw the huge American flag still flying above the fort and was inspired to pen "The Star-Spangled Banner."

Rapid growth in the early 19th century resulted from the opening of the National Road and then the nation's first railroad, the Baltimore & Ohio.

Politics was a preoccupation in those days, and the city hosted many national party conventions. At least seven presidents and three losing candidates were nominated here. Edgar Allan Poe's mysterious death in the city may have been at the hands of shady electioneers.

Untouched physically by the Civil War, effects came later when Southerners flooded in to rebuild their fortunes, and commerce was disrupted by the loss of Southern markets. A disastrous fire in 1904 destroyed 140 acres of the business district, but the city recovered rapidly and, during the two World Wars, was a major shipbuilding and naval repair center.

In the 1950s and early 1960s, Baltimore was the victim of apathy and the general decay that struck the industrial Northeast. But the city fought back, replacing hundreds of acres of slums, rotting wharves and warehouses with gleaming new office plazas, parks and public buildings. The Inner Harbor was transformed into a huge public area with shops, museums, restaurants and frequent concerts and festivals. Millions of tourists and proud Baltimoreans flock downtown to enjoy the sights and activities.

Famous residents and native sons include Babe Ruth, Edgar Allan Poe, H.L. Mencken, Mother Elizabeth Ann Seton, Eubie Blake, Ogden Nash, Thurgood Marshall, Wallis Warfield Simpson, who became the Duchess of Windsor, and more recent sports legends Brooks Robinson, Johnny Unitas and Jim Palmer.

Transportation

Airport. See BALTIMORE/WASHINGTON INTL AIRPORT AREA.

Car Rental Agencies. See IMPORTANT TOLL-FREE NUMBERS.

Public Transportation. Bus & subway (Mass Transit Administration), phone 410/539-5000.

Rail Passenger Service. Amtrak 800/872-7245; MARC (commuter train serving Baltimore & Washington, DC) 800/325-RAIL or 410/291-4267.

What to See and Do

B & O Railroad Museum. The museum includes the Mount Clare Station (1851), site of the nation's first passenger station, and the roundhouse (1884); original tracks and wooden turntable are fully preserved. Collection includes over 120 full-sized train cars. (Daily; closed Easter, Thanksgiving, Dec 25). 901 W Pratt St, at Poppleton St. Phone 410/752-2490. ¢¢¢

Babe Ruth Birthplace/Baseball Center. Renovated house where Babe Ruth was born. Features memorabilia of Babe Ruth, Orioles and Maryland baseball; 25-min movie of the "Sultan of Swat" and many other audiovisual displays. (Daily) 216 Emory St. Phone 410/727-1539. ¢¢

Baltimore Maritime Museum. USS *Torsk,* WWII submarine, Coast Guard cutter *Taney* and lightship *Chesapeake.* (Daily) Pier 3, Pratt St, Inner Harbor area. Phone 410/396-5528. ¢¢

Baltimore Museum of Art. Variety of collections, including American paintings, period rooms; African and Oceanian art. Noted for Cone collection of French Post-Impressionists, including Matisse and Picasso; Cheney miniature rooms; modern art wing; sculpture gardens; museum cafe and shop. (Wed-Sun; closed major hols) 10 Art Museum Dr near N Charles & 31st Sts. Phone 410/396-7100 or 410/396-7101. ¢¢¢

Baltimore Museum of Industry. Exhibits trace the growth of Baltimore as an industrial center. Turn-of-the-century machine shop, print shop and garment loft. Hands-on exhibits; children's activities. Restored tugboat on waterfront behind museum. (Thurs-Sun; limited hrs) Phone 410/727-4808. ¢¢

Baltimore Streetcar Museum. Eleven electric streetcars and two horsecars used in city between 1859 and 1963; 1¼-mi rides (fee). (June-Oct, Sat & Sun afternoons; rest of yr, Sun afternoons only; also open Memorial Day, July 4, Labor Day) 1901 Falls Rd, under North Ave Bridge. Phone 410/547-0264. ¢¢

Baltimore Zoo. Main zoo has collection of more than 1,500 animals. Includes 3-acre African elephant park; 6-acre African watering hole; hippo and African flamingo exhibit; 8-acre children's zoo (daily); track train & carousel (Apr-Sept; fee). Zoo (daily exc Dec 25). Druid Hill Park. Phone 410/366-5466. ¢¢¢

Basilica of the National Shrine of the Assumption. Now a co-cathedral, this was the first Roman Catholic cathedral in the US. Bishop John Carroll, head of the diocese of Baltimore from its establishment in 1789, blessed the cornerstone in 1806. The church was dedicated in 1821. Architectural design by B. H. Latrobe. Tours (2nd & 4th Sun each month or by appt). (Daily) Cathedral & Mulberry Sts, downtown. Phone 410/727-3565.

Battle Monument (1815). Memorial to those who fell defending the city in the War of 1812. Calvert & Fayette Sts.

Charles Center. Business area with European-style plazas, part of an overhead walkway system, shops, restaurants and outdoor activities. Prize-winning office building by Mies van der Rohe borders center plaza. Bounded by Charles, Liberty, Saratoga & Lombard Sts, downtown. Also here is

   Baltimore Center for the Performing Arts-Morris Mechanic Theater. Hosts Broadway productions. Hopkins Plaza. For schedule, fees phone 410/625-4230.

Church Home and Hospital. Edgar Allan Poe died here in 1849. Broadway & Fairmount Ave.

City Court House (1900). On steps is statue of Cecil Calvert, brother of Leonard and founder of Maryland as the second Lord Baltimore. St Paul & Fayette Sts, downtown.

City Hall. Post-Civil War architecture, restored to original detail. 100 N Holliday St, downtown. Tours by appt, Phone 410/396-3100. **Free**

City of Baltimore Conservatory. This graceful building (ca 1885) houses a large variety of tropical plants. Special shows during Easter, Nov & Christmas. (Thurs-Sun) Druid Hill Park. Phone 410/396-0180. **Free**

Cylburn Arboretum. Marked nature trails. Nature museum, ornithological room, horticultural library in restored mansion; shade and formal gardens, All-American Selection Garden, Garden of the Senses. (Daily) 4915 Greenspring Ave. Phone 410/396-0180. **Free**

Edgar Allan Poe Grave. Baltimore's oldest cemeteries also contain the graves of many prominent early Marylanders. Tour of catacombs by appt

28TH ST

7

FALLS RD

25

HOWARD ST

CHARLES ST

ST PAUL ST

CALVERT ST

45

147

NORTH AV

1

AISQUITH ST

HARFORD AV

HARFORD RD

GAY AV

LAFAYETTE AV

LANVALE ST

83

5

2 2

UNIVERSITY OF BALTIMORE

4

4

MT ROYAL AV

PRESTON

GREENMOUNT AV

ST

PRESTON ST

BIDDLE ST

MC CULLOH ST

DRUID HILL AV

PRESTON ST

CALVERT ST

CENTRAL AV

3

M L KING JR BLVD

ST MARY ST

MADISON ST

83

MONUMENT ST

SOJOURNER DOUGLASS COLLEGE

JOHNS HOPKINS HOSPITAL

ENSOR ST

ORLEANS ST

FRANKLIN ST

ORLEANS ST VIADUCT

40

MULBERRY ST

2

FAYETTE ST

CHURCH HOSPITAL CORP

GREENE ST

PACA ST

CENTRAL AREA

N

FAYETTE ST

BALTIMORE ARENA

COMMUNITY COLLEGE

GAY ST

LITTLE ITALY

UNIV OF MD MED SYSTEM

LOMBARD ST

E FALLS AV

FALLS BLVD

TRK 3

PRATT ST

INNER HARBOR

EASTERN AV

CONWAY ST

LIGHT ST

FELL'S POINT

LEE ST

2

Inner Harbor

KEY HWY

BALTIMORE NEIGHBORHOODS

0   0.25   0.5 mile

0.25   0.5 km

© 2000, Rand McNally

LOCUST POINT

(Apr-Nov, 1st & 3rd Fri & Sat). At Westminster Hall & Burying Ground and Catacombs, Fayette & Greene Sts, downtown. ¢¢

Edgar Allan Poe House (ca 1830). Poe's home from 1832-1835. (Apr-July & Oct-mid-Dec, Wed-Sat, afternoons; Aug & Sept, Sat afternoon only) Also offered are tours of Westminster Cemetery and Catacombs (evenings, by appt; fee). 203 N Amity St, off 900 blk W Lexington St, downtown. Phone 410/396-7932. ¢

Enoch Pratt Free Library. City's public library. H.L. Mencken & Edgar Allan Poe collections. (Oct-Apr, daily exc Fri; rest of yr, Mon-Thurs & Sat; closed hols) 400 Cathedral St, at Franklin St, downtown. Phone 410/396-5430 or -3557.

Federal Hill. View of city harbor and skyline. Named after a celebration that occurred here in 1788 to mark Maryland's ratification of the Constitution. Warren St & Battery Ave, Inner Harbor area.

Fell's Point. Shipbuilding and maritime center, this neighborhood dates back to 1730; approx 350 original residential structures. Working tugboats and tankers can be observed from docks. Broadway, S of Fleet St to the harbor.

First Unitarian Church (1817). William Ellery Channing preached a sermon here that hastened the establishment of the Unitarian denomination. Example of Classic Revival architecture. Charles & Franklin Sts, in Mt Vernon Place area. Phone 410/685-2330.

Fort McHenry National Monument and Historic Shrine. The flag flying over this five-pointed, star-shaped brick fort inspired Francis Scott Key to write the poem in 1814 that later became the lyrics to the national anthem. Named for James McHenry, Secretary of War (1796-1800). Replica flagpole on 1814 site. Restored powder magazine, guardroom, officers' quarters and barracks all contain exhibits. Cannons of War of 1812 and Civil War periods. Guided activities (mid-June-Aug, daily). The Fort McHenry Guard, in period uniform, reenacts life at the garrison (mid-June-Aug, Sat & Sun afternoons). Military ceremony (July-Aug, some Sun evenings). Visitor Center has exhibit area, film, gift shop. Special exhibits for visually and hearing impaired. (Daily; closed Jan 1, Dec 25) E end of Fort Ave. Phone 410/962-4299. ¢

   Narrated cruises. on the *Baltimore Patriot* depart from Inner Harbor Finger Pier to Fort McHenry and Fells Point (Memorial Day-Labor Day). Also departures from Fort McHenry and Fells Point. For other tours contact Maryland Tours, Inc. Round-trip. ¢¢

Gunpowder Falls State Park. Approx 17,000 acres, located in Gunpowder River Valley. **Hammerman Area,** E on US 40, right onto Ebenezer Rd, 5 mi to park entrance in Chase, is a developed day-use area. Offers swimming beach, windsurfing beach, boating, marina (Dundee Creek), picnicking, playground. Other areas offer hiking/biking trails, canoeing, trout fishing. Standard fees. Phone 410/592-2897.

Harbor cruises. Depart from Inner Harbor.

   MV *Lady Baltimore.* Round-trip cruises to Annapolis (June-Aug, Wed); also cruises to the Chesapeake & Delaware Canal (3 selected Sun in Oct). *Bay Lady* has lunch and dinner cruises (Apr-Oct, daily; limited schedule rest of yr). West Bulkhead, 301 Light St. Phone 410/727-3113 or 800/695-LADY. ¢¢¢¢¢

   Baltimore Patriot has 90-min tours around Baltimore harbor. (Apr-Oct, daily). ¢¢¢

Harborplace. European-style marketplace comprised of two glass-enclosed pavilions; one featuring many eateries, including waterside cafes and restaurants, the other housing dozens of specialty shops arranged in Parisian style along a colonnade. Overhead walkway leads to **The Gallery at Harborplace**, with many additional top-name shops and eateries. Free summer concerts along waterfront. (Daily; closed Thanksgiving, Dec 25) Light & Pratt Sts, Inner Harbor area. Phone 410/332-4191.

Holocaust Memorial. Simple stone memorial to the victims of the Holocaust. Water & Gay Sts, downtown.

Jewish Historical Society of Maryland. Buildings include Lloyd St Synagogue (1845), the oldest in Maryland; B'nai Israel Synagogue (1876); Jewish Museum of Maryland. (Tues-Fri & Sun afternoons; or by appt; closed Jewish hols) Research archives (Mon-Fri, by appt). 15 Lloyd St, downtown. Phone 410/732-6400. ¢

Johns Hopkins Medical Institutions (1889). Widely known as a leading medical school, research center and teaching hospital. Victorian buildings. Broadway & Monument St.

Johns Hopkins University (1876). (4,600 students) Modern buildings in Georgian style on wooded 126-acre campus. Distinguished research school founded by wealthy merchant of the city. Charles & 34th Sts, 2 mi N. Phone 410/516-8000. On grounds are

   Bufano Sculpture Garden. A wooded retreat with animals sculpted by artist Beniamino Bufano. Dunning Park, behind Mudd Hall. **Free**

   Evergreen House. On 26 wooded acres; features Classical-revival architecture and formal garden. Contains the Library (35,000 volumes). Post-Impressionist paintings, Japanese and Chinese collections and Tiffany glass. Tours (daily). 4545 N Charles St, approx 2 mi N of Homewood campus. Phone 410/516-0341. ¢¢

   Homewood House Museum. Former country home (1801) of Charles Carroll, Jr, whose father was a signer of the Declaration of Independence; period furnishings. (Tues-Sat, also Sun afternoons) Guided tours (hourly). 3400 N Charles St near 34th St. Phone 410/516-5589. ¢¢

Lacrosse Hall of Fame Museum. Team trophies, display of lacrosse artifacts and memorabilia; videotapes of championship games. (Mon-Fri; Sat during lacrosse season; closed hols) 113 W University Pkwy. Phone 410/235-6882. ¢

Joseph Meyerhoff Symphony Hall. Permanent residence of the Baltimore Symphony Orchestra. 1212 Cathedral St. Phone 410/783-8000 or 410/783-8100.

Lexington Market. In continuous operation since 1782, this famous indoor marketplace houses more than 140 stalls run by independent merchants. (Daily exc Sun; closed major hols) 400 W Lexington St, between Eutaw & Paca Sts, downtown. Phone 410/685-6169. **Free**

Lovely Lane Museum. Permanent and changing exhibits of items of Methodist church history since 1760. Guided tours (Mon-Fri; also Sun after services and by appt; closed hols). 2200 St Paul St. Phone 410/889-4458. **Free**

Maryland Historical Society Library of Maryland. Original manuscript of "Star-Spangled Banner" is displayed; extensive displays of Maryland silver, furniture and painting; changing exhibits; maritime museum. Also within the museum is the **Darnall Young Peoples Museum**, a gallery with "hands-on" exhibits. Museum and gallery (Oct-Apr, daily exc Mon; rest of yr, Tues-Sun). Library (Tues-Sat). Museum free on Wed. 201 W Monument St, between Park Ave & Howard St, in Mt Vernon Place area. Phone 410/685-3750. ¢¢

Maryland Institute, College of Art (1826). (880 students) Institute hosts frequent contemporary art exhibitions. Cafeteria. Campus distinguished by recycled buildings and white marble Italianate Main Building. (Daily) Main building 1300 Mt Royal Ave, at Lanvale St. Phone 410/669-9200.

Maryland Science Center & Davis Planetarium. Home of the Maryland Academy of Sciences, the oldest scientific institution in the state. Features exhibits in areas such as energy, physics, the Chesapeake Bay, optical illusions & television production. Planetarium. Includes IMAX theater. Science demonstrations. (Daily; closed Thanksgiving, Dec 25) 601 Light St, Inner Harbor area. Phone 410/685-5225 (recording). ¢¢¢

Minnie V. Chesapeake Bay skipjack built in 1906. Harbor tours under sail (open wkends). Docks near Pier 1, Pratt St, Inner Harbor area. Phone 410/685-0295. ¢¢¢¢

Morgan State University (1867). (5,100 students) The James E. Lewis Museum of Art has changing exhibits (Mon-Fri; wkends by appt; closed hols). Cold Spring Lane & Hillen Rd. Phone 443/885-3333.

Mother Seton House. Home of St Elizabeth Ann Bayley Seton from 1808-1809. Here she established forerunner of the parochial school system. She also established an order of nuns here that eventually became the Daughters & Sisters of Charity in the US and Canada. (Sat & Sun afternoons, also by appt; closed Jan 1, Easter, Dec 25) 600 N Paca St, downtown. Phone 410/523-3443. **Free**

Mount Clare Museum House (1760). Oldest mansion in Baltimore, former home of Charles Carroll, barrister. 18th-century furnishings. Guided tours on the hr. (Daily exc Mon; closed some hols) In Carroll Park at 1500 Washington Blvd. Phone 410/837-3262. ¢¢

Mount Vernon Place United Methodist Church (ca 1850). Brownstone with balcony and grillwork extending entire width of house; spiral staircase suspended from 3 floors; library with century-old painting on ceiling; drawing room. (Mon-Fri; closed hols and Mon after Easter) 10 E Mt Vernon Place. Phone 410/685-5290. **Free**

MPT (Maryland Public Television). Tours of state's television network studios. (By appt) Phone 410/356-5600 or 800/223-3MPT (surrounding states). **Free**

⭐ **National Aquarium.** One of the most advanced facilities in US. Exhibits include a South American rain forest, Atlantic coral reef, shark tank; houses 5,000 specimens of 500 different types of mammals, fish, birds, reptiles, amphibians, invertebrates and plants. (Daily; closed Thanksgiving, Dec 25) Pier 3, 501 E Pratt St, Inner Harbor area. Phone 410/576-3800. ¢¢¢¢ Visitors cross an enclosed skywalk to reach the adj wing, which house

Marine Mammal Pavilion. This unique structure features a 1,300-seat amphitheater surrounding a 1.2-million-gallon pool, which houses Atlantic bottlenose dolphins; underwater viewing areas enable visitors to also observe the mammals from below the surface. (Daily) Special video programs about dolphins and whales; educational arcade with computerized video screens and other participatory exhibits around the upper deck of the pavilion. A visitor service area is located in the atrium. Gift shop. Cafe. A life-size replica of a humpback whale spans two levels of the atrium. A Discovery Room houses a collection of marine artifacts. The Resource Center is designed as an aquatic learning center for school visitors; a library boasts an extensive collection of marine science material. One ticket for admission to both buildings. Pier 4.

Old Otterbein United Methodist Church (1785-1786). Fine Georgian architecture; mother church of United Brethren. Tours of historic building (Apr-Oct, Sat). Conway & Sharp Sts, Inner Harbor area. Phone 410/685-4703.

Old Town Mall. This 150-yr-old, brick-lined commercial area has been beautifully refurbished; closed to vehicular traffic. 400 & 500 blks of N Gay St. Nearby is

Stirling Street "Homesteading." First community urban "homesteading" venture in the US. Renovated homes date back to the 1830s. Original façades have been maintained; the interior rehabilitation ranges in style from the antique to the avant garde. 1000 blk of Monument St, 1 blk W of mall.

Otterbein "Homesteading." The original neighborhood dates back to 1785. Houses have been restored. Area around S Sharp St, Inner Harbor area.

Patterson Park. Defenses here helped stop British attack in 1814. Breastworks, artillery pieces are displayed. Baltimore St, Eastern & Patterson Park Aves.

Peabody Institute of the Johns Hopkins University (1857). (550 students) Founded by philanthropist George Peabody; now affiliated with Johns Hopkins. Research and reference collection in library accessible to the public (Mon-Fri; closed hols). The Miriam A. Friedberg Concert Hall seats 800. The Conservatory holds orchestra concerts, recitals and operas. In Mt Vernon Place area. Box office Phone 410/659-8124.

Pier 6 Concert Pavilion. Summertime outdoor concerts and plays at the water's edge. Some covered seating. (June-Sept, evenings) (See SEASONAL EVENTS) Pier 6, Inner Harbor area. Phone 410/625-3100 for schedule. ¢¢¢¢¢

Professional sports.

American League baseball (Baltimore Orioles). Camden Yards, 333 W Camden St. Phone 410/685-9800.

NFL (Baltimore Ravens). Football Stadium at Camden Yards, 1101 Russell St. Phone 410/654-6200.

Public Works Museum & Streetscape. Museum exhibits the history and artifacts of public works. Located in historic sewage pumping station. Streetscape sculpture outside depicts the various utility lines and ducts under a typical city street, in a walk-through model. (Daily exc Mon) 751 Eastern Ave, at Inner Harbor East. Phone 410/396-5565. ¢¢

Sherwood Gardens. More than 6 acres in size, the gardens reach their peak of splendor in late Apr & early May, when thousands of tulips, azaleas and flowering shrubs bloom. Stratford Rd & Greenway, located in the residential community of Guilford in northern Baltimore.

Star-Spangled Banner Flag House and 1812 Museum. The banner (30 by 42 ft) with 15 stars and 15 stripes that Key saw "by the dawn's early light" over Ft McHenry was hand-sewn here by Mary Young Pickersgill. The actual flag is in the Smithsonian. House (1793) is authentically restored and furnished in the Federal period. 1812 Museum contains relics, documents, weapons, memorabilia; audiovisual program; garden. Focal

point of the garden is a stone map of the US; every state is represented by a stone native to and cut in the shape of that state. (Daily exc Sun; closed some hols) 844 E Pratt St, at Albemarle St, downtown. Phone 410/837-1793. ¢¢

Theaters.

Cockpit in Court Summer Theatre. (See SEASONAL EVENTS)

Vagabond Players. Oldest continuously operating "little theater" in US. Recent Broadway shows, revivals and original scripts are performed. (Fri-Sun) 806 S Broadway. Box office phone 410/563-9135.

Top of the World. Observation deck and museum on the 27th floor of the World Trade Center, which was designed by I.M. Pei. Exhibits describe the city's history, famous residents and the activities of the port. (Daily) World Trade Center, Pratt St, Inner Harbor area. ¢

University of Maryland at Baltimore. (5,000 students) The 32-acre downtown campus includes 6 professional schools; the University of Maryland Medical System and the Graduate School. Davidge Hall (1812) is the oldest medical teaching building in continuous use in the Western Hemisphere. Lombard, Greene & Redwood Sts, downtown. Phone 410/706-7820.

Walters Art Gallery. City-owned fine arts collection of paintings, sculpture, arms, armor, jewelry and manuscripts from antiquity through the 19th century. (Daily exc Mon; closed major hols) 600 N Charles St, at Centre St, in Mt Vernon Place area. Phone 410/547-9000. ¢¢

Washington Monument (1815-1842). First major monument to honor George Washington. Museum in base; view city from top. Other monuments nearby honor Lafayette, Chief Justice Roger Brooke Taney, philanthropist George Peabody, lawyer Severn Teackle Wallis and Revolutionary War hero John Eager Howard. Charles & Monument Sts, in Mt Vernon Place area.

Annual Events

ACC Crafts Fair. Convention Center. Featuring more than 800 artisans. Late Feb.

Maryland House and Garden Pilgrimage. More than 100 homes and gardens throughout the state are open. To purchase tour book contact 1105-A Providence Rd, 21286; phone 410/821-6933. Late Apr-early May.

Maryland Preakness Celebration. Statewide festival; events include hot air balloon festival, parade, steeplechase, celebrity golf tournament, block parties and schooner race. Phone 410/837-3030. 10 days preceding Preakness Stakes (see SEASONAL EVENTS). Early to mid-May.

Harbor Expo. Middle Branch and Canton Waterfront. Boat parades; seafood festival; entertainment; events. Phone 888/225-8466. Mid-June.

Artscape. Salute to the arts & culture. Phone 410/396-4575. 3 days July.

New Year's Eve Extravaganza. Convention Center and Inner Harbor. Parties, entertainment, big bands, fireworks.

Seasonal Events

Pimlico Race Course. Hayward & Winner Aves, 2 mi W of Jones Falls Expy. Thoroughbred racing. **The Preakness**, the $500,000 middle jewel in Thoroughbred racing's Triple Crown, has been run here yearly since 1873 and is held the 3rd Sat in May. All seats reserved Preakness Day. Phone 410/542-9400. Late Mar-early June & early Aug-early Oct.

Cockpit in Court Summer Theatre. 7201 Rossville Blvd, use Beltway (I-695) exit 34, in Baltimore County. Theater in residence at Essex Community College. Four separate theaters offer a diverse collection of plays, including Broadway productions, contemporary drama, revues and Shakespeare. Box office phone 410/780-6369. Mid-June-mid-Aug.

Pier 6 Concert Pavilion. Evening concerts featuring big names in jazz, pop, classical and country music. For schedule phone 410/625-3100. Late June-Sept.

Showcase of Nations Ethnic Festivals. Presenting the food, music and crafts of a different culture each wkend. Various downtown locations. Phone 410/752-8632. June-Sept.

Additional Visitor Information

Maps, brochures and calendars of events are available at the Baltimore Area Visitors Center, 301 E Pratt St, Constellation Pier, 21202; phone 410/837-INFO or 800/282-6632.

Baltimore/Washington Intl Airport Area

For additional accommodations, see BALTIMORE/WASHINGTON INTL AIRPORT AREA, which follows BALTIMORE.

City Neighborhoods

Many of the restaurants, unrated dining establishments and some lodgings listed under Baltimore include neighborhoods as well as exact street addresses. Geographic descriptions of these areas are given.

Central Area. South of Mt Royal Ave, west of I-83, north of the Inner Harbor and Pratt St and east of Martin Luther King Jr Blvd and Greene St. **North of Central Area:** North of Chase. **East of Central Area:** East of I-83.

Fell's Point. Waterfront area east of Inner Harbor; south of Eastern Ave, west of Wolfe St and east of Caroline St.

Inner Harbor. Waterfront area south of Central Area at Pratt St, west of Jones Fall Pkwy and east of Light St.

Little Italy. East of Inner Harbor; south of Lombard St, west of Caroline St, north of Lancaster St and the waterfront and east of Jones Fall Pkwy.

Motels

✓★ **CHRISTLEN MOTEL.** 8733 Pulaski Hwy (21237), I-695 exit 35B, east of Central Area. 410/687-1740. 28 rms. S $32-$38; D $38-$42; each addl $5. Crib $5. TV; cable (premium). Restaurant adj open 24 hrs. Ck-out 11 am. Some refrigerators. Cr cds: A, C, D, DS, MC, V.

D ⊠ 🔥

★ **DAYS INN.** 5801 Baltimore Natl Pike (21228), on US 40, just E of I-695 exit 15A, west of Central Area. 410/744-5000; FAX 410/788-5197; res: 800/329-7466. 98 rms, 3 story. S, D $55-$75; under 12 free. Crib free. TV; cable (premium). Pool; lifeguard. Complimentary continental bkfst. Restaurant 7 am-1 pm, 5-10 pm. Ck-out noon. Coin lndry. Meeting rms. Business servs avail. Cr cds: A, C, D, DS, MC, V.

D ⊠ ✈ ⊠ 🔥 SC

★★ **HAMPTON INN.** 8225 Town Center Dr (21236), east of Central Area. 410/931-2200; FAX 410/931-2215. 127 rms, 4 story, 16 suites. S, D $89; suites $109; under 18 free. Crib $10. TV; cable (premium). Complimentary continental bkfst. Coffee in rms. Restaurant nearby. Ck-out noon. Meeting rms. Business center. In-rm modem link. Exercise equipt. Health club privileges. Heated pool; lifeguard. Wet bar in suites. Refrigerators, microwaves avail. Cr cds: A, C, D, DS, MC, V.

D ⊠ ✈ ⊠ 🔥 SC ♣

★★ **HOLIDAY INN.** 1800 Belmont Ave (21244), I-695 exit 17, north of Central Area. 410/265-1400; FAX 410/281-9569; res: 800/465-4329. 135 rms, 2 story. S, D $59-$83. Crib free. Pet accepted. TV; cable (premium). Pool; lifeguard. Restaurant 6 am-2 pm, 5-10 pm; Sat, Sun from 7 am. Rm serv. Bar 5 pm-midnight. Ck-out noon. Meeting rms. Business servs avail. In-rm modem link. Valet serv. Sundries. Health club privileges. Some refrigerators; microwaves avail. Cr cds: A, C, D, DS, ER, JCB, MC, V.

D 🐾 ⊠ ⊠ 🔥 SC

✓★ **SUSSE CHALET INN.** 4 Philadelphia Ct (21237), I-695 exit 34, north of Central Area. 410/574-8100; FAX 410/574-8204; res: 800/524-2538. 132 rms, 5 story. S $56.70; D $61.70; each addl $3. Crib free. TV; cable (premium). Pool; lifeguard. Complimentary continental bkfst. Restaurant nearby. Ck-out 11 am. Coin lndry. Business servs avail. Sundries. Microwaves avail. Cr cds: A, C, D, DS, MC, V.

D ⊠ ⊠ 🔥 SC

Motor Hotels

✓★ **BEST INN.** 5701 Baltimore National Pike (21228), ½ mi E of I-695 exit 15A, west of Central Area. 410/747-8900; FAX 410/744-3522; res: 800/237-8466. 145 rms, 7 story. S $40-$70; D $48-$75; each addl $8; under 18 free. Crib free. TV; cable (premium), VCR avail (movies). Pool; whirlpool, lifeguard. Ck-out 11 am. Coin lndry. Meeting rms. Business servs avail. Sundries. Some refrigerators. Balconies. Cr cds: A, C, D, DS, ER, JCB, MC, V.

D ⊠ ⊠ 🔥 SC

★★ **BEST WESTERN HOTEL & CONFRENCE CENTER.** 5625 Odonnell St (21224), I-95 exit 57, east of Central Area. 410/633-9500; FAX 410/633-4314; res: 800/633-9511. 175 rms, 12 story. S, D $89-$109; each addl $10; suites $129-$229. Crib avail. TV; cable (premium). Indoor pool; lifeguard. Coffee in rms. Restaurant 6:30 am-10 pm. Rm serv. Bar. Ck-out noon. Coin lndry. Meeting rms. Business servs avail. In-rm modem link. Gift shop. Bus depot transportation. Exercise equipt; sauna. Game rm. Microwaves avail. Cr cds: A, C, D, DS, MC, V.

D ⊠ ✈ ⊠ 🔥 SC

★ **DAYS INN INNER HARBOR HOTEL.** 100 Hopkins Pl (21201), in Central Area. 410/576-1000; FAX 410/576-9437; res: 800/432-9755. 250 rms, 9 story. S $90-$120; D $100-$130; each addl $10; suites $140-$180; under 12 free; higher rates special events. Crib free. Garage $8.50. TV; cable (premium). Pool; poolside serv, lifeguard. Restaurant 6:30 am-10 pm. Rm serv. Bar. Ck-out 11 am. Meeting rms. Business center. Bellhops. Concierge. Sundries. Health club privileges. Some refrigerators; microwaves avail. Cr cds: A, C, D, DS, MC, V.

D ⊠ ⊠ 🔥 SC ♣

★★★ **RADISSON HOTEL CROSS KEYS.** 5100 Falls Rd (21210), north of Central Area. 410/532-6900; FAX 410/532-2403; res: 800/532-5397. E-mail reservations@crosskeysinn.com; web www.crosskeysinn.com. 148 rms, 4 story. S, D $139-$189; each addl $15; suites $225-$425; under 17 free; wkend rates. Crib free. TV; cable (premium). Pool; poolside serv, lifeguard. Complimentary coffee in rms. Restaurant 6:30 am-11 pm. Rm serv. Bar 11 am-midnight. Ck-out noon. Meeting rms. Business servs avail. In-rm modem link. Exercise equipt. Shopping arcade. Barber, beauty shop. Tennis privileges. Health club privileges. Bathrm phones. Some private balconies. Cr cds: A, C, D, DS, MC, V.

D ⊱ ⊠ ✈ ⊠ 🔥 SC

Hotels

★★★ **BROOKSHIRE INNER HARBOR SUITE HOTEL.** 120 E Lombard St (21202), Inner Harbor. 410/625-1300; FAX 410/625-0912; res: 800/647-0013. 90 suites, 12 story. S $170-$305; D $190-$325; each addl $20; children free; wkend rates. Crib free. TV; cable. Coffee in rms. Restaurant 6:30-10 am, 5-9 pm. Bar 5-10 pm. Ck-out noon. Meeting rms. Concierge. Health club privileges. Bathrm phones, refrigerators, minibars; microwaves avail. Cr cds: A, C, D, DS, MC, V.

D ⊠ 🔥 SC

★★★ **CLARION HOTEL.** 612 Cathedral St (21201), at Mt Vernon Place, north of Central Area. 410/727-7101; FAX 410/789-3312; res: 800/292-5500. 103 rms, 14 story. S, D $114-$154; each addl $10; suites $189-$350; under 18 free; wkend rates; package plans. Crib free. Valet parking $12. TV; cable (premium), VCR avail (movies). Pool privileges. Restaurants 6:30 am-11 pm. Bar. Ck-out 11 am. Meeting rms. In-rm modem link. Concierge. Health club privileges. Some in-rm whirlpools. Restored hotel built in 1927. Marble floors, stairs in lobby. Period furnishings, artwork, crystal chandeliers. Cr cds: A, C, D, DS, ER, JCB, MC, V.

D ⊠ 🔥 SC

★★★ **DOUBLETREE INN AT THE COLLONADE.** 4 W University Pkwy (21218), Charles St N to University Pkwy, north of Central area. 410/235-5400; FAX 410/235-5572; res: 800/222-8733. Web www.double treehotel.com. 125 units, 3 story, 31 suites. S, D $129-$175; each addl

$15; suites $159-$475; family rates; wkend plans. Crib free. Pet accepted. TV; cable (premium). Indoor pool; whirlpool, poolside serv, lifeguard. Coffee in rms. Restaurant 6 am-11 pm (also see POLO GRILL). Rm serv to 10 pm. Ck-out noon. Meeting rm. Business center. In-rm modem link. Gift shop. Barber, beauty shop. Exercise equipt. Some wet bars; microwaves avail. Balconies. Biedermeier-inspired furnishings; extensive collection of 18th-century European masters. Adj to Johns Hopkins University. Cr cds: A, C, D, DS, ER, JCB, MC, V.

★★★ **HARBOR COURT HOTEL.** *550 Light St (21202), Inner Harbor.* 410/234-0550; FAX 410/659-5925; res: 800/824-0076. Web www.harbor.com. 203 rms, 8 story, 25 suites. S $205-$245; D $220-$260; suites $375-$2,000; under 18 free; wkend rates; some package plans. Crib free. Covered parking: self-park $15; valet $18. TV; cable (premium), VCR avail. Heated pool; whirlpool, poolside serv, lifeguard. Restaurant 7 am-11 pm (also see HAMPTON'S). Rm serv 24 hrs. Bar 11-2 am; entertainment exc Sun. Ck-out noon. Meeting rms. Business center. In-rm modem link. Concierge. Airport transportation. Tennis. Exercise rm; sauna. Massage. Racquetball. Lawn games. Bathrm phones, refrigerators. Elegant retreat located on Inner Harbor; panoramic view of city. Cr cds: A, C, D, DS, ER, JCB, MC, V.

★★★ **HILTON HOTEL & TOWERS.** *20 W Baltimore St (21201), in Central Area.* 410/539-8400; FAX 410/625-1060. 419 rms, 23 story. S $189; D $209; each addl $15; suites $275-$400; kit. units $600-$800; under 17 free; wkend rates. Crib free. Valet parking $15. TV; cable. Restaurants 6:30 am-10 pm. Bar 11-2 am. Ck-out noon. Meeting rms. In-rm modem link. Exercise equipt; sauna. Whirlpool. Health club privileges. Microwaves avail. Historic landmark; near harbor. Cr cds: A, C, D, DS, ER, MC, V.

★★ **HOLIDAY INN-INNER HARBOR.** *301 W Lombard St (21201), in Central Area.* 410/685-3500; FAX 410/727-6169; res: 800/465-4329. 375 rms; 10, 13 story. Apr-Sept: S $139; D $149; each addl $10; suites $275; under 19 free; lower rates rest of yr. Crib free. Pet accepted, some restrictions. Garage parking $6. TV; cable (premium). Indoor pool; lifeguard. Complimentary coffee in rms. Restaurant 6:30 am-11 pm. Bar 11-1 am. Ck-out noon. Convention facilities. Gift shop. Exercise equipt; sauna. Cr cds: A, C, D, DS, ER, JCB, MC, V.

★★★ **HYATT REGENCY.** *300 Light St (21202), Inner Harbor.* 410/528-1234; FAX 410/685-3362; res: 800/233-1234. Web www.travel web.com/hyatt.html. 486 rms, 14 story. S $195; D $220; each addl $25; suites $350-$1,200; under 18 free; wkend plan. Crib free. Valet parking $14. TV; cable (premium). Pool; whirlpool, lifeguard. Restaurant 6:30-1 am. Bar 11:30-2 am; entertainment Fri, Sat. Ck-out noon. Convention facilities. Business center. In-rm modem link. Concierge. Gift shop. Tennis. Exercise rm. Putting green. Basketball ½ court. Minibars; refrigerators avail. Luxury level. Cr cds: A, C, D, DS, ER, JCB, MC, V.

★★★ **MARRIOTT INNER HARBOR.** *110 S Eutaw St (21201), Inner Harbor.* 410/962-0202; FAX 410/625-7892; res: 800/228-9290. Web www.marriott.com. 525 units, 10 story. S, D $209; suites $195-$650; under 18 free; wkend rates. Crib free. Covered parking $8. TV; cable (premium), VCR avail. Indoor pool; whirlpool. Restaurant 6 am-10 pm. Bar noon-2 am; entertainment. Ck-out noon. Convention facilities. Business center. In-rm modem link. Concierge. Exercise equipt; sauna. Opp baseball stadium at Camden Yards. Luxury level. Cr cds: A, C, D, DS, ER, JCB, MC, V.

★★★ **OMNI INNER HARBOR HOTEL.** *101 W Fayette St (21201), Inner Harbor.* 410/752-1100; FAX 410/625-9646; res: 800/843-6664. 707 rms in 2 bldgs, 23, 27 story. S, D $149-$249; each addl $20; suites $200-$999; under 17 free; wkend rates. Crib free. Garage $9; valet parking $15. TV; cable (premium). Pool; poolside serv. Coffee in rms.

Restaurant 6:30 am-midnight. Bars noon-2 am. Ck-out noon. Convention facilities. Business center. In-rm modem link. Exercise equipt; some refrigerators; microwaves avail. Cr cds: A, C, D, DS, ER, MC, V.

★★★ **RENAISSANCE HARBORPLACE HOTEL.** *202 E Pratt St (21202), Inner Harbor.* 410/547-1200; FAX 410/539-5780; res: 800/468-3571. Web www.renaissancehotels.com. 622 rms, 12 story. S $215-$285; D $235-$305; each addl $20; suites $450-$3,000; under 18 free; wkend rates. Parking $10; valet $14. Crib free. TV; cable (premium), VCR avail. Indoor pool; whirlpool, poolside serv, lifeguard. Coffee in rms. Restaurant 6:30 am-11 pm. Rm serv 24 hrs. Bar 11-1:30 am; entertainment. Ck-out noon. Convention facilities. Business center. In-rm modem link. Concierge. Shopping arcade. Exercise equipt; sauna. Health club privileges. Minibars; bathrm phones. Luxury level. Cr cds: A, C, D, DS, ER, JCB, MC, V.

★★★ **SHERATON INNER HARBOR HOTEL.** *300 S Charles St (21201), Inner Harbor.* 410/962-8300; FAX 410/962-8211; res: 800/325-3535. E-mail resdept@erols.com; web www.ittsheraton.com. 337 rms, 15 story. Mar-June, Sept-Dec: S, D $170-$230; each addl $15; suites $425-$1,400; under 17 free; wkly, wkend rates; lower rates rest of yr. Crib free. Covered parking $12, valet parking $19. TV; cable (premium), VCR avail (movies). Indoor pool; lifeguard. Restaurant 6:30 am-11 pm. Bar 11:30-2 am. Ck-out noon. Convention facilities. Business center. In-rm modem link. Concierge. Gift shop. Exercise equipt; sauna. Health club privileges. Minibars; some bathrm phones, refrigerators. Cr cds: A, C, D, DS, ER, JCB, MC, V.

✓★★ **TREMONT HOTEL.** *8 E Pleasant St (21202), in Central Area.* 410/576-1200; FAX 410/244-1154; res: 800/873-6668. 58 kit. suites, 13 story. S $109-$135; D $129-$155; each addl $20; under 16 free; wkend rates. Crib free. Pet accepted; $5. Valet parking $12. Pool privileges. TV; cable, VCR avail. Complimentary continental bkfst. Restaurant 5-9 pm. Bar to 10 pm. Ck-out noon. Meeting rms. Business servs avail. Health club privileges. Microwaves. Cr cds: A, C, D, DS, MC, V.

Inns

✓★★★ **ABERCROMBIE BADGER BED & BREAKFAST.** *58 W Biddle St (21201), west of Central Area.* 410/244-7227; FAX 410/244-8415. 12 rms, 4 story. S $79; D $105-$145. TV; cable. Complimentary continental bkfst. Restaurant 11 am-10 pm; Fri, Sat to midnight; closed Mon. Bar to midnight; Fri, Sat to 2 am. Ck-out 11 am, ck-in 4 pm. Business servs avail. Turn-of-the-century building; many antique furnishings. Cr cds: A, C, D, DS, MC, V.

★★★ **ADMIRAL FELL INN.** *888 S Broadway, Historic Fell's Pt (21231), in Fell's Point.* 410/522-7377; FAX 410/522-0707; res: 800/292-4667. E-mail mobil@admiralfell.com; web www.admiralfell.com. 80 rms, 5 story. S $115-$145; D $135-$195; each addl $20; suites $220-$395; under 16 free; wkly rates. Pet accepted, some restrictions. TV; cable (premium). Complimentary continental bkfst. Dining rm noon-10 pm. Bar to 2 am. Ck-out 11 am, ck-in 4 pm. Meeting rms. Health club privileges. Some in-rm whirlpools. Cr cds: A, C, MC, V.

★★★ **CELIE'S WATERFRONT BED & BREAKFAST.** *1714 Thames St (21231), in Fell's Point.* 410/522-2323; FAX 410/522-2324; res: 800/432-0184. E-mail celies@aol.com; web www.bbonline.com/md/celies. 7 rms, 1 with shower only, 3 story. S $100-$175; D $115-$200; hol, wkend rates. Children over 9 yrs only. TV; cable, VCR. Complimentary continental bkfst. Complimentary coffee in rms. Restaurant nearby. Ck-out 11 am, ck-in 3-6 pm. Business servs avail. In-rm modem link. Health club privileges. Refrigerators; some in-rm whirlpools, fireplaces. On harbor; many antiques. Roof deck. Totally nonsmoking. Cr cds: A, C, DS, MC, V.

★ ★ ★ **HOPKINS INN.** 3404 Saint Paul St (21218), north of Central Area. 410/235-8600; FAX 410/235-7051. 25 rms, 4 story. S, D $100-$140; wkly, monthly rates. Covered parking $6. TV. Complimentary continental bkfst. Restaurant nearby. Ck-out 11 am, ck-in 3 pm. Meeting rms. Business servs avail. 1920's Spanish-revival building. Rms individually furnished in variety of styles. Totally nonsmoking. Cr cds: A, C, D, DS, MC, V.

★ ★ ★ **INN AT GOVERNMENT HOUSE.** 1125 N Calvert St (21202), north of Central Area. 410/539-0566; FAX 410/539-0567. 18 rms, 4 story. S, D $125-$150; wkly rates; Preakness (2-day min). TV. Complimentary continental bkfst; afternoon refreshments. Restaurant nearby. Ck-out noon, ck-in 3-8 pm. Business servs avail. Part of complex of several Federal and Victorian mansions and town houses (1888). Totally nonsmoking. Cr cds: A, C, D, DS, MC, V.

★ ★ **INN AT HENDERSON'S WHARF.** 1000 Fell St (21231), in Fell's Point. 410/522-7777; FAX 410/522-7087; res: 800/522-2088. E-mail sales@hendersonswharf.com; web www.hendersonswharf.com. 38 rms. Apr-Nov: S, D $120-$160; kit. suites $400; under 18 free; higher rates special events; lower rates rest of yr. TV; cable (premium). Complimentary continental bkfst. Restaurant nearby. Ck-out noon, ck-in 3 pm. Coin lndry. Meeting rms. Business servs avail. In-rm modem link. Valet serv. Exercise equipt. Some refrigerators. On waterfront; dockage avail. 19th-century tobacco warehouse. Cr cds: A, C, D, MC, V.

★ ★ ★ **MR MOLE BED & BREAKFAST.** 1601 Bolton St (21217), north of Central Area. 410/728-1179; FAX 410/728-3379. 5 rms, 5 story, 2 suites. S, D $105-$135; suites $135-$165; 2-day min wkends. Children over 12 yrs only. Complimentary bkfst. Restaurant nearby. Ck-out 11 am, ck-in 4-6 pm. Business servs avail. In-rm modem link. Totally nonsmoking. Cr cds: A, C, D, DS, MC, V.

Restaurants

★ ★ **ANGELINA'S.** 7135 Harford Rd (21234), north of Central Area. 410/444-5545. E-mail angelinacc@aol.com; web www.crabcake.com. Hrs: 11:30 am-10 pm; Fri, Sat to 11:30 pm. Closed Mon; Thanksgiving, Dec 25. Italian, seafood menu. Bar. Semi-a la carte: lunch $5-$16.95, dinner $9-$29. Child's meals. Specializes in crab cakes, seafood. Entertainment Fri. Cr cds: A, C, DS, MC, V.

★ **BERTHA'S.** 734 S Broadway (21231), in Fell's Point. 410/327-0426. E-mail berthas@ix.netcom.com. Hrs: 11:30 am-11 pm; Fri, Sat to midnight; Sun brunch to 2 pm. Closed major hols. Res required for Scottish afternoon tea (Mon-Sat). Bar. Semi-a la carte: lunch, dinner $4.95-$19.25. Sun brunch $7.95-$8.50. Specializes in mussels, seafood. Eclectic decor. Historic 19th-century building. Cr cds: C, MC, V.

★ ★ ★ **BOCCACCIO.** 925 Eastern Ave (21231), Little Italy. 410/234-1322. Hrs: 11:30 am-2:30 pm, 5-11 pm; Sat from 5 pm; Sun 3-10 pm. Closed Thanksgiving, Dec 25. Res required eves. Italian menu. Bar. Semi-a la carte: lunch $9.75-$15.75, dinner $13.50-$28.50. Specializes in veal, seafood, pasta. Formal decor. Cr cds: A, C, D, MC, V.

★ **CAFE HON.** 1002 W 36th St (21211), north of Central Area. 410/243-1230. Web www.cafehon.com. Hrs: 7 am-10 pm; Sat from 9 am; Sun 3-9 pm; Sun brunch 9 am-3 pm. Closed most major hols. Bar. Semi-a la carte: bkfst $1.25-$5.95, lunch, dinner $4.25-$14.95. Sun brunch $1.50-$6.50. Child's meals. Specialties: crab cakes, meatloaf. Eclectic cafe reminiscent of 1930s Baltimore soda fountain. Totally nonsmoking. Cr cds: A, C, MC, V.

★ ★ **CHIAPPARELLI'S.** 237 S High St (21202), Little Italy. 410/837-0309. E-mail jagger@erols.com. Hrs: 11 am-10 pm; Fri, Sat to midnight. Closed Thanksgiving, Dec 25. Res accepted. Italian menu. A la carte: lunch $7-$14, dinner $10-$25. Child's meals. Specialty: Piatto Napolitano. Valet parking after 5 pm. Built 1870; original brick walls, oak paneling. 7 dining rms on 2 levels. Family-owned. Cr cds: A, C, D, DS, MC, V.

★ ★ **CITY LIGHTS.** 301 Light St (21202), Light St Pavilion, Inner Harbor. 410/244-8811. Hrs: 11:30 am-10 pm; Fri to 11 pm; Sat to midnight; Sun to 9 pm. Closed Thanksgiving, Dec 24, 25. Res accepted. Bar. A la carte entrees: lunch, dinner $5-$18. Child's meals. Specializes in Chesapeake Bay seafood. Own desserts. Outdoor dining. Cr cds: A, C, D, DS, JCB, MC, V.

★ ★ ★ **DALESIO'S.** 829 Eastern Ave (21202), Little Italy. 410/539-1965. Hrs: 11:30 am-3 pm, 5-10 pm; Sun 4-9 pm. Closed Thanksgiving. Res accepted. Northern Italian menu. Bar. A la carte entrees: lunch $5.95-$9.95, dinner $10.95-$21.95. Specializes in Northern Italian spa cuisine. Own cakes, pasta. Outdoor dining. Cr cds: A, C, MC, V.

★ ★ **GERMANO'S TRATTORIA.** 300 S High St (21202), Little Italy. 410/752-4515. Hrs: 11:30 am-11 pm; Fri, Sat to midnight. Closed Thanksgiving, Dec 25. Res accepted. Italian menu. Bar. Semi-a la carte: lunch $5.95-$9.95, dinner $7.50-$22. Child's meals. Specializes in Tuscan cuisine and seafood. Cr cds: A, C, D, DS, MC, V.

★ ★ ★ **HAMPTON'S.** (See Harbor Court Hotel) 410/234-0550. This hotel dining room's setting is similar to an 18th-century mansion. Specializes in seafood, regional dishes. Own pastries. Hrs: 5:30-11 pm; Sun to 10 pm; Sun brunch 10:30 am-3 pm. Closed Mon. Res required. Serv bar. Extensive wine list. A la carte entrees: dinner $23-$36. Vegetarian prix fixe dinner: $36-$49. Sun brunch $19.95-$27.95. Valet parking. Jacket. Totally nonsmoking. Cr cds: A, C, D, DS, ER, JCB, MC, V.

★ ★ ★ **HAUSSNER'S.** 3244 Eastern Ave (21224), east of Central Area. 410/327-8365. Hrs: 11 am-10 pm. Closed Sun, Mon; Dec 25. German, Amer menu. Bar. Semi-a la carte: lunch, dinner $8-$24.50. Specializes in seafood. Own baking. Braille menu. Extensive dining room display of original 19th-century artwork. Old-world atmosphere. Family-owned. Cr cds: A, C, D, DS, MC, V.

★ **HENNINGER'S TAVERN.** 1812 Bank St (21231), in Fell's Point. 410/342-2172. Hrs: 5-10 pm; Fri, Sat to 11 pm. Closed Sun, Mon; Jan 1, Dec 25. Bar to 1 am. A la carte entrees: dinner $12.75-$18.95. Specializes in seafood. Late 1800s atmosphere. Cr cds: A, C, D, JCB, MC, V.

✓ ★ ★ **IKAROS.** 4805 Eastern Ave (21224), east of Central Area. 410/633-3750. Hrs: 11 am-10 pm; Fri, Sat to 11 pm. Closed Tues; Thanksgiving, Dec 25. Greek, Amer menu. Serv bar. Semi-a la carte: lunch $4-$9, dinner $8-$15. Specializes in lamb, squid, fresh whole fish. Cr cds: A, C, D, DS, MC, V.

★★ **JEANNIER'S.** *105 W 39th St (21211), north of Central Area.* 410/889-3303. E-mail tr_ jeannier@juno.com. Hrs: noon-2:30 pm, 5:30-9:30 pm; Fri to 10 pm; Sat 5:30-10 pm; early-bird dinner 5:30-7 pm. Closed Sun; most major hols. French, continental menu. Bar noon-11 pm. A la carte entrees: lunch $6-$11, dinner $13.95-$25. Complete meals: dinner $14-$25. Specializes in seafood, country-French cuisine. Own desserts. Country chateau decor. Cr cds: A, C, D, MC, V.

D

★★ **JOHN STEVEN LTD.** *1800 Thames St (21231), in Fell's Point.* 410/327-5561. Hrs: 11 am-11 pm; Fri, Sat to midnight. Res accepted. Bar to 2 am. A la carte entrees: lunch $6-$11, dinner $7-$21. Specializes in seafood, sushi. Outdoor dining. Located in building built 1838. Cr cds: A, C, D, DS, MC, V.

D

★★★ **JOY AMERICA CAFE.** *800 Key Hwy (21230), in American Visionary Art Museum, Inner Harbor.* 410/244-6500. Web www.joyamerica.com. Hrs: 11:30 am-2:30 pm, 5:30-10 pm; Sun brunch 11 am-4 pm. Closed Mon; Labor Day, Thanksgiving, Dec 25. Res accepted. Contemporary Amer menu. Bar. Semi-a la carte: lunch $9-$15, dinner $19-$28.50. Sun brunch $11.50-$14. Child's meals. Specialties: chicken and dried cherry dim sum, Thai-grilled rack of lamb. Outdoor dining. View of city and Inner Harbor. Totally nonsmoking. Cr cds: A, C, D, MC, V.

D

★★ **KARSON'S INN.** *5100 Holabird Ave (21224), east of Central Area.* 410/631-5400. Hrs: 11 am-9:15 pm; Sat from 4 pm; Sun 11 am-8:15 pm. Closed Mon; Thanksgiving, Dec 25. Res accepted; required hols. Bar. Semi-a la carte: lunch $6.95-$11.50, dinner $10.95-$32. Child's meals. Specializes in steak, seafood. Parking. Family-owned. Cr cds: A, C, DS, MC, V.

D ☒

★★ **KAWASAKI.** *413 N Charles St (21201), in Central Area.* 410/659-7600. Hrs: 11:30-2:30 pm, 5-11 pm; Fri to midnight; Sat 5-midnight. Closed Sun; most major hols. Japanese menu. Bar. A la carte entrees: lunch, dinner $2.50-$9. Semi-a la carte: lunch $5.95-$9.50, dinner $9.50-$18. Specializes in Japanese seafood, sushi rolls. In townhouse; Japanese decor. Cr cds: A, C, D, JCB, MC, V.

★★ **LA SCALA RESTAURANT.** *411 S High St (21202), in Little Italy.* 410/783-9209. Hrs: 4:30-10 pm; Fri, Sat to 11 pm; Sun 2-10 pm. Closed Jan 1, Thanksgiving, Dec 25. Res accepted. Italian menu. Bar. Semi-a la carte: dinner $9.95-$29.95. Specializes in veal, pasta, seafood. Contemporary decor. Cr cds: A, C, D, DS, MC, V.

☒

★★ **MORGAN MILLARD.** *4800 Roland Ave (21210), north of Central Area.* 410/889-0030. Hrs: 11:30 am-9:30 pm; Fri, Sat to 10:30 pm; Sun 11 am-8:30 pm; Sun brunch to 3 pm. Closed most major hols. Res accepted (dinner). Regional Amer menu. Bar. Semi-a la carte: lunch $5.95-$11.50, dinner $5.95-$22. Sun brunch $6.95-$12.95. Child's meals. Specialties: pan-fried catfish, barbecued duck breast. Own baking. In historic Roland Park area; local artwork and music featured. Totally nonsmoking. Cr cds: A, C, MC, V.

D

★★ **MT WASHINGTON TAVERN.** *5700 Newbury St (21209), I-83 N, exit Northern Pkwy E, W at Falls Rd, W onto Kelly Ave Bridge, E on Sungrave, 1 blk to Newbury, north of Central Area.* 410/367-6903. Hrs: 11:30 am-10 pm; Sat to 11 pm; Sun brunch to 3 pm. Closed Dec 25. Res accepted. Bar. Semi-a la carte: lunch $5.95-$12.95, dinner $12.95-$22.95. Sun brunch $5.95-$12.95. Child's meals. Specializes in Angus beef, veal chops, shrimp. Entertainment Wed, Sat. Outdoor dining. Tavern atmosphere has varied dining areas. Cr cds: A, C, D, MC, V.

D ♥

★★ **OBRYCKI'S CRAB HOUSE.** *1727 E Pratt St (21231), in Fell's Point.* 410/732-6399. Web www.obryckis.com. Hrs: noon-11 pm; Sun to 9:30 pm. Closed mid-Dec-Mar. Bar. Semi-a la carte: lunch $5.50-$17.95, dinner $13.25-$27.95. Child's meals. Specializes in crab. Parking. Family-owned. Cr cds: A, C, D, DS, MC, V.

D ☒

★★ **PIERPOINT.** *1822 Aliceanna St (21231), in Fell's Point.* 410/675-2080. Hrs: 11:30 am-2:30 pm, 5:30-9:30 pm; Fri to 10:30 pm; Sat 5:30-11 pm; Sun 4-9:30 pm. Closed Mon; Jan 1, July 4, Dec 25. Res accepted. Bar. A la carte entrees: lunch $5.95-$8.95, dinner $5.95-$24. Specializes in Maryland cuisine. Contemporary decor. Cr cds: A, C, MC, V.

D

★★★ **POLO GRILL.** *(See Doubletree Inn at the Colonnade)* 410/235-8200. Hrs: 6:30-10 am, 11:30 am-4 pm, 5:30-11 pm; Fri to midnight; Sat 7-10:30 am, 11:30 am-4 pm, 5:30 pm-midnight; Sun 7-10:30 am, 11 am-2:30 pm, 5:30-10 pm. Res accepted. A la carte entrees: lunch $5.95-$19.50, dinner $10.95-$36.95. Complete meals: bkfst $7.50-$7.95. Specializes in seafood, pasta. Valet parking. English hunt decor. Cr cds: A, C, D, DS, ER, JCB, MC, V.

D

★★★ **PRIME RIB.** *1101 N Calvert St (21202), in Central Area.* 410/539-1804. Hrs: 5 pm-midnight; Sun 4-11 pm. Closed Thanksgiving. Res accepted. Bar. Wine list. A la carte entrees: dinner $20-$25. Specializes in steak, seafood, lamb. Pianist. Parking. Black laquered walls. Paintings and prints displayed. Jacket. Family-owned. Cr cds: A, C, D, MC, V.

D ☒

★★ **ROCCO CAPRICCIO.** *846 Fawn St (21202), Little Italy.* 410/685-2710. Hrs: 11:30 am-10:30 pm; Fri, Sat to 11:30 pm. Closed Thanksgiving, Dec 25. Res accepted. Northern Italian menu. Bar. Semi-a la carte: lunch $6.25-$12, dinner $9.95-$28. Child's meals. Specialties: fettucine frutta de mare (white or red), veal Capriccio. Own pasta. Cr cds: A, C, D, DS, MC, V.

★★★ **RUBY LOUNGE.** *802 N Charles St (21201), in Central Area.* 410/539-8051. Hrs: 5:30-11 pm; Fri, Sat to midnight. Closed Sun, Mon; also most major hols. Res accepted. Bar. A la carte entrees: dinner $9.95-$15.95. Specializes in duck, pork, seafood. Valet parking. Casual decor. Cr cds: A, C, MC.

★★★ **RUTH'S CHRIS STEAK HOUSE.** *600 Water St (21202), in Central Area.* 410/783-0033. E-mail serioussteaks.com. Hrs: 5-10 pm; Fri, Sat to 11 pm. Closed Thanksgiving, Dec 25. Res accepted. Bar. A la carte entrees: dinner $15.95-$28.95. Specializes in steaks, seafood. Free valet parking. Upscale furnishing. Cr cds: A, C, D, DS, ER, JCB, MC, V.

D ☒

★★★ **SPIKE & CHARLIE'S.** *1225 Cathedral St (21201), north of Central Area.* 410/752-8144. Hrs: 5:30-10 pm; Fri, Sat to midnight. Closed Mon; most major hols. Res accepted. Bar. Semi-a la carte: dinner $8-$26. Specializes in seafood. Own baking. Contemporary decor. Cr cds: A, C, D, DS, MC, V.

D ☒

★★★ **TIO PEPE.** *10 E Franklin St (21202), in Central Area.* 410/539-4675. Hrs: 11:30 am-2:30 pm, 5-10:30 pm; Fri to 11:30 pm; Sat 5-11:30 pm; Sun 4-10:30 pm. Closed most major hols. Res required. Spanish, continental menu. Bar. Wine cellar. Semi-a la carte: lunch $9-$14, dinner $13.75-$24. Specialties: shrimp in garlic sauce, suckling pig. Spanish casa atmosphere. Jacket. Cr cds: A, C, D, DS, MC, V.

D

★★ **VELLEGGIA'S.** *829 E Pratt St (21202), Little Italy. 410/685-2620.* Hrs: 11 am-11 pm; Fri to midnight; Sat to 1 am. Closed Dec 24, 25. Res accepted. Italian menu. Bar. A la carte entrees: lunch $4.95-$9.95, dinner $9.25-$19.95. Child's meals. Specializes in veal, seafood. Own pasta. Family-owned. Cr cds: A, C, D, MC, V.

[D] [≜]

✓★ **WATER STREET EXCHANGE.** *110 Water St, in Central Area. 410/332-4060.* Hrs: 11:30 am-8 pm; Mon to 3 pm; Tues to 6 pm; Sat from 5:30. Closed Sun; major hols. Res accepted. Bar to 2 am. Semi-a la carte: lunch $5.95-$13, dinner $13-$26. Specializes in pasta, seafood. Outdoor dining. Victorian decor. Cr cds: A, C, D, DS, MC, V.

[≜]

★ **WATERFRONT HOTEL.** *1710 Thames St (21231), in Fell's Point. 410/327-4886.* Hrs: 11 am-10 pm; Fri, Sat to 11 pm. Closed Dec 25. Res accepted. Continental menu. Bar 10-2 am. Semi-a la carte: lunch $4.50-$9.95, dinner $11.95-$20. Child's meals. Specializes in seafood, beef. Restored building (1771) located on waterfront; 3-story brick fireplace, stained-glass windows. Cr cds: A, C, D, MC, V.

[≜]

✓★ **WAYNE'S BAR-B-QUE.** *201 Pratt St (21202), Inner Harbor. 410/539-3810.* Hrs: 8 am-11 pm; Fri, Sat to midnight. Closed Thanksgiving. Res accepted. Bar to 2 am. A la carte entrees: bkfst $4.50-$7.95, lunch, dinner $5-$12.95. Child's meals. Specializes in barbecue dishes, desserts. Outdoor dining. View of harbor. Cr cds: A, C, DS, MC, V.

[D] [SC] [≜]

★★ **WILD MUSHROOM.** *641 S Montford Ave (21224), in Central Area. 410/675-4225.* Hrs: 11:30-1 am. Closed Sun; Jan 1, Thanksgiving, Dec 25. Bar. A la carte entrees: lunch $4.95-$12.95, dinner $6.95-$25. Specializes in mushroom-driven dishes. Contemporary decor. Cr cds: A, C, D, DS, JCB, MC, V.

Unrated Dining Spot

LOUIE'S THE BOOKSTORE CAFE. *518 N Charles St, in Central Area. 410/962-1224.* Hrs: 11:30-12:30 am; Mon to midnight; Fri, Sat to 2 am; Sun 10:30 am-midnight; Sun brunch to 3 pm. Closed major hols. Bar. A la carte: lunch $3.50-$10.95, dinner $3.95-$16.95. Sun brunch $3.25-$9.95. Specializes in international bistro fare. Outdoor dining. Chamber music. Original artwork. Cr cds: A, C, MC, V.

[D] [≜]

Baltimore/Washington Intl Airport Area (C-7)

(See also Baltimore; also see District of Columbia)

Services and Information

Information: 410/859-7100.

Lost and Found: 410/859-7387.

Weather: 410/936-1212.

Cash Machines: Main Terminal, Pier C.

Airlines: Air Aruba, Air Canada, Air Jamaica, America West, American, British Airways, Continental, Delta, El Al, Icelandair, Midway, Northwest, Southwest, TWA, United, USAir.

Motels

★★ **COURTYARD BY MARRIOTT.** *1671 W Nursery Rd (21090), approx 1 mi N on Nursery Rd. 410/859-8855; FAX 410/859-5068; res: 800/321-2211.* Web www.courtyard.com. 149 rms, 3 story. Apr-Nov: S, D $104-$114; suites $123-$134; under 10 free; lower rates rest of yr. TV; cable (premium). Indoor pool; whirlpool, lifeguard. Complimentary coffee in rms. Restaurant 6:30-10:30 am, 5-10 pm; Sat, Sun 7 am-noon. Bar 4-10 pm. Ck-out noon. Meeting rms. Business servs avail. Coin lndry. Free airport transportation. Exercise equipt. Some refrigerators. Cr cds: A, C, D, DS, MC, V.

[D] [≈] [🚶] [✈] [⊠] [🔥] [SC]

✓★ **DAYS INN.** *6600 Ritchie Hwy (21061), I-195 to I-695, E to MD 2 (Ritchie Hwy). 410/761-8300; FAX 410/760-4966; res: 800/329-7466.* 100 rms, 3 story. S, D $75; each addl $10; under 18 free. Crib free. Pet accepted, some restrictions. TV; cable (premium). Pool; lifeguard. Restaurant 6 am-2 pm, 5-10 pm; Sat, Sun from 7 am. Rm serv. Bar 4 pm-midnight. Ck-out noon. Meeting rms. In-rm modem link. Valet serv. Health club privileges. Microwaves avail. Mall opp. Cr cds: A, C, D, DS, ER, JCB, MC, V.

[D] [🐾] [≈] [⊠] [🔥] [SC]

★★ **HAMPTON INN.** *6617 Governor Ritchie Hwy (21061), I-695, exit 3B, in Governor Plaza Shopping Ctr. 410/761-7666; FAX 410/761-0253; res: 800/426-7866.* 116 rms, 5 story. S $92; D $99; suites $110; under 18 free; higher rates special events. Crib free. TV; cable (premium). Complimentary continental bkfst. Restaurant adj open 24 hrs. Ck-out noon. Meeting rms. Business servs avail. In-rm modem links. Valet serv. Sundries. Health club privileges. Microwaves avail. Cr cds: A, C, D, DS, MC, V.

[D] [⊠] [🔥] [SC]

Motor Hotels

✓★★ **BEST WESTERN BALTIMORE WASHINGTON AIR-PORT.** *6755 Dorsey Rd (21075), I-295 S to MD 176. 410/796-3300; FAX 410/379-0471; res: 800/528-1234.* 134 rms, 4 story. S $69; D $74; each addl $5; under 18 free. Crib free. TV; cable (premium), VCR avail. Indoor pool; whirlpool. Complimentary coffee in lobby. Restaurant adj 7 am-11 pm; Sat, Sun 8 am-10 pm. Ck-out noon. Meeting rms. In-rm modem link. Valet serv. Airport transportation. Exercise equipt; sauna. Cr cds: A, C, D, DS, ER, MC, V.

[D] [≈] [🚶] [✈] [⊠] [🔥] [SC]

★★ **COMFORT INN AIRPORT.** *6921 Baltimore Annapolis Blvd (21225), N on MD 170 to Baltimore Annapolis Blvd. 410/789-9100; FAX 410/355-2854.* 188 rms, 6 story. S $79; D $89; each addl $8; suites $125-$225; studio rms $79-$89; under 12 free; wkend rates. Crib free. Pet accepted. TV; cable (premium), VCR avail. Complimentary bkfst buffet. Restaurant 7 am-11 pm. Bar 11 am-midnight. Ck-out 11 am. Meeting rms. Business servs avail. In-rm modem link. Bellhops. Valet serv. Airport transportation. Exercise equipt; sauna. Whirlpool. Game rm. Microwaves avail. Cr cds: A, C, D, DS, ER, JCB, MC, V.

[D] [🐾] [🚶] [✈] [⊠] [🔥] [SC]

✓★ **HAMPTON INN.** *829 Elkridge Landing Rd (21090), From I-95 or I-295 take I-195E to exit 1A (MD 170N). 410/850-0600; FAX 410/691-2119; res: 800/426-7866.* 139 rms, 5 story. S $79; D $85; under 18 free. Crib free. Pet accepted. TV; cable (premium). Complimentary continental bkfst. Restaurant nearby. Ck-out noon. Meeting rms. In-rm modem link. Valet serv. Free airport transportation. Microwaves avail. Cr cds: A, C, D, DS, ER, JCB, MC, V.

[D] [🐾] [✈] [⊠] [🔥] [SC]

★★★ **SHERATON INTERNATIONAL HOTEL BMW.** *7032 Elm Rd (21240), N of terminal. 410/859-3300; FAX 410/859-0565; res: 800/325-3535.* Web www.sheraton.com. 196 rms, 2 story. S $129-$139; D $129-$149; each addl $10; suites $145-$175; under 16 free; wkend rates. Crib free. TV; cable (premium). Pool; poolside serv, lifeguard. Complimentary continental bkfst. Coffee in rms. Restaurant 6:30 am-10:30 pm. Rm serv 24 hrs. Bar 11-2 am; entertainment. Ck-out noon. Meeting rms. Business servs avail. In-rm modem link. Bellhops. Sundries. Gift shop. Airport transportation. Exercise equipt. Cr cds: A, C, D, DS, MC, V.

⬛ ⬛ ⬛ ⬛ ⬛ ⬛ SC

★ **SUSSE CHALET INN.** *1734 W Nursery Rd (21090). 410/859-2333; FAX 410/859-2357; res: 800/258-1980.* 130 rms, 5 story. S, D $68.70-$75.70; each addl $7; suites $89.70-$99.70; under 18 free. Crib free. TV; cable (premium). Pool; lifeguard. Complimentary continental bkfst. Restaurant nearby. Ck-out 11 am. Coin lndry. Business servs avail. In-rm modem link. Airport, RR station transportation. Exercise equipt. Microwaves avail. Cr cds: A, C, D, DS, MC, V.

⬛ ⬛ ⬛ ⬛ ⬛ ⬛ SC

Hotels

★★★ **DOUBLETREE GUEST SUITES HOTEL.** *1300 Concourse Dr (21090), N on MD 170 to Elkridge Landing Rd, NW 1½ mi to Winterson Rd, W to Concourse Dr; or I-295 to W Nursery Rd exit, then to Winterson Rd. 410/850-0747; FAX 410/859-0816; res: 800/528-0444.* Web www.doubletreehotels.com. 251 suites, 8 story. S $99-$160; D $109-$170; each addl $10; under 18 free; wkend rates. Crib free. TV; cable (premium). Indoor pool; whirlpool, lifeguard. Complimentary coffee in rms. Restaurant 6:30 am-10 pm; wkends to 11 pm. Bar 11-1 am. Ck-out noon. Convention facilities. Business servs avail. In-rm modem link. Gift shop. Airport transportation. Exercise equipt; sauna. Health club privileges. Bathrm phones, refrigerators, wet bars; microwaves avail. Cr cds: A, C, D, DS, MC, V.

⬛ ⬛ ⬛ ⬛ ⬛ ⬛ SC

★★★ **MARRIOTT BALTIMORE-WASHINGTON INTERNATIONAL AIRPORT.** *1743 W Nursery Rd (21240), approx 1 mi N on Nursery Rd. 410/859-8300; FAX 410/691-4555; res: 800/228-9290.* 310 rms, 10 story. S, D $99-$179; each addl $15; suites $143-$350; under 18 free. Crib free. TV; cable (premium). Indoor pool; whirlpool. Complimentary coffee in lobby. Restaurant 6:30 am-10 pm. Bar 4 pm-1:30 am. Ck-out noon. Convention facilities. Business servs avail. Free airport transportation. Exercise equipt. Health club privileges. Cr cds: A, C, D, DS, ER, JCB, MC, V.

⬛ ⬛ ⬛ ⬛ ⬛ ⬛ SC

Bethesda (C-6)

(See also District of Columbia)

Pop 62,936 **Elev** 305 ft **Area Code** 240 & 301 **Web** www.bccchamber.org
Information The Greater Bethesda-Chevy Chase Chamber of Commerce, Landow Bldg, 7910 Woodmont Ave, Suite 1204, 20814; 301/652-4900

A suburb of Washington, DC, Bethesda is the home of both the National Institutes of Health, research arm of the Public Health Service, and Bethesda Naval Hospital.

What to See and Do

Cabin John Regional Park. This 551-acre park has playgrounds, miniature train ride; nature center; concerts (summer evenings; free); tennis courts, game fields, ice rink, nature trails, picnicking. Fee for some activities. (Daily) Approx 3 mi N on MD 355 then W on Tuckerman Lane. Phone 301/299-0024.

Clara Barton National Historic Site. 3 mi W via MD 191, Goldsboro Rd in Glen Echo (see DISTRICT OF COLUMBIA).

National Library of Medicine. World's largest biomedical library; rare books, manuscripts, prints; medical art displays. (Daily exc Sun; closed hols & Sat before Mon hols) Visitors center & guided tour (Mon-Fri, 1 departure each day). 8600 Rockville Pike. Phone 301/496-6308. **Free**

Motor Hotel

★★ **AMERICAN INN OF BETHESDA.** *8130 Wisconsin Ave (20814). 301/656-9300; FAX 301/656-2907.* E-mail innkeeper@american-inn.com; web www.american-inn.com. 76 rms, 5 story. S $126; D $136; each addl $5; under 18 free. Crib free. TV; cable (premium), VCR avail. Pool; lifeguard. Complimentary continental bkfst. Restaurant 11:30 am-10 pm; Fri, Sat to midnight; Sun to 10 pm. Ck-out 12:30 pm. Coin lndry. Meeting rms. Business center. Sundries. Valet serv. Health club privileges. Some refrigerators. Cr cds: A, C, D, DS, MC, V.

⬛ ⬛ ⬛ ⬛ SC ⬛

Hotels

✓★★ **HOLIDAY INN.** *5520 Wisconsin Ave (20815), S on Wisconsin Ave. 301/656-1500; FAX 301/656-5045; res: 800/465-4329.* E-mail cornel@pop.net; web www.holidayinn.com. 215 rms, 12 story. S, D $89-$159; each addl $10; suites $169; under 18 free. Crib free. Pet accepted, some restrictions; $50. TV; cable (premium), VCR avail. Pool. Complimentary coffee in rms. Restaurant 6:30 am-11 pm. Bar. Ck-out noon. Free lndry facilities. Meeting rms. Business center. In-rm modem link. Gift shop. Health club privileges. Bathrm phones; microwaves avail. Cr cds: A, C, D, DS, ER, JCB, MC, V.

⬛ ⬛ ⬛ ⬛ ⬛ SC ⬛

★★★ **HYATT REGENCY.** *1 Bethesda Metro Ctr (20814). 301/657-1234; FAX 301/657-6478; res: 800/233-1234.* Web www.hyatt.com. 381 rms, 12 story. S $225; D $250; each addl $25; suites $200-$600; under 18 free; wkend rates. Crib free. Covered parking $10; valet $12. TV; cable (premium), VCR avail. Indoor pool; lifeguard. Restaurant 6:30 am-11:30 pm. Bar 11:30-12:30 am. Ck-out noon. Convention facilities. Business center. In-rm modem link. Gift shop. Exercise equipt; sauna. Bathrm phones. Private patios, balconies. 12-story atrium lobby; extensive collection of artwork. Luxury level. Cr cds: A, C, D, DS, ER, JCB, MC, V.

⬛ ⬛ ⬛ ⬛ ⬛ SC ⬛

★★★ **MARRIOTT HOTEL.** *5151 Pooks Hill Rd (20814), 1 blk S of I-495 exit 34. 301/897-9400; FAX 301/897-0192; res: 800/228-9290.* 407 rms, 4-16 story. S $199; D $219; suites $300-$750; under 18 free; wkend plan. Crib free. TV; cable (premium), VCR avail. Indoor/outdoor pool; whirlpool, poolside serv, lifeguard. Coffee in rms. Restaurants 6:30 am-10 pm. Rm serv to 1 am. Bar 11-1 am; Fri, Sat to 2 am, entertainment Fri, Sat. Ck-out noon. Guest lndry. Convention facilities. Business center. In-rm modem link. Gift shops. Lighted tennis. Exercise equipt; sauna. Game rm. Microwaves avail. Some balconies. On 18 landscaped acres. Luxury level. Cr cds: A, C, D, DS, ER, JCB, MC, V.

⬛ ⬛ ⬛ ⬛ ⬛ ⬛ SC ⬛

★★★ **MARRIOTT SUITES.** *6711 Democracy Blvd (20817). 301/897-5600; FAX 301/530-1427; res: 800/228-9290.* Web www.marriott.com. 274 suites, 11 story. Suites $190-$220; family rates. Crib free. TV; cable (premium), VCR avail. Indoor/outdoor pool; whirlpool, poolside serv, lifeguard. Complimentary coffee in rms. Restaurant 6:30 am-10:30 pm. Bar noon-midnight. Ck-out 11 am. Meeting rms. Business center. In-rm modem link. RR station transportation. Exercise equipt. Wet bars; microwaves avail. Balconies. Cr cds: A, C, D, DS, ER, JCB, MC, V.

⬛ ⬛ ⬛ ⬛ ⬛ ⬛ SC ⬛

★★★ **RESIDENCE INN BY MARRIOTT.** *7335 Wisconsin Ave (20814). 301/718-0200; FAX 301/718-0679; res: 800/331-3131.* Web www.marriott.com. 187 kit suites, 13 story. S, D $189-$299; under 16 free; wkend, wkly, monthly rates. Crib free. Pet accepted; $100 & $5/day. Valet parking $12. TV; cable (premium), VCR avail (movies). Pool; lifeguard. Complimentary continental bkfst. Complimentary coffee in rms. Restaurant adj 6:30 am-midnight. Ck-out noon. Coin lndry. Meeting rms. Business servs avail. Exercise equipt. Rec rm. Microwaves. Cr cds: A, C, D, DS, JCB, MC, V.

⊡ 🐾 ≈ 🏃 🛟 🔥 SC

Restaurants

★★★ **ANDALUCIA DE BETHESDA.** 4931 Elm St (20814). 301/907-0052. Hrs: 11:30 am-2:30 pm, 5:30-10 pm; Fri, Sat to 11 pm; Sun 5-9:30 pm. Closed some major hols. Res accepted; required Fri, Sat dinner. Spanish menu. Bar. Wine list. Semi-a la carte: lunch $7.25-$10.95, dinner $13.95-$22.95. Specialties: zarzuela Mediterraneo, mero en salsa verde, paella para dos. Own desserts. Classical guitar Sun-Thurs. Totally nonsmoking. Cr cds: A, C, D, DS, MC, V.

⊡

✓★ **AUSTIN GRILL.** 7278 Woodmont Ave (20814), at Elm St. 301/656-1366. E-mail austingrill@aol.com; web www.austingrill.com. Hrs: 11:30 am-11 pm; Mon to 10 pm; Fri to midnight; Sat 11 am-midnight; Sun 11 am-10 pm; Sat, Sun brunch to 3 pm. Closed Thanksgiving, Dec 24, 25. Tex-Mex menu. Bar. Semi-a la carte: lunch $6-$9, dinner $6-$14. Sat, Sun brunch $5-$7. Child's meals. Specializes in chicken, fresh seafood, vegetarian dishes. Outdoor dining. Contemporary Southwestern motif. Totally nonsmoking. Cr cds: A, C, D, DS, MC, V.

⊡

★★ **BACCHUS BETHESDA.** 7945 Norfolk Ave (20814). 301/657-1722. Hrs: noon-2 pm, 6-10 pm; Fri to 10:30 pm; Sat 6-10:30 pm; Sun 6-10 pm. Closed Thanksgiving, Dec 25. Res accepted; required Fri, Sat. Lebanese menu. Serv bar. Semi-a la carte: lunch $4-$9, dinner $12.25-$16.25. Specialties: falafel, shish kebab. Valet parking (dinner). Outdoor dining. Cr cds: A, C; MC, V.

⊡

✓★★ **BOMBAY DINING.** 4931 Cordell Ave (20814). 301/656-3373. Hrs: 11:30 am-2:30 pm, 5:30-10 pm; Sat, Sun noon-3 pm, 5:30-10:30 pm. Res accepted. Indian menu. Bar. Semi-a la carte: lunch, dinner $7.95-$15.95. Sat, Sun brunch $9.95. Specializes in tandoori, curries, vegetables. Salad bar. Valet parking (wkends). Cr cds: A, C, D, DS, MC, V.

⊡

★★ **BUON GIORNO.** 8003 Norfolk Ave (20814). 301/652-1400. Hrs: 11:30 am-2:30 pm, 5:30-10 pm; Fri to 10:30 pm; Sat 5:30-10:30 pm; Sun 5:30-10 pm. Closed Mon; Jan 1, Thanksgiving, Dec 25; also mid-Aug-mid-Sept. Res accepted; required Fri, Sat. Italian menu. Serv bar. Semi-a la carte: lunch $8.95-$10.95, dinner $12.95-$20.95. Specialties: trenette alla Genovese, pappardelle alla contadina, fresh fish. Own pasta. Valet parking (dinner). Totally nonsmoking. Cr cds: A, C, D, DS, MC, V.

⊡

★★★ **CAFE BETHESDA.** 5027 Wilson Lane (20814), at Cordell Ave. 301/657-3383. Hrs: 11:30 am-2 pm, 5:30-9 pm; Fri to 10 pm; Sat 5:30-10 pm; Sun 5:30-9 pm. Closed most major hols. Res accepted; required Fri, Sat. French menu. Wine, beer. Semi-a la carte: lunch $8-$12, dinner $14-$25. Specializes in rack of lamb, seafood, veal. Valet parking. Outdoor dining. Atmosphere of French country inn. Totally nonsmoking. Cr cds: A, C, D, MC, V.

✓★ **CAPITAL WRAPPS.** 4733 Bethesda Ave (20814). 301/654-0262. Hrs: 11:30 am-8 pm; Fri, Sat to 9 pm. Closed Sun; major hols. Southwestern menu. Beer, wine. A la carte entrees: lunch, dinner $4.95-$6.25. Child's meals. Specializes in international foods wrapped in tortillas. Outdoor dining. Mediterranean open market atmosphere. Totally nonsmoking. Cr cds: C, MC, V.

⊡

★★★ **CESCO TRATTORIA.** 4871 Cordell Ave (20814). 301/654-8333. Web www.robertodonna/cesco.com. Hrs: 11:30 am-2 pm, 5:30-10 pm; Fri to 11 pm; Sat 5:30-11 pm; Sun 5-9 pm. Closed major hols. Res accepted; required Fri, Sat dinner. Italian menu. Bar. Wine list. A la carte entrees: lunch $10-$13.95, dinner $11.95-$21.95. Specializes in fresh seafood, Tuscan cuisine, pasta. Own pasta. Valet parking (dinner). Outdoor dining. Contemporary Italian trattoria atmosphere. Cr cds: A, C, MC, V.

★★ **COTTONWOOD CAFE.** 4844 Cordell Ave (20814). 301/656-4844. Web www.cottonwood-cafe.com. Hrs: 11:30 am-10 pm; Fri, Sat to 11 pm; Sun from 5:30 pm. Closed most major hols. Res accepted. Southwestern menu. Bar. Semi-a la carte: lunch $5.95-$7, dinner $12.65-$20.95. Specializes in grilled meats, seafood. Valet parking (dinner). Southwestern atmosphere. Mural of adobe village. Cr cds: A, C, D, MC, V.

⊡ ♥

★★ **DELRAY VIETNAMESE GARDEN.** 4918 Delray Ave (20814). 301/986-0606. Hrs: 11:30 am-2:30 pm, 5-10 pm; Sat, Sun 5-10 pm. Closed major hols. Res required Fri, Sat (dinner). Vietnamese menu. Bar. A la carte entrees: lunch $5.95-$12.75, dinner $7.95-$12.75. Specialties: pinecone fish, nid d'amour, curry. Valet parking wkends. Outdoor dining. Country inn decor. Cr cds: A, C, MC, V.

⊡

✓★★ **FOONG LIN.** 7710 Norfolk Ave (20814). 301/656-3427. Hrs: 11 am-10:30 pm; Fri, Sat to 11 pm. Closed Thanksgiving. Res accepted. Chinese menu. Bar. Semi-a la carte: lunch $3.95-$7.50, dinner $7.25-$19.95. Specialties: fresh fish, Peking duckling, crispy beef. Cr cds: A, C, DS, MC, V.

⊡ ♥

★★ **FRASCATI RISTORANTE ITALIANO.** 4806 Rugby Ave (20814). 301/652-9514. E-mail ilfrascati@aol.com. Hrs: 11 am-2:30 pm, 4-10:30 pm; Sat from 5 pm; Sun 4-9:30 pm; early-bird dinner Tues-Fri, Sun 4-6:30 pm. Closed Mon; Jan 1, Easter, Dec 25. Res accepted; required Fri, Sat. Italian menu. Semi-a la carte: lunch $4.75-$6.95, dinner $9.75-$16.95. Child's meals. Specializes in fresh fish, veal, pasta. Outdoor dining. Totally nonsmoking. Cr cds: A, C, D, DS, MC, V.

⊡

★★ **HAANDI FINE INDIAN CUSINE.** 4904 Fairmont Ave (20814). 301/718-0121. Hrs: 11:30 am-2:30 pm, 5-10 pm; Fri, Sat to 10:30 pm. Res accepted. Indian menu. Bar. Semi-a la carte: lunch $4.95-$10.95, dinner $7.95-$14.95. Buffet: lunch $7.95. Specialties: tandoori dishes, vegetarian dishes, murg makhini. Totally nonsmoking. Cr cds: A, C, D, MC, V.

⊡

★★ **IL RITROVO.** 4838 Rugby Ave (20814). 301/986-1447. Hrs: 11:30 am-2:30 pm, 5:30-11 pm; Sat from 5:30 pm. Closed Sun; most major hols. Res accepted Sat, Sun. Mediterranean menu. Bar. Semi-a la carte: lunch $3.95-$15.95, dinner $8.95-$17.95. Specializes in fresh seafood. Own baking, pasta. Outdoor dining. Mediterranean decor. Cr cds: A, C, D, DS, MC, V.

⊡ ⊟

★★ **JEAN-MICHEL.** 10223 Old Georgetown Rd (20814). 301/564-4910. Hrs: 11:30 am-2:30 pm, 5:30-10 pm; Sat from 5:30 pm; Sun 5:30-8:30 pm. Closed most major hols; also Sun July-Aug. Res accepted. French menu. Serv bar. Semi-a la carte: lunch $9.50-$13.25, dinner $12.95-$21.75. Specialties: mussels marinieres, venison with chestnut puree & cranberry jelly. French decor. Cr cds: A, C, D, MC, V.

⊡

★★★ **LA FERME.** 7101 Brookville Rd (20815), E on MD 186. 301/986-5255. Hrs: noon-2 pm, 6-10 pm; Sat from 6 pm; Sun 5-9 pm. Closed Mon; Dec 25. Res accepted; required Fri, Sat dinner. French menu. Serv bar. Wine cellar. Semi-a la carte: lunch $7.25-$10.75, dinner $15.75-$22.75. Specialties: duck with turnips & apple cider; lobster, shrimp, scallops and grouper in saffron broth; boneless breast of chicken. Pianist. Outdoor dining. Country inn decor. Cr cds: A, C, D, MC, V.

⊡

★★ **LA MICHE.** *7905 Norfolk Ave (20814). 301/986-0707.* Hrs: 11:30 am-2 pm, 6-9:45 pm; Mon, Sat from 6 pm; Sun 5:30-8 pm. Closed major hols. Res required Fri, Sat. French menu. Serv bar. A la carte entrees: lunch $6-$16, dinner $13-$24. Specialties: souffles, fricassee of lobster, grilled breast of duck. Valet parking (dinner). Outdoor dining. French country decor. Cr cds: A, C, D, MC, V.

D

★★★ **LE VIEUX LOGIS.** *7925 Old Georgetown Rd (20814). 301/652-6816.* Hrs: 5:30-10 pm; hrs vary Nov-Dec. Closed Sun; Jan 1, Dec 25. Res accepted; required Sat. French, Amer menu. Serv bar. Wine list. Semi-a la carte: lunch $7-$15, dinner $16-$24. Specialties: roasted Long Island duckling, grilled Norwegian salmon. Free valet parking. Outdoor dining. Rustic French inn atmosphere. Cr cds: A, C, D, DS, MC, V.

D ♥

✓★ **MATUBA JAPANESE.** *4918 Cordell Ave (20814). 301/652-7449.* Hrs: 11:30 am-2:30 pm, 5-10 pm; Fri to 10:30 pm; Sat noon-3 pm, 5-10:30 pm; Sun 5-10 pm. Japanese menu. Wine, beer. Semi-a la carte: lunch $4.95-$9.95, dinner $6.95-$11.95. Specialties: sushi, chicken teriyaki. Casual decor. Totally nonsmoking. Cr cds: A, C, MC, V.

D

✓★★ **MONTGOMERY'S GRILLE.** *7200 Wisconsin Ave (20814), 4 mi S on I-270 exit Wisconsin Ave, at Bethesda Ave. 301/654-3595.* Hrs: 11:30 am-10 pm; Thurs to 11 pm; Fri, Sat to midnight; Sun from 10 am; Sun brunch to 2 pm. Closed Thanksgiving, Dec 25. Bar to 12:30 am; Fri, Sat to 1:30 am. Semi-a la carte: lunch $5.95-$8.95, dinner $7.95-$14.95. Sun brunch $12.95. Child's meals. Specializes in pasta, fresh grilled seafood, crab cakes. Own baking. Outdoor dining. American pub atmosphere with antique bar, bronze-framed windows, hand-carved woodwork. Totally nonsmoking. Cr cds: A, C, D, DS, MC, V.

D ♥

✓★★ **NAM'S OF BETHESDA.** *4928 Cordell Ave (20814). 301/652-2635.* Hrs: 11:30 am-2:30 pm, 5:30-11 pm; Sat 5-11 pm; Sun 5-9:30 pm. Closed Thanksgiving, Dec 25. Res accepted. Vietnamese menu. Bar. Semi-a la carte: lunch $5.50-$8.50, dinner $7.50-$10.95. Specializes in chicken, beef, pork. Contemporary decor. Cr cds: A, C, MC, V.

D

★★ **O'DONNELL'S.** *8301 Wisconsin Ave (20814). 301/656-6200.* Hrs: 11:30 am-10 pm; Sun noon-9 pm. Closed Dec 25. Res accepted. Bar. Semi-a la carte: lunch $5.50-$12.95, dinner $13.95-$21.95. Child's meals. Specializes in seafood. Outdoor dining on patio. Nautical theme. Family-owned. Cr cds: A, C, D, DS, MC, V.

D ⬓

★ **ORIGINAL PANCAKE HOUSE.** *7703 Woodmont Ave (20814). 301/986-0285.* E-mail orgnlpanke@aol.com. Hrs: 7 am-3 pm. Closed Dec 25. A la carte entrees: bkfst, lunch $3.95-$7.95. Child's meals. Specializes in crepes, waffles, pancakes. Casual dining. Cr cds: A, C, MC, V.

D

★ **RAKU-AN ASIAN DINER.** *7240 Woodmont Ave (20814). 301/718-8680.* Hrs: 11:30 am-10 pm; Fri, Sat to 10:30 pm; Sun to 9 pm. Closed Thanksgiving, Dec 25. Pan-Asian menu. Serv bar. Semi-a la carte: lunch $2.35-$9.25. A la carte entrees: dinner $2.35-$13.25. Child's meals. Specializes in noodles, wraps, stir fry. Own desserts. Outdoor dining. Casual decor with Oriental flair. Totally nonsmoking. Cr cds: A, C, MC, V.

D

★★ **RED TOMATO CAFE.** *4910 St Elmo Ave (20814). 301/652-4499.* Hrs: 11:30 am-9:30 pm; Thurs to 10 pm; Fri, Sat to 11 pm; Sun 4:30-9 pm. Closed Jan 1, Thanksgiving, Dec 25. Res accepted Sun-Thurs. Italian, Amer menu. Serv bar. A la carte entrees: lunch $3.95-

$10.95, dinner $5.95-$15.95. Specializes in pasta, pizza. Valet parking Thurs-Sat. Colorful, contemporary pizzeria; large mural, wood-burning pizza oven. Totally nonsmoking. Cr cds: A, C, D, DS, MC, V.

D

★★ **ROCK BOTTOM BREWERY.** *7900 Norfolk Ave (20814). 301/652-1311.* Web www.rockbottom.com. Hrs: 11-1 am; Fri, Sat to 2 am. Bar. Semi-a la carte: lunch $6.50-$9.95, dinner $8.50-$17.95. Specializes in enchiladas, hamburgers, pizza. Own baking. Musicians Sat, Sun. Valet parking (dinner). Outdoor dining. American brew pub atmosphere with open kitchen, microbrewery, wood-burning pizza oven. Cr cds: A, C, D, MC, V.

D

★★★ **RUTH'S CHRIS STEAKHOUSE.** *7315 Wisconsin Ave (20814). 301/652-7877.* Hrs: 5-10:30 pm; Sun 4-9:30 pm. Closed Thanksgiving, Dec 25. Res accepted; required Fri, Sat. Serv bar. Wine list. A la carte entrees: dinner $18.95-$29.95. Specializes in beef, lobster, fresh seafood. Own desserts. Pianist Thurs-Sat. Valet parking. Intimate, club-like atmosphere; artwork. Totally nonsmoking. Cr cds: A, C, D, DS, MC, V.

D

★★★ **TARA THAI.** *4828 Bethesda Ave (20814). 301/657-0488.* Web www.tarathai.com. Hrs: 11:30 am-3 pm, 5-10 pm; Fri to 11 pm; Sat noon-3:30 pm, 5-11 pm; Sun noon-3:30 pm, 5-10 pm. Closed July 4, Thanksgiving. Thai menu. Bar. Semi-a la carte: lunch $4.95-$7.95, dinner $6.95-$15.95. Specialties: grilled whole rock fish, crispy whole flounder. Underwater theme. Totally nonsmoking. Cr cds: A, C, D, DS, MC, V.

D

✓★★ **TEL-AVIV CAFE.** *4869 Cordell Ave (20814). 301/718-9068.* Hrs: 11:30 am-midnight; Mon to 11 pm; Sat to 1 am; Sun 4:30-11 pm. Closed Yom Kippur, Passover. Mediterranean menu. Bar to 1 am; Fri, Sat to 2 am. Semi-a la carte: lunch, dinner $6.95-$15.95. Specialities: lamb shank, kafta kabob, kosher dishes. Own baking. Entertainment Tues, Sat. Outdoor dining. Contemporary Mediterranean decor. Cr cds: A, C, D, DS, MC, V.

D

✓★ **THAI PLACE.** *4828 Cordell Ave (20814). 301/951-0535.* Hrs: 11 am-3 pm, 5-10 pm; Fri, Sat to 10:30 pm; Sun 11 am-10 pm. Thai menu. Serv bar. Semi-a la carte: lunch $5.75-$6.50, dinner $7.50-$12. Specializes in steamed fish, Thai cuisine. Cr cds: A, C, DS, MC, V.

D

★★ **THYME SQUARE.** *4735 Bethesda Ave (20814). 301/657-9077.* Hrs: 11 am-10 pm; Fri, Sat to 11 pm. Closed Dec 24, 25. Res accepted; required Thurs-Sun dinner. Bar. Semi-a la carte: lunch $5.95-$10.95, dinner $6.95-$18.95. Specializes in seasonal Amer dishes, vegetarian dishes, fresh seafood. Contemporary decor with extensive murals; open kitchen. Totally nonsmoking. Cr cds: A, C, MC, V.

★★★ **TRAGARA.** *4935 Cordell Ave (20814). 301/951-4935.* Hrs: 11:30 am-2:30 pm, 5:30-10:30 pm; Sat from 5:30 pm; Sun 5-9 pm. Closed major hols. Res accepted; required Fri, Sat. Italian menu. Semi-a la carte: lunch $8.95-$15.95. A la carte entrees: dinner $15.95-$25. Specialties: veal scaloppini, linguine with Maine lobster, lamb chops sauteed with herbs and mustard. Own baking, pastas. Valet parking (dinner). Italian marble, original paintings, chandelier. Cr cds: A, C, D, MC, V.

D

Unrated Dining Spot

BETHESDA CRAB HOUSE. *4958 Bethesda Ave (20814). 301/652-3382.* Hrs: 9 am-midnight. Closed Dec 25. Res accepted. Wine, beer. A la carte entrees: lunch, dinner $10-$30. Specializes in spiced shrimp, steamed crab, crabcakes. Outdoor dining. Rustic decor; established 1961. Cr cds: C, MC, V.

Boonsboro (Washington County) (B-5)

(See also Frederick, Hagerstown)

Settled 1787 **Pop** 2,445 **Elev** 591 ft **Area Code** 301 **Zip** 21713
E-mail info@marylandmemories.org **Web** www.marylandmemories.org
Information Hagerstown/Washington County Convention and Visitors Bureau, 16 Public Sq, Hagerstown 21740; 301/791-3246

What to See and Do

Antietam National Battlefield (see). 8 mi SW on MD 34.

Crystal Grottoes Caverns. Limestone caverns may be viewed from walkways. Picnicking. Guided tours (Apr-Oct, daily; rest of yr, by appt). 1 mi SW on MD 34. Phone 301/432-6336. ¢¢¢

Gathland State Park. 140 acres. A site once owned by George Townsend, Civil War reporter. Monument built in 1896 to honor Civil War correspondents. Visitor center contains original papers. Picnicking. Walking tour. Winter sports. 8 mi S off MD 67, then 1 mi E, W of Burkittsville off MD 17. Park schedule varies, Phone 301/791-4767.

Washington Monument State Park. 147 acres. A 34-ft tower of native stone (1827) was first completed monument to honor George Washington. Views of nearby battlefields, two states (PA & WV). History Center displays firearms and Civil War mementos (by appt). The Appalachian Trail leads through the park; hiking and picnicking. 3 mi SE off US 40A. Park schedule varies, Phone 301/791-4767. **Free**

Restaurant

★★ **OLD SOUTH MOUNTAIN INN.** *6132 Old National Pike (21713). 301/371-5400.* Web www.marylandrestaurants.org/ram.guide/old south.html. Hrs: 5-9 pm; Sat 11:30 am-2:30 pm, 4-10 pm; Sun 10:30 am-8 pm, brunch to 2 pm. Closed Mon; Dec 25. Res accepted; required Sat, Sun. Bar. Semi-a la carte: lunch $5-$11, dinner $14-$28. Sun brunch $12.95. Child's meals. Specialties: crab cakes, prime rib. Outdoor dining. Founded in 1732; was once a stagecoach stop. Totally nonsmoking. Cr cds: A, C, D, MC, V.

Bowie (C-7)

(See also College Park, Silver Spring; also see District of Columbia)

Pop 37,589 **Elev** 150 ft **Area Code** 240 & 301
Information Greater Bowie Chamber of Commerce, 6770 Race Track Rd, Hilltop Plaza, 20715; 301/262-0920. Information is also available from Prince George's Conference & Visitors Bureau, 9475 Lottsford Rd, #130, Landover 20785; 301/925-8300

What to See and Do

Belair Mansion. Georgian-style home (ca 1745) was home of Governor Samuel Ogle in the 1700s; later owned by the Woodward family, prominent racehorse breeders in the first half of the 20th century. Tours. (Sun, groups by appt; closed Jan) 12207 Tulip Grove Dr. Phone 301/262-6200. **Donation**

Belair Stable. Part of famed Belair Stud, one of the premier Thoroughbred racing stables of the '30s, '40s and '50s. Was home to two Triple Crown winners-Gallant Fox and Omaha-and the 1955 Horse of the Year, Nashua. (May, June, Sept, Oct, Sun only) 2835 Belair Dr. Phone 301/262-6200. **Free**

Marietta Manor. A modest Federal-style plantation house built by Gabriel Duvall, an associate justice of the US Supreme Court (1811-1835). Tours. (Mar-Dec, Sun afternoons; also by appt) 3 mi W in Glenn Dale, at 5626 Bell Station Rd. Phone 301/464-5291. ¢

Annual Event

Heritage Day. Belair Mansion & Stable. Performance by Congress's Own Regiment; tour of stables and grounds; battle reenactments; demonstrations of colonial crafts. Phone 301/262-6200. 3rd Sun May.

Cambridge (D-8)

(See also Easton, Salisbury)

Founded 1684 **Pop** 11,514 **Elev** 14 ft **Area Code** 410 & 443 **Zip** 21613
E-mail chamber@shore.intercom.net **Web** www.bluecrab.org/dorchester
Information Dorchester Chamber of Commerce, 528 Poplar St; 410/228-3575 or 800/522-TOUR (Dorchester Tourism)

On the Eastern Shore, Cambridge is Maryland's second-largest deep-water port. Boating and fishing opportunities are found in the Choptank and Honga rivers and Chesapeake, Tar and Fishing bays.

What to See and Do

Blackwater National Wildlife Refuge. Over 20,000 acres of rich tidal marsh, freshwater ponds and woodlands. One of the chief wintering areas for Canada geese and ducks using the Atlantic Flyway; in fall, as many as 33,000 geese and 17,000 ducks swell the bird population. Also a haven for the bald eagle, the Delmarva fox squirrel and the peregrine falcon, all three of which are endangered species. Scenic drive, woodland trails, observation tower. Visitor center (Sept-May, daily; rest of yr, Mon-Fri; closed hols and Labor Day wkend). Golden Age, Golden Eagle and Golden Access passports (see MAKING THE MOST OF YOUR TRIP). 12 mi S via MD 16, 335. Phone 410/228-2677. Per vehicle ¢¢; Per hiker or cyclist ¢

Old Trinity Church, Dorchester Parish (ca 1675). One of the oldest churches in US still holding regular services; faithful restoration of interior. (By appt) 8 mi SW on MD 16 in Church Creek. Phone 410/228-2940. **Free**

Annual Events

National Outdoor Show. Goose and duck calling, log sawing, crab picking, trap setting contests; entertainment. Phone 800/522-TOUR. Last wkend Feb.

Antique Aircraft Fly-In. Dorchester Heritage Museum, 5 mi W on MD 343 at 1904 Horne Point Rd. Old and new planes on display. Phone 410/228-5530 or 410/228-1899 or 800/522-TOUR. 3rd wkend May.

Motel

★ **FOREST HILLS MOTEL.** *2901 Crain Hwy (20774), 8 mi S on US 301.* 301/627-3969; FAX 301/627-4058. 13 rms, shower only. Apr-Oct: S $42-$44; D $46-$49; under 13 free; lower rates rest of yr. Crib free. Pet accepted. TV. Complimentary coffee in rms. Ck-out 11 am. Some refrigerators. Picnic tables. Cr cds: A, C, D, DS, MC, V.

⊠ 🐾 🔥 SC

Chesapeake Bay Bridge Area (C-7)

The majestic twin spans of the Chesapeake Bay Bridge carry visitors to the Eastern Shore, a patchwork of small picturesque towns, lighthouses and fishing villages tucked away from the city. Scenic rivers and bays, wildlife, gardens and wildflowers fill the countryside. The main attractions of any visit, however, are the many fine inns and the restaurants specializing in local seafood.

What to See and Do

Wye Oak State Park. Official state tree of Maryland is in this 29-acre park; it is the largest white oak in the US (108 ft high, 28 ft around) and believed to be over 400 yrs old; a new tree has been started from an acorn. A restored 18th-century one-room schoolhouse and the Old Wye Mill (late 1600s) are nearby. E on US 50 to Wye Mills. Phone 410/820-1668.

Motel

★★ **COMFORT INN.** *3101 Main St (21638), E via US 50, then S after Kent Narrows Bridge (exit 42).* 410/827-6767; FAX 410/827-8626; res: 800/228-5150. 86 units, 4 story, 9 kit. suites. Apr-Nov: S $66-$126; D $76-$140; each addl $8; kit. suites $125-$200; under 18 free; higher rates special events; lower rates rest of yr. Crib free. TV; cable (premium). Indoor pool; whirlpool. Complimentary continental bkfst. Complimentary coffee in rms. Restaurant nearby. Ck-out 11 am. Coin lndry. Meeting rms. Business servs avail. Exercise equipt; sauna. Refrigerators, microwaves. Cr cds: A, C, D, DS, ER, JCB, MC, V.

D 🏊 🏋 🔥 🔥 SC

Motor Hotel

✓★★ **COMFORT SUITES.** *160 Scheeler Rd (21666), US 301 to Chestertown exit.* 410/810-0555; FAX 410/810-0286. Web www.chestertown.com/comfortsuites. 53 suites, 3 story. Apr-Nov: S, D $69.95-$109.95; under 18 free; lower rates rest of yr. Crib avail. TV; cable. Indoor pool. Complimentary continental bkfst. Restaurant nearby. Ck-out 11 am. Meeting rms. Business servs avail. Coin lndry. Health club privileges. Refrigerators, microwaves. Cr cds: A, C, D, DS, MC, V.

D 🏊 🔥 🔥 SC

Inns

★★ **HUNTINGFIELD MANOR.** *4928 Eastern Neck Rd (21661), 2 mi S on MD 20/445.* 410/639-7779; FAX 410/639-2924; res: 800/720-8788. E-mail manorlord@juno.com; web www.huntingfield.com. 6 rms, 2 story. No rm phones. S, D $85-$125; each addl $25; under 3 free. Pet accepted. Complimentary continental bkfst. Restaurant nearby. Ck-out noon, ck-in 2 pm. Telescope-type house on a working farm that dates back to the middle 1600s. Cr cds: A, C, MC, V.

D 🐾 🔥 🔥

★★★ **IMPERIAL HOTEL.** *208 High St (21620), US 301 to Chestertown exit.* 410/778-5000; FAX 410/778-9662. 13 rms, 3 story. S, D $125-$200; suites $200-$250; lower rates wkdays. Crib free. TV; cable (premium), VCR avail. Continental bkfst Tues-Sat. Dining rm 11:45 am-2:30 pm, 5:30-close; Sun brunch 11:30 am-3 pm; closed Mon. Ck-out 11 am, ck-in 3 pm. Meeting rms. Business servs avail. Refrigerator in suites. Built in 1903; Victorian furnishings. Cr cds: A, C, D, DS, MC, V.

D 🔥 🔥

★★★ **INN AT MITCHELL HOUSE.** *8796 Maryland Pkwy (21620), US 301 to Chestertown exit.* 410/778-6500; FAX 410/778-2861. Web www.chestertown.com/mitchell. 5 rms, 2 story. No rm phones. S, D $90-$110; wkends (2-day min). Crib free. TV in parlor. Complimentary full bkfst. Dinner avail Fri, Sat 7 pm; res required. Ck-out noon, ck-in 3 pm. Manor house built in 1743 on 10 acres. Totally nonsmoking. Cr cds: A, C, MC, V.

🐾 🔥 🔥

★★ **KENT MANOR INN.** *500 Kent Manor Dr (21666), US 50/301, S on MD 8.* 410/643-5757; FAX 410/643-8315; res: 800/820-4511. 24 rms, 3 story. S, D $135-$215; lower rates mid-wk. Crib $15. TV. Pool. Complimentary continental bkfst. Restaurant 11:30 am-9 pm; Fri, Sat to 9:30 pm; Sun brunch 10 am-2 pm, 4:30-8 pm. Ck-out 11 am, ck-in 3 pm. Meeting rms. Business servs avail. Built in 1820; antiques. On Thompson Creek. Cr cds: A, C, D, MC, V.

D 🏊 🔥 🔥 SC

★★ **WHITE SWAN TAVERN.** *231 High St (21620), US 301 to Chestertown exit.* 410/778-2300; FAX 410/778-4543. 6 rms, 2 story, 2 suites. No rm phones. S, D $100-$130; suites $140-$150; under 3 free. Crib free. TV in sitting rm. Complimentary continental bkfst. Restaurant nearby. Ck-out noon, ck-in 3 pm. Health club privileges. Refrigerators. Game rm. Former house and tavern built in 1733 and 1793; restored with antique furnishings; museum. Cr cds: C, MC, V.

D 🔥 🔥

Restaurants

★★ **FISHERMAN'S INN & CRAB DECK.** *US 50/301 (21638), E over bridge to exit 42, turn right and continue to end of road.* 410/827-8807. Hrs: 11 am-10 pm. Closed Dec 24, 25. Bar. Semi-a la carte: lunch $4.95-$9.95, dinner $6.95-$21. Specializes in fresh seafood. 2 dining areas; fireplace; display of antique oyster plates. Scenic view of the Kent Narrows of the Eastern Bay. Family-owned. Cr cds: A, C, DS, MC, V.

D 🔥

★ **HARRIS CRAB HOUSE.** *433 Kent Narrows Way N (21638), 4 mi E via US 50/301.* 410/827-9500. Hrs: 11 am-10 pm; Fri, Sat to 11 pm. Closed Thanksgiving, Dec 25. Bar. Semi-a la carte: lunch, dinner $6-$21.95. Specialties: fresh seafood, barbecued ribs & chicken, steamed crabs. Outdoor dining. Gazebo. On waterfront; dockage. Cr cds: C, MC, V.

D SC 🔥

★★★ **NARROWS RESTAURANT.** *3023 Kent Narrows Way S (21638), 4 mi E via US 50/301.* 410/827-8113. Hrs: 11 am-9 pm; summer to 10 pm; Sun brunch to 2 pm. Closed Dec 24, 25. Res accepted. Regional Eastern Shore menu. Bar. Wine list. Semi-a la carte: lunch $6-$12, dinner $12.75-$25. Sun brunch $9.75. Child's meals. Specializes in seafood, traditional Maryland recipes. Waterfront dining. View of the Narrows. Cr cds: A, C, D, MC, V.

D

★★ **OLD WHARF INN.** *Cannon St (21620), US 50 to Chestertown exit, on Chester River.* 410/778-3566. Hrs: 11 am-9 pm; Fri, Sat to 10 pm; Sun from 10 am; Sun brunch to 3 pm. Closed Dec 25. Bar. Semi-a la carte: lunch $3-$8, dinner $7.25-$19.95. Sun brunch $2.50-$12.25. Child's meals. Specializes in fresh seafood, steak, salad. Outdoor dining. View of river. Cr cds: A, C, MC, V.

[D] [🍴] [♥]

✓★ **WATERMAN'S CRAB HOUSE.** *Sharp St Wharf (21661), US 301 to MD 213, N to MD 20 to Rock Hall.* 410/639-2261. Hrs: 11 am-9 pm; Fri, Sat to 10 pm. Closed Thanksgiving; also Dec-Feb. Bar. Semi-a la carte: lunch, dinner $8.99-$16.95. Child's meals. Specializes in seafood, crabs, ribs. Outdoor dining. On Rock Hall Harbor. Cr cds: A, C, DS, MC, V.

[D] [SC] [🍴]

Chesapeake and Ohio Canal National Historical Park (A-2 - C-6)

As early as 1754, the enterprising George Washington, only in his twenties, proposed a system of navigation along the Potomac River valley. His Potowmack Canal Company, organized in 1785, cleared obstructions and built skirting canals to facilitate the transportation of goods from settlements beyond the Allegheny Mountains to the lower Potomac River towns.

The eventual inadequacy of these improvements and the renowned success of the Erie Canal spurred the formation in 1828 of the Chesapeake and Ohio Canal Company, whose purpose was to connect Georgetown with the Ohio Valley by river and canal. On July 4, 1828, President John Quincy Adams led the traditional groundbreaking ceremony declaring, "To subdue the earth is preeminently the purpose of this undertaking." Unfortunately, the earth was not easily subdued. President Adams bent his shovel after several attempts before breaking into an energetic frenzy and successfully getting a shovelful of dirt.

The difficulty of the groundbreaking ceremony foreshadowed the canal's short-lived future as a major transportation artery. Completed in 1850 as far as Cumberland, MD (184½ miles from Georgetown), the waterway was used extensively for the transportation of coal, flour, grain and lumber. Financial and legal difficulties, the decline of commerce after the Civil War, the Baltimore and Ohio Railroad and the advent of improved roads cut deeply into the commerce of the waterway, and it gradually faded into obsolescence. The canal still had limited commercial use as late as 1924, when a flood destroyed many of the canal locks and nothing was restored.

The unfortunate demise of the C & O Canal is now a blessing for hikers, canoeists and bikers, who can find access to the towpath along the banks of the waterway. Remaining as one of the least altered of old American canals, the Chesapeake and Ohio is flanked by ample foliage throughout most of its 20,239 acres.

Many points of interest can be seen along the waterway. Exhibits are offered in Cumberland, Georgetown, Hancock and Williamsport and at a museum near the Great Falls of the Potomac. At the Great Falls there are interpretive programs, including self-guiding trails, picnic facilities and a working lock. Mule-drawn canal boat rides are offered April-October at Georgetown and Great Falls (fee). Camping for hikers and bikers is available throughout the park.

For information about the canal contact the Chief of Visitor Services, C & O Canal National Historical Park, PO Box 4, Sharpsburg, MD 21782; 301/739-4200. Visitor centers are located in Cumberland, Georgetown, Great Falls, Hancock and Williamsport.

Cockeysville (B-7)

(See also Baltimore, Towson)

Pop 18,668 **Elev** 260 ft **Area Code** 410 **Zip** 21030
Information Baltimore County Chamber of Commerce, 102 W Pennsylvania Ave, Ste 402, Towson 21204; 410/825-6200

What to See and Do

⭐ **Ladew Topiary Gardens.** Extensive topiary gardens on 22 acres; 15 flower gardens. Also here is the Manor House (fee), with English antiques, fox-hunting memorabilia, paintings, unusual china, reconstructed Elizabethan room; Oval Library housing more than 3,000 volumes; carriage museum; cafe; gift shop. (Mid-Apr-Oct, daily exc Mon) 3535 Jarrettsville Pike, 5 mi E on MD 143 to Sunnybrook, then 6 mi N on MD 146. Phone 410/557-9466. Gardens ¢¢¢; Combination gardens and house ¢¢¢

Annual Event

Point-to-point Steeplechase. Three well-known meets on consecutive wkends: **My Lady's Manor.** In Monkton. Mid-Apr. **Grand National.** In Butler; phone 410/666-7777. Mid-Apr. **Maryland Hunt Cup.** In Glyndon; phone 410/666-7777. Late Apr.

Motel

★★ **COURTYARD BY MARRIOTT.** *221 International Cir (21030), exit 20-A from I-83.* 410/584-7070; FAX 410/584-8151; res: 800/765-4543. 146 rms, 3 story, 12 suites. S $72; D $76; suites $92-$99. Crib free. TV; cable (premium). Complimentary coffee in rms. Restaurant 6:30-10:30 am, 5-9:30 pm. Rm serv from 5 pm. Bar 4-10 pm Mon-Fri. Ck-out noon. Meeting rms. Business servs avail. In-rm modem link. Valet serv. Sundries. Coin lndry. Exercise equipt. Indoor pool; whirlpool, lifeguard. Refrigerator in suites. Balconies. Cr cds: A, C, D, DS, MC, V.

[D] [≈] [✕] [⊠] [🔥] [SC]

Motor Hotel

★★★ **MARRIOTT INN.** *245 Shawan Rd (21031), I-83 exit 20-A.* 410/785-7000; FAX 410/785-0341; res: 800/228-9290. Web www.marriott.com. 390 rms, 4 story. Mar-Nov: S $129; D $149; suites $179-$350; under 12 free; wkend rates. Pet accepted, some restrictions. TV; cable (premium). Coffee in rms. Restaurant 6:30 am-10 pm; Fri to 11 pm; Sat 7 am-11 pm; Sun from 7 am. Rm serv. Bar 3 pm-1 am. Ck-out noon. Convention facilities. Business center. In-rm modem link. Bellhops. Valet serv. Concierge. Gift shop. Tennis. Exercise equipt. Heated indoor/outdoor pool; wading pool, whirlpool, poolside serv. Refrigerator in suites. Luxury level. Cr cds: A, C, D, DS, JCB, MC, V.

[D] [🐾] [⚷] [≈] [✕] [⊠] [🔥] [SC] [✕]

Restaurants

★★★★ **OREGON GRILL.** *245 Shawan Rd.* 410/771-0505. Hrs: lunch 11:30 am-4 pm, dinner 5 pm-10 pm, Fri, Sat until 11 pm. Brunch 11 am-3 pm, Sun dinner 4-10 pm. Res recommended. American menu. Wine cellar. A la carte entrees: lunch $7-$16, dinner $18-$32. Specializes crab cakes, lamb, dry aged prime steak, veal. Own pastries. Cr cds: C.

★★★ **THE MILTON INN.** *14833 York Rd (21075), 5 mi N on MD 45.* 410/771-4366. E-mail miltoninn@aol.com; web www.byi.com/md/miltoninn. Hrs: 5:30-9:30 pm; Sun 4-9 pm. Closed some major hols. Res accepted. Bar. Wine cellar. Complete meals: dinner $45. Child's meals. Specializes in seasonal dishes, fresh seafood, poultry. Outdoor dining. Main part of building ca 1820; one section was stagecoach stop ca 1740. English country decor. Cr cds: A, C, D, DS, MC, V.

[D]

★★ **YORK INN.** *10010 York Rd (21030). 410/666-0006.* Hrs: 11-2 am; Sun brunch 9 am-2 pm. Closed Dec 25. Res accepted; required major hols. Continental menu. Bar to 2 am. Semi-a la carte: lunch $5.95-$10.95, dinner $11.95-$25.95. Sun bkfst buffet $6.95. Child's meals. Specializes in seafood, steak. Casual dining. Cr cds: A, C, D, DS, MC, V.

College Park (C-6)

(See also Bowie, Silver Spring; also see District of Columbia)

Pop 21,927 **Elev** 190 ft **Area Code** 240 & 301 **Zip** 20740 **E-mail** visitor_info@co.pg.md.us

Information Prince George's County Conference & Visitors Bureau, 9200 Basil Ct, #101, Largo 20774; 301/925-8300 or 888/925-8300

What to See and Do

College Park Aviation Museum. World's oldest operating airport, started by Wilbur Wright in 1909 to train 2 military officers in the operation of aircraft. First airplane machine gun and radio-navigational aids tested here; first air mail and controlled helicopter flights. Museum (Wed-Sun; closed major hols). 6709 Corporal Frank Scott Dr. Phone 301/864-6029 (recording). **Free**

Greenbelt Park. A 1,100-acre wooded park operated by the National Park Service. Nature trails. Picnicking. Camping (dump station, showers; 7-day limit Memorial Day-Labor Day; 14-day limit rest of yr). Self-registration, first come, first served. Standard fees. 6565 Greenbelt Rd, E off Kenilworth Ave, MD 201 exit 23. Phone 301/344-3948.

NASA/Goddard Visitor Center. Satellites, rockets, capsules and exhibits in all phases of space research. (Daily) SE on I-95 to Baltimore-Washington Pkwy, exit 22-A Greenbelt, then follow signs. For tour information phone 301/286-8981. **Free**

University of Maryland (1865). (35,000 students) Tawes Fine Arts Theater has plays, musicals, concerts, dance, opera and music festivals. Tours. For information phone 301/405-1000.

Motor Hotel

★★★ **COURTYARD BY MARRIOTT.** *6301 Golden Triangle Dr (20770), 4 mi NE on I-495, exit 23. 301/441-3311; FAX 301/441-4978; res: 800/321-2211.* 152 rms, 4 story, 12 suites. S, D $110; each addl $10; suites $124-$134; under 17 free; wkend, wkly rates. Crib free. TV; cable (premium). Indoor pool; whirlpool, lifeguard. Complimentary coffee in rms. Restaurant 6:30-10 am, 5-10 pm; wkends 6:30 am-midnight. Bar 4-10 pm Mon-Thurs. Ck-out noon. Meeting rms. Business servs avail. Bellhops. Valet serv. Sundries. Coin lndry. Exercise equipt. Refrigerator in suites; microwaves avail. Some balconies. Cr cds: A, C, D, DS, MC, V.

Hotels

✓★★★ **HOLIDAY INN.** *4095 Powder Mill Rd (20705), I-95 exit 29B. 301/937-4422; FAX 301/937-4455; res: 800/465-4329.* 206 rms, 9 story. S, D $109-$129; each addl $7; suites $165; under 18 free; wkend rates; higher rates Cherry Blossom. Crib free. TV; cable (premium). Pool; lifeguard. Complimentary coffee in rms. Restaurant 6:30 am-10 pm; wkends from 7 am. Bar. Ck-out noon. Coin lndry. Meeting rms. Business servs avail. In-rm modem link. Gift shop. Exercise equipt. Massage. Game rm. Refrigerator; microwaves avail. Cr cds: A, C, D, DS, JCB, MC, V.

★★★ **HOLIDAY INN.** *10000 Baltimore Ave (20740), I-495/95 exit 25. 301/345-6700; FAX 301/441-4923; res: 800/465-4329.* 222 rms in 2 bldgs, 4 story. S, D $139; under 18 free. Crib free. TV; cable (premium). Indoor pool; whirlpool, lifeguard. Coffee in rms. Restaurant 6:30 am-10 pm.

Bar 11 am-midnight. Ck-out noon. Coin lndry. Meeting rms. Business center. In-rm modem link. Exercise equipt; sauna. Health club privileges. Refrigerators, microwaves avail. Cr cds: A, C, D, DS, ER, MC, V.

★★★ **MARRIOTT GREENBELT.** *6400 Ivy Ln (20770), 2 blks N of I-95 exit 23 (Kenilworth Ave N). 301/441-3700; FAX 301/441-3995; res: 800/228-9290.* 283 rms, 18 story. S, D $149-$179; kit. units (min stay) $139-$184; family, wkend rates. Crib free. TV; cable (premium), VCR avail. 2 pools, 1 indoor; whirlpool, poolside serv, lifeguard. Restaurant 6:30 am-10:30 pm. Bar. Ck-out noon. Coin lndry. Convention facilities. Business center. In-rm modem link. Gift shop. Lighted tennis. Exercise equipt; sauna. Refrigerators, microwaves avail. Luxury level. Cr cds: A, C, D, DS, ER, JCB, MC, V.

Restaurants

✓★★ **ALAMO MEXICAN RESTAURANT INC.** *5508 Kenilworth Ave (20737), S on US 201; 3 mi S of I-95 exit 23. 301/927-8787.* Hrs: 11 am-11 pm. Res accepted. Mexican menu. Bar. Semi-a la carte: lunch $5-$11, dinner $8.30-$12.95. Child's meals. Specializes in tostadas, tacos, enchiladas. Entertainment Fri, Sat. Mexican decor. Cr cds: A, C, MC, V.

★★ **CALVERT HOUSE INN.** *6211 Baltimore Ave (20737), 1 mi S on US 1. 301/864-5220.* Hrs: 11 am-10 pm; Sat from 4 pm; Sun 4-9 pm; early-bird dinner 4-6 pm. Closed some major hols. Res accepted; required Fri, Sat dinner. Bar. Semi-a la carte: lunch $4.50-$10.95, dinner $6.95-$19.95. Child's meals. Specializes in fresh seafood, steak, crab cakes. Tavern atmosphere. Cr cds: A, C, D, DS, MC, V.

★★★ **CHEF'S SECRET.** *5810 Greenbelt Rd (20770). 301/345-6101.* Hrs: 11:30 am-3 pm, 5-9 pm; Fri, Sat to 10 pm; Sun 4-9 pm; early-bird dinner 5-6 pm. Closed Labor Day, Dec 25. Res accepted. Continental menu. Serv bar. Semi-a la carte: lunch $7.95-$14.95, dinner $11.95-$17.95. Specializes in seafood, veal, steak. Own desserts. Cr cds: A, C, D, DS, MC, V.

★ **SANTA FE CAFE.** *4410 Knox Rd (20740), off US 1, on Univ campus. 301/779-1345.* Hrs: 11 am-midnight. Closed Sun; Thanksgiving, Dec 25. Res accepted. Southwestern, Amer menu. Bar to 1:30 am. Semi-a la carte: lunch, dinner $3.95-$9.95. Specializes in fajitas, buffalo wings, pizzas. Outdoor dining. Casual Southwestern decor; murals, buffalo heads, Native American rugs. Cr cds: A, C, DS, MC, V.

Columbia (C-6)

(See also Baltimore)

Pop 75,883 **Elev** 402 ft **Area Code** 410 & 443 **E-mail** hctc@connext.net **Web** www.howardcountymdtour.com

Information Howard County Tourism Council, 8267 Main St, PO Box 9, Ellicott City 21041; 410/313-1900 or 800/288-TRIP

A planned city built on a tract of land larger than Manhattan Island, Columbia is comprised of 11 villages surrounding a central downtown service area. Construction of the city began in 1966.

What to See and Do

Howard County Center of African-American Culture. Contains artifacts and memorabilia depicting images of African-Americans over the last 200 years. Extensive collection of spiritual, jazz and rap music; over 2,000

books and periodicals; hands-on exhibit for children. (Daily; closed major hols) 5434 Vantage Point Rd. Phone 410/715-1921. ¢¢

Maryland Museum of African Art. Masks, sculptured figures, textiles, basketry, household items and musical instruments displayed in a 19th-century manor. (Tues-Fri, also Sun afternoons; closed major hols) 5430 Vantage Point Rd, in Historic Oakland at Town Center. Phone 410/730-7105. ¢

Annual Events

Wine in the Woods. Symphony Woods at Merriweather Post Pavilion. 2-day celebration featuring Maryland wines, gourmet food, entertainment, arts & crafts. Phone 410/313-PARK. 3rd wkend May.

Columbia Festival of Arts. Music, dance, theater, lakeside entertainment. Ten days in mid-June.

Symphony of Lights. Animated lighting displays along a 1½-mi park route. Late Nov-early Jan.

Hotels

★ ★ ★ **HILTON.** *5485 Twin Knolls Rd (21045), at jct US 29 & MD 175.* 410/997-1060; FAX 410/997-0169; res: 800/445-8667. Web www.hilton.com. 152 rms, 4 story. S, D $99-$129; each addl $10; suites $175-$250; under 18 free; wkend plans. Crib free. TV; cable (premium), VCR avail. Indoor pool; whirlpool. Coffee in rms. Restaurant 6:30 am-11 pm. Bar noon-midnight; Fri, Sat to 1 am. Ck-out 11 am. Meeting rms. Business servs avail. In-rm modem link. Exercise equipt; sauna. Microwaves avail. Cr cds: A, C, D, DS, ER, MC, V.

D ⚓ 🏃 ⚡ 🔥 SC

★ ★ **SHERATON.** *10207 Wincopin Cir (21044), opp Columbia Mall.* 410/730-3900; FAX 410/730-1290; res: 800/325-3535. E-mail sales@columbiainn.com; web www.columbiainn.com. 289 rms, 3-10 story. S $115-$130; D $130-$145; each addl $10; suites $250-$375; under 12 free; wkend plan. Crib free. Pet accepted, some restrictions; $75 refundable. TV; cable (premium). Pool; poolside serv (in season), lifeguard. Coffee in rms. Restaurant 7 am-2:30 pm, 5:30-10:30 pm. Bar 4 pm-2 am. Ck-out noon. Lndry facilities. Meeting rms. Business servs avail. In-rm modem link. Gift shop. Tennis privileges. 18-hole golf privileges, greens fee $35-$44. Health club privileges. Some bathrm phones; microwaves avail. Overlooks Lake Kittamaqundi; boat rides, entertainment on lake (summer). Cr cds: A, C, D, DS, MC, V.

D ⚓ 🏃 ⛷ ⚓ 🔥 SC

Restaurants

★ ★ **CLYDE'S.** *10221 Wincopin Circle (21044).* 410/730-2829. Hrs: 11:30-2 am; Sun from 10 am; early-bird dinner Mon-Fri 4:30-6 pm; Sun brunch to 4 pm. Closed Dec 25. Res accepted (dinner). Bar. Semi-a la carte: lunch $7-$13, dinner $10-$18. Sun brunch $6-$11. Child's meals. Specializes in seasonal dishes, salmon, crab. Own baking. Outdoor dining. Bistro atmosphere; etched and stained glass; view of lake. Totally nonsmoking. Cr cds: A, C, D, DS, MC, V.

D

★ ★ ★ **KING'S CONTRIVANCE.** *10150 Shaker Dr (21046).* 410/995-0500. Hrs: 11:30 am-2 pm, 5:30-9 pm; Fri, Sat 5:30-9:30 pm; Sun 4-8 pm. Res accepted; required Dec. Bar. Wine cellar. Semi-a la carte: lunch $8-$14, dinner $14-$26. Specializes in fresh seafood, rack of lamb. Own baking. Enclosed porch dining. Mansion built in 1900. Cr cds: A, C, DS, MC, V.

Crisfield (F-9)

(See also Pocomoke City)

Pop 2,880 **Elev** 4 ft **Area Code** 410 & 443 **Zip** 21817
Information Crisfield Area Chamber of Commerce, PO Box 292; 410/968-2500

What to See and Do

Janes Island State Park. These 3,147 acres are nearly surrounded by Chesapeake Bay and its inlets. Swimming; fishing; boat ramp (rentals). Cabins. Camping. Standard fees. Approx 2 mi NE via MD 413, then 1½ mi N on MD 358. Phone 410/968-1565.

Tyler's Cruises. The *Betty Jo Tyler* and the *Capt Tyler II* make approx one-hr cruises to Smith Island. Bus tour of the two villages comprising the island, with spare time to visit the rest of the island; lunch avail (fee). Tour length approx 4½ hours. (Memorial Day wkend-Oct) Somers Cove Marina. Phone 410/425-2771. ¢¢¢¢¢

Annual Event

National Hard Crab Derby & Fair. Cooking, crab picking, boat docking contests; crab racing; fireworks and parade. Phone 410/968-2500. Fri-Sun, Labor Day wkend.

Motel

★ ★ **PINES.** *127 N Somerset Ave (21817), 3 blks E of MD 413.* 410/968-0900. 40 rms. July-Aug: S $50-$55; D $55-$70; each addl $5; kit. units $15 addl; under 11 free; higher rates: July 4, Labor Day, special events; lower rates rest of yr. TV; cable. Pool. Restaurant nearby. Ck-out 11 am. Gift shop. Picnic area. In scenic, wooded section. Cr cds: C.

⚓ ⚓ 🔥 SC

Cumberland (A-2)

Settled 1750 **Pop** 23,706 **Elev** 688 ft **Area Code** 240 & 301 **Zip** 21502
E-mail tourism@netbiz.net **Web** www.mdmountainside.com
Information Allegany County Convention & Visitors Bureau, Mechanic & Harrison Sts; 301/777-5905 or 800/50-VISIT

Far to the west in the state, Cumberland is nestled between Pennsylvania and West Virginia. The Potomac River and its tributary, Wills Creek, flow peaceably by this onetime western outpost of the colonies.

British General Edward Braddock was sent here to conquer the French and Native Americans in 1755; unprepared for the wilderness, he met with defeat and death. George Washington, who defended the town in that period, felt the main east-west route would pass through Cumberland eventually. In 1833 the National Road (US 40 Alternate) made the town a supply terminus for overland commerce. The road was extended farther west, the B & O Railroad reached here in 1842, and eight years later came the Chesapeake and Ohio Canal (see CHESAPEAKE AND OHIO CANAL NATIONAL HISTORICAL PARK), bringing prosperous business. Today's economy no longer depends on industry alone but includes services and recreational facilities.

What to See and Do

Dans Mountain State Park. 481 acres. Nearby Dans Rock affords a panoramic view of surrounding region from a height of 2,898 ft. Swimming pool (fee); fishing. Picnicking. Playground. Hiking. Sledding. 10 mi W on I-68, then 8 mi S on MD 36, 2 mi SE of Lonaconing. Schedule varies, Phone 301/463-5564 or 301/777-2139.

Fort Cumberland Trail. Walking trail covers several city blocks downtown around the site of Ft Cumberland. Includes boundary markers, narrative plaques.

George Washington's Headquarters (ca 1755). His first military headquarters. Taped narration. In Riverside Park, downtown, on Greene St. **Free**

Green Ridge State Forest. These 38,811 acres of forest land stretch across mountains of Western Maryland and occupy portions of Town Hill, Polish Mt and Green Ridge Mt. Abundant wildlife. Fishing. Boat launch; canoeing. Hiking trails. Camping. Winter sports. C & O Canal runs through here into 3,118-ft Paw-Paw Tunnel. 21 mi E off I-68 at exit 64. Phone 301/478-3124.

History House (ca 1867). Restored 18-rm Victorian house with nine period rooms; medical instruments, costumes; research room. (June-Oct, daily exc Mon; rest of yr, Tues-Sat) 218 Washington St, in Victorian Historic District. Phone 301/777-8678. ¢¢

Rocky Gap State Park. Mountain scenery around 243-acre lake with three swimming beaches. Swimming; fishing; boating (electric motors only; rentals). Nature, hiking trails. Picnicking, cafe. Improved camping (res accepted 1 yr in advance). Winter activities. Resort; 18-hole golf course. Standard fees. (See ANNUAL EVENTS) 6 mi E on I-68, exit 50. Phone 301/777-2138 (camping) or 301/777-2139. Per person ¢

The Narrows. Picturesque 1,000-ft gap through Alleghenies (US 40A) used by pioneers on their way to the West.

Toll Gate House (1836). Built to collect tolls from users of Cumberland Road (National Road); only remaining toll house in state; restored. (Late May-late Oct, Sat & Sun afternoons; other times by appt) Approx 6 mi W on US 40A, in La Vale. Phone 301/777-5905. ¢

Western Maryland Station Center. This 1913 railroad station houses Canal Place Authority, Industrial and Transportation Museum; C & O Canal National Historical Park Visitors Center and Allegany County Visitors Center. (Daily; closed most major hols) Canal St. Phone 301/777-5905. **Free** is also the departure point for

Western Maryland Scenic Railroad. Excursion train makes scenic trip 17 mi to Frostburg and back. (May-Oct, daily exc Mon; Nov-mid-Dec, wkends) For schedule and fees phone 301/759-4400 or 800/TRAIN-50.

Annual Events

Agricultural Expo & Fair. Allegany County Fairgrounds. Poultry, livestock, carnival, entertainment. Phone 301/729-1200. Mid-July.

Drumfest. Greenway Ave Stadium. Drum and bugle corps championship. Phone 301/777-8325. Last Sat July.

Rocky Gap Music Festival. Allegany College. Features bluegrass and country music; children's activities, crafts, workshops. Phone 888/762-5942. Fri-Sun, 1st wkend Aug.

Street Rod Roundup. 6 mi S on MD 220, at fairgrounds. Hundreds of pre-1950 hot-rods on display and in competitions. Phone 301/729-5555. Labor Day wkend.

Motels

★★★ **BEST WESTERN BRADDOCK MOTOR INN.** *1268 National Hwy (21502), 6 mi W on US 40, at jct MD 53; I-68 exit 39 or 40. 301/729-3300; res: 800/528-1234; res: 800/296-6006.* 108 rms, 1-2 story. S $49-$60; D $55-$66; each addl $6; suites $82-$102; under 18 free. TV; cable (premium), VCR avail (movies). Indoor pool; whirlpool, poolside serv. Restaurant 7 am-9 pm. Rm serv. Bar 4:30 pm-midnight; Fri, Sat to 1 am; closed Sun. Ck-out 11 am. Meeting rm. Business servs avail. In-rm modem link. Sundries. Airport transportation. Exercise equipt; sauna. Game rm. Cr cds: A, C, D, DS, MC, V.

D 🏊 🏋 ⌧ 🔥 SC

★★ **COMFORT INN.** *11100 New Georges Creek Rd Sw (21532), 1 mi N of US 40 & I-68, exit 34. 301/689-2050; FAX 301/689-2050; res: 800/638-7949; res: 800/221-2222.* 100 rms, 2 story. May-Oct: S $66-$78; D $71-$83; each addl $5; suites $86; under 18 free; wkly rates; lower rates rest of yr. Crib free. Pet accepted; $10. TV; cable. Complimentary continental bkfst. Restaurant nearby. Ck-out 11 am. Meeting rms. Busi-

ness servs avail. In-rm modem link. 18-hole golf privileges. X-country ski 15 mi. Exercise rm. Pool privileges. Some in-rm whirlpools. Picnic tables. Cr cds: A, C, D, DS, ER, JCB, MC, V.

D 🐾 🏊 🏋 ✈ ⌧ 🔥 SC

✓★ **SUPER 8 MOTEL.** *1301 National Hwy (21502), I-68 exit 39 W. 301/729-6265; FAX 301/729-6265; res: 800/800-8000.* 63 rms, 3 story. S $46.98; D $56.98; each addl $8; suites $64.98-$69.98; under 12 free. Crib free. TV; cable. Complimentary continental bkfst. Restaurant nearby. Ck-out 11 am. Meeting rms. Business servs avail. Cr cds: A, C, D, DS, MC, V.

D ⌧ 🔥 SC

Motor Hotel

★★ **HOLIDAY INN.** *100 S George St (21502), I-68 exit 43C. 301/724-8800; FAX 301/724-4001; res: 800/877-4426.* E-mail cumberlands2@crownam. 130 rms, 6 story. S, D $89; under 18 free. Crib free. Pet accepted. TV; cable (premium), VCR avail. Pool; lifeguard. Restaurant 6:30 am-2 pm, 5-10 pm; Sun from 4 pm. Rm serv. Bar noon-midnight; Sun from 4 pm; entertainment. Ck-out noon. Meeting rms. Business center. In-rm modem link. Sundries. Airport transportation. Cr cds: A, C, D, DS, JCB, MC, V.

D 🐾 🏊 ⌧ 🔥 SC 🏋

Inn

★★★ **INN AT WALNUT BOTTOM.** *120 Greene St (21502), I-68 exit 43A. 301/777-0003; FAX 301/777-8288; res: 800/286-9718.* 12 rms, 4 share bath, 2-3 story, 2 suites. S, D $79-$120; each addl $15; suites $120-$180. Crib avail. TV; cable (premium). Complimentary full bkfst. Restaurant (see OXFORD HOUSE). Ck-out 11 am, ck-in 3 pm. Business servs avail. Health club privileges. Two buildings (1820, 1890). Antiques; period reproductions. Totally nonsmoking. Cr cds: A, C, DS, MC, V.

⌧ 🔥 SC

Restaurants

★★★ **AU PETIT PARIS.** *86 E Main St (21532), I-68, exit 34. 301/689-8946.* Hrs: 6-9:30 pm. Closed Sun, Mon; major hols. Res accepted. French menu. Bar 5:30 pm-midnight. Wine list. Semi-a la carte: dinner $10.50-$35. Child's meals. Specialties: coq au vin, Dover sole. Tableside preparation. Cr cds: A, C, D, DS, MC, V.

D ⌧

★★★ **OXFORD HOUSE.** *(See Inn at Walnut Bottom) 301/777-7101.* Hrs: 11 am-2:30 pm, 5-9:30 pm; Mon, Tues, Sat 5-9:30 pm. Closed Sun; also major hols. Res accepted. Continental menu. Bar. Semi-a la carte: lunch $5-$10, dinner $10.95-$18.95. Specialties: romaine-wrapped salmon, filet of pork, Jaye's gin & juniper gravlax. Own baking. Parking. Victorian decor. Totally nonsmoking. Cr cds: A, C, D, DS, MC, V.

D

✓★★ **WARNER'S GERMAN RESTAURANT.** *McMullen Hwy (21505), US 220S, off I-68. 301/729-2361.* Hrs: 11 am-9 pm; Fri, Sat to 10 pm; Sun noon-7 pm. Closed Mon; Jan 1, July 4, Dec 25. German, Amer menu. Bar. Semi-a la carte: lunch $3.50-$7.95, dinner $8.95-$13.95. Child's meals. Specialties: sauerbraten, bratwurst, bienenstich. Outdoor dining. Old World Bavarian atmosphere; costumed waitresses. Family-owned. Totally nonsmoking. Cr cds: A, C, D, MC, V.

Easton (D-8)

(See also Cambridge, St Michaels)

Settled 1682 **Pop** 9,372 **Elev** 28 ft **Area Code** 410 & 443 **Zip** 21601
Web www.talbotchamber.org
Information Talbot County Chamber of Commerce, PO Box 1366;
410/822-4606

What to See and Do

Historical Society of Talbot County. A 3-gallery museum in a renovated early commercial building; changing exhibits, museum shop. Historic houses: 1810 Federal town house, 1700s Quaker cabinetmaker's cottage, period gardens; tours. (Daily exc Mon) 25 S Washington St. Phone 410/822-0773. Museum **¢¢**; Houses **¢¢**

The Academy of the Arts. Housed in renovated 1820s schoolhouse, Academy exhibits works of local & national artists in permanent collection. Also hosts over 200 visual & performing arts programs annually. (Daily exc Sun) 106 South St. Phone 410/822-0455 or -ARTS (recording). **¢**

Third Haven Friends Meeting House (1682-1684). One of the oldest frame-construction houses of worship in US. (Daily) 405 S Washington St. Phone 410/822-0293. **Free**

Tuckahoe State Park. A 60-acre lake and Tuckahoe Creek provide a secluded atmosphere in this 3,498-acre park. The Adkins Arboretum, 500 acres, propagates trees, plants and shrubs indigenous to Maryland. Fishing, hunting; boating. Hiking. Picnicking. Standard fees. 5 mi N of Queen Anne, off MD 404. For schedule Phone 410/820-1668.

Annual Events

Eastern Shore Chamber Music Festival. Various locations. World-class chamber music; young people's concert. Phone 410/819-0380. 2 wks June.

Tuckahoe Steam & Gas Show and Reunion. 5 mi N via US 50, opp Woodlawn Memorial Park. Old steam and gas engines; antique tractors and cars. Demonstrations in soap and broom making; flour milling. Gas and steam wheat threshing; sawmill working; flea market, crafts, parade, entertainment. Phone 410/643-6123 or 410/820-9868 (during event). Usually wkend after July 4.

Waterfowl Festival. Downtown and various locations in and around town. Exhibits on waterfowl; pictures, carvings; food. Phone 410/822-4606. 1st or 2nd wkend Nov.

Motels

✓ ★ ★ **COMFORT INN.** *8523 Ocean Gtwy (21601). 410/820-8333; FAX 410/820-8436; res: 800/228-5150.* 84 units, 2 story, 15 suites. Mid-Apr-Nov: S, D $79-$99; each addl $8; suites $105; under 18 free; higher rates special events; lower rates rest of yr. Crib free. TV; cable (premium). Pool; whirlpool. Complimentary continental bkfst. Restaurant nearby. Ck-out 11 am. Meeting rms. Business servs avail. In-rm modem link. Sundries. Some refrigerators; microwaves avail. Picnic tables. Cr cds: A, C, D, DS, MC, V.

🅳 ⌘ ▦ 🔥 SC

★ **DAYS INN.** *7018 Ocean Gateway (21601). 410/822-4600; FAX 410/820-9723; res: 800/329-7466.* 80 rms, 2 story. Apr-Nov: S $69-$89; D, suites $79-$102; under 18 free; higher rates Waterfowl Festival; lower rates rest of yr. Crib free. Pet accepted, some restrictions; $8. TV; cable (premium). Complimentary continental bkfst. Ck-out 11 am. Pool; wading pool. Some refrigerators. Cr cds: A, C, D, DS, ER, JCB, MC, V.

🅳 🐾 ⌘ ▦ 🔥 SC

Motor Hotel

★ ★ **HOLIDAY INN EXPRESS.** *8561 Ocean Gateway (21601). 410/819-6500; FAX 410/819-6505; res: 877/327-8661.* Web www.holiday-inn.com. 73 rms, 4 story. Apr-Nov: S, D $109-$129; each addl $8; under 18 free; lower rates rest of yr. Crib free. Pet accepted. TV; cable (premium). Indoor pool; whirlpool. Complimentary continental bkfst. Restaurant adj open 24 hrs. Ck-out 11 am. Meeting rms. Business servs avail. Exercise equipt. Cr cds: A, C, D, DS, MC, V.

🅳 🐾 ⌘ 🏃 ▦ 🔥 SC

Hotel

★ ★ ★ **TIDEWATER INN & CONFERENCE CENTER.** *101 E Dover St (21601). 410/822-1300; FAX 410/820-8847; res: 800/237-8775.* Web www.tidewaterinn.com. 114 rms, 4 story. June-Nov: S $90-$175; D $90-$190; each addl $10; under 13 free; wkly, wkend rates; package plans; higher rates Waterfowl Festival; lower rates rest of yr. Crib free. TV; cable (premium), VCR avail. Pool; poolside serv. Restaurant (see HUNTER'S TAVERN). Bar 11-2 am; entertainment Fri, Sat, Sun brunch. Ck-out noon. Meeting rms. Business center. In-rm modem link. Free valet parking. Airport transportation. Health club privileges. Restored turn-of-the-century hotel. Cr cds: A, C, D, DS, MC, V.

🅳 ⌘ ▦ 🔥 SC 🏃

Inns

★ ★ ★ **ASHBY 1663.** *27448 Ashby Dr (21601). 410/822-4235; FAX 410/822-9288; res: 800/458-3622.* Web www.ashby1663.com. 12 rms, 1-3 story, 5 suites. 9 rm phones. Apr-Nov (2-day min): S, D $265-$475; suites $215-$595; lower rates rest of yr. Children over 12 yrs only. TV; VCR avail. Pool; whirlpool. Sauna. Complimentary full bkfst; afternoon refreshments. Ck-out noon, ck-in 3 pm. Luggage handling. Lighted tennis. Exercise equipt. Some in rm whirlpools. Game rm. Lawn games. Some balconies. Georgian colonial manor house built in 1858; on Miles River. Totally nonsmoking. Cr cds: A, C, MC, V.

⛵ 🎿 ⌘ 🏃 ▦ 🔥

✓ ★ ★ **BISHOPS HOUSE.** *214 Goldsborough St (21601). 410/820-7290; FAX 410/820-7290.* E-mail bishopshouse@skipjack.blue crab.org; web www.traveldata.com/inns/data/bishop.html. 5 rms, 3 story. No rm phone. No elvtr. 2-day min: S $110; D $120; lower rates mid-wk. Children over 13 yrs only. TV; cable (premium) in main rm. Complimentary full bkfst. Restaurant nearby. Ck-out 11 am, ck-in 4-5 pm. Tennis privileges. Golf privileges. Some whirlpools, fireplaces. Built in 1880; antiques, toys, porcelains. Totally nonsmoking. Cr cds: C.

🏃 🎿 ▦ 🔥

★ ★ ★ **ROBERT MORRIS INN.** *314 N Morris St (21654), 11 mi SW on MD 333. 410/226-5111; FAX 410/226-5744.* Web www.robertmorrisinn.com. 35 rms, 13 rms with showers only, 2-3 story, 2 kit. cottages. No rm phones. S, D $100-$240. Children over 10 yrs only. Dining rm 8-10 am, noon-9 pm; winter hrs vary. Bar noon-10 pm. Ck-out noon, ck-in 3 pm. Business servs avail. Golf privileges. Private patios, balconies. Historic house (1710) built by ships' carpenters. Private beach on river. Totally nonsmoking. Cr cds: A, C, MC, V.

🅳 ⛵ 🏃 ▦ 🔥

Restaurants

★ ★ ★ **HUNTER'S TAVERN.** *(See Tidewater Inn Hotel) 410/822-1300.* Web www.tidewaterinn.com. Hrs: 7 am-10 pm; early-bird dinner Mon-Fri 4-6 pm; Sun brunch 9:30 am-2 pm. Res accepted (dinner). Bar; Fri, Sat 11-2 am. Semi-a la carte: bkfst $4.95-$10.50, lunch $6.95-$12.50, dinner $12.95-$24.95. Sun brunch $15.70-$18.80. Specializes in Chesapeake Bay seafood, prime rib, crab cakes. Valet parking. Outdoor dining. Waterfowl theme; carvings and murals. Cr cds: A, C, D, DS, MC, V.

🅳 SC

★ **LEGAL SPIRITS.** *42 E Dover St (21601). 410-820-0033.* Hrs: 11:30 am-10 pm; Fri, Sat to 11 pm; Sun noon-9 pm. Closed most major hols. Bar. Semi-a la carte: lunch $4.25-$9.95, dinner $6.95-$17. Specializes in monster salads, crab cakes, regional seafood. Located in restored 1922 vaudeville theater. Cr cds: A, C, D, DS, MC, V.

Elkton (B-9)

(See also Havre De Grace)

Pop 9,073 **Elev** 30 ft **Area Code** 410 **Zip** 21921
Information Elkton Chamber of Commerce, 101 E Main St; 410/398-1640

What to See and Do

Elk Neck State Forest. Has 3,165 acres. Forest wildlife, particularly white-tailed deer, can be seen; food plots have been established. Hunting. Hiking, bridle trail. Picnicking. Primitive camping. Shooting range. Winter sports. Pets allowed. 4 mi W off MD 7, near North East. Phone 410/287-5675.

Elk Neck State Park. Park has 2,188 acres of sandy beaches, marshlands and heavily wooded bluffs. Swimming; fishing; boating (launch, rentals). Miniature golf (fee). Hiking and nature trails. Picnicking. Concession. Winter sports. Camping; cabins. Standard fees. 14 mi SW via US 40, MD 272, near North East. Phone 410/287-5333.

Motels

✓ ★ **ELKTON LODGE.** *200 Belle Hill Rd (21921), I-95 exit 109A. 410/398-9400; FAX 410/398-9579.* 32 rms, 2 story. S $35-$40; D $42-$50; each addl $4; under 15 free. Crib $5. TV; cable (premium). Restaurant nearby. Ck-out 11 am. Refrigerators; some microwaves. Cr cds: A, C, D, DS, MC, V.

★ **SUTTON MOTEL.** *405 E Pulaski Hwy (21921). 410/398-3830.* 11 rms, shower only. No rm phones. S $31; D $34-$36; each addl $3. Crib $1. Pet accepted, some restrictions. TV. Restaurant nearby. Ck-out 11 am. Cr cds: C.

Inns

★★ **INN AT THE CANAL.** *104 Bohemia Ave (21915), 7 mi S on MD 213. 410/885-5995; FAX 410/885-3585.* 7 rms, 3 story. Apr-Nov: D $75-$130; each addl $25; 2-day min some hols; lower rates rest of yr. Children over 10 yrs only. TV; cable (premium). Complimentary full bkfst; afternoon refreshments. Restaurant nearby. Ck-out 11 am, ck-in 2 pm. Business servs avail. Lawn games. Mansion built 1870; antiques. Overlooks Chesapeake & Delaware Canal. Totally nonsmoking. Cr cds: A, C, D, DS, MC, V.

★ **KITTY KNIGHT HOUSE.** *MD 213 (21930), 20 mi S on MD 213, turn right after drawbridge. 410/648-5777; FAX 410/648-5729.* 11 rms, 3 story. D $75-$125; each addl $10. TV; cable. Complimentary continental bkfst. Dining rm noon-9 pm; Fri, Sat to 10:30 pm. Ck-out 11 am, ck-in 2 pm. Built ca 1755. Antiques. Cr cds: A, C, MC, V.

Restaurant

★★ **SCHAEFER'S CANAL HOUSE.** *208 Bank St (21915), 6 mi S on MD 213. 410/885-2200.* Hrs: 8 am-10 pm; wkend hrs may vary; Sun brunch 10 am-3 pm. Closed Dec 25. Res accepted Sun-Fri. Bar. Semi-a la carte: bkfst $3-$9, lunch $5-$24, dinner $18-$32. Sun brunch $14.95. Child's meals. Specializes in seafood. Outdoor dining. Nautical decor; view of canal. Cr cds: A, C, MC, V.

Ellicott City (B-6)

(See also Baltimore)

Settled 1772 **Pop** 41,396 **Elev** 233 ft **Area Code** 410
E-mail hctc@connext.net **Web** www.howardcountymdtour.com
Information Howard County Tourism Council, 8267 Main St, PO Box 9, 21041; 410/313-1900 or 800/288-TRIP

The town was originally named Ellicott Mills for the three Quaker brothers who founded it as the site of their gristmill. Charles Carroll of Carrollton, whose Doughoregan Manor can still be seen nearby, lent financial help to the Ellicotts and the town eventually became the site of ironworks, rolling mills and the first railroad terminus in the US. The famous Tom Thumb locomotive race with a horse took place near here. Many of the town's original stone houses and log cabins, on hills above the Patapsco River, have been preserved.

What to See and Do

Cider Mill Farm. Cider press operating most days. Bushels of pumpkins, apples and other foods and produce. Hayrides, petting zoo, pony rides, storytelling, crafts, contests, apple-butter making. (Apr-May & mid-Sept-Dec, daily) 5012 Landing Rd, Elkridge, 5 mi SE via MD 29 and MD 103, Ilchester Rd to Landing Rd. Phone 410/788-9595. ¢¢

Ellicott City B & O Railroad Station Museum. Two restored buildings (ca 1830 and 1885) house historic rooms, RR displays and memorabilia, operating HO model RR of the first 13 mi of the B & O track, photographs, dioramas. Full size B & O caboose and museum store. Civil War reenactments of military and civilian life, June-Sept. (May-Sept, daily exc Tues; rest of yr, Fri-Mon) 2711 Maryland Ave, at Main St. Phone 410/461-1944 (recording). ¢¢

Patapsco Valley State Park. Four of the recreation areas located within the 15,000 acres sprawling along the Patapsco River are as follows. Area 1: Glen Artney via South St from MD 1, in Relay; Baltimore County. Picnicking, fishing. Area 2: Hilton Ave, via Rolling Rd, S of Frederick Rd, in Catonsville; Baltimore County. Picnicking, camping. Area 3: Hollofield, adj to US 40, near Ellicott City; Howard County. Scenic overlook, camping. Pets allowed (in camping area). Area 4: McKeldin Area, off Marriottsville Rd; Carroll County. Picnicking, fishing. Hiking trails & pavilions available in all areas. Golden Age Passport (see MAKING THE MOST OF YOUR TRIP). NE and SE of town; 5 mi from I-695 exits 12 and 15, 50 yds from I-195 exit 1. Phone 410/461-5005. ¢¢

Annual Events

Maryland Sheep & Wool Festival. In West Friendship. Sheep breeds and other wool-bearing animals; sheep dog demonstration. Craftsmen sell products related to sheep and wool; spinning, weaving, and sheep-shearing contests; wool dyeing; entertainment. 1st wkend May.

Howard County Fair. In West Friendship. Rides, entertainment, concessions, 4-H exhibits, horse-pulling contests and other events. Mid-Aug.

Restaurant nearby. Ck-out 11 am. Refrigerators; some microwaves. Cr cds: A, C, D, DS, MC, V.

Hotel

★★ **TURF VALLEY HOTEL AND COUNTRY CLUB.** *2700 Turf Valley Rd (21042), approx 8 mi W via US 40.* 410/465-1500; FAX 410/465-8280; res: 800/666-8873; res: 888/833-8873. E-mail tvrcc@aol.com; web www.turfvalley.com. 223 rms, 7 story, 6 villas. Mar-Nov: S $120; D $135; each addl $15; suites $130-$415; villas $650-$700; under 12 free; wkend rates; lower rates rest of yr. Crib free. TV; cable (premium). Indoor/outdoor pool; whirlpool, poolside serv, lifeguard. Restaurant 6:30 am-10 pm. Bar 4:30-11 pm; Fri, Sat to 2 am; entertainment Fri-Sun. Ck-out noon. Convention facilities. Business servs avail. In-rm modem link. Gift shop. Tennis. 54-hole golf, greens fee $37-$52, pro, putting green, driving range. Exercise equipt; steam rm. Spa. Cr cds: A, C, D, DS, MC, V.

Restaurants

★★ **CRAB SHANTY.** *3410 Plumtree Dr & US 40W (21042).* 410/465-9660. Hrs: 11:30 am-2:30 pm, 5-10 pm; Mon, Tues to 9 pm; Sun 2-9 pm. Bar. Semi-a la carte: lunch $2.95-$9.50, dinner $8.75-$18.95. Child's meals. Specializes in seafood. Cr cds: A, C, D, DS, MC, V.

★ **SIDESTREETS.** *8069 Tiber Alley (21043).* 410/461-5577. Hrs: 11:30 am-10 pm; Fri, Sat to 11 pm; Sun 11 am-9 pm; Sun brunch to 2 pm. Closed Thanksgiving, Dec 25. Res accepted Fri, Sat dinner. Seafood menu. Bar. Semi-a la carte: lunch, dinner $5.95-$19.95. Sun brunch $2.95-$7.95. Specializes in Chesapeake Bay seafood. Eclectic decor. Totally nonsmoking. Cr cds: A, C, DS, MC, V.

★★★ **TERSIGUEL'S.** *8293 Main St (21043).* 410/465-4004. Hrs: 11:30 am-2:30 pm, 5-9 pm; Fri to 10 pm; Sat 11:30 am-3:30 pm, 5-10 pm; Sun 11:30 am-3:30 pm, 5-9 pm. Closed Dec 25. Res accepted. French menu. Bar. Wine cellar. Semi-a la carte: lunch $8.95-$19.95, dinner $14.95-$26.95. Prix fixe: lunch $15.95-$25.95, dinner $27.95-$37.95. Specialities: rack of lamb, châteaubriand pour deux. Historic bldg; mementos from Brittany, France. Totally nonsmoking. Cr cds: A, C, D, DS, MC, V.

Emmitsburg (A-5)

(See also Frederick, Hagerstown, Thurmont)

Settled 1785 **Pop** 1,688 **Elev** 449 ft **Area Code** 301 **Zip** 21727
E-mail fredtour@erols.com **Web** www.co.frederick.md.us/tour/tourpage.html
Information Tourism Council of Frederick County, 19 E Church St, Frederick 21701; 301/663-8687 or 800/999-3613

What to See and Do

Mount Saint Mary's College and Seminary (1808). (1,800 students) Oldest independent Catholic college in US. Liberal arts and sciences. 3 mi S on US 15. Phone 301/447-6122. Near campus is the

National Shrine Grotto of Lourdes. Replica of the French shrine is ⅓ the size of the original; oldest replica in the Western Hemisphere. Pangborn Memorial Campanile, constructed of native stone and located at the entrance, is 120 ft tall and is surmounted by a 25-ft bronze gold-leaf statue of the Blessed Virgin Mary. (Apr-Oct, daily; rest of yr, daily exc Mon; closed last 2 wks Jan) **Free**

⭐ **Seton Shrine Center.** National Shrine of Saint Elizabeth Ann Seton, first US female saint, canonized 1975. Includes Stone House (1809), White House (1810), home in which Mother Seton died; slide presentation, basilica, museum and cemetery. (May-Nov, daily; rest of yr, daily exc Mon; closed Dec 25; also last 2 wks Jan) 333 S Seton Ave. Phone 301/447-6606. **Free**

Inn

★★★ **ANTRIM 1844 INC.** *30 Trevanion Rd (21787), approx 10 mi E on MD 140.* 410/756-6812; FAX 410/756-2744; res: 800/858-1844. 21 rms, 2 with shower only, 3 story, 2 suites. No rm phones. S, D $150-$300; suites $300; ski, golf plans; 2-day min wkends, hols; higher rates Dec 31. Pool; whirlpools. Complimentary full bkfst. Complimentary coffee in rms. Restaurant (see ANTRIM 1844). Ck-out 11 am, ck-in 3 pm. Luggage handling. Business servs avail. Airport transportation. Tennis. Putting green. Croquet. Downhill ski 14 mi; x-country 15 mi. Lawn games. Many fireplaces, in-rm whirlpools. Some balconies. Antebellum plantation (1844) built on 25 acres. Elegant antique furnishings, 3-story spiral staircase. Formal gardens and gazebo. Cr cds: A, C, D, DS, MC, V.

Restaurant

★★★ **ANTRIM 1844.** *(See Antrim Inn 1844)* 800/858-1844. Sittings: 7-7:30 pm (hors d'oeuvres served at 6:30 pm). Closed Jan 1. Res required. French, Amer menu. Bar. Wine cellar. Prix fixe: $55. Specialties: wild rockfish with scallop mousse, black Angus tenderloin. Outdoor dining. Refined dining in elegant atmosphere; fireplace, piano. Cr cds: A, C, D, DS, MC, V.

Frederick (B-5)

(See also Hagerstown, Thurmont)

Settled 1745 **Pop** 40,148 **Elev** 290 ft **Area Code** 240 & 301 **Zip** 21701
E-mail fredtour@erols.com **Web** www.co.frederick.md.us/tour/tourpage.html
Information Tourism Council of Frederick County, 19 E Church St; 301/663-8687 or 800/999-3613

Home of dauntless Barbara Fritchie, who reportedly spoke her mind to Stonewall Jackson and his "rebel hordes," Frederick is a town filled with history. Named for Frederick Calvert, 6th Lord Baltimore, it is the seat of one of America's richest agricultural counties. Francis Scott Key and Chief Justice Roger Brooke Taney made their homes here. Court House Square was the scene of several important events during the Revolutionary War, including the famed protest against the Stamp Act, in which an effigy of the stamp distributor was burned.

During the Civil War, Frederick was a focal point for strategic operations by both sides. In the campaign of 1862 the Confederacy's first invasions of the North were made at nearby South Mountain and Sharpsburg, at Antietam Creek. Wounded men by the thousands were cared for here. Troop movements continued for the duration of the war; cavalry skirmishes took place in the streets. In July 1864, the town was forced to pay a $200,000 ransom to Confederate General Jubal Early before he fought the Battle of Monocacy a few miles south. Frederick today is an educational center, tourist attraction, location of Fort Detrick army installation and home of diversified small industry. A 33-block area has been designated a Historic District.

What to See and Do

Barbara Fritchie House and Museum. Exhibits include quilts, clothing made by Fritchie, her rocker and Bible, the bed in which she died and other items; 10-min film; also garden. (Apr-Sept, Thurs-Mon; Oct-Nov, Sat & Sun) 154 W Patrick St. Phone 301/698-0630. ¢¢

Brunswick Museum. Furnishings and clothing interpret life in turn-of-the-century railroad town; large HO model train exhibit; gift shop. Special events held on selected wkends. (June-Sept, Thurs-Sun; Apr-May & Oct-late Dec, Sat & Sun; limited hrs, Phone 301/834-7100. ¢¢

Gambrill State Park. Park has 1,136 acres with two developed areas. Fishing. Nature, hiking trails. Picnicking. Tent & trailer sites (standard fees). Tea room. Two overlooks. (Schedule varies, Phone 301/791-4767.

Historical Society of Frederick County Museum. House, built in early 1800s, shows both Georgian and Federal details; leaded side and fan-lights, Doric columns inside, double porches in rear and boxwood gardens. Portraits of early Frederick residents. Genealogy library (Tues-Sat). (Mon-Sat; also Sun afternoons) 24 E Church St. Phone 301/663-1188. Museum tour ¢

Horse-drawn carriage tours. (Daily, by appt) Phone 301/694-RIDE.

Monocacy National Battlefield. On July 9, 1864, Union General Lew Wallace with 5,000 men delayed General Jubal Early and his 23,000 Confederate soldiers for 24 hours, during which Grant was able to reinforce, and save, Washington, DC. New Jersey, Vermont, Pennsylvania and Confederate monuments mark the area. 3 mi S on MD 355. For tour information phone 301/662-3515. **Free**

Mt Olivet Cemetery (1852). Monuments mark graves of Francis Scott Key and Barbara Fritchie. Flag flies over Key's grave. S end of Market St.

Roger Brooke Taney Home (1799) **and Francis Scott Key Museum.** Chief Justice of Supreme Court from 1835-1864, Taney was chosen by Andrew Jackson to succeed John Marshall. He swore in seven presidents, including Abraham Lincoln, and issued the famous Dred Scott Decision. He is buried in the cemetery of St John's Catholic Church at E 3rd & East Sts. (Apr-Oct, wkends) 121 S Bentz St. Phone 301/663-8687. ¢¢

Rose Hill Manor Children's Museum. Hands-on exhibits of 19th-century family life; carriage museum; colonial herb and fragrant gardens; farm museum; blacksmith shop; log cabin. (Apr-Oct, daily; Nov, Sat & Sun only) 1611 N Market St. Phone 301/694-1648 or 301/694-1650. ¢¢

Schifferstadt (1756). Fine example of German-colonial farmhouse architecture. Tours of architectural museum. Gift shop. (Apr-mid Dec, daily exc Mon; closed Thanksgiving) 1110 Rosemont Ave. Phone 301/663-3885. ¢

Trinity Chapel (1763). Graceful colonial church; Francis Scott Key was baptized here. Steeple houses town clock and ten-bell chimes; chimes play every Sat evening. W Church St, near N Market St. The chapel is now used as Sunday School for

Evangelical Reformed Church. United Church of Christ (1848). Opp Trinity Chapel. A Grecian-style building modeled after the Erechtheum, with two towers resembling Lanterns of Demosthenes. Here Stonewall Jackson slept through pro-Union sermon before Battle of Antietam; Barbara Fritchie was a member. Phone 301/662-2762.

Annual Events

Beyond the Garden Gates Tour. Downtown. Tour historic and contemporary gardens. Phone 301/663-8687. Late May.

Lotus Blossom Festival. Lilypons Water Gardens, 6800 Lilypons Rd, 10 mi S via MD 85. Endless blooms of water lilies and lotus, water garden; arts & crafts, food, entertainment, lectures. Phone 301/874-5133. First double-digit wkend July.

Great Frederick Fair. Frederick county fair. Phone 301/663-5895. Mid-late Sept.

New Market Days. 8 mi E, in New Market. Nostalgic revival of the atmosphere of a 19th-century village; costumed guides, period crafts and events; held in New Market, the town dedicated to being the "Antiques Capital of Maryland." Phone 301/831-6755. Last full wkend Sept.

Fall Festival. Rose Hill Manor. Apple-butter making, music, crafts demonstrations, tractor pull, hay rides, country cooking. Early Oct.

Motel

✓★★ **DAYS INN.** 5646 Buckeystown Pike (21704). 301/694-6600; FAX 301/831-4242; res: 800/329-7466. 119 rms, 2 story. Apr-Oct: S, D $56-$75; under 18 free; lower rates rest of yr. Crib free. TV; cable (pre-

mium). Pool. Playground. Complimentary continental bkfst. Ck-out noon. Meeting rm. Business servs avail. Sundries. Refrigerators, microwaves avail. Cr cds: A, C, D, DS, MC, V.

D ⌇ ⛷ ☼ SC

Motor Hotels

★★ **FAIRFIELD INN.** 5220 Westview Dr (21703). 301/631-2000; FAX 301/631-2100. 105 rms, 3 story. May-mid-Oct: S $69-$82; D $69-$87; higher rates special events. Crib free. TV; cable (premium). Complimentary continental bkfst. Ck-out noon. Business servs avail. Sundries. Exercise equipt. Indoor pool; whirlpool. Health club privileges. Some refrigerators, microwaves. Cr cds: A, C, D, DS, MC, V.

D ⌇ ⛷ ☼ ☼

★★ **HAMPTON INN.** 5311 Buckeystown Pike (21704). 301/698-2500; FAX 301/695-8735; res: 800/426-7866. 160 rms, 6 story. S, D $69-$100; suites $150; under 18 free. Crib free. Pet accepted, some restrictions; fee. TV; cable (premium). Pool; lifeguard. Complimentary continental bkfst. Ck-out noon. Coin lndry. Meeting rms. Business servs avail. In-rm modem link. Sundries. Valet serv. Exercise equipt. Health club privileges. Some refrigerators; microwaves avail. Cr cds: A, C, D, DS, MC, V.

D ⛷ ⌇ ☼ ☼ ☼ SC

Inns

★★ **CATOCTIN INN.** 3619 Buckeystown Pike (21717), 5 mi S on I-270, exit 31B. 301/831-8102; FAX 301/874-2026; res: 800/730-5550. E-mail catoctin@fred.net; web www.catoctininn.fred.net. 20 rms, 3 story, 3 cottages. S, D $85-$125; each addl $10; cottages $150; under 2 free; wkly rates; min stay hols; higher rates: wkends, fall foliage. Crib free. TV; cable (premium), VCR avail (movies). Complimentary full bkfst. Complimentary coffee in rms. Restaurant nearby. Ck-out noon, ck-in by appt. Luggage handling. Meeting rms. Business servs avail. Lawn games. Refrigerators. House built in 1780s; parlour with antique sofas, fireplaces. Cr cds: A, C, D, DS, MC, V.

D ☼ ☼ SC

★★★ **INN AT BUCKEYSTOWN.** 3521 Buckeystown Pike (21717), 5 mi S on MD 85. 301/874-5755; FAX 301/831-1355; res: 800/272-1190. Web www.innbrook.com/buckeystown. 5 rms, 3 story. MAP: S, D $200-$225; suite $225; cottage $250-$300. Children over 12 yrs only. TV avail; cable (premium), VCR avail (movies). Whirlpool. Restaurant (public by res) 7:30 pm sitting; closed Sun-Tues. Setups. Ck-out noon, ck-in 4 pm. Meeting rm. Business servs avail. Downhill ski 20 mi; x-country ski 1 mi. Refrigerators avail; microwaves in cottages. Restored Victorian mansion (1897). Near river. Totally nonsmoking. Cr cds: A, C, MC, V.

⛷ ☼ ☼

★★★ **STONE MANOR.** 5820 Carroll Boyer Rd (21769), US 340 W to Lander Rd exit, in Jefferson take MD 180 S, turn right on Old Middletown Rd, left on Sumantown Rd, left on Carroll Boyer Rd. 301/473-5454; FAX 301/371-5622. E-mail stonemanor@juno.com; web www.stonemanor.com. 6 rms, 2 story, 5 suites. No rm phones. S, D $200; suites $125-$250. TV; VCR avail. Complimentary continental bkfst. Restaurant 11 am-2 pm, 6-9 pm; Sun 11 am-2 pm (brunch), 4-7 pm; closed Mon. Rm serv 24 hrs. Ck-out 11 am, ck-in 2 pm. Business servs avail. Lawn games. Fireplaces. Balconies. On pond. Stone building built in 1760s; on more than 100 acres of wooded area. Totally nonsmoking. Cr cds: A, C, DS, MC, V.

D ☼ ☼ ☼ ☼

★★★ **TURNING POINT INN.** 3406 Urbana Pike (21704), 9 mi S on MD 355, I-270 Ext. 26. 301/831-8232; FAX 301/831-8092. 5 rms, 2 with shower only, 3 story, 2 kit. cottages. S, D $75-$95; kit. cottages $100-$150. TV; cable (premium). Complimentary full bkfst; afternoon refreshments. Dining rm 11:30 am-2 pm, 5:30-9 pm; wkend hrs vary; closed Mon. Ck-out 11 am, ck-in 3 pm. Business servs avail. Built in 1910; antiques. View of Sugarloaf Mt and adj farmland. Cr cds: A, C, D, DS, MC, V.

Restaurants

★★ **BROWN PELICAN.** *5 E Church St (21701). 301/695-5833.* Hrs: 11:30 am-3 pm, 5-9:30 pm; Fri to 10 pm; Sat 5-10 pm; Sun 5-9:30 pm. Closed Jan 1, Thanksgiving, Dec 25; also Super Bowl Sun. Res accepted; required Fri, Sat. Continental menu. Bar. Semi-a la carte: lunch $5.75-$12.95, dinner $12.95-$23.95. Specializes in fresh seafood, pasta, veal. In basement of antebellum bank. Cr cds: A, C, D, DS, MC, V.

★★ **COMUS INN.** *23900 Old Hundred Rd (20842), approx 10 mi S on I-270, S on MD 109, exit 22. 301/253-2522.* Web www.comusinn.com. Hrs: 11 am-9 pm; Sun from 10 am; Sun brunch to 2 pm. Closed Dec 25; also wkdays in winter. Res accepted. Serv bar. Complete meals: lunch $8-$16, dinner $15-$30. Sun brunch $16. Specialties: mesquite-grilled chicken breast, crab cakes. Salad bar. Residence built in 1860 on family farm. View of Sugar Loaf Mt; rural setting. Cr cds: A, C, D, JCB, MC, V.

★★ **GABRIEL'S.** *4730 Ijamsville Rd (21754), E on I-70, exit 59. 301/865-5500.* Web www.gaithersburg.com. Hrs: 6-10 pm; Sun 3-9:30 pm. Closed Mon-Wed; Jan 1. Res accepted; required Fri, Sat. French menu. Serv bar. Semi-a la carte: $16.95-$24.50. Specialties: beef Wellington, salmon coulibac, stuffed breast of chicken Marengo. French provincial inn atmosphere; building constructed in 1862. Family-owned. Cr cds: C, MC, V.

★★ **QUAIL RIDGE INN.** *6212 Ridge Rd (21771), approx 10 mi E on I-70, N on MD 27. 410/549-3218.* Hrs: 11:30 am-9 pm; Mon from 5 pm; Fri, Sat to 9:30 pm; Sun 11 am-8:30 pm; Sun brunch to 2 pm. Closed Mon (Apr-Sept); Dec 25. Res accepted. Italian, Amer menu. Serv bar. Semi-a la carte: lunch $3.75-$8, dinner $8.75-$20.95. Sun brunch $9-$14. Child's meals. Specializes in veal, seafood. Own desserts. Originally a one-rm schoolhouse; intimate dining in scenic rural setting. Cr cds: A, C, D, DS, MC, V.

★★ **TAURASO'S.** *6 East St (21701), Everedy Square. 301/663-6600.* E-mail tauro@aol.com. Hrs: 11 am-10 pm; Fri, Sat to 11 pm. Closed Dec 25. Res accepted. Italian, Amer menu. Bar to midnight. Semi-a la carte: lunch $4.95-$8.95, dinner $7.95-$19.95. Specializes in fresh fish, veal, steak. Outdoor dining. In restored factory building (late 1800s). Cr cds: A, C, D, DS, MC, V.

Gaithersburg (C-6)

(See also Rockville)

Pop 39,542 Elev 508 ft Area Code 240 & 301
Information Chamber of Commerce, 9 Park Ave, 20877; 301/840-1400

What to See and Do

Seneca Creek State Park. Stream valley park of 6,109 acres with 90-acre lake. Historic sites with old mills, an old schoolhouse, stone quarries. Fishing; boating (rentals). Winter sports. Picnicking. Hiking, bicycle and bridle trails. Disk golf. Standard fees. 2½ mi W of I-270 on MD 117. Phone 301/924-2127. ¢

Annual Event

Montgomery County Agricultural Fair. One of the East Coast's leading county fairs; emphasis on agriculture, 4-H activities; animal exhibits, home arts; antique farm equipment; tractor pull, horse pull, demolition derby; rodeo; entertainment. Phone 301/926-3100. Mid-late Aug.

Motel

✓★★ **COMFORT INN AT SHADY GROVE.** *16216 Frederick Rd (20877). 301/330-0023; FAX 301/258-1950; res: 800/228-5150.* E-mail cisg@aol.com. 127 rms, 7 story. Apr-Oct: S, D $49-$109; each addl $10; under 18 free; monthly rates; lower rates rest of yr. Crib free. Pet accepted, some restrictions. TV; cable (premium). Heated pool; lifeguard. Complimentary full bkfst. Coffee in rms. Restaurant adj 11 am-9 pm. Ck-out 11 am. Coin lndry. Meeting rms. Business center. In-rm modem link. Valet serv. Gift shop. Exercise equipt. Health club privileges. Some refrigerators; microwaves. Picnic tables. Cr cds: A, C, D, DS, ER, JCB, MC, V.

Motor Hotels

★★★ **COURTYARD BY MARRIOTT.** *805 Russell Ave (20879). 301/670-0008; FAX 301/948-4538; res: 800/321-2211.* 203 rms, 7 story. S $105; D $115; each addl $10; suites $250; wkend rates. Crib free. TV; cable (premium), VCR avail. Pool; whirlpool, lifeguard. Coffee in rms. Restaurant 6-10 am, 5:30-9:30 pm; Sat 7-11 am; Sun 7 am-noon. Bar 5 pm-midnight. Ck-out noon. Business servs avail. In-rm modem link. Valet serv. Lighted tennis. Exercise equipt; steam rm. Some refrigerators, microwaves. Some balconies. Cr cds: A, C, D, DS, JCB, MC, V.

✓★★ **HAMPTON INN.** *20260 Goldenrod Ln (20876), I-270, exit 15 A. 301/428-1300; FAX 301/428-9034; res: 800/426-7866.* 178 rms, 6 story, 16 kit. units. S, D $95-$105; kit. units $129; suites $199; under 18 free; wkend rates. Crib free. TV; cable (premium). Pool. Complimentary continental bkfst. Restaurant 11 am-11 pm. Ck-out noon. Coin lndry. Meeting rms. Business servs avail. Valet serv. Sundries. Exercise equipt; sauna. Health club privileges. Microwaves avail. Cr cds: A, C, D, DS, MC, V.

★★★ **HOLIDAY INN.** *2 Montgomery Village Ave (20879). 301/948-8900; FAX 301/258-1940; res: 800/465-4329.* 301 rms, 2-8 story. S $114-$124; D $124-$149; suites $300-$350; kit. units $119-$139; under 18 free. Crib free. Pet accepted, some restrictions. TV; cable (premium). Indoor pool; whirlpool, poolside serv, lifeguard. Coffee in rms. Restaurant 6:30 am-10 pm. Rm serv to midnight. Bar noon-midnight. Ck-out noon. Coin lndry. Convention facilities. Business center. In-rm modem link. Bellhops. Gift shop. Exercise equipt. Game rm. Some refrigerators; microwaves avail. Balconies. Cr cds: A, C, D, DS, JCB, MC, V.

Hotels

★★ **HILTON.** *620 Perry Pkwy (20877), 1 blk E of I-270 exit 11. 301/977-8900; FAX 301/869-8597; res: 800/445-8667; res: 800/599-5111.* Web www.hilton.com. 301 rms, 12 story. S, D $115-$155; suites $325; under 18 free; wkend rates. Crib free. Pet accepted, some restrictions. TV; cable (premium). Indoor/outdoor pool. Restaurant 6:30 am-11 pm; wkends from 7 am. Bars 11-1 am. Convention facilities. Business servs avail. In-rm modem link. Exercise equipt. Health club privileges. Refrigerators avail. Some private patios, balconies. Adj to Lake Forest shopping center. Cr cds: A, C, D, DS, ER, JCB, MC, V.

★★★ **MARRIOTT WASHINGTONIAN CENTER.** *9751 Washingtonian Blvd (20878). 301/590-0044; FAX 301/212-6155; res: 800/228-9290.* Web www.marriott.com. 284 rms, 11 story. S, D $164; suites $250; under 18 free; wkend rates. Crib free. TV; cable (premium). Indoor pool;

whirlpool, poolside serv, lifeguard. Restaurant 6:30 am-11 pm; wkend hrs vary. Bar 4 pm-midnight. Ck-out noon. Convention facilities. Business center. In-rm modem link. Concierge. Gift shop. Exercise equipt; sauna. Health club privileges. Luxury level. Cr cds: A, C, D, DS, ER, JCB, MC, V.

Restaurants

★ **CHRIS' STEAK HOUSE.** 201 E Diamond Ave (20877). 301/869-6116. Hrs: 11 am-midnight. Closed Sun; also most major hols. Bar. Semi-a la carte: lunch $3.95-$8.50, dinner $6.50-$18. Child's meals. Specializes in beef, pork, seafood. Football memorabilia. Cr cds: C, MC, V.

★★ **FLAMING PIT.** 18701 N Frederick Ave (20879). 301/977-0700. Hrs: 11:30 am-10 pm; Fri to 11 pm; Sat 4-11 pm; Sun 5-10 pm; early-bird dinner Mon-Fri 4-7 pm. Closed some major hols. Res accepted; required Fri, Sat. Bar to midnight; Fri, Sat to 1 am. Semi-a la carte: lunch $6.95-$12.95, dinner $13.95-$29.95. Child's meals. Specializes in prime rib, lamb, fresh seafood. Pianist. Skylight; hanging baskets. Original antique fireplaces. Cr cds: A, C, D, MC, V.

★★ **GOLDEN BULL GRAND CAFE.** 7 Dalamar St (20877), I-270 exit 11. 301/948-3666. Hrs: 11 am-3 pm, 4:30-10 pm; Fri, Sat to 11 pm; Sun noon-10 pm; early-bird dinner 4:30-6:30 pm, Sun noon-4 pm. Closed Dec 25. Bar 11 am-11 pm. Semi-a la carte: lunch $5.50-$10.95, dinner $9.95-$29.95. Child's meals. Specializes in beef, seafood. Salad bar. Cr cds: A, C, D, DS, MC, V.

✓★ **IL FORNO PIZZERIA.** 8941 Westland Dr (20877). 301/977-5900. Hrs: 11 am-10 pm; Fri, Sat to 11 pm. Closed major hols. Italian menu. Wine, beer. A la carte entrees: lunch $4.45-$7.95, dinner $10-$15.95. Specializes in pizza, pasta. Outdoor dining. Casual decor. Cr cds: C, MC, V.

★★ **LE PARADIS.** 347 Muddy Branch Rd (20878). 301/208-9493. Hrs: 11:30 am-2:30 pm, 5:30-10 pm. Closed Sun; major hols. Res accepted; required Fri, Sat. French menu. Wine list. A la carte entrees: lunch $6.95-$12.95, dinner $15.95-$22.95. Prix fixe: lunch $12.50, dinner $16.95. Specialties: lobster with ginger key lime sauce, black Angus steak with portobello mushroom. Bistro decor. Totally nonsmoking. Cr cds: A, C, D, DS, MC, V.

★★ **OLDE TOWNE TAVERN & BREWING CO.** 227 E Diamond Ave (20877), in Olde Town. 301/948-4200. Hrs: noon-1 am; Fri, Sat to 2 am; early-bird dinner Mon-Fri 4-7 pm. Closed Thanksgiving, Dec 25. Res accepted; required Fri, Sat dinner. Semi-a la carte: lunch $4.95-$15.95, dinner $8.95-$17.95. Child's meals. Specializes in beef, pasta, seafood. Musicians Fri, Sat. Brew pub in historic Belt Bldg (1896); 2-level dining area. Totally nonsmoking. Cr cds: A, C, D, MC, V.

✓★★ **PEKING CHEERS.** 519 Quince Orchard Rd (20878). 301/216-2090. Hrs: 11 am-10:30 pm; Fri, Sat to 11 pm. Res accepted. Chinese menu. Serv bar. Semi-a la carte: lunch $4.25-$5.50, dinner $5.95-$11.95. Specialties: Peking duck, sesame chicken, crispy beef. Casual decor; large murals. Totally nonsmoking. Cr cds: A, C, DS, MC, V.

✓★ **PEKING SUPREME.** 19204 Montgomery Village Ave (20886). 301/963-8088. Hrs: 11:30 am-9:45 pm; Fri, Sat to 10:45 pm. Closed Thanksgiving. Chinese menu. Bar. Semi-a la carte: lunch $4.50-$5.50, dinner $6.95-$11.95. Specialties: Peking-style chicken, crispy beef. Art deco decor. Cr cds: A, C, D, DS, MC, V.

★ **ROY'S PLACE.** 2 E Diamond Ave (20877). 301/948-5548. Hrs: 11 am-11 pm; Fri, Sat to midnight; Sun from 11:30 am. Closed Thanksgiving, Dec 24, 25. Bar. A la carte entrees: lunch, dinner $4.50-$14. Specializes in extensive sandwich selection. 1920s tavern atmosphere; Tiffany-style lamps, beamed ceiling, period posters. Family-owned. Cr cds: A, C, D, DS, MC, V.

✓★★ **SIR WALTER RALEIGH.** 19100 Montgomery Village Ave (20886). 301/258-0576. Hrs: 11:30 am-2 pm, 5-9 pm; Fri to 10 pm; Sat 5-10 pm; Sun 4-8:30 pm. Closed Dec 25. Bar. Semi-a la carte: lunch $7-$11, dinner $10.95-$19.95. Child's meals. Specializes in prime rib, seafood, crab cakes. Salad bar. Brick fireplaces. Cr cds: A, C, D, DS, MC, V.

Grantsville (A-1)

(See also Cumberland, Oakland)

Pop 505 **Elev** 2,300 ft **Area Code** 301 **Zip** 21536
E-mail info@garrettchamber.com **Web** www.garrettchamber.com
Information Garrett County Chamber of Commerce, 15 Visitors Center Dr, McHenry 21541; 301/387-4386

What to See and Do

New Germany State Park. A 13-acre lake built on site of a once prosperous milling center. Swimming; fishing; boating. Nature, hiking trails. Winter sports. Picnicking, playground, concession. Improved campsites, cabins (fee). 5 mi S. Phone 301/895-5453. Admission (wkends & hols) per person ¢

Savage River State Forest. Largest of Maryland's state forests comprises about 52,800 acres of near wilderness. A strategic watershed area, the northern hardwood forest surrounds the Savage River Dam. Fishing, hunting. Hiking trails. Winter sports. Primitive camping (permit required). S on Chestnut Ridge Rd. Phone 301/895-5453.

Springs Museum. Depicts life of settlers of Casselman Valley; 18th-century farming tools, fossil collection, other exhibits. (Memorial Day-mid-Oct, Wed-Sat afternoons) 2 mi N via MD 669, PA 669 in Springs, PA. Phone 814/662-4158. ¢

Spruce Forest Artisan Village. Original log cabins plus other historic buildings serve as studios for a potter, internationally recognized bird carver, weaver, spinner, stained-glass maker and other artisans. Buildings (daily exc Sun). Special events (summer; fee). Restaurant (see). (See ANNUAL EVENTS) 1 mi E on US 40, near Penn Alps. Phone 301/895-3332. **Free**

Annual Events

Spruce Forest Summerfest and Quilt Show. Spruce Forest Artisan Village. More than 200 quilts on display; more than 70 craftspeople demonstrate their various skills. Phone 301/895-3332. 2nd full Thurs, Fri & Sat wkend July.

Springs Folk Festival. On grounds of Springs Museum (see). Pennsylvania Dutch food, music. Phone 814/662-4158. 1st Fri & Sat Oct.

Restaurant

✓★★ **PENN ALPS.** 125 Casselman Rd (21536), 1 mi on US 40 at Casselman River Bridge. 301/895-5985. Hrs: 7 am-8 pm; Sun brunch 10 am-3 pm. Closed Dec 24, 25. Complete meals: bkfst $2.50-$6.95, lunch $4-$7.95, dinner $8.75-$15.95. Sun brunch $8.95. Child's meals. Specializes in Dutch cooking. Salad bar. Colonial decor; 1818 stagecoach stop. Totally nonsmoking. Cr cds: C, DS, MC, V.

Hagerstown (A-4)

(See also Boonsboro, Frederick, Thurmont)

Settled 1762 **Pop** 35,445 **Elev** 552 ft **Area Code** 240 & 301 **Zip** 21740
E-mail info@marylandmemories.org **Web** www.marylandmemories.org
Information Hagerstown/Washington County Tourism Office, 16 Public Sq;
301/791-3246 or 800/228-7829

Within the city of Hagerstown, there is a walking tour with points of interest marked on downtown sidewalks and walking paths in city parks. South Prospect Street is one of the city's oldest neighborhoods, listed on the National Register of Historic Places. The tree-lined street is graced by homes dating back to the early 1800s.

What to See and Do

Antietam National Battlefield (see). 11 mi S on MD 65.

Ft Frederick State Park. Erected in 1756, during French and Indian War, the fort is considered a fine example of a pre-Revolutionary stone fort. Overlooks Chesapeake and Ohio Canal National Historical Park (see); barracks, interior and wall of fort restored; military reenactments throughout year. Fishing; boating (rentals). Nature & hiking trails. Picnicking (shelter), playground. Unimproved camping. Museum, orientation film, historical programs. Standard fees. Winter hours may vary. 18 mi W of jct I-81 & I-70 to Big Pool, then 1 mi SE via MD 56, unnumbered road. Phone 301/842-2155.

Greenbrier State Park. The Appalachian Trail passes near this 1,275-acre park and its 42-acre man-made lake. Swimming (Memorial Day-Labor Day, daily); fishing; boating (rentals; no gas motors). Nature, hiking trails. Picnicking. Standard fees. 6 mi E via US 40. Phone 301/791-4767. ¢-¢¢

Hagerstown Roundhouse Museum. Museum houses photographic exhibits of the 7 railroads of Hagerstown; historic railroad memorabilia, tools and equipment; archives of maps, books, papers and related items. Gift shop. (Fri-Sun afternoons) (See ANNUAL EVENTS) 300 S Burhans Blvd, across the tracks from City Park. Phone 301/739-4665. ¢

Jonathan Hager House and Museum (1739). Stone house in park setting; authentic 18th-century furnishings. (Apr-Dec, daily exc Mon) 110 Key St, in City Park. Phone 301/739-8393. ¢¢

Miller House. Washington County Historical Society Headquarters. Federal town house (ca 1820); 3-story spiral staircase; period furnishings; garden; clock, doll and Bell pottery collections; Chesapeake & Ohio Canal and Civil War exhibits; 19th-century country store display. (Apr-Dec, Wed-Sat; closed major hols; also 1st 2 wks Dec) 135 W Washington St. Phone 301/797-8782. ¢¢

Washington County Museum of Fine Arts. Paintings, sculpture, changing exhibits; concerts, lectures. (Daily exc Mon; closed major hols) 91 Key St in City Park, S on US 11 (Virginia Ave). Phone 301/739-5727. **Free**

Annual Events

Hagerstown Railroad Heritage Days. Special events centered on the Roundhouse Museum. For information and schedule phone 301/739-4665. Early May.

Halfway Park Days. Helicopter rides, antique cars, dance bands, flea market, food. Late May.

Jonathan Hager Frontier Craft Day. Colonial crafts demonstrated and exhibited. Bluegrass music; food. 1st wkend Aug.

Leitersburg Peach Festival. Peach-related edibles, farmers' market, bluegrass music. 2nd wkend Aug.

Williamsport C & O Canal Days. Arts and crafts, Indian Village, National Park Service activities; food. Late Aug.

Alsatia Mummers Halloween Parade Festival. Sat, wkend closest to Halloween.

Motel

✓ ★★ **DAYS INN.** 900 Dual Hwy (21740), I-81 exit 6A. 301/739-9050; FAX 301/739-8347; res: 800/422-2754. 140 rms, 2 story. May-Oct: S $48-$58; D $54-$65; each addl $5; under 18 free; wkend rates; lower rates rest of yr. TV; cable (premium). Playground. Pool. Complimentary continental bkfst. Restaurant 6:30 am-2 pm, 5-9 pm. Bar 4:30-9:30 pm. Ck-out noon. Coin lndry. Meeting rms. Business servs avail. Refrigerators avail. Cr cds: A, C, D, DS, JCB, MC, V.

🄳 ⬙ ⬙ ⬙ SC

Motor Hotels

★★★ **HOWARD JOHNSON PLAZA HOTEL.** 1718 Underpass Way (21740), at I-81 exit 5. 301/797-2500; FAX 301/797-6209; res: 800/826-4534. 164 units, 6 story. S $63; D $68; each addl $8; suites $75-$89; under 18 free. Crib free. TV; cable (premium), VCR avail. Indoor pool; whirlpool; lifeguard. Complimentary coffee in rms. Restaurant 6:30 am-9 pm. Rm serv. Bar 11 am-11 pm. Ck-out noon. Meeting rms. Business servs avail. In-rm modem link. Valet serv. Free airport transportation. Exercise equipt; sauna. Refrigerators. Cr cds: A, C, D, DS, JCB, MC, V.

🄳 ⬙ 🯄 ⬙ ⬙ ⬙ SC

★★ **RAMADA INN.** 901 Dual Hwy (21740), I-70 exit 32B. 301/733-5100; FAX 301/733-9192; res: 800/272-6232. E-mail dave learn@aol.com; web nfris.com/~ramada/. 210 rms, 5 story. S $62-$69; D $67-$74; each addl $5; suites $95-$200; under 18 free. Crib free. TV; cable (premium). Indoor pool. Restaurant 6:30 am-9:30 pm; Sun to 9 pm. Rm serv. Bar noon-2 am. Ck-out 11 am. Coin lndry. Meeting rms. Business servs avail. Free airport transportation. Exercise equipt. Some refrigerators, in-rm whirlpools. Cr cds: A, C, D, DS, MC, V.

🄳 ⬙ 🯄 🯄 ⬙ ⬙ SC

★★★ **SHERATON FOUR POINTS HOTEL.** 1910 Dual Hwy (21740), I-70 exit 32B. 301/790-3010; FAX 301/733-4559; res: 800/325-3535. 108 rms, 2 story. S $60-$75; D $64-$79; each addl $6; suites $150; under 18 free. Crib $6. Pet accepted; $50 deposit. TV; cable (premium). Pool; whirlpool. Complimentary continental bkfst. Restaurant 6:30 am-10 pm; Sat, Sun 7 am-9 pm. Rm serv. Bar 11-2 am. Ck-out noon. Meeting rms. Business servs avail. Bellhops. Valet serv. Sundries. Free airport transportation. Exercise equipt; sauna. Microwaves avail. Cr cds: A, C, D, DS, MC, V.

🄳 🯄 ⬙ 🯄 ⬙ ⬙ SC

✓ ★★ **VENICE INN.** 431 Dual Hwy (21740), I-70 exit 32B, I-81 exit 6A. 301/733-0830; FAX 301/733-4978; res: 800/283-6423. 220 rms, 2-5 story. Apr-Oct: S $58-$68; D $63-$73; each addl $6; suites $125-$250; under 18 free; lower rates rest of yr. Crib $6. Pet accepted, some restrictions. TV; cable (premium), VCR (movies). Pool. Complimentary coffee in lobby. Restaurant 6 am-10:30 pm. Rm serv. Bar; entertainment Tues-Sat. Ck-out noon. Meeting rms. Bellhops. Valet serv. Beauty shop. Airport transportation. Game rm. Golf adj. Exercise equipt. Refrigerators, microwaves avail. Whirlpool in suites. Cr cds: A, C, D, DS, MC, V.

🄳 🯄 ⬙ 🯄 ⬙ ⬙ SC

Inn

★★★ **BEAVER CREEK HOUSE BED & BREAKFAST.** 20432 Beaver Creek Rd (21740), 4 mi E on I-70, exit 32A or 35, in village of Beaver Creek. 301/797-4764; FAX 301/797-4978. 5 rms, 2 with shower only. No rm phones. S $75-$85; D $85-$95; lower rates mid-wk. Children over 10 yrs only. TV in sitting rm. Complimentary full bkfst; afternoon refreshments. Ck-out 11 am, ck-in 1 pm. Turn-of-the-century country home located in historic village; antique furnishings and family memorabilia; parlor with fireplace; library/sitting rm; scenic view of South Mountain. Cr cds: A, C, MC, V.

⬙ ⬙

Restaurants

✓★ **JUNCTION 808.** *808 Noland Dr (21740), at jct US 11. 301/791-3639.* Hrs: 6 am-8:30 pm. Closed Sun; also July 4, Dec 24-26. Res accepted. Semi-a la carte: bkfst $1.50-$4.95, lunch $2.50-$4.25, dinner $4.95-$10.95. Child's meals. Specialties: lasagne, Cajun steak. Own pies. Located near railroad tracks. Railroad-theme decor and tapes of actual trains; model trains circle the room at the ceiling. Totally nonsmoking. Cr cds: C.

[SC]

★★ **RED HORSE STEAK HOUSE.** *1800 Dual Hwy US 40 (21740), I-70 exit 32B. 301/733-3788.* E-mail RCJATRH@aol.com. Hrs: 4-10 pm; Sun to 9 pm. Closed major hols. Res accepted. Bar. Semi-a la carte: dinner $9.75-$19.95. Child's meals. Specializes in prime rib, broiled seafood, steak. Open-hearth grill. Western-style atmosphere. Family-owned. Cr cds: C, D, MC, V.

[D] [⊒]

✓★★ **RICHARDSON'S.** *710 Dual Hwy US 40W (21740). 301/733-3660.* Hrs: 7 am-10 pm; Fri, Sat to 11 pm. Closed Dec 24 evening, Dec 25. Res accepted. Bar. Semi-a la carte: bkfst $1.95-$4.95, lunch $2.95-$6.95, dinner $5.95-$14.95. Buffet: bkfst $4.95, lunch $4.99, dinner $8.95-$18.95. Child's meals. Specializes in fried chicken, seafood, crab cakes. Salad bar. Own pies, cakes. 3 dining areas; railroad theme, memorabilia. Cr cds: C, DS, MC, V.

[D] [SC]

Havre de Grace (B-8)

(See also Aberdeen, Elkton)

Settled 1658 **Pop** 8,952 **Elev** 52 ft **Area Code** 410 & 443 **Zip** 21078
Information Chamber of Commerce, 224 N Washington St, PO Box 339; 410/939-3303 or 800/851-7756

What to See and Do

Concord Point Lighthouse (1827). Built of granite, considered the oldest continually used lighthouse on the East Coast. It was automated in 1928. (May-Oct, wkends & hols only) At foot of Lafayette St.   **Free**

Decoy Museum. Houses a collection of hand-carved waterfowl decoys and interprets this art form as it applies to the heritage of Chesapeake Bay. (Daily; closed Jan 1, Thanksgiving, Dec 25) (See ANNUAL EVENTS) Giles & Market Sts, at the bay.   ¢

Susquehanna State Park. A 2,639-acre park. Fishing. Boat launch. Nature, riding and hiking trails. Cross-country skiing. Picnicking. Camping (May-Sept; fee). Schedule varies, phone 410/557-7994. In the park is

Steppingstone Museum. Self-guided tour of museum grounds includes sites of a once working Harford County farm; farmhouse is furnished as a turn-of-the-century country home; nearby shops and barn hold many displays and exhibits of the 1880-1920 period; demonstrations of rural arts and crafts of the period. Also here are blacksmith, woodworking, cooper and dairy shops. (May-1st Sun Oct, Sat & Sun afternoons) Special events held throughout the year (see ANNUAL EVENTS). 461 Quaker Bottom Rd. Phone 410/939-2299.   ¢-¢¢

Annual Events

Decoy Festival. Decoys on display, auction. Carving, gunning & calling contests. Refreshments. Phone 410/939-3739. Fri-Sun 1st wkend May.

Fall Harvest Festival & Craft Show. Steppingstone Museum. Features activities related to the harvest and preparation for winter: apple pressing, scarecrow stuffing and other events. Entertainment. Phone 410/939-2299. Last full wkend Sept.

Inn

★★★ **VANDIVER INN.** *301 S Union Ave (21078). 410/939-5200; FAX 410/939-5202; res: 800/245-1655.* 9 rms, 3 story. S, D $75-$105; wkly rates. TV in parlor. Complimentary full bkfst. Ck-in 4-7 pm. Some fireplaces. Some balconies. Queen Anne-style mansion (1886) with antique furnishings. Chesapeake Bay 2 blks. Cr cds: A, C, DS, MC, V.

[D] [⊠] [🔥] [SC]

Restaurants

✓★★ **BAYOU.** *927 Pulaski Hwy US 40 (21078). 410/939-3565.* Hrs: 11:30 am-10 pm. Closed Dec 24-26. Res accepted; required hols. Semi-a la carte: lunch $3-$6.25, dinner $7.50-$13.50. Child's meals. Specializes in seafood, veal. Cr cds: A, C, D, MC, V.

[D] [⊒]

★★ **CRAZY SWEDE.** *400 N Union Ave (21078). 410/939-5440.* Hrs: 11-2 am; Sun brunch 10 am-2:30 pm. Closed Thanksgiving, Dec 25. Res accepted; required Fri & Sat. Continental menu. Bar. Semi-a la carte: lunch $4.25-$6.95, dinner $11.95-$21. Sun brunch $3.50-$9. Child's meals. Specializes in seafood. Cr cds: A, C, D, MC, V.

[D]

La Plata (D-6)

(See also Waldorf; also see District of Columbia)

Pop 5,841 **Elev** 193 ft **Area Code** 301 **Zip** 20646
Information Charles County Chamber of Commerce, 6360 Crain Hwy, phone; 301/932-6500; or the Dept of Tourism, 301/645-0558

What to See and Do

Doncaster Demonstration Forest. Heavily forested with yellow poplar, sweet gum, red and white oaks, and pine throughout its 1,477 acres. Hunting; 13 mi of hiking trails, bridle trails; picnic area. Cross-country skiing. 13 mi W on MD 6, near Doncaster. Phone 301/934-2282.

Port Tobacco. Infrared aerial photography and archaeological excavation revealed the site of one of the oldest continuously inhabited English settlements in North America. Appearing as a Native American village on Captain John Smith's map of the area (1608), the area was colonized by the English as early as 1638. The town was chartered in 1727, and the first courthouse was erected in 1729. Among the remaining buildings are the Chimney House (1765) and Stagg Hall (1732), an original colonial home still a private residence, Burch (Catslide) House (1700), the reconstructed Quenzel Store, house and a Federal period courthouse, with the Port Tobacco Museum on the second floor; archeological items on display, replicas of colonial houses; Civil War and John Wilkes Booth exhibits, 30-min audiovisual film of *The Story of Port Tobacco.* (Apr-Dec, Sat & Sun afternoons) 3 mi SW on MD 6. Phone 301/934-4313.   ¢

Smallwood State Park. Restored home of Revolutionary General William Smallwood. Guided tour and historical program during summer. Hiking. Picnicking. Marina. Boating (launch, rentals). Fishing. Retreat House. Park (daily). Standard fees. 16 mi W via MD 225, 224, near Rison. Phone 301/743-7613. Wkends   ¢

Motel

✓★★ **BEST WESTERN.** *6900 Crain Hwy; Rte 301 (20646). 301/934-4900; FAX 301/934-5389; res: 800/528-1234.* 73 rms, 2 story, 8 suites. S, D $57-$67; each addl $5; suites $90-$105; under 13 free. Crib free. TV; cable (premium), VCR avail. Pool. Complimentary continental bkfst. Restaurant adj 11 am-11 pm. Ck-out noon. Coin lndry. Meeting rm. Business servs avail. Exercise equipt. Refrigerators, microwaves. Picnic table. Cr cds: A, C, D, DS, MC, V.

D ⊷ ✕ ⬚ ♨ SC

Laurel (C-6)

(See also Bowie, College Park, Silver Spring; also see District of Columbia)

Pop 19,438 **Elev** 160 ft **Area Code** 240 & 301
Information Corridor Information Centers, PO Box 288, Savage 20763; 301/490-2444. There are 2 information centers open daily except holidays at the northbound and southbound rest areas on I-195 just outside of Laurel

What to See and Do

Montpelier Mansion (ca 1780). Built and owned for generations by Maryland's Snowden family; Georgian architecture. George Washington and Abigail Adams were among its early visitors. On the grounds are boxwood gardens, an 18th-century herb garden and a small summer house. Tours; purchase ticket in gift shop. (Mar-Nov, Sun afternoons; groups by appt; closed major hols) Candlelight tours held in early Dec. 3 mi SE on MD 197 at Muirkirk. Phone 301/953-1376. ¢¢

National Wildlife Visitor Center. 12,750-acre national wildlife refuge and research area. Interactive exhibits focus on global environmental issues, migratory birds, wildlife habitats and endangered species. Tram tours avail of surrounding forests and lakes (weather permitting; fee). Trails. Gift shop. (Daily; closed Dec 25) 10901 Scarlet Tanager Loop. Phone 301/497-5760. **Free**

Seasonal Event

Thoroughbred racing. Laurel Race Course, on MD 198. Entrances accessible from northbound or southbound on US 1, I-95 or from Baltimore-Washington Pkwy, MD 198 exit. Phone 301/725-0400 or 800/638-1859 for current racing schedule.

Motel

★★ **HOLIDAY INN.** 3400 Fort Meade Rd (20724), MD 198 & Baltimore/Washington Pkwy. 301/498-0900; FAX 301/498-3203; res: 800/477-7410. 166 rms, 2 story. S, D $84-$114; each addl $10; under 18 free. Crib free. TV; cable (premium), VCR avail. Pool; lifeguard. Complimentary coffee in rms. Restaurant 6:30 am-2 pm, 5-10 pm. Rm serv from 7 am. Bar 4 pm-midnight. Ck-out 11 am. Coin lndry. Meeting rms. Business servs avail. In-rm modem link. Valet serv. Exercise equipt. Health club privileges. Refrigerators, microwaves avail. Cr cds: A, C, D, DS, ER, JCB, MC, V.

D ⊷ ✕ ⬚ ♨ SC

Motor Hotel

★★ **COMFORT SUITES.** 14402 Laurel Pl (20707), US 1 at Laurel Lakes Center. 301/206-2600; FAX 301/725-0056; res: 800/628-7760. Web www.comfortsuiteslaurel.com. 119 rms, 5 story. S, D $80-$100; each addl $10; suites $95-$125; under 18 free; wkly, wkend rates; higher rates: cherry blossom, Memorial Day wkend. Crib free. Pet accepted; $50 refundable. TV; cable (premium). Indoor pool; whirlpool, lifeguard. Complimentary continental bkfst. Complimentary coffee in rms. Restaurant nearby. Ck-out noon. Coin lndry. Meeting rms. Business servs avail. Sundries. Valet serv. Airport transportation. Exercise equipt. Refrigerators, microwaves. Cr cds: A, C, D, DS, ER, JCB, MC, V.

D 🐾 ⊷ ✕ ⬚ ♨ SC

Leonardtown (E-7)

(See also St Mary's City; also see District of Columbia)

Pop 1,475 **Elev** 87 ft **Area Code** 301 **Zip** 20650 **E-mail** stmcdecd@mail. ameritel.net **Web** www.somd.lib.md.us/STMA/government/stmcdecd.html
Information St Mary's County Division of Tourism, 23115 Leonard Hall Dr, PO Box 653; 301/475-4411 or 800/327-9023.

What to See and Do

Calvert Marine Museum. Museum complex with exhibits relating to the culture and marine environment of Chesapeake Bay and Patuxent River estuary; fossils of marine life; estuarine biology displays, aquariums, touch-tank; maritime history exhibits, including boat-building gallery. Also here is the restored Drum Point Lighthouse, built 1883; ½ mi S is the JC Lore Oyster House, with exhibits on the area's seafood industry. Gift shop. (Daily; closed Jan 1, Thanksgiving, Dec 25) 1 mi SE on MD 5, then 11 mi NE on MD 4, cross bridge and turn right on Solomons Island Rd; follow signs. Phone 410/326-2042. Main exhibit building ¢¢

Old Jail Museum. Local historical exhibits housed in old jail; also a genealogy library for researchers. A cannon from Leonard Calvert's ship, the Ark, is mounted in front. (Tues-Sat; closed hols; also last wk Dec) 11 Court House Dr. Phone 301/475-2467. **Free**

Sotterley Plantation (ca 1715). Overlooks Patuxent River. Working plantation; house in original condition. Chinese Chippendale staircase, antiques, original pine paneling in three rooms. Farming exhibit. (Grounds open May-Oct, daily exc Mon; individual tours of manor house on wkends; group tours by appt only) 9 mi E on MD 245. Phone 301/373-2280. ¢¢¢

St Clements Island-Potomac River Museum. Maryland colonists first landed on the island in 1634. Exhibits trace amlost 400 yrs of local history and pre-history. Museum includes Little Red School House (ca 1821) and country store. Picnic area; fishing and crabbing. (Late Mar-Sept, Mon-Fri, also Sat, Sun afternoons; rest of yr, Wed-Sun afternoons; closed major hols) 5 mi W via MD 234 to Clements, then 9 mi S on MD 242, in Colton Point. Phone 301/769-2222. ¢

Annual Events

St Mary's County Fair. Midway, seafood, horse shows. Phone 301/475-2707. Late Sept.

Blessing of the Fleet & Historical Pageant. St Clements Island, Potomac River Museum. Celebration commemorates first Roman Catholic Mass held on Maryland soil and Governor Leonard Calvert's proclamation of religious freedom. Blessing of oyster and clam fishing fleets. Folk dances, historical exhibits, concerts. Boat rides to the island. Phone 301/769-2222. 1st wkend Oct.

St Mary's County Oyster Festival. County Fairgrounds. National oyster shucking contest; oyster cook-off, seafood and crafts. Phone 301/863-5015. 3rd wkend Oct.

Oakland (Garrett Co) (B-1)

Settled 1851 **Pop** 1,741 **Elev** 2,384 ft **Area Code** 301 **Zip** 21550
E-mail info@garrettchamber.com **Web** www.garrettchamber.com
Information Garrett County Chamber of Commerce, 200 S Third St; 301/334-1948

What to See and Do

Backbone Mt. Highest point in the state (3,360 ft). 8 mi S on US 219, then W on US 50.

Deep Creek Lake State Park. Approx 1,800 acres with 3,900-acre man-made lake. Swimming, bathhouse; fishing, boating (rowboat rentals). Nature, hiking trails. Picnicking (shelters), playground, concession.

Improved campsites (fee). From I-68, 10 mi SE off US 219. For general information and camping reservations Phone 301/387-5563 (reservations accepted up to 1 yr in advance). Entrance for day-use area, per pers. ¢

Garrett State Forest. Approx 6,800 acres. The forest contains much wildlife. Fishing, hunting. Hiking and riding trails. Winter activities. Primitive camping. Forestry demonstration area. 5 mi NW on County 20. Phone 301/334-2038. Within the forest are

Herrington Manor State Park. Well-developed 365-acre park with housekeeping cabins, 53-acre lake. Swimming, fishing, boating (launch, rentals). Hiking trails. Concession. Picnicking. Cross-country skiing (rentals). Interpretive programs (summer). No pets. Standard fees. Phone 301/334-9180.

Swallow Falls State Park. Surrounding 257 acres, the Youghiogheny River tumbles along the park's boundaries, passing through shaded rocky gorges and over sunny rapids. Muddy Creek produces a 52-ft waterfall. Here the last remaining stand of virgin hemlock dwarfs visitors. Fishing. Nature trails, hiking. Picnicking. Improved campsites. Pets at registered campsites only. Standard fees. Phone 301/334-9180.

Potomac State Forest. More than 10,685 acres for hiking, riding and hunting. Primitive camping. Timber is harvested regularly here and the area is important in the management of watershed and wildlife programs. 9 mi SE off MD 560, along Potomac River. Phone 301/334-2038.

Annual Events

Winterfest. Deep Creek Lake in McHenry. Ski races, parade, fireworks. Late Feb and early Mar.

McHenry Highland Festival. Deep Creek Lake. Traditional Scottish and Celtic festival. 1st Sat June.

Garrett County Fair. McHenry Fairgrounds. Early Aug.

Autumn Glory Festival. Celebrates fall foliage. Features arts and crafts, five-string banjo contest, state fiddle contest, western Maryland tournament of bands, parades, antique show. Phone 301/334-1948. Mid-Oct.

Motels

✓ ★ ★ **ALPINE VILLAGE.** 19638 Garrett Hwy (21550), 7 mi N on US 219. 301/387-5534; FAX 301/334-0726; res: 800/343-5253. 29 motel rms, 2 story, 8 kits., 14 kit. chalets. June-Sept: S, D $60-$80; each addl $5; kit. units, studio rms $70; chalets for 1-6, $575-$750/wk; lower rates rest of yr. Crib free. TV; cable. Heated pool; wading pool. Restaurant 5-11 pm; Sun from 4 pm. Bar 5-11 pm. Ck-out 11 am. Downhill/x-country ski 5 mi. On lake; private sand beach; dock. Some private patios. Picnic table, grills. Cr cds: A, C, D, DS, MC, V.

★ **LAKE SIDE MOTOR COURT.** 19956 Garrett Hwy (21550), 8 mi N on US 219. 301/387-5566. 10 rms, 1 cottage. Mid-June-Labor Day: S, D $64; each addl $4; cottage for 2-6, $468-$900/wk; MAP avail; lower rates May-mid-June, after Labor Day-Oct. Closed rest of yr. TV; cable. Pool privileges. Playground. Restaurant adj 7 am-2 pm, 5-9:30 pm. Ck-out 11 am. Refrigerators. Picnic area, grills. Overlooks lake; private swimming beach; dock. Cr cds: A, C, D, DS, MC, V.

★ **WILL O THE WISP.** 20160 Garrett Hwy (21550), 9 mi N on US 219. 301/387-5503; FAX 301/387-4999; res: 301/387-4911. 10 rms. May-Oct: S, D $62; each addl $4; cottage for 2-6, $468-$900/wk; MAP avail. Closed rest of yr. Crib free. TV. Pool privileges. Restaurant adj 7 am-2 pm, 5-9:30 pm. Ck-out 11 am. On lake; private beach; dock. Picnic tables. Cr cds: A, C, D, DS, MC, V.

Inns

★ ★ ★ **CARMEL COVE BED & BREAKFAST.** 105 Monastery Way (21550), off MD 219, on Glendale Rd. 301/387-0067; FAX 301/387-2394. E-mail carmelcove@aol.com; web carmelcoveinn.com. 10 rms, 5 with shower only, 2 story, 3 suites. S, D $80-$140; suites $120-$140; ski plans; package plans; wkends, hols (2-3 day min). Children over 12 yrs only. TV in common rm; cable (premium), VCR (movies). Complimentary full bkfst. Ck-out 11 am, ck-in 4-9 pm. In-rm modem link. Luggage handling. Concierge serv. Gift shop. Tennis. X-country ski 10 mi. Game rm. Rec rm. In-rm whirlpool, fireplace in suites. Some balconies. Picnic tables, grills. On lake. Built in 1945. Totally nonsmoking. Cr cds: C, DS, MC, V.

★ ★ ★ **HALEY FARM BED & BREAKFAST.** 16766 Garrett Hwy (21550), 5 mi N on MD 219. 301/387-9050; res: 888/231-3276. E-mail kgillespie@haleyfarm.com; web www.haleyfarm. com. 9 rms, 7 with A/C, 2 story, 3 kit. suites. Rm phone in 2 suites only. S, D $100-$120; each addl $25; suites $140-$160; kit. units $170-$190; golf rates; package plans; wkends, hols (2-3 day min). Children over 12 yrs only. TV in suites; cable (premium), VCR (movies). Complimentary full bkfst; afternoon refreshments. Ck-out noon, ck-in 3 pm. Concierge serv. Gift shop. Downhill ski 5 mi; x-country ski on site. Bicycles. Sauna. Fireplaces; in-rm whirlpool, refrigerators in suite; microwaves avail. Some balconies. Picnic tables, grills. Built in 1923; formerly a working farm. Totally nonsmoking. Cr cds: A, C, DS, MC, V.

Restaurants

★ ★ **POINT VIEW INN.** Deep Creek Dr (21541), 8 mi N on US 219. 301/387-5555. Hrs: 8 am-10 pm; Sun to 9 pm. Closed Easter, Dec 25. Res accepted. Bar 11-2 am. Semi-a la carte: bkfst $3-$6, lunch $5.75-$8.50, dinner $7.50-$21.95. Child's meals. Specialities: crab cakes, prime rib. Entertainment wkends. Patio dining. Elevated dining areas with view of Deep Creek Lake. Cr cds: A, C, MC, V.

★ ★ **SILVER TREE HARBOR SEAFOOD BAR.** 19638 Garrett Hwy (21550), 8 blks N on Glendale Rd. 301/387-5524. Hrs: 5-10 pm; Sat to 11 pm. Italian, Amer menu. Bar to 2 am. Semi-a la carte: dinner $5.99-$24.95. Child's meals. Specializes in pasta, seafood, steak. 1890s decor. Stone fireplaces. View of lake. Cr cds: A, C, D, DS, MC, V.

Ocean City (E-10)

Founded 1869 **Pop** 5,146 **Elev** 7 ft **Area Code** 410 **Zip** 21842
Information Chamber of Commerce, 12320 Ocean Gateway; 410/213-0552

Deep-sea fishing is highly regarded in Maryland's only Atlantic Ocean resort. The white sand beach, three-mile boardwalk, amusements, golf courses and boating draw thousands of visitors every summer.

What to See and Do

❌ **Assateague Island National Seashore.** A 37-mi barrier strand that supports an intricate ecosystem, Assateague is also known for its population of ponies, Sika deer (miniature Oriental elk) and, in autumn, the migratory peregrine falcon. Campground (fee; Phone 410/641-3030); hike-in and canoe-in campsites and day-use facilities; conducted walks and demonstrations in summer. Visitor center (daily; closed winter hols). 1 mi W on US 50, then 7 mi S on MD 611. For further information phone 410/641-1441. For camping reservations phone 800/365-2267. (See CHINCOTEAGUE, VA) Per vehicle ¢¢ Also on the island is

Assateague State Park. Has 755 acres with 2 mi of ocean frontage and gentle, sloping beaches. Swimming, fishing. Boat launch. Picnicking, concession (summer). Bicycle, hiking trails. Camping (Apr-Oct). Standard fees (summer). For reservations, contact 7307 Stephen Decatur Hwy, Berlin 21811. Phone 410/641-2120. Entrance fee (Memorial Day-Labor Day) ¢

Annual Event

Fishing contests and tournaments. Many held throughout the yr. For exact dates contact the Chamber of Commerce.

Seasonal Event

Harness racing. Ocean Downs. 4 mi W on US 50. Nightly exc Mon. Children with adult only. Phone 410/641-0600. Late July-Labor Day.

Motels

★ ★ **BEST WESTERN FLAGSHIP OCEANFRONT.** 2600 Baltimore Ave (21842), 26th & Oceanfront. 410/289-3384; FAX 410/289-1743; res: 800/528-1234; res: 800/837-3585. E-mail bwestern@beachinn.net; web www.ocean-city.com/bestwestern.htm. 93 rms, 3 story. Late June-late Aug (3-day min wkends): S, D $179-$189; under 13 free; lower rates rest of yr. Closed 2 wks Dec & wkdays Dec 26-Feb 14. Crib free. TV; cable (premium), VCR (free movies). 2 pools, 1 indoor; wading pool, whirlpool, poolside serv. Dinner buffet avail May-Sept. Ck-out 11 am. Guest lndry. Business servs avail. Lighted tennis. Exercise equipt; sauna. Game rm. Rec rm. Many kit. units. Cr cds: A, C, D, DS, MC, V.

[D] [icons]

★ ★ **CASTLE IN THE SAND HOTEL.** 3701 Atlantic Ave (21842), Oceanfront at 37th St. 410/289-6846; FAX 410/289-9446; res: 800/552-7263. E-mail castle@beachin.net; web www.beachin.net/~castle. 36 rms, 5 story, 27 cottages, 108 kit. units. Early July-late Aug: S, D $165-$182; each addl $8; kit. units $165-$205; cottages $750-$1,295/wk; under 12 free; lower rates mid-Apr-early July & late Aug-late Oct. Closed rest of yr. Crib $5. TV; cable (premium). Pool; lifeguard. Supervised child's activities (June-Aug); ages 3-12. Restaurant 7:30 am-midnight. Bar 11-2 am; entertainment wkends. Ck-out 11 am. Meeting rm. Business servs avail. In-rm modem link. Bellhops. Free airport transportation. Game rm. Refrigerators. Some balconies. Cr cds: A, C, D, DS, MC, V.

[D] [icons]

✓ ★ **EXECUTIVE MOTEL.** 30th St & Baltimore Ave (21842). 410/289-3101; res: 800/638-1600. Web www.ocean-city/executive. 47 rms, 3 story. No elvtr. Memorial Day wkend, July-Labor Day (3-day min wkends): S, D $78-$88; each addl $6; under 6 free; lower rates late May-June, after Labor Day-mid-Sept. Closed rest of yr. Crib $6. TV; cable. Restaurant nearby. Ck-out 11 am. Refrigerators. Cr cds: C, MC, V.

[D] [icon]

★ **GATEWAY RESORT HOTEL.** 4800 Coastal Hwy (21842). 410/524-6500; FAX 410/524-5374; res: 800/382-2582. E-mail gateway@beach.com. 59 kit. units, 3 story. July-mid-Aug: S, D $195-$230; each addl $10; suites $1,195-$1,285/wk; under 6 free; higher rates hol wkends; lower rates rest of yr. Crib $10. TV; cable (premium). Pool; wading pool, whirlpool, lifeguard (summer). Playground. Complimentary coffee in rms. Restaurant 11-2 am. Rm serv. Bar; entertainment. Ck-out 11 am. Coin lndry. Business servs avail. Health club privileges. Lawn games. Balconies. Picnic tables. On ocean, swimming beach. Cr cds: A, C, D, DS, MC, V.

[icons]

★ ★ **HOWARD JOHNSON OCEANFRONT.** 24th St & Boardwalk (21842), Oceanfront & 24th St. 410/289-6401; FAX 410/289-2365. Web www.ocean-city.com/lodging/howardjohnsons. 72 units, 4 story, 26 kits. Late June-Aug: S, D $135-$175; each addl $10; kit. units $165-$185; under 18 free; lower rates Mar-June, Sept-Oct. Closed rest of yr. Crib free. TV; cable (premium). Heated pool; whirlpool. Complimentary coffee in lobby. Restaurant 7 am-6 pm. Ck-out 11 am. Business servs avail. Bellhops. Refrigerators. Balconies. On beach. Cr cds: A, C, D, DS, MC, V.

[D] [icons] SC

★ **NASSAU MOTEL.** 6002 Coastal Hwy (21842). 410/524-6451. E-mail nassauocm@aol.com. 62 rms, 3 story, 42 kits. No elvtr. July-late Aug: S, D $102-$120; each addl $6; higher rates wkends; lower rates Apr-June, late Aug-Oct. Closed rest of yr. Crib $5. TV; cable (premium).

Pool. Coffee in rms. Restaurant opp 6 am-11 pm. Ck-out 11 am. Refrigerators, microwaves. Grills. Sun deck. On ocean, beach. Cr cds: A, C, DS, MC, V.

[D] [icons]

★ ★ **QUALITY INN.** 5400 Coastal Hwy (21843), Oceanfront & 54th St. 410/524-7200; FAX 410/723-0018; res: 800/228-5050; res: 800/837-3586. 126 kit. units, 3-5 story. Memorial Day-Labor Day: kit. units $79-$239; each addl $7; under 6 free; wkly rates; package plans; higher rates hols; lower rates rest of yr. Crib free. TV; cable (premium), VCR (movies). 2 pools, 1 indoor; wading pool, whirlpool. Playground. Restaurant 8 am-9 pm. Bar 11 am-11 pm. Ck-out 11 am. Free lndry facilities. Business servs avail. In-rm modem link. Bellhops (summer). Tennis. Exercise equipt; saunas. Game rm. Lawn games. Private patios, balconies. Picnic tables, grills. On ocean, swimming beach. Tropical atrium. Cr cds: A, C, D, DS, ER, JCB, MC, V.

[D] [icons]

★ ★ **QUALITY INN.** 3301 Atlantic Ave (21843), at Oceanfront. 410/289-1234; res: 800/228-5050. 109 units, 5 story, 92 kits., 15 suites. June-Aug: S, D $158-$235; suites $250-$330; lower rates rest of yr. Crib $5. TV; cable, VCR (movies). 2 pools, 1 indoor; wading pool, whirlpool. Restaurant 7:30 am-2 pm. Restaurant nearby. Ck-out 11 am. Sundries. Coin lndry. Business servs avail. Gift shop. Exercise equipt; sauna. Game rm. Some in-rm whirlpools. Balconies. Cr cds: A, C, D, DS, MC, V.

[D] [icons] SC

★ ★ **RAMADA LIMITED OCEANFRONT.** Oceanfront & 32nd St (21842), 32nd St at oceanfront. 410/289-6444; FAX 410/289-0108; res: 800/837-3589. 76 kit. units, 3 story. No elvtr. July-Aug: S, D $174-$189; each addl $7; surcharge off-season wkends; lower rates rest of yr. Crib free. TV; cable (premium), VCR (movies). Pool; wading pool. Complimentary continental bkfst. Complimentary coffee in lobby. Ck-out 11 am. Guest lndry. Balconies overlook beach. Picnic area. Cr cds: A, C, D, DS, ER, MC, V.

[D] [icons]

★ **SAFARI MOTEL.** 1-13th St (21842). 410/289-6411; res: 800/787-2183. 46 rms in 2 bldgs, 3 & 4 story. July-Aug: S, D $119; under 14 free; lower rates mid-Apr-June, Sept-Oct. Closed rest of yr. Crib free. Pet accepted, some restrictions; $9/day. TV; cable (premium). Restaurant opp from 8 am. Ck-out 11 am. Bellhops. Balconies. On ocean. Cr cds: A, C, D, DS, MC, V.

[icons]

✓ ★ **SAHARA MOTEL.** 19th St & Boardwalk (21842). 410/289-8101; FAX 410/289-2894; res: 800/638-1600. Web www.saharamotel.com. 161 rms in 4 bldgs, 3 & 4 story, 5 kits. Elvtr in Tower bldg. Late June-mid-Sept: S, D $78-$140; each addl $6; kit. units $102-$138; lower rates late Apr-late June, late Sept. Closed rest of yr. Crib $6. TV. 2 pools. Restaurant 6 am-3 pm. Ck-out 11 am. Refrigerators. Some balconies. On beach. Cr cds: C, MC, V.

[D] [icons]

★ **TIDES MOTEL.** 7100 Coastal Hwy (21843). 410/524-7100; FAX 410/289-3039; res: 800/638-1600. 54 kit. units, 3 story. Late June-late Aug: S, D $99; each addl $6; under 6 free; higher rates: wkends & hols (3-day min), July-Aug wkdays (2-day min), Memorial Day & Labor Day; lower rates May-late June & Sept. Closed rest of yr. Crib $5. TV; cable. Pool. Coffee in rms. Restaurant nearby. Ck-out 11 am. Bellhops (in season). Some balconies. Cr cds: C, MC, V.

[D] [icons]

Motor Hotels

★ **CAYMAN SUITES.** 125th St Coastal Hwy (21842). 410/250-7600; FAX 410/250-7603; res: 800/546-0042. Web www.ocean-city.com/caymansuites. 57 suites. July-Aug: suites $179-$209; each addl $10; under 16 free; wkly, mid-wk rates; lower rates rest of yr. Closed Jan,

Feb. Crib $6. TV; cable (premium). Indoor pool. Complimentary coffee in lobby. Ck-out 11 am. Meeting rms. Business servs avail. Bellhops (in season). Exercise equipt. Microwaves. Balconies. Near ocean beach. Cr cds: A, C, DS, MC, V.

★★ COMFORT INN. 507 Atlantic Ave (21842), 5th St and Boardwalk. 410/289-5155; FAX 410/289-6547; res: 800/228-5150. Web www.comfortinnboardwalk.com. 84 kit. units in 2 bldgs, 5 story. June-Aug: S, D $164-$209; each addl $10; under 12 free; lower rates Mar-May, Sept-Nov. Closed rest of yr. Crib free. TV; cable (premium). 2 pools, 1 indoor. Complimentary continental bkfst. Restaurant nearby. Ck-out 11 am. Bellhops. Balconies. On ocean. Cr cds: A, C, D, DS, ER, JCB, MC, V.

★★ HOLIDAY INN OCEANFRONT. 6600 Coastal Hwy (21842), Oceanfront & 67th St. 410/524-1600; FAX 410/524-1135; res: 800/465-4329; res: 800/638-2106. 216 kit. units, 8 story. Memorial Day-Labor Day: S, D $160-$250; each addl $9; under 19 free; higher rates hol wkends; golf plans; lower rates rest of yr. Crib free. TV; cable (premium). 2 pools, 1 indoor; wading pools, whirlpool, poolside serv. Supervised child's activities (June-Aug); ages 5-9. Restaurant 7-11:30 am, 5-11 pm. Rm serv. Bar 5-midnight. Ck-out 11 am. Free lndry facilities. Meeting rms. Business servs avail. In-rm modem link. Bellhops. Tennis. Exercise equipt; sauna. Game rm. Balconies. Picnic tables. On ocean. Cr cds: A, C, D, DS, ER, JCB, MC, V.

★★ PHILLIPS BEACH PLAZA HOTEL. 1301 N Boardwalk (21842), Boardwalk at 13th St. 410/289-9121; FAX 410/289-3041; res: 800/492-5834. 96 units, 5 story, 26 kits., 8 3-bedrm kit. suites. July-late Aug: S, D $119-$174; each addl $20; kit. units $154-$194; kit. suites $200-$230; $20 surcharge wkends; package plans; lower rates rest of yr. Crib $10. TV; cable. Restaurant 8 am-1 pm, 5-9:30 pm. Bar 5 pm-2 am; entertainment 6-11 pm. Ck-out 11 am. Business servs avail. Bellhops. Shopping arcade. On ocean. Cr cds: A, C, D, DS, MC, V.

Hotels

★★★ COCONUT MALORIE HOTEL RESORT. 200 59th St. (21842), on Isle of Wight Bay, 59th St exit. 410/723-6100; FAX 410/524-9327; res: 800/767-6060. E-mail ocmalorie@beachin.net; web www.coconutmalorie.com. 85 units, 5 story, 52 suites. Memorial Day-Labor Day: S, D $164-$290; each addl $15; wkly rates; lower rates rest of yr. Crib $15. TV; cable (premium), VCR avail. Pool; poolside serv. Complimentary coffee in rms. Restaurant adj 11 am-11 pm. Ck-out noon. Meeting rms. Business servs avail. In-rm modem link. Concierge. Health club privileges. Refrigerators; many bathrm phones. Balconies. Original Haitian art; antique collection. Footbridge over marsh to dining facilities. Cr cds: A, C, D, MC, V.

★★★★ LIGHTHOUSE CLUB HOTEL. 56th St In-the Bay (21842), on Isle of Wight Bay. 410/524-5400; FAX 410/524-3928; res: 888/371-5400. E-mail island@dmv.com; web www. fagers.com. Rooms are wedge-shaped with spectacular views of the bay in this luxuriously appointed hotel, which was designed to resemble an archetypal Chesapeake Bay lighthouse. 23 rms, 3 story. No elvtr. Mid-June-Labor Day (2-day min): S, D $184-$285; each addl $15; wkly rates; lower rates rest of yr. Crib $15. TV; cable (premium), VCR. Pool privileges. Complimentary continental bkfst. Complimentary coffee in rms. Restaurant adj 11 am-11 pm. Bar 11-2 am; entertainment. Ck-out noon. Meeting rm. Business servs avail. In-rm modem link. Health club privileges. Bathrm phones, in-rm whirlpools, refrigerators, wet bars; some fireplaces. Balconies. Cr cds: A, C, D, DS, MC, V.

★★★ PRINCESS ROYALE OCEANFRONT HOTEL. 9100 Coastal Hwy (21842), 3 mi N on Coastal Hwy. 410/524-7777; FAX 410/524-7787; res: 800/476-9253. E-mail princess@dmv.com; web www.princessroyale.com. 310 kit. suites, 5 story. Mid-June-Labor Day: D $109-$299; under 12 free; wkly rates; golf plans; lower rates rest of yr. Crib $10. TV; cable. Indoor pool; whirlpool, poolside serv. Complimentary coffee in rms. Restaurant 7-2 am. Bar 11-2 am; entertainment. Ck-out 11 am. Coin lndry. Convention facilities. Business center. Gift shop. Beauty shop. Lighted tennis. 18-hole golf privileges, pro, putting green, driving range. Exercise equipt; sauna. Health club privileges. Game rm. Some in-rm whirlpools. Balconies. On ocean; swimming beach, ocean deck, private boardwalk. Most suites with ocean view. Cr cds: A, C, D, DS, MC, V.

★★★ SHERATON FONTAINEBLEAU HOTEL. 10100 Coastal Hwy (21842). 410/524-3535; FAX 410/524-3834; res: 800/638-2100. Web www.sheratonoc.com. 250 rms, 16 story, 8 kits. June-Aug: S, D $230-$300; each addl $15; suites, kit. units $350; studio rms $320; condos $1,600-$2,700/wkly; under 17 free; higher rates hol wkends (3-day min); lower rates rest of yr. Crib $15. Pet accepted; $20/day. TV; cable (premium), VCR avail. Heated pool; whirlpool, poolside serv in season, lifeguard. Coffee in rms. Restaurant 7 am-11 pm. Bar to 2 am; entertainment. Ck-out 11 am. Meeting rms. Business center. In-rm modem link. Beauty shop. Airport, bus depot transportation. Tennis privileges. Golf privileges. Exercise equipt; sauna, steam rm. Game rm. Refrigerators. Balconies. On ocean, beach. Cr cds: A, C, D, DS, ER, JCB, MC, V.

Inns

★★★ BERLIN ATLANTIC HOTEL. 2 N Main St (21811), 8 mi W on MD 50 to MD 113, S to Berlin, right on Bay St to Main St. 410/641-0189; FAX 410/641-4928; res: 800/814-7672. Web www.atbeach.com/lodging/md/hotel/atlantic. 17 rms, 5 with shower only, 3 story. S, D $75-$140; golf plans. Crib free. TV; cable. Complimentary full bkfst. Dining rm 6-9 pm; Fri, Sat to 10 pm. Bar noon-1 am. Ck-out 11 am, ck-in 3 pm. 18-hole golf privileges, greens fee $30-$35, pro, putting green. Porch on each floor. Restored Victorian hotel (1895); antiques. 2nd-floor parlor. Cr cds: A, C, MC, V.

★★ MERRY SHERWOOD PLANTATION. 8909 Worcester Hwy (21811), 8 mi W on US 50, then 3 mi S on MD 113. 410/641-2112; FAX 410/641-9528; res: 800/660-0358. Web www.atbeach.com/lodging/md/hotel/merrysherwood. 8 rms, 6 with bath. No rm phones. Mid-May-mid-Oct: S, D $150-$175; lower rates rest of yr. Children over 8 yrs only. Complimentary full bkfst; afternoon refreshments. Restaurant nearby. Ck-out 11 am, ck-in 2 pm. Some fireplaces. Built in 1859; on grounds of former plantation; large variety of trees and shrubs. Totally nonsmoking. Cr cds: C, MC, V.

Restaurants

★★ BONFIRE. 71st St & Coastal Hwy (21842). 410/524-7171. Hrs: 5-10 pm; from 4 pm in season; early-bird dinner 4-5 pm. Closed Mon-Thurs in winter. Res accepted. Bar to 2 am. Semi-a la carte: dinner $14.95-$26.95. Seafood buffet $21.95. Child's meals. Specializes in steak, prime rib, seafood. Cr cds: A, C, D, MC, V.

★★ EMBERS. 2305 Philadelphia Ave (21842), at 24th St. 410/289-3322. E-mail ocembers@aol.com; web www.embers.com. Hrs: 2-10 pm; also 8 am-noon Memorial Day wkend-Labor Day. Closed Dec-Feb. Res accepted. Bar to 2 am. Buffet: bkfst $7.99. Semi-a la carte: dinner $14-$25. Seafood buffet $22.95. Child's meals. Specializes in fresh seafood, steak, prime rib. Family-owned. Cr cds: A, C, DS, MC, V.

★★★ **FAGER'S ISLAND.** *201 60th St (21842), in the Bay.* *410/524-5500.* E-mail island@dmv.com; web www.fagers.com. Hrs: 11 am-12am. Res accepted. Bar. Semi-a la carte: lunch $3.75-$10.95, dinner $17-$25. Specializes in seafood, beef, Pacific rim dishes. Entertainment. View of bay. Oudoor dining in season. Cr cds: A, C, D, DS, MC, V.

D

★★ **HANNA'S MARINA DECK.** *306 Dorchester St (21842).* *410/289-4411.* Hrs: 11 am-11 pm. Closed mid-Oct-Easter. Bar. Semi-a la carte: lunch $4.95-$7.95, dinner $7.95-$27.95. Child's meals. Specializes in fish, lobster. On waterfront. Cr cds: A, C, DS, MC, V.

D

★★★ **HARRISON'S HARBOR WATCH.** *806 S Boardwalk (21842). 410/289-5121.* Hrs: 5-10 pm; July-Aug from 11:30 am. Closed Mon-Thurs Dec-Mar. Res accepted. Bar. Wine list. Semi-a la carte: dinner $8.95-$24.95. Child's meals. Specializes in fresh seafood, fish. Raw bar. Own breads. View of inlet overlooking Assateague Island. Cr cds: A, C, D, DS, ER, MC, V.

D

★★★ **HOBBIT.** *81st St & Bay (21842). 410/524-8100.* Hrs: 11 am-midnight; early-bird dinner 5-6 pm. Closed Dec 24-25. Res accepted. Contemporary Amer menu. Bar. Wine list. Semi-a la carte: lunch $3.95-$10.95, dinner $15.95-$24.95. Child's meals. Specializes in beef, veal, seafood. Own baking. Outdoor dining. View of bay. Family-owned. Cr cds: A, C, DS, MC, V.

D

★★ **OCEAN CLUB.** *49th St at Oceanfront (21842). 410/524-7500.* Hrs: 11-2 am; early-bird dinner 5-7 pm. Closed Dec 25; Mon, Tues off-season; also 2 wks in Jan. Res accepted. Bar. Semi-a la carte: bkfst $3.95-$9.95, lunch $4.25-$10, dinner $12.95-$26.95. Child's meals. Specializes in seafood. Entertainment Apr-Oct; rest of yr, Wed-Sun. Outdoor dining. On ocean. Cr cds: A, C, D, DS, MC, V.

SC

★★ **PHILLIPS CRAB HOUSE.** *2004 Philadelphia Ave at 21st (21842). 410/289-6821.* Web www.ocean-city/phillips. Hrs: noon-10 pm. Closed Nov-Mar. Serv bar. Semi-a la carte: lunch, dinner $4-$25. Seafood buffet $21.95. Child's meals. Specializes in crab dishes, fresh seafood. Family-owned. Cr cds: A, C, D, DS, MC, V.

D

★★ **PHILLIPS SEAFOOD HOUSE.** *14101 Coastal Hwy (21842), at 141st St. 410/250-1200.* Hrs: noon-10 pm; Fri, Sat to 11 pm; off-season 5-9 pm. Closed last wk Nov-Feb. Bar to 2 am. Semi-a la carte: lunch $4.95-$8.95, dinner $8.95-$22.95. Child's meals. Specializes in fresh seafood, crab, lobster. Pianist exc Mon; off-season Thurs-Sun. Cr cds: A, C, D, DS, MC, V.

D

Pikesville (B-7)

(See also Baltimore)

Pop 24,815 **Area Code** 410 **Zip** 21208

Motels

✓★ **COMFORT INN.** *10 Wooded Way (21208), at I-695 exit 20. 410/484-7700; FAX 410/653-1516; res: 800/732-2458.* 103 rms, 2-3 story. No elvtr. S, D $59-$89; under 18 free; wkly, monthly rates. Crib free. Pet accepted. TV; cable (premium). Pool; wading pool, lifeguard. Complimentary continental bkfst. Coffee in rms. Restaurant adj 6:30 am-11:30

pm. Ck-out 11 am. Coin lndry. Meeting rms. Business servs avail. In-rm modem link. Valet serv Mon-Fri. Health club privileges. Microwaves avail. Cr cds: A, C, D, DS, ER, JCB, MC, V.

D

★ **RAMADA INN.** *1721 Reisterstown Rd (21208), at I-695 exit 20S. 410/486-5600; FAX 410/484-9377; res: 800/272-7232.* Web www.holiday-inn.com. 108 rms, 2 story. S, D $69; under 18 free; higher rates Preakness. Crib free. Pet accepted. TV; cable (premium). Pool; poolside serv, lifeguard. Restaurant 6 am-1 pm, 5-10 pm; Sat, Sun from 7 am. Rm serv. Bar 5 pm-midnight. Ck-out noon. Meeting rms. Business servs avail. Valet serv. Health club privileges. Some refrigerators; microwaves avail. Cr cds: A, C, D, DS, ER, JCB, MC, V.

D

Motor Hotel

★★★ **HILTON.** *1726 Reisterstown Rd (21208), at I-695 exit 20S. 410/653-1100; FAX 410/415-6231; res: 800/445-8667.* E-mail pikhi_ds@hilton.com; web www.hilton.com. 171 rms, 5 story. S $99-$154; D $102-$164; each addl $15; suites $300-$399; wkend plans; family rates. Crib $10. TV; cable (premium), VCR avail (movies). Pool; lifeguard. Coffee in rms. Restaurant 7 am-11 pm. Rm serv. Bar 11-1 am. Ck-out noon. Meeting rms. Business servs avail. Bellhops. Valet serv. Gift shop. Barber, beauty shop. Airport transportation. Tennis privileges. Exercise equipt. Bathrm phones; microwaves avail. Cr cds: A, C, D, DS, ER, MC, V.

D

Inn

★★★ **GRAMERCY BED & BREAKFAST.** *1400 Greenspring Valley Rd (21153), I-695 exit 23N, Falls Rd to 2nd light, left on Greenspring Valley Rd. 410/486-2405; FAX 410/486-1765; res: 800/553-3404.* Web www.angelfire.com/md/pomykala. 10 rms, 3 story, 2 suites. S, D $155-$260; each addl $25; suites $250. Crib $10. TV; VCR (movies). Pool. Complimentary full bkfst. Ck-out noon, ck-in 3 pm. Business servs avail. In-rm modem link. Tennis. Lawn games. Picnic tables. Mansion (1902) on 45-acre wooded estate. Flower, herb gardens. Totally nonsmoking. Cr cds: A, C, DS, MC, V.

Restaurants

★★ **DUE.** *25 Crossroads Dr (21117), I-695, exit 20. 410/356-4147.* Hrs: 5:30-10 pm; Fri, Sat to 11 pm; Sun 5-9 pm. Closed most major hols. Res accepted. Italian menu. Bar. A la carte entrees: dinner $9.95-$24.95. Specializes in pasta, veal, chicken. Comtemporary decor. Cr cds: A, C, D, MC, V.

D

★★★ **LINWOOD'S CAFE.** *25 Crossroads Dr (21117), I-695, exit 20. 410/356-3030.* Hrs: 11:30 am-3 pm, 5:30-10 pm; Fri, Sat to 11 pm; Sun 5-9 pm. Closed most major hols. Res accepted; required Fri, Sat. Bar. A la carte entrees: lunch $4.95-$14.95, dinner $9.95-$27.95. Specializes in chicken, seafood, steak. Formal decor. Cr cds: A, C, D, MC, V.

D

★★ **PUFFINS.** *1000 Reisterstown Rd (21208), at Sherwood Ave. 410/486-8811.* Hrs: noon-2:30 pm, 5:30-close; Sun 5-8:30 pm. Closed most major hols. Res accepted Fri, Sat dinner. Bar. Semi-a la carte: lunch $6-$9.75, dinner $13-$21. Specializes in vegetarian, chicken, seafood dishes. Own breads. Modern decor; artwork. Totally nonsmoking. Cr cds: A, C, D, MC, V.

D

Pocomoke City (F-9)

(See also Crisfield)

Founded 1670 **Pop** 3,922 **Elev** 22 ft **Area Code** 410 & 443 **Zip** 21851
Information Pocomoke Chamber of Commerce, City Hall, 2nd floor, Clarke Ave & Vine St, PO Box 356; 410/957-1919

Motel

✓★★ **QUALITY INN.** *825 Ocean Hwy (21851), 2½ mi S on US 13.* 410/957-1300; FAX 410/957-9329; res: 800/228-5151. 64 rms. Memorial Day-Labor Day: S $60-$75; D $65-$82; each addl $5; under 18 free; higher rates Pony Penning. Crib free. Pet accepted. TV; cable (premium). Pool; wading pool. Complimentary continental bkfst. Ck-out 11 am. Business servs avail. In-rm modem link. Some in-rm whirlpools, refrigerators. Picnic tables, grills. Cr cds: A, C, D, DS, ER, JCB, MC, V.

Inn

★★ **RIVER HOUSE INN.** *201 E Market St (21863), 10 mi NE on Business US 113.* 410/632-2722; FAX 410/632-2866. E-mail riverinn@shore.intercom.net. 8 rms, 2 with shower only, 3 story, 1 suite, 1 guest house. No elvtrs. No rm phones. Apr-Oct: S, D $100-$175; each addl $20; suite $100; guest house $160; under 16 free; golf rates; package plans; wkends (2-day min); lower rates rest of yr. Pet accepted, some restrictions. 18-hole golf privileges, greens fee, pro. Lawn games. Some refrigerators, microwaves. In-rm whirlpool in suite. Fireplaces. On river. Built in 1860. Totally nonsmoking. Cr cds: A, C, DS, MC, V.

Restaurant

★ **UPPER DECK.** *1245 Ocean Hwy (21851), 2 mi S of US 113.* 410/957-3166. Hrs: 11 am-10 pm; Sun noon-9 pm. Res accepted. Bar to 11 am; Sun to 10 pm. Semi-a la carte: lunch $4.95-$5.95, dinner $7.50-$20. Child's meals. Specializes in local seafood, steak. Own desserts. Antiques. Cr cds: C, MC, V.

Rockville (C-6)

(See also Gaithersburg)

Pop 44,835 **Elev** 451 ft **Area Code** 240 & 301 **E-mail** rccchamber@aol.com **Web** www.rockvillechamber.org
Information Chamber of Commerce, 250 Hungerford Dr, Suite L10, 20850; 301/424-9300

Second-largest city in the state of Maryland, Rockville is the seat of Montgomery County, located at the north edge of the District of Columbia. The Great Falls of the Potomac are 9 miles south off MD 189. This series of small falls was pretty but unnavigable, so the Chesapeake and Ohio Canal (see CHESAPEAKE AND OHIO CANAL NATIONAL HISTORICAL PARK) was built from Washington, DC, to Cumberland to simplify travel. Stone locks and levels are still visible. The graves of F. Scott and Zelda Fitzgerald are in St Mary's Cemetery.

What to See and Do

Beall-Dawson House (1815). Federal architecture; period furnishings; library; museum shop; 19th-century doctor's office. Tours guided by docents. (Tues-Sat; also 1st Sun of month; closed major hols) 103 W Montgomery Ave. Phone 301/762-1492. ¢

Annual Event

Hometown Holidays. Family entertainment. Memorial Day wkend.

Motel

★★★ **COURTYARD BY MARRIOTT.** *2500 Research Blvd (20850).* 301/670-6700; FAX 301/670-9023; res: 800/321-2211. Web www.marriott.com. 147 rms, 2 story, 13 suites. S, D $120-$135; suites $135-$145; under 12 free; wkly rates. Crib free. TV; cable (premium). Indoor pool; whirlpool, lifeguard. Complimentary coffee. Restaurant 6:30 am-2 pm, 5-10 pm; Sat 7-11 am; Sun 7 am-2 pm. Rm serv 5-10 pm. Bar 5-11 pm. Ck-out 1 pm. Coin lndry. Meeting rms. Business servs avail. In-rm modem link. Valet serv. Sundries. Exercise equipt. Balconies. Refrigerators avail. Cr cds: A, C, D, DS, MC, V.

Motor Hotels

★★★ **QUALITY SUITES.** *3 Research Ct (20850), 3 mi N on I-270, exit 8.* 301/840-0200; FAX 301/258-0160; res: 800/228-5151. 124 rms, 3 story, 66 kit. suites. S, D $99.95-$129.95; each addl $10; kit. suites $109.95-$139.95; under 18 free; wkend rates. Crib free. TV; cable (premium), VCR avail. Complimentary full bkfst. Complimentary coffee in rms. Restaurant nearby. Ck-out noon. Meeting rms. Business center. Valet serv. Sundries. Gift shop. Coin lndry. Exercise equipt. Pool; lifeguard. Refrigerators, microwaves, wet bars. Cr cds: A, C, D, DS, MC, V.

★★★ **WOODFIN SUITES HOTEL.** *1380 Piccard Dr (20850), I-270 exit 8.* 301/590-9880; FAX 301/590-9614; res: 800/237-8811. 203 suites, 3 story. S, D $165-$230; each addl $15; 2-bedrm suites $275; under 12 free. Crib free. Pet accepted, some restrictions. TV; cable (premium). Pool; whirlpool, lifeguard. Complimentary full bkfst. Restaurant 6-9 am, wkends 7-10 am. Bar 5-10 pm Mon-Thurs. Ck-out noon. Meeting rms. Business center. In-rm modem link. Valet serv. Sundries. Exercise equipt. Refrigerators, microwaves. Cr cds: A, C, D, DS, ER, JCB, MC, V.

Hotel

★★★ **DOUBLETREE.** *1750 Rockville Pike (20852).* 301/468-1100; FAX 301/468-0163; res: 800/222-8733. 315 rms, 8 story. S, D $159-$169; each addl $10; suites $195-$325; under 19 free; wkly, wkend rates. Crib free. TV; cable (premium). Indoor/outdoor pool; whirlpool, lifeguard. Coffee in rms. Restaurant 6 am-11 pm. Bar from 11 am; Fri, Sat to 1 am. Ck-out noon. Convention facilities. Business center. In-rm modem link. Gift shop. Beauty shop. Covered valet parking. Exercise equipt: sauna. Game rm. Refrigerators, microwaves avail. 8-story atrium; 20-ft waterfall. Gazebo. Luxury level. Cr cds: A, C, D, DS, ER, JCB, MC, V.

Restaurants

✓★ **A & J.** *1319-c Rockville Pike (20852), Woodmont Station shopping center.* 301/251-7878. Hrs: 11:30 am-9 pm; Fri, Sat to 9:30 pm. Chinese menu. A la carte entrees: lunch $4.85-$9, dinner $6.25-$9. Specializes in Northern Chinese dim sum. Casual decor. Totally nonsmoking. Cr cds: C.

✓★★ **ADDIE'S RESTAURANT.** *11120 Rockville Pike (20852).* 301/881-0081. Hrs: 11:30 am-2:30 pm, 5:30-9:30 pm; Fri to 10 pm; Sat noon to 3 pm, 5:30-10 pm. Closed Sun; Jan 1, Thanksgiving, Dec 25. Res accepted Mon-Thurs dinner. Regional Amer menu. Bar. Semi-a la carte:

lunch $6.50-$10.95, dinner $11.95-$20. Child's meals. Specializes in seasonal American dishes. Own pastries. Outdoor dining. Eclectic decor; collection of whimsical clocks; wood-burning grill. Cr cds: A, C, D, MC, V.

D

★★ **ANDALUCIA.** *12300 Wilkens Ave (20852). 301/770-1880.* Hrs: 11:30 am-2:30 pm, 5:30-10 pm; Sat 5:30-10:30 pm; Sun 4:30-9:30 pm. Closed Mon; Jan 1. Res accepted; required Fri, Sat dinner. Spanish menu. Serv bar. A la carte entrees: lunch $7.50-$10.95, dinner $12.50-$19.95. Specialties: paella Valenciana, zarzuela costa del sol, fresh seafood. Own desserts. Entertainment Thurs. Mediterranean decor; many plants. Totally nonsmoking. Cr cds: A, C, D, DS, MC, V.

✓★★ **BENJARONG THAI RESTAURANT.** *855 Rockville Pike # C (20852), Wintergreen shopping center. 301/424-5533.* Hrs: 11:30 am-3 pm, 5-9:30 pm; Fri, Sat to 10:30 pm; Sun 5-9:30 pm. Closed most major hols. Res accepted. Thai menu. Bar. Semi-a la carte: lunch $5.95-$7.95, dinner $7.95-$11.95. Specialties: pad thai, chicken satay. Thai decor. Cr cds: A, C, D, DS, MC, V.

D

✓★★ **BOMBAY BISTRO.** *98 W Montgomery Ave (20850). 301/762-8798.* Hrs: 11 am-2:30 pm, 5-9:30 pm; Fri, Sat to 10 pm; Sun noon-3 pm, 5-9:30 pm. Closed Thanksgiving, Labor Day. Indian menu. Wine, beer. A la carte entrees: lunch, dinner $6.95-$15.95. Buffet lunch: $6.95-$8.95. Specializes in vegetarian, tandoori dishes. Casual decor. Cr cds: A, C, D, DS, MC, V.

D

★★ **COPELAND'S OF NEW ORLEANS.** *1584 Rockville Pike (20852). 301/230-0968.* E-mail store8@vni.net. Hrs: 11 am-midnight. Closed Dec 25. Bar. Semi-a la carte: lunch $6-$12, dinner $7-$15. Child's meals. Specializes in seafood, Creole & Cajun dishes. Art deco decor. Cr cds: A, C, D, DS, MC, V.

D

★★ **IL PIZZICO.** *15209 Frederick Rd (20850). 301/309-0610.* Hrs: 11 am-2:30 pm, 5-9:30 pm; Fri to 10 pm; Sat 5-10 pm. Closed Sun; most major hols. Italian menu. Bar. Semi-a la carte: lunch $6.95-$10.95, dinner $8.95-$13.95. Specializes in pasta, seafood. Italian decor. Cr cds: A, C, MC, V.

D

★★★ **NORMANDIE FARM.** *10710 Falls Rd (20854), 3½ mi SW on MD 189, I-270 exit 5. 301/983-8838.* Hrs: 11:30 am-2:30 pm, 6-10 pm; Sun 5-9 pm; Sun brunch 11 am-2 pm. Closed Mon. Res accepted. French menu. Bar. Semi-a la carte: lunch $6.50-$12.50, dinner $14-$25. Sun brunch $18.50. Specializes in seafood, veal. Entertainment Thur-Sat. French provincial decor. Cr cds: A, C, DS, MC, V.

D

★★★ **OLD ANGLER'S INN.** *10801 Macarthur Blvd (20854), approx 8 mi S on MD 189, I-270 Exit 5. 301/299-9097.* Web www.oldanglersinn.com. Hrs: noon-2:30 pm, 6-10:30 pm. Closed Mon. Bar. Wine list. A la carte entrees: lunch $12-$16, dinner $22-$29. Prix fixe: dinner $55-$75. Specializes in seafood, lamb. Patio dining overlooking wooded area. Stone inn (1860); fireplace. Family-owned. Cr cds: A, C, D, MC, V.

♥

✓★ **RED HOT & BLUE.** *16811 Crabbs Branch Way (20855), in Grove Shopping Center. 301/948-7333.* Hrs: 11 am-10 pm; Fri to 11 pm; Sat noon-11 pm; Sun from noon. Closed Thanksgiving, Dec 25. Bar. Semi-a la carte: lunch, dinner $5.99-$13.99. Child's meals. Specializes in Memphis pit barbecue, ribs. Outdoor dining. Casual decor; blues memorabilia. Totally nonsmoking. Cr cds: A, C, MC, V.

D

✓★ **RICCIUTI'S.** *3308 Olney-sandy Spring Rd (20832), 9 mi NE on MD 108. 301/570-3388.* Hrs: 11:30 am-9 pm; Fri, Sat to 10 pm; Sun 4-9 pm. Closed major hols. Italian menu. Wine, beer. Semi-a la carte: lunch

$3.95-$5.50, dinner $5.25-$10.75. Child's meals. Specialties: calzone, stromboli, chocolate pizza. Outdoor dining. Italian decor. Totally nonsmoking. Cr cds: A, C, DS, MC, V.

✓★ **SEVEN SEAS.** *1776 E Jefferson St (20852). 301/770-5020.* Hrs: 11:30-1 am. Closed Thanksgiving. Res accepted. Chinese, Japanese menu. Bar. Semi-a la carte: lunch $3.95-$6.50, dinner $7.25-$16.95. Specializes in Szechwan, Taiwan, Shanghai cuisine. Sushi bar. Chinese artwork. Cr cds: A, C, DS, MC, V.

D

✓★ **SILVER DINER.** *11806 Rockville Pike MD 355 (20852), in Mid-Pike Plaza. 301/770-0333.* Web www.silverdiner.com. Hrs: 7-2 am; Fri, Sat to 3 am; early-bird dinner Mon-Fri 4-6 pm. Closed Dec 25. Serv bar. Semi-a la carte: bkfst $3.99-$5.99, lunch $5.99-$7.99, dinner $5.99-$9.99. Child's meals. Specialties: meatloaf, chicken-pot pie, turkey. 1950s-style diner with jukeboxes. Servers dressed in period clothing. Cr cds: A, C, D, DS, MC, V.

D SC

★★ **TASTE OF SAIGON.** *410 Hungerford Dr (20850). 301/424-7222.* Hrs: 11 am-10 pm; Fri, Sat to 11 pm; Sun 11 am-9:30 pm. Closed Thanksgiving, Dec 25. Res accepted. Vietnamese menu. Bar. A la carte entrees: lunch $5.95-$14.95, dinner $7.95-$16.95. Specialties: black pepper soft shell crab and shrimp, pepper Saigon steak. Outdoor dining. Contemporary decor. Cr cds: A, C, D, DS, MC, V.

D

★★ **THAT'S AMORE.** *15201 Shady Grove Rd (20850). 301/670-9666.* Hrs: 11:30 am-10:30 pm; Fri to midnight; Sat 4 pm-midnight; Sun 4-9:30 pm. Closed Labor Day, Thanksgiving, Dec 25. Italian menu. Bar. A la carte entrees: lunch $5.95-$9.95, dinner $18-$22. Specializes in pasta, veal, chicken. Stained-glass windows. Early 20th-century mens club atmosphere. Cr cds: A, C, D, DS, MC, V.

D

✓★★ **WURZBURG HAUS.** *7236 Muncaster Mill Rd (20855), in Red Mill Shopping Center. 301/330-0402.* Hrs: 11:30 am-9 pm; Fri to 10 pm; Sat noon-9 pm; Sun noon-9 pm. German menu. Wine, beer. A la carte entrees: lunch $6.75-$12.95, dinner $9.95-$14.75. Child's meals. Specializes in schnitzel, wurst. Accordionist Fri-Sun. 2 dining areas. German, Austrian atmosphere; collection of beer steins. Cr cds: A, C, D, DS, MC, V.

D

Unrated Dining Spot

HARD TIMES CAFE. *1117 Nelson St (20850), in Woodley Garden Shopping Center. 301/294-9720.* E-mail htcrock@aol.com. Hrs: 11:30 am-10 pm; Fri, Sat to 11 pm; Sun noon-9 pm. Closed Thanksgiving, Dec 25. Bar. A la carte entrees: lunch, dinner $4.50-$6. Child's meals. Specializes in chili, vegetarian dishes. Cr cds: A, C, MC, V.

D

Salisbury (E-9)

(See also Ocean City)

Founded 1732 **Pop** 20,592 **Elev** 33 ft **Area Code** 410 & 443 **Zip** 21801 **E-mail** wicotour@shore.intercom.net **Web** www.co.wicomico.md.us/tourism

Information Wicomico County Convention & Visitors Bureau, 8480 Ocean Hwy, Delmar 21875; 410/548-4914 or 800/332-TOUR. Information is also available from the Chamber of Commerce, 300 E Main St, PO Box 510, 21803; 410/749-0144

"Central City of the Eastern Shore" and of the Delmarva Peninsula, Salisbury has a marina on the Wicomico River providing access to Chesapeake Bay. It lies within 30 miles of duck-hunting and deep-sea fishing. Gasoline pumps, hydraulic lifts, canned and frozen foods, seafood and poultry come from this area.

What to See and Do

Mason-Dixon Line Marker. Bears coats of arms of Lord Baltimore and William Penn. 5 mi N on US 13, 13A, then 7 mi W on MD 467.

Poplar Hill Mansion (ca 1805). Example of Georgian and Federal-style architecture; palladium and bull's-eye windows; large brass box locks on doors, woodwork, mantels and fireplaces. Period furniture; country garden. (Usually Sun afternoons; Tues-Sat by appt) Phone 410/749-1776. ¢

Princess Anne. This town was the home of Samuel Chase, signer of the Declaration of Independence. Buildings of the Colonial and Federal periods are of architectural interest. 13 mi SW on US 13.

Salisbury Zoological Park. Natural habitats for almost 400 mammals, birds and reptiles. Major exhibits include bears, monkeys, jaguars, bison, waterfowl. Also exotic plants. (Daily) 755 S Park Dr. Phone 410/548-3188. Donation

The Nassawango Iron Furnace. One of the oldest industrial sites in Maryland and one of the earliest hot-blast mechanisms still intact. The stack was restored in 1966; archaeological excavations were made and a canal, a dike and a portion of the old waterwheel used in the manufacturing process were found. The remains of the area are undergoing restoration. (Apr-Oct, daily) 16 mi S via MD 12 to Old Furnace Rd. Phone 410/632-2032. ¢¢   Surrounding the iron furnace is

Furnace Town. This 1840s industrial village occupies 22 acres around the iron furnace and also includes six historic structures; a working 19th-century blacksmith shop and broom-making shop has demonstrations on selected days; a museum and company store; archaeological excavations; a nature trail and picnic area. Special events take place throughout the season. (Same days & fees as furnace)

Ward Museum of Wildfowl Art. Displays include the history of decoy and wildfowl carving in North America; wildfowl habitats; contemporary wildfowl art. Changing exhibits. Gift shop. (Mon-Sat, also Sun afternoons) 909 S Schumaker Dr, at Beaglin Park Dr. Phone 410/742-4988, ext 100.   ¢¢

Motels

✓ ★ ★ **COMFORT INN.** 2701 N Salisbury Blvd (21801), 4½ mi N on US 13. 410/543-4666; FAX 410/749-2639; res: 800/638-7949. 96 units, 2 story, 24 suites. Mid-May-mid-Sept: S $74.95-$97.95; D $85.95-$108.95; each addl $8; suites $97.95-$120.95; under 18 free; higher rates wkends; lower rates rest of yr. Crib avail. Pet accepted. TV; cable (premium). Pool privileges. Complimentary continental bkfst. Restaurant nearby. Ck-out 11 am. Meeting rm. Business servs avail. Lawn games. Refrigerator, wet bar avail. Picnic table, grills. Cr cds: A, C, D, DS, ER, JCB, MC, V.

D 🐾 ≈ 🔥 SC

★ ★ **HOWARD JOHNSON.** 2625 N Salisbury Blvd (21801), 3 mi N on US 13. 410/742-7194; FAX 410/742-5194; res: 800/465-4329. Web www.hojo.com. 123 rms, 2 story. Mid-June-mid-Sept: S $49-$99; D $49-$107; each addl $8; under 18 free; lower rates rest of yr. Crib free. Pet accepted, some restrictions. TV; cable (premium). Pool. Complimentary bkfst buffet. Restaurant 6:30-9:30 am. Bar 4:30 pm-midnight. Ck-out 11 am. Coin lndry. Meeting rms. Business servs avail. Health club privileges. Cr cds: A, C, D, DS, MC, V.

D 🐾 ≈ 🔥 SC

Motor Hotel

★ ★ **RAMADA INN CONFERENCE CENTER.** 300 S Salisbury Blvd (21801). 410/546-4400; FAX 410/546-2528; res: 888/800-7617. E-mail ramadasalis@aol.com. 156 rms, 5 story. July-Aug: S, D $87-$135; each addl $10; under 18 free; lower rates rest of yr. Crib free. Pet accepted. TV; cable (premium). Indoor pool. Coffee in rms. Restaurant 6:30 am-2:30 pm, 5:30-10 pm; wkends from 7 am. Rm serv. Bar 4 pm-2

am; wkends from noon. Ck-out noon. Meeting rms. Business servs avail. Bellhops. Free airport transportation. Health club privileges. On river. Cr cds: A, C, D, DS, MC, V.

D 🐾 ≈ 🏖 🔥 SC

Inn

★ ★ ★ **WATERLOO COUNTRY INN.** 28822 Mt Vernon Rd (21853), 15 mi S on US 13, 3 mi W on MD 362. 410/651-0883; FAX 410/651-5592. E-mail waterloo@shore.intercom.net. 5 rms, 3 story, 2 suites. Apr-Oct: S, D $125-$175; suites $205-$225; wkends, hols (2-day min); lower rates rest of yr. Closed Jan-Feb. Children over 9 yrs only. TV; cable. Complimentary full bkfst. Ck-out 11 am, ck-in 2 pm. Luggage handling. Golf privileges, greens fee $60, pro, putting green. Pool; whirlpool. In-rm whirlpool, fireplace in suites. Picnic tables. Built in 1750; on 317 acres. Totally nonsmoking. Cr cds: A, C, MC, V.

D 🐾 🏇 🏖 ≈ 🔥 🐾

Silver Spring (C-6)

(See also Bowie, College Park, Rockville; also see District of Columbia)

Pop 76,046 **Elev** 350 ft **Area Code** 240 & 301
Information Chamber of Commerce, 8601 Georgia Ave, Suite 203, 20910; 301/565-3777

What to See and Do

Brookside Gardens. A 50-acre display garden with two conservatories, flowering displays; variety of flowering plants in eight gardens; educational programs. (Daily; closed Dec 25) N on MD 97, right on Randolph Rd, right on Glenallan Ave, in Wheaton. Phone 301/949-8230.   **Free**

National Capital Trolley Museum. Rides on old-time American and European trolleys; exhibits depict history of streetcars. Special events during yr. (July-Aug, Sat-Sun & Wed; rest of yr, Sat & Sun only; also open Memorial Day, July 4, Labor Day) Northwest Branch Park, about 7 mi N on Bonifant Rd, just off MD 650 in Layhill. Phone 301/384-6088. Museum   **Free**; Rides   ¢¢

Motel

★ ★ ★ **COURTYARD BY MARRIOTT.** 12521 Prosperity Dr (20904), 6 mi NE on US 29, then E on Cherry Hill Rd to Prosperity Dr. 301/680-8500; FAX 301/680-9232; res: 800/321-2211. 146 units, 3 story. S $114; D $124; suites $140-$150; wkly, wkend rates. Crib free. TV; cable (premium). Indoor pool; whirlpool, lifeguard. Complimentary coffee in rms. Restaurant 6:30-10 am, 5-10 pm; Sat, Sun 7 am-1 pm. Bar Mon-Fri 4-10 pm. Ck-out noon. Coin lndry. Meeting rms. Business servs avail. In-rm modem link. Valet serv. Sundries. Exercise equipt. Health club privileges. Refrigerators, microwaves avail. Cr cds: A, C, D, DS, ER, JCB, MC, V.

D ≈ 🏇 🏖 🔥 SC

Restaurants

★ ★ **BLAIR MANSION INN.** 7711 Eastern Ave (20912). 301/588-1688. Hrs: 11:30 am-9 pm; Sat from 5 pm; Sun from 2 pm. Closed Mon. Res accepted. Continental, Amer menu. Bar. Semi-a la carte: lunch $5.95-$9.95, dinner $9.95-$19.95. Specializes in poultry, beef, crab. Murder mystery dinners Thurs-Sun. 1890s Victorian mansion; gaslight chandelier, 7 fireplaces. Family-owned. Totally nonsmoking. Cr cds: A, C, D, DS, MC, V.

★ ★ **CRISFIELD AT LEE PLAZA.** 8606 Colesville Rd MD 29 (20910), ground floor of high rise building, in Lee Plaza. 301/588-1572. Hrs: 11:30 am-10 pm; Fri to 11 pm; Sat 4-11 pm; Sun 2-9:30 pm. Closed

Thanksgiving, Dec 25. Res accepted; required Fri, Sat. Bar. Semi-a la carte: lunch $5.95-$15.95, dinner $14.95-$17.95. Child's meals. Specializes in seafood, shrimp, crab. Art deco decor. Cr cds: A, C, D, DS, MC, V.

★ ★ ★ MRS. K'S TOLL HOUSE. *9201 Colesville Rd (20910). 301/589-3500.* Hrs: 11:30 am-2:30 pm, 5-9 pm; Fri, Sat to 9:30 pm; Sun 11 am-9 pm; Sun brunch to 1 pm. Closed Mon; Dec 25. Serv bar. Complete meals: lunch $11.95, dinner $17.95-$25.50. Sun brunch $15.75. Specializes in regional American cuisine. Century-old tollhouse; antique china, glass. Gardens. Totally nonsmoking. Cr cds: A, C, D, DS, MC, V.

★ VICINO RESTAURANTE ITALIANO. *959 Sligo Ave (20910). 301/588-3372.* Hrs: 11:30 am-10:30 pm; Mon to 9:30 pm; Sun 1-9:30 pm. Closed some major hols. Italian menu. Wine, beer. A la carte entrees: lunch, dinner $6.50-$12. Child's meals. Specializes in pizza, pasta, seafood. Outdoor dining. Casual Italian neighborhood decor. Totally nonsmoking. Cr cds: C, MC, V.

St Mary's City (E-7)

(See also Leonardtown, Waldorf; also see District of Columbia)

Settled 1634 **Pop** 1,300 (est) **Elev** 36 ft **Area Code** 240 & 301 **Zip** 20686 **E-mail** stmcdecd@mail.ameritel.net **Web** www.somd.lib.md.us/stma/government/stmcdecd.html

Information St Mary's County Division of Tourism, 23115 Leonard Hall Dr, PO Box 653, Leonardtown 20650; 301/475-4411 or 800/327-9023

Maryland's first colonists bought a Native American village on this site upon their arrival in the New World under Leonard Calvert. The settlement was the capital and hub of the area until 1694, when the colonial capital was moved to Annapolis. The town gradually disappeared. The city and county are still rich in historical attractions.

What to See and Do

Historic St Mary's City. Outdoor museum at site of Maryland's 1st capital (1634) includes reconstructed State House (1676), replica of the original capital bldg; other exhibits include the *Maryland Dove*, replica of a 17th-century ship, and archaeological exhibits. Also seasonal living history programs, a 17th-century tobacco plantation, reconstructed 17th-century inn; visitor center, outdoor cafe. Visitor center (daily; closed Jan 1, Thanksgiving, Dec 25); outdoor museum (4th wkend Mar-Nov, Wed-Sun). MD 5 & Rosecroft Rd. Phone 301/862-0990 or 800/SMC-1634. ¢¢¢ Also here is

Margaret Brent Memorial. Gazebo overlooking the river; memorial to the woman who, being a wealthy landowner, requested the right to vote in the Maryland Assembly in 1648, in order to settle Leonard Calvert's affairs after his death.

Leonard Calvert Monument. Monument to Maryland's first colonial governor. Trinity Churchyard.

Point Lookout State Park. Site of the Confederate Monument, the only memorial erected by the US government to honor the POWs who died in the Point Lookout Prison Camp during the Civil War (3,384 died here). Swimming, fishing, boating, hiking. Picnicking; improved camping (Apr-Oct; self-contained camping units yr round). Nature center. Civil War museum. Standard fees. (May-Sept, wkends) 13 mi S on MD 5. Phone 301/872-5688. Day-use entrance fee (May-Oct) ¢¢

Annual Events

Maryland Days. Boat rides, seafood, 17th-century militia musters. 3rd wkend Mar.

Crab Festival. Steamed crabs, other seafood and nonseafood dishes. Arts and crafts, antique and classic car show. 1st Sun June.

Restaurant

✓ ★ **ALOHA RESTAURANT.** *2025 State Route 235 (20619), 11 mi NW on MD 235, in shopping center. 301/862-4838.* Hrs: 10:30 am-10 pm; Fri to 11 pm; Sat noon-11 pm; Sun noon-9:30 pm. Closed Thanksgiving, Dec 25. Chinese, Japanese menu. Bar. Semi-a la carte: lunch $4.25-$5.25, dinner $5.95-$19. Complete meals: lunch $4.95, dinner $7.25-$9.95. Buffet: lunch $5.99, dinner $7.99. Child's meals. Specializes in Szechwan, Hunan dishes. Sushi bar. Polynesian atmosphere. Cr cds: A, C, DS, MC, V.

Unrated Dining Spot

EVANS SEAFOOD. *16680 Piney Point Rd (20674), S on MD 5, approx 10 mi S on MD 249. 301/994-2299.* Hrs: 4-10 pm; Sat from noon; Sun noon-9 pm. Closed Mon. Bar. Semi-a la carte: lunch $5.50-$13.95, dinner $8.95-$21.95. Child's meals. Specializes in steak, seafood. View of the Potomac River. Family-owned. Cr cds: C, MC, V.

St Michaels (D-8)

Pop 1,301 **Elev** 7 ft **Area Code** 410 **Zip** 21663 **Web** www.bluecrab.org/st.michaels

Information Talbot County Chamber of Commerce, PO Box 1366, Easton 21601; 410/822-4606

Chartered in 1804, St Michaels has become a boating and tourist center with its abundance of shops, marinas, restaurants, bed-and-breakfasts and country inns. It is a town with many Federal- and Victorian-period buildings.

What to See and Do

Chesapeake Bay Maritime Museum. Waterside museum consists of 9 buildings. Includes historic lighthouse, floating exhibits, boat-building shop with working exhibit, ship models, small boats; paintings; waterfowl exhibits; workboats and mechanical propulsion. Special events throughout the year (see ANNUAL EVENT). (Daily) Mill St. Phone 410/745-2916. ¢¢¢

St Mary's Square. Public square laid out in 1770 by Englishman James Braddock. Several buildings date to the early 1800s, including the Cannonball House and Dr. Miller's Farmhouse. The Ship's Carpenter Bell was cast in 1842; across from the bell stand 2 cannons, one dating from the Revolution, the other from the War of 1812. Also here is

St Mary's Square Museum. Mid-19th-century home of "half-timber" construction; one of the earliest buildings in St Michaels. Exhibits of historical and local interest. (1st wkend May-last wkend Oct, Sat & Sun; also by appt) Inquire about the town walking tour brochures. Contact the Town Office, Phone 410/745-9535.

The Footbridge. Only remaining bridge of three that once connected the town with areas across the harbor. Joins Navy Point to Cherry St.

The *Patriot*. A 1-hr narrated cruise on Miles River. Four trips daily. (Apr-Oct) Berthed at Chesapeake Bay Maritime Museum. Phone 410/745-3100. ¢¢¢

Annual Event

Mid-Atlantic Maritime Festival. Chesapeake Bay Maritime Museum. Nautical celebration with fly-fishing demonstration, skipjack races, boat building contest, boat parade, seafood festival cooking contest. Phone 410/745-2916 or 410/822-5553. 3 days mid-May.

Motor Hotel

✓★★ **BEST WESTERN/SAINT MICHAELS MOTOR INN.** *1228 S Talbot St (21663).* 410/745-3333; FAX 410/745-2906; res: 800/528-1234. 93 rms, 2 story. May-mid-Nov: S $75-$96; D $87-$107; each addl $8; under 18 free; lower rates rest of yr. TV; cable (premium). 2 pools. Complimentary continental bkfst. Restaurant adj 11 am-11 pm. Ck-out 11 am. Meeting rms. Business servs avail. Cr cds: A, C, D, DS, MC, V.

D ⌷ ⌷ 🔥 SC

Hotel

★★★ **ST MICHAELS HARBOUR INN & MARINA.** *101 N Harbor Rd (21663).* 410/745-9001; FAX 410/745-9150; res: 800/955-9001. E-mail harbour@friend.ly.net; web www.harbourinn.com. 46 units, 3 story, 38 suites. May-Oct: S, D, suites $169-$429; under 18 free; higher rates wkends (2-day min); lower rates rest of yr. Crib $10. TV; cable (premium). Pool; whirlpool; poolside serv. Coffee in rms. Restaurant (see WINDOWS). Bar 11 am-10 pm. Ck-out noon. Coin lndry. Meeting rms. Business servs avail. Gift shop. Exercise equipt. Health club privileges. Refrigerator in suites; some in-rm whirlpools. Some balconies. Picnic tables. 60-slip marina. Cr cds: A, C, D, DS, MC, V.

D ⌷ 🏃 ⌷ 🔥 SC

Resort

★★ **HARBOURTOWNE GOLF RESORT & CONFERENCE CENTER.** *Rte 33 & Martingham Dr (21663), 3 mi W on MD 33.* 410/745-9066; FAX 410/745-9124; res: 800/446-9066. Web www.harbortowne.com. 111 rms, 1-2 story. Mar-Nov: S, D $155-$175; each addl $10; suites $225-$250; under 12 free; golf plans; lower rates rest of yr. TV; cable (premium), VCR avail. Crib free. Pool; poolside serv, lifeguard. Dining rm 7 am-10 pm. Ck-out 11 am, ck-in 3 pm. Grocery, package store 3 mi. Meeting rms. Business center. In-rm modem link. Tennis. 18-hole golf, greens fee $55, pro, putting green, driving range. Exercise equipt. Bicycles. Paddle boats. Lawn games. Private patios, balconies. Refrigerators. Some fireplaces. Cr cds: A, C, D, DS, MC, V.

D ⌷ ⌷ 🎿 ⌷ 🏃 ⌷ 🔥 SC ⌷

Inns

★ **BLACK WALNUT POINT INN INC.** *Black Walnut Point Rd (21671), 15 mi W on MD 33.* 410/886-2452; FAX 410/886-2053. Web www.tilghmanisland.com/blackwalnut. 7 rms, 6 with shower only, 3 bldgs, main bldg 3 story. No rm phones. D $120-$135; each addl $20; kit. unit $150. Adults only. TV in sitting rm. Pool; whirlpool. Complimentary continental bkfst; afternoon refreshments. Ck-out 11 am, ck-in 2-7 pm. Business servs avail. Lighted tennis. Lawn games. Balconies. Picnic tables, grills. On Cheasapeake Bay. Built in 1843; hand-hewn beams. Cr cds: C, MC, V.

⌷ 🎿 ⌷ ⌷ 🔥 SC

★★★ **CHESAPEAKE WOOD DUCK INN.** *Gibsontown Rd at Dogwood Harbor (21671), approx 11 mi W on MD 33.* 410/886-2070; FAX 410/886-2263. E-mail woodduck@bluecrab.org; web www.woodduckinn.com. 7 rms, 2 with shower only, 3 story. No rm phones. No elvtr. Apr-Nov: S, D $125-$155; suites $165-$205; lower rates rest of yr. Children over 14 yrs only. TV, cable, in main rm; VCR. Complimentary full bkfst. Restaurant nearby. Ck-out 11 am, ck-in 4-7 pm. Business servs avail. Luggage handling. Water sport privileges. Built in 1890. Fireplace. Totally nonsmoking. Cr cds: C, MC, V.

⌷ ⌷ ⌷ SC

✓★★★★ **INN AT PERRY CABIN.** *308 Watkins Ln (21663).* 410/745-5178; FAX 410/745-3348; res: 800/722-2949. E-mail perrycbn@friend.ly.net; web www.ashley-house.com. This white dormered farmhouse, built on the banks of the Miles River in the late 18th century, was refurbished by Sir Bernard Ashley to showcase the designs of his late wife, Laura Ashley, and has the ambience of an English country house. 41

rms, 3 story, 6 suites. S, D $295-$695; suites $695. Children over 10 yrs only. TV; cable (premium), VCR avail (movies). Indoor pool; whirlpool. Complimentary full bkfst. Dining rm (see ASHLEY ROOM). Rm serv. Ck-out noon, ck-in 3 pm. Business center. In-rm modem link. Luggage handling. Valet serv. Concierge serv. Tennis. Golf privileges. Exercise equipt; sauna, steam rm. Massage. Health club privileges. Rec rm. Lawn games. Dockage. Cr cds: A, C, D, MC, V.

D ⌷ ⌷ 🎿 ⌷ ⌷ 🏃 ⌷ ⌷ 🏃

★★★ **LAZYJACK INN.** *5907 Tilghman Island Rd (21671), approx 15 mi W on MD 33.* 410/886-2215; FAX 410/886-2635; res: 800/690-5080. E-mail mrichards@skipjack.bluecrab.org; web www.lazyjack.com. 4 rms, 2 with shower only, 2 story. No rm phones. Apr-mid-Nov: S, D $130-$205; lower rates rest of yr. Children over 12 yrs only. Complimentary full bkfst; afternoon refreshments. TV, VCR in main rm. Restaurant nearby. Ck-out 11 am, ck-in 4-7 pm. Luggage handling. Some in-rm whirlpools. Historic waterfront bldg (1855); furnished with antiques. Private yacht for charter. Totally nonsmoking. Cr cds: C, MC, V.

⌷ 🔥 SC

★★★ **PARSONAGE INN.** *210 N Talbot (21663), edge of historic district.* 410/745-5519; res: 800/394-5519. Web www.bestinns.net. 8 rms, 7 with shower only, 2 story. No rm phones. May-Oct: D $110-$172; lower rates rest of yr. Crib free. Complimentary full bkfst. Restaurant adj 5-10 pm. Ck-out 11 am, ck-in 2-7 pm. Health club privileges. Balconies. Picnic table, grill. Built in 1883 as a private residence; later used as a parsonage. Restored and furnished with period reproductions; unique architecture. Totally nonsmoking. Cr cds: C, MC, V.

D ⌷ ⌷ 🔥 SC

★★★ **WADES POINT INN.** *Wades Point Rd (21663), 5 mi W via MD 33, right on Wades Point Rd, in McDaniel.* 410/745-2500; FAX 410/745-3443; res: 888/923-3466. E-mail wadesinn@ wadespoint.com; web www.wadespoint.com. 24 rms, 6 share bath, 12 A/C, 2-3 story, 4 kits. No rm phones. D $95-$230; each addl $10; kit. units $230; under 12 free. Crib free. Complimentary continental bkfst. Restaurant nearby. Ck-out 11 am, ck-in 2-8 pm. Business servs avail. Balconies. Picnic tables. Main building (1819) with new guest house (1989) built in same style. Both buildings surrounded by fields and Chesapeake Bay. Located on 120 acres; flower gardens, woods with nature trail. Totally nonsmoking. Cr cds: C, MC, V.

D ⌷ ⌷ 🔥 SC

Restaurants

★★★ **208 TALBOT.** *208 N Talbot St (21663).* 410/745-3838. Web www.208talbot.com. Hrs: 5-10 pm; Sun 5-9 pm; Sun brunch 11 am-2 pm. Closed Mon, Tues; Dec 24, 25. Res accepted; required wkends. Bar. Semi-a la carte: dinner $21-$26. Prix fixe: Sat dinner $48. Sun brunch $9.50-$15.50. Specializes in fresh seafood, rack of lamb. Own pastries, ice cream. Casual gourmet dining in a renovated mid-1800s brick house; many antiques; original fireplace. Cr cds: C, DS, MC, V.

★★★ **ASHLEY ROOM.** *(See Inn at Perry Cabin)* 410/745-2200. E-mail perrycbn@friendly.net; web www.ashley-house.com. Hrs: 8-10:30 am, 12:30-2:30 pm, 6-10 pm; afternoon tea 3-5 pm. Res accepted. Serv bar. Wine list. Prix fixe: bkfst $27.50, lunch $30, 5-course dinner $65. High tea $19.50. Specializes in classical cuisine. Menu changes daily. Own herb garden. Own baking. Valet parking. English country-style dining rm with fireplace; French doors open to terrace overlooking bay. Totally nonsmoking. Cr cds: A, C, D, MC, V.

D

✓★ **CHESAPEAKE LANDING SEAFOOD.** *23713 St Michaels Rd (21663), 3 mi W on MD 33.* 410/745-9600. Hrs: 11 am-9 pm; early-bird dinner 4-6 pm (Mon-Fri). Closed Dec 25. Res accepted. Serv bar. Semi-a la carte: lunch $2.75-$8.25, dinner $8.95-$16.95. Child's meals. Specializes in seafood, steak, chicken. Parking. Totally nonsmoking. Cr cds: A, C, DS, MC, V.

D

★★ **MICHAEL RORK'S TOWN DOCK.** *125 Mulberry St (21663),* at the harbor, in public dock area. *410/884-0103.* Hrs: 11 am-9 pm; Fri, Sat to 10 pm; early-bird dinner Sun-Fri 3:30-5:30 pm; Sun brunch to 3 pm. Closed Dec 25; also Wed Jan-Mar. Res accepted. Bar. Semi-a la carte: lunch $5.95-$10.95, dinner $16.95-$24.95. Sun brunch $13.95. Child's meals. Specializes in fresh seafood, Eastern Shore cuisine. Outdoor dining. Nightclub on 2nd floor; entertainment Fri, Sat evenings. 4-level dining; harbor view. Cr cds: A, C, D, DS, MC, V.

★★ **OSPREY AT TILGHMAN ISLAND.** *6136 Tilghman Island Rd (21671), 11 mi W on MD 33. 410/886-2330.* Hrs: 11:30 am-9 pm; Fri-Sun to 9:30 pm. Closed Thanksgiving, Dec 25. Res required Fri-Sun (dinner). Bar to 2 am. Semi-a la carte: lunch, dinner $13.95-$19.95. Child's meals. Specializes in seafood, sandwiches, pizza. Parking. Outdoor dining. View of bay. Casual dining. Totally nonsmoking. Cr cds: C, D, DS, MC, V.

✓★ **ST MICHAELS CRAB HOUSE.** *305 Mulberry St (21663). 410/745-3737.* Hrs: 11 am-10 pm; Fri, Sat to 11 pm. Closed mid-Dec-early Mar. Res accepted. Bar. Semi-a la carte: lunch $4.95-$10.95, dinner $9.95-$17.95. Child's meals. Specializes in fresh seafood, beef, chicken. Outdoor dining. Overlooks harbor. Cr cds: C, DS, MC, V.

★★★ **WINDOWS.** *(See St. Michaels Harbour Inn & Marina Hotel) 410/745-5102.* E-mail harbour@friend.ly.net; web www.harbourinn.com. Hrs: 7 am-9 pm; Oct-May to 10 pm. Closed Mon, Tues (Dec-mid-Mar). Res accepted. Bar. Wine list. Semi-a la carte: bkfst $5.95-$9.95, lunch $5.95-$11.95, dinner $14.95-$22.95. Specializes in seafood, steaks, chicken. Cr cds: A, C, D, DS, MC, V.

Thurmont (B-5)

(See also Frederick, Hagerstown)

Settled 1751 **Pop** 3,398 **Elev** 523 ft **Area Code** 301 **Zip** 21788
E-mail fredtour@erols.com **Web** www.co.frederick.md.us
Information Tourism Council of Frederick County, 19 E Church St, Frederick 21701; 301/663-8687 or 800/999-3613

What to See and Do

Catoctin Mountain National Park. A 5,770-acre area on a spur of the Blue Ridge Mountains. Self-guided nature trails; restored whiskey still; fishing, picnicking; camping (mid-Apr-mid-Nov; fee), cabins (mid-Apr-Oct; fee). Park (daily). A unit of the National Park Service. 3 mi W on MD 77. Phone 301/663-9330. **Free**

Cunningham Falls State Park. 4,950 acres in the Catoctin Mountains. Two recreation areas: Houck, 5 mi W of town, has swimming, fishing, boating (rentals); picnicking, camping; hiking trails lead to 78-ft falls and scenic overlooks. Manor Area, 3 mi S of town on US 15, has picnicking, camping, playground. Trout fishing in Big Hunting Creek. Ruins of Iron Masters Mansion and the industrial village that surrounded it are also here. (See ANNUAL EVENTS) Standard fees. Phone 301/271-7574.

Annual Events

Maple Syrup Demonstration. At Cunningham Falls State Park. Tree tapping, sap boiling; carriage rides; food; children's storytelling corner. Usually 2nd & 3rd wkend Mar.

Catoctin Colorfest. Fall foliage; arts & crafts show. Phone 301/271-4432. 2nd wkend Oct.

Motel

★★★ **COZY COUNTRY INN THURMONT.** *103 Frederick Rd (21788). 301/271-4301; FAX 301/271-4301.* 21 units, 3 with shower only, 2 story, 5 cottages. May-Oct: S, D $46-$130; each addl $5; cottages $46-$110; under 12 free; wkly rates. Crib avail. Pet accepted. TV; cable (premium), VCR avail. Complimentary continental bkfst Mon-Fri. Complimentary coffee in rms. Restaurant 11 am-9 pm; Sat, Sun from 8 am. Rm serv. Bar 11 am-10 pm. Meeting rms. Business servs avail. In-rm modem link. Gift shop. Downhill ski 12 mi; x-country ski 4 mi. Refrigerators; some minibars; microwaves avail. Balconies. Picnic tables. Near Camp David; visiting dignitaries have stayed here. Cr cds: A, C, DS, MC, V.

Restaurant

✓★★ **COZY.** *105 Frederick Rd MD 806 (21788), 3 blks E of US 15. 301/271-7373.* Hrs: 11 am-8:45 pm; Fri to 9:15 pm; Sat 8 am-9:15 pm; Sun 8 am-8:45 pm. Closed Dec 24, 25. Res accepted. Bar. Buffet: bkfst $5.99, lunch $5.59-$15.25, dinner $8.50-$15.25. Semi-a la carte: lunch $4.29-$5.99, dinner $8.19-$12.79. Child's meals. Specializes in fresh fish, poultry, chicken. Own desserts. Outdoor dining. Family-owned. Cr cds: A, C, MC, V.

Towson (B-7)

(See also Baltimore)

Pop 49,445 **Elev** 465 ft **Area Code** 410 & 443 **Zip** 21204
Information Baltimore County Chamber of Commerce, 102 W Pennsylvania Ave, Ste 402; 410/825-6200

What to See and Do

Fire Museum of Maryland. More than 60 pieces of antique fire-fighting equipment; includes motorized and hand/horse-drawn units from 1822-1957. (May, Sept-Oct, wkends; June-Aug, daily) 1301 York Rd, 1 blk N of I-695 exit 26B, in Lutherville. Phone 410/321-7500. ¢¢

Hampton National Historic Site. Includes ornate Georgian mansion (ca 1790) (tours), formal gardens and plantation outbuildings. Gift shop. (Daily; closed Jan 1, Thanksgiving, Dec 25) Tea room open for luncheon (daily exc Mon; closed 6 wks mid-Jan-early Mar). 535 Hampton Lane, ½ mi off Dulaney Valley Rd; I-695 exit 27B. Phone 410/823-1309. ¢¢

Soldiers Delight Natural Environment Area. This 1,725-acre park has 19th-century chrome mines; restored log cabin; scenic overlook; hiking, nature trails; picnicking (at visitor center only). It is the only undisturbed serpentine barren in the state. Pets must be on leash. 7 mi W on I-695, then W on MD 26, then 5 mi N on Deerpark Rd to overlook. Phone 410/922-3044.

Towson State University (1866). (15,000 students) On campus are three art galleries, including Holtzman Art Gallery, with an extensive collection of art media (Sept-May, Tues-Sat). Concerts and sporting events are held in the Towson Center. York Rd. For information on entertainment & events Phone 410/830-ARTS.

Annual Event

State Fair. Timonium Fairgrounds, 3 mi N on York Rd, in Timonium. Ten-day festival of home arts; entertainment, midway; agricultural demonstrations, Thoroughbred horse racing, livestock presentations. Phone 410/252-0200. Aug 26-Sept 4.

Motor Hotel

★ ★ ★ **HOLIDAY INN SELECT.** *2004 Greenspring Dr (21093), I-83 exit 16.* 410/252-7373; FAX 410/561-0182; res: 800/465-4329. 250 rms, 5 story. S, D $119-$149; each addl $10; suites $259-$368; family, wkly, wkend, hol rates. Crib free. TV; cable (premium). Indoor/outdoor pool; whirlpool. Restaurant 6 am-10 pm. Bars; entertainment. Ck-out noon. Coin lndry. Meeting rms. Business servs avail. In-rm modem link. Bellhops. Gift shop. Valet serv. Exercise equipt. Microwaves avail. Cr cds: A, C, D, DS, JCB, MC, V.

D ⚊ 🕴 🛏 🔥 SC

Hotels

✓ ★ ★ **DAYS INN.** *9615 Deereco Rd (21093), I-83 exit 17, Padonia Rd.* 410/560-1000; FAX 410/561-3918; res: 800/235-3297. Web www.daysinn.com. 146 rms, 7 story. Apr-Nov: S $49.95-$85; D $55-$90; each addl $5; suites $100-$140; family, hol rates; lower rates rest of yr. Crib avail. TV; cable (premium), VCR. Pool. Complimentary continental bkfst. Restaurant open 24 hrs. Rm serv 7 am-10 pm. Bar. Ck-out 11 am. Guest lndry. Meeting rms. Business servs avail. In-rm modem link. Exercise equipt. Game rm. Refrigerators; microwaves avail. Cr cds: A, C, D, DS, JCB, MC, V.

D ⚊ 🕴 🛏 🔥 SC

★ ★ ★ **SHERATON BALTIMORE NORTH HOTEL.** *903 Dulaney Valley Rd (21204), I-695 exit 27A.* 410/321-7400; FAX 410/296-9534; res: 800/433-7619. E-mail SBNTowson@aol.com; web www.sheratonbaltimore.com. 284 units, 12 story. S, D $109-$179; each addl $12; suites $350-$450; under 17 free; wkend plans; higher rates Preakness. Crib free. TV; cable (premium). Indoor pool; whirlpool, poolside serv, lifeguard. Coffee in rms. Restaurant 6:30 am-10:30 pm. Bar 11:30-1 am; entertainment. Ck-out noon. Convention facilities. Business center. In-rm modem link. Gift shop. Free valet parking. Exercise equipt; sauna. Health club privileges. Refrigerators, microwaves avail. Cr cds: A, C, D, DS, MC, V.

D ⚊ 🕴 🛏 🔥 SC 🚶

Restaurants

★ ★ **CAFE TROIA.** *28 W Allegheny Ave (21204).* 410/337-0133. E-mail ctroia@earthlink.net. Hrs: 11 am-3 pm, 5-10 pm; Mon 5-10 pm; Fri to 11 pm; Sat 5-11 pm; Sun 5-9 pm. Res accepted. Italian menu. Bar. Semi-a la carte: lunch $4-$12, dinner $9-$22. Specializes in regional Italian dishes. Outdoor dining. Cr cds: A, C, D, MC, V.

D �‗

✓ ★ ★ ★ **LIBERATORE'S RISTORANTE.** *9515 Deereco Rd (21093), N on MD 45 to I-695, W on I-695, exit 25.* 410/561-3300. Hrs: 11 am-10 pm; Fri, Sat to 11 pm; Sun 3-10 pm. Closed most major hols. Res accepted. Italian menu. Bar. A la carte entrees: lunch, dinner $3.95-$14.95. Specializes in pasta, chicken, seafood. Pianist Thurs-Sat. Italian decor. Cr cds: A, C, D, DS, MC, V.

D

★ ★ **PEERCE'S PLANTATION.** *12460 Dulaney Valley Rd (21131), 6 mi N of I-695 exit 27 N.* 410/252-3100. Hrs: 11:30 am-3 pm, 5-10 pm; Fri, Sat to 11 pm; Sun 5-9 pm; Sun brunch 11:30 am-2 pm. Closed Dec 25. Res accepted. Continental menu. Bar 11:30-2 am. Semi-a la carte: lunch $6.25-$15, dinner $15.95-$25.95. Sun brunch $6.25-$12.95. Child's meals. Specialties: rack of lamb, filet Chesapeake. Valet parking. Outdoor dining. Antebellum decor. Scenic view of countryside overlooking Loch Raven Reservoir. Family-owned. Jacket. Cr cds: A, C, D, DS, MC, V.

D SC �‗

★ ★ **ROTHWELL'S GRILLE.** *106 W Padonia Rd (21093).* 410/252-0600. Hrs: 11:30 am-midnight; Sat, Sun from 5 pm. Closed most major hols. Res accepted (dinner). Bar. Semi-a la carte: lunch $6-$12, din-

ner $9-$19. Specializes in fresh meats and fish cooked on wood burning grill. Own baking. Outdoor dining. Casual atmosphere. Cr cds: A, C, D, DS, MC, V.

D �‗

★ ★ **THAT'S AMORE.** *720 Kennilworth Dr (21204).* 410/825-5255. Hrs: 11:30 am-10:30 pm; Fri to midnight; Sat 4 pm-midnight; Sun 4-9:30 pm. Closed Labor Day, Thanksgiving, Dec 25. Italian menu. Bar. A la carte entrees: lunch $3.50-$10.95, dinner $16-$22. Specializes in seafood. Outdoor dining. Italian vineyard setting. Cr cds: A, C, D, DS, MC, V.

D ➼

Waldorf (D-6)

(See also La Plata; also see District of Columbia)

Pop 15,058 **Elev** 215 ft **Area Code** 301 **E-mail** tourism@govt.co.charles.md.us **Web** www.govt.co.charles.md.us
Information Tourism Director, PO Box B, La Plata 20646; 301/645-0558 or 800/766-3386

What to See and Do

Cedarville State Forest. Includes 3,697 acres of woodland, once home of the Piscataway, who settled around the Zekiah Swamp. Fishing, hunting. Nature, hiking trails. Picnicking. Standard fees. 4 mi E off US 301 on Cedarville Rd. Schedule varies, Phone 301/856-8987 or 410/974-3771.

Farmer's Market and Auction. Nearby Amish farms offer fresh baked goods and produce (auction Wed) for sale; more than 90 shops. Antique dealers. (Wed & Sat) 13 mi SE on MD 5. Phone 301/884-3108.

✪ **John Wilkes Booth Escape Route.** After shooting Abraham Lincoln on Apr 14, 1865, John Wilkes Booth fled south into Maryland to rendezvous with his accomplice, David Herold, at

Surratt House and Tavern (1852), where they recovered arms they had hidden there. Though she may have been innocent, Mary Surratt was hanged for conspiracy. Eight period rooms, museum; guides in period costumes; Dec candlelight tours; special events and exhibits throughout the year. (Mar-mid-Dec, Thurs-Sun) 9110 Brandywine Rd, Clinton (then Surrattsville). Phone 301/868-1121. ¢ Booth and Herold next stopped at

Dr. Samuel A. Mudd House Museum (ca 1830). Where Dr. Mudd set Booth's broken leg, unaware that Booth had just shot the president. Mudd was convicted and imprisoned for life, but pardoned four years later by President Andrew Johnson. Tours conducted by costumed docents, some of whom are Dr. Mudd's descendants. (Apr-Nov, Sat-Sun afternoons & Wed 11 am-3 pm; closed Easter Sun, Thanksgiving) From US 301, take MD 5, then left on MD 205, turn right on Poplar Hill Rd approx 4 mi, right on Dr Samuel Mudd Rd, continue to house; sign at entrance. Phone 301/934-8464 or 301/645-6870. ¢¢

Booth and Herold continued south, crossed the Potomac River and were captured at Garrett's farm, Virginia, on Apr 26; Booth was killed. (See ANNUAL EVENT)

Maryland Indian Cultural Center. Exhibits reflect diverse tribal structures, art, lodging construction and cultures of Native Americans. (Tues, Thurs, Sun afternoons) 16816 Country Ln. Phone 301/372-1932. **Free**

Annual Event

John Wilkes Booth Escape Route Tour. Day-long bus tour of Booth's route from Ford's Theatre, Washington, through southern Maryland to site of Garrett's farm, Virginia, with expert commentary. For reservations phone 301/868-1121. Mid-Apr and early Sept.

Motels

★ **DAYS INN.** *US 301 (20603). 301/932-9200; FAX 301/843-9816; res: 800/329-7466.* 100 rms, 3 story. S, D $65-$75; suite $119-$135. each addl $5; under 18 free. Crib free. Pet accepted; $10. TV; cable (premium). Complimentary continental bkfst. Coffee in rms. Restaurant adj 11 am-10 pm. Ck-out 11 am. Coin lndry. Meeting rm. Business servs avail. Some in-rm whirlpools, refrigerators. Cr cds: A, C, D, DS, ER, JCB, MC, V.

D ⮔ ⮞ ⮙ 🔥 SC

★★★ **HOLIDAY INN.** *45 Saint Patricks Dr (20603). 301/645-8200; FAX 301/843-7945; res: 800/465-4329; res: 800/645-8277.* E-mail hldyinn@erols.com. 192 rms, 3 story, 8 kit. units. S, D $69-$74; each addl $6; suites, kit. units $70-$90; under 19 free. Crib free. TV; cable (premium). Pool; lifeguard. Complimentary coffee in rms. Restaurant 6:30 am-10 pm. Rm serv. Bar noon-11 pm. Ck-out 11 am. Coin lndry. Meeting rms. Business servs avail. In-rm modem link. Bellhops. Valet serv. Beauty shop. Health club privileges. Refrigerators, microwaves avail. Cr cds: A, C, D, DS, JCB, MC, V.

D ⮞ ⮙ 🔥 SC

✓★ **HOWARD JOHNSON EXPRESS INN.** *3125 Crain Hwy (20603). 301/932-5090; FAX 301/932-5090; res: 800/826-4534.* Web www.howardjohnsons.com. 109 rms. S, D $55-$65; suites, kit. units $60-$65; under 18 free. Crib free. Pet accepted; $10. TV; cable (premium), VCR (movies). Pool. Complimentary continental bkfst. Coffee in rms. Restaurant adj 11 am-10 pm. Ck-out noon. Meeting rms. Business servs avail. Health club privileges. Refrigerators, microwaves avail. Picnic tables, grills. Cr cds: A, C, D, DS, JCB, MC, V.

D ⮔ ⮞ ⮙ 🔥 SC

Westminster (B-6)

(See also Baltimore, Frederick)

Founded 1764 **Pop** 13,068 **Elev** 717 ft **Area Code** 410 & 443

Westminster, a Union supply depot at the Battle of Gettysburg, saw scattered action before the battle. It is the county seat of Carroll County, first in the US to offer complete rural free delivery mail service (started in 1899 with four two-horse wagons).

Motel

★★ **COMFORT INN.** *451 Wmc Dr (21158), adj to Western Maryland College. 410/857-1900; FAX 410/857-9584.* 101 rms, 1-2 story. May-June: S $69-$89; D $69-$159; each addl $10; under 18 free; wkly rates; monthly rates; higher rates: WMC parents wkend, graduation, Dec 31; lower rates rest of yr. Crib free. Pet accepted, some restrictions; $25 refundable. TV; cable. Pool; whirlpool. Complimentary continental bkfst. Ck-out 11 am. Meeting rms. Business servs avail. Valet serv. Tennis privileges. Golf privileges. Some in-rm whirlpools; microwaves avail. Cr cds: A, C, D, DS, ER, JCB, MC, V.

D ⮔ 🏋 ⛷ ⮞ ⮙ 🔥 SC

Restaurants

✓★ **BAUGHER'S.** *289 W Main St (21158). 410/848-7413.* Hrs: 7:30 am-9 pm. Closed most major hols. Semi-a la carte: bkfst $1.30-$3.75, lunch, dinner $1-$10.50. Specializes in Baugher's own farm-raised beef, ham, chicken. Own ice cream. Country-style restaurant; adj to farmer's market. Family-owned. Cr cds: C, DS, MC, V.

D ⮕

★★ **CHAMELEON.** *32 W Main St (21157). 410/751-2422.* Hrs: noon-11 pm; Sun 4-8:30 pm. Closed Mon; some major hols. Contemporary Amer menu. Bar to 1 am. Semi-a la carte: lunch $3.50-$7.50, dinner $9-$20. Specializes in fresh seafood, vegetarian and pasta dishes. Own baking, pasta. Contemporary cafe atmosphere; displays modern art by local artists. Cr cds: A, C, D, DS, MC, V.

D

★★ **JOHANSSON'S.** *4 W Main St (21157). 410/876-0101.* Hrs: 11 am-11 pm; Sat to midnight; Sun to 10 pm. Closed major hols. Res accepted; required Fri, Sat dinner. Bar to 1 am. Semi-a la carte: lunch $5.95-$8.95, dinner $11.95-$17.95. Child's meals. Specializes in veal, beef, fresh seafood. Musicians Fri. Outdoor dining. English pub atmosphere, originally a nickel-and-dime store; colored-glass artwork. Cr cds: A, C, DS, MC, V.

D ⮕

★★ **RUDY'S 2900.** *2900 Baltimore Blvd (21048), 8 mi E on US 140. 410/833-5777.* Hrs: 11:30 am-2:30 pm, 5:30-10 pm; Fri to 11 pm; Sat 5:30-11 pm; Sun 4-9 pm. Closed Mon; most major hols. Res accepted; required Fri, Sat dinner. Continental menu. Bar to 10:30 pm. Semi-a la carte: lunch $5.95-$11.95, dinner $9.95-$24.95. Specialties: roast duckling with plum sauce, grilled pork chop with fennel-flavored sausage, grouper in potato crust with red wine butter. Own pastries. Vocalist Wed. European decor; French impressionist oil paintings. Cr cds: A, C, D, DS, MC, V.

D ♥

New Jersey

Population: 7,730,188
Land area: 7,504 square miles
Elevation: 0–1,803 feet
Highest point: High Point Mountain (Sussex County)
Entered union: Third of original 13 states (December 18, 1787)
Capital: Trenton
Motto: Liberty and prosperity
Nickname: Garden State
State flower: Purple violet
State bird: Eastern goldfinch
State tree: Red oak
Time zone: Eastern
Web: www.state.nj.us/travel

Tree-shaded 18th-century towns and history-hallowed grounds, on which Revolutionary battles were fought, make this state one of dignified beauty and democratic tradition. More than 800 lakes and ponds, 100 rivers and streams and 1,400 miles of freshly stocked trout streams are scattered throughout its wooded, scenic northwest corner. The swampy meadows west of the New Jersey Turnpike have been reclaimed and transformed into commercial and industrial areas. The Meadowlands, a multimillion-dollar sports complex, offers horse racing, the NY Giants and the NY Jets NFL football teams, the NJ Devils NHL hockey team and the NJ Nets NBA basketball team. The coastline, stretching 127 miles from Sandy Hook to Cape May, offers excellent swimming and ocean fishing.

George Washington spent a quarter of his time here as commander-in-chief of the Revolutionary Army. On Christmas night in 1776, he crossed the Delaware and surprised the Hessians at Trenton. A few days later, he marched to Princeton and defeated three British regiments. He then spent the winter in Morristown, where the memories of his campaign are preserved in a national historical park.

New Jersey often is associated only with its factories, oil refineries, research laboratories and industrial towns. But history buffs, hunters, anglers, scenery lovers and amateur beachcombers need only to wander a short distance from its industrial areas to find whatever they like best.

When to Go/Climate

Moderate temperatures in spring and fall make these the best times to visit New Jersey. Summers can be hot and humid; winters can be bitterly cold, particularly in the inland mountain areas. Beaches are lovely, and coastal temperatures are often 5°F lower in summer and higher in winter than inland areas.

AVERAGE HIGH/LOW TEMPERATURES (F)

ATLANTIC CITY

Jan 40/27	**May** 66/54	**Sept** 74/62
Feb 42/29	**Jun** 74/62	**Oct** 64/51
Mar 49/36	**July** 80/68	**Nov** 55/42
Apr 57/44	**Aug** 80/68	**Dec** 46/33

NEWARK

Jan 38/23	**May** 72/53	**Sept** 78/60
Feb 41/25	**June** 82/63	**Oct** 67/48
Mar 51/33	**July** 87/69	**Nov** 55/39
Apr 62/43	**Aug** 85/67	**Dec** 43/29

Parks and Recreation Finder

Directions to and information about the parks and recreation areas below are given under their respective town/city sections. Please refer to those sections for details.

NATIONAL PARK AND RECREATION AREAS

Key to abbreviations. I.H.S. = International Historic Site; I.P.M. = International Peace Memorial; N.B. = National Battlefield; N.B.P. = National Battlefield Park; N.B.C. = National Battlefield & Cemetery; N.C. = National Conservation Area; N.E.M. = National Expansion Memorial; N.F. = National Forest; N.G. = National Grassland; N.H.P. = National Historical Park; N.H.C.= National Heritage Corridor; N.H.S. = National Historic Site; N.L. = National Lakeshore; N.M. = National Monument; N.M.P. = National Military Park; N.Mem = National Memorial; N.P. = National Park; N.Pres. = National Preserve; N.R. = National Recreational Area; N.R.R. = National Recreational River; N.Riv. = National River; N.S. = National Seashore; N.S.R. = National Scenic Riverway; N.S.T. = National Scenic Trail; N.Sc. = National Scientific Reserve; N.V.M. = National Volcanic Monument.

Place Name	Listed Under
Edison N.H.S.	WEST ORANGE
Morristown N.H.	same
Sandy Hook Unit of Gateway N.R.	same

STATE PARK AND RECREATION AREAS

Key to abbreviations. I.P. = Interstate Park; S.A.P. = State Archaeological Park; S.B. = State Beach; S.C. = State Conservation Area; S.C.P. = State Conservation Park; S.Cp. = State Campground; S.F. = State Forest; S.G. = State Garden; S.H.A. = State Historic Area; S.H.P. = State Historic Park; S.H.S. = State Historic Site; S.M.P. = State Marine Park; S.N.A. = State

Natural Area; S.P. = State Park; S.P.C. = State Public Campground; S.R. = State Reserve; S.R.A. = State Recreation Area; S.Res. = State Reservoir; S.Res.P. = State Resort Park; S.R.P. = State Rustic Park.

Place Name	Listed Under
Allaire S.P.	same
Allamuchy Mountain S.P. (Stephens Section)	HACKETTSTOWN
Barnegat Lighthouse S.P.	LONG BEACH ISLAND
Cheesequake S.P.	MATAWAN
Fort Mott S.P.	SALEM
High Point S.P.	same
Hopatcong S.P.	LAKE HOPATCONG
Island Beach S.P.	SEASIDE PARK
Liberty S.P.	JERSEY CITY
Parvin S.P.	BRIDGETON
Ringwood S.P.	same
Round Valley S.P.	CLINTON
Spruce Run S.R.A.	CLINTON
Stokes S.F.	BRANCHVILLE
Swartswood S.P.	BRANCHVILLE
Washington Crossing S.P.	TRENTON
Wharton S.F.	BATSTO

Water-related activities, hiking, riding, various sports, picnicking, camping and visitor centers are available in many of these areas. There is a $1/person (12–62 yrs) walk-in/bicycle fee in some areas; there is a parking fee ($2–$7) in many areas. In most areas, fees are collected Memorial Day wkend–Labor Day wkend; fees collected yr-round at Island Beach (see SEASIDE PARK). No pets in bathing, camping areas or buildings; in other day-use areas, pets must be attended and kept on a six-foot leash.

Bathing at inland beaches, Memorial Day–Labor Day; at ocean beaches from mid-June; cabins ($20–$100); campsites ($10–$12), lean-tos ($15); reservations accepted ($7, nonrefundable). Most areas are wildlife sanctuaries. In addition, 1,700 acres of Palisades Interstate Parks (see) on the Hudson are in New Jersey. There are also more than 20 state-owned historic sites (clearly marked); some with museums and guides. For detailed information contact Division of Parks and Forestry, CN 404, Trenton 08625; 609/984-0370.

SKI AREAS

Place Name	Listed Under
Campgaw Mountain Ski Area	RAMSEY
Craigmeur Ski Area	NEWFOUNDLAND
Vernon Valley/Great Gorge Ski Area	VERNON

FISHING & HUNTING

Fishing opportunities abound in New Jersey's fresh and salt waters. No license is required for deep-sea or surf fishing along the 127-mile coastline; *however,* a license is required for taking shellfish. Nonresident clam license: $20; under age 14, $2. A license is required for freshwater fishing for everyone over 14 years of age. Nonresident fishing license: $25.25; nonresident trout stamp: $15.50; 7-day nonresident vacation fishing license: $16.50.

Hunting licenses are required for everyone over 10 years of age. Firearm or bow & arrow: nonresident, $100 each; small game only: nonresident, 2-day, $27.50; nonresident, 1-day, $7.75 (for commercial or semi-wild preserves only). Juveniles 10–13 with licensee over 21, $3. Woodcock stamp, $2.75; pheasant & quail stamp, $22 (for wildlife management areas only). Hunter Education Course or a previous year's resident license required to purchase license. For information contact Department of Environmental Protection, Division of Fish, Game and Wildlife, PO Box 400, Trenton 08625-0400; 609/292-2965.

Driving Information

Safety belts are mandatory for all persons in front seat of vehicle. Children under 5 years must be in an approved passenger restraint anywhere in vehicle; ages 18 months–5 years may use a regulation safety belt in back seat; however, in front seat, children must use an approved safety seat; children under 18 months must use an approved safety seat anywhere in vehicle. For further information phone 609/633-9300.

INTERSTATE HIGHWAY SYSTEM

The following alphabetical listing of New Jersey towns in *Mobil Travel Guide* shows that these cities are within 10 miles of the indicated Interstate highways. A highway map should be checked, however, for the nearest exit.

Highway Number	Cities/Towns within 10 miles
Interstate 78	Clinton, Plainfield, Scotch Plains, Somerville, Union.
Interstate 80	Fort Lee, Hackensack, Hackettstown, Paramus, Parsippany, Rockaway, Saddle Brook, Wayne.
Interstate 95	Elizabeth, Fort Lee, Newark, Trenton, Woodbridge.

Additional Visitor Information

The State Division of Travel and Tourism, PO Box 820, Trenton 08625-0820, phone 609/292-2470 or 800/JERSEY-7, publishes a variety of materials for travelers. There are also two periodicals: *New Jersey Monthly* (write Subscription Dept, Box 936, Farmingdale, NY 11737); *New Jersey Outdoors* (write Dept of Environmental Protection & Energy, CN-402, Trenton 08625).

There are eight tourist welcome centers and numerous information centers in New Jersey. At these centers visitors will find information racks with brochures to help plan trips to points of interest. For a publication with the locations of the centers contact the State Division of Travel and Tourism.

CALENDAR HIGHLIGHTS

APRIL

Tulip Festival (Cape May). Celebrate Dutch heritage with ethnic foods and dancing, craft show, street fair, garden and house tours. Phone 609/884-5508.

JUNE

Sea & Sky Festival (Cape May). Sample Cape May's variety of seafood while colorful kites and Blues music fill the air. Phone 609/884-5508.

IBM/USET Festival of Champions (Somerville). Hamilton Farm. Competition of three Olympic equestrian disciplines. Phone 908/234-0555.

JULY

Night in Venice (Ocean City). Decorated boat parade. Contact Public Relations Dept 609/525-9300 or 800/BEACH-NJ.

SEPTEMBER

Victorian Faire (Bridgeton). Victorian Bridgeton is re-created through music, games and contests, street vendors, crafts, costumes and city tours. Phone 609/451-9208.

OCTOBER

Atlantic City Marathon (Atlantic City). Phone 609/822-6911.

DECEMBER

Reenactment of Crossing of the Delaware (Trenton). Washington Crossing State Park. Departs PA side on the afternoon of Dec 25.

Allaire State Park (E-5)

(See also Asbury Park, Freehold)

(On County 524 in Howell and Wall Townships)

Allaire State Park has more than 3,000 acres and offers a fishing pond for children under 14; multiuse trails; picnic facilities, playground; camping (dump station, summer); and the opportunity to visit a historic 19th-century village (see below). Park (daily). Standard fees when village buildings are open. For more information contact PO Box 220, Farmingdale 07727; 732/938-2371. Parking fee (Memorial Day–Labor Day, wkends)   ¢¢

What to See and Do

Historic Allaire Village. In 1822, James Allaire bought this site as a source of bog ore for his ironworks. The furnace also produced cast-iron items such as hollow-ware pots and kettles, stoves, sadirons and pipes for New York City's waterworks. Today, visitors can explore the bakery, general store, blacksmith and carpentry shops, workmen's houses, the community church and other buildings still much as they were in 1836. Village grounds and Center (all yr); village buildings (May–Labor Day, wkends); special events (Feb–Dec). For information phone 732/938-2253.   **Free**

> **Train Rides.** Narrow-gauge steam locomotive rides (mid-June–Labor Day, daily; Apr–mid-June & after Labor Day–Nov, Sat & Sun). Phone 732/938-5524.   ¢

Asbury Park (E-6)

Settled 1871 **Pop** 16,799 **Elev** 21 ft **Area Code** 732 **Zip** 07712

Information Greater Asbury Park Chamber of Commerce, 100 Lake Ave, PO Box 649; 732/775-7676

This popular shore resort was bought in 1871 by New York brush manufacturer James A. Bradley and named for Francis Asbury, first American Bishop of the Methodist Episcopal Church. Bradley established a town for temperance advocates and good neighbors. The beach and the three lakes proved so attractive that, by 1874, Asbury Park had grown into a borough, and by 1897, a city. It is the home of the famous boardwalk, Convention Hall and Paramount Theatre. In September 1934, the SS *Morro Castle* was grounded off this beach and burned with a loss of 122 lives. Asbury Park became the birthplace of a favorite sweet when a local confectioner introduced "saltwater taffy" and watched the sales curve rise with the tide. Today, this is a popular resort area for swimming and fishing.

What to See and Do

Long Branch Historical Museum (Church of the Presidents). Presidents Grant, Garfield, Arthur, McKinley, Hayes, Harrison and Wilson worshiped here. Museum contains items of interest from post-Civil War to the present; also records, pictures, relics of period between the Civil War and World War I when the resort was the playground of notables. (By appt) 3 mi N at 1260 Ocean Ave in Elberon section of Long Branch. Phone 732/229-0600 or 732/222-9879.   **Free**

Annual Event

Jazz Fest. Phone 732/775-7676 or 732/502-5728. July.

Seasonal Events

Horse racing. Monmouth Park. Oceanport Ave in Oceanport via NJ 35 N to NJ 36; or via Garden State Pkwy exit 105, then E on NJ 36. Thoroughbred racing. Phone 732/222-5100. Wed-Sun, Memorial Day–Labor Day.

Metro Lyric Opera Series. At the Paramount Theater on the Boardwalk. Phone 908/531-2378 for schedule, information. Sat evenings, July–Aug.

Restaurants

★ ★ **CHRISTIE'S.** *1 English Lane (07712), N of Asbury Park Circle, off NJ 35.* 732/776-8558. Hrs: 11:30 am-10 pm; Sat 5 pm-midnight; Sun from 4 pm. Closed Mon; Dec 25. Res accepted. Bar. Semi-a la carte: lunch, dinner $8.95-$22.95. Child's meals. Specialties: lobster and scallops in curry sauce, sirlion steak with sweet madiera sauce. Entertainment. Valet parking. Cr cds: C, MC, V.

D ⚓

★ ★ **MOONSTRUCK.** *68 Lake Ave (07756), ½ mi S on NJ 71.* 732/988-0123. Web members.aol.com/raspmoon. Hrs: 5-10 pm; Sat to 10:30 pm; Sun to 9:30 pm. Closed Mon, Tues; some major hols; also Jan-mid-Feb. Italian, Mediterranean menu. A la carte entrees: dinner $10.95-$22.95. Specialties: Mediterranean antipasto, grilled Asian shrimp, raspberry chicken. Own pastries. Outdoor dining. Two-level dining in casual cafe atmosphere. Cr cds: C, MC, V.

Atlantic City (J-4)

(See also Ocean City)

Settled 1854 **Pop** 37,986 **Elev** 8 ft **Area Code** 609 **E-mail** accvavisitors info@worldnet.att.net **Web** www.atlanticcitynj.com

Information Atlantic City Convention & Visitors Authority, 2314 Pacific Ave, 08401; 609/449-7147, 888/ACVISIT or; 800/BOARDWALK

Honeymooners, conventioneers, Miss America and some 37 million annual visitors have made Atlantic City the best-known New Jersey beach resort. Built on Absecon Island, it is shielded by the curve of the coast from battering northeastern storms while the nearby Gulf Stream warms its waters, helping to make it a year-round resort. A 60-foot-wide boardwalk extends along five miles of beaches. Hand-pushed wicker rolling chairs take visitors up and down the Boardwalk. Absecon Lighthouse ("Old Ab"), a well-known landmark, was first lit in 1857 and now stands in an uptown city park. The game of Monopoly uses Atlantic City street names.

What to See and Do

Amusement piers.

> **The Shops on Ocean One.** A 900-ft, 3-deck shopping pier houses shops, food court & restaurants. (Daily) Boardwalk at Arkansas Ave. Phone 609/347-8082.

> **Garden Pier.** Atlantic City Art Center and Atlantic City Historical Museum are located here. (Daily) Boardwalk & New Jersey Ave. Phone 609/347-5844.   **Free**

Convention Center. Seats 22,000; one of the world's largest pipe organs. Can accommodate small meetings as well as large conventions, sports events; site of the annual Miss America Pageant. Phone 609/348-7000.

Edwin B. Forsythe National Wildlife Refuge, Brigantine Division. Auto-tour route; interpretive nature trails (daily). Over the years, more than 200 species of birds have been observed at this 40,000-acre refuge. Public-use area has an 8-mi wildlife drive through diversified wetlands and uplands habitat; most popular in the spring and fall, during the course of the waterbird migration, and at sunset, when the birds roost for the evening. Refuge headquarters (Mon–Fri). 9 mi N on US 9. Contact PO Box 72, Great Creek Rd, Oceanville 08231; phone 609/652-1665. Per vehicle   ¢¢

Fishing. Surf fishing and deep-sea fishing. License may be required, check locally. Charter boats (Mar–Nov). Many tournaments are scheduled. Contact Atlantic City Party and Charter Boat Assn. Phone 609/645-4001.

Historic Gardner's Basin. An eight-acre, sea-oriented park featuring the working lobstermen; US Coast Guard Lightship; speed boat belonging to Guy Lombardo. Educational aquarium with local species. Picnicking. (Daily) 800 New Hampshire Ave, at N end of city. Phone 609/348-2880.

Historic Town of Smithville and the Village Greene at Smithville. (1787). Restored 18th-century village with specialty shops and restaurants.

Also carousel, horse-drawn carriage rides, train ride, paddle boats and miniature golf (Apr–Oct, fee for some activities). Village (daily). Special events throughout the yr. 7 mi W on US 30 to Absecon, then 6 mi N on US 9, at Moss Mill Rd. Phone 609/652-7777 or 609/652-0440.

Lucy, the Margate Elephant. Only elephant in the world you can walk through and come out alive. Guided tour and exhibit inside this six-story elephant-shaped building. Built 1881; spiral stairs in Lucy's legs lead to main hall & observation area on her back. Gift shop. Concession. Free outdoor concerts (July–Aug, Thurs evenings). (Mid-June–Labor Day, daily; Apr–mid-June & Sept–Oct, Sat & Sun only) S via Atlantic Ave in Margate. Phone 609/823-6473. ¢¢

Marine Mammal Stranding Center & Museum. One of few marine mammal rescue and rehabilitation centers in US. Injured dolphins, turtles and other marine animals are brought to center for treatment. Museum offers exhibits on mammal species; recuperating animals can be viewed at center. Dolphin & whale watch tours avail (fee; res required). (Memorial Day–Labor Day, daily; rest of yr, wkends only; closed some hols) Over bridge and 2 mi N, at 3625 Atlantic-Brigantine Blvd. Phone 609/266-0538. **Donation**

Noyes Museum. Rotating and permanent exhibits of American art; collection of working bird decoys. (Wed–Sun; closed major hols) Admission free Fri. 12 mi NW via US 9, on Lily Lake Rd in Oceanville. Phone 609/652-8848. ¢¢

Recreation areas. Beach (Memorial Day–mid-Sept; free), surfing at special areas (daily); boating. Bicycling and rolling chairs on Boardwalk (daily); golf, tennis.

Renault Winery. Guided tour (approx 1 hr) includes wine-aging cellars; press room; antique wine-making equipment; free wine tasting (daily). Restaurant (Fri–Sun; res recommended); garden cafe (daily exc Sun). 16 mi W on US 30 in Egg Harbor City. Phone 609/965-2111. Tour ¢

Storybook Land. More than 50 storybook buildings and displays depicting children's stories; live animals; rides; picnic area, playground, concession. (May–mid-Sept, daily; Mar–Apr & mid-Sept–Thanksgiving, Sat & Sun only) Christmas Fantasy with Lights and visiting with Mr. and Mrs. Santa (Thanksgiving–Dec 30, nightly). Admission includes attractions & unlimited rides. 10 mi W via US 40, 322. Phone 609/641-7847. ¢¢¢

Annual Events

Boardwalk National Professional Fine Arts Show. Phone 609/347-5844. June.

LPGA Atlantic City Classic. Phone 609/927-7888. Late June.

Miss America Pageant. Convention Center. Usually 1st or 2nd wkend after Labor Day.

Indian Summer Boardwalk Art & Craft Show. Phone 609/347-5837. Usually 3rd wkend Sept.

Atlantic City Marathon. Phone 609/822-6911. Mid-Oct.

Motels

★★ **BEST WESTERN INN.** *8029 Black Horse Pike (08232), 2 mi W on US 40 & 322.* 609/641-3546; FAX 609/641-4329; res: 800/528-1234; res: 800/999-9466. 110 rms, 2 story. July-mid-Sept: S, D $85-$125; each addl $10; under 17 free; lower rates rest of yr. Crib free. TV; cable (premium), VCR avail. Pool; wading pool. Supervised child's activities (June-Aug) ages 8-15. Restaurant 7 am-10 pm. Serv bar. Ck-out 11 am. Coin lndry. Meeting rms. Business servs avail. Airport transportation. Indoor & outdoor tennis, pro. Exercise rm; sauna. On bay. Cr cds: A, C, D, DS, MC, V.

D 🐾 🏖 👤 ⛷ 🔥 SC

✓★★ **COMFORT INN NORTH.** *405 E Absecon Blvd (08201), 3 mi W on US 30.* 609/646-5000; FAX 609/383-8744; res: 800/228-2800. Web www.fairfieldinn.com. 200 rms, 6 story. S, D $46-$129; each addl $10; suites $75-$199; under 18 free. Crib free. TV; cable (premium). Pool. Complimentary continental bkfst. Restaurant nearby. Ck-out 11 am. Meeting rms. Business servs avail. In-rm modem link. Cr cds: A, C, D, DS, MC, V.

D 🏖 🛏 🔥 SC

★★ **HAMPTON INN.** *240 E White Horse Pike (08201), 7 mi W on US 30.* 609/652-2500; FAX 609/652-2212; res: 800/426-7866; res: 800/446-6066. Web www.hamptoninn.com. 129 rms, 4 story. Memorial Day-Labor Day: S, D $65-$109; suites $92-$146; under 18 free; higher rates hols; lower rates rest of yr. Crib free. TV; cable (premium), VCR avail. Pool; whirlpool, lifeguard. Complimentary continental bkfst. Restaurant adj open 24 hrs. Ck-out 11 am. Coin lndry. Meeting rms. Business servs avail. In-rm modem link. Free airport transportation. Cr cds: A, C, D, DS, MC, V.

D 🏖 🛏 🔥 SC

★★ **HAMPTON INN WEST.** *7079 Black Horse Pike (08232), 2 mi W on US 40 & 322.* 609/484-1900; FAX 609/383-0731; res: 800/426-7866; res: 800/926-7866. Web www.hamptoninn.com. 143 rms, 6 story. June-Sept: S, D $65-$135; family rates; higher rates: hols (2-day min). Crib free. TV; cable (premium). Complimentary continental bkfst. Coffee in rms. Ck-out 11 am. Meeting rm. Business servs avail. Cr cds: A, C, D, DS, MC, V.

D 🛏 🔥 SC

✓★ **SUPER 8 MOTEL.** *229 E Rte 30; 633 White Horse Pike (08201), 7 mi W on US 30.* 609/652-2477; FAX 609/748-0666; res: 800/800-8000. Web www.super8.com. 58 rms, 2 story. July 4-Aug: S, D $55-$125; suites $80-$150; under 12 free; lower rates rest of yr. TV; cable (premium). Complimentary coffee in lobby. Restaurant opp open 24 hrs. Ck-out noon. Business servs avail. Refrigerators avail. Cr cds: A, C, D, DS, MC, V.

D 🛏 🔥 SC

Motor Hotel

★ **DAYS INN.** *6708 Tilton Rd (08234), Atlantic City Expwy to Garden State Pkwy, exit 36.* 609/641-4500; FAX 609/645-8295; res: 800/329-7466. 117 rms, 5 story. July-mid-Sept: S, D $69-$169; each addl $5; suites $89-$189; kit. unit $99-$200; under 13 free; family rates; package plans; higher rates special events; lower rates rest of yr. Crib free. TV; cable (premium), VCR avail. Complimentary continental bkfst. Restaurant adj 7 am-midnight. Ck-out 11 am. Meeting rms. Business servs avail. In-rm modem link. Coin lndry. Exercise equipt. Pool; lifeguard. Playground. Game rm. Some refrigerators, microwaves. Picnic tables. Cr cds: A, C, D, DS, JCB, MC, V.

D 🏖 👤 🛏 🔥 SC

Hotels

★★★★ **BALLY'S PARK PLACE CASINO HOTEL & TOWER.** *Park Pl & Boardwalk (08401).* 609/340-2000; FAX 609/340-4713; res: 800/225-5977. Web www.bally.com. The two buildings composing this hotel are emblematic of Atlantic City present and past; there is the new hexagonal tower with a glitzy 93-foot escalator at its core, and the old Denis Hotel, built of stone, with a mansard roof and guest rooms decorated in art-deco style. 1,268 rms, 49 story. Mid-June-Sept: S, D $95-$245; each addl $15; under 18 free; lower rates rest of yr. Crib free. TV; cable (premium), VCR avail. 2 pools, 1 indoor; whirlpool, poolside serv, lifeguard. Restaurants open 24 hrs. Bars. Ck-out noon. Convention facilities. Business servs avail. In-rm modem link. Barber, beauty shop. Valet parking; self-park garage. Exercise rm; sauna, steam rm. Massage. Bathrm phones; refrigerators avail. On beach. Cr cds: A, C, D, DS, MC, V.

D 🏖 👤 🔥

★★★ **CAESARS ATLANTIC CITY.** *2100 Pacific & Arkansas Aves (08401).* 609/348-4411; FAX 609/343-2405; res: 800/223-7277. Web www.caesars.com. 1,138 rms, 20 story. June-Labor Day: S, D $130-$300; each addl $15; lower rates rest of yr. Crib avail. TV; cable (premium), VCR avail (movies). Pool; whirlpool, lifeguard. Restaurants open 24 hrs. Bars open 24 hrs. Ck-out noon. Convention facilities. Business servs avail.

Shopping arcade. Barber, beauty shop. Airport transportation. Tennis. Exercise equipt; steam rm, sauna. Massage. Microwaves avail. On ocean. Cr cds: A, C, D, DS, MC, V.

⊡ ⤢ ⛵ 🕴 ⊠ 🔥

★★ **CLARIDGE CASINO & HOTEL.** *Boardwalk & Indiana Rd (08401).* 609/340-3400; FAX 609/340-3875; res: 800/257-8585. 504 rms, 24 story. July-early Sept: S, D $130-$165; each addl $10; under 12 free; lower rates rest of yr. TV; cable (premium). Indoor pool; whirlpool, lifeguard. Restaurant open 24 hrs. Rm serv 24 hrs. Bar open 24 hrs. Ck-out noon. Meeting rms. Business servs avail. Concierge. Beauty shop. Exercise rm; sauna, steam rm. Refrigerators. On ocean. Cr cds: A, C, D, DS, MC, V.

⊡ ⛵ 🕴 ⊠ 🔥

✓★ **COMFORT INN.** *539 E Absecon Blvd (08201), 3 mi W on US 30.* 609/641-7272; FAX 609/646-3286; res: 800/638-7949; res: 800/233-4656. 205 rms, 7 story. S, D $54-$150; each addl $10; under 18 free. Crib avail. TV; cable (premium). Complimentary continental bkfst. Ck-out noon. Meeting rms. Business servs avail. Cr cds: A, C, D, DS, MC, V.

⊡ ⊠ 🔥 SC

★★★ **HARRAH'S SHOWBOAT CASINO & HOTEL.** *801 Boardwalk (08401).* 609/343-4000; FAX 609/343-3409; res: 800/621-0200. 755 rms, 25 story. July-mid-Sept: S, D $140-$180; each addl $15; suites $200-$472; under 12 free; lower rates rest of yr. Crib free. TV; cable (premium), VCR avail. Pool; whirlpool, lifeguard. Supervised child's activities. Restaurant open 24 hrs. Bar open 24 hrs; entertainment. Ck-out noon. Convention facilities. Business servs avail. Beauty shop. Airport transportation. Bowling center. Game rm. Exercise rm; sauna. Bathrm phones. Some refrigerators. Some balconies. On ocean; ocean view from most rms. Cr cds: A, C, D, DS, MC, V.

⊡ ⛵ 🕴 ⊠ 🔥

★★★ **HILTON CASINO RESORT.** *Boston & The Boardwalk (21717).* 609/347-7111; FAX 609/640-1083; res: 800/257-8677. Web www.hilton.com. 803 rms, 22 story. Late June-Sept: S, D $125-$255; each addl $20; suites $210-$400; under 12 free; lower rates rest of yr. Crib free. TV; cable (premium), VCR avail. Indoor pool; whirlpool, poolside serv, lifeguard. Free supervised child's activities (June-Aug). Restaurant, bar noon-2 am. Entertainment. Ck-out noon. Convention facilities. Business servs avail. Concierge. Barber, beauty shop. Valet parking. Exercise rm; sauna. Game rm. Bathrm phones. On beach. Cr cds: A, C, D, DS, MC, V.

⊡ ⛵ 🕴 ⊠

★★ **HOLIDAY INN BOARDWALK.** *111 S. Chelsea Ave (08401).* 609/348-2200; FAX 609/345-5110; res: 800/548-3030; res: 800/598-3030. 220 rms, 21 story. Mid-June-Labor Day: S, D $98-$179; each addl $15; under 19 free; lower rates rest of yr. Crib avail. TV; cable (premium). Pool; poolside serv. Restaurant 7 am-10 pm. Bar 11:30-2 am. Ck-out 11 am. Meeting rms. Business servs avail. In-rm modem link. Health club privileges. On ocean. Cr cds: A, C, D, DS, JCB, MC, V.

⊡ ⛵ ⊠ 🔥 SC

★★★ **RESORTS CASINO HOTEL.** *1133 Boardwalk & North Carolina Ave. (08401).* 609/344-6000; FAX 609/340-7684; res: 800/336-6378. Web www.resortsac.com. 662 rms, 15 story. July-Labor Day: S, D $70-$225; each addl $10; lower rates rest of yr. Crib free. TV; cable. Indoor/outdoor pool; whirlpool. Restaurants open 24 hrs. Bars open 24 hrs. Ck-out noon. Convention facilities. Business servs avail. In-rm modem link. Concierge. Shopping arcade. Valet parking. Airport transportation. Exercise equipt; steam rm, sauna. Game rm. Bathrm phones. Some balconies. First casino in Atlantic City. Cr cds: A, C, D, DS, JCB, MC, V.

⊡ ⛵ 🕴 ⊠ 🔥

★★ **THE SANDS HOTEL & CASINO IN ATLANTIC CITY.** *Indiana Ave & Brighton Park (08401).* 609/441-4000; FAX 609/441-4180; res: 800/257-8580. Web www.acsands.com. 534 rms, 21 story. July-Sept: S, D $99-$259; each addl $15; under 18 free; package plans; lower rates rest of yr. Crib free. TV; cable (premium), VCR avail. Restaurants (see BRIGHTON STEAKHOUSE and CHINA MOON). Bar open 24 hrs; enter-

tainment. Ck-out noon. Convention facilities. Business servs avail. Concierge. Beauty shop. Valet, garage parking. Airport transportation. Exercise equipt; sauna. On ocean. Cr cds: A, C, D, DS, MC, V.

⊡ 🕴 ⊠ 🖐 SC

★★★ **TROPICANA CASINO & RESORT.** *Brighton Ave & The Boardwalk (08401).* 609/340-4398; FAX 609/343-5211; res: 800/843-8767. Web www.tropicana.net. 1,624 rms, 23 story. Mid-June-Sept: S, D $105-$225; under 18 free; lower rates rest of yr. TV; cable (premium). 2 pools, 1 indoor; whirlpool, poolside serv, lifeguard. Restaurants open 24 hrs. Bars open 24 hrs. Ck-out noon. Business center. In-rm modem link. Shopping arcade. Barber, beauty shop. Valet, garage parking. Lighted tennis. Exercise rm; sauna. Some bathrm phones. On ocean. Cr cds: A, C, D, DS, MC, V.

⊡ ⤢ ⛵ 🕴 ⊠ 🖐 🕴

★★★ **TRUMP MARINA.** *601 Huron Ave (08401).* 609/441-2000; FAX 609/441-8541; res: 800/777-8477. Web www.trumpmarina.com. With its helicopter service and the state's largest marina, this hotel caters to a sophisticated clientele. Decoration begins with an open atrium lobby with black granite accents. It also hosts major sports and entertainment events. 728 rms, 27 story. July-mid-Sept: S, D $150-$225; each addl $15; suites $175-$275; under 12 free; package plans; lower rates rest of yr. Crib free. TV; cable (premium), VCR avail. Pool; wading pool, whirlpool, poolside serv, lifeguard. Restaurants open 24 hrs. Bars; entertainment. Ck-out noon. Convention facilities. Business servs avail. In-rm modem link. Shopping arcade. Barber, beauty shop. Garage parking. Lighted tennis. Exercise rm; sauna, steam rm. Massage. Health club privileges. Basketball. Lawn games. Game rm. On ocean inlet. Cr cds: A, C, D, DS, JCB, MC, V.

⊡ ⬤ 🚲 ⤢ ⛵ 🕴 🕴 ⊠ 🔥

★★★ **TRUMP PLAZA HOTEL & CASINO.** *Boardwalk & Mississippi Ave (08401).* 609/441-6000; FAX 609/441-7881; res: 800/677-7378. 904 rms, 38 story. June-Sept: S, D $200-$245; each addl $10; under 16 free; lower rates rest of yr. Crib avail. TV; cable (premium), VCR avail. Indoor pool; whirlpool, lifeguard. Restaurants open 24 hrs. Bar; entertainment. Ck-out noon. Business servs avail. In-rm modem link. Concierge. Shopping arcade. Beauty shop. Garage parking. Tennis. Golf privileges. Exercise rm; sauna, steam rm. Massage. Game rm. Bathrm phones. On ocean. Cr cds: A, C, D, DS, MC, V.

⊡ 🕴 🕴 ⤢ ⛵ 🕴 ⊠ 🔥

★★★ **TRUMP TAJ MAHAL CASINO RESORT.** *1000 Boardwalk (08401), at Virginia Ave.* 609/449-1000; FAX 609/449-6818; res: 800/825-8786. Web www.trumptaj.com. 1,250 rms, 52 story, 246 suites. July-Labor Day: S, D $195-$295; each addl $25; suites $325-$650; lower rates rest of yr. Crib free. TV; cable (premium). Indoor pool; whirlpool, poolside serv, lifeguard. Restaurant open 24 hrs. Bar; entertainment. Ck-out noon. Convention facilities. Business center. Concierge. Shopping arcade. Barber, beauty shop. Valet parking. Exercise rm; sauna, steam rm. Massage. Spa. Casino. Game rm. Bicycles avail. Refrigerators avail. Cr cds: A, C, D, DS, MC, V.

⊡ ⛵ 🕴 ⊠ 🔥 🕴

Resort

★★★ **SEAVIEW MARRIOTT RESORT.** *401 S New York Rd (08201), 7 mi W on US 9, just N of Absecon.* 609/748-1990; FAX 609/652-2307; res: 800/922-8000. Web www.marriott.com. 297 rms; 3 story. May-Nov: S, D $199-$275; suites $250-$700; under 18 free; golf, package plans; lower rates rest of yr. Crib free. TV; cable (premium), VCR avail (free movies). 2 pools, 1 indoor; whirlpool, poolside serv, lifeguard. Dining rm 6:30 am-10 pm. Rm serv. Box lunches. Snack bar. Bar noon-2 am. Ck-out 12:30 pm, ck-in 4 pm. Coin lndry. Convention facilities. Business center. In-rm modem link. Gift shop. Sports dir. 8 tennis courts, 4 lighted, pro. 36-hole golf, pro, 9-hole putting green; golf school. Rec rm. Game rm. Exercise equipt; sauna. Basketball. Volleyball. Minibars; refrigerator, fireplace in suites. Driving ranges. Located on 670-acre estate. Cr cds: A, C, D, DS, ER, JCB, MC, V.

Restaurants

★ ★ ★ **BRIGHTON STEAKHOUSE.** *(See Sands Hotel Casino) 609/441-4300.* Web www.arsands.com. Hrs: 6-10 pm; Fri, Sat to 10:30 pm; Sun brunch 10 am-2 pm. Closed Tues, Wed. Res required. American menu. Bar noon-midnight. Wine list. A la carte entrees: dinner $18-$48. Sun brunch $26.95. Specialties: chateaubriand, pepper-seared tuna, Brighton seafood harvest. Tropical decor. Cr cds: A, C, D, DS, MC, V.

★ **CAPTAIN YOUNG'S SEAFOOD EMPORIUM.** *1 Atlantic Ocean (08401), on 3rd floor of The Shops on Ocean One Mall. 609/344-2001.* Hrs: 11:30 am-9 pm; Sat to 10 pm. Closed Thanksgiving, Dec 25. Bar. Semi-a la carte: lunch $6.25-$9.95, dinner $13.95-$19.95. Specializes in fresh fish, fresh lobster, crab legs. Overlooks beach and Boardwalk. Cr cds: A, C, D, DS, MC, V.

★ ★ **CHEF VOLA'S.** *111 S Albion Place (08401). 609/345-2022.* Hrs: 6-10 pm. Closed Mon; Thanksgiving, Dec 24, 25. Res required. Italian menu. A la carte entrees: dinner $13.95-$30. Specializes in steak, veal. Italian decor. Photographs of celebrities. Cr cds: C.

★ ★ ★ **CHINA MOON.** *(See Sands Hotel Casino) 609/441-4100.* Web www.acsands.com. Hrs: 6-10 pm; Fri-Sun to 10:30 pm. Closed Wed, Thurs. Res required. Chinese menu. Bar noon-midnight. Wine list. A la carte entrees: dinner $14.95-$42. Specialties: China Moon chicken, Dragon Phoenix, filet with mixed vegetables. Own baking. Elegant decor; gold Chinese script accents black walls. Cr cds: A, C, D, DS, MC, V.

★ ★ **DOCK'S OYSTER HOUSE.** *2405 Atlantic Ave (08401). 609/345-0092.* Hrs: 5-10:30 pm. Closed Mon; also Jan, Dec. Res accepted. Bar. Semi-a la carte: dinner $13.95-$29. Child's meals. Specialties: imperial crab, oyster stew. Pianist Thurs-Sat. Parking. Casual atmosphere in family-owned restaurant since 1897. Cr cds: A, C, D, MC, V.

★ **GRABELS RESTAURANT LOUNGE.** *3901 Atlantic Ave (08401). 609/344-9263.* Hrs: 3 pm-7 am. Closed Dec 24. Res accepted. Continental menu. Bar. Semi-a la carte: dinner $4.95-$21.95. Child's meals. Specialties: veal rollintine, black Angus New York strip, crab cakes. Pianist Wed-Sun. Modern decor; casual dining. Family-owned. Cr cds: C, MC, V.

✓ ★ **HARLEY DAWN DINER.** *1402 Blackhorse Pike (08037), 20 mi W on US 322. 609/567-6084.* Web www.njra.com. Hrs: 6 am-10 pm. Closed Dec 25. Semi-a la carte: bkfst $1.75-$7.95, lunch $2.25-$5.95, dinner $6.95-$12.95. Child's meals. Specialties: chicken & broccoli Harley Dawn-style, broiled crab cakes, eggs Benedict. Own breads. Authentic diner atmosphere. Cr cds: A, C, DS, MC, V.

★ ★ **OLD WATERWAY INN.** *1660 W Riverside Dr (08401). 609/347-1793.* Hrs: 5-11 pm. Closed Mon, Tues, Oct-Apr. Res accepted. Bar. Semi-a la carte: dinner $15-$24. Child's meals. Specializes in fresh seafood and Cajun specialities. Own pasta. Outdoor dining. Nautical decor. On waterfront; view of skyline. Cr cds: A, C, D, MC, V.

★ ★ ★ **RAM'S HEAD INN.** *9 W White Horse Pike (08201), on US 30 at Garden State Pkwy exit 40S. 609/652-1700.* Web www.ramsheadinn.com. Hrs: noon-3 pm, 5-9:30 pm; Sat 5-10 pm; Sun 1:30-7:30 pm; hrs vary by season. Res accepted. Closed Mon; Labor Day, Dec 24. Continental menu. Bar. Semi-a la carte: lunch $7.25-$12.95, dinner $16.95-$25.95. Child's meals. Specializes in colonial Amer dishes, fresh southern New Jersey seafood. Menu changes seasonally. Own baking. Pianist. Valet parking. Outdoor dining. Colonial decor; gallery with paintings, plants. Jacket (dinner). Cr cds: A, C, D, DS, MC, V.

★ ★ ★ **RENAULT WINERY.** *72 N Bremen Ave (08215), 16 mi W on US 30. 609/965-2111.* E-mail wine@renaultwinery.com; Web www.renaultwinery.com. Hrs: 5-9 pm; Sun brunch 10:30 am-2:30 pm. Closed Mon-Thurs; Dec 25. Res required. Wine list. Complete meals: dinner $27.95-$31.95. Sun brunch $14.95. Specializes in fresh seafood, poultry, beef. Menu changes wkly. Pianist/guitarist. Parking. Elegant dining in eclectic Methode Champenoise rm of winery founded in 1864. Cr cds: A, C, D, MC, V.

★ ★ **SCANNICCHIO'S.** *119 S California Ave (08401). 609/348-6378.* Web www.atlantic/city/online.com/scannicchios. Hrs: 4 pm-midnight. Closed most major hols. Res required wkends. Italian menu. Bar. A la carte entrees: dinner $10.95-$19.95. Specializes in veal, fresh seafood. Intimate ambiance. Cr cds: A, C, D, DS, MC, V.

★ ★ **STEVE COOKIE'S BY THE BAY.** *9700 Amherst Ave (08402), on Margate waterfront. 609/823-1163.* Hrs: 5-10 pm; Sat to 11 pm; Sat, Sun 10 am-3 pm. Closed Dec 24, Dec 25. Res accepted. Contemporary Amer menu. Bar 3 pm-1 am. A la carte entrees: dinner $12-$27. Sat, Sun brunch $4-$10. Child's meals. Specialties: crab cakes, char-grilled filet mignon, steamed whole Maine lobster. Jazz. Parking. View of bay & marina. Fireplaces. Casual dining. Cr cds: A, C, D, DS, MC, V.

✓ ★ **SUNSET DOCK.** *9707 Amherst Ave (08402), 5 mi S on Amherst Ave on the bay. 609/487-3010.* Hrs: 8-4 am. Bar. Semi-a la carte: bkfst $2.75-$7.95, lunch $4.95-$12.95, dinner $10.95-$18.95. Specializes in fresh seafood, hand-cut steaks. Outdoor dining. Overlooks bay, marina. Cr cds: C, MC, V.

Unrated Dining Spot

IRISH PUB AND INN. *St James Place & Boardwalk. 609/344-9063.* Open 24 hrs. Irish, Amer menu. Bar. A la carte entrees: lunch $1.95-$3.95, dinner $2.95-$6.25. Complete meals: dinner $5.50. Specialty: Dublin beef stew. Irish balladeer Thurs-Sun (summer). Patio dining. Informal, Irish pub atmosphere. Cr cds: C.

Batsto (H-4)

(See also Atlantic City)

Area Code 609 **Zip** 08037

(Approx 10 mi E of Hammonton)

The Batsto Iron Works, established in 1766, made munitions for the Revolutionary Army from the bog iron ore found nearby. Its furnaces shut down for the last time in 1848. Eighteen years later, Joseph Wharton, whose immense estate totaled nearly 100,000 acres, bought the land. In 1954, the state of New Jersey bought nearly 150 square miles of land in this area, including the entire Wharton tract, for a state forest.

What to See and Do

Batsto State Historic Site. Restored early 19th-century iron and glass-making community. General store, gristmill, blacksmith shop, wheelwright shop, sawmill, workers' houses and visitor center are open seasonally to the public. Guided tours of the mansion (fee). Parking fee (Memorial Day–Labor Day, wkends & hols). For further information and hrs phone 609/561-3262.　**Free**

Wharton State Forest. Crossed by NJ 542, 563. Streams wind through 110,000 acres of wilderness. Swimming; fishing, hunting; canoeing. Limited picnicking. Tent & trailer sites, cabins. Standard fees. Along US 206 near Atsion. Phone 609/561-3262. Also here is

Atsion Recreation Area. Swimming; canoeing. Picnicking. Camping. Standard fees. For information phone 609/268-0444.

Beach Haven

(see Long Beach Island)

Restaurant

★★ **LEEWARD ROOM.** (See Engleside Inn) 609/492-5116. Hrs: 8 am-noon, 5-10 pm; Sun brunch 8 am-1:30 pm. Closed Dec 25. Res accepted. Japanese menu. Bar 5 pm-1 am. A la carte entrees: bkfst $2.25-$9.50, lunch $2-$10. Semi-a la carte: dinner $10-$26. Sun brunch $13.95. Child's meals. Specialties: lobster roll, salmon Oscar, prime rib. Parking. Outdoor dining. Nautical decor. Sushi bar. Cr cds: A, C, D, DS, MC, V.

ⒹⓈ

Bernardsville (C-4)

(See also Morristown)

Pop 6,597 **Elev** 400 ft **Area Code** 908 **Zip** 07924

What to See and Do

Great Swamp National Wildlife Refuge. Nature trails, boardwalk. Observation blind; wilderness area. More than 200 species of birds, fish, reptiles, frogs, ducks, geese and fox may be seen in this 7,300-acre refuge. Headquarters (Mon–Fri; closed hols). Trails and information booth (daily, dawn–dusk). 1 mi N on US 202, W on N Maple Ave, 2 mi E on Madisonville Rd, then 1½ mi NE on Lee's Hill Rd, then right on Long Hill Rd. Phone 973/425-1222.　**Free**

Morristown National Historical Park. (see). Approx 5 mi N on US 2.

Hotel

★★★ **SOMMERSET HILLS HOTEL.** 200 Liberty Corner Rd (07059), SW on I-287 to I-78E, exit 33 (Martinsville-Bernardsville). 908/647-6700; FAX 908/647-8053; res: 800/688-0700. E-mail shhotel@aol.com; Web www.shh.com. 111 units, 4 story. S $105-$180; D $105-$190; each addl $10; suites $250-$310; kits. $145-$185. Crib free. Pet accepted. TV; cable (premium). Pool; poolside serv. Restaurant 6:30 am-11 pm. Bar 11:30-2 am. Ck-out noon. Meeting rms. Business center. In-rm modem link. Concierge. Gift shop. Tennis privileges. 18-hole golf privileges, pro, putting green, driving range. Exercise equipt. Microwaves avail. Nestled in the Watchung Mountains near the crossroads of historical Liberty Corner. Cr cds: A, C, D, MC, V.

Ⓓ🏊🎿⛷🏃🏊🎿🏊ⓈⒸ🚶

Inn

★★★★ **BERNARDS INN.** 27 Mine Brook Rd (07924). 908/766-0002; FAX 908/766-4604; res: 888/766-0002. E-mail info@bernardsinn.com; Web www.bernardsinn.com. This completely renovated inn, built in 1907, offers plush accommodations and gracious hospitality. 20 rms, 5 story, 4 suites. S, D $115-$190; suites $190-$215. Crib $10. TV; cable (premium). Complimentary continental bkfst. Restaurant (see THE BERNARDS INN). Rm serv. Bar. Ck-out 11 am, ck-in 4 pm. Business servs avail. In-rm modem link. Luggage handling. Concierge serv. Massage. Health club privileges. Cr cds: A, C, D, MC, V.

Ⓓ🖹🔥

Restaurants

★★★ **GIRAFE.** 95 Morristown Rd (07924), I-287 exit 30B, W to US 202S. 908/221-0017. Hrs: 11:30 am-2 pm, 5:30-9 pm; Fri to 10 pm; Sat 5:30-10 pm. Sun 4-8 pm. Closed major hols. Res accepted. Wine cellar. A la carte entrees: lunch $6.50-$12.50, dinner $16-$28. Specializes in pasta, fresh fish, desserts. Own baking. Cr cds: A, C, D, MC, V.

Ⓓ🖹

★★★ **LE PETIT CHATEAU.** 121 Claramont Rd (07924). 908/766-4544. Hrs: 11:30 am-10:30 pm; Sat 5 pm-midnight; Sun 4-9:30 pm. Closed Mon; Dec 25. Res accepted. French menu. Bar. Wine cellar. A la carte entrees: lunch $10.95-$14.95, dinner $18.95-$29.95. Specialties: duck confit, shrimp with portabello & asparagus, flounder with petit croutons. Harpist Sat. Parking. Private wine cellar dining rm. Jacket. Cr cds: A, C, DS, MC, V.

Ⓓ

★★★ **THE BERNARDS INN.** (See The Bernards Inn) 908/766-0002. E-mail info@bernardsinn.com; Web www.bernardsinn.com. Hrs: 11:30 am-3 pm, 5:30-10 pm; Fri, Sat to 11 pm. Closed Sun; some major hols. Res accepted, required Fri, Sat. Bar. Wine list. A la carte entrees: lunch $9-$13, dinner $21-$32. Specializes in rack of lamb, veal medallion, creme brulee. Pianist Tues-Sat. Outdoor dining. Elegant dining, turn-of-the-century ambiance. Jacket (dinner). Cr cds: A, C, D, MC, V.

Ⓓ🖹

Bordentown (E-4)

(See also Trenton)

Settled 1682 **Pop** 4,341 **Elev** 72 ft **Area Code** 609 **Zip** 08505

Information Historical Society Visitors Center, Old City Hall, 13 Crosswicks St, PO Box 182; 609/298-1740

A long and honorable history has left an indelible stamp on this town. Bordentown was once a busy shipping center and a key stop on the Delaware and Raritan Canal. In January 1778, Bordentown citizens filled numerous kegs with gun powder and sent them down the Delaware River to Philadelphia hoping to blow up the British fleet stationed there. But the plan was discovered, and British troops intercepted the kegs and discharged them. In 1816, Joseph Bonaparte, exiled king of Spain and brother of Napoleon, bought 1,500 acres and settled here.

What to See and Do

Clara Barton Schoolhouse. Building was in use as a school in Revolutionary days. In 1851, Clara Barton, founder of the American Red Cross, established one of the first free public schools in the country in this building. (By appt) 142 Crosswicks St. Phone 609/298-0676.　**Free**

Motel

★ **DAYS INN.** *1073 US Hwy 206 N (08505), just N of NJ Tpke exit 7. 609/298-6100; FAX 609/298-7509; res: 800/329-7466.* Web www.daysinn.com. 131 rms, 2 story. S, D $95-$105; each addl $10; under 12 free. Crib free. Pet accepted. TV; cable. Pool; lifeguard. Restaurant 6:30-10 am, 5-9 pm. Rm serv. Bar 5 pm-1:30 am. Ck-out 11 am. Coin lndry. Meeting rms. Business servs avail. Sundries. Cr cds: A, C, D, DS, JCB, MC, V.

Branchville (B-3)

(See also Vernon)

Pop 851 **Elev** 529 ft **Area Code** 201 **Zip** 07826
Information Sussex County Chamber of Commerce, 120 Hampton House Rd, Newton 07860; 201/579-1811

This town in Sussex County is near many attractions in New Jersey's scenic northwest corner.

What to See and Do

Peters Valley. Historic buildings in the Delaware Water Gap National Recreation Area (see DELAWARE WATER GAP, PA) serve as residences and studios for professional craftspeople and summer crafts workshops in blacksmithing, ceramics, fine metals, photography, fibers and woodworking. Contemporary craft store (Thurs-Sun). Studios (June–Aug, Fri–Sat, Sun afternoons). 8 mi NW via US 206, County 560, then S on County 615. Phone 201/948-5200.   **Free**

Space Farms Zoo & Museum. Collection of more than 500 wild animals; early American museum in main building, addl museums on grounds; picnic area, concession; gift shop. Zoo and museum (May–Oct, daily). 6 mi N on County 519. Phone 201/875-5800 or 201/875-3223.   ¢¢¢

Stokes State Forest. Located on the Kittatinny Ridge, this 15,482-acre forest includes some of the finest mountain country in New Jersey. Swimming; fishing, hunting. Picnicking. Camping. Scenic views from Sunrise Mt; Tillman Ravine, a natural gorge, is in the southern corner of the park. Standard fees. 4 mi N on US 206. Phone 201/948-3820.

Swartswood State Park. A 1,470-acre park on Swartswood Lake. Swimming (Memorial Day-Labor Day), bathhouse; fishing, hunting; boating (rentals, Memorial Day-Labor Day). Picnicking, concession. Camping. Standard fees. 2 mi S on County 519, then continue 2 mi on County 627, left 3 mi on County 521 to Swartswood, left 1 mi on County 622, right on County 619, ½ mi to park entrance. Phone 201/383-5230.

Annual Event

Peters Valley Craft Fair. Peters Valley. More than 150 juried exhibitors; demonstrations, music, food. Last wknd Sept.

Bridgeton (H-2)

(See also Millville)

Settled 1686 **Pop** 18,942 **Elev** 40 ft **Area Code** 609 **Zip** 08302 **E-mail** njbridge@aol.com

Information Bridgeton-Cumberland Tourist Association, 50 E Broad St; 609/451-4802 or 800/319-3379

The city of Bridgeton has been recognized as New Jersey's largest historic district, with more than 2,200 registered historical landmarks. There are

many styles of architecture here, some of which date back nearly 300 years.

What to See and Do

City Park. A 1,100-acre wooded area with swimming (protected beaches, Memorial Day–Labor Day); fishing; boating (floating dock), canoeing. Picnic grounds, recreation center. Zoo. (Daily) W Commerce St & Mayor Aitken Dr off NJ 49. Phone 609/451-9208. Also here is

New Sweden Farmstead Museum. Reconstruction of first permanent European settlement in Delaware Valley. Seven log buildings including smokehouse/sauna; horse barn, cow and goat barn, threshing barn; storage house; blacksmith shop; family residence with period furnishings. Costumed guides. (May–Labor Day, Wed–Sat, also Sun afternoons) Phone 609/455-9785.   ¢¢

George J. Woodruff Museum of Indian Artifacts. Approx 20,000 local Native American artifacts, some up to 10,000 yrs old; clay pots, pipes, implements. (Mon–Fri afternoons; also by appt; closed some major hols) Bridgeton Free Public Library, 150 E Commerce St. Phone 609/451-2620.   **Free**

Gibbon House (1730). Site of New Jersey's only 18th-century tea burning party; genealogical research library (Mar–Dec, Wed & Sun). Events scheduled throughout yr. Gibbon House (early Apr–late Nov, daily exc Mon; closed Sun in July, Aug); tours (wkdays). 7 mi SW in Greenwich, on Ye Greate St. Phone 609/455-4055 or 609/451-8454.   **Donation**

Old Broad St Church (1792). Outstanding example of Georgian architecture, with Palladian window, high-backed wooden pews, wine glass pulpit, brick-paved aisles and brass lamps that once held whale oil. W Broad St & West Ave.

Parvin State Park. This 1,125-acre park offers swimming, bathhouse; fishing; boating, canoeing (rentals). Picnicking, concessions, playgrounds. Camping (dump station), cabins. Standard fees. 7 mi NE off NJ 77, near Centerton. Phone 609/358-8616.

Annual Event

Victorian Faire. Victorian Bridgeton is re-created through music, games and contests, street vendors, crafts, costumes and city tours. Phone 609/451-9208. Labor Day wknd.

Seasonal Event

Concerts. Riverfront. Performances by ragtime, military, country & western bands and others. Sun nights. Phone 609/451-9208. Nine wks July–Aug.

Burlington (F-3)

(See also Bordentown, Mount Holly; also see Philadelphia, PA)

Settled 1677 **Pop** 9,835 **Elev** 13 ft **Area Code** 609 **Zip** 08016
Information Burlington County Chamber of Commerce, Northwestern Mutual Life Bldg, 2311 Rte 541; 609/386-1012; or write to PO Box 2006, Willingboro 08046

In 1774 Burlington, along with New York, Philadelphia and Boston, was a thriving port. A Quaker settlement, it was one of the first to provide public education. A 1682 Act of Assembly gave Matinicunk (now Burlington) Island in the Delaware River to the town with the stipulation that the revenue it generated would be used for public schools; that act is still upheld. Burlington was the capital of West Jersey; the legislature met here, and in the East Jersey capital of Perth Amboy, from 1681 until after the Revolution. In 1776, the Provincial Congress adopted the state constitution here.

What to See and Do

Burlington County Historical Society. The society maintains **D.B. Pugh Library,** in the Corson-Poley Center, genealogical and historical holdings; **James Fenimore Cooper House** (ca 1780), birthplace of the famous author, now the society headquarters; **Bard-How House** (ca 1740) with period furnishings; **Capt James Lawrence House,** birthplace of the commander of the *Chesapeake* during the War of 1812 and speaker of the immortal words "Don't give up the ship," contains 1812 objects and costume display. Tour of historic houses (Sun–Thurs afternoons). 457 High St. Phone 609/386-4773. ¢¢

Friends Meeting House (1784). (By appt) High St in 300 blk. Phone 609/387-3875. ¢¢

Historic tours. Guided walking tours of 33 historic sites (1685–1829), eight of which are open to the public. (Daily; no tours Easter, Dec 25) Leave foot of High St. Phone 609/386-3993. ¢¢

Old St Mary's Church (1703). The oldest Episcopal Church building in the state. (By appt) W Broad & Wood Sts. Phone 609/386-0902.

Thomas Revell House (1685). The oldest building in Burlington County. Included in Burlington County Historical Society home tour (see). (By appt and during Wood Street Fair; see ANNUAL EVENT) 213 Wood St. Phone 609/386-3993. **Free**

Annual Event

Wood Street Fair. Re-creation of colonial fair; crafts, antiques exhibits; food; entertainment. 1st Sat after Labor Day.

Restaurant

★★★ **CAFE GALLERY.** *219 High St (08016). 609/386-6150.* Hrs: 11:30 am-10 pm; Fri, Sat to 11 pm; Sun brunch 11:30 am-3 pm. Closed most major hols. Res accepted. Continental menu. Bar. Semi-a la carte: lunch $5.75-$9.75, dinner $14.50-$19.75. Sun brunch $16.75. Child's meals. Specializes in fresh seafood. Outdoor dining. Restored Colonial building overlooking Delaware River. Cr cds: A, C, D, MC, V.

Caldwell (C-5)

(See also Newark, Newark Intl Airport Area)

Pop 7,549 **Elev** 411 ft **Area Code** 973 **Zip** 07006

What to See and Do

Grover Cleveland Birthplace State Historic Site. Built in 1832, this building served as the parsonage of the First Presbyterian Church. It is the birthplace of President Grover Cleveland, the only president born in New Jersey. He lived here from 1837–1841. (Wed–Sat, also Sun afternoons; closed Jan 1, Thanksgiving, Dec 25, all state hols; res recommended) 207 Bloomfield Ave. Phone 973/226-1810. **Free**

Camden (F-2)

(See also Cherry Hill; also see Philadelphia, PA)

Settled 1681 **Pop** 87,492 **Elev** 23 ft **Area Code** 856

Camden's growth as the leading industrial, marketing and transportation center of southern New Jersey dates from post-Civil War days. Its location across the Delaware River from Philadelphia prompted large companies such as Campbell Soup (national headquarters) to establish plants here. Walt Whitman spent the last 20 years of his life in Camden.

What to See and Do

Camden County Historical Society–Pomona Hall (1726/1788). Brick Georgian house that belonged to descendants of William Cooper, an early Camden settler; period furnishings. Museum exhibits focus on regional history and include antique glass, lamps, toys and early hand tools; fire-fighting equipment; Victor Talking Machines. Library (fee) has more than 20,000 books, as well as maps (17th century–present), newspapers (18th–20th century), oral history tapes, photographs and genealogical material. (Tues, Thurs, Sun; closed major hols, also Aug) Park Blvd at Euclid Ave. Phone 856/964-3333. Museum ¢

New Jersey State Aquarium. Features one of the largest "open ocean" tanks in the country. Other highlights include an underwater research station, aquatic nursery and the opportunity to touch sharks, rays and starfish in special tanks and pools. Gift shop. Cafeteria. (Daily; closed some hols) 1 Riverside Dr, I-676 exit Mickle Blvd. Phone 856/365-3300. ¢¢¢

Tomb of Walt Whitman. The "good gray poet's" vault, designed by the poet himself, is of rough-cut stone with a grillwork door. Harleigh Cemetery, Haddon Ave & Vesper Blvd.

Walt Whitman Cultural Arts Center. Poetry readings, concerts and plays (Oct–May). Children's theater (late June–Aug, Fri). Art gallery; statuary. Center (Mon–Fri). 2nd & Cooper Sts. For schedule and fees phone 856/964-8300.

 Walt Whitman House State Historic Site. The last residence of the poet and the only house he ever owned; he lived here from 1884 until his death on Mar 26, 1892. Contains original furnishings, books and mementos. (Wed–Sat, also Sun afternoons) 330 Mickle Blvd. Phone 856/964-5383. **Free**

Cape May (K-3)

(See also Wildwood & Wildwood Crest)

Settled 1631 **Pop** 4,668 **Elev** 14 ft **Area Code** 609 **Zip** 08204 **E-mail** ccgcm@aol.com **Web** www.capemaychamber.com

Information Chamber of Commerce, PO Box 556, phone 609/884-5508; or the Welcome Center at 405 Lafayette St, phone 609/884-9562

Cape May, the nation's oldest seashore resort, is located on the southernmost tip of the state surrounded by the Atlantic Ocean and Delaware Bay. Popular with Philadelphia and New York society since 1766, Cape May has been host to Presidents Lincoln, Grant, Pierce, Buchanan and Harrison, as well as notables such as John Wanamaker and Horace Greeley. The entire town has been proclaimed a National Historic Landmark because it has more than 600 Victorian homes and buildings, many of which have been restored. The downtown Washington Street Victorian Mall features three blocks of shops and restaurants. Four miles of beaches and a 1¼-mile paved promenade offer vacationers varied entertainment. "Cape May diamonds," often found on the shores of Delaware Bay by visitors, are actually pure quartz, rounded by the waves.

What to See and Do

Cape May-Lewes (DE) Ferry. Sole connection between southern terminus of Garden State Pkwy and US 13 (Ocean Hwy) on the Delmarva Peninsula. 16-mi, 70-min trip across Delaware Bay. (Daily) For schedule Phone 800/64-FERRY (Cape May Terminal) or 302/645-6313 (Lewes Terminal). Per vehicle ¢¢¢¢

Emlen Physick Estate (1879). Authentically restored 18-rm Victorian mansion designed by Frank Furness. Mansion is also headquarters for the Mid-Atlantic Center for the Arts. (Apr–Nov, daily; rest of yr, Tues–Thurs & Sat–Sun) 1048 Washington St. Phone 609/884-5404. ¢¢

Historic Cold Spring Village (1879). Restored 1870 South Jersey farm village. Craft shops; spinning, blacksmithing, weaving, pottery, broom making, ship modeling demonstrations; folk art; bakery and food shops; restaurant. (June–Sept, daily) 3 mi N via US 109. Phone 609/898-2300. ¢¢

Swimming, fishing, boating. Beaches with lifeguards (fee). Fishing is very good at the confluence of the Atlantic and Delaware Bay. A large harbor holds boats of all sizes; excellent for sailboating and other small-boat activity.

Tours. The Mid-Atlantic Center for the Arts offers the following tours. For further information contact PO Box 340; phone 609/884-5404.

Cape May INNteriors Tour & Tea. Features a different group of houses each week, visiting five or more bed & breakfast inns and guesthouses. Innkeepers greet guests and describe experiences. (Summer, Mon; rest of yr, Sat; no tours Dec–Jan) ¢¢¢¢

Combination Tours. Approx 2 hrs; includes trolley tour and guided tour of Physick House. (June–Oct, daily; rest of yr, Sat & Sun) Begin at Emlen Physick Estate. (see) Phone for schedule. ¢¢¢

Mansions by Gaslight. Three-hr tour begins at Emlen Physick Estate. Visits four Victorian landmarks: Emlen Physick House (see), the Abbey (1869), Mainstay Inn (1872) and Humphrey Hughes House (1903); shuttle bus between houses. (Mid-June–Sept, Wed evenings; rest of yr, hol & special tours) ¢¢¢¢

Ocean Walk Tours. A 1½-hr guided tour of Cape May's beaches. Guide discusses marine life and history of the beaches, including legends of buried treasure. (May–Sept, Tues–Sat) Begins at Promenade & Beach Dr. ¢¢

Trolleys. Half-hr tours on enclosed trolley bus or open-air carriage; three routes beginning at Ocean St opp the Washington St Mall. (June–Oct, daily; reduced schedule rest of yr; no tours Thanksgiving) ¢¢

Walking Tours of the Historic District. Begin at Information Booth on Washington St Mall at Ocean St. Three 1½-hr guided tours give historical insight into the customs and traditions of the Victorians and their ornate architecture. (June–Sept, daily; reduced schedule rest of yr) ¢¢

Annual Events

Tulip Festival. Celebrate Dutch heritage with ethnic foods and dancing, craft show, street fair, garden and house tours. Phone 609/884-5508. Apr.

Sea & Sky Festival. Sample Cape May's variety of seafood while colorful kites and blues music fill the air. Phone 609/884-5508. June.

Promenade Art Exhibit. July.

Victorian Week. Tours, antiques, crafts, period fashion shows. Mid-Oct.

Motels

★★ **AVONDALE BY THE SEA.** *Beach Ave & Gurney St (08204). 609/884-2332; FAX 609/884-2073; res: 800/676-7030.* Web www.capenet.com/capemay/avondale. 46 rms, 3 story, 18 suites. Late July-early Sept: S, D $154-$189; each addl $15; suites $164-$192; kit. units $184-$200; package plans; wkends (2-day min); lower rates rest of yr. Crib free. TV; cable. Complimentary continental bkfst. Restaurant adj 8 am-9 pm. Ck-out 11 am. Concierge. Pool. Refrigerators avail. Balconies. Opp ocean. Cr cds: A, C, DS, MC, V.

⬛🏊🔲🔥

★★ **COACHMANS MOTOR INN.** *205 Beach Dr 15 (08204). 609/884-8463.* Web www.capenet.com/capemay/coachman. 65 rms, 3 story, 45 kits. No elvtr. Late June-Labor Day (3-day min hols): S, D $140-$185; each addl $15-20; kit. units $145-$185; lower rates rest of yr. Crib free. TV. Pool; wading pool. Restaurant 7:30 am-10 pm. Bar; entertainment. Ck-out 11 am. Coin lndry. Tennis. Lawn games. Basketball. Sun deck. On ocean. Cr cds: A, C, MC, V.

🎾🏊🔥

★★ **LAMERE BEACHFRONT MOTOR INN.** *1317 Beach Dr (08204). 609/884-9000; FAX 609/884-5004.* Web www.capenet.com/capemay/lamer. 93 rms, 4 story, 14 kits. July-Labor Day: S $118-$136; D $136-$195; each addl $15; kit. units to 5, $160-$170; lower rates May-June, after Labor Day-mid-Oct. Closed rest of yr. TV; VCR avail (movies). Pool; wading pool. Restaurant 5-10 pm. Ck-out 11 am. Coin lndry. Business servs avail. Miniature golf. Some microwaves. Bicycles. Picnic tables, grill. On ocean. Cr cds: A, C, D, DS, MC, V.

⬛🏊🔲🔥

★★ **MOUNT VERNON MOTEL.** *300 Beach Ave & 1st Ave. (08204). 609/884-4665.* Web www.capenet.com/capemay/mtvernon. 25 units, 2 story, 12 kits. July-Labor Day: S, D $145; each addl $12-15; kit.

units $148; lower rates Apr-June, after Labor Day-Oct. Closed rest of yr. Crib avail. TV; cable (premium). Pool; wading pool. Restaurant adj 8 am-midnight. Ck-out 11 am. Refrigerators; some microwaves. Sun deck. Opp ocean. Cr cds: C.

🏊🔥

★★ **PERIWINKLE INN.** *1039 Beach Ave (08204). 609/884-9200; FAX 609/884-4177.* Web www.capenet.com/capemay/prwnkl. 50 rms, 3 story, 14 kits. July-Aug: S, D $130-$152; each addl $15; suites, kit. units $161-$205; lower rates mid-Apr-June, Sept-mid-Oct. Closed rest of yr. Crib free. TV; cable (premium). Pool; wading pool. Restaurant adj 7 am-10 pm. Ck-out 11 am. Refrigerators; some microwaves. Balconies. Grills. On ocean. Cr cds: C.

⬛🏊🔥

Motor Hotels

★★ **GRAND HOTEL.** *1045 Beach Ave (08204). 609/884-5611; FAX 609/884-4344; res: 800/257-8550.* Web www.capenet.com/capenet/grand. 160 rms, 5 story, 30 suites, 40 kit. units. Late July-Aug: S, D $127-$137; each addl $10; suites $164-$267; kit. units $151-$267; family rates; package plans; lower rates rest of yr. Crib $9. TV; cable. Restaurant 8 am-10 pm. Bar noon-1 am; entertainment Fri, Sat. Ck-out 11 am. Meeting rms. Business servs avail. Sundries. Gift shop. Beauty shop. Coin lndry. Sauna. Indoor/outdoor pool; wading pool, whirlpool, poolside serv, lifeguard. Game rm. Refrigerators; many microwaves. Balconies. Picnic tables, grills. Cr cds: A, C, D, DS, MC, V.

⬛🏊🔲🔥

★★ **MARQUIS DE LAFAYETTE.** *501 Beach Ave (08204). 609/884-3500; FAX 609/884-0669; res: 800/257-0432.* 73 units, 6 story, 43 kits. July-Labor Day: S, D $209-$249; each addl $18; kit. units $259-$339; under 8 free; wkend rates; lower rates rest of yr. Crib avail. Pet accepted, some restrictions; $20/day. TV. Pool; poolside serv. Complimentary full bkfst. Restaurant (see TOP OF THE MARQ). Bar; entertainment. Ck-out 1 pm. Coin lndry. Meeting rms. Business servs avail. Bellhops. Valet serv. Balconies. On ocean. Cr cds: A, C, DS, MC, V.

🐾🏊🔲🔥 SC

★★ **MONTREAL INN.** *1019 Beach Dr (08204). 609/884-7011; FAX 609/884-4559; res: 800/525-7011.* E-mail montrealin@aol.com/ Web www.capemayfun.com. 70 units, 4 story, 42 kits. Mid-June-mid-Sept: S, D, suites $90-$140; each addl $6-$9; kit. units $140-$165; lower rates Mar-mid-June, mid-Sept-Dec. Closed rest of yr. Crib free. TV; cable (premium). Heated pool; wading pool, whirlpool, poolside serv, lifeguard. Restaurant 8 am-11 pm. Rm serv. Bar from 11 am. Ck-out 11 am. Coin lndry. Business servs avail. In-rm modem link. Valet serv. Free airport transportation. Putting green, miniature golf. Exercise equipt; sauna. Game rm. Refrigerators; many microwaves. Balconies. Picnic tables, grills. On ocean. Cr cds: A, C, DS, MC, V.

🏊🚶🔲🔥

Hotel

★ **INN OF CAPE MAY.** *7 Ocean St at Beach Drive (08204). 609/884-5555; FAX 609/884-3871; res: 800/582-5933.* 69 rms, 5 story. No rm phones. July-Aug: S, D $98-$275; each addl $20; MAP avail; package plans; lower rates mid-May-June, Sept-mid-Nov. Closed rest of yr. Crib avail. TV; cable. Pool; poolside serv. Restaurant (see ALEATHEA'S). No rm serv. Bar 11-1 am. Ck-out 1 pm. Meeting rms. Business servs avail. On ocean. Opened 1894; antiques. Cr cds: A, C, D, DS, MC, V.

🏊🔥

Inns

★ **ABIGAIL ADAMS BED & BREAKFAST.** *12 Jackson St (08204). 609/884-1371; res: 888/827-4354.* 5 rms, 3 with A/C, 2 air-cooled, 2 share bath, 3 story. No elvtr. No rm phones. Apr-Oct: S, D $125-$185;

each addl $25; wkends, hols (3-4 day min); lower rates rest of yr. Children over 12 yrs only. TV in some rms; cable. Complimentary full bkfst; afternoon refreshments. Restaurant opp 8 am-10 pm. Ck-out 11 am, ck-in 2 pm. Luggage handling. Street parking. 100 ft from beach. Built in 1892. Victorian inn; antiques. Totally nonsmoking. Cr cds: A, C, MC, V.

⊠ 🔥

★★★ **ANGEL OF THE SEA.** *5 Trenton Ave (08204). 609/884-3369; FAX 609/884-3331; res: 800/848-3369.* Web www.angelofthe sea.com. 27 rms, 3 story. A/C July, Aug only. No elvtr. No rm phones. June-Oct: S, D $135-$285; each addl $50; lower rates rest of yr. Children over 8 yrs only. TV; cable (premium), VCR avail. Complimentary full bkfst; afternoon refreshments. Ck-out 11 am, ck-in 2 pm. Business servs avail. Concierge serv. Gift shop. Free airport transportation. Some balconies. Picnic tables. Authentic Victorian house (1850). Located opp ocean, swimming beach. Totally nonsmoking. Cr cds: C, MC, V.

⊠ 🔥

✓★★ **CARROLL VILLA HOTEL.** *19 Jackson St (08204). 609/884-9619; FAX 609/884-0264.* E-mail mbatter@cyberenet.com; Web www.beachcomer.com/capemay. 22 rms, 3 story. Memorial Day-mid-Sept: S $95-$160; D $103-$167; each addl $20; under 2 free; wkly rates; hols, wkends (2-3-day min); lower rates rest of yr. Crib avail. TV in parlor. Complimentary full bkfst. Restaurant (see MAD BATTER). Ck-out 11 am, ck-in 2 pm. Business servs avail. Victorian inn (1882); antiques. Cr cds: A, C, D, DS, MC, V.

⊠ 🔥

★★ **COLUMNS BY THE SEA BED & BREAKFAST.** *1513 Beach Dr (08204). 609/884-2228; FAX 609/884-4789.* Web www.columns. com. 11 air-cooled rms, 3 story. No rm phones. July-Aug: S $150-$260; D $160-$275; each addl $40; wkly rates; lower rates rest of yr. Children over 7 yrs only. TV; cable. Complimentary full bkfst; afternoon refreshments. Restaurant nearby. Ck-out 11:30 am, ck-in 2 pm. Bicycles. Library. Refrigerators. Victorian furnishings; antiques. On beach. Totally nonsmoking. Cr cds: C, MC, V.

⊠ 🔥 SC

★★★ **MAINSTAY INN.** *635 Columbia Ave (08204). 609/884-8690.* Web www.mainstayinn.com. 9 rms, 3 story, 7 suites. Mar-Dec (2-to-3-day min): S, D $95-$255; each addl $35. Complimentary full bkfst; afternoon refreshments. Ck-out 11 am, ck-in 2 pm. Lawn games. Some balconies. Beach passes. Built in 1872 as a gentlemen's gambling house. Victorian decor; antiques; 14-ft ceilings. Veranda. Totally nonsmoking. Cr cds: C.

D ⊠ 🔥

★★★ **QUEEN VICTORIA.** *102 Ocean St (08204). 609/884-8702.* E-mail qvn@bellatlantic.com; Web www.queenvictoria.com. 17 rms, 3 story, 6 suites. June-Sept: S $180-$220; D $190-$240; each addl $25; suites $245-$280; lower rates rest of yr. TV; VCR avail. Complimentary full bkfst; afternoon refreshments. Ck-out 11 am; ck-in 3 pm. Bicycles, beach passes. Whirlpool in suites. Restored Victorian villas; rms individually decorated with Victorian antiques. Cr cds: C, MC, V.

D ⊠ 🔥

★★ **QUEENS HOTEL.** *601 Columbia Ave (08204). 609/884-1613.* Web www.queenvictoria.com. 11 rms, 3 story, 2 suites. No elvtr. Mid-June-mid-Sept: S $90-$185; D $100-$220; each addl $25; suites $155-$250; wkend, wkly rates; wkends, hols (3-day min); lower rates rest of yr. Crib free. TV; cable, VCR avail. Complimentary coffee in rms. Restaurant nearby. Ck-out 11 am; ck-in 3 pm. Meeting rms. Concierge serv. Bicycles. Refrigerators; some microwaves. Some balconies. 1 blk to ocean. Totally nonsmoking. Cr cds: C, MC, V.

⊠ 🔥

★★★ **THE ABBEY BED & BREAKFAST.** *34 Gurney St (08204), at Columbia Ave. 609/884-4506; FAX 609/884-2379.* Web www.beachcomber.com. 14 rms in 2 bldgs, 3 story. No rm phones. Apr-Dec: S, D $100-$275. Closed rest of yr. Children over 12 yrs only. Compli-

mentary full bkfst; afternoon refreshments. Ck-out 11 am, ck-in after 2 pm. Lawn games. Picnic table. Beach passes, chairs, towels. Refrigerators. Gothic-style inn with 60-ft tower; main house built 1869; cottage built 1873. Stenciled and ruby glass arched windows; library, antiques. Cr cds: C, DS, MC, V.

⊠ 🔥

★★★ **THE SOUTHERN MANSION.** *720 Washington St (08204). 609/884-7171; FAX 609/898-0492; res: 800/381-3888.* E-mail mansion@jersey.com; Web www.southernmansion.com. 24 rms, 3 story. July-Dec: S $150-$295; D $175-$350; each addl $35; suite $175-$350; family rates; lower rates rest of yr. Children over 8 yrs only. TV; cable, VCR avail. Complimentary full bkfst. Ck-out 11 am, ck-in 3 pm. Business servs avail. In-rm modem link. Luggage handling. Concierge serv. Massage. Lawn games. Picnic tables. Built in 1863; 5,000 sq ft of verandahs, terraces & solariums; mid-19th century antiques. Totally nonsmoking. Cr cds: A, C, MC, V.

D ⊠ 🔥

★★ **VICTORIAN LACE INN.** *901 Stockton Ave (08204). 609/884-1772; FAX 609/884-0983.* 5 rms, 2 with shower only, 3 story. July-Aug: S, D $100-$195; each addl $10-15; lower rates Mar-June, Sept-Dec. Closed early Jan-mid-Feb. TV; cable, VCR. Complimentary full bkfst. Restaurant nearby. Ck-out 10 am, ck-in 2 pm. Refrigerators, microwaves, fireplaces. Built in 1869; antiques. Totally nonsmoking. Cr cds: C.

⊠ 🔥

★★★ **VIRGINIA HOTEL.** *25 Jackson St (08204), in historic district. 609/884-5700; FAX 609/884-1236; res: 800/732-4236.* Web www.virginiahotel.com. 24 rms, 3 story. No elvtr. Memorial Day-Labor Day: S, D $120-$295; each addl $20; under 5 free; wkly rates; lower rates rest of yr. Crib free. TV; VCR (movies $2). Complimentary continental bkfst. Dining rm (see EBBITT ROOM). Rm serv. Bar 5 pm-midnight; Sat, Sun from noon. Ck-out noon, ck-in 3 pm. Meeting rms. Business servs avail. In-rm modem link. Luggage handling. Concierge serv. Health club privileges. In-rm whirlpools. Balconies. Built 1879; restored. Antique and modern furnishing; amenities. Ocean view from veranda. Cr cds: A, C, D, DS, MC, V.

🔥

Restaurants

★★ **410 BANK STREET RESTAURANT.** *410 Bank St (08204), adj to Welcome Center. 609/884-2127.* Web www.beachcomber.com. Hrs: 5-10:30 pm. Closed Nov-Apr. Res accepted. Louisana French menu. Setups. A la carte entrees: dinner $22-$28. Child's meals. Specializes in grilled fish steaks and prime meats. Porch and garden dining. Restored 1840 Cape May residence. Island atmosphere. Cr cds: A, C, D, DS, MC, V.

★ **ALEATHEA'S.** *(See Inn of Cape May) 609/884-5555.* Hrs: 8 am-noon, 5-10 pm; early-bird dinner 5-6 pm (seasonal). Closed most major hols; also Sept-mid-May. Res accepted. Bar to 11 pm. Semi-a la carte: bkfst $3-$15, dinner $14-$32. Child's meals. Specialties: grilled filet mignon, grilled swordfish, baked salmon. Parking. Property built in 1894; view of ocean. Cr cds: C.

★★ **ALEXANDER'S INN.** *653 Washington St (08204). 609/884-2555.* Web www.alexandersinn.com. Hrs: 6-10 pm; Sun brunch 10 am-1 pm. Closed Mon, Tues; Jan 1, Thanksgiving, Dec 25. Res accepted. French menu. Setups. Semi-a la carte: dinner $27.95-$39.95. Complete meals: dinner $39.95-$57.95. Specializes in rack of lamb, rabbit, Angus beef. Own ice cream. Victorian decor; antiques. Cr cds: A, C, D, DS, MC, V.

★★★ **EBBITT ROOM.** *(See Virginia) 609/884-5700.* E-mail virginia@jerseycape.com; Web www.virginiahotel.com. American Cuisine with Asain influences. Specialities: Pan-seared yellowfin tuna in seasame crust with crisp rice paper, grilled rack of lamb w/white bean cassoulet & peach chutney, oven roast lobster monkfish wrapped in wonton with dual tabasco butter sauces. Hours: 5:30-9:30 pm; Fri, Sat to 10 pm. Res accepted. Valet Parking. Bar. A la carte: dinner $24-$28. Child's meals. Extensive wine list. Pianist; nightly in season, weekends off-season. Intimate Victorian dining rm. Totally nonsmoking. Cr cds: A, C, D, DS, MC, V.

★★ **FRESCOS.** *412 Bank St (08204), 1 blk behind Victorian Mall, adj to Welcome Center.* 609/884-0366. Web www.beachcomber.com. Hrs: 5-10:30 pm. Closed Nov-Apr. Res accepted. Italian menu. A la carte entrees: dinner $15-$23.95. Child's meals. Specializes in fresh seafood, pasta, veal. Outdoor dining. 3 dining areas in restored Victorian summer cottage. Cr cds: A, C, D, DS, MC, V.

D

★★ **LOBSTER HOUSE.** *Fisherman's Wharf (08204), turn E just S of bridge at end of Garden State Pkwy.* 609/884-8296. Hrs: 11:30 am-3 pm, 4:30-10 pm; Sun from 4 pm; winter hrs vary. Closed Thanksgiving, Dec 24-25. Bar. Semi-a la carte: lunch $5.75-$12.50, dinner $15.95-$38.95. Child's meals. Specializes in fresh fish, lobster, crabmeat. Parking. Outdoor dining. On wharf; nautical decor. Fireplace. Raw seafood bars in main bar & dock. Cr cds: A, C, DS, MC, V.

D

★★ **MAD BATTER.** *(See Carroll Villa Hotel)* 609/884-5970. E-mail MBatter@cyberenet.com; Web www.beachcomer.com/capemay. Hrs: 8 am-2:30 pm, 5:30-10 pm; Fri, Sat to 10:30 pm. Closed Jan. Res accepted dinner. Contemporary Amer menu. Setups. A la carte entrees: bkfst, lunch $5-$11, dinner $15-$25. Child's meals. Specializes in fresh seafood, desserts. Outdoor dining. Victorian inn (1882). Cr cds: A, C, D, DS, MC, V.

★★ **MERION INN.** *106 Decatur St (08204).* 609/884-8363. Hrs: noon-2:30 pm, 5-10 pm, early-bird dinner 5-6 pm. Closed Jan-Mar; also Mon-Thurs Apr-May & mid-Oct-Dec. Res accepted. Bar. Semi-a la carte: lunch $5.95-$15.95, dinner $14.95-$32.95. Child's meals. Specializes in stuffed lobster tail, fresh grilled fish, steak. Own desserts. Outdoor dining. Turn-of-the-century Victorian decor. Built 1885. Family-owned. Cr cds: A, C, D, DS, MC, V.

★★ **PEACHES AT SUNSET.** *1 Sunset Blvd W (08204).* 609/898-0100. Hrs: 4:30-10 pm. Closed Dec 25; also Mon-Thurs Oct-May. Res accepted. Pacific Rim cuisine. Semi-a la carte: dinner $17.95-$27.95. Child's meals. Specialties: sea bass with mango salsa, rack of lamb. Free parking. Outdoor dining. Local artwork displayed. Totally nonsmoking. Cr cds: A, C, D, DS, MC, V.

D

★ **RUSTY NAIL BAR AND GRILL.** *205 Beach Dr (08204).* 609/884-0220. Web www.capenet.com/capemay/coachmall. Hrs: 7:30-1 am. Closed Nov-mid-Apr. Bar. Complete meals: bkfst $5-$8.50, lunch $6.50-$10. Semi-a la carte: dinner $9.25-$22. Child's meals. Specializes in crab cake, prime rib, lemon chicken. Beach decor. Cr cds: A, C, MC, V.

D

★★ **TOP OF THE MARQ.** *(See Marquis De Lafayette)* 609/884-3500. Hrs: 5-10 pm. Closed Dec 24, 25. Res accepted. Bar. Complete meals: dinner $12.95-$43. Child's meals. Specializes in lobster, beef tenderloin. Pianist. Valet parking in season. Victorian setting with view of Atlantic. Cr cds: A, C, D, DS, MC, V.

★★★ **WASHINGTON INN.** *801 Washington St (08204).* 609/884-5697. Web www.washingtoninn.com. Hrs: 5-10 pm; hrs may vary wkends & off season. Closed Thanksgiving, Dec 24-25. Res accepted; required Sat. Continental menu. Bar. Wine cellar. Semi-a la carte: dinner $17.95-$25.95. Child's meals. Specializes in steak, veal, fresh seafood. Own baking. Patio dining. Former plantation house (1848). Fireside dining. Cr cds: A, C, D, DS, MC, V.

D

★★ **WATERS EDGE RESTAURANT.** *Beach & Pittsburgh Aves (08204).* 609/884-1717. E-mail neilre@jerseycape.com. Hrs: 5-11 pm; hrs vary off season. Closed Thanksgiving, Dec 25. Res accepted. Bar. A la carte entrees: dinner $19-$28. Child's meals. Specializes in fresh local seafood, free range veal, Angus steak. Contemporary decor. Patio dining, ocean view. Cr cds: A, C, D, DS, MC, V.

D

Cape May Court House (K-3)

(See also Cape May, Stone Harbor, Wildwood & Wildwood Crest)

Pop 4,426 **Elev** 18 ft **Area Code** 609 **Zip** 08210 **Web** www.cmccofc.com
Information Cape May County Chamber of Commerce, PO Box 74; 609/465-7181

To be accurately named, this county seat would have to be called Cape May Court Houses, for there are two of them—one is a white, 19th-century building now used as a meeting hall.

What to See and Do

Cape May County Historical Museum. Period dining room (predating 1820), 18th-century kitchen, doctor's room, military room with Merrimac flag, Cape May diamonds. Barn exhibits; whaling implements; Indian artifacts; pioneer tools; lens from Cape May Point Lighthouse. Genealogical library. (Mid-June–Labor Day wkend, daily exc Sun; after Labor Day–Nov & Apr–mid-June, Tues–Sat; Dec–Mar, Sat only) Shore Rd, 1 mi N on US 9. Phone 609/465-3535. ¢

Cape May County Park. Zoo has over 100 types of animals. Jogging path, bike trail; tennis courts. Picnicking, playground. (Daily) On US 9 at Crest Haven Rd. Phone 609/465-5271. **Donation**

Leaming's Run Gardens. Amid 20 acres of lawns, ponds and ferneries are 25 gardens, each with a separate theme. Eighteenth-century colonial farm grows tobacco and cotton; farm animals. (Mid-May–mid-Oct, daily) Approx 4 mi N on US 9, between Pkwy exits 13 & 17 in Swainton. Phone 609/465-5871. ¢¢

Victorian houses. Fine examples of 19th-century architecture located in the area. Information can be obtained at the Chamber of Commerce Information Center, Crest Haven Rd & Garden State Pkwy, milepost 11 (Easter–mid-Oct, daily; rest of yr, Mon–Fri; closed hols).

Motel

★ **HY-LAND MOTOR INN.** *38 E Mechanic St (08210).* 609/465-7305; FAX 609/465-8776. 34 rms, 24 with shower only, 2 story. Mid-June-Sept: S, D $75-$85; each addl $10; suite $100-$125; kits $90-$125; under 10 free; lower rates rest of yr. Crib $5. TV; cable. Pool. Restaurant nearby. Ck-out 11 am. Business servs avail. Picnic tables, grill. Cr cds: A, C, MC, V.

D

Inn

★★★ **DOCTORS INN AT KINGS GRANT.** *2 N Main St (08210).* 609/463-9330; FAX 609/463-9650. 6 rms, 3 story. June-Oct: D, suites $135-$170; lower rates rest of yr. TV; cable. Complimentary full bkfst. Ck-out 11 am, ck-in 2 pm. Some refrigerators. Built in 1854; pays tribute to physicians and teachers who ministered to the community. Totally nonsmoking. Cr cds: A, C, MC, V.

D

Chatham (C-4)

Pop 8,007 **Elev** 244 ft **Area Code** 973 **Zip** 07928
Information Township of Chatham, 58 Meyersville Rd. 973/635-4600

What to See and Do

Great Swamp National Wildlife Refuge. SW of city (see BERNARDSVILLE).

Restaurant

★★★★ **RESTAURANT SERENADE.** *6 Roosevelt Ave (07928). 973/701-0303.* Hrs: noon-2 pm, 6-9:30 pm; Sat 5:30-10 pm. Closed Sun; most major hols. Res accepted, required Sat. Bar. Wine list. A la carte entrees: lunch $8-$15, dinner $17-$28. Specializes in contemporary French cuisine. Jacket. Cr cds: A, C, D, DS, MC, V.

Cherry Hill (F-3)

(See also Camden, Haddonfield)

Pop 69,319 **Elev** 30 ft **Area Code** 856
E-mail chamber@cherryhillnj.com **Web** www.cherryhillnj.com
Information Chamber of Commerce, 1060 Kings Hwy N, Suite 200, 08034; 856/667-1600

What to See and Do

Barclay Farmstead. One of the earliest properties settled in what is now Cherry Hill; origins traced to 1684. The township-owned site consists of 32 acres of open space; restored Federal-style farmhouse; operating forge barn; corn crib; Victorian spring house. Grounds (all yr); house tours (Tues–Fri, also Sun in fall & spring; and by appt). 209 Barclay Lane. Phone 856/795-6225. ¢

Motels

✓★★ **DAYS INN.** *550 Fellowship Rd (08054), NJ 73 at NJ Tpke exit 4. 856/235-7400; FAX 856/778-9729; res: 800/329-7466; res: 800/228-5151.* 150 rms, 2 story. S, D $52-$99; each addl $10; under 12 free. Crib free. TV; cable (premium). Pool. Restaurant 7 am-11 pm. Rm serv. Bar 11-2 am. Ck-out noon. Coin lndry. Meeting rms. Business servs avail. In-rm modem link. Valet serv. Exercise equipt. Health club privileges. Refrigerators, microwaves avail. Cr cds: A, C, D, DS, MC, V.

★★ **HAMPTON INN.** *121 Laurel Oak Rd (08043), I-295, exit 32, 2 mi E NJ 561. 856/346-4500; FAX 856/346-2402; res: 800/426-7866.* 122 rms, 50 with shower only, 4 story. S, D $88-$95; under 18 free. Crib avail. Pet accepted. TV; cable (premium), VCR avail. Pool. Complimentary continental bkfst. Restaurant adj 11 am-11 pm. Ck-out noon. Business servs avail. In-rm modem link. Health club privileges. Refrigerators, microwaves avail. Cr cds: A, C, D, DS, MC, V.

✓★ **MCINTOSH INN.** *1132 Rte 73 & Church Rd (08054), on NJ 73, ¼ mi E of NJ Tpke exit 4. 856/234-7194; FAX 856/231-8516; res: 800/444-2775.* 91 rms, 2 story. S, D $50.95-$65.95. Crib free. TV; cable (premium). Complimentary continental bkfst. Restaurant adj open 24 hrs. Ck-out 11 am. Business servs avail. Refrigerators, microwaves avail. Cr cds: A, C, D, MC, V.

Motor Hotel

★★ **THE LANDMARK INN.** *531 Rte 38 W (08052), at jct NJ 73, 38, ½ mi N of I-295, 1 mi N of NJ Tpke exit 4. 856/235-6400; FAX 856/727-1027.* 106 suites, 3 story. S $85-$115; D $95-$135; each addl $5; under 18 free. Crib free. TV; cable (premium); VCR (movies). Pool; wading pool, lifeguard. Playground. Complimentary bkfst. Complimentary coffee in rms. Restaurant 6:30 am-10 pm; Sat, Sun 8 am-noon, 5-11 pm. Rm serv. Bar; entertainment Fri, Sat. Ck-out 11 am. Coin lndry. Meeting rms. In-rm modem link. Sundries. Exercise equipt; sauna. Refrigerators, microwaves. Private patios, balconies. Cr cds: A, C, D, DS, MC, V.

Hotels

★★★ **FOUR POINTS BY SHERATON.** *1450 Rte 70E (08034), NJ 70 & I-295. 856/428-2300; FAX 856/354-7662; res: 800/257-8262.* E-mail www.fourptsch@aol.com. 213 rms, 4 story. S $98-$139; D $108-$159; each addl $10; under 18 free; wkend rates. Crib free. TV; cable (premium), VCR avail. Pool. Coffee in rms. Restaurant (see MORGAN'S). Bar 11-2 am. Ck-out noon. Meeting rms. Business servs avail. In-rm modem link. Gift shop. Airport transportation. Tennis. Exercise equipt. Health club privileges. Microwaves avail. Cr cds: A, C, D, DS, ER, MC, V.

★★★ **HILTON HOTEL.** *2349 W Marlton Pike (08002). 856/665-6666; FAX 856/662-3676.* Web www.cherryhilton.com. 408 rms, 14 story. S $119-$209; D $129-$219; each addl $10; suites $350-$650; under 14 free. Crib free. Pet accepted. TV; cable (premium), VCR avail. Pool; wading pool. Coffee in rms. Restaurant 6 am-11 pm. Bar 11-1 am. Ck-out noon. Convention facilities. Business center. In-rm modem link. Valet serv. Exercise equipt. Some refrigerators; microwaves avail. Cr cds: A, C, D, DS, JCB, MC, V.

★★ **HOLIDAY INN.** *Rte 70 & Sayer Ave (08034), 3 mi W of I-295, 7 mi W of NJ Tpke exit 4, opp Garden State Racetrack. 856/663-5300; FAX 856/663-5300; res: 800/465-4329.* 186 rms, 6 story. S, D $99-$109; each addl $8; under 19 free. Crib free. Pet accepted. TV; cable (premium), VCR avail. 2 pools, 1 indoor; wading pool. Restaurant (see RED HOT & BLUE). Bar 11 am-11 pm. Ck-out noon. Coin lndry. Meeting rms. Business servs avail. In-rm modem link. Valet serv. Exercise equipt; sauna. Microwaves avail. Cr cds: A, C, D, DS, ER, JCB, MC, V.

★★★ **RADISSON HOTEL.** *915 Rte 73N (08054), ½ mi N of NJ Tpke exit 4 on NJ 73N. 856/234-7300; FAX 856/802-3912.* Web www.radisson.com. 283 rms, 10 story. S, D $99-$109; suites $250-$350; under 17 free. Crib free. TV; cable (premium). Pool, lifeguard. Restaurant 6:30 am-10 pm; Sat, Sun from 7 am. Bar. Ck-out noon. Coin lndry. Convention facilities. Business servs avail. In-rm modem link. Gift shop. Lighted tennis. Golf privileges. Exercise equipt. Health club privileges. Game rm. Some in-rm whirlpools, refrigerators; microwaves avail. Picnic tables. Some private patios, balconies. Luxury level. Cr cds: A, C, D, DS, JCB, MC, V.

Restaurants

✓★ **BROOKLAWN DINER & RESTAURANT.** *Highway 130 (08030), S on NJ 130. 856/742-0035.* Hrs: open 24 hrs. Closed Dec 25. Res accepted. Greek, Amer menu. Bar 11 am-10 pm; Sun from 1 pm. Semi-a la carte: bkfst $1.90-$5.20, lunch $4.50-$5.50, dinner $5.95-$13.50. Buffet: bkfst $5.65. Child's meals. Specialties: prime rib, Greek-style lamb stew, lunch soup & salad special. Parking. American diner; chrome exterior. Totally nonsmoking. Cr cds: A, C, DS, MC, V.

✓★★ **CAFFE LA BELLA.** *61 E Main St (08057), I-295 N. 856/234-7755.* Hrs: 10:30 am-2:30 pm, 4:30-9 pm; Fri, Sat to 9:30 pm; Mon 10:30 am-2:30 pm; Sun 8:30 am-2 pm, 4:30-9 pm; Sun brunch 10 am-2 pm. Closed most major hols; also Super Bowl Sun. Res required Fri, Sat (dinner). Italian menu. Semi-a la carte: lunch $4.25-$9.95, dinner $10.95-$19.95. Sun brunch $10.95. Child's meals. Specialties: cioppino, chicken continental, veal romano. Harpist Tues, Wed, Sun. Parking. Casual, intimate dining. Totally nonsmoking. Cr cds: C, MC, V.

✓★ **GOLDEN EAGLE DINER.** *NJ 73S At I-295 (08052), 1 mi W of NJ Tpke exit 4. 856/235-8550.* Hrs: 6 am-midnight; Fri, Sat to 4 am. Res accepted. Bar from 11 am. Semi-a la carte: bkfst $1.99-$6, lunch $5.25-$6.95, dinner $7.95-$13.95. Child's meals. Specializes in prime rib, seafood. Salad bar. Parking. Cr cds: A, C, DS, MC, V.

[SC] [icon]

★★★ **LA CAMPAGNE.** *312 Kresson Rd (08034), US 70 to NJ 154S. 856/429-7647.* Web www.lacampagne.com. Hrs: 11:30 am-2:30 pm, 5-10 pm; Sun brunch 10 am-2 pm. Closed Mon. Res accepted. French menu. Semi-a la carte: lunch $7.50-$15, dinner $25-$29.50. Sun brunch $10.95-$19.95. Child's meals. Specializes in rack of lamb, seafood, duck. Outdoor dining. Country French decor. Cr cds: A, C, D, MC, V.

[D] [icon]

★★ **LOS AMIGOS MEXICAN RESTAURANT.** *461 N Rte 73 (08091), S on NJ 41, then 7 mi SE on NJ 561. 856/767-5216.* E-mail losamigos@hotmail.com; web www.losamigosrest.com. Hrs: 5-10 pm; Fri to 11 pm; Sat 3-11 pm; Sun from 3 pm. Closed Mon; some hols. Southwestern menu. Bar. A la carte entrees: dinner $9.95-$20.95. Child's meals. Specialties: Southwestern crab cakes, tabasco tequila shrimp. Outdoor dining. Fiesta atmosphere; Mexican cantina decor. Family-owned. Cr cds: A, C, D, MC, V.

[icon]

★★ **MELANGE CAFE.** *1601 Chapel Ave (08002). 856/663-7339.* Web www.digitalcitydining.aol.com. Hrs: 11 am-10 pm; Fri to 11 pm; Sat 4-11 pm; Sun from 4 pm. Closed Mon; also July 4, Thanksgiving, Dec 25. Res accepted. Italian, Louisiana menu. A la carte entrees: lunch $9-$12, dinner $16-$24. Child's meals. Specialties: pan-smoked tomato crab bisque, jambalaya, seafood etouffee. Parking. Outdoor dining. Upscale casual dining. Cr cds: A, C, D, DS, MC, V.

[D]

★★ **MORGAN'S FOOD & SPIRITS.** *(See Four Points by Sheraton) 856/427-0427.* Hrs: 6:30 am-11 pm; Sat, Sun 7 am-midnight; Sun brunch 10 am-2 pm; early-bird dinner 4-6 pm (Mon-Fri). Res accepted. Bar 11:30-1 am; Fri, Sat to 2 am; Sun to midnight. Semi-a la carte: bkfst $4.50-$9.95, lunch $4.25-$9.95, dinner $8.95-$18.95. Buffet: dinner $13.95-$15.95. Sun brunch $17.95. Child's meals. Specialties: chicken focaccia, salmon with lobster sauce, roast prime rib. Parking. Casual dining; antique decorated dining rm. Cr cds: A, C, D, DS, MC, V.

[D] [SC] [icon]

✓★ **OLD HICKORY SMOKE HOUSE TX BBQ.** *848 Rte 73 S (08009), I-295W to US 30, SE 8 mi to jct NJ 73. 856/753-1323.* Hrs: 11 am-9 pm; Fri, Sat to 10 pm; Sun noon-8 pm. Closed some major hols. Res accepted. Semi-a la carte: lunch, dinner $5.25-$15.95. Child's meals. Specializes in barbecue ribs, chicken, beef. Own baking. Outdoor dining. Old-style Texas barbecue. Cr cds: A, C, MC, V.

[D] [SC] [icon]

✓★ **RED HOT & BLUE.** *(See Holiday Inn) 856/665-7427.* Hrs: 11 am-10 pm; Fri to 11 pm; Sat to midnight; Sun from noon. Closed Easter, Thanksgiving, Dec 25. Res accepted (dinner). Bar; Fri, Sat to 2 am. Semi-a la carte: lunch, dinner $5.50-$13. Child's meals. Specialties: pulled pork, barbecued pork ribs, beef brisket. Blues Fri, Sat. Casual, Memphis-style barbecue. Cr cds: A, C, D, DS, MC, V.

[D] [icon]

★★ **SIRI'S THAI FRENCH CUISINE.** *2117 Route 70W (08002). 856/663-6781.* Hrs: 11:30 am-10 pm; Fri, Sat to 11 pm. Closed some major hols. Res accepted. Thai, French menu. A la carte entrees: lunch $9-$15, dinner $12-$24.95. Specialties: seafood medley, rack of lamb, crispy duck. Parking. Thai decor. Totally nonsmoking. Cr cds: A, C, D, MC, V.

[D]

Clifton (C-5)

Pop 71,742 **Elev** 70 ft **Area Code** 973 **E-mail** staff@njrcc.org **Web** www.njrcc.org
Information North Jersey Regional Chamber of Commerce, 1033 US 46E, PO Box 110, 07011; 973/470-9300

What to See and Do

Hamilton House Museum. Early 19th-century sandstone farmhouse with period furniture; country store; exhibits. Open-hearth cooking demonstrations by costumed guides. (Mar–Dec, Sun afternoons; closed hol wkends) 971 Valley Rd. Phone 973/744-5707. **Free**

Motel

★★ **HOWARD JOHNSON LODGE.** *680 W Rte 3 (07014), NJ Tpke exit 16W. 973/471-3800; FAX 973/471-2128; res: 800/446-4656.* E-mail www.hojo.com. 116 rms, 4 story. S $84-$114, D $94-$124; each addl $10; under 18 free; wkend rates. Crib free. Pet accepted, some restrictions. TV; cable (premium). Pool; lifeguard. Complimentary continental bkfst. Restaurant 7 am-11 pm. Bar 4 pm-2 am. Ck-out noon. Meeting rm. Business servs avail. In-rm modem link. Sundries. Refrigerators, microwaves avail. Private patios, balconies. Cr cds: A, C, D, DS, ER, JCB, MC, V.

[D] [icons] [SC]

Motor Hotel

★★ **RAMADA INN.** *265 Rte 3E (07014). 973/778-6500; FAX 973/778-8724; res: 800/272-6232; res: 800/772-2816.* 183 rms, 4 story. S, D $99-$149; each addl $10; suites $200; kit units $150; under 12 free; wkend rates. Crib free. Pet accepted. TV; cable (premium). Indoor pool. Restaurant 6:30 am-10 pm; wkends from 7 am. Rm serv. Bar; entertainment. Ck-out noon. Meeting rms. Business servs avail. Sundries. Gift shop. Exercise equipt; sauna. Some refrigerators; microwaves avail. Cr cds: A, C, D, DS, ER, JCB, MC, V.

[D] [icons] [SC]

Clinton (C-3)

(See also Flemington)

Pop 2,054 **Elev** 195 ft **Area Code** 908 **Zip** 08809

What to See and Do

Hunterdon Historical Museum. Four-story gristmill (ca 1810). Ten-acre park houses education center, quarry and lime kilns, blacksmith shop, general store, one-room schoolhouse, log cabin, machinery sheds, herb garden. Also home of Clinton's landmark red mill. Gift shop. (Apr–Oct, daily exc Mon) Outdoor concerts some Sat evenings in summer (fee). 56 Main St, off I-78. Phone 908/735-4101. **¢¢**

Round Valley State Park. A 4,003-acre park. Swimming; fishing; boating. Picnicking, concession (Memorial Day-Labor Day). Wilderness camping (access to campsites via hiking or boating only). Standard fees. Off US 22, E of jct I-78; follow signs. Phone 908/236-6355.

Spruce Run State Recreation Area. A 1,961-acre park. Swimming; fishing; boating (launch, rentals). Picnicking, concession. Camping (Apr–Oct). Standard fees. 3 mi NW off NJ 31. Phone 908/638-8572.

Motor Hotel

★★ **HOLIDAY INN SELECT.** *111 Rte 173 (08809), I-78 exit 15, then W on NJ 173.* 908/735-5111; FAX 908/730-9768; res: 800/465-4329. 142 units, 5 story. S $125-$145; D $133-$153; each addl $8; suites $145-$160; under 18 free; wkend rates. Crib free. TV; cable (premium). Indoor pool. Coffee in rms. Restaurant 6:30 am-11 pm. Rm serv. Bar 3 pm-midnight; entertainment Tues-Sat. Ck-out noon. Meeting rms. Business center. In-rm modem link. Sundries. Exercise equipt. Microwaves avail. Some balconies. Cr cds: A, C, D, DS, MC, V.

⊡ ⨂ 🏃 🏊 🔥 SC 🏃

Inn

★★ **STEWART INN.** *708 S Main St (08886), I-78 exit 4.* 908/479-6060; FAX 908/479-4211. 7 rms, 2 story. S, D $95-$135; suite $125-$135. Children over 12 yrs only. TV; VCR avail. Pool. Complimentary full bkfst. Restaurant nearby. Ck-out 11 am, ck-in 3 pm. Business servs avail. Picnic tables, grills. Stone manor house built in 1770s, set amidst 16 acres of lawns, gardens, woods, stream and pasture. Trout stream, barns and outbuildings with farm animals. Totally nonsmoking. Cr cds: A, C, MC, V.

🏊 ⨂ 🏊 🔥

Restaurant

★★ **CLINTON HOUSE.** *2 W Main St (08809).* 908/730-9300. Hrs: 11:30 am-2:30 pm, 5-9:30 pm. Closed Dec 25. Res accepted. Bar to midnight. Semi-a la carte: lunch $6.95-$21.95, dinner $16.95-$26. Child's meals. Specializes in beef, seafood. Built 1743; former stagecoach stop. Family-owned. Cr cds: A, C, D, DS, MC, V.

⊡ 🍽

Eatontown (E-5)

(See also Red Bank)

Pop 13,800 **Elev** 46 ft **Area Code** 732 **Zip** 07724

Motels

✓ ★ **RED ROOF INN.** *11 Center Plz (07724), off Garden State Pkwy exit 105.* 732/389-4646; FAX 732/389-4509; res: 800/843-7663. 119 rms, 3 story. May-Labor Day: S, D $85-$89; each addl $7; under 18 free; lower rates rest of yr. Crib free. Pet accepted, some restrictions. TV; cable (premium). Restaurant nearby. Ck-out noon. Cr cds: A, C, D, DS, MC, V.

★★ **RESIDENCE INN BY MARRIOTT.** *90 Park Rd (07724), off Garden State Pkwy exit 105, on Hope Rd, then 1st left on Park Rd.* 732/389-8100; FAX 732/389-1573; res: 800/331-3131. 96 kit. suites. S, D $135-$145. Crib free. Pet accepted. TV; cable (premium), VCR avail. Pool; whirlpool. Complimentary continental bkfst. Restaurant nearby. Ck-out

noon. Coin lndry. Meeting rms. Business servs avail. In-rm modem link. Valet serv. Health club privileges. Microwaves. Balconies. Picnic tables, grills. Cr cds: A, C, D, DS, JCB, MC, V.

⊡ 🐾 ⨂ 🏊 🔥 SC

Motor Hotel

★★★ **HOLIDAY INN.** *700 Hope Rd (07724), at Garden State Pkwy exit 105.* 732/544-9300; FAX 732/544-0570; res: 800/465-4329; res: 800/253-7739. 171 rms, 5 story. S, D $85-$139; each addl $10; suites $115-$225; wkend rates. Crib free. TV; cable (premium). Pool; poolside serv. Restaurant 6:30 am-11 pm. Rm serv. Bar 11:30-2 am. Ck-out noon. Lndry facilities. Meeting rms. Business servs avail. In-rm modem link. Bellhops. Valet serv. Gift shop. Exercise equipt; sauna. Refrigerators, microwaves avail. Cr cds: A, C, D, DS, MC, V.

⊡ ⨂ 🏃 🏊 🔥 SC

Hotels

★★★ **OCEAN PLACE CONFERENCE RESORT.** *1 Ocean Blvd (07740), Garden State Pkwy exit 105, E on NJ 36.* 732/571-4000; FAX 732/571-3314; res: 800/445-8667. E-mail oceanplace.hilton@worldnet.att.net; Web www.hilton.com/hotels/lbrophf.shtml. 254 rms, 12 story. Memorial Day-Labor Day: S $170-$205; D $190-$225; each addl $20; suites $350-$1,000; family, wkend rates; lower rates rest of yr. Crib free. TV; cable (premium), VCR avail. 2 pools, 1 indoor; whirlpools, poolside serv, lifeguard. Supervised child's activities (mid-May-early Sept), ages 3-12. Restaurants 6:30 am-10 pm; Sat, Sun from 7 am. Bar 11-2 am; entertainment. Ck-out noon. Convention facilities. Business center. In-rm modem link. Concierge. Shopping arcade. Barber, beauty shop. Free garage parking. RR station transportation. Lighted tennis. Exercise rm; sauna, steam rm. Massage. Balconies. On ocean. Cr cds: A, C, D, DS, ER, MC, V.

⊡ 🐾 ⨂ 🏃 🏃 🏊 🔥 SC 🏃

★★★ **SHERATON.** *Sheraton Eatontown Htl And Conf. Center (07724), off Garden State Pkwy exit 105, at Industrial Way E.* 732/542-6500; FAX 732/542-6607; res: 800/544-5064. 208 rms, 6 story. May-Sept: S $154-$164; D $164-$174; each addl $15; suites $364; wkend rates; lower rates rest of yr. Crib free. TV; cable (premium). Indoor/outdoor pool; whirlpool. Restaurant 6:30 am-11 pm. Bar. Ck-out noon. Meeting rms. Business servs avail. In-rm modem link. Gift shop. Coin lndry. Exercise equipt. Health club privileges. Refrigerators, microwaves avail. Cr cds: A, C, D, DS, MC, V.

⊡ ⨂ 🏃 🏊 🔥 SC

Restaurants

★★ **JOE & MAGGIE'S BISTRO.** *591 Broadway (07740), Garden State Pkwy exit 205, NJ 36E.* 732/571-8848. Hrs: 11:30 am-2:30 pm, 4-10 pm; Fri, Sat to 11 pm; Sun to 9 pm; early-bird dinner 4-6 pm (Mon-Thurs). Closed Thanksgiving, Dec 25; also day after Labor Day, Super Bowl Sun. Res required Sat (dinner). Contemporary Amer menu. Bar. A la carte entrees: lunch $5.95-$10.95, dinner $15-$25. Specialties: grilled lamb chops, filet mignon. Street parking. Casual dining; bistro atmosphere. Cr cds: A, C, D, MC, V.

⊡

★★ **MUMFORD RESTAURANT.** *45 Atlantic Ave (07740), E on NJ 71.* 732/222-2657. Hrs: 5-10 pm; Fri, Sat to 11 pm; Sun 4-10 pm. Closed Mon; most major hols. Res accepted. Semi-a la carte: dinner $18-$25. Child's meals. Specializes in fresh seafood, organic vegetables. Art deco setting. Cr cds: A, C, MC, V.

⊡

Edison (D-4)

(See also Woodbridge)

Pop 88,680 **Elev** 95 ft **Area Code** 732
Information Chamber of Commerce, PO Box 2103, 08818-2103; 732/494-0300.

Although Thomas A. Edison's house here has been destroyed, Edison State Park and the Edison Memorial Tower stand in tribute to the great American inventor. Here, on December 6, 1877, the 30-year-old Edison invented the phonograph. Two years later, he perfected the first practical incandescent light, designing and constructing various kinds of electrical equipment we now take for granted. His workshop has been moved to the Ford Museum in Dearborn, Michigan. Edison also built the first electric railway locomotive here in 1880; it ran 1½ miles over the fields of Pumptown.

What to See and Do

Edison Memorial Tower. A 131-ft tower topped by a 13-ft-high electric light bulb stands on the spot where the first incandescent bulb was made. Museum contains some of Edison's inventions (Memorial Day–Labor Day, daily exc Mon; rest of yr, Wed–Sun afternoons). Christie St, ½ mi SW of Garden State Pkwy exit 131 off NJ 27 in Edison State Park. Phone 732/549-3299. **Free**

Motor Hotel

★★★ **CLARION HOTEL & TOWERS.** *2055 Lincoln Hwy (08817), ½ mi S of I-287 on NJ 27. 732/287-3500; FAX 732/287-3500; res: 800/252-7466.* 169 rms, 5 story. S, D $119-$149; each addl $10; under 18 free; wkend rates. Crib free. TV; cable (premium). Complimentary continental bkfst. Coffee in rms. Restaurant 7 am-10:30 pm; Fri, Sat to 11 pm. Rm serv. Bar 11-1 am. Ck-out noon. Meeting rms. Business center. In-rm modem link. Bellhops. Gift shop. Exercise equipt. Refrigerators; microwaves avail. Luxury level. Cr cds: A, C, D, DS, MC, V.

Hotel

★★★ **SHERATON EDISON HOTEL RARITAN CENTER.** *125 Raritan Center Pkwy (08837). 732/225-8300; FAX 732/225-0037; res: 800/465-4329.* 274 rms, 12 story. S, D $150-$175; suites $325; under 12 free; wkend rates. Crib free. Pet accepted; fee. TV; cable (premium). Indoor pool; whirlpool. Complimentary coffee in rms. Restaurant 6 am-2 pm, 5-10 pm. Bar. Ck-out noon. Coin lndry. Convention facilities. Business servs avail. In-rm modem link. Concierge. Gift shop. Exercise equipt; sauna. Game rm. Cr cds: A, C, D, DS, MC, V.

Restaurants

★★ **CHARLIE BROWN'S.** *222 Plainfield Rd (08820). 732/494-6135.* Web www.charliebrowns.com. Hrs: 11:30 am-10 pm; Fri, Sat to 10:30 pm; Sun to 9 pm. Closed Dec 25. Bar to 2 am. Semi-a la carte: lunch $4.95-$8.45, dinner $9.75-$16.99. Child's meals. Specialties: prime rib, filet mignon, grilled salmon. Outdoor dining. Rustic American decor; stained glass windows; casual setting. Cr cds: A, C, D, MC, V.

★★ **MOGHUL RESTAURANT.** *1665-195 Oaktree Centre (08820). 732/549-5050.* Web www.powerpg.com/nj1//moghul1. Hrs: noon-3 pm, 5:30-10:30 pm; Fri, Sat to 11 pm; brunch noon-3 pm. Closed Mon. Res accepted. North Indian menu. Setups. A la carte entrees: lunch, dinner $8.95-$15.95. Brunch: wkdays $7.95, wkends $9.95. Specializes in chicken, lamb, shrimp. Parking. Elegant decor; Indian artifacts. Cr cds: A, C, D, DS, MC, V.

Elizabeth (C-5)

(See also Jersey City, Newark, Newark Intl Airport Area)

Settled 1664 **Pop** 110,002 **Elev** 36 ft **Area Code** 908
Information Union County Chamber of Commerce, 135 Jefferson Ave, PO Box 300, 07207; 908/352-0900

More than 1,200 manufacturing industries are located in Elizabeth and Union County. Long before the Revolution, Elizabeth was not only the capital of New Jersey, but also a thriving industrial town. The first Colonial Assembly met here from 1669 to 1692. Princeton University began in Elizabeth in 1746 as the College of New Jersey. More than 20 pre-Revolutionary buildings still stand. Many noteworthy people were citizens of Elizabeth: William Livingston, first governor of New Jersey; Elias Boudinot, first president of the Continental Congress; Alexander Hamilton; Aaron Burr; General Winfield Scott; John Philip Holland, builder of the first successful submarine; and Admiral William J. Halsey. The Elizabeth-Port Authority Marine Terminal is the largest container port in the US.

What to See and Do

Boxwood Hall State Historic Site. Home of Elias Boudinot, lawyer, diplomat, president (1783) of the Continental Congress and director of the US Mint. Boudinot entertained George Washington here on April 23, 1789, when Washington was on his way to his inauguration. (Daily exc Sun; closed Jan 1, Thanksgiving, Dec 25) 1073 E Jersey St, 1½ blks W of US 1. Phone 973/648-4540.

First Presbyterian Church and Graveyard. The first General Assembly of New Jersey convened in an earlier building in 1668. The burned-out church was rebuilt in 1785–1787, and again in 1949. The Rev. James Caldwell was an early pastor. Alexander Hamilton and Aaron Burr attended an academy where the parish house now stands. Broad St & Caldwell Pl.

Warinanco Park. One of the largest Union County parks. Fishing; boating (rentals June–Sept, daily). Running track; parcourse fitness circuit; tennis (late Apr–early Oct); handball; horseshoes. Indoor ice-skating (early Oct–early Apr, daily). Henry S Chatfield Memorial Garden features tulip blooms each spring; azaleas and Japanese cherry trees; summer and fall flower displays. Some fees. St Georges, border of Elizabeth and Roselle. Phone 908/527-4900. **Free**

Flemington (D-3)

(See also Clinton, Somerville)

Settled 1738 **Pop** 4,047 **Elev** 160 ft **Area Code** 908 **Zip** 08822
Information Hunterdon County Chamber of Commerce, 2200 Rte 31, Suite 15, Lebanon 08833; 908/735-5955

Originally a farming community, Flemington became a center for the production of pottery and cut glass at the turn of the century.

What to See and Do

Black River & Western Railroad. Excursion ride on old steam train, 11-mi round trip to Ringoes. Picnic area; museum. (July–Aug, Thurs–Sun; Apr–June & Sept–Nov, Sat, Sun & hols) Center Shopping Area. Phone 908/782-9600. **¢¢¢**

County Courthouse (1828). For 46 days in 1935, world attention was focused on this Greek-revival building where Bruno Hauptmann was tried for the kidnapping and murder of the Lindbergh baby. Main St.

Fleming Castle (1756). Typical 2-story Colonial house built as a residence and inn by Samuel Fleming, for whom the town is named. DAR headquarters. (By appt) 5 Bonnell St. Phone 908/782-6472 (days) or 908/782-4655 (evenings). **Donation**

Kase Cemetery. John Philip Kase, Flemington's first settler, purchased a tract from William Penn. His family's crumbling gravestones date from 1774 to 1856. Kase's Native American friend, Chief Tuccamirgan, is also memorialized here. Bonnell St, W of Fleming Castle.

Volendam Windmill Museum. Named after a town in the northern Netherlands, this is an authentic reproduction of an old-time wind-driven mill used for grinding raw grain into flour. Mill stands 60 ft high with sail arms stretching 86 ft. Museum contains old milling and farm tools. (June–Sept, Sat & Sun afternoons; closed hols) Approx 21 mi NW via NJ 12, County 519 to Adamic Hill Rd in Milford, follow signs. Phone 908/995-4365. **¢¢**

Annual Event

Flemington Agricultural Fair. Phone 908/782-2413. Late Aug–early Sept.

Seasonal Event

Stock-car racing. Flemington Fair Speedway. Sat, Apr–Nov.

Motel

★ **RAMADA INN.** Rte 202; Rte 31 (08822), ½ mi S of jct NJ 31. 908/782-7472; FAX 908/782-1975; res: 800/272-6232. 104 rms, 2 story, 24 kits. S $95; D $103; each addl $10; suites $125; kit. units $114. Crib avail. Pet accepted. TV; cable (premium). Pool. Complimentary coffee in lobby. Restaurant 6:30 am-10 pm. Bar. Ck-out noon. Valet serv. Coin lndry. Meeting rms. In-rm modem link. Microwaves avail. Cr cds: A, C, D, DS, MC, V.

Restaurants

★★★ **HARVEST MOON INN.** 1039 Old York Rd (08551), US 202S to US 179. 908/806-6020. Web www.harvestmooninn.com. Hrs: 11:30 am-2:30 pm, 5-9:30 pm; Fri to 10 pm; Sat 5-10 pm; Sun 1-8 pm; early-bird dinner Tues-Fri 5-6 pm. Closed Mon; most major hols. Res accepted. Bar. Semi-a la carte: lunch $5.95-$12.95, dinner $16-$26. Complete meal: dinner $19.97. Specialty: pan-seared tuna. Own baking. Piano bar Fri, Sat. Stone building (ca 1811) with two fireplaces. Cr cds: A, C, DS, MC, V.

★★ **UNION HOTEL.** 76 Main St (08822). 908/788-7474. Hrs: 11 am-10 pm; Sun noon-8 pm. Closed some major hols. Res accepted. Bar to 2 am. Semi-a la carte: lunch $6-$9.50, dinner $13-$17.50. Child's meals. Specializes in fresh fish, steak. Entertainment Tues, Fri, Sat. In ornate Victorian hotel (1878) opp historical county courthouse. Cr cds: A, C, MC, V.

Forked River (G-5)

(See also Toms River)

Pop 4,243 **Elev** 19 ft **Area Code** 609 **Zip** 08731

Restaurant

★★ **CAPTAIN'S INN.** East Lacey Rd (08731), ½ mi E of US 9, Garden State Pkwy exit 74S, 69N. 609/693-3351. Hrs: 11:45 am-10 pm. Closed Dec 25. Continental menu. Bar. Semi-a la carte: lunch from $3.95, dinner $10.95-$19.95. Child's meals. Specialties: crab Imperial, steak au poivre, lobster. Entertainment Fri-Sun eves. Docking. Built in 1831. Overlooks river. Cr cds: A, C, D, MC, V.

Fort Lee (C-6)

(See also Hackensack)

Pop 31,997 **Elev** 314 ft **Area Code** 201 **Zip** 07024
Information Greater Fort Lee Chamber of Commerce, 2357 Lemoine Ave; 201/944-7575

North and south of the George Washington Bridge, Fort Lee is named for General Charles Lee, who served in the Revolutionary Army under George Washington. Its rocky bluff achieved fame as the cliff from which Pearl White hung in the early movie serial "The Adventures of Pearl White." From 1907 to 1916, 21 companies and seven studios produced motion pictures in Fort Lee. Stars such as Mary Pickford, Mabel Normand, Theda Bara and Clara Kimball Young made movies here.

What to See and Do

Fort Lee Historic Park. (See PALISADES INTERSTATE PARKS)

Motor Hotel

★★ **HOLIDAY INN.** 2339 Rte 4 (07024). 201/944-5000; FAX 201/944-0623; res: 800/329-7466. E-mail ftlee@concentric.net. 175 rms, 6 story. S $71-$100; D $81-$100; each addl $10; under 18 free. Crib free. TV; cable. Pool. Restaurant 7 am-1 pm. Rm serv. Bar 5 pm-midnight; closed Sun. Ck-out noon. Meeting rms. Business servs avail. Sundries. Cr cds: A, C, D, DS, JCB, MC, V.

Hotels

★★★ **HILTON.** 2117 Rte 4 Eastbound (07024), at jct I-95 Fort Lee exit. 201/461-9000; FAX 201/585-9807; res: 800/932-3322. 235 rms, 15 story. S, D $139-$189; under 12 free. Crib free. TV; cable (premium), VCR avail. Indoor pool; whirlpool. Coffee in rms. Restaurant 6:30 am-10:30 pm. Rm serv. Bars 11-1 am. Ck-out noon. Meeting rms. Business center. In-rm modem link. Bellhops. Valet serv. Concierge. Gift shop. Covered parking. Exercise equipt; sauna. Cr cds: A, C, D, DS, ER, JCB, MC, V.

★★★ **RADISSON HOTEL.** 401 S Van Brunt St (07631), NJ 4W exit Van Brunt St. 201/871-2020; FAX 201/871-7116; res: 800/333-3333. 192 rms, 9 story. Late Nov-mid Dec: S, D $145-$165; suites $185-$275; wkend rates; lower rates rest of yr. Crib free. Pet accepted, some restrictions. TV; cable (premium), VCR avail. Coffee in rms. Restaurant 6:30 am-10 pm. Bar 11:30-1 am. Ck-out noon. Meeting rms. Business center.

Concierge. Coin lndry. Exercise equipt. Indoor pool. Some bathrm phones; refrigerators, microwaves avail. Luxury level. Cr cds: A, C, D, DS, ER, JCB, MC, V.

D ⚇ ⌖ 🏋 ⤢ 🔥 SC 🚶

Freehold (E-5)

(See also Eatontown, Hightstown, Lakewood)

Founded 1715 **Pop** 10,742 **Elev** 154 ft **Area Code** 732 **Zip** 07728
E-mail admin@wmchamber.com **Web** www.wmchamber.com
Information Western Monmouth Chamber of Commerce, 36 W Main St; 732/462-3030

George Washington and the Revolutionary Army defeated the British under General Sir Henry Clinton at the Battle of Monmouth near here on June 28, 1778. Molly Hays carried water to artillerymen in a pitcher and from that day on she has been known as "Molly Pitcher." Formerly known as Monmouth Courthouse, Freehold is the seat of Monmouth County.

What to See and Do

Covenhoven House. Eighteenth-century house with period furnishings; once occupied by General Sir Henry Clinton prior to the Battle of Monmouth in 1778. (May–Oct, Tues, Thurs, Sat & Sun afternoons) 150 W Main St. Phone 732/462-1466. ¢

Monmouth County Historical Museum and Library. Headquarters of Monmouth County Historical Assn. Large rooms and galleries with 17th-, 18th- and early 19th-century furniture; collections of silver, ceramics, paintings; attic museum with toys, dolls, doll houses; Civil and Revolutionary War weapons. Museum (Tues–Sat, also Sun afternoons); library (Wed–Sat; both closed major hols). 70 Court St. Phone 732/462-1466. ¢

Turkey Swamp Park. An 890-acre park with fishing; boating (rentals). Hiking trails. Ice-skating. Picnicking (shelter), playfields. Camping (Mar–Nov; fee; electric & water hookups). Special events. 2 mi SW off I-195, exit 22, County 524 to Georgia Rd. Phone 732/462-7286. **Free**

Seasonal Event

Harness racing. Freehold Raceway, jct US 9, NJ 33. Phone 732/462-3800. Daily exc Sun, mid-Aug–May.

Motor Hotels

★ **COLTS NECK INN HOTEL.** *6 Rte 537 W (07722), W on NJ 537, at jct NJ 34.* 732/409-1200; FAX 732/431-6640. 49 rms, 2 story. S $65; D $85; each addl $10; suites $150; under 12 free. TV; cable (premium), VCR avail. Complimentary continental bkfst. Restaurant adj 11:30 am-10 pm. Bar. Ck-out 11 am. Meeting rms. Business servs avail. Refrigerators, microwaves avail. Cr cds: A, C, MC, V.

D ⤢ 🔥 SC

★★ **FREEHOLD GARDENS HOTEL.** *50 Gibson Pl (07728), 1 mi W on NJ 537.* 732/780-3870; FAX 732/780-8725. 114 rms, 5 story. S, D $69-$90; each addl $10; under 13 free; higher rates late May-early Sept. Crib free. Pet accepted, some restrictions. TV; cable. Pool. Complimentary continental bkfst. Restaurant 5-11 pm. Entertainment Fri, Sat. Ck-out noon. Meeting rms. Business servs avail. Health club privileges. Refrigerators avail. Cr cds: A, C, D, MC, V.

D ⚇ ⤢ ⤢ 🔥 SC

Restaurant

★ **GOLDEN BELL DINER INC.** *3320 US Highway 9 (07728).* 732/462-7259. Hrs: 6 am-midnight; Fri, Sat open 24 hrs. Italian, Amer menu. Semi-a la carte: lunch $4.95-$8.25, dinner $7-$23. A la carte

entrees: lunch $4.95-$8.25, dinner $7.95-$19.95. Child's meals. Specialties: Golden Bell fisherman's platter, tropical waffle, chicken salad in pita bread. Green house atrium. Cr cds: A, C, D, DS, MC, V.

D SC ⤢

Gateway National Recreation Area (Sandy Hook Unit) (D-6)

(See also Red Bank)

(5 mi E of Atlantic Highlands on NJ 36)

Sandy Hook is a barrier peninsula that was first sighted by the crew of Henry Hudson's *Half Moon* (1609). It once was (1692) owned by Richard Hartshorne, an English Quaker, but has been government property since the 18th century. Fort Hancock (1895) was an important harbor defense from the Spanish-American War through the cold war era. Among Sandy Hook's most significant features are the Sandy Hook Lighthouse (1764), the oldest operating lighthouse in the US, and the US Army Proving Ground (1874-1919), the army's first new-weapons testing site.

The park offers swimming (lifeguards in summer), fishing, guided and self-guided walks, picnicking and a concession. Visitors are advised to obtain literature at the Visitor Center (daily). There is no charge for entrance and activities scheduled by the National Park Service. Parking fee, Memorial Day wkend–Labor Day. (Daily, sunrise–sunset; some facilities closed in winter) For further information contact Superintendent, PO Box 530, Fort Hancock 07732; 732/872-5970.

What to See and Do

Twin Lights State Historic Site (1862). A lighthouse built to guide ships into New York harbor; now a marine museum operated by the State Park Service. (May–Oct, daily; rest of yr, Wed–Sun) White House Rd. Phone 732/872-1814. **Donation**

Restaurants

★★ **BAHR'S RESTAURANT & MARINA.** *2 Bay Ave (07732), Garden State Pkwy exit 117, then NJ 36E to Highlands Bridge.* 732/872-1245. E-mail jay@bahrs.com; Web www.bahrs.com. Hrs: 11:30 am-9:30 pm; Fri, Sat to 10:30 pm; Sun brunch 11 am-2:30 pm. Closed Dec 25. Bar. A la carte entrees: lunch, dinner $12.95-$25.95. Sun brunch $5-$9.95. Child's meals. Specializes in fresh seafood. On waterfront; scenic view of the channel. Family-owned. Cr cds: A, C, D, DS, MC, V.

D ⤢

★★ **DORIS & ED'S.** *348 Shore Dr (07732).* 732/872-1565. E-mail if@doris-and-eds.com; Web www.doris-and-eds.com. Hrs: 5-10 pm; Sat to 11 pm; Sun 3-10 pm. Closed Mon, Tues; also Jan-Feb. Res accepted. Semi-a la carte: dinner $21-$29. Child's meals. Specialties: grilled tuna with wasabi mayonnaise, sauteed red snapper with fresh rock shrimp. View of Sandy Hook Bay. Cr cds: A, C, D, MC, V.

D

Gibbstown (G-2)

Pop 3,902 **Elev** 15 ft **Area Code** 609 **Zip** 08027

Information Township of Greenwich, 420 Washington St; 609/423-1038 or 609/423-4913

What to See and Do

Hunter-Lawrence-Jessup House (1765). Headquarters of Gloucester County Historical Society. Museum contains 16 rms of furnishings and memorabilia from 17th- to 19th-century New Jersey. (Wed & Fri afternoons, also 1st & 3rd Mon afternoon of each month; closed hols) Approx 7 mi NW via NJ 45, County 534 in Woodbury at 58 N Broad St. Phone 609/845-7881. ¢

Nothnagle Home (1638-1643). America's oldest log house. (By appt) 406 Swedesboro Rd. Phone 609/423-0916. **Free**

Motor Hotel

★ ★ ★ **HOLIDAY INN SELECT.** *1 Pureland Dr (08085), 3 mi S at I-295, exit 10.* 609/467-3322; FAX 609/467-3031; res: 800/465-4329. 149 rms, 4 story. S, D $79-$129; each addl $10; suites $149-$189; under 18 free. Crib free. TV; cable (premium), VCR avail. Indoor pool; whirlpool; poolside serv. Coffee in rms. Restaurant 6:30 am-10 pm. Rm serv. Bar 11 am-midnight; entertainment Mon-Fri. Ck-out noon. Coin lndry. Meeting rms. Business servs avail. In-rm modem link. Bellhops. Valet serv. Sundries. Exercise equipt. Game rm. Some refrigerators. Some balconies. Cr cds: A, C, D, DS, JCB, MC, V.

D ≈ ⚡ ≥ ≋ 🔥 SC

Hackensack (C-5)

(See also Fort Lee, Paterson)

Settled 1647 **Pop** 37,049 **Elev** 20 ft **Area Code** 201

Information Chamber of Commerce, 190 Main St, 07601; 201/489-3700

Hackensack was officially known as New Barbados until 1921, when it received its charter under its present name, thought to be derived from the Native American word *Hacquinsacq*. The influence of the original Dutch settlers who established a trading post here remained strong even after British conquest. A strategic point during the Revolution, the city contains a number of historical sites from that era. Hackensack is the hub for industry, business and government in Bergen County. Edward Williams College is located here.

What to See and Do

Steuben House State Historic Site (1713). Museum of the Bergen County Historical Society. Enlarged in 1752 as home of Jan and his wife, Annetie Zabriskie. The house was confiscated during the Revolutionary War because the Zabriskies were Loyalists; it was given to Baron von Steuben, by the state of New Jersey, as a reward for his military services. The baron later sold it back to the original owners. Colonial furniture, glassware, china; Native American artifacts. (Wed–Sat & Sun afternoons; closed Jan 1, Thanksgiving, Dec 25) Approx ¼ mi N of NJ 4, at 1209 Main St in River Edge, overlooking river. Phone 201/487-1739.

The Church on the Green. Organized in 1686, the original building was built in 1696 (13 monogrammed stones preserved in east wall), and rebuilt in 1791 in Stone Dutch architectural style. It is the oldest church building in Bergen County. Museum contains pictures, books and colonial items. Enoch Poor, a Revolutionary War general, is buried in the cemetery. Tours (wkdays on request). 42 Court St, NE corner of the Green, S end of Main St, opp County Court House. Phone 201/845-0957. **Free**

USS *Ling* **Submarine.** Restored World War II fleet submarine; New Jersey Naval Museum. (Wed–Sun; closed most major hols) Docked at Court & River Sts. Phone 201/342-3268. ¢¢

Motel

★ ★ **BEST WESTERN ORITANI.** *414 Hackensack Ave (07601).* 201/488-8900; FAX 201/488-5456. Web www.bestwestern.com/best.html. 99 units, 4 story. S, D $90-$140. Crib $8. TV; cable (premium). Pool; sauna. Complimentary continental bkfst. Restaurant noon-2:30 pm, 5:30-10 pm. Bar noon-2:30 pm, 5:30-10:30 pm. Ck-out noon. Meeting rms. Business servs avail. Valet serv. Sundries. Exercise equipt. Cr cds: A, C, D, DS, MC, V.

≈ ⚡ ≥ 🔥 SC

Hotels

★ ★ ★ **GLENPOINTE MARRIOTT.** *100 Frank W Burr Blvd (07666), at I-80 & I-95.* 201/836-0600; FAX 201/836-0638; res: 800/228-9290. Web www.marriott.com. 341 rms, 15 story. S, D $160-$190; suites $300-$650; wkend rates. Crib free. TV; cable (premium), VCR avail. Indoor pool; whirlpool. Coffee in rms. Restaurant 6:30 am-10 pm. Bar 11-1 am. Ck-out noon. Business center. In-rm modem link. Concierge. Exercise rm; sauna. Bathrm phones, refrigerators. Cr cds: A, C, D, DS, ER, JCB, MC, V.

D ⚡ ≈ ⚡ ≥ 🔥 SC ⚡

★ ★ ★ **HILTON.** *650 Terrace Ave (07604), At jct NJ 17N, I-80.* 201/288-6100; FAX 201/288-4717; res: 800/ HILTONS. E-mail jpear@cybernex.net; Web www.crownplaza.com. 355 rms, 12 story. S, D $159-$199; each addl $20; suites $220-$500; under 17 free; wkend rates. Crib free. Pet accepted. TV; cable (premium), VCR avail. Heated pool; poolside serv. Restaurant 6:30 am-11 pm. Bars 11-1:30 am, Sat to 2:30 am. Ck-out 1 pm. Convention facilities. Business center. In-rm modem link. Gift shop. Exercise equipt; sauna. Luxury level. Cr cds: A, C, D, DS, ER, MC, V.

D ⚡ ≈ ⚡ ≥ 🔥 SC ⚡

Restaurant

★ ★ ★ **STONY HILL INN.** *231 Polifly Rd (07601), I-80 jct NJ 17N.* 201/342-4085. Hrs: 11:30 am-3 pm, 5:30-10:30 pm; Sat from 5:30 pm; Sun 2-10 pm. Closed Dec 25. Continental menu. Bar to midnight. Wine cellar. A la carte entrees: lunch $12.95-$21, dinner $15.95-$29.95. Specializes in continental cusine. Own pastries. Entertainment Fri, Sat. Landmark house (1818); period furnishings. Jacket. Cr cds: A, C, D, MC, V.

D ≥

Hackettstown (C-3)

Settled ca 1760 **Pop** 8,120 **Elev** 571 ft **Area Code** 908 **Zip** 07840

Information Town Hall, 215 Stiger St; 908/852-3130

First called Helm's Mills and then Musconetcong, citizens renamed the town for Samuel Hackett, the largest local landowner. His popularity increased when he provided unlimited free drinks at the christening of a new hotel. Hackettstown is located in the Musconetcong Valley between Schooleys and Upper Pohatcong mountains.

What to See and Do

Allamuchy Mountain State Park, Stephens Section. Allamuchy Mountain State Park (7,263 acres) is divided into three sections. The Stephens Section (482 acres) is developed; the rest (Allamuchy) is natural. Hunting. Fishing in Musconetcong River. Hiking. Picnicking, playground. Camping. Standard fees. Willow Grove St, 1½ mi N of US 46. Phone 908/852-3790 (Stephens).

Land of Make Believe. Amusement park at foot of Jenny Jump Mountain includes the Himalaya Ride; Old McDonald's Farm; the Red Baron airplane; Santa Claus at the North Pole; a Civil War train; a maze; water activities; hayrides; picnic grove; fudge factory. (Mid-June–Labor Day, daily; Memorial Day wkend–mid-June, wkends; Sept, wkend after Labor Day) I-80 exit 12, on County 611, in Hope. Phone 908/459-5100. ¢¢¢¢

Inn

★★ **INN AT MILLRACE POND.** *313 Johnsonberg Rd (07844), off I-80 exit 12, then 1 mi S to NJ 519, then E. 908/459-4884; FAX 908/459-5276; res: 800/746-6467.* E-mail millrace@epix.net. 17 rms, 2 story, 4 bldgs. S, D $95-$165; each addl $20. TV in some rms; cable. Complimentary bkfst. Restaurant 5-9 pm; Sun 4-7:30 pm. Ck-out noon, ck-in 3 pm. Meeting rms. Business servs avail. Airport transportation. Tennis. Library. Colonial gristmill (1769). Rms individually decorated with colonial-style furniture and period reproductions. Cr cds: A, C, D, DS, MC, V.

Haddonfield (F-3)

(See also Camden, Cherry Hill)

Settled ca 1713 **Pop** 11,628 **Elev** 95 ft **Area Code** 856 **Zip** 08033
Information Visitor/Information Center, 114 Kings Hwy E; 856/216-7253

Named for Elizabeth Haddon, a Quaker girl of 20 whose father sent her here from England in 1701 to develop 400 acres of land. This assertive young woman built a house, started a colony and proposed to a Quaker missionary who promptly married her. The "Theologian's Tale" in Longfellow's *Tales of a Wayside Inn* celebrates Elizabeth Haddon's romance with the missionary.

What to See and Do

Greenfield Hall. Haddonfield's Historical Society headquarters in old Gill House (1747–1841) contains personal items of Elizabeth Haddon; furniture; costumes; doll collection. Boxwood garden; library on local history. On grounds is a house (ca 1735) once owned by Elizabeth Haddon. (Mon–Fri, mornings, other days by appt; closed Aug) 343 King's Hwy E (NJ 41). Phone 856/429-7375. ¢
Indian King Tavern Museum State Historic Site. Built as an inn; state legislatures met here frequently, passing a bill (1777) substituting "State" for "Colony" in all state papers. Colonial furnishings. Guided tours. (Wed–Sun; closed Jan 1, Thanksgiving, Dec 25; also Wed if following Mon or Tues hol) 233 King's Hwy E. Phone 856/429-6792. **Donation**
The Site of the Elizabeth Haddon House. Isaac Wood built this house in 1842, on the foundation of Elizabeth Haddon's 1713 brick mansion, immediately after it was destroyed by fire. The original brew house Elizabeth built (1713) and the English yew trees she brought over in 1712 are in the yard. Private residence; not open to the public. Wood Lane & Merion Ave.

High Point State Park (A-4)

(7 mi NW of Sussex on NJ 23)

High Point's elevation (1,803 ft), the highest point in New Jersey, gave this 15,000-acre park its name. The spot is marked by a 220-foot stone war memorial. The view is magnificent, overlooking Tri-State—the point where New Jersey, New York and Pennsylvania meet—with the Catskill Mountains to the north, the Pocono Mountains to the west, and hills, valleys and lakes all around. Elsewhere in the forests of this Kittatinny Mountain park are facilities for swimming; fishing; boating. Nature center. Picnicking. Tent camping (no trailers). Standard fees. Phone 973/875-4800.

Hightstown (E-4)

Pop 5,126 **Elev** 84 ft **Area Code** 609 **Zip** 08520

Motor Hotel

★★ **RAMADA INN.** *399 Monmouth St (08520), NJ Turnpike, exit 8. 609/448-7000; FAX 609/443-6227; res: 800/272-6232.* 200 rms, 4 story. Mid-June-Aug: S, D $85-$115; each addl $10; suite $139-$199; under 12 free; lower rates rest of yr. Crib free. TV; cable (premium). Pool. Restaurant opp 7 am-10 pm. Bar 5 pm-1 am. Ck-out noon. Meeting rms. Business servs avail. Coin lndry. Exercise equipt; sauna. Cr cds: A, C, D, DS, MC, V.

Restaurant

★★ **FORSGATE COUNTRY CLUB.** *Forsgate Dr (08831), at NJ Tpke, exit 8A. 732/521-0070.* E-mail utgrant@ix.netcom.com; Web www.forsgatecc.com. Hrs: 11:30 am-2 pm, 5-9 pm; Sat from 6 pm; Sun brunch from 10:30 am. Closed Mon; Jan 1, Dec 25. Bar. A la carte entrees: lunch $7.50-$18, dinner $8-$27. Sun brunch $22.95. Specializes in regional American dishes. Country club atmosphere; view of golf course. Cr cds: A, C, D, MC, V.

Hillsdale (B-5)

(See also Montvale, Paramus)

Pop 9,750 **Elev** 83 ft **Area Code** 201 **Zip** 07642

Motor Hotel

★★★ **HILTON.** *200 Tice Blvd (07675), N on I-76, exit 171, W on Glen Rd, E on Chestnut Ridge Rd, W on Tice Blvd. 201/391-3600; FAX 201/391-4572; res: 800/932-3322; res: 800/445-8667.* 334 rms, 4 story. S, D $109-$189; each addl $15; suites $325-$450; under 18 free; wkend, wkly, hol rates. Crib free. TV; cable (premium). Complimentary coffee in rms. Restaurant 6:30 am-11 pm. Rm serv. Bar 11:30-12:30 am. Ck-out noon. Convention facilities. Business center. In-rm modem link. Bellhops. Concierge. Sundries. Gift shop. Coin lndry. Airport, RR station transportation. Tennis. Exercise equipt; sauna. Massage. 2 pools, 1 indoor/outdoor; pool, whirlpool, poolside serv, lifeguard. Refrigerators, microwaves avail. Cr cds: A, C, D, DS, JCB, MC, V.

Hoboken (C-5)

(See also Jersey City, Secaucus)

Settled 1640 **Pop** 33,397 **Elev** 5 ft **Area Code** 201 **Zip** 07030
Information Hoboken Community Development, 94 Washington St; 201/420-2013

In the early 19th century, beer gardens and other amusement centers dotted the Hoboken shore, enticing New Yorkers across the Hudson. John Jacob Astor, Washington Irving, William Cullen Bryant and Martin Van Buren were among the fashionable visitors. By the second half of the century, industries and shipping began to encroach on the fun. In 1928–1929, Christopher Morley and Cleon Throckmorton presented revivals of *After Dark* and *The Black Crook* to enchanted New Yorkers. Hoboken is connected to Manhattan by the PATH rapid–transit system.

What to See and Do

Stevens Institute of Technology (1870). (3,600 students) A leading college of engineering, science, computer science management and the humanities; also a center for research. Campus tours. Castle Point, E of Hudson St between 5th & 9th Sts. Phone 201/216-5105. On campus are

Davidson Laboratory. One of the largest privately owned hydrodynamic labs of its kind in the world. Testing site for models of ships, hydrofoils, the America's Cup participants and the Apollo command capsule. (Limited public access) W end of campus. Phone 201/216-5290.

Samuel C. Williams Library (1969). Special collections include set of facsimiles of every drawing by Leonardo da Vinci; library of 3,000 volumes by and about da Vinci; Alexander Calder mobile; the Frederick Winslow Taylor Collection of Scientific Management. (Academic yr) Phone 201/216-5198.

Stevens Center (1962). The 14-story hub of campus. Excellent view of Manhattan from George Washington Bridge to the Verrazano Bridge.

Restaurants

★ **ARTHUR'S TAVERN.** *237 Washington St (07030), at 3rd St. 201/656-5009.* Hrs: 11:30 am-11 pm; Fri, Sat to midnight; Sun 2-10 pm. Closed Thanksgiving, Dec 25. Bars. A la carte entrees: lunch $3.95-$11.95, dinner $3.95-$20.95. Specialties: 24-oz Delmonico steak, Maine lobster. Built 1850; old tavern decor, stained glass. Cr cds: A, C, D, DS, MC, V.

D   🏷️

★★ **BAJA MEXICAN CUISINE.** *104 14th St (07030). 201/653-0610.* Hrs: 5-10:30 pm; Fri, Sat noon-11:30 pm; Sun noon-10 pm. Closed Jan 1, Thanksgiving, Dec 25. Res accepted. Mexican menu. Bar. Semi-a la carte: lunch, dinner $3.95-$17.95. Specialties: parrillada a la baja, alambre veracruz, enchiladas a la parrilla. Southwestern decor. Cr cds: A, C, D, DS, MC, V.

🏷️

✓ ★ **CAFE MICHELINA.** *423 Bloomfield St (07030). 201/659-3663.* Hrs: 11 am-10 pm; Fri to midnight; Sat 3-11 pm; Sun 3-9:30 pm. Closed Mon; most major hols. Italian menu. A la carte entrees: lunch, dinner $7.95-$13.95. Specialties: chicken portobello with marcella sauce, lobster ravioli, chicken Michelina. Italian decor. Cr cds: A, C.

D   🏷️

★ **GRIMALDI'S.** *133 Clinton St (07030). 201/792-0800.* Hrs: noon-11 pm; Sat, Sun from 2 pm; Tues, Wed from 5 pm. Closed Mon; Easter, Thanksgiving, Dec 25. Italian menu. A la carte entrees: lunch, dinner $11-$16. Specialties: roasted sweet red peppers, sausage pizza, mushroom pizza. Outdoor dining. Cozy, Italian atmosphere; brick oven; two-level dining area. Cr cds: A, C, MC, V.

🏷️

✓ ★ **MARGHERITAS'S.** *740 Washington St (07030). 201/222-2400.* Hrs: 11:30 am-10:30 pm; Fri, Sat to 11:30 pm; Sun 1-9:30 pm. Closed Mon; Easter, Thanksgiving, Dec 25. Italian menu. A la carte entrees: lunch $4.95-$7.95. Semi-a la carte: dinner $9.95-$15.95. Specialties: ravioli mondella, chicken Carol, shrimp fra diavolo. Own desserts. Italian decor. Cr cds: C, MC, V.

D   🏷️

★ **ODD FELLOWS.** *80 River St (07030). 201/656-9009.* Web www.oddfellowsrest.com. Hrs: 11:30 am-10:30 pm; Thurs-Sat to 11 pm; Sun to 4 pm (brunch). Closed Thanksgiving, Dec 25. Creole/Cajun menu. Bar. Semi-a la carte: lunch $7.95-$11.95, dinner $7.95-$16.95. Sun

brunch $9. Specialties: catfish, jambalaya, crawfish etouffee. Blues Thurs, Sun. Outdoor dining. Authentic French Quarter decor; exposed brick walls, tiled tabletops. Cr cds: A, C, MC, V.

D   🏷️

Ho-Ho-Kus (B-5)

(See also Paramus)

Pop 3,935 **Elev** 111 ft **Area Code** 201 **Zip** 07423
Information Borough of Ho-Ho-Kus, 333 Warren Ave; 201/652-4400

In colonial times, Ho-Ho-Kus was known as Hoppertown. Its present name is derived from the Chihohokies, who also had a settlement on this spot.

What to See and Do

The Hermitage. Stone Victorian house of Gothic-revival architecture superimposed on original 18th-century house. Its span of history includes ownership by the Rosencrantz family for more than 150 yrs. Grounds consist of five wooded acres, including a second stone Victorian house. Costumed docents conduct tours of site and the Hermitage. Clothing exhibit (June–Sept). Special events held throughout the yr. Tours phone 201/445-8311 for exact schedule, including events and productions. ¢¢

Jackson (F-5)

(See also Lakewood, Toms River)

Pop 33,233 **Elev** 138 ft **Area Code** 732 **Zip** 08527 **E-mail** jacksonnj chamber@juno.com
Information Chamber of Commerce, PO Box A-C; 732/363-1080

What to See and Do

Six Flags Great Adventure Theme Park/Six Flags Wild Safari Animal Park. A family entertainment center, including 350-acre drive-through safari park with more than 1,200 free-roaming animals from 6 continents; 125–acre theme park featuring more than 100 rides, shows and attractions. (Late Mar–late Oct; schedule varies). On Rte 537, 1 mi S of I-195. Phone 732/928-1821. ¢¢¢¢¢

Jersey City (C-5)

(See also Newark, Newark Intl Airport Area)

Settled 1629 **Pop** 228,537 **Elev** 11 ft **Area Code** 201
Information Jersey City Cultural Affairs, 1 Chapel Ave, 07305; 201/547-5522

Jersey City's location on the Hudson River, due west of the southern end of Manhattan Island, has aided its growth to such a degree that it is now the second-largest city in New Jersey. New Yorkers across the bay tell time by the Colgate-Palmolive Clock at 105 Hudson St; the dial is 50 feet across, and the minute hand, weighing 2,200 pounds, moves 23 inches each minute. Jersey City's major links with New York are the 8,557-foot Holland Tunnel, which is 72 feet below water level; the Port Authority Trans-Hudson (PATH) rapid–transit system; and New York Waterways Ferries, which run between Exchange Place, the city's Financial District and the World Financial Center in lower Manhattan.

What to See and Do

Liberty State Park. Offers breathtaking view of New York City skyline; flag display including state, historic and US flags; swimming pool (fee); boat launch; fitness course; picnic area. Historic railroad terminal has been partially restored. The Interpretive Center houses an exhibit area; adj to the Center is a 60-acre natural area consisting mostly of salt marsh. Nature trails and observation points complement this wildlife habitat. (Daily) Off NJ Tpke, exit 14B; on the New York Harbor, less than 2,000 ft from the Statue of Liberty. Boat tours and ferry service to Ellis Island and Statue of Liberty are avail; for schedule and general information, phone 201/915-3400. Also in park is

 Liberty Science Center. Four-story structure encompasses Environment, Health and Invention exhibit areas that feature more than 250 hands-on exhibits. Geodesic dome houses OMNI Theater with a six-story screen. (Late Apr–Labor Day, daily; rest of yr, daily exc Mon; closed Jan 1, Thanksgiving, Dec 25) 251 Phillip St. Phone 201/451-0006. Exhibits and OMNI Theater combined ticket ¢¢¢¢

Motor Hotel

★★ **QUALITY INN.** *180 12th St (07310), at entrance to Holland Tunnel.* 201/653-0300; FAX 201/659-1963. 150 rms, 3 story. No elvtr. S $82-$89; D $87-$99; each addl $5; under 18 free. Crib free. TV; cable (premium). Pool. Restaurant 7 am-10 pm; Sun 7 am-2 pm. Rm serv. Bar 11 am-10 pm; Sat from 5 pm; Sun noon-2 pm. Ck-out 11 am. Meeting rms. Health club privileges. Cr cds: A, C, D, DS, MC, V.

🏊 🔜 🐾 SC

Lake Hopatcong (B-4)

(Approx 15 mi N and W of Dover via NJ 15 & unnumbered road)

Area Code 973

The largest lake in New Jersey, Hopatcong's popularity as a resort is second only to the seacoast spots. It covers 2,443 acres and has a hilly shoreline of approximately 40 miles. The area offers swimming, stocked fishing and boating.

What to See and Do

Hopatcong State Park. A 113-acre park with swimming, bathhouse; fishing. Picnicking, playground, concession. Historic museum (Sun afternoons). Standard fees. SW shore of lake, in Landing. Phone 973/398-7010.

Motel

★★ **DAYS INN.** *1691 W US Hwy 46 (07852), on US 46W at I-80 exit 27.* 973/347-5100; FAX 973/347-6356; res: 800/329-7466. 100 rms, 2 story. S, D $85; each addl $10; under 15 free. Crib free. TV. Pool; lifeguard. Complimentary continental bkfst. Restaurant 11:30 am-9:30 pm; Sun 8 am-1 pm. Rm serv. Bar 4 pm-2 am; entertainment Fri, Sat. Ck-out 11 am. Coin lndry. Meeting rms. Business servs avail. Sundries. 2 tennis courts. Refrigerators, microwaves avail. Cr cds: A, C, DS, MC, V.

🅳 🐾 🏊 🔜 🔥 SC

Motor Hotel

★★★ **FOUR POINTS HOTEL BY SHERATON.** *15 Howard Blvd (07856), I-80 exit 30.* 973/770-2000; FAX 973/770-1287; res: 800/325-3535. 124 rms, 5 story. S, D $130-$140; each addl $10; suites $140-$160; under 18 free; wkend rates. Crib free. Pet accepted. TV; cable (premium). Indoor pool. Coffee in rms. Restaurant 6:30 am-10 pm. Rm serv. Bar 11-2

am; entertainment Wed, Sat. Ck-out noon. Meeting rms. Business servs avail. Valet serv. Exercise equipt. Refrigerators, microwaves avail. Cr cds: A, C, D, DS, MC, V.

🅳 🐾 🏊 🏃 🔜 🔥 SC

Lakewood (F-5)

(See also Toms River)

Settled 1800 **Pop** 26,095 **Elev** 67 ft **Area Code** 732 **Zip** 08701
Information Chamber of Commerce, PO Box 656; 908/363-0012

A well-known winter resort in the 1890s, many socially prominent New Yorkers such as the Astors, the Goulds, the Rhinelanders, the Rockefellers and the Vanderbilts maintained large homes on the shores of Lake Carasaljo.

What to See and Do

Ocean County Park #1. The 325-acre former Rockefeller estate. Lake swimming; children's fishing lake. Tennis, platform tennis. Picnicking (grills), playground, athletic fields. (Daily) Entrance fee (July–Aug, wkends). 659 Ocean Ave, 1 mi E on NJ 88. Phone 732/370-7380. Per vehicle ¢

Motel

★★ **BEST WESTERN LEISURE INN.** *1600 Hwy 70 (08701), Garden State Pkwy exit 88.* 732/367-0900; FAX 732/370-4928; res: 800/528-1234. 105 rms, 2 story. Memorial Day-Sept: S, D $75-$115; each addl $10; lower rates rest of yr. Crib free. Pet accepted; some restrictions. TV; cable (premium). Pool. Restaurant 7 am-10 pm. Bar 6-11 pm. Ck-out 11 am. Coin lndry. Meeting rm. Business servs avail. In-rm modem link. Refrigerators avail. Cr cds: A, C, D, DS, MC, V.

🐾 🏊 🔜 🔥 SC

Lambertville (E-3)

(See also Trenton)

Settled 1705 **Pop** 3,927 **Elev** 76 ft **Area Code** 609 **Zip** 08530
Information Lambertville Area Chamber of Commerce, 4 S Union St; 609/397-0055

What to See and Do

John Holcombe House. Washington stayed here just before crossing the Delaware. Privately owned residence. 260 N Main St.

Marshall House (1816). James Marshall, who first discovered gold at Sutter's Mill in California in 1848, lived here until 1834. Period furnishings; memorabilia of Lambertville; small museum collection. (May–mid-Oct, wkends or by appt) 62 Bridge St. Phone 609/397-0770. **Free**

Inns

★★ **CHIMNEY HILL BED & BREAKFAST.** *207 Goat Hill Rd (08530), just off NJ 179 & 29.* 609/397-1516; FAX 609/397-9353; res: 800/211-4667. Web www.chimneyhill.com. 8 rms, 3 story. S, D $95-$215; wkly rates; some lower rates mid-wk. Children over 12 yrs only. Complimentary full bkfst; afternoon refreshments. Ck-out 11 am, ck-in 3 pm. Business servs avail. Downhill ski ½ mi. Picnic tables. Elegant stone and frame manor house built in 1820; furnishings are antiques and period reproductions. Cr cds: A, C, MC, V.

★★★ **INN AT LAMBERTVILLE STATION.** *11 Bridge St (08530). 609/397-8300; FAX 609/397-4262; res: 800/524-1091.* 45 units, 3 story. S, D $85-$95; each addl $15; suites $135. Crib avail. TV; cable (premium). Complimentary continental bkfst. Dining rm 11:30 am-10 pm. Ck-out noon. Meeting rms. Business servs avail. Health club privileges. Fireplace in suites. View of Delaware River. Victorian antiques. Cr cds: A, C, D, MC, V.

★★ **WOOLVERTON INN.** *6 Woolverton Rd (08559). 609/397-0802; FAX 609/397-4936; res: 888/264-6648.* E-mail woolbandb@aol.com; Web www.woolvertonbnb.com. 10 rms, 3 with shower only, 2 story, 2 suites. May-Sept: S, D $90-$140; each addl $35; suites $120-$190; wkends, hols (2-3 day min). Complimentary full bkfst; afternoon refreshments. Restaurant nearby. Ck-out 11 am, ck-in 3-8 pm. Meeting rms. In-rm whirlpool in suites. Totally nonsmoking. Cr cds: A, C, MC, V.

Restaurants

★★ **ANTON'S AT THE SWAN.** *43 S Main St (08530). 609/397-1960.* Hrs: 6-10 pm; Mon to 9 pm; Sun 4:30-8 pm. Closed Mon; also Jan 1, Dec 25. Res accepted. Contemporary Amer menu. Bar 4 pm-1 am; Sun 2-11 pm. A la carte entrees: dinner $23-$29. Menu changes monthly. Parking. Local artists display work. Cr cds: A, C, MC, V.

★★ **LAMBERTVILLE STATION.** *11 Bridge St (08530). 609/397-8300.* Web www.lambertvillestation.com. Hrs: 11:30 am-3 pm, 4-10 pm; Fri, Sat to 11 pm; early-bird dinner Mon-Thurs 4-6:30 pm, Fri to 6 pm; Sun brunch 10:30 am-3 pm. Res accepted. Bar. Semi-a la carte: lunch $6.95-$12.50, dinner $13.50-$22.50. Sun brunch $7.25-$11.50. Child's meals. Specializes in rack of lamb, elk. Jazz Sat, Sun. Renovated railroad station with 3 dining areas; 1 dining rm is an old station platform. Victorian-style decor. Cr cds: A, C, D, MC, V.

Livingston (C-5)

Pop 26,609 **Elev** 307 ft **Area Code** 973 **Zip** 07039

This suburban community in southwestern Essex County is named for William Livingston, the first governor of New Jersey.

Restaurant

★★ **AFTON.** *2 Hanover Rd (07039), 4½ mi E of I-287 at Columbia Tpke, NJ 510. 973/377-1871.* Hrs: 11:30 am-2:30 pm, 5-9 pm; Sun noon-8 pm; Sun brunch 11 am-2 pm. Closed Mon; Dec 25. Bar to 11 pm. Complete meals: lunch $7.95-$12.95, dinner $13.50-$18.50. Sun brunch $12.95. Specializes in prime rib, seafood. Family-owned. Cr cds: A, C, D, MC, V.

Long Beach Island (G-5 - H-5)

Area Code 609 **E-mail** sochamber@aol.com **Web** www.nealcomm.com/lbi/index.htm

Information Southern Ocean County Chamber of Commerce, 265 W 9th St, Ship Bottom 08008; 609/494-7211 or 800/292-6372

Six miles out to sea, this island is separated from the New Jersey mainland by Barnegat and Little Egg Harbor bays. NJ 72, going east from Manahawkin on the mainland, enters the island at Ship Bottom. The island is no more than three blocks wide in some places, and extends 18 miles from historic Barnegat Lighthouse to the north. It includes towns such as Loveladies, Harvey Cedars, Surf City, Ship Bottom, Brant Beach and the Beach Havens at the southern tip. The island is a popular family resort with excellent fishing, boating and other water sports. For swimming, the bay is calm, while the ocean offers a vigorous surf.

Tales are told of pirate coins buried on the island, and, over the years, silver and gold pieces occasionally have turned up. Whether they are part of pirate treasure or the refuse of shipwrecks remains a mystery.

What to See and Do

Barnegat Lighthouse State Park. Barnegat Lighthouse, a 167-ft red and white tower, was engineered by General George G. Meade and completed in 1858; 217-step spiral staircase leading to lookout offering spectacular view. Fishing. Picnicking. Park (daily); lighthouse (Memorial Day–Labor Day, daily; May & Labor Day–Oct, wkends only). Standard fees. At N end of island. Phone 609/494-2016.

Fantasy Island Amusement Park. Family-oriented amusement park featuring rides and games; adult casino arcade. (June–Aug, daily; May & Sept, wkends; schedule varies, Phone 609/492-4000.

Seasonal Event

Surflight Theatre. Engleside & Beach Aves, Beach Haven. Broadway musicals nightly. Children's theater, Wed–Sat. Phone 609/492-9477. May–mid-Oct.

Motels

★★★ **ENGLESIDE INN.** *30 Engleside Ave (08008), 7 mi S of NJ 72. 609/492-1251; FAX 609/492-9175; res: 800/762-2214.* 72 units, 3 story, 37 kits. No elvtr. July-Labor Day: S, D $150-$225; each addl $12; suites $220-$299; kit. units $165-$225; lower rates rest of yr. Crib avail. Pet accepted, some restrictions. TV; cable, VCR (movies $2). Pool; poolside serv (in season), lifeguard. Restaurant. Bar. Ck-out 11 am. Meeting rms. Business servs avail. Sundries. Exercise equipt. Refrigerators. Private patios, balconies. On beach. Cr cds: A, C, D, DS, MC, V.

★ **SANDPIPER MOTEL.** *10 Long Beach Blvd (08008), NJ 72E to end. 609/494-6909; FAX 609/361-2246.* 20 rms, shower only. July-Aug: S, D $85-$125; each addl $5; wkly rates; higher rates wkends & hols (3-day min); lower rates May-June & Sept-Oct. Closed rest of yr. TV; cable. Pool. Restaurant adj 4-10 pm. Ck-out 11 am. Refrigerators. Ocean 1 blk. Cr cds: A, C, MC, V.

★ **SPRAY BEACH MOTOR INN.** *200 E 24th St (08008), 5½ mi S of NJ 72. 609/492-1501; FAX 609/492-0504.* 88 rms, 3 story, 10 kits. Late June-Labor Day: S, D $160-$205; each addl $10; kit. units $155-$195; lower rates rest of yr. Closed Jan. Crib $7. TV; cable, VCR avail. Heated pool; lifeguard. Restaurant 8 am-2:30 pm, 5-10 pm. Bar 10:30-2 am; entertainment wkends, hols in season. Ck-out noon. Business servs avail. Sundries. Refrigerators. On beach. Cr cds: A, C, MC, V.

Inn

★ ★ ★ **AMBER STREET INN BED & BREAKFAST.** *118 Amber St (08008), Garden State Pkwy, exit 63. 609/492-1611; FAX 609/492-9165.* Web www.bbianj.com/amber. 6 rms, 3 story. Mid-May-mid-Sept: S, D $110-$165; each addl $10; suites $125-$165; lower rates rest of yr. Children over 10 yrs only. TV in parlor. Complimentary full bkfst. Restaurant adj 7 am-10 pm. Ck-out 11 am, ck-in 3 pm. Built in 1885; antiques. Totally non-smoking. Cr cds: C, MC, V.

Restaurants

✓ ★ ★ **BUCKALEW'S.** *101 N Bay Ave (08008). 609/492-1065.* Hrs: 11:30-1:30 am; Sat to 3 am. Closed Dec 25. Res accepted. Continental menu. Bar. Semi-a la carte: bkfst $3.95-$8.95, lunch $3.95-$7.95, dinner $13.95-$19.95. Child's meals. Specialties: crab cakes, black & blue tuna, portabella mushroom sandwich. Bands Tues-Sat. Parking. Cr cds: A, C, D, MC, V.

D

★ ★ **TUCKER'S.** *101 N Bay Ave (08008), Engleside Ave & West St. 609/492-2300.* Web www.southernocean.com. Hrs: 11:30-2 am; early-bird dinner (seasonal) 5-6 pm. Closed Dec 25. Bar. A la carte entrees: lunch $5.95-$11.95, dinner $5.95-$19.95. Child's meals. Specialties: prime rib, crab penne, chicken & biscuits. Entertainment wkends. Parking. Outdoor dining. Cr cds: A, C, D, DS, MC, V.

D

Madison (C-4)

(See also Chatham, Morristown)

Settled ca 1685 **Pop** 15,850 **Elev** 261 ft **Area Code** 973 **Zip** 07940
Information Chamber of Commerce, 155 Main St, PO Box 152; 973/377-7830

For many years, the quiet suburban town of Madison was called the "Rose City" because of the thousands of bouquets produced in its many greenhouses.

What to See and Do

Drew University (1867). (2,100 students) A 186-acre wooded campus west of town. College of Liberal Arts, Theological School and Graduate School. On campus are a Neoclassical administration building (1833), the United Methodist Archives and History Center and the Rose Memorial Library containing Nestorian Cross collection, government and UN documents and manuscripts and memorabilia of early Methodism. Tours (phone 973/408-3252 for schedule). Madison Ave, NJ 24. Phone 973/408-3000.

Fairleigh Dickinson University-Florham-Madison Campus (1958). (3,889 students) (1 of 3 campuses) On site of Twombly Estate (1895); many original buildings still in use. Friendship Library houses numerous special collections including Harry A. Chesler collection of comic art, archives of the Outdoor Advertising Assn of America and collections devoted to printing and the graphic arts. (Academic yr, Mon-Fri; closed school hols) Tours of campus by appt. 285 Madison Ave, NJ 24. Phone 973/593-8500.

Museum of Early Trades and Crafts. Hands-on look at 18th- & 19th-century artisans. Special events include Bottle Hill Craft Festival (Oct). Tours. (Tues-Sat, also Sun afternoons; closed major hols) Main St (NJ 124) at Green Village Rd. Phone 973/377-2982. ¢¢

Seasonal Event

New Jersey Shakespeare Festival. In residence at Drew University. Professional theater company. Includes Shakespearean, classic and modern plays; special guest attractions and classic films. For schedule, reservations phone 973/408-5600. Mid-May-Sept.

Matawan (E-5)

(See also Freehold)

Pop 9,270 **Elev** 55 ft **Area Code** 732 **Zip** 07747
Information Matawan-Aberdeen Chamber of Commerce, PO Box 522; 732/290-1125

What to See and Do

Cheesequake State Park. This 1,300-acre park offers swimming, bathhouse; fishing. Nature tours. Picnicking, playground, concession. Camping (fee; dump station). Standard fees. Garden State Pkwy, exit 120, right at 1st traffic light and right at next traffic light onto Gordon Rd, ¼ mi to entrance. Phone 732/566-2161.

Seasonal Event

Concerts. Garden State Arts Center, at Telegraph Hill Park on the Garden State Pkwy, exit 116. A 5,302-seat amphitheater; lawn area seats 4,500-5,500. Contemporary, classical, pop and rock concerts. Phone 732/442-9200. Mid-June-Sept.

Motels

★ **HAZLET HOTEL.** *2870 Rte 35 (07730), 2 mi S of Garden State Pkwy exit 117. 732/264-2400; FAX 732/739-9735; res: 877/650-2640.* 120 rms, 2 story. S, D $72-$119; each addl $10; under 18 free. Crib free. TV; cable (premium). Pool; lifeguard. Restaurant 6:30 am-10 pm. Ck-out noon. Meeting rms. Business servs avail. Health club privileges. Refrigerators avail. Cr cds: A, C, D, DS, JCB, MC, V.

D ⌖ ⌖ ⌖ SC

✓ ★ ★ **WELLESLEY INN.** *3215 State Rte 35 (07730), 1 mi S of Garden State Pkwy, exit 117, S on NJ 35. 732/888-2800; FAX 732/888-2902; res: 800/444-8888.* 89 rms, 3 story. S $63-$129; D $65-$129; each addl $5; under 18 free. Crib free. Pet accepted, some restrictions; $5. TV; cable (premium). Complimentary continental bkfst. Restaurant nearby. Ck-out 11 am. Business servs avail. Health club privileges. Refrigerators, microwaves avail. Cr cds: A, C, D, DS, JCB, MC, V.

D ⌖ ⌖ ⌖ SC

Restaurant

★ ★ **BUTTONWOOD MANOR.** *845 NJ 34 (07747). 732/566-6220.* Hrs: 11:30 am-10 pm; Sat to 11 pm; Sun noon-9 pm. Res accepted. Bar. Semi-a la carte: lunch $5.25-$9.95, dinner $11.95-$24.95. Child's meals. Specializes in duckling, steak, fresh seafood. Entertainment Fri, Sat. Lakeside dining. Cr cds: A, C, MC, V.

D

Metuchen

(see Woodbridge)

Millburn (C-5)

(See also Newark, Newark Intl Airport Area, Union)

Settled 1720s **Pop** 18,630 **Elev** 140 ft **Area Code** 973 **Zip** 07041 **E-mail** mshcc@millburn.com **Web** www.millburn.com

Information Chamber of Commerce, 343 Millburn Ave, PO Box 651; 973/379-1198

Once bristling with paper mills and hat factories, Millburn today boasts a thriving downtown with a regional theater, a quiet residential area and direct access to New York City.

What to See and Do

Cora Hartshorn Arboretum and Bird Sanctuary. A 17-acre sanctuary with nature trails; guided walks. Stone House Museum with nature exhibits (late Sept–mid-June, Tues, Thurs & Sat). Grounds (daily). 2 mi W on Forest Dr in Short Hills. Phone 973/376-3587. **Free**

Paper Mill Playhouse. State Theater of New Jersey. A variety of plays, musicals and children's theater (Wed–Sun); matinees (Thurs, Sat & Sun). Brookside Dr. Phone 973/376-4343 (box office) or 973/379-3636 (information).

Hotel

★★★★ **HILTON.** *41 John F Kennedy Pkwy (07078), 3 mi W at jct NJ 24 Livingston exit, JFK Pkwy, opp Mall at Short Hills. 973/379-0100; FAX 973/379-6870; res: 800/445-8667.* Web www.spaatshorthills.com. Less than an hour's drive from mid-Manhattan, this elegant suburban hotel offers many facilities of a fine resort. The hotel is located across from the Mall at Short Hills with branches of many of the nation's top stores. 301 rms, 7 story, 37 suites. S $160-$280; D $160-$295; each addl $30; suites $310-$775; family, wknd rates. Crib free. TV; cable (premium), VCR avail. 2 pools, 1 indoor; whirlpool, lifeguard. Restaurant 6:30 am-10:30 pm (also see THE DINING ROOM). Rm serv 24 hrs. Bar 11:30-1:30 am; entertainment. Ck-out 1 pm. Convention facilities. Business center. In-rm modem link. Concierge. Gift shop. Beauty shop. Valet parking. Tennis privileges. Exercise rm; sauna, steam rm. Massage. Spa. Refrigerator in suites. Microwaves avail. Luxury level. Cr cds: A, C, D, DS, ER, JCB, MC, V.

⊡ 🏌 ⚓ 🏃 ✕ 🔥 SC 🎿

Restaurants

★★ **CAFE MAIN.** *40 Main St (07041), downtown near Paper Mill Playhouse. 973/467-2222.* Hrs: 11:30 am-11 pm. Res accepted. Bar to 2 am. A la carte entrees: lunch $5.95-$8.95, dinner $8.95-$21.95. Specializes in seafood, steak, pasta. Own desserts. Seasonal menu; wine tasting dinners. Storefront location; cafe decor. Cr cds: A, C, D, MC, V.

⊡ SC ⊟

★★★ **THE DINING ROOM.** *(See Hilton at Short Hills Hotel) 973/379-0100.* Hrs: 6-10:30 pm. Closed Sun. Bar. Complete meals: 3-course dinner $62, 4-course dinner $72. Specializes in seafood, game, veal. Seasonal menu. Own pastries. Harpist. Valet parking. English drawing room atmosphere. Jacket. Cr cds: A, C, D, DS, ER, JCB, MC, V.

⊡ ♥

Millville (H-3)

(See also Bridgeton)

Pop 25,992 **Elev** 37 ft **Area Code** 609 **Zip** 08332 **E-mail** chamber@xes.com **Web** www.millvillechamber.com

Information Chamber of Commerce, 25 E Main St, PO Box 831; 609/825-2600

What to See and Do

Wheaton Village. Tranquil lifestyle of an 1888 South Jersey glass town. Buildings include Museum of American Glass, which houses an extensive glass collection; working factory where demonstrations of glassmaking are given; general store; restored train station; 1876 one-rm schoolhouse. Crafts demonstrations, arcade, shops. Restaurant, hotel. Self-guided tours. (Apr–Dec, daily; closed major hols) 2 mi NE via County 552. Phone 609/825-6800. ¢¢¢

Motel

★★ **COUNTRY INN - WHEATON VILLAGE.** *1125 Village Dr (08332). 609/825-3100; FAX 609/825-1317; res: 800/456-4000.* 100 rms, 2 story. S, D $75; each addl $5; suites $125-$130; under 18 free. Crib free. TV; cable (premium). Heated pool. Restaurant 7 am-9 pm; Fri, Sat to 10 pm. Bar 11-1 am. Meeting rms. Business servs avail. Health club privileges. Game rm. Some refrigerators. Cr cds: A, C, D, DS, MC, V.

⊡ ⚓ ⊠ 🔥 SC

Montclair (C-5)

(See also Newark, Newark Intl Airport Area)

Settled 1666 **Pop** 37,729 **Elev** 337 ft **Area Code** 973 **E-mail** office@montclairchamber.org **Web** www.montclairchamber.org

Information Chamber of Commerce, 26 Park St, Suite 2025, 07042; 973/744-7660

Originally a part of Newark, the area that includes Montclair was purchased from Native Americans in 1678 for "two guns, three coats and thirteen cans of rum." The first settlers were English farmers from Connecticut who came here to form a Puritan church of their own. Shortly after, Dutch from Hackensack arrived, and two communities were created: Cranetown and Speertown. The two communities later were absorbed into West Bloomfield.

During the Revolutionary War, First Mountain served as a lookout point and as a barrier, preventing the British from crossing into the Upper Passaic valley. In the early 1800s, manufacturing began, new roads opened and the area grew. In 1856–1857, a rail controversy arose: West Bloomfield citizens wanted a rail connection with New York City; Bloomfield residents saw no need for it. In 1868, the two towns separated and West Bloomfield became Montclair. This railroad helped to make Montclair the suburban, residential town it is today. One of the town's schools is named for painter George Inness, who once lived here.

What to See and Do

Eagle Rock Reservation. ½ mi W on Bloomfield Ave, then S on Prospect Ave to Eagle Rock Ave in West Orange (see).

Israel Crane House (1796). Federal mansion with period rooms; working 18th-century kitchen; school room; special exhibits during the year. Country Store & Post Office have authentic items; old-time crafts demonstrations. Research library. (Sept–June, Sun afternoons; other times by appt; costumed tours Sun only) 110 Orange Rd. Phone 973/744-1796. ¢¢

Presby Iris Gardens. Height of bloom in late May or early June. In Mountainside Park, on Upper Mountain Ave in Upper Montclair. Phone 973/783-5974.

The Montclair Art Museum. American art; Native American gallery; changing exhibits. (Daily exc Mon; closed major hols) Gallery lectures (Sun). Concerts; jazz; film series. 3 S Mountain Ave at Bloomfield Ave. Phone 973/746-5555. **¢¢**

Seasonal Event

Summerfun Theater Inc. Weiss Arts Center, Montclair-Kimberley Academy, Lloyd Rd. Professional summer stock company presents six productions. Phone 973/256-0576. Tues–Sat, mid-June–mid-Aug.

Montvale (B-5)

Pop 6,946 **Elev** 187 ft **Area Code** 201 **Zip** 07645

Motel

★★ **HOLIDAY INN.** 100 Chestnut Ridge Rd (07645). 201/391-7700; FAX 201/391-6648; res: 800/465-4329. 190 rms, 3 story. S, D $79-$175; each addl $10; under 18 free; wkend rates. Crib free. TV; cable (premium). Pool; poolside serv. Restaurant 6:30 am-10 pm; Sat from 5:30 pm. Rm serv. Bar 11:30-2 am; entertainment. Ck-out noon. Meeting rms. Business servs avail. In-rm modem link. Bellhops. Valet serv. Exercise equipt. Microwaves avail. Cr cds: A, C, D, DS, JCB, MC, V.

⧆ 🗅 ⇌ 🏋 🛥 🔥 SC

Hotel

★★★ **MARRIOTT HOTEL.** 300 Brae Blvd (07656), Garden State Pkwy exit 172N (Grand Ave). 201/307-0800; FAX 201/307-0859; res: 800/228-9290. Web www.marriott.com. 289 units, 4 story. S, D $79-$175; suites $275; under 18 free; wkly, wkend rates. Crib avail. TV; cable (premium); VCR avail. Indoor/outdoor pool; whirlpool, poolside serv. Restaurant 6:30 am-10 pm. Bars 4:30 pm-2 am. Ck-out noon. Meeting rms. Business center. In-rm modem link. Concierge. Gift shop. Exercise equipt; sauna. Refrigerators avail. Many private patios, balconies. Luxury level. Cr cds: A, C, D, DS, JCB, MC, V.

🗅 ⇌ 🖈 🏋 🛥 🔥 SC 🏃

Restaurant

★★ **VALENTINO'S.** 103 Spring Valley Rd (07645), Garden State Pkwy exit 172. 201/391-2230. Hrs: 11:30 am-2:30 pm, 5-10 pm; Fri to 11 pm, Sat 5-11 pm. Closed Sun; some major hols. Res accepted. Italian menu. Bar. A la carte entrees: lunch $8.95-$15.95, dinner $14.95-$25.95. Specializes in veal, pasta, fish. Cr cds: A, C, D, DS, MC, V.

Moorestown

(see Camden)

Morristown (C-4)

(See also Madison)

Settled ca 1710 **Pop** 16,189 **Elev** 327 ft **Area Code** 973 **Web** www.visitors.morris.nj.us
Information Historic Morris Visitors Center, 6 Court St, 07960; 973/631-5151

Today, Morristown is primarily residential, but the iron industry, so desperately needed during the Revolutionary War, was responsible for the development of the town and the surrounding county. George Washington and his army spent two winters here, operating throughout the area until the fall of 1781. The first successful experiments with the telegraph were made in Morristown by Samuel F.B. Morse and Stephen Vail. Cartoonist Thomas Nast, writers Bret Harte and Frank Stockton and millionaire Otto Kahn all lived here. Morristown rises to a 597-foot peak at Fort Nonsense; the Whippany River runs through the town.

What to See and Do

Acorn Hall (1853). Victorian Italianate house; original furnishings; reference library; restored garden. (Mar–Dec, Thurs & Sun, limited hrs; closed major hols) 68 Morris Ave. Phone 973/267-3465. **¢¢**

Fosterfields Historical Farm. Turn-of-the-century living-history farm (200 acres). Self-guided trail; displays; audiovisual presentations; workshops; farming demonstrations; restored Gothic-revival house. Visitors Center. (Apr–Oct, Wed–Sun) 73 Kahdena Rd. Phone 973/326-7645. **¢¢-¢¢¢**

Frelinghuysen Arboretum. Features 127 acres of forest and open fields; natural and formal gardens; spring and fall bulb displays; labeled collections of trees and shrubs; Braille trail; gift shop. Grounds (daily). 1½ mi NE via Morris Ave, Whippany Rd; entrance from E Hanover Ave. Phone 973/326-7600. **Free**

Historic Speedwell. Home and factory of Stephen Vail, iron master, who in 1818 manufactured the engine for the SS *Savannah*, first steamship to cross the Atlantic. In 1838, Alfred Vail (Stephen's son) and Samuel F.B. Morse perfected the telegraph and first publicly demonstrated it here in the factory. Displays include period furnishings in the mansion, exhibit on Speedwell Iron Works, exhibits on history of the telegraph; water wheel, carriage house & granary. Gift shop. Picnic area. (May–Sept, hrs vary; closed July 4) 333 Speedwell Ave. Phone 973/540-0211. **¢¢**

Macculloch Hall Historical Museum. Restored 1810 house and garden; home of George P. Macculloch, initiator of the Morris Canal, and his descendants for more than 140 yrs. American, European decorative arts from the 18th and 19th centuries. Illustrations by Thomas Nast. Garden. (Wed, Thurs & Sun afternoons; closed hols) 45 Macculloch Ave. Phone 973/538-2404. **¢¢**

Morris Museum. Art, science and history exhibits; permanent and changing. Musical, theatrical events; lectures and films. (Mon-Sat, also Sun afternoons; closed major hols) Free admission Thurs afternoons. 6 Normandy Heights Rd. Phone 973/538-0454. **¢¢**

Morristown National Historical Park (see). Approx 3 mi S on US 202.

Schuyler-Hamilton House (1760). Former home of Dr. Jabez Campfield. Alexander Hamilton courted Betsy Schuyler here. Period furniture; colonial garden. (Tues & Sun afternoons; other times by appt; closed Easter, Dec 25) 5 Olyphant Pl. Phone 973/267-4039. **¢**

Motel

★★ **BEST WESTERN.** 270 South St (07960). 973/540-1700; FAX 973/267-0241; res: 800/528-1234; res: 800/688-4646. Web www.bestwestern.com/best.html. 60 rms, 3 story, 14 kits. S $99-$119; D $109-$129; each addl $10; kit. units $110-$120; under 12 free; wkend rates. Crib $10. TV; cable (premium); VCR avail (movies). Ck-out noon. Coin lndry. In-rm modem link. Airport transportation. Exercise equipt; sauna. Colonial decor. Cr cds: A, C, D, DS, MC, V.

🗅 🏋 🛥 🔥 SC

Motor Hotel

★★★ **HAMILTON PARK CONFERENCE CENTER.** *175 Park Ave (07932), SE on NJ 24.* 973/377-2424; FAX 973/377-9560; res: 800/321-6000. Web www.dolce.com. 219 rms, 5 story. S, D $185; family, wkend, hol rates. Crib avail. TV; cable (premium), VCR avail. Indoor/outdoor pool; whirlpool, poolside serv, lifeguard. Restaurant 6:45 am-10 pm. Rm serv. Bar; entertainment Thur-Sat. Ck-out noon. Convention facilities. Business center. In-rm modem link. Bellhops. Concierge. Sundries. Lighted tennis. Exercise rm; sauna. Massage. Raquetball. Basketball. Lawn games. Cr cds: A, C, D, DS, MC, V.

⊡ 🏌 🏊 🏋 🍴 🔥 🐾 🏃

Hotels

★★★ **HEADQUARTERS PLAZA.** *3 Headquarters Plz (07960).* 973/898-9100; FAX 973/292-0112; res: 800/225-1941. Web www.travel-web.com/thisco/lri. 256 rms, 16 story. S, D $170-$190; each addl $20; under 12 free; wkend rates. Crib free. TV; cable (premium). Indoor pool privileges. Restaurant 6:30 am-1 am. Bar 11 am-1 am. Ck-out noon. Meeting rms. Business center. In-rm modem link. Shopping arcade. Health club privileges. Microwaves avail. Luxury level. Cr cds: A, C, D, MC, V.

⊡ 🏌 🌊 🔥 SC 🏃

★★★ **MADISON HOTEL.** *One Convent Rd (07960), at Madison Ave (NJ 24).* 973/285-1800; FAX 973/540-8566; res: 800/526-0729. 192 rms, 4 story. S $160-$200; D $180-$200; under 18 free; wkend rates. Crib avail. TV; cable (premium). Indoor pool; whirlpool, poolside serv. Complimentary continental bkfst. Coffee in rms. Restaurants 6:30 am-11 pm. Bar 11-2 am; entertainment. Ck-out noon. Meeting rms. Business center. In-rm modem link. Concierge. Airport transportation. Tennis privileges. Golf privileges. Exercise equipt. Some bathrm phones; microwaves avail. Cr cds: A, C, D, DS, MC, V.

⊡ 🎾 🏌 🌊 🏋 🏃 🌊 🔥 SC 🏃

Restaurant

★★ **ROD'S 1890S RESTAURANT.** *NJ 124 (07961), approx 1½ mi E on NJ 124.* 973/539-6666. Hrs: 11:30 am-11 pm; early-bird dinner 4:30-6 pm; Sun brunch 11 am-3 pm. Closed Dec 25. Bar. Semi-a la carte: lunch $7.95-$15.95, dinner $15.95-$29.95. Sun brunch $10.50-$15.95. Child's meals. Specializes in prime beef, seafood. Entertainment Wed-Sat. Valet parking. Display of authentic Victorian antiques. Family-owned. Cr cds: A, C, D, DS, MC, V.

⊡ 🍴

Morristown National Historical Park (C-4)

(See also Bernardsville, Morristown)

(Approx 3 mi S of Morristown on US 202)

This national historical park, the first to be established and maintained by the federal government, was created by an Act of Congress in 1933. Its three units cover more than 1,600 acres, all but Jockey Hollow and the NJ Brigade Area being within Morristown's limits. The main body of the Continental Army stayed here in the winter of 1779–1780.

Headquarters and museum (daily); Jockey Hollow buildings (summer, daily; rest of yr schedule varies, phone ahead; closed Jan 1, Thanksgiving, Dec 25). For further information contact Chief of Interpretation, Washington Pl, Morristown 07960; 973/539-2085.

What to See and Do

Ft Nonsense. Its name came long after residents had forgotten the real reason for earthworks constructed here in 1777. Overlook commemorates fortifications, which were built at Washington's order to defend military supplies stored in the village. Ann St.   **Free**

Historical Museum. Contains Washington memorabilia; period weapons and 18th-century artifacts; audiovisual programs. Washington Pl, directly to the rear of Ford Mansion.   ¢   Admission includes

Ford Mansion. One of the finest early houses in Morristown was built in 1772–1774 by Colonel Jacob Ford, Jr, who produced gunpowder for American troops during the Revolution. His widow rented the house to the army for General and Mrs. Washington when the Continental Army spent the winter of 1779–1780 here.

Jockey Hollow. The site of the Continental Army's winter quarters in 1779–1780 and the 1781 mutiny of the Pennsylvania Line. Signs indicate locations of various brigades. There are typical log huts and an officer's hut among other landmarks. Demonstrations of military and colonial farm life (summer). Visitor center has exhibits and audiovisual programs. 5 mi SW of Morristown.   **Free**

Wick House. Farmer Henry Wick lived here with his wife and daughter. Used as quarters by Major General Arthur St Clair in 1779–1780. Restored with period furnishings. Jockey Hollow.   **Free**

Mount Holly (F-3)

(See also Burlington)

Settled 1676 **Pop** 10,639 **Elev** 52 ft **Area Code** 609 **Zip** 08060

The mountain that gives this old Quaker town its name is only 183 feet high. For two months in 1779, Mount Holly was the capital of the state; today, it is the seat of Burlington County.

What to See and Do

John Woolman Memorial (1783). John Woolman, the noted Quaker abolitionist whose *Journal* is still appreciated today, owned the property on which this small, 3-story red brick house was built; garden. Picnicking. (Fri; also by appt) 99 Branch St, ½ mi E. Phone 609/267-3226. **Donation**

Mansion at Smithville (1840). Victorian mansion and village of inventor/entrepreneur Hezekiah B. Smith; home of the "Star" hi-wheel bicycle. Guided tours (May–Oct, Wed & Sun). Victorian Christmas tours (Dec; fee). On NJ 537, ½ mi W of US 206. Phone 609/265-5068.   ¢¢

Mount Holly Library. Chartered in 1765 by King George III, the library is currently housed in Georgian mansion built in 1830. Historic Lyceum contains original crystal chandeliers, blue marble fireplaces, boxwood gardens; archives date to original 1765 collection. (July-Aug, Tues-Thurs; rest of yr, Mon-Sat, limited hrs) 307 High St. Phone 609/267-7111.   **Free**

Motel

★★ **HOWARD JOHNSON INN.** *Rte 541 & NJ Tpke Exit 5 (08060), on NJ 541 at NJ Tpke exit 5.* 609/267-6550; FAX 609/267-2575; res: 800/446-4656. Web www.hojo.com. 90 rms, 2 story. S $58-$95; D $60-$102; each addl $7; under 12 free. Crib free. Pet accepted. TV; cable (premium), VCR avail. Pool; lifeguard, sauna. Playground. Coffee in rms. Restaurant 6 am-11 pm. Bar 5-11 pm. Ck-out noon. Meeting rms. Cr cds: A, C, D, DS, ER, MC, V.

⊡ 🐾 🌊 🏋 🌊 🔥 SC

Motor Hotel

✓ ★★ **QUALITY INN.** *21 Cookstown Road (08511), NJ 537E to McGuire Access Rd.* 609/723-6500; FAX 609/723-7895; res: 800/329-7466. 100 rms, 2 story. May-Sept: S, D $99; each addl $10; suites $125-$175; under 16 free; higher rates hols; lower rates rest of yr. Crib free. TV;

cable. Pool. Complimentary full bkfst. Restaurant 11 am-10 pm. Ck-out 11 am. Business servs avail. Refrigerators avail. Cr cds: A, C, D, DS, JCB, MC, V.

Inn

✓★★ **ISAAC HILLIARD HOUSE BED & BREAKFAST.** *31 Hanover St (08068), E on NJ 38 to S Pemberton Rd, E on Hanover.* 609/894-0756; FAX 609/894-7899; res: 800/371-0756. E-mail ppaul@city com.com. 4 rms, 2 story, 1 suite. S $65-$90; D $75-$100; each addl $20; suite $120-$140. TV; cable. Pool. Complimentary full bkfst. Restaurant nearby. Ck-out 11 am, ck-in 3 pm. Victorian house built in mid-18th century. Cr cds: A, C, DS, MC, V.

Restaurants

★★★ **BEAU RIVAGE.** *128 Taunton Blvd (08055), S on NJ 541, just S of Tuckerton Rd.* 609/983-1999. Web www.beaurivage.com. Hrs: 11:30 am-2:30 pm, 5:30-9:30 pm; Sat from 5:30 pm; Sun 4-8 pm. Closed Mon; most major hols; also 2 wks before Labor Day. Res accepted. French menu. Serv bar. Wine cellar. A la carte entrees: lunch $12.50-$15, dinner $20-$25. Specialties: beef Wellington, wild game, souffles. Own pastries. 2 dining areas, 1 upstairs. Parking; valet wkends. Jacket (dinner). Cr cds: A, C, D, MC, V.

★★★ **BRADDOCK'S TAVERN.** *39 S Main St (08055), S on NJ 541.* 609/654-1604. Hrs: 11:30 am-2:30 pm, 5-10 pm; Sun 11 am-2:30 pm, 4-9 pm. Closed Jan 1, Dec 25. Res accepted. Bar to 2 am. Semi-a la carte: lunch $5.75-$8.95, dinner $16.95-$26.95. Sun brunch $15.95. Child's meals. Specializes in fresh seafood, beef, veal. Own baking. Cr cds: A, C, D, DS, MC, V.

✓★★ **CHARLEY'S OTHER BROTHER.** *NJ 537 (08060), ½ mi W of US 206.* 609/261-1555. Hrs: 11:30 am-2:30 pm, 5-9:30 pm; Fri, Sat to 10:30 pm; Sun 4-9 pm. Closed Dec 25. Res accepted. Bar. Semi-a la carte: lunch $5.95-$7.95, dinner $13.95-$16.95. Child's meals. Specializes in fresh seafood, steak, prime rib. Country setting; tiffany lamps. Cr cds: A, C, D, DS, MC, V.

Newark (C-5)

(See also Elizabeth, Jersey City)

Services and Information

Settled 1666 **Pop** 275,221 **Elev** 146 ft **Area Code** 973 **E-mail** lindamonize@msn.com **Web** www.state.nj.us/travel

Information Gateway Tourism Council Inc, PO Box 602, Little Ferry, 07643; 201/641-7632

Once a strict Puritan settlement, Newark has grown to become the largest city in the state and one of the country's leading manufacturing cities. Major insurance firms and banks have large offices in Newark, dominating the city's financial life. Newark was the birthplace of Stephen Crane (1871-1900), author of *The Red Badge of Courage,* and Mary Mapes Dodge (1838-1905), author of the children's book *Hans Brinker, or the Silver Skates.* Newark is also an educational center with Newark College of Rutgers University, College of Medicine and Dentistry of New Jersey, New Jersey Institute of Technology, Seton Hall Law School and Essex County College.

Transportation

Airport. See NEWARK INTL AIRPORT AREA.
Car Rental Agencies. See IMPORTANT TOLL-FREE NUMBERS.
Public Transportation. Trains, buses (NJ Transit), phone 973/491-9400.
Rail Passenger Service. Amtrak 800/872-7245.

What to See and Do

Minor Basilica of the Sacred Heart. French Gothic in design, it resembles the cathedral at Rheims. Hand-carved reredos. (Daily) 89 Ridge St, at Clifton & 6th Aves. **Donation**

New Jersey Historical Society. Museum with collections of paintings, prints, furniture, decorative arts; period rm; special exhibitions. Reference and research library of state and local history; manuscripts, documents, maps. (Tues–Sat) 52 Park Pl. **Free**

New Jersey Performing Arts Center. Home of the New Jersey Symphony Orchestra and host to many other performances. One Center St. For ticket information phone 888/GO-NJPAC.

Old Plume House. Now the rectory of the adjoining House of Prayer Episcopal Church, it is thought to have been standing as early as 1710, which would make it the oldest building in Newark. 407 Broad St. Phone 973/483-8202.

Symphony Hall (1925). A 2,811-seat auditorium; home of New Jersey State Opera and the New Jersey Symphony Orchestra; also here is the famous Terrace Ballroom. 1030 Broad St. Phone 973/643-4550 or 973/643-8009 (box office).

The Newark Museum. Museum of art and science, with changing exhibitions. American paintings and sculpture; American and European decorative arts; classical art; the arts of Asia, the Americas and the Pacific; numismatics and the natural sciences. Also here are the Junior Museum, Mini Zoo, Dreyfuss Planetarium, Garden, with its 1784 schoolhouse and the Newark Fire Museum. Special programs, lectures, concerts; cafe (lunch). (Wed–Sun, afternoons; closed some major hols) 49 Washington St. Phone 973/596-6550. **Free**

The Wars of America. Sculptured bronze group by Gutzon Borglum features 42 human figures representing soldiers in the major conflicts in US history. Military Park, bounded by Broad St, Park Pl, Rector St, Raymond Blvd. Other works by Borglum are

> **Bridge Memorial.** This sculpture of a Native American and a Puritan stands on the site of a colonial marketplace. N of Washington Park (Broad St, Washington Pl & Washington St).

> **Statue of Abraham Lincoln.** Essex County Courthouse, Springfield Ave & Market St.

Newark Intl Airport Area

For additional accommodations, see NEWARK INTL AIRPORT AREA, which follows NEWARK.

Motor Hotel

★★★ **HILTON GATEWAY.** *Gateway Ctr Raymond Blvd (07102), in Gateway Center.* 973/622-5000; FAX 973/824-2188; res: 800/932-3322. 253 rms, 10 story. S, D $169-$199; each addl $10; suites $239-$350; under 18 free; wkend rates. TV; cable (premium), VCR avail. Pool; lifeguard. Restaurant 6:30 am-10 pm; Sat, Sun 7 am-10 pm. Rm serv. Bar 11:30 am-midnight; Fri, Sat to 1 am. Ck-out noon. Meeting rms. Business center. Bellhops. Valet serv. Shopping arcade. Garage parking; $8. Free airport transportation. Exercise equipt. Luxury level. Cr cds: A, C, D, DS, MC, V.

Newark Intl Airport Area (C-5)

(See also Newark)

Services and Information

Information: 201/961-6000 or 800/247-7433.

Lost and Found: 201/961-6230.

Airlines: Aeroperu, Air Aruba, Air Canada, Air France, Air Jamaica, Alitalia, America West, American, Avianca, British Airways, Carnival, Colgan Air, Continental, Czech Arlns, Delta, El Al, Eva Airways, Kiwi Intl, Korean Air, Lot, Lufthansa, Mexicana, Midway Arlns, Midwest Express, Northwest, Philippine Arlns, SAS, Swissair, Tap Air Portugal, TWA, United, USAir, Virgin Atlantic, Western Pacific Arlns.

Motels

★★★ **COURTYARD BY MARRIOTT.** *600 US Rte 1 & 9S (07114), NJ Tpke exit 14, S on US 1 & 9S.* 973/643-8500; FAX 973/648-0662; res: 800/321-2211. 146 rms, 3 story. S, D $149-$159; suites $179-$189; children free; package plans. Crib free. TV; cable (premium), VCR avail. Indoor pool; whirlpool. Complimentary coffee in rms. Restaurant 6 am-10 pm. Rm serv. Bar 5-11 pm. Ck-out noon. Coin lndry. Meeting rms. Business servs avail. Valet serv. Sundries. Free airport transportation. Exercise equipt. Health club privileges. Microwave, refrigerator in suites. Some balconies. Cr cds: A, C, D, DS, MC, V.

✓★★ **DAYS INN AIRPORT.** *450 Rte 1 S (near Haynes Ave) (07114), Off NJ Tpke exit 14, S on US 1 & 9S.* 973/242-0900; FAX 973/242-8480; res: 800/432-9755. 191 rms, 8 story. S, D $69.95-$104.95; each addl $5; suites $99-$175; wkend rates. TV; cable (premium). Restaurant 6:30 am-midnight. Bar. Ck-out noon. Coin lndry. Meeting rms. Business servs avail. Free airport transportation. Exercise equipt. Microwaves avail. Cr cds: A, C, D, DS, JCB, MC, V.

✓★ **HOWARD JOHNSON.** *20 Frontage Rd (07114), Off NJ Tpke exit 14.* 973/344-1500; FAX 973/344-3311; res: 800/446-4656. 171 rms, 3 story. S, D $69.99-$99.99; under 12 free. Crib free. TV; cable (premium). Coffee in rms. Restaurant open 24 hrs; Fri, Sat 6-1 am. Ck-out noon. Coin lndry. Meeting rms. Business servs avail. In-rm modem link. Gift shop. Free airport transportation. Cr cds: A, C, D, DS, MC, V.

Motor Hotel

★★ **HOLIDAY INN.** *160 Frontage Rd (07114), Off NJ Tpke exit 14, opp N terminal; use Frontage Rd.* 973/589-1000; FAX 973/589-2799. 234 rms, 10 story. S, D $149-$229; under 18 free; wkend rates by res. Crib free. TV; cable (premium). Pool; lifeguard. Restaurant 6 am-midnight. Rm serv. Bar 11-2 am. Ck-out noon. Meeting rms. Business servs avail. In-rm modem link. Bellhops. Sundries. Gift shop. Free airport transportation. Exercise equipt. Cr cds: A, C, D, DS, JCB, MC, V.

Hotels

★★★ **MARRIOTT HOTEL AIRPORT.** *Newark International Airport (07114), on airport grounds; follow signs for main terminal.* 973/623-0006; FAX 973/623-7618; res: 800/228-9290. 590 rms, 10 story. S, D $199-$229; suites $450-$550; under 18 free; wkend rates. Crib free. TV; cable (premium), VCR avail. Indoor/outdoor pool; whirlpool, poolside serv. Restaurants 6 am-11 pm. Rm serv 24 hrs. Bars 11:30-1:30 am. Ck-out noon. Convention facilities. Business center. Concierge. Free airport transportation. Exercise equipt; sauna. Some refrigerators. Luxury level. Cr cds: A, C, D, DS, ER, JCB, MC, V.

★★★ **NEWARK AIRPORT HILTON.** *1170 Spring St (07201), off NJ Tpke exit 13A.* 908/351-3900; FAX 908/351-9556; res: 800/445-8667. Web www.hilton.com/hilton. 375 rms, 12 story. S, D $164-$209; each addl $10; suites $295-$650; under 18 free; wkend rates. Crib free. TV; cable (premium), VCR avail. Indoor pool; whirlpool. Coffee in rms. Restaurant 6:30 am-11 pm. Rm serv 24 hrs. Bar 4 pm-2 am. Ck-out noon. Convention facilities. Business center. In-rm modem link. Gift shop. Free airport, RR station transportation. Valet parking. Exercise equipt; sauna. Cr cds: A, C, D, DS, ER, JCB, MC, V.

★★★ **RADISSON HOTEL.** *128 Frontage Rd (07114), Off NJ Tpke exit 14; use Frontage Rd.* 973/690-5500; FAX 973/465-7195; res: 800/333-3333. 502 rms, 12 story. S, D $175; each addl $10; suites $395-$495; under 18 free; wkend rates. Crib free. TV; cable (premium). Indoor pool; whirlpool. Coffee in rms. Restaurants 6:30 am-11 pm. Bar 2 pm-2 am. Ck-out noon. Convention facilities. Business center. In-rm modem link. Concierge. Gift shop. Free airport transportation. Exercise equipt. Game rm. Refrigerators avail. Balconies. Atrium. Luxury level. Cr cds: A, C, D, DS, MC, V.

★ **TRAVELODGE.** *50 Park Pl (20036).* 973/622-1000; FAX 973/622-6410; res: 800/569-2400; res: 800/578-7878. Web www.travelodge.com. 169 rms, 12 story. S $90; D $110; suites $275-$375; under 16 free; wkend rates. Crib avail. TV; cable (premium), VCR avail. Complimentary coffee in rms. Restaurant 7 am-11 pm. No rm serv. Bar 4 pm-midnight; entertainment Thurs. Ck-out noon. Meeting rms. Business servs avail. In-rm modem link. Gift shop. Coin lndry. Free airport, RR station transportation. Exercise equipt. In-rm whirlpool, refrigerator, minibar in suites. Cr cds: A, C, D, DS, ER, JCB, MC, V.

New Brunswick (D-4)

Settled 1681 **Pop** 41,711 **Elev** 42 ft **Area Code** 732

Information Middlesex County Regional Chamber of Commerce, One Distribution Way, Ste 101, Monmouth Junction 08852; 732/821-1700

New Brunswick, the seat of Middlesex County, is on the south bank of the Raritan River. It is both a college town and a diversified commercial and retail city. Rutgers University, the eighth-oldest institution of higher learning in the country and the only state university with a colonial charter, was founded in 1766 as Queens College, and opened in 1771 with a faculty of one—aged 18. Livingston College, Cook College and Douglass College (for women), all part of the university, are also located here. One of New Brunswick's most important industries is Johnson and Johnson; its company headquarters are located downtown. Joyce Kilmer, the poet, was born in New Brunswick; his house, at 17 Joyce Kilmer Avenue, is open to visitors.

What to See and Do

Buccleuch Mansion. Built in 1739 by Anthony White, son-in-law of Lewis Morris, a colonial governor of New Jersey. Period rooms. (June–Oct, Sun afternoons; closed hols) Under 10 only with adult. George St & Easton Ave, in 78-acre Buccleuch Park. Phone 732/745-5094.   **Free**

Crossroads Theatre. Professional African-American theater company offering plays, musicals, touring programs and workshops. (Sept–May, Wed–Sun) 7 Livingston Ave. For schedule, information phone 732/249-5560.

George Street Playhouse. Regional theater; seven-show season of plays and musicals; touring Outreach program for students. A 367-seat house. Stage II Theater; cafe; cabaret. (Daily) 9 Livingston Ave. Phone 732/246-7717 (box office, daily exc Mon).

Hungarian Heritage Center. Museum of changing exhibits that focus on Hungarian folk life, fine and folk art; library, archives. (Daily exc Mon; closed major hols) 300 Somerset St. Phone 732/846-5777. **Donation**

Rutgers University Display Gardens. Features extensive display of American holly. (Daily) Ryder's Lane (US 1). Phone 732/932-8451. **Free**

Rutgers–The State University (1766). (49,000 students) Multiple campuses include 26 colleges serving students at all levels through postdoctoral studies; main campus on College Ave. Phone 732/932-1766 (general information) or 732/932-7881 (campus tours). On campus are

Geology Museum. Displays of New Jersey minerals; dinosaur; mammals, including a mastodon; Egyptian exhibit with mummy. (Mon–Fri; closed hols) Phone 732/932-7243. **Free**

Jane Voorhees Zimmerli Art Museum. Paintings from early 16th century through the present; changing exhibits. (Tues–Fri, also Sat & Sun afternoons; closed major hols) George & Hamilton Sts. Phone 732/932-7237. **Donation**

Annual Event

Middlesex County Fair. Cranbury-South River Rd, in East Brunswick. Aug.

Seasonal Event

Rutgers SummerFest. Rutgers Arts Center. Features music, dance, visual arts exhibits and theater performances. July.

Motel

✓ ★★ **MCINTOSH INN.** *764 State Rte 18 (08816), 6 mi S on NJ 18, 4 mi off NJ Tpke exit 9.* 732/238-4900; FAX 732/257-2023; res: 800/444-2705; res: 800/444-2775. 107 rms, 2 story. S $54.95-$61.95; D $60.95-$67.95; each addl $3. TV; cable (premium). Complimentary continental bkfst. Restaurant adj open 24 hrs. Ck-out 11 am. Business servs avail. Cr cds: A, C, D, MC, V.

D ⊠ 🔥 SC

Motor Hotels

★★ **HOLIDAY INN.** *195 Davidson Ave (08873), off NJ 527 at I-287 exit 10.* 732/356-1700; FAX 732/356-0939; res: 800/922-0645. 284 rms, 6 story. S, D $85-$129; under 12 free; wkend rates. Crib free. Pet accepted. TV; cable (premium). Pool; poolside serv, lifeguard. Coffee in rms. Restaurant 6:30 am-2 pm, 5-10:30 pm. Rm serv. Bar 11:30-1 am. Ck-out noon. Convention facilities. Business center. In-rm modem link. Bellhops. Valet serv. Sundries. Gift shop. Exercise equipt. Health club privileges. Microwaves avail. Cr cds: A, C, D, DS, ER, JCB, MC, V.

D 🐾 ⊠ 🏋 🏊 🔥 SC 🛏

★★ **MADISON SUITES HOTEL.** *11 Cedar Grove Ln (08873), ½ mi SE of I-287 exit 10, just off Easton Ave.* 732/563-1000; FAX 732/563-0352; res: 800/372-9099. 83 suites, 2 story. Suites $99-$120; under 18 free; wkend rates. TV; cable (premium). Complimentary continental bkfst. Ck-out noon. Meeting rms. Business servs avail. In-rm modem link. Valet serv. Coin lndry. Health club privileges. Refrigerators, microwaves. Cr cds: A, C, D, DS, MC, V.

D ⊠ 🔥 SC

★★ **RAMADA INN.** *195 Hwy 18 (08816), at Eggers St & NJ Tpke exit 9.* 732/828-6900; FAX 732/937-4838; res: 800/272-6232. 137 rms, 4 story. S, D $75-$155; each addl $10; under 18 free. Crib free. TV; cable (premium). Pool. Coffee in rms. Restaurant 6:30 am-10:30 pm. Rm

serv. Bar 11:30 am-midnight; entertainment Fri, Sat. Ck-out noon. Meeting rms. Business center. Valet serv. Exercise equipt. Health club privileges. Microwaves avail. Cr cds: A, C, D, DS, ER, JCB, MC, V.

D ⊠ 🏋 🏊 🔥 SC 🛏

Hotels

★★★ **DOUBLETREE HOTEL.** *200 Atrium Dr (08873), off I-287 Easton Ave exit 10, left on Davidson Ave.* 732/469-2600; FAX 732/560-8043; res: 800/528-0444. 360 rms, 6 story. S, D $89-$164; each addl $10; suites $175-$375; family, wkend rates. Crib free. TV; cable (premium), VCR avail. 2 pools, 1 indoor; whirlpool, poolside serv, lifeguard. Restaurant 6:30 am-2 pm; dining rm 5:30-10 pm. Bar 2 pm-1:30 am; entertainment. Ck-out noon. Business center. In-rm modem link. Gift shop. Tennis. Exercise equipt. Refrigerator in suites; microwaves avail. Private patios. Cr cds: A, C, D, DS, ER, JCB, MC, V.

D 🏌 ⊠ 🏋 ⛷ 🔥 🍴 SC 🛏

★★★ **EAST BRUNSWICK HILTON AND TOWERS.** *3 Tower Center Blvd (08816), off I-95 exit 9.* 732/828-2000; FAX 732/828-6958; res: 800/445-8667. E-mail bhtsales@injersey.com; Web www.hilton.com. 405 rms, 15 story. S $125-$205; D $145-$225; each addl $20; suites $430-$620; under 18 free; wkend rates. Crib free. TV; cable (premium), VCR avail. Indoor pool; whirlpool. Coffee in rms. Restaurant 6:30 am-10:30 pm. Rm serv 24 hrs. Bar 11 am-midnight; wkends to 2 am. Ck-out noon. Convention facilities. Business center. In-rm modem link. Concierge. Gift shop. Airport transportation. Exercise equipt; sauna. Some bathrm phones, minibars; refrigerators, microwaves avail. Luxury level. Cr cds: A, C, D, DS, ER, MC, V.

D ⊠ 🏋 🏊 🔥 SC 🛏

★★★ **EMBASSY SUITES HOTEL.** *121 Centennial Ave (08854), off I-287 exit 9.* 732/980-0500; FAX 732/980-9473; res: 800/362-2779. Web www.embassysuites.com. 224 suites, 5 story. Suites $185; each addl $20; under 18 free; wkend rates. Crib free. TV; cable (premium). Indoor pool; whirlpool. Complimentary full bkfst. Coffee in rms. Restaurant 11:30 am-2 pm, 5-10 pm. Bar to midnight. Ck-out noon. Coin lndry. Meeting rms. Business servs avail. In-rm modem link. Gift shop. Exercise equipt; sauna. Health club privileges. Game rm. Lawn games. Refrigerators, microwaves. Atrium. Cr cds: A, C, D, DS, JCB, MC, V.

D ⊠ 🏋 🏊 🔥 SC

★★★ **HYATT REGENCY.** *2 Albany St (08901).* 732/873-1234; FAX 732/873-1382; res: 800/233-1234. Web www.hyatt.com. 286 rms, 6 story. S $180; D $205; suites $270-$700; under 18 free; wkend rates. Crib free. TV; cable (premium). Indoor pool; whirlpool. Coffee in rms. Restaurant (see 2 ALBANY). Bar 11-1 am; pianist Thurs-Sat. Ck-out noon. Convention facilities. Business center. In-rm modem link. Gift shop. Garage. Tennis. Exercise equipt; sauna. Refrigerators avail. Some balconies. Cr cds: A, C, D, DS, JCB, MC, V.

D 🏌 ⊠ 🏋 🏊 🔥 SC 🛏

★★★ **MARRIOTT SOMERSET.** *110 Davidson Ave (08873), I-287 exit 10.* 732/560-0500; FAX 732/560-3669; res: 800/228-9290. Web www.marriott.com. 440 rms, 11 story. S, D $139; each addl $15; under 18 free; wkend rates. Crib free. TV; cable (premium), VCR avail. Indoor/outdoor pool; whirlpool, poolside serv (summer). Restaurant 6:30 am-10 pm. Bar 11:30 am-midnight; Fri, Sat to 2 am. Ck-out 11 am. Meeting rms. Business center. In-rm modem link. Concierge. Gift shop. Tennis. Exercise rm; sauna. Refrigerators, microwaves avail. Some balconies. Cr cds: A, C, D, DS, JCB, MC, V.

D 🏌 ⊠ 🏋 🏊 🔥 SC 🛏

Restaurants

★★ **2 ALBANY.** *(See Hyatt Regency)* 732/873-6600. Web www.hyatt.com. Hrs: 6:30 am-11 pm; Sun brunch 10:30 am-2 pm; early-bird dinner 4:30-6:30 pm (seasonal, Thurs-Sat). Res accepted. Mediterranean, Amer menu. Semi-a la carte: bkfst $4.95-$8.95, lunch

$4.95-$11.95, dinner $16.95-$21.95. Bkfst buffet $9.95. Sun brunch $23.95. Child's meals. Specializes in beef, chicken. Piano Thurs-Sat. Parking. Cr cds: A, C, D, DS.

D SC ⌐ ♥

★★ **ANTONIA'S.** *40 Livingston Ave (08901). 732/828-7080.* Hrs: 11 am-2 pm, 5-9 pm; Mon 11 am-2 pm. Closed Sat, Sun; also major hols. Res accepted. Italian menu. Bar. A la carte entrees: lunch $6.75-$7.95, dinner $8.25-$9.75. Child's meals. Specializes in pasta, eggplant. Parking. Patriotic decor; turn-of-the-century pictures. Cr cds: A, C, DS, MC, V.

D ⌐

★★★ **LA FONTANA.** *120 Albany St (08901). 732/249-7500.* Hrs: 11:30 am-2:30 pm, 5-10 pm; Fri to 11 pm; Sat 5-11 pm. Closed Sun. Res accepted. Italian menu. Bar. Wine cellar. A la carte entrees: lunch $15, dinner $22-$28. Child's meals. Specializes in aristocratic-style Italian cuisine. Valet parking. 1920s Old World elegance. Jacket. Cr cds: A, C, D, MC, V.

D

★★ **MAKEDA ETHIOPIAN RESTAURANT.** *338 George St (08901). 732/545-5115.* Hrs: 11:30 am-10:30 pm; Fri, Sat to midnight; Sun 1-10 pm. Closed Jan 1, Thanksgiving, Dec 25. Res accepted. Ethiopian menu. Bar 11:30-2 am. A la carte entrees: lunch $4-$25, dinner $6-$36. Specializes in Ethiopian cuisine. Music Thurs-Sun. Elegant atmosphere with authentic Ethiopian-style seating. Cr cds: A, C, D, DS, MC, V.

D SC ⌐

✓★ **MARITA'S CANTINA.** *1 Penn Plaza (08901). 732/247-3840.* Hrs: 11:30-2 am; Sun 3-11:30 pm. Closed Easter, Thanksgiving, Dec 25. Res accepted. Mexican menu. Bar to 2 am. Semi-a la carte: lunch, dinner $4.95-$11.95. Child's meals. Specializes in Mexican cuisine. Own desserts. Entertainment Thurs. Outdoor dining. Cr cds: A, C, D, MC, V.

D ⌐

★★ **NAPOLITANO'S.** *19 Dennis St (08901). 732/249-1551.* Hrs: 11:30-1 am; Fri to 2 am; Sat 5:30 pm-2 am; Sun 4-9 pm. Closed Jan 1, July 4, Dec 25. Res accepted. Italian menu. Bar. A la carte entrees: lunch $7-$12, dinner $10-$21. Specializes in homemade pasta. Piano, guitar Fri, Sat. Street parking. Antiques. Cr cds: A, C, D, MC, V.

D

★ **RUSTY NAIL.** *US 130 S (08902), 4 mi S on US 130, 1½ mi S of jct US 1 & US 130. 732/821-4141.* Hrs: 11:30 am-10 pm; Sun from noon pm. Res accepted. Bar to 2 am. Semi-a la carte: lunch $4.25-$7.25, dinner $9.95-$16.95. Child's meals. Specializes in prime roast beef. Cr cds: A, C, D, DS, MC, V.

D ⌐

★★★ **STAGE LEFT: AN AMERICAN CAFE.** *5 Livingston Ave (08901). 732/828-4444.* Web www.stageleft.com. Hrs: 5-11 pm; Fri 11:30 am-2 pm, 5-11 pm; early-bird dinner 5:30-7 pm. Closed Mon; also Jan 1, Memorial Day, Dec 25. Res accepted. Bar to 2 am. Wine cellar. A la carte entrees: lunch $9.95-$15.95, dinner $18.95-$26.95. Complete meal: dinner $29. Specializes in chicken, beef, seafood. Valet parking. Outdoor dining. Romantic atmosphere; unique art. Mahogany art deco bar. Cr cds: A, C, D, DS, MC, V.

D ⌐

✓★★ **SZECHWAN GOURMET.** *3 Livingston Ave (08901). 732/846-7878.* Hrs: 11:30-2 am; summer hrs to 11:30 pm. Closed Thanksgiving. Chinese menu. Setups. Semi-a la carte: lunch $4.50-$6.50, dinner $4.50-$13.95. Specialty: General Tso's two treasures of jumbo shrimp & chicken. Street parking. Cr cds: A, C, DS, MC, V.

⌐

★★ **TERESA'S.** *48 Easton Ave (08901). 732/545-3737.* Hrs: 11 am-11 pm; Fri to midnight; Sun 4-10 pm. Closed Easter, Thanksgiving, Dec 25. Res accepted. Italian menu. Bar to 2 am. A la carte entrees: lunch $7-$11, dinner $11-$21. Child's meals. Specializes in seafood, pasta. Street parking. Outdoor dining. Cr cds: A, C, D, MC, V.

D ⌐

★★★ **THE FROG AND THE PEACH.** *29 Dennis St (08901), at Hiram Square. 732/846-3216.* Web www.frogandpeach.com. Hrs: 11:30 am-2:30 pm, 5:30-10:30 pm; Sat from 5:30 pm; Sun 4:30-9:30 pm. Closed most major hols. Res accepted. Bar to midnight. Wine list. A la carte entrees: lunch $9-$15.50, dinner $19.50-$34.50. Child's meals. Specialties: pastrami-cured smoked salmon, proscuitto wrapped tuna. Own baking. Outdoor dining. In renovated industrial bldg with antique bar, stained glass. Cr cds: A, C, D, DS, MC, V.

D

★★ **THE OLD BAY.** *61-63 Church St (08901). 732/246-3111.* E-mail oldbay@aol.com; Web oldbay.com. Hrs: 11:30 am-9:30 pm; Sun 5-9 pm; early-bird dinner 5-6 pm (seasonal). Closed most major hols. Res accepted. French creole menu. Bar to 2 am. Semi-a la carte: lunch $5.45-$8.95, dinner $14.95-$25.95. Specializes in seafood, steaks. Entertainment Thurs-Sat. Street parking. Outdoor dining. Cr cds: A, C, D, MC, V.

D

Newfoundland (B-4)

(See also Paterson, Wayne)

Pop 900 (est) **Elev** 756 ft **Area Code** 973 **Zip** 07435

What to See and Do

Craigmeur Ski Area. Area has double chairlift, T-bar, rope tow; patrol, school, rentals; snowmaking; restaurant, cafeteria, bar. Four runs, longest run 1¼ mi; vertical drop 250 ft. (Dec–Mar, daily) 2 mi S on Green Pond Rd (NJ 513) off NJ 23. Phone 973/697-4500. ¢¢¢¢¢

Ocean City (J-4)

Pop 15,512 **Elev** 4 ft **Area Code** 609 **Zip** 08226
Information Public Relations Dept, City of Ocean City, 9th & Asbury Ave; 609/525-9300

Families from all over the country come to this popular resort year after year, as do conventions and religious conferences. In accordance with its founder's instructions, liquor cannot be sold here. Ocean City is an island that lies between the Atlantic Ocean and Great Egg Harbor. It has eight miles of beaches, more than two miles of boardwalk, an enclosed entertainment auditorium on the boardwalk, and excellent swimming, fishing, boating, golf and tennis.

What to See and Do

Historic House. Furnishings and fashions circa 1920–1930. Tours. (Apr–Dec, daily exc Sun) 1139 Wesley Ave. Phone 609/399-1801. **Donation**

Ocean City Historical Museum. Victorian furnishings and fashions; doll exhibit; local shipwreck; historical Ocean City photographic exhibit; gift shop. (Apr–Dec, Mon–Fri, also Sat afternoons; rest of yr, Tues–Sat afternoons) 1735 Simpson Ave, at 17th St. Phone 609/399-1801. **Donation**

Annual Events

Flower Show. Music Pier. June.

Night in Venice. Decorated boat parade. Mid-July.

Baseball Card Convention. Late July.

Hermit Crab Race, Miss Crustacean Contest. 6th St Beach. Crab beauty pageant, races. Phone 609/525-9300 or 800/BEACH-NJ. Early Aug.

Boardwalk Art Show. International and regional artists. Aug.

Seasonal Event

Concerts. Music Pier. Pops orchestra and dance band. Sun–Wed. Late June–Sept.

Motels

★★★ **BEACH CLUB HOTEL.** *1280 Boardwalk Ave (08226), at 13th St.* 609/399-8555; FAX 609/398-4379. E-mail impbcwd@aol; web www.roccplex.com/beach club/welcome.html. 82 rms, 3 story. Mid-June-Labor Day: S, D $190-$262; each addl $10; higher rates wknds, May-mid-June, Labor Day-Nov. Closed rest of yr. Crib free. TV; cable (premium). Pool; wading pool, lifeguard. Restaurant 7 am-9 pm. Rm serv. Ck-out 11 am. Coin lndry. Business servs avail. Bellhops. Golf privileges. Health club privileges. Refrigerators. Balconies. Sun deck. On beach. Cr cds: A, C, MC, V.

⬛⬛⬛⬛⬛ SC

★ **DAYS INN.** *7th & Boarddwalk (08226).* 609/398-2200; FAX 609/391-2050; res: 800/329-7466. Web www.daysinn.com. 80 rms, 4 story, 39 kit. suites. June-Aug: S, D $55-$200; each addl $15; kit. suites $70-$215; wkly rates; higher rates sporting events; lower rates Apr-May & Sept-Oct. Closed rest of yr. Crib free. TV; cable, VCR avail (movies). Heated pool; lifeguard. Restaurant nearby. Ck-out 11 am. Coin lndry. Business servs avail. Bellhops. Balconies. Cr cds: A, C, D, DS, MC, V.

⬛⬛⬛⬛⬛ SC

★★ **FORUM MOTOR INN.** *800 E 8th St & Atlantic Ave (08226).* 609/399-8700; FAX 609/399-8704. 61 rms, 2-3 story. July-Aug (3-day min): S, D $62-$204; each addl $8; some wknd rates; lower rates Apr-May, Sept-Oct. Closed rest of yr. Crib avail. TV; cable (premium). Heated pool; wading pool, lifeguard. Ck-out noon. Coin lndry. Business servs avail. Game rm. Rec rm. Refrigerators. Picnic tables. Sun deck. Cr cds: C, MC, V.

⬛⬛ ⬛

★ **HARRIS HOUSE.** *1201 Ocean Ave & 12th St (08226).* 609/399-7800; FAX 609/398-8082. 74 rms, 2 story. Late June-Aug: S, D $160; each addl $10; under 12 free; wkly rates; higher rates hols (3-day min); lower rates late Aug-late Oct & Apr-late June; closed rest of yr. Crib free. TV; cable. Heated pool; lifeguard. Complimentary coffee in lobby. Restaurant adj 6 am-9 pm. Ck-out 11 am. Business servs avail. Refrigerators, microwaves avail. On beach. Cr cds: A, C, DS, MC, V.

⬛⬛⬛⬛⬛

★★ **IMPALA ISLAND INN.** *1001 Ocean Avenue (08226), 10th St at Ocean Ave.* 609/399-7500; FAX 609/398-4379. E-mail impbcwd@aol; Web www.rccplex.com/impalisland/welcome.html. 109 units in 2 bldgs, 2 story. July-Aug; S, D $140-$175; kit. units $1,300-$1,800/wk; lower rates rest of yr. Crib free. TV; cable. 2 pools, 1 heated; wading pool, lifeguard. Restaurant 7 am-9 pm. Rm serv. Ck-out 11 am. Meeting rms. Business servs avail. Refrigerators. Sun deck. Cr cds: A, C, MC, V.

⬛⬛⬛⬛ SC

★ **PAVILION.** *801 Atlantic Ave (08226).* 609/399-2600; FAX 609/814-0456. E-mail pavilionoc@aol.com; web www.pavilionmotor lodge.com. 80 rms, 3 story. Early July-early Sept (3-day min wknds): S, D $125-$135; kit. units $150; lower rates Mar-June & early Sept-Nov; closed rest of yr. Crib avail. TV; cable (premium), VCR avail (movies). Heated pool; wading pool, poolside serv, lifeguard. Restaurant 7:30 am-9 pm. Rm serv. Ck-out 11 am. Coin lndry. Business servs avail. Refrigerators. On beach. Cr cds: A, C, DS, MC, V.

⬛⬛⬛⬛ SC

★★ **RESIDENCE INN BY MARRIOTT.** *900 Mays Landing Rd (08244), 3 mi NW on NJ 52, then W on Mays Landing Rd; E of Garden State Pkwy exits 29N, 30S.* 609/927-6400; FAX 609/926-0145; res: 800/331-3131. Web www.adnetinn.com/residence. 120 kit. suites, 2 story. Memorial Day-Labor Day: S, D $160-$240; each addl $10; under 12 free; wkly rates; lower rates rest of yr. Pet accepted. TV; cable, VCR avail (movies). Heated pool; lifeguard. Complimentary continental bkfst. Ck-out 11 am. Coin lndry. Meeting rms. Business servs avail. In-rm modem link. Valet serv. Golf privileges. Health club privileges. Rec rm. Microwaves. Some private patios, balconies. Picnic tables, grills. Cr cds: A, C, D, DS, JCB, MC, V.

⬛⬛⬛⬛⬛⬛⬛ SC

Motor Hotels

★★ **PIER 4 HOTEL.** *The Bay & Broadway Ave. (21030).* 609/927-9141; FAX 609/653-2752; res: 888/927-9141. E-mail pier4fh@aol.com. 72 rms, 4 story, 8 suites. Apr-Dec: S, D $59-$159; each addl $15; suites $89-$189; under 14 free; wkly rates; golf plans; wknds, hols (2-day min); higher rates special events; lower rates rest of yr. Crib free. TV; cable. Complimentary continental bkfst. Complimentary coffee in rms. Restaurant adj 11-1 am. Ck-out 11 am. Meeting rms. Business servs avail. Coin lndry. Golf privileges. Exercise equipt. Health club privileges. Heated pool; poolside serv. Rec rm. Refrigerators, microwaves. On bay. Cr cds: A, C, D, DS, MC, V.

⬛⬛⬛⬛⬛⬛⬛⬛ SC

★★ **PORT-O-CALL HOTEL.** *1510 Boardwalk (08226).* 609/399-8812; FAX 609/399-0387; res: 800/334-4546. Web clever.net/wwwmall/portocall. 99 rms, 9 story. June-Sept: S, D $170-$285; each addl $15; penthouse apt $325-$650; under 18 free; lower rates rest of yr. Crib free. TV; cable (premium). Pool; lifeguard. Free supervised child's activities (June-Aug). Coffee in rms. Restaurant 7 am-2 pm, 5-8 pm; Sun 9:30 am-1:30 pm, 5-8 pm. Rm serv. Ck-out 11 am. Coin lndry. Meeting rms. Business servs avail. In-rm modem link. Bellhops. Sundries. Airport transportation. Golf privileges. Exercise rm; sauna. Refrigerators. Balconies, grills. On ocean. Cr cds: A, C, D, DS, MC, V.

⬛⬛⬛⬛⬛⬛⬛⬛ SC

★★ **WILD DUNES INN.** *801 10th St (08226).* 609/399-2910; FAX 609/398-4379. Web www.ochotels.com. 28 suites, 2 story. S, D $203-$215; wkends, hols (3-day min). Crib free. TV; cable. Restaurant nearby. Ck-out 10 am. Coin lndry. Heated pool; wading pool, lifeguard. Refrigerators, microwaves. Cr cds: A, C, MC, V.

⬛⬛⬛⬛

Inn

★★★ **SERENDIPITY BED & BREAKFAST.** *712 E 9th St (08226).* 609/399-1554; FAX 609/399-1527; res: 800/842-8544; res: 800/842-8544. E-mail serendipitynj@prodigy.net; web www.bbonline.com/nj/serendipity/. 6 rms, 2 share bath, 3 story. No rm phones. July 4-Labor Day: S, D $75-$139; higher rates hols (3-day min); lower rates rest of yr. Children over 10 yrs only. TV; cable. Complimentary full bkfst. Restaurant opp 7 am-9 pm. Ck-out 11 am, ck-in 2 pm. Luggage handling. Picnic tables. Renovated inn built 1912. Totally nonsmoking. Cr cds: A, C, DS, MC, V.

⬛⬛

Restaurants

★★ **CRAB TRAP.** *Somers Pt Circle (08226), 1 mi E of Garden State Pkwy exit 30.* 609/927-7377. Hrs: 11-2 am. Closed Dec 24, 25. Bar. Semi-a la carte: lunch $5.75-$8.95, dinner $11.25-$27.95. Child's meals. Specialties: stuffed lobster tail, prime rib. Entertainment. Nautical decor. On the bay. Family-owned. Cr cds: A, C, D, DS, MC, V.

D ⬜

★★ **DEAUVILLE INN.** *201 Willard Rd (08248), 6 mi E on Garden State Pkwy.* 609/263-2080. Hrs: noon-midnight; summer hrs vary; early-bird dinner 4-6 pm. Closed Dec 25, 26. Bar. Semi-a la carte: lunch $3.95-$12, dinner $8.50-$24. Child's meals. Specializes in fresh seafood, steak, veal. Valet parking. Outdoor dining overlooking bay. Cr cds: A, C, MC, V.

D ⬜

✓★ **GREGORY'S.** *900 Shore Rd (08244), NJ 152S, approximately 4 mi.* 609/927-6665. Hrs: 11-2 am; early-bird dinner 4-6 pm (Mon-Fri). Res accepted. Continental menu. Bar. Semi-a la carte: lunch $4.50-$9, dinner $6.95-$21.50. Child's meals. Specialties: steamed lobster, Jersey crab cakes, pan-seared salmon. Soft rock Mon, Fri. Parking. Family-owned since 1946. Cr cds: A, C, D, MC, V.

★★ **MAC'S.** *908 Shore Rd (08244), 1 blk N of Somers Pt Circle.* 609/927-4360. Hrs: 3:30-11 pm. Closed Dec 25. Res accepted. Italian, Amer menu. Bar. Semi-a la carte: dinner $9.95-$29.95. Child's meals. Specializes in seafood, steak. Family-owned. Cr cds: A, C, DS, MC, V.

D ⬜

Palisades Interstate Parks (B-6)

(See also Fort Lee, Hackensack)

(Reached via Palisades Interstate Pkwy, starting at New Jersey end of George Washington Bridge; US 9W, NJ/NY 17, Dewey Thrwy exit 13)

This 81,067-acre system of conservation and recreation areas extends along the west side of the Hudson River from the George Washington Bridge at Fort Lee, NJ (see), to Saugerties, NY. Its main unit is the 51,679-acre tract of Bear Mountain and Harriman (NY) state parks; the two are contiguous.

Bear Mountain (5,066 acres) extends westward from the Hudson River opposite Peekskill. Only 45 mi from New York City via the Palisades Interstate Parkway, this is one of the most popular recreation areas, with year-round facilities, mostly for one-day visits. Area includes swimming pool (Memorial Day-Labor Day; fee), bathhouse; fishing, game fields; boating on Hessian Lake. Nature trails. Cafeteria. Inn. Ice-skating (late Oct-mid-Mar; fee); square dances in July and August.

Perkins Memorial Drive leads to the top of Bear Mountain, where there is a picnic area and a sightseeing tower. Near the site of Fort Clinton, just west of Bear Mountain Bridge, is the Trailside Museum, with exhibits of local flora, fauna, geology and history (daily; fee).

Harriman (46,613 acres), southwest of Bear Mountain, includes much wilder country with several lakes. Swimming beaches (Lakes Tiorati, Welch and Sebago); fishing; boating. Hiking, biking. Picnicking. Miles of scenic drives. Tent camping (Lake Welch), cabins (Lake Sebago).

Many smaller parks are located in the New Jersey section of the park system.

Alpine Area (12 acres). This area has fishing; boat basin. Hiking. Picnicking, concession (seasonal). Outdoor concerts in summer. (Daily, weather permitting) Off Henry Hudson Dr, E of Alpine.

Englewood-Bloomers Area (13 acres). This area offers fishing; boat basin. Hiking. Picnicking, concession (seasonal). (Daily, weather permitting) Off Henry Hudson Dr, E of jct Palisades Interstate Pkwy & NJ 505 in Englewood Cliffs.

Ross Dock (14 acres). Near the southern end of the park system, this area has fishing; boat-launching ramp. Hiking. Picnicking, playgrounds. (Apr-mid-Nov, daily, weather permitting) Off Henry Hudson Dr, N of George Washington Bridge.

Fort Lee Historic Park. This 33-acre facility presents the story of Washington's retreat from Fort Lee in 1776. Visitor's Center/Museum (Mar-Dec, Wed-Sun) offers two floors of exhibits; audiovisual displays; a short film; general information; special events. On grounds (daily, daylight hrs) are 18th-century soldiers' hut, reconstructed gun batteries, a rifle parapet; overlooks with scenic views of the George Washington Bridge, the Palisades, the Hudson River and the New York skyline. Gift shop. Parking fee (May-Sept, daily; Apr & Oct-mid-Nov, wknds & hols). No pets, bicycles or fires. Hudson Ter. Phone 201/461-1776. ¢¢

There are fees for parking and special events. For further information on the New Jersey section contact Palisades Interstate Park Commission, PO Box 155, Alpine 07620; 201/768-1360. Further information on the New York section can be obtained from Palisades Interstate Park Commission, Administration Bldg, Bear Mountain, NY 10911; 914/786-2701.

Paramus (B-5)

Settled 1660 **Pop** 25,067 **Elev** 58 ft **Area Code** 201 **Zip** 07652 **Web** www.paramuschamber.com

Information Chamber of Commerce, 58 E Midland Ave, PO Box 325; 201/261-3344

This old Dutch farm community was an important hub of transportation as long ago as the Revolutionary War; western Paramus became headquarters for the Continental Army as a result. Paramus has grown as a residential community from 4,000 inhabitants in 1946 to its present size.

What to See and Do

Bergen Museum of Art & Science. Features Dwarkskill and Hackensack mastodons; nature room; birds and minerals of Bergen County; Native American artifacts; galleries with changing exhibits. (Daily exc Mon; closed major hols) 327 E Ridgewood Ave at Farview Ave. Phone 201/265-1248. ¢¢

New Jersey Children's Museum. Interactive displays in 30 rms. Includes aviation, firefighting, TV studio, hospital. Gift shop. (Daily; closed some hols) 599 Industrial Ave. Phone 201/262-5151. ¢¢¢

Schoolhouse Museum. Exhibits in 1873 schoolhouse depict life from colonial times through 19th century, with emphasis on local history. Native American relics; early maps; Dutch genealogies; farm implements; doll and toy displays; clothing. Tours (by appt). (May-late Oct, Sun afternoons; closed hols) 650 E Glen Ave, at NJ 17, in Ridgewood. Phone 201/652-4584 or 201/447-3242 (recording). **Free**

Van Saun County Park. Fishing lake. Bike trail; tennis (fee); horseshoes, shuffleboard. Ice-skating, sledding. Picnicking, concession, playgrounds, ball fields (permit). Zoo; train, pony rides (fees). Garden surrounding historic Washington Spring; farmyard. Park (daily). 216 Forest Ave, 1½ mi N of NJ 4. Phone 201/262-2627 or 201/262-3771 (zoo). **Free**

Motor Hotel

★★ **RADISSON HOTEL.** *601 From Rd (07652), adj to Paramus Park Mall, Garden State Pkwy exit 165.* 201/262-6900; FAX 201/262-4955; res: 800/333-3333. Web www.radisson.com. 119 rms, 2 story. S, D $145; each addl $10; wknd rates. Crib free. Pet accepted, some restrictions. TV; cable (premium). Pool. Complimentary coffee in rms. Restaurant 6:30 am-10 pm; Sat, Sun from 7 am. Rm serv. Bar. Ck-out noon. Coin lndry. Meeting rms. Business servs avail. In-rm modem link. Health club privileges. Refrigerators. Cr cds: A, C, D, DS, ER, JCB, MC, V.

D 🖐 ⬜ 🛋 🔥 SC

Parsippany (C-4)

Pop 48,478 Elev 282 ft Area Code 973 Zip 07054

Motels

✓★ **HOWARD JOHNSON EXPRESS INN.** *625 Rte 46E (07054).* 973/882-8600; FAX 973/882-3493; res: 800/446-4656. Web www.hojo.com. 117 rms, 3 story. S $59.95; D $64.95-$74.95; under 18 free; wkly rates. Crib free. Pet accepted. TV; cable (premium). Complimentary continental bkfst. Restaurant nearby. Ck-out noon. Coin lndry. Meeting rm. Business servs avail. Refrigerators, microwaves avail. Cr cds: A, C, D, DS, ER, JCB, MC, V.

D 🐕 🏊 🔥 SC

★★ **HOWARD JOHNSON INN.** *1255 R 10 (08244), I-80 to I-287S exit 39B (NJ 10).* 973/539-8350; FAX 973/539-9338; res: 800/446-4656. Web www.hojo.com. 108 rms, 2 story. S $89-$99; D $99-$109; each addl $10; under 18 free; family, wkend, wkly, hol rates. Crib free. Pet accepted, some restrictions. TV; cable (premium). Complimentary continental bkfst. Restaurant 11 am-10 pm. Ck-out noon. Meeting rms. Business servs avail. Valet serv. Coin lndry. Pool. Refrigerators, microwaves avail. Cr cds: A, C, D, DS, JCB, MC, V.

D 🐕 🏊 🔥 SC

Motor Hotels

★★ **HAMPTON INN.** *3535 Rte 46E, at Cherry Hill Rd (07054).* 973/263-0095; FAX 973/263-6133; res: 800/426-7866. Web www.hampton-inn.com. 100 rms, 4 story, 18 kits. S, D $120; kit. units $135; under 18 free; wkend rates. Crib free. TV; cable (premium). Complimentary continental bkfst. Rm serv. Ck-out noon. Business center. Valet serv (exc wkends). Exercise equipt; sauna. Refrigerators, microwaves avail. Cr cds: A, C, D, DS, ER, MC, V.

D 🏋 🏊 🔥 SC 🚶

★★ **HOLIDAY INN.** *707 Rte 46 (07054), I-80 exit 45 (E) or exit 47 (W).* 973/263-2000; FAX 973/299-9029; res: 800/465-4329. Web www.holiday.com. 178 rms, 4 story. S, D $89-$99; suites $119-$129; under 18 free; lower rates wkends. Crib free. TV; cable (premium). Pool. Restaurant 7 am-11 pm. Ck-out noon. Coin lndry. Meeting rms. Business servs avail. Sundries. Exercise equipt. Health club privileges. Microwaves avail. Cr cds: A, C, D, DS, JCB, MC, V.

D 🏊 🏋 🔥 SC

Hotel

★★★ **HILTON.** *1 Hilton Ct (07054), jct NJ 10 & I-287.* 973/267-7373; FAX 973/984-6853; res: 800/445-8667. Web www.hilton.com. 510 rms, 6 story. S $165-$195; D $175-$205; each addl $20; suites $350-$675; family, wkend rates. Crib free. Pet accepted, some restrictions. TV; cable (premium), VCR avail. Indoor/outdoor pool; whirlpool. Playground. Coffee in rms. Restaurants 6:30 am-11 pm; wkends from 7 am. Rm serv Mon-Thurs 6:30-2 am. Bar 11-2 am; entertainment. Ck-out noon. Convention facilities. Business center. In-rm modem link. Airport transportation. Tennis. Exercise equipt. Basketball court. Some bathrm phones; wet bar, refrigerator in suites. Cr cds: A, C, D, DS, ER, JCB, MC, V.

D 🐕 🏋 🏊 🏋 🏊 🔥 SC 🏋

Restaurant

✓★★ **BLACK BULL INN.** *60 Rte 46 (07046), I-80 exit 42 (W) or 39 (E).* 973/335-8585. Hrs: 11 am-11 pm; Fri, Sat to midnight. Bar. Semi-a la carte: lunch $4.95-$11.95, dinner $4.95-$17.95. Child's meals. Specializes in steak, prime rib, fish. Entertainment Fri, Sat. English Tudor atmosphere. Cr cds: A, C, DS, MC, V.

D SC 🍴

Paterson (B-5)

(See also Clifton, Wayne)

Settled 1711 Pop 140,891 Elev 100 ft Area Code 973
Information Great Falls Visitor Center, 65 McBride Ave Ext, across from the Great Falls, 07501-1715, phone; 973/279-9587; or the Special Events Office, 72 McBride Ave, 07501, phone 973/523-9201

Named after Governor William Paterson, this city owes its present and historic eminence as an industrial city to Alexander Hamilton. He was the first man to realize the possibility of harnessing the Great Falls of the Passaic River for industrial purposes. As secretary of the Treasury, he helped form the Society for Establishing Useful Manufactures in 1791 and, a year later, was instrumental in choosing Paterson as the site of its initial ventures. Paterson was the country's major silk-producing town in the late 1800s. Today, it is a diversified industrial center. The area surrounding the Great Falls is now being restored and preserved as a historic district. Paterson is the seat of Passaic County.

What to See and Do

American Labor Museum–Botto House National Landmark. The history of the working class is presented through restored period rooms, changing exhibits and ethnic gardens. Tours, seminars and workshops are offered. (Wed–Sat; closed major hols exc Labor Day) 83 Norwood St in Haledon. Phone 973/595-7953. ¢

Garret Mountain Reservation. A 570-acre woodland park on a 502-ft-high plateau. Fishing pond (stocked with trout); boat dock, rowboats, paddleboats. Trails, stables. Picnic groves. Rifle Camp Rd & Mountain Ave. Phone 973/881-4832. **Free**

★ **Great Falls Historic District.** Includes 77-ft-high falls, park and picnic area, renovated raceway system, restored 19th-century buildings. McBride Ave Ext & Spruce St. For further information and tours phone 973/279-9587. **Free**   Also here is

Paterson Museum. Contains shell of original 14-ft submarine invented by John P. Holland in 1878; also his second submarine (31 ft), built in 1881. Paterson-Colt gun collection (1836–1840); mineral display; exhibits on Paterson history, including the silk and locomotive industries; two locomotives; Curtiss-Wright airplane engines; changing art exhibits. (Daily exc Mon; closed hols) Thomas Rogers Bldg, 2 Market St. Phone 973/881-3874. **Donation**

Lambert Castle. Built by an immigrant who rose to wealth as a silk manufacturer. The 1893 castle of brownstone and granite houses a local-history museum; two restored period rooms; changing exhibits; library (by appt). (Wed–Sun, afternoons; closed most major hols) 3 Valley Rd. Phone 973/881-2761. ¢

Rifle Camp Park. This 158-acre park is 584 ft above sea level. Includes nature and geology trails, nature center with astronomical observatory; walking paths, fitness course. Picnic areas. Rifle Camp Rd in West Paterson. **Free**

Plainfield (D-4)

Settled 1685 **Pop** 46,567 **Elev** 118 ft **Area Code** 908 **E-mail** cjcc@erols.com **Web** www.erols.com/cjcc

Information Central Jersey Chamber of Commerce, 120 W 7th St, #217, 07060; 908/754-7250

Plainfield, directly south of the Watchung Mountains, is actually the center of a group of associated towns: Scotch Plains (see), Watchung, North and South Plainfield, Fanwood, Green Brook, Warren Township, Dunellen, Middlesex and Piscataway, all of which are mainly residential. Plainfield is also home to a number of industries.

What to See and Do

Drake House Museum (1746). General Washington's headquarters in 1777; now the Plainfield Historical Society headquarters. Period furnishings; diorama depicts Battle for the Watchungs. (Sat afternoons) 602 W Front St. Phone 908/755-5831. ¢

Motor Hotel

★★ **HOLIDAY INN.** 4701 Stelton Rd (07080), at jct NJ 529, I-287. 908/753-5500; FAX 908/753-5500; res: 800/465-4329. Web www.holidayinn.com. 173 rms, 4 story. S, D $89-$109; under 12 free; wknd rates. Crib free. Pet accepted, some restrictions. TV; cable (premium). Indoor pool; whirlpool, lifeguard. Coffee in rms. Restaurant 6:30 am-midnight. Rm serv. Bar. Ck-out 1 pm. Coin lndry. Meeting rms. Business servs avail. In-rm modem link. Valet serv. Exercise equipt; sauna. Refrigerators; microwaves avail. Cr cds: A, C, D, DS, MC, V.

Princeton (E-4)

(See also Trenton)

Settled 1685 **Pop** 12,016 **Elev** 215 ft **Area Code** 609 **E-mail** ccpa@ix.netcom.com **Web** www.princetonchamber.org

Information Chamber of Commerce, 216 Rockingham Row PO Box 431, 08540; 609/520-1776

In 1776, the first State Legislature of New Jersey met in Princeton University's Nassau Hall. Washington and his troops surprised and defeated a superior British Army in the 1777 Battle of Princeton. From June to November 1783, Princeton was the new nation's capital. Around the same time, Washington was staying at Rockingham in nearby Rocky Hill, where he wrote and delivered his famous "Farewell Orders to the Armies."

Princeton's life is greatly influenced by the university, which opened here in 1756; at that time it was known as the College of New Jersey. In 1896, on the 150th anniversary of its charter, the institution became Princeton University. Woodrow Wilson, the first president of the university who was not a clergyman, held the office from 1902 to 1910. Princeton is also the home of the Institute for Advanced Study, where Albert Einstein spent the last years of his life.

What to See and Do

Bainbridge House (ca 1766). Birthplace of commander of the USS *Constitution* during War of 1812. Changing exhibits on Princeton history; research library (Tues, Sat; fee), photo archives. Museum shops. Also offers walking tours of historic district (Sun; fee). 158 Nassau St. For schedule phone 609/921-6748. **Free**

Kuser Farm Mansion and Park. Farm and 1890s summer mansion of Fred Kuser; more than 20 rms open; many original furnishings. Grounds

consist of 22 acres with original buildings including coachman's house, chicken house; tennis pavilion; clay tennis court. Park with picnic areas; quoit courts, lawn bowling, walking trails; formal garden, gazebo. Tours (May–Nov, Thurs–Sun; Feb–Apr, Sat & Sun; limited hrs, call for schedule and hol closings); self-guided tour maps of grounds. Special programs, lectures and video evenings throughout the yr. 10 mi SE via US 206, I-295 to Olden Ave in Hamilton, then ½ mi W to Newkirk Ave. Phone 609/890-3630. **Free**

Morven (ca 1750). House of Richard Stockton, signer of the Declaration of Independence. Used as a Revolutionary headquarters; was frequently visited by General Washington and other colonial leaders. 55 Stockton St. Phone 609/683-4495 for schedule.

Princeton Battle Monument. The work of Frederick W. MacMonnies, this 50-ft block of Indiana limestone commemorates the famous 1777 battle when George Washington defeated the British. On Monument Dr, off Stockton St, near Morven.

Princeton Cemetery. Buried in the Presidents' Plot are 11 university presidents, including Aaron Burr Sr, Jonathan Edwards and John Witherspoon. Monument to Grover Cleveland and grave of Paul Tulane, in whose honor Tulane University was named. Witherspoon & Wiggins Sts.

Princeton University (1746). (4,500 undergraduate students, 1,650 graduate students) An Ivy League college that has been coeducational since 1969. A campus guide service shows the visitor points of interest on the main campus; for tour information phone 609/258-3603. (Daily; closed major hols). On campus are

McCarter Theatre. Professional repertory company performs classical and modern drama; concerts; ballet; other special programs yr-round. Phone 609/683-8000 (box office).

Nassau Hall (1756). Provided all college facilities, classrooms, dormitories, library and prayer hall for about 50 yrs. New Jersey's first legislature met here in 1776, and the Continental Congress met here in 1783, when Princeton was the capital. During the Revolution, it served as a barracks and hospital for Continental and British troops.

The Putnam Sculptures. One of the largest modern outdoor sculpture showcases in the country, with 19 sculptures on display throughout the campus, including pieces by Picasso, Moore, Noguchi, Calder and Lipchitz.

Woodrow Wilson School of Public and International Affairs. Designed by Minoru Yamasaki; reflecting pool and "Fountain of Freedom" by James Fitzgerald.

Rockingham State Historic Site. On this 5-acre site are 3 buildings: a kitchen, a wash house and the main building. This was Washington's headquarters Aug 23–Nov 10, 1783, where he wrote his "Farewell Orders to the Armies"; 10 rms with period furnishings. (Wed–Sat, also Sun afternoons; closed most major hols) 4 mi N on US 206, then 2 mi E on County 518 in Rocky Hill. Phone 609/921-8835. **Free**

Motels

✓★ **DAYS INN.** 4191 US 1 (08852), 2 mi N on US 1. 732/329-4555; FAX 732/329-1041; res: 800/329-7466. Web www.hotelusa.com. 73 rms, 2 story, 7 suites. S $44.95-$59.95; D $59.95-$99.95; each addl $10; suites $150.95; under 12 free. Crib free. TV; cable, VCR avail (movies). Restaurant 6:30-10:30 am. Ck-out 11 am. Business servs avail. Refrigerators, microwaves avail. Cr cds: A, C, D, DS, JCB, MC, V.

★★ **RESIDENCE INN BY MARRIOTT.** 4225 Rte 1 (08543), 4 mi NE, just S of Raymond Rd on US 1. 732/329-9600; FAX 732/329-8422; res: 800/331-3131. Web www.pacpub.com/residence. 208 kit. suites, 2 story. S, D $149-$199; under 18 free; wkly, wkend rates. Crib free. Pet accepted, some restrictions. $10. TV; cable (premium). Heated pool; whirlpool. Complimentary continental bkfst. Ck-out noon. Coin lndry. Meeting rm. Business servs avail. Valet serv. Health club privileges. Microwaves; many fireplaces. Balconies. Picnic tables, grills. Cr cds: A, C, D, DS, JCB, MC, V.

Motor Hotels

★ ★ ★ **HOLIDAY INN.** *4355 Rte 1 (08540), at Ridge Rd.* 609/452-2400; FAX 609/452-2494; res: 800/465-4329. E-mail holidayin npt@erols.com. 242 rms, 6 story. S, D $179; each addl $10; suites from $225; under 18 free; wkend rates. Crib free. Pet accepted. TV; cable (premium). Indoor pool. Restaurant 6:30 am-11 pm. Bar 11-1 am. Ck-out noon. Meeting rms. Business servs avail. Gift shop. Exercise equipt. Health club privileges. Refrigerators, microwaves avail. Cr cds: A, C, D, DS, MC, V.

D 🐾 🏊 🏋 🐕 🔥 SC

★ ★ **NOVOTEL HOTEL.** *100 Independence Way (08540), jct NJ 522, US 1.* 609/520-1200; FAX 609/520-0594; res: 800/221-4542; res: 800/668-6835. E-mail prinmail@aol.com. 180 rms, 4 story. S, D, suites $169; under 16 free; wkend rates. Crib free. Pet accepted, some restrictions. TV; cable (premium), VCR avail. Pool; whirlpool. Restaurant 6 am-10:30 pm. Rm serv. Bar. Ck-out 1 pm. Coin lndry. Meeting rms. Business servs avail. In-rm modem link. Valet serv. Free RR station transportation. Exercise equipt. Microwaves avail. Cr cds: A, C, D, DS, JCB, MC, V.

D 🐾 🏊 🏋 🐕 🔥 SC

Hotels

★ ★ ★ **HYATT REGENCY.** *102 Carnegie Ctr (08540), 2 mi E on US 1, at Alexander Rd.* 609/987-1234; FAX 609/987-2584; res: 800/233-1234. 348 rms, 4 story. S $89-$179; D $89-$204; suites $200-$575; under 18 free; wkend rates. Crib free. TV; cable (premium), VCR avail. Indoor/outdoor pool; whirlpool, poolside serv. Restaurant 6:30 am-10:30 pm. Bar 11-2 am; entertainment Fri-Sun. Ck-out noon. Business center. In-rm modem link. Gift shop. Airport transportation. Tennis. Exercise equipt; sauna. Health club privileges. Some bathrm phones; microwaves avail. Cr cds: A, C, D, DS, ER, JCB, MC, V.

D 🏊 🏋 🐕 🔥 SC 🚶

★ ★ ★ **MARRIOTT.** *201 Village Blvd (08540), in Forrestal Village, 8 mi S of NJ Tpke exit 9.* 609/452-7900; FAX 609/452-1223; res: 800/228-9290. Web www.marriott.com. 294 units, 6 story. S, D $164-$184; under 18 free; some wkend rates. Crib free. TV; cable (premium), VCR avail. Indoor/outdoor pool; whirlpool, poolside serv, lifeguard. Coffee in rms. Restaurant 6:30 am-11 pm. Bar noon-2 am; entertainment. Ck-out 11 am. Coin lndry. Meeting rms. Business center. In-rm modem link. Concierge. Gift shop. Tennis. Exercise equipt. Health club privileges. Refrigerators avail. Some private patios, balconies. Shopping center adj. Cr cds: A, C, D, DS, ER, JCB, MC, V.

D 🏊 🏋 🐕 🔥 SC 🚶

★ ★ ★ **NASSAU INN.** *10 Palmer Sq (08542).* 609/921-7500; FAX 609/921-2684; res: 800/862-7728. E-mail lorginjam@aol.com; Web www.nassauinn.com. 216 rms, 5 story. S $139-$189; D $159-$209; each addl $20; suites $325-$780; under 13 free. Crib free. Pet accepted. TV; cable (premium). Restaurant 7 am-10 pm. Bar 4 pm-1 am; entertainment Fri, Sat. Ck-out noon. Business center. In-rm modem link. Exercise equipt. Refrigerators avail. Colonial atmosphere. Beamed ceilings, fireplaces in public rms. Cr cds: A, C, D, MC, V.

D 🐾 🏋 🔥 🚶

★ ★ ★ **THE FORRESTAL AT PRINCETON HOTEL.** *100 College Rd E (08540), off US 1, in Princeton Forrestal Center.* 609/452-7800; FAX 609/452-7883; res: 800/222-1131. Web www.forrestal.com. 290 rms, 3-4 story. S, D $125-$185; each addl $10; suites $275-$650; under 18 free; wkend rates. Crib free. TV; cable (premium), VCR avail. Indoor pool; whirlpool. Restaurant 7 am-10 pm. Bars 11-1 am. Ck-out noon. Convention facilities. Business center. In-rm modem link. Gift shop. Free valet parking. Airport transportation. Lighted tennis. Exercise equipt; sauna. Lawn games. Minibars. Contemporary design and furnishings. On 25 wooded acres. Luxury level. Cr cds: A, C, D, DS, MC, V.

D 🐾 🏊 🏋 🍴 🐕 🔥 SC 🚶

Inn

★ ★ **PEACOCK INN.** *20 Bayard Ln (08540).* 609/924-1707; FAX 609/924-0788. 17 rms, some share bath, 3 story. S, D $115-$150; higher rates: graduations, reunions. Pet accepted. TV in some rms, lobby; cable (premium). Complimentary bkfst buffet. Dining rm 11:45 am-2:30 pm, 5:30-9:30 pm. Ck-out noon, ck-in 2 pm. Business servs avail. Historic late Georgian colonial house, built in 1775 and relocated from Nassau St to its present site. Antique furnishings; rms individually decorated. 2 blks from Princeton Univ campus. Cr cds: A, C, MC, V.

🐾 🐕 🔥

Restaurants

★ ★ **ALCHEMIST AND BARRISTER.** *28 Witherspoon (08540).* 609/924-5555. Web www.alchemistandbarrister.com/. Hrs: 11:30 am-2:30 pm, 5-10 pm; Fri, Sat to 10:30 pm; Sun 11:30 am-3 pm (brunch), 5-10 pm. Closed Jan 1, July 4, Dec 25. Res accepted. Bar to 2 am. Semi-a la carte: lunch $7-$13, dinner $17-$26. Sun brunch $7.95-$13. Specializes in seafood, steak. Outdoor dining. Colonial decor. Cr cds: A, C, MC, V.

D

★ **ANNEX RESTAURANT.** *128½ Nassau St (08542).* 609/921-7555. Web www.powerpgs/#1/annex. Hrs: 11 am-10 pm; early-bird dinner Mon-Thurs 3:30-5:30 pm. Closed Sun; most major hols. Continental menu. Bar to 1 am. Semi-a la carte: lunch $4.50-$23, dinner $6.25-$23. Child's meals. Specialties: steak Diane, chicken a la cacciatori, baked stuffed sole with crabmeat. Casual atmosphere. Family-owned. Cr cds: A, C, D, MC, V.

◻

★ ★ **GOOD TIME CHARLEY'S.** *40 Main St (08528), 2 mi N on NJ 27.* 609/924-7405. Web www.gtcharleys.com. Hrs: 11:30-1 am. Closed Dec 25; also lunch major hols. Res accepted. Bar to 2 am. Semi-a la carte: lunch $5.95-$9.95, dinner $11.95-$21.95. Specializes in prime rib, fresh seafood. Musicians Fri, Sat. Victorian decor. Tiffany lamps; posters. Cr cds: A, C, D, DS, MC, V.

D ◻

✓ ★ ★ **RUSTY SCUPPER.** *378 Alexander Rd (08540).* 609/921-3276. Hrs: 11:30 am-2:30 pm, 5-10 pm; Fri, Sat to 11 pm; Sun 1-9 pm. Closed Dec 25. Res accepted. Bar 11:30-1 am; Sat, Sun from 1:30 pm. Semi-a la carte: lunch $6.25-$16.95, dinner $16.95-$33.95. Child's meals. Specializes in seafood, prime rib, steak. Salad bar. Outdoor dining. Cr cds: A, C, D, DS, MC, V.

D ◻

Ramsey (B-5)

Pop 13,228 **Elev** 373 ft **Area Code** 201 **Zip** 07446

What to See and Do

Campgaw Mountain Ski Area. Two double chairlifts, T-bar; patrol, school, rentals; snowmaking; cafeteria. Eight runs, longest run 1,760 ft; vertical drop 275 ft. (Early Dec–mid-Mar, daily) Lighted cross-country trails; half-pipe; cross-country and snowboard rentals. NJ 17 N, exit NJ 202 Suffern, 1.6 mi S on NJ 202, left on Darlington Ave 1 blk, stay to right, 1 mi on Campgaw Rd in Mahwah. Phone 201/327-7800. ¢¢¢¢¢

Darlington Swim Area. Two lakes provide swimming (fee); fishing (in 1 lake). Tennis, handball; shuffleboard, horseshoes. Picnicking (pavilion), playground. Park (Apr–Nov). 600 Darlington Ave in Mahwah; follow signs on NJ 17 or 208 N. For opening swim date phone 201/646-2680 or 201/327-3500. Park admission during swim season ¢¢

James A McFaul Environmental Center. An 81-acre wildlife sanctuary including museum with natural history displays, lectures, film programs (Tues, Sat & Sun afternoons); woodland trail; waterfowl pond; picnic area. Arboretum and perennial gardens. (Daily; closed morning wkends & major hols) 3 mi NW off NJ 208 on Crescent Ave in Wyckoff. Phone 201/891-5571. **Free**

Motel

★★ **WELLESLEY INN.** *946 Rte 17N (07981). 201/934-9250; FAX 201/934-9719; res: 800/444-8888.* 89 rms, 3 story. S $80-$85; D $85-$94; each addl $5; under 18 free; wkend, monthly rates. Crib free. Pet accepted, some restrictions; $3. TV; cable (premium). Complimentary continental bkfst. Complimentary coffee in rms. Restaurant adj open 24 hrs. Ck-out 11 am. Business servs avail. Health club privileges. Refrigerators, microwaves avail. Cr cds: A, C, D, DS, ER, JCB, MC, V.

[symbols]

Motor Hotel

✓ ★★ **RAMADA INN.** *180 Rte 17S (07430), S of US 202 on NJ 17. 201/529-5880; FAX 201/529-4767; res: 800/272-6232.* 128 rms, 4 story. S, D $94-$121; each addl $10; suites $120-$190; under 16 free. Crib free. TV; cable (premium). Indoor pool. Restaurant 6:30 am-11 pm. Rm serv. Bar. Ck-out noon. Coin lndry. Meeting rms. Business servs avail. In-rm modem link. Valet serv. Sundries. Exercise equipt. Microwaves avail. Cr cds: A, C, D, DS, ER, JCB, MC, V.

[symbols]

Hotel

★★★ **SHERATON CROSSROADS HOTEL.** *1 International Blvd, Rte 17 (07495), jct I-87, I-287, NJ 17. 201/529-1660; FAX 201/529-4709; res: 800/325-3535.* 225 units, 14-22 story. S, D $150-$160; each addl $10; suites $260-$750; under 18 free; wkend rates. Crib free. Pet accepted, some restrictions. TV; cable (premium). Indoor pool. Restaurant 6:30 am-11 pm. Bar noon-2 am; entertainment exc Sun. Ck-out noon. Convention facilities. Business center. Concierge. Shopping arcade. Covered parking. Tennis. Exercise equipt; sauna. Refrigerators, microwaves avail. Luxury level. Cr cds: A, C, D, DS, ER, JCB, MC, V.

[symbols]

Restaurant

★★★ **CAFE PANACHE.** *130 E Main St (07446). 201/934-0030.* Hrs: noon-2 pm, 5-9 pm; Mon to 8 pm; Fri to 10 pm; Sat 5:30-10 pm. Closed Sun; also Easter, Dec 24, 25. Res accepted. French, northern Italian menu. Setups. Semi-a la carte: lunch $10-$16, dinner $22-$30. Own baking. Guitar, classical music Wed-Thurs. Parking. Totally nonsmoking. Cr cds: A, C, D, MC, V.

[symbol]

Red Bank (E-5)

Pop 10,636 **Elev** 35 ft **Area Code** 732 **Zip** 07701

Red Bank, a historic community on the shores of the Navesink River, includes a central business area with shops, restaurants, brokerage firms and an antique center.

What to See and Do

Allen House (ca 1750). Lower floor restored as tavern of the Revolutionary period; two upstairs galleries have historical exhibits. (Days same as Holmes House) 2 mi S on NJ 35, at jct Sycamore Ave in Shrewsbury. Phone 732/462-1466. ¢

Holmes-Hendrickson House (ca 1750). A 14-rm Dutch Colonial farmhouse with period furnishings. (May–Sept, Tues, Thurs, Sat & Sun afternoons; closed hols) Longstreet Rd in Holmdel, W on NJ 520. Phone 732/462-1466. ¢

Monmouth Museum. Changing exhibits of art, science, nature and cultural history; children's hands-on wing. (Daily exc Mon; closed hols) 5 mi W on Newman Springs Rd; on campus of Brookdale Community College in Lincroft. Phone 732/747-2266. ¢¢

Motel

★★ **COURTYARD BY MARRIOTT.** *245 Half Mile Rd (07701), off Garden State Pkwy exit 109. 732/530-5552; FAX 732/530-5756; res: 800/321-2211.* 146 rms, 3 story. S $119-$129; D $145-$155; wkend rates. Crib free. TV; cable (premium). Indoor pool; whirlpool. Complimentary coffee in rms. Restaurant 6:30-10 am, 6-10 pm. Bar 6-11 pm. Ck-out noon. Coin lndry. Meeting rms. Business servs avail. In-rm modem link. Valet serv. Exercise equipt. Some refrigerators; microwaves avail. Balconies. Cr cds: A, C, D, DS, MC, V.

[symbols]

Restaurants

★★★ **LA FROMAGERIE.** *26 Ridge Rd (07760), 7 mi E of Garden State Pkwy exit 109, east on Newman Springs Rd, turn left on Brood St, turn right on Harding Rd, 4 ½ mi on left. 732/842-8088.* Web www.fromagerierestaurant.com. Hrs: 11:30 am-2:30 pm, 5-10 pm; Fri to 11 pm; Sat 5-11 pm; Sun from 4 pm. Closed Dec 25. Res accepted. French menu. Bar. Wine cellar. Semi-a la carte: lunch $9.95-$13.95, dinner $24.50-$32.50. Specialties: smoked duck with baked lentils, grilled swordfish with roasted red pepper coulis, rack of lamb. Own baking. Valet parking. Family-owned. Jacket. Cr cds: A, C, D, MC, V.

[symbol]

★★★ **MOLLY PITCHER INN.** *88 Riverside Ave (07701), in Molly Pitcher Inn. 732/747-2500.* Web www.redbank.commollypitcher. Hrs: 6:30-10:30 am, 11:30 am-3 pm, 5-9 pm; Sat 8-10:30 am, 11:30 am-3 pm, 5-10 pm; Sun 8-10 am, 11 am-2:30 pm (brunch), 5-9 pm. Res accepted. Bar 11:30-2 am. Wine list. A la carte entrees: bkfst $2.95-$12.95, lunch $4.95-$12.95. Semi-a la carte: dinner $6-$30. Sun brunch $23.95. Child's meals. Specialties: Molly Pitcher chicken pot pie, crab cakes, coriander tuna. Pianist Fri-Sun. Elegant European decor with panoramic views of Navesink River. Jacket (dinner). Cr cds: A, C, D, MC, V.

[symbols]

★★★ **SHADOWBROOK.** *Rt 35S (07701), just off NJ 35, 2 mi SE of Garden State Pkwy exit 109. 732/747-0200.* E-mail shadowbrook@shadowbrook.com; Web www.shadowbrook.com. Hrs: 5:30-9 pm; Sat to 10 pm; Sun 3-9 pm. Closed Mon; Dec 24. Res accepted. Bar. Semi-a la carte: dinner $20-$33. Child's meals. Specialties: seafood Fra Diavolo, rack of lamb, veal Francaise. Valet parking. Fireplace; in Georgian mansion; Victorian antiques. Formal gardens. Family-owned. Jacket. Cr cds: A, C, D, MC, V.

[symbols]

★★★ **THE RAVEN & THE PEACH.** *740 River Rd (07704), exit 109 from Garden State Pkwy to Half-Mile Rd to West Front St into River Rd. 732/747-4666.* Hrs: 11:30 am-2:30 pm, 5:30-10 pm; Fri, Sat to 11 pm. Closed Dec 25. Res accepted. Contemporary French menu. Bar. Wine cellar. A la carte entrees: lunch $8.50-$15.50, dinner $22.50-$31.50. Child's meals. Specialties: seasame-roasted rack of lamb, black-peppered seared sushi, tuna. Piano Wed-Sun. Valet parking. Outdoor dining. Modern French atmosphere. Cr cds: A, C, MC, V.

Ringwood State Park (B-5)

(See also Wayne)

(On the New Jersey, New York border)

Ringwood State Park lies in upper Passaic County, near the town of Ringwood, within the heart of the Ramapo Mountains. Consisting of 6,196 acres, the park is reached by Rte 23 and 511 from the west and Rte 17 and Sloatsburg Rd from the east.

Ringwood Manor Section. This section features a 51-rm mansion containing a collection of Americana; relics of iron-making days (1740); formal gardens. Interpretive tours. Fishing in Ringwood River. Picnic facilities nearby. Tours (Wed–Sun).

Shepherd Lake Section. A 541-acre wooded area has trap and skeet shooting all year (fee). The 74-acre Shepherd Lake provides a swimming beach and bathhouse; fishing; boating (ramp). Also available is picnicking (tables & grills).

Skylands Section. Located here is a 44-rm mansion modeled after an English baronial house (open to the public on select days). The gardens (90 acres) surrounding the manor house comprise the only botanical garden in the state park system (guided tours upon request, phone 973/962-7527). This 1,119-acre section also offers fishing, hunting. Hiking; mountain biking.

Standard fees are charged for each section Memorial Day-Labor Day. Phone 973/962-7031.

Rockaway (B-4)

Pop 6,243 **Elev** 534 ft **Area Code** 973 **Zip** 07866

Motels

★★ **HOWARD JOHNSON INN.** *14 Green Pond Rd (07866), I-80 exit 37, left.* 973/625-1200; FAX 973/625-1686. Web www.hojo.com. 64 rms, 2 story. S, D $79-$99; each addl $10. Crib free. TV; cable (premium). Pool; wading pool. Complimentary continental bkfst (Mon-Fri). Restaurant 6:30-2 am. Rm serv. Bar. Ck-out noon. Business servs avail. Some refrigerators; microwaves avail. Balconies. Cr cds: A, C, D, DS, MC, V.

[D] [icons] SC

★ **MOUNTAIN INN OF ROCKAWAY.** *156 US Hwy 46 (07866), approx 3 mi off I-80 exit 42W.* 973/627-8310; FAX 973/627-0556; res: 800/537-3732. 86 rms, 2 story, 16 kits. (no ovens). S, D $50-$85; each addl $5; kit. units $85; under 12 free; wkend rates. Crib free. TV. Pool. Complimentary continental bkfst. Restaurant 5-11 pm. Bar. Ck-out 11 am. Coin lndry. Meeting rms. Business servs avail. Valet serv. Cr cds: A, C, D, DS, MC, V.

[D] [icons] SC

Rutherford (C-5)

Pop 17,790 **Elev** 100 ft **Area Code** 201

What to See and Do

Fairleigh Dickinson University–Rutherford Campus (1942). (2,300 students) On campus is the Kingsland House (1670), in which George Washington stayed in August 1783; and the Castle, an 1888 copy of Chateau d'Amboise in France. W Passaic & Montross Aves. Phone 201/692-7032.

Professional sports.

NBA (New Jersey Nets). Continental Airlines Arena, 50 NJ 120 in East Rutherford. Phone 201/935-8888.

NHL (New Jersey Devils). Continental Airlines Arena, 50 NJ 120 in East Rutherford. Phone 201/935-6050.

Motel

★★ **QUALITY INN.** *10 Polito Ave (07071), jct NJ 3 & NJ 17, Lyndhurst Serv Rd exit off NJ 17S.* 201/933-9800; FAX 201/933-0658; res: 800/468-3588. 150 rms, 2 story. S $59-$89; D $65-$99; each addl $6; under 18 free; wkend rates. Crib free. TV; cable (premium), VCR (movies). Pool; lifeguard. Restaurant 6:30 am-10 pm. Rm serv. Bar 11-2 am. Ck-out noon. Coin lndry. Meeting rms. Business servs avail. In-rm modem link. Sundries. Airport transportation. Exercise equipt. Health club privileges. Microwaves avail. Stadium, racetrack opp. Cr cds: A, C, D, DS, ER, JCB, MC, V.

[D] [icons] SC

Motor Hotel

★★ **FAIRFIELD INN.** *850 Rte 120 Patterson Plank Rd (07073), on NJ 120, ¼ mi E of NJ 17.* 201/507-5222; FAX 201/507-0744; res: 800/228-2800. Web www.marriott.com/fairfieldinn. 140 rms, 5 story. S, D $89-$110. Crib avail. TV; cable (premium). Ck-out noon. Meeting rm. Business servs avail. In-rm modem link. Exercise equipt. Refrigerators avail. Cr cds: A, C, D, DS, MC, V.

[D] [icons] SC

Hotels

★★ **NOVOTEL MEADOWLANDS HOTEL.** *1 Polito Ave (07071), NJ 17S.* 201/896-6666; FAX 201/896-1309; res: 800/882-3252; res: 800/668-6735. E-mail meadmail@aol.com; Web www.novotel.com. 219 rms, 6 story. S $169; D $179; each addl $10; under 18 free; family, wkend, hol rates. Crib free. Pet accepted, some restrictions. TV; cable (premium). Complimentary coffee in lobby. Restaurant 6:30 am-midnight. Bar 5 pm-1 am. Ck-out 1 pm. Meeting rms. Business center. In-rm modem link. Coin lndry. Exercise rm; sauna. Health club privileges. Indoor pool; whirlpool. Refrigerators, microwaves avail. Cr cds: A, C, D, DS, ER, JCB, MC, V.

[D] [icons] SC

★★★ **SHERATON MEADOWLANDS HOTEL.** *2 Meadowlands Plz (07073), ¼ mi E of NJ Tpke exit 16W, opp Meadowlands Sports Complex.* 201/896-0500; FAX 201/896-9696; res: 800/325-3535. E-mail edgar.lagos@ittsheraton.com; Web www.ittsheraton.com. 425 units, 21 story. S, D $130-$189; each addl $20; suites $250-$600; under 18 free; wkend rates. Crib free. Pet accepted, some restrictions. TV; cable (premium), VCR avail. Indoor pool; whirlpool, poolside serv. Restaurant 6:30 am-11 pm. Bars noon-2 am. Ck-out 1 pm. Convention facilities. Business center. In-rm modem link. Concierge. Gift shop. Exercise equipt; sauna. Bathrm phone, wet bar in suites. Cr cds: A, C, D, DS, ER, MC, V.

[D] [icons] SC

Restaurants

★★ **ROMANISSIMO.** *1 Hoboken Rd (07073), NJ 17S exit Paterson Plank Rd, follow signs.* 201/939-1128. Hrs: 11:30 am-11 pm; Sat 5 pm-midnight; Sun 2-10 pm. Res accepted. Country Italian menu. Bar. A la carte entrees: lunch $10.95-$14.95, dinner $12.95-$20. Specializes in rabbit, seafood. Singer Fri, Sat. Valet parking. Glass enclosed patio. Contemporary decor. Cr cds: A, C, D, MC, V.

★★★ **SONOMA GRILL.** *64 Hoboken Rd (07073).* 201/507-8989. Hrs: 11:30 am-2:30 pm, 5-10 pm; Fri to 11 pm; Sat 5-11 pm. Closed Sun; some major hols. Res accepted. Bar. Wine cellar. A la carte entrees:

lunch $7.95-$15.95, dinner $8.95-$29.95. Specialties: grilled fresh tuna with black olives, grilled marinated pork chop on Chinese noodles, grilled certified California grill-style, one antique with stained glass and tin ceiling. Cr cds: A, C, D, MC, V.

D

Saddle Brook (B-5)

Pop 13,296 **Elev** 90 ft **Area Code** 201 **Zip** 07663

Motor Hotel

★★ **RAMADA INN.** *375 W Passaic St (07662), at Garden State Pkwy exit 160N.* 201/845-3400; FAX 201/845-0412; res: 800/344-7666. 173 rms, 5 story. S $95-$119; D $105-$135; each addl $10; suites $150; wkend rates. Crib free. TV; cable. Indoor pool. Restaurant 6:30 am-11 pm; wkends from 7 am. Rm serv. Bar 11-2 am; entertainment Thurs-Sat. Ck-out noon. Coin lndry. Meeting rms. Business servs avail. Valet serv. Sundries. Exercise equipt. Cr cds: A, C, D, DS, ER, JCB, MC, V.

D ⟰ 🏃 ⟱ 🔥 SC

Hotels

★★ **HOLIDAY INN & CONFERENCE CENTER.** *50 Kenney Pl (07663), at jct Garden State Pkwy exit 159, I-80 exit 62.* 201/843-0600; FAX 201/843-2822; res: 800/465-4329. E-mail hisb201@aol.com. 144 rms, 12 story. S, D $119-$149; each addl $10; under 18 free; wkend rates. Crib free. TV; cable (premium). Pool. Coffee in rms. Restaurant 6:30 am-10 pm, wkends from 7 am. Bar 11 am-midnight. Ck-out noon. Meeting rms. Business servs avail. In-rm modem link. Exercise equipt. Cr cds: A, C, D, DS, MC, V.

D ⟰ 🏃 ⟱ 🔥 SC

★★★ **MARRIOTT HOTEL.** *Garden State Pkwy & I-80 (07663), Garden State Pkwy exit 159.* 201/843-9500; FAX 201/843-7760; res: 800/228-9290. 221 rms, 12 story. S, D $130; suites $300-$450; wkend rates. Crib free. TV; cable (premium). 2 pools, 1 indoor; whirlpool, poolside serv, lifeguard. Restaurant 6:30 am-10 pm; Fri, Sat to 11 pm; Sun 7 am-10 pm. Bar 11:30-1 am. Ck-out noon. Meeting rms. Business center. Free parking. Exercise equipt; sauna. Refrigerators avail. Cr cds: A, C, D, DS, ER, JCB, MC, V.

D ⟰ 🏃 ⟱ 🔥 SC 🏃

Salem (H-1)

(See also Wilmington, DE)

Founded ca 1675 **Pop** 6,883 **Elev** 19 ft **Area Code** 609 **Zip** 08079
Information Salem County Chamber of Commerce, 104 Market St; 609/935-1415

Salem is said to be the oldest English settlement on the Delaware River. The town and its surrounding area have more than sixty 18th-century houses and buildings, as well as many points of historical interest. In the Friends Burying Ground on Broadway is the 600-year-old Salem Oak, under which John Fenwick, the town's founder, signed a treaty with the Lenni-Lenape tribe.

What to See and Do

Alexander Grant House (1721). Headquarters of Salem County Historical Society. Twenty rooms with period furniture; Wistarburg glass; Native American relics; dolls; paintings; genealogy library; stone barn. (Tues–Fri afternoons; also open 2nd Sat afternoon of each month) 79–83 Market St. Phone 609/935-5004. ¢¢

Fort Mott State Park. A 104-acre park at Finns Point; established in 1837 as a defense of the port of Philadelphia. North of the park is Finns Point National Cemetery, where more than 2,500 Union and Confederate soldiers are buried. Fishing; boating. Picnicking, playground; overlook. Ft Mott Rd. Phone 609/935-3218.

Seasonal Event

Cowtown Rodeo. 12 mi NE on NJ 45, then 3 mi W on US 40, near Woodstown. PRCA sanctioned. Phone 609/769-3200. Sat evenings, late May–mid-Sept.

Inn

✓★ **BROWNS HISTORIC HOME BED & BREAKFAST.** *41 Market St (08079).* 609/935-8595. 6 rms, 3 with bath, 2 story. S $65; D $95; kit. unit $200-$300/wk. Adults only. TV; cable (premium). Complimentary full bkfst. Restaurant nearby. Ck-out noon, ck-in 2 pm. Business servs avail. Health club privileges. Refrigerators. Pre-revolutionary house (pre-1738) in historic district. Totally nonsmoking. Cr cds: A, C, DS, MC, V.

⟱ 🔥 SC

Sandy Hook

(see Gateway National Recreation Area)

Scotch Plains (C-4)

(See also Plainfield)

Settled 1684 **Pop** 21,160 **Elev** 119 ft **Area Code** 908 **Zip** 07076

What to See and Do

Watchung Reservation. A 2,000-wooded-acre reservation in the Watchung Mts including the 25-acre Surprise Lake. Nature trails, bridle trails. Ice-skating. Picnic areas, playground. Ten-acre nursery and rhododendron display garden. 1 mi NE. Phone 908/527-4900. Also here is

Trailside Nature and Science Center. Nature exhibits; special programs; planetarium shows (Sun; separate shows for preschoolers; fee). Museum (late Mar–mid-Nov, daily; rest of yr, wkends only; closed some hols). Visitor Center with live reptile exhibit (daily, afternoons). Gift shop. Grounds (daily). 452 New Providence Rd in Mountainside. Phone 908/789-3670. **Free**

Motel

★★ **BEST WESTERN WESTFIELD INN.** *435 North Ave W (07090), 3½ mi W on NJ 28; W of Garden State Pkwy exit 137.* 908/654-5600; FAX 908/654-6483; res: 800/688-5454. 40 rms, 3 story, 15 kits. S $98-$125; D $108-$135; each addl $10; kit. units $112-$125; under 18 free. Crib free. TV; cable (premium). Complimentary continental bkfst. Restaurant noon-10 pm. Ck-out 11 am. Coin lndry. Meeting rm. Valet serv. Health club privileges. Cr cds: A, C, D, DS, MC, V.

D ⟱ 🔥 SC

Restaurant

★★★ **STAGE HOUSE INN.** *366 Park Ave (07076). 908/322-4224.* E-mail stageinn@aol.com; Web www.stagehouseinn.com. Hrs: 11:30 am-2:30 pm, 5:30-10 pm; Sun 4-8 pm. Closed Mon; Dec 25. Bar. A la carte entrees: lunch $8-$18, dinner $21-$29. Specialties: charlotte of Maine crab, pan roasted cod with crispy potatoes, peas & black truffle sauce. Outdoor dining. Cr cds: A, C, D, DS, MC, V.

Seaside Park (F-5)

Pop 1,871 **Elev** 6 ft **Area Code** 732 **Zip** 08752

What to See and Do

Island Beach State Park. This strip of land (3,002 acres) is across the water, N of Long Beach Island (see) and faces Barnegat Lighthouse. There are two natural areas (Northern Area and Southern Area) and a recreational zone in the center. Excellent swimming and fishing in Atlantic Ocean (seasonal). Nature tours. Picnicking. (Daily) Standard fees. S on Central Ave. Phone 732/793-0506.

Motel

★★ **WINDJAMMER MOTOR INN.** *1st Ave & Central Ave (08752). 732/830-2555.* 39 rms, 3 story, 24 kits. June-Sept: S, D $95-$130; each addl $10; kit. units $130; lower rates rest of yr. Crib $5. TV; cable. Heated pool; poolside serv. Restaurant 8 am-7 pm. Bar from 11 am. Ck-out 11 am. Coin lndry. Beach privileges. Cr cds: A, C, MC, V.

Secaucus (C-5)

Pop 14,061 **Elev** 12 ft **Area Code** 201

Motor Hotel

★★ **HOLIDAY INN HARMON MEADOW.** *300 Plaza Dr (07094). 201/348-2000; FAX 201/348-6035; res: 800/465-4329; res: 800/222-2676.* 160 rms, 8 story. S, D $115-$170; each addl $10; suites $175-$225; under 18 free; wkend, monthly rates. Crib free. TV; cable (premium). Valet parking $3. Restaurant 7 am-11 pm. Rm serv. Bar. Ck-out noon. Coin lndry. Meeting rms. In-rm modem link. Bellhops. Gift shop. Exercise equipt. Refrigerators. Health club privileges. Luxury level. Cr cds: A, C, D, DS, JCB, MC, V.

Hotels

★★ **CROWNE PLAZA.** *2 Harmon Plz (07094), NJ Tpke exit 16W, Meadowlands Pkwy. 201/348-6900; FAX 201/348-4436; res: 800/445-8667.* Web www.bristolhotel.com. 301 rms, 14 story. S, D $109-$169; each addl $10; suites $190-$350; family, wkend rates. Crib free. TV; cable (premium). Pool; whirlpool; poolside serv. Coffee in rms. Restaurant 6:30 am-11 pm; Sat, Sun from 7 am. Bars 11-2 am. Ck-out 11 am. Convention facilities. Business servs avail. In-rm modem link. Concierge. Gift shop. Valet parking avail. Exercise equipt; sauna. Some refrigerators; microwaves avail. Cr cds: A, C, D, DS, MC, V.

★★★ **EMBASSY SUITES.** *455 Plz Dr (07094). 201/864-7300; FAX 201/864-5391; res: 800/362-2779.* Web www.promus.comm. 261 suites, 9 story. S, D $199-$259; each addl $25; under 12 free; wkend rates. Crib free. TV; cable (premium), VCR avail. Indoor pool. Complimentary full bkfst. Restaurant 11:30 am-10 pm. Bar noon-midnight. Ck-out noon. Coin lndry. Meeting rms. Business center. In-rm modem link. Gift shop. Airport transportation. Exercise equipt; sauna. Health club privileges. Refrigerators, microwaves. Cr cds: A, C, D, DS, ER, JCB, MC, V.

★★★ **RADISSON.** *350 Rte 3W (07102). 201/863-8700; FAX 201/863-6209; res: 800/654-2000; res: 800/624-8631.* Web www.radisson.com. 151 suites, 9 story. S $179-$239; D $189-$249; under 12 free; wkend, monthly rates. Crib avail. Pet accepted, some restrictions. TV; cable (premium), VCR avail. Complimentary coffee in rms. Restaurant 7 am-10 pm. Bar noon-midnight. Ck-out noon. Meeting rms. Business servs avail. In-rm modem link. Coin lndry. Airport, RR station transportation. Exercise equipt. Health club privileges. Indoor pool. Refrigerators, wet bars; microwaves avail. Cr cds: A, C, D, DS, JCB, MC, V.

★★★ **RAMADA SUITE HOTEL LINCOLN HARBOR.** *500 Harbor Blvd (07087). 201/617-5600; FAX 201/617-5627; res: 800/272-6232; res: 800/831-6262.* Web www.ramada.com. 244 suites, 10 story. Mar-Dec: S $189-$279; D $209-$269; each addl $20; under 18 free; family rates; package plans; lower rates rest of yr. Crib free. Pet accepted. TV; cable (premium), VCR avail. Complimentary continental bkfst. Complimentary coffee in rms. Restaurant 11:30 am-10 pm. Rm serv from 7 am. Bar from noon. Ck-out noon. Meeting rms. Business center. In-rm modem link. Concierge. Gift shop. Exercise equipt. Indoor pool. Refrigerators, microwaves, wet bars. On river. Cr cds: A, C, D, DS, ER, JCB, MC, V.

Ship Bottom

(see Long Beach Island)

Somerset

(see New Brunswick)

Somerville (D-4)

(See also New Brunswick)

Pop 11,632 **Elev** 54 ft **Area Code** 908 **Zip** 08876 **Web** www.somersetcountychamber.org

Information Somerset County Chamber of Commerce, 64 W End Ave, PO Box 833; 908/725-1552

What to See and Do

Duke Gardens. Features 11 gardens under glass, including colonial, desert, Italian, Oriental, English and tropical (closed Jan 1, Thanksgiving, Dec 25); 45-min guided tour (Oct–May, daily). No high heels, no cameras. On US 206, about 1¼ mi S of Somerville Circle. Res required; contact Duke Gardens Foundation (Mon–Fri), Phone 908/722-3700. ¢¢-¢¢¢

Golf House-USGA Museum and Library. Georgian colonial mansion originally designed as private residence by John Russel Pope, now houses exhibits tracing the evolution of golf. Equipment and artifacts donated by golf's greatest champions, including Bobby Jones, Byron Nelson, Jack Nicklaus and Arnold Palmer. Interactive displays. Library with over 10,000 volumes on golf. USGA Research and Test Center, featuring the USGA's ball-testing robot "Iron Byron," is adj. (Daily; closed Jan 1, Easter, Thanksgiving, Dec 25) US 287 to Rte 512, in Far Hills. Phone 800/223-0041. **Free**

Old Dutch Parsonage State Historic Site (1751). Moved from its original location, this brick building was the home of the Rev Jacob Hardenbergh from 1758 to 1781. He founded Queens College, now Rutgers University, while residing in this building. Some furnishings and memorabilia on display. (Wed–Sun; closed hols; hrs may vary) Phone 908/725-1015.

Wallace House State Historic Site. General and Mrs. Washington made their headquarters here immediately after the house was built in 1778, while the army was stationed at Camp Middlebrook. Period furnishings. (Wed–Sun; closed hols; hrs may vary) Phone 908/725-1015.

Annual Event

IBM/USET Festival of Champions. Hamilton Farm, 10 mi N on US 206 in Bedminster. Competition of 3 Olympic equestrian disciplines. Phone 908/234-1251. Mid- or late June.

Motel

★ **DAYS INN EXECUTIVE.** *118 US Hwy 206 (08876), 3 mi S on US 206.* 908/685-9000; FAX 908/685-0601; res: 800/329-7466. 100 rms, 2 story. S, D $100-$150; each addl $5; suites $125-$175; under 17 free. Crib free. TV; cable. Complimentary continental bkfst. Ck-out 11 am. In-rm modem link. Valet serv. Pool. Exercise equipt. Some refrigerators; microwaves avail. Cr cds: A, C, D, DS, MC, V.

D ⌖ 🐾 🖼 🔥 SC

Restaurants

★ **A LA PIETRA.** *1979 Washington Valley Rd (08836), 3 mi N on NJ 525.* 732/469-9040. Hrs: 11 am-3 pm, 5-10 pm; Sat from 5 pm; Sun from 4 pm. Closed Mon; also Jan 1, Thanksgiving, Dec 25. Res accepted Fri, Sat. Italian menu. Semi-a la carte: lunch $7-$10, dinner $10-$20. Child's meals. Specializes in pasta, veal, chicken. Trattoria atmosphere. Cr cds: A, C, D, MC, V.

D 🖼

★★★ **RYLAND INN.** *US 22W (08888), 8 mi W on US 22 from Somerville Circle.* 908/534-4011. Web www.powerpg.com/njl1/ryland. Dine in one of five dining rooms of this 200-year-old Victorian manor house set on 55 sweeping acres complete with a six-acre vegetable garden. Contemporary French menu. Specialties: veal chop with asparagus and morels, warm lobster tarte, grilled foie gras with banyuls sauce. Hrs: 11:30 am-2 pm, 5:30-9 pm; Fri to 10 pm; Sat 5:30-10 pm; Sun 4-9 pm. Closed Mon; also 1st wk in Jan. Res accepted. Bar. Wine cellar. A la carte entrees: lunch $13-$16, dinner $26-$36. Eight-course tasting menu: dinner $85. Valet parking. Cigar rm. Organic garden. Jacket. Cr cds: A, C, D, DS, MC, V.

D 🖼

Spring Lake (E-5)

(See also Asbury Park)

Pop 3,499 **Elev** 25 ft **Area Code** 732 **Zip** 07762

Motels

★ **BELMAR MOTOR LODGE.** *910 State Rte 35 10th Ave (34222), 1 mi N on NJ 35.* 732/681-6600. 55 rms, 2 story. Memorial Day-Labor Day: S, D $88-$115; each addl $10; under 14 free; higher rates hols

(3-day min); lower rates rest of yr. Crib $3. TV; cable (premium). Pool. Restaurant adj open 24 hrs. Ck-out 11 am. Coin lndry. Opp Belmar Marine Basin. Cr cds: A, C, D, MC, V.

🏊 🖼 🔥 SC

★ **COMFORT INN.** *1909 Hwy 35 (07719), Garden State Pkwy exit 98.* 732/449-6146; FAX 732/449-6556; res: 800/638-7949. 70 rms, 2 story. Mid-June-Labor Day: S, D $96.25-$175; each addl $10; suites from $150; lower rates rest of yr. Crib $5. TV. Pool; lifeguard. Complimentary continental bkfst. Meeting rm. Business servs avail. In-rm modem link. Exercise equipt. Refrigerator, microwave in suites. Cr cds: A, C, D, DS, ER, JCB, MC, V.

D 🏊 🐾 🖼 🔥 SC

★ **DOOLANS MOTOR LODGE.** *700 Hwy 71 (07762), 4 mi E of Garden State Pkwy exit 98.* 732/449-3666; FAX 732/449-2601. 60 rms, 3 story. Memorial Day-Labor Day: S, D $80-$150; each addl $15; lower rates rest of yr. Crib $5. TV; cable (premium). Pool; lifeguard. Complimentary continental bkfst. Restaurant 8-10 am, noon-3 pm, 4:30-10 pm; closed for lunch Sat. Bar; entertainment Wed-Sun. Ck-out 11 am. Meeting rms. Cr cds: A, C, D, DS, MC, V.

D 🏊 🔥

★ **MARINER'S COVE MOTOR INN.** *50 Broadway (08742), NJ 35S.* 732/899-0060; FAX 732/701-0260. 24 rms, 2 story. Memorial Day-Labor Day: S, D $122-$160; each addl $15; under 16 free; family rates; package plans; wkends, hols (2-3 day min). TV; cable. Restaurant adj 6 am-9 pm. Ck-out 11 am, ck-in 2 pm. Pool. Refrigerators. Cr cds: A, C, MC, V.

🏊 🔥

★ **POINT BEACH MOTEL.** *Ocean Ave & Trenton Ave (08742), Garden State Parkway exit 98.* 732/892-5100. 24 rms, 2 story. July-Labor Day: S, D $129-$160; each addl $10; under 8 free; higher rates hols; lower rates rest of yr. Closed Oct-Apr. Crib $10. TV; cable. Heated pool; wading pool. Ck-out 11 am. Refrigerators; microwaves avail. Opp Atlantic Ocean. Cr cds: C, DS, MC, V.

D 🏊 🔥

★ **TRAVELODGE.** *1916 Hwy 35 (07719), 2 mi W on Rte 524, then N on NJ 35.* 732/974-8400; FAX 732/974-8401; res: 800/578-7878. 52 rms, 2 with shower only. S $44-$124; D $54-$159; each addl $5-$10; under 16 free; higher rates some hol wkends. Crib free. TV; cable (premium). Pool. Complimentary continental bkfst. Complimentary coffee in rms. Ck-out 11 am. Business servs avail. Refrigerators. Cr cds: A, C, D, DS, MC, V.

D 🏊 🖼 🔥 SC

Hotels

★★ **BREAKERS HOTEL.** *1507 Ocean Ave (07762).* 732/449-7700; FAX 732/449-0161. Web www.breakershotel.com. 67 units. Mid-June-Labor Day (hol wkends 5-day min): S, D $160-$320; each addl $30; lower rates rest of yr. Crib free. TV. Pool; whirlpool, poolside serv, lifeguard. Restaurant 8 am-4 pm, 4:30-10 pm. Ck-out noon. Meeting rms. Business servs avail. Refrigerators. Restored Victorian oceanfront hotel. Cr cds: A, C, D, MC, V.

🏊 🔥

★★★ **HEWITT WELLINGTON HOTEL.** *200 Monmouth Ave (07762).* 732/974-1212; FAX 732/974-2338. 29 rms, 3 story, 17 suites. Late June-Labor Day: S, D $140-$250; each addl $40; suites $210-$270; wkly rates; higher rates: wkends (2-day min), hols (3-day min); lower rates rest of yr. Children over 12 yrs only. TV; cable. Heated pool. Coffee in rms. Restaurant 5:30-11 pm. Ck-out 11 am. Meeting rm. Business servs avail. In-rm modem link. Refrigerators. Some balconies. On lake. Renovated Victorian hotel (1880). Cr cds: A, C, DS, MC, V.

🏊 🔥 SC

Inns

★ ★ **ASHLING COTTAGE.** *106 Sussex Ave (07762), Garden State Parkway exit 98.* 732/449-3553; FAX 732/974-0831; res: 800/274-5464; res: 888/274-5464. E-mail ashling@lonekeep.com; Web www.bbianj.com/ashling. 10 rms, 2 share bath, 3 story. No rm phones. Mid-June-mid-Sept (2-day min): S $98-$169; D $103-$174; hols (3-night min); lower rates Apr-mid-June & mid-Sept-Dec; closed rest of yr. TV in lobby, VCR avail (movies). Complimentary full bkfst. Restaurant nearby. Ck-out 11 am, ck-in 1 pm. Business servs avail. Concierge serv. Free RR station, bus depot transportation. Bicycles. Picnic tables. Victorian-style frame house (1877). Antiques. Totally nonsmoking. Cr cds: C.

★ ★ ★ **BAY HEAD GABLES.** *200 Main Ave (08742), S on NJ 35.* 732/892-9844; FAX 732/295-2196; res: 800/984-9536. E-mail bhgables@monmouth.com; Web www.bayheadgables.com. 11 rms, 3 story. June-Labor Day: S $110-$165; D $120-$175; wkly rates; higher rates wkends (2-3-day min); open wkends only Apr-June & Labor Day-Dec. Closed rest of yr. TV in sitting rm; cable. Complimentary full bkfst. Restaurant nearby. Ck-out 11 am, ck-in 1 pm. Designed by Stanford White in 1914. Totally nonsmoking. Cr cds: A, C, DS, MC, V.

★ ★ ★ **CHATEAU INN.** *500 Warren Ave & 5th Ave (07762).* 732/974-2000; FAX 732/974-0007. Web www.chateauinn.com. 38 rms, 2 story. Late June-Labor Day: S $109-$225; D $150-$165; each addl $15; suites $190-$225; lower rates rest of yr. TV; cable (premium), VCR (movies). Beach, pool privileges. Meeting rm. Business servs avail. Health club privileges. Bicycles. Refrigerators; some fireplaces; microwaves avail. Private patios. Renovated Victorian hotel (1888). Overlooks parks, lake. Cr cds: A, C, D, DS, MC, V.

★ ★ **INN AT THE SHORE.** *301 4th Ave (07719), 1 mi N on NJ 35.* 732/681-3762; FAX 201/945-2944. E-mail tomvolker@aol.com; Web www.bbianj.com/innattheshore. 12 rms, 9 share baths. May-Sept: S, D $65-$125; each addl $20; under 12 free; wkly rates; lower rates rest of yr. Crib free. Complimentary continental bkfst. Restaurant nearby. Ck-out noon, ck-in 2 pm. Luggage handling. Refrigerator, microwave avail. Victorian-style ambience in house built in 1888; many antiques. Cr cds: A, C, MC, V.

★ ★ **NORMANDY INN.** *21 Tuttle Ave (07762), Garden State Pkwy exit 98.* 732/449-7172; FAX 732/449-1070; res: 800/449-1888. E-mail normandy@bellatlantic.net; Web www.normandyinn.com. 19 rms, 3 story. June-Sept: S $98-$190; D $131-$315; each addl $20; lower rates rest of yr. Crib avail. TV avail; VCR avail. Complimentary full bkfst. Business servs avail. Bicycles. Some fireplaces. Porches. Built as private residence in 1888; 19th-century antiques. Cr cds: A, C, D, DS, MC, V.

★ ★ **THE SANDPIPER INN.** *7 Atlantic Ave (07762).* 732/449-6060; FAX 732/449-8409; res: 800/824-2779. E-mail ubhappy@cyber comm.net; Web www.sandpiperinn.com. 15 rms, 8 with shower only, 4 story. Mid-June-early Sept: S, D $175-$250; each addl $50; lower rates rest of yr. Children over 16 yrs only. TV; cable. Indoor pool. Complimentary continental bkfst; afternoon refreshments. Dining rm (see SANDPIPER). Ck-out noon, ck-in 2 pm. Business servs avail. Refrigerators. Opp beach. Victorian inn built 1888; casual atmosphere in elegant surroundings. Cr cds: C, DS, MC, V.

★ ★ **WHITE LILAC INN.** *414 Central Ave (07762).* 732/449-0211. Web www.whitelilac.com. 10 rms, 2 share bath, 2½ story. No rm phones. S, D $99-$159; wkly rates; wkends (2-day min); hols (3-day min). Closed Jan. Children over 14 yrs only. TV in some rms; cable (premium).

Complimentary full bkfst. Ck-out 11 am, ck-in 2 pm. Free RR station transportation. Some fireplaces. Southern accent; built in 1880. Cr cds: A, C, DS, MC, V.

Restaurants

★ ★ ★ **DEGUSTARE.** *1969 NJ 34S (07719), on NJ 34S exit 98 from Parkway S.* 732/974-0606. Hrs: 11:30 am-10 pm; Fri to 11 pm; Sat 5-11 pm; Sun 10:30 am-9 pm; Sun brunch 10:30 am-2:30 pm. Closed Dec 25. Res accepted. Contemporary Amer menu. Setups. A la carte entrees: lunch $5.95-$10.95, dinner $14.95-$24.95. Lunch buffet $9.50. Sun brunch $17.95. Child's meals. Specialties: veal osso bucco, potato-crusted Chilean sea bass, Australian herb crusted rack of lamb. Jazz, piano Thurs-Sun. Valet parking. Sushi bar. Cigars. Cr cds: A, C, DS, MC, V.

✓ ★ **FAMILY TREE TAVERN.** *2420 Highway 35 (08736), 3 mi S on NJ 35.* 732/528-5950. Hrs: 11:30 am-11 pm. Continental menu. Bar to 2 am. Semi-a la carte: lunch $3-$7.95, dinner $11.95-$17.95. Child's meals. Specialties: coconut shrimp, chicken Elizabeth, tournedos Diane. Pianist Fri, Sat evenings. Casual, family atmosphere. Cr cds: A, C, D, DS, MC, V.

★ ★ **HEAT WAVE CAFE.** *513 Main St (08742).* 732/714-8881. Hrs: 5-10 pm. Closed Mon; Jan 1, Thanksgiving, Dec 25. Res accepted. A la carte entrees: dinner $18.95-$25.95. Street parking. Outdoor dining. Totally nonsmoking. Cr cds: A, C, DS, MC, V.

★ ★ **MARLINS CAFE.** *1901 Ocean Ave (08742), NJ 35 S to Point Pleasant Beach in Bay Head.* 732/714-8035. Hrs: noon-2 am; early-bird dinner 4-7 pm (Mon-Fri). Continental, Amer menu. Bar. Semi-a la carte: lunch $4.95-$19.95, dinner $7.95-$19.95. Specialty: Chilean sea bass. Own baking. Child's meals. Parking. Cr cds: A, C, MC, V.

★ ★ ★ **OLD MILL INN.** *Old Mill Rd (07762), Garden State Pkwy exit 98.* 732/449-1800. Web www.powerpg.com/nji/oldmill. Hrs: 11:30 am-10 pm; Fri, Sat to 11 pm; Sun to 9 pm; early-bird dinner Mon-Fri 2:30-6 pm; Sun brunch 11 am-3 pm. Closed Dec 24; Mon (Sept-May). Res accepted. Bar. Semi-a la carte: lunch $6.95-$14.95, dinner $18.95-$35.95. Sun brunch $9.95-$19.95. Child's meals. Specializes in seafood, steak. Own baking. Entertainment Fri, Sat. Valet parking. Outdoor dining. Lakeside view. Cr cds: A, C, D, MC, V.

✓ ★ ★ **SANDPIPER.** *(See The Sandpiper Inn)* 732/449-4700. Hrs: 11:30 am-3 pm, 5-11 pm; early-bird dinner to 6:30 pm; Sun brunch 11 am-2 pm. Res accepted. American contemporary menu. Setups. Semi-a la carte: lunch $6.50-$9.50, dinner $13.95-$22.95. Complete meals: lunch $6.50-$11.95, dinner $13.95-$21.95. Sun brunch $14.95. Child's meals. Specialties: pistachio-encrusted halibut, chicken and shrimp forestiere. Own baking. Pianist Sat. Candlelit dining in Victorian setting. Cr cds: C, D, MC, V.

★ ★ **TESAURO'S.** *401 Broadway (08742), NJ 35 to Broadway.* 732/892-2090. Hrs: 4:30-10 pm; early-bird dinner 4:30-7 pm (seasonal, Tues-Thurs). Closed Mon; also Thanksgiving, Dec 25. Res accepted. Italian menu. Bar. A la carte entrees: dinner $10.50-$17.95. Specialties: veal saltimbocca, chicken & sausage, lobster & shrimp fra'diavolo. Guitarist Fri, Sat. Valet parking. Outdoor dining. Family-owned since 1967. Festive atmosphere. Fireplace. Cr cds: A, C, D, MC, V.

Stanhope (B-4)

(See also Lake Hoptacong, Rockaway)

Pop 3,393 **Elev** 882 ft **Area Code** 973 **Zip** 07874

What to See and Do

Waterloo Village Restoration. Known as the Andover Forge during the Revolutionary War, it was once a busy town on the Morris Canal. The 18th-century buildings include Stagecoach Inn, houses and craft barns, grist mill, apothecary shop, general store. Music festival during summer (fee). (Mid-Apr–mid-Nov, Wed–Sun; closed Thanksgiving, Dec 25) I-80 exit 25; follow signs. Phone 973/347-0900. ¢¢¢

Inns

★★ **CROSSED KEYS BED & BREAKFAST.** *289 Peguest Rd (07821), NJ 80 to exit 19 to NJ 517N, left on NJ 603.* 973/786-6661; FAX 973/786-1636; res: 973/786-6320. Web www.bbianj.com. 5 rms, 2 share bath, 2 story, 1 cottage. S, D $125-$175; each addl $25; cottage $175; wkends, hols (2-day min). TV; cable. Complimentary full bkfst. Ck-out 11 am, ck-in after 2 pm. Game rm. Lawn games. Some fireplaces. Totally nonsmoking. Cr cds: A, C, D, DS, MC, V.

★★★ **WOODEN DUCK BED & BREAKFAST.** *140 Goodale Rd (07860), I-80 exit 25 to US 206N, E on Goodale Rd.* 973/300-0395; FAX 973/300-0395. Web www.bbianj.com.woodenduck. 7 rms, 2 story, 1 guest house. S, D $100-$150; hols (2-day min). Children over 12 yrs only. TV; cable, VCR (movies). Complimentary full bkfst. Ck-out 11 am, ck-in 2 pm. Business servs avail. In-rm modem link. Luggage handling. Gift shop. Downhill ski 20 mi; x-country ski on site. Pool. Game rm. Lawn games. Picnic tables. On 17 acres. Totally nonsmoking. Cr cds: A, C, DS, MC, V.

Restaurant

★★ **THE BLACK FOREST INN.** *249 US 206N (07874).* 973/347-3344. Web www.powerpg.com/nji/blackforest. Hrs: 11:30 am-2 pm, 5-10 pm; Sun 1-9 pm. Closed Tues; Jan 1, Dec 24, 25. Res accepted. German, continental menu. Bar. A la carte entrees: lunch $8.75-$15.50, dinner $16.75-$22.50. Specializes in veal, seafood. Classic European elegance. Cr cds: A, C, D, MC, V.

Stone Harbor (K-3)

Pop 1,025 **Elev** 5 ft **Area Code** 609 **Zip** 08247

Information Stone Harbor Chamber of Commerce, PO Box 422, phone 609/368-6101; or the Cape May County Chamber of Commerce, PO Box 74, Cape May Court House 08210, phone 609/465-7181

What to See and Do

Wetlands Institute. Environmental center focusing on coastal ecology. Also includes observation tower; marsh trail; aquarium; films and guided walks (July & Aug, daily). Bookstore. (Mid-May–mid-Oct, daily; rest of yr, Tues–Sat; closed Easter, July 4, Thanksgiving; also 2 wks late Dec–early Jan) 3 mi E off Garden State Pkwy exit 10, on Stone Harbor Blvd. Phone 609/368-1211. ¢¢

Annual Events

Sail into Summer Boat Show. Pleasure boating, family entertainment, musicians, food. Phone 609/368-6101. 1st wkend May.

Wings 'n Water Festival. Arts and crafts, decoys; entertainment; seafood. Phone 609/368-1211. 3rd full wkend Sept.

Motel

★★ **DESERT SANDS RESORT COMPLEX.** *79th St & Dune Dr (08202), off Garden State Pkwy exit 13.* 609/368-5133; FAX 609/368-1849. 90 units, 3 story, 15 suites, 31 kits. July-Aug: S, D $115-140; each addl $10; suites $137-$150; kits. $150-$180; wkly rates; higher rates hols; lower rates mid-Apr-June, Sept-Oct. Closed rest of yr. Crib avail. TV; cable. 2 pools, 1 indoor; whirlpool, lifeguard. Restaurant 8:30 am-10 pm. Bar noon-midnight. Ck-out 11 am. Coin lndry. Meeting rms. Business servs avail. Exercise equipt. Refrigerators; microwaves avail. Cr cds: C, MC, V.

Motor Hotel

★★★ **AVALON GOLDEN INN.** *7849 Dune Dr (08202), off Garden State Pkwy exit 10.* 609/368-5155; FAX 609/368-6112. E-mail allison@goldeninn.com; Web www.goldeninn.com. 160 rms, 3 story, 76 kits. June-Labor Day: S, D $169-$259; each addl $15; suites $245-$345; kit. units $214-$275; under 12 free; lower rates rest of yr. Crib avail. TV; cable (premium), VCR (movies). Heated pool; wading pool, poolside serv, lifeguard. Supervised child's activities (mid-June-late Sept). Restaurant 8 am-11 pm. Rm serv. Bar 11-2 am; entertainment wkends. Ck-out 11 am. Meeting rms. Business servs avail. In-rm modem link. Bellhops. Tennis privileges. Golf privileges. Health club privileges. Refrigerators. Balconies. Picnic tables. On beach. Cr cds: C, MC, V.

Restaurant

★★ **MIRAGE RESTAURANT.** *(See Desert Sand Resort Complex)* 609/368-1919. E-mail themirage@desertsand.com; Web www.desertsand.com. Hrs: 8 am-1 pm, 5-9:30 pm. Closed Nov-Mar. Res accepted (dinner). Continental menu. Bar. A la carte entrees: bkfst $3.95-$8.95, dinner $7.95-$25.95. Child's meals. Specialties: mixed grill, veal Bianca. Own pastries. Pianist Fri-Sun. Casual, contemporary decor. Cr cds: C, MC, V.

Toms River (F-5)

Pop 7,524 **Elev** 40 ft **Area Code** 732

Information Toms River–Ocean County Chamber of Commerce, 1200 Hooper Ave, 08753; 908/349-0220

What to See and Do

Cooper Environmental Center. A 500-acre facility with 3-mi bay front. Boat tours (summer; free). Ten miles of marked trails. Picnicking (grills), playground. Nature center. (Daily) 1170 Cattus Island Blvd, E on NJ 37 to Fischer Blvd, follow signs. Phone 732/270-6960. **Free**

Motels

★★ **HOLIDAY INN.** *290 Rte 37E (08753).* 732/244-4000; FAX 732/244-4000; res: 800/465-4329. Web www.holidayinn.com. 123 rms, 4 story. Memorial Day-Labor Day: S, D $109-$124; each addl $10; higher rates wkends; lower rates rest of yr. Crib free. Pet accepted. TV; cable (premium). Indoor pool; whirlpool, poolside serv. Restaurant 6:30 am-10 pm.

Rm serv. Bar 11-2 am; entertainment. Ck-out noon. Coin lndry. Valet serv. Meeting rms. Business servs avail. Sauna. Game rm. Refrigerators. Cr cds: A, C, D, DS, JCB, MC, V.

★★ **HOWARD JOHNSON.** *955 Hooper Ave (08753). 732/244-1000; FAX 732/505-3194; res: 800/654-2000; res: 800/446-4656.* Web www.hojo.com. 96 rms, 2 story. S $75-$120; D $85-$140; each addl $10; under 18 free; higher rates some hols. Crib free. Pet accepted, some restrictions; $10. TV; cable, VCR avail (movies). Indoor/outdoor pool. Restaurant 11 am-9 pm. Bar. Ck-out noon. Meeting rms. Business servs avail. In-rm modem link. Cr cds: A, C, D, DS, MC, V.

★★ **QUALITY INN.** *815 W Rte 37 (08755), Garden State Pkwy exit 82A. 732/341-2400; FAX 732/341-6469; res: 800/424-6423; res: 800/228-5151.* E-mail htlman@ameri-com.com; web www.qualityinntr.com. 100 rms, 2 story. Memorial Day-Labor Day: S, D $75-$129; each addl $10; suites $129-$229; under 18 free; lower rates rest of yr. Crib free. TV; cable. Pool; poolside serv, lifeguard. Playground. Complimentary continental bkfst. Coffee in rms. Restaurant noon-8 pm. Rm serv. Bar; entertainment. Ck-out 11 am. Meeting rms. Business servs avail. In-rm modem link. Valet serv. Sundries. Airport transportation. Exercise equipt; sauna. Refrigerators avail. Cr cds: A, C, D, DS, JCB, MC, V.

Motor Hotel

★★ **RAMADA INN.** *2373 Rte 9 (08755), at jct NJ 70. 732/905-2626; FAX 732/905-8735; res: 800/272-6232.* 154 rms, 3 story, 48 kits. Memorial Day-Labor Day: S, D $82-$125; each addl $10; suites $119-$159; under 12 free; lower rates rest of yr. Crib free. TV; cable (premium). Pool; whirlpool, lifeguard. Complimentary continental bkfst. Restaurant 7 am-10 pm. Rm serv. Bar. Ck-out noon. Coin lndry. Meeting rms. Business servs avail. In-rm modem link. Sundries. Tennis. Exercise equipt. Game rm. Refrigerators avail. Cr cds: A, C, D, DS, MC, V.

Restaurant

✓★ **THE TAVERN.** *N Main St (08753), 1 mi N on NJ 166, just N of NJ 37. 732/349-8778.* Hrs: 11:30-1 am; Sun to midnight. Closed Dec 25. Bar. Complete meals: lunch $3.95-$9.95. A la carte entrees: dinner $5.95-$14.95. Child's meals. Specializes in steak, seafood, selected Italian dishes. Cr cds: A, C, D, MC, V.

Trenton (E-3)

(See also Princeton)

Settled 1679 **Pop** 88,675 **Elev** 50 ft **Area Code** 609

Information Mercer County Chamber of Commerce, 214 W State St, 08608-1002; 609/393-4143

The capital of New Jersey since 1790, Trenton is one of the fastest-growing business and industrial areas in the country and a leading rubber-manufacturing center since colonial times. After crossing the Delaware on December 26, 1776, George Washington attacked the British-held town eight miles to the northwest.

What to See and Do

New Jersey State Museum. (Daily exc Mon). 205 W State St, adj Capitol. Phone 609/292-6464. Includes

Auditorium. Lectures; films; music; children's theater. Some fees. Phone 609/292-6308.

Main Building. Fine art, cultural history, archaeology and natural science exhibits. (Daily exc Mon; closed state hols) **Free**

Planetarium. One of few Intermediate Space Transit planetaria (duplicates motions of space vehicles) in the world. Programs (wkends; July–Aug, daily exc Mon). Over 4 yrs only exc children's programs. Tickets one-half hr in advance. Phone 609/292-6333. ¢

Sesame Place. A family play park. 6 mi NW via NJ 29, then 8 mi SW on I-95 to Langhorne (see BRISTOL, PA).

The Old Barracks Museum. One of the finest examples of colonial barracks in the US. Built in 1758–1759, it housed British, Hessian and Continental troops during the Revolution. Museum contains restored soldiers' squad rm; antique furniture; ceramics; firearms; dioramas. Guides in period costumes. (Daily; closed most major hols & Dec 24) Barrack St, opp W Front St. Phone 609/396-1776. ¢

Trenton State College (1855). (6,150 students) A 250-acre wooded campus with 2 lakes. Tours of campus. 4 mi N on NJ 31. Phone 609/771-1855. On campus is the

College Art Gallery. (Feb–May & Sept–Dec, daily exc Sat; closed hols) Phone 609/771-2198. **Free**

 Washington Crossing State Park. (See WASHINGTON CROSSING STATE PARK, PA) This 841-acre park commemorates the famous crossing on Christmas night, 1776, by the Continental Army, under the command of General George Washington. Continental Lane, at the park, is the road over which Washington's army began its march to Trenton, December 25, 1776. Nature tours. Picnicking, playground. Visitor center and nature center (Wed–Sun); open-air summer theater (fee). Standard fees. (See ANNUAL EVENTS) 8 mi NW on NJ 29. Phone 609/737-0623. Also in the park is

Ferry House State Historic Site. Building sheltered Washington and some of his men on Dec 25, 1776, after they had crossed the Delaware from the Pennsylvania side. It is believed that the strategy to be used for the attack on Trenton was discussed here. Restored as a living history colonial farmhouse; special programs throughout the yr. (Wed–Sun) Phone 609/737-2515.

William Trent House (1719). Trenton's oldest house is an example of Queen Anne architecture. It was the home of Chief Justice William Trent, for whom the city was named. Colonial garden; period furnishings. (Daily, limited hrs; closed major hols) 15 Market St. Phone 609/989-3027. ¢¢

Annual Events

Trenton Kennel Club Dog Show. Mercer County Central Park. Early May.

Heritage Days. 1st wkend June.

Reenactment of Crossing of the Delaware. Washington Crossing State Park. Departs PA side on the afternoon of Dec 25.

Motel

★ **HOWARD JOHNSON LODGE.** *2991 Brunswick Pike (08648), 5 mi N on US 1. 609/896-1100; FAX 609/895-1325; res: 800/654-2000; res: 800/446-4656.* 104 rms, 2 story. S $62.50-$84.50; D $68.50-$84.50; each addl $10; under 18 free; higher rates special events. Crib free. Pet accepted. TV; cable (premium). Pool. Complimentary continental bkfst. Restaurant open 24 hrs. Ck-out noon. Meeting rm. Business servs avail. In-rm modem link. Valet serv. Sundries. Private patios, balconies. Cr cds: A, C, D, DS, JCB, MC, V.

Restaurants

★★ **DIAMONDS.** *132 Kent (08611), in Chambersburg district. 609/393-1000.* Web www.diamonds.inter.net. Hrs: 11:30 am-2:30 pm, 4:30 pm-midnight; Sat from 4:30 pm; Sun from 3:30 pm. Closed major hols. Res accepted. Italian menu. Bar 11-2 am. Semi-a la carte: lunch $7-$15, dinner $16-$33. Specializes in seafood, steak, veal. Valet parking. Italian decor. Cr cds: A, C, D, DS, MC, V.

★★ **LA GONDOLA.** *762 Roebling Ave (08611). 609/392-0600.* Hrs: 11:30 am-3 pm, 4:30-10 pm; Fri to 11 pm; Sat 4:30-11 pm. Closed Sun; some major hols. Res accepted. Italian menu. Bar. Semi-a la carte: lunch $4.95-$9.95, dinner $12.95-$23.95. Child's meals. Specialties: saltimbocca alla Gondola, fettine di pollo al carciofetto. Five dining rms. Dining in wine cellar. Mediterranean decor. Cr cds: A, C, D, MC, V.

★★ **LARRY PERONI'S WATERFRONT.** *1140 River Rd (08628), 7 mi NW on NJ 29, ½ mi N of Scudder's Falls Bridge, I-95, exit 1. 609/882-0303.* Hrs: 11:30 am-9 pm; Sat 4-11 pm. Closed Dec 25. Res accepted. Continental menu. Bar. Semi-a la carte: lunch $4.95-$7.95, dinner $11.95-$18.95. Specializes in veal, beef, seafood. Outdoor dining. Paneled dining rms, fireplaces. Spacious grounds. Cr cds: A, C, D, DS, MC, V.

★★ **MARSILIO'S RESTAURANT.** *541 Roebling Ave (08611), in Chambersburg district. 609/695-1916.* Hrs: 11:30 am-2 pm, 5-10 pm; Fri, Sat to 11 pm. Closed Sun; most major hols. Res accepted. Italian menu. Bar. Semi-a la carte: lunch $6.45-$19.95, dinner $12.95-$26. Child's meals. Specializes in veal, chicken. Italian decor. Cr cds: A, C, MC, V.

D

Vernon (A-4)

Pop 1,696 **Elev** 564 ft **Area Code** 973 **Zip** 07462
Information Vernon Township Municipal Bldg, 21 Church St; 201/764-4055

What to See and Do

Action Park. Theme park includes 75 self-operative rides, shows and attractions. Action park has more than 40 water rides, including river rides and Tidal Wave Pool; also Grand Prix race cars, bungee jumping, miniature golf, children's park; food, picnic area. 3 daily shows, wkend festival series. (Mid-June–Labor Day, daily; late May–mid-June, Thurs–Sun) NJ 94. Phone 973/827-2000. ¢¢¢¢¢ Also here is

Vernon Valley/Great Gorge Ski Resort. Resort has 1 triple, 14 double chairlifts; 3 rope tows; school, rentals; 100% snowmaking; cafeterias, restaurants, bars, night club; nursery. 52 runs; vertical drop 1,040 ft. (Dec–Mar, daily) Night skiing. Health spa, country club (daily). NJ 94. Phone 973/827-3900 (ski conditions) or 973/827-2000 (general information & fees). ¢¢¢¢¢

Inn

✓ ★★ **APPLE VALLEY INN.** *967 Rte 517 (07418), SW on NJ 94 & N NJ 517. 973/764-3735; FAX 973/764-1050.* Web www.applevalleyinn.com. 7 rms, 5 share bath, 3 story. No elvtr. S, D $70-$90; each addl $20. Premium cable TV in common rm; VCR avail (movies). Complimentary full bkfst. Ck-out 11 am, ck-in before 9 pm. Pool. Built in 1831; antiques. Cr cds: C, MC, V.

≈ ⚡ SC

Wayne (B-5)

Pop 47,025 **Elev** 200 ft **Area Code** 973 **Zip** 07470 **E-mail** mfoster@ tricounty.org **Web** www.tricounty.org
Information Tri-County Chamber of Commerce, 2055 Hamburg Tpke; 973/831-7788

Wayne is the home of William Paterson University of New Jersey (1855).

What to See and Do

Dey Mansion (ca 1740). Restoration of Washington's headquarters (1780); period furnishings. Guided tours. Picnic tables. (Wed–Sun; closed major hols) 199 Totowa Rd. Phone 973/696-1776. ¢

Terhune Memorial Park (Sunnybank). Estate of the late Albert Payson Terhune, author of *Lad, a Dog* and many other books about his collies. Scenic garden; picnic area, playground. (Daily) 2½ mi N on US 202N. Phone 973/694-1800. **Free**

Van Riper-Hopper (Wayne) Museum (ca 1786). Dutch Colonial farmhouse with 18th- and 19th-century furnishings; local historical objects; herb garden; bird sanctuary. 533 Berdan Ave. Phone 973/694-7192 for schedule and fees. Also here is

Mead Van Duyne House. Restored Dutch farmhouse.

Motels

★★ **HOLIDAY INN.** *334 Rte 46 East (07470), on Service Rd, I-80 exit S Verona. 973/256-7000; FAX 973/890-5406; res: 800/465-4329.* 140 rms, 2 story. S, D $75-$94; under 18 free. Crib free. TV; cable (premium). Pool; poolside serv, lifeguard. Restaurant 6:30 am-2 pm, 5-10 pm. Rm serv. Bar 11-2 am; 5 pm-12:30 am; entertainment. Ck-out noon. Meeting rms. In-rm modem link. Valet serv. Sundries. Health club privileges. Miniature golf. Microwaves avail. Cr cds: A, C, D, DS, JCB, MC, V.

D ≈ ⋈ 🔥 SC

✓ ★ **HOWARD JOHNSON.** *1850 Rte 23 & Ratzer Rd (07470). 973/696-8050; FAX 973/696-0682; res: 800/446-4656.* 149 rms, 2 story. S $109-$118; D $119-$128; each addl $10; under 16 free. Crib free. Pet accepted, some restrictions. TV; cable (premium). Pool. Complimentary continental bkfst. Ck-out noon. Coin lndry. Business servs avail. In-rm modem link. Valet serv. Some refrigerators; microwaves avail. Private patios, balconies. Cr cds: A, C, D, DS, JCB, MC, V.

D 🐾 ≈ ⋈ 🔥 SC

Motor Hotels

★★★ **FAIRFIELD EXECUTIVE INN.** *216-234 Rte 46E (07446), NJ 23S, exit 53 to I-80W. 973/575-7700; FAX 973/575-4653; res: 800/528-1234.* 171 rms, 4 story. S, D $85-$166; each addl $13; suites $114-$166; under 16 free; family, wkend, wkly, hol rates. Crib free. Pet accepted, some restrictions. TV; cable (premium), VCR avail (movies). Complimentary full bkfst. Complimentary coffee in rms. Restaurant 6 am-11 pm. Rm serv. Bar 11-1:30 am; entertainment Thurs-Sun. Ck-out noon. Meeting rms. Business center. In-rm modem link. Bellhops. Valet serv. Sundries. Coin lndry. Exercise equipt; sauna. Health club privileges. Indoor pool; whirlpool, poolside serv. Game rm. Rec rm. Refrigerators; some in-rm whirlpools; wet bar in suites; microwaves avail. Cr cds: A, C, D, DS, MC, V.

D 🐾 ≈ 🏋 ⋈ 🔥 SC 🚶

★★ **HOLIDAY INN TOTOWA.** *1 Rte 46W (07512), on US 46 just E of Union Blvd in Totowa. 973/785-9000; FAX 973/785-3031; res: 800/443-5943.* 155 rms, 5 story. S, D $89-$129; each addl $6; under 18 free. Crib free. TV; cable (premium), VCR avail. Pool. Complimentary bkfst. Coffee in rms. Restaurant 6:30 am-11 pm Mon-Fri. Rm serv. Ck-out noon.

Meeting rms. Business servs avail. In-rm modem link. Bellhops. Valet serv. Sundries. Exercise equipt. Indoor parking. Refrigerators. Cr cds: A, C, D, DS, JCB, MC, V.

⊡ ⌇ ⚹ ⊠ ⚿ SC

★★★ **RADISSON.** *690 Rte 46E (07004), ½ mi W of jct NJ 23. 973/227-9200; FAX 973/227-4308; res: 800/333-3333.* 204 rms, 5 story, 61 suites. S $185-$195; D $195-$215; each addl $10; suites $195-$425; under 18 free. Crib $10. TV; cable (premium), VCR avail. Indoor pool. Restaurant 6:30 am-10 pm. Rm serv. Bar 11-1:30 am; entertainment Thurs-Sat. Ck-out noon. Meeting rms. Business center. In-rm modem link. Bellhops. Gift shop. Exercise equipt; sauna. Bathrm phones. In-rm whirlpools; some refrigerators; microwaves avail. Cr cds: A, C, D, DS, ER, JCB, MC, V.

⊡ ⌇ ⚹ ⊠ ⚿ SC ⚶

West Orange (C-5)

(See also Newark, Newark Intl Airport Area)

Pop 39,103 **Elev** 368 ft **Area Code** 973 **Zip** 07052 **Web** www.westorange.com

Information West Orange Chamber of Commerce, PO Box 83; 973/731-0360

What to See and Do

Eagle Rock Reservation. A 644-ft elevation in the Orange Mts; visitors see a heavily populated area that stretches from the Passaic River Valley east to New York City. Hiking trails; restaurant. Picnicking. Bridle paths. (Daily) NW via Main St & Eagle Rock Ave. Phone 973/268-3500 or 973/731-3000.

⭐ **Edison National Historic Site.** Main St & Lakeside Ave. Phone 973/736-5050.

   Edison Laboratory. Built by Edison in 1887, it was his laboratory for 44 years. During that time, he was granted more than half of his 1,093 patents (an all-time record). Here he perfected the phonograph, motion picture camera and electric storage battery. One-hr lab tour (no video cameras, strollers) includes the chemistry lab and library; demonstrations of early phonographs. Visitor center has exhibits; films (daily; closed Jan 1, Thanksgiving, Dec 25). Phone 973/736-5050. ¢

Turtle Back Zoo. This 16-acre park features animals in natural surroundings; sea lion pool; miniature train ride (1 mi). Picnicking, concessions. Gift shop (hrs vary). (Daily; closed Jan 1, Thanksgiving, Dec 24, 25, 31; limited schedule Dec-Jan) 560 Northfield Ave, 3 mi W on I-280, exit 10, in South Mountain Reservation. Phone 973/731-5800. ¢¢¢ Adj is

   South Mountain Arena. Indoor ice rink. Hockey games, special events. Phone 973/731-3828.

Restaurants

★★★ **HIGHLAWN PAVILION.** *Eagle Rock Reservation (07052). 973/731-3463.* Web www.powerpg.com/njl/highlawn. Hrs: noon-3 pm, 5:30-10 pm; Fri to 11:30 pm; Sat 5-11:30 pm; Sun 5-9 pm. Closed Dec 24. Res accepted. Bar to midnight. A la carte entrees: lunch $8-$16.50, dinner $15.95-$28.75. Specializes in veal chop, steak, fresh seafood. Oyster bar. Pianist Thurs-Sat. Valet parking. Outdoor dining. Located in county park on top of mountain; view of NY skyline. Food preparation visible from dining rm. Jacket. Cr cds: A, C, D, DS, MC, V.

⊡

★★★ **THE MANOR.** *111 Prospect Ave (07052), I-280 exit 8B. 973/325-1400.* E-mail manor111@aol.com; Web www.the-manor.com. Hrs: noon-2:30 pm, 6-10 pm; Sat 6 pm-midnight; Sun to 8:30 pm. Closed Mon; Dec 24. Continental menu. Bar to 2 am. Wine cellar. A la carte entrees: lunch $9.50-$15, dinner $23-$30. Lobster buffet Tues-Fri $36.95; Sat

$39.95. Buffet: Wed (lunch) $19.95; Sun $31.95. Specialties: rack of lamb, Dover sole, beef Wellington. Own baking. Pianist Tue-Sun; band, vocalist Fri, Sat. Jacket. View of formal gardens. Cr cds: A, C, D, DS, MC, V.

⊡

Wildwood & Wildwood Crest (K-3)

(See also Cape May)

Pop Wildwood 4,484; Wildwood Crest 3,631 **Elev** 8 ft **Area Code** 609 **Zip** 08260 **E-mail** gwcc@bellatlantic.net **Web** www.gwcoc.com

Information Greater Wildwood Chamber of Commerce, PO Box 823; 609/729-4000

Wildwood's busy boardwalk extends for approximately two miles along the five miles of protected sandy beach it shares with North Wildwood and Wildwood Crest, two neighboring resorts. The area offers swimming, waterskiing, ocean and bay fishing, boating, sailing, bicycling, golf, tennis and shuffleboard.

What to See and Do

Boat trips. Sightseeing and whale-watching cruises aboard *Big Flamingo.* (Apr-Nov, daily) Capt Sinn's Dock, 6006 Park Blvd in Wildwood Crest. For schedule, fees, phone 609/522-3934. Also aboard the *Big Blue Sightseer.* (June-Sept, daily) 4500 Park Blvd in Wildwood. Phone 609/522-2919.

Motels

★ **AQUARIUS MOTOR INN.** *4712 Ocean Ave (08260). 609/729-0054; res: 800/982-1831.* 28 rms, 4 story. S, D $110-$159; under 18 free; wkly, wkend rates; lower rates Apr-June & Sept-Oct. Closed rest of yr. Crib free. TV; cable (premium). Heated pool; wading pool. Complimentary coffee in lobby. Restaurant opp 7 am-11 pm. Ck-out 10 am. Coin lndry. Business servs avail. Refrigerators, microwaves. Balconies. Picnic tables. Opp beach. Cr cds: A, C, DS, MC, V.

⌇ ⚿ SC

★★ **ARMADA BY-THE-SEA.** *6503 Ocean Ave (08260), on beach. 609/729-3000; FAX 609/729-7472; res: 800/399-3001.* 56 rms, 5 story, 40 kits. Mid-July-Aug: up to 4 persons $145-$166; each addl $10; kit. units up to 4 persons $163-$166; some lower rates rest of yr. Closed Oct-mid-Apr. Crib $5. TV; VCR avail (movies). Heated pool; wading pool. Restaurant nearby. Ck-out 11 am. Coin lndry. Meeting rms. Business servs avail. Sundries. Game rm. Refrigerators, microwaves. Balconies. Picnic tables, grill. Sun decks. Cr cds: A, C, DS, MC, V.

⊡ ⌇ ⚿

★★ **ASTRONAUT MOTEL.** *511 E Stockton Rd (08260), on beach. 609/522-6981; FAX 609/523-1927.* Web www.beachcomber.com. 33 kit. units, 3 story. No elvtr. July-early Sept: up to 6 persons $134-$180; lower rates Apr-June, early Sept-mid-Oct. Closed rest of yr. TV. Pool; wading pool. Restaurant nearby. Ck-out 11 am. Coin lndry. Sundries. Shuffleboard. Refrigerators, microwaves. Sun decks. Picnic tables, grills. Cr cds: C, DS, MC, V.

⌇ ⚿

★★ **ATTACHE MOTEL.** *5707 Ocean Ave (08260), on beach. 609/522-0241; FAX 609/523-8379.* Web www.beachcomber.com/. 42 rms, 3 story, 26 kits. Mid-July-late Aug: up to 4 persons $130-$175; each addl $10; kit. units for 4 persons $130-$215; family rates; lower rates mid-Apr-mid-July, late Aug-mid-Oct. Closed rest of yr. Crib avail. TV; cable, VCR avail. Heated pool; wading pool. Restaurant nearby. Ck-out 11 am. Guest lndry. Business servs avail. Refrigerators, microwaves. Some balconies. Picnic tables, grills. Cr cds: A, C, MC, V.

⊠ 🔥

★★ **CAPE COD INN.** *6109 Atlantic Ave (08260). 609/522-1177; FAX 609/729-2353.* E-mail www.ccmotel@bellatlantic.net. 50 units, 3 story, 27 kits. Mid-July-mid-Aug: S, D $110; each addl $10; kits. $120; family rates; higher rates wkends, hols (3-day min); lower rates May-June, mid-Aug-Sept. Closed rest of yr. TV; cable (premium). Pool; wading pool. Restaurant nearby. Ck-out 10 am. Coin lndry. Meeting rm. Business servs avail. Sundries. Game rm. Miniature golf. Refrigerators, microwaves. Picnic tables. Cr cds: A, C, DS, MC, V.

D ⊠ ⊠ 🔥

✓★★ **CARIBBEAN MOTEL.** *5600 Ocean Ave (08260), at Buttercup Rd. 609/522-8292; res: 800/457-7040.* 30 rms, 2 story, 9 kits. July-Labor Day: up to 4 persons $94-$106; kit. units for 4 persons $99-$120; lower rates May-June, after Labor Day-Sept. Closed rest of yr. Crib avail. TV; cable. Heated pool; wading pool, lifeguard. Complimentary coffee in rms. Restaurant opp 7 am-10 pm. Ck-out 11 am. Coin lndry. Game rm. Lawn games. Refrigerators; some microwaves. Sun deck. Picnic tables, grills. Cr cds: C, MC, V.

⊠ 🔥

★★ **CRUSADER OCEAN FRONT RESORT.** *6101 Cardinal Rd (08260), at Cardinal Rd, on beach. 609/522-6991; FAX 609/522-2280; res: 800/462-3260.* E-mail CrusaderWC@aol.com; web www.jerseyshore-online.com/crusader. 61 units, 3 story, 54 suites, 37 kits. July-Aug: S, D $141-$202; each addl $12; kit. units $166-$202; lower rates Apr-June & Sept-Oct. Closed Nov-Mar. Crib avail. TV; cable (premium), VCR avail. Heated pool; wading pool, lifeguard. Sauna. Restaurant 7 am-8 pm. Ck-out 11 am. Coin lndry. Meeting rms. Business servs avail. Sundries. Gift shop. Game rm. Refrigerators, microwaves. Some balconies. Picnic tables. Ocean beach; boardwalk. Cr cds: A, C, MC, V.

D ⊠ ⊠ 🔥

★★ **FLEUR DE LIS MOTEL.** *6105 Ocean Ave (08260), at Sweetbriar. 609/522-0123; FAX 609/523-0893.* E-mail fleur@cybernet.net; Web www.fleurdelismotel.com. 44 rms, 3 story, 32 kits. Mid-July-late Aug: S, D $100-$116; each addl $10; kits. $140-$170; higher rates wkends (3-day min); lower rates mid-Apr-mid-July & Sept-mid-Oct. Closed rest of yr. Crib $5. TV; cable. Pool; wading pool. Restaurant adj 7 am-9 pm. Ck-out 11 am. Coin lndry. Business servs avail. Game rm. Refrigerators, microwaves. On beach. Cr cds: C, MC, V.

⊠ ⊠ 🔥

✓★★ **IMPERIAL 500 MOTEL.** *6601 Atlantic Ave (08260). 609/522-6063; FAX 609/522-7643; res: 800/522-1255.* 45 rms, 3 story, 26 kits. No elvtr. July-Labor Day: S, D for 4, $100-$110; each addl $10; kit. units $115; lower rates May-June, after Labor Day-Sept. Closed rest of yr. Crib avail. TV; cable. Heated pool; wading pool. Restaurant nearby. Ck-out 11 am. Coin lndry. Meeting rm. Business servs avail. Sundries. Shuffleboard. Rec rm. Lawn games. Refrigerators, microwaves. Sun deck. Picnic tables, grills. Cr cds: C, DS, MC, V.

⊠ 🔥

★ **IVANHOE MOTEL & APARTMENTS.** *430 E 21st Ave (08260). 609/522-5874; FAX 609/523-2323.* 40 rms, 2 story. July-Aug: S, D $90-$150; each addl $10-$15; family, wkly rates; lower rates rest of yr. Crib $8. TV; cable (premium). Heated pools; wading pool. Coffee in rms. Restaurant nearby. Ck-out 10 am. Coin lndry. Meeting rms. Business servs avail. Refrigerators, microwaves. Some balconies. Opp beach. Cr cds: A, C, D, DS, MC, V.

⊠ ⊠ 🔥 SC

★★ **JOLLY ROGER MOTEL.** *6805 Atlantic Ave (08260). 609/522-6915; FAX 609/729-2051; res: 800/337-5232.* 74 rms, 3 story. Mid-July-mid-Aug: S, D $102-$121; each addl $7; kits. $112-$158; under 5 free; wkends, hols (3-day min); lower rates mid-May, late Aug-late Sept.

Closed rest of yr. Crib $10. TV; cable. Pool; wading pool, lifeguard. Supervised child's activities (July-Aug), ages 4-16. Restaurant nearby. Ck-out 11 am. Coin lndry. Meeting rms. Tennis. Game rm. Refrigerators; some microwaves. Balconies, grills. Picnic tables. Cr cds: C, MC, V.

🏄 ⊠ 🔥

★★ **LE VOYAGEUR MOTEL.** *232 E Andrews Ave (08260). 609/522-6407; FAX 609/523-1834; res: 800/348-0846.* Web www.wildwoods.orglevoyageur. 33 rms, 3 story, 14 kits. July-Aug: S, D $74; each addl $10; suites $97; kits. $107; under 5 free; wkly, hol rates; lower rates Apr-June, Sept-Oct. Closed rest of yr. Crib $9. TV; cable. Heated pool; wading pool. Restaurant nearby. Ck-out 10:30 am. Coin lndry. Meeting rm. Game rm. Refrigerators; many microwaves. Balconies. Picnic tables. Cr cds: A, C, MC, V.

D ⊠ 🔥

★ **MADRID OCEAN RESORT.** *427 E Miami Ave (08260), on beach. 609/729-1600; FAX 609/729-8483.* E-mail lindaworld@aol.com; Web www.beachcomber.com. 54 rms, 5 story, 24 kits. July-Labor Day: S, D $110-$150; each addl $10; suites $140; kit. units up to 4 persons $150; higher rates wkends; lower rates mid-May-June, after Labor Day-Sept. Closed rest of yr. Crib avail. TV. Heated pool; wading pool. Restaurant 7:30 am-9 pm. Ck-out 11 am. Coin lndry. Business servs avail. Sundries. Rec rm. Sun deck. Refrigerators; microwaves avail. All oceanfront rms. Cr cds: A, C, MC, V.

⊠ 🔥

★★ **NASSAU INN.** *6201 Ocean Ave at Sweetbriar Rd (08260), at Sweetbriar. 609/729-9077; FAX 609/729-2208; res: 800/336-9077.* Web www.wildwoods.com/nassau. 56 rms, 5 story. July-early Sept: S, D $105-$180; each addl $10; kits. $145-$170; family rates; package plans; lower rates early Sept-mid-Oct & May-June. Closed rest of yr. Crib $9. TV; cable. Heated pool; wading pool. Restaurant adj 7 am-9 pm. Ck-out 11 am. Coin lndry. Business servs avail. Game rm. Refrigerators; many microwaves. On beach. Cr cds: C, DS, MC, V.

⊠ 🔥

✓★ **NEW COMPASS MOTEL.** *6501 Atlantic Ave (08260). 609/522-6948.* 50 rms, 3 story, 25 kits. July-Aug: S, D $98-$122; each addl $10; family rates; wkly, wkend rates; higher rates hols (3-day min); lower rates May-June, Sept-Oct. Closed rest of yr. Crib $10. TV; cable. Heated pool; wading pool. Complimentary coffee in rms. Restaurant nearby. Ck-out 11 am. Meeting rms. Business servs avail. Refrigerators; many microwaves. Cr cds: A, C, DS, MC, V.

⊠ ⊠ 🔥

★★ **OCEAN HOLIDAY MOTOR INN.** *6501 Ocean Ave (08260), on beach. 609/729-2900; FAX 609/523-1024; res: 800/321-6232.* Web www.beachcomber.com. 56 rms, 5 story, 51 kits. July-Aug: S, D $70-$120; each addl $10; kit. units (up to 4 persons) $100-$255; hol wkends (3-day min); lower rates Apr-June, Sept-Oct. Closed rest of yr. Crib $5. TV; cable (premium), VCR avail. Pool; wading pool. Restaurant nearby. Ck-out 11 am. Coin lndry. Meeting rms. Business servs avail. Sundries. Game rm. Refrigerators, microwaves. Some private patios, balconies. Picnic tables, grills. Cr cds: A, C, MC, V.

D ⊠ 🔥

★ **OCEANVIEW MOTEL.** *7201 Ocean Ave (08260). 609/522-6656; FAX 609/522-6793; res: 800/647-6656.* Web www.beachcomber.com/wwcrest.ocview.html. 110 rms, 4 story, 36 suites, 61 kit. units. July-Aug: S, D $105-$145; each addl $10; suites $130-$150; kit. units $130-$160; family rates; package plans; lower rates May-June, Sept-Oct. Closed rest of yr. Crib $9. TV; cable (premium). Restaurant opp 7 am-9 pm. Ck-out 11 am. Business servs avail. Coin lndry. Heated pool; wading pool, lifeguard. Miniature golf. Playground. Supervised child's activities (late June-early Sept). Game rm. Refrigerators. Picnic tables, grills. On beach. Cr cds: C, DS, MC, V.

D ⊠ 🔥

★★★ **PAN AMERICAN HOTEL.** *5901 Ocean Ave (08260), on beach.* 609/522-6936; FAX 609/522-6937. E-mail panamericaninfo@ morey-sandcastles.com; web www.morey-sandcastles.com. 78 rms, 4 story, 39 kits. Early July-early Sept $165-$175; each addl $12; suites $195-$200; kit. units $175-$185; lower rates mid-May-early June, early Sept-mid-Oct. Closed rest of yr. Crib free. TV; VCR avail. Heated pool; wading pool, lifeguard. Sauna. Free supervised child's activities (mid-June-Labor Day), ages 4-10. Restaurant 7:30 am-8 pm. Rm serv. Ck-out 11 am. Meeting rm. Coin lndry. Business servs avail. Sundries. Rec rm. Refrigerators; some microwaves. Sun deck. Balconies. Cr cds: C, MC, V.

★ **PANORAMIC MOTEL & APARTMENTS.** *2101 Surf Ave (08260).* 609/522-1181. 25 rms, 2 story. July-Sept: S, D $98-$150; each addl $10-$15; family, wkly rates; lower rates rest of yr. Crib $8. TV; cable (premium). Heated pool; wading pool. Complimentary coffee in rms. Restaurant nearby. Ck-out 10 am. Coin lndry. Meeting rms. Business servs avail. Refrigerators, microwaves. Some balconies. On beach. Cr cds: A, C, D, DS, MC, V.

★★★ **PORT ROYAL HOTEL.** *6801 Ocean Ave (08260), on beach.* 609/729-2000; FAX 609/729-2051. E-mail portroyalinfo@morey-sandcastles.com; web www.morey-sandcastles.com. 100 rms, 6 story, 50 kits. Late June-Labor Day: S, D $160-$170; each addl $12; kit. units for 4 persons $190-$205; lower rates May-late June, after Labor Day-mid-Oct. Closed rest of yr. Crib avail. TV; VCR avail. Heated pool; wading pool, sauna. Free supervised child's activities (mid-June-Labor Day), ages 3-10. Restaurant 8 am-8 pm in season. Ck-out 11 am. Coin lndry. Meeting rm (off-season). Business servs avail. Sundries. Rec rm, game rm in season. Some microwaves. Balconies. Cr cds: C, MC, V.

★ **ROYAL HAWAIIAN RESORT MOTEL.** *501 E Orchid Rd (08260).* 609/522-3414; FAX 609/522-1316. 88 rms, 5 story, 56 kits. Mid-July-Aug: S, D $99-$169; suites, kit. units for 4 $139-$229; each addl $10; lower rates mid-May-mid-July, Sept-Oct. Closed rest of yr. Crib avail. TV; cable (premium). Pool; wading pool, lifeguard. Playground. Ck-out 11 am. Coin lndry. Business servs avail. Valet serv. Rec rm. Exercise equipt; sauna. Refrigerators, microwaves. Balconies. Sun deck. Grills. On ocean. Cr cds: A, C, DS, MC, V.

Motor Hotels

★★ **ADVENTURE MOTOR INN.** *5401 Ocean Ave (08260).* 609/729-1200; FAX 609/729-3935; res: 800/232-7873. Web www.adventurerinn.com. 104 rms, 6 story. July-early Sept: S, D $140-$330; each addl $12; under 3 free; higher rates wkends (3-day min); lower rates early-Sept-Oct & mid-Apr-June. Closed rest of yr. Crib $8. TV; cable. Heated pool; wading pool, lifeguard. Restaurant 7 am-8 pm. Rm serv. Ck-out 11 am. Coin lndry. Meeting rms. Business servs avail. Sundries. Gift shop. Game rm. Refrigerators; microwaves avail. On beach. Cr cds: C, DS, MC, V.

★★ **BRISTOL PLAZA MOTOR INN.** *6407 Ocean Ave (08260).* 609/729-1234; FAX 609/729-5835; res: 800/433-9731. 55 rms, 5 story, 41 kits. Mid-July-late Aug: S, D (up to 4) $131-$184; family rates; wkly, wkend, hol rates; lower rates May-mid-July & late Aug-Oct. Closed rest of yr. Crib $10. TV; cable. Heated pool; wading pool. Sauna. Complimentary coffee in rms. Restaurant nearby. Ck-out 11 am. Coin lndry. Business servs avail. Refrigerators; many microwaves. Balconies. Picnic tables. Opp ocean. Cr cds: A, C, DS, MC, V.

★★★ **EL CORONADO MOTOR INN.** *8501 Atlantic Ave (08260), on beach.* 609/729-1000; FAX 609/729-6557; res: 800/227-5302. Web www.elcoronado.com. 113 rms, 6 story, 63 kit. suites. July-Aug: S, D $130-$140; each addl $10; kit. suites $158-$240; under 12 free; wkly, wkend (3-night min), hol rates; lower rates May-June & Sept-Oct. Closed rest of yr. Crib avail. TV; cable (premium). Pool; wading pool, whirlpool, poolside serv, lifeguard. Sauna. Supervised child's activities (July-Aug). Restaurant 7 am-4 pm. Ck-out 11 am. Coin lndry. Meeting rms. Business servs avail. In-rm modem link. Gift shop. Game rm. Refrigerators, microwaves. Balconies. Cr cds: A, C, DS, MC, V.

Inn

★★★ **CANDLELIGHT INN.** *2310 Central Ave (08260).* 609/522-6200; FAX 609/522-6125; res: 800/992-2632. E-mail inn4pd@aol.com; Web www.candlelight-inn.com. 10 rms, 8 with A/C, 4 story. No rm phones. May-Oct: S $85-$150; D $100-$260; lower rates rest of yr. Complimentary full bkfst; afternoon refreshments. Ck-out 11 am, ck-in 1 pm. Business servs avail. Whirlpool, sun deck. Lawn games. Health club privileges. Some in-rm whirlpools, microwaves, fireplaces. Grills. Queen Anne/Victorian-style house (ca 1905); restored. Antique furnishings. Large porch with swing and hammocks. Totally nonsmoking. Cr cds: A, C, DS, MC, V.

Restaurants

★★ **CAPTAIN'S TABLE.** *Hollywood at Oceanfront (08260).* 609/522-2939. Hrs: 8 am-noon, 4:30-10 pm. Closed mid-Oct-Mother's Day. Buffet: bkfst $3.95-$8.50. Semi-a la carte: dinner $9.95-$23.95. Child's meals. Specializes in Maine lobster, steak. Nautical decor; ocean view. Family-owned. Cr cds: A, C, D, DS, MC, V.

★★ **GARFIELD'S GIARDINO RISTORANTE.** *9204 Atlantic Ave (08260), Holly Beach Station.* 609/729-0120. Hrs: 11:30-3 am; July, Aug 4-11 pm; winter hrs vary. Res accepted. Italian, seafood menu. Bar. Complete meals: dinner $6.95-$19.95. Child's meals. Specializes in fresh seafood, veal, poultry. Entertainment July, Aug. 2 dining areas in garden setting. Cr cds: A, C, D, DS, MC, V.

★★ **LUIGI'S.** *4119 Pacific Ave (08260).* 609/522-8571. Hrs: 4 pm-1 am; early-bird dinner 4-6 pm. Closed mid-Oct-Easter. Res accepted. Italian, Amer menu. Bar. Semi-a la carte: dinner $8.95-$18.95. Child's meals. Specializes in veal, fresh fish, pasta. European-style dining. Family-owned. Cr cds: A, C, DS, MC, V.

★ **MENZ RESTAURANT & SEAFOOD.** *985 NJ 47S (08242), 5 mi NE.* 609/886-5691. Hrs: 4-9 pm; Sun from 2 pm. Closed winter months. Res accepted. A la carte entrees: dinner $8.95-$31.95. Child's meals. Specializes in seafood. Antique decor; music boxes, clocks, stained glass. Cr cds: C, MC, V.

Woodbridge (D-5)

Settled 1664 **Pop** 93,086 **Elev** 21 ft **Area Code** 732 **Zip** 07095
Information Chamber of Commerce Visitor Center, 52 Main St; 732/636-4040

Here, where the first cloverleaf interchange in the US was constructed in 1929, cross two of the country's busiest roads—the Garden State Pkwy and the New Jersey Tpke. Also in Woodbridge are seaway and river port areas visited by thousands of vessels annually.

What to See and Do

Barron Arts Center. Built in 1877 in Romanesque-revival style. Originally the first free public library in Middlesex County, now an arts and cultural center with art exhibits; workshops; lectures; poetry sessions; concerts; special events. Gallery (Mon–Fri; closed hols). 582 Rahway Ave. Phone 732/634-0413. **Free**

Hotels

★★★ **HILTON.** *120 Wood Ave S (08830), W of Garden State Pkwy exit 131A.* 732/494-6200; FAX 732/603-7777; res: 800/445-8667. Web www.hilton.com. 200 rms, 7-11 story. S $90-$165; D $90-$180; each addl $15; under 18 free; wkend rates. Crib free. TV; cable (premium), VCR. Indoor pool; whirlpool, lifeguard. Restaurant 6 am-midnight; dining rms 11 am-10 pm. Bar noon-1 am; entertainment. Meeting rms. Business center. In-rm modem link. Gift shop. Exercise rm. Bathrm phones. Cr cds: A, C, D, DS, MC, V.

D ⌹ ✗ ⋈ 🐾 SC 🚶

★★★ **SHERATON.** *515 Rte 1S (08830), US 1 at Gill Ln, ½ mi N of Garden State Pkwy exit 130.* 732/634-3600; FAX 732/634-0258; res: 800/544-5064. E-mail iahdecicco@aol.com. 253 rms, 7 story. S, D $180; each addl $10; suites $265; under 12 free; wkend rates. Crib free. TV; cable (premium). 2 pools, 1 indoor; whirlpool, poolside serv. Restaurants 6:30-11 pm. Bar 11-1 am. Ck-out noon. Convention facilities. Business center. In-rm modem link. Gift shop. RR station transportation. Exercise equipt. Health club privileges. Game rm. Microwaves avail. 40-ft atrium lobby, marble fountain. Luxury level. Cr cds: A, C, D, DS, ER, JCB, MC, V.

D ⌹ ✗ ⋈ 🐾 SC 🚶

North Carolina

Population: 6,628,637
Land area: 48,843 square miles
Elevation: 0–6,684 feet
Highest point: Mount Mitchell (Yancey County)
Entered union: Twelfth of original 13 states (November 21, 1789)
Capital: Raleigh
Motto: To be rather than to seem
Nickname: Tar Heel State, Old North State
State flower: American dogwood
State bird: Cardinal
State tree: Pine
State fair: October 13-22, 2000, in Raleigh
Time zone: Eastern

North Carolina, besides being a wonderful place for a vacation, is a cross section of America—a state of magnificent variety with three distinctive regions: the coast, the heartland and the mountains. Its elevation ranges from sea level to 6,684 feet atop Mt Mitchell in the Black Mountain Range of the Appalachians. It has descendants of English, German, Scottish, Irish and African immigrants. It has Quakers, Moravians, Episcopalians and Calvinists. It produces two-thirds of our flue-cured tobacco, as well as cotton, peanuts and vegetables on its farms. Fabrics, furniture and many other products are made in its factories. It also has one of the finest state university systems in the nation with campuses at Chapel Hill, Raleigh, Greensboro, Charlotte, Asheville and Wilmington.

In 1585, the first English settlement was unsuccessfully started on Roanoke Island. Another attempt at settlement was made in 1587—but the colony disappeared, leaving only the crudely scratched word "CROATOAN" on a tree—perhaps referring to the Croatan Indians who may have killed the colonists or absorbed them into their own culture, leaving behind one of history's great mysteries. Here, in the Great Smoky Mountains, lived the Cherokee before the government drove them westward to Oklahoma over the Trail of Tears, on which a third of them died. Descendants of many members of this tribe, who hid in the inaccessible rocky coves and forests, still live here. Some "mountain people," isolated, independent, still singing songs dating back to Elizabethan England, also live here. Few North Carolinians owned slaves, very few owned many, and, early on, the state accepted free blacks (in 1860 there were 30,463) as a part of the community.

Citizens take pride in being called "Tar Heels." During the Civil War, North Carolinians returning from the front were taunted by a troop from another state who had "retreated" a good deal earlier. The Carolinians declared that Jefferson Davis had decided to bring up all the tar from North Carolina to use on the heels of the other regiment to make them "stick better in the next fight." General Lee, hearing of the incident, said, "God bless the Tar Heel boys."

Individual and democratic from the beginning, this state refused to ratify the Constitution until the Bill of Rights had been added. Its western citizens strongly supported the Union in 1860. It did not join the Confederate States of America until after Fort Sumter had been fired upon and Lincoln had called for volunteers. Its independence was then challenged, and it furnished one-fifth of the soldiers of the Southern armies even though its population was only one-ninth of the Confederacy's. Eighty-four engagements (most of them small) were fought on its soil. Jealous of its rights, North Carolina resisted the authority of Confederate Army officers from Virginia and loudly protested many of the policies of Jefferson Davis; but its 125,000 men fought furiously, and 40,000 of them died for what they believed was right. For years after the Civil War, North Carolina was a poverty-stricken state, although it suffered less from the inroads of carpetbaggers than did many of its neighbors.

The state seems designed for vacationers. Beautiful mountains and flowering plants, lake and ocean swimming and boating, hunting and fishing, superb golf courses, old towns, festivals, pageantry and parks are a few of the state's many attractions.

When to Go/Climate

North Carolina has the most varied climate of any state on the east coast. Subtropical temperatures on the coast are contrasted by a medium continental climate in the western mountain areas. Fall is hurricane season along the coast; winter in the western mountains can be snowy and cold. Fall foliage is magnificent in September and October; March and April are marked by blooming dogwood and azaleas.

AVERAGE HIGH/LOW TEMPERATURES (°F)

CAPE HATTERAS

Jan 52/37	May 74/60	Sept 81/68
Feb 53/38	June 81/68	Oct 72/58
Mar 60/44	July 85/72	Nov 65/49
Apr 67/51	Aug 85/72	Dec 57/41

RALEIGH

Jan 49/29	May 79/55	Sept 81/61
Feb 53/31	June 85/64	Oct 72/48
Mar 62/39	July 88/68	Nov 63/40
Apr 72/46	Aug 87/68	Dec 53/32

Parks and Recreation Finder

Directions to and information about the parks and recreation areas below are given under their respective town/city sections. Please refer to those sections for details.

NATIONAL PARK AND RECREATION AREAS

Key to abbreviations. I.H.S. = International Historic Site; I.P.M. = International Peace Memorial; N.B. = National Battlefield; N.B.P. = National Battlefield Park; N.B.C. = National Battlefield & Cemetery; N.C.A. = National Conservation Area; N.E.M. = National Expansion Memorial; N.F. = National Forest; N.G. = National Grassland; N.H.P. = National Historical Park; N.H.S. = National Historic Site. N.M.P. = National Military Park; N.Mem. = National Memorial; N.P. = National Park; N.Pres. = National Preserve; N.R.A. = National Recreational Area; N.R.R. = National Recreational River; N.Riv. = National River; N.S. = National Seashore; N.S.R. = National Scenic Riverway; N.S.T. = National Scenic Trail; N.Sc. = National Scientific Reserve; N.V.M. = National Volcanic Monument.

Place Name	Listed Under
Cape Hatteras N.S.	same
Cape Lookout N.S.	BEAUFORT
Carl Sandburg Home N.H.S.	HENDERSONVILLE
Croatan N.F.	NEW BERN
Fort Raleigh N.H.S.	same
Great Smoky Mountains N.P.	same
Guilford Courthouse N.M.P.	GREENSBORO
Moores Creek N.B.	WILMINGTON
Nantahala N.F.	FRANKLIN
Pisgah N.F.	BREVARD
Wright Brothers N.Mem.	KILL DEVIL HILLS

STATE PARK AND RECREATION AREAS

Key to abbreviations. I.P. = Interstate Park; S.A.P. = State Archaeological Park; S.B. = State Beach; S.C.A. = State Conservation Area; S.C.P. = State Conservation Park; S.Cp. = State Campground; S.F. = State Forest; S.G. = State Garden; S.H.A. = State Historic Area; S.H.P. = State Historic Park; S.H.S. = State Historic Site; S.M.P. = State Marine Park; S.N.A. = State Natural Area; S.P. = State Park; S.P.C. = State Public Campground; S.R. = State Reserve; S.R.A. = State Recreation Area; S.Res.P. = State Resort Park; S.R.P. = State Rustic Park.

Place Name	Listed Under
Carolina Beach S.P.	WILMINGTON
Cliffs of the Neuse S.P.	GOLDSBORO
Duke Power S.P.	STATESVILLE
Fort Macon S.P.	MOREHEAD CITY
Hanging Rock S.P.	WINSTON-SALEM
Jones Lake S.P.	LUMBERTON
Kerr Reservoir	HENDERSON
Merchant's Millpond S.P.	EDENTON
Morrow Mountain S.P.	ALBEMARLE
Mt Mitchell S.P.	LITTLE SWITZERLAND
Pilot Mountain S.P.	PILOT MOUNTAIN
Raven Rock S.P.	SANFORD
Stone Mountain S.P.	WILKESBORO
William B. Umstead S.P.	RALEIGH

Water-related activities, hiking, riding, various other sports, picnicking and visitor centers, as well as camping, are available in many of these areas. Parks are open daily: June–Aug, 8 am–9 pm; Apr–May & Sept to 8 pm; Mar & Oct to 7 pm; Nov–Feb to 6 pm. Most parks have picnicking and hiking. Swimming ($3; 6–12, $2; under 3 free) and concessions open Memorial Day–Labor Day. Admission and parking free (exc reservoirs; $4); canoe and boat rentals ($3/hr first hr, $1/hr thereafter); fishing. Campgrounds: open all yr, limited facilities in winter; family of 6 for $12/day; hookups $5 more; primitive sites $8/day; youth group tent camping $1/person ($8 min). Senior citizen discounts offered. Dogs on leash only. Campgrounds are on first-come, first-served basis; reservations are allowed for minimum of 7 days, maximum of 14 days; write the Park Superintendent.

Information, including a comprehensive brochure, may be obtained from the Division of Parks & Recreation, Dept of Environment, Health and Natural Resources, 1615 MSC, Raleigh 27699-1615; 919/733-7275 or 919/733-4181.

SKI AREAS

Place Name	Listed Under
Appalachian Ski Mountain	BLOWING ROCK
Cataloochee Ski Area	MAGGIE VALLEY
Fairfield Sapphire Valley Ski Area	CASHIERS
Scaly Mountain Ski Area	HIGHLANDS
Ski Beech	BANNER ELK

CALENDAR HIGHLIGHTS

APRIL

North Carolina Azalea Festival (Wilmington). Garden and home tours, horse show, celebrity entertainers, pageants, parade, street fair. Phone 910/763-0905.

Greater Greensboro Chrysler Classic Golf Tournament (Greensboro). Top golfers compete for more than $1.8 million on PGA circuit. For more information, contact Convention & Visitors Bureau, 336/274-2282 or 800/344-2282.

Springfest (Charlotte). Three-day festival in uptown offers food, live entertainment.

MAY

Gliding Spectacular (Nags Head, Outer Banks). Hang gliding competition, novice through advanced. Spectacular flying and fun events. Phone 252/441-4124.

Artsplosure Spring Arts Festival (Raleigh). Moore Square and City Market. Citywide celebration of the arts. Showcase for regional dance, music, theater performances by nationally known artists; outdoor arts and crafts show; children's activities. Phone 919/832-8699.

JUNE

Rogallo Kite Festival (Nags Head, Outer Banks). Competition for homebuilt kites; stunt kite performances, demonstrations; kite auction. Phone 252/441-4124.

"Singing on the Mountain" (Linville). On the slopes of Grandfather Mountain. All-day program of modern and traditional gospel music featuring top groups and nationally known speakers. Concessions or bring your own food.

JULY

Mountain Dance and Folk Festival (Asheville). Civic Center. Folk songs and ballads. Finest of its kind for devotees of the five-string banjo, gut-string fiddle, clogging and smooth dancing. Phone 828/258-6107 or 800/257-5583.

SEPTEMBER

CenterFest (Durham). Downtown. Two-day event with over 250 artists and craftsmen; musicians, jugglers and clowns; continuous entertainment from three stages. Phone 919/560-2722.

Bull Durham Blues Festival (Durham). Historic Durham Athletic Park. Celebrates the blues with performances held at the location where *Bull Durham* was filmed. Phone 919/683-1709.

OCTOBER

Southern Highland Craft Guild Fair (Asheville). Civic Center. More than 175 craftsmen from nine Southern states exhibit and demonstrate their skills. Folk and contemporary entertainment daily. Phone 828/298-7928.

State Fair (Raleigh). State Fairgrounds. Phone 919/733-2145 or 919/821-7400.

| Sugar Mt Ski Area | BANNER ELK |
| Wolf Laurel Ski Resort | ASHEVILLE |

FISHING & HUNTING

Nonresident fishing license $30; daily license $10; 3-day license $15. Nonresident 6-day and basic hunting license $50. Nonresident trapping license $100. Nonresident comprehensive fishing license (includes basic fishing, trout and trout waters on gamelands) $30; 3-day license $15; daily license $10. Waterfowl stamp (mandatory) $5.

For latest regulations contact License Section, Wildlife Resources Commission, Archdale Building, 512 N Salisbury St, Raleigh 27604-1188; 919/662-4370.

Driving Information

Safety belts are mandatory for all persons in front seat of vehicle. Children under 6 years must be in an approved child passenger restraint system anywhere in vehicle; ages 3–6 may use a regulation safety belt; children under 3 years must use an approved child passenger restraint system. For further information phone 919/733-7952.

INTERSTATE HIGHWAY SYSTEM

The following alphabetical listing of North Carolina towns in *Mobil Travel Guide* shows that these cities are within 10 miles of the indicated Interstate highways. A highway map should, however, be checked for the nearest exit.

Highway Number	Cities/Towns within 10 miles
Interstate 26	Asheville, Columbus, Hendersonville, Tryon.
Interstate 40	Asheville, Burlington, Durham, Greensboro, Hickory, Maggie Valley, Marion, Morganton, Raleigh, Statesville, Waynesville, Wilmington, Winston-Salem.
Interstate 77	Charlotte, Cornelius, Dobson, Statesville.
Interstate 85	Burlington, Charlotte, Concord, Durham, Gastonia, Greensboro, Henderson, High Point, Lexington, Salisbury.
Interstate 95	Dunn, Fayetteville, Lumberton, Roanoke Rapids, Rocky Mount, Smithfield, Wilson.

Additional Visitor Information

The North Carolina Gazetteer, by William S. Powell (University of North Carolina Press, Chapel Hill, 1968) lists over 20,000 entries that will enable the reader to find any place in the state, as well as information about size, history and derivation of name. The Travel and Tourism Division, 301 N Wilmington, Raleigh 27601, 800/VISIT-NC, has free travel information, including brochures.

North Carolina Welcome Center locations are: I-85 North, Box 156, Norlina 27563; I-85 South, Box 830, Kings Mountain 28086; I-95 North, Box 52, Roanoke Rapids 27870; I-40, Box 809, Waynesville 28786; I-95 South, Box 518, Rowland 28383; I-26, Box 249, Columbus 28722; I-77 North, Box 1066, Dobson 27017; and I-77 South, Box 410724, Charlotte 28241–0724.

Ahoskie (A-9)

Pop 4,391 **Elev** 53 ft **Area Code** 252 **Zip** 27910

Motel

✓ ★ **TOMAHAWK MOTEL INC.** *601 Academy St N (27910).* *252/332-3194; FAX 252/332-3194.* 58 rms. S $34.85; D $44.85. TV; cable. Restaurant opp 6 am-8:30 pm. Ck-out 11 am. Business servs avail. Cr cds: A, C, D, DS, MC, V.

🔥 **SC**

Motor Hotel

★ **AHOSKIE INN.** *Rte 2 Box 3501 (27910), jct NC 11 & 561.* *252/332-4165; FAX 252/333-1632; res: 800/272-3262; res: 800/582-3220.* Web www.welcome.to/ahoskieinn.com. 98 rms, 2 story. S $47; D $56; each addl $10; suites $161; under 18 free. TV; cable (premium). Indoor pool. Coffee in rms. Restaurant 6 am-2 pm, 5:30-9 pm. Bar; entertainment Sat. Ck-out noon. Meeting rms. Business servs avail. In-rm modem link. Valet serv. Lawn games. Cr cds: A, C, D, DS, MC, V.

D 🏊 🛏 🔥 **SC**

Restaurant

✓ ★ **WHITLEY'S BARBECUE.** *Highway 11 S (27855), 1¼ mi S on NC 11 (Beechwood Blvd).* *252/398-4884.* Hrs: 11 am-9 pm; Sun buffet noon-4 pm. Closed Mon; also July 4, Christmas week. Res accepted. Wine, beer. Semi-a la carte: lunch, dinner $5-$15. Sun buffet $10.95-$12.95. Specializes in seafood, chicken, pork. Own desserts. Parking. Outdoor dining. Family dining. Family-owned since 1963. Cr cds: C.

Albemarle (B-5)

(See also Concord)

Founded 1857 **Pop** 14,939 **Elev** 455 ft **Area Code** 704 **Zip** 28001
Information Stanly County Chamber of Commerce, 116 E North St, PO Box 909, 28002; 704/982-8116

Albemarle is in the gently rolling hills of the Uwharrie Mountains, in the Piedmont section of the state. It manufactures textiles, aircraft tires, automotive parts and aluminum.

What to See and Do

Cotton Patch Gold Mine. Site of first gold lode deposit in state. Prospecting; concessions, picnic facilities. Camping (hookups). (Daily exc Mon, closed hols). 3 mi W off NC 740 on Gurley Rd. Phone 704/463-5797. ¢¢¢

Morrow Mountain State Park. Approx 4,700 acres of hilly forested terrain, touched on two sides by Lake Tillery. Swimming pool, bathhouse; fishing; boating (rentals, launching). Natural history museum. Nature trails, hiking, riding. Picnic facilities, concessions. Camping (no hookups); 6 cabins, families only (Mar–Nov; advance res required). Standard fees. 7 mi E off NC 740, on Morrow Mountain Rd. Phone 704/982-4402.

Stanly Museum and Visitor Center. Originally built as a 3-rm log cabin in the 1850s, the Snuggs House has been enlarged and houses period artifacts. Research rm. (Tues–Fri; also wkends by appt; closed hols) Also on lot is Marks House, town's oldest bldg (1850s) once used as residence/law office. 245 E Main St. Phone 704/983-7316. **Free**

Town Creek Indian Mound State Historic Site. Reconstructed 14th-century Native American ceremonial center with stockade, temples and mortuary. Visitor center, audiovisual shows, exhibits (Apr–Oct, daily; rest of yr, daily exc Mon; closed hols in winter). Picnic area. 11 mi S on US 52, then 12 mi E on NC 731 to Town Creek Mound Rd. Phone 910/439-6802. **Free**

Motel

✓ ★ **COMFORT INN.** 735 Hwy 27 E (28001). 704/983-6990; FAX 704/983-5597; res: 800/638-7949. 80 rms, 2 story. S $59.95-$69.95; D $63.95-$74.95; each addl $6; under 18 free; higher rates during races. Crib free. TV; cable (premium). Complimentary continental bkfst. Restaurant nearby. Ck-out noon. Meeting rms. Business servs avail. Pool. Some refrigerators. Cr cds: A, C, D, DS, ER, JCB, MC, V.

D ⛱ ⛷ 🐾 SC

Asheboro (B-6)

(See also Greensboro, High Point, Lexington)

Founded 1779 **Pop** 16,362 **Elev** 844 ft **Area Code** 336 **Zip** 27203 **E-mail** chamber@asheboro.com **Web** www.chamber.asheboro.com **Information** Randolph Tourism Development Authority, 317 E Dixie Dr, PO Box 4774; 336/626-0364 or 800/626-2672

Situated in the agriculturally and industrially rich Piedmont and the timber-covered Uwharrie Mountains, Asheboro has for over a century served as the seat of Randolph County. Planked roads, covered bridges and the waters of the Deep and Uwharrie rivers provided the impetus for industrial development late in the 19th century. Asheboro is in the heart of North Carolina's pottery-making country.

What to See and Do

North Carolina Zoological Park. North American region exhibits span over 200 acres; African habitats cover over 300 acres and feature 9 outdoor exhibits; Forest Aviary; African Pavilion. (Daily) 6 mi S on NC 159. Phone 800/488-0444. ¢¢¢

Seagrove Area Potteries. Over 80 artists practice traditional hand-turning of pottery. Shops. (Daily) 10 mi S on US 73/74 phone 336/626-0364. **Free**

Annual Event

Asheboro Fall Festival. Arts, crafts, food, parade, music, entertainment. 1st wkend Oct.

Motel

✓ ★★ **DAYS INN.** 999 Albemarle Road (27203), at jct NC 49, US 220 Bypass. 336/629-2101; FAX 336/626-7944; res: 800/329-7466 or 800/222-0519. 136 rms, 2 story. S $46-$80; D $64-$78; each addl $4; suites $125. Crib free. TV; cable (premium). Pool. Ck-out 11 am. Meeting rms. Business servs avail. Valet serv. Health club privileges. Cr cds: A, C, D, DS, MC, V.

D ⛱ ⛷ 🐾 SC

Asheville (B-3)

(See also Maggie Valley, Waynesville)

Settled 1794 **Pop** 61,607 **Elev** 2,134 ft **Area Code** 828 **E-mail** cvb@ashevillechamber.org **Web** www.ashevillechamber.org **Information** Convention & Visitors Bureau, 151 Haywood St, PO Box 1010, 28802-1010; 828/258-6101 or 800/257-1300

Thomas Wolfe came from Asheville, the seat of Buncombe County, as did the expression "bunkum" (nonsense). A local congressman, when asked why he had been so evasive during a masterful oration in which he said nothing, replied, "I did it for Buncombe." Wolfe wrote often of his hill-rimmed home, shrewdly observant of the people and life of Asheville.

Asheville is a vacation headquarters in the Blue Ridge Mountains, as well as a marketing and industrial city. It is the North Carolina city nearest Great Smoky Mountains National Park (see) and attracts many of the park's visitors with its annual mountain fetes, local handicrafts and summer theaters. It is the headquarters for the Uwharrie National Forest, Pisgah National Forest (see BREVARD), Nantahala National Forest (see FRANKLIN) and Croatan National Forest (see NEW BERN). The Blue Ridge Parkway brings many travelers to Asheville on their way south from the Shenandoah Valley of Virginia.

For further information about Croatan, Nantahala, Pisgah and Uwharrie national forests contact the US Forest Service, 828/257-4202.

What to See and Do

Asheville Community Theatre. Comedies, musicals and dramas performed throughout yr. 35 E Walnut St. Phone 828/254-1320 for schedule. ¢¢¢-¢¢¢¢

⊠ **Biltmore Estate.** The 8,000-acre country estate incl 75 acres of formal gardens, numerous varieties of azaleas and roses and the 250-rm chateau (85 rms are open for viewing), which is the largest house ever built in the New World. George W. Vanderbilt commissioned Richard Morris Hunt to design the house, which was begun in 1890 and finished in 1895. Materials and furnishings were brought from many parts of Europe and Asia; a private railroad was built to transport them to the site. Life here was lived in the grand manner. Vanderbilt employed Gifford Pinchot, later Governor of Pennsylvania and famous for forestry and conservation achievements, to manage his forests. Biltmore was the site of the first US forestry school. Much of the original estate is now part of Pisgah National Forest. Tours of the estate include gardens, conservatory and winery facilities; tasting. Three restaurants on grounds. (Daily; closed Thanksgiving, Dec 25) Guidebook (fee) is recommended. S on US 25, 3 blks N of I-40 exit 50. Phone 828/255-1700 or 800/543-2961. ¢¢¢¢

Biltmore Homespun Shops. At the turn of the century, Mrs. George W. Vanderbilt opened a school to keep alive the skills of hand-dyeing, spinning and hand-weaving wool into cloth. The business still has the old machinery and handlooms. An antique automobile museum and the North Carolina Homespun Museum are in an 11-acre park adjoining Grove Park Inn Resort. (Apr-Oct, daily; rest of yr, daily exc Sun; closed Jan 1, Thanksgiving, Dec 25) Grovewood Rd, near Macon Ave, 2 mi NE. Phone 828/253-7651. **Free**

Botanical Gardens of Asheville. A 10-acre tract with thousands of flowers, trees and shrubs native to southern Appalachia; 125-yr-old "dog trot" log cabin. (Daily) On campus of Univ of North Carolina. Phone 828/252-5190. **Free**

Chimney Rock Park. Towering granite monolith Chimney Rock affords 75-mi view; 3 hiking trails lead to 404-ft Hickory Nut Falls, Moonshiner's Cave, Devil's Head balancing rock, Nature's Showerbath. Trails, stairs and catwalks; picnic areas, playground; nature center; observation lounge with snack bar, gift shop. 26-story elevator shaft through granite. (Daily, weather permitting; closed Jan 1, Dec 25) 25 mi SE on US 74, just past jct US 64, NC 9. Phone 828/625-9611 or 800/277-9611. ¢¢¢

Folk Art Center. Home of the Southern Highland Craft Guild. Stone and timber structure; home of Blue Ridge Pkwy info center; craft exhibits, demonstrations, workshops, related programs. (Daily; closed Jan 1, Thanksgiving, Dec 25) 5 mi E on US 70, then ½ mi N on the Blue Ridge Pkwy to Milepost 382. Phone 828/298-7928. (See ANNUAL EVENTS) **Free**

Graves of Thomas Wolfe (1900-1938) and **O. Henry** (William Sydney Porter) (1862-1910). Entrance on Birch St off Pearson Dr. Riverside Cemetery.

Mt Mitchell State Park. 27 mi NE on Blue Ridge Pkwy, then 5 mi N on NC 128 (see LITTLE SWITZERLAND).

Pack Place Education, Arts and Science Center. This 92,000 square-ft complex features multiple museums and exhibit galleries as well as a state-of-the-art theater. A permanent exhibit entitled "Here Is the Square..."

describes the history of Asheville. Restaurant (lunch only); gift shop. (Tues–Sat, also some Sun afternoons; closed Jan 1, Thanksgiving, Dec 24–25) 2 S Pack Square. For general info, phone 828/257-4500. Includes

Asheville Art Museum. Permanent collection and changing exhibits. Phone 828/253-3227. **¢¢**

Colburn Gem and Mineral Museum. Displays of 1,000 minerals from around the world; incl info on mineral locations in the state. Phone 828/254-7162. **¢¢**

Diana Wortham Theatre. This 500-seat theater hosts local, regional and national companies. For box office info, phone 828/257-4530.

The Health Adventure. Extensive collection of imaginative, educational exhibits on the human body; incl a talking transparent woman, a bicycle-pedaling skeleton and an opportunity to hear sound of your own heartbeat. Also on premises is Creative PlaySpace, a special exhibit for young children. Phone 828/254-6373. **¢¢**

YMI Cultural Center. Galleries featuring permanent and rotating exhibts on African American art. Phone 828/252-4614. **¢¢**

River rafting. Nantahala Outdoor Center. Offers various trips on the Nantahala, French Broad, Ocee, Nolichucky and Chattooga rivers ranging from 1½ to 6 hrs. For info and reservations, contact 1377 US 19W, Bryson City 28713-9114; phone 800/232-7238. **¢¢¢¢**

Thomas Wolfe Memorial. The state maintains the Wolfe boardinghouse as a literary shrine, restored and furnished to appear as it did in 1916. In Asheville it is known as the Old Kentucky Home. In *Look Homeward, Angel* it was referred to as "Dixieland"; Asheville was "Altamont." Visitor center with exhibit. (Apr–Oct, daily; rest of yr, daily exc Mon; closed major hols) 48 Spruce St, between Woodfin & Walnut Sts. Phone 828/253-8304. **¢**

Western North Carolina Nature Center. Live animals, children's petting barnyard, natural history exhibits, nature trail, educational programs. (Memorial Day–Labor Day, daily; rest of yr, Tues–Sat and Sun afternoons) Gashes Creek Rd, 3 mi E on NC 81. Phone 828/298-5600. **¢¢**

Wolf Laurel Ski Resort. Quad, double chairlifts, Mitey-mite; patrol, school, rentals; snowmaking; restaurant. Longest run ¾ mi; vertical drop 700 ft. (Mid-Dec–mid-Mar, daily) 27 mi N off US 23. Phone 828/689-4111. **¢¢¢¢**

Zebulon B. Vance Birthplace State Historic Site. Log house (reconstructed 1961) and outbuildings on site where Civil War governor of North Carolina grew up. Honors Vance family, which was deeply involved with early history of state. Visitor center, exhibits. Picnic area. (Apr–Oct, daily; rest of yr, daily exc Mon; closed some hols) 9 mi N on US 19/23, exit New-Stock Rd, then 6 mi N on Reems Creek Rd in Weaverville. Phone 828/645-6706. **Free**

Annual Events

Shindig-on-the-Green. College & Spruce Sts., In front of City Hall. Mountain fiddling, dulcimer players, singing, square dancing. Phone 828/258-6109. Sat eves, July–Labor Day exc last wkend July.

Mountain Dance and Folk Festival. Civic Center. Folk songs and ballads. Finest of its kind for devotees of the 5-string banjo, gut-string fiddle, clogging and smooth dancing. Phone 828/258-6107. July 4 wkend.

Southern Highland Craft Guild Fair. Civic Center, Haywood St, just off I-240. More than 175 craftsmen from 9 Southern states exhibit and demonstrate their skills. Folk and contemporary entertainment daily. Phone 828/298-7928. 3rd wkend July, 3rd wkend Oct.

World Gee Haw Whimmy Diddle Competition. Folk Art Center. Competitions, demonstrations, storytelling, music, dance. Early Aug.

Seasonal Event

Shakespeare in the Park. Montford Park Players. Phone 828/254-4540. Wkends early June–late Aug.

Motels

✓★ **AMERICAN COURT MOTEL.** *85 Merrimon Ave (28801). 828/253-4427; FAX 828/253-2507; res: 800/233-3582.* E-mail tom@americancourt.com; web www.americancourt.com. 22 rms. S $52; D $58–$72;

each addl $3; under 18 free. TV; cable. Pool. Complimentary coffee. Restaurant nearby. Ck-out 11 am. Coin lndry. Refrigerators. Cr cds: A, C, D, DS, MC, V.

▱ ⌇ 🔥 SC

✓★ **BEST INNS.** *1435 Tunnel Rd (28805). 828/298-4000; FAX 828/298-4000; res: 800/237-8466.* 84 rms, 3 story. May-Nov: S $49.88–$55.88; D $56.88–$65.88; each addl $7–$10; under 18 free; lower rates rest of yr. Crib free. TV; cable (premium), VCR avail (movies $4). Heated pool. Complimentary continental bkfst. Complimentary coffee in lobby. Restaurant nearby. Ck-out 1 pm. Business servs avail. Some refrigerators. Cr cds: A, C, D, DS, MC, V.

D ▱ ⌇ 🔥 SC

★★ **COMFORT SUITES.** *890 Brevard Rd (28806), I-26 exit 2. 828/665-4000; FAX 828/665-9082; res: 800/422-6005.* 125 suites, 5 story. May-Oct: suites $69-$109; each addl $6; under 18 free; lower rates rest of yr. Crib free. Pet accepted; $20. TV; cable (premium). Pool; whirlpool. Complimentary continental bkfst. Coffee in rms. Restaurant nearby. Ck-out noon. Coin lndry. Meeting rms. Business servs avail. In-rm modem link. Free airport transportation. Exercise equipt. Refrigerators. Cr cds: A, C, D, DS, ER, JCB, MC, V.

D 🐾 ▱ 🏋 ⌇ 🔥 SC

★★ **FOREST MANOR MOTOR LODGE.** *866 Hendersonville Rd (28803), on US 25, 1 mi S of I-40 exit 50. 828/274-3531; FAX 828/274-3036; res: 800/866-3531.* Web www.ashevillechamber.org. 21 rms. July, Aug & Oct: D $79-$139; kit. units $695-$795/wk; lower rates rest of yr. Crib $5. TV; cable. Heated pool. Complimentary continental bkfst. Restaurant nearby. Ck-out 11 am. Business servs avail. Tennis privileges. Golf privileges. Health club privileges. Lawn games. On 4 wooded acres. Cr cds: A, C, DS, MC, V.

🏋 🎿 ▱ ⌇ 🔥

★★ **HAMPTON INN.** *204 Tunnel Rd (28805), I-240 exit 6 & 7, US 70 to Tunnel Rd. 828/255-9220; FAX 828/254-4303; res: 800/426-7866.* 120 rms, 5 story. June-Oct: S $69-$119; D $79-$119; suites $95-$225; under 18 free; higher rates special events; lower rates rest of yr. Crib free. TV; cable (premium). Indoor pool; whirlpool. Complimentary continental bkfst. Coffee in rms. Restaurant nearby. Ck-out noon. Meeting rms. Business servs avail. Exercise equipt; sauna. Refrigerators, microwaves avail. Cr cds: A, C, D, DS, MC, V.

D ▱ 🏋 ⌇ 🔥

★★ **HAMPTON INN.** *1 Rocky Ridge Rd (28806), jct I-26 & NC 191. 828/667-2022; FAX 828/665-9680; res: 800/426-7866.* 121 rms, 5 story. June-Oct: S $69-$119; D $79-$119; suites $145; under 18 free. Crib free. TV; cable (premium). Indoor pool; whirlpool. Complimentary continental bkfst. Coffee in rms. Ck-out noon. Meeting rms. Business servs avail. In-rm modem link. Free airport transportation. Exercise equipt; sauna. Refrigerator in suites. Cr cds: A, C, D, DS, MC, V.

D ▱ 🏋 ⌇ 🔥 SC

★★ **HOWARD JOHNSON BILTMORE INN.** *190 Hendersonville Rd (28803). 828/274-2300; FAX 828/274-2304; res: 800/446-4656.* 68 rms, 2 story. Apr-Oct: S $54-$149; D $64-$149; each addl $8; higher rates: special events wkends & autumn foliage; lower rates rest of yr. Crib free. TV; cable (premium). Pool. Restaurant 6:30 am-1:30 pm, 5:30-8:30 pm; Sat, Sun from 7 am. Ck-out noon. Meeting rms. Business servs avail. Private patios, balconies. Cr cds: A, C, D, DS, JCB, MC, V.

D ▱ ⌇ 🔥 SC

★★ **MOUNTAIN SPRINGS CABINS.** *Hwy 151 (28715), I-40 W to exit 44, 5 mi S on US 151. 828/665-1004; FAX 828/667-1581.* E-mail mtnsprings@ioa.com; web loa.com/home/mtnsprings. 15 kit. cottages, 1-2 story. S, D $90-$165; each addl $20. Crib free. TV, cable. Ck-out 10 am. Lawn games. Microwaves. Picnic tables, outdoor grills. On mountain stream. Cr cds: C, MC, V.

✔ ★ **RED ROOF INN.** 16 Crowell Rd (28806), I-40 exit 44. 828/667-9803; FAX 828/667-9810; res: 800/843-7663. 109 rms, 3 story. May-Oct: S $65.99; D $69.99; under 18 free; lower rates rest of yr. Pet accepted, some restrictions. TV; cable (premium). Complimentary coffee in lobby. Restaurant opp open 24 hrs. Ck-out noon. Business servs avail. Cr cds: A, C, D, DS, MC, V.

Motor Hotels

★ ★ **BEST WESTERN ASHEVILLE BILTMORE.** 22 Woodfin St (28801), 1 blk off I-240 at Merrimon Ave exit. 828/253-1851; FAX 828/252-9205; res: 800/528-1234. 150 rms, 5 story. June-Oct: S, D $65-$89; under 18 free; lower rates rest of yr. Crib free. TV; cable (premium). Heated pool. Complimentary coffee in rms. Restaurant 6:30-10 am; Sat, Sun 7-11 am. Bar 5 pm-1 am. Ck-out noon. Meeting rm. Business servs avail. In-rm modem link. Exercise equipt. Health club privileges. Cr cds: A, C, D, DS, MC, V.

★ ★ ★ **HOLIDAY INN.** 1 Holiday Inn Dr (28806). 828/254-3211; FAX 828/285-2688; res: 800/733-3211. Web www.sunspree.com. 277 rms, 5 story. May-Oct: S, D $89-$135; each addl $12; suites $195-$275; family rates; ski, golf plans; lower rates rest of yr. Crib free. TV; cable (premium). 2 pools, 1 heated; wading pool. Supervised child's activities (May-Oct); ages 3-15. Playground. Restaurant 6:30 am-10 pm. Rm serv. Bar. Ck-out noon. Convention facilities. Business servs avail. Gift shop. Bellhops. Valet serv. Indoor & outdoor tennis, pro. 18-hole golf, pro, putting green. Exercise equipt. Health club privileges. Refrigerators; some wet bars; microwaves avail. Private patios, balconies. Near shopping center. Cr cds: A, C, D, DS, ER, JCB, MC, V.

★ ★ ★ **QUALITY INN BILTMORE.** 115 Hendersonville Rd (28803). 828/274-1800; FAX 828/274-5960; res: 800/228-5151. E-mail bilt sarms@ioa.com. 160 rms, 5 story, 20 suites. Apr-Oct: S, D $95-$107; each addl $8; suites $110-$150; under 18 free; lower rates rest of yr. Crib free. TV; cable (premium). Pool. Complimentary coffee in rms. Restaurant 6:30 am-10 pm. Rm serv. Bar 5-11 pm. Ck-out noon. Meeting rms. Business servs avail. Bellhops. Valet serv. Health club privileges. Some refrigerators. Cr cds: A, C, D, DS, MC, V.

Hotels

★ ★ ★ **HAYWOOD PARK HOTEL.** 1 Battery Park Ave (28801). 828/252-2522; FAX 828/253-0481; res: 800/228-2522. Web www.hay woodpark.com. 33 suites, 4 story. S $130-$245; D $155-$295; each addl $15; under 18 free. TV; cable (premium), VCR. Complimentary continental bkfst. Restaurant 11 am-9:30 pm (also see 23 PAGE). Bar. Ck-out noon. Meeting rms. Business servs avail. In-rm modem link. Shopping arcade. Free valet parking. Exercise equipt; sauna. Bathrm phones, refrigerators; some in-rm whirlpools. Cr cds: A, C, D, DS, MC, V.

★ ★ **RADISSON HOTEL.** 1 Thomas Wolfe Plz (28801). 828/252-8211; FAX 828/254-1374; res: 800/333-3333. Web www.radis-son.com/asheville. 281 rms, 12 story. Apr-mid-Nov: S $89-$119; D $99-$139; each addl $10; suites $165-$225; under 18 free; lower rates rest of yr. Crib free. TV; cable (premium), VCR avail. Pool. Restaurant 6:30 am-10 pm. Bar 11am-1 am. Ck-out noon. Convention facilities. Business servs avail. In-rm modem link. Concierge. Gift shop. Exercise equipt. Game rm. Minibars; refrigerators avail. Cr cds: A, C, D, DS, MC, V.

Resorts

GROVE PARK INN RESORT. 290 Macon Ave (28804). 828/252-2711; FAX 828/253-7053; res: 800/438-5800. Web www.grove

parkinn.com. Unrated due to renovation. 510 rms, 6-11 story. Apr-Dec: S, D $125-$230; each addl $25; suites $450; under 16 free; golf plans; lower rates rest of yr. Crib free. TV; cable (premium), VCR avail. 2 heated pools, 1 indoor; whirlpool, lifeguard. Supervised child's activities; ages 3-16. Restaurants 6:30 am-midnight (also see HORIZONS). Rm serv. Bar from 11 am; entertainment. Ck-out 11 am, ck-in 4 pm. Convention facilities. Business center. Bellhops. Valet serv. Shopping arcade. 9 lighted tennis courts, 3 indoor. Golf, greens fee $75 (incl cart), nine holes $37.50, putting green. Rec rm. Exercise rm; sauna. Raquetball & squash courts. Massage. Luxury level. Cr cds: A, C, D, DS, JCB, MC, V.

✔ ★ **PISGAH INN.** Blue Ridge Pkwy (28786), Enka-Candler exit off I-40, S on US 19/23 4 mi to Candler, left on NC 151, 9 mi to ranch. 828/235-8228; FAX 828/648-9719. 48 units. May-Oct: AP: S $55-$125/person, $300-$700/wk; D $55-$85/person, $300-$475/wk; family rates. Closed rest of yr. Crib free. TV. Heated pool. Playground. Dining rm: bkfst 8 am, lunch 12:30 pm, dinner 5:30 pm. Ck-out 11 am, ck-in 2 pm. Coin lndry. Meeting rms. Gift shop. Airport, bus depot transportation. Tennis. Hiking trails. Rec rm. Lawn games. Entertainment. Cr cds: C.

Inns

★ ★ **ADAMS CAIRN BRAE BED & BREAKFAST.** 217 Patton Mountain Rd (28804). 828/252-9219. E-mail cairnbrae@compuserv.com; web www.ourworld.compuserve.com/homepages/mrichardson/. 3 rms, 1 with shower only, 2 story, 2 suites. No rm phones. S $85-$100; D $95-$120; each addl $20; suites $120. Children over 10 yrs only. TV in sitting rm; cable (premium). Complimentary full bkfst; afternoon refreshments. Ck-out 11 am, ck-in 3 pm. Rec rm. Picnic tables. Situated along mountainside. Totally nonsmoking. Cr cds: C, DS, MC, V.

★ ★ **ALBEMARLE INN.** 86 Edgemont Rd (28801). 828/255-0027; FAX 828/236-3397; res: 800/621-7435. Web www.albemarle inn.com. 11 rms, 3 story. S, D $95-$170; each addl $25. Children over 9 yrs only. TV; cable. Pool. Complimentary full bkfst; afternoon refreshments. Ck-out 11 am, ck-in 3 pm. Luggage handling. Greek-revival mansion built 1909; many antiques. Totally nonsmoking. Cr cds: C, DS, MC, V.

★ ★ **APPLEWOOD MANOR INN BED & BREAKFAST.** 62 Cumberland Cir (28801), 1 mi N on I-240, exit 4-C. 828/254-2244; FAX 828/254-0899; res: 800/442-2197. Web comscape.com/apple. 4 rms, 2 with shower only, 1 kit. cottage, 2 story. No rm phones. S $90-$110; D $95-$115; each addl $20; kit. cottage $105-$110; hols (2-day min). Children over 12 yrs only. TV in kit. cottage; cable. Complimentary full bkfst; afternoon refreshments. Ck-out 11 am, ck-in 3-7 pm. Business servs avail. Lawn games. Many fireplaces. Many balconies. Colonial turn-of-the-century home built in 1910; antiques. Totally nonsmoking. Cr cds: C, MC, V.

★ ★ ★ **BEAUFORT HOUSE.** 61 N Liberty St (28801). 828/254-8334; FAX 828/251-2082; res: 800/261-2221. Web www.beaufort house.com. 11 rms, 1 shower only, 3 story, 1 suite. Apr-Dec: S, D $95-$185; suite $195; call ahead for wkend rates (2-day min); lower rates rest of yr. Children over 10 yrs only. TV; cable, VCR (movies). Complimentary full bkfst. Restaurant nearby. Ck-out 11 am, ck-in 3-7 pm. Luggage handling. Exercise equipt. Many in-rm whirlpools, fireplaces. Built in 1894. Victorian decor; antiques. Totally nonsmoking. Cr cds: C, MC, V.

★ ★ ★ **CEDAR CREST.** 674 Biltmore Ave (28803). 828/252-1389; FAX 828/253-7667; res: 800/252-0310. 9 rms, 3 story, 2 cottage suites. S, D $130-$170; each addl $20; suites $130-$220. Children over

10 yrs only. Complimentary full bkfst. Ck-out 11 am, ck-in 3-10 pm. Business servs avail. Lawn games. Balconies. Historic inn (1890); antiques. Flower gardens. Cr cds: A, C, D, DS, MC, V.

★ **CORNER OAK MANOR.** *53 Saint Dunstans Rd (28803). 828/253-3525; FAX 828/253-3525.* E-mail vineguy@aol.com; web www.bbonline.com/nc/corneroak. 4 rms, 2 story, 1 kit. unit. No rm phones. S $75; D $100-$115; kit. unit $145. Children over 12 yrs only. Complimentary full bkfst. Ck-out 11 am, ck-in 3 pm. Whirlpool on terrace. Picnic tables. English Tudor home (1920); antiques. Totally nonsmoking. Cr cds: A, C, DS, MC, V.

✓★★ **FLINT STREET INNS.** *116 Flint St (28801). 704/253-6723.* Web www.bbonline/nc/flintstreet. 8 rms in 2 bldgs, 2 story. S $80; D $100; each addl $25. Complimentary full bkfst; afternoon refreshments. Ck-out 11 am, ck-in noon-8 pm. Cr cds: A, C, DS, ER, MC, V.

★★★ **LION AND THE ROSE.** *276 Montford Ave (28636). 828/255-7673; FAX 828/285-9810; res: 800/546-6988.* E-mail lion-rose@a-o.com; web www.a-o.com/lion-rose. 5 rms, 3 story. No rm phones. No elvtr. S, D $115-$195; each addl $35. Children over 12 yrs only. Complimentary full bkfst; afternoon refreshments. Restaurant nearby. Ck-out 11 am, ck-in 3 pm. Luggage handling. Health club privileges. Georgian house built in 1895; antiques. Totally nonsmoking. Cr cds: A, C, DS, MC, V.

★★★ **OWLS NEST INN.** *2630 Smokey Park Hwy (28715), W on I-40, exit 37. 828/665-8325; FAX 828/667-2539; res: 800/665-8868.* Web www.circle.net.owlsnest. 4 rms, 1 suite, 3 story. No rm phones. No elvtr. S $80-$135; D $95-$165; each addl $15. Children over 12 yrs only. Complimentary full bkfst. Restaurant nearby. Ck-out 11 am, ck-in 3-7 pm. Luggage handling. Victorian house built in 1885; antiques. Totally nonsmoking. Cr cds: C, DS, MC, V.

★★★★ **RICHMOND HILL INN.** *87 Richmond Hill Dr (28806). 828/252-7313; FAX 828/252-8726; res: 800/545-9238.* Web www.richmond hillinn.com. 36 rms, 3 story, 7 cottages. S, D $135-$385; each addl $20. Crib $15. TV; cable (premium). Complimentary full bkfst; afternoon refreshments. Coffee in rms. Dining rms (see GABRIELLE'S). Ck-out 11 am, ck-in 3 pm. Business servs avail. Gift shop. Exercise equipt. Croquet courts. Queen Anne-style architecture; library, grand entrance hall. Former congressman's residence. Cr cds: A, C, MC, V.

★★ **THE OLD REYNOLDS MANSION.** *100 Reynolds Hts (28804). 828/254-0496; res: 800/709-0496.* 10 rms, 8 with bath, 3 story. No rm phones. S, D $60-$115; cottage suite $110-$120. Closed Sun-Thurs Nov-June. Pool. Complimentary continental bkfst; afternoon refreshments. Restaurant nearby. Ck-out 11 am, ck-in 3 pm. Antebellum mansion (1855) on hill overlooking mountains; antiques, verandas. Cr cds: C.

Restaurants

★★★ **23 PAGE RESTAURANT.** *(See Haywood Park Hotel) 828/252-3685.* Hrs: 5:30-10 pm. Closed some major hols. Res accepted. Continental menu. Bar. Wine list. A la carte entrees: dinner $15.95-$28.95. Child's meals. Specializes in seafood, desserts, pasta. Intimate dining. Cr cds: A, C, D, DS, MC, V.

★★ **DA VINCENZO RISTORANTE.** *10 N Market St (28801). 828/254-4698.* Hrs: 11:30 am-2 pm; 5:30-11 pm; Sat from 5:30 pm; Sun

5:30-9 pm. Closed major hols. Res accepted. Italian, continental menu. Bar. Semi-a la carte: lunch $3.95-$7.95, dinner $9-$27. Child's meals. Specializes in veal, pasta, seafood. Entertainment. Cr cds: A, C, DS, MC, V.

★★ **FINE FRIENDS.** *946 Merrimon Ave (28804), in Northland Shopping Center. 828/253-6649.* Hrs: 11:30 am-9 pm; Fri, Sat to 10 pm; Sun brunch 11:30 am-3:30 pm. Closed Thanksgiving, Dec 24, 25. Res accepted. Bar to midnight. Semi-a la carte: lunch $5.95-$10.95, dinner $10.95-$16.95. Sun brunch $6-$8. Child's meals. Specializes in seafood, beef, pasta. Own desserts. Cr cds: A, C, D, DS, MC, V.

★★★ **GABRIELLE'S.** *(See Richmond Hill Inn) 828/252-7313.* Hrs: 6-10 pm. Res accepted. Wine list. Semi-a la carte: dinner $25-$42. Child's meals. Specializes in fresh fish, game, beef. Own pasta. Pianist Thurs-Mon. Valet parking. Formal dining. Jacket. Totally nonsmoking. Cr cds: A, C, MC, V.

★★ **GREENERY.** *148 Tunnel Rd (28803). 828/253-2809.* Hrs: 5-10 pm. Closed Jan 1. Res accepted. Bar. Semi-a la carte: dinner $14.95-$24.95. Specialties: Maryland crabcakes, mountain trout. Cr cds: A, C, MC, V.

★★★ **HORIZONS.** *(See Grove Park Inn Resort) 828/252-2711.* Web www.groveparkinn.com. Hrs: 6:30-9:30 pm. Closed Sun. Res accepted. Contemporary Amer menu. Serv bar. Wine list. Semi-a la carte: dinner $21-$36. Complete meals: dinner $58. Specialties: Lone star ostrich au poivre, double breast of free range chicken, mixed grill of American wild game. Piano Tue-Sat. Valet parking. Formal dining in elegant setting with mountain views. Jacket. Totally nonsmoking. Cr cds: A, C, D, DS, JCB, MC, V.

★★ **MARKET PLACE ON WALL STREET.** *20 Wall St (28801). 828/252-4162.* Hrs: 6-9:30 pm. Closed Sun; some major hols. Res accepted. Bar. A la carte entrees: dinner $12.50-$27.95. Child's meals. Specializes in seafood, veal, lamb. Outdoor dining. 3 formal dining areas. Totally nonsmoking. Cr cds: A, C, D, MC, V.

✓★ **MCGUFFEY'S INC.** *13 Kenilworth Knoll (28805). 828/252-3300.* Hrs: 11 am-2 am; Sun brunch to 4 pm. Closed Thanksgiving, Dec 25. Bar. Semi-a la carte: lunch $4.99-$8.99, dinner $6.99-$15. Sun brunch $4.99-$10.99. Specializes in beef, seafood, chicken. Cr cds: A, C, D, DS, MC, V.

★★ **WINDMILL EUROPEAN GRILL.** *85 Tunnel Rd (28805), at Innsbruck Mall. 828/253-5285.* Hrs: 5:30-9:30 pm; Fri, Sat to 10 pm. Closed Sun, Mon; Jan 1, Dec 25. Res accepted. Continental menu. Bar. Semi-a la carte: dinner $10.99-$21.99. Specializes in beef, chicken, seafood. Cr cds: A, C, DS, MC, V.

Unrated Dining Spot

MOUNTAIN SMOKE HOUSE. *20 Spruce St (28801). 828/253-4871.* Hrs: 5:30-11 pm; Fri, Sat to midnight; Apr-May hrs vary. Closed Jan-Mar. Res accepted. Bar. Semi-a la carte: dinner $7.95-$16.95. Child's meals. Specializes in barbecued chopped pork, herb-smoked chicken, barbecued ribs. Bluegrass band, clogging. Casual, family atmosphere. Cr cds: A, C, D, DS, MC, V.

Atlantic Beach

(see Morehead City)

Banner Elk (A-3)

(See also Blowing Rock, Boone, Linville)

Pop 933 **Elev** 3,739 ft **Area Code** 828 **Zip** 28604 **E-mail** beacc@skybest.com **Web** www.banner-elk.com

Information Chamber of Commerce, PO Box 335; 828/898-5605

What to See and Do

Grandfather Mountain. 3 mi N via US 221 (see LINVILLE).
Skiing.

Ski Beech. Quad chairlift, 6 double chairlifts, J-bar, rope tow; patrol, school, rentals; snowmaking, ice-skating; restaurant, cafeteria; nursery, shopping. Vertical drop 830 ft. (Mid-Nov–mid-Mar, daily) 3 mi N on NC 184. Phone 828/387-2011. ¢¢¢¢¢

Sugar Mt. Five chairlifts, 2 T-bars, rope tow; patrol, school, rentals; snowmaking; children's program; lodging, cafeteria; nursery. (Mid-Nov–mid-Mar, daily) Off NC 184. Phone 828/898-4521. ¢¢¢¢¢

Motels

★★ **HOLIDAY INN.** *1615 Tynecastle Hwy (NC 184) (28604), 1 mi S on NC 184 between NC 194 and NC 105.* 828/898-4571; FAX 828/898-8437; res: 877/877-4553. 101 rms, 2 story. Dec-Feb: S, D $64.99-$99.99; under 18 free; ski plans; lower rates rest of yr. Crib free. TV; cable (premium). Pool. Restaurant 7 am-2 pm, 6-9 pm. Rm serv. Ck-out noon. Meeting rms. Business servs avail. Downhill/x-country ski 1 mi. Cr cds: A, C, D, DS, MC, V.

D ⊁ ⊠ ⊠ ⊁ SC

★ **PINNACLE INN.** *301 Pinnacle Inn Rd (28604), off NC 184.* 828/387-2231; FAX 828/387-3742; res: 800/405-7888. 242 kits, 3 story. No elvtr. Mid-Nov-mid-Mar: kit. units $75-$170; lower rates rest of yr. Crib $5. TV; cable. Indoor pool; whirlpool. Sauna. Free supervised child's activities (mid-June-mid-Sept). Restaurant nearby. Ck-out 10 am. Coin lndry. Meeting rms. Business servs avail. Tennis. Downhill ski ½ mi. Game rm. Fireplaces. Balconies. Picnic tables, grills. Cr cds: A, C, MC, V.

⊠ ⊁ ⊁ ⊠ ⊼ ⊁

Inn

✓★★ **ARCHER'S MOUNTAIN INN.** *2489 Beech Mountain Pkwy (28604).* 828/898-9004; FAX 828/898-9007. Web www.archersinn.com. 15 rms, 2 story. Mid-Dec-mid-Mar: S, D $75-$200; each addl $10; lower rates rest of yr. Crib free. TV; cable, VCR some rms. Complimentary full bkfst. Coffee in rms. Restaurant (see JACKALOPE'S VIEW). Swimming privileges. Ck-out 11 am, ck-in 3 pm. Tennis privileges. Golf privileges. Downhill ski 2 mi. Fireplaces; many refrigerators. Many balconies. Rustic decor. Cr cds: C, DS, MC, V.

⊠ ⊁⊀ ⊁ ⊠ ⊁

Restaurant

★★ **JACKALOPE'S VIEW.** *(See Archers Inn)* 828/898-9004. Web www.archersinn.com. Hrs: 5-9:30 pm; Fri, Sat to 10 pm. Closed Mon. Res accepted. No A/C. Continental menu. Bar. Semi-a la carte: dinner $10-

$20. Child's meals. Specializes in steak, seafood, wild game. Own baking. Outdoor dining. Floor-to-ceiling windows overlook mountains, patio; artwork by local artists. Totally nonsmoking. Cr cds: C, DS, MC, V.

D

Beaufort (C-9)

(See also Morehead City)

Pop 3,808 **Elev** 7 ft **Area Code** 252 **Zip** 28516 **E-mail** vaction@sunnync.com **Web** www.sunnync.com

Information Carteret County Tourism Development Bureau, PO Box 1406, Morehead City 28557; 252/726-8148 or 800/SUNNY-NC

Beaufort, dating from the colonial era, is a seaport with more than 125 historic houses and sites.

What to See and Do

Beaufort Historic Site. Old Burying Ground, 1829 restored Old Jail, restored houses (1767–1830), courthouse (ca 1796), apothecary shop, art gallery and gift shop. Obtain additional info, self-guided walking tour map from Beaufort Historical Assn, Inc, 138 Turner St, PO Box 1709. (Daily exc Sun; closed some major hols) Phone 252/728-5225. Admission to 6 bldgs open to the public ¢¢

Cape Lookout National Seashore. This unit of the National Park System, on the outer banks of North Carolina, extends 55 mi S from Ocracoke Inlet and incl unspoiled barrier islands. There are no roads or bridges; access is by boat only (fee). Ferries from Beaufort, Harkers Island, Davis, Atlantic and Ocracoke (Apr–Nov). Excellent fishing and shell collecting; primitive camping; interpretive programs (seasonal). Lighthouse (1859) at Cape Lookout is still operational. Phone 252/728-2250.

North Carolina Maritime Museum and Watercraft Center. Natural and maritime history exhibits, field trips; special programs in maritime and coastal natural history. (Daily; closed Jan 1, Thanksgiving, Dec 25) 315 Front St. Phone 252/728-7317. **Free**

Annual Events

Beaufort by the Sea Music Festival. Late Apr.

Old Homes Tour and Antiques Show. Private homes and historic public bldgs; Carteret County Militia; bus tours and tours of old burying ground; historical crafts. Sponsored by the Beaufort Historical Assn, Inc, PO Box 1709. Phone 919/728-5225. Last wkend June.

Inns

★★ **DELAMAR INN.** *217 Turner St (28516).* 919/728-4300; res: 800/349-5823. Web www.bbonline.com/nc/ncbbi. 3 rms, 2 with shower only, 2 story. No rm phones. May-Sept: D $82-$120; lower rates rest of yr. Children over 10 yrs only. Complimentary continental bkfst; afternoon refreshments. Restaurant nearby. Ck-out 11 am, ck-in 1 pm. Business servs avail. Built 1865; first and second floor porches. Many antiques. Totally nonsmoking. Cr cds: C, MC, V.

⊠ ⊁ SC

★★ **PECAN TREE INN.** *116 Queen St (28516).* 252/728-6733. Web www.pecantree.com. 7 rms, 5 with shower only, 2 story. No rm phones. Apr-Sept: D $90-$135; each addl $15; wkly rates; lower rates rest of yr. Children over 12 yrs only. Complimentary continental bkfst. Restaurant adj 11 am-10 pm. Ck-out 11 am, ck-in 2 pm. Game rm. Built 1866. Many antiques. Totally nonsmoking. Cr cds: C, DS, MC, V.

⊠ ⊁

★★ **THE CEDARS INN BY THE SEA.** *305 Front St (28516).* 252/728-7036; FAX 252/728-1685. Web www.cedarsinn.com. 6 rms, 5 suites, 2 story. Mid-Apr-mid-Oct: S, D $95-$125; suites $125-$165; lower rates rest of yr. Children over 9 yrs only. TV; cable. Complimentary full bkfst. Ck-out 11 am, ck-in 3 pm. Private patios, balconies. Historic house (ca 1770) overlooking river; antiques. Cr cds: A, C, DS, MC, V.

Restaurant

✓★★ **LOUGHRY'S LANDING.** *510 Front St (28516), on the Waterfront.* 252/728-7541. E-mail loughry@brnd.clis.com; web www.loughryslanding.com. Hrs: 11:30 am-9 pm; hrs may vary Nov-Feb. Bar. A la carte entrees: lunch $3.75-$7.95, dinner $8.75-$15.95. Child's meals. Specializes in fresh local seafood, pasta. Overlooks harbor. Cr cds: A, C, D, DS, MC, V.

Blowing Rock (A-4)

(See also Banner Elk, Boone, Linville)

Founded 1889 **Pop** 1,257 **Elev** 4,000 ft **Area Code** 828 **Zip** 28605 **Web** www.blowingrock.com/northcarolina
Information Chamber of Commerce, PO Box 406; 828/295-7851 or 800/295-7851

On the Blue Ridge Parkway, Blowing Rock was named, based on Native American folklore, for the cliff near town where lightweight objects thrown outward are swept back to their origin by the wind. It has been a resort area for more than 100 years; a wide variety of recreational facilities and shops can be found nearby.

What to See and Do

Blowing Rock. Cliff (4,000 ft) hangs over Johns River Gorge 2,000–3,000 ft below. Scenic views of Grandfather, Grandmother, Table Rock and Hawksbill mountains. Observation deck. Gift shop. (Apr–Nov, daily) 2 mi SE on US 321. Phone 828/295-7111. ¢¢

Julian Price Memorial Park. Boating (hand-powered only, rentals). Picnicking. Camping (trailer facilities, no hookups; June–Oct only; fee). Amphitheater; evening interpretive programs (May–Oct). Park open yr-round (weather permitting). SW via US 221 & Blue Ridge Pkwy. Phone 828/295-7591 or 828/963-5911. **Free**

Moses H. Cone Memorial Park. Former summer estate of textile magnate. Bridle paths, 2 lakes; 25 mi of hiking and cross-country skiing trails. (May–Oct, daily) On Blue Ridge Pkwy. Phone 828/295-7591. **Free**

Parkway Craft Center. Demonstrations of weaving, wood carving, pottery, jewelry making, other crafts. (May–Oct, daily) Handcrafted items for sale. Phone 828/295-7938. **Free**

Mystery Hill. Educational exhibits explore science, optical illusion and natural phenomena. Features TouchTown, Mystery House, Hall of Mystery and BubbleRama. Gift shop. (Daily; closed Thanksgiving, Dec 25) N on US 321. Phone 828/264-2792. ¢¢

Skiing.

Appalachian Ski Mountain. Quad & 2 double chairlifts, 2 rope tows, 1 handle-pull tow; patrol; French-Swiss Ski College; Ski-Wee children's program; equipment rentals; 100% snowmaking; restaurant; 8 runs; longest run 2,700 ft; vertical drop 365 ft. (Thanksgiving–mid-Mar, daily & nightly; closed Dec 24 eve–Dec 25) Night skiing (all slopes lighted); half-day and twilight rates. 3 mi N on US 321, near Blueridge Pkwy intersection. Phone 828/295-7828 or 800/322-2373 (res). ¢¢¢¢¢

Tweetsie Railroad. A 3-mi excursion, with mock holdup and raid, on old narrow-gauge railroad; Western Town with variety show at Tweetsie Palace; country fair, petting zoo; craft village; chairlift to Mouse Mt Picnic Area. (May–Oct, limited hrs) 4 mi N on US 321. Phone 828/264-9061. ¢¢¢¢

Annual Event

Tour of Homes. 4th Fri July.

Motels

★ **ALPINE VILLAGE INN.** *297 Sunset Dr (28605).* 828/295-7206. 15 rms, 14 with shower only. June-Oct: S, D $45-$79; each addl $6; under 12 free; hol wkends (2-day min); lower rates rest of yr. Crib $2. TV; cable. Complimentary coffee in lobby. Restaurant adj. 7 am-9 pm. Ck-out 11 am. Refrigerators avail. Cr cds: A, C, DS, MC, V.

★★ **BLOWING ROCK INN.** *788 N Main St (28605), ¼ mi N on US 221/321 Business.* 828/295-7921. 24 rms. July-Nov: S, D $69-$84; each addl $5; lower rates early-mid-Nov, Apr-May; also 1-bedrm villas avail. Closed Dec-Mar. TV; cable. Heated pool. Complimentary coffee on porch. Restaurant nearby. Ck-out 11 am. Picnic tables. Cr cds: A, C, DS, MC, V.

★★ **CLIFF DWELLERS INN.** *116 Lakeview Ter (28605), 1 mi S, Blue Ridge Pkwy exit for US 321, across from Shoppes on the Pkwy.* 828/295-3121; FAX 828/295-3121; res: 800/322-7380. E-mail cliffdwellers@boone.net; web www.cliffdwellers.com. 20 rms, 3 story, 3 suites, 2 kit. units. No elvtr. Mid-May-early Nov: S, D $95-$115; each addl $5; suites, kit. units $155-$245; under 12 free; lower rates rest of yr. Closed Dec-Apr exc wkends, Christmas hol. Crib $5. TV; cable. Heated pool; whirlpool. Complimentary coffee in rms. Restaurant nearby. Ck-out 11 am. Refrigerators; microwaves avail. Balconies. View of mountains. Cr cds: C, D, MC, V.

✓★ **HOMESTEAD INN.** *153 Morris St (28605).* 828/295-9559; FAX 828/295-9551. E-mail homesteadinn@appstate.campus.mci.net. 15 rms. Early June-Oct: S, D $47-$69; each addl $5; family, wkday, wkly rates; lower rates rest of yr. Crib free. TV; cable. Playground. Coffee in lobby. Restaurant nearby. Ck-out 11 am. Downhill ski 4 mi. Refrigerators, microwaves avail. Picnic tables, grills. Cr cds: A, C, DS, MC, V.

Resorts

★★★ **CHETOLA RESORT.** *N Main St (28605).* 828/295-5500; FAX 828/295-5529; res: 800/243-8652. Web www.chetola.com. 104 rms, 1-3 story, 62 condos. May-Dec: S, D $125-$214; condos $160-$365; wkly rates; lower rates rest of yr. Crib $5. TV; cable (premium); VCR avail. Indoor pool; whirlpool. Playground. Supervised child's activities (June-Aug); ages 5-12. Dining rm (public by res) 8-10 am, 11:30 am-2 pm, 5:30-8:30 pm. Ck-out 11 am, ck-in 3 pm. Coin lndry. Meeting rms. Business servs avail. Grocery, package store ½ mi. Sports dir. Lighted tennis. Golf privileges. Boating, fishing. Downhill/x-country ski 3 mi. Exercise equipt; sauna. Massage. Hiking. Bicycles. Soc dir. Entertainment. Racquetball court. Game rm. Refrigerators. Some private balconies. Picnic tables, grills. Seven-acre lake. Adj to Moses Cone Natl Park. Cr cds: A, C, DS, MC, V.

★★★ **HOUNDS EARS LODGE & CLUB.** *Rt 3, Hwy 105 S (28607), 7 mi W, ½ mi off NC 105.* 828/963-4321; FAX 828/963-8030. Web www.houndears.com. 29 rms in lodge & club house, 2 story. MAP, mid-June-Oct: S $150; D $270; each addl $48; suites $290-$330; under 11, $55; lower rates rest of yr. Serv charge 17%. TV; cable (premium), VCR avail. Heated pool; poolside serv, lifeguard. Free supervised child's activities (June-Sept); ages 8-16. Dining rm 7-10 am, noon-2:30 pm, 6:30-9:30 pm (res required). Rm serv. Bar; entertainment. Ck-out 11 am, ck-in 1:30 pm. Meeting rms. Business servs avail. Bellhops. Valet serv. 6 tennis courts, pro. 18-hole golf, greens fee $38, pro. Exercise equipt; sauna. Cr cds: A, C, MC, V.

Inns

★★ **CRIPPEN'S COUNTRY INN.** *239 Sunset Dr (28605).* *828/295-3487; FAX 828/295-0388.* Web www.crippens.com. 8 rms, 2 with shower only, 3 story, 1 guest house. May-Dec: S, D $129; each addl $25; guest house $159; hols (2-day min); lower rates rest of yr. TV in common rm; cable (premium). Complimentary continental bkfst. Restaurant (see CRIPPEN'S). Rm serv 6-10 pm. Ck-out 11 am, ck-in 3 pm. Business servs avail. Luggage handling. Built in 1931. Totally nonsmoking. Cr cds: A, C, DS, MC, V.

✓★★★ **INN AT RAGGED GARDENS.** *203 Sunset (28605).* *828/295-9703.* Web www.ragged-gardens.com. 12 rms, 5 with A/C, 3 story. S, D $125-$200. Children over 12 yrs only. Complimentary full bkfst; afternoon refreshments. Ck-out 11 am, ck-in after 3 pm. Fireplaces, in-rm whirlpools. Balconies. Built in 1900; gardens. Totally nonsmoking. Cr cds: C, MC, V.

★★ **MAPLE LODGE.** *152 Sunset Dr (28605). 828/295-3331; FAX 828/295-9986.* E-mail innkeeper@maplelodge.net; web www.maple lodge.net. 11 rms, some A/C, 2 story. No rm phones. No elvtr. S, D $90-$140; each addl $20; suite $140; wkends (2-day min). Closed Jan, Feb. Children over 12 yrs only. Some TVs. Complimentary full bkfst; afternoon refreshments. Restaurant opp 11 am-10 pm. Ck-out 11 am, ck-in 3-9 pm. Luggage handling. Downhill ski 5 mi; x-country ski 2 mi. Some refrigerators. Antiques. Totally nonsmoking. Cr cds: A, C, D, DS, MC, V.

★★★ **MEADOWBROOK INN.** *152 Sunset Dr (28605). 704/295-4300; FAX 704/295-4300; res: 800/456-5456.* Web www.meadow brook-inn.com. 61 rms, 2-3 story. S, D $119-$139; each addl $10; suites $139-$259; under 12 free; ski plans. TV; cable, VCR avail. Indoor pool; whirlpool. Complimentary continental bkfst. Dining rm 6-9 pm. Bar. Ck-out 11 am, ck-in 3 pm. Meeting rms. Business servs avail. Downhill ski 3 mi. Exercise equipt. European style country inn. Cr cds: A, C, D, DS, MC, V.

Restaurants

★★ **BEST CELLAR INC.** *Highway 321 & Blowing Rock Rd (28605), behind Food Lion Shopping Center. 828/295-3466.* Hrs: 5:30-10 pm; Dec-Apr to 9:30. Closed Sun (May-Nov); also Tues, Wed (Dec-Apr). Res accepted. No A/C. Continental menu. Serv bar. Semi-a la carte: dinner $15.95-$21.95. Specialties: roast duckling, Sterling Silver beef, banana cream pie. Valet parking. Rustic decor; pine floor, stone walls, 3 fireplaces. Cr cds: A, C, D, MC, V.

★★★ **CRIPPEN'S.** *(See Crippen's Country Inn) 828/295-3487.* Web www.crippens.com. Hrs: 6-9 pm; Fri to 10 pm; Sat 5-10 pm. Closed Mon; most major hols; also Super Bowl Sun. Res accepted. Continental menu. Bar 5:30-10:30 pm. Semi-a la carte: dinner $16.95-$33. Child's meals. Specialties: grilled Maine lobster, grilled North Carolina ostrich, horseradish-encrusted salmon. Own pasta. Parking. Semi-formal, spacious dining area. Totally nonsmoking. Cr cds: A, C, DS, MC, V.

★★ **RIVERWOOD.** *7179 Valley Blvd (28605), ½ mi S of Blue Ridge Pkwy. 828/295-4162.* Web blowingrock.com/northcarolina/river woodrestaurant. Hrs: 6 pm-closing; Sat from 5:30 pm; winter hrs vary. Closed Sun. Res accepted. Bar. Semi-a la carte: dinner $13.95-$23.95. Specialties: stuffed rainbow trout, marinated beef tenderloin. Own desserts. Totally nonsmoking. Cr cds: C, DS, MC, V.

★★ **TWIG'S.** *US 321 Bypass (28605). 828/295-5050.* Hrs: 5:30-9:30 pm; Fri, Sat to 10 pm. Closed Mon; Dec 24-25. Res accepted.

Regional Amer menu. Bar 5:30 pm-2 am. Semi-a la carte: dinner $13.95-$21.95. Specializes in crab cakes, lamb, fresh seafood. Porch dining (summer). Cr cds: A, C, DS, MC, V.

Blue Ridge Parkway

(see Virginia)

Boone (A-4)

(See also Banner Elk, Blowing Rock, Linville)

Settled 1772 **Pop** 12,915 **Elev** 3,266 ft **Area Code** 828 **Zip** 28607 **E-mail** chamber@boone.net **Web** www.boonechamber.com

Information Convention & Visitors Bureau, 208 Howard St, 28607-4032, 828/262-3516 or 800/852-9506; or North Carolina High Country Host, 1700 Blowing Rock Rd, 828/264-1299 or 800/438-7500

Boone, the seat of Watauga County, was named for Daniel Boone, who had a cabin and hunted here in the 1760s. This "Heart of the High Country" sprawls over a long valley, which provides a natural pass through the hills. Watauga County boasts several industrial firms providing its economic base, in addition to tourism, agriculture and Appalachian State University. Mountain crafts are featured in a variety of craft fairs, festivals and shops.

What to See and Do

Appalachian State University (1899). (11,500 students) Offers 90 undergraduate and 12 graduate majors. Dark Sky Observatory. Atop Blue Ridge Mtns. Phone 828/262-2000 or 828/262-2179. (See SEASONAL EVENTS) Opp is

Appalachian Cultural Museum. Regional museum presents an overview of the Blue Ridge area. Exhibits incl Native American artifacts, exhibit on Daniel Boone, mountain music and the environment. Gift shop. (Tues-Sat, also Sun afternoons) Univ Hall Dr. Phone 828/262-3117. **Free**

Daniel Boone Native Gardens. Native plants in informal setting; Squire Boone Cabin, wishing well, fern garden. (May–Sept, daily; Oct, wkends) Horn in the West Dr, 1 mi E off US 421, adj to Daniel Boone Amphitheatre (see SEASONAL EVENTS). Phone 828/264-6390. ¢

Seasonal Events

Horn in the West. Daniel Boone Amphitheatre, 1 mi E off US 421. Outdoor drama depicts Daniel Boone and settlers of the mountain during the Revolutionary War. Nightly exc Mon. Contact PO Box 295; 828/264-2120. Mid-June–mid-Aug.

An Appalachian Summer. Appalachian State Univ. Concerts, drama, art exhibits. Phone 800/841-2787.

Motels

★ **ECONO LODGE.** *Rr 6 Box 46 (28607), 3 mi S on NC 105. 828/264-4133; FAX 828/262-0101; res: 800/560-5942.* 101 rms, 4 story. Mid-June-late Oct, late Dec-Feb: S, D $52-$89; each addl $3; under 18 free; lower rates rest of yr. Crib free. TV; cable (premium). Indoor pool. Complimentary continental bkfst. Restaurant nearby. Ck-out 11 am. Business servs avail. Downhill/x-country ski 8 mi. Game rm. Cr cds: A, C, D, DS, MC, V.

✓★★ HOLIDAY INN EXPRESS. *1855 Blowing Rock Rd (28607). 828/264-2451; FAX 828/265-3861; res: 800/465-4329; res: 888/733-6867.* E-mail holidayinn@boone.mail.net; web www.holidayinn.com. 138 rms, 2 story. June-Oct, ski season: S, D $69-$109; each addl $8; under 18 free; lower rates rest of yr. Crib free. TV; cable (premium), VCR avail. Heated pool. Complimentary continental bkfst. Coffee in rms. Ck-out 11 am. Coin lndry. Meeting rms. Business servs avail. In-rm modem link. Exercise equipt. Downhill ski 5 mi. Cr cds: A, C, D, DS, JCB, MC, V.

⬜ 🏊 ➤ 🏕 🛏 🔥 SC

Motor Hotel

★★ HAMPTON INN. *208 Linville Rd (28607). 828/264-0077; FAX 828/264-4600; res: 800/426-7866.* 95 rms, 5 story. June-Oct: S, D $89-$119; under 18 free; golf plan; lower rates rest of yr. Crib free. TV; cable (premium), VCR avail. Indoor pool. Complimentary continental bkfst. Restaurant adj 11 am-10 pm. Ck-out 11 am. Meeting rms. Business servs avail. Health club privileges. Cr cds: A, C, D, DS, ER, JCB, MC, V.

⬜ ➤ 🛏 🔥 SC

Hotel

★★★ QUALITY INN & CONVENTION CENTER. *949 Blowing Rock Rd (28607), 1 mi S at jct US 321, NC 105. 828/262-0020; FAX 828/262-0020; res: 800/903-8209.* Web www.qualityinnboone.com. 132 rms, 7 story. Mid-June-mid-Nov: S $90; D $95; each addl $8; suites $90-$165; under 18 free; ski, golf packages; higher rates late Dec-Feb; lower rates rest of yr. TV; cable (premium). Indoor pool. Restaurant 7 am-2 pm, 5:30-10 pm. Bar 5 pm-1 am. Ck-out 11 am. Guest lndry. Meeting rms. Business servs avail. Golf privileges. Downhill ski 8 mi; x-country ski 9 mi. Exercise equipt. Health club privileges. Refrigerator in suites. Cr cds: A, C, D, DS, ER, JCB, MC, V.

⬜ ➤ 🎿 ➤ 🏕 🛏 🔥 SC

Inn

★★★ LOVILL HOUSE INN. *404 Old Bristol Rd (28607), just off US 421N. 828/264-4204; res: 800/849-9466.* E-mail innkeeper@lovillhouseinn.com; web www.lovillhouseinn.com. 5 rms, 2 story. No A/C. S, D $115-$175; each addl $25. Closed Mar, 2 wks Sept. Children over 12 yrs only. TV; cable. Complimentary full bkfst. Ck-out noon, ck-in 3 pm. Concierge serv. Luggage handling. Downhill/x-country ski 8 mi. Picnic tables. Restored country farmhouse built 1875; grounds include gardens, stream with waterfall. Totally nonsmoking. Cr cds: C, MC, V.

➤ 🛏 🔥

Restaurants

✓★ DAN'L BOONE INN. *130 Hardin St (28607), at jct US 421 & US 321. 828/264-8657.* Hrs: 11:30 am-9 pm; Sat, Sun from 8 am; Nov-May from 5 pm. Closed 2 days at Christmas. Family style: bkfst $6.95, lunch, dinner $11.95. Specialty: fried chicken. In one of oldest buildings in Boone; country atmosphere. Family-owned. Cr cds: C.

⬜

★★ MAKOTO. *2124 Blowing Rock Rd (28607). 828/264-7976.* E-mail tedmac@appstate.campusmci.net. Hrs: 11 am-2 pm, 5-10 pm. Closed Thanksgiving, Dec 25. Japanese menu. Serv bar. Complete meals: lunch $3.95-$9.95, dinner $8.50-$22.95. Serv charge 15%. Child's meals. Specializes in seafood, beef, poultry. Sushi bar Fri, Sat. Tableside preparation. Cr cds: A, C, D, DS, MC, V.

⬜

Brevard (B-2)

(See also Asheville, Hendersonville)

Settled 1861 **Pop** 5,388 **Elev** 2,230 ft **Area Code** 828 **Zip** 28712
E-mail brevchamber@citcom.net
Information Chamber of Commerce, PO Box 589; 828/883-3700 or 800/648-4523

An industrial and mountain resort center near the entrance to Pisgah National Forest, Brevard has several industries, including Sterling Diagnostic Imaging, Inc, Coats American Company and the Ecusta division of P.H. Glatfelter.

What to See and Do

Mt Pisgah (5,749 ft). Blue Ridge Pkwy, US 276 to within 1 mi of summit, trail rest of way.

Pisgah National Forest. A 499,816-acre, 4-district forest. The Cradle of Forestry Visitor Center (summer, daily; fee) is at site of first forestry school in the US. The forest surrounds Mt Mitchell State Park (see LITTLE SWITZERLAND), which contains the highest point in the US east of the Mississippi (6,684 ft). Linville Gorge Wilderness is 10,975 acres of precipitous cliffs and cascading falls (permit required May–Oct for overnight camping, contact the Grandfather Ranger District in MARION). Wiseman's View looks into Linville Gorge. Shining Rock Wilderness contains 18,500 acres of rugged alpine scenery. The forest shares with Cherokee National Forest in Tennessee the 6,286-ft Roan Mtn, with its purple rhododendron and stands of spruce and fir. Offers swimming and boating sites; good fishing for trout, bass and perch; hunting for deer, bear and small game; miles of hiking and riding trails; picnic sites; campgrounds (fee). NW of town, via US 276. For further info contact the Supervisor, 100 Otis St, Box 2750, Asheville 28802; Phone 828/257-4200.

Annual Events

Festival of the Arts. Music, crafts, art, sporting events. 2nd wk July.

Twilight Tour on Main. Horse & buggy rides, entertainment, refreshments. 1st Sat Dec.

Seasonal Event

Summer Festival of Music. Brevard Music Center. Whittington-Pfhol Auditorium. More than 50 programs presented, incl symphonic, choral, chamber, recital; musical comedy and operatic performances; guest artists. Mon–Sat eves; Sun afternoons. Contact Box 312; 828/884-2019 or 828/884-2011. Late June–early Aug.

Motels

★ IMPERIAL MOTOR LODGE. *Hwy 64 & 276 N (28712), ½ mi N on US 64, 276. 828/884-2887; FAX 828/883-9811; res: 800/869-3335.* 95 rms, 1-2 story. June-Oct: S, D $45-$85; each addl $5; under 12 free; lower rates rest of yr. Crib $5. TV; cable (premium). Pool. Complimentary continental bkfst. Restaurant opp 6 am-midnight. Ck-out 11:30 am. Refrigerators. Grill. Cr cds: A, C, D, DS, MC, V.

⬜ ➤ 🛏 🔥 SC

★ SUNSET MOTEL. *415 S Broad St (28712). 828/884-9106; FAX 828/883-4919.* 18 rms. June-Oct: S $50; D $60; each addl $5; lower rates rest of yr. Pet accepted, some restrictions. TV; cable. Restaurant opp 11 am-10 pm. Ck-out 11 am. Refrigerators. Cr cds: A, C, D, DS, MC, V.

 🐾 🛏 🔥

Bryson City (B-2)

(See also Cherokee, Franklin, Waynesville)

Pop 1,145 **Elev** 1,736 ft **Area Code** 828 **Zip** 28713 **E-mail** chamber@greatsmokies.com **Web** www.greatsmokies.com

Information Chamber of Commerce, PO Box 509; 828/488-3681 or 800/867-9246

At the confluence of the Little Tennessee and Tuckasegee rivers, Bryson City is also at the entrance to Great Smoky Mountains National Park. Fontana Lake, part of the TVA system, is nearby. Industries include textiles.

What to See and Do

Fontana Dam (see). 35 mi SW on US 19 & NC 28.

Great Smoky Mountains National Park (see). 8 mi N on US 19.

Great Smoky Mountains Railway. 4½-hr rail excursions to Nantahala Gorge aboard diesel or steam locomotives. 1-hr layover; view whitewater sports. Special excursions throughout yr (fees, dates vary). (Mar-Nov) For info contact PO Box 397, Dillsboro 28725-0397; phone 800/872-4681 ext R. ¢¢¢¢

Whitewater Rafting. Rolling Thunder River Co. Guided raft, canoe, kayak trips through Smoky Mtns; day and overnight. (Apr–Oct) Res suggested. 10 mi W on US 19S/74W, at Nantahala Gorge. For info, fees, contact Rolling Thunder River Co, Box 88, Almond 28702; phone 828/488-2030 or 800/344-5838. ¢¢¢¢

Motel

★ **BUDGET HOST INN.** *5280 Ela Rd N (28713).* 828/488-2284; FAX 828/488-2284. 21 rms, 1 cottage. No rm phones. Mid-June-Oct: S, D $68; kit. cottage $160; lower rates May-mid-June. Closed rest of yr. TV; cable. Pool. Coffee in rms. Ck-out 11 am. Cr cds: C, DS, MC, V.

Inns

★★ **CHALET INN.** *285 Lone Oak Dr (28789), 14 mi E on US 74/441.* 828/586-0251; res: 800/789-8024. E-mail chaletinn@wcu.campus.mci.net; web www.bbonline.com/nc/chaletinn. 6 rms, 2 with shower only, 2 story, 2 suites. No rm phones. S, D $75-$98; suites $120-$150; wkend rates: hols (3-day min); higher rates hols, July-Aug, Oct. Children over 12 yrs only. Complimentary full bkfst. Complimentary coffee in rms. Ck-out 10:30 am, ck-in 3 pm. Luggage handling. 18-hole golf privileges, greens fee $32, pro, putting green, driving range. Lawn games. Fireplace in suites. Balconies. Picnic tables, grills. European ambience in Blue Ridge Mts. Totally nonsmoking. Cr cds: C, MC, V.

★ **FOLKESTONE INN.** *101 Folkestone Rd (28713).* 828/488-2730; FAX 828/488-0722; res: 888/812-3385. E-mail innkeeper@folkestone.com; web www.folkestone.com. 10 rms, 3 story. No A/C. No rm phones. S, D $98; each addl $10. Complimentary full bkfst. Ck-out 11 am, ck-in 3 pm. Business servs avail. Game rm. Lawn games. Some balconies. Picnic tables. Built 1926; restored country farmhouse. Cr cds: A, C, DS, MC, V.

★★ **HEMLOCK INN.** *911 Galbriath Creek Rd (28713), 3 mi NE, 1 mi N of US 19.* 828/488-2885; FAX 828/488-8985. Web www.innbook.com/hemlock.html. 25 rms, 4 kit. units (1-3-bedrm). No A/C. MAP, mid-Apr-Oct: D $130-$148; each addl $20-$39; kit. cottage for 2, $148-

$178. Closed rest of yr. Dining rm (public by res) 8:30 am & 6 pm sittings; Sun 8:30 am & 12:30 pm sittings. Ck-out 11 am, ck-in 1 pm. Game rm. Lawn games. Early Amer decor; mountain view. Cr cds: C, DS, MC, V.

Burlington (A-6)

(See also Greensboro, High Point)

Settled ca 1700 **Pop** 39,498 **Elev** 656 ft **Area Code** 336 **E-mail** visitor@netpath.net **Web** www.netpath.net/visitor

Information Burlington/Alamance County Convention & Visitors Bureau, PO Drawer 519, 27216; 336/570-1444 or 800/637-3804

In 1837, E. M. Holt converted his father's gristmill on Alamance Creek into a textile mill. The Alamance Mill produced the first commercially dyed plaids south of the Potomac, changing the face of the textile industry in the South.

What to See and Do

Alamance Battleground State Historic Site. On May 16, 1771, a 2-hr battle was fought here between the colonial militia under Royal Governor Tryon and about 2,000 rebellious "Regulators." The latter were defeated. Restored log house; visitor center, exhibits, audiovisual presentation; picnic area. (Apr–Oct, daily; rest of yr, daily exc Mon; closed most major hols) 6 mi SW on NC 62. Phone 336/227-4785. **Free**

Alamance County Historical Museum. 19th-century house-museum depicts life of textile pioneer E. M. Holt. Period rms, audiovisual presentations. Rotating exhibits feature antique clothing and toys, Native American artifacts, traditional pottery and local history pieces. Docent-guided tours. (Daily exc Mon) 5 mi S on NC 62. Phone 336/226-8254. **Free**

Dentzel Menagerie Carousel (ca 1910). Rare hand-carved carousel; restored. (Apr–Oct, daily exc Mon) S Main, at Church St in City Park. Phone 336/222-5030. ¢

Lake Cammack Park and Marina. An 800-acre city reservoir. Waterskiing; fishing; boating. Picnic area, playground. (Daily exc Thurs; days vary winter) 6 mi N on Union Ridge Rd, off NC 62. Phone 336/421-3872. ¢

Annual Events

Antiques Fair. 3-day event where antiques are sold and auctioned. March.

Hospice League Horizons Balloon Fest. Hot-air-balloon race, air show, parachuting, music. Phone 800/637-3804. May.

Seasonal Event

The Sword of Peace Summer Outdoor Drama. 18 mi SW via I-85, Liberty-49S exit, then NC 49S and NC 1005 to Snow Camp. Repertory outdoor theater (eves) and summer arts festival; 150-yr-old and 200-yr-old bldgs converted into museums, craft gallery and cane mill. Thurs–Sat. Contact PO Box 535, Snow Camp 27349; 910/376-6948 or 800/726-5115. Late June–late Aug.

Motels

★ **COMFORT INN.** *I-85 & Sr 49 (27215), I-85, exit 145.* 336/227-3681; FAX 336/570-0900. 127 rms, 2 story. S $57-$88; D $61-$88; each addl $4; under 18 free; higher rates Furniture Market. Crib free. Pet accepted, some restrictions. TV; cable (premium). Pool; wading pool. Complimentary continental bkfst. Complimentary coffee in rms. Restaurant adj 11 am-11 pm. Ck-out noon. Coin lndry. Meeting rms. Business servs avail. Valet serv. Some refrigerators; microwaves avail. Cr cds: A, C, D, DS, JCB, MC, V.

★★ **HAMPTON INN.** *2701 Kirkpatrick Rd (27215), I-85, exit 141.* 336/584-4447; FAX 336/721-1325. 116 rms, 4 story. S $60-$65; D $65-$70; suites $92; under 18 free; higher rates Furniture Market (Apr & Oct). Crib free. TV; cable (premium). Pool; whirlpool. Complimentary continental bkfst. Restaurant adj 5-10 pm. Ck-out noon. Meeting rms. Business servs avail. Exercise equipt; sauna. Cr cds: A, C, D, DS, MC, V.

D ➰ 🏋 ➰ 🔥 SC

✓★ **KIRKS MOTOR COURT INC.** *1155 N Church St (27217).* 336/228-1383; FAX 336/228-9786. 102 rms, 1-2 story, 14 kits. S $28-$36; D $36-$44; each addl $6; kit. units $245-$285/wk; under 12 free. Crib $4. TV; cable. Pool; wading pool. Restaurant nearby. Ck-out 11 am. Meeting rms. Business servs avail. Valet serv. Sundries. Cr cds: C, MC, V.

D ➰ ➰ 🔥

★★ **RAMADA INN.** *2703 Ramada Rd (27215), at jct I-85.* 336/227-5541; FAX 910/570-2701; res: 800/272-6232. 138 rms, 2 story. S $59; D $65; each addl $6; under 18 free; higher rates: Furniture Market, special events. Crib free. TV; cable (premium). Pool. Restaurant 6 am-2 pm. Bar 5-10 pm; closed Sun. Ck-out noon. Convention facilities. Business servs avail. Health club privileges. Cr cds: A, C, D, DS, MC, V.

D ➰ ➰ 🔥 SC

✓★ **RED ROOF INN.** *2133 W Hanford Rd (27215), I-85 exit 145.* 336/227-1270; FAX 336/227-1702; res: 800/329-7466. 122 rms, 2 story. S $44; D $49; each addl $5; under 12 free. Crib avail. TV. Pool. Complimentary continental bkfst. Restaurant adj 6 am-11 pm; Fri, Sat to 1 am. Ck-out noon. Meeting rms. Business servs avail. Valet serv. Health club privileges. Cr cds: A, C, D, DS, ER, JCB, MC, V.

D ➰ ➰ 🔥 SC

Restaurant

✓★ **HURSEY'S PIG PICKIN' BAR-B-Q.** *1834 S Church St (27215).* 336/226-1694. Hrs: 11 am-9 pm. Closed Sun; Dec 25. Semi-a la carte: lunch, dinner $3.50-$7.50. Child's meals. Specializes in wood-cooked pit barbecue. Rustic decor. Family-owned since 1949. Cr cds: C.

D ➰

Burnsville (A-3)

(See also Asheville, Little Switzerland)

Pop 1,482 **Elev** 2,814 ft **Area Code** 828 **Zip** 28714 **E-mail** info@yancey chamber.com **Web** www.yanceychamber.com/nc

Information Yancey County Chamber of Commerce, 106 W Main St; 828/682-7413 or 800/948-1632

A Ranger District office of the Pisgah National Forest (see BREVARD) is located here.

Annual Events

Mt Mitchell Crafts Fair. Town Square. 1st Fri & Sat Aug.
Old Time Days. Town Square. Early Oct.

Inn

★★ **HISTORIC NU WRAY INN.** *102 Town Sq, US 19E (28714), Town Square.* 828/682-2329; FAX 828/682-1113; res: 800/368-9729. E-mail nuwrayinn@aol.com; web www.nuwrayinn.com. 26 rms, 3 story. No A/C. No rm phones. S $65-$85; D $75-$95; suites $90; each addl

$10; MAP avail. TV in most rms; cable (premium). Dining rm sittings (May-Oct): 8:30 am, 6 pm; Sun 1 pm; times vary rest of yr. Ck-out 11 am, ck-in after 3 pm. Inn built in 1833. Cr cds: A, C, DS, MC, V.

D ➰ 🔥

Buxton (Outer Banks) (B-10)

Pop 3,250 **Elev** 10 ft **Area Code** 252 **Zip** 27920

This town is on Hatteras Island, part of the Outer Banks (see). It is surrounded by Cape Hatteras National Seashore (see).

Motels

★ **CAPE HATTERAS MOTEL.** *Hwy 12 (27920).* 252/995-5611; FAX 252/995-4303; res: 800/995-0711. 6 motel rms, 1-2 story, 30 kit. units. No rm phones. Mid June-Labor Day: S, D $105-$110; kit. units $130-$190; lower rates rest of yr. Crib $3. TV; cable (premium). Pool; whirlpool. Ck-out 11 am, kit units 10 am. Cr cds: A, C, DS, MC, V.

🐾 ➰ 🔥

★★ **COMFORT INN.** *Rte 12 & Old Lighthouse Rd (27920), near Cape Hatteras lighthouse.* 252/995-6100; FAX 252/995-5444; res: 800/432-1441. 60 rms, 2 story. Mid-June-mid-Sept: S, D $92-$125; each addl $5; under 18 free; lower rates rest of yr. Crib free. TV; cable (premium). Pool. Complimentary continental bkfst. Restaurant nearby. Ck-out 11 am. Business servs avail. In-rm modem link. Guest lndry. Refrigerators, microwaves. Near beach. Cr cds: A, C, D, DS, JCB, MC, V.

D 🐾 ➰ ➰ 🔥 SC

✓★ **FALCON MOTEL.** *Rte 12 (27920).* 252/995-5968; res: 800/635-6911. 30 rms, 5 kits. No rm phones. Memorial Day-Labor Day: S, D $63-$75; kits. $70-$90; under 6 free; wkly rates; lower rates Labor Day-mid-Dec. Closed rest of yr. Crib free. TV; cable (premium). Pool. Restaurant opp 6:30-11 am, 5-9:30 pm. Ck-out 11 am. Refrigerators avail. Picnic tables. Bicycles avail. Near ocean. Cr cds: C, MC, V.

➰ ➰ 🔥 SC

Restaurant

✓★ **TIDES.** *NC 12 (27920).* 252/995-5988. Hrs: 6-11:30 am, 5:30-9:30 pm. Closed Dec-Mar. Wine, beer. Semi-a la carte: bkfst $2.50-$5.50, dinner $7.50-$18.50. Specializes in seafood, steak. Nautical decor. Cr cds: C, MC, V.

D ➰

Cape Hatteras National Seashore (B-10)

(See also Buxton, Hatteras, Kill Devil Hills, Nags Head, Ocracoke)

(Enter from Cedar Island or Swan Quarter toll ferry. Reservations advised. Free ferry from Ocracoke Island to Hatteras Island.)

This thin strand stretches for 75 miles along the Outer Banks (see), threaded between the windy, pounding Atlantic and shallow Pamlico Sound. Nags Head (see) is the northern limit of the recreational area, which has three sections (separated by inlets): Bodie (pronounced *body*), Hatteras (largest of the barrier islands) and Ocracoke, the most picturesque. Bounded on three sides by the park, but separate from it, are the villages of Rodanthe, Waves, Salvo, Avon, Buxton, Frisco, Hatteras and Ocracoke. Although the area is noted for long expanses of sand beaches, wildflowers bloom most of the year. There are also stands of yaupon (holly), loblolly pine and live oak. Several freshwater ponds are found on Bodie, Hatteras and Ocracoke Islands. Many migratory and non-migratory waterfowl winter here, including gadwalls, greater snow and Canada geese, loons, grebes and herons.

There is an information station at Whalebone Junction (Memorial Day–Labor Day, daily), south of Nags Head. Near Bodie Island Lighthouse is a bird observation platform, a nature trail and a visitor center (Good Friday-Columbus Day, daily) with natural history exhibits. There are also visitor centers with history exhibits at Ocracoke (same hours), Bodie Island Lighthouse (same hours), and the Cape Hatteras Lighthouse at Buxton (daily; closed December 25).

(Do not drive off the highways—you are likely to get stuck.)

Sport fishing, boating, sailing, swimming (recommended only at protected beaches); picnicking and camping (fee), also waterfowl hunting in season under regulation.

For further information contact the Superintendent, Rte 1, Box 675, Manteo 27954; or phone the Hatteras Island Visitor Center, 252/995-4474.

Cashiers (B-2)

(See also Franklin, Highlands)

Pop 1,200 **Elev** 3,486 ft **Area Code** 828 **Zip** 28717 **Web** www.cashiers-nc.com

Information Cashiers Area Chamber of Commerce, PO Box 238; 828/743-5191

High in the Blue Ridge Mountains, this well-known summer resort area offers scenic drives on twisting mountain roads, hiking trails, views, waterfalls, lake sports, fishing and other recreational activities.

What to See and Do

Fairfield Sapphire Valley Ski Area. Chairlift, rope tow; patrol, school, snowmaking. Longest run 2,400 ft; vertical drop 425 ft. (Mid-Dec–mid-Mar, daily) Night skiing (exc Sun). Evening, half-day rates. Other seasons: swimming, fishing, boating; hiking, horseback riding; golf, tennis; recreation center. Restaurants, inn. 3 mi E on US 64. Phone 828/743-3441. ¢¢¢¢¢

Lake Thorpe. Fishing, swimming, waterskiing. Boats may be rented at Glenville (on lake) or launched from here. 5 mi N on NC 107.

Motels

★ **LAURELWOOD MOUNTAIN INN.** *58 107 N (28717). 828/743-9939; FAX 828/743-5300; res: 800/346-6846.* E-mail laurelwd@dnet.net; web www.dnet.net/laurelwood. 22 rms, 10 with shower only, 3 A/C, 1-2 story. May-Oct: S, D $62-$135; under 12 free; wkly rates; wkends, hols (2-day min); lower rates rest of yr. Crib free. TV; cable. Complimentary coffee in rms. Restaurant opp 6:30 am-10 pm. Ck-out 11 am. Playground. Refrigerators; some in-rm whirlpools, microwaves. Some balconies. Picnic tables, grills. Cr cds: A, C, D, DS, MC, V.

★ **OAKMONT LODGE.** *173 Oakmont St (28717), ½ mi N of jct US 64. 828/743-2298.* 20 rms, 2 cabins. No A/C. June-Oct: S, D $62-$69; each addl $5; kit. cottages $94-$115. Crib free. TV; cable. Restaurant 11:30 am-9 pm. Ck-out 11 am. Downhill ski 2 mi. Cr cds: C, MC, V.

Resorts

★ ★ ★ **FAIRFIELD SAPPHIRE VALLEY.** *4000 US Hwy 64 W (28774), 3 mi E. 828/743-3441; FAX 828/743-2169; res: 800/533-8268.* 160 villas (summer), 100 villas (winter), 1-2 story. S, D $90; kit. villas $90-

$260; wkly rates; ski, golf, tennis plans. Crib $3. TV; cable, VCR avail. Indoor/outdoor pool; whirlpool. Playground. Supervised child's activities (June-mid-Aug); ages 6-12. Dining rm 11 am-9 pm. Ck-out 10 am, ck-in 4 pm. Sports dir. Lighted tennis, pro. 18-hole golf, driving range. Private beach; boats (no motors). Downhill ski 1 mi. Miniature golf. Lawn games. Soc dir; entertainment. Exercise equipt; sauna. Refrigerators, fireplaces; microwaves avail. Whirlpool in some villas. 5,700 acres in mountain setting; on lake. Gardens, extensive lawns. Cr cds: A, C, DS, MC, V.

★ ★ ★ **HIGH HAMPTON INN & COUNTRY CLUB.** *Hwy 107 S (28717), 2 mi S on NC 107. 828/743-2411; FAX 828/743-5991; res: 800/334-2551.* Web www.highhamptoninn.com. 34 rms in 3-story inn, 15 cottages, 37 golf villas. No A/C. AP, July-Aug: S $94-$103; D $164-$198; each addl $57; golf villas (3-day min) $206-$385; wkly rates; golf, tennis plans; higher rates July-Aug. Closed late Nov-April. Crib free. Pet accepted, some restrictions. TV rm; cable. Supervised child's activities (June-Labor Day); ages 3-12. Complimentary afternoon refreshments. Dining rm 7-9:30 am, noon-2:15 pm, 6:30-8:15 pm. Box lunches, buffets. Ck-out 1 pm, ck-in 3 pm. Coin lndry. Business servs avail. Valet serv. Gift shop. Airport transportation. Sports dir. 18-hole golf, greens fee $29, pro, 2 putting greens, driving range. Exercise equipt. Boats, dockage. Archery. Trail guides. Bicycle rentals. Outdoor, indoor games. Soc dir; entertainment, movies. Rec rm, library. Lawn games. Kennels. 1,400-acre mountain estate, 2 lakes. Cr cds: A, C, DS, MC, V.

Inns

★ ★ ★ **INNISFREE VICTORIAN INN.** *7 Lakeside Knoll (28736), 6 mi N on NC 107. 828/743-2946.* 10 rms, 1 & 2 story. No A/C. Some rm phones. June-Oct: S, D $150-$290; lower rates rest of yr. Adults only. TV in some rms; cable. Complimentary full bkfst; afternoon refreshments. Complimentary coffee in rms. Ck-out 11 am, ck-in 2:30 pm. Business servs avail. Luggage handling. Concierge serv. Tennis privileges. Golf privileges. Game rm. Refrigerators, minibars; some fireplaces. Balconies. 1 blk from Lake Glenville. Built 1989 in Victorian style and furnished with antiques. Totally nonsmoking. Cr cds: A, C, DS, MC, V.

★ ★ ★ **THE GREYSTONE INN.** *Greystone Ln (28747), 8 mi E on US 64. 828/966-4700; FAX 828/862-5689; res: 800/824-5766.* 33 rms, 3 story, 17 A/C. May-Oct: S, D $280-$430; each addl $85; family rates; lower rates Apr, Nov, Dec. Open wkends Jan-Mar. Crib free. TV; cable (premium), VCR. Pool. Supervised child's activities (June-Aug); ages 5-14. Complimentary full bkfst; afternoon refreshments. Restaurant adj 8-10 am, 6:30-9:30 pm. Ck-out noon, ck-in 3 pm. Business servs avail. Luggage handling. Concierge serv. Tennis, pro. 18-hole golf, greens fee $45, putting green, driving range. Massage. Refrigerators, minibars. Balconies. Picnic tables. On swimming beach. Cr cds: C, MC, V.

Cedar Island (C-9)

Pop 333 (est) **Elev** 7 ft **Area Code** 919 **Zip** 28520

There is daily ferry service from Cedar Island to Ocracoke (see).

Motel

✓ ★ **DRIFTWOOD MOTEL & RESTAURANT.** *Hwy 12 (28520), on NC 12 N at Cedar Island-Ocracoke ferry terminal. 252/225-*

4861; FAX 252/225-1113. 37 rms. May-mid-Oct: S $40; D $50; each addl $4; under 12 free; lower rates rest of yr. Crib free. TV; cable (premium). Restaurant 5-8:30 pm. Ck-out noon. On ocean. Cr cds: C, DS, MC, V.

⬛⬛⬛⬛⬛

Chapel Hill (B-6)

(See also Durham, Raleigh)

Founded 1793 **Pop** 38,719 **Elev** 487 ft **Area Code** 919
E-mail chamber@cpl.mindspring.com **Web** www.herald-sun.com/cchamber

Information Chapel Hill-Carrboro Chamber of Commerce, 104 S Estes Dr, PO Box 2897, 27515; 919/967-7075

The community of Chapel Hill is centered around the University of North Carolina, the oldest state university in the US. This school has been a leader in American education for more than 170 years and is now part of a "research triangle," together with Duke University at Durham and North Carolina State University at Raleigh. Despite heavy losses of faculty and students to the Civil War, the school remained open until the years of Reconstruction, 1870–1875. During the next decade the university was reborn.

What to See and Do

Chapel of the Cross (1842–1848). Antebellum Gothic-revival Episcopal church. (Daily, exc Sat) 304 E Franklin St, adj to Morehead Planetarium. Phone 919/929-2193.

Horace Williams House. Historic house is home to the Chapel Hill Preservation Society; changing art exhibits, chamber music concerts. Guided tours. (Mon-Fri, also Sun afternoons; closed hols & first 2 wks Aug) 610 Rosemary St. Phone 919/942-7818. **Free**

North Carolina Botanical Garden. Approx 600 acres; variety of trees and plants of southeastern US; wildflower areas, herb gardens. Nature trails (daily). (Mid-Mar–mid-Nov, daily; rest of yr, Mon–Fri) Old Mason Farm Rd and US 15/501 Bypass. Phone 919/962-0522. **Free**

University of North Carolina at Chapel Hill (1795). (Approx 24,000 students) This institution, the first state university in the country, is on a 720-acre campus and has more than 200 bldgs. On campus are

Coker Arboretum. Covers 5 acres. Extensive collection of ornamental plants and shrubs. Cameron Ave & Raleigh St.

Davie Poplar. Ancient ivy-covered tree named for the "father of the university," William Richardson Davie; more than 200 yrs old. N of Old Well.

Kenan Stadium (1927). Seats 52,000; in wooded natural bowl. Behind Bell Tower.

Memorial Hall (1930). White columns front this structure dedicated to war dead, honored alumni and university benefactors. James K. Polk, class of 1818, has a commemorative tablet here. He graduated first in his class and became the 11th President of the US. Opp New West.

Morehead-Patterson Memorial Bell Tower (1930). A 172-ft Italian Renaissance campanile; concert chimes. The 12 bells range in weight from 300 lbs to almost 2 tons. Popular tunes are rung daily.

Morehead Planetarium. Offers indoor star-gazing, art gallery with permanent and changing exhibits, scientific exhibits; rare Zeiss instrument. Shows (daily; closed Dec 24, 25). Rose garden has mammoth sundial showing time around the world. E Franklin St. Phone 919/549-6863. Shows ¢¢

Old East. Oldest state university bldg in the country; cornerstone laid in 1793. Matched by Old West (1823). Still being used as a residence hall. E of Old Well.

Old Well. Long the unofficial symbol of the University, this well was the only source of water here for nearly a century. The present "Greek temple" structure dates from 1897. Cameron Ave in center of campus.

Paul Green Theater (1978). PlayMakers Repertory Company. Named for one of the first dramatic arts students at the University. Green is known as the father of American outdoor drama. (Sept–May) (For further info on the University, phone 919/962-1630.).

Playmakers Theater (1851). Greek-revival temple was designed as a combination library and ballrm.

South (Main) Building. Cornerstone laid in 1798 but bldg not completed until 1814, during which time the boys lived inside the roofless walls in little huts. Future President James K. Polk lived here from 1814–1818. Opp Old Well.

Wilson Library. Houses special collections. Incl North Carolina Collection Gallery; historic rms, texts and artifacts. Also here is the Southern Historical Collection, featuring manuscripts, rare books and photographs. (Daily) Phone 919/962-0114.

Motels

★ ★ **BEST WESTERN UNIVERSITY INN.** Hwy 54 (27515), 2 mi E on NC 54, ¼ mi E of US 15/501 Bypass. 919/932-3000; FAX 919/968-6513; res: 800/528-1234. 84 rms, 1-2 story. S, D $75-$110. Crib $5. TV; cable (premium), VCR avail (movies). Pool. Complimentary continental bkfst. Ck-out noon. Business servs avail. Health club privileges. Refrigerators avail. Cr cds: A, C, D, DS, MC, V.

⬛⬛⬛⬛⬛

✓★ ★ **HAMPTON INN.** 1740 Hwy 15/501 (27514). 919/968-3000; FAX 919/929-0322; res: 800/426-7866. 122 rms, 2 story. S $67-$89; D $69-$97; under 18 free. Crib free. TV; cable (premium), VCR avail. Pool. Complimentary continental bkfst. Coffee in rms. Restaurant nearby. Ck-out noon. Meeting rm. Business servs avail. Health club privileges. Cr cds: A, C, D, DS, MC, V.

⬛⬛⬛⬛⬛

★ ★ **HOLIDAY INN.** 1301 N Fordham Blvd (27514), 2 mi S of I-40 exit 270 on 15-501S, at Eastgate Shopping Center. 919/929-2171; FAX 919/929-5736; res: 800/465-4329. 135 rms, 2 story. S, D $69-$119; each addl $6; higher rates: football season (2-day min), graduation (3-day min). Crib free. TV; cable (premium). Pool. Restaurant 6:30-10 am, 4-9 pm. Rm serv. Bar 5-11 pm. Ck-out noon. Meeting rms. Business servs avail. In-rm modem link. Cr cds: A, C, D, DS, JCB, MC, V.

⬛⬛⬛⬛⬛

Hotels

★ ★ **SHERATON HOTEL.** 1 Europa Dr (27514). 919/968-4900; FAX 919/968-3520; res: 800/843-6664. Web www.citysearch.com. 168 rms, 4 story. S, D $169; each addl $10; suites $195-$275; under 16 free. Crib $10. TV; cable (premium). Pool. Restaurant 6:30 am-2 pm, 4-10 pm. Bar 4 pm-1 am. Meeting rms. Business servs avail. Concierge. Gift shop. Exercise equipt. Health club privileges. Private patios, balconies. Cr cds: A, C, D, DS, MC, V.

⬛⬛⬛⬛⬛⬛

★ ★ ★ **THE CAROLINA INN.** 211 Pittsboro St (27516), on University of North Carolina's campus. 919/933-2001; FAX 919/962-3400; res: 800/962-8519. Web www.citysearch.com/rdu/carolinainn. 184 rms, 3 story. S, D $139-$169; each addl $10-$15; suites $239-$289; under 18 free; higher rates special events. Crib free. Valet parking $10. TV; cable (premium). Complimentary coffee in lobby. Restaurant (see CAROLINA CROSSROADS). Bar 11 am-midnight. Ck-out noon. Coin lndry. Meeting rms. Business servs avail. In-rm modem link. Concierge. Gift shop. Tennis privileges. Golf privileges. Exercise equipt. Health club privileges. Cr cds: A, C, D, DS, ER, JCB, MC, V.

⬛⬛⬛⬛⬛⬛⬛

★ ★ ★ **THE SIENA HOTEL.** 1505 E Franklin St (27514). 919/929-4000; FAX 919/968-8527; res: 800/223-7379. Web www.siena hotel.com. 80 rms, 4 story, 12 suites. S, D $155; each addl $10; suites $185-$250; under 17 free; higher rates: football games, graduation. Crib free. Pet accepted; $50 refundable. TV; cable (premium). VCR avail. Complimentary full bkfst. Restaurant (see IL PALIO). Bar noon-midnight; entertainment. Ck-out noon. Meeting rms. Business servs avail. In-rm modem link. Concierge. Airport transportation. Tennis privileges. Golf privileges, greens fee $25-$110. Exercise equipt. Health club privileges. Bathrm phones; some refrigerators. Picnic tables. Cr cds: A, C, D, JCB, MC, V.

D 🐾 🏊 ⛷ 🏋 ≈ 🐾 SC

Inns

✓ ★ ★ ★ ★ ★ **FEARRINGTON HOUSE.** 2000 Fearrington Village Center (27312), 8 mi S on US 15/501. 919/542-2121; FAX 919/542-4202. E-mail fhouse@fearrington.com; web www.fearrington.com. This English-style country inn on an old farm is decorated with chintz, original art and pinewood antiques. A courtyard and fountain welcome visitors at the entrance. 31 rms, 2 story. S, D $165-$200; suites $225-$325. TV; cable (premium), VCR avail. Pool; whirlpool. Complimentary full bkfst; afternoon refreshments. Dining rm (see FEARRINGTON HOUSE). Rm serv 24 hrs. Liquor, beer, wine. Ck-out noon, ck-in 3 pm. Meeting rms. Business servs avail. Tennis. Golf privileges. Exercise equipt. Lawn games. Totally non-smoking. Cr cds: A, C, MC, V.

D 🏋 ⛷ ≈ ✈ 🐾 ≋ 🐾

★ **INN AT BINGHAM SCHOOL.** 6720 Mebane Oaks Rd (27514), 12 mi W on NC 54. 919/563-5583; FAX 919/563-9826; res: 800/566-5583. E-mail fdeprez@aol.com; web www.virtualcities.com. 5 rms, 2 with shower only, 2 story. S $65-$110; D $75-$120; each addl $15; suites $120; under 5 free. TV. Complimentary full bkfst. Restaurant nearby. Ck-out 11 am, ck-in 3 pm. A combination of Greek and Federal styles; antiques. Cr cds: A, C, DS, MC, V.

≈ 🐾 SC

Restaurants

★ ★ **AURORA.** 200 Greensboro St (27510), Carr Mill Shopping Center. 919/942-2400. Hrs: 11:30 am-2 pm, 6-10 pm; Sat, Sun from 6 pm. Closed some major hols. Res accepted. Northern Italian menu. Bar. Semi-a la carte: lunch $3.95-$8.95, dinner $8.95-$17.95. Daily menu. Own pasta. In renovated textile mill. Cr cds: A, C, D, MC, V.

D SC 🍴

★ ★ ★ **CAROLINA CROSSROADS.** (See The Carolina Inn) 919/918-2777. Web www.citysearch.com/rdu/carolinainn. Hrs: 6:30 am-10 pm; brunch 10:30 am-2 pm. Res accepted. Contemporary Amer menu. Bar 11 am-11 pm. Wine list. Semi-a la carte: bkfst $6.95-$11.95. A la carte entrees: lunch $6.50-$12.50, dinner $15-$24. Buffet: lunch $8.95. Brunch $16.95. Child's meals. Specialties: white shrimp & grits, grilled pork rib chop. Salad bar (lunch only). Piano Fri. Valet parking. French country decor; prints, plants. Totally nonsmoking. Cr cds: A, C, D, DS, ER, JCB, MC, V.

D

★ ★ ★ **FEARRINGTON HOUSE.** (See Fearrington House Inn) 919/542-2121. E-mail fhouse@fearrington.com; web www.fearrington.com. Each dining area in this restaurant features a different decor, from the airy garden rooms with large windows to the more formal interior room with a fireplace. Service is attentive and courteous no matter where you are seated. Specialties: roast duck breast, rice paper wrapped yellowfin tuna, maple glazed smoked quail. Own baking. Hrs: 6-9 pm; Sun to 8 pm. Closed Mon. Res required. Wine list. Complete meals: dinner $59. Totally nonsmoking. Cr cds: A, C, MC, V.

D

★ ★ ★ **IL PALIO.** (See The Siena Hotel) 919/929-4000. Web www.sienahotel.com. Hrs: 6:30-10 am, 11:30 am-2 pm, 6-10 pm; Sun brunch 11:30 am-2 pm. Res accepted. Continental menu. Bar. Wine cellar. Semi-a la carte: bkfst $7.50-$10, lunch $7.50-$18, dinner $17.95-$24. Sun brunch $16.95. Specialty: osso bucco. Own pasta. Entertainment. Mediter-

ranean decor with Northern Italian emphasis; much artwork, wall ornamentation, flower arrangements. Totally nonsmoking. Cr cds: A, C, D, JCB, MC, V.

D SC

★ ★ **LA RESIDENCE.** 202 W Rosemary St (27516). 919/967-2506. E-mail larez@juno.com. Hrs: 6-9:30 pm; Sun to 8:30 pm. Closed Mon; July 4, Dec 24, 25. Res accepted. French, Amer menu. Bar. A la carte entrees: dinner $15.95-$24.95. Specializes in local seafood, duckling, wild game. Outdoor dining. Cr cds: A, C, D, MC, V.

D 🍴

✓ ★ **SQUID'S.** 1201 N Fordham Blvd (US 15/501 Bypass) (27514). 919/942-8757. Hrs: 5-9:30 pm; Fri, Sat to 10 pm; Sun to 9 pm. Closed Jan 1, Thanksgiving, Dec 24, 25. Bar. Semi-a la carte: dinner $9-$15. Child's meals. Specializes in fresh seafood. Oyster bar. Cr cds: A, C, D, DS, MC, V.

D SC

★ **THE WILD TURTLE.** 220 W Rosemary St (27516). 919/932-4841. Web www.citysearch.com/rdu/thewildturtle. Hrs: 6-10 pm. Closed Sun; major hols. Res accepted. Bar. A la carte entrees: dinner $9.95-$17.95. Specializes in beef, chicken, lamb. Outdoor dining. Intimate dining in turn-of-the-century bungalow; tapestries, fireplaces; original fixtures. Cr cds: A, C, MC, V.

Charlotte (B-5)

(See also Gastonia; also see Rock Hill, SC)

Settled 1748 **Pop** 395,934 **Elev** 700 ft **Area Code** 704
Information Convention & Visitors Bureau, 122 E Stonewall St, 28202; 704/331-2700 or 800/231-4636

The Carolinas' largest metropolis, Charlotte grew quickly as a regional retail, financial and distribution center and became the nation's leader in the textile industry. General Cornwallis occupied the town for a short time in 1780 but met such determined resistance that he called it a "hornet's nest," a name that has been applied with pride on the city seal and by several local groups. Gold was discovered here in 1799, and the region around Charlotte was the nation's major gold producer until the California gold rush in 1848. There was a US Mint here between 1837–1861. The last Confederate Cabinet meeting was held here in 1865.

Chiefly agricultural and dependent on slave labor in antebellum days, the region took eagerly to industry after Appomattox. Abundant water power for electricity from the Catawba River has been a principal reason for its rapid growth. Today, Charlotte is among the largest banking centers in the country.

Transportation

Charlotte/Douglas Intl Airport. Information 704/359-4013; lost and found 704/359-4012.
Car Rental Agencies. See IMPORTANT TOLL-FREE NUMBERS.
Public Transportation. Buses (Charlotte Transit System), phone 704/336-3366.
Rail Passenger Service. Amtrak 800/872-7245.

What to See and Do

Charlotte Coliseum. This 23,000-seat arena hosts various sports events as well as family shows and concerts. 100 Paul Buck Blvd. For schedule info phone 704/357-4700.
Discovery Place. Hands-on science museum features aquarium; also science circus, life center, rain forest, collections gallery; Omnimax theater; Space Voyager Planetarium; major traveling exhibits. (Daily; closed

Thanksgiving, Dec 25) 301 N Tryon St. Phone 704/372-6261 or 800/935-0553. ¢¢¢

James K. Polk Memorial State Historic Site. Replica of log cabin and outbuildings at birthsite of 11th President of the US. Visitor center with exhibits, film. Guided tour. (Apr–Nov, Mon–Sat, also Sun afternoons; rest of yr, Tues–Sat, also Sun afternoons; closed major hols) 308 S Polk St, in Pineville (1½ mi S of Exit 65B on I-485). Phone 704/889-7145.   **Free**

Latta Plantation Park. Approx 1,000-acre nature preserve on Mt Island Lake. Interpretive Center, Carolina Raptor Center, Audubon Sanctuary, Equestrian Center (fees for each). Bridle paths, hiking trails, fishing, picnicking, canoe access. (Daily) 12 mi NW via I-77, exit 16B (Sunset Rd W), right at Beattie's Ford Rd 5 mi, then left at Sample Rd. Phone 704/875-1391.   **Free**   Also here is

Latta Place (ca 1800). Restored Federal-style plantation house, original storehouse, log slave house replica; barns, farm animals; kitchen garden, cotton field. (Daily exc Mon; closed most major hols) Phone 704/875-2312.   ¢

Mint Museum of Art. First Branch US Mint operated here 1837–1861 and 1867–1913, and in 1933 it was chartered as an art museum. Collections incl European and American art from Renaissance to contemporary; fine pottery and porcelain collection; maps; period costumes; survey collection of pre-Columbian and African artifacts; exhibition of coins. (Daily exc Mon; closed Jan 1, Thanksgiving, Dec 25) 2730 Randolph Rd. Phone 704/337-2000.   ¢¢

Mint Museum of Craft & Design. 220 N Tryon St. Phone 704/337-2000.

Nature Museum. Live Animal Rm, nature trail, puppet theater; earth science hall. (Daily; closed Thanksgiving, Dec 25) 1658 Sterling Rd. Phone 704/372-6261.   ¢

Ovens Auditorium. Shows by touring Broadway companies (fall–late spring); musicals; symphony. 2700 E Independence Blvd, 5 mi E on US 74. Phone 704/372-3600 for schedule.

Paramount's Carowinds. 100-acre family theme park has over 40 rides, shows and attractions incl 12-acre water entertainment complex Water-Works; Animation Station children's area; DROP ZONE stunt tower; roller-coasters. 13,000-seat Paladium Amphitheater hosts special events. Campground (all yr). (June–late Aug, daily; Mar–May & Sept–Oct, wkends) Exit 90 off I-77, at state line. Phone 704/588-2600, 803/548-5300 or 800/888-4386.   ¢¢¢¢

Professional sports.

NBA (Charlotte Hornets). Charlotte Coliseum, 100 Paul Buck Blvd. Phone 704/357-0252.

NFL (Carolina Panthers). Ericsson Stadium, 800 S Mint St. Phone 704/358-7000.

Spirit Square Center for the Arts. Exhibitions by well-known contemporary artists; studio art classes (fee); performances (fee). Parking fee. 345 N College St. Phone 704/372-9664 or 704/372-1000 (box office).

The Charlotte Museum of History and Alexander Homesite. Incl Hezekiah Alexander House (1774), oldest dwelling still standing in Mecklenburg County; 2-story springhouse; working log kitchen. Tours (fee). (Tues–Fri, also Sat & Sun afternoons; closed major hols) 3500 Shamrock Dr. Phone 704/568-1774.   **Free**

University of North Carolina at Charlotte (1946). (15,000 students) Beautiful landscaping and blooming plants (Mar–Nov); rhododendron garden (blooms Apr–May); ornamental garden, public greenhouse with rainforest and orchid collection. Sculpture garden. Rare Book Room and panoramic view of campus, 10th floor of library (Mon–Fri; closed hols). Walking-tour guide and map. NE off I-85. Phone 704/547-4286.

Annual Events

Springfest. 3-day festival in uptown, offers food, live entertainment. Last wkend Apr.

Festival in the Park. Freedom Park. Arts and crafts, entertainment. Phone 704/338-1060. 6 days mid-Sept.

Seasonal Events

Symphony. Charlotte Symphony Orchestra, Inc. Phone 704/332-6136. Performs yr-round.

Theatre Charlotte. 501 Queens Rd. Classic and Broadway plays. Features 6 productions a yr on alternate months beginning in Sept. Thurs–Sat eves. Phone 704/376-3777.

Opera. Opera Carolina. Phone 704/332-7177. Oct–Apr.

Auto racing. Charlotte Motor Speedway. 12 mi N on US 29 or off I-85 exit 49 Speedway Blvd. Coca-Cola 600 Winston Cup stock car race (Memorial Day wkend); Mello Yello 500 Winston Cup stock car race (early Oct); Spring AutoFair car show & flea market (mid-Apr); Fall AutoFair (mid-Sept). Phone 704/455-3200.

Motels

✓★ **COMFORT INN.** 4040 S I-85 at Little Rock Rd (28208), exit 32 (Little Rock Rd), near Douglas Intl Airport. 704/394-4111; FAX 704/394-4111; res: 800/392-4005. 118 rms, 2 story. S $65; D $75; each addl $5; under 18 free; higher rates stock car races. Crib free. TV; cable (premium). Pool. Complimentary continental bkfst. Bar 5-11 pm. Ck-out 11 am. Meeting rms. Business servs avail. Free airport transportation. Exercise equipt. Refrigerators, microwaves avail. Cr cds: A, C, D, DS, MC, V.

D ≥ 🏋 ✈ 🏊 🔥 SC

✓★ **COMFORT INN UNCC.** 5111 N I-85 Sugar Creek Rd. (28269). 704/598-0007; FAX 704/319-2683; res: 800/882-3835. 87 rms, 2 story. S $49.95-$69.95; D $59.95-$79.95; each addl $6; under 18 free; higher rates special events. Crib free. TV; cable (premium). Pool; whirlpool. Complimentary continental bkfst. Restaurant nearby. Ck-out 11 am. Meeting rms. Business servs avail. Valet serv. Exercise equipt. Refrigerators, microwaves avail. Cr cds: A, C, D, DS, ER, JCB, MC, V.

D ≥ 🏋 🏊 🔥 SC

★★★ **COURTYARD BY MARRIOTT.** 800 Arrowood Rd (28217), I-77 exit 3. 704/527-5055; FAX 704/525-5848; res: 800/228-9290. 146 rms, 3 story. S, D $89-$99; wkend rates; under 6 free. Crib free. TV; cable (premium). Pool; whirlpool. Coffee in rms. Bar 5-10 pm. Ck-out noon. Coin lndry. Meeting rms. Business servs avail. Valet serv. Exercise equipt. Some refrigerators. Private patios, balconies. Cr cds: A, C, D, DS, MC, V.

D ≥ 🏋 🏊 🔥 SC

★★★ **COURTYARD BY MARRIOTT.** 333 W W.T. Harris Blvd (28262), I-85 North, exit 45-A. 704/549-4888; FAX 704/549-4946; res: 800/321-2211. 152 rms, 4 story. S $99; D $109; suites $109; under 12 free; wkend rates; higher rates special events. Crib free. TV; cable (premium). Pool; whirlpool. Complimentary coffee in rms. Bar. Ck-out noon. Coin lndry. Meeting rms. Business servs avail. In-rm modem link. Exercise equipt. Refrigerator in suites. Near University of NC. Cr cds: A, C, D, DS, MC, V.

D ≥ 🏋 🏊 🔥 SC

✓★ **FAIRFIELD INN BY MARRIOTT.** 5415 N I-85 Service Rd (28262), I-85 exit 41. 704/596-2999; FAX 704/596-3329; res: 800/228-2800. 133 rms, 3 story. S, D $49; under 18 free; lower rates wkends; higher rates special events. Crib free. TV; cable (premium). Pool. Complimentary continental bkfst. Restaurant nearby. Ck-out noon. Business servs avail. Cr cds: A, C, D, DS, MC, V.

D ≥ 🏊 🔥 SC

★★ **HAMPTON INN.** 440 Griffith Rd (28217), approx 6 mi S via I-77, Tyvola Rd exit 5. 704/525-0747; FAX 704/522-0968; res: 800/426-7866. 161 rms, 4 story. S $72; D $80-$85; under 18 free. Crib free. TV; cable (premium). Pool. Complimentary continental bkfst. Ck-out noon. Meeting rms. Business servs avail. Valet serv. Airport transportation. Exercise equipt; sauna. Microwaves avail. Cr cds: A, C, D, DS, MC, V.

D ≥ 🏋 🏊 🔥 SC

✓★ **INNKEEPER COLISEUM.** 305 Archdale Dr (28217). 704/525-3033; FAX 704/525-3033; res: 800/822-9899. 69 rms, 2 story. S $45.99; D $45.99-$55.99; each addl $5; under 16 free; higher rates special events. Crib free. TV; cable (premium). Pool. Complimentary continental bkfst. Restaurant nearby. Ck-out noon. Business servs avail. Microwaves avail. Cr cds: A, C, D, DS, MC, V.

D 🔲 🏊 🔥 SC

★★ **LA QUINTA INN.** *7900 Nations Ford Rd (28217), S via I-77 to exit 4.* 704/522-7110; FAX 704/521-9778; res: 800/687-6667. Web www.laquinta.com. 118 rms, 3 story. S, D $66-$74; each addl $7; under 18 free; higher rates: auto race wkends, special events. Crib free. Pet accepted, some restrictions. TV; cable (premium). Heated pool. Continental bkfst. Restaurant adj open 24 hrs. Ck-out noon. Business servs avail. Valet serv. Health club privileges. Microwaves avail. Cr cds: A, C, D, DS, MC, V.

D 🐾 🏊 🔥 SC

✓★ **RED ROOF INN.** *131 Red Roof Dr (28217), I-77 S to exit 4 (Nations Ford Rd).* 704/529-1020; FAX 704/529-1054; res: 800/843-7663. E-mail 124@redroofinn.com. 115 rms, 3 story. S $36-$41; D $41-$47; up to 5, $59; under 18 free. Crib free. Pet accepted, some restrictions. TV; cable (premium). Complimentary coffee in lobby. Ck-out noon. Business servs avail. Health club privileges. Cr cds: A, C, D, DS, MC, V.

D 🐾 🏊 🔥

★★ **RESIDENCE INN BY MARRIOTT.** *5816 Westpark Dr (28217), off I-77S at Tyvola Rd exit 5.* 704/527-8110; FAX 704/521-8282; res: 800/331-3131. E-mail charlotte-062@rfsmgmt.com. 80 kit. suites, 1-2 story. S, D $115-$169. Crib free. Pet accepted; $10/day. TV; cable (premium). Heated pool; whirlpool. Complimentary continental bkfst. Restaurant adj 7 am-10 pm. Coin lndry. Ck-out noon. Business servs avail. Valet serv. Health club privileges. Lawn games. Microwaves. Private patios, balconies. Cr cds: A, C, D, DS, MC, V.

D 🐾 🏊 🔥 SC

✓★ **RODEWAY INN.** *1416 W Sugar Creek Rd (28262).* 704/597-5074; FAX 704/597-5074; res: 800/638-7949. 56 rms, 2 story. S $40.95-$48.95; D $46.95-$54.95; each addl $5; higher rates special events; under 12 free. Crib free. TV; cable (premium). Pool. Complimentary continental bkfst. Restaurant adj open 24 hrs. Ck-out 11 am. Cr cds: A, C, D, DS, MC, V.

D 🏊 🔥 SC

Motor Hotels

★★ **HOLIDAY INN.** *212 W Woodlawn Rd (28217), at I-77S exit 6A.* 704/525-8356; FAX 704/522-0671; res: 800/847-7829. E-mail holidaywoodlawn@travelbase.com; web www.travelbase.com/destinations/charlotte/holiday-woodlawn. 425 rms, 4 story. S, D $89-$99; suites $180; under 18 free; wkend rates; higher rates special events. Crib free. TV; cable (premium). Pool. Restaurant 6 am-10 pm. Rm serv. Bar 4 pm-1 am; entertainment. Ck-out noon. Meeting rms. Business servs avail. In-rm modem link. Bellhops. Valet serv. Sundries. Gift shop. Free airport transportation. Exercise equipt. Refrigerator in suites. Cr cds: A, C, D, DS, JCB, MC, V.

D 🏊 🏋 🔥 SC

★★ **HOLIDAY INN.** *2707 Little Rock Rd (28214).* 704/394-4301; FAX 704/394-1844; res: 800/647- STAY. 215 rms, 4 story. S $69; D $69-$79; suites $109; under 18 free; higher rates race wkends. Crib avail. TV; cable (premium). Complimentary continental bkfst. Complimentary coffee in rms. Restaurant 6 am-11 pm. Rm serv 7 am-10:30 pm. Bar 2 pm-1 am; entertainment Fri, Sat. Ck-out noon. Meeting rms. Business servs avail. Bellhops. Free airport transportation. Exercise equipt; sauna. Heated pool. Game rm. In-rm whirlpool, refrigerator, microwave in suites. Cr cds: A, C, D, DS, MC, V.

D 🐾 🏋 🏊 🔥 SC

★★★ **SHERATON PLAZA HOTEL.** *3315 I-85 Billy Graham Pkwy (28208), at Billy Graham Pkwy, near Douglas Intl Airport, I-85 exit 33.* 704/392-1200; FAX 704/393-2207; res: 800/325-2529. 222 rms, 8 story. S, D $119-$135; each addl $10; suites $150-$175; under 16 free; wkend rates. Crib free. Pet accepted. TV; cable (premium). Indoor/outdoor pool; whirlpool, poolside serv. Coffee in rms. Restaurant 6:30 am-10:30 pm. Rm serv. Bar 11 am-midnight; entertainment Thurs-Sat. Ck-out noon. Meeting rms. Business servs avail. Bellhops. Valet serv. Gift shop. Guest lndry. Free airport transportation. Exercise equipt; sauna. Bathrm phones; microwaves avail. Cr cds: A, C, D, DS, JCB, MC, V.

D 🐾 🏊 🏋 🏊 🔥 SC

★★ **SUMMERFIELD SUITES HOTEL.** *4920 S Tryon St (28217).* 704/525-2600; FAX 704/521-9932; res: 800/833-4353. 135 kit. suites, 5 story. Kit. suites $119-$169; under 18 free; wkend rates; higher rates race wkend. Crib free. Pet accepted; $50. TV; cable (premium), VCR (movies). Complimentary continental bkfst. Complimentary coffee in rms. Ck-out noon. Meeting rms. In-rm modem link. Free airport transportation. Exercise equipt. Pool; whirlpool. Game rm. Refrigerators, microwaves. Picnic tables, grills. Totally nonsmoking. Cr cds: A, C, D, DS, JCB, MC, V.

D 🐾 🏊 🏋 🔥 SC

★★★ **WYNDHAM GARDEN HOTEL.** *2600 Yorkmont Rd (28208), off Billy Graham Pkwy at Tyvola Rd & Coliseum exit.* 704/357-9100; FAX 704/357-9159; res: 800/822-4200. 173 rms, 3 story. S $119; D $129; each addl $10; suites $129-$149; under 12 free; wkend rates; higher rates special events. Crib free. TV; cable (premium), VCR avail. Heated pool; whirlpool. Complimentary coffee in rms. Restaurant 6:30 am-2:30 pm, 5-10 pm. Rm serv from 5 pm. Bar 4 pm-midnight. Ck-out noon. Meeting rms. Business servs avail. In-rm modem link. Bellhops. Valet serv. Free airport transportation. Exercise equipt. Refrigerator in some suites. Cr cds: A, C, D, DS, MC, V.

D 🏊 🏋 🏊 🔥 SC

Hotels

★★★ **ADAM'S MARK HOTEL.** *555 S McDowell St (28204), at jct US 74 & US 77.* 704/372-4100; FAX 704/348-4646; res: 800/444-2326. 615 rms, 18 story. S, D $99-$155; each addl $15; suites $125-$450; under 18 free. Crib free. TV; cable (premium). Heated pools, 1 indoor; whirlpool. Restaurant (see BRAVO). Bars 11-1 am; entertainment. Ck-out noon. Convention facilities. Concierge. Gift shop. Exercise equipt; sauna. Health club privileges. Raquetball courts. Wet bar in some suites. Opp park. Cr cds: A, C, D, DS, ER, MC, V.

D 🏊 🏋 🏊 🔥 SC

★★ **DOUBLETREE HOTEL.** *895 W Trade St (28202).* 704/347-0070; FAX 704/347-0267; res: 800/222-8733. 187 rms, 8 story. S $150; D $165; each addl $15; under 18 free; wkend rates; higher rates auto races (May & Oct). TV; cable (premium). Pool; whirlpool. Coffee in rms. Restaurant 6:30 am-11 pm. Bar 5 pm-midnight. Ck-out 1 pm. Meeting rms. Exercise equipt; sauna. Health club privileges. Refrigerators. Cr cds: A, C, D, DS, JCB, MC, V.

D 🏊 🏋 🏊 🔥 SC

★★ **DUNHILL HOTEL.** *237 N Tryon St (28202).* 704/332-4141; FAX 704/376-4117; res: 800/354-4141. E-mail rjm@msn.com. 60 rms, 10 story. S, D $99-$300; wkend rates; higher rates special events. Crib free. TV; cable (premium). Restaurant 6:30 am-10:30 pm. Bar. Ck-out noon. Meeting rms. Business servs avail. In-rm modem link. Concierge. Free garage parking. Health club privileges. Refrigerators. European-style hotel built in 1929; 18th-century furnishings, original artwork. Cr cds: A, C, D, DS, MC, V.

D 🏊 🔥 SC

★★★ **EMBASSY SUITES HOTEL.** *4800 S Tryon St (28217).* 704/527-8400; FAX 704/527-7035; res: 800/362-2779. Web www.embassy-charlotte.com. 274 suites, 8 story. Suites $159-$179; each addl $20; under 12 free; wkend rates; higher rates special events. Crib free. TV; cable (premium). Indoor pool; whirlpool, poolside serv. Complimentary full bkfst. Complimentary coffee in rms. Restaurant 11 am-11 pm. Bar 10-2 am; entertainment. Ck-out noon. Coin lndry. Convention facilities. Business center. In-rm modem link. Gift shop. Covered parking. Free airport transportation. Exercise equipt; sauna. Refrigerators, microwaves, wet bars; some bathrm phones. Cr cds: A, C, D, DS, MC, V.

D ⊠ ⫞ ⫞ ⫞ ⫞ SC ⫞

★★★ **HILTON AT UNIVERSTY PLACE.** 8629 J M Keynes Dr (28262), off I-85, exit 45A (Harris Blvd). 704/547-7444; FAX 704/549-9708; res: 800/445-8667. E-mail hiltonuniversity@travelbase.com; web www.travelbase.com/destinations/charlotte/hilton-univ. 243 rms, 12 story. S, D $89-$179; each addl $15; wkend rates. Crib $15. Pet accepted; $50. TV; cable. Pool; poolside serv. Restaurant 6:30 am-10 pm. Bar 11-2 am. Ck-out noon. Meeting rms. Business servs avail. In-rm modem link. Exercise equipt. Microwaves avail. Cr cds: A, C, D, DS, MC, V.

D ⫞ ⫞ ⫞ ⫞ ⫞ SC

★★★ **HILTON CHARLOTTE & TOWERS.** 222 E 3rd St (28202). 704/377-1500; FAX 704/377-4143. 407 rms, 22 story. S $175, D $195; each addl $25; suites $195-$600; under 18 free; wkend rates. Crib free. Garage parking; valet $18. TV; cable (premium), VCR avail. Pool privileges. Restaurant 6:30 am-11 pm. Bar 11-1:30 am. Ck-out noon. Convention facilities. Business center. In-rm modem link. Shopping arcade. Airport transportation. Tennis privileges. Golf privileges. Health club privileges. Minibars; some bathrm phones; refrigerators avail. Wet bar in suites. Luxury level. Cr cds: A, C, D, DS, JCB, MC, V.

D ⫞ ⫞ ⫞ ⫞ ⫞ SC ⫞

★★★ **HILTON HOTEL EXECUTIVE PARK.** 5624 Westpark Dr (28217), I-77 exit 5. 704/527-9616; FAX 704/527-4278; res: 800/445-8667. 178 rms, 7 story, 34 suites. S $135; D $145; each addl $10; suites $155; under 18 free. Crib free. Pet accepted; $50 deposit & $15/day. TV; cable (premium), VCR avail. Pool; whirlpool. Restaurant 6:30 am-2 pm, 5-10 pm. Bar 2 pm-midnight. Ck-out noon. Meeting rms. Business servs avail. Free airport transportation. Exercise equipt. Microwaves avail. Refrigerator in suites. Cr cds: A, C, D, DS, MC, V.

D ⫞ ⫞ ⫞ ⫞ ⫞ SC

★★★ **HYATT AT SOUTH PARK.** 5501 Carnegie Blvd (28209), opp South Park Mall. 704/554-1234; FAX 704/554-8319; res: 800/228-9000. 262 rms, 7 story. S $175; D $200; suites $375-$550; lower rates wkends; under 18 free. Crib free. TV; cable (premium). Indoor pool; poolside serv. Restaurant 6 am-10:30 pm. Rm serv 24 hrs. Bar 4 pm-1 am. Ck-out noon. Convention facilities. Business center. Gift shop. Free valet parking. Airport transportation. Exercise equipt; sauna. Refrigerators avail. Some balconies. Cr cds: A, C, D, DS, ER, JCB, MC, V.

D ⫞ ⫞ ⫞ ⫞ SC ⫞

★★★ **MARRIOTT HOTEL.** 100 W Trade St (28202). 704/333-9000; FAX 704/342-3419; res: 800/228-9290. 434 rms, 19 story. S $149; D $159; suites $375-$650; under 12 free; wkend rates. Crib free. Covered parking, valet $16. TV; cable (premium), VCR avail. Heated pool; whirlpool. Restaurant 6:30 am-10 pm. Bar 11:30-1 am. Ck-out noon. Guest lndry. Convention facilities. Business center. In-rm modem link. Concierge. Gift shop. Airport transportation. Exercise equipt. Refrigerators, microwaves avail. Shopping adj. Luxury level. Cr cds: A, C, D, DS, ER, JCB, MC, V.

D ⫞ ⫞ ⫞ ⫞ ⫞ SC ⫞

★★ **OMNI.** 101 S Tryon St (28280), at jct Trade & Tryon Sts. 704/377-0400; FAX 704/347-0649; res: 800/601-8400. 365 rms, 15 story. S, D $159; each addl $10; suites $219-$325; under 18 free; wkend rates. Crib free. Pet accepted, some restrictions. TV; cable (premium), VCR avail. Pool; poolside serv. Coffee in rms. Restaurant 6:30 am-10:30 pm. Bar 11 am-midnight. Ck-out noon. Convention facilities. Business center. Concierge. Shopping arcade. Barber, beauty shop. Covered parking. Exercise equipt; sauna. Refrigerator, wet bar in suites. Luxury level. Cr cds: A, C, D, DS, MC, V.

D ⫞ ⫞ ⫞ ⫞ ⫞ SC ⫞

★★★★ **PARK HOTEL, THE.** 2200 Rexford Rd (28211). 704/364-8220; FAX 704/365-4712; res: 800/334-0331. Web www.theparkhotel.com. Marble, brass and traditional patterns, cast in rich colors, are used throughout the hotel's public areas and in the well-appointed guest rooms.

192 rms, 6 story. S $139-$220; D $149-$240; each addl $15; suites $350-$650; under 18 free; wkend rates. Crib free. TV; cable (premium), VCR avail. Heated pool; whirlpool, poolside serv. Restaurant (see MORRO-CROFTS). Rm serv 24 hrs. Bars 11-2 am; entertainment. Ck-out noon. Meeting rms. Business center. In-rm modem link. Concierge. Free valet parking. Airport, RR station, bus depot transportation. Tennis privileges. Golf privileges. Exercise equipt; steam rm. Health club privileges. Some refrigerators; microwaves avail. Cr cds: A, C, D, DS, JCB, MC, V.

D ⫞ ⫞ ⫞ ⫞ ⫞ ⫞ SC ⫞

★★★ **SOUTHPARK SUITE HOTEL.** 6300 Morrison Blvd (28211), near South Park Mall. 704/364-2400; FAX 704/362-0203; res: 800/647-8483. E-mail spsh@vnet.net; web www.vnet.net/southpark. 208 kit. suites, 3-6 story. S, D $93-$189; under 18 free; wkend rates. Crib avail. TV; cable (premium). Pool; whirlpool, poolside serv. Restaurant 6:30 am-2 pm, 5:30-10:30 pm. Bar 4 pm-midnight. Ck-out noon. Lndry facilities. Meeting rms. Business center. Gift shop. Exercise equipt; sauna. Health club privileges. Microwaves. Private patios, balconies. Cr cds: A, C, D, DS, MC, V.

D ⫞ ⫞ ⫞ ⫞ SC ⫞

Restaurants

★★★ **BRAVO RISTORANTE & LOUNGE.** (See Adam's Mark) 704/372-5440. Hrs: 5:30-10 pm; Fri, Sat to 10:30 pm; Sun brunch 11 am-3 pm. Res accepted. Italian menu. Bar. Semi-a la carte: dinner $15.25-$24.50 Sun brunch $18.95. Specializes in fresh seafood, pasta, chicken. Singing waiters. Italian decor. Cr cds: A, C, D, DS, ER, MC, V.

D ⫞

★★★ **EPICUREAN.** 1324 East Blvd (28203). 704/377-4529. Hrs: 6-10 pm. Closed Sun; major hols; also 1st 2 wks July. Res accepted. Bar. Wine list. Semi-a la carte: dinner $16.95-$35.95. Child's meals. Specializes in prime steaks, fresh seafood, lamb. Own baking. Family-owned. Cr cds: A, C, D, MC, V.

⫞

★★ **FISHMARKET, THE.** 6631 Morrison Blvd (28211). 704/365-0883. Hrs: 11:30 am-2 pm, 6-10 pm; Sat from 6 pm; Sun 6-9 pm. Closed major hols. Res accepted. Bar 4-11 pm. Semi-a la carte: lunch $5.95-$10.95, dinner $15.95-$32.95. Specializes in seafood, pasta, desserts. Cr cds: A, C, D, DS, MC, V.

D ⫞

★★ **HEREFORD BARN STEAK HOUSE.** 4320 N I-85 (28206), on service road between Sugar Creek Rd & Graham St. 704/596-0854. Hrs: 5-10 pm; Fri, Sat to 11 pm. Closed Sun, Mon; major hols. Serv bar. Semi-a la carte: dinner $9.95-$29.95. Child's meals. Specializes in steak, prime rib, chicken. Country-barn decor; farm implements; fireplace. Family-owned. Cr cds: A, C, D, MC, V.

SC ⫞

★★★ **LA BIBLIOTHEQUE.** 1901 Roxborough Rd (28211), in Roxborough office bldg. 704/365-5000. Web www.labibliotheque.com. Hrs: 11:30 am-2:30 pm, 5:30-10:30 pm; Sat from 5:30 pm. Closed Sun; Jan 1, Thanksgiving, Dec 25. Res accepted. French-American menu. Serv bar. A la carte entrees: lunch $7.95-$11.95, dinner $14-$35. Specializes in seafood, beef, veal. Pianist Tues-Sat. Terrace dining. Traditional decor; oil paintings. Jacket (dinner). Cr cds: A, C, D, DS, MC, V.

D ⫞

★★★ **LAMP LIGHTER.** 1065 E Morehead St (28204). 704/372-5343. Hrs: 5:30-10 pm; Fri, Sat to 10:30 pm. Closed Jan 1, Thanksgiving, Dec 25. Res accepted. Continental menu. Bar. Wine list. Semi-a la carte: dinner $15.95-$29.95. Specializes in fresh seafood, wild game, ostrich. Own baking. Valet parking. In Spanish-colonial house built 1926. Jacket. Cr cds: A, C, D, MC, V.

D ⫞

★★ **MCNINCH HOUSE.** *511 N Church St (28202). 704/332-6159.* Hrs: 6:30 pm-12:30 am. Closed Mon, Sun; also major hols. Res required. French, continental menu. Bar. Complete meal: dinner $78. Serv charge 20%. Specialties: rack of lamb, crab cakes, white chocolate mousse with macadamia nuts. Valet parking. In 100-yr-old Victorian house. Cr cds: A, C, MC, V.

D ⌷

★★★ **MORROCROFTS.** *(See The Park Hotel) 704/364-8220.* Hrs: 6:30 am-11 pm; early-bird dinner 5-6:30 pm; Sun brunch 10:30 am-2 pm. Res accepted. Continental menu. Bar 11-1 am. Wine list. Semi-a la carte: bkfst $2.50-$9.95, lunch $4.95-$14.95, dinner $15.95-$27.95. Sun brunch $16.95-$29.95. Child's meals. Specializes in fresh seafood, regional cuisine. Own baking. Pianist. Valet parking. Outdoor dining. English club decor. Cr cds: A, C, D, DS, JCB, MC, V.

D ⌷

★★★ **PATOU BISTRO.** *2400 Park Rd Suite M (28203). 704/376-2233.* Hrs: 11:30 am-2:30 pm, 5-10:30 pm. Closed Sun; also major hols. Res accepted. French menu. Bar. Wine cellar. Semi-a la carte: lunch $5-$9, dinner $10-$18. Specialties: seafood waterzooi, snails in roquefort sauce, confit of duck. Parking. Outdoor dining. Bistro decor; black/white photos. Cr cds: A, C, DS, MC, V.

D ⌷

★ **RANCH HOUSE.** *5614 Wilkinson Blvd (28208). 704/399-5411.* Hrs: 5-11 pm. Closed Sun; major hols. Serv bar. Semi-a la carte: dinner: $9.75-$20.75. Child's meals. Specializes in steak, seafood, chicken. Western decor. Family-owned. Cr cds: A, C, D, DS, MC, V.

⌷

★★★ **TOWNHOUSE.** *1011 Providence Rd (28270). 704/335-1546.* E-mail townhouse2@aol.com. Hrs: 5-9 pm. Closed some major hols. Res accepted. Bar from 5 pm. Wine list. Semi-a la carte: dinner $19.50-$30. Specializes in fowl, beef, seafood. Own baking, pasta. 18th-century English decor. Cr cds: A, C, D, DS, JCB, MC, V.

D ⌷

Cherokee *(B-2)*

(See also Bryson City, Maggie Valley, Waynesville)

Pop 8,519 **Elev** 1,991 ft **Area Code** 828 **Zip** 28719 **E-mail** chero@dmet.net **Web** www.cherokee-nc.co

Information Cherokee Travel and Promotion, PO Box 460; 828/497-9195 or 800/438-1601

This is the capital of the Eastern Band of the Cherokee, who live on the Qualla Reservation at the edge of Great Smoky Mountains National Park (see) and the Blue Ridge Parkway. The reservation is the largest east of the Mississippi. These descendants of members of the tribe who avoided being driven to Oklahoma over the "Trail of Tears" are progressive in their ideas, yet determined to maintain their ancient traditions.

What to See and Do

Cherokee Heritage Museum and Gallery. Interpretive center features Cherokee culture and history. Gift shop. (Daily; closed 3 wks late Dec–early Jan) On US 441 and Big Cove Rd, in Saunooke's Village. Phone 828/497-3211. ¢¢

Museum of the Cherokee Indian. Arts and crafts, audiovisual displays, portraits, prehistoric artifacts. (Daily; closed Jan 1, Thanksgiving, Dec 25) On US 441 at Drama Rd, on Cherokee Reservation. Phone 828/497-3481. ¢¢

Oconaluftee Indian Village. Replica of Native American village of more than 250 yrs ago. Incl 7-sided council house; lectures; herb garden; craft demonstrations. Guided tours (Mid-May–late Oct, daily). ½ mi N on US 441, adj to Mountainside Theater. Phone 828/497-2111. ¢¢¢

Santa's Land. Christmas theme park featuring Santa Claus and helpers; rides; zoo; entertainment, incl magic show; lake with pedal boats; primitive crafts; snack shops, picnic area, play areas; gardens. (Early May–late Oct, daily) 3 mi E on US 19N. Phone 828/497-9191. ¢¢¢¢

Seasonal Event

Unto These Hills. Mountainside Theater. On US 441, ½ mi from jct US 19. Kermit Hunter drama re-creating the history of Cherokee Nation from 1540–1838; in natural amphitheater. Nightly exc Sun. Phone 828/497-2111. Mid-June–late Aug.

Motels

★★ **BEST WESTERN.** *441 N & Aquoni Rd (28719). 828/497-2020; FAX 828/497-3903; res: 800/528-1234.* 152 rms, 2 story. Late May-Oct: S, D $85; each addl $6; under 12 free; lower rates rest of yr. Crib free. TV; cable (premium). Pool; wading pool. Restaurant 7 am-9 pm. Rm serv. Ck-out 11 am. Coin lndry. Meeting rms. Business servs avail. Sundries. Cr cds: A, C, D, DS, MC, V.

D ⌷ ⌷ ⌷ ⌷ SC

★★ **COMFORT INN.** *US 19 S (28719), ½ mi W of jct US 441 & 19. 828/497-2411; FAX 828/497-6555; res: 800/228-5150.* 87 rms, 2 story. Late May-Oct: S, D $59-$109; each addl $8; under 18 free; lower rates Apr-late May & Nov-Dec. Closed rest of yr. Crib $2. TV; cable (premium). Pool; whirlpool. Complimentary continental bkfst. Restaurant nearby. Ck-out 11 am. Meeting rm. Business servs avail. Some refrigerators. On river. Cr cds: A, C, D, DS, JCB, MC, V.

D ⌷ ⌷ ⌷ ⌷ ⌷ SC

✓★ **COOL WATERS MOTEL.** *US Hwy 19 N (28719), 1½ mi E. 828/497-3855; FAX 828/497-3855.* 50 rms. Mid-June-Oct: S, D $42-$70; lower rates rest of yr. Crib $3. TV; cable. Pool; wading pool. Restaurant opp 6:30 am-9 pm. Ck-out 11 am. Tennis. Some patios. Picnic tables, grills. On stream; trout pond. Cr cds: C, DS, MC, V.

⌷ ⌷ ⌷ ⌷ ⌷

★ **CRAIG'S MOTEL.** *Hwy 19 (28719). 828/497-3821; FAX 828/497-3821; res: 800/560-6869.* 30 rms. S, D $49-$63; each addl $5; higher rates: hols, wkends, fall foliage season. TV; cable (premium). Pool. Playground. Restaurant 7 am-10 pm. Ck-out 11 am. On stream; picnic tables nearby. Cr cds: A, C, DS, MC, V.

⌷ ⌷ ⌷ ⌷ SC

★★ **DAYS INN.** *Hwy 19 N (28719). 828/497-9171; FAX 828/497-3424; res: 800/329-7466.* 58 rms, 1-2 story. Mid-June-Labor Day, Oct: S, D $65-$90; each addl $3; lower rates rest of yr. Crib free. TV; cable (premium). Pool; wading pool. Playground. Restaurant adj 7 am-noon, 5-9 pm. Ck-out 11 am. Cr cds: A, C, D, DS, JCB, MC, V.

⌷ ⌷ ⌷ ⌷ SC

★★★ **HOLIDAY INN.** *US Hwy 19 S (28719), 1 mi W. 828/497-9181; FAX 828/497-5973; res: 800/465-4329.* 154 rms, 2 story. Mid-June-Oct: S, D $66-$100; each addl $6; under 19 free; lower rates rest of yr. Crib free. TV; cable (premium). 2 pools, 1 indoor; wading pool, whirlpool. Sauna. Playground. Coffee in rms. Restaurant 7-11 am, 5-9 pm. Rm serv. Ck-out 11 am. Coin lndry. Meeting rm. Sundries. Gift shop. Game rm. Cr cds: A, C, D, DS, JCB, MC, V.

D ⌷ ⌷ ⌷ SC

★ **PIONEER MOTEL & COTTAGES.** *Highway 19 S (28719). 828/497-2271.* 21 rms, 6 kit. cottages. Mid-June-Labor Day, Oct: S, D $48-$68; each addl $5; cottages $75-$150; under 12 free; lower rates Apr-mid-June, Sept. Closed rest of yr. Crib free. TV; cable (premium). Pool. Complimentary coffee in lobby. Restaurant nearby. Ck-out 11 am. At river. Cr cds: A, C, DS, MC, V.

⌷ ⌷ ⌷ ⌷ ⌷ SC

Cherryville (B-4)

(See also Gastonia, Shelby)

Founded 1881 **Pop** 4,756 **Elev** 960 ft **Area Code** 704 **Zip** 28021
Information Chamber of Commerce, 301 E Main St, PO Box 305;
704/435-3451 or 704/435-4200

Customs of Cherryville's original German settlers still live on in this town
nestled in the rolling hills of the Piedmont.

Annual Event

Shooting in the New Year. Old rite to bring fertility to fruit trees and for
good luck in the coming yr. Men chant blessings and fire black-powder
muzzleloaders as they go from home to home New Year's Eve until dusk,
Jan 1.

Concord (Cabarrus Co) (B-5)

(See also Albemarle, Charlotte)

Pop 27,347 **Elev** 704 ft **Area Code** 704 **Zip** 28026
Information Chamber of Commerce, 23 Union St N, PO Box 1029;
704/782-4111

Concord was founded by Scottish-Irish and German-Dutch settlers and
received its name when the two factions settled a dispute regarding the
location of the county seat. An early textile area in the South, Concord continues to lead in dyeing, finishing and weaving of hosiery and knitted textiles.

What to See and Do

Reed Gold Mine State Historic Site. First documented discovery of gold
in the US (1799) occurred here. Panning area (Apr–Oct, daily; fee); underground mine tours, history trail; working machinery, demonstrations,
exhibits, visitor center; film; picnicking. (Apr–Oct, Mon–Sat, also Sun afternoons; rest of yr, Tues–Sat, also Sun afternoons) 10 mi SE on US 601 and
NC 200 to Georgeville, then 2 mi S on NC 1100. Phone 704/786-8337.
Free

Motels

★ COLONIAL INN. *1325 Concord Pkwy N. (28025),* ¾ *mi
NW on US 29/601 Concord exit.* 704/782-2146; FAX 704/786-9856. 65
rms. S $42; D $52. Crib $6. TV; cable (premium). Pool. Complimentary cof-
fee in lobby. Restaurant adj 6 am-midnight. Ck-out 11 am. Meeting rms.
Lawn games. Cr cds: A, C, D, DS, MC, V.

D ≈ � 🔥 SC

✓ **★★ COMFORT INN.** *3100 Cloverleaf Pkwy (28081).* 704/786-
3100; FAX 704/784-3114; res: 800/638-7949. 71 rms, 2 story. S, D $58.95;
each addl $5; suites $72.95; under 18 free; higher rates: auto races, horse
shows. Crib $5. TV; cable (premium), VCR avail (movies). Pool. Compli-
mentary continental bkfst. Complimentary coffee in rms. Restaurant adj 11
am-11 pm. Ck-out 11 am. Coin lndry. Meeting rms. Business servs avail.
Health club privileges. Many refrigerators. Cr cds: A, C, D, DS, ER, JCB,
MC, V.

D ≈ ⇥ 🔥 SC

Cornelius (B-4)

(See also Charlotte, Statesville)

Founded 1893 **Pop** 2,581 **Elev** 831 ft **Area Code** 704 **Zip** 28031
E-mail NMeckCofC1@aol.com **Web** www.lakenorman.org
Information North Mecklenburg Chamber & Visitors Center, PO Box 760;
704/892-1922

A dispute between two cotton companies in Davidson during the late 1800s
led to one of the firms relocating south of the city limits and establishing a
new town. Originally called Liverpool, the community changed its name to
Cornelius in honor of an investor.

What to See and Do

Lake Norman. The state's largest freshwater lake (32,510 acres); created
by Cowans Ford Dam, a Duke Power project on the Catawba River. 8 public access areas. NW of town. Phone 704/382-8587.

Annual Event

LakeFest. County Park. Entertainment, dog show, Art in the Park, concessions. KidzFest, petting zoo, magic shows, face painting. Phone
704/892-1922. 2nd wkend mid-Sept.

Motels

★★ BEST WESTERN LAKE NORMAN. *19608 Liverpool
Pkwy (28031).* 704/896-0660; FAX 704/896-8633; res: 800/528-1234. 80
rms, 4 story, 10 suites. S $65.95; D $72.95; each addl $7; suites $89.95-
$99.95; under 15 free; higher rates special events. Crib free. TV; cable
(premium), VCR avail (movies $6). Pool. Complimentary continental bkfst.
Restaurant nearby. Ck-out 11 am. Meeting rms. Business servs avail. Exercise equipt. Refrigerators, microwaves avail. Cr cds: A, C, D, DS, MC, V.

D ≈ ⇥ ⇥ 🔥 SC

★★ COMFORT INN LAKE NORMAN. *20740 Torrence
Chapel Rd (28031), 1 mi W on I-77, exit 28.* 704/892-3500; FAX 704/892-
6473; res: 800/848-9751. 90 rms, 2-3 story. S, D $71.95; suites $125-$175;
under 18 free; wkend, hol, wkly rates; higher rates special events. Crib
free. TV; cable (premium), VCR avail (movies). Pool. Complimentary continental bkfst. Complimentary coffee in rms. Restaurant nearby. Ck-out 11
am. Coin lndry. Meeting rm. Business servs avail. Health club privileges.
Refrigerators. Microwaves avail. Cr cds: A, C, D, DS, ER, JCB, MC, V.

D ≈ ⇥ 🔥 SC

✓ **★★ HAMPTON INN.** *19501 Statesville Rd (28031), I-77 exit
28.* 704/892-9900; FAX 704/896-7488; res: 800/426-7866. Web www.hamp
ton-inn.com. 117 rms, 5 story. S, D $74-$79; under 18 free; higher rates
wkends, special events. Crib free. TV; cable (premium). Pool. Complimentary continental bkfst. Restaurant adj 6 am-10 pm. Ck-out noon. Meeting rm. Business servs avail. Exercise equipt. Some refrigerators. Cr cds:
A, C, D, DS, MC, V.

D ≈ ⇥ ⇥ 🔥 SC

★★ HOLIDAY INN EXPRESS. *14135 Statesville Rd (28078),
5 mi S on I-77, exit 23.* 704/875-1165; FAX 704/875-1894; res: 800/465-
4329. 60 rms, 2 story. S $66; D $71; each addl $5; suites $90; under 16
free; higher rates sports events. Crib free. TV; cable (premium). Pool. Complimentary continental bkfst. Restaurant nearby. Ck-out 11 am. Meeting
rms. Business servs avail. Some refrigerators. Microwaves avail. Cr cds: A,
C, D, DS, JCB, MC, V.

D ≈ ⇥ 🔥 SC

★★ LAKE NORMAN HOLIDAY INN. *19901 Holiday Ln
(28031), jct NC 73 & I-77 exit 28.* 704/892-9120; FAX 704/892-3854; res:
800/465-4329. 119 rms, 2 story. S, D $84; under 18 free; higher rates spe-
cial events. Crib free. Pet accepted; $25. TV; cable (premium). Pool. Com-

plimentary coffee in rms. Restaurant 6 am-10 pm. Rm serv. Bar 4:30 pm-midnight. Ck-out 11 am. Coin lndry. Meeting rms. Exercise equipt. Some refrigerators, microwaves. Cr cds: A, C, D, DS, JCB, MC, V.

Inn

★★ **DAVIDSON VILLAGE INN.** 117 Depot St (28036), 1 mi N on I-77, exit 30. 704/892-8044; FAX 704/896-2184; res: 800/892-0796. E-mail dvi@charlotte.infi.net. 18 rms, 3 story, 4 suites. S, D $100-$110; suites $115-$125; under 16 free; wkends, hols (2-day min); higher rates special events. Crib free. TV; cable (premium). VCR avail. Complimentary continental bkfst. Restaurant adj 11 am-10 pm. Rm serv. Ck-out 11 am, ck-in 3 pm. Business servs avail. Luggage handling. Valet serv. Health club privileges. Refrigerator, microwave, wet bar in suites; microwaves avail. Cr cds: C.

Restaurants

✓★ **CAPTAIN'S GALLEY.** 105 Statesville Rd # J (28078), 2 mi S on I-77, exit 23. 704/875-6038. Hrs: 11 am-9 pm; Fri to 10 pm; Sat noon-10 pm. Closed Sun; most major hols. Semi-a la carte: lunch $3.75-$10, dinner $4.95-$16. Child's meals. Specializes in seafood. Own baking. Nautical decor; wall murals. Family-owned since 1978. Cr cds: C.

★★ **KOBE JAPANESE HOUSE OF STEAK & SEAFOOD.** 20465 Chartwell Center Dr (28031). 704/896-7778. Hrs: 11:30 am-2 pm, 5-10 pm; Sat 5-11 pm; Sun from 5 pm; early-bird dinner Mon-Fri 5-6 pm. Closed Thanksgiving, Dec 25. Res accepted. Japanese menu. Bar. Semi-a la carte: lunch $5.95-$14.95, dinner $9.95-$24.95. Serv charge 15%. Child's meals. Specializes in teppanyaki preparation, Kobe beef, seafood. Sushi bar (dinner). Japanese decor. Cr cds: A, C, D, DS, MC, V.

★★ **LAKESIDE AT HOLIDAY MARINA.** 20210 Henderson Rd (28031). 704/896-8985. Hrs: 11:30 am-10 pm; Fri & Sat to 11 pm. Closed Jan 1, Thanksgiving, Dec 25. Bar. Semi-a la carte: lunch, dinner $5.95-$17.95. Child's meals. Specializes in seafood, pasta, steak. Outdoor dining overlooking Lake Norman. Marina decor. Cr cds: A, C, D, DS, MC, V.

★ **RAINBOW DELI & CAFE.** 8301 Magnolia Estates Dr (28078), 5 mi S on I-77. 704/896-0091. Hrs: 11 am-10 pm; Sun to 9 pm. Sun brunch 11 am-3 pm. Closed Thanksgiving, Dec 25. Italian, Amer menu. Bar to 2 am. Semi-a la carte: lunch $2.50-$6.95, dinner $4.95-$16.95. Sun brunch $4.75-$9.95. Child's meals. Specializes in seafood, pasta, steak. Patio dining. Art deco theme. Cr cds: A, C, D, MC, V.

Dunn (B-7)

(See also Fayetteville, Goldsboro)

Pop 8,336 **Elev** 213 ft **Area Code** 910 **Zip** 28334

What to See and Do

Bentonville Battleground State Historic Site. Biggest battle on North Carolina soil, Mar 19–21, 1865. It was the last organized attempt to stop Gen William Tecumseh Sherman after he left Atlanta. A month later, the rebel cause was lost; Lee surrendered at Appomattox Apr 9; Lincoln was shot Apr 14; and Johnston surrendered Apr 26. The restored Harper House was used as a hospital to treat wounded of both sides. Reconstructed and original trenches; history trail with exhibits. Picnic area. Visitor center, audiovisual show. (Apr–Oct, daily; rest of yr, daily exc Mon; closed Jan 1,

Thanksgiving, Dec 24–25) 15 mi E via NC 55 to Newton Grove, 3 mi N via US 701 to NC 1008, then 3 mi E. Phone 910/594-0789.   **Free**

Motels

✓★ **BEST WESTERN.** 603 Springbranch Rd (28334), I-95, exit 72. 910/892-2162; FAX 910/892-3010; res: 800/528-1234. 142 rms, 2 story. S, D $29.99-$52.99; family rates. Crib $5. Pet accepted. TV; cable (premium). Pool. Restaurant 5-10 am, 5:30-9:30 pm. Ck-out 11 am. Business servs avail. Cr cds: A, C, D, DS, MC, V.

✓★ **EXPRESS INN.** 1125 E Broad St (28334). 910/892-1293; FAX 910/891-1038. 105 rms, 2 story. May-Sept: D $44.95-$54.95; D $44.95-$65.95; under 18 free; higher rates special events; lower rates rest of yr. Pet accepted. TV; cable (premium). Complimentary continental bkfst. Restaurant 5-10 pm. Ck-out 11 am. Meeting rm. Business servs avail. Pool. Some refrigerators. Cr cds: A, C, D, DS, MC, V.

★ **RAMADA INN.** 1011 E Cumberland St (28335), I-95 exit 73. 910/892-8101; FAX 910/892-2836; res: 800/272-6232. 100 rms, 2 story. S $39-$59; D $49-$69; each addl $6; under 18 free. Crib free. Pet accepted. TV; cable (premium). Pool. Restaurant 6:30 am-2 pm, 5-9 pm. Rm serv. Ck-out noon. Meeting rms. Business servs avail. In-rm modem link. Valet serv. Some refrigerators. Cr cds: A, C, D, DS, JCB, MC, V.

Durham (A-7)

(See also Chapel Hill, Raleigh)

Founded 1853 **Pop** 136,611 **Elev** 406 ft **Area Code** 919 **E-mail** visit@durham-cvb.com **Web** dcvb.durham.nc.us

Information Convention & Visitors Bureau, 101 E Morgan St, 27701; 800/772-2855

Durham's sparkle has brought it near-top national ranking in numerous livability studies. Known for excellence in medicine, education, research and industry, Durham is also a recreational and cultural center in the rolling Piedmont region.

In 1924, an endowment from James B. Duke, head of the American Tobacco Company, helped establish Duke University as a leader among the nation's institutions of higher learning. North Carolina Central University makes its home here. In the 1950s, Durham County was chosen as the site of Research Triangle Park, a planned scientific research center that includes the Environmental Protection Agency, the National Institute for Environmental Health Sciences, IBM Corporation, the Glaxo Wellcome Company and others. Duke University Medical Center, Durham Regional Hospital and several other outstanding medical institutions here have earned Durham the title "City of Medicine, USA."

What to See and Do

Bennett Place State Historic Site. Site of signing (Apr 26, 1865) of surrender of Confederate General Johnston to Union General Sherman, one of the last and most significant of the Confederate surrenders. Reconstructed Bennett homestead. Picnicking. Visitor Center, exhibits, audiovisual show. (Apr–Oct, daily; rest of yr, daily exc Mon; closed major hols) Just SW of jct I-85 exit 173 & US 70. Phone 919/383-4345.   **Free**

Duke Homestead State Historic Site (1852). Ancestral home of Duke family; first Duke tobacco factory; curing barn; outbuildings; farm crops. Tobacco Museum, exhibits, film; furnishings of period. Tours. (Apr–Oct, daily; rest of yr, daily exc Mon; closed major hols) 2828 Duke Homestead Rd, ½ mi N of jct I-85, Guess Rd. Phone 919/477-5498.   **Free**

Duke University (1838). (10,000 students) Two campuses, East and West, on 8,000 acres. Incl original Trinity College. The West Campus, occupied since 1930, is the showplace of the university. 919/684-8111. On campus are

Art Museum. (Daily exc Mon; closed hols) East Campus, off W Main St. Phone 919/684-5135.   **Free**

Duke Chapel. Beautiful Gothic-style chapel with a carillon of 50 bells in its 210-ft tower; 5,000-pipe Flentrop organ. (Daily) Chapel Dr to main quadrangle. Phone 919/684-2572.

Duke Libraries. Most comprehensive in the South, with more than 4 million volumes and more than 7 million manuscripts. Large Confederate imprint collection; Walt Whitman manuscripts. Phone 919/684-3009.

Duke Medical Center. Research and teaching complex. Treats more than one-half million patients annually. Phone 919/684-8111 for info.

Duke's Wallace Wade Stadium. (33,941 capacity) and the 8,564-seat Cameron Indoor Stadium. Home of the Duke Blue Devils.

Sarah P. Duke Gardens. 55 acres of landscaped gardens, pine forest. Continuous display. (Daily) Main entrance on Anderson St. Phone 919/684-3698.   **Free**

Historic Stagville Center. State-owned historic property, once part of the Bennehan-Cameron plantation; several historic 18th- and 19th-century plantation bldgs on 71 acres of land. (Mon–Fri; closed hols) 7 mi NE via Roxboro Rd and Old Oxford Hwy. Phone 919/620-0120.   **Free**

North Carolina Museum of Life and Science. North Carolina wildlife; hands-on science exhibits; aerospace, weather and geology collections; train ride; farmyard; science park; discovery rms; Butterfly House. Picnic area. (Daily; closed Jan 1, Thanksgiving, Dec 25) 433 Murray Ave. Phone 919/220-5429.   ¢¢¢

West Point on the Eno. A 371-acre park along the scenic Eno River; restored farmhouse (1850); working gristmill; museum of photography; blacksmith shop. Picnicking; fishing, hiking, boating; environmental programs (fee). Park (daily). Mill, farmhouse, museum (Mar–Dec, Sat & Sun). I-85, Duke St exit then 3½ mi N. Phone 919/471-1623.   **Free**

Annual Events

CenterFest. Downtown. 2-day event with over 250 artists and craftsmen; musicians, jugglers and clowns; continuous entertainment from 3 stages. Phone 919/560-2722. Sept.

Bull Durham Blues Festival. Historic Durham Athletic Park. Celebrates the blues with performances held at the location where *Bull Durham* was filmed. Phone 919/683-1709. Wkend mid-Sept.

Seasonal Event

American Dance Festival. Page Auditorium and Reynolds Industries Theater, Duke University, West Campus. Six-weeks of performances by the finest of both major and emerging modern dance companies from the US and abroad. Contact the Festival at PO Box 6097, College Station 22708; 919/684-6402. June–July.

Motels

★ **BEST WESTERN INN.** *5400 US 70; I-85 (27705), jct I-85 exit 170 & US 70W.* 919/383-2508; FAX 919/383-7316; res: 800/528-1234. 31 rms. S, D $58-$72; each addl $10; under 12 free. Crib $10. Pet accepted. TV; cable (premium). Pool. Playground. Coffee in rms. Complimentary continental bkfst. Ck-out noon. Business servs avail. Refrigerators. Picnic tables, grills. Cr cds: A, C, D, DS, ER, JCB, MC, V.

D 🐾 ⛵ 🖎 🔥 SC

★★ **COMFORT INN UNIVERSITY.** *3508 Mt Moriah Rd (27707).* 919/490-4949; FAX 919/419-0535; res: 800/228-5150; res: 800/221-2222. E-mail duroinn@qte.net.com. 138 rms, 4 story, 18 suites. S, D $69-$75; each addl $6; suites $119-$149; under 16 free; higher rates special events. Crib free. TV; cable (premium). Pool; whirlpool. Complimentary continental bkfst. Complimentary coffee in lobby. Restaurant nearby. Ck-out noon. Coin lndry. Meeting rms. Business servs avail. Exercise equipt; sauna. Cr cds: A, C, D, DS, MC, V.

D ⛵ 🕴 🖎 🔥 SC

★★ **COURTYARD.** *1815 Front St (27705).* 919/309-1500; FAX 919/383-8189. 146 rms, 4 story. Apr-Nov: S $79.97-$109.95; D $89.95-$119.95; each addl $10; suites $109.95-$169.95; under 18 free; package plans; higher rates special events; lower rates rest of yr. Crib free. TV; cable (premium). Complimentary coffee in rms. Restaurant nearby. Ck-out noon. Meeting rms. Business servs avail. In-rm modem link. Sundries. Coin lndry. Exercise equipt. Health club privileges. Pool. Refrigerator in suites. Some balconies. Cr cds: A, C, D, DS, JCB, MC, V.

D ⛵ 🕴 🖎 🔥 SC

✓ ★ **FAIRFIELD INN BY MARRIOTT.** *3710 Hillsborough Rd (27705).* 919/382-3388; FAX 919/382-3388; res: 800/228-2800. 135 rms, 3 story. S, D $59-$65; each addl $3; under 18 free. Crib free. TV; cable (premium). Pool. Complimentary continental bkfst. Ck-out noon. Business servs avail. Cr cds: A, C, D, DS, MC, V.

D ⛵ 🖎 🔥 SC

✓ ★ **RED ROOF INN.** *1915 North Pointe Drive (27705), I-40 exit 175.* 919/471-9882; FAX 919/477-0512; res: 800/843-7663. Web www.redroofinn.com. 120 rms, 3 story. S $47.99-$61.99; D $50.99-$63.99. Crib free. Pet accepted, some restrictions. TV; cable (premium). Complimentary coffee in lobby. Restaurant nearby. Ck-out noon. Business servs avail. Cr cds: A, C, D, DS, MC, V.

D 🐾 🖎 🔥 SC

Motor Hotels

★★ **HAWTHORN SUITES.** *300 Meredith Dr (27713), I-40 exit 278.* 919/361-1234; FAX 919/361-1213; res: 800/527-1133. E-mail beaver1@bellsouth.net; web www.citysearch.com/rdu/hawthornesuites. 100 kit. suites, 2-3 story. S, D $135-$150; 2-bedrm suites $169-$189. Crib free. TV; cable (premium). Pool. Complimentary continental bkfst. Coffee in rms. Ck-out noon. Meeting rms. Business servs avail. Free airport transportation. Health club privileges. Private patios. Cr cds: A, C, D, DS, MC, V.

D ⛵ 🖎 🔥 SC

★★★ **REGAL UNIVERSITY HOTEL.** *2800 Campus Walk Ave (27705).* 919/383-8575; FAX 919/383-8495; res: 800/222-8888. E-mail rusales@e.net. 315 rms, 4 story. S, D $99-$185; each addl $15; suites $190-$375; under 18 free. Crib $10. TV; cable (premium). Complimentary continental bkfst. Coffee in rms. Heated pool; whirlpool, poolside serv. Restaurant 6:30 am-2 pm, 5-10:30 pm. Bar 11:30 am-midnight. Ck-out 11 am. Meeting rms. Business servs avail. Bellhops. Concierge. Free airport transportation. Exercise equipt. Refrigerator in suites; microwaves avail. Luxury level. Cr cds: A, C, D, DS, MC, V.

D ⛵ 🕴 🖎 🔥 SC

Hotels

★★★ **DOUBLETREE GUEST SUITES.** *2515 Meridian Pkwy (27713), 1 blk N of I-40 exit 278, near Research Triangle Park.* 919/361-4660; FAX 919/361-2256; res: 800/528-0444; res: 800/365-9876. Web www.citysearch.com/rdu/doubletreeguest. 203 suites, 7 story. Suites $144-$175; under 18 free; wkend rates. Crib free. TV; cable (premium). VCR avail. 2 heated pools, 1 indoor; whirlpool. Complimentary coffee in rms. Restaurant 6:30 am-10 pm. Bar 11 am-midnight. Ck-out noon. Coin lndry. Meeting rms. Business center. Free airport transportation. Lighted tennis. Sauna. Refrigerators; microwaves avail. Private patios, balconies. Small lake adj; paddleboat rentals. Cr cds: A, C, D, DS, ER, JCB, MC, V.

D 🏋 ⛵ 🎿 🖎 🔥 SC 🏃

★★★ **HILTON.** *3800 Hillsborough Rd (27705).* 919/383-8033; FAX 919/383-4287; res: 800/445-8667. Web www.hilton.com. 194 rms, 6 story. S $79-$139; D $79-$149; each addl $10; suites $129-$349; family rates. Crib free. TV; cable (premium). Pool; whirlpool. Coffee in rms. Restaurant 6 am-10 pm. Bar 2 pm-1 am; Sun to 11 pm. Ck-out noon. Meeting rms. Business center. In-rm modem link. Exercise equipt; sauna. Health club privileges. Some bathrm phones. Cr cds: A, C, D, DS, ER, MC, V.

D 🏊 🍴 🔚 🔥 SC 🏃

★★★ **MARRIOTT HOTEL.** *201 Foster St (27701). 919/768-6000; FAX 919/768-6037.* Web www.citysearch.com. 187 rms, 10 story. S, D $79-$149; suites $199-$209. Crib free. TV; cable (premium). Swimming privileges. Coffee in rms. Restaurant 6:30-10:30 am, 11:30 am-2 pm, 5-10 pm. Bar 2 pm-midnight. Ck-out noon. Meeting rms. Business center. Gift shop. Exercise equipt. Health club privileges. Cr cds: A, C, D, DS, JCB, MC, V.

D 🍴 🔚 🔥 SC 🏃

★★★ **SHERATON IMPERIAL HOTEL & CONVENTION CENTER.** *4700 Emperor Blvd (27703), 1 blk S of I-40 exit 282. 919/941-5050; FAX 919/941-9109.* Web www.sheratonrtp.com. 331 rms, 10 story. S, D $100-$175; each addl $10; suites $180-$225; under 18 free; wkend rates. TV; cable (premium). Heated pool; whirlpool, poolside serv. Coffee in rms. Restaurant 6:30 am-10 pm. Bar 11 am-midnight. Ck-out noon. Convention facilities. Business center. Concierge. Gift shop. Free valet parking. Free airport transportation. Lighted tennis. Exercise rm; sauna, steam rm. Massage. Some bathrm phones; refrigerator in suites. Luxury level. Cr cds: A, C, D, DS, MC, V.

D 🏌 🏊 🍴 🔚 🔥 SC 🏃

★★★★ **WASHINGTON DUKE INN.** *3001 Cameron Blvd (27706). 919/490-0999; FAX 919/688-0105; res: 800/443-3853.* E-mail wdi@netmar.com; web www.washingtondukeinn.com. On the campus of Duke University, this luxurious hotel overlooks the Robert Trent Jones golf course. Memorabilia belonging to the Duke family, for whom the hotel and university are named, is on display in the public rooms. The bar is called the Bull Durham. 171 rms, 5 story. S, D $170-$315; each addl $20; suites $435-$725; under 17 free; golf plans. Crib free. TV; cable (premium), VCR avail. Heated pool. Complimentary coffee in lobby. Restaurant 7 am-10 pm. Bar 11:30 am-midnight; Sun brunch, 2 sittings: 11:30 am & 1:30 pm. Ck-out noon. Meeting rms. Business center. In-rm modem link. Concierge. Gift shop. Airport transportation. Lighted tennis, pro. 18-hole golf, greens fee $55-$80, pro, putting green, driving range. Health club privileges. Refrigerators avail. Cr cds: A, C, D, DS, MC, V.

D 🏌 🏊 🍴 🔚 🔥 SC 🏃

★★ **WYNDHAM GARDEN HOTEL.** *4620 S Miami Blvd (27703), 10 mi SE on I-40, exit 281, near Research Triangle Park. 919/941-6066; FAX 919/941-6363; res: 800/528-1234; res: 800/972-0264.* 172 rms, 7 story. S, D $129-$159; each addl $10; suites $160-$210; under 16 free; wkend rates. Crib free. TV; cable (premium). Pool; whirlpool. Complimentary coffee in rms. Restaurant 6:30-10 am, 11 am-2:30 pm, 5-10 pm; Sat 7 am-2:30 pm, 5-10 pm. Bar 5 pm-midnight; Fri, Sat to 11 pm. Ck-out noon. Meeting rms. Business servs avail. In-rm modem link. Free airport transportation. Exercise equipt. Some refrigerators, microwaves. Cr cds: A, C, D, DS, MC, V.

D 🏊 🍴 🔚 🔥 SC

Inns

★★ **ARROWHEAD INN BED & BREAKFAST.** *106 Mason Rd (27712), US 501, 7 mi N of I-85. 919/477-8430; FAX 919/471-9538; res: 800/528-2207.* Web www.arrowhead.com. 5 rms, 2 story, 4 suites. S, D $100-$130; each addl $20; suites $150-$225. TV; VCR. Complimentary full bkfst. Ck-out flexible. Meeting rms. Business servs avail. In-rm modem link. Game rm. Lawn games. Many fireplaces; in-rm whirlpool some suites. Patio tables. In colonial house (1775) and converted carriage house; on 4 acres. Cr cds: A, C, D, DS, MC, V.

D 🔚 🔥

★ **HILLSBOROUGH HOUSE INN.** *209 E Tryon St (27278), 15 mi W on I-85. 919/644-1600; FAX 919/644-1308; res: 800/616-1660.* Web www.citysearch.com/rdu/hillsboroughinn. 6 rms, 2 story. No rm phones. S, D $95-$125; suite $200. Children over 10 yrs only. TV in sitting

rm; cable (premium). Pool. Complimentary bkfst. Restaurant nearby. Ck-out 11 am, ck-in 3 pm. Portions of this large frame house date to circa 1790; decor includes work by local artists. On 7 acres. Totally nonsmoking. Cr cds: A, C, DS, MC, V.

🏊 🔚 🔥 🏠

Restaurants

✓★ **BULLOCK'S BBQ.** *3330 Quebec (27705). 919/383-3211.* Hrs: 11:30 am-8 pm. Closed Sun, Mon; 2 wks July, 1 wk Christmas. Semi-a la carte: lunch, dinner $5-$9. Child's meals. Specializes in barbecued pork, seafood, chicken. Family-owned for over 50 yrs. Cr cds: C.

D 🔚

★★★ **FAIRVIEW.** *(See Washington Duke Inn) 919/493-6699.* E-mail wdi@netmar.com; web www.washingtondukeinn.com. Hrs: 7-10:30 am, 11:30 am-2 pm, 5:30-10 pm; Sun brunch sittings 11:30 am & 1:30 pm. Res accepted. Contemporary Amer menu. Bar 11:30 am-midnight. Wine cellar. Semi-a la carte: bkfst $7.95-$12.95, lunch $7.95-$20.95, dinner $16.95-$32. Sun brunch $18.95. Child's meals. Specializes in seasonal seafood, pan-seared veal chops, game. Own desserts. Pianist Thurs-Sat, Sun brunch. Valet parking. Outdoor dining. Formal atmosphere; view of grounds and 18th green. Totally nonsmoking. Cr cds: A, C, D, DS, MC, V.

D ♥

★★★ **MAGNOLIA GRILL.** *1002 9th St (27705). 919/286-3609.* Hrs: 6-9:30 pm; Fri to 10 pm; Sat 5:30-10 pm. Closed Sun, Mon; major hols. Res accepted. Bar from 5:30 pm. Wine list. A la carte entrees: dinner $13-$21. Specializes in seasonal cuisine. Local artwork on display. Cr cds: C, MC, V.

D

★★ **PAPA'S GRILL.** *1821 Hillandale Rd (27705), in Loehmann's Plaza at Croasdaile. 919/383-8502.* Hrs: 11:30 am-2:30 pm, 5-10 pm; Fri to 10:30 pm; Sat 5-10:30 pm. Closed Thanksgiving, Dec 25. Res accepted. Greek, Mediterranean menu. Bar. Semi-a la carte: lunch $5.95-$10.95, dinner $7.50-$26.95. Specializes in chicken, lamb, beef. Own baking. Cr cds: A, C, D, DS, MC, V.

D 🔚

★★ **PARIZADE.** *2200 W Main St (27705). 919/286-9712.* Hrs: 11:30 am-2:30 pm, 5:30-10 pm; Fri, Sat to 11 pm; Sun to 9 pm. Closed Dec 25. Res accepted. Mediterranean menu. Bar. Semi-a la carte: lunch $5.95-$10.95, dinner $8.95-$25. Specializes in beef, chicken, duck. Outdoor dining. Semi-formal dining in Mediterranean atmosphere. Cr cds: A, C, D, DS, MC, V.

D

✓★ **SHANGHAI.** *3433 Hillsborough Rd (27705), in shopping center. 919/383-7581.* Hrs: 11:30 am-2:30 pm, 5-9:30 pm; Fri, Sat 5-10:30 pm. Closed Thanksgiving, Dec 25. Res accepted. Chinese menu. Bar. Semi-a la carte: lunch $4.75-$6, dinner $7.95-$17.25. Specializes in seafood, chicken, pork. Oriental decor. Cr cds: A, C, D, DS, MC, V.

D SC 🔚

Edenton (A-9)

Settled 1658 **Pop** 5,268 **Elev** 16 ft **Area Code** 252 **Zip** 27932
E-mail nicholls@interpath.com **Web** www.edenton.com

Information Chamber of Commerce, 116 E King St, PO Box 245,; 252/482-3400; or Historic Edenton, 108 N Broad St, PO Box 474, 252/482-2637

This is one of the oldest communities in North Carolina and was the capital of the colony for more than 22 years. The women of Edenton staged their own Revolutionary tea party on October 25, 1774, signing a resolution protesting British injustice. A bronze teapot, at the west side of the Courthouse Green, commemorates the event.

The seat of Chowan County, Edenton is now an important industrial town and marketing place. It is a charming town with the graciousness of the Old South and many houses and buildings that date back to the 1700s. Joseph Hewes, a signer of the Declaration of Independence, lived here.

What to See and Do

Historic Edenton. Tour of historic properties, which may be seen individually or as a group; allow 2½ to 3 hrs for complete tour. (Apr–Dec, daily; rest of yr, daily exc Mon; closed some major hols; also day after Thanksgiving, 3 days at Christmas) Phone 252/482-2637. ¢¢

    Chowan County Courthouse (1767). A fine example of Georgian architecture, in continuous use since built. E King & Court Sts.

    Cupola House (1758). Considered an outstanding example of Jacobean architecture. Formal garden restored from 1769 map of Edenton. W Water & S Broad Sts.

    Historic Edenton Visitor Center. Audiovisual program (free), exhibits, visitor info, gift shop, tickets for guided tours of Historic Edenton. 108 N Broad St.

    James Iredell House (1800/1827). Home of early attorney general of North Carolina who was appointed by George Washington to first US Supreme Court. E Church St.

    St Paul's Episcopal Church (1736). A charming church with many old gravestones in its yard; 3 colonial governors are buried here. W Church & Broad Sts.

Merchant's Millpond State Park. This 2,900-acre swamp forest is dominated by massive gum and cypress trees. Pond fishing, canoeing (rentals). Nature trails. Picnicking. Developed and primitive camping. Interpretive program. Standard fees. 25 mi N on NC 32, 5 mi N of Gatesville on SR 1403. Contact Superintendent, Rte 1, Box 141-A, Gatesville 27938; phone 252/357-1191.

Newbold-White House (1730). This brick structure was a meeting place for the proprietary government of North Carolina. (Mar–Dec, daily exc Sun) 15 mi N on US 17 Bypass to Hertford, SE on SR 1336. Phone 252/426-7567. ¢

Other historic buildings are shown in a guidebook published by the Edenton Woman's Club and sold at Historic Edenton Visitor Center ($4). Since most houses are not open to the public, we suggest calling the Historic Edenton Visitor Center for further info. Phone 252/482-2637.

Somerset Place State Historic Site. Original plantation, one of the largest in North Carolina, encompassed more than 100,000 acres. First primary crop was rice, which gave way to corn. Mansion and outbuildings built (ca 1830). (Daily exc Mon; closed Jan 1, Thanksgiving, Dec 24–25) 18 mi SE via NC 32, US 64 to Creswell, then 7 mi S; on Lake Phelps in Pettigrew State Park. Phone 252/797-4560. **Free**

Inns

✓ ★ ★ **CAPTAINS QUARTERS INN.** *202 W Queen St (27932). 252/482-8945; res: 800/482-8945.* E-mail captqtrinn@coastalnet.com; web www.captainquartersinn.com. 8 rms, 2 story. S $55-$65; D $80-$95; suites $80. Children over 8 yrs only. TV; cable, VCR avail. Complimentary full bkfst. Restaurant nearby. Ck-out 11 am, ck-in 3-10 pm. Golf privileges. Tennis privileges. Bicycles avail. Built in 1907; antiques. Totally nonsmoking. Cr cds: C, MC, V.

🄳 ❌ 🎿 🏊 🔥 🎿

★ **GOVERNOR EDEN INN.** *304 N Broad St (27932). 252/482-2072; FAX 252/482-3613.* 4 rms, 2 story. No rm phones. S $60; D $80. TV; cable (premium). Complimentary full bkfst. Ck-out 11 am, ck-in 2 pm. Built 1906; antiques. Neoclassical design; Ionic columns, oval portals. Totally nonsmoking. Cr cds: C.

🏊 🔥 SC

★ ★ ★ **LORDS PROPRIETORS.** *300 N Broad St (27932). 252/482-3641; FAX 252/482-2432.* E-mail reserv@lordspropedentan.com; web www.lordspropendantan.com. 20 rms in 3 buildings, 2 story. S, D

$185-$235; each addl $20, lower rates Sun-Mon. TV; cable (premium), VCR (movies). Pool privileges. Ck-out 11 am, ck-in 1 pm. Meeting rm. Business servs avail. Gift shop. Library. Three adj restored homes furnished with antiques. Cr cds: C.

🄳 ❌ 🔥 🐾

★ ★ **TRESTLE HOUSE INN.** *632 Soundside Rd (27932), 4 mi S on NC 32, turn right on Soundside Rd.* 919/482-2282; FAX 919/482-7003; res: 800/645-8466. E-mail thinn@coastalnet.com; web www.edenton.com/trestlehouse. 5 rms, 2 story. No rm phones. S $60-$70; D $80-$100; each addl $15; wkly rates. TV; cable, VCR avail (movies). Complimentary full bkfst; afternoon refreshments. Ck-out 11 am, ck-in 2 pm. Business servs avail. Tennis privileges. 18-hole golf privileges. Picnic tables. Private lake fed by Albermarle Sound. Some antiques. Totally nonsmoking. Cr cds: A, C, MC, V.

🛆 🏋 🎿 🎿 🏊 🔥 SC

Elizabeth City (A-9)

Settled ca 1665 **Pop** 14,292 **Elev** 18 ft **Area Code** 252 **Zip** 27909
E-mail ecacc@interpath.com **Web** www.elizcity.com/G-O-E/chamber
Information Elizabeth City Area Chamber of Commerce, 502 E Ehringhaus St, PO Box 426; 252/335-4365

A town with a freshwater harbor on the Pasquotank River and accessible to the ocean, Elizabeth City has seen seafaring activity since the middle of the 17th century. The town was chartered in 1793 at the narrows of the river as Redding, and renamed Elizabeth City in 1801. The Dismal Swamp Canal, dug in 1793, provided a critical north-south transportation route and brought prosperity to Elizabeth City. Shipyards, warehouses, fisheries, tanneries, sawmills and other industries flourished along with commission merchants, artisans and navigators; trading occurred with Norfolk, the West Indies, New England, New York and Charleston.

Although captured in the Civil War, Elizabeth City sustained minor damage. Today, many antebellum homes still stand alongside the historic homes and commercial buildings of the late 19th and early 20th centuries, a testament to the vitality of the community. Wood, agriculture, small specialty industries and the United States Coast Guard contribute to the area's steady economic growth. The town also welcomes boating traffic from the Intracoastal Waterway, and is a coveted location for sport fishing and hunting. It serves as a gateway to Nags Head and Cape Hatteras National Seashore (see).

What to See and Do

Historic District. A 30-blk area in the city center, contains largest number of antebellum commercial bldgs in the state. Tour brochures avail at Chamber of Commerce.

Museum of the Albemarle. Regional historical displays; Native American exhibits; local artifacts, incl decoys, fire engines; changing exhibits. (Daily exc Mon; closed state hols) 3 mi SW on US 17. Phone 252/335-1453. **Free**

Annual Events

RiverSpree. Water events, arts, crafts, live entertainment. Late May.
Albemarle Craftsman's Fair. Late Oct.
Mistletoe Show. Crafts, wood carvings. 2nd wkend Nov.

Motels

★ **COMFORT INN.** *306 S Hughes Blvd; (27909).* 252/338-8900; FAX 252/338-6420; res: 800/638-7949. 80 rms, 5 story, 28 suites. S, D $55-$95; each addl $8; suites $65-$105; under 18 free; higher rates hol wkends. Crib free. TV; cable (premium), VCR avail (movies). Pool.

Complimentary continental bkfst. Restaurant nearby. Ck-out 11 am. Business servs avail. In-rm modem link. Refrigerator in suites. Cr cds: A, C, D, DS, MC, V.

D ⊟ ⊡ 🔥 SC

★★ **HAMPTON INN.** *402 Halstead Blvd (27909). 252/333-1800; FAX 252/333-1801; res: 800/426-7866.* 101 rms, 5 story, 10 suites. S, D $56-$80; suites $85-$120; under 18 free. Crib free. TV; cable. Complimentary continental bkfst. Complimentary coffee in rms. Restaurant nearby 6:30 am-10 pm. Ck-out 11 am. Meeting rms. Business servs avail. In-rm modem link. Valet serv. Sundries. Health club privileges. Pool. Some in-rm whirlpools; refrigerator in suites. Cr cds: A, C, D, DS, MC, V.

D ⊡ 🔥 SC

★★ **HOLIDAY INN.** *522 S Hughes Blvd (27909). 252/338-3951; FAX 252/338-6225.* 158 rms, 2 story. S $60-$75; D $65-$75; each addl $6; under 19 free. Crib free. TV; cable (premium). Pool. Complimentary continental bkfst. Coffee in rms. Restaurant 6:30-10 am, 5-10 pm. Rm serv (dinner only). Bar 5 pm-midnight. Ck-out noon. Coin lndry. Meeting rms. Business servs avail. In-rm modem link. Exercise equipt. Health club privileges. Cr cds: A, C, D, DS, JCB, MC, V.

D ⊟ 🏊 ⊡ 🔥 SC

Restaurant

✓★ **MARINA RESTAURANT.** *Camden Causeway (27909), ½ mi E on US 158. 252/335-7307.* Hrs: 5-10 pm; Sun 11 am-9 pm. Closed Mon; Jan 1, Thanksgiving, Dec 25. Serv bar. Semi-a la carte: lunch, dinner $5-$14.95. Child's meals. Specializes in steak, seafood. Overlooks Pasquotank River. Outdoor dining. Cr cds: C, MC, V.

D ⊟

Fayetteville (C-7)

(See also Goldsboro)

Founded 1739 **Pop** 75,695 **Elev** 102 ft **Area Code** 910 **E-mail** facvb@ fayettevillenc.com **Web** facvb.com

Information Convention & Visitors Bureau, 245 Person St, 28301; 910/483-5311 or 800/255-8217

In 1783 the towns of Cross Creek and Campbellton merged and were renamed Fayetteville for the Marquis de Lafayette, becoming the first US city to thus honor him. It was the site of North Carolina's Constitutional Convention in 1787 and the capital of the state from 1789–1793. By 1831 it had become a busy commercial city.

Fayetteville is the state's farthest inland port, at the head of navigation on the Cape Fear River, with an 8-foot-deep channel connecting it to the Intracoastal Waterway. Fayetteville State University (1867) and Methodist College (1956) are located here. In 1985, Fayetteville received the All-America City Award. Today, it's a center for retail, manufacturing and conventions, as well as the home of Ft Bragg and Pope Air Force Base.

What to See and Do

Cape Fear Botanical Garden. On 85 acres overlooking Cross Creek and the Cape Fear River. Wildflowers, oaks, native plants. Nature trails. (Mid-Dec-mid-Feb, daily exc Sun; rest of yr, daily; closed hols) 536 N Eastern Blvd. Phone 910/486-0221. ¢

First Presbyterian Church. Classic Southern colonial-style architecture and whale-oil chandeliers. Among contributors to the original bldg (destroyed by fire in 1831) were James Monroe and John Quincy Adams. Tours (by appt only). Bow & Ann Sts. Phone 910/483-0121.

Fort Bragg and Pope AFB. 10 mi NW on NC 24. Here are

82nd Airborne Div War Memorial Museum. Weapons, relics of the First & Second World Wars, Vietnam; library; gift shop. (Daily exc Mon; closed Jan 1, Dec 25) Ardennes St. Phone 910/432-3443. **Free**

John F. Kennedy Special Warfare Museum. Guerrilla warfare weapons. (Daily exc Mon; closed some major hols). Ardennes St. (Bldg #D-2502) Phone 910/432-1533. **Free**

Parachute Jumps. For schedule info phone 910/396-6366.

(For further info, contact the Public Affairs Office, Ft Bragg & XVIII Airborne Corps, Ft Bragg 28307-5000; Phone 910/396-2920 or 910/396-5620.)

Museum of the Cape Fear. Retraces the regional cultural history from prehistoric Indian artifacts through 20th century. A branch of the North Carolina Museum of History. (Daily exc Mon; closed hols) 801 Arsenal Ave. Phone 910/486-1330. **Free**

Annual Events

Dogwood Festival. Late Apr.

Pope AFB/Fort Bragg Joint Open House & Air Show. Aerial demonstrations, aircraft and equipment displays, military drill team performances. Phone 910/394-4183. Aug. or Sept.

Motels

★★ **COMFORT INN.** *1922 Skibo Rd (28314), off US 401 Bypass. 910/867-1777; FAX 910/867-0325; res: 800/537-2268.* 176 rms, 4 story. S, D $50-$69; each addl $6; suites $75-$135; under 16 free. Crib free. TV; cable (premium). Pool. Complimentary continental bkfst. Restaurant nearby. Coin lndry. Ck-out noon. Business servs avail. Health club privileges. Bathrm phone, refrigerator in suites. Cr cds: A, C, D, DS, ER, MC, V.

D ⊟ ⊡ 🔥 SC

✓★★ **COMFORT INN.** *1957 Cedar Creek Rd (27893). 910/323-8333; FAX 910/323-3946; res: 800/621-6596.* Web www.hotelchoice.com. 120 rms, 2 story. S $60-$70; D $65-$75; each addl $6; under 18 free. Crib free. Pet accepted. TV; cable (premium). Pool. Coffee in rms. Complimentary bkfst buffet. Restaurant adj 6 am-midnight. Ck-out noon. Meeting rms. Business servs avail. Valet serv. Exercise equipt. Refrigerators, microwaves. Cr cds: A, C, D, DS, ER, JCB, MC, V.

D 🐾 ⊟ 🏊 ⊡ 🔥 SC

✓★ **DAYS INN.** *2065 Cedar Creek Rd (28301). 910/483-6191; FAX 910/483-4113; res: 800/329-7466 or 800/621-6594.* 122 rms, 2 story. S $39-$49; D $45-$55; each addl $6; under 12 free. Crib free. TV; cable (premium). Pool. Complimentary continental bkfst. Restaurant 24 hrs. Ck-out 11 am. Meeting rms. Business servs avail. Game rm. Cr cds: A, C, D, DS, ER, JCB, MC, V.

D ⊟ ⊡ 🔥 SC

★★ **DAYS INN.** *1706 Skibo Rd. (28303). 910/867-6777; FAX 910/864-9541; res: 800/329-7466.* E-mail daysinnnc@aol.com; web members.aol.com/daysinnnc. 54 rms, 4 story, 28 suites. Mar-Aug: S $58-$88; D $62-$92; each addl $6; suites $60-$95; under 17 free; package plans; lower rates rest of yr. Crib free. TV; cable (premium), VCR avail (movies). Complimentary continental bkfst. Complimentary coffee in rms. Restaurant adj 6 am-midnight. Ck-out 11 am. Meeting rms. Business servs avail. In-rm modem link. Pool. Many refrigerators, microwaves. Cr cds: A, C, D, DS, ER, JCB, MC, V.

D ⊟ ⊡ 🔥 SC

★ **ECONO LODGE.** *1952 Cedar Creek Rd (28306), Jct NC 210 & US 53; I-95 exit 49. 910/433-2100; FAX 910/433-2009; res: 800/446-0650.* 150 rms, 2 story. S $46.95-$54.95; D $49.95-$59.95; each addl $5; under 18 free. Crib free. TV; cable (premium). Pool. Complimentary continental bkfst. Restaurant nearby. Ck-out noon. Business servs avail. Cr cds: A, C, D, DS, ER, JCB, MC, V.

D ⊟ ⊡ 🔥 SC

✓★ **FAIRFIELD INN BY MARRIOTT.** *562 Cross Creek Mall (28303).* 910/487-1400; FAX 910/487-1400; res: 800/228-2800. 134 rms, 3 story. S $49-$69; D $55.95-$69.95; each addl $6; under 18 free. Crib free. TV; cable (premium). Pool. Complimentary continental bkfst. Restaurant nearby. Ck-out noon. Business servs avail. In-rm modem link. Valet serv. Cr cds: A, C, D, DS, MC, V.

D ☒ ☒ ☒ SC

★★ **HAMPTON INN.** *1922 Cedar Creek Rd (28301),* at I-95 exit 49. 910/323-0011; FAX 910/323-8764; res: 800/426-7866. 122 rms, 2 story. S $59; D $65; under 18 free. Crib free. TV; cable (premium). Pool. Complimentary continental bkfst. Restaurant nearby. Ck-out noon. Business servs avail. In-rm modem link. Valet serv. Cr cds: A, C, D, DS, MC, V.

D ☒ ☒ ☒ SC

★★ **HOLIDAY INN.** *1944 Cedar Creek Rd (28301), I-95 exit 49.* 336/323-1600; FAX 910/323-0691; res: 800/465-4329. 198 rms, 2 story. Mar-Nov: S, D $69-$109; each addl $5; kits. $89-$125; under 12 free; lower rates rest of yr. Crib free. TV; cable (premium). Indoor pool; whirlpool. Complimentary coffee in rms. Restaurant 6:30 am-2 pm, 5-10 pm. Rm serv. Bar. Ck-out noon. Coin lndry. Meeting rms. Business servs avail. In-rm modem link. Bellhops. Free airport transportation. Exercise equipt. Game rm. Cr cds: A, C, D, DS, ER, JCB, MC, V.

D ☒ ⚹ ☒ ☒ SC

✓★ **HOWARD JOHNSON.** *218 Eastern Blvd (28301).* 910/483-1113; FAX 910/483-3366; res: 800/446-4656. 134 units, 2 story, 12 kits. S, D $35.95-$49.95; kit. units avail; wkly rates. TV; cable. Pool. Complimentary coffee. Restaurant 11 am-9 pm. Ck-out noon. Business servs avail. In-rm modem link. Bathrm phones. Cr cds: A, C, D, DS, MC, V.

D ☒ ☒ ☒ SC

★★ **QUALITY INN AMBASSADOR.** *2035 Eastern Blvd (28306),* jct I-95 Business, US 301S. 910/485-8135; FAX 910/485-8682; res: 800/638-7949; res: 800/828-2346. 62 rms. S $52; D $68; each addl $6; under 18 free; golf plans. Crib $6. TV; cable (premium). Pool. Playground. Restaurant 6 am-9 pm. Ck-out noon. Meeting rms. Business servs avail. Picnic tables. Cr cds: A, C, D, DS, JCB, MC, V.

☒ ☒ ☒ SC

Motor Hotels

★★ **CLARION PLAZA HOTEL.** *1965 Cedar Creek Rd (28301),* I-95 exit 49. 910/323-8282; FAX 910/323-4039; res: 800/253-7808. 168 rms, 4 story. S, D $59-$69; each addl $6; suites $69-$79; under 18 free; golf plans. Crib free. TV; cable (premium). Indoor/outdoor pool; whirlpool. Complimentary bkfst buffet. Coffee in rms. Restaurant 6 am-2 pm, 5-9 pm. Rm serv. Bar. Ck-out noon. Meeting rms. Business center. Exercise equipt; sauna, steam rm. Some private patios. Luxury level. Cr cds: A, C, D, DS, JCB, MC, V.

D ☒ ⚹ ☒ ☒ SC ⚹

★★★ **HOLIDAY INN.** *1707 Owen Dr (28304).* 910/323-0111; FAX 910/484-9444; res: 800/325-0211. E-mail hotel4u@fayettevillenc.com; web www.fayettevillenc.com/bordeaux. 290 units, 6 story. S, D $88; suites $180; each addl $10; under 18 free. Golf pkg. Crib free. TV; cable (premium). Pool. Restaurant 6 am-2 pm, 5-10 pm; Fri, Sat 6-3:30 am, Sun to 9:30 pm. Bar 4 pm-midnight, Sat to 1 am. Ck-out 11 am. Convention facilities. Business servs avail. In-rm modem link. Some covered parking. Free airport transportation. Exercise equipt. Private patios, balconies. Luxury level. Cr cds: A, C, D, DS, MC, V.

D ☒ ⚹ ☒ ☒ SC

Restaurants

✓★ **CANTON STATION.** *301 N McPherson Church Rd (28303).* 910/864-5555. Hrs: 11 am-2:30 pm, 5-10 pm; Sat from noon-10 pm; Sun noon-9 pm. Res accepted. Cantonese menu. Bar. Semi-a la carte:

lunch $3.50-$5.15, dinner $7.10-$14.95. Buffet: lunch $5.15, dinner $7.10. Specializes in seafood, pork, chicken. Chinese decor. Cr cds: A, C, DS, MC, V.

D ☒

★★ **DE LAFAYETTE.** *6112 Cliffdale Rd (28314).* 910/868-4600. Hrs: 5 pm-midnight. Closed Sun, Mon; some major hols. Res accepted. Continental menu. Bar. A la carte entrees: dinner $12-$26. Specializes in French & Creole cooking. Piano, jazz quartet Fri. Formal dining rms with views of lake. French decor. Cr cds: A, C, D, DS, MC, V.

D ☒

★★ **NEW LOBSTER HOUSE INC.** *448 Person St (28301).* 910/485-8866. Hrs: 11:30 am-2 pm, 5:30-10 pm; Fri to 11 pm; Sat 5-11 pm. Closed some major hols. Res accepted. Bar. Semi-a la carte: lunch $4.75-$7.95, dinner $10.95-$66. Specializes in lobster, seafood, steak. Intimate dining in formal atmosphere. Cr cds: A, C, DS, MC, V.

D ☒

✓★ **SQUIRE'S PUB.** *482 N McPherson Church Rd (28303).* 910/860-0660. Web www.thesquirespub.com. Hrs: 11 am-10 pm; Fri, Sat to 11 pm; Sun noon-9 pm. Closed Thanksgiving, Dec 24, 25. English menu. Bar. Semi-a la carte: lunch $4.95-$10.95, dinner $4.95-$15.95. Child's meals. Specialties: fish n' chips, shepherd's pie, Welsh rarebit. Parking. British pub atmosphere & decor; stained glass, dart boards. Cr cds: A, C, DS, MC, V.

D ☒

★★ **TRIO CAFE.** *201 S McPherson Church Rd (28303).* 910/868-2443. Hrs: from 5 pm. Closed Dec 25. Res accepted. Mediterranean menu. Bar. A la carte entrees: dinner $8.50-$24.50. Specializes in steaks, fresh pasta, fresh seafood. Parking. Outdoor dining. Open kitchen; art-deco decor. Cr cds: A, C, D, DS, MC, V.

D ☒

Fontana Dam (B-1)

(See also Bryson City)

Founded 1947 **Pop** 130 (est) **Elev** 2,900 ft **Area Code** 704 **Zip** 28733

At the southwest corner of Great Smoky Mountains National Park, this village was originally built for the construction crew that worked on the Fontana Dam project. The 480-foot dam is crossed by the Appalachian Trail. The region is now a resort area, with swimming, fishing, boating, hiking and horseback riding centering around Fontana Lake, 30 miles long.

Fort Raleigh National Historic Site (A-10)

(See also Cape Hatteras National Seashore, Kill Devil Hills, Nags Head; Outer Banks)

(Off US 64, 3 mi N of Manteo)

The first English colony in America was attempted here on Roanoke Island in 1585. Virginia Dare, born here August 18, 1587, was the first child of English parents born in what is now the United States.

Governor John White left the island for England a few days after Virginia's birth, intending to return shortly with supplies. He was detained by the war with Spain and did not get back until August, 1590. The colony had disappeared, leaving behind only the mysterious word "CROATOAN" cut into a tree or post.

What happened to the colonists is unknown, though some believe that the present-day Lumbee Indians of Robeson County descend from them. Fort Raleigh has been excavated and the fort built by the colonists reconstructed. The Lindsay Warren Visitor Center has relics, an audiovisual program and exhibits. Park and Visitor Center (daily; closed Dec 25). For further information, contact Fort Raleigh National Historic Site, Rte 1, Box 675, Manteo 27954; 252/473-5772. **Free**

Seasonal Event

***The Lost Colony* Outdoor Drama.** Waterside Theater, 3 mi NW of Manteo on US 64/264. Outdoor drama by Pulitzer Prize winner Paul Green about the first English colony established in the New World, whose curious disappearance remains a mystery to this day. Nightly exc Sat. Reservations advised. Contact 1409 US 64, Manteo 27954; 919/473-3414 or 800/488-5012. Mid-June–late Aug.

Franklin (Macon Co) (B-2)

(See also Cashiers, Highlands)

Pop 2,873 **Elev** 2,133 ft **Area Code** 828 **Zip** 28734 **E-mail** facc@ franklin-chamber.com **Web** www.franklin-chamber.com
Information Chamber of Commerce, 425 Porter St; 828/524-3161 or 800/336-7829

Home of the Cowee Valley ruby mines, Franklin attracts rockhounds who often find interesting gems in surface mines. Franklin is surrounded by waterfalls, mountain lakes and streams that offer excellent fishing for trout and bass, or boating, tubing and swimming. Around the county are 420,000 acres of the Nantahala National Forest, which offers hiking trails, camping and fishing. A Ranger District office is located here. The Appalachian Trail bisects the western part of the county through Standing Indian Wildlife Management area and over Wayah Bald Mountain.

What to See and Do

Franklin Gem and Mineral Museum. Gems & minerals; Native American artifacts, fossils; fluorescent mineral display. (May–Oct, daily) 2 W Main St, in the Old Jail. Phone 828/369-7831. **Free**

Gem mines. There are more than a dozen mines in the area, most offering assistance and equipment for beginners. For a complete list of mines contact the Chamber of Commerce.

Macon County Historical Museum. Artifacts, documents depicting early history of Macon County; genealogical material. (Apr–Oct, Mon–Fri, also Sat mornings) 6 W Main St. Phone 828/524-9758. **Free**

Nantahala National Forest. Nantahala, a Native American name meaning Land of the Noonday Sun, refers to Nantahala Gorge, so deep and narrow that the sun reaches the bottom only at noonday. Scenic drives through the Southern Appalachians, sparkling waterfalls, incl the Whitewater Falls—a series of cascades dropping 411 ft within a distance of 500 ft—and the 17,013-acre Joyce Kilmer-Slickrock Wilderness (see ROBBINSVILLE), with more than 100 species of trees native to the region are part of this 518,560-acre forest. Hiking; swimming; fishing for bass and trout; hunting for deer, wild boar, turkey and ruffed grouse; boating; camping (fee). W of town. For further info contact the District Ranger, 100 Otis St, PO Box 2750, Asheville 28802; phone 828/524-6441.

Perry's Water Garden. Water park with 4½-acre sunken garden, waterfall, hundreds of water lilies and other flowers, wishing well, trails, picnicking. (Mid-May–Labor Day, daily) 8 mi NW on NC 28 to Cowee Creek Rd, then E 2 mi to Leatherman Gap Rd. Phone 828/524-3264. **Free**

Scottish Tartans Museum. American extension of Scottish Tartans Society in Edinburgh, Scotland. Exhibits trace heritage of Scottish Tartan and traditional Scottish dress. Research library. Gift shop. (Daily; closed Jan 1, Easter, Dec 25) W. C. Burrell Bldg, 95 E Main St. Phone 828/524-7472. ¢

Annual Events

Macon County Gemboree. Jewelry and gem exhibits, ruby mining, field trips. Late July.
Macon County Fair. Mid-Sept.

Motels

✓ ★ **COUNTRY INN TOWN-MOTEL.** *277 E Main St (28734). 828/524-4451; FAX 828/524-0703; res: 800/233-7555.* 46 rms. S $34-$37; D $42-$45; each addl $5; under 12 free; higher rates fall foliage season. Crib $5. TV; cable. Pool. Ck-out 11 am. Sundries. Health club privileges. On Little Tennessee River. Cr cds: A, C, DS, MC, V.

⊞ ⊠ 🔥 SC

★ **DAYS INN.** *1320 E Main St (28734), US 441/23N, 1 mi N. 828/524-6491; FAX 828/369-9636; res: 800/329-7466.* 41 rms. May-Oct: S, D $54-$95; each addl $5; higher rates: Gemboree, Labor Day wkend, Oct; lower rates rest of yr. Pet accepted. TV; cable (premium). Pool. Complimentary continental bkfst. Restaurant opp 7 am-11 pm. Business servs avail. Microwaves avail. Scenic view of mountains. Cr cds: A, C, D, DS, MC, V.

D 🐾 ⊞ ⊠ 🔥 SC

Inn

✓ ★ **HERITAGE INN.** *43 Heritage Hollow Dr (28734), ½ mi W off N Main St. 828/524-4150; res: 888/524-4150.* E-mail heritage@dnet. net; web www.intertekweb.com/heritage. 6 rms, 2 kit. units. No rm phones. Mar-Nov: S $65, D $75; lower rates rest of yr. Children over 14 yrs only. TV in common rm; cable, VCR avail (movies). Complimentary full bkfst. Restaurant adj 11 am-7 pm. Ck-out 10 am, ck-in 2 pm. Microwaves avail. Southern hospitality atmosphere. Totally nonsmoking. Cr cds: C, MC, V.

⊠ 🔥

Restaurants

★ ★ **FROG & OWL KITCHEN.** *46 E Main St (28734). 704/349-4112.* Hrs: 11 am-2 pm, 5-9 pm. Closed Sun, Mon. French menu. Semi-a la carte: lunch $5-$7, dinner $10.95-$18.95. Specializes in duck, fresh seafood, pasta. Intimate dining. Family-owned. Totally nonsmoking. Cr cds: C, MC, V.

✓ ★ **GAZEBO CAFE.** *103 Heritage Hollow (28734). 704/524-8783.* Hrs: 11 am-7 pm; Sun noon-4 pm. Closed some major hols; late Oct-May. Semi-a la carte: lunch, dinner $3.95-$5.95. Child's meals. Specializes in deli and specialty sandwiches, soups. Own pasta. Entire restaurant is outdoors; three different patio levels for dining. Cr cds: C.

D ⊟

Gastonia (B-4)

(See also Charlotte)

Pop 54,732 **Elev** 816 ft **Area Code** 704 **E-mail** 76660.334@compuserve. com **Web** www.gaston.org
Information Gaston County Travel and Tourism, 2551 Pembroke, PO Box 2339, 28054; 704/867-2170 or 800/849-9994

This is an industrial town in the Piedmont, turning out textiles, textile machinery and supplies. In addition, Gastonia produces chain saws, plastics, oil seals, lithium, automotive parts, trucks and truck parts.

What to See and Do

Gaston County Museum of Art & History. Sculpture, paintings, Gaston County artifacts and documents, carriage and sleigh collection, textile history exhibit. 19th-century parlors. Located in Hoffman Hotel (1852) and Dallas Depot (1901). (Daily exc Mon; closed hols) 6 mi N via US 321, Dallas exit. Phone 704/922-7681.   **Free**

Lake Wylie. Artificial lake formed by Duke Power Co development; fishing, swimming, waterskiing; marina. S on NC 274. Phone 803/831-2101.

Schiele Museum of Natural History and Planetarium. Habitat settings showcasing more than 75,000 mounted birds, mammals, reptiles, fish; rocks and minerals, Native American arts & crafts, forestry exhibits; 28-acre nature park. Major exhibits on the Southeast and North Carolina; special exhibits and events, films. Restored mid-1700s pioneer farm with living history programs. Hall of Natural History, Hall of Earth and Man. Also here is Catawba Indian Village, with re-created dwellings from 1500s to 1900s. Planetarium programs & Cinema 360 Wide-Screen science films (fee) phone 704/866-6900. Museum   **Free**; Planetarium   ¢

Motel

★★ **HAMPTON INN.** *1859 Remount Rd (28054), I-85 exit New Hope Rd.* 704/866-9090; FAX 704/866-7070; res: 800/426-7866. 109 rms, 5 story. S, D $64-$71; under 12 free. Crib free. TV; cable (premium). Pool. Complimentary continental bkfst. Coffee in rms. Restaurant adj open 24 hrs. Ck-out noon. Meeting rm. Cr cds: A, C, D, DS, MC, V.

D ⛖ ⊠ 🔥

Goldsboro (B-8)

Pop 40,709 **Elev** 121 ft **Area Code** 919 **E-mail** wccc@esn.net
Web www.entrsft.com/wayne

Information Wayne County Chamber of Commerce, PO Box 1107, 27533–1107; 919/734-2241

Center of the bright-leaf tobacco belt, Goldsboro is also the seat of Wayne County and home of Seymour Johnson Air Force Base. Poultry production and tobacco warehousing and processing are important industries. There are also many food, wood product and textile plants here.

What to See and Do

Cliffs of the Neuse State Park. Over 700 acres on Neuse River. Swimming, bathhouse; fishing; boating (rowboat rentals). Nature trails. Picnicking. Tent & trailer sites (mid-Mar–Nov; fee). Museum, interpretive center. Standard fees. 14 mi SE, off NC 111. Contact Superintendent, 345A Park Entrance Rd, Seven Springs 28578; Phone 919/778-6234.

Governor Charles B. Aycock Birthplace State Historic Site. Mid-1800s farmhouse and outbuildings; audiovisual presentation in one-rm school (1893); exhibits in visitor center portray life of the "educational governor." Picnicking. (Apr–Oct, daily; rest of yr, daily exc Mon; closed most major hols) 12 mi N, off US 117 just S of Fremont. Phone 919/242-5581.   **Free**

Motels

✓★ **BEST WESTERN GOLDSBORO.** *801 US Hwy 70 Byp E (27534).* 919/735-7911; FAX 919/735-5030; res: 800/528-1234. E-mail western@pindigital.net. 116 rms, 2 story. S $50.95-$55.95; D $58.95-$68.95; each addl $5; suites $85-$95; under 12 free; wkly rates. Crib free. Pet accepted, some restrictions; $10. TV; cable (premium). Complimentary continental bkfst. Complimentary coffee in rms. Restaurant 11 am-2 pm, 5-9 pm. Rm serv. Bar 5 pm-1 am. Ck-out noon. Meeting rms. Business servs avail. In-rm modem link. Sundries. Coin lndry. Exercise equipt. Pool. Refrigerator, microwave in suites; microwaves avail. Cr cds: A, C, D, DS, MC, V.

D ⛟ ⛖ 🧍 ⊠ 🔥 SC

✓★ **DAYS INN.** *2000 Wayne Memorial Dr (27534).* 919/734-9471; FAX 919/736-2623; res: 800/329-7466. 121 rms, 2 story. S $46-$52; D $49-$54; each addl $4. Crib free. Pet accepted. TV; cable. Pool. Restaurant 6 am-9 pm; Sun to 4 pm. Ck-out 11 am. Business servs avail. Sundries. Exercise equipt. Health club privileges. Some refrigerators, microwaves. Cr cds: A, C, D, DS, MC, V.

D ⛟ ⛖ 🧍 ⊠ 🔥 SC

★★ **HAMPTON INN.** *905 N Spence Ave (27534).* 919/778-1800; FAX 919/778-5891; res: 800/426-7866. 111 rms, 4 story. S, D $58-$68; each addl $6; suites $141; under 18 free. Crib free. TV; cable (premium). Pool. Complimentary continental bkfst. Coffee in rms. Restaurant adj 9 am-midnight. Ck-out noon. Meeting rms. Business servs avail. In-rm modem link. Coin lndry. Exercise equipt. Some refrigerators. Cr cds: A, C, D, DS, JCB, MC, V.

D ⛖ 🧍 ⊠ 🔥

★★ **QUALITY INN & SUITES.** *708 US Hwy 70 (27534), 1½ mi NE on US 13, 70 Bypass.* 919/735-7901; FAX 919/734-2946; res: 800/228-5151. 108 rms, 2 story. S $58-$78; D $64-$78; each addl $6; suites $99-$135; under 12 free. Pet accepted. TV; cable (premium). Pool. Restaurant 6-9 am, 5-10 pm. Rm serv. Bar 5-11 pm; wkends to 1 am. Ck-out noon. Meeting rms. Business servs avail. In-rm modem link. Exercise equipt. Health club privileges. Cr cds: A, C, D, DS, MC, V.

D ⛟ ⛖ 🧍 ⊠ 🔥 SC

✓★ **RAMADA INN.** *808 W Grantham St (27530), jct US 70 & US 117S.* 919/736-4590; FAX 919/735-3218. 128 rms, 2 story. S $39-$74; D $43-$79; suites from $85; under 18 free. Crib free. Pet accepted. TV; cable (premium). Pool. Restaurant 5 am-10 pm. Rm serv. Bar 5 pm-2 am; entertainment Fri, Sat. Ck-out noon. Coin lndry. Meeting rms. Business servs avail. In-rm modem link. Valet serv. Sundries. Health club privileges. Game rm. Some refrigerators, microwaves. Picnic table. Cr cds: A, C, D, DS, JCB, MC, V.

D ⛟ ⛖ ⊠ 🔥

Motor Hotel

★★ **HOLIDAY INN EXPRESS.** *909 N Spence Ave (27534).* 919/751-1999; FAX 919/751-1506; res: 800/465-4329. 122 rms, 5 story. S, D $60-$75; each addl $6; suites $100-$140; under 18 free. TV; cable (premium). Pool. Complimentary continental bkfst. Coffee in rms. Restaurant adj. Ck-out noon. Sundries. Business servs avail. In-rm modem link. Exercise equipt. Health club privileges. Cr cds: A, C, D, DS, JCB, MC, V.

D ⛖ 🧍 ⊠ 🔥 SC

Restaurant

★ **CAPTAIN BOB'S SEAFOOD.** *430 N Berkeley Blvd (27534), across from Eastgate Shopping Center.* 919/778-8332. Hrs: 11 am-9 pm; Fri to 9:30 pm; Sat 4-9:30 pm; Sun 11 am-8 pm. Closed Mon; Thanksgiving, Dec 25. Res accepted Tues-Fri. Semi-a la carte: lunch $3.99-$5.25, dinner $5.95-$9.25. Child's meals. Specializes in seafood, char-grilled steak. Salad bar. Nautical decor. Cr cds: C, MC, V.

D SC ⊠

Great Smoky Mountains National Park (B-1 - B-2)

(See also Bryson City, Cherokee, Fontana Dam, Maggie)

(50 mi W of Asheville off US 19)

The Appalachian Mountains, product of a slow upthrusting of ancient sediments that took place more than 200 million years ago, stand tall and regal in this 800-square-mile area. Red spruce, basswood, eastern hemlock, yellow birch, white ash, cucumber trees, silverbells, Fraser fir, tulip poplar, red maple and Fraser magnolias tower above hundreds of other species of flowering plants. Perhaps the most spectacular of these are the purple rhododendron, mountain laurel and flame azalea, in bloom from early June to mid-July.

The moist climate has helped make this a rich wilderness. From early spring to late fall the "coves" (as the open valleys surrounded by peaks are called) and forest floors are covered with a succession of flowers with colorful variety. Summer brings heavy showers, days that are warm (although 15° to 20° cooler than in the valleys below) and cool nights. Autumn is breathtaking as the deciduous trees change color. Winter brings snow, occasionally heavy, and fog over the mountains. Winter is a very good time to visit the park; but be aware of temporary road closures.

Half in North Carolina and half in Tennessee, with the Appalachian Trail following the state line along the ridge for 70 miles, this is a place to hike. In the lowlands are the cabins, barns and mills of the mountain people whose ancestors came years ago from England and Scotland. It is also a place to see the descendants of the once-mighty Cherokee Nation, whose ancestors hid in the mountains from the soldiers in the winter of 1838–1839 to avoid being driven over the Trail of Tears to Oklahoma. This is the tribe of Sequoyah, the brilliant chief who invented a written alphabet for the Cherokee people.

Stop first at one of the 3 visitor centers: Oconaluftee Center in North Carolina, 2 miles north of Cherokee on Newfound Gap Road, designated US 441 outside of park (daily; closed Dec 25; phone 423/436-1200); Sugarlands, in Tennessee, 2 miles southwest of Gatlinburg (daily; closed Dec 25; phone 423/436-1200); or Cades Cove, in Tennessee, 10 miles SW of Townsend (daily, closed Dec 25; phone 423/436-1200). All have exhibits and information about the park. There are hundreds of miles of foot trails and bridle paths. Camping is popular; ask at any visitor center for locations and regulations. There are developed campgrounds (fee). For reservations at Elkmont, Cades Cove or Smokemont phone 800/365-CAMP; reservations are not taken for other sites.

The views from Newfound Gap and the observation tower at Clingmans Dome (closed in winter) are spectacular. Cades Cove is an outdoor museum reflecting the life of the original mountain people, about 25 miles west of Sugarlands. It has log cabins and barns. Park naturalists conduct campfire programs and hikes during the summer. There are also self-guided nature trails. LeConte Lodge, reached only by foot or horseback, is an accommodation within the park; phone 423/429-5704 (late Mar–mid-Nov).

Fishing is permitted with a TN or NC state fishing license. Obtain list of regulations at visitor centers and campgrounds. The park is a wildlife sanctuary; any disturbance of plant or animal life is forbidden. Dogs and cats are not permitted on trails but may be brought in if kept on leash or other physical restrictive controls. Never feed, tease or frighten bears; always give them a wide berth, as they can inflict serious injury. Watch bears from car with the windows closed. Park (daily). For the disabled, there is an all-access trail, the Sugarland Valley Nature Trail, equipped with special interpretive exhibits. Accessibility information is available at the visitor centers. **Free**

For information contact the Superintendent, Great Smoky Mountains National Park, 107 Park Headquarters Rd, Gatlinburg, TN 37738; 423/436-1200.

Greensboro (A-6)

(See also Burlington, High Point)

Founded 1808 **Pop** 183,521 **Elev** 841 ft **Area Code** 336 **E-mail** gso@greensboronc.org **Web** www.greensboronc.org

Information Greensboro Area Convention & Visitors Bureau, 317 S Greene St, 27401; 336/274-2282 or 800/344-2282

William Sydney Porter (O. Henry) was born and raised near Greensboro, a diversified Piedmont industrial city whose products are typical of North Carolina: textiles, cigarettes, machinery and electronic components. It was settled by Quakers, Germans and the Scotch-Irish with a zeal for political, religious and economic freedom. Men from this region fought in the Revolution and the War of 1812, and turned to the Confederacy in 1861. It was in Greensboro, the rebel supply depot, that Jefferson Davis met General Johnston after Richmond fell in 1865 and agreed on surrender terms. Today it is an educational, manufacturing and distribution center.

What to See and Do

Charlotte Hawkins Brown Memorial State Historic Site. North Carolina's first state historic site, honoring the achievements of African-American education in the state. In 1902, C.H. Brown, granddaughter of former slaves, founded Palmer Memorial Institute, which became one of the finest preparatory schools for blacks in the nation. Guided tours of historic campus (several bldgs being restored), visitor center, audiovisual program. Picnicking. (Apr–Oct, daily; rest of yr, daily exc Mon; closed some hols) 10 mi E on I-85 to exit 135, then ½ mi W on US 70. Phone 336/449-4846. **Free**

★ **Chinqua-Penn Plantation.** English-style country house, extensive formal and rose gardens; 27 rms contain furnishings, art objects from around the world; no pets; picnic area. (Mar–Dec, Tues–Sat, also Sun afternoons; closed July 4, Thanksgiving, Dec 25) 20 mi N on US 29, exit Hwy 14, 3 mi NW on Wentworth Rd. Phone 336/349-4576. **¢¢¢**

Greensboro Historical Museum. Housed in 19th-century church; exhibits on First Lady Dolley Madison, author O. Henry; military history, incl Revolutionary Battle of Guilford Courthouse; 1960s lunch counter sit-ins; decorative arts; vintage autos; period furnishings. (Daily exc Mon; closed most hols) 130 Summit Ave. Phone 336/373-2043. **Free**

Guilford College (1837). (1,300 students) Oldest coed college in the South. Beautiful wooded 340-acre campus with Georgian-style bldgs and a unique solar-energy fieldhouse. Quaker archives dating from 1680 (Tues–Fri, by appt; closed some hols). Official home of Eastern Music Festival (June–Aug). 5800 W Friendly Ave, 2 mi N of I-40. Phone 336/316-2000 or 336/316-2264 (archives).

Guilford Courthouse National Military Park. On Mar 15, 1781, Lord Cornwallis won a costly victory that was one link in a series of events that led to his surrender at Yorktown in Oct of the same yr. After destroying a quarter of the enemy troops, General Nathanael Greene (for whom the city is named) made a successful retreat and then severely hampered the British plan of subduing the Southern colonies. The 220-acre park, established in 1917, has monuments marking important locations and honoring those who fought here; two signers of the Declaration of Independence, John Penn and William Hooper, are also buried here. Self-guided auto tour; walking trails. The visitor center has a museum housing Revolutionary War weapons, other items; 20-min film. (Daily; closed Jan 1, Dec 25) 6 mi NW and ¼ mi E off US 220 on New Garden Rd. For additional info contact the Superintendent, 2332 New Garden Rd, 27429-0806; phone 336/288-1776. **Free**

Hagan-Stone Park. Swimming; fishing. Hiking. Picnicking, playground. Camping (hookups, dump station). Park (all yr). Some fees. Pets on leash only. 6 mi S on US 421, then 2 mi W on Hagan-Stone Park Rd. Phone 336/674-0472.

Natural Science Center of Greensboro, Inc. Natural science museum with zoo, trails and indoor exhibits incl geology, paleontology, aquarium, herpetarium and science & technology. Kid's Alley, an exploratorium for young children. Planetarium shows; inquire for schedule. Some fees. (Daily; closed major hols) 4301 Lawndale Dr. Phone 336/288-3769. **¢¢**

University of North Carolina at Greensboro (1891). (13,000 students) 1000 Spring Garden St. Phone 336/334-5243 (Admissions) 336/334-5000 (Main). On campus is

Weatherspoon Art Gallery. Permanent collection of over 4,000 contemporary paintings, graphic arts, sculpture. (Daily exc Mon; closed school hols) Anne and Benjamin Cone Bldg. Phone 336/334-5770. **Free**

Annual Event

Greater Greensboro Chrysler Classic Golf Tournament. Top golfers compete for more than $2.2 million on PGA circuit. Mid–late Apr.

Motels

★ **COMFORT INN.** *2001 Veasley St (27407). 336/294-6220; FAX 336/294-6220; res: 800/638-7949.* 123 rms, 2 story. S $57-$62; D $62-$65; each addl $5; under 16 free; higher rates special events. Crib free. TV; cable (premium). Pool. Complimentary continental bkfst. Ck-out noon. Meeting rm. Business servs avail. Health club privileges. Some refrigerators. Cr cds: A, C, D, DS, MC, V.

D ⛱ 🏊 🔥 SC

✓ ★★ **DAYS INN.** *120 Seneca Rd (27406), I-85 & S Elm. 336/275-9571; FAX 336/275-9571; res: 800/329-7466.* 122 rms, 2 story. S $45-$58; D $48-$64; each addl $6; family rates. Crib free. TV; cable. Pool; wading pool. Playground. Complimentary continental bkfst. Ck-out 11 am. Cr cds: A, C, D, DS, MC, V.

D ⛱ 🏊 🔥 SC

★★ **FAIRFIELD INN BY MARRIOTT.** *2003 Athena Ct (27407). 336/294-9922; FAX 336/294-9922; res: 800/228-2800.* 135 rms, 3 story. S $49.95; D $54.95; each addl $3; under 18 free. Crib free. TV; cable (premium). Pool. Complimentary continental bkfst. Restaurant nearby. Ck-out noon. Business servs avail. Cr cds: A, C, D, DS, MC, V.

D ⛱ 🏊 🔥 SC

★★ **HAMPTON INN FOUR SEASONS.** *2004 Veasley St (27407). 336/854-8600; FAX 910/854-8741; res: 800/426-7866.* 121 rms, 2 story. S $59; D $65-$73; under 18 free. Crib free. Pet accepted, some restrictions. TV; cable (premium). Pool. Complimentary continental bkfst. Meeting rm. Business servs avail. Cr cds: A, C, D, DS, JCB, MC, V.

D 🐾 ⛱ 🏊 🔥 SC

★★ **RAMADA INN-AIRPORT.** *7067 Albert Pick Rd (27409), near Piedmont Triad Airport. 336/668-2431; FAX 336/668-7012; res: 800/272-6232.* 170 rms, 2 story. S, D $74-$78; each addl $8; higher rates special events. Crib free. TV; cable (premium). Pool; poolside serv. Sauna. Restaurant 7-10 am, 11:30 am-2 pm, 5-10 pm; Sat 7-10 am, 5-10 pm; Sun 7-10 am. Rm serv. Bar 4 pm-midnight. Ck-out noon. Meeting rms. Business servs avail. Bellhops. Valet serv. Free airport transportation. Cr cds: A, C, D, DS, JCB, MC, V.

D ⛱ ✈ 🏊 🔥 SC

✓ ★ **TRAVELODGE.** *2112 W Meadowview Rd (27403). 336/292-2020; FAX 336/852-3476; res: 800/578-7878.* 108 rms, 2 story. S, D $49-$64; each addl $5; under 17 free; higher rates golf tournament. Crib free. TV; cable (premium). Pool. Complimentary coffee in rms. Restaurant adj 11 am-10 pm. Ck-out noon. Meeting rms. Business servs avail. Cr cds: A, C, D, DS, MC, V.

D ⛱ 🏊 🔥 SC

Motor Hotels

★★ **AMERISUITES.** *1619 Stanley Rd (27407). 336/852-1443; FAX 336/854-9339; res: 800/833-1516.* 126 suites, 6 story. S, D $80-$109; each addl $5; under 12 free; wkend rates; golf plans; higher rates special events. Crib free. TV; cable (premium), VCR. Complimentary continental bkfst. Complimentary coffee in rms. Restaurant nearby. Ck-out 11 am. Meeting rms. Business center. In-rm modem link. Free airport, RR station transportation. Golf privileges. Exercise equipt. Heated pool. Refrigerators, microwaves, wet bars. Cr cds: A, C, D, DS, ER, JCB, MC, V.

D 🏋 ⛱ 🏃 🏊 🔥 SC 🏌

★★★ **HOLIDAY INN FOUR SEASONS.** *3121 High Point Rd (27407), I-40 exit 217A in Four Seasons Mall. 336/292-9161; FAX 336/292-1407; res: 800/242-6556.* Web www.kourycenter.com. 986 rms, 28 story. S $130-$140; D $140-$150; each addl $10; under 18 free; higher rates special events. Crib free. TV; cable (premium). Indoor/outdoor pool; whirlpool, wading pool, poolside serv. Restaurants 6 am-midnight. Rm serv. Bars 11-1 am, Sun from 1 pm; entertainment. Ck-out noon. Convention facilities.

Business center. Bellhops. Valet serv. Gift shop. Free airport transportation. Golf privileges. Raquetball courts. Exercise equipt; sauna. Cr cds: A, C, D, DS, JCB, MC, V.

D 🏋 ⛱ 🏃 🏊 🔥 🏌

★★ **PARK LANE HOTEL.** *3005 High Point Rd (27403). 336/294-4565; FAX 336/294-0572.* 161 rms, 4 story. S $70-$80; D $76-$86; each addl $10; suites $130; under 16 free. Crib free. TV; cable (premium). Pool. Complimentary continental bkfst. Restaurant 6-10 am, 5-9:30 pm; wkends 7-11 am. Rm serv. Bar 4:30-10 pm. Ck-out noon. Coin lndry. Meeting rms. Business servs avail. In-rm modem link. Sundries. Free airport transportation. Exercise equipt; sauna. Health club privileges. Some in-rm whirlpools; refrigerator, wet bar in suites; microwaves avail. Cr cds: A, C, D, DS, MC, V.

D ⛱ 🏃 ✈ 🏊 🔥

Hotels

★★★ **BILTMORE HOTEL.** *111 W Washington St (27401). 336/272-3474; FAX 336/275-2523; res: 800/033-20303.* 25 rms. S, D $75-$110; under 18 free. Crib free. TV; cable (premium). Complimentary continental bkfst. Ck-out noon. Meeting rm. Business center. Concierge. Airport transportation. Refrigerators, wet bars. Built 1895. Cr cds: A, C, D, DS, MC, V.

🏊 🔥 SC 🏌

★★★ **EMBASSY SUITES HOTEL.** *204 Centreport Dr (27409), near Piedmont Triad Airport. 336/668-4535; FAX 336/668-3901.* 221 suites, 7 story. Suites $79-$214; under 16 free. Crib free. TV; cable (premium), VCR avail. Indoor pool; whirlpool. Complimentary full bkfst. Restaurant 6 am-10 pm. Bar 4 pm-midnight. Ck-out noon. Coin lndry. Meeting rms. Business center. Gift shop. Free airport transportation. Exercise equipt; sauna. Game rm. Refrigerators, wet bars. Microwaves avail. Balconies. Atrium lobby; glass elevators. Cr cds: A, C, D, DS, JCB, MC, V.

D ⛱ 🏃 ✈ 🏊 🔥 SC 🏌

★★★ **HILTON.** *304 N Greene St (27401). 336/379-8000; FAX 336/275-2810.* Web www.hilton.com. 281 rms, 11 story. S, D $109-$139; suites $185-$450; under 17 free; wkend rates. Crib free. TV; cable (premium). Indoor pool; whirlpool. Supervised child's activities; ages 6 months-15 yrs. Restaurant 6:30 am-10 pm. Bar 4 pm-1 am. Ck-out 11 am. Convention facilities. Covered parking. Exercise rm; sauna. Refrigerator in suites. Luxury level. Cr cds: A, C, D, DS, JCB, MC, V.

D ⛱ 🏃 🏊 🔥 SC

★★★ **MARRIOTT AIRPORT HOTEL.** *1 Marriott Dr (27409), I-40 exit 210, at Piedmont Triad Airport. 336/852-6450; FAX 336/665-6522; res: 800/228-9290.* 299 rms. S, D $114; suites $175-$250; under 16 free. Crib free. TV; cable (premium). Indoor/outdoor pool; whirlpool, poolside serv. Restaurant 6 am-10 pm. Bar 11:30-2 am. Ck-out noon. Coin lndry. Convention facilities. Business servs avail. In-rm modem link. Gift shop. Free airport transportation. Lighted tennis. Exercise equipt. Lawn games. Luxury level. Cr cds: A, C, D, DS, JCB, MC, V.

D 🏋 ⛱ 🏃 ✈ 🏊 🔥 SC

Restaurant

★★★ **GATE CITY CHOP HOUSE.** *106 S Holden St (27407). 336/294-9977.* Hrs: 11:30 am-10 pm; Sat 4:30-10:30 pm. Closed Sun; some major hols. Res accepted. Bar. Wine list. Semi-a la carte: lunch $5.95-$8.95, dinner $13.95-$31.95. Child's meals. Specializes in Angus beef, grilled fish, chops. Salad bar. Outdoor dining. Five dining areas; circular oak bar. Cr cds: A, C, D, DS, MC, V.

D 🍽

Greenville (B-8)

(See also Washington, Williamston)

Founded 1786 **Pop** 44,972 **Elev** 55 ft **Area Code** 252 **E-mail** green villenc@globalad.com **Web** www.globalad.com/greenvillenc

Information Greenville-Pitt County Convention and Visitors Bureau, 525 S Evans St, PO Box 8027, 27835-8027; 252/752-8044 or 800/537-5564

An educational, cultural, commercial and medical center, Greenville is one of the towns named for General Nathanael Greene, a hero of the American Revolutionary War.

What to See and Do

East Carolina University (1907). (17,600 students) Jenkins Fine Arts Center, ECU Music School and Gray Art Gallery offer many cultural events to the public. E side of town. Medical Center campus, W side of town. Phone 252/328-6131.

East Carolina Village of Yesteryear. Restoration and preservation of small-town life (1840-1940) within Pitt County and eastern North Carolina. The area contains a general store, railroad depot, museum, farmhouse, chicken house and schoolhouse. (Wkends) 2 mi N via US 264. Phone 252/758-6385. ¢

Greenville Museum of Art. Collections emphasize North Carolina contemporary fine arts and drawings, also paintings and prints of the period 1900-1945. (Tues–Fri, also Sun afternoons; closed major hols) 802 Evans St. Phone 252/758-1946. **Donation**

River Park North Science & Nature Center. A 309-acre park with 4 lakes and 1.2 mi of Tar River water frontage. Science center near park entrance offers hands-on exhibits. Fishing, boating (ramp; no gas motors), pedal boats. Picnicking. (Daily exc Mon; closed most major hols) 5 mi N on Mumford Rd. Phone 252/830-4561. ¢

Motels

✓★ **FAIRFIELD INN BY MARRIOTT.** *821 S Memorial Dr (27834).* 252/758-5544; FAX 252/758-1416; res: 800/228-2800; res: 800/758-5544. 114 rms, 2 story. S, D $46-$85; under 16 free. Crib free. TV; cable (premium), VCR avail. Pool. Complimentary continental bkfst. Restaurant adj open 24 hrs. Business servs avail. In-rm modem link. Valet serv. Free airport transportation. Health club privileges. Cr cds: A, C, D, DS, MC, V.

⬜ 🏊 ✈ 🖼 🐾 SC

★★ **HAMPTON INN.** *3439 S Memorial Dr (27834).* 252/355-2521; FAX 252/355-0262; res: 800/426-7866. 121 rms, 2 story. S $49-$52; D $52-$59; under 18 free. Crib free. TV; cable (premium). Pool. Complimentary continental bkfst. Restaurant nearby. Ck-out noon. Meeting rm. Business servs avail. In-rm modem link. Cr cds: A, C, D, DS, MC, V.

⬜ 🏊 🖼 🔥 SC

✓★ **SUPER 8 MOTEL.** *1004 S Memorial Dr (27834).* 252/758-8888; FAX 252/758-0523; res: 800/800-8000. 52 rms, 2 story. S $37.99-$40.99; D $44.99-47.99; each addl $5; under 12 free. Crib free. TV; cable (premium). Complimentary coffee in lobby. Ck-out 11 am. Business servs avail. Cr cds: A, C, D, DS, MC, V.

⬜ 🖼 🔥 SC

Hotels

★★★ **HILTON INN.** *207 SW Greenville Blvd (27834).* 252/355-5000; FAX 252/355-5099. E-mail wmichael@greenvillenc.com; web www.hilton.com. 141 rms, 6 story. S, D $89-$114; each addl $10; suites $175-$275; under 18 free. Crib free. TV; cable (premium), VCR avail. Pool; whirlpool, poolside serv. Coffee in rms. Restaurant 6:30 am-10:30 pm. Bar 11-2 am. Ck-out noon. Meeting rms. Business center. In-rm modem link. Airport transportation. Exercise equipt. Refrigerator in suites. Cr cds: A, C, D, DS, ER, JCB, MC, V.

⬜ 🏊 🏃 ✈ 🖼 🐾 SC 🏃

★★ **RAMADA PLAZA.** *203 W Greenville Blvd (27834).* 252/355-8300; FAX 252/756-3553; res: 800/272-6232; res: 800/228-2828. 192 rms, 4 story. S, D $54-$84; each addl $6; suites $100-$120; under 12 free. Crib free. TV; cable (premium). Pool. Restaurant 6:30-9:30 am, 11:30 am-1:30 pm, 6-9 pm. Bar 5 pm-2 am; entertainment. Ck-out noon. Meeting rms. Business servs avail. Exercise equipt. Cr cds: A, C, D, DS, JCB, MC, V.

⬜ 🏊 🏃 🖼 🐾 SC

Restaurants

★★ **BEEF BARN.** *400 St Andrews Dr (27834).* 252/756-1161. Hrs: 11:30 am-2 pm, 5-9:30 pm. Closed some major hols. Res accepted. Bar. Semi-a la carte: lunch $4.25-$7.25, dinner $8.95-$25.95. Child's meals. Specializes in beef, steak, seafood. Salad bar. Antiques. Family-owned. Cr cds: A, C, D, DS, MC, V.

⬜ 🖼

✓★ **PARKER'S BAR-B-QUE.** *3109 Memorial Dr (27834).* 252/756-2388. Hrs: 9 am-9 pm. Closed Thanksgiving, Dec 25; also 1 wk mid-June. Res accepted. Semi-a la carte: lunch, dinner $5.50-$8.50. Child's meals. Specializes in pork barbecue, fried chicken. Outdoor dining. Family-owned. Cr cds: C.

⬜ SC 🖼

Hatteras (Outer Banks) (B-10)

Pop 1,660 **Elev** 2 ft **Area Code** 919 **Zip** 27943

This Hatteras Island fishing village on the Outer Banks (see) was settled, it is said, by shipwrecked sailors from Devon, England. The Devon accent is indeed heard here and on the islands of Ocracoke and Manteo. There are ferries south to Ocracoke (see).

Motels

★ **HATTERAS MARLIN MOTEL.** *Hwy 12 (27943).* 252/986-2141; FAX 252/986-2436. 32 rms, 2 story, 5 kits. May-early Sept: S $48, D $54; each addl $5; kit. units $58; under 6 free; lower rates rest of yr. Crib free. TV; cable. Pool. Restaurant nearby. Ck-out 11 am. Business servs avail. Sun deck. Picnic tables. Cr cds: C, MC, V.

🏊 🐾

★★ **HOLIDAY INN EXPRESS.** *58822 Hwy 12 (27943).* 252/986-1110; FAX 252/986-1131; res: 800/361-1590. 72 rms, 2 story, 32 suites. May-Labor Day: S, D $69-$149; suites $89-$169; under 18 free; hols (3-day min); lower rates rest of yr. Crib free. TV; cable (premium). Complimentary continental bkfst. Restaurant nearby. Ck-out 11 am. Business servs avail. In-rm modem link. Guest lndry. Pool. Refrigerators, microwaves. Balcony with suites. On beach. Cr cds: A, C, D, DS, JCB, MC, V.

⬜ 🐕 🏊 🖼 🐾 SC

★ **SEA GULL MOTEL.** *Hwy 12 (27943).* 252/986-2550; FAX 252/986-2525. Web www.seagullhatteras.com. 45 rms, 1-2 story, 10 kits. Mid-May-mid-Sept: S, D $60-$90; each addl $5; kit. units $70-$100; under

5 free. Closed Dec-Feb. Crib $5. TV; cable. Pool; wading pool. Restaurant opp 6 am-9 pm. Ck-out 11 am. Many microwaves, refrigerators. Picnic tables. Grills. Beach adj. Cr cds: C, DS, MC, V.

🅓 ⚓ 🏊 🖼 🔥

Restaurant

★★ **CHANNEL BASS RESTAURANT.** *57571 NC Hwy 12 (27943), 8 mi S of lighthouse, 1 mi N of ferry docks.* 252/986-2250. Hrs: 5:30-9:30 pm. Closed Dec. Res accepted. Semi-a la carte: dinner $8.95-$27. Child's meals. Specializes in seafood, pies. On channel; nautical decor. Family-owned. Cr cds: C, DS, MC, V.

🅓 🍽

Henderson (A-7)

Founded 1840 **Pop** 15,655 **Elev** 509 ft **Area Code** 252 **Zip** 27536 **E-mail** vctourism@gloryroad.net **Web** www.kerrlake-nc.com
Information Vance County Tourism Department, 943 K-West Andrews Ave; 252/438-2222

Tobacco has historically been the major crop in Vance County, of which Henderson is the seat. Manufacture and processing of textiles, hosiery, furniture, food, tobacco, mobile homes and glass containers are local industries. Tourism helps drive the economy.

What to See and Do

Kerr Reservoir. Part of the development of the Roanoke River Basin by the US Army Corps of Engineers. Approx 800 mi of shoreline and 50,000 acres of water. Swimming, waterskiing; fishing; boating, several private marinas. Picnicking. Camping (fee). Seven state recreation areas around lake, some open only Apr–Oct. (Daily) State camping areas (water and electric hookups in all exc some sites in Bullocksville; standard fees). 6 mi N off I-85. For reservations phone 252/438-7791.

Annual Events

Governor's Cup Regatta. Kerr Lake. 2 days mid-June.

Parade of Lights on Water. Kerr Lake. Fireworks, entertainment. Labor Day wkend.

Seasonal Event

Tobacco auctions. Held at 7 warehouses. Inquire at Chamber of Commerce. Sept–Nov.

Motels

★ **HOWARD JOHNSON INN.** *I-85 & Parham Rd (27536), Parham Rd at jct US 1, 158 & I-85.* 252/492-7001; FAX 252/438-2389; res: 800/654-2000. Web www.hojo.inn. 98 rms, 2 story. S $49-$60; D $54-$66; each addl $6; under 18 free. Crib free. TV; cable (premium). Pool. Complimentary continental bkfst. Ck-out noon. Meeting rms. Business servs avail. In-rm modem link. Sundries. Balconies; some private patios. Cr cds: A, C, D, DS, MC, V.

🅓 🏊 🖼 🔥 SC

★ **QUALITY INN.** *I-85 & Parham Rd (27536), 1¼ mi N on US 1, 158 at jct I-85 exit 215.* 252/492-1126; FAX 252/492-2575. 156 rms, 2 story. S $48-$61; D $49-$84; each addl $6; under 19 free. Pet accepted. TV; cable (premium). Pool; wading pool. Complimentary continental bkfst. Coffee in rms. Bar 11 am-11 pm. Ck-out 11 am. Meeting rms. Business servs avail. In-rm modem link. Sundries. Cr cds: A, C, D, DS, MC, V.

🅓 🐾 🏊 🖼 🔥 SC

Hendersonville (B-3)

(See also Asheville, Brevard)

Pop 7,284 **Elev** 2,146 ft **Area Code** 828 **E-mail** chamber@henderson villenc.org **Web** www.hendersonvillenc.org
Information Chamber of Commerce, 330 N King St, 28792; 828/692-1413

The county seat of Henderson County, Hendersonville is well-known as a summer resort colony and popular retirement community. Manufacturing, agriculture and tourism help make up the county's balanced economy.

What to See and Do

⭐ **Carl Sandburg Home National Historic Site** (Connemara). The famous poet's 264-acre farm residence is maintained as it was when Sandburg and his family lived here from 1945 until his death in 1967. On grounds are house and bldgs for animals as well as a visitor center. (Daily; closed Dec 25) 1928 Little River Rd, 3 mi S on US 25, in Flat Rock. For further info contact the Superintendent, Flat Rock 28731; Phone 828/693-4178. Tours ¢¢

Holmes State Forest. Managed forest designed to facilitate better understanding of the value of forests in our lives. Features "talking trees" with recorded narration about site and forest history. Picnicking. Camping (res required). (Mid-Mar–Nov, daily exc Mon) SW on Crab Creek Rd. For reservations or info contact Rte 4, Box 308; Phone 828/692-0100. **Free**

Jump-Off Rock. Panoramic view from atop Jump-Off Mountain. 5th Ave, 6 mi W.

Annual Event

North Carolina Apple Festival. Labor Day wkend.

Seasonal Event

Flat Rock Playhouse. 3½ mi S on US 25 in Flat Rock. Outstanding professional theater since 1939; State Theater of North Carolina since 1961. Vagabond Players offer 8 Broadway and London productions in 15 wks. Wed–Sat eves; Thurs, Sat, Sun matinees. For reservations phone 828/693-0731. Late May–early Sept.

Motels

★ **COMFORT INN.** *206 Mitchell Dr (28792).* 828/693-8800; FAX 828/693-8800; res: 800/638-7949. 85 rms, 2 story. June-Oct: S $55.95; D $69; each addl $10; under 18 free; higher rates wkends; lower rates rest of yr. Crib free. Pet accepted. TV; cable, VCR. Pool. Complimentary continental bkfst. Coffee in rms. Restaurant nearby. Ck-out 11 am. Meeting rm. Business servs avail. In-rm modem link. Refrigerators, microwaves avail. Cr cds: A, C, D, DS, JCB, MC, V.

🅓 🐾 🏊 🖼 🔥 SC

★★ **HAMPTON INN.** *155 Sugarloaf Rd (28792).* 828/697-2333; FAX 828/693-5280; res: 800/426-7866. 119 rms, 4 story. June-Oct: S $61-$72; D $71-$82; under 18 free; higher rates wkends (June-Aug, Oct); lower rates rest of yr. Crib free. TV; cable (premium). Pool. Complimentary continental bkfst. Coffee in rms. Ck-out noon. Business servs avail. In-rm modem link. Cr cds: A, C, D, DS, MC, V.

🅓 🏊 🖼 🔥 SC

★★★ **QUALITY INN.** *201 Sugarloaf Rd (28792), at jct I-26 & US 64.* 828/692-7231; FAX 828/693-9905; res: 800/581-4745. 150 rms, 2 story. June-Oct: S, D $65-$100; each addl $6; under 18 free; higher rates wkends; lower rates rest of yr. Crib free. TV; cable (premium), VCR avail. Heated indoor pool; whirlpool. Sauna. Playground. Complimentary continental bkfst. Restaurant 7-10 am, 5-10 pm. Ck-out 11 am. Meeting rms.

Business servs avail. In-rm modem link. Valet serv. Sundries. Free airport transportation. Rec rm. Some refrigerators. Cr cds: A, C, D, DS, JCB, MC, V.

⬛ ⬛ ⬛ ⬛ ⬛

Inns

★★★ **CHALET CLUB.** *532 Washburn Rd (28746), 13 mi NE on US 64, then 8 mi E on US 64/74.* 828/625-9315; FAX 828/625-9373; res: 800/336-3309. Web www.chaletclub.com. 21 rms, 1-2 story, 7 cottages. Apr, June-Aug, Oct, AP: S, D $84-$90; cottages $87-$92; golf plans; package plans; lower rates rest of yr. Crib free. TV in common rm. Ck-out 11 am, ck-in varies. Coin lndry. Tennis privileges. Exercise equipt. Pool. Refrigerators, fireplaces. Built in 1927. Cr cds: C, MC, V.

⬛ ⬛ ⬛ ⬛ ⬛

★★ **ECHO MOUNTAIN INN.** *2849 Laurel Park Hwy (28739).* 828/693-9626; FAX 828/697-2047; res: 888/234-6466. 37 units, 2 story, 8 kits. May-Oct: S, D $75-$175; kit. suites $95-$135; each addl $10; lower rates rest of yr. Crib $10. TV; cable. Pool. Complimentary continental bkfst. Restaurant 5-9:30 pm; closed Sun, Mon. Bar. Ck-out 11 am, ck-in 2 pm. Meeting rm. Business servs avail. On mountain top. Built 1896; stone & frame structure. Totally nonsmoking. Cr cds: A, C, MC, V.

⬛ ⬛ ⬛ ⬛

★★ **LAKE LURE INN.** *Hwy 64 & 74A (28746), 13 mi NE on US 64, 8 mi E on US 64/74A.* 704/625-2525; FAX 704/625-9655; res: 800/277-5873. E-mail lakelureinn@wncguide.com; web www.wncguide.com/rutherford/lakelureinn. 50 rms, 3 story. Mid-Mar-Nov: S, D $109-$150; each addl $10; under 12 free; lower rates rest of yr. Crib free. TV; cable (premium). Pool. Complimentary continental bkfst. Dining rm 11 am-2 pm, 5-9 pm; Sun 11 am-2:30 pm. Bar. Ck-out 11 am, ck-in 3 pm. Business servs avail. Golf privileges. On lake; view of Blue Ridge Mts. Mediterranean-style hostelry (1927). Cr cds: A, C, D, DS, MC, V.

⬛ ⬛ ⬛ ⬛ ⬛

★★★ **LODGE ON LAKE LURE BED & BREAKFAST INN.** *361 Charlotte Dr (28746), 13 mi NE on US 64, then 8 mi E on US 64/74.* 828/625-2789; FAX 828/625-2421; res: 800/733-2785. E-mail info@lodge onlakelure.com; web www.lodgeonlakelure.com. 14 rms, 7 with shower only, 2 story. No rm phones. Apr-mid-Nov: S, D $99-$149; each addl $15; wkends (2-day min); lower rates rest of yr. Crib free. TV; cable, VCR avail (movies). Complimentary full bkfst; afternoon refreshments. Restaurant nearby. Ck-out 11 am. Business servs avail. Concierge serv. Tennis privileges. 18-hole golf privileges. Picnic tables, grills. On lake. Built in 1930. Totally nonsmoking. Cr cds: A, C, DS, MC, V.

⬛ ⬛ ⬛ ⬛ ⬛ ⬛

★★ **WAVERLY INN.** *783 N Main St (28792).* 828/693-9193; FAX 828/692-1010; res: 800/537-8195. E-mail innkeeper@waverlyinn.com; web www.waverlyinn.com. 15 rms, 3 story. S $89-$149; each addl $20; under 12 free; wkly rates. Crib free. TV; cable, VCR avail (free movies). Complimentary full bkfst; afternoon refreshments. Restaurant nearby. Ck-out 11 am, ck-in after 1 pm. Business servs avail. Golf privileges. Game rm. Restored guest house (1898); Victorian decor, upstairs sun porch. Cr cds: A, C, DS, MC, V.

⬛ ⬛

★★ **WOODFIELD INN.** *2905 Greenville Hwy US 25 (28731), 3 mi S on US 25.* 828/693-6016; FAX 828/693-0437; res: 800/533-6016. Web www.woodfieldinn.com. 17 rms, 3 story. S, D $89-$149. Complimentary full bkfst. Ck-out 11 am. Tennis. Nature trail. Built 1852; antiques. Cr cds: A, C, DS, MC, V.

⬛ ⬛ ⬛

Cottage Colony

★★ **HIGHLAND LAKE CANTEEN.** *180 Highland Lake Dr (28731), I-26 exit 22, then W on Upward Rd to Highland Lake Rd.* 828/697-9314; FAX 828/696-8951; res: 800/762-1376. Web www.highlandlake.com. 36 rms, 1-3 story, 11 cottages, 6 kit. units. Apr-Oct: S $89-$140; D $99-$202; each addl $50; under 16 free; wkends (2-day min); lower rates rest of yr. Crib free. TV; cable (premium). Complimentary coffee in rms. Restaurant 7 am-8:30 pm. Box lunches. Picnic. Bar from 11:30 am; entertainment Sat, Sun. Ck-out 11 am, ck-in 3 pm. Grocery ½ mi. Coin lndry 2 mi. Package store 2 mi. Meeting rms. Business center. Concierge. 9-hole golf privileges adj. Boats. Hiking. Lawn games. Rec rm. Steam rm. Pool; lifeguard. Playground. Supervised child's activities (June-Sept); ages 5-12. Some fireplaces. Picnic tables, grills. On lake. Totally nonsmoking. Cr cds: A, C, DS, MC, V.

⬛ ⬛ ⬛ ⬛ ⬛ ⬛ ⬛ ⬛

Restaurants

★★★ **EXPRESSIONS.** *114 N Main St (28792).* 828/693-8516. Hrs: 6-9 pm. Closed Sun; most major hols; also mid-Jan-mid-Feb. Res accepted. Bar. Wine cellar. Semi-a la carte: dinner $13.95-$24.50. Child's meals. Specializes in beef, crab cakes, fish. Fine dining in subdued atmosphere. Totally nonsmoking. Cr cds: C, D, MC, V.

⬛

★★★ **SINBAD RESTAURANT.** *133 4th Ave E (28792).* 828/696-2039. Hrs: 11 am-2 pm, 5-9 pm. Closed Mon, Sun; also Jan 1, Thanksgiving, Dec 25. Res accepted. Mediterranean menu. Bar. Wine cellar. Semi-a la carte: lunch $3.95-$6.95, dinner $11.95-$19.95. Specializes in Lebanon, Greece, Indian dishes. Parking. Traditional Middle East decor. Totally nonsmoking. Cr cds: A, C, DS, MC, V.

⬛

Hickory (B-4)

(See also Statesville)

Pop 28,301 **Elev** 1,163 ft **Area Code** 704
Information Catawba County Chamber of Commerce, 470 US 70 SW, PO Box 1828, 28603; 704/328-6111

Nationally known brands of furniture and hosiery are produced here, as are ceramics and electronic equipment.

What to See and Do

Arts Center of Catawba Valley. 243 3rd Ave NE. Here are

Catawba Science Center. Interactive exhibits feature life, earth, medical and physical sciences. Also changing exhibits. (Daily exc Mon; closed hols) Phone 704/322-8169. ¢

Hickory Museum of Art. American realist 19th- & 20th-century art, incl works by Gilbert Stuart; Hudson River School, Thos. Cole to Homer Martin; American Impressionists; European, Oriental and pre-Columbian pieces; changing exhibits quarterly. (Daily exc Mon; closed Easter, Dec 25) Phone 704/327-8576. **Free**

Bunker Hill Covered Bridge. One of only two remaining covered bridges in state. Built in 1895, it spans Lyle's Creek. Nature trail, picnicking. On US 70, approx 10 mi E. Phone 704/465-0383.

Catawba County Museum of History. Exhibits incl a fire engine (1919), country doctor's office (1920), Waugh Cabin (1839), Barringer Cabin (1759), blacksmith shop (1870) and an agriculture exhibit. (Sun, Tues–Fri; closed major hols) 3 mi S, Courthouse Square, in Newton. Phone 704/465-0383. **Free**

Lake Hickory. A 4,100-acre lake with 105-mi shoreline; created by the Oxford Dam on the Catawba River. Boating, fishing, swimming, marinas. 4 mi N.

Lenoir-Rhyne College (1891). (Approx 1,700 students) Observatory (Sept–Apr, eves, weather permitting). Concerts, athletic contests, dramatic productions, art exhibits, convocation programs and other special events throughout the academic yr. 8th St & 7th Ave NE. Phone 704/328-1741.

Murray's Mill (1890). Overshot waterwheel; working machinery; milling museum and demonstrations. Country store (1890), folk art gallery (1880). (Thurs–Sun; closed major hols). 10 mi E via I-40, in Catawba. Phone 704/465-0383. ¢

Seasonal Event

Auto racing. Hickory Motor Speedway. 4 mi E on US 70. Stock car racing. For schedule, prices phone 704/464-3655. Mid-Mar–early Oct.

Motels

★★ **COMFORT SUITES.** *1125 13th Ave Dr SE (28602), off I-40 exit 125.* 828/323-1211; FAX 828/322-4395; res: 800/742-7026. 114 suites, 2 story, 12 kits. S $74-$100; D $81-$100; each addl $10; under 18 free. Crib free. TV; cable (premium). Pool. Complimentary full bkfst. Coffee in rms. Restaurant adj 6:30 am-11 pm. Ck-out 11 am. Coin lndry. Meeting rms. Business servs avail. In-rm modem link. Exercise equipt. Refrigerators, microwaves, wet bars. Cr cds: A, C, D, DS, JCB, MC, V.

D 🏊 🏋 🖼 🐾 SC

★★ **HAMPTON INN.** *1520 13th Ave Dr SE (28602).* 828/323-1150; FAX 828/324-8979; res: 800/426-7866. E-mail hckpco@hihotel.com. 119 rms, 2 story. S $62-$65; D $68-$71; under 18 free. Crib free. TV; cable. Pool. Complimentary continental bkfst. Restaurant adj 6 am-8 pm. Ck-out noon. Business servs avail. In-rm modem link. Cr cds: A, C, D, DS, MC, V.

D 🏊 🖼 🔥 SC

★★★ **HOLIDAY INN SELECT.** *1385 Lenoir Rhyne Blvd SE (28602), I-40 exit 125.* 828/323-1000; FAX 828/322-4275; res: 800/465-4329. 200 rms, 2 story. S, D $89-$109; under 19 free. Crib $6. TV; cable (premium). Indoor pool; whirlpool. Complimentary coffee in rms. Restaurant 6 am-11 pm. Rm serv. Bar 4:30 pm-1 am; Sun to midnight. Ck-out noon. Coin lndry. Meeting rms. Business servs avail. In-rm modem link. Valet serv. Exercise equipt; sauna. Some refrigerators. Balconies. Cr cds: A, C, D, DS, JCB, MC, V.

D 🏊 🏋 🖼 🐾 SC

✓★ **RED ROOF INN.** *1184 Lenoir Rhyne Blvd SE (28602).* 828/323-1500; FAX 828/323-1509; res: 800/843-7663. 108 rms, 2 story. S $38-$48; D $45-$55; each addl $7; under 18 free. Crib free. Pet accepted, some restrictions. TV. Complimentary coffee in lobby. Restaurant adj. Ck-out noon. In-rm modem link. Cr cds: A, C, D, DS, MC, V.

D 🏊 🐾 🖼 🔥

✓★ **SLEEP INN.** *1179 13th Ave Dr SE (28602).* 828/323-1140; FAX 828/324-6203; res: 800/424-6423. 100 rms, shower only, 3 story. S $55-$62; D $62-$109; each addl $7; under 18 free. Crib free. TV; cable, VCR avail (movies). Swimming privileges. Complimentary continental bkfst. Restaurant adj open 24 hrs. Ck-out 11 am. Guest lndry. Business servs avail. In-rm modem link. Cr cds: A, C, D, DS, ER, JCB, MC, V.

D 🖼 🐾 SC

Inn

★★ **HICKORY BED & BREAKFAST.** *464 7th SW St (28602).* 828/324-0548; FAX 828/324-0443. E-mail hickory b+b@conninc.com. 4 rms, 2 story. Rm phones avail. S, D $85-$105. Children over 12 yrs only. TV in sitting rm. Pool. Complimentary full bkfst. Ck-out 11 am, ck-in 4 pm. Built in 1908; Georgian-style architecture; antiques. Totally nonsmoking. Cr cds: A, C, DS, MC, V.

🏊 🖼 🔥

Restaurants

★★ **1859 CAFE.** *443 2nd Ave SW (28602).* 828/322-1859. Hrs: 5-10 pm. Closed Sun; some major hols. Res accepted. Bar. Semi-a la carte: dinner $14.50-$22.95. Specializes in fresh seafood, prime beef, pasta. Entertainment Fri, Sat. Outdoor dining. 3 dining rms in converted house. Cr cds: A, C, D, DS, MC, V.

★★★ **VINTAGE HOUSE RESTAURANT.** *271 3rd Ave NW (28601).* 828/324-1210. Hrs: 11:30 am-2 pm, 6-9 pm; Fri, Sat to 10 pm. Closed Sun; also major hols. Res accepted. Contemporary Amer menu. Bar. Wine cellar. Semi-a la carte: lunch $5.95-$8.95, dinner $15-$20. Child's meals. Specialties: osso bucco, mountain trout with lobster, lump crab cakes. Parking. Cr cds: A, C, MC, V.

High Point (A-5)

(See also Burlington, Greensboro, Lexington)

Founded 1859 **Pop** 69,496 **Elev** 939 ft **Area Code** 336 **E-mail** hpcvb@highpoint.org **Web** www.highpoint.org

Information Convention and Visitors Bureau, 300 S Main St, PO Box 2273, 27261; 336/884-5255 or 800/720-5255

Furniture and hosiery are the products that make High Point prosperous. The city rests on the highest point along the North Carolina and Midland Railroad, which the state built in 1853. The plank road (finished in 1854), stretching 130 miles from Salem to Fayetteville, made it a center of trade; mileposts on this road had carved numbers instead of painted ones so travelers could feel their way at night.

What to See and Do

Furniture Discovery Center. Nation's only museum of modern day furniture manufacturing. Hands-on displays; miniatures; hall of fame; special exhibits. (Apr–Oct, daily; rest of yr, daily exc Mon; closed hols) 101 W Green Dr. Phone 336/887-3876. ¢¢

Peterson Doll and Miniature Museum. Collection of more than 2,000 dolls and related artifacts from around the world, some dating back to the 15th century. (Apr–Oct, daily; Nov–Mar, daily exc Mon; closed holidays) Main & Green Sts. Phone 336/885-3655 or 336/887-3876. ¢¢

World's Largest Chest of Drawers. Bldg designed to look like a 19th-century dresser; symbolizes city's position as a furniture center. Built in 1926. 508 N Hamilton St. Phone 336/883-2016. **Free**

Annual Events

Gas Boat Drag Championships. Oak Hollow Lake. One of several World Series Championship races. Phone 336/883-2016. 4th wkend July.

Day in the Park. City Lake Park. Arts and crafts, rides, entertainment. Phone 336/889-2787. Late Sept.

Seasonal Event

North Carolina Shakespeare Festival. 220 E Commerce Ave, High Point Theatre. Season incl 3 productions and *A Christmas Carol*. Phone 336/841-6273 or 336/841-2273. Aug–Oct & Dec.

Motor Hotel

★★ **RAMADA INN.** *236 S Main St (27260).* 336/886-7011; FAX 336/886-5595; res: 800/272-6232. 165 rms, 2-6 story. S, D $62-$68; each addl $10; suites $115-$135; under 18 free; higher rates Furniture Market. Crib free. Pet accepted. TV; cable (premium). Pool. Restaurant 7 am-2 pm, 5-10 pm. Rm serv. Bar 5-11 pm. Ck-out noon. Coin lndry. Meeting rms. Business servs avail. Barber. Many poolside rms with balcony. Cr cds: A, C, D, DS, MC, V.

D 🐾 ⛱ 🏊 🔥 **SC**

Hotel

★★ **RADISSON HOTEL.** *135 S Main St (27260). 336/889-8888; FAX 336/885-2737; res: 800/333-3333.* 252 rms, 8 story. S, D $109-$140; each addl $10; suites $225-$275; higher rates special events. Crib free. Garage parking $3. Pet accepted. TV; cable (premium). Restaurant 6:30 am-2:30 pm, 5-10 pm. Bar 3-11 pm. Ck-out noon. Meeting rms. In-rm modem link. Gift shop. Free airport transportation. Exercise equipt. Indoor pool; whirlpool, poolside serv. Some refrigerators, wet bars. Cr cds: A, C, D, DS, ER, JCB, MC, V.

D 🐾 ⛱ 🏋 🏊 🔥 **SC**

Inn

★★ **BOULDIN HOUSE BED & BREAKFAST.** *4332 Archdale Rd (27263), 2 mi S on I-85, exit 111. 336/431-4909; FAX 336/431-4914; res: 800/739-1816.* E-mail lmiller582@aol.com; web www.bbonline.com/nc/bouldin. 4 rms. No rm phones. S, D $85-$110; each addl $25; higher rates Furniture Market. Children over 12 yrs only. TV in common rm; cable, VCR avail (movies). Complimentary full bkfst. Complimentary coffee in rms. Ck-out 11 am, ck-in 5-7 pm. Business servs avail. Luggage handling. Fireplaces. Grills. Built in 1918. Totally nonsmoking. Cr cds: A, C, DS, MC, V.

🏊 🔥

Restaurant

★★ **J BASUL NOBLE'S RESTAURANT.** *114 S Main St (27260). 336/889-3354.* Hrs: 6-11 pm. Closed Sun; major hols. Res accepted. French, Amer menu. Bar to midnight. A la carte entrees: dinner $10.95-$24.95. Specializes in beef, veal, seafood. Jazz combo Thurs-Sat. Cr cds: A, C, D, MC, V.

D 🏊

Highlands (C-2)

(See also Cashiers, Franklin)

Pop 948 **Elev** 3,835 ft **Area Code** 828 **Zip** 28741
Information Chamber of Commerce, PO Box 404; 828/526-2112

Highlands is a summer resort near the Georgia state line. Many unusual plants are part of the primeval rain forest preserve. Completely encircled by Nantahala National Forest (see FRANKLIN), the area surrounding the town is called "land of the waterfalls." A Ranger District office is located here.

What to See and Do

Bridal Veil Falls, Dry Falls. Behind Dry Falls the visitor may stand and look through to the Cullasaja River without getting wet. Also Lower Cullasaja Falls. The road here was cut from vertical cliffs and overlooks the river 250 ft below. NW of town on US 64, NC 28.

Highlands Nature Center. Cherokee artifacts, minerals of North Carolina; local flora and fauna, botanical garden; nature trail, hikes, lectures, movies. (Late May–Labor Day, daily exc Sun) E Main St (Horse Cove Rd), ½ mi E of jct US 64, NC 28, on grounds of Highlands Biological Station. Phone 828/526-2623. **Free**

Scaly Mountain Ski Area. Chairlift, rope tow; patrol, school, rentals; snowmaking; cafeteria. Longest run 2,200 ft; vertical drop 225 ft. (Mid-Dec–early

Mar, daily) Half-day rates. 7 mi S on NC 106. Phone 828/526-3737. ¢¢¢¢¢

Motels

★★ **HIGHLAND'S SUITE HOTEL.** *205 E Main St (28741). 828/526-4502; FAX 828/526-4840; res: 800/221-5076.* 28 suites, 2 story. Late June-early Sept, Oct-early Nov: S, D $141-$161; under 15 free; higher rates wkends, hols (2-day min); lower rates rest of yr. Crib free. TV; cable. Complimentary continental bkfst. Complimentary coffee in rms. Restaurant opp 7 am-9 pm. Ck-out noon. Meeting rms. Business servs avail. Bellhops. Minibars, microwaves, fireplaces. Balconies. Cr cds: A, C, MC, V.

D 🏊 🔥

★★ **MOUNTAIN HIGH MOTEL.** *200 Main St (28741). 828/526-2790; FAX 828/526-2750.* 55 rms, 1-2 story. June-Labor Day, Oct: S, D $93-$175; under 18 free; higher rates: wkends, hols; lower rates rest of yr. Crib $5. Pet accepted. TV; cable (premium). Complimentary continental bkfst. Restaurant opp 7:15 am-9:30 pm. Ck-out noon. Meeting rms. Business servs avail. Downhill ski 7 mi. Some bathrm phones, in-rm whirlpools, refrigerators, fireplaces; microwaves avail. Balconies. Picnic tables. Cr cds: A, C, DS, MC, V.

D 🐾 ⛱ 🏊 🔥

Inn

★★ **HIGHLANDS INN & KELSEY PLACE RESTAURANTS.** *4th & E Main St (28741). 828/526-9380; FAX 828/526-9380; res: 800/964-6955;* 30 rms, 3 story. Apr-Nov: S, D $89-$99; suites $99-$125; wkly rates. Closed rest of yr. TV; cable. Complimentary continental bkfst. Ck-out 11 am, ck-in 4 pm. Balconies. Built in 1880; antiques. Cr cds: A, C, MC, V.

D 🏊 🔥

Restaurants

★★ **NICK'S CALICO COTTAGE.** *NC 28 At Satulah Rd (28741), 4 blks S on NC 28. 828/526-2706.* Hrs: 11 am-3 pm, 5:30-10 pm. Closed Jan-Feb. Res accepted. Continental menu. Semi-a la carte: lunch $5.95-$11.95, dinner $10.95-$29.95. Child's meals. Specializes in veal, prime rib, seafood. Cr cds: C, MC, V.

D 🏊

★★ **ON THE VERANDAH.** *1536 Franklin Rd (28741), at Sequoyah Lake. 828/526-2338.* E-mail otv@dnet.net; web www.ontheverandah.com. Hrs: 6-10 pm; Sun brunch noon-2:30 pm. Closed Jan-Mar. Res accepted. No A/C. Setups. Semi-a la carte: dinner $15.50-$25. Sun brunch $18. Specializes in pasta, seafood. Pianist. Vaulted ceiling; contemporary rustic decor. Cr cds: C, MC, V.

D 🏊

Jacksonville (C-8)

Pop 30,013 **Elev** 15 ft **Area Code** 910

This town is on the edge of the New River Marine Base (Camp Lejeune). There is excellent fishing nearby.

Motel

★★ **HAMPTON INN.** *474 Western Blvd (28546). 910/347-6500; FAX 910/347-6858; res: 800/426-7866.* 120 rms, 2 story. S, D $63-$78; higher rates wkends. Crib free. TV; cable (premium). Pool.

Complimentary continental bkfst. Restaurant adj 11 am-11 pm. Ck-out noon. Coin lndry. Meeting rms. Business servs avail. In-rm modem link. Sundries. Health club privileges. Cr cds: A, C, D, DS, MC, V.

D ⌖ ⌖ ⌖ SC

Motor Hotel

★★ **HOLIDAY INN EXPRESS.** *2115 Hwy 17 N (28546). 910/347-1900; FAX 910/347-7593; res: 800/465-4329.* E-mail holin exp@onslowonline.net; web www.holidayinn.onslowonline.net. 118 rms, 4 story. S $60-$65; D $65-$70; each addl $5; under 18 free. Crib free. Pet accepted. TV; cable (premium). Pool. Complimentary continental bkfst. Coffee in rms. Ck-out 11 am. Coin lndry. Business center. In-rm modem link. Valet serv. Some refrigerators. Cr cds: A, C, D, DS, JCB, MC, V.

D ⌖ ⌖ ⌖ ⌖ SC ⌖ ⌖

Jefferson (A-4)

(See also Boone)

Founded 1800 **Pop** 1,300 **Elev** 2,960 ft **Area Code** 336 **Zip** 28640 **E-mail** ashechamber@skybest.com **Web** www.ashechamber.com

Information Ashe County Chamber of Commerce, PO Box 31, West Jefferson 28694; 336/246-9550

What to See and Do

Ashe County Cheese Factory. North Carolina's only cheese factory. Viewing of cheese production; samples. (Daily exc Sun; closed some major hols, also Dec 26) 2 mi S on NC 194, in West Jefferson. Phone 336/246-2501 or 800/445-1378. **Free**

Mt Jefferson State Park. National natural landmark; excellent view of Blue Ridge Mtns. Approx 500 acres. Hiking, nature trails. Picnicking. No camping avail. 1 mi S off US 221, at summit of Mt Jefferson. Phone 336/246-9653.

Motel

★★ **BEST WESTERN ELDRETH INN.** *829 E Main St (28640), US 221 & NC 88. 336/246-8845; FAX 336/246-9109; res: 800/221-8802.* 48 rms, 1-2 story. Mid-May-Dec: S $56-$67; D $60-$74; each addl $6; lower rates rest of yr. Crib free. TV; cable. Restaurant 6 am-9 pm; Sun to 3 pm. Rm serv. Ck-out 11 am. Meeting rms. Exercise equipt; sauna. Some refrigerators, microwaves. Cr cds: A, C, D, DS, MC, V.

⌖ ⌖ ⌖ SC

Inn

★★★ **GLENDALE SPRINGS INN.** *7414 NC Highway 16 S (28629), 8 mi SE on NC 16. 336/982-2103; FAX 336/982-4036; res: 800/287-1206.* Web glendalespringinn.com. 9 rms, 2 story, 1 guest house. No rm phones. S, D $85-$115; each addl $10; guest house $115. TV; cable, VCR avail (movies). Complimentary full bkfst. Restaurant 11 am-2 pm, 5-9 pm. Ck-out 11 am, ck-in 2 pm. Business servs avail. 18-hole golf privileges. Some in-rm whirlpools. Built in 1898; Victorian decor. Totally nonsmoking. Cr cds: A, C, DS, MC, V.

D ⌖ ⌖ ⌖

Kill Devil Hills (Outer Banks) (A-10)

(See also Manteo, Nags Head)

Pop 4,238 **Elev** 20 ft **Area Code** 252 **Zip** 27948 **E-mail** dctb-admin@ outer-banks.com **Web** www.outer-banks.com/visitor-info/

Information Dare County Tourist Bureau, 704 US 64/264, PO Box 399, Manteo 27954; 252/473-2138 or 800/446-6262.

Although the name Kitty Hawk is usually associated with the Wright Brothers, their early flying experiments took place on and near these dunes on the Outer Banks (see).

What to See and Do

✪ **Wright Brothers National Memorial.** Field where first powered flight took place, Dec 17, 1903, is marked showing takeoff point and landing places. The living quarters and hangar bldgs used by the Wrights during their experiments have been reconstructed. The visitor center has reproductions of 1902 glider and 1903 flyer with exhibits on story of their invention. 3,000-ft airstrip. (Daily; closed Dec 25) Off US 158, between mileposts 7 & 8. Phone 252/441-7430. ¢¢

Motels

✓★ **BEACH HAVEN MOTEL.** *4104 Virginia Dare Trail (27949), NC 12 milepost 4. 252/261-4785; res: 888/559-0506.* Web www.outerbanks.cityinformation.com/beachhaven. 6 rms. Early July-Labor Day: S, D $69-$112; each addl $6; wknd rates; higher rates hols (3-day min); lower rates Apr-June & Sept-Oct. Closed rest of yr. Crib free. TV; cable. Complimentary coffee in rms. Restaurant nearby. Ck-out 10 am. Coin lndry. Refrigerators, microwaves. Swimming beach. Grills. Cr cds: A, C, MC, V.

⌖ ⌖ ⌖ SC

★★ **COMFORT INN.** *401 N Virginia Dare Trail (27948), NC 12 milepost 8. 252/480-2600; FAX 252/480-2873; res: 800/638-7949 or 800/854-5286.* 121 rms, 3 story. Memorial Day-Labor Day: S, D $117-$180; each addl $5; under 18 free; lower rates rest of yr. Crib free. TV; cable (premium). Pool. Complimentary continental bkfst. Complimentary coffee in rms. Ck-out 11 am. Coin lndry. Business servs avail. Some refrigerators. Balconies. On ocean; swimming beach. Cr cds: A, C, D, DS, MC, V.

D ⌖ ⌖ ⌖ ⌖ SC

★ **DAYS INN-OCEANFRONT.** *101 N Virginia Dare Trail (27948), NC 12 milepost 8.5. 252/441-7211; FAX 252/441-8080; res: 800/329-7466.* E-mail days-inn-ocnside@outerbanks.com. 52 units, 2 story, 15 kits. Mid-June-early Sept: S, D $90-$105; each addl $5; kit. units $125-$160; higher rates: hols, wknds; lower rates mid-Sept-mid-June. Crib free. TV; cable (premium). Pool. Complimentary continental bkfst. Ck-out 11 am. Business servs avail. In-rm modem link. Refrigerators. On swimming beach. Volleyball. Cr cds: A, C, D, DS, JCB, MC, V.

⌖ ⌖ ⌖ ⌖ SC

★★ **RAMADA INN.** *1701 S Virginia Dare Trail (27948), milepost 9.5, NC 12. 252/441-2151; FAX 252/441-1830; res: 800/635-1824.* 172 rms, 5 story. Memorial Day-Labor Day: D $97-$197; each addl $10; under 18 free; lower rates rest of yr. Crib free. Pet accepted; $5/day. TV; cable, VCR avail (free movies). Indoor pool; whirlpool. Coffee in rms. Restaurant 7-11 am, 11:30 am-2 pm, 5-10 pm. Rm serv. Bar; entertainment wkends (in season). Ck-out 11 am. Meeting rms. Business servs avail. In-rm modem link. Refrigerators, microwaves. Private balconies. Lawn games. Cr cds: A, C, D, DS, JCB, MC, V.

D ⌖ ⌖ ⌖ ⌖ ⌖ SC

Motor Hotels

★★ **BEST WESTERN OCEAN REEF SUITES.** *107 Virginia Dare Trail (27948).* 252/441-1611; FAX 252/441-1482; res: 800/528-1234. Web www.bestwestern.com. 70 kit. suites, 5 story. May-Sept: kit. suites (up to 6) $154-$190; each addl $10; under 17 free; lower rates rest of yr. Crib $5. TV; cable, VCR avail (movies). Heated pool; whirlpool. Restaurant 7 am-9 pm. Ck-out 11 am. Business servs avail. Exercise equipt; sauna, steam rm. Private patios, balconies. Cr cds: A, C, D, DS, JCB, MC, V.

[D][⚓][≈][🏃][≋][🔥][SC]

★★ **HOLIDAY INN.** *1601 Virginia Dare Trail (27948), on NC 12 between mileposts 9 & 10.* 252/441-6333; FAX 252/441-7779; res: 800/465-4329; res: 800/843-1249. 105 rms, 4 story. May-Sept: S, D $139-$190; each addl $10; under 19 free; lower rates rest of yr. Crib free. TV; cable. Pool; whirlpool, wading pool. Restaurant 7-11 am, 5:30-9 pm. Rm serv. Bar 5:30 pm-1:30 am; entertainment. Ck-out 11 am. Coin lndry. Meeting rms. Business servs avail. In-rm modem link. Refrigerators, microwaves. Private patios, balconies. Oceanfront deck. On beach; many oceanfront rms. Cr cds: A, C, D, DS, JCB, MC, V.

[D][⚓][≈][≋][🔥][SC]

★★ **NAGGS HEAD BEACH.** *804 N Virginia Daretrail (27948).* 252/441-0411; FAX 252/441-7811; res: 800/338-7761. 96 rms, 4 story. Mid-June-early Sept: S, D $78-$100; under 18 free; higher rates hol wknds; lower rates rest of yr. Crib free. Pet accepted. TV; cable (premium). Pool. Complimentary continental bkfst. Ck-out 11 am. Refrigerators. Many balconies. Cr cds: A, C, D, DS, MC, V.

[D][🐾][⚓][≈][≋][🔥][SC]

Inn

✓ ★ **CYPRESS HOUSE B&B.** *500 N Virginia Dare Trl (27948), on NC 12, milepost 8.* 252/441-6127; FAX 252/441-2009; res: 800/554-2764. Web www.cypresshouseinn.com. 6 rms, 2 story. No rm phones. June-Aug: S, D $110; lower rates Apr-May & Sept-Oct. Closed rest of yr. Children over 13 yrs only. TV; cable. Complimentary continental bkfst. Ck-out 11 am, ck-in 3 pm. Sitting rm. Near swimming beach. Totally non-smoking. Cr cds: A, C, MC, V.

[≈][🔥][SC]

Restaurants

✓ ★★ **FLYING FISH CAFE.** *2003 Croatan Hwy (27948).* 252/441-6894. E-mail gwp3@beachlink.com. Hrs: 11:30 am-4 pm, 5-10 pm; early-bird dinner 5-6 pm. Res accepted. Seafood menu. Bar. Semi-a la carte: lunch $3.95-$6.95, dinner $9.95-$17.95. Child's meals. Specializes in seafood prepared Mediterranean style, pasta. Own baking. Parking. Outdoor dining. Cr cds: A, C, DS, MC, V.

[D][≈]

★ **JOLLY ROGER.** *1836 N Virginia Dare Trail (27948), on NC 12 between mileposts 6.5 & 7.* 252/441-6530. E-mail mardud@beachlink.com. Hrs: 6 am-10 pm. Bar. Semi-a la carte: bkfst $1.50-$8, lunch $2-$8, dinner $7.95-$29.95. Specializes in seafood, pasta, beef. Cr cds: A, C, D, DS, MC, V.

[D][SC][≈]

★★ **PORT O' CALL.** *504 Virginia Dare Trail (27948).* 919/441-8001. Hrs: 5-10 pm; Sun brunch 9:30 am-1:30 pm. Closed Jan-mid-Mar. Res accepted. Bar. Semi-a la carte: dinner $9.95-$34.95. Child's meals. Specializes in seafood, beef, pasta. Entertainment. Turn-of-the-century Victorian decor. Gift shop, antiques, art gallery. Cr cds: A, C, DS, MC, V.

[D][≈]

Kinston (B-8)

Pop 25,295 **Elev** 44 ft **Area Code** 252 **Zip** 28501

What to See and Do

CSS *Neuse* State Historic Site. Remains of Confederate ironclad gunboat sunk by her crew in 1865 and not raised until 1963. Visitor center relates story of the *Neuse* through an audio show, artifacts recovered from the gunboat; photographs; memorial has exhibits on life of Caswell, first elected governor of the state of North Carolina. Picnicking. (Apr–Oct, daily; rest of yr, daily exc Mon; closed major hols) 1 mi W on US 70A. Phone 252/522-2091. **Free**

Motels

★★ **BEST WESTERN RIVERVIEW.** *208 E New Bern Rd (28504).* 252/527-4155; FAX 252/527-2900; res: 800/528-1234. Web www.holiday.com. 100 rms, 2 story. S, D $47-$69; each addl $5. Crib free. TV; cable (premium). Pool; wading pool. Restaurant 6 am-2 pm, 5:30-10 pm. Rm serv. Bar 5 pm-1 am. Ck-out noon. Meeting rms. Business center. In-rm modem link. Cr cds: A, C, D, DS, JCB, MC, V.

[D][≈][≋][🔥][SC][🏃]

✓ ★ **COMFORT INN.** *200 W Newbern Rd (28504).* 252/527-3200; FAX 252/527-3200; res: 800/638-7949. 60 rms, 2 story. Apr-Sept: S, D $52-$60; each addl $5; suites $65; under 18 free; lower rates rest of yr. Crib $5. TV; cable (premium); VCR avail. Pool: Complimentary continental bkfst. Coffee in rms. Restaurant nearby. Ck-out noon. Meeting rms. Business center. Exercise equipt; sauna. Refrigerators, microwaves. Cr cds: A, C, D, DS, MC, V.

[D][≈][🏃][≋][🔥][SC][🏃]

Motor Hotel

★★ **HAMPTON INN.** *1382 NC 258 S (28501).* 252/523-1400; FAX 252/523-1326; res: 800/250-5370. 123 rms, 4 story. June-late Sept: S $54-$59; D $59-$64; under 17 free; lower rates rest of yr. Crib free. Pet accepted. TV; cable (premium). Pool. Complimentary continental bkfst. Ck-out noon. Meeting rms. Business servs avail. Some refrigerators. Cr cds: A, C, D, DS, MC, V.

[D][🐾][≈][≋][🔥][SC]

Kitty Hawk (Outer Banks)

(see Kill Devil Hills)

Laurinburg (C-6)

(See also Pinehurst, Southern Pines)

Settled (ca 1700) **Pop** 11,643 **Elev** 227 ft **Area Code** 910
E-mail scotcoc@carolina.net **Web** www.NCSEorg/scotland
Information Laurinburg-Scotland County Area Chamber of Commerce, 606 Atkinson St, PO Box 1025, 28353; 910/276-7420

Laurinburg is the seat of Scotland County, named for its early Scottish Highland settlers. Industrial development has expanded this agricultural center's economy.

What to See and Do

St Andrews Presbyterian College (1958). (800 students) Contemporary-style bldgs on an 800-acre campus around a 70-acre lake. Mosaic tile wall depicts story of humankind. S city limits. Phone 910/277-5000. On campus are

Science Center. Features interdisciplinary laboratory, guides. (Sept–May and summer session, Mon–Fri; other times by appt) **Free**

Vardell Art Gallery. (Mid-Sept–May, Mon–Fri; closed school hols) Vardell Bldg. Phone 910/277-5000, ext 5023. **Free**

Motels

✓ ★ ★ **COMFORT INN.** *1705 401 Byp S (28352), 1 mi S of US 74 on US 15/401.* 910/277-7788; FAX 910/277-7229; res: 800/526-8169. 80 rms, 2 story. S $59-$99; D $59-$110; each addl $8; under 18 free; family rates; higher rates: special events, Rockingham Races. Crib free. TV; cable (premium), VCR avail. Pool. Complimentary continental bkfst. Restaurant adj 5:30-9:30 pm. Ck-out noon. Meeting rms. Business servs avail. Sundries. Exercise equipt. Some in-rm whirlpools, refrigerators. Cr cds: A, C, D, DS, JCB, MC, V.

[D] [≈] [⊀] [⊠] [♨] [SC]

✓ ★ **PINE ACRES LODGE.** *US Hwy 15 & 401 S Byp (28352), US 15, 401 S Bypass.* 910/276-1531; FAX 910/277-1481. 74 rms. S, D $22.50-$40; each addl $6. TV; cable (premium). Pool; wading pool. Complimentary continental bkfst. Restaurant nearby. Ck-out 11 am. Refrigerators. Cr cds: A, C, D, DS, MC, V.

[D] [≈] [⊠] [♨]

Restaurant

✓ ★ **CHAMPS FINE FOODS & SPIRITS.** *1500 US Hwy 401 S (28352).* 910/276-4386. Hrs: 4 pm-1 am. Closed Easter, July 4, Dec 25. Res accepted. Bar. Semi-a la carte: dinner $9-$19.95. Child's meals. Specializes in sandwiches, seafood, beef. Salad bar. Decorated with ACC colleges memorabilia. Cr cds: A, C, DS, MC, V.

[D] [SC] [⊣]

Lenoir (A-4)

(See also Blowing Rock)

Pop 14,192 **Elev** 1,182 ft **Area Code** 828 **Zip** 28645

Motel

★ ★ **RAMADA LIMITED.** *142 Wilkesboro Blvd SE (28645).* 828/758-4403; FAX 828/758-4403. 100 rms, 2 story. S, D $55-$65; each addl $10; under 19 free. Crib free. TV. Pool. Complimentary continental bkfst. Ck-out 11 am. Meeting rms. Cr cds: A, C, D, DS, JCB, MC, V.

[D] [≈] [⊠] [♨] [SC]

Lexington (B-5)

(See also Asheboro, High Point, Winston-Salem)

Settled 1750 **Pop** 16,581 **Elev** 809 ft **Area Code** 336 **Zip** 27292
E-mail lexingtonnc@infoave.net **Web** web.infoave.net/~lexingtonnc
Information Chamber of Commerce, 16 E Center St, PO Box C, 27293; 336/248-5929

In 1775, settlers learned of the battle of Lexington in Massachusetts and decided to name this town for it. Local industry is diversified and includes furniture making, textiles and clothing, food processing, electronics, ceramics, machinery and fiberglass. Native to the area is traditional pork barbecue, which can be found in many local restaurants.

What to See and Do

High Rock Lake. Its 300-mi shoreline is a center for water sports in the piedmont. 10 mi SW on US 70 or S on NC 8.

Old Davidson County Courthouse (1858). Greek-revival bldg facing the town square; old courtrm houses museum of local history. (Tues–Fri, also Sun afternoons; closed hols) Center of city. Phone 336/242-2035. **Free**

Linville (A-3)

(See also Banner Elk, Blowing Rock, Boone)

Pop 244 (est) **Elev** 3,669 ft **Area Code** 828 **Zip** 28646

Linville is in the heart of a ruggedly beautiful resort area. Several miles to the south, just off the Blue Ridge Parkway, is scenic Linville Falls, cascading down the steep Linville Gorge, designated a national wilderness. Visible from vantage points in this area are the mysterious Brown Mountain lights.

What to See and Do

✪ **Grandfather Mountain** (5,964 ft). Highest peak in the Blue Ridge, with spectacular views, rugged rock formations; 1-mi-high swinging bridge; bald eagles, deer, cougars, black bears, bear cubs and others in natural habitats. Hiking trails, picnic areas. Museum with exhibits on local animals, birds, flowers, geology; restaurant; gift shop. (Daily; winter, open weather permitting; closed Thanksgiving, Dec 25) 2 mi NE via US 221, 1 mi S of jct Blue Ridge Pkwy & US 221. Phone 828/733-4337. ¢¢¢

Annual Events

Grandfather Mountain Nature Photography Weekend. Grandfather Mtn. Nationally known photographers give illustrated lectures; nature photography contest; picnic dinner. Preregistration required. Late may-early June.

"Singing on the Mountain." On the slopes of Grandfather Mtn. All-day program of modern and traditional gospel music featuring top groups and nationally known speakers. Concessions or bring your own food. 4th Sun June.

Grandfather Mountain Highland Games. MacRae Meadows, on US 221 at Grandfather Mtn. Gathering of members of over 100 Scottish clans and societies to view or participate in traditional Scottish sports, track-and-field events, mountain marathon; highland dancing, piping and drumming; ceremonies and pageantry. Mid July.

Lodge

★ ★ ★ ★ **ESEEOLA LODGE.** *175 Linville Ave (US 221 & NC 105) (28646), 2 mi W of Blue Ridge Pkwy.* 828/733-4311; FAX 828/733-3227; res: 800/742-6717. E-mail eseeola@skybest.com; web www.eseeola.com. This rustic lakeside lodge, built in the late 1880s, is the focal point of the village. Its interiors are richly detailed with chestnut paneling and stonework. 29 rms, 2 story. Mid-May-mid-Oct: S $200-$250; D $250-$300; each addl $50. Closed rest of yr. Crib free. TV; cable. Pool; lifeguard. Supervised child's activities (mid-June-mid-Aug). Coffee in rms. Dining rm (public by res) 7:30-9:30 am, 11:30 am-2:30 pm, 7-9 pm (jacket at dinner). Rm serv. Box lunches. Bar. Ck-out noon. Business servs avail. Tennis. 18-hole golf, greens fee $65 (incl cart), pro, putting green. Exercise rm. Massage. Croquet court. Rec rm. Soc dir. Boating, trout fishing. Cr cds: C, MC, V.

 [⛷] [🏌] [🚴] [≈] [⊀] [🎣] [♨]

Little Switzerland (B-3)

(See also Burnsville, Linville, Morganton)

Founded 1910 **Pop** 200 (est) **Elev** 3,500 ft **Area Code** 704 **Zip** 28749
E-mail info@mitchell-county.com **Web** www.mitchell-county.com/north-carolina

Information Mitchell County Chamber of Commerce, Rte 1, Box 796, Spruce Pine 28777; 704/765-9483 or 800/227-3912

A restful summer resort amid the high mountains of western Carolina, Little Switzerland is bisected by the Blue Ridge Parkway.

What to See and Do

Emerald Village. Historical area incl mines; North Carolina Mining Museum; Main Street 1920s Mining Community Museum; Gemstone Mine, where visitors can prospect for gems under shaded flumes (fee; equipment furnished); Mechanical Music Maker Museum; waterfall and scenic overlook; shops and deli. (Daily; closed some major hols) NW on County 1100 (McKinney Mine Rd), at Blue Ridge Pkwy milepost 334. Phone 704/765-6463. ¢¢

Mt Mitchell State Park. Adj Pisgah National Forest; natural national landmark. Road leads to summit (6,684 ft; highest point E of the Mississippi River) for incomparable views. Trails. Picnicking, restaurant, refreshment stands. Small tent camping area. Observation tower, museum. Standard fees. 20 mi S on Blue Ridge Pkwy, then N on NC 128. Phone 704/675-4611.

Museum of North Carolina Minerals. Mineral exhibits of the state. (May–Nov, daily; rest of yr, Wed–Sun; closed Jan 1, Thanksgiving, Dec 24–26) At jct Blue Ridge Pkwy, NC 226. Phone 704/765-2761. **Free**

Motels

★★ **BIG LYNN LODGE.** *Hwy 226A (28749),* 1½ mi W on NC 226A. 828/765-4257; FAX 828/765-0301; res: 800/654-5232. 26 rms, some A/C, 2 story, 4 suites, 12 cottages. Mid-Apr-early Nov: S $72-$125; D $83-$125; each addl $23; suites $125; wkly rates; EP rates rest of yr. TV in lounge. Restaurant 7:30-9 am, 6-7:30 pm. Ck-out 11 am. Coin lndry. Bellhops. Sundries. Rec rm; player piano. Lawn games. Hiking trails. Library. Cr cds: C, MC, V.

⊠ 🔥 SC

★ **PINEBRIDGE INN.** *101 Pinebridge Ave (28777),* 3 mi S on NC 226, off Summit St. 828/765-5543; FAX 828/765-5543; res: 800/356-5059. 46 rms, 3 story. S, D $44-$68; suites $83-$125; kit. unit $135; under 12 free; ski plans; golf plans; package plans. Crib $10. TV; cable. Ck-out noon. Meeting rm. Business servs avail. Tennis privileges. Golf privileges. Downhill/x-country ski 19 mi. Health club privileges. Picnic tables. Cr cds: A, C, DS, MC, V.

🅳 🏊 🏌 🎿 ⊠ 🔥 SC

Lodges

★ **ALPINE INN.** *Hwy 226A (28749),* Blue Ridge Pkwy milepost 334, then S on NC 226A. 828/765-5380; FAX 828/765-5380; res: 828/765-1961. 14 rms, 11 with shower only, 2-3 story. No A/C. No rm phones. S, D $38-$52; kit. $60; wkly rates. Closed Dec-Mar. TV in sitting rm. Complimentary coffee in lobby. Ck-out noon. Balconies. Picnic tables. On Grassy Mt. Cr cds: C, MC, V.

🔥

★★★ **CHALET SWITZERLAND INN.** *226A Blue Ridge Pkwy (28749),* Blue Ridge Pkwy at milepost 334. 828/765-2153; FAX 828/765-0049; res: 800/654-4026. 60 units, 8 with A/C, 2 story. May-Oct: S, D $75-$100; each addl $15; suites $110; family rates. Closed rest of yr. TV; cable (premium). Pool. Complimentary full bkfst. Dining rm 7:30-9:30 am, 11:30

am-2 pm, 5:30-9:30 pm. Ck-out 11 am. Meeting rms. Business servs avail. Sundries. Tennis. Balconies. Picnic tables. Mountain view. Cr cds: A, C, MC, V.

🏌 🏊 ⊠ 🔥 SC

Lumberton (C-7)

Founded 1787 **Pop** 18,601 **Elev** 137 ft **Area Code** 910 **Zip** 28358
E-mail lluke@vacationtime.com **Web** www.i95travel.org

Information Visitors Bureau, 3431 Lackey St, 28358; 910/739-9999 or 800/359-6971

Lumberton is the county seat of Robeson County and the home of many industries, including one of the largest tobacco marketing centers in the state. Hunting for quail, duck, dove and rabbit is excellent in the area. Pembroke, to the northwest, is the population center for some 30,000 Lumbee Native Americans, believed by some historians to include descendants of the "lost colonists" (see FORT RALEIGH NATIONAL HISTORIC SITE).

What to See and Do

Jones Lake State Park. More than 2,200 acres with swimming; fishing; boating. Interpretive trails. Picnicking. Primitive camping (mid-Mar–Nov). Standard fees. 25 mi E on NC 41 to Elizabethtown, then 4 mi N on NC 242. Phone 910/588-4550.

One-rm schoolhouse. Restored early American furnished classrm. (Mon–Fri; closed hols) **Free**

Annual Event

Scottish Highland Games. Celebration of Scottish heritage with music; dancing; competitions; childrens events. Phone 910/843-5000. First wkend Oct.

Motels

✓★ **COMFORT INN.** *3070 Roberts Ave (28360).* 910/739-4800; FAX 910/738-5299; res: 800/638-7949; res: 800/566-5252. 65 rms, 2 story. S $49.95-$65; D $52.95-$65; each addl $5; suites $75-$85; under 18 free; higher rates special events. Crib $5. TV; cable (premium), VCR avail (movies). Complimentary continental bkfst. Complimentary coffee in rms. Restaurant nearby. Ck-out 11 am. Business servs avail. In-rm modem link. Exercise equipt. Pool. Refrigerators, microwaves. Cr cds: A, C, D, DS, MC, V.

🅳 🏊 🏌 ⊠ 🔥 SC

★★ **COMFORT SUITES.** *215 Wintergreen Dr (28358).* 910/739-8800; FAX 910/739-0027; res: 800/228-5150. E-mail comfort@nconline.com; web www.webmar.com/comfort. 93 suites, 4 story. Suites $65-$95; each addl $5; under 18 free. Crib free. TV; cable (premium), VCR avail. Pool. Complimentary continental bkfst. Coffee in rms. Restaurant nearby. Ck-out 11 am. Coin lndry. Meeting rms. Business servs avail. In-rm modem link. Exercise equipt; sauna. Health club privileges. Refrigerators; microwaves avail. Cr cds: A, C, D, DS, JCB, MC, V.

🅳 🏊 🏌 ⊠ 🔥 SC

✓★★ **COUNTRY INN AND SUITES.** *3621 Dawn Dr (28358).* 910/738-2481; FAX 910/738-8260; res: 800/524-9999; res: 800/456-4000. Web www.countryinn.com. 53 rms, 4 story, 10 suites. June-Sept: S $45.95-$65.95; D $50.95-$80.95; each addl $7; suites $65.95-$85.95; under 12 free; higher rates special events; lower rates rest of yr. Crib $7. TV; cable (premium). Complimentary continental bkfst. Complimentary coffee in rms. Restaurant nearby. Ck-out noon. Business servs avail. In-rm modem link. Sundries. Coin lndry. Exercise equipt. Pool. Refrigerator, microwave in suites. Cr cds: A, C, D, DS, MC, V.

🅳 🏊 🏌 ⊠ 🔥 SC

✓ ★ **FAIRFIELD INN.** *3361 Lackey St (28360). 910/739-8444; FAX 910/739-8466; res: 800/228-2800.* 105 rms, 3 story. May-Sept: S, D $39.95-$59.95; suites $59-$99; lower rates rest of yr. Crib free. TV; cable (premium). Pool. Complimentary continental bkfst. Restaurant adj 6 am-10 pm. Ck-out noon. Business servs avail. Refrigerator in suites. Cr cds: A, C, D, DS, MC, V.

D ⊠ ⊠ ⊛ SC

★★ **HAMPTON INN.** *201 Wintergreen Dr (28358). 910/738-3332; FAX 910/739-8671; res: 800/426-7866.* E-mail hamptoninn@juno.com. 68 rms, 2 story. S, D $62-$69; suites $99. Crib free. TV; cable (premium), VCR avail in suites. Pool. Complimentary continental bkfst. Coffee in rms. Restaurant adj open 24 hrs. Ck-out 11 am. Meeting rms. Business servs avail. Coin lndry. Exercise equipt. Refrigerators, microwaves. Cr cds: A, C, D, DS, MC, V.

D ⊠ 🛇 ⊠ ⊛ SC

★★ **HOLIDAY INN.** *5201 Fayetteville Rd (28358). 910/671-1166; FAX 910/671-1166; res: 800/465-4329.* 108 rms, 2 story. S, D $55-$70; each addl $6; under 18 free. Crib free. TV; cable (premium). Pool. Restaurant open 24 hrs. Rm serv. Ck-out noon. Meeting rms. Business servs avail. In-rm modem link. Health club privileges. Cr cds: A, C, D, DS, MC, V.

D ⊠ 🛇 ⊠ SC

✓ ★★ **QUALITY INN AND SUITES.** *3608 Kahn Dr (28358). 910/738-8261; FAX 910/671-9075; res: 800/638-7949.* 120 rms, 2 story. Late Apr-mid-Sept: S, D $49.95-$65; each addl $6; suites $65-$79; under 17 free; higher rates special events; lower rates rest of yr. Crib free. Pet accepted. TV; cable. Pool. Complimentary continental bkfst. Restaurant 6 am-10 pm. Bar 5 pm-midnight. Ck-out noon. Meeting rms. Business servs avail. Health club privileges. Refrigerator, microwave in suites. Cr cds: A, C, D, DS, ER, MC, V.

D ⊠ 🐾 ⊠ 🛇 ⊠ SC

Restaurant

★★ **JOHNS RESTAURANT.** *4880 Kahn Dr (28358). 910/738-4709.* Hrs: 5:30-10 pm. Closed Sun & Mon; major hols. Res accepted. Continental menu. Bar. Semi-a la carte: dinner $10.50-$22.95. Specializes in beef, seafood, prime rib. Cr cds: A, C, D, DS, MC, V.

⊠

Maggie Valley (B-2)

(See also Asheville, Cherokee, Waynesville)

Pop 185 **Elev** 3,020 ft **Area Code** 828 **Zip** 28751 **Web** www.maggievalley usa.com

Information CVB Chamber of Commerce, 2487 Soco Rd, PO Box 87; 828/926-1686 or 800/785-8259

In 1909, Henry Setzer decided the expanding community of Plott needed a post office. He submitted the names of his three daughters to the Postmaster General, who selected Maggie, then age 14. Lying in the shadow of the Great Smoky Mountains National Park (see), the town is four miles from the Soco Gap entrance to the Blue Ridge Parkway and has become a year-round resort area.

What to See and Do

Cataloochee Ski Area. Double chairlift, T-bar, rope tow; patrol, school, rentals; snowmaking; half-day and twilight rates; cafeteria, bar. Longest run 5,400 ft; vertical drop 740 ft. (Dec-mid-Mar, daily) 4 mi N via US 19 to Fie Top Rd. Phone 828/926-0285 or 800/768-0285. ¢¢¢¢

Ghost Town in the Sky. Chairlift, incline railway or shuttle to top of mountain; shows, rides, gun fights, shops; food. (Early May-late Oct, daily) On US 19. Phone 828/926-1140 or 800/GHOSTOWN. ¢¢¢¢

Lindsey Miniature Village. Over 120 miniature bldgs, many historical, in garden setting. Doll shop. (Mid-Apr-early-Jan, daily; limited hrs after Labor Day) 1110 Soco Rd. Phone 828/926-6277 or 828/298-4586. ¢¢

Soco Gardens Zoo. A 2½-acre zoo with more than 25 different species of animals, incl exotic birds, alligators, bears, snow leopards, monkeys, jaguar and wallabies. Reptile house; poisonous and non-poisonous snake shows. Guided tours. Gift shop. (May-Oct, daily) 3578 Soco Rd. Phone 828/926-1746. ¢¢

Stompin Ground. Bluegrass and country music; clogging; exhibition dancers; square dancing (audience participation). (May-Oct, nightly) 3116 Soco Rd. Phone 828/926-1288. ¢¢¢

Annual Events

International Folk Festival. Premier folk groups from over 10 countries demonstrate their cultural heritage through lively music and costumed dance. Phone 828/452-2997. 11 days late July.

Clogging Hall of Fame. World class cloggers from all across US compete. Oct.

Motels

★★ **BEST WESTERN MOUNTAIN BROOK INN.** *3811 Soco Road (28751), on US 19. 828/926-3962; FAX 828/926-2947; res: 800/528-1234.* 48 rms, 2 story. May-Oct: S, D $49-$99; each addl $8; under 12 free; ski plans; higher rates special events; lower rates rest of yr. Crib free. TV; cable (premium). Pool; whirlpool. Complimentary continental bkfst. Coffee in rms. Restaurant adj 7:30 am-8 pm. Ck-out 11 am. Meeting rms. Business servs avail. Sundries. 18-hole golf privileges, greens fee $50, putting green, driving range. Refrigerators, microwaves. Picnic tables. Cr cds: A, C, D, DS, MC, V.

D 🛇 ⊠ ⊠ ⊛ SC

★ **CARDINAL INN.** *3735 Soco Rd (28751), on US 19. 828/926-0422; FAX 828/926-2570; res: 800/826-0422.* E-mail berg@ primeline.com. 8 rms, 2 kit. units. Apr-Oct: S, D $30-$70; each addl $5; kits. $40-$80; under 6 free; wkly rates; hols (2-day min); higher rates special events. Crib free. TV; cable (premium), VCR avail. Complimentary coffee in lobby. Restaurant nearby. Ck-out 11 am. Picnic tables. Cr cds: A, C, DS, MC, V.

D ⊠ ⊛

★★ **COMFORT INN.** *3282 Soco Rd (28751), on US 19. 828/926-9106; FAX 828/926-9106; res: 800/228-5150.* 68 rms, 2 story. June-Oct: S $55-$99; D $65-$99; each addl $10; under 18 free; lower rates rest of yr. Crib free. TV; cable (premium). Pool. Complimentary continental bkfst. Complimentary coffee. Restaurant opp 7 am-10 pm. Ck-out 11 am. Whirlpool in some suites. Cr cds: A, C, D, DS, MC, V.

D ⊠ ⊠ ⊛ SC

★★ **JOHNATHAN CREEK INN.** *4324 Soco Rd (28751), on US 19. 828/926-1232; FAX 828/926-9750; res: 800/577-7812.* Web maggie-valley.nc./us/www/jonathan/. 42 rms, 2 story. Late May-early Sept, Oct: S, D $65-$109; each addl $5; under 16 free; higher rates: Memorial Day, July 4, Labor Day; lower rates rest of yr. Crib free. TV; cable. Indoor pool. Coffee in rms. Restaurant opp 7 am-noon. Ck-out 11 am. Refrigerators; some in-rm whirlpools; microwaves avail. Some balconies. Cr cds: A, C, DS, MC, V.

D 🛇 ⊠ ⊠ ⊛ SC

✓ ★ **RIVERLET MOTEL & REST.** *4102 Soco Rd (28751), 4½ mi W on US 19. 828/926-1900; res: 800/691-9952; res: 800/691-9952.* 21 rms. July-Labor Day & Oct: S, D $25-$90; lower rates rest of yr. Crib free. TV; cable (premium). Pool. Ck-out 11 am. Overlooks 2 streams. Cr cds: C, DS, MC, V.

🛇 ⊠ ⊠ ⊛ SC

★ **ROCKY WATERS MOTEL.** *4898 Soco Rd (28751), 1½ mi W on US 19, 3 mi E of Blue Ridge Pkwy, Soco exit.* 828/926-1585; res: 888/224-4882. 32 rms, 2 kits. Mid-June-Labor Day, Oct: S $55; D $75; kit. units $85; lower rates May-mid-June, after Labor Day-Sept. Closed rest of yr. Crib free. TV; cable. Heated pool; wading pool. Playground. Complimentary coffee. Restaurant nearby. Ck-out 11 am. Lawn games. Some refrigerators. Picnic tables, grill. Rear porches overlook mountain brook. Cr cds: A, C, DS, MC, V.

⬧ ⬧ ⬧ **SC**

★ **STONY CREEK MOTEL.** *4494 Soco Rd (28751).* 828/926-1996. 20 rms, 1-2 story. June-Oct: S $40-$80; D $50-$80; each addl $5; lower rates rest of yr. Crib free. TV; cable (premium). Complimentary coffee in lobby. Restaurant nearby. Ck-out 11 am. Some refrigerators. Picnic tables. Stream runs through back of property. Cr cds: C, MC, V.

D ⬧ ⬧ ⬧

Guest Ranch

★★★ **CATALOOCHEE SKI AREA.** *119 Ranch Dr (28751), 3 mi NE of US 19.* 828/926-0285; FAX 828/926-9249; res: 800/868-1401. 15 rms in two 2-story lodges, 11 cabins, 2 suites. No A/C. July, Aug, Oct & Dec: S $125-$140; D $130-$250; each addl $55-$60; suites, kit. cottages $190-$210; lower rates rest of yr. Crib free. Serv charge 17%. Supervised child's activities (June-Aug); ages 6-16. Box lunches, cookouts. Beer, wine, setups. Ck-out 11 am, ck-in 3 pm. Business servs avail. Tennis. Downhill ski 1 mi. Whirlpool. Lawn games. Card rm. Mountain music entertainment. Fireplace in lobby, cottages, some rms. 5,000-ft elevation. 1,000-acre working ranch; Appalachian stone barn (1870) remodeled to ranch house. Cr cds: A, C, MC, V.

D ⬧ ⬧ ⬧ ⬧ ⬧ ⬧

Restaurant

★★ **J ARTHUR'S.** *801 Soco Rd (28751), on US 19S.* 828/926-1817. Hrs: 5-9:30 pm. Closed Thanksgiving, Dec 25. Bar. Semi-a la carte: dinner $9.25-$24.95. Child's meals. Specializes in steak, fresh seafood. Own desserts. Loft dining area. Cr cds: A, C, D, MC, V.

D

Manteo (A-10)

(See also Kill Devil Hills, Nags Head)

Pop 991 **Elev** 5 ft **Area Code** 252 **Zip** 27954 **E-mail** dctb-admin@outer-banks.com **Web** www.outer-banks.com/visitor-info/
Information Dare County Tourist Bureau, 704 US 64/264, PO Box 399; 252/473-2138 or 800/446-6262

Fishing in the waters off Manteo is excellent. A large sport fishing fleet is available for booking at Oregon Inlet as well as on Roanoke Island.

What to See and Do

Elizabeth II **State Historic Site.** Representative 16th-century sailing vessel similar to those that brought the first English colonists to the New World more than 400 yrs ago. Living history interpretation (summer). Visitor center with exhibits and audiovisual program. (Apr–Oct, daily; rest of yr, daily exc Mon; closed some major hols) Manteo waterfront. Phone 252/473-1144. ¢¢

Elizabethan Gardens. These 10½ acres incl Great Lawn, Sunken Garden, Queen's Rose Garden, herb garden, 16th-century gazebo with thatched roof, ancient garden statuary. Plants bloom all yr: spring peak (mid-Apr); summer peak (mid-July); fall peak (mid-Oct); and winter peak

(mid-Feb). Gate House Reception Center displays period furniture, English portraits, coat of arms. (Daily; closed Jan 1, Dec 25) 3 mi N on US 64/264, on Roanoke Island. Phone 252/473-3234. ¢¢

Fort Raleigh National Historic Site (see). 3 mi N via US 64.

North Carolina Aquarium on Roanoke Island. Aquarium and marine-oriented educational and research facility. Public aquaria and exhibits, films and educational programs. (Daily; closed Jan 1, Thanksgiving, Dec 25) 3 mi N via US 64/264, Airport Rd exit. Phone 252/473-3493. ¢¢

Seasonal Event

The Lost Colony. Drama by Paul Green (see FORT RALEIGH NATIONAL HISTORIC SITE).

Inn

★★★ **TRANQUIL HOUSE.** *Queen Eizabeth St (27954).* 252/473-1404; FAX 252/473-1526; res: 800/458-7069. E-mail djust1587@aol.com; web www.tranquilinn.com. 25 rms, 3 story. Memorial Day-Labor Day: S, D $129-$179; suites $179; wkly rates; lower rates rest of yr. Crib $10. TV; cable (premium). Complimentary continental bkfst; afternoon refreshments. Restaurant 5-10 pm. Ck-out 11 am, ck-in 3 pm. Business servs avail. Bicycles. Built in style of a 19th-century Outer Banks inn; cypress woodwork, beveled glass doors, observation tower. On bay; overlooks marina. Cr cds: A, C, DS, MC, V.

D ⬧ ⬧ ⬧ **SC**

Restaurants

✓★★ **CLARA'S SEAFOOD GRILL.** *Queen Elizabeth Ave (27954), on the waterfront.* 252/473-1727; FAX 252/473-1723. Hrs: 11:30 am-9 pm; summer hrs vary. Closed Thanksgiving, Dec 25; also Jan, Feb. Bar. Semi-a la carte: lunch, dinner $3.95-$17.95. Child's meals. Specializes in fresh seafood, beef, pasta. 3 dining rms with view of bay. Art-deco decor. Cr cds: A, C, DS, MC, V.

D ⬧

★★ **QUEEN ANNE'S REVENGE.** *1064 Old Wharf Rd (27981), S on NC 345.* 252/473-5466. Hrs: 5-9 pm. Closed Tues; Dec 24-25. Wine, beer. Semi-a la carte: dinner $13-$25. Child's meals. Specializes in fresh seafood. Artwork. Cr cds: A, C, D, DS, MC, V.

D ⬧

Marion (B-3)

(See also Little Switzerland, Morganton)

Founded 1843 **Pop** 4,765 **Elev** 1,395 ft **Area Code** 704 **Zip** 28752
Permits for the Linville Gorge Wilderness of the Pisgah National Forest (see BREVARD) can be obtained at the Grandfather Ranger District Office (Rte 1 Box 110A; 704/652-2144), located here.

What to See and Do

Linville Caverns. Beneath Humpback Mtn. ½-hr guided tours. Gift shop. (Mar–Nov, daily; rest of yr, wkends only) 17 mi N on US 221. Phone 704/756-4171. ¢¢

Morehead City (C-9)

(See also Beaufort)

Founded 1857 **Pop** 6,046 **Elev** 16 ft **Area Code** 252 **Zip** 28557
E-mail vacation@sunnync.com **Web** www.sunnync.com

Information Carteret County Tourism Development Bureau, PO Box 1406; 252/726-8148 or 800/SUNNY-NC

Just across the Intracoastal Waterway from Beaufort, Morehead City is the largest town in Carteret County and a year-round resort town. It is involved in both sport and commercial fishing. The port accommodates oceangoing vessels and charter boats.

What to See and Do

Carteret County Museum. Paintings and artifacts from the 19th century. (Tues–Sat) 100 Wallace Rd. Phone 252/247-7533.   **Free**

Fishing. Onshore and offshore; charter boats avail. Gulfstream fishing for marlin, amberjack, dolphin, mackerel, bluefish.

Fort Macon State Park. This restored fort, built in 1834, was originally used as a harbor defense. Beach (lifeguards in summer), bathhouse (fee); surf fishing; hiking, nature trails. Museum; interpretive program (summer); battle reenactments. Snack bar. 2 mi E of Atlantic Beach, on Bogue Banks. Phone 252/726-3775.   **Free**

Town of Atlantic Beach. Swimming, fishing, boating; boardwalk. Across the bridge from Morehead.

Annual Events

Big Rock Blue Marlin Tournament. Largest tournament of its kind on the East Coast. Fishing for blue marlin; cash awards; registration required. Phone 252/247-3575. Six days early June.

Atlantic Beach King Mackerel Tournament. Phone 252/247-2334. Mid-Sept.

North Carolina Seafood Festival. Seafood, arts and crafts, music. Phone 252/726-NCSF. First wkend Oct.

Motels

★★ **BEST WESTERN BUCCANEER.** *2806 Arendell St (28557).* 252/726-3115; FAX 252/726-3864; res: 800/682-4982. Web www.bestwestern.com. 91 rms, 3 story. May-Aug: S, D $65-$92; each addl $5; under 18 free; lower rates rest of yr. Crib free. TV; cable (premium). Pool. Complimentary full bkfst. Restaurant adj 6 am-10 pm. Ck-out noon. Meeting rms. Business servs avail. Refrigerators; some in-rm whirlpools. Cr cds: A, C, D, DS, MC, V.

[D] [≈] [⊠] [🐾] [SC]

✓★★ **COMFORT INN.** *3100 Arendell St (28557).* 252/247-3434; FAX 252/247-4411; res: 800/422-5404. E-mail comfort@moreheadhotels. com; web www.moreheadhotels.com. 101 rms, 2 story. Apr-Aug: S $50-$95; D $55-$100; each addl $5; under 18 free; lower rates rest of yr. Crib $5. TV; cable (premium), VCR avail. Pool. Complimentary continental bkfst. Restaurant adj 6 am-11 pm. Ck-out 11 am. Meeting rm. Business servs avail. Some refrigerators. Cr cds: A, C, D, DS, ER, JCB, MC, V.

[D] [≈] [⊠] [🔥] [SC]

★ **DAYS INN AND SUITES.** *602 W Fort Macon Rd (28512),* S on Atlantic Beach Bridge, then ½ mi W on Fort Macon Rd (NC 58). 252/247-6400; FAX 252/247-2264; res: 800/329-7466; res: 800/972-3297. 90 rms, 2 story. May-Sept: S, D $84-$135; under 12 free; package plans; lower rates rest of yr. Crib free. TV; cable. Pool. Complimentary continental bkfst. Restaurant nearby. Ck-out noon. Coin lndry. Business servs avail. In-rm modem link. Refrigerators; microwaves avail. Balconies. Picnic tables. Ocean nearby. Cr cds: A, C, D, DS, MC, V.

[D] [🐾] [≈] [⊠] [🐾] [SC]

✓★ **ECONO LODGE.** *3410 Bridges St (28557).* 252/247-2940; FAX 252/247-0746; res: 800/533-7556. Web ww.moreheadhotels. com. 56 rms, 2 story. June-Aug: S, D $48-$85; each addl $5; under 19 free; wkly rates; lower rates rest of yr. Crib $5. TV; cable (premium). Pool; wading pool. Complimentary continental bkfst. Restaurant nearby. Ck-out 11 am. Meeting rms. Business servs avail. In-rm modem link. Cr cds: A, C, D, DS, MC, V.

[D] [≈] [⊠] [🐾] [SC]

★★ **HAMPTON INN.** *4035 Arendell St (28557).* 252/240-2300; FAX 252/240-2311; res: 800/467-9375. Web www.hamptoninn-suites.com. 119 rms, 4 story. Memorial Day-Labor Day: S, D $70-$125; suites $100-$125; under 18 free; higher rates wkends; lower rates rest of yr. Crib free. TV; cable (premium). Pool. Complimentary continental bkfst. Coffee in rms. Restaurant nearby. Ck-out 11 am. Meeting rms. Business servs avail. Exercise equipt. Health club privileges. Cr cds: A, C, D, DS, MC, V.

[D] [🐾] [≈] [🏃] [⊠] [🐾] [SC]

★ **SEAHAWK MOTOR LODGE.** *105 Salter Path Rd (28512),* S on US 70, then W on NC 58. 252/726-4146; res: 800/682-6898. Web www. insiders.com/crystalcoast/test_ads/seahawk/index.htm. 36 rms, 2 story. May-Labor Day: S, D $97-$120; kit. cottages $130; villas $1,600/wk; under 16 free; 3-day min hol wkends; lower rates rest of yr. TV; cable (premium). Pool. Restaurant 7:30 am-2 pm. Rm serv. Ck-out 11 am. Refrigerators. Some balconies, patios. On ocean; swimming beach. Cr cds: C, MC, V.

[🐾] [≈] [🔥] [🐾]

★ **WINDJAMMER INN.** *Salter Path Rd (28512),* S on US 70, then 3 mi W on NC 58. 252/247-7123; FAX 252/247-0133. 45 rms, 5 story. May-Sept: S, D $92-$125; under 12 free; wkly rates; lower rates rest of yr. Crib free. TV; cable (premium). Pool. Complimentary coffee in lobby. Restaurant nearby. Ck-out 11 am. Bathrm phones, refrigerators. Balconies. On beach. Cr cds: A, C, DS, MC, V.

[D] [🐾] [≈] [⊠] [🐾]

Motor Hotel

★★ **CRYSTAL COAST.** *109 Salter Path Rd (28512),* 3 mi W on NC 58. 252/726-2544; FAX 252/726-6570; res: 800/733-7888. 114 rms, 5 story. May-Aug: S, D $129-$189; each addl $10; under 18 free; golf plans; lower rates rest of yr. Crib free. TV; cable (premium). Pool; wading pool. Restaurant 7 am-1 pm, 5:30-9 pm. Rm serv. Bar 5-10 pm. Ck-out 11 am. Meeting rms. Business servs avail. In-rm modem link. Tennis privileges. Golf privileges. Private patios, balconies. Picnic tables. On beach. Cr cds: A, C, D, DS, JCB, MC, V.

[D] [🐾] [🍴] [🏃] [≈] [🐾] [SC]

Hotel

★★★ **SHERATON HOTEL.** *2717 W Fort Macon Rd (28512),* 3 mi W on NC 58. 252/240-1155; FAX 252/240-1452; res: 800/624-8875. 200 rms, 9 story. Mid-May-Labor Day: S, D $135-$165; each addl $15; suites $210-$235; under 18 free; lower rates rest of yr. Crib free. TV; cable (premium). Indoor/outdoor pool; whirlpool, poolside serv. Supervised child's activities (Memorial Day-Labor Day). Complimentary coffee in rms. Restaurant 6:30 am-2 pm, 5-10:30 pm. Bar 5 pm-2 am; entertainment. Ck-out noon. Meeting rms. Business servs avail. Gift shop. Exercise equipt. Refrigerators, microwaves. Balconies. On ocean. Cr cds: A, C, D, DS, ER, JCB, MC, V.

[D] [🐾] [≈] [🏃] [⊠] [🔥] [SC]

Inns

★★ **EMERALD ISLE INN & BED & BREAKFAST.** *502 Ocean Dr (28594),* 13 mi S US 58. 252/354-3222; FAX 252/354-3222. Web www4.coastalnet.com/emeraldisleinn. 4 rms, 2 story. Mid-May-Labor Day: S, D, suites $125-$160; each addl $15; under 6 free; lower rates rest of yr.

Complimentary full bkfst. Restaurant nearby. Ck-out 11 am, ck-in 3 pm. Luggage handling. On Bogue Banks. Totally nonsmoking. Cr cds: C, MC, V.

⬛⬛⬛

★★ **HARBOR LIGHT GUEST HOUSE.** *332 Live Oak Dr (28584), 20 mi S on NC 24/58.* 252/393-6868; FAX 252/393-6868; res: 800/624-8439. Web www.emeraldisle.net/harborlight.htm. 9 rms, 3 story. No rm phones. Apr-Oct: S, D $75-$100; suites $125-$200. Children over 16 yrs only. TV; cable. Complimentary full bkfst. Restaurant nearby. Ck-out 11 am, ck-in 3 pm. Luggage handling. Golf privileges. Tennis privileges. Health club privileges. Refrigerators; some in-rm whirlpools, fireplaces. Balconies. Overlooks Bogue Sound. Totally nonsmoking. Cr cds: A, C, MC, V.

⬛⬛⬛⬛⬛⬛

Restaurants

★★ **ANCHOR INN.** *109 N 28th St (28557).* 252/726-2156. Hrs: 6 am-1:30 pm, 5-10 pm; Sat 6 am-noon, 5-11 pm; Sun 6 am-1 pm, 5-10 pm. Closed Dec 24-25. Res accepted. Bar 5-11 pm; Fri, Sat to midnight. Semi-a la carte: bkfst $3-$7, dinner $8.95-$27. Child's meals. Specializes in black Angus beef, fresh local seafood, chicken. Rattan furniture, ceiling fans, paintings. Cr cds: A, C, DS, MC, V.

⬛⬛⬛⬛

★ **CAPTAIN BILL'S WATERFRONT.** *701 Evans St (28557).* 252/726-2166. Hrs: 11 am-9 pm; Fri, Sat to 10 pm. Semi-a la carte: lunch $4.95-$18.95, dinner $6.95-$18.95. Child's meals. Specializes in seafood, pie. Gift shop. On Bogue Sound; overlooks fishing fleet. Cr cds: C, DS, MC, V.

⬛⬛

★ **CHARTER RESTAURANT.** *405 Evans St (28557).* 252/726-9036. Hrs: 11:30 am-10 pm; winter hrs vary. Closed Thanksgiving, Dec 25. Serv bar. A la carte entrees: lunch $4.95-$7.95, dinner $9.95-$29. Child's meals. Specializes in crab cakes, seafood. Salad bar. Nautical decor. View of waterfront. Cr cds: C, MC, V.

⬛⬛⬛

★ **MRS WILLIS.** *3114 Bridges St (28557).* 252/726-3741. Hrs: 11:30 am-9:30 pm. Closed Dec 24-30. Res accepted. Bar 5 pm-2 am. Semi-a la carte: lunch $3-$5, dinner $5-$20. Child's meals. Specializes in fresh seafood, beef. Parking. Three dining rms. Family-owned. Cr cds: A, C, DS, MC, V.

⬛⬛

★ **SANITARY FISH MARKET.** *501 Evans St (28557).* 252/247-3111. Hrs: 11 am-8:30 pm; May-Sept to 9 pm. Closed Dec-Jan. Semi-a la carte: lunch $4.50-$21.95, dinner $7.95-$21.95. Child's meals. Specializes in fresh seafood, steaks, and chicken. Overlooks water, fishing fleet, state port. Family-owned. Cr cds: C, DS, MC, V.

⬛⬛⬛

Morganton (B-3)

(See also Little Switzerland, Marion)

Pop 15,085 **Elev** 1,182 ft **Area Code** 828 **Zip** 28655 **E-mail** bcttc@hci.net **Web** www.hci.net/~bcttc/

Information Burke County Travel & Tourism, 102 E Union St, Courthouse Sq; 828/433-6793

This is the seat of Burke County and a manufacturing town producing furniture, textiles, shoes, chemicals, electronics, clothing and other products.

In 1893, the county became a haven for the Waldenses, a religious group from the French-Italian Alps that was seeking freedom and space to expand outside their alpine homeland.

What to See and Do

Boating, fishing, swimming. Lake James. 8 mi W on NC 126. **Lake Rhodhiss.** 10 mi E off US 70.

Boat tours. Tours of Lake James on 38-ft pontoon *Harbor Queen*. Departs Mountain Harbor Marina. Phone 828/584-0666. ¢¢¢

Annual Events

Waldensian Celebration of the Glorious Return. On I-40, exit 112 in Valdese. Commemoration of the end of persecution during the reign of Louis XIV; ethnic games, arts and crafts, dances, food. Phone 828/879-2129. Mid-Aug.

Historic Morganton Festival. Downtown. Arts, crafts, ethnic foods, band concert. Phone 828/438-5280. Mid-Sept.

Seasonal Event

From This Day Forward. Church St, Valdese. Outdoor historical drama depicting hardships of the Waldenses and their struggle for religious freedom. Phone 800/743-8398. Thurs-Sun eves. Mid-July–mid-Aug.

Motels

★★ **HOLIDAY INN.** *2400 S Sterling St (28655), 1 mi SE on NC 18, at I-40.* 828/437-0171; FAX 828/437-0171; res: 800/465-4329. 135 rms, 2 story. S, D $69-$89; each addl $6; under 19 free. Crib free. TV; cable (premium). Pool. Restaurant 6 am-2 pm, 5-10 pm. Rm serv. Bar 5 pm-midnight; Sun from 6 pm. Ck-out noon. Meeting rms. Business servs avail. In-rm modem link. Valet serv. Cr cds: A, C, D, DS, JCB, MC, V.

⬛⬛⬛⬛⬛⬛

✓★ **SLEEP INN.** *2400A S Sterling St (28655).* 828/433-9000; FAX 828/433-9000; res: 800/638-7949. 61 rms, shower only, 2 story. S $49; D $55; each addl $6; under 18 free; higher rates wkends. Crib free. TV; cable (premium). Swimming privileges. Complimentary continental bkfst. Complimentary coffee in rms. Restaurant adj 6 am-10 pm. Ck-out 11 am. In-rm modem link. Valet serv. Refrigerators avail. Cr cds: A, C, D, DS, JCB, MC, V.

⬛⬛⬛⬛

Inn

✓★ **RICHMOND INN BED & BREAKFAST.** *51 Pine Ave (28777), E on US 19.* 828/765-6993. 7 rms, 2 story. No A/C. No rm phone. Apr-Dec: S $45-$60; D $55-70; each addl $10; under 10 free; lower rates rest of yr. Complimentary full bkfst. Restaurant nearby. Ck-out 11 am, ck-in 4 pm. Luggage handling. Totally nonsmoking. Cr cds: C, DS, MC, V.

⬛⬛⬛

Nags Head (Outer Banks) (A-10)

(See also Kill Devil Hills, Manteo)

Pop 1,838 **Elev** 10 ft **Area Code** 252 **Zip** 27959 **E-mail** dctd-admin@outer-banks.com **Web** www.outer-banks.com/visitor-info/

Information Dare County Tourist Bureau, 704 US 64/264, PO Box 399, Manteo 27954; 252/473-2138 or 800/446-6262.

This is a year-round fishing and beachcombing town on the Outer Banks (see), just south of Kill Devil Hills. There are fishing piers and boats for rent. Swimming is good in summer. A museum is located at Jockey's Ridge State Park, which boasts one of the largest sand dunes on the East Coast.

The soft sand dunes and Atlantic breezes make this a popular area for hang gliding. Offshore, partly buried in the drifting sand, are many wrecks of both old sailing ships and more modern vessels.

Cape Hatteras National Seashore (see) is south of Nags Head.

Annual Events

Gliding Spectacular. Hang gliding competition, novice through advanced. Spectacular flying and fun events. Phone 252/441-4124. 2nd wkend May.

Rogallo Kite Festival. Competition for homebuilt kites; stunt kite performances, demonstrations; kite auction. Phone 252/441-4124. 1st wkend June.

Motels

✓★ **BEACON MOTOR LODGE.** 2617 S Virgina Dare Trail (27959), on the oceanfront at milepost 11. 252/441-5501; FAX 252/441-2178; res: 800/441-4804. Web www.beacon.com. 47 rms, 1-2 story, 20 kits. Late May-early Sept: S, D $80-$100; each addl $10; suites $700-$800/wk; kit. units $650/wk; kit. cottages $700-$1,000/wk; higher rates hols, wkends; lower rates mid-Mar-late May, early Sept-Oct. Closed rest of yr. Crib $3. TV; cable (premium). Pool; 2 wading pools. Playground. Restaurant nearby. Ck-out 11 am. Coin lndry. Business servs avail. In-rm modem link. Refrigerators, microwaves. Picnic tables, grill. Sun deck. Beach. Cr cds: A, C, D, DS, MC, V.

★ **BLUE HERRON MOTEL.** 6811 Virginia Dare Trail (27959). 252/441-7447. 30 rms, 3 story, 13 kits. No elvtr. June-Labor Day: D $91-$100; each addl $5; kit. units $96-$105; lower rates rest of yr. Crib $2. TV; cable. 2 pools, 1 indoor; whirlpool. Complimentary coffee in rms. Restaurant nearby. Ck-out 11 am. Refrigerators, microwaves. Porches, balconies overlook private beach. Cr cds: C, DS, MC, V.

★ **COMFORT INN.** 8031 Old Oregon Inlet Rd (27959). 252/441-6315; FAX 252/441-6315; res: 800/334-3302. 105 rms, 7 story. June-Labor Day: D $128-$170; each addl $10; under 17 free; higher rates hols (3-day min); lower rates rest of yr. Crib free. TV; cable. Pool; wading pool. Complimentary continental bkfst. Restaurant nearby. Ck-out 11 am. Meeting rms. Business servs avail. Refrigerators, microwaves. Ocean view balconies. Swimming beach. Cr cds: A, C, D, DS, MC, V.

✓★★ **ISLANDER MOTEL.** 7001 Virginia Dare Trail (27959), on US 158 Business, near milepost 16. 252/441-6229; FAX 252/480-3883. Web www.islandermotel.com. 24 rms, 3 story, 6 kits. No elvtr. Mid-June-early Sept: D, kit. units $103; each addl $10; lower rates Apr-mid-June, early Sept-Oct. Closed rest of yr. Crib free. TV; cable. Pool. Coffee in rms. Restaurant nearby. Ck-out 11 am. Coin lndry. Business center. Refrigerators. Private patios, balconies. Picnic table, grill. On beach. Cr cds: A, C, MC, V.

★★ **QUALITY INN.** 7123 S Virginia Dare Trail (27959), 3½ mi S on US 158 Business at milepost 16.5. 252/441-7191; FAX 252/441-1961; res: 800/440-4386. 111 rms, 1-3 story. Memorial Day-Labor Day: S, D $90-$150; each addl $10; under 18 free; lower rates rest of yr. Crib free. TV; cable (premium), VCR avail (movies). Pool; wading pool. Ck-out 11 am. Business servs avail. Most rms with balcony overlook ocean. Some rms across street. Cr cds: A, C, D, DS, ER, JCB, MC, V.

★★ **SEA FOAM MOTEL.** 7111 S Virginia Dare Trail (27959). 252/441-7320; FAX 252/441-7324. Web www.seafoam.com. 51 rms, 2 story, 18 kits., three 2-bedrm kit. cottages, 1 apt. Late May-early Sept: D $77-$95; each addl $5; kit. units $525-$630/wk; kit. cottages $725/wk; apt. $675/wk; under 12 free; lower rates Mar-Memorial Day, Labor Day-mid-Dec. Closed rest of yr. Crib $5. TV; cable (premium). Pool. Playground. Restaurant adj 5-10 pm. Ck-out 11 am. Airport transportation. Lawn games. Refrigerators. Some private patios, balconies. Picnic tables, grills. Playground. Beach. Cr cds: A, C, MC, V.

★★ **SURF SIDE MOTEL.** 6701 S Virginia Dare Trail (27959), milepost 16. 252/441-2105; FAX 252/441-2456; res: 800/552-7873. E-mail surfside@pinn.net; web wwwinsider.com/outerbanks/wwwads/surfside/index.htm. 76 rms, 5 story, 14 suites. Mid-June-early Sept: S, D $104-$139; each addl $10; suites $169-$209; kit. units $169-$209; under 13 free; higher rates hol wkends; lower rates rest of yr. Crib $5. TV; cable. 2 pools, 1 indoor; whirlpool. Complimentary continental bkfst. Restaurant nearby. Ck-out 11 am. Coin lndry. Meeting rms. Business servs avail. Game rm. Refrigerators, microwaves. Balconies. On beach. Cr cds: A, C, DS, MC, V.

Motor Hotel

★★ **NAGS HEAD INN.** 4701 S Virginia Dare Trail (27959). 252/441-0454; FAX 252/441-0454; res: 800/327-8881. 100 rms, 5 story. Late May-Labor Day: S, D $99-$190; each addl $10; suites $239; wkly rates; lower rates rest of yr. Crib $5. TV; cable (premium). Indoor/outdoor pool; whirlpool. Complimentary coffee in lobby. Restaurant nearby. Ck-out 11 am. Business servs avail. In-rm modem link. Refrigerators. Balconies. On ocean, swimming beach. Cr cds: A, C, DS, MC, V.

Inn

★★★ **FIRST COLONY INN.** 6720 S Virginia Dare Trail (27959). 252/441-2343; FAX 252/441-9234; res: 800/368-9390. E-mail innkeeper@firstcolonyinn.com; web www.firstcolonyinn.com. 26 rms, 3 story, 4 kits. Memorial Day-Labor Day: S, D $145-$275; each addl $30; lower rates rest of yr. Crib free. TV; cable, VCR avail (free movies). Pool. Complimentary full bkfst; afternoon refreshments. Complimentary coffee in rms. Restaurant nearby. Ck-out 11 am, ck-in 3 pm. Business servs avail. In-rm modem link. Concierge serv. Picnic tables, grills. Two-story veranda; overlooks ocean. On 5 acres of landscaped grounds. Totally nonsmoking. Cr cds: A, C, DS, MC, V.

Restaurants

★★ **OWENS'.** 7114 S Virginia Dare Trail (27959). 252/441-7309. Web www.owensrestaurant.com. Hrs: 5-10 pm. Closed Jan-mid-Feb. Bar to midnight. Semi-a la carte: dinner $13.95-$18.95. Child's meals. Specializes in crab cakes, grilled fish, whole Maine lobster. Jazz in summer. Parking. Historic artifacts of US Lifesaving Service (forerunner of US Coast Guard) on display; uniforms, log books, photographs. Family-owned. Cr cds: A, C, DS, MC, V.

★★ **PENGUIN ISLE.** 6708 S Croatan Hwy US 158 (27959), milepost 16. 252/441-2637. Hrs: 5-10 pm; early-bird dinner to 6 pm. Closed Dec 24-25. Bar 5 pm-midnight. Semi-a la carte: dinner $9.95-$22.95. Child's meals. Specializes in seafood, Black Angus beef. Entertainment Thurs-Sat. Nautical decor. View of sound. Cr cds: A, C, D, DS, MC, V.

★★ **WINDMILL POINT RESTAURANT.** US 158 (27959), at milepost 16. 252/441-1535. Hrs: 4:30-10 pm. Bar. Semi-a la carte: dinner $13.95-$20.95. Child's meals. Specializes in seafood, veal, pasta. Features memorabilia of SS United States. Cr cds: A, C, D, DS, MC, V.

New Bern (B-9)

(See also Kinston)

Settled 1710 **Pop** 17,363 **Elev** 15 ft **Area Code** 252 **E-mail** tourism@ cravencounty.com **Web** www4.coastalnet.com/cvb

Information Visitor Information Center, 314 S Front St, PO Box 1413, 28560; 252/637-9400 or 800/437-5767

The first settlers in this, one of North Carolina's earliest towns, were Germans and Swiss seeking political and religious freedom in the New World. The name Bern came from the city in Switzerland. Many Georgian and Federal-style buildings give New Bern an architectural ambiance unique in North Carolina. Many of these homes can be visited during April and October.

Swimming, boating and freshwater and saltwater fishing can be enjoyed on the Neuse and Trent rivers. A Ranger District office of the Croatan National Forest is located here.

What to See and Do

Attmore-Oliver House (ca 1790). This house, headquarters for the New Bern Historical Society, exhibits 18th- and 19th-century furnishings and historical objects, incl Civil War artifacts, doll collection. (Early Apr–mid-Dec, Tues–Sat; also by appt; closed July 4, Thanksgiving, Dec 25) 510 Pollock St. Phone 252/638-8558.   **Free**

Croatan National Forest. A unique coastal forest (157,724 acres), with many estuaries and waterways; northernmost habitat of the alligator. Pocosins (Native American for "swamp on a hill") have many unusual dwarf and insect-eating plants. Swimming, boating and fishing in Neuse River; hunting for deer, bear, turkey, quail and migratory waterfowl; picnicking; camping (fee). SE via US 17, 70. For further info contact the Forest Supervisor, 100 Otis St, PO Box 2750, Asheville 28802, phone 828/257-4200; or the District Ranger, 141 E Fisher Ave, 28560, phone 252/638-5628.

New Bern Firemen's Museum. Antique firefighting equipment, relics and pictures, 1917 double-size ladder trucks and engines, 1913 pumper. (Daily; closed some major hols) 410 Hancock St, off US 17, 70 Business. Phone 252/636-4087. ¢

⭐ **Tryon Palace Historic Sites & Gardens.** Built in 1767–1770 by the Royal Governor, William Tryon, this "most beautiful building in the colonial Americas" burned by accident in 1798 and lay in ruins until rebuilt between 1952–1959. It served as the colonial and first state capitol. Reconstruction, furnishings and 18th-century English gardens are beautiful and authentic. Docent-guided tours (daily; closed Jan 1, Thanksgiving, Dec 24–26). Also self-guided garden tours. 610 Pollock St, S end of George St, 1 blk S of US 17, 70 Business, NC 55. Phone 800/767-1560. Combination ticket incl admission to all historic sites and gardens that are part of the Tryon Palace. Combination ticket ¢¢¢¢   On grounds are

Dixon-Stevenson House (ca 1830). Early Federal architecture reflects maritime history of the area in its interior woodwork and widow's walk. Furnished in Federal and Empire antiques.

John Wright Stanly House (ca 1780). Georgian-style house, furnished with 18th-century American antiques. Elegant interior woodwork. Formal gardens typical of the period.

New Bern Academy (ca 1810). 4 blks from Tryon Palace complex, in the historic residential district. Major surviving landmark of an educational institution founded in the 1760s, the Academy is restored as a self-guided museum of New Bern Civil War history, early education and local architecture. Phone 252/514-4874.

Motels

⭐⭐ **COMFORT SUITES RIVERFRONT PARK.** *218 E Front St (28560). 252/636-0022; FAX 252/636-0051; res: 800/638-7949.* Web www.insiders.com. 100 rms, 4 story. Apr-Oct: S $69-$104; D $74-$129; under 18 free; lower rates rest of yr. Crib free. TV; cable (premium), VCR avail. Pool; whirlpool. Complimentary continental bkfst. Coffee in rms.

Restaurant nearby. Ck-out noon. Meeting rms. Business servs avail. Tennis privileges. Health club privileges. Refrigerators, microwaves. Cr cds: A, C, D, DS, ER, JCB, MC, V.

🄳 🛉 🏌 🏊 🛄 🔥 SC

✓⭐⭐ **HAMPTON INN.** *200 Hotel Dr (28562). 252/637-2111; FAX 252/637-2000; res: 800/448-8288.* Web www.hamptoninn.com/hi/ newbern. 101 rms, 4 story. S, D $57-$80; under 18 free; higher rates wkends. Crib free. TV; cable (premium). Pool. Complimentary continental bkfst. Coffee in rms. Restaurant nearby. Ck-out noon. Meeting rms. Business servs avail. In-rm modem link. Exercise equipt. Health club privileges. Cr cds: A, C, D, DS, MC, V.

🄳 🏊 🏌 🛄 🔥 SC

Hotel

⭐⭐⭐ **SHERATON HOTEL & MARINA.** *100 Middle St (28563). 252/638-3585; FAX 252/638-8112; res: 800/326-3745.* Web www.sheraton newbern.com. 172 rms, 5 story. S, D $95-$135; each addl $10; suites $195; under 17 free. Crib free. Pet accepted. TV; cable (premium). Pool. Coffee in rms. Restaurant 6:30 am-2 pm, 5-10 pm. Bar noon-2 am; entertainment Fri, Sat. Ck-out noon. Meeting rms. Business center. In-rm modem link. Free airport transportation. Golf privileges. Exercise equipt. Health club privileges. Refrigerators. Balconies. On river; marina facilities. Cr cds: A, C, D, DS, MC, V.

🄳 🐾 🛉 🏌 🏊 🏌 ✈ 🛄 🔥 SC 🚶

Inns

⭐⭐ **AERIE BED & BREAKFAST.** *509 Pollock St (28562). 252/636-5553; FAX 252/514-2157; res: 800/849-5553.* E-mail aerie@ cconnect.net. 7 rms, 2 story. S $60; D $89-99; under 6 free. TV; cable. Complimentary full bkfst. Ck-out 11 am, ck-in 3 pm. Business servs avail. Airport transportation. Health club privileges. Victorian house built in 1880; antiques. One blk E of Tryon Palace. Cr cds: A, C, DS, MC, V.

🛄 🔥 SC

⭐⭐ **HARMONY HOUSE.** *215 Pollock St (28560). 252/636-3810; FAX 252/636-3810; res: 800/636-3113.* E-mail harmony@ccconnect. net; web www.harmonyhouseinn.com. 10 rms, 2 story. S $70; D $89-$99; suites $140; each addl $20. TV; cable (premium). Complimentary full bkfst; afternoon refreshments. Ck-out 11 am, ck-in 3 pm. Business servs avail. In-rm modem link. Free airport transportation. Health club privileges. Some in-rm whirlpools. Greek-revival house built in 1850; antiques, artwork. Cr cds: A, C, D, DS, MC, V.

🛄 🔥 SC

⭐ **INN AT ORIENTAL.** *508 Church St (28571), approx 25 mi E on NC 55. 252/249-1078; FAX 252/248-1201; res: 800/485-7174.* E-mail orientalinn@pamlico-nc.com; web www.pamlico-nc.com/oinn. 8 rms, 2 story. No rm phones. May-Nov: S, D $75-$110; each addl $15; lower rates rest of yr. Complimentary full bkfst. Restaurant nearby. Ck-out 11 am, ck-in 3 pm. Built in 1840; antiques. Totally nonsmoking. Cr cds: A, C, MC, V.

🄳 🛄 🔥 SC

⭐⭐ **KINGS ARMS BED & BREAKFAST INN.** *212 Pollock St (28560). 252/638-4409; FAX 252/638-2191; res: 800/872-9306.* 8 rms, 3 story. S, D $60-$90; each addl $10; under 10 free. TV; cable. Complimentary full bkfst; afternoon refreshments. Ck-out 11 am, ck-in 3 pm. Business servs avail. In-rm modem link. Valet serv. Airport transportation. Tennis privileges. Golf privileges. In restored house (ca 1848); antiques, canopied beds. Cr cds: A, C, MC, V.

🏌 🏌 🛄 🔥 SC

⭐ **NEW BERN HOUSE INN.** *709 Broad St (28560). 252/636-2250; res: 800/842-7688.* 7 rms, 3 story. S $68; D $88. Children over 12 yrs only. TV in sitting rm; cable. Complimentary full bkfst. Restaurant nearby. Ck-out 11 am, ck-in 2 pm. Free airport transportation. Colonial-revival house (1923); porch. Totally nonsmoking. Cr cds: A, C, MC, V.

Restaurants

✓ ★ **FRED & CLAIRE'S RESTAURANT.** *247 Craven St (28560). 252/638-5426.* Hrs: 11 am-7 pm; Fri to 8 pm; Sat to 3 pm. Closed Sun; some major hols. Res accepted. Wine, beer. Semi-a la carte: lunch $1.50-$7.25, dinner $5.95-$9.95. Specializes in casserole dishes, quiche, soups. Housed in historic building (1870). Casual dining. Cr cds: C.

★ ★ ★ **HARVEY MANSION RESTAURANT.** *221 Tryon Palace Dr (28560). 252/638-3205.* Web www.innplace.com. Hrs: 6-10 pm. Closed Dec 24-25. Res accepted. International menu. Bar. Semi-a la carte: dinner $12.95-$25.95. Specializes in seafood, beef, veal. In 18th-century mansion near confluence of Trent & Neuse Rivers. Cr cds: A, C, D, DS, MC, V.

★ ★ ★ **HENDERSON HOUSE.** *216 Pollock St (28560). 252/637-4784.* Hrs: 6-9 pm. Closed Sun, Mon. Res accepted. Semi-a la carte: dinner $17.95-$28.95. Specializes in veal, Angus beef, seafood. Restored house built in 1810. Totally nonsmoking. Cr cds: A, C, DS, MC, V.

★ **SCALZO ITALIAN RESTAURANT.** *415 Broad St (28560). 252/633-9898.* Hrs: 5-10 pm. Closed Sun; Jan 1, Dec 25. Res accepted. Italian menu. Wine, beer. Semi-a la carte: dinner $9.95-$21.95. Child's meals. Specializes in chicken, veal, beef. Three dining areas. Prints, murals of Italian scenes. Cr cds: A, C, MC, V.

Ocracoke (Outer Banks) (B-10)

(See also Buxton)

Pop 658 (est) **Elev** 6 ft **Area Code** 919 **Zip** 27960

Settled in the 17th century, Ocracoke was, according to legend, once used as headquarters by the pirate Blackbeard. On the Outer Banks (see), Ocracoke offers excellent fishing and hunting for wildfowl. The lighthouse, built in 1823, is still in use. One of the visitor centers for Cape Hatteras National Seashore (see) is here.

What to See and Do

Cedar Island to Ocracoke Ferry Service. (Winter & summer, daily) **Swan Quarter to Ocracoke.** (All yr, daily) Ferries are crowded; there may be a wait. Reservations are recommended; they may be made up to one yr in advance by phone or in person at the ferry terminal: Ocracoke 919/928-3841; Cedar Island 919/225-3551; Swan Quarter 919/926-1111; or phone 800/BY-FERRY. Reservations are void if vehicle is not in loading lane at least 30 min before departure.
Ocracoke to Hatteras Ferry. Northward across Hatteras Inlet.

Motels

★ ★ **ANCHORAGE INN.** *Hwy 12 (27960). 252/928-1101; FAX 252/928-6322.* Web www.theanchorageinn.com. 35 rms, 4 story. May-Oct: S, D $89-$115; higher rates special events; lower rates rest of yr. Crib $5.

Pet accepted. TV; cable (premium). Pool. Complimentary continental bkfst. Ck-out 11 am. Business servs avail. Balconies. Picnic tables, grill. Marina. Cr cds: A, C, D, DS, MC, V.

★ **BLUFF SHOAL MOTEL.** *Hwy 12 (27960). 252/928-4301; res: 800/292-2304.* 8 rms. Memorial Day-Labor Day: S, D $70-$80, each addl $8; under 12 free; lower rates rest of yr. Crib free. TV; cable (premium). Restaurant opp 7 am-10 pm. Ck-out 11 am. Refrigerators. On Silver Lake. Cr cds: C, DS, MC, V.

★ **BOYETTE HOUSE.** *Hwy 12 (27960), 1½ blks from harbor in village. 252/928-4261; FAX 252/928-4901; res: 800/928-4261.* Web www.boyettehouse.com. 22 rms, 3 story, 2 suites. Mid-May-Oct: S, D $60-$110; suites $155-$175; each addl $4-$8; lower rates rest of yr. Crib free. TV, cable (premium). Whirlpool. Restaurant adj 7 am-9 pm. Ck-out 11 am. Exercise equipt. Near beach; swimming. Cr cds: C, DS, MC, V.

✓ ★ **OCRACOKE ISLAND INN.** *100 Lighthouse Rd (27960), on NC 12. 252/928-4351; FAX 252/928-4352; res: 877/456-3466.* Web www.ocracoke-island-inn.com. 35 rms, 2-3 story, 4 suites. No elvtr. Late May-late Sept: D $49-$99; each addl $5; suites $80-$100 (3-day min); cottages $675/wk; lower rates rest of yr. Crib free. Pet accepted. TV; cable (premium). Heated pool. Restaurant 7-11 am, 5-8:30 pm. Ck-out 11 am. Free airport transportation. Private patios. Near beach. Built in 1901; antiques. Cr cds: C, DS, MC, V.

★ **PONY ISLAND MOTEL & REST INC.** *Hwy 12 (27960). 252/928-4411; FAX 252/928-2522.* 50 rms, 9 kits. Memorial Day-Labor Day: S, D $80-$95; each addl $5; kit. units, suites $85-$140; cottages $700-$850/wk; lower rates rest of yr. TV; cable (premium). Pool. Restaurant adj 7-11 am, 5-9 pm. Ck-out 11 am. Business servs avail. Picnic tables, grills. Bicycle rentals. Cr cds: C, DS, MC, V.

Inn

★ ★ **BERKLEY CENTER COUNTRY INN.** *Hwy 12 (27960), near south ferry docks. 252/928-5911.* Web www.berkleymanor.com. 12 rms in 2 bldgs, 2 story. No rm phones. S, D $125-$135; each addl $20; suites $155-$175. TV in sitting rm; cable (premium). Complimentary full bkfst. Restaurant nearby. Ck-out 11 am, ck-in 2 pm. Some in-rm whirlpools. Library, sitting rm. Caribbean plantation style furnishing. Cr cds: A, C, DS, MC, V.

Restaurants

★ ★ **BACK PORCH RESTAURANT.** *Hwy 12 (27960). 252/928-6401.* Hrs: 5-9:30 pm. Closed mid Nov-mid Mar. Wine, beer. Semi-a la carte: dinner $7.95-$19.50. Child's meals. Specializes in crab cakes, fresh fish. Porch dining. Cr cds: C, MC, V.

✓ ★ **ISLAND INN RESTAURANT.** *NC 12 (27960). 252/928-7821.* Web www.ocracoke-island-inn.com. Hrs: 7-11 am, 5-8:30 pm. Closed Dec-Feb. Semi-a la carte: bkfst $2.95-$8.95, dinner $8.95-$15.95. Child's meals. Specialties: clam chowder, prime rib. Nautical decor. Cr cds: C, DS, MC, V.

Outer Banks (A-10 - B-10)

E-mail chamber@outer-banks.com **Web** www.outer-banks.com/chamber
Information Chamber of Commerce, PO Box 1757, Kill Devil Hills 27948;
252/441-8144

The Outer Banks are a chain of narrow, sandy islands stretching 175 miles
from Cape Lookout to Back Bay, Virginia. Parts of the chain are 30 miles
from the mainland. Cape Hatteras is about 75 miles from the southern end.
The islands may be reached by bridge from Point Harbor and Manteo or by
ferry from Cedar Island and Swan Quarter to Ocracoke (see).

The following Outer Banks areas are included in the *Mobil Travel Guide*.
For information on any one of them, see the individual alphabetical listing:
Buxton, Cape Hatteras National Seashore, Hatteras, Kill Devil Hills, Nags
Head, Ocracoke.

Inn

★★★ **SANDERLING INN & RESTAURANT.** *1461 Duck Rd
(27949), closest airport is Norfolk airport & is 2-hr drive from resort.*
252/261-4111; FAX 252/261-1638; res: 800/701-4111. Web www.sander
linginn.com. 87 rooms, 3 bldgs. Nov 1-May 1 S,D $123-$198; suites $274
+ up. May 2-Oct 31 S,D $214-$294; suites $375 + up. Crib. Wet bar, refrig,
kit. TV, radio. Concierge. Health club. Restaurant. Bar. Room serv. 4 tennis courts; indoor whirlpool; indoor pool; priv saunas; massage therapy;
gift shop; sailing center; jet skiing, fishing, jog trail. Cr cds: A, C, D, DS,
MC, V.

D [icons]

Pilot Mountain (A-5)

Pop 1,181 **Elev** 1,152 ft **Area Code** 910 **Zip** 27041

What to See and Do

Pilot Mountain State Park. More than 3,700 acres; hard-surfaced road
up mountain to parking. Foot trail to base of rocky knob; extensive view.
Canoeing and rafting on the Yadkin River. Nature and riding trails. Picnicking. Camping. Standard fees. 4 mi S on US 52. Phone 910/325-2355.

Motel

✓★★ **RAMADA INN.** *Hwy 52 & Hwy 268 (27041). 336/368-
2237; FAX 336/368-1212.* 68 rms, 2 story. S $51.95-$56.95; D $56.95-
$64.95; each addl $5; under 12 free. Crib free. TV; cable (premium), VCR
avail. Pool. Complimentary continental bkfst. Restaurant 6:30 am-9:30 pm.
Ck-out 11 am. Meeting rms. Business servs avail. In-rm modem link. Valet
serv. Exercise equipt. Microwaves avail. View of mountain. Cr cds: A, C,
D, DS, MC, V.

D [icons] SC

Inn

★★★ **PINE RIDGE INN.** *2893 W Pine St (27030), NW on US 52
then W on NC 89. 336/789-5034; FAX 336/786-9039.* 6 rms, 2 story. S, D
$60-$100; each addl $10; cottage $110. Crib $10. TV; cable, VCR avail.
Pool. Complimentary full bkfst; afternoon refreshments. Restaurant 7:00-
8:30 am, 11 am-2 pm, 5-9 pm. Ck-out 11 am, ck-in 2 pm. Lawn games.
English manor (1949); antique furnishings. Cr cds: A, C, DS, MC, V.

[icons] SC

Pinehurst (B-6)

(See also Southern Pines)

Founded 1895 **Pop** 5,103 **Elev** 529 ft **Area Code** 910 **Zip** 28374
E-mail cvb4golf@mindspring.com **Web** www.homeofgolf.com
Information Convention & Visitors Bureau, PO Box 2270, Southern Pines
28388; 910/692-3330 or 800/346-5362

A famous year-round resort village, Pinehurst preserves an era steeped
both in tradition and golfing excellence. Its New England style was
designed over 100 years ago by the firm of Frederick Law Olmsted, which
also designed New York's Central Park and landscaped Asheville's Biltmore Estate. Handsome estates and other residences, mostly styled in
Georgian colonial, dot the village. The Pinehurst Resort and Country Club
has eight 18-hole golf courses, a 200-acre lake, 24 tennis courts and other
recreational facilities that are open to members as well as to guests staying there.

What to See and Do

Sandhills Horticultural Gardens. 25 acres incl Ebersole Holly Garden;
Rose Garden; Conifer Garden; Hillside Garden with bridges, waterfalls and
gazebo; Desmond Native Wetland Trail Garden, a nature conservancy and
bird sanctuary; and Sir Walter Raleigh Garden, a one-acre formal English
garden. Docent-guided group tours (by appt only). (Daily) 2200 Airport Rd,
Sandhills Community College. Phone 910/695-3882.   **Free**

Motel

★★ **COMFORT INN.** *9801 US Hwy 15-501 (28374). 910/215-
5500; FAX 910/215-5535; res: 800/831-0541.* 80 rms, 2 story. Mid-Feb-
Nov: S $78; D $84; each addl $6; suites $118-$125; under 18 free; lower
rates rest of yr. Crib free. TV; cable (premium). Pool. Complimentary continental bkfst. Restaurant nearby. Ck-out noon. Meeting rms. Valet serv.
Coin lndry. Exercise equipt. Health club privileges. Some refrigerators. Cr
cds: A, C, D, DS, MC, V.

D [icons] SC

Inns

★★ **MAGNOLIA INN.** *65 Magnolia Rd (28374), jct Magnolia &
Chinquapin Rds. 910/295-6900; FAX 910/215-0858; res: 800/526-5562.*
E-mail magnolia@pinehurst.net. 11 rms, 3 story. No rm phones. Mar-May,
Oct-Nov: S $85-$100; D $110-$150; family, wkly rates; lower
rates rest of yr. Crib free. TV; cable. Pool. Complimentary full bkfst. Dining
rm 11:30 am-2:30 pm, 6-9:30 pm. bar. Ck-out noon, ck-in 2 pm. Meeting
rm. Business servs avail. Golf privileges. Health club privileges. Restored,
turn-of-the-century inn; Victorian decor, antiques, veranda. Cr cds: A, C,
MC, V.

[icons]

★ **PINE CREST INN.** *Dogwood Rd (28370). 910/295-6121;
FAX 910/295-4880; res: 800/371-2545.* E-mail frontdesk@pinecrestinn
pinehurst.com; web www.pinecrestinnpinehurst.com. 40 rms, 3 story. MAP,
Mar-May & early Sept-Nov: S $85-$115; D $140-$180; under 12 free; lower
rates rest of yr. Crib free. TV; cable (premium). Dining rm 7-9 am, 7-9 pm.
Bar Wed-Sat. Ck-out noon, ck-in 2 pm. Tennis privileges. 18-hole golf priv-
ileges. Health club privileges. Golf decor and artifacts in lobby. Cr cds: A,
C, D, DS, MC, V.

[icons]

★★★★ **PINEHURST RESORT/COUNTRY CLUB.** *Carolina Vista
Dr (28374). 910/295-6811; FAX 910/295-1339; res: 800/487-4653.* Web
www.pinehurst.info@ourclub.com. Since 1895 this sprawling, genteel
property has been the belle of the South with gorgeous landscaping,

sweeping verandas and genteel service. The addition of a world class golf course early in the century and award-winning creative Southern cuisine completes the experience. 549 rms, 4 fl. Prices: S $179-$1,125. D $320-$817. Cribs. TV/cable. Concierge. Valet. Pool. Exercise room. Business center. Restaurants: Carolina Dining Room The 1895 Donald Ross Grill. Handicap. 8 golf courses. 24 tennis courts. 200 acre lake & marina. Cr cds: A, C, D, DS, MC, V.

Restaurant

★ **COVES.** *1181 Market Square (28374), across from Holly Inn.* 910/295-3400. Hrs: 11:30 am-9 pm. Res accepted. Bar 11:30 am-midnight. Semi-a la carte: lunch $3.95-$8.95, dinner $3.95-$20. Specializes in seafood, pasta, veal. Nautical decor. Cr cds: A, C, MC, V.

Raleigh (B-7)

(See also Chapel Hill, Durham)

Founded 1792 **Pop** 207,951 **Elev** 363 ft **Area Code** 919 **E-mail** visit@raleighcvb.org **Web** www.raleighcvb.org

Information Greater Raleigh Convention & Visitors Bureau, One Hannover Square, 421 Fayetteville St Mall, Ste 1505, PO Box 1879, 27602-1879; 919/834-5900 or 800/849-8499

The capital of North Carolina, Raleigh is also known as a center of education and high-technology research. It still retains the flavor of a relaxed residential town with two centuries of history. Fine residences coexist with apartment houses and modern shopping centers; rural areas with meadows and plowed fields can be found within a few miles.

Named for Sir Walter Raleigh, the town was laid out in 1792, following a resolution by the North Carolina General Assembly that an "unalterable seat of government" should be established within 10 miles of Isaac Hunter's tavern. The founders were able to find a site just four miles from the tavern. The site was laid off in a square. Lots within and just outside the city were sold as residences, which helped finance the capitol building and the governor's residence. Both structures were subsequently destroyed (the capitol by fire in 1831, the governor's residence by Union troops during the Civil War). Their replacements remain standing today. Fortunately, many of the lovely homes and gardens of the antebellum period have survived.

Like much of North Carolina, Raleigh was sprinkled with Union sympathizers until Fort Sumter was fired upon. Lincoln's call for volunteers was regarded as an insult, and North Carolina joined the Confederacy. Raleigh surrendered quietly to General Sherman in April, 1865. During Reconstruction, carpetbaggers and scalawags controlled the Assembly, voted themselves exorbitant salaries, set up a bar in the capitol and left permanent nicks in the capitol steps from the whiskey barrels rolled up for the thirsty legislators.

Located within 15 miles of Raleigh is the Research Triangle Park, a 6,800-acre research and development center with more than 50 companies. Complementing these facilities are the resources of three major universities that form the triangle region—North Carolina State University, Duke University in Durham and the University of North Carolina at Chapel Hill.

What to See and Do

Capital Area Visitor Center. Info center; brochures. Tours may be scheduled to the State Capitol, the North Carolina Executive Mansion, the State Legislative Bldg, historic sites and other attractions. (Daily; closed Jan 1, Thanksgiving, Dec 25, 26) 301 N Blount St. Phone 919/733-3456. **Free**

Falls Lake State Recreation Area. Man-made lake built as a reservoir and for flood control. Approx 38,000 acres of land and water offer swim-

ming beach, waterskiing; fishing; boating (ramps). Hiking. Picnicking (shelters), playground. Three state recreation areas in vicinity. 12 mi N via NC 50. Phone 919/676-1027. Per vehicle **¢¢**

JC Raulston Arboretum at NC State University. Eight acres of gardens featuring more than 5,000 diverse trees and shrubs from around the world. (Daily) 4301 Beryl Rd. Phone 919/515-3132. **Free**

Mordecai Historic Park. Preserved plantation home (1785 and 1826) with many original furnishings, noted for its neoclassical architecture; early Raleigh office bldg, St Mark's chapel, Badger-Iredell Law Office, 1830s herb garden. Also house in which Andrew Johnson, 17th president of the US, was born. Guided tours. (Daily exc Tues; closed hols) Mimosa St & Wake Forest Rd. Phone 919/834-4844. **¢¢**

North Carolina Museum of Art. European and American painting and sculpture; Egyptian, Greek, Roman, African and pre-Columbian objects; Judaica collection; changing exhibits. Amphitheatre. Restaurant. (Daily exc Mon; closed some hols) 2110 Blue Ridge Rd. Phone 919/839-6262. **Free**

North Carolina Museum of History. Four innovative exhibits convey the state's history. Gift shop; auditorium. (Daily exc Mon) 5 E Edenton St. Phone 919/715-0200. **Free**

Pullen Park. Scenic 72-acre park in the heart of downtown featuring 1911 carousel, train ride, paddle boats, indoor aquatic center, ball fields, tennis courts, playground and picnic shelters. (Daily) 520 Ashe Ave. Phone 919/831-6468. Admission **Free**; Rides **¢**

State Capitol (1840). A simple, stately Greek-revival style bldg. Statues of honored sons and daughters decorate the grounds. The old legislative chambers, in use until 1963, have been restored to their 1840s appearance, as have the old state library rm and the state geologist's office. (Daily; closed Jan 1, Thanksgiving, late Dec) Capitol Square. Phone 919/733-4994 or 919/733-3456. **Free**

State Legislative Building. First bldg constructed to house a state general assembly (1963); designed by Edward Durell Stone in a blend of modern and classical styles. Tours of chambers may incl view of legislators at work. (Daily; closed Jan 1, Thanksgiving, Dec 25) Corner of Salisbury & Jones Sts. Phone 919/733-7928. **Free**

State Museum of Natural Sciences. Exhibits depict natural history of state; "Freshwater Wetlands" exhibit. (Daily; closed hols) 11 W. Jones St Bicentennial Plaza (opening 4-story facility 4/2000) Phone 919/733-7450 or 877/4NATSCI Toll-Free. **Free**

William B. Umstead State Park. On 5,377 acres with a 55-acre lake. Fishing; boating. Hiking, riding. Picnicking. Camping (Mar–mid-Dec, Thurs–Sun). Nature study. **Reedy Creek Section**, 10 mi NW off I-40. Approx 1,800 acres. Fishing. Hiking, riding. Picnicking. Nature study. Crabtree Creek Section, 10 mi NW on US 70. Phone 919/571-4170 (Reedy Creek). Hrs vary. Standard fees for boat rentals and camping.

Annual Events

Artsplosure Spring Arts Festival. Moore Square and City Market. Citywide celebration of the arts. Showcase for regional dance, music, theater performances by nationally known artists; outdoor arts and crafts show; children's activities. For further info phone 919/832-8699. Mid-May.

State Fair. State Fairgrounds. 5 mi W on US 1, then 1 mi W on NC 54. For further info contact 1025 Blue Ridge Blvd, 27607; 919/733-2145 or 919/821-7400. Oct 13-22.

Motels

★ **COMFORT INN NORTH.** *2910 Capital Blvd (27604).* 919/878-9550; FAX 919/876-5457. Web www.citysearch.com/rdu.comfort innnorth. 149 rms, 2-4 story. S $54-$59; D $64-$69; each addl $5; kit. suite $89-$94; higher rates state fair. Crib free. TV; cable (premium). Pool. Complimentary continental bkfst. Restaurant nearby. Ck-out noon. Coin lndry. Meeting rms. Business servs avail. Some refrigerators. Cr cds: A, C, D, DS, ER, JCB, MC, V.

★ **COMFORT INN SOUTH.** *1602 Mechanical Blvd (27529).* 919/779-7888; FAX 919/779-4603; res: 800/638-7949; res: 800/970-5432. 60 rms, 2 story. S, D $59-$89; each addl $5; suites $89-$99; under 12 free. Crib $7. TV; cable (premium); VCR avail. Pool. Complimentary continental bkfst. Coffee in rms. Restaurant opp 11 am-10 pm. Ck-out 11 am. Meeting rms. Exercise equipt; sauna. Microwaves; refrigerators. Cr cds: A, C, D, DS, MC, V.

D ⊠ 🏃 ⊠ 🔥 SC

★★ **COURTYARD BY MARRIOTT.** *1041 Wake Towne Dr (27609).* 919/821-3400; FAX 919/821-1209; res: 800/321-2211. 153 rms, 4 story, 13 suites. S $65-$99; D $109; suites $85-$122; under 12 free; wknd rates. Crib free. TV; cable (premium). VCR avail. Pool; whirlpool. Complimentary coffee in rms. Restaurant 6:30-10 am; Sat, Sun 7 am-noon. Bar 4-11 pm. Ck-out noon. Coin lndry. Meeting rms. In-rm modem link. Valet serv. Exercise equipt. Health club privileges. Refrigerator in suites; microwaves avail. Some balconies. Cr cds: A, C, D, DS, MC, V.

D ⊠ 🏃 ⊠ 🔥 SC

★ **DAYS INN.** *3901 S Wilmington St (27603).* 919/772-8900; FAX 919/772-1536; res: 800/329-7466. 103 rms, 3 story. S, D $49-$79; each addl $5; under 12 free. Crib free. TV; cable (premium). Pool. Complimentary continental bkfst. Coffee in rms. Restaurant adj open 24 hrs. Ck-out 11 am. Business servs avail. Some refrigerators, microwaves. Cr cds: A, C, D, DS, MC, V.

D ⊠ ⊠ 🔥 SC

✓★ **FAIRFIELD INN NORTHEAST.** *2641 Appliance Ct (27604).* 919/856-9800; FAX 919/856-9800; res: 800/228-2800. Web www.fairfieldinn.com. 132 rms, 3 story. S $49-$59; D $54-$59; each addl $5; under 18 free. Crib free. TV; cable (premium). Pool. Complimentary continental bkfst. Restaurant nearby. Ck-out noon. Business servs avail. In-rm modem link. Valet serv. Cr cds: A, C, D, DS, MC, V.

D ⊠ ⊠ 🔥 SC

★★ **HAMPTON INN.** *1001 Wake Towne Dr (27609).* 919/828-1813; FAX 919/834-2672; res: 800/426-7866. Web www.hampton-inn.com. 130 rms, 5 story. S $65-$75; D $70-$80; under 18 free; wknd rates. Crib free. TV; cable (premium). Pool. Complimentary continental bkfst. Coffee in rms. Restaurant nearby. Ck-out noon. Meeting rm. Business servs avail. In-rm modem link. Valet serv. Sundries. Health club privileges. Cr cds: A, C, D, DS, MC, V.

D ⊠ ⊠ 🔥 SC

★★ **HAMPTON INN RALEIGH DURHAM AIRPORT.** *1010 Airport Blvd (18977), Approx 10 mi W on NC 54.* 919/462-1620; FAX 919/462-3217. 102 rms, 4 story. S, D $89-$99; under 18 free. Crib free. TV; cable (premium). Pool. Complimentary continental bkfst. Restaurant nearby. Ck-out noon. Business servs avail. Free airport transportation. Health club privileges. Cr cds: A, C, D, DS, MC, V.

D ⊠ ✈ ⊠ 🔥 SC

★★ **PLANTATION INN RESORT.** *6401 Capital Blvd (27616), 9 mi NE on US 1.* 919/876-1411; FAX 919/790-7093; res: 800/992-9662. 94 rms, 2 story. S, D $59-$79; suites $75-$100. Crib free. TV; cable (premium). VCR avail. Pool; wading pool, poolside serv. Playground. Complimentary continental bkfst. Restaurant 6:30-10:30 am, 11:30 am-2:30 pm, 5-11 pm. Rm serv. Ck-out noon. Meeting rms. Business servs avail. In-rm modem link. Bellhops. Airport transportation. Putting green. Health club privileges. Some refrigerators. Picnic tables. Greek-revival detailing. Cr cds: A, C, D, MC, V.

D 🐾 ⊠ ⊠ 🔥 SC

✓★ **RED ROOF INN.** *3520 Maitland Dr (27610).* 919/231-0200; FAX 919/231-0228; res: 800/843-7663. 115 rms, 3 story. S $41.99-$46.99; D $50.99; each addl $5; under 18 free. Crib $5. Pet accepted. TV; cable (premium). Complimentary coffee in lobby. Restaurant adj 6 am-10 pm. Ck-out noon. Health club privileges. Cr cds: A, C, D, DS, MC, V.

D 🐾 ⊠

✓★ **RED ROOF INN OF NORTH RALEIGH.** *3201 Wake Forest Rd (27609).* 919/878-9310; FAX 919/790-1451; res: 800/716-6406. 148 rms, 2 story. S, D $45.99-$59.99; under 18 free. Crib free. Pet accepted,

some restrictions; $25 deposit. TV; cable (premium). Pool. Complimentary continental bkfst. Restaurant adj open 24 hrs. Ck-out 11 am. Meeting rm. Picnic tables, grill. Cr cds: A, C, D, DS, MC, V.

D 🐾 ⊠ ⊠ 🔥 SC

★★ **RESIDENCE INN BY MARRIOTT.** *1000 Navaho Dr (27609).* 919/878-6100; FAX 919/876-4117; res: 800/331-3131. 144 kit. suites, 1-2 story. S, D $119-$154; wkly, monthly rates. Crib free. Pet accepted, some restrictions; $200. TV; cable (premium). Heated pool; whirlpool. Complimentary continental bkfst. Coffee in rms. Ck-out noon. Coin lndry. Meeting rm. Business servs avail. In-rm modem link. Valet serv. Health club privileges. Refrigerators, microwaves; some bathrm phones. Private patios, balconies. Picnic tables, grills. Cr cds: A, C, D, DS, JCB, MC, V.

D 🐾 ⊠ ⊠ 🔥 SC

Motor Hotels

★★ **COURTYARD BY MARRIOTT.** *2001 Hospitality Ct (27560).* 919/467-9444; FAX 919/467-9332; res: 800/321-2211. 152 rms, 4 story. S $109-$115; D $119-$125; each addl $10; suites $125-$135; under 18 free; higher rates special events. Crib free. TV; cable (premium). Complimentary coffee in rms. Restaurant 6-10 am, 5-10 pm. Rm serv. Ck-out noon. Meeting rms. Business servs avail. In-rm modem link. Valet serv. Sundries. Coin lndry. Free airport transportation. Exercise equipt. Pool; whirlpool. Refrigerator, microwave in suites. Some balconies. Cr cds: A, C, D, DS, MC, V.

D ⊠ 🏃 ✈ ⊠ 🔥 SC

★★ **CRABTREE SUMMIT HOTEL.** *3908 Arrow Dr (27612).* 919/782-6868; FAX 919/881-9340; res: 800/521-7521. 88 rms, 4 story, 7 suites. S, D $98-$150; suites $125-$150; wkend rates. Crib free. TV; cable (premium). Pool. Complimentary full bkfst. Restaurant nearby. Ck-out noon. Meeting rms. Business servs avail. In-rm modem link. Free airport, RR station, bus depot transportation. Exercise equipt. Refrigerators, wet bars. Cr cds: A, C, D, DS, ER, JCB, MC, V.

D ⊠ 🏃 ⊠ 🔥

★★ **HAMPTON INN CRABTREE.** *6209 Glenwood Ave (27612).* 919/782-1112; FAX 919/782-9119. Web www.hamptoninn.com. 141 rms, 6 story, 17 suites. S $80-$84; D $85-$89; suites $99-$149; under 18 free; wkend rates; higher rates special events. Crib free. TV; cable (premium). Complimentary continental bkfst. Restaurant adj 11 am-11 pm. Ck-out noon. Meeting rms. Business servs avail. In-rm modem link. Free airport transportation. Exercise equipt; sauna. Pool. Some in-rm whirlpools, wet bars; bathroom phone, refrigerator, microwave in suites. Some balconies. Cr cds: A, C, D, DS, MC, V.

D ⊠ 🏃 ⊠ 🔥 SC

★★ **QUALITY SUITES.** *4400 Capital Blvd (27604).* 919/876-2211; FAX 919/790-1352; res: 800/543-5497. Web www.sunbursthospitality.com. 114 suites, 3 story. S, D $69-$139; under 18 free; wkend rates. Crib free. TV; cable (premium), VCR (movies). Pool. Complimentary full bkfst. Complimentary coffee in rms. Restaurant adj 11 am-11 pm. Ck-out noon. Meeting rms. Business servs avail. In-rm modem link. Valet serv. Exercise equipt. Bathrm phones, refrigerators, microwaves, minibars. Cr cds: A, C, D, DS, ER, JCB, MC, V.

D ⊠ 🏃 ⊠ 🔥 SC

★★★ **VELVET CLOAK INN.** *1505 Hillsborough St (27605), in university area, west of downtown.* 919/828-0333; FAX 919/828-2656; res: 800/662-8829. 171 rms, 5 story. S, D $69-$117; each addl $10; suites $95-$290; under 18 free; wknd rates. Crib free. TV; cable (premium), VCR avail. Indoor/outdoor pool. Complimentary afternoon refreshments. Restaurant (see CHARTER ROOM). Rm serv. Bar 4:30 pm-midnight. Ck-out noon. Meeting rms. Business servs avail. Bellhops. Concierge. Sundries. Free airport transportation. Health club privileges. Bathrm phones; microwave in suites. Cr cds: A, C, D, DS, ER, JCB, MC, V.

D ⊠ ⊠ 🔥 SC

Hotels

★★ **BROWNESTONE HOTEL & CONFERENCE.** *1707 Hillsborough St (27605).* 919/828-0811; FAX 919/834-0904. Web www.brownstonehotel.com. 192 rms, 9 story. S, D $69-$125; each addl $10. Crib free. TV; cable (premium). Pool. Coffee in rms. Restaurant 6:30 am-2 pm; Sat, Sun 7 am-3 pm. Bar 5-11 pm; closed Sun. Ck-out 1 pm. Meeting rms. Business servs avail. Free airport transportation. Balconies. Cr cds: A, C, D, DS, MC, V.

D ≈ ⊠ 🔥 SC

★★★ **EMBASSY SUITES HOTEL.** *4700 Creedmoor Rd (27612).* 919/881-0000; FAX 919/782-7225; res: 800/362-2779. Web www.embassy-suites.com. 225 suites, 9 story. Suites $124-$184; under 12 free; wkend rates. Crib free. TV; cable (premium). Indoor pool; whirlpool. Complimentary full bkfst. Coffee im rms. Restaurant 11 am-11 pm. Bar to 1 am. Ck-out noon. Meeting rms. Business servs avail. In-rm modem link. Gift shop. Free covered parking. Airport transportation. Exercise equipt; sauna. Health club privileges. Refrigerators, microwaves. Cr cds: A, C, D, DS, JCB, MC, V.

D ≈ 🕇 ⊠ 🔥 SC

★★★ **FOUR POINTS HOTEL.** *4501 Creedmoor Rd (27612).* 919/787-7111; FAX 919/783-0024. 317 rms, 4-10 story. S $65-$130; D $95-$140; each addl $10; suites $110-$160; under 18 free; wkend rates. Crib free. TV; cable (premium), VCR avail. Indoor pool. Restaurant 6:30 am-10:30 pm; Sat, Sun from 7:30 pm. Bar 4 pm-midnight. Ck-out noon. Convention facilities. Business center. In-rm modem link. Concierge. Gift shop. Free airport transportation. Exercise equipt. Health club privileges. Luxury level. Cr cds: A, C, D, DS, JCB, MC, V.

D ≈ 🕇 ✈ ⊠ 🔥 SC 🚶

★★★ **HILTON NORTH RALEIGH.** *3415 Wake Forest Rd (27609).* 919/872-2323; FAX 919/876-0890; res: 800/445-8667. 338 units, 6 story. S $99-$160; D $109-$170; each addl $10; suites $135-$450; wkend rates. Crib free. TV; cable (premium), VCR avail. Indoor pool; whirlpool. Restaurant 6:30 am-10 pm. Bars 11-2 am; entertainment. Ck-out noon. Convention facilities. Business center. In-rm modem link. Gift shop. Free airport transportation. Exercise equipt. Luxury level. Cr cds: A, C, D, DS, ER, MC, V.

D ≈ 🕇 ⊠ 🔥 SC 🚶

★★ **HOLIDAY INN.** *320 Hillsborough St (27603).* 919/832-0501; FAX 919/833-1631; res: 800/465-4329. 202 rms, 20 story. S, D $74-$99; each addl $5; suites $139; under 18 free; wkend rates. Crib free. TV; cable (premium). Pool. Restaurant 6:30 am-2 pm, 5:30-10 pm; Sat 7 am-1 pm; Sun 6:30 am-2 pm. Bar 4 pm-2 am. Ck-out noon. Meeting rms. Business servs avail. In-rm modem link. Free garage parking. Exercise equipt. Health club privileges. Balconies. Cr cds: A, C, D, DS, MC, V.

D ≈ 🕇 ⊠ 🔥 SC

★★ **HOLIDAY INN.** *4100 Glenwood Ave (27612).* 919/782-8600; FAX 919/782-7213. 176 rms, 12 story. S, D $99-$109; under 12 free. Crib free. Pet accepted. TV; cable (premium). Pool. Restaurant 6:30 am-11 pm. Bar 4 pm-midnight. Ck-out noon. Meeting rms. Business servs avail. In-rm modem link. Airport, RR station, bus depot transportation. Exercise equipt. Health club privileges. Cr cds: A, C, D, DS, JCB, MC, V.

D 🐾 ≈ 🕇 ⊠ 🔥 SC

★★ **HOMEWOOD SUITES.** *5400 Edwards Mill Rd (27612).* 919/785-1131; FAX 919/781-3119; res: 800/225-5463. Web www.homewood-suites.com. 137 suites, 7 story. S, D $89-$169; wkends, hols (2-day min). Crib free. TV; cable (premium). Complimentary full bkfst. Complimentary coffee in rms. Restaurant adj 11 am-9 pm. Ck-out noon. Meeting rms. Business servs avail. In-rm modem link. Shopping arcade. Coin lndry. Free airport transportation. Exercise equipt. Pool. Refrigerators, microwaves. Some balconies. Cr cds: A, C, D, DS, MC, V.

D ≈ 🕇 ⊠ 🔥 SC

★★★ **MARRIOTT.** *4500 Marriott Dr (27612), on US 70W opp Crabtree Valley Mall.* 919/781-7000; FAX 919/781-3059; res: 800/228-9290. Web www.marriott.com/marriott/nc//46.htm. 375 rms, 6 story. S, D $129-$139; wkend plans. Crib free. TV; cable (premium). Indoor/outdoor pool; whirlpool, poolside serv. Restaurant 6:30 am-2 pm, 5-10 pm; Sat, Sun 7 am-2 pm, 5-11 pm. Ck-out noon. Convention facilities. Business center. In-rm modem link. Concierge. Exercise equipt. Health club privileges. Free airport transportation. Balconies. Luxury level. Cr cds: A, C, D, DS, JCB, MC, V.

D ≈ 🕇 ⊠ 🔥 SC 🚶

Inn

★★ **OAKWOOD INN BED & BREAKFAST.** *411 N Bloodworth St (27604).* 919/832-9712; FAX 919/836-9263; res: 800/267-9712. E-mail oakwoodbb@aol.com; web members.aol.com/oakwood.bb/. 6 rms, 2 story. S $75-$120; D $85-$130. TV, cable. Complimentary full bkfst; afternoon refreshments. Ck-out 11:30 am, ck-in 3 pm. Meeting rm. In-rm modem link. Fireplaces. Historic district; built 1871. Cr cds: A, C, D, DS, MC, V.

⊠ 🔥 SC

Restaurants

★★ **42 STREET OYSTER BAR & SEAFOOD.** *508 W Jones St (27603).* 919/831-2811. Hrs: 11:30 am-11 pm; Sat from 5 pm; Sun 5-10 pm. Closed Jan 1, Thanksgiving, Dec 24 & 25. Res accepted. Bar. Semi-a la carte: lunch $5.95-$10.95, dinner $10.95-$49.95. Child's meals. Specializes in fresh fish, beef, chicken. Rhythm & blues, jazz bands Thurs-Sat. Oyster bar. Nautical decor. Cr cds: A, C, D, MC, V.

D ⊠

★★★ **ANGUS BARN LTD.** *9401 Glenwood Ave (27612), 12½ mi NW on US 70.* 919/787-3505. E-mail angusbarn@aol.com; web www.angusbarn.com. Hrs: 5-11 pm; Sun to 10 pm. Closed Jan 1, Thanksgiving, Dec 24, 25. Res accepted Sun-Fri. Bar 4 pm-midnight. Wine list. Semi-a la carte: dinner $14.95-$47.95. Child's meals. Specializes in prime rib, charcoal-broiled steak, seafood. Own baking. Valet parking. Farm decor; fireplaces; Colt revolver display. Family-owned. Cr cds: A, C, D, DS, MC, V.

D ⊠

✓★★ **CASA CARBONE RISTORANTE.** *6019-a Glenwood Ave (27612).* 919/781-8750. Hrs: 5-10 pm; Sun from 4 pm. Closed Mon; also major hols. Italian menu. Serv bar. Semi-a la carte: dinner $7-$15. Child's meals. Specializes in veal, pasta. Own desserts. Mediterranean decor. Cr cds: A, C, D, DS, MC, V.

D SC ⊠

★★★ **CHARTER ROOM.** *(See Velvet Cloak Inn Motor Hotel)* 919/828-0333. Hrs: 6:30 am-10 pm; Sat, Sun from 7:30 am; Sun brunch 11:30 am-2 pm. Res accepted. Contemporary Amer menu. Bar 4:30 pm-midnight. Wine list. Semi-a la carte: bkfst $2-$10, lunch $6.95-$13.95, dinner $7.95-$27.95. Sun brunch $12.95. Specializes in chicken, steak, seafood. Child's meals. Valet parking. Cr cds: A, C, D, DS, ER, JCB, MC, V.

D

✓★ **COURTNEY'S.** *407 E Six Forks Rd (27609).* 919/834-3613. Hrs: 7 am-2:30 pm. Closed Thanksgiving, Dec 25. Semi-a la carte: bkst, lunch $5.50-$6.95. Child's meals. Specializes in omelettes. Cr cds: C, MC, V.

D ⊠

✓★★ **IRREGARDLESS CAFE.** *901 W Morgan (27603).* 919/833-9920. Web www.citysearch.com. Hrs: 11:30 am-2:30 pm, 5:30-9:30 pm; Fri to 10 pm; Sat 5:30-10 pm; Sun brunch 10 am-2:30 pm. Bar. Semi-a la carte: lunch $4-$8, dinner $8-$16. Sun brunch $7.95-$9.75. Specializes in chicken, seafood, vegetarian dishes. Jazz, folk, classical musician. Totally nonsmoking. Cr cds: A, C, DS, MC, V.

D

★ **JEAN CLAUDE'S CAFE.** 6112 Falls Of Neuse Rd (27609), in North Ridge Shopping Center. 919/872-6224. E-mail larryfree man@worldnet.att.net; web www.jeanclaudes.com. Hrs: 11 am-2 pm, 5:30-9 pm; Fri, Sat to 9:30 pm. Closed Sun; some major hols. French, Amer menu. Wine, beer. Semi-a la carte: lunch $4.95-$8.99, dinner $8-$24. Child's meals. Specialties: beef tenderloin, salmon in puff pastry, rack of lamb. Two dining rms with French decor. Totally nonsmoking. Cr cds: A, C, D, DS, MC, V.

D

✓ ★ **LAS MARGARITAS.** 231 Timber Dr (27529), 20 mi E on US 70, in Timber Crossing Shopping Center. 919/662-1030. Hrs: 11 am-2:30 pm, 5-10 pm; Fri 11 am-11 pm; Sat noon-11 pm; Sun noon-10 pm. Closed major hols. Res accepted. Mexican menu. Bar. Semi-a la carte: lunch $3.75-$5.95, dinner $6.10-$9.25. Child's meals. Specializes in fajitas, seafood, margaritas. Parking. Contemporary atmosphere. Cr cds: A, C, D, DS, MC, V.

D

✓ ★ ★ **PEKING GARDEN.** 126 Millbrook Rd (27609), in Colony Shopping Ctr. 919/848-4663. Hrs: 11:30 am-2:30 pm, 5-10 pm. Chinese menu. Bar. A la carte entrees: lunch $4.95-$10, dinner $7.95-$20. Specializes in Chinese cuisine. Modern decor with Chinese accents. Cr cds: A, C, DS, MC, V.

D

★ ★ ★ **SIMPSON'S.** 5625 Creedmoor Rd (27612), in Creedmore Crossing Shopping Center. 919/783-8818. Web www.citysearch.com/rdu/simpsonsbeef.com. Hrs: 5-10 pm; Fri, Sat to 11 pm. Closed Sun; most major hols. Res accepted. Bar. Semi-a la carte: dinner $9.95-$45.95. Child's meals. Specializes in grilled fish, steak, prime rib. Pianist wkdays, jazz wkends. Formal dining in spacious surroundings. Cr cds: A, C, D, DS, MC, V.

D

★ ★ **VINNIE'S STEAKHOUSE & TAVERN.** 7440 Six Forks Rd (27615). 919/847-7319. Web www.vinnies.com. Hrs: 5 pm-midnight. Closed some major hols. Bar. A la carte entrees: dinner $15-$55. Specializes in steak, seafood. Club decor. Cr cds: A, C, D, MC, V.

D

★ ★ **WINSTON'S GRILLE.** 6401 Falls of Neuse Rd (27615), in Sutton Square Shopping Center. 919/790-0700. Hrs: 11 am-10 pm; Fri, Sat to 11 pm; Sun brunch to 3 pm. Closed some major hols. Res accepted. Bar. A la carte entrees: lunch $4.95-$9.95, dinner $9.95-$22.95. Sun brunch $4.95-$10.95. Child's meals. Specializes in beef, seafood, pasta. Outdoor dining. Cr cds: A, C, D, DS, MC, V.

D

Roanoke Rapids (A-8)

Pop 15,722 **Elev** 170 ft **Area Code** 252 **Zip** 27870 **E-mail** hctlr@coastal net.com **Web** www.visithalifax.com

Information Halifax County Tourism Development Authority, PO Box 144; 252/535-1687 or 800/522-4282

What to See and Do

Historic Halifax State Historic Site. The Halifax Resolves, first formal sanction of American independence, were adopted here Apr 12, 1776. Bldgs incl Owens House (1760), Burgess Law Office, Eagle Tavern (1790), Sally-Billy House, clerk's office, jail, Montfort Archaeology Exhibit Center. Other features are Magazine Spring, garden and churchyard. Visitor center; audiovisual programs, exhibits. (Apr–Oct, daily; rest of yr, daily exc Mon; closed some hols) Historical dramas presented in summer (fee). 9 mi SE off US 301 or S on I-95 exit 168. Phone 252/583-7191. **Free**

Lake Gaston. A 34-mi-long, 20,300-acre lake has fishing, boating (ramps); picnicking. 10 mi W via US 158 and NC 1214.

Roanoke Rapids Lake. Covers 5,000 acres. Launching facilities. NW edge of town.

Motels

✓ ★ **COMFORT INN.** I-95 N & Rte 46 (27870), At I-95 exit 176. 252/537-1011; FAX 252/537-9258; res: 800/832-8375. 100 rms, 2 story. S, D $48-$60; each addl $5; under 18 free. Crib free. TV; cable (premium). Pool. Complimentary continental bkfst. Restaurant 6:30 am-9 pm. Ck-out 11 am. Business servs avail. Gift shop. Cr cds: A, C, D, DS, MC, V.

D SC

★ ★ **HAMPTON INN.** 1914 Weldon Rd (27870), I-95 exit 173. 252/537-7555; FAX 252/537-9852; res: 800/426-7866. 124 rms, 2 story. S $58-$70; D $65-$75; under 18 free. Crib free. TV; cable (premium). Pool. Complimentary continental bkfst. Coffee in rms. Restaurant adj 6 am-10 pm. Ck-out noon. Meeting rms. Business servs avail. In-rm modem link. Health club privileges. Picnic tables, grills. Cr cds: A, C, D, DS, MC, V.

D SC

Robbinsville (B-1)

(See also Bryson City, Fontana Dam)

Pop 709 **Elev** 2,064 ft **Area Code** 828 **Zip** 28771

A Ranger District office of the Nantahala National Forest (see FRANKLIN) is located here.

What to See and Do

Joyce Kilmer-Slickrock Wilderness. A 17,013-acre area within Nantahala National Forest (see FRANKLIN). More than 100 species of trees native to region; trails through forest to view prime specimens. Located within the area is the Joyce Kilmer Memorial Forest, a 3,840-acre stand of virgin timber dedicated to the author of the poem "Trees"; and a National Recreation Trail. 13 mi NW via US 129, SR 1116 & 1127. Inquire at District Ranger Office (mid-Apr–Oct, wkends & hols), N off US 129; phone 828/479-6431. **Free**

Motel

★ **TAPOCO LODGE.** Route 72 Box A-1 (28771), 15 mi N on US 129. 828/498-2435; res: 800/822-5083. Web www.tapocolodge.com. 24 rms, 3 story. AP: S $80; D $124; each addl $40; under 3 free. Closed Dec-Mar. Crib free. TV in main rm; cable. Coffee in rms. Restaurant 8 am-8 pm. Ck-out 10 am. Meeting rms. Gift shop. Lighted tennis. Playground. Game rm. Rec rm. Cr cds: A, C, DS, MC, V.

Lodge

★ ★ **SNOWBIRD MOUNTAIN LODGE.** 275 Santeetlah Rd (28771), 12 mi NW, off US 129. 828/479-3433; FAX 828/479-3473; res: 800/941-9290. E-mail snbdmtnldg@aol.com; web www.snowbirdlodge.com. 22 rms, 2 story. No A/C. No rm phones. Mid-Apr-early Nov: D $125-$200. Closed rest of yr. Children over 12 yrs only. Dining rm (by res only) 8-9:30 am, 6-8 pm. Setups. Ck-out 10 am, ck-in 1 pm. Hiking trails. Lawn games. 100 acres atop mountain; stone lodge with great room; adj to Joyce Kilmer Memorial Forest. Cr cds: C, MC, V.

D

Rocky Mount (A-8)

(See also Wilson)

Settled 1840 **Pop** 48,997 **Elev** 120 ft **Area Code** 252
Information Chamber of Commerce, 2501 Sunset Ave, PO Box 392, 27802; 252/442-5111

This is one of the country's largest bright-leaf tobacco marts. Cotton products in the form of yarn, bolts of fabric and ready-to-wear clothing flow from the mills. The factories produce fertilizer, furniture, chemicals, metal products, lumber and pharmaceuticals. Rocky Mount is also the home of Hardee's Food Systems.

What to See and Do

Children's Museum. Incl touch tank, greenhouse; live animal collection, exhibits. (Daily; closed Thanksgiving, Dec 25) 1610 Gay St, Sunset Park, off US 64, 301 Bypass. Phone 252/972-1167 or 252/972-1168. ¢

Seasonal Event

Tobacco auctions. Numerous warehouses. Inquire locally. Aug–mid-Nov.

Motels

★ **CARLETON HOUSE INN.** *215 N Church St (27804). 252/977-0410; FAX 252/985-2115.* 42 rms, 2 story. S $42-$49; D $49-$56; suites $75; under 16 free. Crib free. TV; cable (premium). Pool. Coffee in rms. Restaurant 6:30 am-9 pm; Sat 7 am-noon, 5-10 pm; Sun 7:30-10:30 am, 11:30 am-2 pm, 5-8 pm. Ck-out noon. Meeting rm. Business servs avail. Sundries. Health club privileges. Cr cds: A, C, MC, V.

⊟ ⇲ 🐾 SC

✓★ **FAIRFIELD INN BY MARRIOTT.** *1200 Benvenue Rd (27804). 252/972-9400; FAX 252/972-9400; res: 800/228-2800.* Web www.fairfieldinn.com. 104 rms, 3 story. D $55.95-$62.95; under 18 free. Crib free. TV; cable (premium). Pool. Complimentary continental bkfst. Ck-out noon. Business servs avail. In-rm modem link. Cr cds: A, C, D, DS, MC, V.

D ⊟ ⇲ 🐾 SC

★★ **HAMPTON INN.** *530 N Winstead Ave (27804). 252/937-6333; FAX 252/937-4333; res: 800/426-7866.* Web www.hamptoninn.com. 124 rms, 4 story. S, D $62-$70; suites $89; under 18 free. Crib free. TV; cable (premium). Pool. Complimentary continental bkfst. Restaurant opp 6 am-9 pm. Ck-out noon. Meeting rms. Business servs avail. Health club privileges. Volleyball. Basketball. Cr cds: A, C, D, DS, MC, V.

D ⊟ ⇲ 🐾 SC

Motor Hotels

★★ **HOLIDAY INN.** *651 Winstead Ave (27804), 1 mi E of I-95, exit 138. 252/937-6888; FAX 252/937-4788; res: 800/465-4329; res: 888/543-2255.* Web www.gateway.com. 171 rms, 4 story. S, D $75-$90; each addl $6; suites $99-$125; under 12 free. Crib free. TV; cable (premium). Pool. Restaurant 6:30-11 am, 11:30 am-10 pm. Rm serv. Bar. Ck-out noon. Meeting rms. Business servs avail. Bellhops. Exercise equipt. Refrigerator in suites. Cr cds: A, C, D, DS, ER, JCB, MC, V.

D ⇲ 🏃 ⇲ 🐾 SC

★★ **HOLIDAY INN DORTCHES** *I-95; 5350 Dortches Blvd (27804). 252/937-6300; FAX 252/937-6312; res: 800/465-4329; res: 888/937-4938.* 154 rms, 2 story. S, D $61.95-$67.95; under 18 free. Crib free. TV; cable (premium). Pool. Complimentary coffee in rms. Restaurant

6 am-2 pm, 4:30-10 pm. Ck-out noon. Meeting rms. Business servs avail. Coin lndry. Health club privileges. Some refrigerators. Cr cds: A, C, D, DS, MC, V.

D ⇲ ⇲ 🐾 SC

Salisbury (B-5)

(See also Concord, Lexington, Statesville)

Founded 1753 **Pop** 23,087 **Elev** 746 ft **Area Code** 704 **Zip** 28144
E-mail visitorinfo@co.rowan.nc.us **Web** www.visitsalisburync.com.
Information Rowan County Convention & Visitors Bureau, PO Box 4044, 28145; 704/638-3100 or 800/332-2343. Visit the Visitor Information Center at 132 E Innes for brochures, maps and audio tape tours

A trading, cultural and judicial center since 1753, it is here that Daniel Boone spent his youth and Andrew Jackson studied law. Salisbury's wide, shady streets were twice taken over by military troops. The first time was by Lord Cornwallis during the Revolutionary War, and the Civil War brought General Stoneman. During the Civil War, Salisbury was the site of a Confederate prison for Union soldiers where 5,000 died; they are buried here in the National Cemetery. Among the dead was Robert Livingstone, Union soldier and son of African missionary David Livingstone. Livingstone College was named for the father. Catawba College and Rowan-Cabarrus Community College complete Salisbury's triad of higher learning.

What to See and Do

Dan Nicholas Park. This 330-acre park has lake with fishing; paddleboats (fee). Hiking, nature trail; tennis, miniature golf (fee). Picnicking. Camping hookups (fee). Outdoor theater; two nature museums; petting zoo; carousel; miniature train ride. Park (all yr). 2 mi N on I-85, to exit 79, then 6 mi SE. Phone 704/636-0154 or 704/636-2089.   **Free**

Dr. Josephus Hall House (1820). Large antebellum house set amid giant oaks and century-old boxwoods; contains most of its original Federal and Victorian furnishings. House was used as Union commander's headquarters following Civil War. (Sat & Sun afternoons) 226 S Jackson. Phone 704/636-0103 or -1502.   ¢¢

N.C. Transportation Museum. Once the steam locomotive repair facility for Southern Railway, now a transportation museum, railroad yards and shops. Back shop and 37-stall Bob Julian Roundhouse (1924). Rolling stock incl 6 engines (steam and diesel); restored luxury private cars; freight cars, trolley, passenger coaches. Train ride (seasonal; fee). Visitor Center, 2 exhibit bldgs, audiovisual show. (Apr–Oct, daily; rest of yr, daily exc Mon; closed Jan 1, Thanksgiving, Dec 24–25) 2 mi NE via I-85, in Spencer. Phone 704/636-2889.   **Free**

Old Stone House (1766). Built of hand-laid granite with walls 2-ft thick. Restored (1966); authentically furnished; family burial ground opp. (Apr–Nov, Sat & Sun afternoons) 4 mi SE, off US 52 in Granite Quarry. Phone 704/633-5946.   ¢¢

Poets & Dreamers Garden. Formal, Biblical and Shakespearean gardens; fountain, sundial. Tomb of founder Joseph Charles Price in garden. On campus of Livingstone College.

Utzman-Chambers House. In Federal Town House Museum (1819). Period rms, authentic regional furniture; 19th-century garden. (Thurs–Sun, afternoons; closed legal hols, Dec 24) 116 S Jackson St. Phone 704/633-5946.   ¢¢

Waterworks Visual Arts Center. Adaptive restoration of former Salisbury Waterworks into arts center. Changing exhibits; studios, classes; courtyard; sensory garden. Guided tours. (Daily; closed legal hols). 1 Water St. Phone 704/636-1882.   **Free**

Motels

★★ **HAMPTON INN.** *1001 Klumack Rd (28147), I-85 exit 75. 704/637-8000; FAX 704/639-9995; res: 800/426-7866.* 121 rms, 4 story. S

$59; D $64; suites $95; under 18 free; higher rates: Furniture Market, auto racing events. Crib free. Pet accepted, some restrictions. TV; cable (premium). Pool. Complimentary continental bkfst. Restaurant adj 11 am-11 pm. Ck-out noon. Meeting rms. Business servs avail. Health club privileges. Refrigerator in suites. Cr cds: A, C, D, DS, MC, V.

D ⬛ ⬛ ⬛ ⬛ SC

★★★ **HOLIDAY INN.** *530 Jake Alexander Blvd (28145), I-85 exit 75. 704/638-0311; FAX 704/637-9152; res: 800/465-4329.* E-mail slbnc@aol.com. 181 rms, 3 story. S $63-$88; D $67-$90; each addl $6; suites $95-$125; under 18 free; higher rates special events. Crib free. TV; cable (premium). Indoor/outdoor pool. Restaurant 7 am-2 pm, 6-9 pm. Rm serv. Bar 5 pm-1 am; Sat from 6 pm; entertainment Fri, Sat. Ck-out noon. Business servs avail. Bellhops. Valet serv. Exercise equipt. Refrigerator avail in suites. Cr cds: A, C, D, DS, JCB, MC, V.

D ⬛ ⬛ ⬛ ⬛ SC

Sanford (B-6)

Pop 14,475 **Elev** 375 ft **Area Code** 919 **Zip** 27330

What to See and Do

House in the Horseshoe State Historic Site. House (ca 1770) was the residence of North Carolina Governor Benjamin Williams; site of a Revolutionary War skirmish. (Apr–Oct, daily; rest of yr, daily exc Mon; closed some major hols) 12 mi W on NC 42 to Carbonton, then 5 mi S on SR 1644. Phone 910/947-2051. **Free**

Raven Rock State Park. A 2,990-acre park characterized by 152-ft outcrop of rock jutting over Cape Fear River. Fishing. Nature trails, interpretive programs. Picnicking. Primitive camping. Standard hrs, fees. 18 mi S on US 421. Phone 910/893-4888.

Motels

✓★★ **COMFORT INN.** *1403 N Horner Blvd (27330). 919/774-6411; FAX 919/774-7018; res: 800/424-6423.* 122 rms, 2 story. S $50-$56; D $54-$60; suites $85-$105; under 18 free. Crib free. TV; cable (premium). Pool. Complimentary full bkfst. Restaurant nearby. Meeting rms. Coin lndry. Exercise equipt; sauna. Some refrigerators. Cr cds: A, C, D, DS, MC, V.

D ⬛ ⬛ ⬛ ⬛ SC

✓★ **PALOMINO MOTEL.** *1508 Westover Dr (27331), 2½ mi on US 1, US 15/501 Bypass. 919/776-7531; FAX 919/776-9670; res: 800/641-6060.* 92 rms. S $34-$42; D $44-$48; each addl $2; suites $108. Crib $5. Pet accepted. TV; cable (premium). Pool; whirlpool. Playground. Restaurant 6 am-9 pm. Bar 4-11 pm. Ck-out noon. Meeting rms. Golf privileges. Exercise equipt; sauna. Picnic tables, grill. Cr cds: A, C, D, DS, MC, V.

D ⬛ ⬛ ⬛ ⬛ ⬛ ⬛ ⬛ SC

Shelby (B-4)

(See also Gastonia)

Pop 14,669 **Elev** 853 ft **Area Code** 704 **E-mail** edc@countynt2.co.cleveland.nc.us **Web** www.co.cleveland.nc.us

Information Cleveland County Economic Development, 311 E Marion St, PO Box 1210, 28151; 704/484-4999 or 800/480-8687

Seat of Cleveland County, this town in the Piedmont boasts of diversified industry and agriculture. It is named for Colonel Isaac Shelby, hero of the Battle of Kings Mountain in the Revolutionary War. (See KINGS MOUN-

TAIN NATIONAL MILITARY PARK, SC.) The town celebrates its heritage and culture with special events, fairs and historic preservation.

What to See and Do

Central Shelby Historic District Walking Tour. 2-hr self-guided tour encompasses much of original area established in 1841. Features 38 architecturally significant structures ca 1850s. For info phone 704/481-1842.

Motel

★★ **DAYS INN.** *1431 W Dixon Blvd (28152). 704/482-6721; FAX 704/480-1423; res: 800/892-3845.* 97 rms, 2 story. S $50; D $54; each addl $5; under 12 free. Crib free. TV; cable (premium). Pool. Complimentary continental bkfst. Restaurant 11 am-2 pm, 5-9 pm. Rm serv. Ck-out noon. Meeting rms. Cr cds: A, C, D, DS, MC, V.

D ⬛ ⬛ ⬛ SC

Inn

★★★ **INN AT WEBBLEY.** *403 S Washington St (28151). 704/481-1403; FAX 704/487-0619; res: 800/852-2346.* E-mail omgiii@bell south.net. 8 rms, 3 story. S, D $195-$250; children over 12 yrs only. TV; cable (premium). Complimentary full bkfst. Dining rm (guest only) 6-10 pm. Ck-out noon, ck-in 3 pm. Business center. In-rm modem link. Exercise equipt. Golf privileges. Grand piano in library. Colonial-revival house built in 1852; antiques. Landscaped grounds with gardens. Cr cds: C, DS, MC, V.

⬛ ⬛ ⬛ ⬛ ⬛

Smithfield (B-7)

(See also Dunn, Goldsboro, Raleigh)

Pop 7,540 **Elev** 153 ft **Area Code** 919 **Zip** 27577

Motels

★ **COMFORT INN.** *1705 Industrial Park Dr (27576), approx 5 mi N on US 301. 919/965-5200; FAX 919/965-5200; res: 800/638-7949; res: 800/228-5150.* Web www.comfortinn.com. 80 rms, 2 story. S $51-$85, D $55-$85; each addl $5, suites $85; under 15 free. Crib $5. TV; cable (premium), VCR avail. Pool; whirlpool. Complimentary continental bkfst. Restaurant nearby. Ck-out 11 am. Business servs avail. Exercise equipt. Some refrigerators, microwaves. Cr cds: A, C, D, DS, MC, V.

D ⬛ ⬛ ⬛ ⬛ SC

✓★ **MASTERS ECONOMY INN.** *318 US Hwy 70E (33316). 919/965-3771; FAX 919/965-5565; res: 800/633-3434.* Web www.masters-inns.com. 119 rms, 2 story. S $31.95, D $35.95; each addl $4; under 18 free. Crib $6. TV; cable (premium). Pool. Ck-out noon. Meeting rms. Business servs avail. Cr cds: A, C, D, DS, MC, V.

D ⬛ ⬛ ⬛ ⬛ SC

South Brunswick Islands (D-7)

(See also Southport; also see Myrtle Beach, SC)

E-mail sbicc1@nccoast.net **Web** www.weblync.com/sbi_chamber

Information Chamber of Commerce, PO Box 1380, Shallotte 28459; 910/754-6644 or 800/426-6644

The South Brunswick Islands offer wide, gently sloping beaches and beautiful scenery. Located just 50 miles from the Gulf Stream, the region has a subtropical climate and mild temperatures. Resort activities are plentiful and include fishing, swimming, tennis and golf. Shallotte is the hub of the area that includes Holden, Ocean Isle and Sunset beaches. The islands are reached by bridges across the Intracoastal Waterway.

Annual Events

A Day at the Docks. Holden Beach. Blessing of the fleet, arts & crafts, bobble race. Late Mar.

King Classic King Mackerel Tournament. Holden Beach. Early Sept.

North Carolina Oyster Festival. In Shallotte. Arts and crafts, music, sports, oyster-shucking contest. 3rd wkend Oct.

Motor Hotel

★★ **CLARION INN - THE WINDS OCEANFRONT.** *310 E 1st St (28469), 1½ mi N of jct NC 904 & E First St. 910/579-6275; FAX 910/579-2884; res: 800/334-3581.* E-mail info@thewinds.com; web www.thewinds.com. 72 units, 4 story, 45 suites, 58 kit. units, 6 houses (1-4 bedrm). No elvtr. Early June-late Aug: S, D $114-$207; each addl $15; suites, kits. $164-$412; houses $481-$544; under 18 free; lower rates rest of yr. Crib $5. TV; cable. Pool; whirlpool, poolside serv. Complimentary bkfst buffet. Complimentary coffee in rms. Ck-out 11 am. Coin lndry. Meeting rms. Business servs avail. In-rm modem link. Tennis privileges. 18-hole golf privileges, pro, putting green, driving range. Exercise equipt. Rec rm. Lawn games. Bicycle rental. Refrigerators, wet bars. Balconies. Picnic tables, grills. On beach. Cr cds: A, C, D, DS, ER, JCB, MC, V.

Southern Pines (B-6)

(See also Pinehurst)

Pop 9,129 **Elev** 512 ft **Area Code** 910 **Zip** 28387 **E-mail** cvb4golf@mindspring.com **Web** www.homeofgolf.com

Information Convention & Visitors Bureau, PO Box 2270, 28388; 910/692-3330 or 800/346-5362

The Sandhills, among fine longleaf and loblolly pines, are famed for golf and horses. Known as "sand country," it first gained popularity as a resort in the 1880s, but the enthusiasm for golf in the 1920s fueled Southern Pines' growth as a recreational and resort area. The area is still steeped in tradition and history, with golf and equestrian activities as popular as ever.

What to See and Do

Shaw House. Antebellum house of simple and sturdy style is lightened by unusual mantels of carved cypress. Guided tours (mid-Jan–June & Sept–mid-Dec, Fri & Sat afternoons). Also on premises are Britt Sanders Cabin and Garner House. SW Broad St and Morganton Rd. Phone 910/692-2051. ¢

Weymouth Woods-Sandhills Nature Preserve. Excellent examples of Sandhills ecology. Hiking trails along pine-covered "sandridges." Natural history museum. (Daily; closed Dec 25) 3 mi SE on Indiana Ave, then N on Ft Bragg Rd. Phone 910/692-2167. **Free**

Annual Event

House and Garden Tour. Conducted by Southern Pines Garden Club. Mid-Apr.

Motels

★★ **HAMPTON INN.** *1675 US Hwy 1 S (28387). 910/692-9266; FAX 910/692-9298; res: 800/333-9266.* 126 rms, 2 story. Mar-May, Sept-Nov: S, D $64-$89; under 18 free; golf plan; higher rates: wkends, special events; lower rates rest of yr. Crib free. TV; cable (premium), VCR avail. Pool. Complimentary continental bkfst. Coffee in rms. Restaurant nearby. Ck-out noon. Coin lndry. Meeting rm. Business servs avail. Valet serv. Golf privileges. Health club privileges. Cr cds: A, C, D, DS, MC, V.

★★★ **HOLIDAY INN.** *US Hwy 1 (28387), at Morganton Rd. 910/692-8585; FAX 910/692-5213; res: 800/465-4329.* E-mail holiday@pinehurst.net; web www.pinehurst.net/~holiday. 158 rms, 2 story. Mar-Oct: S $69-$89; D $79-$99; each addl $10; suites $140-$175; studio rms $69-$79; under 18 free; lower rates rest of yr. Crib free. TV; cable (premium). Pool. Restaurant 6:30 am-9:30 pm. Rm serv. Bar 4 pm-midnight. Ck-out noon. Meeting rms. Business center. In-rm modem link. Valet serv. Tennis. Golf privileges. Exercise equipt. Health club privileges. Game rm. Cr cds: A, C, D, DS, ER, JCB, MC, V.

Resorts

★★★ **MID PINES INN & GOLF CLUB.** *1010 Midland Rd (28387). 910/692-2114; FAX 910/692-4615.* E-mail midpines@golfnc.com; web www.golfnc.com/midpines. 112 rms in 3-story hotel, 6 golf villas, 10 lakeside villas. Mar-May, Sept-Nov: S, D $140-$210; each addl $10; under 12 free; golf, tennis plans; lower rates rest of yr. TV; cable, VCR avail. Pool. Coffee in rms. Dining rm (public by res) 6:30-9 am, noon-2:30 pm, 6:30-8:30 pm. Box lunches; snack bar. Rm serv in hotel. Bar 11 am-11 pm. Ck-out 11 am, ck-in 2 pm. Meeting rms. Business center. Airport transportation. Lighted tennis. 18-hole golf, greens fee $70-$140, pro lessons, putting green. Health club privileges. Lawn games. Rec rm. Minibars; some refrigerators. Cr cds: A, C, D, DS, MC, V.

★★★ **PINE NEEDLES LODGES/COUNTRY CLUB.** *1005 Midland Rd (28387), On NC 2, 1 mi W of jct US 1. 910/692-7111; FAX 910/692-5349; res: 800/747-7272.* Web www.golfnc.com/pineneedles. 71 rms in 10 lodges, 2 story, mid-Mar-mid-June & mid-Sept-mid-Nov: S, D $135-$230/person; under 4 free; golf plans; lower rates rest of yr. Crib free. TV; cable (premium). Heated pool; poolside serv. Complimentary coffee in rms. Dining rm 7-9 am, 11:30 am-2:30 pm, 7-8:30 pm. Box lunches. Snack bar. Picnics. Rm serv. Bar noon-11 pm. Ck-out 11 am, ck-in 2 pm. Meeting rms. Business servs avail. In-rm modem link. Bellhops. Valet serv. Lighted grass tennis. 18-hole golf, greens fee $70-$100, pro, putting green, driving range. Health club privileges. Bicycles (rentals). Lawn games. Rec rm. Game rm. Some refrigerators. Balconies. Family-owned golf resort with course designed in 1927 by renowned golf course architect Donald Ross. Cr cds: A, C, MC, V.

Restaurants

★★ **LA TERRACE.** *270 SW Broad St (28387). 910/692-5622.* Hrs: 11:30 am-2 pm, 6-10 pm. Closed Sun; Jan 1, Dec 25. Res accepted. Continental menu. Serv bar. A la carte entrees: lunch $7.25-$9.75, dinner $13.50-$25.95. Specializes in seafood, lamb, Angus beef. Outdoor dining. Intimate dining in formal atmosphere. Cr cds: C, MC, V.

★ **SQUIRE'S PUB.** *1720 US Highway 1 S (28387). 910/695-1161.* Hrs: 11 am-10 pm; Fri, Sat to 11 pm. Closed Sun; Thanksgiving, Dec 24 & 25. British menu. Bar. Semi-a la carte: lunch $4.95-$10.95, dinner $4.95-$15.95. Child's meals. Specialties: fish and chips, shepherd's pie, Welsh rabbit. 5 dining areas. English decor. Cr cds: C, DS, MC, V.

✓★ **VITO'S RISTORANTE & PIZZERIA.** *311 SE Broad St (28387), off US 1.* 910/692-7815. Hrs: 5-9:30 pm; Fri, Sat to 10 pm; Sun to 9 pm. Closed Mon; major hols. Italian menu. Semi-a la carte: dinner $5-$15. Child's meals. Specializes in veal, chicken. Italian decor. Cr cds: C.

D ⊒ ♥

Southport (D-8)

(See also South Brunswick Islands, Wilmington)

Founded 1792 **Pop** 2,369 **Elev** 22 ft **Area Code** 910 **Zip** 28461
E-mail chamber@southport.net **Web** www.southport.net/chamber.html
Information Southport-Oak Island Area Chamber of Commerce, 4841 Long Beach Rd SE; 910/457-6964 or 800/457-6964

Saltwater and freshwater fishing are very good in the vicinity of Cape Fear. Deep-sea charter boats are available at Southport, Long Beach and Shallotte Point. There is a good yacht harbor facility for small boats and yachts, a municipal pier, three ocean piers, as well as several beaches and golf courses nearby.

Fort Johnston (1764) was the first fort built in North Carolina. With Fort Fisher and Fort Caswell (1825), it guarded the mouth of the Cape Fear River during the Civil War, making it possible for blockade runners to reach Wilmington. Fort Johnston (restored) is the residence of the Commanding Officer of the Sunny Point Military Ocean Terminal.

What to See and Do

Brunswick Town-Fort Anderson State Historic Site. Brunswick, founded in 1726, thrived as a major port exporting tar and lumber. Fearing a British attack, its citizens fled when the Revolution began; in 1776 the town was burned by British sailors. Twenty-three foundations have been excavated. Built across part of the town are the Civil War earthworks of Ft Anderson, which held out for 30 days after the fall of Ft Fisher in 1865. Visitor Center, exhibits, audiovisual show; marked historical trailside exhibits; nature trail, picnic area. (Apr–Oct, daily; rest of yr, daily exc Mon; closed some major hols) 14 mi N on NC 133, then 5 mi S on Plantation Rd. Phone 910/371-6613. **Free**

Carolina Power & Light Company Visitors Center. Audiovisual presentations show history of energy & its use; nuclear reactor model. Picnic area. (Tues-Thurs) 2 mi N on NC 87. Phone 910/457-6041. **Free**

Ferry Service. Southport to Fort Fisher. Approx 30-min crossing. For schedule and fee info phone 910/457-6942 (local service) or 800/293-3779 (NC Dept of Transportation).

Fort Fisher State Historic Site. The largest earthworks fort in the Confederacy; until the last few months of the Civil War, it kept Wilmington open to blockade runners. Some of the heaviest naval bombardment of land fortifications took place here on Dec 24–25, 1864 and Jan 13–15, 1865. Tours. Visitor Center has exhibits, audiovisual shows. Reconstructed gun emplacement. Picnic area. (Apr–Oct, daily; rest of yr, daily exc Mon; closed some major hols) 6 mi E via US 421, ferry. Phone 910/458-5538. **Free**

Long Beach Scenic Walkway. Crosses several important wetland communities; viewing of maritime forests, wetland birds, marsh animals and seacoast fowl. E at 20th St SE and 19th Place, across Davis Canal in Long Beach. Phone 910/278-5518.

Maritime Museum. Houses memorabilia pertaining to the history of the lower Cape Fear area. (Tues-Sat; closed some hols) 116 N Howe St. Phone 910/457-0003. ¢

Annual Events

Robert Ruark Chili Cook Off. Easter wknd.

US Open King Mackerel Tournament. 1st wknd Oct.

Inns

★★ **LOIS JANE'S RIVERVIEW INN.** *106 W Bay St (28461).* 910/457-6701; FAX 910/457-6701. 4 rms, 2 share bath, 2 story. No rm phones. May-Sept: S, D $75-$100; lower rates rest of yr. TV; cable. Complimentary full bkfst; refreshments. Restaurant opp 11:30 am-9 pm. Ck-out 11 am, ck-in 3 pm. Built in 1892; antiques. Cr cds: C, MC, V.

⊵ ♨

★★ **THEODOSIA'S BED & BREAKFAST.** *2 Keelson Row (28461), take Bald Head Island ferry to facility.* 910/457-6563; FAX 910/457-6055; res: 800/656-1812. Web www.southport.net/theodosia.html. 10 rms, 7 with shower only, 3 story, 1 suite, 1 guest house. Mar-Oct: S $135-$180; D $150-$195; each addl $25; suites $185; guest house $150; under 5 free; wknds, hols (2-3 day min); lower rates rest of yr. TV; cable (premium), VCR avail. Complimentary full bkfst. Restaurant adj 7 am-10 pm. Ck-out 11:30 am, ck-in 3 pm. Valet serv. Free ferry transportation. Lighted tennis. 18-hole golf, greens fee $50, pro, putting green, driving range. Pool privileges. In-rm whirlpool in suite. Balconies. Antiques. Totally nonsmoking. Cr cds: C, MC, V.

D 🎿 🏌 🎾 ⊵ ♨

Restaurant

✓★ **SANDFIDDLER SEAFOOD RESTAURANT.** *1643 N Howe St (28461), near jct NC 87.* 910/457-6588. Hrs: 11 am-2 pm, 5-9 pm; Sat from 5 pm; Sun buffet 11:30 am-2 pm. Closed some major hols. Semi-a la carte: lunch $2.95-$14.95, dinner $4.95-$26.95. Sun buffet $8.95. Child's meals. Specializes in seafood, prime rib. Nautical decor. Cr cds: C, MC, V.

D ⊒

Statesville (B-4)

(See also Cornelius, Hickory, Salisbury)

Founded 1789 **Pop** 17,567 **Elev** 923 ft **Area Code** 704 **Zip** 28677
Information Greater Statesville Chamber of Commerce, 115 E Front St, PO Box 1064, 28687; 704/873-2892

Statesville is a community of many small, diversified industries, including furniture, apparel, metalworking and textiles. Iredell County, of which Statesville is the seat, is known for its dairy and beef cattle.

What to See and Do

Duke Power State Park. On Lake Norman (see CORNELIUS); 1,500 acres. Swimming; fishing; boating (ramp, rentals). Nature trails. Picnicking. Tent and trailer sites. Standard fees. 10 mi S via I-77, US 21. Phone 704/528-6350.

Fort Dobbs State Historic Site. Named for Royal Governor Arthur Dobbs, the now-vanished fort was built during the French and Indian War to protect settlers. Exhibits, nature trails, excavations. (Apr–Oct, daily; rest of yr, daily exc Mon; closed some major hols, also wknds Dec–Feb) N via I-40, US 21, State Rd 1930, then 1½ mi W. Phone 704/873-5866. **Free**

Annual Events

Carolina Dogwood Festival. Apr.

Tar Heel Classic Horse Show. Early May.

Iredell County Fair. 1 wk beginning Labor Day.

National Balloon Rally. 3rd wknd Sept.

Motel

★ **FAIRFIELD INN.** *1505 E Broad St (28677). 704/878-2091; FAX 704/873-1368; res: 800/228-2800.* 117 rms, 2 story. S $56; D $61; each addl $5; under 17 free. Crib free. TV; cable. Pool. Complimentary continental bkfst. Restaurant nearby. Ck-out noon. Business servs avail. Cr cds: A, C, D, DS, MC, V.

✓ ★ ★ **HAMPTON INN.** *715 Sullivan Rd (28677). 704/878-2721; FAX 704/873-6694; res: 800/426-7866.* 122 rms, 2 story. S $59-$69; D $64-$74; under 18 free; higher rates: wkends, special events. Crib free. TV; cable (premium). Pool. Complimentary continental bkfst. Ck-out 11 am. Meeting rm. Business servs avail. In-rm modem link. Cr cds: A, C, D, DS, MC, V.

★ ★ ★ **HOLIDAY INN.** *1215 Gardner Bagnal Blvd (28677). 704/878-9691; FAX 704/873-6927; res: 800/465-4329.* 134 rms, 2 story. S, D $77-$84; under 18 free; higher rates special events. Crib free. TV; cable (premium). Pool. Coffee in rms. Restaurant 6:30 am-2 pm, 5-9 pm. Rm serv. Bar 5 pm-2 am. Ck-out noon. Meeting rms. Business servs avail. In-rm modem link. Guest lndry. Exercise equipt. Cr cds: A, C, D, DS, JCB, MC, V.

✓ ★ **RED ROOF INN.** *1508 E Broad St (28625). 704/878-2051; FAX 704/872-3885; res: 800/843-7663.* 115 rms, 3 story. S $42.99-$45.99; D $49.99-$58.99; each addl $5; under 18 free. Crib free. TV; cable. Complimentary coffee in lobby. Restaurant nearby. Ck-out noon. Cr cds: A, C, DS, MC, V.

Inn

★ ★ ★ **HIDDEN CRYSTAL INN.** *471 Sulphur Springs Rd (22209), 17 mi NW on US 64. 828/632-0063; FAX 828/632-3562; res: 800/439-1639.* 12 rms, 2 share bath, 2 story. S, D $75-$115; each addl $15; suites $160. Crib free. TV; cable. Pool. Complimentary full bkfst. Restaurant 11:30 am-2 pm, 5-9 pm; Sun 11 am-2 pm. Ck-out 10:30 am, ck-in 2 pm. Luggage handling. Business servs avail. Colonial house built in 1930s. Totally nonsmoking. Cr cds: A, C, MC, V.

Tryon (B-3)

(See also Hendersonville)

Pop 1,680 **Elev** 1,085 ft **Area Code** 828 **Zip** 28782 **E-mail** visitpolk@teleplex.net **Web** www.teleplex.net/visitpolk/index.htm
Information Polk County Travel & Tourism, Visitor Information, 425 N Trade St; 828/859-8300 or 800/440-7848

On the southern slope of the Blue Ridge Mountains in the "thermal belt," almost at the South Carolina border, Tryon was named for Royal Governor William Tryon, who held office during the Revolution. The Fine Arts Center is the focal point for much of the cultural life of the community.

What to See and Do

Foothills Equestrian Nature Center (FENCE). 300-acre nature preserve has 5 mi of riding and hiking trails; wildlife programs; bird and nature walks. Host to many equestrian events. (Daily) 500 Hunting Country Rd. Phone 828/859-9021. **Free**

White Oak Mountain. Scenic drive around the mountain. Turn off onto Houston Rd at Columbus and take dirt road, which winds around mountain.

Annual Events

Steeplechase Races. 3rd wkend Apr.
Blue Ridge Barbecue. Music festival, arts & crafts. June.

Inn

★ ★ ★ **PINE CREST INN.** *200 Pinecrest Ln (28782). 828/859-9135; FAX 828/859-9135; res: 800/633-3001.* Web www.pinecrestinn.com. 4 rms in main bldg, 30 rms in 9 cottages, 1-2 story, 10 suites. S, D $160-$200; each addl $35; cottage rms $160-$185; suites $180-$540; under 12 free. Crib free. TV; cable; VCR (movies free). Complimentary continental bkfst; afternoon refreshments. Restaurant (see PINE CREST INN). Rm serv. Ck-out 11 am, ck-in 3 pm. Business servs avail. Tennis privileges. Golf privileges. Lawn games. Situated on 3 acres in the foothills of the Blue Ridge Mountains; library, stone fireplaces; some rms with equestrian, hunt club theme. Cr cds: A, C, DS, MC, V.

Restaurant

★ ★ ★ **PINE CREST INN.** *(See Pine Crest Inn) 828/859-9135.* Web www.pinecrest.com. Hrs: 8-9:30 am, 6-9 pm. Closed Sun. Res accepted. Continental menu. Bar. Wine cellar. Semi-a la carte: bkfst $5-$10, dinner $17-$26. Specialties: crab cakes, rack of lamb, creme brulee. Outdoor dining. Elegant, rustic decor in the style of a Colonial tavern; heavy pine tables, beamed ceiling, stone fireplace. Cr cds: A, C, DS, MC, V.

Warsaw (C-7)

Pop 2,859 **Elev** 160 ft **Area Code** 910 **Zip** 28398

What to See and Do

Duplin Wine Cellars. Largest winery in state. Videotape, tour, wine-tasting, retail outlet. (Daily exc Sun; closed most hols) 2 mi S via US 117; off I-40 exit 380. Phone 910/289-3888. **Free**

Motel

★ **THE COUNTRY SQUIRE & VINTAGE INN.** *748 NC Hwy 24 & 50 (28349). 910/296-1831; FAX 910/296-1431; res: 877/830-1602.* 12 rms. S $58; D $65; each addl $15; under 12 free; wkend rates. TV. Complimentary continental bkfst. Restaurant 11:30 am-2 pm, 5:30-10 pm; Fri, Sat from 5:30 pm. Ck-out 11 am. Golf privileges. English gardens; gazebos. Cr cds: A, C, D, MC, V.

Restaurant

★ ★ **COUNTRY SQUIRE.** *748 NC Highway 24 50 (28398). 910/296-1727.* Hrs: 11:30 am-2 pm, 5:30-10 pm; Fri, Sat 5:30-11 pm; Sun noon-2 pm, 5:30-10 pm. Closed Thanksgiving, Dec 24, 25. Res accepted. Bar. Semi-a la carte: lunch $3.50-$12.75, dinner $10.95-$34.95. Child's meals. Specializes in beef, poultry. Five dining rms with historical themes. Gardens. Cr cds: A, C, D, MC, V.

Washington (B-9)

(See also Greenville)

Founded 1776 **Pop** 9,075 **Elev** 14 ft **Area Code** 252 **Zip** 27889
Information Chamber of Commerce, PO Box 665; 252/946-9168

First American village named for the first president, Washington was rebuilt on the ashes left by evacuating Union troops in April 1864. The rebels lost the town in March 1862, and, because it was an important saltwater port, tried to retake it for two years. Evidence of the shelling and burning can be seen in the stone foundations on Water St. Water sports, including sailing, yachting, fishing and swimming, are popular.

What to See and Do

Bath State Historic Site. Oldest incorporated town in state (1705). Bldgs incl Bonner House (ca 1820), Van Der Veer House (ca 1790) and Palmer-Marsh House (ca 1745). (Apr–Oct, daily; rest of yr, daily exc Mon; closed some major hols) St Thomas Episcopal Church (ca 1735) (daily; free). Visitor Center, film. Picnic area. 14 mi E on US 264 & NC 92. Phone 252/923-3971. ¢

Annual Event

Washington Summer Festival. Beach music street dance, ski show, arts and crafts, children's rides. 3 days last full wkend July.

Motels

✓★ **COMFORT INN.** 1636 Carolina Ave (27889), US 17N. 252/946-4444; FAX 252/946-2563; res: 800/424-6423; res: 800/228-5150. 56 rms, 2 story. S, D $55; each addl $5; under 18 free. Crib free. TV; cable (premium). Pool. Complimentary continental bkfst. Restaurant adj 6 am-10 pm. Ck-out noon. Business servs avail. In-rm modem link. Exercise equipt. Refrigerators avail. Cr cds: A, C, D, DS, JCB, MC, V.

⬛ 🏊 🏋 ⬛ 🐾 SC

★ **DAYS INN.** 916 Carolina Ave (27889). 252/946-6141; FAX 252/946-6167; res: 800/329-7466. 72 rms, 2 story. S $38-$65; D $42-$75; each addl $5; under 12 free. Crib free. TV; cable (premium). Pool. Bar 4 pm-2 am; entertainment wknds. Ck-out 11 am. Business servs avail. In-rm modem link. Cr cds: A, C, D, DS, JCB, MC, V.

⬛ 🏊 ⬛ 🔥 SC

Inns

★★ **PAMLICO HOUSE BED & BREAKFAST.** 400 E Main St (27889). 252/946-7184; FAX 252/946-9944; res: 800/948-8507. E-mail pamlicohouse@coastalnet.com; web www.bbonline.com/nc/pamlico. 4 rms, 2 story. S $65-$75; D $75-$85; each addl $15. Children over 6 yrs only. TV; cable. Complimentary full bkfst. Ck-out 11 am, ck-in 3 pm. Former rector's house (1906); antiques, library. Cr cds: A, C, DS, MC, V.

⬛ 🐾

✓★★ **RIVER FOREST MANOR.** 738 E Main St (27810), approx 30 mi E on US 264 at marina on Intracoastal Waterway. 252/943-2151; FAX 252/943-6628; res: 800/346-2151. 11 rms, 2 story. S, D $50-$85. TV; cable (premium). Pool; whirlpool. Complimentary continental bkfst. Restaurant (see RIVER FOREST MANOR). Ck-out 11 am, ck-in 2 pm. Business servs avail. Gift shop. Airport transportation. Tennis. View of river. 1899 building, antique furnishings. Golf carts avail for touring town. Cr cds: A, C, MC, V.

⬛ 🏌 🏊 🔥

Restaurant

★★ **RIVER FOREST MANOR.** *(See River Forest Manor Inn)* 252/943-2151. Hrs: 6-8:30 pm; Sun brunch 11 am-2 pm. Bar. Dinner buffet $15.95. Sun brunch $6.95. Specialties: crabmeat casserole, pickled sausages, oyster fritters. Salad bar. Classical Greek-revival house built 1899. Cr cds: A, C, MC, V.

⬛

Waynesville (B-2)

(See also Asheville, Cherokee, Maggie Valley)

Pop 6,758 **Elev** 2,644 ft **Area Code** 704 **Zip** 28786
Information Visitor & Lodging Information, 1233 N Main St, Ste I-40; 800/334-9036

Popular with tourists, this area offers mountain trails for riding and hiking, superb scenery, golf and fishing in cool mountain streams. Waynesville is 26 miles from the Cherokee Indian Reservation (see CHEROKEE) and Great Smoky Mountains National Park (see). Maggie Valley (see), about six miles northwest, is in a particularly attractive area.

Resort

★★★ **WAYNESVILLE COUNTRY CLUB INN.** 176 Country Club Dr (28786), 1½ mi W on US 23/74 Bypass off I-40. 828/456-3551; FAX 828/456-3555; res: 800/627-6250. 94 rms, eight 1-bedrm cottages, 1-2 story. May-Oct: S $110-$155; D $148-$184; cottages $184-$220; each addl $50; lower rates rest of yr. TV; cable. Pool. Dining rm 7-9:15 am, 10 am-4 pm, 6:30-8:30 pm. Bar 4-10 pm; entertainment Tues, Wed, Fri, Sat. Ck-out noon. Meeting rms. Business servs avail. Bellhops. Airport transportation. Tennis. 27-hole golf, greens fee $13-$23, pro. Downhill ski 20 mi. Balconies. Cr cds: C, MC, V.

🏊 🏌 🎿 🏊 ⬛ 🐾

Inns

★★ **BALSAM MOUNTAIN INN.** Seven Springs Dr (28707), 7 mi W on US 74W Balsam exit. 704/456-9498; FAX 704/452-1405; res: 800/224-9498. E-mail merrily@dnet.net; web www.aski.net/ncmark/balsam.htm. 50 rms, 21 with shower only, 3 story, 8 suites. No A/C. No rm phones. June-Oct, winter wkends: S, D $95; each addl $15; suites $115-$150; wkend, hol rates (2-day min); lower rates rest of yr. Crib free. Complimentary coffee in library. Dining rm 8-9:30 am, 6-7:30 pm; Sun noon-2 pm; wkend hrs vary. Ck-out 11 am, ck-in 3 pm. Meeting rm. Business servs avail. Gift shop. Restored, turn-of-the-century inn nestled on scenic mountainside. Near Great Smoky Mountain Scenic Railway. Cr cds: C, DS, MC, V.

⬛ 🍴 🔥 SC

★ **GRANDVIEW LODGE.** 466 Lickstone Rd (28786). 704/456-5212; FAX 704/452-5432; res: 800/255-7826. E-mail sarnold@haywood.main.nc.us; web www.bbonline.com/nc/grandview. 9 rms, 5 with shower only, 1-2 story, 2 kit. suites. No rm phones. MAP: S $80; D $105-$110; each addl $30; kit. suites $115; family, wkly rates. TV; cable; VCR avail. Dining rm, sittings: 8 am, 6 pm; also 1 pm Sun. Ck-out 10 am, ck-in 1 pm. 27-hole golf privileges. Game rm. Lawn games. Some refrigerators. Picnic tables. Built 1890; restored mountain guest lodge. Totally nonsmoking. Cr cds: C.

🏌 🏊 🔥

★★★ **OLD STONE INN.** 109 Dolan Rd (28786). 828/456-3333; res: 800/432-8499. Web www.bbonline.com/nc/oldstone. 22 rms, 1-2 story.

No A/C. No rm phones. S $74-$124; D $89-$139; avail TV; cable (premium). Dining rm 8-9 am, 6-8 pm. Ck-out 11 am, ck-in 3 pm. Porches. Cr cds: C, DS, MC, V.

★ ★ ★ ★ **THE SWAG.** *Hemphill Rd (28786), W on US 19, then 2.3 mi N on US 276 to Hemphill Rd, then left for 4 mi, follow sign up private driveway. 828/926-0430; FAX 828/926-2036.* Web www.theswag.com. This mountaintop inn, decorated with early American crafts and furniture, was constructed out of six authentic log structures, including an old church, which were transported from their sites to their present setting on 250 wooded acres. 16 rms, 1-2 story. 3 cabins. Mid-May-Oct: S, D $235-$490; each addl $80; higher rates: wkends, hols (2-3-day min), fall foliage. Closed rest of yr. Children over 7 yrs only. Coffee, tea in rms. Dining rm (public by res), 2 sittings: noon & 7 pm. Ck-out 11 am, ck-in 3 pm. Business servs avail. Gift shop. Underground raquetball court. Badminton, croquet court. Sauna. Whirlpool. Massage. Fireplaces. Balconies. Library, video collection. Swimming pond with swinging bridge. Walking trails. Cr cds: A, C, DS, MC, V.

★ ★ ★ **WINDSONG A MOUNTAIN INN.** *459 Rockcliffe Ln (28721), I-40, exit 24, then 3 mi N on NC 209, then 2½ mi W on Riverside Dr, then 1 mi N on Ferguson Cove Loop. 828/627-6111; FAX 828/627-8080.* E-mail 100263.375@compuserv.com; web www.bbonline.com/nc/windsong. 5 rms, 2 story. No A/C. Rm phones avail. S, D $130-$155; guest house $160-$185; each addl $20. Children over 12 yrs only. TV; VCR (movies avail). Heated pool. Complimentary full bkfst. Ck-out 11 am, ck-in 3-6 pm. Tennis. Game rm. Balconies. Grills. Contemporary log house on mountainside; fireplace and special theme decor in rms. Totally nonsmoking. Cr cds: C, DS, MC, V.

★ ★ ★ **YELLOW HOUSE ON PLOT CREEK RD.** *89 Oakview Dr (28786). 828/452-0991; FAX 828/452-1140; res: 800/563-1236.* Web www.bbonline.com/nc/yellowhouse. 6 rms, 1 with shower only, 3 story. 4 suites. No A/C. S $115-$220; D $125-$230; each addl $20; suites $150-$230; golf plans; wkends, hols (2-day min); higher rates special events. Children over 12 yrs only. TV in common rm; cable. Complimentary full bkfst. Complimentary coffee in rms. Ck-out 11 am, ck-in 2 pm. Business servs avail. Luggage handling. Tennis privileges. 18-hole golf privileges, greens fee $45, pro, putting green, driving range. Fireplaces, refrigerators; some in-rm whirlpools, minibars, wet bars. Some balconies. House on 2½ acres of lawns and gardens built in 1885. Totally nonsmoking. Cr cds: C, MC, V.

Wilkesboro (A-4)

(See also Jefferson)

Settled 1779 **Pop** 2,573 **Elev** 1,042 ft **Area Code** 910 **Zip** 28697

What to See and Do

Stone Mountain State Park. A 13,500-acre natural landmark with waterfalls and wooded areas. The mountain, in the center of the park, is a 600-ft dome-shaped granite mass measuring 6 mi in circumference. The park is popular for mountain climbing. There are 17 mi of designated trout streams. Extensive nature, hiking trails. Picnicking. Developed and primitive camping (dump station). Interpretive program in summer. Standard fees. 25 mi NE on NC 18, SR 1002. Phone 910/957-8185.

Motel

★ ★ **ADDISON MOTEL.** *Hwy 421 N (28697), 2 mi N on US 421. 336/838-1000; FAX 336/667-7458; res: 800/672-7218.* 115 rms, 2

story. S $53.99-$56.99; D $58.99-$61.99; each addl $5; under 18 free; higher rates special events. Crib free. TV; cable (premium). Pool. Coffee in lobby. Complimentary continental bkfst. Restaurant adj 6 am-11 pm; Fri, Sat to 1 am. Ck-out 11 am. Meeting rm. Business servs avail. Health club privileges. Some refrigerators. Cr cds: A, C, D, DS, MC, V.

Williamston (B-9)

(See also Washington)

Pop 5,503 **Elev** 80 ft **Area Code** 252 **Zip** 27892

What to See and Do

Hope Plantation. Two-hr guided tour of Georgian plantation house (ca 1800) built by Governor David Stone. Period furnishings; outbuildings; gardens. (Mon–Sat, also Sun afternoons) US 13 to Windsor, then 4 mi W on NC 308. Phone 252/794-3140.   ¢¢¢   Included in admission is

King-Bazemore House (1763). Tour of this unique colonial-style house with gambrel roof, dormer windows and solid brick ends. Period furnishings; outbuildings; gardens.

Motels

✓ ★ **COMFORT INN.** *100 East Blvd (27892), Jct US 17 & US 13/64. 252/792-8400; FAX 252/809-4800; res: 800/827-8400.* 59 rms, 2 story. S $56; D $60; each addl $5; suites $60-$64; under 18 free. Crib free. Pet accepted. TV; cable (premium). Complimentary continental bkfst. Restaurant nearby. Ck-out noon. Business servs avail. Exercise equipt. Cr cds: A, C, D, DS, ER, JCB, MC, V.

★ ★ **HOLIDAY INN MOTEL.** *101 East Blvd (27892), 1 mi S on US 17. 252/792-3184; FAX 252/792-9003; res: 800/792-3101.* 100 rms, 2 story. S, D $59-$65; each addl $5; under 18 free. Crib free. Pet accepted. TV; cable (premium). Pool. Restaurant 6 am-9 pm. Rm serv. Bar 5 pm-midnight. Ck-out noon. Meeting rms. Business servs avail. In-rm modem link. Cr cds: A, C, D, DS, JCB, MC, V.

Wilmington (D-8)

(See also Southport, Wrightsville Beach)

Settled 1732 **Pop** 55,530 **Elev** 25 ft **Area Code** 910 **E-mail** info@cape-fear.nc.us; **Web** www.cape-fear.nc.us

Information Cape Fear Coast Convention & Visitors Bureau, 24 N 3rd St, 28401; 910/341-4030 or 800/222-4757

Chief port of North Carolina, Wilmington is the region's major trade and retail center. Manufacturing, tourism and port-oriented business lead the area's growth.

Patriots who defied the Crown in the Revolution were led by William Hooper, signer of the Declaration of Independence. In 1765, eight years before the Boston Tea Party, the citizens of Wilmington kept the British from unloading their stamps for the Stamp Act. Cornwallis held the town for almost a year in 1781 as his main base of operation. After the battle of Guilford Courthouse, the Lord General came back to Wilmington before heading for Yorktown and defeat.

During the Civil War, blockade runners brought fortunes in goods past Federal ships lying off Cape Fear, making Wilmington the Confederacy's chief port until January, 1865, when it fell. Wilmington was North Carolina's biggest town until 1910, when railroad-fed industries of the inland Piedmont area outgrew the limited facilities of the harbor. The channel, harbor and expanded port facilities bring goods from throughout the world to the area.

What to See and Do

Battleship *North Carolina*. World War II vessel moored on west bank of Cape Fear River. Tour of museum, gun turrets, galley, bridge, sick bay, engine rm, wheelhouse. (Daily) Jct of US 74/76, 17 & 421. Phone 910/251-5797. ¢¢¢

Bellamy Mansion Museum of History and Design Arts. Restored 1859 landmark home has exhibits featuring history, restoration, southern architecture and regional design arts. Tours. (Wed-Sun) 5th & Market Sts. Phone 910/251-3700. ¢¢

Burgwin-Wright House (1770). Restored colonial town house built on foundation of abandoned town jail. British General Cornwallis had his headquarters here during April, 1781. Eighteenth-century furnishings and garden. Tours. (Tues-Sat; closed some major hols; also Jan & wk of Dec 25) 224 Market St, at 3rd St. Phone 910/762-0570. ¢¢

Cape Fear Museum. Interprets social and natural history of Lower Cape Fear. Changing exhibits. (Daily exc Mon; closed major hols) 814 Market St. Phone 910/341-7413. ¢

Carolina Beach State Park. This 700-acre park is a naturalist's delight; the rare Venus' flytrap as well as 5 other species of insect-eating plants grow here. Fishing; boating (ramps, marina). Picnicking, concession. Nature, hiking trails. Camping (dump station). Naturalist program. Standard fees. 15 mi S off US 421. Phone 910/458-8206 or marina 910/458-7770.

Cotton Exchange. Specialty shops and restaurants in historic bldgs on Cape Fear River. (Daily; some stores closed Sun, closed some major hols) N Front St. Phone 910/343-9896.

Greenfield Gardens. A 150-acre municipal park with 180-acre lake, 5-mi scenic drive; canoe and paddleboat rentals (Apr–Oct); bike path; fragrance garden; amphitheater; picnicking; nature trail. (Daily) 2½ mi S on US 421. Phone 910/341-7855. **Free**

Moores Creek National Battlefield. In 1776 the loosely knit colonists took sides against each other—patriots versus loyalists. Colonels Moore, Lillington and Caswell, with the blessing of the Continental Congress, broke up the loyalist forces, captured the leaders and seized gold and quantities of weapons. The action defeated British hopes of an early invasion through the South and encouraged North Carolina to be the first colony to instruct its delegates to vote for independence in Philadelphia. The 86-acre park has a visitor center near entrance to explain the battle. Picnic area. (Daily; closed Jan 1, Dec 25) 17 mi N on US 421, then 3 mi W on NC 210. Phone 910/283-5591. **Free**

North Carolina Aquarium/Fort Fisher. 15 aquariums of North Carolina native sea life; marine exhibits, films, workshops, programs; nature trails. (Daily; closed Jan 1, Thanksgiving, Dec 25) 21 mi S on US 421, in Kure Beach. Phone 910/458-8257. ¢¢

Orton Plantation Gardens. 20 acres. Formerly a rice plantation, now beautiful gardens with ancient oaks, magnolias, ornamental plants, lawn and water scenes; rice fields now a waterfowl refuge. Antebellum Orton House (not open), begun in 1730, can be seen from garden paths. Overlooks Cape Fear River. (Mar–Nov, daily) 18 mi S on NC 133. Phone 910/371-6851. ¢¢¢

Poplar Grove Plantation (ca 1850). Restored Greek-revival plantation; manor house, smokehouse, tenant house, blacksmith, weaver; also country store. Guided tours (daily; closed Thanksgiving, also late Dec–Jan). 14 mi NE on US 17. Phone 910/686-9989 or 910/686-4868. ¢¢¢

Sightseeing cruises.

Henrietta II **Paddlewheel Riverboat Cruises.** 1½-hr narrated sightseeing cruise down Cape Fear River to North Carolina State Port. (June–Aug, 2 cruises daily exc Mon; Apr–May, Sept–Oct, 1 cruise daily exc Mon) Dinner cruises (Apr–Dec, Fri and Sat; June–Aug, Wed–Sat). Downtown at riverfront. For reservations phone 910/343-1611 or 800/676-0162. ¢¢¢

Captain J.N. Maffitt **River Cruises.** 5-mi narrated sightseeing cruise covering Wilmington's harbor life and points of interest. Also "river taxi"

service (addl fee) from Battleship *North Carolina*. (May–Sept, daily) Located at the foot of Market St. Phone 910/343-1611 or 800/676-0162. ¢¢

St John's Museum of Art. Collection of Mary Cassatt prints; paintings and works on paper, Jugtown Pottery, sculpture. Changing exhibits; lectures; educational programs. (Daily exc Mon; closed hols) 114 Orange St. Phone 910/763-0281. ¢

Wilmington Railroad Museum. Exhibits on railroading past and present, centering on the Atlantic Coast Line and other Southeastern rail lines. HO scale regional history exhibit on 2nd floor; outside are ACL steam locomotive and caboose for on-board viewing. (Daily; closed Jan 1, Thanksgiving, Dec 25) 501 Nutt St. Phone 910/763-2634. ¢¢

Annual Events

North Carolina Azalea Festival. Garden and home tours, horse show, celebrity entertainers, pageants, parade, street fair. Early Apr.

Riverfest. Arts and crafts, music, dancing and entertainment; boat rides; raft regatta; street fair. Phone 910/452-6862. 1st full wkend Oct.

Motels

★★★ **COURTYARD BY MARRIOTT.** *151 Van Campen Dr (28001), near New Hanover Regional Airport.* 910/395-8224; FAX 910/452-5569. 128 rms, 2 story. Mid-May-mid-Oct: S, D $79-$119; suites $99-$159; under 18 free; wkends (2-day min); higher rates special events; lower rates rest of yr. Crib free. TV; cable (premium). Complimentary coffee in rms. Restaurant 6:30-10 am; Sat, Sun 7-11 am. Bar 5-11 pm. Ck-out noon. Meeting rms. Business servs avail. In-rm modem link. Valet serv. Coin lndry. Exercise equipt. Pool; whirlpool. Some bathrm phones, in-rm whirlpools, refrigerators, microwaves, wet bars. Some balconies. Cr cds: A, C, D, DS, MC, V.

D ➡ ✗ ⊠ 🔥 SC

✓★ **DAYS INN.** *5040 Market St (28405).* 910/799-6300; FAX 910/791-7414; res: 800/329-7466. 122 rms, 2 story. S $42-$85; D $48-$85; each addl $4; under 12 free; family rates; higher rates: Azalea Festival, Riverfest, summer hols, wkends. Crib free. TV; cable (premium). Pool. Restaurant 6 am-8:45 pm. Ck-out 11 am. Business servs avail. Sundries. Picnic tables, grills. Cr cds: A, C, D, DS, JCB, MC, V.

D ➡ ⊠ 🔥 SC

★★ **DOCKSIDER INN.** *Hwy 421 S, 202 N Fort Fisher Blvd (28449), 20 mi S on US 421.* 910/458-4200; FAX 910/458-6468; res: 800/383-8111. E-mail beachnow@bellsouth.net; web www.docksiderinn.com. 34 rms, 3 story, 15 kits. Memorial Day-Labor Day: S, D $135-$175; kits. $99-$149; under 18 free; wkends, hols (2-, 3-day min); lower rates rest of yr. Crib free. TV; cable. Pool. Coffee in rms. Restaurant nearby. Ck-out 11 am. Refrigerators, microwaves. On beach. Cr cds: A, C, D, DS, MC, V.

D ♿ ➡ 🔥 SC

★ **FAIRFIELD INN.** *306 S College Rd (28403).* 910/392-6767; FAX 910/392-2144; res: 800/228-2800. 134 rms, 3 story. Apr-Sept: S, D $57.95-$95.95; each addl $3; under 18 free; lower rates rest of yr. Crib free. TV; cable (premium). Pool. Complimentary continental bkfst. Restaurant nearby. Ck-out noon. Meeting rms. Business servs avail. Cr cds: A, C, D, DS, MC, V.

D ➡ ⊠ 🔥 SC

★★ **HAMPTON INN.** *5107 Market St (28405).* 910/395-5045; FAX 910/799-1974; res: 800/426-7866. Web www.hampton.com. 118 rms, 2 story. Apr-Sept: S $75; D $99; under 18 free; lower rates rest of yr. Crib free. TV; cable (premium). Pool. Complimentary continental bkfst. Coffee in rms. Restaurant nearby. Ck-out noon. Meeting rm. Business servs avail. In-rm modem link. Cr cds: A, C, D, DS, MC, V.

D ➡ ⊠ 🔥 SC

★★ **HOLIDAY INN.** *4903 Market St (28405).* 910/799-1440; FAX 910/799-2683; res: 800/465-4329; res: 800/782-9061. 232 rms, 2 story. Mar-Oct: S, D $70-$140; under 12 free; lower rates rest of yr. Crib free. Pet accepted. TV; cable (premium). Pool; poolside serv. Complimentary full bkfst. Restaurant 6 am-1 pm, 5-10 pm. Rm serv. Bar 5 pm-2 am. Ck-out noon. Coin lndry. Meeting rms. Business servs avail. In-rm modem link. Valet serv. Sundries. Free airport transportation. Exercise equipt. Some in-rm whirlpools. Cr cds: A, C, D, DS, JCB, MC, V.

[icons]

★ **HOWARD JOHNSON EXPRESS INN.** *3901 Market St (28403). 910/343-1727; res: 800/654-2000.* 80 rms. Apr-Labor Day: S, D $70; each addl $5; under 16 free; lower rates rest of yr. Crib free. TV; cable (premium). Complimentary coffee in lobby. Restaurant nearby. Ck-out 11 am. Business servs avail. Microwaves avail. Cr cds: A, C, D, DS, MC, V.

[icons]

✓★★ **RAMADA INN CONFERENCE CENTER.** *5001 Market St (28405). 910/799-1730; FAX 910/799-1730; res: 800/433-7144; res: 800/272-6232.* 100 rms, 2 story. Apr-Sept: S, D $44-$125; under 18 free; golf plans; lower rates rest of yr. Crib free. TV; cable (premium). Pool. Complimentary full bkfst Mon-Fri. Restaurant 6 am-2 pm, 5-10 pm. Rm serv. Bar 5 pm-2 am; entertainment. Ck-out noon. Meeting rms. Business servs avail. Free airport transportation. Some refrigerators. Cr cds: A, C, D, DS, MC, V.

[icons]

✓★ **SLEEP INN.** *5225 Market St (28405). 910/313-6665; FAX 910/313-2679.* Web www.choicehotels.com. 104 rms, 3 story. S, D $59-$89; under 18 free; hols (2-day min). Crib free. TV; cable (premium), VCR avail. Complimentary continental bkfst. Restaurant nearby. Ck-out 11 am. Meeting rms. Business servs avail. In-rm modem link. Valet serv. Exercise equipt. Pool. Cr cds: A, C, D, DS, JCB, MC, V.

[icons]

Motor Hotels

★★ **4 POINTS HOTEL.** *5032 Market St (28405). 910/392-1101; FAX 910/397-0698; res: 800/833-4721.* 124 rms, 5 story. S, D $59-$109; each addl $10; suites $85-$250; under 18 free; wknd rates; higher rates: Azalea Festival, Memorial Day, July 4, Labor Day. Crib free. TV; cable (premium). Indoor pool; whirlpool. Restaurant 6 am-2 pm, 5-10 pm. Rm serv. Bar. Ck-out noon. Meeting rms. Business servs avail. Bellhops. Exercise equipt; sauna. Refrigerator in suites. Microwaves avail. Cr cds: A, C, D, DS, MC, V.

[icons]

★★ **COMFORT INN.** *151 S College Rd (28403). 910/791-4841; FAX 910/790-9100; res: 800/221-2222.* 146 rms, 6 story. S, D $55-$120; each addl $7; suites $125; under 18 free. Crib free. TV; cable (premium). Pool. Complimentary continental bkfst. Restaurant nearby. Ck-out noon. Meeting rms. Business servs avail. Valet serv. Cr cds: A, C, D, DS, MC, V.

[icons]

Hotels

★★★ **HILTON RIVERSIDE.** *301 N Water St (28401). 910/763-5900; FAX 910/763-0038; res: 800/445-8667.* Web www.wilmington hilton.com. 178 rms, 9 story. S, D $99-$179; each addl $10; suites $179-$340; under 18 free. Crib free. Pet accepted. TV; cable (premium). Pool; whirlpool. Complimentary coffee in rms. Restaurant 6:30 am-10:30 pm. Bar 4 pm-midnight. Ck-out noon. Meeting rms. Business servs avail. In-rm modem link. Gift shop. Free airport transporation. Exercise equipt. Boat dock. Luxury level. Cr cds: A, C, D, DS, ER, JCB, MC, V.

[icons]

★★ **HOLIDAY INN.** *160 Vancampen Blvd (28403). 910/392-3227; FAX 910/395-9907; res: 800/465-4329.* 131 rms, 5 story. S, D $99-$139; each addl $10; suites $119-$159; under 19 free. Crib free. TV; cable

(premium). Pool. Complimentary continental bkfst. Restaurant nearby. Ck-out noon. Meeting rms. Business servs avail. Coin lndry. Exercise equipt. Refrigerator in suites; microwaves avail. Cr cds: A, C, D, DS, JCB, MC, V.

[icons]

Inns

★★ **CATHERINES INN.** *410 S Front St (28401). 910/251-0863; FAX 910/772-9550; res: 800/476-7723.* 5 rms, 2 story. S $75-$87.50; D $85-$110; each addl $20. Children over 10 yrs only. TV; cable (premium). Complimentary full bkfst. Restaurant nearby. Ck-out 11 am, ck-in 3-6 pm. Luggage handling. Built in 1883; antiques. Totally nonsmoking. Cr cds: A, C, MC, V.

[icons]

★★ **CURRAN HOUSE.** *312 S 3rd St (28401). 910/763-6603; FAX 910/763-5116; res: 800/763-6603.* Web www.bbonline.com/nc/curran. 3 rms, 2 story. S, D $75-$119; hols (2-day min). Children over 12 yrs only. TV; cable (premium), VCR (free movies). Complimentary full bkfst. Ck-out 11 am, ck-in 3-6 pm. Business servs avail. Free airport transportation. Lawn games. Refrigerators avail. Original building from 1837, addition made in 1885. Totally nonsmoking. Cr cds: A, C, MC, V.

[icons]

★★★ **DARLINGS BY THE SEA.** *329 Atlantic Ave (28449), 15 mi S on US 421. 910/458-8887; FAX 910/458-6468; res: 800/383-8111.* E-mail beachnow@bellsouth.net; web www.darlingsbythesea.com. 5 suites, 3 story. Memorial Day-Labor Day: suites $189-$219; wkends (2-day min); lower rates rest of yr. Adults only. TV; cable (premium), VCR. Complimentary continental bkfst. Complimentary coffee in rms. Restaurant nearby. Ck-out 11 am, ck-in 2 pm. Business servs avail. In-rm modem link. Concierge serv. Exercise equipt. Bathrm phones, in-rm whirlpools, refrigerators, microwaves, wet bars. Balconies. On ocean. Cr cds: A, C, D, DS, ER, MC, V.

[icons]

★★ **FRONT STREET INN.** *215 S Front St (28401). 910/762-6442; FAX 910/762-8991.* Web frontstreetinn.wilm.net. 9 rms, 2 story. S, D $89-$165; under 16 free; wkly rates. Crib free. TV; cable (premium), VCR avail. Complimentary continental bkfst. Complimentary coffee in rms. Restaurant nearby. Ck-out 11 am, ck-in 4 pm. Business servs avail. In-rm modem link. Luggage handling. Exercise equipt. Game rm. Refrigerators; microwaves avail. Balconies. Brick building (1923) that once housed Salvation Army. Cr cds: A, C, D, DS, MC, V.

[icons]

★★★ **GRAYSTONE INN.** *100 S 3rd St (28401). 910/763-2000; FAX 910/763-5555; res: 888/763-4773.* Web www.graystoneinn.com. 7 rms, 3 story. S, D $105-$180; each addl $15; suites $155-$280. Children over 12 only. TV avail; cable (premium). Complimentary full bkfst. Restaurant nearby. Ck-out 11 am, ck-in 4 pm. Library, game rm. Built in 1906; antiques. Cr cds: A, C, D, DS, MC, V.

[icons]

★★★ **ROSEHILL INN.** *114 S 3rd St (28401). 910/815-0250; FAX 910/815-0350; res: 800/815-0250.* E-mail rose hill@rosehill.com; web www.rosehill.com. 6 rms, 4 with shower only, 2 story. Mar-Oct: S, D $129-$195; each addl $25; package plans; higher rates special events; lower rates rest of yr. Children over 12 yrs only. TV; cable, VCR (movies). Complimentary full bkfst. Complimentary coffee in rms. Restaurant nearby. Ck-out 11 am, ck-in 4 pm. Business center. In-rm modem link. Luggage handling. Valet serv. Street parking. Massage. Built in 1848; antiques. Elegant atmosphere; Victorian home. Totally nonsmoking. Cr cds: A, C, DS, MC, V.

[icons]

★★ **TAYLOR HOUSE INN.** *14 N 7th St (28401). 910/763-7581; res: 800/382-9982.* 5 rms, 2 story. S, D $95-$110; wkends (2-day min). Complimentary full bkfst; afternoon refreshments. Ck-out 10:30 am, ck-in 4-7 pm. Free airport transportation. Built in 1905; many fireplaces, antiques. Totally nonsmoking. Cr cds: A, C, MC, V.

⊠ 🔥

★★★ **THE INN AT ST. THOMAS COURT.** *101 S 2nd St (28401).* 910/343-1800; FAX 910/251-1149; res: 800/525-0909. E-mail theinn@wilm.net; web www.ego.net/us/nc/ilm/stthomas. 40 suites, 1-3 story. Apr-Oct: S, D $135-$275; 2-bedrm suites $210; lower rates rest of yr. TV; cable (premium), VCR (free movies). Complimentary continental bkfst. Complimentary coffee in rms. Restaurant nearby. Ck-out 11 am, ck-in 3 pm. Meeting rm. Business servs avail. In-rm modem link. Luggage handling. Valet serv. Concierge serv. Microwaves. Balconies. Renovated commercial building (1906) in historic district; entrance court, library, antiques. Cr cds: A, C, D, DS, MC, V.

D ⊠ 🔥 🏃

★★★ **THE VERANDAS.** *202 Nun St (28401).* 910/251-2212; FAX 910/251-8932. Web www.verandas.com. 8 rms, 3 story. No elvtr. S $120; D $120-$175; wkends (2-day min); hols (3-day min). Children over 12 yrs only. TV; cable, VCR avail (movies). Complimentary full bkfst. Ck-out 11 am, ck-in 4 pm. Business servs avail. In-rm modem link. Luggage handling. Street parking. Built in 1854; antiques. Verandas. Totally nonsmoking. Cr cds: A, C, DS, MC, V.

⊠ 🔥

★★ **THE WORTH HOUSE.** *412 S 3rd St (28401).* 910/762-8562; FAX 910/763-2173; res: 800/340-8559. E-mail worthhse@wilmington.net; web www.bbonline.com/nc/worth. 7 rms, 3 story. Mar-Oct: S $80-$120; D $85-$125; each addl $20; lower rates rest of yr. Children over 8 yrs only. TV in sitting rm; cable (premium), VCR (movies). Complimentary full bkfst. Ck-out 11 am, ck-in 4-7 pm. Victorian house (1893) in historic district. Totally nonsmoking. Cr cds: A, C, MC, V.

⊠ 🏃 SC

Restaurants

✓★ **CAFFE PHOENIX.** *9 S Front St (28401).* 910/343-1395. Hrs: 11:30 am-10:30 pm; Fri, Sat to 11 pm; Sun 5-10:30 pm. Closed most major hols. Mediterranean menu. Bar. Semi-a la carte: lunch $6-$8, dinner $13-$25. Child's meals. Specializes in pasta, grilled seafood. Outdoor dining. Casual decor. Cr cds: A, C, D, DS, MC, V.

D ⟷

★ **COTTAGE RESTAURANT.** *1 N Lake Park Blvd (28428), 15 mi S on US 421.* 910/458-4383. Hrs: 11:30 am-3 pm, 5:30 pm to close. Closed Sun; major hols; also Dec 26. Res accepted. Seafood menu. Bar. Semi-a la carte: lunch $4.95-$8.95, dinner $7.50-$18.95. Child's meals. Specializes in mix and match pasta, seafood, appetizers. Street parking. Outdoor dining. In old restored beach cottage. Cr cds: A, C, DS, MC, V.

D ⟷

✓★ **DRAGON GARDEN.** *341-52 S College Rd (28403), Univ Commons.* 910/452-0708. Hrs: 11 am-2:30 pm, 5-9:30 pm; Fri, Sat to 10:30 pm; Sun to 9 pm. Closed Thanksgiving, Dec 24, 25. Res accepted. Chinese menu. Bar. Semi-a la carte: lunch $4-$6, dinner $5-$12. Specializes in Hunan, Szechuan, and Mandarin dishes. Chinese decor with many artifacts. Cr cds: A, C, DS, MC, V.

D ⟷

✓★ **EDDIE ROMANELLI'S.** *5400 Oleander Dr (28403).* 910/799-7000. Hrs: 11:30-2 am; Sun, Mon to 11 pm. Closed Thanksgiving, Dec 25. Italian, Amer menu. Bar. Semi-a la carte: lunch $3.95-$7.95, dinner $8.95-$18.95. Child's meals. Specializes in marinated steak, prime rib, pasta. Parking. Beamed ceiling with skylight. Cr cds: A, C, MC, V.

D ⟷

★★ **ELIJAHS RESTAURANT.** *2 Ann St (28401).* 910/343-1448. Hrs: 11:30 am-3 pm, 5-10 pm; Fri, Sat 5-11 pm; Sun brunch to 3 pm. Closed Jan 1, Thanksgiving, Dec 25. Bar to midnight. Semi-a la carte:

lunch $5.95-$9.95, dinner $9.95-$22.95. Sun brunch $4.95-$7.95. Child's meals. Specialties: chowder, hot crab dip. Pianist Sun brunch. Outdoor dining. View of river. Nautical decor; former maritime museum. Cr cds: A, C, DS, MC, V.

D

★ **FREDDIE'S.** *111 K Ave (28449), 15 mi S on US 421.* 910/458-5979. Hrs: 5-10 pm; early-bird dinner 5-6 pm. Closed Jan 1, Thanksgiving, Dec 25. Italian, Amer menu. Bar. Semi-a la carte: dinner $8.95-$18.95. Child's meals. Specialties: 4-layer lasagna, Freddie's special chop, chicken cacciatore. Street parking. Murals. Cr cds: A, C, MC, V.

D ⟷

★★ **HARVEST MOON.** *5704 Oleander Dr (28403).* 910/792-0172. Web www.beachline.com. Hrs: 5:30-10 pm; Fri, Sat to 10:30 pm. Closed most major hols. Res accepted. Bar. Semi-a la carte: dinner $10.95-$22.95. Child's meals. Specializes in beef, seafood. Mediterranean decor. Cr cds: A, C, D, DS, MC, V.

D

✓★★ **HIERONYMUS SEAFOOD.** *5035 Market St (28405).* 910/392-6313. Hrs: 11:30 am-10 pm; Apr-Sept Fri, Sat to 11 pm. Closed Jan 1, Thanksgiving, Dec 24, 25. Res accepted. Bar to 2 am. Semi-a la carte: lunch $3.95-$10.95, dinner $4.95-$18.95. Child's meals. Specializes in seafood, prime rib, chicken. Outdoor dining. Oyster bar in lounge. Nautical decor. Cr cds: A, C, D, DS, MC, V.

D SC ⟷

✓★★ **MARKET STREET CASUAL DINING.** *6309 Market St (28405).* 910/395-2488. Hrs: 5-11 pm. Closed Thanksgiving, Dec 25; also Super Bowl Sun. Bar to 1 am. Semi-a la carte: dinner $4.95-$14.95. Specializes in grilled seafood, steak, pasta. Cr cds: A, C, DS, MC, V.

D ⟷

✓★ **OH! BRIAN'S.** *4311 Oleander Dr (28403).* 910/791-1477. Hrs: 11 am-10 pm; Fri, Sat to 11 pm. Closed Thanksgiving, Dec 25. Res accepted Sun-Thur. Bar to 1 am. Semi-a la carte: lunch $3.95-$6.95, dinner $4.95-$16.95. Child's meals. Specializes in ribs, chicken, salads. Atrium. Cr cds: A, C, MC, V.

D ⟷

★★ **PILOT HOUSE.** *2 Ann St (28401), Chandler's Wharf on waterfront.* 910/343-0200. Hrs: 11:30 am-3 pm, 5-10 pm; Fri, Sat to 11 pm; Sun brunch to 3 pm. Closed Jan 1, Dec 24, 25. Res accepted. A la carte entrees: lunch $2.95-$9.95, dinner $10.95-$24.95. Child's meals. Specialties: crab melt sandwich, Caribbean fudge pie. Own bread. Parking. Outdoor dining. Located in restored area of waterfront; built in 1870. Cr cds: A, C, DS, MC, V.

D

★★ **PORT CITY CHOP HOUSE.** *1981 Eastwood Rd (28405).* 910/256-4955. Hrs: 11:30 am-10 pm; Fri to 10:30 pm; Sat 4-10:30 pm. Closed Sun; Thanksgiving, Dec 25. Res accepted. Bar. Semi-a la carte: lunch $5-$10, dinner $13.95-$33.95. Child's meals. Specializes in Angus beef, grilled fish, lamb chops. Outdoor dining. Contemporary decor with brick and light woods; open kitchen area. Cr cds: A, C, D, DS, MC, V.

D ⟷

★ **RUCKERJOHN'S.** *5511 Carolina Beach Rd (28412), on US 421.* 910/452-1212. Hrs: 11 am-10 pm; Fri, Sat to 11 pm. Closed Thanksgiving, Dec 25. Bar. Semi-a la carte: lunch $4.50-$6.50, dinner $5.95-$14.95. Child's meals. Specializes in beef, pasta, seafood. Casual, friendly atmosphere. Cr cds: A, C, MC, V.

D ⟷

★★ **VINNIE'S.** *1900 Eastwood Rd (28403), in Lumina Station.* 910/256-0995. Web www.vinnies.com. Hrs: 11:30 am-2:30 pm, 5 pm-close; Sat, Sun from 5 pm. Closed Jan 1, Dec 25. Bar from 4 pm. Semi-a la carte: lunch $3.95-$9.95, dinner $10.95-$49.95. Specializes in prime rib, seafood. Own pasta. Outdoor dining. Entertainment Thurs-Sat. Semi-formal club decor; mahogany woodwork, framed caricatures. Cr cds: A, C, D, DS, MC, V.

D ⊒

★ **WATER STREET.** *5 S Water St (28401). 910/343-0042.* Hrs: 11:30 am-midnight. Closed Thanksgiving, Dec 25. Res accepted. Bar. Semi-a la carte: lunch $4.95-$9.95, dinner $7.95-$15.95. Specializes in seafood, sandwiches, soups. Entertainment Wed-Sun. Outdoor dining. Riverfront dining in old warehouse. Cr cds: A, C, MC, V.

D ⊒

Unrated Dining Spot

★ **DOXEY'S MARKET & CAFE.** *1319 Military Cut-off Rd (28403). 910/256-9952.* Hrs: 9 am-7 pm; Sun noon-6 pm. Closed most major hols. Semi-a la carte: lunch, dinner $3-$7. Specializes in soups, salads, sandwiches. Salad bar. Cr cds: A, C, DS, MC, V.

D

Wilson (B-8)

(See also Rocky Mount)

Pop 36,930 **Elev** 145 ft **Area Code** 252

Located just off I-95, midway between New York and Florida, Wilson is a convenient rest stop for road-weary travelers. It is one of the Southeast's leading antique markets and is said to have one of the nation's largest tobacco markets.

Motels

✓ ★ ★ **BEST WESTERN LA SAMMANA.** *817-a SW Ward Blvd (27893). 252/237-8700; FAX 252/237-8092; res: 800/528-1234.* 83 rms, 2 story. S, D $59; each addl $5; suites $95-$105; under 12 free; golf plans; hols (2-day min); higher rates special events. Crib $5. TV; cable, VCR avail. Complimentary continental bkfst. Complimentary coffee in rms. Restaurant adj 11 am-10 pm. Ck-out 11 am. Meeting rms. Business servs avail. In-rm modem link. Valet serv. Pool. Refrigerators; many microwaves; bathrm phone in suites. Cr cds: A, C, D, DS, JCB, MC, V.

D ⇌ ⊒ 🔥 SC

✓ ★ ★ **COMFORT INN.** *4941 US Hwy 264 W (28403). 252/291-6400; FAX 252/291-7744; res: 800/228-5150.* 76 rms, 2 story. S, D $55-$65; each addl $6; suites $75-$125; under 18 free. Crib free. TV; cable (premium), VCR avail. Pool. Complimentary continental bkfst. Restaurant adj 6 am-10 pm. Ck-out 11 am. Meeting rms. Business servs avail. In-rm modem link. Some refrigerators. Cr cds: A, C, D, DS, MC, V.

D ⇌ ⊒ 🐾 SC

★ ★ **HAMPTON INN.** *1801 S Tarboro (27893), 6 mi E of I-95, exit 121. 252/291-2323; FAX 252/291-7696.* 100 rms, 2 story. S, D $57-$64; under 18 free. Crib free. TV; cable (premium). Pool. Complimentary continental bkfst. Coffee in rms. Restaurant nearby. Ck-out 11 am. Meeting rm. Business center. In-rm modem link. Health club privileges. Cr cds: A, C, D, DS, MC, V.

D ⇌ ⊒ 🔥 SC ⚲

★ **HOLIDAY INN.** *1815 Hwy 301 S (22033). 252/243-5111; FAX 252/291-9697; res: 800/465-4329; res: 800/329-7466.* 100 rms, 2 story. S, D $51.14; each addl $5; under 12 free. Crib free. Pet accepted,

some restrictions; $10. TV; cable (premium). Pool. Complimentary continental bkfst. Coffee in rms. Bar. Ck-out noon. Meeting rms. Business servs avail. Cr cds: A, C, D, DS, JCB, MC, V.

D 🐾 ⇌ ⊒ 🔥 🐾 SC

✓ ★ **MICROTEL INN.** *5013 Hayes Place (27896). 252/234-0444; FAX 252/234-0065; res: 888/771-7171.* 62 rms, 2 story. S $39.95-$54.95; D $41.95-$56.95; suites $64.94-$84.95; under 18 free; golf plans. TV; cable (premium). Complimentary coffee in lobby. Restaurant nearby. Ck-out 11 am. Business servs avail. In-rm modem link. Coin lndry. Cr cds: A, C, D, DS, MC, V.

D ⊒ 🐾 SC

Inn

★ ★ **MISS BETTY'S BED & BREAKFAST INN.** *600 W Nash St (27893). 252/243-4447; FAX 252/243-4447; res: 800/258-2058.* 14 rms, 3 with shower only, 2 story, 3 suites. S $50-$65; D $60-$90. Adults only. TV; cable (premium), VCR avail. Complimentary full bkfst. Restaurant opp 6 am-10 pm. Ck-out 11 am, ck-in 3 pm. Business servs avail. In-rm modem link. Health club privileges. Three restored houses (1858 & 1943). Many antiques. Totally nonsmoking. Cr cds: A, C, D, DS, MC, V.

D ⊒ 🐾

Winston-Salem (A-5)

(See also Greensboro, High Point, Lexington)

Founded Salem: 1766; Winston: 1849; combined as Winston-Salem: 1913 **Pop** 143,485 **Elev** 912 ft **Area Code** 336
Information Convention and Visitors Bureau, PO Box 1409, 27102; 336/777-3796 or 800/331-7018

First in industry in the Carolinas and one of the South's chief cities, Winston-Salem is a combination of two communities. Salem, with the traditions of its Moravian founders, and Winston, an industrial center, matured together. Tobacco markets, large banks and arts & crafts galleries contribute to this thriving community.

What to See and Do

Hanging Rock State Park. Approx 6,200 acres in Sauratown Mts. Lake swimming, bathhouse; fishing; boating (rentals). Nature trails. Picnicking, concession. Tent & trailer sites, 6 family cabins (Mar–Nov, by res only). Observation tower. Standard fees. 32 mi N, between NC 66 & 89 near Danbury. Phone 336/593-8480.

Historic Bethabara Park. Site of first Moravian settlement in North Carolina (1753); restored bldgs incl Gemeinhaus (1788), Potter's House (1782), Buttner House (1803); reconstructed palisade fort (1756–1763); stabilized archaeological foundations of original settlement and God's Acre (graveyard); reconstructed community gardens (1759). Visitor center; exhibits, slide show. Nature trails. Picnicking. (Apr–Nov, daily; walking tour all yr) 2147 Bethabara Rd. Phone 336/924-8191. **Free**

Historic Old Salem (1766). Restoration of a planned community which Moravians, with their Old World skills, made the 18th-century trade and cultural center of North Carolina's Piedmont. Many of the sturdy structures built for practical living have been restored and furnished with original or period pieces. Early crafts are demonstrated throughout the town. Here also is an original Tannenberg organ in working condition. A number of houses are privately occupied. 9 houses plus outbuildings are open to the public. Tours (self-guided) start at Visitor Center on Old Salem Rd. Special events are held during the yr. (Daily; no tours Thanksgiving, Dec 24 & 25) S of business district on Old Salem Rd. Phone 336/721-7300. Ticket to all bldgs (exc museum) ¢¢¢¢ In the old village are

Museum of Early Southern Decorative Arts. Twenty-one period rms and 6 galleries (1690–1820), with decorative arts of Maryland, Virginia,

Georgia, Kentucky, Tennessee and the Carolinas. (Daily; closed Thanksgiving, Dec 24 & 25) 924 S Main St. Phone 336/721-7360. Museum ¢¢¢; Combination ticket incl Old Salem ¢¢¢¢¢

Salem Academy and College (1772). (1,100 women) When founded by the Moravians, it was the only school of its kind for women in the South. The Fine Arts Center offers art exhibits, lectures, films, concerts and plays (mid-Sept–mid-May, daily; eves during special events; some fees). Church St, on Salem Sq in Old Salem. Campus tours on request; phone 336/721-2702.

R.J. Reynolds Tobacco Company, Whitaker Park Cigarette Plant. Guided tours (Mon–Fri; closed hols) 1100 Reynolds Blvd. Phone 336/741-5718. **Free**

Reynolda House, Museum of American Art. On estate of the late R.J. Reynolds of the tobacco dynasty. American paintings, original furniture, art objects, costume collection. Adj is Reynolda Gardens, 125 acres of open fields and naturalized woodlands; formal gardens, greenhouse. (Tues–Sat, also Sun afternoons; closed Jan 1, Thanksgiving, Dec 25) Approx 2 mi N on University Pkwy, then ½ mi E on Coliseum Dr then N on Reynolda Rd. 2250 Reynolda Rd. Phone 336/725-5325. ¢¢¢

SciWorks. Hands-on exhibits of physical and natural sciences; planetarium; 31-acre outdoor environmental park and nature trails. (Daily; closed Jan 1, Easter, Thanksgiving, Dec 25) 400 W Hanes Mill Rd at US 52N. Phone 336/767-6730. ¢¢¢

Southeastern Center for Contemporary Art. Exhibits by contemporary artists from across the country with accompanying educational programs. (Daily exc Mon; closed hols) 750 Marguerite Dr. Phone 336/725-1904. ¢¢

Tanglewood Park. Swimming; fishing; boating (paddleboats, canoes); horseback riding; golf, miniature golf, tennis; nature trail. Picnicking, playgrounds. Camping (fee); accommodations. Deer park. Steeplechase (early May). (Daily) 12 mi SW off I-40, in Clemmons. (Exit 182) Phone 336/778-6300. Per vehicle ¢

Wake Forest University (1834). (5,600 students) On campus are Fine Arts Center, Museum of Anthropology; also Reynolda Village, a complex of shops, offices & restaurants. Bowman Gray School of Medicine is on Medical Center Blvd. 3 mi NW off Reynolda Rd. 1834 Wake Forest Rd. Phone 336/759-5000 or 336/758-5000.

Motels

✓★★ **COURTYARD BY MARRIOTT.** 3111 University Pkwy (27105). 336/727-1277; FAX 336/722-8219; res: 800/321-2211. 124 rms, 2 story. S, D $75; under 18 free; higher rates graduation (May). Crib free. TV; cable (premium). Pool; whirlpool. Complimentary coffee in lobby. Resturant nearby. Ck-out noon. Coin lndry. Business servs avail. Exercise equipt. Health club privileges. Cr cds: A, C, D, DS, MC, V.

D ⚓ 🕴 🔀 🔥 SC

★ **DAYS INN.** 3330 Silas Creek Pkwy (27103), I-40 Wake Forest exit. 336/760-4770; FAX 336/760-1085; res: 800/329-7466. 135 rms, 5 story. S $52-$54; D $57-$60; each addl $5; under 17 free. Crib free. TV; cable (premium). Pool; whirlpool. Complimentary continental bkfst. Ck-out noon. Meeting rms. Business servs avail. Health club privileges. Cr cds: A, C, D, DS, MC, V.

D ⚓ 🔀 🐾 SC

✓★★ **HAMPTON INN.** 5719 University Pkwy (27105). 336/767-9009; FAX 336/661-0448; res: 800/426-6786. 117 rms, 2 story. S $60-$65; D $65-$70; under 18 free. Crib free. TV; cable (premium). Pool. Complimentary continental bkfst. Restaurant adj 6 am-10 pm. Ck-out noon. Meeting rms. Business servs avail. In-rm modem link. Cr cds: A, C, D, DS, MC, V.

D ⚓ 🔀 🐾 SC

★★ **HAMPTON INN.** 1990 Hampton Inn Ct (27103), I-40 exit 189, at Stradford Rd. 336/760-1660; FAX 336/768-9168; res: 800/426-7866. 131 rms, 5 story. S, D $63-$120; each addl $6; under 18 free; higher

rates special events. TV; cable (premium). Pool. Complimentary continental bkfst. Ck-out noon. Meeting rms. Business servs avail. Exercise equipt. Some refrigerators. Minibars. Cr cds: A, C, D, DS, MC, V.

D ⚓ 🕴 🔀 🐾 SC

★★ **RESIDENCE INN BY MARRIOTT.** 7835 N Point Blvd (27106). 336/759-0777; FAX 336/759-9671; res: 800/331-3131. 88 kit. suites, 2 story. S, D $89-$129; under 18 free; wkly rates. Crib free. Pet accepted; $75-$150. TV; cable (premium). Heated pool; whirlpool. Complimentary continental bkfst. Complimentary coffee in rms. Ck-out noon. Coin lndry. Valet serv. Health club privileges. Refrigerators, microwaves. Picnic tables, grills. Cr cds: A, C, D, DS, JCB, MC, V.

D 🐾 ⚓ 🔀 🔀 SC

Hotels

★★★ **ADAM'S MARK PLAZA.** 425 N Cherry St (27101). 336/725-3500; FAX 336/721-2240; res: 800/444-2326. Web www.adamsmark.com. 605 rms, 17 story. S, D $79-$180; suites $275-$550; under 18 free; wknd rates. Crib free. Garage $6. TV; cable (premium). VCR avail. Indoor pool; poolside serv. Restaurants 6:30 am-11 pm. Rm serv 24 hrs. Bar 11:30-1 am; entertainment Fri-Sat. Ck-out 1 pm. Convention facilities. Business servs avail. In-rm modem link. Concierge. Gift shop. Exercise equipt; sauna. Health club privileges. Game rm. Refrigerator in suites. Local art displayed. Luxury level. Cr cds: A, C, D, DS, MC, V.

D ⚓ 🕴 🔀 🐾 SC

★★★ **HOLIDAY INN SELECT.** 5790 University Pkwy (27105). 336/767-9595; FAX 336/744-1888; 150 rms, 6 story. S, D $86; suites $99; under 18 free; wkend rates; higher rates. Crib free. TV; cable (premium). VCR avail. Pool. Restaurant 6:30 am-2 pm, 5:30-10 pm. Bar; entertainment. Ck-out noon. Meeting rms. Business servs avail. Exercise equipt. Health club privileges. Some refrigerators, minibars. Cr cds: A, C, D, DS, JCB, MC, V.

D ⚓ 🕴 🔀 🐾 SC

Inns

★★ **AUGUSTUS T ZEVELY INN.** 803 S Main St (27101). 336/748-9299; FAX 336/721-2211; res: 800/928-9299. Web www.travelguides.com/bb/zevely/. 12 rms, 3 story. S, D $80-$135; each addl $15; suite $205; higher rates special events. Children over 12 yrs only. Pet accepted. TV; cable (premium). Complimentary continental bkfst; complimentary full bkfst on wkends. Restaurant opp 11:30 am-9 pm. Ck-out 11:30 am, ck-in 3-9 pm. Business servs avail. Health club privileges. Some in-rm whirlpools, refrigerators, fireplaces. Some balconies. Built in 1844; restored to its mid-19th century appearance. Moravian ambience. Cr cds: A, C, MC, V.

D 🐾 🔀 🔀

★★★ **BROOKSTOWN INN.** 200 Brookstown Ave (27101). 336/725-1120; FAX 336/773-0147; res: 800/845-4262. Web getawaysmag.com. 71 units, 4 story. S $90-$125; D, suites $105-$135; each addl $20; under 12 free. Crib free. TV; cable (premium). Complimentary continental bkfst; afternoon refreshments. Coffee in rms. Ck-out noon, ck-in 2 pm. Business servs avail. In-rm modem link. Exercise equipt. Health club privileges. Restored brick cotton mill (1837); antiques, handmade quilts. Cr cds: A, C, D, MC, V.

D 🕴 🔀 🐾 SC

★★ **COLONEL LUDLOW INN.** 434 Summit & W 5th (27101). 336/777-1887; FAX 336/777-0518; res: 800/301-1887. E-mail innkeeper@bbinn.com; web www.bbinn.com. 10 rms, 2 story, 1 suite. S $75; D, suite $139-$209; higher rates special events. TV; cable (premium), VCR (movies). Complimentary full bkfst. Complimentary coffee in rms. Restaurant adj 5-10 pm. Ck-out 11:30 am, ck-in 3 pm. Business servs avail. In-rm modem link. Concierge serv. Valet serv. Exercise equipt. In-rm whirlpools, refrigerators, microwaves. Balconies. Victorian homes built in 1887 & 1895; restored and converted. Cr cds: A, C, DS, MC, V.

✓ ★★ **TANGLEWOOD PARK.** *434 Summit & W 5th (27012), 12 mi SW on US 158, I-40 exit 182, in Tanglewood Park.* 336/778-6300; FAX 336/778-6379. 18 rms in lodge, 10 rms in manor house, 2 story. S $35-$95; D $45-$107. Crib $3. TV. Pool; wading pool, lifeguard. Complimentary continental bkfst. Ck-out noon, ck-in 2 pm. Meeting rms. Tennis. Golf. Facilities of Tanglewood Park avail. Cr cds: A, C, D, MC, V.

Restaurants

★★ **OLD SALEM TAVERN.** *736 S Main St (27101).* 336/748-8585. Hrs: 11:30 am-2 pm, 5-9 pm; Fri, Sat to 9:30 pm; Sun to 2 pm. Closed Jan 1, Dec 25. Serv bar. Semi-a la carte: lunch $4.75-$7.50, dinner $13-$20. Child's meals. Specialties: roast duck, rack of lamb. Outdoor dining. Cr cds: A, C, DS, MC, V.

★★ **RYAN'S STEAK CHOPS & SEAFOOD.** *719 Coliseum Dr (27106).* 336/724-6132. Hrs: 5-10 pm; Fri & Sat to 10:30 pm. Closed Sun; Jan 1, Thanksgiving, Dec 24, 25. Res accepted. Continental menu. Bar 4:30-11:45 pm. Semi-a la carte: dinner $15.25-$34.95. Own soup, some desserts. Specializes in beef, seafood. Wooded setting. Cr cds: A, C, D, MC, V.

★★ **STALEY'S CHARCOAL STEAK HOUSE.** *2000 Reynolda Rd (27106).* 336/723-8631. Hrs: 5-10 pm; Fri, Sat to 11 pm. Closed Sun; major hols. Res accepted. Serv bar. Semi-a la carte: dinner $11.95-$39.95. Child's meals. Specialties: prime rib, shish kebab. Fountain at entrance. Cr cds: A, C, MC, V.

★★ **VINEYARD RESTAURANT.** *120 Reynolda Village (27106).* 336/748-0269. Hrs: 5-10 pm. Closed Sun; most major hols. Bar. Semi-a la carte: dinner $10-$19. Child's meals. Specializes in beef, seafood, vegetarian dishes. Outdoor dining. Entertainment Wed-Sat. Casual, contemporary atmosphere. Cr cds: A, C, MC, V.

★★ **ZEVELY HOUSE.** *901 W 4th St (27101).* 336/725-6666. Hrs: 5:30-9 pm; Sun brunch 11 am-2 pm. Closed Mon; some major hols. Res accepted. Bar. Semi-a la carte: dinner $12.95-$21. Sun brunch $6.95-$11. Child's meals. Specialties: potato cakes with smoked salmon & caviar, chicken pie, mixed grill. Outdoor dining. Antiques, fireplace in older brick house. Cr cds: A, C, D, MC, V.

Wrightsville Beach (D-8)

(See also Wilmington)

Pop 2,937 **Elev** 7 ft **Area Code** 910 **Zip** 28480

A very pleasant family-oriented resort town, Wrightsville Beach offers swimming, surfing, fishing and boating. The public park has facilities for tennis, basketball, soccer, softball, volleyball, shuffleboard and other sports.

Motels

★ **ONE SOUTH LUMINA MOTEL.** *1 S Lumina Ave (28480).* 910/256-9100; FAX 910/509-1639; res: 800/421-3255. 17 kit. suites, 3 story. Memorial Day-Labor Day: D $145-$210; each addl $10; wkly rates; lower rates rest of yr. TV; cable. Pool. Coffee in rms. Restaurant nearby. Ck-out 11 am. Guest lndry. Microwaves. Balconies. On swimming beach. Cr cds: A, C, D, DS, ER, JCB, MC, V.

★ **SILVER GULL MOTEL.** *20 E Salisbury St (28480).* 910/256-3728; FAX 910/256-2909; res: 800/842-8894. Web www.beach online.com. 32 kit. units, 3 story. June-Labor Day: S, D $135-$220; each addl $7; lower rates rest of yr. Crib $7. TV; cable. Ck-out 11 am. Coin lndry. Balconies. On ocean. Cr cds: A, C, DS, MC, V.

★★ **SURF MOTEL.** *711 S Lumina Ave (28480).* 910/256-2275; FAX 910/256-1206. 45 kit. suites, 4 story. Late May-early Sept: S, D $150-$215; each addl $10; wkly rates; wkend rates rest of yr. Crib $10. TV; cable. Pool. Coffee in rms. Restaurant adj 11 am-10 pm. Ck-out 11:30 am. Coin lndry. Balconies. Swimming beach. Cr cds: A, C, DS, MC, V.

★ **WATERWAY LODGE.** *7246 Wrightsville Ave (28403).* 910/256-3771; FAX 910/256-6916; res: 800/677-3771. 42 units, 4 story. May-Sept: S, D $90-$115; each addl $10; kits. $100-$130; under 12 free; wkly rates; higher rates wkends (2-day min); lower rates rest of yr. Crib free. Pet accepted; $15. TV; cable (premium). Pool. Coffee in rms. Restaurant opp 11 am-10 pm. Ck-out 11:30 am. Business servs avail. Refrigerators, microwaves. Cr cds: A, C, DS, MC, V.

Motor Hotel

★★★ **BLOCKADE RUNNER RESORT & HOTEL.** *275 Waynick Blvd (28480), ¼ mi S on US 76.* 910/256-2251; FAX 910/256-2251; res: 800/722-5809. Web www.blockade-runner.com. 150 rms, 7 story. Mid-May-mid-Sept: S, D $189-$289; each addl $25; suites $290-$375; under 12 free; lower rates rest of yr. Crib free. TV; cable. Heated pool; whirlpool, lifeguard. Supervised child's activities (June-Labor Day); ages 5-12. Coffee in rms. Restaurant (see OCEAN TERRACE). Rm serv 6:30 am-midnight. Bar; entertainment. Ck-out 11:30 am. Meeting rms. Business servs avail. Free airport transportation. Tennis privileges. Golf privileges. Exercise equipt; sauna, steam rm. Sailboat rentals. Private balconies. On ocean. Cr cds: A, C, D, DS, MC, V.

Hotel

★★ **HAMPTON INN & SUITES LANDFALL.** *1989 Eastwood Rd (28403), 4 mi E on US 74.* 910/256-9600; FAX 910/256-1996; res: 877/256-9600. Web www.landfallparkhotel.com. 120 rms, 4 story, 30 kit. suites. May-Sept: S, D $119; suites $169-$349; under 18 free; wkly rates; golf plans; wkends (2-day min); higher rates special events; lower rates rest of yr. Crib free. Pet accepted; $25. TV; cable (premium). Complimentary continental bkfst. Restaurant adj 11 am-11 pm. Bar 4:30-10 pm. Ck-out 11 am. Coin lndry. Meeting rms. Business servs avail. In-rm modem link. Concierge. Gift shop. 18-hole golf privileges, greens fee $75, pro, putting green, driving range. Exercise equipt. Pool; poolside serv. Some in-rm whirlpools, fireplaces; refrigerator, microwave, wet bar in kit. suites. Picnic tables, grills. Cr cds: A, C, D, DS, JCB, MC, V.

Inn

★ **THE COTTAGE.** *225 S Lumina Ave (28480).* 910/256-2251; FAX 910/256-5502; res: 800/541-1161. Web www.blockade-runner.

com. 13 rms, 2 story. Mid-May-mid-Sept: S, D $89-$235; each addl $25; under 12 free; lower rates rest of yr. Crib free. TV in sitting rm. Pool; whirlpool. Complimentary full bkfst. Restaurant adj 6:30 am-10 pm. Ck-out 11:30 am, ck-in 3 pm. Exercise equipt; sauna. Former boarding house. Totally nonsmoking. Cr cds: A, C, D, DS, MC, V.

Restaurants

★★ **BRIDGE TENDER.** *1414 Airle Rd (28480), at Wrightsville Beach Bridge. 910/256-4519.* Hrs: 11:30 am-2 pm, 5:30-10 pm; Fri to 11 pm; Sat 5-11 pm. Closed Sun; Jan 1, Thanksgiving, Dec 25. Bar. Semi-a la carte: lunch $5.95-$8.95, dinner $13.95-$23.95. Specializes in seafood, beef. View of waterway, marina. Cr cds: A, C, D, DS, MC, V.

★ **CLARENCE FOSTER'S.** *22 N Lumina Ave (28480). 910/256-0224.* Hrs: 5:30-10 pm. Closed Dec 25. Amer menu. Bar to 2 am. Semi-a la carte: dinner $6.75-$19.95. Specializes in seafood. Intimate dining; artwork on display. Cr cds: A, C, MC, V.

✓ ★ **DOCKSIDE.** *1308 Airlie Rd (28480). 910/256-2752.* Hrs: 11 am-9:30 pm; wkends to 10 pm. Closed Thanksgiving, Dec 24-25. Bar. Semi-a la carte: lunch $1.75-$9.95, dinner $7.95-$17.95. Specializes in grilled seafood, pasta. Outdoor dining. Casual dining. Overlooks dock, waterway; docking facilities. Cr cds: C, DS, MC, V.

★★ **KING NEPTUNE.** *11 N Lumina Ave on US 76 (28480). 910/256-2525.* Hrs: 5-10 pm; Sun 5:30-9:30 pm. Closed Thanksgiving, Dec 25. Caribbean menu. Bar to 2 am. Semi-a la carte: dinner $9.95-$20.95. Child's meals. Specializes in prime rib, seafood. Caribbean decor. Cr cds: A, C, MC, V.

★★ **OCEAN TERRACE.** *(See Blockade Runner)* 910/256-2251. Web www.blockade-runner.com. Hrs: 6:30 am-midnight; Sun brunch 11:30 am-2:30 pm. Closed wk of Dec 25. Res accepted. Bar. Semi-a la carte: bkfst $10.95, lunch $7-$14, dinner $15-$32. Sun brunch $14.95. Child's meals. Specializes in seafood, pasta. Pianist Fri, Sat; jazz Sun brunch. Parking. Oceanfront outdoor dining. Cr cds: A, C, D, DS, MC, V.

★★ **OCEANIC RESTAURANT & GRILL.** *703 S Lumina Ave (28480). 910/256-5551.* Hrs: 11:30 am-11 pm; Sun 4-11 pm; Sun brunch 10 am-2 pm. Closed Jan 1, Thanksgiving, Dec 25. Bar. Semi-a la carte: lunch $4.95-$10.95, dinner $10.95-$21.95. Sun brunch $4.75-$9.95. Child's meals. Specializes in seafood. Parking. Outdoor dining. Panoramic view of ocean. Cr cds: A, C, MC, V.

★★ **PUSSER'S LANDING.** *4 Marina St (28480). 910/256-2002.* Hrs: deck dining 11:30 am-10:30 pm; upper dining level from 5:30 pm. Closed Dec 25. Res accepted (upper dining level). Bar to midnight. Semi-a la carte: lunch $5.75-$15.95, dinner (upper dining level) $13.95-$20.95. Child's meals. Specializes in seafood, Caribbean fare, steaks. Entertainment Fri, Sun evenings. Beach resort atmosphere; dock. Cr cds: A, C, DS, MC, V.

✓ ★★ **RIALTO.** *530 Causeway Dr (28480), in The Landing Shopping Center. 910/256-1099.* Hrs: 5-10 pm; Fri, Sat to 11 pm. Closed Jan 1, Thanksgiving, Dec 25. Bar. Semi-a la carte: dinner $9.50-$18. Child's meals. Specializes in seafood, pasta. Cr cds: A, C, D, DS, MC, V.

Pennsylvania

Population: 11,881,643
Land area: 44,892 square miles
Elevation: 0–3,213 feet
Highest point: Mount Davis (Somerset County)
Entered union: Second of original 13 states (December 12, 1787)
Capital: Harrisburg
Motto: Virtue, liberty and independence
Nickname: Keystone State
State flower: Mountain laurel
State bird: Ruffed grouse
State tree: Eastern hemlock
State fair: (Pennsylvania State Farm Show), January 8-13, 2000, in Harrisburg
Time zone: Eastern
Web: www.state.pa.us

From its easternmost tip near Bordentown, New Jersey, to its straight western boundary with Ohio and West Virginia, Pennsylvania's 300-mile giant stride across the country covers a mountain-and-farm, river-and-stream, mine-and-mill topography. Its cities, people and resources are just as diverse. Philadelphia is a great city in the eastern part of the state, a treasure house of tradition and historical shrines; Pittsburgh is a great city in the western part, a mighty arsenal of industry. In this state are the Pennsylvania Dutch, their barns painted with vivid hex signs; here also are steel mills. Pennsylvania miners dig nearly all the anthracite coal in the US and still work some of the oldest iron mines in the country. Oil employees work more than 19,000 producing wells, and 55,000 farm families make up 20 percent of the Pennsylvania work force.

Pennsylvania, the keystone of the original 13 states, remains one of the keystones in modern America. A leader in steel and coal production, the state also is a leader in cigar leaf tobacco, apples, grapes, ice cream, chocolate products, mushrooms (nearly half of the US total) and soft drinks, plus factory and farm machinery, electronics equipment, scientific instruments, watches, textile machines, railroad cars, ships, assorted metal products and electrical machinery. This fifth most populous state is also a major factor in national politics.

Pennsylvania has been a keystone of culture. The first serious music in the colonies was heard in Bethlehem; today, it resounds throughout the state—Pittsburgh has an acclaimed symphony, as does Philadelphia. There are 140 institutions of higher learning (including the oldest medical school in the US at the University of Pennsylvania), celebrated art galleries and hundreds of museums.

Despite its size, all of Pennsylvania is within the motorist's grasp. Its 44,000 miles of state highways, including the 470-mile Pennsylvania Turnpike (pioneer of superhighways), plus 69,363 miles of other roads make up one of the largest road networks in the nation.

Swedes made the first settlement on this fertile land at Tinicum Island in the Delaware River in 1643. The territory became Dutch in 1655 and British in 1664. After Charles II granted William Penn a charter that made him proprietor of "Pennsilvania," this Quaker statesman landed here in 1682 and invested the land with his money, leadership and fellow Quakers. The Swedes, Finns and Dutch already in the new land were granted citizen-ship; soon came Welsh, Germans, Scots, Irish and French Huguenots. Of these, the Germans left the strongest imprint on the state's personality. Commercial, agricultural and industrial growth came quickly, and all these resources were contributed to the Revolution. In Pennsylvania, Washington camped at Valley Forge, the Declaration of Independence was signed and the Constitution drafted.

With Philadelphia the capital of the new nation, tides of pioneers pushed west and north to develop far corners of the state. The Civil War brought fresh industrial development, and for the past century Pennsylvania has continued to develop at an ever-quickening industrial pace. Today the Keystone State is an empire of industry and a storehouse of historic traditions.

When to Go/Climate

Pennsylvania's lowlands and hill country enjoy typical east-coast seasonal temperatures—hot, humid summers; relatively mild winters; crisp falls; and wet springs. The mountains, however, experience short summers and cold, snowy winters.

AVERAGE HIGH/LOW TEMPERATURES (°F)

PHILADELPHIA

Jan 38/23	May 73/53	Sept 78/59
Feb 41/25	June 82/62	Oct 66/47
Mar 52/33	July 86/67	Nov 55/38
Apr 63/42	Aug 85/66	Dec 43/28

PITTSBURGH

Jan 34/19	May 71/48	Sept 74/54
Feb 37/20	June 79/57	Oct 63/42
Mar 49/30	July 83/62	Nov 50/34
Apr 60/39	Aug 81/60	Dec 39/24

Parks and Recreation Finder

Directions to and information about the parks and recreation areas below are given under their respective town/city sections. Please refer to those sections for details.

NATIONAL PARK AND RECREATION AREAS

Key to abbreviations. I.H.S. = International Historic Site; I.P.M. = International Peace Memorial; N.B. = National Battlefield; N.B.P. = National Battlefield Park; N.B.C. = National Battlefield & Cemetery; N.C. = National Conservation Area; N.E.M. = National Expansion Memorial; N.F. = National Forest; N.G. = National Grassland; N.H. = National Historical Park; N.H.C. = National Heritage Corridor; N.H.S. = National Historic Site; N.L. = National Lakeshore; N.M. = National Monument; N.M.P. = National Military Park; N.Mem. = National Memorial; N.P. = National Park; N.Pres. = National Preserve; N.R. = National Recreational Area; N.R.R. = National Recreational River; N.Riv. = National River; N.S. = National Seashore; N.S.R. = National Scenic Riverway; N.S.T. = National Scenic Trail; N.Sc. = National Scientific Reserve; N.V.M. = National Volcanic Monument.

Place Name	Listed Under
Allegheny N.F.	WARREN
Allegheny Portage Railroad N.H.S.	EBENSBURG
Delaware Water Gap N.R.	same
Edgar Allan Poe N.H.S.	PHILADELPHIA
Eisenhower N.H.S.	same
Fort Necessity National Battlefield	UNIONTOWN
Friendship Hill N.H.S.	UNIONTOWN
Gettysburg N.M.P.	same
Hopewell Furnace N.H.S.	same
Independence N.H.	PHILADELPHIA
Johnstown Flood N.Mem.	JOHNSTOWN
Steamtown N.H.S.	SCRANTON
Thaddeus Kosciuszko N.Mem.	PHILADELPHIA
Valley Forge N.P.	same

STATE PARK AND RECREATION AREAS

Key to abbreviations. I.P. = Interstate Park; S.A.P. = State Archaeological Park; S.B. = State Beach; S.C. = State Conservation Area; S.C.P. = State Conservation Park; S.Cp. = State Campground; S.F. = State Forest; S.G. = State Garden; S.H.A. = State Historic Area; S.H.P. = State Historic Park; S.H.S. = State Historic Site; S.M.P. = State Marine Park; S.N.A. = State Natural Area; S.P. = State Park; S.P.C. = State Public Campground; S.R. = State Reserve; S.R.A. = State Recreation Area; S.Res. = State Reservoir; S.Res.P. = State Resort Park; S.R.P. = State Rustic Park.

Place Name	Listed Under
Bald Eagle S.P.	LOCK HAVEN
Bendigo S.P.	KANE
Blue Knob S.P.	BEDFORD
Black Moshannon S.P.	BELLEFONTE
Caledonia S.P.	CHAMBERSBURG
Canoe Creek S.P.	ALTOONA
Chapman S.P.	WARREN
Clear Creek S.P.	BROOKVILLE
Codorus S.P.	HANOVER
Cook Forest S.P.	CLARION
Fort Washington S.P.	FORT WASHINGTON
French Creek S.P.	POTTSTOWN
Gifford Pinchot S.P.	YORK
Gouldsboro S.P.	MOUNT POCONO
Greenwood Furnace S.P.	LEWISTOWN
Hickory Run S.P.	WHITE HAVEN
Hills Creek S.P.	MANSFIELD
Kettle Creek S.P.	LOCK HAVEN
Kinzua Bridge S.P.	KANE

CALENDAR HIGHLIGHTS

JANUARY
Pennsylvania State Farm Show (Harrisburg). State fair. Phone 717/787-5373.

FEBRUARY
Chocolate Lovers' Extravaganza (Hershey). Hotel Hershey. Everything chocolate—tasting & sampling, chef-taught classes, decorating instruction, and more. For reservations, phone 800/533-3131.

MAY
Devon Horse Show (Philadelphia). Horse Show Grounds in Devon. One of America's leading equestrian events. More than 1,200 horses compete; country fair; antique carriage drive. Phone 610/964-0550.

JUNE
Three Rivers Arts Festival (Pittsburgh). Point State Park. Juried, original works of local and national artists; paintings, photography, sculpture, crafts and videos; artists' market in outdoor plazas. Ongoing performances include music, dance and performance art. Special art projects; film festival; food; children's activities. Phone 412/281-8723.

CoreStates US Pro Cycling Championship (Philadelphia). Longest single-day cycling event in the country—156 miles.

JULY
Civil War Heritage Days (Gettysburg). Lectures by historians; Civil War collectors' show; entertainment; Civil War book show; firefighters' festival; fireworks. For information, phone Convention & Visitors Bureau 717/334-6274.

Folk Festival (Kutztown). Festival grounds. Celebration of Pennsylvania Dutch folk culture; quilts, music, dancing and food of Plain and Fancy Dutch. Craftspeople make baskets, brooms, rugs, toleware and other handcrafts. Phone 215/679-9610.

AUGUST
Das Awkscht Festival (Allentown). Macungie Memorial Park. 2,500 antique, classic and special-interest autos; arts and crafts; antique toy show, entertainment, food, fireworks. Phone 610/967-2317.

Musikfest (Bethlehem). Nine sites in downtown historic area. Nine-day festival celebrating Bethlehem's rich musical and ethnic heritage. More than 600 performances of all types of music from folk to rock. Phone 610/861-0678.

SEPTEMBER
Ligonier Highland Games and Gathering of the Clans of Scotland (Ligonier). Idlewild Park. Sports; massed pipe bands, Highland dancing competitions, Scottish fiddling; sheep dog, wool spinning and weaving demonstrations; genealogy booth; Scottish fair. Phone 724/238-3666.

Wine Country Harvest Festival (North East). Gravel Pit Park and Gibson Park. Arts and crafts, bands, buses to wineries, food. Phone 814/725-4262.

DECEMBER
Army-Navy Football Game (Philadelphia). John F. Kennedy Memorial Stadium or Veterans Stadium.

The Crossing. Washington Crossing Historical Park (Bucks Co.) Reenactment of George Washington's crossing of the Delaware River. Phone 215/493-4076.

Place Name	Listed Under
Kooser S.P.	SOMERSET
Laurel Hill S.P.	SOMERSET
Little Pine S.P.	WILLIAMSPORT
McConnell's Mill S.P.	NEW CASTLE
Moraine S.P.	BUTLER
Ohiopyle S.P.	UNIONTOWN
Ole Bull S.P.	GALETON
Parker Dam S.P.	CLEARFIELD
Pine Grove Furnace S.P.	CARLISLE
Presque Isle S.P.	ERIE
Prince Gallitzin S.P.	ALTOONA
Promised Land S.P.	HAWLEY
Pymatuning S.P.	CONNEAUT LAKE
Raccoon Creek S.P.	AMBRIDGE
Reeds Gap S.P.	LEWISTOWN
Ridley Creek S.P.	MEDIA
S.B. Elliott S.P.	CLEARFIELD
Shawnee S.P.	BEDFORD
Sizerville S.P.	PORT ALLEGANY
Tobyhanna S.P.	MOUNT POCONO
Whipple Dam S.P.	STATE COLLEGE
Yellow Creek S.P.	INDIANA

Water-related activities, hiking, riding, various other sports, picnicking and environmental interpretive centers, as well as camping, are available in many of these areas. More than 116 state parks and four environmental centers are scattered throughout the commonwealth. 57 campgrounds offer camping. Seven are open all year; the rest are open from 2nd Fri Apr–3rd Sun Oct or Dec. Occupancy is limited to two consecutive weeks; $9-$14 resident, $11-$16 nonresident/night (primitive areas); $11-$17 resident, $13-$19 nonresident/night (modern areas). Cabins (daily and weekly rentals spring, fall & winter; 1 wk only, Fri after Memorial Day–Fri before Labor Day). Boat launching (yearly) $10 resident, $15 nonresident. No pets allowed in overnight areas. Write to Bureau of State Parks, PO Box 8551, Harrisburg 17105-8551, for detailed information. Cabin reservations are made by calling the park directly. For other state park information, phone 888/PA-PARKS.

SKI AREAS

Place Name	Listed Under
Alpine Mountain Ski Area	STROUDSBURG
Big Boulder Ski Area	WHITE HAVEN
Blue Mountain Ski Area	ALLENTOWN
Blue Knob Ski Area	BEDFORD
Boyce Park Ski Area	PITTSBURGH
Camelback Ski Area	TANNERSVILLE
Doe Mountain Ski Area	ALLENTOWN
Elk Mt Ski Center	CARBONDALE
Hidden Valley Ski Area	SOMERSET
Jack Frost Ski Area	WHITE HAVEN
Montage Ski Area	SCRANTON
Mount Airy Lodge Ski Area	MOUNT POCONO
Mount Tone Ski Resort	CARBONDALE
Mountain View Ski Area	EDINBORO
Seven Springs Mt Resort Ski Area	DONEGAL
Shawnee Mountain Ski Area	SHAWNEE ON DELAWARE
Ski Denton/Denton Hill Ski Area	GALETON
Ski Liberty Ski Area	GETTYSBURG
Ski Roundtop Ski Area	YORK
Ski Sawmill Resort	WELLSBORO
Spring Mountain Ski Area	LIMERICK
Tanglwood Ski Area	HAWLEY

FISHING

Pennsylvania is one of the country's leading states in the amount of waters open to public and private fishing. There are nearly 5,000 miles of trout streams stocked annually and many thousands of miles of warm-water streams plus thousands of acres of lakes with walleye, panfish, muskellunge, and bass. Nonresident fishing license is $35; 3-day tourist license is $15; 7-day tourist license is $30. A $5.50 trout/salmon stamp also is required (for trout fishing only). Write to Pennsylvania Fish and Boat Commission, PO Box 67000, Harrisburg 17106-7000, or phone 717/657-4518, for the annual "Summary of Fishing Regulations and Laws" as well as maps and other useful information.

HUNTING

A license is required to hunt, take, trap or kill any wild bird or animal in the state. Nonresident hunting license, $80.75; children 12–16, $40.75. The license tag must be displayed on the back of outer garment, between the shoulders, at all times. For big-game and turkey hunting and small-game hunting in the fall, 250 square inches of fluorescent orange must be worn on the head, chest and back combined. For the "Official Digest, Pennsylvania Hunting and Trapping Regulations," contact the Pennsylvania Game Commission, 2001 Elmerton Ave, Harrisburg 17110-9797; 717/787-4250.

Driving Information

Safety belts are mandatory for all persons in front seat of vehicle. Children under 4 years must be in an approved passenger restraint anywhere in vehicle; age 4 and older may use a regulation safety belt; ages 1–3 may use a regulation safety belt in back seat only. Children under 4 years must use an approved safety seat in front seat; under age 1 must use an approved safety seat anywhere in the vehicle. For further information phone 717/787-6853.

INTERSTATE HIGHWAY SYSTEM

The following alphabetical listing of Pennsylvania towns in *Mobil Travel Guide* shows that these cities are within 10 miles of the indicated Interstate highways. A highway map should, however, be checked for the nearest exit.

Highway Number	Cities/Towns within 10 miles
Interstate 70	Bedford, Breezewood, Donegal, Greensburg, New Stanton, Somerset, Washington.
Interstate 78	Allentown, Bethlehem, Easton, Hamburg, Kutztown, Lebanon, Shartlesville.
Interstate 79	Conneaut Lake, Edinboro, Erie, Harmony, Meadville, Mercer, Pittsburgh, Washington.
Interstate 80	Bellefonte, Bloomsburg, Brookville, Clarion, Clearfield, Danville, Du Bois, Hazleton, Lewisburg, Lock Haven, Mercer, Mount Pocono, Sharon, Shawnee on Delaware, Stroudsburg, Tannersville, White Haven.
Interstate 81	Ashland, Carlisle, Chambersburg, Harrisburg, Hazleton, Scranton, Wilkes-Barre.
Interstate 83	Harrisburg, York.
Interstate 84	Milford, Scranton.
Interstate 90	Erie, North East.
Interstate 95	Bristol, Philadelphia.

Additional Visitor Information

A free visitors guide is available by calling 800/VISIT-PA, at the Pennsylvania Office of Travel, Tourism and Film Promotion, Dept of Community & Economic Development, PO Box 61, Warrendale 15086.

There are 14 state-run traveler information centers in Pennsylvania; visitors who stop by will find information and brochures most helpful in planning stops at points of interest. Their locations are as follows: I-79 Edinboro (southbound), 1 mile south of the Edinboro exit; I-81 Greencastle (northbound), 1 mile north of the Pennsylvania/Maryland border; I-95 Linwood (northbound), ½ mile north of the Pennsylvania/Delaware border; I-70 Warfordsburg (westbound), 1 mile from the Pennsylvania/Maryland border; I-80 West Middlesex (eastbound), ½ mile east of the Pennsylvania/Ohio border; Neshaminy Welcome Center, Mile Marker 351 (westbound) on the Pennsylvania Turnpike, 7 miles west of the Pennsylvania/New Jersey border, located inside the plaza building; I-78 Easton (westbound), 1 mile west of the Pennsylvania/New Jersey border; Sideling Hill Welcome Center, Mile Marker 172 (eastbound and westbound) on the Pennsylvania Turnpike, 10 miles east of the Breezewood exit, located inside the plaza building; I-81 Lenox (southbound), 4 miles south of the Lenox exit 64; I-83 Shrewsbury (northbound), ½ mile north of the Pennsylvania/Maryland border; Zelienople Welcome Center, Mile Marker 21 (eastbound), 21 miles east of the Pennsylvania/Ohio border, located inside the plaza building; I-79 northbound, north of PA/WV line; I-70 Washington County, east of PA/WV line.

Ride with Me—Pennsylvania, Interstate 81 is a 90-minute audio cassette tape that provides information on points of interest along I-81, from New York to Maryland. Topics such as the history of the Pennsylvania Dutch, notable battlegrounds and areas related to the Civil War and anthracite coal miners are discussed. Contact RWM Associates, PO Box 1324, Bethesda, MD 20817; 301/299-7817.

Allentown (D-9)

(See also Bethlehem, Easton, Kutztown, Quakertown)

Founded 1762 **Pop** 105,090 **Elev** 364 ft **Area Code** 484 & 610
Information Lehigh Valley Convention & Visitors Bureau, PO Box 20785, Lehigh Valley 18002-0785; 610/882-9200

Allentown, situated in the heart of Pennsylvania Dutch country, is conveniently accessible via a network of major highways. Allentown was originally incorporated as Northampton. The city later took the name of its founder, William Allen, a Chief Justice of Pennsylvania. Allentown was greatly influenced by the Pennsylvania Germans who settled the surrounding countryside and helped the city become the business hub for a rich agricultural community.

What to See and Do

Cedar Crest College (1867). (1,700 women) An 84-acre campus that incl nationally registered William F. Curtis Arboretum (tours); chapel with stained-glass windows portraying outstanding women in history; art galleries, sculpture gardens, museum and theater. Campus tours. 100 College Dr. Phone 610/437-4471. **Free**

Dorney Park and Wildwater Kingdom. Theme park/water park featuring more than 100 rides and attractions, antique wooden carousel, 4 world-class roller coasters, incl Steel Force—the longest, tallest, fastest steel roller coaster on the East Coast; 11 water slides; Berenstain Bear Country; midway games and entertainment; public picnic facility adjacent to the park. **Wildwater Kingdom** is one of the top seasonal water parks in the country. Dorney Park (May–Oct). Water park (mid-May–Sept). Operating hrs may vary. 3830 Dorney Park Rd. Phone 610/395-3724. ¢¢¢¢¢

Frank Buchman House. Constructed in 1892, this 3-story row house, typical of Allentown's inner city, is an example of Victorian architecture; period rms. (Sat & Sun afternoons; also by appt) 117 N 11th St. Phone 610/435-4664. **Free**

George Taylor House and Park (1768). House of a signer of the Declaration of Independence; 18th-century restoration period rms; museum; walled garden. Guided tours. (June–Oct, Sat & Sun afternoons; also by appt) 4 mi N off US 22, at Lehigh & Poplar Sts in Catasauqua. Phone 610/435-4664. **Free**

Haines Mill Museum (ca 1760). Operating gristmill (reconstructed 1909); exhibits portray the development and importance of the gristmill in rural America. (May–Sept, Sat & Sun afternoons; also hols & by appt) 3 mi W

via Hamilton St, at 3600 Dorney Park Rd (Cetronia). Phone 610/435-4664. **Free**

Lehigh County Museum. Exhibits illustrate economic, social and cultural history of the county. (Mon–Sat, Sun afternoons; closed hols) Old Courthouse, 5th & Hamilton Sts. Phone 610/435-4664. **Free**

Liberty Bell Shrine. Reconstructed Zion's church has shrine in basement area where Liberty Bell was hidden in 1777; contains a full-size replica of the original bell; a 46-ft mural depicts the journey of the bell; other historical exhibits, art collection. (Mon–Sat afternoons; closed most major hols) 622 Hamilton, at Church St. Phone 610/435-4232. **Free**

Lock Ridge Furnace Museum. Exhibits on the development of the US iron and steel industry; emphasis on the anthracite-coal-heated iron industry. Located in a reconstructed 19th-century iron furnace. (May–Sept, Sat & Sun afternoons; also by appt) 525 Franklin St in Alburtis. Phone 610/435-4664. **Free**

Muhlenberg College (1848). (1,700 students) Founded by the Lutheran Church to honor patriarch of Lutheranism in America. On campus is the Gideon F. Egner Memorial Chapel, an example of Gothic architecture. Also here is the Center for the Arts, a dramatic bldg designed by renowned architect Philip Johnson, which houses the Muhlenberg Theater Association. Campus tours. Chew & 26th Sts. Phone 610/821-3230.

Saylor Park Cement Industry Museum. Exhibits on the historical development of the cement industry and its role in modern society. Located in rebuilt cement kilns. (May–Sept, Sat & Sun afternoons; also hols & by appt) 245 N 2nd in Coplay. Phone 610/435-4664. **Free**

Skiing.

Blue Mountain. 7 chairlifts, T-bar; school, rentals; snowmaking; cafeteria, bar, lodge. Vertical drop 1,082 ft. Also 20 trails with day and night skiing. (Dec–Apr, daily) 17 mi N via PA 145, Treichlers exit, at "Y" turn right to Cherryville, and on to Danielsville, to top of Blue Mt. Phone 610/826-7700 or 800/235-2226 (in PA, ski report). ¢¢¢¢¢

Doe Mountain. 4 chairlifts, T-bar, 2 rope tows; 15 slopes; patrol, school, rentals; snowmaking; night skiing and snowboarding; restaurant, cafeteria, bar; nursery. Longest run 1½ mi; vertical drop 500 ft. (Dec–mid-Mar, daily) 12 mi SW, 4½ mi off PA 100, just N of Hereford. Phone 610/682-7100. ¢¢¢¢¢

Trexler Memorial Park. Spring outdoor bulb display (Apr–May). **Gross Memorial Rose Garden** (at peak 2nd wk June) and **Old-Fashioned Garden**, Cedar Pkwy (June–Aug). **Trout Nursery** and Fish-for-Fun stream, Lehigh Pkwy; picnic areas. **West Park**, 16th and Turner. Band concerts (June–Aug). Cedar Crest Blvd & Broadway. Phone 610/437-7628. **Free**

Trexler-Lehigh County Game Preserve. A 1,200-acre zoo, petting farm and wilderness tour that is home to more than 350 animals. Scenic overlooks; picnic area. (Memorial Day–Labor Day, daily; April–May & Sept–Oct, wkends) 4 mi W on US 22, then 6 mi N on US 309, near Schnecksville. Phone 610/799-4171. ¢¢

Trout Hall (1770). Oldest house in city, Georgian colonial; restored. Period rms, museum. Guided tours (Apr–Nov, Tues–Sun afternoons; also by appt; closed most major hols) 414 Walnut St. Phone 610/435-4664. **Free**

Troxell-Steckel House and Farm Museum (1756). Stone house is an example of German medieval architecture. Period rms; museum. Swiss-style bank barn adj has exhibits of farm implements, carriages and sleighs. Guided tours. (June–Oct, Sat & Sun afternoons; also by appt) 6 mi N on PA 145, then 1 mi W on PA 329, at 4229 Reliance St in Egypt. Phone 610/435-4664. **Free**

Annual Events

Mayfair. Allentown parks. Family arts festival with 150 free musical performances; crafts and food. Phone 610/437-6900. Thurs–Mon, Memorial Day wkend.

Das Awkscht Fescht. Macungie Memorial Park. 2,500 antique, classic and special-interest autos; arts and crafts; antique toy show, entertainment, food, fireworks. Phone 610/967-2317. 1st wkend Aug.

Drum Corps International–Eastern Regional Championship. J. Birney Crum Stadium, 21st & Linden Sts. Drum and bugle corps competition. Phone 610/966-5344. Early Aug.

Great Allentown Fair. Fairgrounds. 17th & Chew Sts. Farm and commercial exhibits, rides, games, food, entertainment. Phone 610/435-SHOW. Late Aug–early Sept.

Super Sunday. Hamilton Street Mall. Arts and crafts, food, entertainment. Mid-Sept.

Motels

★ **ALLENWOOD MOTEL.** *1058 Hausman Rd (18104).* 610/395-3707; FAX 610/530-8166. 21 rms. S, D, studio rms $45-$50; each addl $5. Crib free. Pet accepted. TV; cable. Restaurant nearby. Ck-out 11 am. Cr cds: A, C, DS, MC, V.

★★ **COMFORT SUITES.** *3712 Hamilton Blvd (18103).* 610/437-9100; FAX 610/437-0221; res: 800/228-5150. 122 suites, 4 story. Suites $105-$130; each addl $10; under 18 free. Crib free. TV; cable. Complimentary continental bkfst. Restaurant 7-2 am. Rm serv. Bar; entertainment Thurs-Sat. Ck-out noon. Meeting rms. Business servs avail. In-rm modem link. Sundries. Free airport, RR station, bus depot transportation. Exercise equipt. Refrigerators. Cr cds: A, C, D, DS, ER, JCB, MC, V.

✓★ **DAYS INN.** *1151 Bulldog Dr (18104).* 610/395-3731; FAX 610/395-9899; res: 800/329-7466; res: 888/395-5200. Web www.lilly days.com. 282 rms, 2 story. May-Oct: S $79.95; D $109; each addl $6; suites $109-$129; under 18 free; wkly rates; package plans; higher rates local festivals; lower rates rest of yr. Crib free. TV; cable. Pool; poolside serv, lifeguard. Playground. Restaurant 6:30 am-10 pm. Bar 2 pm-1 am. Ck-out noon. Coin lndry. Convention facilities. Business servs avail. Sundries. Free airport, bus depot transportation. Game rm. Lawn games. Some refrigerators. Some balconies. Cr cds: A, C, D, DS, MC, V.

★★ **HAMPTON INN.** *7471 Keebler Way (18106), I-78 exit 14A, S on PA 100.* 610/391-1500; FAX 610/391-0386; res: 800/426-7866. 124 rms, 5 story. S, D $89-$129; under 18 free; higher rates special events. Crib free. TV; cable. Complimentary continental bkfst. Restaurant nearby. Ck-out noon. Meeting rms. Business servs avail. Free airport transportation. Exercise equipt; sauna. Cr cds: A, C, D, DS, MC, V.

✓★ **HOLIDAY INN EXPRESS.** *1715 Plaza Ln (18104).* 610/435-7880; FAX 610/432-2555; res: 800/465-4329. 82 rms, 4 story. S, D $74-$95; each addl $5; under 18 free. Crib free. Pet accepted; $5. TV; cable. Complimentary continental bkfst. Restaurant nearby. Ck-out 11 am. Business servs avail. Cr cds: A, C, D, DS, MC, V.

Motor Hotel

★★ **SHERATON INN.** *3400 Airport Rd (18103), 5 mi E on US 22.* 610/266-1000; FAX 610/266-1888; res: 800/325-3535. 147 rms, 3 story, 30 suites. S $99; D $109; each addl $10; suites $115-$145; under 13 free; higher rates NASCAR races. Crib free. Pet accepted. TV; cable (premium), VCR avail. Indoor pool; whirlpool, lifeguard. Complimentary coffee in rms. Restaurant 6:30 am-10 pm. Rm serv. Bar 11-2 am, entertainment Tues-Sun. Ck-out noon. Meeting rm. Business servs avail. In-rm modem link. Bellhops. Sundries. Valet serv. Free airport transportation. Exercise equipt; sauna. Some refrigerators. Cr cds: A, C, D, DS, MC, V.

Hotel

★★★ **HILTON HOTEL.** *904 Hamilton Mall (18101).* 610/433-2221; FAX 610/433-6455; res: 800/999-7784. 224 rms, 9 story. S $125; D $135; each addl $10; suites $145-$250; under 18 free; wkend rates.

Crib free. TV; cable. Heated pool; lifeguard. Restaurant 6:30 am-10 pm. Bar 11-2 am. Ck-out 11 am. Meeting rms. Business servs avail. In-rm modem link. Free airport transportation. Exercise equipt; sauna. Cr cds: A, C, D, DS, ER, JCB, MC, V.

Inn

★★★ **THE GLASBERN INN.** *2141 Packhouse Rd (18051), Approx 10 mi W on I-78, exit PA 100 N, W on Main St, N on Church St to Pack House Rd.* 610/285-4723; FAX 610/285-2862. Web www.glas bern.com. 24 rms, 2 story, 17 suites. S $100-$155; D $120-$355; each addl $20; suites, kit units $120-$355; 2-night min special wkends, hols. Crib avail. TV; cable, VCR (movies). Heated pool. Complimentary full bkfst. Dining rm (public by res) 6-8 pm. Ck-out noon, ck-in 4 pm. Meeting rm. Business servs avail. Exercise equipt. Many whirlpools, fireplaces. Farmhouse, barn, gate house and carriage house built in late 1800s; antiques. Cr cds: A, C, MC, V.

Restaurants

★★★ **APPENNINO.** *3079 Willow St (18104), at Cedar Crest Blvd, 2½ mi N of PA 22 on Cedar Crest.* 610/799-2727. Hrs: 5:30-10 pm. Closed Sun; major hols. Res accepted. Northern Italian menu. Bar. Wine list. A la carte entrees: dinner $17-$30. Specialties: veal Valdostana, filet of sole in green sauce with shrimp. Own desserts. Restored hotel (1800s); imported Italian lamps, chandeliers and tapestry on chairs. Jacket. Cr cds: A, C, D, DS, MC, V.

★★ **BAY LEAF RESTAURANT.** *935 E Hamilton St (18103).* 610/433-4211. Hrs: 11:30 am-2 pm, 5-10 pm. Closed Sun; also major hols. Res accepted. Bar. A la carte entrees: lunch $7.95, dinner $13.95-$24.95. Specializes in seafood, steak, lamb. Street parking. Thai pictures. Cr cds: A, C, MC, V.

★★ **FEDERAL GRILL.** *536 E Hamilton St (18103).* 610/776-7600. E-mail info@federalgrill.com; web www.federalgrill.com. Hrs: 11 am-midnight; Sat, Sun brunch 11 am-3 pm. Closed most major hols. Res required Fri, Sat. Bar. A la carte entrees: lunch $5-$15, dinner $13-$24. Brunch $8-$15. Specializes in seafood, pasta. Parking. Outdoor dining. Cigar bar. Cr cds: A, C, D, DS, MC, V.

★★★ **THE FARMHOUSE.** *1449 Chestnut St (18049), 7 mi SE off 78, exit 17.* 610/967-6225. Web thefarmhouse.com. Hrs: 5-9 pm. Closed Sun. Res accepted. Contemporary Amer menu. Bar 5-11 pm. Wine list. A la carte entrees: dinner $16-$23. Specialties: creme brûlee, saffron risotto. Parking. Outdoor dining. In 1830 farmhouse. Cr cds: A, C, D, DS, MC, V.

Altoona (E-4)

(See also Ebensburg)

Founded 1849 **Pop** 51,881 **Elev** 1,170 ft **Area Code** 814
E-mail amcvb@aol.com **Web** www.alleghenymountains.com
Information Allegheny Mountains Convention & Visitors Bureau, Logan Valley Mall, Rte 220 & Goods Ln, 16602; 814/943-4183 or 800/84-ALTOONA

The rough, high Alleghenies ring this city, which was founded by the Pennsylvania Railroad. Altoona expanded rapidly after 1852, when the difficult task of spanning the Alleghenies with track, linking Philadelphia and Pittsburgh, was completed. The railroad shops still offer substantial employment for residents of the city and Blair County, but new and diversified industries now provide the economic base.

What to See and Do

Allegheny Portage Railroad National Site. View authentic Lemon House and original rebuilt Engine House; learn how canal boats were taken over the Allegheny Mts before the Horseshoe Curve was built. (Daily; closed Dec 25) In Cresson. Phone 814/886-6150. ¢¢¢

Baker Mansion Museum (1844-1848). Stone Greek-revival house of early ironmaster; now occupied by Blair County Historical Society. Hand-carved Belgian furniture of the period; transportation exhibits, gun collection, clothing, housewares. (Memorial Day–Labor Day, daily exc Mon; mid-Apr–Memorial Day & Labor Day–Oct, Sat & Sun; closed hols) 3500 Oak Lane. Phone 814/942-3916. ¢¢

Bland's Park. More than 30 rides and attractions incl antique carousel, miniature golf and pony rides. Also here are arcade games, picnic pavilions and restaurant. (May-Sept, daily exc Mon) 10 mi N, on US 220 in Tipton. Phone 814/684-3538. All-day ride pass ¢¢¢

Canoe Creek State Park. Approx 950-acre park features 155-acre lake. Swimming beach; fishing; boating (launches, rentals). Hiking. Picnicking (reservations for pavilion). Cross-country skiing, sledding, ice boating, ice skating. Cabins. Standard fees. 12 mi E via US 22. Phone 814/695-6807.

Fort Roberdeau. Reconstructed Revolutionary War fort with horizontal logs, contains lead smelter, blacksmith shop, lead miners' hut, barracks, storehouse, officers' quarters, powder magazine. Costumed guides; wknd reenactments. Visitor center. Picnicking, nature trails. (Mid-May–early Oct, daily exc Mon) 8 mi NE via US 220, Kettle St exit onto PA 1013. Phone 814/946-0048. ¢¢

Horseshoe Curve Visitors Center. World-famous engineering feat, carrying main-line Conrail and Amtrak trains around western grade of 91 ft per mi. Curve is 2,375 ft long and has a central angle of 220 degrees. Funicular runs between interpretive center and observation area. Gift shop. (May–Oct, daily; rest of yr, daily exc Mon) 5 mi W via well-marked, unnumbered road. Phone 814/946-0834. ¢¢

Lakemont Park. An amusement park with more than 30 rides and attractions; home of the nation's oldest wooden roller coaster; water park, miniature golf, entertainment. (May-Sept, daily) 700 Park Ave, Frankstown Rd & I-99. Phone 814/949-7275. All-day ride pass ¢¢¢

Prince Gallitzin State Park. Approx 6,200 acres; 26 mi of shoreline on 1,600-acre lake. Swimming beach; fishing; boating (rentals, mooring, launching), marina. Hiking trails, horseback riding. Cross-country skiing, snowmobiling, ice skating, ice fishing. Picnicking, snack bar, store, laundry facilities. Tent & trailer sites, cabins. Nature center; interpretive program. Standard fees. 8 mi NW on PA 36, then 1¼ mi NW off PA 53, then W on SR 1026. Phone 814/674-1000 or 814/674-1007 for reservations.

Railroader's Memorial Museum. Exhibits feature railroad artifacts, art and theme displays. Railroad rolling stock, steam and electric locomotive collections. (May–Oct, daily; rest of yr, daily exc Mon) 1300 9th Ave. Phone 814/946-0834. ¢¢

Wopsononock Mt. Lookout provides view of 6-county area from height of 2,580 ft; offers one of the best views in the state. 6 mi NW on Juniata Gap Rd.

Annual Events

Blair County Arts Festival. Penn State Altoona Campus. Arts, crafts, hobbies on display. Mid-May.

Keystone Country Festival. Lakemont Park. Arts & crafts, continuous music; food. Contact Convention & Visitors Bureau for details. Wkend after Labor Day.

Railfest. 1300 9th Ave. A celebration of Altoona's rich rail heritage. Phone 814/946-0834. Early Oct.

Motor Hotel

★★★ **RAMADA INN.** 1 Sheraton Dr (16601), 5 mi S on US 220. 814/946-1631; FAX 814/946-0785. 215 rms, 2-3 story. S, D $55-$85; each addl $5; suites $80-$140; under 18 free; some wkend rates; higher rates: football games, ski season. Crib $5. Pet accepted. TV; cable (premium), VCR avail. Indoor pool; wading pool, whirlpool, lifeguard. Complimentary continental bkfst. Restaurants 6:30 am-2:30 pm, 5:30-10 pm; Sat to 11 pm. Rm serv. Bar 11-2 am. Ck-out noon. Meeting rms. Business center. In-rm modem link. Bellhops. Valet serv. Gift shop. Airport transportation. 18-hole golf privileges. Downhill ski 20 mi. Exercise equipt. Rec rm. Microwaves avail. Cr cds: A, C, D, DS, JCB, MC, V.

Restaurants

★★★ **ALLEGRO.** 3926 Broad Ave (16601). 814/946-5216. Web www.lazerlink.com/brian/allegro. Hrs: 4-9:30 pm; Sat to 10 pm. Closed Sun; major hols. Res accepted. Italian, Amer menu. Bar. Wine list. Semi-a la carte: dinner $10.95-$25.50. Child's meals. Specializes in veal, seafood. Own baking, sauces, pasta. Cr cds: A, C, D, DS, MC, V.

✓★★ **HOUSE OF CHANG PEKING II.** 601 Logan Blvd (16602). 814/942-3322. Hrs: 11:30 am-10 pm; Sun to 9 pm. Closed Thanksgiving, Dec 25. Chinese menu. Bar. Semi-a la carte: lunch $4.45-$6.25, dinner $6.50-$16.50. Buffet: lunch (Sun) $7.45. Child's meals. Specialties: Peking shrimp, subgum wonton. Oriental decor. Cr cds: A, C, MC, V.

Ambridge (D-1)

(See also Beaver Falls, Pittsburgh)

Founded 1901 **Pop** 8,133 **Elev** 751 ft **Area Code** 724 **Zip** 15003

Information Beaver County Tourist Promotion Agency, 215B Ninth St, Monaca 15061-2028; 724/728-0212 or 800/342-8192

Founded by and taking its name from the American Bridge Co, this city rests on part of the site of Old Economy Village. In 1825, under the leadership of George Rapp, the Harmony Society established a communal pietistic colony that for many decades was important in the industrial life and development of western Pennsylvania. Despite its spiritual emphasis, Old Economy Village enjoyed a great material prosperity; farms were productive, craft shops were busy and factories made textiles widely acclaimed for their quality. Surplus funds financed railroads and industrial enterprises throughout the upper Ohio Valley. After celibacy was adopted and unwise investments were made, the community's productivity decreased. Officially dissolved in 1905, the remains of the community were taken over by the Commonwealth of Pennsylvania in 1916.

What to See and Do

⚑ **Old Economy Village.** Seventeen original Harmony Society bldgs located on 6 acres, restored and filled with furnishings of the period. Included are the communal leader's 32-rm Great House, the Feast Hall, the Grotto in the Gardens, wine cellars, a 5-story granary, shops, dwellings and community kitchens. Cobblestone streets link the bldgs. Special festivals and events. (Daily exc Mon; closed hols) 14th & Church Sts. Phone 724/266-4500. ¢¢

Raccoon Creek State Park. Approx 7,300 acres. Swimming beach; fishing, hunting; boating (rentals, mooring, launching). Hiking, horseback riding. Cross-country skiing, sledding, snowmobiling, ice skating, ice fishing. Snack bar. Tent & trailer sites. Nature & historical centers. Standard fees. 9 mi W on PA 151, then 7 mi S on PA 18, near Frankfort Springs. Phone 724/899-2200.

Annual Event

Nationality Days. Ethnic cultural displays, foods; native music, dancing. Mid-May.

Ashland (D-8)

(See also Hazleton)

Pop 3,859 **Elev** 1,000 ft **Area Code** 717 **Zip** 17921 **E-mail** tourism@ schylkill.org **Web** www.schylkill.org

Information Schuylkill County Visitors Bureau, 91 S Progress Ave, Pottsville 17901; 717/622-7700 or 800/765-7282

What to See and Do

Museum of Anthracite Mining. Museum on geology and technology of mining "hard" coal. (May–Oct, Mon–Sat, also Sun afternoons; rest of yr, Tues–Sat, also Sun afternoons; closed hols) Pine & 17th Sts. Phone 717/875-4708. ¢¢

Pioneer Tunnel Coal Mine and Steam Lokie Ride. Tour and explanation of mining in original coal mine tunnel; indoor temperature 52°F. Narrow-gauge steam train ride; picnic park. (Memorial Day–Oct, daily; May, wkends) 19th & Oak Sts. Phone 717/875-3850 or 717/875-3301. Mine tour ¢¢; Train ride ¢¢

Beaver Falls (D-1)

(See also Ambridge, Harmony)

Founded 1806 **Pop** 10,687 **Elev** 800 ft **Area Code** 724 **Zip** 15010

Information Beaver County Tourist Promotion Agency, 215B Ninth St, Monaca 15061-2028; 724/728-0212 or 800/342-8192

Founded as Brighton, the town changed its name for the falls in the Beaver River. The plates from which US currency is printed are made in Beaver Falls. Geneva College (1848) is located here.

Motels

✓★ **BEAVER VALLEY MOTEL.** *7257 Big Beaver Blvd (15010), ½ mi N of PA Tpke exit 2. 724/843-0630; FAX 724/843-1610; res: 800/400-8312.* 27 rms. S $39.60-$44; D $47-$52; each addl $6; kit units $225/wk; under 18 free; Crib free. TV; cable (premium). Complimentary coffee in lobby. Ck-out 11 am. Business servs avail. Cr cds: A, C, DS, MC, V.

★ **CONLEY INN.** *Big Beaver Blvd; RR 18 (15010), ¼ mi S of PA Tpke exit 2. 724/843-9300; FAX 724/843-9039; res: 800/345-6819; res: 800/345-6819.* 54 rms. S $45; D $55; each addl $10; under 12 free; wkly, monthly rates. Pet accepted. TV; cable. Restaurant 5:30-10 pm. Bar. Ck-out 11 am. Meeting rms. Business servs avail. Refrigerators. Cr cds: A, C, D, DS, MC, V.

Motor Hotel

★★★ **HOLIDAY INN.** *7195 Eastwood Rd (15010), PA 18N at PA Tpke exit 2. 724/846-3700; FAX 724/846-7008; res: 800/465-4329; res: 800/613-1490.* 156 rms, 3 story. S, D $89; under 18 free. Crib free. Pet accepted. TV. Indoor pool; whirlpool, poolside serv, lifeguard. Coffee in rms. Restaurant 6:30 am-2 pm, 5-10 pm. Rm serv. Bar 11-2 am. Ck-out noon. Meeting rms. Business servs avail. In-rm modem link. Valet serv. Sauna. Miniature golf. Game rm. Cr cds: A, C, D, DS, JCB, MC, V.

Restaurant

★★★ **WOODEN ANGEL.** *308 Leopard Lane (15009), from jct PA 51 & 68, ½ mi N on PA 51, ¼ mi W on Leopard Lane. 724/774-7880.* E-mail woodang@ccia.com; web www.novard.com/sebastian. Hrs: 11:30 am-11 pm; Sat from 5 pm. Closed Sun, Mon; major hols exc Mother's Day. Res accepted. Bar. Wine cellar. Semi-a la carte: lunch $6.75-$15.75, dinner $16-$28. Specializes in rack of lamb, fresh seafood. Own baking. Cr cds: A, C, D, DS, MC, V.

Bedford (F-4)

Settled 1751 **Pop** 3,137 **Elev** 1,106 ft **Area Code** 814 **Zip** 15522 **E-mail** dtice@bedford.net **Web** www.bedfordcounty.net

Information Bedford County Conference & Visitors Bureau, 141 S Juliana St; 814/623-1771 or 800/765-3331

Fort Bedford was a major frontier outpost in pre-Revolutionary War days. After the war it became an important stopover along the route of western migration and has remained so up until the present. Garrett Pendergrass, the second settler here, built Pendergrass's Tavern, which figures in a number of novels by Hervey Allen.

What to See and Do

Bedford County Courthouse. Federal-style bldg constructed in 1828 has unique hanging spiral staircase; oldest courthouse still in operation in PA. (Mon–Fri; closed hols) S Juliana St. Phone 814/623-4807. **Free**

Blue Knob Ski Area. 2 triple, 2 double chairlifts, 3 platter pulls; patrol, school, rentals; snowmaking; bar, cafeteria; nursery. Longest run approx 2 mi; vertical drop 1,072 ft. (Dec–Mar, daily) Half-day rates avail. Phone 814/239-5111 or 800/458-3403 (snow conditions). ¢¢¢¢¢

Fort Bedford Park and Museum. Log blockhouse, erected during Bedford's bicentennial. Contains large-scale replica of original fort, displays of colonial antiques and relics, Native American artifacts. (May–late Oct, daily) Ft Bedford Dr, N end of Juliana St, park along Raystown River. Phone 814/623-8891. ¢¢

Old Bedford Village. More than 40 authentic log and frame structures (1750–1851) house historical exhibits; crafts demonstrations; operating pioneer farm. Many special events throughout the yr. (1st Sat May–last Sun Oct, daily exc Wed) 1 mi N on US Business 220N. Phone 814/623-1156. ¢¢¢

State parks.

Shawnee. Approx 450-acre lake surrounded by 3,840 acres. Swimming beach; fishing, hunting; boating (rentals, mooring, launching). Cross-country skiing, snowmobiling, sledding, ice skating, ice fishing. Picnicking, playfield, snack bar. Camping; tent & trailer sites. Standard fees. 8 mi W on US 30. Phone 814/733-4218.

Blue Knob. Approx 6,000 acres. Swimming pool; fishing, hunting. Hiking. Cross-country skiing, snowmobiling, sledding. Picnicking, playfield. Camping (mid-Apr–mid-Oct). Standard fees. 10 mi N on US 220, then 8 mi NW on PA 869. Phone 814/276-3576.

Annual Events

Civil War Reenactment. Old Bedford Village. Early Sept.

Fall Foliage Festival Days. Entertainment, ethnic foods, antique cars, more than 350 craft booths. 1st 2 full wkends Oct.

Motels

✓★★★ **BEST WESTERN.** *Rte 240 (15522), 2 mi N via US 220 Business, PA Tpke exit 11. 814/623-9006; FAX 814/623-7120; res: 800/752-8592.* Web www.bestwestern.com/best.html. 105 rms, 2 story. Apr-Oct: S $49.95; D $59.95; suites $67.95; each addl $10; under 18 free;

lower rates rest of yr. Crib free. Pet accepted, some restrictions; $50. TV; cable (premium), VCR avail (movies). Pool; whirlpool, lifeguard. Restaurant 6:30-11 am, 5-10 pm; Sat, Sun 6:30 am-10 pm. Bar 5 pm-midnight. Ck-out noon. Meeting rms. Gift shop. Exercise equipt; sauna. Game rm. Cr cds: A, C, D, DS, MC, V.

★ **ECONO LODGE.** *141 Hillcrest Dr. (15522). 814/623-5174; FAX 814/623-5455.* Web www.hotelchoice.com. 32 rms, 2 story. May-Oct: S $42-$58; D $46-$65; each addl $6; under 18 free; ski plans; higher rates special events; lower rates rest of yr. Crib free. Pet accepted. TV; cable (premium). Bar 4 pm-midnight. Ck-out 11 am. Downhill ski 15 mi. Game rm. Cr cds: A, C, D, DS, JCB, MC, V.

★★★ **QUALITY INN.** *RR 2 (15522), 2 mi N on US 220 Business, 1 blk N of PA Tpke exit 11. 814/623-5188; FAX 814/623-0049; res: 800/228-5050.* Web www.qualityinn.com. 66 rms. May-Nov: S $57-$63; D $63-$69; each addl $6; under 18 free; lower rates rest of yr. Crib $4. Pet accepted, some restrictions. TV; cable (premium). Pool. Complimentary continental bkfst. Restaurant 7 am-10 pm. Bar 11 am-11 pm. Ck-out 11 am. Meeting rms. Business servs avail. Downhill ski 20 mi. Cr cds: A, C, D, DS, ER, JCB, MC, V.

Restaurant

★★ **ED'S STEAK HOUSE.** *Us 22 (15522), 2 mi N on US 220 Business, ¼ mi N of PA Tpke exit 11. 814/623-8894.* Hrs: 7 am-9 pm; Fri, Sat to 10 pm. Closed Thanksgiving, Dec 25. Res accepted. Bar. Semi-a la carte: bkfst $2.59-$4.59, lunch $2.99-$5.99, dinner $6.59-$14.99. Child's meals. Specializes in steak, seafood. Family-owned. Cr cds: A, C, MC, V.

Bellefonte (D-5)

(See also State College)

Settled 1770 **Pop** 6,358 **Elev** 809 ft **Area Code** 814 **Zip** 16823
E-mail countyseat@aol.com **Web** iul.com/bellefonte
Information Bellefonte Intervalley Area Chamber of Commerce, Train Station, 320 W High St; 814/355-2917

When the exiled French minister Talleyrand saw the Big Spring here in 1794, his exclamation—"Beautiful fountain"—gave the town its name. Bellefonte is perched on seven hills at the southeast base of Bald Eagle Mountain.

What to See and Do

Black Moshannon State Park. Approx 3,450 acres. Swimming beach; fishing, hunting; boating (rentals, mooring, launching). Hiking. Cross-country skiing, snowmobiling, ice skating, ice fishing, ice boating. Picnicking, snack bar. Tent & trailer sites, cabins. Interpretive program. Standard fees. N via PA 144/150, SW via US 220, then approx 12 mi W on PA 504. Phone 814/342-5960.

Centre County Library and Historical Museum. Local historical museum incl central Pennsylvania historical and genealogical books, records. (Daily exc Sun; closed hols) 200 N Allegheny St. Phone 814/355-1516.   **Free**

Restaurant

★★ **GAMBLE MILL TAVERN.** *160 Dunlap St (16823), at Lamb St Bridge. 814/355-7764.* Web www.statecollege.com. Hrs: 11:30

am-2 pm, 5-8 pm. Closed Sun; Thanksgiving, Dec 25. Res accepted. Continental menu. Bar. A la carte entrees: lunch $6-$10, dinner $12.50-$24. Specializes in fresh seafood, veal, duck. Own desserts. Restored mill (1786); rustic early American decor. Cr cds: C, DS, MC, V.

Bethlehem (D-9)

(See also Allentown, Easton, Quakertown)

Founded 1741 **Pop** 71,428 **Elev** 340 ft **Area Code** 484 & 610
E-mail BTA@itw.com **Web** info@bethtour.org
Information Bethlehem Tourism Authority, 52 W Broad St, 18018; 610/868-1513 or 800/360-8687

The city is famous throughout the world for Bethlehem Steel products and is also well known for its Bach Festival, for Lehigh University (1865), Moravian College (1807), Musikfest, its historic district and as "America's Christmas city."

Moravians, members of a very old Protestant denomination that came here to the banks of the Lehigh River, assembled on Christmas Eve 1741 in the only building, a log house that was part stable. Singing a hymn that praised Bethlehem, they found a name for their village. The musical heritage, too, dates from this moment; string quartets and symphonies were heard here before any other place in the colonies.

The opening of the Lehigh Canal in 1829 started industrialization of the area and development of the borough of South Bethlehem (1865), which was incorporated into the city of Bethlehem in 1917.

What to See and Do

Brethren's House (1748). Early residence and shop area for single men of the Moravian Community. Used as a general hospital by the Continental Army during the Revolutionary War. Now serves Moravian College as its Center for Music and Art. Church & Main Sts. Phone 610/861-3916.

Central Moravian Church (1806). Federal-style with hand-carved detail, considered foremost Moravian church in the US. Noted for its music, incl a trombone choir in existence since 1754. May be toured only in combination with Moravian Museum community walking tour. Main & W Church Sts.

God's Acre (1742–1910). Old Moravian cemetery following Moravian tradition that all gravestones are laid flat, indicating that all are equal in the sight of God. May be toured only in combination with Moravian Museum community walking tour. Market St.

Hill-to-Hill Bridge. Joins old and new parts of the city and provides excellent view of historic area, river and Bethlehem Steel plant. Main St, PA 378 over Lehigh River.

Historic Bethlehem Inc's 18th-Century Industrial Quarter. Guided tours (July-Aug, Sat; late Nov-late Dec, wkends). (See ANNUAL EVENTS) Ohio Rd & Main St (pedestrian entrance); Old York Rd & Union Blvd (parking lot entrance). Phone 610/691-0603. Tour of area includes

Goundie House (1810). Restored Federal-style brick house has period-furnished rms and interpretive exhibits. 501 Main St.

Luckenbach Mill (1869). Restored gristmill contains contemporary craft gallery and museum shop; also the offices of Bethlehem Area Chamber of Commerce and Historic Bethlehem Inc. Interpretive display here is incl in guided tour.

Springhouse (1764). Reconstruction on site of original spring that served Moravian community as a water source from the time of settlement in 1741 until 1912.

Tannery (1761). Exhibits Moravian crafts, trades and industries. Includes a working model of the original oil mill.

Waterworks (1762) with reconstructed 18-ft wooden waterwheel and pumping mechanisms.

Kemerer Museum of Decorative Arts. Exhibits incl art, Bohemian glass, toys, prints, china; regional German folk art from 1750–1900; Federal furniture; period rm settings. (Daily exc Mon; closed hols) 427 N New St. Phone 610/691-0603. ¢¢

Lost River Caverns. Stalagmites, stalactites, other formations. Picnic area; Gilman Museum with rocks and minerals, ancient and modern armor; also jungle garden (free). 30-min guided tours. (Daily; closed Jan 1, Thanksgiving, Dec 25) Durham St, 3 mi SE via PA 412 in Hellertown. Phone 610/838-8767. Tours ¢¢¢

Moravian Museum (Gemein Haus) (1741). This five-story log bldg is the oldest structure in the city; docents interpret the history and culture of early Bethlehem and the Moravians. 2 tours avail: 45-min tour of museum only; a 2-hr walking tour of the community incl the museum, Old Chapel, Central Moravian Church, God's Acre and a walk down historic Church St. (Tues–Sat; closed Good Friday, Holy Saturday, most major hols & Jan) 66 W Church St. Phone 610/867-0173. Museum ¢¢; Walking tour ¢¢¢

Old Chapel (1751). Once called the "Indian chapel" because so many Native Americans attended the services, this stone structure, the second church for the Moravian congregation, is still used frequently. May be toured only in combination with Moravian Museum community walking tour. Heckewelder Place, adjoining Moravian Museum.

Annual Events

Shad Festival. Historic Bethlehem Inc's 18th-century Industrial Quarter. Old-fashioned planked shad bake (res required for dinner), exhibits, demonstrations. Phone 610/691-0603. 1st Sun May.

Bach Festival. Packer Church, Lehigh University campus. One of the country's outstanding musical events. Famous artists and the Bach Choir of Bethlehem participate. Phone 610/866-4382. Mid–late May.

Moravian College Alumni Association Antiques Show. Johnston Hall, Moravian College Campus. Phone 610/861-1366. Early June.

Musikfest. Nine-day festival celebrating Bethlehem's rich musical and ethnic heritage. More than 600 performances (most free) of all types of music incl folk, big-band, jazz, Bach, country-western, chamber, classical, gospel, rock, swing; held at 9 different sites in downtown historic area. Also children's activities. Phone 610/861-0678. Late Aug.

Christmas. Bethlehem continues more than 2 centuries of Christmas tradition with candlelight, music and a number of special events. Moravians sing their own Christmas songs intermingled with Mozart and Handel. A huge "Star of Bethlehem" shines from the top of South Mt and the Hill-to-Hill Bridge has special lighting. The community "Putzes," a Moravian version of nativity scenes, are open to the public daily. Thousands of people post their Christmas cards from Bethlehem. Night Light Tours of city's Christmas displays and historical areas are offered (Dec) by the Bethlehem Tourism Authority. Reservations suggested. Phone 610/868-1513 or 800/360-8687. Thanksgiving–Jan 1.

Live Bethlehem Christmas Pageant. Scores of volunteers, garbed in biblical costumes, and live animals (incl camels, horses, donkey and sheep) join together to re-create the nativity story; narrated. Phone 610/867-2893. 1st wkend Dec.

Motels

★★ **COMFORT INN.** 3191 Highfield Dr (18020), US 22 exit 191. 610/865-6300; FAX 610/865-5074; res: 800/732-2500. 116 rms, 2½ story. S $59-$80; D $66-$86; each addl $6; under 18 free; ski plan. Crib free. Pet accepted. TV; cable, VCR (movies $5). Complimentary continental bkfst. Restaurant adj. Bar noon-2 am; entertainment Fri, Sat. Ck-out noon. Business servs avail. Valet serv. Cr cds: A, C, D, DS, ER, JCB, MC, V.

[D] [icons] SC

★★★ **HOLIDAY INN.** Rte 512 & Rte 22; 3560 Bath Pike (18017). 610/866-5800; FAX 610/867-9120; res: 800/465-4329. 192 rms, 2 story. S $110-$115; D $120-$125; each addl $10; under 18 free. Crib free. TV; cable. Pool; wading pool, lifeguard. Restaurant 6:30 am-10 pm. Rm serv. Bar 11-2 am. Ck-out noon. Meeting rms. Business center. In-rm modem link. Valet serv. Gift shop. Free airport, bus depot transportation. Exercise equipt. Cr cds: A, C, D, DS, MC, V.

[D] [icons] SC

Inn

★★★ **WYDNOR HALL INN.** 3612 Old Philadelphia Pike (18015). 610/867-6851; FAX 610/866-2062; res: 800/839-0020. 5 rms, 3 story, 2 suites. No elvtr. S $100-$130; D $110-$140; each addl $10; suites $120-$130; wkend rates; wkend, hols (1-3 day min); higher rates special events. TV. Complimentary continental bkfst. Ck-out 11 am, ck-in 2-8 pm. Built in 1895. European-style inn; antiques. Totally nonsmoking. Cr cds: A, C, DS, MC, V.

Restaurants

★★ **CAFE.** 221 W Broad St (18018). 610/866-1686. Hrs: 11 am-2 pm, 5-9 pm. Closed Mon, Sun. Res required Fri, Sat (dinner). International menu. Semi-a la carte: lunch $6-$7, dinner $14-$21. Specializes in fresh seafood, Thai cuisine, French pastries. Piano Fri, Sat. Totally nonsmoking. Cr cds: A, C, D, MC, V.

★★★ **CAFE LUIGI.** 2915 Schoenersville Rd (18017). 610/694-8853. Hrs: 4-10 pm. Closed Mon, Sun; also most major hols. Res required Fri, Sat. Italian menu. Setups. A la carte entrees: dinner $11.95-$19.95. Child's meals. Specialties: pasta alla basta, penne alla dante, chicken alla cognac. Parking. Pictures. Totally nonsmoking. Cr cds: A, C, D, DS, MC, V.

[D]

★★ **CANDLELIGHT INN.** 4431 Easton Ave (18020), US 22 exit 191. 610/691-7777. Hrs: 11 am-10 pm; Sat from 4 pm; Sun from 10 am. Closed some major hols. Res accepted. Continental menu. Bar. Semi-a la carte: lunch $5.95-$8.95, dinner $8.95-$19.95. Child's meals. Specializes in prime rib, steak, seafood. Contemporary decor. Cr cds: A, C, D, DS, MC, V.

[D]

✓★★ **EASTERN CHINESE RESTAURANT INC.** 3926 Linden St (18020). 610/868-0299. Hrs: 11 am-10 pm. Closed Thanksgiving. Res required Fri, Sat (dinner). Chinese menu. Liquor, wine, beer. Semi-a la carte: lunch $6-$8, dinner $10-$15. Specializes in chicken, seafood, beef. Parking. Chinese decor. Cr cds: A, C, D, DS, MC, V.

[D] [icon]

★★★ **INN OF THE FALCON.** 1740 Seidersville Rd (18015). 610/868-6505. Hrs: 5-9:30 pm. Closed Sun; also major hols. Res required. International menu. Bar. Wine list. A la carte entrees: dinner $15-$24. Specialties: seafood strudel, salmon chaine, filet nouveau. Parking. Building was built in 1800s. Antiques, fireplaces. Cr cds: A, C, DS, MC, V.

[D]

★★★ **MAIN STREET DEPOT RESTAURANT.** 61 W Lehigh St (18018). 610/868-7123. Hrs: 11:30 am-2 pm, 4:30-9:30 pm. Closed Sun; also many major hols. Res required Fri, Sat (dinner). Bar to midnight. A la carte entrees: lunch $4.50-$7, dinner $15-$27. Specialties: veal ala Jessica, Norwegian chicken, salmon Adria. Parking. 1873 Victorian railway station; old train pictures, gas chandeliers. Family-owned since 1979. Cr cds: C, MC, V.

[D] [icon]

★★ **MINSI TRAIL INN.** 626 Stefko Blvd (18017). 610/691-5613. Web www.minsitrailinn.com. Hrs: 11 am-9 pm; Sun brunch 11 am-3 pm. Closed some major hols. Res required Fri, Sat (dinner). Greek, Amer menu. Bar. A la carte entrees: lunch $5.95-$9.95, dinner $8.95-$18.95. Sun brunch $10.95. Child's meals. Specializes in seafood, veal, beef. Parking. Totally nonsmoking. Cr cds: C, MC, V.

[D]

Bird-in-Hand (F-8)

(See also Ephrata, Lancaster)

Pop 700 (est) **Elev** 358 ft **Area Code** 717 **Zip** 17505
Web www.800padutch.com

Information Pennsylvania Dutch Convention and Visitors Bureau, 501 Greenfield Rd, Lancaster 17601; 717/299-8901 or 800/723-8824

This Pennsylvania Dutch farming village got its name from the signboard of an early inn.

What to See and Do

Amish Village. Reconstructed and original bldgs incl blacksmith shop, schoolhouse, operating smokehouse; livestock. Guided tours of Amish farmhouse. (Mar–Dec, daily; rest of yr, most wkends; closed wk of Thanksgiving, also Dec 25) 1 mi W on PA 340, then 3 mi S on PA 896. Phone 717/687-8511.

Bird-in-Hand Farmers' Market. Indoor market with a wide variety of Pennsylvania Dutch foods and gifts. (July–Oct, Wed–Sat; Apr–June & Nov, Wed, Fri & Sat; rest of yr, Fri & Sat; closed Jan 1, Thanksgiving, Dec 25) On PA 340 & Maple Ave. Phone 717/393-9674.

Folk Craft Center & Museum. Early 18th-century bldgs display tools, household implements, stoneware pottery, toys, Stiegel glass, quilts, coverlets and early Pennsylvania Dutch memorabilia; log cabin loom house (1762); herb and ornamental gardens; turn-of-the-century woodworking and print shops; audiovisual presentation. (Apr–Nov, daily) 1½ mi W on PA 340, then N on Mt Sidney Rd, in Witmer. Phone 717/397-3609. ¢¢

The People's Place. Arts and heritage center features three-screen documentary on the Amish; interpretive museum with hands-on exhibits; Amish quilt museum. Also bookstore, art gallery. (Daily exc Sun; closed Jan 1, Thanksgiving, Dec 25) 5 mi E on PA 340, on Main St in Intercourse. Phone 717/768-7171. ¢¢—¢¢¢

Weavertown One-Room Schoolhouse. Life-size animated re-creation of activities at a one-rm schoolhouse. (Early April–Oct, daily; Mar & Nov, wkends) 1 mi E via PA 340. Phone 717/768-3976 or 717/291-1888 (winter). ¢¢

Motel

★★★ **BIRD-IN-HAND FAMILY INN.** *2740 Old Philadelphia Pike (17505). 717/768-8271; FAX 717/768-1117; res: 800/537-2535.* E-mail smucker@bird-in-hand.com; web www.bird-in-hand.com. 100 rms, 1-2 story. May-Nov: S $60-$88; D $74-$90; each addl $8; under 16 free; higher rates wkends; lower rates rest of yr. Crib $6. TV; cable, VCR avail (movies). 2 pools, 1 indoor. Playground. Complimentary coffee in rms. Restaurant 6 am-9 pm. Ck-out 11 am. Coin lndry. Meeting rms. Business servs avail. In-rm modem link. Sundries. Lighted tennis. Game rm. Refrigerators; microwaves avail. Picnic tables. Cr cds: A, C, D, DS, MC, V.

Inns

★★★ **GREYSTONE MANOR BED & BREAKFAST.** *2658 Old Philadelphia Pike (17505), on S side of PA 340. 717/393-4233; FAX 717/393-0616.* Web www.800padutch.com/greystone.html. 13 rms, 3 story, 6 suites. No rm phones. S $70-$90; D $75-$95; each addl $15; suites $95-$135; under 2 free; min stay hols, wkends. Closed Jan. Children in Carriage House only. TV. Complimentary full bkfst. Ck-out 11 am, ck-in 3 pm. Balconies. Picnic tables. Victorian mansion built in 1883; Carriage House was once a barn (1880s). Authentic antique furnishings, original woodwork, cut crystal doors. Totally nonsmoking. Cr cds: C, MC, V.

★★★ **VILLAGE INN.** *2695 Old Philadelphia Pike (17505). 717/293-8369; FAX 717/768-1117; res: 800/914-2473; res: 800/914-2439.*

Web www.yourinfo.com/lanco/smucker/birdhand.html. 11 units, 3 story, 6 suites. Mid-June-Nov: S, D $79-$99; each addl $10; suites $109-$139; under 4 free; lower rates rest of yr. Closed early Dec-early Feb. Crib free. TV; cable. Pool privileges. Complimentary continental bkfst. Restaurant nearby. Ck-out noon, ck-in 3 pm. Tennis privileges. Built in 1734 to serve as inn on Old Philadelphia Pike. Interior Victorian in ambience. Cr cds: A, C, DS, MC, V.

Restaurants

✓★★ **AMISH BARN RESTAURANT & GIFT.** *3029 Old Philadelphia Pike (17505). 717/768-8886.* Hrs: 8 am-7 pm; summer to 9 pm. Res accepted exc hols. Pennsylvania Dutch menu. A la carte entrees: bkfst $3-$5.25, lunch $3.95-$6, dinner $5.95-$13.95. Child's meals. Specialties: apple dumplings, shoofly pie. Courtyard patio dining. Rustic Amish decor. Family-owned. Cr cds: A, C, DS, MC, V.

★ **PLAIN & FANCY FARM.** *3121 Old Philadelphia Pike (17505). 717/768-4400.* Hrs: 11:30 am-8 pm; Sun noon-7 pm. Res accepted. Pennsylvania Dutch cuisine. Closed Dec 24, 25. Complete meals: lunch, dinner $14.95. Child's meals. Specializes in family-style food. Authentic Amish homestead. Buggy rides avail 8 am-dusk. Variety of specialty shops. Family-owned. Totally nonsmoking. Cr cds: A, C, DS, MC, V.

Bloomsburg (D-7)

(See also Danville)

Settled 1802 **Pop** 12,439 **Elev** 530 ft **Area Code** 717 **Zip** 17815
E-mail cmtpa@bwkip.com **Web** www.bwkip.com/~cmtpa
Information Columbia-Montour Tourist Promotion Agency, 121 Papermill Rd; 570/784-8279 or 800/847-4810

Situated on the north bank of the Susquehanna River, Bloomsburg is the seat of Columbia County. The town was a center of mining, transportation and industry during the 19th and early 20th centuries. Although manufacturing continues to be the largest employer here, Bloomsburg retains the relaxed atmosphere of earlier days with its lovely scenery and many covered bridges. In nearby Orangeville, nine miles west on PA 487, Fishing Creek offers trout, bass and pickerel.

The only incorporated town in the state (all the others are boroughs or cities), Bloomsburg has silk and rayon manufacturers; it also produces architectural aluminum, processed foods and electronic products. During the Civil War, Union troops came here to crush the "Fishing Creek Confederacy," a group of alleged draft dodgers who were reportedly building fortifications; no fort was found, and the men were released. One of the "Molly Maguire" murder trials was held here. (The Molly Maguires was a miners' society seeking improved conditions through force and violence.)

What to See and Do

Bloomsburg University of Pennsylvania (1839). (6,600 students) On campus are Carver Hall (1867); the Harvey A. Andruss Library (1966); Haas Center for the Arts (1967) with 2,000-seat auditorium and art gallery; McCormick Center for Human Services (1985); Redman Stadium and Nelson Field House. Tours (academic yr, Mon-Fri). E 2nd St. Phone 570/389-4316.

Columbia County Historical Society. Museum and Edwin M. Barton Library with local history exhibits, pioneer items. (Apr–Oct, Thurs–Sat; closed major hols) 6 mi N on PA 487; 410 Main St, in Orangeville. Phone 570/683-6011. Museum tour **Free**; Library research/hr ¢

Historic District. More than 650 structures spanning architectural styles ranging from Georgian to art deco. Center of town. Phone 570/784-7703.

Twin Covered Bridges. Believed to be only twin covered bridges in US. More than 20 other covered bridges are in the area. 10 mi N on PA 487.

Annual Events

Bloomsburg Fair. Fairgrounds, W side of town. Fair held since 1854. Agricultural and industrial exhibits; harness racing. 8 days late Sept.

Covered Bridge & Arts Festival. I-80, exit 35. Tours of covered bridges; apple butter boil, weaving; old-fashioned arts & crafts. Early Oct.

Seasonal Event

Bloomsburg Theatre Ensemble. Alvina Krause Theatre, 226 Center St. Three to four wks of performances for each of six plays. For info contact BTE, PO Box 66; 570/784-8181. Main stage Oct–June (special performances rest of yr).

Motels

✓ ★ **BUDGET HOST PATRIOT INN.** *6305 New Berwick Hwy (17815).* 570/387-1776; FAX 570/387-9611; res: 800/873-1180. 48 rms. S $42-$48; D $48-$55; each addl $6; under 18 free. Crib free. TV; cable, VCR avail (movies). Restaurant adj 11 am-9 pm. Bar from 4 pm. Ck-out noon. Meeting rms. Business servs avail. Health club privileges. Some refrigerators. Cr cds: A, C, D, DS, MC, V.

D ⌷ ⌷ ⌷ SC

★★ **INN AT BUCKHORN.** *5 Buckhorn Rd (17815),* I-80 at Buckhorn exit 34. 570/784-5300; FAX 570/387-0367; res: 888/754-6600. 120 rms, 2 story. S $45-$65; D $50-$70; each addl $5; under 18 free. Crib $5. Pet accepted. TV; cable. Coffee in lobby. Restaurant adj 6 am-10 pm. Bar 7-2 am, Sun from 11 am. Ck-out 11 am. Business servs avail. Sundries. Balconies. Cr cds: A, C, D, DS, ER, JCB, MC, V.

⌷ ⌷ ⌷ SC

Inns

★★★ **INN AT TURKEY HILL.** *991 Central Rd (17815),* at I-80 exit 35. 570/387-1500; FAX 570/784-3718. 18 rms, 2 story. S $87, D $92; each addl $15; suites $115-$185; under 12 free. Pet accepted. $15. TV; cable. Complimentary continental bkfst. Dining rm 5-9 pm. Rm serv. Bar. Ck-out noon, ck-in 2 pm. Business servs avail. In-rm modem link. Airport, bus depot transportation. Fireplace in some rms. Elegant antiques. Old homestead (1839); guest rooms overlook landscaped courtyard; gazebo, lily pond. Cr cds: A, C, D, DS, MC, V.

D ⌷ ⌷ ⌷ SC

★★ **MAGEE'S MAIN STREET INN.** *20 W Main St (17815).* 570/784-3500; FAX 570/784-5517; res: 800/331-9815. 43 rms, 3 story. S $57-$79; D $66-$87; each addl $3.95-$7.95; under 6 free. Pet accepted. TV; cable. Complimentary full bkfst. Dining rm 7 am-midnight. Bar 11-1 am, Sun to 11 pm. Ck-out noon. Meeting rms. Business servs avail. Cr cds: A, C, D, DS, MC, V.

⌷ ⌷ ⌷ SC

Bradford (B-4)

(See also Kane, Warren)

Settled 1827 **Pop** 9,625 **Elev** 1,442 ft **Area Code** 814 **Zip** 16701
Information Bradford Area Chamber of Commerce, 10 Main St, PO Box 135; 814/368-7115

When oil was discovered here the price of land jumped from about six cents to $1,000 an acre; wells appeared on front lawns, in backyards, even in a cemetery. An oil exchange was established in 1877, two years after the first producing well was brought in. Diversified industry now provides the city's economic base. A Ranger District office of the Allegheny National Forest (see WARREN) is located here.

What to See and Do

Bradford Landmark Society. Headquartered in restored bakery; local history exhibits, period rms. (Mon, Wed & Fri; closed hols) 45 E Corydon St. Phone 814/362-3906. **Free**

Crook Farm (1848). Original home of Erastus and Betsy Crook; being restored to the 1870s period. (May–Sept, Tues–Fri afternoons, also Sat by appt; closed hols) (See ANNUAL EVENT) On Seaward Ave extension near the Tuna Crossroad. Phone 814/362-3906. ¢ Includes

Old One-Room Schoolhouse #8 (1880). Authentic structure where classes are still held occasionally.

Old Barn (ca 1870). Identical to the original; moved to Crook Farm in 1981 and rebuilt on the site of the original barn.

Carpenter Shop (ca 1870). Reconstruction of original; old hand tools.

Annual Event

Crook Farm Country Fair. Crook Farm. Arts and crafts, exhibits, entertainment, food. Last wkend Aug.

Motels

✓ ★ **DE SOTO HOLIDAY HOUSE.** *515 S Ave (16701).* 814/362-4511; FAX 814/362-1699. 70 rms, 2-3 story. No elvtr. S $39-$49; D $47-$53; each addl $4. Crib free. TV; cable. Heated pool; whirlpool. Sauna. Playground. Restaurant 7 am-10 pm; Sun to 8 pm. Bar 11-2 am; entertainment. Ck-out noon. Meeting rms. Business servs avail. Sundries. Rec rm. Driving range, miniature golf, batting cages. Cr cds: A, C, D, DS, MC, V.

⌷ ⌷ ⌷

★★ **HOWARD JOHNSON MOTOR LODGE.** *100 S Davis St (16701),* US 219 exits Elm & Forman Sts. 814/362-4501; FAX 814/362-2709; res: 800/654-2000. E-mail hojo@penn.com; web www.hojobradford.com. 120 rms, 3 story. S $64-$74; D $69-$79; each addl $10; under 12 free. Crib free. TV; cable (premium). Heated pool; lifeguard. Restaurant 6:30 am-2 pm, 5-10 pm. Bar 3 pm-1 am. Ck-out noon. Meeting rms. Business servs avail. Valet serv. Health club privileges. Cr cds: A, C, D, DS, JCB, MC, V.

D ⌷ ⌷ ⌷ SC

Inn

★★★ **GLENDORN - A LODGE IN THE COUNTRY.** *1032 W Corydon (75062),* approx 5 mi from downtown area. 814/362-6511; FAX 814/368-9923; res: 800/843-8568. E-mail glendorn@penn.com; web www.glendorn.com. 12 units, 2 story (main lodge), 4 suites, 6 cabins. AP: S $285-$485; D $345-$545; each addl $100; cabins $445-$1,545; wkend rates; 2-day min hols. Closed Jan. Children over 12 yrs only. TV. Heated pool. Sittings: 9:30 am bkfst, 1 pm lunch, 7:30 pm dinner. Ck-out 2 pm, ck-in 11 am. Luggage handling. Business servs avail. Tennis. Golf privileges. X-country ski on site. Exercise equipt. Game rm. Lawn games. Some refrigerators. Cr cds: A, C, MC, V.

⌷ ⌷ ⌷ ⌷ ⌷ ⌷ ⌷ ⌷

Breezewood (F-4)

(See also Bedford, Chambersburg)

Pop 180 (est) **Elev** 1,356 ft **Area Code** 814 **Zip** 15533

Motels

★★ **BEST WESTERN PLAZA MOTOR LODGE.** *Rte 30 (15533), jct I-70, 1 blk W of PA Tpke exit 12.* 814/735-4352; FAX 814/735-3036; res: 800/528-1234. Web www.bestwestern.com/best.html. 89 rms, 2 story. S $37-$42; D $43-$52; each addl $7. Crib $7. TV; cable (premium). Pool. Restaurant 7 am-10 pm. Ck-out 11 am. Meeting rm. Cr cds: A, C, D, DS, MC, V.

D 🖾 🖾 🖾 SC

★★ **QUALITY INN BREEZE MANOR.** *16621 Lincoln Hwy (15533), E on US 30, 1 blk E of I-70 & PA Tpke exit 12.* 814/735-4311; FAX 814/735-3433; res: 800/721-4311. Web www.qualityinn.com. 50 rms, 1-2 story. May-Nov: S $43-$76; D $48-$76; each addl $5; family rates; lower rates rest of yr. Crib $5. TV; cable (premium). Heated pool; wading pool, lifeguard. Playground. Restaurant opp open 24 hrs. Ck-out noon. Coin lndry. Business servs avail. Sundries. Cr cds: A, C, D, DS, ER, JCB, MC, V.

D 🖾 🖾 🖾 SC

★★★ **RAMADA INN.** *US Rte 30 & I-70 (15533).* 814/735-4005; FAX 814/735-3228; res: 814/535-4025. 125 rms, 2 story. Apr-Oct: S $57; D $79; under 18 free; lower rates rest of yr. Crib avail. Pet accepted, some restrictions. TV; cable (premium), VCR avail (movies). Indoor pool. Playground. Restaurant 6:30 am-10 pm. Rm serv. Bar 4 pm-midnight. Ck-out noon. Meeting rms. Business center. In-rm modem link. Gift shop. Golf privileges. Exercise equipt. Game rm. Some in-rm whirlpool. Picnic tables. Cr cds: A, C, D, DS, JCB, MC, V.

D 🐾 🛏 🖾 🏋 🖾 🔥 SC 🚶

Bristol (Bucks Co) (E-10) 🐎

(See also Philadelphia)

Settled 1697 **Pop** 10,405 **Elev** 20 ft **Area Code** 215 & 267 **Zip** 19007 **E-mail** buckscountycvb@buckscountycvb.org **Web** www.buckscounty cvb.org

Information Bucks County Conference and Visitors Bureau, Inc, 152 Swamp Rd, Doylestown 18901; 215/345-4552 or 800/836-BUCKS

Bristol, founded in 1681, was the main thoroughfare from Philadelphia to New York. It has been frequented by famous visitors including Joseph Bonaparte, brother of Napoleon and General Lafayette. There are homes dating from the 1700s; most of these have been restored.

What to See and Do

Grave of Captain John Green. Grave of US Navy captain who piloted the *Columbia* around the world in 1787–1789 on first such voyage by vessel flying American flag. St James Protestant Episcopal Church Burial Ground. Cedar & Walnut Sts.

Historic Fallsington. Restored 17th-, 18th- & 19th-century bldgs. Self-guided walking tour of 17th-century log house, 18th-century schoolmaster's house, Burges-Lippincott house, tavern. Also museum store. Tours. (See ANNUAL EVENT) (Mid-May–Oct, daily; closed some hols) 4 Yardley Ave, Fallsington, 5 mi N of PA Tpke, off PA 13. Phone 215/295-6567. ¢¢

Pennsbury Manor. Reconstruction of William Penn's 17th-century country manor; formal and kitchen gardens; livestock. Craft demonstrations; hands-on workshops. (Daily exc Mon; closed some hols) 5 mi NE at 400 Pennsbury Memorial Rd, off Bordentown Rd. Phone 215/946-0400. ¢¢

Sesame Place. Family theme park combines fun with learning. More than 50 outdoor physical play activities develop skills and coordination with kid-powered units. The indoor interactive and science galleries offer games to challenge the mind. Sesame Food Factory: visible kitchen-in-the-round serves wholesome favorites. Mr. Hooper's Emporium: complete shop for all Sesame Street items. Sesame Island area with Caribbean theme; water activities incl Big Bird's Rambling River and Sky Splash. Musical revue with Sesame Street characters. (May–Labor Day, daily; after Labor Day–late Oct, wkends only) Approx 7 mi N, near Oxford Valley Mall (Langhorne), just N of Philadelphia off I-95 between Philadelphia and Trenton, NJ. Phone 215/752-7070. ¢¢¢¢

Annual Event

Fallsington Day. In Fallsington. Outdoor fair; restored bldgs open; colonial craft demonstrations; entertainment. 2nd Sat Oct.

Brookville (C-3)

(See also Clarion)

Settled 1830 **Pop** 4,184 **Elev** 1,269 ft **Area Code** 814 **Zip** 15825 **Information** Brookville Area Chamber of Commerce, 70 Pickering St; 814/849-8448

What to See and Do

Clear Creek State Park. Approx 1,600 acres. Swimming beach; fishing; canoeing. Hiking trails. Cross-country skiing. Picnicking, playing field. Camping, cabins (dump station). Nature center; interpretive activities. Standard fees. 8 mi N on PA 36, then 4 mi NE on PA 949. For info contact Park Manager, RD 1, Box 82, Sigel 15860; Phone 814/752-2368.

Annual Event

Western Pennsylvania Laurel Festival. Phone 814/849-2024. 3rd wk June.

Motels

★★ **DAYS INN.** *US 322 & I-80 Exit 13 (15825).* 814/849-8001; FAX 814/849-9647; res: 800/329-7466. 118 rms, 3 story. S $40-$60; D $45-$85; each addl $5; under 18 free; higher rates hunting season. Crib free. Pet accepted. TV; cable. Heated pool; wading pool, whirlpool, poolside serv, lifeguard. Restaurant 6-10 am, 4:30-10 pm; winter from 7 am. Bar 5 pm-midnight; closed Sun. Ck-out noon. Coin lndry. Business servs avail. X-country ski 17 mi. Game rm. Cr cds: A, C, D, DS, MC, V.

D 🐾 ✕ 🛏 🖾 🔥 SC

✓★ **HOLIDAY INN.** *235 Allegheny Blvd (15825), I-80 exit 13.* 814/849-8381; FAX 814/849-8386; res: 800/465-4329. 68 rms, 3 story. S $50-$60; D $57-$67; each addl $7; under 12 free; higher rates hunting season. Crib free. Pet accepted. TV; cable (premium). Complimentary continental bkfst. Restaurant adj 11 am-11 pm. Ck-out noon. Coin lndry. Meeting rm. Business servs avail. Sundries. Private patios, balconies. Cr cds: A, C, D, DS, MC, V.

D 🐾 🖾 🔥 SC

Restaurant

✓★★ **MEETING PLACE.** *209 Main St (15825).* 814/849-2557. E-mail meetingplace@ncentral.com. Hrs: 8 am-9 pm; Sat from 9 am; Sun 10 am-7:30 pm. Closed some major hols. Res accepted. Bar. Semi-a la carte: bkfst $2-$5, lunch $2.75-$7, dinner $4.95-$12. Child's meals. Specializes in salads, chicken, seafood. Restored Victorian building (1871); casual dining. Cr cds: A, C, DS, MC, V.

Bucks County (E-9 - E-10)

E-mail buckscountycvb@buckscountycvb.org **Web** www.buckscounty cvb.org

Information Bucks County Conference and Visitors Bureau, Inc, 152 Swamp Rd, Doylestown 18901; 215/345-4552 or 800/836-BUCKS

Bucks County's great natural resources, location and waterway transportation were known to the Leni-Lenape centuries ago. Dutch explorers, followed by Swedes, English Quakers and Germans, began to take possession of the area in the 1600s. William Penn established his country estate in this area in the 17th century.

The county's historic importance is highlighted in the central section—it was here that General George Washington crossed the Delaware River with the Continental Army during the Revolution. More recently, artists and writers have settled in and around New Hope, giving rise to the village's fame as an art center. Bucks County's scenic beauty and rich history make it a popular tourist spot.

Following are the places in Bucks County included in the *Mobil Travel Guide.* For full information on any one of them, see the individual alphabetical listing. Bristol, Doylestown, New Hope, Quakertown, Washington Crossing Historic Park.

Bushkill (C-10)

(See also Milford)

Pop 900 (est) **Elev** 365 ft **Area Code** 570 **Zip** 18324 **E-mail** pocomts@ poconos.org **Web** www.poconos.org

Information Pocono Mts Vacation Bureau, 1004 Main St, Stroudsburg 18360; 570/424-6050; for free brochures phone 800/POCONOS.

What to See and Do

Bushkill Falls. Largest series of falls in Pocono Mts. Main falls have 100-ft drop. Scenic gorge. Fishing; boating. Picnicking. Wildlife exhibit of mounted animals and birds of Pennsylvania. (Apr–mid-Nov, daily) 2 mi N off US 209 on local road. Phone 570/588-6682. ¢¢¢

Delaware Water Gap (see). 15 mi W on US 209.

Pocono Indian Museum. Traces history of the Delaware through displays of artifacts, weapons and tools. Gift shop. (Daily; closed Thanksgiving, Dec 25) 3 mi S on US 209. Phone 570/588-9338 or 570/588-9164. ¢¢

Butler (D-2)

(See also Harmony, Pittsburgh)

Settled 1793 **Pop** 15,714 **Elev** 1,077 ft **Area Code** 724 **Zip** 16003 **E-mail** chamber@isrv.com

Information Butler County Tourist Promotion Agency, 201 S Main St, PO Box 1082; 724/283-2222 or 888/741-6772

This is a manufacturing city nestled amid rolling hills that were owned by Robert Morris of Philadelphia, financier of the American Revolution. The city and county are named for General Richard Butler, who died in the St Clair Indian Expedition. During the 1930s, the Butler-based American Austin Company—later called American Bantam Company—pioneered the development of small, lightweight cars in America and invented the prototype of the jeep.

What to See and Do

Cooper Cabin (ca 1810). A family homestead on 4 acres with heirlooms and memorabilia; spinning house, spring house, tool shed. Self-guided nature trail and herb garden; live history demonstrations and tours. (June-Sept, Sun afternoons, also by appt) 199 Cooper Rd, in Cabot. Phone 724/283-8116. ¢

Jennings Environmental Education Center. Blazing Star, a relict prairie wildflower, blooms profusely here late July–early Aug. Trails, guided walks, interpretive center; picnicking. (Memorial Day–Labor Day, daily; rest of yr, Mon–Fri, some Sun) 12 mi N, at jct PA 8, 528, 173. Phone 724/794-6011. **Free**

Moraine State Park. A 3,225-acre lake in a 16,180-acre park. Swimming beaches; fishing, hunting; boating (rentals, mooring, launching, marina). Hiking, bicycle trails (rentals), horseback riding. Cross-country skiing, snowmobiling, sledding, ice skating, ice fishing, ice boating. Picnicking, playground, snack bar, restaurant. Cabin rentals. Waterfowl observation area; interpretive programs. Pontoon boat tours. 12 mi NW on US 422. Phone 724/368-8811. **Free**

Motels

★★ **CONLEY RESORT INN.** 740 Pittsburgh Rd (16002), exit 4 off PA Tpke on PA SR 8N. 724/586-7711; FAX 724/586-2944; res: 800/344-7303. 56 rms, 2-3 story, 10 kits. No elvtr. S $62-$65; D $84-$99; each addl $10; under 18 free; golf plans. Crib free. TV. Indoor pool; whirlpool, lifeguard. Sauna. Restaurant 7 am-10 pm. Rm serv. Bar 11-2 am; Sun to midnight. Ck-out 1 pm. Meeting rms. Business servs avail. Sundries. Rec rm. Tennis. 18-hole golf, greens fee $20-$32, putting green. X-country ski on site. Game rm. 150-ft indoor water slide. Cr cds: A, C, D, DS, MC, V.

★★ **DAYS INN.** 139 Pittsburgh Rd (16001). 724/287-6761; FAX 724/287-4307; res: 800/329-7466. 139 rms, 2 story. S $56-$72; D $62-$77; each addl $6; family rates; golf package plan. Crib free. Pet accepted. TV; cable. Indoor pool; whirlpool, lifeguard. Coffee in rms. Restaurant 6 am-10 pm. Rm serv. Bar 3 pm-2 am; Sun 1 pm-midnight; entertainment. Ck-out 11 am. Coin lndry. Meeting rms. Business servs avail. Valet serv. Sundries. Exercise equipt. Game rm. Cr cds: A, C, D, DS, MC, V.

✓★ **MC KEE'S MOTEL.** 930 New Castle Rd (16001), 6 mi W. 724/865-2272. 22 rms. S $29.68-$33.92; D $32.86-$39.22; kit units $47.70; under 5 free; wkly rates. TV; cable. Ck-out 11 am. Cr cds: A, C, DS, MC, V.

Inn

★★★ **APPLEBUTTER INN.** 666 Centreville Pike (16057), 15 mi N on US 8 to US 173, N to Slippery Rock. 412/794-1844; FAX 412/794-3319; res: 888/275-3466; res: 888/275-3466. Web www.pathway.net/ applebutterinn. 11 rms, 2 story. S $59-$79; D $79-$125; each addl $15; higher rates wknds. Adults only. TV. Complimentary full bkfst. Ck-out 11 am, ck-in 3-8 pm; Fri, Sat 3-10 pm. Sitting rm. Massage. Restored brick farmhouse (1844) furnished with antiques; addition added 1988. Totally nonsmoking. Cr cds: A, C, MC, V.

Canadensis (C-9)

Pop 1,200 (est) **Area Code** 570 **Zip** 18325

What to See and Do

Holley Ross Pottery. 20-min guided tours with demonstration of pottery making (Mon-Fri). Swinging bridge, park, sawdust trails. (May–mid-Dec, daily) S on PA 390, NW on PA 447, on PA 191N in La Anna. Phone 570/676-3248. **Free**

Resort

★★ **SKYTOP LODGE.** 1 Skytop (18357), 3 mi N on PA 390. 570/595-7401; FAX 570/595-9618; res: 800/345-7759. 167 rms, 1-4 story, 40 cottages. May-Oct, AP: S $190-$275; D $230-$390; each addl $45; cottages $345-$390; under 18 free; family, wkend, hol rates; ski, golf plans; 3-day min wkends, hols; higher rates some hols; lower rates rest of yr. Crib free. 2 pools, 1 indoor; wading pool, whirlpool, poolside serv, lifeguard. Playground. Supervised child's activities; ages 4-10. Dining rm. Rm serv. Box lunches, picnics. Bar noon-midnight. Ck-out 1 pm, ck-in 3 pm. Gift shop. Grocery, coin lndry 3-5 mi. Bellhops. Valet serv. Meeting rms. Business servs avail. Sports dir. Tennis, pro. 18-hole golf, pro, greens fee $40, putting green, driving range. Downhill/x-country ski on site. Boats. Sleighing, tobogganing. Hiking. Bicycle rentals. Lawn games. Soc dir. Rec rm. Game rm. Exercise rm; sauna, steam rm. Massage. Fishing guides, clean and store. Refrigerators in cottages. Picnic tables. On beach. Cr cds: A, C, D, DS, MC, V.

Inns

★★★ **BROOLVIEW MANOR.** PA 447 (18325), 1 mi S on PA 447. 570/595-2451; FAX 570/595-5065; res: 800/585-7974. 10 rms, 2-3 story, suite. No rm phones. MAP: S $100-$140, D $110-$150; each addl $20; suite $150; hol wkends (2-day min). Children over 12 yrs only. Complimentary full bkfst. Coffee in library. Ck-out 11 am, Ck-in 3-7 pm. Picnic tables. Totally nonsmoking. Cr cds: A, C, D, DS, MC, V.

★★★ **CRESCENT LODGE INC.** 940 Paradise Valley (18326), S on PA 191 to PA 447. 570/595-7486; FAX 570/595-3452. 12 lodge rms, 4 motel rms, 9 suites, 6 cottages (some with kit.). Mid-June-mid-Sept: S, D $85-$185; each addl $15; suites $172-$275; kit cottages $1,000-$1,150/wk; EP, MAP, wkly rates; ski plans; lower rates rest of yr. TV; cable. Heated pool. Complimentary continental bkfst (exc summer). Restaurant (see CRESCENT LODGE). Bar. Ck-out 11 am, ck-in 2 pm. Business servs avail. Free bus depot transportation. Gift shop. Tennis. Downhill/x-country ski 5 mi. Fitness trail. Lawn games. Some refrigerators; whirlpool in suites. Varied accommodations. Private patios. Picnic tables. Same owners more than 40 yrs. Cr cds: A, C, D, DS, MC, V.

★★ **PINE KNOB INN.** RR 447 (18325). 570/595-2532; FAX 570/595-6429; res: 800/426-1460. 28 units, 19 baths. No rm phones. MAP: S $79-$95; D $158-$190. TV in library; cable. Ck-out 11 am, ck-in 2 pm. Tennis. Downhill/x-country ski 5 mi. Lawn games. Pre-Civil War period inn (1847); antiques. Cr cds: A, C, DS, MC, V.

★ **PUMP HOUSE INN.** Skytop Rd. (18325). 570/595-7501. 8 rms, 2 story. S, D $65-$100; each addl $5; suites $85-$100. Complimentary continental bkfst. Restaurant (see PUMP HOUSE INN). Ck-out 11 am, ck-in 2 pm. Built as stagecoach stop in 1842; furnished in country decor antiques. Cr cds: C, D, MC, V.

Restaurants

★★ **CRESCENT LODGE.** (See Crescent Lodge Inn) 570/595-7486. Hrs: 5:30-10 pm; Sun to 9 pm. Closed Dec 25; also Mon-Tues from Jan-May. Res accepted. Continental menu. Bar 4 pm-midnight. A la carte entrees: dinner $16.95-$28.95. Specializes in seafood, veal, chicken. Pianist Sat. Family-owned. Cr cds: A, C, D, DS, MC, V.

★★★ **PUMP HOUSE INN.** (See Pump House Inn) 570/595-7501. Hrs: 5-9 pm; Sun 2:30-8:30 pm. Closed Mon; Dec 25. Res accepted. French, Amer menu. Bar. Wine list. Semi-a la carte: dinner $13.95-$24.95. Specialties: roast rack of lamb, shrimp in beer batter, chocolate mousse. Own breads. Country inn (1842). Cr cds: C, D, MC, V.

Carbondale (C-9)

(See also Hawley, Scranton)

Founded 1822 **Pop** 10,664 **Elev** 1,070 ft **Area Code** 570 **Zip** 18407 **E-mail** pntvb@epix.net **Web** www.visitnepa.org

Information Pennsylvania Northeast Territory Visitors Bureau, 100 Terminal Rd, Ste 216, Avoca 18641; 570/457-1320 or 800/22-WELCOME

Carbondale, located in the heart of the northeast Pocono area, has excellent sports facilities. There are 33 lakes within an 8-mile radius and 201 more lakes within 25 miles. One of the first railroad lines in the country was built to haul coal from Carbondale.

What to See and Do

Merli-Sarnoski Park. Covers 850 acres of woodlands with 40-acre lake. Swimming beach (lifeguards); fishing (seasonal); boating (launch). Hiking trails. Winter activities incl cross-country skiing, ice skating, ice fishing. Picnicking. (Daily) ½ mi off PA 106. Phone 570/876-1714.

Skiing.

Elk Mt Ski Center. At an elevation of 2,693 ft, this is eastern Pennsylvania's highest mountain. Five double chairlifts; patrol, school, rentals; cafeteria, restaurant, bar. Longest run 2 mi; vertical drop 1,000 ft. (Early Dec–late Mar, daily) Half-day rate. NW on PA 106, E on PA 374. Phone 570/679-2611 or 800/233-4131 (East Coast states, for snow conditions). ¢¢¢¢¢

Mount Tone Ski Resort. Triple chairlift, T-bar, double rope tow, mighty mite; school, rentals; snowmaking; cafeteria; lodge. Vertical drop 450 ft. (Late Dec–mid-Mar) Two mountains, 11 trails; also night skiing, cross-country trails. N via PA 171, E via PA 370 to Lakewood, then S on PA 247 to Lake Como, follow signs. Phone 570/798-2707. ¢¢¢¢¢

Carlisle (E-6)

(See also Harrisburg)

Settled 1720 **Pop** 18,419 **Elev** 478 ft **Area Code** 717 **Zip** 17013 **E-mail** info@carlislechamber.org **Web** www.carlislechamber.org

Information Greater Area Chamber of Commerce, 212 N Hanover St, PO Box 572; 717/243-4515

In the historically strategic Cumberland Valley, Carlisle was a vital point for Native American fighting during the Revolutionary and Civil wars.

Carlisle Barracks is one of the oldest military posts in America. Soldiers mounted guard here as early as 1750 to protect the frontier. From here began British campaigns that drove the French from the Ohio Valley and, in 1763, the march to relieve Fort Pitt. In 1794 President Washington reviewed troops assembled to march against the "Whiskey Rebels." Troops went from the Barracks to the Mexican and Civil wars. The famous

Carlisle Indian Industrial School, first nonreservation school, was here until 1918. The Barracks was reopened in 1920 as the Medical Field Service School. It is now the home of the US Army War College.

George Ross, James Wilson and James Smith, all signers of the Declaration of Independence, lived in Carlisle, as did Molly Pitcher.

What to See and Do

Carlisle Barracks. Army War College, senior school in US Army's educational system. Includes the US Army Military History Institute and Hessian Powder Magazine Museum (1777), built by prisoners captured at the Battle of Trenton. The Carlisle Indian Industrial School (1879–1918) was one of the first institutions of higher learning for Native Americans. Also incl the Omar Bradley Museum, containing a collection of personal and military memorabilia of the five-star general. Jim Thorpe and other famous Native American athletes studied here. Military History Institute and the Omar Bradley Museum (Mon–Fri; closed federal hols). Post/grounds (daily; closed federal hols). 1 mi N on US 11. Phone 717/245-3611. **Free**

Cumberland County Historical Society and Hamilton Library Association. Woodcarvings, furniture, silver, tools, redware, ironware, tall-case clocks, coverlets, paintings by local artisans; mementos of the Carlisle Indian School; special exhibits and programs. Library contains books, tax lists, early photographs, genealogical material. (Daily exc Sun; closed hols) 21 N Pitt St. Phone 717/249-7610. Museum **Free**; Library (nonmembers) ¢¢

Dickinson College (1773). (1,900 students) Tenth college chartered in US; President James Buchanan was a graduate. On campus is "Old West" (1804), a bldg registered as a National Historic Landmark that was designed by Benjamin Henry Latrobe, one of the designers of the Capitol in Washington. Tours of campus. W High St (US 11). Phone 717/243-5121. Also here is

The Trout Gallery. Permanent and temporary exhibits. (Sept–mid-June, Tues–Sat) Emil R. Weiss Center for the Arts. Phone 717/245-1711. **Free**

Grave of "Molly Pitcher" (Mary Ludwig Hays McCauley). Soldiers in the Battle of Monmouth (June 1778) gave Molly her nickname because of her devotion to her husband and others who were fighting by bringing them pitchers of water. When her husband was wounded, Molly took his place at a cannon and continued fighting for him. In Old Graveyard, E South St.

Huntsdale Fish Hatchery. Springs and mountain stream fill tanks and ponds of brown, rainbow and palomino trout, muskellunge and walleye; visitor center. (Daily) 10 mi SW in Huntsdale. Phone 717/486-3419. **Free**

Pine Grove Furnace State Park. Pre-Revolutionary iron, slate and brick works were in this area. Approx 696 acres. Swimming beaches; fishing, hunting; boating (rentals, mooring, launching). Hiking, bicycling (rentals). Cross-country skiing, ice skating, ice fishing. Picnicking, snack bar, store. Tent & trailer sites. Visitor center. Lodging avail (Phone 717/486-7575). Standard fees. 10 mi SW on I-81, exit 11, then 8 mi S on PA 233. Park office phone 717/486-7174.

Annual Events

Summerfair. Downtown Carlisle. Early July.

Art Festival and Octoberfest. Oct.

Motels

✓★★ **APPALACHIAN TRAIL INN.** 1825 Harrisburg Pike (17013), off I-81S exit 17E. 717/245-2242; FAX 717/258-4881; res: 800/445-6715. 200 rms, 2 story. Apr-Oct: S $42-$52; D $47-$57; each addl $5; suites $85-$125; under 12 free; higher rates car shows; lower rates rest of yr. Crib free. TV; cable (premium). Restaurant 5-2 am. Ck-out noon. Business servs avail. Downhill ski 16 mi. Picnic tables. Cr cds: A, C, D, DS, ER, MC, V.

D ⚡ ➠ ≋ 🔥 SC

★★ **BEST WESTERN.** 1245 Harrisburg Pike (17013). 717/243-5411; FAX 717/243-0778; res: 800/528-1234. E-mail bestinn@aol.com. 130 rms, 2 story. S $46.50-$64.50; D $63.50-$77.50; each addl $7; suites $68.50-$140; under 18 free. Crib free. TV; cable (premium),

VCR avail (movies). Pool; lifeguard. Restaurant 6:30 am-9 pm. Bar 5 pm-1 am. Ck-out noon. Meeting rms. Valet serv. Sundries. Health club privileges. Microwaves avail. Cr cds: A, C, D, DS, ER, MC, V.

D ➠ ≋ 🔥 SC

★★★ **CLARION INN & CONVENTION CENTER.** 1700 Harrisburg Pike (17013), I-81 exit 17, I-76 exit 16. 717/243-1717; FAX 717/243-6648; res: 800/692-7315. 270 rms. S $62; D $67; each addl $5; suites $110-$173; under 18 free. Crib $10. Pet accepted. TV; cable (premium), VCR avail (movies). Indoor pool; whirlpool. Sauna. Restaurant 7 am-9 pm. Rm serv. Bar 11-2 am. Ck-out 11 am. Meeting rms. Business servs avail. In-rm modem link. Sundries. Gift shop. Tennis. Refrigerators; microwaves avail. Cr cds: A, C, D, DS, ER, MC, V.

D 🐾 🏊 ➠ ≋ 🔥 SC

★★ **DAYS INN.** 101 Alexander Spring Rd (17013), I-81 exit 13. 717/258-4147; FAX 717/258-1207; res: 800/329-7466. Web www.daysinn.com. 130 rms, 3 story. S $55-$80; D $60-$80; suites $85-$125; each addl $5; under 18 free; higher rates special events. Crib free. TV; cable, VCR avail (movies). Pool; lifeguard. Complimentary continental bkfst. Restaurant nearby. Ck-out noon. Coin lndry. Meeting rm. Business servs avail. Sundries. Airport transportation. Exercise equipt. Game rm. Some refrigerators. Cr cds: A, C, D, DS, JCB, MC, V.

D ➠ 🏃 ≋ 🔥 SC

★★★ **HOLIDAY INN.** 1450 Harrisburg Pike (17103), just off I-81, exit 17. 717/245-2400; FAX 717/245-9070; res: 800/465-4329. 100 rms, 2 story. S, D $79; each addl $10; under 18 free; higher rates special events. Crib free. Pet accepted. TV; cable (premium), VCR avail. Pool; lifeguard. Restaurant 6:30 am-2 pm, 5-10 pm. Rm serv. Bar 11 am-midnight. Ck-out noon. Coin lndry. Meeting rms. Business servs avail. In-rm modem link. Valet serv. Health club privileges. Cr cds: A, C, D, DS, JCB, MC, V.

D 🐾 ➠ ≋ 🔥 SC

★★ **QUALITY INN.** 1255 Harrisburg Pike (17013), US 11 at I-81. 717/243-6000; FAX 717/258-4123; res: 800/654-2000. 96 rms, 2 story. S, D $62.99; each addl $5; under 18 free; higher rates special events. Crib free. Pet accepted. TV; cable (premium). Pool; wading pool. Complimentary continental bkfst. Coffee in rms. Restaurant adj open 24 hrs. Bar 5 pm-midnight. Ck-out noon. Coin lndry. Meeting rm. Business servs avail. Valet serv. Refrigerators, microwaves avail. Cr cds: A, C, D, DS, MC, V.

D 🐾 ➠ ≋ 🔥 SC

★ **SUPER 8 MOTEL.** 1800 Harrisburg Pike (17013), on US 11, N of I-81 exit 17. 717/249-7000; FAX 717/249-9070; res: 800/800-8000. 112 rms, 2 story, 16 kits. S $40-$80; D $45-$90; kits. $58; under 12 free; higher rates special events. Crib free. TV; cable. Complimentary coffee in lobby. Restaurant nearby. Ck-out 11 am. Coin lndry. Microwaves avail. Cr cds: A, C, D, DS, MC, V.

D ≋ 🔥 SC

Resort

★★★ **ALLENBERRY RESORT INN.** 1559 Boiling Springs Rd (17007), 6 mi SE. 717/258-3211; FAX 717/258-1464. 69 rms in lodges, 1 cottage (3-bedrm). S $89; D $109; each addl $15; suites $225; cottage $295; under 17 free; package plans. Crib free. TV. Pool; wading pool, whirlpool, lifeguard. Dining rm 8-10 am, 11 am-2 pm, 5-9 pm (also see CARRIAGE ROOM). Bar 11 am-midnight. Ck-out noon. Meeting rms. Business servs avail. Airport transportation. Lighted tennis. Professional theater. On 57 wooded acres, 200-yr-old trees; several remodeled limestone buildings date from 1785, 1812. On Yellow Breeches Creek. Cr cds: A, C, DS, MC, V.

D ⚓ 🏃 ➠ ≋ 🔥 SC

Restaurants

★★ **BOILING SPRINGS TAVERN.** *Front & First Sts (17007), 6 mi SE on PA 174, on town square.* 717/258-3614. E-mail bst368@aol.com. Hrs: 11:30 am-10 pm. Closed Sun, Mon; major hols. Res accepted. Continental menu. Bar. Semi-a la carte: lunch $4.95-$9.95, dinner $9.95-$20.95. Child's meals. Specializes in fresh seafood, aged Western steak. Old stone structure (1832), originally an inn. Colonial decor. Cr cds: A, C, MC, V.

D ⊟

★★★ **CALIFORNIA CAFE.** *38 W Pomfret St (17013).* 717/249-2028. Hrs: 11 am-9 pm. Closed major hols. Res accepted. French, California menu. Serv bar. Semi-a la carte: lunch $4.45-$9.45. Complete meals: dinner $13.95-$19.95. Specialties: escalope de veau aux artichauts, poulet grille chasseur. 1859 fire station building; French and Florentine artwork in addition to artwork from local gallery. Cr cds: A, C, D, DS, MC, V.

D

★★ **CARRIAGE ROOM AT ALLENBERRY.** *(See Allenberry Inn)* 717/258-3211. Hrs: 5 pm-midnight; Sun-Tues to 9 pm. Closed mid-Nov-Mar. Res accepted. Bar to midnight. Semi-a la carte: dinner $19-$26. Specializes in crab cakes, steak, prime rib. Salad bar. Guitarist Thurs-Sat. Colonial decor. Cr cds: A, C, DS, MC, V.

D SC ⊟

Chambersburg (F-5)

Settled 1730 **Pop** 16,647 **Elev** 621 ft **Area Code** 717 **Zip** 17201
E-mail chambersburg@chamber.org **Web** www.chambersburg.org
Information Chamber of Commerce, 75 S Second St; 717/264-7101. Information is also available at the Visitors Station, 1235 Lincoln Way E; 717/261-1200

Named for Colonel Benjamin Chambers, a Scottish-Irish pioneer, this is an industrial county seat amid peach and apple orchards. John Brown had his headquarters here. During the Civil War, Confederate cavalry burned down the town, destroying 537 buildings after the citizens refused to pay an indemnity of $100,000.

What to See and Do

Caledonia State Park. Confederate General Jubal A. Early came through here during the Civil War and destroyed an iron furnace, which had been producing arms for the Union armies. Approx 1,100 acres. Swimming pool (fee); fishing. Nature, hiking trails; bicycling, 18-hole golf course. Cross-country skiing. Picnicking, playground, snack bar. Tent & trailer sites. Standard fees. (See ANNUAL and SEASONAL EVENTS) 10 mi E on US 30. Phone 717/352-2161.

Capitol Theatre. This 1927 movie house presents performances ranging from classical concerts to big bands; theatrical presentations. Features a 1928 Moller pipe organ. Call for performances and fees. 159 S Main St. Phone 717/263-0202.

The Old Jail. Jail complex (1818) restored and renovated for use as the Kittochtinny Historical Society's Museum and Library. An 1880 cell block houses community cultural activities, art and historical exhibits; other events. Also on grounds are Colonial, Fragrance and Japanese gardens; 19th-century barn; agricultural museum. Cultural programs (May-Oct). Tours (May-Nov, Thurs-Sat). 175 E King St. Phone 717/264-6364 or 717/264-1667. **Free**

Annual Events

ChambersFest. Caledonia State Park. Civil War festival with crafts, food, reenactments, parade of pets. Phone 717/264-7101. July.

Franklin County Fair. Arts and crafts displays, needlework, home and dairy products, state turkey-calling contest, tractor pull, agricultural and livestock exhibits, entertainment. Phone 717/369-4100. 3rd full wk Aug.

Seasonal Event

Totem Pole Playhouse. Caledonia State Park. Resident professional theater company performs dramas, comedies and musicals in 453-seat proscenium theater. Tues-Sun eves; matinees Wed, Sat-Sun. Phone 717/352-2164. June-Aug.

Motels

✓★ **DAYS INN.** *30 Falling Spring Rd (17201), I-81 exit 6.* 717/263-1288; FAX 717/263-6514; res: 800/329-7466. Web www.daysinn.com. 107 rms, 3 story. Apr-Oct: S $46-$60; D $51-$65; each addl $7; suites $70-$85; under 17 free; lower rates rest of yr. Crib free. Pet accepted. TV; cable (premium). Complimentary continental bkfst. Restaurant adj 6 am-11 pm. Ck-out 11 am. Business servs avail. Downhill ski 15 mi. Cr cds: A, C, D, DS, MC, V.

D 🐾 ⊠ ⊠ 🔥 SC

★★ **HAMPTON INN.** *955 Lesher Rd (17201), ¼ mi off I-81 exit 5.* 717/261-9185; FAX 717/261-1984; res: 800/426-7866. 124 rms, 3 story. May-Oct: S, D $64-$72; under 18 free; higher rates special events; lower rates rest of yr. Crib free. TV; cable (premium). Complimentary continental bkfst. Coffee in rms. Restaurant adj 6 am-11 pm. Ck-out noon. Meeting rms. Business servs avail. In-rm modem link. Sundries. Exercise equipt. Refrigerators. Cr cds: A, C, D, DS, MC, V.

D 🏋 ⊠ 🔥 SC

★★★ **QUALITY INN AND SUITES.** *1095 Wayne Ave (17201), I-81 exit 5.* 717/263-3400; FAX 717/263-8386; res: 800/465-4329. 139 rms, 2 story. Apr-Oct: S $59; D $66; each adl $7; under 19 free; wkend rates; golf plan; lower rates rest of yr. Crib free. Pet accepted, some restrictions. TV; cable, VCR avail. Pool; poolside serv, lifeguard. Restaurant 6 am-2 pm, 5-10 pm. Rm serv. Bar. Ck-out noon. Meeting rms. Business servs avail. Some in-rm modem links. Bellhops. Sundries. Valet serv. 18-hole golf privileges. Health club privileges. Cr cds: A, C, D, DS, JCB, MC, V.

D 🐾 🏋 ⊠ ⊠ 🔥 SC

✓★★ **TRAVELODGE.** *565 Lincoln Way E (17201), I-81 exit 6.* 717/264-4187; FAX 717/264-2446; res: 800/578-7878. 52 rms, 3 story. S $39-$49; D $45-$57; each addl $7; under 18 free. Crib free. Pet accepted, some restrictions. TV; cable (premium). Coffee in rms. Restaurant 6 am-2 pm, 4:30-9:30 pm. Rm serv. Bar 11 am-2 pm, 4:30-9:30 pm. Ck-out noon. Meeting rm. Health club privileges. Refrigerators avail. Some balconies. Cr cds: A, C, D, DS, ER, JCB, MC, V.

D 🐾 ⊠ 🔥 SC

Inns

★★★ **MERCERSBURG INN.** *405 S Main St (17236), 13 mi S on I-81, then 11 mi W on PA 16.* 717/328-5231; FAX 717/328-3403. 15 rms, 3 story. S, D $120-$235; each addl $25. TV in game rm. Complimentary full bkfst. Restaurant (see MERCERSBURG INN). Rm serv. Ck-out 11 am, ck-in 3 pm. Some fireplaces. Some balconies. Totally nonsmoking. Cr cds: C, DS, MC, V.

⊠ 🔥

★★ **PENN NATIONAL INN & GOLF CLUB.** *3809 Anthony Hwy (17237), E on PA 30, then S on PA 997.* 717/352-2400; FAX 717/352-3926; res: 800/231-0080. Web www.penngolf.com. 36 rms, 4 in manor house, 2 story. Mid-Apr-Oct: S $80-$100; D $90-$110; each addl $10-$15; under 18 free; golf plan; monthly rates; lower rates rest of yr. Crib free. Pet accepted, some restrictions. TV; cable. Heated pool. Playground. Coffee in rms. Restaurant (Apr-Oct) 7 am-7 pm. Ck-out 11 am, ck-in 2 pm. Business servs avail. Tennis. 18-hole golf course, greens fee $25-$45, putting green, driving range. Refrigerators; microwaves avail. Georgian-style manor house built 1847, additions built 1989. Cr cds: A, C, DS, MC, V.

⬚ ◖ ⅄ ⅃ ⅂ ⤢ ⅃ ⧄ ⧄ SC

Restaurants

★★ COPPER KETTLE. *1049 Lincoln Way E US 30 (17201), 2 blks W of I-81 exit 6. 717/264-3109.* Hrs: 5-9:30 pm; Fri, Sat to 10 pm. Closed Sun; major hols. Res accepted; required Fri, Sat. Bar to midnight. Semi-a la carte: dinner $8-$21.50. Child's meals. Specializes in seafood, steak, prime rib. Early Amer decor; antiques. Cr cds: A, C, D, DS, MC, V.

⤢

★★★ MERCERSBURG INN. *(See Mercersburg Inn) 717/328-5231.* Sitting: 5:30-8:30 pm. Closed Sun-Wed; Dec 24-25. Res required. Bar. Complete meals: 5-course dinner $45. Specialties: pan-seared venison with red currant glace de veau, cornbread crusted salmon chive ravioli, lobster ravioli. Cr cds: C, DS, MC, V.

Chester (F-9)

(See also Kennett Square, King of Prussia, Media, Philadelphia, West Chester)

Settled 1643 **Pop** 41,856 **Elev** 20 ft **Area Code** 484 & 610 **E-mail** delcocvb@ libertynet.org **Web** www.delcocvb.org

Information Delaware County Convention & Tourist Bureau, 200 E State St, Suite 100, Media 19063; 610/565-3679 or 800/343-3983

The oldest settlement in the state, Chester was established by the Swedish Trading Company as Upland. William Penn came to Upland in 1682 to begin colonization of the land granted to him by King Charles II. He renamed the settlement in honor of Chester, a Quaker center in Cheshire, England. The first Assembly here adopted Penn's Framework of Government, enacted the first laws and organized the county of Chester—from which Delaware County broke off in 1789. On the Delaware River, 15 miles southwest of Philadelphia, Chester is a busy port and home of shipyards where every type of vessel has been built for the navy and merchant marine.

What to See and Do

Caleb Pusey Home, Landingford Plantation (1683). Built for manager and agent of Penn's mill; only remaining house in state visited by William Penn. Period furniture. Also on 27 acres of original plantation are a log house (1790), stone schoolhouse-museum (1849) and herb garden. (May–Sept, Sat & Sun afternoons; also by appt; closed hols) 15 Race St, in Upland, 2 mi W. Phone 610/874-5665. ¢

Morton Homestead (ca 1655). Two-part log house built by ancestors of John Morton, signer of Declaration of Independence. Contemporary outdoor exhibits on Pennsylvania's Swedish Period, log-house construction, Morton family. (Wed-Sat) 4 mi NE on US 13, then SW on PA 420, at 100 Lincoln Ave in Prospect Park. Phone 610/583-7221. ¢

Penn Memorial Landing Stone. Marks spot where William Penn first landed Oct 28, 1682. Front & Penn Sts.

Swarthmore College (1864). (1,320 students) Coeducational; on wooded 330-acre campus are Friends Historical Library and Peace Collection; an art gallery; concert hall; performing arts center; observatory; grassy, terraced amphitheater; Friends Meeting House; Scott Arboretum, a collection of trees, shrubs and herbaceous plants throughout campus. Symposia, exhibits, music and dance programs are open to the public. 4 mi N on PA 320, in Swarthmore. Phone 610/328-8000.

Widener University (1821). (8,700 students) On campus are Old Main, a national historic landmark, and the University Art Museum, with a permanent collection of 19th- & 20th-century American Impressionist and European academic art as well as contemporary exhibits (Sept–May, Tues–Sat; June & Aug, Mon–Thurs; closed July). Also here is Wolfgram Memorial

Library. Campus tours. 14th & Chestnut Sts, 1 University Pl. Phone 610/499-4000.

Clarion (C-3)

Founded 1839 **Pop** 6,457 **Elev** 1,491 ft **Area Code** 814 **Zip** 16214 **E-mail** commerce@penn.com **Web** www.clarionpa.com

Information Clarion Area Chamber of Business and Industry, 41 S Fifth Ave; 814/226-9161

Once the forests were so thick and tall here that, according to tradition, the wind in the treetops sounded like a distant clarion. That's how the town, county and river got their names. Today many campers and sports and outdoors enthusiasts enjoy the beauty and recreation that the Clarion area offers.

What to See and Do

Clarion County Historical Society. Museum housed in mid-19th century Sutton-Ditz house. Contains exhibits on county industry and business; Victorian bedrm and parlor; genealogical and historical library (researchers may call ahead for appt other than regular hrs); changing exhibits. (Apr–Dec, Tues, Thurs & Fri afternoons; closed hols) 18 Grant St. Phone 814/226-4450. **Free**

Cook Forest State Park. Approx 6,700 acres. Swimming pool (fee); fishing, hunting. Hiking, bicycling, horseback riding. Cross-country skiing (rentals), snowmobiling, sledding, ice skating. Picnicking. Tent & trailer sites, cabins (rentals). Nature & historical center. Standard fees. 11 mi NE on Clarion to Cook Forest Rd, then 3 mi S on PA 36. Phone 814/744-8407.

Tionesta Reservoir. 5 mi NW on US 322, then 20 mi NW on PA 66, in Allegheny National Forest (see WARREN).

Annual Events

Spring Fling. Concerts, food concessions, games, entertainment. Early May.

Autumn Leaf Festival. Parade, carnival, autorama, scholarship pageants, concerts, flea market, craft shows. Sept 25-Oct 3.

Motels

★★ DAYS INN. *Rte 68 & I-80 (16214), exit 9N. 814/226-8682; FAX 814/226-8372; res: 800/329-7466.* 150 rms, 2 story. S $46-$56; D $51-$61; each addl $5; under 18 free; tennis, golf, ski plans; higher rates: Autumn Leaf Festival, hunting season. Crib free. Pet accepted. TV; cable (premium). Heated pool; lifeguard. Complimentary continental bkfst. Restaurant 6 am-2 pm, 5-10 pm. Rm serv. Bar 5 pm-2 am; entertainment. Ck-out noon. Coin lndry. Meeting rms. Business servs avail. Sundries. Golf privileges. Health club privileges. Cr cds: A, C, D, DS, JCB, MC, V.

⬚ ◖ ⅃ ⅂ ⤢ ⧄ ⧄ SC

★★★ HOLIDAY INN. *I-80 & Rte 68 (16214). 814/226-8850; FAX 814/226-9055; res: 800/596-1313.* Web www.holiday.com. 122 rms, 2 story. S, D $69-$94; suites $149; under 20 free. Crib free. Pet accepted. TV; cable (premium), VCR avail (movies). Indoor pool; lifeguard. Sauna. Coffee in rms. Restaurant 6:30 am-10 pm. Rm serv. Bar 4 pm-1 am. Ck-out noon. Meeting rms. Business servs avail. In-rm modem link. Airport transportation. 18-hole golf privileges, greens fee $14-$28, putting green. Game rm. Indoor balconies. Cr cds: A, C, D, DS, JCB, MC, V.

⬚ ◖ ⅃ ⅂ ⤢ ⧄ ⧄ SC

✓★ SUPER 8. *I-80 & Rte 68 (16214), I-80 exit 9. 814/226-4550; FAX 814/227-2337; res: 800/800-8000.* 99 rms, 9 kits. S, D $45-$90; each addl $5; under 18 free; wkly, monthly rates (winter). Crib free. Pet accepted. TV; cable (premium), VCR avail (movies). Pool. Complimentary continental bkfst. Coffee in rms. Restaurant adj open 24 hrs. Ck-out noon. Business servs avail. In-rm modem link. Cr cds: A, C, D, DS, MC, V.

Restaurant

✓ ★ ★ **CLARION CLIPPER.** On PA 68N (16214), ½ mi N of I-80 exit 9. 814/226-7950. Hrs: 6:30 am-10 pm. Closed Thanksgiving, Dec 25. Bar noon-midnight. Semi-a la carte: bkfst $2.50-$4.75, lunch $3.50-$5.75, dinner $5.50-$13. Child's meals. Specializes in steak, seafood. Salad bar. Exterior modeled after steamboats that operated on the Allegheny and Ohio Rivers in 1848. Cr cds: A, C, D, DS, MC, V.

D SC ⬚

Clearfield (Clearfield Co) (D-4)

Settled 1805 **Pop** 6,633 **Elev** 1,109 ft **Area Code** 814 **Zip** 16830
Information Clearfield Chamber of Commerce, 125 E Market St, PO Box 250; 814/765-7567

The old and important Native American town of Chinklacamoose occupied this site until it was burned in 1757. Coal and clay mining and more than 20 diversified plants producing school supplies, firebrick, fur products, precision instruments, electronic products and sportswear now occupy what used to be cleared fields. Easy access to other parts of the state and rich river bottom land led to the establishment of the county seat here.

What to See and Do

State parks.
S.B. Elliott. Approx 300 acres in the heart of the Moshannon State Forest; entirely wooded; display of mountain laurel in season. Fishing in small mountain streams surrounding the park. Hiking. Snowmobile trails. Tent & trailer sites, cabins. Standard fees. 9 mi N, off PA 153, just N of I-80 exit 18. Phone 814/765-7271 or 814/765-0630.
Parker Dam. Approx 950 acres in Moshannon State Forest. Swimming beach; fishing; boating (launch, rentals). Hiking. Cross-country skiing, snowmobiling, sledding, ice skating, ice fishing. Snack bar. Tent & trailer sites (electric hookups), cabins. Nature center. Standard fees. 14 mi NW on PA 153, 6 mi off I-80 exit 18, then 2 mi E on unnumbered road. Phone 814/765-0630.

Annual Events

Central Counties Concerned Sportsmen Annual Show. Clearfield County Fairgrounds. Phone 814/765-9495. Fri-Sun mid-Mar.
Laurel Tour. Late June–early July.
High Country Arts & Craft Fair. S.B. Elliott State Park. Phone 814/765-9804. Sun after July 4.
Clearfield County Fair. Phone 814/765-4629. Late July–early Aug.

Motel

★ **DAYS INN.** Rte 879 (16830), PA 879 & I-80 exit 19. 814/765-5381; FAX 814/765-7885; res: 800/329-7466. 119 rms, 2 story. S $40-$60; D $46-$80; each addl $6; under 18 free; higher rates special events. Crib free. Pet accepted. TV, VCR avail (movies). Pool; lifeguard. Complimentary continental bkfst. Ck-out noon. Meeting rms. Business servs avail. In-rm modem link. Exercise equipt. Some refrigerators. Cr cds: A, C, D, DS, MC, V.

Conneaut Lake (B-1)

(See also Edinboro, Meadville)

Pop 699 **Elev** 1,100 ft **Area Code** 814 **Zip** 16316 **E-mail** welcome@ visitcrawford.org **Web** www.visitcrawford.org
Information Crawford County Convention & Visitors Bureau, 242½ Chestnut St, Meadville 16335; 814/333-1258 or 800/332-2338

Located on the largest natural lake in Pennsylvania (929 acres), this resort town has swimming, boating and excellent fishing for perch, muskellunge, walleye, bass and crappie.

What to See and Do

Conneaut Cellars Winery. Tours and tastings. (May–Dec, daily; rest of yr, daily exc Mon; closed most major hols) 12005 Conneaut Lake Rd. Phone 814/382-3999. **Free**
Pymatuning Spillway. Part of Pymatuning State Park. When fish are fed bread, they flock so thickly that ducks walk on them. NW via US 6 on N end of reservoir. Phone 724/932-3141. **Free**
Pymatuning State Park. Approx 21,100 acres with 17-mi lake. Swimming beach; fishing, hunting; boating (rentals, mooring, launching, marina). Hiking. Cross-country skiing, snowmobiling, sledding, ice skating. Picnicking, playground, snack bar. Tent & trailer areas along shore. Cabins. Waterfowl museum and refuge; fish hatchery. Standard fees. SW via US 322, 1 mi W of Jamestown. Phone 724/932-3141.
Pymatuning Visitors Center. Part of Pennsylvania Game Commission; birds and animals indigenous to Pymatuning Reservoir area; bald eagle's nest visible from museum. Educational and interpretive programs. (Apr-mid Oct, daily) 9 mi W on US 285, then N on Hartstown-Linesville Rd. Phone 814/683-5545. **Free**

Connellsville (F-2)

(See also New Stanton, Uniontown)

Pop 9,229 **Elev** 885 ft **Area Code** 724 **Zip** 15425
Information Greater Connellsville Chamber of Commerce, 923 W Crawford Ave; 724/628-5500

Located in an area visited by George Washington and where he owned land, the region has many references to him in place names. The restored Crawford Cabin near the river was the home of Colonel William Crawford, surveyor of these properties and Washington's surveying pupil.

Northwest of town in Perryopolis are many historic restorations. The town square is named for Washington, who some believe planned the design of the town.

What to See and Do

⭐ **Fallingwater (Kaufmann Conservation on Bear Run).** One of the most famous structures of the 20th century, Fallingwater, designed by Frank Lloyd Wright in 1936, is cantilevered on 3 levels over a waterfall; interior features Wright-designed furniture, textiles, lighting, as well as sculpture by modern masters; extensive grounds are heavily wooded and planted with rhododendron, which blooms in early July. Visitor center with self-guided orientation program; concession; gift shop. Guided tours (Apr–mid-Nov, daily exc Mon; winter, Sat–Sun). No children under 10; child-care center. No pets. Res required. 8 mi E on PA 711, then 8 mi S on PA 381, near Mill Run. Phone 724/329-8501. ¢¢¢-¢¢¢¢
Linden Hall (1913). Conference and convention center in mountaintop mansion, situated in picturesque Laurel Highlands. Golf, tennis, fishing, swimming, walking trail. Guided tours of mansion (Mar–Dec, Mon-Fri; wkends by appt). 4 mi S on PA 201, then 1 mi N on PA 819, left on River

Rd in Dawson. Phone 724/529-7543, 724/529-2882 or 412/461-2424. ¢¢¢

Motel

★ **MELODY MOTOR LODGE.** *1607 Morrell Ave (15425).* *724/628-9600.* 46 rms. S, D $34-$47; higher rates Labor Day wkend. Crib $5. Pet accepted, some restrictions. TV; cable. Restaurant adj 6 am-10 pm. Ck-out 11 am. Picnic tables. Cr cds: A, C, DS, MC, V.

Inn

✓★★ **NEWMYER HOUSE.** *507 S Pittsburgh St (15425).* *412/626-0141.* E-mail smidcap@cvzoom.net; web www.bbonline.com/pa/ newmyer. 4 rms, 1 with shower only, 3 story. No rm phones. S $60; D $75; each addl $10; June-Labor Day wkends (2-day min). Children over 12 yrs only. TV in common rm; cable, VCR avail (movies). Complimentary full bkfst. Ck-out 11 am, ck-in 3 pm. Downhill/x-country ski 20 mi. Many fireplaces. Restored Queen Anne-style mansion built in 1892; antiques. Cr cds: C, MC, V.

Coraopolis

(see Pittsburgh Intl Airport Area)

Cornwall (E-8)

See also Ephrata, Hershey, Lancaster, Lebanon, Manheim)

Settled 1732 **Pop** 3,231 **Elev** 680 ft **Area Code** 717 **Zip** 17016 **Web** www.parrvb.com

Information Pennsylvania Rainbow Region Vacation Bureau, 625 Quentin Rd, PO Box 329, Lebanon 17042; 717/272-8555

The Cornwall Ore Banks were a major source of magnetic iron ore for nearly 250 years.

What to See and Do

Cornwall Iron Furnace. In operation 1742–1883. Open pit mine; 19th-century Miners Village still occupied. Furnace bldg houses "great wheel" and 19th-century steam engine. Visitor center, exhibits, book store. (Daily exc Mon; closed most hols) Rexmont Rd at Boyd St. Phone 717/272-9711. ¢¢

Historic Schaefferstown. An 18th-century farm established by Swiss-German settlers. Village square with authentic log and stone and half-timber bldgs; site of first waterworks in US (1758), still in operation. Schaeffer Farm Museum has Swiss Bank House and Barn (1737); early farm tools; colonial farm garden. The museum N of the Square has antiques and artifacts of settlers. (See ANNUAL EVENTS) House and museum (open during festivals; also June–Sept, by appt). 6 mi SE of Lebanon at jct PA 419, 501, 897. Phone 717/949-2244. ¢¢

Annual Events

Historic Schaefferstown Events. Events during the yr incl **Cherry Fair,** 4th Sat June; **Folk Festival,** mid-July; **Harvest Fair & Horse Plowing Contest,** 2nd wkend Sept.

Danville (D-7)

(See also Bloomsburg, Lewisburg)

Pop 5,165 **Elev** 490 ft **Area Code** 570 **Zip** 17821 **E-mail** danville@ sunlink.net **Web** www.sunlink.net/~danville

Information Danville Area Chamber of Commerce, 206 Walnut St; 570/275-5200

What to See and Do

Joseph Priestley House (1794). American house of the 18th-century Englishman and Unitarian theologian who, in 1774, was first to isolate the element oxygen. (By appt) SW via US 11 in Northumberland at 472 Priestley Ave. Phone 570/473-9474. ¢¢

PP & L Montour Preserve. Fishing; boating (no gasoline motors) on 165-acre Lake Chillisquaque. Hiking and nature trails. Picnicking. Birds of prey exhibit in visitors center; scheduled programs (fee for some). From I-80 exit 33, then PA 54W to Washingtonville, and NE on local roads. Phone 570/437-3131. **Free**

Motel

✓★★ **DANVILLE MOTOR LODGE.** *15 Valley West Rd (17821),* *I-80 exit 33.* *570/275-5100; FAX 570/275-1886.* 77 rms, 2 story. Apr-Oct: S $45-$55; D $50-$65; each addl $5; under 18 free; lower rates rest of yr. Crib free. TV; cable. Pool. Restaurant adj 6:30 am-10 pm. Ck-out noon. Coin lndry. Meeting rms. Business servs avail. In-rm modem link. Game rm. Cr cds: A, C, D, DS, ER, JCB, MC, V.

[D] 〰 〰 〰 SC

Inn

★★★ **PINE BARN INN.** *1 Pine Barn Pl (17821).* *570/275-2071;* *FAX 570/275-3248; res:* 800/627-2276. 65 rms, 1-2 story. S $42-$65; D $46-$75; each addl $2; under 16 free. Crib $5. TV; cable. Restaurant (see PINE BARN INN). Rm serv. Bar 11 am-midnight, Sun 1-8 pm. Ck-out 1 pm. Meeting rms. Business servs avail. Valet serv. Gift shop. Geisinger Medical Center adj. Cr cds: A, C, D, DS, MC, V.

[D] 〰 〰

Restaurant

★★ **PINE BARN INN.** *(See Pine Barn Inn)* 717/275-2071. Hrs: 7 am-10 pm; Sun 8 am-8 pm; Sun brunch 11 am-2 pm. Closed major hols. Res accepted. Bar 11 am-midnight; Sun 1-8 pm. Semi-a la carte: bkfst $3.50-$6.50, lunch $4.50-$9.50, dinner $12-$26. Sun brunch $5-$13. Child's meals. Specializes in New England seafood, steak. Salad bar. Outdoor dining. Converted 19th-century barn. Fireplace. Family-owned. Cr cds: A, C, D, DS, MC, V.

Delaware Water Gap (C-10)

(See also Milford, Pocono Mountains, Stroudsburg)

It is difficult to believe that the quiet Delaware River could carve a path through the Kittatinny Mountains, which are nearly a quarter of a mile high at this point. Conflicting geological theories account for this natural phenomenon, which is part of a national recreation area. The prevailing theory is that the mountains were formed after the advent of the river, rising up from the earth so slowly that the course of the Delaware was never altered.

Despite the speculation about the origin of the gap, there is no doubt about the area's recreational value. A relatively unspoiled area along the river boundary between Pennsylvania and New Jersey, stretching approximately 35 miles from Matamoras to an area just south of I-80, the site of the Delaware Water Gap is managed by the National Park Service.

Trails and overlooks (year round) offer scenic views. Also here are canoeing and boating, hunting and fishing; camping is nearby at the Dingmans Campground within the recreation area. Swimming and picnicking at Smithfield and Milford beaches. Dingmans Falls and Silver Thread Falls, two of the highest waterfalls in the Poconos, are near here (see MILFORD). Several 19th-century buildings are in the area, including Millbrook Village (several buildings open May–Oct) and Peters Valley (see BRANCHVILLE, NJ). The visitors center is located off I-80 in New Jersey, at Kittatinny Point (Apr–Nov, daily; rest of yr, Sat & Sun only; closed Jan 1, Dec 25), phone 908/496-4458 or 717/588-2451. Park headquarters are in Bushkill, PA. Phone 717/588-2451.

Denver/Adamstown (E-8)

(See also Ephrata, Lancaster, Reading)

Pop Denver 2,861; Adamstown 1,108 **Elev** Denver 380 ft; Adamstown 500 ft **Area Code** 717 **Zip** Denver 17517; Adamstown 19501 **Web** www.800padutch.com

Information Pennsylvania Dutch Convention and Visitors Bureau, 501 Greenfield Rd, Lancaster 17601; 717/299-8901 or 800/PADUTCH

Located near a Pennsylvania Turnpike exit, Denver and Adamstown are in the center of an active antique marketing area, which preserves its Pennsylvania German heritage.

What to See and Do

Stoudt's Black Angus. More than 350 dealers display quality antiques for sale. (Sun) Along PA 272 from PA Tpke exit 21 to just beyond Adamstown. Phone 717/484-4385.

Seasonal Event

Bavarian Summer Fest. Oom-pah bands, schuhplattler dance groups; Oktoberfest atmosphere. Includes special events, German folklore, German food, displays, shops. SW via PA 272 in Adamstown at Black Angus Bier Garten. Phone 717/484-4385 (wkends). Fri–Sun, early Aug-Labor Day; Sun only Oct.

Motels

★★★ **BLACK HORSE LODGE & SUITES.** *2180 N Reading Rd (17517), jct PA Tpke exit 21 & US 272. 717/336-7563; FAX 717/336-1110; res: 800/610-3805.* 74 rms, 2 story. Mid-Apr-mid-Nov: S $59-$129; D $69-$139; under 13 free; suites $100-$250; wkly, monthly rates; golf plans; lower rates rest of yr. Crib free. Pet accepted, some restrictions. TV; cable. Pool. Complimentary full bkfst. Complimentary coffee in rms. Restaurant from 4 pm; Sun from 11 am. Bar to 11 pm. Ck-out noon. Coin lndry. Business servs avail. Golf privileges. Many refrigerators; some bathrm phones; microwaves avail. Private patios, balconies. Picnic tables, grills. Cr cds: A, C, D, DS, MC, V.

★★★ **HOLIDAY INN.** *1 Denver Rd (17517), US 272, US 222, PA Tpke exit 21. 717/336-7541; FAX 717/336-0515; res: 800/437-5711.* E-mail hilanc@postoffice.ptd.net. 110 rms, 2 story. June-Oct: S, D $89; each addl $8; under 18 free; higher rates special events; lower rates rest of yr. Crib free. TV; cable (premium), VCR avail (movies). Pool; poolside

serv, lifeguard. Restaurant 6:30 am-2 pm, 5-10 pm. Rm serv. Bar 5-10 pm. Ck-out noon. Coin lndry. Meeting rms. Business servs avail. In-rm modem link. Valet serv. Golf privileges. Cr cds: A, C, D, DS, JCB, MC, V.

Inn

★★★ **INN OF ADAMSTOWN.** *62 W Main St (19501). 717/484-0800; FAX 717/484-1384; res: 800/594-4808.* E-mail info@adamstown. com; web www.adamstown.com. 4 rms, 2 with shower only, 2 story. Rm phones avail. S $63-$108; D $70-$130; wkends (2-day min). Children over 12 yrs only. TV in some rms; cable. Complimentary continental bkfst; afternoon refreshments. Restaurant nearby. Ck-out 10 am, ck-in 3-6 pm. Luggage handling. Valet serv. Concierge serv. Health club privileges. Some in-rm whirlpools, fireplaces. Patio. Picnic tables. Built in 1925; Victorian decor; antiques, family heirlooms. Totally nonsmoking. Cr cds: C, MC, V.

Restaurant

★★★ **BLACK HORSE.** *2170 N Reading Rd (17517), 1 mi N of Tpke exit 21, on PA 272. 717/336-6555.* Hrs: 5-10 pm; Sun 11:30 am-9 pm. Closed Dec 25. Res accepted. Bar 4-11 pm; Sun 11 am-10 pm. Wine cellar. Semi-a la carte: dinner $14-$30. Child's meals. Specializes in certified Angus beef, fresh seafood, gourmet desserts. Own pasta. Casual yet elegant decor with stained-glass windows, antique chandeliers, artwork. Cr cds: A, C, D, DS, MC, V.

Donegal (E-3)

(See also Connellsville, Greensburg, Ligonier, Somerset)

Pop 212 **Elev** 1,814 ft **Area Code** 724 **Zip** 15628

What to See and Do

Seven Springs Mountain Resort Ski Area. 2 quad, 7 triple, 2 double chairlifts, 7 rope tows; patrol, school, rentals; snowmaking; cafeteria, restaurant, bar; lodge. Longest run 1¼ mi; vertical drop 750 ft. Night skiing. (Dec–Mar, daily) Alpine slide (May–Sept, daily). Hotel and conference center; summer activities incl 18-hole golf, tennis, swimming. 12 mi SE of PA Tpke exit 9 on Champion-Trent Rd. Phone 814/352-7777. Lift ¢¢¢¢¢

Motel

★ **DAYS INN.** *Rte 31 (15628), PA Tpke, exit 9. 724/593-7536; FAX 724/593-6165; res: 800/329-7466.* Web www.daysinn.com. 50 rms, 20 with shower only. S, D $59-$72; each addl $6; under 12 free; higher rates special events. TV; cable (premium). Heated pool. Complimentary continental bkfst. Restaurant nearby. Ck-out 11 am. Downhill/x-country ski 9 mi. Lawn games. Picnic tables. Cr cds: A, C, MC, V.

Resort

★★★ **SEVEN SPRINGS MOUNTAIN RESORT.** *RD 1 (15622), on County Line Rd, 12 mi SE of PA Tpke exit 9. 814/352-7777; FAX 814/352-7911; res: 800/452-2223.* Web www.7springs.com. 385 rms in 10 story lodge; 20 kit chalets, cabins, 1-4 bedrm, 2 story. Lodge: S, D $155; each addl $50; under 17 free; suites $420; kit chalets $525; package plans; cabins for 6-25, $520-$895/wk; also daily rates (2-day min); wkend rates. Crib free. Maid serv avail in chalets, cabins $5/bed. TV; VCR avail.

Heated indoor/outdoor pools (open to public); wading pool, poolside serv, lifeguard. Playground. Free supervised child's activities. Dining rm 7 am-10 pm (also see HELEN'S). Snack bar; box lunches. Bar 11-2 am. Ck-out noon, ck-in 5 pm. Coin lndry. Convention facilities. Business servs avail. Bellhops. Shopping arcade. Beauty shop. Airport transportation. Sports dir. Tennis. Golf, greens fee $65.90, pro, putting green, driving range. Miniature golf. Downhill ski on site. Outdoor games. Hay rides. Mountain bikes avail. Soc dir; dancing, entertainment. Rec rm. Bowling. Indoor roller skating. Exercise equipt; sauna, steam rm. Wet bar in suites. Many private patios, balconies. Cr cds: C, DS, MC, V.

Restaurants

★★★ **HELEN'S.** *(See Seven Springs)* 814/352-7777. Web www.7springs.com. Hrs: 6-10 pm; also lunch during ski season. Res required. Continental menu. Bar. A la carte entrees: dinner $19-$30. Specialties: Dover sole, chicken Frangelica, lamb Helena. Totally nonsmoking. Cr cds: C, DS, MC, V.

Ⓓ

★★★ **NINO BARSOTTI'S RESTAURANT.** *Rte 31 (15666), 8 mi E on PA 31.* 724/547-2900. Hrs: 11 am-3 pm, 5-10 pm; Sat to 11 pm; Sun to 9 pm; Sun brunch 11:30 am-2 pm. Closed Mon; most major hols. Res accepted Fri, Sat. Italian, Amer menu. Bar. Semi-a la carte: lunch $4.95-$9.45, dinner $7.45-$23.45. Sun brunch $7.95. Child's meals. Specializes in fresh seafood, steak. Own desserts. Salad bar. Own pasta. Valet parking. Family-owned. Cr cds: A, C, D, DS, MC, V.

Ⓓ 🍽

Downingtown (F-9)

(See also King of Prussia, West Chester)

Settled 1702 **Pop** 7,749 **Elev** 244 ft **Area Code** 484 & 610 **Zip** 19335 **Web** www.brandywinevalley.com
Information Chester County Tourist Bureau, 601 Westtown Rd, Ste 170, West Chester 19382; 610/344-6365 or 800/228-9933

Settled by emigrants from Birmingham, England, Downingtown honors Thomas Downing, who erected a log cabin here in 1702. The borough was first called Milltown, after the mill built here by Roger Hunt in 1765. The town, with its many historically interesting homes, retains much of its colonial charm. Jacob Eichholtz, a leading early American portrait artist, was born here.

What to See and Do

Hibernia County Park. Once the center of an iron works community, it is now the largest of the county parks, encompassing 800 acres of woodlands and meadows. The west branch of the Brandywine Creek, Birch Run and a pond are stocked with trout; hiking trails; picnicking; tent & trailer camping (dump station). Park features Hibernia Mansion; portions of house date from 1798, period furnishings. Tours of mansion (Memorial Day–Labor Day, Sun; fee). From US 30 Bypass take PA 82 approx 2 mi N to Cedar Knoll Rd, then left 1¼ mi to park entrance on left. Phone 610/384-0290. **Free**

Historic Yellow Springs. From its beginnings as a fashionable spa, this historic village has been everything from a Revolutionary hospital to an art school. Countryside covers 145 acres with bldgs, medicinal herb garden and mineral springs. Events and educational programs throughout the yr (some fees). Self-guided tour. Office (Mon–Fri). 10 mi NE via PA 113, NW on Yellow Springs Rd. Phone 610/827-7414.

Valley Forge National Historical Park. (see). 10 mi E on I-76.

Annual Events

Old Fiddlers' Picnic. Hibernia County Park. 2nd Sat Aug.

jHibernia Mansion Christmas Tours. Hibernia County Park. 1st wk Dec.

Motor Hotel

★★ **BEST WESTERN.** *815 N Pottstown Pike (19341), N on PA 113 to PA 100, 1 mi S of PA Tpke exit 23.* 610/363-1100; FAX 610/524-2329; res: 800/465-4329. Web www.bestwestern.com. 225 rms, 4 story. S, D $109; under 18 free. Crib free. Pet accepted. TV; cable (premium). 2 pools, 1 indoor; poolside serv, lifeguard. Coffee in rms. Restaurant (see Arthur's Restaurant). Rm serv. Bar 2 pm-2 am. Ck-out 11 am. Coin lndry. Meeting rms. Business servs avail. In-rm modem link. Valet serv. Gift shop. Airport transportation. Health club privileges. Refrigerators, microwaves avail. Picnic tables. Cr cds: A, C, D, DS, ER, JCB, MC, V.

Ⓓ 🐾 ≈ ⇙ 🖾 SC

Restaurants

★★ **ARTHUR'S RESTAURANT.** *(See Best Western)* 610/363-1100. Web www.bestwestern.com. Hrs: 6:30 am-2 pm, 5:30-10 pm; Sat 7 am-2 pm, 5:30-10 pm; Sun 7 am-1 pm. Res accepted. Bar 11:30-2 am. A la carte entrees: bkfst $3.50-$7, lunch $4.95-$9, dinner $7.99-$20. Lunch buffet $7.99. Child's meals. Specialties: salmon Rockefeller, filet of tenderloin. Jazz Mon. Parking. Outdoor dining. Family-owned since 1971. Cr cds: A, C, D, DS, JCB, MC, V.

Ⓓ SC 🍽

★★★ **VICKERS.** *Gordon Dr (19341), PA Tpke exit 23.* 610/363-7998. Hrs: 11:30 am-2 pm, 5:30-10:30 pm; Sat from 5:30 pm. Closed Sun; major hols. Res accepted; required Sat. French, continental menu. Bar. Semi-a la carte: lunch $6.50-$14.95, dinner $19.95-$29.95. Specialties: beef Wellington, Dover sole, rack of lamb. Own desserts. Pianist Fri, Sat. Authentic farmhouse, built 1823. Cr cds: A, C, D, MC, V.

Ⓓ 🍽

Doylestown (Bucks Co) (E-10)

(See also Philadelphia, Quakertown)

Settled 1735 **Pop** 8,575 **Elev** 340 ft **Area Code** 215 **Zip** 18901 **E-mail** buckscountycvb@buckscountycvb.org **Web** www.buckscounty cvb.org
Information Bucks County Conference and Visitors Bureau, 152 Swamp Rd; 215/345-4552 or 800/836-2825

Doylestown is the county seat of historic and colorful Bucks County.

What to See and Do

Covered bridges. Descriptive list, map of 11 bridges in Bucks County may be obtained at Bucks County Tourist Commission.

James A. Michener Art Museum. Changing exhibitions of 20th-century American art, contemporary crafts and sculpture garden. Located in restored old Bucks County jail. (Daily exc Mon; closed major hols) 138 S Pine St. Phone 215/340-9800. ¢¢

Mercer Mile. Three reinforced-concrete structures built between 1910–1916 within a one-mi radius by Dr. Henry Chapman Mercer, archaeologist, historian, world traveler and tile maker. They include

Fonthill Museum. Concrete castle of Henry Chapman Mercer (1856–1930) displays his collection of tiles and prints from around the world. Guided tours (times vary; phone 215/348-9461). ¢¢

Mercer Museum of the Bucks County Historical Society. Collection of over 50,000 early American artifacts and tools. Changing exhibits gallery. (Daily; closed Jan 1, Thanksgiving, Dec 25) 84 S Pine St. Phone 215/345-0210. ¢¢

Moravian Pottery and Tile Works. Restored and established as a living history museum; tiles are handcrafted on premises. Slide show and self-guided tour explain ceramic process and history of Mercer's work, which appears in bldgs all over the country. (Daily; closed some hols) 130 Swamp Rd. Phone 215/345-6722. ¢¢

⭐ **Pearl S. Buck House** (1835). House of Pulitzer and Nobel Prize winning author Pearl S. Buck. Original furnishings incl desk at which *The Good Earth* was written; memorabilia, Chinese artifacts. Picnicking on grounds. Gift shop. One-hr guided tours (Mar–Dec, daily exc Mon; closed most major hols). 520 Dublin Rd, 8 mi NW via PA 611, 313 in Hilltown Township. Phone 215/249-0100. ¢¢

Motor Hotel

★★★ **COMFORT INN.** 678 Bethlehem Pike (18936), S on US 202. 215/361-3600; FAX 215/361-7949; res: 800/228-5150. 84 rms, 3 story. S $90.95-$129.95; D $95.95-$129.95; each addl $5; suites $124.95-$129.95; under 18 free. Crib free. TV; cable, VCR avail (movies). Complimentary continental bkfst. Coffee in rms. Restaurant nearby. Ck-out 11 am. Coin lndry. Meeting rm. Business servs avail. In-rm modem link. Valet serv. Health club privileges. Microwaves avail. Refrigerator, wet bar in suites. Cr cds: A, C, D, DS, MC, V.

Inns

★★★ **HIGHLAND FARMS BED & BREAKFAST.** 70 East Rd (18901), 1½ mi N on US 202, exit East Rd. 215/340-1354. Web www.web/comm.com/highland. 4 rms, 3 story, 2 suites. 1 rm phone. S, D $135-$195; each addl $25; suites $175-$195. Children over 12 yrs only. TV in common rm; cable, VCR avail (movies). Pool. Complimentary full bkfst. Ck-out 11 am, ck-in 3:30 pm. In-rm modem link. Tennis. Downhill ski 4 mi; x-country ski on-site. Many fireplaces. Picnic tables, grills. Built in 1800; antiques. Was home to Oscar Hammerstein, Broadway lyricist. Totally nonsmoking. Cr cds: C, MC, V.

★★★ **PINE TREE FARM BED & BREAKFAST.** 2155 Lower State Rd (18901). 215/348-0632. 4 rms, 3 story. S, D $160-$180; wkends (2-day min), hols (3-day min). Children over 16 yrs only. Pool. Complimentary full bkfst; afternoon refreshments. Ck-out 11 am, ck-in 4 pm. Tennis. Solarium. 16-acre country estate built 1730; antiques. Totally nonsmoking. Cr cds: C.

★★ **SIGN SORREL HORSE.** 4424 Old Easton Rd (18901). 215/230-9999; FAX 215/230-8053. 5 rms, 2 with shower only, 2 story, 2 suites. No rm phones. S, D $85-$175; wkends (2-day min). Complimentary continental bkfst. Complimentary coffee in rms. Restaurant (see SIGN OF THE SORREL HORSE). Ck-out 11 am, ck-in 4 pm. Luggage handling. Free airport, RR station transportation. Lawn games. Picnic tables. On river. Built as a grist-mill (1714); antiques. Totally nonsmoking. Cr cds: A, C, D, MC, V.

★★ **THE INN AT FORDHOOK FARM.** 105 New Britain Rd (18901). 215/345-1766; FAX 215/345-1791. 7 rms, 2 with shower only, 2 share bath, 3 story. Many rm phones. S, D $100-$300; each addl $20; wkends (2-day min). Children over 12 yrs only. 2 TVs; VCR avail (movies). Complimentary full bkfst. Ck-out 11 am, ck-in 3 pm. Meeting rms. Business servs avail. X-country ski on site. Lawn games. Balconies. Picnic tables. On 60 acres of woods and meadows; many antiques. Totally nonsmoking. Cr cds: A, C, MC, V.

Restaurants

★★ **BLACK WALNUT.** 80 W State St (18901). 215/348-0708. Hrs: noon-2:30 pm, 5:30-9 pm; Fri to 9:30 pm; Sat 5:30-9:30 pm; Sun 5-8:30 pm. Closed Mon; also most major hols. Res required Sat (dinner). Continental menu. A la carte entrees: lunch $10-$15, dinner $35-$42. Specialties: foie gras, galette of goat cheese, beef tenderloin with 1,000 peppercorns. Parking. Outdoor dining. In historic 1846 town; garden. Totally nonsmoking. Cr cds: C, DS, MC, V.

✓★ **LOS SARAPES.** 17 Moyer Rd (18914), 3 mi S on US 202, exit Moyer Rd. 215/822-8858. E-mail sarapes@ix.netcom.com; web www.lossarapes.com. Hrs: 11 am-9 pm; Fri, Sat to 10 pm; Sun from 4 pm. Closed Mon; major hols. Res accepted. Mexican menu. Bar. Semi-a la carte: lunch, dinner $4.50-$14. Specialties: tampiquena, mole poblano, pescado a la Veracruzana. Own desserts. Outdoor dining. Casual Mexican decor. Totally nonsmoking. Cr cds: A, C, DS, MC, V.

★★ **RUSSELL'S 96 WEST.** 96 W State St (18901). 215/345-8746. Hrs: 11:30 am-2 pm, 5:30-9:30 pm; Sat 5:30-9:30 pm; Sun brunch 10 am-2 pm. Closed major hols. Res accepted. French, Amer menu. Bar. A la carte entrees: lunch $7-$12, dinner $17-$29. Sun brunch $15.95. Specialties: New Zealand rack of lamb, Norwegian salmon, Peking duck breast. Outdoor dining. Intimate dining. Cr cds: A, C, D, DS, MC, V.

★★★ **SIGN OF THE SORREL HORSE.** (See Sign Sorrel Horse) 215/230-9999. Hrs: 5:30-9:30 pm. Closed Mon, Tues; Dec 25; also 2 wks Mar. Res accepted. French, Amer menu. Bar. A la carte entrees: dinner $15.95-$28. Prix fixe: dinner $55. Specialties: Swedish elk, kangaroo, ostrich. Outdoor dining. Guest rms avail. Located in historic gristmill (1714). Cr cds: A, C, D, MC, V.

Du Bois (C-4)

(See also Clearfield)

Settled 1865 **Pop** 8,286 **Elev** 1,420 ft **Area Code** 814 **Zip** 15801 **Web** www.ds.psu.edu~dacc

Information Du Bois Area Chamber of Commerce, 33 N Brady St; 814/371-5010

At the entrance to the lowest pass of the Allegheny Range, Du Bois is a transportation center—once the apex of huge lumbering operations. Destroyed by fire in 1888, the town was rebuilt on the ashes of the old community and today ranks as one of the 12 major trading centers in the state.

Motels

✓★★ **BEST WESTERN INN & CONFERENCE CENTER.** 82 N Park Pl (15801), between I-80 exits 16 & 17 on SR 219 and SR 255. 814/371-6200; FAX 814/371-4608. 60 rms, 3 story. S $47-$57; D $53-$63; each addl $6; under 18 free. Crib free. TV; cable. Playground. Complimentary continental bkfst. Restaurant nearby. Ck-out 11 am. Business servs avail. Sundries. Golf privileges. Health club privileges. Picnic tables. Cr cds: A, C, D, DS, MC, V.

✓★★ **HAMPTON INN.** RR 8 Box 3A (15801), I-80 exit 17. 814/375-1000; FAX 814/375-4668; res: 800/426-7866. 96 rms, 3 story. S $59-$64; D $64; kit suite $95; under 18 free; wkly, wkend, hol rates; ski, golf plans; 2-day min Penn State football games. Crib free. TV; cable (premium), VCR avail. Indoor pool; whirlpool. Complimentary continental bkfst. Complimentary coffee in rms. Restaurant adj open 24 hrs. Ck-out noon. Meeting rms. Business servs avail. Valet serv. Downhill/x-country ski 1 mi. Exercise equipt. Health club privileges. Refrigerators avail. Cr cds: A, C, D, DS, MC, V.

⊡ 🎿 🏊 🎎 🛶 🔥 SC

★★★ **HOLIDAY INN.** *US 219 & I-80 (15801), US 219 & I-80 exit 16.* 814/371-5100; *FAX* 814/375-0230; *res:* 800/959-3412; *res:* 800/959-3412. E-mail holidayd@penn.com. 160 rms, 2 story. S $72-$77; D $78-$84; each addl $6; studio rms $75; under 18 free. Pet accepted. TV; cable (premium), VCR avail. Pool; wading, poolside serv, lifeguard. Complimentary coffee in rms. Restaurant 7 am-2 pm, 5-10 pm. Rm serv. Bar 5 pm-1 am. Ck-out noon. Coin lndry. Meeting rms. Business servs avail. In-rm modem link. Bellhops. Free airport transportation. Health club privileges. Cr cds: A, C, D, DS, JCB, MC, V.

⊡ 🛶 🏊 🎎 🔥 SC

★★ **RAMADA INN.** *I-80 And Rte 255 (15801).* 814/371-7070; *FAX* 814/371-1055; *res:* 800/272-6232; *res:* 800/272-6232. Web www.ramada.com. 96 rms, 2-3 story. No elvtr. S $53-$65; D $59-$75; each addl $10; suites $80-$150; under 18 free. Crib free. Pet accepted. TV; cable (premium), VCR avail. Indoor pool; poolside serv. Restaurant 6:30 am-1:30 pm, 5:30-10 pm. Rm serv. Bar 5 pm-2 am; entertainment exc Sun. Ck-out noon. Meeting rms. Business servs avail. Airport transportation. Golf privileges, pro. Health club privileges. Cr cds: A, C, D, DS, JCB, MC, V.

⊡ 🛶 🎎 🏊 🎎 🔥 SC

Inn

★★★ **TOWN HOUSE MOTOR INN.** *138 Center St (15857), 31 mi NE on PA 255N.* 814/781-1556; *FAX* 814/834-4449; *res:* 800/852-9180. 53 rms, 3 story. S $48-$90; D $53-$97; each addl $7. Crib $7. TV; cable (premium). Complimentary continental bkfst. Complimentary coffee in rms. Restaurant 6:30 am-2 pm, 5-9 pm; Sat from 5 pm; closed Sun. Rm serv. Ck-out 11 am. Meeting rms. Business servs avail. In-rm modem link. Exercise equipt. Fireplaces. Picnic tables. Stained glass, antiques in 7 historic (1890s) townhouses. Cr cds: A, C, D, DS, MC, V.

⊡ 🎎 🎎 🔥 🐾

Easton (D-9)

(See also Allentown, Bethlehem)

Founded 1752 **Pop** 26,276 **Elev** 300 ft **Area Code** 484 & 610 **Zip** 18042 **E-mail** tracc@silo.com **Web** silo.com/tracc
Information Two Rivers Area Chamber of Commerce, 1 S 3rd St, PO Box 637, 18044-0637; 610/253-4211

Named by Thomas Penn, one of the proprietors, for the English birthplace of his bride, Easton today is the gateway to the great industrial Lehigh Valley. Lafayette College, with its beautiful campus, and the historic Great Square are of interest. Easton, the seat of Northampton County, is part of a larger metropolitan area, the Lehigh Valley, which also includes Allentown and Bethlehem.

What to See and Do

Canal Museum. Exhibits incl photographs, models, documents and artifacts from the era of mule-drawn canal boats in the 1800s; electronic map and audiovisual programs. (Daily exc Mon; closed Jan 1, Thanksgiving, Dec 25; open Mon hols) PA 611, 1 mi S of US 22, Two Rivers Landing. Phone 610/250-6700. ¢¢¢ Admission includes

The Crayola Factory. See how crayons & markers are created. Visit Crayola Hall of Fame; enjoy dozens of interactive exhibits featuring the wonders of light and color. Same location and schedule as Canal Museum. Phone 610/515-8000.

"The Great Square." Center of business district. Now called Center Square. Dominated by Soldiers' and Sailors' Monument. Bronze marker shows replica of Old Courthouse, which stood until 1862 on land rented from the Penns for one red rose a year. From Old Courthouse steps, the Declaration of Independence was read on July 8, 1776, when the Easton Flag, the first Stars and Stripes of the united colonies, was unfurled here.

Hugh Moore Park. Restored Lehigh Canal, locks and locktender's house; mule-drawn canal boat rides (early May–Labor Day, daily; early-late Sept, wkends). Also hiking, picnicking; boat rentals in park. Park (daily). S 25th St, 2 mi S of US 22. Phone 610/250-6700. Boat rides ¢¢

Lafayette College (1826). (2,000 students) Bronze statue of Lafayette by Daniel Chester French in front of college chapel; American historical portrait collection in Kirby Hall of Civil Rights. Tour of campus. N side of town. Phone 610/250-5000.

Northampton County Historical Society. Changing exhibits; library; museum. (By appt) 101-107 S 4th St, diagonally opp Parsons-Taylor House. Phone 610/253-1222. Museum ¢; Library ¢¢

Restaurants

★★ **MANDARIN TANG.** *25th St Shopping Center (18045).* 610/258-5697. Hrs: 11:30 am-10 pm; Fri, Sat to 11 pm. Closed Thanksgiving. Res accepted Fri-Sun. Chinese menu. Semi-a la carte: lunch $3.95-$5.50, dinner $5-$16.95. Specialties: mandarin orange beef, General Tso's chicken. Chinese decor. Cr cds: A, C, D, MC, V.

★★ **PEARLY BAKER'S ALE HOUSE.** *11 Center Square (18042).* 610/253-9949. Hrs: 11:30 am-10 pm. Closed Mon; also many major hols. Res required Fri, Sat (dinner). International menu. Bar to 2 am. A la carte entrees: lunch $6-$9, dinner $14-$19. Child's meals. Entertainment Fri. Specializes in international cuisine. Outdoor dining. Austrian chandelier in main dining rm. Cr cds: A, C, MC, V.

⊡

Ebensburg (E-4)

(See also Altoona, Johnstown)

Pop 3,872 **Elev** 2,140 ft **Area Code** 814 **Zip** 15931 **E-mail** jstcvb@visitjohnstownpa.com **Web** www.visitjohnstownpa.com
Information Greater Johnstown/Cambria County Convention & Visitors Bureau, 111 Market St, Johnstown 15901-1608; 814/536-7993 or 800/237-8590

What to See and Do

Allegheny Portage Railroad National Historic Site. Remains of railroad built 1831–1834 to link east and west divisions of the Pennsylvania Mainline Canal. Cars were pulled up 10 inclined planes by ropes powered by steam engines. Horses or locomotives pulled the cars over the level stretches of the 36-mi route across the Alleghenies from Hollidaysburg to Johnstown. The Skew Arch Bridge, an engine house exhibit, and the Lemon House, a historic tavern, help tell the story of the Allegheny Portage Railroad. A visitor center (daily; closed Dec 25) has exhibits and a 20-min film. There are ranger-led programs (summer, daily) and costumed demonstrations (summer); picnic area (daily); hiking & cross-country trails. 12 mi E on US 22. Phone 814/886-6150. ¢

Portage Station Museum. This historic station was once a stop on the Pennsylvania Railroad. The first floor, with its original lighting fixtures, oak wainscoting and woodwork, contains the Master's Office and waiting rm. Exhibits on the second floor incl artifacts from the Mainline Mining Museum. (Wed, Sat & Sun afternoons) 400 Lee St, in Portage. Phone 814/736-8918 or 814/736-4343. **Free**

Edinboro (B-2)

(See also Erie, Meadville)

Pop 7,736 **Elev** 1,210 ft **Area Code** 814 **Zip** 16412

This is a resort town on Edinboro Lake and the home of Edinboro State College.

What to See and Do

Mountain View Ski Area. 2 T-bars, Pomalift; patrol, school, rentals; snow-making; cafeteria. Longest run 2,800 ft; vertical drop 350 ft. (Dec–Mar, daily) Half-day and evening rates. 4 mi E on US 6N, then 3 mi S on PA 86, in Cambridge Springs. Phone 814/734-1641. ¢¢¢¢

Motel

★★★ **RAMADA INN.** *401 W Plum St (16412), off I-79 exit 38, 6N. 814/734-5650; FAX 814/734-7532; res: 888/449-0344; res: 888/449-0344.* 105 rms, 2 story. S, D $80-$90; each addl $10; package plans. Crib free. Pet accepted. TV. Indoor pool. Sauna. Restaurant 6 am-10 pm. Rm serv. Bars 11:30-2 am; entertainment. Ck-out noon. Coin lndry. Meeting rms. Business servs avail. 18-hole golf adj, greens fee $18-$24, putting green. Downhill ski 7 mi. Cr cds: A, C, D, DS, MC, V.

D 🐾 🛥 🏊 🍽 🏄 🏌 🐾 SC

Inn

★★★ **RIVERSIDE INN.** *1 Fountain Ave (16403), at US 6/19 & PA 99S. 814/398-4645; FAX 814/398-8161; res: 800/964-5173.* Web www.theriversideinn.com. 74 rms, 3 story. S $50-$70; D $65-$95; each addl $10; suites $100; under 5 free. Closed Jan-mid-Apr. TV in suites & sitting rm. Pool. Complimentary full bkfst. Dining rm 11:30 am-2 pm, 5:30-8:30 pm; Fri, Sat to 10 pm; Sun 11 am-2 pm, 5:30-8:30 pm. Dinner theater on wkends, matinees wkdays. Bar. Ck-out 11 am, ck-in 3 pm. Business servs avail. Tennis privileges. Golf privileges. Lawn games. Victorian inn (1885) overlooking French Creek. Cr cds: C, DS, MC, V.

D 🐾 🏌 🏊 🍽 🏄 🔥

Ephrata (E-8)

(See also Bird-in-Hand, Denver/Adamstown, Lancaster, Lebanon, Reading)

Settled 1732 **Pop** 12,133 **Elev** 380 ft **Area Code** 717 **Zip** 17522
E-mail ephcoc@ptd.net **Web** www.ephrata-area.org
Information Chamber of Commerce, 77 Park Ave, Ste 1; 717/738-9010

What to See and Do

Ephrata Cloister. Buildings stand as a monument to an unusual religious experiment. In 1732 Conrad Beissel, a German Seventh-Day Baptist, began to lead a hermit's life here; within a few years he established a religious community of recluses, with a Brotherhood, a Sisterhood and a group of married "householders." The members of the solitary order dressed in concealing white habits; the bldgs (1735–1749) were without adornment, the halls were narrow, the doorways were low and board benches served as beds and wooden blocks as pillows. Their religious zeal and charity, however, proved to be their undoing. After the Battle of Brandy-wine, the cloistered community nursed the Revolutionary sick and wounded, but contracted typhus, which decimated their numbers. Celibacy also contributed to the decline of the community, but the Society was not formally dissolved until 1934. Surviving and restored bldgs incl the Sisters'

House, Chapel, Almonry and 8 others. Craft demonstrations (summer). (Daily; closed some hols) 632 W Main St. Phone 717/733-6600. ¢¢

Museum and Library of the Historical Society of Cocalico Valley. Italianate Victorian mansion contains period displays; historical exhibits; genealogical and historical research library (fee) on Cocalico Valley area and residents. (Mon, Wed, Thurs, Sat) 249 W Main St. Phone 717/733-1616. **Free**

Annual Event

Street Fair. One of largest in state. Last full wk Sept.

Inns

★★★ **DONECKERS.** *318-324 N State Street (17522). 717/738-9502; FAX 717/738-9502.* 12 rms, 3 story, 2 carriage house suites. S $61-$81; D $69-$89; each addl $10; suites $149-$185; package plans. Crib $8. TV in sitting rm; cable. Complimentary continental bkfst. Restaurant nearby. Ck-out 11 am, ck-in 3 pm. Health club privileges. Microwaves avail. Restored clockmaker's house (1777). Antiques. Hand-cut stenciling. Cr cds: A, C, D, DS, MC, V.

D 🔥

✓ ★★★ **DONECKERS THE GUESTHOUSE.** *318 N State St (17522). 717/738-9502; FAX 717/738-9554.* E-mail customerservice@doneckers.com; web www.doneckers.com. 19 rms, 2 story. S $57-$87; D $65-$95; each addl $10; suites $155-$175. Crib $8. Complimentary continental bkfst. Restaurant (see DONECKERS). Ck-out 11 am, ck-in 3 pm. Health club privileges. Some balconies. Mansion furnished with antiques. Cr cds: A, C, D, DS, MC, V.

D 🏄 🔥

★★★ **SMITHTON BED & BREAKFAST COUNTRY INN.** *900 W Main St (17522), at S Academy Dr. 717/733-6094.* 8 rms, 2 story. S $75-$115; D $85-$155; each addl $20-$35; suites $145-$175. Complimentary full bkfst. Restaurant nearby. Ck-out noon, ck-in 3:30 pm. Concierge. Some in-rm whirlpools. Historic stone inn (1763); fireplaces, antiques. Totally nonsmoking. Cr cds: A, C, MC, V.

D 🏄 🔥

Restaurant

★★★ **DONECKERS.** *(See Doneckers The Guesthouse) 717/738-9501.* E-mail customerservice@doneckers.com; web www.doneckers.com. Hrs: 11 am-10 pm. Closed Wed, Sun; major hols. Res accepted. Bar. Wine list. French, Amer menu. A la carte entrees: lunch $6.95-$13.75, dinner $7.50-$29. Child's meals. Specialties: Dover sole with strawberry sauce, steak au poivre. Own baking. Elegant French decor. Cr cds: A, C, D, DS, MC, V.

D

Erie (A-2)

(See also North East)

Settled 1753 **Pop** 108,718 **Elev** 744 ft **Area Code** 814
E-mail Erie-Chamber@erie.net **Web** www.eriepa.com
Information Erie Area Chamber of Commerce, 109 Boston Store Pl, 16501-2312; 814/454-7191

Third-largest city in the state and only Great Lakes port in Pennsylvania, Erie has a fine natural harbor on Lake Erie, which is protected and bounded by Presque Isle peninsula, the site of many historic events. Greater Erie is also one of the nation's mighty industrial centers, with more than 750 highly diversified manufacturing firms and several large industrial parks. The lake and city take their name from the Eriez tribe, who were killed by the Seneca about 1654.

On the south shore of Presque Isle Bay, Commodore Oliver Hazard Perry built his fleet, floated the ships across the sandbars and fought the British in the Battle of Lake Erie (1813). Fort Presque Isle, built by the French in 1753 and destroyed by them in 1759, was rebuilt by the English, burned by Native Americans and rebuilt again in 1794 by Americans.

What to See and Do

Bicentennial Tower. Commemorating Erie's 200th birthday, this 187-ft tower features 2 observation decks with aerial view of city, bay, Lake Erie. Concessions in tower lobby. (May-Oct, daily; rest of yr, call for schedule; closed some hols) Free admission Tues. Erie's Bayfront, at the foot of State St. Phone 814/455-6055. ¢

Erie Art Museum. Temporary art exhibits in a variety of media; regional artwork and lectures in the restored Greek-revival Old Customs House (1839). Art classes, concerts, lectures and workshops are also offered. (Tues–Sat, also Sun afternoons; closed major hols) Free admission Wed. 411 State St. Phone 814/459-5477. ¢

Erie Historical Museum & Planetarium. Housed in 1890s Victorian mansion. Museum features regional history and decorative arts exhibits; multimedia presentations on regional maritime history; restored period rms; changing exhibits (Tues–Sun afternoons; closed most hols). Also planetarium with shows (Sun afternoons). 356 W 6th St. Phone 814/871-5790. Museum ¢; Planetarium ¢

Erie Zoo. Zoo houses more than 300 animals, incl gorillas, polar bears and giraffes; children's zoo (May–Sept); 1-mi tour of grounds on Safariland Express Train (fee). Indoor ice rink (Sept–Mar, Phone 814/868-3651). Zoo (daily). 3 mi N of I-90 State St exit 7. Phone 814/864-4091. Zoo ¢¢

Firefighters Historical Museum. More than 1,300 items of firefighting memorabilia are displayed in the old #4 Firehouse. Exhibits incl fire apparatus dating from 1823, alarm systems, uniforms, badges, ribbons, helmets, nozzles, fire marks and fire extinguishers; fire safety films are shown in the Hay Loft Theater. (May–Oct, Sat & Sun) 428 Chestnut St. Phone 814/456-5969. ¢

Gridley's Grave. Final resting place of Captain Charles Vernon Gridley, to whom, at the Battle of Manila Bay in 1898, Admiral Dewey said, "You may fire when ready, Gridley." Gridley died in Japan; his body was returned here for burial. Four old Spanish cannons from Manila Harbor, built in 1777, guard the grave. Offers view of peninsula, Lake Erie and entrance to Erie Harbor from cliff by Gridley Circle. Lakeside Cemetery, 1718 E Lake Rd. Phone 814/459-8200.

Land Lighthouse. (1866). The first lighthouse on the Great Lakes was constructed on this site in 1813. Foot of Dunn Blvd. Phone 814/452-3937.

Misery Bay. State monument to Perry; named after Perry defeated British and the fleet suffered cold and privations of a bitter winter. NE corner of Presque Isle Bay.

Presque Isle State Park. Peninsula stretches 7 mi into Lake Erie and curves back toward city. Approx 3,200 acres of recreation and conservation areas. Swimming; fishing; boating (rentals, mooring, launching, marina). Hiking, birding, trails. Cross-country skiing, ice skating, ice fishing, ice boating. Picnicking, concessions. Visitor center, environmental education and interpretive programs. N off PA 832. Phone 814/833-7424.

Waldameer Park & Water World. Rides, midway, kiddieland, water park, picnic area, food, dance pavilion. (Memorial Day–Labor Day, daily exc Mon; open Mon hols) 220 Peninsula Drive, at entrance to Presque Isle State Park. Phone 814/838-3591. ¢¢¢¢

Wayne Memorial Blockhouse. Replica of blockhouse in which General Anthony Wayne died Dec 15, 1796, after becoming ill on a voyage from Detroit. He was buried at the foot of the flagpole; later, his son had the body disinterred and the remains moved to Radnor. (Memorial Day–Labor Day, daily) On grounds of State Soldiers' and Sailors' Home, 560 E 3rd St. Phone 814/871-4531. **Free**

Motels

★ ★ **COMFORT INN.** 8051 Peach St (16509); I-90E exit 6. 814/866-6666; FAX 814/864-1367; res: 800/221-2222. 110 rms, 2 story, 50 suites. Mid-May-Sept: S $80-$99; D $90-$120; each addl $6; suites $95-$125; under 18 free; higher rates hol wkends; lower rates rest of yr. Crib free. TV; cable (premium), VCR (movies). Heated pool; whirlpool, lifeguard. Complimentary continental bkfst. Coffee in rms. Restaurant adj 6 am-midnight. Ck-out noon. Meeting rm. Business servs avail. In-rm modem link. Free airport transportation. Exercise equipt. Refrigerator, wet bar in suites. Some balconies. Cr cds: A, C, D, DS, JCB, MC, V.

D ⤶ ✕ ≥≤ ♨ SC

★ ★ **ECONO LODGE.** 8050 Peach St (16509), I-90E exit 6. 814/866-5544; FAX 814/864-6218; res: 800/638-7949. 97 rms, 3 story. Late May-Oct: S $79-$109; D $89.95-$149; each addl $10; higher rates special events; lower rates rest of yr. Crib free. TV; cable, VCR (movies). Indoor pool; whirlpool. Complimentary continental bkfst. Restaurant adj 7-2 am. Ck-out noon. Meeting rms. Business servs avail. In-rm modem link. Sundries. Free airport transportation. Exercise equipt. Some refrigerators, wet bars. Cr cds: A, C, D, DS, JCB, MC, V.

D ⤶ ✕ ≥≤ ♨ SC

✓ ★ ★ **GLASS HOUSE INN.** 3202 W 26th St (16506). 814/833-7751; FAX 814/833-4222; res: 800/956-7222. Web www.velocity.net/~g hilel. 30 rms. June-Labor Day: S, D $65-$92; each addl $7; family rates; lower rates rest of yr. Crib $4. TV; cable (premium), VCR avail (movies). Heated pool. Complimentary continental bkfst. Restaurant nearby. Ck-out 11 am. In-rm modem link. Sundries. Gift shop. Downhill/x-country ski 20 mi. Cr cds: A, C, D, DS, MC, V.

⤶ ⤶ ≥≤ ♨

✓ ★ ★ **HAMPTON INN.** 3041 W 12th St (16505). 814/835-4200; FAX 814/835-5212; res: 800/426-7866. 100 rms, 3 story. S $71-$105; D $78-$105; under 18 free. Crib avail. TV; cable (premium). Heated pool. Complimentary continental bkfst. Restaurant nearby 7 am-10:30 pm. Ck-out noon. Business servs avail. Valet serv. Cr cds: A, C, D, DS, MC, V.

D ⤶ ≥≤ ♨ SC

★ **MOTEL 6.** 7875 Peach St (16509), jct I-90 & US 19, exit 6. 814/864-4811; FAX 814/868-1277; res: 800/542-7674. 83 rms, 2 story. Late May-Sept: S $59-$89; D $69-$99; each addl $10; under 18 free; package plan; some lower rates rest of yr. Crib free. Pet accepted. TV; cable. Indoor pool; wading pool. Complimentary coffee. Restaurant nearby. Ck-out noon. Business servs avail. Coin lndry. Valet serv. Free airport transportation. Exercise equipt; sauna. Private patios, balconies. Cr cds: A, C, D, DS, ER, JCB, MC, V.

D ⤶ ⤶ ≥≤ ✕ ≥≤ ♨ SC

★ ★ ★ **RAMADA INN.** 6101 Wattsburg Rd (16509). 814/825-3100; FAX 814/825-0857; res: 800/272-6232; res: 800/374-1875. E-mail ramadaerie@aol.com. 122 rms, 2 story. July-Sept: S, D $80-$90; each addl $8; suites $90-$120; under 18 free; ski, wkend plans; lower rates rest of yr. Crib free. TV; cable (premium), VCR (movies). Heated pool; wading pool, whirlpool, lifeguard. Restaurant 6:30 am-1 pm, 5-10 pm. Rm serv. Bar 5 pm-2 am. Ck-out noon. Meeting rms. Business center. In-rm modem link. Sundries. Downhill ski 15 mi. Exercise equipt. Game rm. Cr cds: A, C, D, DS, JCB, MC, V.

D ⤶ ⤶ ≥≤ ✕ ≥≤ ♨ SC ✕

Motor Hotels

★ ★ ★ **BEL AIRE HOTEL COMPLEX.** 2800 W 8th St (16505). 814/833-1116; FAX 814/838-3242; res: 800/888-8781. Web www.bel-aire-hotel.com. 151 rms, 3 story. Mid-June-mid-Sept: S, D $95-$100; each addl $10; suites $125-$200; under 19 free; lower rates rest of yr. Crib $10. TV; cable. Indoor pool; whirlpool. Complimentary coffee in rms. Restaurant 6 am-11 pm. Bar 11-2 am; Sun to midnight. Ck-out noon. Meeting rms. In-rm modem link. Valet serv. Sundries. Exercise equipt; sauna. Private patios, balconies. Cr cds: A, C, D, DS, MC, V.

D ⤶ ✕ ≥≤ ♨

★ ★ ★ **HOLIDAY INN.** 18 W 18th St (16501). 814/456-2961; FAX 814/456-7067; res: 800/465-4329; res: 800/832-9101. 133 rms, 4 story. Memorial Day-Labor Day: S, D $69-$94; each addl $6; under 18 free; lower rates rest of yr. Crib free. TV; cable (premium). Heated pool; poolside serv. Complimentary full bkfst. Coffee in rms. Restaurant 6:30 am-10 pm. Rm serv. Bar 11:30-2 am. Ck-out noon. Lndry facilities. Meeting rms. Business center. In-rm modem link. Bellhops. Valet serv. Free airport transportation. Exercise equipt. Health club privileges. Cr cds: A, C, D, DS, JCB, MC, V.

★★ **QUALITY INN.** 8040 Perry Hwy (16509), exit 7 off I-90. 814/864-4911; FAX 814/864-3743; res: 800/550-8040. 107 rms, 2 story. S, D $49-$109; each addl $6; under 18 free. Crib free. Pet accepted. TV; cable. Heated pool. Restaurant 6:30 am-10 pm. Rm serv. Bar 11-1 am. Ck-out 11 am. Meeting rms. Business center. In-rm modem link. Bellhops. Valet serv. Free airport, RR station transportation. Health club privileges. Cr cds: A, C, D, DS, JCB, MC, V.

★ **SUPER 8.** 8040 B Perry Hwy (16509). 814/864-9200; FAX 814/868-4973. Web www.super8.com. 93 rms, 4 story. Apr-Oct: S, D $39-$89; under 18 free; family rates; package plans; higher rates special events; lower rates rest of yr. Crib free. Pet accepted, some restrictions. TV; cable (premium). Complimentary continental bkfst. Restaurant adj 6:30 am-10 pm. Ck-out 11 am. Business servs avail. In-rm modem link. Bellhops. Valet serv. Coin lndry. Airport transportation. Pool privileges. Game rm. Some refrigerators, microwaves. Cr cds: A, C, D, DS, ER, MC, V.

Restaurant

★★ **PUFFERBELLY.** 414 French St (16507). 814/454-1557. Hrs: 11:30 am-9:30 pm; Fri, Sat to 11 pm; Sun to 8 pm; Sun brunch to 3 pm. Closed major hols. Res accepted. Bar. Semi-a la carte: lunch $3.95-$6, dinner $8.95-$15.95. Sun brunch $9.95. Specializes in regional cuisine, steak, seafood. Outdoor dining. Restored firehouse (1907). Cr cds: A, C, DS, MC, V.

Fort Washington (E-9)

Pop 3,699 Elev 250 ft Area Code 215 Zip 19034 E-mail info@ valleyforge.org Web www.valleyforge.org
Information Valley Forge Convention & Visitors Bureau, 600 W Germantown Pike, Suite 130, Plymouth Meeting 19462; 610/834-1550

What to See and Do

Fort Washington State Park. Commemorates the site of Washington's northern defense line against the British in 1777. Fishing. Hiking, ball fields. Picnicking. 500 Bethlehem Pike. Phone 215/646-2942.

Hope Lodge (ca 1745). Colonial Georgian mansion; headquarters for Surgeon General John Cochran after Battle of Germantown. Historic furnishings, paintings, ceramics. (Daily exc Mon; closed most hols) 1 mi S, 553 Bethlehem Pike. Phone 215/646-1595. ¢¢

The Highlands (1796). Late-Georgian mansion on 43 acres built by Anthony Morris, active in both state and federal government. Formal gardens and crenelated walls built ca 1845. Tours (by appt). (Mon–Fri) 7001 Sheaff Lane. Phone 215/641-2687. ¢

Restaurant

✓ ★★ **PALACE OF ASIA.** 285 Commerce Dr (19034). 215/646-2133. Hrs: 11:30 am-11 pm; Sat, Sun brunch to 3:30 pm. Closed Dec 24. Res required Fri-Sun dinner. Indian menu. Bar. Semi-a la carte: lunch

$6.25-$7.95, dinner $7.95-$15.95. Sat, Sun brunch $3.50-$8.25. Specializes in vegetarian & curry dishes. Own baking. Authentic Indian atmosphere. Cr cds: A, C, D, DS, MC, V.

Franklin (Venango Co) (C-2)

(See also Meadville, Oil City, Titusville)

Settled 1787 Pop 7,329 Elev 1,020 ft Area Code 814 Zip 16323
E-mail chamber@franklin-pa.org Web www.franklin-pa.org
Information Franklin Area Chamber of Commerce, 1259 Liberty St; 814/432-5823

A series of French and British forts was erected in this area. The last one, Fort Franklin, was razed by local settlers who used the stone and timber in their own buildings. Old Garrison took its place in 1796 and later served as the Venango County Jail. In 1859, James Evans, a blacksmith, made tools to drill an oil well that brought an oil boom to the area. For years, oil was dominant in the area's industries.

What to See and Do

DeBence Antique Music World. Features nickelodeons, band organs, calliopes, German organs, a variety of music boxes, many other items. Unique "see and hear" museum. Guided tours. (Jan-mid-Mar, Thurs-Sat; mid-Mar-Dec, daily exc Mon; closed hols) 1261 Liberty St. Phone 814/432-5668. ¢¢¢

Hoge-Osmer House (ca 1865). Museum owned by Venango County Historical Society; houses displays of materials and artifacts relating to Venango County history; period furnishings, research library. House open (May–Dec, Tues–Thurs & Sat; rest of yr, Sat; closed major hols). Inquire for genealogy library hrs. Corner of South Park & Elk Sts. Phone 814/437-2275. **Free**

Pioneer Cemetery (1795–1879). Self-guided walking tour booklets can be purchased at the Chamber of Commerce. Otter & 15th Sts.

Venango County Court House (1868). Unique styling; contains display of Native American artifacts. (Mon–Fri; closed hols) 12th & Liberty Sts. Phone 814/432-9500.

Annual Events

Rocky Grove Fair. July.

Applefest. Apple pie baking contest; arts & crafts; entertainment; classic car show. Kids Korner. 5-km race; horse-drawn buggy rides. Phone 814/432-5823. 1st full wkend Oct.

Seasonal Event

Franklin Silver Cornet Band Concerts. City Park. Thurs, mid-June–Aug.

Motor Hotel

★★★ **FRANKLIN INN.** 1421 Liberty St (16323). 814/437-3031; FAX 814/437-1901; res: 800/535-4052. 85 rms, 6 story. Apr-Sept: S $65; D $70; each addl $5; under 18 free; wkly, monthly rates; lower rates rest of yr. Pet accepted, some restrictions. TV; cable. Complimentary continental bkfst. Restaurant 6 am-2 pm, 5-10 pm; Sun 7 am-2 pm. Bar. Ck-out 11 am. Business servs avail. Valet serv. Barber, beauty shop. Free airport, bus depot transportation. Exercise equipt. Health club privileges. Some refrigerators. Cr cds: A, C, D, DS, MC, V.

Inns

✓ ★★ **LAMBERTON HOUSE BED & BREAKFAST.** *1331 Otter St (16323).* 814/432-7908. 6 rms, 2 story, 2 share bath, 3 with shower only. No rm phones. S $45-$75, D $50-$75; each addl $10; under 8 free; wkly rates. Crib free. TV in drawing room; VCR. Complimentary full bkfst. Restaurant nearby 7 am-11 pm. Ck-out 11 am, ck-in 3 pm. Health club privileges. Historic building (1874). Cr cds: C, MC, V.

★★ **QUO VADIS BED & BREAKFAST.** *1501 Liberty St (16323), near Chess-Lamberton Airport, Rte 8, 15 mi N of I-80, Exit 3.* 814/432-4208; FAX 814/797-1162; res: 800/360-6598. 6 rms, 3 story. S, D $60-$80; each addl $10; wkly rates. TV in sitting rm. Complimentary full bkfst. Restaurant nearby. Ck-out 11 am, ck-in 4-9 pm. Victorian mansion (1867); detailed woodwork, heirloom antiques. Totally nonsmoking. Cr cds: A, C, MC, V.

Galeton (B-6)

(See also Wellsboro)

Pop 1,370 **Elev** 1,325 ft **Area Code** 814 **Zip** 16922
Information Potter County Recreation, PO Box 245, Coudersport 16915; 814/435-2290 or 888-POTTER2

What to See and Do

Ole Bull State Park. At upper reaches of the Kettle Creek. Site of unsuccessful effort by the famous Norwegian violinist, Ole Bornemann Bull, to establish a colony called "New Norway." Approx 125 acres. Swimming beach; fishing, hunting. Hiking. Cross-country skiing, snowmobiling. Tent & trailer sites (electric hookups). Interpretive program. Standard fees. 18 mi SW on PA 144. Phone 814/435-5000.

Pennsylvania Lumber Museum. Exhibits on lumbering and its techniques, forest industries and products; reconstructed lumber camp and sawmill; restored locomotive and log-loader; nature trails, picnicking. Slide show in visitor center. (Apr-Nov, daily; closed hols) (See ANNUAL EVENTS) 10 mi W on US 6. Phone 814/435-2652. ¢¢

Ski Denton/Denton Hill. Triple, double chairlifts, 2 Pomalifts; patrol, school, rentals; snowmaking; cafeteria, restaurant; lodge, cabins. Longest run 1 mi; vertical drop 650 ft. (Dec-Mar, daily) 100 mi of cross-country trails; night skiing; camping. (See ANNUAL EVENTS) 10 mi W on US 6. Phone 814/435-2115. ¢¢¢¢¢

Annual Events

Bark Peeler's Convention. On grounds of Pennsylvania Lumber Museum. Re-creation of old-time festival held by lumber camp workers celebrating the end of the work year. Features many demonstrations, incl cross-cut sawing, hewing, bark peeling; entertainment; period music; exhibits. Phone 814/435-2652. Early July.

Woodsmen's Carnival. Cherry Springs State Park, 12 mi SW on West Branch Rd. Horse-pulling and woodcutting competitions; food; displays. Phone 814/435-5010. First full wkend Aug.

Bowhunter's Festival. Denton Hill. Wkend late Aug.

Germania Old Home Day. 7 mi SE via PA 144 in Germania. Food, dancing, events, games, entertainment. Phone 814/435-8881. Early Sept.

Gettysburg (F-6)

(See also Hanover, York)

Founded 1798 **Pop** 7,025 **Elev** 560 ft **Area Code** 717 **Zip** 17325
Web www.gettysburg.com
Information Convention & Visitors Bureau, 35 Carlisle St; 717/334-6274

Because of the historical nature of this area and the many attractions in this town, visitors may want to stop in at the Gettysburg Convention & Visitors Bureau for complete information about bus tours, guide service (including a tape-recorded and self-guided tour) and help in planning their visit here.

What to See and Do

A. Lincoln's Place. Live portrayal of the 16th president; 45 min. (Mid-June–Labor Day, Mon–Fri) 213 Steinwehr Ave. For reservations phone 717/334-6049 or 717/334-8003. ¢¢¢

Confederate States Armory and Museum. Displays of Confederate weapons used in the Battle of Gettysburg. Included are collection of swords, small arms, memorabilia. (June-mid-Aug, daily; mid-Aug-late Nov, Fri-Mon) 529 Baltimore St. ¢

"The Conflict." A triple-screen program depicts the Civil War and battle at Gettysburg in 7 different 50-min programs. Multiple projectors blend camera, artwork of the period and modern panoramic photography with narration. Military bookshop. Abraham Lincoln performances (mid-June–Labor Day, Mon–Fri eves). (Daily; closed Thanksgiving, Dec 25) 213 Steinwehr Ave. Phone 717/334-8003. The Conflict ¢¢; Lincoln performance ¢¢¢

Eisenhower National Historic Site (see GETTYSBURG NATIONAL MILITARY PARK).

General Lee's Headquarters. Robert E. Lee planned Confederate strategy for the Gettysburg battle in this house; contains collection of historical items from the battle. (Mid-Mar–mid-Nov, daily) 401 Buford Ave. Phone 717/334-3141. ¢¢

Gettysburg Battle Theatre. Miniature battlefield with 25,000 figures; 30-min multimedia program showing battle strategy. (Mar–Nov, daily) 571 Steinwehr Ave. Phone 717/334-6100. ¢¢¢

Gettysburg College (1832). (2,000 students) Liberal arts; oldest Lutheran-affiliated college in US. Pennsylvania Hall was used as Civil War hospital; Eisenhower House and statue on grounds. Tour of campus. 3 blks NW of Lincoln Sq off US 15 Business N. Phone 717/337-6000.

Gettysburg National Military Park (see).

Gettysburg Scenic Rail Tours. A 16-mi round trip to Biglerville on steam train. Also charter trips and special runs. (July–Aug, daily; May–June & Sept–Oct, Thurs–Sun; Apr, Sat & Sun) Washington St. Phone 717/334-6932. ¢¢¢

Ghosts of Gettysburg Candlelight Walking Tours. Armed with tales from Mark Nesbitt's *Ghosts of Gettysburg* books, knowledgeable guides lead 1¼-hr tours through sections of town that were bloody battlefields 130 yrs ago. (June-Oct, daily eves; Apr, May, Nov, wkend eves) Tours depart from gallery at 271 Baltimore St. For reservations phone 717/337-0445. ¢¢¢

Hall of Presidents and First Ladies. Costumed life-size wax figures of all the presidents; reproductions of their wives' inaugural gowns; "The Eisenhowers at Gettysburg" exhibit. (Mid-Mar–Nov, daily) 789 Baltimore St, adj National Cemetery. Phone 717/334-5717. ¢¢

Land of Little Horses. A variety of performing horses—all in miniature. Continuous entertainment; indoor arena; exotic animal races. Saddle and wagon rides. Picnic area, snack bar, gift shop. (May-late Aug, daily; Apr, Sept, Oct, wkends) 5 mi W off US 30, on Knoxlyn Rd to Glenwood Dr; follow signs. Phone 717/334-7259. ¢¢¢

Lincoln Room Museum. Preserved bedrm in Wills House; collection of Lincoln items; huge plaque inscribed with Gettysburg Address, audiovisual display. (Mar-Nov, daily; rest of yr, Mon-Fri) 12 Lincoln Sq. Phone 717/334-8188. ¢¢

Lutheran Theological Seminary (1826). (250 students) Oldest Lutheran seminary in US; cupola on campus used as Confederate lookout during battle. Old Dorm, now home of Adams County Historical Society, served as hospital for both Union and Confederate soldiers. Confederate Ave, 1 mi W of Lincoln Sq on US 30. Phone 717/334-6286.

National Civil War Wax Museum. Highlights Civil War era and Battle of Gettysburg. (Mar–Nov, daily; rest of yr, Sat & Sun; closed Jan 1, Thanksgiving, Dec 25) 297 Steinwehr Ave. Phone 717/334-6245. ¢¢

National Tower. Four observation decks (two enclosed) on 300-ft-high tower permit 360° view of battlefield; 12-min sight-and-sound program, displays; landscaped grounds, picnicking. Braille and text for visually or hearing impaired; also nine translations. (Apr–Oct, daily; Nov, wkends only; Mar, inquire for date) 1 mi S via US 97. Phone 717/334-6754. ¢¢

Ski Liberty. 2 quad, 3 double chairlifts, J-bar, handle tow; patrol, school, rentals; snowmaking; cafeteria, restaurant, bar; nursery, lodge. Longest run approx 1 mi; vertical drop 600 ft. (Dec–Mar, daily) 9 mi W on PA 116, in Carroll Valley. Phone 717/642-8282. ¢¢¢¢

Soldiers' National Museum. Dioramas of major battles, with sound; Civil War collection. (Mar–Nov, daily; schedule may vary) 777 Baltimore St. Phone 717/334-4890. ¢¢¢

The Lincoln Train Museum. Museum features more than 1,000 model trains and railroad memorabilia; Lincoln Train Ride—simulated trip of 20 mi. (Mar–Nov, daily) ½ mi S via US 15 on Steinwehr Ave. Phone 717/334-5678. ¢¢¢

Annual Events

Apple Blossom Festival. South Mountain Fairgrounds, 8 mi NW. Early May.

Civil War Heritage Days. Lectures by historians; Civil War collectors' show; entertainment; Civil War book show; firefighters' festival; fireworks. Late June-early July.

Apple Harvest Festival. South Mountain Fairgrounds. Demonstrations; arts and crafts; guided tours of orchard, mountain areas. 1st & 2nd wkends Oct.

Motels

✓ ★★ **BEST INN.** 301 Steinwehr Ave (17325). 717/334-1188; FAX 717/334-1188; res: 800/654-2000; res: 800/446-4656. Web www.get tys burg.com. 77 rms, 2 story. Apr-Oct: S, D $59-$99; under 18 free; lower rates rest of yr. Crib free. Pet accepted, some restrictions. TV; cable (premium), VCR avail. Pool; lifeguard. Coffee in rms. Restaurant adj 6:30 am-11 pm. Bar 4 pm-1 am; closed Sun. Ck-out noon. Sundries. Free bus depot transportation. Downhill ski 9 mi; x-country ski adj. Private patios. Sun deck. Cr cds: A, C, D, DS, MC, V.

D 🐾 ➤ ⚓ ⊠ 🔥 SC

★★ **COLLEGE MOTEL.** 345 Carlisle St (17325), opp Gettysburg College. 717/334-6731; res: 800/367-6731. Web www.gettysburg.com. 21 rms. Mid-June-Labor Day: S, D $76; each addl $10; higher rates: wkends, graduation, parents' wkend; lower rates rest of yr. TV; cable. Pool; lifeguard. Restaurant nearby. Ck-out 11 am. Cr cds: A, C, MC, V.

⚓ 🔥 SC

★ **COLONIAL MOTEL.** 157 Carlisle St (17325). 717/334-3126; res: 800/367-6731. Web www.gettysburg.com. 30 rms, 2 story. Early June-early Sept: S, D $68-$82; each addl $5; under 17 free; higher rates special events; lower rates rest of yr. Crib free. TV; cable (premium). Complimentary coffee in lobby. Restaurant nearby. Ck-out 11 am. Cr cds: A, C, MC, V.

🔥 SC

★★ **COMFORT INN.** 871 York Rd (17325). 717/337-2400; FAX 717/337-0831; res: 800/221-2222. Web www.gettysburg.com. 81 rms, 2 story. June-Aug: S $77-$82; D $87-$90; each addl $6; under 18 free; higher rates: antique car show, college events; lower rates rest of yr. Crib free. TV; cable (premium). Indoor pool; whirlpool. Complimentary continental bkfst. Restaurant nearby. Ck-out 11 am. Business servs avail. In-rm modem link. Some in-rm whirlpools; refrigerator in suites. Cr cds: A, C, D, DS, ER, JCB, MC, V.

D ⚓ ➤ ⊠ 🔥 SC

★★ **CROSS KEYS MOTOR INN RESTAURANT.** 6110 York Rd (17350), at jct US 30 & PA 94. 717/624-7778; FAX 717/624-7941. 64 rms, 4 story. Apr-Sept: S $39-$63; D $49-$73; each addl $5; under 12 free; wkly rates; higher rates special events. Crib free. TV; cable, VCR avail (movies). Restaurants 6 am-10 pm; Fri, Sat to 11 pm. Rm serv. Bar 4 pm-2 am. Ck-out 11 am. Meeting rms. Business servs avail. Gift shop. Golf privileges. Downhill ski 15 mi. Some in-rm whirlpools. Cr cds: A, C, DS, MC, V.

➤ 🎿 ⚓ ⊠ 🔥 SC

★★ **HOLIDAY INN.** 869 York Rd (15628). 717/337-1400; FAX 717/337-0159; res: 800/465-4329. Web gettysburg.com. 51 rms, 2 story. Apr-Oct: S $79-$99; D $89-$109; each addl $10; suites $109-$129; under 19 free; higher rates special events; lower rates rest of yr. Crib free. TV; cable (premium). Indoor pool; lifeguard, whirlpool. Complimentary continental bkfst. Restaurant adj open 24 hrs. Ck-out 11 am. In-rm modem link. Downhill ski 8 mi. Picnic tables. Cr cds: A, C, D, DS, MC, V.

D ⚓ ➤ ⚓ ⊠ 🔥 SC

★ **HOMESTEAD MOTOR LODGE.** 1650 York Rd (17325). 717/334-3866. 10 rms. June-Oct: S, D $45-$65; each addl $8; lower rates Apr-May, Nov. Closed rest of yr. TV. Restaurant nearby. Ck-out 10 am. Downhill ski 8 mi. Totally nonsmoking. Cr cds: A, C, DS, MC, V.

➤ ⊠ 🔥

★★ **QUALITY INN.** 401 Buford Ave (17325). 717/334-3141; FAX 717/334-1813; res: 800/228-5050. Web www.gettysburg.com. 41 rms. June-early Sept: S, D $69-$89; each addl $5; under 17 free; lower rates rest of yr. Crib $3. TV; VCR avail. Pool. Restaurant 7 am-9 pm. Bar from noon. Ck-out noon. Business servs avail. Downhill ski 6 mi. General Lee's Headquarters (museum) adj. Cr cds: A, C, D, DS, ER, JCB, MC, V.

D ➤ ⚓ ⊠ 🔥 SC

★★★ **QUALITY INN MOTOR LODGE.** 380 Steinwehr Ave (17325). 717/334-1103; FAX 717/334-1103; res: 800/228-5151; res: 800/228-5151. E-mail gburgqi@mail.cvn.net; web www.gettysburg.com. 109 rms, 2 story. Apr-Oct: S, D $69-$107; suite $97-$135; under 16 free; lower rates rest of yr. Crib free. Pet accepted, some restrictions. TV; cable (premium), VCR avail. 2 pools, 1 indoor; lifeguard. Coffee in rms. Restaurant opp 6 am-11 pm. Bar 6 pm-1 am. Ck-out noon. Coin lndry. Meeting rm. Gift shop. Free bus depot transportation. Putting green. Downhill/x-country ski 8 mi. Exercise equipt; sauna. Balconies. Cr cds: A, C, D, DS, MC, V.

D 🐾 ➤ ⚓ 🏋 ⊠ 🔥 SC

✓ ★ **RED CARPET INN.** 2450 Emmitsburg Rd (17325), 4 mi S on US 15 Business, at edge of National Military Park. 717/334-1345; FAX 717/334-5026; res: 800/336-1345; res: 800/336-1345. Web www.get tysburg.com. 25 rms. Apr-early Nov: S, D $35-$69; suites $58-$85; higher rates: spring, fall wkends, college, area events; lower rates rest of yr. Crib $5. TV; cable (premium). Pool. Complimentary coffee. Restaurant nearby. Ck-out 11 am. Microwaves avail. Picnic tables, grills. Cr cds: A, C, D, DS, MC, V.

⚓ ⊠ 🔥 SC

Motor Hotel

★★ **DAYS INN.** 865 York Rd (17325). 717/334-0030; FAX 717/337-1002; res: 800/329-7466. Web www.gettysburg.com. 112 rms, 5 story. Apr-Oct: S $59-$98; D $69-$108; each addl $5; under 18 free; ski plans; higher rates special events; lower rates rest of yr. Crib free. TV; cable (premium), VCR avail. Heated pool; lifeguard. Complimentary coffee in lobby. Restaurant adj 6 am-11 pm. Ck-out noon. Coin lndry. Meeting rms. Business servs avail. In-rm modem link. Valet serv. Sundries. Downhill ski 10 mi. Exercise equipt. Game rm. Microwaves avail. Cr cds: A, C, D, DS, JCB, MC, V.

[D] [≈] [✕] [⊠] [🔥] [SC]

Hotel

★★★ **BEST WESTERN INN.** *1 Lincoln Sq (17325), US 15 & 30.* 717/337-2000; FAX 717/337-2075; res: 800/528-1234. Web www.apci.net/~getty. 83 rms, 6 story, 23 suites. Mid-June-Oct: S, D $88-$125; each addl $5; suites $125-$150; under 16 free; higher rates: graduation, homecoming; lower rates rest of yr. Crib free. TV; cable, VCR avail (movies). Pool; whirlpool, poolside serv, lifeguard. Restaurant 7-10:30 am, 5-9 pm. Bar from 5 pm. Ck-out 11 am. Meeting rms. Business center. In-rm modem link. Free garage parking. Tennis privileges. Downhill ski 8 mi. Some refrigerators. Established 1797. Cr cds: A, C, D, DS, MC, V.

[D] [≈] [✓] [≈] [⊠] [🔥] [SC] [✕]

Inns

★★★ **BALADERRY INN.** *40 Hospital Rd (17325), at edge of battlefield.* 717/337-1342; FAX 717/337-1342; res: 800/220-0025. E-mail baladerry@mail.wideopen.net; web www.baladerryinn.com. 8 rms, 7 with shower only, 2 story. S $84-$102; D $94-$112; each addl $15; 2-day min wkends Apr-Nov. Children over 14 yrs only. TV in common area; VCR. Complimentary full bkfst. Ck-out 11 am, ck-in 2 pm. Tennis. Golf privileges. Downhill ski 10 mi; x-country ski adj. Built in 1812; used as a field hospital during the Civil War battle of Gettysburg. Restored; furnished with antiques and reproductions. Cr cds: A, C, D, DS, MC, V.

[✕] [≈] [✕] [✕] [⊠] [🔥] [SC]

★★★ **BATTLEFIELD BED & BREAKFAST INN.** *2264 Emmitsburg Rd (17325).* 717/334-8804; FAX 717/334-7330; res: 888/766-3897. Web www.gettysburg.com. 8 rms, 2 story. No rm phones. Apr-Nov: S $77-$107; D $90-$137; each addl $10; suite $149-$159; 2-day min hols, wkends; lower rates rest of yr. Crib free. TV in sitting rm; VCR. Complimentary full bkfst; afternoon refreshments. Ck-out 11:30 am, ck-in 2 pm. Luggage handling. Concierge serv. Business servs avail. Downhill ski 10 mi. Lawn games. Carriage rides. Fireplaces. Restored 1809 farmhouse famous for living history activities. Totally nonsmoking. Cr cds: A, C, D, DS, MC, V.

[≈] [✕] [⊠] [🔥]

★★ **BRAFFERTON INN.** *44 York St (17325).* 717/337-3423. Web www.gettysburg.com. 10 rms, 2 story, 2 suites. No rm phones. S, D $75-$125; each addl $10; suites $120-$125; higher rates special events. TV in suites. Complimentary full bkfst. Restaurant nearby. Ck-out 11 am, ck-in 2 pm. First house built in town (1786); antiques. Cr cds: A, C, DS, MC, V.

[⊠] [🔥]

★★★ **FARNSWORTH HOUSE INN.** *401 Baltimore St (17325), at corner of South St.* 717/334-8838; FAX 717/334-5862. E-mail farnhaus@cvn.net; web www.gettysburgaddress.com. 10 rms, 2 story. No rm phones. Apr-Oct: S $85/ D $95; each addl $10. TV in some rms, sitting rm; cable. Complimentary full bkfst. Restaurant (see FARNSWORTH HOUSE). Ck-out 11 am, ck-in 3 pm. Business servs avail. Concierge serv. Luggage handling. Downhill ski 7 mi; x-country ski ¼ mi. Some in-rm whirlpools. Historic house (1810), restored to its 1863 appearance. The uppermost level of the inn was once used by Confederate sharpshooters; more than 100 bullet holes still remain in the south wall of the inn. Daily tours. Cr cds: A, C, DS, MC, V.

[⚡] [≈] [⊠] [🔥]

★★★ **GASLIGHT INN.** *33 E Middle St (17325).* 717/337-9100; FAX 717/337-9616. E-mail gaslight@mail.cvn.net. 9 rms, 8 with shower only, 3 story. S, D $95-$135; each addl $20; 2-day min hol wkends. Children over 10 yrs only. TV; cable, VCR (free movies). Complimentary full

bkfst; afternoon refreshments. Dining rm 6-8 pm (by res only). Restaurant nearby. Ck-out 11 am, ck-in 3 pm. Concierge serv. Luggage handling. Business servs avail. In-rm modem link. Tennis privileges. Golf privileges. Downhill ski 6 mi; x-country ski 1 mi. Health club privileges. Balconies. Italianate house (1872) with original exterior trim. Rms decorated and named in theme of flowers. Cr cds: A, C, DS, MC, V.

[D] [≈] [✕] [✕] [⊠] [🔥]

★★ **GETTYSTOWN INN BED & BREAKFAST.** *89 Steinwehr Ave (17325).* 717/334-2100; FAX 717/334-6905. E-mail info@dobbin house.com; web www.dobbinhouse.com. 5 rms, 2 story, 1 suite. No rm phones. Mar-Nov: S $79-$99, D $85-$105; each addl $6; suite $105; under 12 free; wkly rates; higher rates: hols (2-day min), special events; lower rates rest of yr. TV in some rms; cable. Complimentary full bkfst. Restaurant (see DOBBIN HOUSE). Ck-out 10 am, ck-in 2 pm. Downhill ski 7 mi; x-country ski 1 mi. Refrigerators. Renovated 1860s home; antiques. Overlooks site of Abraham Lincoln's Gettysburg Address. Totally nonsmoking. Cr cds: A, C, MC, V.

[⊠] [⊠] [🔥] [SC]

★★★ **JAMES GETTYS HOTEL.** *27 Chambersburg St (17325).* 717/337-1334; FAX 717/334-2103. E-mail jghotel@mail.cvn.net; web www.jamesgettyshotel.com. 11 kit suites, 4 story. Mid-Mar-Nov: kit suites $115-$135; each addl $15; under 12 free; lower rates rest of yr. Crib free. TV; cable, VCR avail. Complimentary continental bkfst. Complimentary coffee in rms. Restaurant adj 11:30 am-5 pm. Ck-out 11 am, ck-in 3 pm. Business servs avail. Luggage handling. Concierge serv. Gift shop. Guest lndry. Downhill ski 10 mi; x-country ski 1 mi. Refrigerators, microwaves, wet bars. Built in 1804. Totally nonsmoking. Cr cds: A, C, DS, MC, V.

[D] [⊠] [🔥]

★★ **OLD APPLEFORD INN.** *218 Carlisle St (17325).* 717/337-1711; FAX 717/334-6228; res: 800/275-3373. E-mail jwiley@ cvn.net; web www.virtualcities.com. 10 rms, 6 with shower only, 3 story. No rm phones. Apr-Oct: S $80-$95; D $105-$120; suite $115-$150; 2-day min wkends, hols, special events; lower rates rest of yr. Children over 8 yrs only. Complimentary full bkfst; afternoon refreshments. Restaurant nearby. Ck-out 11 am, ck-in 2 pm. Concierge serv. Downhill ski 7 mi; x-country ski 15 mi. Health club privileges. Victorian mansion (1867); many antiques. Totally nonsmoking. Cr cds: A, C, DS, MC, V.

[≈] [⊠] [🔥]

★★★ **THE HERR TAVERN & PUBLIC HOUSE.** *900 Chambersburg Rd (17325).* 717/334-4332; FAX 717/334-3332; res: 800/362-9849. E-mail herrtav@cvn.net; web www.herrtavern.com. 12 rms, 3 story. S, D $90-$170. Children over 12 yrs only. TV; cable, VCR (movies). Complimentary full bkfst. Restaurant (see HERR TAVERN & PUBLICK HOUSE). Rm serv. Ck-out 11 am, ck-in 4 pm. Luggage handling. Downhill ski 5 mi. Some in-rm whirlpools. Built in 1815, antiques; served as Confederate hospital. Totally nonsmoking. Cr cds: A, C, DS, MC, V.

[≈] [⊠] [🔥]

Restaurants

★★★ **DOBBIN HOUSE.** *(See Gettystown Inn)* 717/334-2100. E-mail info@dobbinhouse.com; web www.dobbinhouse.com. Hrs: 11:30 am-11 pm. Closed Jan 1, Thanksgiving, Dec 25. Res accepted. Continental menu. Bar. Semi-a la carte: lunch $4.95-$15.95, dinner $15.95-$29.95. Child's meals. Specializes in 1700s recipes, fresh seafood, large selection of meats. Own baking. Oldest building in Gettysburg; built 1776. Totally nonsmoking. Cr cds: A, C, MC, V.

[D]

★★★ **FARNSWORTH HOUSE.** *(See Farnsworth House Inn)* 717/334-8838. E-mail farnhaus@cvn.net; web www.visitgettysburgaddress.com. Hrs: 5-9 pm. Closed Jan 1, Thanksgiving, Dec 25. Res accepted. Bar to midnight. Semi-a la carte: dinner $12.95-$18. Child's meals. Specialties: peanut soup, game pie, pumpkin fritters. Outdoor dining. Built in 1810; tour avail. Cr cds: A, C, DS, MC, V.

★ **GINGERBREAD MAN.** *217 Steinwehr Ave (17325).* *717/334-1100.* Hrs: 11 am-11 pm; Sun to 10 pm. Closed Jan 1, Dec 25. Varied menu. Bar. Semi-a la carte: lunch $4-$7, dinner $6.95-$12.95. Child's meals. Specializes in NY-style deli sandwiches, Mexican dishes, fresh Maryland crabcakes. Casual, lively atmosphere. Cr cds: A, C, D, DS, MC, V.

D ⬛

★★ **HERR TAVERN & PUBLICK HOUSE.** *(See The Herr Tavern & Publick House) 717/334-4332.* E-mail herrtav@cvn.net; web www.her tavern.com. Hrs: 11 am-9 pm; Sun from 5 pm. Closed Jan 1, Dec 24, 25. Res accepted. Continental menu. Bar. Semi-a la carte: lunch $3.49-$8.49, dinner $13-$20. Specialties: blackened prime rib, chicken Chesapeake, seafood pasta. Child's meals. Restored antebellum tavern with period art and antiques. Cr cds: A, C, DS, MC, V.

D

✓★★ **STONEHENGE.** *985 Baltimore Pike (17325).* *717/334-9227.* Hrs: 11 am-10 pm. Closed Jan 1, Dec 24, 25. Res accepted. Continental menu. Bar to 2 am. Semi-a la carte: lunch $2.95-$6.95, dinner $5.95-$19.95. Child's meals. Specialties: Cajun prime rib, crab cakes, veal Marsala. Intimate dining; fresh flowers. Cr cds: A, C, MC, V.

D ⬛

Gettysburg National Military Park (F-6)

(See also Gettysburg, Hanover)

The hallowed battlefield of Gettysburg, scene of one of the most decisive battles of the Civil War and immortalized by Lincoln's Gettysburg Address, is preserved by the National Park Service. The town itself is still a college community, as it was more than a hundred years ago on July 1, 2 and 3, 1863, when General Robert E. Lee led his Confederate Army in its greatest invasion of the North. The defending Northerners under Union General George Meade repulsed the Southern assault after three days of fierce fighting, which left 51,000 men dead, wounded or missing.

The Gettysburg National Military Park has more than 35 miles of roads through 5,900 acres of the battlefield area. There are more than 1,300 monuments, markers and tablets of granite and bronze; 400 cannons are also located on the field.

Visitors may wish to tour the battlefield with a Battlefield Guide, licensed by the National Park Service (two-hour tour; fee). The guides escort visitors to all points of interest and sketch the movement of troops and details of the battle. Or visitors may wish to first orient themselves at the Electric Map at the Visitor Center; then using the park folder, the battlefield can be toured without a guide. Audio cassettes are also available for self-guided tours.

The late President Dwight D. Eisenhower's retirement farm, a National Historic Site, adjoins the battlefield. It is open to the public on a limited-tour basis. All visitors must obtain tour tickets at the tour information center, located at the lobby of the Visitor Center-Electric Map building. Transportation to the farm is by shuttle (fee). For further information contact Gettysburg National Military Park, 97 Taneytown Rd, Gettysburg 17325; 717/334-1124.

What to See and Do

The Angle. Spot where Pickett's Charge was repulsed on July 3, referred to as "high water mark" of the Confederacy.

Cyclorama Center. Adj to visitor center. Instructive film and exhibits: 356-ft Cyclorama painting of Pickett's Charge. (Daily) ¢¢

Culp's Hill. Site of longest sustained fighting during battle.

Devil's Den. Stronghold of Confederate sharpshooters following its capture during action on the 2nd day.

East Cemetery Hill. Rallying point for Union forces on 1st day of battle. Scene of fierce fighting on evening of 2nd day.

Eisenhower National Historic Site. Farm and home of the 34th President of the United States and his wife, Mamie. Tour of grounds and home (1½-2 hrs). Self-guided tours explore the farm and skeet range. Reception Center houses exhibits and bookstore; 11-min video is shown. Access to site is by shuttle only, from the National Park Service Visitor Center at 97 Taneytown Rd. (Apr-Oct, daily; rest of yr Wed-Sun; closed Thanksgiving, Dec 25, also Jan) Phone 717/334-4474 (advance tickets) or 717/338-9114 (Info). ¢¢¢

The Eternal Light Peace Memorial. On Oak Ridge. Erected in 1938 and dedicated by President Roosevelt to "peace eternal in a nation united."

The Gettysburg National Cemetery. Site of Lincoln's Gettysburg Address.

Little Round Top. Key Union position during 2nd and 3rd days of battle.

Memorials to State Units. Includes Pennsylvania State Monument, with names of more than 34,500 Pennsylvanian soldiers who participated in the battle.

Seminary Ridge. Main Confederate battle line.

⭐ **Visitor Center–Electric Map–Gettysburg Museum of the Civil War.** Visits to the park should begin here. Park information, incl a self-guided auto tour, and guides may be obtained at the center. Story of battle told on 750-sq-ft electric map surrounded by 525 seats (every 45 min; fee). Gettysburg Museum of the Civil War has an extensive collection of Civil War relics (free). (Daily; closed Jan 1, Thanksgiving, Dec 25) On PA 134. Electric map. ¢¢ Obtain tickets here for

Whitworth Guns on Oak Hill. Only breech-loading cannon used here.

The Wheatfield and Peach Orchard. Scene of heavy Union and Confederate losses on the second day of fighting.

Gibsonia

(see Pittsburgh)

Greensburg (E-2)

(See also Connellsville, Donegal, Ligonier, New Stanton)

Founded 1785 **Pop** 16,318 **Elev** 1,099 ft **Area Code** 724 **Zip** 15601 **E-mail** lhvb@laurelhighlands.org **Web** www.laurelhighlands.org

Information Laurel Highlands Visitors Bureau, 120 E Main St, Ligonier 15658; 724/238-5661

Greensburg was named for Revolutionary General Nathanael Greene.

What to See and Do

Bushy Run Battlefield. Here Colonel Henry Bouquet defeated united Native American forces during Pontiac's War on Aug 5 & 6, 1763. The battle lifted the siege of Fort Pitt and was the turning point of the war. Picnicking, park (free); hiking trails. Visitor center exhibits depict battle (Wed–Sun; closed most hols). NW on PA 993. Phone 724/527-5584. ¢¢

Historic Hanna's Town. Costumed tour guide tells story of Hanna's Town, site of first court west of Alleghenies. Includes reconstructed courthouse, tavern, jail and stockaded fort; picnic area. (June–Aug, daily exc Mon; May, Sept & Oct, wkends only) 3 mi NE via US 119. Phone 724/836-1800. ¢

Lincoln Highway Heritage Corridor. 140-mi stretch of US 30 extending from Greensburg to Chambersburg. Pass through and explore countless historical and recreational areas. Driving guide avail (fee) from Lincoln Highway Heritage Corridor, PO Box 386; Phone 724/668-8330. Guide ¢

Westmoreland County Courthouse. Building in style of Italian Renaissance; restored in 1982. (Mon–Fri; closed hols) Main & Pittsburgh Sts. Phone 724/830-3000.

Westmoreland Museum of American Art. 18th-, 19th- and early 20th-century American paintings, sculpture, furniture and decorative arts. 19th- and early 20th-century southwestern Pennsylvania paintings. Extensive toy collection. Lectures, guided tours. (Tues–Sat, also Sun afternoons; closed hols) 221 N Main St. Phone 724/837-1500. **Free**

Motels

★★ **COMFORT INN.** *1129 E Pittsburgh St (15601), PA Tpke exit 7, E on PA 30.* 724/838-0260; FAX 724/834-3442; res: 800/228-5150. Web www.comfortinn.com. 77 rms, 3 story. S $66-$110; D $76-$110; each addl $5; suites $81-$147; under 18 free; higher rates special events. Crib free. TV; cable (premium), VCR avail (movies). Heated pool. Complimentary continental bkfst. Restaurant nearby. Ck-out 11 am. Meeting rm. Business servs avail. Valet serv. Health club privileges. Some in-rm whirlpools, refrigerators, wet bars; microwaves avail. Cr cds: A, C, D, DS, ER, JCB, MC, V.

D ⊷ ⊠ 🐾 SC

✓ ★ **KNIGHTS INN.** *1215 S Main St (15601), at jct US 119 & US 30.* 724/836-7100; FAX 724/837-5390; res: 800/843-5644. 110 rms, 10 suites, 11 kits. May-Oct: S $47.95-$57.95; D $56.95-$73.95; each addl $7; kit units $63.95-$75.95; under 18 free; lower rates rest of yr. Crib free. TV; cable (premium), VCR avail. Pool. Complimentary coffee in lobby. Restaurant adj 6 am-11 pm. Ck-out noon. Meeting rm. In-rm modem link. Guest lndry. Refrigerators, microwaves avail. Cr cds: A, C, D, DS, MC, V.

⊷ ⊠ 🐾 SC

★★★ **SHERATON FOUR POINTS HOTEL.** *100 Sheraton Dr; Rte 30 E (15601).* 724/836-6060; FAX 724/834-5640. E-mail jsupko@aol.com; web www.sheraton.com. 146 rms, 2 story. S $66-$80; D $71-$85; each addl $5; suites $110-$250; under 17 free; package plans. Crib free. TV; cable (premium), VCR avail. Indoor pool. Sauna. Restaurant 6:30 am-2 pm, 5-10 pm. Bar 11-2 am; entertainment. Ck-out noon. Meeting rms. Business servs avail. Bellhops. Valet serv. Sundries. Free RR station, bus depot transportation. 9-hole golf course, greens fee, pro shop, putting green. Exercise equipt. Some refrigerators. Shopping mall opp. Cr cds: A, C, D, DS, JCB, MC, V.

D 🍴 ⊷ ✈ ⊠ 🔥 SC

Motor Hotel

★★★ **MOUNTAIN VIEW INN.** *1001 Village Dr (15601), 13 mi NE of PA Tpke exit 7.* 724/834-5300; FAX 724/834-5304; res: 800/537-8709. Web www.mountainviewinn.com. 97 rms. S $59-$135; D $69-$135; suites $150-$275. TV; cable (premium), VCR avail. Pool. Complimentary continental bkfst. Coffee in rms. Restaurant 7 am-2 pm, 5-9 pm; wkend hrs vary. Rm serv 7:30 am-11 pm. Bar 11 am-midnight; Fri, Sat to 1 am; Sun noon-8 pm. Ck-out 11 am. Meeting rms. Business servs avail. In-rm modem link. Sundries. Exercise equipt. Health club privileges. Antique decor; English and herb gardens; gazebo. Cr cds: A, C, D, DS, MC, V.

D ⊷ ✈ ⊠ 🐾 SC

Restaurant

★★ **CARBONE'S.** *US 119 (15624), 6 mi N on US 119.* 724/834-3430. E-mail carbones@carbonepasta.com; web www.carbonepasta.com. Hrs: 4:30-9 pm; Fri, Sat to 10 pm. Closed Sun; major hols. Res accepted. Italian, Amer menu. Semi-a la carte: dinner $8.95-$16.95. Child's meals. Specialties: angel pie, antipasto, braciole. Mediterranean decor. Family-owned. Cr cds: A, C, D, DS, MC, V.

D ⊠

Hamburg (E-8)

(See also Kutztown, Reading, Shartlesville)

Founded 1779 **Pop** 3,987 **Elev** 373 ft **Area Code** 484 & 610 **Zip** 19526 **E-mail** rdgberks@ptd.net **Web** www.readingberkspa.com

Information Reading/Berks County Visitors Bureau, 352 Penn St, Reading 19602; 610/375-4085 or 800/443-6610

Situated on the banks of the Schuylkill River, Hamburg is a center for one of the finest farming sections in Pennsylvania. The town's industries include the manufacture of brooms, iron and steel castings, knitwear and soft-drink products.

What to See and Do

Blue Rocks. Covers 90 acres; pool; fishing (stocked pond); picnicking, 2 pavilions; hiking, Appalachian Trail; camping, trailer facilities (fee; hookups addl). Game rm. 5 mi E on I-78 to Lenhartsville, then 2 mi N on PA 143. Phone 610/756-6366. Park ¢

Hawk Mountain Sanctuary. Hawk, eagle flights visible with binoculars from lookouts mid-Aug–Nov; museum, bookstore. (Daily; closed Jan 1, Thanksgiving, Dec 25) 11 mi N via PA 61 & 895; follow signs. Phone 610/756-6961. ¢¢

Wanamaker, Kempton & Southern, Inc. A 6-mi, 40-min round trip on steam or diesel train along the Ontelaunee Creek at the foot of Hawk Mountain. Model railroad (Sun), antique shop. Snack bar, picnic area. Steam train (July-Aug & Oct, Sat & Sun afternoons; May & June, Sun afternoons). Diesel train (June & Sept, 1st & 3rd Sat afternoons only). Also special events throughout the yr. 5 mi E on I-78 to Lenhartsville exit, then 5 mi N on PA 143 to Kempton. Phone 610/756-6469. ¢¢

Hanover (F-7)

(See also Gettysburg, York)

Founded 1763 **Pop** 14,399 **Elev** 609 ft **Area Code** 717 **Zip** 17331 **E-mail** lascad@netrax.net **Web** www.cvn.net/~hanoverareachamber

Information Hanover Area Chamber of Commerce, 146 Carlisle St; 717/637-6130

Known in early days as "McAllisterstown" (for founder Colonel Richard McAllister) and "Rogue's Harbor" (for lack of law enforcement), Hanover is in the rich Conewago Valley. Here, on June 30, 1863, Confederate General J.E.B. Stuart's cavalry tangled with Union forces under Generals Kilpatrick and Custer. The battle prevented Stuart from reaching Gettysburg in time to function as "the eyes of Lee's army."

Among the products of the town's diversified industry are books, wirecloth, yarns, furniture, industrial machinery, textiles and foods, including snack foods.

What to See and Do

Codorus State Park. Approx 3,300 acres. Swimming pool; fishing in 1,275-acre Lake Marburg, hunting; boating (rentals, mooring, launching, marina). Hiking, bridle trails. Cross-country skiing, snowmobiling, sledding, ice skating, ice boating, ice fishing. Picnicking, playground, snack bar. Tent & trailer sites. Standard fees. 3 mi E on PA 216. Phone 717/637-2816.

Conewago Chapel (1741). Oldest stone Catholic church in the US. Designated Sacred Heart Basilica in 1962. Cemetery dates from 1752. (Daily) 30 Basilica Dr, 2 mi W on PA 116, then 2 mi N. Phone 717/637-2721. **Free**

Neas House Museum. Neas House (ca 1783), restored Georgian mansion, serves as local history museum. (May–Nov, Tues–Fri) Special events (spring, summer, late Dec). 113 W Chestnut St. Phone 717/632-3207. **Free**

Utz Quality Foods, Inc. Producers of potato chips and snack foods. Glass-enclosed tour gallery overlooks production area; push-to-talk audio program and closed-circuit TV monitors. (Mon–Thurs; closed major hols) 900 High St. Phone 717/637-6644. **Free**

Inn

★ ★ ★ **BEECHMONT BED & BREAKFAST INN.** *315 Broadway (17331). 717/632-3013; res: 800/553-7009.* 7 rms, 2 story, 3 suites. S, D $80-$95; suites $115-$135. Children over 12 yrs only. Complimentary full bkfst; afternoon refreshments. Restaurant nearby. Ck-out 11 am, ck-in 3 pm. Microwaves avail. Federal period house (1834); landscaped courtyard. Cr cds: A, C, DS, MC, V.

⊠ 🐾 SC

Harmony (D-1)

(See also Butler, Pittsburgh)

Founded 1804 **Pop** 1,054 **Elev** 925 ft **Area Code** 724 **Zip** 16037
E-mail chamber@isrv.com
Information Butler County Tourist Promotion Agency, 201 S Main St, PO Box 1082, Butler 16003; 724/283-2222 or 888/741-6772

First settlement of George Rapp's Harmony Society, Harmony served the colony only until 1814. More than 100 of the original group are buried in Harmonists Cemetery, southeast of town. Several of the Rappite Society's sturdy brick houses still stand in the village.

What to See and Do

Harmony Museum (1809). Exhibits depict early life under Harmonists and Mennonites; regional history. The Harmony Society was one of America's most successful experiments in communal living. Harmony was the society's first home (1804). Tour. (June–Sept, daily afternoons; rest of yr, Mon, Wed, Fri, also Sun afternoons) 218 Mercer St. Phone 724/452-7341. ¢¢

Annual Events

Dankfest. Pioneer craft festival held on grounds of Harmony Museum (see). Crafts, entertainment, tours, refreshments. Contact museum for schedule. Late Aug.

Christmas Open House. Candlelight tour of Harmony Museum, Wagner House and Ziegler log house. Entertainment, refreshments. Contact museum for schedule. Early Dec.

Harrisburg (E-7)

(See also Carlisle, Hershey, York)

Settled 1718 **Pop** 52,376 **Elev** 360 ft **Area Code** 717 **E-mail** CRchamber@SQ-Alliance.org **Web** www.hbgchamber.com
Information Capital Region Chamber of Commerce, 3211 N Front St, 17110-1342, phone; 717/232-4099; or the Harrisburg-Hershey-Carlisle Tourism & Convention Bureau, 25 N Front St, 17101, phone 717/231-7788

This midstate metropolis is graced by what many consider the finest capitol building in the nation. Its riverside park (known as City Island), Italian Lake, unique museum and beautiful Forum are the showplaces; commerce, industry and politics keep the city going.

The site was viewed in 1615 by Etienne Brulé on a trip down the Susquehanna, but more than a century passed before John Harris, the first settler, opened his trading post here. His son established the town in 1785. It became the seat of state government in 1812; the cornerstone of the first capitol building was laid in 1819.

What to See and Do

Capitol Hill buildings. N 3rd & Walnut Sts. Phone 717/787-6810 or 800/868-7672. Clustered in a 45-acre complex, the major bldgs are

The Capitol (dedicated 1906). Italian Renaissance bldg covers 2 acres, has 651 rms; 26,000-ton, 272-ft dome, imitating that of St Peter's in Rome, dominates city skyline. Includes murals by Abbey and Okley. Tours (daily; closed most major hols). Main entrance, 3rd & State Sts. **Free**

Finance Building. Ceiling murals by Maragliotti, Eugene Savage; mural in south vestibule illustrates *The Collection of Taxes.* (Mon–Fri)

Forum Building. Includes auditorium below constellation-bedecked ceiling; walls review man's progress through time. Main lobby boasts a Maragliotti ceiling. General and law libraries.

North Office Building. Map inscribed on main lobby floor shows state highways, seals of Pennsylvania cities.

South Office Building. Colorful murals by Edward Trumbull depict *Penn's Treaty with the Indians* and *The Industries of Pittsburgh.*

The State Museum of Pennsylvania. A six-story circular bldg housing 4 stories of galleries, authentic early country store, Native American life exhibit, technological and industrial exhibits, collection of antique autos and period carriages; planetarium; natural history and geology exhibits and one of world's largest framed paintings, Rothermel's *The Battle of Gettysburg.* Planetarium has public shows (Sat & Sun; fee). (Daily exc Mon; closed most hols) N of Capitol Bldg, 3rd & North Sts. Phone 717/787-4978. **Free**

Dauphin County Courthouse. Seven imposing courtrms; outline map on floor of main foyer pictures borough and township boundaries. (Mon–Fri; closed hols) Front & Market Sts. Phone 717/255-2741.

Fort Hunter Park. Historic 37-acre property; site of British-built fort erected in 1754 to combat mounting threats prior to the French and Indian War. In 1787 the land was purchased and became a farm that eventually grew into a self-sufficient village. The Pennsylvania Canal runs through the park; on the grounds are historic buttonwood trees dating from William Penn's time; a 19th-century boxwood garden; herb gardens; paths along the banks of the Susquehanna River; picnic area. Also here are an ice house, springhouse (ca 1800), Centennial barn (1876), and corncrib (1880). Also on the grounds, but not open to the public because of restoration, are the old tavern (1800), blacksmith shop (1890) and stone stable. 6 mi N on N Front St. Outstanding feature of park is

Fort Hunter Mansion. Federal-style stone mansion, built in 3 sections. Front stone portions were built in 1786 and 1814; rear wooden portion built in 1870. Spacious mansion displays period furnishings, clothing, toys and other artifacts. Guided tours. (May–Dec, daily exc Mon) 5300 N Front St, in park. Phone 717/599-5751. ¢¢

Indian Echo Caverns. Stalagmite and stalactite formations. Picnicking, playground. (Daily, schedule varies; closed Jan 1, Thanksgiving, Dec 25) 10 mi E on US 322, 422, in Hummelstown. Phone 717/566-8131. ¢¢¢

Italian Lake. Bordered with flowers, shrubs and shade trees in summer. N 3rd & Division Sts.

John Harris Mansion. Home of city's founder, now Historical Society of Dauphin County headquarters. Stone house has 19th-century furnishings, library (Mon–Thurs; fee), collection of county artifacts. Tours (Mon–Fri). 219 S Front St. Phone 717/233-3462. ¢¢¢

Museum of Scientific Discovery. Hands-on exhibits demonstrating various scientific and math principles; daily programs. (Daily exc Mon; closed most major hols) 3rd & Walnut Sts, 1st level, Strawberry Sq. ¢¢

Penn National Race Course. Live yr-round Thoroughbred racing (Wed, Fri-Sun). Nation wide simulcasts (daily). Terrace dining rm; gift shop. NE via I-81, exit 28, in Grantville. Phone 717/469-2211. ¢¢

Reservoir Park. View of E end of city, five nearby counties. Walnut & N 19th Sts.

Riverfront Park. 4 mi along Susquehanna River, with park promenade flanking Front St, concrete walk along river.

Rockville Bridge (1902). A 3,810-ft stone-arch bridge; 48 spans carry 4 tracks of Penn Central Railroad main line. 4 mi N on US 22.

Annual Events

Kipona. Boating and water-related activities. Labor Day wkend.

Pennsylvania State Farm Show. State fair. Phone 717/787-5373. Jan 8-13.

Pennsylvania National Horse Show. Phone 717/975-3677. 10 days mid-Oct.

Motels

★ **BAYMONT INN.** 200 N Mountain Rd (17112), I-81 exit 26. 717/540-9339; FAX 717/540-9486; res: 800/428-3438. Web www.budgetel.com. 66 rms, 3 story, 8 suites. Apr-Oct: S $57.95-$70.95; D $63.95-$76.95; suites $66.95-$80.95; under 19 free; lower rates rest of yr. Crib free. Pet accepted. TV; cable (premium), VCR avail. Complimentary continental bkfst. Complimentary coffee in rms. Restaurant nearby. Ck-out noon. Coin lndry. Meeting rms. Business center. In-rm modem link. Sundries. Refrigerator, microwaves in suites. Cr cds: A, C, D, DS, MC, V.

D 🐾 🏊 🔌 🔥 SC 🚶

★★ **BEST WESTERN COUNTRY OVEN.** 300 N Mountain Rd (17112), I-81 exit 26. 717/652-7180; FAX 717/541-8991; res: 800/528-1234. Web www.bestwestern.com/best.html. 49 rms, 2 story. S $50-$80; D $50-$85; each addl $3; under 13 free. Crib $5. Pet accepted. TV; cable (premium). Restaurant 6:30 am-9 pm. Bar 11 am-11 pm. Ck-out 11 am. Business servs avail. In-rm modem link. Sundries. Microwaves avail. Cr cds: A, C, D, DS, MC, V.

🐾 🔌 🔥 SC

★★ **COMFORT INN EAST.** 4021 Union Deposit Rd (17109), I-83 exit 29. 717/561-8100; FAX 717/561-1357; res: 800/253-1409. 115 rms, 5 story. June-Oct: S, D $79-$109; under 18 free; higher rates car shows; lower rates rest of yr. Crib free. Pet accepted. TV; cable (premium). Heated pool; lifeguard. Complimentary continental bkfst. Coffee in rms. Restaurant adj 6 am-10 pm. Ck-out noon. Coin lndry. Meeting rms. Business servs avail. Free airport, RR station transportation. Health club privileges. Microwaves avail. Cr cds: A, C, D, DS, ER, JCB, MC, V.

D 🐾 🏊 🔌 🔥 SC

✓★ **DAYS INN.** 3919 N Front St (17110), I-81, exit 22N. 717/233-3100; FAX 717/233-6415; res: 800/329-7466. 116 rms, 3 story. S $54.99-$69.99; D $54.99-$74.99; each addl $5; under 12 free; higher rates: car shows, farm show. Crib free. TV; cable. Pool; lifeguard. Playground. Complimentary continental bkfst. Restaurant nearby. Ck-out noon. Coin lndry. Business servs avail. In-rm modem link. Exercise equipt. Refrigerators, microwaves avail. Picnic tables. Cr cds: A, C, D, DS, JCB, MC, V.

D 🏊 🔥 🔌 🔥 SC

★★ **HAMPTON INN.** 4950 Ritter Rd (17055), 8 mi SW on PA 641. 717/691-1300; FAX 717/691-9692; res: 800/426-7866. 129 rms, 4 story. S $79-$84; D $88-$93; under 18 free; ski plan. Crib free. TV; cable (premium), VCR avail. Heated pool; whirlpool; lifeguard. Complimentary continental bkfst. Restaurant adj 11 am-11 pm. Ck-out 11 am. Coin lndry. Meeting rms. Business center. In-rm modem link. Downhill ski 20 mi. Exercise equipt. Health club privileges. Microwaves avail. Cr cds: A, C, D, DS, MC, V.

D 🏊 🔌 🔥 SC 🚶

★★ **HAMPTON INN.** 4230 Union Deposit Rd (17111), I-83 exit 29. 717/545-9595; FAX 717/545-0607; res: 800/426-7866. Web www.hampton-inn.com. 145 rms, 5 story. S $68-$80; D $75-$86; under 18 free; higher rates auto shows. Crib avail. TV; cable (premium). Heated pool; whirlpool; lifeguard. Complimentary continental bkfst. Restaurant adj

open 24 hrs. Ck-out noon. Coin lndry. Meeting rms. Business servs avail. Valet serv. Golf privileges. Downhill ski 15 mi. Exercise equipt. Health club privileges. Microwaves avail. Cr cds: A, C, D, DS, MC, V.

D 🔌 🏊 🔌 🔥 SC

✓★★★ **HOLIDAY INN.** 148 Sheraton Dr (17070), S on I-83, W on I-283. 717/774-2721; FAX 717/774-2485. 196 rms, 2 story. May-Oct: S, D $59-$99; each addl $10; suites $160; under 18 free; family, wkend, hol rates; ski plans; higher rates special events; lower rates rest of yr. Crib free. Pet accepted, some restrictions; $10. TV; cable (premium). Indoor pool; whirlpool. Restaurant 6:30 am-2 pm, 5-9 pm; Fri, Sat to 10 pm. Rm serv. Bar 5 pm-2 am; entertainment. Ck-out 11 am. Meeting rms. Business center. In-rm modem link. Bellhops. Valet serv. Coin lndry. Free airport, RR station transportation. Exercise equipt. Health club privileges. Game rm. Refrigerators, microwaves avail. Some balconies. Picnic tables, grills. Luxury level. Cr cds: A, C, D, DS, JCB, MC, V.

D 🐾 🏊 🔌 🔥 SC 🚶

★★ **HOLIDAY INN.** 5401 Carlisle Pike (17055), W on I-81 exit 18 S. 717/697-0321; FAX 717/697-7594; res: 800/772-7829. 218 rms, 2 story. Feb-Oct: S $93; D $103; each addl $10; under 18 free; wkly rates; higher rates special events; lower rates rest of yr. Crib free. Pet accepted, some restrictions; $50 deposit. TV; cable (premium). Complimentary continental bkfst. Complimentary coffee in rms. Restaurant 6:30 am-9 pm. Rm serv. Bar 5 pm-2 am; entertainment. Ck-out noon. Meeting rms. Business servs avail. Coin lndry. Exercise equipt. Miniature golf. Heated indoor/outdoor pool; lifeguard. Some in-rm whirlpools; microwaves avail. Picnic tables, grills. Cr cds: A, C, D, DS, JCB, MC, V.

D 🐾 🏊 🔌 🔥 SC

★★ **HOWARD JOHNSON MOTOR LODGE.** 473 Eisenhower Blvd (17111), I-283 exit 1. 717/564-4730; FAX 717/564-4840. E-mail hkharrisburg@intereach.net. 176 rms, 2 story. S $55-$79; D $62-$89; each addl $8; under 17 free; higher rates Hershey Antique Auto Show. Crib free. TV; cable (premium). Pool; wading pool. Restaurant 5 am-midnight. Bar from 11 am. Ck-out noon. Meeting rms. Business center. Valet serv. Sundries. Free airport, RR station transportation. Exercise equipt. Microwaves avail. Private patios, balconies. Cr cds: A, C, D, DS, ER, MC, V.

D 🏊 🔌 🔥 SC 🚶

★★★ **RADISSON PENN HARRIS HOTEL.** 1150 Camp Hill Byp (17011), S on US 15, Camp Hill Bypass; 6 mi N of PA Turnpike exit 17. 717/763-7117; FAX 717/763-4518; res: 800/333-3333. 250 rms, 2-3 story. No elvtr. S $69-$119; D $79-$139; each addl $10; suites $225-$400; under 18 free. Crib free. Pet accepted. TV; cable (premium). Pool; poolside serv, lifeguard. Coffee in rms. Restaurant 6:30 am-10 pm. Rm serv. Bar noon-2 am. Ck-out 11 am. Convention facilities. Business center. In-rm modem link. Valet serv. Bellhops. Free airport transportation. Exercise equipt. Some refrigerators. Cr cds: A, C, D, DS, MC, V.

D 🐾 🏊 🔌 🔥 SC 🚶

✓★ **RED ROOF INN.** 400 Corp Cir. (17110), I-81 exit 24. 717/657-1445; FAX 717/657-2775; res: 800/843-7663. 110 rms, 2 story. S $34-$44; D $44-$62; under 18 free. Crib free. Pet accepted. TV; cable (premium). Complimentary coffee in lobby. Restaurant nearby. Ck-out noon. Business servs avail. In-rm modem link. Cr cds: A, C, D, DS, MC, V.

D 🐾 🔌 🔥 SC

Motor Hotels

★★★ **HOLIDAY INN.** 4751 Lindle Rd (17111), jct I-283 & PA 441 exit 1. 717/939-7841; FAX 717/939-9317; res: 800/465-4329. 300 rms, 4 story. S $109-139; D $121-$151; each addl $12; under 19 free. Crib free. TV; cable (premium). 2 pools, 1 indoor; whirlpool, poolside serv, lifeguard. Restaurant 7 am-2 pm, 5-10 pm. Rm serv 7 am-10 pm. Bar 11-2 am. Ck-out 10 am. Valet serv. Convention facilities. Business servs avail. Free airport transportation. Lighted tennis. Putting green. Exercise equipt; sauna. Health club privileges. Game rm. Private patios, balconies. Cr cds: A, C, D, DS, JCB, MC, V.

★★★ **MARRIOTT.** *4650 Lindle Rd (17111). jct I-283 & PA 441.* *717/564-5511; FAX 717/564-2476; res: 800/343-5982.* E-mail 105616. 1760@compuserve.com. 348 rms, 10 story. S, D $80-$159; each addl $14; suites $225; under 18 free. Crib free. TV; cable (premium), VCR avail. Indoor/outdoor pool; whirlpool, poolside serv, lifeguard. Restaurant 6 am-midnight. Rm serv. Bar to 2 am; entertainment. Ck-out noon. Convention facilities. Business servs avail. In-rm modem link. Bellhops. Valet serv. Sundries. Gift shop. Free airport transportation. Exercise equipt; sauna. Game rm. Balconies. Luxury level. Cr cds: A, C, D, DS, ER, MC, V.

★★★ **SHERATON INN.** *800 E Park Dr (17111). I-83 exit 29.* *717/561-2800; FAX 717/561-8398; res: 800/644-3144.* 174 rms, 3 story. S $86-$105; D $96-$115; each addl $10; suites $145-$165; under 18 free. Crib free. Pet accepted, some restrictions. TV; cable (premium). Heated pool; whirlpool, lifeguard. Restaurant 6:30 am-10 pm. Rm serv. Bar 11-2 am. Ck-out noon. Meeting rms. Business servs avail. In-rm modem link. Bellhops. Valet serv. Shopping arcade. Free airport transportation. Golf privileges. Exercise rm; sauna. Game rm. Cr cds: A, C, D, DS, MC, V.

Hotels

★★★ **HILTON HOTEL.** *1 N 2nd St (17101). 717/233-6000;* *FAX 717/233-6271; res: 800/445-8667.* 341 rms, 15 story. S, D $99-$164; each addl $10; suites $200-$500; wkend rates. Crib avail. TV; cable (premium). Indoor pool. Restaurant 6:30 am-11 pm. Bar 11-1 am; entertainment. Ck-out noon. Convention facilities. Business servs avail. In-rm modem link. Concierge. Valet parking. Free airport transportation. Exercise equipt. Health club privileges. Minibars, refrigerators; microwaves avail. Luxury level. Cr cds: A, C, D, DS, ER, MC, V.

★★★ **RAMADA INN.** *23 S 2nd St (17101). 717/234-5021; FAX* *717/234-2347; res: 800/272-6232.* Web www.ramada.com/ramada.html. 254 rms, 10 story. S $75-$95; D $85-$105; each addl $10; studio rms $78-$90; suites $145; under 19 free. TV; cable (premium), VCR avail (movies). Indoor pool. Restaurant 6:30 am-2 pm, 5-10 pm. Bar 4:30 pm-1 am. Ck-out noon. Meeting rms. Business servs avail. In-rm modem links. Gift shop. Airport transportation. Exercise equipt. Microwaves avail. Rooftop patio. Cr cds: A, C, D, DS, ER, JCB, MC, V.

★★★ **WYNDHAM GARDEN HOTEL.** *765 Eisenhower Blvd* *(17111), I-283 exit 1. 717/558-9500; FAX 717/558-8956; res: 800/528-1234; res: 800/253-0238.* 167 rms, 6 story. May-Oct: S, D $89-$119; each addl $10; suites $150; under 19 free; ski plans; wkend rates; higher rates car shows; lower rates rest of yr. Crib free. Pet accepted. TV; cable (premium). Heated pool; lifeguard. Coffee in rms. Restaurant 6 am-2:30 pm, 5-10 pm. Bar 4 pm-midnight. Ck-out noon. Meeting rms. Business servs avail. In-rm modem link. Free airport, RR station, bus depot transportation. Downhill ski 20 mi. Exercise equipt. Health club privileges. Refrigerator in suites; microwaves avail. Cr cds: A, C, D, DS, ER, JCB, MC, V.

Restaurants

★★★ **ALFRED'S VICTORIAN RESTAURANT.** *38 N Union St* *(17057), E on I-83, then S on I-283, then SE on PA 230 to PA 441.* *717/944-5373.* Hrs: 11:30 am-2 pm, 5-10 pm; Sat from 5 pm; Sun 3-9 pm. Closed some major hols. Res accepted. Italian, continental menu. Bar. Wine list. Semi-a la carte: lunch $5-$12.50, dinner $9.95-$27.95. Spe-

cializes in homemade pastas, hand-cut steaks, seafood. Own baking, pasta. Tableside cooking. Patio dining. Victorian mansion; antique chandeliers, furnishings; floor-to-ceiling windows; fireplaces. Family-owned. Cr cds: A, C, D, DS, MC, V.

★★ **MANADA HILL INN.** *128 N Hershey Rd (17112).* *717/652-0400.* Hrs: 4-9 pm; Fri-Sat to 10 pm; Sun 11 am-8 pm; Sun brunch to 2:30 pm. Closed Dec 25. Res accepted. Continental menu. Bar to 11 pm. Semi-a la carte: dinner $8.25-$19.95. Sun brunch $11.50. Child's meals. Specializes in fresh seafood, prime rib. Restored house; artwork, antique brass chandeliers. 3 dining rms. Cr cds: A, C, D, DS, MC, V.

Hawley (C-9)

(See also Milford, Scranton)

Settled 1827 **Pop** 1,244 **Elev** 920 ft **Area Code** 570 **Zip** 18428
E-mail pocomts@poconos.org **Web** www.poconos.org
Information Pocono Mts Vacation Bureau, 1004 Main St, Stroudsburg 18360; 570/424-6050; for brochures phone 800/POCONOS.

A major attraction in this Pocono resort area is man-made Lake Wallenpaupack, offering summer recreation on the lake as well as winter recreation nearby.

What to See and Do

Claws 'N Paws Wild Animal Park. A zoo in the woods with more than 100 species of exotic animals. Petting zoo with tame deer, lambs and goats. Farmyard area. Parrot, reptile shows; zookeeper talks (schedule varies). Picnicking, snack bar. (May–Oct, daily) 12 mi W via PA 590, near Lake Wallenpaupack. Phone 570/698-6154. ¢¢¢

Gravity Coach. Car used on Pennsylvania Gravity Railroad (22 inclined planes between Hawley and Scranton, 1850–1885). W of town on US 6.

Lake Wallenpaupack. One of the largest man-made lakes in state (5,600 acres), formed by damming of Wallenpaupack Creek. Swimming beach (Memorial Day-day before Labor Day; fee); fishing, boating, water sports; ice fishing; camping. Information center, ½ mi NW on US 6 at PA 507 (mid-May-Oct, daily; rest of yr, Thurs-Mon; closed Easter, Thanksgiving, Dec 25). Phone 570/226-2141. **Free**

Pennsylvania Power & Light Co. Hydroelectric facilities, dam; recreation area. Visitor center near lake has exhibits. Superintendent's office has info on region (Mon-Fri); observation point. (Daily) Approx 1½ mi E on US 6. Phone 570/226-3702. **Free**

Promised Land State Park. Approx 2,950 acres. Swimming beach; fishing; boating (rentals, mooring, launch). Hiking. Cross-country skiing, snowmobiling, ice skating, ice fishing. Picnicking, snack bar. Tent & trailer sites, cabins. Nature center, interpretive program. 12 mi S on PA 390. Phone 570/676-3428. Camping ¢¢¢¢–¢¢¢¢¢

Skiing. Tanglwood. 2 double chairlifts, 2 T-bars, rope tow, beginner lift; patrol, school, rentals; snowmaking; cafeteria, bar; nursery. Longest run 1 mi; vertical drop 415 ft. Night skiing. (Early Dec–late Mar, daily) Half-day rates. 4 mi S via PA 390, off I-84 in Tafton. Phone 570/226-7669 or 888/226-SNOW. ¢¢¢¢¢

Motel

✓★ **GRESHAM'S LAKE VIEW MOTEL.** *Rte 6 (18428), 2 mi* *E on US 6. 570/226-4621; FAX 570/226-1857; res: 888/845-6760.* 21 rms, 2 story. S, D $68-$73; each addl $5; under 5 free; wkly rates; ski plans;

lower rates off-season. Crib free. TV; cable. Complimentary coffee in lobby. Restaurant nearby. Ck-out 11 am. Downhill/x-country ski 2½ mi. Balconies. Overlooks Lake Wallenpaupack. Cr cds: A, C, DS, MC, V.

🄳 🏊 🔥

Resort

★★★ **COVE HAVEN HONEYMOON RESORT.** *RR 590 (18438), 8 mi W on PA 590.* 570/226-4506; FAX 570/226-4697; res: 800/233-4141. 282 units, 3 story. MAP: D $180-$320; wkly rates. Adults only. TV, VCR avail (movies $5). Indoor/outdoor pools; whirlpool, poolside serv. Bars 11:30-1:30 am; entertainment. Ck-out 11 am. Coin lndry. Gift shop. Free bus depot transportation. Indoor tennis. Racquetball. Driving range, indoor miniature golf. Boats, waterskiing. Snowmobiling. Soc dir. Indoor ice skating and roller skating. Rec rm. Game rm. Exercise equipt; saunas. Refrigerators, some balconies. On lake. Cr cds: A, C, D, DS, MC, V.

🄳 🚴 🏊 🎿 ⛷ 🛶 🔥 SC

Inns

★ **FALLS PORT INN & RESTAURANT.** *330 Main Ave (18428).* 570/226-2600; FAX 570/226-6409. 9 rms, 5 share bath, 2 story. No rm phones. May-Labor Day: S, D $75-$95; under 2 free; wknd, hol rates (2-day min); ski plans; lower rates rest of yr. Crib free. 2 TVs; cable, VCR avail. Complimentary continental bkfst. Restaurant 11:30 am-9 pm. Rm serv. Ck-out 11 am, ck-in 1 pm. Downhill/x-country ski 9 mi. Built in 1902 as an inn. Cr cds: A, C, MC, V.

🄳 🏊 🛶 🔥

✓★★★ **ROEBLING INN ON THE DELAWARE.** *155 Scenic Dr (18435), 15 mi E on PA 590.* 570/685-7900; FAX 570/685-1718. 6 rms, 2 story. 4 rms with shower only, 1 rm with kit July-Aug, AP: S $70-$90, D $75-$95, each addl $10, kit unit $85-$105. Wkly rates. Min stay wknds, hols. Lower rates rest of yr. TV; cable. Complimentary full bkfst. Restaurant nearby 7 am-9 pm. Ck-out 11:30 am, ck-in 2:30 pm. Luggage handling. Business servs avail. Tennis privileges 1 mi. Downhill/x-country ski 5 mi. Refrigerators. On river. Cr cds: A, C, DS, MC, V.

🄳 🚴 ⛷ 🛶 🔥

★★★ **SETTLERS INN AT BINGHAM PARK.** *4 Main Ave (18428).* 570/226-2448; FAX 570/226-1874; res: 800/833-8527. 18 rms, 2 story, 5 suites. S $58-$75; D $83-$113; each addl $15; suites $113-$153; under 12 free. Crib $10. Complimentary full bkfst. Restaurant (see THE SETTLERS INN). Ck-out noon, ck-in 1 pm. Business servs avail. In-rm modem link. Airport transportation. Downhill ski 8 mi; x-country ski 1 mi. Golf course nearby. Bingham Park opp. Tudor-revival manor (1927); stone fireplace, sitting rooms with many antiques. Totally nonsmoking. Cr cds: A, C, DS, MC, V.

🄳 🚴 🛶 🔥 SC

Restaurants

★ **EHRHARDT'S LAKESIDE.** *On PA 507 (18428), 1 mi S of US 6.* 570/226-2124. Hrs: 11 am-10 pm; Sun from 9 am; Sun brunch to 12:30 pm. Closed Thanksgiving, Dec 25. Res accepted. Bar. Semi-a la carte: lunch $2.50-$10, dinner $9-$20. Sun brunch $7.95. Child's meals. Specializes in steak, seafood. Tri-level dining area; overlooks lake. Cr cds: A, C, DS, MC, V.

🄳 ♥

★★★ **THE SETTLERS INN.** *(See The Settlers Inn)* 570/226-2993. Hrs: 11:30 am-2 pm, 5-9 pm; Sun brunch to 2 pm. Closed Dec 23-25. Res accepted wknds and July-Aug. Bar. A la carte entrees: lunch $5-$11, dinner $13-$20. Sun brunch $5.95-$10.95. Child's meals. Specializes in pheasant, seafood, trout. Pianist Fri, Sat. Dining rm of Tudor-style hotel constructed in 1920s. Cr cds: A, C, DS, MC, V.

🄳

Hazleton (D-8)

(See also Ashland, Bloomsburg, Jim Thorpe, Wilkes-Barre)

Settled 1809 **Pop** 24,730 **Elev** 1,660 ft **Area Code** 570 **Zip** 18201
E-mail hazchamb@ptdprolog.net **Web** hazlechamber.org
Information Greater Hazleton Chamber of Commerce, 1 S Church St, Ste 200; 570/455-1508

On top of Spring Mountain, Hazleton calls itself the highest city in Pennsylvania. Rich agricultural land surrounds Hazleton, and its early and rapid economic growth was spurred by the rich anthracite coal reserves found in the area. Although coal dominated the town's economy during the 19th century, today there are many diversified industries located here, producing building materials, textiles, office furniture, business forms, foods and food containers, boxes, heavy fabricated steel, plastics, electronic parts and other products.

What to See and Do

Eckley Miners' Village. (Pennsylvania Anthracite Museum Complex). Mining coal patch town (1850s) portrays life in the anthracite region until about 1940. Walking tour (Memorial Day–Labor Day; fee). (Daily; closed some hols) 10 mi NE off PA 940, near Freeland. Phone 570/636-2070. ¢¢

National Shrine of the Sacred Heart. Large outdoor shrine incl stations of the cross and crucifixion scene; picnic area. (Mar–Oct, daily) 1½ mi NE on US 309, PA 940, in Harleigh section of Hazleton. Phone 570/455-1162. **Free**

Motels

★★ **BEST WESTERN GENETTI MOTOR LODGE.** *32nd & N Church St (18201), 2 mi N on PA 309.* 570/454-2494; FAX 570/455-7793; res: 800/528-1234. 89 rms, 3 story. June-Oct: S $55-$65; D $65-$75; each addl $7; suites $130-$150; under 12 free; higher rates special events; lower rates rest of yr. Crib free. TV; cable, VCR avail (movies). Heated pool; lifeguard. Playground. Complimentary continental bkfst. Ck-out 11 am. Coin lndry. Business servs avail. Valet serv. Sundries. Bus depot transportation. Cr cds: A, C, D, DS, MC, V.

🏊 🛶 🔥 SC

★★ **RAMADA INN.** *Rte 309 N (18201), 1½ mi N on PA 309.* 717/455-2061; FAX 717/455-9387; res: 800/465-4329. 107 rms, 2 story. S, D, studio rms $72; under 18 free. Crib free. Pet accepted. TV; cable. Pool; lifeguard. Restaurant 6 am-10 pm. Rm serv. Bar 5 pm-2 am. Ck-out noon. Meeting rms. Business servs avail. In-rm modem link. Bellhops. Sundries. Cr cds: A, C, D, DS, ER, JCB, MC, V.

🄳 🐾 🏊 ⛷ 🔥 SC

Restaurants

★★★ **SCATTON'S.** *1008 N Vine St. (18201).* 717/455-6630. Hrs: 5-10 pm; Thurs 11:30 am-2 pm, 5-10 pm. Closed Sun; Jan 1, Thanksgiving, Dec 25. Northern Italian menu. Bar. Semi-a la carte: lunch $3.50-$11.25, dinner $10.50-$24.75. Specializes in fresh seafood, veal, pasta. Casual; collection of antique prints. Cr cds: A, C, D, MC, V.

🄳

✓★ **TOM'S KITCHEN.** *PA 93 (18219), 6 mi NW on PA 93.* 717/788-3808. Hrs: 7 am-8 pm; Sun from 8 am. Closed most major hols. Semi-a la carte: bkfst $3.45-$4.25, lunch $2.75-$3.75, dinner $5.25-$9.95. Child's meals. Specialties: roast turkey platter, stuffed breast of chicken. Family-style restaurant. Family-owned. Totally nonsmoking. Cr cds: C.

🄳

Hershey (E-7)

(See also Cornwall, Harrisburg, Lebanon)

Founded 1903 **Pop** 11,860 **Elev** 420 ft **Area Code** 717 **Zip** 17033
Web www.800hershey.com

Information Hersheypark, 100 W Hersheypark Dr; 800/HERSHEY (information) or 800/533-3311 (reservations)

One of America's most fascinating success stories, this planned community takes its name from founder M.S. Hershey, who established his world-famous chocolate factory here in 1903, then built a town around it. The streets have names like Chocolate and Cocoa, and streetlights are shaped like chocolate kisses. But there's more than chocolate here. Today, Hershey is known as one of the most diverse entertainment and resort areas in the eastern US. Hershey is also known as the "golf capital of Pennsylvania" and has a number of well-known golf courses.

What to See and Do

Founders Hall. Campus center of Milton Hershey School, noted for its striking rotunda. (Daily; closed hols) Phone 717/520-2000.

Hershey Gardens. From mid-June to first frost, 8,000 rose plants bloom on 23 acres. Tulip garden (mid-Apr–mid-May); chrysanthemums and annuals; butterfly house featuring 400-500 butterflies; 6 theme gardens. (Mid-Apr–Oct, daily) Hotel Rd. Phone 717/534-3492. ¢¢

Hershey Museum. Pennsylvania German, Native American, Eskimo collections; displays of Stiegel glass; "Apostolic Clock" depicting life of Christ; Milton Hershey history. (Daily; closed Jan 1, Thanksgiving, Dec 25) Near entrance to Hersheypark. Phone 717/534-3439. ¢¢ Adj is

Hersheypark Arena. Capacity 10,000; professional hockey, basketball, ice skating, variety shows, concerts. Phone 717/534-3911.

☑ **Hershey's Chocolate World.** Tour via automated conveyance; simulates steps of chocolate production from cacao bean plantations through chocolate making in Hershey. Also tropical gardens, shopping village. (Daily; closed most major hols) Entrance adj to Hersheypark. Phone 717/534-4900. **Free**

Hersheypark Stadium/Star Pavilion. Stadium seats 25,000, Star Pavilion seats 7,200; sports and entertainment events. Phone 717/534-3911.

Hersheypark. 110-acre theme park incl Rhine Land, Tudor Square, Dutch crafts barn; more than 50 rides incl 6 roller coasters; live family shows. (Mid-May–Labor Day, daily; May & Sept, selected wknds) Entrance on Hersheypark Dr (PA 39). Phone 800/HERSHEY. ¢¢¢¢ Also here is

ZooAmerica. An 11-acre environmental zoo depicting 5 climatic regions of North America; home to more than 200 animals. (Daily; closed some major hols) Combination admission with Hersheypark avail. Phone 717/534-3860. Separate admission ¢¢

Seltzer's Lebanon Bologna Co. Outdoor wooden smokehouses since 1902. Video tours. (Daily exc Sun; closed hols) 230 N College St, 3 blks N of US 422, in Palmyra. Phone 717/838-6336. **Free**

Annual Events

Chocolate Lovers' Weekend. Feb.

Hersheypark Balloonfest. Oct.

Antique Automobile Club. National fall rally. 2nd wkend Oct.

Christmas in Hershey. Mid-Nov–Dec.

Motels

★ **ADDEY'S INN OF HERSHEY.** *150 E Governor Rd (17033). 717/533-2591; FAX 717/533-2591.* E-mail addeysinn@aol.com; web www.go2pa.com/addeys_inn. 12 rms. May-Labor Day: S, D $89; each addl $5; lower rates rest of yr. Crib $5. TV; cable (premium). Complimentary coffee in lobby. Ck-out 11 am. Picnic tables. Cr cds: A, C, DS, MC, V.

⬜ ⬜ SC

★★ **BEST WESTERN INN.** *150 E Governor Rd (17033). 717/533-5665; FAX 717/533-5675; res: 800/233-0338.* Web www.bestwestern.com/best.html. 123 rms, 3 story. No elvtr. May-Aug: S, D $99-$159; each addl $10; under 17 free; wkly rates; higher rates special events; lower rates rest of yr. Crib $2. TV; cable (premium), VCR avail (movies). Heated pool; whirlpool. Complimentary continental bkfst. Restaurant nearby. Ck-out noon. Coin lndry. Meeting rms. Business servs avail. In-rm modem link. Valet serv. Game rm. Refrigerators; microwaves avail. Cr cds: A, C, D, DS, ER, MC, V.

D ⬜ ⬜ ⬜ ⬜ SC

✓ ★★ **DAYS INN.** *350 W Chocolate Ave (17033). 717/534-2162; FAX 717/533-6409; res: 800/329-7466.* Web www.travelweb.com/travel. 75 rms, 4 story. Late June-Aug: S $119-$139; D $129-$149; each addl $6; under 18 free; higher rates antique car shows; lower rates rest of yr. Crib free. TV; cable, VCR avail (movies). Complimentary continental bkfst. Restaurant opp 11:30 am-10 pm. Ck-out 11 am. Valet serv. Free RR station, bus depot transportation. Health club privileges. Some refrigerators; microwaves avail. Cr cds: A, C, D, DS, JCB, MC, V.

D ⬜ ⬜ SC

★★★ **HERSHEY LODGE & CONVENTION CENTER.** *W Chocolate Ave & University Dr (17033), at University Dr. 717/533-3311; FAX 717/533-9642; res: 800/437-7439.* Web www.800hershey.com/~herco. 457 rms, 1-2 story. May-Labor Day: S $130-$157; D $136-$163; each addl $15; suites $250-$425; under 18 free; package plans; lower rates rest of yr. Crib free. TV; cable (premium). 2 pools, 1 indoor; wading pool, whirlpool, poolside serv, lifeguard. Playground. Free supervised child's activities (May-early Sept, late Nov-Jan 1). Complimentary coffee in rms. Restaurant 7 am-10 pm; also dining rm. Bar 11-2 am; entertainment. Ck-out 11 am. Convention facilities. Business servs avail. In-rm modem link. Valet serv. Sundries. Gift shop. Free airport transportation. Lighted tennis. 18-hole golf privileges, greens fee $60-$120, miniature golf. Exercise equipt; sauna. Rec rm. Cinema. Cr cds: A, C, D, DS, MC, V.

D ⬜ ⬜ ⬜ ⬜ ⬜ ⬜ ⬜ ⬜ SC

✓ ★★ **MILTON MOTEL.** *1733 E Chocolate Ave (17033). 717/533-4533; FAX 717/533-0369.* 34 rms, 2 story. Mid-May-Labor Day: S $49-$76; D $66-$99; each addl $5; wkly rates Sept-May; higher rates hol wkends; lower rates rest of yr. Crib $6. TV; cable (premium), VCR avail. Heated pool. Restaurant adj 11-2 am. Ck-out 11 am. Business servs avail. In-rm modem link. Game rm. Refrigerators, microwaves avail. Cr cds: A, C, D, DS, MC, V.

⬜ ⬜ ⬜ SC

★ **RODEWAY INN & SUITES.** *43 W Areba Ave (17033). 717/533-7054; FAX 717/533-3405; res: 800/638-7949.* Web www.rodeway.com. 22 rms, 2 story, 11 kits. Mid-June-early Sept: S $79-$198; D $89-$129; each addl $10; kits. $125-$198; under 18 free; lower rates rest of yr. Crib free. TV; cable. Indoor pool. Complimentary continental bkfst. Complimentary coffee in rms. Restaurant nearby. Ck-out 11 am. Business servs avail. In-rm modem link. Refrigerators; microwaves avail. Cr cds: A, C, D, DS, MC, V.

⬜ ⬜ ⬜ SC

✓ ★ **SIMMONS MOTEL.** *355 W Chocolate Ave (17033), 2½ blks W of town square. 717/533-9177; FAX 717/533-3605.* E-mail simmons355@aol.com; web www.superpages.gte.net. 32 rms, 2 story. June-Oct: S $55-$85; D $65-$95; each addl $5; apts (1-3 bedrm) $110-$185; kit units $95-$110; wkly, family rates; higher rates antique car show; lower rates rest of yr. Crib free. TV; cable (premium), VCR avail. Complimentary coffee in lobby. Restaurant nearby. Ck-out 11 am. Business servs avail. Health club privileges. Many refrigerators; microwaves avail. Picnic tables, grills. Cr cds: A, C, DS, MC, V.

⬜ ⬜ SC

✓ ★★ **SPINNERS MOTOR INN.** *845 E Chocolate Ave (17033). 717/533-9157; FAX 717/534-1189.* Web www.visithe.com. 52 rms, 6 with shower only, 2 story. May-mid-Oct: S $65-$95; D $69-$109; each addl $5; suites $89-$139; under 2 free; golf plans; wkends, hols (2-day min); higher rates special events; lower rates rest of yr. Crib $6. TV; cable (premium), VCR avail (movies). Heated pool. Complimentary continental bkfst. Restaurant (see CATHERINE'S). Bar. Ck-out 11 am. Business servs avail. Game rms. Some refrigerators, microwaves. Some balconies. Picnic tables. Cr cds: A, C, D, DS, MC, V.

★★ **WHITE ROSE MOTEL.** *1060 E Chocolate Ave (17033). 717/533-9876; FAX 717/533-6923.* E-mail whiterose@worldnet.att.net; web www.800hershey.com. 24 rms, 2 story. July-Aug: S, D $108; under 18 free; lower rates rest of yr. Crib $5. TV; cable (premium). Heated pool; lifeguard. Coffee in rms. Restaurant nearby. Ck-out 11 am. Business servs avail. In-rm modem link. Gift shop. Health club privileges. Refrigerators. Private patios, balconies. Picnic tables. Totally nonsmoking. Cr cds: A, C, DS, MC, V.

Motor Hotel

★★★ **HOLIDAY INN.** *604 Station Rd (17028), N on PA 743 to I-81, exit 28. 717/469-0661; FAX 717/469-7755; res: 800/465-4329.* E-mail info@stayholiday.com; web www.stayholiday.com. 195 rms, 4 story. Memorial Day-mid-Oct: S $119-$179; D $129-$189; each addl $10; suites $195-$295; under 19 free; lower rates rest of yr. Crib free. Pet accepted. TV; cable. 2 pools, 1 indoor; whirlpool. Restaurant 6:30 am-10 pm. Rm serv. Bar 11-2 am; entertainment. Ck-out noon. Coin lndry. Meeting rms. Business center. In-rm modem link. Bellhops. Valet serv. Gift shop. Airport, RR station, bus depot transportation. Exercise equipt; sauna. Lawn games. Microwaves avail. Balconies. Cr cds: A, C, D, DS, ER, JCB, MC, V.

Resort

✓★★★★ **THE HOTEL HERSHEY.** *Hotel Rd (17033), off US 322/422. 717/533-2171; FAX 717/534-8887; res: 800/533-3131.* Web www.800hershey.com/-herco. 235 rms, 5 story. MAP, Apr-Oct: S $231-$293; D $289-$351; each addl $75; under 3 free; EP avail; package plans; lower rates rest of yr. Crib free. Valet Parking. TV; cable, VCR avail. Indoor and outdoor pools, wading pool, whirlpool, lifeguard. Supervised child's nursery; age 3-16. Restaurants (Circular Dining Room and The Fountain Cafe) 7 am-11 pm. Rm serv 24 hrs. Bar 11-1 am; Sat entertainment. Ck-out noon, ck-in after 4 pm. Conference facilities. Business center. Bellhops. Valet serv. Gift shop. Fitness Center and Spa, sauna. Massage. 2 tennis courts. Basketball court. 9-hole golf, greens fee $19-$22, putting green. Nature trails. Bicycle rentals. Lawn games. Basketball court. Carriage rides. X-country ski on site. Extensive gardens, landscaping; scenic hilltop location. Cr cds: A, C, D, DS, MC, V.

Inn

★★ **PINEHURST INN BED & BREAKFAST.** *50 NE Dr (17033), on PA 743 off Hersheypark Dr & Park Ave. 717/533-2603; FAX 717/534-2639; res: 800/743-9140.* 15 rms, some share bath, 2 story. No rm phones. S, D $45-$75; each addl $5; 2-day min hols. TV in sitting rm. Complimentary full bkfst. Ck-out 11 am. Airport transportation. Health club privileges. Brick mansion built by Milton Hershey for orphaned boys. Totally nonsmoking. Cr cds: C, MC, V.

Restaurants

★★ **CATHERINE'S AT SPINNER'S.** *(See Spinner's Inn) 717/533-9050.* Hrs: 4-10 pm. Closed Sun, Mon; some major hols. Res

accepted. Bar. Semi-a la carte: dinner $10-$24. Child's meals. Specializes in steak, fresh seafood, pasta. Own baking. Elegant decor with chandelier, portraits of historical figures. Cr cds: A, C, D, DS, MC, V.

★★ **DIMITRI'S.** *1311 E Chocolate Ave (17033). 717/533-3403.* Hrs: 11 am-11 pm. Closed Jan 1, Dec 25. Res accepted. Greek, continental menu. Bar to 2 am. Semi-a la carte: lunch $3.95-$7.95, dinner $6.95-$21.95. Child's meals. Specializes in seafood, steak. Cr cds: C, MC, V.

★★ **UNION CANAL HOUSE.** *107 S Hanover St (17033), in Union Deposit Village. 717/566-0054.* Hrs: 5-10 pm. Closed Sun; major hols. Res accepted. Continental menu. Bar. Semi-a la carte: dinner $8.95-$29.95. Child's meals. Specialties: roast duckling, Angus beef, lump crab cakes. Three dining areas; fireplace, memorabilia from 1800s. Family-owned. Cr cds: A, C, D, MC, V.

Honesdale (C-9)

(See also Hawley, Scranton)

Founded 1826 **Pop** 4,972 **Elev** 980 ft **Area Code** 570 **Zip** 18431
E-mail nand@ezaccess.net
Information Wayne County Chamber of Commerce, 303 Commercial St; 570/253-1960 or 800/433-9008

Named in honor of Philip Hone, a mayor of New York City and first president of the Delaware & Hudson Canal Co, Honesdale was for many years the world's largest coal storage center, transshipping millions of tons of anthracite. A gravity railroad brought coal here in winter; in spring it was reshipped by canal boats to tidewater. The *Stourbridge Lion,* first steam locomotive to operate in the US (1829), was used by the Delaware & Hudson Canal Co, but when the rail bed proved too weak, mule power replaced the steam engine. Today, Honesdale manufactures textile products, business forms and furniture and is surrounded by dairy farms in the beautiful rolling countryside.

What to See and Do

Replica of the *Stourbridge Lion* (original is in Smithsonian Institution). First steam locomotive to operate in the US (1829). Main St.

Stourbridge Rail Excursions. Scenic rail excursions from Honesdale to Lackawaxen, centering on the change of seasons, with entertainment and activities. Contact the Chamber of Commerce for schedule, fees.

Triple W Riding Stable. 181-acre horse ranch in the NE range of Pocono Mtns. Variety of trail rides for beginners or advanced riders; ½- and full-day trips; overnight camping trips. Hay & sleigh rides (seasonal; by appt). (Daily) US 6 through Hawley, left at post office, 3½ mi to "Triple W" sign, turn right. Phone 570/226-2620. ¢¢¢¢¢

Wayne County Historical Society Museum. Dorflinger glass collection. (Apr-Dec, daily; rest of yr, Tues, Thurs, Sat; closed some hols) 810 Main St. Phone 570/253-3240. ¢

Annual Event

Wayne County Fair. Exhibits, livestock, horse racing. 1st full wk Aug.

Hopewell Furnace National Historic Site (E-8)

(See also Pottstown, Reading)

(15 mi SE of Reading via US 422, PA 82 to Birdsboro, then SE on Birdsboro-Warwick Rd/PA 345; 10 mi NE of Tpke Morgantown Interchange)

Hopewell, an early industrial community, was built around a charcoal-burning cold-blast furnace, which made pig iron and many other iron products from 1771 to 1883. Nearby mines and forests supplied ore and charcoal for the furnace. The National Park Service has restored the buildings, and interpretive programs emphasize the community's role in the history of American industry. Hopewell is surrounded by the approximately 7,330-acre French Creek State Park (see POTTSTOWN).

The Visitor Center has a museum and audiovisual program on ironmaking and community life. Self-guided tour includes: charcoal house, where fuel for furnace was stored; anthracite furnace ruin; waterwheel and blast machinery; casting house, where 16 moulders produced up to 5,000 stoves annually; cold-blast charcoal-burning furnace; blacksmith shop; tenant houses; barn for horses and mules transporting charcoal, ore, iron products to market; office store, which was source of staples, clothing and house furnishings; springhouse, which supplied "refrigeration"; ironmaster's house, home of proprietor or manager. Stove moulding and casting demonstrations (late June–Labor Day; fee). Captioned slide program for the hearing impaired; Braille map and large-print pamphlets for the visually impaired; wheelchair access. (Daily; closed winter hols) For further information contact the Superintendent, 2 Mark Bird Lane, Elverson 19520; 610/582-8773 or 610/582-2093 (TDD). ¢¢

Huntingdon (E-5)

(See also Altoona, Orbisonia)

Founded 1767 **Pop** 6,843 **Elev** 643 ft **Area Code** 814 **Zip** 16652
E-mail rcvb@raystown.org **Web** www.raystown.org
Information Raystown County Visitors Bureau, 241 Mifflin St; 814/643-3577 or 888/RAYSTOWN

Founded on the site of an Oneida village in the Juniata Valley, Huntingdon was first called Standing Stone—for a 14-foot etched stone pillar venerated by Native Americans.

What to See and Do

Indian Caverns. A 1-mi guided tour; extensive scenic beauty and authentic Native American history; relic rm contains artifacts, tablet of picture writing; picnic area. (Apr–Oct, daily) 13 mi NW via US 22, PA 45 in Spruce Creek. Phone 814/632-7578 or 814/632-8333. ¢¢¢

Lincoln Caverns. The 1-hr tour of two caves incl Frozen Niagara, Diamond Cascade; visitors' center & gift shop. (Apr-Nov, daily; Mar & Dec, wkends only) 3 mi W on US 22. Phone 814/643-0268. ¢¢¢

Raystown Lake. Large man-made lake, with 110 mi of shoreline. Swimming; fishing, hunting; boating. Hiking. Picnicking, restaurant. Camping. Observation area. Fee for some activities. 7 mi S on PA 26, follow signs to Hesston. Phone 814/658-3405.

Swigart Auto Museum. Changing exhibits of American steam, gas, electric autos. Large collection of nameplates, license plates and auto memorabilia; picnic area. (Memorial Day-Oct, daily) 4 mi E on US 22. Phone 814/643-0885. ¢¢

Annual Event

Hartslog Day. 7 mi NW via US 22, in Alexandria. Heritage festival incl crafts, food, music, games. 2nd Sat Oct.

Motels

★★ **DAYS INN.** *22 S 4th St (16652), 4th St at US 22.* 814/643-3934; FAX 814/643-3005. 76 rms, 3 story. S $44-$56; D $49-$61; each addl $5; under 13 free; higher rates special events. Crib free. Pet accepted; $5. TV; cable. Restaurant 6 am-10 pm; Fri, Sat to 11 pm. Bar 4:30 pm-2 am. Ck-out 11 am. Meeting rms. Business servs avail. In-rm modem link. Valet serv. Sundries. Microwaves avail. Cr cds: A, C, D, DS, MC, V.

✓★★ **HUNTINGDON MOTOR INN.** *US 22 & Rte 26 (16652), US 22 & PA 26.* 814/643-1133; FAX 814/643-1331. 48 rms, 2 story. S $37-$40; D $46-$52; each addl $4. Crib free. Pet accepted, some restrictions. TV; cable. Restaurant 7 am-9 pm. Bar 4:30 pm-2 am. Ck-out 11 pm. Meeting rms. Business servs avail. In-rm modem link. Microwaves avail. Balconies. Cr cds: A, C, D, DS, MC, V.

Indiana (D-3)

(See also Johnstown)

Founded 1805 **Pop** 15,174 **Elev** 1,310 ft **Area Code** 724 **Zip** 15701
Web www.indiana-co-pa-tourism.org
Information Indiana County Tourist Bureau, 1019 Philadelphia St; 724/463-7505

Named after the Native American population in the area, this borough was established on 250 acres donated for a county seat by George Clymer of Philadelphia, a signer of the Declaration of Independence. Indiana University of Pennsylvania (1875) is located here. This is also the birthplace of actor Jimmy Stewart.

What to See and Do

County parks. Blue Spruce. Covers 420 acres. Fishing for bass, perch, catfish and crappie; boating (rowboat, canoe rentals). Winter sports area. Picnicking, grills, playground. (Daily) 6 mi N off PA 110. **Pine Ridge.** Covers 630 acres. Trout fishing. Hiking, nature study. Picnicking. (Daily) SW via US 22 near Blairsville. **Hemlock Lake.** Covers 200 acres. Fishing, small game hunting. Hiking. ice skating. Nature study, photography. W on PA 286 near Rossiter. (Daily) For general info phone 724/463-8636 (park commission).

Jimmy Stewart Museum. Highlights the namesake's accomplishments on film, radio and TV. His roles as a military hero, civic leader, family man and world citizen are woven into displays, film presentations and gallery talks. 52-seat vintage theater. (Daily) Indiana Public Library Bldg, 3rd floor, corner of 9th & Philadelphia Sts. Phone 412/349-6112 or 800/83-JIMMY. ¢¢

Yellow Creek State Park. Approx 3,000 acres. Swimming beach; fishing, hunting; boating. Hiking. Cross-country skiing, snowmobiling, sledding, ice skating, ice fishing, ice boating. Picnicking, playground. Standard fees. 12 mi E via US 422. Phone 724/357-7913.

Motels

★★ **BEST WESTERN INN.** *1545 Wayne Ave (15701).* 724/349-9620; FAX 724/349-2620; res: 888/299-9620; res: 888/299-9620. 107 rms, 2 story. S $55-$65; D $60-$70; each addl $5; under 12 free;

higher rates special university events. Crib free. TV; cable (premium). Heated pool. Coffee in rms. Restaurant 6:30 am-1:30 pm; Sun from 8 am. Ck-out noon. Meeting rms. In-rm modem link. Cr cds: A, C, D, DS, MC, V.

★★★ **HOLIDAY INN.** *1395 Wayne Ave (15701). 724/463-3561; FAX 724/463-8006; res: 800/477-3561; res: 800/477-3561.* 159 rms, 2 story. S, D $79-$89; suites $149; family, wkend rates; golf plans; higher rates university events. Crib free. Pet accepted. TV; cable (premium). Indoor pool; whirlpool, poolside serv, lifeguard. Complimentary full bkfst. Coffee in rms. Restaurant 6:30 am-10 pm; Sat, Sun from 7 am. Rm serv. Bar 4 pm-2 am; entertainment. Ck-out noon. Meeting rms. Business servs avail. In-rm modem link. Miniature golf. Game rm. Sauna. Health club privileges. Cr cds: A, C, D, DS, MC, V.

Jenkintown (F-10)

(See also Fort Washington, Philadelphia, Willow Grove)

Pop 4,574 **Elev** 250 ft **Area Code** 215 **Zip** 19046 **E-mail** info@valley forge.org **Web** www.valleyforge.org

Information Valley Forge Convention & Visitors Bureau, 600 W Germantown Pike, Suite 130, Plymouth Meeting 19462; 610/834-1550

What to See and Do

Abington Art Center. Contemporary art, sculpture garden (daily, dawn to dusk), gallery and gallery shop. (Tues-Sat) Located in historic Alverthorpe Manor. 515 Meetinghouse Rd. Phone 215/887-4882. **Free**

Beth Sholom Synagogue. The only synagogue designed by Frank Lloyd Wright. (By appt) Old York & Foxcroft Rds, 1 mi S, in Elkins Park. Phone 215/887-1342. **Free**

Restaurants

★★ **JOHNNY MOTT'S.** *8460 Limekiln Pike Bldg #1 (19095), jct PA 309 & Greenwood Ave. 215/887-1263.* Hrs: 11:30 am-2 pm, 4:30-10 pm; Sat 4:30-11 pm; Sun 4:30-9 pm. Closed Jan 1, Dec 25. Res accepted. Continental, seafood menu. Bar. Semi-a la carte: lunch $5.95-$8.50, dinner $14.95-$23.95. Specialities: seafood pescatore, lobster diablo, loin veal chop. Valet parking. Cr cds: A, C, D, MC, V.

✓★★ **STAZI MILANO.** *Township Line & Greenwood Ave (19046), in Jenkintown RR station. 215/885-9000.* Hrs: 11:30 am-3 pm, 4-9:30 pm; Fri, Sat 5-10:30 pm; Sun 4-9 pm; early-bird dinner Mon-Thurs 4-6 pm. Italian menu. Bar to midnight; Fri, Sat to 1 am. Semi-a la carte: lunch $6.95-$10.95, dinner $6.95-$17.95. Specializes in pasta, beef, chicken. In 1931 RR station; mahogany railings. Cr cds: A, C, D, MC, V.

Jim Thorpe (D-9)

(See also Hazleton)

Settled 1815 **Pop** 5,048 **Elev** 600 ft **Area Code** 570 **Zip** 18229
Information Carbon County Tourist Promotion Agency Information Center, PO Box 90; 570/325-3673 or 888/JIM-THORPE

The twin towns, Mauch Chunk (Bear Mountain) and East Mauch Chunk, built on the sides of a narrow gorge of the Lehigh River, merged in 1954 and adopted the name of Jim Thorpe, the great Native American athlete. This, together with a "nickel-a-week" plan whereby each man, woman and child paid five cents to promote the community and attract industry, gave the area (formerly dependent on coal mining) a new lease on economic life. Little has changed in appearance after more than a century; a walking tour will reveal 19th-century architecture.

What to See and Do

Asa Packer Mansion. Former showplace home of founder of Lehigh Valley Railroad and Lehigh University, one of state's wealthiest men. Packer's house, treasures and money were left to the borough. (June–Oct, daily; Apr–May, wkends) Packer Hill. Phone 570/325-3229. ¢¢ Adj is

Jim Thorpe Memorial. A 20-ton granite mausoleum built in memory of the 1912 Olympic champion. 1 mi E on PA 903.

Old Jail Museum. Built in 1871, the Old Jail, which was an active prison until Jan 1995, contains 28 original cells, warden's living quarters and 16 dungeon cells. Famous for hangings of Molly Maguires; one Molly, to claim his innocence, placed his hand on his cell wall and said his hand print would remain forever as a sign of his innocence. The hand print is still on the wall of Cell 17. (Late May-early Nov) 128 W Broadway. Phone 570/325-5259. ¢¢

Stone Row. 16 townhouses built by Asa Packer for the engineers on his railroad; reminiscent of Philadelphia's Elfreth's Alley. Some are stores open to the public. Race St, downtown. Also here is

St Mark's Church. Has Tiffany windows and copy of reredos from Windsor Castle. (June–Oct, daily; Apr–May, wkends) Phone 570/325-2241. ¢¢

Whitewater rafting. On upper and lower gorges of Lehigh River.

Pocono Whitewater Adventures. Also bike tours. (Mar–Nov, daily) 8 mi NE of Jim Thorpe Bridge on PA 903. For info, reservations, phone 570/325-3655. ¢¢¢¢¢

Jim Thorpe River Adventures, Inc. (Mar–Nov, daily) Coalport Rd, NE via PA 903. For info, reservations, phone 570/325-2570 or 570/325-4960. ¢¢¢¢

Annual Events

Laurel Blossom Festival. Arts & crafts, entertainment, food, steam train rides. 2nd wkend June.

Fall Foliage Festival. Arts & crafts, food, entertainment. Scenic 3-hr train rides. 2nd wkend Oct.

Inns

★★ **HARRY PACKER MANSION.** *Packer Hill (18229), Packer Hill. 570/325-8566.* E-mail mystery@murdermansion.com; web www.murdermansion.com. 13 rms, 2 share bath, 2 with shower only, 3 story, 3 suites. S, D $75-$150; package plans; wkends, hols (2-day min); higher rates special events. Children over 12 yrs only. Pet accepted. TV in some rms; VCR (movies). Complimentary full bkfst; afternoon refreshments. Ck-out 11 am, ck-in 4 pm. Luggage handling. Valet serv. Concierge serv. Built in 1871; a second empire mansion used as a model for the haunted mansion in Disney World. Cr cds: A, C, MC, V.

★★★ **INN AT JIM THORPE.** *24 Broadway (18229). 717/325-2599; FAX 717/325-9145; res: 800/329-2599.* 27 rms, 4 story. S $70-$90; D $70-$110; each addl $10. Crib free. TV; cable. Complimentary continental bkfst. Dining rm 11:30 am-9 pm. Bar 11:30-2 am; entertainment Sat. Ck-out 11 am, ck-in 2 pm. Business servs avail. Victorian-era hotel (1864), with ornamental-iron galleries, hosted Buffalo Bill, Thomas Edison, John D. Rockefeller, and Presidents Grant & Taft. Restored with period furnishings. Cr cds: A, C, D, DS, MC, V.

Johnstown (E-3)

(See also Ebensburg, Ligonier)

Settled 1800 **Pop** 28,134 **Elev** 1,180 ft **Area Code** 814
E-mail jstcvb@visitjohnstownpa.com **Web** www.visitjohnstownpa.com
Information Greater Johnstown/Cambria County Convention & Visitors Bureau, 111 Market St, 15901-1608; 814/536-7993 or 800/237-8590

On May 31, 1889, a break in the South Fork Dam that impounded an old reservoir 10 miles east of the city poured a wall of water onto the city in the disastrous "Johnstown Flood." The death toll rose to 2,209 and property damage totaled $17 million. The city has been flooded 22 times since 1850, most recently in 1977.

Founded by a Swiss Mennonite, Joseph Johns, the city today is the center of Cambria County's iron and steel industry, producing iron and steel bars, railroad cars, parts and railroad supplies.

What to See and Do

Conemaugh Gap. Gorge, 7 mi long and 1,700 ft deep, cuts between Laurel Hill Ridge and Chestnut Ridge. Located at the W end of the city.

Grandview Cemetery. 777 unidentified victims of the 1889 flood are buried under blank headstones in the "Unknown Plot." 1 mi W on PA 271, in Westmont. Phone 814/535-2652.

Inclined Plane Railway. Joins Johnstown and Westmont. Ride is on steep (72% grade) passenger incline 500-ft ascent. Counterbalanced cable cars take 50 passengers and 2 automobiles each. (Daily; closed Jan 1, Dec 25) Vine St & Roosevelt Blvd. Phone 814/536-1816. ¢¢

Johnstown Flood Museum. Museum depicts history of Johnstown, with permanent exhibits on 1889 Johnstown Flood; Academy Award-winning film, photographs, artifacts, memorabilia. (Daily; closed some hols) 304 Washington St. Phone 814/539-1889. ¢¢

Johnstown Flood National Memorial. Commemorates 1889 Johnstown Flood; preserved remnants of the South Fork Dam. Visitor center with exhibits, 30-min movie (daily; closed Dec 25). Jct US 219, PA 869. Phone 814/495-4643. ¢

Motels

✓★★ **COMFORT INN.** *455 Theatre Dr (15904), US 219 exit Elton Rd.* 814/266-3678; FAX 814/266-9783; res: 800/228-5150. 117 rms, 5 story, 27 suites. S $57-$63; D $63-$69; each addl $6; suites $84-$91; kit units $94-$99; under 18 free; monthly rates; higher rates special events. Crib free. Pet accepted; $6. TV; cable, VCR (movies). Indoor pool; whirlpool, lifeguard. Complimentary continental bkfst. Restaurant nearby. Ck-out noon. Coin lndry. Meeting rms. Business center. In-rm modem link. Sundries. Free airport transportation. Exercise equipt. Health club privileges. Refrigerator, wet bar in suites; microwaves avail. Picnic table, grill. Cr cds: A, C, D, DS, ER, JCB, MC, V.

D 🐾 ⌨ 🏋 🔁 🔥 SC 🚶

✓★ **SLEEP INN.** *453 Theatre Dr (15904).* 814/262-9292; FAX 814/262-0486. 62 rms, 58 with shower only, 3 story. S $49-$55; D $55-$61; under 18 free; wkly rates; higher rates: Labor Day, sporting events. Crib free. Pet accepted, some restrictions; $6. TV; cable (premium). Complimentary continental bkfst. Restaurant adj 11 am-9 pm. Ck-out noon. Meeting rm. Business servs avail. In-rm modem link. Airport transportation. Refrigerators, microwaves avail. Cr cds: A, C, D, DS, ER, JCB, MC, V.

D 🐾 🔁 🔥 SC

Hotel

★★ **HOLIDAY INN.** *250 Market St (15901), US 219 exit 56W.* 814/535-7777; FAX 814/535-7777; res: 800/443-5663. 164 rms, 6 story. S, D $72-$89; suites $238-$290; under 18 free. Crib free. Pet accepted,

some restrictions. TV; cable (premium). Indoor pool; whirlpool, poolside serv, lifeguard. Coffee in rms. Restaurant 7 am-10 pm. Bar 4 pm-midnight. Ck-out noon. Meeting rms. Business center. In-rm modem link. Airport transportation. Exercise equipt; sauna. Health club privileges. Cr cds: A, C, D, DS, JCB, MC, V.

D 🐾 ⌨ 🏋 🔁 🔥 SC 🚶

Restaurant

★★ **SURF N'TURF.** *100 Valley Pike (15905).* 814/536-9250. Hrs: 4-10 pm; Sun 11 am-8 pm. Closed Dec 25. Bar. Semi-a la carte: dinner $8.95-$32.95. Child's meals. Specializes in seafood, steak. Salad bar. Pianist Sat. Cr cds: A, C, D, DS, MC, V.

D

Kane (B-4)

(See also Clarion, Warren)

Settled 1864 **Pop** 4,590 **Elev** 2,000 ft **Area Code** 814 **Zip** 16735
Information Seneca Highlands Tourist Association, Jct 770 W & US 219, PO Box H, Custer City 16725; 814/368-9370

Situated on a lofty plateau, Kane offers hunting, fishing and abundant winter sports. Summers are cool and winters are bracing. Allegheny National Forest is to the north, west and south; there are scenic drives through 4,000 acres of virgin timber. General Thomas L. Kane of "Mormon War" fame settled here and laid out the community, which prospered as a lumber and railroad town. General Ulysses Grant was once arrested here for fishing without a license.

What to See and Do

Bendigo State Park. Approx 100 acres. Swimming pool; fishing. Sledding. Standard fees. 9 mi SE on PA 321, then 7 mi S on US 219, then 3 mi NE on unnumbered road. Phone 814/965-2646.

Kinzua Bridge State Park. An approx 300-acre park surrounds Kinzua Bridge. When built in 1882, the bridge was the highest railroad bridge in the world, taking its 2,053-ft span 301 ft above the Kinzua Creek. Overlooks, picnicking. (Daily) 12 mi E via US 6 in Mt Jewett. Phone 814/965-2646. **Free**

Thomas L. Kane Memorial Chapel (1878). Built as a chapel for the new town under the direction of General Kane, a Civil War hero and humanitarian who championed the persecuted Mormons. Visitor center incl film of General Kane's life; small museum. (Tues-Sat) 30 Chestnut St. Phone 814/837-9729. **Free**

Twin Lakes. Swimming (fee); fishing. Hiking. Picnicking. Camping (fee). 8 mi S of E Kane on PA 321, then 2 mi N on Forest Rd 191, in Allegheny National Forest. Phone 814/723-5150.

Kempton

(see Hamburg)

Kennett Square (F-9)

(See also West Chester; also see Wilmington, DE)

Settled 1705 **Pop** 5,218 **Elev** 370 ft **Area Code** 484 & 610 **Zip** 19348 **Web** www.brandywinevalley.com

Information Chester County Tourist Bureau, 601 Westtown Rd, Ste 170, West Chester 19382, phone; 610/344-6365 or 800/228-9933; or the Southeastern Chester County Chamber of Commerce, 206 E State St, PO Box 395, phone 610/444-0774

What to See and Do

Barns-Brinton House (1714). Authentically restored 18th-century tavern, now a house museum furnished in the period. Guides in colonial costume offer interpretive tours; domestic art demonstrations. (June–Aug, Sat–Sun; also by appt) 5½ mi NE on US 1, in Chadds Ford. Phone 610/388-7376. ¢

Brandywine Battlefield. Includes Lafayette's quarters and Washington's headquarters. Here, and around Chadds Ford, the Battle of the Brandywine (1777) took place—a decisive battle for Washington. Visitor center with exhibits; tours of historic bldgs; museum shop. Picnicking. (Daily exc Mon; closed some hols) 2 mi W of jct US 1, 202, near Chadds Ford. Phone 610/459-3342. House tours ¢¢

Brandywine River Museum. Converted 19th-century gristmill houses largest collection of paintings by Andrew Wyeth and other Wyeth family members; also collections of American illustration, still life and landscape painting. Nature trail; wildflower gardens; restaurant, museum shop, guided tours. (Daily; closed Dec 25) 7 mi NE on US 1, in Chadds Ford. Phone 610/388-2700. ¢¢

Chaddsford Winery. Tours of boutique winery, housed in renovated old barn; view of production process; tasting room. Tours; tastings. (Schedule varies) 5 mi NE on US 1, in Chadds Ford. Phone 610/388-6221. ¢¢

John Chads House. Stone bldg (ca 1725) is fine example of early 18th-century Pennsylvania architecture; authentically restored and furnished as a house museum. Narrated tours by guides in colonial costume; baking demonstrations in beehive oven. (May–Sept, Sat–Sun; also by appt) 7 mi NE via US 1, then ¼ mi N on PA 100, in Chadds Ford. Phone 610/388-7376. ¢

★ **Longwood Gardens.** Longwood was the estate of Pierre S. du Pont, chairman of the board of both Du Pont Chemicals and General Motors, who designed the 1,050 acres of gardens around Peirce's Park, a grove of trees planted in 1798. Estate incl the original grove; the Peirce-du Pont House (1730); a variety of exterior gardens, incl the rose, peony, wisteria, idea, hillside, heath, water lily and topiary gardens; the Italian Water Garden, Open Air Theatre and Main Fountain Garden, which together feature more than 1,700 water jets; and the neoclassical conservatories, nearly 4 acres under glass, housing indoor gardens that are among the most spectacular in the world. Display of color-illuminated fountains (Memorial Day wkend–Sept, Tues, Thurs & Sat eves). Organ concerts, orchestral concerts, plays, holiday displays, horticultural lectures (schedules at visitor center). Restaurant (see THE TERRACE); picnic areas; museum shop. (Daily) 3 mi NE on US 1. Phone 610/388-1000. ¢¢¢

Phillips Mushroom Museum. Museum explains history, lore and mystique of mushrooms through motion picture, diorama, slides and exhibits. Gift shop. (Daily; closed some major hols) 2 mi NE on US 1. Phone 610/388-6082. ¢

Motel

★ **LONGWOOD INN.** *815 E Baltimore Pike (19348).* *610/444-3515; FAX 610/444-4285.* 28 rms. S $74; D $80; each addl $6; under 12 free; wkly rates (winter). Crib free. TV; VCR avail. Ck-out noon. Business servs avail. Cr cds: A, C, D, DS, MC, V.

D ⊠ 🔥 SC

Motor Hotel

★★★ **MENDENHALL HOTEL.** *Rte 52 (19357), 3 mi N on US 1.* *610/388-1181; FAX 610/388-1184.* E-mail hionis@aol.com; web www.mendenhallinn.com. 70 rms, 3 story. S $105; D $115; each addl $20; suites $150-$199; under 12 free. Crib free. TV; cable (premium), VCR avail (free movies). Complimentary continental bkfst. Rm serv. Bar from 11:30 am. Ck-out noon. Meeting rms. Business center. In-rm modem link. Bellhops. Valet serv. Concierge. Airport transportation. Exercise equipt. Bathrm phones, minibars. Cr cds: A, C, D, DS, MC, V.

D ⊀ ⊠ ⊠ 🔥 SC ⊀

Inns

★★★ **BRANDYWINE RIVER HOTEL.** *US 1 & SR 100 (19317), Approx 5 mi N on US 1.* *610/388-1200; FAX 610/388-1200.* 40 rms, 2 story, 10 suites. S, D $125-$169; each addl $10; suites $149-$169. Crib free. Pet accepted, some restrictions. TV; cable. Complimentary continental bkfst; afternoon refreshments. Restaurant adj 11:30 am-10 pm. Ck-out 11 am, ck-in 2 pm. Meeting rms. Business servs avail. Exercise equipt. Bathrm phones; refrigerator in suites. Specialty shops on site. Cr cds: A, C, D, DS, MC, V.

D 🐾 ⊀ ⊠ 🔥 SC

★★★ **FAIRVILLE INN.** *506 Kennett Pike (19357), 2 mi S of US 1 on PA 52.* *610/388-5900; FAX 610/388-5902.* Web www.innbook.com. 15 rms, 2 story. S, D $135-$195; each addl $15. Adults only. TV; cable. Complimentary continental bkfst. Ck-out 11 am, ck-in after 3 pm. Business servs avail. Some fireplaces. Private patios, balconies. Built in 1826; antiques, period decor. View of surrounding countryside. Totally nonsmoking. Cr cds: A, C, DS, MC, V.

D ⅙ ⊠ 🔥

★★ **SCARLETT HOUSE BED & BREAKFAST.** *503 W State St (19348).* *610/444-9592; FAX 610/925-0373; res: 800/820-9592.* E-mail janes10575@aol.com; web www.traveldata.com/cnns/data/scarlett.html. 4 rms, 2 with bath, 2 story, 1 suite. Rm phones avail. S, D $85-$135; suite $135; golf packages. TV; cable (premium). Complimentary full bkfst. Restaurants nearby. Ck-out 11 am, ck-in 4-6 pm. Street parking. American Foursquare house built in 1910; Victorian decor. 3 sitting rms. Fireplaces. Totally nonsmoking. Cr cds: A, C, DS, MC, V.

⊠ 🔥

Restaurants

★★ **KENNETT SQUARE INN.** *201 E State St (19348).* *610/444-5687.* Hrs: 11:30 am-2:30 pm, 5:30-10 pm; Sun 5-9 pm; Mon, Tues to 9 pm. Closed Jan 1, Dec 25. Res accepted. Bar 11:30-2 am. Semi-a la carte: lunch $4.50-$10, dinner $10.95-$25.95. Specializes in fresh mushroom dishes. Pianist Sat. Restored country inn (1835). Cr cds: A, C, D, MC, V.

D ⊡

★★★ **MENDENHALL INN.** *PA 52 (19357), 3 mi N on US 1 to PA 52S.* *610/388-1181.* E-mail hionis@aol.com; web www.mendenhallinn.com. Hrs: 11:30 am-2:30 pm, 5-10 pm; Sun 4-8 pm; Sun brunch 10 am-2 pm. Closed Dec 25. Res required. Continental menu. Bar. Wine cellar. Semi-a la carte: lunch $6-$15, dinner $18-$29. Sun brunch $22.95. Child's meals. Specializes in veal, seafood, wild game. Pianist, harpist. Valet parking. Country inn; colonial decor. Cr cds: A, C, D, DS, MC, V.

D ⊡

✓ ★★★ **TERRACE RESTAURANT.** *Longwood Gardens (19348).* *610/388-6771.* Hrs: 11 am-4 pm; dinner hrs same as Longwood Gardens; wkend hrs vary; Dec to 7:30 pm. Cafeteria 10 am-4 pm; wkend hrs vary; Jan, Feb 10 am-3 pm; Dec 10 am-8 pm. Dining rm closed Jan-Mar. Res accepted. Bar. Semi-a la carte: lunch $6.95-$13.95, dinner $9.95-$18.95. Child's meals. Specialties: crab cakes, mushroom strudel. Salad bar.

Cafeteria avg ck: lunch, dinner $8. Outdoor dining. Admission to Long-wood Gardens required. Cr cds: A, C, MC, V.

D

King of Prussia (F-9)

(See also Norristown, Philadelphia, West Chester)

Settled early 1700s **Pop** 18,406 **Elev** 200 ft **Area Code** 484 & 610 **Zip** 19406 **E-mail** info@valleyforge.org **Web** www.valleyforge.org

Information Valley Forge Convention & Visitors Bureau, 600 W German-town Pike, Suite 130, Plymouth Meeting 19462; 610/834-1550

Originally named Reeseville for the Welsh family that owned the land, the town changed its name to that of the local inn, which is still standing. The area around the town is full of historic interest.

What to See and Do

Harriton House (1704). Early American domestic architecture of the Philadelphia area. Originally 700-acre estate, now 16½ acres. House of Charles Thomson, Secretary of the Continental Congresses; restored to early 18th-century period. Nature park. (Wed–Sat; Sun by appt; closed hols) 6 mi SE via Old Gulph Rd to Harriton Rd, in Bryn Mawr. Phone 610/525-0201. ¢

Mill Grove (1762). Includes 175-acre wildlife sanctuary, developed around the first American home of ornithologist John James Audubon, now a museum. Prints, incl complete elephant folio. Hiking trails. (Tues–Sat, also Sun afternoons; closed Jan 1, Thanksgiving, Dec 25) 5 mi NW via US 422 & Audubon Rd, N of Valley Forge National Historic Park, on Pawlings Rd, in Audubon. Phone 610/666-5593. **Free**

Swiss Pines. Japanese gardens featuring azalea and rhododendron collection; ponds, waterfalls, winding pathway; herb and groundcover garden. Children under 12 yrs not permitted. (Mid-Apr–Nov, Mon–Fri, also Sat mornings; closed hols & inclement weather) 6 mi SW via PA 202, Great Valley exit, on Charlestown Rd in Malvern. Phone 610/933-6916. **Free**

Valley Forge National Historical Park (see). Just W of town.

Motels

★★★ **BEST WESTERN INN.** *127 S Gulph Rd; Rte 202 N (19406), jct US 202, I-76, PA Tpk.* 610/265-4500; FAX 610/354-8905; res: 800/528-1234. Web www.bestwestern.com/pa/kingofprussia. 168 units, 2 story. S, D $95-$115; each addl $10; under 12 free. Crib free. TV; cable (premium). Pool. Complimentary continental bkfst. Restaurants adj. Ck-out noon. Coin lndry. Business servs avail. In-rm modem link. Valet serv. Airport transportation. Health club privileges. Some bathrm phones. Private patios, balconies. Cr cds: A, C, D, DS, MC, V.

D ⛱ 🏊 🔥 SC

★★★ **COURTYARD BY MARRIOTT VALLEY FORGE.** *1100 Drummers Ln (19087), S on US 202, Warner Rd exit.* 610/687-6700; FAX 610/687-1149; res: 800/321-2211. Web www.courtyard.com/phlva. 150 rms, 2 story. S, D $79-$144; suites $169; under 16 free; wkly, wkend rates. TV; cable (premium). Indoor pool; whirlpool. Complimentary coffee in rms. Restaurant 5-10 pm Mon-Thur; 7-11 am Sat-Sun. Rm serv Sun-Thurs. Bar 5-10 pm. Ck-out 1 pm. Coin lndry. Meeting rms. Business center. In-rm modem link. Valet serv. Sundries. Exercise equipt. Refrigerator, microwaves avail. Many balconies. Cr cds: A, C, D, DS, MC, V.

D ⛱ 🏊 🔥 SC 🏃

✓ ★ **MCINTOSH INN.** *260 N Gulph Rd (19406).* 610/768-9500; FAX 610/768-0225; res: 800/444-2775. 210 rms, 7 story. S $64.95; D $64.95-$74.95; each addl $5. Crib free. TV; cable (premium). Complimentary continental bkfst. Restaurant adj open 24 hrs. Ck-out 11 am.

Business servs avail. In-rm modem link. Valet serv Mon-Fri. Refrigerators, microwaves avail. Cr cds: A, C, D, MC, V.

D 🏊 🔥 SC

Motor Hotels

✓ ★★ **COMFORT INN.** *550 W Dekalb Pike (19406).* 610/962-0700; FAX 610/962-0218; res: 800/222-0222. 121 rms, 5 story. S, D $85-$139; under 18 free; wkend rates. Crib free. TV; cable (premium), VCR avail. Complimentary continental bkfst. Ck-out noon. Coin lndry. Meeting rm. Business servs avail. Concierge. Airport transportation. Exercise equipt. Bathrm phones, minibars. Cr cds: A, C, D, DS, ER, JCB, MC, V.

D 🏃 🏊 🔥 SC

★★★ **HOLIDAY INN.** *260 Mall Blvd (19406), Exit 24 I-76, US 202N to Mall Blvd.* 610/265-7500; FAX 610/265-4076; res: 800/465-4329. 225 rms, 5 story. S, D $135; each addl $10; under 19 free. Crib free. TV; cable (premium). Restaurant 6:30 am-9:30 pm. Rm serv. Bar 11-2 am. Ck-out 11 am. Meeting rms. Business center. In-rm modem link. Bellhops. Valet serv. Gift shop. Barber, beauty shop. Health club privileges. Pool privileges. Microwaves avail. Cr cds: A, C, D, DS, ER, JCB, MC, V.

D 🏊 🔥 SC 🏃

★★ **HOMEWOOD SUITES.** *12 E Swedesford Rd (19355), 10 mi S on US 202, exit PA 29.* 610/296-3500; FAX 610/296-1941; res: 800/225-5466. E-mail homewoodsuites@aol.com; web www.homewood-suites.com. 123 suites, 4 story. May-Nov: suites $134-$194; under 18 free; lower rates rest of yr. Crib avail. Pet accepted, some restrictions; $150. TV; cable (premium), VCR. Complimentary continental bkfst. Complimentary coffee in rms. Rm serv to 10 pm. Ck-out noon. Meeting rms. Business servs avail. In-rm modem link. Bellhops. Valet serv. Sundries. Coin lndry. Exercise equipt. Indoor pool; whirlpool, lifeguard. Refrigerators, microwaves. Picnic tables, grills. Cr cds: A, C, D, DS, JCB, MC, V.

D 🐾 🏊 🏃 🏊 🔥 SC

Hotels

★★★ **HILTON.** *251 W Dekalb Pike (19406).* 610/337-1200; FAX 610/337-2224; res: 800/879-8372. Web www.hilton.com. 340 rms, 9 story. S, D $110-$139; each addl $10; suites $139-$500; under 18 free; wkend rates. Crib free. TV; cable (premium), VCR avail. Indoor/outdoor pool; whirlpool, lifeguard. Restaurants 6:30 am-11 pm. Bars 11:30-2 am. Ck-out noon. Meeting rms. Business center. In-rm modem link. Concierge. Gift shop. Garage parking. Airport, bus depot transportation. Exercise equipt; sauna. Luxury level. Cr cds: A, C, D, DS, ER, JCB, MC, V.

D 🏊 🏃 🏊 🏊 SC 🏃

★★★ **MARRIOTT SUITES.** *888 Chesterbrook Blvd (19087), I-76 exit 26B to US 202S, at Chesterbrook exit.* 610/647-6700; FAX 610/889-9420; res: 800/228-9290. 229 suites, 5 story. Suites $149-$199; each addl $20; under 16 free; wkend rates. Crib free. TV; cable (premium), VCR avail. Indoor pool; whirlpool, lifeguard. Coffee in rms. Restaurant (see TOWN AND COUNTRY GRILLE). Bar 11:30 am-midnight; wkends to 1 am. Ck-out noon. Meeting rms. Business servs avail. In-rm modem link. Gift shop. Airport, RR station, bus depot transportation. Tennis privileges. Exercise equipt; sauna. Refrigerators, bathrm phones; microwaves avail. Cr cds: A, C, D, DS, JCB, MC, V.

D 🎾 🏊 🏃 🏊 🔥 SC

★★★ **SHERATON VALLEY FORGE HOTEL.** *1160 1st Ave (19406).* 610/337-2000; FAX 610/768-3222; res: 800/325-3535. Web www.sheratonvalleyforge.com. 489 rms, 15 story. S, D $140-$180; each addl $12; suites $175-$275. Crib. TV; cable, VCR avail. Heated pool; whirlpool, poolside serv, lifeguard. Coffee in rms. Restaurant 6:30 am-11:30 pm; wkends to midnight. Bars 11-2 am; entertainment. Ck-out noon. Convention facilities. Business center. In-rm modem link. Concierge. Airport, RR station, bus depot transportation. Exercise equipt; sauna. Wet bar in suites; microwaves avail. Cr cds: A, C, D, DS, ER, JCB, MC, V.

⊡ 🛥 🏃 🎿 ✈ 🛶 🔥 SC 🎣

★ ★ ★ **WAYNE HOTEL.** *139 E Lancaster Ave (19087), S on US 202, S on PA 252 to US 30; from Blue Rte (I-476), exit 5 to US 30W.* 610/687-5000; FAX 610/687-8387; res: 800/962-5850. 38 rms, 6 story. S, D $125-$159; each addl $10; suites $159-$189; under 12 free; wkend rates. Crib free. TV; cable (premium). Pool. Complimentary continental bkfst. Restaurant (see TAQUET). Bar 11:30 am-midnight. Ck-out noon. Meeting rms. Business servs avail. In-rm modem link. Concierge. Airport, RR station transportation. Health club privileges. Microwaves avail. Restored Victorian building (1906) with ornate furnishings, antiques. Cr cds: A, C, D, DS, MC, V.

⊡ 🛥 🛶 🔥 SC

Restaurants

★ ★ **BARON'S INNE.** *499 N Gulph Rd (19406).* 610/265-2550. Web www.baronsinne.com. Hrs: 11 am-2:30 pm, 5-10 pm. Closed Sun; major hols; also first wk in July. Res accepted. Bar 11 am-10 pm; Sat 5-10 pm. A la carte entrees: lunch $7-$13, dinner $16-$25. Specializes in steak, seafood. Piano Fri, Sat. Parking. Antique chandeliers and furniture. Cr cds: A, C, D, MC, V.

⊡ 🛶 ♥

★ ★ **LA FOURCHETTE.** *110 N Wayne Ave (19087), S on US 202, S on PA 252, E on US 30.* 610/687-8333. Hrs: 11:30 am-2 pm; Sat from 5:30 pm; Sun brunch 11 am-2 pm. Closed major hols. Res accepted. Classical French menu. Bar 6 pm-midnight. Wine cellar. A la carte entrees: dinner $18-$28. Sun brunch $12.50-$18.75. Specializes in seafood, lamb, game. Own pastries. Formal atmosphere. Cr cds: A, C, D, DS, MC, V.

⊡ 🛶 ♥

✓ ★ ★ **LOTUS INN.** *402 W Swedesford Rd (19312), S on US 202, exit Devon, left on Valley Forge Rd, right on PA 252 ½ mi.* 610/725-8888. Web www.lotus-inn.com. Hrs: 11:30 am-10 pm; Fri to 11 pm; Sat noon-11 pm; Sun from noon; Sun brunch to 3 pm. Closed Thanksgiving. Res accepted; required Fri-Sun. Chinese, Japanese menu. Bar. Semi-a la carte: lunch $5.95-$14.95, dinner $5.95-$18.95. Sun brunch $9.95. Child's meals. Specialties: sushi, sashimi, General Tso's chicken. Oriental decor; sushi bar. Cr cds: A, C, D, DS, MC, V.

⊡ 🛶

★ ★ ★ **SAMUELS.** *503 W Lancaster Ave (19087), S on US 202, S on PA 252, E on US 30.* 610/687-2840. E-mail eaglenes@ix.netcom.com. Hrs: 11:30 am-2:30 pm, 6-10 pm. Res accepted. Contemporary Amer menu. Bar. Wine list. A la carte entrees: lunch $7-$14, dinner $18-$27. Specializes in beef, chicken. Own desserts. Jazz Fri, Sat. Outdoor dining. Cr cds: A, C, D, DS, MC, V.

⊡ 🛶

★ ★ ★ **TAQUET.** *(See Wayne Hotel)* 610/687-5005. Web www.taquet.com. Hrs: 11:30 am-2:30 pm, 5:30-10 pm; Fri, Sat to 10:30 pm. Closed Sun; Jan 1, Dec 25. Res accepted. French menu. Bar. Wine list. Semi-a la carte: lunch $10-$22.50, dinner $12.75-$24.75. Specializes in venison, seasonal fish, duck. Outdoor dining. Victorian decor. Chef-owned. Cr cds: A, C, D, DS, MC, V.

⊡ 🛶 ♥

★ ★ ★ **TOWN AND COUNTRY GRILLE.** *(See Marriott Suites)* 610/647-6700. Hrs: 7 am-2 pm, 5-10 pm; Fri, Sat to 11 pm. Res accepted. Bar. A la carte entrees: bkfst, lunch $6.95-$10.95, dinner $13.95-$22.95. Buffet: bkfst, lunch $8.95-$9.95. Sun brunch $11.95. Child's meals. Specializes in pasta, grilled steak, seafood. Salad bar (lunch buffet). Country furnishings. View of Valley Forge National Park. Cr cds: A, C, D, DS, JCB, MC, V.

⊡ SC ♥

★ ★ ★ **VILLA STRAFFORD.** *115 Strafford Ave (19087), S on US 202, S on PA 252, E on US 30.* 610/964-1116. Hrs: 11:30 am-2:30 pm, 5:30-9:30 pm. Closed Sun; Jan 1. Res accepted. Continental menu. Bar. Wine cellar. A la carte entrees: lunch $9-$14, dinner $16.95-$27.95. Specialties: rack of lamb, Dover sole. Own pasta, desserts. Jazz Fri-Sat. Mansion built in 1909. Cr cds: A, C, D, MC, V.

⊡ 🛶

✓ ★ ★ **WILD ONION.** *900 Conestoga Rd (19010), I-476, exit 5.* 610/527-4826. Hrs: 11:30 am-11 pm. Res accepted. Bar to 2 am. Semi-a la carte: lunch $5.25-$7.95, dinner $8.95-$18.95. Child's meals. Specializes in fresh seafood, in-season produce. Cr cds: A, C, D, DS, MC, V.

🛶

Kulpsville (E-9)

(See also Norristown, Philadelphia)

Pop 1,200 (est) **Elev** 290 ft **Area Code** 215 & 267 **Zip** 19443
E-mail info@ valleyforge.org **Web** www.valleyforge.org
Information Valley Forge Country Convention & Visitors Bureau, 600 W Germantown Pike, Suite 130, Plymouth Meeting 19462; 610/834-1550

What to See and Do

Morgan Log House (1695). Built by the grandfather of General Daniel Morgan and Daniel Boone, this is the oldest and finest surviving medieval-style log house in the country. Partially restored; authentic early 18th-century furnishings. Guided tours (late Apr–Nov, wkends; other times by appt). E on PA 63, then N on Troxel Rd, E on Snyder Rd and N on Weikel Rd; house is on Weikel Rd, between Snyder & Allentown Rds. Phone 215/368-2480. ¢¢

Restaurant

★ ★ **MAINLAND INN.** *17 Main St (19451).* 215/256-8500. Hrs: 11:30 am-2:30 pm, 5:30-9 pm; Fri to 9:30 pm; Sat 5:30-9:30 pm; Sun (brunch) 11 am-2 pm, 5-8 pm. Closed most major hols. Res accepted. Bar. A la carte entrees: lunch $7-$14, dinner $18-$25. Sun brunch $16.95. Specializes in seafood, lamb, game (in season). Parking. Cr cds: A, C, D, MC, V.

⊡

Kutztown (E-9)

(See also Allentown, Hamburg, Pennsylvania Dutch Area, Reading)

Founded 1771 **Pop** 4,704 **Elev** 417 ft **Area Code** 484 & 610 **Zip** 19530

Home of a popular folk festival, Kutztown is named for its founder, George Kutz. The town's population includes many descendants of the Pennsylvania Germans.

What to See and Do

Crystal Cave Park. Discovered in 1871; crystal formations, stalactites, stalagmites, natural bridges—all enhanced by indirect lighting. Also museum (July-Sept); nature trail; miniature golf (July-Sept; fee); theater. Cafe, rock shop, gift shop. Tours (Mar–Nov, daily). 3 mi NW off US 222. Phone 610/683-6765. ¢¢¢

Annual Event

Folk Festival. Festival grounds. Celebration of Pennsylvania Dutch folk culture; quilts, music, dancing and food of Plain and Fancy Dutch. Craftspeople make baskets, brooms, rugs, toleware and other handcrafts. Phone 610/683-8707. Late June–early July.

Restaurant

★★ **NEW SMITHVILLE COUNTRY INN.** *10425 Old Rte 22 (19530), I-78 exit 13.* 610/285-2987. Hrs: 11 am-11 pm; Sun 8 am-10 pm. Closed Memorial Day, Labor Day. Res accepted. Bar. Semi-a la carte: bkfst $2.25-$6.75, lunch $4.95-$7.25, dinner $9.25-$14.50. Child's meals. Specializes in prime rib, soups, salads. Originally a post office and general store; fireplace, antiques. Cr cds: A, C, MC, V.

Lancaster (F-8)

(See also Bird-in-Hand, Cornwall, Ephrata, Lebanon, Reading, Wrightsville, York)

Settled 1721 **Pop** 55,551 **Elev** 380 ft **Area Code** 717
Web www.800padutch.com
Information Pennsylvania Dutch Convention & Visitors Bureau, 501 Greenfield Rd, 17601; 717/299-8901 or 800/723-8824

Lancaster blends the industrial modern, the colonial past and the Pennsylvania Dutch present. It is the heart of the Pennsylvania Dutch Area (see), one of the East's most colorful tourist attractions. To fully appreciate the area, visitors should leave the main highways and travel on country roads, which Amish buggies share with automobiles. Lancaster was an important provisioning area for the armies of the French and Indian War and the Revolution. Its craftsmen turned out fine guns, which brought the city fame as the "arsenal of the Colonies." When Congress, fleeing from Philadelphia, paused here, September 27, 1777, the city was the national capital for one day. It was the state capital from 1799-1812.

What to See and Do

Amish Farm and House. Typical Amish farm in operation. Lecture on the Amish and tour through early 19th-century stone bldgs furnished and decorated as old-order Amish household; waterwheels, windmill, hand-dug well, carriages, spring wagon, sleighs. (Daily; closed Dec 25) 4½ mi E via US 30. Phone 717/394-6185. ¢¢¢

✪ **Bube's Brewery.** Historic brewery, built before the Civil War, is the only brewery left in the country that has remained intact since the mid-1800s; now operates as a restaurant (see THE CATACOMBS–ALOIS'S–THE BOTTLING WORKS). Guided tours take visitors 43 ft below the street into the brewery's aging vaults and passages, which were built from a cave and were part of what became known as the underground railroad; narrator tells about the history of the brewery and explains methods of producing beer in a Victorian-age brewery. Historic tours (Memorial Day-Labor Day, daily). Restaurants are open all yr (free tour incl with reservations for the Catacombs Restaurant). 102 N Market St, in Mount Joy. Phone 717/653-2056. **Free**

Candy Americana Museum. Antique candy-production equipment, confectionery molds, unusual candy containers; outlet store. (Daily exc Sun; closed Labor Day, Thanksgiving, Dec 25 & 26) 5 mi N via PA 501 at Wilbur Chocolate Co, 48 N Broad St, in Lititz. Phone 717/626-3249. **Free**

Choo-Choo Barn, Traintown, USA. A 1,700-sq-ft layout of Lancaster County in miniature, featuring 16 operating trains and more than 130 animated and automated figures and vehicles. Gift shop. Picnicking. (Apr-Dec, daily; closed most major hols) E via US 30, then SE on PA 741, in Strasburg. Phone 717/687-7911. ¢¢

Dutch Wonderland. Family fun park with rides, botanical gardens, diving shows, shops. Monorail (fee). (Memorial Day-Labor Day, daily; Easter-Memorial Day & after Labor Day-Oct, Sat & Sun) 4 mi E via US 30. Phone 717/291-1888. ¢¢¢¢¢ Adj is

National Wax Museum of Lancaster County. Figures re-create Lancaster County's history from the 1700s to present. (Daily; closed Dec 25) Phone 717/393-3679. ¢¢¢

Franklin and Marshall College (1787) (1,810 students). Liberal arts college. Rothman Gallery showcases Pennsylvania-German artifacts: quilts, Fraktur and stoneware. More than 200 varieties of trees, plants and shrubs on grounds. Tours of campus. College Ave. Phone 717/291-3981. Also here are

North Museum of Natural History and Science. General science and natural history; planetarium shows (Sat & Sun, also by appt); children's Discovery Room; film series; monthly art exhibits (Tues-Sun). Phone 717/291-3941. Planetarium shows ¢

Joseph R. Grundy Observatory. Holds 11-inch refractor and 16-inch reflecting telescope demonstrations. Phone 717/291-4136. **Free**

Fulton Opera House (1852). One of the oldest American theaters; many legendary people have performed here. It is believed that more than one ghost haunts the theater's Victorian interior. Professional regional theater; home of community theater, opera and symphony organizations. 12 N Prince St. Phone 717/394-7133. ¢-¢¢¢¢¢

Gast Classic Motorcars Museum. Collection of 50 favorite antique & classic cars in changing display. Self-guided tours. (Daily; closed most hols) 5 mi SE via US 30, in Strasburg. Phone 717/687-9500. ¢¢¢

Hans Herr House (1719). Example of medieval Germanic architecture; served as early Mennonite meeting house and colonial residence of the Herr family. Mennonite rural life exhibit; blacksmith shop. House tours. (Apr-Dec, daily exc Sun; closed major hols) 1849 Hans Herr Dr, in Willow Street. Phone 717/464-4438. ¢¢

Heritage Center Museum of Lancaster County (1795). Houses examples of early Lancaster County arts and crafts. Furniture, tall clocks, quilts, needlework, silver, pewter, Fraktur, rifles. (Mid-Apr-early Jan, Tues-Sat) Penn Square. Phone 717/299-6440. **Free**

Historic Rock Ford (1794). Preserved home of General Edward Hand, Revolutionary War commander and member of Continental Congress. (Apr-Oct, Tues-Fri & Sun) 2 mi S on Rock Ford Rd, off S Duke St at Lancaster County Park. Phone 717/392-7223. ¢¢ Fees include

Kauffman Museum. Collection of folk art & crafts; antique pewter, rifles, copper and tinware collections housed in restored 18th-century barn. (Apr-Oct, Sun, also by appt)

James Buchanan's Wheatland (1828). Residence of President James Buchanan from 1848-1868; restored Federal mansion with period rms containing American Empire and Victorian furniture and decorative arts. Tours by costumed guides (Apr-Nov, daily). Christmas candlelight tours (early Dec). 1120 Marietta Ave, 1½ mi W on PA 23. Phone 717/392-8721. ¢¢¢

Landis Valley Museum. Interprets Pennsylvania German rural life. Largest collection of Pennsylvania German objects in US; craft and living history demonstrations (May-Oct; see ANNUAL EVENTS); farmsteads, tavern, country store among other exhibit bldgs. (Mar-Dec, daily exc Mon; closed most hols) 2451 Kissel Hill Rd, 2 ½ mi N, off PA 272. Phone 717/569-0401 or -9312. ¢¢¢

Mennonite Information Center. Tourist info; interpretation of Mennonite and Amish origins, beliefs. Free video. (Daily exc Sun; closed Jan 1, Thanksgiving, Dec 25) E on US 30, 2209 Millstream Rd. Phone 717/299-0954. **Free** Also here is

Hebrew Tabernacle Reproduction. Tours (daily exc Sun; closed Jan 1, Thanksgiving, Dec 25). ¢¢

Mill Bridge Village. Restored historic colonial mill village with operating water-powered gristmill (1738); covered bridge; country crafts incl broommaking, quilting, candlemaking, blacksmithing; quilt log cabin; Amish kitchen exhibit; music boxes and nickelodeons; horse-drawn hay & carriage rides; 1890s playground; picnicking. Amish house and schoolhouse tour avail. Oktoberfest (Oct wkends). Camp resort (early Apr-Oct, daily; fee). Village (early Apr-Nov, daily). S Ronks Rd, 4 mi E of jct US 30E, PA 462 in Strasburg. Phone 717/687-8181 or 800/645-2744. ¢¢¢

Muddy Run Recreation Park of Philadelphia Electric Co. Covers 700 acres with 100-acre lake for boating (no power boats), rentals; fishing; picnicking, playgrounds, snack bar, concession; camping. Park (Apr-early Nov). 11 mi S on PA 272, then 3½ mi SW on PA 372. Phone 717/284-4325. Also here is

Muddy Run Information Center of Philadelphia Electric Co. Energy and environmental center; exhibits and movies; illustrated talks periodically. (Tues-Sat) Phone 717/284-2538 for schedule.   **Free**

National Toy Train Museum. Trains from the 1880s to present; 5 operating layouts; movies; rare, unusual and specialty trains. (May-Oct, daily; Apr & Nov-Dec, Sat & Sun) E via US 30, PA 896, 741, to Paradise Lane, in Strasburg. Phone 717/687-8976.   ¢¢

Robert Fulton Birthplace. Robert Fulton, a great inventor and accomplished artist, is best known for having built the steamboat *Clermont,* which, in 1807, successfully made a trip up the Hudson River against winds and strong current. This little stone house, where Fulton was born, was nearly destroyed by fire about 1822; now refurbished. (June-Labor Day, Sat & Sun) 14 mi S via PA 222. Phone 717/548-2679.   ¢

Sightseeing tours.

Abe's Buggy Rides. A tour through Amish country in an Amish family carriage. (Daily exc Sun) 6 mi E on PA 340, at 2596 Old Philadelphia Pike, Bird-in-Hand. Phone 717/392-1794.   ¢¢¢

Amish Country Tours. Tours of Amish farmlands and Philadelphia. Phone 717/768-3600.   ¢¢¢¢¢

Brunswick Tours. Private guide and auto tape tours. 2249 Lincoln Hwy E, at National Wax Museum. Phone 717/397-7541.   ¢¢¢¢-¢¢¢¢¢

Historic Lancaster Walking Tour. A 90-min tour of historic downtown area. Costumed guide narrates 50 points of architectural or historic interest covering 6 sq blks. (Apr-Oct, 2 tours daily Fri & Sat, 1 tour daily Sun-Thurs; rest of yr, by appt) 100 S Queen St. Phone 717/392-1776.   ¢¢

Strasburg Railroad. Railroad runs 4½ mi to Paradise. Picnic stop. This 160-yr-old line uses late 19th-century coaches, various steam locomotives. (Apr-Oct, daily; winter, wkends) 8 mi SE via US 30, PA 896, 741, in Strasburg. Phone 717/687-7522.   ¢¢¢   Adj is

Railroad Museum of Pennsylvania. More than 50 locomotives, freight and passenger cars dating from 1825; audiovisual exhibits; railroading memorabilia. Picnicking. (Mar–Oct, daily; rest of yr, daily exc Mon; closed some hols) Phone 717/687-8628.   ¢¢¢

Sturgis Pretzel House. First US commercial pretzel bakery (1861), restored as museum. Early equipment (also modern plant); pretzel-making demonstrations, visitors may try twisting pretzels; outlet store. (Daily exc Sun; closed Jan 1, Thanksgiving, Dec 25) 9 mi N via PA 501, 772 at 219 E Main St, in Lititz. Phone 717/626-4354.   ¢

The Watch and Clock Museum. National Association of Watch and Clock Collectors living museum of timepieces and related tools and memorabilia. Over 8,000 items representing the 1600s to the present. Extensive research library. Special exhibitions. (May–Sept, Tues–Sat, also Sun afternoons; winter schedule varies; closed major hols) 12 mi W via US 30, at 514 Poplar St in Columbia. Phone 717/684-8261.   ¢¢

Twin Brook Winery. Estate winery housed in a restored 19th-century barn offers wine tasting, tours of wine-making facilities, visits to the vineyard; picnic areas. Outdoor concerts (late June–mid-Sept, Sat eves; fee); special events throughout the yr. (Apr–Dec, Mon–Sat, also Sun afternoons; rest of yr, Tues–Sat, also Sun afternoons) 17 mi E via US 30, S on PA 41, E on Strasburg Rd, located in Gap at 5697 Strasburg Rd. Phone 717/442-4915.

Annual Events

Sheep Shearing. Amish Farm and House. Phone 717/394-6185. Last Thurs & Fri Apr, 1st Fri Oct.

Old Fashioned Sunday. At Wheatland. Festivities incl entertainment, magic show and 19th-century activities. Phone 717/392-8721. Mid-May.

Harvest Days. Landis Valley Museum. Demonstrations of more than 80 traditional craft and harvest time activities. Phone 717/569-0401. Columbus Day wkend.

Victorian Christmas Week. On grounds of Wheatland. Phone 717/392-8721. Early Dec.

Seasonal Event

Music at Gretna. 15 mi N via PA 72, in Mt Gretna. Chamber music and jazz; well-known artists. Phone 717/964-3836. Mid-June–early Sept.

Motels

✓★★ **COUNTRY LIVING INN.** *2406 Old Philadelphia Pike (17602). 717/295-7295; FAX 717/295-0994.* Web www.padutch.welcome. com/ctryliv.html. 34 rms, 2 story. July-Oct: S, D $79-$99; each addl $8; higher rates hol wkends; lower rates rest of yr. Crib free. TV; cable (premium). Restaurant nearby. Ck-out noon. Whirlpool in suite. Cr cds: C, MC, V.

🛎 🔥

★★ **DAYS INN.** *30 Keller Ave (17601). 717/299-5700; FAX 717/295-3727; res: 800/329-7466.* Web www.800padutch.com/daysinnl.html. 193 rms, 2-3 story. S $76-$81; D $88-$91; each addl $10; under 12 free. Crib free. TV; cable (premium). 2 pools, 1 indoor; wading pool, lifeguard. Playground. Restaurant 7-11 am, 5-9 pm. Bar noon-midnight. Ck-out noon. Coin lndry. Meeting rms. Business servs avail. Tennis. Game rm. Some refrigerators. Balconies. Cr cds: A, C, D, DS, MC, V.

🏸 🌊 🐟 ⇩ 🔥 SC

✓★★ **GARDEN SPOT MOTEL.** *2291 Lincoln Hwy E (17602). 717/394-4736; FAX 717/299-6339.* 19 rms. S $35-$55; D $40-$62; each addl $5; under 5 free; higher rates hols. Closed Dec-Mar. Crib $4. TV; cable. Restaurant 7:30-11 am. Ck-out 11:30 am. Gift shop. Cr cds: A, C, DS, MC, V.

🛎 🔥

★★ **HERSHEY FARM MOTOR INN.** *240 Hartman Bridge Rd (17070), 1½ mi S of US 30. 717/687-8635; FAX 717/687-8638; res: 800/ 827-8635.* E-mail eby.fam@epix.net; web www.800padutch/hersheyf.html. 59 rms, 2 story. June-Aug: S $84; D $89; each addl $8; suites $104-$109; under 16 free; wkly rates; lower rates rest of yr. Crib free. TV; cable (premium). Complimentary full bkfst. Restaurant adj 8 am-7 pm; Sat, Sun to 8 pm. Ck-out 11 am. Meeting rms. Business servs avail. Gift shop. Pool. Playground. Some in-rm whirlpools; refrigerators avail. Some balconies. Cr cds: C, DS, MC, V.

🌊 🛎 🥾 SC

★★★ **HILTON GARDEN INN.** *101 Granite Run Dr (17601). 717/560-0880; FAX 717/560-5400; res: 800/445-8667.* E-mail hilton@ redrose.net; web www.hilton.com. 156 rms, 2 story. May-Oct: S $119-$149; D $124-$154; family rates; lower rates rest of yr. TV; cable (premium). Indoor pool; whirlpool, lifeguard. Complimentary coffee in rms. Restaurant 6:30 am-2 pm, 5-10 pm. Bar 11:30 am-midnight. Coin lndry. Meeting rms. Business center. In-rm modem link. Sundries. Exercise equipt. Cr cds: A, C, D, DS, MC, V.

D 🌊 🥾 ⇩ 🔥 SC 🏃

★★ **HOWARD JOHNSON INN.** *2100 Lincoln Hwy (17602). 717/397-7781; FAX 717/397-6340; res: 800/446-4656.* Web www.hojo. com. 112 rms, 2 story. June-Oct: S $48-$75; D $68-$88; each addl $7; higher rates major hols; lower rates rest of yr. Crib free. TV; cable (premium). Indoor pool. Complimentary continental bkfst. Coffee in rms. Restaurant 11 am-midnight. Bar from 11 am. Ck-out 11 am. Meeting rms. Business servs avail. Shopping arcade. Private patios, balconies. Cr cds: A, C, D, DS, MC, V.

D 🌊 ⇩ 🔥 SC

★★ **RAMADA INN.** *1492 Lititz Pike (17601). 717/393-0771; FAX 717/299-6238.* 160 rms, 2 story. May-Oct: S, D $95; under 12 free; 2-day min stay hols; lower rates rest of yr. Crib free. TV; cable. Pool. Restaurant 6 am-2 pm, 5-10 pm, Sat, Sun 7 am-2 pm. Rm serv. Bar 5 pm-midnight. Ck-out noon. Meeting rms. Business servs avail. In-rm modem link. Bellhops. Valet serv. Sundries. Health club privileges. Game rm. Some refrigerators. Balconies. Cr cds: A, C, D, DS, ER, JCB, MC, V.

D 🌊 ⇩ 🔥 SC

★★ **RAMADA INN.** *2250 Lincoln Hwy E (17602), Rte 30 E. 717/393-5499; FAX 717/293-1014; res: 800/867-2623.* Web www.ramada. com/ramada.html. 166 rms, 5 story. Mid-June-Oct: S, D $84-$129; each addl $10; under 18 free; lower rates rest of yr. Crib free. Pet accepted, some restrictions. TV; cable. 2 pools, 1 indoor. Sauna. Playground. Ck-out 11 am. Coin lndry. Meeting rms. Business servs avail. In-rm modem link. Free airport transportation. Tennis. 27-hole golf privileges, pro, putting green, driving range. Health club privileges. Game rm. Lawn games. Refrigerators. Balconies. Picnic tables. Cr cds: A, C, D, DS, ER, JCB, MC, V.

D ◆ ⚓ ⛷ ≈ ⊠ 🔥 SC

★★ **ROCKVALE VILLAGE INN.** *24 S Willowdale Dr (17602). 717/293-9500; FAX 717/293-8558; res: 800/524-3817.* 113 rms, 2 story. Late June-Nov: S, D $79-$109; each addl $8; under 12 free; lower rates rest of yr. Crib free. TV; cable (premium). Pool; lifeguard. Restaurant 7 am-2 pm. Bar noon-midnight. Ck-out 11 am. Meeting rm. Business servs avail. Cr cds: A, C, DS, MC, V.

D ≈ ⊠ 🔥 SC

✓★★ **WESTFIELD MOTOR INN.** *2929 Hempland Rd (17601), US 30W exit Centerville Rd. 717/397-9300; FAX 717/295-9240; res: 800/547-1395.* 84 rms, 2 story. S, D $49-$79; each addl $5; suites $79-$89; under 18 free. Crib free. TV; cable, VCR avail. Pool; lifeguard. Complimentary continental bkfst. Restaurant nearby. Ck-out 11 am. Coin lndry. Business servs avail. Some refrigerators; microwaves avail. Cr cds: A, C, D, DS, MC, V.

D ≈ ⊠ 🔥 SC

Motor Hotels

★★★ **BEST WESTERN EDEN RESORT INN AND CONFERENCE CENTER.** *222 Eden Rd (17601). 717/569-6444; FAX 717/569-4208; res: 800/533-5634.* E-mail eden@edenresort.com; web www.eden resort.com. 274 rms, 3 story. June-Nov: S, D $125-$139; each addl $10; suites $129-$249; under 18 free; varied lower rates rest of yr. Crib free. Pet accepted. TV; cable (premium). 2 pools, 1 indoor; whirlpool, poolside serv, lifeguard. Playground. Restaurant 6:30 am-11 pm; wknds to midnight. Rm serv. Bar 11-2 am; entertainment. Ck-out noon. Meeting rms. Business center. In-rm modem link. Valet serv. Free airport transportation. Gift shop. Lighted tennis. Exercise equipt; saunas. Lawn games. Microwaves avail. Some balconies. Cr cds: A, C, D, DS, MC, V.

D ◆ ⛷ ≈ ⅟ ⊠ 🔥 SC ☂

★★ **HOLIDAY INN.** *521 Greenfield Rd (17601), opp Tourist Bureau. 717/299-2551; FAX 717/397-0220; res: 800/465-4329.* E-mail hivisitor@aol.com. 189 rms, 4 story. Early May-Nov: S, D $79-$109; under 18 free; lower rates rest of yr. Crib free. TV; cable (premium). 2 pools, 1 indoor. Restaurant 6:30 am-2 pm, 5-10 pm. Rm serv. Bar 4 pm-2 am. Ck-out noon. Meeting rms. Business servs avail. In-rm modem link. Valet serv. Sundries. Tennis. Exercise equipt. Health club privileges. Microwaves avail. Cr cds: A, C, D, DS, ER, JCB, MC, V.

D ⛷ ≈ ⅟ ⊠ 🔥 SC

Hotel

✓★★ **BRUNSWICK HOTEL.** *N Queen St & Chestnut St (17608), at jct Chestnut & Queen Sts. 717/397-4801; FAX 717/397-4991; res: 800/233-0182.* E-mail hblanc@lancnews.info.net; web www.hotel brunswick.com. 222 rms, 7 story. S $62-$78; D $72-$86; each addl $6; under 17 free; monthly, wkly, wkend rates; lower rates Nov-Apr. Crib free. Pet accepted; $100. TV; cable, VCR avail (movies). Indoor pool; lifeguard. Restaurant 7 am-1:30 pm, 5:30-9 pm. Bar; entertainment. Ck-out noon. Coin lndry. Meeting rms. Business servs avail. Free garage parking. Exercise equipt. Refrigerators avail. Cr cds: A, C, D, DS, MC, V.

D ◆ ≈ ⅟ ⊠ 🔥 SC

Resort

★★★ **WILLOW VALLEY FAMILY RESORT.** *2416 Willow St Pike. (17602), 3 mi S on Rte 222. 717/464-2711; FAX 717/464-4784; res:*

800/444-1714. E-mail info@willowvalley.com; web www.willowval.com. 352 rms, 5 story. Mid-June-early Sept, hol wkends: S, D $109-$149; each addl $10; ages 6-12, $5; under 6 free; lower rates rest of yr. Crib free. TV; cable, VCR avail (movies). 3 pools, 2 indoor; whirlpool, lifeguard. Playgrounds. Coffee in rms. Restaurants 6 am-9 pm. Ck-out noon. Free guest lndry. Meeting rms. Business servs avail. Shopping arcade. Free airport, RR station, bus depot transportation. Lighted tennis. 9-hole golf, putting green. Exercise equipt; sauna. Game rm. Some private patios, balconies. Country view; large landscaped grounds. Cr cds: A, C, D, DS, MC, V.

D ⅟ ⛷ ≈ ⅟ ⊠ 🔥 SC

Inns

★★★ **ALDEN HOUSE BED & BREAKFAST.** *62 E Main St (17543), N on PA 501. 717/627-3363; FAX 717/627-5428; res: 800/584-0753.* E-mail inn@aldenhouse.com; web www.alden house.com. 5 rms, shower only, 2 story, 3 suites. No rm phones. S $75; D $85; each addl $20; suites $105-$120; wkends (2-day min); higher rates special events. Children over 10 yrs only. TV; cable. Complimentary full bkfst. Restaurant nearby. Ck-out 11 am, ck-in after 3 pm. Luggage handling. Concierge serv. Microwaves avail. Some balconies. Built in 1850. Totally nonsmoking. Cr cds: C, MC, V.

⊠ 🔥

★★ **AUSTRALIAN WALKABOUT INN BED & BREAKFAST.** *837 Village Rd (17537), 4 mi S on PA 741, off US 222. 717/464-0707; FAX 717/464-2501.* Web www.bbonline.com/pa/walkabout/index.html. 5 rms, 3 story, 3 suites. No rm phones. May-Nov: S $89-$135; D $99-$149; each addl $25; suites $139-$199; lower rates rest of yr. Adults only. TV; cable (premium). Whirlpools. Complimentary full bkfst. Ck-out 10 am, ck-in 3-8 pm. Lawn games. Some balconies. Picnic tables. Brick house with wraparound porch built in 1925. Totally nonsmoking. Cr cds: A, C, MC, V.

⊠ 🔥

★★★ **CAMERON ESTATE INN.** *1855 Mansion Ln (17552), 15 mi W on PA 283, Rheems exit, Colebrook Rd to Donegal Springs Rd. 717/653-1773; FAX 717/653-9432; res: 888/722-6376.* E-mail ceii@paonline.com; web www.bbhost.com/cameronestate. 17 rms, 3 story. S, D $125-$200. Children over 14 yrs only. Complimentary full bkfst. Ck-out 11 am, ck-in 3 pm. Meeting rms. In-rm modem link. Business center. Brick Federal structure (1805) on 15-acre estate; was acquired as a country house, then rebuilt and expanded by Simon Cameron–political kingmaker, US Senator and Abraham Lincoln's first Secretary of War. Totally nonsmoking. Cr cds: A, C, D, DS, MC, V.

D 🔥 ☂

★★★ **GENERAL SUTTER INN.** *14 E Main St (17543), 6 mi N via PA 501, on the Square. 717/626-2115; FAX 717/626-0992.* 14 rms, 3 story. S, D $75-$100. Crib $5. Pet accepted. TV; cable. Dining rm 7 am-9 pm; Sun 8 am-8 pm. Bar 11 am-11 pm. Ck-out noon, ck-in 3 pm. Spacious brick-lined patio. Built in 1764; antique country and Victorian furniture. Fireplace in parlor. Cr cds: A, C, DS, MC, V.

🐾 🔥

★★★ **HISTORIC STRASBURG INN.** *1 Historic Dr Rt. 896 (17579), 8 mi SE via US 30, PA 896. 717/687-7691; FAX 717/687-6098; res: 800/872-0201.* E-mail strassinn@800padutch.com; web www.800pa dutch.com/strasinn.html. 101 rms in 5 bldgs, 2 story. Apr-Nov: S, D $119-$129; each addl $15; suites $159-$199; under 12 free; lower rates rest of yr. Crib $15. Pet accepted; $15. TV; cable, VCR avail (movies). Heated pool; whirlpool. Playground. Complimentary full bkfst. Restaurant (see WASHINGTON HOUSE). Bar 11:30 am-11 pm. Ck-out noon. Meeting rms. Business servs avail. Gift shop. Exercise equipt; sauna. Lawn games. Balconies. Hot air balloon rides on property (58 acres). Cr cds: A, C, D, DS, MC, V.

D ◆ ≈ ⅟ ⊠ 🔥 SC

★★★ **KING'S COTTAGE BED & BREAKFAST.** *1049 E King St (17602). 717/397-1017; FAX 717/397-3447; res: 800/747-8717.* Web www.bbonline.com/pa/kingscottage/. 9 rms. Rm phones avail. S, D $100-

$135. Children over 12 yrs only. TV; cable in library. Complimentary full bkfst; afternoon refreshments. Restaurant nearby. Ck-out 11 am, ck-in 4 pm. Restored Spanish/mission-style house (1913); library, antiques, fireplaces. Totally nonsmoking. Cr cds: C, DS, MC, V.

★★ **O'FLAHERTYS DINGELDEIN HOUSE.** *1105 E King St (17602), on PA 462.* 717/293-1723; FAX 717/293-1947; res: 800/779-7765. E-mail oflahbb@lancnews.infi.net; web www.800padutch.com/ofhouse.html. 5 rms, 2 share bath, 3 story, 1 suite. No rm phones. S, D $80-$100; each addl $15; suite $110; wkends, hols (2-3 day min). Crib free. TV in common rm; cable (premium), VCR avail (movies). Complimentary full bkfst; afternoon refreshments. Ck-out 11 am, ck-in 2:30 pm. Luggage handling. Free airport, RR station transportation. Playground. Dutch colonial mansion built in 1912. Totally nonsmoking. Cr cds: C, DS, MC, V.

★★★ **SWISS WOODS BED & BREAKFAST.** *500 Blantz Rd (17543), N on PA 501, W on Brubaker Valley Rd, N on Blantz Rd.* 717/627-3358; FAX 717/627-3483; res: 800/594-8018. E-mail swiss woods@prodigy.net. 7 rms, 2 story, 1 suite. Apr-Dec: S $80-$130; D $95-$150; each addl $15; suite $135; wkends, hols (2-3 day min); lower rates rest of yr. Children over 12 yrs only. TV in suite and common rm; VCR avail. Complimentary full bkfst. Complimentary coffee in rms. Ck-out 11 am, ck-in 3-7 pm. Luggage handling. Concierge serv. Gift shop. Some in-rm whirlpools; refrigerator, fireplace in suite. Some balconies. Picnic tables. Built to resemble Swiss chalet. Totally nonsmoking. Cr cds: A, C, DS, MC, V.

★★ **ZAHM GEORGE HOUSE BED & BREAKFAST.** *6070 Main St (17520).* 717/569-6026. 4 rms, 3 with shower only, 2 story, 1 suite. No rm phones. S $65-$80; D $65-$85; each addl $10; suites $85; wkly rates; wkends, hols (2-day min). Children over 12 yrs only. Complimentary bkfst. Restaurant nearby. Ck-out 11 am, ck-in 4-7 pm. Luggage handling. Picnic tables, grills. Built in 1856; restored Federal-period mansion. Totally nonsmoking. Cr cds: C, MC, V.

Restaurants

★★ **CATACOMBS AT BUBE'S BREWERY.** *102 N Market St (17552), W on PA 283, exit Mount Joy, 2 mi W on PA 230, turn right at third light.* 717/653-2056. Web www.lancaster.net/bubes. Hrs: 11 am-2 pm, 5:30-9 pm; Fri, Sat to 10 pm; Sun 4:30-9 pm. Closed some major hols. Res accepted. Continental menu. Bar. Semi-a la carte: lunch $2.95-$7.45. Complete meals: dinner $15.95-$26.95. Specializes in shrimp, roast duck. Entertainment Fri, Sat. Outdoor dining. In old Victorian hotel and brewery (1876); dining areas are located in original bottling plant, original dining rms of the hotel portion (Victorian decor) and below ground, in the cellars (medieval atmosphere, costumes, entertainment). Guided tours. Cr cds: A, C, DS, MC, V.

★★ **D & S BRASSERIE.** *1679 Lincoln Hwy E (17602).* 717/299-1694. Hrs: 11:30 am-midnight; Sat 4 pm-1 am; Sun 4-10 pm. Closed Thanksgiving, Dec 25. Res accepted. Continental menu. Bar. Semi-a la carte: lunch $3.75-$8.95, dinner $8.95-$33. Specializes in prime rib, pasta, seafood. Outdoor dining. House built in 1925; original woodwork, fireplaces. Cr cds: A, C, D, DS, MC, V.

★★★ **GROFF'S FARM RESTAURANT & GOLF.** *650 Pinkerton Rd (17552), 11 mi SW via US 30, PA 283 (1st Mt Joy exit) and PA 772 to Pinkerton Rd, 1 mi S.* 717/653-2048. Hrs: 11:30 am-1:30 pm, 5-7:30 pm; Sat 11:30 am-1:30 pm, sittings 5 & 8 pm; Sun brunch 10 am-2 pm. Closed Dec 24-26; also wkdays Jan-mid-Feb. Res required. Serv bar. Wine list. A la carte entrees: lunch $2.50-$7.50, dinner $12.50-$25. Complete meals:

dinner $16-$24. Child's meals. Specialties: chicken Stoltzfus, home-cured ham. Own pastries. Located in farmhouse built in 1756. Family-owned. Cr cds: C, D, DS, MC, V.

★★★ **HAYDN ZUG'S.** *1987 State St (17520), N on PA 72.* 717/569-5746. Hrs: 11:30 am-2 pm, 5-9 pm; Sat from 5 pm. Closed Sun, Mon; most major hols. Res accepted. Bar 5-9 pm. Wine cellar. A la carte entrees: lunch $4.25-$10.95, dinner $10.75-$27.95. Specialties: cheesy chowder, grilled lamb tenderloin, Norwegian chicken. Own pastries. Colonial setting. Family-operated. Cr cds: A, C, D, DS, MC, V.

★★★ **LOG CABIN.** *11 Lehoy Forest Dr (17540), 6 mi NW off PA 272.* 717/626-1181. Hrs: 5-10 pm; Sun 4-9 pm. Closed major hols. Res accepted. Bar. Wine cellar. Semi-a la carte: dinner $15-$35. Child's meals. Specializes in charcoal-broiled steak, fresh seafood. Own baking. Log cabin in woods; paintings, fireplace. Entry through covered "kissing" bridge. Cr cds: A, C, D, MC, V.

✓ ★★★ **OLDE GREENFIELD INN.** *595 Greenfield Rd (17601).* 717/393-0668. E-mail rhottenst@aol.com; web www.find-dining.com/greenfield. Hrs: 11 am-2 pm, 5-10 pm; Mon from 5 pm; Sat 8 am-2 pm (brunch), 5-10 pm; Sun 8 am-2 pm (brunch). Closed some major hols. Res accepted. Bar. Wine cellar. Semi-a la carte: bkfst $4.95-$9.95, lunch $4.95-$8.45, dinner $10.95-$20.95. Sat, Sun brunch $4.95-$12.95. Child's meals. Specializes in steak, seafood, pasta. Own baking, pasta. Pianist Fri, Sat, hols. Outdoor dining. In restored stone farmhouse; dining avail on balcony and in wine cellar. Cr cds: A, C, D, DS, MC, V.

★★ **WASHINGTON HOUSE RESTAURANT.** *(See Historic Strasburg Inn)* 717/687-9211. Hrs: 7 am-2 pm, 5-9:30 pm; Sun 7 am-9:30 pm. Res accepted. French menu. Bar 11:30 am-10 pm. A la carte entrees: lunch $5.25-$12.50, dinner $19.95-$26.95. Buffet: bkfst $6.95, lunch $9.95. Sun brunch $16.95. Child's meals. Specialties: crab cakes, medallions de filet, grillade de bouef. Outdoor dining. Colonial decor. Cr cds: A, C, D, DS, MC, V.

Lebanon (E-7)

(See also Cornwall, Ephrata, Hershey, Lancaster, Pennsylvania Dutch Area)

Founded 1756 **Pop** 24,800 **Elev** 460 ft **Area Code** 717 **Zip** 17042 **Web** www.parrvb.com

Information Pennsylvania Rainbow Region Vacation Bureau, 625 Quentin Rd, PO Box 329; 717/272-8555

This industrial city, steeped in German traditions, is the marketplace for colorful Lebanon County. Many Hessians were confined here after the Battle of Trenton. Today, Lebanon bologna factories and food processing are important to the city's economy. Master planning for redevelopment of city and county combines with the traditional atmosphere to make this a charming community.

What to See and Do

Coleman Memorial Park. This 100-acre former estate has swimming pool (Memorial Day–Labor Day, daily; fee), tennis courts, athletic fields, picnic facilities. Fee for some activities. Park (daily). 2 mi N on PA 72, W Maple St. Phone 717/228-4470. **Free**

Fort Zeller. One of state's oldest existing forts; originally built of logs, rebuilt of stone in 1745; has 12-ft-wide Queen Anne fireplace in kitchen.

(By appt) 11 mi E on US 422, then S on PA 419, in Newmanstown. Phone 610/589-4301. **Donation**

Middlecreek Wildlife Management Area. A 5,144-acre tract provides refuge for waterfowl, forest and farmland wildlife. Permit and open hunting areas, inquire at visitor center for regulations. Fishing; boating (mid-May–mid-Sept). Hiking. Picnicking. Visitor center (Mar–Nov, daily exc Mon). Braille trail for the visually impaired. 11 mi SE on PA 897 to Kleinfeltersville, then 1 mi S. Phone 717/733-1512. **Free**

Stoevers Dam Recreational Area. A 153-acre park with 52-acre lake for fishing; boating (electric motors only), canoeing. A 1½-mi trail for jogging, hiking, bicycling. Primitive camping (permit only; fee). Nature trails; nature barn (Apr–Oct, daily exc Mon; winter, by appt). Community park (daily). 2 mi N on PA 343, Miller St. Phone 717/228-4470. **Free**

Stoy Museum of the Lebanon County Historical Society. Local historical museum containing 30 permanent rm and shop displays on 3 floors of house built in 1773 and used as first county courthouse; research library. Tours. (Daily exc Sat; closed Sun & Mon of hol wkends) 924 Cumberland St. Phone 717/272-1473. ¢¢

The Daniel Weaver Company. Manufacturers, since 1885, of Weaver's Famous Lebanon Bologna and other wood-smoked gourmet meats; smoked in 100-yr-old outdoor smokehouses. Samples. Tours. (Daily exc Sun) 15th Ave & Weavertown Rd. Phone 717/274-6100 or 800/WEAVERS. **Free**

Motel

★★★ **LANTERN LODGE MOTOR INN.** *411 N College St (17067), 7 mi E on PA 501 at US 422.* 717/866-6536; FAX 717/866-6536; res: 800/262-5564. 80 rms, 2 story. S $54-$66; D $60-$90; each addl $10; suites $110-$225; cottage $150-$200. Crib free. TV; cable, VCR avail. Playground. Complimentary coffee in rms. Restaurant 7 am-10 pm. Rm serv. Ck-out 11 am. Meeting rms. Business servs avail. Bellhops. Barber, beauty shop. Valet serv. Sundries. Tennis. Early Amer decor. Cr cds: A, C, D, DS, MC, V.

D ⬛ ⬛ ⬛ ⬛ SC

Motor Hotel

★★★ **QUALITY INN.** *625 Quentin Rd (17042), on PA 72.* 717/273-6771; FAX 717/273-4882; res: 800/228-5050; res: 800/228-5151. 56 hotel rms, 74 motel rms, 5 story. Late May-Oct: S $78-$110; D $83-$120; each addl $7; under 18 free; lower rates rest of yr. Crib free. TV; cable. Pool; lifeguard. Restaurant 6 am-9 pm. Rm serv. Bar 11-2 am; entertainment. Ck-out noon. Meeting rms. Business servs avail. Sundries. Barber. Game rm. Cr cds: A, C, D, DS, ER, JCB, MC, V.

D ⬛ ⬛ ⬛ SC

Inn

★★ **SWATARA CREEK INN.** *RR 2 Box 692 (19464), US 81, exit 29.* 717/865-3259. 10 rms, 2 with shower only, 3 story, 1 suite. No rm phones. Apr-Nov: S $45-$70; D $55-$80; suite $115; family rates; Hershey car show (3-day min); lower rates rest of yr. Complimentary full bkfst. Complimentary coffee in sitting rm. Restaurant nearby. Ck-out 11 am, ck-in 3 pm. Concierge serv. Gift shop. Refrigerator on 2nd floor. Some balconies. Picnic tables. Victorian mansion built in 1860; country setting. Cr cds: A, C, D, DS, MC, V.

D ⬛ ⬛ SC

Lewisburg (D-7)

(See also Danville, Williamsport)

Settled 1785 **Pop** 5,785 **Elev** 460 ft **Area Code** 570 **Zip** 17837
E-mail svvb@svvb.com **Web** www.svvb.com
Information Susquehanna Valley Visitors Bureau, RR3, 219-D Hafer Rd; 570/524-7234 or 800/525-7320

Home of Bucknell University (1846), this college community also has light industry. The Native American village of Old Muncy Town was located nearby before the region was opened by Ludwig (Lewis) Doerr.

What to See and Do

Fort Augusta (1757). Museum collection of Northumberland County Historical Society. (Mon, Wed, Fri & Sat) 9 mi SE on PA 147, in Sunbury, at 1150 N Front St. Phone 570/286-4083. **Free**

Packwood House Museum. A 3-story, 27-rm log and frame bldg begun in the late 18th century. Former hostelry houses a wide-ranging collection of Americana, period furnishings, textiles and decorative arts. Changing exhibits; museum shop. Tours. (Daily exc Mon; closed hols) 15 N Water St. Phone 570/524-0323. ¢¢

Slifer House Museum. Elaborate 3-story, 20-rm Victorian mansion. First and second floors have been restored, complete with Victorian parlor, dining room, library, 5 bedrms and the summer kitchen exhibit rm. (Apr–late Dec, daily exc Mon; rest of yr, Tues–Fri afternoons, also by appt; closed hols) 1 mi N, on grounds of Lewisburg United Methodist Homes. Phone 570/524-2245. ¢¢

Walnut Acres Organic Farms. Working organic farm; bakery; cannery; Farm Store with farm-grown items. Self-guided farm tours (daily). Guided plant tours (Mon-Fri; closed hols). (Daily; closed hols) 12 mi SW on PA 45, 7 mi S on PA 104 to Penns Creek. Phone 800/433-3998. **Free**

Motels

★★★ **BEST WESTERN CUPBOARD INN.** *Rte 15 N (17837), I-80 exit 30A, 5 mi S on US 15.* 570/524-5500; FAX 570/524-4291; res: 800/528-1234. 106 rms, 3 story. S $68-$99; D $75-$105; each addl $6; suites $105-$149; under 18 free; higher rates university events. Crib free. TV; cable. Heated pool; lifeguard. Complimentary continental bkfst. Restaurant adj 7 am-9 pm. Ck-out 11 am. Coin lndry. Meeting rms. Business servs avail. Exercise equipt. Game rm. Refrigerator in suites. Cr cds: A, C, D, DS, MC, V.

D ⬛ ⬛ ⬛ ⬛ SC

★★ **DAYS INN.** *US Rte 15 (17837), On US 15, 1 blk S of jct PA 192.* 570/523-1171; FAX 570/524-4667; res: 800/329-7466. 108 rms, 2 story. S $55-$69; D $61-$69; each addl $6; under 16 free. Crib free. TV; cable, VCR avail (movies). Pool; lifeguard. Restaurant adj open 24 hrs. Ck-out noon. Business servs avail. In-rm modem link. Exercise equipt. Cr cds: A, C, D, DS, MC, V.

⬛ ⬛ ⬛ ⬛ SC

Restaurant

✓★★ **COUNTRY CUPBOARD.** *Hafer Rd US 15 (17837), 5 mi S of I-80 exit 30A.* 570/523-3211. Hrs: 7 am-9 pm. Closed Dec 25. Res accepted Mon-Fri. Semi-a la carte: bkfst $2.25-$5.50, lunch, dinner $4.99-$10.99. Buffet: bkfst (Sat, Sun), lunch (Mon-Sat) $5.99, dinner $8.99-$10.99. Child's meals. Specializes in poultry, ham. Country dining. Totally nonsmoking. Cr cds: C, DS, MC, V.

D

Lewistown (E-6)

Settled 1754 **Pop** 9,341 **Elev** 520 ft **Area Code** 717
E-mail jvacc@acsworld.net
Information Juniata Valley Area Chamber of Commerce, 3 W Monument Sq, 17044; 717/248-6713

Surrounded by rich farmland and beautiful forested mountain ranges, Lewistown lies in the scenic Juniata River Valley, in the heart of central Pennsylvania. Lewistown retains the charm of its rustic surroundings, which yearly attract thousands of sportsmen and outdoor enthusiasts to the area's fine hunting, fishing and camping facilities. A large Amish population, which thrives on the farmland of the Kishacoquillas Valley, has contributed greatly to the area's culture and heritage.

What to See and Do

Brookmere Farm Vineyards. In 19th-century stone & wood barn. Winery tour, wine tasting; picnicking. (Mar–Dec, Mon–Sat, also Sun afternoons; rest of yr, daily exc Sun; closed hols) Approx 5 mi N via US 322, then SW on PA 655, near Belleville. Phone 717/935-5380. **Free**

Greenwood Furnace State Park. Remains of Greenwood Works, last iron furnace to operate in area (ca 1833–1904); restored stack. Approx 400 acres. Swimming beach; fishing. Hiking. Snowmobiling, ice skating, ice fishing. Picnicking, playground, snack bar, store. Tent & trailer sites. Visitor center, interpretive program. Standard fees. 5 mi N on US 322, then 9 mi W on PA 655, then NW on PA 305. Phone 814/667-1800.

Reeds Gap State Park. Approx 200 acres. Swimming pool; fishing. Hiking. Picnicking, snack bar, store. Tent sites only. 8 mi N off US 322 & unnumbered road. Phone 717/667-3622. Camping   ¢¢¢—¢¢¢¢

Motel

✓★★ **CLARION INN.** 13015 Ferguson Valley Rd (17009), just off US 322 at Burnham exit. 717/248-4961; FAX 717/242-3013; res: 800/252-7466. 119 rms, 2 story. S, D $59; each addl $5; under 18 free. Crib free. Pet accepted. TV; cable (premium). Pool; poolside serv, lifeguard. Restaurant 6 am-2 pm, 5-10 pm. Rm serv. Bar 4 pm-midnight. Ck-out noon. Meeting rms. In-rm modem link. Valet serv. Cr cds: A, C, D, DS, MC, V.

D ⊁ ⊠ ⊠ ⊠ SC

Ligonier (E-3)

(See also Donegal, Greensburg, Johnstown)

Founded 1816 **Pop** 1,638 **Elev** 1,200 ft **Area Code** 724 **Zip** 15658
E-mail ligonier@ligonier.com **Web** www.ligonier.com
Information Ligonier Valley Chamber of Commerce, Town Hall, 120 E Main St; 724/238-4200

Fort Ligonier, built in 1758 by the British, was the scene of one of the key battles of the French and Indian War. It also served as a supply base during Pontiac's War in 1763.

What to See and Do

Compass Inn Museum. A 1799 stagecoach stop; original log and stone inn authentically restored and furnished; log barn houses Conestoga wagon and stagecoach; cookhouse with beehive oven and fireplace; blacksmith shop contains working forge. (May–Oct, daily exc Mon) 3 mi E on US 30, in Laughlintown. Phone 724/238-4983.   ¢¢

Fort Ligonier. Reconstructed 18th-century British fort; incl bldgs with period furnishings. Museum houses outstanding French and Indian War

collection, 18th-century artifacts; introductory film. (Apr–Oct, daily) (See ANNUAL EVENTS) S Market St, on US 30, PA 711. Phone 724/238-9701.   ¢¢

Idlewild Park. Amusement rides; entertainment; picnicking; children's play area; water park. (Memorial Day–late Aug, daily exc Mon) 2 mi W on US 30. Phone 724/238-3666.   ¢¢¢¢   Adj is

  Story Book Forest. Children's park with animals, people and bldgs portraying nursery rhymes. (Memorial Day–late Aug, daily exc Mon) Phone 724/238-3666. Admission incl with Idlewild Park.

St Vincent Archabbey and College (1846) (1,000 students). Includes Benedictine monastery, seminary and coeducational liberal arts college. St Vincent Theatre has performances at theater-in-the-round; for schedule phone 412/537-8900. Free self-guided tape tours. 8 mi W on US 30, in Latrobe. Phone 724/537-4560.

Annual Events

Ligonier Ice Fest. Professional ice sculptures on the Diamond and in front of businesses; collegiate ice-carving competition. Super Bowl wkend Jan.

Ligonier Highland Games and Gathering of the Clans of Scotland. Idlewild Park. Sports; massed pipe bands, Highland dancing competitions; Scottish fiddling; sheep dog, wool spinning and weaving demonstrations; genealogy booth, Scottish fair. Phone 724/238-3666. 1st Sat after Labor Day.

Fort Ligonier Days. Living history program of the French and Indian War. Parade; 150 juried crafters, food and special events. Usually 2nd wkend Oct.

Seasonal Event

Mountain Playhouse. 11 mi SE on US 30, then ½ mi N on US 985, in Jennerstown. Phone 814/629-9201. Broadway shows in restored gristmill (1805). Matinees and evening performances. Late May–mid-Oct.

Motels

✓★ **FORT LIGONIER MOTOR LODGE.** 11 Rte 30 E (15658), 2 blks S on US 30, jct PA 711. 724/238-6677; FAX 717/746-1217. 35 rms, 2 story. May-Oct: S, D $55-$80; each addl $6; higher rates: wkends, special events; lower rates rest of yr. Crib $4. TV; cable. Pool. Complimentary coffee. Restaurant nearby. Ck-out 11 am. Sundries. Downhill/x-country ski 7 mi. Picnic tables. Trout stream. Cr cds: A, C, MC, V.

⚓ ⊁ ⊠ ⊠ ⊠

★★★ **RAMADA INN.** 216 W Loyalhanna St (15658). 724/238-9545; FAX 724/238-9803; res: 800/272-6232. E-mail goramada@aol.com; web www.goramada.com. 66 rms, 3 story. S, D $65-$95; each addl $6; suites $95-$150; under 12 free; ski plans. Crib free. TV; cable (premium). VCR avail. Pool. Restaurant 6:30 am-10 pm. Rm serv. Bar 4 pm-2 am. Ck-out noon. Meeting rms. Business servs avail. In-rm modem link. Health club privileges. Cr cds: A, C, MC, V.

D ⊠ ⊠ ⊠ SC

Limerick (E-9)

(See also Norristown, Pottstown, Reading)

Pop 800 (est) **Elev** 302 ft **Area Code** 484 & 610 **Zip** 19468
E-mail info@ valleyforge.org **Web** www.valleyforge.org
Information Valley Forge Convention & Visitors Bureau, 600 W Germantown Pike, Suite 130, Plymouth Meeting 19462; 610/834-1550

What to See and Do

Spring Mountain Ski Area. Triple, 3 double chairlifts, 2 rope tows; patrol; school, rentals; snowmaking; cafeteria. Longest run ½ mi; vertical drop 450

ft. Also camping avail (fee; hookups). (Mid-Dec–mid-Mar, daily) 6 mi N, off PA 29 near Schwenksville. Phone 610/287-7900. ¢¢¢¢

Restaurant

✓★★★ **GYPSY ROSE.** *505 Bridge Rd PA 113 (19426), 4 mi S on US 422, exit PA 113, then N 2 mi.* 610/489-1600. Hrs: 11:30 am-10 pm; Fri, Sat to 11 pm; Sun 11 am-9 pm; Sun brunch to 2 pm. Closed some major hols. Res accepted. Bar 11-2 am. Semi-a la carte: lunch $7-$12, dinner $7-$22. Sun brunch $13. Child's meals. Specialties: chicken Philadelphia, Maryland crab cakes. Own baking. Outdoor dining. Farmhouse (1725); views of creek and landscaped garden. Cr cds: A, C, DS, MC, V.

Lock Haven (C-6)

(See also Williamsport)

Founded 1833 **Pop** 9,230 **Elev** 564 ft **Area Code** 570 **Zip** 17745
Information Clinton County Tourist Promotion Agency, Court House Annex, 151 Susquehanna Ave; 570/893-4037

Founded on the site of pre-Revolutionary Fort Reed, the community takes its name from two sources. The lock of the Pennsylvania Canal once crossed the West Branch of the Susquehanna River here, and the town was once a "haven" for the rafts and lumberjacks of nearby logging camps. Near the geographic center of the state, the town today is a center of commerce and small industry.

What to See and Do

Bucktail Natural Area. Scenic area extends from mountain rim to mountain rim for 75 mi from Lock Haven N to Renovo and W to Emporium. Connecting the 3 towns and weaving through the park is PA 120, an outstanding drive through mountain scenery. Historic site W of Renovo commemorates Bucktail Trail, which served pioneers and Civil War volunteers. Fishing.

Bull Run School House (1899). Only remaining one-rm schoolhouse in county; fully restored with all of its original equipment, incl double desks, schoolmaster's and recitation desks, Waterbury clock, bell. (Hrs vary) Phone 570/893-4037. **Free**

Fin, Fur & Feather Wildlife Museum. Personal collection of animals from across the globe. More than 500 animals are mounted on display. Gift shop (yr-round, daily). (Late June-Oct, daily; rest of yr, Fri–Sun, also by appt; closed Dec 25) 18 mi N via PA 664. Phone 570/769-6620 (gift shop) or 570/769-6482. ¢¢

Hyner View. At 2,000 ft, "Laurel Drive to the top of the world" provides panoramic view of valley, river, highway and forest. Site of state and national hang-gliding competitions. 22 mi NW on PA 120.

State parks.
Bald Eagle. A 1,730-acre lake on approx 5,900 acres. Swimming beach; fishing, hunting; boating (rentals, mooring, launching, marina). Hiking. Sledding, ice skating, ice boating. Picnicking, playground, snack bar, store. Tent & trailer sites. Standard fees. 13 mi SW off PA 150. Phone 570/625-2775.

Kettle Creek. Approx 1,600 acres. Winds through beautiful valley developed as tourist area. Swimming beach; fishing, hunting; boating (mooring, launching). Hiking. Bridle trail. Snowmobiling, sledding, ice skating. Picnicking, playground. Tent & trailer sites (electric hookups). Standard fees. 35 mi NW on PA 120 to Westport, then 7 mi N on SR 4001. Phone 570/923-6004.

The Heisey Museum. Victorian house-museum; early 1800s kitchen; ice house containing logging, farming and canal artifacts. (Tues–Fri; also by appt) 362 E Water St. Phone 570/748-7254. **Donation**

Annual Event

Flaming Foliage Festival. 29 mi NW on PA 120, in Renovo. Includes parade, craft show and contest for festival queen. Phone 570/923-2411. 2nd wkend Oct.

Inn

★★ **VICTORIAN INN BED & BREAKFAST.** *402 E Water St (17745).* 570/748-8688; FAX 570/748-2444. 13 rms, 2 with shower only, 2 share bath, 2 story. S $55-$60; D $60-$65; each addl $10. Adults only. Pet accepted. TV. Complimentary full bkfst. Restaurant nearby. Ck-out 1 pm, ck-in 2 pm. Health club privileges. Built in 1859; garden atrium. Cr cds: A, C, D, DS, MC, V.

Manheim (E-8)

(See also Cornwall, Lancaster, Lebanon)

Founded 1762 **Pop** 5,011 **Elev** 400 ft **Area Code** 717 **Zip** 17545
E-mail MACC@redrose.net **Web** www.redrose.net/macc
Information Manheim Area Chamber of Commerce, 210 S Charlotte St; 717/665-6330

Baron Henry William Stiegel founded Manheim and started manufacturing the flint glassware that bore his name. In 1770 he owned the town; by 1774 he was in debtor's prison, the victim of his own generosity and his poor choice of business associates. After his imprisonment, he made a meager living teaching here.

What to See and Do

✪ **Mt Hope Estate & Winery.** Restored sandstone mansion was originally built in the Federal style (ca 1800), then increased its size to 32 rms from an extension built in 1895, which changed the house's style to Victorian. Turrets, winding walnut staircase, hand-painted 18-ft ceilings, Egyptian marble fireplaces, grand ballroom, crystal chandeliers; greenhouse, solarium, gardens. Vineyards on grounds; wine tasting in billiards rm. (Daily; closed Jan 1, Thanksgiving, Dec 25) (See SEASONAL EVENT) ½ mi S of exit 20 at jct PA 72 & PA Tpke. Phone 717/665-7021. ¢¢

Zion Lutheran Church (1891). Victorian Gothic structure built on site of original church; Stiegel donated the ground (1772) in exchange for one red rose from the congregation every yr. (Mon–Fri) 2 S Hazel St, 1 blk E of PA 72. Phone 717/665-5880.

Annual Event

Rose Festival. Celebration during which Stiegel descendant accepts annual rent of one red rose for church grounds. 2nd Sun June.

Seasonal Event

Pennsylvania Renaissance Faire. Mt Hope Estate & Winery. A 16th-century village is created in the acres of gardens surrounding the mansion. Eleven stages incl a jousting arena with capacity of 6,000. Highlights incl medieval jousting tournament, trial and dunking, human chess match, knighthood ceremonies. Wkends, Aug–mid-Oct.

Mansfield (B-6)

(See also Wellsboro)

Pop 3,538 **Elev** 1,120 ft **Area Code** 570 **Zip** 16933
E-mail mwwacc@epix.net **Web** www.epix.net~mwwacc/
Information Wellsboro Area Chamber of Commerce, 114 Main St, PO Box 733, Wellsboro 16901; 570/724-1926

What to See and Do

Cowanesque Lake. Same facilities as Tioga-Hammond Lakes. (May–Sept) 15 mi N on US 15 to Lawrenceville, then 3½ mi W on Bliss Rd. Phone 570/835-5281.

Hills Creek State Park. Approx 400 acres. Swimming beach; fishing for muskellunge, largemouth bass, walleye in Hills Creek Lake; boating (rentals, mooring, launching). Hiking. Sledding, ice skating, ice fishing. Picnicking, playground, snack bar, store. Tent & trailer sites, cabins. Interpretive program. Standard fees. 6 mi W, then N on unnumbered road. Phone 570/724-4246.

Tioga-Hammond Lakes. Twin lakes and dams for flood control and recreation. Swimming; fishing, hunting; boating. Trails. Picnicking. Camping (fee; some sites free). (Late Apr–Dec) 10 mi N on US 15, then 7 mi SW on PA 287. Phone 570/835-5281.

Motel

★★ **COMFORT INN.** *300 Gateway Dr (16933). 570/662-3000; FAX 570/662-2551; res: 800/822-5470.* 100 rms, 2 story. S $49-$75; D $59-$85; each addl $6; under 18 free; golf plans; higher rates seasonal events. Crib avail. Pet accepted. TV; cable. Complimentary continental bkfst. Ck-out noon. Business servs avail. Exercise equipt. Cr cds: A, C, D, DS, ER, JCB, MC, V.

Meadville (B-2)

(See also Conneaut Lake, Franklin)

Settled 1788 **Pop** 14,318 **Elev** 1,100 ft **Area Code** 814 **Zip** 16335
E-mail welcome@visitcrawford.org **Web** www.visitcrawford.org
Information Crawford County Convention & Visitors Bureau, 242½ Chestnut St; 814/333-1258 or 800/332-2338

David Mead—Revolutionary War ensign, tavernkeeper and major-general in the War of 1812—and his brothers established Mead's Settlement in 1788. Colonel Lewis Walker started manufacture of hookless slide fasteners here; since 1923 these fasteners (now known as "zippers") have been the leading local industry. The city is also a major producer of yarn and thread and is home to many tool-and-die manufacturers.

What to See and Do

Allegheny College (1815) (1,850 students). Bentley Hall (1820) is a fine example of Federalist architecture. Also on campus are Bowman, Penelec & Megahan Art Galleries (Phone 814/332-4365 for schedule). Library has colonial, Ida Tarbell and Lincoln collections. Tours of campus. N Main St. Phone 814/332-3100.

Baldwin-Reynolds House Museum (1841-1843). Restored mansion of Henry Baldwin, congressman and US Supreme Court justice. First and second floors refurbished in period; basement exhibits 19th-century kitchen and Land Office. Also on grounds is 1890 doctor's office. Elaborate landscaping on 3-acre grounds feature pond and icehouse. Tours (Late May–Labor Day, Wed-Sun). 639 Terrace St. Phone 814/724-6080. ¢¢

Colonel Crawford Park. Within park is Woodcock Creek Lake. Swimming (fee); fishing, hunting; boating. Nature trail. Picnicking. Camping (fee). Park (Memorial Day–Labor Day, daily). 6 mi NE via PA 86, PA 198. Phone 814/724-6879 (summer) or 814/333-7372 (Memorial Day-Labor Day). Camping per night. ¢¢¢

Erie National Wildlife Refuge. Over 250 species of birds, as well as woodchuck, white-tailed deer, fox, beaver and muskrat are found on this 8,750-acre refuge. Fishing and hunting permitted; regulations at refuge office. Nature and ski trails; overlook; photo blind. Office, 10 mi E on the outskirts of the village of Guys Mills (Mon–Fri). Refuge (daily). 10 mi E on PA 27. Phone 814/789-3585. **Free**

Annual Event

Crawford County Fair. 3rd wk Aug.

Motel

★★ **DAYS INN.** *18360 Conneaut Lake Rd (16335), I-79 exit 36A. 814/337-4264; FAX 814/337-7304; res: 800/329-7466.* 163 rms, 2 story. S $65-$85; D $70-$86; each addl $6; under 18 free; higher rates special events. Crib free. Pet accepted. TV; cable (premium), VCR avail (movies). Indoor pool; whirlpool. Restaurant 7 am-2 pm, 5-10 pm; Sun 7 am-2 pm. Bar 3 pm-2 am. Ck-out 11 am. Coin lndry. Meeting rms. Business servs avail. Cr cds: A, C, D, DS, JCB, MC, V.

Media (F-9)

(See also Chester, Kennett Square, King of Prussia, Philadelphia, West Chester)

Pop 5,957 **Elev** 300 ft **Area Code** 484 & 610 **E-mail** delcocvb@liberty net.org **Web** www.delcocvb.org
Information Delaware County Convention & Visitors Bureau, 200 E State St, Suite 100, 19063; 610/565-3679 or 800/343-3983

What to See and Do

Franklin Mint Museum. Houses original works by Andrew Wyeth and Norman Rockwell; collectibles on display, incl books, dolls, jewelry, furniture; artworks in porcelain, bronze, pewter, crystal and precious metals; one of the world's largest private mints. (Daily; closed major hols) 4 mi SW on US 1. Phone 610/459-6168. **Free**

Newlin Mill Park. Park with operating stone gristmill (1704), furnished miller's house (1739), springhouse, blacksmith shop; milling exhibit. Tours, picnicking, fishing, nature trails. (Daily) 7 mi SW via US 1, in Glen Mills. Phone 610/459-2359. Guided tour ¢

Ridley Creek State Park. Approx 2,600 acres of woodlands and meadows. Fishing. Hiking, bicycling. Sledding. Picnicking, playground. S on US 1, then N on PA 352. Phone 610/892-3900. Within park is

   Colonial Pennsylvania Plantation. A 200-yr-old farm is a living history museum that re-creates the life of a typical farm family of the late 1700s. Period tools and methods are used to perform seasonal and daily chores. Tours (Tues–Sat, by appt). Visitors may participate in some activities. (Mid-Apr–Nov, Sat & Sun) Phone 610/566-1725. ¢¢

Tyler Arboretum. 650 acres of ornamental and native plants. Outdoor "living museum" with a 20-mi system of trails; special fragrant garden and bird garden; notable trees planted in the 1800s; bookstore. Guided walks and educational programs each wk; phone 610/566-5431. ¢¢

Restaurants

★★★ **D'IGNAZIO'S TOWNE HOUSE.** *117 Veterans Square (19063). 610/566-6141.* Hrs: 11:30 am-3 pm, 4:30-10 pm; Fri, Sat to 10:30 pm; Sun 4-8:30 pm. Closed some major hols. Res accepted. Bar to midnight; Fri, Sat to 1 am; Sun 4-9 pm. Wine cellar. A la carte entrees: lunch $6-$12, dinner $10-$20. Child's meals. Specializes in prime rib, seafood, Italian specialties. Pianist Tues-Sat. Singing maitre'd. Many stone fireplaces; extensive collection of memorabilia, antiques and personal photographs. Family-owned. Cr cds: A, C, DS, MC, V.

✓ ★ **PACKY'S PUB.** *113 W State St (19063). 610/891-0810.* Hrs: 11:30-2 am; Sat, Sun from noon; Sat, Sun brunch to 4 pm; summer hrs vary. Res accepted Sun-Thurs. Bar. Semi-a la carte: lunch $5-$8, dinner $7-$15. Sat, Sun brunch $5-$8. Specializes in home-cooked roast pork, giant burgers, pub salads. Musicians Fri, Sat. Pub atmosphere. Cr cds: A, C, DS, MC, V.

Mercer (C-1)

(See also Franklin)

Settled 1795 **Pop** 2,444 **Elev** 1,270 ft **Area Code** 724 **Zip** 16137
Information Mercer Area Chamber of Commerce, PO Box 473; 724/662-4185

What to See and Do

Magoffin House Museum (1821). Houses collection of Native American artifacts, pioneer tools, furniture, children's toys, clothing; military items. Some original furnishings; memorabilia. Special collection of artifacts from John Goodsell's trip to the North Pole with Peary in 1908-1909, as well as early maps, historic records; restored print shop. Office of Mercer County Historical Society is located in the **Anderson House**, just off Court House Sq. (Tues–Sat; closed hols) 119 S Pitt St. Phone 724/662-3490.   **Free**

Wendell August Forge, Inc. Creators of hand-hammered aluminum, bronze, copper, pewter, sterling silver and glass and crystal items handcut on stone wheel lathe; also limited-edition collectors' items. Gift shop. Self-guided tours (15–30 min). (Daily; closed hols) 10 mi SE on PA 58, in Grove City at 620 Madison Ave. Phone 724/458-8360.   **Free**

Annual Event

Penn's Woods West—Folk & Arts Festival. Mercer Area High School, W Butler St. Fine arts and country crafts. 130 artisans, live entertainment and demonstrations, children's activities, home-cooked foods. Phone 412/662-1490. Mid Feb.

Motel

★ ★ ★ **HOWARD JOHNSON INN.** *835 Perry Hwy (16137), Rte 19S, just off I-80 exit 2. 724/748-3030; FAX 724/748-3484; res: 800/542-7674.* 102 rms, 2 story. S $67; D $71-$74; each addl $6; suites $105-$125; under 18 free; higher rates special events. Crib free. Pet accepted. TV; cable (premium), VCR avail. Heated pool; lifeguard. Playground. Coffee in rms. Restaurant 6 am-midnight. Rm serv. Bar. Ck-out noon. Coin lndry. Meeting rms. Business servs avail. In-rm modem link. Bellhops. Bus depot transportation. Exercise equipt; sauna. Private patios, balconies. Amish craft shop in lobby. Cr cds: A, C, D, DS, MC, V.

Restaurant

✓ ★ ★ **TIMBERS RESTAURANT & LOUNGE.** *101 Timber Ln (16137), on US 62. 724/662-4533.* Hrs: 3-10 pm; Fri, Sat 11:30 am-11 pm;

Sun 11 am-8 pm. Closed Mon; major hols. Bar. Complete meals: dinner $6.95-$13.95. Child's meals. Specializes in seafood, prime rib. Rustic atmosphere; in converted barn (1872). Cr cds: A, C, DS, MC, V.

Milford (C-10)

(See also Bushkill, Delaware Water Gap)

Settled 1733 **Pop** 1,064 **Elev** 503 ft **Area Code** 570 **Zip** 18337
E-mail pocomts@poconos.org **Web** www.poconos.org
Information Pocono Mts Vacation Bureau, 1004 Main St, Stroudsburg 18360; 570/424-6050; for free brochures phone 800/POCONOS.

The borough of Milford was settled by Thomas Quick, a Hollander. Governor Gifford Pinchot, noted forester and conservationist, lived here. His house, Grey Towers, is near the town.

What to See and Do

Canoeing, rafting, kayaking and tubing. Kittatinny Canoes. Trips travel down the Delaware River. Camping. (Mid-Apr–Oct, daily) S to Dingmans Ferry via US 209, then ½ mi E via PA 739 S, at Dingmans Ferry toll bridge. Phone 570/828-2338 or 800/FLOAT-KC.   ¢¢¢¢¢

Dingmans Falls & Silver Thread Falls. Part of Delaware Water Gap National Recreation Area (see). Two of the highest waterfalls in the Pocono Mts; many rhododendrons bloom in July. 8 mi S & W on US 209 near Dingmans Ferry. Phone 570/588-2451.   **Free**

Grey Towers (1886). A 100-acre estate originally built as summer house for philanthropist James W. Pinchot; became residence of his son, Gifford Pinchot, "father of American conservation," governor of Pennsylvania and first chief of USDA Forest Service. Now site of Pinchot Institute for Conservation Studies. Tours. (Memorial Day–Labor Day, daily; after Labor Day–Veterans Day, Fri–Mon afternoons; rest of yr, by appt; occasionally closed for conferences) Phone 570/296-6401. **Donation**

Motels

★ ★ ★ **BEST WESTERN INN.** *120 Rte 6; Rte 209 (18336), 6 mi E on I-84, exit 11. 570/491-2400; FAX 570/491-2422; res: 800/308-2378.* 108 rms, 4 story. May-Oct: S $69-$75; D $77-$85; each addl $6; suites $115-$125; under 12 free; lower rates rest of yr. Crib free. Pet accepted. TV; cable. Indoor pool; lifeguard. Sauna. Restaurant 6:30 am-9 pm; Fri, Sat to 10 pm; Sun from 7 am. Bar 4-11 pm; entertainment. Ck-out 11 am. Coin lndry. Meeting rms. Business servs avail. In-rm modem link. Sundries. Gift shop. Game rm. Lawn games. Cr cds: A, C, D, DS, MC, V.

✓ ★ ★ **MYER MOTEL.** *600 Rte 6 & Rte 209 (18337), ¼ mi E on US 6, PA 209. 570/296-7223; res: 800/764-6937.* 19 cottages, 1 kit S $40-$50; D $45-$70; each addl $5; kit unit $90. Crib free. Pet accepted, some restrictions. TV; cable. Restaurant nearby. Ck-out 11 am. Lawn games. Refrigerators. Picnic tables, grills. Cr cds: A, C, D, DS, MC, V.

Inns

★ **BLACK WALNUT BED & BREAKFAST COUNTRY INN.** *179 Fire Tower Rd (18337), Firetower Rd, 2 mi E off US 6, I-84 exit 10, 1 mi, follow signs. 570/296-6322; FAX 570/296-7696.* 12 rms, 8 with bathrm, 2 story. No A/C. D $60-$100; hols (2-day min). TV in sitting rm; movies. Dining rm 8:30-10 am; 5:30-9 pm; closed Mon-Thur. Ck-out

11 am, ck-in 3 pm. Rec rm. Tudor-style stone house; marble fireplace; some antiques. 160-acre estate on the bank of a 5-acre stocked pond; paddleboats, rowboats. Cr cds: A, C, MC, V.

★★★ **CLIFF PARK INN.** *155 Cliff Park Rd (18337), 1 ½ mi W of PA 6, on 6th St to Cliff Park Rd.* 570/296-6491; FAX 570/296-3982; res: 800/225-6535. 18 rms, 1-3 story. S $82.50-$140; D $95-$205; EP, MAP avail; wkend rates. Dining rm 8-10 am, noon-3 pm, 6-9 pm. Business servs avail. In-rm modem link. 9-hole golf, greens fee $6-$13, pro, putting green, rentals. X-country ski; rentals. Hiking trails. Near Delaware River. Classic country inn; originally a farmhouse built 1820. Some fireplaces. Screened porches. Cr cds: A, C, D, DS, MC, V.

★★ **PINE HILL FARM BED & BREAKFAST.** *Cummins Hill Rd (18337), 2½ mi N on US 6, PA 209 (Broad St); left on Cummins Hill Rd; turn at the first Pine Hill Farm sign and continue on a 1-mi climb on a public access road.* 570/296-7395. 3 rms in main house, 2 story, 2 suites in adj cottage. No rm phones. S $75-$100; D $85-$110; each addl $25; suites $100-$110; hols (2-night min). Adults only. TV in some rms and sitting rm. Complimentary full bkfst. Ck-out 11 am, ck-in 3 pm. Bellman. X-country ski on site. Main house was the original farmhouse (ca 1870); fireplace, many antique furnishings. Located atop hill overlooking the Delaware River. Includes 268 acres of fields and forests, with 5 mi of 1800s logging trails for walking, birdwatching. Cr cds: C, DS, MC, V.

Monroeville

(see Pittsburgh)

Mount Pocono (C-9)

(See also Pocono Mountains)

Pop 1,795 **Elev** 1,840 ft **Area Code** 570 **Zip** 18344
E-mail pocomts@poconos.org **Web** www.poconos.org
Information Pocono Mts Vacation Bureau, Inc, 1004 Main St, Stroudsburg 18360; 570/424-6050; for brochures phone 800/POCONOS.

One of the many thriving resort communities in the heart of the Pocono Mountains, Mount Pocono offers recreation year round in nearby parks, lakes and ski areas.

What to See and Do

Gouldsboro State Park. 2,800 acres; 250-acre lake. Swimming beach; fishing, hunting; boating (rentals, mooring, launching). Hiking. ice skating, ice fishing. Standard fees. 10 mi N on PA 611 & I-380, then NE on PA 507. Phone 570/894-8336.

Memorytown, USA. Old-time village incl hex shop, country store, store with artifacts; ice-cream parlor; paddle-boats, mini-raceway, fishing; entertainment; lodging, picnic area, restaurant and tavern. Summer festivals. Fee for some activities. (June–Sept, daily; Mar–May, Fri–Sun) 2 mi E via PA 940. Phone 570/839-1680.   **Free**

Mount Airy Lodge Ski Area. 2 double chairlifts; patrol, school, rentals; snowmaking; cafeteria, restaurant, bar; nursery, lodge. Longest run 1,800 ft; vertical drop 240 ft. Also cross-country trails. (Mid-Dec–late Mar) Just E of town via PA 940. Phone 570/839-8811.   ¢¢¢¢¢

Pocono Knob. Excellent view of surrounding countryside. 1½ mi E on Knob Rd.

Tobyhanna State Park. Approx 5,440 acres with 170-acre lake. Swimming beach; fishing, hunting; boating (rentals, mooring, launching). Hiking, biking. Cross-country skiing. Snowmobiling, ice skating, ice fishing. Tent & trailer sites. Standard fees. 5 mi N on PA 611, then NE on PA 423. Phone 570/894-8336.

Motels

✓★ **HAMPTON INN.** *Rte 940 E (18344), 1 ½ mi E on PA 940.* 570/839-2119; FAX 570/839-6982. 14 rms. No rm phones. S $45-$50; D $55-$65; each addl $8. TV; cable. Pool. Restaurant 5-10 pm; wkends to 11 pm; closed Tues. Ck-out 11 am. Cr cds: A, C, D, MC, V.

★★ **MEMORYTOWN.** *Hc 1 Box 10 (18344).* 570/839-1680; FAX 570/839-5846. E-mail memorytown@aol.com. 30 rms, all with shower only. No A/C. No rm phones. May-Oct: S $109; D $118-$138; each addl $70; family rates; package plans; hols 2-day min; higher rates special events; lower rates rest of yr. Pet accepted. TV; cable. Complimentary continental bkfst; full bkfst wkends. Restaurant 11 am-8 pm. Ck-out 11 am, ck-in 3 pm. Gift shop. Downhill ski 10 mi; x-country ski on site. Playground. Game rm. Lawn games. Some fireplaces. Picnic tables. On lake. Built in 1890; antiques. Country store, farmhouse on premises. Cr cds: A, C, D, DS, MC, V.

★★ **SUPER 8 MOTEL.** *Rte 611 (18344), 1½ mi S on PA 611.* 570/839-7728; FAX 570/839-7729; res: 800/800-8000. 37 rms. May-Sept: S $58-$135; D $65-$135; each addl $5; lower rates rest of yr. Crib free. TV; cable. Pool; whirlpool. Playground. Restaurant 6 am-10 pm. Ck-out 11 am. Business servs avail. Sundries. Downhill ski 5 mi. Private patios, picnic tables. Cr cds: A, C, D, DS, MC, V.

Resorts

★★★ **CAESARS PARADISE STREAM.** *Rte 940 (18344), 3 mi E on PA 940.* 570/839-8881; FAX 570/839-1842; res: 800/233-4141. 164 rms. MAP: D $260-$335; wkly rates. Couples only. TV; cable, VCR avail (movies $5). 2 pools, 1 indoor; whirlpool, poolside serv, lifeguard. Rm serv limited hrs. Snack bar. Bar noon-2 am. Ck-out 11 am, ck-in 3 pm. Business servs avail. Concierge. Grocery, package store. Sundries. Bus depot transportation. Tennis. Miniature golf. Bicycles. Boats, paddleboats. Snowmobiles available. Lawn games. Soc dir; entertainment. Game rm. Exercise equipt; sauna. Hiking trails. Archery. Some fireplaces. Cr cds: A, C, D, DS, MC, V.

★★★ **POCONO MANOR INN & GOLF CLUB.** *Route 314 (18349), on PA 314, 2 mi W of PA 611 in Pocono Manor.* 570/839-7111; FAX 570/839-0708; res: 800/233-8150. Web www.poconomanor.com. 190 rms in inn, 65 in 2 lodges. MAP: S $119; D $198; each addl $50; under 8 free; higher rates special events. Crib $7. Serv charge. TV. Indoor/outdoor pool; poolside serv, lifeguard. Free supervised child's activities. Dining rm (public by res) 7:30-9 am, noon-1 pm, 6:30-8:30 pm. Rm serv. Box lunches, snacks. Bar 11-2 am. Ck-out 11 am, ck-in 4 pm. Business servs avail. In-rm modem link. Bellhops. Grocery, package store 2 mi. Bus depot transportation. Sports dir. Tennis, pro. 36-hole golf, pro, putting green, driving range. Trapshooting. Artificial ice rink, sleigh rides. Indoor, outdoor games. Bicycles. Soc dir. Entertainment. Rec rm; library. Exercise equipt; sauna. Extra fee for some activities. On 3,100-acre mountain estate. Cr cds: A, C, D, MC, V.

Inns

★★★ **FRENCH MANOR.** *Rte 191 S , Huckleberry Rd (18460), N on PA 196, E on PA 423, then continue N on PA 191, left on Huckleberry Rd.* 570/676-3244; FAX 570/676-9786; res: 800/523-8200. 9 rms, 3 story. No rm phones. S, D $165-$180. Adults only. TV in sitting rm. Indoor pool privileges. Dining rm (public by res; jacket required) 8:30-10 am, noon-2 pm, 6-9 pm. Rm serv. Ck-out 11 am, ck-in 2 pm. Airport, bus depot transportation. X-country ski on premises. French chateau-style; Spanish slate roof; patio; 38-ft high dining rm with beamed ceilings; Great Hall has 2 floor-to-ceiling fireplaces. Antiques. Cr cds: A, C, DS, MC, V.

★★★ **STERLING INN.** *RR 191 (18460), N on PA 196, E on PA 423, N on PA 191.* 570/676-3311; FAX 570/676-9786; res: 800/523-8200. 54 units, 3 story, 16 suites, 4 cottages. MAP: S $75-$95, D $140-$160; suites, cottages $190-$220; family, wkly rates; ski, golf plans; lower rates mid-wk. Crib $10. TV in some rms; cable. Indoor pool; whirlpool. Dining rm 8-10 am, noon-1:30 pm, 6-8:30 pm. Ck-out 11 am, ck-in 2 pm. Business servs avail. Airport, bus depot transportation. Tennis. Downhill ski 10 mi; x-country ski on site, rentals. Sleigh rides. Rec rm. Lawn games. On lake. Built in 1850s; country and Victorian suites. Some fireplaces. Cr cds: A, C, DS, MC, V.

Restaurants

★ **TAVERN BY THE LAKE.** *HC 1, Box 10 (18344).* 570/839-1680. E-mail memorytown@aol.com. Hrs: 11 am-8 pm; Fri to midnight; Sat to 2 am. Res required Sat (dinner). Bar. A la carte entrees: lunch, dinner $5.50-$16.95. Specializes in chili, beef, chicken. Country music Fri-Sun. Parking. Outdoor dining. Cr cds: A, C, D, DS, MC, V.

★ **TOKYO TEAHOUSE.** *RR 940 (18346), 3 mi W, off I-380 exit 8.* 570/839-8880. Hrs: 11:30 am-10 pm. Closed Tues in July, Aug. Res accepted. Japanese menu. Semi-a la carte: lunch $4.95-$7, dinner $7.25-$19.95. Specialties: sushi, steak takiki. Cr cds: A, C, D, DS, MC, V.

New Castle (D-1))

(See also Beaver Falls, Harmony)

Settled 1798 **Pop** 28,334 **Elev** 860 ft **Area Code** 724
E-mail tourlc@ncconnect.com **Web** www.lawrencecounty.com/tourism
Information Lawrence County Tourist Promotion Agency, Celli Central Station, 229 S Jefferson, 16101; 724/654-8408

At the junction of the Shenango, Mahoning and Beaver rivers, this was long an important Native American trading center; the Delawares used it as their capital. Today, the fireworks and plastics industries have become an integral part of the community.

What to See and Do

Greer House. Turn-of-the-century restored mansion houses the Lawrence County Historical Society. Museum has extensive Shenango China and Castleton China collections, Sports Hall of Fame, fireworks rm. Archives; workshops and speakers. (Wed, Sun; also by appt) 408 N Jefferson. Phone 724/658-4022. **Donation**

Hoyt Institute of Fine Arts. Cultural arts center housed in 2 early 20th-century mansions on 4 acres of landscaped grounds; permanent art collection, changing exhibits, period rms, performing arts programs, classes. Tours. (Tues-Sat; closed major hols) 124 E Leasure Ave. Phone 724/652-2882. **Donation**

Living Treasures Animal Park. Pet and feed over 100 species from around the world. (Memorial Day-Labor Day, daily; May, Sept, Oct, wkends) On US 422. Phone 724/924-9571. ¢¢¢

McConnell's Mill State Park. Approx 2,500 acres. Century-old mill surrounded by beautiful landscape and scenery. Fishing, hunting; whitewater boating. Hiking. Picnicking, store. Historical center, interpretive program. Standard fees. 12 mi E via US 422. Phone 724/368-8091 or 724/368-8811.

Scottish Rite Cathedral. On hillside, six 32-ft columns dominate city's skyline. Large auditorium; cathedral; ballrm. Local Masonic headquarters. Tours (by appt). Highland & Lincoln Aves. Phone 724/654-6683. ¢

Motel

✓★★ **COMFORT INN.** *1740 New Butler Rd (16101), 11 mi W on US 422 Business.* 724/658-7700; FAX 724/658-7727; res: 800/228-5150. 79 rms, 2 story, 13 suites. S $66-$72; D $78-$88; each addl $6; suites $96-$124; under 18 free; wkly, wkend rates; higher rates: July 4, Dec 31. Crib free. Pet accepted, some restrictions; $6/day. TV; cable. Complimentary continental bkfst. Restaurant nearby. Ck-out noon. Meeting rm. Business servs avail. Valet serv. Exercise equipt; sauna. Some refrigerators. Cr cds: A, C, D, DS, JCB, MC, V.

New Hope (Bucks Co) (E-10)

(See also Doylestown; also see Lambertville & Trenton, NJ)

Founded 1681 **Pop** 1,400 **Elev** 76 ft **Area Code** 215 & 267 **Zip** 18938
E-mail buckscountycvb@buckscountycvb.org
Web www.buckscountycvb.org
Information Information Center, 1 W Mechanic St, PO Box 633, phone 215/862-5880 or Bucks County Conference and Visitors Bureau, Inc, 152 Swamp Rd, Doylestown 18901, phone 215/345-4552 or 800/836-2825

The river village of New Hope was originally the largest part of a 1,000-acre land grant from William Penn to Thomas Woolrich of Shalford, England. In the 20th century, the area gained fame as the home of artists, literary and theatrical personalities.

What to See and Do

Bucks County River Country. On the Delaware River; two- to four-hr canoeing, rafting, tubing and kayaking trips; one-day outings to full vacation trips. (Apr–Oct) Bucks County River Country, PO Box 6, Point Pleasant 18950. Phone 215/297-5000. ¢¢¢—¢¢¢¢¢

Coryell's Ferry. Passenger and charter rides aboard the *Major William C. Barnett*, a 65-ft Mississippi-style, stern-wheel riverboat, on the Delaware River. (Memorial Day-Labor Day, daily; call for extended season) 22 S Main St. Phone 215/862-2050. ¢¢

Ghost Tours. Follow a lantern-led walk to learn about the area's ghosts. (Sept-Nov, Fri & Sat eves; June-Aug, Sat eve only) Main & Ferry Sts. Phone 215/957-9988. ¢¢¢

New Hope & Ivyland Railroad. A 9-mi, 50-min narrated train ride through Bucks County. Reading Railroad passenger coaches from the 1920s depart from restored 1890 New Hope Station. Gift shop. (Early Apr–Nov, daily; Dec, special Santa Train Fri–Sun; rest of yr, wkends) W Bridge St, adj to Delaware Canal. Phone 215/862-2332. ¢¢¢

Parry Barn (1784). Owned by New Hope Historical Society; operated as commercial art gallery. S Main St, opp mansion. **Free**

Parry Mansion Museum (1784). Restored stone house built by Benjamin Parry, prosperous merchant and mill owner. Eleven rms on view, restored and furnished to depict period styles from late 18th to early 20th centuries. (May–Dec, Fri–Sun; also by appt) S Main & Ferry Sts. Phone 215/862-5652 or 215/862-5460. ¢¢

Peddler's Village. 18th-century-style village featuring over 70 specialty shops, 8 restaurants, 60-rm inn (see INNS), festivals and craft competitions throughout the yr (see ANNUAL EVENTS). 42 acres with landscaped gardens and walkways. (Daily) 5 mi S on US 202 in Lahaska. Phone 215/794-4000. Also in village is

Carousel World. Learn about history of the carousel in turn-of-the-century park. Antique carousel rides. Gift shop. (Daily) Phone 215/794-8960. Carousel rides ¢

Washington Crossing Historical Park (see). 7 mi S on PA 32.

Annual Events

Teddy Bear's Picnic. Peddler's Village. Teddy bear vendors, parades, competitions. "Bear clinic" for hurt bears. Appraisals. Music. Phone 215/794-4000. Mid-July.

Scarecrow Festival. Peddler's Village. Scarecrow making, pumpkin painting. Jack-O-Lantern & Gourd Art Contest. Square dancing, entertainment. Phone 215/794-4000. Mid-Sept.

New Hope Arts and Crafts Festival. Contemporary & traditional crafts. Painting, photography, sculpture. Phone 215/862-5880. Early Oct.

Inns

★★★ **1740 HOUSE.** *3390 River Rd (18933), 7 mi N on PA 32.* 215/297-5661; FAX 215/297-5956. 24 rms. Wkends (Sat 2-day min), hols (3-4-day min): D $113; lower rates wkdays. Pool. Complimentary buffet bkfst. Ck-out noon, ck-in 2 pm. Meeting rms. Business servs avail. Balconies. Overlooks Delaware River. Cr cds: C.

★★★ **AARON BURR HOUSE.** *80 W Bridge St (18938).* 215/862-2343; FAX 215/862-2570. Web www.travelguide.com/bb/aaronburr. 5 rms, 2 story, 2 suites. S, D $80-$150; each addl $20; suite $160-$205; wkly rates; lower rates mid-wk. Pet accepted. TV in sitting rm; cable, VCR avail. Swimming privileges. Complimentary full bkfst; afternoon refreshments. Restaurant nearby. Ck-out 11 am, ck-in 2 pm. Meeting rm. Business servs avail. Concierge. Free bus depot transportation. Downhill ski 2 mi; x-country ski adj. Tennis privileges. Golf privileges. Health club privileges. Lawn games. Fireplace in suites. Built in 1873; some antiques. Screened flagstone patio. Totally nonsmoking. Cr cds: C, MC, V.

★★★ **BARLEY SHEAF FARM BED & BREAKFAST.** *5281 York Rd (18928), approx 7 mi S on US 202.* 215/794-5104; FAX 215/794-5332. E-mail barleysheaf@netreach.net; web www.netreach.net/~barley sheaf. 12 rms, 3 story. Rm phones avail. July-Oct, wkends: D $140-$255; each addl $20; lower rates rest of yr. TV in sitting rm; cable, VCR avail. Pool. Complimentary full bkfst; afternoon refreshments. Ck-out 11 am, ck-in 2 pm. Meeting rms. Business servs avail. In-rm modem link. Lawn games. Thirty-acre farmhouse; built in 1740. Totally nonsmoking. Cr cds: A, C, MC, V.

★★★ **CENTRE BRIDGE INN.** *2998 N Iver Rd (18938), PA 32 & PA 263.* 215/862-2048; FAX 215/862-3244. E-mail centreinn@aol.com; web www.letsmakeplans.com/centrebridgeinn. 9 rms, 2 story. No rm phones. D $80-$150; each addl $15. TV; cable. Complimentary continental bkfst. Restaurant (see CENTRE BRIDGE). Bar. Ck-out noon, ck-in 3 pm. Business servs avail. Sitting rm and terrace overlook river. Fireplace; antiques. Cr cds: A, C, MC, V.

★★★ **EVERMAY ON THE DELAWARE.** *889 River Rd (18920), 13 mi N on PA 32.* 610/294-9100; FAX 610/294-8249. E-mail moffly@evermay.com; web www.evermay.com. 16 rms, 4 story. No elvtrs. S $95-$150; D $115-$195; suite $250; guest house $150; wkends (2-day min). Children over 13 yrs only. TV in common rm; cable, VCR avail. Complimentary continental bkfst. Restaurant (see EVERMAY ON-THE-DELAWARE). Ck-out noon, ck-in 2 pm. Business servs avail. In-rm modem link.

X-country ski on-site. Game rm. Rec rm. Lawn games. Some fireplaces. On river. Built in 1790; classic Federal structure with Victorian antiques. On 25 acres. Totally nonsmoking. Cr cds: C, MC, V.

★★★ **FOX & HOUND BED & BREAKFAST OF NEW HOPE.** *246 W Bridge St (18938).* 215/862-5082; FAX 215/862-5082; res: 800/862-5082. Web www.visitbucks.com/foxandhound. 8 rms, 3 story. Some rm phones. S, D $65-$170; wkend rates. Children over 12 yrs only. Pet accepted. TV avail; cable. Complimentary continental bkfst; full bkfst on wkends. Restaurant nearby. Ck-out 11 am, ck-in 1:30 pm. Business servs avail. Luggage handling. Free bus depot transportation. Health club privileges. Picnic tables. Stone manor house built in 1850. Cr cds: A, C, MC, V.

★★★ **GOLDEN PHEASANT INN.** *763 River Rd (18920), 13 mi N on PA 32.* 610/294-9595; FAX 610/294-9882; res: 800/830-4474. Web www.goldenpheasant.com. 6 rms, 3 with shower only, 2 story, kit suite. No rm phones. MAP: S, D $85-$155; each addl $10; suite $125-$155; wkly rates; hols (3-day min). Pet accepted; $10. Complimentary continental bkfst. Coffee in rms. Restaurant (see GOLDEN PHEASANT INN). Ck-out 11 am, ck-in 2 pm. Meeting rms. Cr cds: A, C, D, DS, MC, V.

★★★ **GOLDEN PLOUGH INN.** *SR 202 (18931), 5 mi S on US 202, in Peddler's Village.* 215/794-4004; FAX 215/794-4008. Web www.peddlersvillage.com. 65 units in 7 bldgs, 2-3 story, 24 suites. S, D $109-$325; each addl $15; suites $225-$325. Crib free. TV; cable. Complimentary continental bkfst. Complimentary coffee in rms. Restaurant (see SPOTTED HOG). Ck-out 11 am, ck-in 3 pm. Meeting rms. Business servs avail. In-rm modem link. Health club privileges. Refrigerators; some in-rm whirlpools. Some balconies. Country decor; antiques. Cr cds: A, C, D, DS, MC, V.

★★★ **HOLLILEIF BED & BREAKFAST.** *677 Durham Rd; SR 413 (18940), S on PA 232, approx ½ mi S on PA 413.* 215/598-3100. E-mail hollileif@aol.com; web www.bbhost.com/hollileif. 5 rms, 3 story. No rm phones. D $85-$160; each addl $20. TV in some rms; cable, VCR avail (free movies). Complimentary full bkfst; afternoon refreshments. Ck-out 11:30 am, ck-in 3 pm. Business servs avail. Lawn games. 18th-century house; antiques, fireplace. Totally nonsmoking. Cr cds: A, C, DS, MC, V.

★★ **HOTEL DU VILLAGE.** *2535 N River Rd. (18938), N River Rd (PA 32) & Phillips Mill Rd.* 215/862-9911; FAX 215/862-9788. 20 rms, 2 story. No rm phones. S, D $85-$100; each addl $5; wkly rates. Pool. Complimentary continental bkfst. Dining rm (see HOTEL DU VILLAGE). Bar. Ck-out 11 am, ck-in after 2 pm. Tennis. Small Tudor-style country inn on spacious grounds; former estate. Cr cds: A, C, D.

★ **INN AT PHILLIPS MILL.** *2590 N River Rd (18938), 1½ mi N on PA 32.* 215/862-2984. 4 rms, 3 story, 1 suite. D $80; suite $90. Closed Jan. Pool. Dining rm (see INN AT PHILLIPS MILL). Rm serv. Ck-out 1 pm, ck-in 2 pm. Gift shop. Built in 1750 as stone barn; antiques, fireplaces. Cr cds: C.

★★★ **INN TO THE WOODS.** *150 Glenwood Dr (18977), 6 mi S on PA 32.* 215/493-1974; FAX 215/493-7592; res: 800/982-7619. E-mail intowoods@aol.com; web www.inn-bucks.com. 6 rms, 3 story, 1 suite. S, D $95-$210; each addl $25; suite $140-$210; wkend plans (2-day min). Children over 10 yrs only. TV; cable, VCR avail (movies). Complimentary full bkfst; afternoon refreshments. Ck-out 11 am, ck-in 2 pm. Luggage handling. Concierge serv. Business servs avail. In-rm modem link. X-country ski 1 mi. Whirlpool. Some fireplaces. On 10 acres of forest with hiking trails. Totally nonsmoking. Cr cds: A, C, DS, MC, V.

🖼️🖼️🖼️

★ **LOGAN INN.** *10 W Ferry St (18938), at Main St.* 215/862-2300; FAX 215/862-3931. Web www.letsmakeplans.com/loganinn. 16 rms, 10 with shower only, 3 story. S, D $75-$150; each addl $17; under 3 free; wkly, wkday rates; hols (3-day min). Crib avail. TV; cable. Complimentary continental bkfst. Restaurant 11 am-11 pm. Ck-out noon, ck-in 3-10 pm. Downhill/x-country ski 5 mi. On canal; built in 1722. One of the oldest inns in US. Cr cds: A, C, D, DS, MC, V.

🖼️🖼️🖼️🖼️

★★★ **MANSION INN.** *9 S Main St (18938), center of town.* 215/862-1231; FAX 215/862-0277. E-mail mansion@pil.net; web www.the mansion.com. 9 rms, 3 story, 5 suites. No elvtr. D $160-$225; suites $205-$305; min stay 2-3 days. Children over 16 yrs only. TV; cable (premium). Pool. Complimentary full bkfst. Complimentary coffee delivered to rms. Restaurant nearby. Ck-out 11 am, ck-in 2 pm. Business servs avail. In-rm modem link. Luggage handling. Concierge serv. X-country ski 15 mi. Health club privileges. Some in-rm whirlpools, fireplaces. Built (1865); Victorian decor. Totally nonsmoking. Cr cds: A, C, MC, V.

🖼️🖼️🖼️🖼️

★★★ **PINEAPPLE HILL BED & BREAKFAST.** *1324 River Rd (18938), 4 mi S on PA 32.* 215/862-9571; FAX 215/862-1790. Web www.pineapplehill.com. 8 rms, 3 with shower only, 3 story, 3 suites. May-Dec: S $75-$135; D $85-$145; each addl $30; suites $115-$165; wkly rates; wkends (2-day min); package plans; lower rates rest of yr. TV; cable, VCR avail (movies). Pool. Complimentary full bkfst; afternoon refreshments. Complimentary coffee in rms. Ck-out 11 am, ck-in 3 pm. Luggage handling. Concierge serv. Business servs avail. X-country ski on site. Health club privileges. Lawn games. Balconies. Picnic tables. On river. Built in 1790. Totally nonsmoking. Cr cds: A, C, DS, MC, V.

🖼️🖼️🖼️🖼️🖼️🖼️ SC

★★★ **TATTERSALL INN.** *N River Rd (18950), 8 mi N on PA 32.* 215/297-8233; FAX 215/297-5093; res: 800/297-4988. E-mail nrhg17a@prodigy.net; web www.bbhost.com/tattersall_inn. 6 rms, 2 story, 2 suites. S $60-$99; D $70-$130; each addl $15; suites $99-$130. TV in sitting rm. Complimentary full bkfst; afternoon refreshments. Restaurant nearby. Ck-out noon, ck-in 2 pm. Business servs avail. Some fireplaces. House (1740); porches, marble fireplace, antiques. Cr cds: A, C, DS, MC, V.

🖼️🖼️🖼️ SC

✓ ★★★ **WEDGWOOD INN.** *111 W Bridge St (18938).* 215/862-2570; FAX 215/862-2570. Web www.travelguides.com/bb/wedgwood. 12 rms, 2 story. Some rm phones. S $75-$120; D $105-$175; each addl $20; suites $150-$225. Pet accepted. Swimming privileges. Complimentary full bkfst; afternoon refreshments. Ck-out 11 am, ck-in 3 pm. Concierge serv. Meeting rm. Business servs avail. Health club privileges. Tennis privileges. Golf privileges. Lawn games. Some fireplaces; microwaves avail. Picnic tables, grills. Carriage rides. Built 1870; antiques, large Wedgwood collection. Totally nonsmoking. Cr cds: A, C, MC, V.

D🖼️🖼️🖼️🖼️🖼️🖼️ SC

★★★ **WHITEHALL INN.** *1370 Pineville Rd (18938).* 215/598-7945; res: 888/379-4483. Web www.innbrook.com/whitehal.html. 5 rms, 3 story, 1 suite. No rm phones. S, D $140-$195; suite $195; wkends, hols (2-3-day min). Complimentary full bkfst; afternoon refreshments. Ck-out 11 am, ck-in after 3 pm. Business servs avail. Luggage handling. Concierge serv. 18-hole golf privileges, pro, putting green, driving range. Downhill ski 7 mi; x-country ski on-site. Health club privileges. Pool. Lawn games. Many fireplaces. Picnic tables. Built in 1794; set on 12 rolling acres. Antiques. Totally nonsmoking. Cr cds: A, C, D, DS, MC, V.

🖼️🖼️🖼️🖼️🖼️🖼️

Restaurants

★★ **CENTRE BRIDGE INN.** *(See Centre Bridge Inn)* 215/862-9139. E-mail centreinn@aol.com; web www.letsmakeplans.com/centre bridgeinn. Hrs: 5:30-9:30 pm; Fri, Sat to 10 pm; Sun brunch 11:30 am-2:30 pm; dinner 3:30-9 pm. Closed Dec 25. Res accepted Fri-Sun. Continental menu. Bar. Semi-a la carte: dinner $18.95-$26.95. Sun brunch $20. Specializes in lamb, salmon, crab cakes. Entertainment Sat. Valet parking Sat. Outdoor dining. Stone fireplace. Patio overlooks canal, river. Cr cds: A, C, MC, V.

SC 🖼️

✓ ★★ **COCK N' BULL RESTAURANT.** *Routes 202 & 263 (18931), S on US 202, in Peddler's Village.* 215/794-4010. Web www.ped dlersville.com. Hrs: 11 am-3 pm, 5-9 pm; Fri to 10 pm; Sat 4-10 pm; Sun 4-8 pm; Sun brunch 9:30 am-2:30 pm. Closed Jan 1, Dec 25. Res accepted (dinner). Bar. Semi-a la carte: lunch $4.95-$10.95, dinner $11.25-$24.95. Sun brunch $14.95. Specialties: country chicken pie, beef Burgundy. Salad bar. Family-owned. Cr cds: A, C, D, DS, MC, V.

D 🖼️

★★★ **CUTTALOSSA INN.** *3498 River Rd/PA 32 (18933), 6 mi N on PA 32.* 215/297-5082. E-mail cutta@dynanet.com; web www.ans data.com/cutta/. Hrs: 11 am-2 pm, 5:30-9 pm; Fri, Sat 5:30-10 pm. Closed Sun; Jan 1, Dec 24, 25. Bar. Complete meals: lunch $6-$15, dinner $18-$28. Specializes in seafood. Entertainment in summer exc Mon. Outdoor dining. Built 1750; overlooks waterfall and wooden bridge. Cr cds: A, C, MC, V.

🖼️

★★★ **EVERMAY ON-THE-DELAWARE.** *(See Evermay on-the-Delaware)* 610/294-9100. E-mail moffly@evermay.com; web www.eve rmay.com. Hrs: 7:30-11 pm. Closed Mon-Thurs. Res required. Bar. Wine cellar. Complete meal: $62. Specialties: poached Norwegian salmon with citrus buerre blanc, contrefilet of beef with port wine reduction. Menu changes daily. Jacket. Cr cds: C, MC, V.

D

★★ **FORAGER HOUSE RESTAURANT.** *1600 River Rd (18938).* 215/862-9477. E-mail table42pls@aol.com. Hrs: 5-10 pm; Fri to 11 pm; Sat noon-11 pm; Sun noon-9 pm. Closed Tues; Jan 1, Thanksgiving, Dec 25. Res accepted; required Sat dinner. Contemporary Amer menu. Bar. A la carte entrees: lunch, dinner $13.95-$21.95. Child's meals. Specialties: Thai chicken curry, grilled salmon, seared sea scallops. Own pastries, ice cream. Cabaret Fri. Outdoor dining. Contemporary decor with local artists' works; woodburning oven. Cr cds: A, C, D, DS, MC, V.

D 🖼️

★★★ **GOLDEN PHEASANT INN.** *(See Golden Pheasant Inn)* 610/294-9595. Web www.goldenpheasant.com. Hrs: 5:30-10 pm; Sun 11 am-9 pm. Sun brunch 11 am-3 pm. Closed Mon. Res accepted. French menu. Bar. Wine cellar. A la carte entrees: dinner $18.95-$24.95. Sun brunch $18.95. Specialties: roast lamb, crabmeat Brittany, steak au poivre. Own baking. Restored 1857 inn; dining rm in solarium, overlooks canal. Cr cds: A, C, D, DS, MC, V.

🖼️

★★ **HOTEL DU VILLAGE.** *(See Hotel du Village)* 215/862-9911. Hrs: 5:30-9 pm; Fri, Sat to 10:30 pm; Sun 3-9 pm. Closed Mon, Tues; Dec 25; also Sun-Wed Jan. Res accepted. French menu. Bar. A la carte entrees: dinner $14-$20. Specialties: filet of beef Bearnaise, sweetbreads. English manor house; elegant dining. Cr cds: A, C, D.

D 🖼️

★★ **INN AT PHILLIPS MILL.** *(See Inn at Phillips Mill)* 215/862-9919. Hrs: 5:30-9:30 pm; Fri, Sat to 10 pm. Closed Dec 25; also Jan. Res accepted, required Sat. French country menu. Setups. A la carte entrees: $14.50-$24. Specialties: sole bonne femme, filet de boeuf rochambeau, Muscovy duck with cranberry sauce. Entertainment Fri, Sun. Outdoor dining in garden setting. Jacket. Cr cds: C.

★★★ **JEAN PIERRE'S.** *101 S State St (18940), State St & Centre Ave, 3 mi from I-95 exit 30.* 215/968-6201. Web www.letsmakeplans.com/jeanpierre. Hrs: 11:30 am-2 pm, 5:30-9:30 pm; Sun 11:30 am-2 pm (brunch), 4:30-8 pm. Closed Mon; Jan 1, Dec 25. Res accepted. French menu. Wine cellar. Prix fixe: lunch $19.50. A la carte entrees: dinner $22-$29. Specializes in imported fish, rack of lamb, fresh game. Own pastries. Built in 1747. Fireplaces. Cr cds: A, C, D, DS, MC, V.

[◻]

★★ **JENNY'S RESTAURANT.** *US 202 & Street Rd (18931), 5 mi S on US 202, in Peddler's Village.* 215/794-4020. Web www.peddlersvillage.com. Hrs: 11 am-9 pm; Mon to 3 pm; Fri, Sat to 10 pm; Sun 4:30-8 pm; Sun brunch 10 am-3 pm. Closed Dec 25. Res accepted. Continental menu. Bar. A la carte entrees: lunch $4.95-$9.95, dinner $15.95-$24.95. Sun brunch $5.25-$9.95. Specialties: lobster ravioli, filet Chesterfield, mushrooms Pennsylvania. Jazz, blues Fri, Sat. Cr cds: A, C, D, DS, MC, V.

[SC] [◻]

★★★ **ODETTE'S.** *S River Rd (18938), 1 mi S on PA 32.* 215/862-2432. Hrs: 11:30-2 am; Sun brunch 10:30 am-1:30 pm. Res accepted; required hols. Continental menu. Bar. Wine list. A la carte entrees: lunch $7.50-$10, dinner $15-$24. Sun brunch $15.95. Child's meals. Specializes in veal chops, salmon. Pianist. Valet parking. Built in 1794 as bargeman's inn; overlooks Delaware River; memorabilia of Odette Myrtil Logan of South Pacific fame. Cr cds: A, C, D, DS, MC, V.

[D] [◻]

★ **SPOTTED HOG.** *(See Golden Plough Inn)* 215/794-4030. Web www.peddlersvillage.com. Hrs: 7 am-11 pm; Sun to 9 pm. Closed Thanksgiving, Dec 25. Bar to midnight; Fri, Sat to 1 am; Sun to 10 pm. A la carte entrees: bkfst $2.95-$7.25, lunch, dinner $3.25-$18.95. Child's meals. Specializes in stir-fry, pizza, calzones. Cr cds: A, C, D, DS, MC, V.

[D] [◻]

New Stanton (E-2)

(See also Connellsville, Greensburg)

Pop 2,081 **Elev** 980 ft **Area Code** 724 **Zip** 15672
E-mail lhvb@ laurelhighlands.org **Web** www.laurelhighlands.org
Information Laurel Highlands Visitors Bureau, Town Hall, 120 E Main St, Ligonier 15658; 724/238-5661

What to See and Do

L.E. Smith Glass Co. Reproductions of several styles of antique handcrafted glass. Children under 6 yrs not admitted. (Mon–Fri; closed 1st 2 wks July) 6 mi SE via US 119, PA 31, in Mt Pleasant, 1900 Liberty St. Phone 724/547-3544 for tour schedule. **Free**

Motels

★★ **DAYS INN.** *127 W Byers Ave (15672).* 724/925-3591; FAX 724/925-9859; res: 800/329-7466. 135 rms, 3 story. S $47-$55; D $49-$60; each addl $6; under 18 free. Crib free. TV; cable (premium). Pool; lifeguard. Restaurant 6-11 am, 4-10 pm; Sat, Sun from 7 am. Bar 4 pm-midnight; entertainment. Ck-out 11 am. Coin lndry. Meeting rms. Business servs avail. Sundries. Exercise equipt. Microwaves avail. Cr cds: A, C, DS, MC, V.

[D] [⊷] [大] [◻] [🐾] [SC]

✓★★ **HOWARD JOHNSON INN.** *112 W Byers Ave (15672), 1 blk S off US 119, ¼ mi SW of PA Tpke exit 8.* 724/925-3511; FAX 724/925-3511; res: 800/446-4656. 87 rms, 2 story. Mid-May-Sept: S $38-$79; D $45-$79; each addl $5; under 18 free; lower rates rest of yr. Crib free. TV; cable (premium), VCR avail (movies). Heated pool. Playground. Complimentary continental bkfst. Coffee in rms. Restaurant adj open 24 hrs. Ck-out noon. Business servs avail. In-rm modem link. Valet serv. Refrigerators, microwaves avail. Cr cds: A, C, D, DS, MC, V.

[D] [⊷] [◻] [🐾] [SC]

Norristown (E-9)

(See also King of Prussia, Kulpsville, Philadelphia)

Founded 1704 **Pop** 30,749 **Elev** 130 ft **Area Code** 484 & 610
E-mail info@valleyforge.org **Web** www.valleyforge.org
Information Valley Forge Convention and Visitors Bureau, 600 W Germantown Pike, Suite 130, Plymouth Meeting 19462; 610/834-1550

William Penn, Jr, owner of the 7,600-acre tract around Norristown, sold it to Isaac Norris and William Trent for 50¢ an acre in 1704. It became a crossroads for colonial merchants and soldiers; Washington's army camped nearby. Dutch, German, Swedish, Welsh and English immigrants left their mark on the city. Today Norristown, still a transportation hub, houses many industries and serves as a county government center.

What to See and Do

Elmwood Park Zoo. Features extensive North American waterfowl area; cougars, bobcats, bison, elk; outdoor aviary; birds of prey; children's zoo barn; museum with exhibit on animal senses. (Daily; closed Jan 1, Thanksgiving, Dec 25) Harding Blvd, off US 202. Phone 610/277-3825. **¢¢**

Peter Wentz Farmstead. Restored and furnished mid-18th-century country mansion, twice used by Washington during the Pennsylvania campaign. More than 70 acres with demonstration field and orchard crops of the period. Slide presentation; costumed interpreters; reconstructed 1744 barn with farm animals. (Daily exc Mon; closed Jan 1, Thanksgiving, Dec 25, also 2nd wk Sept) 10 mi NW via US 202, W via PA 73 on Schultz Rd, in Worcester. Phone 610/584-5104. **Free**

Valley Forge National Historical Park (see). NW on US 422 to Trooper, then S.

Inn

★★★ **WILLIAM PENN INN.** *US 202 & Sumneytown Pke (19436), 5 mi N on US 202.* 215/699-9272; FAX 215/699-4808. Web www.philanet.com/wmpenn/. 4 rms, 2 story, 3 suites. S, D $115-$150; suites $135-$180. TV; cable (premium). Complimentary continental bkfst. Restaurant (see WILLIAM PENN INN). Rm serv 5-10 pm. Ck-out 11 am, ck-in 1 pm. Business servs avail. In-rm modem link. Luggage handling. Refrigerators, minibars. Continuous operation since 1714; antiques. Totally nonsmoking. Cr cds: A, C, D, DS, MC, V.

[D] [◻] [🐾]

Restaurants

★★★ **THE JEFFERSON HOUSE.** *2519 Dekalb Pike (19401).* 610/275-3407. Web www.weddings-delual.com/jeffersonhouse. Hrs: 11:30 am-2:30 pm, 4:30-10 pm; Sun noon-8 pm; Sun brunch to 4 pm; early-bird dinner Mon-Sat 4-6 pm. Closed most major hols. Res accepted.

Contemporary Amer menu. Bar to 2 am. Wine cellar. Semi-a la carte: lunch $5.50-$16.95, dinner $12.50-$32. Child's meals. Specializes in pastas, prime meats. Jazz, blues Fri in season. Manor-house set on extensive, landscaped grounds; former Buckland estate. Family-owned. Cr cds: A, C, D, MC, V.

★★★ **WILLIAM PENN INN.** *(See William Penn Inn)* 215/699-9272. Web www.philanet.com/wmpenn. Hrs: 11:30 am-3 pm, 5-10 pm; Fri, Sat to 11 pm; Sun 2-8 pm; early-bird dinner Mon-Sat 5-6:30 pm; Sun brunch 10:30 am-2 pm. Closed Dec 25. Res accepted. Continental menu. Bar. Semi-a la carte: lunch $5.25-$15, dinner $18-$30. Sun brunch $17.95. Specializes in seafood, roast rack of lamb, prime rib. Own pastries. Salad bar. Harpist, pianist Tues-Sun. Originally built as a tavern (1714); antiques. Guest rms avail. Cr cds: A, C, D, DS, MC, V.

North East (A-2)

(See also Erie)

Settled 1794 **Pop** 4,617 **Elev** 801 ft **Area Code** 814 **Zip** 16428
Information Chamber of Commerce, 21 S Lake St; 814/725-4262

In 1778, when Pennsylvania bought from the federal government the tract containing North East, the state gained 46 miles of Lake Erie frontage, a fine harbor and some of the best Concord grape country in the nation.

What to See and Do

Winery tours.

Heritage Wine Cellars. Guided tours; wine tastings. (Daily; closed some hols) 12162 E Main Rd. Phone 814/725-8015.   **Free**

Mazza Vineyards. Guided tours; wine tastings. (Daily; closed some hols) 11815 E Lake Rd. Phone 814/725-8695.   **Free**

Penn-Shore Vineyards and Winery. Guided tours; wine tastings. (Daily; closed some hols) 10225 E Lake Rd. Phone 814/725-8688.   **Free**

Annual Events

Cherry Festival. Concessions, rides, games, parade. Mid-July.

Wine Country Harvest Festival. Gravel Pit Park and Gibson Park. Arts and crafts, bands, buses to wineries, food. Phone 814/725-4262. Last full wkend Sept.

Oil City (C-2)

(See also Franklin, Titusville)

Pop 11,949 **Elev** 1,000 ft **Area Code** 814 **Zip** 16301

Spreading on both sides of Oil Creek and the Allegheny River, Oil City was born of the oil boom. Oil refining and the manufacture of oil machinery are its major occupations today. Nearby are natural gas fields. Seven miles northwest stood the famous oil-boom town of Pithole. In 1865 it expanded from a single farmhouse to a population of more than 10,000 in 5 months, as its first oil well brought in 250 barrels a day.

Motor Hotel

★★ **HOLIDAY INN.** *1 Seneca St (16301), at State St Bridge.* 814/677-1221; FAX 814/677-0492; res: 800/465-4329. E-mail holiday@

blink.net. 106 rms, 5 story. S, D $65; each addl $5; suites $75-$99; family rates. Crib free. Pet accepted. TV; cable. Heated pool. Coffee in rms. Restaurant 6:30 am-2 pm, 5-9 pm. Rm serv. Bar 5 pm-2 am, Sun from 1 pm. Ck-out noon. Meeting rms. Business servs avail. In-rm modem link. Bellhops. Valet serv. X-country ski 2 mi. Health club privileges. Cr cds: A, C, D, DS, MC, V.

Orbisonia (E-5)

(See also Chambersburg, Huntingdon)

Pop 447 **Elev** 640 ft **Area Code** 814 **Zip** 17243

What to See and Do

East Broad Top Railroad. The oldest surviving narrow-gauge railroad east of the Rockies. Train ride (70 min); fascinating old equipment, bldgs. Picnic area. (June–Oct, wkends only) On US 522. Phone 814/447-3011. ¢¢¢   Opp is

Rockhill Trolley Museum. Old-time trolleys; car barn and restoration shop tours. A 2-mi ride on Shade Gap Electric Railway. Gift shop. (Memorial Day–Oct, wkends) ½ mi W off US 522, on PA 994, in Rockhill Furnace. Phone 814/447-9576.   ¢¢

Pennsylvania Dutch Area (E-8 - F-8)

(See also Allentown, Bird-in-Hand, Ephrata, Kutztown, Lancaster, Lebanon, Manheim, Reading)

Web www.800padutch.com

Information Pennsylvania Dutch Convention & Visitors Bureau, 501 Greenfield Rd, Lancaster 17601; 717/299-8901 or 800/PADUTCH. There is also a downtown visitor center, at 100 S Queen St in the Lancaster Chamber of Commerce & Industry Building, which provides brochures, maps and other general information; also another on US 272 near PA Tpke exit 21.

From the Rhineland and Palatinate of Germany came great migrations of settlers to Pennsylvania in the 18th century, first near Philadelphia and then moving west. Because they retained their customs and speech and developed beautiful and bountiful farms, the Pennsylvania Dutch (corruption of the German *Deutsch*) country is one of the state's greatest tourist attractions. There are all degrees of conservatism among these descendants of German immigrants, ranging from the Amish to the Brethren, but all share tremendous vigor, family devotion, love of the Bible and belief in thrift and hard work.

Many of the "plain people"—the Amish, Old Order Mennonites and Brethren (Dunkards)—live today much as they did a century ago. Married men wear beards, black coats and low-crowned black hats; women wear bonnets and long, simple dresses. They drive horses and buggies instead of cars, work long hours in the fields, shun the use of modern farm machinery and turn to the Bible for guidance. Despite their refusal to use machinery they are master farmers. (They were among the first to rotate crops and practice modern fertilization methods.) Their harvests are consistently among the best in the country.

Many of the Amish regard photographs as "graven images"; visitors should not take pictures of individuals without their permission.

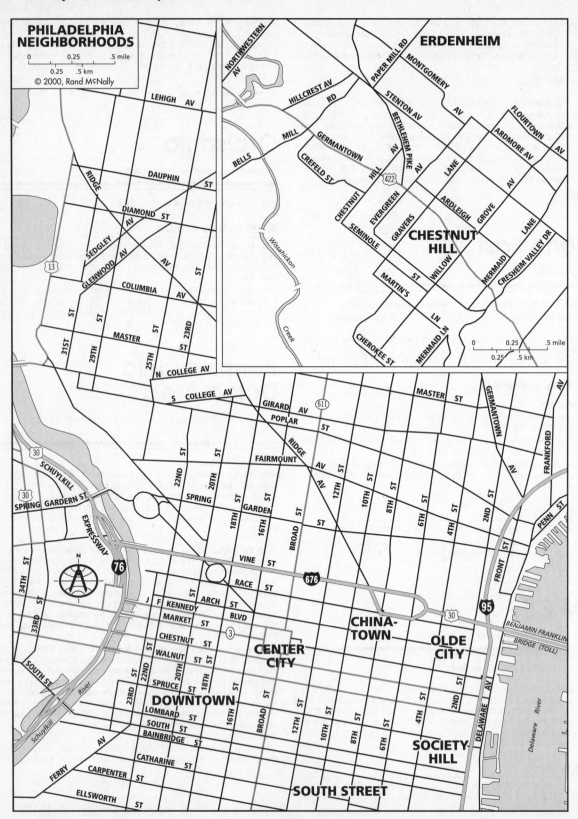

PHILADELPHIA NEIGHBORHOODS

0   0.25   .5 mile
0.25   .5 km
© 2000, Rand McNally

LEHIGH   AV

DAUPHIN   ST

DIAMOND   ST

RIDGE

SEDGLEY   AV

GLENWOOD   AV

COLUMBIA   AV

MASTER

31ST   ST

29TH   ST

25TH   ST

23RD   ST

N   COLLEGE   AV

13

ERDENHEIM

NORTHWESTERN   AV

HILLCREST   AV

RD

PAPER MILL RD

MONTGOMERY

STENTON   AV

AV

GERMANTOWN   AV

BELLS

MILL

CREFELD ST

BETHLEHEM PIKE

HILL   AV

422

FLOURTOWN

ARDMORE   AV

AV

LANE

ARDLEIGH   AV

GROVE

CHESTNUT

EVERGREEN

GRAVERS

CHESTNUT HILL

SEMINOLE

WILLOW

MERMAID

CRESHEIM VALLEY DR

LANE

Wissahickon

MARTIN'S

ST

LN

Creek

CHEROKEE ST

MERMAID LN

0   0.25   .5 mile
0.25   .5 km

S   COLLEGE   AV

GIRARD   AV

611

MASTER   ST

GERMANTOWN   AV

POPLAR   ST

RIDGE

FAIRMOUNT

AV

22ND   ST

20TH   ST

12TH   ST

10TH   ST

8TH   ST

9TH   ST

4TH   ST

2ND   ST

FRANKFORD   AV

SCHUYLKILL

30

SPRING

18TH   ST

16TH   ST

GARDEN   ST

BROAD   ST

PENN   ST

30

SPRING   GARDEN   ST

EXPRESSWAY

VINE   ST

76

RACE   ST

676

95

34TH   ST

33RD   ST

ARCH   ST

KENNEDY

J F

BLVD

30

BENJAMIN FRANKLIN

MARKET   ST

CHINA-TOWN

BRIDGE (TOLL)

CHESTNUT   ST

3

OLDE CITY

CENTER CITY

WALNUT   ST

22ND   ST

20TH   ST

18TH   ST

SOUTH   ST

SPRUCE   ST

DELAWARE   AV

23RD   ST

DOWNTOWN

River

LOMBARD   ST

16TH   ST

BROAD   ST

12TH   ST

10TH   ST

8TH   ST

6TH   ST

4TH   ST

2ND   ST

Delaware   River

SOUTH   ST

Schuylkill   River

BAINBRIDGE   ST

AV

CATHARINE   ST

SOCIETY-HILL

FERRY

CARPENTER   ST

ELLSWORTH   ST

SOUTH STREET

Philadelphia (F-10)

Founded 1682 **Pop** 1,585,577 **Elev** 45 ft **Area Code** 215 & 267
Web www.libertynet.org/phila-visitor
Information Visitors Center, 1525 JFK Blvd, 19103; 215/636-1666 or 800/537-7676

Suburbs Bristol, Chester, Fort Washington, Jenkintown, Kennett Square, King of Prussia, Media, Norristown, West Chester, Willow Grove; also Wilmington, DE and Camden, NJ. (See individual alphabetical listings.)

The nation's first capital has experienced a rebirth in the past few decades. Philadelphia has successfully blended its historic past with an electricity of modern times, all the while keeping an eye on the future. In the mid-18th century it was the second-largest city in the English-speaking world. Now, nearing the end of the 20th century, Philadelphia is the second-largest city on the East Coast and the fifth largest in the country. Here, in William Penn's City of Brotherly Love, the Declaration of Independence was written and adopted, the Constitution was molded and signed, the Liberty Bell was rung, Betsy Ross was said to have sewn her flag and Washington served most of his years as president.

This is the city of "firsts," including the first American hospital, medical college, women's medical college, bank, paper mill, steamboat, zoo, sugar refinery, daily newspaper, US Mint and public school for black children (1750).

The first Quakers, who came here in 1681, lived in caves dug into the banks of the Delaware River. During the first year, 80 houses were raised; by the following year, William Penn's "greene countrie towne" was a city of 600 buildings. The Quakers prospered in trade and commerce, and Philadelphia became the leading port in the colonies. Its leading citizen for many years was Benjamin Franklin—statesman, scientist, diplomat, writer, inventor and publisher.

The fires of colonial indignation burned hot and early in Philadelphia. Soon after the Boston tea party, a protest rally of 8,000 Philadelphians frightened off a British tea ship. In May 1774, when Paul Revere rode from Boston to Philadelphia to report that Boston's harbor had been closed, all of Philadelphia went into mourning. The 1st and 2nd Continental Congresses convened here, and Philadelphia became headquarters of the Revolution. After the Declaration of Independence was composed and accepted by Congress, the city gave men, factories and shipyards to the cause. But British General Howe and 18,000 soldiers poured in on September 26, 1777, to spend a comfortable and social winter here while Washington's troops endured the bitter winter at Valley Forge. When the British evacuated the city, Congress returned. Philadelphia continued as the seat of government until 1800, except for a short period when New York City held the honor. The Constitution of the United States was written here; President George Washington graced the city's halls and streets.

Since those historic days, Philadelphia has figured importantly in the politics, economy and culture of the country. Here national conventions have nominated presidents. During four wars the city has served as an arsenal and a shipyard. More than 1,400 churches and synagogues grace the city. There are more than 25 colleges, universities and professional schools in Philadelphia as well. Fine restaurants are in abundance, along with an exciting nightlife to top off an evening. Entertainment is offered by the world-renowned Philadelphia Orchestra, theaters, college and professional sports, outstanding parks, recreation centers and playgrounds. Shoppers may browse major department stores, hundreds of specialty shops and antique shopping areas.

Between the Delaware River and 9th Street for 10 blocks lies a history-rich part of Philadelphia. Here are the shrines of American liberty: Independence Hall, the Liberty Bell Pavilion and many other historical sites in and around Independence National Historical Park.

Transportation

Car Rental Agencies. See IMPORTANT TOLL-FREE NUMBERS.
Public Transportation. Subway and elevated trains, commuter trains, buses, trolleys (SEPTA), phone 215/580-7800.
Rail Passenger Service. Amtrak 800/872-7245.

Airport Information

Philadelphia Intl Airport. Information 215/937-6800 or 800/PHL-GATE; lost and found 215/937-6888; weather 215/936-1212.

What to See and Do

Academy of Music (1857). City's opera house and concert hall; home of Philadelphia Orchestra, Philly Pops, Opera Company of Philadelphia and Pennsylvania Ballet (see SEASONAL EVENTS). Broad & Locust Sts. Phone 215/893-1935.

Academy of Natural Sciences Museum (1812). Dinosaurs, Egyptian mummies, animal displays in natural habitats, live animal programs, hands-on children's museum. (Daily; closed Jan 1, Thanksgiving, Dec 25) 1900 Benjamin Franklin Pkwy. Phone 215/299-1000. ¢¢¢

African-American Museum. Built to house and interpret African-American culture. Changing exhibits; public events incl lectures, workshops, films and concerts. (Daily exc Mon; closed Jan 1, Thanksgiving, Dec 25) 701 Arch St. Phone 215/574-0380. ¢¢

American Swedish Historical Museum. From tapestries to technology, the museum celebrates Swedish influence on American life. Special exhibits on the New Sweden Colony. Research library, collections. (Daily exc Mon; closed hols) 1900 Pattison Ave. Phone 215/389-1776. ¢

Arch Street Meetinghouse (1804). Perhaps the largest Friends meetinghouse in the world. Exhibits, slide show, tours. (Daily exc Sun; closed Jan 1, Thanksgiving, Dec 25) 320 Arch St. Phone 215/627-2667. **Donation**

Balch Institute for Ethnic Studies. A multicultural library, archive, museum and education center that promotes intergroup understanding using education; 300 yrs of US immigration are documented here. Features "Peopling of Pennsylvania," as well as changing exhibits. (Mon–Sat; closed hols) 18 S 7th St. Phone 215/925-8090. **Free**

Betsy Ross House. Where the famous seamstress is said to have made the first American flag. Upholsterer's shop, memorabilia. Flag Day ceremonies, June 14. (Daily until Labor Day; closed Jan 1, Thanksgiving, Dec 25) 239 Arch St. Phone 215/627-5343. **Donation**

Burial Ground of Congregation Mikveh Israel (1738). Graves of Haym Salomon, Revolutionary War financier, and Rebecca Gratz, probable model for "Rebecca" of Sir Walter Scott's *Ivanhoe*. Spruce & 8th Sts.

Christ Church (Episcopal). Patriots, Loyalists and heroes have worshiped here since 1695. Sit in pews once occupied by Washington, Franklin and Betsy Ross. (Mar–Dec, daily; rest of yr, Wed–Sun; closed Jan 1, Thanksgiving, Dec 25) 2nd St between Market & Arch Sts. Phone 215/922-1695.

Christ Church Burial Ground. Resting place of Benjamin Franklin, his wife, Deborah, and four other signers of the Declaration of Independence. (Mid-Apr–mid-Oct, daily) 5th & Arch Sts. Phone 215/922-1695.

City Hall. (Mon–Fri; closed hols) Broad & Market Sts. Tours avail. Phone 215/686-2840.

Civil War Library and Museum. Four-story brick 19th-century town house filled with 18,000 books and periodicals dealing with events leading up to the American Civil War, the war itself and early Reconstruction. Unique collection of arms, uniforms, flags of the period, memorabilia and artifacts begun in 1888 by former officers of the Union Army. Exhibits on Lincoln, Grant and Meade; also the Navy Room and the Armory. (Tues-Sat; closed hols) 1805 Pine St. Phone 215/735-8196. ¢¢

Edgar Allan Poe National Historic Site. Where Poe lived before his move to New York in 1844. The site is the nation's memorial to the literary genius of Edgar Allan Poe. Exhibits, slide show, tours and special programs. (June-Oct, daily; rest of yr, Wed-Sun; closed Jan 1, Dec 25) 532 N 7th, at Spring Garden St. Phone 215/597-8780. **Free**

Elfreth's Alley. Oldest continuously residential street in America, with 30 houses dating from 1728-1836 (see ANNUAL EVENTS). At #126 is the mid-18th-century **Museum House;** period furnishings, historical exhibit. (Tues-Sun; Jan, wkends only) Off 2nd St between Arch & Race Sts. Phone 215/574-0560. Museum ¢

★ **Fairmount Park.** Covers 8,700 acres. Begins at Philadelphia Museum of Art, extends NW on both sides of Wissahickon Creek and Schuylkill River. Phone 215/685-0000. In park are

Boat House Row. Used by collegiate and club oarsmen. Schuylkill River is scene of many nationally important crew competitions; crews practice all spring and summer during early morning and afternoon. On E bank of river. Phone 215/978-6919 for rowing, regatta schedules.

Colonial Mansions. Handsome 18th-century dwellings in varying architectural styles, authentically preserved and furnished, incl Mount Pleasant (1761) (daily exc Mon); Cedar Grove (1756) (daily exc Mon); Strawberry Mansion (1797) (daily exc Mon); Sweetbriar (1797) (daily exc Tues); Lemon Hill (1799) (Wed–Sun); Woodford (1756) (daily exc Mon); Laurel Hill (1760) (Wed–Sun). Further details and guided tours from Park Houses office at Philadelphia Museum of Art. Phone 215/684-7922. Each house ¢

Japanese Exhibition House. Re-creates a bit of Japan, complete with garden, pond, bridge. (May-Labor Day, daily exc Mon; Labor Day-Oct, Sat & Sun) Fairmount Park Horticulture Ctr. Phone 215/878-5097. ¢

Philadelphia Zoo. America's first zoo. More than 1,700 animals, many in natural surroundings; TREEHOUSE (fee); waterfowl collection; bear country; five-acre African plains exhibit; reptile house; bird house; carnivore kingdom; children's zoo. Picnic areas; concession. Guided tours by appt. Main zoo (daily; closed Jan 1, Thanksgiving, Dec 24, 25, 31). 3400 W Girard Ave. Phone 215/243-1100. ¢¢

Robin Hood Dell East. (See SEASONAL EVENTS)

Fireman's Hall Museum. Collection of antique firefighting equipment; displays and exhibits of fire dept history since its beginning in 1736; library. (Tues–Sat; closed hols) 147 N 2nd St. Phone 215/923-1438. **Donation**

Fort Mifflin. Site of a 7-wk siege during the Revolutionary War. Served as a military installation until 1959. Guided tours (Apr–Nov, Wed–Sun). From the airport, follow Island Ave toward the Delaware River, follow brown and white signs. Phone 215/492-1881. ¢¢

Franklin Institute Science Museum. Science Center incl exhibits on trains, shipmaking, astronomy, bioscience, communications, aviation and electricity; highlights incl a Baldwin #60000 locomotive and a giant walkthrough heart. **Mandell Futures Center** is dedicated to the science and technology shaping the 21st century; it explores such areas as space, earth, health and computers. Also here are **Benjamin Franklin National Memorial, Fels Planetarium** and the four-story screen of the **Tuttleman Omniverse Theater** (30-40-min films). (Daily; closed major hols) 20th St & Ben Franklin Pkwy. Phone 215/448-1200. ¢¢¢

Free Library. Large central library with over 9 million indexed items in all fields. Rare books, maps, theater scripts and orchestral scores; automobile reference collections; changing exhibits. (Memorial Day–Labor Day, daily exc Sun; rest of yr, daily; closed hols) Logan Sq, 19th & Vine Sts. Phone 215/686-5322. **Free**

Germantown.

Cliveden (1767). A 2½-story stone Georgian house of individual design built as summer home by Benjamin Chew, Chief Justice of colonial Pennsylvania. On Oct 4, 1777, British soldiers used house as a fortress to repulse Washington's attempt to recapture Philadelphia. Used as Chew family residence for 200 yrs; many original furnishings. A National Trust for Historic Preservation property. (Apr–Dec, Thurs-Sun afternoons; closed Easter, Thanksgiving, Dec 25) 6401 Germantown Ave, between Johnson & Cliveden Sts. www.cliveden.org. Phone 215/848-1777. ¢¢¢

Deshler-Morris House (1772–1773). Residence of President Washington in the summers of 1793, 1794; period furnishings, garden. (Apr–Nov, Tues-Sat; rest of yr, by appt; closed most hols) 5442 Germantown Ave. Phone 215/596-1748. ¢

Stenton House (1723–1730). Mansion built by James Logan, secretary to William Penn. Excellent example of Pennsylvania colonial architecture, furnished with 18th- and 19th-century antiques. General Washington spent Aug 13, 1777, here; General Sir William Howe headquartered here for the Battle of Germantown. Colonial barn, gardens, kitchen. (Apr–Dec, Tues–Sat afternoons; rest of yr, by appt; closed hols) 18th St between Courtland St & Windrim Ave. Phone 215/329-7312. ¢¢

Gloria Dei Church National Historic Site ("Old Swedes") (1700). State's oldest church. Memorial to John Hanson, President of the United States under Articles of Confederation. (Daily) Columbus Blvd & Christian St, 8 blks S of Chestnut. Phone 215/389-1513.

Haverford College (1833) (1,100 students). Founded by members of the Society of Friends. The 216-acre campus incl Founders Hall; James P. Magill Library; Arboretum; Morris Cricket Library and Collection (by appt

only; Phone 610/896-1162). Tours of arboretum and campus. 10 mi W on US 30, in Haverford. Phone 610/896-1000.

Historical Society of Pennsylvania. Museum exhibit features first draft of Constitution, 500 artifacts and manuscripts plus video tours of turn-of-the-century urban and suburban neighborhoods. Research library and archives house historical and genealogical collections. (Tues–Sat; closed hols) 1300 Locust St. Phone 215/732-6200. ¢¢

Historic Bartram's Garden. Pre-Revolutionary home of John Bartram, royal botanist to the colonies under George III, naturalist and plant explorer. The 18th-century stone farmhouse (fee), barn, stable and cider mill overlook the Schuylkill River. Museum shop. (Apr–Dec, daily; rest of yr, Wed–Fri afternoons; closed hols) 54th St & Lindbergh Blvd. Phone 215/729-5281. House tour ¢; Combination house & garden tour ¢¢

⭐ **Independence National Historical Park.** The park has been called "America's most historic square mile." The Visitor Center at 3rd & Chestnut Sts has a tour map, information on all park activities and attractions and a 30-min film entitled *Independence*. An exhibit to mark the 200th anniversary of the United States Constitution, "Promise of Permanency," is composed of an interactive computer system with 16 touch-sensitive monitors that inform visitors of the meaning of the federal Constitution, how it has endured for 2 centuries, and its relevance to modern America. For info phone 215/597-8974. Unless otherwise indicated, all historic sites and museums in the park are open daily and are free. They include

Independence Square. (known as State House Yard in colonial times). Bounded by Chestnut, Walnut, 5th & 6th Sts. Contains Independence Hall, Congress Hall, Old City Hall and Philosophical Hall.

Independence Mall. Extends 3 blks N of the Square. The tree-lined walks add to the ambience while viewing the Square's Georgian structures. On the mall is a glass pavilion housing the Liberty Bell.

Declaration House. Reconstructed house on site of writing of Declaration of Independence by Thomas Jefferson; 2 rms Jefferson rented have been reproduced. Short orientation and movie about Jefferson, his philosophy on the common man, and history of the house. 701 Market St.

Liberty Bell Pavilion. The Liberty Bell, created to commemorate the 50th anniversary of the Charter of Privileges granted by William Penn to his colony in 1701, bears the inscription, "Proclaim liberty throughout all the land unto all the inhabitants thereof" (Leviticus, chapter 25). It was rung at public occasions thereafter, incl the first reading of the Declaration of Independence on July 8, 1776, and was last rung formally on Washington's birthday in 1846. The bell got its name from 19th-century antislavery groups who adopted it as a symbol of their cause. At 12:01 am on Jan 1, 1976, it was moved across the street from its original home in Independence Hall to its own glass structure. The Liberty Bell faces

Independence Hall (1732). Site of the adoption of the Declaration of Independence. First used as the Pennsylvania State House, it housed the Second Continental Congress, 1775-1783, and the Constitutional Convention in 1787—when the Constitution of the United States was written. Admission by tour only. Chestnut St between 5th & 6th Sts. Beside Independence Hall is

Congress Hall. Congress met here during the last decade of the 18th century. House of Representatives and Senate chambers are restored. 6th & Chestnut Sts. On the other side of Independence Hall is

Old City Hall (1789). Built as City Hall, but was also home of first US Supreme Court, 1791-1800. Exterior restored. Interior depicts the judicial phase of the bldg. Chestnut & 5th Sts. Nearby is

Philosophical Hall (1785-1789). Home of the American Philosophical Society, oldest learned society in America (1743), founded by Benjamin Franklin. Not open to public. 5th St side of Square. Across 5th St is

Library Hall. Reconstruction of Library Company of Philadelphia bldg (1789-1790) is occupied by library of American Philosophical Society. Open to scholars. (Mon–Fri) 5th & Library Sts. To the E is

The Second Bank of the United States (1824-1841). Was also used as US Custom House (1845-1934). Now houses Portrait Gallery. 420 Chestnut St, between 4th & 5th Sts. One blk NE is

Franklin Court. The site of Benjamin Franklin's house has been developed as a tribute to him; area incl working printing office and bindery, underground museum with multimedia exhibits, archaeological exhibit and the B. Free Franklin Post Office. Between Market & Chestnut Sts, in block bounded by 3rd & 4th Sts. One-half blk S is

Carpenters' Hall (1770). Constructed as guild hall; meeting site of first Continental Congress (1774). Historical museum since 1857; still operated by Carpenters Co. Contains original chairs; exhibits of early tools. (Daily exc Mon) 320 Chestnut St. Adj is

New Hall Military Museum. This reconstruction houses the US Marine Corps Memorial Museum, featuring exhibits on the early history of the Marines and the Army-Navy Museum. 4th & Chestnut Sts, in Carpenters' Court. Also in Carpenters' Court is

Museum Shop (Pemberton House). Reconstruction of Quaker merchant's house; now shop with items relating to historic sites. Nearby is

The First Bank of the United States (1797-1811). Organized by Alexander Hamilton; country's oldest bank bldg; exterior restored. Closed to public. 3rd St between Walnut & Chestnut Sts. Walk approx ½ blk S to

Bishop White House (1786-1787). House of Bishop William White, first Episcopal Bishop of Pennsylvania. Restored and furnished. Tours. Free tickets at park's Visitor Center. 309 Walnut St. One blk W is

Todd House (1775). House of Dolley Payne Todd, who later married James Madison and became First Lady; 18th-century furnishings depict middle-class Quaker family life. Tours. Free tickets at park's Visitor Center. 4th & Walnut Sts. Retrace steps 1 blk to

The Merchant's Exchange. Designed by William Strickland, one of the East's finest examples of Greek revival architecture. Exterior restored; now houses regional offices of the National Park Service. Closed to public. 3rd & Walnut Sts. Proceed E on Dock St.

Thaddeus Kosciuszko National Memorial. House of Polish patriot during his second visit to US (1797-1798). He was one of the 18th century's greatest champions of American and Polish freedom and one of the first volunteers to come to the aid of the American Revolutionary Army. Exterior and 2nd-floor bedrm have been restored. (Daily) 3rd & Pine Sts.

For further info about the park, contact Visitor Center, 3rd & Chestnut Sts, 19106; phone 215/597-8974 (voice), 215/597-1785 (TDD) or 215/597-8974 (recording).

Independence Seaport Museum. Ship models, figureheads, whaling equipment, paintings. Exhibits illustrate maritime history of Delaware Bay and River, life of a sailor; special exhibits. Waterfront facility at Penn's Landing houses boat-building workshop and small gallery. (Daily; closed hols) 211 S Columbus Blvd. Phone 215/925-5439. ¢¢

John Heinz National Wildlife Refuge at Tinicum. Largest remaining freshwater tidal wetland in the state, protecting more than 1,000 acres of wildlife habitat. Area was first diked by Swedish farmers in 1643; Dutch farmers and the colonial government added dikes during the Revolutionary War. More than 280 species of birds and 13 resident mammal species. Hiking, bicycling, nature observation, canoeing on Darby Creek, fishing. (Daily) S via I-95, W PA 291 exit, right on Bartram Ave, left on 84th St, left on Lindbergh Blvd, at 86th & Lindbergh Blvd. Phone 215/365-3118 or 610/521-0662. **Free**

Morris Arboretum of the University of Pennsylvania (1887). Public garden; more than 1,600 types of native and exotic trees and shrubs on 166 acres; special garden areas include swan pond, rose garden and Japanese gardens. Tours (Sat & Sun afternoon; one each day) (Daily; closed Dec 24–Jan 1) Approx 12 mi NW in Chestnut Hill; entrance on Northwestern Ave, between Stenton & Germantown Ave. Phone 215/247-5777. ¢¢

Mummer's Museum. Participatory exhibits and displays highlighting the history and tradition of the Mummers Parade (see ANNUAL EVENTS). Costumes and videotapes of past parades. Free outdoor string band concerts (May-Sept, Tues eves, weather permitting); 20 string bands, different every wk. (Sept-June, Tues-Sat, also Sun afternoons; rest of yr, daily exc Sun; closed major hols) 1100 S 2nd St & Washington Ave. Phone 215/336-3050. ¢¢

Museum of American Art of the Pennsylvania Academy of Fine Arts. Oldest art museum and school in US; housed in restored Victorian bldg by architect Frank Furness. Outstanding permanent collection of 3 centuries of American art; rotating exhibits. Guided tours (Mon–Fri; closed major hols). 118 N Broad St. Phone 215/972-7600. ¢¢¢

Mütter Museum. In the College of Physicians of Philadelphia. Medical antiques and memorabilia; anatomical and pathological specimens and models. (Daily exc Sun; closed hols) 19 S 22nd St. Phone 215/563-3737. ¢¢

National Museum of American Jewish History. Exhibit portrays the American Jewish experience from 1654 to the present; changing exhibits; art, artifacts; audiovisual display. (Daily exc Sat; limited hrs Fri & Sun; closed Jan 1, Thanksgiving, also Jewish hols) Independence Mall East, 55 N 5th St. Phone 215/923-3811. ¢¢

Old Pine St Presbyterian Church (1768). Colonial church and graveyard, renovated in 1850s in Greek revival style. 412 Pine St, at 4th St. Phone 215/925-8051.

Old St George's United Methodist Church (1769). Oldest Methodist Church in continuous service in US. Colonial architecture; collection of Methodist memorabilia; has only Bishop Asbury Bible and John Wesley Chalice Cup in America. (Daily) 235 N 4th St. Phone 215/925-7788.

Old St Mary's Church (1763). Commodore John Barry, "father of the US Navy," is interred in graveyard behind the city's first Catholic cathedral. (Daily) 252 S 4th St, between Locust & Spruce Sts. Phone 215/923-7930.

Penn's Landing. Columbus Blvd & Spruce St. Here are

   Gazela **of Philadelphia** (1883). Portuguese square-rigger tall ship. (June-Sept, Sat & Sun) Columbus Blvd & Chestnut St. Phone 215/218-0110. **Donation**

   USS *Olympia.* Commodore Dewey's flagship during Spanish-American War; restored. Naval museum has weapons, uniforms, ship models, naval relics of all periods. Also here is World War II submarine **USS** *Becuna.* (Daily; closed Jan 1, Dec 25) Phone 215/925-5439. *Olympia* and *Becuna* ¢¢

Pennsylvania Hospital (1751). First in country, founded by Benjamin Franklin. 8th & Spruce Sts.

Pentimenti Gallery. Exhibiting works of art in all modes ranging from figurative to abstract by local, regional and international artists. (Daily) 133 N 3rd St. Phone 215/625-9990.

Philadelphia History Museum—The Atwater Kent. Hundreds of fascinating artifacts, toys and miniatures, maps, prints, paintings and photographs reflecting the city's social and cultural history. (Wed–Mon; closed hols) 15 S 7th St. Phone 215/684-7500. ¢

Philadelphia Museum of Art. Over 200 galleries with collections of paintings, graphics, sculpture; period rms, medieval cloister, Indian temple, Chinese palace hall, Japanese teahouse; armor collection. American wing incl rural Pennsylvania Dutch crafts, Shaker furniture, and paintings of early American artists such as Gilbert Stuart and Thomas Eakins. Free guided tours. (Tues–Sun, also Wed eves; closed legal hols) Free admission Sun mornings. 26th St & Benjamin Franklin Pkwy. Phone 215/684-7500. ¢¢¢

Please Touch Museum for Children. Unique museum designed especially for children 1-7 yrs old. Hands-on exhibits, incl "Sendak," "Super-Market Science," "Studio PTM" and "Science Park." (Daily; closed Jan 1, Thanksgiving, Dec 25) 210 N 21st St. Phone 215/963-0667. ¢¢¢

Professional sports.

   National League baseball (Philadelphia Phillies). Veterans Stadium, Broad St & Pattison Ave. Phone 215/463-6000.

   NBA (Philadelphia 76ers). First Union Center, Broad St & Pattison Ave. Phone 215/339-7600.

   NFL (Philadelphia Eagles). Veterans Stadium, Broad St & Pattison Ave. Phone 215/463-2500.

   NHL (Philadelphia Flyers). First Union Center, Broad St & Pattison Ave. Phone 215/465-4500.

Rodin Museum. Largest collection of Rodin sculpture outside Paris. (Daily exc Mon; closed legal hols) 22nd St & Franklin Pkwy. Phone 215/563-1948. **Donation**

Rosenbach Museum and Library. This 19th-century townhouse has permanent and changing exhibits of fine and decorative arts; collection incl 18th- and 19th-century English and French prints, 18th-century American silver, historical manuscripts and American and British literature collection, incl a *Canterbury Tales* manuscript. (Daily exc Mon; closed hols, also Aug) 2010 DeLancey Pl. Phone 215/732-1600. Tours ¢¢

St Peter's Church (Episcopal) (1761). Georgian colonial architecture; numerous famous people buried in churchyard. 3rd & Pine Sts. Phone 215/925-5968 for appt.

Schuylkill Center for Environmental Education. A 500-acre natural area with more than 7 miles of trails; discovery rm; gift shop/bookstore. (Daily; closed hols) 9 mi NW, at 8480 Hagy's Mill Rd. Phone 215/482-7300. ¢¢

Sesame Place. 20 mi NE via I-95 to Levittown exit (25E). Follow signs for Oxford Valley Mall on the US 1 Bypass. (See BRISTOL)

Shopping.

Antique Row. Dozens of antique, third-world craft and curio shops. From 9th to 17th Sts along Pine St.

Italian Market. Historical outdoor food mall sells fresh foods, cookware and clothing. Also here are restaurants and South Philly cheesesteaks. (Daily) 9th St between Christian & Wharton Sts.

Jeweler's Row. Largest jewelry district in the country other than New York City. More than 300 shops, incl wholesalers and diamond cutters. 7th & Sansom Sts.

South St. Nearly 150 hip shops, boutiques and galleries line either side of the street. Broad St at Walnut.

The Bourse (1893-1895). Restored Victorian bldg houses shops and restaurants. 5th St, across from Liberty Bell Pavilion.

The Gallery. Concentration of 250 shops and restaurants in four-level mall with glass elevators, trees, fountains and benches. 10th & Market Sts. Phone 215/925-7162.

The Shops at the Bellevue. Beaux-arts architecture of the former Bellevue Stratford Hotel has been preserved and transformed; it now contains offices, a hotel and a four-level shopping area centered around an atrium court. (Daily exc Sun) Broad St at Walnut. Phone 215/875-8350.

Sightseeing tours.

Centipede Tours. Candlelight strolls (1½ hrs) through historic Philadelphia and Society Hill areas led by guides in 18th-century dress; begins and ends at City Tavern. (Mid-May–mid-Oct, Mon–Fri) Reservations preferred. 1315 Walnut St. Phone 215/735-3123. ¢¢

Gray Line bus tours. For info, reservations, contact 3101 E Orthodox St, 19137; Phone 215/744-1100 or 800/220-3133.

Philadelphia Carriage Company. Guided tours via horse-drawn carriage covering Society Hill and other historic areas; begin and end in front of Independence Hall & Liberty Bell Pavilion. (Daily, weather permitting; closed Dec 25) 500 N 13th St. Phone 215/922-6840. ¢¢¢¢-¢¢¢¢¢

Society Hill Area. This historic area, the name of which is derived from the Free Society of Traders, was created by William Penn as the city's original land company and has undergone extensive renewal of its historic bldgs. Area bounded approx by Front, Walnut, 7th & Lombard Sts. In this area are

Athenaeum of Philadelphia. Landmark example of Italian Renaissance architecture (1845-1847); restored bldg has American neoclassical-style decorative arts, paintings, sculpture; research library; furniture and art from the collection of Joseph Bonaparte, King of Spain and older brother of Napoleon; changing exhibits of architectural drawings, photos and rare books. (Mon–Fri; closed hols) 219 S 6th St. Phone 215/925-2688. **Free**

Physick House (1786). House of Dr. Philip Sung Physick, "father of American surgery," from 1815-1837. Restored Federal-style house with period furnishings; garden. (Thurs-Sun afternoons) 321 S 4th St. For tour schedule phone 215/925-7866. ¢¢

Powel House (1765). Georgian town house of Samuel Powel, last colonial mayor of Philadelphia and first mayor under the new republic. Period furnishings, silver and porcelain; garden. Tours (Thurs-Sun afternoons; closed most hols). 244 S 3rd St. For tour schedule phone 215/627-0364. ¢¢

Temple University (1884) (33,000 students). Undergraduate, professional and research school. Walking tours of campus. Cecil B. Moore Ave & Broad St. Phone 215/204-8551.

University of Pennsylvania (1740) (23,000 students). On campus are the restored Fisher Fine Arts Library (phone 215/898-8325), Annenberg Center for performing arts (phone 215/898-6791); University Museum of Archaeology and Anthropology and Institute of Contemporary Art, located at 36th & Sansom Sts (daily exc Mon; phone 215/898-7108; fee). Chestnut to Pine Sts & 32nd to 40th Sts. For info phone 215/898-5000.

University of Pennsylvania Museum of Archaeology & Anthropology. World-famous archaeological and ethnological collections developed from the museum's own expeditions, gifts and purchases; features Chinese, Near Eastern, Greek, ancient Egyptian, African, Pacific, and North, Middle & South American materials; library. Restaurant, shops. (Daily exc Mon; closed hols, also Sun in summer) 33rd & Spruce Sts. Phone 215/898-4000. ¢¢

US Mint. Produces coins of all denominations. Gallery affords visitors an elevated view of the coinage operations. Medal making may also be observed. Audiovisual, self-guided tours. Rittenhouse Room on the mezzanine contains historic coins, medals and other exhibits. (July–Aug, daily; rest of yr, Mon–Fri; closed Jan 1, Thanksgiving, Dec 25) On Independence Mall at 5th & Arch Sts. Phone 215/408-0114. **Free**

Wagner Free Institute of Science. Victorian science museum with more than 50,000 specimens illustrating the various branches of the natural sciences. Dinosaur bones, fossils, reptiles and rare species are all mounted in the Victorian style. Reference library and research archives. (Tues–Fri) Montgomery & 17th Sts. Phone 215/763-6529. **Free**

Walnut Street Theatre (1809). America's oldest theater. The Walnut Mainstage offers musicals, classical and contemporary plays. Two studio theaters provide a forum for new and avant-garde works. 9th & Walnut Sts. Phone 215/574-3550.

Washington Square. Walnut St from 6th St, where hundreds of Revolutionary War soldiers and victims of the yellow fever epidemic are buried. Life-size statue of Washington has tomb of Revolutionary War's Unknown Soldier at its feet. Across the street is

Philadelphia Savings Fund Society Building (1816). Site of oldest savings bank in US. Not open to public. Walnut & 8th Sts.

Annual Events

Mummers Parade. An 8-hr spectacle along Broad St. Jan 1.

PECO Energy Jazz Festival. Jazz concerts around the city. Phone 800/537-7676. 4 days mid-Feb.

"The Book and the Cook." Sample fine cuisine as world-famous cook book authors team up with the city's most respected chefs to create culinary delights. Wine tastings, market tours, film festival. Phone 215/686-3662. Early Mar.

Philadelphia Open House. House and garden tours in different neighborhoods; distinguished selection of over 150 private homes, gardens, historic sites. Many tours incl lunches, candlelight dinners or high teas. Phone 215/928-1188. Late Apr–mid-May.

Devon Horse Show. Approx 20 mi NW via US 30, at Horse Show Grounds, in Devon. One of America's leading equestrian events. More than 1,200 horses compete; country fair; antique carriage drive. Phone 610/964-0550. 9 days beginning Memorial Day wkend.

Elfreth's Alley Fete Days. Homes open to public, costumed guides, demonstrations of colonial crafts; food, entertainment. 1st wkend June.

CoreStates US Pro Cycling Championship. At 156 mi, it's the longest (and richest) single-day cycling event in the country. Mid-June.

Thanksgiving Day Parade. Giant floats; celebrities.

Army-Navy Football Game. John F. Kennedy Memorial Stadium or Veterans Stadium. 1st Sat Dec.

Fairmount Park Historical Christmas Tours. Period decorations in 18th-century mansions. Phone 215/684-7922. Early Dec.

Seasonal Events

American Music Theater Festival. Repertory incl new opera, musical comedy, cabaret-style shows, revues and experimental works. Main stage productions Mar–June.

Head House Open Air Craft Market. Pine & 2nd Sts, in Society Hill area in Head House Square. Crafts demonstrations, children's workshops. Sat & Sun, June–Aug.

Mann Center for the Performing Arts. 52nd St & Parkside Ave, West Fairmount Park. Philadelphia Orchestra performs late June–July, Mon, Wed & Thurs. Also popular music attractions. Phone 215/546-7900. June–Sept.

Robin Hood Dell East. 33rd & Ridge Sts, in Fairmount Park. Top stars in outdoor popular music concerts. Phone 215/685-9560. July–Aug.

Performing arts.

Philadelphia Orchestra. Academy of Music. Phone 215/893-1900. Sept–May. Also Mann Music Center (see above), late June–late July.

Philadelphia Theatre Company. Plays and Players Theatre, 1714 Delancey St. Four contemporary American plays per season. Phone 215/568-1920. Oct–June.

Pennsylvania Ballet. Performs at Merriam Theatre and at Academy of Music. Phone 215/551-7000.

The Opera Company of Philadelphia. Academy of Music. Phone 215/928-2100. Oct–Apr.

Horse racing. Flat racing at Philadelphia Park, Richlieu & Street Rds in Bensalem. For schedule phone 215/639-9000.

Additional Visitor Information

The Visitors Center of the Philadelphia Convention and Visitors Bureau, 16th St & John F. Kennedy Blvd, 19102, has tourist information and maps (daily; closed Thanksgiving, Dec 25). Phone 215/636-1666 or 800/537-7676.

There is also a visitor center at 3rd & Chestnut Sts, operated by the National Park Service. (Daily) Phone 215/597-8975 or 215/597-8974 for information on park attractions.

City Neighborhoods

Many of the restaurants, unrated dining establishments and some lodgings listed under Philadelphia include neighborhoods as well as exact street addresses. Geographic descriptions of these areas are given.

Center City. Area of Downtown around city hall; south of Kennedy Blvd, west of Juniper St, north of S Penn Square and east of 15th St.

Chestnut Hill. South of Stenton Ave, west and north of Cresheim Valley Dr and east of Fairmount Park; along Germantown Ave.

Chinatown. North-central area of Downtown; south of Vine St, west of 8th St, north of Arch St and east of 11th St.

Downtown. South of Spring Garden St, west of I-95, north of South St and east of the Schuylkill River. **North of Downtown:** North of Spring Garden St. **South of Downtown:** South of South St. **West of Downtown:** West of Schuylkill River.

Old City. Area of Downtown south of I-676, west of the Delaware River, north of Chestnut St and east of Independence Mall.

Society Hill. Southeast side of Downtown; south of Walnut St, west of Front St, north of Lombard St and east of 7th St.

South Street. Downtown area; South St between 10th St on the west and the Delaware River on the east; also north to Pine St and south to Bainbridge St.

Motels

★★ **BEST WESTERN HOTEL.** *11580 Roosevelt Blvd (19116), north of downtown.* 215/464-9500; FAX 215/464-8511; res: 800/528-1234. 100 rms, 2 story. S, D $70-$125; under 18 free; package plans. Crib free. TV; cable (premium). Pool; lifeguard. Playground. Complimentary continental bkfst. Bar from 5 pm. Ck-out 11 am. Coin lndry. Meeting rms. Business servs avail. Exercise equipt. Lawn games. Some bathrm phones, refrigerators. Many balconies. Picnic tables. Cr cds: A, C, D, DS, JCB, MC, V.

⬛ ⬛ ⬛ ⬛ ⬛ SC

✓★★ **COMFORT INN.** *3660 Street Rd (19020), N on I-95 to Street Rd W exit, 3 mi W.* 215/245-0100; FAX 215/245-1851; res: 800/228-5150; res: 800/458-6886. 141 units, 3 story. S $75-$109; D $85-$150; each addl $10; suites $125; family rates. Crib free. Pet accepted, some restrictions. TV; cable (premium). Complimentary continental bkfst. Restaurant nearby. Bar 4 pm-2 am; entertainment. Ck-out noon. Meeting rms. Business servs avail. In-rm modem link. Gift shop. Exercise equipt. Some in-rm whirlpools. Cr cds: A, C, D, DS, ER, JCB, MC, V.

⬛ ⬛ ⬛ ⬛ ⬛ SC

Motor Hotels

✓★★ **BEST WESTERN CENTER CITY HOTEL.** *501 N 22nd St (19130), in Center City.* 215/568-8300; FAX 215/557-0259; res: 800/528-1234. 183 rms, 3 story. S $109-$119; D $119-$139; each addl $10; suites $150; under 18 free; family rates. Pet accepted, some restrictions. TV; cable (premium), VCR avail. Pool; lifeguard. Restaurant 6:30 am-10:30 pm. Bar 11-2 am. Ck-out noon. Meeting rms. Business servs avail. In-rm modem link. Valet serv. Gift shop. Exercise equipt. Cr cds: A, C, D, DS, MC, V.

⬛ ⬛ ⬛ ⬛ ⬛ ⬛ SC

★★★ **CLUB HOTEL BY DOUBLETREE.** *9461 Roosevelt Blvd (19114), north of downtown.* 215/671-9600; FAX 215/464-7759; res: 800/354-4332. Web www.doubletreehotels.com. 188 rms, 6 story. S, D $79-$119; each addl $10; suites $150; under 17 free; wkend rates. Crib free. TV; cable, VCR avail. Indoor pool. Restaurant 6 am-11 pm. Bar 5-11 pm. Ck-out 11 am. Coin lndry. Meeting rms. Business center. In-rm modem link. Valet serv. Sundries. Gift shop. Exercise equipt. Health club privileges. Some refrigerators; microwaves avail. Cr cds: A, C, D, DS, MC, V.

⬛ ⬛ ⬛ ⬛ ⬛ ⬛ SC ⬛

✓★★★ **SHERATON PHILADELPHIA AIRPORT HOTEL.** *4101 Island Ave (19153), near Intl Airport, south of downtown.* 215/492-0400; FAX 215/365-6035. Web www.fourpoints.com. 177 rms, 5 story. S, D $169; each addl $15; under 18 free. Crib free. TV; cable (premium), VCR avail. Pool. Coffee in rms. Restaurant 6 am-2 pm, 5 pm-midnight; Sat to noon. Rm serv. Bar 1 pm-midnight. Ck-out noon. Coin lndry. Meeting rms. Business servs avail. Valet serv. Free airport transportation. Health club privileges. Refrigerators, microwaves avail. Cr cds: A, C, D, DS, MC, V.

⬛ ⬛ ⬛ ⬛ ⬛ ⬛ SC

Hotels

★★★ **ADAM'S MARK HOTEL.** *4000 City Line Monument Rd; (19131), west of downtown.* 215/581-5000; FAX 215/581-5069; res: 800/444-2326. Web www.adamsmark.com. 515 rms, 23 story. S $99-$219; D $99-$235; each addl $15; suites $179-$925; under 18 free; wkend, wkly rates. Crib free. TV; cable, VCR avail. Indoor/outdoor pool; whirlpool, poolside serv. Restaurant (see THE MARKER). Bars; entertainment. Ck-out noon. Convention facilities. Business center. In-rm modem link. Shopping arcade. Barber, beauty shop. Airport, RR station, bus depot transportation. Exercise equipt; sauna, steam rm. Refrigerators. Cr cds: A, C, D, DS, MC, V.

⬛ ⬛ ⬛ ⬛ ⬛ ⬛ SC ⬛

★★ **AIRPORT TOWER HOTEL.** *2015 Penrose Ave (19145), in Packer Park subdivision, near Intl Airport, south of downtown.* 215/755-6500; FAX 215/465-5517; res: 800/537-8483. E-mail towerhtl@aol.com. 224 rms, 17 story. S $99-$129; D $109-$139; each addl $10; under 18 free; wkly, wkend, hol rates; higher rates special events. Crib free. Pet accepted, some restrictions; $35. TV; cable (premium). Heated pool; wading pool, poolside serv. Complimentary coffee in rms. Restaurant 6:30 am-10 pm. Bar 11-2 am. Ck-out noon. Coin lndry. Meeting rms. Business servs avail. In-rm modem link. Gift shop. Free airport, RR station transportation. Tennis privileges. 18-hole golf privileges. Exercise equipt. Some refrigerators; microwaves avail. Cr cds: A, C, D, DS, ER, JCB, MC, V.

⬛ ⬛ ⬛ ⬛ ⬛ ⬛ ⬛ ⬛ SC

✓★★ **COMFORT INN.** *100 N Christopher Columbus Blvd (19106), downtown.* 215/627-7900; FAX 215/238-0809; res: 800/228-5150. 185 rms, 10 story. S, D $99-$129; each addl $10; suites $160; under 18 free; higher rates some hols. Crib free. TV. Complimentary continental bkfst. Coffee in rms. Restaurant nearby. Bar 5 pm-2 am. Ck-out noon. Meeting rms. Business servs avail. In-rm modem link. Airport, RR station, bus depot transportation. Health club privileges. View of Delaware River. Cr cds: A, C, D, DS, ER, JCB, MC, V.

⬛ ⬛ ⬛ SC

★ ★ ★ **DOUBLETREE GUEST SUITES.** *640 W Germantown Pike (19462), W on I-76, exit I-476N to Germantown Pike West exit, right on Hickory Rd.* 610/834-8300; FAX 610/834-7813; res: 800/222-8733. Web www.doubletreehotels.com. 252 suites, 7 story. S, D $230-$250; family, wkend rates. Crib $10. TV; cable (premium), VCR avail. Indoor pool; whirlpool, wading pool, poolside serv, lifeguard. Restaurant 6:30 am-10 pm. Bar. Ck-out noon. Coin lndry. Meeting rms. Business servs avail. In-rm modem link. Gift shop. Airport, RR station, bus depot transportation. Exercise equipt; sauna. Bathrm phones, refrigerators, minibars; microwaves avail. Some private patios, balconies. Cr cds: A, C, D, DS, MC, V.

D ⛱ 🏃 🏋 ➰ 🔥 SC

★ ★ ★ **DOUBLETREE HOTEL.** *Broad St & Locust St (19107), downtown.* 215/893-1600; FAX 215/893-1663; res: 800/222-8733. Web www.doubletree.com. 427 rms, 26 story. S $160-$195; D $185-$209; each addl $15; suites $250-$500; under 18 free; wkend rates; higher rates New Year's hols. Crib free. Garage $13, valet $17. TV; cable (premium), VCR avail. Indoor pool; whirlpool. Coffee in rms. Restaurant 6:30 am-11 pm; Fri, Sat to midnight. Bar to 1 am. Ck-out noon. Convention facilities. Business servs avail. In-rm modem link. Concierge. Gift shop. Airport transportation. Exercise equipt; sauna, steam rm. Health club privileges. Luxury level. Cr cds: A, C, D, DS, ER, JCB, MC, V.

D ⛱ 🏃 🏋 ➰ 🔥 SC

★ ★ ★ ★ **FOUR SEASONS HOTEL.** *1 Logan Square (19103), in center of Museum District, on Logan Circle, downtown.* 215/963-1500; FAX 215/963-9506; res: 800/332-3442. Web www.fshr.com. This elegant eight-story hotel has a magnificent setting on Logan Circle, reminiscent of the Place de la Concorde in Paris. Guest rooms are large and uncluttered, and the spacious marble lobby has an indoor garden with a fountain that makes it easy to forget that this is the heart of a large city. 371 rms, 8 story. S $290-$355; D $330-$395; each addl $30; suites $400-$2,600; under 18 free; wkend rates. Pet accepted. Garage $24. TV; cable (premium), VCR avail. Indoor pool; whirlpool, poolside serv, lifeguard. Restaurants 6:30-1 am; Sat, Sun from 7 am (also see FOUNTAIN and SWANN CAFE; and see SWANN LOUNGE, Unrated Dining). Rm serv 24 hrs. Bar 11-2 am; pianist. Ck-out 1 pm. Convention facilities. Business center. In-rm modem link. Concierge. Beauty shop. Exercise rm; sauna. Massage. Minibars; microwaves avail. Some balconies. Cr cds: A, C, D, ER, JCB, MC, V.

D 🐾 ⛱ 🏃 ➰ 🔥 🏃

★ ★ ★ **FRANKLIN PLAZA HOTEL.** *2 Franklin Blvd (19103), jct 17th & Race Sts, downtown.* 215/448-2000; FAX 215/448-2864; res: 800/996-3426. E-mail franklinplaza@wyndham.com; web www.wyndham.com. 758 rms, 26 story. S $185-$218; D $215-$225; each addl $20; suites $400-$1,300; under 18 free; wkend rates. Crib free. Pet accepted, some restrictions. Garage $15. TV; cable (premium), VCR avail. Indoor pool; whirlpool, poolside serv. Complimentary coffee in rms. Restaurant 6 am-11 pm. Bars 11-1 am. Ck-out noon. Convention facilities. Business center. In-rm modem link. Drugstore. Barber, beauty shop. Tennis. Exercise rm; sauna, steam rm. Massage. Refrigerators; microwaves avail. Cr cds: A, C, D, DS, ER, JCB, MC, V.

D 🐾 🏋 ⛱ 🏃 ➰ 🔥 SC 🏃

★ ★ ★ **HILTON AIRPORT.** *4509 Island Ave (19153), at Intl Airport, south of downtown.* 215/365-4150; FAX 215/365-3875; res: 800/228-9290. 330 rms, 9 story. S, D $109-$149; suites $325; studio rms $150; under 18 free; wkend rates. Crib free. Pet accepted, some restrictions. TV; cable (premium). Indoor pool; whirlpool. Restaurant 6 am-11 pm. Rm serv 24 hrs. Bar 11-2 am. Ck-out noon. Meeting rms. Business center. In-rm modem link. Gift shop. Free airport transportation. Exercise equipt. Luxury level. Cr cds: A, C, D, DS, ER, MC, V.

D 🐾 ⛱ 🏃 ✈ ➰ 🔥 SC 🏃

★ ★ ★ **HOLIDAY INN.** *1800 Market St (19103), in Center City.* 215/561-7500; FAX 215/561-4484; res: 800/HOLIDAY. Web www.holidayinnselect-phila.com. 445 rms, 25 story. S $175-$215; D $185-$225; each addl $10; suites $450; under 19 free; wkend rates. Crib free. Pet accepted. Garage fee. TV; cable (premium), VCR avail. Pool. Restaurant 6 am-2 am. Bar from 11 am. Ck-out noon. Coin lndry. Convention facilities. In-rm modem link. Concierge. Gift shop. Airport transportation. Exercise equipt. Health club privileges. Microwaves avail. Cr cds: A, C, D, DS, ER, JCB, MC, V.

D 🐾 ⛱ 🏃 ➰ 🔥 SC

★ ★ **HOLIDAY INN.** *400 Arch St (19106), downtown.* 215/923-8660; FAX 215/923-4633; res: 800/843-2355. 364 rms, 8 story. S, D $99-$169; each addl $10; suites $275-$300; under 19 free; wkend rates. Garage $10. Crib free. Pet accepted. TV; cable (premium), VCR avail. Rooftop pool; lifeguard. Restaurant 6:30 am-10 pm. Bar 11-1 am, Sun from noon. Ck-out 11 am. Coin lndry. Meeting rms. Business center. Sundries. Gift shop. Health club privileges. Cr cds: A, C, D, DS, JCB, MC, V.

D 🐾 ⛱ ➰ 🔥 SC 🏃

★ ★ **HOLIDAY INN EXPRESS.** *1305-11 Walnut St (19107), downtown.* 215/735-9300; FAX 215/732-2682; res: 800/465-4329. E-mail midtown@erols.com; web www.libertynet.org/iha/holidayinn. 166 rms, 20 story. S $120-$145; D $130-$155; each addl $10; under 19 free. Crib free. Garage $12.75. TV; cable (premium). Pool. Complimentary continental bkfst. Ck-out 1 pm. Meeting rms. Business servs avail. In-rm modem link. Concierge. Health club privileges. Cr cds: A, C, D, DS, JCB, MC, V.

D ⛱ ➰ 🔥 SC

✓ ★ ★ ★ **KORMAN SUITES.** *2001 Hamilton St (19130), just off the Pkwy, museum area, in Center City.* 215/569-7000; FAX 215/496-0138; res: 888/456-7626. 150 suites, 25 story. S $109-$169, D $139-$189; under 18 free; wkend rates. Crib free. TV; cable (premium). Pool; whirlpool, poolside serv, lifeguard. Complimentary coffee. Restaurant 6:30-2 am. Bar. Ck-out 11 am. Convention facilities. Business servs avail. In-rm modem link. Gift shop. Barber, beauty shop. Free garage parking. Exercise equipt. Microwaves. Landscaped Japanese sculpture garden. In museum district. Cr cds: A, C, D, MC, V.

D ⛱ 🏃 ➰ 🔥 SC

★ ★ ★ **LATHAM HOTEL.** *135 S 17th St (19103), at Walnut St, downtown.* 215/563-7474; FAX 215/568-0110; res: 800/528-1877. E-mail jlittle@lathamhotel.com; web www.lathamhotel.com. 139 rms, 14 story. S, D $195-$245; each addl $20; suites $350 & $450; under 18 free; wkend, hol rates. Crib free. Valet parking $14. TV; cable (premium), VCR avail (movies). Pool privileges. Restaurant 6:30 am-10:30 pm. Bar 11:30-2 am. Ck-out noon. Meeting rms. Business center. In-rm modem link. Concierge. Exercise equipt. Health club privileges. Many minibars. European ambience in intimate, boutique-style hotel. Cr cds: A, C, D, DS, ER, JCB, MC, V.

D 🏋 ➰ 🔥 SC 🏃

★ ★ ★ **MARRIOTT.** *111 Crawford Ave (19428), 11 mi W on I-76, exit 29.* 610/941-5600; FAX 610/940-1060; res: 800/237-3639. 286 rms, 17 story. S $179-$189; D $199-$209; each addl $30; suites $375; wkend, hol rates. Crib free. TV; cable (premium), VCR avail. Indoor pool; whirlpool, poolside serv, lifeguard. Restaurant 6 am-11 pm. Bar. Ck-out 1 pm. Convention facilities. Business servs avail. In-rm modem link. Concierge. Gift shop. Airport, RR station transportation. Exercise rm; sauna. Microwaves avail. 1 blk from Schuylkill River. Atrium deck. Luxury level. Cr cds: A, C, D, DS, MC, V.

D ⛱ 🏃 ✈ ➰ 🔥 SC

★ ★ ★ **MARRIOTT.** *1201 Market St (19107), in Center City.* 215/625-2900; FAX 215/625-6000; res: 800/228-9290. Web www.marriott.com. 1,198 rms, 23 story, 56 suites. S $189-$230; D $210-$270; suites $375-$1,000; under 12 free; wkend, hol rates. Crib free. Valet parking $23. TV; cable (premium), VCR avail. Indoor pool; wading pool, whirlpool. Restaurants 6:30-1:30 am. Bar 11-2 am. Ck-out noon. Coin lndry. Convention facilities. Business center. In-rm modem link. Concierge. Shopping arcade. Beauty shop. Exercise equipt; sauna. Refrigerator in suites; microwaves avail. Connected to shopping mall. Luxury level. Cr cds: A, C, D, DS, ER, JCB, MC, V.

D ⊠ 🏃 ⊠ 🔥 SC 🏃

★★★ **OMNI HOTEL AT INDEPENDENCE PARK.** *4th & Chestnut Sts (19106), on Independence Park, adj to Independence Hall, in Olde City.* 215/925-0000; FAX 215/925-1263. 150 rms, 14 story. S $249; D $269; each addl $20; suites from $340; under 18 free; wkend rates. Garage, valet parking (fees). TV; cable (premium), VCR avail. Indoor pool; whirlpool. Restaurant (see AZALEA). Rm serv 24 hrs. Bar 3-11 pm; entertainment Tues-Sat. Ck-out 11 am. Meeting rms. Business center. In-rm modem link. Concierge. Gift shop. Exercise equipt; sauna. Massage. Bathrm phones, minibars; microwaves avail. Cr cds: A, C, D, DS, ER, JCB, MC, V.

D ⊠ 🏃 ⊠ 🔥 SC 🏃

★★★ **PARK HYATT PHILADELPHIA AT THE BELLEVUE.** *Broad & Walnut Sts (19102), downtown.* 215/893-1234; FAX 215/893-9868; res: 800/223-1234. Web www.hyatt.com. 170 rms, 7 story. S $225-$325; D $250-$350; suites $350-$1,800; under 18 free; special plans. Crib free. Garage $14, valet $21. TV; cable (premium), VCR. Indoor pool privileges; whirlpool. Restaurants 7 am-11 pm (also see THE FOUNDERS). Rm serv 24 hrs. Bar 11-1 am. Ck-out 1 pm. Business center. In-rm modem link. Concierge. Shopping arcade. Barber, beauty shop. Tennis privileges. Golf privileges. Health club privileges. Massage. Bathrm phones, minibars. Conservatory atrium. Cr cds: A, C, D, DS, ER, JCB, MC, V.

D 🖫 🎿 ⊠ 🔥 SC

★★★ **PENN'S VIEW INN.** *14 N Front St (19106), in Olde City.* 215/922-7600; FAX 215/922-7642; res: 800/331-7634. 40 rms, 5 story. S, D $115-$200; under 12 free; wkend rates. Crib free. TV; cable, VCR avail. Complimentary continental bkfst. Dining rm (see RISTORANTE PANORAMA). Ck-out noon, ck-in 4 pm. Meeting rms. Business servs avail. In-rm modem link. Concierge. Airport, RR station, bus depot transportation. Health club privileges. Some in-rm whirlpools, fireplaces. Overlooks Delaware River. Built 1828; Old World elegance. Cr cds: A, C, D, ER, JCB, MC, V.

D ⊠ 🔥 SC

★★★ **RADISSON HOTEL.** *500 Stevens Dr (19113), at Intl Airport (US 291), south of downtown.* 610/521-5900; FAX 610/521-4362; res: 800/333-3333. E-mail radssnphl@aol.com; web www.radisson.com. 353 rms, 12 story. S $155; D $165; each addl $10; suites $175; under 18 free; wkend packages. Crib free. TV; cable. Indoor pool; whirlpool, poolside serv. Restaurant 6:30 am-2 pm, 5-11 pm. Bars 2 pm-midnight. Ck-out noon. Meeting rms. Business center. In-rm modem link. Gift shop. Free airport transportation. Exercise equipt. Game rm. Microwaves avail. Atrium. Cr cds: A, C, D, DS, ER, MC, V.

D ⊠ 🏃 🎿 ⊠ 🔥 SC 🏃

★★ **RADISSON HOTEL.** *2400 Old Lincoln Hwy (19053), N on I-95, exit 24.* 215/638-8300; FAX 215/638-4377; res: 800/333-3333. 282 rms, 6 story. S $129; D $139; each addl $10; suites $209-$309; under 18 free; family rates. TV; cable, VCR avail. Complimentary coffee in rms. Restaurant 6:30 am-10 pm; Sun 7 am-noon, 5-10 pm. Bar noon-2 am; entertainment. Ck-out noon. Convention facilities. Business servs avail. In-rm modem link. Concierge. Gift shop. Barber, beauty shop. Coin lndry. Exercise equipt. Indoor/outdoor pool; poolside serv, lifeguard. Game rm. Some refrigerators; wet bars. Atrium. Cr cds: A, C, D, DS, ER, JCB, MC, V.

D ⊠ 🏃 ⊠ 🔥 SC

★★★ **RADNOR HOTEL.** *591 E Lancaster Ave (19087), 17 mi W on US 30, ¼ mi W of Blue Rte (I-476) exit 5.* 610/688-5800; FAX 610/341-3299; res: 800/537-3000. E-mail iprevost@radnorhotel.com; web www.radnorhotel.com. 170 rms, 4 story. S $145-$160; D $155-$170; each addl $10; suites $220; under 16 free. Crib free. TV; cable (premium), VCR avail. Pool; wading pool, lifeguard. Restaurant (see ABBEY GRILL). Rm serv 24 hrs. Bar 11-2 am; entertainment wkends. Ck-out noon. Meeting rms. Business center. In-rm modem link. Airport transportation. Exercise equipt. Health club privileges. Game rm. Microwaves avail. Luxury level. Cr cds: A, C, D, DS, ER, JCB, MC, V.

D ⊠ 🏃 ⊠ 🔥 SC 🏃

★★★ **SHERATON SOCIETY HILL HOTEL.** *One Dock St (19106), in Society Hill.* 215/238-6000; FAX 215/922-2709; res: 888/345-7333. Web www.ITTsheraton.com. 365 units, 4 story. S, D $169-$250; suites $450-$3,000; under 17 free; wkend rates. Crib free. Pet accepted. Covered parking (fee). TV; cable (premium), VCR avail. Indoor pool; whirlpool, wading pool, poolside serv. Coffee in rms. Restaurants 6:30 am-2 pm, 5-10 pm. Rm serv 24 hrs. Bar noon-2 am. Ck-out noon. Convention facilities. Business servs avail. In-rm modem link. Concierge. Shopping arcade. Exercise rm; sauna. Massage. Minibars; some refrigerators. Cr cds: A, C, D, DS, ER, JCB, MC, V.

D 🐾 ⊠ 🏃 ⊠ 🔥 SC

★★★ **ST. REGIS HOTEL PHILADELPHIA.** *17th & Chestnut Sts (19103), at Liberty Place, downtown.* 215/563-1600; FAX 215/567-2822. Web www.ritzcarlton.com. Unrated for 2000 due to renovation. 290 rms, 15 story. S, D $245-$355; suites $395-$1,250; wkend rates. Crib free. Pet accepted. Garage (fee). TV; cable (premium), VCR avail. Restaurant (see THE GRILL). Rm serv 24 hrs. Bar 11-1 am; pianist. Ck-out noon. Meeting rms. Business center. In-rm modem link. Concierge. Gift shop. Airport, RR station transportation. Exercise equipt; sauna. Massage. Health club privileges. Bathrm phones, minibars. Cr cds: A, C, D, DS, ER, JCB, MC, V.

D 🐾 🏃 ⊠ 🔥 🏃

★★★★ **THE RITTENHOUSE HOTEL.** *210 W Rittenhouse Sq (19103), downtown.* 215/546-9000; FAX 215/732-3364; res: 800/635-1042. E-mail hotel@rittenhouse.com; web www.rittenhousehotel.com. Subdued elegance and superior, intimate service are the hallmarks of the lower floors of a residential building on fashionable Rittenhouse Square, a verdant park in central Philadelphia. The hotel is suitable for business travelers, family vacationers and honeymooners. 133 rms, 9 story. S, D $330-$355; suites $525-$1,400; wkend rates. Crib free. Pet accepted. Garage; valet parking $25. TV; cable (premium), VCR (movies avail). Indoor pool; poolside serv. Restaurants (see NICHOLAS NICKOLAS, NICK'S and TREETOPS). Rm serv 24 hrs. Bar; entertainment. Ck-out 1 pm. Meeting rms. Business center. In-rm modem link. Concierge. Barber, beauty shop. Tennis privileges. Golf privileges. Exercise rm; sauna, steam rm. Massage. Bathrm phones, minibars; microwaves avail. Cr cds: A, C, D, DS, MC, V.

D 🐾 🎿 🏊 ⊠ 🏃 ⊠ 🔥 🏃

★★★ **WARWICK HOTEL.** *1701 Locust St (19103), downtown.* 215/735-6000; FAX 215/790-7766; res: 800/523-4210. 180 rms, 20 story, 20 kits. S $165-$185; D $195-$200; each addl $15; suites $185-$390; studio rms $185; apt $195; under 12 free; wkend rates. Crib free. Garage (fee). TV; cable (premium), VCR avail. Restaurant 6:30 am-midnight. Bar 11-2 am. Ck-out noon. Meeting rms. Business servs avail. In-rm modem link. Concierge. Barber, beauty shop. Health club privileges. Cr cds: A, C, D, DS, MC, V.

D ⊠ 🔥 SC

★★★ **WESTIN SUITES HOTEL.** *4101 Island Ave (19153), at I-95 Island Ave exit, near Intl Airport, south of downtown.* 215/365-6600; FAX 215/492-9858; res: 800/222-8733. E-mail gcordero@starlodge.com; web www.westin.com. 251 suites, 8 story. S, D $185-$205; each addl $15; under 18 free; wkend rates. Crib free. TV; cable (premium), VCR avail. Indoor pool; whirlpool, lifeguard. Coffee in rms. Restaurant 6 am-11 pm. Bar noon-2 am. Ck-out noon. Meeting rms. Business center. In-rm modem link. Gift shop. Free airport transportation. Exercise equipt; sauna, steam rm. Bathrm phones, refrigerators, minibars; microwaves avail. Cr cds: A, C, D, DS, JCB, MC, V.

Inns

✓★ **BED & BREAKFAST CENTER CITY.** 1804 Pine St (19103), in Center City. 215/735-1137; FAX 215/735-0582; res: 800/354-8401. Web travelguides.com/bb/reserve/. 8 rms, 5 share bath, 4 story, 3 suites. No rm phones. S, D $60-$100; suites $95. Crib avail. TV in common rm; cable (premium), VCR avail (movies). Complimentary full bkfst. Restaurant nearby. Ck-out, ck-in times vary. Business servs avail. Luggage handling. Concierge serv. Street parking. Many fireplaces; microwaves avail. Built in 1868. Victorian decor; antiques. Totally nonsmoking. Cr cds: A, C, DS, MC, V.

★ **RODEWAY INN.** 1208 Walnut St (19107), in Center City. 215/546-7000; FAX 215/546-7573; res: 800/887-1776. E-mail murrayorgn@aol.com. 25 rms, 22 with shower only, 7 story, 6 suites. S, D $95; each addl $15; suites $125. Crib free. Parking adj $9. TV; cable. Complimentary continental bkfst; afternoon refreshments. Restaurant nearby. Ck-out noon, ck-in 3 pm. Luggage handling. Business servs avail. In-rm modem link. Health club privileges. Built in 1890s; early American decor. Walking distance from Pennsylvania Convention Center. Cr cds: A, C, D, DS, MC, V.

★★ **TEN-ELEVEN CLINTON.** 1011 Clinton St (19107), downtown. 215/923-8144; FAX 215/923-5757. E-mail 1011@concentric.net. 8 rms, 3 story, 7 kit units. No elvtrs. S, D, kit units $125-$175; each addl $15; wkends 2-day min. Crib free. Pet accepted, some restrictions. TV; cable, VCR (movies). Complimentary continental bkfst. Complimentary coffee in rms. Restaurant nearby. Ck-out noon, ck-in 3 pm. Business servs avail. In-rm modem link. Luggage handling. Concierge serv. Coin lndry. Street parking. Health club privileges. Some fireplaces. Some balconies. Built in 1836; enclosed courtyard. Totally nonsmoking. Cr cds: A, C, MC, V.

✓★★ **THOMAS BOND HOUSE.** 129 S 2nd St (19106), in Olde City. 215/923-8523; FAX 215/923-8504; res: 800/845-2663. Web www.libertynet.org/phila-visitor. 12 rms, 4 story, 2 suites. No elvtr. S, D $95-$175; each addl $15; suites $175. TV. Complimentary continental bkfst; afternoon refreshments. Restaurants nearby. Ck-out noon, ck-in 3-9 pm. Business servs avail. Airport transportation. Health club privileges. Library/sitting rm; antiques. Restored guest house (1769) built by Dr Thomas Bond, founder of the country's first public hospital. Individually decorated rms. Totally nonsmoking. Cr cds: A, C, D, DS, MC, V.

Restaurants

★★★ **ABBEY GRILL.** (See Radnor Hotel) 610/341-3165. Web www.radnorhotel.com. Hrs: 6:30 am-10 pm; wkends to 11 pm; Sun brunch 10 am-2 pm. Res accepted; required hols. Bar to 2 am. Wine list. Semi-a la carte: lunch $5.95-$12.95, dinner $12.95-$19.95. Sun brunch $19.95. Child's meals. Specializes in ostrich, salmon. Entertainment Fri. Parking. Outdoor dining. Cr cds: A, C, D, DS, ER, JCB, MC, V.

★★ **ARROYO GRILLE.** 1 Leverington Ave (19127), 6 mi W on I-76, exit 31, right at 1st light, left on Main St, left on Leverington. 215/487-1400. Web www.arroyogrille.com. Hrs: 11-2 am; Sun brunch to 3 pm. Closed Thanksgiving. Res accepted. Southwestern menu. Bar. A la carte entrees: lunch $5-$12, dinner $13-$22. Sun brunch $17.95. Child's meals. Specializes in smokehouse barbecue, margaritas. Own baking.

pasta. Musicians Wed-Sun. Parking. Outdoor dining. Southwestern decor with woodburning fireplace; two-level dining area. Cr cds: A, C, DS, MC, V.

★★ **ASSAGGI ITALIANI.** 935 Ellsworth St (19147), south of downtown. 215/339-0700. Hrs: 5:30-10 pm; Fri, Sat to 11 pm; Sun 4-9 pm. Closed Mon; most major hols. Res accepted. Tuscan menu. Bar. A la carte entrees: dinner $8.50-$21. Specializes in pasta, grilled fish, veal dishes. Own baking. Italian decor. Cr cds: A, C, D, MC, V.

★★★ **AZALEA.** (See Omni Hotel at Independence Park) 215/931-4270. Hrs: 7 am-2:30 pm, 5:30-10 pm; wkends to 11 pm; Sun brunch 11 am-2 pm. Res accepted. Bar. Wine list. A la carte entrees: bkfst $8.95-$17, lunch $8.75-$16.50, dinner $12.50-$19.50. Sun brunch $23.95. Specialties: Chilean sea bass, Norwegian salmon, duck. Valet parking. Cr cds: A, C, D, DS, ER, JCB, MC, V.

★ **BERLENGAS.** 4926 N 5th St (19120), north of downtown. 215/324-3240. Hrs: noon-10 pm. Closed Wed. Res required Fri-Sun dinner. Portuguese menu. Bar 10 am-midnight. A la carte entrees: lunch, dinner $11-$25. Specializes in seafood. Jacket. Intimate atmosphere. Cr cds: C, MC, V.

★★ **BIG FISH.** 140 Moorehead Ave (19428), 11 mi W on I-76, exit 29. 610/834-7224. Hrs: 11:30 am-10 pm; Fri, Sat to 11 pm, Sun noon-9 pm. Res accepted. Bar. Semi-a la carte: lunch $7-$15, dinner $10-$23. Child's meals. Specializes in fresh seafood. Free parking. Nautical decor. Cr cds: A, C, D, DS, MC, V.

★★★ **BONAPARTE RESTAURANT.** 260 S Broad St (19102), downtown. 215/893-9100. Hrs: 5-10 pm; Fri, Sat to 11 pm. Closed major hols. Res accepted. Contemporary menu. Bar. Wine list. A la carte entrees: dinner $16.50-$24. Specialities: gold tomato barbequed monkfish, steak Napoleon. Valet parking. Entertainment Sat. Modern decor with old-world charm. Cr cds: A, C, D, MC, V.

★★ **BOOKBINDER'S 15TH STREET SEAFOOD HOUSE.** 215 S 15th St (19102), in Center City. 215/545-1137. Hrs: 11:30 am-10 pm; Sat 4-11 pm; Sun 3-10 pm. Closed Thanksgiving, Dec 25. Res accepted. Bar. Semi-a la carte: lunch $6-$13.50, dinner $15.95-$24.95. Child's meals. Specializes in seafood, steak. Own pastries. Family-owned since 1893. Cr cds: A, C, D, DS, MC, V.

★★★★ **BRASSERIE PERRIER.** 1619 Walnut St (19102), downtown. 215/568-3000. E-mail saugustine@brasserieperrier.com; web www.brasserieperrier.com. Original paintings and sculpture complement the art-deco decor of this elegant restaurant. Eclectic menu. Specializes in pasta, fresh seafood. Hrs: 11:30 am-2:30 pm, 5:30-11 pm. Closed most major hols. Res required. Bar to 1 am. Wine cellar. Complete meal: 3-course lunch $25. Semi-a la carte: dinner $19-$35. Valet parking. Totally nonsmoking. Cr cds: A, C, DS, MC, V.

✓★★ **BRIDGET FOY'S SOUTH STREET GRILL.** 200 South St (19147), near Head House Square, in South Street Area. 215/922-1813. E-mail 28696@msn.com; web www.bridgetfoys.com. Hrs: 11:30 am-10:30 pm; Fri, Sat to midnight. Closed Thanksgiving, Dec 25. Res accepted. Bar to 2 am. A la carte entrees: lunch $6.95-$12.95, dinner $11.95-$19.95. Specializes in grilled fish, meat. Valet parking wkends. Outdoor dining. Cr cds: A, C, D, DS, MC, V.

★★ **CIBO.** *603 S 3rd St (19147), in South Street Area.* 215/625-5700. Hrs: 5-10 pm; Fri, Sat to 11:30 pm. Res accepted Fri, Sat. Bar to 2 am. A la carte entrees: dinner $8.50-$18. Specialties: steak frites, grilled tuna, braised veal cheeks. Outdoor dining. European bistro decor. Cr cds: A, C, D, MC, V.

D

★★★ **CIBOULETTE.** *200 S Broad St (19102), downtown.* 215/790-1210. Hrs: 5:30-9 pm; Fri, Sat to 10:30 pm. Closed Sun; most major hols. Res accepted; required Sat. French Provençal menu. Bar. Wine cellar. A la carte entrees (appetizer portions): $6-$18. Specialties: roasted Maine lobster, black sea bass, loin of veal. Own desserts. Valet parking. French Renaissance-style architecture; display of local artists; original mosaic tile floor; one rm with ceiling mural. Cr cds: A, C, MC, V.

D

★★★ **CIRCA.** *1518 Walnut St (19102), downtown.* 215/545-6800. Web www.circarestaurant.com. Hrs: 11:30 am-2:30 pm, 5-10 pm; Thurs, Sat to 11 pm; Mon from 5 pm; Sun 4:30-9 pm. Closed Jan 1, Dec 25. Res accepted. Bar. Wine list. Semi-a la carte: lunch $8-$15, dinner $13.25-$24. Child's meals. Specialties: roast Chilean sea bass, fire grilled spice-rubbed filet mignon, crazy E's BBQ pork loin chop. Valet parking. Former bank lobby; cathedral ceilings. Seating in authentic bank vault. Cr cds: A, C, D, MC, V.

D

★★ **CITY TAVERN.** *138 S 2nd St At Walnut (19106), in Society Hill area.* 215/413-1443. E-mail citytav@axs2000.net; web www.citytavern.com. Hrs: 11:30 am-10:30 pm. Res accepted. Bar. Semi-a la carte: lunch $8.95-$16.95, dinner $17.95-$32.95. Child's meals. Specializes in fresh fish, poultry, meats. Entertainment Sat. Outdoor dining (in season). Historic colonial tavern (1773). Cr cds: A, C, D, DS, MC, V.

D

★★ **COYOTE CROSSING.** *800 Spring Mill Ave (19428), 15 mi W on I-76, exit Conshohocken.* 610/825-3000. E-mail dreamer@worldlynx.net; web www.coyotecrossing.com. Hrs: 11:30 am-2:30 pm, 5-9 pm; Fri to 10:30 pm; Sat 4:30-10:30 pm; Sun from 4:30 pm. Closed Jan 1, July 4, Dec 25. Southwestern menu. Bar. A la carte entrees: lunch $6.75-$9.95, dinner $11.95-$18.95. Specialties: homemade stuffed crepes, filet mignon, enchiladas. Own baking. Outdoor dining. Modern Southwestern decor. Cr cds: A, C, D, DS, MC, V.

D

★★ **CUVEE NOTRE DAME.** *1701 Green St (19130), downtown.* 215/765-2777. Hrs: 11:30-2 am; Sun brunch 11:30 am-2:30 pm. Closed Thanksgiving, Dec 25. Res accepted. Belgian menu. Bar. A la carte entrees: lunch $5, dinner $15-$21. Sun brunch $15. Child's meals. Specializes in mussels, duck. Outdoor dining. Belgian atmosphere. Cr cds: A, C, D, DS, MC, V.

D

★★★ **DEUX CHEMINEES.** *1221 Locust St (19107), downtown.* 215/790-0200. Hrs: 5:30-8:30 pm; Sat to 9 pm. Closed Sun, Mon; major hols. Res accepted. French menu. Serv bar. Wine cellar. Prix fixe: dinner $75. Specialties: rack of lamb, crab soup. Menu changes daily. Own baking. Chef-owned. Totally nonsmoking. Cr cds: A, C, D, MC, V.

♥

★★ **DICKENS INN.** *Head House Square (19147), on 2nd St, in Society Hill.* 215/928-9307. E-mail box51@dickensinn.com; web www.dickensinn.com. Hrs: 11:30 am-3 pm, 5-10 pm; Sat to 10:30 pm; Sun 4:30-9 pm; Sun brunch 11 am-2:30 pm. Closed Mon; Jan 1, Dec 25. Res accepted. Continental menu. Bar 11:30-2 am; Mon from 5 pm. A la carte entrees: lunch $4.75-$10.75, dinner $13.95-$24. Sun brunch $6-$8.50.

Child's meals. Specialties: beef Wellington, fish & chips. In historic Harper House (1788); Victorian decor; artwork imported from England. Cr cds: A, C, D, DS, MC, V.

D

★ **DIMITRI'S.** *795 S 3rd St (19147), south of downtown.* 215/625-0556. Hrs: 5:30-11 pm; Sun 5-10 pm. Closed Easter, Thanksgiving, Dec 24, 25. Mediterranean menu. Setups. A la carte entrees: $12-$20. Specializes in seafood, lamb. Cr cds: C.

★★★ **DINARDO'S.** *312 Race St (19106), in Olde City.* 215/925-5115. Web www.menusonline.com. Hrs: 11 am-10 pm; Fri, Sat to 11 pm; Sun 3-9 pm. Closed Easter, Thanksgiving, Dec 25. Bar. Semi-a la carte: lunch $5-$10, dinner $12-$25. Child's meals. Specializes in seafood. Historic bldg (1740). Cr cds: A, C, D, MC, V.

D

✓★★ **DOCK STREET BREWERY.** *2 Logan Square (19103), at 18th & Cherry Sts, downtown.* 215/496-0413. Web www.dockstreet.com. Hrs: 11:30 am-midnight; Fri to 2 am; Sat noon-2 am; Sun noon-11 pm. Closed Labor Day, Dec 25. Res accepted. Bar. A la carte entrees: lunch $7.95-$10.50, dinner $8.95-$22.95. Specializes in beef, chicken, seafood. Entertainment Fri, Sat. Brewery tanks; beer brewed on premises, tours avail. Dart board and billiard tables. Cr cds: A, C, D, DS, MC, V.

D

★★ **FELICIA'S.** *1148 S 11th St (19147), south of downtown.* 215/755-9656. Hrs: 11:30-2 am. Closed Mon; most major hols. Res accepted; required Fri-Sun. Italian menu. Bar. Semi-a la carte: $6.95-$12.50, dinner $11.95-$21.95. Specialties: seafood ravioli, ricotta gnocci, veal chop. Own desserts. Valet parking. Cr cds: A, C, D, DS, MC, V.

D

✓★★ **FISHER'S SEAFOOD.** *7312 Castor Ave (19152), north of downtown.* 215/725-6201. Hrs: 11 am-9 pm; Fri, Sat to 10 pm; Sun noon-9 pm. Closed Mon; Labor Day, Thanksgiving, Dec 25. Res accepted. Bar. Semi-a la carte: lunch $3.25-$6.95, dinner $6.25-$12.95. Complete meals: lunch $4.95-$9.20, dinner $9.95-$15.95. Specializes in seafood, stir-fried dishes. Parking. Three large dining areas, individually decorated. Family-owned. Cr cds: C, DS, MC, V.

D ♥

★★ **FLYING FISH.** *8142 Germantown Ave (19118), in Chestnut Hill.* 215/247-0707. Hrs: 11:30 am-2:30 pm, 5:30-9 pm; Mon from 5:30 pm; Fri, Sat noon-2:30 pm, 5:30-10 pm. Closed Sun; some major hols. Bar. A la carte entrees: lunch $6.50-$8.75, dinner $13-$22. Child's meals. Specializes in seafood, clam bake (summer). Own pasta, pastries, ice cream. Totally nonsmoking. Cr cds: C, MC, V.

D

★★ **FORK.** *306 Market St (19106), in Olde City.* 215/625-9425. Hrs: 11:30 am-2:30 pm, 5:30-10:30 pm; Thurs, Fri to 11:30 pm. Sat 5:30-11:30 pm; Sun 11 am-2:30 pm. Closed Mon; also some major hols. Res accepted. Contemporary Amer menu. Bar 11:30-2 am. A la carte entrees: lunch $6-$9, dinner $11-$18.50. Sun brunch $6-$9. Child's meals. Specialties: Greek marinated lamb chops, Chilean sea bass with dill pinenut crust. Street parking. Outdoor dining. Modern American bistro atmosphere. Cr cds: A, C, D, DS, MC, V.

D

★★★★ **FOUNTAIN.** *(See Four Seasons Hotel)* 215/ 963-1500. Web www.fshr.com. This elegant, luxurious restaurant, nestled in the lavish yet dignified lobby of the Four Seasons, maintains the atmosphere of a private club. Continental menu with Provençal influence. Specialties: foie gras with duck confit, vension chop with prune chutney, Dover sole. Own baking. Hrs: 6:30 am-2:30 pm, 6-10:30 pm; Sun brunch 11 am-2:30 pm. Res accepted. Bar to 2 am. Wine cellar. A la carte entrees: bkfst $12-

$20, lunch $22-$32, dinner $32-$40. Prix fixe: 4-course dinner $85. Sun brunch $36-$45. Child's meals. Entertainment. Valet parking. Jacket (dinner). Cr cds: A, C, D, DS, MC, V.

★★ **ISABELLA'S.** *6516 Castor Ave (19149), I-95N, exit Cottman Ave, north of downtown.* 215/533-0356. Hrs: 5:30-9 pm; Fri, Sat to 9:30 pm; Sun to 8 pm. Closed Mon; Easter, Thanksgiving, Dec 25. Res required. French, Italian menu. Bar. Semi-a-la carte: dinner $17-$25. Child's meals. Specialties: shrimp and crab risotto cakes, potato gnocchi, grilled whole striped bass. Own baking. Intimate atmosphere; modern European decor. Cr cds: A, C, D, MC, V.

★★ **ITALIAN BISTRO.** *211 S Broad St (19107), downtown.* 215/731-0700. Hrs: 11:30 am-11 pm; wkends 12:30 pm-midnight. Closed Thanksgiving, Dec 25. Res accepted. Bar. Complete meals: lunch $5.50-$6.25. Semi-a la carte entrees: dinner $8-$18. Child's meals. Specializes in Northern Italian dishes, brick oven pizza. Own pasta, desserts. Cr cds: A, C, D, DS, MC, V.

★★★★ **JAKE'S.** *3365 Main St (33365).* 215/483-0444. Web www.jakes-restaurant.com. Paintings by local artists complement the eclectic, sophisticated decor of this Philadelphia favorite. The menu, by owner Bruce Cooper, is also suitably inventive while maintaining a firm sense of control and bearing in French technique. American Continental cuisine. Specialties: crab cakes, veal, lobster. Hrs: 11:30 am-2:30 pm, 5-10:30 pm; Sun brunch 10:30 am-2:30 pm. Prices $19.95-$29.95. Nonsmoking. Res reqd. Valet. Cr cds: A, D, MC, V.

★★ **JOSEPH POON.** *1002 Arch St (19107), in Chinatown.* 215/928-9333. E-mail joepoon@aol.com. Hrs: 11:30 am-10:30 pm; Fri to 11:30 pm; Sat 2:30-11:30 pm; Sun from 2:30 pm; early-bird dinner 3-6 pm Tues-Thurs. Closed Mon; Thanksgiving, Dec 25; also Chinese New Year's. Res accepted. Bar. A la carte entrees: lunch $7.50-$13.95, dinner $5-$18. Complete meal: lunch $10. Child's meals. Specializes in duck, lobster, fish. Parking. Cr cds: A, C, D, DS, MC, V.

★★★ **KANSAS CITY PRIME.** *4417 Main St (19127), off I-76, exit 31.* 215/482-3700. Web www.kansascityprime.com. Hrs: 5:30-11 pm; Fri, Sat to midnight; Sun 5-10 pm. Closed Thanksgiving. Res accepted. Bar to 2 am. A la carte entrees: dinner $17-$31. Specializes in aged prime beef, grilled seafood. Contemporary decor. Cr cds: A, C, D, DS, JCB, MC, V.

★★ **KNAVE OF HEARTS.** *230 South St (19147), in South Street Area.* 215/922-3956. Hrs: noon-4 pm, 5:30-10:30 pm; Fri, Sat to 11:30 pm; Sun 5-10 pm; Sun brunch 11 am-4 pm. Closed Dec 25. Res accepted. Bar. A la carte entrees: lunch $5-$9, dinner $13-$18. Sun brunch $12.50-$13.50. Specialties: chicken coco loco, grilled tuna, filet mignon. Cr cds: A, C, MC, V.

★★★★ **LA FAMIGLIA.** *8 S Front St (19106), in Olde City.* 215/922-2803. Hrs: noon-2 pm, 5:30-9:30 pm; Sat 5:30-10 pm; Sun 5-9 pm. Closed Mon; major hols; also last wk Aug. Res required. Italian menu. Bar. Wine cellar. A la carte entrees: lunch $12.95-$19.95, dinner $24-$40. Specializes in veal, fresh fish, pasta. Own desserts. Built in 1878 in one of city's first blocks of buildings. Jacket. Cr cds: A, C, D, MC, V.

★★ **LAUREN'S.** *PA 420 & Morton Ave (19070), I-95, exit 9A, N on PA 420.* 610/543-3033. Hrs: 5-9:30 pm; Sat from 5 pm; Sun 4-8 pm.

Closed Mon; some major hols. Res accepted. American fusion menu. Semi-a la carte: dinner $12-$19. Specializes in fresh seafood. Jazz Fri, Sat. Parking. Cr cds: A, C, D, DS, MC, V.

★★★ **LE BAR LYONNAIS.** *1523 Walnut St (19102), downstairs at Le Bec Fin, downtown.* 215/567-1000. Web www.lebecfin.com. Hrs: 11:30 am-1:30 pm, 6-9 pm; Sat 6-9:30 pm. Closed Sun; major hols. French bistro menu. Bar. A la carte entrees: lunch, dinner $12-$25. Specialties: escargots au champagne, galette de crabe, thon au poivres. Valet parking (dinner). Elegant bistro atmosphere; original art. Cr cds: A, C, D, DS, MC, V.

★★ **LE BAR NOSTRADAMUS.** *1701 Green St (19130), downtown.* 215/765-3360. Hrs: 5 pm-2 am. Closed Thanksgiving, Dec 25. Res accepted. Belgian steakhouse menu. Bar. A la carte entrees: dinner $15-$21. Specializes in steaks, chops. Casual atmosphere; humorous artwork, brick fireplace. Cr cds: A, C, D, DS, MC, V.

★★★★ **LE BEC-FIN.** *1523 Walnut St (19102), downtown.* 215/567-1000. Web www.lebecfin.com. There's probably no better French cuisine outside France than at this fine dining room decorated in Louis XVI style with crystal chandeliers, red silk wallpaper and gilt mirrors. The prix-fixe dinner is steep, but it includes six superb courses featuring a broad choice of delicately prepared appetizers, fish, meats and desserts. French menu. Specializes in seasonal dishes. Own baking. Sittings: lunch 11:30 am & 1:30 pm, dinner 6 & 9 pm; Fri & Sat dinner 6 & 9:30 pm. Closed Sun; major hols. Res required. Bar to 1 am. Wine cellar. Prix fixe: lunch $36, dinner $118. Valet parking (dinner). Chef-owned. Jacket. Cr cds: A, C, D, DS, MC, V.

★★★ **LE COLONIAL.** *1623 Walnut St (19103), downtown.* 215/851-1623. Hrs: 11:30 am-2:30 pm, 5-11 pm; Mon to 10 pm; Fri to 11:30 pm; Sat 5-11:30 pm; Sun 5-10 pm; early-bird dinner 5-6 pm (exc Sun). Res accepted. Vietnamese menu. Bar 4:30-11:30 pm. A la carte entrees: lunch $12-$16.50, dinner $12-$18.50. Specialties: Saigon snapper, roasted duck, filet mignon. Valet parking. French colonial ambiance & decor. Cr cds: A, C, D, MC, V.

★★★ **MARKER RESTAURANT & LOUNGE.** *(See Adam's Mark)* 215/581-5010. Hrs: 11 am-2:30 pm, 5:30-10 pm; Fri to 11 pm; Sat, Sun 5:30-11 pm; Sun brunch 10:30 am-2:30 pm. Closed some major hols. Res accepted. Contemporary Amer menu. Bar. Wine cellar. Semi-a la carte: lunch $8.95-$13.95, dinner $17.95-$25.95. Sun brunch $22.95. Specialties: lemon mint-cured salmon, wasabi and citrus-crusted tuna mignon, lavender-honey and apple cider-glazed duck. Own baking, pasta. Pianist. Formal French and English decor with stained glass, tapestries, stone fireplace and gold-plated chandelier. Jacket. Cr cds: A, C, D, DS, MC, V.

★★ **MICHAEL'S.** *824 S 8th St (19147), south of downtown.* 215/922-3986. Web www.michaelsristorante.com. Hrs: 5-11 pm; Sun 3-10 pm. Closed Mon. Res accepted. Italian menu. Bar. A la carte entrees: dinner $12.95-$21.95. Child's meals. Specialties: veal chop, gnocchi. Valet parking. Exposed brick, stucco walls; statuary in alcoves. Bronze, glass chandeliers. Cr cds: A, C, D, DS, MC, V.

★★★ **MONTE CARLO LIVING ROOM.** *2nd & South Sts (19147), in South Street Area.* 215/925-2220. E-mail info@montecarlo livingroom.com; web www.montecarlolivingroom.com. Hrs: 6-10:30 pm; Fri, Sat 5:30-11 pm; Sun 5-9 pm. Closed major hols. Res accepted. Northern Italian menu. Bar. Wine cellar. A la carte entrees: dinner $28-$40. Degustation dinner $65. Specializes in fresh fish, veal, beef. Daily menu. Own pastries. Mediterranean decor. Jacket. Cr cds: A, C, D, MC, V.

✓★★★ **MOONSTRUCK.** *7955 Oxford Ave (19111), north of downtown.* 215/725-6000. Hrs: 5-9 pm; Fri, Sat to 10 pm; Sun 4:30-8 pm. Closed Jan 1, July 4, Dec 25. Italian menu. Wine cellar. Semi-a la carte: dinner $14-$20. Specializes in veal dishes, seafood. Own pasta, pastries. Parking. Cr cds: A, C, D, MC, V.

[D] [🍴]

★★★ **MOSHULU.** *Pier 34 (19147), in South Street Area.* 215/923-2500. Web wwwmoshulu.com. Hrs: 11:30 am-3 pm, 5:30-10 pm; Sun 11 am-2 pm (brunch), 5:30-10 pm. Closed Jan 1, Dec 25. Res accepted. Continental menu. Bar to midnight. Wine cellar. Semi-a la carte: lunch $7-$14, dinner $18-$28. Sun brunch $20-$26. Specializes in steak, seafood. Entertainment Wed-Sat. Valet parking. Outdoor dining. Restored 400-ft sailing ship (1904); turn-of-the-century nautical decor with mahogany paneling and brass trim. Jacket. Cr cds: A, C, D, DS, MC, V.

[D] [🍴] [♥]

★ **NAIS CUISINE.** *13-17 W Benedict Ave (19083), I-476, exit 3.* 610/789-5983. Hrs: 5-9 pm; wkends to 10 pm. Res accepted; required Fri, Sat. French menu with Thai influence. A la carte entrees: $13.25-$23.50. Specialties: roast duckling, steamed salmon stuffed with crab meat, snow pea salad. Cr cds: A, C, DS, MC, V.

[🍴]

★★★ **NICHOLAS NICKOLAS.** *(See The Rittenhouse)* 215/546-8440. Web www.harman-nickolas.com. Hrs: 5:30-10:30 pm; Fri, Sat to 11 pm. Closed Sun. Res accepted; required Sat. Continental menu. Bar 11:30-2 am; Sat from 5 pm. Wine cellar. A la carte entrees: dinner $19-$46. Specialties: Chilean sea bass, veal chops, chicken Yanni. Pianist. Valet parking. Modern decor; view of Rittenhouse Square. Totally non-smoking. Cr cds: A, C, D, DS, MC, V.

[D] [♥]

✓★★★ **NICK'S.** *(See The Rittenhouse)* 215/546-8440. Web www.harman-nickolas.com. Hrs: 11:30-2 am. Bar from 5:30 pm. Semi-a la carte: lunch, dinner $13.50-$14.95. Specializes in portobello sandwiches, blue plate special, salads. Pianist. Valet parking. Piano and sports bar; large aquarium. Cr cds: A, C, D, DS, MC, V.

[D]

★★★ **OLD ORIGINAL BOOKBINDER'S.** *125 Walnut St (19106), in Society Hill.* 215/925-7027. E-mail johnny@lobsters.com; web www.oldbookbinders.com. Hrs: 11:45 am-10 pm; Sat from 4:30 pm; Sun 3-9 pm. Closed Thanksgiving, Dec 25. Res accepted. Bars. Wine list. Complete meals: lunch $7.95-$11, dinner $16.95-$35. Child's meals. Specializes in lobster, snapper soup, steaks. Own desserts. Valet parking. Established 1865; in historic bldg. Family-owned. Cr cds: A, C, D, DS, MC, V.

[D] [🍴] [♥]

★★★ **OPUS 251.** *251 S 18th St (19103), downtown.* 215/735-6787. Web www.nitescene.com/opus251. Hrs: 11 am-2:30 pm, 5-10 pm; Fri, Sat to 11 pm; Sun to 9 pm; Sun brunch to 3 pm. Closed Mon; Memorial Day, Thanksgiving, Dec 25. Res required (dinner). Bar. Wine cellar. Semi-a la carte: lunch $4.75-$10.75, dinner $14-$24.50. Sun brunch $15-$27. Specialties: lemon lavender-glazed Muscovy duck steak, black sesame-crusted Ahi tuna, truffled fettuccini. Own baking, ice cream. Valet parking. Outdoor dining. Casually elegant dining in Philadelphia Art Alliance; arched windows, European garden. Cr cds: A, C, D, MC, V.

[D] [🍴]

★★★ **OVERTURES.** *609 E Passyunk Ave (19147), in South Street Area.* 215/627-3455. Hrs: 6-10:30 pm; Sun 5-9:30 pm. Closed Mon; hols. Res accepted; required Fri, Sat. Mediterranean menu. Setups. A la carte entrees: $10-$28. Prix fixe: $45. Specialties: sauteed veal sweetbreads in port, roast saddle of lamb. Own desserts. Cr cds: A, C, D, MC, V.

[🍴]

✓★★ **PEACOCK ON THE PARKWAY.** *1700 Benjamin Franklin Pkwy (19103), downtown.* 215/569-8888. Hrs: 11:30 am-3 pm, 5:30-10 pm; Sat from 5:30 pm. Closed Sun. Continental menu. Prix fixe: lunch $10, dinner $15. Semi-a la carte: dinner $11.95-$18.95. Child's meals. Specialties: lobster, shrimp and scallops over portabello mushroom; shish kebob mix; crispy duck with wild berries. Own baking. Valet parking. Outdoor dining. Three-level dining area overlooks parkway; casual dining. Cr cds: A, C, D, MC, V.

[D] [🍴]

★★ **PHILADELPHIA FISH.** *207 Chestnut St (19106), in Olde City.* 215/625-8605. Hrs: 11:30 am-10 pm; Fri to midnight; Sat noon-midnight; Sun 3-10 pm. Closed Thanksgiving, Dec 25. Res accepted. Seafood menu. Bar to 2 am. A la carte entrees: lunch $7-$10, dinner $14-$19. Child's meals. Specialties: oven-roast Chilean sea bass, grilled ahi tuna, four-spiced seared jumbo lump crab cakes. Street parking. Outdoor dining. Cr cds: A, C, D, MC, V.

[D] [🍴] [♥]

★★★ **PHILIPPE ON LOCUST.** *1644 Locust St.* 215/735-7551; FAX 215/735-7609. Web www.locustclub.com/. French-Asian cuisine. Hrs: 11:30 am-midnight Mon-Sat. Closed Sat & maj hols. Bar/lounge. Live entertainment Wed-Sat. Valet. Res pref. Cr cds: A, C, D, DS, MC, V.

★★ **PLOUGH & THE STARS.** *123 Chestnut St (19106), in Olde City.* 215/733-0300. E-mail amadan1@aol.com. Hrs: 11:30-2 am. Res accepted. Contemporary Irish menu. Bar. A la carte entrees: lunch $6.50-$9, dinner $13.75-$18.75. Child's meals. Specialties: striped bass, duck with pear, warm sea scallop salad. Irish music Sun. Street parking. Outdoor dining. Irish atmosphere. Cr cds: A, C, D, DS, MC, V.

[D] [🍴]

★★ **POMPANO GRILLE.** *701 E Passyunk Ave (19147), at 5th & Bainbridge, in South Street Area.* 215/923-7676. Hrs: 5 pm-2 am. Closed Dec 25. Res accepted. Fusion menu. Bar. A la carte entrees: dinner $14-$19. Complete meals: dinner $25-$30. Specializes in shrimp, crab cakes. Own baking. Musicians Fri, Sat. Valet parking. Outdoor dining. Converted bank bldg has large windows and three dining levels. Cr cds: A, C, D, DS, MC, V.

[D] [🍴]

★★ **PROVENCE.** *379 Lancaster Ave (19041), I 76 W to City Line Ave, to US 30W (Lancaster Ave).* 610/896-0400. Hrs: 11:30 am-2:30 pm, 5:30-9:30 pm; Fri, Sat to 10:30 pm; Sun to 9 pm; Sun brunch to 2:30 pm. Closed most major hols. Res accepted; required dinner. French Provençale menu. Bar. A la carte entrees: lunch $6.75-$10.75, dinner $13.25-$18.75. Sun brunch $18. Child's meals. Specialties: rack of lamb, seared yellowfin tuna, escargot with argula cream sauce. Own baking, pasta. Cr cds: A, C, D, MC, V.

[🍴] [♥]

✓★★ **RANGOON BURMESE RESTAURANT.** *112 N 9th St (19107), in Chinatown.* 215/829-8939. Hrs: 11:30 am-9 pm; Fri to 10 pm; Sat 1-10 pm; Sun from 1 pm. Closed Mon; Thanksgiving. Res accepted. Burmese menu. Bar. Semi-a la carte: lunch $4.50-$12.50, dinner $8.50-$12.50. Specializes in salads, curry dishes, appetizers. Authentic Burmese atmosphere. Totally nonsmoking. Cr cds: C, MC, V.

[D]

★★ **RISTORANTE ALBERTO.** *1415 City Line Ave (19096), I-76 W to City Line Ave exit.* 610/896-0275. Hrs: 11:30 am-2:30 pm, 5-10 pm; Fri, Sat 5-11 pm; Sun from 4 pm. Closed Jan 1, Thanksgiving, Dec 25. Res accepted; required Fri, Sat. Northern Italian menu. Bar. A la carte entrees: lunch $5.95-$11.95; dinner $12.95-$22.95. Specialties: grilled Dover sole, double veal chop. Own pasta. Valet parking. Display of wine bottles; original art. Cr cds: A, C, D, MC, V.

[D] [🍴]

★★★ **RISTORANTE PANORAMA.** *(See Penn's View Hotel)* 215/922-7800. Hrs: noon-2:30 pm, 5:30-10 pm; Fri to 11 pm; Sat 5:30-

11 pm; Sun 5-9 pm. Closed most major hols. Res accepted, required wkends. Italian menu. Bar. Wine list. A la carte entrees: lunch, dinner $15.50-$23.95. Child's meals. Specializes in veal, seafood. Own pasta. Parking. Cr cds: A, C, D, ER, JCB, MC, V.

★ **RIVER CITY DINER.** *3722 Main St (19127), 6 mi W on I-76, exit 31, at Ridge & Main.* 215/483-7500. E-mail mainstr@ axs2000.net; web www.rivercitydiner.com. Hrs: 8 am-midnight; Fri, Sat to 4 am. Bar. A la carte entrees: bkfst, lunch, dinner $4-$12. Child's meals. Specialties: chicken-in-a-pot, grilled River City Caesar salad, Kansas City meatloaf. Outdoor dining. Dramatic diner decor with stainless steel, glass and granite. Cr cds: A, C, D, DS, MC, V.

★★★ **ROCOCO.** *123 Chestnut St (19106), in Olde City.* 215/629-1100. Hrs: 5-11 pm; Fri, Sat to midnight. Closed Sun; Dec 25. Res accepted. Eclectic menu. Bar to 2 am. Wine cellar. Semi-a la carte: dinner $14-$24. Specializes in seafood, beef, lamb. Valet parking. European decor in converted bank bldg; cathedral ceiling. Cr cds: A, C, D, MC, V.

★★★ **ROUGE 99.** *205 S. 18th St (19103).* 215/732-6622. Hrs: lunch 11:30 am-1pm, dinner 5 pm-1am, Bar until 2 am. No res accepted. American/French menu. Wine list. A la carte entrees: lunch $10-$12, dinner $19-$24. Specializes burgers, fresh fish, rack of lamb, tuna tartare. Own pastries. Cr cds: A, D, MC, V.

✓★★ **SERRANO.** *20 S 2nd St (19106), in Olde City.* 215/928-0770. Web www.tinangel.com. Hrs: 5-10:30 pm; Fri, Sat to 11:30 pm; Sun 4-10 pm. Closed major hols. Res accepted. International menu. Bar. A la carte entrees: dinner $10-$20. Specialties: Vietnamese happy family, Malaysian pork chops. Own desserts. Entertainment Wed-Sat. Theatrical decor with puppets and tapestries from around the world. Cr cds: A, C, D, DS, MC, V.

★★★ **SIGGIE'S L'AUBERGE.** *101 Ford St (19428), 15 mi W on I-76, exit 28B.* 610/828-6262. Hrs: 5:30-10 pm; Fri, Sat to 11 pm. Closed Sun; major hols. Res required. French continental menu. Bar. A la carte entrees: dinner $19-$29. Specialties: crisp shrimp with fruit sauce, jumbo lump crab cakes, sea bass. Valet parking. Rustic French decor. Cr cds: A, C, D, MC, V.

✓★★ **SONOMA.** *4411 Main St (19127), 6 mi W on I-76, exit 31, at Main & Gay Sts.* 215/483-9400. Hrs: 11 am-11 pm; Fri, Sat to midnight; early-bird dinner Sun-Thurs 5-6 pm; Sun brunch to 4 pm. Continental menu. Bar to 2 am. Semi-a la carte: lunch, dinner $6.50-$14. Sun brunch $6-$12. Child's meals. Specialties: refried risotto, honey-lavender hickory-roasted salmon, garlic-grilled ribeye steak. Own baking, pasta. Valet parking. Outdoor dining. Modern, eclectic decor; revolving art display. Cr cds: A, C, D, DS, MC, V.

✓★ **SOUTH STREET DINER.** *140 South St (19147), in South Street Area.* 215/627-5258. Open 24 hrs. Closed Dec 25. Bar. Semi-a la carte: bkfst $4.50-$7, lunch $5-$7.50, dinner $8.50-$10.50. Child's meals. Specializes in bkfst dishes, Greek dishes, meats. Own pasta. Outdoor dining. Patio and sports bar. Cr cds: A, C, D, MC, V.

★★★★ **STRIPED BASS.** *1500 Walnut St (19102), in Center City.* 215/732-4444. This stylish, highly popular, fish-and-seafood-only restaurant is in a striking former bank building with marble columns. The creative menu is accompanied by a broad international selection of wines by the bottle and glass. Specializes in fresh seafood, shellfish. Menu changes daily. Hrs: 11:30 am-2:30 pm, 5-11 pm; Fri to 11:30 pm; Sat 5-

11:30 pm; Sun 11 am-2:30 pm, 5-10 pm. Closed major hols. Res required. Bar. Wine cellar. Prix fixe: lunch $24, 5-course dinner $85. A la carte entrees: dinner $30-$50. Valet parking. Cr cds: A, C, D, MC, V.

★★★★ **SUSANNA FOO.** *1512 Walnut St (19102), downtown.* 215/545-2666. Web www.susannafoo.com. Fresh ingredients and cooking techniques from around the world come together here in chef Susanna Foo's unique cuisine. Silk lanterns and bouquets of orchids create a romantic setting. Chinese, French menu. Specialties: crispy duck, soft-shell crabs, hundred corner crab cake. Hrs: 11:30 am-2:30 pm, 5-10 pm; Fri, Sat to 11 pm; Sun 5-9 pm. Closed some major hols. Res accepted; required Sat. Bar. Wine cellar. A la carte entrees: lunch $10-$18, dinner $18-$30. Valet parking. Jacket. Cr cds: A, C, D, MC, V.

★★★ **SWANN CAFE.** *(See Four Seasons Hotel)* 215/963-1500. Web www.fshr.com. Hrs: 11:30-1 am; Sun 10 am-midnight; Sun brunch to 3 pm. Res accepted. French menu. Bar. Wine cellar. A la carte entrees: lunch, dinner $14-$25. Sun brunch $45. Child's meals. Specialties: steak pomfrite; osso bucco; shrimp, crab and scallop salad. Own baking, pasta. Entertainment. Valet parking. Outdoor dining. Intimate atmosphere; luxurious decor uses mahogany, silk and large chandeliers. Cr cds: A, C, D, DS, MC, V.

★★★ **THE FOUNDERS.** *(See Park Hyatt Philadelphia at the Bellevue)* 215/790-2814. Web www.hyatt.com. Hrs: 6:30 am-2:30 pm, 5-11 pm; Sat, Sun brunch 10:30 am-3 pm. Res accepted. French, Asian menu. Bar 11-2 am. Wine cellar. Complete meals: bkfst $9.50-$12.50, dinner $45-$70. A la carte entrees: lunch $9.50-$16.50, dinner $24-$36. Sat, Sun brunch $34.50. Specialties: filet de boeuf a la Moelle, red snapper en papillote. Entertainment. Valet parking. Rotunda with sweeping views of city. Elegant turn-of-the-century decor. Jacket (dinner). Cr cds: A, C, D, DS, ER, JCB, MC, V.

★★★ **THE GARDEN.** *1617 Spruce St (19103), downtown.* 215/546-4455. Web www.thegardenrestaurant.com. Hrs: 11:30 am-1:30 pm, 5:30-9:30 pm; Mon, Sat from 5:30 pm. Closed Sun; major hols. Res accepted. Continental menu. Bar. Wine list. A la carte entrees: lunch $10.95-$24.95, dinner $16.95-$25.95. Specializes in fresh seafood, aged prime beef. Valet parking. Spacious outdoor dining. City skyline views. Cr cds: A, C, D, MC, V.

★★★ **THE GRILL.** *(See St. Regis Hotel Philadelphia)* 215/563-1600. Web www.ritzcarlton.com. Hrs: 6:30 am-2:30 pm; 5:30-10:30 pm; Sat, Sun from 5:30 pm. Res accepted. Eclectic menu. Bar. Semi-a la carte: bkfst $7-$18, lunch $12-$28. A la carte entrees: dinner $19-$40. Specializes in fresh fish, poultry. Valet parking. Club atmosphere. Cr cds: A, C, D, DS, ER, JCB, MC, V.

★★ **THE PALM.** *200 S Broad St (19102), downtown.* 215/546-7256. Hrs: 11:30 am-11 pm; Sat from 5 pm; Sun 4:30-9 pm. Closed most major hols. Res accepted. Bar. A la carte entrees: lunch $7.50-$18, dinner $16.50-$40. Specializes in fresh seafood, prime aged beef, lamb chops. Valet parking. Counterpart of famous New York restaurant. Caricatures of celebrities. Cr cds: A, C, D, MC, V.

★★★ **THE SALOON.** *750 S 7th St (19148), in South Street area.* 215/627-1811. Hrs: 11:30 am-2 pm, 5-10 pm; Sat to midnight. Closed Sun; hols. Res accepted. Italian menu. Bar. Wine list. A la carte entrees: lunch, dinner $18-$28. Specializes in veal, steak, seafood. Parking. Family-owned. Cr cds: A, C, MC, V.

★★★ **TOSCANA CUCINA RUSTICA.** *24 N Merion Ave (19010), 15 mi W on I-76, exit City Ave to US 30 (Lancaster Ave) to N Merion Ave.* 610/527-7700. Hrs: 11:30 am-2:30 pm, 5:30-10 pm; Fri to 11 pm; Sat 5:30-11 pm; Sun from 5:30 pm. Closed Thanksgiving, Dec 25. Res accepted. Tuscan Italian menu. Bar. Wine cellar. A la carte entrees: lunch $7-$13, dinner $12.95-$25. Specializes in grilled meats, wafer-thin-crusted brick-oven pizza. Own baking, pasta. Wine list offers over 550 selections. Totally nonsmoking. Cr cds: A, C.

D ⊟

★★★ **TREETOPS.** *(See The Rittenhouse Hotel)* 215/790-2534. Web www.treetopsrestaurant.com. Hrs: 6:30 am-10:30 pm; Sat, Sun from 7 pm. Res accepted. Regional Amer menu. Bar 11:30-1 am. Wine list. Semi-a la carte: lunch $11-$20, dinner $20-$35. Specializes in seafood, steak, veal. Seasonal menu. Own pastries. Valet parking. Casual decor. Overlooks park. Cr cds: A, C, D, DS, MC, V.

D ⊟ ♥

★★ **UMBRIA RESTAURANT.** *7131 Germantown Ave (19119), north of downtown.* 215/242-6470. Hrs: 6-9 pm. Closed Mon; major hols. Res accepted. Eclectic menu. A la carte entrees: dinner $16.95-$24.95. Specialties: filet au poivre, curried lamb, soft-shelled crabs in season. Blackboard menu changes daily. Totally nonsmoking. Cr cds: C.

✓★ **VANG'S GARDEN.** *121 N 11th St (19107), in Chinatown.* 215/923-2438. Hrs: 10 am-10 pm. Closed Thanksgiving. Vietnamese menu. Semi-a la carte: lunch, dinner $3.75-$7.95. Specialties: charbroiled beef, barbecued beef on rice noodles, sauteed chicken with lemon grass. Adj to convention center. Cr cds: A, C, DS, MC, V.

⊟

★ **VEGA GRILL.** *4141 Main St (19127), 9 mi W on I-76, exit 31.* 215/487-9600. Hrs: 5 pm-2 am. Closed some major hols. Contemporary Latin Amer menu. Bar 4:30 pm-2 am. A la carte entrees: dinner $12-$18. Child's meals. Specializes in South American meat and fish. Outdoor dining. Neighborhood tavern atmosphere. Cr cds: A, C, MC, V.

⊟

★★★ **VETRI.** *1312 Spruce St (19107).* 215/732-3478; FAX 215/732-3487. Italian cuisine. Specialties: homemade pasta, fresh fish, onion crepe in white truffle sauce. Hrs: Mon-Sat 6 pm-midnight. Closed Sun and some hol (call). Prices $25-$32 entrees; degustation menu 5 course $65, 7 course $90. Res reqd. Cr cds: A, C.

★★ **WHITE DOG CAFE.** *3420 Sansom St (19104), downtown.* 215/386-9224. Hrs: 11:30 am-2:30 pm, 5:30-10 pm; Fri, Sat 5:30-11 pm; Sun 5-10 pm; Sat, Sun brunch 11 am-2:30 pm. Closed Thanksgiving, Dec 25. Res accepted. Bar. A la carte entrees: lunch $7.50-$11, dinner $14-$20. Sat, Sun brunch $7-$11. Child's meals. Specializes in beef, chicken. Own desserts. Entertainment Wed-Sun. Outdoor dining. Former house (ca 1870) of author Madame Blavatsky, founder of the Theosophical Society. Cr cds: A, C, D, DS, MC, V.

D ⊟

✓★★ **ZOCALO.** *3600 Lancaster Ave (19104), west of downtown in University City.* 215/895-0139. E-mail zoc3600@aol.com. Hrs: noon-10 pm; Fri to 11 pm; Sat 5:30-11 pm; Sun 5-9:30 pm. Closed major hols. Res accepted. Contemporary Mexican menu. Bar. Semi-a la carte: lunch $6-$13, dinner $10-$19. Specializes in handmade corn tortillas. Parking. Outdoor dining. Cr cds: A, C, D, DS, MC, V.

D ⊟

Unrated Dining Spots

FAMOUS 4TH ST DELICATESSEN. *700 S 4th St (19147), south of downtown.* 215/922-3274. E-mail cookies@voicenet.com; web www.famousdeli.net. Hrs: 7 am-6 pm; Sun to 4 pm. Closed Rosh Hashana, Yom Kippur. Delicatessen fare. A la carte entrees: bkfst $2-$9,

lunch $3.50-$10. Specializes in chocolate chip cookies, fresh roasted turkey, corned beef. Antique telephones. Family-owned for more than 75 yrs. Cr cds: A, C, D, MC, V.

★★★ **ROLLER'S.** *8705 Germantown Ave (19118), in Top-of-the-Hill Plaza, in Chestnut Hill.* 215/242-1771. Hrs: 11:30 am-2:30 pm, 5:30-9 pm; Fri to 10 pm; Sat noon-2:30 pm, 5:30-10 pm; Sun 5-9 pm; Sun brunch 11 am-2:30 pm. Closed Mon; most major hols. Bar. Semi-a la carte: lunch $6-$11, dinner $16-$24. Sun brunch $6-$10. Specializes in fresh fish, veal, duck. Parking. Outdoor dining. Modern cafe atmosphere. Totally nonsmoking. Cr cds: C.

★★ **SASSAFRAS.** *48 S 2nd St (19106), in Olde City.* 215/925-2317. Hrs: noon-midnight; Fri, Sat to 1 am. Sun to 9 pm. Closed major hols. Bar. A la carte entrees: dinner $5-$18. Specializes in salads, omelettes, grilled fish. Cr cds: A, C, D, MC, V.

⊟

★★★ **SWANN LOUNGE.** *(See Four Seasons Hotel)* 215/963-1500. Hrs: 11:30 am-2:30 pm; tea 3-5 pm; Sun brunch 11 am-2:30 pm; Viennese buffet Fri, Sat 9-11 pm. Res accepted. Bar 11:30-1 am; Fri, Sat to 2 am. Buffet: bkfst $9.75-$14, lunch $12-$21. Afternoon tea $12. Sun brunch $24. Viennese buffet $11. Specializes in English tea service with sandwiches & cakes. Valet parking. Outdoor dining (lunch). Elegant atmosphere. Cr cds: A, C, D, DS, ER, JCB, MC, V.

D ⊟

★★★ **THE RESTAURANT SCHOOL.** *4207 Walnut St (19104), near University of Pennsylvania, west of downtown.* 215/222-4200. Web therestaurantschool.com. Hrs: 5:30-10 pm. Closed Sun, Mon; also during student breaks. Res accepted. Continental menu. Complete meals: dinner $13.50. Seasonal menu. Own baking. Parking. Bakery shop on premises. Unique dining experience in a "restaurant school." Consists of 2 buildings; a restored 1856 mansion is linked by a large atrium dining area to a new building housing the kitchen and classrooms. Cr cds: A, C, D, DS, MC, V.

Pittsburgh (E-2)

(See also Ambridge, Beaver Falls, Connellsville, New Stanton, Washington)

Settled 1758 **Pop** 369,879 **Elev** 760 ft **Area Code** 412
E-mail info@gpcvb.org **Web** www.pittsburgh-cvb.org

Information Greater Pittsburgh Convention & Visitors Bureau, 425 6th Ave. 30th Floor 15219; 800/366-0093

Pittsburgh has had a remarkable renaissance to become one of the most spectacular civic redevelopments in America, with modern buildings, clean parks and community pride. In fact, it has been named "all-America city" by the National Civic League. The new Pittsburgh is a result of a rare combination of capital-labor cooperation, public-private support, enlightened political leadership and imaginative, venturesome community planning. Its $1-billion international airport was designed to be the most user-friendly in the country.

After massive war production, Pittsburgh labored to eliminate the 1930s image of an unsophisticated mill town. During the 1950s and 1960s, Renaissance I began, a $500-million program to clean the city's air and develop new structures, such as Gateway Center, the Civic Arena and Point State Park. The late 1970s and early 1980s ushered in Renaissance II, a $3-billion expansion program reflecting the movement away from industry and toward high technology.

Today, Pittsburgh has completed this dramatic shift from industry to a diversified base including high technology, health care, finance and education, and continues its transition to a services-oriented city.

Pittsburgh's cultural personality is expressed by the Pittsburgh Symphony Orchestra, Pittsburgh Opera, Pittsburgh Ballet, Phipps Conservatory and The Carnegie Museums of Pittsburgh, which include the Museum of Natural History and Museum of Art. The city has 25 parks, 45 "parklets," 60 recreation centers and 27 swimming pools.

Born of frontier warfare in the shadow of Fort Pitt, the city is named after the elder William Pitt, the great British statesman. Its militarily strategic position was an important commercial asset and Pittsburgh soon became a busy river port and transit point for the western flow of pioneers.

Industry grew out of the West's need for manufactured goods; foundries and rolling mills were soon producing nails, axes, frying pans and shovels. The Civil War added tremendous impetus to industry; by the end of the war, Pittsburgh was producing ½ the steel and ⅓ of the glass made in the country. Such captains of industry and finance as Thomas Mellon, Andrew Carnegie and Henry Clay Frick built their industrial empires in Pittsburgh. The American Federation of Labor was born here (1881); the city has been the scene of historic clashes between labor and management.

World War I brought a fresh boom to the cit, as well as changes in its industrial character. It was a vast arsenal for the Allies during World War II.

Transportation

Airport. See PITTSBURGH INTL AIRPORT AREA.

Car Rental Agencies. See IMPORTANT TOLL-FREE NUMBERS.

Public Transportation. Subway and surface trains, buses (Port Authority of Allegheny County), phone 412/442-2000.

Rail Passenger Service. Amtrak 800/872-7245.

What to See and Do

Alcoa Building. Pioneer in aluminum for skyscraper construction, exterior work was done from inside; no scaffolding was required. Draped in aluminum waffle, 30 stories high; it is considered to be one of the country's most daring experiments in skyscraper design. 425 6th Ave.

Allegheny County Courthouse. One of the country's outstanding Romanesque-style bldgs, the two square-city-block structure was designed by Henry Hobson Richardson in 1884. (Mon–Fri; closed hols) Grant St & 5th Ave.   **Free**

Andy Warhol Museum. The most comprehensive single-artist museum in the world. More than 500 works. (Wed–Sun) 117 Sandusky St. Phone 412/237-8300.   ¢¢

Benedum Center for the Performing Arts. Expansion and restoration of the Stanley Theater, a movie palace built in 1928. Gilded plasterwork, 500,000-piece crystal chandelier and a 9-story addition to backstage area make this an exceptional auditorium with one of the largest stages in the country. The center is home to Pittsburgh Ballet Theatre, the Pittsburgh Dance Council, the Pittsburgh Opera and Civic Light Opera. Free guided tours (by appt). Penn & 7th Aves, at 719 Liberty Ave. Phone 412/456-6666.

Boyce Park Ski Area. Beginner–intermediate slopes; 2 double chairlifts; 2 Pomalifts; patrol, school, rentals; snowmaking; cafeteria. Longest run, ¼ mi; vertical drop, 175 ft. (Dec–Feb, daily) 18 mi E on I-376 to Plum exit (16B); follow signs to park. Phone 724/733-4656 or 412/733-4665 (snow conditions; 24-hr recording).   ¢¢¢¢

Carnegie Mellon University (1900) (7,900 students). Founded by Andrew Carnegie. Composed of 7 colleges. Tours of campus. Adj to Schenley Park. Phone 412/268-2000 or 412/268-5052.

Civic Arena. $22-million all-weather amphitheater accommodates 17,500 people. Retractable roof can fold up within 2½ min. In Golden Triangle.

County parks. South Park, 12 mi S on PA 88. **North Park,** 14 mi N on PA 19. **Boyce Park,** 14 mi E on I-376, US 22. **Settler's Cabin Park,** 9 mi W on I-279, US 22. Swimming; fishing; boating. Bicycling (rentals), ball fields; golf, tennis. Cross-country skiing, ice skating (winter, daily). Picnicking. Parks open daily. Fees for activities. Attractions for each park vary; Phone 412/350-2455 county park info (permits) or 412/835-4809 (administration south park).

⭐ **Fallingwater.** 27 mi S on PA 51, 10 mi E on PA 201 to Connellsville, 8 mi E on PA 711, then 8 mi S on PA 381, near Mill Run. (See CONNELLSVILLE)

Frick Park. Covers 476 acres, largely in natural state; nature trails wind through ravines and over hills; also nature center (2005 Beechwood Blvd), tennis courts, picnic areas, playgrounds. Park (daily). Beechwood Blvd & English Lane. Phone 412/422-6536.   **Free**

Gateway Center. Complex incl 4 skyscrapers of Equitable Life Assurance Society. Equitable Plaza, a 2-acre open-air garden over underground parking garage, has lovely walks, 3 fountains, more than 90 types of trees and 100 varieties of shrubs and seasonal flowers. (Mon–Fri; closed major hols) Covers 23 acres adj to Point State Park. Phone 412/392-6000.

Hartwood (1929). A 629-acre re-creation of English country estate; Tudor mansion with many antiques; formal gardens, stables. Tours (daily exc Mon; closed hols & 1 wk late Nov). Also music and theater events during summer. 12 mi N via PA 8, at 215 Saxonburg Blvd. For info and tour reservations, phone 412/767-9200.   ¢¢

⭐ **Inclines** (hill-climbing trolleys). Travel to top of Mt Washington for excellent view of Golden Triangle, where the Allegheny and Monongahela Rivers join to form the Ohio River.

Monongahela Incline. Panoramic views from observation deck. (Daily) Station on W Carson St near Station Square & Smithfield St Bridge. Phone 412/442-2000.   ¢

Duquesne Incline. Built 1877; restored and run by community effort; observation deck. (Daily) Free parking at lower station. Lower station, W Carson St, opposite the fountain, SW of Fort Pitt Bridge; upper station, 1220 Grandview Ave, in restaurant area. Phone 412/381-1665.   ¢

James L. Kelso Bible Lands Museum. Artifacts and displays from the ancient Near East, especially Palestine. (Sept–May, Wed; also by appt) 616 N Highland, on grounds of Pittsburgh Theological Seminary. Phone 412/362-5610.   **Free**

Kennywood Park. Combines modern rides with rides from traditional streetcar parks, popular at the turn of the century. **Lost Kennywood**, with lagoon, Victorian-era bldgs, shopping. Gardens, picnic groves. (Mid-May–Labor Day, daily) 8 mi SE on PA 837, 4800 Kennywood Blvd, in W Mifflin. Phone 412/461-0500.   ¢¢¢¢

National Aviary in Pittsburgh. The Aviary is home to one of the world's premier bird collections and is the only indoor bird facility independent of a larger zoo in North America. A veritable jungle of colorful, amusing and exotic birds. (Daily; closed Jan 1, Thanksgiving, Dec 25) Allegheny Commons West, approx 1 mi W of downtown. Phone 412/323-7235.   ¢¢

Photo Antiquities. Photo gallery and museum. Selections from 100,000 antique photographic images. (Mon-Sat; closed major hols) 531 E Ohio. Phone 412/231-7881 or 800/474-6862.   ¢¢

Pittsburgh Children's Museum. Hands-on exhibits. Hands-on silkscreen studio; storytelling; regularly scheduled puppet shows; live performances; 2-story museum. (Tues–Sat, also Sun afternoons) 10 Childrens' Way. Phone 412/322-5058. Tues, Wed, Fri–Sun   ¢¢;   Thurs   ¢

Point State Park. "Point" where the Allegheny and Monongahela rivers meet to form the Ohio; 36 acres. Giant fountain symbolizes joining of rivers. There are military drills with fifes and drums, muskets and cannon (May–Labor Day; some Sun afternoons). Foot of Ft Duquesne & Ft Pitt Blvds. Phone 412/471-0235. In the park are

Block House of Fort Pitt. Last remaining bldg of original fort (1767). (Daily exc Mon)   **Free**

Fort Pitt Museum. Built on part of original fort. Exhibits on early Pittsburgh and Fort Pitt; military struggles between France and Britain for western Pennsylvania and the Old Northwest Territory. (Daily exc Mon; closed some hols) 101 Commonwealth Place. Phone 412/281-9284.   ¢¢

PPG Place. Designed by Philip Johnson, this is Pittsburgh's most popular Renaissance II bldg. PPG Place consists of 6 separate bldgs designed in a postmodern, Gothic skyscraper style. Shopping and a food court can be found in Two PPG Place. Market Square.

Professional sports.

National League Baseball (Pittsburgh Pirates). Three Rivers Stadium, 600 Stadium Circle. Phone 412/323-5000.

NFL (Pittsburgh Steelers). Three Rivers Stadium, 600 Stadium Circle. Phone 412/323-0300.

NHL (Pittsburgh Penguins). Civic Arena, 300 Auditorium Pl. Phone 412/642-1300.

Millvale

40TH ST BRIDGE

31ST ST BRIDGE

HERRS ISLAND

MARSHALL AV

19

FEDERAL ST

SPRING GARDEN AV

OHIO

ST

40TH ST

BUTLER ST

279

HERRON AVENUE

River

ALLEGHENY AV

WEST NORTH AV

N COMMONS

E COMMONS

EAST OHIO ST

CHESTNUT ST

28

Allegheny

PENN AV

LIBERTY AV

BLVD

HERRON

W COMMONS

Lake Elizabeth

AV

579

16TH ST BRIDGE

16TH ST

BIGELOW

AMTRAK

380

AMERICAN LUNG ASSOC

CENTRE AV

CARRILLO ST

ROBINSON ST

UNIVERSITY OF PITTSBURGH

RIDGE

S COMMONS

ALLEGHENY CTR MALL

VETERANS BRIDGE

Bedford Reservoir

5TH AV

THREE RIVERS STADIUM

9TH ST BRIDGE

7TH ST BRIDGE

6TH ST BRIDGE

11TH

AV

FORT DUQUESNE BRIDGE (VIADUCT)

PENN STATION

CENTRE AV

CARLOW COLLEGE

FORBES

Ohio River

GATEWAY CENTER

PENN LIBERTY AV

7TH AV

CIVIC ARENA

5TH

AV

OAKLAND

837

10

9

DOWNTOWN

FORBES AV

885

DUQUESNE INCLINE PLANE

7

FORT PITT BRIDGE (VIADUCT)

8

2

22 30

GRANT ST

DUQUESNE UNIV

MERCY HOSP

ARMSTRONG TUNNEL

THE BOULEVARD OF THE ALLIES

6

PENN

BATES ST

WEST CARSON ST

AMTRAK

376

STATION SQUARE

SMITHFIELD ST BRIDGE

LIBERTY BRIDGE

10TH ST BRIDGE

885

5

LINCOLN PARKWAY

7

FORT PITT TUNNELS

MERRIMAC ST

P.J. McARDLE

Monongahela

BRADY ST

BIRMINGHAM BRIDGE

AMTRAK

River

WOODRUFF ST

RDWY

10TH ST

SOUTHSIDE

E CARSON ST

TRK 19

ARLINGTON AV

18TH ST

837

MOUNT WASHINGTON

51

AMTRAK

SAW MILL RUN

ARLINGTON AV

18TH ST

N

SAW MILL Run

BROWNSVILLE ROAD

Mt. Oliver

BLVD

BECKS RUN ROAD

Riverview Park. Covers 251 acres. Swimming pool (mid-June–Labor Day, daily, fee); tennis courts (Apr–Nov, daily); picnic shelter (May–Sept, permit required). Also playgrounds, parklet; nature, jogging trail. Fee for some activities. 2 mi N on US 19. **Free** In the park is

Allegheny Observatory. Slides, tour of bldg. Maintained by University of Pittsburgh. Children under 12 yrs only with adult. Reservation required. (Apr–Oct, Thurs–Fri; closed hols) Center of park, entrance on Riverview Ave off US 19. Phone 412/321-2400. **Free**

Rodef Shalom Biblical Botanical Garden. The natural world of ancient Israel is re-created here in settings that specialize in plants of the Bible. A waterfall, desert and stream all help simulate the areas of the Jordan, Lake Kineret and the Dead Sea. Tours (by appt). Special programs and exhibits. (June–mid-Sept, daily exc Fri; Sat hrs limited) 4905 5th Ave. Phone 412/621-6566. **Free**

Sandcastle Water Park. The city's down-by-the-riverside water park has 15 slides, adult & kiddie pools; boardwalk; food. (1st Sat June–Labor Day, daily; closed hols) Approx 5 mi SE of downtown via I-376 & PA 837. Phone 412/462-6666. All-day slide pass ¢¢¢¢

Schenley Park. Covers 456 acres; picnic areas; 18-hole golf course, lighted tennis courts; swimming pool; ice skating (winter); softball fields, running track; nature trails; bandstand (summer; free). Fee for some activities. (Daily) Forbes Ave, adj Carnegie-Mellon University. **Free** Also in park is

Phipps Conservatory. Constantly changing array of flowers; tropical gardens; outstanding orchid collection. Children's Discovery Garden with interactive learning opportunities. Seasonal flower shows (see SEASONAL EVENTS). (Daily) Phone 412/622-6914. ¢¢

Sightseeing tours.

Gray Line bus tours. For info and reservations contact 110 Lenzner Ct, Sewickley 15143; Phone 412/741-2720, 412/761-7000 or 800/342-2349.

Guided Bus and Walking Tours. Offered through the Pittsburgh History and Landmarks Foundation. For info and reservations, phone 412/471-5808. ¢¢¢

Soldiers and Sailors Memorial Hall and Military History Museum. Auditorium has Lincoln's Gettysburg Address inscribed above stage; flags, weapons, uniforms, memorabilia from US wars. (Mon–Fri, also Sat & Sun afternoons; closed most major hols) 5th Ave & Bigelow Blvd. Phone 412/621-4253. **Free**

Station Square. This 40-acre area features shopping, dining and entertainment in and among the historic bldgs of the P & LE Railroad (see RESTAURANTS). Shopping in warehouses that once held loaded railroad boxcars. (Daily; closed some hols) 450 Landmarks Bldg, 1 Station Sq, along Monongahela River across from downtown, via Smithfield St Bridge. Phone 412/471-5808.

The Carnegie Science Center. Learning and entertainment complex has over 40,000 sq ft of exhibit galleries that demonstrate how human activities are affected by science and technology. USS *Requin,* moored in front of the center, is a World War II diesel-electric submarine; tours (40 min) demonstrate the electronic, visual and voice communication devices on board. Henry Buhl Jr Planetarium and Observatory is a technologically sophisticated interactive planetarium with control panels at every seat. Also here are 350-seat OMNIMAX Theater and Health Sciences Amphitheater. Restaurant, gift shop. (Daily; closed Dec 25) One Allegheny Ave, adj to Three Rivers Stadium on Ohio River. For combination ticket prices and info phone 412/237-3400. Submarine ¢¢; Exhibits and planetarium ¢¢¢; OMNIMAX Theater ¢¢¢

★ **The Carnegie Museums of Pittsburgh.** Public complex built by industrialist Andrew Carnegie. (Daily exc Mon; closed hols) 4400 Forbes Ave. Phone 412/622-3360. ¢¢ Includes

Library of Pittsburgh. Central branch contains more than 4½ million books. Houses first department of science and technology established in a US public library.

Museum of Art. Possibly America's first modern art museum, as Carnegie urged the gallery to exhibit works dated after 1896. Collection of Impressionist and Post-Impressionist paintings; Hall of Sculpture; Hall of Architecture; films, videos.

Museum of Natural History. Houses one of the most complete collections of dinosaur fossils. Exhibits incl Dinosaur Hall, Polar World, Hill-

man Hall of Minerals and Gems, Walton Hall of Ancient Egypt; changing exhibits.

Music Hall. Home to the Mendelssohn Choir, the Pittsburgh Chamber Music Society and the River City Brass Band. Elaborate gilt and marble foyer; walls of French eschallion, 24 pillars made of green stone and a gold baroque ceiling.

★ **The Frick Art and Historical Center.** Museum complex built on grounds of estate once belonging to industrialist Henry Clay Frick; gardens, carriage house museum, greenhouse, cafe and restored children's playhouse that now serves as a visitor's center. (Daily exc Mon; closed some major hols) Between Reynolds St & Penn Ave, along S Homewood Ave. For tour schedule and info, phone 412/371-0600. **Free** Also on grounds are

Clayton, the Henry Clay Frick Home. A restored 4-story Victorian mansion with 23 rms; only remaining house of area in East End once known as "millionaire's row." Some original decor and personal mementos of the Fricks. Tours; reservation recommended. 7227 Reynolds St. ¢¢

The Frick Art Museum. Collection of Helen Clay Frick, daughter of Henry Clay Frick, incl Italian Renaissance, Flemish and French 18th-century paintings and decorative arts. Italian and French furniture, Renaissance bronzes, tapestries, Chinese porcelains. Also changing exhibits; concerts, lectures. 7227 Reynolds St. Phone 412/371-0600. **Free**

The Pittsburgh Zoo. Over 70 acres containing over 6,000 animals, children's farm (late May–Oct), discovery pavilion, reptile house, tropical and Asian forests, African savanna and aqua zoo. Merry-go-round and train rides (fee). Highland Park covers 75 acres and has tennis courts, picnic grounds, shelters (some require permit), twin reservoirs, swimming pool (fee). (Daily; closed Dec 25) NE on Highland Ave in Highland Park area. Phone 412/665-3639. ¢¢¢

The Senator John Heinz Regional History Center. In Chatauqua Ice Warehouse (1898). Preserves 300 yrs of region's history with artifacts and extensive collection of archives, photos. Houses the Historical Society of Western Pennsylvania. Library (Tues-Sat). (Daily; closed Jan 1, Thanksgiving, Dec 25) 1212 Smallman St. Phone 412/454-6000. ¢¢¢

Tour—Ed Mine. Complete underground coal mining operation; sawmill; furnished log house (1789); old company store; historical mine museum; shelters; playground. (May–Labor Day wk, daily) 20 mi NW via PA 28 (Allegheny Valley Expy) to Tarentum, then ¼ mi W via Red Belt W. Phone 724/224-4720. ¢¢¢

Two Mellon Bank Center. Formerly the Union Trust Bldg, its Flemish-Gothic style was modeled after a library in Louvain, Belgium. Interior has a glass rotunda. Grant St & 5th Ave.

University of Pittsburgh (1787) (33,000 students). Tours of Nationality Rooms in Cathedral of Learning (wkends; fee). Campus of 70 bldgs on 125 acres. 5th Ave & Bigelow Blvd. Phone 412/624-4141. Buildings include

Cathedral of Learning (1935). Unique skyscraper of classrms, stretching its Gothic-moderne architecture 42 floors high (535 ft); vantage point on 36th floor. Surrounding a 3-story Gothic commons rm are an Early American Rm and 24 Nationality Rms, each reflecting the distinctive culture of the ethnic group that created and furnished it. Tours (daily; closed Jan 1, Dec 24, 25, 31). Phone 412/624-6000. Tours ¢

Heinz Chapel. Tall stained-glass windows; French Gothic architecture. (Daily exc Sat; closed hols) E of Cathedral of Learning. Phone 412/624-4157. **Free**

Henry Clay Frick Fine Arts Building. Glass-enclosed cloister; changing exhibits; art reference library. (Sept–mid-June, daily; rest of yr, Mon–Fri; closed univ hols, also Dec 24–Jan 2) Schenley Plaza. Phone 412/648-2400. **Free**

Stephen Foster Memorial. Auditorium/theater. Collection of Pittsburgh-born composer's music and memorabilia. Said to be one of the most elaborate memorials ever built to a musician. (Mon–Sat, also Sun afternoons; closed hols) Phone 412/624-4100.

USX Tower. Once known as the US Steel Bldg; 64 stories high; the tallest bldg in Pittsburgh. Ten exposed triangular columns and an exterior paneling of steel make up its construction. Grant St & 7th Ave.

Annual Events

Folk Festival. Pittsburgh Expo Mart, Monroeville. Foods of many nations; arts and crafts; folk music, dancing. Memorial Day wkend.

Three Rivers Arts Festival. Point State Park, Gateway Center, USX Tower, PPG Place. Juried, original works of local and national artists: paintings, photography, sculpture, crafts and videos; artists' market in outdoor plazas. Ongoing performances incl music, dance and performance art. Special art projects; film festival; food; children's activities. Phone 412/281-8723. Early–mid-June.

Pittsburgh/Shop 'N Save Three Rivers Regatta. Point State Park. Water, land and air events; water shows and speedboat races. Last wkend July & 1st wkend Aug.

Pittsburgh Irish Festival. I.C. Light Amphitheatre, Station Square. Irish foods, dances and entertainment. Phone 412/661-1221. Early or mid-Sept.

Seasonal Events

Phipps Conservatory Flower Shows. Schenley Park. Phone 412/622-6914. Spring, summer, fall and hols.

Concerts. Pittsburgh Symphony Orchestra. Heinz Hall for the Performing Arts, 600 Penn Ave. Phone 412/392-4900. Sept–May.

Pittsburgh Public Theater. City's largest resident professional company. 621 Penn Ave. Sept–June.

Additional Visitor Information

For additional information about Pittsburgh, contact the Greater Pittsburgh Convention and Visitors Bureau, 425 6th Ave, 30th Floor, 15219 (Mon–Fri); 412/281-7711 or 800/366-0093. A Visitor Information Center is along Liberty Ave, adj to 4 Gateway Center (Mar–Dec, daily; rest of yr, daily exc Sun). Other centers can be found in the Carnegie Library's Mt Washington branch, and on the University of Pittsburgh's campus, Log Cabin, Forbes Ave. For a schedule of events in Pittsburgh, 24-hr visitor information, phone 800/366-0093.

Pittsburgh Intl Airport Area

For additional accommodations, see PITTSBURGH INTL AIRPORT AREA, which follows PITTSBURGH.

City Neighborhoods

Many of the restaurants, unrated dining establishments and some lodgings listed under Pittsburgh include neighborhoods as well as exact street addresses. Geographic descriptions of these areas are given.

Downtown. South of the Allegheny River, west of I-579, north of the Monongahela River and east of Point State Park. **North of Downtown:** North of Allegheny River. **South of Downtown:** South of Monongahela River. **East of Downtown:** East of US 579.

Mount Washington. Across the Monongahela River south of Downtown; north of Saw Mill Run Blvd, south of West Carson St, east of Hallock and west of Beltzhoover.

Oakland. East of Downtown; centered on and around 5th Ave between Bellefield St on the north and Halket St on the south.

South Side. Across the Monongahela River south of Downtown; Station Square area east of the Liberty Bridge, west of S 27th St and north of Mary St.

Motels

★★ **CLUBHOUSE INN & SUITES.** 5311 Campbells Run Rd (15205), jct I-279 & PA 60, exit Moon Run, west of downtown. 412/788-8400; FAX 412/788-2577; res: 800/258-2466. Web www.clubhouse inn.com. 152 rms, 3 story. 26 suites. S $85; D $95; each addl $10; suites $100; under 18 free; lower rates Fri, Sat. Crib free. TV; cable (premium). Heated pool; whirlpool. Complimentary buffet bkfst. Restaurant adj 11 am-

11 pm. Ck-out noon. Coin lndry. Meeting rms. Business servs avail. In-rm modem link. Free airport transportation. Exercise equipt. Some microwaves; refrigerator in suites. Cr cds: A, C, D, DS, MC, V.

D ⛱ 🏃 ⊠ 🔥 SC

✓★★ **HAMPTON INN.** 555 Trumbull Dr (15205), across river, west of downtown. 412/922-0100; FAX 412/921-7631; res: 800/426-7866. Web www.hampton-inn.com. 135 rms, 6 story. June-Nov: S $69-$79; D $79; under 18 free; wknd rates; lower rates rest of yr. Pet accepted. TV; cable (premium). Complimentary continental bkfst. Coffee in rms. Restaurant nearby. Ck-out noon. Meeting rms. Business servs avail. In-rm modem link. Valet serv. Free airport transportation. Health club privileges. Picnic tables. Cr cds: A, C, D, DS, MC, V.

D 🐾 ⛱ ⊠ 🔥 SC

✓★★ **HAMPTON INN.** 1550 Lebanon Church Rd (15236), S on US 51, south of downtown. 412/650-1000; FAX 412/650-1001; res: 800/527-1133. 70 rms, 3 story. S $79-$94; D $84-$99; under 18 free; higher rates: hols, football games. Crib free. TV; cable (premium). VCR avail (movies). Restaurant nearby. Ck-out noon. Meeting rms. Business servs avail. In-rm modem link. Valet serv. Concierge. Heated pool; lifeguard. Some in-rm whirlpools, refrigerators, microwaves. Cr cds: A, C, D, DS, JCB, MC, V.

D ⛱ ⊠ 🔥 SC

★★ **HAWTHORN SUITES.** 700 Mansfield Ave (15205), at Noblestown Rd, I-279 exit 4, south of downtown. 412/279-6300; FAX 412/279-4993; res: 800/331-3131; res: 800/527-1133. E-mail tn009665@psinet.com; web www.hawthorn.com. 151 suites, 2 story. S $89-$119; D $119-$149; wkly, monthly rates. Crib free. Pet accepted, some restrictions; $50 and $6/day. TV; cable (premium). Pool; whirlpool, lifeguard. Complimentary full bkfst. Ck-out noon. Meeting rms. Business servs avail. Airport, RR station, bus depot transportation. Health club privileges. Refrigerators, microwaves, fireplaces. Private patios, balconies. Picnic tables, grills. Chalet-style buildings. Cr cds: A, C, D, DS, JCB, MC, V.

D 🐾 ⛱ ⊠ 🔥 SC

★★★ **HOLIDAY INN.** 401 Holiday Dr (15220), west of downtown. 412/922-8100; FAX 412/922-6511; res: 800/465-4329. 200 rms, 4 story. S, D $104-$148; each addl $10; under 18 free. Crib free. Pet accepted. TV; cable, VCR avail. Heated pool; poolside serv, lifeguard. Restaurant 6:30 am-10 pm; Fri, Sat to 11 pm. Rm serv. Bar 11-2 am; Sun from 1 pm; entertainment. Ck-out noon. Meeting rms. Business servs avail. In-rm modem link. Valet serv. Sundries. Free airport transportation. Tennis privileges. Golf privileges. Exercise equipt. Health club privileges. Private patios. Cr cds: A, C, D, DS, JCB, MC, V.

D 🐾 🍴 🏊 🏃 ⊠ 🔥 SC

★★★ **HOLIDAY INN.** 180 Gamma Dr (15238), PA 28 exit 10, north of downtown. 412/963-0600; FAX 412/963-7852; res: 800/465-4329. 223 rms, 2 story. S $99; D $100; suites $120-$150; under 18 free. TV; cable (premium). Heated pool; pooside serv, lifeguard. Coffee in rms. Restaurant 6 am-10 pm; Sat, Sun from 7 am. Rm serv. Bar 11-2 am; Sun 1 pm-1 am. Ck-out 11 am. Meeting rms. Business servs avail. In-rm modem link. Bellhops. Valet serv. Airport transportation. Exercise equipt. Refrigerator in suites; microwaves avail. Cr cds: A, C, D, DS, JCB, MC, V.

D ⛱ 🏃 ⊠ 🔥 SC

✓★ **RED ROOF INN.** 6404 Steubenville Pike (15205), south of downtown. 412/787-7870; FAX 412/787-8392; res: 800/843-7663. 120 rms, 2 story. S, D $53.99-$59.99; under 18 free. Crib free. Pet accepted, some restrictions. TV; cable (premium). Complimentary morning coffee. Restaurant adj open 24 hrs. Ck-out noon. Business servs avail. Cr cds: A, C, D, DS, MC, V.

D 🐾 ⊠ 🔥

Motor Hotels

✓★★★ **BEST WESTERN PARKWAY CENTER.** 875 Greentree Rd (15220), adj Parkway Center Mall, west of downtown. 412/922-7070; FAX 412/922-4949; res: 800/528-1234. E-mail bwpci@usaor.net. 138 rms, 6 story, 44 kits. S, D $64-$89; kit units $79-$89; under 12 free; wkend rates. Crib free. TV; cable (premium). Indoor pool; lifeguard. Complimentary bkfst. Ck-out noon. Coin lndry. Meeting rms. Business servs avail. In-rm modem link, Bellhops. Valet serv. Sundries. Free airport transportation. Exercise equipt; sauna. Rec rm. Microwaves avail. Cr cds: A, C, D, DS, ER, MC, V.

D ⚓ ⛄ ⛷ 🔥 SC

★★★ **HOLIDAY INN.** 164 Fort Couch Rd (15241), south of downtown. 412/833-5300; FAX 412/839-8539; res: 800/465-4329. Web www.hionline.com. 210 rms, 8 story. S, D $79; each addl $10; suites $120-$130; under 18 free; wkend rates. Crib free. Pet accepted, some restrictions. TV; cable (premium), VCR avail. Pool; poolside serv, lifeguard. Coffee in rms. Restaurant 6:30 am-11 pm; Sat, Sun from 7 am. Rm serv. Bar 11-2 am; entertainment Tues-Sat. Ck-out noon. Meeting rms. Business servs avail. In-rm modem link. Bellhops. Valet serv. Shopping arcade. Airport transportation. Health club privileges. Game rm. Microwaves avail. Balconies. Cr cds: A, C, D, DS, ER, JCB, MC, V.

D 🐕 ⛄ ⛄ 🔥 SC

★★★ **HOLIDAY INN.** 4859 McKnight Rd (15237), 5 mi N on I-279, exit 18, north of downtown. 412/366-5200; FAX 412/366-5682; res: 800/465-4329. 147 rms, 7 story, 19 suites. S, D $99-$109; each addl $10; suites $109-$139; under 18 free. Crib free. TV; cable (premium). Heated pool; poolside serv, lifeguard. Complimentary coffee in rms. Restaurant 6:30 am-10 pm; Sun from 7 am. Rm serv. Bar 11 am-11 pm; entertainment Sat. Ck-out noon. Coin lndry. Meeting rms. Business servs avail. In-rm modem link. Valet serv. Sundries. Health club privileges. Refrigerator in suites; microwaves avail. Cr cds: A, C, D, DS, MC, V.

D ⛄ ⛄ 🔥 SC

★★ **HOLIDAY INN.** 2750 Mosside Blvd (15146), approx 7 mi E on I-376, exit 16A, at PA 48 & US 22 Business. 412/372-1022; FAX 412/373-4065; res: 800/465-4329. 189 rms, 4 story. S, D $69-$129; each addl $10; under 19 free; package plans. Crib free. Pet accepted. TV; cable (premium). Pool. Complimentary coffee in rms. Restaurant 6:30 am-2 pm, 5-10 pm. Rm serv. Bar 11-2 am; entertainment Sun. Ck-out noon. Coin lndry. Meeting rms. Business servs avail. In-rm modem link. Valet serv. Sundries. Exercise equipt. Health club privileges. Some in-rm whirlpools; microwaves avail. Cr cds: A, C, D, DS, ER, MC, V.

D 🐕 ⛄ ⛷ ⛄ 🔥 SC

★★★ **HOLIDAY INN.** 915 Brinton Rd (15221), east of downtown. 412/247-2700; FAX 412/371-9619; res: 800/465-4323. 180 rms, 11 story. Apr-Oct: S, D $99-$129; suites $150; under 18 free; wkend, hol rates; lower rates rest of yr. Crib free. Pet accepted. TV; cable (premium). Indoor pool; lifeguard. Coffee in rms. Restaurant 6:30 am-10 pm. Rm serv. Bar 4 pm-1 am; entertainment Fri, Sat. Ck-out noon. Coin lndry. Meeting rms. Business servs avail. Valet serv. Health club privileges. Some refrigerators; microwaves avail. Cr cds: A, C, D, DS, ER, JCB, MC, V.

D 🐕 ⛄ ⛄ 🔥 SC

★★★ **MARRIOTT.** 101 Marriott Dr (15205), across river, west of downtown. 412/922-8400; FAX 412/922-8981; res: 800/525-5902. Web www.marriott.com. 467 rms, 7 story. S $99-$164; D $114-$179; each addl $15; suites $200-$375; under 18 free; wkend rates; package plans. Crib free. Pet accepted. TV; cable (premium), VCR avail. 3 pools, 1 indoor; whirlpool, poolside serv, lifeguard. Restaurant 6:30 am-midnight. Rm serv. Bar 11-2 am; entertainment. Ck-out noon. Meeting rms. Business servs avail. In-rm modem link. Bellhops. Valet serv. Sundries. Gift shop. Barber, beauty shop. Free airport transportation. Indoor tennis privileges. Exercise equipt; sauna, steam rm. Health club privileges. Rec rm. Many minibars. Luxury level. Cr cds: A, C, D, DS, ER, MC, V.

D 🐕 ⛷ ⛄ ⛷ ⛄ 🔥 SC

★★★ **RADISSON HOTEL.** 699 Rodi Rd (15235), at jct PA 791 & I-376, east of downtown. 412/244-1600; FAX 412/829-2334; res: 800/272-6232. 152 rms, 3 story. No elvtr. S $112-$122; D $122-$132; each addl $10; under 18 free; wkend plan. Crib free. TV; cable, VCR avail. 2 heated pools, 1 indoor; whirlpool, poolside serv, lifeguard. Sauna. Restaurant 6:30 am-2 pm, 5:30-10 pm; Fri, Sat 6-11 pm. Rm serv 7 am-11 pm. Bar 4:30 pm-midnight; Fri to 1 am; Sat noon-1 am; Sun 4:30-11 pm; entertainment Fri, Sat. Ck-out 11 am. Meeting rms. Business servs avail. In-rm modem link. Bellhops. Valet serv. Sundries. Airport transportation. Lighted tennis. Health club privileges. Private patios, balconies. Cr cds: A, C, D, DS, JCB, MC, V.

D ⛷ ⛄ ⛄ 🔥 SC

Hotels

★★★ **DOUBLETREE HOTEL.** 1000 Penn Ave (15222), downtown. 412/281-3700; FAX 412/227-4500; res: 800/578-0444. Web www.doubletreehotel.com. 616 rms, 26 story. S $125-$180; D $145-$215; each addl $20; suites $255-$1,550; family rates; wkend rates. Crib free. Pet accepted. TV; cable (premium). Indoor pool; whirlpool. Coffee in rms. Restaurants 6:30 am-2:30 pm, 5-10:30 pm; Fri, Sat to 11 pm. Rm serv 24 hrs. Bar 11-2 am. Ck-out noon. Convention facilities. Business center. In-rm modem link. Concierge. Shopping arcade. Exercise rm; sauna, steam rm. Refrigerators; many bathrm phones. Cr cds: A, C, D, DS, ER, JCB, MC, V.

D 🐕 ⛄ ⛷ ⛄ 🔥 SC 🚶

★★★ **HILTON HOTEL.** 600 Commonwealth Pl (15222), at Point State Park, downtown. 412/391-4600; FAX 412/594-5161; res: 800/445-8667. 713 rms, 24 story. S $154-$219; D $179-$244; each addl $20; suites $355; studio rms $109; under 12 free; wkend plans. Crib free. Pet accepted, some restrictions. TV; cable (premium), VCR avail. Coffee in rms. Restaurant 6:30 am-11:30 pm. Bars 11-2 am; entertainment. Ck-out noon. Meeting rms. Business center. In-rm modem link. Concierge. Drugstore. Garage; valet parking. Airport transportation. Exercise equipt. Minibars; some bathrm phones, refrigerators. Luxury level. Cr cds: A, C, D, DS, ER, JCB, MC, V.

D 🐕 ⛷ ⛄ 🔥 SC 🚶

★★★ **RAMADA PLAZA SUITES & CONFERENCE CENTER.** 1 Bigelow Sq (15219), downtown. 412/281-5800; FAX 412/281-8467; res: 800/225-5858. Web www.idp.com/pit/rps. 311 kit suites, 20 story. S, D $139-$199; each addl $10; under 16 free; package plans. Crib free. TV; cable, VCR avail. Complimentary continental bkfst. Complimentary coffee in rms. Restaurant 6:30-1 am; wkends 7 am-midnight. Bar 11-1 am. Ck-out noon. Convention facilities. Business center. In-rm modem link. Grocery store. Beauty shop. Coin lndry. Exercise rm; sauna. Indoor pool. Cr cds: A, C, D, DS, JCB, MC, V.

D ⛄ ⛷ ⛄ 🔥 SC 🚶

★★★ **SHERATON HOTEL.** 7 Station Square Dr (15219), on South Side. 412/261-2000; FAX 412/261-2932; res: 800/255-7488. 292 rms, 15 story. S $149-$170; D $149-$185; each addl $15; suites $225-$600; under 18 free; wkend rates. Crib free. TV; cable (premium), VCR avail. Indoor pool; whirlpool, lifeguard. Coffee in rms. Restaurant 6 am-midnight. Bar 11-2 am; entertainment. Ck-out noon. Meeting rms. Business center. In-rm modem link. Shopping arcade. RR station, bus depot transportation. Exercise equipt. Health club privileges. On riverfront. Luxury level. Cr cds: A, C, D, DS, ER, JCB, MC, V.

D ⛄ ⛷ ⛄ 🔥 SC 🚶

★★★ **WESTIN WILLIAM PENN HOTEL.** 530 William Penn Pl (15219), on Mellon Square, downtown. 412/281-7100; FAX 412/553-5252. 595 rms, 24 story. S, D $204-$214; each addl $20; suites $399-$2,200; under 18 free; wkend rates. Crib free. Pet accepted. Valet parking $19.50. TV; cable (premium), VCR avail. Restaurant 6:30 am-10 pm (also see TERRACE ROOM, Unrated Dining). Rm serv 24 hrs. Bar 11-2 am; entertainment. Ck-out 1 pm. Convention facilities. Business center. Gift shop.

Barber shop. Airport, RR station, bus depot transportation. Exercise equipt. Health club privileges. Historic, landmark hotel. Cr cds: A, C, D, DS, ER, JCB, MC, V.

★★★ **WYNDHAM GARDEN HOTEL.** *1 Wyndham Cir (15275), off PA 60, exit Montour Run Rd, west of downtown.* 724/695-0002; FAX 724/695-7262; res: 800/996-3426. Web www.wyndham.com. 140 rms, 4 story. S $109; D $119; each addl $10; suites $109-$119; under 18 free; wkend, hol rates. Crib free. TV; cable (premium). Pool; wading pool, lifeguard. Complimentary coffee in rms. Restaurant 6:30 am-2 pm, 5-10 pm. Bar 4 pm-midnight. Ck-out noon. Meeting rms. Business center. In-rm modem link. Free airport transportation. Exercise equipt. Some refrigerators. Cr cds: A, C, D, DS, ER, JCB, MC, V.

Inns

★★★ **APPLETREE BED & BREAKFAST.** *703 S Negley Ave (15232), east of downtown.* 412/661-0631. Web deskshop.lm.com/appletree-bb/. 4 rms, 2 story, suite. MAP: S, D $105-$140; suite $140; wkend plans; hols (2-3 day min). Children over 12 yrs only. TV; VCR. Complimentary full bkfst. Ck-out 11 am, ck-in 3-6 pm. Concierge serv. Luggage handling. Business servs avail. In-rm modem link. Health club privileges. Fireplaces. Totally nonsmoking. Historic building (1884). Cr cds: A, C, DS, MC, V.

★★★ **INN AT OAKMONT.** *300 Rte 909 (15139), 15 mi NE on PA 28, adj to golf course.* 412/828-0410; FAX 412/828-1358. Web www.bnb.lm.com. 8 rms, 1 with shower only, 2 story. S $100-$120; D $130-$140; each addl $10. TV; VCR avail. Complimentary full bkfst. Coffee in library. Restaurant nearby. Ck-out 11 am, ck-in 2 pm. Concierge serv. Business servs avail. 18-hole golf privileges. Exercise equipt. Balconies. Many antiques. Totally nonsmoking. Cr cds: A, C, DS, MC, V.

★★★ **PRIORY INN.** *614 Pressley St (15212), north of downtown.* 412/231-3338; FAX 412/231-4838. Web www.sgi.net/thepriory/. 24 rms, 3 story. S $65-$100; D $103-$120; each addl $10; suites $110-$143; under 7 free; lower rates wkends. TV; cable. Complimentary continental bkfst; refreshments. Ck-out 11 am, wkends noon, ck-in 3 pm. Meeting rms. Business servs avail. Previously a haven for Benedictine monks (1888). European-style inn with fountain and floral arrangements in courtyard. Cr cds: A, C, D, DS, MC, V.

★★★ **SHADYSIDE BED & BREAKFAST.** *5516 Maple Hts Rd (15232), east of downtown; I-279 exit 13.* 412/683-6501; FAX 412/683-7228. Web www.bnb.lm.com. 8 rms, 2 share bath, 3 story. No elvtr. MAP: S, D $115-$140. TV in sitting rm; cable (premium), VCR, (movies). Complimentary continental bkfst. Restaurant nearby. Ck-out noon, ck-in 3 pm. Concierge serv. Luggage handling. Health club privileges. Microwaves avail. Billiard rm, library. Cr cds: A, C, D, DS, MC, V.

Restaurants

★★ **1902 LANDMARK TAVERN.** *24 Market St (15222), downtown.* 412/471-1902. Hrs: 11:30 am-11 pm; Fri, Sat to midnight. Closed Sun; major hols. Res accepted. Italian-American menu. Bar to 2 am. Semi-a la carte: lunch $5.95-$11.50, dinner $10.95-$22. Specializes in steaks, fresh seafood, oyster bar. Valet parking (dinner). Restored tavern (1902); ornate tin ceiling, original tiles. Cr cds: A, C, D, DS, MC, V.

★★ **BENIHANA.** *2100 Greentree Rd (15220), south of downtown.* 412/276-2100. Hrs: 11:30 am-2 pm, 5:30-10 pm; Fri to 11 pm; Sat 5-

11:30 pm; Sun 4:30-9 pm. Res accepted. Japanese menu. Bar. Semi-a la carte: lunch $5.95-$12.50, dinner $12.95-$27.95. Child's meals. Specializes in hibachi chicken, steak, seafood. Japanese garden. Cr cds: A, C, D, DS, MC, V.

✓★ **BRITISH BICYCLE CLUB.** *923 Penn Ave (15222), downtown.* 412/391-9623. Hrs: 10 am-10 pm. Closed Sat, Sun; major hols. Res accepted. Bar. Semi-a la carte: lunch $4.75-$8.75, dinner $4.75-$15.95. Specializes in prime rib, steak salad, steak. English pub atmosphere. Cr cds: A, C, D, DS, MC, V.

★★★ **CAFE ALLEGRO.** *51 S 12th St (15203), on South Side.* 412/481-7788. Hrs: 5-11 pm. Closed major hols. Res accepted. Italian menu. Bar. Wine list. Semi-a la carte: dinner $17-$23. Child's meals. Specialties: pasta del sole, seafood arrabbiata, grilled veal medallions. Valet parking. Ambience of Riviera cafe; artwork. Cr cds: A, C, D, MC, V.

★★ **CAFE AT THE FRICK.** *7227 Reynolds St (15208), at the Frick Art and Historical Center, east of downtown.* 412/371-0600. Hrs: 11 am-5 pm; Sun noon-6 pm; high tea from 3 pm. Closed Mon; most major hols. Semi-a la carte: lunch $7.95-$10. Specializes in salads, desserts. Outdoor dining. View of garden and Frick estate. Totally nonsmoking. Cr cds: C, DS, MC, V.

★★★ **CARLTON.** *1 Mellon Bank Center (15219), on grounds of Mellon Bank Center Commercial Bldg, at Grant St, downtown.* 412/391-4099. Hrs: 11:30 am-2:30 pm, 5-10 pm; Fri to 11 pm; Sat 5-11 pm. Closed Sun; major hols. Res accepted. Continental menu. Bar. Wine list. Semi-a la carte: lunch $9.95-$14.95, dinner $19.95-$25.95. Child's meals. Specializes in charcoal-grilled seafood, prime steak, veal. Own pastries. Parking. Cr cds: A, C, D, DS, MC, V.

★★★ **CARMASSI'S TUSCANY GRILL.** *711 Penn Ave (15222), downtown.* 412/281-6644. Hrs: 11 am-10 pm; Sat from 4:30 pm; Sun 4:30-8 pm. Closed hols. Res accepted. Northern Italian menu. Bar. Semi-a la carte: lunch $9-$12, dinner $17-$25. Child's meals. Specialties: veal a'la lucca, penne arrabiatta. Italian art on display. Cr cds: A, C, D, DS, MC, V.

★★★ **CASBAH.** *229 S Highland Ave (15206), in Shadyside, east of downtown.* 412/661-5656. Hrs: 11:30 am-2:30 pm, 5-11 pm; Sat, Sun 11 am-2 pm, 5-10 pm. Closed most major hols. Res accepted. Mediterranean menu. Bar. Wine list. Semi-a la carte: lunch $5.50-$12, dinner $15-$25. Specialties: lamb mixed grill, roasted vegetable tagine, Mahi Mahi and grape leaves. Cr cds: A, C, D, DS, MC, V.

✓★★ **CHEESE CELLAR RESTAURANT & BAR.** *25 Station Sq (15219), Station Square (Smithfield & Carson Sts), on South Side.* 412/471-3355. Hrs: 11:30 am-midnight; Fri, Sat to 1 am; Sun 10:30 am-11 pm. Closed Thanksgiving, Dec 25. Res accepted Sun-Thurs. Continental menu. Bar to 2 am. Semi-a la carte: Sun bkfst $5.95-$6.50, lunch, dinner $4.95-$13.95. Child's meals. Specialty: cheese and chocolate fondue. Outdoor dining. Rustic decor. Cr cds: A, C, D, DS, MC, V.

✓★★ **CHINA PALACE.** *5440 Walnut St (15232), in Shadyside, east of downtown.* 412/687-7423. Hrs: 11:30 am-10 pm; Fri, Sat to 11 pm; Sun 2-9 pm. Closed July 4, Labor Day, Thanksgiving. Chinese menu. Bar. Semi-a la carte: lunch $4.95-$5.50, dinner $6.95-$16.95. Specialties: crispy walnut shrimp, orange beef, lemon chicken. Cr cds: A, C, D, DS, MC, V.

★ ★ ★ **CLIFFSIDE.** *1208 Grandview Ave (15211), on Mt Washington.* 412/431-6996. Hrs: 5-10 pm; Fri, Sat to 11 pm. Closed major hols. Res accepted. Continental menu. Bar. Semi-a la carte: dinner $16-$24. Child's meals. Specializes in fresh seafood, chicken, veal. Pianist. Valet parking. Contemporary decor in older building (1897). Cr cds: A, C, D, DS, JCB, MC, V.

★ ★ ★ **COLONY.** *Greentree & Cochran Rds (15220), south of downtown.* 412/561-2060. Hrs: 5-10:30 pm; Sun 4-9 pm. Res accepted. Continental menu. Bar 4 pm-1 am. Wine list. Complete meals: dinner $21-$42. Specializes in fresh seafood, pork tenderloin, prime Angus steaks. Own baking. Pianist, vocalist Fri, Sat. Valet parking. Family-owned. Jacket. Cr cds: A, C, D, DS, JCB, MC, V.

★ ★ ★ **COMMON PLEA.** *308 Ross St (15219), downtown.* 412/281-5140. Hrs: 11:30 am-2:30 pm, 5-10 pm; Sat 5-10 pm. Closed Sun; major hols. Res accepted. Bar. Wine list. Complete meals: lunch $6.95-$10.75, dinner $18.25-$28. Specializes in seafood, veal, chicken. Own baking. Valet parking (dinner). Courtroom decor. Family-owned. Cr cds: A, C, D, MC, V.

★ ★ ★ **D'IMPERIO'S.** *3412 Wm Penn Hwy (15235), east of downtown.* 412/823-4800. Hrs: 11:30 am-3 pm, 5-11 pm; Mon, Sat from 5 pm. Closed Sun; most major hols. Res accepted; required wkends. Italian, Amer menu. Bar. Semi-a la carte: dinner $13.50-$28. Child's meals. Specialties: shrimp Sorrento, lobster sausage, veal Genovese. Own bread. Pianist. Parking. Different displays of artwork in each dining rm. Cr cds: A, C, D, DS, MC, V.

★ ★ **GEORGETOWNE INN.** *1230 Grandview Ave (15211), on Mt Washington.* 412/481-4424. Hrs: 11 am-3 pm, 5 pm-midnight; Fri, Sat to 1 am; Sun 4-10 pm. Closed most hols. Res accepted. Bar. Semi-a la carte: lunch $5.50-$15.95, dinner $13.95-$31.95. Specializes in steak, fresh seafood. Panoramic view of city. Cr cds: A, C, D, DS, MC, V.

★ ★ ★ **GRAND CONCOURSE.** *1 Station Square (15219), jct Carson & Smithfield Sts, on South Side.* 412/261-1717. Hrs: 11:30 am-2:30 pm, 4:30-10 pm; Sat 4:30-11 pm; Sun 4:30-10 pm; early-bird dinner 4:30-6 pm; Sun brunch 10 am-2:30 pm. Closed Dec 25. Res accepted. Continental menu. Bar 11:30-2 am; Sun 11 am-10 pm. Wine list. Semi-a la carte: lunch $6-$12, dinner $10-$30. Sun brunch $16.95. Child's meals. Specializes in seafood, steak, pasta. Own baking, pasta. Pianist. Converted railroad station. Braille menu. Outdoor dining. Cr cds: A, C, D, DS, MC, V.

★ ★ **INDIA GARDEN.** *328 Atwood St (15213), in Oakland.* 412/682-3000. Hrs: 11:30 am-2:30 pm, 5-10 pm. Res accepted. Northern Indian menu. Setups. A la carte entrees: $6.95-$13.95. Buffet: lunch $6.95. Specialties: tandoori chicken, chicken tekka masala, vegetable korma. Indian decor, chairs. Cr cds: A, C, DS, MC, V.

✓ ★ ★ **JIMMY TSANG'S.** *5700 Centre Ave (15206), at Negley, in Kennilworth Bldg, east of downtown.* 412/661-4226. Hrs: 11:30 am-10 pm; Fri, Sat to 11 pm; Sun 3:30-9 pm; early-bird dinner Mon-Sat 3-6 pm. Closed July 4, Thanksgiving. Chinese menu. Bar. A la carte: lunch $4.95-$5.75, dinner $7.95-$9.95. Specialties: Peking duck, honey chicken, Mongolian beef. Oriental decor, artwork. Cr cds: A, C, D, MC, V.

★ ★ **JUNO TRATTORIA.** *301 Grant St (15219), downtown.* 412/392-0225. Hrs: 11 am-10 pm; Fri, Sat to 11 pm. Closed Sun; most major hols. Italian menu. Bar. Semi-a la carte: lunch $6-$12, dinner $12-$16. Specializes in pastas, salads, seafood. Cr cds: A, C, D, DS, MC, V.

★ ★ **KAYA.** *2000 Smallman St (15222), in Strip District, east of downtown.* 412/261-6565. Web bigburrito.com. Hrs: 11:30 am-11 pm; Fri, Sat to midnight; Sun to 9 pm. Closed some major hols. Carribean menu. Bar. Semi-a la carte: lunch $6.25-$8.95, dinner $6.25-$16.95. Specialties: Jamaican jerk chicken wings, grilled alligator, salmon. Outdoor dining. Cr cds: A, C, D, DS, MC, V.

★ ★ ★ **LE MONT.** *1114 Grandview Ave (15211), on Mt Washington.* 412/431-3100. E-mail info@le-mont.com; web www.le-mont.com. Hrs: 5-11:30 pm; Sun 4-10 pm. Closed major hols. Res accepted. Contemporary Amer menu. Bar to midnight. Wine list. A la carte entrees: dinner $18.95-$46. Specializes in variety of wild game dishes, flaming desserts. Own baking. Pianist Fri, Sat. Valet parking. Atop Mt Washington; panoramic view of city. Cr cds: A, C, D, DS, JCB, MC, V.

★ ★ ★ **LE POMMIER.** *2104 E Carson St (15203), on South Side.* 412/431-1901. E-mail lepommier@lepommier.com; web www.le pommier.com. Hrs: 5:30-9:30 pm; Fri, Sat to 10:30 pm. Closed Mon, Sun; some major hols. Res accepted. French menu. Bar. Wine cellar. A la carte entrees: dinner $14-$28. Specializes in seasonal French country fare. Own baking. Valet parking Fri, Sat. Located in oldest storefront in area (1863). Outdoor dining in season. Country French decor. Cr cds: A, C, D, DS, MC, V.

★ ★ ★ **LONDON GRILLE.** *1500 Washington Rd (15228), US 19S, in Galleria Mall, south of downtown.* 412/563-3400. Hrs: 11:30 am-10 pm; Fri, Sat to 11:30 pm; Sun noon-9 pm. Closed Dec 25. British menu. Bar. Wine list. Semi-a la carte: lunch $7.95-$11.95; dinner $17.95-$25.95. Specialties: prime rib, beef Wellington. Patio dining. 4 dining rooms. Cr cds: A, C, D, DS, MC, V.

✓ ★ **MAX & ERMA'S.** *5533 Walnut St (15232), in Shadyside, east of downtown.* 412/681-5775. Hrs: 11:30 am-11 pm; Fri, Sat to midnight; Sun to 10 pm. Closed Thanksgiving, Dec 25. Bar. Semi-a la carte: lunch $6-$10, dinner $8-$14. Specializes in steak, ribs, pasta. Cr cds: A, C, D, DS, MC, V.

✓ ★ ★ **MAX'S ALLEGHENY TAVERN.** *Middle & Suisman Sts (15212), north of downtown.* 412/231-1899. Hrs: 11 am-midnight; Sun to 10 pm. Closed most major hols. German menu. Bar. A la carte entrees: lunch $4.25-$7.95, dinner $5.95-$13.95. Specialties: jagerschnitzel, kase spatzle, sauerbraten. Tavern with German memorabilia and collection of photographs. Cr cds: A, C, D, DS, MC, V.

★ ★ **PASTA PIATTO.** *736 Bellefonte St (15232), in Shadyside, east of downtown.* 412/621-5547. Hrs: 11:30 am-3 pm, 4:30-10 pm; Wed, Thurs to 10:30 pm; Fri, Sat to 11 pm; Sun 4-9 pm. Closed major hols. Northern Italian menu. Bar. Semi-a la carte: lunch $5-$10, dinner $10.95-$22.95. Child's meals. Specializes in homemade pasta, veal, seafood. Cr cds: A, C, MC, V.

✓ ★ ★ **PENN BREWERY.** *800 Vinial St Troy Hill (15212), north of downtown.* 412/237-9402. Hrs: 11 am-midnight. Closed Sun; hols. German menu. Bar. Semi-a la carte: lunch $4.50-$8.50, dinner $8.50-$15.95.

Child's meals. Specialties: Wienerschnitzel, sauerbraten, chicken Berlin. Entertainment Tues-Sat. Outdoor dining. Restored 19th-century brewery, German beer hall-style communal dining. Cr cds: A, C, DS, MC, V.

★★★ **PICCOLO MONDO.** *661 Andersen Dr (15220), Bldg 7, Foster Plaza, Green Tree, south of downtown.* 412/922-0920. Web www.piccolo-mondo.com. Hrs: 11:30 am-10 pm; Sat to 4-11 pm. Closed Sun exc Mother's Day; some hols. Res accepted. Northern Italian menu. Bar. Wine list. Semi-a la carte: lunch $7.50-$13, dinner $14-$24. Child's meals. Specializes in fresh fish, veal. Own desserts. Parking. Jacket. Cr cds: A, C, D, DS, MC, V.

★★★ **POLI.** *2607 Murray Ave (15217), east of downtown.* 412/521-6400. Hrs: 11:30 am-11 pm; Sun 1-9:30 pm; early-bird dinner Tues-Fri 3-5:30 pm. Closed Mon; Thanksgiving, Dec 25. Bar. Semi-a la carte: lunch $5.50-$10.95, dinner $15-$25. Child's meals. Specializes in fresh seafood, Italian cuisine. Own baking. Valet parking. Family-owned. Cr cds: A, C, D, DS, MC, V.

✓★ **PRIMANTI BROS.** *46 18th St (15222), in Strip District, east of downtown.* 412/263-2142. Hrs: open 24 hrs. Closed Dec 25. Italian, Amer menu. Wine, beer. Semi-a la carte: $3.75-$4.25. Specializes in deli sandwiches with fries and cole slaw inside, soups. Family-owned. Cr cds: C.

★★★ **RICO'S.** *1 Rico Lane (15237), off Evergreen Rd in North Hills, north of downtown.* 412/931-1989. Hrs: 11:45 am-2:45 pm, 4-10:30 pm; Fri, Sat 4-11:30 pm. Closed Sun; most major hols. Italian, Amer menu. Bar to midnight. Wine cellar. Semi-a la carte: lunch $7.50-$12.50, dinner $15.50-$28. Specializes in fresh seafood, veal. Valet parking. Old World atmosphere; Italian lithographs. Jacket. Cr cds: A, C, D, DS, MC, V.

✓★★ **SEVENTH STREET GRILLE.** *130 7th St (15222), downtown.* 412/338-0303. Hrs: 11:30 am-9 pm; Fri, Sat to 11 pm; Sun to 8 pm. Closed most major hols. Res accepted. Continental menu. Bar. Semi-a la carte: lunch $5.95-$15.95, dinner $7.95-$22.95. Specializes in grilled seafood, prime rib, specialty beers. Cr cds: A, C, D, DS, MC, V.

★★ **SOBA LOUNGE.** *5847 Ellsworth Ave (15232), east of downtown.* 412/362-5656. Hrs: 5-10 pm; Fri, Sat to 11 pm. Closed Thanksgiving. Res accepted. Pan-Asian menu. Bars. Semi-a la carte: dinner $12-$30. Specialties: pork and vegetarian dumplings, wok-seared salmon, zaru soba noodles. Own noodles. Music. Outdoor dining. Three dining levels; eclectic decor; original artwork. Cr cds: A, C, D, DS, MC, V.

✓★★ **SUSHI TWO.** *2122 E Carson St (15203), south of downtown.* 412/431-7874. Hrs: 11:30 am-3 pm, 5-10 pm; Fri to 11:30 pm; Sat 11:30 am-11 pm; Sun 1-9 pm. Closed Labor Day. Res accepted. Japanese menu. Bar. Semi-a la carte: lunch $5.50-$10.95, dinner $9.95-$18.95. Specializes in traditional Japanese dishes. Valet parking Fri, Sat. Contemporary Japanese decor. Cr cds: A, C, D, DS, MC, V.

★★★ **TAMBELLINI'S.** *PA 51 (15226), south of downtown.* 412/481-1118. E-mail seafood@teleroma.lm.com; web www.tamb.lm.com. Hrs: 11:30 am-10 pm. Closed Sun; Jan 1, Thanksgiving, Dec 25. Res accepted. Continental menu. Bar. Semi-a la carte: lunch $7.95-$8.50, dinner $13.95-$27.50. Complete meals: dinner $21.95. Child's meals. Specializes in seafood, pasta, steak. Valet parking. Modern decor. Cr cds: A, C, D, MC, V.

✓★★ **TESSARO'S.** *4601 Liberty Ave (15224), at Taylor St, east of downtown.* 412/682-6809. Hrs: 11 am-midnight. Closed Sun; Jan 1, Thanksgiving, Dec 25. Mexican, Amer menu. Bar. Semi-a la carte: lunch $5-$10, dinner $12-$15. Specializes in hamburgers, fresh seafood. Own pasta. Casual decor has pressed tin ceiling (ca early 1900s), ceiling fans, fireplaces. Cr cds: A, C, D, DS, MC, V.

✓★★ **THAI PLACE.** *809 Bellefonte St (15232), in Shadyside, east of downtown.* 412/687-8586. Hrs: 11:30 am-10 pm; Fri to 10:30 pm; Sat noon-11 pm; Sun noon-9:30 pm; Mon from 4:30 pm. Thai menu. Bar. A la carte entrees: lunch $5.50-$7.50, dinner $7.50-$17.95. Specializes in authentic Thai cuisine. Outdoor dining. Asian art. Cr cds: A, C, D, DS, MC, V.

✓★★ **THE CHURCH BREW WORKS.** *3525 Liberty Ave (15201), north of downtown.* 412/688-8200. E-mail churchbrew@ juno.com; web www.churchbrew.com. Hrs: 11:30 am-midnight; Fri, Sat to 1 am; Sun noon-10 pm. Closed Jan 1, Thanksgiving, Dec 25. Regional Amer menu. Bar. Semi-a la carte: lunch $5.75-$7.95, dinner $13.95-$19.95. Specialties: buffalo steak, wood-fired oven pizza, Pittsburgh pierogie. Own pasta. Outdoor dining. Brewpub in 1902 church; vaulted ceiling, stained-glass windows. Cr cds: A, C, D, DS, MC, V.

★★★ **TIN ANGEL.** *1200 Grandview Ave (15211), on Mt Washington.* 412/381-1919. Hrs: 5-10 pm. Closed Sun; hols. Res accepted. Bar. Wine list. Complete meals: $26.95-$46.95. Specialties: sole baretone, black forest filet. Panoramic view of city. Jacket. Family-owned. Cr cds: A, C, D, DS, MC, V.

★★★ **TOP OF THE TRIANGLE.** *600 Grant St (15219), on 62nd floor of USX Tower, downtown.* 412/471-4100. Hrs: 11:30 am-3 pm, 5:30-10 pm; Sat noon-3 pm, 5:30-11 pm; Sun 4-9 pm. Closed most major hols. Res accepted. Bar to 1 am. Wine list. Semi-a la carte: lunch $6.95-$14.95, dinner $18.95-$29.95. Child's meals. Specialties: prime-aged New York strip steak, cioppino. Pianist Sat. Parking. Panoramic view of city. Cr cds: A, C, D, DS, MC, V.

✓★ **VERMONT FLATBREAD CO.** *2701 Penn Ave (15222), east of downtown.* 412/434-1220. Hrs: 11 am-10 pm; Fri, Sat to 11 pm. Closed Sun. Bar. Semi-a la carte: lunch $5.95-$7.50, dinner $5.95-$8.25. Child's meals. Specialties: maple-sugar flatbread, Italian grilled sandwich, sweet stuffed peppers with chorizo sausage. Own baking, pasta. Street parking. Rustic Vermont decor with skylights. Cr cds: C, D, DS, MC, V.

★★★ **VIAGGIO'S.** *2302 Carson St (15203), on South Side.* 412/488-0646. Hrs: 11 am-11 pm; Fri to 2 am; Sat 5 pm-2 am; Sun 4-10 pm. Closed Memorial Day, Thanksgiving, Dec 25. Res required Sat (dinner). Classic Venetian menu. Bar. Semi-a la carte: lunch $5.95-$10.95, dinner $12.95-$23.95. Child's meals. Specialties: osso bucco, pistachio-encrusted ahi tuna, frutti di mare. Jazz, swing & pop Wed-Sat. Valet parking. Venetian setting; casual elegance. Cr cds: A, C, D, MC, V.

Unrated Dining Spots

DAVE AND ANDY'S ICE CREAM PARLOR. *207 Atwood St (15213), in Oakland.* 412/681-9906. Hrs: 11:30 am-10 pm; Sat, Sun from noon. Closed major hols. Specialties: homemade ice cream (fresh daily), homemade cones. 1930s look; some counters. Cr cds: C.

PIZZERIA UNO. *333 Penn Center Blvd (15146), 15 mi E on US 376, Penn Center Blvd exit.* 412/824-8667. Hrs: 11 am-11 pm; Fri, Sat to 12:30 am; Sun noon-10 pm. Closed Thanksgiving, Dec 25. Italian,

Amer menu. Bar. Semi-a la carte: lunch $3.95-$8.95, dinner $4.95-$10.95. Specialty: deep-dish pizza. Parking. Casual dining. Cr cds: A, C, DS, MC, V.

⊡ ⊠

TERRACE ROOM. *(See Westin William Penn Hotel) 412/553-5235.* Hrs: tea 2:30-5:30 pm. English custom tea serv. Bar. A la carte items also avail. Specializes in tea, finger sandwiches, pastries. Pianist. Parking avail opp Lobby room; Georgian decor. Cr cds: A, C, D, DS, ER, JCB, MC, V.

⊡ ⊠

Pittsburgh Intl Airport Area (E-1)

(See also Pittsburgh)

Services and Information

Information: 412/472-3525 or -3526.

Lost and Found: 412/472-3500.

Weather: 412/936-1212.

Cash Machines: Landside Terminal, entrance; Airside Terminal, throughout concourses in Passenger Service Centers.

Airlines: American, British Airways, Continental, Delta, Northwest, TWA, United, USAir.

Motels

★ **HAMPTON INN.** *1420 Beers School Rd (15108), N on PA Business 60. 412/264-0020; FAX 412/264-3220; res: 800/426-7866.* 129 rms, 5 story. S $69; D $74; under 18 free. Crib free. Pet accepted. TV; cable (premium). Complimentary continental bkfst. Coffee in rms. Restaurant adj 6 am-10 pm. Ck-out noon. Meeting rms. Business servs avail. Valet serv. Free airport transportation. Health club privileges. Cr cds: A, C, D, DS, ER, MC, V.

⊡ 🐾 ⊠ 🔥 SC

★★ **LA QUINTA INN.** *1433 Beers School Rd (15108), N on Business PA 60. 412/269-0400; FAX 412/269-9258; res: 800/687-6667.* 127 rms, 3 story. S $59-$75; D $64-$80; suites $99; under 18 free. Crib free. Pet accepted. TV; cable. Heated pool; lifeguard. Complimentary continental bkfst. Coffee in rms. Restaurant adj 6 am-11 pm. Ck-out noon. Coin lndry. Business servs avail. In-rm modem link. Valet serv. Sundries. Free airport transportation. Cr cds: A, C, D, DS, MC, V.

⊡ 🐾 ⊠ ⊠ 🔥 SC

✓★★ **PITTSBURGH PLAZA.** *1500 Beers School Rd (15108), I-79 Bus 60 exit to Beers School Rd. 412/264-7900; FAX 412/262-3229.* 193 rms, 2 story. S, D $49.99-$59.99; under 18 free. Pet accepted; $50 refundable. TV; cable (premium), VCR avail. Complimentary continental bkfst. Restaurant adj open 24 hrs. Ck-out noon. Meeting rms. Business servs avail. In-rm modem link. Valet serv. Sundries. Free airport transportation. Exercise equipt. Some refrigerators. Some balconies. Cr cds: A, C, D, DS, MC, V.

🐾 🛪 ⊠ 🔥 SC

✓★ **RED ROOF INN.** *1454 Beers School Rd (15108), N on Bus PA 60. 412/264-5678; FAX 412/264-8034; res: 800/843-7663.* 119 rms, 3 story. S $49.99-$59.99; D $54-$64; each addl $6; under 18 free.

Crib free. Pet accepted. TV; cable (premium). Restaurant opp 6 am-10 pm. Ck-out noon. Coin lndry. Meeting rm. Business servs avail. Valet serv. Free airport transportation. Cr cds: A, C, D, DS, MC, V.

⊡ 🐾 ⊠ 🔥 SC

Hotels

★★★ **CLARION ROYCE HOTEL.** *1160 Thorn Run Rd (15108), N on Bus Rte 60, exit Thorn Run Rd. 412/262-2400; FAX 412/264-9373; res: 800/627-6373.* 193 rms, 9 story. S $69-$129; D $69-$139; each addl $10; suites $109-$149; under 18 free; wkend rates. Crib free. Pet accepted. TV; cable (premium). Pool; lifeguard. Coffee in rms. Restaurant 6 am-2 pm, 5-11 pm; Sat, Sun 7 am-11 pm. Bar 11-2 am; entertainment wkends. Ck-out noon. Meeting rms. Business center. In-rm modem link. Concierge. Airport transportation. Exercise equipt. Luxury Level. Cr cds: A, C, D, DS, MC, V.

⊡ 🐾 ⊠ 🛪 🛩 ⊠ 🔥 SC 🛶

★★★ **MARRIOTT.** *777 Aten Rd (15108), S on PA 60, exit Montour Run Rd. 412/788-8800; FAX 412/788-0743; res: 800/328-9297.* 314 rms, 14 story. S, D $69-$169; each addl $15; suites $175-$425; family, wkly rates. Crib free. Pet accepted. TV; cable (premium). 2 pools, 1 indoor; whirlpool, poolside serv, lifeguard. Restaurant 6:30 am-11 pm. Bar 11-1 am. Ck-out noon. Convention facilities. Business center. In-rm modem link. Concierge. Shopping arcade. Free airport, bus depot transportation. Exercise equipt; sauna. Some refrigerators. Luxury level. Cr cds: A, C, D, DS, ER, JCB, MC, V.

⊡ 🐾 ⊠ 🛪 🛶 ⊠ 🔥 SC 🛶

Restaurant

★★★ **HYEHOLDE.** *190 Hyeholde Dr (15108), PA Bus N 60 to Beers School Rd, right on Beaver Grade Rd, left on Coraopolis Hts Rd. 412/264-3116.* Hrs: 11:30 am-2 pm, 5-10 pm; Sat from 5 pm. Closed Sun exc Mother's Day; major hols. Res accepted. Continental menu. Serv bar. Wine list. Complete meals: lunch $9.50-$13, dinner $18.50-$36. Specializes in lamb, fresh trout. Own baking. Valet parking. Patio dining. Herb garden. Country French decor; fireplaces; estate grounds. Cr cds: A, C, DS, MC, V.

⊡ ⊠

Pocono Mountains (C-9)

(See also Bushkill, Canadensis, Hawley, Milford, Mount Pocono, Shawnee on Delaware)

E-mail pocomts@poconos.org **Web** www.poconos.org

Information Pocono Mts Vacation Bureau, 1004 Main St, Stroudsburg 18360; 717/424-6050; for free brochures phone 800/POCONOS.

(Northeast Pennsylvania resort area)

The Pocono Mountains area in northeast Pennsylvania extends north from Wind Gap and Delaware Water Gap into Pike, Carbon, Monroe and Wayne counties. Within its 2,400 square miles almost every form of recreation can be found.

This scenic country with 500 lakes, including Lake Wallenpaupack (see HAWLEY), has hundreds of accommodations and is a well-established resort area. Visitors, many of whom return year after year, take advantage of the large plush resorts, smaller family-run resorts, housekeeping cottage resorts, camping resorts, country inns and bed & breakfasts. There is primitive, forested country for those who wish to rough it. For the hunter there are deer, bear, wildcat and fox. For the freshwater angler there are black bass, trout, pickerel and walleye.

Summer offers boating, swimming, hiking, horseback riding, mountain biking, golf, theaters and a host of other diversions. In the autumn there is a magnificent display of foliage as well as heritage festivals and country fairs. The first snowfall brings skiing, snowboarding, snow tubing, ice skating, sleigh rides, tobogganing and snowmobiling.

The name "Pocono" was probably taken from the Native American "pocohanne," meaning a stream between the mountains. Settled in the mid-1700s, the Poconos yielded iron and, later, coal. The lakes and forest still retain their charm. The land "between the mountains" is as inviting as it always has been.

Port Allegany (B-4)

(See also Bradford)

Settled 1816 **Pop** 2,391 **Elev** 1,481 ft **Area Code** 814 **Zip** 16743
Information Chamber of Commerce, 22 Church St; 814/642-2181

Native Americans called this spot "canoe place" because here on the portage route between the Allegheny and Susquehanna headwaters they paused to build canoes. Early settlers followed their route. Soon after the town was established, lumbering operations reached their peak; later industrial expansion included coal mining and tanning. In the late 1890s, the borough became the center of a boom resulting from the discovery of natural gas and glass sand.

What to See and Do

Eldred World War II Museum. Exhibits incl battle maps, posters, dioramas with narrative, video history. Centerpiece is "Remembering the Women Behind the Front Lines" exhibit. Library. (Tue, Thur, Sat, Sun) 15 mi N on PA 155, 5 mi N on PA 446, in Eldred. Phone 814/225-2220. **Free**

Sizerville State Park. Approx 385 acres. Swimming pool; fishing, hunting. Cross-country skiing, snowmobiling. Picnicking, playground, snack bar. Tent & trailer sites. Standard fees. 19 mi S on PA 155, in Sizerville. Phone 814/486-5605.

Motel

★ **MIDTOWN MOTEL.** *111 N Main St (16743).* 814/642-2575. 25 rms, 2 story. S $40-$49; D $44-$54; each addl $5. Crib $5. TV; cable (premium). Restaurant opp 6 am-11 pm. Ck-out 11 am. Cr cds: A, C, D, DS, MC, V.

Pottstown (E-9)

(See also Limerick, Norristown, Reading)

Settled 1701 **Pop** 21,831 **Elev** 160 ft **Area Code** 610 **Zip** 19464
E-mail tcacc@ptdprolog.net **Web** www.tricopa.com
Information TriCounty Area Chamber of Commerce, 135 High St; 610/326-2900

An iron forge operating in 1714 at Manatawny Creek, about three miles north of Pottstown, was the first industrial establishment in the state. The borough was established by John Potts, an ironmaster, on land William Penn had earlier deeded to his son, John. Today the community is the commercial and cultural hub for an area with a population of 130,000. Nearly 200 modern industries are located here.

What to See and Do

Boyertown Museum of Historic Vehicles. Collection of over 100 antique autos, trucks, sleighs, buggies and bicycles. Also incl the Hill, which was among the first gasoline-powered cars. (Daily exc Mon) 7 mi N via PA 100, 73, in Boyertown, on Warwick St. Phone 610/367-2090. ¢¢

French Creek State Park. Approx 7,330 acres, two lakes. Boating (rentals, mooring, launching), fishing. Swimming pool. Hiking. Ice fishing. Picnicking. Tent & trailer sites, cabins. Standard fees. 9 mi W on PA 724, then 4 mi S on PA 345. Phone 610/582-9680. Also here is

Hopewell Furnace National Historic Site (see).

Merritt's Museum of Childhood. Antique toys, costumed figures, furnishings; Native American relics; gift shop in lobby. (Daily; closed major hols) 1 mi W on US 422, in Douglassville. Phone 610/385-3408. ¢¢ Admission includes

Mary Merritt Doll Museum. Antique dolls and toys dating from 1725 to 1900. (Daily; closed major hols) Phone 610/385-3809.

Pottsgrove Manor (1752). Newly-restored house of John Potts, 18th-century ironmaster and founder of Pottstown; outstanding example of early Georgian architecture and furniture. Includes recently discovered slave quarters and Potts's office. Slide orientation. Museum shop. (Daily exc Mon; closed major hols) W King St & PA 100. Phone 610/326-4014. **Free**

Ringing Rocks Park. Roller-skating (Fri–Sun; fee); nature trails, picnicking, interesting rock formations. (Daily) 3 mi N off PA 663. Phone 610/323-6560. **Free**

Annual Event

Duryea Day Antique & Classic Auto Show. Boyertown Community Park. Antique autos, trucks and other vehicles; displays, arts & crafts, flea market with automotive memorabilia, activities, Pennsylvania Dutch food. Labor Day wkend.

Motels

★★ **COMFORT INN.** *Rte 100 & Shoemaker Rd (19464).* 610/326-5000; FAX 610/970-7230; res: 800/879-2477. E-mail pottstown bc@crownam.com. 121 rms, 4 story. S, D $79-$109; each addl $7; under 18 free; golf plans; wkend rates. Crib free. Pet accepted. TV; cable (premium). Heated pool; lifeguard. Complimentary continental bkfst. Restaurant adj 6 am-11 pm. Rm serv. Ck-out noon. Coin lndry. Meeting rms. Business servs avail. In-rm modem link. Free bus depot transportation. Health club privileges. Refrigerators, microwaves avail. Cr cds: A, C, D, DS, ER, JCB, MC, V.

D ➤ ≈ ⚞ ⊠ 🔥 SC

★★ **HOLIDAY INN EXPRESS.** *1600 Industrial Hwy (19464), at Armand Hammer Blvd exit.* 610/327-3300; FAX 610/327-9447; res: 800/386-0031. 120 rms, 4 story. S, D $69; each addl $5; suites $122; under 19 free; wkly, hol rates; higher rates special events. Crib free. Pet accepted. TV; cable (premium); VCR avail (movies). Pool. Complimentary continental bkfst. Complimentary coffee in rms. Restaurant adj open 24 hrs. Rm serv 24 hrs. Ck-out noon. Meeting rms. Business servs avail. In-rm modem link. Sundries. Valet serv. Health club privileges. Refrigerators, microwaves avail. Cr cds: A, C, D, DS, JCB, MC, V.

D ➤ ≈ ⊠ 🐾 SC

Inn

★★★ **TWIN TURRETS INN.** *11 E Philadelphia Ave (19512), 7 mi N on US 100, then 1 mi W on PA 73.* 610/367-4513; FAX 610/369-7898; res: 877/877-7897. E-mail turrets@netjunction.com; web www.netjunction.com/twinturrets. 10 rms, 3 story. S, D $95-$120; each addl $15; wkly rates. Children over 12 yrs preferred. TV; cable (premium), VCR avail. Complimentary full bkfst; afternoon refreshments. Restaurant nearby. Ck-out 11 am, ck-in 1 pm. Luggage handling. Business center.

Health club privileges. Original Boyer mansion built in 1850; antiques and original art. Flower gardens with fountain. Totally nonsmoking. Cr cds: A, C, DS, MC, V.

Restaurants

★★★ **CAB FRYE'S TAVERN.** *914 Gravel Pike (18070), 10 mi N on PA 100, exit PA 29 S.* 215/679-9935. Web www.regiononline.com ~cab fryes/. Hrs: 11:30 am-2 pm, 5-10 pm; Mon, Tues, Sat 5-10 pm. Closed Sun; also major hols. Res required Fri, Sat (dinner). Continental menu. Bar from 4 pm. Wine cellar. A la carte entrees: lunch $5-$9, dinner $13-$22. Child's meals. Specialties: Scottish lobster, Dover sole, wild game. Parking. Outdoor dining. Old stage coach stop; countryside atmosphere. Antiques. Cr cds: A, C, DS, MC, V.

★★★ **COVENTRY FORGE INN.** *3360 Coventryville Rd (19465), 5 mi S on PA 100, 1½ mi W on PA 23 in Coventryville.* 610/469-6222. Hrs: 5:30-9 pm; Sat 5-10 pm. Res accepted. Closed Mon, Sun exc Mother's Day; Jan 1, Dec 25. French menu. Bar. Wine cellar. A la carte entrees: dinner $16.95-$25.95. Prix fixe: (Sat) dinner $39.50. Specialties: carre d'agneau Provençal, escalopes de veau. Own baking. Built in 1717; antiques. Cr cds: A, C, D, MC, V.

★★★ **GRACIE'S 21ST CENTURY CAFE.** *PO Box 333 (19548), 3.4 mi N on Manatawny Rd.* 610/323-4004. Hrs: 5:30-10:30 pm. Closed Mon, Tues, Sun; also major hols. Res required Sat (dinner). Contemporary Amer menu. Bar from 5:30 pm. Wine cellar. A la carte entrees: dinner $21.50-$31.50. Specialties: rasta pasta, quail in rose petal sauce, sushi quality seared tuna. Jazz Fri, Sat. Valet parking. Outdoor dining. Ultra modern facility. Cr cds: A, C, D, MC, V.

Quakertown (Bucks Co) (E-9)

(See also Allentown, Bethlehem, Doylestown, Pottstown)

Founded 1715 **Pop** 8,982 **Elev** 500 ft **Area Code** 215 & 267 **Zip** 18951 **E-mail** ubchamber@enter.net **Web** ubcc.org

Information Upper Bucks County Chamber of Commerce, 320 W Broad St, phone; 215/536-3211 or Bucks County Conference and Visitors Bureau, 152 Swamp Rd, Doylestown 18901, phone 215/345-4552 or 800/836-2825

Once a station on the "underground railroad," Quakertown today still retains some of its colonial appearance. In 1798, angered by what they considered an unfair federal tax and incited by one John Fries, Quakertown housewives started greeting tax assessors with pans of hot water. The "hot water" rebellion cooled down when federal troops arrived, but the town switched parties (from Federalist to Jeffersonian) almost en masse.

What to See and Do

Mennonite Heritage Center. An interpretive video and exhibits incl quilts, Pennsylvania German Fraktur, furniture, books, deeds and clothing show the history of local Mennonites through 3 centuries. (Daily exc Mon) 4 mi S of PA 309 on PA 113, in Harleysville, 565 Yoder Rd. Phone 215/256-3020. **Donation**

Restaurants

★ **LA PIAZZA CAFE.** *1408 W Broad St (18951).* 610/536-2452. Hrs: 11 am-11 pm. Closed most major hols. Res required Fri, Sat (dinner). Italian menu. A la carte entrees: lunch $5.95, dinner $7.50-$12.95. Buffet: lunch $7.95, dinner $10.95. Child's meals. Specializes in chicken, pizza, pasta. Parking. Cr cds: A, C, D, DS, MC, V.

★★★ **WASHINGTON HOUSE.** *136 N Main St (18960).* 215/257-3000. Hrs: 11 am-2:30 pm, 5-9 pm; Fri to 10:30 pm; Sat noon-2 pm, 5-10:30 pm; Sun (brunch) 10 am-2 pm, 4-8 pm; early-bird dinner 5-6 pm; Sun from 4 pm. Closed most major hols. Res accepted. Bar to midnight. A la carte entrees: lunch $6-$12, dinner $12-$20. Sun brunch $13.95. Child's meals. Specializes in fresh fish, chicken, beef. Harpist Mon (eve). Parking. Restored Victorian building. Antiques, artwork. Romantic atmosphere. Cr cds: C, MC, V.

Reading (E-8)

(See also Denver/Adamstown, Hamburg, Kutztown, Lancaster, Pottstown)

Founded 1748 **Pop** 78,380 **Elev** 260 ft **Area Code** 484 & 610 **E-mail** rdgberks@ptd.net **Web** www.readingberkspa.com

Information Reading & Berks County Visitors Bureau, 352 Penn St 19602; 610/375-4085 or 800/443-6610

A city of railroads and industry famous for its superb pretzels, Reading (RED-ing) was the second community in the United States to vote a Socialist government into office; however, the city has not had such a government for many years. Love of music and the thrift and vigor of the "Dutch" are reflected in the character of this unofficial capital of Pennsylvania Dutch Land.

William Penn purchased the land now occupied by Reading from the Lenni-Lenape Native Americans and settled his two sons, Thomas and Richard, on it. They named it Reading (fern meadow) for their home in England. During the Revolution, the citizens of Reading mustered troops for the Continental army, forged cannon and provided a depot for military supplies and a prison for Hessians and British. The hundreds of skilled German craftspeople, plus canal and railroad transportation, ignited Reading's industrial development. Today some of the world's leading industries continue to headquarter here.

What to See and Do

Berks County Heritage Center. Historical interpretive complex. Here are the Gruber Wagon Works (1882), where finely crafted wagons were produced for farm and industry; Wertz's Red Bridge (1867), the longest single-span covered bridge in the state; Deppen Cemetery, with graves of Irish workers who died of "swamp fever" while building the Union Canal; C. Howard Hiester Canal Center, with its collection of canal artifacts. Tours of wagon works and canal center; orientation slide program. (May–Oct, daily exc Mon) 4 mi N via PA 183, then W onto Red Bridge Rd, in Bern Twp. Phone 610/374-8839 or 610/372-8939. ¢¢

Conrad Weiser Homestead (1729). Restored and furnished house of colonial "ambassador" to the Iroquois nation; springhouse; gravesite; visitor center; picnicking in 26-acre park. (Apr-Oct, daily exc Mon) 14 mi W via US 422. Phone 610/589-2934. Homestead ¢¢ Grounds **Free**

Daniel Boone Homestead. Birthplace of Daniel Boone in 1734. Approx 570 acres; incl Boone House, barn, blacksmith shop and sawmill. Picnicking. Nature trails. Youth camping. Visitor's center. (Daily exc Mon; closed some hols) 7 mi E on US 422 to Baumstown, then N on Boone Rd. Phone 610/582-4900. ¢¢

Historical Society of Berks County. Local history exhibits; decorative arts, antiques, transportation displays. (Tues–Sat; closed most hols) 940 Centre Ave. Phone 610/375-4375. ¢¢

Koziar's Christmas Village. Valley set aglow with over 500,000 Christmas lights; Wishing Well Lane; 2 barns filled with handmade items, decorations; theme exhibits, Santa's Post Office. (Thanksgiving–Dec) 12 mi N via PA 183, in Bernville, 782 Christmas Village Rd. Phone 610/488-1110. ¢¢¢

Mid-Atlantic Air Museum. Aviation museum dedicated to the preservation of vintage aircraft; planes are restored to flying condition by volunteers. Collection of 40 airplanes and helicopters; 20 on public display, incl Martin 4-0-4 airliners, B-25 bomber and others. (Daily; closed Jan 1, Thanksgiving, Dec 25) Reading Regional Airport, at PA 183 & Van Reed Rd. Phone 610/372-7333. ¢¢

Outlet Shopping. More than 300 factory outlet stores can be found at 5 different shopping complexes. For more info, contact Visitors Bureau; Phone 610/375-4085 or 800/443-6610.

Reading Public Museum and Art Gallery. In 25-acre Museum Park with stream. Exhibits of art and science. (Tues–Sun; closed most major hols) 500 Museum Rd. Phone 610/371-5850. ¢¢ Adj is

Planetarium. For schedule and info, phone 610/371-5854. ¢¢

Motels

★★★ **BEST WESTERN INN.** *4635 Perkiomen Ave (19606). 610/779-2345; FAX 610/779-8348; res: 800/828-2830.* 71 rms, 2 story. May-Nov: S $58-$83; D $63-$88; each addl $5; under 18 free; lower rates rest of yr. Crib $5. Pet accepted, some restrictions; $5. TV; cable. Pool; lifeguard. Restaurant (see ANTIQUE AIRPLANE). Rm serv. Bar 11-2 am. Ck-out noon. Coin lndry. Meeting rms. Business servs avail. Valet serv. Sundries. Health club privileges. Lawn games. Microwaves avail. Balconies. Cr cds: A, C, D, DS, ER, MC, V.

D 🐾 🏊 🏝 🔥 SC

✓★ **COMFORT INN.** *2200 Stacey Dr (19605). 610/371-0500; FAX 610/478-9421; res: 800/228-5150.* Web www.comfortinn.com. 60 rms, 2 story. Apr-Oct: S $55-$70; D $55-$75; each addl $5; under 18 free; wkly rates; higher rates: car & antique shows; lower rates rest of yr. Crib free. TV; cable (premium), VCR. Complimentary continental bkfst. Restaurant nearby. Ck-out 11 am. Meeting rms. Business servs avail. In-rm modem link. Valet serv. Free airport transportation. Exercise equipt. Some refrigerators; microwaves avail. Cr cds: A, C, D, DS, ER, JCB, MC, V.

D 🏋 🏝 🔥 SC

✓★ **ECONO LODGE INN OUTLET VILLAGE.** *635 Spring St (19610). 610/378-5105; FAX 610/373-3181.* 84 rms, 4 story. Mar-Nov: S, D $58-$85; each addl $5; under 18 free; higher rates: Keystone Nationals, antique wkends; lower rates rest of yr. Crib free. Pet accepted; $5/day. TV; cable (premium). Complimentary continental bkfst. Restaurant adj 7 am-10 pm. Ck-out 11 am. Business servs. Sundries. Coin lndry. Exercise equipt. Many refrigerators, microwaves. Cr cds: A, C, D, DS, MC, V.

D 🐾 🏋 🏝 🔥 SC

★★★ **INN AT READING.** *1040 N Park Rd (19610), 3 mi W, just off US 422 at Warren St Bypass. 610/372-7811; FAX 610/372-4545; res: 800/383-9713.* E-mail innatreading@msn.com; web www.innatreading.com. 250 rms, 1-2 story. S, D $79-$129; suites $99-$129; each addl $10; under 18 free; some wkend rates. Crib free. TV; cable (premium). Pool; poolside serv, lifeguard. Restaurant 6:30 am-10 pm. Rm serv. Bar 11-1 am; entertainment. Ck-out 11 am. Meeting rms. Business center. In-rm modem link. Bellhops. Valet serv. Free airport, bus depot transportation. Exercise equipt. Refrigerators. Picnic tables. Cr cds: A, C, D, DS, MC, V.

D 🏊 🏋 🏝 🔥 SC 🚶

★★ **RAMADA INN AT THE OUTLETS.** *2545 N 5th St Hwy (19605), at Warren St Bypass. 610/929-4741; FAX 610/929-5237; res: 800/465-4329; res: 888/929-9234.* 138 rms, 2 story. S $55-$175; D $60-$175; each addl $10; under 18 free; some wkend rates. Crib free. TV; cable (premium). Pool. Coffee in rms. Restaurant 6:30-10:30 am, 5-9 pm.

Rm serv. Bar 5-11:30 pm. Ck-out noon. Meeting rms. Business servs avail. In-rm modem link. Valet serv. Sundries. Refrigerators, microwaves. Cr cds: A, C, D, DS, JCB, MC, V.

D 🏊 🏝 🔥 SC

Motor Hotels

★★★ **HOLIDAY INN.** *230 Cherry Ln US (19543), PA Tpke exit 22. 610/286-3000; FAX 610/286-0520; res: 800/339-0264.* E-mail himorga@ibm.net; web www.gfhotels.com/himorgantown. 191 rms, 4 story. S $79-$99; D $89-$109; each addl $5; under 18 free. Crib $10. Pet accepted, some restrictions. TV; cable (premium). Indoor pool; whirlpool. Coffee in rms. Restaurant 6:30 am-2 pm, 5-10 pm; Sat, Sun from 5 pm. Rm serv. Bar 5 pm-1 am. Ck-out noon. Meeting rms. Business center. In-rm modem link. Sundries. Exercise equipt. Some refrigerators. Cr cds: A, C, D, DS, JCB, MC, V.

D 🐾 🏊 🏋 🏝 🔥 SC 🚶

★★★ **SHERATON INN.** *1741 W Papermill Rd (19610), US 422 W, Papermill Rd exit. 610/376-3811; FAX 610/375-7562; res: 800/325-3535.* Web sheratonreadingpa.com. 254 rms, 5 story. S, D $79-$139; each addl $10; suites $185-$195; studio rms $140-$150; under 18 free; some wkend rates. Crib free. Pet accepted; $50. TV; cable (premium), VCR avail. Indoor pool; whirlpool, poolside serv, lifeguard. Coffee in rms. Restaurant 6:30 am-10:30 pm. Rm serv. Bar 11:30-2 am; entertainment. Ck-out noon. Meeting rms. Business servs avail. In-rm modem link. Bellhops. Gift shop. Free airport, bus depot transportation. Putting green. Exercise equipt; sauna. Massage. Health club privileges. Some bathrm phones; microwaves avail. Cr cds: A, C, D, DS, JCB, MC, V.

D 🐾 🏊 🏋 🏝 🔥 SC

Restaurants

✓★★ **ALPENHOF BAVARIAN.** *903 Morgantown Rd (19607), 1¼ mi S of jct US 222. 610/373-1624.* Hrs: 11:30 am-2 pm, 5-8:30 pm; Mon to 2 pm; Sat to 9 pm; Sun 11:30 am-7 pm. Closed Jan 1, Dec 25. Res accepted. German, Amer menu. Bar. Semi-a la carte: lunch $3.45-$6.95, dinner $8.75-$19.95. Specialties: schnitzel, sauerbraten. Outdoor dining. Bavarian Gasthaus with authentic decor. Family-owned. Cr cds: A, C, MC, V.

🏝

★★ **ANTIQUE AIRPLANE.** *(See Best Western Dutch Colony Inn) 610/779-2345.* Hrs: 7 am-3 pm, 5-9:30 pm; Sun to 3 pm. Closed Jan 1, Dec 25. Res accepted. Bar. Semi-a la carte: bkfst $2.95-$4.95, lunch $3.99-$5.95, dinner $6.95-$17.95. Child's meals. Specializes in seafood, steak. Salad bar. Casual elegance; aviation theme. Cr cds: A, C, D, DS, ER, MC, V.

★★★ **GREEN HILLS INN.** *2444 Morgantown Rd (19607). 610/777-9611.* Hrs: 5-9 pm. Closed Sun. Res accepted. French menu. Wine cellar. A la carte entrees: dinner $16.95-$27.95. Specialties: herb-crusted rack of lamb, boneless squab with honey ginger glaze, warm Valrhona chocolate souffle. Family-owned. Cr cds: A, C, DS, JCB, MC, V.

D

★★★ **MOSELEM SPRINGS INN.** *RD 4 Box 4035 (19522), 12 mi N on US 222. 610/944-8213.* Hrs: 11:30 am-9 pm; Fri, Sat to 10 pm; Sun, hols to 8 pm. Closed Dec 24, 25. Res accepted. Pennsylvania Dutch menu. Bar. Semi-a la carte: lunch $6-$12.95, dinner $11.25-$20. Child's meals. Specializes in smoked meats, fresh seafood. Built in 1852; six distinct dining areas with individual decor, including the elegant Presidential Room. Cr cds: A, C, D, DS, MC, V.

D SC 🏝

Scranton (C-9)

(See also Carbondale, Pocono Mountains, Wilkes-Barre)

Settled 1771 **Pop** 81,805 **Elev** 754 ft **Area Code** 570
E-mail pntvb@epix.net **Web** www.visitnepa.org
Information Northeast Pennsylvania Convention and Visitors Bureau, 300 Penn Ave, 18503; 570/963-6363 or 800/22-WELCOME

The first settlers here found a Monsey Native American village on the site. In 1840, George and Seldon Scranton built five iron furnaces using the revolutionary method of firing with anthracite coal instead of charcoal. Manufacture of iron and steel remained an important industry until 1901, when the mills moved to Lake Erie to ease transportation problems.

After World War II, Scranton thoroughly revamped its economy when faced with depletion of the anthracite coal mines, which for more than a century had fired its forges. Scranton's redevelopment drew nationwide attention and served as a model for problem cities elsewhere. Today, Scranton is the home of electronic and printing industries and is host to several major trucking firm terminals.

What to See and Do

Catlin House (1912). Headquarters of Lackawanna Historical Society; period furnishings (colonial-1900s), historic exhibits, antiques; research library (fee). (Tues–Fri, also Sat afternoons; closed hols) 232 Monroe Ave. Phone 570/344-3841.   **Free**

Lackawanna County Stadium. Open-air stadium/civic arena seats 11,000. Home of AAA baseball, high school and college football and marching band competitions. (Apr–Nov) Exit 51 off I-81, Montage Mountain Rd. For schedule phone 570/969-2255.   ¢¢-¢¢¢

Montage Ski Area. Quad, double, 3 triple chairlifts; school, rentals; snowmaking; bar, restaurant; lodge. Vertical drop 1,000 ft. Night skiing. More than 130 acres of trails set in 400 acres of mountainside. (Early Dec–late Mar, daily) Summer activities incl water slides, batting cages, amphitheater (late June–Labor Day). S on I-81, exit 51, follow signs. Phone 570/969-7669.   ¢¢¢¢¢

Nay Aug Park. More than 35 acres with memorials to pioneer days. Picnicking, swimming pool (fee), walking trail, refreshment stands and the "Pioneer," a gravity railroad car dating back to 1850; wkend concerts (summer). (Daily) Arthur Ave & Mulberry St in E Scranton. Phone 570/348-4186. In park is

Anthracite Heritage Museum. History and culture of anthracite region. Other affiliated parts of the complex are the Iron Furnaces; Museum of Anthracite Mining (see ASHLAND), with emphasis on technology of the industry, and the 19th-century miners' village of Eckley, near Hazleton (see). (Daily; closed some hols) Keyser Ave in McDade Park. Phone 570/963-4804.   ¢¢

Everhart Museum. Permanent collections incl 19th- and 20th-century American art; Dorflinger glass; Native American, Oriental and primitive art; natural history displays, incl Dinosaur Hall. Gift shop. (Daily exc Mon; closed some hols) Phone 570/346-8370.   **Donation**

Lackawanna Coal Mine Tour. Underground coal mine 300 ft below ground shows world of anthracite miners. Conditions are authentic (damp, dark, slippery and cold); dress appropriately. Above-ground facilities incl a "shifting shanty" exhibit rm with photo-mural graphic displays, mine artifacts and video presentations; gift shop; restaurant. (Apr–Nov, daily; closed Thanksgiving) McDade Park. Phone 570/963-MINE or 800/238-7245.   ¢¢¢

Scranton Iron Furnaces. Partially restored site of 4 anthracite-fired iron furnaces built 1848-1857 and used until 1902. Visitor center, outdoor exhibits. Self-guided tours (daily). Guided tours (late May-early Sept, Mon-Thurs). 159 Cedar Ave. Phone 570/963-3208.   **Free**

Steamtown National Historic Site. Site with large collection of steam locomotives and other memorabilia located in an authentic freight yard. Steam train ride through yard (Memorial Day–Dec; daily). 25-mi train excursion (June–Oct, Sat & Sun). 150 S Washington Ave (mailing address), Lackawanna & Cliff Sts (location). Phone 888/693-9391 (tickets). Excursion.   ¢¢¢

Motels

★★ **DAYS INN.** *1226 O'Neill Hwy (18512), 4 mi N on I-81, exit 55A.* 717/348-6101; FAX 717/348-5064; res: 888/246-3297. 90 rms, 4 story. S $59.99-$83.99; D $61.99-$99.99; suites $78.99-$99.99; under 17 free; wkend, hol rates; higher rates Pocono NASCAR. Crib free. Pet accepted; $3. TV; cable (premium), VCR avail. Complimentary continental bkfst. Restaurant adj open 24 hrs. Ck-out 11 am. Business servs avail. Valet serv. Refrigerators. Cr cds: A, C, D, DS, ER, MC, V.

D ⊷ ≋ ≊ 🔥 SC

★★ **HAMPTON INN.** *22 Montage Mountain Rd (18507), near Avoco Intl Airport.* 570/342-7002; FAX 570/342-7012; res: 800/426-7866. 129 rms, 4 story. S $72-$82; D $77-$87; suites $90-$175; under 19 free; wkend rates; ski plans; higher rates: NASCAR, hols. Crib free. TV; cable (premium). Indoor pool; whirlpool. Complimentary continental bkfst. Ck-out noon. Meeting rms. Business servs avail. Valet serv. Sundries. Free airport, bus depot transportation. Downhill ski 2 mi. Exercise equipt. Picnic tables. Cr cds: A, C, D, DS, MC, V.

D ≊ ≋ 🏃 ✈ ≊ 🔥 SC

★★★ **HOLIDAY INN.** *200 Tigue St (18512), I-380 exit 1, just E of I-81.* 570/343-4771; FAX 570/343-5171; res: 800/465-4329. 139 rms, 2-3 story. S, D $79-$89; each addl $10; suites $145-$175; under 18 free; some wkend rates; ski plan. Crib free. Pet accepted. TV; cable. Pool. Restaurant 6:30 am-10 pm. Rm serv. Bar noon-2 am. Ck-out noon. Meeting rms. Business servs avail. In-rm modem link. Valet serv. Cr cds: A, C, D, DS, ER, JCB, MC, V.

D ⊷ ≋ ≊ 🔥 SC

Motor Hotels

★★ **CLARION INN.** *300 Meadow Ave (18505).* 570/344-9811; FAX 570/344-7799; res: 800/347-1551. 125 rms, 6 story. S $59-$69; D $69-$79; each addl $10; suites $135-$150; under 13 free; higher rates special events. Crib free. TV; cable (premium). Pool; lifeguard. Restaurant 6 am-10 pm. Rm serv. Bar 11-2 am; entertainment Tues-Sun. Ck-out noon. Meeting rms. Business servs avail. Valet serv. Free airport, bus depot transportation. Cr cds: A, C, D, DS, MC, V.

D ≊ ≋ 🔥 SC

★★★ **INN AT NICHOLS VILLAGE.** *1101 Northern Blvd (18411), 3 mi N on I-81, exit 58.* 570/587-1135; FAX 570/586-7140; res: 800/642-2215. 135 rms, 4 story. S, D $98-$150; each addl $10; under 18 free. Crib free. TV; cable. Indoor pool; lifeguard. Restaurant 6 am-10 pm. Rm serv. Bar 5-11 pm. Ck-out noon. Meeting rms. Business servs avail. In-rm modem link. Sundries. Free airport transportation. Exercise equipt; sauna. Rec rm. 12 acres include over 1,000 rhododendrons; forest land. Cr cds: A, C, D, DS, MC, V.

D ≊ 🏃 ≋ 🔥 SC

Hotel

★★★ **RADISSON HOTEL.** *700 Lackawanna Ave (18503), I-81 exit 53.* 717/342-8300; FAX 717/342-0380; res: 800/333-3333. 145 rms, 6 story. S $99; D $109; each addl $10; suites $119-$300; studio rms $109; package plans. Crib free. TV; cable. Restaurant 7 am-10 pm. Bar 11-2 am. Ck-out noon. Meeting rms. Business servs avail. In-rm modem link. Gift shop. Free airport, bus depot transportation. Downhill/x-country ski 4 mi. Exercise equipt; sauna, steam rm. Whirlpool. Some refrigerators. In-rm whirlpools. Located in historic Lackawanna RR station building. Cr cds: A, C, D, DS, JCB, MC, V.

D ≊ 🏃 ≋ 🔥 SC

Resort

✓★★ **SHADOWBROOK RESORT.** *Rte 6 E (18657), 25 mi NW on US 6.* 717/836-2151; FAX 717/836-5655; res: 800/955-0295. 55 rms, 2 story. S $50-$85; D $60-$95; each addl $12; kit units $80-$90; under 12 free. Crib $8/day. TV; cable (premium). Pool; poolside serv, lifeguard. Complimentary continental bkfst. Restaurant 6 am-10 pm. Rm serv 5-8 pm. Box lunches, picnics. Bar 11-2 am; entertainment Wed, Fri-Sun. Ck-out noon, ck-in 2 pm. Gift shop. Grocery, coin lndry 2 mi. Meeting rms. Business servs avail. Sports dir. 18-hole golf, pro. Hiking. Game rm. Exercise rm; sauna, steam rm. Some refrigerators. Balconies. Picnic tables. Cr cds: A, C, D, DS, MC, V.

Restaurants

★ **COOPER'S SEAFOOD HOUSE.** *701 N Washington Ave (18509).* 717/346-6883. Hrs: 11 am-midnight. Closed major hols. Bar 4 pm-1 am; Sun to 11 pm. Complete meals: lunch $5.99-$9.99, dinner $9.99-$28.99. Child's meals. Specializes in seafood. Pianist, vocalist exc Mon. Nautical decor. Cr cds: A, C, DS, MC, V.

★ **FIREPLACE RESTAURANT.** *RR 6 (18657), 15 mi N on US 11, W on US 6, 3 mi W of Tunkhannock.* 717/836-9662. Hrs: 11 am-10 pm; Fri, Sat to 11 pm. Closed Dec 25. Bar. A la carte entrees: lunch, dinner $2-$21.95. Child's meals. Specializes in beef, chicken. Cr cds: A, C, D, MC, V.

Shamokin Dam (D-7)

Settled 1790 **Pop** 1,690 **Elev** 500 ft **Area Code** 570 **Zip** 17876

Motel

★ **INN OF SHAMOKIN DAM.** *Rte 11 & Rte 15 (17876).* 570/743-1111; FAX 570/743-1190; res: 800/329-7466. 151 rms, 2 story. S $50-$60; D $55-$70; each addl $5; under 18 free. Crib free. Pet accepted. TV; cable. Pool; lifeguard. Restaurant 7 am-9 pm. Bar from 5 pm; Ck-out noon. Meeting rms. Business servs avail. In-rm modem link. Valet serv. Sundries. Cr cds: A, C, D, DS, JCB, MC, V.

Inn

★★★ **INN AT OLDE NEW BERLIN.** *321 Market St (17855), 8 mi W on PA 304.* 570/966-0321; FAX 570/966-9557; res: 800/797-2350. Web www.newberlin-inn.com. 5 rms, 3 with shower only, 2 story. MAP: S, D $85-$175; each addl $20; higher rates special events. Crib $5. Complimentary full bkfst. Restaurant 10 am-2 pm, 4:30-8:30 pm; closed Mon, Tues. Ck-out noon, ck-in 3 pm. Gift shop. Garden setting. Cr cds: C, DS, MC, V.

Sharon (C-1)

(See also Mercer)

Settled 1802 **Pop** 17,493 **Elev** 998 ft **Area Code** 724 **Zip** 16146 **Web** www.merlink.org
Information Mercer County Convention & Visitors Bureau, 835 Perry Hwy, Mercer 16137; 724/748-5315 or 800/637-2370

In the heart of the rich Shenango Valley, Sharon is a busy industrial city that started with a lonely mill on the banks of the Shenango River. Steel, fabrication of steel products and manufacture of electric transformers are a major part of the economy. The Shenango Dam and its reservoir are northeast of town, near Sharpsville, and offer many recreational activities.

What to See and Do

Shenango Lake. Swimming, waterskiing; fishing, hunting; boating (ramps). Picnicking. More than 300 tent & trailer sites (mid-May–Labor Day; rest of Sept, reduced number of sites; electric hookups addl). 6 mi N of I-80, PA 18. Phone 724/646-1115 (camping); 724/962-7746 or 724/646-1124 (general info). Camping per night. ¢¢¢-¢¢¢¢

Annual Event

The Small Ships Review. Downtown. Parade of ships, entertainment, fireworks, food. Phone 724/981-3123. July.

Motel

★ **COLLINS MOTEL.** *4036 E State St (16148), 4 mi E on US 62.* 724/981-6150. 13 rms, shower only. S $39-$49; D $42-$55; each addl $6; higher rates special events. Crib $6. TV; cable. Restaurant nearby. Ck-out 10 am. Gift shop. 9-hole golf privileges. Some refrigerators. Cr cds: C, MC, V.

Inn

★★★ **TARA—A COUNTRY INN.** *2844 Lake Rd. (16113), I-80 exit 1N, 7 mi on PA 18N exit PA 258.* 724/962-2992; FAX 724/962-3250; res: 800/782-2803. Web www.countryinns.com. 27 rms, 2 story. MAP: S, D $180-$450; wkly rates; package plans; higher rates Sat. Adults only. TV; cable. 2 pools, 1 indoor. Dining rms 11 am-8 pm. Ck-out noon, ck-in 3 pm. Meeting rm. Business center. In-rm modem link. Croquet court. Some in-rm whirlpools. Antebellum mansion dates from 1854; formal gardens. Cr cds: A, C, DS, MC, V.

Restaurants

✓★★ **HOT ROD CAFE AND TULLY'S GRILLE.** *101 Chestnut St. (16146).* 724/981-3123. Web www.lubewings.com. Hrs: 4 pm-2 am. Hot Rod Cafe closed Mon. Bar. Semi-a la carte: dinner $8.99-$15.99. Child's meals. Specializes in char-grilled steak. Entertainment Thurs-Sun. Outdoor dining. 3 dining rooms in a converted, restored railroad depot. Family-owned. Cr cds: A, C, D, DS, MC, V.

★ **QUAKER STEAK & LUBE.** *101 Chestnut St (16146).* 724/981-7221. Web www.lubewings.com. Hrs: 11-1 am; Thurs-Sat to 2 am; Sun noon-1 am. Bar. Semi-a la carte: lunch $3.99-$12, dinner $5.50-$18. Child's meals. Specializes in chicken wings, steak, burgers. Outdoor dining. Former gas station; vintage automobiles, license plates, memorabilia. Casual dining. Cr cds: A, C, D, DS, MC, V.

Shartlesville (E-8)

(See also Hamburg, Reading)

Pop 300 (est) **Elev** 560 ft **Area Code** 484 & 610 **Zip** 19554

What to See and Do

Roadside America. This miniature "village" consists of O-gauge trains, villages and scenes, with 66 miniature displays re-creating 200 yrs of life in rural America. Started in 1903, displays now cover 6,000 sq ft. (Daily; closed Dec 25) Just off US 22, Shartlesville exit at I-78. Phone 610/488-6241. ¢¢

Restaurants

★ **BLUE MOUNTAIN FAMILY RESTAURANT.** *I-78 (19554), exit 8.* 610/488-0353. Hrs: 6:30 am-10 pm. Closed Jan 1, Dec 25. Res accepted. Continental menu. Bar. Semi-a la carte: bkfst $1.95-$4.95, lunch $2.75-$6.95, dinner $5.95-$12.95. Child's meals. Specializes in fresh seafood, Greek, Italian dishes. Salad bar. Own baking. Cr cds: A, C, MC, V.

D SC 🖼

★ **HAAG'S HOTEL RESTAURANT.** *Main & Third Sts (19554).* 610/488-6692. Hrs: 7:30 am-7:30 pm. Closed Dec 25. Res accepted. Bar 11:00 am-midnight. Complete meals: bkfst $1.75-$6.50, lunch $4.75-$7, dinner $7-$13. Buffet: bkfst $6.50, lunch, dinner $13. Specializes in Pennsylvania Dutch cooking, family style dinners. Own pies. In former hotel (1914); early-American decor. Cr cds: C, MC, V.

Shawnee on Delaware (D-10)

(See also Bushkill, Stroudsburg)

Pop 400 (est) **Elev** 320 ft **Area Code** 570 **Zip** 18356
E-mail pocomts@poconos.org **Web** www.poconos.org
Information Pocono Mts Vacation Bureau Inc, 1004 Main St, Stroudsburg 18360; 570/424-6050; for free brochures phone 800/POCONOS.

What to See and Do

Delaware Water Gap (see). 6 mi E along Delaware River.

Shawnee Mountain Ski Area. 9 chairlifts; patrol, school, rentals; snowmaking; cafeteria, bar; nursery. 23 slopes and trails; longest run 1 mi; vertical drop 700 ft. (Dec–Mar, daily) Night skiing. Half-day rates. 6 mi N of I-80, exit 52, follow signs. Phone 570/421-7231 or 800/233-4218 (ski report). ¢¢¢¢¢

Shawnee Place Play & Water Park. Kids can jump in a pool of plastic balls, swing on a cable glide, climb on cargo nets, glide down waterslides and splash in a wading pool. Magic shows, picnics, video games, snack bar. (Mid-June-early Sept, daily; Late May-mid-June, wkends only). I-80, exit 52, Rte 209 N and follow signs. Phone 570/421-7231. ¢¢¢

Resort

★★ **SHAWNEE INN.** *1 River Rd (18356), E on I-80, exit 52.* 570/424-4000; FAX 570/424-9168; res: 800/742-9633. 103 rms, 3 story. MAP, May-Oct: S $129; D $179; suites $50 addl; kit units (Nov-Apr) $120; EP: S, D $89-$115; under 8 free; some wkly, wkend rates; higher rates Christmas hols; lower rates rest of yr. Crib free. Serv charge 10%. TV; cable, VCR avail. 4 pools, 1 indoor; wading pool, lifeguard. Playground. Supervised child's activities. Dining rm 7 am-9 pm. Snack bar. Picnics.

Bar hrs vary. Ck-out noon, ck-in 4 pm. Coin lndry. Grocery, package store 4 mi. Meeting rms. Lighted tennis, pro (summer). 27-hole golf, pro, putting green, driving range, miniature golf. Downhill/x-country ski 3 mi. Lawn games. Soc dir; entertainment. Rec rm. Game rm. Cr cds: A, C, D, DS, MC, V.

D 🛶 ⛷ 🎿 ⛷ 🎿 🏊 🏃 🔥 SC

Somerset (F-3)

(See also Johnstown, Ligonier)

Settled 1773 **Pop** 6,454 **Elev** 2,190 ft **Area Code** 814 **Zip** 15501
E-mail somchmbr@shol.com **Web** www.shol.com/smrst/somrst.htm
Information Somerset County Chamber of Commerce, 601 N Center Ave; 814/445-6431

Somerset, a county seat, is also the marketing place for farms, lumber mills and coal mines in the area. James Whitcomb Riley described the countryside in his poem *'Mongst the Hills of Somerset.* The county offers fishing, swimming, boating, hiking, biking, camping, skiing and ice skating.

What to See and Do

Hidden Valley Ski Area. 8 lifts; patrol, school, rentals; snowmaking; cafeteria, restaurant, bars; nursery. Longest run 5,280 ft; vertical drop 610 ft; 16 slopes (Dec-Mar, daily). 30 mi of cross-country trails (rentals). Shuttle service. Conference center, lodging. Yr-round facilities, activities. 12 mi W of PA Tpke Somerset exit 10; 8 mi E of PA Tpke Donegal exit 9, on PA 31. Phone 814/443-8000. ¢¢¢¢¢

Mt Davis. Highest point in state (3,213 ft). 26 mi S on US 219 to Salisbury, then W on unnumbered road. Phone 724/238-9533.

Somerset Historical Center. Museum exhibits on rural life; outdoor display incl log house, log barn, covered bridge, sugarhouse. Bus tour (fee). (Wed-Sun; closed most hols) 5 mi N on PA 985. Phone 814/445-6077. ¢¢

State parks.

Laurel Hill. Approx 3,900 acres. Swimming beach, snack bar; hunting; boating (mooring, launching). Hiking. Snowmobiling, ice fishing. Picnicking. Tent and trailer sites. Standard fees. 8 mi W on PA 31, then SW on unnumbered road. Phone 814/445-7725.

Kooser. Approx 220 acres. Four-acre lake with fishing; swimming beach (Memorial Day-Labor Day). Cross-country skiing, sledding. Picnicking. Tent and trailer sites, cabins. Standard fees. 9 mi NW on PA 31. Phone 814/445-8673.

Annual Events

Maple Festival. Festival Park in Meyersdale. Phone 814/634-0213. Apr.

Somerfest. Laurel Arts/Phillip Dressler Center for the Arts. German festival: dancing, competitions, entertainment, food, tours. Phone 814/443-2433. Mid–July.

Mountain Craft Days. Somerset Historical Center. More than 150 traditional craft demonstrations; antique exhibits; entertainment. Phone 814/445-6077. Early Sept.

Farmers' and Threshermen's Jubilee. 9 mi SW via PA 281, in New Centerville. Equipment demonstrations; tractor-pulling, horseshoe pitching, tobacco-spitting contests; antique car show and flea market; food. Phone 814/926-3142. Early Sept.

Springs Folk Festival. On PA 669, in Springs. Crafts demonstrations incl bread baking, wheat weaving, basket and broom making, candle dipping, quilt stitching; entertainment featuring banjo and fiddle music; pioneer exhibits on forest trail; maple sugaring, apple butter boiling, log hewing; museum adj with antique tools, furnishings, historical artifacts. Phone 814/662-4158 or 814/662-4298. Early Oct.

Motels

✓★ **BUDGET HOST INN.** 799 N Center Ave (15501). 814/445-7988; FAX 814/445-7988; res: 800/283-4678. 28 rms, 2 story. S $33-$35; D $45-$55; each addl $5. Crib $4. Pet accepted. TV; cable (premium). Complimentary coffee in lobby. Restaurant nearby. Ck-out 11 am. Downhill ski 10 mi; x-country ski 13 mi. Cr cds: A, C, D, DS, MC, V.

✓★ **DOLLAR INN.** 1146 N Center Ave (15501), PA 601. 814/445-2977; FAX 814/443-6205; res: 800/250-1505. 15 rms. S $25-$40; D $30-$50; each addl $5; under 10 free; wkly, wkend rates; higher rates special events. Crib $5. Pet accepted, some restrictions; $5. TV; cable (premium). Complimentary coffee in lobby. Restaurant nearby. Ck-out 11 am. Business servs avail. Some refrigerators. Cr cds: A, C, D, DS, MC, V.

★★ **ECONOMY INN.** 1138 North Center Ave (15501), PA Tpke exit 10. 814/445-4144; FAX 814/445-3763. 19 rms. S $30-$45; D $40-$95; each addl $5; under 12 free; higher rates: special events, ski season. TV; cable (premium), VCR. Indoor pool. Playground. Complimentary continental bkfst. Restaurant nearby. Ck-out 11 am. Coin lndry. Exercise equipt. Game rm. Refrigerators, microwaves. Cr cds: A, C, DS, MC, V.

✓★ **KNIGHTS INN.** 585 Ramada Rd (15501), exit 10 off I-70/76, at PA Tpke entrance. 814/445-8933; FAX 814/443-9745; res: 800/843-5644. 112 rms, 10 kit units. S $39.95-$59.95; D $46.95-$69.95; each addl $10; kit units $43.95-$52.95; under 18 free; wkly rates; higher rates Dec-Mar wkends. Crib free. Pet accepted, some restrictions. TV; cable (premium), VCR avail (movies). Pool. Complimentary coffee in lobby. Restaurant nearby. Ck-out noon. Coin lndry. Business servs avail. Downhill ski 15 mi. Cr cds: A, C, D, DS, MC, V.

Motor Hotel

★★★ **RAMADA INN.** Pennsylvania Tpke Rte 70 & Rte 76 (15501), At PA Tpke exit 10. 814/443-4646; FAX 814/445-7539; res: 800/228-2828. 152 rms, 2 story. S $64-$78; D $74-$88; each addl $10; suites $95-$125; under 18 free; some wkend rates. Crib free. Pet accepted. TV; cable (premium). Indoor pool; whirlpool, poolside serv, lifeguard. Sauna. Restaurant 6:30 am-2 pm, 5-10 pm; Sun 7-11 am. Rm serv. Bar 2 pm-2 am; Sun to 9 pm; entertainment Tues-Sat. Ck-out noon. Meeting rms. Business servs avail. Bellhops. Valet serv. Sundries. Downhill/x-country ski 12 mi. Health club privileges. Game rm. Cr cds: A, C, D, DS, JCB, MC, V.

Resort

★★★ **HIDDEN VALLEY RESORT CONFERENCE CENTER.** 1 Craighead Dr (15502), PA Tpke exit 9, (then 8 mi E on PA 31) or exit 10 (then 12 mi W on PA 31). 814/443-6454; FAX 814/443-1907; res: 800/458-0175. Web www.hiddenvalleyresort.com. 206 units, some A/C, 2-3 story. Mid-Dec-mid-Mar: S $120-$180; D $222-$350; each addl $30; under 13 free; ski, golf packages; MAP avail; lower rates rest of yr. Crib free. TV; cable (premium). 4 pools, 1 indoor; whirlpool, lifeguard. Playground. Supervised child's activities (June-Sept). Dining rms 7 am-10 pm. Bars 11-1 am; entertainment. Ck-out noon, ck-in 4 pm. Grocery. Package store. Convention facilities. Business servs avail. Bellhops. Valet serv. Gift shop. Airport transportation. Sports dir. Lighted tennis, pro. 18-hole golf, greens fee $49-$59, pro, putting green, driving range. Boats. Downhill/

x-country ski on site. Hiking. Soc dir. Exercise equipt; sauna. Fireplaces; microwaves avail. Balconies. Picnic tables. Located in scenic Laurel Highlands mountain area. Cr cds: A, C, D, DS, MC, V.

Inns

★★★ **BAYBERRY INN BED & BREAKFAST.** 611 N Center Ave (15501), on PA 601. 814/445-8471. 11 rms, shower only, 2 story. No A/C. No rm phones. S $40-$50; D $45-$55; each addl $10; suite $75; min stay some hol wkends. Children over 12 yrs only. TV in sitting rm; VCR. Complimentary continental bkfst; afternoon refreshments. Restaurant nearby. Ck-out 11 am, ck-in 3 pm. Luggage handling. Concierge serv. Downhill/x-country ski 18 mi. Brick house built 1902. Cr cds: A, C, DS, MC, V.

★★★ **INN AT GEORGIAN PLACE.** 800 Georgian Place Dr (15501). 814/443-1043; FAX 814/443-6220. 11 rms, 3 story, 2 suites. S, D $95-$145; each addl $10; suites $170-$185. Children over 5 yrs only. Pet accepted, some restrictions. TV; cable (premium), VCR (movies). Complimentary full bkfst. Restaurant noon-4 pm. Rm serv. Ck-out noon, ck-in 3 pm. Business servs avail. Luggage handling. Valet serv. Concierge serv. Downhill/x-country ski 12 mi. Some fireplaces. Georgian mansion built in 1915; chandeliers, marble foyer. Cr cds: A, C, D, DS, MC, V.

Restaurants

★ **COUNTRY COTTAGE RESTAURANT.** 2817 New Centerville Rd (15557), 7 mi S on PA 281, near New Centerville. 814/926-4078. Hrs: 10:30 am-9 pm. Closed major hols. Res accepted. Semi-a la carte: bkfst $2.50-$4.25, lunch $2.50-$4.50, dinner $4.95-$6.95. Child's meals. Specialties: pot pies, roast turkey, grilled chicken salad. Own pies. Country decor; gift shop with local products and crafts. Cr cds: C.

★★ **OAKHURST TEA ROOM.** 2409 Glades Pike (15501), 6 mi W on PA 31. 814/443-2897. Hrs: 11 am-10 pm; Sun to 8 pm. Closed Mon; Dec 25. Bar. Semi-a la carte: lunch $3-$7. Complete meals: lunch, dinner $10.95-$28.95. Buffet (Tues-Sat): lunch $6.95, dinner $10.95. Sun brunch $8.95. Child's meals. Specializes in waffles, own noodles in chicken broth. Salad bar. Outdoor dining. Early Amer decor. Fireplace. Family-owned. Cr cds: A, C, DS, MC, V.

★★ **PINE GRILL.** 800 N Center Ave (15501). 814/445-2102. Hrs: 7 am-10 pm. Closed Dec 25. Res accepted. Bar. Semi-a la carte: bkfst $1.50-$4.50, lunch $3-$14.50. Child's meals. Specializes in fresh seafood, grilled steak, gourmet pasta. Early Amer decor; artwork. Opened 1941. Cr cds: A, C, MC, V.

State College (D-5)

(See also Bellefonte)

Settled 1859 **Pop** 38,923 **Elev** 1,154 ft **Area Code** 814
E-mail cccvb@visitpennstate.org **Web** www.visitpennstate.org
Information Centre County Convention & Visitors Bureau, 1402 S Atherton St, 16801; 814/231-1400 or 800/358-5466

The home of Pennsylvania State University and principally concerned with services to this institution, this borough is near the geographic center of the state. In the beautiful Nittany Valley, State College is surrounded by farmland famous for its production of oats and swine. Iron ore was discovered just east of town in 1790, and many iron furnaces later sprang up.

What to See and Do

Columbus Chapel—Boal Mansion Museum. The mansion has been the Boal family home since 1789 and incl original furnishings, china, tools and weapons. Colonel Theodore Davis Boal, who outfitted his own troop for World War I, lived here. The 16th-century chapel belonged to the family of Christopher Columbus in Spain and was brought here in 1909 by Boal relatives. It contains religious items and Renaissance and Baroque art, as well as an admiral's desk and explorer's cross that belonged to Columbus himself. Summer concerts on grounds. (Daily exc Mon) 4 mi E on US 322, in Boalsburg. Phone 814/466-6210. Mansion ¢¢

Mount Nittany Vineyard & Winery. Stone-faced, chalet-style bldg nestled on southern slopes of Mt Nittany. Tasting rm offers variety of wines and view of large pond, vineyard and mountains. Group tastings (by appt). (Fri-Sun; closed major hols, also Jan) 7 mi E on US 322, E on PA 45, N on Linden Hall Rd. Phone 814/466-6373. **Free**

Penn's Cave. A 1-hr, 1-mi boat trip through cavern; stalactites, stalagmites; plus walk-through wildlife sanctuary. Picnic area; airplane rides; visitor center; gift shop, restaurant. (Mid-Feb–Nov, daily) NE on PA 26, SE on PA 144, then 5 mi E of Centre Hall on PA 192. Phone 814/364-1664. ¢¢¢

Pennsylvania Military Museum. On grounds of 28th Division Shrine; dioramas; battle exhibits and equipment from the Revolutionary War to the present. Audiovisual program; military bookstore. (Daily exc Mon; closed some hols) 4 mi E on US 322, in Boalsburg. Phone 814/466-6263. ¢¢

Pennsylvania State University (1855) (39,000 students). Approx 290 major bldgs on a 5,005-acre campus; it is the land grant institution of Pennsylvania. On US 322 in University Park. Phone 814/865-4700. On campus are

"Ag Hill," The College of Agriculture. Showplace for state's dairy industry incl the dairy center, off Park Rd near stadium, with 5 herds of cows, automatic milking equipment (daily). The creamery, Curtain Rd, has retail salesroom for cheeses, milk, cream, ice cream (daily; closed major hols). Also flower test gardens off Park Rd near East Halls (July–Sept). **Free**

Earth and Mineral Sciences Museum. Exhibitions of ores, gems and fossils; automated displays; art gallery. (Mon–Fri; closed major hols) Steidle Bldg on Pollock Rd. Phone 814/865-6427. **Free**

Old Main (1929). Present bldg, on site of original Old Main (1863), uses many of the original stones; topped by lofty bell tower. Here are Henry Varnum Poor's land grant frescoes. (Mon–Fri; closed major hols) E of Mall near Pollock Rd. Phone 814/865-7517. **Free**

Whipple Dam State Park. Approx 250 acres. Swimming beach; fishing, hunting; boating (launching, mooring). Hiking. Snowmobiling, ice skating, ice fishing. Picnicking, snack bar. Standard fees. 10 mi S on PA 26, then 1 mi E on unnumbered road. Phone 814/667-3808.

Annual Events

Memorial Day Celebration. In Boalsburg. Celebrate the holiday in the birthplace of Memorial Day. Phone 814/231-1400.

Central Pennsylvania Festival of the Arts. Open-air display of visual and performing arts; indoor exhibits; demonstrations of arts and crafts; food booths. Phone 814/237-3682. Mid-July.

Centre County Grange Fair. PA 144S, at Grange Park in Centre Hall. Exhibits, livestock show, rides, concessions, entertainment. Phone 814/364-9674. Last wk Aug.

Motels

★★★ **AUTOPORT MOTEL & RESTAURANT.** *1405 S Atherton St (16801). 814/237-7666; FAX 814/237-7456; res: 800/932-7678.* E-mail autoport@lazerlink; web www.autoport.statecollege.com. 86 rms, 3 story, 12 kit units. S $55-$65; D $59-$69; each addl $5; suites $69-$85; under 16 free; wkly, wkend rates; higher rates special events. Crib free. TV; cable (premium), VCR avail (movies). Heated pool; lifeguard. Restaurant 6 am-11 pm; dining rm 11:30 am-2 pm, 5-10 pm. Bar 11-2 am; Sun to mid-

night; entertainment Wed-Sat. Ck-out 11 am. Coin lndry. Meeting rms. Business servs avail. In-rm modem link. Sundries. Downhill ski 4 mi. Rms vary. Cr cds: A, C, D, DS, MC, V.

⧉ 🏊 🏊 🛶 🔥 SC

★★ **HAMPTON INN.** *1101 E College Ave (16801). 814/231-1590; FAX 814/238-7320; res: 800/426-7866.* Web www.hampton-inn.com. 121 rms, 3 story. S $59-$74; D $66-$81; suites $71-$78; under 18 free; ski, golf plans. Crib free. TV; cable (premium). Heated pool; lifeguard. Complimentary continental bkfst. Restaurant adj. Meeting rm. Valet serv. Sundries. Airport transportation. Downhill/x-country ski 5 mi. Picnic tables. Cr cds: A, C, D, DS, ER, MC, V.

⧉ 🏊 🏊 🛶 🔥 SC

★★★ **RAMADA INN.** *1450 S Atherton St (16801). 814/238-3001; FAX 814/237-1345; res: 800/465-4329.* Web www.goramada.com. 288 rms, 2 story. S $72-$79; D $78-$85; each addl $7; suites $175; under 19 free. Crib free. Pet accepted. TV; cable (premium). 2 pools; lifeguard. Restaurant 7 am-10 pm; Fri, Sat to 11 pm. Rm serv. Bar 11 am-midnight. Ck-out noon. Meeting rms. Business servs avail. In-rm modem link. Exercise equipt. Health club privileges. Game rm. Microwaves avail. Cr cds: A, C, D, DS, JCB, MC, V.

⧉ 🐾 🏊 🏃 🛶 🔥 SC

✓ ★ **RODEWAY INN.** *1040 N Atherton St (16803). 814/238-6783; FAX 814/238-4519; res: 800/228-2000.* 29 rms, 3 with shower only, 2 story. S $39-$69; D $44-$69; each addl $5; under 16 free; wkly rates; higher rates special events. Crib $6. TV; cable. Complimentary coffee in lobby. Restaurant nearby. Ck-out 11 am. Some refrigerators. Cr cds: A, C, D, DS, JCB, MC, V.

🛶 🔥 SC

★ **STEVENS MOTEL.** *1275 N Atherton St (16803). 814/238-2438; FAX 814/238-7548.* 18 rms, 17 with shower only, 2 story. S $33-$38; D $38-$48; each addl $4; family rates; higher rates special events (2-day min). Crib $4. TV; cable (premium). Complimentary coffee in lobby. Restaurant adj 6 am-midnight. Ck-out 11 am. Downhill ski 4 mi; x-country ski 1 mi. Cr cds: A, C, D, DS, MC, V.

🏊 🛶 🔥 SC

Motor Hotel

★★ **DAYS INN.** *240 S Pugh St (16801). 814/238-8454; FAX 814/237-1607; res: 800/258-3297.* 184 rms, 6 story. S $59-$115; D $69-$115; each addl $10; suites $150; under 18 free; some wkend rates; higher rates special events. Crib free. Pet accepted, some restrictions; $10. TV; cable Indoor pool; lifeguard. Complimentary continental bkfst Mon-Fri. Restaurant 6:30 am-midnight; Sun from 7 am. Rm serv. Bar 11-2 am; entertainment. Ck-out noon. Meeting rms. Business center. In-rm modem link. Bellhops. Valet serv. Sundries. Free airport transportation. Exercise rm; sauna. Rec rm. Game rm. Refrigerators avail. Cr cds: A, C, D, DS, MC, V.

🐾 🏊 🏃 🛶 🔥 SC 🏃

Hotel

★★★ **ATHERTON HOTEL.** *125 S Atherton St (US 322 Business) (16801). 814/231-2100; FAX 814/237-1130; res: 800/832-0132.* E-mail atherton97@aol.com; web www.atherton.statecollege.com. 150 rms, 7 story. S $75-$95; D $85-$105; each addl $10; suites $165; under 18 free; higher rates special events. Crib free. TV; cable (premium). Restaurant 5 am-10 pm. Bar 2 pm-2 am. Ck-out noon. Meeting rms. Business servs avail. In-rm modem link. Valet serv. Free garage parking. Free airport, bus depot transportation. Tennis privileges. Golf privileges. Downhill ski 6 mi. Health club privileges. Some in-rm whirlpools; refrigerator, microwave in suites. Cr cds: A, C, D, DS, ER, MC, V.

⧉ 🏊 🍴 💈 🛶 🔥 SC

Resort

★★★ **TOFTREES RESORT.** *1 Country Club Ln (16803). 814/ 234-8000; FAX 814/238-4404; res: 800/242-3551.* 113 units, 3 story, 22 suites. Apr–mid-Oct: S $99-$150; D $125-$170; each addl $15; suites $150-$250; AP, MAP avail; golf plans; some wknd rates; lower rates rest of yr. Crib avail. TV; cable (premium), VCR avail. Heated pool; lifeguard. Dining rms 6:30 am-10 pm. Bar from 11 am; entertainment. Ck-out noon, ck-in 3 pm. Business servs avail. In-rm modem link. Free airport transportation. Tennis, pro. 18-hole golf, pro, putting green, driving range. Exercise equipt. Refrigerators; microwaves avail. Balconies. Mediterranean decor. Cr cds: A, C, D, DS, MC, V.

⬛❄⬛⬛⬛⬛⬛⬛ SC

Inns

★★★ **CARNEGIE HOUSE.** *100 Cricklewood Dr (16803), near Penn State Univ Park Airport. 814/234-2424; FAX 814/231-1299; res: 800/229-5033.* E-mail carnhouse@aol.com; web www.cmagic.com/ch/. 22 rms, 2-3 story. S, D $125-$175; suites $250-$275; under 6 free. TV; cable (premium), VCR. Complimentary continental bkfst. Dining rm 6:30-10 am, 11:30 am-1:30 pm, 5:30-9 pm. Ck-out 11 am, ck-in 3 pm. Business servs avail. In-rm modem link. Luggage handling. Gift shop. Free airport transportation. Downhill ski 6 mi; x-country ski adj. Minibar; some microwaves. Decor and ambiance reminiscent of Scotland. Cr cds: A, C, MC, V.

⬛⬛⬛⬛

★★★ **NITTANY LION INN.** *200 W Park Ave (16803), on Penn State campus. 814/865-8500; FAX 814/865-8501; res: 800/233-7505.* E-mail jwp4@psu.edu. 237 rms, 3 story. S $85-$95; D $95-$105; each addl $10; suites $160-$190; under 12 free; golf plan. Crib free. TV; cable, VCR avail. Dining rm 6:45 am-9 pm. Bar 11:30-1 am. Ck-out noon, ck-in 3 pm. Meeting rms. Business servs avail. In-rm modem link. Valet serv. Free airport transportation. Exercise equipt. Cr cds: A, C, D, DS, MC, V.

⬛⬛⬛⬛

Restaurants

✓★★ **TAVERN RESTAURANT.** *220 E College Ave (16801). 814/238-6116.* Web www.thetavern.com. Hrs: 5-10:30 pm; Sun to 8:30 pm. Closed major hols. Res accepted Sun-Thurs. Bar 4 pm-12:30 am. Semi-a la carte: dinner $6.95-$16.95. Child's meals. Specializes in fresh veal dishes, fresh seafood. Classical music. Colonial decor; large collection of original Pennsylvania prints. Cr cds: A, C, D, DS, MC, V.

⬛⬛

★★★ **VICTORIAN MANOR.** *901 Pike St, 1¾ mi E on US 322, then 2 mi NE via East Branch Rd. 814/238-5534.* Hrs: 5-9 pm. Closed Mon; Jan 1, Memorial Day, Labor Day, Dec 25. Res accepted; required wkends. Continental menu. Wine list. Semi-a la carte: dinner $11.95-$28.45. Prix fixe: 3-course dinner $16.50. Specialties: rack of lamb, filet of salmon. Own pastries. Historic building (1891). Victorian decor. Totally nonsmoking. Cr cds: A, C, D, DS, MC, V.

⬛⬛

Stroudsburg (D-9)

(See also Easton, Pocono Mountains)

Settled 1769 **Pop** 5,312 **Elev** 430 ft **Area Code** 570 **Zip** 18360
E-mail pocomts@poconos.org **Web** www.poconos.org
Information Pocono Mts Vacation Bureau, Inc, 1004 Main St; phone 570/424-6050; for free brochures phone 800/POCONOS.

This is a center for the Pocono Mountains resort area and the surrounding rural community. It is the Monroe County seat.

What to See and Do

Alpine Mountain Ski Area. 2 quad, 1 double chairlift; patrol, school, rentals; snowmaking; restaurant, bar; child-care center. Vertical drop 500 ft. 20 trails & slopes. (Dec–Mar, daily) 6 mi N via PA 191, 447N, just outside Analomink. Phone 570/595-2150 or 800/233-8240. ¢¢¢¢¢

Canoeing. Canoe trips on the Delaware River; equipment provided; also transportation to and from the river. (May–Oct) Contact Chamberlain Canoes, PO Box 155, Minisink Hills 18341; Phone 570/421-0180. ¢¢¢¢—¢¢¢¢¢

Delaware Water Gap (see). 3½ mi E on PA 611, I-80.

Quiet Valley Living Historical Farm. A log house (1765) with kitchen and parlor added 1892; 12 other original or reconstructed bldgs. Demonstrations of seasonal farm activities. Farm animals, garden, gift shop. Guided tours with costumed guides, 1½-2 hrs. (Late June–Labor Day, daily exc Mon) 3½ mi SW on US 209 Business, then 1½ mi S (follow signs). Phone 570/992-6161. ¢¢¢

Stroud Mansion (18th century). Built by founder of city; houses Historical Society of Monroe County. Historical artifacts, genealogical records. Tours. (Tues–Fri, also Sun afternoons; closed major hols) 9th & Main Sts. Phone 570/421-7703. ¢

Motels

★★ **BEST WESTERN POCONO INN.** *570/421-2200; FAX 570/421-5561; res: 888/508-2378.* 90 rms, 4 story. S, D $74-$109; each addl $10; higher rates special events. Crib free. TV; cable, VCR avail (movies). Indoor pool; whirlpools. Restaurant (see CHOP HOUSE). Rm serv. Bar 11:30-2 am; entertainment. Ck-out 11 am. Meeting rms. Business servs avail. Game rm. Cr cds: A, C, D, DS, ER, JCB, MC, V.

⬛⬛⬛ SC

✓★ **BUDGET MOTEL.** *I-80 Exit 51 (18301), E on I-80, exit 51. 570/424-5451; FAX 570/424-0389; res: 800/233-8144.* 115 rms, 2-3 story. No elvtr. S $33.90-48; D $48-$66; higher rates: special events, hols, some wkends. Crib free. Pet accepted; $20 deposit. TV; cable, VCR avail (movies). Restaurant 7-11 am, 5-10 pm. Bar 4 pm-midnight. Ck-out 11 am. Business servs avail. In-rm modem link. Game rm. Cr cds: A, C, D, DS, MC, V.

⬛⬛⬛⬛

✓★★ **SHANNON INN.** *US Rte 209 & State Rte 447 (18301), 4 mi E on I-80. 570/424-1951; FAX 570/424-7782; res: 800/424-8052.* 120 rms, 2 story. S $60-$90; D $65-$95; each addl $5; under 18 free; 2-day min hols; higher rates NASCAR races. Crib free. TV; cable. Indoor pool. Complimentary continental bkfst. Restaurant 4 pm-2 am. Rm serv. Bar; entertainment Fri, Sat. Ck-out 11 am. Coin lndry. Meeting rms. Business servs avail. In-rm modem link. Valet serv. Sundries. Downhill/x-country ski 4 mi. Some refrigerators. Picnic tables. Cr cds: A, C, D, DS, MC, V.

⬛⬛⬛⬛ SC

★★ **SHERATON FOUR POINTS HOTEL.** *1220 W Main St (18360), I-80 exit 48. 570/424-1930; FAX 570/424-5909; res: 800/777-5453.* 133 rms, 2 story. S, D $85-$99; each addl $10; suites $120-$130; under 18 free; some wkend rates. Crib free. TV; cable. Pool; poolside serv. Sauna. Restaurant 7 am-10 pm. Rm serv. Bars 11-2 am; entertainment. Ck-out 11 am. Meeting rms. Business servs avail. In-rm modem link. Bellhops. Sundries. Game rm. Balconies. Cr cds: A, C, D, DS, MC, V.

⬛⬛⬛ SC

Resort

★★★ **CAESARS POCONO PALACE RESORT.** *Rte 209, PO Box 1400 (18335), 6 mi N on US 209, exit 52 I-80. 570/588-6692; FAX 570/588-0754; res: 800/233-4141.* 189 units, 155 suites. MAP: S, D, suites $195-$350; wkly rates. Adults only. TV; cable, VCR avail (movies

$5). 2 pools, 1 indoor; whirlpool. Dining rm 8:30-11 am; 6-8 pm. Rm serv 11-2 am. Bar from 11:30 am; entertainment. Ck-out 11 am, ck in 3 pm. Business servs avail. Gift shop. 9-hole golf, pro, putting green, driving range. Marina; paddle boats, waterskiing. Downhill ski 3 mi; x-country on site. Snowmobiles, ice skating. Softball field. Volleyball. Archery. Lawn games. Rec rm. Game rm. Exercise equipt; sauna. Refrigerators. Some balconies. On lake. Cr cds: A, C, D, DS, MC, V.

Restaurants

✓ ★ **ARLINGTON DINER.** *834 N 9th St (18360). 570/421-2329.* Hrs: 6 am-10 pm; Fri, Sat to 11 pm; Sun 7 am-10 pm. Closed Jan 1, Thanksgiving, Dec 25. Semi-a la carte: bkfst $2.50-$6.40, lunch $3-$6, dinner $5.75-$11.50. Child's meals. Specializes in pudding, homemade pies. Cr cds: C.

★ **BEAVER HOUSE.** *1001 N 9th St (18360). 570/424-1020.* Hrs: 11:30 am-9:30 pm; Sat to 10:30 pm; Sun noon-8 pm. Closed Dec 25. Res accepted. Bar. Complete meals: lunch $4.95-$8.95, dinner $12.50-$31.95. Specializes in seafood, prime rib. Many antiques; Tiffany lamps, trophies, bottles, stained glass, clocks. Family-owned. Cr cds: A, C, D, DS, MC, V.

D

★ **CHOP HOUSE OF STROUDSBURG.** (See Best Western Pocono Inn) *570/421-2200.* Hrs: 11 am-10 pm; Fri, Sat to 11 pm. Bar. Semi-a la carte: lunch $3.95-$9.95, dinner $8.95-$23.95. Specialties: captain's seafood platter, Kansas City steak. Salad bar. Family-owned. Cr cds: A, C, D, DS, MC, V.

D SC

✓ ★ **LEE'S RESTAURANT.** *PA 611 (18321), 6 mi SE on PA 715, exit 46B. 570/421-1212.* Hrs: noon-9 pm; Sat 2-10 pm; Sun 1-9:30 pm. Closed Thanksgiving. Res required Fri-Sun. Chinese, Japanese menu. Bar. A la carte entrees: lunch, dinner $6.50-$12.95. Specializes in steak dishes. Salad bar. Sushi bar. Oriental decor. Cr cds: A, C, MC, V.

D

★★ **STONEBAR INN.** *Rte 9 Box 9255 (18360). 570/992-6634.* Hrs: 5-10 pm; Fri, Sat to 11 pm; Sun from 4 pm. Closed most major hols. Res required Fri, Sat. Bar. A la carte entrees: dinner $12.95-$25.95. Child's meals. Specializes in beef, seafood, game. Guitarist Wed. Parking. Outdoor dining. Fireside dining. Intimate dining; Tiffany-style lamps. Cr cds: A, C, DS, MC, V.

D

Unrated Dining Spot

DANSBURY DEPOT. *50 Crystal St (18360), E on I-80, exit 51. 570/476-0500.* Hrs: 11 am-10 pm; Fri, Sat to 11 pm; Sun to 9 pm. Closed Thanksgiving, Dec 25. Continental menu. Bar. Semi-a la carte: lunch $4-$6, dinner $8-$14. Child's meals. Specializes in steak, seafood. Converted railroad station depot and freight house, built in 1864. Railroad memorabilia. Small trains move around the room, overhead on the walls. Cr cds: A, C, D, DS, MC, V.

D

Tannersville (D-9)

(See also Pocono Mountains, Stroudsburg)

Pop 1,200 (est) **Elev** 890 ft **Area Code** 570 **Zip** 18372
E-mail pocomts@poconos.org **Web** www.poconos.org
Information Pocono Mts Vacation Bureau Inc, 1004 Main St, Stroudsburg 18360; 570/424-6050; for free brochures phone 800/POCONOS.

What to See and Do

Camelback Ski Area. 2 quad, 3 triple, 7 double chairlifts; patrol, school, rentals; snowmaking; cafeteria, restaurant, bar; nursery. Longest run 1 mi; vertical drop 800 ft. (Mid-Dec–late Mar, daily) 33 trails. Alpine slide, water slide, swimming pool, bumper boats, entertainment (mid-June-Labor Day, daily; mid-May-mid-June & Labor Day-Oct, wkends only). Single & combination tickets. 3½ mi W off I-80, exit 45, in Big Pocono State Park. Phone 570/629-1661 or 800/233-8100 (mid-Atlantic states, ski report). ¢¢¢¢

Resort

★★ **CAESARS POCONO RESORTS.** *Rte 611, Brookdale Rd (18355), 3 mi N on PA 611. 570/839-8844; FAX 570/839-2414; res: 800/233-4141.* 127 rms in 8 bldgs, 1-2 story. June-Sept, MAP: S $106-$215; D $190-$250; each addl $55; suites $230-$360; under 5 free; wkly plans; hol plans (3-day min); higher rates hols & theme wkends; lower rates rest of yr. Crib free. TV; cable, VCR avail (movies). 2 pools, 1 indoor; wading pool, whirlpool, poolside serv, lifeguard. Playground. Supervised child's activities (seasonal); from 5 yrs. Complimentary coffee in lobby. Restaurant 8:30-11:30 am, 5:30-8 pm. Rm serv. Box lunches, picnics. Bar noon-2 am; entertainment. Ck-out 11 am, ck-in 3 pm. Gift shop. Grocery. Coin lndry. Meeting rms. Business servs avail. Valet serv. Sports dir. Lighted tennis. 9-hole golf privileges, putting green, driving range. Beach, boats. Downhill ski 3 mi; x-country ski 17 mi. Snowmobiles, sleighing, tobogganing. Hiking. Bicycles. Lawn games. Soc dir. Rec rm. Game rm. Exercise rm; sauna. Massage. Some refrigerators. Balconies. Picnic tables. On lake. Cr cds: A, C, D, DS, MC, V.

D ⬆ 🏊 🎿 ⛸ 🎣 🏃 ⛷ 🏹 🔥 SC

Titusville (B-2)

(See also Franklin, Meadville, Oil City)

Settled 1796 **Pop** 6,434 **Elev** 1,199 ft **Area Code** 814 **Zip** 16354
Information Titusville Area Chamber of Commerce, 202 W Central Ave; 814/827-2941

Titusville spreads from the banks of Oil Creek, so-called because of the oil that appeared on its surface. Edwin L. Drake drilled the first successful oil well in the world on August 27, 1859. Overnight, Titusville became the center of the worldwide oil industry.

What to See and Do

Drake Well Museum. Site of world's first oil well; operating replica of Drake derrick and engine house; picnic area. Features dioramas, working models, life-size exhibits depicting history of oil. (May-Oct, daily; Nov-Apr, Tues-Sat, also Sun afternoons) 1 mi SE of PA 8. Phone 814/827-2797. ¢¢

Resort

★★ **CROSS CREEK RESORT.** *RD 3 Box 152 (16354), 4½ mi S on PA 8. 814/827-9611; FAX 814/827-2062; res: 800/461-3173.* Web www.crosscreekresort.com. 94 rms, 1-2 story. May-Oct: S $95-$110; D

$100-$120; each addl $10; suites $120-$140; under 12 free; golf plan; lower rates rest of yr. Crib free. TV; cable. Heated pool; lifeguard. Restaurant 7 am-2 pm, 6-10 pm. Bar 11-2 am; entertainment. Ck-out 2 pm. Meeting rms. In-rm modem link. Gift shop. Tennis. 27-hole golf, greens fee $28-$33, putting green. Some private patios, balconies. Cr cds: A, C, D, DS, MC, V.

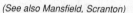

Inn

✓ ★ ★ ★ **MCMULLEN HOUSE BED & BREAKFAST.** *430 E Main St (16354). 814/827-1592.* 5 rms, 2 story, 4 with shower only. No elvtr. No rm phones. MAP: S $46-$48; D $56-$58; family rates. Crib free. TV rm; cable (premium). Complimentary continental bkfst. Coffee in library. Restaurant nearby. Ck-out noon, ck-in 3:30 pm. Luggage handling. Picnic tables. Restored Italianate mansion (1870). Cr cds: C, D, MC, V.

Towanda (B-7)

(See also Mansfield, Scranton)

Settled 1794 **Pop** 3,242 **Elev** 737 ft **Area Code** 570 **Zip** 18848
E-mail emvb@epix.net **Web** www.endlessmountains.org
Information Endless Mountains Visitors Bureau, 712 Rte 6E, Tunkhannock 18657-9232; 570/836-5431 or 800/769-8999

On the north branch of the Susquehanna River, Towanda takes its name from a Native American word meaning "where we bury the dead."

In 1793 the Asylum Company purchased 1,600 acres of these wild valleys as a refuge for Marie Antoinette of France, should she escape to America. "La Grande Maison," a queenly house, was built. French noblemen settled here, and a thriving community (called Azilum) was planned. The colony was unsuccessful and most of its founders returned to France. Many of their descendants, however, still live in Bradford County.

What to See and Do

David Wilmot's Burial Place. Congressman (1845-1851), senator (1861-1863), leader of the Free Soil Party, Wilmot introduced the Wilmot Proviso in Congress, which would have required the US to outlaw slavery in any lands purchased from Mexico. This was an important factor in the dissension between North and South that led to the Civil War. Riverside Cemetery, William St between Chestnut & Walnut Sts.

French Azilum. Site of colony for refugees from the French Revolution (1793-1803). Three cabins with crafts, tool exhibits; log cabin museum (1793); Laporte House (1836), built by son of one of colony's founders, reflects elegant French influence. Special events. Guided tours. (June-Aug, Wed-Sun; May, Sept-Oct, Sat & Sun) 8 mi SE via US 6, PA 187. Phone 570/265-3376. ¢¢

Tioga Point Museum. Mementos of French Azilum; Civil War, Stephen Foster and Native American exhibits; historical displays of early canals and steam railroad. (Tues, Thurs & Sat, hrs vary; closed major hols) 17 mi N off US 220, on PA 199, Spalding Memorial Bldg, 724 S Main St in Athens. Phone 570/888-7225. **Donation**

Valley Railroad Museum. Century-old Lehigh Valley passenger station houses museum with displays of railroad memorabilia and railroad exhibit of Lehigh Valley in miniature; gift shop. (Daily exc Mon; closed major hols) 15 mi N off US 220, in Sayre on S Lehigh Ave. Phone 570/888-1881. ¢¢

Motel

✓ ★ **TOWANDA MOTEL & RESTAURANT.** *383 York Ave (18848). 570/265-2178; FAX 570/265-9060.* 48 rms. S $39-$65; D $43-$70; each addl $5; under 12 free. Crib $3.50. Pet accepted. TV; cable.

Pool. Restaurant 6 am-9:30 pm; Sat, Sun from 7 am. Bar 3 pm-2 am. Ck-out noon. Meeting rms. Business servs avail. Sundries. Cr cds: A, C, D, DS, MC, V.

Motor Hotel

★ ★ ★ **BEST WESTERN GRAND VICTORIA INN.** *255 Spring St (18840), approx 15 mi N on US 220, E on NY 17, exit 61, S on PA 199. 570/888-7711; FAX 570/888-0541; res: 800/627-7972.* 100 rms, 4 story. S $83-$86; D $93-$96; each addl $10; suites $154; under 12 free; wkend package. Crib $10. TV; cable. Indoor pool; whirlpool, lifeguard. Complimentary coffee in rms. Restaurant 6:30 am-9 pm; Fri, Sat to 10 pm. Rm serv. Bar; entertainment Fri, Sat. Ck-out 11 am. Meeting rms. Business servs avail. In-rm modem link. Sundries. Tennis. 18-hole golf privileges. Exercise rm; sauna, steam rm. Balconies. Cr cds: A, C, D, DS, MC, V.

Uniontown (F-2)

(See also Connellsville)

Settled 1768 **Pop** 12,034 **Elev** 999 ft **Area Code** 724 **Zip** 15401
E-mail lhvb@laurelhighlands.org **Web** www.laurelhighlands.org
Information Laurel Highlands Visitors Bureau, 120 E Main St, Ligonier 15658; 724/238-5661

Coal and its byproducts made Uniontown prosperous; with the decline in coal mining the city has developed a more diversified economic base. First known as Union, this city has been the Fayette County seat since 1784. General Lafayette and his son, George Washington de Lafayette, came on a visit after the Revolutionary War and were welcomed by Albert Gallatin, one-time senator and secretary of the Treasury. Uniontown was a hotbed of the Whiskey Rebellion, and federal troops were sent here in 1794.

What to See and Do

Braddock's Grave. Granite monument marks burial place of British General Edward Braddock, who was wounded in battle with French and Native American forces on July 9, 1755, and died 4 days later.

Fort Necessity National Battlefield (1754). The site of Washington's first major battle and the opening battle of the French and Indian War (1754). This land was known as the Great Meadows. A portion was later purchased by Washington, who owned it until his death. A replica of the original fort was built on the site following an archaeological survey in 1953. Picnic area (mid-spring–late fall). 11 mi SE on US 40. Phone 724/329-5512. ¢ Nearby and incl in the admission fee are

Mt Washington Tavern. Restored as historic stagecoach inn; furnishings, exhibits of 1827-1855. (Daily; closed Dec 25) 1 mi W on US 40 is

Visitor Center. Exhibits on battle at Great Meadows; audiovisual program. (Daily; closed Dec 25) Overlooking Fort Necessity is

Friendship Hill National Historic Site. Preserves the restored home of Albert Gallatin, a Swiss immigrant who served his adopted country, in public and private life, for nearly 7 decades. Gallatin made significant contributions to our young republic in the fields of finance, politics, diplomacy and scholarship. He is best known as Treasury Secretary under Jefferson and Madison. Exhibits, audiovisual program, and audio tour provide info on Gallatin. (Daily; closed Dec 25) 15 mi S on US 119 to PA 166. Phone 724/329-5512 or 724/725-9190. **Free**

Jumonville Glen. Site of the skirmish between British and French forces that led to the battle at Fort Necessity. (Mid-Apr–mid-Oct) 7 mi from Ft Necessity, 2½ mi N of US 40 on Summit Rd.

Laurel Caverns. Colored lighting; unusual formations. Indoor miniature golf. Guided tours. Exploring trips. (May–Oct, daily) 5 mi SE on US 40, then 5 mi S on marked road. Phone 724/438-3003. Tours ¢¢¢

Ohiopyle State Park. Approx 18,700 acres of overlooks, waterfalls. Fishing, hunting; whitewater boating. Hiking, bicycling. Cross-country skiing, snowmobiling, sledding. Picnicking, playground, snack bar. Tent & trailer sites. Nature center, interpretive program. Standard fees. 10 mi SE on US 40, then 6 mi NE off PA 381. Phone 724/329-8591.

River tours. Whitewater rafting on the Youghiogheny River; some of the wildest and most scenic in the eastern US. Cost incl equipment and professional guides. Age limits are imposed because of level of difficulty.

Laurel Highlands River Tours. For info contact PO Box 107, Dept PM, Ohiopyle 15470; phone 724/329-8531 or 800/472-3846. ¢¢¢¢¢

Mountain Streams & Trails Outfitters. Also on the Gauley, Big Sandy, Cheat and Tygart's Valley rivers. For info contact Manager, PO Box 106, Ohiopyle 15470; phone 724/329-8810. Also rentals of whitewater rafts, canoes, trail bikes; for info contact Ohiopyle Recreational Rentals, PO Box 4, Ohiopyle 15470; 724/329-8810 or 800/723-8669. ¢¢¢¢¢

White Water Adventurers. For info contact Director, PO Box 31, Ohiopyle 15470; phone 800/WWA-RAFT. ¢¢¢¢¢

Wilderness Voyagers. Trips on the lower and middle Youghiogheny. Also bicycle, canoe rentals; kayak and canoe lessons. For info contact PO Box 97, Ohiopyle 15470; phone 800/272-4141. ¢¢¢¢¢

Motels

★★★ **HOLIDAY INN.** 700 W Main St (15401). 412/438-5543; FAX 412/437-3505; res: 800/465-4329; res: 800/258-7238. 179 rms, 2 story. S $75-$99; D $77-$99; suites $145-$175; under 18 free; package plans; higher rates Labor Day wkend. Crib free. Pet accepted, some restrictions. TV; cable (premium), VCR avail. Indoor pool; whirlpool, poolside serv, lifeguard. Sauna. Coffee in rms. Restaurant 6:30 am-2 pm, 4:30-10 pm. Rm serv from 7 am. Bar 3 pm-2 am; entertainment. Ck-out 11 am. Meeting rms. Business servs avail. In-rm modem link. Valet serv. Sundries. Lighted tennis. Miniature golf. Rec rm. Game rm. Lawn games. Microwaves avail. Some balconies. Cr cds: A, C, D, DS, JCB, MC, V.

🅳 ⬛⬛⬛⬛⬛ SC

✓★★ **LODGE AT CHALK HILL.** Rte 40E (15421), 9 mi E on US 40. 724/438-0168; FAX 724/438-1685; res: 800/833-4283. Web thelodge.uniontown.com. 60 units, 6 suites, 6 kit units. May-Nov: S $60-$73; D $72-$78; each addl $10; suites $143-$167; kit units $77-$93; under 14 free; higher rates: July 4, Memorial Day, Labor Day, Dec 31; lower rates rest of yr. Crib free. Pet accepted, some restrictions; $10. TV; cable (premium), VCR avail. Complimentary continental bkfst. Restaurant opp 7 am-9 pm. Ck-out noon. Meeting rms. Business servs avail. Balconies. Picnic tables. On Lake Lenore. Cr cds: A, C, DS, MC, V.

🅳 ⬛⬛⬛⬛⬛ SC

Resorts

★★★ **NEMACOLIN WOODLANDS RESORT.** 1001 Lafayette Dr (15437), 12 mi E on US 40. 724/329-8555; FAX 724/329-6153; res: 800/422-2736. 220 rms, 4 & 5 story, 60 condo units (1-2 bedrm). May-Oct: S, D $215; each addl $25; suites $345-$1,500; kit condos $245; under 17 free; AP, MAP avail; wkly rates; golf plans; lower rates rest of yr. Crib free. TV; cable (premium), VCR avail. 4 pools, 2 indoor; whirlpools, poolside serv, lifeguard. Playground. Supervised child's activities; ages 4-12. Dining rm 6 am-midnight. Box lunches, snack bar, picnics. Rm serv 24 hrs. Bar noon-2 am; entertainment. Ck-out noon, ck-in 3 pm. Lndry facilities in condos. Convention facilities. Business servs avail. In-rm modem link. Bellhops. Valet serv. Concierge. Gift shop. Sports dir. Lighted tennis, pro. Two 18-hole golf courses, greens fee (incl cart) $69-$109 , pro, 2 putting greens, driving range. Boats. Downhill/x-country ski on site. Sleighing, tobogganing. Equestrian center; surrey rides all yr. Hiking. Bicycle rentals. Miniature golf. Lawn games. Social dir. Rec rm. Game rm. Exercise rm; saunas. Massage. Bathrm phones, minibars; many refrigerators; some

wet bars. Microwave in condos. Balconies. Private collection of art and antiques. Situated on 1,250 acres with 7 lakes; landing strip. Cr cds: A, C, D, MC, V.

🅳 ⬛⬛⬛⬛⬛⬛⬛⬛⬛⬛ SC

★★★ **SUMMIT INN RESORT.** 101 Skyline Dr (15437), 6 mi E on US 40. 724/438-8594; FAX 724/438-3917; res: 800/433-8594. E-mail summit@hhs.net; web www.hhs.net/summit. 100 rms, 3 story. No elvtr. July-Labor Day: S $82-$110; D $92-$120; suites $135-$185; family rates; golf plan, MAP avail (2-day min); some wkend rates; lower rates mid-Apr-June, after Labor Day-early Nov. Closed rest of yr. Crib $10. TV; cable, VCR avail (movies). Indoor/outdoor pool; whirlpool, lifeguard. Dining rm (public by res) 8-11 am, noon-3 pm, 5-9 pm. Rm serv. Box lunches, snacks. Bar 11-1 am. Ck-out noon, ck-in 4 pm. Business servs avail. Grocery, package store 3 mi. Gift shop. Tennis. 9-hole golf, greens fee $8.50, pro, putting green. Exercise equipt. Rec rm. Soc dir; entertainment. Picnic tables, grills. Built in 1907. Atop Mt Summit. Cr cds: A, C, DS, MC, V.

🅳 ⬛⬛⬛⬛⬛⬛ SC

Inns

★★★ **BED & BREAKFAST INN OF THE PRINCESS.** 181 W Main St (15401). 724/425-0120; FAX 724/438-0809. 5 rms, 2 story. May-Oct: S $62.50; D $85-$125; under 18 free; wkend rates; wkends 2-day min; higher rates special events; lower rates rest of yr. Crib free. Pet accepted, some restrictions. TV; cable (premium), VCR avail (movies). Complimentary full bkfst. Restaurant 8 am-7 pm. Ck-out, ck-in varies. In-rm modem link. Luggage handling. Valet serv. Concierge serv. Gift shop. Some in-rm whirlpools, fireplaces. Built in 1880. Cr cds: C, MC, V.

🅳 ⬛⬛⬛⬛ SC

★★★ **INNE AT WATSON'S CHOICE.** 234 Balinger Rd (15401), 5 mi W on PA 21, in Village of Balsinger. 724/437-4999; res: 888/820-5380. Web www.watsonschoice.com. 7 rms, shower only, 2 story. S, D $89-$125; each addl $20; wkly rates; wkends, hols (2-day min). Adults only. TV in common rm; cable (premium), VCR avail (movies). Complimentary full bkfst. Complimentary coffee in rms. Ck-out 11 am, ck-in after 3 pm. Luggage handling. Concierge serv. Gift shop. Guest lndry. Golf privileges. Downhill ski 10 mi; x-country ski 10 mi. Many fireplaces. Picnic tables, grills. Built in 1820; German architecture. Totally nonsmoking. Cr cds: A, C, DS, MC, V.

🅳 ⬛⬛⬛⬛⬛

Restaurants

★★★ **CHEZ GARARD FRENCH RESTAURANT.** US 40E Business (15445). 724/437-9001. Web www.hhs.net/bedandb/. Hrs: 11:30 am-2 pm, 5:30-9 pm; Sun brunch 11:30 am-2 pm. Closed Tues; most major hols. Res accepted. French menu. Bar. Wine list. Semi-a la carte: lunch $6-$10, dinner $10-$22. Prix fixe: lunch $16.50, dinner $35-$47. Sun brunch $18. Child's meals. Specialties: champagne gratined onion soup, Dover sole meuniere, creme brulee. Own baking. Outdoor dining. Renovated 1790 stone house with country French decor, fireplaces. Cr cds: C, MC, V.

🅳

★★★ **COAL BARON RESTAURANT.** RD 6 (15401), 6 mi W on US 40. 724/439-0111. Hrs: 4-11 pm; Sun noon-8 pm. Closed Mon; Dec 24-25. Res accepted. Continental menu. Bar. Wine list. Complete meals: dinner $14-$20.95. Child's meals. Specialties: veal saltimbocca, entrecôte maître d'hôtel, seafood. Own baking. Valet parking. Jacket. Cr cds: A, C, D, DS, MC, V.

★★ **SUN PORCH.** US 40E (15445). 724/439-5734. Hrs: 11 am-8 pm; Sat 4-9 pm. Closed Mon; Dec 24, 25. Res accepted. Semi-a la carte: lunch $4.50-$8, dinner $7-$12. Buffet: dinner $8.50-$10.50. Child's meals. Specializes in fresh seafood, beef, poultry. Salad bar. Many plants; country garden atmosphere. Cr cds: C, D, DS, MC, V.

Valley Forge National Historical Park (E-9)

(See also King of Prussia, Philadelphia)

Web www.nps.gov/vafo

Information Superintendent, PO Box 953, Valley Forge 19482; 610/783-1077

(3 mi N of PA Tpke Interchange 24)

From December 19, 1777, to June 19, 1778, General George Washington and his Continental Army were camped here. Of those 12,000 soldiers that Washington brought to Valley Forge, 2,000 would die of disease in camp. However, due to active recruiting, the overall numbers of the army grew to 20,000. The national park is a 3,600-acre memorial to their trial and success. The park itself is scenic at any time of the year. A marked tour route offers the visitor a chance to see the primary encampment facilities; other roads provide a beautiful drive and a chance to view other historical features. (Daily; closed Dec 25)

What to See and Do

National Memorial Arch. Built in 1917 to commemorate Washington's army. Inscribed in the arch is a quote of General Washington: "Naked and starving as they are, we cannot enough admire the incomparable patience and fidelity of the soldiery."

Soldier Life Program. Interpreters present programs detailing camp life of the Continental Army soldier (offered at various times during the yr).

Tours.

  Auto Tape Tour. Self-guided tour dramatizes Washington's winter encampment. (2-hr tape rental, May–Oct, daily) Bookstore. Phone 610/783-5788. ¢¢¢

  Bus Tour. Narrated tour (approx 90 min) incl stops at historic sites. (June–Labor Day, tour departures every ½-hr; Labor Day–Oct, wkends only) Tours leave from Visitor Center. Phone 610/783-5788. ¢¢¢

Visitor Center. Information, exhibits, audiovisual program, tour maps. Bus tours depart from here. (Daily) Jct PA 23 & N Gulph Rd, just inside park. Phone 610/783-1077.

Washington Headquarters. Park staff provide info about the house where Washington lived for 6 months and which served as military headquarters for the Continental Army during that time. (Daily) Fee charged Apr–Nov ¢

Washington Memorial Chapel. Private property within park boundaries. Stained-glass windows depict the story of the New World, its discovery and development; hand-carved oak choir stalls, Pews of the Patriots, and Roof of the Republic bearing the State Seal of all the states. Also part of the chapel is the 58 cast-bell Washington Memorial National Carillon, with bells honoring states and territories. On PA 23. Phone 610/783-0120. Adj is

  Museum of the Valley Forge Historical Society. Relics of the winter at Valley Forge. (Daily; closed Easter, Thanksgiving, Dec 25) Phone 610/783-0535. ¢

Restaurants

  ★ ★ **COLUMBIA HOTEL.** *148 Bridge St (19460), 6 mi NW off PA 23. 610/933-9973.* Hrs: 11:30 am-2:30 pm, 5-10 pm. Closed Sun. Res accepted. Bar to midnight. A la carte entrees: lunch $5.95-$12.95, dinner $15.95-$25.95. Child's meals. Specializes in fresh Maine & Florida fish, Angus beef. Own desserts. Built in 1892. Cr cds: A, C, D, MC, V.

  ★ ★ ★ **KENNEDY-SUPPLEE MANSION.** *1100 W Valley Forge Rd, PA 23 (19406), opp visitors center to Valley Forge National Historical Park. 610/337-3777.* Hrs: 11:30 am-2 pm, 5:30-11 pm; Sat from 5:30 pm. Closed Sun; some major hols. Res accepted. Continental menu. Bar; pianist Fri, Sat. A la carte entrees: lunch $8-$16, dinner $22-$30. Specializes in French, northern Italian cuisine. Valet parking. 8 dining rooms in 1850s mansion. Crystal chandeliers, original artwork. Jacket (dinner). Cr cds: A, C, D, MC, V.

  ★ ★ ★ **KIMBERTON INN.** *Kimberton Rd (19442), PA 23W to PA 113S. 610/933-8148.* Hrs: 5:30-9:30 pm; Sun to 8:30 pm; Sun brunch 11 am-2 pm. Res accepted. Continental menu. Bar. Wine list. Semi-a la carte: dinner $17.95-$21.95. Sun brunch $17.95. Specializes in fresh seafood. Own desserts. Harpist or pianist. Tavern (1796) on 4½ acres of gardens. Cr cds: A, C, D, DS, MC, V.

  ★ ★ ★ **SEVEN STARS INN.** *PA 23 & Hoffecker Rd (19460), 10 mi W on PA 23. 610/495-5205.* Hrs: 4:30-10 pm; wkends to 11 pm; Sun 3-7 pm. Closed Mon; most major hols. Res accepted. Bar. Wine list. Complete meals: dinner $19.95-$27.95. Child's meals. Specializes in prime rib, seafood, veal. Colonial inn decor. Cr cds: A, C, D, MC, V.

Warren (B-3)

Founded 1795 **Pop** 11,122 **Elev** 1,200 ft **Area Code** 814 **Zip** 16365

Information Warren County Chamber of Commerce, 315 2nd Ave, PO Box 942; 814/723-3050; or Travel Northern Alleghenies, 315 Second St, at the point, PO Box 804, 814/726-1222

At the junction of the Allegheny and Conewango rivers, Warren is the headquarters and gateway of the famous Allegheny National Forest. Named for General Joseph Warren, American patriot killed in the Battle of Bunker Hill, the town was once the point where great flotillas of logs were formed for the journey to Pittsburgh or Cincinnati.

What to See and Do

Allegheny National Forest. More than 510,000 acres S & E on US 6, 62, located in Warren, Forest, McKean and Elk counties. Black bear, whitetail deer and wild turkey, a diversity of small birds and mammals; streams and reservoirs with trout, walleye, muskellunge, northern pike and bass; rugged hills, quiet valleys, open meadows, dense forest. These lures, plus swimming, boating, hiking, camping and picnicking facilities, draw more than 2 million visitors a yr. Hundreds of campsites; fees are charged at some recreation sites. For info contact Supervisor, US Forest Service, PO Box 847, phone 814/723-5150; or Reservoir Area Office/Bradford District, phone 814/362-4613 or 814/368-8116 (TTY). In forest are

  Buckaloons Recreation Area. Site of former Native American village on the banks of the Allegheny River. Boat launching. Picnicking. Camping (fee). Seneca Interpretive Trail. 6 mi W on US 6. Phone 814/362-4613 or 814/368-8116 (TTY).

  Kinzua Dam and Allegheny Reservoir. Dam (179 ft high, 1,897 ft long) with 27-mi-long lake. Swimming; fishing; boating (ramps, rentals; fees). Picnicking, overlooks. Camping (fee). Kinzua Dam Visitor Center has displays. Kinzua Point Information Center, 4 mi NE of dam, phone 814/726-1291. Some fees. 3 mi SE on US 6, then 6 mi E on PA 59. *(It is possible that the PA 59 bridge, 1½ mi E of Kinzua Dam, will be closed;*

phone ahead for info.) Phone 814/726-0661, 814/362-4613 or 814/726-0164 (24-hr fishing hotline).

Chapman State Park. Approx 800 acres. Lake and creek stocked with trout and bass. Swimming beach; fishing, hunting; boating (rentals, mooring, launching). Hiking. Cross-country skiing, snowmobiling, sledding, ice skating, ice fishing. Picnicking, snack bar. Tent & trailer sites avail (some with electric; fee). Interpretive program. 7 mi SE on US 6, then W at light in Clarendon. Phone 814/723-0250. Camping   ¢¢¢-¢¢¢¢

Washington (E-1)

Founded 1781 **Pop** 15,864 **Elev** 1,120 ft **Area Code** 724 **Zip** 15301
E-mail info@washpatourism.org **Web** www.washpatourism.org

Information Washington County Tourism Promotion Agency, Franklin Mall, 1500 W Chestnut St; 724/228-5520 or 800/531-4114

Originally a Native American village known as Catfish Camp, the village of Bassettown became Washington during the Revolution. During the Whiskey Rebellion the town was a center of protest against the new federal government's tax; arrival of federal troops quieted the rebellious farmers. Washington and Jefferson College (1781) is located here.

What to See and Do

David Bradford House (1788). Restored frontier home of a leader of the Whiskey Rebellion. (May–late Dec, Wed–Sat, limited hrs, also Sun afternoons) 175 S Main St. For fee info phone 724/222-3604.

Ladbroke at the Meadows. Harness racing. Parimutuel betting. (Tues, Thurs-Sun eves) Simulcasts (daily). 4 mi N on US 19. Phone 724/225-9300.

LeMoyne House (1812). Abolitionist's home, built by the LeMoyne family, was a stop on the underground railroad; period furnishings, paintings, library; gardens; museum shop. Administered by Washington County Historical Society. (Feb–Dec, daily exc Mon) 49 E Maiden St. Phone 724/225-6740. **Free.**

Meadowcroft Museum of Rural Life. A 200-acre outdoor museum complex that preserves the history of life on the land in Western Pennsylvania. General store, restored log houses, one-rm schoolhouse, blacksmith shop and archaeology exhibit. (May–Oct, Wed–Sun) 19 mi NW via PA 18, 50, in Avella. Phone 724/587-3412.   ¢¢¢

Pennsylvania Trolley Museum. Museum displays incl more than 35 trolley cars dating from 1894. Scenic trolley ride; car barn and trolley-restoration shop; visitor's center and gift shop with exhibit, video presentation and picnic area. (June–Aug, daily; May & Sept–Oct, wkends) I-79 N, exit 8 (Meadowlands), follow signs. Phone 724/228-9256.   ¢¢

Motels

★ **MOTEL 6.** *1283 Motel 6 Dr (15301). I-70 at US 19, exit 7A.* 724/223-8040; FAX 724/228-6445; res: 800/722-7220; res: 800/843-5644. 102 rms. S $35.99; D $42.39; each addl $6; under 18 free. Crib free. Pet accepted. TV; cable (premium). Pool. Complimentary coffee in lobby. Restaurant adj open 24 hrs. Ck-out noon. Cr cds: A, C, D, DS, ER, MC, V.

D 🐕 🐾 🖂 🔥 SC

✓ ★ **RED ROOF INN.** *1399 W Chestnut St (15301).* 724/228-5750; FAX 724/228-5865; res: 800/843-7663. 110 rms, 2 story. May-Oct: S $35.99-$45.99; D $42.99-$64.99; each addl $6; under 18 free; lower rates rest of yr. Crib free. Pet accepted, some restrictions. TV; cable (premium). Complimentary coffee in lobby. Restaurant adj open 24 hrs. Ck-out noon. Cr cds: A, C, D, DS, MC, V.

D 🐕 🖂 🔥

★ **WASHINTON MOTOR INN.** *1385 W Chestnut St (15301), on US 40.* 724/222-6500; FAX 724/222-7671; res: 888/735-6500.

62 rms, 1-2 story. S $40-$60; D $48-$68; each addl $6; under 18 free; higher rates special events. Crib free. TV; cable (premium). Complimentary continental bkfst. Restaurant adj open 24 hrs. Ck-out 11 am. Business servs avail. Bellhops. Airport transportation. Picnic tables. Cr cds: A, C, D, DS, MC, V.

D 🖂 🔥 SC

Motor Hotel

★★★ **HOLIDAY INN MEADOWLANDS.** *340 Race Track Rd (15301), I-79 exit 8B.* 724/222-6200; FAX 724/228-0709; res: 800/465-4329. 138 rms, 7 story. S, D $99-$109; each addl $6; under 18 free. Crib free. Pet accepted, some restrictions. TV; cable (premium), VCR avail. Pool; whirlpool, poolside serv, lifeguard. Restaurant 6:30 am-10 pm. Rm serv. Bars 11-2 am; entertainment. Ck-out noon. Meeting rms. Business servs avail. In-rm modem link. Airport transportation. Exercise equipt; sauna. Microwaves avail. Private patios. Meadows Racetrack adj. Cr cds: A, C, D, DS, ER, JCB, MC, V.

D 🐾 🏊 ✈ 🖂 🔥 SC

Washington Crossing Historic Park (Bucks Co) (E-10)

(See also Doylestown, New Hope, Philadelphia, PA; also see Trenton, NJ)

Information Superintendent, PO Box 103, Washington Crossing 18977; 215/493-4076
(Two sections: Bowman's Hill, 2 mi S of New Hope on PA 32, and Washington Crossing, 7 mi S of New Hope on PA 32)

In a blinding snowstorm on Christmas night 1776, George Washington and 2,400 soldiers crossed the Delaware River from the Pennsylvania shore and marched to Trenton, surprising the celebrating Hessian mercenaries and capturing the city. Washington's feat was a turning point of the Revolutionary War. Park (daily exc Mon; closed some hols). Phone 215/493-4076.   ¢¢

What to See and Do

BOWMAN'S HILL

Memorial Flagstaff. Marks graves of unknown Continentals who died during encampment.

Wildflower Preserve. Adj park; 2 mi of native wildflower trails. (Daily) Phone 215/862-2924.

WASHINGTON CROSSING

Area of Embarkation. Marked by tall granite shaft supporting Washington's statue.

Concentration Valley. Where Washington assembled troops for raid on Trenton.

McConkey Ferry Inn (1752). At Washington Crossing; restored as historic house. Sold in 1777 to Benjamin Taylor, whose descendants established the 19th-century village of Taylorsville.

Memorial Building. Near Point of Embarkation. Houses copy of Emanuel Leutze's painting, *Washington Crossing the Delaware*. Movie shown 5 times daily. Phone 215/493-4076.

Annual Event

The Crossing. Re-enactment of Washington's crossing of the Delaware River, Christmas night in 1776. Phone 215/493-4076. Dec.

Wellsboro (B-6)

(See also Galeton, Mansfield)

Settled 1799 **Pop** 3,430 **Elev** 1,311 ft **Area Code** 570 **Zip** 16901
E-mail mwwacc@epix.net **Web** www.epix.net~mwwacc/
Information Wellsboro Area Chamber of Commerce, 114 Main St, PO Box 733; 570/724-1926

Wellsboro is the gateway to Pennsylvania's "canyon country." Settled largely by New Englanders, it is sustained by an assortment of industries. The area yields coal, natural gas, hardwoods, maple syrup and farm products.

What to See and Do

Auto tours. There are more than a million acres of forests, mountains and streams to be explored. The Wellsboro Area Chamber of Commerce has published a map of three tours.

Red Arrow Tour follows PA 660 SW 10 mi from Wellsboro to Leonard Harrison State Park. Lookout Point, near the parking area, has large picnic area nearby. Path winds 1 mi from park to bottom of gorge, through shady glens, past waterfalls.

White Arrow Tour leads from the Switchbacks (1½ mi W of Bradley Wales Park), 3 mi S to Leetonia, once a prosperous lumber village, now occupied by State Forest Rangers; then W & N to Cushman View, Wilson Point Rd, Lee Fire Tower, Cedar Run Mountain Rd & US 6; approx 75 mi.

Yellow Arrow Tour leads from Leonard Harrison State Park, back on PA 660, NW on PA 362, then ¼ mi W on US 6 to Colton Point Rd for views of the canyon and Four Mile Run Country. At Colton Point State Park (observation points, picnic shelters, fireplaces) the arrows follow Pine Creek S on old lumbering railroad tracks, converted into roadways called the "Switchbacks," to Bradley Wales Park overlooking Tiadaghton, the next lookout point on Pine Creek. From here continue S on W Rim Rd to Blackwell, NE on PA 414 to Morris, then N on PA 287 to Wellsboro—a circle of 65 mi.

Robinson House Museum (ca 1820). Houses turn-of-the-century artifacts; genealogical library. (Mon-Fri afternoons) 120 Main St. Contact Tioga County Historical Society, PO Box 724; phone 570/724-6116. **Free**

Ski Sawmill Resort. Chairlift, 3 T-bars; patrol, school, rentals; snowmaking; cafeteria, restaurant, bar. Longest run 3,250 ft; vertical drop 515 ft. (Dec–Mar, daily) Yr-round activities. Oregon Hill Rd, 16 mi S via PA 287. Phone 800/532-SNOW. ¢¢¢-¢¢¢¢¢

Annual Event

Pennsylvania State Laurel Festival. Week-long event incl parade of floats, marching musical and precision units, antique cars, laurel queen contestants; crowning of the queen; arts and crafts; children's pet and hobby parade, exhibits and displays. Mid-June.

Motels

✓ ★ **CANYON MOTEL.** *18 East Ave (16901).* 570/724-1681; FAX 570/724-1681; res: 800/255-2718. 28 rms. S $28-$45; D $32-$49; each addl $5; under 12 free; golf, ski package plans. Crib $5. Pet accepted. TV; cable. Heated pool; lifeguard. Playground. Complimentary continental bkfst. Restaurant nearby. Ck-out 11 am. Business servs avail. In-rm modem link. Downhill/x-country ski 17 mi. Refrigerators. Picnic tables, grills. Cr cds: A, C, D, DS, MC, V.

★ ★ **PENN WELLS LODGE.** *4 Main St (16901).* 717/724-3463; FAX 717/724-2270; res: 800/545-2446. 55 rms, 2 story. S $53-$61; D $61-$69; each addl $5; under 18 free. Crib $5. TV; cable. Indoor pool; whirlpool, lifeguard. Playground. Restaurant nearby. Ck-out noon. Business servs avail. Downhill/x-country ski 17 mi. Exercise rm; sauna. Community-owned. Cr cds: A, C, D, DS, MC, V.

★ **SHERWOOD MOTEL.** *2 Main St (16901).* 717/724-3424; FAX 717/724-5658; res: 800/628-5802. 32 rms, 1-2 story. S $37; D $49-$54; each addl $5; under 10 free; golf, ski package plans. Crib $5. Pet accepted; $5. TV; cable. Heated pool; lifeguard. Playground. Complimentary coffee. Restaurant nearby. Ck-out 11 am. Business servs avail. In-rm modem link. Downhill/x-country ski 17 mi. Refrigerators. Cr cds: A, C, D, DS, MC, V.

Hotel

★ **PENN WELLS HOTEL & LODGE.** *62 Main St (16901).* 570/724-2111; FAX 570/724-3703; res: 800/545-2446. 73 rms. Late May-Oct, hunting season: S $30-$40; D $40-$49; each addl $5; suites $55-$60; under 18 free; golf plans; lower rates rest of yr. Crib $5. TV; cable. Indoor pool; whirlpool. Playground. Restaurant 7 am-1:30 pm, 5-10 pm. Bar 11:30-1 am; entertainment Fri, Sat. Ck-out noon. Meeting rms. Business servs avail. Downhill/x-country ski 17 mi. Exercise rm; sauna. Built in 1869; high ceilings, oak & cherry woodwork, antiques, early Americana. Community-owned. Cr cds: A, C, D, DS, MC, V.

Inn

★ ★ **KALTENBACH'S BED & BREAKFAST.** *Stony Fork Rd (16901),* 2 mi W on Kelsey St, S on Stony Fork Rd. 570/724-4954; res: 800/772-4954; res: 800/722-4954. 10 rms, 2 suites, 1 rm with shared bath. 5 rm phones. S $35; D $70; suites $125; under age 6 free; golf, ski plans; wknds, hols (2-day min); lower rates Jan-April. TV; cable (premium). Playground. Complimentary full bkfst; afternoon refreshments. Restaurant nearby 11 am-10 pm. Ck-out 11 am, ck-in noon. 18-hole golf privileges 2 mi, greens fee $35, putting green, driving range, pro. Downhill ski 12 mi; x-country ski 20 mi. Totally nonsmoking. Cr cds: A, C, D, DS, MC, V.

West Chester (F-9)

(See also Chester, Kennett Square, King of Prussia, Media, Philadelphia)

Founded 1788 **Pop** 18,041 **Elev** 459 ft **Area Code** 484 & 610
Web www.brandywinevalley.com
Information Chester County Tourist Bureau, 601 Westtown Rd, Suite 170, 19382; 610/344-6365 or 800/228-9933

In the heart of three Pennsylvania Revolutionary War historic sites—Brandywine, Paoli and Valley Forge—West Chester today is a university and residential community, with fine examples of Greek revival and Victorian architecture.

What to See and Do

Brinton 1704 House. Stone house built by Quaker farmer William Brinton, authentically restored and furnished. (May–Oct, Sat, Sun; also by appt) 5 mi S just off US 202, Oakland Rd, in Dilworthtown. Phone 302/478-2853. ¢

Motel

✓ ★ **ABBEY GREEN MOTOR LODGE.** *1036 Wilmington Pike (19382). 610/692-3310; FAX 610/431-0811.* E-mail ireland@epix.net; web www.abbeygreen.com. 18 rms. S $49-$59; D $59-$69; each addl $5; cottages with kit $59-$69; wkly rates. Crib free. Pet accepted. TV; cable (premium). Restaurant nearby. Ck-out 11 am. Business servs avail. Gift shop. Refrigerators; some fireplaces; microwaves avail. Picnic tables, grill. Cr cds: A, C, D, DS, MC, V.

Motor Hotel

★★★ **HOLIDAY INN.** *943 S High St (19382), at US 202. 610/692-1900; FAX 610/436-0159; res: 800/465-4329.* 143 rms, 3 story. S, D $85-$105; each addl $10; suites $109-$129; kit suites $129-$149; under 17 free. Crib free. TV; cable (premium), VCR avail. Pool; lifeguard. Restaurant 6:30 am-10 pm. Rm serv. Bar 4 pm-2 am. Ck-out noon. Coin lndry. Meeting rms. Business servs avail. In-rm modem link. Valet serv. Airport transportation. Lawn games. Exercise equipt. Microwaves avail. Cr cds: A, C, D, DS, MC, V.

Hotel

★★★ **BEST WESTERN.** *Rte 322 & Rte 1 (16803), 6 mi S on US 202, then 3 mi N on US 1. 610/358-9400; FAX 610/358-9381; res: 800/522-0070.* Web www.concordville.com. 116 rms, 5 story, 25 suites. S $110; D $125; each addl $15; suites $160-$195; under 12 free. Crib free. TV; cable, VCR avail. Indoor pool; whirlpool, lifeguard. Complimentary continental bkfst. Restaurant (see CONCORDVILLE INN). Bar. Ck-out noon. Meeting rms. Business servs avail. In-rm modem link. Gift shop. Beauty shop; spa. Valet serv. Exercise rm; sauna. Refrigerator in suites, mini bars. Cr cds: A, C, D, DS, MC, V.

Inn

★★★ **DULING–KURTZ HOUSE & COUNTRY INN.** *146 S Whitford Rd (19341), N on PA 100, ½ mi W on US 30. 610/524-1830; FAX 610/524-6258.* 15 rms, 3 story, 5 suites. S, D $55-$120; each addl $25; suites $79-$120; higher rates Fri, Sat & hols. TV; cable. Complimentary continental bkfst. Restaurant (see DULING–KURTZ HOUSE). Rm serv. Ck-out 11 am, ck-in 3 pm. Business servs avail. Built in 1783; period furniture, antiques, sitting rm. Cr cds: A, C, D, DS, MC, V.

Restaurants

★★★ **CONCORDVILLE INN.** *(See Best Western Concordville) 610/459-2230.* Web www.concordville.com. Hrs: 11 am-10 pm; Sun to 8 pm; early-bird dinner 4-5:30 pm. Closed Dec 25. Res accepted. Continental menu. Bar to 2 am. Wine cellar. Semi-a la carte: lunch $5.50-$9.95; dinner $14.95-$24.95. Child's meals. Specialties: crab imperial, crab cakes, prime rib. Outdoor dining. Family-owned. Cr cds: A, C, D, DS, MC, V.

★★★ **DULING–KURTZ HOUSE.** *(See Duling–Kurtz House Inn) 610/524-1830.* Hrs: 11:30 am-10 pm; Sat from 5 pm; Sun 3-9 pm. Res accepted. French, continental menu. Bar. Wine list. A la carte entrees: lunch $6.95-$13.95, dinner $16.50-$29.75. Specialties: hickory smoked buffalo, lobster crepes, Oyster Lafayette. Valet parking Fri, Sat. 7 dining rms. Country inn atmosphere; formal gardens with gazebo. Fireplaces. Cr cds: A, C, D, DS, MC, V.

★★★ **LENAPE INN.** *Jct PA 52 & 100 (19382), 5 mi S on PA 52. 610/793-2005.* Hrs: 11:30 am-11 pm; Sun from 2 pm. Closed Mon. Res accepted. Continental menu. Bar. Wine list. Semi-a la carte: lunch $6.50-$15.95, dinner $15-$29.95. Child's meals. Specialties: Wienerschnitzel, roast rack of lamb a la Bretonne, sirloin steak au Poivre. Elegant dining overlooking Brandywine River. Cathedral ceilings, chandeliers, fireplace. Cr cds: A, C, D, DS, MC, V.

THE DILWORTHTOWN INN DINING ROOM. *1390 Old Wilmington Pike (19382), 1 mi S of PA 926. 610/399-1390.* E-mail info@dilworthtown.com; web www.dilworthtown.com. Hrs: 5:30-10 pm; Sun 3-9 pm. Closed Jan 1, Dec 25. Res required. Bar. Wine cellar. Semi-a la carte: dinner $18-$25. Specializes in seafood, game, beef. Outdoor dining. Entertainment Fri, Sat. Fifteen dining rms in restored colonial house (1758). Authentic period decor. Cr cds: A, C, D, DS, MC, V.

West Middlesex (C-1)

Pop 982 **Elev** 840 ft **Area Code** 724 **Zip** 16159

Motels

★★ **HOLIDAY INN.** *3200 S Hermitage Rd (16159), N on PA 60, at jct I-80 exit 1N. 724/981-1530; FAX 724/981-1518; res: 800/465-4329.* 180 rms, 3 story. S, D $79.95; under 19 free; golf plans. Crib free. Pet accepted. TV; cable (premium). Heated pool; poolside serv, lifeguard. Playground. Restaurant 6:30 am-10 pm; Dec-Mar 6:30 am-2 pm, 5-10 pm. Rm serv. Bar 11-2 am; entertainment. Ck-out 11 am. Coin lndry. Meeting rms. Business servs avail. In-rm modem link. Valet serv. Game rm. Cr cds: A, C, D, DS, ER, JCB, MC, V.

★★★ **RADISSON HOTEL SHARON.** *I-80 & Rte 18 (16159). 724/528-2501; FAX 724/528-2306; res: 800/333-3333; res: 800/358-7260.* 153 rms, 3 story. S $80-$90; D $88-$98; each addl $8; suites $150-$200; under 12 free; wkend rates. Crib free. Pet accepted. TV; cable. Indoor pool; whirlpool, poolside serv, lifeguard. Restaurant 6:30 am-10 pm. Rm serv. Bar 11-2 am; entertainment Wed, Fri, Sat. Ck-out 11 am. Coin lndry. Meeting rms. Business servs avail. Bellhops. Valet serv. Gift shop. Sundries. Exercise equipt; sauna. Game rm. In-rm whirlpools; refrigerator in suites. Cr cds: A, C, D, DS, MC, V.

Restaurant

★★ **THE TAVERN.** *108 N Market St (16142), 3 mi S on PA 60, 5 mi E on PA 208. 724/946-2020.* Hrs: 11:30 am-2 pm, 5-8 pm; Sun noon-6:30 pm. Closed Tues; July 4, Thanksgiving, Dec 25. Res required. Complete meals: lunch $9-$13, dinner $11-$18.50. Specialties: stuffed pork chops, creamed chicken & biscuits, baked chicken. Country decor; built in 1840. Cr cds: A, C, DS, MC, V.

White Haven (D-9)

(See also Hazleton, Jim Thorpe, Pocono Mountains, Wilkes-Barre)

Pop 1,132 **Elev** 1,221 ft **Area Code** 570 **Zip** 18661
E-mail pocomts@poconos.org **Web** www.poconos.org
Information Pocono Mts Vacation Bureau, 1004 Main St, Stroudsburg 18360, phone; 570/424-6050; for free brochures phone 800/POCONOS.

What to See and Do

Hickory Run State Park. Approx 15,500 acres of scenic area. Swimming beach; fishing, hunting. Hiking. Cross-country skiing, snowmobiling, sledding, ice skating, ice fishing. Picnicking, playground, snack bar, store. Tent & trailer sites. Standard fees. 6 mi S on PA 534 off I-80 exit 41. Phone 570/443-0400.

Skiing.

Big Boulder. 5 double, 2 triple chairlifts; patrol, school, rentals; snowmaking; cafeteria, bar; nursery, lodge. Night skiing. Longest run approx ¾ mi; vertical drop 475 ft. (Dec–Mar, daily) 1 mi E off PA 903 in Lake Harmony. Phone 570/722-0100. ¢¢¢¢¢

Jack Frost. 2 triple, 5 double chairlifts; patrol, school, rentals; snowmaking; cafeteria, restaurant, bar; nursery. Longest run approx ½ mi; vertical drop 600 ft. (Dec–Mar, daily) Half-day rate. 6 mi E on PA 940. Phone 570/443-8425. ¢¢¢¢¢

Motels

★ **POCONO MOUNTAIN LODGE.** *Rte 940 (18661), Jct PA 940 & I-80.* 570/443-8461; FAX 570/443-7988; res: 800/443-4049. 123 rms, 6 story. S, D $70; each addl $10; under 18 free; ski plans. Crib free. TV; cable. Pool. Restaurant adj 6 am-midnight. Bar 11-2 am. Ck-out noon. Meeting rms. Business servs avail. Downhill/x-country ski 4 mi. Hiking trails. Game rm. Cr cds: A, C, D, DS, MC, V.

★★★ **RAMADA INN.** *Rte 940 (18624), 4 mi E on I-80, exit 42.* 570/443-8471; FAX 570/443-0326; res: 800/251-2610. 138 rms, 4 story, 2 suites. Jan-Feb & mid-June-Columbus Day: S $90-$120; D $95-$130; each addl $10; under 18 free; higher rates NASCAR races; lower rates rest of yr. Crib free. Pet accepted; $50 deposit. TV; cable. Indoor pool; poolside serv, lifeguard. Sauna. Complimentary coffee in lobby. Restaurant 7 am-10 pm. Rm serv. Bar 4 pm-midnight. Ck-out noon. Meeting rm. Business servs avail. Gift shop. Valet serv. Coin lndry. Airport transportation. Golf privileges, greens fee $40, pro, putting green, driving range. Downhill/x-country ski 4 mi. Game rm. Lawn games. Some refrigerators. Picnic tables. Cr cds: A, C, D, DS, JCB, MC, V.

Resort

★★★ **MOUNTAIN LAUREL RESORT.** *I-80 at PA Tpke NE Ext (18661), 4 mi E on PA 940 at jct PA Tpke exit 35 & I-80 exit 42.* 570/443-8411; FAX 570/443-5518; res: 800/255-7625. 250 rms, 3 story. MAP: S $134; D $188/person; each addl $10; suites $150; under 13 free; golf plan; some wkend rates; higher rates hols. Crib free. TV; cable, VCR avail (movies). 2 pools, 1 indoor; whirlpool, poolside serv, lifeguard. Playground. Supervised child's activities. Dining rm 6-9 pm. Box lunches, snacks, picnics. Bar 11-2 am; entertainment. Ck-out noon, ck-in 4 pm. Coin lndry. Meeting rms. Business center. Airport, RR station, bus depot transportation. Sports dir. 4 lighted tennis courts. 18-hole golf, greens fee from $44 (incl cart), driving range, putting green, miniature golf. Archery. Downhill ski 5 mi. Soc dir; entertainment. Nursery. Movies. Game rm. Exercise rm; sauna. Picnic tables. Cr cds: A, C, D, DS, MC, V.

Restaurant

✓★★★ **POWERHOUSE RESTAURANT.** *I-80 Exit 40 (18661), 1 mi E on I-80, exit 40.* 570/443-4480. Hrs: 4-10 pm; Sun noon-10 pm. Closed Dec 24, 25. Res accepted. Italian, Amer menu. Bar. Semi-a la carte: $11.95-$15.95. Specialties: veal marsala, shrimp & crab fracaise. Located in old power plant. Cr cds: A, C, DS, MC, V.

Ⓓ

Wilkes-Barre (C-8)

(See also Hazleton, Pocono Mountains, Scranton, White Haven)

Founded 1769 **Pop** 47,523 **Elev** 550 ft **Area Code** 570
Information Pennsylvania's Northeast Territory Visitors Bureau, 100 Terminal Rd, Ste 216, Avoca 18641; 570/457-1320

Named in honor of two members of British Parliament who championed individual rights and supported the colonies, Wilkes-Barre (WILKS-berry) and the Wyoming Valley were settled by pioneers from Connecticut. Pennsylvania and Connecticut waged the Pennamite-Yankee War, the first phase ending in 1771 with Connecticut in control of the valley. It was later resumed until Connecticut relinquished its claims in 1800. Wilkes-Barre was burned by Native Americans and Tories during the Revolution and again by Connecticut settlers protesting the Decree of Trenton (1782), in which Congress favored Pennsylvania's claim to the territory. Discovery of anthracite coal in the valley sparked the town's growth after Judge Jesse Fell demonstrated that anthracite could be burned in a grate without forced draft.

Motels

★★ **HAMPTON INN.** *1063 Hwy 315 (18702).* 570/825-3838; FAX 570/825-8775; res: 800/426-7866. 123 rms, 5 story. May-Oct: S $55-$65; D $65-$75; under 18 free; ski plans; higher rates: car races, Dec 31; lower rates rest of yr. Crib free. Pet accepted. TV; cable. Complimentary continental bkfst. Restaurant adj 7 am-11 pm. Ck-out noon. Meeting rm. Business servs avail. In-rm modem link. Valet serv Mon-Fri. Downhill ski 10 mi. Cr cds: A, C, D, DS, ER, MC, V.

Ⓓ

★★ **HOLIDAY INN.** *880 Kidder St (18702), at PA 309.* 570/824-8901; FAX 570/824-9310; res: 888/466-9272. 120 rms, 2 story. S, D $69-$120; each addl $10; studio rms $75; package plans. Pet accepted. TV; cable. Pool; wading pool, poolside serv. Restaurant 6:30-1 am. Rm serv. Bar noon-2 am. Ck-out noon. Meeting rms. Business servs avail. In-rm modem link. Bellhops. Sundries. Downhill ski 10 mi. Cr cds: A, C, D, DS, ER, JCB, MC, V.

Ⓓ

Motor Hotel

★★★ **THE WOODLANDS INN & RESORT.** *1073 Hwy 315 (18702).* 570/824-9831; FAX 570/824-8865; res: 800/762-2222. 179 rms, 9 story, 25 apts. S $69-$107; D $79-$107; each addl $10; package plans; wkend rates. Crib $5. TV; cable. 2 pools, 1 indoor; whirlpool, poolside serv, lifeguard. Restaurant 7 am-11 pm. Rm serv. Bar 11-2 am; entertainment, dancing. Ck-out noon. Meeting rms. Business servs avail. Bellhops. Sundries. Barber, beauty shop. Free airport transportation. Lighted tennis. Exercise rm; sauna. Game rm. Rec rm. Lawn games. Private patios, balconies. Cr cds: A, C, D, DS, MC, V.

Ⓓ

Hotel

★★★ **BEST WESTERN EAST MOUNTAIN INN.** *2400 E End Blvd (18702), I-81 exit 47A.* 570/822-1011; FAX 570/822-6072; res: 800/528-1234. 156 rms, 7 story, 24 suites. S $87-$92; D $92-$97; each addl $5; suites $115-$120; under 13 free; ski, golf plans; higher rates special events. Crib free. TV; cable, VCR avail (movies). Indoor pool; whirlpool, poolside serv, lifeguard. Restaurant 6 am-11 pm. Bar 11-1 am; entertainment Tue-Sun. Ck-out noon. Coin lndry. Meeting rms. Business servs avail. In-rm modem link. Free airport, RR station, bus depot transportation. Tennis privileges. Downhill ski 10 mi. Exercise equipt; sauna. Game rm. Refrigerator, wet bar in suites. Balconies. Cr cds: A, C, D, DS, ER, MC, V.

⬛ 🏂 🏌 🏊 🏋 ⛵ 🔥 **SC**

Inn

★★ **PONDA ROWLAND BED & BREAKFAST.** *RR 1 Box 349 (18612), 5 mi N on US 11, 10 mi N on PA 309.* 570/639-3245; FAX 570/639-5531; res: 800/854-3286. 5 rms, 2 story. No rm phones. S, D $70-$95; each addl $25; under 3 free; 2-day min hols. Crib free. 2 cable TVs. Playground. Complimentary full bkfst. Complimentary coffee in rms. Ck-out noon, ck-in 1 pm. Business servs avail. Refrigerators. Picnic tables. On 130-acre farm. Country antiques. Totally nonsmoking. Cr cds: A, C, DS, MC, V.

🐾 ⛵ 🔥

Restaurant

★★★ **SABER ROOM.** *94 Butler St (18702).* 717/829-5743. Hrs: 11 am-2:30 pm, 5-11 pm; Sat from 5 pm. Closed Sun, Easter, July 4. Res accepted, required hols. Continental menu. Bar. Wine list. A la carte entrees: lunch $3.95-$8.95, dinner $10.95-$21.95. Specializes in veal, seafood. Family-owned. Cr cds: A, C, D, MC, V.

⬛

Williamsport (C-7)

(See also Lewisburg, Lock Haven)

Settled 1795 **Pop** 31,933 **Elev** 528 ft **Area Code** 570 **Zip** 17701
Information Lycoming County Tourist Promotion Agency, 454 Pine St; 800/358-9900

Now famous as the birthplace of Little League baseball, Williamsport once was known as the "lumber capital of the world." In 1870, a log boom extended seven miles up the Susquehanna River; 300 million feet of sawed lumber were produced each year. When the timber was exhausted the city developed diversified industry and remained prosperous. The historic district of Williamsport, known as "millionaires row," includes homes of former lumber barons.

What to See and Do

Hiawatha. Sightseeing trips down Susquehanna River aboard replica of an old-fashioned paddlewheel riverboat. Public cruises (May–Oct, daily exc Mon). I-180 Reach Rd exit, in Susquehanna State Park. For schedule and fee info, phone 800/358-9900.

Little League Baseball International Headquarters. Summer baseball camp and Little League World Series Stadium are here. (Mon–Fri; closed hols) 1 mi S on US 15. Phone 570/326-1921. **Free** Adj is

Little League Baseball Museum. (Daily; closed Jan 1, Thanksgiving, Dec 25) 1 mi S on US 15. Phone 570/326-3607. **¢¢**

Little Pine State Park. Approx 2,000 acres. Swimming beach; fishing, hunting; boating (ramps, mooring). Cross-country skiing, snowmobiling, sledding, ice skating, ice fishing. Picnicking, playground, store. Tent & trailer sites. Interpretive program. 15 mi SW via US 220, then 13 mi N via PA 44 & Legislative Rte 4001. Phone 570/753-6000. Camping **¢¢¢-¢¢¢¢**

Lycoming County Historical Museum. Exhibits on regional history from 10,000 B.C. to present. Exhibits incl Native American, frontier era; canals; steam fire engine & hose cart; military history; general store; blacksmith shop; woodworker's shop; gristmill; crafts & industry; Victorian parlor and furnished period rms; wildlife; sports & Little League; lumber business. (May–Oct, daily; rest of yr, daily exc Sun; closed major hols) 858 W 4th St. Phone 570/326-3326. **¢¢** Within museum is

Shempp Toy Train Collection. Extensive toy train collection. More than 350 train sets on display, incl the entire Lionel collection. Two detailed running displays allow visitors to start trains, blow whistles. Twelve unique trains incl an American Flyer #3117 and Lionel "Super #381."

Annual Events

Victorian Sunday. House tours, flower show, entertainment. 2nd Sun June.

Lycoming County Fair. 20 mi SE via US 220, at Hughesville Fairgrounds. More than 50 acres of amusements, commercial displays, livestock judging, demolition derbies, grandstand entertainment, food. Mid-July.

Little League World Series. Teams from all over the world compete. 3rd wk Aug.

Motels

✓★ **ECONO LODGE.** *2401 E 3rd St (17701), at US 220.* 570/326-1501; FAX 570/326-9776; res: 800/553-2666. 99 rms, 2 story. S $45-$50; D $50-$55; each addl $5; higher rates Little League World Series. Crib free. Pet accepted. TV; cable (premium). Complimentary coffee in lobby. Restaurant 6 am-8 pm. Bar 6 pm-2 am; entertainment Tues-Sat. Ck-out noon. Meeting rms. Business servs avail. Valet serv. Cr cds: A, C, D, DS, ER, JCB, MC, V.

⬛ 🐾 ⛵ 🔥 **SC**

★★ **HOLIDAY INN.** *1840 E 3rd St (17701).* 570/326-1981; FAX 570/323-9590; res: 800/326-9572. 170 rms, 2 story. S, D $64-$79; each addl $10; under 18 free; higher rates Little League World Series. Crib free. Pet accepted, some restrictions. TV; cable. Pool; lifeguard. Restaurant 6:30-1 am. Rm serv. Bar 11-1:30 am. Ck-out 11 am. Coin lndry. Meeting rms. Business servs avail. In-rm modem link. Cr cds: A, C, D, DS, JCB, MC, V.

⬛ 🐾 🏊 ⛵ 🔥 **SC**

★★ **QUALITY INN.** *234 Montgomery Pike (17702).* 570/323-9801; FAX 570/322-5231; res: 800/221-2222. 115 rms, 3 story. No elvtr. S $55; D $61; each addl $7; suites $85-$90; under 18 free. Crib $4. TV; cable. Pool; poolside serv, lifeguard. Restaurant 6:30 am-1:30 pm, 5-10 pm. Rm serv. Bar 4:30 pm-2 am; entertainment Wed, Fri, Sat. Ck-out noon. Business servs avail. Valet serv. Sundries. Airport, bus depot transportation. Game rm. Cr cds: A, C, D, DS, ER, JCB, MC, V.

⬛ 🏊 ⛵ 🔥 **SC**

Motor Hotel

★★★ **SHERATON INN.** *100 Pine St (17701), at jct PA 220 & US 15.* 570/327-8231; FAX 570/322-2957; res: 800/325-3535. 148 rms, 5 story. S, D $85-$95; suites $150; under 18 free. Crib free. TV; cable. Indoor pool. Restaurant 6:30 am-10 pm. Rm serv. Bar 11:30-2 am; DJ Tues-Sat. Ck-out noon. Meeting rms. Business servs avail. Bellhops. Free airport transportation. Downhill/x-country ski 18 mi. Some refrigerators. Whirlpool in suites. Cr cds: A, C, D, DS, MC, V.

⬛ 🐾 🏂 🏊 ⛵ 🔥 **SC**

Hotel

✓★★★ **GENETTI HOTEL & SUITES.** *200 W 4th St (17701), downtown.* 570/326-6600; FAX 570/326-5006; res: 800/321-1388. 206 rms, 10 story, 42 suites. S $29.95-$59, D $35.95-$65.95, each addl $6, suites $75.95-$139; under 10 free; higher rates Little League World Series. Wkly rates; golf plans. Crib free. Pet accepted. TV; cable (premium), VCR avail. Pool; poolside serv. Restaurant 6:30 am-10 pm. Bar 11-2 am; entertainment Fri, Sat. Ck-out 11 am. Meeting rm. Business servs avail. Barber, beauty shop. Coin lndry. Free airport transportation. Downhill ski, 20 mi. Exercise equipt. Some refrigerators. Cr cds: A, C, D, MC, V.

Inns

★★★ **REIGHARD HOUSE BED & BREAKFAST INN.** *1323 E 3rd St (17701).* 570/326-3593; FAX 570/323-4734; res: 800/326-8335. 6 rms, 2 story. S $58-$68; D $58-$78; each addl $10. Closed Dec 20-Jan 1. Crib $5. TV; cable. Pool privileges. Complimentary full bkfst; afternoon refreshments. Complimentary coffee in rms. Restaurant nearby. Ck-out 11 am, ck-in 3 pm. Business servs avail. In-rm modem link. Free airport, bus depot transportation. X-country ski 8 mi. Health club privileges. Brick and stone mansion (1905); music rm, library; oak & cherry millwork, paneling. Once used as state police barracks. Cr cds: A, C, D, MC, V.

★★ **SHADY LANE BED & BREAKFAST.** *Allegheny Ave (17731), I-180 to US 220.* 570/525-3394; FAX 570/525-3581; res: 800/524-1248. 7 rms. No AC. No rm phones. MAP: S $60; D $75; each addl $15; wkends (2-day min). Children over 12 yrs only. TV rm; cable. Complimentary full bkfst; afternoon refreshments. Restaurant nearby. Ck-out 11 am, ck-in 2 pm. Tennis privileges. 18-hole golf privileges, greens fee $44-$64, putting green, driving range. X-country ski 2 mi. Picnic tables. Totally nonsmoking. Cr cds: C.

Willow Grove (F-10)

(See also Philadelphia)

Pop 35 (est) **Elev** 310 ft **Area Code** 215 & 267 **Zip** 19090

What to See and Do

Bryn Athyn Cathedral. Outstanding example of Gothic architecture. Free guided tours (Apr–Nov, daily). 3 mi N of PA Tpke, exit 27 on PA 611N, then 4 mi E on County Line Rd to PA 232, in Bryn Athyn. Phone 215/947-0266. On grounds adj is

Glencairn Museum. Romanesque-style bldg features medieval sculpture and one of the largest privately owned collections of stained glass in the world; also Egyptian, Greek, Roman, ancient Near East and Native American collections. (Mon–Fri by appt) 1001 Cathedral Rd, at PA 232. Phone 215/938-2600. ¢¢

Graeme Park (1722). A fine example of Georgian architecture; stone house built by Sir William Keith, colonial governor of colony 1717-1726. Tours. (Wed–Sun; closed some hols) 5 mi N on PA 611. Phone 215/343-0965. ¢¢

Motels

★★★ **COURTYARD BY MARRIOTT.** *2350 Easton Rd (19090), PA Tpke exit 27.* 215/830-0550; FAX 215/830-0572; res: 800/321-2211. 149 rms, 3 story. S, D $159; suites $170-$180; wkly, wkend rates. Crib free. TV; cable (premium), VCR avail (movies). Indoor pool; whirlpool. Complimentary coffee in rms. Restaurant 6:30-10 am; Sat, Sun 7-11:30 am. Bar 5-10 pm Mon-Sat. Ck-out noon. Coin lndry. Meeting rms. Business servs avail. In-rm modem link. Valet serv. Airport transportation. Exercise equipt. Refrigerators; microwaves avail. Cr cds: A, C, D, DS, MC, V.

★★ **HAMPTON INN.** *1500 Easton Rd (19090), PA Tpke, exit 27, S on PA 611.* 215/659-3535; FAX 215/659-4040. 150 rms, 5 story. S, D $119-$139; under 18 free; wkend rates. Crib free. TV; cable (premium). Complimentary continental bkfst. Restaurants nearby. Ck-out noon. Meeting rms. Business servs avail. In-rm modem link. Valet. Airport transportation. Exercise equipt; sauna. Health club privileges. Some refrigerators; microwaves avail. Cr cds: A, C, D, DS, MC, V.

Inn

★★★ **JOSEPH AMBLER INN.** *1005 Horsham Rd (19454), 2 mi N on Easton Rd, 7 mi W on Horsham Rd.* 215/362-7500; FAX 215/361-5924. E-mail jai@philanet.com; web philanet.com/jai. 37 rms, 2-3 story. S $88-$190; D $98-$200; each addl $15. TV; VCR avail. Complimentary full bkfst. Restaurant (see JOSEPH AMBLER INN). Ck-out 11 am, ck-in 3 pm. Business center. In-rm modem link. Private parking. Some in-rm whirlpools. Four buildings built 1734-1820; antiques. Cr cds: A, C, D, DS, MC, V.

Restaurants

★★ **CASABLANCA.** *1111 Easton Rd (18976), 6 mi N on PA 611.* 215/343-7715. Hrs: 5-1 am. Res required. Moroccan menu. Setups. Complete meal: 7-course dinner $22. Child's meals. Specialties: Moroccan salad platter, cous cous with mint tea, rabbit. Belly dancers Fri-Sun. Parking. Traditional Moroccan atmosphere. Cr cds: A, C, D, DS, MC, V.

★★★ **JOSEPH AMBLER INN.** *(See Joseph Ambler Inn)* 215/362-7500. E-mail jai@philanet.com; web philanet.com/jai. Hrs: 6-10 pm; Sat from 5 pm; Sun 5-9 pm. Res accepted. Bar 5-11 pm. Semi-a la carte: dinner $18.95-$26.95. Specialties: rack of lamb, crab cakes, salmon en croute. Entertainment Fri. Outdoor dining. In 1820s stone barn. Cr cds: A, C, D, DS, MC, V.

★★ **OTTO'S BRAUHAUS.** *233 Easton Rd (19044), PA Tpke exit 27, ½ mi N on PA 611.* 215/675-1864. Hrs: 7 am-10 pm; early-bird dinner 3-5:30 pm. Closed Dec 25. Res accepted. German, Amer menu. Bar 11 am-midnight. Semi-a la carte: bkfst $3-$8, lunch $5-$11, dinner $9-$20. Child's meals. Specialties: sauerbraten, Wienerschnitzel. Own desserts. Outdoor dining. Musicians Fri, Sat (summer). Large German beer garden. Cr cds: A, C, D, DS, MC, V.

Wrightsville (York Co) (F-7)

(See also Bird-in-Hand, Lancaster, Pennsylvania Dutch Area, York)

Pop 2,396 **Elev** 306 ft **Area Code** 717 **Zip** 17368
E-mail adruck@yorkpa.org **Web** www.yorkpa.org

Information York County Visitors Information Center, 1618 Toronita St, York 17402; 717/848-4000 or 800/673-2429

What to See and Do

Donegal Mills Plantation & Inn (1800). Historic village and resort dating from 1736. Mansion, bakehouse, gardens; restaurant and lodging (yr-round). Plantation tours (Mar-Dec, Sat & Sun afternoons). 5 mi N via US 30, PA 441, 772, in Mt Joy (Lancaster Co). Phone 717/653-2168. Tours ¢¢

Restaurant

★★★ **ACCOMAC INN.** *6330 S River Dr (17368). 717/252-1521.* E-mail accomac@net-works.net; web www.accomac.com. Hrs: 5:30-9:30 pm; Sun 4-8:30 pm; Sun brunch 11 am-2:30 pm. Closed Dec 25. Res accepted; required wkends. Continental, French menu. Bar. Wine list. Semi-a la carte: dinner $16-$32. Sun brunch $22.95-$28.95. Specialties: roast duckling, steak Diane. Own pastries. Porch dining. Reconstructed historic building (1775) on banks of river. Cr cds: A, C, MC, V.

York (F-7)

(See also Hanover, Harrisburg, Lancaster, Pennsylvania Dutch Area, Wrightsville)

Founded 1741 **Pop** 42,192 **Elev** 400 ft **Area Code** 717
E-mail adruck@yorkpa.org **Web** www.yorkpa.org
Information Convention and Visitors Bureau, 1 Market Way East, 17401, phone 800/673-2429; or the Visitors Information Center, 1618 Toronita St, 17402, phone 717/843-6660

York claims to be the first capital of the United States. The Continental Congress met here in 1777 and adopted the Articles of Confederation, using the phrase "United States of America" for the first time. The first Pennsylvania town founded west of the Susquehanna River, York was and is still based on an agricultural and industrial economy. The city is dotted with 17 historical markers and 35 brass or bronze tablets marking historical events or places. There are over 10 recreation areas in the county.

What to See and Do

Bob Hoffman Weightlifting Hall of Fame. Weightlifting section honors Olympic weightlifters, powerlifters, bodybuilders and strongmen; displays incl samples of Iron Game artifacts, memorabilia and photos. (Daily exc Sun; closed hols) 4 mi N via I-83, exit 11; at York Barbell Co corporate headquarters. Phone 717/767-6481. **Free**

Central Market House. Opened in March 1888. Over 70 vendors offer fresh produce, homemade baked goods, regional handcrafts and specialty items. (Tues, Thurs, Sat; closed hols) 34 W Philadelphia St. Phone 717/848-2243. **Free**

Fire Museum of York County. Turn-of-the-century firehouse preserves 2 centuries of firefighting history; from leather bucket brigades to hand-drawn hose carts and pumps, horse-drawn equipment and finally to motorized equipment; artifacts and memorabilia; fire chief's office and firefighter's sleeping quarters are re-created, complete with brass slide pole. (Apr–Oct, Sat & 2nd Sun every month; also by appt; closed hols) 757 W Market St. Phone 717/843-0464. ¢

Friends Meeting House (1766). Original virgin pine paneling; restored. Regular meetings are still held here. (By appt) 135 W Philadelphia St. Phone 717/843-2285. **Free**

Gifford Pinchot State Park. Approx 2,300 acres; 340-acre lake. Fishing, hunting; boating (rentals, mooring, launching). Hiking. Cross-country skiing, ice skating, ice fishing, ice boating. Picnicking, store. Tent & trailer sites, cabins. Nature center, interpretive center. Standard fees. 14 mi NW on PA 74 to Rossville, then NE on PA 177. Phone 717/432-5011.

Harley-Davidson, Inc. Guided tour through the motorcycle assembly plant and the Rodney Gott Antique Motorcycle Museum. Children under 12 and cameras not permitted on plant tour. Plant and museum combination tour

(Mon–Fri); museum tour (Sat). 1425 Eden Rd, 2 mi E on US 30. Schedule may vary; phone 717/848-1177. **Free**

Historical Society of York County. Includes library with genealogical records (daily exc Sun; fee for nonmembers). Museum features exhibits on the history of York County. Combination ticket for all historic sites maintained by the society. (Daily; closed most major hols) 250 E Market St. Phone 717/848-1587. Museum ¢; Combination ticket ¢¢¢ Sites include

Bonham House (ca 1875). Historic house reflects life in late 19th century. (By appt; closed most hols) 152 E Market St. Phone 717/848-1587. ¢

General Gates' House (1751). It was here that Lafayette gave a toast to Washington, marking the end of a movement to replace him. Also here are **Golden Plough Tavern** (1741), one of the earliest bldgs in York, which reflects the Germanic background of many of the settlers in its furnishings and half-timber architecture, and the **Bobb Log House** (1811), furnished with painted and grained furniture. (Daily; closed most major hols) 157 W Market St (enter on N Pershing Ave). ¢¢

Ski Roundtop. Triple, 5 double chairlifts, 2 J-bars, 2 pony lifts; patrol, school, rentals; snowmaking; cafeteria; nursery. Longest run 4,100 ft; vertical drop 600 ft. (Mid-Nov–mid-Mar, daily) 12 mi NW on PA 74, then ½ N on PA 177 to Mt Airy Rd, then to Roundtop Rd, follow signs. Phone 717/432-9631 or 800/767-4766 (snow report). ¢¢¢¢¢

Warrington Friends Meeting House (1769; expanded in 1782). Fine example of early Quaker meeting house. 14 mi NW on PA 74.

York County Colonial Court House. Replica of 1754 original. Exhibits incl multimedia presentation of Continental Congress's adoption of the Articles of Confederation, audiovisual story of 1777-1778 historic events; original printer's copy of Articles of Confederation, historic documents and artifacts. Tours. (Daily) W Market & Pershing Aves. Phone 717/848-1587. ¢

Annual Event

River Walk Art Festival. Along Codorus Creek at York County Colonial Court House. Late Aug.

Motels

★ **BEST WESTERN INN.** *1415 Kenneth Rd (17404). 717/767-6931; FAX 717/767-6938; res: 800/528-1234.* 105 rms, 3 story. S $57-$83; D $68-$93; each addl $5; under 18 free. Crib free. TV; cable (premium), VCR avail (movies). Complimentary continental bkfst. Restaurant adj 11 am-midnight. Ck-out noon. Meeting rms. In-rm modem link. Health club privileges. Some refrigerators; microwaves avail. Cr cds: A, C, D, DS, JCB, MC, V.

✓ ★ **BUDGET HOST INN.** *1162 Haines Rd (17402), I-83 exit 7. 717/755-1068; FAX 717/757-5571; res: 800/283-4678.* E-mail pmentx pres@aol.com. 40 rms, 1-2 story. S $34-$35; D $36-$50; each addl $4; under 12 free. Crib $2. TV; cable, VCR avail (movies $5). Coffee in rms. Restaurant adj open 24 hrs. Ck-out 11 am. Some refrigerators; microwaves avail. Cr cds: A, C, D, DS, MC, V.

★★ **HAMPTON INN.** *1550 Mt Zion Rd (17402), at US 30E, near Galleria Mall. 717/840-1500; FAX 717/840-1567; res: 800/426-7866.* Web www.hampton-inn.com. 144 rms, 5 story. S $79-$83; D $87-$91; suites, kit units $95-$103; under 18 free. Crib free. TV; cable (premium), VCR avail. Heated pool. Coffee in rms. Complimentary continental bkfst. Restaurant adj 6 am-10 pm. Ck-out 11 am. Coin lndry. Meeting rms. In-rm modem link. Sundries. Exercise equipt. Refrigerator in suites. Picnic tables. Cr cds: A, C, D, DS, MC, V.

★★★ **HOLIDAY INN.** *334 Arsenal Rd (17402), at Toronita St. 717/845-5671; FAX 717/845-1898; res: 800/465-4329.* 100 rms, 2 story. S, D $69-$79; under 18 free. Crib free. TV; cable (premium). Pool. Restaurant 6 am-2 pm, 5:30-10 pm. Rm serv. Bar 5 pm-midnight. Meeting rms. Business servs avail. Valet serv. Sundries. Health club privileges. Microwaves avail. Cr cds: A, C, D, DS, ER, JCB, MC, V.

★★★ **RAMADA INN.** *2600 E Market St (17402). 717/755-1966; FAX 717/755-6936; res: 800/465-4329.* 120 rms, 2 story. S, D, studio rms $69-$79; under 18 free. Crib free. TV; cable (premium). Pool; lifeguard. Restaurant 6 am-2 pm, 5:30-10 pm. Rm serv 7:30 am-9:30 pm. Bar 4 pm-midnight. Ck-out noon. Business servs avail. In-rm modem link. Valet serv. Sundries. Free airport transportation. Health club privileges. Refrigerators, microwaves avail. Cr cds: A, C, D, DS, JCB, MC, V.

Motor Hotel

★★★ **HOLIDAY INN.** *2000 Loucks Rd (17404), at West Manchester Mall. 717/846-9500; FAX 717/764-5038; res: 800/465-4329.* 181 rms, 2 story. S, D $72-$98; under 18 free. Crib $10. Pet accepted. TV; cable (premium). 2 pools, 1 indoor; whirlpool, poolside serv, lifeguard. Playground. Restaurant 6:30 am-9:30 pm. Rm serv. Bar 3 pm-2 am. Ck-out 11 am. Meeting rms. Business servs avail. Bellhops. Valet serv. Miniature golf. Exercise equipt; sauna. Cr cds: A, C, D, DS, JCB, MC, V.

Hotel

★★★ **YORKTOWNE HOTEL.** *48 E Market St (17405), E Market & Duke Sts. 717/848-1111; FAX 717/854-7678; res: 800/233-9323.* 162 rms, 8 story. S $52-$89; D $59-$96; each addl $7; suites $95-$225. Crib free. TV; cable (premium). Restaurants 6:30-2 am. Bar from 11 am. Ck-out noon. Meeting rms. Business servs avail. In-rm modem link. Gift shop. Barber. Free valet parking. Airport transportation. Exercise equipt. Health club privileges. Some in-rm whirlpools; microwaves avail. Cr cds: A, C, D, DS, MC, V.

Restaurants

★★ **SAN CARLO'S.** *333 Arsenal Rd US 30 (17402), I-83 exit 9E. 717/854-2028.* Hrs: 4-9:30 pm; Fri, Sat to 10 pm. Res accepted. Continental menu. Bar. Semi-a la carte: dinner $9.95-$18.95. Child's meals. Specializes in fresh seafood, prime rib, veal. Entertainment. Renovated 175-yr-old barn; original fieldstone walls. Cr cds: A, C, D, DS, MC, V.

★★★ **THE ALTLAND HOUSE.** *US 30 & PA 194 (17301), W on US 30. 717/259-9535.* Web www.altlandhouse.com. Hrs: 11 am-10 pm; Mon to 9 pm; Fri, Sat to 11 pm; Sun 11:30 am-9 pm; Sun brunch to 2 pm. Closed Dec 24, 25. Res accepted. Bar. Semi-a la carte: lunch $3.50-$22.95, dinner $7.50-$27.95. Sun brunch $12.95. Child's meals. Specializes in crab cakes, desserts. Cr cds: A, C, DS, MC, V.

South Carolina

Population: 3,497,800
Land area: 30,207 square miles
Elevation: 0-3,560 feet
Highest point: Sassafras Mountain (Pickens County)
Entered union: Eighth of original 13 states (May 23, 1788)
Capital: Columbia
Motto: Prepared in mind and resources; While I breathe, I hope
Nickname: Palmetto State
State flower: Carolina yellow jessamine
State bird: Carolina wren
State tree: Palmetto
State fair: October 5-15, 2000, in Columbia
Time zone: Eastern
Web: www.prt.state.sc.us/sc

In South Carolina, the modern age has neither masked the romance of the Old South nor overshadowed the powerful events of colonial and Confederate times. This state's turbulent and romantic history tells a story that remains deeply ingrained in the history of the United States.

Spanish explorers made the first attempt to settle in present-day South Carolina in 1526, less than 35 years after the Europeans discovered America. A severe winter, hostile natives and disease proved too much for the Spanish to overcome, and the settlement was abandoned. A group of French Huguenots, led by Jean Ribaut, landed near the site of present-day Parris Island Marine Corps Base in 1562. The French colony might have been a success, had not Ribaut's return to the colony from France on business been delayed. The remaining colonists, fearing they had been abandoned, built a craft and sailed for home. Light winds stranded their boat at sea, and they faced the danger of starvation until a passing English ship rescued them.

The task of settlement fell to the English, whose challenge to Spanish control of the New World eventually met with success. A land grant from England's King Charles II gave the Carolinas to eight English noblemen (still known today as the "Lords Proprietors"). In 1670, the English arrived at Albemarle Point and established Charles Towne, the first successful European settlement in the Carolinas.

During the Revolutionary War, almost 200 battles and skirmishes were fought in South Carolina. The first overt act of revolution occurred at Fort Charlotte on July 12, 1775; this was the first British property seized by American Revolutionary forces. On December 20, 1860, South Carolina became the first state to secede from the Union. The initial clash of the Civil War also occurred on South Carolina soil; the bombardment of Fort Sumter in 1861 resulted in its seizure by Confederate forces, which maintained possession until the evacuation of Charleston in 1865. Bloodied, impoverished and blackened by the fires of General Sherman's march to the sea, South Carolina emerged from the difficult Reconstruction days and was readmitted to the Union in 1868.

For most of the period since the Civil War, South Carolina has had economic problems, but in recent years these have eased as industry has been attracted by hospitable communities and favorable tax rates. From town to town, throughout the state, diversified industries have brought with them greater prosperity. Power projects have been created by damming the Santee, Saluda, Savannah and other rivers. Four atomic energy plants provide commercial energy. Tourism, the state's second-largest industry, continues to grow.

A temperate climate makes South Carolina an attractive all-year resort. The cool upland western area merges into a subtropical seacoast. South Carolina is a major producer of tobacco, cotton, pine lumber, corn, oats, sweet potatoes, soybeans, peanuts, peaches, melons, beef cattle and hogs.

When to Go/Climate

South Carolina enjoys a moderate climate. Summers, however, especially in the low country and along the coast, can be uncomfortably hot and humid. The barrier islands and upcountry elevations provide summer havens from the blistering heat. Early spring and late fall are good times to visit, with comfortable temperatures and moderate rainfall.

AVERAGE HIGH/LOW TEMPERATURES (°F)

CHARLESTON

Jan 56/41	May 80/66	Sept 83/71
Feb 59/43	June 85/72	Oct 75/61
Mar 65/50	July 88/75	Nov 67/52
Apr 73/58	Aug 87/75	Dec 60/45

GREENVILLE

Jan 50/30	May 80/56	Sept 81/61
Feb 54/32	June 86/64	Oct 72/49
Mar 64/40	July 88/68	Nov 63/41
Apr 72/48	Aug 87/67	Dec 53/33

Parks and Recreation Finder

Directions to and information about the parks and recreation areas below are given under their respective town/city sections. Please refer to those sections for details.

NATIONAL PARK AND RECREATION AREAS

Key to abbreviations. I.H.S. = International Historic Site; I.P.M. = International Peace Memorial; N.B. = National Battlefield; N.B.P. = National Battlefield Park; N.B.C. = National Battlefield & Cemetery; N.C. = National Conservation Area; N.E.M. = National Expansion Memorial; N.F. = National Forest; N.G. = National Grassland; N.H. = National Historical Park; N.H.C. = National Heritage Corridor; N.H.S. = National Historic Site; N.L. = National Lakeshore; N.M. = National Monument; N.M.P. = National Military Park; N.Mem. = National Memorial; N.P. = National Park; N.Pres. = National Preserve; N.R. = National Recreational Area; N.R.R. = National Recreational River; N.Riv. = National River; N.S. = National Seashore; N.S.R. = National Scenic Riverway; N.S.T. = National Scenic Trail; N.Sc. = National Scientific Reserve; N.V.M. = National Volcanic Monument.

Place Name	Listed Under
Congaree Swamp N.M.	COLUMBIA
Cowpens N.B.	GAFFNEY
Fort Sumter N.M.	same
Francis Marion N.F.	CHARLESTON
Kings Mountain N.M.P.	same
Ninety Six N.H.S.	GREENWOOD
Sumter N.F.	GREENWOOD

STATE PARK AND RECREATION AREAS

Key to abbreviations. I.P. = Interstate Park; S.A.P. = State Archaeological Park; S.B. = State Beach; S.C. = State Conservation Area; S.C.P. = State Conservation Park; S.Cp. = State Campground; S.F. = State Forest; S.G. = State Garden; S.H.A. = State Historic Area; S.H.P. = State Historic Park; S.H.S. = State Historic Site; S.M.P. = State Marine Park; S.N.A. = State Natural Area; S.P. = State Park; S.P.C. = State Public Campground; S.R. = State Reserve; S.R.A. = State Recreation Area; S.Res. = State Reservoir; S.Res.P. = State Resort Park; S.R.P. = State Rustic Park.

Place Name	Listed Under
Aiken S.P.	AIKEN
Andrew Jackson S.P.	ROCK HILL
Baker Creek S.P.	GREENWOOD
Barnwell S.P.	ALLENDALE
Caesar's Head S.P.	GREENVILLE
Cheraw S.P.	CHERAW
Chester S.P.	CHESTER
Colleton S.P.	WALTERBORO
Croft S.P.	SPARTANBURG
Dreher Island S.P.	NEWBERRY
Edisto Beach S.P.	CHARLESTON
Hickory Knob Resort S.Res.P.	GREENWOOD
Hunting Island S.P.	BEAUFORT
Huntington Beach S.P.	GEORGETOWN
Kings Mountain S.P.	KINGS MOUNTAIN NATIONAL MILITARY PARK
Lake Greenwood S.P.	GREENWOOD
Lake Hartwell S.P.	ANDERSON
Lake Wateree S.P.	CAMDEN
Landsford Canal S.P.	ROCK HILL
Lee S.P.	HARTSVILLE
Little Pee Dee S.P.	DILLON
Lynches River S.P.	FLORENCE
Myrtle Beach S.P.	MYRTLE BEACH
N.R Goodale S.P.	CAMDEN
Oconee S.P.	CLEMSON
Old Dorchester S.P.	CHARLESTON
Paris Mountain S.P.	GREENVILLE
Poinsett S.P.	SUMTER
River Bridge S.P.	ALLENDALE
Sadlers Creek S.P.	ANDERSON
Santee S.P.	SANTEE
Sesquicentennial S.P.	COLUMBIA
Table Rock S.P.	GREENVILLE
Woods Bay S.P.	FLORENCE

Water-related activities, hiking, various other sports, picnicking and visitor centers, as well as camping, are available in many of these areas. Cabins are located at Barnwell, Cheraw, Devils Fork, Dreher Island, Edisto Beach, Givhans Ferry, Hickory Knob Resort, Hunting Island, Keowee-Toxaway, Myrtle Beach, Oconee, Poinsett, Santee and Table Rock. No pets in cabins. Cabin reservations made at individual parks. Camping: 14-day maximum; reservations accepted only at Calhoun Falls, Devils Fork, Dreher Island, Edisto Beach, Hunting Island, Huntington Beach, Lake

Hartwell, Myrtle Beach, Oconee, Santee and Table Rock; $10-$20/night; pets on leash only. Not all state parks are open every day; hours of operation also vary. Contact Columbia office or individual park before making final trip plans. Daily parking fee at major coastal parks in summer, $3-$15. Swimming fee at inland parks with supervised areas & bathhouses (early June-late Aug), $2; age 3-12, $1.50; ocean swimming free. Fees subject to change. For cabin rates and further information contact Department of Parks, Recreation & Tourism, Edgar A. Brown Bldg, 1205 Pendleton St, Columbia 29201; 803/734-0156 or 888/88-PARKS.

FISHING & HUNTING

There is no closed fishing season; well-stocked lakes and rivers are close at hand in all parts of the state. Surf casting and deep-sea fishing can be enjoyed all along the Atlantic shore. Mountain streams offer trout fishing. Nonresident freshwater license: $35; seven-day nonresident license: $11. Saltwater stamp: $5.50. No license or permit required of children under 16. Fees subject to change.

Quail, dove, wild turkey, white-tailed deer, rabbit, squirrel and fox are all legal quarry. Nonresident annual license: $75; ten-day (consecutive) license: $50; three-day (consecutive) license: $25; wildlife management area permit: $76. Nonresident big game permit for deer, turkey and bear: $80. State duck stamp: $5.50. Fees subject to change. For further hunting and fishing information contact South Carolina Department of Natural Resources, PO Box 167, Columbia 29202; 803/734-3888 (general information) or 803/734-3886 (wildlife and freshwater fisheries).

Driving Information

Safety belts are mandatory for all persons anywhere in vehicle. Children must be in an approved safety seat or wear a safety belt. For further information phone 803/737-8340.

INTERSTATE HIGHWAY SYSTEM

The following alphabetical listing of South Carolina towns in *Mobil Travel Guide* shows that these cities are within 10 miles of the indicated Interstate highways. A highway map should, however, be checked for the nearest exit.

Highway Number	Cities/Towns within 10 miles
Interstate 20	Aiken, Camden, Columbia, Darlington, Florence.
Interstate 26	Charleston, Clinton, Columbia, Newberry, Orangeburg, Spartanburg.
Interstate 77	Columbia, Rock Hill.
Interstate 85	Anderson, Clemson, Gaffney, Greenville, Spartanburg.
Interstate 95	Darlington, Dillon, Florence, Hardeeville, Santee, Walterboro.

Additional Visitor Information

For additional information on South Carolina contact the Department of Parks, Recreation & Tourism, 1205 Pendleton St, Columbia 29201; 803/734-0122 or 888/88-PARKS (Toll-Free).

There are ten travel information centers in South Carolina; visitors will find the information provided at these stops useful for planning travel and making lodging reservations in the state. Their locations are: at the eastern end of the state, on I-95 on the SC/NC border; in the eastern coastal region on US 17 on SC/NC border; in the southern section on US 301 on the SC/GA border, and on I-95 on SC/GA border; in midstate center on the southbound side of I-95 near Santee; on the southwestern side on I-20 on the SC/GA border; in the western part of the state on I-85 on the SC/GA border; located in the northwestern part of the state are centers on I-85 on the SC/NC border and on I-26 on the SC/NC border; in the northern part of the state on I-77 on the SC/NC border, and also at the State House Tour and Information Center located in Columbia.

Aiken (D-3)

(See also Allendale, Orangeburg)

Founded 1834 **Pop** 19,872 **Elev** 476 ft **Area Code** 803
E-mail chamber@aiken.net **Web** www.chamber.aiken.net
Information Chamber of Commerce, 121 Richland Ave E, PO Box 892, 29802; 803/641-1111

Aiken is a popular social and sports center in the winter months, providing flat-racing training, steeplechase and harness racing, polo, fox hunts, drag hunts, tennis and golf. The University of South Carolina–Aiken is located here.

What to See and Do

Aiken County Historical Museum. Period rm settings and displays in late-1800s home. Log cabin (1808) and one-rm schoolhouse (1890) on grounds. Special features incl an archaeology exhibit and a 1950s drug store. Museum store. (Tues-Fri, also Sat & Sun afternoons; closed hols) 433 Newberry St SW. Phone 803/642-2015. **Donation**

Aiken State Park. Approx 1,000 acres on the South Edisto River. Swimming; fishing; boating (rentals). Nature trail. Picnicking (shelters), playground. Camping (hookups, dump station). Standard fees. 16 mi E, on unnumbered road between US 78 & SC 4. Phone 803/649-2857.

Hopeland Gardens. A 14-acre public garden on former estate; terraces, reflecting pools, continuous blooms; sculptures. Garden trail for the visually impaired. Summer concert series (May-Aug, Mon eves). (Daily) Whiskey Rd & Dupree Pl. Phone 803/642-7630. **Free** Also here is

Thoroughbred Racing Hall of Fame. Enshrinement of champion horses trained and wintered in Aiken. (Oct-May, daily exc Mon) Phone 803/642-7630. **Free**

Redcliffe. On 350 acres. Built in 1850s by James Henry Hammond. Greek-revival mansion furnished with family pieces, Southern antiques, art collection, historic documents and books. Picnic area. (Thurs-Mon) 15 mi SE off US 278, near Beech Island. Phone 803/827-1473. Mansion ¢

Annual Events

Triple Crown. 3 events: trials (Aiken Training Track), steeplechase (Clark Field), harness race (Aiken Mile Track). 3 consecutive Sat Mar.

Lobster Race. Aiken restaurants provide seafood fare. Festivities incl lobster races, beach music and other activities. Phone 803/648-4981. May.

Seasonal Event

Polo games. Whitney Field. Sun afternoons. Feb-July, & Sept-Nov.

Motel

✓★★ **RAMADA INN.** *110 Frontage Rd (29801), at jct SC 19, I-20 exit 18.* 803/502-0000; FAX 803/502-0005; res: 800/272-6232. 110 units, 2 story. S, D $49-$53; each addl $6; under 18 free; higher rates Masters Golf Tournament. Crib free. Pet accepted, some restrictions. TV; cable (premium), VCR avail. Pool; wading pool. Restaurant 6:30-9:30 am, 6-10 pm; closed Sun. Rm serv. Bar 5-10 pm. Ck-out noon. Meeting rms. Business servs avail. Refrigerators, microwaves avail. Cr cds: A, C, D, DS, ER, JCB, MC, V.

D 🐾 ⚲ ⛆ 🔥 SC

Inn

★★★ **WILLCOX INN.** *100 Colleton Ave & Whiskey Rd (29801).* 803/649-1377; FAX 803/643-0971; res: 800/368-1047. 24 rms, 3 story, 6 suites. S, D $95; suites $105-$135; package plans; higher rates Masters Golf Tournament. TV; cable (premium), VCR avail. Restaurant 7 am-2 pm, 6-9 pm. Rm serv. Bar; entertainment Fri, Sat. Ck-out noon, ck-in 3 pm.

Meeting rm. Business servs avail. Golf privileges. Health club privileges. Refrigerators. English country decor. Built 1898; antique furnishings. Cr cds: A, C, D, DS, MC, V.

D 🐾 ⊠ 🔥

Allendale (E-4)

(See also Aiken, Orangeburg, Walterboro)

Pop 4,410 **Elev** 191 ft **Area Code** 803 **Zip** 29810
Information Chamber of Commerce, PO Box 517; 803/584-0082

Moved six miles in 1872 to its present site to be on the old Port Royal Railroad line, Allendale is an agricultural town with access to the lush hunting and fishing areas of the Savannah River Valley. More than 130 commercial farms with an average size in excess of 1,000 acres—the largest in the state—surround the town.

What to See and Do

Barnwell State Park. Approx 300 acres preserved in natural state with an abundance of trees, flowers. Boating (rentals); fishing. Nature trails. Picnicking (shelters), barbecue pit, playground. Camping, cabins. Standard fees. 17 mi N on US 278 to Barnwell, then 7 mi N on SC 3. Phone 803/284-2212.

Rivers Bridge State Park. Approx 400 acres on site of Civil War skirmish. River fishing. Nature trails. Picnicking (shelters), playground, recreation building. Camping (hookups, dump station). Standard fees. 15 mi E off US 641. Phone 803/267-3675 or -3621.

Anderson (C-3)

(See also Clemson, Greenville, Greenwood)

Founded 1826 **Pop** 26,184 **Elev** 770 ft **Area Code** 864
E-mail aacoc@carol.net
Information Anderson Area Chamber of Commerce, 706 E Greenville St, PO Box 1568, 29622; 864/226-3454

Textile mills and fiberglass plants lead an array of diversified industries that team with the products of the surrounding farmland to make Anderson a lively business center. The town was created as the seat of Anderson County; both were named for General Robert Anderson, who fought in the Revolutionary War.

What to See and Do

Agricultural Museum. Antique farming equipment, tools, pre-Eli Whitney cotton gin. (By appt) On US 76. Phone 864/646-3782. **Free**

Hartwell Dam and Lake. This is a 56,000-acre reservoir with a 962-mi shoreline created by a dam on the Savannah River. Swimming, waterskiing; boating (81 ramps, 5 marinas); fishing. Picnicking (shelters). Camping (Mar-Nov; some all yr; hookups, dump station). Fee for some activities. W & S of town via US 29. Phone 706/376-4788 or 888/893-0678. On lake are

  Lake Hartwell State Park. Located on 680 acres along Lake Hartwell. Swimming; fishing; boating (ramps). Nature trail. Picnicking (shelter), playground, store. Camping (hookups, dump station), laundry. (Daily) Standard fees. S on I-85 exit 1. Phone 864/972-3352.

  Sadlers Creek State Park. On 395 acres. Lake fishing; boating (ramps). Nature trails. Picnicking (shelters), playground. Camping (hookups, dump station). Standard fees. (Daily) 13 mi SW off I-85 & SC 187. Phone 864/226-8950.

"The Old Reformer." Cannon used by both British and Americans during Revolution; was fired in 1860 when Ordinance of Secession was signed. In front of courthouse, Main & Whitner Sts.

Pendleton Historic District. Settled in 1790, this town was the seat of what is now Anderson, Oconee and Pickens counties. There are self-guided tours (free), 2½-hr guided group tours (by appt, fee) or auto/walking tape tours (cassette, also in French; fee) of 45 historic homes and bldgs. The Pendleton District Historical and Recreational Commission, 125 E Queen St, PO Box 565, phone 864/646-3782, has tour info (Mon-Fri; closed hols). Research library, Hunter's Store (ca 1850) across from village green; arts and crafts shop; visitor center (Mon-Fri; closed hols). 7 mi NW of I-85 off US 76. On Pendleton Town Square are

  Historic homes. Two of the many beautiful homes in the area are Ashtabula and Woodburn. (Apr-Oct, Sun; also by appt) Phone 864/646-3782. Per house ¢¢

  Pendleton Farmers' Society Building (1826). Begun as the courthouse, bought and completed by Farmers' Society. Believed to be oldest Farmers' Society bldg in continuous use in America.

Annual Event

Anderson County Fair. Mid-Sept.

Motels

★★ **HOLIDAY INN.** *3025 N Main St (29621), I-85 exit 19A, on US 76.* 864/226-6051; FAX 864/964-9145; res: 800/272-6232. 130 rms, 2 story. S $59-$64; D $65-$70; each addl $6; under 18 free; higher rates Clemson Univ football games. Crib free. Pet accepted, some restrictions. TV; cable. Pool. Complimentary coffee in rms. Restaurant 6:30 am-10 pm. Rm serv. Bar 5 pm-midnight. Ck-out noon. Coin lndry. Meeting rms. Business servs avail. In-rm modem link. Valet serv. Health club privileges. Refrigerators, microwaves avail. Cr cds: A, C, D, DS, MC, V.

D 🐾 ⊠ ⊠ 🔥 SC

✓ ★★ **LA QUINTA INN.** *3430 N Main St (29621).* 864/225-3721; FAX 864/225-7789; res: 800/687-6667. 100 rms, 2 story. S $58-$65; D $64-$71; each addl $7; under 18 free. Crib free. TV; cable. Pool. Complimentary continental bkfst. Ck-out noon. Meeting rms. Business servs avail. In-rm modem link. Cr cds: A, C, D, DS, JCB, MC, V.

⊠ 🔥 SC

★ **SUPER 8 MOTEL.** *3302 Cinema Ave (29621).* 864/225-8384; FAX 864/225-8384. 62 rms, 3 story. No elvtr. S $34.88-$38.88; D $40.88-$48.88; each addl after 3, $4; under 12 free; higher rates Clemson football wkends, special events. TV. Complimentary coffee. Restaurant nearby. Ck-out 11 am. Cr cds: A, C, D, DS, MC, V.

D ⊠ ⊠ 🔥 SC

Beaufort (F-5)

(See also Charleston, Hardeeville, Hilton Head Island, Kiawah Island, Walterboro)

Founded 1710 **Pop** 9,576 **Elev** 11 ft **Area Code** 843 **Zip** 29902
E-mail chamber@lslc.net **Web** www.beaufortsc.org
Information Greater Beaufort Chamber of Commerce, 1106 Carteret St, PO Box 910, 29901-0910; 843/524-3163

The atmosphere of antebellum days is preserved in this old town's gracious houses and churches. Second oldest town in the state, Beaufort (BEW-fort) looks to the sea from Port Royal Island, one of 64 islands that comprise the county. Tourism and the military are major sources of income in this community.

Spanish explorers first noted the harbor in 1514-1515. In 1526, colonists from Spain made an unsuccessful attempt to settle the area. In 1562, a group of Frenchmen established the first Protestant colony on the continent, which also failed. English and Scottish attempts followed, with success finally coming when the present city was laid out and named for the Duke of Beaufort. The town was almost completely destroyed by Native Americans in 1715, captured by the British in the Revolution and menaced by British cannon in 1812. Nearly the entire population evacuated Beaufort when it was captured by Northern troops during the Civil War.

What to See and Do

Beaufort Museum. Collections of antique guns, fossils, paintings, arrowheads, Civil War relics. (Mon & Tues, Thurs-Sat; closed major hols) 713 Craven St, in the Beaufort Arsenal (1795). Phone 843/525-7077. ¢

Hunting Island State Park. A 5,000-acre barrier island in a semitropical setting; beaches, forest, marshes; lighthouse. Swimming, ocean fishing. Nature trails. Picnicking (shelters), playground, boardwalk; concession. Camping (hookups, dump station), cabins. Recreation & nature programs. Standard fees (higher rates Apr-Nov). 16 mi SE on US 21. Phone 843/838-2011.

John Mark Verdier House Museum (ca 1790). Federal period house once known as the Lafayette Bldg; the Marquis de Lafayette is said to have spoken here from the piazza in 1825. (Tues-Sat; closed Thanksgiving, Dec 25) 801 Bay St. Phone 843/524-6334. ¢¢

Marine Corps Air Station. Home of Marine Aircraft Groups MACS-5, MWSS-273, MALS-31 and CSSD-23. Windshield tours avail. Phone 843/522-7201 or -7203. **Free**

National Cemetery (1863). More than 11,000 interments, incl Confederate and Union soldiers. Boundary St.

Parris Island. Famous US Marine Corps Recruit Depot. Visitor Center in Bldg 283; Museum in War Memorial Bldg. Ribaut Monument is memorial to Jean Ribaut, French Huguenot founder of Charlesfort (1562); Iwo Jima monument; monument to Spanish settlement of Santa Elena (1521). Historic driving & narrated bus tours depart from Visitor Center (driving tours, daily; bus tours, Sat-Wed). (Daily) 10 mi S. Phone 843/525-3650. **Free**

St Helena's Episcopal Church (1712). Still in use; tombstones from surrounding burial ground became operating tables when church was used as a hospital during the Civil War. Silver communion set in church donated in 1734 by Capt John Bull in memory of his wife, who was captured by Native Americans. (Daily exc Sun) 507 Newcastle St, at North St. Phone 843/522-1712.

US Naval Hospital. On grounds are ruins of Fort Frederick (1731), one of largest "tabby" (cement & oyster shell) forts in US. 4 mi S on SC 802, between Beaufort & Port Royal, an early French settlement.

Annual Events

Beaufort Water Festival. Along waterfront at harbor. Includes parade, water show, boat races, concerts, dance. Phone 843/524-0600. Mid-July.

Fall Tour of Homes and Gardens. Contact Historic Beaufort Foundation, PO Box 11, 29901; 843/524-6334. Early Oct.

Beaufort Shrimp Festival. Waterfront. Bridge Run, shrimp recipe tastings, frogmore stew contest, Bless'en de Fleet. Phone 843/524-3163. Mid-Oct.

Motel

★★ **BEST WESTERN.** 1015 Bay St (29902), in historic district. 843/522-2090; FAX 843/521-4858; res: 800/528-1234. 43 rms, 2 story. Mid-Feb-Nov: S, D $80-$99; each addl $10; under 12 free; higher rates special events; lower rates rest of yr. Crib free. TV; cable (premium). Pool. Complimentary continental bkfst. Restaurant nearby. Ck-out 11 am. Meeting rms. Business servs avail. In-rm modem link. Exercise equipt. Bicycle rentals. Opp bay. Cr cds: A, C, D, DS, MC, V.

🏊 🧖 ⛷ 🔥 SC

Motor Hotel

✓ ★★★ **HOLIDAY INN.** 2001 Boundary St; Hwy 21 & Ribaut Rd. (29902). 843/524-2144; FAX 843/524-2144; res: 800/465-4329. 152 rms, 4 story. S, D $74; each addl $8; under 19 free. Crib free. TV; cable (premium). Pool. Coffee in rms. Restaurant 6:30 am-2 pm, 5:30-9 pm. Rm serv.

Bar 5-11 pm; Sat to midnight. Meeting rms. Business servs avail. In-rm modem link. Valet serv Mon-Fri. Golf privileges. Refrigerators, microwaves avail. Cr cds: A, C, D, DS, JCB, MC, V.

D 🧖 🏊 ⛷ 🔥 SC

Inns

★★★ **BEAUFORT INN & RESTAURANT.** 809 Port Republic St (29902). 843/521-9000; FAX 843/521-9500. 7 rms, 3 story, 4 suites, 1 cottage. S, D $125-$160; suites $175-$195; cottage $300. Children over 8 yrs in inn only. TV; cable, VCR (movies). Complimentary full bkfst. Complimentary coffee in rms. Restaurant (see BEAUFORT INN). Ck-out 11 am, ck-in 3-10 pm. Luggage handling. Concierge serv. Business servs avail. In-rm modem link. Tennis privileges. Golf privileges. Refrigerators. Some balconies. Built in 1897; double verandas. Totally nonsmoking. Cr cds: A, C, DS, MC, V.

D 🧖 🔥 ⛷ 🏊 🦌

✓ ★★★★ **RHETT HOUSE INN & FINE DINING.** 1009 Craven St (29902). 843/524-9030; FAX 843/524-1310; res: 888/480-9530. E-mail rhetthse@hargray.com; web www.innbook.com/ rhett/html. Reminiscent of a grand plantation house, this Greek-revival townhouse, replete with galleries and gardens, is furnished with antiques and Oriental rugs. 17 rms, 3 story. S, D $125-$225; each addl $25. Children over 5 yrs only. TV; VCR avail. Swimming privileges. Complimentary full bkfst; continental bkfst avail in rms; afternoon refreshments. Ck-out 11 am, ck-in 3 pm. Business servs avail. Tennis privileges, pro. 18-hole golf privileges. Health club privileges. Some fireplaces. Bicycles. Cr cds: A, C, MC, V.

🧖 ⛷ ⛷ 🔥 🦌

★★ **TWO SUNS INN BED & BREAKFAST.** 1705 Bay St (29902), in historic district. 843/522-1122; FAX 843/522-1122; res: 800/532-4244. E-mail 2suns@islc.net; web www.twosunsinn.com. 6 rms, 3 story. Mar-Nov: S $105-$128; D $128-$151; each addl $23; lower rates rest of yr. Children over 12 yrs only. TV avail. Complimentary full bkfst; afternoon refreshments. Restaurant nearby. Ck-out noon, ck-in 3 pm. Business servs avail. Lawn games. Neoclassic-revival house (1917). Veranda overlooks bay. Totally nonsmoking. Cr cds: A, C, D, DS, MC, V.

D ⛷ 🔥 SC

Restaurant

★★★ **BEAUFORT INN.** (See Beaufort Inn) 843/521-9000. Specializes in fresh seafood, veal, game. Hrs: 5-10 pm; Sun brunch 10 am-2 pm. Closed Dec 24-25. Res accepted. Wine list. Semi-a la carte: dinner $17.95-$26.95. Sun brunch $6.95-$14.95. Outdoor dining. Cr cds: A, C, DS, MC, V.

D ⛷

Bennettsville (C-6)

(See also Cheraw, Darlington, Dillon, Florence, Hartsville)

Founded 1819 **Pop** 9,345 **Elev** 150 ft **Area Code** 803 **Zip** 29512

Information Marlboro County Chamber of Commerce, 300 W Main St, PO Box 458; 803/479-3941

Near the geographic center of the Carolinas, Bennettsville radiates highway spokes in every direction. Founded by Welsh settlers, and now the seat of Marlboro County, it has diversified industry including paper and electrical products, textiles and farm equipment. Agriculture is still important; cotton is the leading crop.

What to See and Do

Jennings–Brown House Restoration (1826). Served as headquarters for Union troops when Bennettsville was captured in 1865. The restored house is furnished with antiques pre-dating 1860. (Mon-Fri, also by appt; closed hols) 119 S Marlboro St. Phone 803/479-5624. ¢

Lake Wallace. A 500-acre lake with separate sections for swimming (June-Labor Day), waterskiing; fishing; boating. Waterfowl refuge. At N edge of city, off Country Club Dr. Phone 803/479-3941.

Camden (D-5)

(See also Columbia, Sumter)

Settled 1732 **Pop** 6,696 **Elev** 213 ft **Area Code** 803 **Zip** 29020
E-mail www.camden@camden.net **Web** www.camden-sc.org
Information Kershaw County Chamber of Commerce and Visitor Center, 724 S Broad St, PO Box 605; 803/432-2525 or 800/968-4037

The oldest inland town in the state, Camden was named after Lord Camden, defender of colonial rights. During the Revolution General Cornwallis occupied Camden and made it the principal British garrison in the state and the interior command post for the South. Although several battles were fought in and near the town, including the Battle of Camden, the town was never recaptured by the Americans. Instead, it was evacuated and burned by the British in 1781. Camden contributed six generals to the Confederate cause and served as a storehouse, a hospital for the wounded and a haven of refuge until captured by General Sherman in 1865.

Today, Camden is famous for its history and equestrian sports—horseback riding, horse shows, hunt meets, polo and steeplechase races. There are 200 miles of bridle paths in the area and three racetracks; Springdale Course is an extremely difficult and exciting steeplechase run.

What to See and Do

Bethesda Presbyterian Church (1820). Called House of Five Porches; steeple in rear. Designed by the architect of the Washington Monument, Robert Mills; church is considered a masterpiece. (Daily exc Sun) On US 1, 502 DeKalb St. In front of church is

    DeKalb Monument. German-born hero of Battle of Camden is buried here; monument consists of modest shaft with a base of 24 granite blocks, one for each state in the Union at that time. General Lafayette laid the cornerstone on Mar 9, 1825.

Camden Antique District. Offers all varieties of antiques in over 13 stores, some housing over 35 dealers. (Daily; closed hols) Downtown, bounded by King, DeKalb, Campbell & Fair Sts. Phone 803/432-2525.

Hampton Park. Named for Confederate general who later became governor. Flagstones used in crosswalks were once part of the sidewalks of old Camden and are said to have been brought over as ballast in British ships. Lyttleton St near US 1.

Historic Camden Revolutionary War Park. Archaeological site of South Carolina's oldest inland town. Visitor area incl two early 19th-century log cabins and a restored 18th-century town house. Trails lead to the reconstructed foundation of a pre-Revolutionary War powder magazine, Kershaw–Cornwallis House, and two reconstructed British fortifications. Picnicking, nature trail, historical film. Self-guided and guided tours. (See ANNUAL EVENTS) . (Daily exc Mon; closed some major hols) S Broad St (US 521 S). Phone 803/432-9841. ¢¢

Lake Wateree State Park. Approx 200 acres. Fishing; boating (ramp), bait shop. Nature trail. Picnicking, store. Camping (hookups, dump station). Standard fees. S on US 1, E on SC 34, then N on US 21 to SC 41, continue W. Phone 803/482-6401.

N.R. Goodale State Park. Approx 700 acres. Lake swimming; boating (rentals); fishing. 9-hole golf course. Picnicking (shelters); recreation bldg. Standard fees. 2 mi NW off US 1 on Old Wire Rd. Phone 803/432-2772.

Quaker Cemetery. Buried here are Richard Kirkland, who gained fame in the Battle of Marye's Hill by risking death to take water to dying Union

troops; two of the three residents of the county who won Congressional Medals of Honor prior to World War II; and Dr. George Todd, brother-in-law of Abraham Lincoln. Broad & Meeting Sts, SW edge of town.

Rectory Square. Pantheon; six columns serve as memorial to Camden's six generals of the Confederacy. Chesnut & Lyttleton Sts.

Annual Events

Carolina Downhome Blues Festival & Fine Arts. Center of Kershaw County. Phone 803/425-7676. Mid-Oct.

Revolutionary War Field Days. Broad St. Historic Camden Revolutionary War Site. Two-day Revolutionary War encampment, festivities, battle re-enactments. Phone 803/432-9841. 1st wkend in Nov.

Horse racing. Springdale Race Course. 200 Knights Hill Rd. Phone 803/432-6513. Carolina Cup Steeplechase, early Apr. Colonial Cup International Steeplechase, mid-Nov.

Motels

✓ ★ ★ **COLONY INN.** 2020 W Dekalb St (29020). 803/432-5508; FAX 803/432-0920; res: 800/356-9801. 53 rms, 2 story. S $45-$55; D $55; each addl $3. Crib $5. Pet accepted, some restrictions; $10. TV; cable. Pool. Restaurant 5:30-11 am. Ck-out 11 am. Valet serv. Cr cds: A, C, D, DS, MC, V.

 D 🐾 ➟ ⇟ 🔥 SC

★ ★ ★ **HOLIDAY INN OF CAMDEN.** 850 Hwy 1 S (29078), 3 mi S on US 1/601. 803/438-9441; FAX 803/438-5784; res: 800/465-4329. 117 rms, 2 story. S $59-$89; D $64-$94; each addl $5; under 18 free. Crib free. TV; cable (premium). Pool; wading pool. Complimentary full bkfst. Coffee in rms. Restaurant 6:30-9:30 am, 5-10 pm. Rm serv. Bar 5 pm-midnight. Ck-out 11 am. Meeting rms. Business servs avail. In-rm modem link. Valet serv. Health club privileges. Some in-rm whirlpools; refrigerators, microwaves avail. Cr cds: A, C, D, DS, MC, V.

D ➟ ⇟ 🔥 SC

★ ★ **THE INN AT CAMDEN (LUGOFF).** 928 Hwy 1 S (29078). 803/438-4961; FAX 803/438-4961; res: 877/843-4667. 84 rms, 2 story. S $48; D $53; each addl $5; under 18 free. Crib free. TV; cable. Pool. Restaurant adj 6 am-11 pm; Fri, Sat to 1 am. Ck-out noon. Meeting rm. Microwaves avail. Cr cds: A, C, D, DS, MC, V.

D ➟ ⇟ 🔥 SC

Inn

★ ★ **GREENLEAF INN.** 1308 Broad St (29020). 803/425-1806; FAX 803/425-5853; res: 800/437-5874. 11 rms, 2 story. S $55-$65; D $65-$75; each addl $10; suite $65-$75; under 12 free. TV; cable (premium). Complimentary continental bkfst. Dining rm 6-10 pm; closed Wed, Sun. Ck-out 11 am, ck-in 2 pm. Health club privileges. Built in 1810. Cr cds: A, C, MC, V.

🔥 SC

Restaurants

★ ★ **LILFREDS OF CAMDEN.** 8425 Main St (29128). 803/432-7063. Specializes in fresh seafood, black Angus beef. Hrs: 6-10 pm. Closed Sun-Tues; some major hols. Res accepted. Semi-a la carte: dinner $13.95-$21.95. Rustic decor. Cr cds: C, MC, V.

➟

★ ★ **LUCY'S.** 1043 Broad St (29020). 803/432-9096. Specializes in seafood, veal, beef. Own bread. Menu changes seasonally. Hrs: 11:30 am-2:30 pm, 5:30-10 pm; Fri to 10:30 pm; Sat 5:30-10:30 pm. Closed Sun, Mon; Jan 1, Dec 25. Res accepted. Bar. Semi-a la carte: lunch $5.95-$8.95, dinner $10.95-$21.95. Historic antique bar. Cr cds: A, C, MC, V.

 D ➟

★ ★ MILL POND RESTAURANT. *84 Boykin Mill Rd (29128),*
S on US 521, S on SC 261. 803/424-0261. Contemporary Amer menu.
Specializes in seafood, Angus beef. Hrs: 5-10 pm; Fri, Sat to 11 pm.
Closed Sun, Mon; Jan 1, Dec 25; also first wk July. Res accepted. Bar.
Semi-a la carte: dinner $17.95-$28.95. Rustic country decor; brick fire-
place. Cr cds: C, MC, V.

Charleston (E-5)

(See also Beaufort, Kiawah Island, Walterboro)

Founded 1670 **Pop** 80,414 **Elev** 9 ft **Area Code** 843
Web www.charlestoncvb.com
Information Visitor Reception and Transportation Center, 375 Meeting St,
PO Box 975, 29402; 843/853-8000 or 800/868-8118

This aristocratic and storied American city lives up to its reputation for
cultivated manners. Charleston's homes, historic shrines, old churches,
lovely gardens, winding streets and intricate iron lace gateways exude
charm and dignity.

Charleston enjoys international and coastal commerce in the fine harbor formed, according to local opinion, where the "Ashley and Cooper
rivers unite to form the Atlantic Ocean." The strategic harbor, inlets and sea
islands provide recreational retreats.

The Charleston of today is the survivor of siege, flood, hurricane and
epidemic. Capital of the province until 1786, its history and that of South
Carolina are almost the same. Charleston received colonists from the Old
World and sent them into the wilderness. The city served as the personifi-
cation of Europe's luxury and culture in the New World.

The first permanent settlement in the Carolinas, Charles Towne, as
it was first called, was established as a tiny colony, westward across the
Ashley River, by Anthony Ashley Cooper, Earl of Shaftesbury. At the same
time, he established the only American nobility in history, with barons, land-
graves (dukes) and caciques (earls), each owning great plantations.

This nobility lasted less than 50 years, but it was the foundation for an
aristocratic tradition that still exists, even though the rice and indigo that
made the early Charleston people rich are gone. Colonists from Barbados,
England and Ireland came to enlarge the settlement in 1670, and by 1680
the colony moved across the river to become a city-state. Although many
of the colonists went on to the Carolina Lowcountry and established grand
plantations, every year on the traditional date of May 10, the planters and
their families moved back to Charleston to escape the mosquitoes and
malarial heat. From spring to frost, these planters created a season of
dancing, sport, musicales, theater and socials. Commerce and plantations
provided the prosperity on which the city's cosmopolitan graces were
based. Charleston founded the first playhouse designed solely for presentation of drama, the first museum, the first public school in the colony, the
first municipal college in America and the first fire insurance company on
the continent. (It was a victim the next year of a fire that destroyed half the
city.) The city became famous throughout the world as "a flourishing capital of wealth and ease."

The First Provincial Congress of South Carolina met in Charleston in
1775 and prepared the city to repulse a British attack on June 28, 1776.
But in 1780 the city was captured and for two and a half years was occupied by the enemy. Charleston was almost the last point in the state to be
cleared of British troops. With peace came great prosperity, but rivalry
between small farmers of the interior and merchants and plantation owners
of the Lowlands resulted in removal of the capital to Columbia.

The convention that authored the Ordinance of Secession came to
Charleston to pass that declaration; the Civil War then began with the bombardment of Fort Sumter by Fort Johnson. A long siege followed, including the gallant defense of Fort Sumter (1863-1865), blockade running, the
first submarine warfare, evacuation after Sherman had demolished Columbia and, finally, bombardment of the city by the Union Army.

What to See and Do

Aiken–Rhett House (1817). Home of Governor William Aiken (1833-
1887). Enlarged in Greek revival style (1833-1836); subsequent additions
(1858) created some of the finest rms in Charleston, incl a Rococo revival
art gallery. Many original furnishings from 1833. (Daily; closed most hols)
48 Elizabeth St, corner of Judith St. Phone 843/724-8481. ¢¢¢ Combination ticket (addl fee) incl Nathaniel Russell House.

Boat trips.

Fort Sumter Tours. Tour (2¼ hrs) through Charleston harbor to
Ft Sumter (see). (Daily; closed Dec 25) Also 2-hr Charleston harbor tour,
3-hr *Spirit of Charleston* dinner cruise. Municipal Marina, Lockwood Blvd
& Patriots Point, Mt Pleasant. Phone 843/722-1691. ¢¢¢¢ Dinner
cruise ¢¢¢¢¢

Gray Line Water Tours. Tours (approx 2 hrs) of harbor, US Naval Base,
view of forts, other points of interest. City Municipal Marina, Lockwood
Blvd. For info, reservations contact PO Box 861, 29402-0861; phone
843/722-1112. ¢¢¢

Boone Hall Plantation (1681). A 738-acre estate with 9 original slave
houses and ginhouse (ca 1750), pecan grove, ½-mi "Avenue of Oaks."
Several rms in the house are open to the public. (Daily; closed Thanksgiving, Dec 25) 8 mi N off US 17 on Long Point Rd in Mt Pleasant. Phone
843/884-4371. ¢¢¢

Chamber of Commerce. Building was once the South Carolina Railway
Warehouse, home of one of the nation's first steam locomotives. Organized in 1773, the Chamber of Commerce (phone 843/577-2510) is one of
the oldest city commercial organizations in the country. Also houses the
Charleston Area Convention & Visitors Bureau. 81 Mary St.

Charles Towne Landing. Unusual 664-acre park on site of state's first
permanent English settlement (1670). Reconstructed fortifications in original settlement area; replica of *Adventure,* 17th-century trading vessel;
1670 experimental crop garden; formal gardens; nature trails; Colonial Village; 20-acre animal forest. Also featured is a 30-min movie, *Carolina.*
Tram tours and bicycle rentals. Picnicking, playground; restaurant. (Daily;
closed Dec 24, 25) 1500 Old Town Rd, on SC 171. Phone 843/852-
4200. ¢¢

Cypress Gardens. Consists of 163 acres with giant cypresses, blackwa-
ter swamp, azaleas, camellias, dogwoods, daffodils. Boat trips. Picnic area.
Free parking. Gift shop. (Daily; closed Thanksgiving, Dec 25) 24 mi N off
US 52, between Goose Creek & Moncks Corner. Phone 843/553-0515.
¢¢¢

Drayton Hall. One of the oldest surviving pre-Revolutionary War plantation houses (1738) in the area, this Georgian Palladian house is surrounded by live oaks and is located on the Ashley River. Held in the
Drayton family for 7 generations, the mansion has been maintained in vir-
tually its original condition. A National Trust for Historic Preservation property. Tours (hrly). (Daily; closed Jan 1, Thanksgiving, Dec 25) 9 mi NW via
SC 61 (Old Ashley River Rd). Phone 843/766-0188. ¢¢¢

Edisto Beach State Park. Approx 1,200 acres. 1½ mi of beach; shell collecting is very good here. Ocean swimming, fishing. Nature trail. Picnic
area (shelters); gift shop. Camping (higher fees Apr-Labor Day); cabins.
Standard fees. 21 mi W on US 17, then 29 mi S on SC 174. Phone
843/869-2756.

Folly Beach County Park. Approx 4,000 ft of ocean frontage and 2,000 ft
of river frontage. There is a 600-ft section of beach for swimming (Apr-
Sept); lifeguards. Dressing areas, outdoor showers; picnic areas; concessions; shelter. (Daily) S via SC 171 on W end of Folly Island. Phone
843/588-2426. Per vehicle ¢¢

Fort Sumter National Monument (see).

Francis Beidler Forest. National Audubon Society Sanctuary. Boardwalk
½ mi into the center of a beautiful blackwater swamp; close-up view of one
of the largest stands of old-growth bald cypress and tupelo gum forest in
the world. Self-guided tour. Visitor center, slide show. Canoe trips, night
walks (in season, by res only; fee). (Daily exc Mon; closed Jan 1, Thanksgiving, Dec 24, 25, 31) No pets, food facilities or camping. Four Holes
Swamp. 40 mi NW via I-26W to exit 187, then S on SC 27 to US 78, then
W to US 178, follow signs. Phone 843/462-2150. ¢¢

Francis Marion National Forest. Early colonial settlements, plantations;
lakes, moss-hung oaks, flowering trees and shrubs on 250,000 acres.
Camping, picnicking, boating, fishing, hiking, horseback riding, motor-

cycling, rifle ranges, hunting. Fees may be charged at recreation sites. Headquarters are in Columbia (Mon-Fri). (Daily) NE via US 17 & 17A, SC 41. Phone 843/336-3248.

Hampton Park. Historic park with camellias and azaleas in spring, roses in summer; 1-mi nature trail; Charleston's mounted horse patrol stables. Rutledge Ave & Cleveland St. Phone 843/724-7321. **Free**

Joseph Manigault House (1803). Outstanding example of Adam-style architecture. Features Charleston antiques, silver; curving staircase. (Daily; closed most hols) 350 Meeting St. Phone 843/723-2926. ¢¢ Combination ticket (addl fee) includes Heyward–Washington House and Charleston Museum.

Kahal Kadosh Beth Elohim (1840). Founded in 1749; first Reform Jewish congregation in America (1824). Museum. Gift shop. (Mon-Fri mornings; closed all Jewish hols) 90 Hasell St. Phone 843/723-1090. **Donation**

⊠ **Magnolia Plantation and Gardens.** Internationally famous gardens are America's oldest (ca 1680); now covering 50 acres with camellias, azaleas, magnolias and hundreds of other flowering species. Azaleas best mid-Mar-Apr; camellias best mid-Nov-Mar. Also on grounds is a 125-acre waterfowl refuge; tri-level observation tower, 16th-century maze, 18th-century herb garden; biblical gardens; topiary; nature trails; petting zoo; canoe and bicycle rentals; picnicking. Gift shop, snack shop; orientation theater. Plantation home and local art gallery (addl fee). (Daily) 10 mi NW on SC 61. Phone 843/571-1266. ¢¢-¢¢¢ Through Magnolia Plantation, enter

Audubon Swamp Garden. Boardwalks, bridges and dikes make this 60-acre blackwater cypress and tupelo swamp accessible to visitors. Home to all local species of wildlife, this colorful area is planted with hundreds of varieties of local and exotic flowering shrubs. (Daily) Phone 843/571-1266. ¢¢

Medical University of South Carolina (1824). (2,200 students) Oldest medical school in the South. 171 Ashley Ave. Phone 843/792-3621. On campus is

Waring Historical Medical Library & Macaulay Museum of Dental History. (Mon-Fri; closed hols) Phone 843/792-2288. **Free**

Middleton Place Gardens, House & Stableyards. Once home of Arthur Middleton, signer of the Declaration of Independence, Middleton Place encompasses America's oldest landscaped gardens, the Plantation Stableyards and the restored House Museum. The gardens, laid out in 1741, highlight ornamental butterfly lakes, sweeping terraces and a wide variety of flora and fauna. The Stableyards feature numerous craftspeople demonstrating skills necessary for a self-sufficient 18th-century plantation. House (addl fee). Guided tours (addl fee). Special events incl Starlight Pops (May), Spoleto Finale (mid-June), Plantation Days (Nov) and Plantation Christmas (Dec). (Daily) 14 mi NW on SC 61. Phone 843/556-6020. ¢¢¢¢

Old Dorchester State Park. Congregationalists from Massachusetts established a village in 1696 at the head of the Ashley River. It grew as a trading center until 1752, when there was a general exodus of Congregationalists to Georgia in a search for plentiful land and a better climate. By 1780 the once-thriving town was occupied by the British and had only 40 houses and a church. In late 1781, Col Wade Hampton advanced against Dorchester. The British did not wait for the attack but instead destroyed the town and retreated to Charleston. Remains of the church tower and Fort Dorchester may be seen; 97-acre area has been partially excavated. Fishing. Picnicking. Drawings, artifacts in interpretive bldg. (Thurs-Mon) 19 mi NW on SC 642. Phone 843/873-1740. **Free**

Palmetto Islands County Park. Nature-oriented park in tropical setting. Bicycle paths, marsh boardwalks, picnicking and grills throughout park. Two-acre pond. Canoe trails. Pedal boat, canoe & bicycle rentals. BigToy Playground. 50-ft observation tower with play area. Interpretive trails. Natural swimming facility with sand bottom. Fishing supplies; concession. (Daily; closed Jan 1, Thanksgiving, Dec 24 & 25) N on US 17, ½ mi past Snee Farm, then left on Long Point Rd. Phone 843/884-0832. ¢

Patriots Point Naval and Maritime Museum. Home of the WWII aircraft carrier *Yorktown;* also submarine *Clamagore,* destroyer *Laffey,* Coast Guard cutter *Ingham* and the Medal of Honor Museum. Vintage military aircraft and weapons on display. Living and working areas of ships tour. Gift shop. (Daily) Located on Charleston Harbor, in Mt Pleasant (at foot of Cooper River Bridges). Phone 843/884-2727. ¢¢¢

Sightseeing tours.

Charleston Carriage Co. Offers narrated, horse-drawn carriage tours of Old Charleston (1 hr). Free shuttle service from visitor center. (Daily; closed Thanksgiving, Dec 25) 14 Hayne St. Phone 843/577-0042. ¢¢¢¢

Gray Line bus tours. For info, reservations contact PO Box 219, 29402-0219; phone 843/722-4444.

Palmetto Carriage Tours. One-hr tour through Old Charleston by horse- & mule-drawn carriages. Tours originate at Rainbow Market. Shuttle van from visitor center (free). (Daily; closed Dec 25) 40 N Market St. Phone 843/723-8145. ¢¢¢¢

St John's Lutheran Church (1817). Congregation established in 1742. Steeple, wrought-iron gates, churchyard fence, graves of interest. Interior restored. Pastor John Bachman (1815-1874), who coauthored *Quadrupeds of America* with Audubon, is buried beneath the altar in the church nave. (Mon-Fri; also Sun worship) Archdale & Clifford Sts. Phone 843/723-2426.

St Mary's Church (1838). Mother church for Catholic dioceses of Carolinas and Georgia. Congregation established in 1789. Stained-glass windows, paintings. (Daily) 89 Hasell St, between King & Meeting Sts. Phone 843/722-7696.

The Charleston Museum (1773). Oldest museum in US. Cultural, historical, natural history collections; children's "Discovery Me" rm; decorative arts exhibits. (Daily; closed some hols) 360 Meeting St, at John St. Phone 843/722-2996. ¢¢¢ Combination ticket (addl fee) incl Heyward–Washington House and Joseph Manigault House.

The Citadel, Military College of South Carolina (1842) (2,000 uniformed cadets). Originally located near city's pre-Revolutionary War rampart, the college moved to its present site in 1922. Dress parades (academic yr, Fri). Moultrie & Rutledge Aves, near Hampton Park. Phone 843/953-5006. On campus is

The Citadel Archives Museum. Exhibits depict history of the South Carolina Corps of Cadets at The Citadel. (Academic yr, afternoons) Phone 843/953-6846. **Free**

Unitarian Church (1772). Second-oldest church in the city; under restoration. Fan tracery ceiling; interior modeled after Henry VII Chapel, Westminster Abbey. (Mon-Fri) 4 Archdale St. Phone 843/723-4617.

⊠ **Walking tour of Old Charleston.**

White Point Gardens. View of harbor, city, Fort Sumter National Monument (see) and Fort Moultrie. Murray Blvd & E Battery, at foot of peninsula. Walk N on E Battery ½ blk to

Edmondston-Alston House (ca 1825). Built by wealthy merchant and wharf owner, remodeled by next owner, an important rice planter, beginning in 1838; Greek-revival style. Uninterrupted view across harbor. Documents, engravings, portraits, original furnishings, elaborate woodwork. Guided tours (daily; closed Jan 1, Thanksgiving, Dec 25). 21 E Battery. Phone 843/722-7171. ¢¢¢ Continue N on E Battery (which becomes E Bay St) 8 blks past Rainbow Row (14 houses dating from the mid-18th century, each painted a different color) to Broad St and the

Old Exchange & Provost Dungeon (1771). Built by the British with material brought from England, this was the last bldg constructed by them on colonial soil in Charleston prior to the Revolutionary War; served as an exchange and a customs house. Used as a prison during the Revolutionary War. Original seawall of Charleston preserved in dungeon. Extensively restored; site of many important historical events. 122 E Bay St. Phone 843/727-2165. ¢¢¢ Follow Broad St to Church St and turn S; walk past Catfish Row (made famous in *Porgy and Bess*) to

Heyward–Washington House (1772). Once owned by Thomas Heyward Jr, signer of Declaration of Independence and host to George Washington during his visit in 1791. Period pieces of exquisite design and craftsmanship; Charleston-made furniture; house is a classic example of a Georgian town house. Garden laid out with shrubs, plants that grew in city in Washington's time; carriage house, kitchen. (Daily; closed most hols) 87 Church St. Phone 843/722-0354. ¢¢¢ Combination ticket (addl fee) incl the Charleston Museum and Joseph Manigault House. Walk N on Church St to

Huguenot Church (1845). Third bldg on this site; rebuilt on site of earlier structure burned in 1796. Congregation founded 1681. Only church in US using Calvinist Huguenot liturgy; services were in French until 1928. 136 Church St, at Queen St. Phone 843/722-4385. Continue N to

St Philip's Church (Episcopal) (1838). Lofty steeple held mariner's light, was target for Union guns. Late Georgian architecture. Third bldg used by St Philip's parish. First Anglican parish (1670) south of Virginia. John C. Calhoun and other notables buried in churchyard. 142 Church St. Phone 843/722-7734. From here walk N to Cumberland St then W to

The Powder Magazine (ca 1710). Part of city's original fortifications, oldest public bldg remaining. Used in Revolutionary War. Walls of this 8-gabled structure are 32 inches thick. Now houses historic colonial museum. (Mon-Sat, also Sun afternoons; closed Jan 1, Thanksgiving, Dec 25) 79 Cumberland St. Phone 843/805-6730. ¢ Walk W to Meeting St, then 1 blk S to

Gibbes Museum of Art. Permanent collection of American paintings, miniatures, Japanese wood block prints; changing exhibits. (Tues-Sat, also Sun & Mon afternoons; closed hols) 135 Meeting St. Phone 843/722-2706. ¢¢ Walk S to

City Hall Art Gallery (1801). On the site of colonial marketplace, first housed Bank of United States; became City Hall in 1818. Superb picture gallery on 2nd floor resulted from custom of commissioning artists to paint famous visitors; incl portrait of Washington by John Trumbull, considered one of the best of the general in his later yrs; painting of President Monroe by Samuel F.B. Morse. Tours. (Mon-Fri; closed hols) 80 Broad St, at Meeting St. Phone 843/724-3799. **Free** On next blk is

St Michael's Church (1752). Steeple rises 186 ft; tower has four-faced clock in operation since 1764. Steeple bells were captured by the British, returned after the Revolution, sent to Columbia during the Civil War and partly destroyed by the fire there. Later they were sent back to England, recast in the original molds and returned in 1867. (Mon-Fri; closed hols and periodically for maintenance) Meeting & Broad Sts. Phone 843/723-0603. 2 blks S is

Nathaniel Russell House (1808). Home of wealthy merchant; example of Adam-style architecture; free-flying staircase, oval drawing rms, period furnishings. (Daily; closed Dec 25) 51 Meeting St. Phone 843/724-8481. Combination ticket incl. Aiken-Rhett House (see) ¢¢¢ Nearby are

Sword Gates. Gates represent one of the best examples of wrought-iron art, with 2 spears joining at center of broadsword to form cross. (Private) 32 Legare (la-GREE) St.

Annual Events

Southeastern Wildlife Exposition. Eighteen downtown historical locations. More than 500 exhibitors display wildlife art, carvings, antique collections and crafts for sale. Phone 843/723-1748. Mid-Feb.

Festival of Houses & Gardens. Many of the city's finest private residences (ca 1710-1850) and gardens are open to visitors. Afternoon & candlelight tours; res recommended. Phone 843/723-1623. Mid-Mar–mid-Apr.

Spoleto Festival USA. Internationally acclaimed counterpart to the arts festival in Spoleto, Italy, founded by Gian Carlo Menotti; incl opera, ballet, dance, visual arts, theater, chamber music, jazz, symphonic and choral performances and much more. Piccolo Spoleto, running concurrent with the main festival, has performances by local and regional artists. Phone 843/722-2764. Late May–mid-June.

Fall House & Garden Candlelight Tours. Evening tours of privately owned houses and gardens in the Historic District (fee). Phone 843/722-4630. Late Sept-late Oct.

Additional Visitor Information

The Charleston Visitor Reception and Transportation Center, 375 Meeting St, has information on other points of interest, tours, campsites, fishing trips, cultural, special and annual events, maps and self-guided walking tour of the city. (Daily; closed Jan 1, Thanksgiving, Dec 25) Contact PO Box 975, 29402; 843/853-8000. For city bus service information phone SCE & G at 843/747-0922; for DASH, Downtown Area Shuttle, phone 803/577-6970, ext 500.

Forever Charleston, a multimedia presentation about the city, is shown every half hr at the Visitor Center.

Motels

★★ **BEST WESTERN—KING CHARLES INN.** *237 Meeting St (29401).* 843/723-7451; FAX 843/723-2041; res: 800/528-1234. 91 rms, 3 story. Mar-Oct: S, D $99-$199; each addl $10; under 12 free; higher rates wkends; lower rates rest of yr. Crib free. TV; cable. Pool. Restaurant nearby. Ck-out noon. Business servs avail. Bellhops. Valet serv. Cr cds: A, C, D, DS, MC, V.

★ **DAYS INN.** *2998 W Montague Ave (29418), near Intl Airport.* 843/747-4101; FAX 843/566-0378; res: 800/329-7466. 147 rms, 2 story. S $45-$65; D $50-$72; each addl $6; under 12 free. Crib free. Pet accepted; $6. TV; cable (premium). Pool. Playground. Restaurant 6 am-9 pm. Ck-out noon. Coin lndry. Business servs avail. Some refrigerators, microwaves. Cr cds: A, C, D, DS, ER, MC, V.

✓★★ **HAMPTON INN.** *11 Ashley Point Dr (29407).* 843/556-5200; FAX 843/571-5499; res: 800/426-7866. 177 rms, 4 story. S $75-$99; D $85-$115; under 18 free; higher rates wkends, special events. Crib free. Pet accepted. TV; cable (premium). Pool. Complimentary continental bkfst. Restaurant adj 11 am-11 pm. Ck-out noon. Coin lndry. Meeting rm. Business servs avail. In-rm modem link. Valet serv. Golf privileges. Health club privileges. Opp Ashley River; marina. Cr cds: A, C, D, DS, MC, V.

✓★★ **HAMPTON INN & SUITES.** *1104 Isle of Palms Connector (29464), Hwy 17 N and Isle of Palms connection.* 843/856-3900; FAX 843/881-6277. 121 rms, 3 story, 40 kit. suites. S $79-$109; D $89-$119; kit. suites $99-$139; higher rates hols. Crib free. TV; cable (premium), VCR (movies) avail in suites. Restaurant adj 6 am-10 pm. Ck-out noon. Meeting rms. Business servs avail. In-rm modem link. Sundries. Gift shop. Guest lndry. Exercise equipt. Pool. Refrigerator, microwave, wet bar in suites. Cr cds: A, C, D, DS, MC, V.

✓★ **KNIGHTS INN.** *2355 Aviation Ave (29406).* 843/744-4900; FAX 843/745-0668; res: 800/845-1927 or 800/722-7220. 242 rms, 2 story, 31 kits. S $29.95-$45; D $35-$45; each addl $3; suites $75; kit. units $55. Crib $3. TV; cable (premium). 2 pools. Complimentary continental bkfst. Ck-out noon. Coin lndry. Business servs avail. Airport transportation. Some refrigerators, microwaves. Lawn games. Cr cds: A, C, D, DS, MC, V.

★★ **LA QUINTA.** *2499 La Quinta Ln (29420), at I-26N exit 209.* 843/797-8181; FAX 843/569-1608; res: 800/687-6667. Web www.laquinta.com. 122 rms, 2 suites, 2 story. S $60-$70; D $70-$80; each addl $10; suites $90-$100; under 18 free; higher rates wkends. Crib free. Pet accepted. TV; cable (premium). Pool. Complimentary continental bkfst. Restaurant adj 6 am-11 pm. Ck-out noon. Business servs avail. In-rm modem link. Valet serv. Refrigerators, microwaves avail. Picnic tables, grill. Cr cds: A, C, D, DS, MC, V.

✓★ **LANDS INN.** *2545 Savannah Hwy (29414).* 843/763-8885; FAX 843/556-9536. 57 rms, 2 story. Mar-Oct: S $59-$69; D $69-$79; each addl $10; under 16 free; higher rates wkends; lower rates rest of yr. Crib free. Pet accepted; $10. TV; cable. Complimentary continental bkfst. Restaurant nearby. Rm serv open 24 hrs. Ck-out 11 am. Business servs avail. Pool. On river. Cr cds: A, C, DS, MC, V.

★★ **RAMADA INN COLISEUM.** *2934 W Montague Ave (29418), 7 mi NW at I-26.* 843/744-8281; FAX 843/744-6230. 155 rms, 2 story. Mid-Mar-Oct: S $59-$89; D $68-$89; each addl $10; under 18 free; lower rates rest of yr. TV; cable. Pool. Coffee in rms. Restaurant 6-11 am, 11:30 am-2 pm, 5:30-9 pm. Rm serv lunch, dinner. Bar 5-11 pm. Ck-out noon. Business servs avail. In-rm modem link. Valet serv. Free airport transportation. Some refrigerators. Cr cds: A, C, D, DS, MC, V.

✓★ **RED ROOF INN.** *7480 Northwoods Blvd (29406), I-26 to exit 209.* 843/572-9100; FAX 843/572-0061; res: 800/843-7663. 109 rms, 2 story. S $39-$51; D $44-$57; each addl $7; under 18 free. Crib free. Pet accepted, some restrictions. TV; cable (premium). Complimentary coffee in lobby. Restaurant nearby. Ck-out noon. Microwaves, refrigerators avail. Cr cds: A, C, D, DS, MC, V.

[D] [symbols] SC

★★ **SHEM CREEK INN.** *1401 Shrimp Boat Ln (87501), approx 5 mi E on US 17/701, S on US Business 17 to Mt. Pleasant.* 843/881-1000; FAX 843/849-6969; res: 800/523-4951. 50 rms, 2 story. Mid-Feb-Nov: S, D $89-$175; under 18 free; higher rates special events; lower rates rest of yr. Crib free. TV; cable. Pool. Complimentary continental bkfst. Complimentary coffee in rms. Restaurant adj 4:30 am-10 pm. Ck-out 11 am. Meeting rms. Business servs avail. Health club privileges. Refrigerators, microwaves avail. Cr cds: A, C, D, DS, MC, V.

[D] [symbols] SC

★★★ **TOWN & COUNTRY MOTOR INN.** *2008 Savannah Hwy (29407).* 843/571-1000; FAX 843/766-9444; res: 800/334-6660. 124 rms, 2 story. 20 kits. Mar-Nov: S $69; D $89; each addl $7; suites $109-$189; kit. units $7 addl; under 18 free; lower rates rest of yr. Crib free. TV; cable (premium). 2 pools, 1 indoor; whirlpool. Restaurant 6:30 am-10 pm. Bar 3 pm-midnight. Ck-out noon. Coin lndry. Meeting rms. Business servs avail. In-rm modem link. Valet serv. Golf privileges, pro. Exercise equipt; sauna. Racquetball court. Some refrigerators. Cr cds: A, C, D, DS, MC, V.

[D] [symbols] SC

Lodge

★★ **MIDDLETON INN.** *4290 Ashley River Rd (29414), 14 mi W.* 843/556-0500; FAX 803/556-0500; res: 800/543-4774. 55 rms, 2-3 story. S, D $99-$169; each addl $20. Crib free. TV; cable. Pool. Coffee in rms. Complimentary bkfst. Meeting rms. Business servs avail. Tennis. Golf privileges. Kayak, swamp tours. Refrigerators, fireplaces. On 7,000 acres overlooking river, former rice fields; free admission to nearby Middleton Place Gardens. Cr cds: A, C, MC, V.

[symbols] SC

Motor Hotels

★★ **BEST WESTERN.** *7401 Northwoods Blvd (29406), NW on I-26.* 843/572-2200; FAX 843/863-8316; res: 800/528-1234. E-mail northwoodatrium@mindspring.com. 197 rms, 4 story. S $64-$94; D $69-$99; each addl $5; under 18 free. Crib free. TV; cable (premium). 2 pools, 1 indoor; whirlpool, poolside serv. Complimentary bkfst buffet. Restaurant 6:30 am-2 pm, 5-10:30 pm. Rm serv. Bar 5 pm-1 am; closed Sun. Ck-out 11 am. Meeting rms. Business servs avail. Bellhops. Valet serv. Free airport, RR station, bus depot transportation. Exercise equipt; sauna. Game rm. Refrigerators, microwaves avail. Cr cds: A, C, D, DS, MC, V.

[D] [symbols] SC

★★ **DOUBLETREE GUEST SUITES.** *181 Church St (29401).* 843/577-2644; FAX 843/577-2697; res: 800/222-8733. E-mail hawthorn@awod.com; web www.hawthorn.com. 182 rms, 5 story, 125 kit. suites. Mar-mid-June, Sept-mid-Nov: S, D $129-$210; wkly rates; higher rates wkends; lower rates rest of yr. Crib free. Pet accepted, some restrictions; $125 and $10/day. TV; cable (premium), VCR. Whirlpool. Complimentary full bkfst. Complimentary coffee in rms. Restaurant nearby. Ck-out noon. Coin lndry. Meeting rms. Business servs avail. In-rm modem link. Bellhops. Valet serv. Exercise equipt. Microwaves, wet bars. In historic market area. Cr cds: A, C, D, DS, JCB, MC, V.

[D] [symbols] SC

★★ **HAMPTON INN.** *345 Meeting St (29403).* 843/723-4000; FAX 843/722-3725; res: 800/426-7866. 171 rms, 5 story. Mid-Feb-early Nov: S $99; D $109; suites $150; under 18 free; higher rates wkends, special events; lower rates rest of yr. Crib free. Garage $9. TV; cable (premium). Pool. Complimentary continental bkfst. Restaurant nearby. Rm serv. Ck-out noon. Meeting rms. Business servs avail. In-rm modem link.

Bellhops. Concierge. Valet serv. Health club privileges. Some refrigerators, microwaves avail. Cr cds: A, C, D, DS, MC, V.

[D] [symbols] SC

★★★ **HILTON CHARLESTON HARBOR RESORT.** *20 Patriots Point Rd (29464).* 843/856-0028; FAX 843/856-8333; res: 888/856-0028. Web www.hilton.com. 131 rms, 4 story. Mid-Feb-June: S, D $125-$150; each addl $15; suites $225-$400; under 18 free; higher rates wkends; lower rates rest of yr. Crib free. TV; cable (premium). Complimentary coffee in rms. Restaurant 6 am-2 pm, 4-10 pm. Rm serv. Bar 11 am-midnight. Ck-out noon. Meeting rms. Business servs avail. In-rm modem link. Bellhops. Concierge. 18-hole golf privileges. Exercise equipt. Pool; whirlpool. Refrigerator in suites. Many balconies. On river. Cr cds: A, C, D, DS, ER, MC, V.

[D] [symbols] SC

★★ **HOLIDAY INN.** *301 Savannah Hwy (29407).* 843/556-7100; FAX 843/556-6176; res: 800/465-4329. 181 rms, 14 story. S $79-$139; D $85-$145; under 19 free. Crib free. TV; cable (premium). Pool. Restaurant 6:30 am-2 pm, 5-10 pm. Rm serv. Bar 1 pm-1 am. Ck-out noon. Coin lndry. Business servs avail. In-rm modem link. Bellhops. Valet serv. Exercise equipt. Health club privileges. Balconies. On river. Cr cds: A, C, D, DS, JCB, MC, V.

[D] [symbols] SC

★★★ **QUALITY SUITES HOTEL.** *5225 N Arco Ln (29418).* 843/747-7300; FAX 843/747-6324; res: 800/747-7300. 168 suites, 5 story. Mar-mid-June: S $89-$175; D $99-$175; each addl $10; under 18 free; lower rates rest of yr. Crib free. TV; cable, VCR. Pool. Complimentary full bkfst. Coffee in rms. Restaurant nearby. Ck-out noon. Coin lndry. Meeting rms. Business servs avail. In-rm modem link. Gift shop. Free airport transportation. Exercise equipt. Health club privileges. Refrigerators, microwaves, wet bars; some bathrm phones. Many balconies. Cr cds: A, C, D, DS, ER, JCB, MC, V.

[D] [symbols] SC

★★ **RADISSON INN.** *5991 Rivers Ave (29406), jct Aviation Ave & I-26.* 843/744-2501; FAX 843/744-2501; res: 800/333-3333. 158 rms, 8 story. S $75-$110; D $85-$120; each addl $10; under 17 free. Crib free. TV; cable. Pool; whirlpool. Restaurant 6 am-10:30 pm. Rm serv. Bar noon-2 am; Sun 5 pm-midnight; entertainment. Ck-out noon. Meeting rms. Business servs avail. In-rm modem link. Bellhops. Valet serv. Free airport transportation. Health club privileges. Refrigerators, microwaves avail. Cr cds: A, C, D, DS, ER, JCB, MC, V.

[D] [symbols] SC

Hotels

★★★ **BOARDWALK INN.** *5757 Palm Blvd (29451).* 843/886-6000; FAX 843/886-2916. E-mail wilddunes@awod.com; web www.wilddunes.com. 93 rms, 5 story, 9 suites. June-Sept: S, D $129-$199; suites $250-$325; under 18 free; wkends, hols (3-day min); lower rates rest of yr. Crib free. TV; cable (premium), VCR avail (movies). Complimentary coffee in rms. Restaurant 6:30 am-11 pm. Bar 11 am-midnight. Ck-out 11 am. Meeting rms. Business center. In-rm modem link. Concierge. Gift shop. Beauty shop. Lighted tennis, pro. 36-hole golf, greens fee $39-$145, pro, putting green, driving range. Exercise rm; sauna. Massage. Indoor pool; wading pool, poolside serv. Playground. Supervised child's activities (June-Sept); ages 3-12. Lawn games. Refrigerators, minibars. Balconies. On beach. Cr cds: A, C, D, DS, MC, V.

[D] [symbols] SC

✓★★★★ **CHARLESTON PLACE.** *130 Market St (29401).* 843/722-4900; FAX 843/722-0728; res: 800/611-5545. Web www.charleston-place.com. This graceful structure is in the city's historic district near a fashionable shopping area. The lobby contains antiques, a magnificent hand-blown Venetian chandelier and Italian marble floors. 440 rms, 8 story. S $295; D $315; each addl $20; suites $375-$2,000; under 18 free. Crib free. Garage $9, valet parking $13. TV; cable (premium). Indoor/outdoor pool; whirlpool, poolside serv. Supervised child's activities (June-Aug). Restaurants 6:30 am-10 pm (also see CHARLESTON GRILL). Rm serv 24 hrs.

Bar 11:30-1 am; entertainment. Ck-out noon. Convention facilities. Business center. In-rm modem link. Concierge. Shopping arcade. Tennis privileges. Golf privileges. Exercise rm; sauna. Massage. Some balconies. Luxury level. Cr cds: A, C, D, DS, MC, V.

★★★ **EMBASSY SUITES.** *337 Meeting St (29403). 843/723-6900; FAX 843/723-6938; res: 800/362-2779.* 153 suites, 5 story. Mid-Mar-early June, late Sept-late Nov: S, D $169-$269; each addl $10; under 18 free; higher rates Southeastern Wildlife Exposition, Bridge Run; lower rates rest of yr. Crib free. Valet parking $11; garage $9. TV; cable (premium). Complimentary full bkfst. Restaurant nearby. Bar 4-11 pm. Ck-out noon. Meeting rms. Business servs avail. In-rm modem link. Gift shop. Coin lndry. Exercise equipt. Pool. Refrigerators, microwaves, wet bars; some in-rm whirlpools. Cr cds: A, C, D, DS, MC, V.

★★★ **FRANCIS MARION WESTIN.** *387 King St (29403). 843/722-0600; FAX 843/723-4633; res: 800/937-8461 or 800/433-3733.* 226 rms, 12 story, 66 suites. Mid-Feb-May, Sept-Oct: S, D $119-$159; each addl $10; suites $159-$209; under 12 free; higher rates wkends, Southeastern Wildlife Exposition, Bridge Run; lower rates rest of yr. Crib free. Garage $9, valet $12. TV; cable (premium). Restaurant 6:30 am-10 pm. Bar 11 am-10 pm. Ck-out noon. Meeting rms. Business servs avail. In-rm modem link. Concierge. Gift shop. Exercise equipt. Massage. European-style historic hotel; view of harbor. Cr cds: A, C, D, DS, MC, V.

★★★ **HILTON HOTEL.** *4770 Goer Dr (29406), 8 mi W on I-26 exit Montague Ave. 843/747-1900; FAX 843/744-6108.* E-mail hilton@charleston.net; web www.charleston.net/com/hilton. 296 rms, 8 story. Mid-Feb-May, mid-Sept-Nov: S $79-$129; D $94-$144; suites $159-$300; under 18 free; wkend rates; lower rates rest of yr. Crib free. TV; cable (premium). Indoor/outdoor pool; whirlpool. Restaurant 6:30 am-10 pm; Sat, Sun from 7 am. Bar; entertainment. Ck-out noon. Convention facilities. Business center. In-rm modem link. Gift shop. Free airport transportation. Tennis privileges. Golf privileges. Exercise equipt. Refrigerators, microwaves avail. Landscaped grounds. Cr cds: A, C, D, DS, ER, JCB, MC, V.

★★★ **THE MILLS HOUSE.** *115 Meeting St (29401), at Queen St. 843/577-2400; FAX 843/722-2112; res: 800/874-9600.* 214 rms, 7 story. Mid-Mar–mid-June, mid-Sept–mid-Nov: S, D $195; each addl $20; under 19 free; lower rates rest of yr. Crib free. Garage $9. TV; cable (premium). Pool. Restaurant (see BARBADOES ROOM). Bar 11-2 am. Ck-out 11 am. Meeting rms. Business servs avail. In-rm modem link. Concierge. Health club privileges. Reconstruction of 19th-century inn; many antiques; reproduction furnishings. Cr cds: A, C, D, DS, MC, V.

Resorts

★★★ **SEABROOK ISLAND.** *1002 Landfall Way (29455), 23 mi SE off US 17. 843/768-2500; FAX 843/768-4922; res: 800/845-2475.* E-mail resort@charleston.net; web www.seabrookresort.com. 170 kit. villas, 1-2 story. Mid-Mar–mid Aug: 1-bedrm $165-$240; 2-bedrm $205-$315; 3-bedrm $230-$375; package plans; lower rates rest of yr. Crib $5. TV; cable, VCR avail. 7 pools; wading pool, lifeguard. Supervised child's activities (Memorial Day–Labor Day). Dining rm 7 am-9 pm. Bar from 11 am. Ck-out 11 am, ck-in 4 pm. Business center. Grocery. Convention facilities. Tennis, pro. 36-hole golf, greens fee $55-$100, pro, putting green, driving range. Private beach. Sailboat. Deep-sea fishing. Bicycles. Horseback riding. Exercise equipt. Health club privileges. Entertainment. Game rm. Refrigerators, microwaves; some fireplaces. Private patios, balconies. Sunset cruises avail. Cr cds: A, C, D, DS, MC, V.

★★★ **WILD DUNES RESORT.** *5757 Palm Blvd. (29451), E on US 17, N on SC 703. 843/886-6000; FAX 843/886-2916; res: 800/845-8880.* E-mail wilddunes@awod.com; web www.wilddunes.com. 320 kit.

villas, 1-5 story, 24 cottages. June-Sept: kit. villas, cottages $125-$375; wkly rates; golf plans; lower rates rest of yr. Crib $10. TV; cable (premium). Pools; wading pool, whirlpool, poolside serv, lifeguard. Free supervised child's activities (June-mid-Sept). Teen club. Dining rm 7 am-midnight. Box lunches, snack bar, picnics. Bar 7 am-midnight; entertainment Tues-Sat. Ck-out 11 am, ck-in 4 pm. Lndry facilities. Grocery. Package store. Convention facilities. Business center. Valet serv. Beauty shop. Gift shop. Sports dir. Lighted tennis, pro. 36-hole golf course, greens fee $39-$145, pro, putting green, driving range. Exercise rm. Swimming beach, boats. Bicycle rentals. Lawn games. Soc dir. Fishing guides. Microwaves. Balconies. Picnic tables. On beach. Cr cds: A, C, DS, MC, V.

Inns

★★★ **ANCHORAGE INN.** *26 Vendue Range (29401), in historic district. 843/723-8300; FAX 843/723-9543; res: 800/421-2952.* Web www.insiders.com. 17 rms, 2 story, 2 suites. Mid-Mar-mid-June, Sept-Nov: D $125-$199; suites $255; lower rates rest of yr. Garage parking $6/day. TV; cable (premium). Complimentary continental bkfst; afternoon refreshments. Restaurant nearby. Ck-out 11 am, ck-in 3 pm. Business servs avail. Concierge serv. Antiques. Library/sitting rm. Renovated antebellum warehouse adj to harbor, Waterfront Park; individually decorated rms. Cr cds: A, C, MC, V.

★★ **ASHLEY INN BED & BREAKFAST.** *201 Ashley Ave (29403). 843/723-1848; FAX 843/579-9080; res: 800/581-6658.* E-mail ashley@cchat.com; web www.cchat.com/ashley. 6 rms, 5 with shower only, 1 suite, 3 story. Early Mar-Nov: S, D $98-$150; suite $160; lower rates rest of yr. Children over 10 yrs only. TV; cable (premium). Complimentary full bkfst; afternoon refreshments. Ck-out 11 am, ck-in 3 pm. Business servs avail. Bicycles. Built 1832; antiques. Garden with fish pond, fountain. Totally nonsmoking. Cr cds: A, C, DS, MC, V.

★★★ **BARKSDALE HOUSE INN.** *27 George St (29401), in historic district. 843/577-4800; FAX 843/853-0482.* 14 rms, 3 story. Mar-Oct: S, D $80-$195; each addl $10; lower rates rest of yr. Children over 10 yrs only. TV; cable (premium). Complimentary continental bkfst; afternoon refreshments. Restaurant nearby. Ck-out 11 am, ck-in 3 pm. Business servs avail. Health club privileges. Townhouse built in 1778; porches, courtyard in rear. Cr cds: C, MC, V.

★★★ **BATTERY CARRIAGE HOUSE INN.** *20 S Battery St (73401). 843/727-3100; FAX 843/727-3130; res: 800/775-5575.* Web www.charleston-inns.com. 11 rms, 4 with shower only, 2 story. Mar-mid-June, mid-Sept-mid-Nov: S, D $149-$199; each addl $15; higher rates wkends (2-day min); lower rates rest of yr. Children over 12 yrs only. TV; cable (premium). Complimentary continental bkfst. Complimentary coffee in rms. Ck-out noon, ck-in 3 pm. Concierge serv. Street parking. On Battery Park, harbor. Cr cds: A, C, DS, MC, V.

★★ **CANNONBORO INN BED & BREAKFAST.** *184 Ashley Ave (29403). 843/723-8572; FAX 843/723-8007; res: 800/235-8039.* E-mail cannon@cchat.com; web www.cchat.com.cannon. 7 rms, 4 with shower only, 2 story, 1 suite. Early Mar-Nov: S, D $98-$155; each addl $25; suite $180; lower rates rest of yr. Children over 10 yrs only. TV. Complimentary full bkfst; afternoon refreshments. Restaurant nearby. Ck-out 10 am, ck-in 3 pm. Business servs avail. Refrigerators avail. Bicycles. Second-story porch. Some Victorian furnishings; antiques. Totally nonsmoking. Cr cds: A, C, DS, MC, V.

★★★ **HARBOURVIEW INN.** *2 Vendue Range (29401). 843/853-8439; FAX 843/853-4034; res: 888/853-8439.* Web www.awod.com/gallery/business/cmh/hvi/index.html. 52 rms, 4 story. Mid-Mar-June, Oct-Nov: S $119-$159; D $129-$169; suites $219; lower rates rest of yr. Crib avail. TV; cable (premium). Complimentary continental bkfst;

afternoon refreshments. Restaurant nearby. Ck-out noon, ck-in 3 pm. Business servs avail. In-rm modem link. Luggage handling. Valet serv. Parking $6. Some in-rm whirlpools, fireplaces. Some balconies. Opp harbor. Cr cds: A, C, D, DS, MC, V.

D ⬛ ⬛ SC

★★★ **INDIGO INN.** 1 Maiden Ln (29401). 843/577-5900; FAX 843/577-0378; res: 800/845-7639. E-mail indigoinn@crabnet.net; web www.aesir.com/indigoinn. 40 rms, 3 story. Mar-June, Sept-Nov: S $140; D $155; each addl $10; under 12 free; higher rates wkends; lower rates rest of yr. Crib $10. Pet accepted; $20. TV; cable (premium). Complimentary continental bkfst; afternoon refreshments. Restaurant nearby. Ck-out noon, ck-in 3 pm. Business servs avail. In-rm modem link. Luggage handling. Valet serv. Health club privileges. Parking. Built in 1850; courtyard. Cr cds: A, C, D, DS, MC, V.

⬛ ⬛

★★★ **JOHN RUTLEDGE HOUSE INN.** 116 Broad St (29401). 843/723-7999; FAX 843/720-2615; res: 800/476-9741. 19 rms, 2-3 story, 3 suites. Mid-Mar-mid-June, mid-Sept-Oct: S $180-$240; D $200-$260; each addl $20; suites $310; under 12 free; lower rates rest of yr. Crib free. TV; cable (premium). Complimentary continental bkfst; afternoon refreshments. Restaurant nearby. Ck-out noon, ck-in 4 pm. Business servs avail. In-rm modem link. Luggage handling. Valet serv. Concierge serv. Health club privileges. Stocked refrigerators, fireplaces. Cr cds: A, C, D, DS, MC, V.

⬛ ⬛ SC

★ **KING GEORGE THE FOURTH INN.** 32 George St (29401). 843/723-9339; FAX 843/723-7749; res: 888/723-1667. Web www.bbonline.com/sc/kinggeorge/. 10 rms, 5 with shower only, 2 share bath, 4 story, 4 suites. No elvtr. Mid-Feb-early June, Oct-Nov: S, D $89-$139; each addl $10; suites $135-$155; wkends (2-day min); lower rates rest of yr. TV. Complimentary continental bkfst. Complimentary coffee in rms. Restaurant nearby. Ck-out 11 am, ck-in 1-6 pm. Luggage handling. Refrigerators, fireplaces. Built in 1790s; Federal style. Totally nonsmoking. Cr cds: C, MC, V.

⬛ ⬛

★★★ **KINGS COURTYARD INN.** 198 King St (29401). 843/723-7000; FAX 843/720-2608. 41 rms, 3 story. Mid-Mar-early June, mid-Sept-Oct: S $135-$175; D $155-$195; each addl $20; suites $240; under 12 free; lower rates rest of yr. Crib free. TV; cable (premium). Complimentary continental bkfst. Dining rm 7-10 am; Sat, Sun to 11 am. Rm serv. Serv bar. Ck-out noon, ck-in 3 pm. Meeting rms. Business servs avail. In-rm modem link. Luggage handling. Concierge serv. Whirlpool. Health club privileges. Refrigerators, fireplaces. Built in 1853; 2 inner courtyards. Cr cds: A, C, DS, MC, V.

D ⬛ ⬛ SC

✓★★ **LAUREL HILL PLANTATION BED & BREAKFAST.** 8913 N Hwy 17 (29458), 30 mi N on SC 17. 843/887-3708; res: 888/887-3708. Web bbonline.com/sc/laurelhill/. 4 rms, 3 story. No elvtrs. No rm phones. Feb-May, Sept-Oct: S, D $95-$115; each addl $15; lower rates rest of yr. TV in some rms. Complimentary full bkfst. Ck-out 11 am, ck-in 4-7 pm. On creek. Totally nonsmoking. Cr cds: A, C, D, DS, MC, V.

⬛ ⬛ ⬛

★★★ **LODGE ALLEY INN.** 195 E Bay St (29401). 843/722-1611; FAX 843/577-7497; res: 800/845-1004. 95 rms, 4 story, 50 kit. units. Mid-Mar-early June, early Sept-early Nov: S, D $145-$179; each addl $15; kit. suites $155-$349; under 12 free; package plans; lower rates rest of yr. Crib free. TV; cable (premium). Complimentary coffee; refreshments. Dining rm 7-10:30 am, 11:30 am-2:30 pm, 6-10 pm; Sun to 2:30 pm. Rm serv to 10:30 am. Bar 11:30 am-midnight; closed Sun; entertainment spring, fall. Ck-out noon, ck-in 4 pm. Business servs avail. Luggage handling. Valet serv. Health club privileges. Refrigerators, minibars; some fireplaces. Some balconies. Built in 1773; antiques. Courtyard gardens with fountain. Cr cds: A, C, MC, V.

⬛

★★★ **MAISON DU PRÉ.** 317 E Bay St (29401). 843/723-8691; FAX 843/723-3722; res: 800/844-4667. Web www.maisondupre.com. 15 rms, 1-3 story, 1 kit. Early Feb-mid-June, Sept-mid-Nov: S, D $98-$165; suites $160-$200; carriage house with kit. $160; lower rates rest of yr. Crib free. TV; cable. Complimentary continental bkfst. Ck-out noon, ck-in 2 pm. Built in 1804. Composed of 3 single Charleston houses and 2 carriage houses with porches. 3 fountains. Cr cds: C, DS, MC, V.

⬛ ⬛

★★★ **MEETING STREET INN.** 173 Meeting St (29401), in heart of downtown historic district. 843/723-1882; FAX 843/577-0851; res: 800/842-8022. Web www.aesir.com/meetingstreet/. 56 rms, 4 story. Mid-Mar-early June, mid-Sept-Oct: S, D $109-$210; each addl $10; under 13 free; lower rates rest of yr. Crib free. Parking $6. TV; cable (premium). Whirlpool. Complimentary continental bkfst; afternoon refreshments. Bar noon-11 pm, closed Sun. Ck-out noon, ck-in 3 pm. Business servs avail. Luggage handling. Health club privileges. Walking tours. Refrigerators avail. Courtyard with fountain. Opp Old City Market. Cr cds: A, C, D, DS, MC, V.

D ⬛ SC

★★★ **PLANTERS INN.** 112 N Market St (29401). 843/722-2345; FAX 843/577-2125; res: 800/845-7082. E-mail plantersinn@charleston.net; web www.plantersinn.com. 56 rms, 4 story, 6 suites. Mid-March-mid-June, mid-Sept-mid-Nov: S, D $160-$250; suites $300-$450; lower rates rest of yr. Crib free. TV; cable (premium). Complimentary continental bkfst; afternoon refreshments. Restaurant (see PENINSULA GRILL). Ck-out noon, ck-in 3 pm. Meeting rm. Business servs avail. In-rm modem link. Luggage handling. Concierge serv. Health club privileges. Massage. Many antiques. Cr cds: A, C, D, DS, MC, V.

D ⬛

★★★ **QUEEN VICTORIA INN.** 208 King St (29401). 843/720-2944; FAX 843/720-2930; res: 800/933-5464. 18 rms, 3 story, 4 suites. Mar-mid-June, Sept-Nov: S $165; D $185; each addl $20; suites $235; under 12 free; lower rates rest of yr. Crib free. TV; cable (premium). Complimentary continental bkfst; afternoon refreshments. Restaurant adj 8 am-3 pm. Ck-out noon, ck-in 3 pm. Business servs avail. In-rm modem link. Luggage handling. Concierge serv. Health club privileges. Massage. Refrigerators. Romanesque-style building (1889). Cr cds: C, D, DS, MC, V.

⬛ ⬛ SC

★★ **RUTLEDGE VICTORIAN GUESTHOUSES.** 114 Rutledge Ave (29401). 843/722-7551; FAX 843/727-0065; res: 888/722-7553. Web www.bbonline.com/sc/rutledge. 11 rms, 7 with shower only, 3 share bath, 4 story. No elvtr. Mid-Sept-Nov, Mar-mid-June: S $59; D $89-$159; 2-bedrm kit. cottage $190; each addl $20. Children over 12 yrs only. TV. Complimentary continental bkfst; afternoon refreshments. Restaurant nearby. Ck-out 11 am, ck-in 2-6 pm. Luggage handling. Concierge serv. Parking. Bathrm phones, fireplaces; some refrigerators. Built in 1880; Italianate architecture; antiques. Totally nonsmoking. Cr cds: C, MC, V.

⬛ ⬛

★★★ **VENDUE INN.** 19 Vendue Range (29401). 843/577-7970; FAX 843/577-2913; res: 800/845-7900. Web www.charleston.net/com/vendueinn. 22 rms, 3 story, 23 suites. Mid-Mar-mid-June, mid-Sept-Nov: S $130-$150; D $155-$165; each addl $15; suites $175-$235; lower rates rest of yr. TV. Complimentary full bkfst; afternoon refreshments. Restaurant 6-10 pm. Bar 11:30 am-9 pm. Ck-out noon, ck-in 3 pm. Meeting rm. Business servs avail. In-rm modem link. Luggage handling. Valet serv. Concierge serv. Exercise equipt. Fireplace in suites. Located in 1824 structure. Rooftop terrace overlooking harbor. Cr cds: A, C, D, DS, MC, V.

D ⬛ ⬛ ⬛

★★★ **WENTWORTH MANSION.** 149 Wentworth St (29401). 843/853-1896; FAX 843/720-5290; res: 888/466-1886. Web www.wentworthmansion.com. 21 rms, 4 story, 7 suites. S $225-$425; D $275-$475; each addl $50; suites $475-$675; under 12 free. Crib free. TV; cable, VCR avail (movies). Complimentary full bkfst; afternoon refreshments. Restaurant 5-11 pm. Rm serv 24 hrs. Ck-out noon. Business center. In-rm modem link. Luggage handling. Valet serv. Concierge serv. Valet parking. Golf privileges. Health club privileges. In-rm whirlpools, refrigerators; many fire-places. Built in 1886. Second Empire mansion. Totally nonsmoking. Cr cds: A, C, D, DS, MC, V.

★★★★ **WOODLANDS RESORT & INN.** *125 Parsons Rd (29483), approx 20 mi N on I-26, exit 199A, 2 mi W on US 17A, N on SC 165 to Parsons Rd.* 843/875-2600; FAX 843/875-2603; res: 800/774-9999. Web www.woodlandsinn.com. This English country house hotel nestled in 42 low-country acres offers tennis, croquet, swimming and entertainment. Guest rooms are sumptuously appointed with sitting areas, fireplaces, heated towel racks and whirlpool baths. A full-service, state-of-the-art spa offers everything from massage to mud masks and aromatherapy. 19 rms, 3 story. S, D $225-$335. TV; cable (premium), VCR (movies). Pool; pool-side serv. Restaurant (see THE DINING ROOM AT WOODLANDS). Rm serv 7:30 am-10 pm. Bar 11:30 am-midnight; closed Sun. Ck-out noon, ck-in 3 pm. Luggage handling. Concierge serv. Meeting rms. Business servs avail. Lighted tennis. Golf privileges, pro. Lawn games. Bicycles. Massage. Totally nonsmoking. Cr cds: A, C, D, DS, MC, V.

Restaurants

★★ **82 QUEEN.** *82 Queen St (29401).* 843/722-4428. Specializes in seafood, regional low-country dishes. Hrs: 11:30 am-4 pm, 6-10 pm; Fri, Sat to 10:30 pm. Res accepted. Bar to 2 am. Semi-a la carte: lunch $6.50-$10.95, dinner $16-$22. Outdoor dining. Located in 1800s bldg. Cr cds: A, C, D, MC, V.

★★ **ANSON.** *12 Anson St (29401).* 843/577-0551. Hrs: 5:30-11 pm; Fri, Sat to midnight. Res accepted. Bar. A la carte entrees: dinner $14.95-$24.95. Specializes in fresh seafood, chops. Bi-level dining. Decor reminiscent of Lowcountry plantation homes. Cr cds: A, C, D, DS, MC, V.

★ **AW SHUCKS.** *70 State St (29401).* 843/723-1151. Hrs: 11 am-10 pm; Fri, Sat to 11 pm. Closed Thanksgiving, Dec 25. Bar. Semi-a la carte: lunch $5.99-$9.99, dinner $9.99-$14.99. Specializes in seafood. Salad bar. Casual rustic decor. Cr cds: A, C, DS, MC, V.

★★★ **BARBADOES ROOM.** *(See Mills House Hotel)* 843/577-2400. Hrs: 6:30 am-2 pm, 5:30-10 pm; Sun brunch 11 am-2 pm. Res accepted. Continental menu. Bar 11-2 am. Wine list. Semi-a la carte: bkfst $5.95-$8.95, lunch $5.95-$9.95, dinner $14.95-$24.95. Buffet: bkfst $8.95. Sun brunch $16.95. Specializes in seafood. Own baking. Pianist evenings. Valet parking. Cr cds: A, C, D, DS, MC, V.

★★★ **BEAUMONT'S CAFE.** *12 Cumberland St (29401).* 843/577-5500. Hrs: 11:30 am-3 pm, 5-11 pm. Closed Dec 25; Sun in Aug. Res accepted. French, Mediterranean menu. Bar. Semi-a la carte: lunch $5.25-$12.95, dinner $6.95-$21.75. Specialties: bouillabaisse, foie gras, duck. View of courtyard. Outdoor dining. Cr cds: A, C, D, DS, MC, V.

★★ **BLOSSOM CAFE.** *171 E Bay St (29401).* 843/722-9200. Hrs: 11:30 am-11 pm; Fri, Sat to midnight; Sun from 11 am. Closed Jan 1, Dec 25. Res accepted. Mediterranean, Amer menu. Bar. Semi-a la carte: lunch, dinner $6.25-$21.95. Child's meals. Specialties: oak-roasted salmon, pizzas cooked in wood-burning oven. Outdoor dining. Modern decor. Cr cds: A, C, MC, V.

✓★★ **BRIX.** *415 Mill St (29414), on Shem Creek.* 843/881-2246. Hrs: 5:30-10 pm; Sun brunch 10:30 am-2 pm. Closed Jan 1, Dec 25. Res accepted. French menu. Bar. Wine cellar. Semi-a la carte: dinner $8-$16.75. Sun brunch varies. Specializes in seafood, veal, beef. Child's meals. Parking. Fireplace. Cr cds: A, C, MC, V.

★★ **CAROLINA'S.** *10 Exchange St (29401).* 843/724-3800. Hrs: 5:30 pm to closing; Sun from 5 pm. Res accepted. Bar from 5 pm. Semi-a la carte: dinner $7.95-$25.95. Specializes in grilled seafood, pasta, regional cuisine. Own baking. Cr cds: A, C, D, DS, MC, V.

★★★ **CHARLESTON GRILL.** *(See Charleston Place)* 843/577-4522. The club-like atmosphere of this hotel dining room features mahogany-paneled walls, green marble floors and dim, romantic lighting. Specializes in game, beef, fresh local seafood. Own baking, soups. Hrs: 6-11 pm. Res accepted. Bar 4 pm-midnight. Wine cellar. A la carte entrees: dinner $16-$29. Valet parking. Jazz trio. Cr cds: A, C, D, MC, V.

✓★★★ **ELLIOTT'S ON THE SQUARE.** *387 King St (29403), Francis Marion.* 843/724-8888. Hrs: 6:30 am-10 am, 11:30 am-3 pm, 5:30-9:30 pm; Sat, Sun 6:30-11 am, 11:30 am-3 pm, 5:30-9:30 pm. Res accepted. Contemporary Amer menu. Bar. Semi-a la carte: bkfst $3.95-$7.95, lunch $5.95-$11.50, dinner $17-$19.95. Specializes in fresh seafood. Valet parking. Art deco decor. Cr cds: A, C, D, DS, MC, V.

★★★ **FULTON FIVE.** *5 Fulton St (29401).* 843/853-5555. Hrs: 5:30 pm to closing. Closed Sun; also late Aug-1st wk Sept. Res accepted. Northern Italian menu. Bar. Wine cellar. Semi-a la carte: dinner $12-$24. Specialties: risotto, antipasto spoleto, lemon sherbet with campari. Own baking. Street parking. Intimate atmosphere; European decor. Cr cds: A, C, D, MC, V.

★★ **GARIBALDI'S.** *49 S Market St (29401).* 843/723-7153. Hrs: 6-11 pm. Closed Dec 25. Italian menu. Serv bar. Semi-a la carte: dinner $7.95-19.95. Specializes in fresh seafood, pasta, veal. Own desserts. Outdoor dining. Bistro atmosphere; in center of historic Charleston Market. Cr cds: A, C, MC, V.

★★ **J BISTRO.** *819 Coleman Blvd (29464).* 843/971-7778. Hrs: 5-10 pm; Fri, Sat to 11 pm; Sun brunch 10:30 am-2:30 pm. Closed Mon; most major hols. Bar. Semi-a la carte: dinner $6-$18. Sun brunch $12. Specializes in pork chops, seafood. Two-level dining area. Casual decor. Cr cds: A, C, D, MC, V.

★★ **MAGNOLIAS.** *185 E Bay St (29401).* 843/577-7771. Hrs: 11:30 am-11 pm; Fri, Sat to midnight. Closed Jan 1, Dec 25. Res accepted. Bar. Semi-a la carte: lunch $7.50-$17.50, dinner $8.25-$21.95. Specialties: pan-fried chicken livers, spicy shrimp and sausage, veal meatloaf. Contemporary decor within historic structure; overlooks Lodge Alley. Cr cds: A, C, D, MC, V.

★★ **MARKET EAST BISTRO.** *14 N Market St (29401).* 843/577-5080. Hrs: 10:30 am-11 pm. Closed Jan 1, July 4. Res accepted. Continental menu. Bar. Semi-a la carte: lunch $6.75-$10.25, dinner $8.50-$15.95. Child's meals. Specialties: bistro crabcake with lobster coulis, Moroccan cous cous with seafood. Outdoor dining. Bistro atmosphere. Cr cds: A, C, D, DS, MC, V.

★★★ **MCCRADY'S TAVERN.** *2 Unity Alley (29401).* 843/577-0025. Hrs: 11:30 am-2:30 pm, 5-11 pm; Fri, Sat to midnight. Closed Sun; some major hols. Bar. Semi-a la carte: lunch $5.95-$9.95, dinner $7.95-$19. Specializes in seafood, pasta, veal. Historic tavern (1778). Cr cds: A, C, D, MC, V.

★ **ONE-EYED PARROT.** *1130 Ocean Blvd (29451), E on US 17B to SC 703, then S.* 843/886-4360. Hrs: 5-10 pm; Fri, Sat to 11 pm. Closed Thanksgiving, Dec 25. Caribbean menu. Bar. Semi-a la carte: dinner $6.95-$16.99. Child's meals. Specializes in seafood, beef. Entertainment Fri-Sun. Second floor dining rm overlooking ocean; terrace dining. Cr cds: A, C, D, DS, MC, V.

✓★ **PAPILLONS RESTAURANT.** *32 N Market St (29401). 843/723-6510.* Hrs: 11 am-10 pm; Fri, Sat to 11 pm; Sun to 9 pm. Mediterranean menu. Semi-a la carte: lunch $5.95-$8.95, dinner $8.95-$12.95. Buffet: lunch $5.95. Specializes in pasta, calzones, wood-burning oven pizza. Own pastries. Trattoria atmosphere. Cr cds: A, C, DS, MC, V.

★★★ **PENINSULA GRILL.** *(See Planters) 843/723-0700.* Hrs: 5:30-10 pm; Fri, Sat to 11 pm. Res accepted. Regional Amer menu. Bar from 4 pm. Wine cellar. Semi-a la carte: dinner $15-$27. Child's meals. Specialties: wild mushroom grits, pistachio-crusted sea bass, benne seed-crusted rack of New Zealand lamb. Own pastries. Outdoor dining. Elegant atmosphere reminiscent of 1940s supper club. Cr cds: A, C, DS, MC, V.

★★ **POOGAN'S PORCH.** *72 Queen St (29401), in historic district. 843/577-2337.* Hrs: 11:30 am-2:30 pm, 5:30-10 pm; Sat, Sun brunch 10:30 am-2:30 pm. Res accepted. Regional low-country cuisine. Bar. Semi-a la carte: lunch $4.95-$7.95, dinner $9.95-$17.95. Specialties: Cajun shrimp, bread pudding, shrimp creole. Outdoor dining. Restored house (1891); fireplace, garden rm. Intimate dining. Cr cds: A, C, MC, V.

★★★ **RESTAURANT MILLION.** *2 Unity Alley (29401). 843/577-3141.* Hrs: 6:30-10 pm. Closed Sun, Mon; Jan 1, July 4, Dec 25. Res accepted. French menu. Bar. Semi-a la carte: dinner $27-$33. Prix fixe: dinner $38. Specializes in seafood, rack of lamb, rabbit. Tapestry, fireplaces. Jacket. Cr cds: A, C, D, MC, V.

★★ **SARACEN RESTAURANT.** *141 E Bay St (29401). 843/723-6242.* Hrs: 6-10 pm. Closed Sun, Mon; some major hols. Res accepted. Eclectic menu. Bar 5 pm-2 am. Semi-a la carte: dinner $11-$25. Child's meals. Specializes in fresh seafood, beef, pork. Own baking. Jazz Fri, Sat seasonal. Street, garage parking. Former bank bldg (1853) combines Moorish, Persian, Hindu and Gothic architecture. On National Register of Historic Places. Cr cds: A, C, D, JCB, MC, V.

✓★★ **SERMET'S CORNER.** *276 King St (29401). 843/853-7775.* Hrs: 11 am-10 pm; Fri, Sat to 11 pm. Res accepted. Mediterranean menu. Bar. Semi-a la carte: lunch $7.75-$9, dinner $11-$17. Child's meals. Specialties: citrus-crusted salmon, pork tenderloin, grilled calamari. Street parking. Cr cds: A, C, MC, V.

★★ **SLIGHTLY NORTH OF BROAD.** *192 E Bay St (29401). 843/723-3424.* Hrs: 11:30 am-3 pm, 5:30-10 pm; Sat, Sun from 5:30 pm. Closed maj hols. Bar. Regional Southern menu. A la carte entrees: lunch $6.75-$10.95, dinner $8.50-$18.95. Child's meals. Specializes in seafood, pasta, beef. Open kitchen. Cr cds: A, C, D, DS, MC, V.

✓★★ **SLIGHTLY UP THE CREEK.** *130 Mill St (29464). 843/884-5005.* Hrs: from 5:30 pm; brunch 10:30 am-2:30 pm (in season). Closed Jan 1, Dec 25. Res accepted. Contemporary Amer menu. Bar. Semi-a la carte: dinner $6.50-$18.50. Brunch $4.75-$12. Child's meals. Specialties: grilled barbecued tuna, fried oysters in golden ginger citrus sauce. Parking. Outdoor dining. Cr cds: A, C, D, DS, MC, V.

★★ **SUPPER AT STACKS.** *101 Pitt St (29464). 843/884-7009.* Hrs: 6-10 pm. Closed Sun, Mon; some major hols. Regional Amer menu. Serv bar. Complete meals: dinner $29. Specializes in roast duck, fresh fish, beef tenderloin. Menu changes daily. Formal dining rm reminiscent of 18th-century Williamsburg, VA. Cr cds: A, C, MC, V.

★★★ **THE DINING ROOM AT WOODLANDS.** *(See Woodlands Resort & Inn) 843/875-2600.* Hrs: 7-10 am, 11 am-2:30 pm, 6-10 pm. Res accepted. Regional contemporary menu. Bar noon-midnight. Wine cellar. Semi-a la carte: bkfst $4.75-$18, lunch $7-$18. Complete meals: dinner $48-$65. Specialties: seafood, lamb, beef. Valet parking. Outdoor dining. Elegant decor. Terrace view. Jacket (dinner). Cr cds: A, C, D, DS, MC, V.

Unrated Dining Spot

LOUIS'S. *200 Meeting Street at Pinckney (29401). 843/853-2550.* Web www.louisrestaurant.com. Low country cuisine. Specialty: crab cakes. Mon-Sun 6-11 pm; $18-$24. Child's meals. Valet parking. Bar. Res pref. Cr cds: A, C, D, DS, MC, V.

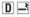

Cheraw (C-6)

(See also Bennettsville, Camden, Darlington, Florence, Hartsville)

Settled 1740 **Pop** 5,505 **Elev** 150 ft **Area Code** 843 **Zip** 29520
Information Chamber of Commerce, 221 Market St; 843/537-8425 or 843/537-7681

Profiting in commerce from both Carolinas, Cheraw grew rapidly when the Pee Dee River was opened for traffic. It is said that the town owes its many trees to an ordinance that required every person seen intoxicated in public to go out into the woods and fetch a tree for planting within the town.

What to See and Do

Carolina Sandhills National Wildlife Refuge. Approx 46,000 acres house almost 300 species of birds, mammals, reptiles and amphibians. Auto-tour route, hiking trails and observation towers avail. Fishing, hunting permitted. Interpretive displays avail at headquarters (on US 1, 4 mi NE of McBee). (Mon-Fri, during daylight) Approx 20 mi SW on US 1. Phone 843/335-8401. **Free**

Cheraw State Park. Located on 7,361 acres of gently rolling green sandhills. Lake swimming; boating (rentals); fishing. Nature trails; 18-hole golf. Picnicking (shelters); playground; recreation bldg. Camping; cabins (hookups, dump station). Standard fees. Unusually cool in hot-weather periods. 4 mi SW on US 52. Phone 843/537-2215 or 800/868-9630.

★ **Historic District.** Comprises 214 acres downtown and contains more than 50 antebellum homes and public bldgs, plus structures dating from later periods. The Town Green (ca 1768) is the site of the small Lyceum Museum (ca 1820). Other notable bldgs are Town Hall (ca 1858), Market Hall (ca 1837) and the Inglis-McIver Law Office (ca 1810). Free brochures on the district are avail at the Chamber office on the Green and at some local shops. Picnicking. Self-guided tours. Phone 843/537-7681.

Old St David's Episcopal Church (1768). Restored to 1820s period; last Anglican parish established in the state prior to the Revolutionary War. Used as a hospital by British during Revolution, later by Union Army during Civil War; about 50 British soldiers are buried in the churchyard. Tours (by appt); for self-tours, pick up keys at Chamber of Commerce, 221 Market St; phone 843/537-7681. Front & Church Sts. Phone 843/537-8425. **Free**

Annual Event

Spring Festival. Family Fun Run; tours; arts &crafts shows; Confederate reenactments; entertainment, trolley rides, car show. Phone 843/537-8420. Early Apr.

Motel

★ **INN CHERAW.** *321 2nd St (29520). 843/537-2011; FAX 843/537-0227; res: 800/535-8709.* 50 rms, 2 story. S $36-$60; D $40-$65; each addl $5; kit. units $45-$60; under 6 free; golf plans; higher rates NASCAR races. Crib free. Pet accepted, some restrictions. TV; cable (premium), VCR. Complimentary continental bkfst. Complimentary coffee in rms. Restaurant adj 11 am-9 pm. Ck-out 11 am. Meeting rms. Valet serv. Refrigerators; microwaves avail. Cr cds: A, C, D, DS, MC, V.

Inn

★★ **SPEARS GUEST HOUSE.** *228 Huger St (29520). 843/ 537-1094; FAX 843/537-0302; res: 888/424-3729.* 4 rms. S, D $56-$75; wkly, monthly rates. TV; cable (premium). Complimentary continental bkfst. Complimentary coffee in rms. Ck-out noon, ck-in 4 pm. Federal-style house built in 1845; antiques. Cr cds: A, C, MC, V.

Chester (C-4)

(See also Rock Hill)

Settled 1755 **Pop** 7,158 **Elev** 485 ft **Area Code** 803 **Zip** 29706
Information Chester County Chamber of Commerce, 109 Gadsden St, PO Box 489; 803/581-4142

Seat of Chester County, this town was named by settlers from Pennsylvania. Aaron Burr, guarded here in 1807 while under arrest for treason, broke away and climbed a high rock. After haranguing a surprised crowd, he was recaptured.

What to See and Do

Chester State Park. Approx 500 acres. Lake fishing; boating. Nature trail. Picnicking (shelters); recreation bldg. Camping (hookups, dump station). Equestrian show ring. Standard fees. 3 mi SW on SC 72. Phone 803/385-2680.

Clemson (C-2)

(See also Anderson, Greenville)

Founded 1889 **Pop** 11,096 **Elev** 850 ft **Area Code** 864 **Zip** 29631
E-mail clemcham@clemsonchamber.org
Web www.clemsonchamber.org
Information Clemson Area Chamber of Commerce, PO Box 1622, 29633; 864/654-1200 or 800/542-0746

Home of Clemson University, this community also hosts vacationers attracted to the huge lake that Hartwell Dam has formed on the Savannah River.

What to See and Do

Clemson University (1889) (17,000 students). Named for Thomas G. Clemson, son-in-law of John C. Calhoun, who bequeathed the bulk of his estate, Fort Hill, for establishment of a scientific college. 11 mi NW of I-85 at jct US 76, SC 93. Phone 864/656-3311 or -2061. On this 1,400 acre campus are

 Fort Hill (1803). Mansion on 1,100 acres acquired by Calhoun during his first term as vice president. House has many original furnishings belonging to Calhoun, Clemson. (Daily; closed some major hols) Phone 864/656-2475.   **Free**

 Hanover House (1716). This French Huguenot house was moved here from its original site near Pinopolis to prevent submersion in Lake Moultrie. (Wkends). Phone 864/656-2241.   **Free**

 State Botanical Gardens. This 250-acre area incl azalea and camelia trails, ornamental plantings, large collection of shrubs; dwarf conifer flower and turf display gardens; wildflower pioneer and bog garden is labeled in Braille. (Daily) E side of campus. Phone 864/656-3405.   **Free**

Oconee State Park. Approx 1,100 acres of park nestled in the foothills of the Blue Ridge and surrounded by Sumter National Forest (see GREENWOOD). Lake swimming, lifeguard (summer); boating (rentals); fishing.

Nature, hiking trails; recreation bldg; recreation & nature programs (summer); carpet golf. Picnicking (shelters), playground, concession, restaurant. Camping (hookups, dump station), cabins. Standard fees. 20 mi NW of town, 12 mi NW of Walhalla on SC 107. Phone 864/638-5353.

Raft trips. Guided whitewater rafting trips on the Chattooga National Wild and Scenic River. Res required. Also canoe and kayak clinics and overnight trips. (Mar-Oct, daily) 34 mi NW on US 76 in Long Creek. Phone 800/451-9972.

World of Energy. Three-dimensional displays on the "Story of Energy," with exhibits on hydro, coal and nuclear production of electricity; also displays on radiation and supplemental energy sources. Computer games; films. Overlooks Lake Keowee and one of the world's largest nuclear generating plants. Tour of the control rm training simulator. Picnic area and boat dock adj. (Daily; closed Jan 1, Thanksgiving, Dec 24 & 25) 12 mi NW on SC 130, 123. Phone 864/885-4600 or 800/777-1004.   **Free**

Annual Event

Clemson Fest. Entertainment, arts & crafts, children's activities. Boat parade & contest precedes fireworks display. Phone 864/646-6110. July 4.

Motels

✓★ **COMFORT INN.** *1305 Tiger Blvd (29633).* 864/653-3600; FAX 864/654-3123; res: 800/228-5150. 122 rms, 4 story. S, D $50-$65; each addl $6; suites $79-$150; under 18 free. Crib free. TV; cable. Pool; whirlpool. Complimentary continental bkfst. Restaurant nearby. Ck-out noon. Meeting rms. In-rm modem link. Valet serv. Exercise equipt; sauna. Cr cds: A, C, D, DS, MC, V.

★★ **HOLIDAY INN.** *894 Tiger Blvd (29631), 1½ mi E on US 123.* 864/654-4450; FAX 864/654-8451; res: 888/442-0422. 220 rms, 2 story. S, D $57-$63; each addl $5; suites $129; under 19 free; higher rates football wkends. Crib free. Pet accepted. TV; cable (premium). Pool. Coffee in rms. Restaurant 6:30 am-2 pm, 5:30-8:30 pm. Bar 4 pm-midnight; closed Sun. Ck-out noon. Coin lndry. Meeting rms. Business servs avail. In-rm modem link. Valet serv. Golf privileges. Health club privileges. On lake. Cr cds: A, C, D, DS, JCB, MC, V.

★★ **RAMADA INN.** *US Hwy 76 & 123 (29633), SC 76 & US 123.* 864/654-7501; FAX 864/654-7301; res: 800/654-7501. 149 rms, 4 story. S $49-$58; D $54-$65; suites $125-$150; under 18 free; wkend rates; higher rates: football wkends, special events. Crib free. TV; cable (premium). Indoor pool; whirlpool. Sauna. Restaurant 6:30 am-2 pm, 5-10 pm. Rm serv. Bar exc Sun. Ck-out 11 am. Meeting rms. Valet serv. Golf privileges. Some refrigerators. Cr cds: A, C, D, DS, MC, V.

Inn

✓★★ **SUNRISE FARM BED & BREAKFAST INN.** *325 Sunrise Dr (29676), 1 mi E of SC 130.* 864/944-0121; FAX 864/944-6195; res: 888/991-0121. E-mail sfbb@bellsouth.net; web www.bbonline.com/sc/ sunrise farm. 6 rms, 2 story, 1 suite, 2 cottages. Rm phones in cottages. S $70; D $80-$85; each addl $10; suite $120; cottages $85-$100. Crib avail. TV; VCR (movies). Complimentary full bkfst. Complimentary coffee in rms. Restaurant nearby 6 am-8 pm. Ck-out 11 am, ck-in 3-6 pm. Business servs avail. 18-hole golf privileges. Refrigerator in cottages. Built in 1890; Victorian country farmhouse. Totally nonsmoking. Cr cds: C, MC, V.

Clinton (C-3)

(See also Greenville, Greenwood, Newberry, Spartanburg)

Pop 7,987 **Elev** 680 ft **Area Code** 864 **Zip** 29325
E-mail lcchamber@prtcnet.com
Information Laurens County Chamber of Commerce, PO Box 248, Laurens 29360; 864/833-2716

In 1865, Clinton was "a mudhole surrounded by barrooms," according to the young Reverend William Jacobs, who not only rid the town of barrooms but founded a library, orphanage, high school and Presbyterian College (1880). A young attorney by the name of Henry Clinton Young was hired by the townspeople to help lay out the streets, hence the town came to be named for his middle name.

What to See and Do

Rose Hill (ca 1825). Forty-four acres. Located in Rose Hill State Park, this restored cotton plantation was the home of William H. Gist, known as South Carolina's secession governor. The Federal-style house with 1860 furnishings sits on a gently rising knoll amid boxwoods and roses. House (Sat & Sun; also by appt). Grounds (Thurs-Mon). Picnic area, nature trail. 15 mi E on SC 72, 2 mi N on SC 176, then W on Sardis Rd. Phone 864/427-5966. Museum ¢; Grounds **Free**

Motels

✓ ★ **DAYS INN.** *12374 Hwy 56 N (29325), exit 52.* 864/833-6600; FAX 864/833-6600; res: 800/329-7466. 59 rms, 2 story. S $42-$45; D $49-$50; each addl $5; suites $80; under 17 free. Crib free. Pet accepted. TV; cable (premium). Pool. Complimentary continental bkfst. Restaurant adj 6:30 am-10 pm. Ck-out 11 am. Coin lndry. Meeting rms. Exercise equipt; sauna. Some refrigerators, microwaves. Cr cds: A, C, D, DS, MC, V.

D 🐾 ➤ 🏋 ➤ 🔥 SC

★★ **RAMADA INN.** *US Hwy 56 & I-26 (29325), exit 52.* 864/833-4900; FAX 864/833-4916. 102 rms, 2 story. S, D $65. TV; cable (premium). Pool. Restaurant 6:30 am-2 pm, 5-9 pm; Sat 6:30-10 am, 5-9 pm; Sun to 2 pm. Rm serv. Bar 5 pm-midnight. Ck-out noon. Lndry facilities. Meeting rms. Business servs avail. Sundries. Exercise equipt. Refrigerators avail. Cr cds: A, C, D, DS, MC, V.

D ➤ 🏋 ➤ 🔥 SC

Columbia (D-4)

(See also Camden, Newberry, Orangeburg, Sumter)

Founded 1786 **Pop** 98,052 **Elev** 213 ft **Area Code** 803
Web www.columbiasc.net
Information Columbia Metropolitan Visitors Center, 1012 Gervais St, 29201; 803/254-0479 or 800/264-4884

The broad-boulevarded capital of South Carolina is not only the state's political and governmental capital, but also its wholesale and retail trade center. Located within three miles of the geographic center of the state, Columbia was laid out as the capital as a compromise between the contending Up Country and Low Country farmers. The city rarely departs from a checkerboard pattern; the streets are sometimes 150 feet wide, originally planned that way to discourage malaria.

The General Assembly met for the first time in the State House in Columbia on January 4, 1790. George Washington was a guest here during his Southern tour the next year. On December 17, 1860, a convention assembled in Columbia's First Baptist Church and drew up the Ordinance of Secession, setting off a chain of events that terminated, for the city, on February 17, 1865, when General William T. Sherman's troops occupied Columbia and reduced it to ashes. An area of 84 blocks and 1,386 buildings was destroyed; on Main Street only the unfinished new statehouse and the home of the French consul were spared. From these ashes, a city of stately buildings has risen.

The economy of the city is based on trade, industry, finance and government.

Since 1801, when the South Carolina College, now the University of South Carolina, was established here, the city has been an educational center; today it is the site of nine schools of higher education.

Columbia is the headquarters for the Francis Marion National Forest (see CHARLESTON) and the Sumter National Forest (see GREENWOOD).

What to See and Do

Columbia Museum of Art. Galleries house Renaissance paintings from the collection of Samuel H. Kress; 19th- and 20th-century American, emphasizing the Southeast, and European paintings; changing exhibitions drawn from permanent collection and from objects on loan. Concerts, films, lectures and special events accenting exhibitions. (Daily exc Mon; closed most major hols) Main & Hampton Sts. Phone 803/799-2810. ¢¢

Confederate Relic Room and Museum. Relic collection from the Colonial period through the space age, with special emphasis on South Carolina's Confederate period. (Mon-Fri, also 1st Sat of month) 920 Sumter St. Phone 803/898-8095. **Free**

Congaree Swamp National Monument. Old-growth, bottomland hardwood forest, approximately 22,200 acres. Trees and waters teem with wildlife. Fishing, canoeing; hiking trails, boardwalks; public contact station; primitive camping (by permit). (Daily; closed Dec 25) 20 mi SE off SC 48. Phone 803/776-4396. **Free**

First Baptist Church (1859). First Secession Convention, which marked the beginning of the Civil War, met here Dec 17, 1860. (Daily exc Sat; closed hols) 1306 Hampton St. Phone 803/256-4251.

First Presbyterian Church (1853). First congregation organized in Columbia (1795); President Woodrow Wilson's parents are buried in churchyard. (Daily) 1324 Marion St, at Lady St. Phone 803/799-9062.

Fort Jackson. The most active entry training center for US Army, with 16,000 soldiers assigned. Museum on Jackson Blvd has displays on history of fort and of today's army. (Tues-Sat; closed hols) E edge of city, between I-20 & US 76. Phone 803/751-7419 or 803/751-7355. **Free**

Governor's Mansion (1855). Built as officers' quarters for the Arsenal Academy. Tours (Tues-Thurs). Res required. 800 Richland St. Phone 803/737-1710. **Free**

Hampton–Preston Mansion (1818). Purchased by Wade Hampton I; occupied by the Hamptons and the family of his daughter, Mrs. John Preston. In February 1865, it served as headquarters for Union General J.A. Logan. Many Hampton family furnishings and decorative arts of the antebellum period. (Daily exc Mon; closed most major hols) 1615 Blanding St. Phone 803/252-1770. ¢¢

Lake Murray. Lake is 41 mi long, with 520-mi shoreline; impounded by Saluda Dam for hydroelectric purposes. Swimming, waterskiing; boating, fishing; picnicking; camping (fee). Marina in White Rock, 17 mi NW, phone 803/749-1554. 15 mi NW via I-26, Irmo exit. For further info phone 803/781-5940.

Lexington County Museum Complex. Historic restoration from mid-1800s; depicts life of area farmer. Period country furnishings, textiles, decorative arts. Spinning and weaving demonstrations. (Daily exc Mon; closed hols) 10 mi W via US 378 at Fox St in Lexington. Phone 803/359-8369. ¢

Riverbanks Zoological Park & Botanical Garden. Exhibits of animals in nonrestrictive natural habitat areas; aquarium-reptile complex with diving demonstrations; birdhouse with daily rainstorm; demonstrations at Riverbanks Farm; penguin and sea lion feedings. (Daily; closed Thanksgiving, Dec 25) 500 Wildlife Pkwy. Phone 803/779-8717. ¢¢¢

Robert Mills Historic House (1823) **& Park.** One of a few residences designed by Robert Mills, Federal architect and designer of the Washington Monument; mantels, art, furnishings of Regency period. (Daily exc Mon; closed most major hols) 1616 Blanding St. Phone 803/252-1770. ¢¢

Sesquicentennial State Park. On 1,445 acres. Log house (1756). Interpretive center. Lake swimming, bathhouse; boating (rentals), fishing. Nature, exercise trails. Picnicking (shelters), playground. Recreation bldg. Camping (hookups, dump station). Swimming & boating (Memorial Day-Labor Day). Standard fees. 13 mi NE on US 1. Phone 803/788-2706.

South Carolina Archives Building. Historical and genealogical research facility with documents dating from 1671; changing exhibits. Research rm (Tues-Sat, also Sun afternoons; closed state hols). Tours (by appt). 8301 Parklane Rd. Phone 803/896-6219 or 803/898-4921. **Free**

South Carolina State Museum. Located in world's first fully-electric textile mill (1894); exhibits on art, natural history, cultural history and science & technology with emphasis on contributions by South Carolinians; numerous hands-on exhibits; dioramas. Included is a center dedicated to Nobel Prize winner Charles Townes, who helped develop the laser. Gift shop. (Mon-Sat, also Sun afternoons; closed Easter, Thanksgiving, Dec 25, also morning of Jan 1) 301 Gervais St. Phone 803/898-4921. **¢¢**

Town Theatre. One of the oldest (since 1919) community theater groups in the US. Broadway plays and musicals. Tours (by appt). Performances (late Sept-late May; also summer show). 1012 Sumter St. For tour schedule, ticket info phone 803/799-2510.

Trinity Cathedral (Episcopal) (1846). Reproduction of Yorkminster, England; the oldest church bldg in Columbia and one of the largest Episcopal congregations in the US. Hiram Powers baptismal font, box pews, English stained glass. Three Wade Hamptons (politically prominent South Carolina family) are buried in the churchyard; graves of 7 governors and 6 bishops are also here. In 1977 it became the Cathedral Parish of the Episcopal Diocese of Upper South Carolina. (Spring & fall, Mon-Fri, limited hrs) 1100 Sumter St, at Senate St, opp statehouse. Phone 803/771-7300. **Free**

University of South Carolina (1801) (26,000 students). Located downtown. For campus tour info stop at the University of South Carolina Visitor Center. (Daily exc Sun) Pendleton & Assemby Sts. Phone 803/777-0169 (exc SC) or 800/922-9755. Points of interest include

Carolina Coliseum. Houses Gamecock Basketball and other sports events, concerts, exhibitions, trade shows, circuses and other entertainment. Assembly & Blossom Sts.

Koger Center for the Arts. Contemporary structure houses center for the performing arts. Diverse musical, theatrical and dance programs. Assembly & Greene Sts.

McKissick Museum. Houses Bernard M. Baruch Silver Gallery with antique European silver, J. Harry Howard gemstone collection, Laurence L. Smith Mineral Library, Catawba Native American pottery collection, Southern Folk Art, historical collections, Art Gallery, Education Museum, Broadcasting Archives. (Daily; closed major hols, also Dec 24) At the head of the Horseshoe. Phone 803/777-7251. **Free**

The Horseshoe. Original campus area. Ten of the 11 bldgs on the quadrangle date back to the 19th century and are listed in the National Register of Historic Places. Monument erected in 1827 was designed by Robert Mills. Off Sumter St.

Woodrow Wilson Boyhood Home (1872). Built by Wilson's father; items associated with Wilson's family and career. (Daily exc Mon; closed most major hols) 1705 Hampton St. Phone 803/252-1770. **¢¢**

Annual Event

South Carolina State Fair. Fairgrounds, 1200 Rosewood Dr. Agricultural, floral, home, craft, livestock and commercial exhibits. Entertainment, shows, carnival. Phone 803/799-3387. Oct 5-15.

Motels

✓ ★ **BAYMONT INN & SUITES.** *1538 Horseshoe Dr (29223), exit 74 to Horseshoe Dr.* 803/736-6400; FAX 803/788-7875; res: 800/301-0200. 102 rms, 3 story. S $35.95-$43.95; D $42.95-$49.95. Crib free. TV; cable (premium). Pool. Complimentary continental bkfst. Coffee in rms. Restaurant adj open 24 hrs. Ck-out noon. Coin lndry. Meeting rm. Business servs avail. In-rm modem link. Valet serv. Microwaves. Cr cds: A, C, D, DS, MC, V.

D ⊠ ⊠ ⊠ SC

★★ **COLUMBIA RESIDENCE INN.** *150 Stoneridge Dr (29210), off I-126 Greystone Blvd exit.* 803/779-7000; FAX 803/779-0408; res: 800/331-3131. 128 kit. suites, 2 story. S $99; D $109-$134; family rates. Crib free. Pet accepted, some restrictions. TV; cable (premium). Pool; whirlpool. Complimentary continental bkfst. Complimentary coffee in rms. Ck-out noon. Coin lndry. Meeting rms. Business servs avail. In-rm modem link. Valet serv. Exercise equipt. Microwaves; some fireplaces. Some grills. Cr cds: A, C, D, DS, JCB, MC, V.

D ⊠ ⊠ ⊠ ⊠ ⊠ SC

★ **COLUMBIA WEST TRAVELODGE.** *2210 Bush River Rd (29210), at I-20.* 803/798-9665; FAX 803/798-4876; res: 800/378-7878. 108 rms, 3 story. S $49.95; D $54.95; each addl $5; under 18 free. Crib free. Pet accepted. TV; cable (premium). Pool. Coffee in rms. Restaurant opp 6 am-10 pm. Ck-out 11 am. Meeting rms. Business servs avail. Valet serv. Guest lndry. Health club privileges. Refrigerators, microwaves avail. Cr cds: A, C, D, DS, ER, JCB, MC, V.

D ⊠ ⊠ ⊠ ⊠ SC

★★★ **COURTYARD BY MARRIOTT.** *347 Zimalcrest Dr (29210), off I-20.* 803/731-2300; FAX 803/772-6965; res: 800/321-2211. 149 units, 3 story. S $84; suites $98; wkend rates. Crib free. TV; cable (premium). Pool; whirlpool. Coffee in rms. Restaurant 6:30-10 am; wkends 7-11 am. Bar 5-10 pm (Mon-Sat). Ck-out noon. Coin lndry. Meeting rms. Business servs avail. In-rm modem link. Valet serv. Exercise equipt. Refrigerators avail. Cr cds: A, C, D, DS, MC, V.

D ⊠ ⊠ ⊠ ⊠ SC

★★ **HAMPTON INN.** *1094 Chris Dr (29169).* 803/791-8940; FAX 803/739-2291; res: 800/426-7866. 121 rms, 4 story. S, D $57-$71; under 18 free. Crib free. TV; cable (premium). Pool. Complimentary continental bkfst. Business servs avail. In-rm modem link. Cr cds: A, C, D, DS, MC, V.

D ⊠ ⊠ ⊠ SC

★★ **HAMPTON INN.** *1551 Barbara Ln (17572).* 803/865-8000; FAX 803/865-8046; res: 800/426-7866. 111 rms, 5 story, 18 suites. Late-May-Aug: S $68; D $73; suites $92-$97; under 18 free; higher rates special events; lower rates rest of yr. Crib free. TV; cable (premium), VCR avail. Complimentary continental bkfst. Complimentary coffee in rms. Restaurant opp 11 am-11 pm. Ck-out noon. Meeting rm. Business servs avail. In-rm modem link. Exercise equipt. Pool. Health club privileges. Some in-rm whirlpools; refrigerator, microwave, wet bar in suites. Cr cds: A, C, D, DS, MC, V.

D ⊠ ⊠ ⊠ ⊠ SC

★★★ **HOLIDAY INN NORTHEAST.** *7510 Two Notch Rd (29223), at I-20.* 803/736-3000; FAX 803/736-6399; res: 800/465-4329. 253 rms, 2 story. S, D $69; each addl $6; under 12 free; wkend rates. Crib free. Pet accepted. TV; cable (premium). Indoor/outdoor pool; whirlpool, poolside serv. Complimentary bkfst. Restaurant 6:30-10:30 am, 5-10 pm. Rm serv. Bar 5 pm-midnight. Ck-out 11 am. Coin lndry. Meeting rms. Business servs avail. In-rm modem link. Sauna. Health club privileges. Game rm. Courtyard. Cr cds: A, C, D, DS, MC, V.

D ⊠ ⊠ ⊠ ⊠ SC

★★ **LA QUINTA INN.** *1335 Garner Ln (29210).* 803/798-9590; FAX 803/751-5574; res: 800/639-7667. 120 rms, 2 story. S $53; D $59; each addl $6; under 18 free. Crib free. TV; cable (premium). Pool. Complimentary continental bkfst. Restaurant adj 4-11 pm. Ck-out noon. Meeting rms. Business servs avail. Valet serv. Cr cds: A, C, D, DS, MC, V.

D ⊠ ⊠ ⊠ SC

★★ **RAMADA LIMITED NORTHWEST.** *773 Saint Andrews Rd (29210), I-26, exit 106.* 803/772-7275; FAX 803/750-1877; res: 800/465-4329. 101 rms, 2 story. S, D $50-$65; family rates. Crib free. TV; cable (premium). Pool. Complimentary continental bkfst. Restaurant adj 10:30 am-10 pm. Ck-out noon. Meeting rms. Business servs avail. Valet serv. Health club privileges. Cr cds: A, C, D, DS, JCB, MC, V.

D ⊠ ⊠ ⊠ ⊠ SC

✓ ★ **RED ROOF INN.** *7580 Two Notch Rd (29223), at I-20 Two Notch Rd exit.* 803/736-0850; FAX 803/736-4270; res: 800/843-7663. 108 rms, 2 story. S $40.99; D $46.99; each addl $6; under 18 free. Crib free. TV; cable (premium). Complimentary coffee in lobby. Restaurant adj 6 am-10 pm. Business servs avail. In-rm modem link. Cr cds: A, C, D, DS, MC, V.

Motor Hotels

✓ ★ ★ **AMERISUITES.** *7525 Two Notch Rd (29223), at I-20.* 803/736-6666; FAX 803/788-6011; res: 800/833-1516. 112 suites, 6 story. S, D $69-$109; each addl $5; under 16 free; wknd rates. Crib free. TV; cable (premium), VCR. Pool. Complimentary continental bkfst. Coffee in rms. Restaurant nearby. Ck-out noon. Meeting rms. Business center. Valet serv. Exercise equipt. Refrigerators, microwaves. Cr cds: A, C, D, DS, MC, V.

★ ★ ★ **RAMADA PLAZA HOTEL.** *8105 Two Notch Rd (29223), at I-77.* 803/736-5600; FAX 803/736-1241; res: 800/272-6232. 187 units, 6 story. S $66.75; D $74.25; suites $112.50-$142.50; under 18 free; golf plan. Crib $6. Pet accepted, some restrictions. TV; cable. Pool; whirlpool. Coffee in rms. Restaurant 6:30 am-10 pm. Rm serv. Bar 6:30-10 pm. Ck-out noon. Convention facilities. Business servs avail. In-rm modem link. Bellhops. Valet serv. 18-hole golf privileges. Exercise equipt; sauna. Refrigerator, microwave in suites. Cr cds: A, C, D, DS, ER, MC, V.

★ ★ ★ **WHITNEY HOTEL.** *700 Woodrow St (29205).* 803/252-0845; FAX 803/771-0495; res: 800/637-4008. E-mail robin@scsn.net; web www.whitneyhotel.com. 74 kit. suites, 7 story. 1-bedrm $119; 2-bedrm $139. TV; cable (premium). Pool. Complimentary continental bkfst. Restaurant nearby. Ck-out noon. Meeting rms. Business servs avail. Valet serv. Free airport transportation. Health club privileges. Microwaves. Balconies. In residential area. Cr cds: A, C, D, DS, MC, V.

Hotels

★ ★ ★ **ADAM'S MARK HOTEL.** *1200 Hampton St (29201).* 803/771-7000; FAX 803/254-2911; res: 800/444-2326. 301 rms, 13 story. S $129; D $139; each addl $10; suites $225-$450; under 18 free; wknd rates. Crib free. Pet accepted; $50 deposit. TV; cable. Indoor pool; whirlpool. Restaurants 6 am-midnight. Bar 11:30-1 am. Ck-out noon. Convention facilities. Business servs avail. In-rm modem link. Airport transportation. Exercise equipt. Some refrigerators. Some balconies. Cr cds: A, C, D, DS, ER, JCB, MC, V.

★ ★ ★ **COLUMBIA SHERATON.** *2100 Bush River Rd (29210).* 803/731-0300; FAX 803/731-2839; res: 800/325-3535; res: 800/325-3535. 237 rms, 5 story. S $109; D $119; each addl $10; suites $129-$350; under 17 free. Crib free. TV; cable (premium). 2 pools, 1 indoor; whirlpool. Coffee in rms. Restaurant 6:30 am-10:30 pm. Bars; entertainment. Meeting rms. Business center. In-rm modem link. Gift shop. Free airport transportation. Exercise equipt; sauna. Some refrigerators; bathrm phone in suites. Some balconies. Luxury level. Cr cds: A, C, D, DS, ER, MC, V.

★ ★ ★ **EMBASSY SUITES.** *200 Stoneridge Dr (29210), on I-126 at Greystone Blvd exit.* 803/252-8700; FAX 803/256-8749; res: 800/362-2779. 214 suites, 7 story. S $99-$139; D $109-$149; under 17 free; wknd rates. Crib free. TV; cable (premium). Indoor pool; whirlpool. Complimentary full bkfst. Complimentary coffee in rms. Restaurant 11 am-10 pm; Fri, Sat to 11 pm. Bar 2-11 pm; Fri, Sat to midnight. Ck-out noon. Coin lndry. Meeting rms. Business servs avail. In-rm modem link. Gift shop. Free airport transportation. Exercise equipt; sauna. Microwaves, refrigerators. Atrium lobby; glass-enclosed elvtr. Cr cds: A, C, D, DS, MC, V.

Inns

★ ★ ★ **CLAUSSEN'S INN.** *2003 Greene St (29205).* 803/765-0440; FAX 803/799-7924; res: 800/622-3382. 29 units, 2 story. S $100-$115; D, suites $115-$130; each addl $10; under 12 free. Crib free. TV; cable. Complimentary continental bkfst; afternoon refrshmts. Ck-out noon, ck-in 3 pm. Meeting rms. Health club privileges. Whirlpool. Refrigerators avail. Private patios. In renovated bakery (1928). Cr cds: A, C, MC, V.

★ ★ ★ **RICHLAND STREET BED & BREAKFAST.** *1425 Richland St (29201).* 803/779-7001; FAX 803/256-3725; res: 800/779-7011. 8 rms, 2 story, 1 suite. S $79-$110; D $79-$130; each addl $10; suite $140. Children over 12 yrs only. TV; cable. Complimentary continental bkfst; afternoon refreshments. Restaurant nearby. Ck-out 11 am, ck-in 4 pm. Health club privileges. Modern building (1992) in Victorian style. Totally nonsmoking. Cr cds: A, C, MC, V.

Restaurants

★ ★ **AL'S UPSTAIRS.** *304 Meeting St, 1 mi W on US 1, in National Register Bldg.* 803/794-7404. Hrs: 5-10 pm. Closed Sun; some major hols. Res accepted. Italian menu. Bar. Semi-a la carte: dinner $11.95-$19.95. Specializes in veal, pasta, fresh fish. Parking. Overlooks river. Views of Columbia's skyline. Cr cds: A, C, D, MC, V.

✓ ★ ★ **BLUE MARLIN SEAFOOD KITCHEN.** *1200 Lincoln St (29201).* 803/799-3838. Hrs: 11:30 am-2 pm, 5-10 pm; Sat 5-11 pm; Sun from 5 pm. Closed Jan 1, Dec 25. Regional Amer menu. Bar. Semi-a la carte: lunch $5.95-$7.45, dinner $9.95-$14.95. Child's meals. Specialties: shrimp and grits, oyster skillet bienville, blackened catfish. Own pastries. Outdoor dining. Nautical decor in former passenger train station. Cr cds: A, C, D, MC, V.

★ ★ **GARIBALDI'S.** *2013 Greene St (29205).* 803/771-8888. Hrs: 5:30-10:30 pm; Fri, Sat to 11 pm. Res accepted. Italian menu. Bar. A la carte entrees: dinner $6.95-$21.95. Specializes in fish, steak, pasta. Valet parking. Art deco furnishings. Cr cds: A, C, MC, V.

★ ★ **HAMPTON STREET VINEYARD.** *1207 Hampton St (29201).* 803/252-0850. Hrs: 11:30 am-2 pm, 6-10 pm; Sat from 6 pm. Closed Sun; Jan 1, July 4, Dec 25. Res accepted. Bar. Semi-a la carte: lunch $6.25-$8.75, dinner $12.50-$18.75. Specializes in seafood, veal, duck. Own desserts. Street parking. In historic Sylvan Bldg (1871); bistro atmosphere; French posters adorn walls. Cr cds: A, C, DS, MC, V.

★ ★ **HENNESSY'S.** *1649 Main St (29201).* 803/799-8280. Web www.scbell.com. Hrs: 11:30 am-2:30 pm, 6-10 pm; Sat from 6 pm. Closed Sun; hols. Res accepted. Continental menu. Bar. Semi-a la carte: lunch $4.95-$8.95, dinner $12.95-$23.95. Specializes in steak, poultry, fresh seafood. Converted hardware store. Cr cds: A, C, D, DS, MC, V.

★ ★ **RISTORANTE DIVINO.** *4423 Devine St (29205).* 803/799-4550. Hrs: 5:30-10 pm. Closed Sun, Mon; Jan 1, Dec 25. Res accepted. Northern Italian menu. Serv bar. Semi-a la carte: dinner $12.95-$17.75. Specializes in seafood, pasta, veal. Casual, intimate dining. Totally nonsmoking. Cr cds: A, C, MC, V.

✓ ★ ★ **VISTA BREWING & BISTRO.** *936 Gervais St (29201).* 803/799-2739. Hrs: 11-1 am. Closed Sun; Dec 25. Res accepted. French bistro menu. Bar. Semi-a la carte: lunch $5.95-$6.95, dinner $14.95-$17.50. Specialties: lobster ravioli with saffron sauce, herb-encrusted salmon, honey-roasted pork loin. Jazz Tues. Brewing equipt on view; casual decor. Cr cds: A, C, D, DS, MC, V.

D ⊡

Darlington (D-6)

(See also Cheraw, Florence; also see Bennettsville, Hartsville)

Founded 1798 **Pop** 7,311 **Elev** 157 ft **Area Code** 843 **Zip** 29532
Information Greater Darlington Chamber of Commerce, PO Box 274; 843/393-2641

Darlington is situated in one of the most fertile sections of the state. Along with its agricultural economy, the area has diversified industry. Darlington was a pioneer in the culture and marketing of tobacco as a cash crop and has a large tobacco market. It is the home of what is said to be the nation's largest automobile auction market and is a stock car racing center.

What to See and Do

NMPA Stock Car Hall of Fame/Joe Weatherly Stock Car Museum. Museum is said to house largest collection of race cars in the world. Major automotive companies have displays tracing the evolution of the racing stock car and accessories from 1950 to present; cars, engines and trophies of famous drivers. (Daily; closed Dec 25) 1 mi W on SC 34 at Darlington Raceway, the oldest superspeedway in the country. Phone 843/395-8821. ¢¢

Annual Events

TranSouth Financial 400. Darlington Raceway. Late-model stock car race. Late Mar.

Southern 500. Darlington Raceway. 500-mi stock car classic; also beauty pageant, "Southern 500" Festival parade; golf tournament. Preceded by 2 days of trials. Labor Day wkend.

Dillon (C-6)

(See also Bennettsville, Darlington, Florence)

Settled 1887 **Pop** 6,829 **Elev** 115 ft **Area Code** 803 **Zip** 29536

Industrial growth and diversification characterize this town. The county seat, Dillon also serves as a shipping center for farm produce.

What to See and Do

Little Pee Dee State Park. Approx 800 acres on Little Pee Dee River. Boating (rentals); fishing (bream). Nature trails. Picnicking (shelters); playground. Camping (hookups, dump station). Standard fees. 11 mi SE between SC 9 & 57, near I-95. Phone 803/774-8872.

Inn

★★★ **ABINGDON MANOR.** *307 Church St (29565), S on I-95, exit 181, 6 mi E.* 843/752-5090; FAX 843/752-6034; res: 888/752-5090. E-mail abingdon@southtech.net; web www.bbonline.com/sc/abingdon. 5 rms, 2 story, 1 suite. Rm phones avail. S, D $105; each addl $25; suites $140. Children over 12 yrs only. TV; cable (premium), VCR (movies). Whirlpool. Complimentary full bkfst. Ck-out 11 am, ck-in 3 pm. Business servs avail. Luggage handling. Valet serv. Concierge serv. Exercise equipt. Some balconies. Greek Revival mansion built in 1902. Totally nonsmoking. Cr cds: A, C, D, DS, MC, V.

🏃 ⊠ 🔥

Florence (D-6)

(See also Darlington, Dillon, Hartsville)

Settled 1890 **Pop** 29,813 **Elev** 149 ft **Area Code** 843
Information Greater Florence Chamber of Commerce, 610 W Palmetto St, PO Box 948, 29503; 843/665-0515

Since extensive railroad shops and yards were established here by the Atlantic coastline, this community has grown from a sparsely settled crossroads into a major retail and wholesale distribution center. The economy is no longer dependent on agriculture; a balance of farm and industry has been attained. Florence is also the home of Francis Marion College and Florence–Darlington Technical College.

What to See and Do

Air & Missile Museum. Display of 38 aircraft and missiles incl jets, cargo plane, Bomarc missile, Titan I missile, German V2 rocket, B-47 bomber; Alan Shepard's *Apollo* space suit; heat tiles from space shuttle *Columbia*. Approximately 2,000 displays in bldg. (Daily) Airport entrance, 2 mi E on US 76/301 or from I-95 exit 170, follow signs. Phone 843/665-5118. ¢¢

Beauty Trail. 12-mi trail within city featuring beautiful gardens (usually best in Apr). **Free**

City parks.

    Lucas Park. Picnicking, playground; tennis courts. Rose gardens, camellias, azaleas, rhododendrons; lighted fountain. Santee Dr and Azalea Ln. **Free**

    Jeffries Creek Nature Park. Fishing. Nature trails. Picnicking, playground. Deberry Blvd. **Free**

    McLeod Park. Swimming pool (fee), fishing pond. Lighted tennis; basketball courts, ball fields. Picnicking, playground. Santiago Dr.

Florence Museum. Art, history and science exhibits. Southwest Native American pottery; Oriental & African collections; Catawba pottery; furniture gallery of mixed periods; South Carolina Hall of History. (Daily exc Mon; closed major hols) 558 Spruce St, at Graham St. Phone 843/662-3351. **Free**

Lynches River State Park. Approx 650 acres. Located on old stagecoach route. Swimming pool (fee); fishing. Nature trail, bird-watching. Picnicking; playground, community bldg. Primitive camping. 15 mi S off US 52. Phone 843/389-2785.

National Military Cemetery. Burial ground for Union soldiers who died here in prison. S on US 52/301 to Cherokee Rd.

Timrod Park. One-rm schoolhouse in which Henry Timrod, Poet Laureate of the Confederacy, taught. Playgrounds, picnic areas, barbecue pits; lighted tennis courts. Azalea display in spring. Test rose gardens. Nature trails; fitness station, jogging trail. Special fitness court for the disabled. (Daily) Timrod Park Dr & S Coit St. Phone 843/665-3253. **Free**

Woods Bay State Park. Approx 1,500 acres of unique natural area with an abundance of wildlife, incl alligators, in a "Carolina Bay" (an elliptical, swampy depression mostly underwater). Lake fishing, canoe trail (rentals). Picnic area (shelter). Boardwalk for nature and wildlife observation. 24 mi SW, off US 301 & I-95. Phone 843/659-4445.

Annual Event

Arts Alive. Francis Marion University. Arts, crafts, music, dance, theater, demonstrations, exhibits. Phone 843/661-1225. Apr.

Motels

★ **COMFORT INN.** *1916 W Lucas St (29502), jct I-95 & US 52.* 843/665-4558; FAX 843/665-4558; res: 800/228-5150. 162 rms, 2 story. S $49; D $59; each addl $6; under 18 free. Crib free. TV; cable (premium). Pool; whirlpool. Complimentary continental bkfst. Coffee in rms. Restaurant adj. Ck-out 11 am. Meeting rms. Exercise equipt. Some in-rm whirlpools; refrigerators, microwaves avail. Cr cds: A, C, D, DS, MC, V.

D ⊠ 🏃 ⊠ 🔥 SC

✓★ **DAYS INN NORTH.** *2111 W Lucas St (29501), jct I-95 & US 52.* 843/665-4444; FAX 843/665-4444; res: 800/489-4344. 103 rms, 2 story. S, D $38-$75; under 12 free; higher rates: race wkends, hols. Crib free. Pet accepted, some restrictions. TV; cable (premium). Pool; whirlpool. Complimentary continental bkfst. Restaurant adj 6 am-midnight. Ck-out 11 am. Meeting rms. Business servs avail. Exercise equipt; sauna. Some in-rm whirlpools, refrigerators, microwaves. Cr cds: A, C, D, DS, MC, V.

D ⌨ 🏊 🛷 ⊠ 🔥 SC

★★ **RAMADA INN.** *2038 W Lucas St (29221).* 843/669-4241; FAX 843/665-8883; res: 800/272-6232. 179 rms, 2 story. S, D $54-$75; each addl $6; suites $85-$150; under 18 free; higher rates special events. Crib free. Pet accepted, some restrictions. TV; cable (premium). Pool; whirlpool. Restaurant 6:30 am-2 pm, 5-10 pm. Rm serv. Bar; entertainment. Ck-out noon. Meeting rms. Business servs avail. Free airport transportation. Exercise equipt. Refrigerators, microwaves avail. Cr cds: A, C, D, DS, ER, JCB, MC, V.

D ⌨ 🏊 🛷 ⊠ 🔥 SC

✓★ **RED ROOF INN.** *2690 David H Mcleod Blvd (29501).* 843/678-9000; FAX 843/667-1267; res: 800/843-7663. E-mail i0178@redroof.com. 112 rms, 2 story. S $36.99; D $43.99-$52.99; each addl $5; under 18 free; higher rates special events. Crib free. Pet accepted. TV; cable (premium). Complimentary coffee in lobby. Restaurant adj open 24 hrs. Ck-out noon. Business servs avail. Cr cds: A, C, D, DS, MC, V.

D ⌨ ⊠ 🔥 SC

✓★★ **TRAVELERS INN.** *1914 W Lucas St (29501), jct I-95 & US 52 exit 164.* 843/665-2575; FAX 843/661-0700; res: 800/847-7666. 168 rms, 2 story, 24 suites. S $35.95; D $48.95; each addl $7; suites $51.95-$59.95; under 18 free. TV; cable (premium). Pool; whirlpool. Complimentary full bkfst. Restaurant open 24 hrs. Bar 5 pm-2 am; entertainment exc Sun. Ck-out 11 am. Business servs avail. In-rm modem link. Exercise equipt. Refrigerators, microwaves avail. Cr cds: A, C, D, DS, MC, V.

D ⌨ 🛷 ⊠ 🔥 SC

Fort Sumter National Monument (F-6)

(See also Charleston, Kiawah Island)

On an island in Charleston harbor. Accessible by private boat or by Fort Sumter tour boat, leaving City Marina, Lockwood Blvd, Charleston (see) and from Patriots Point Naval Museum, Mt Pleasant.

The national monument includes Fort Sumter, located three miles southeast of Charleston at the harbor entrance, and Fort Moultrie, located one mile east of Fort Sumter on Sullivan's Island. Fort Moultrie is reached via US 17 to SC 703; turn right and follow signs. Fort Moultrie was originally built in 1776 of sand and palmetto logs. Colonel William Moultrie's forces drove British ships from Charleston Harbor at Fort Moultrie in June 1776. The present Fort Moultrie was completed in 1809 and was garrisoned by Union forces in late 1860, when these forces were moved to Fort Sumter.

South Carolina, first state to secede, passed its Ordinance of Secession December 20, 1860. Surrender of Fort Sumter was demanded on April 11, 1861. This demand was refused by Major Robert Anderson, in command of Union forces at the fort. At 4:30 am, April 12, Confederate firing began, and the fort was surrendered after 34 hours of intense bombardment. This attack compelled President Lincoln to call for 75,000 volunteers to put down the rebellion, thus beginning the Civil War. Fort Sumter and Fort Moultrie have been modified through the years. Both were active through World War II.

Fort Moultrie has been restored by the National Park Service; Visitor Center has an audiovisual program depicting the evolution of seacoast defense. Self-guided tour. (Daily; closed Dec 25) ¢

Fort Sumter's ruins have been partially excavated, and a museum has been established. (Daily; closed Dec 25) Contact the Superintendent, 1214 Middle St, Sullivan's Island 29482; 843/883-3123 or -3124. Daily tour boat (fee). **Free**

Gaffney (C-4)

(See also Rock Hill, Spartanburg; also see Charlotte, NC)

Settled 1803 **Pop** 13,145 **Elev** 779 ft **Area Code** 864 **Zip** 29340
Information Cherokee County Chamber of Commerce, 225 S Limestone St; 864/489-5721

Once a prosperous resort town where plantation owners sought to cure malaria attacks with the supposedly therapeutic waters of the limestone springs, Gaffney is now a textile and metalworking center and the home of a variety of other industries and agricultural products, particularly peaches. On I-85, just outside of town, stands the Gaffney Peachoid (1981), an elevated tank that resembles a gigantic peach and holds a million-gallon water supply.

What to See and Do

Carolina Factory Shops. An open-air, village-style manufacturers' outlet. Contains 235,000 sq ft of space featuring 65 outlet shops. (Daily) 1 Factory Shops Blvd., at exit 90 off I85. Phone 864-902-0096.

Cowpens National Battlefield. Scene of victory of General Daniel Morgan's American Army over superior British forces on Jan 17, 1781. The British suffered 110 men killed, 200 wounded, and 550 captured, while the American losses were minimal. This victory was followed by the Battle of Guilford Courthouse; then the forces moved on to Yorktown, where Cornwallis was forced to surrender. An 843-acre tract with exhibits, Information and Visitor Center, self-guided tour road and walking trail with audio stations, and restored 1830 historic house. Slide program (fee). Picnicking (shelters). (Daily; closed Jan 1, Dec 25) 11 mi NW on SC 11, ½ mi from jct SC 110. Phone 864/461-2828. **Free**

Kings Mountain National Military Park (see). 20 mi NE off I-85.

Annual Event

South Carolina Peach Festival. Arts & crafts, sports events, entertainment. Mid-July.

Motel

✓★ COMFORT INN. *143 Corono Dr (29341), exit 92.* 864/487-4200; FAX 864/487-4637. 83 rms, 2 story. S $62; D $68; each addl $5; under 18 free; higher rates special events. Crib free. TV; cable (premium). Pool. Complimentary continental bkfst. Ck-out 11 am. Meeting rms. Exercise equipt. Refrigerators, microwaves. Cr cds: A, C, D, DS, MC, V.

D 🏊 🛷 ⊠ 🔥 SC

Georgetown (E-6)

(See also Myrtle Beach)

Founded 1729 **Pop** 9,517 **Elev** 10 ft **Area Code** 843 **Zip** 29440
E-mail geocofc@sccoast.net **Web** tidelands.com
Information Georgetown County Chamber of Commerce, PO Box 1776, 29442; 843/546-8436 or 800/777-7705

A seaport throughout its long history, Georgetown enjoyed a resurgence of ship traffic following the deepening of the channel and the building of a new cargo dock. The shore of Winyah Bay, on which Georgetown is situated, was the site of the first European settlement on the North American mainland outside of Mexico. In 1526 a group of Spaniards settled here, only to be driven out within a year by disease and Native American attacks. Rice and indigo plantations were established along nearby rivers about 1700. Georgetown was founded by Rev. Elisha Screven, son of the first Baptists in the South; the city was finally laid out to honor King George II of England. It became increasingly important as an export center with quantities of lumber and naval stores, rice and indigo. Lafayette landed near here to join the American cause in the Revolution. The city was later occupied by British troops. Known as a sawmill city during the first three decades of the 20th century, Georgetown currently boasts several manufacturing industries as well as a thriving tourist economy.

What to See and Do

Brookgreen Gardens. On site of former rice and indigo plantations; more than 500 pieces of American sculpture in garden; boxwood, massive moss-hung oaks, native plants; wildlife park with native animals. Picnicking. (Daily; closed Dec 25) 18 mi N on US 17, 3 mi S of Murrells Inlet. Phone 803/237-4218. ¢¢¢

Captain Sandy's Plantation Tours. Leaves from Harborwalk Seaport. For schedule phone 803/527-4106. ¢¢¢¢¢

Fishing. Charter boats from docks. Channel fishing for bass or deep-sea fishing for barracuda, amberjack, albacore, bonito, mackerel. (Apr-Nov)

Hampton Plantation State Park. Restored 18th-century mansion was centerpiece of large rice plantation; ancestral home of Rutledge family. Guided tours, special programs. (Thurs-Mon) 1950 Rutledge Rd, McClellanville; 20 mi S off US 17. Phone 803/546-9361. Mansion ¢

Harold Kaminski House (ca 1760). Pre-Revolutionary house furnished with antiques. Tours. (Daily; closed legal hols) 1003 Front St. Phone 803/546-7706. ¢¢

Hopsewee Plantation (ca 1740). Preserved rice plantation house on North Santee River. Birthplace of Thomas Lynch, Jr, signer of Declaration of Independence. Grounds (daily). House (Mar-Nov, Tues-Fri; rest of yr, by appt). 12 mi S on US 17. Phone 803/546-7891. ¢¢

Huntington Beach State Park. Approx 2,500 acres. Ocean swimming; surf fishing. Hiking, nature trails; marsh boardwalk. Picnicking (shelters); playground; concession. Camping. Standard fees (higher Apr-Sept). 17 mi N on US 17, 3 mi S of Murrells Inlet. Phone 803/237-4440. ¢¢ Also here is

   Atalaya. Former home and studio of sculptress Anna Hyatt Huntington. (June-Labor Day; daily) Art festival (mid-late Sept). ¢

Prince George Winyah Church (ca 1750). English stained-glass window behind altar was originally a part of St Mary's Chapel for Negroes at Hagley Plantation on Waccamaw. In continuous use except during Revolutionary and Civil wars. Tours. (Mar-Oct, Mon-Fri) Broad & Highmarket Sts. Phone 803/546-4358. **Free**

Town Clock Building (rebuilt 1842). Tablet marks landing of Lafayette at North Island in 1777; Federal troops came ashore on the dock, at the rear of bldg, in an attempt to capture the town. Front & Screven Sts. Inside is

   Rice Museum. Maps, dioramas, film, artifacts and exhibits depict development and production of crop that was once the basis of Georgetown's economy. (Daily exc Sun; closed hols) Phone 803/546-7423. ¢

Motel

★★ **CLARION CAROLINIAN INN.** 706 Church St (29440). 843/546-5191; FAX 843/546-1514; res: 800/722-4667. 89 rms, 1-2 story. May-Aug: S $48-$75; D $54-$75; each addl $10; under 18 free; higher rates hols; lower rates rest of yr. Crib $5. TV; cable (premium). Pool. Complimentary continental bkfst. Restaurant 4-9 pm; closed Sun. Ck-out 11 am. Meeting rms. Business servs avail. In-rm modem link. Cr cds: A, C, D, DS, JCB, MC, V.

⌨ 🔄 🔥 SC

Inns

★★★ **ALEXANDRA'S INN.** 620 Prince St (29440). 843/527-0233; FAX 843/520-0718; res: 888/557-0233. Web www.alexandras

inn.com. 6 rms, 2 with shower only, 1-2 story, 1 guest house. S, D $95-$135; guest house $135; guest house 3-day min. TV; cable (premium), VCR avail. Complimentary full bkfst. Restaurant nearby. Ck-out 11 am, ck-in 3-7 pm. Business servs avail. Luggage handling. Pool. Some in-rm whirlpools, fireplaces. Built in 1880; Greek revival. Totally nonsmoking. Cr cds: A, C, MC, V.

⌨ 🔄 🔥

★★★ **KINGS INN.** 230 Broad St (29440). 843/527-6937; FAX 843/527-6937; res: 800/251-8805. Web www.bbonline.com/sc/kingsinn. 7 rms, 2 story. S, D $85-$125. TV in common rm; cable. Pool. Complimentary full bkfst. Restaurant nearby. Ck-out 11 am, ck-in 3 pm. Luggage handling. Street parking. Tennis privileges. Game rm. Federal style; antiques. Totally nonsmoking. Cr cds: A, C, MC, V.

🎾 ⌨ 🔄

★★ **SEAVIEW INN.** 414 Myrtle Ave (29585), N on US 17. 843/237-4253; FAX 843/237-7909. E-mail Pawleys252@aol.com. 20 rms, 14 air-cooled, all share bath, 2 story. No rm phones. Mid-Apr-Oct, AP: S $109-$135; D $168-$220; each addl $50; wkly rates. Closed rest of yr. Children over 3 yrs only. Ck-out 11 am, ck-in noon. Built in 1930s. On beach; view of ocean. Cr cds: C.

👍 🔥

✓★★ **SHAW HOUSE BED & BREAKFAST.** 613 Cypress Court (29440). 843/546-9663. 4 rms, 2 story. S $55, D $65-$70. Crib free. TV; cable. Complimentary full bkfst; afternoon refreshments. Ck-out 1 pm, ck-in after 1 pm. Tennis privileges. Golf privileges. Greek-revival architecture; overlooks Willowbank Marsh. Antiques. Cr cds: C.

🎿 🎾 🔄 🔥 SC

Restaurants

★★ **COMMUNITY HOUSE RESTAURANT.** US 17 S (29585), 20 mi S on US 17 S. 843/237-8353. Hrs: 6-10 pm. Res accepted. Northern Italian menu. Bar. Wine list. Semi-a la carte: dinner $10.95-$21.95. Child's meals. Specializes in fresh local seafood, veal, pasta. Own baking, pasta. In old schoolhouse bldg (1932); country decor. Cr cds: C, DS, MC, V.

D 🔄

★★ **RICE PADDY.** 819 Front St (29440). 843/546-2021. Hrs: 11:30 am-2:30 pm, 6-10 pm. Closed Sun. Res accepted. Bar. Wine list. Semi-a la carte: lunch $5.50-$9.95, dinner $15.95-$23.95. Specializes in seafood, lamb, veal. Local art displayed. Overlooks Sampit River. Cr cds: A, C, DS, MC, V.

🔄

★★ **RIVER ROOM.** 801 Front St (29440). 843/527-4110. Hrs: 11 am-2:30 pm, 5-10 pm. Closed Sun; Jan 1, Thanksgiving, Dec 24, 25. Bar. Semi-a la carte: lunch $4.75-$11.95, dinner $9.95-$19.95. Child's meals. Specialties: grilled local fish, crab cakes, shrimp and grits. Own desserts. Restored dry goods store (1880s); view of river. Cr cds: A, C, MC, V.

D 🔄

Greenville (C-3)

(See also Anderson, Clemson, Clinton, Spartanburg)

Founded 1797 **Pop** 58,282 **Elev** 966 ft **Area Code** 864
E-mail visit@greenvillesc.org **Web** greatergreenville.com

Information Convention & Visitors Center, 206 S Main St, City Hall Bldg, PO Box 10527, 29603; 864/233-0461 or 800/717-0023

Greenville has several hundred manufacturing plants producing clothing, nylon, chemicals, plastic film and machinery. It is best known for its numerous textile plants. Yet the town is also well named—beautiful trees line the streets, and there are many forested parks in the area. The Reedy River, passing over falls in the heart of Greenville, originally provided the city's power. Pleasant streets now border the twisting sylvan stream.

What to See and Do

Bob Jones University (1927) (5,000 students). During academic yr, university offers vesper concerts (twice/month, Sun). Multimedia presentation (daily; closed hols). Tours. At jct US 29, SC 291. Phone 864/242-5100. On campus are

Bob Jones University Collection of Religious Art. Houses collection of rare biblical material and collection of sacred art, incl works by Botticelli, Veronese, Rembrandt, Rubens. Under 6 yrs not permitted. (Daily exc Mon; closed Jan 1, July 4, Dec 20-25) **Free**

Mack Memorial Library. Contains Archives Room and Jerusalem Chamber, display area for the university's collection of rare Bibles.

Confederate History Museum. Permanent collection of American art, featuring historical and contemporary works. Changing exhibits incl painting, sculpture, photography. Lectures, tours. (Daily exc Mon; closed most hols) 420 College St. Phone 864/271-7570. **Free**

Greenville Zoo. Wildlife from around the world are displayed in natural, open-air exhibits. Picnicking, concessions. Lighted tennis courts, ball field; nature, jogging, hiking and bicycle trails; park. (Daily; closed Jan 1, Thanksgiving, Dec 25) Children under 13 must be accompanied by an adult. 150 Cleveland Park Dr. Phone 864/467-4300. ¢¢

State parks.

Caesar's Head. Approx 7,000 acres. At 3,208 ft above sea level, the park overlooks a valley of almost impenetrable brush and dense forest. One side of the mountain resembles Caesar's head. Raven Cliff Falls. Scenic overlook. Hiking trails. Picnicking (shelter). Trailside camping, store, special programs. Standard fees. 30 mi NW via US 276. Phone 864/836-6115.

Paris Mountain. Approx 1,000 acres with 3 lakes. Thick forest setting with swiftly flowing streams. Lake swimming; fishing; pedal boats (rentals). Nature, hiking trail. Picnicking, playground. Camping (hookups, dump station). Standard fees. 6 mi N off US 276 & SC 253. Phone 864/244-5565.

Table Rock. Approx 3,000 acres. Extends over Table Rock Mt (elev 3,124 ft) and valleys. Lake swimming; fishing; boating, canoeing (rentals). Hiking trail; carpet golf. Picnicking, restaurant, store. Camping (hookups, dump station), cabins; recreation bldg. Nature center; nature & recreation programs. Standard fees. 16 mi N on US 25, then 15 mi W on SC 11. Phone 864/878-9813.

Annual Event

Freedom Weekend Aloft. More than 200 hot air balloonists compete. Phone 864/232-3700. Memorial Day or July 4 wkend.

Motels

★★★ **COURTYARD BY MARRIOTT.** 70 Orchard Park Dr (29615). 864/234-0300; FAX 864/234-0296; res: 800/321-2211. 146 rms, 3 story. S, D $89.95; suites $99.95. Crib free. TV; cable (premium). Heated pool; whirlpool. Complimentary coffee in rms. Restaurant 6:30-10:30 am; Sat, Sun 7-11 am. Coin lndry. Meeting rms. Business servs avail. Valet serv. Exercise equipt. Refrigerator, microwave in suites. Cr cds: A, C, D, DS, MC, V.

✓★ **DAYS INN.** 831 Congaree Rd (29607). 864/288-6221; FAX 864/288-2778; res: 800/329-7466. 124 rms, 5 story. S, D $59-$69; each addl $5; under 18 free; higher rates special events. Crib free. TV; cable (premium). Pool. Complimentary continental bkfst. Restaurant nearby. Ck-out 11 am. Meeting rms. In-rm modem link. Health club privileges. Cr cds: A, C, D, DS, MC, V.

✓★★ **FAIRFIELD INN BY MARRIOTT.** 60 Roper Mountain Rd (29607), I-385 exit 37. 864/297-9996; FAX 864/297-9965; res: 800/228-2800. 132 rms, 3 story. S, D $56; under 18 free. Crib free. TV; cable (premium). Pool. Complimentary continental bkfst. Restaurant nearby. Ck-out noon. Business servs avail. In-rm modem link. Health club privileges. Cr cds: A, C, D, DS, MC, V.

★★ **GUEST HOUSE SUITES INN.** 48 Mcprice Ct (29615). 864/297-0099; FAX 864/288-8203; res: 800/214-8378. 96 kit. suites, 2 story. S, D $99-$119; wkly, monthly rates. Crib free. Pet accepted, some restrictions; $100. TV; cable (premium). Pool; whirlpool. Complimentary continental bkfst. Restaurant adj 6-2 am. Ck-out noon. Meeting rms. Business servs. Private patios, balconies. Cr cds: A, C, D, DS, JCB, MC, V.

★★ **HAMPTON INN.** 246 Congaree Rd (29607), off I-385. 864/288-1200; FAX 864/288-5667; res: 800/426-7866. 123 rms, 4 story. S $59-$67; D $59-$75; under 18 free. Crib free. TV; cable (premium). Pool. Complimentary continental bkfst. Ck-out noon. Meeting rm. Business servs avail. In-rm modem link. Health club privileges. Cr cds: A, C, D, DS, MC, V.

★★ **LA QUINTA INN.** 31 Old Country Rd (29607). 864/297-3500; FAX 864/458-9818; res: 800/639-7667. 122 rms, 2 story. S $57; D $63; under 18 free. Crib free. Pet accepted. TV; cable (premium). Pool. Complimentary continental bkfst. Restaurant adj 6 am-10 pm. Ck-out noon. Coin lndry. Business servs avail. Valet serv. Cr cds: A, C, D, DS, MC, V.

★ **QUALITY INN.** 50 Orchard Park Dr (29615). 864/297-9000; FAX 864/297-8292; res: 800/221-2222. 147 rms, 2 story. S $49; D $58; each addl $6; suites $75; under 18 free; higher rates Textile Show. Crib $6. TV; cable. Pool. Complimentary continental bkfst. Complimentary coffee in rms. Ck-out noon. Meeting rms. Valet serv. Health club privileges. Cr cds: A, C, D, DS, JCB, MC, V.

✓★ **SUPER 8 MOTEL.** 1515 Hwy 101 S (29650). 864/848-1626; FAX 864/848-3092; res: 800/800-8000. 61 rms, 2 story, 6 suites. S $45; D $45-$50; suites $80-$90; under 12 free; higher rates special events. Crib free. TV; cable (premium). Complimentary continental bkfst. Restaurant nearby. Ck-out 11 am. Business servs avail. In-rm modem link. Pool. Some refrigerators, microwaves. Cr cds: A, C, D, DS, MC, V.

Motor Hotel

★★ **HOLIDAY INN.** 4295 Augusta Rd (29605), I-85 exit 46-A. 864/277-8921; FAX 864/299-6066; res: 800/465-4329. E-mail holiday85@worldnet.att.net. 154 rms, 5 story. S, D $74; suites $79; under 18 free; higher rates special events. Crib free. TV; cable (premium). Pool. Complimentary coffee in rms. Restaurant 7 am-2 pm, 5-10 pm. Rm serv. Bar 4 pm-midnight. Ck-out noon. Meeting rms. Business servs avail. In-rm modem link. Bellhops. Valet serv. Free airport transportation. Golf privileges. Cr cds: A, C, D, DS, ER, JCB, MC, V.

Hotels

★★★ **CROWNE PLAZA.** 851 Congaree Rd (29607). 864/297-6300; FAX 864/234-0747; res: 800/227-6963. 208 rms, 6 story. S $119.95; D $129.95; each addl $10; under 18 free; wknd rates. TV; cable (premium). Indoor pool; whirlpool, poolside serv. Coffee in rms. Restaurant 6:30 am-10 pm. Bar 11-2 am; closed Sun. Ck-out noon. Meeting rms. Business servs avail. In-rm modem link. Free airport transportation. Exercise equipt. Some refrigerators. Cr cds: A, C, D, DS, JCB, MC, V.

★★★ **EMBASSY SUITES HOTEL.** *670 Verdae Blvd (29607), I-85, exit 48B.* 864/676-9090; FAX 864/676-0669; res: 800/362-2779. 268 suites, 9 story. S $129; D $139; each addl $10; under 18 free; wkend rates. Crib free. TV; cable (premium). 2 pools, 1 indoor; whirlpool. Complimentary full bkfst. Complimentary coffee in rms. Restaurant 11 am-10 pm. Bar 11 am-midnight. Coin lndry. Convention facilities. Business center. In-rm modem link. Gift shop. Free airport transportation. Tennis privileges. 18-hole golf privileges, greens fee $44, pro, putting green, driving range. Exercise equipt; sauna. Refrigerators. Cr cds: A, C, D, DS, JCB, MC, V.

★★★ **HILTON HOTEL & TOWERS.** *45 W Orchard Park Dr (29615).* 864/232-4747; FAX 864/235-6248; res: 800/445-8667. 256 rms, 9 story. S $144; D $164; suites $250-$400; family, wkend rates. Crib free. TV; cable. Indoor pool; whirlpool, poolside serv. Restaurant 6 am-11 pm. Bar 4:30 pm-2 am. Ck-out noon. Convention facilities. Business center. In-rm modem link. Concierge. Gift shop. Airport, RR station, bus depot transportation. Exercise equipt; sauna. Refrigerator in suites. Luxury level. Cr cds: A, C, D, DS, ER, MC, V.

★★ **HYATT REGENCY.** *220 N Main St (29601).* 864/235-1234; FAX 864/232-7584; res: 800/233-1234. 327 rms, 8 story. S $135; D $160; each addl $25; suites $195-$500; under 18 free; wkend rates. Crib free. Covered parking $5; valet $9. TV; cable (premium). Pool; whirlpool, poolside serv. Restaurants 6:30 am-11 pm. Bar; closed Sun. Ck-out noon. Convention facilities. Business center. In-rm modem link. Shopping arcade. Free airport transportation. Indoor tennis privileges. Golf privileges. Exercise equipt. Health club privileges. Cr cds: A, C, D, DS, JCB, MC, V.

★★★ **MARRIOTT HOTEL.** *1 Pkwy E (29615), near Greenville/Spartanburg Airport.* 864/297-0300; FAX 864/281-0801; res: 800/228-9290. 204 rms, 7 story. S, D $129; each addl $10; under 18 free; higher rates Textile Show. Crib free. TV; cable (premium), VCR avail. 2 pools, 1 indoor; whirlpool, poolside serv. Coffee in rms. Restaurant 6:30 am-10 pm. Bar 3:30 pm-1 am; Sat to midnight; closed Sun; entertainment. Ck-out noon. Convention facilities. Business center. In-rm modem link. Concierge. Free airport transportation. Tennis privileges. 18-hole golf privileges. Exercise equipt; sauna. Luxury level. Cr cds: A, C, D, DS, ER, JCB, MC, V.

Restaurants

★★ **858.** *18 E North St (29601).* 864/242-8883. Hrs: 5-10 pm; Thur-Sat to 11 pm. Closed Sun; major hols. Res accepted. Bar. Semi-a la carte: dinner $13-$29. Specialties: potato-crusted grouper, sauteed macadamia pepper chicken. Free valet parking. Grand piano in dining rm. Cr cds: A, C, D, DS, MC, V.

★ **BISTRO EUROPA.** *219 N Main St (29601).* 864/467-9975. Hrs: 11:30 am-3 pm, 5-10 pm; Fri to 11 pm; Sat 11:30 am-3:30 pm, 5:30-11 pm. Closed Sun; major hols. Bar. Semi-a la carte: lunch $6.95-$8.95, dinner $6.95-$18.95. Specialties: pepper-crusted tenderloin, bistro catch. Outdoor dining. Bistro decor. Cr cds: A, C, D, DS, MC, V.

★★★ **NIPPON CENTER YAGOTO.** *500 Congaree Rd (29607), in Nippon Center Yagoto.* 864/288-8471. Hrs: 6-9:30 pm. Closed Sun; major hols. Res accepted. Japanese menu. Bar. Wine cellar. A la carte entrees: dinner $13-$28. Complete meals: dinner $34.50-$39. Specializes in sushi, sashimi. Sushi bar. Tatami rm. Housed in Japanese cultural center. Tours, tea ceremonies avail by appt. Cr cds: A, C, D, DS, JCB, MC, V.

★★ **OPEN HEARTH.** *2801 Wade Hampton Blvd (29687), 5 mi N on US 29.* 864/244-2665. Hrs: 5:30-10:30 pm. Closed Sun; major hols. Res accepted. Bar. Semi-a la carte: dinner $9.95-$25.95. Child's meals.

Specializes in aged steak, fresh seafood. Family-owned. Cr cds: A, C, D, DS, MC, V.

★★★ **SEVEN OAKS.** *104 Broadus Ave (29601).* 864/232-1895. Hrs: 6-9:30 pm. Closed Sun; some major hols. Res accepted. Continental menu. Serv bar. Wine cellar. A la carte entrees: dinner $16.95-$26. Specializes in fresh seafood, lamb, beef. Own baking. Outdoor dining. Beautifully restored 1895 mansion; eight fireplaces. Cr cds: A, C, D, DS, MC, V.

★★★ **STAX'S PEPPERMILL.** *30 Orchard Pk Dr (29615).* 864/288-9320. Hrs: 5:30-10:30 pm; Fri, Sat to 11:30 pm. Closed Sun; most major hols. Res accepted. Continental menu. Bar. Wine list. Semi-a la carte: dinner $14-$31.50. Specializes in lamb, beef, fresh fish. Own baking. Entertainment Wed-Sat. Outdoor dining. Tableside preparation. Cr cds: A, C, D, MC, V.

★★ **TAHOE SOUTH.** *1 College St (29687).* 864/235-7166. Hrs: 6-10 pm; Fri, Sat to 11 pm. Closed Sun, Mon; also major hols. Southwestern menu. Bar from 5 pm. Semi-a la carte: dinner $9.95-$18.95. Child's meals. Specialties: chile rellenos, pork loin Tahoe supreme. Western decor. Cr cds: A, C, MC, V.

✓ ★★ **TERRACE.** *100 Villa Rd (29615).* 864/242-3804. Hrs: 11:30 am-2 pm, 6-9 pm; Mon 6-9 pm; Fri 11:30 am-2 pm, 6-10 pm; Sat 6-10 pm. Closed Sun; also most major hols. Res accepted. Continental menu. Bar. Semi-a la carte: lunch $5.95-$9.95, dinner $10.95-$19.95. Child's meals. Specializes in beef, chicken, seafood. Jazz Thurs-Sat. Parking. Cr cds: A, C, DS, MC, V.

★★ **VINCE PERONE'S.** *1 E Antrim Dr (29607).* 864/239-2100. Hrs: 11:30 am-2:30 pm, 5-10 pm; Fri, Sat to 11 pm. Closed Sun; major hols. Italian, Amer menu. Semi-a la carte: lunch $4.95-$7.99, dinner $8.99-$17.99. Child's meals. Specializes in fresh seafood, pasta. Cr cds: A, C, D, DS, MC, V.

Greenwood (D-3)

(See also Clinton, Newberry)

Settled 1830 **Pop** 20,807 **Elev** 665 ft **Area Code** 864
E-mail chamber@greenwood.net
Information Chamber of Commerce, PO Box 980, 29648; 864/223-8431

At the junction of highways and railways, Greenwood was originally the plantation of Green Wood; it later became known as the community of Woodville and finally adopted its present name. Greenwood's Main Street is one of the widest (316 feet) in the nation. The town enjoys diversified industry.

What to See and Do

J. Strom Thurmond Lake. Formed by damming of Savannah River. Fishing; boating (ramps). Picnicking (shelters). Campgrounds (fees). (Daily) 30 mi SW via US 221, 378. Phone 864/333-2476 or 706/722-3770. **Free**
Ninety-Six National Historic Site. Site of old Ninety-Six, an early village in South Carolina backcountry, so named because of its distance of 96 mi from the Cherokee Village of Keowee on the Cherokee Path. Site of the South's first land battle of the Revolutionary War in 1775, and of the 28-day siege of Ninety-Six in 1781. The earthworks of the British-built Star Fort remain, along with reconstructed siegeworks and other fortifications of the period. Visitor center; museum, video presentation. Also here are

subsurface remains of 2 village complexes, a trading post/plantation complex and a network of 18th-century roads. (Daily; closed Jan 1, Dec 25) 9 mi E on SC 34 to present town of Ninety Six, then 2 mi S on SC 248. Phone 864/543-4068. **Free**

State parks.

Baker Creek. Approx 1,300 acres. Lake swimming, bathhouse; lake fishing; boating (ramps). Nature, bridle trails; carpet golf. Picnicking, playground, camping (dump station). Standard fees. 28 mi SW via US 221, US 378W. Phone 864/443-2457 or 864/443-5886.

Hickory Knob Resort. On 1,091 acres. Waterskiing; lake fishing, supplies; boating (ramps, rentals). Nature trails; 18-hole golf course, putting green, field archery course, skeet range, field trial area. Playground, restaurant. Camping (hookups, dump station); lodge, cabins. Recreation and nature programs. Convention facilities. Standard fees. 32 mi SW via US 221, US 378W. Phone 800/491-1764.

Lake Greenwood. On 914 acres bordering Greenwood Lake, which is 20 mi long, 2 mi wide. Waterskiing; lake fishing, bait shop; boating (ramps). Nature trails. Picnicking (shelters), store. Camping (hookups, dump station). Recreation bldg. Standard fees. 13 mi E on SC 34, then N on SC 702. Phone 864/543-3535.

Sumter National Forest. Approx 353,000 acres in the Piedmont Plateau and the Blue Ridge Mts. Miles of trails through pine and hardwood forest; canoeing, whitewater trips, swimming, trout fishing; hunting for deer, turkey, quail; picnicking, camping. Fees may be charged at recreation sites. In three sections: SW via US 221; NW via SC 28; and NE via SC 72. Phone 864/561-4000.

The Museum. Features a nostalgic "street" lined with houses, shops. Displays of minerals, mounted animal heads, Native American artifacts, ethnographic materials. Art gallery with regional art, traveling exhibits. (Tues-Fri, also Sat afternoons; closed major hols) 106 Main St. Phone 864/229-7093. **Free**

Annual Event

South Carolina Festival of Flowers. Arts & crafts, photography display, musical groups, golf & tennis tournaments, theater, water show, Railroad Historical Exhibit, flower shows, Park Seed Flower Day. Phone 864/223-8411. 3rd wkend June.

Motels

★ **COMFORT INN.** *1215 Ne Hwy 72 Byp (29649). 864/223-2838; FAX 864/942-0119; res: 800/221-2222.* 83 rms, 2 story. S $52-$60; D $57-$71; suites $100; under 12 free. Crib free. TV; cable (premium). Pool; whirlpool. Complimentary continental bkfst. Complimentary coffee in rms. Restaurant nearby. Ck-out noon. Meeting rms. Business servs avail. Valet serv. Exercise equipt. Refrigerators, microwaves. Cr cds: A, C, D, DS, ER, JCB, MC, V.

D ⊷ ⚡ ⊠ 🔥 SC

✓★ **EXTENDED STAY.** *919 Montague Ave (29649), US 25N & SC 72 Bypass. 864/223-3979; FAX 864/223-3297; res: 800/575-0133.* 100 rms, 2 story. S $35-$44; D $40-$49; each addl $5. TV; cable (premium). Pool. Complimentary bkfst. Bar 5 am-10 pm. Ck-out 11 am. Meeting rms. Business servs avail. In-rm modem link. Cr cds: A, C, D, DS, MC, V.

D ⊷ ⊠ 🔥 SC

★★ **RAMADA INN.** *1014 Montague Ave (29649). 864/223-4231; FAX 864/223-6911; res: 800/272-6232.* 100 rms, 2 story. S, D $65; each addl $6; under 19 free. Crib free. TV; cable (premium). Pool. Complimentary coffee in lobby. Restaurant 6-9 am, 6-9 pm; Sat, Sun 7-10 am. Rm serv. Bar 6-10 pm; closed Sun. Ck-out noon. Coin lndry. Meeting rms. Business servs avail. In-rm modem link. Valet serv. Cr cds: A, C, D, DS, JCB, MC, V.

D ⊷ ⊠ 🔥 SC

Inns

★★ **BELMONT INN.** *106 E Pickens St (29620), E on SC 72. 864/459-9625; FAX 864/459-9625; res: 877/459-8118.* 25 rms, 3 story. S,

D $69-$99; higher rates wkends. Crib free. TV, cable (premium). Complimentary continental bkfst. Dining rm 5:30-9 pm. Bar 4:30 pm-midnight. Ck-out noon, ck-in 3 pm. Business servs avail. Restored historic bldg (1903). Period reproduction; antique furnishings. Cr cds: A, C, DS, MC, V.

★★★ **INN ON THE SQUARE.** *104 Ct St (29646), at Main St. 864/223-4488; FAX 864/223-7067; res: 800/231-9109.* Web www.innon thesquare.com. 48 rms, 3 story. S, D $72-$80. Crib $15. TV; cable (premium). Pool. Complimentary full bkfst; afternoon refreshments. Dining rm 6:30-10 am, 11:30 am-2 pm, 5:30-10 pm; wkend hrs vary. Rm serv. Ck-out 11 am, ck-in 2 pm. Business servs avail. Atrium. Rms furnished with 18th-century reproductions. Cr cds: A, C, D, DS, MC, V.

D ⊷ ⊠ 🔥

Restaurant

★ **BLAZER'S.** *US 221E & SC 72E (29649), 8 mi E on SC 72. 864/223-1917.* Hrs: 5-10 pm. Closed Sun, Mon; Jan 1, Thanksgiving, Dec 24-25. Bar. Semi-a la carte: dinner $7.95-$14.95. Child's meals. Specializes in fresh seafood, steak, ribs. Overlooks Lake Greenwood. Cr cds: A, C, DS, MC, V.

⊠

Hardeeville (F-4)

(See also Beaufort, Hilton Head Island)

Pop 1,583 **Elev** 80 ft **Area Code** 803 **Zip** 29927

What to See and Do

Savannah National Wildlife Refuge. Approx 25,600 acres. More than half the acreage consists of bottomland hardwoods reminiscent of the great cypress/tupelo swamps that once extended along the Carolina and Georgia Low Country. Argent Swamp can only be reached by boat; wild azaleas, iris, spider lilies & other flowers bloom in succession, beginning in spring. Laurel Hill Wildlife Dr, open to cars, allows viewing of wildlife, especially waterfowl (Dec-Feb). Migrating songbirds are abundant in spring and fall. Tupelo Swamp Walk (mid-Mar-Sept) is best for bird watchers and photographers. (Daily; some areas closed Oct-Nov for hunting; impoundments N of US 17 closed Nov-mid-Mar; Laurel Hill Dr hrs posted at gate) 17 mi S via US 17. Phone 912/652-4415. **Free**

Motels

✓★★ **HOWARD JOHNSON INN.** *I-95 & US 17 (29927). 843/784-2271; FAX 843/784-2271; res: 800/654-2000.* 126 rms, 2 story. S $33-$50; D $37-$55; each addl $5; under 18 free. Crib free. Pet accepted; $5. TV; cable (premium). Pool; wading pool. Restaurant 7-10 am, 11 am-2 pm, 5-9 pm. Ck-out noon. Business servs avail. Private patios, balconies. Cr cds: A, C, D, DS, MC, V.

D ⊷ 🐾 ⊠ 🔥 SC

★ **SCOTTISH INN.** *Hwy 17 & I-95 (29927), at I-95 exit 5. 843/784-2151; FAX 843/784-3026; res: 800/800-8000.* 100 rms, 2 story. S $28.95; D $35.86; each addl $5. Crib free. TV; cable. Pool. Coffee in lobby. Ck-out 11 am. Coin lndry. Cr cds: A, C, D, DS, MC, V.

D ⊷ ⊠ 🔥 SC

Hartsville (C-5)

(See also Bennettsville, Camden, Cheraw, Darlington, Florence)

Settled 1760 **Pop** 8,372 **Elev** 200 ft **Area Code** 843 **Zip** 29550
E-mail tourhart@aol.com **Web** www.hartsvillesc.com
Information Chamber of Commerce, 214 N 5th St, PO Box 578, 29551;
843/332-6401

From a crossroads store, Hartsville has become a vigorous trading center, raising crops of cotton, soybeans, tobacco and oats, and boasts fifteen major manufacturers—including makers of consumer packaging, plastic bags, fertilizer, roller bearings, boats, brass, textiles and paper. The town developed from what was once the Hart plantation and the pioneer store established by Major James Lide Coker, a Harvard graduate who founded a series of businesses here and built a railroad to the town.

What to See and Do

H. B. Robinson Nuclear Information Center. Located at site of first commercial nuclear plant in Southeast. Exhibits explain generation of electricity, nuclear power and energy use. (Mon-Fri; closed hols) 4 mi NW at jct SC 151/23. Phone 843/857-1000. **Free**

Hartsville Museum. Housed in restored post office; changing exhibits of local history, arts & crafts. (Daily exc Sun; closed hols) 222 N 5th St. Phone 843/383-3005. **Free**

Kalmia Gardens of Coker College. A 30-acre botanical garden. Walking trails through blackwater swamp, mountain laurel thickets, pine-oak-holly uplands and a beech bluff. Plantings of azaleas, camellias and other ornamentals complement native plants. (Daily) Approx 2½ mi W on Carolina Ave. Phone 843/383-8145. **Free**

Lee State Park. Approx 2,500 acres on Lynches River. Lake swimming; river fishing, boating (pedal boat rentals). Nature trails; horse trails, show ring, stable (no rentals). Picnicking (shelters), playground. Camping (hookups, dump station). Recreation bldg. Standard fees. 16 mi SW via US 15, 3 mi S on SC 341, then 2 mi E off I-20 exit 123. Phone 803/428-3833.

Hilton Head Island (F-5)

(See also Beaufort, Hardeeville)

Pop 23,694 **Elev** 15 ft **Area Code** 843
Information Chamber of Commerce, PO Box 5647, 29938; 843/785-3673

This year-round resort island, the development of which began in 1956, is reached by a bridge on US 278. The island is bordered by one of the few remaining unpolluted marine estuaries on the East Coast and is the largest sea island between New Jersey and Florida. Its growth was rapid; there are 12 miles of beaches and the climate is delightful. There are numerous golf courses and tennis courts, swimming, miles of bicycle paths, horseback riding, four nature preserves and deep-sea, sound and dockside fishing. Facilities also include nine marinas and a paved 3,700-foot airstrip with parallel taxiway. There are more than 3,000 hotel and motel rooms, more than 6,000 homes/villas/condos on the rental market, more than 200 restaurants and 28 shopping centers. For the less athletic, there are many art galleries and numerous sporting and cultural events.

Annual Events

Springfest. Food, wine and seafood festivals. Sports events. Concerts, shows and house tours. Phone 843/686-4944. Mar.

Family Circle Magazine Cup Tennis Tournament. Sea Pines Racquet Club. Phone 843/363-3500. Late Mar-early Apr.

MCI Heritage Classic. Harbour Town Golf Links. Top PGA golfers. Phone 843/671-2448. Mid-Apr.

Hilton Head Island Celebrity Golf Tournament. Palmetto Hall, Indigo Run & Sea Pines Plantation. Phone 843/842-7711. Labor Day wkend.

St Luke's Tour of Homes. Tour of distinctive contemporary houses. Phone 843/785-4099. Oct.

Motels

★★ **BEST WESTERN INN AT HILTON HEAD.** *40 Waterside Dr (29928).* 843/842-8888; FAX 843/842-5948; res: 888/813-2560. 92 rms, 3 story. Mar-early Sept: S $85; D $90; each addl $5; under 19 free; lower rates rest of yr. Crib free. TV; cable (premium). Complimentary continental bkfst. Restaurant adj 11-2 am. Ck-out 11 am. Business servs avail. In-rm modem link. Valet serv. Health club privileges. Pool. Refrigerators avail. Cr cds: A, C, D, DS, JCB, MC, V.

D ≥ ⊠ ☼ SC

✓★ **FAIRFIELD INN.** *9 Marina Side Dr (29928).* 843/842-4800; FAX 843/842-4800; res: 800/833-6334. 119 rms, 3 story, 14 suites. Apr-mid-Sept: S $66; D $73; suites $83-$89; under 18 free; golf plans; higher rates wkends; lower rates rest of yr. Crib free. TV; cable (premium). Complimentary continental bkfst. Restaurant nearby. Ck-out 11 am. Business servs avail. In-rm modem link. Golf privileges. Miniature golf adj. Health club privileges. Refrigerator in suites. Picnic tables, grills. Cr cds: A, C, D, DS, MC, V.

D ⅟ ≥ ⊠ ☼ SC

★★ **HAMPTON INN.** *1 Dillon Rd (29926).* 843/681-7900; FAX 843/681-4330; res: 800/426-7866. 124 rms, 2 story, 20 suites, 12 kit. units. Mar-Sept: S $79-$99; D $84-$104; suites, kit. units $94-$124; under 18 free; lower rates rest of yr. Crib free. TV; cable (premium). Pool. Complimentary continental bkfst. Restaurant nearby. Ck-out noon. Coin lndry. Meeting rms. Business servs avail. In-rm modem link. Free airport transportation. Tennis privileges, pro. 18-hole golf privileges. Exercise equipt. Some refrigerators, microwaves. Cr cds: A, C, D, DS, ER, JCB, MC, V.

D ⅟ ⌂ ≥ ⊠ ☼ SC

✓★ **RED ROOF INN-HILTON HEAD.** *5 Regency Pkwy (29928), off US 278.* 843/686-6808; FAX 843/842-3352. 112 rms, 2 story. June-Sept: S, D $64.99-$69.99; suites $89.99-$139.99; family rates; wkend rates; higher rates hols; lower rates rest of yr. Crib free. TV; cable (premium). Pool. Restaurant adj 5-10 pm. Ck-out noon. Business servs avail. Some refrigerators, microwaves. Cr cds: A, C, D, DS, MC, V.

D ≥ ⊠ ☼

Motor Hotel

★★ **HOLIDAY INN.** *1 S Forest Beach Dr (29938).* 843/785-5126; FAX 843/785-6678; res: 800/423-9897. E-mail hi.hilton.head.4010@servicohotels.com. 201 rms, 5 story. Mid-Mar–mid-Oct: S, D $159-$229; each addl $10; under 18 free; lower rates rest of yr. Crib free. TV; cable (premium). Heated pool; wading pool; poolside serv. Supervised child's activities (Memorial Day-Labor Day). Coffee in rms. Restaurant 7 am-10 pm. Rm serv. Bar 11 am-10 pm. Ck-out 11 am. Coin lndry. Meeting rms. Business servs avail. In-rm modem link. Valet serv. Bellhops. Tennis privileges. Golf privileges. Refrigerators. Patios. On beach. Cr cds: A, C, D, DS, ER, JCB, MC, V.

D ⅟ ⌂ ≥ ⊠ ☼ SC

Hotel

★★ **RESIDENCE MARRIOTT INN.** *12 Park Ln (29928), off US 278.* 843/686-5700; FAX 843/686-3952. Web www.radisson.com. 156 kit. suites, 3 story. Mar-Nov: S, D $119-$169; under 18 free; family rates; golf plans; lower rates rest of yr. Crib free. TV; cable (premium). Pool; whirlpool. Complimentary continental bkfst. Restaurant adj 5-1 am. Ck-out noon. Coin lndry. Business servs avail. Free airport transportation. Lighted tennis. Golf privileges. Bicycles. Fireplaces, microwaves. Private patios, balconies. Picnic tables. Cr cds: A, C, D, DS, MC, V.

🅳 ⛷ 🛷 ⚓ ⛵ 🔥 SC

Resorts

★★★ **CROWNE PLAZA RESORT.** *130 Shipyard Dr (29928), in Shipyard Plantation.* 843/842-2400; FAX 843/842-6503; res: 800/341-1881. E-mail info@crowneplazaresort.com; web www.crowneplaza resort.com. 340 rms, 5 story. Early Mar-Nov: S, D $189-$269; suites $350-$495; family rates, golf plans; lower rates rest of yr. TV; cable (premium). Pools, 1 indoor; wading pool, whirlpools, poolside serv. Supervised child's activities (mid-Mar to late-Apr; Memorial Day-Labor Day); ages 3-19. Coffee in rms. Dining rms 6 am-midnight. Box lunches. Snack bar. Rm serv. Bar 11-2 am. Ck-out noon, ck-in 4 pm. Coin lndry. Convention facilities. Business center. In-rm modem link. Valet serv. Concierge. Gift shop. Lighted tennis, pro. 27-hole golf, greens fee $45-$89, pro, putting green, driving range. Boats, sailboats. Bicycle rentals. Entertainment. Exercise rm; sauna. Fishing guides, storage. Some refrigerators; microwaves avail. Private patios, balconies. Cr cds: A, C, D, DS, MC, V.

🅳 ⛷ ⛷ 🛷 ⚓ 🏃 ⛵ 🔥 SC 🏃

★★★ **DISNEY HILTON HEAD ISLAND RESORT.** *22 Harborside Ln (29928).* 843/341-4000; FAX 843/341-4130; res: 800/341-2616. Web www.dvc-resorts.com. 102 kit. units, 2 story. Mid-June-mid-Aug: S, D $175-$490; golf plans; lower rates rest of yr. Crib free. TV; cable (premium); VCR (movies). Heated pools; wading pool, whirlpool, poolside serv, lifeguard. Supervised children's activities; ages 3-16. Restaurant nearby. Ck-out 11 am, ck-in 4 pm. Gift, grocery shop. Guest lndry. Concierge. Valet serv. Lighted tennis, pro. Three 18-hole golf courses, putting green, driving range. Boats. Bicycle rental. Exercise equipt. Lawn games. Microwaves. Balconies. Fishing pier. Cr cds: A, C, MC, V.

🅳 ⛷ ⛷ 🛷 ⚓ 🏃 ⛵ 🔥

★★★ **HILTON OCEANFRONT RESORT.** *23 Ocean Ln (29928), on Palmetto Dunes.* 843/341-8000; FAX 843/341-8033; res: 800/845-8001. E-mail hiltonhh@hargray.com. 296 kit. units, 5 story, 28 suites. Apr-Aug: S, D $134-$239; each addl $15; suites $225-$400; under 18 free; golf, tennis plans; lower rates rest of yr. Crib free. TV; cable (premium). 2 pools, 1 heated; whirlpools, wading pool, poolside serv. Playground. Supervised child's activities (Mar-Oct); ages 4-11. Dining rm 6:30 am-11 pm (to 10 pm off-season). Rm serv. Bar 5 pm-2 am; entertainment exc Mon. Ck-out 11 am, ck-in 4 pm. Coin lndry. Convention facilities. Business center. In-rm modem link. Valet serv. Concierge. Lighted tennis, pro. Three 18-hole golf courses, greens fee $65-$89, pro. Lawn games. Exercise rm; sauna. Balconies. On ocean. Poolside entertainment (Apr-Oct). Cr cds: A, C, D, DS, MC, V.

🅳 ⛷ ⛷ 🛷 ⚓ 🏃 ⛵ 🔥 SC 🏃

★★ **HYATT REGENCY.** *1 Hyatt Circle at Palmetto Dunes (29928), on US 278, in Palmetto Dunes area.* 843/785-1234; FAX 843/842-4695. Web www.hyatt.com. 505 rms, 10 story. Mar-mid-Nov: S, D $200-$285; each addl $25; suites $400-$975; under 18 free; package plans; lower rates rest of yr. Crib free. Valet parking $8/night. TV; cable (premium), VCR avail. 2 pools, 1 indoor; whirlpool, wading pool, poolside serv. Supervised child's activities (Memorial Day-Labor Day); ages 3-18. Dining rm (see HEMINGWAY'S). Rm serv 6-2 am. Bars 11:30-1 am, Sun from 1 pm; entertainment. Ck-out noon, ck-in 4 pm. Meeting rms. Business center. In-rm modem link. Bellhops. Valet serv. Gift shops. Barber, beauty shop. Tennis. Three 18-hole golf courses, putting green. Canoes, sailboats. Bicycle rentals. Exercise equipt; sauna. Massage. Private patios, balconies. Luxury level. Cr cds: A, C, D, DS, JCB, MC, V.

🅳 ⛷ ⛷ 🛷 ⚓ 🏃 ⛵ 🔥 SC 🏃

★★★ **PALMETTO DUNES RESORT.** *Wm Hilton Pkwy (29938), 7 mi SE of Byrnes Bridge, off US 278.* 843/785-7300; FAX 843/686-2877; res: 800/845-6130. E-mail sdmpdr@aol.com. 480 villas, 1-5 story. Mar-Labor Day: S, D $125-$436; family rates; lower rates rest of yr. Crib avail. TV; cable. Pools; wading pool. Playground. Supervised child's activities (June-mid-Aug); ages 4-12. Dining rms 7 am-10 pm. Rm serv. Bars to 2 am. Ck-out 10 am, ck-in 4 pm. Grocery. Package store 1 mi. Meeting

rms. Business servs avail. Valet serv. Lighted tennis. 5 golf courses, greens fee $43-$95, putting green, driving range. Boats, rowboats, canoes, sailboats. Microwaves; some fireplaces. Private patios, balconies. Picnic tables. Private beach. 4,300-ft airstrip 4 mi. Cr cds: A, C, D, DS, MC, V.

♿ ⛷ ⛷ 🛷 ⚓ ⛵ 🔥

★★★ **SEA PINES PLANTATION.** *Wm Hilton Pkwy (29928).* 843/785-3333; FAX 843/842-1475; res: 800/732-7463. Web www.sea pines.com. 400 kit. suites in villas, 1-5 story, 60 houses. June-Aug: 1-4 bedrm units $145-$300; wkly rates; golf, tennis packages; lower rates rest of yr. TV; cable, VCR. Pools, wading pools, poolside serv. Playgrounds. Supervised child's activities (June-Aug); ages 4-12. Restaurants 6:30 am-10 pm. Snack bars. Cookouts. Bars. Ck-out 10 am, ck-in 4 pm. Guest lndry. Grocery, package store. Convention facilities. Business center. Bellhops. Concierge. Sports dir. Lighted tennis, pro. Three 18-hole golf courses, greens fee $65-$180, putting green, driving range. Exercise rm. Sailboat instruction, charter boats, jet skis, windsurfing. Bicycles. Entertainment. Microwaves; some fireplaces. Screened porch in some houses and villas. On 5,000 acres; 605-acre forest, wildlife preserve. Cr cds: A, C, D, DS, MC, V.

♿ ⛷ ⛷ ⛷ ⚓ 🏃 🏃 ⛵ 🔥 SC 🏃

★★★ **WESTIN RESORT HILTON HEAD.** *2 Grasslawn Ave (29928).* 843/681-4000; FAX 843/681-1087; res: 800/228-3000. Web www.westin.com. 412 rms, 5 story; 99 villas (2-, 3- and 4-bedrm). Late Mar-early Nov: S, D $250-$350; suites from $355; villas $280-$325; under 18 free; tennis, golf plans; lower rates rest of yr. Serv charge $6/day. TV; cable (premium), VCR avail. 3 pools, 1 indoor; whirlpool, poolside serv. Playground. Supervised child's activities (Memorial Day-Labor Day, major hols). Dining rm 6 am-10 pm. Rm serv 24 hrs. Bars 3 pm-2 am; entertainment (seasonal). Ck-out noon, ck-in 4 pm. Meeting rms. Business center. In-rm modem link. Concierge. Valet parking. Free airport transportation. Tennis, pro. 54-hole golf, greens fee (incl cart) $60-$90, putting green, driving range. Lawn games. Exercise rm; sauna, steam rm. Massage. Bathrm phones, refrigerators. Cr cds: A, C, D, DS, ER, JCB, MC, V.

🅳 ♿ ⛷ ⛷ 🛷 ⚓ 🏃 ⛵ 🔥 🏃

Inn

★★★ **MAIN STREET INN.** *2200 Main St (29926).* 843/681-3001; FAX 843/681-5541; res: 800/471-3001. E-mail mainstreetinn@digitel.net; web mainstreetinn.com. 34 rms, 3 story. Mid-Mar-mid-Nov: S, D $185-$300; each addl $15; lower rates rest of yr. Children over 12 yrs only. TV; cable (premium), VCR avail. Complimentary full bkfst. Restaurant nearby. Rm serv 24 hrs. Ck-out 11 am, ck-in 3 pm. Business servs avail. In-rm modem link. Luggage handling. Valet serv. Concierge serv. 18-hole golf privileges. Massage. Heated pool; whirlpool. Refrigerators; some in-rm whirlpools, fireplaces. Some balconies. French period antiques. Gardens. Totally nonsmoking. Cr cds: A, C, DS, MC, V.

🅳 ⚓ ⛵ 🔥 🧍

Restaurants

★★ **ALEXANDER'S.** *76 Queens Folly Rd (29928), in Palmetto Dunes area.* 843/785-4999. Hrs: 5-10 pm. Res accepted. Bar. A la carte entrees: dinner $16-$23.95. Child's meals. Specializes in fresh local seafood, steak, lamb. Own desserts. Parking. Garden rm decor. Overlooks lagoon. Cr cds: A, C, DS, MC, V.

🅳

★★ **CAFE EUROPA.** *Lighthouse in Harbour Town (29928).* 843/671-3399. Hrs: 9 am-2:30 pm, 5:30-10 pm. Closed Nov-mid-Feb. Res accepted. Serv bar. Semi-a la carte: bkfst $6-$8, lunch $6-$10, dinner $14-$20. Child's meals. Specialty: baked shrimp Daufuskie. Own pastries. Parking. Outdoor dining. Cr cds: A, C, MC, V.

🅳

★★★ **CHARLIE'S L'ETOILE VERTE.** *807 William Hilton Pkwy #1000 (29928).* 843/785-9277. Hrs: 11:30 am-2 pm, 6-9 pm. Closed Sun, Mon; most major hols. Res accepted (dinner). French menu. Bar. Wine cellar. Semi-a la carte: lunch $7.50-$10, dinner $19-$27. Specialties: salmon in parmesan crust, rack of lamb, grilled pompano with mango vinaigrette. Own baking. Bright, eclectic decor with French artwork on walls; fresh flowers; menu changes daily. Totally nonsmoking. Cr cds: A, C, DS, MC, V.

[D] [img]

✓★ **DAMON'S THE PLACE FOR RIBS.** Hwy 278 Bldg B (29928), Hwy 278. 843/785-6677. Hrs: 11:30 am-10 pm. Bar. Semi-a la carte: lunch $4.95-$13.99, dinner $6.99-$15.99. Child's meals. Specializes in barbecued ribs, onion loaf, steak. Parking. Outdoor dining (lunch). Casual atmosphere. Cr cds: A, C, D, DS, MC, V.

[D] [img]

★★★ **GASLIGHT 2000.** 303 Market Place (29928), in Park Plaza shopping center. 843/785-5814. Hrs: 11:30 am-2 pm, 6-10 pm; Sat from 6 pm. Closed Sun. Res accepted. French menu. Serv bar. Semi-a la carte: lunch $8.95-$10.95, dinner $19.50-$26. Specialties: quenelles of snapper, Dover sole, beef Wellington. Own baking. Parking. Cr cds: A, C, MC, V.

[img]

★★★ **HARBOURMASTER'S.** Shelter Cove Harbor (29938). 843/785-3030. Hrs: from 5 pm. Closed Sun; Dec 25; also Jan. Res accepted. Continental menu. Bar. Wine cellar. Semi-a la carte: dinner $14.95-$24.95. Specialties: potato-crusted grouper, blackened tuna mango chutney, rack of lamb. Parking. Tableside preparation. Outdoor dining. View of yacht harbor. Cr cds: A, C, D, MC, V.

[D]

★★ **HEMINGWAY'S.** (See Hyatt Regency Hilton Head Resort) 843/785-1234. Hrs: 5-11 pm; early-bird dinner 5-6:30 pm; Sun brunch 10 am-2 pm. Res accepted. Bar 4 pm-midnight; entertainment (exc Mon). Semi-a la carte: dinner $18-$26. Sun brunch $20.95. Specializes in fresh seafood, steak. Valet parking. Cr cds: A, C, D, DS, JCB, MC, V.

[D] [img]

✓★★ **HOFBRAUHAUS RESTAURANT.** Pope Ave & Executive Park (29928). 843/785-3663. Hrs: 5-10 pm; early-bird dinner 5-6:30 pm. Res accepted. German menu. Bar. Semi-a la carte: dinner $9.95-$17.25. Serv charge 15%. Child's meals. Specialties: roast young duckling, sauerbraten, Wienerschnitzel. Entertainment. Festive German decor; stained-glass windows, stein and mug collection. Cr cds: A, C, MC, V.

[D] [img]

✓★ **HUDSON'S ON THE DOCKS.** 1 Hudson Rd (29926), 1 mi N off US 278. 843/342-3636. Hrs: 11 am-10 pm. Closed Jan 1, Thanksgiving, Dec 24, 25. Bar. Semi-a la carte: lunch $5.95-$11.95, dinner $12.95-$21.95. Child's meals. Specializes in fresh seafood, live Maine lobster. Magician (Memorial Day-Labor Day). Parking. Gift shop. Outdoor dining. On Intracoastal Waterway; near boat docks. Cr cds: A, C, D, MC, V.

[D] [img]

★ **KINGFISHER.** 18 Harbourside Ln (29928), off US 278, on Shelter Cove Harbour. 843/785-4442. Web www.hiltonheadisland.com. Hrs: 5-10 pm. Closed Dec 25. Res accepted. Bar. Semi-a la carte: dinner $11-$21.95. Child's meals. Specializes in seafood. Guitarist in season. Parking. Outdoor dining. Windows overlook harbor and marshes. Cr cds: A, C, DS, MC, V.

[D] [img]

★★ **LA POLA'S.** 103 Executive Ctr, Unit A (29928), in Shelter Cove Harbor. 843/842-6400. Web www.hiltonheadisland.com. Hrs: 5-10 pm. Closed Jan. Res accepted. Italian, Amer menu. Bar. Semi-a la carte: dinner $10.95-$22.95. Child's meals. Specializes in fresh fish, veal, black Angus steak. Own desserts. Parking. Screened dining porch. Overlooks Shelter Cove Harbor. . Cr cds: C.

★★ **LITTLE VENICE.** Shelter Cove (29928). 843/785-3300. Hrs: noon-2:30 pm, 5-10 pm. Closed Dec 25; also Jan. Res accepted. Italian menu. Bar. Semi-a la carte: lunch $6.95-$7.95, dinner $13.95-$19.95. Specialties: veal chop, zuppa di pesce, chicken a la Fiorentina. Parking.

Outdoor dining. Overlooks marina. Trattoria atmosphere. Cr cds: A, C, D, DS, MC, V.

[img]

✓★ **LONGHORN STEAK HOUSE.** 841 US Hwy 278, Unit A (29928), in South Island Square. 843/686-4056. Hrs: 11 am-10 pm; Fri to 10:30 pm; Sat noon-10:30 pm; Sun 4-10:30 pm. Closed Thanksgiving, Dec 25. Bar. Semi-a la carte: lunch $6.25-$9.99, dinner $7.95-$18.99. Child's meals. Specializes in steak, salmon, chili. Country-Western decor. Cr cds: A, C, D, DS, JCB, MC, V.

[D] [img]

★★ **NENO IL TOSCANO.** 105 Festival Ctr (29928). 843/342-2400. Hrs: 11:30 am-2 pm, 6 pm to closing; Sat from 6 pm. Closed Sun; Jan 1, Easter, Dec 25. Res accepted. Italian menu. Bar. Semi-a la carte: lunch $8.95-$9.95, dinner $13.95-$24.95. Specializes in pasta, beef, chicken. Own baking. European decor with 2-level dining area; marble-and-mahogany bar. Totally nonsmoking. Cr cds: A, C, MC, V.

[D]

★★ **OLD OYSTER FACTORY.** 101 Marshland Rd (29928). 843/681-6040. Hrs: 5-10 pm. Closed Thanksgiving, Dec 25. Bar. Semi-a la carte: dinner $9.95-$21.95. Child's meals. Specializes in fresh seafood, local oysters, steak. Guitarist, vocalist in season. Parking. Overlooks creek, marshes. Cr cds: A, C, D, DS, MC, V.

[D] [SC]

★★★ **PRIMO.** At Orleans Plaza (29928), Orleans Plaza. 843/785-2343. Hrs: 6 pm to closing. Closed Thanksgiving, Dec 25; also Super Bowl Sun. Res accepted. Contemporary Italian menu. Bar. Semi-a la carte: dinner $10.95-$24.95. Specializes in fresh pasta, char-grilled seafood, veal. Own baking, pasta. Parking. Italian cafe atmosphere. Cr cds: A, C, DS, MC, V.

[D] [img]

✓★ **REILLEY'S.** 7d Greenwood Dr (29928), in Gallery of Shops. 843/842-4414. Hrs: 11:30 am-11 pm; Sat, Sun brunch 11:30 am-2:30 pm. Closed Dec 25. Bar to 2 am. Semi-a la carte: lunch, dinner $5.95-$19.95. Sun brunch $5.75-$8.95. Child's meals. Specialties: cottage pie, corned beef and cabbage, fish and chips. Own ice cream. Irish pub atmosphere; sports memorabilia. Outdoor dining. Cr cds: A, C, MC, V.

[D] [SC] [img]

★★ **SCOTT'S FISH MARKET.** Shelter Cove Harbour (29928). 843/785-7575. Hrs: 4:30-10 pm. Closed Sun; some major hols; also Jan. Bar. Semi-a la carte: dinner $15-$20. Specializes in fresh local seafood. Parking. Outdoor dining. Nautical decor. View of harbor. Cr cds: A, C, D, DS, MC, V.

[D]

Kiawah Island (F-5)

(See also Beaufort, Charleston)

Pop 718 **Area Code** 843 **E-mail** kiawahres@aol.com **Web** kiawah-island.com

Information Visitor Center, 22 Beachwalker Dr, 29455; 843/768-5116 or -5117

Kiawah Island (KEE-a-wah) is one of the richest natural environments in the Middle Atlantic states. The island is a model for maintaining ecological balance while allowing human habitation. Named for the Native Americans who once hunted and fished here, the island is separated from the mainland by the Kiawah River and a mile-wide salt marsh.

Extensive environmental study has helped to preserve nature while also providing for human needs. Separate resort areas and private residential neighborhoods have been planned to provide a minimum of automobile traffic and leave much of the island untouched. The Kiawah Island Resort offers activities like golf, tennis and nature programs that take advantage of the island's natural beauty.

Resort

✓★★★ **KIAWAH ISLAND RESORTS.** *12 Kiawah Beach Dr (29455), at W end of Kiawah Island, off Kiawah Beach Dr. 843/768-2121; FAX 843/768-9339; res: 800/654-2924.* 610 rms, 3 story, 460 villas and houses (1-4 bedrms). Mar-Nov: S, D $135-$225; villas $175-$500; under 18 free; wkly rates; package plans; lower rates rest of yr. Crib free. TV; cable (premium). 7 pools, 1 heated; wading pool, poolside serv, lifeguard. Playground. Supervised child's activities (Easter-Labor Day); ages 3-19. Coffee in rms. Dining rms 6:30 am-11 pm. Snack bar, picnics. Rm serv. Bar 11-1 am; entertainment (in season). Ck-out noon, ck-in 4 pm. Grocery. Package store 3 mi. Meeting rms. Business center. Bellhops. Valet serv. Concierge. Gift shop. Lighted tennis, pro. Four 18-hole golf courses, greens fee $105-$185, pro, driving range. Swimming beach; boats. Canoe trips. Bicycle rentals. Nature walks. Exercise rm. Lawn games. Rec rm. Game rm. Many wet bars, microwaves. On ocean; marina. Cr cds: A, C, D, DS, MC, V.

🛇 🛆 🛆 🛆 🛆 🛆 🛆 🛆 SC 🛆

Inn

★★★ **CASSINA POINT PLANTATION BED & BREAKFAST.** *1642 Clark Rd (29438), SC 174, exit Indigo Hill Rd. 843/869-2535; FAX 843/869-2535.* Web www.bbonline.com/sc/cassina. 4 rms, 2 share bath, 4 story. No rm phones. S $90; D $115; each addl $25. Children over 10 yrs only. TV in parlor. Complimentary full bkfst. Restaurant nearby. Ck-out 10 am, ck-in 2 pm. Canoe, kayak rentals. Plantation built in 1847 was later used by Federal troops during the Civil War. Totally nonsmoking. Cr cds: C.

🛆 🛆 🛆

Restaurant

★★★ **OLD POST OFFICE RESTAURANT.** *1442 Hwy 174 (29438). 843/869-2339.* Hrs: 6-10 pm. Closed Sun, Mon; some major hols. Res accepted. Regional Amer menu. Bar 5-11 pm. Wine cellar. Semi-a la carte: dinner $17-$20. Specializes in seafood. Own baking. Former post office bldg; old mail boxes in entry; local artwork on walls. Cr cds: C, MC, V.

D 🛆

Kings Mountain National Military Park (B-4)

(See also Gaffney, Rock Hill, Spartanburg; also see Charlotte, NC)

(20 mi NE of Gaffney off I-85, near Grover, NC)

On these 3,950 rugged acres, a fierce attack by Carolina, Georgia and Virginia frontiersmen in October 1780 broke up Britain's southern campaign. The mountain men and other patriots were faced with the invasion of their homes by advancing Tories. After traveling more than 200 miles, the Americans surrounded and attacked Cornwallis's left wing, which was encamped atop Kings Mountain spur and under the command of Major Patrick Ferguson. Although untrained in formal warfare, American patriots killed, wounded or captured Ferguson's entire force of 1,104 Tories. Twenty-eight patriots were killed and 62 were wounded. The battle led to renewed American resistance and American victory at Yorktown. Near the center of the park is the battlefield ridge with several monuments, including the Centennial Monument, dedicated in 1880, and the US Monument, erected in 1909. The visitor center has exhibits and a film. Self-guided trail

leads to main features of battlefield. (Daily; closed Jan 1, Thanksgiving, Dec 25) Contact Superintendent, PO Box 40, Kings Mountain, NC 28086; 864/936-7921. **Free**

King's Mountain State Park on SC 161, adj to S edge of national military park, has 6,141 acres of scenic drives; living history farm; 2 lakes. Swimming; fishing; boating. Nature, hiking, bridle trails; carpet golf. Picnicking (shelters), store. Camping. Interpretive center. Standard fees. Phone 803/222-3209.

Myrtle Beach (D-7)

(See also Georgetown)

Pop 24,848 **Elev** 30 ft **Area Code** 843 **Web** www.myrtlebeachlive.com
Information Myrtle Beach Area Chamber of Commerce, 1200 N Oak St, PO Box 2115, 29578; 843/626-7444 or 800/356-3016

With the Gulf Stream only a few miles offshore and dunes to shelter miles of white sand, Myrtle Beach is one of the most popular seaside resorts on the Atlantic coast. Swimming, fishing, golf, tennis and boardwalk amusements combine to lure millions of vacationers each summer. The many myrtle trees in the area give this resort its name.

What to See and Do

✪ **"The Grand Strand."** Sixty mi of beach from the North Carolina border south to Georgetown. Camping; fishing; golf, tennis; amusement parks.

Myrtle Beach State Park. Approx 300 acres. Ocean and pool swimming; surf fishing (supplies avail). Nature trail. Picnicking (shelters), playground, stores. Camping, cabins. Interpretive center. Standard fees (higher rates Apr-Sept). 3 mi S on US 17 Business. Phone 843/238-5325.

Annual Event

Sun Fun Festival. More than 60 seaside entertainment events, incl parades. 1st wk June.

Motels

★★ **CHESTERFIELD INN & MOTOR LODGE.** *700 N Ocean Blvd (29577). 843/448-3177; FAX 843/626-4736; res: 800/392-3869.* 32 inn rms, 26 motel rms, 3 story, 6 kits. Mid-June-late Aug, MAP: D $123-$145; each addl $31; kit. units $107; family rates; golf plans; lower rates Feb-mid-June, late Aug-Dec. Closed rest of yr. Crib free. TV; cable. Pool. Complimentary coffee in lobby. Restaurant 7:30-10 am, 5:30-7:30 pm. Ck-out 11 am. Golf privileges. Refrigerators. Balconies. On beach. Cr cds: A, C, DS, MC, V.

🛆 🛆 🛆 SC

★★ **FAIRFIELD INN BY MARRIOTT.** *1350 Paradise Circle (29577). 843/444-8097; FAX 843/444-8394; res: 800/217-1511.* E-mail stay@thefairfieldinn.com; web www.thefairfieldinn.com. 111 rms, 4 story. Mid-June-Sept: S $85-$105; D $93-$113; summer wkends, hols (2-4 day min); higher rates bike week; lower rates rest of yr. Crib free. TV; cable (premium). Complimentary continental bkfst. Ck-out noon. Meeting rm. Business servs avail. In-rm modem link. Valet serv. Sundries. Golf privileges. Health club privileges. Heated pool; whirlpool. Some in-rm whirlpools. Cr cds: A, C, D, DS, MC, V.

D 🛆 🛆 🛆 🛆 SC

★★ **HAMPTON INN.** *4709 N Kings Hwy (29577), jct US 17 & 48th Ave N. 843/449-7635; FAX 843/449-1528; res: 888/916-2001 or 800/833-1360.* Web www.mbhampton.com. 152 rms, 4 story. Memorial Day-Labor Day: S $99; D $105; higher rates: wkends, Easter, July 4; lower rates rest of yr. Crib free. TV; cable (premium). Indoor pool. Complimentary continental bkfst. Coffee in rms. Restaurant adj 6 am-midnight. Ck-out 11 am. Meeting rms. Business servs avail. In-rm modem link. Valet serv.

Guest lndry. Tennis and golf privileges. Health club privileges. Miniature golf adj. Some refrigerators; microwaves avail. Cr cds: A, C, D, DS, MC, V.

D 🛏️ 🧖 👤 🏊 🔥 SC

★★ **HAMPTON INN.** *1140 Celebrity Circle (29577). 843/916-0600; FAX 843/946-6308; res: 800/916-2001.* E-mail broadwayhi@worldnet.att.net; web www.hampton-inn.com. 141 rms, 8 story. June-Aug: S $109; D $119-$299; under 14 free; higher rates wknds, hols; lower rates rest of yr. Crib free. TV; cable (premium). Complimentary continental bkfst. Complimentary coffee in rms. Restaurant adj 11 am-10 pm. Bar 4:30-10:30 pm. Ck-out 11 am. Meeting rms. Business center. In-rm modem link. Free airport transportation. Exercise equipt; sauna. 2 pools, 1 indoor; whirlpool. Refrigerators, microwaves; some in-rm whirlpools. Some balconies. Cr cds: A, C, D, DS, MC, V.

D 🏊 👤 🧖 🔥 SC 🎿

★★ **HAMPTON INN NORTHWOOD.** *620 75th Ave N (29572). 843/497-0077; FAX 843/497-8845; res: 800/543-4286.* E-mail hampton innnorthwood@worldnet.att.net; web www.mbhampton.com. 122 rms, 5 story, 20 suites. June-Labor Day: S $109-$129; D $119-$159; suites $149-$219; golf plans; lower rates rest of yr. Crib free. TV; cable (premium), VCR avail. Indoor pool; whirlpool. Complimentary continental bkfst. Complimentary coffee in rms. Restaurant adj 11-1 am. Ck-out 11 am. Meeting rms. Business servs avail. In-rm modem link. Coin lndry. Exercise equipt; sauna. Refrigerators, microwaves; some in-rm whirlpools; wet bar in suites. Cr cds: A, C, D, DS, MC, V.

D 🏊 👤 🧖 🔥 SC

✓★ **PALM CREST MOTEL.** *701 S Ocean Blvd (29577). 843/448-7141; FAX 843/444-4799; res: 800/487-9233.* 41 units, 3 story, 38 kits. No elvtr. Early June-late Aug: S, D $57-$78; each addl $10; kit. units $78-$82; 1 to 2-bedrm units $89-$129; wkly rates; golf, tennis plans; lower rates rest of yr. Crib $5. TV; cable. Pool; wading pool. Restaurant adj 6:30 am-10:30 pm. Ck-out 11 am. Coin lndry. Free airport transportation. Tennis privileges. Golf privileges. Microwaves avail. Picnic tables, grills. Cr cds: C, DS, MC, V.

👤 🧖 🏊 🔥

✓★ **SUPER 8 MOTEL.** *1591 N Hwy 17 (29582). 843/249-7339; FAX 843/249-7339; res: 800/800-8000 or 888/249-8819.* E-mail dsam53@aol.com. 61 rms, 2 story. June-Aug: S $65; D $70; each addl $5; suites $80-$85; under 12 free; higher rates: hols, special events; lower rates rest of yr. Crib free. TV; cable (premium). Complimentary continental bkfst. Restaurant adj 11 am-10 pm. Ck-out 11 am. Business servs avail. In-rm modem link. Exercise equipt. Indoor pool; whirlpool. Some refrigerators, microwaves. Cr cds: A, C, D, DS, MC, V.

D 🏊 👤 🧖 🔥 SC

✓★ **VIKING MOTEL.** *1811 S Ocean Blvd (29577). 843/448-4355; FAX 843/448-6174; res: 800/334-4876.* E-mail viking@sccoast.net; web www.seasideproperties.com. 76 units, 5 story, 67 kits. June-Aug: S, D $65-$87; each addl $7; kit. units $65-$92; 2-rm kit. apts. $83-$106; family, wkly rates; higher rates: wknds, hols, special events; lower rates rest of yr. Crib free. TV; cable. Pool; wading pool. Restaurant nearby. Ck-out 11 am. Coin lndry. Business servs avail. Tennis privileges. Golf privileges. Refrigerators. Some private patios, balconies. On beach. Cr cds: A, C, D, DS, MC, V.

👤 🧖 🏊 🔥

Motor Hotels

★★ **BEST WESTERN DAYTON HOUSE.** *2400 N Ocean Blvd (29577). 843/448-2441; FAX 843/448-5957; res: 800/258-7963.* 323 kit. units, 5-16 story. June-Aug: S, D $89-$159; each addl $10; under 12 free; wkly rates; golf plans; higher rates wknds; lower rates rest of yr. Crib $5. TV; cable (premium). Heated indoor/outdoor pool; whirlpools. Complimentary coffee in lobby. Restaurant adj 6-11 am. Ck-out 11 am. Coin lndry. Golf privileges. Exercise equipt; sauna. Refrigerators, microwaves. Balconies. On beach. Cr cds: A, C, D, DS, MC, V.

👤 🧖 🏊 🔥 SC

★★ **CARIBBEAN RESORTS & VILLAS.** *3000 N Ocean Blvd (29577), at 30th Ave N. 843/448-7181; FAX 843/448-3224.* E-mail caribr@sccoast.net; web www.caribbeanresort.com. 278 rms, 5-14 story, 38 kits., 195 kit. suites. Early June-late Aug: D $79-$122; each addl $6; kit. units $84-$123; kit. suites $153; wkly rates; golf plans; higher rates: hols, special events; lower rates rest of yr. Crib free. TV; cable (premium). Supervised child's activities (mid-June-early Sept); ages 5-13. Heated pool; whirlpool. Coffee in lobby. Restaurant adj 6 am-10 pm. Ck-out 11 am. Guest lndry. Business servs avail. Golf privileges. Lawn games. Game rm. Refrigerators. Balconies. On beach. Cr cds: A, C, D, DS, MC, V.

👤 🏊 🔥 SC

★★ **COMPASS COVE.** *2311 S Ocean Blvd (29578). 843/448-8373; FAX 843/448-5444; res: 800/228-9894.* E-mail swpfox@aol.com; web www.swampfox.com. 377 units, 5-16 story, 296 kits. June-late Aug: S, D $99-$119; each addl $8; kit. units $109-$134; 1-bedrm suites $154-$164; 2-bedrm penthouses $235-$260; under 17 free; wkly rates; golf plans; lower rates rest of yr. Crib free. TV, cable (premium). 7 pools, 2 indoor; wading pool, whirlpool. Sauna. Supervised child's activities (mid-June-mid-Aug); ages 5-11. Restaurant 6 am-9 pm. Ck-out 11 am. Coin lndry. Meeting rms. Business servs avail. Bellhops. Tennis and golf privileges. Health club privileges. Refrigerators; microwaves avail. Balconies. Picnic tables, grills. On beach. Cr cds: A, C, D, DS, ER, JCB, MC, V.

D 🛏️ 👤 🧖 🏊 🔥 SC

★★★ **HOLIDAY INN.** *415 S Ocean Blvd (29577). 843/448-4481; FAX 843/448-0086; res: 800/845-0313.* Web www.hioceanfront.com. 306 rms, 8 story. Mid-May-Aug: S, D $99-$149; each addl $10; under 18 free; lower rates rest of yr. Crib free. TV; cable (premium). 2 pools, 1 indoor; whirlpool, poolside serv. Supervised child's activities (Memorial Day-Labor Day); ages 3-12. Coffee in rms. Restaurant 6 am-10 pm. Bars 1 pm-midnight; entertainment. Ck-out 11 am. Coin lndry. Convention facilities. Gift shop. Tennis privileges. Golf privileges. Exercise equipt; sauna. Game rm. On beach. Cr cds: A, C, D, DS, ER, JCB, MC, V.

D 🛏️ 👤 🧖 🏊 👤 🔥 SC

★★ **LA QUINTA INN & SUITES.** *1561 21st Ave N (29577). 843/916-8801; FAX 843/916-8701; res: 800/687-6667.* 128 rms, 4 story. Memorial Day-Labor Day: S, D $135-$153; each addl $7; suites $153; under 18 free; lower rates rest of yr. Crib free. Pet accepted, some restrictions. TV; cable (premium). Complimentary continental bkfst; coffee in rms. Restaurant nearby. Rm serv 11 am-10 pm. Ck-out noon. Meeting rm. Business servs avail. Guest lndry. Exercise equipt. Heated pool; whirlpool. Some refrigerators, microwaves. Cr cds: A, C, D, DS, MC, V.

D 🐾 🏊 👤 🧖 🔥 SC

★★★ **PAN AMERICA MOTOR INN.** *5300 N Ocean Blvd (29577). 843/449-7411; FAX 843/449-6031; res: 800/845-4501.* Web www.panamericanresort.com. 85 kit. units, 6 story. Early June-mid-Aug: S, D $115; each addl $8; 1-bedrm apts $129; golf plans; family rates; lower rates rest of yr. Crib free. TV; cable. Heated pool. Coffee in rms. Restaurant 7-11 am. Rm serv. Ck-out 11 am. Guest lndry. Business servs avail. Bellhops. Tennis. Golf privileges. Exercise equipt. Refrigerators, microwaves. Private patios, balconies. On beach. Cr cds: C, DS, MC, V.

👤 🧖 🏊 👤 🔥

★★★ **SEA ISLAND INN ON THE BEACH.** *6000 N Ocean Blvd (29577). 843/449-6406; FAX 843/449-4102; res: 800/548-0767.* Web www.seaislandinn.com. 112 units, 5 story, 46 kits. Early June-late Aug: D $118-$133; each addl $10; kit. units $124-$139; under 12 free; MAP avail; lower rates rest of yr. Crib free. TV; cable (premium). Heated pool; 2 wading pools. Restaurant 7:30-10 am, 5:30-8 pm. Rm serv. Ck-out 11 am. Meeting rms. Bellhops. Valet serv. Free airport transportation. Tennis privileges. Golf privileges. Refrigerators; some microwaves. Balconies. On ocean; swimming beach. Cr cds: A, C, DS, MC, V.

♿ 👤 🧖 🏊 🔥

★★ **ST JOHN'S INN.** *6803 N Ocean Blvd (29572). 843/449-5251; FAX 843/449-3306; res: 800/845-0624.* 90 rms, 3 story, 28 kits. June-Labor Day: D $95; each addl $5; kit. units $102; under 12 free; golf plan; higher rates hols; lower rates rest of yr. Crib avail. Pet accepted, some restrictions. TV; cable. Pool; whirlpool. Restaurant 7-11 am. Ck-out 11 am. Meeting rm. Lawn games. Refrigerators. Private patios, balconies. Bathrm phones. Beach opp. Cr cds: A, C, DS, MC, V.

[icons] D ⟐ ⟐ ⟐ ⟐ SC

✓★ **SURF & DUNES MOTOR INN.** *2201 S Ocean Blvd (29578). 843/448-1755; FAX 843/444-9360; res: 800/845-2109.* 129 units, 3-7 story, 80 kits. Mid-May-late Oct: S, D $36-$109; each addl $5; kit. units $50-$125; under 18 free; package plans; higher rates: Easter wk, all hol wkends in season; lower rates rest of yr. Crib free. TV; cable (premium). 3 pools, 1 indoor; whirlpool. Playground. Restaurant nearby. Ck-out 11 am. Coin lndry. Business servs avail. Lighted tennis. Golf privileges. Exercise equipt; sauna. Game rm. Lawn games. Refrigerators, microwaves. Some balconies. On beach. Cr cds: A, C, DS, MC, V.

[icons] ⟐ ⟐ ⟐ ⟐ ⟐ SC

Hotels

★★ **BEACH COLONY RESORT.** *5308 N Ocean Blvd (29577). 843/449-4010; FAX 843/449-2810; res: 800/222-2141.* E-mail www.bch colony@sccoast.net. 222 kit. suites, 22 story. Mid-June-mid-Aug: 1-bedrm $162; 2-bedrm $1,700/wk; 3-bedrm $1,940/wk; 4-bedrm $2,230/wk; lower rates rest of yr. Crib free. TV; cable. 3 pools, 1 indoor; wading pool, whirlpools, poolside serv. Free supervised child's activities (Memorial Day-Labor Day); ages 6-12. Restaurant (see FUSCO'S). Bar 5 pm-1 am. Ck-out 11 am. Coin lndry. Meeting rms. Free covered parking. Tennis privileges. Golf privileges. Exercise equipt; sauna. Microwaves. Balconies. On ocean, beach. Cr cds: A, C, D, DS, MC, V.

[icons] ⟐ ⟐ ⟐ ⟐ ⟐ ⟐ SC

★★ **BEACH COVE RESORT.** *4800 S Ocean Blvd (29582). 843/918-9000; FAX 843/918-8399; res: 800/331-6533.* E-mail bchcove@sccoast.net; web www.beachcove.com. 315 kit. units, 16 story. Late May-mid-Aug: kit. units for up to 6, $148-$295; each addl $10; 2-bedrm condos $1,878/wk; under 18 free; wkly rates; lower rates rest of yr. Crib $5. TV; cable. 4 pools, 1 indoor; 3 whirlpools, poolside serv. Sauna. Supervised child's activities (Memorial Day-Labor Day); ages 3-12. Restaurant 7-10:30 am, 5-10 pm. Bar. Ck-out 11 am. Meeting rms. Business servs avail. Tennis privileges. Game rm. Microwaves. Private patios, balconies. On ocean; beach. Cr cds: A, C, DS, MC, V.

[icons] D ⟐ ⟐ ⟐ ⟐ ⟐ SC

★★ **CARAVELLE RESORT HOTEL.** *6900 N Ocean Blvd (29572). 843/918-8000; FAX 843/918-8199; res: 800/845-0893.* Web www.thecaravelle.com. 360 rms, 4-15 story, 220 villas, 1-3 bedrm. June-Aug: S, D $90-$126; suites $107-$158; villas $98-$268; lower rates rest of yr. Crib free. TV; cable. 8 pools, 2 indoor; whirlpool, poolside serv. Free supervised child's activities (Memorial Day-Labor Day); ages 4-16. Restaurant 7-10 am, 6-9 pm. Rm serv. Ck-out 11 am. Coin lndry. Meeting rms. Business servs avail. Bellhops. Free airport, bus depot transportation. Golf privileges. Exercise equipt; sauna. Rec rm. Refrigerators, microwaves. Balconies. On beach. Cr cds: A, C, DS, MC, V.

[icons] ⟐ ⟐ ⟐ ⟐ ⟐ SC

★★ **DUNES VILLAGE RESORT.** *5200 N Ocean Blvd (29578), at 52nd Ave. 843/449-5275; FAX 843/449-5275; res: 800/648-3539.* 93 rms, 8 story. Mid-June-mid-Aug: D $115; each addl $8; kit. apts $129; under 14 free; wkly rates; lower rates rest of yr. Crib free. TV; cable, VCR avail (movies). 2 pools, 1 indoor; whirlpool. Restaurant 7-10 am, also noon-2 pm June-Aug. Ck-out 11 am. Guest lndry. Tennis. Golf privileges. Exercise equipt. Refrigerators, microwaves avail. Balconies. On beach. Cr cds: C, DS, MC, V.

[icons] D ⟐ ⟐ ⟐ ⟐ ⟐

★★★ **EMBASSY SUITES—KINGSTON PLANTATION.** *9800 Lake Dr (29572). 843/449-0006; FAX 843/497-1017; res: 800/876-0010.* Web www.kingstonplantation.com. 255 kit. suites, 20 story. Memorial Day-Labor Day: suites $209-$289; each addl $20; condos, villas $159-$359; under 18 free; lower rates rest of yr. Crib free. TV; cable (premium), VCR. 7 pools, 1 indoor; wading pool, whirlpool, poolside serv. Supervised child's activities (June-Aug); ages 5-12. Complimentary full bkfst. Restaurant

6 am-10 pm. Bar 10-1 am; entertainment Wed-Sun. Ck-out noon. Convention facilities. Business center. In-rm modem link. Concierge. Gift shop. Lighted tennis, pro. Golf privileges. Exercise rm; sauna. Massage. Refrigerators, microwaves. On ocean. Cr cds: A, C, D, DS, MC, V. .

[icons] D ⟐ ⟐ ⟐ ⟐ ⟐ ⟐ SC ⟐

★★★ **MYRTLE BEACH MARTINIQUE RESORT HOTEL.** *7100 N Ocean Blvd (29577). 843/449-4441; FAX 843/497-3041; res: 800/542-0048.* E-mail martinq@sccoast.net; web www.mbmartinique.com. 203 units, 17 story, 92 kits. Mid-June-late Aug: D $139; each addl $10; suites $167-$386; kit. units $149; under 18 free; lower rates rest of yr. Crib free. TV; cable (premium). 2 pools, 1 indoor; whirlpool, poolside serv. Supervised child's activities (mid-June-mid-Aug); ages 5-12. Complimentary coffee in rms. Restaurant 7 am-2 pm, 5-9 pm. Bar 4 pm-2 am; entertainment in season. Ck-out 11 am. Free lndry facilities. Meeting rms. Business servs avail. Golf privileges. Exercise equipt; sauna. Refrigerators, microwaves. Balconies. On ocean, beach. Cr cds: A, C, D, DS, MC, V.

[icons] D ⟐ ⟐ ⟐ ⟐ ⟐ SC

★★ **OCEAN DUNES RESORT & VILLAS.** *201 74th Ave N (29578). 843/449-7441; FAX 843/449-0558; res: 800/845-0635.* E-mail sands@sccoast.net; web www.sandsresorts.com. 138 rms, 8-15 story, 10 townhouses, 45 villas (2-bedrm), 165 tower suites (1-bedrm). Mid-June-mid-Aug: S, D $126-$140; villas $228; suites $138; townhouses $292; advance deposit required for 1-day stay; golf plan; lower rates rest of yr. Crib free. TV; cable. 5 pools, 1 indoor, 1 heated; whirlpool, poolside serv. Free supervised child's activities (Memorial Day-Labor Day); ages 5-12. Restaurant 7-10 am, 6-10 pm. Bar 4 pm-1 am; entertainment. Ck-out 11 am. Coin lndry. Convention facilities. Business servs avail. In-rm modem link. Concierge. Gift shop. Beauty shop. Free airport transportation. Tennis and golf privileges; pro shop. Exercise & steam rms. Game rm. Refrigerators; microwaves avail. Balconies. On beach. Cr cds: A, C, D, DS, MC, V.

[icons] ⟐ ⟐ ⟐ ⟐ ⟐ SC

★★ **OCEAN DUNES RESORT & VILLAS.** *201 75th Ave N (29578). 843/449-7441; FAX 843/449-0558; res: 800/845-0635.* E-mail sands@sccoast.net; web www.sandsresorts.com. 308 units, 12 story. Mid-June-mid-Aug: S, D $140; each addl $10; suites $136-$268; kit. units $149; under 18 free; golf plans; higher rates hols; lower rates rest of yr. Crib free. TV; cable. Indoor/outdoor pool; whirlpool. Supervised child's activities (Memorial Day-Labor Day); ages 5-12. Restaurant 6 am-10 pm. Bar 4 pm-1 am. Ck-out 11 am. Coin lndry. Meeting rms. Business servs avail. In-rm modem link. Grocery store. Free airport transportation. Tennis privileges. Golf privileges. Exercise rm. Game rm. Refrigerators; microwaves avail. Balconies. On beach. Cr cds: A, C, DS, MC, V.

[icons] ⟐ ⟐ ⟐ ⟐ ⟐ ⟐ SC

★ **OCEAN FOREST PLAZA.** *5523 N Ocean Blvd (29577). 843/497-0044; FAX 843/497-3051; res: 800/522-0818.* E-mail ofplaza@sccoast.net; web www.oceanforest.com. 190 kit. suites, 23 story. Memorial Day-Labor Day: 1-bedrm $82-$139; 2-bedrm $139-$229; under 18 free; wkly rates; golf plans; higher rates hols; lower rates rest of yr. Crib free. TV; cable. 2 pools, 1 indoor; whirlpool, steam rm, poolside serv. Sauna. Supervised child's activities (Memorial Day-Labor Day); ages 5-12. Restaurant 7 am-2 pm. Bar 5-11 pm. Ck-out 11 am. Meeting rms. Gift shop. Golf privileges. Game rm. Microwaves. Balconies. Opp beach. Cr cds: A, C, D, DS, MC, V.

[icons] ⟐ ⟐ ⟐ ⟐ SC

✓★★ **SEA MIST RESORT.** *1200 S Ocean Blvd (29577). 843/448-1551; FAX 843/448-5858; res: 800/732-6478.* E-mail seamist@sccoast.net; web www.seamist.com. 827 rms, 2-16 story, 552 kits. Mid-June-late Aug: S, D $80.50-$133; each addl $6; kit. units $99.50-$145; 2-4 bedrm suites $875-$3,250/wk; under 15 free; golf plans; lower rates rest of yr. Crib $7. TV; cable (premium). 10 pools, 1 indoor/outdoor; wading pools, whirlpool. Playground. Supervised child's activities (mid-June-mid-Aug); ages 4-12. Restaurant 5-10 am. No rm serv. Ck-out 11 am. Coin lndry. Convention facilities. Business servs avail. Gift shop. Lighted tennis. Golf privileges. Sauna, steam rm. Game rm. Children's water park. Many refrigerators. Some private patios, balconies. Picnic tables, grills. On beach. Cr cds: A, C, D, DS, MC, V.

[icons]

★★★ **SHERATON HOTEL.** *2701 S Ocean Blvd (29577). 843/448-2518; FAX 843/448-1506; res: 800/992-1055.* E-mail sheraton@ sccoast.net; web www.sheratonresort.com. 219 rms, 16 story, 57 kits. Late May-late Aug: S, D $148-$170; suites $223; kits. $148; under 18 free; golf plans; lower rates rest of yr. Crib free. TV; cable (premium). 2 pools, 1 indoor. Supervised child's activities (June-Aug); ages 2-12. Restaurant 7-11 am, noon-2 pm, 5:30-10 pm. Bar. Ck-out 11 am. Guest lndry. Meeting rms. Business center. Gift shop. Free airport transportation. Tennis privileges. Golf privileges. Exercise equipt; sauna. Massage. Game rm. Refrigerators; microwaves avail. Balconies. On oceanfront beach. Cr cds: A, C, D, DS, ER, JCB, MC, V.

[icons]

★★★ **THE BREAKERS RESORT HOTEL.** *2006 N Ocean Blvd (29577). 843/626-5000; FAX 843/626-5001; res: 800/845-0688 or 800/953-1135.* E-mail breakers@sccoast.net; web www.breakers.com. 398 units in 4 bldgs, 11, 15, 18 story, 98 kit. suites, 77 kits. June-Aug: D $103-$116; each addl $8; 1-, 2-bedrm kit. suites $137-$202; kit. units $108-$129; under 16 free; wkly rates; golf, tennis plans; lower rates rest of yr. Crib free. TV; cable. 3 pools, 1 indoor/outdoor; wading pool, whirlpool, poolside serv. Free supervised child's activities (June-Labor Day); ages 6-14. Restaurant 7-11 am, 5:30-9 pm. Bar 5 pm-2 am; entertainment. Ck-out 11 am. Coin lndry. Meeting rms. Free airport transportation. Tennis and golf privileges. Deep-sea fishing. Exercise equipt; sauna. Refrigerators; microwaves avail. Private patios; balconies. On ocean. Cr cds: A, C, D, DS, MC, V.

[icons]

Inns

★★ **BRUSTMAN HOUSE BED & BREAKFAST.** *400 25th Ave S (29577). 843/448-7699; FAX 843/626-2478; res: 800/448-7699.* E-mail wcbrustman@worldnet.att.net; web home.att.net/~wcbrustman. 5 rms, 2 story, 1 kit. suite. Memorial Day-Labor Day: S $60-$90; D $65-$100; each addl $20; kit. suite $135; wkends (2-day min), hols (3-day min); lower rates rest of yr. TV; cable (premium), VCR avail. Complimentary full bkfst; afternoon refreshments. Restaurant nearby. Ck-out 11 am, ck-in 2 pm. Business center. Concierge serv. Many in-rm whirlpools. Scandinavian furnishings. Totally nonsmoking. Cr cds: A, C, MC, V.

[icons]

✓★★ **SERENDIPITY INN.** *407 71st Ave N (29572). 843/449-5268; FAX 843/449-3998; res: 800/762-3229.* 14 rms, 2 story, 2 suites, 6 kits. June-Aug: S, D $77-$99; suites $129; kits. $99-$129; lower rates rest of yr. Crib free. TV; cable. Heated pool; whirlpool. Complimentary continental bkfst. Restaurant adj 6 am-2 pm, 5-10 pm. Ck-out 11 am, ck-in 2 pm. Golf privileges. Lawn games. Refrigerators; microwaves avail. Balconies. Picnic tables, grills. Library/sitting rm; antiques. Beach nearby. Cr cds: C, MC, V.

[icons]

★★★ **THE CYPRESS INN.** *16 Elm St (29526). 834/248-8199; FAX 843/248-0329; res: 800/575-5307.* Web www.bbonline.com/sc/cypress/. 12 rms, 3 story. No elvtrs. June-Aug: S, D $105-$145; higher rates wkends; lower rates rest of yr. TV; cable, VCR avail (movies). Complimentary full bkfst; refreshments. Restaurant nearby. Ck-out 11 am, ck-in 4 pm. Business servs avail. In-rm modem link. Luggage handling. Valet serv. Concierge serv. Gift shop. Lighted tennis privileges, pro. 18-hole golf privileges. Massage. Many in-rm whirlpools; some fireplaces. Totally nonsmoking. Cr cds: A, C, D, MC, V.

[icons]

Restaurants

★ **CAGNEY'S OLD PLACE.** *9911 N Kings Hwy US 17 (29577). 843/449-3824.* Hrs: 5-11 pm. Closed Sun; also mid-Dec-2nd wk Feb. Bar. Semi-a la carte: dinner $11.95-$18.95. Specializes in seafood,

chicken, prime rib. Entertainment wkends. Nostalgic decor. Cr cds: A, C, DS, MC, V.

[icons]

★★ **CAPTAIN DAVE'S DOCKSIDE.** *US 17 Business (29576), 12 mi S on US 17. 843/651-5850.* Web www.webs4you.com/dockside/. Hrs: 11:30 am-2:30 pm, 5-10 pm; Sun, Mon from 5 pm. Low country menu. Bar. Semi-a la carte: lunch $5.95-$15.95, dinner $12-$25. Child's meals. Specializes in fresh seafood, aged beef. Outdoor dining. Nautical decor. View of marsh. Cr cds: C, DS, MC, V.

[icons]

★★ **COLLECTORS CAFE.** *7726 N King's Hwy (29572). 843/449-9370.* Hrs: 6-10 pm. Closed Sun; also most major hols. Res accepted. Mediterranean menu. Bar. Semi-a la carte: dinner $14.95-$21.95. Child's meals. Specialties: pan-sauteed crab cakes, grilled filet of beef, cajun spiced shrimp. Parking. International art on walls (for sale). Cr cds: A, C, D, DS, MC, V.

[icons]

✓★ **DAMON'S THE PLACE FOR RIBS.** *4810 Hwy 17 S (29582), Approx 15 mi N on US 17, in Barefoot Landing shopping center. 843/272-5107.* Web www.ribsribsribs.com. Hrs: 11 am-10 pm. Closed Dec 25. Bar. Semi-a la carte: lunch $4.50-$6.99, dinner $8.50-$19.99. Child's meals. Specializes in onion loaf, prime rib, steak. Overlooks lagoon. Cr cds: A, C, D, MC, V.

[icons]

★★ **FUSCO'S RESTAURANT.** *(See Beach Colony) 843/449-4010.* Hrs: 6-10 am, 4-10 pm; Sun 6 am-2 pm, 4-10 pm; hrs vary June-Aug. Closed 1st wk Jan. Res accepted. Italian menu. Bar 4 pm-1 am. Semi-a la carte: bkfst $4.50-$5.45, dinner $12.95-$21.95. Child's meals. Specializes in seafood, pasta, veal. Own baking. Casual atmosphere; overlooks pool and ocean. Cr cds: A, C, D, DS, MC, V.

[icons]

★★ **JOE'S BAR & GRILL.** *810 Conway Ave (29582), approx 15 mi N on US 17. 843/272-4666.* Hrs: 5-10 pm. Closed Thanksgiving, Dec 25. Res accepted. Bar. Semi-a la carte: dinner $13.95-$25.95. Child's meals. Specialties: steak au poivre, veal Marsala, lobster tail. Outdoor dining. Overlooks marsh. Cr cds: A, C, DS, MC, V.

[icons]

✓★★★ **LATIF'S BAKERY & CAFE.** *503 61st Ave (29577). 843/449-1716.* Hrs: 8 am-4 pm, 5-9:30 pm; Mon to 4 pm; Sun brunch 10 am-3 pm. Continental menu. Bar. Semi-a la carte: lunch $5.95-$9.95, dinner $12.95-$15.95. Sun brunch $4.75-$9.95. Specialties: Chinese chicken salad, triple mochá torte. Outdoor dining. French bistro atmosphere. Cr cds: A, C, DS, MC, V.

[icons]

★ **LONGHORN STEAKHOUSE.** *7604 N Kings Hwy US 17 (29572). 843/449-7013.* Hrs: 5-10 pm. Closed Thanksgiving; also 1 wk during Christmas season. Bar. Semi-a la carte: dinner $10.95-$36.95. Child's meals. Specializes in choice steaks, seafood. Salad bar. Western decor. Family-owned. Cr cds: A, C, D, DS, MC, V.

[icons]

★★ **OAK HARBOUR.** *1407 13th Ave N (29582), 16 mi N on US 17, at Vereen's Marina. 843/249-4737.* Hrs: 5-9:30 pm. Closed Thanksgiving, Dec 25. Res accepted. Bar 4-11 pm. Semi-a la carte: dinner $13.95-$19.25. Child's meals. Specializes in prime rib, fresh seafood, veal. Outdoor dining. Overlooks marina. Cr cds: A, C, D, DS, MC, V.

[icons]

✓★ **ROSA LINDA'S CAFE.** *4713 Hwy 17 S (29582), approx 6 mi N on US 17. 843/272-6823.* Hrs: 3-10 pm; Fri-Sun from noon. Closed Dec, Jan. Bar. Semi-a la carte: lunch $3.95-$6.95, dinner $6.50-$14.50.

Child's meals. Specialties: fajitas, pasta, pizza. Mexican/Italian atmosphere. Cr cds: A, C, D, DS, MC, V.

★★ SEA CAPTAIN'S HOUSE. *3000 N Ocean Blvd (29577). 843/448-8082.* Hrs: 6-10:30 am, 11:30 am-2:30 pm, 5-10 pm. Serv bar. Semi-a la carte: bkfst $4.50-$8.95, lunch, dinner $5.50-$29. Child's meals. Specializes in fresh seafood, steaks, homemade pies. Sea captain's house design; flowering shrubs. Ocean view. Cr cds: A, C, DS, MC, V.

★ SHENANIGAN'S. *10131 N Kings Hwy US 17 (29572). 843/272-1171.* Hrs: 4-10:30 pm; Fri, Sat to 11 pm; Sun to 10:30 pm. Closed Dec 25. Bar. Semi-a la carte: dinner $7.95-$31.95. Specializes in steak, prime rib. Cr cds: A, C, D, DS, MC, V.

★★ TONY'S. *1407 US 17 (29582), 15 mi N on US 17. 843/ 249-1314.* Hrs: 5-10 pm. Closed Dec-Jan; also Sun Sept-May. Italian menu. Bar. Semi-a la carte: dinner $8.95-$29.50. Child's meals. Specializes in pasta, pizza, seafood, veal. Contemporary Mediterranean decor. Family-owned. Cr cds: A, C, D, DS, MC, V.

Newberry (D-4)

(See also Clinton, Columbia, Greenwood)

Pop 10,542 **Elev** 500 ft **Area Code** 803 **Zip** 29108

What to See and Do

Dreher Island State Park. Approx 340 acres. Three islands with 12-mi shoreline. Lake swimming; fishing (supplies); boating (ramps, rental slips). Nature trail. Picnicking (shelters), playground, recreation bldg, store. Camping (hookups, dump station; higher fees for lakefront campsites in summer). Standard fees. 20 mi SE via US 76 to Chapin, then 9 mi SW via unnumbered road. Phone 803/364-4152 or 803/364-3530.

Sumter National Forest. N via SC 121, US 176 (see GREENWOOD).

Motel

✓★ BEST WESTERN INN. *11701 S Carolina Hwy 34 (29108), at jct I-26 & Hwy 34, exit 74. 803/276-5850; FAX 803/276-9851; res: 800/ 528-1234.* 116 rms, 1-2 story. S $37.95; D $42.95-$47.95; each addl $5; under 12 free. Crib free. TV, cable (premium). Pool. Complimentary continental bkfst. Bar 6 pm-midnight. Ck-out 11 am. Meeting rms. Business servs avail. Exercise equipt. Cr cds: A, C, D, DS, MC, V.

Orangeburg (E-4)

(See also Aiken, Santee)

Settled 1730s **Pop** 13,739 **Elev** 245 ft **Area Code** 803 **Zip** 29115
Information Orangeburg County Chamber of Commerce, 1570 John C. Calhoun Dr, Box 328, 29116-0328; 803/534-6821

Named for the Prince of Orange, this community is the seat of Orangeburg County, one of the most prosperous farm areas in the state. Manufacturing plants for wood products, ball bearings, textiles, textile equipment, chemicals, hand tools and lawn mowers are all located within the county.

What to See and Do

Edisto Memorial Gardens. City-owned 110-acre site. Seasonal flowers bloom all yr; more than 3,200 rose bushes, camellias, azaleas; also many flowering trees. Gardens (daily). Wetlands boardwalk park. Tennis courts, picnic areas, shelters nearby, playground. S on US 301, within city limits, alongside N Edisto River. Phone 803/533-6020.   **Free**

South Carolina State University (1896) (5,000 students). 300 College St NE. Phone 803/536-7000. On campus is

I.P. Stanback Museum and Planetarium. Museum has changing exhibits (Sept-May, Mon-Fri; closed hols). Planetarium shows (Oct-Apr, 2nd & 4th Sun; closed hols). Phone 803/536-7174 for reservations. Shows. ¢

Annual Event

Orangeburg County Fair. Fairgrounds. Late Sept-early Oct.

Motels

✓★ DAYS INN. *3691 Saint Matthews Rd (29115), on US 601N. 803/531-2590; FAX 803/531-2829; res: 800/329-7466.* 75 rms. S $45-$50; D $50-$60; each addl $7; under 12 free. Crib free. TV; cable (premium). Pool. Complimentary continental bkfst. Ck-out 11 am. Some refrigerators; microwaves avail. Cr cds: A, C, D, DS, MC, V.

★★ HOLIDAY INN. *1415 John C Calhoun Dr (29118). 803/531-4600; FAX 803/516-0187.* 160 rms, 2 story. S $68-$78; D $76-$86; each addl $8; under 19 free. Crib free. Pet accepted. TV; cable (premium). Heated pool. Restaurant 6:30 am-2 pm, 5:30-9 pm; Sat, Sun from 7 am. Bar; closed Sun. Ck-out noon. Meeting rms. Business servs avail. In-rm modem link. Valet serv. Cr cds: A, C, D, DS, JCB, MC, V.

Rock Hill (C-4)

(See also Chester, Gaffney; also see Charlotte, NC)

Founded 1852 **Pop** 41,643 **Elev** 667 ft **Area Code** 803
E-mail yccvb@cetlink.net **Web** www.yccvb.com
Information York County Convention & Visitors Bureau, 201 E Main St, PO Box 11377, 29731; 803/329-5200 or; 800/866-5200

Both a college and an industrial town, Rock Hill takes its name from the flint rock that had to be cut through when a railroad was built through town.

What to See and Do

Andrew Jackson State Park. Approx 360 acres. Lake fishing; boating (rentals). Nature trail. Picnicking (shelters), playground. Camping. Recreation bldg, outdoor amphitheater. Log house museum contains documents, exhibits of Jackson lore. One-rm school with exhibits. Standard fees. 9 mi N on US 521. Phone 803/285-3344.

Catawba Cultural Center. Located on the Catawba Indian Reservation, this center strives to preserve the heritage of the Catawba's culture. Tours and programs demonstrating the Catawba's culture and heritage are avail (by appt). Gift shop. (Mon-Sat; closed major hols) 1536 Tom Steven Rd. Phone 803/328-2427.   **Free**

Glencairn Garden. Municipally-owned 6 acres of colorful azaleas, dogwood, redbud, crepe myrtle, boxwood; pool, fountain (daily). 725 Crest St. Phone 803/329-5620.   **Free**

Historic Brattonsville. Learn about local history in this restored village of over 2 dozen structures, incl Backwoodsman Cabin, Colonel Bratton Home (ca 1780), Homestead House (ca 1823) and Brick Kitchen. Gift shop. Guided tours (by appt). Self-guided audio tour. (Mar-Nov, Tues-Sat, also

Sun afternoons; closed hols) SW via SC 322, at 1444 Brattonsville Rd near McConnells. Phone 803/684-2327. ¢¢

Kings Mountain State Park (See KINGS MOUNTAIN NATIONAL MILITARY PARK.)

Lake Wylie. Created by Duke Power Co. dam on the Catawba River. Freshwater fishing, boating, waterskiing, swimming; 12,455 acres. N on SC 274. Phone 704/382-8587.

Landsford Canal State Park. Approx 250 acres. Site of canal built in 1820s; locks, stone bridges. Trail parallels canals. Picnicking (shelter), community bldg. (Thurs-Mon) 15 mi S off US 21. Phone 803/789-5800.

Museum of York County. Contains a large collection of mounted African hoofed mammals; large African artifacts collection. Hall of Western Hemisphere contains mounted animals from North and South America. Art galleries & planetarium. Catawba pottery sold here. Nature trail, picnic area. (Daily; closed Thanksgiving, Dec 25) Mt Gallant Rd, 7 mi NW, off I-77 exit 82 A. Phone 800/968-2726. ¢¢

Winthrop University (1886) (5,000 students). Coeducational. 100 undergraduate and graduate programs. Concerts, lectures, sports, plays; art galleries. Large lake and recreational area. Oakland Ave. Phone 803/323-2236.

Annual Event

"Come-See-Me." Art shows, tour of houses, entertainment, road race, concerts. 10 days early Apr.

Motels

★★ **COMFORT INN.** 3725 Ave of The Carolinas (29708), N on I-77, exit 90. 803/548-5200; FAX 803/548-6692; res: 800/228-5150. E-mail ft.mill071@rfsmgmt.com. 155 rms, 4 story. S $65-$95; D $75-$105; suites, kit. unit $130-$160; under 18 free; higher rates race weekends. Crib free. TV; cable (premium). Pool. Complimentary continental bkfst. Restaurant adj 6 am-10 pm. Ck-out 11 am. Meeting rms. In-rm modem link. Valet serv. Exercise equipt. Refrigerator in suites. Cr cds: A, C, D, DS, ER, JCB, MC, V.

D ⌦ 🏋 🏊 🔥 SC

✓★★ **COUNTRY INN & SUITES.** 865 Patriot Pkwy (29730). 803/329-5151; FAX 803/329-5811; res: 800/456-4000. 43 rms, 3 story, 6 suites. S, D $69; suites $99; under 18 free; higher rates special events. Crib free. TV; cable (premium). Complimentary continental bkfst. Complimentary coffee in rms. Restaurant nearby. Ck-out noon. Meeting rms. Business servs avail. In-rm modem link. Exercise equipt. Pool. Refrigerators, microwaves. Wet bar in suites. Cr cds: A, C, D, DS, MC, V.

D ⌦ 🏋 🏊 🔥 SC

★ **DAYS INN.** 914 Riverview Rd (29730). 803/329-6581; FAX 803/366-4472; res: 800/329-7466. 113 rms, 3 story. S $45-$125; D $50-$150; each addl $5; higher rates wkends, special events. Crib free. TV; cable (premium). Pool. Complimentary continental bkfst. Restaurant 6-9 am. Ck-out 11 am. Meeting rms. Business servs avail. Cr cds: A, C, D, DS, ER, JCB, MC, V.

D ⌦ 🏊 🔥 SC

★ **DAYS INN.** 3482 Carowinds Blvd (29715), approx 5 mi N on I-77 exit 90. 803/548-8000; FAX 803/548-6058; res: 800/329-7466. 119 rms, 2 story. Apr-Sept: S $45-$70; D $50-$75; each addl $5; higher rates special events; lower rates rest of yr. Crib free. Pet accepted. TV; cable (premium), VCR avail. Pool. Complimentary continental bkfst. Restaurant adj open 24 hrs. Ck-out 11 am. Cr cds: A, C, D, DS, MC, V.

D 🐾 ⌦ 🏊 🔥 SC

✓★ **ECONO LODGE.** 962 Riverview Rd (29730), I-77 exit 82B. 803/329-3232; FAX 803/329-3232; res: 800/553-2666. 106 rms, 2 story. S $36.95; D $43.45; each addl $5; under 18 free; higher rates wkends, special events. TV; cable (premium). Complimentary continental bkfst. Restaurant adj open 24 hrs. Ck-out 11 am. Business servs avail. Cr cds: A, C, D, DS, ER, JCB, MC, V.

D 🏊 🔥 SC

★★ **HOLIDAY INN.** 2640 N Cherry Rd (29730), at jct I-77, US 21N. 803/329-1122; FAX 803/329-1072; res: 800/465-4329. 125 rms, 2 story. S, D $79; each addl $5; suites $95-$150; under 18 free. Crib free. Pet accepted, some restrictions; deposit. TV; cable (premium). Pool. Coffee in rms. Restaurant 6:30 am-10 pm, Sat to 9 pm. Ck-out noon. Coin lndry. Business servs avail. In-rm modem link. Airport transportation. Cr cds: A, C, D, DS, JCB, MC, V.

D 🐾 ⌦ 🏊 🔥 SC

Motor Hotel

✓★★ **HAMPTON INN.** 2111 Tabor Dr (29730). 803/325-1100; FAX 803/325-7814; res: 800/426-7866. E-mail rhhampton@rhtc.net. 162 rms, 5 story, 33 suites. S $75; D $79; suites $99-$149; under 18 free; higher rates special events. Crib avail. TV; cable (premium), VCR avail. Complimentary continental bkfst. Complimentary coffee in rms. Restaurant nearby. Ck-out 11 am. Meeting rms. Business center. In-rm modem link. Coin lndry. Exercise equipt; sauna. Pool. Refrigerator, microwave in suites. Cr cds: A, C, D, DS, MC, V.

D 🏊 🏋 🔥 SC 🚶

Hotel

★★ **RAMADA HOTEL CAROWINDS.** 225 Carowinds Blvd (29715), I-77 Carowinds exit. 803/548-2400; FAX 803/548-6382; res: 800/237-8753. 208 rms, 11 story. S, D $71-$85; each addl $10; under 18 free; higher rates race wkends. Crib free. Pet accepted. TV; cable (premium). Pool. Complimentary continental bkfst. Restaurant 6:30 am-2 pm, 5-10 pm; Fri, Sat to 11 pm. Bar 4:30-11 pm. Ck-out noon. Coin lndry. Meeting rms. Business center. In-rm modem link. Free airport transportation. Exercise equipt. Tennis. Cr cds: A, C, D, DS, JCB, MC, V.

D 🐾 🏋 🏊 🏋 🔥 SC 🚶

Inn

✓★★ **EAST MAIN GUEST HOUSE.** 600 E Main St (29730). 803/366-1161; FAX 803/366-1161. 4 rms, 2 story. S $59; D $59-$79. Children over 12 yrs only. TV; cable, VCR avail. Complimentary continental bkfst. Restaurant nearby. Ck-out noon, ck-in 3 pm. Luggage handling. 18-hole golf privileges. Some fireplaces. Built in 1910. Totally nonsmoking. Cr cds: C, MC, V.

🏊 🔥

Restaurant

✓★ **TAM'S TAVERN.** 1027 Oakland Ave (29732). 803/329-2226. Hrs: 11 am-3 pm, 5-10 pm; Fri, Sat to 10:30 pm. Closed Sun; also major hols. Res accepted. Bar to 11 pm. Semi-a la carte: lunch $4.95-$6.95, dinner $5.95-$16.95. Child's meals. Specializes in seafood, beef. Parking. Cr cds: A, C, D, DS, MC, V.

D 🍴

Santee (E-5)

(See also Orangeburg)

Pop 638 **Elev** 250 ft **Area Code** 803 **Zip** 29142
E-mail tourscc@oburg.net **Web** www.santeecoopercountry.org
Information Santee-Cooper Country, PO Drawer 40; 803/854-2131 or 800/227-8510 outside SC

This community serves as the gateway to the Santee-Cooper Lakes recreation area, created by the Pinopolis and Santee dams on the Santee and

Cooper rivers. There are numerous marinas and campgrounds on the Santee–Cooper lakes.

What to See and Do

Eutaw Springs Battlefield Site. Site where ragged colonials fought the British on Sept 8, 1781, in what is considered to be the last major engagement in South Carolina; both sides claimed victory. Three acres maintained by state. No facilities. 12 mi SE off SC 6. **Free**

Fort Watson Battle Site and Indian Mound. A 48-ft-high mound; site of Revolutionary War battle Apr 15-23, 1781, during which Gen Francis Marion attacked and captured a British fortification, its garrison, supplies and ammunition. Three acres maintained by state. No facilities. Observation point has view of Santee–Cooper waters. 4 mi N, 1 mi off US 15/301, on Lake Marion. **Free**

Santee National Wildlife Refuge. Attracts many geese and ducks during winter. Observation tower, self-guided nature trail; visitor info center with exhibits (Mon-Fri; closed hols). Seasonal hunting and fishing, wildlife observation and photography. 4 mi N on US 15/301 or exit 102 from I-95. Phone 803/478-2217. **Free**

Santee State Park. Approx 2,500 acres. Lake swimming; fishing (supplies avail); boating (ramp, rentals, dock). Scenic lake tours. Nature trails; tennis. Picnicking (shelters), playground, restaurant, groceries. Camping, cabins (higher fees for lakefront sites), primitive camping. Interpretive center, recreation building. Standard fees. 3 mi NW off SC 6, on shores of Lake Marion. Phone 803/854-2408.

Motels

★★ **BEST WESTERN INN.** *Hwy 6 (29142), I-95 exit 98 E.* 803/854-3089; FAX 803/854-3093; res: 800/528-1234. 108 rms. S $50-$60; D $50-$65; under 12 free. Crib $4. TV; cable (premium). Heated pool. Complimentary continental bkfst. Restaurant 5-9:30 pm. Ck-out 11 am. Business servs avail. Some in-rm whirlpools. 18-hole golf privileges. Cr cds: A, C, D, DS, MC, V.

🅳 🍴 🏊 🖇 🔥 SC

✓★ **DAYS INN.** *9074 Old #6 Hwy (29142).* 803/854-2175; FAX 803/854-2835; res: 800/329-7466. 119 rms, 2 story. S $30-$50; D $40-$60; each addl $6; under 12 free; golf plans. Crib free. Pet accepted, some restrictions; $6. TV; cable (premium). Pool. Playground. Complimentary full bkfst. Restaurant 6-10 am, 5-9 pm. Ck-out noon. Guest lndry. Business servs avail. 18-hole golf privileges. Refrigerators avail. Cr cds: A, C, D, DS, MC, V.

🐾 🍴 🏊 🖇 🔥 SC

Spartanburg (C-3)

(See also Clinton, Gaffney, Greenville)

Founded 1785 **Pop** 43,467 **Elev** 816 ft **Area Code** 864
Information Convention & Visitors Bureau, 105 N Pine St, PO Box 1636, 29304; 864/594-5050

An array of highways and railroads feeds agricultural products into, and moves manufactured products out of, heavily industrialized Spartanburg. Textiles and peaches are the leading products. The Spartan Regiment of South Carolina militia, heroes of the Battle at Cowpens, gave both the county and its seat their names.

What to See and Do

Croft State Park. On part of old Camp Croft military area. Approx 7,000 acres. Swimming pool (fee); lake fishing. Nature, exercise trails; bridle trail (no rentals); stable, show ring; tennis. Picnicking (shelters), playground. Camping (hookups, dump station). Standard fees. 3 mi SE on SC 56. Phone 864/585-1283.

Regional Museum. Exhibits depict up-country history of state; Pardo Stone (1567), doll collections, Native American artifacts. (Daily exc Mon; closed hols) 501 Otis Blvd, at Pine St. Phone 864/596-3501. ¢

The Arts Council of Spartanburg. Permanent and changing exhibits; classes in visual and performing arts. (Daily; closed most hols) 385 S Spring St. Phone 864/583-2776. **Free**

Walnut Grove Plantation (1765). Restored girlhood home of Kate Moore Barry, Revolutionary heroine; period furniture; schoolhouse, kitchen, doctor's office, other bldgs; family cemetery; herb gardens with "dipping well." (Apr-Oct, daily exc Mon; rest of yr, Sun only; closed some hols) 8 mi SE near jct I-26, US 221. Phone 864/576-6546. ¢¢

Annual Event

Piedmont Interstate Fair. Art exhibit, livestock and flower shows, needlecraft and food displays; auto race. Phone 864/582-7042. 2nd full wk Oct.

Motels

★★ **COMFORT INN.** *2070 New Cut Rd (29303).* 864/576-2992; FAX 864/576-2992; res: 800/638-7949. 99 rms, 2 story. S $45-$55; D $55-$85; each addl $6; suites $125; under 18 free. Crib free. TV; cable. Pool. Complimentary continental bkfst. Ck-out 11 am. Refrigerators, microwaves avail. Cr cds: A, C, D, DS, ER, JCB, MC, V.

🅳 🏊 🖇 🔥 SC

★★ **DAYS INN.** *1000 Hearon Cir (29303), at jct I-85 & I-585.* 864/503-9048; FAX 864/503-0576; res: 800/329-7466. 138 rms, 2-3 story. No elvtr. S $58-$64; D $64-$68; each addl $7. Crib free. TV. Pool. Coffee in rms. Restaurant 6-10:30 am. Rm serv. Bar 5 pm-2 am; entertainment exc Sun. Ck-out noon. Meeting rms. Business servs avail. Bellhops. Valet serv. Cr cds: A, C, D, DS, JCB, MC, V.

🅳 🏊 🖇 🔥 SC

★★ **HAMPTON INN.** *4930 College Dr (29301).* 864/576-6080; FAX 864/587-8901; res: 800/426-7866. 110 rms, 2 story. S $55-$57; D $60-$62; under 18 free. Crib free. TV; cable. Pool. Complimentary continental bkfst. Ck-out noon. Meeting rm. Business servs avail. Cr cds: A, C, D, DS, MC, V.

🅳 🏊 🖇 🔥 SC

★★★ **RAMADA INN.** *200 International Dr (29303), jct I-26 & I-85 exit 71.* 864/576-5220; FAX 864/574-1243; res: 800/972-7511. 224 rms, 3 story. S $59-$89; D $64-$94; under 18 free. Crib free. TV. Indoor pool; whirlpool, wading pool, poolside serv. Restaurant 6:30 am-2 pm, 5:30-10 pm. Rm serv. Bar; entertainment exc Sun. Ck-out noon. Coin lndry. Meeting rms. Business servs avail. In-rm modem link. Bellhops. Valet serv. Exercise equipt; sauna. Rec rm. Cr cds: A, C, D, DS, JCB, MC, V.

🅳 🏊 🍴 🖇 🔥 SC

Motor Hotel

★★ **QUALITY HOTEL INN & CONFERENCE CENTER.** *7136 Asheville Hwy (29303).* 864/503-0780; FAX 864/503-0780; res: 800/221-2222. 143 rms, 6 story. S, D $59; each addl $10; suites $135; under 18 free. Crib free. Pet accepted. TV; cable (premium). Pool; poolside serv. Coffee in rms. Restaurant 6:30 am-2 pm, 5-10 pm. Bar 4 pm-midnight. Ck-out noon. Meeting rms. Business servs avail. In-rm modem link. Valet serv. Exercise equipt. Refrigerators avail. Cr cds: A, C, D, DS, JCB, MC, V.

🐾 🏊 🍴 🖇 🔥 SC

Sumter (D-5)

(See also Camden, Columbia)

Settled 1785 **Pop** 36,933 **Elev** 173 ft **Area Code** 803
E-mail sumter@usc.net **Web** www.sumter.sc.us

Information Convention & Visitors Bureau, 32 E Calhoun St, PO Box 1449, 29150; 803/778-5434 or 800/688-4748

Long the center of a prosperous agricultural area, Sumter has, in recent years, become an industrial center. Both the city and county are named for General Thomas Sumter, the "fighting gamecock" of the Revolutionary War. As a tourism spot, Sumter offers a unique contrast of antebellum mansions and modern facilities. Shaw Air Force Base, headquarters of the 9th Air Force and the 363rd Tactical Fighter Wing, is nearby.

What to See and Do

Church of the Holy Cross (1850). Built of *pise de terre* (rammed earth); unusual architectural design and construction. Also noted for stained-glass windows set to catch rays of the rising sun. Many notable South Carolinians from the 1700s are buried in the church cemetery, incl Joel R. Poinsett. 10 mi W via US 76, exit at SC 261, in Stateburg. Phone 803/494-8101.

Opera House. The Opera House stands today not only as a symbol of the past, but as an active sign of the ongoing progressive spirit of the people of Sumter. The 600-seat auditorium is used for concerts, school events and other local happenings. Fees vary for booked activities. (By appt only; closed hols) 21 N Main St. Phone 803/436-2500 or 800/688-4748.   **Free**

Poinsett State Park. Approx 1,000 acres of mountains, swamps. Named for Joel Poinsett, who introduced the poinsettia (which originated in Mexico) to the US. Spanish moss, mountain laurel, rhododendron. Lake swimming; fishing; boating (rentals). Hiking, nature trails;. Picnicking (shelters), playground. Primitive & improved camping (dump station), cabins. Nature center; programs. Standard fees. 18 mi SW via SC 763, 261. Phone 803/494-8177.

Sumter County Museum. Two-story Edwardian house depicting Victorian lifestyle; period rms, historical exhibits, war memorabilia, economic and cultural artifacts, artwork and archives (genealogical research). Museum surrounded by formal gardens designed by Robert Marvin; several outdoor exhibits of farm implements, rural life; carriage house. (Daily exc Mon; closed hols) 122 N Washington St. Phone 803/775-0908.   **Donation**

Sumter Gallery of Art. Located in the historic Elizabeth White house, regional artwork features paintings, drawings, sculpture, photography and pottery; permanent collection of touchable works for the blind; changing exhibits. (Tues-Sun afternoons; closed hols & July) 421 N Main St. Phone 803/775-0543.   **Free**

Swan Lake Iris Gardens. Covers 150 acres; Kaempferi and Japanese iris; seasonal plantings, nature trails; ancient cypress, oak and pine trees; 45-acre lake with all 8 species of swan. Picnicking, playground. (Daily) Home to the Iris Festival held every May. (See ANNUAL EVENTS) W Liberty St.   **Free**

Annual Events

Sumter Iris Festival. Fireworks display, parade, art show, golf & tennis tournaments, barbecue cook-off, local talent exhibition, square dance, iris gardens display. Late May.

Fall Fiesta of Arts. Swan Lake Gardens. Features visual & performing arts, concerts. Phone 803/436-2258. 3rd wkend Oct.

Motels

★ ★ ★ **HOLIDAY INN.** *2390 Broad St (29150). 803/469-9001; FAX 803/469-9070; res: 800/465-4329.* 124 rms, 2 story. S, D $59-$79; each addl $6; under 19 free. Crib free. TV; cable (premium). Pool. Complimentary bkfst buffet. Coffee in rms. Restaurant 6-9 am, 5:30-10 pm; Sat, Sun 6:30-10 am, 5:30-10 pm. Rm serv. Ck-out noon. Meeting rms. Busi-

ness center. In-rm modem link. Valet serv. Tennis privileges. Exercise equipt. Microwaves avail. Cr cds: A, C, D, DS, JCB, MC, V.

★ ★ **RAMADA INN.** *226 N Washington St (29151), on US 76/378/521. 803/775-2323; FAX 803/773-9500; res: 800/272-6232.* 125 rms in 2 buildings, 2-3 story. S $49-$89; D $59-$89; each addl $9; under 18 free; golf plans. Crib free. Pet accepted, some restrictions. TV; cable (premium). Pool. Complimentary bkfst buffet. Coffee in rms. Restaurant 6:30 am-2 pm, 6-9 pm. Rm serv. Bar 5 pm-midnight; closed Sun. Ck-out noon. Meeting rms. Business servs avail. In-rm modem link. Health club privileges. Refrigerators, microwaves avail. Cr cds: A, C, D, DS, ER, JCB, MC, V.

★ **TRAVELERS INN.** *378 Broad St (29150). 803/469-9210; FAX 803/469-4306; res: 800/304-6389.* 104 rms. S $32.95; D $35.95-$40.95; each addl $5; higher rates: hol wkends, special events. Crib free. TV; cable (premium). Pool. Complimentary continental bkfst. Ck-out 11 am. Cr cds: A, C, D, DS, MC, V.

Inns

★ ★ **BED & BREAKFAST OF SUMTER.** *6 Park Ave (29150). 803/773-2903; FAX 803/775-6943; res: 888/786-8372.* Web www.bbonline.com/sc/sumter. 5 rms, 2 story. No rm phones. S $65; D $75. TV in common rm; cable. Complimentary full bkfst. Ck-out 11 am, ck-in 3-6 pm. Some fireplaces. Built in 1897; prairie home style with Victorian decor. Totally nonsmoking. Cr cds: C, DS, MC, V.

✓ ★ ★ ★ **MAGNOLIA HOUSE BED & BREAKFAST.** *230 Church St (29150). 803/775-6694; res: 888/666-0296.* E-mail magnoliahouse@sumter.net. 4 rms, 2 story, 1 suite. S $65; D $75; suite $125. Crib free. Pet accepted, some restrictions. TV; cable, VCR avail (movies). Complimentary full bkfst; afternoon refreshments. Ck-out 11 am, ck-in 3 pm. Luggage handling. Built in 1907; Greek revival. Totally nonsmoking. Cr cds: A, C, D, MC, V.

Walterboro (E-5)

(See also Beaufort, Charleston)

Settled 1784 **Pop** 5,492 **Elev** 69 ft **Area Code** 843 **Zip** 29488
E-mail chamber@lowcountry.com **Web** www.pride-net.com

Information Walterboro-Colleton Chamber of Commerce, 109 Benson St, PO Box 426; 843/549-9595

Settled in 1784 by Charleston plantation owners as a summer resort area, Walterboro has retained its charm of yesterday despite its growth. The town boasts a casual pace and rural lifestyle where people can enjoy fishing and hunting, early-19th-century architectural designs, plantations, and beach and recreational facilities.

What to See and Do

Colleton County Courthouse. Building designed by Robert Mills; first public nullification meeting in state was held in 1828. Hampton St and Jefferies Blvd.

Colleton State Park. On 35 acres; tree-shaded area on banks of Edisto River. Canoeing (dock); river fishing. Nature trails. Picnicking (shelters). Camping (hookups, dump station). Standard fees. 11 mi N on US 15. Phone 843/538-8206.

Old Colleton County Jail (1855). Neo-Gothic structure resembles a castle; home to the Colleton Museum and the Chamber of Commerce. Served as Walterboro jail until 1937. Jefferies Blvd. Phone 843/549-2303.

South Carolina Artisans Center. Features handcrafted art and gifts by regional artists. Craftspeople demonstrate their skills. Educational programs and special events also offered. (Daily; closed hols) 334 Wichman St in Hickory Valley Historic District. Phone 843/549-0011.   **Free**

Annual Events

Mount Carmel Herb Festival. Mt Carmel Rd. Features weed walks, herb walks, cook with herbs, herb gardening; sale of herbs, soaps, candles; music. Phone 843/538-3505. Mar.

Rice Festival. Entertainment, parade, arts & crafts; street dances, soapbox derby. Phone 803/549-1079. Last full wkend Apr.

Edisto Riverfest. Colleton State Park. Canoe & kayak trips, river rafting, music, displays and workshops. For info contact SC Dept of Parks, Recreation and Tourism, 1205 Pendleton St, Columbia, SC 29201; 803/734-0156. June.

Motels

★ **ECONO LODGE.** *1145 Sniders Hwy (29488), I-95 & SC 63. 843/538-3830; FAX 843/538-3341.* 100 rms, 1-2 story. S, D $32.95-$65; each addl $5; under 18 free. Crib free. TV, cable (premium). Complimentary continental bkfst. Coffee in rms. Restaurant opp open 6 am-11 pm. Ck-out 11 am. Cr cds: A, C, DS, MC, V.

D ⊠ 🔥 SC

★★ **HOLIDAY INN.** *1236 Sniders Hwy (29488). 843/538-5473; FAX 843/538-5473; res: 800/465-4329.* 171 rms, 2 story. S, D $65; under 18 free. Crib free. Pet accepted. TV, cable (premium). Pool; wading pool. Complimentary full bkfst. Restaurant 6 am-2 pm, 5-10 pm. Rm serv. Ck-out noon. Meeting rms. Business servs avail. Valet serv. Cr cds: A, C, D, DS, MC, V.

D 🐾 ≈ ⊠ 🔥 SC

★ **TOWN & COUNTRY INN.** *97 Downs Ln (29488), at jct SC 63, I-95 exit 53. 843/538-5911; FAX 843/538-5911; res: 800/757-1237.* 96 rms, 2 story. S $26.95-$29.95; D $36.95; each addl $4; under 18 free. Crib free. Pet accepted. TV; cable. Pool. Playground. Complimentary continental bkfst. Restaurant 6 am-10 pm. Ck-out 11 am. Business servs avail. Private patios, balconies. Cr cds: A, C, D, DS, MC, V.

D 🐾 ≈ ⊠ 🔥 SC

Virginia

Population: 6,377,000
Land area: 40,815 square miles
Elevation: 0-5,729 feet
Highest point: Mt Rogers (Between Smyth, Grayson Counties)
Entered union: Tenth of original 13 states (June 25, 1788)
Capital: Richmond
Motto: Thus always to tyrants
Nickname: Old Dominion
State flower: American dogwood
State bird: Cardinal
State fair: September 21-October 1, 2000, in Richmond
Time zone: Eastern
Web: www.virginia.org

Settled by Elizabethans and named for their Virgin Queen, the first of the Southern states still retains a degree of the graceful courtliness that reached its peak just before the Civil War. Evidence of strong ties with the past are apparent in the Old Dominion. More than 1,600 historical markers dot its 55,000 miles of paved roads. More than 100 historic buildings are open all year; hundreds more welcome visitors during the statewide Historic Garden Week (usually the last week in April).

Permanent English settlement of America began in Jamestown in 1607 and started a long line of Virginia "firsts": the first legislative assembly in the Western Hemisphere (1619); the first armed rebellion against royal government (Bacon's Rebellion, 1676); the first stirring debates, in Williamsburg and Richmond, which left pre-Revolutionary America echoing Patrick Henry's inflammatory "Give me liberty, or give me death!" Records show that America's first Thanksgiving was held December 4, 1619, on the site of what is now Berkeley Plantation.

To Virginia the nation owes its most cherished documents—Thomas Jefferson's Declaration of Independence, George Mason's Bill of Rights, James Madison's Constitution. From here came George Washington to lead the Revolution and to become the first of eight US presidents to hail from Virginia.

Ironically, the state so passionately involved in creating a new nation was very nearly the means of its destruction. Virginia was the spiritual and physical capital of the Confederacy; the Army of Northern Virginia was the Confederacy's most powerful weapon; General Robert E. Lee its greatest commander. More than half the fighting of the Civil War took place in Virginia; and here, in the quaint little village of Appomattox Court House, the war finally came to an end.

When chartered in 1609, the Virginia territory included about one-tenth of what is now the United States; the present state ranks 36th in size, but the remaining area is remarkably diverse. Tidewater Virginia—the coastal plain—is low, almost flat, arable land cut by rivers and bays into a magnificent system of natural harbors. It was vital to commerce and agriculture in the early days. Today it is still important commercially (the Hampton Roads port is one of the world's great naval and shipbuilding bases) and a perennial lure to vacationers as well.

Inland lies the gentle rolling Piedmont, covering about half the state. Here is Virginia's leading tobacco area; it also produces apples, corn, wheat, hay and dairy products. The world's largest single-unit textile plant is in Danville; the Piedmont also manufactures shoes, furniture, paper products, clay and glass, chemicals and transportation equipment.

West of the Piedmont rise the Blue Ridge Mountains; high, rugged upland plateaus occur to the south. Further west is the Valley of Virginia, a series of fertile valleys. Best known is the Shenandoah, which contains some of the richest—and once bloodiest—land in the nation. Civil War fighting swept the valley for four years; Winchester changed hands 72 times.

To the southwest are the Appalachian Plateaus, a rugged, forested region of coal mines. Here the splendid outdoor drama, the *Trail of the Lonesome Pine,* romanticized by the novelist John Fox, is performed.

For the vacationer today, the state offers colonial and Civil War history at every turn, seashore and mountain recreation the year round, such natural oddities as caverns in the west and the Dismal Swamp in the southeast, and the Skyline Drive (see SHENANDOAH NATIONAL PARK), one of the loveliest scenic drives in the East.

When to Go/Climate

Virginia summers can be hot and humid, marked by brief, powerful thunderstorms; winter snows are common in the mountains. Moderate temperatures, light rainfall, verdant flowering gardens, and brilliant foliage make spring and fall the best seasons to visit.

AVERAGE HIGH/LOW TEMPERATURES (°F)

RICHMOND

Jan 46/26	**May** 78/54	**Sept** 81/59
Feb 49/28	**June** 85/63	**Oct** 71/47
Mar 60/36	**July** 88/68	**Nov** 61/38
Apr 70/45	**Aug** 87/66	**Dec** 50/30

ROANOKE

Jan 44/25	**May** 76/53	**Sept** 79/57
Feb 47/27	**June** 83/60	**Oct** 68/45
Mar 58/36	**July** 86/65	**Nov** 58/37
Apr 67/44	**Aug** 85/64	**Dec** 48/29

Parks and Recreation Finder

Directions to and information about the parks and recreation areas below are given under their respective town/city sections. Please refer to those sections for details.

CALENDAR HIGHLIGHTS

FEBRUARY

Mobil Invitational Track & Field Meet (Fairfax). George Mason University campus. For more information, phone Visitors Center 703/550-2450.

APRIL

International Azalea Festival (Norfolk). Downtown & Norfolk Botanical Garden. To honor NATO. Parade, coronation ceremony, air show (held at Norfolk Naval Air Station), events, concerts, fair, ball, entertainment. Phone 757/664-6620.

Garden Week (Charlottesville). Some fine private homes and gardens in the area are open. For more information, phone Garden Club of Virginia/Richmond headquarters 804/644-7776.

Garden Week in Historic Lexington (Lexington). Tour of homes and gardens in the Lexington, Rockbridge County area. Phone 540/463-3777.

MAY

Jamestown Weekend (Jamestown, Colonial National Historical Park). Original Jamestown site. Commemorates arrival of first settlers in 1607; special tours and activities. Phone 757/229-1733.

JUNE

Natural Chimneys Jousting Tournament (Harrisonburg). Natural Chimneys Regional Park. America's oldest continuous sporting event, held annually since 1821. "Knights" armed with lances charge down an 80-yard track and attempt to spear three small rings suspended from posts. Phone 540/350-2510.

JULY

Red Cross Waterfront Festival (Alexandria). Commemorates Alexandria's maritime heritage. Features "tall ships," blessing of the fleet, river cruises, races, arts & crafts, exhibits, food, variety of music; fireworks. Phone 703/549-8300.

Pony Penning (Chincoteague). The "wild" ponies are rounded up on Assateague Island, then swim the inlet to Chincoteague, where foals are sold at auction before the ponies swim back to Assateague. Carnival amusements. For more information, phone Chincoteague Chamber of Commerce, 757/336-6161.

SEPTEMBER

Publick Times (Williamsburg). Colonial Williamsburg. Re-creation of colonial market days; contests, crafts, auctions, military encampment. Phone 757/220-7645 or 800/246-2099.

Virginia State Fair (Richmond). Animal and 4-H contests, music, horse show, carnival. Phone 804/228-3200.

OCTOBER

Blue Ridge Folklife Festival (Martinsville). Blue Ridge Farm Museum. Gospel, blues and string band music; traditional regional crafts; regional foods; quilt show, antique autos, steam & gas-powered farm equipment. Sports events include horse-pulling & log-skidding contests, coon-dog swimming and treeing contests. Phone 540/365-4415.

DECEMBER

Christmas Candlelight Tour (Fredericksburg). Historic homes open to the public; carriage rides; Christmas decorations and refreshments of the colonial period. Contact Visitor Center, 540/373-1776 or 800/678-4748.

NATIONAL PARK AND RECREATION AREAS

Key to abbreviations. I.H.S. = International Historic Site; I.P.M.=International Peace Memorial; N.B. = National Battlefield; N.B.P. = National Battlefield Park; N.B.C. = National Battlefield & Cemetery; N.C. = National Conservation Area; N.E.M. = National Expansion Memorial; N.F. = National Forest; N.G. = National Grassland; N.H. = National Historical Park; N.H.C. = National Heritage Corridor; N.H.S. = National Historic Site; N.L. = National Lakeshore; N.M. = National Monument; N.M.P. = National Military Park; N.Mem. = National Memorial; N.P. = National Park; N.Pres. = National Preserve; N.R. = National Recreational Area; N.R.R. = National Recreational River; N.Riv. = National River; N.S. = National Seashore; N.S.R. = National Scenic Riverway; N.S.T. = National Scenic Trail; N.Sc. = National Scientific Reserve; N.V.M. = National Volcanic Monument.

Place Name	Listed Under
Appomattox Court House N.H.	same
Assateague Island N.S.	CHINCOTEAGUE
Blue Ridge Parkway	same
Booker T. Washington N.M.	same
George Washington Birthplace N.M.	same
Breaks I.P.	same
Cape Henry Memorial	same
Colonial N.H.	same
Colonial Parkway	same
Fredericksburg & Spotsylvania N.M.P.	same
George Washington and Jefferson N.F.	HARRISONBURG
Jamestown	same
Manassas N.B.P.	same
Petersburg N.B.	same
Prince William Forest Park	TRIANGLE
Richmond N.B.P.	same
Robert E. Lee N.Mem.	ARLINGTON COUNTY
Shenandoah N.P.	same
Wolf Trap Farm Park for the Performing Arts	FAIRFAX
Yorktown N.B.	YORKTOWN

STATE PARK AND RECREATION AREAS

Key to abbreviations. I.P. = Interstate Park; S.A.P. = State Archaeological Park; S.B. = State Beach; S.C. = State Conservation Area; S.C.P. = State Conservation Park; S.Cp. = State Campground; S.F. = State Forest; S.G. = State Garden; S.H.A. = State Historic Area; S.H.P. = State Historic Park; S.H.S. = State Historic Site; S.M.P. = State Marine Park; S.N.A. = State Natural Area; S.P. = State Park; S.P.C. = State Public Campground; S.R. = State Reserve; S.R.A. = State Recreation Area; S.Res. = State Reservoir; S.Res.P. = State Resort Park; S.R.P. = State Rustic Park.

Place Name	Listed Under
Chippokes Plantation S.P.	SURRY
Claytor Lake S.P.	RADFORD
Douthat S.P.	CLIFTON FORGE
Fairy Stone S.P.	MARTINSVILLE
First Landing/Seashore S.P.	VIRGINIA BEACH
Grayson Highlands S.P.	ABINGDON
Holliday Lake S.P.	APPOMATTOX COURT HOUSE N.H.
Hungry Mother S.P.	MARION
Natural Tunnel S.P.	BIG STONE GAP
Occoneechee S.P.	CLARKSVILLE
Pocahontas S.P.	RICHMOND
Sky Meadows S.P.	FRONT ROYAL
Staunton River S.P.	SOUTH BOSTON
Twin Lakes S.P.	KEYSVILLE
Westmoreland S.P.	MONTROSS
York River S.P.	WILLIAMSBURG

Water-related activities, hiking, various other sports, picnicking and visitor centers, as well as camping, are available in many of these areas. State park facilities and services are operated on a seasonal basis. Parking for noncampers, $1.50-$2.50/car/day, Memorial Day-Labor Day. Admission to State Historical Parks $1.25; children $1. Swimming, boat rentals, cafes and concessions, Memorial Day-Labor Day; fees for activities. Pets are allowed in camping and cabins, but must be kept inside at night. At all other times pets must be on a 6-ft leash. Facilities for the disabled at many parks.

Tent and trailer campgrounds are available in 19 state parks generally from Mar-Nov; maximum stay is two weeks. $10.50/site/night, $19.25 at Seashore (up to 6 persons, 1 vehicle); electricity and water $15/site/night where available. Reservations may be made 180 days-1 wk in advance (see below for addresses). Seven parks offer housekeeping cabins (May-Sept). Douthat (see CLIFTON FORGE) has a guest lodge for 15. Reservations for campsites are accepted beginning late March. Campsite and cabin reservations may be made by phoning 800/933-PARK or 804/225-3867. Booklets with details on each park may be obtained from the Virginia Dept of Conservation & Recreation, 203 Governor St, Ste 302, Richmond 23219. A campground directory is available from Virginia Tourism Corporation, 901 E Byrd St, Richmond 23219; 804/786-4484.

SKI AREAS

Place Name	Listed Under
Bryce Resort	BASYE
Homestead Ski Area	HOT SPRINGS
Wintergreen Resort	CHARLOTTESVILLE

FISHING AND HUNTING

Saltwater fishing on ocean, bay, river or creek is a major sport. Virginia is blessed with many miles of shoreline: 120 miles on the Atlantic Ocean, 300 miles on Chesapeake Bay, and 1,300 miles of tidal shores. There is no closed season for saltwater fishing except striped bass. There are some species size and bag limits. No license is required to fish in ocean waters or seaside of the eastern shore, but a license is required to fish in the Chesapeake and tidal tributaries. Information concerning size limits and bag limits on saltwater game fish may be obtained from the Virginia Marine Resources Commission, PO Box 756, Newport News 23607; phone 800/937-9247. The Commonwealth of Virginia sponsors an annual Saltwater Fishing Awards Program (see VIRGINIA BEACH), open to the public. Contact Virginia Saltwater Fishing Tournament, 968 S Oriole Dr, Ste 102, Virginia Beach 23451; 757/491-5160.

Freshwater fishing is excellent in many of the state's large reservoirs and rivers for such species as largemouth and smallmouth bass, landlocked striped bass, muskie and a wide variety of pan fish. Lake Anna, Smith Mt Lake, Lake Gaston, James River, Lake Moomaw & Buggs Island Lake are nationally known for excellent bass and landlocked striped bass fishing. Nonresident license: $30; $30 additional for license for trout in designated stocked waters. Five-day license to fish state-wide, $6; other special fees. Fishing in a national forest requires an additional fishing/hunting stamp, $3.

Hunting for upland game and migratory waterfowl in season. Nonresident license: $60; three-day license: $30; bear, deer, turkey, $60 additional; nonresident muzzle-loader license, $25; nonresident special archery license to hunt during special archery season, $25. Hunting in a national forest requires an additional fishing/hunting stamp, $3. There is a 50¢ issuance fee for all licenses. For fishing and hunting regulations and information write Department of Game and Inland Fisheries, 4010 W Broad St, Richmond 23230 or phone 804/367-1000.

Driving Information

Safety belts are mandatory for all persons in front seat of vehicle. Children under 4 years must be in an approved safety seat anywhere in vehicle. For further information phone 804/367-6081 or 804/367-0538 (VA).

INTERSTATE HIGHWAY SYSTEM

The following alphabetical listing of Virginia towns in *Mobil Travel Guide* shows that these cities are within 10 miles of the indicated Interstate highways. A highway map should, however, be checked for the nearest exit.

Highway Number	Cities/Towns within 10 miles
Interstate 64	Ashland, Charlottesville, Chesapeake, Clifton Forge, Covington, Hampton, Jamestown, Lexington, Newport News, Norfolk, Portsmouth, Richmond, Staunton, Virginia Beach, Waynesboro, Williamsburg, Yorktown.
Interstate 66	Alexandria, Arlington County, Fairfax, Falls Church, Front Royal, Manassas, McLean.
Interstate 77	Wytheville.
Interstate 81	Abingdon, Blacksburg, Bristol, Front Royal, Harrisonburg, Lexington, Marion, Natural Bridge, New Market, Radford, Roanoke, Salem, Staunton, Strasburg, Winchester, Woodstock, Wytheville.
Interstate 85	Petersburg, South Hill.
Interstate 95	Alexandria, Arlington County, Ashland, Emporia, Fairfax, Falls Church, Fredericksburg, Hopewell, McLean, Mount Vernon, Petersburg, Richmond, Springfield, Triangle.

Additional Visitor Information

Recreational and tourist information, including travel guide, brochures and maps, is available from the Virginia Tourism Corporation, 901 E Byrd St, Richmond 23219; phone 804/786-4484 or 800/932-5827. Virginia Department of Transportation, 1401 E Broad St, Richmond 23219, phone 804/786-2838, offers an official state map.

There are 10 welcome information centers in Virginia at the following locations: the northern end of the state, on I-81 in Clear Brook, and on I-66 in Manassas; at the northeastern side, on I-95 in Fredericksburg; around the bay area on the eastern side, on US 13 in New Church; around the southerly border, on I-95 in Skippers, and on I-85 in Bracey; in the southwest part of the state, on I-81 in Bristol, and I-77 in Lambsburg; and on the western side, on I-64 in Covington, and on I-77 in Rocky Gap.

Abingdon (F-3)

(See also Bristol, Marion)

Settled ca 1770 **Pop** 7,003 **Elev** 2,069 ft **Area Code** 540 **Zip** 24210

Information Abingdon Convention & Visitors Bureau, 335 Cummings St; 800/435-3344

Daniel Boone passed through this area in 1760 and dubbed it Wolf Hill after a pack of wolves from a nearby cave disturbed his dogs. Wolf Hill had long been a crossing for buffalo and Native Americans; Boone later used it for his own family's westward migration. Later, Black's Fort was built here, and the community adopted that name. Now known as Abingdon, this summer resort in the Virginia Highlands, just north of Tennessee, is the Washington County seat, Virginia's largest burley tobacco market and a livestock auction center.

What to See and Do

Grayson Highlands State Park. Within this 4,935-acre park are rugged peaks, some more than 5,000 ft; alpine scenery. Hiking, horse trails, picnicking, camping, visitor center, interpretive programs, pioneer life displays (June-Aug). Adj to Mount Rogers National Recreation Area (see MARION). (Daily) Standard fees. 35 mi SE on US 58. Phone 540/579-7092.

White's Mill. Old grist mill and general store, still in operation. (Wed-Sat) 12291 White's Mill Rd. Phone 540/676-0285. ¢

Annual Event

Virginia Highlands Festival. Exhibits, demonstrations of rustic handicrafts; plays, musical entertainment; historical reenactments; historic house tours, antique market. Early-mid Aug.

Seasonal Event

Barter Theatre. Main St, on US 11 off I-81, in former Town Hall. America's oldest, longest-running professional repertory theater. Founded during the Depression on the theory that residents would barter their abundant crops for first-rate professional entertainment. Designated State Theatre of Virginia in 1946. Phone 540/628-3991. Barter Players perform Mar-Dec. Children's theater June-Aug.

Motels

★ **ALPINE MOTEL.** 882 E Main St (24212). 540/628-3178; FAX 540/628-4247. 19 rms. S, D $38-$56; each addl $5; under 12 free; higher rates special events. Crib $2. TV; cable. Restaurant nearby. Ck-out 11 am. Business servs avail. View of mountains. Cr cds: A, C, DS, MC, V.

✓★★ **COMFORT INN.** 170 Old Jonesboro Rd (24210), jct I-81 exit 14, VA 140. 540/676-2222; FAX 540/676-2222; res: 800/228-5150; res: 800/228-5150. 80 rms, 2 story. S, D $55-$150; each addl $6; under 18 free; higher rates special events. Crib free. TV; cable (premium), VCR avail. Pool. Complimentary continental bkfst. Ck-out noon. Business servs avail. Cr cds: A, C, D, DS, ER, JCB, MC, V.

★★ **EMPIRE MOTOR LODGE ABINGDON.** 887 Empire Dr Sw (24210), I-81 exit 19. 540/628-7131; FAX 540/628-7158. 105 rms, 2 story. S, D $38-$48; each addl $2; under 12 free; higher rates special events. Crib $5. TV; cable (premium). Restaurant 7 am-10 pm. Ck-out 11 am. Business servs avail. Balconies. Cr cds: A, C, MC, V.

Inn

★★★★ **MARTHA WASHINGTON INN.** 150 W Main St (24210). 540/628-3161; FAX 540/628-8885; res: 800/533-1014. Web www.camberleyhotel.com. Built as a private home in 1832, this historic inn became a girls' school after the Civil War and an inn in the 1930s. Today it is filled with antiques that recall its vivid past. 61 rms. S, D $149-$159; each addl $10; suites $185-$300; under 12 free; higher rates special events. Crib free. TV; cable (premium), VCR avail. Pool privileges. Dining rm (see THE DINING ROOM). Rm serv. Bar 5 pm-midnight. Ck-out 11 am, ck-in 3 pm. Meeting rms. Business servs avail. Luggage handling. Airport transportation. Tennis privileges. Golf privileges. Health club privileges. Bathrm phone in suites. Cr cds: A, C, D, DS, MC, V.

Restaurants

★★★ **THE DINING ROOM.** (See Martha Washington Inn) 540/628-3161. Hrs: 6:30-10 am, 11:30 am-2 pm, 5-9 pm; Fri to 10 pm; Sat 7-10 am, 11:30 am-2 pm, 5-10 pm; Sun 7-10 am, 5-9 pm; Sun brunch 11:30 am-2 pm. Res accepted. Bar. Semi-a la carte: bkfst $4-$8, lunch $6-$9.95, dinner $15-$25. Sun brunch $16.95. Specialties: Virginia trout, tenderloin of beef. Own baking. Cr cds: A, C, D, DS, MC, V.

★★ **THE TAVERN.** 222 E Main St (24210). 540/628-1118. Hrs: 11 am-10 pm. Closed Dec 25. Res accepted. Continental menu. Bar. Semi-a la carte: lunch $5.95-$7.25, dinner $12.95-$22.95. Specialties: Kassler rippchen, Wienerschnitzel, stuffed filet mignon. Two-story building (1779); colonial decor with fireplace in each of the three dining rms. Cr cds: A, C, MC, V.

Alexandria (C-8)

(See also Arlington County, Fairfax, Falls Church; also see District of Columbia)

Settled 1670 **Pop** 111,183 **Elev** 52 ft **Area Code** 703
Information Convention/Visitors Association, 221 King St, 22314-3209; 703/838-4200

A group of English and Scottish merchants established a tobacco warehouse at the junction of Hunting Creek and the "Potowmack" River in the 1740s. The little settlement prospered and 17 years later John West, Jr, surveyor, and his young assistant, George Washington, arrived and "laid off in streets and 84 half-acre lots" the town of Alexandria. Among the first buyers, on the July morning in 1749 when the lots were offered for public sale, were Lawrence Washington and his brother Augustus, William Ramsay, the Honorable William Fairfax and John Carlyle. Erecting handsome town houses, these gentlemen soon brought a lively and cosmopolitan air to Alexandria, with parties, balls and horse racing. It was also the hometown of George Mason and Robert E. Lee and home to George Washington.

In 1789, Virginia ceded Alexandria to the District of Columbia, but in 1846 the still-Southern-oriented citizens asked to return to the Old Dominion, which Congress allowed.

In the Civil War, Alexandria was cut off from the Confederacy when Union troops occupied the town to protect Potomac River navigation. Safe behind Union lines, the city escaped the dreadful destruction experienced by many other Southern towns. After the war, even with seven railroads centering here for transfer of freight, Alexandria declined as a center of commerce and was in trade doldrums until about 1914, when the Alexandria shipyards were reopened and the Naval Torpedo Station was built. Today it has developed into a trade, commerce, transportation and science center. More than 250 national associations are based here.

What to See and Do

Alexandria Black History Resource Center. Photographs, letters, documents and artifacts relate history of African-Americans in Alexandria. (Tues-Sat; closed hols) 638 N Alfred St. Phone 703/838-4356. **Donation**

Fort Ward Museum and Historic Site. Restored Union Fort from Civil War; museum contains Civil War collection. Museum (daily exc Mon; closed Jan 1, Thanksgiving, Dec 25). Park, picnicking (daily to sunset). 4801 W Braddock Rd. Phone 703/838-4848. **Free**

George Washington Masonic National Memorial. American Freemasons' memorial to their most prominent member, this 333-ft-high structure houses a large collection of objects that belonged to George Washington, which were collected by his family or the masonic lodge where he served as the first master. Guided tours explore a replica of Alexandria-Washington Lodge's first hall, a library, museum and an observation deck on the top floor. (Daily; closed Jan 1, Thanksgiving, Dec 25) 101 Callahan Dr, Shooter's Hill, W end of King St. Phone 703/683-2007. **Free**

Gunston Hall (1755-1759). The 550-acre estate of George Mason, framer of the Constitution, father of the Bill of Rights. Restored 18th-century mansion with period furnishings; reconstructed outbuildings; museum; boxwood gardens on grounds; nature trail; picnic area; gift shop. (Daily; closed Jan 1, Thanksgiving, Dec 25) 18 mi S on US 1, then 4 mi E on VA 242 in Lorton at 10709 Gunston Rd. Phone 703/550-9220. ¢¢

Mount Vernon (see). 9 mi S on Mt Vernon Memorial Hwy.

Pohick Bay Regional Park. Near Gunston Hall. Activities in this 1,000-acre park include swimming (Memorial Day-Labor Day); 18-hole golf; miniature and Frisbee golf; boating (ramp, rentals; fee); camping (7-day limit; electric hookups avail; fee), picnicking. Park (all yr). Fee charged for activities. 6501 Pohick Bay Dr, in Lorton. Phone 703/339-6104. Admission per vehicle (nonresidents only) ¢¢

Pohick Episcopal Church (1774). The colonial parish church of Mt Vernon and Gunston Hall. Built under supervision of George Mason and George Washington; original walls; interior fully restored. (Daily) 9301 Richmond Hwy, 16 mi S on US 1 in Lorton. Phone 703/550-9449. **Free**

Sightseeing boat tours. Tours of Alexandria waterfront. Contact the Potomac Riverboat Co; phone 703/684-0580. ¢¢¢

The Athenaeum. Greek-revival house (1851) built as a bank, now houses Fine Arts Assn. Art shows, dance performances. (Wed-Sat & Sun afternoons; closed hols) 201 Prince St. Phone 703/548-0035.

Torpedo Factory Arts Center. Renovated munitions plant houses artists' center with more than 160 professional artists of various media. Studios, cooperative galleries, school. Also home of Alexandria Archaeology offices, lab, museum; phone 703/838-4399. (Daily; closed most major hols) 105 N Union St. Phone 703/838-4565. **Free**

☑ **Walking tour of historic sites.**

Start at Visitors Center in **Ramsay House** (ca 1725). Oldest house in Alexandria and later used as a tavern, grocery store and cigar factory. Here you can obtain special events information and a free visitors guide. You may also purchase "block tickets" here, good for reduced admission to five of the city's historic properties. Video shown with translations available in 18 languages. Guided walking tours, conducted by costumed guides, depart from here (spring-fall, weather permitting). The Bureau also issues free parking permits, tour and highway maps, hotel, dining and shopping information. (Daily; closed Jan 1, Thanksgiving, Dec 25) 221 King St, at Fairfax St. Phone 703/838-4200. 1 blk N on Fairfax St is

Carlyle House (1753). This stately stone mansion, built in Palladian style, was the site of a 1755 meeting between Gen Edward Braddock and five British colonial governors to plan the early campaigns of the French and Indian War. (Daily exc Mon; closed Jan 1, Thanksgiving, Dec 24, 25) 121 N Fairfax St. Phone 703/549-2997. ¢¢ 1½ blks S on Fairfax St is

Stabler-Leadbeater Apothecary Museum (1792). Largest collection of apothecary glass in its original setting in the country; more than 1,000 apothecary bottles. Original building is now a museum of early pharmacy; collection of old prescriptions, patent medicines, scales, other 18th-century pharmacy items. George Washington, Robert E. Lee and John Calhoun were regular customers. (Daily; closed Jan 1, Thanksgiving, Dec 25) 105 S Fairfax St. Phone 703/836-3713. ¢ 2 blks S on Fairfax St is

Old Presbyterian Meeting House (1774). Tomb of the unknown soldier of the Revolution is in churchyard. (Mon-Fri) 321 S Fairfax St. Phone 703/549-6670. **Free** ½ blk N, then 3 blks W on Duke St is

Lafayette House. Fine example of Federal architecture. House was loaned to Lafayette for his last visit to America (1825). (Private) 301 Asaph St. Walk 2 blks N to Prince St, then left on Prince St to SW corner of Prince & Washington Sts to

The Lyceum. Museum, exhibitions; Virginia travel information (limited). (Daily; closed Jan 1, Thanksgiving, Dec 25) 201 S Washington St. Phone 703/838-4994. **Free** Go 2 blks N on Washington St to

Christ Church (1773). Washington and Robert E. Lee were pewholders. Fine Palladian window; interior balcony; wrought-brass and crystal chandelier brought from England. Structure is extensively restored but little changed since it was built. Exhibit, gift shop at Columbus St entrance. (Mon-Sat, also Sun afternoons; closed Jan 1, Labor Day, Thanksgiving, Dec 25; also for weddings, funerals) 118 N Washington St. Phone 703/549-1450. **Donation** 1 blk E on Cameron St is

Home of General Henry (Light Horse Harry) Lee. (Private) 611 Cameron St. 3 blks N, 1 blk W, then left on Washington St is

Lee-Fendall House (1785). Built by Phillip Richard Fendall and lived in by Lee family for 118 yrs. Both George Washington and Revolutionary War hero "Light Horse Harry" Lee were frequent visitors to the house. Remodeled in 1850, the house is furnished with Lee family belongings. (Daily exc Mon, wkend hrs may vary; closed major hols) 614 Oronoco St. Phone 703/548-1789. ¢¢ Proceed N, turn right on Oronoco St, ½ blk E to

Boyhood Home of Robert E. Lee. Federal-style architecture; antique furnishings and paintings. Famous guests included Washington and Lafayette. (Daily) 607 Oronoco St. Phone 703/548-8454. ¢¢ 3 blks E, then 3 blks S on Royal St is

Gadsby's Tavern Museum (1770, 1792). Famous hostelry, frequented by Washington and other patriots. Combines two 18th-century buildings; interesting architecture. (Daily exc Mon; closed major hols) 134 N Royal St. Phone 703/838-4242. ¢¢

Doorways to Old Virginia. Offers guided walking tours of historic district. (Apr-Oct, daily) Departs from Ramsay House. Phone 703/548-0100. ¢¢

Annual Events

George Washington Birthday Celebrations. Events include race, Revolutionary War reenactment; climaxed by the birthday parade on federal holiday. Feb.

House tours. Fine colonial and Federal-style houses are opened to the public: Cook's tour of kitchens (early Apr); Historic Garden Week (Apr); Hospital Auxiliary Tour of Historic Houses (Sept); Scottish Christmas Walk (Dec). Tickets, addl information at Alexandria Convention/Visitors Association; 703/838-4200.

Red Cross Waterfront Festival. Commemorates Alexandria's maritime heritage. Features "tall ships," blessing of the fleet, river cruises, races, arts & crafts, exhibits, food, variety of music; fireworks. Phone 703/549-8300. June.

Virginia Scottish Games. Athletic competition, Highland dance and music, antique cars, displays, food. Phone 703/838-4200. 4th wkend July.

Scottish Christmas Walk. Parade, house tour, concerts, greens and heather sales, dinner dance to emphasize city's Scottish origins. 1st Sat Dec.

Motels

★★ **BEST WESTERN.** *615 1st St (22314), near National Airport.* 703/739-2222; FAX 703/549-2568; res: 800/528-1234. 151 rms, 2 story. Apr-June, Sept-Oct: S $89; D $99; each addl $10; kits. $109; under 18 free; wkend, hol rates; lower rates rest of yr. Crib free. Pet accepted; $50 deposit & $10/day. TV; cable (premium). Pool; lifeguard. Complimentary continental bkfst. Restaurant adj 6:30 am-11 pm. Ck-out noon. Meeting rms. Business servs avail. In-rm modem link. Sundries. Valet serv. Free airport transportation. Health club privileges. Cr cds: A, C, D, DS, MC, V.

D 🔧 ➰ ✈ 🖎 🔥 SC

★★ **BEST WESTERN MOUNT VERNON.** *8751 Richmond Hwy (22309).* 703/360-1300; FAX 703/799-7713; res: 800/528-1234. 132 rms, 5 story. Mar-Oct: S $77-$82; D $82-$87; each addl $5; suites $110-$120; under 18 free; lower rates rest of yr. Crib free. TV; cable (premium). Complimentary continental bkfst. Restaurant nearby. Ck-out 11 am. Meeting rm. Business servs avail. Valet serv. Exercise equipt. Some refrigerators; microwaves avail. Cr cds: A, C, D, DS, MC, V.

D 🏋 🖎 🔥 SC

✓★★ **COMFORT INN.** *7212 Richmond Hwy (22306).* 703/765-9000; FAX 703/765-2325; res: 800/228-5150; res: 800/433-2546. 92 rms, 2 story. S $50-$65; D $55-$75; each addl $7; under 17 free; package plans. Crib free. Pet accepted, some restrictions. TV; cable (premium). Pool; lifeguard. Complimentary continental bkfst. Restaurant nearby. Ck-out noon. Meeting rm. Business servs avail. In-rm modem link. Valet serv. Sundries. Refrigerators, microwaves avail. Cr cds: A, C, D, DS, MC, V.

D 🔧 ➰ 🖎 🔥 SC

★★ **HAMPTON INN.** *4800 Leesburg Pike (22302).* 703/671-4800; FAX 703/671-2442; res: 800/426-7866. 130 rms, 4 story. S $95; D $95-$105. Crib free. TV; cable (premium). Pool. Complimentary continental bkfst. Coffee in rms. Ck-out noon. Business servs avail. In-rm modem link. Valet serv. Exercise equipt. Health club privileges. Cr cds: A, C, D, DS, MC, V.

D ➰ 🏋 🖎 🔥 SC

✓ ★ **RED ROOF INN.** *5975 Richmond Hwy (22303). 703/960-5200; FAX 703/960-5209; res: 800/843-7663.* E-mail i0169@redroof.com; web www.redroof.com. 115 rms, 3 story. Apr-Oct: S, D $69.99-$78.99; each addl $5; under 18 free; higher rates special events; lower rates rest of yr. Crib free. Pet accepted, some restrictions. TV; cable (premium). Complimentary coffee in lobby. Restaurant nearby. Ck-out noon. Business servs avail. In-rm modem link. Coin lndry. Valet serv. Cr cds: A, C, D, DS, MC, V.

D 🐾 ⊠ 🔥 SC

✓ ★★ **TRAVELERS MOTEL.** *5916 Richmond Hwy (22303). 703/329-1310; FAX 703/960-9211; res: 800/368-7378.* 30 rms. S $58-$66; D $59.99-$73.99; each addl $5. Crib free. TV; cable (premium). Pool; lifeguard. Complimentary coffee in lobby. Restaurant opp 6 am-11 pm. Ck-out 11 am. Business servs avail. Cr cds: A, C, D, DS, MC, V.

D ⊠ ⊠ 🔥 SC

Motor Hotels

★★★ **COURTYARD.** *2700 Eisenhower Ave (22314). 703/329-2323; FAX 703/329-6853; res: 800/321-2211.* Web www.marriott.com. courtyard.va192. 176 rms, 8 story. Apr-May, Oct-Nov: S $169; D $179; suites $220; under 12 free; higher rates Cherry Blossom Festival; lower rates rest of yr. Crib free. TV; cable (premium). Complimentary coffee in rms. Restaurant 6:30-10 am, 5-10 pm; Sat, Sun 7-11 am, 5-10 pm. Rm serv from 5 pm. Bar 4 pm-midnight. Ck-out noon. Meeting rms. Business servs avail. Valet serv. Sundries. Free RR station transportation. Exercise equipt. Whirlpool. Some refrigerators, microwaves. Some balconies. Cr cds: A, C, D, DS, MC, V.

D 🏃 ⊠ 🔥 SC

★★ **EXECUTIVE CLUB SUITES.** *610 Bashford Ln (22314). 703/739-2582; FAX 703/548-0266.* E-mail carole@dcexeclub.com; web www.dcexeclub.com. 78 kit suites, 3 story. No elvtr. S, D $190-$220; wkend, hol rates. Crib free. Pet accepted, some restrictions. TV; cable (premium). Pool; lifeguard. Complimentary continental bkfst. Complimentary coffee in rms. Restaurant nearby. Ck-out noon. Coin lndry. Meeting rms. Business center. In-rm modem link. Valet serv. Sundries. Free airport transportation. Exercise equipt; sauna. Microwaves. Picnic tables. Cr cds: A, C, D, DS, ER, MC, V.

🐾 ⊠ 🏃 ⊠ 🔥 🏃

★★★ **HOLIDAY INN & SUITES.** *625 1st St (22314), in Old Town Alexandria. 703/548-6300; FAX 703/548-8032; res: 800/465-4329.* 161 rms, 4 story, 17 suites. S, D $149; each addl $10; suites $159-$199; under 18 free; wkend rates. Crib free. TV; cable (premium). Indoor/outdoor pool; whirlpool. Coffee in rms. Restaurant 6:30 am-10 pm. Bar 11 am-midnight. Ck-out noon. Coin lndry. Meeting rm. Business center. In-rm modem link. Bellhops. Free airport transportation. Exercise rm. Microwave, wet bar in suites; refrigerators avail. Cr cds: A, C, D, DS, JCB, MC, V.

D ⊠ 🏃 ✈ ⊠ 🔥 SC 🏃

★★ **HOMEWOOD SUITES HOTEL.** *4850 Leesburg Pike (22302). 703/671-6500; FAX 703/671-9322; res: 800/225-4663.* E-mail homewood_alexva@erols.com; web www.homewoodsuites.com. 105 rms, 5 story. S $129-$139, D $135-$155. Crib free. TV; cable (premium). Pool; whirlpool. Complimentary continental bkfst. Restaurant nearby. Ck-out noon. Meeting rms. Business center. Valet serv. Coin lndry. Exercise equipt. Health club privileges. Game rm. Gift shop. Cr cds: A, C, D, DS, MC, V.

D ⊠ 🏃 ⊠ 🐾 SC

Hotels

★★ **DOUBLETREE GUEST SUITES.** *100 S Reynolds St (22304). 703/370-9600; FAX 703/370-0467; res: 800/528-0444.* 225 kit suites, 9 story. S, D $125-$260; each addl $10; under 18 free; wkend rates. Crib $10. Pet accepted; $10/day. TV; cable (premium). Pool; lifeguard. Complimentary continental bkfst. Restaurant 6:30-9:30 am, 5-10 pm. Bar

from 5 pm. Ck-out noon. Coin lndry. Meeting rms. Business center. Exercise equipt. Health club privileges. Microwaves. Some balconies. Cr cds: A, C, D, DS, MC, V.

D 🐾 ⊠ 🏃 ⊠ 🔥 🏃

★★★ **HILTON ALEXANDRIA MARK CENTER.** *5000 Seminary Rd (22311), 1 blk W of I-395 exit 4. 703/845-1010; FAX 703/845-7662; res: 800/333-3333.* Web www.radisson.com. 495 rms, 30 story. S, D $125-$195; each addl $20; suites $250-$800; under 16 free; wkly rates; wkend packages. Crib free. Covered parking $4/day, valet parking $10. TV; cable (premium), VCR avail (free movies). Indoor/outdoor pool; whirlpool. Coffee in rm. Restaurant 6 am-11 pm. Bars 11-1 am. Ck-out noon. Convention facilities. Business center. In-rm modem link. Gift shop. Barber, beauty shop. Free airport transportation. Tennis. Exercise equipt; sauna. Game rm. Refrigerators; some bathrm phones. Whirlpool in some suites. Located on 50 wooded acres with nature preserve. Luxury level. Cr cds: A, C, D, DS, ER, JCB, MC, V.

D 🏃 🐾 ⊠ 🏃 🏋 ⊠ 🔥 SC 🏃

★★★ **HOLIDAY INN.** *480 King St (22314). 703/549-6080; FAX 703/684-6508; res: 800/465-4329 or 800/368-5047.* E-mail othismta@erols.com; web www.hiselect.com. 227 rms, 6 story. Mar-June, Sept-Oct: S $149-$199; D $169-$209; each addl $20; suites $275-$350; under 18 free; wkend rates; lower rates rest of yr. Crib free. Pet accepted, some restrictions. Garage $7/day. TV; cable (premium). Indoor pool; lifeguard. Complimentary coffee in rms. Restaurant 6:30 am-11 pm. Bars 11 am-midnight. Ck-out noon. Coin lndry. Meeting rms. Business center. In-rm modem link. Concierge. Gift shop. Free airport transportation. Exercise equipt; sauna. Refrigerators, minibars, microwaves avail. Some balconies. Cr cds: A, C, D, DS, ER, JCB, MC, V.

D 🐾 ⊠ 🏃 ⊠ 🔥 SC 🏃

★★ **HOLIDAY INN.** *2460 Eisenhower Ave (22314). 703/960-3400; FAX 703/329-0953; res: 800/465-4329.* E-mail moli@erols.com. 197 rms, 10 story. Mar-early July, mid-Sept-mid-Nov: S $94-$120; D $104-$130; suite $250; each addl $10; under 18 free; wkend, hol rates; lower rates rest of yr. Crib free. TV; cable (premium). Indoor pool. Restaurant 6:30 am-10 pm. Bar 11 am-midnight; entertainment Fri, Sat. Ck-out noon. Coin lndry. Meeting rms. Business servs avail. In-rm modem link. Gift shop. Free airport, RR station transportation. Exercise equipt. Game rm. Refrigerators avail. Cr cds: A, C, D, DS, JCB, MC, V.

D ⊠ 🏃 ⊠ 🔥 SC

★★ **RAMADA PLAZA HOTEL.** *901 N Fairfax St (22314). 703/683-6000; FAX 703/683-7597; res: 800/272-6232.* Web www.ramada.com. 258 rms, 12 story. S, D $139-$179; each addl $10; under 18 free; wkend rates. Crib free. TV; cable (premium). Pool; lifeguard. Coffee in rms. Restaurant 6 am-10 pm. Bar 11-1 am. Ck-out noon. Business servs avail. In-rm modem link. Gift shop. Free airport transportation. Health club privileges. Refrigerators, microwaves avail. Cr cds: A, C, D, DS, MC, V.

D ⊠ ⊠ 🔥 🐾 SC

★★★ **SHERATON SUITES.** *801 N Saint Asaph St (22314). 703/836-4700; FAX 703/548-4514; res: 800/325-3535.* Web www.ittsheraton.com. 247 suites, 10 story. Apr-May: S, D $220; under 12 free; wkend, hol rates; lower rates rest of yr. Crib free. Pet accepted. Garage parking $7. TV; cable (premium). Indoor pool; whirlpool, lifeguard. Complimentary coffee in rms. Restaurant 6:30 am-11 pm; wkends from 7 am. Bar. Ck-out 1 pm. Guest lndry. Meeting rms. Business servs avail. In-rm modem link. Gift shop. Free airport transportation. Exercise equipt. Refrigerators; microwaves avail. Luxury level. Cr cds: A, C, D, DS, ER, JCB, MC, V.

D 🐾 ⊠ 🏃 ✈ ⊠ 🐾 SC 🏃

Inn

★★★★ **MORRISON HOUSE.** *116 S Alfred St (22314), downtown. 703/838-8000; FAX 703/684-6283; res: 800/367-0800.* E-mail mhrasrv@morrisonhouse.com; web www.morrisonhouse.com. This elegant red brick building is furnished in the style of the Federal period throughout. Public rooms include the mahogany-paneled library and a parlor with fireplace. Many of the individually decorated rooms have four-poster beds and fireplaces. 45 rms, 5 story. S, D $195-$315; suites $315-$515; wkend rates. Crib free. Covered parking $10/day. TV; cable (premium), VCR avail (movies $5). Dining rm (see ELYSIUM). Afternoon tea 3-5 pm. Rm serv 24 hrs. Bar 11:30 am-11 pm; Fri, Sat to midnight; entertainment Thurs-Sat. Ck-out noon, ck-in after 3 pm. Meeting rms. Business servs avail. In-rm modem link. Butlers. Health club privileges. Bathrm phones. Cr cds: A, C, D, MC, V.

D ⊠ ⚒

Restaurants

★★ **BILBO BAGGINS.** *208 Queen St (22314), in Old Town Alexandria.* *703/683-0300.* Hrs: 11:30 am-10:30 pm; Sun 11 am-9:30 pm; early-bird dinner Mon-Thurs 5:30-6 pm; Sun brunch 11 am-2:30 pm. Closed Dec 25. Res accepted. Continental menu. Bar. Semi-a la carte: lunch $6.95-$9.95, dinner $10.95-$17.95. Sun brunch $7.95-$9.95. Specialties: Bilbo's bread, Chicken Queen Street, Bilbo's salad. Own baking. Upstairs in 1898 structure; stained glass, skylights. Cr cds: A, C, D, DS, MC, V.

D

★★ **BLUE POINT GRILL.** *600 Franklin St (22314), in Old Town Alexandria.* *703/739-0404.* Hrs: 11:30 am-10 pm; Fri, Sat to 11 pm; Sun 11 am-3 pm (brunch), 5-9 pm. Closed 3-5:30 pm Oct-May; also Dec 25. Res accepted. A la carte entrees: lunch $7-$15, dinner $13.95-$20.95. Sun brunch $8.50-$11.95. Specializes in fresh seafood. Parking. Outdoor dining. Cafe atmosphere; adj to gourmet Sutton Place Market. Cr cds: A, C, DS, MC, V.

D

✓★★ **CALVERT GRILLE.** *3106 Mt Vernon Ave (22305).* *703/836-8425.* E-mail calgrill@ids2.idsonline.com. Hrs: 11:30-12:30 am; Fri to 2 am; Sat from 9:30 am; Sun 9:30 am-9 pm; Sat, Sun brunch to 2 pm. Closed Thanksgiving, Dec 25. Bar. Semi-a la carte: bkfst $2.95-$6.50, lunch $5.25-$8.95, dinner $5.95-$11.95. Sat, Sun brunch $5.95-$10.95. Child's meals. Specializes in baby back ribs, crab cakes, regional dishes. Family-friendly atmosphere. Cr cds: A, C, DS, MC, V.

D ⊟

★★★ **CHART HOUSE.** *1 Cameron St (22314).* *703/684-5080.* Web www.charthouse.com. Hrs: 5-10 pm; Fri, Sat to 11 pm; Sun 10:45 am-2:15 pm, 4-10 pm. Closed Dec 25. Res accepted; required Fri-Sun. Contemporary Amer menu. Bar. Semi-a la carte: dinner $14.95-$32.95. Sun brunch $16.95-$23. Child's meals. Specializes in grilled fresh seafood, aged beef. Views of the Capitol, Potomac River. Cr cds: A, C, D, DS, MC, V.

D ⊟

★★★ **CHEZ ANDREE.** *10 E Glebe Rd (22305).* *703/836-1404.* Hrs: 11 am-2:30 pm, 5-9:30 pm; Sat from 5 pm. Closed Sun; major hols. Res accepted; required Fri, Sat. French menu. Serv bar. Semi-a la carte: lunch $8.95-$15.50, dinner $13.95-$21.95. Prix fixe (Mon, Tues): dinner $24.95. Specialties: salmon Hollandaise, coquilles St-Jacques, duck a l'orange. Parking. French country decor. Family-owned. Cr cds: A, C, D, MC, V.

⊟

✓★★ **COPELAND'S OF NEW ORLEANS.** *4300 King St (22302).* *703/671-7997.* Web www.copelands.com. Hrs: 11 am-10 pm; Fri, Sat to midnight; Sun brunch to 3 pm. Closed Thanksgiving, Dec 25. Cajun, Creole, American menu. Bar. Semi-a la carte: lunch $6.99-$7.95, dinner $6.99-$15.95. Sun brunch $7.95-$10.95. Child's meals. Specializes in seafood. Parking. Outdoor dining. Cr cds: A, C, D, DS, MC, V.

D ⊟

✓★★ **EAST WIND.** *809 King St (22314).* *703/836-1515.* Hrs: 11:30 am-2:30 pm, 5:30-10 pm; Fri to 10:30 pm; Sat 5:30-10:30 pm; Sun 5:30-9:30 pm. Closed major hols. Res accepted. Vietnamese menu. Bar.

Semi-a la carte: lunch $5.95-$7.95, dinner $7.95-$15.50. Specialty: charbroiled shrimp & scallops. Own desserts. Original Vietnamese paintings & panels. Cr cds: A, C, D, DS, MC, V.

D ⊟

✓★★ **ECCO CAFE.** *220 N Lee St (22314), in Old Town.* *703/684-0321.* Web www.eccocafe.com. Hrs: 11 am-11 pm; Mon to 10 pm; Fri, Sat to midnight; Sun 4-10 pm; Sun brunch 11:30 am-3 pm. Closed Thanksgiving, Dec 25. Res accepted Sun-Thurs. Italian, Amer menu. A la carte entrees: lunch $6.95-$9.95, dinner $10.95-$16.95. Sun brunch $7.95-$11.95. Specializes in beef, chicken, pasta. Own baking, pasta. Jazz Sun. In restored 1890s warehouse bldg; eclectic decor. Cr cds: A, C, D, DS, MC, V.

D ⊟ ♥

★★★ **ELYSIUM.** *(See Morrison House) 703/838-8000.* Web www.morrisonhouse.com. Hrs: 6-10 pm; Fri, Sat to 11 pm; Sun brunch noon-2:30 pm. Closed Mon; Jan 1. Res required Fri, Sat. Bar 11:30 am-midnight. Wine list. Prix fixe: dinner $35-$55; Sun brunch $25. Specializes in new American cuisine. Formal Federal-period dining rm. Cr cds: A, C, D, MC, V.

D

✓★ **FACCIA LUNA.** *823 S Washington St (22314), in Old Town.* *703/838-5998.* Hrs: 11:30 am-11 pm; Fri, Sat to midnight; Sun from noon. Closed some major hols. Italian menu. Bar. Semi-a la carte: lunch $4.95-$7, dinner $7-$12. Child's meals. Specializes in pizza, fresh pasta, grinders. Own pasta. Outdoor dining. Contemporary American trattoria with woodburning oven. Totally nonsmoking. Cr cds: A, C, MC, V.

D

★★ **FISH MARKET.** *105 King St (22314), at N Union St, in Old Town Alexandria.* *703/836-5676.* E-mail fishmkt@pop.dn.net. Hrs: 11:15-2 am; Sun to midnight. Closed Thanksgiving, Dec 25. Bar. Semi-a la carte: lunch $3.95-$12.95, dinner $4.25-$16.25. Specializes in Chesapeake Bay-style seafood. Ragtime pianist. Outdoor dining. In restored 18th-century warehouse built of bricks carried to New World as ballast in ship's hold; nautical decor. Cr cds: A, C, D, MC, V.

D ⊟

★★ **GADSBY'S TAVERN.** *138 N Royal St (22314), across from Old Town sidewalk.* *703/548-1288.* Web www.washingtonsidewalk.com. Hrs: 11:30 am-3 pm, 5:30-10 pm; Sun brunch 11 am-3 pm. Closed Jan 1, Dec 25. Res accepted; required Fri, Sat. Semi-a la carte: lunch $6.95-$8.95, dinner $14.95-$22.95. Sun brunch $6.75-$9.95. Child's meals. Specialties: Sally Lunn bread, George Washington's favorite duck, English trifle. Strolling minstrels. Outdoor dining. Built 1792; Georgian architecture; colonial decor & costumes. Gadsby's Tavern Museum adj. Totally nonsmoking. Cr cds: C, D, DS, MC, V.

D

✓★★★ **GERANIO RISTORANTE.** *722 King St (22314), in Old Town Alexandria.* *703/548-0088.* Hrs: 11:30 am-2:30 pm, 6-10:30 pm; Sat from 6 pm; Sun 5:30-9:30 pm. Closed some major hols. Res accepted; required Fri, Sat. Italian menu. Serv bar. Semi-a la carte: lunch $6.95-$10.25, dinner $11.75-$15.50. Specializes in veal, seafood, pasta. Rustic Mediterranean decor. Fireplace, ceramic chandeliers. Cr cds: A, C, D, MC, V.

D ⊟

★★★ **IL PORTO RISTORANTE.** *121 King St (22314), at N Lee St, in Old Town Alexandria.* *703/836-8833.* E-mail finefood@ilporto.com; web www.ilporto.com. Hrs: 11:15 am-midnight. Res accepted. Northern Italian menu. Bar from 6 pm. Semi-a la carte: lunch $3.50-$9.50, dinner $9-$16.75. Child's meals. Specialties: pasta de Venezia, chicken Angelica. Extensive dessert menu. In 18th-century building originally a marine warehouse. Cr cds: A, C, D, MC, V.

★★★ **LA BERGERIE.** *218 N Lee St (22314), 2nd floor of Crilley Warehouse, in Old Town Alexandria.* 703/683-1007. E-mail labergerie@msn.com. Hrs: 11:30 am-2:30 pm, 5:30-10:30 pm. Closed Sun exc Mother's Day; major hols. Res accepted; required Fri, Sat. French, Amer menu. Serv bar. Semi-a la carte: lunch $10.95-$14.95, dinner $14.95-$24.95. Specializes in fresh seafood. Own pastries. Restored 1890s warehouse. Cr cds: A, C, D, DS, MC, V.

D ⎙

★★ **LANDINI BROTHERS.** *115 King St (22314), in Old Town Alexandria.* 703/836-8404. Hrs: 11:30 am-11 pm; Sun 3-10 pm. Closed major hols. Res accepted; required Fri, Sat. Italian menu. Bar. A la carte entrees: lunch $9-$13, dinner $13.50-$24.95. Specializes in veal, pasta, fresh fish. 1790s building. Cr cds: A, C, D, DS, MC, V.

D ⎙

★★★ **LE GAULOIS.** *1106 King St (22314), in Old Town Alexandria.* 703/739-9494. Hrs: 11:30 am-10:30 pm; Fri, Sat to 11 pm. Closed Sun; major hols. Res accepted. French menu. Serv Bar. A la carte entrees: lunch $4.75-$12.50, dinner $5.75-$19.75. Specialty: pot au feu gaulois. Outdoor dining. French provincial decor; fireplace. Cr cds: A, C, D, DS, MC, V.

D ⎙

★★ **LE REFUGE.** *127 N Washington St (22314), in Old Town Alexandria.* 703/548-4661. Hrs: 11:30 am-2:30 pm, 5:30-10 pm; early-bird dinner 5:30-7 pm. Closed Sun; some major hols. Res accepted; required Fri, Sat. French menu. Serv bar. A la carte: lunch $7.95-$12.95, dinner $13.95-$19.95. Complete meals: lunch $10.95. Specialties: bouillabaisse, salmon en crôute, veal Normande. Country French decor. Cr cds: A, C, D, DS, MC, V.

⎙

✓★ **MANGO MIKE'S.** *4111 Duke St (22304), 2 mi W on VA 236.* 703/823-1166. Web www.mangomikes.com. Hrs: 11 am-10 pm; Thurs-Sat to 11 pm; Sun from 10 am; Sun brunch to 2 pm. Closed Thanksgiving, Dec 25. Caribbean menu. Bar to 2 am. Semi-a la carte: lunch $4.95-$10.95, dinner $9.95-$13.95. Sun brunch $9.95. Child's meals. Specialties: jerked chicken, mango barbecue ribs. Own desserts. Caribbean drummer Sun. Outdoor dining. Informal Caribbean atmosphere. Cr cds: A, C, D, DS, MC, V.

⎙

✓★★ **MONROE'S AN AMERICAN TRATTORIA.** *1603 Commonwealth Ave (22301).* 703/548-5792. Hrs: 5-10 pm; Fri, Sat to 11 pm; Sun 5-9 pm; Sun brunch 9:30 am-2 pm. Closed most major hols. Res accepted; required Fri, Sat. Italian menu. Bar. Semi-a la carte: dinner $8.50-$16.95. Sun brunch $3.95-$10.95. Child's meals. Specialties: tonno alla livornese, bow-tie pasta with crab meat, aged Angus beef. Own pastries. Outdoor dining. Contemporary trattoria with large murals. Totally nonsmoking. Cr cds: A, C, MC, V.

D

✓★★ **R T'S RESTAURANT.** *3804 Mount Vernon Ave (22305).* 703/684-6010. Web www.rts.com. Hrs: 11 am-10:30 pm; Fri, Sat to 11 pm; Sun 4-9 pm. Closed some major hols. Res accepted. Creole/Cajun menu. Bar. Semi-a la carte: lunch $5.95-$10.95, dinner $12.95-$19.95. Child's meals. Specialties: Jack Daniel's shrimp, Acadian peppered shrimp, she-crab soup. Cr cds: A, C, D, DS, MC, V.

★★ **SANTA FE EAST.** *110 S Pitt St (22314).* 703/548-6900. Web www.santafeeast.com. Hrs: 11:30 am-10 pm; Fri, Sat to 11 pm; Sun 11 am-10 pm. Closed July 4, Thanksgiving, Dec 25. Res accepted; required Fri, Sat. Southwestern menu. Bar. A la carte entrees: lunch $5.95-$9.95, dinner $8.95-$18.75. Sun brunch $5.25-$7.25. Specialties: chipotle chicken, enchilada Santa Fe, salmon a la plancha. Outdoor dining. Native American art, artifacts. Fountain in courtyard. Fireplaces. In historic (1790) building. Cr cds: A, C, D, MC, V.

D

★★ **SCOTLAND YARD.** *728 King St (22314), in Old Town Alexandria.* 703/683-1742. Hrs: 6-8 pm. Closed Mon; Thanksgiving. Res accepted; required Fri, Sat. Scottish menu. Serv bar. A la carte entrees: dinner $12.95-$18.95. Complete meal: dinner $28.95. Specializes in salmon, lamb, venison. Old Scottish inn (1792); tin ceiling, fireplace. Totally nonsmoking. Cr cds: A, C, MC, V.

D

★★ **SEAPORT INN.** *6 King St (22314).* 703/549-2341. Web washington.digitalcity.com/seaportinn. Hrs: 11:30 am-10 pm; Fri to 11 pm; Sat 11 am-11 pm; Sun brunch to 3 pm. Closed Dec 25. Res accepted; required Fri, Sat. Bar 11:30 am-midnight; Fri, Sat to 2 am. Semi-a la carte: lunch $5.75-$10.95, dinner $11.95-$26.95. Sun brunch $5.75-$8.95. Child's meals. Specialties: shrimp & scallops in wine sauce, crab cakes, bouillabaisse. Entertainment. Fireplaces. In 1765 warehouse originally owned by George Washington's aide-de-camp; overlooks Potomac River. Cr cds: A, C, D, MC, V.

D ⎙

✓★ **SOUTH AUSTIN GRILL.** *801 King St (22314), in Old Town.* 703/684-8969. Web www.austingrill.com. Hrs: 11:30 am-11 pm; Mon to 10 pm; Fri to midnight; Sat 11 am-midnight; Sun 11 am-10 pm; Sat, Sun brunch to 3 pm. Closed Thanksgiving, Dec 24, 25. Tex-Mex menu. Bar. Semi-a la carte: lunch, dinner $6.95-$13.95. Sat, Sun brunch $4.95-$6.95. Child's meals. Specializes in beef, chicken. Own baking. Colorful decor with memorabilia of Austin, TX. Cr cds: A, C, D, DS, MC, V.

D

★★ **TAVERNA CRETEKOU.** *818 King St (22314).* 703/548-8688. Hrs: 11:30 am-2:30 pm, 5-10:30 pm; Sat noon-11 pm; Sun 5-9:30 pm; Sun brunch 11 am-3 pm. Closed Mon; some major hols. Res accepted; required Fri, Sat. Greek menu. Serv bar. A la carte entrees: lunch $6.25-$8.95, dinner $11.95-$21.95. Sun brunch $14.95. Specializes in seafood, lamb. Entertainment Thurs. Outdoor dining. Mediterranean decor; brick patio, arbor. Cr cds: A, C, MC, V.

⎙

✓★★ **TEMPO RESTAURANT.** *4231 Duke St (22304), 2½ mi W on VA 236.* 703/370-7900. Hrs: 11:30 am-2:30 pm, 5:30-10 pm; Sun to 9 pm; Sun brunch to 2:30 pm. Closed most major hols. Res accepted; required Fri, Sat dinner. Italian, French menu. Bar. Semi-a la carte: lunch $8.95-$10.95, dinner $11.95-$16.95. Sun brunch $5.95-$10.95. Specialties: linguine with lobster, lamb chops with fresh herbs. Outdoor dining. Modern decor with cathedral windows, original artwork. Cr cds: A, C, D, DS, JCB, MC, V.

D ⎙

★★ **THAI HUT RESTAURANT.** *408 S Van Dorn St (22304).* 703/823-5357. Hrs: 11 am-10 pm; Fri to 11 pm; Sat noon-11 pm; Sun noon-9:30 pm. Closed Thanksgiving, Dec 25. Thai menu. A la carte entrees: lunch, dinner $6.95-$11.95. Complete meals (Mon-Fri): lunch $5.95. Specialties: curries, pad Thai, drunken noodles. Parking. Modern decor; Thai artwork. Cr cds: A, C, D, MC, V.

D ⎙

✓★ **THE ALAMO.** *100 King St (22314), in Old Town Alexandria, bottom of King & Union St.* 703/739-0555. E-mail fishmkt@pop.dn.net. Hrs: 11:15-2 am. Closed Thanksgiving, Dec 25. Res accepted. Nouvelle Southwestern menu. Bar. Semi-a la carte: lunch $4.95-$8.95, dinner $8.95-$16.95. Specializes in ribs, steak, chicken. Entertainment. In 1871 Corn Exchange Building. Cr cds: A, C, D, MC, V.

D ⎙

✓★★ **UNION STREET PUBLIC HOUSE.** *121 S Union St (22314), between King & Prince Sts, in Old Town Alexandria.* 703/548-1785. Hrs: 11:30 am-10:30 pm; Fri, Sat to 11:30 pm; Sun brunch 11 am-3 pm. Closed Thanksgiving, Dec 25. Bar to 1:15 am. Semi-a la carte: lunch, dinner $5.50-$16.95. Sun brunch $4.95-$8.95. Child's meals. Specialties:

pasta jambalaya, linguine with lobster & smoked scallops, aged Angus beef. Oyster raw bar. In sea captain's house & warehouse (ca 1870). Cr cds: A, C, D, DS, MC, V.

★★★ **VILLA D'ESTE.** *600 Montgomery St (22314), at Montgomery St. 703/549-9477.* Hrs: 11:30 am-2:30 pm, 5-10 pm; Fri, Sat to 10:30 pm; Sun 5-9 pm. Closed major hols. Res accepted; required Fri, Sat. Italian menu. Bar. Wine list. A la carte entrees: lunch $10.95-$13.95, dinner $13.75-$18.75. Specialties: osso buco, lamb shank, veal. Own baking, pasta. Elegant, modern decor. Cr cds: A, C, D, MC, V.

★★ **WHARF RESTAURANT.** *119 King St (22314). 703/836-2834.* Hrs: 11 am-10:30 pm; Fri, Sat to 11 pm. Closed Jan 1, Thanksgiving, Dec 25. Res accepted. Bar. Semi-a la carte: lunch: $5.95-$9.95, dinner $14.95-$21.95. Child's meals. Specializes in Maine lobster, Chesapeake Bay seafood. Late 18th-century building. Cr cds: A, C, D, DS, MC, V.

Unrated Dining Spot

HARD TIMES CAFE. *1404 King St. 703/683-5340.* Hrs: 11 am-10 pm; Fri, Sat to 11 pm; Sun noon-10 pm. Closed some major hols. A la carte entrees: lunch, dinner $3.95-$5.75. Specializes in Texas, Cincinnati and vegetarian-style chili. Country, western music on jukebox. Housed in former church; rustic decor; collection of state flags. Cr cds: A, C, MC, V.

Appomattox Court House National Historical Park (E-7)

(See also Lynchburg)

(3 mi NE of Appomattox on VA 24)

The series of clashes between General Ulysses S. Grant and General Robert E. Lee that started with the Battle of the Wilderness (May 5, 1864) finally ended here on Palm Sunday, April 9, 1865, in the little village of Appomattox Court House.

A week earlier, Lee had evacuated besieged Petersburg and headed west in a desperate attempt to join forces with General Johnston in North Carolina. Ragged and exhausted, decimated by desertions, without supplies and beset by Union forces at every turn, the once-great Army of Northern Virginia launched its last attack at dawn on April 9. By 10 am it was clear that further bloodshed was futile; after some difficulty in getting a message to Grant, the two antagonists met in the parlor of the McLean House. By 3 pm the generous surrender terms had been drafted and signed. The war was over. Three days later, 28,231 Confederate soldiers received their parole here.

The 1,743-acre park includes the village of Appomattox Court House, restored and reconstructed to appear much as it did in 1865. As visitors tour the village, uniformed park rangers or interpreters in period dress answer questions about the people who lived here and the events that took place. (Daily; closed major hols Nov-Feb) Golden Eagle Passport accepted (see MAKING THE MOST OF YOUR TRIP). Audiovisual programs, Braille guide folder, audio guide and large-print folder avail for the hearing and visually impaired. For further information contact the Superintendent, PO Box 218, Appomattox 24522; 804/352-8987. ¢¢

What to See and Do

✪ **Appomattox Court House Bldg.** Reconstructed building houses visitor center, museum; audiovisual slide program (every half hr, 2nd floor). Self-guided tour of village begins here and includes

Clover Hill Tavern and outbuildings (1819). Oldest structure in village; bookstore, restrooms.

Confederate Cemetery.

County jail (1870). Furnished.

Jones Law Office.

McLean House and outbuildings. Reconstruction of house where Gen. Lee and Grant met on Apr 9, 1865. East from house, past the courthouse and about 100 yards along Stage Rd past county jail, is

Meek's Store and Meek's Storehouse. With period furnishings.

Stacking of Arms. On exactly the fourth anniversary of the firing on Ft Sumter, which triggered the outbreak of war, Confederate soldiers laid down their weapons here.

Woodson Law Office. With period furnishings.

Holliday Lake State Park. Approx 250 acres in Buckingham-Appomattox State Forest. Swimming beach, bathhouse; fishing, boating (launch, rentals) on 150-acre lake. Hiking trails. Picnicking, concession. Tent & trailer sites. Visitor center, interpretive programs. Standard fees. Park (daily); most activities, including camping (Memorial Day-Labor Day). 9 mi NE of Appomattox on VA 24, then 6 mi SE via VA 626, 692. Phone 804/248-6308.

Arlington County (Ronald Reagan Washington-National Airport Area) (C-8)

(See also Alexandria, Fairfax, Falls Church, McLean; also see District of Columbia)

Elev 200 ft **Area Code** 703 **E-mail** acvs@us.net **Web** www.co.arlington.va.us

Information Arlington Convention & Visitors Service, 2100 Clarendon Blvd, Suite 318, 22201, phone 703/228-3988; or the Arlington Visitors Center, 735 S 18th St, 22202, phone 703/228-5720 or 800/677-6267

Originally a part of the District of Columbia laid out for the capital in 1791, Arlington County, across the Potomac River from Washington, was returned to Virginia in 1846. The county is the urban center of northern Virginia.

Transportation

Car Rental Agencies. See IMPORTANT TOLL-FREE NUMBERS.

Public Transportation. Subway trains and buses (Metro Transit System), phone 202/962-1234. Information line 202/637-7000.

Rail Passenger Service. Amtrak 800/872-7245.

Airport Information

Ronald Reagan Washington-National Airport: Information 703/417-8000; lost and found 703/417-8560; weather 202/936-1212; cash machines, at Main Terminal, main level near Travelers Aid, and at Interim Terminal, main level near Travelers Aid.

Airlines: America West, American, American Eagle, Continental, Delta, Midwest Express, Northwest, TWA, United, USAir.

What to See and Do

⭐ **Arlington National Cemetery.** The most famous of US national cemeteries was established in 1864. Here are interred more than 200,000 men and women who served their country; two presidents, William Howard Taft, John F. Kennedy; Sen. Robert F. Kennedy; Jacqueline Kennedy Onassis. Guided "tourmobiles" leave from visitor center (fare includes on/off privileges), phone 703/979-0690. (Daily). Tourmobiles ¢¢; Parking ¢¢ Here are

Arlington House, the Robert E. Lee Memorial. National memorial to Robert E. Lee. Built between 1802 and 1818 by George Washington Parke Custis, Martha Washington's grandson and foster son of George Washington. In 1831, his daughter, Mary Anna Randolph Custis, married Lieutenant Robert E. Lee; six of the seven Lee children were born here. As executor of Custis's estate, Lee took extended leave from the US Army and devoted his time to managing and improving the estate. It was the Lee homestead for 30 yrs before the Civil War.

On Apr 20, 1861, following the secession of Virginia, Lee made his decision to stay with Virginia. Within a month, the house was vacated. Some of the family possessions were moved for safekeeping, but most were stolen or destroyed when Union troops occupied the house during the Civil War.

In 1864, when Mrs. Lee could not appear personally to pay property tax, the estate was confiscated by the federal government; a 200-acre section was set aside for a national cemetery. (There is some evidence that indicates that this was done to ensure that the Lee family could never again live on the estate.) G. W. Custis Lee, the general's son, later regained title to the property through a Supreme Court decision and sold it to the US government in 1883 for $150,000.

Restoration of the house to its 1861 appearance was begun in 1925. The Classic-revival house is furnished with authentic pieces of the period, including some Lee family originals. From the grand portico with its six massive, faux-marble Doric columns, there is a panoramic view of Washington, DC. (Daily; closed Jan 1, Dec 25) Phone 703/557-0613. **Free**

Memorial Amphitheatre. This impressive white marble edifice is used for ceremonies, such as Memorial Day, Easter sunrise and Veterans Day services.

The Tomb of the Unknowns. On Nov 11, 1921, the remains of an unknown American soldier of World War I were entombed here. A memorial was erected in 1932 with the inscription "Here rests in honored glory an American soldier known but to God." On Memorial Day 1958, an unknown warrior who died in World War II and another who died in the Korean War were laid beside him. On Memorial Day 1984, an unknown soldier from the Vietnam War was interred here. Sentries stand guard 24 hrs a day; changing of the guard is every hour on the hour Oct-Mar, every 30 min Apr-Sept.

Iwo Jima Statue. Marine Corps War Memorial depicts raising of the flag on Mt Suribachi, Iwo Jima, Feb 23, 1945; this is the largest sculpture ever cast in bronze. Sunset Parade concert with performances by US Marine Drum and Bugle Corps, US Marine Corps Color Guard and the Silent Drill Team (late May-late Aug, Tues evenings). On Arlington Blvd, near Arlington National Cemetery.

The Fashion Centre at Pentagon City. Upscale, 160-store shopping mall with restaurants, movie theaters and adjoining 360-rm hotel; features 115,000-sq-ft glass ceiling in atrium. Off I-395 at jct S Hayes St & Army-Navy Dr, just S of the Pentagon. Phone 703/415-2130.

⭐ **The Newseum.** 72,000-sq-ft interactive museum of news takes visitors behind the scenes to see and experience how and why news is made. Be a reporter or newscaster; relive great news stories through multimedia exhibits; and see today's news as it happens on a block-long video wall. (Wed-Sun; closed hols) 1101 Wilson Blvd. Phone 888/NEWSEUM or 703/284-3700. **Free** On grounds is

Freedom Park. Nearly 1,000 ft in length, park occupies never-used bridge. Features memorial to journalists killed in line of duty and various icons of freedom.

The Pentagon. With some 6 million sq ft of floor area, this is one of the largest office buildings in the world; houses offices of the Department of Defense. Guided tour (1½ hr) with a walk of about 1½ miles includes movie, Hall of Heroes, Flag Corridor, Time/Life Art Collection (Mon-Fri;

closed hols). Tour window located on Concourse near the Metrorail subway or by entering at Corridor One, South Parking entrance. A valid picture ID must be presented at tour registration; visitors must stay on the tour once it begins. Cameras are allowed. Accommodations for the disabled avail with 48-hr advance notice. Bounded by Jefferson Davis Hwy, Washington Blvd & I-395. Phone 703/695-1776. **Free**

Annual Events

Memorial Day Service. Arlington National Cemetery. Presidential wreath-laying ceremony at Tomb of the Unknowns; music. Memorial Day.

Arlington County Fair. Countywide fair; arts, crafts, international foods, children's activities. Phone 703/228-6400. Aug.

Army 10-miler. America's largest 10-mi road race, attracting thousands of military and civilian runners. Phone 202/685-3361. Early Oct.

Motels

✓ ★★ **COMFORT INN BALLSTON.** *1211 N Glebe Rd (22201), at Washington Blvd.* 703/247-3399; FAX 703/524-8739; res: 800/228-5150. E-mail comfortinnbalston@erols.com. 126 rms, 3 story. Mar-Oct: S, D $120; suites $135; under 18 free; wkend rates; lower rates rest of yr. Crib free. TV; cable (premium). Pool privileges. Complimentary continental bkfst. Restaurant 6:30 am-10:30 pm. Rm serv. Bar 4-11 pm. Ck-out 11 am. Meeting rms. Business servs avail. In-rm modem link. Valet serv (Mon-Fri). Sundries. Gift shop. Garage parking. Refrigerators avail. Cr cds: A, C, D, DS, ER, JCB, MC, V.

🅳 ⊠ ⚒ SC

★★★ **EXECUTIVE CLUB SUITES.** *108 S Courthouse (22204).* 703/522-2582; FAX 703/486-2694; res: 800/535-2582. E-mail nicole@dc execlub.com; web www.dcexeclub.com. 74 kit suites, 2-3 story. Mar-Sept: kit suites: $159-$179; wkend, wkly, hol rates; higher rates Cherry Blossom Festival; lower rates rest of yr. Crib free. Pet accepted, some restrictions; $250 deposit ($25 nonrefundable). TV; cable (premium), VCR avail. Pool; whirlpool, lifeguard. Complimentary continental bkfst. Complimentary coffee in rms. Ck-out noon. Meeting rms. Business servs avail. Valet serv. Sundries. Coin lndry. Free airport transportation. Exercise equipt; sauna. Refrigerators, microwaves. Picnic tables, grills. Cr cds: A, C, D, DS, MC, V.

🐾 ⊠ ⚒ ⊠ SC

Motor Hotels

★★★ **COURTYARD BY MARRIOTT.** *1533 Clarendon Blvd (22209).* 703/528-2222; FAX 703/528-1027; res: 800/321-2211. 162 rms, 10 story, 18 suites. Apr-June, Aug-Oct: S $154; D $164; each addl $10; suites $174-$184; under 12 free; wkend rates; lower rates rest of yr. Crib free. Garage parking $6.50 Sun-Thurs; Fri, Sat free. TV; cable (premium). Indoor pool; whirlpool, lifeguard. Complimentary coffee in rms. Restaurant 6:30-10 am, 5-11 pm. Rm serv from 5 pm. Bar from 5 pm. Ck-out noon. Business servs avail. Valet serv. Sundries. Coin lndry. Exercise equipt. Health club privileges. Some refrigerators; microwaves avail. Many balconies. Cr cds: A, C, D, DS, MC, V.

🅳 ⊠ ⚒ ⊠ ⚒ SC

★★ **DAYS INN.** *2000 Jefferson Davis Hwy (22202).* 703/920-8600; FAX 703/920-2840; res: 800/329-7466. 247 rms, 8 story. Mar-June, Sept-Nov: S $127-$160; D $137-$170; each addl $10; under 16 free; wkend, hol rates; lower rates rest of yr. Crib free. TV; cable (premium). Pool; lifeguard. Complimentary coffee in rms. Restaurant 6 am-2 pm, 5-10 pm; wkends 7 am-noon, 5-10 pm. Rm serv. Bar 4:30-10 pm. Ck-out 11 am. Meeting rms. Business servs avail. In-rm modem link. Bellhops. Gift shop. Valet serv. Garage parking. Free airport transportation. Exercise equipt. Cr cds: A, C, D, DS, JCB, MC, V.

🅳 ⊠ ⚒ ⊠ ⚒ SC

★★★ **QUALITY INN IWO JIMA.** *1501 Arlington Blvd (22209), ½ mi W of Iwo Jima Memorial.* 703/524-5000; FAX 703/522-5484; res: 800/228-5151; res: 800/424-1501. E-mail qualityinn@mci.com. 141 rms, 1-3 story. Mar-Nov: S, D $95-$105; each addl $10; wkend, family rates;

higher rates special events; lower rates rest of yr. Crib free. TV; cable (premium), VCR avail. Indoor pool; poolside serv, lifeguard. Restaurant (in season) 6:30 am-10 pm; Sat, Sun from 7 am. Rm serv. Bar. Ck-out noon. Coin lndry. Meeting rms. Business servs avail. In-rm modem link. Bellhops. Sundries. Exercise equipt. Health club privileges. Refrigerators, microwaves avail. Some balconies. Cr cds: A, C, D, DS, ER, JCB, MC, V.

D ⊷ 🖈 🛪 🔥 SC

Hotels

★★ **BEST WESTERN KEY BRIDGE.** *1850 Fort Myer Dr (23692). 703/522-0400; FAX 703/524-5275; res: 800/528-1234; res: 800/539-2743.* 178 rms, 11 story. S $129; D $139; suites $149-$169; under 12 free. Crib free. Pet accepted. TV; cable (premium). Pool. Restaurant 6:30 am-2 pm, 5-10 pm. Ck-out noon. Meeting rms. Business servs avail. Exercise equipt. Health club privileges. Some refrigerators; microwaves avail. Cr cds: A, C, D, DS, MC, V.

D 🐾 ⊷ 🖈 🛪 SC

★★★ **COURTYARD BY MARRIOTT.** *2899 Jefferson Davis Hwy (22202), near Reagan National Airport. 703/549-3434; FAX 703/549-7440; res: 800/321-2211.* 272 rms, 14 story. S, D $154-$169; each addl $15; suites $200-$250; under 12 free. Crib free. Garage parking $9. TV; cable (premium), VCR avail. Indoor pool; whirlpool, lifeguard. Complimentary coffee in rms. Restaurant 6-10 am, 5 pm-midnight; wkends 7 am-noon, 5 pm-midnight. Rm serv 5-10 pm. Bar 4 pm-midnight. Ck-out 1 pm. Coin lndry. Meeting rms. Business servs avail. In-rm modem link. Valet serv. Sundries. Free airport transportation. Exercise equipt. Health club privileges. Some refrigerators, wet bars; microwaves avail. Cr cds: A, C, D, DS, ER, JCB, MC, V.

D ⊷ 🖈 🛪 🔥 SC

★★★ **CRYSTAL CITY MARRIOTT HOTEL.** *1999 Jefferson Davis Hwy (22202). 703/413-5500; FAX 703/413-0192; res: 800/228-9290.* Web www.marriott.com/mcc. 345 rms, 12 story. S $189; D $209; suites $250-$400; under 18 free; wkend rates. Crib free. Valet parking $15/day. TV; cable (premium), VCR avail. Indoor pool; whirlpool, lifeguard. Complimentary coffee in rms. Restaurant 6:30 am-10:30 pm; Sat, Sun from 7 am. Bar 11:30 am-midnight. Ck-out 1 pm. Coin lndry. Convention facilities. Business center. In-rm modem link. Concierge. Gift shop. Free airport transportation. Exercise equipt; sauna. Health club privileges. Luxury level. Cr cds: A, C, D, DS, ER, JCB, MC, V.

D ⊷ 🖈 🛪 🔥 SC 🏃

★★ **DOUBLETREE HOTEL.** *300 Army Navy Dr (22202). 703/416-4100; FAX 703/416-4126; res: 800/222-8733.* Web www.doubletreehotels.com. 632 rms, 15 story, 265 suites. S, D $190; suites $200-$375; under 18 free; wkend rates. Crib free. Pet accepted, some restrictions. Garage $10; valet $12. TV; cable (premium). Indoor pool; lifeguard. Coffee in rms. Restaurant 6:30 am-11 pm. Bar 11-2 am; entertainment. Ck-out noon. Convention facilities. Business center. In-rm modem link. Concierge. Gift shop. Free airport transportation. Exercise rm; sauna. Health club privileges. Bathrm phones; some refrigerators; microwaves avail. Some balconies. Luxury level. Cr cds: A, C, D, DS, ER, JCB, MC, V.

D 🐾 ⊷ 🛪 🔥 SC 🏃

★★★ **EMBASSY SUITES.** *1300 Jefferson Davis Hwy (22202), entrance at 1402 S Eads St, near Reagan National Airport. 703/979-9799; FAX 703/920-5947; res: 800/362-2779.* Web www.embassysuites.com. 267 suites, 11 story. Feb-June, Sept-Nov: S $179-$209; D $189-$219; each addl $10; under 12 free; wkend rates; lower rates rest of yr. Crib free. Parking $10. TV; cable (premium). Heated pool; lifeguard. Complimentary full bkfst. Complimentary coffee in rms. Restaurant 11 am-2 pm, 5-10 pm. Rm serv to midnight. Bar to midnight. Ck-out noon. Meeting rms. Business servs avail. In-rm modem link. Gift shop. Free airport transportation. Exercise equipt. Health club privileges. Refrigerators. Atrium lobby. Cr cds: A, C, D, DS, JCB, MC, V.

D ⊷ 🖈 🛪 🔥 SC

★★★ **HILTON & TOWERS.** *950 N Stafford St (22203), at Fairfax Dr. 703/528-6000; FAX 703/812-5127; res: 800/468-3571.* 209 rms, 7 story. S $180-$200; D $200-$220; suites $240; under 18 free; wkend rates. Crib free. TV; cable (premium). Indoor pool; whirlpool, lifeguard. Restaurant 6:30 am-10 pm. Bar 4 pm-midnight. Ck-out 1 pm. Meeting rms. Business servs avail. In-rm modem link. Concierge. Gift shop. Health club privileges. Metro stop in building. Luxury level. Cr cds: A, C, D, DS, ER, JCB, MC, V.

D ⊷ 🛪 🔥 SC

★★★ **HOLIDAY INN NATIONAL AIRPORT.** *1489 Jefferson Davis Hwy (22202). 703/416-1600; FAX 703/416-1615.* 306 rms, 11 story. S, D $189; each addl $10; suites $199-$209; under 18 free; wkend, hol rates. Crib free. Pet accepted, some restrictions; $25 deposit. Garage $8/day. TV; cable (premium). Pool; lifeguard. Coffee in rms. Restaurant 6 am-10 pm; Sat, Sun from 7 am. Bar 11 am-midnight. Ck-out noon. Meeting rms. Business center. In-rm modem link. Gift shop. Free airport transportation. Exercise equipt. Refrigerators avail. Cr cds: A, C, D, DS, JCB, MC, V.

D 🐾 ⊷ 🖈 🛪 🔥 SC 🏃

★★ **HOWARD JOHNSON PLAZA.** *2650 Jefferson Davis Hwy (22202). 703/684-7200; FAX 703/684-3217; res: 800/446-4656.* 279 rms, 11 story. Apr-July, Sept-Oct: S $89-$159; D $89-$169; under 10 free; suites $210-$230; under 18 free; wkend rates; lower rates rest of yr. Crib free. Garage, in/out parking $9. TV; cable. Complimentary coffee in rms. Restaurant 6 am-11 pm. Bar 4-11 pm. Ck-out noon. Meeting rms. Business center. In-rm modem link. Gift shop. Coin lndry. Free airport, RR station transportation. Exercise equipt. Health club privileges. Pool; lifeguard. Balconies. Cr cds: A, C, D, DS, JCB, MC, V.

D ⊷ 🖈 🛪 🔥 SC 🏃

★★★ **HYATT.** *1325 Wilson Blvd (22209), near Key Bridge at Nash St & Wilson. 703/525-1234; FAX 703/875-3393; res: 800/233-1234.* Web www.hyatt.com. 302 rms, 16 story. S $195; D $225; each addl $25; suites $275-$575; under 12 free; wkend rates. Crib free. Pet accepted, some restrictions. Garage $10/day (Sun-Thurs). TV; cable (premium), VCR avail. Restaurant 6:30 am-midnight. Bars 11:30 am-midnight. Ck-out noon. Free guest lndry. Meeting rms. Business center. In-rm modem link. Gift shop. Exercise equipt. Health club privileges. Metro adj. Cr cds: A, C, D, DS, ER, JCB, MC, V.

D 🐾 🖈 🛪 🔥 SC 🏃

★★★ **HYATT REGENCY.** *2799 Jefferson Davis Hwy (22202), near Reagan National Airport. 703/418-1234; FAX 703/418-1289; res: 800/233-1234.* E-mail wasrc1@erols.com. 685 rms, 20 story. S $189; D $214; each addl $25; suites $350-$725; under 18 free; wkend rates. Crib free. Garage; valet $10/day. TV; cable (premium), VCR avail. Pool; whirlpool, poolside serv, lifeguard. Complimentary coffee in rms. Restaurant 6-2 am. Bar 3 pm-1 am. Ck-out noon. Convention facilities. Business center. In-rm modem link. Concierge. Gift shop. Free airport transportation. Exercise equipt; saunas. Health club privileges. Some refrigerators, wet bars; microwaves avail. Some balconies. Cr cds: A, C, D, DS, ER, JCB, MC, V.

D ⊷ 🖈 🛪 🔥 SC 🏃

★★★ **MARRIOTT CRYSTAL GATEWAY HOTEL.** *1700 Jefferson Davis Hwy (22202), entrance on S Eads St, between 15th & 17th Sts, near National Airport. 703/920-3230; FAX 703/271-5212; res: 800/228-9290.* Web www.marriott.com. 700 units, 16 story. S, D $192-$220; suites $199-$700; under 18 free; wkend rates. Crib free. Pet accepted, some restrictions. Garage $12. TV; cable (premium). Indoor/outdoor pool; whirlpool, lifeguard. Restaurant 6:30-2 am. Bar 11-2 am. Ck-out 1 pm. Convention facilities. Business center. In-rm modem link. Concierge. Free airport transportation. Tennis privileges. Exercise equipt; sauna. Health club privileges. Original artwork. Luxury level. Cr cds: A, C, D, DS, ER, JCB, MC, V.

D 🐾 🖙 ⊷ 🖈 🛪 🔥 SC 🏃

★★★ **MARRIOTT KEY BRIDGE HOTEL.** *1401 Lee Hwy (22209).* 703/524-6400; FAX 703/524-8964; res: 800/228-9290; res: 800/327-9789. Web www.marriott.com/marriott/waskb. 584 rms, 2-14 story. S, D $199-$209; suites $225-$500; wkend rates. Crib free. Garage $8/day. TV; cable (premium), VCR avail. Indoor/outdoor pool; whirlpool, poolside serv, lifeguard. Coffee in rms. Restaurant (see JW'S STEAKHOUSE). Bar noon-2 am; entertainment Thurs-Sat. Ck-out 1 pm. Convention facilities. Business center. In-rm modem link. Concierge. Gift shop. Barber, beauty shop. Exercise equipt; sauna. Health club privileges. Refrigerators, microwaves avail. Some balconies. Overlooks Washington across Potomac River. Luxury level. Cr cds: A, C, D, DS, MC, V.

D ⊠ 🕴 🖺 🔥 SC 🚶

✓ ★★★ **QUALITY HOTEL.** *1200 N Court House Rd (22201).* 703/524-4000; FAX 703/522-6814; res: 800/221-2222; res: 888/987-2555. Web www.qualityhotelarlington.com. 392 rms, 1-10 story. S $69.95-$125.95; D $75.95-$135.95; each addl $10; suites $109.95-$169.95; under 18 free; package plans. Crib free. Pet accepted, some restrictions. TV; cable (premium). Pool; lifeguard. Coffee in rms. Restaurant 6:30 am-2 pm, 5-9:30 pm. Bar 4-10 pm. Ck-out noon. Coin lndry. Convention facilities. Business servs avail. In-rm modem link. Concierge. Gift shop. Exercise equipt; sauna. Microwaves avail. Balconies. Luxury level. Cr cds: A, C, D, DS, ER, JCB, MC, V.

D 🐾 ⊠ 🕴 🖺 🔥 SC

★★★ **RESIDENCE INN BY NAVY.** *550 Army Navy Dr (22202).* 703/413-6630; FAX 703/418-1751; res: 800/331-3131. Web www.residenceinn.com/waspt. 299 kit suites, 17 story. Kit. suites $170-$235; wkend, wkly rates. Crib free. Garage parking $10/day. TV; cable (premium). Indoor pool; whirlpool, lifeguard. Complimentary continental bkfst. Complimentary coffee in rms. Restaurant nearby. No rm serv. Ck-out noon. Meeting rms. Business servs avail. No bellhops. Concierge. Coin lndry. Free airport transportation. Exercise equipt. Health club privileges. Refrigerators, microwaves. Picnic tables. Cr cds: A, C, D, DS, MC, V.

D ⊠ 🕴 ✈ 🖺 🔥 SC

★★★★ **RITZ-CARLTON PENTAGON CITY.** *1250 S Hayes St (22202), in Pentagon City Fashion Centre Mall, near Reagan National Airport.* 703/415-5000; FAX 703/415-5061; res: 800/241-3333. The Persian carpets, fine art and 18th-century antiques of this quiet hotel contrast with its surroundings. Guest rooms are lavishly appointed with silk drapes and Federal-style furnishings and have panoramic views of the Capitol and the Potomac River. 366 rms, 18 story. S, D $279; each addl $20; suites $379-$2,200; under 18 free; wkend rates. Crib free. Valet parking $24. TV; cable (premium), VCR avail (movies). Indoor pool; whirlpool, lifeguard. Afternoon tea 3-5 pm. Restaurant (see THE GRILL). Bar; entertainment. Ck-out noon. Convention facilities. Business center. In-rm modem link. Concierge. Shopping arcade. Tennis privileges. Golf privileges. Exercise rm; sauna, steam rm. Massage. Bathrm phones, minibars; microwaves avail. Luxury level. Cr cds: A, C, D, DS, ER, JCB, MC, V.

D 🏌 🐾 ⊠ 🕴 🖺 🔥 🚶

★★★ **SHERATON CRYSTAL CITY HOTEL.** *1800 Jefferson Davis Hwy (22202), entrance on S Eads St; ½ mi S of I-395 on US 1, near National Airport.* 703/486-1111; FAX 703/769-3970; res: 800/862-7666. E-mail vajoe11@aol.com; web www.erols.com/sheraton/. 197 rms, 15 story. S $145-$195; D $145-$200; each addl $20; under 18 free; wkend rates. Crib free. TV; cable (premium). Pool; lifeguard. Coffee in rms. Restaurant 6:30 am-10 pm; Sat, Sun from 7 am. Bar 11 am-midnight; entertainment, pianist. Ck-out 1 pm. Meeting rms. Business center. In-rm modem link. Gift shop. Free airport transportation. Exercise equipt; sauna. Refrigerators; some bathrm phones. Luxury level. Cr cds: A, C, D, DS, MC, V.

D ⊠ 🕴 ✈ 🖺 🔥 SC 🚶

Restaurants

★★ **ALPINE RESTAURANT.** *4770 Lee Hwy (22207).* 703/528-7600. Hrs: 11:30 am-11 pm; Sun noon-10 pm. Closed most major hols. Res accepted. Italian, continental menu. Bar. Semi-a la carte: lunch $7.45-$10.75, dinner $10.95-$17.95. Specializes in veal, pasta dishes, seafood. Own pasta. Parking. Family-owned. Cr cds: A, C, D, MC, V.

D 🖼

✓ ★★ **BISTRO BISTRO.** *4021 S 28th St (22206).* 703/379-0300. Hrs: 11 am-10 pm; Fri, Sat to 11 pm; early-bird dinner Mon-Thurs 5-6:30 pm; Sun brunch 10:30 am-3 pm. Closed Thanksgiving, Dec 24, 25. Res accepted. Bar to 1:30 am. A la carte entrees: lunch $5.75-$10.95, dinner $9.95-$16.95. Sun brunch $6-$12. Specializes in pasta, seafood. Outdoor dining. Bistro atmosphere, eclectic decor. Cr cds: A, C, D, DS, MC, V.

D 🖼

★ **CAFE DALAT.** *3143 Wilson Blvd (22201), at N Highland St.* 703/276-0935. Hrs: 11 am-9:30 pm; Fri, Sat to 10:30 pm. Closed July 4, Thanksgiving, Dec 25; also Chinese New Year. Vietnamese menu. Serv bar. Semi-a la carte: lunch $4.25, dinner $7.50-$8.95. Buffet: lunch $4.95. Specialties: sugarcane shrimp, grilled lemon chicken. Own desserts. Totally nonsmoking. Cr cds: C, MC, V.

✓ ★★ **CARLYLE GRAND CAFE.** *4000 S 28th St (22206), S on I-395, Shirlington exit.* 703/931-0777. E-mail carlylegrande@greatamericanrest.com. Hrs: 11:30 am-11 pm; Fri, Sat to midnight; Sun brunch 10:30 am-2 pm. Closed Thanksgiving, Dec 25. Bar. Semi-a la carte: lunch $5.95-$11.75, dinner $8.95-$18.95. Sun brunch $4.95-$11.95. Specialties: lobster pot stickers, baby back ribs, smoked salmon filet. Outdoor dining. Totally nonsmoking. Cr cds: A, C, MC, V.

D

✓ ★ **COWBOY CAFE.** *4792 Lee Hwy (22207).* 703/243-8010. E-mail cowboysarlva@erols.com; web www.washingtonpost.com/cowboycafe. Hrs: 11 am-11 pm; Fri to midnight; Sat 9 am-midnight; Sun 9 am-9 pm. Bar to midnight; Fri, Sat to 1 am; Sun 11 am-9 pm. Semi-a la carte: bkfst $2.99-$6.50, lunch, dinner $2.75-$8.25. Specializes in hamburgers, bkfst dishes. Musicians Thurs-Sat. Casual, Western decor. Cr cds: A, C, D, DS, MC, V.

🖼

★ **FACCIA LUNA.** *2909 Wilson Blvd (22201).* 703/276-3099. Hrs: 11 am-11 pm; Fri, Sat to midnight; Sun noon-11 pm. Closed Thanksgiving, Dec 24, 25. Italian menu. Bar. Semi-a la carte: lunch $4.95-$5.95, dinner $7.75-$14.95. Child's meals. Specializes in pasta, pizza. Outdoor dining. Upscale trattoria. Cr cds: A, C, MC, V.

D 🖼

★★★ **JW'S VIEW STEAKHOUSE.** *(See Marriott Key Bridge Hotel)* 703/284-1407. Hrs: 5-10 pm; Fri to 11 pm; Sat 6-11 pm; Sun 5:30-9:30 pm; Sun brunch 10 am-2:30 pm. Closed Jan 1. Res accepted; required July 4. Bar. Wine list. A la carte entrees: dinner $18.95-$28.95. Sun brunch $25.95-$27.95. Specializes in seafood, steak, certified Angus beef. Parking. View of Washington across Potomac. Cr cds: A, C, D, DS, MC, V.

D SC 🖼

★★ **KABUL CARAVAN.** *1725 Wilson Blvd (22209), in Colonial Village Shopping Ctr.* 703/522-8394. Hrs: 11:30 am-2:30 pm, 5:30-11 pm; Sat, Sun from 5:30 pm. Closed Thanksgiving, Dec 25. Res accepted. Afghan menu. Serv bar. Prix fixe dinners for 2-4: $55.95-$115.95. Semi-a la carte: lunch $7.95-$11.95, dinner $10.95-$16.95. Specialties: sauteed pumpkin with yogurt & meat sauce, eggplant & shish kebob. Outdoor dining. Walls covered with Afghan clothing, pictures, rugs, artifacts, jewelry. Cr cds: A, C, MC, V.

D 🖼

★ ★ ★ **LA COTE D'OR CAFE.** *6876 Lee Hwy (22213).* 703/538-3033. Hrs: 11:30 am-3 pm, 5:30-11 pm; Sun brunch 11 am-3 pm. Closed Jan 1, Dec 25. Res accepted. French menu. Bar. Semi-a la carte: lunch $5.95-$12.95, dinner $18.75-$22.95. Sun brunch $7.95-$11.50. Specializes in seafood, veal. Outdoor dining. French decor. Cr cds: A, C, MC, V.

✓ ★ ★ **LITTLE VIET GARDEN.** *3012 Wilson Blvd (22201).* 703/522-9686. Hrs: 11 am-2:30 pm, 5-10 pm; Sat, Sun 11 am-10 pm. Closed Thanksgiving, Dec 25. Vietnamese menu. Bar. Semi-a la carte: lunch $4.95-$6.95, dinner $6.95-$11.95. Specialties: Viet Garden steak, grilled jumbo shrimp. Parking. Outdoor dining. Cr cds: A, C, D, DS, MC, V.

★ **MATUBA JAPANESE RESTAURANT.** *2915 Columbia Pike (22204).* 703/521-2811. Hrs: 11:30 am-2 pm, 5:30-10 pm; Fri, Sat 5:30-10:30 pm; Sun 5:30-10 pm. Res accepted. Japanese menu. Semi-a la carte: lunch $4.95-$8.50, dinner $7-$12.50. Specializes in seafood, poultry. Japanese decor. Cr cds: A, C, MC, V.

✓ ★ ★ **QUEEN BEE.** *3181 Wilson Blvd (22201).* 703/527-3444. Hrs: 11 am-10 pm. Vietnamese menu. Serv bar. Semi-a la carte: lunch $3.95-$7.50, dinner $6.50-$9.95. Specialties: spring roll, Hanoi beef noodle soup, Hanoi-style grilled pork. Totally nonsmoking. Cr cds: A, C, MC, V.

★ **RED HOT & BLUE.** *1600 Wilson Blvd (22209).* 703/276-8833. Hrs: 11 am-10 pm; Fri, Sat to 11 pm. Closed Thanksgiving, Dec 25. Bar. Semi-a la carte: lunch, dinner $4.69-$11.99. Specializes in Memphis pit barbecue dishes. Memphis blues memorabilia. Cr cds: A, C, D, DS, MC, V.

★ ★ **RT'S SEAFOOD KITCHEN.** *2300 Clarendon Blvd (22201).* 703/841-0100. Hrs: 11 am-10:30 pm; Fri, Sat to 11 pm; Sun 4-9:30 pm. Closed Jan 1, July 4, Thanksgiving, Dec 25. Cajun menu. Bar to midnight. Semi-a la carte: lunch $7.95-$10.95, dinner $11.95-$17.95. Child's meals. Specializes in Cajun-style seafood. Outdoor dining. Contemporary decor. Cr cds: A, C, D, DS, MC, V.

✓ ★ **SILVER DINER.** *3200 Wilson Blvd (22201).* 703/812-8600. Hrs: 7 am-midnight; Thurs to 1 am; Fri, Sat to 3 am; Sat, Sun brunch 7 am-2 pm. Closed Dec 25. Wine, beer. Semi-a la carte: bkfst $2.99-$7.99, lunch $4.99-$7.99, dinner $4.99-$11.99. Sat, Sun brunch $5.99-$7.99. Child's meals. Specializes in classic diner food. Own desserts. Reminiscent of 1950s-style diner. Cr cds: A, C, D, DS, MC, V.

★ ★ ★ **THE GRILL.** *(See Ritz-Carlton Pentagon City)* 703/412-2760. Hrs: 6:30 am-10:30 pm; Fri, Sat to 11 pm; Sun brunch 11 am-2:30 pm. Res accepted. Bar. Wine list. Semi-a la carte: bkfst $5-$15, lunch $10-$25, dinner $22-$32. Buffet: bkfst $12-$17. Sun brunch $45. Tea 3-5 pm; $14-$26. Child's meals. Specializes in seasonal Mid-Atlantic cuisine including macrobiotic daily specials. Pianist Fri, Sat eves. Valet parking. English club-like decor and atmosphere. Fireplace. Cr cds: A, C, D, DS, ER, JCB, MC, V.

★ ★ ★ **TIVOLI RESTAURANT.** *1700 N Moore St (22209).* 703/524-8900. Hrs: 11:30 am-2:30 pm, 5:30-10 pm; Sat from 5:30 pm; early-bird dinner Mon-Sat 5:30-6:30 pm. Closed Sun; major hols. Res accepted; required Fri, Sat. Italian menu. Bar 11:30 am-midnight. Semi-a la carte: lunch $8.50-$11.50; dinner $12.50-$23.50. Specializes in pasta, seafood, veal. Contemporary decor. Cr cds: A, C, D, DS, MC, V.

★ ★ **TOM SARRIS' ORLEANS HOUSE.** *1213 Wilson Blvd (22209).* 703/524-2929. Hrs: 11 am-11 pm; Sat from 4 pm; Sun 4-10 pm. Res accepted. Bar. Semi-a la carte: lunch $4.25-$7.95, dinner $8.95-

$14.95. Child's meals. Specializes in prime rib, NY strip steak, seafood. Salad bar. Parking. New Orleans atmosphere; fountains, iron railings, Tiffany lampshades. Family-owned. Cr cds: A, C, D, DS, MC, V.

★ **VILLAGE BISTRO.** *1723 Wilson Blvd (22209).* 703/522-0284. Hrs: 11:30 am-2:30 pm, 5-10:30 pm; Fri, Sat to 11 pm; Sun 5-10 pm; early-bird dinner 5-7 pm. Closed Thanksgiving, Dec 25. Res accepted; required Fri, Sat. Continental menu. Bar. Semi-a la carte: lunch $5.50-$12.95, dinner $7.95-$18.95. Specializes in seafood, pasta. Parking. Outdoor dining. Monet prints on walls. Cr cds: A, C, D, DS, MC, V.

★ ★ **WOO LAE OAK.** *1500 S Joyce St (22202),* on grounds of River House complex. 703/521-3706. Hrs: 11:30 am-10:30 pm. Closed Jan 1. Res accepted. Korean menu. Semi-a la carte: lunch, dinner $8-$20. Specializes in barbecued dishes prepared tableside. Parking. Large, open dining rm; Korean decor. Cr cds: A, C, D, MC, V.

Ashland (E-8)

(See also Richmond)

Founded 1858 **Pop** 5,864 **Elev** 221 ft **Area Code** 804 **Zip** 23005
E-mail pritter@town.ashland.va.us **Web** www.town.va.us
Information Ashland/Hanover Visitor Information Center, 112 N Railroad Ave; 804/752-6766 or 800/897-1479

Ashland was founded when the president of the Richmond, Fredericksburg and Potomac Railroad bought land here. He dug a well, struck mineral water and started a health resort—Slash Cottage (wilderness acres were called "slashes"). A thriving village grew up and took the name of Henry Clay's Kentucky estate. In 1866, the railroad company gave land to the Methodist Church and induced the church to move Randolph-Macon College here. A section of early 1900s houses along the railroad tracks has been set aside as a historic district.

What to See and Do

Paramount's Kings Dominion. A 400-acre family theme park consisting of 6 theme areas, including Hurricane Reef water park; Days of Thunder ride simulator; the Anaconda, a looping roller coaster that passes through an underwater tunnel; also Shockwave stand-up roller coaster; The Outer Limits roller coaster; 33-story likeness of the Eiffel Tower with panoramic view; whitewater raft ride; live entertainment; shops. (June-Labor Day, daily; late Mar-May, after Labor Day-early Oct, wkends only) 1 mi E on VA 54, then 7 mi N on I-95 in Doswell. Phone 804/876-5000. ¢¢¢¢¢

Patrick Henry Home "Scotchtown" (1719). Also girlhood home of Dolley Madison; fine colonial architecture. (May-Oct, Wed-Sat; Apr, wkends; also by appt) 11 mi NW via VA 54, 671, County 685 (Scotchtown Rd), left onto Chiswell Ln. Phone 804/227-3500. ¢¢

Randolph-Macon College (1830). (1,100 students) Coeducational, liberal arts, Methodist-affiliated college. Historic buildings include Washington-Franklin Hall, Old Chapel and Pace Hall. 1 mi W of I-95. Phone 804/752-7305. Campus tours **Free**

Motels

✓ ★ ★ **BEST WESTERN.** *10296 Sliding Hill Rd (23005),* 1 blk W of I-95 Atlee-Elmont exit 86. 804/550-2805; FAX 804/550-3843; res: 800/528-1234. 93 rms, 2 story. Apr-mid-Oct: S $38-$68; D $51-$68; each addl $5; under 12 free; higher rates special events; lower rates rest of yr.

Crib free. TV; cable. Pool. Restaurant 6:30 am-9 pm. Ck-out noon. Coin lndry. Meeting rms. Business servs avail. Exercise equipt. Some balconies. Cr cds: A, C, D, DS, MC, V.

✓★★ **COMFORT INN.** *101 N Cottage Green Dr (23005). 804/752-7777; FAX 804/798-0327; res: 800/228-5150.* 126 rms, 2 story. Memorial Day-Labor Day: S, D $59-$89; each addl $5; suites $120; under 18 free; lower rates rest of yr. Crib free. TV; cable. Pool. Complimentary continental bkfst. Restaurant adj open 24 hrs. Ck-out noon. Coin lndry. Business servs avail. Exercise equipt; sauna. Some refrigerators. Cr cds: A, C, D, DS, JCB, MC, V.

D ⟋ 🏌 ⤢ 🔥 SC

★★ **HOLIDAY INN.** *810 England St (23005), 1 blk W of I-95 exit 92, at jct VA 54. 804/798-4231; FAX 804/798-9074; res: 800/922-4231.* 165 rms, 2 story. S, D $45-$98; under 18 free; higher rates some wkends. Crib free. TV; cable (premium). Pool; wading pool. Restaurant 6 am-10 pm. Rm serv. Bar. Ck-out 11 am. Coin lndry. Meeting rms. Business servs avail. Valet serv. Exercise equipt. Private patios, balconies. Cr cds: A, C, D, DS, ER, JCB, MC, V.

D ⟋ 🏌 ⤢ 🔥 SC

Inn

★★★ **HENRY CLAY INN.** *114 N Railroad Ave (23005), adj to visitors center. 804/798-3100; FAX 804/752-7555; res: 800/343-4565.* 15 rms, 3 story, 1 suite. S, D $90-$115; each addl $15; suite $145; higher rates special events. Crib $15. TV; cable. Complimentary continental bkfst. Dining rm 7-9 am; wkends also 11 am-2:30 pm, 6-9 pm. Ck-out 11 am, ck-in 2 pm. Business servs avail. In-rm modem link. Gift shop. Balconies. Authentic reproduction of Georgian-revival inn. Totally nonsmoking. Cr cds: A, C, MC, V.

D ⤢ 🔥 SC

Restaurants

★★ **IRONHORSE.** *100 S Railroad Ave (23005). 804/752-6410.* Web www.zip2.com/styweekly/ironhorse. Hrs: 11:30 am-2:30 pm, 5:30-9 pm; Mon to 2:30 pm; Fri, Sat to 10 pm. Closed Sun; some major hols; also wk after Jan 1 & wk after July 4. Res accepted. Bar to midnight. Entertainment. Semi-a la carte: lunch $4.95-$8.95, dinner $13.95-$18.95. Specializes in Angus beef, barbecue shrimp, crab cakes. Railroad memorabilia. Cr cds: C, MC, V.

★ **SMOKEY PIG.** *212 S Washington Hwy (23005). 804/798-4590.* Hrs: 11 am-9 pm; Sun from noon. Closed Mon; major hols. Bar. Semi-a la carte: lunch $3.45-$13.99, dinner $3.88-$16.95. Child's meals. Specializes in pit-cooked meats, seafood, ribs. Cr cds: A, C, MC, V.

D ⤢

Basye (C-7)

(See also Luray, New Market, Woodstock)

Pop 200 (est) **Elev** 1,354 ft **Area Code** 540 **Zip** 22810 **E-mail** bryce@ bryceresort.com **Web** www.bryceresort.com
Information Bryce Resort, PO Box 3; 540/856-2121

What to See and Do

Bryce Resort. On VA 263.

Summer. Fishing, swimming, horseback riding, golf, tennis, hiking, boating, grass skiing. Fee for activities.
Winter. Skiing: 2 double chairlifts, 3 rope tows; patrol, school, rentals; snowmaking; ski shop; restaurant, cafeteria, bar. Longest run 3,500 ft; vertical drop 500 ft. (Mid-Dec-mid-Mar, daily) Phone 540/856-2121. ¢¢¢¢¢

Motel

✓★★ **BEST WESTERN.** *250 Conickville Blvd (22842), at I-81 exit 273. 540/477-2911; FAX 540/477-2392; res: 800/528-1234.* 98 rms, 2 story. June-Oct: S $60; D $70; each addl $4; lower rates rest of yr. Crib free. Pet accepted. TV; cable. Pool; wading pool. Playground. Restaurant 6 am-midnight. Bar 5-10 pm. Ck-out 11 am. Meeting rms. Business servs avail. Sundries. Gift shop. Tennis. Game rm. Cr cds: A, C, D, DS, MC, V.

D 🐾 ⟋ ⤢ ⤢ 🔥 SC

Inn

★★★ **WIDOW KIPS COUNTRY INN.** *355 Orchard Dr (22842), approx 9 mi E via VA 263E, then S on VA 698. 540/477-2400; res: 800/478-8714.* E-mail widokips@shantel.net; web www.widowkips.com. 5 rms, showers only; 2 cottages. No rm phones. S $55-$75; D $65-$85; each addl $15, lower rates mid-wk. Pet accepted in cottages. TV in sitting rm, cottages; cable (premium). Pool. Complimentary full bkfst. Picnic lunches avail. Ck-out 11 am, ck-in 3 pm. Some fireplaces. Bicycles. Grill. Federal-style saltbox house (1830) on 7 acres. Victorian furnishings, handmade quilts. Totally nonsmoking. Cr cds: C, MC, V.

🐾 🧺 ⤢ ⤢ 🔥 SC

Big Stone Gap (F-2)

(See also Breaks Interstate Park, Wise)

Founded 1888 **Pop** 4,748 **Elev** 1,488 ft **Area Code** 540 **Zip** 24219
E-mail gaptourism@va-village.com
Information Lonesome Pine Tourist Information Center, 619 Gilley Ave, PO Box 236; 540/523-2060

This rugged mountain country gave John Fox, Jr, his inspiration for *Trail of the Lonesome Pine* and *Little Shepherd of Kingdom Come*. The town lies at the junction of three forks of the Powell River, which cuts a pass through Stone Mountain.

What to See and Do

John Fox, Jr, House & Museum. Occupied from 1888 by the author of *Trail of the Lonesome Pine* and *Little Shepherd of Kingdom Come*, best-selling novels of the early 1900s. Memorabilia and original furnishings. Guided tours (June-Sept, daily exc Mon; Oct, wkends). 117 Shawnee Ave. Phone 540/523-2747 or 540/523-1235. ¢¢

June Tolliver House. Heroine in *Trail of the Lonesome Pine* lived here; period furnishings; now an arts & crafts center; restored 1890 house. (June-late Dec, daily exc Mon) Jerome St and Clinton Ave, jct US 23, 58A. Phone 540/523-1235. **Free**

Natural Tunnel State Park. Consists of 648 acres. Giant hole chiseled through Purchase Ridge by Stock Creek; pinnacles or "chimneys." Railroad and stream are accommodated in this vast tunnel—100 ft or more in diameter, 850 ft long. Tunnel, visitor center with exhibits. Swimming, pool; fishing. Hiking. Picnicking; concession. Camping, tent & trailer sites (Memorial Day-Labor Day). Interpretive programs. Chairlift. Park (daily); tunnel & most activities (Memorial Day-Labor Day; daily). Standard fees. 18 mi SE, off US 23. Phone 540/940-2674.

Southwest Virginia Museum. Four-story mansion contains exhibits dealing with life in southwestern Virginia during original coal boom of the 1890s; also Native Americans of the area and early pioneers. (Memorial Day-

Labor Day, daily; Mar-late May & early Sept-Dec, daily exc Mon; closed hols) W 1st St & Wood Ave. Phone 540/523-1322. ¢

Seasonal Event

Trail of the Lonesome Pine. June Tolliver Playhouse, adj to June Tolliver House. Outdoor musical drama. For reserved seats phone 540/523-1235. Thurs-Sat, late June-Labor Day.

Blacksburg (E-5)

(See also Radford, Roanoke, Salem)

Founded 1798 **Pop** 34,590 **Elev** 2,080 ft **Area Code** 540 **Zip** 24060
E-mail gbcc@bev.net **Web** www.guide.new-river.va.us
Information Blacksburg Regional Chamber of Commerce, 1995 S Main St, Ste 901; 540/522-4503 or 800/288-4061

The George Washington and Jefferson National Forests, which lie to the northwest, provide a colorful backdrop: azaleas, flowering dogwood and redbud in spring and brilliant hardwoods in fall. Virginia Polytechnic Institute and State University is a source of employment for the town. The forests' Blacksburg Ranger District office is located here.

What to See and Do

Mountain Lake. A resort lake, particularly inviting in late June and early July, when azaleas and rhododendron are in bloom. 20 mi NW on US 460, VA 700.

Smithfield Plantation. (1773). Restored pre-Revolutionary house; original woodwork. Home of Colonel William Preston and three governors. Architectural link between Tidewater and Piedmont plantations of Virginia and those of the Mississippi Valley. Grounds restored by the Garden Club of Virginia. (Apr-Nov, Thurs-Sun afternoons) ¼ mi W off US 460 bypass, at VA Tech exit. Phone 540/231-3947. ¢¢

Motels

★★★ **BEST WESTERN.** *900 Plantation Rd (24060).* 540/552-7770; FAX 540/552-6346; res: 800/528-1234. 104 rms, 1-2 story. S $49-$54; D $64-$68; each addl $6; suites $139; under 18 free; higher rates university events. Crib free. TV; cable, VCR avail. Pool; poolside serv. Playground. Restaurant 7 am-10 pm. Rm serv. Bar 4:30 pm-2 am. Ck-out noon. Meeting rms. Business servs avail. Valet serv. Sundries. Tennis. Golf privileges. X-country ski 15 mi. Lawn games. Picnic tables, grills. On 13 acres. Cr cds: A, C, D, DS, MC, V.

D ⊁ ⊀ ⛾ ⇌ ⊀ ⊠ 🕭 SC

★★ **COMFORT INN.** *3705 S Main St (24060).* 540/951-1500; FAX 540/951-1530; res: 800/228-5150. 80 rms, 4 story. S $57-$65; D $62-$67; each addl $5; suite $85; under 18 free; higher rates special events. Crib free. Pet accepted. TV; cable (premium), VCR avail. Pool. Complimentary continental bkfst. Restaurant adj 6 am-10 pm. Ck-out 11 am. Business servs avail. In-rm modem link. Valet serv. Exercise equipt. Microwaves avail. Cr cds: A, C, D, DS, ER, JCB, MC, V.

D 🐾 ⇌ ⊀ ⊠ 🕭 SC

✓ ★★ **DAYS INN.** *3705 S Main St (24068),* 1 blk NE of I-81 exit 118. 540/382-0261; FAX 540/382-0365; res: 800/329-7466. 122 rms, 2 story. S $46-$84; D $54-$84; each addl $5; under 18 free; higher rates: special events. Crib free. Pet accepted. TV; cable (premium). Pool. Playground. Complimentary continental bkfst. Ck-out noon. In-rm modem link. Cr cds: A, C, D, DS, MC, V.

D 🐾 ⇌ ⊠ 🕭 SC

★★★ **FOUR POINTS BY SHERATON.** *900 Price's Fork Rd (24060).* 540/552-7001; FAX 540/552-0827; res: 800/325-3535. 148 rms, 2 story. S, D $89-$169; each addl $10; suites $199; under 18 free. Crib free.

TV; cable (premium). 2 pools, 1 indoor; wading pool. Complimentary coffee in lobby. Restaurant 7 am-2 pm, 5-9 pm. Bar noon-2 am; entertainment. Ck-out noon. Meeting rms. Business servs avail. In-rm modem link. Valet serv. Health club privileges. Tennis. Cr cds: A, C, D, DS, ER, JCB, MC, V.

D ⊁ ⇌ ⊠ 🕭 🐾 SC

★★ **HAMPTON INN.** *50 Hampton Blvd (24073),* S via I-81, exit 118, then E. 540/382-2055; FAX 540/382-4515. 125 rms, 2 story. S $57; D $70; under 18 free; higher rates: wkends, univ graduation, football games. Crib free. TV; cable (premium). Pool. Restaurant opp 6 am-10 pm. Ck-out 11 am. Coin lndry. Business servs avail. Microwave avail. Cr cds: A, C, D, DS, MC, V.

D ⇌ ⊠ 🐾 SC

★★ **RAMADA.** *3503 Holiday Ln (24060).* 540/951-1330; FAX 540/951-4847; res: 800/465-4329. 98 rms, 2 story. S $55-$65; D $60-$70; each addl $5; suites $135; under 12 free; higher rates: univ graduation, football wkends. Crib free. Pet accepted. TV; cable (premium). Pool; wading pool. Restaurant 6:30 am-2 pm, 5-10 pm. Rm serv. Bar. Ck-out noon. Coin lndry. Meeting rm. Business servs avail. Valet serv. Sundries. X-country ski 20 mi. Some in-rm steam baths. Cr cds: A, C, D, DS, JCB, MC, V.

D 🐾 ⊁ ⇌ ⊠ 🐾 SC

Inn

★★★ **OAKS VICTORIAN INN.** *311 E Main St (24073),* S on I-81, exit 114, turn right on Main St approx 2 mi. 540/381-1500; FAX 540/381-3036; res: 800/336-6257. Web www.bbhost.com/theoaksinn. 7 rms, 3 story. S $85-$125; D $115-$150; lower rates Jan-Mar. Children over 14 yrs only. TV; cable (premium). Whirlpool. Complimentary full bkfst; afternoon refreshments. Restaurant nearby. Ck-out noon, ck-in 4 pm. Business servs avail. In-rm modem link. Valet serv. Airport transportation. Health club privileges. Refrigerators; some fireplaces. Balconies. Queen Anne/Victorian residence (1889); period furnishings. Surrounded by 300-yr-old white oak trees. Totally nonsmoking. Cr cds: A, C, DS, MC, V.

⊠ 🕭

Blue Ridge Parkway (F-4-D-6)

(See also Roanoke, Waynesboro)

Elev 649-6,050 ft; avg 3,000 ft

Winding 469 mountainous miles between Shenandoah and Great Smoky Mountains National Parks (about 217 miles are in Virginia), the Blue Ridge Parkway represents a different concept in highway travel. It is not an express highway (speed limit 45 MPH) but a road intended for leisurely travel. All towns are bypassed. Travelers in a hurry would be wise to take state and US routes, where speed limits are higher.

The parkway follows the Blue Ridge Mountains for about 355 miles, then winds through the Craggies, Pisgahs and Balsams to the Great Smokies. Overlooks, picnic and camp sites, visitor centers, nature trails, fishing streams and lakes and points of interest are numerous and well marked.

Accommodations are plentiful in cities and towns along the way. Food availability is limited on the parkway.

The parkway is open all year, but the best time to drive it is between April and November. Some sections are closed by ice and snow for periods in winter and early spring. Fog may be present during wet weather. The higher sections west of Asheville to Great Smoky Mountains National Park and north of Asheville to Mt Mitchell may be closed January through March due to hazardous driving conditions.

For maps, pamphlets and detailed information contact Superintendent, 400 BB&T Bldg, One Pack Sq, Asheville, NC 28801; 828/298-0398.

What to See and Do

(Park visitor facilities are open May-Oct. Numbered concrete posts are located at each mile of the parkway. "Milepost 0" is at Rockfish Gap; MP 469 is just above Cherokee, NC.)

Camping. Tent and trailer sites at Otter Creek, Peaks of Otter, Roanoke Mt, Rocky Knob, Doughton Park, Julian Price Memorial Park, Linville Falls, Crabtree Meadows and Mt Pisgah. (May-Oct) 14-day limit, June-Labor Day. No electricity; pets on leash only; water is shut off with first freeze, usually late Oct. Fee/site/night. Primitive winter camping at Linville Falls when roads are passable.

Craft demonstrations and sales.

Folk Art Center. Craft Guild Headquarters, sales, parkway travel information. Interpretive programs (daily, May-Oct). MP 382.

Northwest Trading Post. Country store sells native handicrafts. MP 258.6.

Parkway Craft Center. MP 294. (See BLOWING ROCK, NC)

Fishing. Rainbow, brook, brown trout and smallmouth bass in streams and lakes. State licenses required.

Interpretive programs. Outdoor talks (mid-June-Labor Day) at Otter Creek (MP 60.8), Peaks of Otter (MP 86), Rocky Knob (MP 169), Doughton Park (MP 241.1), Price Park (MP 297.1), Linville Falls (MP 316.3), Crabtree Meadows (MP 340) and Mt Pisgah (MP 408.6). Obtain schedules at Parkway Visitor Centers.

Riding. 20 mi of trails in Moses H. Cone Memorial Park (MP 292.7). Horses for hire at Blowing Rock, NC.

Self-guided trails. Moderate grades. Walks take from 5 min to 1 hr. Trails on the parkway include

Cascades Trail. Leads to waterfall. MP 272.

Cone Park Trail. Manor house wild garden. MP 294.

Craggy Gardens Trail. Traverses high mountain "gardens." MP 364.6.

Elk Run Trail. Forest, plant, animal community. MP 86.

Flat Rock Trail. Magnificent valley and mountain views. MP 308.3.

Greenstone Trail. Of geologic interest. MP 8.8.

Linville Falls Trail. Views of falls, Linville River Gorge. MP 317.5.

Mabry Mill Trail. Old-time mountain industry. MP 176.

Mountain Farm Trail. Typical mountain farm, reconstructed. MP 5.8.

Richland Balsam Trail. Spruce-fir forests. Highest spot on parkway. MP 431.

Rocky Knob Trail. Leads to overlook of Rock Castle Gorge. MP 168.

Trail of the Trees. Leads to overlook of James River. MP 63.6.

✪ **Visitor Centers.** Exhibits, travel information, interpretive publications. Centers (daily during peak travel season) include

Craggy Gardens Visitor Center. 5,892-ft elevation. Natural history exhibits, naturalist. (Mid-June-Labor Day, daily; May-mid-June, early Sept-Oct, wkends) MP 364.6.

Cumberland Knob Contact Station. Visitor information, publications, park ranger. MP 218.

Folk Art Center. Craft Guild Headquarters, sales, parkway travel information, park ranger. (Daily) MP 382.

Humpback Rocks Visitor Center. Pioneer mountain farm, park ranger. MP 5.8.

James River Wayside. Story of James River and Kanawha Canal, park ranger. MP 63.6.

Linn Cove Information Center. MP 304.

Mabry Mill. Old-time mountain industry, including tannery exhibits, picturesque mill, blacksmith shop. MP 176.

Museum of North Carolina Minerals. (Daily, winter hrs vary; closed hols) MP 331.

Peaks of Otter Visitor Center. Wildlife exhibits, park ranger. MP 86.

Rocky Knob Information Station. Information, exhibits, park ranger. MP 170.

Waterrock Knob Information Center. Panoramic views, visitor information, exhibits, publications. MP 451.2.

Motel

★★★ **PEAKS OF OTTER LODGE MOTEL.** *Mile Marker 86 Blue Ridge Prkwy (24174), on Blue Ridge Pkwy at jct VA 43 (Milepost 86). 540/586-1081; FAX 540/586-4420. Web www.1mall.com/stores/peaks.* 63 rms, 2 story. Mar-Nov: S $67; D $72; each addl $6.25; suites $85-$100; under 16 free; MAP rest of yr. Crib free. TV in lobby. Restaurant (see PEAKS OF OTTER). Bar 5-11 pm. Ck-out noon. Meeting rm. Business servs avail. Sundries. Gift shop. Private patios, balconies. Located on a lake and surrounded by peaks. Scenic view. Cr cds: C, MC, V.

D ⟡ ⚒

Lodge

★★★ **DOE RUN LODGE RESORT & CONFERENCE CENTER.** *Blue Ridge Pkwy (24343), 1/8 mi S of Blue Ridge Pkwy. 540/398-2212; FAX 540/398-2833; res: 800/325-6189. E-mail doerun@tcia.net; web www.doerunlodge.com.* 47 kit suites, 1-2 story. No elvtr. May-Oct: kit suites $119-$250; each addl $18; under 15 free; package plans; lower rates rest of yr. Crib free. Pet accepted; $45 deposit. TV; VCR (movies $3). Heated pool; poolside serv. Sauna. Complimentary coffee in rms. Restaurant (see HIGH COUNTRY). Bar; entertainment Fri, Sat. Ck-out noon. Meeting rms. Business servs avail. Sundries. Lighted tennis. 18-hole golf privileges, greens fee, pro, putting green, driving range. Lawn games. Balconies. Picnic tables. Cr cds: A, C, MC, V.

D ⚒ ⟡ ⚒ ⚒ ⚒ ⚒ ⚒ ⚒ SC

Inn

★★ **THE OSCEOLA MILL COUNTRY INN.** *Hwy 56 (24476), 4 mi W of Blue Ridge Pkwy, Milepost 27, on VA 56. 540/377-6455; FAX 540/377-6455. E-mail osceola@cfw.com.* 12 rms, 1-2 story, 1 cottage. No rm phones. S, D $89-$109; each addl $20; cottage $149-$169; wkly rates. Pool. Complimentary full bkfst. Ck-out 11 am, ck-in 2 pm. Business servs avail. In renovated 1849 mill, mill store and restored 1873 miller's house. Totally nonsmoking. Cr cds: C, MC, V.

D ⚒ ⚒ ⚒

Restaurants

★★ **HIGH COUNTRY.** *(See Doe Run Lodge) 540/398-2212. E-mail doerun@tcia.net; web www.doerunlodge.com.* Hrs: 8 am-10 pm; Sun brunch 11:30 am-2:30 pm. Closed Mon; Dec 25. Res accepted. Bar noon-midnight; closed Sun. Complete meals: bkfst $4.25-$12.95. Semi-a la carte: lunch $4.95-$16.95, dinner $13.95-$25. Specializes in beef, chicken. Entertainment Fri, Sat. Panoramic view of countryside. Cr cds: A, C, MC, V.

D ⚒

✓★★ **PEAKS OF OTTER.** *(See Peaks of Otter Lodge Motel) 540/586-9263. E-mail peaks@aol.com; web www.peaksotter.com.* Hrs: 7:30-10:30 am, 11:30 am-2:30 pm, 5-8:30 pm; Sun brunch noon-8:30 pm. Bar 5-11 pm. Semi-a la carte: bkfst $3-$7.95, lunch $4.50-$8.95, dinner $4.70-$16.95. Sun brunch $10.55. Child's meals. Specialties: prime rib of beef au jus, barbecued "little pig" ribs, whole rainbow trout. Salad bar. Panoramic view of mountains, lake. Rustic decor. Family-owned. Cr cds: C, MC, V.

D ⚒

Booker T. Washington National Monument (E-5)

(See also Roanoke)

(Approx 18 mi S on VA 116 from Roanoke to Burnt Chimney, then continue 6 mi E on VA 122)

The 1861 property inventory of the Burroughs plantation listed, along with household goods and farm implements, the entry "1 Negro boy (Booker)—$400." Freed in 1865, the boy and his family moved to Malden, West Virginia. There, while working at a salt furnace and in coal mines, the youngster learned the alphabet from *Webster's Blueback Spelling Book*. Later, by working at the salt furnace before school, then going to work at the mine after school, he got the rudiments of an education. When he realized that everyone else at the school roll call had two names, he chose Washington for his own.

From Malden, at 16, he started the 500-mile trip to Hampton Institute, where he earned his way. He taught at Malden for 2 years, attended Wayland Seminary and returned to Hampton Institute to teach. In July 1881 he started Tuskegee Institute in Alabama with 30 pupils, two run-down buildings and $2,000 for salaries. When Washington died in 1915, the Institute had 107 buildings, more than 2,000 acres and was assessed at more than $500,000.

The 224-acre monument includes most of the original plantation. A ¼-mile self-guided plantation trail passes reconstructed farm buildings, a slave cabin, crops and animals of the period; there is also a 1½-mile self-guided Jack-O-Lantern Branch nature trail. Picnic facilities. Visitor Center has an audiovisual program, exhibits depicting his life (daily; closed Jan 1, Thanksgiving, Dec 25). Phone 540/721-2094.   **Free**

Inn

★★ **MANOR AT TAYLORS STORE BED & BREAKFAST.** *Rte 1 (24184), 4 mi W on VA 122S.* 540/721-3951; *FAX 540/721-5243; res: 800/248-6267.* E-mail taylors@symweb.com; web www.symweb.com/taylors. 9 rms, 3 story. No rm phones. S, D $85-$180. TV in sitting rm. Whirlpool. Complimentary full bkfst. Ck-out 11 am, ck-in 4 pm. Business servs avail. Exercise equipt. Rec rm. Lawn games. Some balconies. Library, sun rm. On 120 acres with pond. Historic trading post built in 1799, became a post office in 1818. Totally nonsmoking. Cr cds: A, C, MC, V.

🐾 🏊 🏃 🎿 🔥

Breaks Interstate Park (E-3)

(See also Wise)

(8 mi N of Haysi, VA, and 7 mi SE of Elkhorn City, KY, on KY-VA 80)

The "Grand Canyon of the South," where the Russell Fork of the Big Sandy River plunges through the mountains, is the major attraction of this 4,600-acre park on the Virginia-Kentucky border. From the entrance, a paved road winds through an evergreen forest and then skirts the canyon rim. Overlooks provide a spectacular view of the Towers, a ½-mile-long, ⅓-mile-wide pyramid of rocks; the 5-mile-long, 1,600-foot-deep, 250-million-year-old gorge; odd rock formations; caves; springs and a profusion of rhododendron.

The visitor center houses natural and historical exhibits and a coal exhibit (Apr-Oct, daily). Laurel Lake is stocked with bass and bluegill. Picnicking, swimming pool, pedal boats, hiking and bridle trails and playground. Camping (Apr-Oct, fee); cottages (all yr); restaurant, gift shop, conference center. Facilities (Apr-Mid-Dec, daily); park (all yr, daily). For details contact Breaks Interstate Park, PO Box 100, Breaks, 24607;

540/865-4413 or 800/982-5122 (reservations). Memorial Day-Labor Day, per car   ¢; Rest of yr   **Free**

Motel

✓★★ **BREAKS INTERSTATE.** *Rte 1 (24607), on VA 80.* 540/865-4414; *FAX 540/865-5561; res: 800/982-5122.* E-mail bip@mounet.com; web www.breakspark.com. 34 rms, 1-2 story. Apr-Dec: S $66.03; D $74.55; each addl $8; cottages $350/wk. Closed late Dec-Mar. Crib free. TV; cable. Pool; wading pool, lifeguard. Restaurant 7 am-9 pm. Ck-out 11 am. Meeting rm. Sundries. Gift shop. Balconies. Picnic tables, grills. Bicycle rentals. Woodland setting; overlooks Breaks Canyon. Hiking trails, picnic shelters. Cr cds: A, C, DS, MC, V.

🄳 🐾 🏋 🏖 🎿 🔥 **SC**

Bristol (F-3)

(See also Abingdon)

Founded 1771 **Pop** Bristol, VA: 18,426; Bristol, TN: 24,000 (est) **Elev** 1,680 ft **Area Code** 540 (VA); 423 (TN) **Zip** 24201 (VA); 37620 (TN) **E-mail** tourism@bristolchamber.org **Web** www.bristolchamber.org **Information** Chamber of Commerce, 20 Volunteer Pkwy, TN, or PO Box 519, VA 24203; 423/989-4850

Essentially a city in two states, Bristol is actually two cities—Bristol, TN, and Bristol, VA—sharing the same main street and the same personality. Each has its own government and city services. Together they constitute a major shopping center. Named for the English industrial center, Bristol is an important factory town in its own right. These carry on the pioneer tradition of an ironworks, established here about 1784, which made the first nails for use on the frontier.

What to See and Do

Bristol Caverns. Unusual rock formations, seen from lighted, paved walkways winding through caverns and along an underground river. Guided tours every 20 min. Picnic area. (Daily; closed Thanksgiving, Dec 25) 5 mi SE on US 421, off I-81. Phone 423/878-2011.   ¢¢¢

Rocky Mount Historic Site. Features the 2½-story log house (1770) that served, from 1790 to 1792, as capitol under William Blount, governor of the Territory of the United States South of the River Ohio. Restored to its original simplicity; 18th-century furniture. On grounds are restored log kitchen, slave cabin, barn, blacksmith shop and smokehouse. (Daily; closed Thanksgiving, Dec 21-Jan 5; also wkends Jan, Feb) 11 mi SW on US 11E. Phone 423/538-7396.   ¢¢

Seasonal Event

Bristol Motor Speedway. 5 mi S on US 11E. Phone 423/764-1161. Apr, June & Aug.

Motels

★ **BUDGET HOST.** *1209 W State St (24201).* 540/669-5187; *FAX 540/466-5848; res: 800/283-4678.* 24 rms. S, D $28.50-$80; each addl $4; under 12 free; wkly rates. TV; cable (premium). Restaurant nearby. Ck-out 11 am. Business servs avail. Cr cds: A, C, DS, MC, V.

🎿 🔥 **SC**

★★ **COMFORT INN.** *2368 Lee Hwy (24201).* 540/466-3881; *FAX 540/466-6544; res: 800/228-5150 or 800/221-2222.* 60 rms, 2 story. Apr-Oct: S, D $65-$195; each addl $5; suites $125-$225; under 18 free;

higher rates special events; lower rates rest of yr. Crib free. TV; cable (premium). Pool. Complimentary continental bkfst. Restaurant nearby. Ck-out 11 am. Business servs avail. Cr cds: A, C, D, DS, JCB, MC, V.

⬜ 🛏 🖪 🔥 🅂🄲

★★ **RAMADA INN.** *2221 Euclid Ave (24201), at W State St.* 540/669-7171; FAX 540/669-7171. 123 rms, 2 story. S, D $55-$95; each addl $4; under 18 free; higher rates special events. TV; cable. Pool. Restaurant 7 am-2 pm, 5-9 pm. Rm serv. Bar from 5 pm. Ck-out noon. Meeting rms. Business servs avail. Sundries. Microwaves avail. Cr cds: A, C, D, DS, JCB, MC, V.

⬜ 🛏 🖪 🔥 🅂🄲

✓ ★ **RED CARPET INN.** *15589 Lee Hwy (24202), I-81 exit 10.* 540/669-1151; FAX 540/669-1153; res 800/948-6257. 60 rms, 2 story. June-Oct: S, D $48-$74; each addl $5; higher rates special events; lower rates rest of yr. Crib free. Pet accepted, some restrictions. TV; cable (premium). Pool. Ck-out noon. Microwaves avail. Cr cds: A, C, D, DS, MC, V.

🐾 🛏 🖪 🔥 🅂🄲

★ **SUPER 8 MOTEL.** *2139 Lee Hwy (24201), I-81 exit 5.* 540/466-8800; FAX 540/466-8800; res 800/800-8000. 62 rms, 3 story. S, D $46-$64; each addl $6; under 12 free; higher rates car races. Crib free. Pet accepted. TV; cable. Complimentary coffee in lobby. Restaurant nearby. Ck-out 11 am. Business servs avail. Some refrigerators, microwaves. Picnic tables. Cr cds: A, C, D, DS, JCB, MC, V.

⬜ 🐾 🖪 🔥 🅂🄲

Motor Hotel

✓ ★★ **LA QUINTA INN.** *1014 Old Airport Rd (24201).* 540/669-9353; FAX 540/669-6974; res: 800/687-6667. Web www.laquinta.com. 123 rms, 4 story. June-Sept: S $59-$79; D $69-$89; each addl $10; suites $95-$105; under 18 free; higher rates race cars; lower rates rest of yr. Crib free. Pet accepted. TV; cable (premium), VCR avail. Complimentary continental bkfst. Complimentary coffee in rms. Restaurant nearby. Ck-out noon. Meeting rms. Business servs avail. In-rm modem link. Pool. Cr cds: A, C, D, DS, MC, V.

⬜ 🐾 🛏 🖪 🔥 🅂🄲

Restaurants

★ **ATHENS STEAK HOUSE.** *105 Goodson St (24201).* 540/466-8271. Hrs: 4-10:30 pm. Closed Sun; major hols. Greek, Amer menu. Bar. Semi-a la carte: dinner $7.95-$20.45. Specializes in lobster tail, steak. Cr cds: A, C, MC, V.

⬜ 🖪

★★ **VINYARD RESTAURANT.** *603 Gate City Hwy (24201).* 540/466-4244. Hrs: 7 am-10 pm; Fri, Sat to 11 pm. Closed July 4, Dec 24, 25. Res accepted wkends. Italian, Amer menu. Bar. Semi-a la carte: bkfst $3.95-$6.95, lunch $4.95-$7.95. Complete meals: dinner $8.25-$25. Specializes in fresh seafood, veal. Salad bar. Cr cds: A, C, D, DS, MC, V.

⬜ 🖪

Brookneal (F-6)

(See also Lynchburg, South Boston)

Settled ca 1790 **Pop** 1,344 **Elev** 560 ft **Area Code** 804 **Zip** 24528

What to See and Do

Patrick Henry National Memorial (Red Hill). Last home and burial place of Patrick Henry. Restoration of family cottage, cook's cabin, smokehouse,

stable, kitchen. Patrick Henry's law office. Museum and gift shop on grounds. Interpretive video. (Daily; closed Jan 1, Thanksgiving, Dec 25) 3 mi E on VA 40, 2 mi S on VA 600 & 619. Phone 804/376-2044. ¢¢

Cape Charles (E-10)

(See also Hampton, Newport News, Norfolk, Portsmouth, Virginia Beach)

Pop 1,398 **Elev** 10 ft **Area Code** 757 **Zip** 23310 **Web** www.cbbt.com
Information Chesapeake Bay Bridge & Tunnel District, Public Relations Dept, PO Box 111; 757/331-2960, ext 20

The Chesapeake Bay Bridge-Tunnel (17.6 miles long) leads from Cape Charles (12 miles south of the town) to Virginia Beach/Norfolk, VA. There is a scenic stop, gift shop, restaurant and fishing pier (bait avail). **Note:** Noncommercial vehicles entering with compressed gas containers are limited to *(a)* two nonpermanently mounted containers with a maximum individual capacity of 105 lbs water or 45 lbs LP-gas each, or one container with a maximum capacity of 60 lbs LP-gas; or *(b)* not more than 2 permanently mounted containers with a total capacity of 200 gallons water when LP-gas is used as a motor fuel. One-way passenger car toll ¢¢¢

Inns

★★ **BAY AVENUE SUNSET BED & BREAKFAST.** *108 Bay Ave (23310).* 757/331-2424; FAX 757/331-4877; res: 800/331-3113 or 888/422-9283. E-mail info@baysunsetbb.com; web www.baysunsetbb.com. 4 rms, 3 story. No rm phones. Mar-Dec: S, D $85-$105; each addl $20; higher rates hols (2-day min); lower rates rest of yr. Children over 10 yrs only. TV; cable (premium), VCR avail (movies). Complimentary full bkfst. Ck-out 11 am, ck-in 2 pm. Business servs avail. Luggage handling. Bicycles. Victorian house (1915) overlooking Chesapeake Bay. Beach. Totally nonsmoking. Cr cds: A, C, DS, MC, V.

♿ 🖪 🔥

★★ **WILSON-LEE HOUSE BED & BREAKFAST.** *403 Tazewell Ave (23310).* 757/331-1954; FAX 757/331-8133. E-mail wlhbnb@aol.com; web www.wilsonleehouse.com. 6 rms, 4 with shower only. S, D $85-$120; each addl $20; package plans; hols 2-day min. Children over 12 yrs only. Cable TV in common rm, VCR avail (movies). Complimentary full bkfst. Restaurant nearby. Ck-out 11 am, ck-in 4-6 pm. Business servs avail. Luggage handling. Street parking. Built in 1906. Totally nonsmoking. Cr cds: A, C, MC, V.

♿ 🖪 🔥

Restaurants

✓ ★★★ **EASTVILLE MANOR.** *6058 Willow Oak Rd (23347), 7 mi N on US 13, E on VA 631.* 757/678-7378. Hrs: 5:30-9 pm. Closed Sun, Mon; also Tues Sept-May. Res accepted. Contemporary Amer menu. Wine list. A la carte entrees: dinner $11.95-$17.95. Child's meals. Specializes in fresh seafood, beef tenderloin, pasta. Menu changes monthly. Own baking. In 1886 farmhouse; polished wood floors, chandeliers, antiques; landscaped grounds. Cr cds: C, MC, V.

⬜

✓ ★ **LITTLE ITALY.** *10027 Rogers Dr (23413), 15 mi N on US 13, E at Nassawadox stoplight.* 757/442-7831. Hrs: 11 am-8 pm, Fri, Sat to 9 pm; summer hrs vary. Closed Sun; most major hols. Res accepted. Italian menu. Bar. Semi-a la carte: lunch, dinner $2.99-$12.99. Child's meals. Specialties: lasagna, cannolli, tiramisu. Street parking. Former country-style grocery store. Cr cds: C.

⬜ 🖪

Cape Henry Memorial (F-10)

(See also Norfolk, Virginia Beach)

(10 mi E of Norfolk on US 60)

The first English settlers of Jamestown landed here on April 26, 1607. They claimed the land for England, stayed four days, named their landing spot for Henry (then Prince of Wales and oldest son of King James I) and put up a cross.

A cross put up by the Daughters of the American Colonists in 1935 marks the approximate site of the first landing. An interpretive display describes the Battle of the Capes, a sea battle fought between England and France in 1781, a prelude to the Battle of Yorktown. Nearby is Cape Henry Lighthouse, first lighthouse in the United States authorized and built by the federal government (1791). The memorial is in Fort Story Military Reservation.

Charlottesville (D-7)

(See also Waynesboro)

Founded 1762 **Pop** 40,341 **Elev** 480 ft **Area Code** 804 **E-mail** visitor center@ci.charlottesville.va.us

Information Charlottesville/Albemarle Convention & Visitors Bureau, jct I-64 & VA 20, PO Box 178, 22902; 804/977-1783

Thomas Jefferson was born here, as was the University of Virginia, which he founded and designed. Ash Lawn-Highland, which was James Monroe's home, and Monticello are southeast of the city.

In the gently rolling terrain of Albemarle County, Charlottesville is almost at the center of Virginia; it is the trading center for a widespread area. In colonial times, tobacco was the dominant product. Today wheat, beef and dairy herds, riding and race horses, peaches, frozen foods, electronic products, light industry and mountains of native Albemarle pippin apples invigorate the economy.

What to See and Do

Albemarle County Court House. N wing was used in 1820s as a "common temple," shared by Episcopalian, Methodist, Presbyterian and Baptist sects, one Sunday a month to each but with all who wished attending each Sunday. Jefferson, Monroe and Madison worshiped here. Court Square.

⭐ **Ash Lawn-Highland** (1799). Built on a site personally selected by Thomas Jefferson, this 535-acre estate was the home of President James Monroe (1799-1823). The estate is now owned by Monroe's alma mater, the College of William and Mary. This early-19th-century working plantation offers guided tours of the house with Monroe possessions, spinning and weaving demonstrations, old boxwood gardens, peacocks, picnic spots. Special events include Summer Festival (June-Aug) of arts, evening concerts, children's shows (Sat), Plantation Days Wkend, spring and Christmas programs. (Daily; closed Jan 1, Thanksgiving, Dec 25) 4¼ mi SE on County 795. Phone 804/293-9539. ¢¢¢

Historic Michie Tavern (ca 1780). Built on land granted to Patrick Henry's father and later bought by John Michie, this is one of the oldest homesteads remaining in Virginia. Museum illustrates 18th-century tavern life; 1920s preservation perspective on colonial history. Lunch buffet in converted 200-yr-old log house. (Daily; closed Jan 1, Dec 25) 1 mi S on VA 20. Phone 804/977-1234. Museum   ¢¢¢

⭐ **Monticello.** Located on a mountaintop, this is one of the most beautiful estates in Virginia and is considered a classic of American architecture. Monticello was designed by Thomas Jefferson and built over the course of 40 yrs, symbolizing the pleasure he found in "putting up and pulling down." Jefferson moved into the first completed outbuilding of his new home in 1771, though construction continued until 1809. Most of the interior furnishings are original. Tours of the restored orchard, vineyard, 1,000-ft-long vegetable garden and Mulberry Row, once the site of plantation workshops. Jefferson died at Monticello on July 4, 1826, and was buried in the family cemetery. The Thomas Jefferson Memorial Foundation maintains the house and gardens. (Daily; closed Dec 25) 2 mi SE on VA 53. Phone 804/984-9822.   ¢¢¢   Approx 2 mi W of here is

Monticello Visitors Center. Personal and family memorabilia; architectural models and drawings; *Thomas Jefferson: The Pursuit of Liberty,* a 35-minute film, is shown twice daily. (Daily; closed Dec 25) On VA 20S at I-64. Phone 804/984-9822.   **Free**

Monuments.

George Rogers Clark Memorial. Brother of William Clark and soldier on the frontier, this intrepid explorer, who opened up the Northwest Territory, was an Albemarle County native son. W Main St, E of university.

Lewis and Clark Monument. Memorial to Jefferson's secretary, Meriwether Lewis, who explored the Louisiana Territory with his friend William Clark. Midway Park, Ridge & Main Sts.

Robert E. Lee Monument. Jefferson St between 1st & 2nd Sts.

Stonewall Jackson on Little Sorrel. By Charles Keck. Adj courthouse.

Shenandoah National Park (see). 20 mi W on VA 250 to Afton, then N on Skyline Dr.

Sightseeing tour. The Charlottesville/Albemarle Information Center, located on VA 20S in the Monticello Visitors Center Bldg, has information for a walking tour of historic Charlottesville. Phone 804/977-1783.

Skiing. Wintergreen Resort. Five chairlifts; patrol, school, rentals; lodge (see RESORTS); nursery. 10 runs; longest run 4,200 ft; vertical drop 1,000 ft. (1st wkend Dec-3rd wkend Mar, daily) Night skiing. Summer activities include golf, tennis, fishing and boating, horseback riding. W on US 250 to VA 151, then S to VA 664, turn right, follow signs (approx 4½ mi). Phone 804/325-2200.   ¢¢¢¢¢

University of Virginia (1819). (18,100 students) Founded by Thomas Jefferson and built according to his plans. Handsome red-brick buildings with white trim, striking vistas, smooth lawns and ancient trees form the grounds of Jefferson's "academical village." The serpentine walls, one brick thick, which Jefferson designed for strength and beauty, are famous. Room 13, W Range, occupied by Edgar Allan Poe as a student, is displayed for the public. Walking tours start at the Rotunda (daily; closed 3 wks mid-Dec-early Jan). W end of Main St. Phone 804/924-1019. Guided tours   **Free**

Annual Events

Founder's Day (Jefferson's Birthday). Commemorative ceremonies. Mid-Apr.

Dogwood Festival. Parade, lacrosse and golf tournaments, carnival. Nine days mid-Apr.

Garden Week. Some fine private homes and gardens in the area are open. Mid-Apr.

Motels

✓ ★★ **BEST WESTERN.** *1613 Emmet St (22906), jct US 29 and US 250 Bypass.* 804/296-5501; FAX 804/977-6249; res: 800/528-1234. 110 rms, 1-2 story. Mar-Oct: S $51-$55; D $58-$65; each addl $6; under 18 free; family, wkly rates; higher rates graduation; lower rates rest of yr. Crib free. Pet accepted, some restrictions. Complimentary coffee in rms. Restaurant adj 6-10 am. Ck-out noon. Meeting rms. Business servs avail. Bellhops. Sundries. Pool; wading pool. Refrigerators, microwaves avail. Cr cds: A, C, D, DS, ER, JCB, MC, V.

D 🐾 ≋ 🛶 🔥 SC

★★★ **COURTYARD BY MARRIOTT.** *638 Hillsdale Dr (22901).* 804/973-7100; FAX 804/973-7128; res: 800/321-2211. 150 rms, 2-3 story. Mar-late Nov: S, D $72-$85; under 18 free; wkly rates; higher rates graduation; lower rates rest of yr. Crib free. TV; cable (premium). VCR avail. Indoor pool; whirlpool. Complimentary coffee in rms. Bar 5-10 pm. Ck-out noon. Coin lndry. Meeting rms. Business servs avail. In-rm modem link. Sundries. Free airport transportation. Exercise equipt. Some refrigerators; microwaves avail. Balconies. Picnic tables. Cr cds: A, C, D, DS, MC, V.

D ⊠ ✈ ⊠ 🔥 SC

★★ **DAYS INN.** *1600 Emmet St N (22901), near jct US 29 Business & US 250 Bypass.* 804/293-9111; FAX 804/977-2780; res: 800/329-7466. 129 rms, 3 story. S $64-$68; D $74-$78; each addl $10; under 18 free; higher rates special univ events. Crib free. Pet accepted. TV; cable (premium), VCR avail. Pool; wading pool. Restaurant 6:30 am-10 pm; Fri, Sat to 11 pm. Rm serv. Bar 10-1 am. Ck-out noon. Meeting rms. Business servs avail. In-rm modem link. Valet serv. Free airport, RR station, bus depot transportation. Exercise equipt; sauna. Health club privileges. Cr cds: A, C, D, DS, JCB, MC, V.

D 🐾 ⊠ ✈ ⊠ 🔥 ⊠ SC

★★ **HAMPTON INN.** *2035 India Rd (22901).* 804/978-7888; FAX 804/973-0436; res: 800/426-7866. 123 rms, 5 story. S $58-$62; D $62-$70; under 18 free; higher rates univ graduation. Crib free. TV; cable (premium). Pool. Complimentary continental bkfst, coffee. Restaurant nearby. Ck-out noon. Meeting rm. Business servs avail. Bellhops. Sundries. Free airport, RR station, bus depot transportation. Health club privileges. Cr cds: A, C, D, DS, MC, V.

D ⊠ ⊠ 🔥 SC

★★ **HOLIDAY INN.** *1200 5th St Sw (22902), I-64 exit 120.* 804/977-5100; FAX 804/293-5228; res: 800/465-4329. E-mail hdayinn@cville.net. 128 rms, 6 story. S $75-$85; D $75-$95; each addl $10; suites $115-$125; under 18 free; wkend rates; higher rates univ events. Crib free. TV; cable (premium). Pool; wading pool. Complimentary coffee in rms. Restaurant 6:30-10:30 am, 5-10 pm. Rm serv. Bar to 11 pm. Ck-out noon. Meeting rms. Coin lndry. Business center. Bellhops. Valet serv (Mon-Fri). Health club privileges. Game rm. Refrigerators avail. Cr cds: A, C, D, DS, JCB, MC, V.

D ⊠ ✈ 🔥 SC ✈

✓★ **KNIGHTS INN.** *1300 Seminole Trl (22901), US 29N.* 804/973-8133; FAX 804/973-1168; res: 800/843-5644. 115 units. S, D $39-$58; each addl $6; kits. $63; under 18 free; wkly rates. Crib free. Pet accepted, some restrictions. TV; cable (premium), VCR avail (movies). Pool. Complimentary coffee in lobby. Restaurant nearby. Ck-out noon. Meeting rm. Business servs avail. Cr cds: A, C, D, DS, MC, V.

D 🐾 ⊠ ⊠ 🔥 SC

✓★★ **RAMADA INN.** *2097 Inn Dr (22911), I-64, exit 124.* 804/977-3300; FAX 804/977-3300; res: 800/424-6423. 100 rms, 2 story. Apr-Nov: S $50-$55; D $55-$69; each addl $5; under 16 free; higher rates special events; lower rates rest of yr. Crib $5. TV; cable (premium), VCR avail. Complimentary continental bkfst. Complimentary coffee in rms. Restaurant 7 am-10 pm. Rm serv. Bar 11-2 am. Ck-out noon. Meeting rms. Business servs avail. Bellhops. Valet serv. Sundries. Coin lndry. Free airport, RR station, bus depot transportation. 18-hole golf privileges, greens fee $25, pro, putting green. Exercise equipt. Pool. Playground. Game rm. Some in-rm whirlpools, refrigerators, microwaves. Picnic tables, grills. Cr cds: A, C, D, DS, ER, JCB, MC, V.

D 🏊 ⊠ ✈ ⊠ 🔥 SC

Motor Hotels

★ **BEST WESTERN.** *105 Emmet St N (22903), jct US Business 29, US 250.* 804/296-8111; FAX 804/296-3523; res: 800/528-1234. 118 rms, 5 story. S $63-$79; D $73-$89; each addl $8; suites $125; under 18 free; 2-day packages; higher rates univ events. Crib free. Pet accepted. TV; cable (premium). Pool. Complimentary continental bkfst. Coffee in rms. Restaurant 11:30 am-10 pm. Rm serv. Bar to 1 am. Ck-out 1 pm. Meeting rms. Business servs avail. Bellhops. Valet serv. Free airport, RR station, bus depot transportation. Univ of VA opp. Cr cds: A, C, D, DS, MC, V.

D 🐾 ⊠ ⊠ 🔥 SC

★★ **ENGLISH INN OF CHARLOTTESVILLE.** *2000 Morton Dr (22903).* 804/971-9900; FAX 804/977-8008; res: 800/786-5400. 88 units, 3 story, 21 suites. S $69; D $74; each addl $5; suites $75-$80; under 18 free; higher rates: univ graduation, sports events. Crib free. TV; cable (premium). Indoor pool. Complimentary bkfst buffet. Ck-out noon. Meeting rms. Business servs avail. Free airport, RR station, bus depot transportation. Sauna. Refrigerator in suites. Cr cds: A, C, D, DS, MC, V.

D ⊠ ⊠ 🔥 SC

Hotels

★★★ **DOUBLETREE HOTEL.** *2350 Seminole Trl (22901), near Charlottesville-Albemarle Airport.* 804/973-2121; FAX 804/978-7735; res: 800/544-5064. 234 units, 9 story. S, D $65-$135; each addl $10; suites $229-$289; family, wkend rates. Crib $10. TV; cable (premium), VCR avail. Indoor/outdoor pool; whirlpool, poolside serv. Coffee in rms. Restaurant 6:30 am-10 pm. Bar 4 pm-11 pm; entertainment. Ck-out noon. Convention facilities. Business servs avail. In-rm modem link. Free airport, RR station, bus depot transportation. Tennis. Exercise equipt. Some bathrm phones. Refrigerators avail. Cr cds: A, C, D, DS, MC, V.

D ✈ ⊠ ✈ ✈ ⊠ 🔥 SC

★★ **OMNI HOTEL.** *235 W Main St (22902).* 804/971-5500; FAX 804/979-4456; res: 800/843-6664. 204 rms, 7 story. S, D $99-$154; each addl $15; under 18 free; suites $190-$250; wkend rates; higher rates univ events. Crib free. Pet accepted, some restrictions. TV; cable (premium). 2 pools, 1 indoor; whirlpool. Coffee in rms. Restaurant 6:30 am-10 pm. Bar 11-1 am. Ck-out noon. Convention facilities. Business servs avail. Gift shop. Free covered parking. Free airport transportation. Exercise equipt; sauna. Cr cds: A, C, D, DS, JCB, MC, V.

D 🐾 ⊠ ✈ ⊠ 🔥 SC

Resorts

★★★ **BOARS HEAD INN.** *W Rte 250 (22903), Ivy Rd (US 250), 2½ mi W of jct US 29.* 804/296-2181; FAX 804/972-6024; res: 800/476-1988. E-mail bhi@mild.cfw.com; web www.boarsheadinn.com. 173 rms. Apr-Nov: S, D $165-$205; each addl $10; suites $315; under 18 free; lower rates rest of yr. Crib free. TV; cable (premium), VCR avail. 3 pools; poolside serv, lifeguard. Supervised child's activities (mid-June-Labor Day); ages 5-16. Dining rm (see OLD MILL ROOM). Bar 2 pm-midnight; entertainment. Ck-out noon, ck-in 4 pm. Convention facilities. Business center. In-rm modem link. Valet serv Mon-Fri. Concierge. Gift shop. Free airport transportation. Lighted outdoor, indoor tennis, pro. 18-hole golf, driving range. Bicycles. Hot-air ballooning. Exercise equipt; sauna. Some refrigerators. Some private patios, balconies. 2 ponds with ducks, swans & geese. Local landmark; 1834 grist mill. Flower gardens. Local winery tours. Cr cds: A, C, D, DS, MC, V.

D 🏌 🏋 🎿 ⊠ ✈ ✈ ⊠ 🔥 SC ✈

★★★ **WINTERGREEN RESORT.** *Rte 664 (22958), W on US 250 to VA 151S, follow signs.* 804/325-2200; FAX 804/325-8004; res: 800/266-2444. E-mail info@wintergreenresort.com; web www.wintergreenresort.com. 315 kit units, 2-3 story. Late Dec-mid-Mar: S, D $165-$205; family, golf, ski, tennis plans; lower rates rest of yr. Crib avail. TV; cable (premium), VCR avail (movies). 6 pools, 1 indoor; wading pool, whirlpools, lifeguards. Playground. Supervised child's activities (ages 3-12). Restaurants, dining rm 7-10:30 am, 11 am-2 pm, 6-10 pm. Box lunches, snack bar, picnics. Bar. Ck-out noon, ck-in 4 pm. Convention facilities. Business servs avail. Shopping arcade. Airport, RR station transportation. Indoor tennis, pro. Two 18-hole golf courses, greens fee $48-$72, pro, putting green, driving range. Downhill ski on site. Rowboats, canoes. Nature programs. Bicycles. Entertainment, movies. Exercise rm. Massage. Some fireplaces. Private patios, balconies. Picnic tables. Cr cds: A, C, MC, V.

D 🏌 🏋 🎿 ⊠ 🏊 🏋 🚴 ⊠ 🔥 ⊠

Inns

★★ **200 SOUTH STREET INN.** *200 W South St (22902). 804/979-0200; FAX 804/979-4403.* E-mail clancyb@cfw.com; web www.southstreetinn.com. 20 rms, 4 story. S, D $105-$195; each addl $20; suites $195; under 16 free. Crib free. TV. Complimentary continental bkfst. Restaurant nearby. Ck-out 11 am, ck-in 2 pm. Business servs avail. Health club privileges. Some in-rm whirlpools, fireplaces. Built 1853; antiques. Cr cds: A, C, D, MC, V.

[D] [≈] [🔥] [SC]

★★★ **CLIFTON COUNTRY INN.** *1296 Clifton Inn Dr (22911), 5 mi E on I-64, exit 124, 2½ mi E on VA 250, S on VA 729. 804/971-1800; FAX 804/971-7098; res: 888/971-1800.* E-mail reserve@cstone.net; web www.cliftoninn.com. 14 rms, 1-2 story, 8 suites. No rm phones. Mar-June, Sept-Dec: S, D $150-$265; each addl $75-$133; suites $225-$315; wkends (2-day min); lower rates rest of yr. Complimentary full bkfst. Complimentary coffee in rms. Restaurant 6:30-11 pm. Rm serv. Ck-out 11 am, ck-in 3-5 pm. Business servs avail. Luggage handling. Lighted tennis. Downhill/x-country ski 18-20 mi. Pool; whirlpool. Lawn games. Fireplaces. 18th-century manor built in 1799. Totally nonsmoking. Cr cds: C, MC, V.

[D] [⚓] [≈] [🏊] [🔥]

★★★ **INN AT MONTICELLO.** *Rt 20 S; 1188 Scottsville Rd (22902), S on VA 20, past Constitution Rte, near Monticello and Ashlawn-Highlawn. 804/979-3593; FAX 804/296-1344.* E-mail innatmonticello@ mindspring.com; web www.innatmonticello.com. 5 rms, 2 story. No rm phones. S $110; D $125-$145; each addl $25; wkends (2-day min). Children over 12 yrs only. Complimentary full bkfst; afternoon refreshments. Ck-out 11 am, ck-in 3 pm. Business servs avail. Country manor (mid-1800s) filled with period antiques and reproductions. Totally nonsmoking. Cr cds: C, MC, V.

[≈] [🔥]

★★★ **KESWICK HALL AT MONTICELLO.** *701 Club View Dr (22947). 804/979-3440; FAX 804/977-4171; res: 800/274-5391.* E-mail keswick@keswick.com; web www.keswick.com. 48 rms, 1-3 story, 6 suites. Mar-June, Sept-Nov: S, D $250-$595; each addl $50; suites $595; golf plan; special events (2-day min); lower rates rest of yr. Children over 8 yrs only. TV; cable (premium); VCR avail. Indoor/outdoor pool; whirlpool. Complimentary full bkfst; afternoon refreshments. Restaurant (see ASHLEY ROOM). Rm serv 24 hrs. Ck-out noon, ck-in 3 pm. Concierge serv. Luggage handling. Business servs avail. Free airport, RR station transportation. Lighted tennis privileges, pro. 18-hole golf privileges, greens fee $85, pro, putting green, driving range. Exercise rm; sauna. Health club privileges. Game rm. Rec rm. Lawn games. Many balconies. Picnic tables. English country house (1912) on 600-acre estate; designs by Laura Ashley. Cr cds: A, C, D, MC, V.

[D] [⚓] [🏸] [🏊] [🧍] [≈] [🔥]

★★★ **PROSPECT HILL PLANTATION INN.** *2887 Poindexter Rd (23093), 15 mi E on I-64, exit 136, then right to Zion Crossroads, left onto US 250 1 mi E to VA 613, turn left and proceed 3 mi. 540/967-0844; FAX 540/967-0102; res: 800/277-0844.* Web www.innbook.com. 13 rms, 2 with shower only, 2 story, 3 suites. No rm phones. MAP: S $200-$280; D $285-$325; each addl $50; suites $325; under 5 free. Closed Dec 24 eve, Dec 25. Pool. Complimentary full bkfst; afternoon refreshments. Dining rm, 1 sitting: 7 pm; Fri, Sat 8 pm. Ck-out 11 am, ck-in 3 pm. Meeting rm. Business servs avail. Bellhop. Lawn games. Many refrigerators; some in-rm whirlpools. Plantation house built 1732; many antique furnishings; tree-shaded lawns, veranda, gazebo. Cr cds: C, DS, MC, V.

[D] [≈] [🔥] [SC]

★★★ **SILVER THATCH INN.** *3001 Hollymead Dr (22911), near Charlottesville-Albemarle Airport. 804/978-4686; FAX 804/973-6156.* Web www.silverthatch.com. 7 rms, 4 with shower only, 2 story. No rm phones. S, D $125-$160; each addl $25; 2-day min wkends Apr-May, Sept-Nov. Children over 5 yrs only. Pool. Complimentary bkfst; refreshments. Dining rm Tues-Sat 5:30-9 pm. Ck-out 11 am, ck-in 2 pm. Business servs avail. Orig-

inal building dates to 1780 (built by captured Hessian soldiers), additions in 1812 & 1937. Rms are named for Virginia-born presidents. Totally nonsmoking. Cr cds: A, C, D, MC, V.

[≈] [≈] [🔥]

★★★ **TRILLIUM HOUSE.** *Wintergreen Dr (22958), 23½ mi W on I-64 to exit 107, W on US 250, 14 mi S on VA 151, then 4½ mi W on VA 664 to entry gate on grounds of Wintergreen Resort. 804/325-9126; FAX 804/325-1099; res: 800/325-9126.* E-mail Innkeeper@trilliumhouse.com; web www.trilliumhouse.com. 12 rms, 2 story. S $95-$110; D $100-$115; each addl $35; suites $130-$160. Crib $10. TV avail; cable (premium). Pool privileges. Complimentary full bkfst. Dining rm 8-9 am; Fri, Sat 7:30 pm (prix fixe dinner). Serv bar. Ck-out noon, ck-in 3 pm. Business servs avail. In-rm modem link. Tennis privileges. Golf privileges. Downhill ski on site. Health club privileges. Cr cds: C, MC, V.

[D] [⛷] [🏃] [🏸] [≈] [🔥]

Restaurants

★★ **ABERDEEN BARN.** *2018 Holiday Dr (22901). 804/296-4630.* Hrs: 5 pm-midnight; Sun noon-10 pm. Closed Thanksgiving, Dec 25. Res accepted. Bar. Semi-a la carte: dinner $14.95-$32.95. Child's meals. Specializes in prime rib, steak, seafood. Entertainment. Open charcoal hearth. Family-owned. Cr cds: A, C, D, MC, V.

[D] [≈]

★★★ **ASHLEY ROOM.** *(See Keswick Hall) 804/979-3440.* E-mail keswick@keswick.com; web www.keswick.com. Hrs: noon-3 pm, 6-10 pm; Sun to 3 pm (brunch). Res required. Continental menu. Wine cellar. Semi-a la carte: lunch $10.25-$15.50. Complete meal: dinner $58. Sun brunch $25. Specializes in bass, beef, lamb. Own baking. Entertainment Fri-Sun. Valet parking. Elegant dining in Victorian setting; murals, fireplaces, antiques. Family-owned since 1919. Jacket. Totally nonsmoking. Cr cds: A, C, D, MC, V.

[D]

★★ **BERTINES NORTH CARIBBEAN.** *206 S Main St (22727), 27 mi N on US 29. 540/948-3463.* Hrs: 6-9 pm. Closed Tues-Thur; also Easter, Dec 25. Res accepted. Caribbean menu. Wine, beer. Semi-a la carte: dinner $6.85-$19.85. Specialties: jerk chicken, steak on a hot rock, blackened swordfish. Outdoor dining. Caribbean decor. Cr cds: C, D, DS, MC, V.

[D] [SC]

★ **BLUE RIDGE BREWING CO.** *709 W Main St (22903). 804/977-0017.* Hrs: 11:30 am-2 pm, 5-10 pm; Sat 11:30 am-3 pm, 5-10 pm. Sun brunch 11:30 am-3 pm. Closed July 4, Dec 25. Res accepted. Bar 5-10 pm. Semi-a la carte: lunch $4.25-$5.25, dinner $9.25-$15.25. Specialties: Caribbean marinated chicken, marinated NY strip steak, West Indian seafood saute. Within brewery in historic, turn-of-the-century building. Cr cds: A, C, D, MC, V.

[D] [≈]

★★ **C & O RESTAURANT.** *515 E Water St (22902), NW of I-64, exit VA 20N. 804/971-7044.* Hrs: 11:30-2 am; Sat, Sun from 5 pm. Closed some major hols. Res accepted. French, eclectic cuisine. Bar. A la carte entrees: lunch $5-$8, dinner $11-$24. Specializes in regional fresh cooking. Own baking. Cr cds: A, C, MC, V.

[≈]

★★ **CARMELLO'S.** *400 Emmet St (22903). 804/977-5200.* Hrs: 5-10 pm. Closed Jan 1, Dec 25. Res accepted. Northern Italian menu. Bar. Semi-a la carte: dinner $7.95-$16.95. Specializes in veal, pasta, chicken. Cr cds: A, C, D, DS, MC, V.

[D] [≈]

★★ **GOODFELLAS.** *1817 Emmet St (22901). 804/977-6738.* Hrs: 4-10 pm. Closed Mon; Thanksgiving, Dec 25. Res accepted. Bar. Semi-a la carte: dinner $6.95-$18.95. Child's meals. Specializes in pasta, steak, seafood. Own pastries. Dining area has dark woods, green and white accents. Cr cds: A, C, D, DS, MC, V.

D ⬛

★★ **HARDWARE STORE.** *316 E Main St (22902). 804/977-1518.* Hrs: 11 am-9 pm; Fri, Sat to 10 pm; winter hrs vary. Closed Sun; some major hols. Res accepted. Continental menu. Semi-a la carte: lunch $3.50-$7.50, dinner $6.75-$12.95. Specializes in burgers, chicken, sandwiches. Outdoor dining. In 1890s hardware store; vintage signs displayed. Cr cds: A, C, D, MC, V.

D ⬛

★★ **IVY INN.** *2244 Old Ivy Rd (22903). 804/977-1222.* E-mail ivyinn@aol.com. Hrs: 5-10 pm; Sun brunch 11 am-2 pm. Res required. Semi-a la carte: dinner $17-$26. Sun brunch $8-$13. Specializes in regional cuisine. Outdoor dining. Victorian-style house (1804); fireplaces. Totally nonsmoking. Cr cds: C, MC, V.

✓★★ **MAHARAJA INDIAN CUISINE RESTAURANT.** *139 Zan Rd (22901), off US 29N. 804/973-1110.* E-mail aadrad@aol.com. Hrs: noon-2 pm, 5-10 pm; Sat-Mon from 5 pm. Closed Jan 1, Dec 25. Res accepted. Indian menu. Bar. Buffet: lunch $6.99. A la carte entrees: dinner $11.90-$13.90. Specializes in vegetarian dishes, chicken, seafood. Own baking. Outdoor dining. Casual decor; Indian pictures, urns. Totally non-smoking. Cr cds: A, C, D, DS, MC, V.

D SC

★★★ **OLD MILL ROOM.** *(See Boar's Head Inn) 804/972-2230.* Hrs: 7-10 am, 11:30 am-1:30 pm, 6-9 pm; Sat, Sun 7-10:30 am, 11:30 am-1:30 pm; 6-9 pm; Sun brunch 11 am-2 pm. Res accepted. Contemporary Amer menu. Bar 4 pm-midnight. Extensive wine list. Semi-a la carte: bkfst $4.95-$9.50, lunch $6.50-$12, dinner $14-$24. Sun brunch $15.95. Child's meals. Specialties: bison carpaccio, red snapper, rack of lamb. Salad bar. Own baking. Jazz Tues-Sat evening; harpist Sun. Valet parking. Outdoor dining. 19th-century decor with mahogany woodwork, fireplaces, framed artwork. Cr cds: A, C, D, DS, MC, V.

D ⬛

★★ **OREGANO JOE'S.** *1252 Emmet St (22903). 804/971-9308.* Hrs: 11 am-10 pm; Fri to 11 pm; Sat 4-11 pm; Sun from 4 pm. Closed Dec 24, 25. Italian menu. Bar. Semi-a la carte: lunch $4.95-$7.25, dinner $5.95-$12.95. Child's meals. Specialties: veal Parmesan, veal piccata. Casual atmosphere. Cr cds: A, C, D, DS, MC, V.

D ⬛

★★ **ROCOCO'S.** *2001 Commonwealth Dr (22901). 804/971-7371.* Hrs: 11 am-10 pm; Fri to 11 pm; Sat 5-11 pm; Sun 10:30 am-3 pm, 5-10 pm. Closed Thanksgiving, Dec 25. Italian menu. Bar. Semi-a la carte: lunch $4.95-$7.95, dinner $7.95-$19.95. Sun brunch $5.95-$7.95. Child's meals. Specializes in pasta, pizza, mesquite-grilled seafood. Cr cds: A, C, DS, MC, V.

D ⬛

★★ **SCHNITZELHOUSE.** *2208 Fontaine Ave (22903). 804/293-7185.* Hrs: 5-9:30 pm. Closed Sun; major hols; 1 wk Jan, also 1 wk July. Res accepted. Swiss, German menu. Bar. Complete meals: dinner $7.95-$25. Child's meals. Specializes in veal. Parking. Alpine decor. Cr cds: A, C, MC, V.

Chesapeake (F-10)

(See also Norfolk, Portsmouth, Virginia Beach)

Pop 151,976 **Elev** 12 ft **Area Code** 757 **E-mail** pubcomm@city.chesapeake.va.us **Web** www.chesapeake.va.us
Information Public Communications Dept, 306 Cedar Rd, PO Box 15225, 23328; 757/382-6241

This city is located in the heart of the Hampton Roads area, at the northeastern boundary of the Great Dismal Swamp National Wildlife Refuge (see).

What to See and Do

Northwest River Park. Approx 8 mi of hiking/nature trails wind through this 763-acre city park. Fishing; boating, canoeing (ramp, rentals). Picnicking (shelters), playground, 9-hole miniature golf. Camping, tent & trailer sites (Apr-Dec, daily; fee; hookups, dump station). Shuttle tram. (Daily; closed Jan 1, Dec 25) Fragrance trail for the visually impaired. 1733 Indian Creek Rd, off Battlefield Blvd (VA 168). Phone 757/421-3145 or 757/421-7151. **Free**

Annual Event

Chesapeake Jubilee. City Park. National & regional entertainment, carnival, food booths, fireworks. 3rd wkend May.

Motels

★ **DAYS INN.** *1433 N Battlefield Blvd (23320). 757/547-9262; FAX 757/547-4334; res: 800/329-7466.* 90 rms, 2 story. May-Sept: S, D $55-$95; each addl $5; under 12 free; wkly rates (off season); lower rates rest of yr. TV; cable (premium), VCR avail (movies). Pool. Complimentary continental bkfst. Restaurant adj open 24 hrs. Ck-out 11 am. Business servs avail. Health club privileges. Some refrigerators, microwaves. Cr cds: A, C, D, DS, JCB, MC, V.

D ⬛ ⬛ ⬛ ⬛ SC

✓★★ **FAIRFIELD INN.** *1560 Cross Ways Blvd (23320). 757/420-1300; FAX 757/366-0608; res: 800/228-2800.* 113 rms, 3 story. May-Aug: S $52-$70; D $56-$72; under 18 free; higher rates special events. Crib free. TV; cable (premium). Pool. Complimentary continental bkfst. Restaurant nearby. Ck-out noon. Meeting rm. Business center. In-rm modem link. Exercise equipt. Cr cds: A, C, D, DS, MC, V.

D ⬛ ⬛ ⬛ ⬛ SC ⬛

✓★★ **HAMPTON INN.** *701a Woodlake Dr (23320). 757/420-1550; FAX 757/424-7414; res: 800/426-7866.* 119 rms, 4 story. Memorial Day-Labor Day: S, D $65-$85; higher rates summer wkends; lower rates rest of yr. Crib free. TV; cable (premium). Pool. Complimentary continental bkfst. Coffee in rms. Restaurant adj 6:30 am-10 pm. Ck-out noon. Meeting rm. Business servs avail. In-rm modem link. Health club privileges. Microwaves avail. Cr cds: A, C, D, DS, MC, V.

D ⬛ ⬛ ⬛ SC

✓★ **SUPER 8 MOTEL.** *3216 Churchland Blvd (23321). 757/686-8888; FAX 757/686-8888.* 59 rms, 3 story. May-Sept: S $44.88-$50.88; D $56.88-$68.88; each addl $6; suites $68.88-$76.88; under 16 free; wkly rates; higher rates special events; lower rates rest of yr. Crib free. Pet accepted, some restrictions. TV; cable (premium). Complimentary continental bkfst. Restaurant opp 6 am-midnight. Ck-out 11 am. Meeting rms. Business servs avail. In-rm modem link. Cr cds: A, C, D, DS, JCB, MC, V.

D ⬛ ⬛ ⬛ SC

★ **WELLESLEY INN.** *1750 Sara Dr (23320). 757/366-0100; FAX 757/366-0396; res: 800/444-8888.* 106 rms, 4 story. S $80-$110; D $85-$110; each addl $10; suites $100-$140; under 18 free. Crib free. Pet accepted; $5. TV; cable (premium). Pool. Complimentary continental bkfst. Coffee in rms. Restaurant adj 6:30 am-10:30 pm. Ck-out 11 am. Meeting rms. Business servs avail. In-rm modem link. Valet serv. Coin lndry. Health club privileges. Refrigerators, microwaves. Cr cds: A, C, D, DS, ER, JCB, MC, V.

D 🐾 ⌦ ⋈ 🔥 SC

Motor Hotels

★★ **COMFORT SUITES.** *1550 Crossways Blvd (23320). 757/420-1600; FAX 757/420-0099; res: 800/228-5050.* 123 suites, 3 story. Apr-Oct: S, D $65-$100; each addl $7; under 18 free; higher rates: Labor Day, Jubilee; lower rates rest of yr. Crib free. TV; cable (premium), VCR (movies $5). Pool; whirlpool. Complimentary continental bkfst. Coffee in rms. Ck-out 11 am. Meeting rm. Business servs avail. Exercise equipt; sauna. Refrigerators, microwaves. Cr cds: A, C, D, DS, JCB, MC, V.

D ⌦ 🏃 ⋈ 🔥 SC

★★★ **HOLIDAY INN.** *725 Woodlake Dr (23320), I-64 exit 289A, Greenbriar N. 757/523-1500; FAX 757/523-0683; res: 800/465-4329.* Web www.insiders.com/chesapeake-va/wwwads/holidaychesapk/index.htm. 230 units, 7 story. S, D $74-$109; each addl $10; suites $89-$119; under 18 free; higher rates: special events, hols, wkends. TV; cable (premium). Indoor pool; whirlpool. Coffee in rms. Restaurant 6:30 am-10:30 pm. Rm serv. Bar 11 am-midnight. Ck-out noon. Guest lndry. Meeting rms. Business servs avail. In-rm modem link. Bellhops. Sundries. Free airport transportation. Exercise equipt; sauna. Some refrigerators; microwaves avail. Cr cds: A, C, D, DS, JCB, MC, V.

D ⌦ 🏃 ⋈ 🔥 SC

Restaurants

✓ ★ **CARA'S RESTAURANT.** *123 N Battlefield Blvd (23320). 757/548-0006.* Hrs: 11:30 am-10 pm; Fri, Sat to 11:30 pm; Sun noon-9 pm. Closed Thanksgiving, Dec 25. Res accepted. Contemporary Amer menu. Bar. Semi-a la carte: lunch $4.95-$8.50, dinner $9-$16. Child's meals. Specialties: sesame seed chicken with Cumberland sauce, crab cakes, steak Chesapeake. Musicians Wed-Sat. Outdoor dining overlooking wetlands. Cr cds: C, D, DS, MC, V.

D ➟

★★ **KYOTO JAPANESE STEAK HOUSE.** *1412 Greenbriar Pkwy (23320), Suite 129, Crossways center. 757/420-0950.* Hrs: 11 am-2 pm, 5-10 pm; Sun 4-9 pm. Closed July 4, Thanksgiving, Dec 25. Res accepted. Japanese menu. Bar. Semi-a la carte: lunch $4.50-$13, dinner $8.95-$20.95. Child's meals. Specialties: teppanyaki, Kyoto special, sukiyaki. Sushi bar. Original Oriental art. Cr cds: A, C, D, DS, ER, MC, V.

D ➟

★★ **LOCKS POINTE.** *136 N Battlefield Blvd (23320). 757/547-9618.* Hrs: 11:30 am-3 pm, 5-10 pm; Sat from 5 pm; Sun 10:30 am-9 pm; Sun brunch to 3 pm. Closed Mon; Dec 24, 25. Res accepted. Bar 4 pm-1:30 am. Semi-a la carte: lunch $4.50-$6.95, dinner $8.95-$21.95. Sun brunch $7.95. Child's meals. Specializes in fresh seafood. Entertainment wkends. Outdoor dining. On Intracoastal Waterway; dockage. Cr cds: A, C, MC, V.

D ➟

★ **TABOO.** *1036 Volvo Pkwy (23320). 757/548-1996.* Hrs: 11 am-10 pm; Fri to 11 pm; Sat 4-11 pm. Closed Sun; most major hols. Res accepted. Bar. Semi-a la carte: lunch $5.95-$9.95, dinner $8.95-$19.95. Child's meals. Specializes in crab cakes, black Angus steaks, wood-fired pizzas. Own breads. Colorful, contemporary decor. Cr cds: A, C, DS, MC, V.

D SC

Chesapeake and Ohio Canal National Historical Park

(see Maryland)

Chincoteague (D-10)

Founded 1662 **Pop** 3,572 **Elev** 4 ft **Area Code** 757 **Zip** 23336
E-mail pony@shore.intercom.net **Web** www.chincoteaguechamber.com
Information Chamber of Commerce, 6733 Maddox Blvd, PO Box 258; 757/336-6161

Chincoteague oysters, wild ponies and good fishing are the stock in trade of this small island, connected with Chincoteague National Wildlife Refuge by a bridge and to the mainland by 10 miles of highway (VA 175, from US 13), causeways and bridges.

The oysters, many of them grown on the hard sand bottoms off Chincoteague from seed or small oysters brought from natural beds elsewhere, are among the best in the East. Clams and crabs are also plentiful. Commercial fishing has always been the main occupation of the islanders; but now, catering to those who fish for fun is also important economically.

Chincoteague's wild ponies are actually small horses; but when full-grown somewhat larger and more graceful than Shetlands. They are thought to be descended from horses that swam ashore from a wrecked Spanish galleon, their limited growth caused by generations of marsh-grass diet.

What to See and Do

⭐ **Assateague Island.** Accessible by bridge from town. Includes Chincoteague National Wildlife Refuge and Virginia unit of Assateague Island National Seashore. A 37-mi barrier island, Assateague's stretches of ocean and sand dunes, forest and marshes create a natural environment unusual on the East coast. Sika deer, a variety of wildlife and countless birds, including the peregrine falcon (autumn), can be found here, but wild ponies occasionally roaming the marshes offer the most exotic sight for visitors. Nature and auto trails; interpretive programs. Swimming (bathhouse), lifeguards in summer; surf-fishing. Camping; hike-in and canoe-in camp sites and day-use facilities. Picnicking permitted in designated areas; cars are limited to designated roads. No pets allowed. Obtain information at Toms Cove Visitor Center (spring-fall, daily) and at Chincoteague Refuge Visitor Center (daily). Access for disabled to all facilities. For further information contact the Chief of Interpretation, Assateague Island National Seashore, Rte 611, 7206 National Seashore Ln, Berlin, MD 21811; phone 410/641-1441 or 410/641-3030 (camping). (See OCEAN CITY, MD) Also contact Refuge Manager, Chincoteague National Wildlife Refuge, PO Box 62, 23336; 757/336-6122. Per car 4-7 day pass ¢¢

NASA Visitor Center. Showcases world of past, present and future flight. Features Moon rock brought from *Apollo 17* mission; scale models of space probes, satellites and aircraft; displays of current and future NASA projects; full-scale aircraft and rockets; films on space and aeronotics. Model rocket demonstrations (Mar-Nov, 1st Sat; June-Aug also 3rd Sat, weather permitting). Picnic facilities. Gift shop. (July 4-Labor Day, daily; Sept-Nov & Mar-June, Thurs-Mon; closed most hols) 5 mi S on VA 175 on Wallops Island. Phone 757/824-1344 or -2298. **Free**

Oyster and Maritime Museum of Chincoteague. Museum contains diorama, aquarium, shellfish industry interpretation. Also has the Wyle Maddox Library. (May-Aug, daily; Sept-Oct, Sat & Sun) 7125 Maddox Blvd. Phone 757/336-6117. ¢¢

Refuge Waterfowl Museum. Rotating displays of antique decoys and hunting tools. Decoy making and waterfowl art. (Daily; closed Dec 25) 7059 Maddox Blvd. Phone 757/336-5800. ¢¢

Sightseeing tours. Captain Barry's Back Bay Cruises & Expeditions. Include Bird Watch Cruise, Back Bay Expedition, Champagne Sunset Cruise, Moonlight Excursions and Fun Cruise. Trips vary from 1-4 hrs. Reservations recommended. Phone 757/336-6508 for information. ¢¢¢-¢¢¢¢¢

Annual Events

Easter Decoy & Art Festival. Easter wkend.

Chincoteague Power Boat Regatta. Late June.

Pony Penning. The "wild" ponies are rounded up on Assateague Island, then swim the inlet to Chincoteague, where foals are sold at auction before the ponies swim back to Assateague. Carnival amusements. Last Wed & Thurs July.

Oyster Festival. Columbus Day wkend.

Waterfowl Week. National Wildlife Refuge open to vehicles during peak migratory waterfowl populations. Late Nov.

Motels

★ **BIRCHWOOD MOTEL.** 3650 Main St (23336). 757/336-6133; FAX 757/336-6535; res: 800/411-5147. 41 rms. Apr-Nov: S, D $43-$89; each addl $5; kits. $58-$97. Closed rest of yr. Crib $5. TV; cable. Pool. Playground. Complimentary coffee in lobby. Ck-out 11 am. Coin lndry. Refrigerators. Cr cds: C, DS, MC, V.

D ⊠ ⊠ 🔥 SC

✓ ★ ★ **COMFORT INN.** 25287 Lankford Hwy (23418), Four Corner Plaza, at jct VA 179. 757/787-7787; FAX 757/787-4641. 80 units, 2 story, 10 suites. Mid-May-mid-Sept: S $62; D $69; each addl $5; suites $69-$83; under 18 free; lower rates rest of yr. Crib free. TV; cable. Pool. Complimentary continental bkfst. Restaurant adj 11 am-9:30 pm. Ck-out 11 am. Business servs avail. In-rm modem link. Exercise equipt. Refrigerators; microwaves avail. Cr cds: A, C, D, DS, ER, JCB, MC, V.

D ⊠ 🛂 ⊠ 🔥 SC

★ ★ **DRIFTWOOD MOTOR LODGE.** 7105 Maddox Blvd (23336). 757/336-6557; FAX 757/336-6558; res: 800/553-6117. E-mail driftwood@shore.intercom.net. 53 rms, 3 story. Mid-June-early Sept: S, D $86-$91; each addl $7; under 12 free; wkend, hol rates; lower rates rest of yr. Crib $6. TV; cable (premium). Pool. Complimentary coffee in lobby. Restaurant nearby. Ck-out 11 am. Business servs avail. Refrigerators. Private patios, balconies. Picnic tables. At entrance to Assateague Natl Seashore. Cr cds: A, C, D, DS, MC, V.

D ⊠ ⊠ 🔥

★ ★ ★ **ISLAND MOTOR INN.** 4391 Main St (23336). 757/336-3141; FAX 757/336-1483; res: 800/832-2925. E-mail islmoinn@shore.intercom.net. 60 units, 3 story, 16 suites. Mid-June-Labor Day: S, D $92-$150; suites $133-$150; under 16 free; lower rates rest of yr. Crib $5. TV; cable (premium). 2 pools, 1 indoor; whirlpool. Restaurant 6:30-11:30 am. Rm serv. Ck-out 11 am. Guest lndry. Meeting rms. Business servs avail. In-rm modem link. Sundries. Exercise rm. Refrigerators. Bathrm phone in suites. Balconies. Picnic tables, grills. On bay. Cr cds: A, C, D, DS, MC, V.

D 🛂 ⊠ 🛂 ⊠ 🔥 SC

★ **LIGHTHOUSE INN.** 4218 Main St N (23336). 757/336-5091; res: 800/505-5257. 17 rms, 1-2 story. June-Aug: S, D $59-$75; each addl $6; min stays hols, special events; lower rates rest of yr. Crib $6. TV; cable. Pool; whirlpool. Complimentary coffee in rms. Restaurant nearby. Ck-out 11 am. Health club privileges. Refrigerators, microwaves. Picnic tables, grill. Cr cds: C, MC, V.

⊠ ⊠ 🔥 SC

✓ ★ **MARINER MOTEL.** 6273 Maddox Blvd (23336). 757/336-6565; FAX 757/336-5351; res: 800/221-7490. E-mail motel@esva.net; web www.esva.net~motel/. 92 rms, 2 story. Mid-June-mid-Sept: S, D $54-$95; each addl $5; suites $95; under 12 free; wkly rates; hols 2-day min; higher rates special events; lower rates rest of yr. Closed Dec-Feb. Crib $5. TV; cable. Complimentary continental bkfst. Restaurant adj 5-10 pm. Ck-out

11 am. Meeting rms. Business servs avail. Sundries. Coin lndry. Pool. Playground. Many refrigerators; some microwaves. Picnic tables, grills. Cr cds: A, C, D, DS, MC, V.

⊠ ⊠ 🔥

★ ★ **REFUGE MOTOR INN.** 7058 Maddox Blvd (23336). 757/336-5511; FAX 757/336-6134; res: 888/673-3843; res: 888/257-0038. E-mail refugeinn@mailhost.esva.net; web www.chincoteaguechamber.com. 70 units, 2 story, 2 cottages. June-Aug: S, D $88-$103; each addl $5-$8; under 12 free; higher rates special events; lower rates rest of yr. Crib $5. TV; cable. Indoor/outdoor pool; whirlpool. Complimentary coffee in lobby. Ck-out 11 am. Coin lndry. Business servs avail. Gift shop. Bicycle rentals. Exercise equipt; sauna. Refrigerators; some in-rm whirlpools. Picnic tables, grill. Near wildlife refuge. Chincoteague ponies on grounds. Cr cds: A, C, D, DS, MC, V.

D ⊠ 🛂 ⊠ 🔥

★ **SEA SHELL MOTEL.** 3720 Willow St (23336). 757/336-6589; FAX 757/336-0641. 46 rms, 1-2 story. Mid-June-early Sept: S, D $66-$74; each addl $4; suites, kit cottages $550-$600/wk; 2-day min wkends, 3-day min hols; lower rates Apr-mid-June, mid-Sept-Oct, Thanksgiving. Closed rest of yr. Crib $3. TV; cable. Pool. Complimentary coffee in rms. Restaurant nearby. Ck-out 11 am. Business servs avail. Refrigerators; microwaves avail. Picnic tables. Cr cds: A, C, DS, MC, V.

⊠ ⊠ 🔥

✓ ★ **SUNRISE MOTOR INN.** 4491 Chicken City Rd (23336), ½ blk S of Maddox Blvd. 757/336-6671; FAX 757/336-1226; res: 800/673-5211. 24 units, 2 kits. Mid-June-early Sept: S $66; D $70; each addl $5; kit units $540-$575/wk; under 12 free; lower rates mid-Mar-mid-June, early Sept-Nov. Closed rest of yr. Crib free. TV; cable. Pool. Playground. Complimentary coffee in lobby. Restaurant nearby. Ck-out 11 am. Business servs avail. Refrigerators. Picnic tables, grills. Cr cds: A, C, D, DS, MC, V.

D ⊠ 🔥

★ ★ **WATERSIDE MOTOR INN.** 3761 S Main St (23336). 757/336-3434; FAX 757/336-1878. Web www.intercom.net/local/chincoteague/hot/water.html. 45 rms, 3 story. Mid-June-mid-Sept (2-day min): S, D $95-$150; each addl $5; suites (3-day min) $155; under 12 free; lower rates rest of yr. Crib $5. TV; cable (premium). Heated pool; whirlpool. Complimentary coffee in rms. Restaurant nearby. Ck-out 11 am. Coin lndry. Business servs avail. Sundries. Tennis. Exercise equipt. Refrigerators; microwaves avail. Balconies. Picnic tables, grills. On saltwater river; marina. Cr cds: A, C, D, DS, MC, V.

D 🛂 🛂 ⊠ 🛂 ⊠ 🔥

Inns

★ ★ ★ **CEDAR GABLES SEASIDE INN.** 6095 Hopkins Ln (23336). 757/336-6860; FAX 757/336-1291; res: 888/491-2944. E-mail cdrgbl@shore.intercom.net; web www.intercom.net/user/cdrgbl. 4 rms, 3 story, 2 suites. Memorial Day-Labor Day: S, D $150-$175; each addl $25; suites $175; wkends 2-day min, hols 3-day min; lower rates rest of yr. Children over 14 yrs only. TV; cable (premium), VCR (movies). Complimentary full bkfst; refreshments. Complimentary coffee in rms. Ck-out 11 am, ck-in 3 pm. Business servs avail. In-rm modem link. Luggage handling. Gift shop. Heated pool; whirlpool. Bathrm phones, in-rm whirlpools, refrigerators, balconies. Many balconies. Picnic tables, grills. On channel. Contemporary seaside location. Cr cds: A, C, DS, MC, V.

🛂 ⊠ ⊠ 🔥 SC

★ ★ ★ **CHANNEL BASS INN.** 6228 Church St (23336). 757/336-6148; FAX 757/336-0600; res: 800/249-0818. E-mail msmolly@shore.intercom.net. 6 rms, 3 story. June-Sept: S, D $99-$175; suites $175; wkly rates; lower rates mid-Mar-May, Oct, Dec. Closed rest of yr. Children over 8 yrs only. Complimentary full bkfst; afternoon refreshments. Ck-out 11 am, ck-in 2 pm. Built 1892. Assateague Wildlife Refuge nearby. Totally nonsmoking. Cr cds: A, C, MC, V.

⊠ 🔥 SC

★★ **MISS MOLLYS INN.** 4141 Main St (23336). 757/336-6686; FAX 757/336-0600; res: 800/221-5620. E-mail msmolly@shore.intercom.net. 7 rms, 2 share bath, 3 story. Memorial Day-Sept: S $89-$145; D $99-$155; each addl $20; lower rates Mar-late May, Oct-Dec. Closed rest of yr. Children over 8 yrs only wkends. Complimentary full bkfst; afternoon refreshments. Restaurant nearby. Ck-out 11 am, ck-in 2 pm. Business servs avail. Near saltwater bay. In historic building (1886); library, sitting rm; antiques. Marguerite Henry stayed here while writing *Misty of Chincoteague*. Cr cds: A, C, DS, MC, V.

⬜ 🔥

✓★★ **SPINNING WHEEL BED & BREAKFAST.** 31 N St (23417), 32 mi S on US 13, 1 mi W of US 13 on VA 179. 757/787-7311; FAX 757/787-8555. E-mail evergreen@esva.net. 5 rms, all with shower only, 3 story. No rm phones. S, D $75-$95; each addl $10. Closed Nov-Mar. Children over 12 yrs only. Complimentary full bkfst. Ck-out 11 am, ck-in 3 pm. Luggage handling. 18-hole golf privileges, pro, putting green, driving range. Built in 1890s. Folk Victorian inn; antiques. Cr cds: C, DS, MC, V.

🧑 🔥 🦮

★★★ **THE GARDEN & THE SEA INN.** 4188 Nelson Rd (23415), 12 mi NW via VA 175 to US 13, then N to VA 710 (Nelson Rd). 757/824-0672; res: 800/824-0672. E-mail baker@shore.intercom.net; web www.gardenandseainn.com. 6 rms in 2 bldgs. No rm phones. July-Sept: D $75-$165; under 6 free; wkends (2-day min); wkday rates; lower rates mid-Mar-June, Oct-Nov. Closed rest of yr. Pet accepted. Complimentary continental bkfst; afternoon refreshments. Restaurant (see THE GARDEN & THE SEA INN). Ck-out 11 am, ck-in 3 pm. Business servs avail. Luggage handling. Concierge serv. Some in-rm whirlpools. Patio and garden. Built as Bloxom's Tavern (1802) and adj farmhouse. Cr cds: A, C, DS, MC, V.

⬜ 🏖 ⬜ 🔥 🦮

✓★★ **WATSON HOUSE.** 4240 Main St (23336). 757/336-1564; FAX 757/336-5776; res: 800/336-6787. Web www.chincoteague.com/bb/watson. 6 rms, 5 with shower only, 2 story. No rm phones. Memorial Day-Labor Day: S $79-$99; D $89-$109; each addl $15; higher rates: wkends (2-day min), hols (3-day min); lower rates Mar-late May, early Sept-Thanksgiving. Closed rest of yr. Children over 9 yrs only. Complimentary full bkfst; afternoon refreshments. Restaurant nearby. Ck-out 11 am, ck-in 2 pm. Business servs avail. Bicycles. Health club privileges. Victorian residence (1874). Totally nonsmoking. Cr cds: C, MC, V.

⬜ 🦮

Restaurants

★★ **BEACHWAY.** 6455 Maddox Blvd (23336). 757/336-5590. Hrs: 4-10 pm; Fri-Sun from 8 am. Closed Jan-Mar; also Mon-Wed Apr-May. Res accepted. Continental menu. Serv bar. Semi-a la carte: bkfst $3.25-$7.95, lunch $3.95-$8.95, dinner $9.95-$24.95. Child's meals. Specializes in steak, seafood, pasta. Pianist Fri-Sun. Fireplace, solarium. Totally nonsmoking. Cr cds: A, C, D, DS, MC, V.

⬜ SC

✓★ **DON'S SEAFOOD.** 4113 Main St (23336). 757/336-5715. E-mail go2dons@shore.intercom.com. Hrs: 7 am-9 pm. Closed mid-Jan-late Mar. Bar 10 am-10 pm. Semi-a la carte: bkfst $2.95-$3.95, lunch $3.95-$4.95, dinner $9.95-$15.95. Child's meals. Specialties: crab cakes, crab imperial, flounder. Salad bar. Entertainment Wed, Fri, Sat in summer. Parking. View of channel. Family-owned since 1973. Cr cds: C, D, DS, MC, V.

⬜ ⊒

✓★ **LANDMARK CRAB HOUSE.** 6162 N Main St (23336). 757/336-5552. Hrs: 5-10 pm; early-bird dinner 4:30-6 pm. Closed Mon (Sept-May); also Dec 25. Res required Fri, Sat. Seafood menu. Bar to 2 am. Semi-a la carte: dinner $10.95-$17.95. Child's meals. Specializes in seafood, steaks. Salad bar. Piano bar Fri, Sat. Parking. Outdoor dining. On waterfront. Cr cds: A, C, D, DS, MC, V.

⬜ ⊒ ♥

★★ **NONNIE'S RESTAURANT.** 3899 Main St (23336). 757/336-5822. Hrs: 6-9 pm. Closed Sun; also Dec-Easter. Italian, Amer menu. Wine, beer. Semi-a la carte: dinner $8.95-$20.95. Specializes in fresh seafood, pasta. In converted bayside cottage. Cr cds: C, MC, V.

⊒

✓★ **STEAMERS SEAFOOD.** 6251 Maddox Blvd (23336). 757/336-5478. Hrs: 5-9 pm. Closed Nov-Apr. Wine, beer. Semi-a la carte: dinner $10.95-$19.95. Child's meals. Specializes in steamed crabs & shrimp. Nautical theme. Cr cds: C, D, DS, MC, V.

⬜ ⊒

★★★ **THE GARDEN & THE SEA INN.** (See The Garden & The Sea Inn) 757/824-0672. Hrs: 6-9 pm. Closed Mon-Wed; also Dec-Mar. Res accepted. Wine list. A la carte entrees: dinner $14.75-$23. Complete meals: dinner $27.50-$33. Specializes in Northern French cuisine, seafood. Intimate dining rm in historic country inn. Cr cds: A, C, DS, MC, V.

⬜

Clarksville (F-7)

(See also South Boston, South Hill)

Pop 1,243 **Elev** 359 ft **Area Code** 804 **Zip** 23927 **E-mail** clarksville@kerrlake.com **Web** www.kerrlake.com/chamber

Information Clarksville Lake Country Chamber of Commerce, 105 2nd St, PO Box 1017; 804/374-2436

What to See and Do

Occoneechee State Park. Approx 2,700 acres under development; long shoreline on John H. Kerr Reservoir (Buggs Island Lake). Fishing; boat launching. Hiking. Picnic shelters. Tent and trailer sites (hookups, season varies). Amphitheater; interpretive programs. Standard fees. (Daily) 1½ mi E on US 58. Phone 804/374-2210.

Prestwould (1795). Manor house built by Sir Peyton Skipwith; rare French scenic wallpaper; original and period furnishings; restored gardens. (May-Sept, daily; Oct, wkends; rest of yr, by appt) 2 mi N on US 15. Phone 804/374-8672. ¢¢

Annual Events

Native American Heritage Festival and Powwow. Occoneechee State Park. Native American music, dances, crafts. Phone 804/374-2436. 2nd wkend May.

Virginia Lake Festival. Juried arts & crafts show, beach music, dancers, gymnasts. Fun Run, antique car show, sailboat race, hot air balloons. Food vendors. Phone 804/374-2436. 3rd wkend July.

Motels

✓★ **LAKE MOTEL.** 101 Virginia Ave (23927). 804/374-5500; FAX 804/374-0108. E-mail conrad@gc.net; web www.conradusa.com/lakemotel. 84 rms, 2 story, 3 suites. Mid-May-mid-Sept: S, D $53-$68; each addl $5; suites $65-$90; under 12 free; lower rates rest of yr. Pet accepted. TV; cable. Pool. Restaurant adj 6 am-10 pm. Bar 5 pm-1 am. Ck-out 11 am. Meeting rm. Business servs avail. Free airport transportation. Refrigerators avail. Picnic tables, grills. On lake; swimming. Cr cds: A, C, MC, V.

⬜ 🏖 🛶 🛏 🔥 SC

✓★★ **QUALITY INN ON THE LAKE.** *103 2nd St (23927). 804/374-5023; FAX 804/374-7909; res: 800/228-5151.* 50 rms, 2 story, 8 suites. Feb-Oct: S, D $69-$79; each addl $5; suites $79-$95; under 18 free; wkends, hols (2-3 days min); higher rates lake festival; lower rates rest of yr. Crib $5. Pet accepted; $10. TV; cable (premium). Complimentary continental bkfst. Complimentary coffee in rms. Restaurant nearby. Ck-out 11 am. Meeting rms. Business servs avail. In-rm modem link. Valet serv. Sundries. Pool. Refrigerators, microwaves. On lake. Cr cds: A, C, D, DS, MC, V.

Clifton Forge (E-5)

(See also Covington, Lexington, Warm Springs)

Settled 1878 **Pop** 4,679 **Elev** 1,079 ft **Area Code** 540 **Zip** 24422
E-mail ahchamber@aol.com **Web** www.chv.va/alleghanyhighland/
Information Alleghany Highlands Chamber of Commerce, 501 E Ridgeway St; 540/862-4969

The town, named after a tilt-hammer forge that operated profitably for almost a hundred years, is at the southern tip of the Shenadoah Valley just west of the Blue Ridge Parkway.

What to See and Do

C & O Historical Society Archives. Includes C & O Railroad artifacts, old blueprints for cars and engines, books, models, collection of photos. (Daily exc Sun; closed hols) 312 E Ridgeway St, opp terminal bldg. Phone 540/862-2210. **Free**

Douthat State Park. Nearly 4,500 acres, high in the Allegheny Mountains, with 50-acre lake. Swimming beach, bathhouse; trout fishing (fee/day); boating (Memorial Day-Labor Day; rentals, launching, electric motors only). Hiking, self-guided trails. Picnicking, restaurant, concession. Camping (fee), tent & trailer sites (Mar-Sept; no hookups); cabins (all yr). Visitor center, interpretive programs. Standard fees. (Daily) 8 mi N on VA 629. Phone 540/862-7200. **Free**

Iron Gate Gorge. Perpendicular walls of rock rise from banks of Jackson River. James River Div of C & O Railroad and US 220 pass through gorge. Restored chimney of old forge is here. 2 mi S on US 220.

Inn

★★ **LONGDALE INN.** *6209 Longdale Furnace Rd (24422), I-64 exit 35. 540/862-0892; FAX 540/862-3554.* 10 rms, 3 with shower only, 4 share bath, 3 story, 2 suites. No A/C. Rm phones avail. S, D $75-$95; each addl $25; suites $95-$120; wkly rates. Crib $25. Pet accepted. TV in common rm; VCR. Complimentary full bkfst. Ck-out 11 am, ck-in 3 pm. Business servs avail. Gift shop. X-country ski 2 mi. Playground. Game rm. Lawn games. Many fireplaces. Picnic tables, grills. Virginia countryside setting; Victorian inn built in 1873. Totally nonsmoking. Cr cds: A, C, DS, MC, V.

Colonial National Historical Park (E-9)

Made up of four independent areas—Cape Henry Memorial, Colonial Parkway, Jamestown (see all three) and Yorktown Battlefield (see YORKTOWN)—this is where America, as we know it, began. Jamestown, Yorktown and Williamsburg (not a National Park Service area) are connected by the Colonial Parkway. Each of these areas is described in this book under its own name. Abundant in natural as well as historical wealth, the park boundaries enclose more than 9,000 acres of forest woodlands, marshes, shorelines, fields and a large variety of wildlife.

Colonial Parkway (E-9)

(See also Colonial National Historical Park, Jamestown, Williamsburg, Yorktown)

The Colonial Parkway is a 23-mile link between the three towns that formed the "cradle of the nation"—Jamestown, Williamsburg and Yorktown. It starts at the Visitor Center at Jamestown, passes through Williamsburg (the Colonial Williamsburg Information Center is near north underpass entrance) and ends at the Visitor Center in Yorktown.

At turnouts and overlooks along the route, information signs note such historic spots as Glebeland, Kingsmill, Indian Field Creek, Powhatan's Village, Fusilier's Redoubt and others. A free picnic area is provided during the summer at Ringfield Plantation, midway between Williamsburg and Yorktown.

The parkway is free to private vehicles. Commercial vehicles are not permitted. Speed limit is 45 MPH. There are no service stations.

Covington (E-5)

(See also Clifton Forge, Hot Springs)

Founded 1833 **Pop** 6,991 **Elev** 1,245 ft **Area Code** 540 **Zip** 24426
E-mail ahchamber@aol.com **Web** www.chv.va/alleghanyhighland/
Information Alleghany Highlands Chamber of Commerce, 501 E Ridgeway St, Clifton Forge 24422; 540/862-4969

Named for its oldest resident, Covington developed from a small village on the Jackson River. It is located in the western part of Virginia known as the Alleghany Highlands. The James River Ranger District office of the George Washington and Jefferson National Forests is located here.

What to See and Do

Humpback Bridge. Erected in 1857, this 100-ft-long structure was made of hand-hewn oak, held together with locust-wood pins. In use until 1929, it is now maintained as part of a 5-acre state highway wayside and is the only surviving curved-span covered bridge in the US. 3 mi W just off US 60/I-64.

Lake Moomaw. The 12-mi-long lake has a rugged shoreline of more than 43 miles, set off by towering mountains. Surrounded by the Gathright Wildlife Management Area and portions of the George Washington and Jefferson National Forests. Boating, swimming, fishing and waterskiing. Picnicking. Camping (fee). Visitor center. (Apr-Oct, daily) 13 mi N via US 220, VA 687, follow signs to Gathright Dam. Phone 540/962-2214. Per vehicle ¢

Motels

✓★★ **BEST WESTERN MOUNTAIN VIEW.** *820 E Madison St (24426), on US 60 at jct I-64 exit 16. 540/962-4951; FAX 540/965-5714; res: 800/465-4329.* 79 rms, 2 story. S $52-$69; D $66-$79; each addl $8; under 18 free. Crib free. Pet accepted; $10. TV; cable (premium). Pool; wading pool. Coffee in rms. Restaurant 6 am-2 pm, 5-10 pm. Rm serv. Ck-out 11 am. Meeting rms. Business servs avail. In-rm modem link. Bellhops. Valet serv. Some refrigerators. Cr cds: A, C, D, DS, ER, JCB, MC, V.

★★ **COMFORT INN.** *203 Interstate Dr (24426), I-64 exit 16.* 540/962-2141; FAX 540/965-0964; res: 800/228-5150 or 800/228-5160. 99 units, 2 story, 32 suites. S $67-$76; D $76-$86; each addl $9; suites $76-$86; under 18 free. Crib free. Pet accepted; $10. TV; cable (premium), VCR (movies $4). Pool; whirlpool. Restaurant 7 am-midnight. Bar 4 pm-2 am. Ck-out 11 am. Business servs avail. Guest lndry. Sundries. Some refrigerators. Cr cds: A, C, D, DS, ER, JCB, MC, V.

Inn

★★★ **MILTON HALL BED & BREAKFAST INN.** *207 Thorny Ln (24426).* 540/965-0196; FAX 540/962-8232. E-mail HEckert998@aol.com. 6 rms, 2 with shower only, 2 story, 1 suite. Some rm phones. S $75; D $85; each addl $10; suite $130-$140; under 10 free. Pet accepted. TV in some rms, sitting rm; cable (premium). Complimentary full bkfst. Ck-out noon, ck-in 2 pm. Lawn games. Historic country manor house (1874) on 44 acres adj George Washington National Forest. Cr cds: C, DS, MC, V.

Culpeper (D-7)

(See also Orange, Warrenton)

Founded 1748 **Pop** 8,581 **Elev** 430 ft **Area Code** 540 **Zip** 22701
Information Chamber of Commerce, 133 W Davis St; 540/825-8628

Volunteers from Culpeper, Fauquier and Orange Counties marched to Williamsburg in 1777, in answer to Governor Patrick Henry's call to arms. Their flag bore a coiled rattlesnake, with the legends "Don't Tread on Me" and "Liberty or Death."

In the winter of 1862-1863, churches, homes and vacant buildings in Culpeper were turned into hospitals for the wounded from the battles of Cedar Mountain, Kelly's Ford and Brandy Station. Later, the Union Army had headquarters here.

Today, Culpeper is a light-industry and trading center for a five-county area, with a healthy agriculture industry.

What to See and Do

Dominion Wine Cellars. Tours and tasting. (Daily; closed major hols) Winery Ave, 2 mi S on VA 3. Phone 540/825-8772. **Free**

Motels

★ **COMFORT INN.** *890 Willis Ln (22701).* 540/825-4900; FAX 540/825-4904; res: 800/228-5150. 49 rms, 2 story. Apr-Oct: S $65; D $74; each addl $7; under 18 free. Crib free. Pet accepted, some restrictions; $5. TV; cable (premium). Pool. Complimentary continental bkfst. Complimentary coffee in rms. Ck-out 11 am. Business servs avail. In-rm modem link. Refrigerators, microwaves avail. Cr cds: A, C, D, DS, JCB, MC, V.

✓★★ **HOLIDAY INN.** *791 James Madison Rd S (22701), 2½ mi S on US 29.* 540/825-1253; FAX 540/825-7134; res: 800/465-4329. 159 rms, 2 story. S, D $74; under 19 free. Crib free. Pet accepted, some restrictions. TV; cable (premium). Pool; wading pool. Complimentary coffee in rms. Restaurant 6 am-2 pm, 5-10 pm. Rm serv. Bar 2 pm-12:30 am. Ck-out noon. Coin lndry. Meeting rms. Business servs avail. In-rm modem link. Valet serv. Sundries. Refrigerators avail. Cr cds: A, C, D, DS, JCB, MC, V.

Inn

★★★ **FOUNTAIN HALL BED & BREAKFAST.** *609 S East St (22701).* 540/825-8200; FAX 540/825-7716; res: 800/298-4748. E-mail fhbnb@aol.com; web www.fountainhall.com. 6 rms, 2 story, 2 suites. S, D $85-$150; suites $150; Oct, some hols (2-day min). Crib $10. TV; cable (premium), VCR in common rm. Complimentary continental bkfst; afternoon refreshments. Ck-out 11 am, ck-in 2 pm. Business servs avail. In-rm modem link. Health club privileges. Lawn games. Some fireplaces, in-rm whirlpools. Balconies. Picnic tables. Colonial-Revival house (1859). Totally nonsmoking. Cr cds: A, C, D, DS, MC, V.

Guest Ranch

★★ **GRAVES' MOUNTAIN LODGE.** *VA 670 (22743), 20 mi W via US 29, VA 609 & VA 231 to VA 670.* 540/923-4231; FAX 540/923-4312. Web www.gravesmountain.com. 40 rms, 13 cottages, 8 kits. AP, mid-Mar-Nov: S $57-$92; D $65-$98/person; kit cottages $110-$230; higher rates Oct. Closed rest of yr. Crib free. Pet accepted. Pool; wading pool, lifeguard. Playground. Dining rm (public by res) 8:30-9:30 am, 12:30-1:30 pm, 6:30-7:30 pm. Box lunches. Ck-out 11 am, ck-in 3 pm. Coin lndry. Grocery ¼ mi. Meeting rms. Business servs avail. Tennis. Golf privileges, greens fee $45. Lawn games. Rec rm. Some fireplaces; refrigerators, microwaves avail. Picnic tables, grills. Cr cds: C, DS, MC, V.

Restaurant

★★★ **PRINCE MICHEL RESTAURANT.** *US 29S (22725), 10 mi S on US 29.* 540/547-9720. Web www.princemichel.com. Hrs: noon-2 pm, 6-9 pm; Sun 11 am-2:30 pm. Closed Mon-Wed; most major hols; also Dec 25-mid-Jan, mid-June-mid-July. Res accepted. French menu. Serv bar. Wine list. Complete meal: lunch $25-$35; dinner $70, Sat $80. Specialties: venison in red wine sauce, medallions of lamb, hot foie gras with apples. Outdoor dining. Parking. Located at vineyard. Cr cds: A, C, MC, V.

Danville (F-6)

(See also Martinsville, South Boston)

Founded 1792 **Pop** 53,056 **Elev** 500 ft **Area Code** 804
E-mail danchamb@gamewood.net **Web** www.danvillechamber.com
Information Danville Area Chamber of Commerce, 635 Main St, PO Box 1538, 24543; 804/793-5422

This textile and tobacco center blends the leisurely pace of the Old South with the modern tempo of industry. It is one of the nation's largest bright-leaf tobacco auction markets. Dan River Inc houses the largest single-unit textile mill in the world. Other major industries are located here. Nancy Langhorne, Viscountess Astor, the first woman to sit in the British House of Commons, was born in Danville in 1879.

What to See and Do

Chatham. Founded in 1777, this county seat of Pittsylvania County has many historically interesting houses, schools and public buildings: Hargrave Military Academy (1909) with the Owen Cheatham Chapel and Yesteryear Hall (museum); Chatham Hall (1894) with Renaissance Chapel, stained-glass windows of women, and St Francis mural in Commons Building; Old Clerk's Office (1813) restored as museum; Courthouse (1853) in Greek-revival style with delicate plaster ceiling frescoes and portraits; Emmanuel Episcopal Church (1844) with Gothic interior and signed Tiffany windows; Sims-Mitchell House (1860s). Also of interest are the Educational and Cultural Center with planetarium and museum; antique shops, restaurants, trolley diners and the many private houses, several of which offer overnight accommodations. 17 mi N via US 29. Self-guided walking tour information for town and county may be obtained at the Chamber of Commerce, 38 Main St, Chatham 24531; phone 804/432-1650.

Danville Museum of Fine Arts and History. Home of Major W.T. Sutherlin; built 1857. President Jefferson Davis and his cabinet fled to Danville after receiving news of General Lee's retreat from Richmond. It was during this time that the Sutherlin mansion served as the last capitol of the Confederacy. Victorian restoration in historical section of house (parlor, library and Davis bedrm). Rotating art exhibits by national and regional artists. (Tues-Fri, also Sat & Sun afternoons; closed major hols, also Dec 24-Jan 2) 975 Main St. Phone 804/793-5644.   **Free**

Danville Science Center. Hands-on museum for the entire family. Located in a restored Victorian train station. (Daily; closed Thanksgiving, Dec 25) 677 Craghead St. Phone 804/791-5160.   ¢¢

Tobacco auctions. Several huge warehouses ring with the chants of tobacco auctioneers. (Aug-early-Nov, Mon-Thurs; closed Labor Day, Columbus Day, Veterans Day) Phone 804/793-5422.   **Free**

"Wreck of the Old 97" Marker. Site of celebrated train wreck (Sept 27, 1903), made famous by a folk song. On Riverside Dr (US 58) between N Main & Locust Ln overpass.

Annual Events

Festival in the Park. Arts, crafts, entertainment. Phone 804/799-5200. 3rd wkend May.

Danville Harvest Jubilee. Celebration of tobacco harvest season. Phone 804/799-5200. Mid-Sept.

Motels

★★ **HOLIDAY INN EXPRESS.** *2121 Riverside Dr (24540). 804/793-4000; FAX 804/799-5516; res: 800/528-1234.* 98 rms, 3 story. S $58-$60; D $64-$66; each addl $6; under 16 free. Crib free. TV; cable (premium). Pool. Complimentary continental bkfst. Restaurant adj 6 am-10 pm. Ck-out noon. Meeting rm. Business servs avail. Health club privileges. Golf privileges. Bathrm phones; some refrigerators. Deck overlooking river. Cr cds: A, C, D, DS, MC, V.

D ⚓ 🍴 ≈ ⊠ 🔥 SC

✓★ **INNKEEPER MOTOR LODGE.** *3020 Riverside Dr (24541). 804/799-1202; FAX 804/799-9672; res: 800/822-9899.* 118 rms, 2 story. S $40.99-$52.99; D $50.99-$70.99; each addl $5. Crib free. TV; cable (premium). Pool; whirlpool. Complimentary continental bkfst. Restaurant adj 6 am-midnight. Ck-out noon. Business servs avail. Health club privileges. Cr cds: A, C, D, DS, MC, V.

D ≈ ⊠ 🔥 SC

★ **STRATFORD INN.** *2500 Riverside Dr (24540). 804/793-2500; FAX 804/793-6960.* 151 rms, 2 story. S, D $58-$75; each addl $7; suites $93-$165; under 18 free. Crib free. Pet accepted. TV; cable (premium). Heated pool; wading pool, whirlpool. Complimentary full bkfst. Restaurant 6 am-2 pm, 5-10 pm. Rm serv. Bar to midnight. Ck-out noon. Coin lndry. Meeting rms. Business servs avail. In-rm modem link. Valet serv. Sundries. Exercise equipt. Health club privileges. Cr cds: A, C, D, DS, MC, V.

D ✋ ≈ ⊠ 🔥 SC

Motor Hotel

★★ **HOWARD JOHNSON HOTEL.** *100 Tower Dr (24543), at jct US 29N & US 58, adj Piedmont Mall. 804/793-2000; FAX 804/792-4621; res: 800/446-4656.* 118 rms, 6 story, 20 suites. S $69-$74; D $77-$82; each addl $8; suites $89-$97; under 18 free. Crib avail. TV; cable (premium). Pool. Coffee in rms. Restaurant 6:30 am-midnight. Rm serv. Bar from 11 am. Ck-out noon. Coin lndry. Meeting rms. Business servs avail. Valet serv. Health club privileges. Cr cds: A, C, D, DS, JCB, MC, V.

D ≈ ⊠ 🔥 SC

Dulles Intl Airport Area (C-8)

(See also Fairfax)

Services and Information

Information: 703/419-8000.

Lost and Found: 703/572-2954.

Weather: 703/260-0307.

Airlines: Aeroflot, Air Canada, Air France, All Nippon, American, ANA, British Airways, Continental, Continental Express, Delta, Delta Connection, Japan Airlines, KLM, Lufthansa, Northwest, Qantas, Saudi Arabia Airways, Swissair, TACA, Transbrasil, TWA, United, United Express, USAir, Western Pacific.

What to See and Do

Reston Town Center. A 20-acre urban development incorporating elements of a traditional town square. Includes more than 50 retail shops and restaurants, a 13-screen movie theater complex, office space and a 514-rm hotel. (See ANNUAL and SEASONAL EVENTS) Adj Dulles Toll Rd (VA 267) at Reston Pkwy in Reston. Phone 703/709-8500.

Annual Events

Northern Virginia Fine Arts Festival. Reston Town Center (see). Art sale, children's activity area, barbecue. Mid-May.

Taste of the Town. Selected restaurants offer sample-size specialties. Last wkend June.

Oktoberfest. Reston Town Center (see). Biergarten with authentic German music, food. Mid-Sept.

Seasonal Events

Summer Concerts. Reston Town Center (see). Sat evenings June-Aug; also Thurs evenings July.

Fountain Square Ice Rink. Reston Town Center (see). Outdoor public ice rink. Mid-Nov-mid-Mar.

Fountain Square Holiday Celebration. Reston Town Center (see). Choral groups, puppeteers, magicians, ice shows, dancers, parade. Thanksgiving-Dec 24.

Motels

★ **COMFORT INN DULLES INTL. AIRPORT.** *200 Elden St (20170), Dulles Toll Rd exit 12, then left on Baron Cameron Ave (VA 606). 703/437-7555; FAX 703/437-7572; res: 800/228-5160.* 103 rms, 3 story. S, D $119-$169; under 19 free. wkend plans. TV; cable (premium). Complimentary continental bkfst. Complimentary coffee in rms. Restaurant adj 11 am-10 pm. Ck-out 11 am. Meeting rm. Business servs avail. Valet serv. Free airport transportation. Exercise equipt. Refrigerators; microwaves avail. Cr cds: A, C, D, DS, ER, JCB, MC, V.

D 🧍 ✈ ⊠ 🔥 SC

★★★ **COURTYARD BY MARRIOTT.** *3935 Centerview Dr (20151), in Dulles Business Park. 703/709-7100; FAX 703/709-8672; res: 800/321-2211.* 149 rms, 3 story. S $105; D $125; suites $129; under 12 free; wkly rates; higher rates special events. Crib free. TV; cable (premium). Indoor pool; whirlpool, lifeguard. Complimentary coffee in rms. Restaurant 6-10 am; Sat, Sun 7 am-noon. Restaurant opp 11 am-midnight. Rm serv 5-10 pm. Ck-out noon. Coin lndry. Meeting rms. Business servs avail. In-rm modem link. Valet serv. Sundries. Free airport transportation. Exercise equipt. Microwaves avail. Balconies. Picnic tables. Cr cds: A, C, D, DS, MC, V.

D ≈ 🧍 ⊠ 🔥 SC

★★★ **COURTYARD BY MARRIOTT.** *533 Herndon Pkwy (22070), Dulles Toll Rd exit 11.* 703/478-9400; FAX 703/478-3628; res: 800/321-2211. Web www.courtyard.com/iadhc. 146 rms, 3 story. S $129; D $139; suites $149; under 16 free; wknd rates. Crib free. TV; cable (premium). Indoor pool; whirlpool, lifeguard. Complimentary coffee in rms. Restaurant 6-10 am, 5-10 pm; wkends 7-11 am, 5-10 pm. Bar 5-10 pm. Ck-out noon. Coin lndry. Meeting rms. Business servs avail. In-rm modem link. Sundries. Valet serv. Free airport transportation. Exercise equipt. Refrigerators, microwaves avail. Cr cds: A, C, D, DS, MC, V.

D 🏊 🏋 🏖 🔥 SC

★★ **HOLIDAY INN EXPRESS.** *485 Elden St (20170), Dulles Toll Rd exit 10, then E on Elden St.* 703/478-9777; FAX 703/471-4624; res: 800/465-4329. E-mail wasex@bfsaulco.com. 115 rms, 4 story. S, D $99-$129; each addl $6; under 19 free. Crib free. Pet accepted, some restrictions. TV; cable (premium). Complimentary continental bkfst. Complimentary coffee in rms. Restaurant nearby. Ck-out 11 am. Meeting rm. Business center. Valet serv. Free airport transportation. Exercise equipt. Refrigerators, microwaves avail. Cr cds: A, C, D, DS, JCB, MC, V.

D 🐕 🏋 🛫 🏖 🔥 SC 🚶

★★★ **RESIDENCE INN BY MARRIOTT.** *315 Elden St (20170), Dulles Toll Rd exit 12, then left on Baron Cameron Rd (VA 606).* 703/435-0044; FAX 703/437-4007; res: 800/331-3131. Web www.marriott.com. 168 kit units, 2 story. S, D $135-$174; wknd rates. Crib free. Pet accepted; $100 nonrefundable & $6/day. TV; cable (premium), VCR avail (movies). Pool; whirlpool, lifeguard. Playground. Complimentary continental bkfst. Complimentary coffee in rms. Restaurant opp 6:30 am-10 pm. Ck-out noon. Coin lndry. Business servs avail. In-rm modem link. Valet serv. Sundries. Lighted tennis. Health club privileges. Microwaves. Picnic tables, grills. Cr cds: A, C, D, DS, JCB, MC, V.

D 🐕 🏒 🏖 🔥 SC

Motor Hotels

✓ ★ **DAYS INN.** *2200 Centreville Rd (20170), 2 mi E on Dulles Toll Rd, exit 10.* 703/471-6700; FAX 703/742-8965; res: 800/329-7466. E-mail dullesdaysinn@daysinn.com; web www.shirenet.com\daysinn. 205 rms, 4 story. Apr-June, Sept-Oct: S, D $74-$139; each addl $10; under 18 free; wknd, monthly rates; lower rates rest of yr. Crib free. TV; cable (premium). Pool; whirlpool, lifeguard. Complimentary continental bkfst. Restaurant 6-1 am. Bar. Ck-out noon. Business servs avail. In-rm modem link. Bellhops. Sundries. Gift shop. Free airport transportation. Exercise equipt. Cr cds: A, C, D, DS, JCB, MC, V.

D 🏖 🏋 🛫 🏖 🔥 SC

★★★ **HOLIDAY INN DULLES AIRPORT.** *1000 Sully Rd (20166), Dulles Toll Rd exit 9B (US 28/Sully Rd), then 1 mi N.* 703/471-7411; FAX 703/709-0785; res: 800/465-4329. 296 rms, 2 story. S, D $160; suites $179-$209; each addl $10; under 18 free; wknd rates. Crib free. Pet accepted, some restrictions. TV; cable (premium). Indoor pool; whirlpool, lifeguard. Restaurant 6:30 am-10:30 pm. Rm serv to midnight. Bars 11-1:30 am, Sun to midnight; entertainment. Ck-out noon. Coin lndry. Meeting rms. Business center. In-rm modem link. Bellhops. Gift shop. Valet serv. Free airport transportation. Exercise equipt; sauna. Refrigerators, microwaves avail. Game rm. Cr cds: A, C, D, DS, JCB, MC, V.

D 🐕 🏖 🏋 🛫 🏖 🔥 SC 🚶

Hotels

★★★ **HYATT DULLES.** *2300 Dulles Corner Blvd (22071), Dulles Toll Rd exit 9A (VA 28/Sully Rd), then S, left on Frying Pan Rd, left on Horsepen Rd, then left on Dulles Corner Blvd.* 703/713-1234; FAX 703/713-3410; res: 800/223-1234. Web www.hyatt.com. 317 rms, 14 story. S $189; D $214, suites $300-$700; wkly, wknd rates. Crib free. TV; cable (premium), VCR avail. Indoor pool; whirlpool, lifeguard. Restaurant 6 am-

midnight. Bar from noon; pianist. Ck-out noon. Business center. In-rm modem link. Gift shop. Free airport transportation. Exercise equipt; sauna. Refrigerators, microwaves avail. Cr cds: A, C, D, DS, ER, JCB, MC, V.

D 🏊 🏋 🛫 🏖 🔥 SC 🚶

★★★ **HYATT REGENCY.** *1800 President's St (22190), Dulles Toll Rd Reston Pkwy exit 12, at Reston Town Center.* 703/709-1234; FAX 703/709-2291; res: 800/233-1234. Web www.hyatt.com. 514 rms, 12 story. S $215; D $235; each addl $25; suites $275-$550; under 18 free; wknd rates. Crib free. Garage parking; valet (fee). TV; cable (premium), VCR avail. Indoor pool; whirlpool, poolside serv, lifeguard. Restaurant (see MARKET STREET BAR & GRILL). Bar 11:30-2 am; entertainment Fri-Sun. Ck-out noon. Convention facilities. Business center. In-rm modem link. Concierge. Shopping arcade. Free airport transportation. Tennis privileges. Golf privileges. Exercise rm; sauna. Luxury level. Cr cds: A, C, D, DS, ER, JCB, MC, V.

D 🐕 🏖 🏋 🏖 🛫 🏖 🔥 SC 🚶

★★★ **MARRIOTT SUITES.** *13101 Worldgate Dr (20170), Dulles Toll Rd exit 10, in Worldgate Center.* 703/709-0400; FAX 703/709-0426; res: 800/228-9290. Web www.marriott.com. 253 suites, 11 story. S $175; D $190; under 18 free; wknd rates. Crib free. TV; cable (premium), VCR avail. Indoor/outdoor pool; whirlpool, lifeguard. Complimentary coffee in lobby. Restaurant 6:30 am-10:30 pm. Bar to 11 pm. Ck-out noon. Free guest lndry. Meeting rms. Business servs avail. In-rm modem link. Free garage parking. Free airport transportation. Exercise equipt; sauna. Health club privileges. Refrigerators, wet bars; microwaves avail. Cr cds: A, C, D, DS, ER, JCB, MC, V.

D 🏖 🏋 🛫 🏖 🔥 SC

★★★ **WASHINGTON DULLES AIRPORT MARRIOTT.** *45020 Aviation Dr (20166), Dulles Access Rd, at airport.* 703/471-9500; FAX 703/661-8714; res: 800/228-9290. Web www.marriott.com. 367 rms, 3 story. S $154; D $169; each addl $15; suites $275-$300; under 18 free; wknd plans. Crib free. TV; cable (premium), VCR avail. 2 pools, 1 indoor; whirlpool, poolside serv. Restaurant 6 am-midnight; Sat, Sun from 6:30 am. Bar 11:30-1 am. Ck-out noon. Coin lndry. Convention facilities. Business center. In-rm modem link. Concierge. Gift shop. Free airport transportation. Lighted tennis. Exercise equipt. Lawn games. Microwaves avail. Picnic area. On 21 acres with small lake; attractive landscaping. Luxury level. Cr cds: A, C, D, DS, ER, JCB, MC, V.

D 🏖 🏖 🏋 🛫 🏖 🔥 SC 🚶

Resort

★★★ **MARRIOTT'S CONFERENCE CENTER.** *14750 Conference Center Dr (22021), 8 mi S on VA 28.* 703/818-0300; FAX 703/818-3655; res: 800/635-5666; res: 800/635-5666. Web www.marriott.com. 340 rms, 4 story. S $195; D $215; each addl $20; suites $295-$695; under 12 free; MAP, AP avail; wknd rates. Crib free. Pet accepted, some restrictions; $50 deposit. TV; cable (premium), VCR avail. 2 pools, 1 indoor; whirlpool, poolside serv, lifeguard. Complimentary coffee in lobby. Restaurant (see PALM COURT). Rm serv 6-1 am. Box lunches, picnics. Bar 11-1 am; entertainment. Ck-out 1 pm, ck-in 3 pm. Bellhops. Valet serv. Concierge. Gift shop. Convention facilities. Business center. In-rm modem link. Valet parking. Free airport transportation. Sports dir. Lighted tennis, pro. 18-hole golf, greens fee $85. Hiking. Bicycles. Lawn games. Basketball. Exercise rm; sauna, steam rm. Massage. Health club privileges. Minibars; some in-rm whirlpools; refrigerators avail. Balconies. Picnic tables. Cr cds: A, C, D, DS, JCB, MC, V.

D 🐕 🏖 🏖 🏋 🏖 🔥 SC 🚶

Restaurants

★★ **CLYDE'S.** *11905 Market St (20190), 4 mi E on Dulles Toll Rd, exit 12.* 703/787-6601. Hrs: 11 am-midnight; Fri, Sat to 1 am; Sun 10 am-10 pm; early-bird dinner Mon-Fri 4:30-6 pm; Sun brunch to 4 pm. Closed Dec 25. Contemporary Amer menu. Bar to 2 am. Semi-a la carte: lunch $4.95-$10.95, dinner $4.95-$18.50. Sun brunch $4.95-$10.95. Specializes in aged beef, fresh seafood, hamburgers. Own baking, ice cream. Outdoor dining. Contemporary pub decor; toys, art and artifacts reminiscent of youth. Cr cds: A, C, D, DS, MC, V.

★★ **FORTUNE.** *1428 N Point Village Ctr (20194), on VA 602 (Reston Pkwy).* 703/318-8898. Hrs: 11 am-10:30 pm; Fri, Sat to 11:30 pm. Res accepted; required Fri, Sat dinner. Chinese menu. Serv bar. A la carte entrees: lunch $1.95-$5.50, dinner $6.25-$20. Specializes in dim sum, seafood, traditional Hong Kong dishes. Chinese decor. Cr cds: A, C, DS, MC, V.

★★ **IL CIGNO RESTAURANT.** *1617 Washington Plz N (20190), in Lake Anne Shopping Center, off VA 606.* 703/471-0121. Hrs: 11:30 am-2:30 pm, 5:30-10 pm. Closed Sun (exc summer); most major hols. Res accepted; required Fri, Sat. Northern Italian menu. Bar. Semi-a la carte: lunch $8.95-$12.95, dinner 10.95-$18.95. Specializes in fish, veal, pasta. Own baking, pasta, ice cream. Outdoor dining overlooking Lake Anne. Split-level dining rm with original art. Cr cds: A, C, D, MC, V.

★★★ **MARKET STREET BAR & GRILL.** *(See Hyatt Regency)* 703/709-6262. Hrs: 6:30 am-2:30 pm, 5:30-10 pm; Fri, Sat to 10:30 pm; Sun to 9:30 pm. Res accepted; required Fri, Sat. Contemporary Amer, Asian menu. Bar. A la carte entrees: bkfst $4.50-$7.95, lunch $6.95-$14.95, dinner $13.75-$22.75. Sun brunch $17.95. Specializes in seasonal cuisine. Entertainment Fri-Sun. Valet parking. Outdoor dining. Bistro decor. Cr cds: A, C, D, DS, ER, JCB, MC, V.

★★★ **PALM COURT.** *(See Marriott's Conference Center)* 703/818-3522. Hrs: 7 am-2 pm, 6-10 pm; Sun brunch 10 am-2 pm. Res accepted; required Fri, Sat, Sun brunch. Continental menu. Bar 11-1 am. Semi-a la carte: bkfst $4.75-$9.95, lunch $6.95-$15.95. A la carte entrees: dinner $21-$29.95. Prix fixe (Mon-Sat): $40. Sun brunch $30. Child's meals. Specializes in fresh seafood, game. Pianist. Valet parking. Formal decor. Cr cds: A, C, D, DS, JCB, MC, V.

★★★ **RUSSIA HOUSE.** *790 Station St (20170), Dulles Toll Rd exit 10.* 703/787-8880. Hrs: 11:30 am-2:30 pm, 5:30-10 pm; Sat 5:30-10:30 pm; Sun 5-9 pm. Closed most major hols. Res accepted; required Fri, Sat. Continental, Russian menu. Bar. Wine list. Semi-a la carte: lunch $8-$12.95, dinner $14-$21.95. Complete meals (wkends): dinner $25-$45. Specializes in fresh seafood, beef, veal. Pianist, violinist Fri, Sat. Parking. Modern decor highlighted by Russian artwork. Cr cds: A, C, D, DS, MC, V.

✓★★ **SIAM ASIAN BISTRO.** *328 Elden St (20170), Dulles Toll Rd exit 11N.* 703/742-8881. Hrs: 11:30 am-10 pm; Fri to 10:30 pm; Sat noon-10:30 pm; Sun noon-9:30 pm; early-bird dinner Sun-Thurs 4:30-6:30 pm. Closed Dec 25. Res accepted; required Fri, Sat dinner. Asian, Thai menu. Bar. Semi-a la carte: lunch $6.95-$7.95, dinner $9.95-$12.95. Specialties: pad Thai, Thai curry. Own desserts. Outdoor dining. Contemporary Thai decor with light woods, etched glass. Cr cds: A, C, D, MC, V.

★★ **SWEETWATER TAVERN.** *14250 Sweetwater Ln (22020), 9 mi S on VA 28.* 703/449-1100. Hrs: 4:30-11 pm; Mon to 10 pm; Fri, Sat noon-1 am; Sun noon-10 pm; early-bird dinner Mon-Thurs to 6 pm. Closed Thanksgiving, Dec 25. Bar. Semi-a la carte: lunch $4.95-$9.95, dinner $4.95-$16.95. Child's meals. Specializes in hickory-fired Angus beef, fresh seafood, chops. Own baking. Microbrewery. Totally nonsmoking. Cr cds: A, C, MC, V.

✓★ **TORTILLA FACTORY.** *648 Elden St (20172), off Dulles Toll Rd exit 10, Pines Shopping Center.* 703/471-1156. E-mail tortfact@ aol.com. Hrs: 11 am-10 pm; Mon to 9 pm; Fri, Sat to 10:30 pm; Sun noon-

9 pm. Closed most major hols. Res accepted. Mexican menu. Serv bar. Semi-a la carte: lunch $4.75-$6.95, dinner $5-$11.25. Child's meals. Specialties: carne machaca, chimichangas. Own tortillas. Folk music Tues. Cr cds: A, C, D, DS, MC, V.

★ **WINFIELD'S.** *5127 Westfield Blvd (20120), 7 mi S on VA 28, in Sully Station Shopping Center.* 703/803-1040. Hrs: 11 am-midnight; Fri, Sat to 1:30 am; Sun to 9 pm. Closed major hols. Res accepted; required Fri, Sat dinner. Bar. Semi-a la carte: lunch $5.25-$8.50, dinner $7.95-$14.95; Child's meals. Specializes in fresh seafood, steaks. Outdoor dining. Sports bar; informal dining. Cr cds: A, C, D, MC, V.

Emporia (F-8)

Pop 5,306 **Elev** 110 ft **Area Code** 804 **Zip** 23847

Motels

★★ **BEST WESTERN INN.** *1100 W Atlantic St (23847).* 804/634-3200; FAX 804/634-5459; res: 800/528-1234. 99 rms, 2 story. Apr-Sept: S, D $45-$75; each addl $5; under 18 free; lower rates rest of yr. Crib free. Pet accepted. TV; cable (premium). Pool. Complimentary continental bkfst. Restaurant opp 6 am-10 pm. Ck-out 11 am. Meeting rms. Business servs avail. In-rm modem link. Exercise equipt. Some refrigerators, microwaves. Cr cds: A, C, D, DS, MC, V.

★★ **COMFORT INN.** *1411 Skippers Rd (23847), at I-95 exit 8.* 804/348-3282; FAX 804/348-3282; res: 800/228-5150. 96 rms, 2 story. S $48.95-$62.95; D $56.95-$62.95; each addl $4; family rates. Crib $2. Pet accepted. TV; cable (premium). Heated pool. Playground. Complimentary continental bkfst. Restaurant adj 6 am-11 pm; Fri, Sat 5 am-midnight. Business servs avail. In-rm modem link. Cr cds: A, C, D, DS, ER, MC, V.

✓★ **DAYS INN.** *921 W Atlantic St (23847).* 804/634-9481; FAX 804/348-0746; res: 800/329-7466. 122 rms, 2 story. June-Sept: S $45-$55; D $65-$75; each addl $6; under 18 free; lower rates rest of yr. Crib free. Pet accepted. TV; cable (premium). Complimentary full bkfst. Restaurant nearby. Ck-out noon. Business servs avail. Sundries. Coin lndry. Pool. Cr cds: A, C, D, DS, MC, V.

★★ **HAMPTON INN.** *1207 W Atlantic St (23847), off I-95 exit 11B.* 804/634-9200; FAX 804/348-0071; res: 800/426-7866. 115 rms, 2 story. S $59-$65; D $69-$77; under 18 free. Crib free. Pet accepted. TV; cable (premium). Pool. Complimentary continental bkfst. Coffee in rms. Restaurant nearby. Ck-out 11 am. Cr cds: A, C, D, DS, MC, V.

Fairfax (C-8)

(See also Alexandria, Arlington County, Falls Church, McLean; also see District of Columbia)

Pop 19,622 **Elev** 447 ft **Area Code** 703 **E-mail** cvbfceda@mindspring. com **Web** www.visitfairfax.org

Information Fairfax County Convention & Visitors Bureau, 8300 Boone Blvd, Suite 450, Tysons Corner-Vienna 22182; 703/790-3329, 703/550-2450 (visitor center) or 800/7-FAIRFAX

What to See and Do

County parks. For additional information, contact Fairfax County Park Authority, 12055 Government Center Pkwy, Ste 927, 22035; phone 703/324-8700.

Burke Lake. Consists of 888 acres. Fishing, boating (ramp, rentals). Picnicking, playground, concession; miniature train, carousel (summer, daily; early May & late Sept, wkends), 18-hole, par-3 golf course. Camping (May-Sept; 7-day limit). Beaver Cove Nature Trail; fitness trail. Fee for activities. (Daily) 6 mi S on VA 123, in Fairfax Station. Phone 703/323-6601. Day-use fee/vehicle (wkends & hols) ¢¢

Lake Fairfax. Pool; boat rentals, fishing. Picnicking; excursion boat, carousel; miniature train (late May-Labor Day, daily). Camping (Mar-Dec; 7-day limit; electric addl fee). Fee for activities. (Daily) On VA 606 near Leesburg Pike in Reston. Phone 703/471-5415. Nonresident day-use fee/vehicle (wkends & hols) ¢¢

George Mason University (1957). (24,000 students) State-supported, started as branch of University of Virginia. The Performing Arts Center features performances by world-renown performers Fenwick Library maintains the largest collection anywhere of material pertaining to the Federal Theatre Project of the 1930s. The Research Center for the Federal Theatre Project contains 7,000 scripts, including unpublished works by Arthur Miller, sets and costume designs and an oral history collection of interviews with former Federal Theatre personnel. (Mon-Fri; closed hols) 4400 University Dr. Phone 703/993-1000.

Regional parks. Contact Northern Virginia Regional Park Authority, 5400 Ox Rd, Fairfax Station 22039; phone 703/352-5900 or 703/352-3165 (TTY).

Algonkian. Located on the Potomac River, this 800-acre park offers swimming (Memorial Day-Labor Day, fee); fishing; boating (ramp); golf, miniature golf; picnicking; vacation cottages; meeting and reception areas. 6 mi NE on VA 123 to VA 7, then 9 mi NW to Cascades Pkwy N, then 3 mi N near Sterling. Phone 703/450-4655. **Free**

Bull Run. Consists of 5,000 acres. Themed swimming pool (Memorial Day-Labor Day, daily; fee). Camping (1-4 persons, fee; electricity avail; res accepted, phone 703/631-0550). Concession; picnicking, playground; mini-golf; Frisbee golf; public shooting center; nature trail. (Mid-Mar-Dec) From Beltway I-66W, exit at Centreville, W on US 29 3 mi to park sign. Phone 703/631-0550. Admission per vehicle (nonresidents only) ¢¢

Meadowlark Gardens. Lilac, wildflower, herb, hosta and landscaped gardens on 95 acres. Includes 3 ponds; water garden; gazebos; trails. Visitor center. (Daily) 9750 Meadowlark Gardens Ct, 6 mi N off VA 123. Phone 703/255-3631. **Free**

Sully (1794). Restored house of Richard Bland Lee, brother of General "Light Horse Harry" Lee; some original furnishings; kitchen-washhouse, log house store, smokehouse on grounds. Guided tours. (Daily exc Tues; closed Jan 1, Thanksgiving, Dec 25) 10 mi W on US 50, then N on VA 28 (Sully Rd), near Chantilly. Phone 703/437-1794. ¢¢

Annual Events

Mobil Invitational Track & Field Meet. George Mason University campus. Early Feb.

Antique Car Show. Sully. 400 antique cars, flea market and music. June.

Quilt Show. Sully. Quilts for sale, quilting demonstrations and antique quilts on display. Sept.

Seasonal Events

Wolf Trap Farm Park for the Performing Arts. In Vienna, 8 mi NE on VA 123, then W on US 7 to Towlston Rd (Trap Rd), then follow signs. Varied programs include ballet, musicals, opera, classical, jazz and folk music. Filene Center open theater seats 3,800 under cover and 3,000 on the lawn. Picnicking on grounds, all yr. Also free interpretive children's programs, July-Aug. For schedules and prices contact Wolf Trap Foundation, 1624 Trap Rd, Vienna 22182; 703/255-1900. Late May-Sept.

Barns of Wolf Trap Foundation. ¾ mi S of Wolf Trap Farm Park on Trap Rd. A 350-seat theater/conference center with chamber music, recitals, mime, jazz, theater and children's programs. For schedule contact the Barns, 1635 Trap Rd, Vienna 22182; 703/938-2404. Late Sept-early May.

Motels

★★★ **COURTYARD BY MARRIOTT.** *11220 Lee Jackson Memorial Hwy (22030), I-66, exit 57A. 703/273-6161; FAX 703/273-3505.* Web www.courtyard.com. 144 rms, 3 story. S, D $109-$119; suites $134-$154; under 13 free; package plans. Crib free. TV; cable (premium), VCR avail. Indoor pool; whirlpool, lifeguard. Complimentary coffee in rms. Restaurant 6:30-10 am; Sat 7-11 am; Sun 7 am-noon. Bar 5-10 pm. Ck-out noon. Coin lndry. Meeting rms. Business servs avail. In-rm modem link. Valet serv. Sundries. Exercise equipt. Health club privileges. Some refrigerators; microwaves avail. Private patios, balconies. Cr cds: A, C, D, DS, JCB, MC, V.

D ≈ 🏋 🛏 🔥 SC

★★ **HAMPTON INN.** *10860 Lee Jackson Memorial Hwy (22030). 703/385-2600; FAX 703/385-2742.* 86 rms, 5 story. S, D $82-$99; under 18 free. Crib free. TV; cable (premium). Complimentary continental bkfst. Complimentary coffee in rms. Restaurant adj 7 am-11 pm. Ck-out noon. Meeting rms. Business servs avail. In-rm modem link. Exercise equipt. Health club privileges. Some refrigerators, wet bars; microwaves avail. Cr cds: A, C, D, DS, MC, V.

D 🏋 🛏 🔥 SC

Motor Hotel

★★★ **COMFORT INN.** *11180 Main St (22030). 703/591-5900; FAX 703/273-7915; res: 800/228-5150; res: 800/223-1223.* 205 rms, 6 story, 90 kit units. Mid-Mar-mid-Nov: S, D $89-$109; kit units $89-$129; under 18 free; higher rates special events; lower rates rest of yr. Crib free. TV; cable (premium), VCR avail (movies). Complimentary continental bkfst. Complimentary coffee in rms. Restaurant 11 am-10 pm. Rm serv. Bar to 11 pm. Ck-out 11 am. Meeting rms. Business servs avail. Bellhops. Valet serv. Sundries. Gift shop. Coin lndry. Free airport, RR station transportation. Exercise equipt. 2 pools, 1 indoor; lifeguard. Game rm. Some in-rm whirlpools; microwaves avail. Cr cds: A, C, D, DS, JCB, MC, V.

D ≈ 🏋 🛏 🔥 SC

Hotels

★★★ **HOLIDAY INN.** *11787 Lee Jackson Memorial Hwy (22033), I-66, exit 57B. 703/352-2525; FAX 703/352-4471; res: 800/465-4329.* E-mail hifo@erols.com. 312 rms, 6 story. S, D $129-$149; each addl $10; under 19 free; package plans. Crib free. Pet accepted. TV; cable (premium), VCR avail. Indoor pool; lifeguard. Complimentary coffee in rms. Restaurant 6:30 am-midnight. Bar; entertainment. Ck-out noon. Coin lndry. Convention facilities. Business center. In-rm modem link. Concierge. Gift shop. Exercise equipt; sauna. Health club privileges. Game rm. Refrigerators avail. Balconies. Luxury level. Cr cds: A, C, D, DS, ER, JCB, MC, V.

D 🍴 ≈ 🏋 🛏 🔥 SC 🏋

★★★ **HYATT FAIR LAKES.** *12777 Fair Lakes Cir (22033), at I-66 exit 55B. 703/818-1234; FAX 703/818-3140; res: 800/233-1234.* 316 rms, 14 story. S, D $169-$199; each addl $25; suites $199-$475; under 18 free; wkend rates. Crib free. TV; cable (premium), VCR avail. Indoor pool; whirlpool, lifeguard. Restaurant 6:30 am-11 pm; Fri, Sat to midnight. Bar 11:30-1 am; entertainment. Ck-out noon. Convention facilities. Business center. In-rm modem link. Free airport, RR station transportation. Exercise equipt; sauna. Health club privileges. Refrigerators, microwaves avail. Cr cds: A, C, D, DS, ER, JCB, MC, V.

D ≈ 🏋 🛏 🔥 SC 🏋

Inn

★★★ **BAILIWICK INN.** *4023 Chain Bridge Rd (22030). 703/691-2266; FAX 703/934-2112; res: 800/366-7666.* E-mail bailiwick@erols.com; web www.bailiwickinn.com. 14 rms, some with shower only, 4 story. No elvtr. S, D $140-$310. TV; VCR avail. Complimentary full bkfst. Restaurant (see BAILWICK INN). Ck-out 11 am, ck-in 2 pm. Health club privileges. Some in-rm whirlpools, fireplaces. Restored private residence (1800); antiques. The first Civil War skirmish occured here in June of 1861. Totally nonsmoking. Cr cds: A, C, MC, V.

Restaurants

★★ ARTIE'S. *3260 Old Lee Hwy (22030).* 703/273-7600. E-mail artiesrest@aol.com. Hrs: 11:30 am-11 pm; Fri, Sat to midnight; Sun 10:30 am-10 pm; Sun brunch to 3 pm; early-bird dinner Mon-Thurs 5-6 pm. Closed Thanksgiving, Dec 25. Bar. Semi-a la carte: lunch $7.25-$10.25, dinner $8.95-$16.50. Sun brunch $7.25-$9.95. Specializes in steak, seafood, pasta. Parking. Cr cds: A, C, MC, V.

★★★ BAILIWICK INN. *(See Bailiwick Inn)* 703/691-2266. E-mail bailiwick@erols.com. Hrs: Wed, Thurs, Sun seatings 6:30, 7:30, 8:30 pm; Fri, Sat seatings 6, 8:30 pm; Fri lunch noon-2 pm. Closed Mon, Tues. Res required. American menu with Mediterranean influence. A la carte entrees: lunch $12-$18. Complete meals: dinner $45; Fri, Sat $55. Specializes in chicken, beef, seafood. Menu changes bi-weekly. Parking. Patio dining overlooking English garden. In restored inn (1800). Totally nonsmoking. Cr cds: A, C, MC, V.

✓★ BLUE OCEAN. *9440 Main St (22031).* 703/425-7555. Hrs: 11:30 am-2:30 pm, 5-10 pm; Fri to 10:30 pm; Sat noon-2:30 pm, 5-10:30 pm; Sun from 5 pm. Closed most major hols. Res accepted. Japanese menu. Serv bar. Semi-a la carte: lunch $7.95-$9.95, dinner $9.50-$17.95. Specialties: sushi, teriyaki, sukiyaki. Salad bar. Authentic Japanese decor; sushi bar. Cr cds: A, C, D, MC, V.

★★ BOMBAY BISTRO. *3570 Chain Bridge Rd (22030).* 703/359-5810. Hrs: 11:30 am-2:30 pm, 5-10 pm; Fri, Sat to 10:30 pm; Sat, Sun brunch noon-3 pm. Closed Thanksgiving. Indian menu. Bar. A la carte entrees: lunch, dinner $5.95-$11.95. Buffet (Mon-Fri) $6.95. Sat, Sun brunch $8.95. Specializes in tandoori, vegetarian dishes. Outdoor dining. Indian decor. Cr cds: A, C, D, DS, MC, V.

★★ CONNAUGHT PLACE. *10425 North St (22030).* 703/352-5959. Hrs: 11:30 am-2:30 pm, 5-10 pm; Sat noon-3 pm, 5-10 pm; Sun noon-3 pm, 5-9 pm. Closed Thanksgiving, Dec 25. Res accepted. Indian menu. Bar. Semi-a la carte: lunch $5-$11, dinner $6.95-$16.95. Buffet $7.95-$8.95. Sat, Sun brunch $8.95. Specializes in seafood, vegetarian dishes. Sitar Fri, Sat. Middle Eastern decor. Cr cds: A, C, D, MC, V.

★★ HEART-IN-HAND. *7145 Main St (20124), S on VA 123 to Chapel Rd, then W.* 703/830-4111. Hrs: 11 am-2:30 pm, 6-9:30 pm; Sun 5-8 pm; Sun brunch 11 am-2:30 pm. Closed Jan 1, July 4, Dec 25. Res accepted. Semi-a la carte: lunch $5.95-$12.95, dinner $14.95-$22.95. Sun brunch $6.95-$12.95. Specialties: beef Wellington, rack of lamb. Own ice cream. Parking. Outdoor dining. Converted general store (ca 1870). Antique decor; original floors, ceiling fans, antique quilts. Totally nonsmoking. Cr cds: A, C, D, DS, MC, V.

★★★ HERMITAGE INN. *7134 Main St (20124), W on US 29 to Clifton Rd (VA 645), then S.* 703/266-1623. Hrs: 11:30 am-2:30 pm, 5:30-9 pm; Tues from 5:30 pm; Fri, Sat to 10 pm; Sun from 11 am. Closed Mon. Res accepted. French, Mediterranean menu. Serv bar. Semi-a la carte: lunch $5.50-$11.50. Prix fixe: dinner $28-$39. Sun brunch $17.95. Specialties: paella, crepes homard, chateaubriand. Own pastries. Outdoor dining. Located in 1869 clapboard hotel. Cr cds: A, C, D, DS, MC, V.

✓★ P J SKIDOOS RESTAURANT. *9908 Lee Jackson Memorial Hwy (22030).* 703/591-4515. Hrs: 11-2 am; Sun 10 am-9 pm. Closed Thanksgiving, Dec 25. Bar. Semi-a la carte: lunch, dinner $5.50-$12.95. Sun brunch $8.95. Child's meals. Specializes in prime rib, fresh seafood, chicken. Entertainment Tues, Thurs-Sat. Parking. 1890s saloon atmosphere. Cr cds: A, C, MC, V.

Unrated Dining Spot

THE ESPOSITOS/PIZZA 'N PASTA. *9917 Lee Jackson Memorial Hwy (22030).* 703/385-5912. Hrs: 11:30 am-10 pm; Fri to 11 pm; Sat from noon; Sun noon-10 pm. Closed Jan 1, Thanksgiving, Dec 25. Southern Italian menu. Wine, beer. A la carte entrees: lunch, dinner $3.50-$11.50. Semi-a la carte: lunch $5.50-$12.95, dinner $6.25-$13.95. Specialties: pollo cardinale, fettucine alla Romano. Own pasta. Parking. Pizza baked in wood-burning oven imported from Italy. Italian trattoria decor. Cr cds: A, C, D, MC, V.

Falls Church (C-8)

(See also Alexandria, Arlington County, Fairfax, McLean; also see District of Columbia)

Pop 9,578 **Elev** 340 ft **Area Code** 703
Information Greater Falls Church Chamber of Commerce, 417 W Broad St, PO Box 491, 22040-0491; 703/532-1050

Falls Church is a pleasant, cosmopolitan suburb of Washington, DC, just over the Arlington County line, graced with many interesting old houses. This was a crossover point between the North and the South, through which pioneers, armies, adventurers and merchants passed.

What to See and Do

Fountain of Faith. Also in park is a memorial dedicated to the four chaplains—two Protestant, one Jewish, one Catholic—who were aboard the USS *Dorchester* when it was torpedoed off Greenland in 1943. They gave their life jackets to four soldiers on deck who had none. In National Memorial Park.

The Falls Church (Episcopal) (1769). This building replaced the original wooden church built in 1732. Served as a recruiting station during the Revolution; abandoned until 1830; used during the Civil War as a hospital and later as a stable for cavalry horses. Restored according to original plans with gallery additions in 1959. (Daily exc Sat; closed some hols) 115 E Fairfax St at Washington St, on US 29. Phone 703/532-7600. **Free**

Motel

✓★ QUALITY INN. *6650 Arlington Blvd (22042), at I-495 exit 8E.* 703/532-8900; FAX 703/532-7121; res: 800/228-5151. 121 rms. Mar-Sept: S $67-$83; D $70-$85; each addl $5; suites $95; under 18 free; lower rates rest of yr. Crib free. TV; cable (premium). Pool; lifeguard. Restaurant 6:30 am-10 pm; Sat, Sun from 7 am. Ck-out noon. Meeting rms. Business servs avail. Some refrigerators. Cr cds: A, C, D, DS, JCB, MC, V.

Hotel

★★★ FAIRVIEW PARK MARRIOTT. *3111 Fairview Park Dr (22042), at I-495 exit 8A.* 703/849-9400; FAX 703/849-8692; res: 800/228-9290. Web www.marriott.com. 394 rms, 15 story. S $189; D $199; suites $250-$500; under 16 free. Crib free. TV; cable (premium), VCR avail. Indoor/outdoor pool; whirlpool, poolside serv, lifeguard. Coffee in rms.

Restaurant 6:30 am-10 pm; Fri, Sat 7 am-11 pm. Bar 11-2 am. Ck-out noon. Coin lndry. Convention facilities. Business center. In-rm modem link. Concierge. Gift shop. Exercise equipt; sauna. Some bathrm phones. Some balconies. Luxury level. Cr cds: A, C, D, DS, ER, JCB, MC, V.

Restaurants

★★ **BANGKOK ST. GRILL AND NOODLES.** *5872 Leesburg Pike (22041).* 703/379-6707. Hrs: 11:30 am-10 pm; Fri, Sat to 10:30 pm. Closed Thanksgiving. Thai menu. Bar. A la carte entrees: lunch, dinner $6.95-$8.75. Specialties: stir fried noodles, shrimp dumplings, chicken satay. Outdoor dining. Casual Thai decor; arranged like a street scene. Totally nonsmoking. Cr cds: A, C, D, MC, V.

✓★★ **BANGKOK VIENTIANE.** *926 W Broad St # A (22046).* 703/534-0095. Hrs: 11 am-10 pm; wkends to 11 pm. Res accepted. Thai, Laotian menu. Semi-a la carte: lunch $3.95-$8.95, dinner $6.50-$9.25. Lunch buffet $5.95. Specialties: spicy Thai beef noodle, tom yam gung, kaeng seafood combo. Parking. Asian decor. Cr cds: A, C, D, DS, MC, V.

★★★ **DUANGRAT'S.** *5878 Leesburg Pike (22041), adj Glen Forest Shopping Center.* 703/820-5775. Hrs: 11:30 am-2:30 pm, 5-10 pm; Fri to 11 pm; Sat 11:30 am-11 pm; Sun 11:30 am-10 pm. Res accepted. Thai menu. Bar. Semi-a la carte: lunch $6.95-$8.95, dinner $9.95-$18.95. Specialties: pad Thai noodles, Thai curry, crispy fish with chili sauce. Parking. Display of Thai headdresses and masks. Cr cds: A, C, D, MC, V.

✓★★★ **HAANDI FINE INDIAN CUISINE.** *1222 W Broad St VA 7 (22046), in Falls Plaza.* 703/533-3501. Hrs: 11:30 am-2:30 pm, 5-10 pm; wkends to 10:30 pm. Closed Dec 25. Res accepted Sun-Thur. Northern Indian menu. Serv bar. Semi-a la carte: lunch $5.95-$10.95, dinner $7.95-$14.95. Specializes in barbecued meats, chicken, vegetarian dishes. Parking. Totally nonsmoking. Cr cds: A, C, D, MC, V.

✓★★ **PANJSHIR.** *924 W Broad St (22046).* 703/536-4566. Web www.enterit.com/panjshir566.htm. Hrs: 11 am-2 pm, 5-10 pm; Sun 5-9 pm. Closed July 4, Thanksgiving, Dec 25. Afghan menu. Bar. Semi-a la carte: lunch $6.50-$7.25, dinner $9.95-$13.25. Specializes in kebab, palows, vegetarian dishes. Parking. Totally nonsmoking. Cr cds: A, C, D, MC, V.

★★★ **PEKING GOURMET INN.** *6029 Leesburg Pike (22041), 4 mi SE on VA 7 (Leesburg Pike).* 703/671-8088. E-mail ftsui@aol.com. Hrs: 11 am-10:30 pm; Fri, Sat to midnight. Closed Thanksgiving. Res accepted; required Fri, Sat. Northern Chinese menu. Serv bar. Semi-a la carte: lunch $6.25-$13.45, dinner $8.45-$24.95. Specialties: Peking duck, beef Szechuan, striped bass Peking-style. Parking. Oriental antiques and screens; 300-yr-old jade Buddha; original artwork. Favorite of Washington politicians. Cr cds: A, C, MC, V.

★★ **PILIN THAI RESTAURANT.** *116 W Broad St VA 7 (22046).* 703/241-5850. Hrs: 11:30 am-10 pm; Fri, Sat to 11 pm; Sun 5-9 pm. Closed some major hols. Res accepted; required Fri, Sat dinner. Thai menu. Bar. Semi-a la carte: lunch $4.95-$6.95, dinner $7.95-$13.95. Specialties: spicy, crispy catfish; pad Thai; pad gra prow talay. Parking. Cr cds: A, C, D, DS, MC, V.

★★ **SECRET GARDEN BEEWON.** *6678 Arlington Blvd (22042).* 703/533-1004. Hrs: 11-1 am. Closed Jan 1. Res accepted; required Fri, Sat. Korean, Japanese menu. Serv bar. Semi-a la carte: lunch $5.50-$11.95, dinner $8.95-$18. Complete meals: lunch (Mon-Fri) $5.95-$9.95. Specialties: bulgogi, heamul chongol. Sushi bar. Parking. Tableside preparation. Traditional Korean decor. Cr cds: A, C, D, DS, MC, V.

★ **SIR WALTER RALEIGH INN.** *8120 Gatehouse Rd (22042), I-495 exit 8W to VA 650N.* 703/560-6768. Hrs: 11:30 am-2 pm, 5-9 pm; Fri to 10 pm; Sat 5-10 pm; Sun 4-8:30 pm; early-bird dinner 5-6 pm, Sun 4-5 pm. Closed Dec 25. Bar. Semi-a la carte: lunch $5.75-$10.95, dinner $7.95-$17.95. Child's meals. Specializes in steak, seafood. Salad bar. Parking. Cr cds: A, C, D, DS, MC, V.

Farmville (E-7)

(See also Keysville)

Pop 6,046 **Elev** 304 ft **Area Code** 804 **Zip** 23901

Longwood College's Jeffersonian buildings provide architectural interest in downtown Farmville.

What to See and Do

Appomattox Court House National Historical Park (see). 26 mi NW via US 460, VA 24.

Sailor's Creek Battlefield Historic State Park. Site of last major battle of Civil War, which took place on Apr 6, 1865, preceding Lee's surrender at Appomattox by three days. Auto tour. 9 mi E on US 460, then 7 mi NE on VA 307 and 2 mi N on VA 617. Phone 804/392-3435.   **Free**

Motels

✓★★ **COMFORT INN.** *US 15 & US 460 Bypass (23901).* 804/392-8163; FAX 804/392-1966; res: 800/228-5150. 51 rms, 2 story. S $53-$59; D $56-$62; each addl $6; under 18 free; higher rates special events. TV; cable (premium), VCR avail. Pool. Ck-out noon. Business servs avail. Cr cds: A, C, D, DS, ER, MC, V.

✓★ **DAYS INN.** *2011 S Main St (23901), on US 15.* 804/392-6611; FAX 804/392-9774; res: 800/329-7466. 60 rms, 2 story. S $53; $59; under 18 free; family, wkend, wkly rates; higher rates: homecoming wkend, graduation. Crib free. TV; cable (premium). Complimentary continental bkfst. Restaurant opp 11 am-9 pm. Ck-out 11 am. Business servs avail. Valet serv. Sundries. Pool. Picnic tables, grills. Cr cds: A, C, D, DS, ER, MC, V.

Fredericksburg (D-8)

(See also Triangle)

Settled 1727 **Pop** 19,027 **Elev** 61 ft **Area Code** 540 **E-mail** fburg@illuminet.net **Web** www.fredericksburgva.com
Information Visitor Center, 706 Caroline St, 22401; 540/373-1776 or 800/678-4748.

One of the seeds of the American Revolution was planted here when a resolution declaring independence from Great Britain was passed on April 29, 1775. Here is where George Washington went to school, where his sister, Betty, lived and his mother, Mary Ball Washington, lived and died. James Monroe practiced law in town. Guns for the Revolution were manufactured here, and four of the most savage battles of the Civil War were fought nearby.

Captain John Smith visited the area in 1608 and gave glowing reports of its possibilities for settlement. In 1727, the General Assembly directed that

50 acres of "lease-land" be laid out and the town called Fredericksburg, after the Prince of Wales.

Ships from abroad sailed up the Rappahannock River to the harbor—ampler then than now—to exchange their goods for those brought from "upcountry" by the great road wagons and river carriers. The town prospered.

The Civil War left Fredericksburg ravaged. Situated midway between Richmond and Washington, it was recurringly an objective of both sides; the city changed hands seven times, and the casualties were high.

Even so, many buildings put up before 1775 still stand. Proudly aware of their town's place in the country's history, the townspeople keep Fredericksburg inviting with fresh paint, beautiful lawns and well-kept gardens.

What to See and Do

Belmont (The Gari Melchers Estate and Memorial Gallery). Residence from 1916 to 1932 of American-born artist Gari Melchers (1860-1932), best known for his portraits of the famous and wealthy, including Theodore Roosevelt, William Vanderbilt and Andrew Mellon, and as an important impressionist artist of the period. The artist's studio comprises the nation's largest collection of his works, housing more than 1,800 paintings and drawings. The site is a registered National and State Historic Landmark and includes a 27-acre estate, frame house built in the late 18th century and enlarged over the years and a stone studio built by Melchers, which today houses his artwork. Owned by the state of Virginia, Belmont is administered by Mary Washington College. (Daily; closed Jan 1, Thanksgiving, Dec 24, 25, 31) 224 Washington St. Phone 540/654-1843. ¢¢

Fredericksburg and Spotsylvania National Military Park (see).

Mary Washington College (1908). (3,700 students) Liberal arts and sciences including historic preservation, computer science and business administration. Coeducational. Includes 275 acres of open and wooded campus; red-brick, white-pillared buildings. President of the college occupies Brompton (private), a house built in 1830 on land sold to Fielding Lewis in 1760 and expanded by a later owner, Colonel John Lawrence Marye. Campus tours. College Ave. Phone 540/654-1000 or 800/468-5614.

⭐ **Walking or driving tour of Fredericksburg.** Begin at

Visitor Center. Orientation film; information; obtain walking tour brochure and combination tickets here. 706 Caroline St. 3 blks N begin at

Hugh Mercer Apothecary Shop. This 18th-century medical office and pharmacy offers exhibits on the medicine and methods of treatment used by Dr. Hugh Mercer before he left to join the Revolutionary War as brigadier general. Authentic herbs and period medical instruments. (Daily; closed Jan 1, Thanksgiving, Dec 24, 25, 31) 1020 Caroline St. Phone 540/373-3362. ¢¢   Follow Caroline St 3 blks N to

Rising Sun Tavern (ca 1760). Washington's youngest brother, Charles, built this tavern, which became a social and political center and stagecoach stop. Restored and authentically refurnished as an 18th-century tavern; costumed tavern wenches, English and American pewter collection. (Daily; closed Jan 1, Thanksgiving, Dec 24, 25, 31) 1306 Caroline St. Phone 540/371-1494. ¢¢   W to Princess Anne St, 4 blks S is the

Fredericksburg Area Museum (Town Hall) (1814). Museum and cultural center interpret the history of Fredericksburg area from its first settlers to the 20th century. Changing exhibits. Children's events. (Daily; closed Jan 1, Thanksgiving, Dec 25) 907 Princess Anne St. Phone 540/371-3037. ¢¢   Behind Town Hall to the S on Princess Anne St is

St George's Episcopal Church and Churchyard. Patrick Henry, uncle of the orator, was the first rector. Headstones in the churchyard bear the names of illustrious Virginians. (Daily) NE corner of Princess Anne and George Sts. Phone 540/373-4133. 1 blk S to Hanover St is

Fredericksburg Masonic Lodge #4, AF and AM. Washington was initiated into this Lodge Nov 4, 1752; the building, dating from 1812, contains relics of his initiation and membership; authentic Gilbert Stuart portrait; 300-yr-old Bible on which Washington took his Masonic obligation. (Mon-Sat, also Sun afternoons; closed Jan 1, Thanksgiving, Dec 25) Princess Anne & Hanover Sts. Phone 540/373-5885. ¢   Across the street is the

Presbyterian Church (1833). Cannonballs in the front pillar and other damages inflicted in 1862 bombardment. Pews were torn loose and

made into coffins for soldiers. Clara Barton, founder of the American Red Cross, is said to have nursed wounded here. A plaque to her memory is in the churchyard. Open on request (daily exc Sat). SW corner of Princess Anne & George Sts. Phone 540/373-7057. 1 blk W on George St is

Masonic Cemetery. One of nation's oldest Masonic burial grounds. George & Charles Sts. Just N on Charles St is

James Monroe Museum. James Monroe, as a young lawyer, lived and worked in Fredericksburg from 1786 to 1789 and even served on Fredericksburg's City Council. Museum houses one of the nation's largest collections of Monroe memorabilia, articles and original documents. Included are the desk bought in France in 1794 during his years as ambassador and used in the White House for signing of the Monroe Doctrine; formal attire worn at Court of Napoleon; and more than 40 books from Monroe's library. Also garden. The site is a National Historic Landmark. Owned by Commonwealth of Virginia, and administered by Mary Washington College. (Daily; closed Jan 1, Thanksgiving, Dec 24, 25, 31) 908 Charles St. Phone 540/654-1043. ¢¢   Continue N on Charles St to

Old Slave Block. Circular block of sandstone about 3 ft high, from which ladies mounted their horses, and slaves were auctioned in antebellum days. William & Charles Sts. 2 blks N on Charles St is

Mary Washington House. Bought by George for his mother in 1772. She lived here until her death in 1789. Here she was visited by General Lafayette. Some original furnishings. Boxwood garden. (Daily; closed Jan 1, Thanksgiving, Dec 24, 25, 31) 1200 Charles St. Phone 540/373-1569. ¢¢   On Charles St is

St James House. Frame house built in 1760s, antique furnishings, porcelain and silver collections; landscaped gardens. (Open Historic Garden Week in Apr and 1st week in Oct; other times by appt) 1300 Charles St. Phone 540/373-1569. ¢¢   Walk back 1 blk to Lewis St and walk 2 blks W to

Kenmore (1752). Considered one of the finest restorations in Virginia; former home of Col Fielding Lewis, commissioner of Fredericksburg gunnery, who married George Washington's only sister, Betty. On an original grant of 863 acres, Lewis built a magnificent home; three rooms have full decorative molded plaster ceilings. Diorama of 18th-century Fredericksburg. Tea and ginger cookies served free (with paid admission). (Daily; closed Jan, Feb, Thanksgiving, Dec 24, 25, 31) 1201 Washington Ave. Phone 540/373-3381. ¢¢¢   2½ blks N is

Mary Washington Monument. Where Mrs Washington often went to rest and pray and where she is buried. Near "Meditation Rock." 5 blks S on Washington is

Confederate Cemetery. 2,640 Confederate Civil War soldiers are buried here, some in graves marked "Unknown." Washington Ave between Amelia & William Sts.

Annual Events

Historic Garden Week. Private homes open. Usually third wk Apr.

Market Square Fair. Entertainment, crafts demonstrations, food. Mid-May.

Quilt Show. Exhibits at various locations. Demonstrations and sale of old and new quilts. Sept.

Christmas Candlelight Tour. Historic homes open to the public; carriage rides; Christmas decorations and refreshments of the colonial period. 1st wkend Dec.

Motels

✓ ★★ **BEST WESTERN.** 3000 Plank Rd (22401), I-95, exit 130B. 540/786-7404; FAX 540/785-7415; res: 800/528-1234. 76 rms, 2-3 story. Mar-Oct: S $48-$55; D $55-$63; each addl $4; under 12 free; higher rates special events. Crib $2. Pet accepted, some restrictions. TV; cable (premium). Complimentary continental bkfst. Restaurant nearby. Ck-out noon. Coin lndry. Business servs avail. Sundries. Valet serv. Health club privileges. Refrigerators avail. Cr cds: A, C, D, DS, MC, V.

D 🐾 🛰 🔥 SC

★★ **COMFORT INN.** *5422 Jefferson Davis Hwy (22407), I-95 exit 126.* 540/898-5550; FAX 540/891-2861; res: 800/221-2222. 125 rms, 5 story. Mid-Mar-Aug: S, D $62-$74; each addl $6; under 18 free; lower rates rest of yr. Crib free. TV; cable (premium). Indoor pool; whirlpool. Complimentary continental bkfst. Restaurant adj 6 am-10 pm. Ck-out noon. Meeting rms. Business servs avail. In-rm modem link. Sundries. Valet serv. 18-hole golf privileges, greens fee, pro, putting green, driving range. Exercise equipt; sauna. Cr cds: A, C, D, DS, ER, JCB, MC, V.

D ⬚ ⬚ ⬚ ⬚ ⬚ SC

★★ **COMFORT INN NORTH.** *557 Warrenton Rd (22406), jct I-95 exit 133B & US 17N.* 540/371-8900; FAX 540/372-6958; res: 800/428-4888. 80 rms, 3 story, 10 kit units. S, D $62.96-$69.95; kit units $69.95; under 18 free; wkly rates. Crib free. TV; cable (premium). Indoor pool; whirlpool. Complimentary continental bkfst. Restaurant adj open 24 hrs. Ck-out 11 am. Business servs avail. In-rm modem link. Exercise equipt; sauna. Some in-rm whirlpools. Cr cds: A, C, D, DS, JCB, MC, V.

D ⬚ ⬚ ⬚ ⬚ SC

★★★ **HOLIDAY INN NORTH.** *564 Warrenton Rd (22405), at jct US 17, I-95 exit 133/133B.* 540/371-5550; FAX 540/373-3641; res: 800/465-4329. 150 rms, 2 story. June-Aug: S $52; D $67; each addl $5; under 18 free; lower rates rest of yr. Crib free. TV; cable (premium). 2 pools, 1 indoor; whirlpool. Coffee in rms. Restaurant 6-10 am, 5-9:30 pm. Rm serv. Bar 4 pm-2 am; entertainment Fri, Sat. Ck-out noon. Coin lndry. Meeting rms. Business servs avail. Valet serv. Sundries. Exercise equipt. Refrigerators avail. Cr cds: A, C, D, DS, JCB, MC, V.

D ⬚ ⬚ ⬚ ⬚ SC

✓ ★ **RAMADA INN.** *2802 Plank Rd (22404), jct I-95, VA 3W, exit 130B.* 540/786-8361; FAX 540/786-8811; res: 800/272-6232. 129 rms, 2 story. S $45-$57; D $50-$62; each addl $5; suites $75-$100; under 18 free. Crib free. Pet accepted; $25 refundable. TV; cable. Pool. Complimentary coffee in lobby. Restaurant 6 am-10 pm. Rm serv 11 am-9 pm. Ck-out 1 pm. Meeting rms. Business servs avail. In-rm modem link. Valet serv. Sundries. Health club privileges. Cr cds: A, C, D, DS, ER, JCB, MC, V.

D ⬚ ⬚ ⬚ ⬚ SC

Motor Hotels

★★ **HOLIDAY INN.** *5324 Jefferson Davis Hwy (22408), I-95 exit 126.* 540/898-1102; FAX 540/898-2017; res: 800/465-4329. Web www.holidayinnsofredva.com. 195 rms, 2 story. S, D $65-$100; each addl $6; under 18 free. Crib free. Pet accepted. TV; cable (premium). Indoor pool; whirlpool. Coffee in lobby. Restaurant 6:30 am-1 pm, 5-9:30 pm. Rm serv. Bar 4 pm-2 am; entertainment Wed-Sat. Ck-out noon. Coin lndry. Meeting rms. Business servs avail. In-rm modem link. Bellhops. Sundries. Valet serv. Exercise equipt. Game rm. Cr cds: A, C, D, DS, JCB, MC, V.

D ⬚ ⬚ ⬚ ⬚ ⬚ SC

★★★ **SHERATON INN.** *2801 Plank Rd (22404), I-95 exit 130B, jct VA 3.* 540/786-8321; FAX 540/786-3957; res: 800/544-5064; res: 800/682-1049. Web www.sheratoninn.com/fredericksburg. 195 rms, 3 story. S, D $79-$129; each addl $10; suites $150-$275; under 18 free. Crib free. Pet accepted. TV; cable (premium). Pool; wading pool, poolside serv, lifeguard. Complimentary coffee in rms. Restaurant 6:30 am-10 pm. Rm serv. Bar 11:30-2 am; entertainment exc Sun. Ck-out noon. Meeting rms. Business servs avail. Bellhops. Valet serv. Sundries. Gift shop. Airport transportation. Tennis. Golf privileges. Exercise equipt. Health club privileges. Lawn games. Private patios, balconies. Refrigerators avail. Picnic tables. Cr cds: A, C, D, DS, ER, JCB, MC, V.

D ⬚ ⬚ ⬚ ⬚ ⬚ ⬚ SC

Inns

★★ **FREDERICKSBURG COLONIAL INN.** *1707 Princess Anne St (22401).* 540/371-5666; FAX 540/368-1270. 39 rms, 2 story. S, D $55; each addl $6; suites $75-$85; under 12 free. Crib free. TV; cable. Complimentary continental bkfst. Ck-out 11 am, ck-in 2 pm. Meeting rms. Health club privileges. Refrigerators. Built 1928; antiques. Totally nonsmoking. Cr cds: A, C, MC, V.

D ⬚ ⬚ SC

★★ **KENMORE INN.** *1200 Princess Anne St (22401).* 540/371-7622; FAX 540/371-5480; res: 800/437-7622. 12 rms, 2 story. S $85-$115; D $100-$130; each addl $10; suite $175. Crib free. TV in lounge; cable. Complimentary continental bkfst. Dining rm 11:30 am-2:30 pm, 5:30-9:30 pm. Bar 11:30 am-11 pm; Fri, Sat to midnight. Ck-out noon, ck-in 2 pm. Business servs avail. In-rm modem link. Health club privileges. Fireplace, canopy bed in some rms. Refrigerators avail. Structure built late 1700s; in historic district. Cr cds: A, C, D, MC, V.

D ⬚ ⬚ SC

★★ **RICHARD JOHNSTON INN.** *711 Caroline St (22401).* 540/899-7606. 7 rms, 3 story, 2 suites. No rm phones. S, D $95-$125; suites $145. Complimentary continental bkfst. Ck-out 11 am, ck-in 2-8 pm. Built 1787; antiques. In historic district. Totally nonsmoking. Cr cds: A, C, MC, V.

⬚ ⬚

Restaurants

★★ **LA PETITE AUBERGE.** *311 William St (22401).* 540/371-2727. Hrs: 11:30 am-2:30 pm, 5:30-10 pm; early-bird dinner Mon-Thurs 5:30-7 pm. Closed Sun; major hols. Res accepted. French, Amer menu. Bar. Wine list. A la carte entrees: lunch $6.50-$13.95, dinner $9.95-$19.95. Specializes in fresh seafood, seasonal specialties, beef. Outdoor dining. French cafe decor. Cr cds: A, C, D, MC, V.

D

★★★ **OLDE MUDD TAVERN.** *5414 Mudd Tavern Rd (22565), ¼ mi W of I-95 Thornburg exit 118.* 540/582-5250. Hrs: 4-9 pm; Sun noon-8 pm. Closed Mon, Tues; Jan 1, Dec 25; also 1st wk July. Res accepted. Serv bar. Semi-a la carte: dinner $14-$20. Child's meals. Specializes in fresh vegetables, seafood, steak. Own baking. Entertainment Sat. Early Amer decor. Cr cds: C, MC, V.

D SC ⬚

★★★ **RENATO ITALIAN RESTAURANT.** *422 William St (22401).* 540/371-8228. Hrs: 11:30 am-2 pm, 4:30-10 pm; Sat, Sun from 4:30 pm. Closed most major hols. Italian menu. Bar. Semi-a la carte: lunch $5.95-$10.95, dinner $9.95-$24.95. Specializes in seafood, poultry, pasta. Antique chandeliers; fireplace. Cr cds: A, C, MC, V.

D ⬚ ♥

Fredericksburg and Spotsylvania National Military Park (D-8)

(See also Fredericksburg)

(Visitor Center on Old US 1 in Fredericksburg)

Midway between Washington and Richmond, on a good railroad, and protected by the Rappahannock and Rapidan rivers, the Fredericksburg area represented one of the main barriers to Union invasion during the Civil War.

Four major engagements—the heaviest, most concentrated fighting ever seen on this continent—were fought in and around this town between December 1862 and May 1864.

Union General A. E. Burnside, after a hard-won crossing of the Rappahannock, engaged in the Battle of Fredericksburg (December 13, 1862). Damage to the city was severe as Burnside attempted a frontal assault on Lee's Confederate forces entrenched behind a stone wall. The attempt proved suicidal. Burnside retreated across the Rappahannock River and went into winter quarters.

The Battle of Chancellorsville (April 27-May 6, 1863) was another victory for Lee, this time against Union General Joseph Hooker. Outmaneuvered, Hooker also retired across the Rappahannock, and Lee prepared his second invasion of the North. It was during this battle, on May 2, that Stonewall Jackson was mistakenly wounded by his own men; he died eight days later.

The Battle of the Wilderness (May 5-6, 1864) was the first encounter between Lee and Union general Ulysses S. Grant. When bloody fighting finally reached a stalemate, Grant elected to go around Lee, toward Richmond.

Savage fighting in the ensuing Battle of Spotsylvania Court House (May 8-21, 1864) produced no clear-cut victory; again Grant sidestepped and moved on toward Richmond. The relentless attrition of these two battles and the engagements that followed finally destroyed the offensive capabilities of Lee's Army of Northern Virginia.

Some 8,000 park acres include parts of all four battlefields, as well as Fredericksburg National Cemetery, the house at Guinea Station (where Jackson died), Old Salem Church and Chatham Manor. Miles of original trenches and gun pits remain; park roads provide ready access to many of them. (Daily) ¢¢

For further information contact the Superintendent, 120 Chatham Lane, Fredericksburg 22405; 540/371-0802.

What to See and Do

Chancellorsville Visitor Center. Slide program, museum with exhibits; dioramas. (Daily; closed Jan 1, Dec 25) 7 mi W of I-95 on Rte 3. Phone 540/786-2880. ¢¢

Chatham Manor. Georgian brick manor house, owned by a wealthy planter, was converted to Union headquarters during two of the battles of Fredericksburg. The house was eventually used as a hospital where Clara Barton and Walt Whitman nursed the wounded. (Daily; closed Jan 1, Dec 25) phone 540/371-0802. ¢¢

Fredericksburg Visitor Center. Information and directions for various parts of park. Tours should start here. (Daily; closed Jan 1, Dec 25) Lafayette Blvd (US 1) & Sunken Rd. Phone 540/373-6122. Center includes

    Museum. Slide program, diorama, exhibits. (Same days as Visitor Center) **Free**   Across Sunken Rd is

    Fredericksburg National Cemetery. More than 15,000 Federal interments; almost 13,000 unknown.

Old Salem Church (1844). Building used as a field hospital and refugee center. Scene of battle on May 3-4, 1863. 1 mi W of I-95 on VA 3.

Stonewall Jackson Shrine. Plantation office where on May 10, 1863, Confederate general Jackson, ill with pneumonia and with his shattered left arm amputated, murmured, "Let us cross over the river, and rest under the shade of the trees," and died. (Mid-June-Labor Day, daily; Apr-mid-June, after Labor Day-Oct, Fri-Tues; rest of yr, Sat-Mon) 12 mi S on I-95 to Thornburg exit, then 5 mi E on VA 606 to Guinea. Phone 804/633-6076. ¢¢

Front Royal (C-7)

(See also Winchester, Woodstock)

Founded 1788 **Pop** 11,880 **Elev** 567 ft **Area Code** 540 **Zip** 22630
E-mail coc@frontroyal.com **Web** www.frontroyal.com
Information Chamber of Commerce of Front Royal-Warren County, 414 E Main St; 540/635-3185 or 800/338-2576

Once known as Hell Town, for all the wild and reckless spirits it attracted, Front Royal was a frontier stop on the way to eastern markets. The present name is supposed to have originated in the command, "Front the royal oak," given by an English officer to his untrained mountain militia recruits.

Belle Boyd, the Confederate spy, worked here extracting military secrets from Union officers. It is said that she invited General Nathaniel Banks and his officers, whose regiment was occupying the town, to a ball once. Later, she raced on horseback to tell General Jackson what she had learned. Next morning (May 23, 1862), the Confederates attacked and captured nearly all of the Union troops, providing Jackson one of his early victories in the famous Valley Campaign.

Front Royal was a quiet little village until the entrance to the Shenandoah National Park (see) and the beginning of the Skyline Drive opened in 1935, just one mile to the south. With millions of motorists passing through every year, the town has grown rapidly. The production of automotive finishes, limestone and cement contributes to the town's economy, but the tourism industry remains one of its largest.

What to See and Do

Belle Boyd Cottage. Relocated to its present site, the two-story cottage has been restored to reflect life in Front Royal between 1840 and 1860. For a 2-yr period during the Civil War, Belle Boyd stayed in this cottage while visiting relatives and used the opportunity to spy on Union troops occupying the town. This modest dwelling was also used to house wounded soldiers of both armies. (Mid-Apr-Oct, Mon-Fri, wkends by appt; closed hols) 101 Chester St, behind Ivy Lodge. Phone 540/636-1446. ¢

Sky Meadows State Park. A 1,862-acre park. Fishing pond. Hiking, bridle trails. Picnicking. Primitive walk-in camping. Visitor center; programs. (Daily) Standard fees. 20 mi E on US 66, 7 mi N on VA 17. Phone 540/592-3556.

Skyline Caverns. Extensive, rare, intricate flowerlike formations of calcite (anthodites); sound and light presentation; 37-ft waterfall; clear stream stocked with trout (observation only). Electrically lighted; 54°F yr-round. Miniature train provides trip through surrounding wooded area (Mar-mid-Nov, daily, weather permitting). Snack bar; gift shop. Cavern tours start every few minutes. (Daily) 1 mi S on US 340. Phone 540/635-4545 or 800/296-4545. ¢¢¢

Warren Rifles Confederate Museum. Historic relics and memorabilia of War between the States. (Mid-Apr-Oct, daily; rest of yr, by appt) 95 Chester St. Phone 540/636-6982. ¢

Annual Events

Warren County Garden Tour. Garden Club sponsors tours of historic houses and gardens. Last wk Apr.

Virginia Mushroom and Wine Festival. Mushrooms, wine and cheese. Entertainment. 3rd Sat May.

Warren County Fair. Entertainment, livestock exhibits and sale, contests. 1st wk Aug.

Festival of Leaves. Arts and crafts, demonstrations; historic exhibits; parade. 2nd wkend Oct.

Motel

★★ **QUALITY INN.** *10 S Commerce Ave (22630), US 522 Bypass at end of Main St.* 540/635-3161; FAX 540/635-6624; res: 800/821-4488. 107 rms, 3 story. Sept-Oct: S $58-$85; D $68-$85; each addl $9; under 18 free; higher rates special events; lower rates rest of yr. Crib free. TV; cable (premium), VCR avail (movies). Pool. Complimentary coffee in rms. Restaurant 6 am-9 pm; wkends to 10 pm. Ck-out 11 am. Meeting rms. Business servs avail. In-rm modem link. Gift shop. Lawn games. Refrigerators, microwaves avail. Cr cds: A, C, D, DS, ER, MC, V.

Inn

★★★ **CHESTER HOUSE.** *43 Chester St (22630).* 540/635-3937; FAX 540/636-8695; res: 800/621-0441. E-mail chesthse@rma.edu; web www.chesterhouse.com. 6 rms, 2 share bath, 1 with shower only, 2 story, 1 suite. S, D $65-$130; suite $165-$190; special events (2-day min). Children over 12 yrs only. TV in lounge. Complimentary full bkfst; refreshments. Restaurant nearby. Ck-out 11 am, ck-in 3 pm. Business servs avail. Luggage handling. Health club privileges. Lawn games. Guest refrigerator. Picnic tables. Formal gardens with fountain and statuary. Georgian-style mansion built 1905. Cr cds: A, C, MC, V.

Galax (F-4)

(See also Wytheville)

Settled 1904 **Pop** 6,670 **Elev** 2,382 ft **Area Code** 540 **Zip** 24333
E-mail gcgchamber@tcia.net
Information Galax-Carroll-Grayson Chamber of Commerce, 405 N Main St; 540/236-2184

Galax is named for the pretty evergreen with heart-shaped leaves that florists use in various arrangements. It grows in the mountainous regions around Galax and is gathered for sale all over the US. Nearby are three mountain passes: Fancy Gap, Low Gap and Piper's Gap.

What to See and Do

Blue Ridge Parkway (see). 7 mi S.

Jeff Matthews Memorial Museum. Two authentically restored log cabins (1834 & 1860s). Relocated to present site and furnished with items used in the period in which the cabins were inhabited. Also houses collection of photos of Civil War veterans, artifacts and memorabilia of the area; covered wagon; farm implements. Restored log cabin used as a blacksmith's shop. (Wed-Sun) Phone 540/236-7874.   **Free**

Recreation. Swimming, boating, fishing on New River. Hunting and hiking. Canoeing and other activities can be found at

   Cliffview Trading Post. Bike rentals (Tues-Sat; closed Thanksgiving, Dec 25) and horse rentals (Apr-Nov, Tues-Sat); trail rides in New River Trail State Park. Cliffview Rd. Phone 540/238-1530.

Annual Event

Old Fiddler's Convention. Felts Park. Folk songs, bands and dancing. 2nd wk Aug.

George Washington Birthplace National Monument (D-9)

(See also Fredericksburg, Montross)

(38 mi E of Fredericksburg on VA 3, then 2 mi E on VA 204)

George Washington, first child of Augustine and Mary Ball Washington, was born February 11, 1732 (celebrated February 22 according to the new-style calendar) at his father's estate on Popes Creek on the south shore of the Potomac. The family moved in 1735 to Little Hunting Creek Plantation, later called Mt Vernon, then in 1738 to Ferry Farm near Fredericksburg.

The 538-acre monument includes much of the old plantation land. (Daily; closed Jan 1, Dec 25)

What to See and Do

Family burial ground. Site of 1664 home of Colonel John Washington, first Washington in Virginia and great-grandfather of the first president. Washington's ancestors are buried here. 1 mi NW on Bridges Creek.

Memorial House. Original house burned (1779) and was never rebuilt. The Memorial House is not a replica of the original; it represents a composite of typical 18th-century Virginia plantation house. Bricks were handmade from nearby clay. Furnishings are typical of the times. Near house is

   Colonial farm. "Living" farm, designed to show 18th-century Virginia plantation life; livestock, colonial garden, several farm buildings, furnished colonial kitchen, household slave quarters and spinning and weaving room.

Picnic area. ¼ mi N of house.

Visitor Center. Orientation film; museum exhibits. Phone 804/224-1732. ¢

Gloucester (E-9)

(See also Newport News, Williamsburg, Yorktown)

Founded 1769 **Pop** 900 (est) **Elev** 70 ft **Area Code** 804 **Zip** 23061
Information Chamber of Commerce, PO Box 296; 804/693-2425.

In the spring, acres of daffodil blooms make this area a treat for the traveler. This elm-shaded village is the commercial center of Gloucester (GLOSS-ter) County. There are many old landmarks and estates nearby, including the birthplace of Walter Reed, at the jct of VA 614 & 616.

What to See and Do

County Courthouse (18th century). Part of Gloucester Court House Circle Historic District. Portraits of native sons are in the courtroom; plaques memorializing Nathaniel Bacon, leader in the rebellion of 1676, first organized resistance to British authority, and Major Walter Reed, surgeon, conqueror of yellow fever. (Mon-Fri; closed hols) On US 17 Business. Phone 804/693-4042.   **Free**   Nearby are Debtors Prison, the pre-Revolutionary Botetourt Bldg and the

   Roswell Historic Ruins. 3-story Georgian mansion's brickwork was put in place over 250 yrs ago. Majestic ruins hint at projecting pavilions, arched windows and stone-capped chimney stacks. Tours by appt. (Apr-Oct, Sun; winter by appt) Phone 804/693-2585.   **Free**

Virginia Institute of Marine Science, College of William and Mary. Small marine aquarium & museum display sea turtles, local fishes and invertebrates; marine science exhibits, bookstore. (Mon-Fri; closed major hols) Gloucester Point. Phone 804/642-7000.   **Free**

Restaurant

   ★★ **SEAWELL'S ORDINARY RESTAURANT.** *3968 George Washington Hwy (23131), US 17, 5 mi N of Coleman Bridge.* 804/642-3635. Hrs: 11:30 am-3 pm, 5-9:30 pm; Sun brunch 11:30 am-3 pm. Closed Mon; Dec 25. Res accepted. Continental menu. Bar. Semi-a la carte: lunch $4-$12.95, dinner $10.95-$18.95. Sun brunch $8.95-$14.95. Specializes in regional French dishes. Outdoor dining. Built in 1712; became country tavern (1757); was frequented by Washington, Jefferson, Lafayette. Cr cds: A, C, D, MC, V.

Great Dismal Swamp National Wildlife Refuge (F-9)

(See also Chesapeake, Portsmouth)

Harriet Beecher Stowe found Virginia's Dismal Swamp a perfect setting for her antislavery novel *Dred* (1856); modern hunters, fishermen and naturalists find the area fits their ambition just as well. From its northern edge just southwest of Norfolk, the swamp stretches almost due south like a great ribbon, 25 miles long and 11 miles wide. Centuries of decaying organic matter have created layers of peat so deep that fires would sometimes smolder under the surface for weeks.

Creation of the refuge began in 1973, when the Union Camp Corporation donated 49,100 acres of land to the Nature Conservancy, which in turn conveyed it to the Department of Interior. The refuge was officially established through the Dismal Swamp Act of 1974 and is managed for the primary purpose of protecting and preserving a unique ecosystem. The refuge now consists of over 107,000 acres of forested wetlands that have been greatly altered by drainage and logging operations.

Near the center is Lake Drummond, 3,100 acres of juniper water, which is water that combines the juices of gum, cypress and maple with a strong infusion of juniper or white cedar. The chemical mix added by the tree resins results in a water that remains sweet, or fresh, indefinitely. In the days of long sailing voyages, when ordinary water became foul after a few weeks, this "dark water" was highly valued.

The Great Dismal Swamp has also been commercially exploited for its timber, particularly cypress and cedar. A company organized by George Washington and several other businessmen bought a large piece of the swamp and used slave labor to dig the Dismal Swamp Canal, which both facilitated drainage of timber land and provided a transportation route in and out of the swamp.

Animal and bird life continues to abound in this eerie setting. There are white-tailed deer and rarely observed black bear, foxes, bobcats—and a large number of snakes, including copperheads, cottonmouths and rattlesnakes. Birding is popular in the swamp from April-June; the peak of spring migration is mid-April-mid-May.

For further information contact Refuge Manager, PO Box 349, Suffolk 23439-0349; 757/986-3705.

Hampton (F-9)

(See also Newport News, Norfolk, Portsmouth, Virginia Beach)

Settled 1610 **Pop** 133,793 **Elev** 12 ft **Area Code** 757 **E-mail** hct@city.hampton.va.us **Web** www.hampton.va.us/tourism
Information Hampton Visitor Center, 710 Settlers Landing Rd, 23669; 757/727-1102 or 800/800-2202

Hampton is the oldest continuously English-speaking community in the US—Jamestown, settled in 1607, is a national historical park, but not a town. The settlement began at a place then called Kecoughtan, with the building of Fort Algernourne as protection against the Spanish. In the late 1600s and early 1700s, the area was harassed by pirates. Finally, in 1718, the notorious brigand Blackbeard was killed by Lt Robert Maynard, and organized piracy came to an end here.

Hampton was shelled in the Revolutionary War, sacked by the British in the War of 1812 and burned in 1861 by retreating Confederates to prevent its occupation by Union forces. Only the gutted walls of St John's Church survived the fire. The town was rebuilt after the Civil War by its citizens and soldiers. Computer technology, manufacturing, aerospace research and commercial fishing are now big business here.

Langley Air Force Base, headquarters for the Air Combat Command, Fort Monroe, headquarters for the US Army's Training and Doctrine Command, and the NASA Langley Research Center are located here.

What to See and Do

Air Power Park and Aviation History Center. Over 50 indoor and outdoor exhibits feature real fighter aircraft, missiles and rockets; local aviation history and model aircraft exhibits. Picnicking; playground. (Daily; closed Jan 1, Thanksgiving, Dec 25) 413 W Mercury Blvd, US 258. Phone 757/727-1163.   **Free**

Bluebird Gap Farm. This 60-acre farm includes barnyard zoo; indigenous wildlife such as deer and wolves; antique and modern farm equipment and farmhouse artifacts. Picnicking; playground. (Wed-Sun; closed major hols) 60 Pine Chapel Rd. Phone 757/727-6739.   **Free**

Buckroe Beach. Swimming; public park, concerts. Lifeguards (Memorial Day-Labor Day). 4 mi E on VA 351, foot of E Pembroke Ave on Chesapeake Bay. Phone 757/727-6347.   **Free**

Fort Monroe. First fort here was a stockade called Fort Algernourne (1609); second, Fort George, though built of brick, was destroyed by hurricane in 1749; present fort was completed about 1834. 3 mi SE via Mercury Blvd, Ingalls Rd.   **Free**

Casemate Museum. Provides insight on heritage of the fort, Old Point Comfort and of the Army Coast Artillery Corps. Museum offers access to a series of casemates and a walking tour of the fort. Jefferson Davis casemate contains cell in which the Confederacy's president was confined on false charges of plotting against the life of Abraham Lincoln. Museum features Civil War exhibits, military uniforms and assorted artwork, including three original Remington drawings, along with audiovisual programs. Scale models of coast artillery guns and dioramas represent the role of the coast artillery from 1901 to 1946. (Daily; closed Jan 1, Thanksgiving, Dec 25) Phone 757/727-3391.   **Free**

Chapel of the Centurion (1858). This is one of the oldest churches on the Virginia peninsula. Woodrow Wilson worshiped here occasionally.

Hampton Carousel (1920). Completely restored in 1991, antique carousel is housed in its own pavilion and features 48 hand-carved horses. (Apr-Sept, Mon-Sat, also Sun afternoons; Oct-Nov, daily, weather permitting; Dec 1-15, wkends) 602 Settlers Landing Rd, downtown, on waterfront. Phone 757/727-6381 or 757/727-6347 (Parks & Rec Dept).   **¢**

Hampton University (1868). (6,100 students) Founded by Union Brigadier General Samuel Chapman Armstrong, chief of the Freedman's Bureau, to prepare the youth of the South, regardless of color, for the work of organizing and instructing schools in the Southern states; many blacks and Native Americans came to be educated. Now Virginia's only coeducational, nondenominational, 4-yr private college. The Hampton choir is famous. It "sang up" a building, Virginia-Cleveland Hall, in 1870 on a trip through New England and Canada, raising close to $100,000 at concerts. E end of Queen St, ¼ mi off I-64 exit 267. Phone 757/727-5253. On campus are

Emancipation Oak. The Emancipation Proclamation was read here.

Museum. Collection of ethnic art; Native American & African artifacts; contemporary African-American works; paintings by renowned artists. (Daily; closed major and school hols) Huntington Bldg.   **Free**

Miss Hampton II Boat Tours. Narrated 3-hr cruise includes a stop at Fort Wool, a Civil War island fortress. (Apr-Oct) 764 Settlers Landing Rd. Phone 757/722-9102 or 888/757-BOAT.   **¢¢¢¢**

Settlers Landing Monument. Marks approx site of first settlers' landing near Strawberry Banks in 1607. Painting by Sidney King depicts visit to Kecoughtan by colonists en route to Jamestown. (Daily) ½ mi S, on grounds of the Veterans Affairs Medical Center between Hampton River and Mill Creek, off I-64 exit 268.   **Free**

St John's Church (1728) **and Parish Museum.** Fourth site of worship of Episcopal parish established in 1610. Bible dating from 1599; communion silver from 1618; Colonial Vestry Book; taped historical message. (Daily) W Queens Way & Franklin St. Phone 757/722-2567.   **Free**

Virginia Air and Space Center and Hampton Roads History Center. Exhibits show the historical link between Hampton Roads' seafaring past and spacefaring future. Exhibits include 19 full-sized air- and spacecraft, the Apollo 12 Command Module, a moon rock and rare NASA artifacts. Films shown in 283-seat IMAX theater (daily). Gift shop. (Daily; closed Thanksgiving, Dec 25) Downtown, off I-64 exit 267. Phone 757/727-0900 or 800/296-0800.   **¢¢¢**   During summer, take the

NASA Langley Tour. Approx 1½-hr motor tour takes visitors to site where nation's aerospace history began. View NASA wind tunnels and Lunar Landing Research Center. Tours depart from Virginia Air and

Space Center; phone for times. With paid Space Center admission **¢¢**; Tour only **¢¢¢**

Annual Events

Hampton Jazz Festival. Hampton Coliseum. Phone 757/838-4203 (box office). 3 days late June.

Hampton Cup Regatta. Inboard hydroplane races. Phone 800/800-2202. Mid-Aug.

Hampton Bay Days. Arts and crafts, rides, science exhibits; entertainment. Phone 757/727-6122. Mid-Sept.

Motels

★★ COURTYARD BY MARRIOTT. *1917 Coliseum Dr (23666).* 757/838-3300; FAX 757/838-6387; res: 800/321-2211. 146 rms, 3 story. June-Sept: S, D $75-$85; each addl $10; suites $90-$119; under 18 free; higher rates jazz festival; lower rates rest of yr. Crib avail. TV; cable (premium). Heated pool; whirlpool. Complimentary coffee in rms. Bar Mon-Thurs 6-10 pm. Ck-out noon. Coin lndry. Business servs avail. In-rm modem link. Valet serv. Sundries. Exercise equipt. Refrigerator avail in suites. Cr cds: A, C, D, DS, MC, V.

D ⊠ 🕆 ⊠ 🔥 SC

✓ ★ HAMPTON INN. *1813 W.Mercury Blvd (23666).* 757/838-8484; FAX 757/826-0725; res: 800/426-7866. 131 rms, 6 story. S, D $79-$99. Crib free. Pet accepted, some restrictions. TV; cable (premium). Pool privileges. Complimentary continental bkfst. Complimentary coffee in rms. Restaurant adj 6 am-10 pm. Ck-out noon. Business servs avail. In-rm modem link. Exercise equipt. Cr cds: A, C, D, DS, MC, V.

D 🐾 🕆 ⊠ 🔥 SC

★★★ HOLIDAY INN. *1815 W Mercury Blvd (23666).* 757/838-0200; FAX 757/838-4964; res: 800/842-9370; res: 800/842-9370. 320 rms, 2-4 story. S, D $89-$130; suites $125-$225; wkend rates; higher rates Jazz Festival. Crib free. TV; cable (premium). 2 pools, 1 indoor; whirlpool. Coffee in rms. Restaurant 6 am-10 pm. Rm serv to 11 pm. Bar 11 am-midnight. Ck-out 11 am. Coin lndry. Convention facilities. Business center. In-rm modem link. Bellhops. Valet serv. Free airport transportation. Exercise equipt; sauna. Game rm. Some refrigerators. Balconies. Cr cds: A, C, D, DS, ER, JCB, MC, V.

D ⊠ 🕆 ⊠ 🔥 SC 🏃

Hotel

★★★ RADISSON HOTEL. *700 Settlers Lndg Rd (23669),* I-64 exit 267. 757/727-9700; FAX 757/722-4557; res: 800/333-3333. E-mail nossidar@aol.com; web www.radisson.com/hamptonva. 172 rms, 9 story. S, D $89-$125; each addl $10; suites $185-$450; under 18 free; wkend rates; higher rates special events. Crib free. TV; cable (premium). Pool; whirlpool, poolside serv. Restaurant 6:30 am-10 pm. Bar 11-2 am. Coffee in rms. Ck-out noon. Meeting rms. Business servs avail. In-rm modem link. Gift shop. Free airport, RR station, bus depot transportation. Exercise equipt. Some refrigerators. On Hampton River. Luxury level. Cr cds: A, C, D, DS, ER, JCB, MC, V.

D ⊠ 🕆 ⊠ 🔥 SC

Restaurants

★★ FIRE & ICE RESTAURANT. *2040 Coliseum Dr (23666),* in Coliseum Square Shopping Center. 757/826-6698. Hrs: 11 am-10 pm. Closed Sun; hols. Res accepted; required Fri, Sat. Bar. A la carte entrees: lunch $5.25-$9.45, dinner $8.95-$18.95. Specialties: fantasy flat breads, New Orleans-style po' boy sandwiches. Cr cds: A, C, MC, V.

D ⊠

★ SAMMY & NICK'S. *2718 W Mercury Blvd (23666).* 757/838-9100. Hrs: 11 am-11 pm. Sat, Sun from 7 am. Closed Thanksgiving, Dec 25. Res accepted. Bar. Semi-a la carte: bkfst $2-$6.45, lunch, dinner $2.95-$12.95. Child's meals. Specializes in prime rib, steak. Cr cds: A, C, D, DS, MC, V.

D ⊠

Harrisonburg (D-6)

(See also Luray, New Market, Staunton)

Founded 1780 **Pop** 30,707 **Elev** 1,352 ft **Area Code** 540 **Web** www.svta.org/hrcvb

Information Harrisonburg-Rockingham Convention and Visitors Bureau, 10 E Gay St, 22802; 540/434-2319

Originally named Rocktown due to the limestone outcroppings prevalent in the area, Harrisonburg became the county seat of Rockingham County when Thomas Harrison won a race against Mr. Keezle of Keezletown, three miles east. They had raced on horseback to Richmond to file their respective towns for the new county seat. Harrisonburg is noted for good hunting and fishing, recreational opportunities, beautiful scenery and turkeys. The annual production of more than five million turkeys, most of them processed and frozen, has made Rockingham County widely known. This is a college town with three four-year universities. Much of the George Washington and Jefferson National Forests are here.

What to See and Do

Caverns. There are several caverns within 24 mi of Harrisonburg. They include

Grand Caverns Regional Park. Known for its immense underground chambers and spectacular formations. Visited by Union and Confederate troops during the Civil War. Unique shield formations. Electrically lighted; 54°F. Park facilities include swimming pool; tennis courts, miniature golf; picnic pavilions; hiking and bicycle trails. Guided tours. (Apr-Oct, daily; Mar, wkends) 12 mi S on I-81, then 6 mi E on VA 256 in Grottoes. Phone 540/249-5705. **¢¢¢**

Shenandoah Caverns. 24 mi N on US 11. (See NEW MARKET)

Eastern Mennonite University (1917). (1,350 students) Many Mennonites live in this area. On campus is an art gallery, planetarium (shows by appt, free), natural history museum and the Menno Simons Historical Library, containing many 16th-century Mennonite volumes (school yr, daily exc Sun). Campus tours. 2 mi NW on VA 42. Phone 540/432-4000.

Fishing.

Lake Shenandoah. 3 mi E.

Shenandoah River. Good bass fishing.

Silver Lake. 5 mi SW on VA 42 in Dayton.

George Washington and Jefferson National Forests. Consist of approx 1.8 million acres. Hunting for deer, bear, wild turkey, small game; fishing for trout, bluegill and bass; riding trails; camping, picnicking, swimming. Scenic drives past Crabtree Falls, hardwood forests and unusual geologic features. Overlooks of Shenandoah Valley. Part of Appalachian Trail crosses forest. Fees are charged at some recreation sites. Trails for the visually impaired. 10 mi W on US 33. For information contact Forest Headquarters, 5162 Valleypointe Pkwy, Roanoke 24019-3050. Phone 540/265-5100. **Free**

James Madison University (1908). (14,000 students) Interesting old bluestone buildings. Campus tours through Admissions Office. S Main St. Phone 540/568-3621. On campus is

Miller Hall Planetarium and Sawhill Art Gallery. Phone 540/568-3621 for schedules. **Free**

Lincoln Homestead. Brick house, the rear wing of which was built by Abraham Lincoln's grandfather, and where his father was born. Main portion of the house was built about 1800 by Captain Jacob Lincoln. (Private) 9 mi N on VA 42.

Natural Chimneys Regional Park. Seven colorful and massive rock towers rise 120 ft above the plain. Picnic facilities, camping (fee; limited Nov-Feb); bicycle, nature trails; pool; playground. Park (daily). 15 mi SW off VA 42 in Mt Solon. Phone 540/350-2510. Per vehicle ¢¢

Shenandoah National Park (see). 24 mi E on US 33.

Shenandoah Valley Folk Art and Heritage Center. Featured is the Stonewall Jackson Electric Map that depicts his Valley Campaign of 1862. The 12-ft vertical relief map fills an entire wall and lets visitors see and hear the campaign, battle by battle. Also displays of Shenandoah Valley history, artifacts. (Wed-Sat, also Sun afternoons; closed mid-Dec-mid-Jan) 115 Bowman Rd. Phone 540/879-2681. ¢¢

Virginia Quilt Museum. Resource center for the study of quilts and quilting. (Mon, Thurs-Sat, also Sun afternoons; closed major hols) 301 S Main St. Phone 540/433-3818. ¢¢

Annual Events

Natural Chimneys Jousting Tournament. Natural Chimneys Regional Park. America's oldest continuous sporting event, held annually since 1821. "Knights" armed with lances charge down an 80-yard track and attempt to spear 3 small rings suspended from posts. Each knight is allowed 3 rides at the rings, thus, a perfect score is 9 rings. Ties are run off using successively smaller rings. 3rd Sat June & Aug.

Rockingham County Fair. Mid-Aug.

Motels

✓★★ **COMFORT INN.** *1440 E Market St (22801), I-81 exit 247A, on Sheraton Access Rd.* 540/433-6066; FAX 540/433-0793; res: 800/228-5150. 60 rms, 2 story. S, D $70-$80; each addl $10; under 18 free. Crib free. Pet accepted, some restrictions. TV; cable (premium). Pool. Complimentary continental bkfst. Complimentary coffee in rms. Ck-out noon. Business servs avail. Cr cds: A, C, D, DS, ER, JCB, MC, V.

D ⌨ ⇋ 🏊 🔥 SC

★★ **DAYS INN.** *1131 Forest Hill Rd (22801), I-81 exit 245.* 540/433-9353; FAX 540/433-5809; res: 800/329-7466 or 800/457-2792. 89 rms, 4 story. June-Oct: S $55; D $68; each addl $5; under 17 free; ski plan; higher rates special events, wkends (2-day min); lower rates rest of yr. Crib free. Pet accepted; $5/day. TV; cable (premium). Pool; whirlpool. Complimentary continental bkfst. Restaurant adj 11 am-11 pm. Ck-out 11 am. Meeting rms. Business servs avail. Sundries. Valet serv. 27-hole golf privileges, greens fee $30, pro, putting green, driving range. Downhill ski 12 mi. Health club privileges. Refrigerators, microwaves avail. Cr cds: A, C, D, DS, MC, V.

D ⌨ 🎿 🎳 ⇋ 🏊 🔥 SC

★★ **HAMPTON INN.** *85 University Blvd (22801), I-81 exit 247A.* 540/432-1111; FAX 540/432-0748; res: 800/426-7866. E-mail haminn@aol.com. 164 rms, 4 story. May-Oct: S, D $68-$78; under 19 free; higher rates university events; lower rates rest of yr. Crib free. TV; cable (premium). Pool. Complimentary continental bkfst. Complimentary coffee in rms. Restaurant nearby. Ck-out noon. Meeting rms. Business servs avail. In-rm modem link. Valet serv. Sundries. Health club privileges. Refrigerators, microwaves avail. Cr cds: A, C, D, DS, MC, V.

D ⇋ 🏊 🔥 SC

✓★★ **HOWARD JOHNSON.** *605 Port Republic Rd (22801), I-81 exit 245.* 540/434-6771; FAX 540/434-0153; res: 800/654-2000. 134 rms, 2 story. Mar-Nov: S $44.95-$54.95; D $44.95-$59.95; each addl $5; higher rates some univ events; lower rates rest of yr. Crib free. Pet accepted. TV; cable (premium). Pool; wading pool. Restaurant 6 am-9 pm. Ck-out noon. Business servs avail. Refrigerators avail. Private patios, balconies. Cr cds: A, C, D, DS, ER, JCB, MC, V.

D ⌨ ⇋ 🏊 🔥 SC

✓★★ **VILLAGE INN.** *4979 S Valley Pike (22801), on VA 11, 1½ mi N of I-81 exit 240.* 540/434-7355; FAX 540/434-7355; res: 800/736-7355. 36 rms. S $43; D $49-$59; each addl $5; kit units $64. Crib free. Pet accepted. TV; cable (premium). VCR avail (movies). Pool. Playground. Restaurant 7-10 am, 5:30-9 pm; closed Sun. Ck-out noon. Meeting rm. Business servs avail. Sundries. Health club privileges. Lawn games. Many in-rm whirlpools. Picnic tables. Cr cds: A, C, D, DS, MC, V.

D ⌨ ⇋ 🏊 🔥 🛶

Motor Hotel

★★★ **FOUR POINTS BY SHERATON.** *1400 E Market St (22801), off I-81 exit 247A.* 540/433-2521; FAX 540/434-0253; res: 800/708-7037. 140 rms, 5 story. S, D $99-$109; each addl $10; under 18 free. Crib free. Pet accepted. TV; cable (premium). Indoor pool; wading pool, whirlpool, poolside serv. Restaurant 6:30-2 pm, 5-10 pm. Rm serv. Bar 11-2 am; entertainment. Ck-out noon. Meeting rms. Business servs avail. In-rm modem link. Bellhops. Valet serv. Exercise equipt; sauna. Health club privileges. Some bathrm phones; refrigerators, microwaves avail. Cr cds: A, C, D, DS, ER, JCB, MC, V.

D ⌨ ⇋ 🏋 🏊 🔥 🛶 SC

Hopewell (E-8)

(See also Petersburg, Richmond, Surry, Williamsburg)

Founded 1613 **Pop** 23,101 **Elev** 50 ft **Area Code** 804 **Zip** 23860

Information Hopewell Area-Prince George Chamber of Commerce, 210 N 2nd Ave; 804/458-5536

The second permanent English settlement in America has been an important inland port since early times, having a fine channel 28 feet deep and 300 feet wide. It was the birthplace of statesman John Randolph of Roanoke. Edmund Ruffin, an early agricultural chemist who fired the first shot at Fort Sumter, was born near here.

"Cittie Point," at the junction of the James and Appomattox rivers, finally became one of Virginia's big cities during World War I when an E. I. Du Pont de Nemours Company dynamite plant on Hopewell Farm supplied guncotton to the Allies.

What to See and Do

City Point Unit of Petersburg National Battlefield (see). Grant's headquarters during the siege of Petersburg and largest Civil War supply depot. Includes Appomattox Manor, home to one family for 340 yrs; Grant's headquarters were on the front lawn. Many other buildings. (Daily; closed Jan 1, Thanksgiving, Dec 25, also some federal hols) Jct Cedar Ln & Pecan Ave. Phone 804/458-9504. **Free**

Flowerdew Hundred. Outdoor museum on the site of an early English settlement on the south bank of the James River. Originally inhabited by Native Americans, settled by Governor George Yeardley in 1618. Archaeological excavations are in progress. Thousands of artifacts, dating from the prehistoric period through the present, have been found and are on exhibit in the museum. A replicated 19th-century detached kitchen and working 18th-century-style windmill are open to visitors. Exhibits, interpretive tours. Picnicking. (Apr-Nov, daily exc Mon; rest of yr, by appt) 10 mi SE on VA 10. Phone 804/541-8897 or 804/541-8938. ¢¢

Merchants Hope Church (1657). Given the name of a plantation that was named for a barque plying between Virginia and England. The exterior has been called the most beautiful colonial brickwork in America. Oldest operating Protestant church in the country. (Open by request) 6 mi E on VA 10, then ½ mi S on VA 641. Phone 804/458-6197. **Donation**

Annual Events

Prince George County Heritage Fair. Flowerdew Hundred. Arts and crafts; educational exhibits and demonstrations; music, food, children's rides, hayrides. Last wkend Apr.

Hooray for Hopewell Festival. Downtown. Arts and crafts, food, entertainment, children's rides. 3rd wkend Sept.

Motels

★ **HOLIDAY INN EXPRESS.** *4911 Oaklawn Blvd (23860), at jct I-295 & VA 36.* 804/458-1500; FAX 804/458-9151; res: 800/222-3297. 115 rms, 2 story, 50 kit suites. S $50-$75; D $50-$95; each addl $5; kit suites $62-$100; under 18 free; higher rates special events. Crib free. TV; cable, VCR avail (movies). Pool; whirlpool. Complimentary continental bkfst. Restaurant nearby. Ck-out 11 am. Coin lndry. Business servs avail. Exercise equipt; sauna. Refrigerators. Cr cds: A, C, D, DS, JCB, MC, V.

D ☒ 🏃 ⊠ 🔥 SC

✓ ★ **INNKEEPER.** *3952 Courthouse Rd (23860).* 804/458-2600; FAX 804/458-1915; res: 800/466-6337. 104 rms, 3 story. S $52.99-$79.99; D $55.99-$79.99; each addl $5. Crib free. TV; cable. Pool. Complimentary continental bkfst. Restaurant adj 6:30 am-11 pm. Ck-out noon. Coin lndry. Meeting rms. Business servs avail. In-rm modem link. Refrigerators; microwaves avail. Cr cds: A, C, D, DS, MC, V.

D ☒ ⊠ 🐾 SC

Hot Springs (D-5)

(See also Clifton Forge, Covington, Warm Springs)

Pop 300 (est) **Elev** 2,238 ft **Area Code** 540 **Zip** 24445

A Ranger District office of the George Washington and Jefferson National Forests is located here.

What to See and Do

Homestead Ski Area. Double chairlift, T-bar, J-bar, baby rope tow; patrol, school, rentals; snowmaking; cafeteria, bar. Ice curling, ice-skating rink (Thanksgiving-Mar). On US 220. Phone 540/839-7721 (ski information) or 800/336-5771 (resort). ¢¢¢¢-¢¢¢¢¢

Motel

✓ ★ **ROSALOE MOTEL.** *590 N Rte 220 (24445), 3 mi N on US 220.* 540/839-5373. 14 rms, 6 kits. S $38; D $48; each addl $4; kits. $42-$55; family rates. Crib free. TV; cable (premium). Complimentary coffee in rms. Restaurant nearby. Ck-out noon. Downhill ski 3 mi. Refrigerators; microwaves avail. Cr cds: A, C, D, DS, MC, V.

🏃 🐾

Resort

★ ★ ★ ★ **THE HOMESTEAD RESORT.** *US 220 (24445).* 540/839-1766; FAX 540/839-7556; res: 800/838-1766. Web www.thehomestead. com. Famous for its mineral waters since 1766, this luxurious resort is on a 15,000-acre estate. Spacious guest rooms have Victorian decor. 513 units, 4-12 story. Apr-Oct: S, D $212-306; suites $372-$810; family rates; MAP avail; ski, golf, tennis plans; some seasonal rates; some lower rates rest of yr. Serv charges: 15% daily housekeeping and 15% at all dining outlets. Crib free. TV; cable. 2 pools, 1 indoor; lifeguard. Supervised child's activities; ages 3-12. Dining rm 7-10 am, 11:30 am-4 pm, 6-9:30 pm. Afternoon tea. Box lunches, snack bar. Rm serv 7 am-midnight. Bar 11 am-midnight. Ck-out noon, ck-in 4 pm. Convention facilities. Business center. Valet serv. Gift shops. Airport, RR station, bus depot transportation. Sports pros. Tennis. Three 18-hole golf courses, greens fee $100-$150, cart $15/per-

son, putting greens, driving range. Downhill/x-country ski on site. Snowboarding. Skating. Hiking, horseback trails. Skeet & trap shooting. Lawn games. Game rm. Movies. Bowling. Exercise equipt. Spa, mineral pool. Microwaves avail. Cr cds: A, C, D, DS, MC, V.

D 🐾 🏂 🦅 🎿 🎣 ⊠ 🏃 🔥 🚶

Inn

✓ ★ ★ **VINE COTTAGE INN.** *US 220 (24445).* 540/839-2422; FAX 540/839-2422; res: 800/410-9755. E-mail charlton@va.tds.net. 15 rms, 7 share bath, 3 story. No elvtrs. No rm phones. S, D $55-$90; each addl $15-$20; hols 2-day min. Closed 2 wks in Mar. Crib $15. Pet accepted, some restrictions; $25. Cable TV in common rm, VCR avail. Complimentary full bkfst. Restaurant nearby 11 am-10 pm. Ck-out noon, ck-in 3 pm. Luggage handling. Downhill ski 1 mi. Built in 1894; family-oriented Victorian inn. Totally nonsmoking. Cr cds: A, C, DS, MC, V.

🐾 🦅 ⊠ 🔥

Restaurants

✓ ★ **COUNTRY CAFE.** *Rte 2 Box 2b (24445), 2 mi S on US 220.* 540/839-2111. Hrs: 7 am-9 pm; Sun to 2 pm. Closed Mon; Jan 1, Dec 25. Res accepted. Wine, beer. Semi-a la carte: bkfst $3-$6, lunch $4-$5, dinner $7-$15. Child's meals. Specializes in country cooking. Own baking. Country decor with woodburning kitchen stove. Cr cds: C, MC, V.

⊒

★ ★ ★ **SAM SNEAD'S TAVERN.** *Main St (24445).* 540/839-7666. Hrs: 5:30-9:30 pm; Sun to 9 pm. Closed Mon-Wed (Jan-Mar). Res required. Semi-a la carte: dinner $7.95-$24.95. Specializes in fresh mountain trout, Black Angus steaks. Outdoor dining. Rustic decor. Cr cds: A, C, D, DS, MC, V.

D ⊒

Irvington (E-9)

(See also Lancaster)

Pop 496 **Elev** 31 ft **Area Code** 804 **Zip** 22480

What to See and Do

Historic Christ Church (1735). Built by Robert Carter, ancestor of 8 governors of Virginia, 2 presidents, 3 signers of the Declaration of Independence, a chief justice and many others who served the country with distinction. Restored; original structure and furnishings, 3-decker pulpit. Built on site of earlier wooden church (1669); family tombs. Tours. (Apr-Nov, daily) 2½ mi W, off VA 200. Phone 804/438-6855. **Free** On the grounds is

Carter Reception Center. Narrated video presentation; museum with artifacts from Corotoman, home of Robert Carter, and from the church construction; photographs of the restoration. Guides. (Apr-Nov, daily) **Free**

Motel

★ **WHISPERING PINES MOTEL.** *Rte 3 (22578), ¼ mi N on VA 3.* 804/435-1101. 29 rms. S, D $59-$69; each addl $5. Crib $5. TV; cable. Pool; wading pool. Restaurant nearby. Ck-out 11 am. Sundries. Picnic tables. On wooded grounds. Cr cds: A, C, MC, V.

☒ ⊠ 🐾 SC

Resort

★★ **THE TIDES.** *1 St. Andrews Ln (22480), N on VA 200, then W on VA 646, then SW on County 709, follow signs.* 804/438-6000; FAX 804/438-5950; res: 800/843-3746. 60 units. Mid-Mar-Dec: S, D $108-$198; each addl $30; cottages to 2 persons $300; under 18 free; AP, MAP avail; golf plans; higher rates some wkends. Closed rest of yr. Crib free. Pet accepted, some restrictions; $10. TV; cable (premium), VCR avail (free movies). 2 pools, 1 saltwater, 1 heated; poolside erv. Playground. Free supervised child's activities (late June-Labor Day); ages 5-12. Coffee in rms. Dining rm 8-9:30 am, noon-2 pm, 6-10 pm. Bar noon-11 pm. Ck-out 1 pm, ck-in after 3:30 pm. Coin lndry. Meeting rms. Business servs avail. Bellhops. Valet serv. Gift shop. Lighted tennis. 45-hole golf, greens fee $25-$40, pro, putting greens, driving range. Exercise equipt; sauna. Marina, cruises, boat rental. Bicycles. Lawn games. Game rm. Rec rm. Refrigerators. Balconies. Cr cds: C, DS, MC, V.

Jamestown (Colonial National Historical Park) (E-9)

(See also Colonial Parkway, Newport News, Surry, Williamsburg, Yorktown)

Area Code 757 **Zip** 23690

On May 13, 1607, in this unpromising setting, the first permanent English settlement in the New World was founded. From the beginning, characteristics of the early United States were established—self-government, industry, commerce and the plantation system. The 104 men and boys who landed here that day and the people who followed them forecast the varied origins of the American populace. There were English, Germans, Africans, French, Italians, Poles and Irish.

The *Susan Constant* (120 tons), the *Godspeed* (40 tons) and the *Discovery* (20 tons) brought the settlers here after a landing at Cape Henry. Thus, 20 years after the tragic failure to establish a colony at Roanoke Island and 13 years before the Pilgrims landed at Plymouth, Massachusetts, the English succeeded in settling in America.

The landing was not auspicious. Captain John Smith, ablest man in the group, was in chains; most of the others possessed a singular ineptitude for existing in a strange, hostile wilderness. Smith's ability and driving personality soon made him the acknowledged leader. For about a year he kept the bickering at a minimum, and the establishment of a colony was well under way.

The London Company, under whose patronage the colonists had set forth, continued to send "gentlemen" and adventurers to reinforce the colony. The second such shipment (September 1608) elicited the famous "Smith's rude answer" to company demands for gold and assorted riches. He wrote in part, "I entreat you rather send but thirty carpenters, husbandmen, gardeners, fishermen, blacksmiths, masons and diggers up of trees, roots...than a thousand of such as we have: for except we be able both to lodge them and feed them, the most will consume with want of necessaries before they can be made good for anything."

"Good for anything or not, this little band made glass in 1608, introduced the first commercial tobacco cultivation in 1612 and produced the country's first representative legislative body in 1619. In the earliest years, clapboards (some of which were shipped back to England) were made here, and later bricks, fishing nets, pottery, a variety of tools and other items needed in the colony.

The first Africans were brought to the colony in 1619 on a Dutch privateer. They were probably indentured servants, pledged to work until their passage had been paid off. This was a common arrangement at the time.

There was not an easy day for any of the colonists for years. Crops failed, and rats ate the corn. Until John Rolfe married Pocahontas, daughter of Chief Powhatan, in 1614, the Native Americans were suspicious and unfriendly. Disease plagued the settlers. The winter of 1609-1610 was called the "starving time." The 350-person colony was reduced to about 60 emaciated, defeated survivors who decided to give up and return to England. The June 1610 arrival of Lord De la Warre with reinforcements and supplies dissuaded them. Then the colony began to build and hope returned.

When Jamestown became a Royal Colony in 1624, feeling against personal (and often high-handed) government began to mount. By 1676 there was open revolt, led by Nathaniel Bacon, the younger. Bacon's forces finally burned the town, calling it a "stronghold of oppression." It was partially rebuilt, but decline was irrevocable, in part due to the damp, unhealthy climate of the area. The statehouse burned in 1698, and in 1699 the government moved to Middle Plantation and renamed it Williamsburg. By Revolutionary days Jamestown was no longer an active community. About the same time, the James River washed away the sandy isthmus, and the site became an island.

Nothing of the 17th-century settlement remains above ground except the Old Church Tower. Since 1934, however, archaeological exploration by the National Park Service has made the outline of the town clear. Cooperative efforts by the Park Service and the Association for the Preservation of Virginia Antiquities (which owns 22.5 acres of the island, including the Old Church Tower) have exposed foundations and restored streets, property ditches, hedgerows, fences and the James Fort site from 1607. Markers, recorded messages, paintings and monuments are everywhere. Entrance station (daily; closed Dec 25). For further information contact the Superintendent, PO Box 210, Yorktown 23690; 757/898-3400. Jamestown Island entrance fee $5/adult (over age 16); Golden Access, Age and Eagle passports accepted (see MAKING THE MOST OF YOUR TRIP).

What to See and Do

✪ **Colonial National Historical Park.** Recommended as a starting point is the

Visitor Center. Guide leaflets, introductory film and exhibits. Post office. (Daily; closed Dec 25) From here you can walk through

"New Towne." Area where Jamestown expanded around 1620 may be toured along "Back-Streete" and other original streets. Section includes reconstructed foundations indicating sites of Country House, Governor's House, homes of Richard Kemp, builder of one of the first brick houses in America, Henry Hartwell, a founder of College of William and Mary, and Dr. John Pott and William Pierce, who led the "thrusting out" of Gov John Harvey in 1635.

First landing site. Fixed by tradition as point in river, about 200 yards from present seawall, upriver from Old Church Tower.

James Fort site. Excavation of first fort (1607) can be viewed between seawall and Old Church Tower.

Old Church Tower. Only standing ruin of the 17th-century town. Believed to be part of first brick church (1639). Has 3-ft-thick walls of handmade brick.

Memorial Church. Built in 1907 by the National Society of the Colonial Dames of America over foundations of original church. Within are two foundations alleged to be of earlier churches, one from 1617 that housed first assembly.

Tercentenary Monument. Erected by US (1907) to commemorate 300th Jamestown anniversary. Other monuments include Captain John Smith statue (by William Couper), Pocahontas Monument (by William Ordway Partridge), House of Burgesses Monument (listing members of first representative legislative body in America). Located near Jamestown Visitor Center.

Confederate Fort (1861). One of two Civil War fortifications on the island. Near Old Church Tower.

Trails. Three- and 5-mi auto drives provide access to entire area. Visitor center has 45-min auto drive and town-site tape tours available.

Glasshouse. Colonists produced glass here in 1608. Demonstration exhibits, glassblowing (daily; closed Dec 25).

Dale House. Archaeological laboratory. A viewing area is open to the public.

Jamestown Settlement. Living history museum re-creates the first permanent English settlement in New World. Recalls early-17th-century Jamestown with full-scale reproductions of ships which arrived in 1607 and the triangular James Fort. Powhatan Indian Village depicts Native American culture encountered by English colonists. Museum complex features orientation film, changing gallery and three exhibit galleries focusing on the history of Jamestown and the Powhatan. Food service avail. Combination ticket with Yorktown Victory Center (see YORKTOWN) avail. (Daily; closed Jan 1, Dec 25) Adj to historic Jamestown. Phone 757/253-4838. ¢¢¢; Combination ticket ¢¢¢¢

Annual Events

Jamestown Weekend. Jamestown, the original town site. Commemorates arrival of first settlers in 1607; special tours and activities. Mid-May.

First Assembly Day. Jamestown, the original town site. Commemorates first legislative assembly in 1619. Late July.

Keysville (F-7)

Pop 606 **Elev** 642 ft **Area Code** 804 **Zip** 23947

What to See and Do

Twin Lakes State Park. More than 250 acres of state forest; 2 lakes. Swimming, bathhouse; fishing; boating (rentals, launching, electric motors only). Hiking, bicycle, self-guided trails. Picnicking, playground, concession. Camping, hook-ups, tent & trailer sites, cabins (Mar-Dec); pavilion. Standard fees. 15 mi NE on US 360, then 1½ mi NW off VA 613. Phone 804/392-3435.

Motel

✓ ★ **SHELDON'S MOTEL.** 1450 Four Locust Hwy (23947), 1½ mi N on US 15 Business. 804/736-8434; FAX 804/736-9402. E-mail sheldons@hovac.com. 40 rms, 2 story. S $35.95-$50; D $41.95-$50; each addl $6. Crib $6. Pet accepted. TV; cable (premium). Restaurant 6:30 am-10 pm. Ck-out noon. Business servs avail. Some refrigerators; microwaves avail. Cr cds: A, C, DS, MC, V.

D 🐾 📵 🔥

Lancaster (E-9)

(See also Irvington)

Pop 150 (est) **Elev** 89 ft **Area Code** 804 **Zip** 22503

The family of Mary Ball Washington, mother of George Washington, were early settlers of this area. Washington's maternal ancestors are buried in the churchyard of St Mary's Whitechapel Church five miles west of Lancaster.

What to See and Do

Lancaster County Courthouse Historic District. Sycamore trees surround this area around the antebellum courthouse (1860). Marble obelisk is one of the first monuments erected to Confederate soldiers (1872).

Mary Ball Washington Museum and Library Complex. Contains the Old Clerk's Office (1797), the Old Jail (1819), Lancaster House (1800), the headquarters and main museum building. Also Virginia genealogical research center. (Wed-Sat, Tues by appt) Phone 804/462-7280. Museum ¢; Research center ¢¢

St Mary's Whitechapel Church (1740-1741). Church where Mary Ball and her family worshiped; many of the tombstones bear the Ball name. 5 mi W on VA 622.

Inn

★★ **INN AT LEVELFIELD INC.** 10155 Mary Ball Rd (22503), 2 mi E on VA 3, beyond the Courthouse. 804/435-6887; FAX 804/435-7440. 4 rms, 2 story. No rm phones. S $55; D $95; each addl $15. Pool. Complimentary full bkfst. Ck-out 11 am, ck-in 2 pm. Business servs avail. Lawn games. Antiques; hand-made quilts. Antebellum landmark homestead (1857) with double-tiered portico and four massive chimneys; 1,000-ft entrance drive. Located on 54 acres with 12 acres of lawn & 42 acres of timberland bounded by stream. Cr cds: A, C, MC, V.

🏊 📵 🔥 🐾

Leesburg (C-8)

(See also Arlington County, McLean; also see District of Columbia)

Founded 1758 **Pop** 16,202 **Elev** 352 ft **Area Code** 703 **Web** www.visit loudouncova.org

Information Loudoun Tourism Council, 108-D South St SE, 20175; 703/771-2170 or 800/752-6118

Originally named Georgetown for King George II of England, this town was later renamed Leesburg, probably after Francis Lightfoot Lee, a signer of the Declaration of Independence and a local landowner. Leesburg is located in a scenic area of rolling hills, picturesque rural towns and Thoroughbred horse farms, where point-to-point racing and steeplechases are popular.

What to See and Do

Ball's Bluff Battlefield. One of the smallest national cemeteries in US marks site of third armed engagement of Civil War. On Oct 21, 1861, four Union regiments suffered catastrophic losses while surrounded by Confederate forces; the Union commander, a US senator and presidential confidant, was killed here along with half his troops, who were either killed, wounded, captured or drowned while attempting to recross the Potomac River. Oliver Wendell Holmes, Jr, later to become a US Supreme Court justice, was wounded here. N via US 15.

Loudoun Museum. Century-old restored building contains exhibits and memorabilia of the area; audiovisual presentation "A Special Look at Loudoun." Brochures, information about Loudoun County; walking tours; self-guided tour booklets (fee). (Daily; closed Jan 1, Thanksgiving, Dec 25; also Jan) 16 Loudoun St SW. Phone 703/777-7427. **Donation**

Morven Park. Originally the residence of Thomas Swann, early Maryland governor, the estate was enlarged upon by Westmoreland Davis, governor of Virginia from 1918 to 1922. The 1,200-acre park includes a 28-room mansion; boxwood gardens; Winmill Carriage Museum with more than 70 horse-drawn vehicles; Museum of Hounds and Hunting with video presentation and artifacts depicting the history of fox hunting; and Morven Park International Equestrian Center (see ANNUAL EVENTS). (Apr-Oct, Tues-Sun afternoons, also Mon hols) Old Waterford Rd, 1 mi N of Leesburg. Phone 703/777-2414. ¢¢

Oatlands (1803). A 261-acre estate; classical-revival mansion, built by George Carter, was the center of a 5,000-acre plantation; the house was partially remodeled in 1827, which was when the front portico was added. Most of the building materials, including bricks and wood, came from or were made on the estate. Interior, furnished with American, English and French antiques, reflects period between 1897 and 1965, when the house was owned by Mr and Mrs William Corcoran Eustis, prominent Washingtonians. Formal garden has some of the finest boxwood in US. Farm fields provide equestrian area for races and horse shows. (Early Apr-Dec, daily; closed Thanksgiving, Dec 25) 6 mi S on US 15. Phone 703/777-3174.

Vineyard and Winery Tours. For a list of area winery tours contact the Loudoun Tourism Council, 108-D South St SE; phone 800/752-6118.

Waterford. Eighteenth-century Quaker village, designated a National Historic Landmark, has been restored as a residential community. An Annual Homes Tour (1st full wkend Oct) has craft demonstrations, exhibits, traditional music. Waterford Foundation has brochures outlining self-guided walking tours. 3 mi NW on VA 7, ¼ mi on VA 9, then 2 mi N on VA 662. Phone 703/882-3018. **Free**; Brochures ¢

Annual Events

Loudoun Hunt Pony Club Horse Trials. Held at Morven Park International Equestrian Institute, Morven Park. Competition in combined training: dressage, cross-country and stadium jumping. Phone 703/777-2890. Late Mar.

Homes and Gardens Tour. Sponsored by Garden Club of Virginia. Late Apr.

Sheep Dog Trials. Oatlands. May.

Wine Festival. Morven Park. Many wineries participate; includes seminar for home/commercial wine growers; grape-stomping, waiters' race, jousting tournament, music, wine tastings, awards presentations. Phone 202/537-0961. Mid-July.

August Court Days. Reenactment of the opening of the 18th-century judicial court. Festivities resemble a country fair with craft demonstrations, games, entertainers on the street. Phone 703/771-2170 or 800/752-6118. 3rd wkend Aug.

Christmas at Oatlands. Candlelight tours, 1800s decorations, refreshments. Mid-Nov-Dec, Sat evenings.

Motels

✓ ★ **DAYS INN.** *721 E Market St (20176), near Prosperity Shopping Center.* 703/777-6622; FAX 703/777-4119; res: 800/329-7466. 81 rms, 2 story. Mar-Oct: S, D $65; each addl $6; under 12 free; lower rates rest of yr. Crib free. Pet accepted, some restrictions; $6. TV; cable (premium). Complimentary continental bkfst. Restaurant nearby. Ck-out noon. Coin lndry. Business servs avail. Cr cds: A, C, D, DS, JCB, MC, V.

★ ★ ★ **HOLIDAY INN.** *1500 E Market St (20176), on VA 7.* 703/771-9200; FAX 703/771-1575; res: 800/272-6232 or 88/850-8545. E-mail leesburgbo@crownam.com. 126 rms, 2 story. S, D $99-$159; each addl $10; suites $159; under 16 free. Crib free. Pet accepted. TV; cable (premium). Pool. Coffee in rms. Restaurant 6:30 am-2 pm, 5-10 pm. Bar 4 pm-midnight. Ck-out noon. Coin lndry. Meeting rms. Business servs avail. Free airport transportation. Exercise equipt. Colonial mansion (1773). Cr cds: A, C, D, DS, ER, JCB, MC, V.

Hotel

★ ★ ★ **LANSDOWNE CONFERENCE RESORT LEESBURG.** *44050 Woodridge Pkwy (20176), E on VA 7, left onto Lansdowne Blvd, then right onto Woodridge Pkwy.* 703/729-8400; FAX 703/729-4096; res: 800/541-4801. 305 units, 9 story. S $149-$209; D $169-$229; suites $275-$700; under 18 free; wkend rates; golf plans. Crib free. TV; cable (premium). 2 pools, 1 indoor; whirlpool, poolside serv, lifeguard. Supervised child's activities; ages 3-12. Restaurant 6 am-midnight. Bar; entertainment Wed-Sun. Ck-out noon. Convention facilities. Business center. In-rm modem link. Concierge. Gift shop. Airport transportation. Lighted tennis. 18-hole golf, pro, greens fee $85-$95, putting green, driving range. Raquetball. Exercise rm; sauna, steam rm. Massage. Lawn games. Bicycle rentals. Refrigerators avail. Balconies. Picnic tables. Cr cds: A, C, D, DS, MC, V.

Inns

★ ★ **LEESBURG COLONIAL INN.** *19 S King St (20176).* 703/777-5000; FAX 703/777-7000; res: 800/478-8502. 10 rms, 3 story. S $58-$150; D $68-$150; under 10 free. Crib free. Pet accepted, some restrictions. TV; cable. Complimentary full bkfst; afternoon refreshments in library. Restaurant (see Leesburg Colonial Inn). Rm serv. Ck-out noon, ck-in 2 pm. Luggage handling. Free airport transportation. Tennis privileges. Golf privileges. Health club privileges. Picnic tables. Historic building (1759) built of same stone as Capitol in DC. Fireplaces; some in-rm whirlpools. Cr cds: A, C, D, DS, MC, V.

✓ ★ ★ **LITTLE RIVER INN.** *39307 John Mosby Hwy (20105), S on VA 15, then 2 mi W on US 50.* 703/327-6742. 9 units, 3 share bath, 2 story, 3 cottages. Some rm phones. S $65-$80; D $65-$95; each addl $20; cottages $145-$190. Children under 10 yrs in cottages only. Complimentary full bkfst. Pool privileges. Ck-out noon, ck-in 3 pm. Meeting rm. Private patios, balconies. Picnic tables. Built 1810; antiques. In foothills of Bull Run Mts. Cr cds: A, C, MC, V.

★ ★ ★ **NORRIS HOUSE INN.** *108 Loudoun St SW (20175).* 703/777-1806; FAX 703/771-8051; res: 800/644-1806. E-mail inn@norris house.com; web norrishouse.com. 6 rms, all share bath, 3 story. Rm phones avail. S $75-$90; D $90-$105; each addl $25; higher rates wkends (2-day min). Children wkdays only. Complimentary full bkfst; afternoon refreshments. Restaurant nearby. Ck-out noon, ck-in 4-8 pm. Business servs avail. Airport transportation. Lawn games. Picnic tables. Built 1760. Veranda overlooking gardens. Antique furnishings; most rms with fireplace. Totally nonsmoking. Cr cds: A, C, D, DS, MC, V.

Restaurants

✓ ★ ★ **GREEN TREE.** *15 S King St (20175).* 703/777-7246. Hrs: 11:30 am-10 pm; Sun brunch 11:30 am-4 pm. Res accepted. Serv bar. Semi-a la carte: lunch $6.95-$11.95, dinner $14.95-$24.95. Sun brunch $14.95. Specialties: Robert's Delight (beef dish), Jefferson's Delight (calf's liver soaked in milk). Own baking. Authentic 18th-century recipes. Windows open to street. Fireplaces. Strolling musician Fri-Sat. Cr cds: A, C, D, DS, MC, V.

★ ★ **LAUREL BRIGADE INN.** *20 W Market St (20176).* 703/777-1010. Hrs: 11:30 am-2 pm, 5:30-8:30 pm; Fri, Sat to 9 pm; Sun 8 am-11 am, noon-7 pm. Closed Mon. Res accepted; required hols. Serv bar. Semi-a la carte: lunch $4-$10, dinner $9.50-$20. Complete meals: lunch $11-$14.50, dinner $12.50-$25. Child's meals. Specializes in chicken, beef, seafood. Outdoor dining. Oldest section dates from 1759; colonial decor, stone walls, fireplace. Family-owned. Cr cds: A, C, DS, MC, V.

★ ★ **LEESBURG COLONIAL INN.** *(See Leesburg Colonial Inn)* 703/777-5000. Hrs: 11:30 am-10 pm. Res accepted. Continental menu. Bar. Semi-a la carte: lunch $5.95-$10.95, dinner $15.95-$18.95. Child's meals. Specializes in beef, seafood. Outdoor dining. Colonial decor. Cr cds: A, C, D, DS, MC, V.

Lexington (E-6)

(See also Clifton Forge, Natural Bridge)

Founded 1777 **Pop** 6,959 **Elev** 1,060 ft **Area Code** 540 **Zip** 24450
E-mail lexington@rockbridge.net
Information Visitors Bureau, 106 E Washington St; 540/463-3777

Lexington was home to two of the greatest Confederate heroes: Robert E. Lee and Thomas J. "Stonewall" Jackson. Both are buried here. Sam Houston, Cyrus McCormick and James Gibbs (inventor of the sewing machine) were born nearby.

This town, set in rolling country between the Blue Ridge and Allegheny mountains, is the seat of Rockbridge County. Lexington is known for attractive homes, trim farms, fine old mansions and two of the leading educational institutions in the Commonwealth: Washington and Lee University and Virginia Military Institute.

What to See and Do

Goshen Pass. Scenic mountain gorge formed by Maury River. Memorial to Matthew Fontaine Maury is here. 19 mi NW on VA 39.

Lexington Carriage Company. Approx 45-min narrated horse-drawn carriage tours of historic Lexington. Groups of 10 or more by appt only. (Apr-Oct, daily, weather permitting) Tours depart across street from Visitor Center, 106 E Washington St. Phone 540/463-5647. ¢¢¢

Stonewall Jackson House. Only home owned by Confederate General Stonewall Jackson, restored to its appearance of 1859-1861. Many of the furnishings were once owned by Jackson. Interpretive slide presentation and guided tours (½ hr). Restored gardens; shop. (Daily; closed Jan 1, Easter, Thanksgiving, Dec 25) 8 E Washington St. Phone 540/463-2552. ¢¢

Stonewall Jackson Memorial Cemetery. Gen Jackson and more than 100 other Confederate soldiers are buried here. E side of S Main St.

Virginia Horse Center. Sprawling across nearly 400 acres, the Center provides a versatile site for numerous horse-related functions yr-round: shows, clinics, auctions, festivals. Fees vary. VA 11N to VA 39W. For schedule of events, contact PO Box 1051; phone 540/463-2194.

Virginia Military Institute (1839). (1,300 cadets) State military, engineering, sciences and arts college. Stonewall Jackson taught here, as did Matthew Fontaine Maury, famed naval explorer and inventor. George Catlett Marshall, a general of the army and author of the Marshall Plan, was a graduate. Mementos of these men are on display in VMI museum (daily; closed Jan 1, Thanksgiving, Dec 24-31). Dress parade (most Fri afternoons, weather permitting). On US 11. Phone 540/464-7207. **Free** Located on the S end of the parade ground is

George C. Marshall Museum (1964). Displays on life and career of the illustrious military figure and statesman (1880-1959); World War I, electric map and recorded narration of World War II; Marshall Plan; gold medallion awarded with his Nobel Prize for Peace (1953). (Daily; closed Jan 1, Thanksgiving, Dec 25) Faces parade ground of VMI. Phone 540/463-7103. ¢¢

Washington and Lee University (1749). (1,900 students) Liberal arts university situated on an attractive campus with white colonnaded buildings; also includes Washington and Lee Law School. Founded as Augusta Academy in 1749; became Liberty Hall in 1776; its name was changed to Washington Academy in 1798, after receiving 200 shares of James River Canal Company stock from George Washington, and then to Washington College. General Robert E. Lee served as president from 1865-1870; soon after Lee's death in 1870, it became Washington and Lee University. W Washington St. Phone 540/463-8400. Within the university grounds is

Lee Chapel. Robert E. Lee is entombed here. It also houses Lee family crypt and museum, the marble "recumbent statue" of Lee and some of the art collection of Washington and Lee families. Lee's office remains as he left it. (Daily; closed Jan 1, Thanksgiving & following Fri, Dec 24, 25, 31) **Free**

Annual Events

Garden Week in Historic Lexington. Tour of homes and gardens in the Lexington, Rockbridge County area. Phone 540/463-3777. Late Apr.

"Holiday in Lexington." Parade, plays, children's events. Phone 540/463-3777. Early Dec.

Seasonal Event

Lime Kiln Arts' Theater at Lime Kiln. 14 S Randolph St. Professional theatrical productions and concerts in outdoor theater. Phone 540/463-3074. Memorial Day-Labor Day.

Motels

★★★ **BEST WESTERN INN.** *Willow Springs Rd At Hwy 39 (24450).* 540/464-1500; FAX 540/464-1500. 100 rms, 3 story, 10 suites. Apr-Oct: S $69.95-$87.95; D $79.95-$92.95; each addl $8, suites $92.95; under 12 free; higher rates special events; lower rates rest of yr. Crib free. Pet accepted, some restrictions. TV; cable (premium). Indoor/outdoor pool. Complimentary coffee in rms. Restaurant 7 am-10 pm. Rm serv. Bar to midnight. Ck-out 11 am. Coin lndry. Meeting rms. Business servs avail. In-rm modem link. Health club privileges. Refrigerator, microwave in suites. Cr cds: A, C, D, DS, JCB, MC, V.

D ⊕ ⊠ ⊠ ⊠ SC

✓ ★★ **DAYS INN.** *325 W Midland Trail (24450).* 540/463-2143; FAX 540/463-2143; res: 800/329-7466. 53 rms, 10 kit units. S $47.95-$57.95; D $55.95-$65.95; each addl $5. Crib free. Pet accepted, some restrictions. TV; cable (premium). Ck-out 11 am. Business servs avail. Some bathrm phones, refrigerators. Picnic tables. View of mountains. Cr cds: A, C, D, DS, ER, JCB, MC, V.

D ⊕ ⊠ ⊠ SC

★★ **HOLIDAY INN EXPRESS.** *US 11 & I-64 (24450).* 540/463-7351; FAX 540/463-7351; res: 800/465-4329. E-mail dominion@rockbridge.net; web www.rockbridge.net/anderson/index.htp. 72 rms, 2 story. S $75; D $85; each addl $10; under 18 free. Crib free. Pet accepted. TV; cable (premium). Complimentary continental bkfst. Ck-out 11 am. Business servs avail. In-rm modem link. View of mountains. Cr cds: A, C, D, DS, ER, JCB, MC, V.

D ⊕ ⊠ ⊠ SC

★★ **RAMADA INN.** *US 11N (24450).* 540/463-6400; FAX 540/464-3639. 80 rms, 4 story. May-Oct: S $60; D $70; each addl $6; under 19 free; wkly, wkend rates; higher rates special events; lower rates rest of yr. Crib free. Pet accepted. TV; cable (premium). Indoor pool. Restaurant 6 am-2 pm, 5-10 pm. Rm serv. Bar 5-10 pm. Ck-out noon. Meeting rms. Business servs avail. Sundries. Cr cds: A, C, D, DS, ER, JCB, MC, V.

D ⊕ ⊠ ⊠ ⊠ SC

★★ **TRAVELODGE.** *2809 N Lee Hwy; US 11 N (24450),* off exit 195. 540/463-9131; FAX 540/463-7448; res: 800/521-9131. 150 rms, 3 story. May-Oct: S, D $50-$85; each addl $5; under 18 free; lower rates rest of yr. Crib free. TV; cable (premium). Pool. Coffee in rms. Restaurant adj 6 am-9 pm. Ck-out 11 am. Meeting rms. Microwaves avail. Cr cds: A, C, D, DS, MC, V.

D ⊠ ⊠ ⊠ SC

Motor Hotels

★★ **COMFORT INN VIRGINIA HORSE CENTER.** *US 11 & 64 (24450),* at I-64 exit 55, I-81 exit 191. 540/463-7311; FAX 540/463-4590; res: 800/628-1956. E-mail Dominion@Rockbridge.net; web www.rockbridge.net/anderson/index.htp. 80 rms, 4 story. Apr-Nov: S $64.95-$76.95; D $64.95-$85; each addl $5; under 18 free; lower rates rest of yr. Crib free.

Pet accepted. TV; cable (premium). Indoor pool. Complimentary continental bkfst. Restaurant adj 6 am-11 pm. Ck-out 11 am. Coin lndry. Business servs avail. Sundries. Cr cds: A, C, D, DS, ER, JCB, MC, V.

✓ ★★ **HOWARD JOHNSON INN.** 2836 N Lee Hwy (24450), I-81 exit 195, US 11 N. 540/463-9181; FAX 540/464-3448; res: 800/654-2000. E-mail hojo@rockbridge.net. 100 rms, 5 story. S $50-$65; D $55-$75; each addl $7; under 18 free; higher rates special events. Crib free. Pet accepted. TV; cable (premium). Pool. Restaurant 6 am-8 pm. Ck-out noon. Coin lndry. Meeting rm. Business servs avail. Gift shop. Balconies. Private patios. On hill; panoramic view of mountains. Cr cds: A, C, D, DS, ER, JCB, MC, V.

Inns

★★ **ALEXANDER WITHROW INN.** 3 W Washington St (24450). 540/463-2044; FAX 540/463-7262. Web www.innbrook.com. 16 units, 4 story. S $85-$130; D $100-$145; each addl $15; family rates. Crib $5. TV; cable. Pool privileges. Complimentary continental bkfst; afternoon refreshments. Restaurant opp 5:30-9 pm. Ck-out noon, ck-in 2 pm. Business servs avail. Tennis privileges. Refrigerators. Private patios, balconies. Picnic tables. Built 1809; antiques. Cr cds: C, DS, MC, V.

★★ **FASSIFERN BED & BREAKFAST.** 27 Gallery Ln, Hwy 39 (24450), 3 mi N at jct VA 39 & County Rd 750; just N of jct US 11 & I-64 exit 55. 540/463-1013. 4 rms, 2 story. S, D $65-$92. Complimentary full bkfst. Restaurant nearby. Ck-out 11 am, ck-in 3 pm. Restored 1867 house; antiques. Grounds with pond, woods. Near VA Horse Center. Totally nonsmoking. Cr cds: C, MC, V.

★★★ **HUMMINGBIRD INN.** 30 Wood Ln (24439), US 11 N to VA 39 N, turn left, S on Wood Ln. 540/997-9065; FAX 540/997-0289; res: 800/397-3214. E-mail hmgbird@cfw.com; web www. humingbirdinn.com. 5 rms, 2 story. No rm phones. May-Nov: S $75-$105; D $80-$110; wkend rates; MAP avail: wkends (2-day min); lower rates rest of yr. Children over 12 yrs only. Pet accepted; $20. TV in common rm. Complimentary full bkfst. Restaurant nearby. Ck-out 11 am, ck-in 4 pm. Business servs avail. Rec rm. Lawn games. Some in-rm whirlpools, fireplaces. Picnic tables. On river. Victorian Carpenter Gothic villa built in 1780; wraparound verandahs. Totally nonsmoking. Cr cds: A, C, DS, MC, V.

★★★ **INN AT UNION RUN.** 325 Union Run (24450), I-81 exit 191S, or 180N. 540/463-9715; FAX 540/463-3526; res: 800/528-6466. E-mail unionrun@cfw.com; web www.unionrun.com. 8 rms, 2 story. Apr-Nov: S $75-$90; D $85-$125; each addl $20; lower rates rest of yr. Children over 10 yrs only. TV in common rm; cable (premium). Complimentary full bkfst. Restaurant 5-9 pm; closed Sun, Mon. Rm serv. Ck-out 11 am, ck-in 3 pm. Business servs avail. Lawn games. Many in-rm whirlpools. Some balconies. Picnic tables. Federal manor house built in 1883. View of mountains. Cr cds: A, C, MC, V.

★★ **MAPLE HALL COUNTRY INN.** 3111 N Lee Hwy, Rte 11 N (24450), I-81 exit 195, N on US 11. 540/463-6693; FAX 540/463-6693. Web www.virtualcities.com. 21 rms, 9 with shower only, 3 story. S $85-$155; D $100-$165; each addl $15; child under 12, $5. Crib avail. TV in parlor; cable; VCR avail. Pool. Complimentary continental bkfst; afternoon refreshments. Dining rm 5:30-9 pm. Ck-out noon, ck-in 2 pm. Meeting rms. Business servs avail. Tennis. Lawn games. Plantation house built 1850; period furnishings. Cr cds: C, DS, MC, V.

★★★ **STEELES TAVERN MANOR.** US 11 N (24476). 540/377-6444; FAX 540/377-5937; res: 800/743-8666. E-mail hoernlei@cfw.com; web www.steelestavern.com. 5 rms, 2 story. No rm phones. S, D $135-$165; each addl $20. Children over 13 yrs only. TV; VCR (movies). Complimentary full bkfst; afternoon refreshments. Complimentary coffee in rms. Ck-out 11 am, ck-in 3 pm. Business servs avail. Luggage handling. Valet serv. In-rm whirlpools; some fireplaces. Picnic tables. Restored 1916 manor; antiques. On 55 acres. Panoramic view. Cr cds: C, DS, MC, V.

Restaurants

✓ ★ **REDWOOD FAMILY RESTAURANT.** 898 N Lee Hwy (24450). 540/463-2168. Hrs: 7 am-10 pm. Closed Dec 25. Semi-a la carte: bkfst $2.50-$4.50, lunch $3-$6, dinner $4.50-$9. Child's meals. Specializes in seafood, steak, chicken. Family restaurant with home-style cooking; casual atmosphere. Cr cds: C.

★★★ **WILLSON-WALKER HOUSE.** 30 N Main St (24450). 540/463-3020. Web www.webfeat-inc.com/lexingtonfoodanddinner. Hrs: 11:30 am-2:30 pm, 5:30-9 pm. Closed Sun, Mon; Jan 1, Thanksgiving, Dec 24, 25; also Sat lunch Dec-Mar. Res accepted. Serv bar. Wine list. Semi-a la carte: lunch $5-$8, dinner $10-$20. Child's meals. Specializes in pasta, veal, fresh seafood. Outdoor dining. In restored Greek-Revival house (1820) located in downtown historic district; period antiques. Cr cds: A, C, MC, V.

Luray (C-7)

(See also Basye, Front Royal, Harrisonburg, New Market)

Founded 1812 **Pop** 4,587 **Elev** 789 ft **Area Code** 540 **Zip** 22835
E-mail pagecofc@shentel.net **Web** www.luraypage.com
Information Page County Chamber of Commerce, 46 E Main St; 540/743-3915

The name of this town is of French origin; its fame comes from the caverns discovered here in 1878. Luray, at the junction of US 211 and US 340, is 9 miles away from, and within sight of, Shenandoah National Park (see) and Skyline Drive. Headquarters of the park are here. There are three developed recreation areas north and west of town in George Washington and Jefferson National Forests.

What to See and Do

■ **Luray Caverns.** One of the largest caverns in the East. Huge underground rooms (one is 300 ft wide, 500 ft long, with a 140-ft ceiling) connected by natural corridors and paved walkways, are encrusted with colorful rock formations, some delicate as lace, others massive. In one chamber is the world's only "stalacpipe" organ, which produces music of symphonic quality from stone formation. Indirect lighting permits taking color photos within caverns. Temperature is 54°F. One-hr guided tours start about every 20 min. (Daily) W edge of town on US 211. Phone 540/743-6551. ¢¢¢¢ Fee includes

Car and Carriage Museum. Exhibits include 140 restored antique cars, carriages and coaches featuring the history of transportation dating from 1625.

Luray Reptile Center and Dinosaur Park. Features large reptile collection, exotic animals and tropical birds; petting zoo; life-sized dinosaur reproductions. Gift shop. (Mid-Apr-Oct, daily) ½ mi W on US 211. Phone 540/743-4113. ¢¢

Luray Singing Tower. Houses a 47-bell carillon; largest bell weighs 7,640 lbs. Features 45-min recitals by a celebrated carillonneur. (June-Aug, Tues,

Thurs, & Sun evenings; Mar-May & Sept-Oct, wkend afternoons) In park adj caverns. Phone 540/743-6551.   **Free**

Massanutten one-room school. Restored and furnished as it was in the 1800s. Period displays and pictures. (By appt) In Lawn Park. Contact Chamber of Commerce.   **Free**

Shenandoah National Park (see). 9 mi E on US 211, then S on Skyline Dr.

Annual Events

Mayfest Street Festival. Entertainment, crafts. 3rd Sat May.

Page County Heritage Festival. Arts & crafts exhibits. Self-guided tour of churches and old homes. Columbus Day wkend.

Motels

✓★★ **BEST WESTERN INN.** *410 W Main St (22835).* 540/743-6511; FAX 540/743-2917; res: 800/526-0942. 40 rms, 2 story. Apr-Nov: S, D $43-$94.50; each addl $5; under 18 free; lower rates rest of yr. Crib $4. Pet accepted; $20/day. TV; cable (premium). Pool. Playground. Complimentary coffee in rms. Restaurant 6 am-2 pm, 5-9 pm. Rm serv. Ck-out noon. Business servs avail. Lawn games. Cr cds: A, C, D, DS, MC, V.

★★★ **CABINS AT BROOKSIDE.** *2978 US 211 E (22835).* 540/743-5698; FAX 540/743-1326; res: 800/299-2655. Web www.brookside cabins.com. 9 cottages. No rm phones. Feb-Nov: S $75-$145; D $135-$150; each addl $5-$10; kit suite $150-$185; lower rates rest of yr. Crib avail. Complimentary coffee in rms. Restaurant adj 7 am-8:30 pm. Ck-out noon. Sundries. Some fireplaces, in-rm whirlpools; refrigerators avail. Cr cds: A, C, D, DS, MC, V.

★ **LURAY CAVERNS MOTELS.** *832 W Main (22835),* on US 211, opp caverns entrance. 540/743-4531; FAX 540/743-7088. Web www.luraycaverns.com. 64 rms. S, D $57-$74; each addl $7; under 16 free; TV; cable. Pools. Restaurants nearby. Business servs avail. Tennis privileges. Golf privileges. Views of Blue Ridge Mountains. Cr cds: A, C, DS, MC, V.

★★ **MIMSLYN INN.** *401 W Main St (22835).* 540/743-5105; FAX 540/743-2632; res: 800/296-5105. 49 rms, 2 with shower only, 3 story, 11 suites. Mid-June-Oct: S $94; D $104; suites $144-$164; under 18 free; lower rates rest of yr. Crib free. Pet accepted; $10 deposit. TV; cable. Restaurant 7-10 am, 11:30 am-2 pm, 5-9 pm. Ck-out noon. Business servs avail. Gift shop. Health club privileges. Art gallery, antique shop. Built 1930 in style of antebellum mansion. Cr cds: A, C, DS, MC, V.

★★ **RAMADA INN.** *138 Whispering Hill Rd (22835),* 1 mi E on US 211 Bypass, jct VA 656. 540/743-4521; FAX 540/743-6863; res: 800/272-6232. 101 rms, 2 story. Apr-Oct: S, D $69-$130; each addl $5; under 16 free; lower rates rest of yr. Crib free. TV; cable, VCR avail (movies). Pool. Complimentary coffee. Restaurant 6:30 am-2 pm, 5-9 pm. Bar 5 pm-1 am; entertainment wkends. Ck-out noon. Meeting rms. Business servs avail. Health club privileges. Miniature golf. Game rm. Some in-rm whirlpools; refrigerators, microwaves avail. Picnic tables. Cr cds: A, C, D, DS, JCB, MC, V.

Inns

★★★ **JORDAN HOLLOW FARM INN.** *326 Hawksbill Park Rd (22851),* 6½ mi S on US 340 Business, then E on VA 624, N on VA 689, then E on VA 626. 540/778-2285; FAX 540/778-1759; res: 888/418-7000. E-mail jhf@jordanhollows.com. 20 rms in 2 bldgs, 1-2 story. S $85-$130; D $110-$154; each addl $25; under 6 free. Crib free. TV in some rms; cable. Complimentary full bkfst. Dining rm 8:30-10 am, 5:30-9:30 pm. Bar. Ck-out

noon, ck-in 3 pm. Business servs avail. Some in-rm whirlpools. Converted 45-acre horse farm; sundeck with view of Blue Ridge Mts. Totally non-smoking. Cr cds: C, D, DS, MC, V.

★★★ **MAYNEVIEW BED & BREAKFAST.** *439 Mechanic St (22835).* 540/743-7921; FAX 540/743-1191. E-mail mayneviewvu@ chantel.net; web www.mayneview.com. 5 rms, 1 with shower only, 3 story, 1 cottage. No rm phones. No elvtr. S, D $100-$135; cottage (2-day min) $175-$195; under 4 free. Complimentary full bkfst; afternoon refreshments. Restaurant nearby. Ck-out noon, ck-in 3 pm. Luggage handling. Whirlpool. Underground RR stop during the Civil War. Victorian bldg (1865). Cr cds: A, C, DS, MC, V.

★★★ **MILTON HOUSE BED & BREAKFAST.** *113 W Main St (22851),* 7 mi S on US 340 Business. 540/778-2495; FAX 540/778-3451; res: 800/816-3731. E-mail milhouse@shentel.net; web www.nvim.com/miltonhouse. 6 rms, 5 with shower only, 2 story, 1 guest house. No rm phones. S, D $93-$130; guest house $155-$165; package plans; wkends, hols (2-day min). Children over 12 yrs only. TV in some rms; cable (premium), VCR avail. Complimentary full bkfst; afternoon refreshments. Complimentary coffee in rms. Dining rm (public by request only) 6:30-8 pm. Rm serv avail. Ck-out noon, ck-in 3 pm. Business servs avail. Luggage handling. Downhill/x-country ski 18 mi. Fireplaces; some in-rm whirlpools, refrigerators. Picnic tables. Built in 1915; Southern Colonial inn. Antiques. Cr cds: A, C, DS, MC, V.

★★★ **WOODRUFF HOUSE BED & BREAKFAST.** *330 Mechanic St (22835).* 540/743-1494; FAX 540/743-1722. Web www.bbon line.com/va/woodruff. 6 rms in 2 bldgs, 2 with shower only, 3 story. No rm phones. MAP: S, D $98-$195; higher rates Oct. Children over 10 yrs only. Complimentary coffee in rms. Ck-out noon, ck-in 3 pm. Luggage handling. Health club privileges. Some in-rm whirlpools. Victorian house (1830, 1890); antiques. Totally nonsmoking. Cr cds: C, DS, MC, V.

Restaurants

✓★ **BROOKSIDE RESTAURANT.** *2978 US 211 E (22835).* 540/743-5698. Web www.brooksidecabins.com. Hrs: 7 am-8:30 pm; Fri, Sat to 9 pm. Closed mid-Dec-mid-Jan. Res accepted. Wine, beer. Semi-a la carte: bkfst $3-$6, lunch $3.50-$7.50, dinner $7.50-$14.95. Buffet: bkfst (Sat & Sun) $5.95, lunch $5.95, dinner $8.45-$9.45. Child's meals. Specializes in steak, spaghetti, seafood. Salad bar. Own baking. Cr cds: A, C, D, DS, MC, V.

★★ **PARKHURST RESTAURANT.** *2547 US 211 W (22835),* 2 mi W on US 211. 540/743-6009. Hrs: 11 am-10 pm; winter hrs vary. Closed some major hols. Bar. A la carte entrees: dinner $14.95-$17.95. Specializes in steak, fowl, seafood. View of Blue Ridge Mts. Cr cds: A, C, D, DS, MC, V.

Lynchburg (E-6)

Settled 1757 **Pop** 66,049 **Elev** 795 ft **Area Code** 804 **E-mail** realva@ aol.com

Information Visitors Information Center, 12th & Church Sts, 24504; 804/847-1811 or 800/732-5821

Lynchburg is perched on hills overlooking the James River, which was for many years its means of growth. Today the city is home to more than 3,000 businesses and diversified industries. Colleges located here include Lynchburg College, Randolph-Macon Woman's College and Liberty University.

One of the first buildings in the town was a ferryhouse built by John Lynch. The same enterprising young man later built a tobacco warehouse, probably the first one in the country. During the Civil War, Lynchburg was important as a supply base and hospital town. In June of 1864, General Jubal A. Early successfully defended the town from an attack by Union forces. More than 2,200 Confederates are buried in the Confederate Cemetery, located in the Old City Cemetery.

What to See and Do

Anne Spencer House. House of noted poet, only black woman and only Virginian to be included in *Norton Anthology of Modern American and British Poetry*. On grounds is Spencer's writing cottage "Edan Kraal." Many dignitaries have visited here. Museum with artifacts, memorabilia, period antique furnishings; formal garden. (House by appt; gardens daily) 1313 Pierce St. Phone 804/845-1313. ¢

Appomattox Court House Natl Historical Park (see). 21 mi E on US 460.

Blackwater Creek Natural Area. Ruskin Freer Nature Preserve (115 acres) includes trails with plants; athletic area; bikeway winds past wildflower area and historical sites, ending downtown; Creekside Trunk Trail, natural grass trail with typical Piedmont species of plants, moist ravines, north-facing rocky bluffs. (Daily) In the center of the city. **Free**

Fort Early. Defense earthwork for Lynchburg's closest battle during the Civil War. Confederates under General Jubal A. Early turned back forces under General David Hunter in 1864. (Daily) Memorial & Fort Aves. **Free**

Jefferson's Poplar Forest. Designed and built by Thomas Jefferson as a personal retreat; begun in 1806. Restoration in progress; house unfurnished. (Apr-Nov, Wed-Sun & major hols) Just SW of Lynchburg on US 221, then left on VA 811 & left again on VA 661 in Bedford County. Phone 804/525-1806. ¢¢

Old Court House Museum (1855). Restored to original Greek-revival appearance. Three galleries have exhibits on early history of the area, highlighting Quaker settlement and role of tobacco; restored mid-19th-century courtroom. (Daily; closed Jan 1, Thanksgiving, Dec 24, 25) 901 Court St. Phone 804/847-1459. ¢

Pest House Medical Museum. The 1840s white frame medical office of Quaker physician Dr. John Jay Terrell, has been joined with the Pest House quarantine hospital to typify the standard of medicine during the late 1800s. Original medical instruments include an operating table, hypodermic needle, clinical thermometer and chloroform mask. Period furnishings on one side duplicate Dr. Terrell's office during the Civil War; the other represents the quarantine hospital for Confederate soldiers in which Dr. Terrell volunteered to assume responsibility. Window displays with audio description. Tours (by appt). (Daily) Old City Cemetery, 4th & Taylor Sts. Phone 804/847-1465. **Free**

Point of Honor (1815). Restored mansion on Daniel's Hill above the James River, built by Dr. George Cabell, Sr, physician to Patrick Henry. Federal style with octagon-bay facade and finely crafted interior woodwork; period furnishings; gardens and grounds being restored. (Daily; closed Jan 1, Thanksgiving, Dec 24, 25) 112 Cabell St. Phone 804/847-1459. ¢¢

Randolph-Macon Woman's College (1891). (750 women) A 100-acre campus on historic Rivermont Ave near the James River. First college for women in the South granted a Phi Beta Kappa chapter. Campus is interesting mixture of architecture including the Vincent Kling design for the Houston Chapel. Tours (by appt). 2500 Rivermont Ave. Phone 804/947-8000. On campus is

Maier Museum of Art. Collection is representative of 19th- and 20th-century American painting. Artists include Thomas Hart Benton, Edward Hicks, Winslow Homer, James McNeil Whistler, Mary Cassatt and Georgia O'Keeffe. Changing exhibits. (Academic yr, Tues-Sun afternoons) Phone 804/947-8136. **Free**

Riverside Park. (Daily) Rivermont Ave. **Free** In park is

Packet Boat *Marshall.* Mounted on a stone base, this is the boat that carried the remains of Stonewall Jackson home to Lexington; for many years packets were the principal mode of transportation along the James River and Kanawha Canal.

South River Meeting House. Completed in 1798, the stone building remained the site of Quaker worship and activity until the 1840s. John Lynch, the founder of Lynchburg, and other early leaders of the community are buried in the adj historic cemetery. (Daily; closed major hols) 5810 Fort Ave. Phone 804/239-2548. **Free**

Motels

★★ **BEST WESTERN.** *2815 Candlers Mountain Rd (24502).* 804/237-2986; FAX 804/237-2986; res: 800/528-1234. 87 rms, 2-3 story. S $59; D $69; each addl $8; under 12 free; higher rates: homecoming, graduation. Crib free. TV; cable (premium). Pool. Complimentary continental bkfst. Complimentary coffee in rms. Restaurant adj 11 am-midnight. Rm serv. Ck-out 11 am. Meeting rms. Business servs avail. In-rm modem link. Valet serv. Sundries. Health club privileges. Microwaves avail. Cr cds: A, C, D, DS, MC, V.

D ⊠ ⊠ 🐾 SC

★★ **DAYS INN.** *3320 Candlers Mt Rd (24502).* 804/847-8655; FAX 804/846-3297; res: 800/787-3297. E-mail days4u@aol.com. 131 rms, 5 story. S, D $64-$74; each addl $8; under 17 free. Crib free. TV; cable (premium). Pool. Playground. Restaurant 6 am-2 pm, 5 pm-midnight. Rm serv. Ck-out noon. Meeting rms. Business servs avail. In-rm modem link. Valet serv. Sundries. Free airport, RR station, bus depot transportation. Health club privileges. Microwaves avail. Private patios, balconies. Cr cds: A, C, D, DS, JCB, MC, V.

D ⊠ ⊠ 🐾 SC

✓★ **ECONO LODGE INN.** *2400 Stadium Dr (24501), US 29 S Expressway City-Stadium exit.* 804/847-1045; FAX 804/846-0086; res: 800/228-5050. 48 rms, 2 story. S $39.95-$55; D $55-$80. Crib free. TV; cable (premium). Continental bkfst. Restaurant nearby. Ck-out 11 am. Business servs avail. Cr cds: A, C, D, DS, MC, V.

⊠ 🐾 SC

★★ **HAMPTON INN.** *5604 Seminole Ave (24502).* 804/237-2704; FAX 804/239-9183; res: 800/426-7866. 65 rms, 2 story. S $61-$67; D $71-$77; under 18 free; higher rates Randolph-Macon graduation. Crib avail. TV; cable (premium). Complimentary continental bkfst. Restaurant adj 10:30 am-midnight. Ck-out noon. Business servs avail. Health club privileges. Sundries. Cr cds: A, C, D, DS, MC, V.

D ⊠ 🐾 SC

★ **HOWARD JOHNSONS.** *US 29 N (24572), 2 mi N on US 29.* 804/845-7041; FAX 804/845-4718; res: 800/654-2000. 70 rms, 2 story. S, D $46-$77; each addl $7; under 18 free. Crib free. TV; cable (premium). Pool; wading pool. Restaurant 6 am-10 pm. Ck-out noon. Coin lndry. Business servs avail. Valet serv. Sundries. Free airport transportation. Microwaves avail. Private patios, balconies. Cr cds: A, C, D, DS, MC, V.

D ⊠ ⊠ 🐾 SC

✓★★ **INNKEEPER MOTEL.** *5600 Seminole Ave (24501).* 804/237-7771; FAX 804/239-0659; res: 800/466-5337. 104 rms, 3 story. S $49.99-$55.99; D $54.99-$59.99; each addl $5; under 16 free. Crib free. TV; cable (premium). Pool. Complimentary continental bkfst. Restaurant nearby. Ck-out noon. Meeting rm. Valet serv. Health club privileges. Microwaves avail. Cr cds: A, C, D, DS, MC, V.

D ⊠ ⊠ 🐾 SC

Motor Hotels

★★ **COMFORT INN.** *3125 Albert Lankford Drive (24501), US 29, at Odd Fellows Rd.* 804/847-9041; FAX 804/847-8513; res: 800/228-5150. E-mail cilynch@lynchburg.net; web www.guests-inc.com. 120 rms, 5 story. S $71-$85; D $76-$90; each addl $5; suites $151-$170; under 18 free; higher rates: homecoming, graduation. Crib free. Pet accepted. TV; cable (premium), VCR avail. Complimentary full bkfst. Complimentary coffee in rms. Restaurant nearby. Ck-out noon. Meeting rms. Business servs avail. Free airport, RR station transportation. Health club privileges. Pool. Some refrigerators, microwaves. Balconies. Picnic tables, grills. Cr cds: A, C, D, DS, ER, JCB, MC, V.

★★★ **HILTON.** *2900 Chandler's Mountain Rd (24502). 804/237-6333; FAX 804/237-4277; res: 800/445-8667.* 168 rms, 5 story. S $85-$120; D $105-$140; each addl $20; suites $186; family rates. Crib free. TV; cable (premium). Restaurant 6:30 am-2 pm, 5:30-10 pm. Rm serv. Bar 11-1:30 am; entertainment. Ck-out 11 am. Meeting rms. Business center. Bellhops. Valet serv. Sundries. Gift shop. Free airport transportation. Exercise equipt; sauna. Bathrm phone in suites. Microwaves avail. Cr cds: A, C, D, MC, V.

Hotel

★★ **HOLIDAY INN SELECT.** *601 Main St (24505). 804/528-2500; FAX 804/528-0062; res: 800/465-4329.* 243 units, 8 story. S, D $72; each addl $10; suites $85-$110; under 17 free. Crib free. Pet accepted. TV; cable (premium). Pool; poolside serv. Restaurant 6:30 am-10 pm. Bar 3 pm-1 am. Ck-out noon. Meeting rms. Business servs avail. In-rm modem link. Free airport, RR station, bus depot transportation. Exercise equipt. Some bathrm phones, refrigerators; microwaves avail. Cr cds: A, C, D, DS, ER, JCB, MC, V.

Inns

★★★ **1880'S MADISON HOUSE.** *413 Madison St (24504). 804/528-1503; res: 800/828-6422.* E-mail madison@lynchburg.net; web www.bbhost.com/1880s-madison. 4 rms, 2 story. S $79-$99; D $89-$119; each addl $10; suite $109-$119. TV; cable (premium). Complimentary full bkfst. Ck-out 11 am, ck-in 3-6 pm. Free airport, RR station transportation. Some fireplaces. Victorian mansion (1880); antiques. Library features antiques, Civil War collection. Totally nonsmoking. Cr cds: A, C, MC, V.

★★★ **DULWICH MANOR.** *US 60 E (24521), Approx 17 mi N on US 29, then ½ mi E on US 60. 804/386-5461; FAX 804/946-5913.* 6 rms, 4 with bath, 3 story. No rm phones. S $65-$93; D $70-$98; each addl $20; wkly rates. Complimentary full bkfst. Restaurant nearby. Ck-out 11 am, ck-in 3 pm. Whirlpool. English manor house (1912); antique furnishings. Cr cds: C.

★★★ **LYNCHBURG MANSION AND BED & BREAKFAST.** *405 Madison St (24504). 804/528-5400; FAX 804/847-2545; res: 800/352-1199.* E-mail RES50@aol.com; web www.bbonline.com/va/lynchburg. 5 rms, 2 story. S $104-$139; D $109-$144; each addl $25; under 8 free. TV; cable. Complimentary full bkfst. Ck-out 11 am, ck-in 3-6 pm. Some refrigerators, fireplaces. Picnic tables. Spanish/Georgian mansion built 1914; individually decorated rms include the Gilliam Room (traditional English-manor style), and the Bowen Room (Country-French style). The back porch overlooks the landscaped grounds. Totally nonsmoking. Cr cds: A, C, D, MC, V.

Restaurants

★★★ **CAFE FRANCE.** *3225 Old Forest Rd (24501). 804/385-8989.* Hrs: 5:30-10 pm. Closed Sun, Mon; some major hols. Res accepted. Bar. Wine cellar. Semi-a la carte: dinner $10.95-$24.95. Child's meals. Specializes in fresh seafood, lamb, buffalo. Parking. Extensive beer selection. Country French decor. Gourmet wine shop adj. Cr cds: A, C, MC, V.

★★ **CROWN STERLING.** *6120 Fort Ave (24502). 804/239-7744.* Hrs: 5:30-10 pm. Closed Sun; major hols. Res accepted. Bar from 5 pm. Semi-a la carte: dinner $12-$24. Specializes in steak. Salad bar. Parking. Colonial decor. Cr cds: A, C, D, DS, MC, V.

★★ **JEANNE'S RESTAURANT.** *Rte 3 Box 178 D (24504), 8 mi E on US 460. 804/993-2475.* Hrs: 11:30 am-2:30 pm, 4:30-9 pm; wkends to 10 pm; Sun noon-9 pm; Jan-Mar noon-2 pm, 5-9 pm. Closed July 4; also late Dec. Semi-a la carte: lunch $3.95-$9.95, dinner $6.95-$20.95. Child's meals. Specializes in steak, seafood. Salad bar. Own desserts. Parking. Rustic redwood overlooking lake, dining on deck. Cr cds: A, C, DS, MC, V.

★★ **LANDMARK HOUSE.** *6113 Fort Ave (24502). 804/237-1884.* Hrs: 5:30-10 pm; Sat, Sun from 5:30 pm. Closed Mon; some hols. Bar. Semi-a la carte: dinner $6.95-$25.95. Child's meals. Specialties: prime rib, filet mignon. Salad bar. Piano bar. Parking. Cr cds: A, C, D, MC, V.

★★★ **SACHIKO'S.** *126 Old Graves Mill Rd (24502). 804/237-5655.* Hrs: 5:30-10 pm. Closed Sun; some hols. Res accepted. Bar. Semi-a la carte: dinner $10.95-$25. Specializes in new American cuisine. Own baking. Parking. Fireplaces. Cr cds: A, C, MC, V.

✓★ **T.C. TROTTERS.** *2496 Rivermont Ave (24503). 804/846-3545.* Hrs: 11:30 am-10 pm. Closed Mon; Thanksgiving, Dec 25. Res accepted. Bar to 2 am. Semi-a la carte: lunch $6.95-$9.95, dinner $6.95-$19.95. Child's meals. Specializes in fajitas, steak, seafood. Outdoor dining. Cr cds: A, C, MC, V.

Manassas (C-8)

(See also Arlington County, Fairfax, Falls Church, Triangle; also see District of Columbia)

Pop 27,957 **Elev** 321 ft **Area Code** 703 **E-mail** jjensen@mnsinc
Web www.visitpwc.com

Information Prince William County/Manassas Conference & Visitors Bureau, 14420 Bristow Rd, 20112; 703/792-4254 or 800/432-1792

Though the Native Americans who had lived in this area for thousands of years were driven out under a treaty in 1722, settlement remained concentrated along the Potomac River until the coming of the railroad in 1858. The Manassas rail junction was vital to the South, and many troops were stationed along this line of communication. Control of this junction led to two major battles nearby (see MANASSAS (BULL RUN) NATIONAL BATTLEFIELD PARK).

What to See and Do

The Manassas Museum. Museum features collections dealing with Northern Virginia Piedmont history from prehistoric to modern times, with special emphasis on the Civil War. (Daily exc Mon; closed Jan 1, Thanksgiving, Dec 24, 25) 9101 Prince William St. Phone 703/368-1873. ¢

Annual Event

Prince William County Fair. Carnival, entertainment, tractor pull, exhibits, contests. Phone 703/368-0173. Mid-Aug.

Motels

★ ★ **BEST WESTERN.** *10820 Balls Ford Rd (20109), I-66 exit 47A. 703/361-8000; FAX 703/361-8000; res: 800/528-1234.* 121 rms, 2 story. S $54-$89; D $64-$89; each addl $10; under 18 free. Crib free. Pet accepted; $10/day. TV; cable (premium). Pool. Complimentary continental bkfst. Restaurant 5-10 pm; closed Sun. Rm serv. Bar to midnight, Fri, Sat to 2 am; entertainment Tues-Sat. Ck-out 11 am. Meeting rms. Business servs avail. In-rm modem link. Valet serv. Sundries. Health club privileges. Refrigerators, microwaves avail. Cr cds: A, C, D, DS, MC, V.

D ◄ ≈ ⊠ 🔥 SC

✓ ★ ★ **BEST WESTERN INN.** *8640 Mathis Ave (20110). 703/368-7070; FAX 703/368-7292; res: 800/257-7177.* 60 rms, 2 story. Apr-Oct: S, D $59-$79; under 18 free; higher rates: special events, hol wknds; lower rates rest of yr. Crib free. TV; cable (premium). Complimentary continental bkfst. Restaurant adj 4 pm-2 am. Ck-out 11 am. Coin lndry. Business servs avail. Whirlpool. Sauna. Refrigerators, microwaves; some in-rm whirlpools. Cr cds: A, C, D, DS, ER, MC, V.

D ⊠ ⊠ 🔥 SC

★ ★ ★ **COURTYARD BY MARRIOTT.** *10701 Battleview Pkwy (20109), I-66, exit 47B. 703/335-1300; FAX 703/335-9442; res: 800/321-2211.* 149 rms, 3 story. S, D $89-$98; each addl $5; suites $100-$115; under 18 free. Crib free. TV; cable (premium). Indoor pool; whirlpool. Complimentary coffee in rms. Restaurant 6:30-10 am, 5-10 pm; Sat, Sun 7 am-noon. Bar. Ck-out noon. Coin lndry. Meeting rms. Business servs avail. In-rm modem link. Valet serv. Sundries. Exercise equipt. Health club privileges. Refrigerators, microwaves avail. Balconies. Cr cds: A, C, D, DS, MC, V.

D ≈ 🕴 ⊠ 🔥 SC

★ ★ **DAYS INN.** *10653 Balls Ford Rd (20109). 703/368-2800; FAX 703/368-0083; res: 800/329-7466.* 120 rms, 2 story. S $56; D $62; each addl $6; under 18 free. Crib free. TV; cable (premium). Pool. Complimentary continental bkfst. Ck-out 11 am. Coin lndry. Business servs avail. Health club privileges. Refrigerators avail. Cr cds: A, C, D, DS, MC, V.

D ≈ ⊠ 🔥 SC

✓ ★ **RED ROOF INN.** *10610 Automotive Dr (20109), I-66 exit 47A. 703/335-9333; FAX 703/335-9342; res: 800/843-7663.* 119 rms, 3 story. S $52.99-$68.99; D $57.99-$72.99; under 18 free; higher rates: Cherry Blossom, hol wknds. Crib free. Pet accepted, some restrictions. TV; cable (premium). Complimentary coffee in lobby. Restaurant adj 6-2 am. Ck-out noon. Business servs avail. Sundries. Cr cds: A, C, D, DS, MC, V.

D ◄ ⊠ 🔥 SC

✓ ★ **SUPER 8 MOTEL.** *8691 Phoenix Dr (22110), off US 28. 703/369-6323; FAX 703/369-9206; res: 800/800-8000.* 78 rms, 3 story. S $42-$50; D $47-$55; each addl $5; under 18 free. Crib free. TV; cable (premium). Complimentary continental bkfst. Complimentary coffee in rms. Restaurant adj 6 am-11 pm. Ck-out 11 am. Business servs avail. Some in-rm whirlpools; microwaves avail. Cr cds: A, C, D, MC, V.

D ⊠ 🔥 SC

Motor Hotel

★ ★ ★ **HOLIDAY INN.** *10800 Vandor Ln (20109), I-66 exit 47B. 703/335-0000; FAX 703/361-8440; res: 800/465-4329.* 158 rms, 5 story. S $125; D $130; under 12 free. Crib free. Pet accepted, some restrictions; deposit. TV; cable (premium). Pool. Complimentary coffee. Restaurant 6-11 am, 6-11 pm. Rm serv. Bar 4-11 pm; Fri, Sat to midnight. Ck-out noon. Coin lndry. Meeting rms. Business servs avail. In-rm modem link. Valet serv. Exercise equipt. Health club privileges. Refrigerators, microwaves avail. Near Manassas (Bull Run) Battlefield. Cr cds: A, C, D, DS, ER, JCB, MC, V.

D ≈ 🕴 ⊠ 🔥 SC

Restaurants

★ ★ ★ **CARMELLO'S.** *9108 Center St (20110). 703/368-5522.* Hrs: 11:30 am-2:30 pm, 5-10 pm; Sat from 5 pm, Sun 4-9 pm. Closed most major hols. Res accepted. Northern Italian, Portuguese menu. Bar. Semi-a la carte: lunch $7-$11, dinner $12-$20. Child's meals. Specializes in fresh seafood, veal, chicken. Own pasta. Pianist Sat. Located in 2-story brick storefront. Cr cds: A, C, D, DS, MC, V.

D

✓ ★ ★ **HERO'S AMERICAN RESTAURANT.** *9412 Main St (20110), in Old Town. 703/330-1534.* E-mail herosam@aol.com; web www.herosmanassas.com. Hrs: 11 am-10 pm; Thurs-Sat to 12:30 am; Sun from noon. Contemporary Amer menu. Bar to 1:30 am. Semi-a la carte: lunch, dinner $5.25-$18.95. Specializes in fresh seafood, hamburgers, sandwiches. Salad bar. Own desserts, ice cream. Jazz Sat. Outdoor dining. Contemporary American pub; two-level dining; jazz memorabilia. Cr cds: A, C, D, DS, MC, V.

D ⊠

★ ★ ★ **PANINO.** *9116 Mathis Ave (20110), at Manassas Shopping Center. 703/335-2566.* Hrs: 11:30 am-2:30 pm, 5:30-10 pm; Sat from 5:30 pm. Closed Sun; major hols. Res accepted; required Fri, Sat dinner. Northern Italian menu. Serv bar. Wine list. Semi-a la carte: lunch $8.50-$12.50, dinner $9-$19. Specialties: homemade Tuscan bread, seafood ravioli, osso buco. Own baking. Contemporary Italian decor; extensive art collection. Cr cds: A, C, D, DS, MC, V.

D ⊠

Manassas (Bull Run) National Battlefield Park (C-8)

(See also Falls Church, Manassas)

(26 mi SW of Washington, DC, at jct US 29, VA 234)

This 5,000-acre park was the scene of two major Civil War battles. More than 26,000 men were killed or wounded here in struggles for control of a strategically important railroad junction.

The first major land battle of the war (July 21, 1861) was fought here between poorly trained volunteer troops from both North and South. The battle finally resolved itself into a struggle for Henry Hill, where "Stonewall" Jackson earned his nickname. With the outcome in doubt, Confederate reinforcements arrived by railroad from the Shenandoah Valley and turned the battle into a rout.

Thirteen months later (August 28-30, 1862), in the second battle of Manassas, Robert E. Lee outmaneuvered and defeated Union General John Pope and cleared the way for a Confederate invasion of Maryland.

For further information contact Park Superintendent, 6511 Sudley Rd, Manassas 22110; 703/361-1339.

Park (daily; closed Dec 25). ¢

What to See and Do

Chinn House Ruins. The house served as a field hospital in both engagements and marked the left of the Confederate line at First Manassas; also the scene of Longstreet's counterattack at Second Manassas.

Dogan House. An original structure at Groveton, a village around which the battle of Second Manassas was fought.

Stone Bridge. Where Union artillery opened the Battle of First Manassas; it afforded an avenue of escape for the Union troops after both First and Second Manassas.

Stone House. Originally a tavern (ca 1825), used as field hospital in both battles. (Summer, daily)

Unfinished Railroad. Fully graded railroad bed, never completed, behind which Stonewall Jackson's men were positioned during the second battle.

Visitor Center. Hill affords view of much of battlefield. Information; self-guided tours start here (walking tour of First Manassas, directions for driving tour of Second Manassas). Markers throughout park explain various aspects of battles. Ranger-conducted tours (summer). On Henry Hill, just N of I-66 off VA 234. In same building is

Battlefield Museum. Exhibits present stories of battles; audiovisual presentations of background information. (Daily; closed Dec 25)

Marion (F-3)

(See also Abingdon, Wytheville)

Founded 1835 **Pop** 6,630 **Elev** 2,178 ft **Area Code** 540 **Zip** 24354
E-mail smythcofc@netva.com **Web** www.netva.com/smythcoc
Information Chamber of Commerce of Smyth County, 124 W Main St, PO Box 924; 540/783-3161

This popular vacation spot is surrounded by George Washington and Jefferson National Forests, abounding in game and birds, near a state park and high enough to promise an invigorating climate. The seat of Smyth County, it was named for General Francis Marion, known during the American Revolution as the "Swamp Fox."

What to See and Do

George Washington and Jefferson National Forests. (See HARRISONBURG) SE of town via VA 16 is the

Mount Rogers National Recreation Area. A 117,000-acre area that includes Mount Rogers, the state's highest point (5,729 ft), mile-high open meadows known as "balds," and a great variety of animals and plants. Swimming, fishing, hunting, camping (fee at some areas), three visitor centers, approx 400 mi of hiking, bicycle & bridle trails. Mount Rogers Scenic Byway (auto); Virginia Creeper Trail (hikers, bicycles, horses) follows an abandoned railroad grade through spectacular river gorges. Adj to Grayson Highlands State Park (see ABINGDON). (Mid-May-Mid-Sept, daily; rest of yr, Mon-Fri) Some fees. Phone 540/783-5196.

Hungry Mother State Park. More than 2,180 acres amid the mountains with a 108-acre lake; panoramic views. Swimming beach, bathhouse; fishing; boating (rentals, launching, electric motors only). Hiking, self-guided trails; horseback riding (rentals). Picnicking, restaurant, concession. Tent & trailer sites (electrical hookups, late Mar-Dec), cabins (Mar-Dec). Hilltop visitor center, interpretive programs. Standard fees. 3 mi N on VA 16. Phone 540/783-3422. Parking   ¢

Annual Events

Whitetop Ramp Festival. Mid-May.

Hungry Mother Arts and Crafts Festival. Hungry Mother State Park. Mid-July.

Chilhowie Apple Festival. Mid-Sept.

Motel

✓ ★★ **BEST WESTERN INN.** 1424 N Main St (24354). 540/783-3193; FAX 540/783-3193; res: 800/528-1234. 79 rms, 1-2 story. S $54-$68, D $59-$72; under 18 free. Crib free. TV; cable (premium). Pool. Complimentary continental bkfst. Restaurant 5:30-9:30 pm. Rm serv. Bar 5 pm-midnight; closed Sun. Ck-out noon. Meeting rms. Business servs avail. Valet serv. Some microwaves. Cr cds: A, C, D, DS, JCB, MC, V.

⊠ ⇘ ⊯ **SC**

Inn

★ **FOX HILL INN.** 8568 Troutdale Hwy (24378), 20 mi S via VA 16, then follow sign. 540/677-3313; res: 800/874-3313. Web www.bbon line.com/va/foxhill. 8 rms, 2 story. No A/C. No rm phones. S, D $75; each addl $10; under 18 free; wkly rates. Crib free. TV in sitting rm. Complimentary full bkfst. Restaurant nearby. Ck-out 10 am, ck-in 3 pm. X-country ski 5 mi. Situated on mountaintop with panoramic view. On 70 acres of woods & pasture land; wildlife, farm animals; hiking trails. Cr cds: C, DS, MC, V.

⊠ ⇘ ⊯

Martinsville (F-5)

(See also Danville)

Founded 1793 **Pop** 16,162 **Elev** 1,020 ft **Area Code** 540
E-mail mhccoc@neocomm.net **Web** www.neocomm.net/~mhccoc
Information Martinsville-Henry County Chamber of Commerce, 115 Broad St, PO Box 709, 24114; 540/632-6401

Martinsville was named for Joseph Martin, a pioneer who settled here in 1773. Henry County takes its name from Patrick Henry, who lived here. When Henry County Court first opened in October 1776, 640 residents pledged an oath of allegiance to the United States; 40 refused to renounce allegiance to England. Located near the beautiful Blue Ridge Mountains, this community is home to Bassett Furniture and E. I. duPont de Nemours.

What to See and Do

Blue Ridge Farm Museum. Presents the heritage of mountain region through reconstructed farmsteads and "folklife galleries." Authentic buildings from 1800 German-heritage farm, including log house, kitchen, blacksmith shop and barn. Costumed interpreters demonstrate farm and household chores. Special events (fees). (Mid-May-mid-Aug, wkends; rest of yr, by appt) VA 40 in Ferrum. Phone 540/365-4415. ¢¢

Fairy Stone State Park. Consists of 4,570 acres, with a 168-acre lake adjoining Philpott Reservoir. Nestled in the foothills of the Blue Ridge Mountains, this park is named for the "fairy stones" (staurolites) found near the southern tip of its boundary. Swimming beach, bathhouse; fishing; boating (launch, rentals, electric motors only). Hiking, bicycle trails. Picnic shelters, concession, cafe. Tent & trailer sites (dump station, electrical hookups), cabins (Mar-Dec). Visitor center, evening programs. Standard fees. (Daily) 21 mi NW via US 220/VA 57, VA 346. Phone 540/930-2424.

Philpott Lake. State's fourth-largest lake, formed by Philpott Dam, a US Army Corps of Engineers project. Swimming, skindiving; waterskiing, boating, fishing. Hunting, hiking, picnicking; 4 camping areas (Apr-Oct) One area free; some fees. Just NE of Fairy Stone State Park. Phone 540/629-2703.

Virginia Museum of Natural History. State museum focuses on preservation, study and interpretation of Virginia's natural heritage. Features visual and hands-on exhibits; includes a computer-animated triceratops dinosaur and a life-size ground sloth model. Special events during the yr include Earth Day (Apr) and Virginia Indian Festival (Sept). (Daily exc Sun; closed most major hols) 1001 Douglas Ave. Phone 540/666-8600. **Free**

Annual Event

Blue Ridge Folklife Festival. Held at Blue Ridge Farm Museum. Gospel, blues and string band music; traditional regional crafts; regional foods; quilt show, antique autos, steam & gas-powered farm equipment. Sports events include horse-pulling & log-skidding contests, coon-dog swimming and treeing contests. Phone 540/365-4415. Late Oct.

Seasonal Event

Stock car races. Martinsville Speedway. 3 mi S. Phone 540/956-3151. Miller Genuine Draft 300, mid-Mar. Hanes 500, late Apr. Goody's 500, late Sept. Taco Bell 300, mid-Oct.

Motels

✓★★ **BEST WESTERN INN.** *1755 Virginia Ave (24112).* 540/632-5611; FAX 540/632-1168; res: 800/528-1234. 97 rms, 2 story, 20 suites. S $48; D $54; each addl $10; suites $49-$59; under 12 free; package plans. Crib free. Pet accepted. TV, cable (premium). Pool; wading pool. Complimentary coffee in rms. Restaurant 6 am-10 pm; Sat, Sun from 7 am. Rm serv. Bar 4 pm-midnight. Ck-out noon. Coin lndry. Meeting rms. Business servs avail. In-rm modem link. Valet serv. Sundries. Exercise equipt. Microwave avail. Cr cds: A, C, D, DS, ER, MC, V.

✓★★ **DUTCH INN.** *2360 Virginia Ave (24078),* 1¼ mi N on US 220 Business. 540/647-3721; FAX 540/647-4857; res: 800/800-3996. E-mail sgrodens@neocomm.net; web www.dutch-inn.com. 150 rms, 2 story. S $48-$60; D $56-$66; each addl $6; suites $88-$125; studio rms $55-$75; under 16 free; higher rates race wks. Crib free. Pet accepted. TV; cable (premium). Pool; whirlpool, poolside serv. Restaurant 6 am-10:30 pm. Rm serv. Bar 4 pm-midnight; Fri, Sat to 2 am. Ck-out noon. Meeting rms. Business servs avail. In-rm modem link. Valet serv. Sundries. 18-hole golf privileges. Exercise equipt; sauna. Many bathrm phones, refrigerators; microwaves avail. Cr cds: A, C, D, DS, MC, V.

McLean (C-8)

(See also Arlington County, Fairfax, Falls Church, Tysons Corner; also see District of Columbia & Rockville, MD)

Pop 38,168 **Elev** 300 ft **Area Code** 703 **E-mail** cvbfceda@mindspring.com **Web** www.visitfairfax.org

Information Fairfax County Convention & Visitors Bureau, 8300 Boone Blvd, Suite 450, Tysons Corner 22182; 703/790-3329 or 800/7-FAIRFAX

What to See and Do

Claude Moore Colonial Farm. at Turkey Run. Demonstration of 1770s low-income working farm; costumed interpreters work with crops and animals using 18th-century techniques. (Apr-mid-Dec, Wed-Sun weather permitting; closed Thanksgiving) 2 mi E on VA 193 (Georgetown Pike). Phone 703/442-7557. ¢

Colvin Run Mill Park. Tours of historical grist mill. Operating general store, miller's house exhibit, barn and grounds (free). (Mar-Dec, daily exc Tues; rest of yr, wkends; closed Jan 1, Thanksgiving, Dec 25) 3 mi W via VA 123, then 5 mi NW via VA 7, on Colvin Run Rd in Great Falls. Phone 703/759-2771. Tours ¢¢

Evans Farm. Approx 25 acres of farmland. Colonial atmosphere; 18th-century-style building with restaurant. Collection of early American cooking utensils; Robert E. Lee memorabilia. Country store, handcraft and doll shop, old mill. Farm animals for children to feed. (Daily; closed Dec 25) Chain Bridge Rd, on VA 123, 1 mi E of I-495 McLean-VA 123N exit 11. Phone 703/356-8000. **Free**

Restaurants

★★ **CAFE OGGI.** *6671 Old Dominion Dr (22101).* 703/442-7360. Hrs: 11:30 am-2:30 pm, 5:30-10 pm; Sat, Sun from 5:30 pm. Closed major hols. Res accepted; required Fri, Sat dinner. Italian menu. Serv bar. A la carte entrees: lunch $6.95-$11.95, dinner $9.95-$19.95. Specializes in fresh seafood, veal. Own baking, pasta. Cr cds: A, C, D, DS, MC, V.

★★ **CAFE TAJ.** *1379 Beverly Rd (22101), in Market Place Shopping Ctr.* 703/827-0444. Web www.washingtonpost.com/indian restaurants. Hrs: 11:30 am-2:30 pm, 5:30-10 pm; Fri, Sat to 10:30 pm. Closed July 4. Res accepted. Indian menu. Bar. Semi-a la carte: lunch $8.95-$10.95, dinner $8.95-$14.95. Lunch buffet (Mon-Fri) $8.99. Specialties: tandoori chicken tikka, prawns masala. Outdoor dining. Modern decor. Cr cds: A, C, D, DS, MC, V.

★★ **CHARLEY'S PLACE.** *6930 Old Dominion Dr (22101), jct VA 123 & VA 309/738.* 703/893-1034. Hrs: 11 am-10 pm; Fri, Sat to 10:30 pm; Sun 10:30 am-9 pm; early-bird dinner 4-6 pm; Sun brunch 10:30 am-2 pm. Closed Dec 25. Bar to midnight. Semi-a la carte: lunch $5.99-$10.95, dinner $5.99-$18.95. Child's meals. Specializes in steak, pasta, seafood. Outdoor dining. Parking. Fireplaces. Cr cds: A, C, D, DS, MC, V.

★★★ **DANTE.** *1148 Walker Rd (22066).* 703/759-3131. Hrs: 11:30 am-2:30 pm, 5:30-10:30 pm; Sat from 5:30 pm; Sun 4-9 pm. Closed some major hols. Res accepted; required Fri, Sat. Northern Italian menu. Bar. Wine list. A la carte entrees: lunch $9.25-$14.50, dinner $14.50-$22.95. Child's meals. Specialties: grilled Dover sole, grilled veal chops. Own pasta, bread. Parking. Patio dining. Converted country house. Cr cds: A, C, D, DS, MC, V.

★★ **EVANS FARM INN.** *1696 Chain Bridge Rd (22101).* 703/356-8000. Hrs: 11:30 am-9 pm; Sat to 10 pm; Sun from 11 am, brunch to 2 pm. Closed Dec 25. Res accepted; required Fri-Sun. Semi-a la carte: lunch $7.95-$10.95, dinner $14.95-$24.95. Buffet (Mon-Sat): lunch $11.95. Sun brunch $7.25-$12.95. Child's meals. Specializes in ham, fresh seafood, colonial-era cooking. Own baking. Salad bar. Parking. 18th-century-style inn on 21 acres. Family-owned. Cr cds: A, C, D, DS, JCB, MC, V.

★★★ **IL BORGO ITALIAN RESTAURANT.** *1381 Beverly Rd # A (22101), in Market Place Shopping Center.* 703/893-1400. Web www.menusonline.com/cities/wash_dc/desc/ilborgoristorante.shtml. Hrs: 11 am-midnight; Sat from 5 pm; Sun 4-10:30 pm. Closed most major hols. Res accepted; required Fri, Sat dinner. Italian menu. Bar. Wine list. Semi-a la carte: lunch $5.75-$13.50, dinner $12-$17.50. Specializes in veal, pasta, seafood. Pastas, desserts. Cr cds: A, C, D, DS, MC, V.

★★★ **INDIGO AT GREAT FALLS.** *774 Walker Rd (22066), 6 mi W on VA 193, I-495 exit.* 703/759-4650. Hrs: 5:30-10 pm; Sun 5-9 pm. Closed Mon; also Jan 1, July 4, Dec 25. Res required Fri, Sat. Contemporary Amer menu. Bar. Wine list. Semi-a la carte: dinner $16.95-$25.95. Complete meal: dinner $45. Child's meals. Specialties: beef, veal, lamb. Parking. Outdoor dining. Original oil paintings; fireplaces. Totally nonsmoking. Cr cds: A, C, D, DS, MC, V.

★★ **KAZAN RESTAURANT.** *6813 Redmond Dr (22101).* 703/734-1960. Hrs: 11 am-2:30 pm, 5-10 pm; Sat 5-10:30 pm. Closed Sun. Res accepted. Turkish menu. Serv bar. Semi-a la carte: lunch $6.95-$11.95, dinner $11.95-$19.95. Child's meals. Specializes in seafood, lamb. Middle Eastern decor. Totally nonsmoking. Cr cds: A, C, D, MC, V.

★★★ **L'AUBERGE CHEZ FRANCOIS.** *332 Springvale Rd (22066), 4 mi N of jct VA 7 & 674N.* 703/759-3800. Hrs: 5:30-9:30 pm; Sun 1:30-8 pm. Closed Mon; Jan 1, July 4, Dec 25. Res required. French menu. Serv bar. Wine cellar. Table d'hôte: dinner $36-$44. Prix fixe: dinner $25-$26 (Tue-Thur, Sun). Specialties: salmon souffle de l'Auberge; le saute gourmandise Papa Ernest; la choucroute royale garnie comme en Alsace. Own baking, ice cream. Outdoor dining. Chef-owned. Jacket. Totally non-smoking. Cr cds: A, C, D, DS, MC, V.

D

★★ **PULCINELLA.** *6852 Old Dominion Dr (22101).* 703/893-7777. Web www.pulcinella.com. Hrs: 11:30 am-10:45 pm; Sat, Sun from noon. Closed Thanksgiving, Dec 25. Italian menu. Bar. Semi-a la carte: lunch $4.25-$13.95, dinner $6.50-$16.50. Specializes in pasta, chicken. Italian decor. Cr cds: A, C, D, MC, V.

★★★ **SERBIAN CROWN RESTAURANT.** *1141 Walker Rd (22066), 5 mi W on VA 7, then ½ mi N on VA 743.* 703/759-4150. Hrs: 5:30-10 pm; Thurs, Fri noon-2:30 pm; Sun 4-9 pm. Res accepted; required Fri-Sun. Russian, Serbian menu. Bar. Wine list. A la carte entrees: lunch $8.95-$19.50, dinner $17.50-$26. Prix fixe: dinner $26, $39. Specialty: kulebiaka. Extensive vodka selection. Own pastries. Piano bar Tue, Fri, Sat. Gypsy music Wed-Sun. Parking. Intimate atmosphere; antique Russian paintings. Enclosed, heated terrace dining. Family-owned. Cr cds: A, C, D, MC, V.

D

★★ **SITTING DUCK PUB.** *1696 Chain Bridge Rd (22102), lower level of Evans Farm Inn Restaurant.* 703/356-8000. Hrs: 11:30 am-2 pm, 5-11 pm; Sat 5 pm-midnight; Sun 11 am-2 pm. Closed Dec 25. Res accepted. Continental, Amer menu. Bar. Semi-a la carte: lunch $7.95-$10.95, dinner $14.95-$24.95. Sun brunch $7.25-$12.95. Specializes in beef, seafood. Pianist, guitarist Fri-Sun. Parking. Large stone fireplace. Colonial-era prints. Family-owned. Cr cds: A, C, D, DS, JCB, MC, V.

★★ **TACHIBANA.** *6715 Lowell Ave (22101).* 703/847-1771. Hrs: 11:30 am-2 pm, 5-10 pm; Fri to 10:30 pm; Sat noon-2:30 pm, 5-10:30 pm; Sun 12:30-3 pm, 4:30-9 pm. Closed some major hols. Res accepted Mon-Thurs. Japanese menu. Serv bar. Semi-a la carte: lunch $6.50-$15, dinner $8.95-$30. Complete meals: dinner $16.50-$30. Specialties: sushi, sashimi, soft shell crab tempura (in season). Parking. Circular dining rm. Totally nonsmoking. Cr cds: A, C, D, DS, MC, V.

D

Monterey (D-6)

(See also Staunton, Warm Springs)

Pop 222 **Elev** 2,881 ft **Area Code** 540 **Zip** 24465 **E-mail** highcc@cfw.com

Information Highland County Chamber of Commerce, PO Box 223; 540/468-2550

Annual Event

Highland County Maple Festival. Tours of sugar camps producing maple syrup and maple sugar products. Juried craft show; food, entertainment. Phone 540/468-2550. Mid-Mar.

Inn

★★ **HIGHLAND INN.** *Main St (24465), jct of US 220, 250.* 540/468-2143; FAX 540/468-3143; res: 888/466-4682. E-mail highinn@cfw.com; web www.highland-inn.com/. 17 rms, 3 story. No A/C. S, D $55-

$95; suites $79-$95. TV; cable (premium). Dining rm Wed-Sat 6-8 pm; Sun (brunch)11:30 am-2 pm. Bar Mon-Sat 5-8 pm. Ck-out 11 am, ck-in after 2 pm. Meeting rm. Business servs avail. Guest parlor. Porches. Victorian building furnished with period antiques. Built 1904. Cr cds: A, C, DS, MC, V.

Montross (D-9)

Pop 359 **Elev** 149 ft **Area Code** 804 **Zip** 22520

What to See and Do

Stratford Hall Plantation. Boyhood home of Richard Henry Lee and Francis Lightfoot Lee and birthplace of General Robert E. Lee. Center of restored, working plantation is monumental Georgian house, built circa 1735, famous for its uniquely grouped chimney stacks. Interiors span approximately 100-yr period and feature a federal-era parlor and neoclassical paneling in the Great Hall. Flanking dependencies include kitchen, plantation office and gardener's house. Boxwood garden; 18th- & 19th-century carriages; working mill; visitor center with museum, video presentations. Plantation luncheon (daily). (Daily; closed Jan 1, Thanksgiving, Dec 25) 6 mi N on VA 3 to Lerty, then E on VA 214. Phone 804/493-8038. ¢¢¢

Westmoreland State Park. Approx 1,300 acres on Potomac River. Sand beach, swimming pool, bathhouse; fishing, boating (ramp, rentals). Hiking trails. Picnicking, playground, concession. Camping, tent & trailer sites (Mar-Sept; dump station, electrical hookups), cabins (Mar-Dec). Visitor center, evening programs. Standard fees. 5 mi NW on VA 3, then N on VA 347. Phone 804/493-8821.

Mount Vernon (C-8)

(See also Alexandria, Fairfax, Springfield; also see District of Columbia)

Area Code 703 **Zip** 22121
(16 mi S of Washington, DC, on Mt Vernon Memorial Hwy)

What to See and Do

Grist Mill Historical State Park. This mill was reconstructed in 1930 on original foundation of a mill George Washington operated on Dogue Run. Visitor center, programs. (Memorial Day-Labor Day, daily) 3 mi W on VA 235. Phone 703/780-3383. ¢

★ **Mount Vernon.** George Washington brought his gracious and beautiful bride here in 1759 and, with characteristic and ingenious industry, began his plan to become the leading scientific farmer in America. He kept elaborate notes, conferred with many other farmers, tried crop rotation and other new experiments, added to the house, which became a stately Georgian-colonial mansion, and planned for the family that nature unhappily denied him. He and Mrs. Washington brought up her two children by a previous marriage and raised two of her grandchildren.

The nucleus of the existing house was built in approx 1735 by Augustine Washington, George's father. George acquired it in 1754, after the death of his half-brother, Lawrence.

Family, home and farm became the focal point of Washington's life. But he was a great patriot as well as a brilliant planner, and when he was called in 1775 to lead the armies of the country he loved, he did not hesitate. When he had won freedom for his fellow Americans he returned, determined to live as he wished. But 4 yrs later he was called to preside at the Constitutional Convention in Philadelphia and in 1789 became the new nation's first president. From Mar 1797, until his death on Dec 14, 1799, he lived again at Mount Vernon. He and Martha Washington are buried here.

Mount Vernon has been accurately restored to its appearance in the last year of Washington's life, from the paint colors on the walls to the actual arrangement of the furnishings, many of which are original. The estate has been owned and maintained by the Mount Vernon Ladies' Association since 1858 and was, in effect, the nation's first tourist attraction of historic interest. Gift shop, restaurant nearby. (Daily) Phone 703/780-2000. ¢¢¢

Potamac Spirit. Offers round-trip, Potomac River cruises from Washington, DC, to Mount Vernon. The 5-hr excursion is sufficient for a complete tour of house, gardens and tomb (late Mar-early June, 1 trip daily; early June-late Aug, 2 trips daily). Phone 202/554-7447. Excursion with admission to mansion ¢¢¢¢¢

Woodlawn Plantation (1800-1805). In 1799, George Washington gave 2,000 acres of land as a wedding present to Eleanor Parke Custis, his foster daughter, who married his nephew, Major Lawrence Lewis. Dr. William Thornton, first architect of the US Capitol, then designed this mansion. The Lewises entertained such notables as Andrew Jackson, Henry Clay and the Marquis de Lafayette. The house was restored in the early 1900s and later became the residence of a US senator; 19th-century period rooms; many original furnishings. Formal gardens. (Mar-Dec, daily; closed Jan-Feb, Thanksgiving, Dec 25) National Trust for Historic Preservation property. 3 mi W of George Washington Pkwy on US 1. Phone 703/780-4000. ¢¢¢

Frank Lloyd Wright's Pope-Leighey House (1940). Erected in Falls Church in 1940, the house was disassembled (due to the construction of a new highway) and rebuilt at the present site in 1964. Built of cypress, brick and glass, the house is an example of Wright's "Usonian" structures, which he proposed as a prototype of affordable housing for Depression-era middle-income families; original Wright-designed furniture. (Mar-Dec, daily; closed Jan-Feb, Thanksgiving, Dec 25) National Trust for Historic Preservation property. Combination ticket for both houses avail. Phone 703/780-4000. ¢¢¢

Restaurant

★ ★ **MOUNT VERNON INN RESTAURANT.** *On Grounds Of Mount Vernon (22121), S end of George Washington Pkwy.* 703/780-0011. Hrs: 11 am-3:30 pm, 5-9 pm; Sun to 4 pm. Res accepted. Bar. Semi-a la carte: lunch $5.25-$8.50, dinner $12-$23.75. Child's meals. Specializes in mesquite-grilled seafood, game dishes. Own desserts. Waiters in colonial costume. Hand-painted murals of colonial scenes. Cr cds: A, C, DS, MC, V.

D

Natural Bridge (E-6)

(See also Lexington)

Founded 1774 **Pop** 200 (est) **Elev** 1,078 ft **Area Code** 540 **Zip** 24578
E-mail natbrg@aol.com **Web** www.naturalbridgeva.com/nbva/
Information Natural Bridge of Virginia, US 11 & VA 130; PO Box 57; 540/291-2121 or 800/533-1410

Native Americans worshiped at the stone bridge that nature formed across a deep gorge; town and county were both named after it. The limestone arch, 215 feet high, 90 feet long and 150 feet wide in some places, attracted the interest of Thomas Jefferson, who purchased the bridge and 157 surrounding acres from King George III for 20 shillings, about $2.49, in 1774. Fully appreciative of this natural wonder, Jefferson built a cabin for visitors and installed caretakers. His guest book reads like a colonial "Who's Who." Surveyed by George Washington, and painted by many famous artists, the bridge easily accommodates US Highway 11. The Glenwood Ranger District of the George Washington and Jefferson National Forests has its office in Natural Bridge.

What to See and Do

Cave Mountain Lake Recreation Area. Swimming. Picnicking. Camping (fee). (May-Oct) 7 mi S via VA 130, right on VA 759, then right on Forest Service Rd 781 in George Washington and Jefferson National Forests. Phone 540/291-2189 or 540/265-6054. ¢

Natural Bridge. Self-guided tours (1 hr). (Daily) Jct US 11 & VA 130; I-81, exit 175 or 180. Phone 540/291-2121 or 800/533-1410. ¢¢¢ Ticket includes entrance to

Drama of Creation. Musical presentation, viewed from beneath Natural Bridge, includes light show cast under and across arch. (Nightly) Combination tickets can also include

Caverns of Natural Bridge. More than 300 ft below ground on three levels; streams, hanging gardens of formations, flowstone cascade, totem pole, colossal dome and more. One-mi guided tour (1 hr). (Mar-Nov, daily) ¢¢¢

Natural Bridge Wax Museum. Wax figures depicting local history; self-guided factory tours. US 11 & VA 130. (Daily). ¢¢¢

Natural Bridge Zoo. State's largest and most complete zoo with over 400 reptiles, birds and mammals. Petting area; Safari Shop; picnic grounds. (Mar-Nov, daily) I-81 between exits 175 & 180. Phone 540/291-2420. ¢¢¢

Motel

★ **WATTSTULL COURT.** *Rr 1 Box 21 (24066), 8 mi S on US 11; I-81 exit 168.* 540/254-1551. 26 rms. S, D $40-$48; each addl $3. Crib $4. Pet accepted. TV. Pool; wading pool. Restaurant 6 am-10 pm. Ck-out 11 am. Panoramic view of Shenandoah Valley. Cr cds: C, MC, V.

Hotel

✓ ★ ★ **NATURAL BRIDGE.** *US 11 (24578), at jct US 11, VA 130.* 540/291-2121; FAX 540/291-1551; res: 800/533-1410. E-mail natbrg@aol.com; web www.naturalbridgeva.com/nbva. 180 rms in hotel & inn. S, D $59-$129; under 18 free. Crib free. TV; cable. Indoor pool. Restaurant 7 am-9:30 pm. Bar 4-10 pm. Ck-out noon. Meeting rms. Business servs avail. Gift shop. Tennis. Miniature golf. Game rm. Cr cds: A, C, D, DS, MC, V.

New Market (C-7)

(See also Basye, Harrisonburg, Luray)

Settled 1761 **Pop** 1,435 **Elev** 1,060 ft **Area Code** 540 **Zip** 22844
E-mail amy@svta.org **Web** www.svta.org
Information Shenandoah Valley Travel Association, PO Box 1040; 540/740-3132

New Market, situated in the Shenandoah Valley, gained its niche in Virginia history on May 15, 1864, when, in desperation, Confederate General Breckinridge ordered the cadets from Lexington's Virginia Military Institute to join the battle against the forces of General Franz Sigel. The oldest was 20, but they entered the fray fearlessly, taking prisoners and capturing a battery. Their heroism inspired the Confederate defeat of Sigel's seasoned troops.

What to See and Do

Bedrooms of America. Authentic furnishings from William & Mary through Art Deco periods. Antique dolls. Gift shop. (Daily; closed Dec 25) 9386 Congress St, I-81 exit 264. Phone 540/740-3512. ¢

Endless Caverns. Lighted display of unusual rock formations; stalagmites and stalactites, columns, shields, flowstone and limestone pendants, presented in natural color. Temperature 55°F summer & winter. Camping. Guided tours (75 min). (Daily; closed Dec 25) Via I-81, exit 257 or 264, then approx 3 mi on US 11 to entrance. Phone 540/896-CAVE. ¢¢¢

New Market Battlefield State Historical Park. Site of Civil War Battle of New Market (May 15, 1864), in which 257 VMI cadets played a decisive role. Original Bushong farmhouse and outbuildings restored, period furnishings. Hall of Valor; exhibits; films. Scenic overlooks, walking tour. (Daily; closed Jan 1, Thanksgiving, Dec 25) 1 mi N of I-81 exit 264. Phone 540/740-3101. ¢¢ Also here is

New Market Battlefield Military Museum. Located on actual site of Battle of New Market, the museum houses a private collection of more than 2,000 military artifacts and genuine, personal artifacts of the American soldier from 1776 to the present. Includes uniforms, weapons, battlefield diaries, medals, mementos; film (30 min). Bookshop has more than 500 titles, some antique. Union & Confederate troop position markers are on museum grounds. (Mid-Mar-Nov, daily) Rte 305 (Collins Dr), ¼ mi N of I-81 exit 264. Phone 540/740-8065. ¢¢

Shenandoah Caverns. Elevator lowers visitors 220 ft to large subterranean rooms, fascinating rock formations; snack bar, picnic areas. Interior a constant 56°F. (Daily; closed Dec 25) 4 mi N, off I-81 exit 269. Phone 540/477-3115. ¢¢¢

Motels

✓★ **BUDGET INN.** 2192 Old Valley Pike (22844), 1 mi N on US 11; I-81 exit 264. 540/740-3105; FAX 540/740-3108; res: 800/296-6835. 14 rms, 5 with shower only. Mid-Apr-mid-Nov: S $24-$34; D $28-$44; each addl $3; under 12 free; higher rates special events; lower rates rest of yr. Crib $3. Pet accepted, some restrictions. TV; cable (premium). Playground. Complimentary coffee in lobby. Restaurant nearby. Ck-out 11 am. Business servs avail. Refrigerators. Picnic tables. Cr cds: A, C, D, DS, MC, V.

⬛ ⬛ ⬛ ⬛ **SC**

★★ **QUALITY INN SHENANDOAH VALLEY.** 162 W Old Cross Rd (22844), on VA 211 at I-81 exit 264. 540/740-3141; FAX 540/740-3250; res: 800/638-7949. 101 rms, 2 story. May-Oct: S $55-$70; D $70-$85; each addl $6; lower rates rest of yr. Crib free. TV; cable (premium); VCR avail. Pool. Sauna. Playground. Complimentary coffee in rms. Restaurant 6:30 am-9 pm. Rm serv. Ck-out noon. Coin lndry. Meeting rms. Business servs avail. In-rm modem link. Gift shops. Game rm. Miniature golf. Cr cds: A, C, D, DS, ER, MC, V.

D ⬛ ⬛ ⬛ ⬛ **SC**

✓★ **SHENVALEE GOLF RESORT.** 9660 Fairway Dr (22844), I-81 exit 264, at jct US 11. 540/740-3181; FAX 540/740-8931. E-mail shenvale@shentel.net; web www.shenvalee.com. 42 rms, 1-2 story. Apr-Oct: S $55; D $62-$66; each addl $12; under 13 free; golf plan; lower rates rest of yr. Crib free. TV; cable. Pool; wading pool. Restaurant 6:15 am-9 pm; Sun to 8 pm. Bar 4:30 pm-midnight; wkends to 2 am. Ck-out 1 pm. Meeting rms. Business servs avail. Tennis. 27-hole golf privileges, greens fee $22-$25, putting green, driving range. Refrigerators. Balconies. Picnic tables. On 200 acres. Cr cds: A, C, D, DS, MC, V.

D ⬛ ⬛ ⬛ ⬛ ⬛

Newport News (F-9)

(See also Hampton, Norfolk, Portsmouth, Virginia Beach, Yorktown)

Settled 1619 **Pop** 170,045 **Elev** 25 ft **Area Code** 757
Information Visitor Center, 13560 Jefferson Ave, 23603; 757/886-7777 or 888/4-WE-R-FUN

One of the three cities (also see NORFOLK and PORTSMOUTH) that make up the Port of Hampton Roads, Newport News has the world's largest shipbuilding company, Newport News Shipbuilding. Hampton

Roads, 14 miles long and 40 feet deep, formed by the James, York, Elizabeth and Nansemond rivers as they pass into Chesapeake Bay, is one of the world's finest natural harbors. The largest ships are accommodated at Newport News docks; huge tonnages of coal, ore, tobacco and grain are shipped from the port annually. During the two world wars it was a vitally important point of embarkation and supply. The area still has many important defense establishments.

Newport News is located on the historic Virginia Peninsula, between Williamsburg and Virginia Beach. The peninsula contains Hampton, Yorktown, Jamestown and Williamsburg. Some of the earliest landings in this country were here. The name of the town is said to derive from the good "news" of the arrival of Captain Christopher Newport, who brought supplies and additional colonists to the settlement at Jamestown.

What to See and Do

Fort Eustis. Headquarters of US Army Transportation Center. Self-guided auto tour avail; brochures at Public Affairs Office (Bldg 213). NW end of city on Mulberry Island, I-64 exit 250A. Phone 757/878-4920. **Free** On grounds is

US Army Transportation Museum. Depicts development of Army transportation from 1776 to the present; "flying saucer," amphibious vehicles, trucks, helicopters. Gift shop. (Daily exc Mon; closed major hols) Phone 757/878-1115. **Free**

Historic Hilton Village. Listed on the National Register of Historic Places, this village was built between 1918-1920 to provide wartime housing for workers at Newport News Shipbuilding. Architecturally significant neighborhood features 500 English cottage-style homes and antique and specialty shops. I-64 exit 263A, at Warwick Blvd & Main St. Phone 757/886-7777. **Free**

Newport News Park. Facilities of this 8,065-acre park include freshwater fishing; canoes, paddleboats, boat rentals; history, nature trails; bicycle paths (bicycle rentals); archery; arboretum; interpretive center; picnicking; Civil War earthworks; 188 campsites. (All yr) Some fees. Jct VA 105, 143, I-64 exit 250B. Phone 757/888-3333 or 800/203-8322. **Free**; Camping ¢¢¢-¢¢¢¢¢

Peninsula Fine Arts Center. Changing bi-monthly exhibits ranging from national traveling exhibitions to regional artists; classes, workshops and special events. Children's hands-on activity area; museum shop. (Daily; closed Jan 1, Thanksgiving, Dec 24, 25) 101 Museum Dr, I-64 exit 258A. Phone 757/596-8175. **Free**

The Mariners' Museum. Exhibits and displays represent international nautical history; ship models, figureheads, scrimshaw, paintings, decorative arts and small craft. Age of Exploration Gallery chronicles advancements in shipbuilding, ocean navigation and cartography that led to early transoceanic exploration. The Chesapeake Bay Gallery exhibits Native American artifacts, workboats, racing shells, multimedia exhibits, a working steam engine, and hundreds of artifacts and photos that tell the story of this body of water. The Crabtree Collection of Miniature Ships showcases 16 detailed miniatures that illustrate the evolution of the sailing ship. Small craft gallery showcases vessels from five continents. A short film, *Mariner*, introduces the visitor to maritime activities from around the world. Historical interpreters; research library; museum shop. A 550-acre park on the James River features the 5-mi Noland Trail, with 14 pedestrian bridges; picnic area. Special event include Yuletide at The Mariners' (Dec). Guided tours. (Daily; closed Thanksgiving, Dec 25) Warwick Blvd & J Clyde Morris Blvd; 2½ mi off I-64 exit 258A. Phone 757/596-2222 or 800/581-7245. ¢¢

Virginia Living Museum. Exhibits on natural science; wildlife, all native to Virginia, living in natural habitats; indoor & outdoor aviaries; aquariums; wildflower gardens; planetarium with daily shows; observatory; children's hands-on Discovery Center. (Daily; closed Jan 1, Thanksgiving, Dec 24, 25) 524 J Clyde Morris Blvd, I-64 exit 258A. Phone 757/595-1900. ¢¢-¢¢¢

Virginia War Museum. More than 60,000 artifacts, including weapons, uniforms, vehicles, posters, insignia and accoutrements relating to every major US military involvement from the Revolution to the Vietnam War. Military history library and film collection. Civil War tours and educational programs avail. (Mon-Sat, also Sun afternoons; closed Jan 1, Thanksgiving, Dec 25). 9285 Warwick Blvd in Huntington Park, on US 60, I-64 exit 263A. Phone 757/247-8523. ¢

Motel

★★ **COMFORT INN.** 12330 Jefferson Ave (23602), I-64 exit 255A. 757/249-0200; FAX 757/249-4736; res: 800/368-2477. 124 rms, 3 story. S $84; D $94; each addl $7; under 18 free. Crib free. Pet accepted. TV; cable (premium). Pool. Complimentary continental bkfst. Restaurant adj 11 am-midnight. Ck-out noon. Coin lndry. Meeting rms. Business servs avail. In-rm modem link. Free airport transportation. Health club privileges. Some refrigerators. Cr cds: A, C, D, DS, ER, JCB, MC, V.

Motor Hotel

★★ **HAMPTON INN.** 12251 Jefferson Ave (23602), near Intl Airport. 757/249-0001; FAX 757/249-3911; res: 800/426-7866. E-mail hmptstes@visi.net. 120 rms, 4 story, 30 suites. Memorial Day-Labor Day: S, D $79-$89; suites $109-$139; under 18 free; higher rates special events; lower rates rest of yr. Crib free. TV; cable (premium). Complimentary continental bkfst. Coffee in rms. Restaurant opp open 24 hrs. Ck-out noon. Meeting rms. Business center. In-rm modem link. Bellhops. Sundries. Free airport transportation. Pool. Some fireplaces; refrigerator, microwave in suites. Picnic tables, grills. Cr cds: A, C, D, DS, MC, V.

Hotel

★★★ **OMNI HOTEL.** 1000 Omni Blvd (23606). 757/873-6664; FAX 757/873-1732; res: 800/843-6664. 183 rms, 9 story. Memorial Day-Labor Day: S, D $119; lower rates rest of yr. Crib avail. TV; cable (premium), VCR avail. Coffee in rms. Indoor pool; whirlpool, poolside serv. Restaurant 6:30 am-11 pm. Bar 11-2 am; piano bar Mon-Sat. Ck-out noon. Meeting rms. Business center. In-rm modem link. Gift shop. Exercise equipt; sauna. Cr cds: A, C, D, DS, JCB, MC, V.

Restaurants

★★ **BON APPETITE.** 11710 Jefferson Ave (23606), at Oyster Point. 757/873-0644. Hrs: 11 am-2:30 pm, 5-10 pm; Mon to 9 pm; Sat from 5 pm. Closed Sun; major hols. Res accepted. French, Vietnamese menu. Bar. A la carte entrees: lunch $5.25-$6.75, dinner $9.95-$18.95. Specialties: panache de mer, veal Oscar, scallops in oyster sauce. Mediterranean cafe atmosphere. Cr cds: A, C, DS, MC, V.

✓★★ **DAS WALDCAFE.** 12529 Warwick Blvd (23606). 757/930-1781. Hrs: 11:30 am-2 pm, 5-10 pm; Sat from 4 pm; Sun 11:30 am-9 pm. Closed Mon; hols. Res accepted. German menu. Bar. Semi-a la carte: lunch, dinner $3.75-$13.50. Specialties: schnitzel, rouladen, hazelnut cake. Cr cds: A, C, D, MC, V.

★★ **HERMAN'S HARBOR HOUSE.** 663 Deep Creek Rd (23606). 757/930-1000. Hrs: 11:30 am-2:30 pm, 5-10 pm; Sat from 5 pm; Sun brunch 11:30 am-3 pm. Closed Dec 25. Res accepted. Bar. Semi-a la carte: lunch $4.95-$9.95, dinner $8.95-$19.95. Specializes in local seafood, steak. Nautical decor. Cr cds: A, C, DS, MC, V.

★★ **PORT ARTHUR CHINESE RESTAURANT.** 11137 Warwick Blvd (23601). 757/599-6474. Hrs: 11:30 am-10 pm; Fri, Sat to 10:30 pm; Sun noon-10 pm; Sun buffet noon-3 pm, 5:30-9 pm. Closed Thanksgiving, Dec 25. Res accepted. Chinese, Amer menu. Bar. Semi-a la carte:

lunch $3.95-$5.95, dinner $5.95-$14.95. Complete meals: dinner $17.50-$63. Wkend buffet: dinner $7.95. Child's meals. Specialties: Phoenix nest, shrimp kew, Peking duck. Family-owned. Cr cds: A, C, D, DS, MC, V.

Norfolk (F-9)

Founded 1682 **Pop** 261,229 **Elev** 12 ft **Area Code** 757 **E-mail** sales@ norfolkcvb.com **Web** www.norfolk.va.us

Information Norfolk Convention and Visitors Bureau, 232 E Main St, 23510; 757/664-6620 or 800/368-3097

Suburbs Chesapeake, Hampton, Newport News, Portsmouth, Virginia Beach. (See individual alphabetical listings.)

This city is part of the Port of Hampton Roads. It is a bustling trade center and has many historic, cultural and resort areas nearby to attract the tourist. Harbor tours depart from Norfolk's downtown waterfront.

In 1682, the General Assembly bought from Nicholas Wise, a pioneer settler, 50 acres on the Elizabeth River for "ten thousand pounds of tobacco and caske." By 1736 the town that developed was the largest in Virginia. On Jan 1, 1776, Norfolk was shelled by the British and later burned by the colonists to prevent a British takeover. The battle between the *Merrimac* and the *Monitor* in Hampton Roads in March 1862 was followed by the fall of the city to Union forces in May of that year. In 1883, the shipment of the first coal to the port by the Norfolk and Western Railway (now Norfolk Southern) began a new era of prosperity for the city.

Norfolk and Portsmouth, are connected by bridge tunnels and a pedestrian ferry. Norfolk houses the largest naval facility in the world. It is also headquarters for the US Navy's Atlantic Fleet and the North Atlantic Treaty Organization's Allied Command Atlantic. Norfolk has shipbuilding and ship repair companies, consumer and industrial equipment manufacturers and food-processing plants. The city ships coal, tobacco, grain, seafood and vegetables. It is also the region's cultural center; home to the Virginia Opera, Virginia Symphony, the Virginia Waterfront International Arts Festival and Virginia Stage Company.

Old Dominion University (1930), Virginia Wesleyan College (1967) Norfolk State University (1935) and Eastern Virginia Medical School (1973) are located here. This area is also the headquarters for year-round resort activities. Within a 50-mile radius are ocean, bay, river and marsh fishing and hunting; nearby there are 25 miles of good beaches. The 17.6-mile-long Chesapeake Bay Bridge-Tunnel, between Norfolk and the Delmarva Peninsula, opened in 1964; toll for passenger cars is $10, including passengers.

Transportation

Norfolk Intl Airport. Information 757/857-3351; lost and found 757/857-3344; weather 757/666-1212.

Car Rental Agencies. See IMPORTANT TOLL-FREE NUMBERS.

Public Transportation. Buses (Tidewater Regional Transit), phone 757/640-6300.

Rail Passenger Service. Amtrak 800/872-7245.

What to See and Do

Cape Henry Memorial (see) **and Lighthouse.** 10 mi E on US 60.

Chrysler Museum of Art. Art treasures representing nearly every important culture, civilization and historical period of the past 4,000 yrs. Photography gallery; fine collection of Tiffany decorative arts and glass, including the 8,000-piece Chrysler Institute of Glass. (Daily exc Mon; closed some major hols) 245 W Olney Rd, at Mowbray Arch. Phone 757/664-6200. ¢¢

General Douglas MacArthur Memorial. Restored former city hall (1847) where MacArthur is buried. Nine galleries contain memorabilia of his life and military career. There are three other buildings on MacArthur Sq: a theater where a film biography is shown, a gift shop and the library/archives. (Daily; closed Jan 1, Thanksgiving, Dec 25) City Hall Ave & Bank St. Phone 757/441-2965.   **Free**

Hermitage Foundation Museum. Guided tours of fine arts museum in Tudor-style mansion. Collections of tapestries, Chinese bronzes and jade, ancient glass. (Daily; closed Jan 1, Thanksgiving, Dec 25) 7637 North Shore Rd. Phone 757/423-2052. ¢¢

Hunter House Victorian Museum. Built in 1894 and rich in architectural details, the house contains the Hunter family's collection of Victorian furnishings and decorative pieces, including a Renaissance-revival bedchamber suite, a nursery with children's playthings, an inglenook and stained-glass windows; lavish period reproduction floor and wall coverings, lighting fixtures and drapery. Also exhibited is a collection of early-20th-century medical memorabilia. Tours begin every 30 min. (Apr-Dec, Wed-Sat, also Sun afternoons; closed Jan 1, Thanksgiving, Dec 25). 240 W Freemason St. Phone 757/623-9814. ¢¢

Moses Myers House (1792). Excellent example of Georgian architecture; many pieces of original furniture, silver and china. (Apr-Dec, daily exc Mon; rest of yr, Tues-Sat; closed Jan 1, July 4, Thanksgiving, Dec 25) 331 Bank St. Phone 757/664-6283. ¢¢

Nauticus, the National Maritime Center. Interprets aspects from marine biology and ecology to exploration, trade and shipbuilding. Interactive computer exhibits allow visitors to navigate a simulated ocean voyage, design a model ship, pilot a virtual reality submarine and view actual researchers at work in two working marine laboratories. Active US Navy ships and scientific research vessels will periodically moor at Nauticus and be open to visitors. Also 350-seat, 70mm wide-screen theater; shark-petting tank. (May-Sept, daily; rest of yr, daily exc Mon; closed Jan 1, Thanksgiving, Dec 25). One Waterside Dr. Phone 757/664-1000. ¢¢¢ Also here is

Hampton Roads Naval Museum. Interprets the extensive naval history of the Hampton Roads area; includes detailed ship models, period photographs, archaeological artifacts and a superior collection of naval prints and artwork. (Daily; closed Jan 1, Thanksgiving, Dec 25) Phone 757/444-8971. **Free**

Norfolk Botanical Garden. Azaleas, camellias, rhododendrons, roses (May-Oct), dogwoods and hollies on 155 acres. Japanese, Colonial, Perennial and Rose Gardens; Flowering Arboretum; Hill of Nations; Fragrance Garden for the visually impaired; picnicking, restaurant and gift shop; Tropical Pavilion. Flowering displays are best from early Apr-Oct. Gardens (daily; closed special events). Information center (daily; closed Jan 1, Dec 25). Narrated boat ride (30 min) and tram tours (mid-Mar-Labor Day, daily; through Oct wkends, trams only). On Azalea Garden Rd, adj Norfolk Intl Airport. Phone 757/441-5830. ¢¢

Norfolk Naval Base and Norfolk Naval Air Station. The largest naval installation in the world. Tours of designated ships are avail (Sat & Sun); ship visitors should check in at the Naval Base Pass Office on Hampton Blvd, opp Gate 5. Naval base tours are also offered. Tour buses from Tour & Information Office, 9079 Hampton Blvd (Apr-Oct, daily; also, bus tours from downtown at the Waterside). Hampton Blvd & I-564. Phone 757/444-7955 or 757/640-6300. Bus ¢¢

Sightseeing tours.

American Rover. This 135-ft, 3-masted topsail passenger schooner cruises the "smooth waters" of Hampton Roads historical harbor; spacious sun decks; below-deck lounges; concessions. Tour passes historic forts, merchant and US Navy ships. Some tours pass the naval base (inquire for tour schedule). (Apr-mid-Oct, 2- and 3-hr tours daily) Waterside Marina, Waterside Dr exit off I-264. For information, reservations phone 757/627-SAIL. ¢¢¢¢-¢¢¢¢¢

Carrie B Harbor Tours. Replica of 19th-century riverboat takes narrated 90-min tour of naval shipyard and inner harbor (Apr-Oct, daily); narrated 2½-hr tour of naval base (Apr-Oct, daily); 2½-hr sunset cruise to Hampton Roads and naval base (June-Labor Day, daily). Departs from the Waterside. Phone 757/393-4735. (Also see PORTSMOUTH) ¢¢¢¢

Spirit of Norfolk. Harbor cruise aboard 600-passenger cruise ship. Captain's narration highlights the harbor's famous landmarks, including Waterside Festival Marketplace, Portsmouth Naval Hospital, Old Fort Norfolk, Blackbeard's hiding place, Norfolk Naval Base and downtown area's dynamic skyline. Luncheon Cruise (daily exc Mon); Evening Dinner Cruise (daily exc Mon); Moonlight Party Cruise (Fri-Sat, in season). Departs from the Waterside. For schedule, reservations phone 757/627-7771. ¢¢¢¢¢

St Paul's Episcopal Church (1739). Only building to survive burning of Norfolk in 1776. (Tues-Fri, also by appt) 201 St Paul's Blvd, at City Hall Ave. Phone 757/627-4353. **Donation**

Virginia Zoological Park. A combination zoo, park and conservatory. Playground, tennis courts, basketball courts; picnic area, concession. (Daily; closed Jan 1, Dec 25). 3500 Granby St. Phone 757/441-2706 (recording) or 757/441-5227. ¢

Waterside Festival Marketplace. A waterfront pavilion creating a lively marketplace with more than 90 shops, restaurants. (Daily; closed Thanksgiving, Dec 25) 333 Waterside Dr. Bordering the Waterside are the city's marina and dock areas, where harbor tour vessels take on passengers. A brick promenade, skirting the marina, connects the Waterside to

Town Point Park. Home to Norfolk Festevents, the park hosts more than 100 free outdoor concerts, parties, dances, movies and festivals each year. Phone 757/441-2345.

Willoughby-Baylor House (1794). Restored town house with period furnishings; herb and flower garden adj. (By appt; inquire at Moses Myers House) 601 E Freemason St. Phone 757/664-6283. ¢¢

Annual Events

International Azalea Festival. Downtown & Norfolk Botanical Garden. To honor NATO. Parade, coronation ceremony, air show (held at Norfolk Naval Air Station), events, concerts, fair, ball, entertainment. Late-Apr.

Virginia Waterfront International Arts Festival. 18 days of classical & contemporary music, dance, visual arts and theater performances. Phone 757/664-6492. Late Apr-mid-May.

Harborfest. Town Point Park, downtown waterfront on Wayside Dr. Sailboat and speedboat races, tall ships, ship tours, waterskiing, military demonstrations, entertainment, children's activities, fireworks, seafood. 1st full wkend June.

Virginia Children's Festival. Town Point Park. More than 200 educational, creative and interactive activities; entertainment. Early Oct.

Seasonal Events

Virginia Symphony. Chrysler Hall and other select locations. Five series. Phone 757/623-2310 (tickets). Sept-May.

Virginia Opera. Harrison Opera House & other select locations. Statewide opera company; traditional and contemporary works. Features young American artists. Phone 757/623-1223. Oct-Apr.

Virginia Stage Company, Wells Theater. Professional theater performed by nationally known artists. Phone 757/627-1234. Oct-May.

Motels

★★ **BEST WESTERN CENTER INN.** *235 N Military Hwy (23502), jct I-264 & US 13.* 757/461-6600; FAX 757/466-9093; res: 800/237-5517. 152 rms, 2 story. Memorial Day-Labor Day: S $59-$69; D $69-$99; each addl $10; suites $149-$179; under 13 free; higher rates: hols (3-day min), Jazz Festival; lower rates rest of yr. Crib free. TV; cable (premium), VCR avail (movies). 2 pools, 1 indoor; whirlpool. Complimentary coffee in rms. Restaurant 6 am-2 pm, 5-10 pm; Sat, Sun from 7 am. Rm serv. Bar. Ck-out noon. Coin lndry. Meeting rms. Business servs avail. In-rm modem link. Free airport transportation. Exercise equipt; sauna. Many refrigerators; microwaves avail. Picnic tables. Near airport. Cr cds: A, C, D, DS, MC, V.

D ➡ ✕ ➷ 🔥 SC

★ **COMFORT INN.** *8051 Hampton Blvd (23505), adj naval base.* 757/451-0000; FAX 757/451-8394; res: 800/228-5150. E-mail comfnob@tidewaterinnvb.com. 120 rms, 2 story. S, D $59-$80; each addl $5; under 18 free. Crib free. TV; cable (premium). Indoor pool; whirlpool. Complimentary continental bkfst. Restaurant nearby. Ck-out 11 am. Coin lndry. Business servs avail. In-rm modem link. Refrigerators; some microwaves. Cr cds: A, C, D, DS, MC, V.

D ➡ ➷ 🔥 SC

✓★ **ECONO LODGE.** *9601 4th View St (23503).* 757/480-9611; FAX 757/480-1307; res: 800/228-5050. 71 units, 3 story, 22 kits. Mid-May-Labor Day: S $54.95; D $64.95; each addl $5; kit units $69.95; under 18 free; wkly rates; higher rates: some hols, special events; lower rates rest of yr. Pet accepted, some restrictions; $50 deposit. TV; cable (premium), VCR avail (movies). Complimentary continental bkfst. Restaurant nearby. Ck-out 11 am. Business servs avail. Coin lndry. Exercise equipt. Refrigerators. Ocean; fishing pier. Beach adj. Cr cds: A, C, D, DS, JCB, MC, V.

D ⬛ ⬛ ⬛ SC

★★ **HAMPTON INN.** *1450 N Military Hwy (23502).* 757/466-7474; FAX 757/466-0117; res: 800/426-7866. 130 units, 2 story. Late May-early Sept: S $65-$69; D $75; under 18 free; lower rates rest of yr. Crib free. TV; cable (premium). Pool. Coffee in rms. Restaurant opp 7 am-11 pm. Ck-out noon. Business servs avail. In-rm modem link. Valet serv. Free airport transportation. Health club privileges. Cr cds: A, C, D, DS, MC, V.

D ⬛ ⬛ ⬛ SC

★ **HOLIDAY SANDS MOTEL & TOWER.** *1340 E Ocean-view Ave (23503).* 757/583-2621; FAX 757/587-7540; res: 800/525-5156. E-mail holidaysands@worldnet.att.com. 95 units, 2-5 story, 74 kits. Memorial Day-Labor Day: S, D $50-$95; each addl $5; suites $85-$105; kit units $70-$95; under 12 free; lower rates rest of yr. Crib free. Meeting rms. TV; cable (premium). Heated pool. Complimentary continental bkfst. Restaurant nearby. Ck-out 11 am. Business servs avail. Coin lndry. Free airport transportation. Exercise equipt. Refrigerators, microwaves. Private patios, balconies. On beach. Cr cds: A, C, D, DS, MC, V.

D ⬛ ⬛ ⬛ ⬛ ⬛ SC

★ **OLD DOMINION INN.** *4111 Hampton Blvd (23508).* 757/440-5100; FAX 757/423-5238; res: 800/653-9030. 60 rms, 3 story. S, D $70; each addl $5; suites $98-$138; under 12 free; higher rates special events. Crib $5. TV. Complimentary continental bkfst. Restaurant nearby. Ck-out 11 am. Meeting rms. Business servs avail. Refrigerators, microwaves avail. Cr cds: A, C, D, DS, MC, V.

D ⬛ ⬛ SC

✓★ **SUPER 8 MOTEL.** *7940 Shore Dr (23518).* 757/588-7888; FAX 757/588-7888; res: 800/800-8000. 74 units, 3 story, 10 kit units. June-Labor Day: S, D $46.95-$66; suites, kit units $72.88-$89.47; higher rates: July 4, Labor Day; lower rates rest of yr. Crib free. TV; cable (premium). Complimentary continental bkfst. Restaurant nearby. Ck-out 11 am. Business servs avail. Some refrigerators, microwaves. Cr cds: A, C, D, DS, MC, V.

D ⬛ ⬛ SC

Hotels

★★★ **DOUBLETREE CLUB HOTEL.** *880 N Military Hwy (23502), Military Circle Mall.* 757/461-9192; FAX 757/461-8290; res: 800/933-9600. E-mail dbltreeacc@aol.com; web www.doubletreehotel.com. 208 rms, 14 story. S $64-$115; D $74-$123; each addl $10; suites $175; under 18 free; wkend rates. Crib free. TV; cable (premium). Pool. Restaurant 6:30 am-10:30 pm. Bar 11-1 am. Ck-out noon. Meeting rms. Business center. Exercise equipt. Free airport transportation. Microwaves avail. Balconies. Shopping mall adj. Cr cds: A, C, D, DS, ER, JCB, MC, V.

D ⬛ ⬛ ⬛ ⬛ SC ⬛

★★★ **HILTON.** *1500 N Military Hwy (23502), at Northampton Blvd, near Intl Airport.* 757/466-8000; FAX 757/466-8802; res: 800/445-8667. 250 rms, 6 story. S $94-$139; D $104-$149; each addl $15; suites $170-$360; under 18 free; package plans. Crib free. TV; cable (premium). Pool; whirlpool, poolside serv. Coffee in rms. Restaurant 6:30 am-midnight. Bars 4 pm-1 am; entertainment. Ck-out 1 pm. Convention facilities. Business servs avail. In-rm modem link. Gift shop. Beauty shop. Free airport transportation. Lighted tennis. Exercise equipt; sauna. Minibars. Luxury level. Cr cds: A, C, D, DS, ER, JCB, MC, V.

D ⬛ ⬛ ⬛ ⬛ ⬛ ⬛ SC

✓★★ **JAMES MADISON.** *345 Granby St (23510), I-264 exit 9, Waterside Dr.* 757/622-6682; FAX 757/623-5949; res: 888/402-6682. 124 units, 8 story. S, D $70-$150; each addl $10; under 16 free; wkend rates. Crib free. TV; cable (premium). Restaurant 6:30 am-2:30 pm, 4-10 pm. Bar from 4 pm. Ck-out noon. Meeting rms. Business servs avail. In-rm modem link. Health club privileges. Cr cds: A, C, D, DS, MC, V.

D ⬛ ⬛ SC

★★★ **MARRIOT-WATERSIDE.** *235 E Main St (23510).* 757/627-4200; FAX 757/628-6466. 404 rms, 24 story. S, D $109-$165; suites $250-$600. Crib free. Pet accepted; $35. Garage parking $8; valet $10. TV; cable (premium). Indoor pool; whirlpool, poolside serv. Coffee in rms. Restaurant 6-11 am, 5:30-11 pm. Bar 11-1 am. Ck-out noon. Coin lndry. Convention facilities. Business center. In-rm modem link. Concierge. Gift shop. Exercise equipt; sauna. Game rm. Refrigerator, wet bar in suites. Luxury level. Cr cds: A, C, D, DS, ER, JCB, MC, V.

D ⬛ ⬛ ⬛ ⬛ ⬛ SC ⬛

★★★ **OMNI WATERSIDE HOTEL.** *777 Waterside Dr (23510), at St Paul's Blvd and I-264.* 757/622-6664; FAX 757/625-8271; res: 800/325-3535. Web www.sheraton.com. 446 rms, 10 story. S, D $79-$149; each addl $15; suites $200-$600; under 18 free; wkend rates. Crib free. Pet accepted; $35. Valet parking $9.50. TV, cable (premium), VCR avail. Pool; poolside serv. Restaurant 6:30 am-10 pm; wkends to 11 pm. Rm serv to midnight. Bars 11-2 am; entertainment wkends. Ck-out noon. Convention facilities. Business center. In-rm modem link. Gift shop. Health club privileges. Dockage. Some refrigerators. Balconies. Atrium-like lobby. On harbor. Luxury level. Cr cds: A, C, D, DS, JCB, MC, V.

D ⬛ ⬛ ⬛ ⬛ SC ⬛

Inn

★★★ **PAGE HOUSE.** *323 Fairfax Ave (23507).* 757/623-9442; FAX 757/623-9451; res: 800/599-7659. E-mail innkeeper@pagehouseinn.com; web www.pagehouseinn.com. 7 rms, 1 with shower only, 3 story, 3 suites. S, D $110-$135; suites $140-$175. Children under 12 yrs only by res. TV; cable (premium), VCR avail. Complimentary full bkfst. Restaurant nearby. Ck-out 11 am, ck-in 4-6 pm. Business servs avail. In-rm modem link. Some in-rm whirlpools. Refrigerator in suites. Totally restored Georgian-Revival residence (1898) in historic district. Totally nonsmoking. Cr cds: A, C, MC, V.

⬛ ⬛

Restaurants

★★ **FREEMASON ABBEY.** *209 W Freemason St (23510).* 757/622-3966. Web www.cvent.net/restaurants/cvi/freemason/. Hrs: 11:30 am-10 pm; Fri, Sat to 11 pm; Sun brunch 9:30 am-2 pm. Closed Jan 1, Thanksgiving, Dec 25. Bar. Semi-a la carte: lunch $3.95-$9.95, dinner $9.95-$17.95. Sun brunch $5.95-$8.95. Child's meals. Specializes in whole Maine lobster, prime rib. Renovated church (1873); many antiques. Cr cds: A, C, DS, MC, V.

D ⬛

★★★ **LA GALLERIA.** *120 College Place (23510).* 757/623-3939. Hrs: 11:30 am-2:30 pm, 5:30-11:30 pm; Mon to 11 pm; Fri, Sat to midnight. Closed Sun; Thanksgiving, Dec 25. Res accepted. Italian menu. Bar 11:30 am-2:30 pm, 4:30 pm-2 am. Semi-a la carte: lunch $3.95-$7.95, dinner $11.95-$19.95. Child's meals. Specialty: salmon La Galleria. Own baking, pasta. Valet parking. Outdoor dining. Modern decor. Cr cds: A, C, D, MC, V.

D ⬛

★★ **MONASTERY.** *443 Granby St (23510).* 757/625-8193. Hrs: 11:30 am-2:30 pm, 5-10 pm; May-Labor Day from 5 pm. Closed Mon; Easter, Thanksgiving, Dec 25; also July-Aug. Res accepted; required Fri,

Sat. Czech, Eastern European menu. Bar. Semi-a la carte: lunch $2.75-$8.50, dinner $4.75-$21. Specialties: roast duck, Wienerschnitzel, goulash. Antique mirrors, original works by local artists. Cr cds: A, C, D, MC, V.

★ **REGGIE'S BRITISH PUB.** *333 Waterside Dr (23510), at the Waterside.* 757/627-3575. E-mail reggie's@visi.net. Hrs: 11:30 am-11 pm; Fri, Sat to midnight. Closed Thanksgiving, Dec 25. British menu. Bar. Semi-a la carte: lunch $5.95-$7.95, dinner $6.95-$14.25. Specialties: fish & chips, mixed grill, shepherd's pie. Outdoor dining. Entertainment wkends. British Pub decor. Overlooks Elizabeth River. Cr cds: A, C, D, MC, V.

★★★ **SHIP'S CABIN.** *4110 E Ocean View Ave (23518).* 757/362-2526. Hrs: 5:30-9:30 pm; Fri, Sat to 10:30 pm; Sun 5-9 pm. Res accepted. Bar. Wine list. Semi-a la carte: dinner $12.95-$18.95. Specializes in grilled fish & meat. Own baking. Parking. Fireplaces. Outdoor dining. View of Chesapeake Bay. Cr cds: A, C, D, MC, V.

★ **THE BANQUE.** *1849 E Little Creek Rd (23518).* 757/480-3600. Hrs: 6 pm-2 am. Closed Mon; Thanksgiving, Dec 24-25. Res accepted. Bar. A la carte entrees: dinner $5.95-$14.95. Specializes in prime rib, shrimp. Entertainment. Western decor. Cr cds: A, C, DS, MC, V.

✓★ **THE DUMBWAITER.** *117 W Tazewell St (23510).* 757/623-3663. E-mail sydvez@aol.com. Hrs: 4-10:30 pm; Sat, Sun from 5 pm; early-bird dinner Tues-Sat 5-7 pm. Regional Amer menu. Bar. Semi-a la carte: dinner $2.50-$17. Specialties: chicken and mashed potato tart, grilled portobello mushroom, sauteed crab cakes with mango chutney. Menu changes monthly. Jazz Fri, Sat. Eclectic decor features modern artwork. Cr cds: A, C, MC, V.

★★ **THE MAX.** *1421 Colley Ave (23517).* 757/625-0259. Hrs: 11 am-10 pm; Fri, Sat to 2 am; Sun brunch 11 am-2:30 pm. Closed Thanksgiving, Dec 25. Bar. Semi-a la carte: lunch $2.95-$7.95, dinner $2.95-$16.95. Sun brunch $5-$6.95. Child's meals. Specializes in pasta, fresh vegetables, veal. Parking. Outdoor dining. Carnival and novelty items displayed. Cr cds: A, C, D, DS, MC, V.

✓★★ **TODD JURICH'S BISTRO.** *210 W York St (23510).* 757/622-3210. E-mail primethyme@aol.com. Hrs: 11:30 am-2:30 pm, 5:30-10 pm; Fri to 11 pm; Sat 5:30-11 pm. Closed Sun; major hols. Bar. Semi-a la carte: lunch $5-$10, dinner $11.95-$22.95. Specializes in regional cuisine. Own pastries, pasta. Cr cds: A, C, D, MC, V.

✓★★ **UNCLE LOUIE'S.** *132 E Little Creek Rd (23505).* 757/480-1225. E-mail unclouie@erols.com. Hrs: 8 am-11 pm; Fri, Sat to midnight. Closed Thanksgiving, Dec 25. Res accepted. Bar. Semi-a la carte: bkfst $3.50-$6.95, lunch, dinner $3.50-$16.95. Child's meals. Specializes in fresh seafood, prime meats, New York deli sandwiches. Entertainment Wed, Sat. Cr cds: A, C, D, DS, MC, V.

Unrated Dining Spot

DOUMAR'S. *1919 Monticello Ave (23517).* 757/627-4163. Hrs: 8 am-11 pm. Closed Sun; major hols. A la carte entrees: bkfst, lunch, dinner 70¢-$2.30. Ice cream 90¢-$3.40. Specializes in sandwiches, ice cream, hand-rolled cones. Parking. 1950s-style drive-in with addl seating inside. Abe Doumar invented the ice cream cone in 1904; his original cone making machine is on display here. Family-owned. Cr cds: C.

Orange (D-7)

(See also Charlottesville, Culpeper)

Founded 1749 **Pop** 2,582 **Elev** 521 ft **Area Code** 540 **Zip** 22960

This is the seat of Orange County, which was named for William, Prince of Orange, in 1734. Located in the Piedmont (foothills) of the Blue Ridge Mountains, Orange was settled by Germans under the leadership of Alexander Spotswood between 1714 and 1719. This is riding and hunting country, drawing its livelihood from farming, livestock and light industry. There are many antebellum houses in the county.

What to See and Do

James Madison Museum. Exhibits commemorating Madison's life and his contributions to American history; also Orange County history and Hall of Agriculture that includes an 18th-century homestead. (Mar-Nov, daily; rest of yr, Mon-Fri) 129 Caroline St. Phone 540/672-1776. ¢¢

⊠ **Montpelier.** Residence of James Madison, 4th president of US. Madison was the third generation of his family to live on this extensive plantation. He inherited Montpelier and enlarged it twice. After his presidency, he and Dolley Madison retired to the estate, which Mrs. Madison sold, after the president's death, to pay her son's gambling debts. In 1901, the estate was bought by William du Pont, who enlarged the house, added many outbuildings, including a private railroad station, and built greenhouses and planted gardens. Today, under the stewardship of the National Trust for Historic Preservation, a long-term research and preservation project, "The Search for James Madison," has begun. Admission includes a bus tour of the 2,700-acre estate and a guided tour of the mansion. Self-guided tours of arboretum, nature trails and formal garden. (Mar-Dec, daily; rest of yr, wkends; closed Jan 1, Thanksgiving, Dec 25; also 1st Sat Nov) 4 mi SW, on VA 20. Phone 540/672-0006. ¢¢¢

Inns

✓★★★ **HIDDEN INN.** *249 Caroline St (22960), jct US 15, VA 20.* 540/672-3625; FAX 540/672-5029; res: 800/841-1253. 10 rms, 2 story, 4 bldgs. S $59-$89; D $79-$129; each addl $20; suites $139-$169. TV in living rm. Complimentary full bkfst; afternoon refreshments. Ck-out noon, ck-in 3 pm. Business servs avail. Health club privileges. Some in-rm whirlpools. Balconies. Each rm individually decorated; some with canopy bed, fireplace. Late 19th-century residence; on 7½ wooded acres. Totally nonsmoking. Cr cds: A, C, MC, V.

★★ **HOLLADAY HOUSE.** *155 W Main St (22960).* 540/672-4893; FAX 540/672-3028; res: 800/358-4422. E-mail hhbb@summit.net; web www.symweb.com/holladay. 6 rms, 3 story, 2 suites, 1 kit unit. S, D $95-$135; each addl $25; suite $175-$195; kit unit $130-$155; wkly rates. TV in some rms; cable. Complimentary full bkfst. Restaurant adj 7 am-6 pm. Ck-out 11 am, ck-in 4 pm. Business servs avail. Fireplace, whirlpool. Federal-style residence (ca 1830). Totally nonsmoking. Cr cds: A, C, DS, MC, V.

Pearisburg (E-4)

(See also Blacksburg, Radford)

Pop 2,064 **Elev** 1,804 ft **Area Code** 540 **Zip** 24134

What to See and Do

Walnut Flats. Fishing in Dismal Creek; hunting (in season). Hiking. Primitive camping. Dismal Falls and Flat Top Mt are here. 11 mi S on VA 100, then 10½ mi W on VA 42 to County 606, N 1 mi to County 201, 2½ mi. Phone 540/552-4641.   **Free**   Approx ½-mi from Walnut Flats on County 201 is

White Pine Horse Camp. Primitive camping. Horse trails. Phone 540/552-4641.   **Free**

White Rocks Recreation Area. Fishing in Big Stony Creek; hunting (in season). Hiking. Camping (fee). (Apr-Nov) 17 mi E via VA 613, 635 in George Washington and Jefferson National Forests. Phone 540/552-4641.

Pentagon City

(See Arlington County)

Petersburg (E-8)

(See also Hopewell, Richmond)

Settled 1645 **Pop** 38,386 **Elev** 87 ft **Area Code** 804
Information Petersburg Visitors Center, 425 Cockade Alley, 23803; 804/733-2402 or 800/368-3595

This city, Lee's last stand before Appomattox (1864-1865), was settled in 1645 when the General Assembly authorized construction of Fort Henry at the falls of the Appomattox River. In 1784, three separate towns united to become the single city of Petersburg.

British troops under Generals Benedict Arnold and William Phillips occupied the town in 1781; the same year, on May 24, Cornwallis started the journey to his surrender at Yorktown. Between the Revolution and the Civil War, the town was a popular stopping place, with a social life that, for a time, eclipsed that of Richmond.

Physically untouched (though the town sent 17 companies to the front) during the early years of the Civil War, Petersburg in 1864 was the scene of Lee's final struggle against Grant. In April 1865, when Lee's supply routes were finally cut and he was forced to evacuate the city, the Confederacy collapsed. A week later Lee surrendered at Appomattox.

The shattered city made a new start after the war, showing amazing recuperative powers; in 1870, Petersburg had 20 more industries than there had been in 1850. Today, besides being a storehouse of colonial and Civil War history, Petersburg is a thriving industrial city.

What to See and Do

Appomattox River Park. A 137-acre park with canal for canoeing or fishing; access to rapids; picnic area. (Mid-Apr-Oct, daily) W part of town, on River Rd. Phone 804/733-2394.

Blandford Church (1735) and **Cemetery** (1702). Church, since 1901 a memorial to the Confederacy, has 15 Tiffany stained-glass windows. (Daily; closed Jan 1, Thanksgiving, Dec 24, 25) 321 S Crater Rd.   **¢¢**

Centre Hill Mansion (1823). Federal-style mansion visited by Presidents Tyler, Lincoln and Taft. Chandeliers, fine detail carvings; antiques, 1886 Knabe Art grand piano with holly wood inlaid on rosewood. (Daily; closed Jan 1, Thanksgiving, Dec 24, 25) Center Hill.   **¢¢**

Farmers Bank (1817). Banking memorabilia includes original plates and press for printing Confederate currency. Tours depart from Visitors Center, Old Market Sq. (Apr-Oct, daily) 19 Bollingbrook St.   **¢¢**

Fort Lee. Army training center in World Wars I and II. 3 mi NE on VA 36. Here is

Quartermaster Museum. Uniforms, flags, weapons, equestrian equipment from 200 yrs of military service. Civil War and Memorial Rooms. (Daily exc Mon; closed Jan 1, Thanksgiving, Dec 25) Phone 804/734-4203.   **Free**

Lee Memorial Park. Facilities of this 864-acre park include lake (launch fee); fishing (fee; license required); game fields & courts (fee); picnic area. (Daily; lake facilities closed mid-Oct-mid-Apr) S part of town, off Johnson Rd. Phone 804/733-2394. Also here is

USSSA Softball Hall of Fame Museum. Honors outstanding persons in amateur softball. Numerous displays, exhibits, photographs; 7-min film. (Daily; closed hols) 3935 S Crater Rd, 1 mi off I-95. Phone 804/732-4099.   **¢**

Lee's Retreat. 98-mi driving tour follows route of Gen Robert E. Lee's retreat from Petersburg to Appomattox. Roadside pull-overs, signs and audio interpretation at important Civil War sites. For brochures, maps and audio tapes, contact the Petersburg Visitors Center or phone 800/6-RETREAT.   **Free**

Pamplin Park Civil War Site. Site of General Ulysses S. Grant's decisive victory over Confederate forces in 1865. This 120-acre park includes battle trails, reconstructed soldier huts, plantation home Interpretive Center and museum. Guided tours available. (Daily; closed Jan 1, Thanksgiving, Dec 25) 6523 Duncan Rd. Phone 804/861-2408. Also here is

National Museum of the Civil War Soldier. Exhibit on the Civil War's common soldier, one of the country's largest Civil War books. Gift shop; restaurant.

Petersburg National Battlefield (see).

Poplar Grove (Petersburg) National Cemetery. On self-guided tour of Petersburg National Battlefield (see). Of 6,315 graves, 4,110 are unidentified. S off I-85.

Siege Museum. Greek-revival building houses exhibits describing the 10-month Civil War Siege of Petersburg. Film *The Echoes Still Remain*, with Joseph Cotten, is shown every hour on the hour. (Daily; closed Jan 1, Thanksgiving, Dec 24, 25) 15 W Bank St.   **¢¢**

St Paul's Episcopal Church (1856). Lee worshiped here during the siege of Petersburg (1864-1865). Open on request (Mon-Thurs). 110 N Union between W Washington & Tabb Sts. Phone 804/733-3415.

Trapezium House (1817). Built by eccentric Irish bachelor, Charles O'Hara, in the form of a trapezium, with no right angles and no parallel sides. O'Hara is said to have believed the superstition of his West Indian servant, who thought that ghosts and evil spirits inhabited right angles. Tours depart from Siege Museum, 15 W Bank St. (Apr-Oct, daily) Market & High Sts.   **¢¢**

Motels

★★ **DAYS INN.** 12208 S Crater Rd (23805), I-95 exit 45. 804/733-4400; FAX 804/861-9559; res: 800/329-7466. E-mail daysinn@techcom.net; web www.daysinnpetersburg. 155 rms, 2 story. S, D $65-$70; each addl $5; kit suites $75-$80. Crib free. Pet accepted; $5. TV; cable (premium). Coffee in rms. Pool; wading pool. Playground. Restaurant adj 5:30 am-10 pm. Ck-out 11 am. Coin lndry. Meeting rms. Business servs avail. In-rm modem link. Sundries. Putting green. Exercise equipt. Refrigerators, microwaves. Cr cds: A, C, D, DS, ER, JCB, MC, V.

D 🐾 ⇨ ✕ 🐟 ⊵ 🦅 SC

✓ ★★★ **QUALITY INN.** 12205 S Crater Rd (23805), 6 mi S, I-95 exit 45. 804/733-0600; FAX 804/862-4549; res: 800/228-5050. 138 rms, 1-2 story. S, D $45.95-$69.95; each addl $5; under 18 free. Crib $5. Pet accepted; $5. TV; cable (premium). Pool; wading pool. Playground. Restaurant 5:30 am-10 pm. Bar noon-midnight. Ck-out 11 am. Coffee in rms. Coin lndry. Business servs avail. In-rm modem link. Sundries. Lighted tennis. Lawn games. Miniature golf. Some refrigerators. Picnic tables. Cr cds: A, C, D, DS, ER, JCB, MC, V.

Restaurants

✓★ **ALEXANDER'S.** *101 W Bank St (23803). 804/733-7134.* Hrs: 9 am-9 pm; Mon, Tues to 3:30 pm. Closed Sun; Jan 1, Thanksgiving, Dec 25; also wk of July 4. Italian, Greek, Amer menu. Wine, beer. Semi-a la carte: bkfst $1.50-$4, lunch $4.50-$6.50, dinner $6.95-$11.99. Child's meals. Specialties: veal a la Greca, souvlaki, stuffed chicken breast. In old town storefront. Cr cds: C.

✓★ **MELITTA'S GASTHAUS.** *815 S Crater Rd (23803). 804/733-7090.* Hrs: 11 am-2 pm, 5-9 pm; Fri to 10 pm; Sat 5-10 pm. Closed Mon, Sun. Closed major hols. Res accepted. German menu. Bar. A la carte entrees: lunch $2.95-$6.50, dinner $8.50-$15.50. Child's meals. Specialties: rouladen, sauerbraten, schnitzels. Parking. German atmosphere; German folk art. Cr cds: A, C, DS, MC, V.

Petersburg National Battlefield (E-8)

(See also Hopewell, Petersburg, Richmond)

The campaign that spelled doom for the Confederacy occurred in a huge 40-mile semicircle around Richmond and Petersburg, at the price of 70,000 Union and Confederate casualties.

General Grant, after his unsuccessful attempt to take Richmond by frontal assault (at Cold Harbor, June 3, 1864), withdrew and attacked Petersburg. After 4 days of fighting and failing to capture the city, Grant decided to lay siege. Petersburg was the rail center that funneled supplies to Lee and Richmond.

The siege lasted ten months, from June 15, 1864, to April 2, 1865, with the two armies in almost constant contact. When Petersburg finally fell, Lee's surrender was only a week away.

The park, more than 2,700 acres, preserves Union and Confederate fortifications, trenches and gun pits. Another unit of the battlefield, Five Forks Unit, is located 23 miles to the west. Park (daily). There are living history programs daily during summer. Access for the disabled includes several paved trails and ramps to the Visitor Center. For further information contact the Superintendent, 1539 Hickory Hill Rd, Petersburg 23803-4721; 804/732-3531. Golden Eagle, Golden Age and Golden Access Passports honored (see MAKING THE MOST OF YOUR TRIP). Per vehicle ¢¢¢

What to See and Do

Battery 5. Strongest original Confederate position, captured on opening day of battle. From here "the Dictator," a Union mortar, shelled Petersburg, 2 ½ mi away. A similar mortar is nearby.

Battery 8. Confederate artillery position captured and used by Union as Fort Friend.

Battery 9. Confederate position on original line. Site of reconstructed Union camp and living history programs.

City Point Unit. (See HOPEWELL)

Colquitt's Salient. Section of Confederate defense line.

The Crater. Hole remaining after Union troops tunneled beneath Confederate artillery position and exploded four tons of powder (July 30, 1864). The resulting breach in Confederate lines failed as a major breakthrough. Several special monuments in vicinity.

First Maine Monument. Memorial to Maine dead in greatest regimental loss in a single action of the war.

Five Forks Unit. (1,115 acres) This road junction, beyond Lee's extreme right flank, led to the only remaining Confederate supply line, the South Side Railroad. The Battle of Five Forks (Apr 1, 1865) saw Union forces under General Philip H. Sheridan smash Confederates commanded by General George Pickett and gain access to the tracks beyond. On Apr 2, Grant ordered an all-out assault, crumbling Lee's right flank. Only a heroic stand by Confederate forces at Fort Gregg held off the Union advance while Lee evacuated Petersburg on the night of Apr 2. Visitor contact station (summer). Approx 6 mi SW via VA 613 (White Oak Rd), to jct Dinwiddie Courthouse (VA 627) & Wheeler Pond Rd (VA 645). Phone 804/265-8244. **Free**

Fort Haskell. One of the points where Union troops stopped a desperate attempt by Lee to break the siege.

Fort Stedman. Lee's "last grand offensive" concentrated here (Mar 25, 1865). The battle lasted 4 hrs; the Confederates failed to hold their breakthrough.

Gracie's Dam. Site of one of several Confederate dams intended to flood area between lines.

Harrison's Creek. First Grant (June 1864), then Lee (Mar 1865) had advances checked here.

Spring Garden. Heaviest Union artillery concentration during Battle of Crater was along this ridge.

Visitor Center. Information, exhibits; maps for self-guided tours. (Daily; closed Jan 1, Dec 25) Off VA 36.

Portsmouth (F-9)

(See also Chesapeake, Hampton, Newport News, Norfolk, Virginia Beach)

Founded 1752 **Pop** 103,907 **Elev** 15 ft **Area Code** 757 **E-mail** portscvb@ aol.com

Information Portsmouth Convention and Visitors Bureau, 505 Crawford St, Suite 2, 23704; 757/393-5327 or 800/767-8782

Connected to Norfolk by two bridge tunnels and a pedestrian ferry that cross the Elizabeth River, Portsmouth is part of the great Hampton Roads port, unrivaled for commercial shipping and shipbuilding activity. It is also the headquarters of the US Coast Guard Atlantic Fleet.

In Gosport, long a part of Portsmouth, Andrew Sprowle, a Scot, built a marine yard in 1767, which became in turn a British naval repair station and, after the Revolution, a federal navy yard. Now called the Norfolk Naval Shipyard, it is the largest naval shipyard in the world. The *Chesapeake,* sister of the *Constitution* and one of the US Navy's first warships, was built here. So was the *Merrimac,* which was seized by the Confederates, changed into an ironclad in 1861 and rechristened the CSS *Virginia.* The oldest drydock (1831) here is still in use.

What to See and Do

Carrie B Harbor Tours. Replica of 19th-century riverboat makes narrated tour (1½ hrs) of naval shipyard and inner harbor (Apr-Oct, daily); narrated tour (2½ hrs) of naval base and Hampton Roads (Apr-May & Sept-Oct, daily); sunset cruise (2½ hrs) to Hampton Roads and naval base (June-Labor Day, daily). Departs from Portside, 6 Crawford Pkwy. Phone 757/393-4735 for details. (Also see NORFOLK). ¢¢¢¢

Great Dismal Swamp National Wildlife Refuge (see). S on US 17.

Hill House. Headquarters of the Portsmouth Historical Assn. Built in early 1820s, this four-story English-basement-style house (with a raised basement) contains original furnishings collected by generations of the Hill family. In near-original condition, the house has undergone only limited renovation through the yrs. Garden restored. (Apr-Dec, Wed, Sat & Sun) 221 North St. Phone 757/393-5111. ¢

Historic houses. Portsmouth has over 300 yrs of history represented by more than 20 examples of Colonial, Federal and antebellum houses. Among them is the Nivison-Ball House (ca 1730-1750), 417 Middle St, where Andrew Jackson and General Lafayette were entertained. *These houses are private and may be viewed only from the exterior.* Obtain Olde Towne Portsmouth walking tour brochures with map and descriptions of churches, homes and old buildings from the Visitor Center at High St Landing; 757/393-5111.

Monumental United Church (Methodist) (1772). Oldest Methodist congregation in the South; history room. Guided tour (Mon-Fri, by appt; closed hols). Queen & Dinwiddie Sts, 1 blk N of High St. Phone 757/397-1297.

⭐ **The Portsmouth Museums.** Located in a 4-blk radius, the museum complex has facilities housing artistic, educational and historic exhibits. Museums (Tues-Sat; also Sun afternoons; closed Jan 1, Thanksgiving, Dec 25). Phone 757/393-8983. Includes

Children's Museum of Virginia. More than 60 interactive activities in 12 areas; planetarium. (Mid-June-Labor Day, Mon-Sat, also Sun afternoons) 221 High St.   ¢¢

Fine Arts Gallery. Changing exhibits. 420 High St.   ¢

Lightship Museum. Built in 1915, commissioned in 1916 as *Lightship 101,* it served 48 yrs in Virginia, Delaware and Massachusetts. Retired in 1964 and renamed *Portsmouth.* London Slip & Water St.   ¢

Naval Shipyard Museum. Thousands of items of naval equipment, plus flags, uniforms, prints, maps and models, including models of the CSS *Virginia;* the US Ship-of-the-line *Delaware,* built in Portsmouth; and the first ship drydocked in the US. 2 High St, on Elizabeth River.

Trinity Church (Episcopal). Oldest church building (1762) and parish in Portsmouth. Legend says that the church bell cracked while ringing out news of Cornwallis' surrender. It was later recast. Confederate Memorial window. Commodore James Barron, many colonial patriots are buried here. Open on request (Mon-Fri); office behind church in parish hall. 500 Court St. Phone 757/393-0431.

Motel

★ ★ **HOLIDAY INN OLDE TOWNE-PORTSMOUTH.** *8 Crawford Pkwy (23704), on waterfront at Elizabeth River.* 757/393-2573; FAX 757/399-1248; res: 800/465-4329. Web www.holiday.portsmouth.com. 220 rms, 4 story. S $60-$89; D $60-$99; each addl $10; suites $130-$161; studio rms $75-$150; under 19 free; wkend rates; higher rates Harborfest. Crib free. Pet accepted. TV; cable (premium). Pool. Coffee in rms. Restaurant 6:30 am-10 pm. Rm serv. Bar noon-2 am. Ck-out noon. Coin lndry. Meeting rms. Business servs avail. In-rm modem link. Exercise equipt. Refrigerators avail. Dockage, marina adj. Cr cds: A, C, D, DS, JCB, MC, V.

🅳 🐾 ⚓ 🏊 🏕 🔥 SC

Restaurants

✓ ★ ★ **CAFE EUROPA.** *319 High St (23704).* 757/399-6652. Hrs: 11:30 am-2 pm, 5-9:30 pm; Fri, Sat to 10:30 pm. Closed Sun, Mon; most major hols; also mid-Aug-mid-Sept. Res accepted; required Fri, Sat. Continental menu. Bar. Semi-a la carte: lunch $4.50-$12, dinner $9.50-$15.95. Specialties: Russian-style salmon, snail tureen, veal Tuscany. Intimate European atmosphere; Mucha prints. Cr cds: C, MC, V.

🅳 🖼

★ **CIRCLE SEAFOOD RESTAURANT.** *3010 High St (23707).* 757/397-8196. Hrs: 8 am-10 pm; Fri, Sat to 11 pm; Sun brunch noon-9 pm. Res accepted. Bar. Semi-a la carte: bkfst $2.50-$6.50, lunch $3.95-$14.95, dinner $7.95-$19.95. Sun brunch $10.95. Child's meals. Specializes in steak, seafood. Salad bar. Pianist Mon, Wed-Fri. Rotunda dining rm with extensive buffet. Cr cds: C, D, DS, MC, V.

SC 🖼

★ ★ **SCALE O' DE WHALE.** *3515 Shipwright St (23703), off W Norfolk Bridge.* 757/483-2772. Hrs: 11:30 am-2:30 pm, 5-10 pm; Sat from 5:30 pm; Sun 5:30-9:30 pm. Closed major hols. Res accepted. Serv bar. Semi-a la carte: lunch $4.50-$8.25, dinner $9.95-$17.95. Child's

meals. Specializes in seafood, market price lobster, steak. Outdoor dining. At end of pier, dockage. Nautical decor; ship models, antiques, scrimshaw, kerosene lights. Cr cds: A, C, DS, MC, V.

🖼

Radford (E-4)

(See also Blacksburg, Salem)

Settled 1756 **Pop** 15,940 **Elev** 1,820 ft **Area Code** 540 **Zip** 24141
Web www.radford.va.us
Information Chamber of Commerce, 1126 Norwood St; 540/639-2202

What to See and Do

Claytor Lake State Park. Consists of 472 acres in wooded hills adjacent to 5,000-acre lake. Swimming, sand beach, bathhouse; fishing; boating (ramp, rentals, marina). Hiking, bridle trails. Picnicking, concession. Tent and trailer sites (electrical hookups, Apr-Sept); cabins (Mar-early Dec). Visitor center, interpretive programs. Standard fees. Park office and visitor center are in Howe House (1876-1879), built on land once settled by Dunkers (Dunkards), a religious sect that fled persecution in Germany in the 1720s. On VA 660, 6 mi SW, just S of I-81 exit 101. Phone 540/674-5492.

Radford University (1910). (8,500 students) Flossie Martin Gallery in Powell Hall houses visual arts with an emphasis on regional and contemporary; changing exhibits. The Corinna de la Burde Sculpture Court, adjacent to the gallery, is an open-air museum displaying large-scale sculpture through changing exhibitions and permanent installations. Archives in the McConnell Library contain pamphlets, campus information, local history, oral history of Appalachia and rare books. Greenhouse (daily). The Dedmon Center, a recreation-convocation complex, features an air-supported roof, arena seating 5,600; swimming pool; indoor tennis and handball courts. (Daily) On US 11, I-81 exit 109. Phone 540/831-5324.

Seasonal Event

The Long Way Home. Outdoor historical drama by Earl Hobson Smith depicts the true story of Mary Draper Ingles, survivor of the 1755 Draper's Meadow Massacre, and her heroic 850-mi flight to warn settlers of Native American attacks. For reservations contact PO Box 711; 540/639-0679. Thurs-Sun, evenings, Mid-June-Aug.

Motels

★ ★ **BEST WESTERN INN.** *1501 Tyler Ave (24141).* 540/639-3000; FAX 540/633-0251; res: 800/628-1955. 72 rms, 2 story. S $60-$80; D $72-$90; each addl $5; under 18 free; higher rates univ events. Crib free. Pet accepted. TV; cable (premium). Indoor pool; wading pool, whirlpool. Ck-out noon. Business servs avail. Sundries. Exercise equipt; sauna. Bathrm phones; some refrigerators. Cr cds: A, C, D, DS, MC, V.

🅳 🐾 ⚓ 🏕 🏊 🐾 SC

✓ ★ ★ **COMFORT INN.** *Rte 100 (24084), just S of I-81 exit 98 on VA 100.* 540/674-1100; FAX 540/674-2644; res: 800/638-7949. E-mail cidublin@iplus.net. 98 rms, 2 story. S $56-$72; D $61-$78; each addl $6; under 18 free; higher rates univ events. Crib free. TV; cable (premium). Pool. Complimentary continental bkfst. Complimentary coffee in lobby. Restaurant adj 5-10 pm. Ck-out noon. Meeting rm. Business servs avail. Valet serv. Sundries. Some in-rm whirlpools; microwaves avail. Cr cds: A, C, D, DS, ER, JCB, MC, V.

🅳 ⚓ 🏊 🔥 SC

★ **DOGWOOD LODGE.** *7073 Lee Hwy (24141), 2 mi S on US 11. 540/639-9338.* 15 rms. S $26; D $33-$36; each addl $5; higher rates univ events. Crib $5. Pet accepted. TV; cable (premium). Restaurant nearby. Ck-out 11 am. Cr cds: C, DS, MC, V.

✓ ★ **EXECUTIVE MOTEL INC.** *7498 Lee Hwy; Rte 11 W (24141). 540/639-1664; FAX 540/633-1737; res: 888/393-8483.* 27 rms, 13 with shower only, 2 story. Apr-Nov: S $32.50-$36.50; D $36.50-$46.50; under 12 free; higher rates special events; lower rates rest of yr. Crib free. Pet accepted, some restrictions; $4. TV; cable (premium). VCR. Complimentary coffee in lobby. Restaurant adj 6 am-11 pm. Ck-out 11 am. Health club privileges. Refrigerators; microwaves avail. Cr cds: A, C, D, DS, MC, V.

Reston

(see Dulles Intl Airport Area)

Richmond (E-8)

(See also Ashland, Hopewell, Petersburg)

Settled 1607 **Pop** 203,056 **Elev** 150 ft **Area Code** 804 **E-mail** mrcvb tour@aol.com **Web** www.erols.com/richmond

Information Convention and Visitors Bureau, 550 E Marshall St, 23219; 804/782-2777 or 800/370-9004

There have been few dull moments in Richmond's history. Native Americans and settlers fought over the ground on which it now stands. In 1775, Patrick Henry made his "liberty or death" speech in St John's Church, and in 1780 the city was named capital of the state. At that time Virginia extended all the way to the Mississippi. British soldiers plundered it brutally in the Revolution. As the capital of the Confederacy from 1861 to 1865, it was constantly in danger. Finally, in 1865 the city was evacuated, and retreating Confederate soldiers burned the government warehouse; a portion of the rest of the city also went up in flames.

However, Richmond did survive. As Virginia's capital, it proudly exemplifies the modern South. It is a city industrially aggressive yet culturally aware, respectful of its own historical background yet receptive to new trends in architecture and modes of living. Richmond esteems both the oldest monuments and the newest skyscrapers.

Tobacco and tobacco products, paper and paper products, aluminum, chemicals, textiles, printing and publishing and machinery contribute to the city's economy. Richmond is also an educational center; the Virginia Commonwealth University, Virginia Union University and the University of Richmond are based here.

What to See and Do

Agecroft Hall. Half-timbered Tudor manor built in the late 15th century near Manchester, England. Disassembled, brought here and rebuilt during the late 1920s in a spacious setting of formal gardens and grassy terraces overlooking the James River. English furnishings from 16th to 17th centuries. Audiovisual presentation explains history of house. (Daily exc Mon; closed most hols) Cary St exit off I-195, turn onto N Thompson Ave, then right on Cary to Malvern, then left on Cantebury to 4305 Sulgrave Rd. Phone 804/353-4241. ¢¢

✕ Capitol Square. Bounded by Broad, Governor, Bank & 9th Sts, downtown. On Capitol Square are

Equestrian Statue of Washington. By Thomas Crawford; cast in Munich over an 18-yr period. Base features allegorical representations of six famous Revolutionary War figures from Virginia. 9th & Grace Sts.

Governor's Mansion (1813). This two-story Federal-style house was built after the capital was moved from Williamsburg. It is the oldest governor's mansion in the US still in use as a governor's residence. Tours (by appt). E of State Capitol. Phone 804/371-2642. **Free**

State Capitol (1785-1788). Modeled after La Maison Carrée, an ancient Roman temple at Nîmes, France, the Capitol was designed by Thomas Jefferson. In this building, where America's oldest continuous English-speaking legislative bodies still meet, is the famous Houdon statue of Washington. The old Hall of the House of Delegates features the first interior dome in the US; here, Aaron Burr was tried for treason, Virginia ratified the Articles of Secession and Robert E. Lee accepted command of the forces of Virginia; the Confederate Congress also met in the building. (Mon-Sat, also Sun afternoons; closed Jan 1, Thanksgiving, Dec 25) 9th & Grace Sts, Capitol Sq. Phone 804/698-1788. Also on Capitol Sq are

Virginia State Library and Archives. Outstanding collection of books, maps, manuscripts. (Daily exc Sun; closed hols) 800 E Broad St. Phone 804/692-3500. **Free**

Church Hill Historic Area. Neighborhood of 19th-century houses, more than 70 of which predate Civil War. Some Church Hill houses are open Historic Garden Week (see ANNUAL EVENTS). Bounded by Broad, 29th, Main & 21st Sts, E of Capitol Sq. In center of Church Hill is

St John's Episcopal Church (1741). Where Patrick Henry delivered his stirring "liberty or death" speech. Reenactment of Second Virginia Convention (late May-early Sept, Sun). Guided tours. (Daily; closed Jan 1, Easter, Thanksgiving, Dec 24, 25, 31) 25th & Broad Sts. Phone 804/648-5015. ¢ W of Church Hill is

Edgar Allan Poe Museum. Old Stone House portion is thought to be oldest structure in Richmond (1737). Four additional buildings house Poe mementos; James Carling illustrations of "The Raven"; scale model of Richmond of Poe's time; slide presentation of Poe's life in Richmond. Guided tours. (Daily; closed Dec 25). 1914 E Main St. Phone 804/648-5523. ¢¢ E of Church Hill is

Richmond National Battlefield Park (see). Headquarters located at 3215 E Broad St, in Chimborazo Park. Phone 804/226-1981.

City Hall Observation Deck. Eighteenth-floor observation deck offers panoramic view of the city, including Capitol grounds, James River and Revolutionary and Civil War-era buildings contrasted with modern skyscrapers. (Mon-Fri) 900 E Broad St. Phone 804/646-7000. **Free** Across the street is the old City Hall (1886-1894), a restored Gothic-revival building featuring an elaborate central court with arcaded galleries.

Federal Reserve Money Museum. Exhibits of currency, including rare bills; gold and silver bars; money-related artifacts. (Mon-Fri; closed hols) 701 E Byrd St, downtown, on 1st floor of bank. Phone 804/697-8108. **Free**

Hollywood Cemetery (1847). James Monroe, John Tyler, Jefferson Davis, other notables and 18,000 Confederate soldiers are buried here; audiovisual program (Mon-Fri). (Daily) 412 S Cherry St, at Albemarle St. Phone 804/648-8501. **Free**

Jackson Ward. Historic downtown neighborhood that was home to many famous black Richmonders, including Bill "Bojangles" Robinson. Area has numerous 19th-century, Greek-revival and Victorian buildings with ornamental ironwork that rivals the wrought iron of New Orleans. Bounded by I-95, 7th, Broad & Belvidere Sts. Within the ward are

Bill "Bojangles" Robinson Statue. Memorial to the famous dancer, who was born at 915 N 3rd St. Corner of Leigh & Adams Sts.

Black History Museum and Cultural Center. Limited editions, prints, art, photographs; African memorabilia; Sam Gilliam collection. (Tues, Thurs-Sat) 00 Clay St. Phone 804/780-9093. ¢

Maggie Walker National Historic Site. Commemorates life and career of Maggie L. Walker, daughter of former slaves, who overcame great hardships to become successful in banking and insurance; early advocate for women's rights and racial equality. Two-story, red-brick house was home to her family 1904-1934. (Wed-Sun; closed Jan 1, Thanksgiving, Dec 25) 110½ E Leigh St. Phone 804/771-2017. **Free**

John Marshall House (1790). Restored house of famous Supreme Court justice features original woodwork and paneling; family furnishings and mementos. (Daily exc Mon; closed most major hols) Combination ticket avail for Marshall House, Valentine Museum, Museum of the Confederacy,

White House of the Confederacy. 818 E Marshall St. Phone 804/648-7998. Marshall House ¢¢; Combination ticket ¢¢¢

Kanawha Canal Locks. Impressive stone locks were part of nation's first canal system, planned by George Washington. Narrated audiovisual presentation explains workings of locks and canal. Picnic grounds. (Daily) 12th & Byrd Sts, downtown. Phone 804/780-0107 walking tour; or 840/649-2800 cruise tour. **Free**

Meadow Farm Museum. (General Sheppard Crump Memorial Park). Living history farm museum depicting rural life in the 1860s. Orientation center, farmhouse, barn, outbuildings, crop demonstration fields, 1860s doctor's office. Also a 150-acre park with picnic shelters, playground. (Mar-Dec, daily exc Mon) 12 mi NW via I-95N, I-295W, Woodman Rd S exit, at Courtney & Mountain Rds. Phone 804/672-5149. **Free**; Special events ¢

Monumental Church (1812). Located on the Medical College of VA campus of Virginia Commonwealth University. Octagonal domed building designed by Robert Mills, architect of the Washington Monument. Commemorative structure was built on site where many prominent persons, including the governor, perished in a theater fire in 1811. Interior closed. Behind the church is the distinctive Egyptian Building (1845). 1226 E Broad St, N of Capitol Sq.

Museum of the Confederacy. Contains the nation's largest collection of Confederate military and civilian artifacts, including uniforms, equipment, flags, personal belongings of Jefferson Davis, Robert E. Lee and J.E.B. Stuart, documents, manuscripts and artwork. (Daily; closed Jan 1, Thanksgiving, Dec 25) 1201 E Clay St, N of Capitol Sq. Phone 804/649-1861. ¢¢

Parks. For general information contact the Dept of Parks & Recreation; phone 804/780-5733.

William Byrd. Includes 287 acres of groves, artificial lakes, picnic areas. Tennis courts; softball fields; fitness course. Amphitheater (June-Aug). Virginia's World War I memorial, a 240-ft, pink brick carillon tower. Boulevard St & Idlewood Ave. Nearby is

Maymont. Dooley mansion, late Victorian in style, houses art collection and decorative arts exhibits (daily exc Mon; fee). Also here are formal Japanese and Italian gardens, an arboretum, a nature center with wildlife habitat for native species, an aviary, a children's farm and a working carriage collection. (Daily) 1700 Hampton St, at Pennsylvania Ave. Phone 804/358-7166. **Free**

Bryan. A 279-acre park, 20 acres of which are an azalea garden with more than 55,000 plants (best view late Apr-mid-May). Picnic facilities, tennis courts. Bellevue Ave & Hermitage Rd. **Free**

James River. Five sections. Fishing, pedestrian bridges with overlook of James River, whitewater canoe and inner-tube accesses, birdwatching, wildlife sanctuary, self-guided tours, bicycle and hiking trails, visitor center with display, information station, interpretive programs. W 22nd St & Riverside Dr. **Free**

Lewis Ginter Botanical Garden. Victorian-era estate features the Grace Arents Garden and the Henry M. Flagler Perennial Garden; seasonal floral displays; emphasis on daffodils, daylilies, azaleas and rhododendrons. (Daily) 1800 Lakeside Ave, in Lakeside. Phone 804/262-9887. ¢¢

Pocahontas State Park. More than 7,000 acres; Swift Creek Lake. Swimming, pool, bathhouse; fishing; boating (launch, rentals, electric motors only). Hiking trails, bicycle path (rentals). Picnicking, concession. Tent and trailer sites (seasonal), group cabins. Nature center; evening interpretive programs (summer). Standard fees. (Daily) S on US 10, then W on VA 655. Phone 804/796-4255.

Richmond Children's Museum. Exhibits on arts, nature and the world around us designed for children 2-12 yrs old; many hands-on exhibits. (July-Aug, daily; rest of yr, daily exc Mon; closed hols) 740 Navy Hill Dr, downtown. Phone 804/643-5436 or 804/788-4949. ¢¢

Shopping.

6th Street Marketplace. Restored area of shops, restaurants, entertainment. 6th St between Coliseum & Grace St, downtown.

17th Street Market. Farmers market built on site of Native American trading village. Seasonal produce, flowers, holiday greens. (Daily) 17th St between E Main & E Market Sts.

Carytown. Eight blks of shops, restaurants, theaters adjacent to historic Fan neighborhood. W Cary St, between Boulevard St & I-95.

Shockoe Slip. Restored area of historic buildings and gaslit cobblestone streets; shopping, restaurants, galleries. E Cary St between 12th & 14th Sts, downtown.

Sightseeing.

Historic Richmond Tours. Offers guided van tours with pickup at Visitors Center and major hotels (daily); res required. Also guided walking tours (Apr-Oct, daily; fee). For details, reservations phone 804/780-0107. Van tours ¢¢¢¢; Walking tours ¢¢

Paddlewheeler *Annabel Lee.* Departs from Intermediate Terminal. Triple-decked, 350-passenger, 19th-century-style riverboat cruises the James River. Narrated tour; entertainment. Lunch, brunch, dinner and plantation cruises. (Apr-Dec, at least one cruise daily exc Mon) Phone 804/644-5700 or 800/752-7093. ¢¢¢¢¢

Plantation tours. The Richmond-Petersburg-Williamsburg area has many fine old mansions and estates. Some are open most of the yr; others only during Historic Garden Week (see ANNUAL EVENTS). The Metro Richmond Visitors Center has maps, information folders, suggestions. (Daily) 1710 Robin Hood Rd. Phone 804/358-5511.

St Paul's Church (Episcopal). Established in 1843, the church survived the Civil War intact. It was here that Jefferson Davis received news of Lee's retreat from Petersburg to Appomattox. Beginning in 1890, the church added many fine stained-glass windows, including eight from the Tiffany studios. Sanctuary ceiling features decorative plasterwork, interweaving Greek, Hebrew and Christian motifs around a central panel. A Tiffany mosaic of da Vinci's *Last Supper* surmounts the altar. (Daily; closed hols) 9th & Grace Sts, W of Capitol Sq. Phone 804/643-3589.

★ **The Fan** and **Monument Avenue.** Named for the layout of streets that fan out from Monroe Park toward the western part of town. Historical neighborhood has restored antebellum and turn-of-the-century houses, museums, shops, restaurants and famed Monument Ave. The fashionable boulevard, between Lombard and Belmont Sts, is dotted with imposing statues of Generals Lee, Stuart and Jackson, of Jefferson Davis and of Commodore Matthew Fontaine Maury, inventor of the electric torpedo. Bounded by Franklin St & Monument Ave, Boulevard, Main & Belvidere Sts. Within the area are

Science Museum of Virginia. Hands-on museum. Major exhibits include aerospace, computers, electricity, visual perception, physical phenomena and astronomy, giant analemmic sundial and Foucault pendulum. The Ethyl Universe Planetarium Space Theater features Omnimax films and planetarium shows (inquire for schedule). (Mon-Sat, also Sun afternoons; closed Thanksgiving, Dec 25) 2500 W Broad St, N of Monument Ave. Phone 804/367-6552 or 800/659-1727. Museum ¢¢; Museum & theater ¢¢¢

Virginia Historical Society. Comprehensive collection of Virginia history housed in Museum of Virginia History, with permanent and changing exhibits, and Library of Virginia History, with historical and genealogical research facilities. (Mon-Sat, museum also Sun afternoons; closed hols) Kensington & Boulevard Sts. Phone 804/358-4901. ¢¢

Virginia Museum of Fine Arts. America's first state-supported museum of art. Collections of paintings, prints, sculpture from major world cultures; Russian Imperial Easter eggs and jewels by Faberg; decorative arts of the art nouveau and art deco movements; sculpture garden; changing exhibitions. Cafeteria. (Daily exc Mon; closed Jan 1, July 4, Thanksgiving, Dec 25) Boulevard St & Grove Ave. Phone 804/367-0844. ¢¢

Valentine Museum. Traces history of Richmond. Exhibits focus on city life, decorative arts, costumes and textiles, industrial and social history; tour of restored 1812 Wickham House. Lunch served in walled garden (Apr-Oct). (Daily; closed some hols) 1015 E Clay St, N of Capitol Sq. Phone 804/649-0711. ¢¢

Virginia Aviation Museum. Exhibits and artifacts on the history of aviation, with emphasis on Virginia pioneers. (Daily; closed Dec 25) 5701 Huntsman Rd in Sandston, at Richmond Intl Airport. Phone 804/236-3622. ¢¢

Virginia House. A Tudor building constructed of materials from Warwick Priory (built in England in 1125 and rebuilt in 1565 as a residence); moved here in 1925. West wing is modeled after Sulgrave Manor, at one time the home of Lawrence Washington. Furniture, tapestries and paintings from

15th to 20th centuries. Formal gardens. Tours by appt only exc during Historic Garden Week (see ANNUAL EVENTS). (Daily exc Mon; closed major hols) 4301 Sulgrave Rd, ½ mi off VA 147 (Cary St), in Windsor Farms. Phone 804/353-4251. ¢¢

Virginia War Memorial. Honors Virginians who died in WW II, Korean and Vietnam Wars. Mementos of battles; eternal flame; more than 12,000 names engraved on glass and marble walls. (Daily) 621 S Belvidere St, downtown at N end of Robert E. Lee Bridge.   **Free**

White House of the Confederacy. Classical-revival house (1818) used by Jefferson Davis as his official residence during period when Richmond was capital of the Confederacy. Abraham Lincoln met with troops here during the Union occupation of the city. Restored to pre-wartime appearance; original furnishings. (Daily; closed Jan 1, Thanksgiving, Dec 25) 12th & E Clay Sts, N of Capitol Sq. Phone 804/649-1861. ¢¢

Wilton (1753). Georgian mansion built by William Randolph III. Fully paneled, authentic 18th-century furnishings. Headquarters of National Society of Colonial Dames in Virginia. (Daily exc Mon; closed hols) Open during Historic Garden Week (see ANNUAL EVENTS). S Wilton Rd off Cary St, 8 mi W. Phone 804/282-5936. ¢¢

Annual Events

Historic Garden Week in Virginia. Many private houses and gardens of historic or artistic interest are opened for this event, which includes more than 200 houses and gardens throughout the state. Tours. Contact 12 E Franklin St, 23219; 804/644-7776. Mid-late Apr.

June Jubilee. Downtown. Performing and visual arts festival with ethnic foods, African folk dances, music, crafts. 2nd wkend in June.

Virginia State Fair. Animal and 4-H contests, music, horse show, carnival. Phone 804/228-3200. Sept 21-Oct 1.

Richmond Newspapers Marathon. Last Sun Oct.

Motels

★★ **AMERISUITES.** 4100 Cox Rd (23060). 804/747-9644; FAX 804/346-9320; res: 800/833-1516. 126 suites, 6 story. S, D $109-$128; under 18 free. Crib free. TV; cable (premium), VCR. Pool. Complimentary continental bkfst. Restaurant nearby. Ck-out noon. Meeting rms. Business center. Coin lndry. Exercise equipt. Microwaves. Cr cds: A, C, D, DS, MC, V.

★★★ **COURTYARD BY MARRIOTT.** 6400 W Broad St (23230). 804/282-1881; FAX 804/288-2934; res: 800/321-2211. 145 rms, 3 story. S, D $98; suites $125; under 19 free; wkend rates. Crib free. TV; cable (premium). Pool; whirlpool. Coffee in rms. Bar. Ck-out noon. Coin lndry. Business servs avail. In-rm modem link. Valet serv. Sundries. Exercise equipt. Some refrigerators. Cr cds: A, C, D, DS, MC, V.

★ **FAIRFIELD INN.** 7300 W Broad St (23294). 804/672-8621; FAX 804/755-7155; res: 800/228-2800. 124 rms, 2 story. S, D $61-$89; each addl $5; suite $129; under 18 free. Crib free. TV; cable (premium). Complimentary continental bkfst. Restaurant adj 11-2 am. Ck-out noon. Business servs avail. In-rm modem link. Pool. Refrigerator, microwave in suites. Picnic tables. Cr cds: A, C, D, DS, MC, V.

★★ **LA QUINTA INN.** 6910 Midlothian Tpke (23225), at VA 150. 804/745-7100; FAX 804/276-6660; res: 800/687-6667. 130 rms, 3 story. S, D $58-$65; each addl $7; under 18 free. Crib free. Pet accepted, some restrictions. TV; cable (premium). Heated pool. Complimentary continental bkfst. Restaurant adj 6 am-11 pm. Ck-out noon. Meeting rms. Business servs avail. In-rm modem link. Cr cds: A, C, D, DS, ER, JCB, MC, V.

✓ ★ **RED ROOF INN.** 4350 Commerce Rd (23234), south of downtown. 804/271-7240; FAX 804/271-7245; res: 800/843-7663. 108 rms, 2 story. S $35.99-$49.99; D $42.99-$65.99; under 18 free; higher rates race wkends. Pet accepted. TV; cable (premium). Complimentary coffee in lobby. Restaurant nearby. Ck-out noon. Business servs avail. Some refrigerators, microwaves. Cr cds: A, C, D, DS, MC, V.

★★ **RESIDENCE INN BY MARRIOTT.** 2121 Dickens Rd (23230). 804/285-8200; FAX 804/285-2530; res: 800/331-3131. 80 kit suites, 2 story. S, D $119-$159; monthly, wkly, wkend rates. Crib free. Pet accepted, some restrictions; $50 and $5/day. TV; cable (premium), VCR avail (movies). Pool. Complimentary continental bkfst. Ck-out noon. Coin lndry. Meeting rm. Business servs avail. In-rm modem link. Valet serv. Microwaves; many fireplaces. Private patios, balconies. Picnic tables, grills. Cr cds: A, C, D, DS, ER, JCB, MC, V.

Motor Hotels

★★ **HAMPTON INN.** 10800 W Broad St (23060). 804/747-7777; FAX 804/747-7069; res: 800/426-7866. Web www.hampton-inn.com. 136 rms, 5 story. S $86-$96; D $93-$103; each addl $7; under 18 free. Crib free. TV; cable (premium). Complimentary continental bkfst. Restaurant nearby. Ck-out noon. Meeting rms. Business servs avail. In-rm modem link. Bellhops. Exercise equipt. Pool. Picnic table. Cr cds: A, C, D, DS, ER, JCB, MC, V.

★★★ **HOLIDAY INN.** 5203 Williamsburg Rd (23150), near Intl Airport. 804/222-6450; FAX 804/226-4305; res: 800/465-4329. 230 rms, 3-6 story. S, D $84-$99; suites $125; under 19 free. Pet accepted, some restrictions; $20. TV; cable (premium). Pool. Coffee in rms. Restaurant 6 am-11 pm. Rm serv. Bar noon-1 am. Ck-out noon. Meeting rms. Business servs avail. In-rm modem link. Bellhops. Free airport transportation. Health club privileges. Refrigerators, microwaves avail. Cr cds: A, C, D, DS, JCB, MC, V.

★★★ **HYATT.** 6624 W Broad St (23230). 804/285-1234; FAX 804/288-3961; res: 800/228-9000. 372 rms, 3-8 story. S, D $154-$170; suites $200-$475; under 18 free; wkend rates. Crib free. TV; cable (premium), VCR avail. Indoor/outdoor pool; poolside serv. Playground. Coffee in rms. Restaurant 6-10 pm. Rm serv 6 am-midnight. Bar noon-2 am; entertainment. Ck-out noon. Meeting rms. Business center. In-rm modem link. Bellhops. Valet serv. Gift shop. Airport transportation. Lighted tennis. Exercise equipt. Some private patios. Luxury level. Cr cds: A, C, D, DS, ER, JCB, MC, V.

✓ ★★ **QUALITY INN.** 8008 W Broad St (23294). 804/346-0000; FAX 804/346-4547. 194 rms, 6 story. Apr-Oct: S, D $79-$119; each addl $10; under 18 free; lower rates rest of yr. Crib free. TV; cable (premium). Pool. Coffee in rms. Complimentary continental bkfst. Restaurant nearby. Ck-out 11 am. Meeting rms. Business servs avail. In-rm modem link. Microwaves avail. Cr cds: A, C, D, DS, ER, JCB, MC, V.

★★ **RICHMOND AIRPORT HILTON.** 5501 Eubank Rd (23150), near Intl Airport. 804/226-6400; FAX 804/226-1269; res: 800/445-8667. 160 rms, 5 story, 122 suites. S, D $79-$159; each addl $15; family, wkend rates. Crib free. TV; cable (premium). Pool; whirlpool. Coffee in rms. Restaurant 6:30 am-10 pm. Rm serv to midnight. Bar 11 am-midnight. Ck-out noon. Meeting rms. Business servs avail. In-rm modem link. Bellhops. Valet serv. Sundries. Free airport transportation. Exercise equipt. Some balconies. Cr cds: A, C, D, DS, ER, JCB, MC, V.

Hotels

★ ★ ★ **BERKELEY HOTEL.** *1200 E Cary St (23219), in Shockoe Slip area, downtown.* 804/780-1300; FAX 804/648-4728. 55 rms, 6 story. S $125-$160; D $135-$170; each addl $15; under 18 free; wkend rates. Crib free. TV; cable (premium), VCR avail. Pool privileges. Coffee in rms. Restaurant 7 am-2 pm, 6-10 pm; Fri, Sat to 11 pm; Sun to 9 pm. Bar 11:30 am-2 pm, 5:30 pm-midnight. Ck-out noon. Meeting rms. Business servs avail. In-rm modem link. Concierge. Free valet parking. Airport transportation. Health club privileges. Bathrm phones. Cr cds: A, C, D, DS, MC, V.

D 🔌 🔥 SC

★ ★ ★ **CROWNE PLAZA HOTEL.** *555 E Canal St (23219), downtown.* 804/788-0900; FAX 804/788-0791; res: 800/333-3333. 299 rms, 16 story. Apr-June, Sept-Oct: S, D $179-$199; each addl $10; suites $249-$500; under 18 free; wkend rates; lower rates rest of yr. Crib free. TV; cable (premium). Indoor pool; whirlpool. Coffee in rms. Restaurant 6 am-11 pm. Bar 4 pm-1:30 am. Ck-out noon. Convention facilities. Business servs avail. In-rm modem link. Concierge. Gift shop. Exercise equipt. Cr cds: A, C, D, DS, JCB, MC, V.

D 🏊 🍴 🔌 🔥 SC

★ ★ ★ **EMBASSY SUITES.** *2925 Emerywood Pkwy (23294), Commerce Center.* 804/672-8585; FAX 804/672-3749; res: 800/362-2779. 226 suites, 8 story. Suites $119-$185; each addl $20; under 18 free. Crib free. TV; cable (premium). Indoor pool; whirlpool. Complimentary full bkfst. Restaurant 11 am-10 pm. Bar to midnight. Ck-out noon. Coin lndry. Meeting rms. Business center. In-rm modem link. Gift shop. Exercise equipt; sauna, steam rm. Refrigerators, microwaves; wet bar in suites. Cr cds: A, C, D, DS, JCB, MC, V.

D 🏊 🍴 🔌 🔥 SC 🏃

★ ★ ★ **MARRIOTT HOTEL.** *500 E Broad St (23219), downtown.* 804/643-3400; FAX 804/788-1230; res: 800/228-9290. 400 rms, 17 story. S, D $160; each addl $10; suites $200-$700; under 18 free; wkend rates. Crib free. TV; cable (premium). Indoor pool; whirlpool, poolside serv, lifeguard. Coffee in rms. Restaurant 6:30 am-10 pm. Bar 11-1 am. Ck-out noon. Coin lndry. Convention facilities. Business center. In-rm modem link. Concierge. Exercise equipt; sauna. Game rm. Some bathrm phones, refrigerators. Luxury level. Cr cds: A, C, D, DS, JCB, MC, V.

D 🏊 🍴 🔌 🔥 SC 🏃

★ ★ ★ **OMNI HOTEL.** *100 S 12th St (23219), in Shockoe Slip area, downtown.* 804/344-7000; FAX 804/648-6704; res: 800/843-6664. 363 units, 19 story. Mid-Apr-mid-June, mid-Sept-mid-Nov: S $139; D $154; each addl $15; suites $209-$450; under 18 free; package plans; lower rates rest of yr. Crib free. TV; cable (premium). Indoor pool; poolside serv. Coffee in rms. Restaurant 6:30 am-11 pm. Bar noon-1 am; entertainment. Ck-out 1 pm. Convention facilities. Business servs avail. In-rm modem link. Concierge. Shopping arcade. Health club privileges. Minibars. Luxury level. Cr cds: A, C, D, DS, ER, JCB, MC, V.

D 🏊 🔌 🔥 SC

✓ ★ ★ ★ ★ **THE JEFFERSON.** *Franklin & Adams Sts (23220).* 804/788-8000; FAX 804/344-5162; res: 800/424-8014. E-mail sales@jefferson.hotel.com; web www.jefferson.hotel.com. This twin-towered landmark about one-half mile from downtown is an immaculately restored illustration of Richmond's rich history. Some guest rooms are small, but they are well furnished with reproductions and have large, lighted closets and all other facilities necessary for a comfortable stay. 274 rms, 9 story. Apr-mid-June & mid-Sept-early Dec: S $165-$205; D $180-$220; each addl $15; suites $275-$1,000; under 18 free; package plans; lower rates rest of yr. Crib free. Valet parking $11. TV; cable (premium), VCR avail. Restaurant 6:30 am-midnight (also see Lemaire). Rm serv 24 hrs. Bar 11-2 am. Ck-out noon. Meeting rms. Business center. In-rm modem link. Concierge. Shopping arcade. Exercise equipt. Bathrm phones, refrigerators, minibars. Some balconies. Cr cds: A, C, D, DS, ER, JCB, MC, V.

D 🍴 🔌 🔥 SC 🏃

Inns

★ ★ **EMMANUEL HUTZLER HOUSE.** *2036 Monument Ave (23220).* 804/353-6900; FAX 804/355-5053. E-mail be.our.guest@benson house.com; web www.bensonhouse.com. 4 rms, 3 story. S $89-$125; D $95-$155. Children over 12 yrs only. TV; cable. Complimentary full bkfst. Complimentary coffee in library. Restaurant nearby. Ck-out noon, ck-in 4 pm. Luggage handling. Health club privileges. Built 1914; antiques. Totally nonsmoking. Cr cds: A, C, D, DS, MC, V.

🔌 🐾

★ ★ ★ **LINDEN ROW INN.** *100 E Franklin St (23219), entrance at 101 N 1st St, downtown.* 804/783-7000; FAX 804/648-7504; res: 800/348-7424. E-mail lindenrow@erols.com. 70 rms, 4 story, 7 suites. S, D $109-$159; each addl $10; suites $129-$209. TV; cable (premium). Complimentary continental bkfst. Dining rm (public by res) 11 am-2:30 pm, 5:30-10 pm. Rm serv. Ck-out noon, ck-in 3 pm. Business servs avail. In-rm modem link. Bellhops. Valet serv. Concierge. Health club privileges. In block of Greek-Revival row houses (1847) and around courtyard thought to be boyhood playground of Edgar Allan Poe; antique and period furnishings and decor. Cr cds: A, C, D, DS, ER, MC, V.

D 🔌 🔥 SC

★ ★ **MR PATRICK HENRY'S INN.** *2300 E Broad St (23223), in Church Hill Historic District.* 804/644-1322; res: 800/932-2654. 3 rms. Apr-June, Oct-Nov: S $95-$125; D $115-$135; each addl $10; family, wkly, wkend rates; hol wkends (2-day min); higher rates special events; lower rates rest of yr. TV; cable. Complimentary full bkfst. Complimentary coffee in rms. Restaurant (see Mr. Patrick Henry's Inn). Rm serv. Ck-out noon, ck-in 3 pm. Luggage handling. Street parking. Refrigerators. Greek-Revival antebellum row house (ca 1855); garden patio, carriage house. Cr cds: A, C, D, DS, MC, V.

🔥 SC

✓ ★ ★ **WILLIAM CATLIN HOUSE.** *2304 E Broad St (23223), in Church Hill Historic District.* 804/780-3746. 5 rms, 2 share bath, 3 story. No elvtr. S $85, D $95; suites $150. Complimentary full bkfst; afternoon refreshments. Ck-out 11 am, ck-in 3 pm. Balconies. Greek-Revival town house (1845) furnished with antiques, family heirlooms; fireplaces. Spacious veranda overlooks courtyard. Cr cds: C, DS, MC, V.

🔥

Restaurants

★ **AMICI RISTORANTE.** *3343 W Cary St (23221).* 804/353-4700. Hrs: 11:30 am-2:30 pm, 5:30-10 pm; Fri, Sat to 11 pm; Sun from 5:30 pm. Closed major hols. Res accepted. Northern Italian menu. Bar. A la carte entrees: lunch $4-$8.95, dinner $5.95-$18.95. Specializes in pasta, game, seafood. Own breads. Outdoor dining. Cr cds: A, C, MC, V.

🍴

★ **BYRAM'S LOBSTER HOUSE.** *3215 W Broad St (23230).* 804/355-9193. Hrs: 11:30 am-10 pm; Fri, Sat to 11 pm; early-bird dinner Mon-Fri 3:30-6 pm. Closed Jan 1, Dec 25. Res accepted. Continental menu. Bar. Semi-a la carte: lunch $2-$25.95, dinner $7.95-$25.95. Specializes in Maine lobster, crab. Parking. Local artwork, Greek reproductions. Family-owned. Cr cds: A, C, D, DS, MC, V.

D SC 🍴

★ **CAFFE DI PAGLIACCI.** *214 N Lombardy St (23220).* 804/353-3040. Hrs: 5-10 pm; Fri, Sat to 11 pm. Closed Sun; major hols. Res accepted. Italian menu. Bar. Semi-a la carte: $6.95-$14.95. Specializes in pasta, veal. Own desserts. Casual decor. Cr cds: A, C, DS, MC, V.

✓✓ **FAROUK'S HOUSE OF INDIA.** *3033 W Cary St (23221), west of downtown. 804/355-0378.* Hrs: 11:30 am-3 pm, 5:30-10:30 pm. Res accepted. Indian menu. Bar. Semi-a la carte: lunch $4.50-$7.50, dinner $6.95-$12. Buffet: lunch $5.99. Specialties: curries, biryanies, tandoori. Cr cds: C, JCB, MC, V.

★★ **HALF WAY HOUSE.** *10301 Jefferson Davis Hwy (23237), 13 mi S on US 1. 804/275-1760.* Hrs: 11:30 am-2 pm, 5:30-9 pm; Sat, Sun from 5:30 pm. Res accepted. Bar. Semi-a la carte: lunch $8-$17, dinner $17-$32. Specialties: lobster Von Grinegan, filet mignon, colonial chicken & beef pies. Parking. Antique-furnished manor house (1760) was stop on Petersburg stagecoach line until late 19th century; hosted Washington, Lafayette, Patrick Henry, Jefferson, among others. Used as a Union headquarters during 1864 siege of Richmond. Cr cds: A, C, D, DS, MC, V.

✓★★ **INDOCHINE.** *2923 W Cary St (23221). 804/353-5799.* Hrs: 11:30 am-3 pm, 5-10 pm; Sat from 5 pm. Closed Sun; Memorial Day, Dec 25. Res required Fri, Sat dinner. Vietnamese menu. Bar. Semi-a la carte: lunch $7.95, dinner $12.95-$19.95. Specialties: crispy softshell crab; scallops and shrimp in curry sauce; crispy salmon filet with spicy apple-cognac sauce. Own baking. French Colonial atmosphere; greenery throughout. Totally nonsmoking. Cr cds: A, C, D, DS, MC, V.

D

★★ **JAMES RIVER WINE BISTRO.** *1520 W Main St (23220). 804/358-4562.* Hrs: 4-11 pm; Sun brunch 11:30 am-2:30 pm. Closed Dec 25. Res accepted. Regional Amer menu. Bar. Wine cellar. Semi-a la carte: dinner $11-$22.95. Sun brunch $16.95. Child's meals. Specializes in seafood, wood-grilled meats. Own baking. Outdoor dining. Old schoolhouse (ca 1891) complete with brick archways and frosted windows. Cr cds: A, C, DS, MC, V.

D

★★ **KABUTO JAPANESE HOUSE OF STEAK.** *8052 W Broad St (23294). 804/747-9573.* Hrs: 11:30 am-2 pm, 5:30-10 pm; Fri to 10:30 pm; Sat 5-10:30 pm; Sun 4:30-9 pm. Closed Thanksgiving, Dec 25. Res accepted. Japanese menu. Bar. Complete meals: lunch $6-$10.25, dinner $11.50-$23. Child's meals. Specializes in Teppanyaki cooking. Sushi bar. Parking. Japanese-style building. Cr cds: A, C, D, DS, MC, V.

D

★★★ **LA PETITE FRANCE.** *2108 Maywill St (23230). 804/353-8729.* Hrs: 11:30 am-2 pm, 5:30-10 pm; Sat 5:30-11 pm. Closed Sun, Mon; major hols; also last 2 wks Aug. Res accepted. French menu. Serv bar. Wine list. A la carte entrees: lunch $7.95-$10.95, dinner $17.95-$24.50. Child's meals. Specializes in seafood, veal. Family-owned. Jacket (dinner). Cr cds: A, C, D, DS, MC, V.

★★★ **LEMAIRE.** *(See The Jefferson) 804/788-8000.* E-mail sales@jefferson.hotel.com; web www.jefferson.hotel.com. Hrs: 6:30 am-2 pm, 5:30-10:30 pm. Closed Memorial Day. Res accepted. Bar. A la carte entrees: bkfst $2.25-$10.88, lunch $3.50-$13.95, dinner $3.75-$25.95. Buffet: bkfst, lunch $8.95-$11.95. Child's meals. Specializes in regional cuisine. Valet parking. Pianist. Seven small dining rms. Cr cds: A, C, D, DS, ER, JCB, MC, V.

D

★★ **MR. PATRICK HENRY'S INN.** *(See Mr. Patrick Henry's Inn) 804/644-1322.* Hrs: 11:30 am-2:30 pm, 5:30-10 pm. Closed Sun (exc hols); Jan 1, Dec 24-25. Res accepted. Continental menu. Bar. Semi-a la carte: lunch $7.50-$14.50, dinner $17-$24. Specializes in duckling, crab cakes. Own soups. Outdoor dining. In Greek-revival antebellum row house (ca 1855); many antique furnishings. Cr cds: A, C, D, DS, MC, V.

D

✓★ **O'TOOLE'S.** *4800 Forest Hill Ave (23225). 804/233-1781.* Hrs: 11-2 am; Sun to midnight. Closed Dec 24, 25. Bar. Semi-a la carte: lunch $3.75-$8, dinner $4.25-$12.95. Child's meals. Specializes in seafood, steak, barbecued dishes. Pianist. Parking. Irish pub decor. Family-owned. Cr cds: A, C, DS, MC, V.

★★ **PEKING PAVILION.** *1302 E Cary St (23219), in Shockoe Slip historic district, downtown. 804/649-8888.* Hrs: 11:30 am-2:15 pm, 5-9:30 pm; Fri to 10:30 pm; Sat 5-10:30 pm; Sun brunch 11:30 am-2 pm. Closed Thanksgiving. Res accepted. Chinese menu. Bar. Semi-a la carte: lunch $4.85-$7.50, dinner $6.25-$22.50. Sun brunch $8.95. Specialties: Peking duck, seafood delight, chicken imperial. Oriental antiques; teakwood sculpture. Cr cds: A, C, MC, V.

D

★★★ **RUTH'S CHRIS STEAK HOUSE.** *11500 Huguenot Rd (23235), at Bellgrade Plantation House. 804/378-0600.* E-mail rcsh30@aol.com. Hrs: 5-10 pm; Fri, Sat to 11 pm; Sun to 9 pm. Closed some major hols. Res accepted. Bar. A la carte entrees: dinner $17-$30. Specializes in steak, lobster. Organist Tues-Sun. Parking. Outdoor dining. Cr cds: A, C, D, DS, MC, V.

D

★★ **SAM MILLER'S WAREHOUSE RESTAURANT.** *1210 E Cary St (23219), in Shockoe area of downtown. 804/644-5465.* Hrs: 11 am-11 pm; Sun brunch 10 am-5 pm. Res accepted. Bar to 1:30 am. Semi-a la carte: lunch $4.95-$12.50, dinner $14-$26. Sun champagne brunch $6-$13.95. Child's meals. Specializes in fresh seafood, live Maine lobster, prime Western beef. Lobster tank. In historic district; display of antique mirrors. Cr cds: A, C, D, MC, V.

D

★★ **SKILLIGALEE.** *5416 Glenside Dr (23228). 804/672-6200.* E-mail skilligalee@ibm.com; web www.skilligalee.com. Hrs: 11:30 am-4 pm, 5-10 pm; Fri to 10:30 pm; Sat 5-10:30 pm; Sun 5-9 pm. Closed Thanksgiving, Dec 25. Bar. A la carte entrees: lunch $5.95-$11.95, dinner $13.95-$25.95. Child's meals. Specializes in fresh seafood, soups. Raw bar. Own salad dressing. Parking. Nautical decor with fireplace. Family-owned. Cr cds: A, C, D, MC, V.

D

✓★ **TANGLEWOOD ORDINARY RESTAURANT.** *2210 River Rd W (23102), 16 mi W on VA 6 (Patterson Ave). 804/784-7011.* Web www.ordinary.com. Hrs: 5:30-9 pm; Sun noon-7 pm. Closed Mon-Tues; some major hols. Res accepted; required Wed. Traditional Southern menu. Wine, beer. Complete meals: dinner $9. Specializes in chicken, catfish, ham. Casual dining in log cabin building. Collection of *The Saturday Evening Post* dating from 1913. Totally nonsmoking. Cr cds: C.

★★★ **THE FROG AND THE REDNECK.** *1423 E Cary St (23219). 804/648-3764.* E-mail frogneck@mindspring.com; web www.frogandredneck.com. Hrs: 5:30-10 pm; Sat 5-10:30 pm. Closed Sun; major hols. Res accepted. Regional American menu. Bar. Wine list. Semi-a la carte: dinner $9.75-$26.25. Specialties: soft shell crab, jumbo lump crab cakes, buffalo. Contemporary decor, with a touch of Art Deco. Muraled walls. Totally nonsmoking. Cr cds: A, C, D, DS, MC, V.

D

★★★ **TOBACCO COMPANY.** *1201 E Cary St (23219), in Shockoe Slip area, downtown. 804/782-9431.* Hrs: 11:30 am-2:30 pm, 5:30-10:30 pm; Sat 5-11 pm; Sun 10:30 am-2:30 pm, 5:30-10 pm. Closed Jan 1, Dec 25. Res accepted. Bar 11:30-2 am. A la carte entrees: lunch $2.99-$7.95, dinner $12.95-$25.95. Sun brunch $4.95-$15.95. Specializes in prime rib, fresh fish. Own baking. Band exc Sun. In former tobacco warehouse (ca 1880); built around skylighted atrium with antique cage elevator; many unusual antiques. Cr cds: A, C, D, MC, V.

✓ ★ **TRAK'S GREEK & ITALIAN RESTAURANT.** 9115 Quioc-casin Rd (23229). 804/740-1700. Hrs: 11 am-10 pm; Fri, Sat to 11 pm. Closed Sun; also some major hols. Res accepted. Greek, Italian menu. Bar. Semi-a la carte: lunch $5-$7, dinner $10-$15. Child's meals. Specialties: Helen's a la Greek, Mediterranean Lovers, Greek sampler. Parking. Greek artwork. Cr cds: A, C, D, DS, MC, V.

D

★ ★ **YEN CHING.** 6601 Midlothian Tpke (23225). 804/276-7430. Hrs: 11:30 am-10 pm; Sat, Sun to 11 pm. Closed Thanksgiving. Res required. Chinese menu. Bar. Semi-a la carte: lunch, dinner $7-$22. Specializes in Hunan and Szechuan dishes. Parking. Chinese tapestries and art. Cr cds: A, C, MC, V.

D

Richmond National Battlefield Park (E-8)

(See also Ashland, Richmond)

A total of seven Union drives on Richmond, the symbol of secession, were made during the Civil War. Richmond National Battlefield Park, 770 acres in 10 different units, preserves sites of the two efforts that came close to success—McClellan's Peninsula Campaign of 1862 and Grant's attack in 1864.

Of McClellan's campaign, the park includes sites of the Seven Days' Battles at Chickahominy Bluffs, Beaver Dam Creek, Gaines' Mill (Watt House) and Malvern Hill. Grant's campaign is represented by the battlefield at Cold Harbor, where on June 3, 1864, Grant hurled his army at fortified Confederate positions, resulting in 7,000 casualties in less than one hour. Confederate Fort Harrison, Parker's Battery and Drewry's Bluff (Fort Darling) and Union-built Fort Brady are also included. Park (daily).

What to See and Do

Main Visitor Center. Information, exhibits, film, slide program. (Daily; closed Jan 1, Thanksgiving, Dec 25) In Chimborazo City Park. 3215 E Broad St, on US 60E in Richmond. Phone 804/226-1981. **Free** From here start

  Self-guided tour. Auto drive (60 mi) with markers, maps, recorded messages providing background, detailed information for specific places. Visitors may select own route, including all or part of the drive.

Other Visitor Centers. Cold Harbor, 16 mi NE on VA 156 (daily, unstaffed) and Fort Harrison, 10 mi SE on VA 5 & Battlefield Park Rd (June-Aug, daily). **Free**

Roanoke (E-5)

(See also Salem)

Settled 1740 **Pop** 96,397 **Elev** 948 ft **Area Code** 540 **E-mail** rvcvb@rb net; **Web** www.visitroanokeva.com

Information Roanoke Valley Convention & Visitors Bureau, 114 Market St, 24011; 540/342-6025 or 800/635-5535

Roanoke was incorporated in 1882, when it became a junction of the Norfolk and Western Railway and the Shenandoah Valley Railroad. Before that, the town was called Big Lick (salt marshes in the area attracted big game).

It is the cultural, industrial, commercial, convention and medical center for western Virginia. Manufactured products include railroad cars, fabri-cated steel, fabrics, apparel, furniture, flour, wood products, electronic equipment, plastics, cosmetics and locks.

Set in the Shenandoah Valley, between the Blue Ridge and the Allegheny Mountains, it is near the outdoor attractions of the huge George Washington and Jefferson National Forest (see HARRISONBURG) and the Blue Ridge Parkway (see).

What to See and Do

Blue Ridge Pkwy (see). Runs on crest of mountains both N and S of Roanoke. Narrow in parts; limited restaurants. Beautiful seasonal views from overlooks. 6 mi E on US 460 or 3 mi S on US 220.

Center in the Square. Restored 20th-century furniture warehouse housing five independent cultural organizations: three museums, including Art Museum of Western Virginia, and two professional theater companies (see SEASONAL EVENT). (Daily exc Mon; closed major hols) One Market Sq, downtown. Phone 540/342-5700. Art museum **Free** Also here are

  Roanoke Valley History Museum. Permanent exhibits deal with Roanoke history from days of Native Americans to present. Archives, library (by appt). (Daily exc Mon; closed most hols) Phone 540/342-5770. ¢

  Science Museum of Western Virginia. Museum contains hands-on exhibits in the natural and physical sciences: animals of land & ocean, computers, TV weather station. Workshops, programs and classes for children & adults; special exhibits. Hopkins Planetarium shows films. (Daily; closed hols) Phone 540/342-5710. ¢¢

George Washington and Jefferson National Forest (see HARRISONBURG).

Mill Mountain Zoological Park. Zoo sits atop Mill Mt; offers picnic areas with magnificent views of city and valley. (Daily; closed Dec 25) Off US 220/I-581 & Blue Ridge Pkwy. Phone 540/343-3241. ¢¢

Virginia Museum of Transportation. Vehicles from the past and present. Large steam, diesel and electric locomotive collection. Aviation exhibits; model of miniature traveling circus. Hands-on exhibits. (Mar-Dec, daily; rest of yr, daily exc Mon; closed major hols) 303 Norfolk Ave, downtown. Phone 540/342-5670. ¢¢

Virginia's Explore Park. 1,300-acre living history museum and nature center features re-created frontier settlement with interpreters demonstrating 19th-century life. Tutelo Native American Village; 19th-century structures; visitor participation exhibits. 6 mi of hiking trails. Picnic areas. (Apr-Oct, Fri-Mon) Milepost 115 on Blue Ridge Pkwy. Phone 540/427-1800. ¢¢¢

Annual Events

Virginia State Championship Chili Cookoff. City Market. Teams compete to represent Virginia in World Cook-off. Samples, entertainment. For information contact Roanoke Special Events Committee, 210 Reserve Ave SW, 24016; 540/853-2889. 1st Sat May.

Festival in the Park. Art exhibits, crafts, sports, food, parade, entertainment. 2 wkends beginning Fri before Memorial Day.

Seasonal Event

Mill Mountain Theatre. Center in the Square. Musicals, comedies, dramas. Nightly exc Mon; Sat, Sun matinees. For res phone 540/342-5740. Regular season, Oct-Aug.

Motels

✓ ★ **COLONY HOUSE MOTOR LODGE.** 3560 Franklin Rd SW (24014). 540/345-0411; FAX 540/345-0411; res: 800/552-7026. 69 rms, 2 story. S $46; D $58-$68; each addl $5; under 13 free. Crib avail. TV; cable. Complimentary continental bkfst. Restaurant adj 11 am-10 pm. Ck-out 11 am. Meetng rms. Business servs avail. Valet serv. Health club privileges. Pool. Bathrm phone, in-rm whirlpool, refrigerator in suites. Cr cds: A, C, D, DS, MC, V.

D   SC

✓★★ **DAYS INN.** *8118 Plantation Rd (24019), I-81 exit 146. 540/366-0341; FAX 540/366-3935; res: 800/329-7466.* 123 rms, 2 story. S $45-$60; D $55-$65; each addl $6; suites $80; under 12 free. Crib avail. TV; cable (premium), VCR avail. Pool. Restaurant 6-10:30 am, 5-10 pm. Bar 4:30-11 pm. Ck-out noon. Meeting rms. Business servs avail. In-rm modem link. Valet serv. Free airport transportation. Cr cds: A, C, D, DS, JCB, MC, V.

D ☒ ☒ ☒ 🔥 SC

★ **HAMPTON INN.** *3816 Franklin Rd SW (24014). 540/989-4000; FAX 540/989-0250; res: 800/426-7866.* 59 rms, 2 story. May-Nov: S $58-$62; D $68-$72; family rates; higher rates special events. Crib free. TV; cable (premium), VCR avail. Complimentary continental bkfst. Restaurant adj 10:30 am-9 pm; wkends from 8 am. Ck-out 11 am. Coin lndry. Meeting rm. Business servs avail. In-rm modem link. Valet serv. Health club privileges. Some refrigerators, microwaves. Cr cds: A, C, D, DS, MC, V.

D ☒ 🔥 SC

★★ **HAMPTON INN-AIRPORT.** *6621 Thirlane Rd (24019), near Regional Airport. 540/265-2600; FAX 540/366-2091.* 79 rms, 2 story. S $70-$72; D $76-$80; suites $103; under 18 free; higher rates: graduation, sporting events. Crib free. Valet parking $20. TV; cable (premium), VCR. Complimentary coffee in lobby. Restaurant nearby. Ck-out 11 am. Meeting rms. Business servs avail. Valet serv. Sundries. Coin lndry. Free airport transportation. Exercise equipt. Heated pool. Refrigerators, microwaves; some bathrm phones; in-rm whirlpool in suites. Cr cds: A, C, D, DS, MC, V.

D ☒ 🏃 ✈ ☒ 🔥 SC

★★ **HOLIDAY INN.** *6626 Thirlane Rd Nw (24019), near Municipal Airport. 540/366-8861; FAX 540/366-1637; res: 800/465-4329 or 888/337-1385.* Web www.holiday-inn.com/hotels/roaap. 161 rms, 2 story. S, D $74-$85; under 18 free; wkend, special event rates. Crib free. TV; cable (premium), VCR avail. Pool; wading pool. Complimentary coffee in rms. Restaurant 6 am-10 pm. Rm serv. Bar. Ck-out noon. Coin lndry. Meeting rms. Business servs avail. In-rm modem link. Valet serv. Sundries. Airport, bus depot transportation. Tennis privileges. Golf privileges. Health club privileges. Some bathrm phones. Cr cds: A, C, D, DS, JCB, MC, V.

D 🏋 🌄 ☒ ✈ ☒ 🔥 SC

★★ **QUALITY INN.** *501 Orange Ave (24016), at Williamson Rd. 540/342-8961; FAX 540/342-3813; res: 800/465-4329.* 150 rms, 2 story. S, D $60-$80. Crib free. TV; cable (premium), VCR avail. Pool; wading pool. Complimentary bkfst buffet. Coffee in rms. Restaurant 7 am-9 pm. Bar from 5 pm. Ck-out noon. Business servs avail. In-rm modem link. Bellhops. Valet serv. Microwaves avail. Cr cds: A, C, D, DS, ER, JCB, MC, V.

D ☒ ☒ 🔥 SC

★★ **RAMADA INN.** *1927 Franklin Rd SW (24014). 540/343-0121; FAX 540/342-2048; res: 800/272-6232.* 127 rms, 4 story. S $58; D $64; each addl $7; under 18 free; higher rates special events. Pet accepted. TV; cable. Pool. Complimentary full bkfst. Coffee in rms. Restaurant 11:30 am-2:30 pm, 4:30-9:30 pm. Bar 4:30 pm-2 am. Ck-out noon. Coin lndry. Meeting rms. Business servs avail. In-rm modem link. Health club privileges. Sundries. Near river. Cr cds: A, C, D, DS, ER, JCB, MC, V.

D 🐾 ☒ ☒ 🔥 SC

★ **SLEEP INN.** *4045 Electric Rd (24014). 540/772-1500; FAX 540/772-1500; res: 800/628-1929.* 103 rms, shower only, 2 story. No elvtr. S $55.95-$60.95; D $60.95-$65; each addl $6; under 18 free. Crib free. TV; cable (premium), VCR. Complimentary continental bkfst. Restaurant nearby. Ck-out noon. Meeting rm. Business servs avail. In-rm modem link. Valet serv. Health club privileges. Microwaves avail. Cr cds: A, C, D, DS, ER, JCB, MC, V.

D ☒ 🔥 SC

✓★ **TRAVELODGE.** *2444 Lee Hwy S (24175), I-81 exit 150-A. 540/992-6700; FAX 540/992-3991; res: 800/578-7878.* 109 rms. S $45; D $52; each addl $6; kit units $45; under 18 free; wkly rates. Crib free. Pet accepted; $6. TV; cable (premium). Pool. Playground. Complimentary continental bkfst. Coffee in rms. Restaurant nearby. Ck-out 11 am. Meeting rms. Business servs avail. Some refrigerators, microwaves. Cr cds: A, C, D, DS, MC, V.

D 🐾 ☒ ☒ 🔥 SC

Motor Hotels

★★★ **CLARION HOTEL.** *2727 Ferndale Dr NW (24017), near Municipal Airport. 540/362-4500; FAX 540/362-4506; res: 800/228-5050.* 154 rms, 5 story. S $89-$129; D $99-$129; each addl $10; under 18 free; wkend rates. Crib free. Pet accepted; $50 deposit. TV; cable (premium). Indoor/outdoor pool; whirlpool. Restaurant 6 am-10:30 pm. Rm serv. Complimentary coffee in rms. Bar 11:30 am-11 pm. Ck-out noon. Meeting rms. Business servs avail. In-rm modem link. Bellhops. Valet serv. Sundries. Free airport transportation. Lighted tennis. 18-hole golf privileges. Exercise equipt. Bathrm phones. Picnic tables, grills. Cr cds: A, C, D, DS, ER, JCB, MC, V.

D 🐾 🏋 🎾 ☒ 🏃 ✈ ☒ 🔥 SC

★★★ **HOLIDAY INN.** *4468 Starkey Rd (24014). 540/774-4400; FAX 540/774-1195; res: 800/465-4329.* 196 rms, 5 story. S, D $88-$102; suites $128-$153; under 18 free; wkend rates. Crib free. Pet accepted; $10. TV; cable (premium). Pool; poolside serv. Restaurant 6:30 am-10 pm. Rm serv. Bar 4 pm-2 am; entertainment. Ck-out noon. Meeting rms. Business servs avail. In-rm modem link. Bellhops. Valet serv. Concierge. Free airport, bus depot transportation. Golf privileges. Health club privileges. Some wet bars; microwaves avail. Luxury level. Cr cds: A, C, D, DS, JCB, MC, V.

D 🐾 🏋 ☒ ☒ 🔥 SC

Hotels

★★★ **HOTEL ROANOKE & CONFERENCE CENTER.** *110 Shenandoah Ave (24016). 540/985-5900; FAX 540/853-8290; res: 800/222-TREE.* 332 rms, 7 story. S $119-$145; D $129-$155; each addl $10; suites $165-$450; under 18 free; wkend, hol rates; higher rates: graduation, football. Crib free. Valet parking $5. TV; cable (premium). Complimentary coffee in lobby. Restaurant 6:30 am-10 pm; Sat from 7 am; Sun 7 am-9 pm. Bar 11 am-midnight; Fri, Sat to 1 am; entertainment Fri, Sat. Ck-out noon. Convention facilities. Business center. In-rm modem link. Gift shop. Free airport, RR station transportation. Tennis privileges. Golf privileges, pro, putting green, driving range. Exercise equipt. Pool; whirlpool. Some refrigerators, fireplaces. Cr cds: A, C, D, DS, ER, JCB, MC, V.

D 🏋 🌄 ☒ 🏃 ☒ 🔥 SC 🎿

★★★ **MARRIOTT HOTEL.** *2801 Hershberger Rd NW (24017), I-581 exit 3W, near Municipal Airport. 540/563-9300; FAX 540/366-5846; res: 800/228-9290.* Web www.swva.net/roanoke.marriott/. 320 rms, 8 story. S, studio rms $74-$134; D $84-$150; each addl $10; suites $210-$250; under 18 free; golf, wkend rates. Crib free. Pet accepted, some restrictions; $10. TV; cable (premium), VCR avail. 2 pools, 1 indoor; whirlpool, poolside serv. Restaurant 6:30 am-10 pm. Bars 11-1 am. Ck-out noon. Convention facilities. Business servs avail. Concierge. Gift shop. Free airport transportation. Lighted tennis. Exercise equipt; sauna. Some refrigerators. Private patios, balconies. Luxury level. Cr cds: A, C, D, DS, ER, JCB, MC, V.

D 🐾 🎾 🌄 ☒ 🏃 ✈ ☒ 🔥 SC

★★★ **PATRICK HENRY HOTEL.** *617 S Jefferson St (24011). 540/345-8811; FAX 540/342-9908.* E-mail phhotel13@aol.com. 117 kit units, 10 story. S $99; D $109; each addl $10; suites $125-$250; under 18 free; monthly rates. Crib avail. TV; cable (premium). Complimentary continental bkfst. Restaurant 11:30 am-11 pm. Bar 4 pm-2 am. Ck-out noon.

Guest lndry. Meeting rms. Business servs avail. In-rm modem link. Barber, beauty shop. Free airport transportation. Health club privileges. Refrigerators; microwaves avail. Cr cds: A, C, D, DS, ER, JCB, MC, V.

D ⊠ 🔥 SC

Inn

★ ★ **CLAIBORNE HOUSE.** 185 Claiborne Ave (24151), US 220 S, W on VA 40. 540/483-4616; FAX 540/483-4616. 5 rms, 2 story. Some rm phones. S, D $75-$125. TV in some rms; cable (premium). Complimentary full bkfst. Complimentary coffee in rms. Ck-out 11 am, ck-in 3 pm. Business servs avail. Game rm. Built in 1895; Victorian-style decor. Totally nonsmoking. Cr cds: C, MC, V.

⊠ 🔥

Restaurants

★ ★ **BILLY'S RITZ.** 102 Salem Ave SE (24011), at Market St. 540/342-3937. E-mail britz@roanoke.infi.net. Hrs: 5-10:30 pm; Fri, Sat to midnight. Closed most major hols; Jan 1-16. Bar. Semi-a la carte: dinner $8.50-$16. Specializes in steak, pork chops, seafood. Outdoor dining. Three dining areas with eclectic decor. Cr cds: A, C, D, DS, MC, V.

D ⊒

★ ★ **CHARCOAL STEAK HOUSE.** 5225 Williamson Rd (24012). 540/366-3710. Hrs: 11 am-10 pm; Sat from 5 pm; Sun 5-9 pm; Sun brunch 10:30 am-2:30 pm. Closed Mon. Res accepted. Bar. Semi-a la carte: lunch $4.95-$11.50, dinner $9.95-$24. Child's meals. Specializes in prime rib, steak, seafood. Entertainment. Parking. Cr cds: A, C, D, DS, MC, V.

D ⊒

★ ★ **KABUKI JAPANESE STEAK HOUSE.** 3503 Franklin Rd SW (24014). 540/981-0222. Hrs: 5-10:30 pm; Fri, Sat 4:30-11 pm. Closed some major hols; also Jan 2, Super Bowl Sun. Res accepted; required Fri, Sat. Japanese menu. Bar. Complete meals: dinner $10.45-$24.45. Child's meals. Specializes in Teppanyaki cooking. Parking. Japanese antique display. Cr cds: A, C, D, DS, MC, V.

D ⊒

★ ★ ★ **LIBRARY RESTAURANT.** 3117 Franklin Rd (24014), in Piccadilly Square Shopping Ctr. 540/985-0811. Hrs: 6 pm-midnight. Closed Sun; major hols. Res accepted. French, Amer menu. Bar. Wine cellar. Semi-a la carte: dinner $12.95-$24.95. Specialties: roast rack of lamb, Dover sole, steak Diane. Own pastries. Parking. Antique books on display. Jacket. Cr cds: A, C, D, MC, V.

D ⊒

✓ ★ **SUNNYBROOK INN.** 7342 Plantation Rd NW (24019). 540/366-4555. Hrs: 7 am-8 pm; Fri, Sat to 9 pm; Sun to 7 pm. Closed Dec 25. Res accepted. Wine, beer. Semi-a la carte: bkfst $3-$6, lunch $4-$8, dinner $6-$17. Buffet: (Fri, Sat) dinner $12.99-$17.99; (Sun) lunch, dinner $9. Child's meals. Specialties: oysters, country ham, fresh mountain trout. Salad bar. Parking. Outdoor dining. In colonial-revival farmhouse (1912). Cr cds: C, DS, MC, V.

D ⊒

Salem (E-5)

(See also Roanoke)

Founded 1802 **Pop** 23,756 **Elev** 1,060 ft **Area Code** 540 **Zip** 24153 **E-mail** srccham@juno.com
Information Salem/Roanoke County Chamber of Commerce, 9 N College Ave, PO Box 832; 540/387-0267

Salem, part of the industrial complex of the Roanoke Valley, shares with Roanoke the beautiful setting between the Blue Ridge and Allegheny Mountains. Historic markers throughout Salem indicate the city's colonial heritage.

What to See and Do

Dixie Caverns. Stalactites in lofty chambers; modern lighting system makes 45-min tour comfortable as well as interesting. Pottery shop and mineral shop (all yr). Camping facilities (fee). (Daily; closed Dec 25) Off I-81 at exit 132. Phone 540/380-2085. ¢¢¢

Roanoke College (1842). (1,600 students) One of the few Southern colleges to remain open during Civil War. Many historic buildings, some antebellum. Olin Hall, fine arts building, has theater, art gallery and sculptures. Excellent exhibit of paintings, photographs and other items concerning Mary, Queen of Scots (by appt only; phone 540/375-2487). Tours. College Ave, off I-81. Phone 540/375-2282.

Motels

★ ★ **HOLIDAY INN.** 1671 Skyview Rd (24153), I-81 exit 137. 540/389-7061; FAX 540/389-7060; res: 800/465-4329. 102 rms, 3 story. S, D $52-$89; each addl $6; under 19 free. Crib free. TV; cable (premium). Pool; wading pool. Complimentary continental bkfst. Restaurant 6:30 am-2 pm, 5-10 pm. Rm serv. Ck-out noon. Meeting rms. Business servs avail. In-rm modem link. Bellhops. Valet serv. Sundries. Cr cds: A, C, D, DS, ER, JCB, MC, V.

D ⊠ ⊒ 🔥 SC

★ ★ **HOLIDAY INN.** 1535 E Main St (24153). 540/986-1000; FAX 540/986-0355; res: 800/465-4329. 70 rms, 3 story. S $55; D $60-$65; each addl $7; under 19 free. Crib free. TV; cable (premium), VCR avail (movies). Complimentary continental bkfst. Ck-out 11 am. Business servs avail. In-rm modem link. Sundries. Exercise equipt. Refrigerators, microwaves. Cr cds: A, C, D, DS, MC, V.

D 🏋 ⊠ 🔥 SC

✓ ★ ★ **QUALITY INN.** 179 Sheraton Dr (24153). 540/562-1912; FAX 540/562-0507; res: 800/228-5151. 120 rms, 2 story. S $51-$57; D $54-$61; each addl $6; under 18 free. Crib free. Pet accepted, some restrictions; $6. TV; cable (premium), VCR avail. Pool. Complimentary continental bkfst. Coffee in rms. Restaurant 5-9 pm. Bar 5 pm-11 pm. Ck-out 11 am. Meeting rms. Coin lndry. Business servs avail. Airport transportation. Putting green. Exercise equipt. Balconies. Cr cds: A, C, D, DS, ER, JCB, MC, V.

D 🐾 ⊠ 🏋 ⊠ 🔥 SC

Restaurant

★ **SHANGHAI.** 1416 Colorado St (24153). 540/389-4151. Hrs: 11:30 am-10 pm; Fri to 10:30 pm; Sat 5-10:30 pm; Sun from noon; Sun brunch to 2:30 pm. Closed Thanksgiving, Dec 25. Chinese menu. Bar. Semi-a la carte: lunch $2.95-$4.95, dinner $4.95-$8.95. Buffet: lunch $4.50, dinner $6.95. Sun brunch $4.50. Child's meals. Specialties: beef imperial, General Tso's chicken. Chinese decor with mural, vases. Cr cds: A, C, DS, MC, V.

D ⊒

Shenandoah National Park (C-7 - D-7)

(See also Front Royal, Luray, New Market, Waynesboro)

About 450 million years ago the Blue Ridge was at the bottom of a sea. Today it averages about 2,000 feet above sea level; some 300 square miles of the loveliest Blue Ridge area are included in Shenandoah National Park.

The park is 80 miles long and from two to 13 miles wide. Running its full length is the 105-mile Skyline Drive. Main entrances are the North Entrance (Front Royal), from I-66, US 340, US 522 and VA 55; Thornton Gap Entrance (31.5 miles south), from US 211; Swift Run Gap Entrance (65.7 miles south), from US 33; and the South Entrance (Rockfish Gap), from I-64, US 250 and the Blue Ridge Parkway (see). The Drive, twisting and turning along the crest of the Blue Ridge, is one of the finest scenic trips in the East. Approximately 70 overlooks give views of the Blue Ridge, the Piedmont and, to the west, the Shenandoah Valley and the Alleghenies.

The Drive offers much, but the park offers more. Exploration, on foot or horseback, attracts thousands of visitors who return again and again. Most of the area is wooded, predominantly in white, red and chestnut oak, with hickory, birch, maple, hemlock, tulip poplar and nearly 100 other species scattered here and there. At the head of Whiteoak Canyon are hemlocks more than 300 years old. The park bursts with color and contrast in the fall, which makes this season particularly popular with visitors. The park is a sanctuary for deer, bear, fox and bobcat, along with more than 200 varieties of birds.

Accommodations are available in the park, with lodges, motel-type units and cabins at Big Meadows and Skyland, and housekeeping cabins at Lewis Mountain. For reservations and rates (which vary), contact ARAMARK Virginia Sky-Line Co, Inc, PO Box 727, Luray 22835-9051; 800/999-4714. Nearby communities provide a variety of accommodations. In the park, there are restaurants at Panorama, Skyland and Big Meadows; light lunches and groceries are available at Elkwallow, Big Meadows, Lewis Mountain and Loft Mountain Waysides.

The park is open all year; lodge and cabin accommodations, usually Mar-Dec; phone ahead for schedule. Skyline Drive is occasionally closed for short periods during Nov-Mar. As in all national parks, pets must be on a leash. The speed limit is 35 miles per hour. $10/car/week, annual permit $20; Golden Age, Golden Access and Golden Eagle passports accepted (see MAKING THE MOST OF YOUR TRIP).

Park Headquarters is five miles east of Luray on US 211. Detailed information and pamphlets may be obtained by contacting Superintendent, Shenandoah National Park, 3655 US 211E, Luray 22835; 540/999-3500.

What to See and Do

Camping. First-come, first-serve tent and trailer sites (no hookups) at Mathews Arm, Lewis Mountain and Loft Mountain. Big Meadows requires reservations (Phone 800/365-CAMP). 14-day limit. Campers must register and check out. (Spring-fall) Write Park Superintendent, 3655 US 211E, Luray 22835, for information. ¢¢¢¢

Fishing. Trout. Regulations and directions at entrance stations, Dickey Ridge, Panorama, Big Meadows and Loft Mt. State or 5-day nonresident license necessary. ¢¢¢-¢¢¢¢

Hiking. The 500 mi of trails include 101 mi of Appalachian Trail. Along the trail, which winds 2,100 mi from Maine to Georgia, are numerous side trails to mountain tops, waterfalls and secluded valleys. Trail crosses Skyline Drive at several points and can be entered at many overlooks. Overnight backcountry use requires a permit. No open fires are allowed. Regulations and permits may be obtained at any park entrance station, visitor center or at Park HQ. Backcountry may be closed during periods of high fire danger.

Visitor Centers and lodges post schedules of evening programs and ranger-led hikes. Self-guided walks, ranging from ½ to 2 hrs, are at Dickey Ridge (mi 4.6), Skyland (mi 41.7), Big Meadows (mi 51.1), Lewis Mt (mi 57.5) and Loft Mt (mi 79.5).

Interpretive program. Guided walks, illustrated campfire talks. (Usually mid-June-mid-Oct; rest of yr, on a limited basis) Obtain schedule at Park HQ, entrance stations, visitor centers and concessions.

Picnicking. Near Dickey Ridge Visitor Center, Elkwallow, Pinnacles, Big Meadows, Lewis Mountain, South River, Loft Mountain.

★ **Points of special interest on Skyline Drive.** (Mileposts are numbered north to south, starting at Front Royal. Periods of operation are estimated—phone ahead.)

Dickey Ridge Visitor Center. Exhibits, programs, information, book sales; picnic grounds. (usually Apr-Nov, daily) Mile 4.6.

Elkwallow (2,445 ft). Picnic grounds; food, store. (May-Oct, daily) Mile 24.1.

Panorama (2,300 ft). Dining room, gift shop. Trail to Marys Rock. Closed in winter. Mile 31.5, at jct US 211.

Marys Rock Tunnel (2,545 ft). Drive goes through 600 feet of rock (clearance 13 ft). Mile 32.4.

Pinnacles (3,500 ft). Picnic grounds. Mile 36.7.

Skyland (3,680 ft). Accommodations, restaurant, gift shop; guided trail rides; Stony Man Nature Trail. Mile 41.7.

Byrd Visitor Center. Exhibits, information, book sales, orientation programs, maps. (Usually Apr-Nov, daily) Mile 51.

Big Meadows (3,500 ft). Accommodations, restaurant; store, gas; tent and trailer sites; picnic grounds; nature trail. (Usually Apr-Nov) Mile 51.1.

Lewis Mountain (3,390 ft). 1-2 bedroom cabins with heat; tent and trailer sites; picnic grounds, store. (Usually May-Oct) Mile 57.5.

South River (2,940 ft). Picnic grounds, 2½-mi round trip trail to falls. Mile 62.8.

Loft Mountain Information Center. Exhibits, information; programs, nature trail. (Usually May-Nov) Mile 79.5.

Loft Mountain (3,380 ft). Picnicking, camping (May-Oct); wayside facility; gas, store (May-Oct). Mile 79.5.

Riding. Many mi of horseback trails. Trail rides (ponies for children) for rent at Skyland.

Motels

★★ **BIG MEADOWS LODGE.** *Skyline Drive (22835), 19 mi S of US 211, 15 mi N of US 33 on Skyline Dr.* 540/999-2221; FAX 540/999-2011; res: 800/999-4714. 92 units: 62 motel rms, 20 lodge rms, 10 cabins. No A/C. Mid-May-Nov 1: lodge S, D $65-$80; motel S, D $85-$95; cabins $70-$80; suites $130-$140; each addl $5; under 16 free. Closed rest of yr. Crib free. TV in some rms. Playground. Restaurant 7:30-10 am, noon-2 pm, 5:30-8:30 pm. Box lunches. Bar 4-11 pm; entertainment. Ck-out noon. Business servs avail. Gift shop. Private patios, balconies. Panoramic view of Shenandoah Valley. Cr cds: A, C, D, DS, MC, V.

D ⊠ 🔥

✓★★ **SKYLAND LODGE.** *Skyline Drive Shenandoah Natl Park (22835), 10 mi S of US 211, 25 mi N of US 33 on Skyline Dr.* 540/999-2211; FAX 540/999-2231; res: 800/999-4714. 177 rms. No A/C. Apr-Nov: S, D $48-$105; each addl $5; suites $112-$160; under 16 free. Closed rest of yr. Crib free. TV avail. Playground. Coffee in rms. Restaurant 7:30 am-8:30 pm. Box lunches avail. Bar 3-11:30 pm. Ck-out noon. Meeting rms. Business servs avail. Sundries. Gift shop. Private patios. Balconies. Cr cds: A, C, D, DS, MC, V.

D ⚡ ⊠ 🔥

Skyline Drive

(see Shenandoah National Park)

South Boston (F-6)

(See also Clarksville, Danville)

Pop 6,997 **Elev** 407 ft **Area Code** 804 **Zip** 24592

What to See and Do

Staunton River State Park. Approx 1,300 acres of woods, meadows and lengthy shoreline on John H. Kerr Reservoir (Buggs Island Lake). Swimming pool, wading pool, bathhouse; fishing; boating (ramp). Hiking, nature trails; tennis courts. Picnic facilities, shelters; children's playground; concession. Tent & trailer sites, 7 cabins (Mar-Dec). Standard fees. 8 mi NE on VA 304, then 11 mi SE on VA 344. Phone 804/572-4623.

South Hill (F-7)

(See also Clarksville)

Pop 4,217 **Elev** 440 ft **Area Code** 804 **Zip** 23970

Motels

★★ **BEST WESTERN INN.** *I-85 and US 58 (23970), Jct I-85, US 58.* 804/447-3123; FAX 804/447-4237; res: 800/528-1234 or 800/296-3123. E-mail bestwest@msinets.com. 151 rms, 2 story. S $52-$59; D $58-$65; each addl $6; under 19 free. Crib free. Pet accepted. TV; cable (premium). Heated pool; wading pool. Complimentary continental bkfst. Coffee in rms. Restaurant adj open 24 hrs. Bar 5 pm-1 am. Ck-out 11 am. Coin lndry. Meeting rms. Free airport, bus depot transportation. Exercise equipt. Health club privileges. Game rm. Cr cds: A, C, D, DS, JCB, MC, V.

D ⊕ ⊛ ☒ ⊠ ⊠ SC

✓★★ **HAMPTON INN.** *200 Thompson Rd (23970).* 804/447-4600; FAX 804/447-2553; res: 800/426-4329. 55 rms, 3 story, 6 suites. June-Sept: S, D $65-$74; suites $125; under 18 free; lower rates rest of yr. Crib free. TV; cable (premium). Complimentary continental bkfst. Complimentary coffee in rms. Restaurant nearby. Ck-out 11 am. Meeting rms. Business servs avail. In-rm modem link. Sundries. Coin lndry. Exercise equipt. Pool. Some refrigerators, microwaves. Cr cds: A, C, D, DS, MC, V.

D ⊠ ☒ ⊠ ⊠ SC

✓★★ **HOLIDAY INN EXPRESS.** *101 Thompson St (23950).* 804/955-2777; FAX 804/955-2700; res: 800/465-4329. 55 rms, 2 story. Memorial Day-Labor Day: S, D $58-$80; each addl $5; suites $85-$100; under 18 free; lower rates rest of yr. Crib free. TV; cable (premium). Complimentary continental bkfst. Restaurant nearby. Ck-out 11 am. Meeting rm. Business servs avail. In-rm modem link. Sundries. Exercise equipt. Pool. Refrigerators. Cr cds: A, C, D, DS, JCB, MC, V.

D ⊠ ☒ ⊠ ⊠ SC

Springfield (C-8)

(See also Alexandria, Arlington County, Fairfax, Mount Vernon; also see District of Columbia)

Pop 23,706 **Elev** 300 ft **Area Code** 703

Motels

★★ **COMFORT INN.** *6560 Loisdale Ct (22150), I-95 exit 169A.* 703/922-9000; FAX 703/971-6944; res: 800/228-5150. 112 rms, 5 story. S, D $89; under 18 free. Pet accepted. TV; cable (premium). Complimentary continental bkfst. Ck-out noon. Meeting rms. Business servs avail. In-rm modem link. Valet serv. Health club privileges. Refrigerators, microwaves avail. Cr cds: A, C, D, DS, MC, V.

D ⊕ ☒ ⊠ ⊠ SC

✓★★ **DAYS INN.** *6721 Commerce St (22150), I-95 exit 169A.* 703/922-6100; FAX 703/922-0708; res: 800/329-7466. 179 rms, 6 story. Apr-Oct: S, D $62-$105; each addl $6, under 18 free; wkly, monthly rates; lower rates rest of yr. Crib free. TV; cable (premium). Pool; lifeguard. Restaurant 6 am-1 pm, 5-8 pm; Sun to 1 pm. Ck-out noon. Meeting rms. Business servs avail. Valet serv. Health club privileges. Refrigerators avail. Cr cds: A, C, D, DS, ER, MC, V.

D ⊠ ☒ ⊠ ⊠ SC

★ **DAYS INN POTOMAC MILLS.** *14619 Potomac Mills Rd (22192), 10 mi S on I-95, exit 156.* 703/494-4433; FAX 703/385-2627; res: 800/543-2392. E-mail daysinn@pwcweb.com; web www.pwcweb.com/daysinn. 176 rms, 9 story. S $68-$78; D $75-$85; each addl $7; suites $89; under 18 free. Crib free. Pet accepted, some restrictions. TV; cable. Pool; lifeguard. Complimentary continental bkfst. Restaurant adj 6 am-midnight. Ck-out noon. Coin lndry. Meeting rms. Business servs avail. In-rm modem link. Valet serv. Sundries. Exercise equipt. Some refrigerators, minibars. Cr cds: A, C, D, DS, MC, V.

D ⊕ ☒ ☒ ⊠ ⊠ SC

★★ **HAMPTON INN.** *6550 Loisdale Ct (22150).* 703/924-9444; FAX 703/924-0324; res: 800/426-7866. 153 rms, 7 story. Apr-June: S, D $89-$99; under 18 free; lower rates rest of yr. Crib free. Pet accepted. TV; cable (premium). Pool. Complimentary continental bkfst. Restaurant nearby. Ck-out noon. Valet serv. Health club privileges. Some refrigerators; microwaves. Cr cds: A, C, D, DS, MC, V.

D ⊕ ☒ ⊠ ⊠ SC

Hotel

★★★ **HILTON.** *6550 Loisdale Rd (22150), I-95 exit 169A.* 703/971-8900; FAX 703/971-8527; res: 800/445-8667. E-mail guest@springfieldhilton.com. 246 rms, 12 story. Mar-July: S $117; D $127; each addl $10; suites $270; under 18 free; wkend rates; lower rates rest of yr. Crib free. TV; cable (premium), VCR avail. Indoor pool; lifeguard. Complimentary coffee in rms. Restaurant 6:30 am-10 pm. Bar 2 pm-2:30 am; entertainment Thurs-Sat. Ck-out 1 pm. Meeting rms. Business servs avail. In-rm modem link. Concierge. Gift shop. Health club privileges. Some refrigerators. Cr cds: A, C, D, DS, MC, V.

D ☒ ⊠ ⊠ SC

Restaurant

★★ **MIKE'S AMERICAN GRILL.** *6210 Backlick Rd (22150).* 703/644-7100. Hrs: 11:30 am-10:30 pm; Fri, Sat noon-midnight; Sun noon-10 pm. Closed Thanksgiving, Dec 25. Bar. Semi-a la carte: lunch, dinner $8.95-$17.95. Specializes in grilled meats, seafood, vegetarian cuisine. Warehouse decor. Cr cds: A, C, MC, V.

D

Staunton (D-6)

(See also Harrisonburg, Waynesboro)

Settled 1736 **Pop** 24,461 **Elev** 1,385 ft **Area Code** 540 **Zip** 24401
Information Travel Information Center, 1250 Richmond Rd; 540/332-3972 or 800/332-5219

To historians, Staunton (STAN-ton) is known as the birthplace of Woodrow Wilson, and to students of government, as the place where the city-manager plan was first conceived and adopted. Set in fertile Shenandoah Valley fields and orchards, between the Blue Ridge and Allegheny mountain ranges, the area around Staunton produces poultry, livestock and wool. Manufacturing firms in the city make air conditioners, razors, candy and clothing.

A Ranger District office of the George Washington and Jefferson National Forests is located here.

What to See and Do

Augusta Stone Church (1747). Oldest Presbyterian church in continuous use in state. Once used as fort during Native American raids. Museum of early church artifacts (by appt). 7 mi N on US 11 in Ft Defiance. Phone 540/248-2634.

Gypsy Hill Park. Lake stocked with fish; swimming (late May-Labor Day, fee); lighted softball field with concession stand, outdoor basketball courts; tennis; 18-hole golf; picnicking; miniature train ride, playgrounds; fairgrounds. (Daily) Off Churchville & Thornrose Aves. Phone 540/332-3945.

McCormick Memorial Wayside. Cyrus McCormick's first reaper is displayed here. Picnic grounds. (Daily) 16 mi SW via US 11, I-81; 1 mi E of I-81 on VA 606 near Steeles Tavern. Phone 540/377-2255.   **Free**

Museum of American Frontier Culture. Living history museum consists of working farms brought together from England, Germany, Northern Ireland and an American farm. The European farms represent what America's early settlers left; the American farm, from the Valley of Virginia, reflects the blend of the various European influences. Visitors are able to see and take part in life as it was lived on these 17th-, 18th- and 19th-century farmsteads. Costumed interpreters demonstrate daily life at all four sites. Visitor center. (Daily; closed 1st wk Jan, Thanksgiving, Dec 25) I-81 exit 222, US 250 W, first left after stoplight. 1250 Richmond Rd. Phone 540/332-7850.   ¢¢¢

Trinity Episcopal Church (1855). Founded as Augusta Parish Church (1746), original building on this site served as Revolutionary capitol of state for 16 days in 1781. Open on request (Mon-Fri). 120 W Beverley St. Phone 540/886-9132.

⭐ **Woodrow Wilson Birthplace and Presidential Museum.** Restored Greek-revival manse with period furnishings and Wilson family mementos from 1850s; museum building on grounds houses seven-gallery presidential exhibit, "The Life and Times of Woodrow Wilson," and his 1919 Pierce-Arrow limousine. Victorian gardens. (Daily; closed Jan 1, Thanksgiving, Dec 25) 24 N Coalter St, near I-81, I-64 & US 11. Phone 540/885-0897. ¢¢¢

Seasonal Event

Jazz in the Park. Gypsy Hill Park. Thurs nights. July-Aug.

Motels

⭐⭐ **BEST WESTERN INN.** *260 Rowe Rd (24401), I-81, exit 222.* 540/885-1112; FAX 540/885-1112; res: 800/752-9471. 80 rms, 4 story. May-Oct: S $62-$75; D $72-$85; each addl $8; under 18 free; family rates; higher rates: graduation, fall foliage; lower rates rest of yr. Crib free. TV; cable. Complimentary continental bkfst. Complimentary coffee in rms. Restaurant adj 6:30 am-9 pm. Ck-out 11 am. Business servs avail. Valet serv. Sundries. Indoor pool. Some refrigerators. Cr cds: A, C, D, DS, JCB, MC, V.

D ⛹ 🛏 ➶ 🔥 SC

⭐⭐ **COMFORT INN.** *1302 Richmond Ave (24401).* 540/886-5000; FAX 540/886-6643; res: 800/228-5150. 98 rms, 5 story. May-Oct: S $49-$75; D $57-$75; each addl $8; under 18 free; higher rates special events; lower rates rest of yr. Crib avail. Pet accepted, some restrictions. TV; cable (premium). Pool. Complimentary continental bkfst. Complimentary coffee in rms. Restaurant adj open 24 hrs. Ck-out 11 am. Business servs avail. Some refrigerators. Cr cds: A, C, D, DS, ER, JCB, MC, V.

D 🐾 🛏 ➶ 🔥 SC

✓ ⭐ **ECONO LODGE INN.** *I-81 Rte 2 Box 364 (24401), ½ mi S of jct I-81 & I-64 exit 213/213A Greenville.* 540/337-1231; FAX 540/337-0821; res: 800/228-5050 or 800/553-2666. 32 rms, 2 story. May-Nov: S $35-$45; D $45-$75; each addl $6; under 12 free; wkly rates; lower rates rest of yr. Crib free. Pet accepted, some restrictions; $6. TV; cable (premium). Pool; wading pool. Playground. Complimentary continental bkfst. Restaurant nearby. Ck-out 11 am. Refrigerators. Private patios, balconies. Picnic tables. Cr cds: A, C, D, DS, MC, V.

🐾 🛏 ➶ 🔥 SC

⭐⭐ **SHONEY'S MOTOR INN.** *I-81 & US 250 (24402), jct US 250 & I-81 exit 222.* 540/885-3117; FAX 540/885-5620; res: 800/222-2222. 91 rms, 2 story. S $48; D $55; each addl $6; under 18 free. Crib free. TV; cable (premium). Indoor pool; whirlpool. Complimentary continental bkfst. Restaurant 6 am-11 pm; Fri, Sat to 1 am. Ck-out noon. Business servs avail. Valet serv. Sundries. Exercise equipt; sauna. Some in-rm whirlpools. Cr cds: A, C, D, DS, ER, MC, V.

D 🛏 🕴 ➶ 🔥 SC

Motor Hotel

⭐⭐⭐ **HOLIDAY INN.** *I-81; Hwy 275 (24401), I-81 exit 225, Rte 275 at Country Club Rd.* 540/248-6020; FAX 540/248-2902; res: 800/465-4329. E-mail higcc@cfw.com; web www.holidayinnstaunton.com. 116 rms, 4 story. Mid-Mar-mid-Nov: S, D $79-$89; suites $95; under 17 free; golf plans; lower rates rest of yr. Crib free. TV; cable (premium). Indoor/outdoor pool; poolside serv. Restaurant 6 am-10 pm. Rm serv. Bar 4 pm-11 pm; entertainment. Ck-out noon. Meeting rms. Business servs avail. In-rm modem link. Valet serv. Sundries. Free airport transportation. Lighted tennis. 18-hole golf, greens fee $25, pro, putting green, driving range. Exercise equipt. Refrigerator, wet bar in suites. Some balconies. Cr cds: A, C, D, DS, ER, JCB, MC, V.

D 🕴 🏌 🛏 🕴 ➶ 🔥 SC

Inns

⭐⭐ **BELLE GRAE INN.** *515 W Frederick St (24401).* 540/886-5151; FAX 540/886-6641. Web www.bellegrae. 14 rms, 2 story. Some rm phones. S, D $95-$150; each addl $25; suites $140-$170; higher rates wkends. Children over 12 yrs only. TV in most rms. Complimentary full bkfst; afternoon refreshments. Dining rm 7:30-9:30 am, 6-9 pm. Ck-out 11 am, ck-in 3 pm. Meeting rms. Business servs avail. Airport, RR station, bus depot transportation. Tennis privileges. Golf privileges. Fireplaces. Private patios, balconies. 1870s restored Victorian mansion. Each rm individually decorated; antiques. Cr cds: A, C, MC, V.

D 🕴 🏌 ➶ 🔥 SC

✓ ⭐⭐ **BUCKHORN INN.** *2487 Hankey Mountain Hwy (24421), 12 mi W on US 250.* 540/337-6900. 6 rms, 3 story. No rm phones. S $35-$45; D $55-$65; each addl $10. Closed Dec 24, 25. Crib free. Complimentary full bkfst. Restaurant (see Buckhorn Inn). Ck-out 11 am, ck-in 1 pm. Located in Shenandoah Valley of the George Washington National Forest. Restored 1811 inn. Cr cds: C, DS, MC, V.

🔥

⭐⭐ **FREDERICK HOUSE.** *28 N New St (24401).* 540/885-4220; FAX 540/885-5180; res: 800/334-5575. E-mail ejharman@frederick house.com; web www.frederickhouse.com. 19 units, 2 story. 9 suites. S, D $75-$170; each addl $25; suites $95-$170; wkly rates. Crib $10. TV; cable. Complimentary full bkfst. Ck-out 11 am, ck-in 3 pm. Tennis privileges. Golf privileges. Health club privileges. Private patios, balconies. Picnic tables. Encompasses 6 adj townhouses built 1810-1919. Antiques and period furnishings. Mary Baldwin College adj. Totally nonsmoking. Cr cds: A, C, D, DS, MC, V.

★★★ **SAMPSON EAGON INN.** *238 East Beverley St (24401). 540/886-8200; res: 800/597-9722.* E-mail eagoninn@rica.net; web www.eagoninn.com. 5 rms, 1 with shower only, 2 story. S, D $94-$120; each addl $20; wkends (2-day min). Children over 12 yrs only. TV; cable, VCR (free movies). Complimentary full bkfst; afternoon refreshments. Ck-out 11 am, ck-in 4 pm. Business servs avail. Health club privileges. Antiques. Restored antebellum home (1800) adj to Woodrow Wilson birthplace. Cr cds: A, C, MC, V.

★★ **THORNROSE HOUSE.** *531 Thornrose Ave (24401). 540/885-7026; FAX 540/885-6458; res: 800/861-4338.* Web www.bbhsv. org/thornrose. 5 rms, 2 story. No rm phones. S $60-$80; D $70-$90. Complimentary full bkfst. Ck-out 11 am, ck-in 3 pm. Georgian-Revival house (1912); wrap-around veranda. Antiques; four poster and brass beds. Opp park. Totally nonsmoking. Cr cds: A, C, MC, V.

Restaurants

✓★★ **BUCKHORN INN.** *(See Buckhorn Inn)* 540/337-6900. Hrs: 11 am-8 pm; Fri to 9 pm; Sat 9 am-9 pm. Closed Mon; Dec 24, 25; also Tues in Jan, Feb. Semi-a la carte: lunch $4.25-$8. Complete meals: lunch, dinner $4.50-$14.95. Sun brunch $10.95. Child's meals. Specializes in regional country dishes. Salad bar. Located in Colonial-era country inn in Shenandoah Valley. Cr cds: A, C, MC, V.

⊡ SC ⊡

★ **MCCORMICK'S PUB.** *41 N Augusta St (24401). 540/885-3111.* Hrs: 5 pm-midnight; Fri, Sat to 1 am. Closed some major hols. Res accepted. Bar. Semi-a la carte: dinner $6.95-$18.95. Child's meals. Specializes in prime rib, seafood, pasta. In old YMCA building (1915) funded by Cyrus Hall McCormick family. Cr cds: A, C, DS, MC, V.

⊡ ⊡

★ **ROWE'S FAMILY RESTAURANT.** *Rte 4 Box 88 (24401), at I-81 exit 222. 540/886-1833.* Hrs: 7 am-9 pm; Sun to 7 pm. Closed some major hols. Res accepted. Wine, beer. Semi-a la carte: bkfst $2-$5, lunch $3-$6, dinner $5-$13. Child's meals. Specializes in country ham, chicken, catfish. Country atmosphere. Family-owned since 1947. Cr cds: C, DS, MC, V.

⊡

Strasburg (C-7)

(See also Front Royal, Winchester, Woodstock)

Founded 1761 **Pop** 3,762 **Elev** 578 ft **Area Code** 540 **Zip** 22657
Information Chamber of Commerce, PO Box 42; 540/465-3187

Lying at the base of Massanutten Mountain and on the north fork of the Shenandoah River, Strasburg was founded in 1761 by German settlers. Prospering in the early 19th century as a center of trade and flour milling, the village later became identified with the manufacture of high quality pottery, earning the nickname "Pottown" after the Civil War. The town's location on the Manassas Gap Railroad and the Shenandoah Valley Turnpike gave Strasburg a pivotal role in Stonewall Jackson's Campaign of 1862. The first western Virginia town to be served by two railroads, Strasburg became prominent after 1890 as a railroad town, manufacturing center and home of printing and publishing businesses.

Today, Strasburg, located near the entrance to the Skyline Drive, offers historical and cultural museums. It attracts visitors with its antebellum and Victorian architecture and its burgeoning art community. The town calls itself the "antique capital of Virginia " because of its many antique shops.

What to See and Do

Belle Grove (1794). The design of this limestone mansion reflects the influence of Thomas Jefferson. Used as Union headquarters during the Battle of Cedar Creek, Oct 19, 1864. Unusual interior woodwork; herb garden in rear. Guided tours. (Apr-Oct, daily) National Trust for Historic Preservation property. (See ANNUAL EVENTS) 4 mi N on US 11. Phone 540/869-2028. ¢¢

Hupp's Hill Battlefield Park and Study Center. Former campsite for six different Civil War generals' troops, now a museum and hands-on learning center. Artifacts, documents, exhibits. Guided battlefield tours (by appt; fee). (Daily; closed major hols) I-81 to exit 298, S 1 mi on US 11. Phone 540/465-5884. ¢¢

Strasburg Museum. Blacksmith, cooper and potter shop collections; displays from colonial homes; relics from Civil War and railroad eras; Native American artifacts. Housed in Southern Railway Depot. (May-Oct, daily) E King St. Phone 540/465-3175. ¢

Annual Events

Mayfest. Celebration of town's German heritage with parade, entertainment and arts, crafts, antiques and foods fairs. 3rd wkend May.

Battle of Cedar Creek Re-Enactment. Belle Grove. Mid-Oct.

Seasonal Event

Wayside Theatre. Professional performances. Wed-Sun. Res required. On US 11, I-81 exit 302. Phone 540/869-1776. Late May-mid-Oct & Dec.

Inns

★★★ **HOTEL STRASBURG INN.** *213 S Holliday St (22657), 2 mi E of I-81 exit 298. 540/465-9191; FAX 540/465-4788; res: 800/348-8327.* E-mail thehotel@shentel.net; web www.svta.org/thehotel. 29 rms, 17 with shower only, 3 story. S, D $79; suites $112-$175; under 16 free; golf plan. Crib free. TV; cable. Complimentary continental bkfst (Mon-Fri). Restaurant (see Hotel Strasburg). Bar. Ck-out 11 am, ck-in 2 pm. Meeting rm. Business servs avail. Health club privileges. Some in-rm whirlpools. Beach nearby; swimming privileges. Victorian building; antiques. Cr cds: A, C, D, DS, MC, V.

★★★ **WAYSIDE INN.** *7783 Main St (22645), I-81 exit 302. 540/869-1797; FAX 540/869-6038.* Web www.waysideofva.com. 22 rms, 3 story. S, D $95-$145; each addl $20; suites $145; under 12 free. Crib free. TV; cable. Restaurant (see Wilkinson's Tavern). Bar 11 am-midnight. Ck-out 11 am, ck-in 2 pm. Meeting rms. Business servs avail. Boating, swimming nearby. Restored colonial-era bldg; antiques. An inn since 1797. Cr cds: A, C, D, DS, MC, V.

⊡ ⊡ SC

Restaurants

★★★ **HOTEL STRASBURG.** *(See Hotel Strasburg Inn)* 540/465-9191. Hrs: 11:30 am-2:30 pm, 5-9 pm; Fri, Sat 8 am-2:30 pm, 5-10 pm; Sun 8 am-9 pm. Res accepted; required Sat. Continental menu. Bar from 11 am. Semi-a la carte: bkfst $4.95, lunch $5.25-$6.95, dinner $7.95-$18.95. Buffet: bkfst (Sat, Sun) $4.95, lunch (Mon-Fri) $5.95. Sun brunch $8.95. Child's meals. Specialties: Tournedos Jack Daniel's, chicken Shenandoah. Totally nonsmoking. Cr cds: A, C, D, DS, MC, V.

★ ★ **WILKINSON'S TAVERN.** *(See Wayside Inn)* *540/869-1797.* Hrs: 7 am-3 pm, 5-9 pm; Fri, Sat to 10 pm; Sun 8 am-3:30 pm, 5-9 pm; Sun brunch 11:30 am-3:30 pm. Res accepted; required Sat. Bar 11 am-midnight. Semi-a la carte: bkfst $2.75-$6.95, lunch $4.95-$8.95, dinner $14.95-$21.95. Sun brunch $14.95. Child's meals. Specializes in fresh seafood, chicken, vegetarian dishes. In restored Colonial-style inn; many antiques. Cr cds: A, C, D, DS, MC, V.

D �

Suffolk

(see Portsmouth)

Surry (E-9)

(See also Colonial Parkway, Jamestown, Newport News, Williamsburg)

Pop 192 **Elev** 122 ft **Area Code** 757 **Zip** 23883

What to See and Do

Chippokes Plantation State Park. Plantation continuously operated since 1619. Approx 1,600 acres. Swimming pool; fishing; Hiking, bicycle paths; interpretive tour road. Picnicking, concession. Visitor center, programs. Tours of mansion, carriage house, kitchen and formal gardens (Memorial Day-Labor Day, Wed-Sun; Apr-Oct wkends). (See ANNUAL EVENT) Farm & Forestry Museum (Memorial Day-Labor Day, Wed-Sun; Apr-Oct, wkends). Standard fees. 6 mi E via VA 10, 634. Across James River from Jamestown. Phone 757/294-3625 (park) or 757/294-3439 (museum). Farm & Forestry Museum ¢

Annual Event

Pork, Peanut and Pine Festival. Chippokes Plantation. Pork products, peanuts, crafts, pine decorations. 3rd wkend July.

Tangier Island (E-10)

Settled 1666 **Pop** 659 **Elev** 3 ft **Area Code** 757 **Zip** 23440

Bought from Native Americans for two overcoats, Tangier was first settled by a mainland family named West. In 1686 John Crockett moved here with his four sons and four daughters. They were later joined by a few other families. Descendants of these families now populate the island. Life is simple and lacks most urban complexities. Most of the men are fishermen, oystering and clamming in one season, crabbing in another.

This tranquil little island (approximately four miles long) is 12 miles out in Chesapeake Bay. The island offers good duck hunting, fishing, swimming and relaxation. There is an airfield here, and there are excursion boats from Reedville and Onancock, Virginia, and Crisfield, Maryland. Accommodations include a boarding house, Chesapeake House, with seven rooms, family-style meals. Contact PO Box 194; 757/891-2331 for reservations.

Tappahannock (D-9)

(See also Lancaster, Montross, Richmond)

Founded 1680 **Pop** 1,550 **Elev** 22 ft **Area Code** 804 **Zip** 22560

Information Chamber of Commerce, PO Box 481; 804/443-5241

Bartholemew Hoskins patented the first land here in 1645. Following his lead, others came and a small village soon sprang up, known at that time as Hobbes His Hole. Formally chartered in 1682 as New Plymouth, the town was to experience yet another name change. Built around the Rappahannock River, which means "running water," the town port became known as Tappahannock or "on the running water." Four hundred men gathered here in 1765 to protest the Stamp Act.

Today, the area around Prince and Duke streets and Water Lane of Tappahannock has been declared a historic district. Highlights include the beautifully renovated Ritchie House; the Anderton House, once used for the prizing of tobacco into hogsheads; and Scot's Arms Tavern.

Motels

✓ ★ **DAYS INN.** *Tappahannock Blvd (22560), jct US 17, US 360.* 804/443-9200; FAX 804/443-2663; res: 800/329-7466. 60 rms, 2 story. S, D $44-$49; each addl $6; under 12 free. Crib free. TV; cable. Complimentary continental bkfst. Ck-out 11 am. Business servs avail. Cr cds: A, C, D, DS, MC, V.

D ➥ ➦ ➧ SC

★ **SUPER 8 MOTEL.** *US 17 & US 360 (22560), jct US 360, US 17.* 804/443-3888; FAX 804/443-3888; res: 800/800-8000. 43 rms, 2 story. Apr-Sept: S $49.88; D $55.88; each addl $5; under 12 free; lower rates rest of yr. Pet accepted. TV; cable. Complimentary coffee in lobby. Restaurant opp 6 am-11 pm. Ck-out 11 am. Meeting rms. Business servs avail. Some refrigerators. Cr cds: A, C, D, DS, ER, JCB, MC, V.

D ➦ ➥ ➧ ➨ SC

Restaurant

★ ★ **LOWERY'S.** *US 17 (22560).* 804/443-4314. Hrs: 7:30 am-9 pm. Closed Dec 25. Semi-a la carte: bkfst $1.75-$6.75, lunch $3.25-$19, dinner $7-$19. Specializes in fresh local seafood. Own salad dressing. Antique cars on display. Cr cds: A, C, DS, MC, V.

D ➥

Triangle (D-8)

(See also Alexandria, Fredericksburg; also see District of Columbia)

Pop 4,740 **Elev** 150 ft **Area Code** 703 **Zip** 22172 **E-mail** jjensen@mnsinc.com **Web** www.visitpwc.com

Information Prince William County/Manassas Conference & Visitors Bureau, 14420 Bristow Rd, Manassas 20112; 703/792-4254 or 800/432-1792

Quantico Marine Corps Base is three miles east of town.

What to See and Do

Marine Corps Air-Ground Museum. Chronological presentation of the Marine Corps Air-Ground Team's role in American history; artifacts on exhibit include aircraft, engines, armor, tracked & wheeled vehicles, artillery, small arms, uniforms, dioramas and photographs in pre-World War II aviation hangars. (Apr-late Nov, daily exc Mon) 2 mi E, in OCS area on Quantico Marine Corps Base. Phone 703/640-7965.   **Free**

Prince William Forest Park. Consists of 17,000 acres. Hiking, bicycling. Picnicking. Camping (14-day limit; no hookups; fee; group cabins by res only); trailer campground off VA 234 (fee; hookups, showers, lndry). Naturalist programs. (Daily) From I-95, ¼ mi W on VA 619. Phone 703/221-7181. Per vehicle   ¢¢

Tysons Corner (C-8)

(See also Arlington County, Fairfax, Falls Church, McLean; also see District of Columbia)

Pop 13,124 **Area Code** 703 **E-mail** cvbfceda@mindspring.com
Web www.visitfairfax.org

Information Fairfax County Convention & Visitors Bureau, 8300 Boone Blvd, Suite 450, Tysons Corner 22182; 703/790-3329 or 800/7-FAIRFAX

This Virginia suburban area of Washington, DC, is the location of one of the largest shopping centers in the nation.

Motels

★★ **COMFORT INN.** *1587 Spring Hill Rd (22182), 1½ mi W of I-495, exit 10B.* 703/448-8020; FAX 703/448-0343; res: 800/828-3297; res: 800/228-5150. Web www.comfortinntysons.com. 250 rms, 3 story. S, D $115.95-$125.95; each addl $5; suites $125.95-$145.95; under 18 free. Crib free. Pet accepted, some restrictions; $25 deposit. TV; cable (premium). Pool; lifeguard. Complimentary continental bkfst. Coffee in rms. Ck-out noon. Coin lndry. Meeting rms. Business servs avail. In-rm modem link. Valet serv. Free airport transportation. Health club privileges. Refrigerators, microwaves avail. Cr cds: A, C, D, DS, ER, JCB, MC, V.

[icons]

★★★ **RESIDENCE INN BY MARRIOTT.** *8616 Westwood Center Dr (22182), I-495 exit 10B to VA 7, then 2 mi W.* 703/893-0120; FAX 703/790-8896; res: 800/331-3131. 96 kit suites, 2 story. Kit. suites $179-$229; each addl $10; under 18 free; wkend rates. Crib free. Pet accepted; $150 and $5/day. TV; cable (premium). Pool; whirlpool; lifeguard. Complimentary continental bkfst. Restaurant nearby. Ck-out noon. Coin lndry. Meeting rm. Business servs avail. In-rm modem link. Valet serv. Lighted tennis. Health club privileges. Many fireplaces. Picnic tables, grills. Cr cds: A, C, D, DS, MC, V.

[icons]

Hotels

★★★ **EMBASSY SUITES.** *8517 Leesburg Pike (22182), I-495 exit 10B to VA 7, then 2 mi W.* 703/883-0707; FAX 703/883-0694; res: 800/362-2779. Web www.embassysuites.com. 232 suites, 8 story. S, D $169-$189; each addl $10; under 12 free; wkend rates. Crib free. TV; cable (premium). Indoor pool; whirlpool. Complimentary full bkfst. Complimentary coffee in rms. Restaurant 11:30 am-11 pm. Bar. Ck-out noon. Business servs avail. In-rm modem link. Gift shop. Exercise equipt; sauna. Refrigerators, microwaves, wet bars. Cr cds: A, C, D, DS, JCB, MC, V.

[icons]

★★★ **HILTON HOTEL.** *7920 Jones Branch Dr (22102), S on VA 123, turn right at Tysons Blvd, right on Galleria Dr/Westpark Dr, then right on Jones Branch Dr.* 703/847-5000; FAX 703/761-5100; res: 800/932-3322. E-mail mclean_hilton@hilton.com; web www.hilton.com. 458 units, 9 story. S $150-$210; D $170-$230; each addl $20; suites $375-$1,750; package plans. Crib free. TV; cable (premium), VCR avail (free movies). Indoor pool; lifeguard. Complimentary coffee in rms. Restaurant 6:30 am-11 pm. Rm serv 6-2 am. Bar 11-2 am; entertainment. Ck-out noon. Convention facilities. Business center. In-rm modem link. Gift shop. Exercise equipt; sauna. Minibars; refrigerators avail. Atrium lobby; marble floors, fountain. Luxury level. Cr cds: A, C, D, DS, ER, JCB, MC, V.

[icons]

✓★★★ **HOLIDAY INN TYSONS CORNER.** *1960 Chain Bridge Rd (22102), 2 blks W of I-495 exit 11B.* 703/893-2100; FAX 703/356-8218; res: 800/465-4329. 316 rms, 9 story. S, D $179-$194; each addl $15; family rates; wkend rates. Crib free. TV; cable (premium). Indoor pool; whirlpool. Restaurant 6:30 am-10 pm. Bar; entertainment. Ck-out 1 pm.

Conference facilities. Business center. In-rm modem link. Gift shop. Airport transportation. Exercise equipt. Balconies. Cr cds: A, C, D, DS, JCB, MC, V.

[icons]

★★★★ **RITZ-CARLTON TYSONS CORNER.** *1700 Tysons Blvd (22102), N via I-495 exit 11B, connecting to Tysons II Mall.* 703/506-4300; FAX 703/506-2694; res: 800/241-3333. Web www.ritzcarlton.com. A keynote of this hotel is its superb service. The lobby, furnished with antiques and 18th-century oil paintings, sets a tone of comfort and elegance that is carried through in the generously appointed guest rooms. 399 units, 24 story. S, D $170-$260; suites $375-$2,400; under 18 free; monthly rates; wkend family rates; lower rates some wkends. Crib free. Valet parking $16. TV; cable (premium), VCR avail (movies $4). Indoor pool; whirlpool, lifeguard. Restaurant (see The Restaurant). Afternoon tea in lounge. Rm serv 24 hrs. Bar 11:30-1 am; entertainment. Ck-out noon. Convention facilities. Business center. In-rm modem link. Concierge. Gift shop. Beauty shop. Tennis privileges. 18-hole golf privileges, greens fee $75, pro, putting green, driving range. Exercise rm; sauna. Massage. Bathrm phones, minibars; microwaves avail. Luxury level. Cr cds: A, C, D, DS, JCB, MC, V.

[icons]

★★★ **SHERATON PREMIERE TYSONS CORNER.** *8661 Leesburg Pike (22182), I-495 exit 10B, then 2½ mi W on VA 7.* 703/448-1234; FAX 703/893-8193; res: 800/544-5064 or 800/572-7666. E-mail bhubbard@sptc.com; web www.sptc.com. 437 rms, 24 story. S $185-$215; D $205-$235; each addl $20; suites $375-$2,000; under 17 free; wkly rates. Crib free. TV; cable (premium), VCR avail. 2 pools, 1 indoor; whirlpool, poolside serv, lifeguard. Complimentary coffee in rms. Restaurant 6:30 am-midnight. Rm serv 24 hrs. Bars 11-1 am. Ck-out noon. Convention facilities. Business center. In-rm modem link. Concierge. Gift shop. Beauty shop. Free airport transportation. Lighted tennis privileges. 18-hole golf privileges, pro, greens fee. Racquetball. Exercise equipt; sauna. Massage. Health club privileges. Bathrm phones; some refrigerators. Cr cds: A, C, D, DS, ER, JCB, MC, V.

[icons]

★★★ **TYSONS CORNER MARRIOTT.** *8028 Leesburg Pike (22182), 1 blk W of I-495 exit 10W.* 703/734-3200; FAX 703/734-5763; res: 800/228-9290. 390 units, 15 story. S, D $184-$199; suites $375; family rates; wkend packages. Crib free. TV; cable (premium). Indoor pool; whirlpool, poolside serv, lifeguard. Restaurant 6:30 am-11 pm. Bar 4:30 pm-1 am; Fri to 2 am; Sat 7 pm-2 am; closed Sun. Ck-out noon. Convention facilities. Business center. In-rm modem link. Gift shop. Coin lndry. Some covered parking. Exercise equipt; sauna. Refrigerators avail. Luxury level. Cr cds: A, C, D, DS, ER, JCB, MC, V.

[icons]

Restaurants

★★ **AARATHI INDIAN CUISINE.** *409 Maple Ave E (22180), approx 2 mi S on VA 123, in Danor Plaza.* 703/938-0100. Hrs: 11:30 am-2:30 pm, 5:30-10 pm; Fri, Sat to 10:30 pm. Closed July 4, Dec 25. Res accepted; required Fri, Sat dinner. Indian menu. Serv bar. Semi-a la carte: lunch $4.95-$8.50, dinner $4.95-$12.95. Lunch buffet $6.95. Specializes in tandoori, curry and vegetarian dishes. Cr cds: A, C, D, DS, MC, V.

[icons]

★★ **BISTRO 123.** *246 E Maple Ave (22180), 2 mi N of I-66 exit 62.* 703/938-4379. Hrs: 11:30 am-2 pm, 5:30-10 pm; Fri to 10:30 pm; Sat 5:30-10:30 pm. Closed Sun. Res accepted. French menu. Bar. Semi-a la carte: lunch $3.50-$9.95, dinner from $11.95. Complete meals: dinner $34.95. Specialties: pate, lobster bisque, beef. Own desserts. Parking. Outdoor dining. Cr cds: A, C, D, MC, V.

★★ **BONAROTI.** *428 Maple Ave E (22180), 3 mi W on I-495 on VA 123, in Wolf Trappe Shopping Center.* 703/281-7550. Hrs: 11:30 am-3 pm, 5-10:30 pm; Sat 5-11 pm. Closed Sun; some major hols. Res accepted. Italian menu. Bar. Semi-a la carte: lunch $8.95-$13.95, dinner $13.95-$22.95. Child's meals. Specializes in veal, pasta, seafood. Own pastries, pasta. Italian art. Totally nonsmoking. Cr cds: A, C, D, MC, V.

✓★★ **CLYDE'S.** 8332 Leesburg Pike (22182), 10 blks W of I-495 exit 10B on VA 7, then right. 703/734-1901. Web www.clydes.com. Hrs: 11-2 am; Sun brunch 10 am-4 pm. Res accepted. Bar. A la carte entrees: lunch $4.95-$10.95, dinner $6.50-$15.50. Child's meals. Specializes in pasta, seafood, sandwiches. Parking. Original art collection. Cr cds: A, C, D, DS, MC, V.

D SC ⊡

★★ **DA DOMENICO.** 1992 Chain Bridge Rd (22102), 2 blks W of I-495 exit 11B. 703/790-9000. Hrs: 11:30 am-11 pm; Sat from 5 pm. Closed Sun; major hols. Res accepted; required Fri, Sat. Northern Italian menu. Bar. Semi-a la carte: lunch $7.95-$9.95, dinner $9.95-$23.95. Specializes in veal chop, seafood, fresh pasta. Parking. Italian garden decor. Cr cds: A, C, D, DS, MC, V.

⊡

★★ **FEDORA CAFE.** 8521 Leesburg Pike (22182). 703/556-0100. E-mail fedora@erols.com. Hrs: 11:30 am-10:30 pm; Fri, Sat to 11 pm; Sun 10:30 am-2 pm, 4:30-9:30 pm. Res accepted. Bar to 12:30 am. Semi-a la carte: lunch $6.95-$11.95, dinner $8.95-$22.95. Specialties: rotisserie chicken, spit-roasted duck, fresh fish. Own pasta, desserts. Pianist Wed-Fri. Cr cds: A, C, D, DS, MC, V.

D ⊡

★★ **HUNAN LION.** 2070 Chain Bridge Rd (22182), S of I-495 on VA 123, I-495 exit 11B, third light on right. 703/734-9828. Hrs: 11:30 am-10:30 pm; Fri, Sat to 11 pm. Closed Thanksgiving. Res accepted. Chinese menu. Bar. Semi-a la carte: lunch $6-$8, dinner $6-$10.50. Specialties: triple delicacy prawns, orange beef, General Tso's chicken. Parking. Cr cds: A, C, D, DS, MC, V.

D ⊡

★★ **JR'S GOODTIMES.** 8130 Watson St (22102), ½ mi W of I-495 exit 10B. 703/821-0546. E-mail steaks@jrsbeef.com; web www.jrsbeef.com. Hrs: 11:30 am-3 pm, 5-10:30 pm; Fri to 11 pm; Sat 5-11 pm; Sun 5-9 pm. Closed July 4, Thanksgiving, Dec 24, 25. Res accepted; required Fri, Sat. Bar. Semi-a la carte: lunch $5.95-$9.50, dinner $13.50-$19.95. Specializes in sirloin, prime aged beef, fresh seafood. Parking. Western-style chop house. Cr cds: A, C, D, DS, MC, V.

⊡

★★★ **LA PROVENCE.** 144 W Maple Ave (22180), 2½ mi W on VA 123. 703/242-3777. Hrs: 11:30 am-2:30 pm, 5:30-10 pm. Closed Sun; most major hols. Res accepted; required Fri, Sat dinner. French Provençale menu. Serv bar. Wine list. Semi-a la carte: lunch $9.95-$12.95, dinner $15.95-$22.95. Specialties: bouillabaisse, duck confit. Own baking. Large flower murals. Totally nonsmoking. Cr cds: A, C, D, DS, MC, V.

★★★ **LE CANARD.** 132 Branch Rd (22180), VA 123 at Branch Rd, in Danor Shopping Center. 703/281-0070. E-mail http://tigerspaw.com/bite/lecanard.htm; web www.erols.com/bitebyte/lecanard.htm. Hrs: 11:30 am-2:30 pm, 5:30-10:30 pm; Fri to 11 pm; Sat 5:30-11 pm; Sun from 5:30 pm. Res accepted; required Fri, Sat. French menu. Bar to 2 am. Wine list. Semi-a la carte: lunch $9.95-$11.25, dinner $15.95-$24.95. Specializes in fresh seafood, veal, beef. Own pastries. Piano bar. Cr cds: A, C, D, DS, MC, V.

D ⊡

★★ **MARCO POLO.** 245 Maple Ave W (22180), 2½ mi N of I-66 exit 62. 703/281-3922. Hrs: 11:30 am-10:30 pm; Fri, Sat to 11 pm; early-bird dinner Thurs 5:30-7:30 pm. Closed Sun exc Mother's Day. Res accepted. Continental, Northern Italian menu. Serv bar. Semi-a la carte: lunch $6-$9, dinner $11-$18. Buffet: lunch (Tues-Fri) $8.25, dinner (Thurs) $14.50. Specializes in fresh seafood, fresh pasta, veal. Parking. Cr cds: A, C, D, MC, V.

D ⊡

✓★★ **MASQUERADE.** 8601 Westwood Center Dr (22180), I-495 exit 10B, then 2½ mi W on VA 7. 703/848-9476. E-mail kaboudan@aol.com. Hrs: 11 am-11 pm; Fri, Sat to 1 am; Sun from 10:30 am; Sun brunch to 2:30 pm. Res accepted. Contemporary Amer menu. Bar. Semi-a la carte: lunch $6.50-$12.95, dinner $8.95-$16.95. Sun brunch $6.95-$10.95. Child's meals. Specializes in salads, sandwiches, grilled dishes. Parking. Patio dining. Take-out gourmet market. Cr cds: A, C, D, DS, MC, V.

D ⊡

★★★ **MORTON'S OF CHICAGO.** 8075 Leesburg Pike (22182), I-495 exit 10W, then ¼ mi W on VA 7 (Leesburg Pike) on left. 703/883-0800. Web www.mortons.com. Hrs: 11 am-2:30 pm, 5:30-11 pm; Sat from 5:30 pm; Sun 5-10 pm. Closed major hols. Res accepted; required Thurs-Sat. Bar. Wine list. A la carte: lunch $8-$19.95, dinner $19.95-$29.95. Specializes in steak, seafood. Valet parking. Jacket. Cr cds: A, C, D, JCB, MC, V.

D ⊡

★★★ **NIZAM'S RESTAURANT.** 523 Maple Ave W (22180), in Village Green Shopping Ctr. 703/938-8948. Hrs: 11 am-3 pm, 5-10 pm; Sat 5-11 pm; Sun 4-9 pm. Closed Mon; also Jan 1, Thanksgiving, Dec 25. Res accepted; required Fri, Sat. Turkish menu. Serv bar. Semi-a la carte: lunch $5.25-$10.50, dinner $11.95-$17.50. Specializes in beef, lamb, chicken. Turkish artwork. Totally nonsmoking. Cr cds: A, C, DS, MC, V.

D

✓★★ **PANJSHIR II.** 224 W Maple Ave (22180), 3 mi W on I-495, exit 10B on VA 123. 703/281-4183. Hrs: 11:30 am-2 pm, 5-10 pm; Sun 5-9 pm. Closed Jan 1, July 4, Thanksgiving. Res accepted. Afghan menu. Bar. Semi-a la carte: lunch $5.95-$7.25, dinner $9.95-$13.25. Specializes in kebabs, saffron rice, vegetarian dishes. Parking. Cr cds: A, C, D, MC, V.

D ⊡

★★ **PHILLIPS SEAFOOD GRILL.** 8330 Boone Blvd (22182), approx 2 mi S on VA 123, I-495 exit 10A. 703/442-0400. Web www.phillips.com. Hrs: 11:30 am-9 pm; wkends to 10 pm. Closed Dec 25. Res accepted; required Fri, Sat dinner. Bar. Semi-a la carte: lunch $5.95-$9.95, dinner $12.99-$25.99. Prix fixe: lunch, dinner $15.99-$21.99. Child's meals. Specialties: crab cakes, free-range chicken, raw bar. Parking. Outdoor dining. Hickory wood-burning grills. Family-owned. Cr cds: A, C, D, DS, MC, V.

D SC ⊡

★★★ **PRIMI PIATTI.** 8045 Leesburg Pike (22182), W of I-495 exit 10 W B. 703/893-0300. Web www.sidewalk.com. Hrs: 11:30 am-2:30 pm, 5:30-10 pm; Fri to 10:30 pm; Sat 5:30-10:30 pm. Closed Sun; most major hols. Res accepted; required Fri, Sat. Italian menu. Bar. Semi-a la carte: lunch $9-$14.95, dinner $11-$23. Specializes in contemporary Italian cuisine. Valet parking. Outdoor dining. Cr cds: A, C, D, JCB, MC, V.

D

★★ **TARA THAI.** 226 Maple Ave W (22180), approx 2 mi S on VA 123, 2 mi N I-66 exit 62. 703/255-2467. Web www.tarathai.com. Hrs: 11:30 am-3 pm, 5-10 pm; Fri to 11 pm; Sat noon-3:30 pm, 5-11 pm; Sun noon-3:30 pm, 5-10 pm. Closed Dec 25. Res accepted; required Fri, Sat dinner. Thai menu. Bar. Semi-a la carte: lunch $3.95-$7.95, dinner $6.95-$12.95. Specializes in fresh seafood, grilled fish. Parking. Underwater ocean decor. Totally nonsmoking. Cr cds: A, C, D, DS, MC, V.

D

★★ **THAT'S AMORE.** 150 Branch Rd SE (22180), approx 2 mi S on VA 123, I-495 exit 11B. 703/281-7777. Hrs: 11:30 am-10:30 pm; Fri to midnight; Sat 4 pm-midnight; Sun 4-9:30 pm. Closed Labor Day, Thanksgiving, Dec 25. Italian menu. Bar. A la carte entrees: lunch $5.95-$9.95, dinner $15-$38. Specializes in pasta, seafood, chicken. Parking. Cr cds: A, C, D, DS, MC, V.

D ⊡

★ ★ ★ **THE RESTAURANT.** *(See The Ritz-Carlton Tysons Corner Hotel)* 703/506-4300. Hrs: 6:30 am-10 pm; Sat, Sun brunch 11 am-2:30 pm; Sun 1-4:30 pm; Sun brunch 11 am-2:30 pm. Res accepted. Wine list. Semi-a la carte: breakfast $9-$16, lunch $9-$24. A la carte entrees: dinner $18-$40. Sun brunch $45. Child's meals. Specializes in seafood, lamb chops, prime aged beef. Harpist. Valet parking. Cr cds: A, C, D, DS, JCB, MC, V.

⊡ ⬛

✓ ★ **WU'S GARDEN.** *418 Maple Ave E (22180), 3 mi W off I-495 exit 11A.* 703/281-4410. Hrs: 11:30 am-10 pm; Sat noon-11 pm. Closed Thanksgiving. Res accepted. Chinese menu. Bar. Semi-a la carte: lunch $4-$7, dinner $7.95-$12. Specialties: Kung Pao chicken, crispy shrimp with walnuts. Parking. Oriental screens and artwork. Cr cds: A, C, D, DS, MC, V.

⊡ ⬛

Virginia Beach (F-10)

(See also Chesapeake, Hampton, Newport News, Norfolk, Portsmouth)

Pop 393,069 **Elev** 12 ft **Area Code** 757 **E-mail** vabvic@exis.net **Web** www.city.virginia-beach.va.us

Information Visitor Information Center, 2100 Parks Ave, 23451; 757/437-4882 or 800/446-8038

For those who seek year-round recreation, Virginia Beach is the answer. A renovated resort area with a three-mile boardwalk and 28 miles of oceanfront and bay beaches offer visitors myriad activities: surfing, swimming, fishing, boating, waterskiing, in-line skating; bowling, tennis, golf, bicycling; amusement park and arcade games.

After a full day, there's nothing like dinner and a night out. Virginia Beach delivers with many fine restaurants serving fresh seafood, and nightclubs, concerts and theaters catering to all musical tastes. With activities for all ages and hundreds of places to stay in all price ranges, Virginia Beach is one of the most popular resorts on the East Coast.

What to See and Do

Adam Thoroughgood House (ca 1680). One of the oldest remaining brick houses in US; restored, furnished; restored gardens. (Apr-Dec, daily exc Mon; rest of yr, Tues-Sat; closed some major hols) 1636 Parish Rd. Phone 757/460-0007. ¢¢

Association for Research and Enlightenment. Headquarters for study and research of work of psychic Edgar Cayce. Visitor Center has bookstore, library, displays, ESP-testing machine, movie and daily lecture. (Daily; closed Thanksgiving, Dec 25) 67th St & Atlantic Ave. Phone 757/428-3588. **Free**

Contemporary Art Center of Virginia. This 32,000-sq-ft facility is devoted to presentation of 20th-century art through exhibitions, education, performing arts and special events. (Daily; closed major hols) 2200 Parks Ave. Phone 757/425-0000. **Free**

Discovery **Sightseeing Cruise.** Lunch, dinner and sightseeing cruises aboard 80-foot luxury yacht. Reservations required. (May-Oct, daily) 600 Laskin Rd. Phone 757/491-8090 or 757/422-2900. ¢¢¢¢

First Landing/Seashore State Park. More than 2,700 acres with lagoons, cypress trees and sand dunes. Swimming at own risk; fishing; boating (ramp). Hiking, bicycle and self-guided nature trails. Picnicking. Tent & trailer sites (Mar-Nov; fee); 20 cabins (May-Sept). Visitor center, interpretive programs. Access for disabled to nature trail. (Daily) Standard fees. 5 mi N on US 60 at Cape Henry. Phone 757/412-2300. Seasonal parking fee ¢¢

Fishing. In the Lynnhaven and Rudee Inlets for channel bass, speckled trout, spots, croakers, flounder and whiting in season; in the Back Bay area, 18 mi S on VA 615, for largemouth black bass, pickerel and perch. Pier fishing and surf casting from piers jutting into the Atlantic and piers in the Chesapeake Bay. Reef, deep-sea and Gulf Stream fishing from char-

ter boats, for sea bass, weakfish, flounder, cobia, bonito, tuna, marlin, false albacore, blue and dolphin. Lake and stream fishing at Lake Smith, Lake Christine and the inland waterways of the Chesapeake and Albemarle Canal. Crabbing for blue crabs in Lynnhaven waters, Linkhorn Bay and Rudee Inlet. (No license or closed season for saltwater fishing.)

Francis Land House Historic Site and Gardens. Late-18th-century-plantation home features period rooms, special exhibits, gardens and museum gift shop. (Tues-Sat, also Sun afternoons; closed major hols) 3131 Virginia Beach Blvd, on the S side of the boulevard, just E of the Princess Anne Plaza Shopping Center. Phone 757/431-4000. ¢¢

Lynnhaven House (ca 1725). This stately story-and-a-half masonry structure is a well-preserved example of 18th-century architecture and decorative arts. (Limited hrs, phone 757/460-1688. ¢¢

Norwegian Lady Statue. A gift to Virginia Beach from the people of Moss, Norway. The statue commemorates the tragic wreck of the Norwegian bark *Dictator* off the shores of Virginia Beach in 1891. 25th St & Boardwalk.

Ocean Breeze Fun Park. Family fun park includes MotorWorld, with various driving tracks; Wild Water Rapids, a water park with slides, wave pool, rapids, and children's water amusements (late May-early Sept); Shipwreck Golf miniature-golf course; Strike Zone batting cages. (Memorial Day-Labor Day, daily; mid-Apr-May & Sept-Oct, wkends). 849 General Booth Blvd. Phone 757/422-4444 (recording) or 800/678-WILD. Combination ticket ¢¢¢¢¢

Old Cape Henry Lighthouse and Memorial Park. First US-government-built lighthouse (ca 1791). On Fort Story, an active army base. 6 mi N on US 60.

Old Coast Guard Station. Former Life-Saving/Coast Guard Station (1903); visual exhibits of numerous shipwrecks along the Virginia coastline tell of past bravery and disaster. "The War Years" exhibit relates United States Coast Guard efforts during World Wars I and II. Photographs, ship models, artifacts. Gift shop. (Memorial Day-Sept, daily; rest of yr, daily exc Mon; closed Jan 1, Thanksgiving, Dec 25, 31) 24th St & Atlantic Ave. Phone 757/422-1587. ¢¢

Virginia Marine Science Museum. Live animals, interactive exhibits, 6-story screen, 300-seat **IMAX 3-D** theater. Exhibits include ocean aquarium with sharks, large fish; sea turtle aquarium; seal and other habitats; aviary; salt-marsh preserve; touch tank; river room; garden. (Daily; closed Thanksgiving, Dec 25) 717 General Booth Blvd, 2 mi S of resort area. Phone 757/425-FISH. ¢¢¢

Annual Events

Pungo Strawberry Festival. Sat & Sun of Memorial Day wkend.

Boardwalk Art Show. Works by more than 350 artists from US and abroad. 10 days mid-June.

East Coast Surfing Championship. 4th wkend Aug.

Neptune Festival. Last 2 wks Sept.

Seasonal Events

Winter whale-watching boat trips. Phone 757/437-4882. Daily exc Tues, Thurs. Jan-Mar.

Virginia Saltwater Fishing Tournament. The Commonwealth of Virginia sponsors this annual Saltwater Fishing Awards Program. No entry fee or registration requirements; open to everyone who fishes in tournament waters and complies with tournament rules. For information about this program contact Virginia Saltwater Fishing Tournament, 968 S Oriole Dr, Ste 102, 23451; 757/491-5160. Mar-Dec.

Motels

★ ★ **COURTYARD BY MARRIOTT.** *5700 Greenwich Rd (23462).* 757/490-2002; FAX 757/490-0169; res: 800/321-2211. 146 rms, 3 story. Memorial Day-Labor Day: S, D $75-$99; suites $110-$120; under 12 free; wkly, wkend rates; lower rates rest of yr. Crib free. TV; cable (premium). Pool; whirlpool. Coffee in rms. Bar. Ck-out noon. Business servs avail. In-rm modem link. Valet serv. Exercise equipt. Some refrigerators. Cr cds: A, C, D, DS, JCB, MC, V.

✓★★ **FAIRFIELD INN BY MARRIOTT.** *4760 Euclid Rd (23462). 757/499-1935; FAX 757/499-1935; res: 800/228-2800.* 134 rms, 3 story. Mid-May-Labor Day: S, D $62-$95; under 18 free; lower rates rest of yr. Crib free. TV; cable (premium). Pool. Complimentary continental bkfst. Restaurants nearby. Ck-out noon. Business servs avail. In-rm modem link. Cr cds: A, C, D, DS, MC, V.

⊡ ⩫ ⊠ ⚑ SC

✓★★ **HAMPTON INN.** *5793 Greenwich Rd (23462). 757/490-9800; FAX 757/490-3573; res: 800/426-7866.* 122 rms, 4 story. June-Aug: S $64-$76; D $66-$76; under 18 free; higher rates special events; lower rates rest of yr. Crib free. TV; cable (premium). Pool. Complimentary continental bkfst. Coffee in rms. Restaurant adj 6:30 am-11 pm. Ck-out noon. Meeting rm. Business servs avail. In-rm modem link. Exercise equipt. Microwaves avail. Cr cds: A, C, D, DS, MC, V.

⊡ ⩫ 🏋 ⊠ ⚑ SC

★★ **SEA GULL MOTEL.** *2613 Atlantic Ave (23451), on oceanfront. 757/425-5711; FAX 757/425-5710; res: 800/426-4855.* E-mail seagullmotel@worldnet.att.net; web www.vabeach.com/seagull. 51 units, 4 story, 9 kit units. Memorial Day-Labor Day: S, D $120-$138; each addl $10; kit units $130-$155; family, wkly rates; lower rates rest of yr. Crib $5. TV; cable (premium). Indoor pool; whirlpool, poolside serv. Restaurant 7 am-10 pm, seasonal. Rm serv. Bar. Ck-out 11 am. Business servs avail. Refrigerators. On ocean, swimming beach. Cr cds: C, DS, MC, V.

⩫ ⊠ ⚑ SC

Motor Hotels

★★ **COMFORT INN.** *2015 Atlantic Ave (23451). 757/425-8200; FAX 757/425-6521; res: 800/228-5150.* Web www.vbeach.com/hotels/comfort.html. 83 kit suites, 10 story. Mid-June-mid-Aug: S, D $165-$225; each addl $10; under 12 free; lower rates rest of yr. Crib free. TV; cable (premium). Indoor pool; whirlpool. Complimentary continental bkfst. Restaurant adj 6:30 am-10 pm. Ck-out 11 am. Business center. In-rm modem link. Bellhops. Exercise equipt. Refrigerators, microwaves. Private patios. On ocean. Cr cds: A, C, D, DS, ER, JCB, MC, V.

⊡ ⩫ 🏋 ⊠ ⚑ SC 🏃

★★ **COMFORT INN.** *2800 Pacific Ave (23451). 757/428-2203; FAX 757/422-6043; res: 800/441-0684.* E-mail comfortinn@va-beach.com; web www.va-beach.com/comfortinn. 135 rms, 7 story. Memorial Day-Labor Day: S, D $109-$159; each addl $10; under 15 free; family rates; lower rates rest of yr. Crib free. TV; cable (premium). Indoor/outdoor pool; whirlpool. Complimentary continental bkfst. Restaurant opp 11 am-11 pm. Ck-out 11 am. Coin Indry. Meeting rms. Business servs avail. In-rm modem link. Bellhops. Valet serv. Exercise equipt. Game rm. Some refrigerators; microwaves avail. Cr cds: A, C, D, DS, ER, JCB, MC, V.

⊡ ⩫ 🏋 ⊠ ⚑ SC

★★ **DAYS INN.** *3107 Atlantic Ave (23451). 757/428-7233; FAX 757/491-1936; res: 800/292-3297.* 121 units, 8 story. Late June-early Sept: S, D $135-$225; each addl $10; under 12 free; golf plans; lower rates rest of yr. Crib free. Pet accepted; $10. TV; cable (premium). Indoor pool; whirlpool. Restaurant 7-11 am, noon-2 pm, 6-10 pm. Rm serv. Bar from 5 pm. Ck-out 11 am. Coin Indry. Meeting rms. Business servs avail. In-rm modem link. Golf privileges. Some refrigerators; microwaves avail. Balconies. On ocean; beach. Cr cds: A, C, D, DS, MC, V.

⊡ ⩫ 🐕 ⊠ ⊠ ⚑ SC

★★★ **HILTON.** *705 Atlantic Ave (23451). 757/428-8935; FAX 757/425-2769; res: 800/445-8667.* Web www.vabeach-hotels.com/hiltoninn. 120 rms, 6 story. Memorial Day-Labor Day: S $165; D $175; each addl $10; under 18 free; lower rates rest of yr. Crib free. TV; cable (premium), VCR avail. Indoor/outdoor pool; whirlpool, poolside serv. Coffee in rms. Restaurant 7 am-midnight. Rm serv to 10 pm. Bar noon-1:30 am. Ck-

out 11 am. Meeting rms. Business servs avail. In-rm modem link. Bellhops. Valet serv. Exercise equipt; sauna. Lawn games. On ocean; beach. Cr cds: A, C, D, DS, ER, MC, V.

⩫ 🏋 ⊠ ⚑ SC

★★★ **HOLIDAY INN.** *5655 Greenwich Rd (23451), near Norfolk Intl Airport. 757/499-4400; FAX 757/473-0517; res: 800/567-3856.* E-mail hiexec@erols.com; web www.confnet.holiday-inn.com. 328 rms, 6 story. S, D $99-$129; suites $289. Crib free. TV; cable (premium). 2 pools, 1 indoor; whirlpool. Complimentary coffee in rms. Restaurant 6:30 am-10 pm. Rm serv. Bar 11 am-10 pm. Ck-noon. Convention facilities. Business servs avail. In-rm modem link. Bellhops. Concierge. Valet serv. Free airport transportation. Exercise equipt; sauna. Cr cds: A, C, D, DS, ER, JCB, MC, V.

⊡ ⩫ 🏋 ✈ ⊠ ⚑ SC

★★★ **HOLIDAY INN.** *2607 Atlantic Ave (23451). 757/491-6900; FAX 757/491-2125; res: 800/465-4329.* E-mail surfside@vabeach.com; web www.va-beach.com/surfside. 143 rms, 10 story, 18 kit suites. Mid-June-Labor Day: S, D $159-$199; each addl $10; kit suites $199-$219; under 17 free; family rates; wkly rates; higher rates special events. Crib free. TV; cable (premium). Indoor pool; whirlpool. Complimentary coffee in rms. Restaurant 7 am-10 pm. Rm serv. Bar 5-10 pm. Ck-out 11 am. Meeting rms. Business servs avail. In-rm modem link. Bellhops. Valet serv. Coin Indry. Exercise equipt. Refrigerators; some in-rm whirlpools, microwaves. Balconies. On beach. Cr cds: A, C, D, DS, ER, JCB, MC, V.

⊡ 🛥 ⩫ 🏋 ⊠ ⚑ SC

✓★★★ **HOLIDAY INN.** *3900 Atlantic Ave (23451). 757/428-1711; FAX 757/425-5742; res: 800/942-3224.* E-mail sunspree@vabeach.com; web www.vabeach.com/sunspree. 266 rms, 7 story, 55 kits. Mid-June-Labor Day: S, D $149-$189; suites $184-$249; each addl $10; under 19 free. Crib free. TV; cable (premium). Indoor/outdoor pool; poolside serv (summer). Free supervised child's activities (Memorial Day-Labor Day); ages 3-12. Complimentary coffee in rms. Restaurant 6:30 am-2 pm, 5-11 pm (in season), to 10 pm rest of yr. Rm serv. Bar 4-11 pm. Ck-out 11 am. Meeting rms. Business servs avail. Bellhops. Gift shop. Exercise equipt. Refrigerators. Balconies. On ocean. Cr cds: A, C, D, DS, ER, JCB, MC, V.

⊡ ⩫ 🏋 ⊠ ⚑ SC

★★★ **HOLIDAY INN.** *21st & Atlantic Ave (23451). 757/491-1500; FAX 757/491-1945; res: 800/465-4329.* E-mail oceansid@va-beach.com; web www.vabeach.com/oceansid. 150 rms, 12 story. June-Sept: S, D $99-$199; each addl $10; under 18 free; lower rates rest of yr. TV; cable (premium). Indoor pool; whirlpool. Coffee in rms. Restaurant 6:30 am-10 pm. Rm serv. Bar 11 am-10 pm. Ck-out 11 am. Meeting rms. Business servs avail. In-rm modem link. Bellhops. Refrigerators; microwaves avail. Balconies. On ocean; swimming beach. Cr cds: A, C, D, DS, JCB, MC, V.

⊡ 🛥 ⩫ ⊠ ⚑ SC

Hotels

★★★ **CLARION HOTEL PEMBROKE.** *4453 Bonney Rd (23462), VA 44 exit Independence 3B, right on Bonney Rd. 757/473-1700; FAX 757/552-0477; res: 800/847-5202.* 149 rms, 8 story. Memorial Day-Labor Day: S, D $89-$159; each addl $10; suites, studio rms $109-$159; under 12 free; lower rates rest of yr. Crib free. TV; cable (premium). Indoor pool; whirlpool, poolside serv. Complimentary coffee in rms. Restaurant 6:30-10:30 pm; Sat, Sun 7:30-11:30 pm. Bars 5-10 pm. Meeting rms. Business center. In-rm modem link. Exercise equipt; sauna. Some refrigerators, microwaves. Cr cds: A, C, D, DS, ER, JCB, MC, V.

⊡ ⩫ 🏋 ⊠ ⚑ SC 🏃

✓★★★ **DOUBLETREE HOTEL.** *1900 Pavilion Dr (23451). 757/422-8900; FAX 757/425-8460; res: 800/333-3333.* 292 rms, 12 story. Late May-early Sept: S, D $159; each addl $10; suites $165-$395; under 17 free; wkend rates; lower rates rest of yr. Crib free. TV; cable (premium). Indoor pool. Restaurant 6:30 am-2 pm, 5-10 pm. Bar from 4 pm; entertainment. Ck-out 11 am. Convention facilities. Business center. In-rm modem link. Gift shop. Tennis. Exercise equipt; sauna, steam rm. Some refrigerators. Cr cds: A, C, D, DS, ER, JCB, MC, V.

★★ **ECONO LODGE.** *2109 Atlantic Ave (23451).* 757/428-2403; FAX 757/422-2530; res: 800/999-3630. E-mail econo-lodge@va-beach.com; web www.va-beach.com/econo-lodge. 55 rms, 10 story. Memorial Day-Labor Day: S, D $120-$189; each addl $8; kit units $149-$199; under 18 free; lower rates rest of yr. Crib free. TV; cable (premium). Indoor pool. Ck-out 11 am. Business servs avail. In-rm modem link. Free garage parking. Cr cds: A, C, D, DS, ER, JCB, MC, V.

★★★ **FOUNDERS INN & CONFERENCE CENTER.** *5641 Indian River Rd (23464).* 757/424-5511; FAX 757/366-0613; res: 800/926-4466. E-mail founders.inn@cbn.org; web www.foundersinn.com. 249 rms. Memorial Day-Labor Day: S, D $89-$159; each addl $15; suites $159-$700; lower rates rest of yr; family, wkly rates; golf plans. Crib free. TV; cable (premium), VCR avail (movies). 2 pools, 1 indoor; lifeguard (summer). Playground. Supervised child's activities (Memorial Day-Labor Day); ages 3-17. Restaurant 6 am-10 pm; dinner theatre. Rm serv to 11 pm. Ck-out noon. Meeting rms. Business center. In-rm modem link. Concierge. Shopping arcade. Free valet parking. Free airport, bus depot transportation. Lighted tennis, pro. Golf privileges, greens fee $29-59, pro. Exercise rm; sauna. Indoor racquetball court. Lawn games. Bicycle rentals. Bathrm phones, refrigerators. Balconies. Picnic tables. Cr cds: A, C, D, DS, MC, V.

★★★ **OCEAN'S INN.** *2207 Atlantic Ave (23451).* 757/428-5141; FAX 757/422-8436. 111 rms, 14 story. Late May-Labor Day: S, D $130-$142; each addl $8; under 12 free; higher rates Memorial Day wkend; lower rates rest of yr. Crib free. TV; cable (premium). Heated pool; whirlpool. Restaurant 7 am-11 pm (seasonal). Bar 11-2 am. Ck-out 11 am. Business servs avail. In-rm modem link. Coin lndry. Airport transportation. Refrigerators; some microwaves. Private patios; balconies. On beach. Cr cds: A, C, D, DS, ER, JCB, MC, V.

★★★ **RAMADA PLAZA.** *5700 Atlantic Ave (23451).* 757/428-7025; FAX 757/428-2921; res: 800/272-6232. 216 rms, 17 story. May-Sept: S, D $165-$210; suites $230-$280; each addl $10; under 18 free; lower rates rest of yr. TV; cable (premium), VCR avail. Indoor/outdoor pool; whirlpool, poolside serv, lifeguard in season. Supervised child's activities (mid-June-Labor Day); ages 5-11. Coffee in rms. Restaurant 7 am-10 pm. Bar 3 pm-1 am. Ck-out 11 am. Meeting rms. Business center. In-rm modem link. Concierge. Gift shop. Exercise equipt; sauna. Many refrigerators, microwaves. Balconies. On ocean; oceanfront deck, swimming beach. Most rms with ocean view. Luxury level. Video games. Cr cds: A, C, D, DS, ER, JCB, MC, V.

★★★ **VIRGINIA BEACH RESORT HOTEL.** *2800 Shore Dr (23451).* 757/481-9000; FAX 757/496-7429; res: 800/468-2722. E-mail vb-resort@vabeach.com; web www.vabeach.com/va_resort. 295 suites, 8 story. Memorial Day-Labor Day: S, D $165-$344; each addl $10; under 18 free; lower rates rest of yr. Crib free. TV; cable (premium). Indoor/outdoor pool; whirlpool, poolside serv. Supervised child's activities (Memorial Day-Labor Day); ages 4-14. Coffee in rms. Restaurant 6:30 am-11 pm. Bar. Ck-out 11 am. Coin lndry. Convention facilities. Business center. In-rm modem link. Gift shop. Airport, bus depot transportation. Tennis privileges. Golf privileges. Exercise equipt; sauna. Private beach. Bicycles. Refrigerators, microwaves. Balconies. On bay. Cr cds: A, C, D, DS, MC, V.

Inn

★★★ **CHURCH POINT MANOR HOUSE.** *4001 16th St (19710).* 757/460-2657. E-mail cpmanor@aol.com; web www.symweb.com/churchpoint. 10 rms, 6 with shower only, 3 story. Mid-May-mid-Oct: S,

D, guest house $125-$175; each addl $25; lower rates rest of yr. Crib free. TV; cable, VCR avail (movies). Pool. Complimentary full bkfst. Ck-out 11 am, ck-in 3 pm. Luggage handling. Tennis. Bicycles. Game rm. Lawn games. Canoes. Some fireplaces. Some balconies. Picnic tables, grills. Farmhouse built in 1860s; art and antiques. Totally nonsmoking. Cr cds: A, C, D, DS, MC, V.

Restaurants

★★ **ALDO'S RISTORANTE.** *1860 Laskin Rd (23454),* at La Promenade shopping center. 757/491-1111. Hrs: 11 am-11 pm; Fri, Sat to 12:30 am; Sun 4-11 pm. Closed Thanksgiving, Dec 25. Res accepted. Italian menu. Bar. A la carte entrees: lunch, dinner $4.99-$27. Child's meals. Specializes in seafood, pizza. Entertainment Tues-Sat. Outdoor dining. Contemporary decor. Cr cds: A, C, MC, V.

★★ **BLUE PETE'S SEAFOOD & STEAK.** *1400 N Muddy Creek Rd (23456).* 757/426-2005. E-mail soundwavz@series2000.com; web www.bluepetes.com. Hrs: 6-10 pm. Closed Sun. Bar. Semi-a la carte: dinner $7.50-$29.95. Child's meals. Specializes in fresh seafood, biscuits, Angus steak. Own desserts. Parking. Outdoor dining. Located on creek in wooded area. Cr cds: A, C, D, MC, V.

★★ **COASTAL GRILL.** *1427 N Great Neck Rd (23454).* 757/496-3348. Hrs: 5:30-11 pm; Sat 5 pm-midnight; Sun 5-9:30 pm. Closed most major hols. Bar. A la carte entrees: dinner $3.95-$17.95. Child's meals. Specializes in fresh fish, chicken. Parking. Cr cds: A, C, MC, V.

★★ **HENRY'S PLANET SEAFOOD.** *3319 Shore Dr (23451),* at US 60 & E end of Lessner Bridge. 757/481-7300. Hrs: 11-2 am; Nov-Mar 5-11 pm; Sun brunch 10 am-2 pm. Res accepted. Bar. Semi-a la carte: lunch $3.95-$9.95, dinner $9.95-$24.95. Sun brunch $9.95. Child's meals. Specializes in fresh seafood. Lobster tank. Raw bar. Valet parking. Outdoor dining. On Lynnhaven Inlet; 2-story saltwater aquarium in dining area. Cr cds: A, C, D, DS, MC, V.

★★ **IL GIARDINO.** *910 Atlantic Ave (23451),* at 10th St. 757/422-6464. Web www.ilgiardino.com. Hrs: 5-11:30 pm; Fri, Sat to midnight. Closed Thanksgiving, Dec 25. Res accepted. Italian menu. Bar. Semi-a la carte: dinner $9.95-$22.95. Child's meals. Specializes in seafood, veal. Entertainment in season. Valet parking. Outdoor dining. Wood-burning pizza oven. Cr cds: A, C, D, DS, MC, V.

★★★ **LA CARAVELLE.** *1040 Laskin Rd (23451),* 5 blks W of oceanfront. 757/428-2477. Hrs: 5:30-10:30 pm. Res accepted; required Fri, Sat. French, Vietnamese menu. Bar. Wine list. Semi-a la carte: dinner $4.95-$23.95. Specializes in seafood, fowl. Pianist Fri, Sat. Parking. Country French decor. Cr cds: A, C, D, DS, MC, V.

★★★ **LE CHAMBORD.** *324 N Great Neck Rd (23454).* 757/498-1234. Hrs: 11:30 am-3 pm, dinner from 6 pm. Closed Jan 1, Dec 25. Res accepted; required wkend. French, continental menu. Bar. Wine list. Semi-a la carte: lunch $5.95-$8.95, dinner $5.95-$22.95. Specialties: rack of lamb, poached salmon, veal tenderloin. Jazz pianist Fri-Sat. Modern Mediterranean-style decor; fireplaces in lounge area, dining rm. Cr cds: A, C, D, DS, MC, V.

✓★★ **LUCKY STAR.** *1608 Pleasure House Rd (23455).* *757/363-8410.* Hrs: 5:30-10 pm. Closed Sun; some major hols. Res accepted; required Fri, Sat. Bar. A la carte entrees: dinner $5.50-$22. Specialties: tuna Stremberg, Chesapeake Bay crab cakes (in season), bayou banana split. Parking. Local artwork. Totally nonsmoking. Cr cds: C.

★★ **LYNNHAVEN FISH HOUSE.** *2350 Starfish Rd (23451), next to Westminster Canterbury.* *757/481-0003.* Hrs: 11:30 am-10:30 pm. Closed Thanksgiving, Dec 25. Bar. A la carte entrees: lunch $5.95-$10.95, dinner $13.95-$21.95. Child's meals. Specializes in seafood. Lobster tank. Valet parking. On Lynnhaven fishing pier. Cr cds: A, C, D, DS, MC, V.

[D] [⊟]

✓★ **PUNGO GRILL.** *1785 Princess Anne Rd (23456).* *757/426-6655.* Hrs: 11 am-8 pm; Fri, Sat to 9:30 pm. Closed Mon; Thanksgiving, Dec 24, 25; also Jan-Feb. Res accepted. Regional Amer, continental menu. Bar. Semi-a la carte: lunch $4.50-$12.50, dinner $8.95-$18.95. Child's meals. Specializes in Cajun soups, homemade desserts. Parking. Outdoor dining. Dining rm on enclosed porch of 1919 Aladdin House. Cr cds: C, DS, MC, V.

[D] [⊟]

★★ **RUDEE'S.** *227 Mediterranean Ave (23451).* *757/425-1777.* E-mail carter@rudees.com; web www.rudees.com. Hrs: 11 am-midnight. Closed Thanksgiving, Dec 25. Bar. Semi-a la carte: lunch $4.95-$28.95. Sun brunch $4.95-$9.95. Child's meals. Specializes in fresh seafood, shrimp, hand-cut steak. Raw bar. Valet parking. Outdoor dining. Nautical decor; casual atmosphere. On inlet; transient slips avail for boats. Cr cds: A, C, D, DS, MC, V.

[D] [⊟]

✓★ **SAN ANTONIO SAM'S.** *604 Norfolk Ave (23451).* *757/491-0263.* Hrs: 4-11 pm. Closed Dec 24, 25. Tex-Mex menu. Bar. Semi-a la carte: dinner $4.99-$14.99. Child's meals. Specializes in fajitas, ribs, chili. Parking. Casual dining rm in renovated 1898 ice house. Cr cds: A, C, D, DS, MC, V.

[⊟]

★★ **TANDOM'S PINE TREE INN.** *2932 Virginia Beach Blvd (23452).* *757/340-3661.* E-mail tandoms@msn.com; web www.tandoms.com. Hrs: 11:30 am-2:30 pm, 5-9 pm; Fri, Sat to 10 pm; Sun 10:30 am-9 pm; Sun brunch to 2:30 pm. Closed Memorial Day, Labor Day. Res accepted. Bar. Semi-a la carte: lunch $4.95-$9.95, dinner $9.95-$19.95. Sun brunch $7.95-$10.95. Child's meals. Specialties: prime rib, veal Oscar. Salad bar. Pianist. Parking. 1930s style. Cr cds: A, C, D, DS, MC, V.

[⊟]

★★ **THE LIGHTHOUSE.** *1st St & Atlantic Ave (23451).* *757/428-7974.* Hrs: noon-9:30 pm; Sat, Sun from 10 am; Sun brunch to 3 pm; early-bird dinner 5-6:30 pm. Res accepted. Bar. Semi-a la carte: lunch $4.95-$18.95, dinner $6.95-$25.95. Sun brunch $17.95. Child's meals. Specialties: she-crab soup, whole lobster, prime rib. Patio dining. View of ocean or inlet. Family-owned. Cr cds: A, C, D, DS, MC, V.

[D] [SC] [⊟]

★ **WATERMAN'S.** *415 Atlantic Ave (23451).* *757/428-3644.* E-mail mike@watermans.com; web www.watermans.com. Hrs: 11 am-10 pm; Fri, Sat to 11 pm. Closed Thanksgiving, Dec 24 evening, 25. Res accepted. Bar to midnight. A la carte entrees: lunch $5.95-$14.95, dinner $5.95-$22.95. Child's meals. Specializes in seafood, beef. Outdoor dining. Two dining areas, with ocean view. Cr cds: A, C, D, DS, MC, V.

[D] [SC] [⊟]

Unrated Dining Spot

CUISINE AND COMPANY. *3004 Pacific Ave.* *757/428-6700.* Hrs: 9 am-8 pm; summer 9 am-9 pm. Closed Jan 1, Thanksgiving, Dec 25. Continental menu. Wine, beer. A la carte entrees: lunch, dinner $1.25-$12. Specializes in pasta, salads, specialty desserts. Parking. Cr cds: A, C, DS, MC, V.

[D] [♥]

Warm Springs (D-5)

(See also Clifton Forge, Covington, Hot Springs, Monterey)

Pop 425 (est) **Elev** 2,260 ft **Area Code** 540 **Zip** 24484

Nestled at the foot of Little Mountain (3,100 ft), the spring wildflowers or groves of fall foliage make Warm Springs a very scenic spot for sightseeing, hiking or taking the waters. Visitors also enjoy walking tours to view the many historic buildings.

Inn

★★★ **INN AT GRIST MILL SQUARE.** *Rte 645 (24484), 2 blks W of US 220, on VA 619.* *540/839-2231;* FAX *540/839-5770.* E-mail grist@va.tds.net; web www.vainns.com/grist.htm. 17 units, 1 & 2 bedrm. S, D $80-$100; inn apt: S $120; D $140; each addl $10; under 12 free; MAP avail. Crib free. TV; cable. Pool. Sauna. Complimentary continental bkfst. Restaurant (see Waterwheel Restaurant). Bar 5-10 pm. Ck-out noon, ck-in 2 pm. Business servs avail. In-rm modem link. Airport transportation. Tennis. 18-hole golf privileges, pro. Downhill ski 5 mi. Refrigerators, some fireplaces. Private patios. Picnic tables. Consists of 5 restored 19th-century buildings. Cr cds: C, DS, MC, V.

[⚓] [🎿] [⛷] [🏊] [🚣] [🔥]

Restaurant

★★★ **WATERWHEEL RESTAURANT.** *(See Inn at Gristmill Square)* *540/839-2231;* FAX *540/839-5770.* E-mail grist@va.tds.net; web www.vainns.com/grist.htm. Hrs: 6-9 pm; Fri, Sat to 10 pm; Sun brunch 11 am-2 pm. Res accepted. Contemporary Amer menu. Bar. Wine list. Semi-a la carte: dinner $18-$24. Specializes in fresh local trout, veal, home-grown vegetables. Own baking. Parking. In grist mill dating from turn of the century. Totally nonsmoking. Cr cds: C, DS, MC, V.

Warrenton (C-8)

(See also Culpeper, Fairfax, Front Royal, Manassas)

Pop 4,830 **Elev** 560 ft **Area Code** 540 **Zip** 20186 **E-mail** visctr@cross link.net **Web** www.virginia.org

Information Warrenton-Fauquier County Visitor Center, 183A Keith St; 540/347-4414 or 800/820-1021

The seat of Fauquier County, Warrenton was named for General Joseph Warren, who fought at Bunker Hill in the Revolutionary War. The town is situated in the valley of the Piedmont near the foothills of the Blue Ridge Mountains and is known for its cattle and Thoroughbred horse farms. Many old buildings and houses provide for an interesting walking tour of the town.

Seasonal Event

Flying Circus. Flying shows of the barnstorming era, from comedy acts to precision and stunt flying. Rides, picnic area. 7 mi S on US 15/29, then 7 mi SE on US 17 near Bealeton. Phone 540/439-8661. Sun. May-Oct.

Motels

★★ **COMFORT INN.** 7379 Comfort Inn Dr (20187), US 29 Bypass N. 540/349-8900; FAX 540/347-5759; res: 800/228-5150. 97 rms. May-Oct: S, D $59-$79; each addl $8; suites $99-$125; under 18 free; mid-wk rates; lower rates rest of yr. Crib free. Pet accepted, some restrictions; $10/day. TV; cable (premium). Pool. Complimentary continental bkfst. Coffee in rms. Ck-out 11 am. Coin lndry. Meeting rm. Business servs avail. In-rm modem link. Exercise equipt. Health club privileges. Refrigerators; microwaves avail. Whirlpool in some suites. Cr cds: A, C, D, DS, MC, V.

★★ **HAMPTON INN.** 501 Blackwell Rd (20186). 540/349-4200; FAX 540/349-0061; res: 800/426-7866. Web www.hampton-inn.com. 101 rms, 2 story. S, D $64-$79; under 18 free. Crib free. Pet accepted. TV; cable (premium), VCR (movies). Pool. Complimentary continental bkfst. Ck-out noon. Meeting rms. Business servs avail. Coin lndry. Exercise equipt. Refrigerators, microwaves avail. Picnic tables, grill. Cr cds: A, C, D, DS, MC, V.

Restaurant

✓★★ **NAPOLEON'S.** 67 Waterloo St (20186). 540/347-1200. Hrs: 11 am-midnight; Fri, Sat to 1 am. Closed Dec 25. Res accepted. Continental menu. Bar. Semi-a la carte: lunch $5.75-$7.95, dinner $9.95-$16.50. Specializes in veal, fresh fish, hand-cut beef. Outdoor dining. Historic 1838 mansion owned by Confederate General Eppa Hunton. Attractive flower gardens. Cr cds: C, DS, MC, V.

Washington (C-7)

(See also Warrenton)

Founded 1796 **Pop** 198 **Elev** 690 ft **Area Code** 540 **Zip** 22747

The oldest of more than 25 American towns to be named after the first president, this town was surveyed in 1749 by none other than George Washington himself. The streets remain laid out exactly as surveyed, and still bear the names of families who owned the land on which the town was founded. It is romantically rumored that Gay St was named by the 17-year-old Washington after the lovely Gay Fairfax.

The town, seat of Rappahannock County, is situated in the foothills of the Blue Ridge Mountains, which dominate the western horizon.

Inns

★★★ **BLEU ROCK INN.** 12567 Lee Hwy (22747), on US 211. 540/987-3190; FAX 540/987-3193. Web www.innsandouts.com\bleu_rock_inn. 5 rms, 2 story. No rm phones. S, D $125-$195. Closed Mon, Tues; Jan 1, Dec 24, 25. Complimentary full bkfst. Restaurant (see Bleu Rock Inn). Ck-out 11 am, ck-in 3 pm. Business servs avail. Balconies. Restored farmhouse (1899) on lake; rustic setting; vineyard. Cr cds: A, C, D, DS, MC, V.

★★★ **MIDDLETON INN.** 176 Main St (22747). 540/675-2020; FAX 540/675-1050; res: 800/816-8157. E-mail middleinn@shentel.net; web www.middleton-inn.com. 4 rms, 2 with shower only, 2 story, 1 cottage. S, D $195-$375; 2-day min hol wkends, Oct; higher rates Oct. Children over 12 yrs only. TV; cable (premium), VCR avail (movies). Complimen-

tary full bkfst; afternoon refreshments. Restaurant nearby. Ck-out 11 am, ck-in 3 pm. Luggage handling. Business servs avail. Lawn games. Federal house built in 1850; rural setting. Totally nonsmoking. Cr cds: A, C, MC, V.

★★★ **SYCAMORE HILL HOUSE & GARDENS.** 110 Menefee Mt Ln (22747), on US 211, adj to Rappahannock Library. 540/675-3046. 3 rms, 1 with shower only, 2 story. No rm phones. S, D $115-$165; higher rates: wkends, hols, month of Oct (2-day min). Children over 12 yrs only. Complimentary full bkfst; afternoon refreshments. Ck-out 11 am, ck-in 2 pm. Business servs avail. Luggage handling. Lawn games. On top of hill, view of mountains. Gardens. Totally nonsmoking. Cr cds: C, MC, V.

★★★★★ **THE INN AT LITTLE WASHINGTON.** 309 Main St (22747). 540/675-3800; FAX 540/675-3100. The staff at this immaculate, meticulously orchestrated English-style inn, with superb decor and details, spares no effort in pampering guests. What makes a getaway truly memorable is dinner at the restaurant here—one of the country's finest. 14 rms in 2 bldgs, 1 with shower only, 2 story. S, D $290-$495; each addl in suite $50; suites $440-$580; higher rates: Fri, Sat, hols, May & Oct. Inn closed Tues (exc May & Oct); also Dec 24, 25. Complimentary continental bkfst. Restaurant (see The Inn at Little Washington). Rm serv. Bar. Ck-out noon, ck-in 3 pm. Business servs avail. Luggage handling. Gift shop. Airport transportation. Minibars. Some balconies. Bicycles. Cr cds: C, MC, V.

Restaurants

★★★ **BLEU ROCK INN.** (See Bleu Rock Inn) 540/987-3190. Web www.menusonline.com. Hrs: 5:30-9 pm; Sun brunch 11 am-2 pm. Closed Mon, Tues; Dec 25. Res accepted. French, Amer menu. Serv bar. A la carte entrees: dinner $17.95-$24.95. Sun brunch $7.25-$24.95. Specializes in fresh seafood. Outdoor dining. French country decor; fireplaces, antiques. Family-owned. Totally nonsmoking. Cr cds: A, C, D, DS, MC, V.

★★★ **FOUR & TWENTY BLACKBIRDS.** 650 Zachary Taylor Hwy (22627), S on US 522. 540/675-1111. Hrs: 5:30-9 pm; Sun brunch 10 am-2 pm. Closed Mon, Tues; July 4, Dec 25; also 1st 2 wks of Jan and Aug. Res accepted; required Fri, Sat. Serv bar. Semi-a la carte: dinner $16-$22. Sun brunch $8-$12. Specializes in vegetarian dishes, eclectic regional dishes. Own pasta, ice cream. Entertainment. Parking. Originally built in 1910 as a carpenter's shop. Totally nonsmoking. Cr cds: C, MC, V.

★★★★★ **THE INN AT LITTLE WASHINGTON.** (See The Inn at Little Washington) 540/675-3800. Owner/chef Patrick O'Connell demonstrates great creative culinary versatility, utilizing many products of the nearby Virginia countryside. Impeccable service, striking old-world decor, and artful food preparation are found in three dining salons, all with a view of the beautifully landscaped garden. Contemporary Amer cuisine. Specialties: local rabbit braised in pressed apple cider, native wild rockfish pan-roasted. Hrs: 6-9:30 pm; Sat 5:30-10 pm; Sun from 4 pm. Closed Tues (exc May & Oct); also Dec 24, 25. Res accepted; required Fri, Sat. Wine cellar. Prix fixe: dinner $88, Fri, Sun $98, Sat $116. Valet parking. Chef-owned. Cr cds: C, MC, V.

Waynesboro (D-6)

(See also Charlottesville)

Settled ca 1739 **Pop** 18,549 **Elev** 1,300 ft **Area Code** 540 **Zip** 22980
E-mail chamber@cfw.com **Web** www.cfw.com/~chamber
Information Waynesboro Augusta County Chamber of Commerce, 301 W Main St; 540/949-8203

Waynesboro is at the southern end of the Skyline Drive and the northern end of the Blue Ridge Parkway.

What to See and Do

P. Buckley Moss Museum. Museum's exhibits and programs examine the symbolism and aesthetic ideas of one of America's most notable living artists. (Daily; closed hols) 150 P. Buckley Moss Dr. Phone 540/949-6473. **Free**

Shenandoah National Park (see). 1 mi E to Skyline Dr.

Shenandoah Valley Art Center. Art galleries, studios. Working artists; performing arts. (Daily exc Mon) 600 W Main St. Phone 540/949-7662. **Donation**

Sherando Lake Recreation Area. Facilities include 21-acre lake with sand beach and bathhouses. Swimming, fishing. Picnicking. Camping (Apr-Oct, fee). Amphitheater, campfire programs. (Apr-Nov, daily) 16 mi SW on Blue Ridge Pkwy, in George Washington and Jefferson National Forests. Phone 540/942-5965 (summer) or 540/261-6105. Day use   ¢¢

Annual Event

Fall Foliage Festival. 1st & 2nd wkend Oct.

Motels

✓ ★ ★ **COMFORT INN.** *640 W Broad St (22980). 540/942-1171; FAX 540/942-4785; res: 800/228-5150.* 75 rms. S $45-$59; D $52-$69; each addl $5; under 18 free. Crib free. Pet accepted, some restrictions. TV; cable (premium). Pool; wading pool. Coffee in rms. Ck-out noon. Business servs avail. Valet serv. Downhill ski 20 mi. Health club privileges. Microwaves avail. Cr cds: A, C, D, DS, ER, JCB, MC, V.

 ⬛ 🐾 ➤ 🏊 🔥 **SC**

★ **DAYS INN.** *2060 Rosser Ave (22980), I-64 exit 94. 540/943-1101; FAX 540/949-7586; res: 800/329-7466.* 98 rms, 2 story. May-Oct: S $45-$75; D $50-$85; each addl $5; higher rates fall foliage, graduation; lower rates rest of yr. Crib free. Pet accepted; $6. TV; cable (premium). Pool. Restaurant adj 6 am-midnight. Ck-out 11 am. Meeting rms. Business servs avail. Valet serv. Game rm. Lawn games. Microwaves avail. Picnic tables. Cr cds: A, C, D, DS, MC, V.

⬛ 🐾 ➤ 🏊 🔥 **SC**

★ ★ **INN AT AFTON.** *US 250 & I-64 (22980), 4 mi E on US 250 at jct Skyline Dr & I-64 exit 99. 540/942-5201; FAX 540/943-8746; res: 800/860-8559.* Web www.comet.net/nelsoncty. 118 rms, 2-3 story. No elvtr. May-Oct: S $60-$76; D $63-$81; each addl $7; under 18 free; higher rates special events; lower rates rest of yr. Crib free. Pet accepted. TV. Heated pool. Restaurant 7 am-2 pm, 5-10 pm. Rm serv. Bar 5 pm-12:30 am; entertainment Fri, Sat. Ck-out noon. Meeting rms. Business servs avail. Valet serv. Downhill ski 18 mi. Cr cds: A, C, D, DS, JCB, MC, V.

⬛ 🐾 ➤ 🏊 🔥 **SC**

Inn

★ ★ ★ **IRIS INN.** *191 Chinquapin Dr (22980). 540/943-1991; FAX 540/942-2093.* E-mail irisinn@cfw.com; web www.irisinn.com. 9 rms, 2 story. S $75-$90; D $80-$100; each addl $20; suites $130-$140; wkend rates (2-day min). TV. Complimentary full bkfst. Ck-out 11 am, ck-in 3 pm. Balconies. Wooded setting overlooking Shenandoah Valley. Totally nonsmoking. Cr cds: C, MC, V.

⬛ ➤ 🔥 🐾

Williamsburg (E-9)

(See also Colonial Parkway, Jamestown, Newport News, Surry, Yorktown)

Settled 1633 **Pop** 11,530 **Elev** 86 ft **Area Code** 757 **E-mail** wacc@williamsburgcc.com **Web** www.williamsburgcc.com
Information Chamber of Commerce, 201 Penniman Rd, PO Box 3620, 23187; 757/229-6511

After the Native American massacre of 1622, this Virginia colony built a palisade across the peninsula between the James and York rivers. The settlement that grew up around the palisade was called Middle Plantation and is now the site of Colonial Williamsburg.

Middle Plantation figured prominently in Bacon's Rebellion against Governor Berkeley. In 1693, it was chosen as the site of the College of William and Mary, and in 1699, the seat of Virginia government was moved here. The capitol was built to replace the Jamestown statehouse, which had burned the year before. Renamed in honor of William III of England, the new capital gradually became a town of about 200 houses and 1,500 residents. For 81 years, Williamsburg was the political, social and cultural capital of Virginia.

The colony's first successful printing press was established here by William Parks, and in 1736 he published Virginia's first newspaper. The capitol was the scene of such stirring colonial events as Patrick Henry's Stamp Act speech (1765).

The First Continental Congress was called from here by the dissolved House of Burgesses in 1774. Two years later, the Second Continental Congress was boldly led by delegates from Virginia to declare independence; George Mason's Declaration of Rights, which became the basis for the first ten amendments to the Constitution, was adopted here.

Williamsburg's exciting days came to an end in 1780, when the capital was moved to Richmond for greater safety and convenience during the Revolution. For a century and a half it continued as a quiet little college town, its tranquility interrupted briefly by the Civil War. In 1917, when a munitions factory was built near the town and cheap housing for the factory's 15,000 workers was hastily erected, Williamsburg seemed destined to live out its days in ugliness.

In 1926, however, John D. Rockefeller, Jr, and Dr. W.A.R. Goodwin, rector of Bruton Parish Church, who saw the town as a potential treasure house of colonial history, shared the broad vision that inspired the restoration of Williamsburg. For more than 30 years, Rockefeller devoted personal attention to the project and contributed funds to accomplish this nonprofit undertaking.

Today, after many years of archaeological and historical research, the project is near completion. The Historic Area, approximately a mile long and a half-mile wide, encompasses most of the 18th-century capital. Eighty-eight of the original buildings have been restored; 50 major buildings, houses and shops and many smaller outbuildings have been reconstructed on their original sites; 45 of the more historically significant buildings contain more than 200 exhibition rooms, furnished either with original pieces or reproductions and open to the public on regular seasonal schedules.

Visitors stroll Duke of Gloucester Street and mingle with people in 18th-century attire. Craftsmen at about 20 different shops ply such trades as wigmaking and blacksmithing, using materials, tools and techniques of pre-Revolutionary times.

Williamsburg is beautiful year-round. November through March is an excellent time to visit, when it is less crowded and the pace is more leisurely; some holiday weekends may be busy. The Historic Area is closed to private motor vehicles 8 am-10 pm.

What to See and Do

(Please note that Colonial Williamsburg is only a part of the town of Williamsburg. Other attractions are listed for which there are separate admission fees.)

America's Railroads on Parade. More than 4,000-sq-ft of model train layouts. Hands-on exhibits, gift shop. (Daily; closed Jan 1, Thanksgiving, Dec 25) 1915 Pocahontas Trail, in Village Shops at Kingsmill. Phone 757/220-8725. ¢¢

Busch Gardens Williamsburg. European-style themed park on 360 acres features re-created 17th-century German, English, French, Italian, Scottish and Canadian villages. Attractions include more than 30 thrill rides, including Drachen Fire roller coaster, one of the nation's largest; 3-D movie *Haunts of the Olde Country,* with in-theater special effects; live shows, antique carousel, celebrity concerts, miniature of Le Mans racetrack, rides for small children. Themed restaurants; shops. Transportation around the grounds by sky ride or steam train. A computer-operated monorail links the park with the Anheuser-Busch Hospitality Center; brewery tour. Park (mid-May-Labor Day, daily; late Mar-mid-May, wkends; after Labor Day-Oct, Fri-Tues). 3 mi E on US 60. Phone 757/253-3000. ¢¢¢¢¢

Carter's Grove (part of Colonial Williamsburg). This James River site includes the Winthrop Rockefeller Archaeology Museum, the partially reconstructed Wolstenholme Towne and an early-18th-century slave quarter. Also a 1755 mansion, located on 80-ft bluff overlooking the James River, that has been restored to its 1930s splendor. A one-way country road begins here and winds through woods, meadows and marshes back to Williamsburg, or visitors may return via US 60. (Mid-Mar-Dec, daily exc Mon) 7 mi SE. ¢¢¢¢¢

College of William and Mary (1693). (7,000 students) America's second-oldest college (only Harvard is older). Initiated honor system, elective system of studies, schools of law, modern languages; second to have school of medicine (all in 1779). Phi Beta Kappa Society founded here (1776). W end of Duke of Gloucester St. Phone 757/221-4000. On campus are

Earl Gregg Swem Library. Houses College Museum. Large display honoring the college's 300th anniversary. (Mon-Fri; closed most hols)

Muscarelle Museum of Art. Traveling displays and exhibitions from an extensive collection. (Mon-Fri & wkend afternoons; closed Jan 1 & 2, also Easter Sun) Phone 757/221-2700. **Free**

Wren Building. Oldest (1695-1699, restored 1928) academic building in America; designed by the great English architect Sir Christopher Wren. Tours (daily). **Free**

★ **Colonial Williamsburg.**

Colonial Williamsburg Visitor Center. Ticket sales, sightseeing information; orientation film; lodging and dining assistance; bookstore; transportation. Center (daily). Colonial Pkwy & VA 132. Contact the Colonial Williamsburg Foundation, PO Box 1776, 23187; phone 757/220-7645 or 800/246-2099.

Ticket information. An admission ticket is necessary to enjoy the full scope of Colonial Williamsburg. Three types of general admission tickets are available: The **Basic Ticket** provides admission on the Colonial Williamsburg transportation system and entrance to the exhibits in the Historic Area for one day. (This ticket does *not* provide admission to the Governor's Palace, the DeWitt Wallace Decorative Arts Gallery, Carter's Grove or the Abby Aldrich Rockefeller Folk Art Center.) The **Patriot's Pass** (valid one yr) provides admission on the transportation system and entrance to all historic buildings, colonial houses, craft shops, Governor's Palace, Carter's Grove, DeWitt Wallace Decorative Arts Gallery, Abby Aldrich Rockefeller Folk Art Center and historical film. Ticket prices vary. Phone 800/246-2099 for exact prices.

Disabled Visitor Information. Efforts are made to accommodate the disabled while still retaining the authenticity of colonial life. Many buildings have wheelchair access once inside, but it should be noted that most buildings are reached by steps. Visitor Center has a list detailing accessibility of each building; wheelchair ramps may be made avail at some buildings. In addition, there are wheelchair rentals and parking. A hands-on tour of several historic trades may be arranged for the visually impaired and sign language tours are avail with advance notice. Phone 800/246-2099.

Exhibition buildings.

The Capitol. House of Burgesses met here (1704-1779); scene of Patrick Henry's speech against Stamp Act. E end of Duke of Gloucester St. N of capitol, across Nicholson St is

Public Gaol. Where debtors, criminals and pirates (including Blackbeard's crew) were imprisoned. A few steps W and back to Duke of Gloucester St is

Raleigh Tavern. Frequent meeting place for Jefferson, Henry and other Revolutionary patriots; a social center of the Virginia Colony. Opp is

Wetherburn's Tavern. One of the most popular inns of the period.

Governor's Palace and Gardens. Residence of Royal Governor, one of the most elegant mansions in colonial America; set in 10-acre restored gardens. N end of Palace Green. Included in all admission tickets, or by separate ticket ¢¢¢¢¢

Brush-Everard House. Home of early mayor, with programs on slave life. SE is

Peyton Randolph House (1716). Home of president of First Continental Congress. Rochambeau's headquarters prior to Yorktown campaign. SW is

James Geddy House. Once home of a prominent silversmith with working brass, bronze, silver and pewter foundry. Across Palace Green at corner of Prince George St is

Wythe House. Home of George Wythe, America's first law professor, teacher of Jefferson, Clay and Marshall. This was Washington's headquarters before siege of Yorktown, Rochambeau's after.

The Magazine. Arsenal and military storehouse of Virginia Colony; authentic arms exhibited. Duke of Gloucester St, 1 blk E of Palace Green.

Abby Aldrich Rockefeller Folk Art Center. Outstanding collection of American folk art. Items in this collection were created by artists not trained in studio techniques, but who faithfully recorded aspects of everyday life in paintings, sculpture, needlework, ceramics, toys and other media. York St ½ blk SE of capitol. ¢¢¢

Public Hospital. Reconstruction of first public institution in the English colonies devoted exclusively to treatment of mental illness.

DeWitt Wallace Decorative Arts Gallery. Modern museum adjoining Public Hospital, features exhibits, lectures, films and related programs centering on British and American decorative arts of the 17th to early 19th centuries. ¢¢¢

Bruton Parish Church. One of America's oldest Episcopal churches, in continuous use since 1715. Organ recitals (Mar-Dec, Tues & Sat). (Daily; no tours during services) Duke of Gloucester St, just W of Palace Green. Phone 757/229-2891.

Courthouse. County and city business was conducted here from 1770 until 1932. The interior has been carefully restored to its original appearance. Visitors often participate in scheduled reenactments of court sessions. Duke of Gloucester St, E of Palace Green.

Tours and entertainment.

Carriage and wagon rides. A drive through Historic Area in carriage or wagon driven by costumed coachman. General admission ticket holders may make reservations on day of ride at Lumber House ticket office. (Daily, weather permitting) ¢¢¢

Children's Tours. Special programs, tours and experiences exclusively for children and families are offered in the summer.

Evening entertainment. Colonial Williamsburg presents "rollicking 18th-century plays" throughout the yr; wide variety of cultural events, concerts and historical reenactments (fees vary). Chowning's Tavern offers colonial "gambols" (games), music, entertainment and light food and drink (evenings).

Historic trades. Craftsmen in 18th-century costume pursue old trades of apothecary, printer, bookbinder, silversmith, wigmaker, shoemaker, blacksmith, harnessmaker, cabinetmaker, miller, milliner, gunsmith, wheelwright, basketmaker, cook, cooper and carpenter.

Lanthorn Tour. A costumed interpreter conducts evening walking tour of selected shops that are illuminated by candlelight. Tickets may be purchased at any sales location or by phone 800/246-2099. (Mar-Dec, daily) ¢¢¢

Play Booth Theater. Scenes from 18th-century plays in open-air theater. Open to all Colonial Williamsburg ticket holders. (Spring-fall, daily)

Special focus and orientation tours. Orientation tours (30 min) for first-time visitors; special tours (90 min), called history walks, include African American life, gardens, religion and women of Williamsburg. Reservations are avail at any ticket sales location.

Shopping. Superior wares typical of the 18th century are offered in nine restored or reconstructed stores and shops; items include silver, jewelry, herbs, candles, hats and books. Two craft houses sell approved reproductions of the antiques on display in the houses and museums.

Ride with Me to Williamsburg. Informative and entertaining 90-min audiocassette describes events from Williamsburg's colorful colonial, revolutionary and Civil War past. The town's famous restoration is summarized by one of the architects who worked on the project. Contact RWM Associates, PO Box 1324, Bethesda MD 20817; phone 301/299-7817 or 800/840-7433. ¢¢¢¢

York River State Park. A 2,500-acre park along the York River and its related marshes. Includes the Taskinas Creek National Estuarine Research Reserve. Fishing; boating (launch), canoe trips. Hiking, bridle trails. Picnicking. Interpretive center; programs; nature walks. (Daily) Standard fees. 8 mi NW via I-64, exit 231B, then 1 mi N on VA 607 to VA 606E. Phone 757/566-3036.

Annual Events

Antiques Forum. Colonial Williamsburg. Mid-Feb.

Washington's Birthday Celebration. Colonial Williamsburg. President's Day wkend.

Learning Weekend. Colonial Williamsburg. Family-oriented wkend of discovery on a single topic. Mar.

Garden Symposium. Colonial Williamsburg. Lectures and clinics. Last wk Apr.

Prelude to Independence. Colonial Williamsburg. Mid-May.

Publick Times. Colonial Williamsburg. Re-creation of colonial market days; contests, crafts, auctions, military encampment. Labor Day wkend.

Traditional Christmas Activities. Colonial Williamsburg. Featuring grand illumination of city; fireworks. Dec.

Seasonal Events

Colonial Weekends. Package wkends on 18th-century theme, features introductory lecture, guided tours, banquet at Colonial Williamsburg. Jan-early Mar.

18th-Century Comedy. Williamsburg Lodge Auditorium. Sat nights. Mar-Dec.

Military Drill. On Market Square Green. Costumed wkly drill by Williamsburg Independent Company. Mid-Mar-Oct.

Fife-and-Drum Corps. Colonial Williamsburg. Performances in the Historic Area. Sat. Apr-Oct.

Living History Programs. at Colonial Williamsburg. Include *An Assembly, Cross or Crown* and *Cry Witch!* Varying schedule wkly. Spring, summer & fall.

Motels

★ **GOVERNOR'S INN.** 506 N Henry St (23185). 757/229-1000; FAX 757/229-7019; res: 800/447-8679. 200 rms, 3 story. May-Aug: S, D $89; family rates; lower rates rest of yr. Closed Jan-mid-Mar. Crib $8. Pet accepted. TV; cable (premium). Pool. Complimentary coffee. Restaurant nearby. Business servs avail. Sundries. Gift shop. Tennis privileges. Golf privileges. Game rm. Cr cds: A, C, D, DS, MC, V.

D 🐕 🏋️ ⛖ 🏊 🛏 🔥 SC

★★ **HAMPTON INN.** 201 Bypass Rd (23185). 757/220-0880; FAX 757/229-7175; res: 800/426-7866. 122 rms, 4 story. Mid-June-early Sept: S, D $89-$109; lower rates rest of yr, higher rates: July 4, Labor Day. Crib free. TV, cable (premium). Indoor pool; whirlpool. Complimentary continental bkfst. Coffee in rms. Ck-out 11 am. Meeting rm. Business servs avail. Sauna. Game rm. Cr cds: A, C, D, DS, MC, V.

D ⛖ 🛏 🔥 SC

★★ **HOLIDAY INN.** 725 Bypass Rd (23185). 757/220-1776; FAX 757/220-3124; res: 800/465-4329. Web www.holiday-inn1776.com/. 202 rms, 2 story. Mid-June-late Aug: S, D $89-$129; each addl $6; suite $129-$150; under 18 free; lower rates rest of yr. Crib free. TV; cable (premium). Pool; wading pool, poolside serv. Playground. Supervised children's activities (Memorial Day-Labor Day); ages 4-12. Restaurant 7 am-2 pm, 5-10 pm. Rm serv. Bar from 4 pm; Sat, Sun from 1 pm. Ck-out 11 am. Coin lndry. Meeting rms. Business servs avail. Bellhops. Valet serv. Concierge (in season). Sundries. Lighted tennis. Game rm. Lawn games. Picnic tables. Cr cds: A, C, D, DS, JCB, MC, V.

D 🐕 🏋️ ⛖ 🏊 🔥 SC

★ **HOLIDAY INN EXPRESS.** 119 Bypass Rd, Rte 60 Bypass (23185). 757/253-1663; FAX 757/220-9117; res: 800/465-4329. Web www.holiday-express.com. 131 rms, 2 story. Mid-June-Labor Day: S, D $72-$94; each addl $6; under 19 free; lower rates rest of yr. Crib free. TV; cable (premium). Pool. Complimentary continental bkfst. Ck-out 11 am. Meeting rms. Business servs avail. In-rm modem link. Cr cds: A, C, D, DS, ER, JCB, MC, V.

D ⛖ 🏊 🔥 SC

★★★ **MARRIOTT'S MANOR CLUB.** 101 St Andrews Dr (23188). 757/258-1120; FAX 757/258-5705; res: 800/845-5279. 135 kit suites, 3 story. Memorial Day-Labor Day: kit suites $264/day, $1,418/wk; family rates; lower rates rest of yr. Crib free. TV; cable (premium), VCR (movies). 2 pools, 1 indoor; whirlpools. Complimentary coffee in rms. Restaurant 11:30 am-9:30 pm. Ck-out 10 am. Meeting rms. Business servs avail. In-rm modem link. Concierge. Sundries. Gift shop. Lighted tennis. 45-hole golf, greens fee $50-$100, pro, putting green, driving range. Exercise equipt. Massage. In-rm whirlpools, refrigerators, microwaves, fireplaces. Balconies. Grills. Cr cds: A, C, D, DS, MC, V.

D 🏋️ 🚴 🏌️ ⛖ 🏋️ 🏊 🔥

✓★★ **QUALITY INN.** 901 Capitol Landing Rd (23185). 757/229-4444; FAX 757/220-9314; res: 800/638-7949. 94 rms, 1-2 story. May-Oct: S, D $59-$89; suites $89-$109; lower rates rest of yr. Crib free. TV; cable (premium). Pool; wading pool. Restaurant 7 am-10 pm. Ck-out 11 am. Coin lndry. Bellhops. Putting green. Refrigerators, microwaves avail. On 7½ wooded acres with small fishing lake. Cr cds: A, C, D, DS, ER, JCB, MC, V.

D 🦮 ⛖ 🏊 🔥 SC

★ **QUARTERPATH INN.** 620 York St (23185). 757/220-0960; FAX 757/220-1531; res: 800/446-9222. 130 rms, 2 story. Apr-Oct: S, D $62-$75; each addl $6; under 18 free; package plans; lower rates rest of yr. Crib free. Pet accepted, some restrictions. TV; cable (premium). Pool. Restaurant adj 4-10 pm. Ck-out noon. Meeting rm. Business servs avail. Some in-rm whirlpools. Cr cds: A, C, DS, MC, V.

D 🐕 ⛖ 🏊 🔥 SC

★★★ **WILLIAMSBURG WOODLANDS.** Box 1776 (23185), 1 mi SE of I-64, exit 238, opp Visitor Ctr. 757/229-1000; FAX 757/565-8942; res: 800/447-8679. 315 rms. Apr-Dec: S, D $91-$125; each addl $8; golf, tennis packages; lower rates rest of yr. Crib free. TV. 2 pools; wading pool, lifeguard. Playground. Supervised children's activities (mid-June-Aug); ages 5-12. Restaurant (see The Cascades). Ck-out 11 am. Meeting rms. Business servs avail. Bellhops. Valet serv. Sundries. Barber, beauty shop. Tennis. Golf privileges, putting green. Health club privileges. Lawn games. Miniature golf. Picnic tables. Cr cds: A, C, D, DS, MC, V.

D 🏋️ 🚴 ⛖ 🏊 🛏 🔥 SC

Motor Hotels

★★ **COURTYARD BY MARRIOTT.** 470 McLaws Circle (23185). 757/221-0700; FAX 757/221-0741; res: 800/446-9244. 151 rms, 4 story. Memorial Day-Labor Day: S, D $135-145; suites $175-$195; lower rates rest of yr. Crib free. TV; cable (premium). Indoor/outdoor pool; whirlpool. Complimentary coffee in rms. Bar 5-10 pm. Ck-out noon. Coin

Indry. Meeting rms. Business servs avail. In-rm modem link. Valet serv. Concierge. Sundries. Exercise equipt. Game rm. Refrigerator in suites. Balconies. Cr cds: A, C, D, DS, MC, V.

★★ **HOLIDAY INN.** *814 Capitol Landing Rd (23185). 757/229-0200; FAX 757/220-1642; res: 800/465-4329.* E-mail dmeaux@erols.com; web www.holidayinn.com. 139 rms, 3 story. Apr-Oct: S, D $89-$109; each addl $6; under 18 free; wkend rates; golf plan; lower rates rest of yr. Crib free. TV; cable (premium). Indoor pool; whirlpool, poolside serv. Complimentary coffee in rms. Restaurant 7 am-10 pm. Rm serv. Bar 5-11 pm. Ck-out noon. Coin Indry. Meeting rms. Business servs avail. Bellhops. Gift shop. Exercise equipt; sauna. Game rm. Refrigerators, microwaves avail. Cr cds: A, C, D, DS, JCB, MC, V.

★★ **HOWARD JOHNSON HOTEL.** *7135 Pocahontas Trl (23185). 757/229-6900; FAX 757/220-3211; res: 800/841-9100.* E-mail hojohst@hojohst.com; web www.hojohst.com. 100 rms, 4 story. Mid-June-Labor Day (2-day min wkends): S, D $89-$140; suites $120-$150; under 18 free; lower rates rest of yr. Crib free. TV; cable (premium). Pool; wading pool, poolside serv. Complimentary coffee in rms. Restaurant adj 7 am-2 pm. Ck-out noon. Coin Indry. Meeting rms. Business servs avail. Valet serv. Sundries. Health club privileges. Game rms. Cr cds: A, C, D, DS, JCB, MC, V.

★★★ **MARRIOTT.** *50 Kingsmill Rd (23185). 757/220-2500; FAX 757/221-0653; res: 800/288-2662.* Web www.marriott.com. 295 rms, 6 story. Apr-mid-Nov: S, D $129-$200; suites $225-$500; family rates; package plans; lower rates rest of yr. Crib free. TV; cable (premium). Indoor/outdoor pool; whirlpool, poolside serv. Coffee in rms. Restaurant 6:30 am-10:30 pm. Rm serv. Bar. Ck-out noon. Convention facilities. Business center. In-rm modem link. Bellhops. Concierge. Gift shop. Tennis. Exercise equipt; sauna. Game rm. Rec rm. Refrigerators avail. Private patios, balconies. Cr cds: A, C, D, DS, ER, JCB, MC, V.

★★★ **RADISSON FORT MAGRUDER INN.** *6945 Pocahontas Trl (23185). 757/220-2250; FAX 757/220-3215; res: 800/582-1010.* 303 rms, 4 story. Apr-Oct: S $79-$129; D $99-$148; each addl $10; suites $145-$250; under 18 free; lower rates rest of yr. Crib free. TV; cable (premium). 2 pools, 1 indoor; wading pool, whirlpool. Coffee in lobby. Restaurant 6:30 am-10 pm. Rm serv. Bar 11:30-1 am. Ck-out 11 am. Coin Indry. Convention facilities. Business center. Bellhops. Concierge. Gift shop. Lighted tennis. Golf privileges, greens fee $65-$115. Exercise equipt; sauna. Game rm. Bicycles. Refrigerators, some in-rm whirlpools. Balconies; many private patios. Cr cds: A, C, D, DS, MC, V.

Hotels

★★★ **WILLIAMSBURG HOSPITALITY HOUSE.** *415 Richmond Rd (23185). 757/229-4020; FAX 757/229-9557; res: 800/522-2063.* E-mail wcorp52554@aol.com; web www.williamsburghospitalityhouse.com. 297 rms, 4 story. Mid-Mar-Dec: S, D $123-$153; each addl $10; suites $250-$500; under 18 free; wkend rates; golf plan; lower rates rest of yr. Crib free. TV; cable (premium). Heated pool; poolside serv. Restaurant 6:30 am-11 pm. Bar 11:30-1 am. Ck-out noon. Meeting rms. Business servs avail. In-rm modem link. Concierge. Gift shop. Indoor parking. Health club privileges. Cr cds: A, C, D, DS, MC, V.

★★★★ **WILLIAMSBURG INN.** *136 E Francis St (23187), in historic area. 757/220-7978; FAX 757/220-7798.* E-mail conferencesales@cwf.org; web www.history.org. This inn provides elegant English Regency-style accommodations and a wide range of recreational facilities. Rooms are comfortable; furnishings are antiques or Williamsburg reproductions. Public areas are spacious and appealing, and, perhaps best of all, the inn is an easy walk from the 18th-century historic area that made Williamsburg famous. 91 rms, 2 story. S, D $245-$345; suites $410-$750; package plans. Crib $12. TV; cable (premium), VCR avail. 3 pools, 1 indoor; wading pool, whirlpool, poolside serv, lifeguard. Supervised children's activities (July 4-Labor Day); ages 4-12. Restaurant 7 am-10 pm (also see Regency Dining Room). Afternoon tea 4 pm. Rm serv 24 hrs. Bar 11:30 am-11 pm; entertainment. Ck-out noon, ck-in 3 pm. Meeting rms. Business center. In-rm modem link. Airport transportation. Concierge. Tennis, pro. 9-hole & two 18-hole golf courses, greens fee $95, pro, putting green. Exercise equipt; sauna, steam rm. Massage. Lawn games. Bicycle rentals. Card rm. Some refrigerators. Balcony, fireplace in suites. Cr cds: A, C, D, DS, MC, V.

★★★ **WILLIAMSBURG LODGE.** *310 S England St (23185). 757/229-1000; FAX 757/565-8942; res: 800/447-8679.* E-mail conference sales@cwf.org; web www.history.org. 315 rms, 3 story. Mar-Dec: S, D $175-$235; each addl $20; suites $225-$450; lower rates rest of yr. TV, VCR avail. 3 pools; wading pool, whirlpool, poolside serv. Supervised children's activities (Memorial Day-Labor Day); ages 4-12. Complimentary coffee in rms. Restaurant 7 am-10 pm. Bar. Ck-out noon. Meeting rms. Business servs avail. In-rm modem link. Gift shop. Beauty shop. Tennis, pro. 45-hole golf, greens fee $95-$110, pro, putting green. Exercise equipt; sauna. Lawn games. Bicycle rentals. Some fireplaces. Some private patios. Lounge, verandas. Gardens; at edge of Colonial Williamsburg historic district. Cr cds: A, C, D, DS, MC, V.

Resort

✓★★★★ **KINGSMILL RESORT.** *1010 Kingsmill Rd (23185). 757/253-1703; FAX 757/253-3993; res: 800/832-5665.* E-mail reservations@kingsmill.com; web www.kingsmill.com. The weathered-grey buildings and steep, shingled roofs of this resort are typical of those seen frequently in this part of Virginia. 407 rms, 2 story. Mar-Nov: S, D $189-$269; 1-bedrm suites $269-$339; 2-bedrm suites $448-$598; 3-bedrm suites $637-$867; family rates; golf, tennis plans; lower rates rest of yr. Crib free. TV; cable (premium), VCR avail. Indoor/outdoor pools; whirlpool. Supervised children's activities (Memorial Day-Labor Day); ages 5-12. Dining rm 6 am-10 pm. Rm serv to midnight. Bar from 10 am. Ck-out 11 am, ck-in 4 pm. Meeting rms. Business center. In-rm modem link. Concierge. Shopping arcade. Beauty shop. Lighted tennis, pro. Three 18-hole golf courses, one (par 3) golf course, pro, driving range, putting green. Paddle boats. Marina privileges. Racquetball courts. Entertainment. Exercise rm; sauna. Massage. Spa. Some refrigerators, fireplaces. Microwave in suites. Picnic tables, grills. Cr cds: A, C, D, DS, JCB, MC, V.

Inns

★★ **COLONIAL CAPITAL BED & BREAKFAST.** *501 Richmond Rd (23185). 757/229-0233; FAX 757/253-7667; res: 800/776-0570.* E-mail ccbb@widomaker.com; web www.ccbb.com. 5 rms, 3 story. No elvtr. Mid-Mar-Dec: S $85-$110; D $105-$135; each addl $25; suite $150; package plans; lower rates rest of yr. Children over 8 yrs only. Complimentary full bkfst. Restaurant adj 6:30 am-10 pm. Ck-out 11 am, ck-in 2 pm. Built in 1926; antiques. Totally nonsmoking. Cr cds: A, C, DS, MC, V.

★★ **COLONIAL GARDENS INN.** *1109 Jamestown Rd (23185). 757/220-8087; FAX 757/253-1495; res: 800/886-9715; res: 800/886-9715.* E-mail colgdns@widomaker.com; web www.ontheline.com/cgbb. 4 rms, 2 share bath, 2 story, 2 suites. S, D $105-$115; each addl $25; suites $130; wkends, hols (2-3 day min). TV; cable (premium), VCR (movies). Complimentary full bkfst; afternoon refreshments. Complimentary coffee in rms. Restaurant nearby. Ck-out 11 am, ck-in 4-6 pm. In-rm modem link. Luggage handling. Built in 1960; southern design. Antiques. Totally nonsmoking. Cr cds: A, C, MC, V.

★★★ **COLONIAL HOUSES-HISTORIC LOD.** *302-B Francis St (23185)*, in historic area. 757/565-8440; FAX 757/565-8444; res: 800/447-8679. E-mail conferencesales@crw.org.com; web www.history.org. 77 rms in 27 colonial houses and taverns, 1-2 story. Apr-Dec: S, D $215-$225/rm; 2-8 persons $285-$960/house; lower rates rest of yr. Crib $20. TV, cable (premium). Pool privileges. Dining facilities. Ck-out 11 am, ck-in 4 pm. Business center. In-rm modem link. Some of the houses are more than 200 yrs old; furnished in the period. Cr cds: A, C, D, DS, MC, V.

★★★ **EDGEWOOD BED & BREAKFAST.** *4800 John Tyler Memorial (23030)*, 28 mi W on VA 5. 804/829-2962; FAX 804/829-2962. 8 rms, 3 with shower only, 3 story. S, D $120-$198. Children over 12 yrs only. TV; VCR. Pool. Complimentary full bkfst. Restaurant nearby. Ck-out 11:30 am, ck-in 3 pm. Microwaves avail. Once part of the Berkeley Plantation; it has served as a church, post office, and nursing home. Cr cds: A, C, MC, V.

★★ **INDIAN SPRINGS BED & BREAKFAST.** *330 Indian Springs Rd (23030)*. 757/220-0726; FAX 757/220-8924; res: 800/262-9165. Web www.indianspgs@tni.net. 4 rms, 2 story. Rm phone in cottage only. Mid-Mar-Dec: S, D $85-$130; lower rates rest of yr. Crib free. TV; cable. Complimentary full bkfst. Restaurant nearby. Ck-out 11 am, ck-in 3-6 pm. Gardens. Near William and Mary College. Totally nonsmoking. Cr cds: C, MC, V.

★★ **LEGACY OF WILLIAMSBURG BED & BREAKFAST.** *930 Jamestown Rd (23185)*. 757/220-0524; FAX 757/220-2211; res: 800/962-4722. Web www.legacyofwilliamsburgbb.com. 4 rms, 2 story, 3 suites. Mar-Dec: S, D $95; suites $140. Adults only. TV in sitting rm; cable, VCR (free movies). Complimentary full bkfst. Restaurant nearby. Ck-out 10:30 am, ck-in by 5 pm. Business servs avail. Rec rm. Billiards. Some balconies. Built in 18th-century style; period antiques, furnishings; library. Large rear deck overlooks small ravine. Totally nonsmoking. Cr cds: A, C, MC, V.

★★★ **LIBERTY ROSE BED & BREAKFAST.** *1022 Jamestown Rd (23185)*. 757/253-1260; res: 800/545-1825. Web www.libertyrose.com. 4 rms, 2 story. S, D $135-$205; each addl $50. Children over 12 yrs only. TV; VCR (free movies). Complimentary full bkfst; afternoon refreshments. Restaurant nearby. Ck-out 11 am, ck-in 3 pm. Picnic tables. Built 1920; many antiques. Wooded grounds. Totally nonsmoking. Cr cds: A, C, MC, V.

★★ **NORTH BEND PLANTATION BED & BREAKFAST.** *12200 Weyanoke Rd (23030)*, 19 mi W on VA 5. 804/829-5176. 4 rms, 2 story. S $105-$140; D $115-$140; each addl $40. TV. Pool. Complimentary full bkfst. Restaurant nearby. Ck-out 11 am, ck-in 3 pm. Fireplaces. Greek-Revival house (1819); antiques. Cr cds: C, MC, V.

★★ **PINEY GROVE.** *16920 Southall Plantation Ln (23030)*, US 5W to VA 623N. 804/829-2480; FAX 804/829-6888. 4 rms, 2 story, 1 suite. No rm phones. S, D $125-$150; suite $160; hols (2-day min). TV avail in some rms; cable, VCR avail (movies) in common rm. Complimentary full bkfst. Ck-out noon, ck-in 4 pm. Luggage handling. Pool. Lawn games. Refrigerators. 2 historic farmhouses (ca 1800). Totally nonsmoking. Cr cds: C.

✓★ **WAR HILL INN BED & BREAKFAST.** *4560 Longhill Rd (23188)*. 757/565-0248; FAX 757/565-4550; res: 800/743-0248. Web www.ngetaway.com/va/warhill. 5 rms, 2 suites. No rm phones. S, D $75-$165; each addl $15; suites $105-$135. Crib free. TV; cable. Playground. Complimentary full bkfst. Restaurant nearby. Ck-out 11 am, ck-in 4 pm. On a working farm; built 1969 in Colonial style. Totally nonsmoking. Cr cds: C, MC, V.

★★★ **WILLIAMSBURG SAMPLER BED & BREAKFAST.** *922 Jamestown Rd (23185)*. 757/253-0398; FAX 757/253-2669; res: 800/722-1169. E-mail wbgsampler@aol.com. 4 rms, 3 story. Rm phones avail. S, D $100-$150. TV; cable (premium). Complimentary full bkfst. Restaurant nearby. Ck-out 11 am, ck-in 1 pm. Business servs avail. Picnic tables. Plantation-style house; fireplaces, antiques, Colonial-style furnishings; gardens. Near William and Mary College; walking distance to historic area. Totally nonsmoking. Cr cds: C, MC, V.

Restaurants

★★ **ABERDEEN BARN.** *1601 Richmond Rd (23185)*. 757/229-6661. Web www.aberdeen-barn.com. Hrs: 5-9:30 pm; Fri, Sat to 10 pm. Closed Thanksgiving, Dec 25; also 1st 2 wks Jan. Res accepted. Bar. Semi-a la carte: dinner $12.95-$38.95. Child's meals. Specializes in roast prime rib, seafood, baby back ribs. Parking. Open-hearth grill. Barn-like atmosphere; farm implements. Cr cds: A, C, DS, MC, V.

★★ **BERRET'S RESTAURANT.** *199 S Boundary St (23185)*, on Merchant's Square. 757/253-1847. Hrs: 11:30 am-10 pm. Closed Jan 1, Dec 25; also Mon in Jan & Feb. Res accepted. Regional Amer menu. Bar. Semi-a la carte: lunch $3.95-$8, dinner $4.95-$24.50. Child's meals. Specialties: Virginia crab cakes, lobster & crabmeat combo, seafood & herbs baked in parchment. Raw bar. Parking. Outdoor dining. Casual dining rm; fireplace, nautical decor. Cr cds: A, C, DS, MC, V.

★★ **COACH HOUSE TAVERN.** *12604 Harrison Landing Rd (23030)*, approx 25 mi W on VA 5. 804/829-6003. Hrs: 11 am-4 pm; Fri-Sat 6-9 pm; Sun brunch 11 am-4 pm. Closed Dec 25. Res accepted; required Fri-Sat. Bar. Semi-a la carte: lunch $3.95-$14.95. Complete meals: dinner $14-$26. Sun brunch $3.95-$14.95. Child's meals. Specializes in seafood, game, desserts. Parking. In coach house of Berkeley Plantation; view of grounds and plantation house. Cr cds: A, C, D, MC, V.

★★ **DYNASTY.** *1621 Richmond Rd (23185)*. 757/220-8888. E-mail dynasty@wmbg.com; web www.wmbq.com/dynasty. Hrs: noon-midnight; to 10 pm off-season. Res accepted. Chinese menu. Bar. Semi-a la carte: lunch $4.95-$6.95, dinner $6.95-$19.95. Child's meals. Specialties: steamed whole fish, General Zuo's chicken, Peking duck. Parking. Outdoor dining. Large dining area decorated with Chinese screens and art objects. Gift shop. Fish pond. Oriental karaoke. Cr cds: A, C, D, DS, JCB, MC, V.

★★★ **FORDS COLONY RESTAURANT.** *240 Ford's Colony Dr (23188)*, 4 mi W on Long Hill Dr, then left, in clubhouse. 757/258-4107. Hrs: 6-9:30 pm; Sun brunch 11:30 am-2:30 pm. Closed Mon; also early Jan. Res accepted. Regional Amer menu. Bar. Wine cellar. Semi-a la carte: dinner $16-$28. Sun brunch $18.95. Child's meals. Specializes in fresh seafood, rack of lamb. Large floral centerpiece, original artwork, fine china and crystal. Jacket (dinner). Cr cds: A, C, MC, V.

★ **GAZEBO HOUSE OF PANCAKES.** *409 Bypass Rd (23185)*. 757/220-0883. Hrs: 6 am-2 pm. Res accepted. A la carte entrees: bkfst $3.75-$7.75, lunch $2.50-$8.50. Child's meals. Specializes in pancakes, omelettes. Casual decor. Cr cds: C, D, DS, MC, V.

✓★★ **GIUSEPPE'S.** *5601 Richmond Rd (23188)*. 757/565-1977. E-mail dkenn@erols.com; web www.giuseppes.com. Hrs: 11:30 am-2 pm, 5-9 pm; Fri, Sat to 9:30 pm. Closed Sun; major hols. Italian menu.

Bar. Semi-a la carte: lunch, dinner $4.25-$15.95. Child's meals. Specialties: pasta primavera, chicken Provençale. Parking. Patio dining. Cr cds: C, DS, MC, V.

D ⬛

★★ **INDIAN FIELDS TAVERN.** *9220 John Tyler Memorial Hwy (23030), Approx 25 mi W on VA 5.* 804/829-5004. Hrs: 11 am-3:30 pm, 5-9 pm; Fri, Sat to 10 pm. Sun brunch to 3:30 pm. Closed Dec 24, 25; also Mon in Jan. Res accepted. Bar. Semi-a la carte: lunch $5.95-$11.95, dinner $12.95-$29.95. Sun brunch $7-$14.95. Child's meals. Specialties: crab cakes Harrison, bourbon chocolate pecan pie, bread pudding. Parking. Screened porch dining area. Turn-of-the-century farmhouse on working farm. Cr cds: A, C, DS, MC, V.

D ⬛

★★ **JEFFERSON INN.** *1453 Richmond Rd (23185).* 757/229-2296. Hrs: 4-11 pm. Closed Thanksgiving, Dec 24, 25. Res accepted. Italian, continental menu. Semi-a la carte: dinner $8.95-$21.95. Child's meals. Specializes in steak, fresh seafood, Southern favorites. Family-owned. Cr cds: A, C, D, MC, V.

D ⬛

★★ **KING'S ARMS TAVERN.** *Duke Of Gloucester St (23185).* 757/220-7010. Hrs: 11:30 am-2:30 pm, 5-9:30 pm. Closed Tues (Sept, Nov-mid Dec); also mid-Feb-mid-Mar. Res required dinner. Bar. Semi-a la carte: lunch $6.95-$8.50, dinner $17.75-$25.95. Child's meals. Specialties: game pie, peanut soup, Virginia ham. Garden bar serv. Own apple cider. Garden dining. Colonial balladeers. Restored 18th-century tavern; Colonial decor. Cr cds: A, C, D, DS, MC, V.

★★★ **KITCHEN AT POWHATAN.** *3601 Ironbound Rd (23188), on grounds of Powhatan Plantation.* 757/220-0741. Hrs: 5:30-10 pm. Closed Mon. Res accepted. Bar. Semi-a la carte: dinner $15-$28. Prix fixe: dinner $40. Specializes in game, seafood, regional cuisine. Parking. In 1737 structure on grounds of Powhatan Plantation. Cr cds: C, D, MC, V.

⬛

★★★ **LA TRELLIS.** *403 Duke Of Gloucester St (23185), in Merchant's Square.* 757/229-8610. Hrs: 11 am-9:30 pm; Sun brunch to 3 pm. Closed some major hols. Res accepted. Bar 11:30 am-10:30 pm. Semi-a la carte: lunch $5.50-$9.95, dinner $14.50-$24. Sun brunch $5.50-$14.95. Specializes in fresh seafood, pasta. Own ice cream. Entertainment wkends. Outdoor dining under trees. Cr cds: A, C, D, MC, V.

D ⬛

★★★ **LE YACA RESTAURANT.** *1915 Pocahontas Trl #C10 (23185), US 60E in Kingsmill Village shops.* 757/220-3616. Hrs: 11:30 am-2 pm, 6-9:30 pm; Mon from 6 pm. Closed Sun. Res accepted. Southern French menu. Bar. Wine cellar. Semi-a la carte: lunch $6.50-$13.50. Complete meals: dinner $22-$42. Specialties: open-spit leg of lamb, marquise au chocolat. Salad bar (lunch). Own pastries. Cr cds: A, C, D, MC, V.

D ⬛

★ **LOBSTER HOUSE.** *1431 Richmond Rd (23185).* 757/229-7771. Hrs: 4:30-10 pm; Fri, Sat to 11 pm. Res accepted. Continental menu. Bar. A la carte entrees: $11.95-$19.95. Child's meals. Specializes in pasta, seafood. Nautical decor. Cr cds: A, C, MC, V.

D SC ⬛

✓★ **OLD CHICKAHOMINY HOUSE.** *1211 Jamestown Rd (23185), at jct VA 199 & 31.* 757/229-4689. Hrs: 8:30-10:15 am, 11:30 am-2:15 pm. Closed Thanksgiving, Dec 25; also 2 wks mid-Jan. Wine, beer. Semi-a la carte: bkfst $.95-$7.75, lunch $2-$6.98. Specialties: ham on hot biscuits, Brunswick stew, chicken & dumplings. Gift shop. 18th-century stagecoach stop atmosphere. Totally nonsmoking. Cr cds: C, MC, V.

✓★★ **PEKING RESTAURANT.** *122 Waller Mill Rd (23185).* 757/229-2288. E-mail tiao@erols.com. Hrs: 11:30 am-10 pm; Fri, Sat to 11 pm; brunch 11:30 am-2:30 pm; dinner buffet 5:30-8:30 pm. Closed Thanksgiving. Res accepted; required wkends. Chinese menu. Bar. Semi-a la carte: $6.95-$9.95. Buffet: lunch $4.95, dinner $6.95. Sun brunch $4.95. Specialties: General Tso's chicken, Emperor's shrimp, Peking chicken. Cr cds: A, C, D, DS, MC, V.

D ⬛

★★ **PRIME RIB HOUSE.** *1433 Richmond Rd (23185).* 757/229-6823. Hrs: 4:30-10 pm; Fri, Sat to 11 pm. Southwestern menu. Bar. A la carte entrees: dinner $9.95-$17.95. Child's meals. Specializes in prime rib, fresh seafood, Angus steak. Casual decor. Cr cds: A, C, D, DS, MC, V.

D SC ⬛

★★★ **REGENCY DINING ROOM.** *(See Williamsburg Inn Hotel)* 757/229-1000. E-mail conferencesales@cwf.org; web www.history.org. Hrs: 7-10 am, noon-2 pm, 6-9 pm; Sun brunch noon-2 pm. Res accepted. Continental menu. Bar. Wine list. Semi-a la carte: bkfst $9-$14, lunch $10-$17. A la carte entrees: dinner $27-$39. Sun brunch $27.50-$32. Specialties: snapper or veal with crabmeat, rack of lamb. Own baking. Parking. Jacket. Cr cds: A, C, D, DS, MC, V.

D

★★ **SEASON'S CAFE.** *110 S Henry (23185).* 757/259-0018. Hrs: 11 am-10 pm; Fri, Sat to 11 pm. Sun brunch 11 am-3 pm. Closed Dec 25. Res accepted. Continental menu. Bar. Semi-a la carte: lunch $8-$13, dinner $9-$19. Sun brunch $13.95. Child's meals. Specializes in steak, prime rib, pasta. Salad bar. Outdoor dining. Located in former post office. Cr cds: A, C, D, DS, MC, V.

D ⬛

★★ **SHIELDS TAVERN.** *Duke Of Gloucester St (23185).* 757/220-7677. Hrs: 11:30 am-3 pm, 5-9:30 pm; Sun brunch 10 am-2:30 pm. Closed Jan. Res accepted. Bar. Semi-a la carte: lunch $5.95-$12.95, dinner $14.95-$24. Sun brunch $6.25-$10.95. Child's meals. Specialties: filet mignon, cream of crayfish soup. 18th-century balladeers. Outdoor dining. 12 dining rms in authentically restored Colonial building. Totally nonsmoking. Cr cds: A, C, D, DS, MC, V.

D

★ **THAT SEAFOOD PLACE.** *1647 Richmond Rd (23185).* 757/220-3011. Hrs: 11:30 am-2:30 pm, 4:30-9 pm; Fri, Sat 4:30-10 pm; Sun noon-9 pm; summer hrs vary. Closed Dec 25. Res accepted. Bar. Semi-a la carte: lunch $4.95-$6.95, dinner $8.25-$18.50. Child's meals. Specialties: shrimp sampler, sauteed shrimp & scallops. Salad bar. Parking. Outdoor dining. Nautical decor. Cr cds: A, C, D, DS, MC, V.

SC ⬛

★ **THE CASCADES.** *(See Williamsburg Woodlands)* 757/229-1000. Hrs: 7:30-10 am, 11:30 am-2 pm, 5:30-9 pm; Sun brunch 8 am-2 pm. Res accepted. Bar. Semi-a la carte: bkfst $5-$7, lunch $6-$9, dinner $7-$19. Buffet: bkfst $7.50, lunch $6.95. Sun brunch $12.95. Child's meals. Specializes in Chesapeake Bay seafood. Parking. Overlooks ravine with cascading brook; contemporary decor. Cr cds: A, C, D, DS, MC, V.

D ⬛

★★ **WHALING COMPANY.** *494 McLaw Circle (23185).* 757/229-0275. Hrs: 4:30-10 pm; early-bird dinner Sun-Fri 4:30-6 pm. Res accepted. Bar. Semi-a la carte: dinner $9.95-$18.95. Child's meals. Specializes in fresh fish, steaks. Own bread. Parking. Nautical decor. Cr cds: A, C, D, DS, MC, V.

D ⬛

★★ **YORKSHIRE STEAK & SEAFOOD HOUSE.** *700 York St (23185).* 757/229-9790. Web yorkshire-wmbg.com. Hrs: 4-10 pm; summer to 10:30 pm. Closed Dec 25. Res accepted. Bar. Semi-a la carte: dinner $10.95-$22.95. Child's meals. Specialties: shish kebab, prime rib. Parking. In Colonial-style building. Totally nonsmoking. Cr cds: C.

Winchester (C-7)

(See also Front Royal)

Settled 1732 **Pop** 21,947 **Elev** 720 ft **Area Code** 540
Information Winchester-Frederick County Visitor Center, 1360 S Pleasant Valley Rd, 22601; 540/662-4135 or 800/662-1360

This is the oldest colonial city west of the Blue Ridge, a Civil War prize that changed hands 72 times (once, 13 times in a day). Sometimes called the "apple capital of the world," it is located at the northern approach to the Shenandoah Valley.

George Washington, a red-haired 16-year-old, blithely headed for Winchester and his first surveying job in 1748. He began a decade of apprenticeship for the awesome military and political responsibilities he would later assume as a national leader. During the French and Indian Wars, Colonel Washington made the city his defense headquarters while he built Ft Loudoun in Winchester. Washington was elected to his first political office as a representative from Frederick County to the House of Burgesses.

At the intersection of travel routes, both east-west and north-south, Winchester grew and prospered. By the time of the Civil War, it was a major transportation and supply center, strategically located to control both Union approaches to Washington and Confederate supply lines through the Shenandoah Valley. More than 100 minor engagements and 6 battles took place in the vicinity. General Stonewall Jackson had his headquarters here during the winter of 1861-1862. From his headquarters in Winchester, Union General Philip Sheridan started his famous ride to rally his troops at Cedar Creek, 11 miles away, and turn a Confederate victory into a Union rout.

Approximately 3.5 million bushels of apples are harvested annually in Frederick County and are one of Winchester's economic mainstays today. The world's largest apple cold storage plant and one of the world's largest apple processing plants are here.

What to See and Do

Abram's Delight and Log Cabin (1754). Oldest house in city, restored, furnished in 18th-century style; boxwood garden; log cabin, basement kitchen. (Apr-Oct, daily; rest of yr, by appt, weather permitting) Inquire about combination ticket. 1340 S Pleasant Valley Ave. Phone 540/662-6519 or 540/662-6550. ¢¢

First Presbyterian Church of Winchester (1788). Building has been used as a church, a stable by Union troops in Civil War, a public school and an armory; restored in 1941. (Daily) 116 S Loudoun St. Phone 540/662-3824.

Stonewall Jackson's Headquarters. Jackson's headquarters Nov 1861-Mar 1862; now a museum housing Jackson memorabilia and other Confederate items of the war years. (Apr-Oct, daily; rest of yr, by appt, weather permitting) Inquire about combination ticket. 415 N Braddock St. Phone 540/667-3242 or 540/662-6550. ¢¢

The Handley Library and Archives. Completed in 1913, the public library was designed in the Beaux-arts style. The rotunda is crowned on the outside with a copper-covered dome and on the inside by a dome of stained glass. Interesting features of the interior include wrought iron staircases and glass floors. Historical archives are housed on the lower level (nonresident fee). (Daily exc Sun; closed hols) 100 W Piccadilly St. Phone 540/662-9041.

Washington's Office-Museum. Building used by George Washington in 1755-1756 during erection of Ft Loudoun. Housed in this museum are French and Indian, Revolutionary and Civil War relics. (Apr-Oct, daily; rest of yr, by appt, weather permitting) Jct Cork & Braddock Sts. Phone 540/662-4412 or 540/662-6550. ¢

Annual Events

Historic Garden Tour. Open house and gardens in historic Winchester. Phone 540/662-6550. Mid-Apr.

Shenandoah Apple Blossom Festival. Apple Blossom Queen, parades, arts & crafts, band contests, music, food and attractions. Phone 540/662-3863. Late-Apr early May.

Apple Harvest Arts & Crafts. Jim Barnett Park. Pie contests, apple-butter making, music, arts & crafts. 3rd wkend Sept.

Motels

★ ★ **BEST WESTERN LEE-JACKSON.** *711 Millwood Ave (22601).* 540/662-4154; FAX 540/662-2618; res: 800/528-1234. 140 rms, 2 story. Apr-Oct: S $52; D $57; each addl $5; suites $65-$70; kit units $35 (14-day min); under 13 free; lower rates rest of yr. Crib avail. Pet accepted. TV; cable (premium). Pool. Restaurant 6 am-10 pm. Rm serv. Bar 5-10:30 pm. Ck-out noon. Coin lndry. Meeting rms. Business servs avail. Valet serv. Free airport transportation. Health club privileges. Some refrigerators, microwaves. Picnic tables, grills. Cr cds: A, C, D, DS, MC, V.

★ ★ **COMFORT INN.** *167 Town Run Ln (22655), I-81 exit 307.* 540/869-6500; FAX 540/869-2558; res: 800/228-5150. 58 rms, 2 story. S $43-$70; D $49-$80; each addl $6; under 18 free. Crib free. TV; cable (premium), VCR avail (movies). Pool. Complimentary continental bkfst. Restaurant adj 11 am-9 pm. Ck-out noon. Business servs avail. In-rm modem link. Sundries. Refrigerators, microwaves avail. Cr cds: A, C, D, DS, ER, JCB, MC, V.

✓ ★ **ECONO LODGE.** *1593 Martinsburg Pike (22603), I-81 exit 317.* 540/662-4700; FAX 540/665-1762; res: 800/553-2666. 50 rms, 2 story. S $46.95; D $50.95; each addl $5; under 19 free. Crib free. TV; cable (premium). Complimentary continental bkfst. Restaurant nearby. Ck-out 11 am. Business servs avail. In-rm modem link. Cr cds: A, C, D, DS, JCB, MC, V.

★ ★ **HAMPTON INN.** *1655 Apple Blossom Dr (22601), I-81 exit 313, Apple Blossom Mall (US 50 W).* 540/667-8011; FAX 540/667-8033; res: 800/426-7866. 103 rms, 4 story. S, D $60-$67; under 18 free. Crib free. TV; cable (premium). Pool. Complimentary continental bkfst. Restaurant nearby. Ck-out noon. Meeting rms. Business servs avail. In-rm modem link. Valet serv. Golf privileges. Health club privileges. Cr cds: A, C, D, DS, MC, V.

★ ★ **HOLIDAY INN.** *1017 Millwood Pike (22602).* 540/667-3300; FAX 540/722-2730; res: 800/465-4329. 175 rms, 2 story. S, D $49-$79; each addl $6; under 18 free. Crib free. TV; cable. Pool. Restaurant 6:30 am-10 pm. Rm serv. Bar 5:30 pm-midnight. Ck-out noon. Meeting rms. Business servs avail. In-rm modem link. Bellhops. Valet serv. Sundries. Tennis. Health club privileges. Some refrigerators, microwaves. Balconies. Cr cds: A, C, D, DS, JCB, MC, V.

★ ★ **SHONEY'S INN.** *1347 Berryville Ave (22601), jct I-81 & VA 7, exit 315.* 540/665-1700; FAX 540/665-3037; res: 800/222-2222. 98 rms, 4 with shower only, 3 story. May-Oct: S $53; D $58-$61; each addl $5; under 18 free; lower rates rest of yr. Crib free. TV; cable (premium). Indoor pool; whirlpool. Restaurant 6 am-11 pm; Fri, Sat to 1 am. Ck-out noon. Meeting rm. Business servs avail. Sundries. Valet serv. Exercise equipt; sauna. Some in-rm whirlpools, refrigerators, microwaves. Cr cds: A, C, D, DS, ER, MC, V.

✓ ★ ★ **TRAVELODGE.** *160 Front Royal Pike (22602), I-81 exit 313.* 540/665-0685; FAX 540/665-0689; res: 800/578-7878. 149 rms, 3 story. S $46-$63; D $52-$69; each addl $5; suites $125; under 17 free. Crib free. Pet accepted; $5. TV; cable (premium), VCR avail (movies). Heated pool. Complimentary continental bkfst. Complimentary coffee in rms. Restaurant nearby. Ck-out 11 am. Coin lndry. Business servs avail. In-rm modem link. Health club privileges. Refrigerators, microwaves avail. Cr cds: A, C, D, DS, ER, JCB, MC, V.

D 🐾 ⚏ ⚐ 🔥 SC

Inns

★ ★ ★ **ASHBY INN.** 692 Federal St (20130), 18 mi SE on US 50, exit VA 759. 540/592-3900; FAX 540/592-3781. 9 rms, 3 story. Rm phones avail. S, D $130-$200; each addl $20; suite $220. Children over 10 yrs only. TV in some rms. Complimentary full bkfst. Restaurant (see Ashby Inn). Ck-out noon, ck-in 3 pm. Business servs avail. Tennis privileges. Golf privileges. Lawn games. Library/sitting rm. Converted residence (1829) and one-rm schoolhouse; stone fireplace; antique furnishings. Totally nonsmoking. Cr cds: C, MC, V.

🍴 🔥 🔥

★ ★ ★ **L'AUBERGE PROVENÇALE FRENCH COUNTRY INN.** Rte 340 S (22663), 9 mi E on US 50, then 1 mi S on VA 340. 540/837-1375; FAX 540/638-2004; res: 800/638-1702. E-mail cborel@shentel.net; web www.laubergeprovencale.com. 14 rms, 2 story. S $120-$175; D $145-$195; suite $250-$325; each addl $35. Children over 10 yrs only. Complimentary full bkfst. Restaurant (see L'Augerge Provençale). Rm serv to 11 pm. Ck-out 11 am, ck-in 3 pm. Free airport transportation. Tennis privileges. 36-hole golf privileges. Whirlpool. Health club privileges. Balcony. Originally a sheep farm (1753) owned by Lord Fairfax. French country decor. Cr cds: A, C, D, MC, V.

🍴 🔥 ⚏ 🐾 SC

★ ★ ★ **THE INN AT VAUCLUSE SPRING.** 140 Vaucluse Spring Ln (22655), 12 mi S on US 11. 540/869-0200; FAX 540/869-9546; res: 800/869-0525; res: 800/869-0525. 12 rms, 2 story, 2 suites, 2 cottages. No rm phones. S, D $135-$200; each addl $25; suites $135; cottages $210-$250; wkends, hols (2-day min). Children over 10 yrs only. Complimentary full bkfst. Ck-out 11 am, ck-in 3-5 pm. Business center. Luggage handling. Gift shop. X-country ski on site. Pool. Many in-rm whirlpools, fireplaces. Built in 1785; Federal-style decor. On 100 acres. Cr cds: C, MC, V.

D ⚏ ⚏ ⚐ 🔥

★ ★ **THE RIVER HOUSE.** 3075 John Mosby Hwy US 50E & Shennandoah River (22620), 15 mi E on US 50 opp County 622. 540/837-1476; FAX 540/837-2399; res: 800/838-1476. E-mail rvrhouse@visuallink.com; web www.bbhost.com/riverhouse_va. 5 rms, 2 with shower only, 3 story. D $95-$130; higher rates Sat. Closed Jan. Crib $15. TV lounge. Playground. Complimentary brunch. Ck-out noon, ck-in by arrangement. Business servs avail. Tennis privileges. Golf privileges. Fireplaces. On 17-acres at Shenandoah River. Original part of house built 1780 as slave quarters; used as field hospital during Civil War. Cr cds: C, MC, V.

D 🐾 🍴 🔥 🐾 SC

Restaurants

★ ★ ★ **ASHBY INN.** (See Ashby Inn) 540/592-3900. Hrs: 6-9 pm; Sun noon-2:30 pm. Closed Mon, Tues; also major hols. Res required. Serv bar. Semi-a la carte: dinner $17-$25. Sun brunch $21. Specializes in lamb, fresh seafood, crab cakes. Menu changes daily. Outdoor dining. Virginia hunt country atmosphere; antiques. Plank flooring dates back to original inn (1829). Cr cds: C, MC, V.

⚏

★ ★ ★ **L'AUBERGE PROVENÇALE.** (See L'Auberge Provençale Inn) 540/837-1375. E-mail cborel@shentel.net; web www.laubergeprovencale.com. Hrs: 6-10:30 pm; Sun 5-9 pm. Closed Mon, Tues; July 4, Dec 25. Res accepted; required Fri-Sun. French Provençale menu. Bar. Wine cellar. Prix fixe: dinner $65. Specializes in seasonal creations fea-

turing homegrown organic vegetables, fruits & herbs. Outdoor dining. Country inn with extensive art collection. Totally nonsmoking. Cr cds: A, C, D, MC, V.

D

Wise (F-2)

(See also Big Stone Gap, Breaks Interstate Park)

Pop 3,193 **Elev** 2,454 ft **Area Code** 540 **Zip** 24293

What to See and Do

Recreation Areas. In George Washington and Jefferson National Forest (see HARRISONBURG). **High Knob,** 4 mi S on US 23 to Norton, then 3 mi S via VA 619, 1½ mi E on FS Road 238. Camping, swimming, picnicking. Parking fee. **Bark Camp,** 4 mi S on US 23 to Norton, then 6 mi E on US 58A to Tacoma, then 4 mi S off VA 706, 3 mi S on VA 822. Camping, boating, fishing, picnicking. Parking fee. **Cave Springs,** 7 mi W of Big Stone Gap on US 58A, then 1 mi N on VA 622, then 3 mi W on VA 621. Camping (fee). Swimming. Parking fee. **North Fork of Pound Lake,** US 23 to Pound, then W on VA 671. Camping (fee); picnicking, swimming, boat ramp, hiking. Clinch Ranger District office is in Wise. Phone 540/328-2931.

Woodstock (C-7)

(See also Basye, Front Royal, Luray, New Market)

Founded 1761 **Pop** 3,182 **Elev** 780 ft **Area Code** 540 **Zip** 22664
Web www.woodstockva.com/chamber
Information Chamber of Commerce, PO Box 605; 540/459-2542

A German immigrant, Jacob Muller, received a land grant from Lord Fairfax and came here in 1752 with his wife and six children. A few years later he set aside 1,200 acres for a town, first called Müllerstadt, later Woodstock. In a small log church here, John Peter Gabriel Mühlenberg, in January 1776, preached his famous sermon based on Ecclesiastes 3:1-8: "There is a time to every purpose . . a time to war and a time to peace," at the end of which he flung back his vestments to reveal the uniform of a Continental colonel and began to enroll his parishioners in the army that was to overthrow British rule.

The Shenandoah Valley-Herald, a weekly newspaper established in 1817, is still published here.

What to See and Do

Shenandoah County Court House (1792). Oldest courthouse still in use west of the Blue Ridge Mountains; interior restored to original design. (Mon-Fri) Main St.

Shenandoah Vineyards. Valley's first winery. Premium wines; handpicked and processed in the European style. Picnic area. Tours, free tastings available. (Daily; closed Jan 1, Thanksgiving, Dec 25) From I-81 exit 279 at Edinburg, W on VA 675, make first right on VA 686, go 1½ mi to winery. Phone 540/984-8699. **Free**

Woodstock Tower. Panoramic view of seven horseshoe bends of the Shenandoah River. 4 mi E on Mill Rd, crest of Massanutten Mt.

Annual Event

Shenandoah County Fair. One of the oldest county fairs in the state. Harness racing last 4 days. Late Aug-early Sept.

Seasonal Event

Shenandoah Valley Music Festival. Symphony pops, classical, folk, jazz, country and big band concerts. Pavilion and lawn seating. Outdoor pavilion on grounds of historic Orkney Springs Hotel in Orkney Springs. Contact Festival, PO Box 12; 540/459-3396. 4 wkends, mid-July-Labor Day wkend.

Motels

✓ ★ **BUDGET HOST.** 1290 S Main St (22664). 540/459-4086; FAX 540/459-4043; res: 800/283-4678. 43 rms, 1-2 story. S $30; D $37-$40; each addl $5; under 6 free; wkly rates. Crib $5. Pet accepted, some restrictions. TV; cable. Pool. Restaurant 6:30 am-9 pm; Sun from 7 am. Ck-out 11 am. Coin lndry. Business servs avail. Downhill ski 20 mi. Picnic tables. Cr cds: A, C, D, DS, MC, V.

★ ★ **RAMADA INN.** 1130 Motel Dr (22664), I-81 exit 283. 540/459-5000; FAX 540/459-8219; res: 800/272-6232. 124 rms, 3 story. May-Oct: S $62; D $70; each addl $8; under 18 free; lower rates rest of yr. Crib free. TV; cable (premium). Heated pool. Restaurant 7 am-1:30 pm, 5-9 pm. Rm serv. Bar 5 pm-midnight. Ck-out noon. Meeting rms. Business servs avail. Valet serv. Sundries. Some refrigerators. Cr cds: A, C, D, DS, JCB, MC, V.

Inn

★ ★ ★ **INN AT NARROW PASSAGE.** 30 Chapman Landing Rd (22664), US 11 S, 2 mi S of I-81 exit 283. 540/459-8000; FAX 540/459-8001; res: 800/459-8002. Web www.innatnarrowpassage.com. 12 rms, 2 with bath, 2 story. Rm phones avail. S, D $95-$145; each addl $10. TV. Complimentary full bkfst. Ck-out 11 am, ck-in 2 pm. Meeting rms. Business servs avail. Lawn games. On river; canoeing. Historic inn (1740), used as a headquarters by Gen. Stonewall Jackson during Civil War. Totally nonsmoking. Cr cds: C, DS, MC, V.

Restaurants

★ ★ **SPRING HOUSE.** 325 S Main St (22664). 540/459-4755. Hrs: 11 am-9 pm; Fri until 10 pm; Sat 9 am-10 pm; Sun 9 am-9 pm; Sun brunch 10 am-1:30 pm. Closed Jan 1, Dec 25. Res accepted. Bar from 5 pm. Semi-a la carte: bkfst $4.25-$6, lunch $4.25-$7.75, dinner $10-$17.50. Sun brunch $6.50. Child's meals. Salad bar. 5 dining rms include a log lounge. Early American antiques, artifacts. Cr cds: A, C, D, DS, MC, V.

Wytheville (F-4)

(See also Marion)

Founded 1792 **Pop** 8,038 **Elev** 2,284 ft **Area Code** 540 **Zip** 24382 **E-mail** chamber@wytheville.org **Web** www.wytheville.org/chamber

Information Wytheville-Wythe-Bland Chamber of Commerce, 150 Monroe St, PO Box 563; 540/223-3365

With lead mines and the only salt mine in the South nearby, Wytheville was a Union target during the Civil War. One story states a detachment of Union Cavalry attempted to take the town in July, 1863, only to be thwarted by Molly Tynes, who rode 40 miles over the mountains from Rocky Dell to tell the countryside that the Yankees were coming. The alerted home guard turned them away. A transportation center today, Wytheville is a vacationland nestled between the Blue Ridge and Allegheny mountains. Rural Retreat Lake is nearby. Wythe Ranger District office for the George Washington and Jefferson National Forests (see HARRISONBURG) is located here.

What to See and Do

Big Walker Lookout. A 120-ft observation tower at 3,405-ft elevation; swinging bridge. Gift shop; snack bar. (Apr-late May, Thurs-Sun; Memorial Day-Oct, daily exc Mon) 12 mi N on US 52; on Big Walker Mountain Scenic Byway. Phone 540/228-4401. ¢¢

Shot Tower Historical Park (1807). On bluff overlooking New River. One of three shot towers still standing in US; fortress-like stone shaft has 2½-ft-thick walls, rising 75 ft above ground and boring 75 ft below to a water tank. Molten lead was poured through sheet-iron colanders from the tower top; during the 150-ft descent it became globular before hitting the water. Pellets were then sorted by rolling them down an incline; well-formed shot rolled into a receptacle; faulty ones zig-zagged off and were remelted. Visitor center, programs; hiking trails, picnicking. (Memorial Day-Labor Day, daily) Standard fees. At Jackson's Ferry, 6 mi E on I-81, then 7 mi S on US 52; or I-77 S, Poplar Camp exit. Phone 540/699-6778 (New River Trail State Park). Tower. ¢

Wytheville State Fish Hatchery. Approx 150,000 lbs of rainbow trout produced annually. Five-tank aquarium; displays. Self-guided tours. (Daily) 12 mi SE on US 52 to VA 629. Phone 540/637-3212 or 804/525-FISH. **Free**

Annual Event

Chautauqua Festival. Held over a 9-day period. Includes parade, educational events, performing arts, art shows, children's activities, music, food, entertainment. 3rd wk June.

Motels

✓ ★ ★ **COMFORT INN.** 315 Holston Rd (24382), I-81 exit 70. 540/228-4488; FAX 540/228-4092; res: 800/228-5150. 80 rms, 2 story. S $58; D $68; each addl $5; under 18 free. Crib free. TV; cable (premium). Pool. Complimentary continental bkfst. Restaurant nearby. Ck-out 11 am. Business servs avail. Cr cds: A, C, D, DS, ER, JCB, MC, V.

✓ ★ ★ **DAYS INN.** 150 Malin Dr (24382). 540/228-5500; FAX 540/228-6301; res: 800/329-7466. 118 rms, 1-3 story. Apr-Oct: S, D $48-$58; each addl $5; under 17 free; higher rates: hols, Bristol auto races; lower rates rest of yr. Crib free. TV; cable (premium). Complimentary coffee in lobby. Restaurant adj 6 am-midnight. Ck-out noon. Business servs avail. Microwaves avail. View of mountains. Cr cds: A, C, D, DS, MC, V.

★ **ECONO LODGE.** 1160 E Main St (24382). 540/228-5517; FAX 540/228-5517; res: 800/228-5050. 72 rms, 2 story. Apr-Oct: S $35.95-$55.95; D $38.99-$58.99; each addl $5; under 18 free; higher rates special events; lower rates rest of yr. Crib free. TV; cable. Complimentary coffee in lobby. Restaurant adj 11 am-9:30 pm. Ck-out 11 am. Business servs avail. Cr cds: A, C, D, DS, MC, V.

★ ★ **HOLIDAY INN.** 1800 E Main St (24382), I-81 exit 73. 540/228-5483; FAX 540/228-5417; res: 800/465-4329. 199 rms, 1-4 story. Mar-Oct: S $49-$70; D $54-$70; each addl $5; suites $104-$150; under 18 free; wkly rates; higher rates auto races; lower rates rest of yr. Crib free. Pet accepted. TV; cable (premium). Pool; wading pool. Restaurant 6 am-2 pm, 5-9 pm. Rm serv. Bar. Ck-out 11 am. Meeting rms. Business servs avail. Cr cds: A, C, D, DS, JCB, MC, V.

★ ★ **RAMADA INN.** 955 Peppers Ferry Rd (24382), I-77 exit 41 & I-81 exit 72. 540/228-6000; FAX 540/228-6009; res: 800/272-6232. E-mail riwythe@naxs.com; web www.naxs.com/wytheville/ramada. 154 rms, 2 story. S $64-$85; D $69-$85; each addl $5; under 18 free. Crib free. Pet accepted. TV; cable (premium). Pool. Coffee in rms. Restaurant 6:30

am-9 pm. Rm serv. Bar 5-11 pm; Sun 6 pm-midnight. Ck-out noon. Coin lndry. Meeting rms. Business servs avail. Cr cds: A, C, D, DS, ER, JCB, MC, V.

★ **SHENANDOAH INN.** *140 Lithia Rd (24382).* 540/228-3188; FAX 540/228-6458. 100 rms, 1-2 story. S $35-$45; D $43-$60; each addl $6; under 16 free; wkly, wkend, hol rates; higher rates some special events. Crib free. Pet accepted; $5. TV; cable. Complimentary coffee in lobby. Restaurant nearby. Ck-out 11 am. Balconies. Cr cds: A, C, D, DS, MC, V.

★★ **WYTHEVILLE INN.** *355 Nye Rd (24382),* I-77 N exit 41 & I-81 exit 72. 540/228-7300; FAX 540/228-4223; res: 800/228-2000. 99 rms, 2 story. Apr-Oct: S $45-$60; D $50-$66; each addl $6; under 18 free; higher rates special events; lower rates rest of yr. Crib free. Pet accepted. TV, cable (premium). Pool. Complimentary continental bkfst. Ck-out noon. Business servs avail. Valet serv. Microwaves avail. Cr cds: A, C, D, DS, MC, V.

Inn

★★ **BOXWOOD INN BED & BREAKFAST.** *460 E Main St (24382),* I-81 exit 73. 540/228-8911. 6 rms, 2 story. No rm phones. S $54-$64; D $64-$74; each addl $10. TV in some rms; cable. Complimentary full bkfst. Restaurant adj 11 am-10 pm. Ck-out 11 am, ck-in 4 pm. Built 1845 by local businessman as a wedding gift for his daughter. Antiques and period furnishings. Totally nonsmoking. Cr cds: C, MC, V.

Restaurant

★ **LOG HOUSE.** *520 E Main St (24382).* 540/228-4139. Hrs: 11 am-10 pm. Closed Sun; Dec 25. Res accepted. Wine, beer. Semi-a la carte: lunch $2.99-$15.50, dinner $5.55-$16.95. Child's meals. Specialties: beef stew, stuffed chicken breast. Outdoor dining. Colonial motif; built in 1776. Cr cds: A, C, DS, MC, V.

Yorktown (E-9)

(See also Colonial Parkway, Gloucester, Jamestown, Newport News, Williamsburg)

Founded 1691 **Pop** 200 (est) **Elev** 54 ft **Area Code** 757 **Web** www.nps.gov/colo

Information Colonial National Historical Park, PO Box 210, 23690; 757/898-3400.

Free land offered in 1630 to those adventurous enough "to seate and inhabit" the 50-foot bluffs on the south side of the York River "formerly known by ye Indyan name of Chiskiacke," brought about the beginning of settlement. When the Assembly authorized a port, started in 1691, the town slowly expanded and in the following years became a busy shipping center, with prosperity reaching a peak about 1750. From then on, the port declined along with the Tidewater Virginia tobacco trade.

Yorktown's moment in history came in 1781. British commander Cornwallis, after raiding up and down Virginia with minimal resistance from the Marquis de Lafayette, was sent here to establish a naval base in which

supplies and reinforcements could be shipped to him. The Comte de Grasse's French fleet effectively blockaded the British, however, by controlling the mouth of the Chesapeake Bay. At the Battle of the Capes on September 5, 1781, a British fleet sent to investigate the French presence was defeated by the French. Cornwallis found himself bottled up in Yorktown by combined American and French forces under Washington, which arrived on September 28.

Shelling began October 9. The siege of Yorktown ended on Oct 17 with Cornwallis requesting terms of capitulation. On October 19, Cornwallis' troops marched out with flags and arms cased, their bands playing. Then they laid down their arms, bringing the last major battle of the American Revolution to a close.

Yorktown Battlefield, part of Colonial National Historical Park, surrounds the village. Though Yorktown itself is still an active community, many surviving and reconstructed colonial structures supply an 18th-century atmosphere.

What to See and Do

Grace Episcopal Church (1697). Walls of local marl (a mixture of clay, sand and limestone); damaged in 1781, gutted by fire in 1814. A 1649 communion service is still in use. (Daily) Church St. Phone 757/898-3261.

★ **Yorktown Battlefield.** Surrounds and includes part of town. Remains of 1781 British fortifications, modified and strengthened by Confederate forces in Civil War. Reconstructed American and French lines lie beyond. Roads lead to headquarters, encampment areas of Americans, French. Admission fee includes access to Visitor Center, battlefield tour, Moore House and Nelson House. ¢¢ Golden Access, Age and Eagle passports honored (see MAKING THE MOST OF YOUR TRIP). Stop first at

Visitor Center. Information; special exhibits, General Washington's field tents. (Daily; closed Dec 25) E side of town, at end of Colonial Pkwy. Phone 757/898-3400.

Self-guided battlefield tour. Markers, displays aid in visualizing siege. Highlights include headquarters sites of Lafayette, von Steuben, Rochambeau, Washington; American Battery #2; Grand French Battery; a key point is Surrender Field where the British forces laid down their arms.

Moore House. In this 18th-century house, the "Articles of Capitulation" were drafted. These were signed by General Washington in the captured British Redoubt #10 on Oct 19. (Mid-June-mid-Aug, daily; spring & fall, wkends) Located along battlefield tour road. Phone 757/898-3400. W of here on VA 238 is

Yorktown National Civil War Cemetery. 2,183 interments (1,436 unknown).

Yorktown Victory Monument. Elaborately ornamented 95-ft granite column memorializes American-French alliance in Revolution. E end of Main St. Then proceed to

Nelson House. Original restored mansion built by "Scotch Tom" Nelson in the early 1700s. Home of his grandson, Thomas Nelson, Jr, a signer of the Declaration of Independence. Impressive example of Georgian architecture. (Apr-Oct, daily) Nelson & Main Sts.

Yorktown Victory Center. Museum of the American Revolution chronicles the struggle for independence, from the beginnings of colonial unrest to the formation of the new nation. Exhibit galleries, living history Continental Army encampment, and late-18th-century farm. (Daily; closed Jan 1, Dec 25) Combination ticket with Jamestown Settlement (see JAMESTOWN COLONIAL NATIONAL HISTORICAL PARK) avail. ½ mi W on VA 238. Phone 757/253-4838 or 888/593-4682. Museum ¢¢¢; Combination ticket ¢¢¢¢

Annual Event

Yorktown Day. Observance of America's Revolutionary War victory at Yorktown in 1781. Oct 19.

Motels

★★ **DUKE OF YORK MOTOR HOTEL.** *508 Water St (23690). 757/898-3232; FAX 757/898-5922.* 57 rms, 2-3 story. Memorial Day-Labor Day: S, D $74; each addl $10; lower rates rest of yr. TV. Pool. Restaurant (hrs vary). Ck-out noon. Business servs avail. Some refrigerators. Balconies. Opp beach; overlooks river. Cr cds: A, C, D, DS, MC, V.

★ **YORKTOWN MOTOR LODGE.** *8829 George Washington Hwy (23692). 757/898-5451; FAX 757/898-1766; res: 800/950-4003.* 42 rms, 1 story. Memorial Day-Labor Day: S $45-$55; D $55-$75; each addl $5; under 18 free; lower rates rest of yr. Crib $5. TV; cable (premium). Pool. Playground. Restaurant adj 7 am-9 pm. Ck-out 11 am. Business servs avail. Refrigerators, microwaves. Cr cds: A, C, D, DS, MC, V.

Restaurants

★★ **NICK'S SEAFOOD PAVILION.** *324 Water St (23690), On VA 238 (Water St) at S end of bridge. 757/887-5269.* Hrs: 11 am-10 pm. Closed Dec 25. Continental menu. Semi-a la carte: lunch, dinner $7-$35. Child's meals. Specializes in fresh local seafood, lobster, seafood kebab. Grecian atmosphere; art collection. Family-owned. Cr cds: A, C, D, MC, V.

★★ **RIVER'S INN.** *8109 Yacht Haven Dr (23062), 2½ mi N on US 17. 804/642-9942.* Hrs: 11:30 am-3 pm; 5:30-9 pm; Fri, Sat to 10 pm. Closed Dec 25. Res accepted. Seafood menu. Bar. Semi-a la carte: lunch $5-$8, dinner $15-$21. Child's meals. Specialties: pan-fried crab cakes, Chesapeake blue plate, blue cheese salmon. Outdoor dining. View of marina and York River; nautical decor and artwork. Cr cds: A, C, MC, V.

West Virginia

Population: 1,793,477
Land area: 24,282 square miles
Elevation: 240-4,863 feet
Highest point: Spruce Knob (Pendleton County)
Entered union: June 20, 1863 (35th state)
Capital: Charleston
Motto: Mountaineers are always free
Nickname: Mountain State
State flower: Rhododendron
State bird: Cardinal
State tree: Sugar maple
State tree: Mid-August, 2000, in Lewisburg
Time zone: Eastern
Web: www.state.wv.us/tourism

The wild, rugged topography that made settlement of this area difficult in the early days has today made West Virginia a paradise for outdoor enthusiasts. The state's ski industry has taken advantage of the highest total altitude of any state east of the Mississippi River by opening several alpine and nordic ski areas. Outfitters offer excellent whitewater rafting on the state's many turbulent rivers. Rock climbing, caving and hiking are popular in the Monongahela National Forest, and West Virginia also boasts an impressive state park system, as well as extensive hunting and fishing areas.

The nickname "mountain state" gives only a hint of West Virginia's scenic beauty, which is unsurpassed in the East. West Virginia is also a land of proud traditions, with many festivals held throughout the year as tributes to the state's rich heritage. These events include celebrations honoring the state's sternwheel riverboat legacy, its spectacular autumn foliage and even its strawberries, apples and black walnuts.

The occupation of West Virginia began with the Mound Builders, a prehistoric Ohio Valley culture that left behind at least 300 conical earth mounds that challenge the imagination. Many have been worn away by erosion, but excavations in some have revealed elaborately adorned human skeletons and artifacts of amazing beauty and utility.

Pioneers who ventured into western Virginia in the 18th century found fine vistas and forests, curative springs and beautiful rivers. George Washington and his family frequented the soothing mineral waters of Berkeley Springs (see); and White Sulphur Springs (see) later became a popular resort among the colonists. But much of this area was still considered "the wild West" in those days, and life here was not easy.

The Commonwealth of Virginia largely ignored its western citizens—only one governor was elected from the western counties before 1860. When the counties formed their own state during the Civil War, it was the result of many years of strained relations with the parent state. The move had been debated during those years, and the war finally provided the opportunity the counties needed to break away from Virginia. Although many sentiments in the new state remained pro-South, West Virginia's interests were best served by staying with the Union.

The first land battle of the Civil War took place in the western counties (see PHILIPPI) soon after Fort Sumter was fired upon in April 1861. Through the rest of 1861 and into 1862, Union forces under Generals George McClellan and William S. Rosecrans chased the Confederates back toward rebel Virginia. Succeeding battles were fought farther and farther south until major Confederate resistance became impossible. For the rest of the war, Confederate Army activity in the state was limited to destructive lightning raids designed to wreck railroad lines and damage Union supply sources.

The war left West Virginia a new state, but, like other war-ravaged areas, it had suffered heavy losses of life and property. The recovery took many years, but West Virginians eventually rebuilt their state; new industry was developed, railroads were built, and resources like coal, oil and natural gas brought relative prosperity.

Today, West Virginia still is an important source of bituminous coal and a major producer of building stone, timber, glass and chemicals. The state is also the home of such technological wonders as the National Radio Astronomy Observatory (see MARLINTON), where scientists study the universe via radio telescopes, and the New River Gorge Bridge (see GAULEY BRIDGE), the world's longest steel-span bridge.

When to Go/Climate

West Virginia summers are hot and humid, although temperatures in elevated areas rarely top 90°F. Snowfall can range from 10 to 15 feet in some areas. The best time to visit is in spring or fall.

AVERAGE HIGH/LOW TEMPERATURES (°F)

CHARLESTON

Jan 56/41	**May** 80/66	**Sept** 83/71
Feb 59/43	**June** 85/72	**Oct** 75/61
Mar 65/50	**July** 88/75	**Nov** 67/52
Apr 73/58	**Aug** 87/75	**Dec** 60/45

ELKINS

Jan 50/30	**May** 80/56	**Sept** 81/61
Feb 54/32	**June** 86/64	**Oct** 72/49
Mar 64/40	**July** 88/68	**Nov** 63/41
Apr 72/48	**Aug** 87/67	**Dec** 53/33

Parks and Recreation Finder

Directions to and information about the parks and recreation areas below are given under their respective town/city sections. Please refer to those sections for details.

NATIONAL PARK AND RECREATION AREAS

Key to abbreviations. I.H.S. = International Historic Site; I.P.M.= International Peace Memorial; N.B. = National Battlefield; N.B.P. = National Battlefield Park; N.B.C. = National Battlefield & Cemetery; N.C. = National Conservation Area; N.E.M. = National Expansion Memorial; N.F. = National Forest; N.G. = National Grassland; N.H. = National Historical Park; N.H.C. = National Heritage Corridor; N.H.S. = National Historic Site; N.L. = National Lakeshore; N.M. = National Monument; N.M.P. = National Military Park; N.Mem. = National Memorial; N.P. = National Park; N.Pres. = National Preserve; N.R. = National Recreational Area; N.R.R. = National Recreational River; N.Riv. = National River; N.S. = National Seashore; N.S.R. = National Scenic Riverway; N.S.T. = National Scenic Trail; N.Sc. = National Scientific Reserve; N.V.M. = National Volcanic Monument.

Place Name	Listed Under
Gauley River N.R.	SUMMERSVILLE
Harpers Ferry N.H.	HARPERS FERRY
Monongahela N.F.	ELKINS
New River Gorge N.Riv.	HINTON

STATE PARK AND RECREATION AREAS

Key to abbreviations. I.P. = Interstate Park; S.A.P. = State Archaeological Park; S.B. = State Beach; S.C. = State Conservation Area; S.C.P. = State Conservation Park; S.Cp. = State Campground; S.F. = State Forest; S.G. = State Garden; S.H.A. = State Historic Area; S.H.P. = State Historic Park; S.H.S. = State Historic Site; S.M.P. = State Marine Park; S.N.A. = State Natural Area; S.P. = State Park; S.P.C. = State Public Campground; S.R. = State Reserve; S.R.A. = State Recreation Area; S.Res. = State Reservoir; S.Res.P. = State Resort Park; S.R.P. = State Rustic Park.

Place Name	Listed Under
Audra S.P.	BUCKHANNON
Babcock S.P.	BECKLEY
Beartown S.P.	HILLSBORO
Beech Fork S.P.	HUNTINGTON
Berkeley Springs S.P.	BERKELEY SPRINGS
Blackwater Falls S.P.	DAVIS
Blennerhassett Island S.H.P.	PARKERSBURG
Bluestone S.P.	HINTON
Cacapon S.Res.P.	BERKELEY SPRINGS
Camp Creek S.P.	PRINCETON
Canaan Valley S.Res.P.	DAVIS
Carnifex Ferry Battlefield S.P.	SUMMERSVILLE
Cass Scenic Railroad S.P.	MARLINTON
Cathedral S.P.	AURORA
Cedar Creek S.P.	WESTON
Droop Mountain Battlefield S.P.	HILLSBORO
Grave Creek Mound S.P.	WHEELING
Hawks Nest S.P.	GAULEY BRIDGE
Holly River S.P.	WEBSTER SPRINGS
Lost River S.P.	MOOREFIELD
North Bend S.P.	PARKERSBURG
Pinnacle Rock S.P.	BLUEFIELD
Pipestem S.Res.P.	HINTON
Prickett's Fort S.P.	FAIRMONT
Stonewall Jackson Lake S.P.	WESTON
Tomlinson Run S.P.	WEIRTON
Twin Falls S.Res.P.	BECKLEY
Tygart Lake S.P.	GRAFTON
Watoga S.P.	HILLSBORO
Watters Smith Memorial S.P.	CLARKSBURG

Water-related activities, hiking, riding, various other sports, picnicking and visitor centers, as well as camping, are available in many of these areas. There is a small fee for swimming and game court use. Campgrounds with picnic facilities are available in 22 state parks and forests; all have drinking water and sanitary facilities; some have showers, coin laundries, utility hookups; 2-wk limit; $6-$14/night for 6 persons or less, $1 each addl person. Camping season runs from mid-April-October in all parks except Canaan Valley and Pipestem resorts, which are open year round. Campground reservations may be made at Babcock, Beech Fork, Blackwater Falls, Bluestone, Canaan Valley Resort, Cedar Creek, Chief Logan, Holly River, North Bend, Pipestem Resort, Stonewall Jackson Lake, Tomlinson Run, Twin Falls Resort, Tygart Lake and Watoga state parks and at Greenbrier and Kanawha state forests. There is a $5 handling fee; reservations must be made 7-14 days in advance. Camping at all other state parks is on a first-come, first-served basis. Pets on leash only. Many cabins and lodges are available for seasonal or year-round use; 7-day minimum second Monday in June-Labor Day. Most parks are open daily, 8

CALENDAR HIGHLIGHTS

MAY

Webster Springs Woodchopping Festival (Webster Springs). Southeastern World Woodchopping Championships; state championship turkey calling contest, draft horse pull, horse show, fireman's rodeo; arts & crafts; music, parades, concessions.

Vandalia Gathering (Charleston). A festival of traditional arts; craft demonstrations, clogging, gospel music, fiddling, banjo picking, special exhibits. Phone 304/558-0220.

JUNE

Mountain Heritage Arts and Crafts Festival (Harpers Ferry). More than 190 craftspeople and artisans demonstrate quilting, wool spinning, pottery throwing, vegetable dyeing and other crafts; concerts. Also in Sept. Phone 304/725-2055 or 800/624-0577.

JULY

Jamboree in the Hills (Wheeling). A 4-day country music festival featuring more than 30 hours of music; top country stars. Camping is available. Phone 800/624-5456.

AUGUST

State Fair (Lewisburg). Fairgrounds. Exhibitors from a number of other states; horse shows, harness racing. Phone 304/645-1090.

SEPTEMBER

Sternwheel Regatta Festival (Charleston). Sternwheeler and towboat races, parades, contests, hot-air balloon race, fireworks; nationally known entertainers nightly; arts & crafts. Phone 304/348-6419.

Stonewall Jackson Heritage Arts & Crafts Jubilee (Weston). Jackson's Mill State 4-H Conference Center. Mountain crafts, music, dance and food. Phone 304/269-1863.

OCTOBER

Mountain State Forest Festival (Elkins). Some events on campus of Davis & Elkins College. Queen Silvia is crowned; carnival, parades; entertainment; tilting at rings on horseback; sawing and woodchopping contests; marksmanship tests; State Championship Fiddle and Banjo Contest; juried craft fair and art exhibit. Phone 304/636-1824.

Bridge Day (Fayetteville). New River Gorge Bridge. Bridge is opened to pedestrians; parachutists test their skills by jumping off the bridge and floating to the bottom of the gorge. Contact Fayetteville Chamber of Commerce, 304/465-5617.

am-sunset. For information and reservations contact individual parks or phone 800/225-5982 (exc AK and HI).

SKI AREAS

Place Name	Listed Under
Canaan Valley S.Res.P.	DAVIS
Elk River Touring Center	MARLINTON
Oglebay Resort Park	WHEELING
Snowshoe Mt Resort	MARLINTON
Timberline Four Seasons Resort	DAVIS
White Grass Touring Center	DAVIS
WinterPlace Ski Resort	BECKLEY

FISHING & HUNTING

In addition to a million acres of prime federal hunting and fishing land, West Virginia has 48 wildlife management areas. Nonresident statewide fishing license $30; 3-day license $5. Nonresident (exc KY, OH, PA) hunting, basic license, $100; archery deer, muzzleloader deer and turkey stamps $25; 6-day, small-game license $20. Nonresident migratory waterfowl stamp $5. A conservation stamp is required in addition to all regular hunting and fishing licenses (nonresident $5). For further information contact the Division of Natural Resources, Wildlife Resources Section, State Capitol Complex, Building 3, Charleston 25305; 304/558-2771.

Driving Information

Children under 9 must be in an approved passenger restraint anywhere in vehicle; ages 3-8 may use a regulation safety belt; children under 3 yrs must use an approved safety seat. For further information phone 304/746-2121.

INTERSTATE HIGHWAY SYSTEM

The following alphabetical listing of West Virginia towns in *Mobil Travel Guide* shows that these cities are within 10 miles of the indicated interstate highways. A highway map, however, should be checked for the nearest exit.

Highway Number	Cities/Towns within 10 miles
Interstate 64	Beckley, Charleston, Huntington, Lewisburg, Nitro, White Sulphur Springs.
Interstate 70	Wheeling.
Interstate 77	Charleston, Parkersburg, Princeton, Ripley; also see WV Tpke.
Interstate 79	Charleston, Clarksburg, Fairmont, Morgantown, Sutton.
Interstate 81	Martinsburg.

Additional Visitor Information

Travel materials, including information on accommodations, skiing, caving, rock climbing, whitewater rafting and other activities, are available from the West Virginia Division of Tourism, State Capitol Complex, 2101 Washington St E, Charleston 25305; 800/225-5982. The Information & Education Section, Department of Natural Resources, State Capitol, Charleston 25305, publishes a monthly magazine, *Wonderful West Virginia.*

Information on hiking along the completed portion of the Allegheny Trail, including a hiking guide (fee), is available from the West Virginia Scenic Trails Association, 633 West Virginia Ave, Morgantown 26505. The trail runs north-south from the Pennsylvania state line near Coopers Rock State Forest to Peters Mountain, southeast of Lindside, at the Virginia state line.

There are several welcome centers in West Virginia; visitors who stop by will find information and brochures most helpful in planning stops at points of interest. Their locations are as follows: on I-64, westbound near White Sulphur Springs and eastbound near Huntington; on I-81, southbound by the West Virginia/Maryland border and northbound near the West Virginia/Virginia border; on I-79, southbound north of Morgantown; on I-77, southbound near Mineral Wells; on I-70, westbound near the West Virginia/Pennsylvania border. The West Virginia Information Center is located at Harpers Ferry. All centers are open (daily; closed Jan 1, Thanksgiving, Dec 25). Personnel at any of these locations will also assist visitors in making lodging reservations. In addition, information may be obtained at the Capitol Guides Desk in the rotunda of the State Capitol at Charleston (Memorial Day-Labor Day, Mon-Sat, also Sun afternoons).

Aurora (C-6)

(See also Davis, Grafton)

Settled 1787 **Pop** 150 (est) **Elev** 2,641 ft **Area Code** 304 **Zip** 26705

Located at the summit of Cheat Mountain, Aurora offers visitors clean air and high altitude.

What to See and Do

Cathedral State Park. Hiking trails through 132 acres of deep, virgin hemlock forest. Cross-country skiing. Picnicking. Standard hrs. 1 mi E on US 50. Phone 304/735-3771.

Beckley (E-4)

(See also Gauley Bridge, Hinton)

Founded 1838 **Pop** 18,296 **Elev** 2,416 ft **Area Code** 304
E-mail travel@visitwv.org **Web** www.visitwv.org
Information Southern West Virginia Convention & Visitors Bureau, PO Box 1799, 25802; 304/252-2244 or 800/VISIT-WV

The "smokeless coal capital of the world" is a center for more than 200 small mining and farming towns. Beckley is situated on a high plateau surrounded by fertile valleys. During the Civil War, the village was held at various times by both armies; Union troops shelled it in 1863. Coal was found here in 1774, but was not mined until 1890. Smokeless coal became the standard bunker fuel during World War I, and the demand continued for years thereafter. Beckley now serves as a commercial, medical and tourist center.

What to See and Do

Babcock State Park. More than 4,100 acres of rugged mountain scenery with trout stream and waterfalls, views of New River Canyon, rhododendrons (May-July); restored operating gristmill. Swimming pool; lake and stream fishing; boating (rowboat, paddleboat rentals). Hiking trails, horseback riding; game courts (equipment rentals). Cross-country skiing. Picnicking, playground, concession; restaurant (seasonal). Camping (electrical hookups), 26 cabins (rentals, spring & fall). Nature and recreation programs (summer). Standard hrs, fees. (Mid-Apr-Oct) 23 mi NE via US 19 to WV 41, near Landisburg. Phone 304/438-3003 or 800/CALL-WVA.

Beckley Exhibition Coal Mine. Riding tours in coal cars through 1,500 ft of underground passageways, constant 56°F temperature; museum, coal company house, superintendent of coal mines house, church, campground. (Apr-Oct, daily) 1½ mi SE off I-77, exit 44 on Ewart Ave in New River Park. Phone 304/256-1747. ¢¢

Grandview Unit of New River Gorge National River. Nearly 900 wooded acres at the northern end of the New River Gorge National River area (see HINTON); offers spectacular overlooks of New River Gorge and Horseshoe Bend; rhododendron gardens. Hiking trails, game courts (some fees). Cross-country skiing. Picnicking, playgrounds, concession. Outdoor dramas (June-Labor Day, daily exc Mon). 5 mi SE on US 19, then 5 mi NE via Airport, Glen Hedrick & Grandview Rds. Contact Superintendent, PO Box 246, Glen Jean 25846; Phone 304/763-3715 or 304/465-0508.

Lake Stephens. A 303-acre lake with swimming; fishing; boating. Trailer camping (hookups). W of town. Phone 304/934-5323.

Plum Orchard Lake Wildlife Management Area. More than 3,200 acres with rabbit, grouse, squirrel hunting. Also 202-acre lake with more than 6 mi of shoreline; boating; fishing for bass, channel catfish, crappie and bluegill. Picnicking, playground, camping. 11 mi N on I-77 to Pax exit, then E on RR 23. Phone 304/469-9905.

Twin Falls Resort State Park. Approx 4,000 acres with restored pioneer house and farm. Swimming pool. Hiking trails; 18-hole golf course, clubhouse; tennis, game courts. Picnicking, playground, restaurant, lodge. Camping, 13 cabins (equipment rentals). Recreation center, programs. Standard hrs, fees. (Daily) 25 mi SW via WV 16 & WV 54, then W on WV 97, near Maben. Phone 304/294-4000.

Whitewater rafting. Many outfitters offer guided trips on the New and Gauley rivers. For a list of outfitters contact the Southern West Virginia Convention & Visitors Bureau, PO Box 1799, 25802; phone 304/252-2244 or 800/VISIT-WV.

WinterPlace Ski Resort. On southern West Virginia's highest peak. 2 quad, 3 triple, double chairlifts, 2 surface lifts; school, rentals; snowmaking; cafeteria, lounge; restaurants; entertainment; children's program; sporting goods shops. 27 trails. Night skiing. 24 runs; longest run 1¼ mi; vertical drop 603 ft. Snowboard park. (Thanksgiving-late Mar, daily) 17 mi S via I-77 exit 28 (Ghent/Flat Top), follow signs. Phone 304/787-3221 or 800/607-SNOW. ¢¢¢¢

Youth Museum of Southern West Virginia. Hands-on exhibits, planetarium, log house. (May-Labor Day, daily; rest of yr, Tues-Sat) Ewart Ave, in New River Park. Phone 304/252-3730.

Annual Event

Appalachian Festival. Tamarack. Exhibitions and demonstrations of native crafts; entertainment, food. Phone 304/252-7328. Aug.

Seasonal Event

Theatre West Virginia. Cliffside Amphitheatre. Outdoor musical dramas. Grandview Park, W on I-64, exit 129B, follow signs. Contact PO Box 1205, 25802; 304/256-6800 or 800/666-9142. Mid-June-mid-Aug.

Motels

✓ ★ **COMFORT INN.** *1909 Harper Rd (25801).* 304/255-2161; FAX 304/255-2161; res: 800/888-2598 or 888/259-8542. Web wvweb.com/www/cibeckley.html. 130 rms, 3 story. S $60-$90; D $62-$92; under 19 free. Crib free. Pet accepted; $10. TV; cable (premium), VCR avail (movies). Complimentary continental bkfst. Restaurant nearby. Ck-out noon. Coin lndry. Business servs avail. Sundries. Downhill ski 15 mi. Exercise equipt. Some refrigerators, microwaves. Cr cds: A, C, D, DS, ER, JCB, MC, V.

⊡ 🐾 ⛷ 🏋 ⬛ ⬛ SC

★ **HAMPTON INN.** *110 Harper Park Dr (25801), just off I-77.* 304/252-2121; FAX 304/255-6238; res: 800/426-7866. 108 rms, 5 story. S, D $64-$85; each addl $7; under 18 free; higher rates Bridge Day. Crib free. TV; cable (premium). Pool. Complimentary continental bkfst. Restaurant adj. Ck-out noon. Business servs avail. Downhill ski 15 mi. Microwaves avail. Cr cds: A, C, D, DS, MC, V.

⊡ ⛷ ⬛ ⬛ ⬛ SC

★★ **HOLIDAY INN.** *1924 Harper Rd (25801).* 304/255-1511; FAX 304/256-0526; res: 800/465-4329 or 800/233-1466. Web wvweb.com/www/holiday_inn-beckley. 105 rms, 3 story. No elvtr. Apr-Oct: S, D $85-$90; under 19 free; package plans; lower rates rest of yr. Crib free. TV; cable (premium). Pool. Restaurant 6 am-2 pm, 5-10 pm. Rm serv. Bar 3 pm-3 am; Sun to 1 am. Ck-out 1 pm. Free guest lndry. Meeting rms. Business servs avail. In-rm modem link. Downhill ski 15 mi. Some in-rm whirlpools, refrigerators, microwaves. Cr cds: A, C, D, DS, JCB, MC, V.

⊡ ⛷ ⬛ ⬛ ⬛ SC

Berkeley Springs (B-7)

(See also Martinsburg)

Founded 1776 **Pop** 735 (est) **Elev** 612 ft **Area Code** 304 **Zip** 25411
E-mail tbs@intrepid.net **Web** www.berkeleysprings.com
Information Berkeley Springs-Morgan County Chamber of Commerce, 304 Fairfax St; 304/258-3738 or 800/447-8797

Popularized by George Washington, who surveyed the area for Lord Fairfax in 1748, Berkeley Springs is the oldest spa in the nation. Fairfax later granted the land around the springs to Virginia. The town is officially named Bath, for the famous watering place in England, but the post office is Berkeley Springs. The waters, which are piped throughout the town, are fresh and slightly sweet, without the medicinal flavor of most mineral springs. Washington and his family returned again and again. The popularity of the resort reached its peak after the Revolution, becoming something of a summer capital for Washingtonians in the 1830s. But like all resort towns, Berkeley Springs declined as newer, more fashionable spas came into vogue. The Civil War completely destroyed the town's economy. Today, the town is again visited for its healthful waters, spas and charming downtown.

What to See and Do

Berkeley Springs State Park. Famous resort with health baths of all types (fees); five warm springs. Main bathhouse (daily; closed Jan 1, Dec 25). Roman bathhouse with second-floor museum (Memorial Day-mid-Oct, daily). Swimming pool (Memorial Day-Labor Day, daily; fee). Center of town. Phone 304/258-2711 or 304/258-5860. Overlooking park is

The Castle (1886). English-Norman castle, built by Colonel Samuel Taylor Suit for his fiancee, has the flavor of England's famous Berkeley Castle, where King Edward II was murdered in 1327. The battlement tower walls are indented with the cross of St George. The castle is furnished with 17th- and 18th-century antiques and contains a pine-paneled library, carved staircase, interesting collections. Gift shop. Tours. (Daily) Phone 304/258-3274. ¢¢¢

Cacapon Resort State Park. More than 6,100 acres with swimming, sand beach; fishing, boating (rowboat and paddleboat rentals). Hiking, bridle trails, horseback riding; 18-hole golf course, tennis, game courts. Cross-country skiing. Picnicking, playground, concession, restaurant, lodge. No camping; 30 cabins. Nature, recreation programs. Arts & crafts center. Standard hrs, fees. 10 mi S off US 522. Phone 304/258-1022.

Sleepy Creek Wildlife Management Area. Approx 23,000 acres of rugged forest offer wild turkey, deer, grouse and squirrel hunting. Boating, bass fishing on 205-acre lake. Primitive camping (fee). Also 70 miles of hiking trails crossing 2 mountains, several valleys. 15 mi SE, E of US 522. Phone 304/754-3855.

View from Prospect Peak. Potomac River winds through what the National Geographic Society has called one of the nation's outstanding vistas. On WV 9, near town.

Annual Event

Apple Butter Festival. Crafts demonstrations, music, contests. Columbus Day wknd.

Resorts

✓ ★★ **CACAPON STATE PARK.** *RR 1 Box 230 (25411), on US 522, in Cacapon Resort State Park.* 304/258-1022; FAX 304/258-5323; res: 800/225-5982. Web wvweb.com/www/cacapon.html. 49 rms, 2 story, 30 kit. cabins. Apr-Oct: S, D $46-$54; each addl $6; kit. cabins $282-$648/wk; lower rates rest of yr. Crib free in lodge, $5 in cabins. Some TV; cable. Dining rm 7 am-9 pm; winter 8 am-7 pm. Ck-out 10 am, ck-in 4 pm. Meeting rms. Gift shop. Tennis. 18-hole golf, greens fee $13-$24, putting green, driving range. Rec rm. Picnic tables. Near lake; boat rentals, sandy beach. Hiking trails. Naturalist program (Apr-Oct). State-operated. Cr cds: C, D, MC, V.

D [symbols] SC

★★ **COOLFONT RESORT.** *1777 Cold Run Valley Rd; Rte 1 Box 710 (25411), 4 mi W on WV 9, then left on Cold Run Valley Rd. 304/258-4500; FAX 304/258-5499; res: 800/888-8768.* Web www.cool font.com. 22 rms in main bldg, 2 story, 34 cottages. MAP, Oct: S $107-$119; D $168-$188; each addl $84-$94; cottages $198-$238; package plans; fitness plan; wkends, hols (2-3 day min); lower rates rest of yr. Crib $10. Indoor pool; whirlpool. Playground. Supervised child's activities (June-Aug; wkends only rest of yr); ages 5-12. Complimentary coffee in rms. Dining rm 8 am-2 pm, 5:30-8:30 pm; Fri, Sat to 9:30 pm; Sun 8 am-3 pm, 5:30-8 pm. Snacks. Picnics. Bar; entertainment Sat. Ck-out noon, ck-in 4 pm. Gift shop. Coin lndry. Meeting rms. Tennis. Swimming beach; boats. X-country ski on site. Sleighing. Hiking. Lawn games. Exercise equipt; sauna. Massage. Refrigerators; microwaves avail. Some balconies. Picnic tables. Secluded woodland resort on 1,350 acres. Cr cds: C, DS, MC, V.

D [symbols]

Inns

★★★ **COUNTRY INN.** *207 S Washington St (25411). 304/258-2210; FAX 304/258-3986; res: 800/822-6630.* Web wvweb.com/www/coun try_inn/html. 70 rms, 13 share bath, 3 story. S, D $37-$85; each addl $15; suites $80-$145; hol wkends 2-night min; some wkday rates. TV; cable, VCR avail (movies). Dining rm 7-11 am, 11:30 am-2 pm, 5-9 pm; Fri, Sat to 10 pm. Private club 11 am-11 pm; entertainment Sat, Sun. Ck-out noon, ck-in 3 pm. Meeting rms. Business servs avail. Gift shop. Massage. Colonial design. Mineral baths and spa. Cr cds: A, C, D, DS, MC, V.

D [symbols] SC

★★★ **HIGHLAWN INN.** *304 Market St (25411). 304/258-5700; res: 888/290-4163.* Web www.virtualcities.com. 12 rms in 4 bldgs, 2-3 story. No rm phones. S, D $85-$185; whirlpool suite $135. Adults only. TV; cable. Complimentary full bkfst; afternoon refreshments. Ck-out noon, ck-in 2 pm. Health club privileges. Victorian mansion; built 1897. Antiques. Cr cds: C, MC, V.

D [symbols]

Bethany (A-5)

(See also Weirton, Wheeling)

Pop 1,139 **Elev** 932 ft **Area Code** 304 **Zip** 26032

What to See and Do

Bethany College (1840). (800 students) Founded by Alexander Campbell, the leading influence in the 19th-century religious movement that gave rise to the Disciples of Christ, Churches of Christ and Christian Churches. Historic buildings on 300-acre campus include Old Main, styled after the University of Glasgow in Scotland; Pendleton Heights, a 19th-century house used as the college president's residence; Old Bethany Meeting House (1852), Delta Tau Delta Founder's House (1854) and the

Campbell Mansion. A 24-rm house where Campbell lived; antique furnishings. On property is hexagonal brick study, one-room schoolhouse and smokehouse. The Campbell family cemetery, "God's Acre," is across from the mansion. (Apr-Oct, daily exc Mon; rest of yr, by appt) For tour of all buildings, phone 304/829-7285 or 304/829-7000. ¢¢

Bluefield (E-4)

(See also Princeton)

Founded 1889 **Pop** 12,756 **Elev** 2,611 ft **Area Code** 304 **Zip** 24701
E-mail bcvb@bluestonecvb.com **Web** www.bluestonecvb.com
Information Convention & Visitors Bureau, 500 Bland St, PO Box 4099; 304/325-8438 or 800/221-3206

Named for the bluish chicory covering the nearby hills, Bluefield owes its existence to the Pocahontas Coal Field. The town came to life in the 1880s, when the railroad came through to transport the coal. This commercial and industrial center of southern West Virginia is known as nature's "air-conditioned city" because of its altitude—one-half mile above sea level. Bluefield has a sister city by the same name in Virginia, directly across the state line.

What to See and Do

Eastern Regional Coal Archives. Center highlights the history of West Virginia coal fields; exhibits, photographs, mining implements; films, research material. (Mon-Fri afternoons; closed most hols) In Craft Memorial Library, 600 Commerce St. Phone 304/325-3943. **Free**

Panther State Forest. More than 7,800 acres of rugged hills. Swimming pool (Memorial Day-Labor Day); fishing, hunting. Hiking trails. Picnicking, playground, concession. Camping. Standard hrs, fees. 50 mi NW off US 52 near Panther. Phone 304/938-2252.

Pinnacle Rock State Park. The approx 250-acre park contains a 15-acre lake and interesting sandstone formations, which resemble a giant cockscomb. Hiking. Picnicking. Standard hrs, fees. 7 mi NW on US 52. Phone 304/589-5307.

Motels

✓★ **ECONO LODGE.** *3400 Cumberland Rd (24701). 304/327-8171; FAX 304/327-8171; res: 800/228-5050.* 48 rms, 2 story. S $39; D $45; each addl $5; under 18 free. Crib free. Pet accepted; $5. TV; cable. Coffee in lobby. Restaurant nearby. Ck-out 11 am. Business servs avail. Cr cds: A, C, D, DS, MC, V.

D [symbols] SC

★★ **HOLIDAY INN.** *Rte 460 (24701), 3 mi W of I-77, Bluefield exit 1, via US 460/52. 304/325-6170; FAX 304/323-2451; res: 800/465-4329.* Web www.com.holidayinnonthehill.com. 118 rms, 2 story. S, D $85; each addl $10; suites $170; under 18 free. Crib free. Pet accepted. TV; cable (premium), VCR avail. Heated pool; poolside serv. Saunas. Restaurant 6 am-10 pm. Ck-out noon. Meeting rms. In-rm modem link. Gift shop. Valet serv Mon-Fri. Golf privileges. Cr cds: A, C, D, DS, JCB, MC, V.

D [symbols] SC

★★ **RAMADA INN.** *3175 E Cumberland Rd (24701). 304/325-5421; FAX 304/325-6045; res: 800/272-6232.* 98 rms, 2 story. May-early Sept: S $63; D $68; each addl $5; under 18 free; wkend, wkly rates; ski plans; wkends (2-day min); lower rates rest of yr. Crib free. TV; cable (premium), VCR avail. Restaurant 6 am-10 pm. Rm serv. Bar 5 pm-1 am; entertainment Fri, Sat. Ck-out noon. Meeting rms. Business servs avail. Bellhops. Valet serv. Sundries. Exercise equipt; saunas. Indoor pool; whirlpool, poolside serv. Game rm. Rec rm. Some refrigerators; microwaves avail. Cr cds: A, C, D, DS, MC, V.

D [symbols] SC

Restaurant

✓★ **MAYFLOWER I.** *105 Hockman Pike (24605). 540/322-4578.* Seafood menu. Specializes in seafood platters. Hrs: 3-8:30 pm; Sat 2-9 pm; Sun 11:30 am-8 pm. Closed Mon; most major hols. Semi-a la carte: lunch, dinner $5.75-$11. Child's meals. Casual atmosphere with nautical decor. Cr cds: C, MC, V.

D SC ⌐

Buckhannon (C-5)

(See also Elkins, Philippi, Weston)

Settled 1770 **Pop** 5,909 **Elev** 1,433 ft **Area Code** 304 **Zip** 26201
Information Buckhannon-Upshur Chamber of Commerce, 16 S Kanawha St, PO Box 442; 304/472-1722

What to See and Do

Audra State Park. Approx 360 acres offer swimming in a natural mountain stream surrounded by tall timber; bathhouse. Hiking trails. Picnicking, playground, concession. Tent & trailer camping. Standard hrs, fees. 8 mi N on US 119, then 6 mi E on WV 11. Phone 304/457-1162.

Holly River State Park. 8,101 acres and the second largest in WV. Camping. Cabins. Picnicking. Hiking. Standard fees. 32 mi S on WV 20. Phone 304/493-6353.

West Virginia State Wildlife Center. Fenced-in habitats of approx 50 species of birds and animals native to West Virginia, including deer, elk, buffalo, timber wolf, mountain lion and black bear. Loop walkway (1¼ mi). Trout pond. Picnicking, concession. (May-Oct, daily; Apr & Nov, wkends & hols only; Dec-Mar, days vary) 12 mi S on WV 4, 20. Phone 304/924-6211. Apr-Nov. ¢

West Virginia Wesleyan College (1890). (1,600 students) An 80-acre campus featuring Georgian architecture. Wesley Chapel, the largest place of worship in the state, contains a Casavant organ with 1,474 pipes. College Ave & Meade St. Phone 304/473-8000.

Annual Event

West Virginia Strawberry Festival. Parades, dances, exhibits, air show, arts & crafts, other activities. Phone 304/472-9036. Usually wk before Memorial Day.

Motels

★★ **BICENTENNIAL MOTEL.** *88 E Main St (26201). 304/472-5000; FAX 304/472-9159.* 55 rms, 2 story. S $49.95-$55.95; D $55.95-$61.95; each addl $6; under 12 free. Crib free. TV; cable (premium). Pool; wading pool. Playground. Restaurant 6 am-9 pm. Rm serv. Private club 4 pm-midnight. Ck-out noon. Meeting rms. Business servs avail. Sundries. Gift shop. Some refrigerators. Picnic tables, grills. Cr cds: A, C, D, DS, MC, V.

D ⤸ ≋ ⚘ SC

✓★ **CENTENNIAL MOTEL.** *22 N Locust St (26201). 304/472-4100.* 26 rms. S $36.95-$42.95; D $42.95-$48.95; each addl $6; under 12 free. Crib free. Pet accepted. TV; cable. Complimentary coffee. Restaurant nearby. Ck-out noon. Cr cds: A, C, D, DS, MC, V.

🐾 ≋ ⚘ SC

Charleston (D-3)

(See also Nitro)

Settled 1794 **Pop** 57,287 **Elev** 601 ft **Area Code** 304
Web www.charlestonwv.com
Information Convention & Visitors Bureau, Charleston Civic Center, 200 Civic Center Dr, 25301; 304/344-5075 or 800/733-5469

Charleston, capital of the state, is the trading hub for the Great Kanawha Valley, where deposits of coal, oil, natural gas and brine have greatly contributed to this region's national importance as a production center for chemicals and glass. Two institutions of higher learning, West Virginia State College and the University of Charleston, are located in the metropolitan area. Charleston is also the northern terminus of the spectacular West Virginia Turnpike.

Daniel Boone lived around Charleston until 1795. During his residence he was appointed a lieutenant colonel in the county militia in 1789 and was elected to the Virginia assembly the same year. The area became important as a center of salt production in 1824, when steam engines were used to operate brine pumps. After Charleston became the capital of West Virginia in 1885, following a dispute with Wheeling, the town came into its own. During World War I, an increased demand for plate and bottle glass, as well as for high explosives, made Charleston and the nearby town of Nitro (see) boom.

What to See and Do

Coonskin Park. Recreation area includes swimming; fishing for bass and catfish; pedal boating. Hiking trails; 18-hole golf, miniature golf; tennis. Picnicking, playground, concession. (Daily; closed Dec 25; some activities seasonal) Fees for activities. ¾ mi N off WV 114. Phone 304/341-8000.

Elk River Scenic Drive. Beautiful drive along the Elk River from Charleston northeast to Sutton (approx 60 mi). Begins just north of town; take US 119 NE to Clendenin, then WV 4 NE to Rte 19 in Sutton.

Kanawha State Forest. Approx 9,300 acres with swimming pool, bathhouse (Memorial Day-Labor Day); hunting. Hiking, interpretive trail for the disabled. Horseback riding. Cross-country skiing. Picnicking, playground, concession. Camping. Standard hrs, fees. 7 mi S off US 119. Phone 304/558-3500.

State Capitol (1932). One of America's most beautiful state capitols, the building was designed by Cass Gilbert in Italian-Renaissance style. Within the gold-leaf dome, which rises 300 ft above the street, hangs a 10,080-piece, hand-cut imported chandelier weighing more than 2 tons. Guided tours avail. (Daily exc Sun) On river at E Kanawha Blvd between Greenbrier St & California Ave. Phone 304/558-3456 or 800/225-5982. **Free** Across the grounds is the

Governor's Mansion (1925). Beautiful Georgian structure of red Harvard brick with white Corinthian columns. Tours (Thurs & Fri, also by appt). 1716 Kanawha Blvd E. Phone 304/558-3809. **Free**

Sunrise Museum. On 16 acres of wooded grounds with gardens and trails, the museum is housed in two historic mansions (art museum & science museum) built by William MacCorkle, ninth governor of West Virginia. Guided tours by appt. (Wed-Sun; closed major hols) 746 Myrtle Rd, across South Side Bridge. Phone 304/344-8035. ¢¢

Art Museum. American paintings, graphics and sculpture from 19th through 20th centuries; rotating exhibits; films and lectures. ¢¢

Science Museum. Exhibits in natural sciences and technology; nature center with animals; planetarium, programs, lectures. Interactive exhibits, demonstrations. ¢¢

The Cultural Center. The Center houses the Division of Culture and History and Library Commission; West Virginia crafts shop (daily); archives library (daily exc Sun); state museum; special events, changing exhibits. (Daily; closed hols) Next to state capitol, on Greenbrier St. Phone 304/558-0220. **Free** Also here is

Mountain Stage. Live public radio show heard on more than 115 stations nationwide; features jazz, folk, blues and rock. Visitors may watch show; afternoon performances (Sun). Phone 304/342-5757. ¢¢¢

West Virginia State College (1891). (4,635 students) On campus are Davis Fine Arts Bldg with periodic exhibits (daily exc Sun; closed hols); Asian art collection in library (daily; closed hols); and East Hall (1895), formerly president's residence. Tours. 8 mi W via I-64 exit 50, in Institute. Phone 304/766-3000.

Whitewater rafting. Many outfitters offer guided rafting, canoeing and fishing trips on the New and Gauley rivers. For a list of outfitters contact the West Virginia Division of Tourism, Research & Development, 2101 Washington St E, Bldg 17, 25305; phone 800/225-5982.

Annual Events

Vandalia Gathering. A festival of traditional arts; craft demonstrations, clogging, gospel music, fiddling, banjo picking, special exhibits. Phone 304/558-0220. Memorial Day wkend.

Sternwheel Regatta Festival. Sternwheeler and towboat races, parades, contests, hot-air balloon race, fireworks; nationally known entertainers nightly; arts & crafts. Phone 304/348-6419. Late Aug-early Sept.

Motels

✓★★ **DAYS INN.** 6400 SE MacCorkle Ave (25304). 304/925-1010; FAX 304/925-1364; res: 800/304-3809. 147 rms, 2-3 story. S $49.50-$54.50; D $58.50-$63.50; each addl $5; under 12 free. Crib free. Pet accepted, some restrictions. TV; cable (premium). Complimentary continental bkfst. Restaurant nearby. Ck-out noon. Meeting rms. Business servs avail. In-rm modem link. Sundries. Exercise equipt. Pool. Many refrigerators, microwaves. Cr cds: A, C, D, DS, MC, V.

★ **KANAWHA CITY MOTOR LODGE.** 3103 MacCorkle Ave Se (25304). 304/344-2461; FAX 304/345-1419. 50 rms, 2 story. S $51-$55; D $56-$60; each addl $5; kit. units $61; under 18 free. Crib free. TV; cable (premium). Complimentary coffee in lobby. Restaurant nearby. Ck-out noon. Business servs avail. Charleston Memorial Hospital opp. Cr cds: A, C, D, DS, MC, V.

✓★ **RED ROOF INN.** 6305 MacCorkle Ave SE (25304). 304/925-6953; FAX 304/925-8111; res: 800/843-7663. E-mail i0059@redroof.com; web www.redroofinns.com. 108 rms, 2 story. Apr-Oct: S $49.99; D $59.99; each addl $7; under 18 free; higher rates special events; lower rates rest of yr. Crib free. Pet accepted. TV; cable (premium). Complimentary coffee in lobby. Restaurant adj 6 am-10:30 pm. Ck-out noon. Business servs avail. Cr cds: A, C, D, DS, MC, V.

Motor Hotels

★★ **HAMPTON INN.** 1 Virginia St W (25901). 304/343-9300; FAX 304/342-9393. 112 rms, 5 story. S $73-$83; D $78-$88; each addl $5; under 18 free; higher rates basketball tournament. Crib free. TV; cable (premium). Heated pool. Complimentary continental bkfst. Restaurant nearby. Ck-out noon. Meeting rm. Business servs avail. Sundries. Free airport, RR station transportation. Cr cds: A, C, D, DS, MC, V.

★★ **HAMPTON INN.** 1 Preferred Pl (25309). 304/746-4646; FAX 304/746-4665. 104 rms, 6 story. S $76-$130; D $81-$130; each addl $5; under 18 free. Crib free. TV; cable (premium). Indoor pool; whirlpool. Complimentary continental bkfst. Coffee in rms. Restaurant adj 10-1 am. Ck-out noon. Business center. In-rm modem link. Sundries. Coin lndry. Free airport transportation. Exercise equipt. Some in-rm whirlpools, refrigerators, microwaves. Cr cds: A, C, D, DS, MC, V.

★★ **HOLIDAY INN CIVIC CENTER.** 100 Civic Center Dr (25301). 304/345-0600; FAX 304/343-1322. 200 rms, 6 story. S, D $65-$99; under 18 free; wkend rates. Crib free. TV; cable, VCR avail. Pool. Restaurant 6 am-2 pm, 5-10 pm; Sat, Sun from 6:30 am. Rm serv. Bar. Ck-out noon. Coin lndry. Meeting rms. Business servs avail. Bellhops. Valet serv. Free airport transportation. Some refrigerators. Cr cds: A, C, D, DS, JCB, MC, V.

Hotels

★★★ **HOLIDAY INN.** 600 Kanawha Blvd E (25301). 304/344-4092; FAX 304/345-4847; res: 800/465-4329. Web wvweb.com/www/holiday_inn_charleston_house. 256 rms, 12 story. S, D $109-$119; each addl $6; under 18 free; suites $200-$375; wkend rates; package plans. Crib free. Pet accepted. TV; cable (premium), VCR avail. Heated pool. Restaurant 6:30 am-2 pm; dining rm 5-10 pm. Bar 4 pm-2 am; closed Sun. Ck-out noon. Convention facilities. Business servs avail. In-rm modem link. Barber, beauty shop. Gift shop. Garage. Free airport transportation. Exercise equipt. Some wet bars. Some rms with river view. Cr cds: A, C, D, DS, JCB, MC, V.

★★★ **MARRIOTT HOTEL.** 200 Lee St E (25301). 304/345-6500; FAX 304/353-3722; res: 800/228-9290. 352 rms, 16 story. S, D $89-$140; suites $250-$275; under 18 free; wkend rates. Crib free. TV; cable (premium), VCR avail. Indoor pool; whirlpool, poolside serv. Coffee in rms. Restaurant 6:30 am-11 pm; Sun 7 am-10 pm; dining rm 5:30-11 pm. Bar 11-1 am. Ck-out noon. Coin lndry. Free airport transportation. Meeting rms. Business center. Gift shop. Exercise equipt; sauna. Some refrigerators. Luxury level. Many balconies. Cr cds: A, C, D, DS, ER, JCB, MC, V.

Restaurants

★★★ **BLOSSOM DELI.** 904 Quarrier St (25301). 304/345-2233. Hrs: 8 am-9 pm; Mon to 3 pm; Fri to 10 pm; Sat 10 am-3 pm, 5-10 pm. Closed Sun; also major hols. Res accepted (dinner). Eclectic menu. Semi-a la carte: bkfst $1-$2, lunch $5.50-$17.25, dinner $8.25-$17.50. Specialties: create your own pasta, Mediterranean chicken, filet au poivre. Street parking. Decor of 1940s; soda fountain, dairy bar. Totally nonsmoking. Cr cds: A, C, D, DS, MC, V.

★★★ **CAGNEY'S.** 400 Court St (25301). 304/345-3463. Hrs: 11 am-10 pm; Fri, Sat to 11 pm. Closed Thanksgiving, Dec 25. Res accepted. Continental menu. Bar. Semi-a la carte: lunch $6.25-$14.95, dinner $7.55-$21.95. Child's meals. Specialties: cajun chicken pasta, prime rib. Early 1900s decor. Cr cds: A, C, D, DS, MC, V.

★★ **CHEF DAN'S.** 222 Broad St (25301). 304/344-2433. Hrs: 11 am-10 pm; Fri to 11 pm; Sat 4-11 pm. Closed Sun; major hols. Continental menu. Bar. Semi-a la carte: lunch, dinner $3.95-$16.95. Buffet: lunch $8.95. Child's meals. Specializes in pasta, pizza. Bistro decor. Cr cds: A, C, D, DS, MC, V.

★ **FIFTH QUARTER.** 201 Clendenin St (25301). 304/345-2726. Hrs: 11 am-10 pm; Fri and Sat to 11 pm; Sun 11 am-9 pm. Closed Dec 25. Bar. Semi-a la carte: lunch $5.49-$13.50, dinner $9.99-$19.99. Child's meals. Specialty: prime rib. Salad bar. Entertainment midweek. Parking. Rustic decor. Cr cds: A, C, D, DS, MC, V.

★★★ **JOE FAZIO'S.** 1008 Bullitt St (25301). 304/344-3071. Hrs: 5-10:30 pm. Closed Mon; Jan 1, Easter, Dec 24, 25. Res accepted. Italian, Amer menu. Serv bar. Semi-a la carte: dinner $10.95-$19.95. Child's meals. Specializes in veal, chicken, steak. Parking. Family-owned. Cr cds: A, C, D, MC, V.

★★★ **LAURY'S RESTAURANT.** *350 MacCorkle Ave SE (25314).* 304/343-0055. Hrs: 11 am-2 pm, 5-11 pm; Sat 5-10 pm. Closed Sun; major hols. Res accepted. Continental menu. Bar. Semi-a la carte: lunch $4.95-$10.95, dinner $12.95-$49.95. Specialties: châteaubriand, veal, rack of lamb. Entertainment Fri, Sat. Near Kanawha River. Renovated train depot. Cr cds: A, C, D, DS, MC, V.

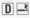

✓★ **SINBAD'S.** *232 7th Ave SW (25303).* 304/744-8091. Hrs: 5-9 pm; Mon 11 am-2 pm; Fri, Sat to 10 pm; Sun brunch 11 am-3 pm. Closed major hols. Res accepted. Middle Eastern menu. Semi-a la carte: dinner $7-$21. Lunch buffet $4.69. Sun brunch $7.95. Specialties: shish kebab, kibbeh, mezze platter. Street parking. Middle Eastern decor. Totally nonsmoking. Cr cds: A, C, D, DS, ER, JCB, MC, V.

★ **STEAK & ALE.** *320 MacCorkle Ave SE (25314).* 304/344-3455. Hrs: 11 am-10 pm; Fri, Sat to 11 pm; Sun to 9 pm. Res accepted. Bar. Semi-a la carte: lunch $5-$13, dinner $9-$23. Child's meals. Specialty: herb crusted prime rib. Salad bar. Casual decor. Cr cds: A, C, D, DS, ER, MC, V.

Charles Town (C-8)

(See also Harpers Ferry, Martinsburg, Shepherdstown; also see Winchester, VA)

Founded 1786 **Pop** 3,122 **Elev** 530 ft **Area Code** 304 **Zip** 25414
E-mail chamber@jeffersoncounty.com **Web** www.jeffersoncounty.com/chamber

Information Jefferson County Chamber of Commerce, 201 Frontage Rd, PO Box 426; 304/725-2055

Charles Town is serene, aristocratic and full of tradition, with orderly, tree-shaded streets and 18th-century houses. It was named for George Washington's youngest brother, Charles, who laid out the town and named most of the streets after members of his family. Charles Washingtons' family lived here for many years. Charles Town is also famed as the place where John Brown was jailed, tried and hanged in 1859 after his raid on Harpers Ferry.

What to See and Do

Charles Town Races and Gaming. Thoroughbred racing; clubhouse, video machines, dining rm. (Wed, Fri-Sun; closed major hols) 1 mi E on US 340. Phone 304/725-7001 or 800/795-7001. **Free**

Jefferson County Courthouse (1836). This red-brick, Georgian-colonial structure was the scene of John Brown's trial, one of three treason trials held in the US before World War II. The courthouse was shelled during the Civil War but was later rebuilt; the original courtroom survived both the shelling and fires and is open to the public. In 1922, leaders of the miners' armed march on Logan City were tried here; one, Walter Allen, was convicted and sentenced to 10 yrs. (Mon-Fri; closed hols) Corner of N George & E Washington Sts. Phone 304/725-9761. **Free**

Jefferson County Museum. Houses John Brown memorabilia, old guns, Civil War artifacts. (Apr-Nov, daily exc Sun) N Samuel & E Washington Sts. Phone 304/725-8628. **Donation**

Site of John Brown Gallows. Marked by pyramid of three stones supposedly taken from Brown's cell in Charles Town jail. At execution, 1,500 troops were massed around the scaffold. Some were commanded by Major Thomas "Stonewall" Jackson; among them was John Wilkes Booth, Virginia militiaman. S Samuel & Hunter Sts.

Tours of Charles Town. Historical walking tours; candlelit tours of Jefferson County Courthouse (evenings); carriage rides. All tours by appt. Phone 304/728-7713. **Free**

Zion Episcopal Church (1852). Buried in cemetery around church are about 75 members of Washington family, as well as many Revolutionary and Confederate soldiers. (Interior, by appt) E Congress between S Mildred & S Church Sts. Phone 304/725-5312.

Annual Events

Founders Day-Washington Heritage. Exhibits, performances, tours. 1st wkend May.

Jefferson County Fair. Livestock show, entertainment, amusement rides, exhibits. Late Aug.

Motels

✓★ **TOWNE HOUSE MOTOR LODGE.** *549 E Washington St (25414).* 304/725-8441; FAX 304/725-5484; res: 800/227-2339. 115 rms, 2-3 story. Mar-mid-Nov: S $30-$45; D $35-$45; each addl $5; suites $90; lower rates rest of yr. Crib free. TV; cable (premium). Pool. Restaurant adj 7 am-8 pm; Fri, Sat to 9 pm. Ck-out 11 am. Meeting rm. Business servs avail. Refrigerators. Cr cds: A, C, D, DS, MC, V.

★ **TURF MOTEL.** *608 E Washington St (25414),* 1 mi E on WV 51. 304/725-2081; FAX 304/728-7605; res: 800/422-8873. 46 rms, 2 story, 6 kits. June-Labor Day: S $32-$61; D $46-$61; each addl $2-$5; suites $80-$160; kit. units $60-$80; lower rates rest of yr. Crib $5. Pet accepted. TV; cable (premium). Pool. Restaurant 6:30 am-9 pm; Fri, Sat to 10 pm. Rm serv. Bar 10-2 am. Ck-out noon. Meeting rms. Business servs avail. Free RR station transportation. Health club privileges. Refrigerators, microwaves avail. Cr cds: A, C, D, DS, MC, V.

Inn

★★★ **HILLBROOK INN.** *RR 2 (25414),* 5 mi SW on WV 13 (Summit Point Rd). 304/725-4223; FAX 304/725-4455; res: 800/304-4223. Web www.hillbrookinn.com. 6 rms, 2 story. S, D $160-$220; higher rates wkends, hols. Dining rm (public by res) dinner (1 sitting) 8 pm. Ck-out noon, ck-in 3 pm. Complimentary full bkfst. Meeting rm. Business servs avail. Lawn games. Some fireplaces. Some balconies. Manor house surrounded by English garden. English country manor decor; eclectic collection of antiques, Oriental rugs, original art. Cr cds: A, C, D, DS, MC, V.

Chesapeake and Ohio Canal National Historical Park

(see Maryland)

Clarksburg (C-5)

(See also Fairmont, Grafton, Weston)

Settled 1773 **Pop** 18,059 **Elev** 1,007 ft **Area Code** 304 **Zip** 26301
E-mail visit@bridgeport-clarksburg.com **Web** www.bridgeport-clarksburg.com

Information Bridgeport-Clarksburg Convention & Visitors Bureau, 109 Platinum Dr, Bridgeport 26330; 304/842-7272 or 800/368-4324

Clarksburg, in the heart of the West Virginia hills, is the trading center for an area of grading lands, coal mines and oil and gas fields. The Criminal Justice Information Services Division of the FBI is located here. During the Civil War it was an important supply base for Union troops. The famous Civil War General "Stonewall" Jackson was born in Clarksburg in 1824. His statue stands before the courthouse.

What to See and Do

North Bend Rail Trail. 71 mi of scenic countryside trails featuring 13 tunnels, numerous bridges and several historic sites. Bike, hike or horseback ride trail from nearby Wilsonburg to North Bend State Park (see PARKERSBURG). I-79, exit 119 to US 50. Phone 304/643-2500 or 800/899-6278.   **Free**

Salem-Teikyo University (1888). (750 students) On campus is the Jennings Randolph Center (by appt; fee), which houses papers and memorabilia of the former senator. 12 mi W in Salem. Phone 304/782-5011 or 304/782-5378. Also here is

> **Fort New Salem.** Collection of 20 log houses from throughout the state were relocated to campus; pioneer history is re-created through crafts and folklore. Special events throughout the year (fee); summer concerts (mid-June-July, Sat evenings). (Memorial Day wkend-Oct, Wed-Sun; Apr-mid-May, Mon-Fri) Phone 304/782-5245.   ¢¢

Stealey-Goff-Vance House (1807). House restored by Harrison County Historical Society as museum with period rooms, antique furniture, tools, Native American artifacts. (May-Sept, Fri, limited hrs) 123 W Main St. Phone 304/842-3073 or 304/624-6512.   ¢

Watters Smith Memorial State Park. More than 500 acres on Duck Creek with visitor center/museum and 19th-century pioneer homestead. Swimming pool (seasonal). Hiking, game courts. Picnicking, playground, concession. Recreation building. Standard hrs, fees. 8 mi S on US 19, then SE on unnumbered road. Phone 304/745-3081.

Annual Event

West Virginia Italian Heritage Festival. Italian arts, music, contests, entertainment. Phone 304/622-7314. Labor Day wkend.

Motels

★★★ HOLIDAY INN. *I-79 & Rte 50 E; 100 Lodgeville Rd (26330), 2½ mi E on US 50E, just E of I-79 exit 119.* 304/842-5411; FAX 304/842-7258; res: 800/465-4329. E-mail hicb@wvholidayinns.com. 160 rms, 2 story. S, D $80-$92; suites $120; under 19 free. Crib free. TV; cable. Pool; wading pool. Restaurant 6 am-2 pm, 5-10 pm; Sat, Sun 6:30 am-2 pm, 5-10 pm. Rm serv. Private club 2 pm-1 am; Sun 5-11 pm. Ck-out noon. Meeting rms. Business servs avail. Valet serv. Sundries. Airport transportation. Cr cds: A, C, D, DS, JCB, MC, V.

D ⊷ ⊠ 🔥 SC

✓★ RAMADA INN. *250 Emily Dr (26301), I-79 exit 119.* 304/623-2600; FAX 304/622-5240. 113 rms, 2 story. S, D $43.95-$59.95; each addl $5; under 18 free. Crib free. TV; cable (premium). Complimentary continental bkfst. Restaurant adj 11 am-10 pm. Ck-out noon. Meeting rms. Business servs avail. Sundries. Cr cds: A, C, D, DS, MC, V.

D ⊠ 🐾 🔥 SC

★ SLEEP INN. *115 Tolley Dr (26330).* 304/842-1919; FAX 304/842-9524; res: 800/638-7949 or 800/221-2222. Web wvonline.com/sleep. 73 rms, 2 story. S $59; D $62; under 18 free. Crib free. Pet accepted. TV; cable (premium). Complimentary continental bkfst. Restaurant nearby. Ck-out 11 am. Meeting rms. Business servs avail. Health club privileges. Microwaves, refrigerators avail. Cr cds: A, C, D, DS, MC, V.

D 🐾 ⊠ 🔥 SC

Restaurants

★★★ JIM REID'S. *1422 Buckhannon Pike (26301), US 50W to Joyce St exit, then ½ mi S on WV 20.* 304/623-4909. Hrs: 11 am-2 pm, 5-10 pm; Sun noon-8 pm. Closed Mon; Jan 1, July 4, Dec 24-26. Res

accepted. Bar. Wine list. Complete meals: lunch $4.25-$6.50, dinner $8.95-$16.95. Child's meals. Specializes in fresh seafood, prime rib, steak. Family-owned. Cr cds: A, C, MC, V.

D ⊷

★★ MINARD'S SPAGHETTI INN. *813 E Pike St (26301).* 304/623-1711. Hrs: 11:30 am-10 pm; Fri, Sat to 11 pm. Closed major hols. Res accepted. Italian menu. Wine, beer. Semi-a la carte: lunch $3.50-$6.75, dinner $5.95-$13. Child's meals. Specializes in steak, spaghetti. Italian decor. Cr cds: A, C, JCB, MC, V.

D SC ⊷

Davis (C-6)

(See also Aurora, Elkins)

Founded 1883 **Pop** 799 **Elev** 3,099 ft **Area Code** 304 **Zip** 26260
Information Potomac Highland Travel Council, 1200 Harrison Ave, Lower Level, Suite A, Elkins 26241; 304/636-8400

Davis, the highest town in the state, was founded by Henry Gassaway Davis, US senator between 1871 and 1883. Senator Davis established the first night train in America (1848). He and his son-in-law, Senator Stephen B. Elkins, became wealthy from coal, lumber and railroading.

What to See and Do

Blackwater Falls State Park. This 1,688-acre park includes deep river gorge with 66-ft falls of dark, amber-colored water. Swimming in lake (fee); bath houses (Memorial Day-Labor Day); fishing; boating (rowboat, paddleboat rentals). Nature trails, horseback riding. Cross-country ski trails, center (rentals, school); sledding. Picnicking, playground, concession, lodge, cabins. Tent & trailer campground. Nature, recreation programs and tours. Paved falls viewing area for the disabled. Standard hrs, fees. 2 mi W off WV 32. Phone 304/259-5216.

Canaan Valley Resort State Park. Approx 6,000 acres includes valley 3,200 ft above sea level, which is surrounded by spectacular mountain peaks. Swimming pool, bathhouse; fishing; boating. Hiking trails; 18-hole golf course, tennis courts. Skiing, ice rink. Playground, lodge, cabins. Camping (dump station). Nature, recreation programs. Standard hrs, fees. 9 mi S on WV 32. Phone 304/866-4121.

Skiing.

> **Canaan Valley Resort State Park.** Quad, 2 triple chairlifts, Pomalift; patrol, school, SKIwee program, rentals; snowmaking; restaurant, cafeteria; lodging, nursery; night skiing (Thurs-Sun). 22 trails, 34 slopes; vertical drop 850 ft. (Dec-Mar, daily) 18 mi of cross-country trails. Chairlift rides (early May-Oct, daily). Special programs for the disabled. Phone 304/866-4121 or 800/622-4121.   ¢¢¢¢¢

> **Timberline Four Seasons Resort.** Triple, 2 double chairlifts; patrol, school, SKIwee program, rentals; snowmaking; restaurant, bar; nursery; lodging, night skiing and special events. 35 slopes and trails; longest run 2 mi, vertical drop 1,000 ft. (Thanksgiving-mid-Apr, daily) Cross-country skiing. Chairlift rides (July-Oct, Sat & Sun, also Mon hols). 8 mi S off WV 32. Phone 304/866-4801 or 800/SNOWING.   ¢¢¢¢

> **White Grass Touring Center.** 36 mi of cross-country trails, some machine-groomed; patrol, school, rentals; snowmaking; restaurant; night skiing; telemark slopes, guided tours. (Late Nov-Mar, daily) 9 mi S on WV 32 to Freeland Rd; ½ mi N of Canaan Valley Resort State Park. Phone 304/866-4114.   ¢¢¢

Whitewater rafting. Many outfitters offer guided trips on the Cheat River. For a list of outfitters contact the West Virginia Division of Tourism, Research & Development, 2101 Washington St E, Bldg 17, Charleston 25305; phone 800/225-5982.

Annual Event

Tucker County Alpine Winter Festival. Governor's Cup ski races. Phone 304/866-4121. 1st wkend Mar.

Motel

✓★★ **BEST WESTERN ALPINE LODGE.** *Williams Ave (26260), On WV 32, near Blackwater Falls State Park entrance. 304/259-5245; FAX 304/259-5168.* 46 rms, 1-2 story. S $50-$52; D $56; each addl $2. Crib $5. TV; cable. Pool. Restaurant 6 am-9 pm. Ck-out 11 am. Coin lndry. Meeting rms. Business servs avail. Sundries. Downhill ski 10 mi; x-country ski 2 mi. Refrigerators. Cr cds: A, C, D, DS, MC, V.

❂ ⚏ 🔥 SC

Resorts

★★ **BLACKWATER LODGE.** *County Rte 29 (26260), 3 mi SW off WV 32 in Blackwater Falls State Park. 304/259-5216; FAX 304/259-5881.* 54 rms in lodge, 1-2 story, 25 kit. cabins (1, 2 & 4 bedrm). S $55; D $63; each addl $6; cabins for 2-8 $77-$108, $462-$648/wk. Crib $4; free in lodge. TV in lodge; cable (premium). Playground. Dining rm 7 am-9 pm. Lodge: ck-out noon, ck-in 3 pm. Cabins: ck-out 10 am, ck-in 4 pm. Coin lndry. Meeting rms. Business servs avail. Tennis. Downhill ski 10 mi; x-country ski on site. Lawn games. Game rm. Picnic tables, grills. All state park facilities avail. Lake swimming. Cr cds: A, C, D, MC, V.

D ⚘ ❂ ⛷ ⚏ 🔥 SC

★★★ **CANAAN VALLEY RESORT & CONFERENCE CENTER.** *Hc 70 Box 330 (26260), via WV 33, then 10 mi N on WV 32 in Canaan Valley Resort State Park. 304/866-4121; FAX 304/866-2172; res: 800/622-4121.* 250 rms, 2 story. Mid-May-mid-Oct, late-Dec-mid-Mar: S $74-$79; D $81-$86; each addl $7; suites $129; 2-4 bedrm cabins $621-$1028/wk; family rates; package plans; lower lodge rates rest of yr. Deposit required. Crib $7; free in lodge. TV; cable (premium). 2 pools, 1 indoor; whirlpool, lifeguard (outside). Playground. Supervised child's activities. Dining rm 7 am-11 pm, noon-2 pm, 5-9 pm. Snack bars; box lunches, picnics. Private club 4 pm-midnight. Ck-out noon, ck-in 4 pm. Grocery 2 mi. Coin lndry. Convention facilities. Business servs avail. Gift shop. Sports dir. Lighted tennis, pro. 18-hole golf, greens fee $30, putting green, driving range, miniature golf. Downhill/x-country ski on site. Naturalist program. Bicycles. Lawn games. Entertainment, movies. Rec rm. Game rm. Exercise equipt; sauna. Fishing privileges. Some refrigerators. Fireplace in cabins. Picnic tables. Camping sites avail. Cr cds: A, C, D, DS, MC, V.

D ⚘ ❂ 🍽 ⛷ ⚏ 🎿 🔥 SC

Elkins (C-5)

(See also Buckhannon, Davis, Philippi)

Founded 1890 **Pop** 7,420 **Elev** 1,830 ft **Area Code** 304 **Zip** 26241
Information Potomac Highland Travel Council, 1200 Harrison Ave, Lower Level, Suite A; 304/636-8400

Elkins was named for US Senator Stephen B. Elkins, an aggressive politician and powerful industrial magnate who was Secretary of War under Benjamin Harrison (1888-1892). This town is in a coal and timber region, and is also a railroad terminus and trade center. Some of the finest scenery in the state can be seen in and around Elkins.

What to See and Do

Bowden National Fish Hatchery. Produces brook, brown and rainbow trout for stocking in state and national forest streams; also striped bass for Chesapeake Bay restoration project. Hatchery (daily). Visitor center (Memorial Day-mid-Oct, daily). 10 mi E on Old US 33. Phone 304/636-2823. **Free**

Monongahela National Forest. This 901,000-acre forest, in the heart of the Alleghenies, has some of the loftiest mountains in the East. Spruce Knob (4,862 ft) is the highest point in the state. Headwaters of the Ohio and Potomac rivers are here. The forest is a meeting ground of northern and southern plant life, with stands of red spruce and northern hardwoods joining with oak, hickory and other southern hardwoods. There are also many interesting secondary and tertiary plants and wildflowers. Several recreation areas, including five wilderness areas, Spruce Knob/Seneca Rocks National Recreation Area, near Petersburg (see), and Blue Bend and Lake Sherwood recreation areas, near White Sulphur Springs (see), are all located within the forest. Swimming; fishing; hunting; boating. Hiking, rock climbing, spelunking. Picnicking. Camping (fee). Fees charged at the more developed recreation sites. Part of the Greenbrier River Trail (see MARLINTON) runs through the southern section of the forest. Forest headquarters are in Elkins; the Cranberry Mountain Visitor Center is near Marlinton (see); and the Seneca Rocks Visitor Center is in Seneca Rocks (see PETERSBURG). Entrance is E of town on US 33. For further information contact Supervisor, US Department of Agriculture Building, 200 Sycamore St; Phone 304/636-1800.

The Old Mill (1877). A grist mill powered by water turbines rather than a waterwheel. It was also used for planing wood and for producing white flour. Today it still uses water power to grind corn, wheat, rye and buckwheat. Observation hive has live bees. West Virginia crafts shop includes rug weaving. (Memorial Day-Labor Day, daily exc Sun) 25 mi E via US 33 to WV 32 N, in Harman. Phone 304/227-4466. **Donation**

Annual Events

Augusta Festival. On campus of Davis & Elkins College, 100 Sycamore St. Celebration of traditional folk life and arts, featuring local and national performers, dances, juried craft fair, storytelling sessions, children's activities and homemade foods. Phone 304/637-1209. Mid-Aug.

Mountain State Forest Festival. Some events on campus of Davis & Elkins College. Queen Silvia is crowned; carnival, parades; entertainment; tilting at rings on horseback; sawing and woodchopping contests; marksmanship tests; State Championship Fiddle and Banjo Contest; juried craft fair and art exhibit. Phone 304/636-1824. Late Sept-early Oct.

Motels

★★ **BEST WESTERN.** *Rte 250/219 S (26241), US 219/250S. 304/636-7711; FAX 304/636-5419.* 63 rms, 2 story. S $41-$45; D $47-$52; each addl $5; suites, kit. suites $67-$77; under 12 free. TV; cable, VCR avail (movies $2). Complimentary coffee in lobby. Restaurant nearby. Ck-out noon. Business servs avail. Sundries. Health club privileges. Cr cds: A, C, D, DS, MC, V.

⚏ 🔥 SC

★★ **ECONO LODGE INN.** *40 Cherry St; Rte 1 Box 15 (26241), near Randolph County Airport. 304/636-5311; FAX 304/636-5311; res: 800/228-5050.* 72 rms, 1-2 story. S $40-$45; D $43-$63; each addl $5; suites $54-$69; kit. units $56-$70; under 18 free; package plans; higher rates Forest Festival. Crib free. TV; cable (premium), VCR avail. Indoor pool; whirlpool. Complimentary continental bkfst. Ck-out 11 am. Coin lndry. Meeting rms. Business servs avail. Some bathrm phones. Picnic tables. Cr cds: A, C, D, DS, MC, V.

D ⚏ ⚏ 🔥 SC

✓★★ **ELKINS MOTOR LODGE INC.** *Harrison Ave (26241), 5 blks W. 304/636-1400; FAX 304/636-6318.* 54 rms. S $38-$44; D $41-$47; each addl $3; suites $60-$70. Crib $3. TV; cable. Restaurant 5-10 pm; Sun to 8 pm. Rm serv. Private club 4:30 pm-1 am. Ck-out noon. Meeting rms. Business servs avail. Free airport transportation. Refrigerators, microwaves avail. Cr cds: A, C, D, DS, MC, V.

D ⚏ 🔥

★ **FOUR SEASONS MOTEL.** *1091 Harrison Ave (26241), on US 33 & 250.* 304/636-1990; FAX 304/636-6475; res: 800/367-7130. 13 rms, 1-2 story. S $30; D $35; each $3; under 12 free; wkly rates. Crib free. TV; cable (premium). Complimentary coffee in lobby. Restaurant nearby. Ck-out 11 am. Cr cds: C, DS, MC, V.

◻ ◻ **SC**

✓★ **SUPER 8 MOTEL.** *350 Beverly Pike; Rte 219 S (26241), 2 mi S on US 219/250, near Randolph County Airport.* 304/636-6500; FAX 304/636-6500. 43 rms, 2 story. S $42.88-$47.88; D $48.88-$53.88; each addl $6; under 12 free; higher rates: Forest Festival, graduation, ski wk. Crib free. TV; cable (premium). Complimentary coffee in lobby. Restaurant opp 7 am-10 pm. Ck-out 11 am. Business servs avail. Health club privileges. Some refrigerators. Cr cds: A, C, D, DS, JCB, MC, V.

D ◻ ◻ **SC**

Inns

★ **THE POST HOUSE BED & BREAKFAST.** *306 Robert E Lee Ave (26241).* 304/636-1792. E-mail jabarlow@juno.com. 5 rms, 2 share bath, 2 story. S $60; D $65; each addl $15; under 15 free. Closed Nov-June. TV; cable. Complimentary continental bkfst. Restaurant nearby. Ck-out 11 am, ck-in 2 pm. Massage. Built in 1936. Cr cds: C.

◻ ◻

★★★ **THE WARFIELD HOUSE.** *318 Buffalo St (26241).* 304/636-4555; res: 888/636-4555. Web www.bbonline.com. 5 air-cooled rms, 2 share bath, 3 story. No rm phones. S $65; D $75; each addl $10; package plans. Children over 12 yrs only. Cable TV in common rm. Complimentary full bkfst. Complimentary coffee in rms. Ck-out 11 am, ck-in 4 pm. Business servs avail. Luggage handling. Street parking. Built in 1901; colonial revival style. Cr cds: C.

◻ ◻ **SC**

Restaurant

★ **CHEAT RIVER INN RESTAURANT.** *US 33E (26241).* 304/636-6265. Hrs: 4-10 pm. Closed Mon. Res accepted. Bar. Semi-a la carte: dinner $8.95-$17. Specializes in seafood. Outdoor dining. Mounted fish on display. Cr cds: C, DS, MC, V.

◻

Fairmont (B-5)

(See also Clarksburg, Morgantown)

Settled 1793 **Pop** 20,210 **Elev** 883 ft **Area Code** 304 **Zip** 26554
E-mail mm@westvirginia.com **Web** www.westvirginia.com/marion
Information Convention & Visitors Bureau of Marion County, 110 Adams St, PO Box 58, 26555-0058; 304/368-1123 or 800/834-7365

Fairmont was a Union supply depot plundered by Confederate cavalry in April 1863. General William Ezra Jones's division swept through town, took 260 prisoners, destroyed the $500,000 bridge across the Monongahela River and raided the governor's residence. After the war, resources in the region were developed, and coal became the mainstay. Today Fairmont manufactures aluminum, mine machinery and other products.

What to See and Do

Fairmont State College (1867). (7,000 students) On campus is a one-room schoolhouse with original desks, books and other artifacts related to early era of education (Apr-Oct, schedule varies; free). Locust Ave. Phone 304/367-4000.

Marion County Museum. Displays of B & O china, five furnished rooms covering 1776-1920s, doll, train and toy collection. (Daily exc Sun; closed hols) Adams St, adj to courthouse. Phone 304/367-5398.   **Free**

Prickett's Fort State Park. Approx 200 acres with reconstructed 18th-century log fort, colonial trade and lifestyle demonstrations by costumed interpreters, outdoor historical drama (July, Wed-Sat). Boating (ramps). Picnicking. Visitor center. Fort and museum (mid-Apr-Oct, daily). Museum (fee). I-79 exit 139, then 2 mi W. Phone 800/CALL-WVA or 304/363-3030 (museum).

Annual Event

Three Rivers Festival. Palatine Park. Entertainment, parade, civil war reenactment, carnival, games. Phone 304/363-2625. 3rd wkend May.

Motels

★★ **COMFORT INN & SUITES.** *1185 Airport Rd (26554), I-79 exit 133.* 304/367-1370; FAX 304/367-1806; res: 800/228-5150. 85 rms, 2 story, 20 suites. S $53; D $57; each addl $5; under 18 free; higher rates special events. Crib free. TV; cable (premium). Complimentary continental bkfst. Complimentary coffee in rms. Restaurant nearby. Ck-out noon. Meeting rms. Business center. In-rm modem link. Sundries. Exercise equipt. Pool. Bathrm phone, refrigerator, microwave in suites. Picnic tables. Cr cds: A, C, D, DS, MC, V.

D ◻ ◻ ◻ **SC** ◻

★★ **HOLIDAY INN.** *930 E Grafton (26554), 1½ mi E on I-79 exit 137.* 304/366-5500; FAX 304/363-3975; res: 800/465-4329. E-mail hif@wvholidayinns.com. 106 rms, 2 story. S, D $50-$95; under 18 free; higher rates: WVU football games, graduation. Crib free. TV; cable, VCR avail. Pool. Restaurant 6 am-2 pm, 5-10 pm. Rm serv. Private club. Ck-out noon. Meeting rms. Business servs avail. In-rm modem link. Bellhops. Valet serv. Sundries. Cr cds: A, C, D, DS, ER, JCB, MC, V.

D ◻ ◻ ◻ **SC**

✓★ **RED ROOF INN.** *50 Middletown Rd (26554), Jct I-79 & US 250.* 304/366-6800; FAX 304/366-6812; res: 800/843-7663. 108 rms, 2 story. S $35.99-$45.99; D $41.99-$51.99; each addl $6; under 18 free. Crib free. TV. Complimentary coffee in lobby. Restaurant nearby. Ck-out noon. Business servs avail. Cr cds: A, C, D, DS, MC, V.

D ◻ ◻ **SC**

Restaurant

✓★★ **MURIALE'S.** *1742 Fairmont Ave (26554), 2 mi S on US 250; 2 mi N of I-79 exit 132.* 304/363-3190. Hrs: 11 am-9 pm; Sun from 10 am. Closed Dec 25. Italian, Amer menu. Bar. Semi-a la carte: lunch $3-$7, dinner $5-$16. Child's meals. Specializes in lasagne, ravioli, steak. Family-owned. Totally nonsmoking. Cr cds: A, C, D, DS, MC, V.

D **SC** ◻

Franklin (C-6)

(See also Petersburg; also see Harrisonburg, VA)

Settled 1794 **Pop** 914 **Elev** 1,731 ft **Area Code** 304 **Zip** 26807
Information Potomac Highland Travel Council, 1200 Harrison Ave, Lower Level, Suite A, Elkins 26241; 304/636-8400

What to See and Do

Seneca Caverns. Caves, which contain magnificent stalagmites and stalactites, were used as a refuge by the Seneca people. (Daily) Approx 17 mi NW on US 33 to Riverton, then 3 mi E. Phone 304/567-2691.   **¢¢¢**

Annual Event

Treasure Mountain Festival. Square dancing, clogging; parade; gospel and mountain music, drama; rifle demonstration, cross-cut sawing contest; children's contests, games; trail rides; craft exhibits; country food. Phone 304/249-5422. 3rd wkend Sept.

Gauley Bridge (D-4)

(See also Beckley, Charleston, Summersville)

Pop 691 **Elev** 680 ft **Area Code** 304 **Zip** 25085
Information Upper Kahawha Valley Chamber of Commerce, PO Box 831, Montgomery 25136; 304/442-5756

This town, at the junction of the New and Gauley rivers, was the key to the Kanawha Valley during the Civil War. In November 1861, Union General W.S. Rosecrans defeated Confederate General John B. Floyd, a victory that assured Union control of western Virginia. Stone piers of the old bridge, which was destroyed by retreating Confederates in 1861, can be seen near the present bridge.

What to See and Do

Contentment Museum Complex (ca 1830). Former residence of Confederate Colonel George W. Imboden contains original woodwork, period furniture, toy collection. Adjacent Fayette County Historical Society Museum features displays of Native American relics, local artifacts, Civil War items; restored one-room schoolhouse. (June-Sept, daily; May, Sun; rest of yr, by appt) 7 mi E on US 60, 1 mi E of Hawks Nest State Park. Phone 304/658-5695 or 304/465-0165. Or contact Fayette County Chamber of Commerce, 800/927-0263. ¢

Hawks Nest State Park. Approx 280 acres on Gauley Mt, with fine views of New River Gorge from rocks 585 ft above the river. A 600-ft aerial tramway carries passengers to canyon floor. Swimming pool; fishing. Hiking trails; tennis. Picnic area, playground, concession, restaurant, lodge. Log museum with early West Virginia artifacts (May-Nov, daily; free). Standard hrs, fees. 6 mi E on US 60. Phone 304/658-5212 or 304/658-5196.

New River Gorge Bridge. A masterpiece of engineering, this four-lane, single-arch, steel-span bridge rises 876 ft above the New River Gorge National River (see HINTON), making it the second-highest bridge in the US, and at 3,030 ft, the longest bridge of its type in the world. Just north of the bridge, on US 19, is the Canyon Rim Visitors Center (daily; closed Dec 25). The visitors center provides 2 overlooks of the bridge and river, a 70-ft descending boardwalk, slide presentation, exhibits and ranger-guided walks (May-Oct). 13 mi SE on US 60, then 6 mi SW on US 19, near Fayetteville. Phone 304/574-2115.

Whitewater rafting. Many outfitters offer guided trips on the New and Gauley rivers. For a list of outfitters contact the West Virginia Division of Tourism, Research & Development, 2101 Washington St E, Bldg 17, Charleston 25305; phone 800/225-5982; or the Fayette County Chamber of Commerce, 310 Oyler Ave, Oak Hill 25901; 800/927-0263.

Annual Event

Bridge Day. New River Gorge Bridge. Bridge is opened to pedestrians; parachutists test their skills by jumping off the bridge and floating to the bottom of gorge. 3rd Sat Oct.

Lodge

★★ **HAWKS NEST STATE PARK LODGE.** *Rte 60 (25812), 8 mi E on US 60, in Hawks Nest State Park.* 304/658-5212; FAX 304/658-4549; res: 800/225-5982. 31 rms, 4 story. Late May-early Sept: S, D $60; each addl $6; suites $66-$80; under 13 free; lower rates rest of yr. Crib

free. TV; cable. Pool. Dining rm 7 am-9 pm; Dec-Feb to 8 pm. Ck-out noon. Meeting rm. Business servs avail. Tennis. Golf privileges. Balconies. View of mountains. 1,100-ft vertical tramway to marina. Cr cds: A, C, D, MC, V.

D ⚓ 🛥 🎿 🏕 ☰ ⛷ 🔥 SC

Inn

★★ **GLEN FERRIS INN.** *US Rte 60 (25090), 1½ mi W on US 60.* 304/632-1111; FAX 304/632-0113. 16 rms. S, D $61-$75; suite $130. TV; cable (premium). Dining rm 6 am-9 pm; Sun from 7 am. Ck-out 11 am. Meeting rm. Business servs avail. Renovated 1840's inn, originally Federal style in design; built by grandson of one of signers of Declaration of Indepedence. Overlooks Kanawha Falls. Cr cds: A, C, DS, MC, V.

D 🔥

Grafton (B-5)

(See also Clarksburg, Fairmont, Morgantown, Philippi)

Founded 1856 **Pop** 5,524 **Elev** 1,004 ft **Area Code** 304 **Zip** 26354
E-mail tvda1@aol.com
Information Grafton-Taylor County Convention & Visitors Bureau, 214 W Main St, Rm 205; 304/265-3938

Mother's Day started in Grafton in 1908 when Anna Jarvis observed the anniversary of her mother's death during a religious service. The idea caught on nationally, and in 1914 President Woodrow Wilson issued a proclamation urging nationwide observance. The International Shrine to Motherhood in the original Mother's Day church is located at 11 E Main Street.

During the Civil War, Grafton was an important railroad center; 4,000 Union troops camped here before the Battle of Philippi in 1861. General McClellan also had his headquarters in the town. The first land soldier killed in the war, T. Bailey Brown, fell at Grafton. He is buried in the Grafton National Cemetery.

What to See and Do

Tygart Lake State Park. This scenic 2,100-acre park contains one of the largest concrete dams east of the Mississippi (1,900 ft by 209 ft). Swimming, waterskiing; fishing; boating (ramp, rentals, marina). Hiking, game courts. Picnic area, playground, concession, lodge. Tent and trailer camping, 10 cabins. Nature and recreation programs, dam tours (summer; phone 304/265-1760). Standard hrs, fees. 2 mi S off US 119, 250. Phone 304/265-3383.

Annual Event

Taylor County Fair. Fairgrounds, US 50. Horse racing, livestock shows, auctions, carnival, crafts. Phone 304/265-4155. Last wk July.

Motels

✓ ★ **CRISLIP MOTOR LODGE.** *300 Moritz Ave (26354), 1 mi NE on US 50, 1 blk W of jct US 119.* 304/265-2100; FAX 304/265-2017. 40 rms, 2 story. S $37; D $46; each addl $5; suites $37-$46. Crib free. TV; cable. Pool. Complimentary coffee in rms. Restaurant nearby. Ck-out 11 am. Business servs avail. Sundries. Cr cds: A, C, D, DS, MC, V.

D 🛥 ☰ 🔥 SC

★★ **TYGART LAKE STATE PARK LODGE.** *Rte 1 (26354), 4 mi S off US 119.* 304/265-6144; FAX 304/265-6147. Web wvweb.com/www/tygart_lake.html. 20 rms, 1 story. May-Oct: S, D $58; each addl $6; cabins $462-$576/wk; under 13 free; golf plans; lower rates Nov, Dec. Closed Jan-Apr. Crib free. TV; cable. Free supervised child's activities

(Memorial Day-Labor Day). Restaurant 8 am-8 pm. Ck-out noon. Meeting rm. Rec rm. Lawn games. Picnic tables. Rms overlook lake. Cr cds: A, C, D, MC, V.

Harpers Ferry (C-8)

(See also Charles Town, Martinsburg, Shepherdstown; also see Frederick, MD)

Settled 1732 **Pop** 308 **Elev** 247 ft **Area Code** 304 **Zip** 25425
E-mail chamber@jeffersoncounty.com **Web** www.jeffersoncounty.com/chamber

Information Jefferson County Chamber of Commerce, 201 Frontage Rd, PO Box 426, Charles Town 25414; 304/725-2055

Harpers Ferry, the scene of abolitionist John Brown's raid in 1859, is at the junction of the Shenandoah and Potomac rivers, where West Virginia, Virginia and Maryland meet. A US armory and rifle factory made this an important town in early Virginia; John Brown had this in mind when he began his insurrection. He and 16 other men seized the armory and arsenal the night of October 16 and took refuge in the engine house of the armory when attacked by local militia. On the morning of the 18th, the engine house was stormed, and Brown was captured by 90 marines from Washington under Brevet Colonel Robert E. Lee and Lt J.E.B. Stuart. Ten of Brown's men were killed, including two of his sons. He was hanged in nearby Charles Town (see) for treason, murder and inciting slaves to rebellion.

When war broke out, Harpers Ferry was a strategic objective for the Confederacy, which considered it the key to Washington. "Stonewall" Jackson captured 12,693 Union prisoners here before the Battle of Antietam in 1862. The town changed hands many times in the war, during which many buildings were damaged. In 1944, Congress authorized a national monument here, setting aside 1,500 acres for that purpose. In 1963, the same area was designated a National Historical Park, now occupying more than 2,200 acres.

What to See and Do

⊠ **Harpers Ferry National Historical Park.** Here the old town has been restored to its 19th-century appearance; exhibits and interpretive presentations explore the park's relation to the water-power industry, the Civil War, John Brown and Storer College, a school established for freed slaves after the war. A Visitor Center is located just off US 340. Visitors should park there; a bus will take them to Lower Town. Contact the Visitor Center, PO Box 65; phone 304/535-6298. Park entrance fee: per person ¢¢; per vehicle ¢¢ A walking tour of the park follows.

Information Center. Restored federalist house built in 1859 by US government as residence for the master armorer of the US Armory. During the Civil War it was used as headquarters by various commanding officers. Also on this street is the site of the US Armory that John Brown attempted to seize; it was destroyed during the Civil War. Farther down Shenandoah St and right under the trestle is S side of Shenandoah St near High St.

The Point. Three states, West Virginia, Virginia and Maryland, and two rivers, the Shenandoah and Potomac, meet at the Blue Ridge Mountains. Back under the trestle is

John Brown's Fort. Where John Brown made his last stand; rebuilt and moved near original site. On Arsenal Square. Across the street is

John Brown Museum. Contains an exhibit and film on John Brown and a 10-min slide presentation on the history of the park. Exiting the museum to the right is High St, which has two Civil War museums and two black history museums. Up the stone steps from High St is

Harper House. Three-story, stone house built between 1775 and 1782 by founder of town; both George Washington and Thomas Jefferson were entertained as overnight guests. Restored and furnished with period pieces. Behind this house is

Marmion Row. Four restored, private houses built 1832-1850. Continue up the hill to the

Ruins of St John's Episcopal Church. Used as a guardhouse and hospital during the Civil War. Approx 100 yards farther is

Jefferson's Rock. From here Thomas Jefferson, in 1783, pronounced the view "one of the most stupendous scenes in nature." Farther along, above the cemetery, is

Lockwood House. (1848). Greek-revival house used as a headquarters, barracks and stable during Civil War; later used as a classroom building by Storer College (1867), which was founded to educate freed men after the war.

Other buildings open to the public during the summer are the dry goods store, provost office and blacksmith shop.

John Brown Wax Museum. Sound and animation depict Brown's exploits, including the raid on Harpers Ferry. (Mid-Mar-early Dec, daily; Jan-Mar, Sat & Sun) High St. Phone 304/535-6342 or 304/535-2792. ¢¢

Whitewater rafting. Many outfitters offer guided trips on the Shenandoah and Potomac rivers. For a list of outfitters contact the West Virginia Division of Tourism, Research & Development, 2101 Washington St E, Bldg 17, Charleston 25305; phone 800/225-5982.

Annual Events

Mountain Heritage Arts and Crafts Festival. More than 190 craftspeople and artisans demonstrate quilting, wool spinning, pottery throwing, vegetable dyeing and other crafts; concerts. 2nd full wkend June & last full wkend Sept.

Election Day 1860. More than 100 people in 19th-century clothing reenact the 1860 presidential election. 2nd Sat Oct.

Old Tyme Christmas. Caroling, musical programs, children's programs, taffy pull, candlelight walk. 1st 2 wkends Dec.

Motel

★★ **COMFORT INN.** *Rte 340 & Union St (25425).* 304/535-6391; FAX 304/535-6395; res: 800/535-9909. 50 rms, 2 story. Apr-Oct: S, D $60-$85; each addl $6; under 18 free; lower rates rest of yr. Crib free. TV; cable, VCR avail (movies). Complimentary continental bkfst. Coffee in rms. Restaurant nearby. Ck-out 11 am. Meeting rms. Business servs avail. Health club privileges. Refrigerators avail. Cr cds: A, C, D, DS, JCB, MC, V.

Hillsboro (D-5)

(See also Marlinton)

Settled 1765 **Pop** 188 **Elev** 2,303 ft **Area Code** 304 **Zip** 24946
Information Potomac Highland Travel Council, 1200 Harrison Ave, Lower Level, Suite A, Elkins 26241; 304/636-8400

Civil War troops marched through Hillsboro, and Confederates camped in town before the decisive Battle of Droop Mountain. Novelist Pearl S. Buck was born in her grandparents' house while her parents, missionaries on leave from China, were visiting.

What to See and Do

Beartown State Park. Approx 110 acres of dense forest with unique rock formations created by erosion; boardwalk with interpretive signs winds through park. Standard hrs. 5 mi S off US 219. Phone 304/653-4254.

Droop Mountain Battlefield State Park. Encompasses approx 285 acres on site where, on Nov 6, 1863, Union forces under General William W. Averell defeated Confederates under General John Echols, destroying the last major rebel resistance in the state. Park features graves, breastworks and monuments. Hiking. Picnic areas, playground. Museum. Battle reenactments (2nd wk Oct, every even yr). Standard hrs. 3 mi S on US 219. Phone 304/653-4254.

☒ **Pearl S. Buck Birthplace Museum** (Stulting House). Birthplace of Pulitzer and Nobel Prize-winning novelist, restored to its 1892 appearance; original and period furniture; memorabilia. Exhibit of antique tools and farm implements in restored barn. Sydenstricker House, home of Buck's father and his ancestors, was moved 40 mi from its original site and restored here. Guided tours. (May-Oct, Mon-Sat, also Sun afternoons) ½ mi N on US 219. Phone 304/653-4430. ¢¢

Watoga State Park. More than 10,100 acres make this West Virginia's largest state park. Watoga, derived from the Cherokee term *watauga*, means "river of islands." It aptly describes the Greenbrier River, which forms several miles of the park's boundary. Swimming pool, bathhouses; fishing; boating on 11-acre Watoga Lake (rentals). Hiking, bridle trails, horseback riding; tennis, game courts. Cross-country skiing. Picnicking, playground, concession, restaurant (seasonal). Tent and trailer camping, 33 cabins. Brooks Memorial Arboretum; nature, recreation programs (summer). Standard hrs, fees. 1 mi N on US 219, then SE. Phone 304/799-4087. Adj to the park is

Calvin Price State Forest. This vast, undeveloped forest has more than 9,400 acres for fishing, deer and small-game hunting, hiking and primitive camping (fee). Phone 304/799-4087.

Hinton (E-4)

(See also Beckley)

Founded 1873 **Pop** 3,433 **Elev** 1,382 ft **Area Code** 304 **Zip** 25951 **E-mail** sccc@inetone.net

Information Summers County Chamber of Commerce, 221 Temple St, PO Box 231; 304/466-5332

Hinton, a railroad town on the banks of the New River, is the seat of Summers County, where the Bluestone and Greenbrier rivers join the scenic and protected New River.

What to See and Do

Bluestone State Park. More than 2,100 acres on Bluestone Lake, which was created by the Bluestone Dam. Swimming pool (Memorial Day-Labor Day), wading pool, bathhouses, waterskiing; fishing; boating (ramps, marina nearby; canoe, rowboat and motorboat rentals). Hiking trails; game courts. Picnicking, playground. Gift shop. Tent & trailer camping (dump station), 25 cabins. Nature, recreation programs (summer). Standard hrs, fees. 5 mi S on WV 20. Phone 304/466-2805.

New River Gorge National River. One of the oldest rivers on the continent, the New River rushes northward through a deep canyon with spectacular scenery. The 52-mi section from Hinton to Fayetteville is popular among outdoor enthusiasts, especially whitewater rafters and hikers. The Hinton Visitor Center is located along the river at WV 3 Bypass (Memorial Day-Labor Day, daily); phone 304/466-0417. A yr-round visitor center is located on US 19 near the New River Gorge Bridge (see GAULEY BRIDGE). For further information and a list of whitewater outfitters contact Superintendent, PO Box 246, Glen Jean 25846; 304/465-0508.

Pipestem Resort State Park. More than 4,000 acres with 3,600-ft aerial tramway to Bluestone River complex. Swimming, bathhouses; fishing; canoeing, paddleboating. Hiking trails, horseback riding; 9- and 18-hole golf courses, miniature golf, tennis, archery, lighted game courts. Cross-country skiing, sledding. Playground, 2 lodges, 4 restaurants. Tent & trailer camping (dump station), 25 cabins. Visitor center; nature, recreation programs. Aerial tramway, arboretum, observation tower. Amphitheater; dances. Standard hrs, fees. 12 mi SW on WV 20. Phone 304/466-1800.

Resort

★★★ **MT CREEK LODGE.** *Pipestem State Park (25979), 12 mi SW via WV 20, in Pipestem Resort State Park, 3 mi from park entrance.* 304/466-1800; FAX 304/466-5679; res: 800/922-5582. E-mail pipestem@

cwv.net. 143 units in 2 bldgs, 7 story, 30 lodge rms, 25 kit. cottages. May-Sept: S $62; D $68; lodge rms (Nov-Mar only): S $46; D $52; each addl $6; under 13 free; suites $72-$94; 2-4 bedrm cottages $575-$754/wk; varied lower rates rest of yr. Crib free. TV; cable (premium), VCR avail (movies $4). 2 pools, 1 indoor; wading pool, lifeguard. Playground. Restaurants (see BLUESTONE DINING ROOM and MOUNTAIN CREEK). Bar (seasonal). Snack bars. Ck-out noon, ck-in 4 pm; cottages ck-out 10 am, ck-in 4 pm. Business servs avail. Grocery 3 mi. Lighted tennis. 18-hole golf. X-country ski on site; sleighing, tobogganing. Exercise equipt; sauna. Lawn games. Soc dir. Rec rm; entertainment in summer. Many balconies. Picnic tables. Mt Creek Lodge (open May-Oct) located at foot of Bluestone Canyon; accessible only by aerial tram. Resort state-owned, operated; all state park facilities avail to guests. Cr cds: A, C, D, MC, V.

🄳 🛉 🛝 🏊 🛎 🎿 🐟 🚶 🛶 🔥 SC

Inn

✓ ★ **PENCE SPRINGS HOTEL.** *Rte 3 (24962), 14 mi E on WV 3.* 304/445-2606; FAX 304/445-2204; res: 800/826-1829. 15 units, 3 story, 1 cottage. Apr-Dec: S $59.50-$89.50; D $69.50-$99.50; cottage $350; under 3 free; wkly rates; lower rates rest of yr. Crib $10. Complimentary full bkfst. Dining rm 8-10 am, 5-9 pm; wkend hrs vary. Bar 5 pm-midnight. Ck-out 11 am, ck-in 1 pm. Meeting rms. Business servs avail. Lawn games. Picnic tables. On high plateau overlooking Greenbrier River valley. Cr cds: A, C, D, DS, MC, V.

🄳 🛝 🛶 🔥 SC

Restaurants

✓ ★★ **BLUESTONE DINING ROOM.** *(See Pipestem)* 304/466-1800. Hrs: 7 am-2 pm, 5:30-9 pm. Wine, beer. Semi-a la carte: bkfst $3.95-$7.95, lunch $5.95-$7.95, dinner $9.95-$15.95. Buffet: bkfst $5.50, lunch $6.95, dinner $9.95. Child's meals. Specializes in seafood, steak, country dishes. Outdoor dining. View of gorge and mts. Cr cds: C, D, DS, MC, V.

🄳 🛎

✓ ★ **KIRK'S.** *Hc 76 Box 3 (25951), WV 20 just below Bluestone Dam.* 304/466-4600. Hrs: 6:30 am-9 pm. Closed Thanksgiving, Dec 25. Semi-a la carte: bkfst, lunch $3-$5, dinner $5-$12.25. Specialties: Kirk's hot dogs, fried chicken, stuffed baked potatoes. Own desserts. Outdoor dining. On New River near Bluestone Resort Park; patio overlooks river. Cr cds: C.

🄳

★★ **MOUNTAIN CREEK.** *(See Pipestem)* 304/466-1800. Hrs: 7 am-2 pm, 5:30-9 pm; Tues, Thurs 7-11 am, 5:30-9 pm; Sat to 10 pm. Closed May-Oct. Res accepted (dinner). French, Amer menu. Bar. Semi-a la carte: bkfst $2.25-$4.50, lunch $4.95, dinner $14.95-$23.95. Child's meals. Specialties: roasted pork filet, rack of lamb, prime rib of beef. Own pastries. Park in Pipestem Resort State Park. Dining rm at 1,000-ft-deep gorge; accessible by tram only. Totally nonsmoking. Cr cds: A, C, MC, V.

★★ **OAK SUPPER CLUB.** *Just N of Pipestem Park Entrance (25951), 12 mi SW on WV 20.* 304/466-4800. Hrs: 5:30-9 pm. Closed Thanksgiving, Dec 25; also Jan-Mar. Res accepted. Bar. Semi-a la carte: dinner $10.95-$24.95. Child's meals. Specializes in pork, duckling, fresh mountain trout. Named for 800 year-old white oak on grounds. Dining rm overlooks mountains. Family-owned. Cr cds: C, MC, V.

🄳

Huntington (D-2)

Founded 1871 **Pop** 54,844 **Elev** 564 ft **Area Code** 304 **E-mail** htgncvb@marshall.edu **Web** wvweb.com/greater_huntington_cvb

Information Cabell-Huntington Convention & Visitors Bureau, PO Box 347, 25708; 304/525-7333 or 800/635-6329

The millionaire president of the Chesapeake & Ohio Railroad, Collis P. Huntington, founded this city and named it for himself. Originally a rail and river terminus, commerce and industry have made it the second-largest city in the state. Thoroughly planned and meticulously laid out, Huntington is protected from the Ohio River by an 11-mile floodwall equipped with 17 pumping stations and 45 gates. Glass, railroad products and metals are important city industries.

What to See and Do

Beech Fork State Park. Nearly 4,000 acres on 720-acre Beech Fork Lake. Fishing; boating (ramp, marina). Hiking trails, physical fitness trail; tennis, game courts. Picnicking. Camping; store. Visitor center; nature, recreation programs (summer). Meeting rms. Standard hrs, fees. Approx 15 mi SE via WV 10, then 7 mi W on Hughes Branch Rd, near Bowen. Phone 304/522-0303.

Camden Park. Amusement park with 27 rides, games, concession; boat and train rides, log flume, miniature golf, roller rink, picnicking. (Mid-Apr-Memorial Day, Sat, Sun; Memorial Day-Labor Day, daily exc Mon) Rides individually priced; also unlimited ride plan. US 60 E. Phone 304/429-4231. ¢¢¢

East Lynn Wildlife Management Area. Almost 23,000 acres used primarily by sportsmen; trails, primitive camping (fee). 15 mi SE via WV 152 & WV 37, near East Lynn. Phone 304/675-0871.

Heritage Village. Restored Victorian B & O Railroad yard surrounding brick courtyard. Restaurant in original passenger station (1887), restored Pullman car, shops in renovated freight and box cars, warehouses. (Daily exc Sun) 11th St & Veterans Memorial Blvd. Phone 304/696-5954. **Free**

Huntington Museum of Art. Museum with American and European paintings, prints and sculpture; Herman P. Dean Firearms Collection; Georgian silver; Oriental prayer rugs; pre-Columbian art; Appalachian folk art; Ohio Valley historical and contemporary glass. Complex includes exhibition galleries, library, studio workshops, amphitheater, auditorium, sculpture garden, observatory, art gallery for young people, nature trails. Free admission Wed. (Tues-Sat, also Sun afternoons; closed some major hols) 2033 McCoy Rd; I-64 exit 8. Phone 304/529-2701. **Donation**

Industrial tours.

Blenko Glass Co, Inc. Famous glass factory; makers of Country Music Award, presidential gifts and original supplier to Colonial Williamsburg. Visitor center (daily; closed hols) has stained glass from nine leading studios; observation gallery for viewing hand-blown glassmaking and blown stained glass. (Mon-Fri; closed hols; also 1st 2 wks July, Dec 25-Jan 1) Museum of Historical Glass; Garden of Glass beside three-acre lake. 16 mi E via US 60, in Milton; I-64 exit 28. Phone 304/743-9081. **Free**

Pilgrim Glass Corp. Observation deck to watch making of hand-blown glassware, including cranberry, cobalt and crystal glass. Gift shop. (Mon-Fri; closed hols, also last wk June & 1st wk July) 5 mi W off I-64 exit 1, adj to Tri-State Airport on Airport Rd, in Ceredo. Phone 304/453-3553. **Free**

Motels

★★★ BEST WESTERN GATEWAY INN. *6007 US Rte 60 (25726). 304/736-8974; FAX 304/736-8974; res: 800/248-2426.* 208 rms, 1-2 story. S, D $70-$90; under 19 free; wkend rates; higher rates special events. Crib free. TV; cable, VCR avail. Indoor pool. Playground. Coffee in rms. Restaurant 7-10 am, 11 am-2 pm, 4-9 pm. Rm serv. Bar; entertainment. Ck-out noon. Coin lndry. Meeting rms. Business servs avail. Bellhops. Valet serv. Barber, beauty shop. Sundries. Lighted tennis. Exercise equipt; sauna. Game rm. Cr cds: A, C, D, DS, JCB, MC, V.

D ✔ ≈ ⫻ ⊠ ⌖ SC

★★ DAYS INN. *5196 Us Rte 60 (25705). 304/733-4477; FAX 304/733-4493; res: 800/694-8999.* 139 rms, 2 story. S $47-$65; D $60-$70; each addl $5; under 16 free. Crib free. Pet accepted, some restrictions. TV; cable (premium). Complimentary continental bkfst. Restaurant nearby.

Ck-out noon. Meeting rms. Business servs avail. In-rm modem link. Sundries. Pool. Many refrigerators, microwaves. Picnic tables, grills. Cr cds: A, C, D, DS, MC, V.

D ✔ ≈ ⊠ ⌖ SC

★ RAMADA INN. *5600 Rte 60 E (25713). 304/736-3451; FAX 304/736-3451.* 120 rms, 3 story. S $42-$54; D $47-$60; each addl $5; suites $54; under 18 free. Crib free. Pet accepted. TV; cable (premium). Pool. Restaurant 4-10 pm. Private club 5 pm-2 am. Ck-out noon. Meeting rms. Business servs avail. Sundries. Free airport transportation. Health club privileges. Private patios, balconies. Cr cds: A, C, D, DS, JCB, MC, V.

D ✔ ≈ ⊠ ⌖ SC

✓ **★ RED ROOF INN.** *5190 US Rte 60 E (25705). 304/733-3737; FAX 304/733-3786; res: 800/843-7663.* E-mail rhubbard@redroof inn.com. 108 rms, 2 story. S $45-$55; D $55-$60; each addl $7; under 18 free. Crib free. Pet accepted. TV; cable. Business servs avail. Refrigerators, microwaves avail. Cr cds: A, C, D, DS, MC, V.

D ✔ ⊠ ⌖ SC

Motor Hotel

★★ UPTOWNER UNIVERSITY PARK. *1415 4th Ave (25701). 304/525-7741; FAX 304/525-3508; res: 800/828-9016.* 138 rms, 4 story. S, D $55-$65; each addl $5; suites $90-$100; under 18 free. Crib free. Pet accepted. TV; cable. Pool; wading pool. Restaurants 6:30 am-10 pm. Rm serv. Bar 4 pm-midnight, Fri, Sat to 1 am. Ck-out noon. Meeting rms. Business servs avail. In-rm modem link. Free airport transportation. Exercise equipt. Cr cds: A, C, D, DS, JCB, MC, V.

D ✔ ≈ ⫻ ⊠ ⌖ SC

Hotel

★★★ RADISSON HOTEL. *1001 3rd Ave (25701). 304/525-1001; FAX 304/525-1048; res: 800/333-3333.* 200 rms, 11 story. S, D $88-$108; each addl $5; suites $160-$377; under 18 free; wkend rates. Crib free. TV; cable (premium). Heated pool; poolside serv. Coffee in rms. Restaurant 6:30 am-11 pm; Fri, Sat to midnight. Bar 3 pm-midnight. Ck-out noon. Meeting rms. Business center. In-rm modem link. Shopping arcade. Valet parking. Airport, RR station, bus depot transportation. Exercise equipt; sauna. On Ohio River. Cr cds: A, C, D, DS, ER, JCB, MC, V.

D ≈ ⫻ ⊠ SC ⌖

Restaurants

✓ **★★ HERITAGE STATION.** *11th St & Veterans Memorial Blvd (25701). 304/523-6373.* Hrs: 11:30 am-9:30 pm; Fri, Sat to 10:30 pm. Closed Sun; Jan 1, Thanksgiving, Dec 25. Res accepted. Bar. Semi-a la carte: lunch, dinner $5.99-$16.99. Specializes in seafood, pasta, steak, burgers. Outdoor dining. Former railroad station built in 1887; memorabilia, antiques. Cr cds: A, C, D, DS, MC, V.

D ➡

★★★ REBELS & REDCOATS TAVERN. *412 W 7th Ave (25701). 304/523-8829.* Hrs: 11:30 am-2:30 pm, 5:30-10 pm; Sat 5:30-11:30 pm. Closed Sun; major hols; also wk of July 4. Res accepted. Continental menu. Bar. Wine cellar. Semi-a la carte: lunch $6-$9, dinner $11-$25. Specialties: veal Oscar, châteaubriand bouquetiere. Colonial decor; fireplace. Family-owned. Cr cds: A, C, D, DS, MC, V.

D ➡

Lewisburg (E-5)

(See also White Sulphur Springs)

Founded 1782 **Pop** 3,598 **Elev** 2,099 ft **Area Code** 304 **Zip** 24901 **Web** wvweb.com/www/lewisburg

Information Lewisburg Visitors Center, 105 Church St; 304/645-1000 or 800/833-2068

At the junction of two important Native American trails, the Seneca (now US 219) and the Kanawha (now US 60), Lewisburg was the site of colonial forts as well as a Civil War battle. The town's 236-acre historic district has more than 60 buildings from the 18th and 19th centuries, in a variety of architectural styles.

What to See and Do

Lost World Caverns. Scenic trail over subterranean rock mountain; prehistoric ocean floor; stalagmites, stalactites; flow stone, ribbons, hex stones. Guided tours (daily; closed some major hols). 1 mi N on Fairview Rd. Phone 304/645-6677. ¢¢¢

North House Museum. Colonial and 19th-century objects and artifacts. (Tues-Sat) 101 W Church St, at Washington. Phone 304/645-3398. ¢¢

Old Stone Presbyterian Church (1796). Original log church (1783) was replaced by present native limestone structure. (Daily) 200 Church St. Phone 304/645-2676. **Free**

Organ Cave. One of the longest caves in the US. 40-mi of mapped passageways. (Daily) 417 Masters Rd, Ronceverte 24970. Phone 304/645-7600.

Annual Event

State Fair. Fairgrounds, 2 mi S on US 219. Exhibitors from a number of other states; horse shows, harness racing. Phone 304/645-1090. Mid-Aug.

Motels

★★ **BRIER INN.** 540 N Jefferson St (24901), jct US 219 & I-64 exit 169. 304/645-7722; FAX 304/645-7865; res: 800/427-4713. 162 units, 2 story. Apr-Oct: S $46; D $51; each addl $5; suites $75-$80; kit. units $65-$70; under 12 free; higher rates state fair; lower rates rest of yr. Crib $5. Pet accepted, some restrictions; $10. TV; cable, VCR avail (movies). Pool. Restaurant 11 am-10 pm; Fri, Sat to 11 pm. Rm serv. Bar 10-2 am; entertainment Fri. Ck-out 11 am. Meeting rms. Business servs avail. In-rm modem link. Exercise rm. Cr cds: A, C, D, DS, MC, V.

D 🐾 ⊠ 🏋 🖂 🐾 SC

✓★ **BUDGET HOST FORT SAVANNAH MOTEL.** 204 N Jefferson St (24901). 304/645-3055; FAX 304/645-3033; res: 800/283-4678. E-mail omb00827.@mall.wunit.edu. 66 rms, 2 story. S $36-$50; D $42-$65; each addl $5; under 18 free. Crib free. Pet accepted; $5. TV; cable. Pool; whirlpool. Restaurant 6 am-10 pm. Rm serv. Ck-out noon. Business servs avail. Airport transportation. Balconies. Cr cds: A, C, D, DS, MC, V.

D 🐾 ⊠ 🖂 🐾 SC

★ **DAYS INN.** 635 N Jefferson St (24901). 304/645-2345; FAX 304/645-5501; res: 800/325-2525. 26 rms. S $48-$65; D $48-$85; each addl $6; higher rates special events. Crib free. Pet accepted, some restrictions; $10. TV; cable (premium). Complimentary coffee in lobby. Restaurant nearby. Ck-out 11 am. Business servs avail. Airport transportation. Health club privileges. Cr cds: A, C, D, DS, MC, V.

🐾 🖂 🐾 SC

Inn

★★★ **GENERAL LEWIS INN.** 301 E Washington St (24901). 304/645-2600; FAX 304/645-2601; res: 800/628-4454. E-mail info@generallewisinn.com; web www.generallewisinn.com. 25 rms, 2 story. S $74-

$94; D $85-$105; each addl $12; higher rates special events; package plans. Crib free. TV; cable. Dining rm 7 am-9 pm. Rm serv. Bar 11 am-9 pm. Ck-out 11 am. Health club privileges. Part of building dates from 1834. Antiques; gardens. Totally nonsmoking. Cr cds: A, C, DS, MC, V.

D 🖂 🐾

Marlinton (D-5)

(See also Hillsboro)

Settled 1749 **Pop** 1,148 **Elev** 2,130 ft **Area Code** 304 **Zip** 24954 **Information** Potomac Highland Travel Council, 1200 Harrison Ave, Lower Level, Suite A. Elkins 26241; 304/636-8400

Marlinton is the seat of Pocahontas County, an area known for its wide variety of outdoor recreational opportunities. A Ranger District office of the Monongahela National Forest (see ELKINS) is located in the town.

What to See and Do

Cass Scenic Railroad State Park. Steam train makes 8-mi round trip (1½ hr) up the mountain to Whittaker (daily) and 22-mi round trip (4½ hr) to top of Bald Knob (daily exc Mon); picnic stopover; dinner trains (some Sat; call for reservation). On 1,089-acre property are 2 museums, a country store and 12 renovated logging camp houses now serving as tourist cottages. Picnicking. Camping. Standard hrs, fees. 5 mi E on WV 39, then 19 mi N on WV 28 to WV 66 in Cass. Phone 304/456-4300. Train ride ¢¢¢¢¢

Cranberry Mountain Visitor Center-Monongahela National Forest. Exhibits, videos and publications on conservation and forest management. (June-Labor Day, daily; Jan-Apr, Oct-Nov, Sat-Sun; May & Sept, Fri-Sun) Approx 7 mi NW of Mill Point via US 219 & WV 39. Phone 304/653-4826 or 304/846-2695 (off-season). **Free** 2 mi W is

Cranberry Glades. A USDA Forest Service botanical area. Approx 750 acres featuring open bog fringed by forest and alder thicket. Boardwalk with interpretive signs. Guided tours leave from visitor center (June-Labor Day, wkends). Glades (all-yr, weather permitting). **Free**

Greenbrier River Trail. Part of the state park system, this 76-mi trail runs along the Greenbrier River from the town of Cass, on the north, through Marlinton to North Caldwell, on the south; passes through small towns, over 35 bridges and through 2 tunnels. Originally the trail was part of the Chesapeake & Ohio RR. Activities include backpacking, bicycling and cross-country skiing; trail also provides access for fishing and canoeing. No developed sites. Phone 304/799-4087.

National Radio Astronomy Observatory. Study of universe by radio telescopes. Slide show, exhibits and 1-hour bus tour of site. (Mid-June-Labor Day wkend, daily; Memorial Day wkend-mid-June & after Labor Day-Oct, Sat & Sun) 5 mi SE on WV 39, then 21 mi N on WV 28, 92 in Green Bank. Phone 304/456-2209. **Free**

Pocahontas County Historical Museum. Displays on history of the county from its beginnings to present. Extensive photo collection. (Early June-Labor Day, daily) On US 219 S, at WV 39. Phone 304/799-4973. ¢

Seneca State Forest. Approx 12,000 acres with fishing and boating on 4-acre lake; hunting. Hiking trails. Picnicking, playground. Camping, 7 rustic cabins. Standard hrs, fees. 5 mi E via WV 39, then 10 mi NE on WV 28. Phone 304/799-6213.

Skiing.

Elk River Touring Center. Features 34 mi of cross-country trails in the Monongahela National Forest; patrol, school, rentals; restaurant; lodging. Night skiing. Guided tours. (All yr, daily) Also guided mountain bike tours, cave tours in season. 16 mi N on US 219, follow signs, near Slatyfork. Phone 304/572-3771. Skiing ¢¢¢¢¢

Snowshoe Mountain Resort. 2 quad, 8 triple, double chairlifts; patrol, school, rentals; snowmaking; restaurants, lodging, nursery, health club, 4 pools. 53 slopes and trails; longest run 6,200 ft; vertical drop 1,500 ft. (Mid-Nov-mid-Apr, daily) Summer activities include horseback riding, fishing, hiking. 26 mi N on US 219, near Slatyfork. Phone 304/572-1000 or 304/572-4636 (ski report). ¢¢¢¢¢

Annual Event

Pioneer Days. Craft exhibits and demonstrations; horse-pulling contests, frog and turtle races; bluegrass and mountain music shows; "4-by-4" pulling; parade; antique car show. Phone 304/799-4315. Early- mid-July.

Martinsburg (B-7)

(See also Berkeley Springs, Charles Town, Harpers Ferry, Shepherd-stown; also see Hagerstown, MD)

Settled 1732 **Pop** 14,073 **Elev** 457 ft **Area Code** 304 **Zip** 25401
E-mail chamber@inrepid.net **Web** wvweb.com/www/berkeley_chamber
Information Martinsburg-Berkeley County Chamber of Commerce, 198 Viking Way; 304/267-4841 or 800/332-9007

Martinsburg is located in the center of an apple- and peach-producing region in the state's eastern panhandle. Because of its strategic location at the entrance to the Shenandoah Valley, the town was the site of several battles during the Civil War. The famous Confederate spy Belle Boyd was a resident. Officially chartered in 1778, Martinsburg is recognized for the preservation of its many 18th- and 19th-century houses and mercantile and industrial buildings.

What to See and Do

General Adam Stephen House (1789). Restored residence of Revolutionary War soldier and surgeon Adam Stephen, founder of Martinsburg. Period furnishings; restored smokehouse and log building. (May-Oct, Sat & Sun, limited hrs; also by appt) 309 E John St. Phone 304/267-4434. **Free** Adj is

Triple-Brick Building. Completed in three sections just after the Civil War, the structure was used to house railroad employees. A museum of local history is located on the top two floors. (May-Oct, Sat & Sun, limited hrs; also by appt) **Free**

Annual Event

Mountain State Apple Harvest Festival. Parade, celebrity breakfast, contests, entertainment, Apple Queen coronation, square dancing, grand ball, arts & crafts show. Phone 304/263-2500. 3rd wkend Oct.

Motels

★★ **COMFORT INN.** *2800 Aikens Ctr (25401), exit 16E. 304/263-6200; FAX 304/267-0995; res: 800/228-5150.* Web wvweb.com/www/comfort_inn_mtsbg.html. 110 rms, 4 story, 11 suites. Apr-Oct: S, D $69; each addl $10; suites $98; under 18 free; wkend, hols rates; lower rates rest of yr. Crib free. TV; cable. Pool. Complimentary continental bkfst. Restaurant adj 11 am-10 pm. Ck-out noon. Coin lndry. Meeting rms. Business servs avail. In-rm modem link. Sundries. Gift shop. Valet serv. Exercise equipt. Game rm. Some refrigerators, microwaves, minibars. Cr cds: A, C, D, DS, JCB, MC, V.

D ⛱ 🏋 🖄 🔥 SC

★★ **COMFORT SUITES.** *Rte 9; E Short Rd (19703), I-81 exit 12, E on US 9. 304/263-8888; FAX 304/263-1540; res: 800/228-5050.* Web wvweb.com/www/comfort_suites. 76 rms, 3 story. May-Oct: S, D $65-$80; each addl $5; under 18 free; lower rates rest of yr. Crib free. TV; cable (premium). Pool; whirlpool. Complimentary continental bkfst. Restaurant nearby. Ck-out 11 am. Meeting rms. Business servs avail. Coin lndry. Golf privileges. Exercise equipt. Refrigerators, microwaves. Cr cds: A, C, D, DS, ER, MC, V.

D 🏋 ⛱ 🖄 🖄 🔥 SC

★ **KNIGHTS INN.** *1599 Edwin Miller Blvd (25401), I-81 exit 16E. 304/267-2211; FAX 304/267-9606; res: 800/843-5644.* 59 rms, 1-2 story, 6 kits. Apr-Dec: S $46.95; D $55; each addl $5; kits. $46.95-$55; under 17 free; lower rates rest of yr. Crib free. Pet accepted. TV; cable (premium), VCR avail. Complimentary coffee in lobby. Restaurant adj 6 am-11 pm. Ck-out noon. Meeting rms. Business servs avail. Sundries. Refrigerators, microwaves avail. Cr cds: A, C, D, DS, MC, V.

D ⛱ 🖄 🔥 🖄 SC

★ **SUPER 8 MOTEL.** *1600 Edwin Miller Blvd (25401), I-81, exit 16E. 304/263-0801; FAX 304/263-0801; res: 800/800-8000.* 43 rms, 3 story. June-Sept: S, D $43.88-$49.88; each addl $6; under 16 free; wkly, wkend rates; higher rates special events; lower rates rest of yr. Crib free. Pet accepted; $20 deposit. TV; cable (premium). Complimentary continental bkfst. Restaurant adj 6 am-11 pm. Ck-out 11 am. Meeting rms. Cr cds: A, C, D, DS, JCB, MC, V.

D ⛱ 🖄 🖄 🔥 SC

Hotel

★★ **HOLIDAY INN.** *301 Foxcroft Ave (25401), I-81 exit 13. 304/267-5500; FAX 304/264-9157; res: 800/465-4329.* 120 rms, 5 story. Apr-Oct: S, D $69-$89; under 17 free; lower rates rest of yr. Crib free. Pet accepted, some restrictions. TV; cable (premium). 2 pools, 1 indoor; whirlpool, lifeguard. Restaurant 6:30 am-10 pm; Sun 7 am-9 pm. Bar 4 pm-1 am. Ck-out noon. Meeting rms. Business servs avail. In-rm modem link. Lighted tennis, pro. Exercise rm; saunas. Lawn games. Some refrigerators. Cr cds: A, C, D, DS, ER, JCB, MC, V.

D ⛱ 🏋 🏊 🏋 🖄 🔥 SC

Resort

★★★ **WOODS RESORT & CONFERENCE CENTER.** *Mountain Lake Rd (25427), 10½ mi W of I-81 exit 16W via WV 9, then left on Mt Lake Rd 2½ mi. 304/754-3358; FAX 304/754-8146; res: 800/248-2222.* Web www.thewoodsresort.com. 60 rms in 3-bldg lodge, 14 kit. cabins. MAP: D $91.50-$111.50/person; EP: S, D $94-$127; each addl $11; kit. cabins $138; under 5 free; wkends 2-night min. Crib free. TV; cable (premium), VCR avail. 3 pools, 1 indoor; wading pools, whirlpool, lifeguard. Supervised child's activities (June-Aug); ages 5-18. Complimentary coffee in lobby. Dining rm 7 am-3 pm, 5-9 pm; Fri 5-10 pm; Sat 3-10 pm; Sun 3-9 pm. Box lunches, picnics. Bar noon-midnight; entertainment Sat. Ck-out noon, ck-in 4 pm. Grocery 2½ mi. Coin lndry. Package store 12 mi. Meeting rms. Business servs avail. Indoor/outdoor lighted tennis. 27-hole golf privileges, greens fee, pro. Exercise equipt; sauna. Lawn games. Refrigerators; some fireplaces. Whirlpools in lodge rms. Private patios. Cr cds: A, C, D, DS, MC, V.

D 🏋 🏋 🏋 🏊 🏋 🖄 🔥

Inn

★★★ **EDGEWOOD MANOR INC.** *RR 2 Box 329 (25413), 10 mi S on I-81, exit 5, 3 mi S on US 11. 304/229-9353.* Web www.wvweb.com/www/edgewood. 6 rms, 2 share bath, 3 story. No rm phones. S, D $95-$145; wkend, wkly, hol rates. Children over 12 yrs only. Complimentary full bkfst; afternoon refreshments. Complimentary coffee in rms. Ck-out noon, ck-in 3 pm. Luggage handling. Rec rm. Lawn games. Fireplaces. Some balconies. Picnic tables. Built in 1839; used as headquarters for Lt Gen Thomas J. Stonewall Jackson and Gen Robert E. Lee. Also used as hospital for both sides in Civil War. Totally nonsmoking. Cr cds: A, C, MC, V.

🖄 🔥 SC

Moorefield (C-6)

(See also Petersburg)

Settled 1777 **Pop** 2,148 **Elev** 821 ft **Area Code** 304 **Zip** 26836
Information Potomac Highland Travel Council, 1200 Harrison Ave, Lower Level, Suite A, Elkins 26241; 304/636-8400

What to See and Do

Lost River State Park. More than 3,700 acres where Lee's White Sulphur Springs was once a famous resort; an original cabin still stands; museum. Swimming pool, wading pool (Memorial Day-Labor Day). Hiking trails, horseback riding; tennis, game courts. Picnicking, playground, restaurant; 24 cabins. Recreation building; nature programs (summer); scenic overlooks. Standard hrs, fees. 18 mi E on WV 55 to Baker, then 13 mi S on WV 259, near Mathias. Phone 304/897-5372 or 800/CALL-WVA.

Annual Event

Hardy County Heritage Weekend. Tours of antebellum houses, medieval jousting, crafts, traditional events. Phone 304/538-6560. Last full wkend Sept.

Morgantown (B-5)

(See also Fairmont)

Settled 1776 **Pop** 25,879 **Elev** 892 ft **Area Code** 304 **Zip** 26505
E-mail cvb@mgtn.com **Web** www.mgtn.com
Information Greater Morgantown Convention & Visitors Bureau, 709 Beechurst Ave; 304/292-5081 or 800/458-7373

Morgantown is both an educational and industrial center. West Virginia University was founded here in 1867, the Morgantown Female Collegiate Institute in 1839. Known internationally for its glass, Morgantown is home to a number of glass plants, which produce wares ranging from lamp parts to decorative paper weights and crystal tableware. The town is also home to a number of research laboratories that are maintained by the federal government.

What to See and Do

Coopers Rock State Forest. More than 12,700 acres. Trout fishing, hunting. Hiking trails to historical sites; Henry Clay iron furnace (1834-1836). Cross-country ski trails. Picnicking, playground, concession. Tent & trailer camping. Standard hrs, fees. 10 mi E on I-68. Phone 304/594-1561. Adj is

Chestnut Ridge Regional Park. Swimming beach; fishing. Tent & trailer camping (hookups, dump station), rustic cabins, lodge (fees). Hiking. Picnicking. Cross-country ski trails (Dec-Feb). Nature center. Park (daily). Phone 304/594-1773.

West Virginia University (1867). (22,712 students) University has 15 colleges. (Tours daily exc Sun; for reservation Phone 304/293-3489). The Visitors Center in the Communications Bldg on Patterson Dr has touch-screen monitors and video presentations about the university and upcoming special events (phone 304/293-6692 for 24-hr event information). Of special interest on the downtown campus are Stewart Hall and the university's original buildings, located on Woodburn Circle. In the Evansdale area of Morgantown are the Creative Arts Center, the 75-acre Cole Arboretum, the 63,500-seat Coliseum and the

Cook-Hayman Pharmacy Museum. Re-creates pharmacy of yesteryear with old patent medicines. (Mon-Fri; wkends by request; closed hols) Health Sciences Center North, Rm 1136. Phone 304/293-5101. **Donation**

Personal Rapid Transit System (PRT). A pioneering transit system, the PRT is the world's first totally automated system. Operating without operators or ticket takers, computer-directed cars travel between university campuses and downtown Morgantown. (Daily exc Sun; may not operate certain hols and univ breaks) Phone 304/293-5011. One-way ¢

Whitewater rafting. Many outfitters offer guided trips on the Cheat and Tygart rivers. For a list of outfitters contact the Greater Morgantown Convention and Visitors Bureau, 709 Beechurst Ave; phone 800/458-7373.

Annual Events

Mason-Dixon Festival. Morgantown Riverfront Park. River parade, boat races, arts & crafts, concessions. Mid-Sept.

Mountaineer Balloon Festival. Morgantown Municipal Airport. Hot-air balloon races, carnival, music, food. Phone 304/296-8356. Mid-Oct.

Motels

★★ **COMFORT INN.** *Rte 9 (26505), at jct US 68, US 119.* 304/296-9364; FAX 304/296-0469; res: 800/638-7949. 81 rms, 2 story. S $45-$100; D $49-$100; each addl $6; suites $80-$125; kit. units $45-$100; under 18 free; higher rates: football wkends, graduation. Crib free. TV; cable (premium), VCR avail. Complimentary continental bkfst. Restaurant adj 11 am-10 pm; Fri, Sat to 2 pm; Sun noon-9 pm. Ck-out noon. Meeting rm. Business servs avail. Sundries. Exercise equipt. Cr cds: A, C, D, DS, MC, V.

🄳 🏌 🐟 🏊 🐾 SC

★ **DAYS INN.** *366 Boyers Ave (26505), 1 mi N on US 19, WV 7.* 304/598-2120; FAX 304/598-3272; res: 800/329-7466. 102 rms, 3 story. Apr-Oct: S $54; D $62; each addl $8; under 12 free; higher rates: football games, graduation; lower rates rest of yr. Crib free. TV; cable (premium), VCR avail. Indoor pool; whirlpool. Complimentary full bkfst. Restaurant 6 am-11 pm; Sun 7 am-noon. Rm serv. Bar 4-11 pm. Ck-out 11 am. Coin lndry. Meeting rm. Business servs avail. Exercise equipt; sauna. Cr cds: A, C, D, DS, MC, V.

🄳 🏊 🏌 🏊 🐾 SC

★ **ECONO LODGE.** *15 Commerce Dr (26507), I-79 exit 152.* 304/296-8774; FAX 304/296-8774; res: 800/553-2666. 81 rms, 2 story. S, D $58; each addl $5; under 18 free. Crib free. TV, VCR avail (movies $5). Restaurant nearby. Ck-out noon. Business servs avail. Cr cds: A, C, D, DS, JCB, MC, V.

🄳 🏊 🐾 SC

✓★ **ECONO LODGE.** *3506 Monongahela Blvd (26505).* 304/599-8181; FAX 304/599-8181. 72 rms, 2 story. S, D $62; higher rates: football wkends, graduation. Crib $5. Pet accepted. TV; VCR avail. Restaurant adj 6 am-midnight. Ck-out 11 am. Meeting rm. Business servs avail. Sundries. Cr cds: A, C, D, DS, MC, V.

🄳 🐾 🏊 🐾 SC

★★ **HAMPTON INN.** *1053 Van Voorhis Rd (26505), I-79 exit 155.* 304/599-1200; FAX 304/598-7331; res: 800/426-7866. 108 rms, 5 story. S $73-$82; D $83-$92; suites $125; under 18 free; higher rates special events. Crib free. TV; cable. Complimentary continental bkfst. Restaurant adj. Ck-out noon. Meeting rms. Business servs avail. In-rm modem link. Health club privileges. Cr cds: A, C, D, DS, MC, V.

🄳 🐾 🏊 🐾 SC

★★ **HOLIDAY INN.** *1400 Saratoga Ave (26505).* 304/599-1680; FAX 304/598-0989; res: 800/465-4329. E-mail him@wvholidayinns.com; web www.wvholidayinns.com. 147 rms, 2-4 story. S, D $49-$99; under 18 free; higher rates: graduation, athletic events. Crib free. Pet accepted. TV; cable. Pool. Restaurant 6-11 am, 5-10 pm. Rm serv. Bar 4 pm-2 am. Ck-out noon. Meeting rms. Business servs avail. Health club privileges. Cr cds: A, C, D, DS, ER, JCB, MC, V.

🄳 🐾 🏊 🏊 🐾 SC

Motor Hotel

★★ **RAMADA INN.** *US Rte 119, I-68 & I-79 (26505), 3 mi S on US 119 at jct US 68 & I-79 exit 148.* 304/296-3431; FAX 304/296-3431; res: 800/834-9766. E-mail innatmtown@aol.com; web www.wvonline.com/ramada. 163 rms, 4 story. S $55-$85; D $60-$85; addl $5; studio rms $100-$185; under 18 free; higher rates: special events, football games, Dec 31, Memorial Day wkend, graduation. Crib free. TV; cable (premium). Pool; lifeguard. Restaurant 6 am-10 pm. Private club 11-2 am; entertainment exc Sun. Ck-out noon. Coin lndry. Meeting rms. Business servs avail. In-rm modem link. Sundries. Gift shop. Free airport transportation. Exercise equipt. Game rm. Cr cds: A, C, D, DS, JCB, MC, V.

Hotel

✓★ **CLARION.** *127 High St (26505).* 304/292-8401; FAX 304/292-8200. 40 rms, 7 story, 27 kit. suites. S, D $40-$50; kit. suites $75-$100; under 12 free; wkly, monthly rates; higher rates: football season, graduation. TV; cable. Ck-out 11 am. Meeting rms. Business servs avail. Some refrigerators. Historic brick hotel (1925). Cr cds: A, C, DS, MC, V.

Resort

★★★ **LAKEVIEW RESORT.** *1 Lakeview Dr (26508), 7 mi N, ¼ mi S off WV 857; ¼ mi N of US 68 exit 10.* 304/594-1111; FAX 304/594-9472; res: 800/624-8300. E-mail peterhornsby@lakeviewresort.com; web www.lakeviewresort.com. 187 rms, 1-3 story. Apr-Nov: S $165; D $175; each addl $10; suites $225-$395; under 18 free; summer, winter rates; golf plans; lower rates rest of yr. Crib free. TV; cable. 4 pools, 2 indoor; wading pool, whirlpool, poolside serv, lifeguard. Dining rms 6:30 am-10 pm. Bar 11-1 am; Sun from 1 pm; entertainment exc Sun. Ck-out 2 pm, ck-in 4 pm. Meeting rms. Business servs avail. Valet serv. Gift shop. Free airport transportation. Indoor/outdoor tennis. Two 18-hole golf courses, greens fee $23-$45, pro. Rec rm. Exercise rm; sauna. Massage. Some refrigerators. On 400 acres. Cr cds: A, C, D, DS, MC, V.

Inn

★ **FIELDCREST MANOR BED & BREAKFAST.** *1440 Stewartstown Rd (26505).* 304/599-2686; FAX 304/599-3796; res: 800/765-0569. E-mail fldcrest@access.mountain.net; web www.pinnaclemall.com/fieldcrestmanor/. 5 rms, 3 story. S $60; D $80; under 10 free; package plans; wkends, hols (2-day min). TV; cable. Complimentary full bkfst. Ck-out 11 am, ck-in 3 pm. Business servs avail. Built in 1900; hillside location. Totally nonsmoking. Cr cds: A, C, MC, V.

Restaurants

✓★★ **ALI-BABA DOWNTOWN RESTAURANT.** *345 High St (26505).* 304/292-4701. E-mail alibaba@etcom.net. Hrs: 11 am-9 pm; Fri, Sat to 10 pm; Sun noon-8 pm. Closed Jan 1, Dec 25. Res accepted. Middle Eastern menu. Res accepted. Bar. Semi-a la carte: lunch $4.50-$7.50, dinner $8-$15.95. Buffets: lunch $5.25, dinner $9.95. Child's meals. Specializes in Middle Eastern salads, vegetarian dishes. Parking. Outdoor dining. Middle Eastern decor. Family-owned since 1978. Cr cds: A, C, DS, MC, V.

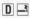

★★ **BACK BAY.** *1869 Mileground (26505), near airport.* 304/296-3027. Hrs: 11 am-9:30 pm; Fri to 10:30 pm; Sat 4-10:30 pm; Sun noon-9 pm. Closed major hols. Bar. Semi-a la carte: lunch $3.95-$7.95, dinner $5.95-$21.95. Specializes in fresh seafood, prime rib, Cajun dishes. Nautical atmosphere. Cr cds: A, C, D, DS, MC, V.

★★ **FLAME STEAK HOUSE.** *76 High St (26505).* 304/296-2976. Hrs: 5-11 pm. Closed major hols. Res accepted. Private club. Complete meals: dinner $6.45-$21.95. Child's meals. Specializes in steak, fresh seafood, Italian dishes. Colonial decor. Family-owned. Cr cds: A, C, D, DS, MC, V.

✓★ **PUGLIONI'S.** *1137 Van Voorhis Rd (26505).* 304/599-7521. Hrs: 11 am-10 pm; Fri, Sat to 11 pm. Closed major hols. Res accepted. Italian menu. Bar. Semi-a la carte: lunch $3.75-$6.95, dinner $7.95-$13.95. Child's meals. Specialties: pasta carbonara, pasta bellagio, chicken putanesca. Own pasta. Parking. Outdoor dining. Cr cds: A, C, DS, MC, V.

Nitro (D-3)

(See also Charleston)

Founded 1918 **Pop** 6,851 **Elev** 604 ft **Area Code** 304 **Zip** 25143
E-mail putnamcounty@newwave.net **Web** www.newwave.net/~putnam county
Information Putnam County Chamber of Commerce, PO Box 553, Teays 25569; 304/757-6510

Nitro experienced explosive growth around a huge smokeless powder plant during World War I, when the town's population reached 35,000 overnight and some 3,400 buildings were erected. When the war ended, the demand for smokeless powder fizzled, and the town dried up; factory buildings were scrapped, and whole houses were shipped down the river. Now a western suburb of Charleston, Nitro produces chemicals.

What to See and Do

Tri-State Greyhound Park. Indoor grandstand, clubhouse, concessions. (Mon-Sat evenings; matinees Sat, Sun & hols) Must be 18 to wager. E via I-64 exit 47A to Goff Mountain Rd, then to Greyhound Dr in Cross Lanes. Phone 304/776-1000.

Waves of Fun. Water park featuring three water slides, wave pool, swimming areas; bathhouse, tube rentals (fee), lockers, concessions. Miniature golf. (Memorial early June, wkends; early June-Labor Day, daily) W via I-64 exit 39, then 3 mi S on WV 34, at Valley Park in Hurricane. Phone 304/562-0518. ¢¢¢

Motels

✓★ **BEST WESTERN.** *4115 1st Ave Nitro (25143).* 304/755-8341; FAX 304/755-2933; res: 800/528-1234. 42 rms, 1-3 story. No elvtr. S, D $45.99-$59.99; each addl $5; under 12 free. Crib $6. TV; cable (premium). Restaurant adj open 24 hrs. Ck-out 11 am. Business servs avail. Cr cds: A, C, D, DS, MC, V.

★★ **COMFORT INN.** *102 Racer Rd. (25313), E on I-64 exit 47 to Goff Mountain Rd.* 304/776-8070; FAX 304/776-6460. 112 rms, 2 story. S $62-$75; D $67-$77; each addl $5; under 18 free. Crib free. TV; cable (premium). Pool; whirlpool. Complimentary continental bkfst. Coffee in rms.

Restaurant adj 7 am-midnight. Bar 4 pm-1 am; Fri, Sat to 2 am. Ck-out noon. Meeting rms. Business servs avail. Sundries. Health club privileges. Microwaves avail. Cr cds: A, C, D, DS, ER, MC, V.

[D] [icons] SC

✓★★ **RAMADA LIMITED.** *419 Hurricane Creek Rd (25526), W on US 60.* 304/562-3346; FAX 304/562-7408; res: 800/726-7016. 147 rms, 2 story. Apr-Sept: S, D $45-$55; each addl $5; under 16 free; wkly rates; higher rates special events; lower rates rest of yr. Crib free. Pet accepted, some restrictions; $5. TV; cable (premium). Pool. Complimentary continental bkfst. Restaurant adj 7 am-10 pm. Ck-out noon. Meeting rms. Business servs avail. Sundries. Some refrigerators; microwaves avail. Picnic tables, grills. Cr cds: A, C, D, DS, JCB, MC, V.

[D] [icons] SC

Restaurants

★ **DIEHL'S.** *152 Main Ave (25143).* 304/755-9353. Hrs: 10:30 am-9 pm; Sun 11 am-8 pm. Closed Mon. Semi-a la carte: lunch $3-$6, dinner $3.50-$7. Specializes in home-cooked meals. Casual decor. Cr cds: C, DS, MC, V.

[D] [icons]

★★★ **WELLINGTON'S.** *#1 Dairy Rd (25159), I-64, Nitro exit.* 304/755-8219. E-mail dfraz11574@aol.com. Hrs: 11 am-2 pm, 5-10 pm; Mon 5-10 pm; Sat 5-10 pm; early-bird dinner 5-6:30 pm. Closed Sun; also most major hols. Res accepted. Continental menu. Bar. Semi-a la carte: lunch $4.95-$9.95, dinner $9.95-$21.95. Lunch buffet $5.50. Specialties: duck Lafayette, beef Wellington, shrimp Napoleon. Piano Fri, Sat. Intimate atmosphere. Totally nonsmoking. Cr cds: A, C, D, DS, MC, V.

[D] [icons]

Parkersburg (C-3)

Settled 1785 **Pop** 33,862 **Elev** 616 ft **Area Code** 304 **Zip** 26101 **E-mail** parkersburg@citynet.net **Web** wvweb.com/www.wvev.com/parkersburg

Information Parkersburg/Wood Co Convention & Visitor's Bureau, 350 7th St; 304/428-1130 or 800/752-4982

In 1770, George Washington came to this area to inspect lands awarded to him by Virginia for his military services. After the Revolution, Blennerhassett Island, in the Ohio River west of Parkersburg, was the scene of the alleged Burr-Blennerhassett plot. Harman Blennerhassett, a wealthy Irishman, built a lavish mansion on this island. After killing Alexander Hamilton in a duel, Aaron Burr came to the island, allegedly with the idea of seizing the Southwest and setting up an empire; Blennerhassett may have agreed to join him. On December 10, 1806, the plot was uncovered. Both men were acquitted of treason but were, in the process, ruined financially. The Blennerhassett mansion burned in 1811, but was later rebuilt.

Today, Parkersburg is the center for many industries, including glass, chemicals, petrochemicals and ferrous and other metals. Fishing is popular in the area, especially below the Belleville and Willow Island locks and dams on the Ohio River.

What to See and Do

Actors Guild Playhouse. Musical, comedic and dramatic performances. (Fri-Sun) 8th & Market Sts. Phone 304/485-1300. ¢¢¢

Blennerhassett Island Historical State Park. A 500-acre island accessible only by sternwheeler. There are self-guided walking tours of the island; horse-drawn wagon rides; tours of the Blennerhassett mansion. Bicycle rentals. Picnicking, concession. (May-Labor Day, daily exc Mon, also hols; Sept-Oct, Thurs-Sun) Tickets avail for boat ride, mansion tour and Blennerhassett Museum. 2 mi S in Ohio River. Phone 304/420-4800. Mansion tour ¢¢

Blennerhassett Museum. Features archaeological and other exhibits relating to history of Blennerhassett Island and Parkersburg area; includes artifacts dating back 12,000 yrs. Theater with video presentation. (May-Oct, daily exc Mon; rest of yr, Sat & Sun; closed Jan 1, Thanksgiving, Dec 25) 2nd & Juliana Sts. Phone 304/420-3000. ¢

City Park. A 55-acre wooded area with the Cooper Log Cabin Museum, which dates from 1804. Swimming pool; fishing; paddle boats. Miniature golf, tennis. Shelters and picnic facilities. Park Ave & 23rd St.

Middleton Doll Company. Tour of vinyl and porcelain doll factory (20 min). Factory store (daily exc Sun). (June-Aug, Tues-Sat; rest of yr, Mon-Fri; closed hols) 2 mi W via US 50, at 1301 Washington Blvd in Belpre, OH. Phone 614/423-1481 or 800/233-7479. **Free**

Mountwood Park. Wooded area with fishing, boating (no gasoline motors); hiking, mountain biking and OHV trails, nature trails; picnic area. 12 mi E via US 50 to Volcano Rd. Phone 304/679-3611. **Free**

North Bend State Park. Approx 1,400 acres in the wide valley of the North Fork of the Hughes River; scenic overlooks of famous horseshoe bend. Swimming pool, bathhouse; fishing. Miniature golf; tennis, game courts. Hiking, bicycle, bridle trail; 71-mi North Bend Rail Trail (see CLARKSBURG). Picnicking, playground, concession, restaurant, lodge. Tent & trailer camping (dump station), eight cabins. Nature, recreation programs. Nature trail for disabled. Standard hrs, fees. 22 mi E on US 50, then 7 mi SE on WV 31, near Cairo. Phone 304/643-2931 or 800/CALL-WVA.

Parkersburg Art Center. Changing exhibits. (Daily exc Mon; closed hols) 220 8th St. Phone 304/485-3859. ¢

Rubles Sternwheelers Riverboat Cruises. To Blennerhassett Island. (Early May-early Sept, daily exc Mon; early Sept-Oct, Thurs-Sun) Depart from Point Park, 2nd & Ann Sts. Phone 614/423-7268. ¢¢

Annual Events

Parkersburg Homecoming. Point Park, just off WV 68 at foot of 2nd St. Riverfront celebration features entertainment, parade, sternwheeler races, waterskiing show, miniature car races, fireworks. Phone 304/422-3588. 3rd wkend Aug.

West Virginia Honey Festival. 4-H Grounds. Honey-related exhibits, baking, food, arts and crafts. Mid-Sept.

Motels

★★★ **HOLIDAY INN.** *Rte 50 & I-77 (26101), 3½ mi E on US 50, at jct I-77.* 304/485-6200; FAX 304/485-6200. 148 rms, 2 story. S, D $59-$70; under 18 free; wkend packages. Crib free. TV. Indoor pool; whirlpool. Restaurant 6 am-9 pm; Sat from 7 am; Sun 7 am-2 pm. Rm serv. Bar 11 am-midnight. Ck-out noon. Coin lndry. Meeting rms. Business servs avail. Bellhops. Game rm. Exercise equipt; sauna. Some refrigerators. Some balconies. Cr cds: A, C, D, DS, JCB, MC, V.

[D] [icons] SC

★★ **NORTH BEND STATE PARK LODGE.** *RR 1 Box 221 (26337), 22 mi E on US 50, then 7 mi SE on WV 31, in North Bend State Park.* 304/643-2931; FAX 304/643-2970; res: 800/225-5982. Web wvweb.com/www/north_bend.html. 29 rms, 2 story, 8 cabins. Memorial Day wkend-Labor Day: S, D $59-$66; each addl $6; 2-3 bedrm cabins $530-$598/wk; under 12 free; lower rates rest of yr. TV. Pool. Free supervised child's activities (June-Aug). Restaurant 7 am-5 pm; Fri, Sat to 8 pm; Sun to 7 pm. Ck-out noon (lodge), 10 am (cabins). Business servs avail. Sundries. Tennis. Picnic tables, grills. On river. View of mountains. State owned, operated. Cr cds: A, C, D, MC, V.

[D] [icons] SC

★ **RED ROOF INN.** *3714 E 7th St (26101).* 304/485-1741; FAX 304/485-1746; res: 800/843-7663. 107 rms, 2 story. S $37-$49; D $44-$67; each addl $5; under 18 free. Crib free. Pet accepted. TV; cable (premium). Ck-out noon. Meeting rms. Business servs avail. In-rm modem link. Cr cds: A, C, D, DS, MC, V.

[D] [icons] SC

Hotel

★★★ **HISTORIC BLENERHASSETT HOTEL.** *320 Market St (26101). 304/422-3131; FAX 304/485-0267; res: 800/262-2536.* Web wvweb.com/www/blennerhassetthotel. 104 rms, 5 story. S, D $69-$79; each addl $6; suites $75-$125; under 18 free. Crib free. Pet accepted. TV; cable (premium), VCR avail. Complimentary full bkfst. Coffee in rms. Restaurant 6 am-10 pm. Bar 11-1 am. Ck-out noon. Meeting rms. Business center. In-rm modem link. Gift shop. Valet parking. Free airport transportation. Health club privileges. Restored Victorian hotel built in 1889. Cr cds: A, C, D, DS, ER, MC, V.

D 🐾 ⇋ 🔥 SC 🏃

Inn

★★★ **WILLIAMS' HOUSE BED & BREAKFAST.** *5406 Grand Central Ave (26105), I-77 exit 179. 304/295-7212; FAX 304/295-7212.* 5 rms, 3 story. No elvtr. Some rm phones. S $50; D $62; each addl $10. Crib free. TV; cable, VCR avail (movies). Complimentary full bkfst. Ck-out 11 am, ck-in 4 pm. Business servs avail. Airport transportation. Exercise equipt. Pool. Lawn games. Microwaves avail. Picnic tables, grills. Built in 1920; antiques. Cr cds: C, MC, V.

⇋ 🏃 🔥

Restaurants

✓★ **MOUNTAINEER FAMILY RESTAURANT.** *4006 E 7th St (26101), at jct US 50 & I-77. 304/422-0101.* Open 24 hrs. Closed Dec 25. Semi-a la carte: bkfst $1.95-$4.95, lunch $1.95-$5.95, dinner $3.95-$11.99. Child's meals. Specializes in steak, seafood, chicken. Cr cds: C.

D SC 🍴 ♥

★★ **POINT OF VIEW.** *Blennerhassett Heights Rd (26101), 3 mi SW via WV 68, Star Ave exit. 304/863-3366.* Hrs: 11:30 am-2 pm, 5-9:30 pm; Fri, Sat 5-10 pm. Closed Sun; major hols. Bar. Semi-a la carte: lunch $4-$8, dinner $10-$22. Child's meals. Specializes in prime rib, fresh seafood, steak. Own baking. View of Blennerhasset Island. Family-owned. Cr cds: A, C, D, DS, MC, V.

🍴

Petersburg (C-6)

(See also Franklin, Moorefield)

Settled 1745 **Pop** 2,360 **Elev** 937 ft **Area Code** 304 **Zip** 26847
Information Potomac Highland Travel Council, 1200 Harrison Ave, Lower Level, Suite A, Elkins 26241; 304/636-8400

A Ranger District office of the Monongahela National Forest (see ELKINS) is located in Petersburg.

What to See and Do

Monongahela National Forest. Recreation area is popular for canoeing, hiking and other outdoor sports. Camping (fee). USDA Forest Service, H659, PO Box 240. Phone 304/257-4488.   **Free**

Smoke Hole Caverns. Caverns were used centuries ago by the Seneca both for shelter and the smoking of meat. During the Civil War, they were used by troops on both sides for storing ammunition. Later, they hid the illegal distillation of corn whiskey. It is claimed the caverns contain the longest ribbon stalactite and the second-highest cave room in the world. Guided tours. Large gift shop with wildlife exhibits; concessions. Tours. (Daily; closed Thanksgiving, Dec 25) 8 mi S on WV 28 & 55. Phone 304/257-4442. ¢¢¢

Motels

★★ **HERMITAGE MOTOR INN.** *203 Virginia Ave (26847). 304/257-1711; FAX 304/257-4330; res: 800/437-6482.* 39 rms, 2 story. S $41-$45; D $47-$51; each addl $6; under 12 free. Crib $6. TV; cable (premium). Pool; whirlpool. Restaurant 11 am-9 pm; Fri, Sat to 10 pm. Ck-out noon. Business servs avail. In-rm modem link. Airport transportation. Health club privileges. Craft shop, bookstore in 1840s inn. Cr cds: A, C, D, DS, MC, V.

D ⇋ ⇋ 🐾 SC

★ **SMOKE HOLE MOTEL & LOG CABINS.** *Rte 28 S; Hc 59 Box 39 (26884), 12 mi S on WV 28/55. 304/257-4442; FAX 304/257-2745; res: 800/828-8478.* Web www.smokehole.com. 13 rms, 3 suites, 35 cottages. S $25-$45; D $45-$55; each addl $10; kit. cottages $79.50-$129.50; family, wkly rates. TV; cable. Pool. Playground. Ck-out 11 am. Gift shop. Lawn games. Refrigerators in cabins. Adj Smoke Hole Caverns. Cr cds: A, C, D, DS, MC, V.

D 🐾 ⇋ 🔥 🐾

Philippi (C-5)

(See also Buckhannon, Clarksburg, Grafton)

Settled 1780 **Pop** 3,132 **Elev** 1,307 ft **Area Code** 304 **Zip** 26416
Information Barbour County Chamber of Commerce, PO Box 5000; 304/457-1958

The first land battle of the Civil War, a running rout of the Confederates known locally as the Philippi Races, was fought here on June 3, 1861. An historical marker on the campus of Alderson-Broaddus College marks the site. The Union attacked to protect the Baltimore & Ohio Railroad, whose main line between Washington and the West ran near the town.

What to See and Do

Barbour County Historical Society Museum. This B & O Railroad station (1911), used until 1956, is now restored as a museum; also local arts & crafts. (May-Oct, daily; rest of yr, by appt) 146 N Main St. For further information contact the Chamber of Commerce.

Covered bridge. Spanning Tygart River since 1852; restored in recent years; believed to be the only two-lane bridge of its type still in daily use on a federal highway (US 250).

Annual Events

Blue & Gray Reunion. Commemorates the first land battle of the Civil War; reenactment, parade, crafts. 1st wkend June.

Barbour County Fair. Fairgrounds, 5 mi SE on US 250. Horse and antique car shows, quilt and livestock exhibits, carnival rides, nightly entertainment, parade and more. Phone 304/457-3254. Wk before Labor Day.

Motel

★ **SUPER 8 MOTEL.** *Rte 2 Box 155 (26416). 304/457-5888; FAX 304/457-5888; res: 800/800-8000.* 40 rms, 2 story. S $49.88-$54.88; D $53.88-$60.88; each addl $6; under 12 free. Crib free. TV; cable (premium). Complimentary coffee in lobby. Restaurant adj 6 am-9 pm. Ck-out 11 am. Business servs avail. Some refrigerators. Cr cds: A, C, D, DS, MC, V.

D ⇋ 🐾 SC

Restaurant

✓★ **PHILIPPI INN.** On US 250S (26416). 304/457-1733. Hrs: 6 am-8 pm; Fri, Sat to 9 pm; Sun from 7 am. Closed Thanksgiving, Dec 25. Res accepted. Semi-a la carte: bkfst, lunch $1.25-$8, dinner $4-$12.10. Child's meals. Specializes in prime rib, steak. Own pies, breads. Family-owned. Cr cds: A, C, DS, MC, V.

D SC ⊟

Point Pleasant (C-3)

(See also Ripley)

Settled 1774 **Pop** 4,996 **Elev** 569 ft **Area Code** 304 **Zip** 25550
Information Mason County Area Chamber of Commerce, 305 Main St; 304/675-1050

On October 10, 1774, British-incited Shawnees under Chief Cornstalk fought a battle here against 1,100 frontiersmen. The colonists won and broke the Native American power in the Ohio Valley. Historians later argued that this, rather than the battle at Lexington, Massachusetts, was the first battle of the Revolutionary War. In 1908, the US Senate rewrote history by recognizing this claim.

What to See and Do

Krodel Park and Lake. A 44-acre park with a replica of Fort Randolph (ca 1775). Fishing (license required); paddle boats (fee). Miniature golf (fee). Playground. Camping (mid-Apr-Oct; fee). 1 mi SE via WV 62/2. Phone 304/675-1068 (seasonal).   **Free**

McClintic Wildlife Management Area. Approx 2,800 acres with primitive camping (fee). Also hunting, fishing (licenses required). 7 mi NE off WV 62. Phone 304/675-0871.

Point Pleasant Battle Monument State Park. An 84-ft granite shaft was erected here in 1909, after the US Senate agreed to a claim made by historians that the first battle of the Revolutionary War was fought here. Park also contains a marker where Joseph Celeron de Bienville buried a leaden plate in 1749, claiming the land for France, and the graves of Chief Cornstalk and "Mad Anne" Bailey, noted pioneer scout. 1 Main St, in Tu-Endie-Wei Park (Native American for "where two rivers meet"). Phone 304/675-0869.   **Free**   Also here is

  Mansion House (1796). Oldest log building in Kanawha Valley, restored as a museum. (May-Oct, daily) Phone 304/675-0869.   **Free**

West Virginia State Farm Museum. Contains more than 30 farm buildings depicting early rural life, including a log church, one-room schoolhouse, kitchen, scale house and 4-unit building. Barn contains mount of one of the largest horses in the world; also animals. (Apr-Nov, daily exc Mon) 4 mi N via WV 62, adj to county fairgrounds. Phone 304/675-5737. **Free**

Annual Event

Mason County Fair. County Fairgrounds. Livestock show, arts & crafts, contests, Nashville entertainers. Phone 304/675-5463. Mid-Aug.

Motel

★★ **LOWE HOTEL.** 401 Main St (25550). 304/675-2260; FAX 304/675-2260. 30 rms, 3 story. S $38; D $42; suites $48-$54. Crib free. TV; cable (premium); VCR avail. Complimentary coffee in lobby. Restaurant nearby. Ck-out noon. Meeting rms. Business servs avail. Some refrigerators. Cr cds: A, C, D, DS, MC, V.

D ⊠ 🔥 SC

Princeton (E-4)

(See also Bluefield)

Settled 1826 **Pop** 7,043 **Elev** 2,446 ft **Area Code** 304 **Zip** 24740
Information Princeton-Mercer County Chamber of Commerce, 910 Oakvale Rd; 304/487-1502

Princeton is the southern terminus of the spectacular 88-mile West Virginia Turnpike and a trade center for an agricultural, industrial and coal mining area.

What to See and Do

Camp Creek State Park. Approx 500 acres. Fishing. Hiking trails, game courts. Picnicking, playgrounds. Camping. Standard hrs, fees. 13 mi N on I-77, exit 20, then 2 mi NW, near Camp Creek. Phone 304/425-9481.

Motels

✓★★ **COMFORT INN.** Ambrose Ln & Rte 460 (24740), Ambrose Lane & US 460W. 304/487-6101; FAX 304/425-7002; res: 800/228-5150. 51 rms, 2 story. S, D $60-$90; each addl $6; under 18 free. Crib free. TV; cable (premium). Complimentary continental bkfst. Restaurant nearby. Ck-out noon. Business servs avail. Downhill ski 20 mi. Whirlpool. Cr cds: A, C, D, DS, MC, V.

D ⊠ 🛏 🔥 SC

★ **DAYS INN.** 347 Meadowfield Ln (24740). 304/425-8100; FAX 304/487-1734; res: 800/329-7466. 122 rms, 2 story. S $58-$63; D $63-$68; kit. units $67-$75; under 16 free. Crib free. Pet accepted. TV; cable. Indoor pool; whirlpool. Complimentary continental bkfst. Restaurant adj 6 am-10 pm. Ck-out 11 am. Business servs avail. Sundries. Downhill ski 15 mi. Cr cds: A, C, D, DS, JCB, MC, V.

D 🐾 🛏 ⊠ 🔥 SC

Restaurant

★ **JOHNSTON'S INN.** On US 460 Old Oakvale Rd (24740). 304/425-7591. Hrs: 6:30 am-10:30 pm; Sun to 10 pm. Closed Thanksgiving, Dec 25. Res accepted. Bar from 11:30 am; Sun 3-10 pm. Semi-a la carte: bkfst $2-$5.50, lunch $5-$7, dinner $8-$15.95. Child's meals. Specializes in steak, seafood, desserts. Salad bar. Own salad dressings. Tiffany lamps, artwork, antiques. Family-owned. Cr cds: A, C, D, DS, MC, V.

SC ⊟

Ripley (C-3)

(See also Point Pleasant)

Settled 1768 **Pop** 3,023 **Elev** 616 ft **Area Code** 304 **Zip** 25271

What to See and Do

Washington's Lands Museum and Park. Housed in converted river lock building and restored Sayre Log House; exhibits trace the pioneer and river history of the area. Park, on the Ohio River, has picnicking and boat launching facilities. Museum (by appt). 6 mi N via I-77 exit 146 to Ravenswood, then 2½ mi S on WV 68. Phone 304/372-5343.   **Donation**

Annual Events

Mountain State Art & Craft Fair. Cedar Lakes Conference Center. Features traditional crafts, art, folk music and foods. Phone 304/372-7860 or 304/372-7866. Early July.

West Virginia Black Walnut Festival. 25 mi E on US 33/119 in Spencer. Parade, carnival, band festival, car show, contests, livestock show, arts & crafts. Phone 304/927-1780. Mid-Oct.

Motels

★★ **BEST WESTERN MCCOYS INN.** *701 Main St (25271), I-77 exit 138.* 304/372-9122; FAX 304/372-4400; res: 800/288-9122. 144 rms, 2 story. S, D $59.95-$63.95; each addl $4; under 12 free. Crib $3. TV; cable. Pool. Complimentary continental bkfst. Restaurant 5-10 pm; Sun 10 am-3 pm. Rm serv. Ck-out 11 am. Coin lndry. Meeting rms. Business servs avail. Sundries. Some in-rm whirlpools, fireplaces. Cr cds: A, C, D, DS, ER, JCB, MC, V.

⬛ 🏊 ⛖ 🔥 SC

✓★★ **HOLIDAY INN EXPRESS.** *1 Hospitality Dr (25271), I-77 exit 138N, near hospital.* 304/372-5000; FAX 304/372-5600; res: 800/465-4329. 65 rms, 2 story. S, D $60-$80; suites $99-$120; under 18 free; higher rates Mountain State Arts & Crafts Fair. Crib free. TV; cable (premium). Complimentary continental bkfst. Restaurant adj 6:30 am-11 pm. Ck-out 11 am. Business servs avail. Cr cds: C.

Shepherdstown (B-8)

(See also Charles Town, Harpers Ferry, Martinsburg; also see Frederick, Hagerstown, MD)

Settled ca 1730 **Pop** 1,287 **Elev** 406 ft **Area Code** 304 **Zip** 25443
E-mail chamber@jeffersoncounty.com **Web** www.jeffersoncounty.com/chamber

Information Jefferson County Chamber of Commerce, 201 Frontage Rd, PO Box 426, Charles Town 25414; 304/725-2055

In 1787, Shepherdstown was the site of the first successful public launching of a steamboat. James Rumsey, inventor of the craft, died, however, before he could exploit his success. Rival claims by John Fitch, and Robert Fulton's commercial success with the *Clermont* 20 years later, have beclouded Rumsey's achievement.

The state's first newspaper was published here in 1790, and Shepherdstown almost became the national capital. (George Washington considered it as a possible site, according to letters in the Library of Congress.) Shepherdstown is also the location of one of the early grist mills, which is believed to have been constructed around 1739 and finally ceased production in 1939. This is the oldest continuously settled town in the state.

What to See and Do

Historic Shepherdstown Museum. Artifacts dating to 1700s, including many items concerning the founding of the town. Guided tours (by appt) (Apr-Oct, daily) In old Entler Hotel (1786), German & Princess Sts. Phone 304/876-0910. **Free** Also avail here are

Guided walking tours of historic sites in Shepherdstown. Phone 304/876-0910. ¢¢

Inns

★★★ **BAVARIAN INN & LODGE.** *Rte 1, Box 30 (25443), ¼ mi N on WV 480 at the Potomac Bridge.* 304/876-2551; FAX 304/876-9355. Web www.wvweb.com/bavarian_inn. 72 rms, 2 in main bldg, 1-3 story, 4 chalets. S, D $85-$165; each addl $10; suites $195-$275; under 12 free; package plans; golf plan. Crib $10. TV; cable (premium), VCR avail. Pool. Complimentary coffee. Dining rm (see BAVARIAN INN AND LODGE RESTAURANT). Bar 5 pm-midnight; Sun from 1 pm. Ck-out noon, ck-in 3

pm. Meeting rms. Business servs avail. In-rm modem link. Luggage handling. Tennis. Golf privileges, putting green. Exercise equipt. In-rm whirlpools, fireplaces. Balconies. Cr cds: A, C, D, DS, MC, V.

⬛ 🏃 ⛖ 🏊 🎾 ⛖ 🔥

★★★ **THOMAS SHEPHERD INN.** *300 W German St (25443).* 304/876-3715; FAX 304/876-3313; res: 888/889-8952. E-mail mrg@intrepid.net; web www.intrepid.net/thomas_shepherd. 7 rms, 2 story. S, D $85-$95; higher rates wkends. Children over 8 yrs only. TV, VCR in sitting rm (movies). Complimentary full bkfst. Restaurant nearby. Ck-out 11 am, ck-in 3 pm. Business servs avail. Tennis privileges. Golf privileges. Fireplaces. Federal-style house (1868) on land originally owned by town founder Thomas Shepherd. Totally nonsmoking. Cr cds: A, C, MC, V.

🏃 ⛖ ⛖ 🐾 SC

Restaurants

★★★ **BAVARIAN INN AND LODGE.** *(See Bavarian Inn and Lodge)* 304/876-2551. Web www.intrepid.net/bavarian_inn. Hrs: 7:30-10:30 am, 11:30 am-2:30 pm, 5-10 pm; Sat from 4 pm; Sun noon-9 pm. Res accepted. German, continental menu. Bar 5 pm-midnight; Sun from 1 pm. Wine list. Semi-a la carte: bkfst $4.50-$9.75, lunch $5.50-$12, dinner $13.50-$22.50. Child's meals. Specializes in veal, game (in season), vegetarian dishes. Own baking. Parking. Entertainment. Fireplaces. Antiques. Overlooks Potomac River. Family-owned. Cr cds: A, C, D, DS, MC, V.

⬛ ⛖

★ **OLD PHARMACY CAFE.** *138 E German St (25443).* 304/876-2085. Hrs: 11 am-9 pm; Fri, Sat to 10 pm. Closed Dec 25, Jan 1. Res accepted. Wine, beer. Semi-a la carte: lunch $5.95-$8.95, dinner $11.95-$18.95. Child's meals. Specializes in gourmet sandwiches, vegetarian dishes, eclectic regional dishes. Street parking. In former pharmacy (1911); many original pieces including a marble soda fountain. Totally nonsmoking. Cr cds: C, D, DS, MC, V.

⬛

★★★ **YELLOW BRICK BANK & LITTLE INN.** *201 German at Princess St (25443), downtown.* 304/876-2208. Hrs: 11:30 am-10 pm; Sun brunch 11 am-4 pm. Closed Thanksgiving, Dec 25. Res accepted. Bar. A la carte entrees: lunch $5-$14, dinner $12-$24. Sun brunch $5-$14. Specializes in seafood, pasta, regional cuisine. Own baking. Street parking. Wood burning oven. In 1910 bank building in historic commercial district. Overnight stays avail. Cr cds: C, D, MC, V.

Summersville (D-4)

(See also Gauley Bridge)

Founded 1824 **Pop** 2,906 **Elev** 1,894 ft **Area Code** 304 **Zip** 26651
Information Chamber of Commerce, 411 Old Main Dr, PO Box 567; 304/872-1588

Twenty-year-old Nancy Hart led a surprise Confederate attack on Summersville in July 1861, captured a Union force and burned the town. She was captured, but her jail guard succumbed to her charms. The guard was then disarmed and killed by the young woman. She escaped to Lee's lines. After the war, she returned to Summersville.

What to See and Do

Carnifex Ferry Battlefield State Park. Here on Sept 10, 1861, 7,000 Union troops under General William S. Rosecrans fought and defeated a lesser number of Confederates under General John B. Floyd. The 156-acre park includes Patteson House Museum (Memorial Day-wkend after Labor Day, Sat, Sun, hols), which displays Civil War relics. Hiking trails. Picnicking; game courts, playgrounds; concession. Civil War reenactment (weekend after Labor Day). Park (May-early Sept, daily). 12 mi W on WV

39, then SE on WV 129, near Kesslers Cross Lanes. Phone 304/872-0825. **Free**

Gauley River National Recreation Area. Designated a federally protected area in Oct 1988, the 25-mi stretch of the Gauley from the Summersville Dam west to just above the town of Swiss is famous for whitewater rafting. There are no developed sites. Large tracts of land along river are privately owned. For further information and a list of whitewater outfitters contact Superintendent, New River Gorge National River, PO Box 246, Glen Jean 25846; phone 304/465-0508.

Summersville Lake. A 2,700-acre lake. Swimming, waterskiing; fishing; boating. Hiking. Picnicking. Battle Run Campground is 3 mi W on WV 129 (fee). (May-Oct, daily) Fee for some activities. 5 mi S on US 19. Phone 304/872-3459.

Annual Events

Nicholas County Fair. 3 mi N at Nicholas County Memorial Park. Midway; flower show; agricultural and crafts exhibits. July.

Nicholas County Potato Festival. Citywide. Includes parades, entertainment, volleyball tournament, arts & crafts show, bed races. 1st full wk Sept.

Motels

✓★ **BEST WESTERN.** *1203 S Broad St (26651). 304/872-6900; FAX 304/872-6908; res: 800/214-9551.* 59 rms, 3 story. April-Oct: S $44-$50; D $49-$55; each addl $5; under 12 free; lower rates rest of yr. Crib free. Pet accepted, some restrictions TV; cable, VCR avail (movies). Complimentary continental bkfst. Restaurant 11 am-10 pm. Bar. Ck-out 11 am. Business servs avail. Microwave avail. Cr cds: A, C, D, DS, ER, JCB, MC, V.

D 🐾 🏊 🔥 SC

★★ **COMFORT INN.** *903 Industrial Dr N (26651), 2 mi N on US 19 at jct WV 41. 304/872-6500; FAX 304/872-3090; res: 800/872-1752.* Web wvweb.com/www/comfort.inn-summersville. 99 rms, 2 story. June-Oct: S $47-$62; D $52-$69; each addl $5-$7; suites $62-$114; under 18 free; lower rates rest of yr. Crib free. Pet accepted, some restrictions; $5. TV; cable (premium), VCR avail (movies). Heated pool; wading pool. Complimentary continental bkfst. Restaurant nearby. Ck-out 11 am. Coin lndry. Meeting rms. Bellhops. Exercise equipt; sauna. Refrigerator in suites. Microwaves avail. Picnic tables. Cr cds: A, C, D, DS, ER, JCB, MC, V.

D 🐾 🏊 🏋 🔥 🐾 SC

★ **SLEEP INN.** *701 Professional Park Dr; 801 Industrial Dr (26651), off US 19. 304/872-4500; FAX 304/872-0288; res: 800/228-5050.* 97 rms, 2 story. June-Oct: S $41-$59; D $46-$67; each addl $5; under 18 free; higher rates special events; lower rates rest of yr. Crib free. Pet accepted, some restrictions; $5. TV; cable (premium), VCR avail (movies). Heated pool. Complimentary continental bkfst. Restaurant adj 11 am-10 pm. Ck-out 11 am. Coin lndry. Meeting rms. Business servs avail. Sundries. Lawn games. Refrigerators, microwaves avail. Cr cds: A, C, D, DS, JCB, MC, V.

D 🐾 🏊 🔥 🐾 SC

Restaurant

★ **COUNTRY ROAD INN.** *Country Rd (26651), 8 mi W on WV 39. 304/872-1620; res: 800/439-8852.* Hrs: 5-8 pm; Fri, Sat to 8:30 pm; Sun 2-6 pm. Closed major hols. Res required. Italian menu. Wine. Complete meals: dinner $14.95-$24.95. Child's meals. Specialties: shrimp scampi, fettucine, lasagne. Own pasta. In restored 19th-century farmhouse; country setting. Cr cds: A, C, DS, MC, V.

Sutton (C-4)

Settled 1826 **Pop** 939 **Elev** 840 ft **Area Code** 304 **Zip** 26601

What to See and Do

Sutton Lake. Dam is one mi E. Swimming in designated areas. Boat launch (fee). Camping (May-Dec; some electric hookups; fees) at Gerald R. Freeman Campground, 16 mi E on WV 15; and at Mill Creek-Bakers Run Area, 16 mi SE on WV 17. Phone 304/765-2816 or 304/765-2705 (recording).

Motor Hotel

★★★ **DAYS INN.** *2000 Sutton Ln (26601), I-79 exit 67. 304/765-5055; FAX 304/765-2067; res: 800/329-7466.* E-mail daysinn@flatwoods.com. 201 units, 5 story. Mar-Nov: S $59.95; D $64.95; each addl $5; suites $125-$150; under 13 free; lower rates rest of yr. Crib free. TV; cable (premium). Indoor pool. Restaurant 5-10 pm; Sun 6-10 am. Bar 5 pm-midnight. Ck-out 11 am. Meeting rms. Business servs avail. In-rm modem link. Sundries. Gift shop. Exercise equipt; sauna. Many balconies. Cr cds: A, C, D, DS, JCB, MC, V.

D 🏊 🏋 🏃 🐾 🔥 SC

Webster Springs (D-5)

Settled 1860 **Pop** 990 (est) **Elev** 1,509 ft **Area Code** 304 **Zip** 26288
Information Mayor's Office, 146 McGraw Ave; 304/847-5411

Once a resort famed for its medicinal "lick" or spring, the town is now a trading center and meeting place for sportsmen.

What to See and Do

Holly River State Park. More than 8,000 acres of heavy forest with excellent trout fishing in Laurel Fork. Swimming pool, bathhouse. Hiking trails to waterfalls and Potato Knob; tennis, game courts. Picnicking, playground; restaurant (seasonal). Camping (dump station), 9 cabins. Nature, recreation programs (summer). Standard hrs, fees. 20 mi N on WV 20 to Hacker Valley, then 1 mi E. Phone 304/493-6353.

Kumbrabow State Forest. More than 9,400 acres of wild, rugged country with trout fishing and deer, turkey and grouse hunting. Hiking trails. Cross-country skiing. Picnicking, playground. Tent & trailer camping, 5 rustic cabins. Standard hrs, fees. 25 mi NE on WV 15, then 5 mi N, near Monterville. Phone 304/335-2219.

Annual Events

Webster Springs Woodchopping Festival. Southeastern World Woodchopping Championships; state championship turkey calling contest, draft horse pull, horse show, fireman's rodeo; arts & crafts, music, parades, concessions. Phone 304/847-7666. Memorial Day wkend.

Webster County Fair. 11 mi S on WV 20 to 4-H Camp Caesar. Rides, agricultural exhibits, entertainers, horse show. Labor Day wk.

Weirton (A-5)

(See also Wheeling; also see Pittsburgh, PA)

Founded 1910 **Pop** 22,124 **Elev** 760 ft **Area Code** 304 **Zip** 26062
Information Chamber of Commerce, 3200 Maine St; 304/748-7212

Weirton has been a steel-producing town since its founding in 1910 by Ernest T. Weir, who also founded the Weirton Steel Company. In 1984, Weirton Steel became the largest employee-owned steel company in the world. Modern plants produce tin plate and hot-rolled, cold-rolled and galvanized steels for containers, automobiles, appliances and other products.

What to See and Do

Mountaineer Racetrack & Resort. Thoroughbred racing on one-mile track; three restaurants. (Thurs-Mon) 12 mi N on WV 2. Phone 304/387-2400.

Tomlinson Run State Park. Approx 1,400 acres. Swimming pool, bathhouse; fishing, boating on 27-acre lake (rowboat and paddleboat rentals). Hiking trails; miniature golf, tennis. Picnicking, playground. Tent & trailer camping (dump station). Nature, recreation programs (summer). Standard hrs, fees. 15 mi N off WV 8. Phone 304/564-3651.

Weirton Steel Corp and Half Moon Industrial Park. Tours of Weirton Steel Corp, Alpo and others. Contact Chamber of Commerce for details, phone 304/748-7212.

Weston (C-5)

(See also Buckhannon, Clarksburg)

Settled 1784 **Pop** 4,994 **Elev** 1,009 ft **Area Code** 304 **Zip** 26452 **E-mail** tour@stonewallcountry.com

Information Lewis County Convention & Visitors Bureau, PO Box 379; 304/269-7328

Surveyed originally by "Stonewall" Jackson's grandfather, Weston today is a center for coal, oil and gas production, as well as the manufacture of glass products. The Weston State Hospital, completed in 1880 and said to be the largest hand-cut stone building in the nation, is located in town.

What to See and Do

Cedar Creek State Park. More than 2,400 acres. Swimming pool, bathhouse; fishing; boating (rentals). Hiking trails; miniature golf; tennis, game courts. Picnicking, playground, concession. Tent & trailer camping (dump station). Park office in restored log cabin. Standard hrs, fees. 31 mi SW off US 33/119, near Glenville. Phone 304/462-7158.

Jackson's Mill State 4-H Conference Center. First camp of its kind in US; with 43 buildings, gardens, swimming pool, amphitheater, interfaith chapel. Picnicking. 4 mi N off US 19. Phone 304/269-5100. Also here is

Jackson's Mill Historic Area. Includes Blaker's Mill, an operating water-powered grist mill; blacksmith shop; McWharten cabin (ca 1700s); Mary Conrad's cabin (ca 1800s); and Jackson's Mill Museum, where "Stonewall" Jackson lived and worked as a boy. Museum represents grist and saw milling agriculture and home arts of the area as practiced 100 yrs ago. (Memorial Day-Labor Day, daily exc Mon; May & after Labor Day-mid-Oct, wkends only) Historic area ¢¢

Stonewall Jackson Lake & Dam. Approx 2,500-acre lake, with over 82 mi of shoreline, created by impounding the waters of the West Fork River. Swimming, scuba diving, waterskiing; fishing; boating (ramps, rentals, marinas). Picnicking. Camping. Visitor center. Just S off I-79 exit 96, follow signs to dam. Phone 304/269-4588 or -0523.

Stonewall Jackson Lake State Park. Approx 3,000 acres. Fishing; boating (launch, marina). Nature, fitness trails. Picnicking; playground. Camping (hookups). Visitor center. Standard hrs, fees. 11 mi S on US 19. Phone 304/269-0523.

Annual Events

Horse show. Trefz Farm, 3 mi E on US 33. Saddle, walking, harness, pony, western and Arabian riding. Phone 304/269-3257. Usually July.

Stonewall Jackson Heritage Arts & Crafts Jubilee. Jackson's Mill State 4-H Conference Center. Mountain crafts, music, dance and food. Phone 304/269-1863. Labor Day wkend.

Motel

✓ ★★ **COMFORT INN.** *Rte 33 E & I-79 (26452), At jct US 33 & I-79.* 304/269-7000; FAX 304/269-7000; res: 800/221-2222. 60 rms, 2 story. S $40-$52; D $46-$58; each addl $6; under 18 free. Crib free. Pet accepted. TV; cable. Heated pool. Restaurant 6 am-9 pm. Bar 5-11 pm. Ck-out noon. Meeting rm. Balconies. Cr cds: A, C, D, DS, ER, JCB, MC, V.

D 🐾 ≈ ⊠ 🔥 SC

Wheeling (A-4)

Settled 1769 **Pop** 34,882 **Elev** 678 ft **Area Code** 304 **Zip** 26003 **E-mail** whcvbwv@access.mountain.net **Web** www.wheelingcvb.com

Information Convention & Visitors Bureau, 1401 Main St; 304/233-7709 or 800/828-3079

Wheeling stands on the site of Fort Henry, built in 1774 by Colonel Ebenezer Zane and his two brothers, who named the fort for Virginia's Governor Patrick Henry. In 1782, the fort was the scene of the final battle of the Revolutionary War, a battle in which the valiant, young pioneer Betty Zane was a heroine. The fort had withstood several Native American and British sieges during the war. However, during the last siege (after the war was officially ended), the defenders of the fort ran out of powder. Betty Zane, sister of the colonel, volunteered to run through the gunfire to the outlying Zane cabin for more. With the powder gathered in her apron, she made the 150-yard trek back to the fort and saved the garrison. Zane Grey, a descendant of the Zanes, wrote a novel about Betty and her exploit.

Today, Wheeling is home to many industries, including producers of steel, iron, tin, chemical products, pottery, glass, paper, tobacco, plastics and coal.

What to See and Do

Grave Creek Mound State Park. Features nation's largest prehistoric Adena burial mound—79 ft high, 900 ft around, 50 ft across the top. Some excavating was done in 1838; exhibits in Delf Norona Museum & Cultural Center (daily; fee). 9 mi S via WV 2, on Jefferson Ave in Moundsville. Phone 304/843-1410.

Jamboree, USA. Live country music shows presented by WWVA Radio since 1933. (Sat) Capitol Music Hall, 1015 Main St. Phone 304/234-0050 or 800/624-5456. ¢¢¢¢

Kruger Street Toy & Train Museum. Collection of antique toys, games and playthings. (Daily; Jan-Apr) 144 Kruger St. Phone 304/242-8133.

Oglebay Resort Park. A 1,500-acre municipal park. Indoor, outdoor swimming pools; fishing, boating on 3-acre Schenk Lake. Three 18-hole golf courses, miniature golf; tennis courts. Picnicking, restaurant, snack shop. Cabins, lodge. Miniature train ride; 65-acre Good Children's Zoo (fee) with animals in natural habitat. Benedum Natural Science Theater; garden center; arboretum with 4 mi of walking paths; greenhouses; observatory. Fee for most activities. 3 mi NE of I-70, on WV 88. Phone 304/243-4000 or 800/624-6988. (See ANNUAL and SEASONAL EVENTS) Also in park is

Mansion House Museum. Period rms, exhibits trace history from 1835 to present. (Daily) Phone 304/242-7272. ¢¢

Site of Fort Henry. Bronze plaque marks location of fort that Betty Zane saved. Main St, near 11th St.

The Artisan Center. Restored 1890s Victorian warehouse houses Nail City Brewing Co, West Virginia's largest brew pub. Wymer's General Store Museum, "Made in Wheeling" crafts and exhibits; artisan demonstrations. (Daily) Heritage Square, 1400 Main St. Phone 304/232-1810. Center. **Free**; Museum ¢¢

West Virginia Independence Hall-Custom House (1859). Site of meeting at which Virginia's secession from the Union was declared unlawful, and the independent state of West Virginia was created. The building, used as a post office, custom office and federal court until 1912, has been restored. It now houses exhibits and events relating to the state's cultural heritage, including an interpretive film and rooms with period furniture. (Mar-Dec, daily; rest of yr, daily exc Sun; closed state hols) 16th & Market Sts. Phone 304/238-1300. **Free**

Wheeling Park. Approx 400 acres. Swimming pool, water slide; boating on Good Lake. Golf, miniature golf, indoor/outdoor tennis. Ice-skating (rentals). Picnicking, playground, refreshment area with video screen and lighted dance floor. Aviary. Fees for activities. (Daily; some facilities seasonal) 5 mi E on US 40. Phone 304/242-3770.

Annual Events

Jamboree in the Hills. 15 mi W off I-70 exit 208 or 213, in St Clairsville, OH. A 4-day country music festival featuring more than 30 hours of music; top country stars. Camping avail. Phone 800/624-5456. 3rd wkend July.

Oglebayfest. Oglebay Resort Park. Country fair, artists' market, fireworks, parade, ethnic foods, contests, square & round dancing, entertainment. Phone 304/243-4000. 1st wkend Oct.

Seasonal Event

City of Lights. Oglebay Resort Park. A 350-acre lighting display featuring lighted buildings, holiday themes with more than 500,000 lights, including 28-foot candy canes and giant swans on Schenk Lake. Winter Fantasy in Good Zoo. Nov-Jan.

Motel

★★ **DAYS INN.** I-70 & Dallas Pike exit 11 (26059), 9 mi E, at I-70 exit 11. 304/547-0610; FAX 304/547-9029; res: 800/329-7466. 106 rms, 2 story. S, D $45-$55; each addl $6; under 18 free. Crib free. Pet accepted. TV; cable (premium), VCR avail. Pool. Bar 5 pm-1 am, closed Sun. Ck-out noon. Meeting rm. Business servs avail. Valet serv. Some in-rm whirlpools. Cr cds: A, C, D, DS, MC, V.

[D] [icons] SC

Motor Hotel

★★ **HAMPTON INN.** 795 National Rd (26003), I-70, exit 24. 304/233-0440; FAX 304/233-2198; res: 800/426-7866. 104 rms, 5 story. S $57-$68; D $62-$73; suites $68-$81; under 18 free; wkends (2-day min). Crib free. TV; cable (premium), VCR avail. Complimentary continental bkfst. Restaurant adj 6:30 am-11 pm. Rm serv. Ck-out noon. Meeting rms. Business servs avail. In-rm modem link. Valet serv. Exercise equipt. Refrigerator, wet bar in suites. Cr cds: A, C, D, DS, MC, V.

[D] [icons] SC

Hotel

✓★ **BEST WESTERN INN.** 949 Main St (26003). 304/233-8500; FAX 304/233-8500; res: 800/528-1234. 80 rms, 5 story. S $46.75-$57.75; D $53.75-$62.75; each addl $8; suites $110.50; under 12 free; higher rates wkends, special events. Crib free. TV; cable (premium). Complimentary continental bkfst. Restaurant 11 am-10 pm; Sat, Sun from 7 am. Bar 11-2 am. Ck-out 11 am. Business servs avail. Free valet parking. Exercise equipt; sauna. Whirlpool. Cr cds: A, C, D, DS, JCB, MC, V.

[icons] SC

Resort

★★★ **OGLEBAY CONFERENCE CENTER.** Oglebay Park (26003), 3 mi NE of I-70 exit 2A. 304/243-4000; FAX 304/243-4070. 204 rms in 2-story lodge, chalets; 49 kit. cottages (2-6 bedrm). S $69-$122; D $110-$150; suites $145-$170; kit. cottages $625-$1,350/wk; golf plans. Crib $5. Pet accepted. TV; cable (premium), VCR avail (movies). 2 pools; 1 indoor; wading pool, whirlpool, poolside serv, lifeguard. Playground. Supervised child's activities (June-Aug); ages 6-12. Dining rm 6:30-10:30

am, noon-2 pm, 5-9 pm. Box lunches, snack bar. Lounge noon-midnight. Rm serv. Ck-out 11 am, ck-in 3 pm. Grocery ½ mi. Package store 2 mi. Meeting rms. Business center. In-rm modem link. Airport, bus depot transportation. 11 lighted tennis courts, pro. Three 18-hole golf courses, greens fee $26-$50, par-3 golf, pro, driving range, miniature golf. Downhill ski ½ mi. Stocked lake. Paddleboats. Lawn games. Children's zoo. Stables. Exercise equipt. Some fireplaces. Some private patios, balconies. Picnic tables, grills. Mansion museum, garden center. Rustic setting in Oglebay Park. Cr cds: A, C, D, DS, MC, V.

[D] [icons] SC [icon]

Restaurants

★★ **ERNIE'S CORK & BOTTLE.** 39 12th St (26003). 304/232-4400. Hrs: 11-3:30 am; major hols from 5 pm. Closed Dec 25. Res accepted. Bar 11-2 am; Sun 5 pm-midnight. Semi-a la carte: lunch $2.95-$7.95, dinner $5.95-$12.95. Specialties: coquille, Greek kebab. Salad bar. Entertainment. New Orleans decor; paddle fans. Family-owned. Cr cds: A, C, D, DS, MC, V.

[D] [icon]

★★★ **ERNIE'S ESQUIRE.** 1 W Bethlehem Blvd (26003), 1¼ mi off I-70 on WV 88S. 304/242-2800. Hrs: 11 am-midnight; Fri to 1 am; Sat to 2 am; Sun to 10:30 pm; Sun brunch to 2 pm. Closed Dec 25. Res accepted. Continental menu. Bar. Wine list. Semi-a la carte: lunch $3.75-$8.95, dinner $8.95-$26.95. Sun brunch $8.95. Child's meals. Specializes in fresh seafood, beef. Own baking. Entertainment Fri, Sat. Valet parking. 6 rms, each with different decor. Family-owned. Cr cds: A, C, D, DS, MC, V.

[D] [icon]

White Sulphur Springs (E-5)

(See also Lewisburg; also see Covington, VA)

Settled 1750 **Pop** 2,779 **Elev** 1,923 ft **Area Code** 304 **Zip** 24986
Information Chamber of Commerce, PO Box 11; 304/536-2500

In the 18th century, White Sulphur Springs became a fashionable destination for rich and famous colonists, who came for the "curative" powers of the mineral waters. It has, for the most part, remained a popular resort ever since. A number of US presidents summered in the town in the days before air conditioning made Washington habitable in hot weather. The John Tylers spent their honeymoon at the famous "Old White" Hotel. In 1913 the Old White Hotel gave way to the present Greenbrier Hotel (see RESORT), where President Wilson honeymooned with the second Mrs. Wilson. During World War II the hotel served as an internment camp for German and Japanese diplomats and, later, as a hospital.

The first golf course in America was laid out near the town in 1884, but the first game was delayed when golf clubs, imported from Scotland, were held for three weeks by customs men, who were suspicious of a game played with "such elongated blackjacks or implements of murder."

What to See and Do

Fishing, swimming, boating, camping, hiking. In Monongahela National Forest (see ELKINS): Blue Bend Recreation Area, 6 mi N on WV 92, then 4 mi W on WV 16/21; Lake Sherwood Recreation Area, 23 mi N via WV 92, then 11 mi NE on WV 14. Phone 304/536-2144. Camping ¢¢¢-¢¢¢¢

Greenbrier State Forest. More than 5,100 acres. Swimming pool (Memorial Day-Labor Day); bass fishing in Greenbrier River; hunting. Hiking trails. Picnicking, playground. Tent & trailer camping, 12 cabins. Nature, recreation programs (summer). Standard hrs, fees. 3 mi W on US 60, then 1½ mi S on Harts Run Rd. Phone 304/536-1944.

Memorial Park. Swimming pool (Memorial Day-Labor Day; fee). Tennis courts, ball fields, track, horseshoe pits, playground. (Daily) Greenbrier Ave.

National Fish Hatchery. Rainbow trout in raceways and ponds. Visitor center has display pool, aquariums and exhibits. (Memorial Day-Labor Day, daily) 400 E Main St, on US 60. Phone 304/536-1361. **Free**

Annual Event

Dandelion Festival. Entertainment, exhibits; arts & crafts. Memorial Day wkend.

Motel

✓★ **OLD WHITE MOTEL.** *865 E Main St (24986). 304/536-2441; FAX 304/536-1836; res: 800/867-2441.* 26 rms; 6 rms with shower only. S $36; D $44; each addl $3; under 12 free; higher rates special events. Crib free. Pet accepted, some restrictions. TV; cable (premium). Pool. Coffee in lobby. Restaurant adj 7:30 am-9 pm. Ck-out noon. Cr cds: A, C, D, DS, MC, V.

Resort

★★★★ **THE GREENBRIER INN.** *300 W Main St (US 60) (24986), ½ mi W on US 60. 304/536-1110; FAX 304/536-7854; res: 800/624-6070.* E-mail tjkbrier@aol.com; web www.greenbrier.com. This elegant, immaculately maintained, 7,000-acre resort has been a popular watering spot for more than 200 years. A huge selection of recreational opportunities is available; falconry and no two guest rooms are alike. 596 rms in hotel, 6 story, 103 guest house rms. MAP, Apr-Oct: S, D, guest rms $210-$292; each addl $125; cottages $339-$399; suites $361-$399; wkend, family rates; tennis, golf plans; lower rates rest of yr. Serv charge $21/person/day. Crib free. TV; cable, VCR avail. 2 pools, 1 indoor; whirlpool, wading pool, poolside serv, lifeguard. Playground. Supervised child's activities. Dining rms 7:30 am-9:30 pm (see THE GREENBRIER MAIN DINING ROOM and THE TAVERN ROOM). Box lunches, snack bar. Rm serv 24 hrs. Bars 11-2 am. Ck-out noon, ck-in 3 pm. Convention facilities. Business center. In-rm modem link. Extensive shopping arcade. Airport, RR station, bus depot transportation. Sports dir. 5 indoor, 15 outdoor tennis courts, pro. Lighted, heated platform tennis. Three 18-hole golf courses, greens fee $135, pro, 2 putting greens, driving range. Canoeing / rafting (seasonal). Ice-skating (seasonal). Horse-drawn sleighing and carriage rides. Stables, English saddles. Fitness trail. Bicycling. Lawn games. Trap and skeet shooting. Hunt club and game preserve. British regulation croquet court. Soc dir; movies, dancing, entertainment. Bowling; indoor games. Extensive exercise rm; sauna, steam rm. Spa. Some refrigerators; microwaves avail; fireplace in cottages. Private patios, balconies. Cr cds: A, C, D, DS, MC, V.

Restaurants

★★★ **THE GREENBRIER MAIN DINING ROOM.** *(See The Greenbrier Resort) 304/536-1110.* E-mail tjkbrier@aol.com; web www.greenbrier.com. Hrs: 7:30-10 am, 6:30-9 pm. Res required. Continental menu. Private club 5 pm-1 am. Wine cellar. Prix fixe: bkfst $20-$25, dinner $80-$90. Serv charge 17.5%; addl serv charge for alcoholic beverages.

Child's meals. Specializes in veal, fresh seafood, vegetarian dishes. Own baking. Chamber music at dinner. Valet parking. Jacket (dinner). Cr cds: A, C, D, DS, MC, V.

★★★ **THE TAVERN ROOM.** *(See The Greenbrier) 304/536-1110.* E-mail tjkbrier@aol.com; web www.greenbrier.com. Hrs: 7-9:30 pm. Closed Nov-Mar. Res required. Continental menu. Bar 7 pm-1 am. Wine cellar. Prix fixe: $100-$105. Serv charge 17.5%. Child's meals. Specializes in fresh seafood, veal, beef. Pianist. Valet parking. Jacket. Cr cds: A, C, D, DS, MC, V.

Williamson (E-3)

Founded 1892 **Pop** 4,154 **Elev** 665 ft **Area Code** 304 **Zip** 25661
Information Tug Valley Chamber of Commerce, 45 E 2nd Ave, PO Box 376; 304/235-5240

The center of the "billion-dollar coal field," Williamson is truly a coal town; the walls of the local Chamber of Commerce building, at the west corner of Courthouse Square, are made of coal. The surrounding Tug River Valley was the scene of the bitter Hatfield-McCoy mountaineer family feud.

What to See and Do

Cabwaylingo State Forest. Approx 8,100 acres. Swimming pool (Memorial Day-Labor Day); fishing, hunting. Hiking trails; game courts. Picnicking, playground, concession. Tent & trailer camping (dump station), 13 cabins. Standard hrs, fees. 38 mi N off US 52, WV 152 near Wilsondale. Phone 304/385-4255.

Matewan. This tiny hamlet was the site of the famous feud between the West Virginia Hatfields and the Kentucky McCoys. On Election Day, Aug 7, 1882, three McCoy sons stabbed and shot Ellison Hatfield. Devil Anse Hatfield avenged his brother by executing the three McCoys. Soon Kentucky bounty hunters made raids into West Virginia to capture the Hatfieds, who retaliated in 1888 by attacking a McCoy homestead. By 1890 the killings had ended but the feud continued to be sensationalized. Later, in 1920, Matewan was the scene of a shootout between union organizers and coal company operators that left 10 dead, including the mayor. 12 mi SW via WV 49. For a walking tour of the area phone 304/426-4239.

Annual Event

King Coal Festival. Entertainment, exhibits; theatrical presentation; country music, square dancing. Mid-Sept.

Appendix A

Restaurant List

Establishment names are listed in alphabetical order followed by a symbol identifying their classification, and then city and state. Establishments affiliated with a chain appear alphabetically under their chain name, followed by the state and city. The symbols for classification are: [R] for restaurants and [U] for unrated dining spots.

1789 RESTAURANT [R] *Washington, DC*

1859 CAFE [R] *Hickory, NC*

1902 LANDMARK TAVERN [R] *Pittsburgh, PA*

2 ALBANY [R] *New Brunswick, NJ*

208 TALBOT [R] *St Michaels, MD*

23 PAGE RESTAURANT [R] *Asheville, NC*

410 BANK STREET RESTAURANT [R] *Cape May, NJ*

42 STREET OYSTER BAR & SEAFOOD [R] *Raleigh, NC*

701 PENNSYLVANIA AVE RESTAURANT [R] *Washington, DC*

82 QUEEN [R] *Charleston, SC*

858 [R] *Greenville, SC*

A & J [R] *Rockville, MD*

A LA PIETRA [R] *Somerville, NJ*

AARATHI INDIAN CUISINE [R] *Tysons Corner, VA*

ABBEY GRILL [R] *Philadelphia, PA*

ABERDEEN BARN, *VA*
[R] *Charlottesville*, [R] *Williamsburg*

ACCOMAC INN [R] *Wrightsville (York Co), PA*

ADDIE'S RESTAURANT [R] *Rockville, MD*

ADITI INDIAN CUISINE [R] *Washington, DC*

AFTON [R] *Livingston, NJ*

AIR TRANSPORT COMMAND [R] *New Castle, DE*

AL'S UPSTAIRS [R] *Columbia, SC*

ALAMO, THE [R] *Alexandria, VA*

ALAMO MEXICAN RESTAURANT INC [R] *College Park, MD*

ALCHEMIST AND BARRISTER [R] *Princeton, NJ*

ALDO'S RISTORANTE [R] *Virginia Beach, VA*

ALEATHEA'S [R] *Cape May, NJ*

ALEXANDER'S, *SC*
[R] *Hilton Head Island*

ALEXANDER'S, *VA*
[R] *Petersburg*

ALEXANDER'S INN [R] *Cape May, NJ*

ALFRED'S VICTORIAN RESTAURANT [R] *Harrisburg, PA*

ALI-BABA DOWNTOWN RESTAURANT [R] *Morgantown, WV*

ALLEGRO [R] *Altoona, PA*

ALOHA RESTAURANT [R] *St Mary's City, MD*

ALPENHOF BAVARIAN [R] *Reading, PA*

ALPINE RESTAURANT [R] *Arlington County (National Airport Area), VA*

ALTLAND HOUSE, THE [R] *York, PA*

AMICI RISTORANTE [R] *Richmond, VA*

AMISH BARN RESTAURANT & GIFT [R] *Bird-in-Hand, PA*

ANCHOR INN [R] *Morehead City, NC*

ANDALUCIA [R] *Rockville, MD*

ANDALUCIA DE BETHESDA [R] *Bethesda, MD*

ANGELINA'S [R] *Baltimore, MD*

ANGUS BARN LTD [R] *Raleigh, NC*

ANNA MARIA'S [R] *Washington, DC*

ANNEX RESTAURANT [R] *Princeton, NJ*

ANSON [R] *Charleston, SC*

ANTIQUE AIRPLANE [R] *Reading, PA*

ANTON'S AT THE SWAN [R] *Lambertville, NJ*

ANTONIA'S [R] *New Brunswick, NJ*

ANTRIM 1844 [R] *Emmitsburg, MD*

APPENNINO [R] *Allentown, PA*

AQUARELLE [R] *Washington, DC*

ARLINGTON DINER [R] *Stroudsburg, PA*

ARMAND'S CHICAGO PIZZERIA [R] *Washington, DC*

ARROYO GRILLE [R] *Philadelphia, PA*

ARSENAL ON THE GREEN [R] *New Castle, DE*

ARTHUR'S RESTAURANT [R] *Downington, PA*

ARTHUR'S TAVERN [R] *Hoboken, NJ*

ARTIE'S [R] *Fairfax, VA*

ASHBY INN [R] *Winchester, VA*

ASHBY'S OYSTER HOUSE [R] *Lewes, DE*

ASHLEY ROOM, *MD*
[R] *St Michaels*

ASHLEY ROOM, *VA*
[R] *Charlottesville*

ASSAGGI ITALIANI [R] *Philadelphia, PA*

ATHENS STEAK HOUSE [R] *Bristol, VA*

AU PETIT PARIS [R] *Cumberland, MD*

AURORA [R] *Chapel Hill, NC*

AUSTIN GRILL, *DC*
[R] *Washington*

AUSTIN GRILL, *MD*
[R] *Bethesda*

AW SHUCKS [R] *Charleston, SC*

AZALEA [R] *Philadelphia, PA*

BACCHUS BETHESDA [R] *Bethesda, MD*

BACCHUS RESTAURANT [R] *Washington, DC*

BACK BAY [R] *Morgantown, WV*

BACK BURNER [R] *Wilmington, DE*

BACK PORCH RESTAURANT [R] *Ocracoke (Outer Banks), NC*

BAHR'S RESTAURANT & MARINA [R] *Gateway National Recreation Area (Sandy Hook Unit), NJ*

BAILIWICK INN [R] *Fairfax, VA*

BAJA MEXICAN CUISINE [R] *Hoboken, NJ*

BANGKOK ST. GRILL AND NOODLES [R] *Falls Church, VA*

BANGKOK VIENTIANE [R] *Falls Church, VA*

BANQUE, THE [R] *Norfolk, VA*

BARBADOES ROOM [R] *Charleston, SC*

BARON'S INNE [R] *King of Prussia, PA*

BAUGHER'S [R] *Westminster, MD*

BAVARIAN INN AND LODGE [R] *Shepherdstown, WV*

BAY LEAF RESTAURANT [R] *Allentown, PA*

BAYOU [R] *Havre De Grace, MD*
BEACHWAY [R] *Chincoteague, VA*
BEAU RIVAGE [R] *Mount Holly, NJ*
BEAUFORT INN [R] *Beaufort, SC*
BEAUMONT'S CAFE [R] *Charleston, SC*
BEAVER HOUSE [R] *Stroudsburg, PA*
BEDUCI [R] *Washington, DC*
BEEF BARN [R] *Greenville, NC*
BENIHANA [R] *Pittsburgh, PA*
BENJARONG THAI RESTAURANT [R]
    Rockville, MD
BERLENGAS [R] *Philadelphia, PA*
BERNARDS INN, THE [R] *Bernardsville,
    NJ*
BERRET'S RESTAURANT [R]
    Williamsburg, VA
BERTHA'S [R] *Baltimore, MD*
BERTINES NORTH CARIBBEAN [R]
    Charlottesville, VA
BEST CELLAR INC [R] *Blowing Rock,
    NC*
BETHESDA CRAB HOUSE [R]
    Bethesda, MD
BIG FISH [R] *Philadelphia, PA*
BILBO BAGGINS [R] *Alexandria, VA*
BILLY MARTIN'S TAVERN [R]
    Washington, DC
BILLY'S RITZ [R] *Roanoke, VA*
BISTRO 123 [R] *Tysons Corner, VA*
BISTRO BISTRO [R] *Arlington County
    (National Airport Area), VA*
BISTRO EUROPA [R] *Greenville, SC*
BISTRO FRANCAIS [R] *Washington,
    DC*
BISTROT LEPIC [R] *Washington, DC*
BLACK BULL INN [R] *Parsippany, NJ*
BLACK FOREST INN, THE [R]
    Stanhope, NJ
BLACK HORSE [R] *Denver/Adamstown,
    PA*
BLACK TRUMPET BISTRO [R]
    Wilmington, DE
BLACK WALNUT [R] *Doylestown (Bucks
    Co), PA*
BLAIR MANSION INN [R] *Silver Spring,
    MD*
BLAZER'S [R] *Greenwood, SC*
BLEU ROCK INN [R] *Washington, VA*
BLOSSOM CAFE [R] *Charleston, SC*
BLOSSOM DELI [R] *Charleston, WV*
BLUE COAT INN [R] *Dover, DE*
BLUE MARLIN SEAFOOD KITCHEN [R]
    Columbia, SC
BLUE MOON [R] *Rehoboth Beach, DE*
BLUE MOUNTAIN FAMILY
    RESTAURANT [R] *Shartlesville,
    PA*
BLUE OCEAN [R] *Fairfax, VA*
BLUE PETE'S SEAFOOD & STEAK [R]
    Virginia Beach, VA
BLUE PLATE [R] *Washington, DC*
BLUE POINT GRILL [R] *Alexandria, VA*
BLUE RIDGE BREWING CO [R]
    Charlottesville, VA

BLUESTONE DINING ROOM [R]
    Hinton, WV
BOCCACCIO [R] *Baltimore, MD*
BOILING SPRINGS TAVERN [R]
    Carlisle, PA
BOMBAY BISTRO, *MD*
    [R] *Rockville*
BOMBAY BISTRO, *VA*
    [R] *Fairfax*
BOMBAY CLUB [R] *Washington, DC*
BOMBAY DINING [R] *Bethesda, MD*
BOMBAY PALACE [R] *Washington, DC*
BON APPETITE [R] *Newport News, VA*
BONAPARTE RESTAURANT [R]
    Philadelphia, PA
BONAROTI [R] *Tysons Corner, VA*
BONFIRE [R] *Ocean City, MD*
BOOKBINDER'S 15TH STREET
    SEAFOOD HOUSE [R]
    Philadelphia, PA
BRADDOCK'S TAVERN [R] *Mount Holly,
    NJ*
BRANDYWINE ROOM [R] *Wilmington,
    DE*
BRASSERIE PERRIER [R] *Philadelphia,
    PA*
BRAVO RISTORANTE & LOUNGE [R]
    Charlotte, NC
BREAD LINE, THE [R] *Washington, DC*
BRIDGE TENDER [R] *Wrightsville
    Beach, NC*
BRIDGET FOY'S SOUTH STREET
    GRILL [R] *Philadelphia, PA*
BRIGHTON STEAKHOUSE [R] *Atlantic
    City, NJ*
BRITISH BICYCLE CLUB [R] *Pittsburgh,
    PA*
BRIX [R] *Charleston, SC*
BROOKLAWN DINER & RESTAURANT
    [R] *Cherry Hill, NJ*
BROOKSIDE RESTAURANT [R] *Luray,
    VA*
BROWN PELICAN [R] *Frederick, MD*
BUA [R] *Washington, DC*
BUCKALEW'S [R] *Long Beach Island,
    NJ*
BUCKHORN INN [R] *Staunton, VA*
BULLOCK'S BBQ [R] *Durham, NC*
BUON GIORNO [R] *Bethesda, MD*
BURMA RESTAURANT [R] *Washington,
    DC*
BUSARA RESTAURANT [R]
    Washington, DC
BUSCH'S CHESAPEAKE INN [R]
    Annapolis, MD
BUTTONWOOD MANOR [R] *Matawan,
    NJ*
BYRAM'S LOBSTER HOUSE [R]
    Richmond, VA
C.F. FOLKS [R] *Washington, DC*
C & O RESTAURANT [R] *Charlottesville,
    VA*
CAB FRYE'S TAVERN [R] *Pottstown, PA*
CAFE [R] *Bethlehem, PA*
CAFE ALLEGRO [R] *Pittsburgh, PA*

CAFE AT THE FRICK [R] *Pittsburgh, PA*
CAFE ATLANTICO [R] *Washington, DC*
CAFE BETHESDA [R] *Bethesda, MD*
CAFE BRETTON [R] *Annapolis, MD*
CAFE DALAT [R] *Arlington County
    (National Airport Area), VA*
CAFE EUROPA, *SC*
    [R] *Hilton Head Island*
CAFE EUROPA, *VA*
    [R] *Portsmouth*
CAFE FRANCE [R] *Lynchburg, VA*
CAFE GALLERY [R] *Burlington, NJ*
CAFE HON [R] *Baltimore, MD*
CAFE LUIGI [R] *Bethlehem, PA*
CAFE MAIN [R] *Millburn, NJ*
CAFE MICHELINA [R] *Hoboken, NJ*
CAFE MILANO [R] *Washington, DC*
CAFE MOZART [R] *Washington, DC*
CAFE NORMANDIE [R] *Annapolis, MD*
CAFE OGGI [R] *McLean, VA*
CAFE PANACHE [R] *Ramsey, NJ*
CAFE TAJ [R] *McLean, VA*
CAFE TROIA [R] *Towson, MD*
CAFFE DI PAGLIACCI [R] *Richmond, VA*
CAFFE LA BELLA [R] *Cherry Hill, NJ*
CAFFE PHOENIX [R] *Wilmington, NC*
CAGNEY'S [R] *Charleston, WV*
CAGNEY'S OLD PLACE [R] *Myrtle
    Beach, SC*
CALIFORNIA CAFE [R] *Carlisle, PA*
CALVERT GRILLE [R] *Alexandria, VA*
CALVERT HOUSE INN [R] *College
    Park, MD*
CANDLELIGHT INN [R] *Bethlehem, PA*
CANTON STATION [R] *Fayetteville, NC*
CAPITAL WRAPPS [R] *Bethesda, MD*
CAPITOL GRILL, THE [R] *Washington,
    DC*
CAPTAIN BILL'S WATERFRONT [R]
    Morehead City, NC
CAPTAIN BOB'S SEAFOOD [R]
    Goldsboro, NC
CAPTAIN DAVE'S DOCKSIDE [R]
    Myrtle Beach, SC
CAPTAIN YOUNG'S SEAFOOD
    EMPORI [R] *Atlantic City, NJ*
CAPTAIN'S GALLEY [R] *Cornelius, NC*
CAPTAIN'S INN [R] *Forked River, NJ*
CAPTAIN'S TABLE [R] *Wildwood &
    Wildwood Crest, NJ*
CARA'S RESTAURANT [R]
    Chesapeake, VA
CARBONE'S [R] *Greensburg, PA*
CARLTON [R] *Pittsburgh, PA*
CARLYLE GRAND CAFE [R] *Arlington
    County (National Airport Area),
    VA*
CARMASSI'S TUSCANY GRILL [R]
    Pittsburgh, PA
CARMELLO'S, *VA*
    [R] *Charlottesville, [R] Manassas*
CAROLINA CROSSROADS [R] *Chapel
    Hill, NC*
CAROLINA'S [R] *Charleston, SC*

CARRIAGE ROOM AT ALLENBERRY [R] *Carlisle, PA*
CARROL'S CREEK [R] *Annapolis, MD*
CASA CARBONE RISTORANTE [R] *Raleigh, NC*
CASABLANCA [R] *Willow Grove, PA*
CASBAH [R] *Pittsburgh, PA*
CASCADES, THE [R] *Williamsburg, VA*
CASHION'S EAT PLACE [R] *Washington, DC*
CATACOMBS AT BUBE'S BREWERY [R] *Lancaster, PA*
CATHERINE'S AT SPINNER'S [R] *Hershey, PA*
CENTRE BRIDGE INN [R] *New Hope (Bucks Co), PA*
CESCO TRATTORIA [R] *Bethesda, MD*
CHAMELEON [R] *Westminster, MD*
CHAMPS FINE FOODS & SPIRITS [R] *Laurinburg, NC*
CHANNEL BASS RESTAURANT [R] *Hatteras (Outer Banks), NC*
CHARCOAL STEAK HOUSE [R] *Roanoke, VA*
CHARLESTON GRILL [R] *Charleston, SC*
CHARLEY'S OTHER BROTHER [R] *Mount Holly, NJ*
CHARLEY'S PLACE [R] *McLean, VA*
CHARLIE BROWN'S [R] *Edison, NJ*
CHARLIE'S L'ETOILE VERTE [R] *Hilton Head Island, SC*
CHART HOUSE [R] *Alexandria, VA*
CHARTER RESTAURANT [R] *Morehead City, NC*
CHARTER ROOM [R] *Raleigh, NC*
CHEAT RIVER INN RESTAURANT [R] *Elkins, WV*
CHEESE CELLAR RESTAURANT & BAR [R] *Pittsburgh, PA*
CHEF DAN'S [R] *Charleston, WV*
CHEF VOLA'S [R] *Atlantic City, NJ*
CHEF'S SECRET [R] *College Park, MD*
CHESAPEAKE LANDING SEAFOOD [R] *St Michaels, MD*
CHEZ ANDREE [R] *Alexandria, VA*
CHEZ GARARD FRENCH RESTAURANT [R] *Uniontown, PA*
CHEZ LA MER [R] *Rehoboth Beach, DE*
CHIAPPARELLI'S [R] *Baltimore, MD*
CHINA MOON [R] *Atlantic City, NJ*
CHINA PALACE [R] *Pittsburgh, PA*
CHOP HOUSE OF STROUDSBURG [R] *Stroudsburg, PA*
CHRIS' STEAK HOUSE [R] *Gaithersburg, MD*
CHRISTIE'S [R] *Asbury Park, NJ*
CHURCH BREW WORKS, THE [R] *Pittsburgh, PA*
CIBO [R] *Philadelphia, PA*
CIBOULETTE [R] *Philadelphia, PA*
CIRCA [R] *Philadelphia, PA*
CIRCLE SEAFOOD RESTAURANT [R] *Portsmouth, VA*
CITRONELLE [R] *Washington, DC*

CITY LIGHTS [R] *Baltimore, MD*
CITY TAVERN [R] *Philadelphia, PA*
CLARA'S SEAFOOD GRILL [R] *Manteo, NC*
CLARENCE FOSTER'S [R] *Wrightsville Beach, NC*
CLARION CLIPPER [R] *Clarion, PA*
CLIFFSIDE [R] *Pittsburgh, PA*
CLINTON HOUSE [R] *Clinton, NJ*
CLYDE'S, DC
    [R] *Washington*
CLYDE'S, MD
    [R] *Columbia*
CLYDE'S, VA
    [R] *Dulles Intl Airport Area*, [R] *Tysons Corner*
COACH HOUSE TAVERN [R] *Williamsburg, VA*
COAL BARON RESTAURANT [R] *Uniontown, PA*
COASTAL GRILL [R] *Virginia Beach, VA*
COCK N' BULL RESTAURANT [R] *New Hope (Bucks Co), PA*
COCO LOCO [R] *Washington, DC*
COLLECTORS CAFE [R] *Myrtle Beach, SC*
COLONY [R] *Pittsburgh, PA*
COLUMBIA HOTEL [R] *Valley Forge National Historical Park, PA*
COLUMBUS INN [R] *Wilmington, DE*
COMMON PLEA [R] *Pittsburgh, PA*
COMMUNITY HOUSE RESTAURANT [R] *Georgetown, SC*
COMUS INN [R] *Frederick, MD*
CONCORDVILLE INN [R] *West Chester, PA*
CONNAUGHT PLACE [R] *Fairfax, VA*
COOPER'S SEAFOOD HOUSE [R] *Scranton, PA*
COPELAND'S OF NEW ORLEANS, MD [R] *Rockville*
COPELAND'S OF NEW ORLEANS, [R] *Alexandria*
COPPER KETTLE [R] *Chambersburg, PA*
COPPI'S VIGORELLI [R] *Washington, DC*
CORINTHIAN [R] *Annapolis, MD*
COTTAGE RESTAURANT [R] *Wilmington, NC*
COTTONWOOD CAFE [R] *Bethesda, MD*
COUNTRY CAFE [R] *Hot Springs, VA*
COUNTRY COTTAGE RESTAURANT [R] *Somerset, PA*
COUNTRY CUPBOARD [R] *Lewisburg, PA*
COUNTRY ROAD INN [R] *Summersville, WV*
COUNTRY SQUIRE [R] *Warsaw, NC*
COURTNEY'S [R] *Raleigh, NC*
COVENTRY FORGE INN [R] *Pottstown, PA*
COVES [R] *Pinehurst, NC*

COWBOY CAFE [R] *Arlington County (National Airport Area), VA*
COYOTE CROSSING [R] *Philadelphia, PA*
COZY [R] *Thurmont, MD*
CRAB SHANTY [R] *Ellicott City, MD*
CRAB TRAP [R] *Ocean City, NJ*
CRAZY SWEDE [R] *Havre De Grace, MD*
CRESCENT LODGE [R] *Canadensis, PA*
CRIPPEN'S [R] *Blowing Rock, NC*
CRISFIELD AT LEE PLAZA [R] *Silver Spring, MD*
CROWN STERLING [R] *Lynchburg, VA*
CUISINE AND COMPANY [R] *Virginia Beach, VA*
CUTTALOSSA INN [R] *New Hope (Bucks Co), PA*
CUVEE NOTREDAME [R] *Philadelphia, PA*
D & S BRASSERIE [R] *Lancaster, PA*
D'IGNAZIO'S TOWNE HOUSE [R] *Media, PA*
D'IMPERIO'S [R] *Pittsburgh, PA*
DA DOMENICO [R] *Tysons Corner, VA*
DA VINCENZO RISTORANTE [R] *Asheville, NC*
DALESIO'S [R] *Baltimore, MD*
DAMON'S THE PLACE FOR RIBS, SC [R] *Hilton Head Island*, [R] *Myrtle Beach*
DAN'L BOONE INN [R] *Boone, NC*
DANSBURY DEPOT [R] *Stroudsburg, PA*
DANTE [R] *McLean, VA*
DAS WALDCAFE [R] *Newport News, VA*
DAVE AND ANDY'S ICE CREAM PARLOR [R] *Pittsburgh, PA*
DE LAFAYETTE [R] *Fayetteville, NC*
DEAUVILLE INN [R] *Ocean City, NJ*
DEGUSTARE [R] *Spring Lake, NJ*
DELRAY VIETNAMESE GARDEN [R] *Bethesda, MD*
DEUX CHEMINEES [R] *Philadelphia, PA*
DIAMONDS [R] *Trenton, NJ*
DICKENS INN [R] *Philadelphia, PA*
DIEHL'S [R] *Nitro, WV*
DILWORTHTOWN INN DINING ROOM, THE [R] *West Chester, PA*
DIMITRI'S, PA
    [R] *Hershey*, [R] *Philadelphia*
DINARDO'S [R] *Philadelphia, PA*
DINARDO'S BY THE SEA [R] *Rehoboth Beach, DE*
DINING ROOM, THE, NJ
    [R] *Millburn*
DINING ROOM, THE, VA
    [R] *Abingdon*
DINING ROOM AT WOODLANDS, THE [R] *Charleston, SC*
DISTRICT CHOPHOUSE [R] *Washington, DC*
DOBBIN HOUSE [R] *Gettysburg, PA*

DOCK STREET BREWERY [R] *Philadelphia, PA*

DOCK'S OYSTER HOUSE [R] *Atlantic City, NJ*

DOCKSIDE [R] *Wrightsville Beach, NC*

DOLCETTO TRATTORIA [R] *Washington, DC*

DON'S SEAFOOD [R] *Chincoteague, VA*

DONECKERS [R] *Ephrata, PA*

DORIS & ED'S [R] *Gateway National Recreation Area (Sandy Hook Unit), NJ*

DOUMAR'S [R] *Norfolk, VA*

DOXEY'S MARKET & CAFE [R] *Wilmington, NC*

DRAGON GARDEN [R] *Wilmington, NC*

DUANGRAT'S [R] *Falls Church, VA*

DUE [R] *Pikesville, MD*

DULING-KURTZ HOUSE [R] *West Chester, PA*

DUMBWAITER, THE [R] *Norfolk, VA*

DYNASTY [R] *Williamsburg, VA*

EAST WIND [R] *Alexandria, VA*

EASTERN CHINESE RESTAURANT INC [R] *Bethlehem, PA*

EASTVILLE MANOR [R] *Cape Charles, VA*

EBBITT ROOM [R] *Cape May, NJ*

ECCO CAFE [R] *Alexandria, VA*

ED'S STEAK HOUSE [R] *Bedford, PA*

EDDIE ROMANELLI'S [R] *Wilmington, NC*

EHRHARDT'S LAKESIDE [R] *Hawley, PA*

EL CARIBE [R] *Washington, DC*

EL CATALAN [R] *Washington, DC*

ELIJAHS RESTAURANT [R] *Wilmington, NC*

ELLIOTT'S ON THE SQUARE [R] *Charleston, SC*

ELYSIUM [R] *Alexandria, VA*

EMBERS [R] *Ocean City, MD*

EPICUREAN [R] *Charlotte, NC*

ERNIE'S CORK & BOTTLE [R] *Wheeling, WV*

ERNIE'S ESQUIRE [R] *Wheeling, WV*

ESPOSITOS/PIZZA 'N PASTA, THE [R] *Fairfax, VA*

EVANS FARM INN [R] *McLean, VA*

EVANS SEAFOOD [R] *St Mary's City, MD*

EVERMAY ON-THE-DELAWARE [R] *New Hope (Bucks Co), PA*

EXPRESSIONS [R] *Hendersonville, NC*

FACCIA LUNA, VA
[R] *Alexandria*, [R] *Arlington County (National Airport Area)*

FAGER'S ISLAND [R] *Ocean City, MD*

FAIRVIEW [R] *Durham, NC*

FAMILY TREE TAVERN [R] *Spring Lake, NJ*

FAMOUS 4TH ST DELICATESSEN [R] *Philadelphia, PA*

FARMHOUSE, THE [R] *Allentown, PA*

FARNSWORTH HOUSE [R] *Gettysburg, PA*

FAROUK'S HOUSE OF INDIA [R] *Richmond, VA*

FEARRINGTON HOUSE [R] *Chapel Hill, NC*

FEDERAL GRILL [R] *Allentown, PA*

FEDORA CAFE [R] *Tysons Corner, VA*

FELICIA'S [R] *Philadelphia, PA*

FIFTH QUARTER [R] *Charleston, WV*

FILOMENA [R] *Washington, DC*

FINE FRIENDS [R] *Asheville, NC*

FIO'S [R] *Washington, DC*

FIRE & ICE RESTAURANT [R] *Hampton, VA*

FIREPLACE RESTAURANT [R] *Scranton, PA*

FISH MARKET [R] *Alexandria, VA*

FISHER'S SEAFOOD [R] *Philadelphia, PA*

FISHERMAN'S INN & CRAB DECK [R] *Chesapeake Bay Bridge Area, MD*

FISHMARKET, THE [R] *Charlotte, NC*

FLAME STEAK HOUSE [R] *Morgantown, WV*

FLAMING PIT [R] *Gaithersburg, MD*

FLYING FISH [R] *Philadelphia, PA*

FLYING FISH CAFE [R] *Kill Devil Hills (Outer Banks), NC*

FOONG LIN [R] *Bethesda, MD*

FORAGER HOUSE RESTAURANT [R] *New Hope (Bucks Co), PA*

FORDS COLONY RESTAURANT [R] *Williamsburg, VA*

FORK [R] *Philadelphia, PA*

FORSGATE COUNTRY CLUB [R] *Hightstown, NJ*

FORTUNE [R] *Dulles Intl Airport Area, VA*

FOUNDERS, THE [R] *Philadelphia, PA*

FOUNTAIN [R] *Philadelphia, PA*

FOUR & TWENTY BLACKBIRDS [R] *Washington, VA*

FOX POINT GRILL [R] *Wilmington, DE*

FRAN O'BRIEN'S STADIUM STEAK HOUSE [R] *Washington, DC*

FRASCATI RISTORANTE ITALIANO [R] *Bethesda, MD*

FRATELLI ITALIAN [R] *Washington, MD*

FRED & CLAIRE'S RESTAURANT [R] *New Bern, NC*

FRED'S [R] *Annapolis, MD*

FREDDIE'S [R] *Wilmington, NC*

FREEMASON ABBEY [R] *Norfolk, VA*

FRESCOS [R] *Cape May, NJ*

FROG AND THE PEACH, THE [R] *New Brunswick, NJ*

FROG AND THE REDNECK, THE [R] *Richmond, VA*

FROG & OWL KITCHEN [R] *Franklin (Macon Co), NC*

FULTON FIVE [R] *Charleston, SC*

FUSCO'S RESTAURANT [R] *Myrtle Beach, SC*

GABRIEL [R] *Washington, DC*

GABRIEL'S [R] *Frederick, MD*

GABRIELLE'S [R] *Asheville, NC*

GADSBY'S TAVERN [R] *Alexandria, VA*

GALILEO RESTAURANT [R] *Washington, DC*

GAMBLE MILL TAVERN [R] *Bellefonte, PA*

GARDEN, THE [R] *Philadelphia, PA*

GARDEN GOURMET [R] *Rehoboth Beach, DE*

GARDEN & THE SEA INN, THE [R] *Chincoteague, VA*

GARFIELD'S GIARDINO RISTORANTE [R] *Wildwood & Wildwood Crest, NJ*

GARIBALDI'S, SC
[R] *Charleston*, [R] *Columbia*

GARRETT'S [R] *Washington, DC*

GASLIGHT 2000 [R] *Hilton Head Island, SC*

GATE CITY CHOP HOUSE [R] *Greensboro, NC*

GAZEBO CAFE [R] *Franklin (Macon Co), NC*

GAZEBO HOUSE OF PANCAKES [R] *Williamsburg, VA*

GEORGETOWNE INN [R] *Pittsburgh, PA*

GEORGIA BROWN'S [R] *Washington, DC*

GERANIO RISTORANTE [R] *Alexandria, VA*

GERARD'S PLACE [R] *Washington, DC*

GERMAINE'S [R] *Washington, DC*

GERMANO'S TRATTORIA [R] *Baltimore, MD*

GILLIGAN'S [R] *Lewes, DE*

GINGERBREAD MAN [R] *Gettysburg, PA*

GIRAFE [R] *Bernardsville, NJ*

GIUSEPPE'S [R] *Williamsburg, VA*

GOLDEN BELL DINER INC [R] *Freehold, NJ*

GOLDEN BULL GRAND CAFE [R] *Gaithersburg, MD*

GOLDEN EAGLE DINER [R] *Cherry Hill, NJ*

GOLDEN PHEASANT INN [R] *New Hope (Bucks Co), PA*

GOLDONI RESTAURANT [R] *Washington, DC*

GOOD TIME CHARLEY'S [R] *Princeton, NJ*

GOODFELLAS [R] *Charlottesville, VA*

GRABELS RESTAURANT LOUNGE [R] *Atlantic City, NJ*

GRACIE'S 21ST CENTURY CAFE [R] *Pottstown, PA*

GRAND CONCOURSE [R] *Pittsburgh, PA*

GREEN HILLS INN [R] *Reading, PA*

GREEN ROOM [R] *Wilmington, DE*

GREEN TREE [R] *Leesburg, VA*

GREENBRIER MAIN DINING ROOM, THE [R] *White Sulphur Springs, WV*
GREENERY [R] *Asheville, NC*
GREENWOOD [R] *Washington, DC*
GREGORY'S [R] *Ocean City, NJ*
GRIFFINS RESTAURANT [R] *Annapolis, MD*
GRILL, THE, *PA*
  [R] *Philadelphia*
GRILL, THE, *VA*
  [R] *Arlington County (National Airport Area)*
GRILL FROM IPANEMA [R] *Washington, DC*
GRIMALDI'S [R] *Hoboken, NJ*
GROFF'S FARM RESTAURANT & GOLF [R] *Lancaster, PA*
GUAPOS MEXICAN CUISINE [R] *Washington, DC*
GUARDS [R] *Washington, DC*
GYPSY ROSE [R] *Limerick, PA*
HAAD THAI [R] *Washington, DC*
HAAG'S HOTEL RESTAURANT [R] *Shartlesville, PA*
HAANDI FINE INDIAN CUISINE [R] *Falls Church, VA*
HAANDI FINE INDIAN CUSINE [R] *Bethesda, MD*
HALF WAY HOUSE [R] *Richmond, VA*
HAMPTON STREET VINEYARD [R] *Columbia, SC*
HAMPTON'S [R] *Baltimore, MD*
HANNA'S MARINA DECK [R] *Ocean City, MD*
HARBOURMASTER'S [R] *Hilton Head Island, SC*
HARD TIMES CAFE, *MD*
  [R] *Rockville*
HARD TIMES CAFE, *VA*
  [R] *Alexandria*
HARDWARE STORE [R] *Charlottesville, VA*
HARLEY DAWN DINER [R] *Atlantic City, NJ*
HARPOON HANNA'S [R] *Fenwick Island, DE*
HARRIS CRAB HOUSE [R] *Chesapeake Bay Bridge Area, MD*
HARRISON'S HARBOR WATCH [R] *Ocean City, MD*
HARRY BROWNE'S [R] *Annapolis, MD*
HARRY'S SAVOY GRILL [R] *Wilmington, DE*
HARVEST MOON [R] *Wilmington, NC*
HARVEST MOON INN [R] *Flemington, NJ*
HARVEY MANSION RESTAURANT [R] *New Bern, NC*
HAUSSNER'S [R] *Baltimore, MD*
HAYDN ZUG'S [R] *Lancaster, PA*
HEART-IN-HAND [R] *Fairfax, VA*
HEAT WAVE CAFE [R] *Spring Lake, NJ*
HELEN'S [R] *Donegal, PA*

HEMINGWAY'S [R] *Hilton Head Island, SC*
HENDERSON HOUSE [R] *New Bern, NC*
HENNESSY'S [R] *Columbia, SC*
HENNINGER'S TAVERN [R] *Baltimore, MD*
HENRY'S PLANET SEAFOOD [R] *Virginia Beach, VA*
HEREFORD BARN STEAK HOUSE [R] *Charlotte, NC*
HERITAGE STATION [R] *Huntington, WV*
HERMAN'S HARBOR HOUSE [R] *Newport News, VA*
HERMITAGE INN [R] *Fairfax, VA*
HERO'S AMERICAN RESTAURANT [R] *Manassas, VA*
HERR TAVERN & PUBLICK HOUSE [R] *Gettysburg, PA*
HIERONYMUS SEAFOOD [R] *Wilmington, NC*
HIGH COUNTRY [R] *Blue Ridge Parkway, VA*
HIGHLAWN PAVILION [R] *West Orange, NJ*
HOBBIT [R] *Ocean City, MD*
HOFBRAUHAUS RESTAURANT [R] *Hilton Head Island, SC*
HOGATES SEAFOOD RESTAURANT [R] *Washington, DC*
HORIZONS [R] *Asheville, NC*
HOT ROD CAFE AND TULLY'S GRILLE [R] *Sharon, PA*
HOTEL DU VILLAGE [R] *New Hope (Bucks Co), PA*
HOTEL STRASBURG [R] *Strasburg, VA*
HOUSE OF CHANG PEKING II [R] *Altoona, PA*
HUDSON'S ON THE DOCKS [R] *Hilton Head Island, SC*
HUNAN CHINATOWN [R] *Washington, DC*
HUNAN LION [R] *Tysons Corner, VA*
HUNTER'S TAVERN [R] *Easton, MD*
HURSEY'S PIG PICKIN' BAR-B-Q [R] *Burlington, NC*
HYEHOLDE [R] *Pittsburgh Intl Airport Area, PA*
I MATTI TRATTORIA [R] *Washington, DC*
IKAROS [R] *Baltimore, MD*
IL BORGO ITALIAN RESTAURANT [R] *McLean, VA*
IL CIGNO RESTAURANT [R] *Dulles Intl Airport Area, VA*
IL FORNO PIZZERIA [R] *Gaithersburg, MD*
IL GIARDINO [R] *Virginia Beach, VA*
IL PALIO [R] *Chapel Hill, NC*
IL PIZZICO [R] *Rockville, MD*
IL PORTO RISTORANTE [R] *Alexandria, VA*
IL RITROVO [R] *Bethesda, MD*

INDIA GARDEN [R] *Pittsburgh, PA*
INDIA PALACE [R] *Wilmington, DE*
INDIAN FIELDS TAVERN [R] *Williamsburg, VA*
INDIGO AT GREAT FALLS [R] *McLean, VA*
INDOCHINE [R] *Richmond, VA*
INN AT LITTLE WASHINGTON, THE [R] *Washington, VA*
INN AT PHILLIPS MILL [R] *New Hope (Bucks Co), PA*
INN OF THE FALCON [R] *Bethlehem, PA*
IRISH EYES [R] *Rehoboth Beach, DE*
IRISH PUB AND INN [R] *Atlantic City, NJ*
IRONHORSE [R] *Ashland, VA*
IRREGARDLESS CAFE [R] *Raleigh, NC*
ISABELLA [R] *Washington, DC*
ISABELLA'S [R] *Philadelphia, PA*
ISLAND INN RESTAURANT [R] *Ocracoke (Outer Banks), NC*
ITALIAN BISTRO [R] *Philadelphia, PA*
IVY INN [R] *Charlottesville, VA*
J ARTHUR'S [R] *Maggie Valley, NC*
J BASUL NOBLE'S RESTAURANT [R] *High Point, NC*
J BISTRO [R] *Charleston, SC*
J.G. COOK'S RIVERVIEW INN [R] *Wilmington, NJ*
J PAUL'S [R] *Washington, DC*
JR'S GOODTIMES [R] *Tysons Corner, VA*
JACKALOPE'S VIEW [R] *Banner Elk, NC*
JAKE'S [R] *Philadelphia, PA*
JALEO [R] *Washington, DC*
JAMES RIVER WINE BISTRO [R] *Richmond, VA*
JEAN CLAUDE'S CAFE [R] *Raleigh, NC*
JEAN PIERRE'S [R] *New Hope (Bucks Co), PA*
JEAN-MICHEL [R] *Bethesda, MD*
JEANNE'S RESTAURANT [R] *Lynchburg, VA*
JEANNIER'S [R] *Baltimore, MD*
JEFFERSON, THE [R] *Washington, DC*
JEFFERSON HOUSE, THE [R] *Norristown, PA*
JEFFERSON INN [R] *Williamsburg, VA*
JENNY'S RESTAURANT [R] *New Hope (Bucks Co), PA*
JIM REID'S [R] *Clarksburg, WV*
JIMMY TSANG'S [R] *Pittsburgh, PA*
JOCKEY CLUB [R] *Washington, DC*
JOE FAZIO'S [R] *Charleston, WV*
JOE & MAGGIE'S BISTRO [R] *Eatontown, NJ*
JOE'S BAR & GRILL [R] *Myrtle Beach, SC*
JOHANSSON'S [R] *Westminster, MD*
JOHN STEVEN LTD [R] *Baltimore, MD*
JOHNNY MOTT'S [R] *Jenkintown, PA*
JOHNS RESTAURANT [R] *Lumberton, NC*

JOHNSTON'S INN [R] *Princeton, WV*
JOLLY ROGER [R] *Kill Devil Hills (Outer Banks), NC*
JOSEPH AMBLER INN [R] *Willow Grove, PA*
JOSEPH POON [R] *Philadelphia, PA*
JOY AMERICA CAFE [R] *Baltimore, MD*
JUNCTION 808 [R] *Hagerstown, MD*
JUNO TRATTORIA [R] *Pittsburgh, PA*
JW'S VIEW STEAKHOUSE [R] *Arlington County (National Airport Area), VA*
KABUKI JAPANESE STEAK HOUSE [R] *Roanoke, VA*
KABUL CARAVAN [R] *Arlington County (National Airport Area), VA*
KABUTO JAPANESE HOUSE OF STEAK [R] *Richmond, VA*
KANSAS CITY PRIME [R] *Philadelphia, PA*
KARSON'S INN [R] *Baltimore, MD*
KAWASAKI [R] *Baltimore, MD*
KAYA [R] *Pittsburgh, PA*
KAZAN RESTAURANT [R] *McLean, VA*
KENNEDY-SUPPLEE MANSION [R] *Valley Forge National Historical Park, PA*
KENNETT SQUARE INN [R] *Kennett Square, PA*
KID SHELLEENS [R] *Wilmington, DE*
KIMBERTON INN [R] *Valley Forge National Historical Park, PA*
KING NEPTUNE [R] *Wrightsville Beach, NC*
KING'S ARMS TAVERN [R] *Williamsburg, VA*
KING'S CONTRIVANCE [R] *Columbia, MD*
KINGFISHER [R] *Hilton Head Island, SC*
KINKEAD'S [R] *Washington, DC*
KIRK'S [R] *Hinton, WV*
KITCHEN AT POWHATAN [R] *Williamsburg, VA*
KLONDIKE KATE'S [R] *Newark, DE*
KNAVE OF HEARTS [R] *Philadelphia, PA*
KOBE JAPANESE HOUSE OF STEAK & SEAFOOD [R] *Cornelius, NC*
KRAMERBOOKS & AFTERWORDS [R] *Washington, DC*
KRAZY KAT'S RESTAURANT [R] *Wilmington, DE*
KRUPIN'S RESTAURANT [R] *Washington, DC*
KUPCHICK'S RESTAURANT [R] *Lewes, DE*
KYOTO JAPANESE STEAK HOUSE [R] *Chesapeake, VA*
L'AUBERGE CHEZ FRANCOIS [R] *McLean, VA*
L'AUBERGE PROVENÇALE [R] *Winchester, VA*
LA BERGERIE [R] *Alexandria, VA*
LA BIBLIOTHEQUE [R] *Charlotte, NC*

LA CAMPAGNE [R] *Cherry Hill, NJ*
LA CARAVELLE [R] *Virginia Beach, VA*
LA CHAUMIERE [R] *Washington, DC*
LA COLLINE [R] *Washington, DC*
LA COTE D'OR CAFE [R] *Arlington County (National Airport Area), VA*
LA FAMIGLIA [R] *Philadelphia, PA*
LA FERME [R] *Bethesda, MD*
LA FONTANA [R] *New Brunswick, NJ*
LA FOURCHETTE, DC [R] *Washington*
LA FOURCHETTE, PA [R] *King of Prussia*
LA FROMAGERIE [R] *Red Bank, NJ*
LA GALLERIA [R] *Norfolk, VA*
LA GONDOLA [R] *Trenton, NJ*
LA LA LAND [R] *Rehoboth Beach, DE*
LA MICHE [R] *Bethesda, MD*
LA PETITE AUBERGE [R] *Fredericksburg, VA*
LA PETITE FRANCE [R] *Richmond, VA*
LA PIAZZA CAFE [R] *Quakertown (Bucks Co), PA*
LA POLA'S [R] *Hilton Head Island, SC*
LA PROVENCE [R] *Tysons Corner, VA*
LA RESIDENCE [R] *Chapel Hill, NC*
LA SCALA RESTAURANT [R] *Baltimore, MD*
LA TERRACE [R] *Southern Pines, NC*
LA TRELLIS [R] *Williamsburg, VA*
LAFAYETTE [R] *Washington, DC*
LAKESIDE AT HOLIDAY MARINA [R] *Cornelius, NC*
LAMBERTVILLE STATION [R] *Lambertville, NJ*
LAMP LIGHTER [R] *Charlotte, NC*
LAMP POST RESTAURANT [R] *Rehoboth Beach, DE*
LANDINI BROTHERS [R] *Alexandria, VA*
LANDMARK CRAB HOUSE [R] *Chincoteague, VA*
LANDMARK HOUSE [R] *Lynchburg, VA*
LARRY PERONI'S WATERFRONT [R] *Trenton, NJ*
LAS MARGARITAS [R] *Raleigh, NC*
LATIF'S BAKERY & CAFE [R] *Myrtle Beach, SC*
LAUREL BRIGADE INN [R] *Leesburg, VA*
LAUREN'S [R] *Philadelphia, PA*
LAURIOL PLAZA [R] *Washington, DC*
LAURY'S RESTAURANT [R] *Charleston, WV*
LAVANDOU [R] *Washington, DC*
LE BAR LYONNAIS [R] *Philadelphia, PA*
LE BAR NOSTRADAMUS [R] *Philadelphia, PA*
LE BEC-FIN [R] *Philadelphia, PA*
LE CANARD [R] *Tysons Corner, VA*
LE CHAMBORD [R] *Virginia Beach, VA*
LE COLONIAL [R] *Philadelphia, PA*
LE GAULOIS [R] *Alexandria, VA*

LE MONT [R] *Pittsburgh, PA*
LE PARADIS [R] *Gaithersburg, MD*
LE PETIT CHATEAU [R] *Bernardsville, NJ*
LE POMMIER [R] *Pittsburgh, PA*
LE REFUGE [R] *Alexandria, VA*
LE VIEUX LOGIS [R] *Bethesda, MD*
LE YACA RESTAURANT [R] *Williamsburg, VA*
LEBANESE TAVERNA [R] *Washington, DC*
LEE'S RESTAURANT [R] *Stroudsburg, PA*
LEESBURG COLONIAL INN [R] *Leesburg, VA*
LEEWARD ROOM [R] *Beach Haven, NJ*
LEGAL SEA FOODS [R] *Washington, DC*
LEGAL SPIRITS [R] *Easton, MD*
LEMAIRE [R] *Richmond, VA*
LENAPE INN [R] *West Chester, PA*
LES HALLES [R] *Washington, DC*
LESPINASSE [R] *Washington, DC*
LEWNES' STEAKHOUSE [R] *Annapolis, MD*
LIBERATORE'S RISTORANTE [R] *Towson, MD*
LIBRARY RESTAURANT [R] *Roanoke, VA*
LIGHTHOUSE [R] *Lewes, DE*
LIGHTHOUSE, THE [R] *Virginia Beach, VA*
LILFREDS OF CAMDEN [R] *Camden, SC*
LINWOOD'S CAFE [R] *Pikesville, MD*
LITTLE ITALY [R] *Cape Charles, VA*
LITTLE VENICE [R] *Hilton Head Island, SC*
LITTLE VIET GARDEN [R] *Arlington County (National Airport Area), VA*
LOBSTER HOUSE, NJ [R] *Cape May*
LOBSTER HOUSE, VA [R] *Williamsburg*
LOCKS POINTE [R] *Chesapeake, VA*
LOG CABIN [R] *Lancaster, PA*
LOG HOUSE [R] *Wytheville, VA*
LONDON GRILLE [R] *Pittsburgh, PA*
LONGHORN STEAK HOUSE [R] *Hilton Head Island, SC*
LONGHORN STEAKHOUSE [R] *Myrtle Beach, SC*
LOS AMIGOS MEXICAN RESTAURANT [R] *Cherry Hill, NJ*
LOS SARAPES [R] *Doylestown (Bucks Co), PA*
LOTUS INN [R] *King of Prussia, PA*
LOUGHRY'S LANDING [R] *Beaufort, NC*
LOUIE'S THE BOOKSTORE CAFE [R] *Baltimore, MD*
LOUIS'S [R] *Charleston, SC*
LOWERY'S [R] *Tappahannock, VA*

LUCKY STAR [R] *VIRGINIA BEACH, VA*
LUCY'S [R] *Camden, SC*
LUIGI'S [R] *Wildwood & Wildwood Crest, NJ*
LUIGINO [R] *Washington, DC*
LYNNHAVEN FISH HOUSE [R] *Virginia Beach, VA*
LYNNHAVEN INN [R] *New Castle, DE*
MAC'S [R] *Ocean City, NJ*
MAD BATTER [R] *Cape May, NJ*
MAGNOLIA GRILL [R] *Durham, NC*
MAGNOLIAS [R] *Charleston, SC*
MAHARAJA INDIAN CUISINE RESTAURANT [R] *Charlottesville, VA*
MAIN STREET DEPOT RESTAURANT [R] *Bethlehem, PA*
MAINLAND INN [R] *Kulpsville, PA*
MAKEDA ETHIOPIAN RESTAURANT [R] *New Brunswick, NJ*
MAKOTO [R] *Boone, NC*
MANADA HILL INN [R] *Harrisburg, PA*
MANDARIN TANG [R] *Easton, PA*
MANGO MIKE'S [R] *Alexandria, VA*
MANOR, THE [R] *West Orange, NJ*
MARCO POLO [R] *Tysons Corner, VA*
MARGHERITAS'S [R] *Hoboken, NJ*
MARINA RESTAURANT [R] *Elizabeth City, NC*
MARITA'S CANTINA [R] *New Brunswick, NJ*
MARKER RESTAURANT & LOUNGE [R] *Philadelphia, PA*
MARKET EAST BISTRO [R] *Charleston, SC*
MARKET INN [R] *Washington, DC*
MARKET PLACE ON WALL STREET, [R] *Asheville, NC*
MARKET STREET BAR & GRILL [R] *Dulles Intl Airport Area, VA*
MARKET STREET CASUAL DINING [R] *Wilmington, NC*
MARLINS CAFE [R] *Spring Lake, NJ*
MARSILIO'S RESTAURANT [R] *Trenton, NJ*
MASQUERADE [R] *Tysons Corner, VA*
MATUBA JAPANESE [R] *Bethesda, MD*
MATUBA JAPANESE RESTAURANT [R] *Arlington County (National Airport Area), VA*
MAX, THE [R] *Norfolk, VA*
MAX & ERMA'S [R] *Pittsburgh, PA*
MAX'S ALLEGHENY TAVERN [R] *Pittsburgh, PA*
MAYFLOWER I [R] *Bluefield, WV*
MCCORMICK & SCHMICK'S [R] *Washington, DC*
MCCORMICK'S PUB [R] *Staunton, VA*
MCCRADY'S TAVERN [R] *Charleston, SC*
MCGUFFEY'S INC [R] *Asheville, NC*
MCNINCH HOUSE [R] *Charlotte, NC*
MEETING PLACE [R] *Brookville, PA*
MELANGE CAFE [R] *Cherry Hill, NJ*

MELITTA'S GASTHAUS [R] *Petersburg, VA*
MELROSE [R] *Washington, DC*
MENDENHALL INN [R] *Kennett Square, PA*
MENZ RESTAURANT & SEAFOOD [R] *Wildwood & Wildwood Crest, NJ*
MERCERSBURG INN [R] *Chambersburg, PA*
MERION INN [R] *Cape May, NJ*
MESKEREM [R] *Washington, DC*
MICHAEL RORK'S TOWN DOCK [R] *St Michaels, MD*
MICHAEL'S [R] *Philadelphia, PA*
MIDDLETON TAVERN [R] *Annapolis, MD*
MIKE'S AMERICAN GRILL [R] *Springfield, VA*
MILL POND RESTAURANT [R] *Camden, SC*
MILTON INN, THE [R] *Cockeysville, MD*
MINARD'S SPAGHETTI INN [R] *Clarksburg, WV*
MINSI TRAIL INN [R] *Bethlehem, PA*
MIRAGE RESTAURANT [R] *Stone Harbor, NJ*
MOGHUL RESTAURANT [R] *Edison, NJ*
MOLLY PITCHER INN [R] *Red Bank, NJ*
MONASTERY [R] *Norfolk, VA*
MONOCLE ON CAPITOL HILL [R] *Washington, DC*
MONROE'S AN AMERICAN TRATTORIA [R] *Alexandria, VA*
MONTE CARLO LIVING ROOM [R] *Philadelphia, PA*
MONTGOMERY'S GRILLE [R] *Bethesda, MD*
MOONSTRUCK, NJ [R] *Asbury Park*
MOONSTRUCK, PA [R] *Philadelphia*
MORGAN MILLARD [R] *Baltimore, MD*
MORGAN'S FOOD & SPIRITS [R] *Cherry Hill, NJ*
MORRISON CLARK RESTAURANT [R] *Washington, DC*
MORROCROFTS [R] *Charlotte, NC*
MORTON'S OF CHICAGO, DC [R] *Washington*
MORTON'S OF CHICAGO, VA [R] *Tysons Corner*
MOSELEM SPRINGS INN [R] *Reading, PA*
MOSHULU [R] *Philadelphia, PA*
MOUNT VERNON INN RESTAURANT [R] *Mount Vernon, VA*
MOUNTAIN CREEK [R] *Hinton, WV*
MOUNTAIN SMOKE HOUSE [R] *Asheville, NC*
MOUNTAINEER FAMILY RESTAURANT [R] *Parkersburg, WV*
MR. PATRICK HENRY'S INN [R] *Richmond, VA*
MR. SMITH'S [R] *Washington, DC*

MR YUNG'S RESTAURANT [R] *Washington, DC*
MRS. K'S TOLL HOUSE [R] *Silver Spring, MD*
MRS WILLIS [R] *Morehead City, NC*
MT WASHINGTON TAVERN [R] *Baltimore, MD*
MUMFORD RESTAURANT [R] *Eatontown, NJ*
MURIALE'S [R] *Fairmont, WV*
MURPHY'S OF D.C [R] *Washington, DC*
MUSIC CITY ROADHOUSE [R] *Washington, DC*
NAIS CUISINE [R] *Philadelphia, PA*
NAM'S OF BETHESDA [R] *Bethesda, MD*
NAPOLEON'S [R] *Warrenton, VA*
NAPOLITANO'S [R] *New Brunswick, NJ*
NARROWS RESTAURANT [R] *Chesapeake Bay Bridge Area, MD*
NATHANS [R] *Washington, DC*
NENO IL TOSCANO [R] *Hilton Head Island, SC*
NEW HEIGHTS [R] *Washington, DC*
NEW LOBSTER HOUSE INC [R] *Fayetteville, NC*
NEW SMITHVILLE COUNTRY INN [R] *Kutztown, PA*
NICHOLAS NICKOLAS [R] *Philadelphia, PA*
NICK'S [R] *Philadelphia, PA*
NICK'S CALICO COTTAGE [R] *Highlands, NC*
NICK'S SEAFOOD PAVILION [R] *Yorktown, VA*
NINO BARSOTTI'S RESTAURANT [R] *Donegal, PA*
NIPPON CENTER YAGOTO [R] *Greenville, SC*
NIZAM'S RESTAURANT [R] *Tysons Corner, VA*
NONNIE'S RESTAURANT [R] *Chincoteague, VA*
NORA [R] *Washington, DC*
NORMANDIE FARM [R] *Rockville, MD*
NORTHWOODS [R] *Annapolis, MD*
O'DONNELL'S [R] *Bethesda, MD*
O'LEARY'S SEAFOOD RESTAURANT [R] *Annapolis, MD*
O'TOOLE'S [R] *Richmond, VA*
OAK HARBOUR [R] *Myrtle Beach, SC*
OAK SUPPER CLUB [R] *Hinton, WV*
OAKHURST TEA ROOM [R] *Somerset, PA*
OBELISK [R] *Washington, DC*
OBRYCKI'S CRAB HOUSE [R] *Baltimore, MD*
OCCIDENTAL GRILL [R] *Washington, DC*
OCEAN CLUB [R] *Ocean City, MD*
OCEAN TERRACE [R] *Wrightsville Beach, NC*
OCEANIC RESTAURANT & GRILL [R] *Wrightsville Beach, NC*

ODD FELLOWS [R] *Hoboken, NJ*

ODETTE'S [R] *New Hope (Bucks Co), PA*

OH! BRIAN'S [R] *Wilmington, NC*

OLD ANGLER'S INN [R] *Rockville, MD*

OLD BAY, THE [R] *New Brunswick, NJ*

OLD CHICKAHOMINY HOUSE [R] *Williamsburg, VA*

OLD EBBITT GRILL [R] *Washington, DC*

OLD EUROPE RESTAURANT & RATHSK [R] *Washington, DC*

OLD HICKORY SMOKE HOUSE TX BBQ [R] *Cherry Hill, NJ*

OLD MILL INN [R] *Spring Lake, NJ*

OLD MILL ROOM [R] *Charlottesville, VA*

OLD ORIGINAL BOOKBINDER'S [R] *Philadelphia, PA*

OLD OYSTER FACTORY [R] *Hilton Head Island, SC*

OLD PHARMACY CAFE [R] *Shepherdstown, WV*

OLD POST OFFICE RESTAURANT [R] *Kiawah Island, SC*

OLD SALEM TAVERN [R] *Winston-Salem, NC*

OLD SOUTH MOUNTAIN INN [R] *Boonsboro (Washington County), MD*

OLD WATERWAY INN [R] *Atlantic City, NJ*

OLD WHARF INN [R] *Chesapeake Bay Bridge Area, MD*

OLDE GREENFIELD INN [R] *Lancaster, PA*

OLDE MUDD TAVERN [R] *Fredericksburg, VA*

OLDE TOWNE TAVERN & BREWING CO [R] *Gaithersburg, MD*

ON THE VERANDAH [R] *Highlands, NC*

ONE EYED PARROT [R] *Charleston, SC*

OPEN HEARTH [R] *Greenville, SC*

OPUS 251 [R] *Philadelphia, PA*

OREGANO JOE'S [R] *Charlottesville, VA*

OREGON GRILL [R] *Cockeysville, MD*

ORIGINAL PANCAKE HOUSE [R] *Bethesda, MD*

OSPREY AT TILGHMAN ISLAND [R] *St Michaels, MD*

OTTO'S BRAUHAUS [R] *Willow Grove, PA*

OVAL ROOM [R] *Washington, DC*

OVERTURES [R] *Philadelphia, PA*

OWENS' [R] *Nags Head (Outer Banks), NC*

OXFORD HOUSE [R] *Cumberland, MD*

P J SKIDOOS RESTAURANT [R] *Fairfax, VA*

PACKY'S PUB [R] *Media, PA*

PALACE OF ASIA [R] *Fort Washington, PA*

PALM, THE [R] *Philadelphia, PA*

PALM COURT [R] *Dulles Intl Airport Area, VA*

PALM RESTAURANT [R] *Washington, DC*

PANINO [R] *Manassas, VA*

PANJSHIR [R] *Falls Church, VA*

PANJSHIR II [R] *Tysons Corner, VA*

PAOLO'S [R] *Washington, DC*

PAPA'S GRILL [R] *Durham, NC*

PAPILLONS RESTAURANT [R] *Charleston, SC*

PARIZADE [R] *Durham, NC*

PARKER'S BAR-B-QUE [R] *Greenville, NC*

PARKHURST RESTAURANT [R] *Luray, VA*

PASTA PIATTO [R] *Pittsburgh, PA*

PATISSERIE-CAFE DIDIER [R] *Washington, DC*

PATOU BISTRO [R] *Charlotte, NC*

PEACHES AT SUNSET [R] *Cape May, NJ*

PEACOCK ON THE PARKWAY [R] *Philadelphia, PA*

PEAKS OF OTTER [R] *Blue Ridge Parkway, VA*

PEARLY BAKER'S ALE HOUSE [R] *Easton, PA*

PEERCE'S PLANTATION [R] *Towson, MD*

PEKING CHEERS [R] *Gaithersburg, MD*

PEKING GARDEN [R] *Raleigh, NC*

PEKING GOURMET INN [R] *Falls Church, VA*

PEKING PAVILION [R] *Richmond, VA*

PEKING RESTAURANT [R] *Williamsburg, VA*

PEKING SUPREME [R] *Gaithersburg, MD*

PENGUIN ISLE [R] *Nags Head (Outer Banks), NC*

PENINSULA GRILL [R] *Charleston, SC*

PENN ALPS [R] *Grantsville, MD*

PENN BREWERY [R] *Pittsburgh, PA*

PESCE [R] *Washington, DC*

PETITTO'S [R] *Washington, DC*

PHILADELPHIA FISH [R] *Philadelphia, PA*

PHILIPPE ON LOCUST [R] *Philadelphia, PA*

PHILIPPI INN [R] *Philippi, WV*

PHILLIPS CRAB HOUSE [R] *Ocean City, MD*

PHILLIPS FLAGSHIP [R] *Washington, DC*

PHILLIPS SEAFOOD GRILL [R] *Tysons Corner, VA*

PHILLIPS SEAFOOD HOUSE [R] *Ocean City, MD*

PICCOLO MONDO, *DE*
   [R] *Wilmington*

PICCOLO MONDO, *PA*
   [R] *Pittsburgh*

PIERPOINT [R] *Baltimore, MD*

PILIN THAI RESTAURANT [R] *Falls Church, VA*

PILOT HOUSE [R] *Wilmington, NC*

PINE BARN INN [R] *Danville, PA*

PINE CREST INN [R] *Tryon, NC*

PINE GRILL [R] *Somerset, PA*

PIZZERIA PARADISO [R] *Washington, DC*

PIZZERIA UNO [R] *Pittsburgh, PA*

PLAIN & FANCY FARM [R] *Bird-in-Hand, PA*

PLOUGH & THE STARS [R] *Philadelphia, PA*

POINT OF VIEW [R] *Parkersburg, WV*

POINT VIEW INN [R] *Oakland (Garrett Co), MD*

POLI [R] *Pittsburgh, PA*

POLO GRILL [R] *Baltimore, MD*

POMPANO GRILLE [R] *Philadelphia, PA*

POOGAN'S PORCH [R] *Charleston, SC*

PORT ARTHUR CHINESE RESTAURANT [R] *Newport News, VA*

PORT CITY CHOP HOUSE [R] *Wilmington, NC*

PORT O' CALL [R] *Kill Devil Hills (Outer Banks), NC*

POSITANO [R] *Wilmington, DE*

POWERHOUSE RESTAURANT [R] *White Haven, PA*

PRIMANTI BROS [R] *Pittsburgh, PA*

PRIME RIB, *DC*
   [R] *Washington*

PRIME RIB, *MD*
   [R] *Baltimore*

PRIME RIB HOUSE [R] *Williamsburg, VA*

PRIMI PIATTI, *DC*
   [R] *Washington*

PRIMI PIATTI, *VA*
   [R] *Tysons Corner*

PRIMO [R] *Hilton Head Island, SC*

PRINCE MICHEL RESTAURANT [R] *Culpeper, VA*

PROVENCE, *DC*
   [R] *Washington*

PROVENCE, *PA*
   [R] *Philadelphia*

PUFFERBELLY [R] *Erie, PA*

PUFFINS [R] *Pikesville, MD*

PUGLIONI'S [R] *Morgantown, WV*

PULCINELLA [R] *McLean, VA*

PUMP HOUSE INN [R] *Canadensis, PA*

PUNGO GRILL [R] *Virginia Beach, VA*

PUSSER'S LANDING [R] *Wrightsville Beach, NC*

QUAIL RIDGE INN [R] *Frederick, MD*

QUAKER STEAK & LUBE [R] *Sharon, PA*

QUEEN ANNE'S REVENGE [R] *Manteo, NC*

QUEEN BEE [R] *Arlington County (National Airport Area), VA*

R T'S RESTAURANT [R] *Alexandria, VA*

RAINBOW DELI & CAFE [R] *Cornelius, NC*

RAKU-AN ASIAN DINER, *DC*
[R] *Washington*
RAKU-AN ASIAN DINER, *MD*
[R] *Bethesda*
RAM'S HEAD INN [R] *Atlantic City, NJ*
RANCH HOUSE [R] *Charlotte, NC*
RANGOON BURMESE RESTAURANT
[R] *Philadelphia, PA*
RAVEN & THE PEACH, THE [R] *Red Bank, NJ*
REBELS & REDCOATS TAVERN [R]
Huntington, WV
RED HORSE STEAK HOUSE [R]
Hagerstown, MD
RED HOT & BLUE, *MD*
[R] *Rockville*
RED HOT & BLUE, *NJ*
[R] *Cherry Hill*
RED HOT & BLUE, *VA*
[R] *Arlington County (National Airport Area)*
RED SAGE RESTAURANT [R]
Washington, DC
RED TOMATO CAFE [R] *Bethesda, MD*
REDWOOD FAMILY RESTAURANT [R]
Lexington, VA
REGENCY DINING ROOM [R]
Williamsburg, VA
REGGIE'S BRITISH PUB [R] *Norfolk, VA*
REILLEY'S [R] *Hilton Head Island, SC*
RENATO ITALIAN RESTAURANT [R]
Fredericksburg, VA
RENAULT WINERY [R] *Atlantic City, NJ*
RESTAURANT, THE [R] *Tysons Corner, VA*
RESTAURANT MILLION [R] *Charleston, SC*
RESTAURANT SCHOOL, THE [R]
Philadelphia, PA
RESTAURANT SERENADE [R]
Chatham, NJ
REYNOLD'S TAVERN [R] *Annapolis, MD*
RIALTO [R] *Wrightsville Beach, NC*
RICCIUTI'S [R] *Rockville, MD*
RICE PADDY [R] *Georgetown, SC*
RICHARDSON'S [R] *Hagerstown, MD*
RICO'S [R] *Pittsburgh, PA*
RISTORANTE ALBERTO [R]
Philadelphia, PA
RISTORANTE DIVINO [R] *Columbia, SC*
RISTORANTE PANORAMA [R]
Philadelphia, PA
RIVER CITY DINER [R] *Philadelphia, PA*
RIVER FOREST MANOR [R]
Washington, NC
RIVER ROOM [R] *Georgetown, SC*
RIVER'S INN [R] *Yorktown, VA*
RIVERWOOD [R] *Blowing Rock, NC*
ROCCO CAPRICCIO [R] *Baltimore, MD*
ROCK BOTTOM BREWERY [R]
Bethesda, MD

ROCOCO [R] *Philadelphia, PA*
ROCOCO'S [R] *Charlottesville, VA*
ROD'S 1890S RESTAURANT [R]
Morristown, NJ
ROLLER'S [R] *Philadelphia, PA*
ROMANISSIMO [R] *Rutherford, NJ*
ROOF TERRACE [R] *Washington, DC*
ROSA LINDA'S CAFE [R] *Myrtle Beach, SC*
ROTHWELL'S GRILLE [R] *Towson, MD*
ROUGE 99 [R] *Philadelphia, PA*
ROWE'S FAMILY RESTAURANT [R]
Staunton, VA
ROY'S PLACE [R] *Gaithersburg, MD*
RT'S SEAFOOD KITCHEN [R] *Arlington County (National Airport Area), VA*
RUBY LOUNGE [R] *Baltimore, MD*
RUCKERJOHN'S [R] *Wilmington, NC*
RUDEE'S [R] *Virginia Beach, VA*
RUDY'S 2900 [R] *Westminster, MD*
RUSSELL'S 96 WEST [R] *Doylestown (Bucks Co), PA*
RUSSIA HOUSE [R] *Dulles Intl Airport Area, VA*
RUSTY NAIL [R] *New Brunswick, NJ*
RUSTY NAIL BAR AND GRILL [R] *Cape May, NJ*
RUSTY RUDDER [R] *Rehoboth Beach, DE*
RUSTY SCUPPER [R] *Princeton, NJ*
RUTH'S CHRIS STEAK HOUSE, *MD*
[R] *Baltimore*
RUTH'S CHRIS STEAK HOUSE, *VA*
[R] *Richmond*
RUTH'S CHRIS STEAKHOUSE [R]
Bethesda, MD
RYAN'S STEAK CHOPS & SEAFOOD
[R] *Winston-Salem, NC*
RYLAND INN [R] *Somerville, NJ*
SABER ROOM [R] *Wilkes-Barre, PA*
SACHIKO'S [R] *Lynchburg, VA*
SAIGON GOURMET [R] *Washington, DC*
SAIGONNAIS [R] *Washington, DC*
SALOON, THE [R] *Philadelphia, PA*
SAM & HARRY'S [R] *Washington, DC*
SAM MILLER'S WAREHOUSE
RESTAURANT [R] *Richmond, VA*
SAM SNEAD'S TAVERN [R] *Hot Springs, VA*
SAMMY & NICK'S [R] *Hampton, VA*
SAMUELS [R] *King of Prussia, PA*
SAN ANTONIO SAM'S [R] *Virginia Beach, VA*
SAN CARLO'S [R] *York, PA*
SANDFIDDLER SEAFOOD
RESTAURANT [R] *Southport, NC*
SANDPIPER [R] *Spring Lake, NJ*
SANITARY FISH MARKET [R]
Morehead City, NC
SANTA FE CAFE [R] *College Park, MD*
SANTA FE EAST [R] *Alexandria, VA*
SARACEN RESTAURANT [R]
Charleston, SC

SASSAFRAS [R] *Philadelphia, PA*
SCALE O' DE WHALE [R] *Portsmouth, VA*
SCALZO ITALIAN RESTAURANT [R]
New Bern, NC
SCANNICCHIO'S [R] *Atlantic City, NJ*
SCATTON'S [R] *Hazleton, PA*
SCHAEFER'S CANAL HOUSE [R]
Elkton, MD
SCHNITZELHOUSE [R] *Charlottesville, VA*
SCOTLAND YARD [R] *Alexandria, VA*
SCOTT'S FISH MARKET [R] *Hilton Head Island, SC*
SEA CAPTAIN'S HOUSE [R] *Myrtle Beach, SC*
SEA CATCH [R] *Washington, DC*
SEAPORT INN [R] *Alexandria, VA*
SEASON'S CAFE [R] *Williamsburg, VA*
SEASONS [R] *Washington, DC*
SEAWELL'S ORDINARY RESTAURANT
[R] *Gloucester, VA*
SECRET GARDEN BEEWON [R] *Falls Church, VA*
SEQUOIA [R] *Washington, DC*
SERBIAN CROWN RESTAURANT [R]
McLean, VA
SERMET'S CORNER [R] *Charleston, SC*
SERRANO [R] *Philadelphia, PA*
SETTLERS INN, THE [R] *Hawley, PA*
SEVEN OAKS [R] *Greenville, SC*
SEVEN SEAS [R] *Rockville, MD*
SEVEN STARS INN [R] *Valley Forge National Historical Park, PA*
SEVENTH STREET GRILLE [R]
Pittsburgh, PA
SHADOWBROOK [R] *Red Bank, NJ*
SHANGHAI, *NC*
[R] *Durham*
SHANGHAI, *VA*
[R] *Salem*
SHENANIGAN'S [R] *Myrtle Beach, SC*
SHIELDS TAVERN [R] *Williamsburg, VA*
SHIP'S CABIN [R] *Norfolk, VA*
SIAM ASIAN BISTRO [R] *Dulles Intl Airport Area, VA*
SIDESTREETS [R] *Ellicott City, MD*
SIENNA [R] *Wilmington, DE*
SIGGIE'S L'AUBERGE [R] *Philadelphia, PA*
SIGN OF THE SORREL HORSE [R]
Doylestown (Bucks Co), PA
SILK PURSE & SOW'S EAR [R]
Wilmington, DE
SILVER DINER, *MD*
[R] *Rockville*
SILVER DINER, *VA*
[R] *Arlington County (National Airport Area)*
SILVER TREE HARBOR SEAFOOD
BAR [R] *Oakland (Garrett Co), MD*
SIMPSON'S [R] *Raleigh, NC*

SINBAD RESTAURANT [R] *Hendersonville, NC*

SINBAD'S [R] *Charleston, WV*

SIR WALTER RALEIGH [R] *Gaithersburg, MD*

SIR WALTER RALEIGH INN [R] *Falls Church, VA*

SIRI'S THAI FRENCH CUISINE [R] *Cherry Hill, NJ*

SITTING DUCK PUB [R] *McLean, VA*

SKILLIGALEE [R] *Richmond, VA*

SLIGHTLY NORTH OF BROAD [R] *Charleston, SC*

SLIGHTLY UP THE CREEK [R] *Charleston, SC*

SMOKEY PIG [R] *Ashland, VA*

SOBA LOUNGE [R] *Pittsburgh, PA*

SONOMA [R] *Philadelphia, PA*

SONOMA GRILL [R] *Rutherford, NJ*

SOSTANZA [R] *Washington, DC*

SOUTH AUSTIN GRILL [R] *Alexandria, VA*

SOUTH STREET DINER [R] *Philadelphia, PA*

SPIKE & CHARLIE'S [R] *Baltimore, MD*

SPOTTED HOG [R] *New Hope (Bucks Co), PA*

SPRING HOUSE [R] *Woodstock, VA*

SQUID'S [R] *Chapel Hill, NC*

SQUIRE'S PUB, *NC*
[R] *Fayetteville*, [R] *Southern Pines*

ST MICHAELS CRAB HOUSE [R] *St Michaels, MD*

STAGE HOUSE INN [R] *Scotch Plains, NJ*

STAGE LEFT: AN AMERICAN CAFE [R] *New Brunswick, NJ*

STALEY'S CHARCOAL STEAK HOUSE [R] *Winston-Salem, NC*

STAX'S PEPPERMILL [R] *Greenville, SC*

STAZI MILANO [R] *Jenkintown, PA*

STEAK & ALE [R] *Charleston, WV*

STEAMERS SEAFOOD [R] *Chincoteague, VA*

STEVE COOKIE'S BY THE BAY [R] *Atlantic City, NJ*

STONEBAR INN [R] *Stroudsburg, PA*

STONEHENGE [R] *Gettysburg, PA*

STONY HILL INN [R] *Hackensack, NJ*

STRIPED BASS [R] *Philadelphia, PA*

SUN PORCH [R] *Uniontown, PA*

SUNNYBROOK INN [R] *Roanoke, VA*

SUNSET DOCK [R] *Atlantic City, NJ*

SUPPER AT STACKS [R] *Charleston, SC*

SURF N'TURF [R] *Johnstown, PA*

SUSANNA FOO [R] *Philadelphia, PA*

SUSHI KO [R] *Washington, DC*

SUSHI TWO [R] *Pittsburgh, PA*

SWANN CAFE [R] *Philadelphia, PA*

SWANN LOUNGE [R] *Philadelphia, PA*

SWEETWATER TAVERN [R] *Dulles Intl Airport Area, VA*

SYDNEY'S SIDE STREET [R] *Rehoboth Beach, DE*

SZECHWAN GOURMET [R] *New Brunswick, NJ*

T.C. TROTTERS [R] *Lynchburg, VA*

TABERNA DEL ALABARDERO [R] *Washington, DC*

TABOO [R] *Chesapeake, VA*

TACHIBANA [R] *McLean, VA*

TAHOE SOUTH [R] *Greenville, SC*

TAM'S TAVERN [R] *Rock Hill, SC*

TAMBELLINI'S [R] *Pittsburgh, PA*

TANDOM'S PINE TREE INN [R] *Virginia Beach, VA*

TANGLEWOOD ORDINARY RESTAURANT [R] *Richmond, VA*

TAQUET [R] *King of Prussia, PA*

TARA THAI, *MD*
[R] *Bethesda*

TARA THAI, *VA*
[R] *Tysons Corner*

TASTE OF SAIGON [R] *Rockville, MD*

TAURASO'S [R] *Frederick, MD*

TAVERN, THE, *NJ*
[R] *Toms River*

TAVERN, THE, *PA*
[R] *West Middlesex*

TAVERN, THE, *VA*
[R] *Abingdon*

TAVERN BY THE LAKE [R] *Mount Pocono, PA*

TAVERN RESTAURANT [R] *State College, PA*

TAVERN ROOM, THE [R] *White Sulphur Springs, WV*

TAVERNA CRETEKOU [R] *Alexandria, VA*

TAVOLA TOSCANA [R] *Wilmington, DE*

TEL-AVIV CAFE [R] *Bethesda, MD*

TEMPO RESTAURANT [R] *Alexandria, VA*

TERESA'S [R] *New Brunswick, NJ*

TERRACE [R] *Greenville, SC*

TERRACE RESTAURANT [R] *Kennett Square, PA*

TERRACE ROOM [R] *Pittsburgh, PA*

TERSIGUEL'S [R] *Ellicott City, MD*

TESAURO'S [R] *Spring Lake, NJ*

TESSARO'S [R] *Pittsburgh, PA*

THAI HUT RESTAURANT [R] *Alexandria, VA*

THAI KINGDOM [R] *Washington, DC*

THAI PLACE, *MD*
[R] *Bethesda*

THAI PLACE, *PA*
[R] *Pittsburgh*

THAT SEAFOOD PLACE [R] *Williamsburg, VA*

THAT'S AMORE, *MD*
[R] *Rockville*, [R] *Towson*

THAT'S AMORE, *VA*
[R] *Tysons Corner*

THOMAS ENGLAND HOUSE [R] *Smyrna, DE*

THYME SQUARE [R] *Bethesda, MD*

TIDES [R] *Buxton (Outer Banks), NC*

TIJUANA TAXI [R] *Rehoboth Beach, DE*

TIMBERS RESTAURANT & LOUNGE [R] *Mercer, PA*

TIN ANGEL [R] *Pittsburgh, PA*

TIO PEPE [R] *Baltimore, MD*

TIVOLI RESTAURANT [R] *Arlington County (National Airport Area), VA*

TOBACCO COMPANY [R] *Richmond, VA*

TODD JURICH'S BISTRO [R] *Norfolk, VA*

TOKYO TEAHOUSE [R] *Mount Pocono, PA*

TOM SARRIS' ORLEANS HOUSE [R] *Arlington County (National Airport Area), VA*

TOM & TERRY'S [R] *Fenwick Island, DE*

TOM'S KITCHEN [R] *Hazleton, PA*

TOMBS [R] *Washington, DC*

TONY CHENG'S MONGOLIAN BARBECUE [R] *Washington, DC*

TONY & JOE'S SEAFOOD PLACE [R] *Washington, DC*

TONY'S [R] *Myrtle Beach, SC*

TOP OF THE MARQ [R] *Cape May, NJ*

TOP OF THE TRIANGLE [R] *Pittsburgh, PA*

TORTILLA FACTORY [R] *Dulles Intl Airport Area, VA*

TOSCANA CUCINA RUSTICA [R] *Philadelphia, PA*

TOWN AND COUNTRY GRILLE [R] *King of Prussia, PA*

TOWNHOUSE [R] *Charlotte, NC*

TRAGARA [R] *Bethesda, MD*

TRAK'S GREEK & ITALIAN RESTAURANT [R] *Richmond, VA*

TREATY OF PARIS RESTAURANT [R] *Annapolis, MD*

TREETOPS [R] *Philadelphia, PA*

TRIO CAFE [R] *Fayetteville, NC*

TUCKER'S [R] *Long Beach Island, NJ*

TWIG'S [R] *Blowing Rock, NC*

TWO QUAIL [R] *Washington, DC*

UMBRIA RESTAURANT [R] *Philadelphia, PA*

UNCLE LOUIE'S [R] *Norfolk, VA*

UNION CANAL HOUSE [R] *Hershey, PA*

UNION HOTEL [R] *Flemington, NJ*

UNION STREET PUBLIC HOUSE [R] *Alexandria, VA*

UPPER DECK [R] *Pocomoke City, MD*

VALENTINO'S [R] *Montvale, NJ*

VANG'S GARDEN [R] *Philadelphia, PA*

VEGA GRILL [R] *Philadelphia, PA*

VELLEGGIA'S [R] *Baltimore, MD*

VERMONT FLATBREAD CO [R] *Pittsburgh, PA*

VESPUCCI'S [R] *Annapolis, MD*

VETRI [R] *Philadelphia, PA*

VIAGGIO'S [R] *Pittsburgh, PA*

VICINO RESTAURANTE ITALIANO [R] *Silver Spring, MD*
VICKERS [R] *Downingtown, PA*
VICTORIAN MANOR [R] *State College, PA*
VIDALIA [R] *Washington, DC*
VILLA D'ESTE [R] *Alexandria, VA*
VILLA FRANCO [R] *Washington, DC*
VILLA STRAFFORD [R] *King of Prussia, PA*
VILLAGE BISTRO [R] *Arlington County (National Airport Area), VA*
VILLAGE INN [R] *Dover, DE*
VINCE PERONE'S [R] *Greenville, SC*
VINCENTE'S [R] *Wilmington, DE*
VINEYARD RESTAURANT [R] *Winston-Salem, NC*
VINNIE'S [R] *Wilmington, NC*
VINNIE'S STEAKHOUSE & TAVERN [R] *Raleigh, NC*
VINTAGE HOUSE RESTAURANT [R] *Hickory, NC*
VINTAGE WINE BISTRO [R] *Washington, DC*
VINYARD RESTAURANT [R] *Bristol, VA*
VISTA BREWING & BISTRO [R] *Columbia, SC*
VITO'S RISTORANTE & PIZZERIA [R] *Southern Pines, NC*
WARNER'S GERMAN RESTAURANT [R] *Cumberland, MD*

WASHINGTON HOUSE [R] *Quakertown (Bucks Co), PA*
WASHINGTON HOUSE RESTAURANT [R] *Lancaster, PA*
WASHINGTON INN [R] *Cape May, NJ*
WATER STREET [R] *Wilmington, NC*
WATER STREET EXCHANGE [R] *Baltimore, MD*
WATERFRONT HOTEL [R] *Baltimore, MD*
WATERMAN'S [R] *Virginia Beach, VA*
WATERMAN'S CRAB HOUSE [R] *Chesapeake Bay Bridge Area, MD*
WATERS EDGE RESTAURANT [R] *Cape May, NJ*
WATERWHEEL RESTAURANT [R] *Warm Springs, VA*
WATERWORKS CAFE [R] *Wilmington, DE*
WAYNE'S BAR-B-QUE [R] *Baltimore, MD*
WAYSIDE INN [R] *Smyrna, DE*
WELLINGTON'S [R] *Nitro, WV*
WHALING COMPANY [R] *Williamsburg, VA*
WHARF RESTAURANT [R] *Alexandria, VA*
WHITE DOG CAFE [R] *Philadelphia, PA*
WHITLEY'S BARBECUE [R] *Ahoskie, NC*
WILD MUSHROOM [R] *Baltimore, MD*

WILD ONION [R] *King of Prussia, PA*
WILD TURTLE, THE [R] *Chapel Hill, NC*
WILKINSON'S TAVERN [R] *Strasburg, VA*
WILLARD ROOM [R] *Washington, DC*
WILLIAM PENN INN [R] *Norristown, PA*
WILLSON-WALKER HOUSE [R] *Lexington, VA*
WINDMILL EUROPEAN GRILL [R] *Asheville, NC*
WINDMILL POINT RESTAURANT [R] *Nags Head (Outer Banks), NC*
WINDOWS [R] *St Michaels, MD*
WINFIELD'S [R] *Dulles Intl Airport Area, VA*
WINSTON'S GRILLE [R] *Raleigh, NC*
WOO LAE OAK [R] *Arlington County (National Airport Area), VA*
WOODEN ANGEL [R] *Beaver Falls, PA*
WU'S GARDEN [R] *Tysons Corner, VA*
WURZBURG HAUS [R] *Rockville, MD*
YELLOW BRICK BANK & LITTLE INN [R] *Shepherdstown, WV*
YEN CHING [R] *Richmond, VA*
YORK INN [R] *Cockeysville, MD*
YORKSHIRE STEAK & SEAFOOD HOUSE [R] *WILLIAMSBURG, VA*
ZED'S ETHIOPIAN [R] *Washington, DC*
ZEVELY HOUSE [R] *Winston-Salem, NC*
ZOCALO [R] *Philadelphia, PA*
ZUKI MOON [R] *Washington, DC*

Appendix B

Lodging List

Establishment names are listed in alphabetical order followed by a symbol identifying their classification, and then city and state. Establishments affiliated with a chain appear alphabetically under their chain name, followed by the state and city. The symbols for classification are: [H] for hotels; [I] for inns; [M] for motels; [L] for lodges; [MH] for motor hotels; [RO] for resorts, guest ranches and cottage colonies.

1740 HOUSE [I] *New Hope (Bucks Co), PA*
1880'S MADISON HOUSE [I] *Lynchburg, VA*
200 SOUTH STREET INN [I] *Charlottesville, VA*
AARON BURR HOUSE [I] *New Hope (Bucks Co), PA*
ABBEY BED & BREAKFAST, THE [I] *Cape May, NJ*
ABBEY GREEN MOTOR LODGE [M] *West Chester, PA*
ABERCROMBIE BADGER BED & BREAKFAST [I] *Baltimore, MD*
ABIGAIL ADAMS BED & BREAKFAST [I] *Cape May, NJ*
ABINGDON MANOR [I] *Dillon, SC*
ADAM'S MARK, *NC*
   [H] *Charlotte,* [H] *Winston-Salem*
ADAM'S MARK, *PA*
   [H] *Philadelphia*
ADAM'S MARK, *SC*
   [H] *Columbia*
ADAMS CAIRN BRAE BED & BREAKFAST [I] *Asheville, NC*
ADAMS OCEANFRONT VILLAS [M] *Rehoboth Beach, DE*
ADDEY'S INN OF HERSHEY [M] *Hershey, PA*
ADDISON MOTEL [M] *Wilkesboro, NC*
ADMIRAL FELL INN [I] *Baltimore, MD*
ADMIRAL MOTEL [M] *Rehoboth Beach, DE*
ADVENTURE MOTOR INN [MH] *Wildwood & Wildwood Crest, NJ*
AERIE BED & BREAKFAST [I] *New Bern, NC*
AHOSKIE INN [MH] *Ahoskie, NC*
AIRPORT TOWER HOTEL [H] *Philadelphia, PA*
ALBEMARLE INN [I] *Asheville, NC*
ALDEN HOUSE BED & BREAKFAST [I] *Lancaster, PA*

ALEXANDER WITHROW INN [I] *Lexington, VA*
ALEXANDRA'S INN [I] *Georgetown, SC*
ALLENBERRY RESORT INN [RO] *Carlisle, PA*
ALLENWOOD MOTEL [M] *Allentown, PA*
ALPINE INN [RO] *Little Switzerland, NC*
ALPINE MOTEL [M] *Abingdon, VA*
ALPINE VILLAGE INN [M] *Blowing Rock, NC*
ALPINE VILLAGE [M] *Oakland (Garrett Co), MD*
AMBER STREET INN BED & BREAKFAST [I] *Long Beach Island, NJ*
AMERICAN COURT MOTEL [M] *Asheville, NC*
AMERICAN INN OF BETHESDA [MH] *Bethesda, MD*
AMERISUITES, *NC*
   [MH] *Greensboro*
AMERISUITES, *SC*
   [MH] *Columbia*
AMERISUITES, *VA*
   [M] *Richmond*
ANCHORAGE INN, *NC*
   [M] *Ocracoke (Outer Banks)*
ANCHORAGE INN, *SC*
   [I] *Charleston*
ANGEL OF THE SEA [I] *Cape May, NJ*
ANGLER'S MOTEL [M] *Lewes, DE*
ANTRIM 1844 INC [I] *Emmitsburg, MD*
APPALACHIAN TRAIL INN [M] *Carlisle, PA*
APPLE VALLEY INN [I] *Vernon, NJ*
APPLEBUTTER INN [I] *Butler, PA*
APPLETREE BED & BREAKFAST [I] *Pittsburgh, PA*
APPLEWOOD MANOR INN BED & BREAKFAST [I] *Asheville, NC*
AQUARIUS MOTOR INN [M] *Wildwood & Wildwood Crest, NJ*

ARCHER'S MOUNTAIN INN [I] *Banner Elk, NC*
ARMADA BY-THE-SEA [M] *Wildwood & Wildwood Crest, NJ*
ARROWHEAD INN BED & BREAKFAST [I] *Durham, NC*
ASHBY 1663 [I] *Easton, MD*
ASHBY INN [I] *Winchester, VA*
ASHLEY INN BED & BREAKFAST [I] *Charleston, SC*
ASHLING COTTAGE [I] *Spring Lake, NJ*
ASTRONAUT MOTEL [M] *Wildwood & Wildwood Crest, NJ*
ATHERTON HOTEL [H] *State College, PA*
ATLANTIC BUDGET INN [M] *Rehoboth Beach, DE*
ATLANTIC VIEW MOTEL [M] *Rehoboth Beach, DE*
ATTACHE MOTEL [M] *Wildwood & Wildwood Crest, NJ*
AUGUSTUS T ZEVELY INN [I] *Winston-Salem, NC*
AUSTRALIAN WALKABOUT INN BED & BREAKFAST [I] *Lancaster, PA*
AUTOPORT MOTEL & RESTAURANT [M] *State College, PA*
AVALON GOLDEN INN [MH] *Stone Harbor, NJ*
AVONDALE BY THE SEA [M] *Cape May, NJ*
BAILIWICK INN [I] *Fairfax, VA*
BALADERRY INN [I] *Gettysburg, PA*
BALLY'S PARK PLACE CASINO HOTEL & TOWER [H] *Atlantic City, NJ*
BALSAM MOUNTAIN INN [I] *Waynesville, NC*
BARKSDALE HOUSE INN [I] *Charleston, SC*
BARLEY SHEAF FARM BED & BREAKFAST [I] *New Hope (Bucks Co), PA*

BATTERY CARRIAGE HOUSE INN [I] *Charleston, SC*
BATTLEFIELD BED & BREAKFAST INN [I] *Gettysburg, PA*
BAVARIAN INN & LODGE [I] *Shepherdstown, WV*
BAY AVENUE SUNSET BED & BREAKFAST [I] *Cape Charles, VA*
BAY HEAD GABLES [I] *Spring Lake, NJ*
BAY RESORT MOTEL [M] *Rehoboth Beach, DE*
BAYBERRY INN BED & BREAKFAST [I] *Somerset, PA*
BAYMONT INN [M] *Harrisburg, PA*
BEACH CLUB HOTEL [M] *Ocean City, NJ*
BEACH COLONY RESORT [H] *Myrtle Beach, SC*
BEACH COVE RESORT [H] *Myrtle Beach, SC*
BEACH HAVEN MOTEL [M] *Kill Devil Hills (Outer Banks), NC*
BEACH VIEW MOTEL [M] *Rehoboth Beach, DE*
BEACON MOTEL [M] *Lewes, DE*
BEACON MOTOR LODGE [M] *Nags Head (Outer Banks), NC*
BEAUFORT HOUSE [I] *Asheville, NC*
BEAUFORT INN & RESTAURANT [I] *Beaufort, SC*
BEAVER CREEK HOUSE BED & BREAKFAST [I] *Hagerstown, MD*
BEAVER VALLEY MOTEL [M] *Beaver Falls, PA*
BED & BREAKFAST CENTER CITY [I] *Philadelphia, PA*
BED & BREAKFAST INN OF THE PRINCESS [I] *Uniontown, PA*
BED & BREAKFAST OF SUMTER [I] *Sumter, SC*
BEECHMONT BED & BREAKFAST INN [I] *Hanover, PA*
BEL AIRE HOTEL COMPLEX [MH] *Erie, PA*
BELLE GRAE INN [I] *Staunton, VA*
BELMAR MOTOR LODGE [M] *Spring Lake, NJ*
BELMONT INN [I] *Greenwood, SC*
BERKELEY HOTEL [H] *Richmond, VA*
BERKLEY CENTER COUNTRY INN [I] *Ocracoke (Outer Banks), NC*
BERLIN ATLANTIC HOTEL [I] *Ocean City, MD*
BERNARDS INN [I] *Bernardsville, NJ*
BEST INN [MH] *Baltimore, MD*
BEST INNS OF AMERICA [M] *Asheville, NC*
BEST WESTERN, *DE*
[M] *Newark*, [M] *Rehoboth Beach*, [M] *Wilmington*
BEST WESTERN, *MD*
[MH] *Baltimore*, [MH] *Baltimore/Washington Intl Airport Area*, [M] *Cumberland*, [MH] *Hagerstown*, [M] *La Plata*, [M] *Ocean City*, [MH] *St Michaels*

BEST WESTERN, *NC*
[MH] *Asheville*, [M] *Chapel Hill*, [MH] *Charlotte*, [M] *Cherokee*, [M] *Cornelius*, [M] *Dunn*, [M] *Durham*, [M] *Goldsboro*, [M] *Jefferson*, [MH] *Kill Devil Hills (Outer Banks)*, [M] *Maggie Valley*, [M] *Morehead City*, [M] *Wilson*
BEST WESTERN, *NJ*
[M] *Atlantic City*, [M] *Hackensack*, [M] *Lakewood*, [M] *Morristown*, [M] *Scotch Plains*, [MH] *Wayne*
BEST WESTERN, *PA*
[M] *Bedford*, [M] *Breezewood*, [M] *Carlisle*, [MH] *Downington*, [M] *Du Bois*, [H] *Gettysburg*, [M] *Harrisburg*, [M] *Hazleton*, [M] *Hershey*, [M] *Indiana*, [M] *King of Prussia*, [MH] *Lancaster*, [M] *Lewisburg*, [M] *Milford*, [M] *Philadelphia*, [MH] *Philadelphia*, [MH] *Pittsburgh*, [M] *Reading*, [M] *Stroudsburg*, [H] *West Chester*, [H] *Wilkes Barre*, [H] *Wilkes-Barre*, [M] *York*
BEST WESTERN, *SC*
[M] *Beaufort*, [M] *Charleston*, [MH] *Charleston*, [M] *Hilton Head Island*, [MH] *Myrtle Beach*, [M] *Newberry*, [M] *Santee*
BEST WESTERN, *VA*
[M] *Alexandria*, [H] *Arlington County (National Airport Area)*, [M] *Ashland*, [M] *Basye*, [M] *Blacksburg*, [M] *Charlottesville*, [MH] *Charlottesville*, [M] *Covington*, [M] *Emporia*, [M] *Fredericksburg*, [M] *Lexington*, [M] *Luray*, [M] *Lynchburg*, [M] *Manassas*, [M] *Marion*, [M] *Martinsville*, [M] *Norfolk*, [M] *Radford*, [M] *South Hill*, [M] *Staunton*, [M] *Winchester*
BEST WESTERN, *WV*
[M] *Davis*, [M] *Elkins*, [M] *Huntington*, [M] *Nitro*, [M] *Ripley*, [M] *Summersville*, [H] *Wheeling*
BEST WESTERN GRAND VICTORIA INN [MH] *Towanda, PA*
BETHANY ARMS [M] *Bethany Beach, DE*
BICENTENNIAL MOTEL [M] *Buckhannon, WV*
BIG LYNN LODGE [M] *Little Switzerland, NC*
BIG MEADOWS LODGE [M] *Shenandoah National Park, VA*
BILTMORE HOTEL [H] *Greensboro, NC*
BIRCHWOOD MOTEL [M] *Chincoteague, VA*
BIRD-IN-HAND FAMILY INN [M] *Bird-in-Hand, PA*
BISHOPS HOUSE [I] *Easton, MD*
BLACK HORSE LODGE & SUITES [M] *Denver/Adamstown, PA*
BLACK WALNUT BED & BREAKFAST COUNTRY INN [I] *Milford, PA*
BLACK WALNUT POINT INN INC [I] *St Michaels, MD*

BLACKWATER LODGE [RO] *Davis, WV*
BLEU ROCK INN [I] *Washington, VA*
BLOCKADE RUNNER RESORT & HOTEL [MH] *Wrightsville Beach, NC*
BLOWING ROCK INN [M] *Blowing Rock, NC*
BLUE HERRON MOTEL [M] *Nags Head (Outer Banks), NC*
BLUFF SHOAL MOTEL [M] *Ocracoke (Outer Banks), NC*
BOARDWALK INN [H] *Charleston, SC*
BOARDWALK PLAZA HOTEL [H] *Rehoboth Beach, DE*
BOARS HEAD INN [RO] *Charlottesville, VA*
BOULDIN HOUSE BED & BREAKFAST [I] *High Point, NC*
BOULEVARD BED & BREAKFAST, THE [I] *Wilmington, DE*
BOXWOOD INN BED & BREAKFAST [I] *Wytheville, VA*
BOYETTE HOUSE [M] *Ocracoke (Outer Banks), NC*
BRAFFERTON INN [I] *Gettysburg, PA*
BRANDYWINE RIVER HOTEL [I] *Kennett Square, PA*
BRANDYWINE SUITES HOTEL [H] *Wilmington, DE*
BREAKERS HOTEL [H] *Spring Lake, NJ*
BREAKERS RESORT HOTEL, THE [H] *Myrtle Beach, SC*
BREAKS INTERSTATE [M] *Breaks Interstate Park, VA*
BRIER INN [M] *Lewisburg, WV*
BRIGHTON SUITES HOTELS [MH] *Rehoboth Beach, DE*
BRISTOL PLAZA MOTOR INN [MH] *Wildwood & Wildwood Crest, NJ*
BROOKSHIRE INNER HARBOR SUITE HOTEL [H] *Baltimore, MD*
BROOKSTOWN INN [I] *Winston-Salem, NC*
BROOLVIEW MANOR [I] *Canadensis, PA*
BROWNESTONE HOTEL & CONFERENCE [H] *Raleigh, NC*
BROWNS HISTORIC HOME BED & BREAKFAST [I] *Salem, NJ*
BRUNSWICK HOTEL [H] *Lancaster, PA*
BRUSTMAN HOUSE BED & BREAKFAST [I] *Myrtle Beach, SC*
BUCKHORN INN [I] *Staunton, VA*
BUDGET HOST, *PA*
[M] *Bloomsburg*, [M] *Somerset*, [M] *York*
BUDGET HOST, *VA*
[M] *Bristol*, [M] *Woodstock*
BUDGET HOST, *WV*
[M] *Lewisburg*
BUDGET HOST INN [M] *Bryson City, NC*
BUDGET INN, *DE*
[M] *Dover*, [M] *Fenwick Island*

BUDGET INN, *VA*
[M] *New Market*
BUDGET MOTEL [M] *Stroudsburg, PA*
BUDGETEL INN [M] *Columbia, SC*
CABINS AT BROOKSIDE [M] *Luray, VA*
CACAPON STATE PARK [RO] *Berkeley Springs, WV*
CAESARS ATLANTIC CITY [H] *Atlantic City, NJ*
CAESARS PARADISE STREAM [RO] *Mount Pocono, PA*
CAESARS POCONO PALACE RESORT [RO] *Stroudsburg, PA*
CAESARS POCONO RESORTS [RO] *Tannersville, PA*
CAMERON ESTATE INN [I] *Lancaster, PA*
CANAAN VALLEY RESORT & CONFERENCE CENTER [RO] *Davis, WV*
CANDLELIGHT INN [I] *Wildwood & Wildwood Crest, NJ*
CANNONBORO INN BED & BREAKFAST [I] *Charleston, SC*
CANTERBURY, THE [H] *Washington, DC*
CANYON MOTEL [M] *Wellsboro, PA*
CAPE COD INN [M] *Wildwood & Wildwood Crest, NJ*
CAPE HATTERAS MOTEL [M] *Buxton (Outer Banks), NC*
CAPITOL HILL SUITES [H] *Washington, DC*
CAPTAINS QUARTERS INN [I] *Edenton, NC*
CARAVELLE RESORT HOTEL [H] *Myrtle Beach, SC*
CARDINAL INN [M] *Maggie Valley, NC*
CARIBBEAN MOTEL [M] *Wildwood & Wildwood Crest, NJ*
CARIBBEAN RESORTS & VILLAS [MH] *Myrtle Beach, SC*
CARLETON HOUSE INN [M] *Rocky Mount, NC*
CARMEL COVE BED & BREAKFAST [I] *Oakland (Garrett Co), MD*
CARNEGIE HOUSE [I] *State College, PA*
CAROLINA INN, THE [H] *Chapel Hill, NC*
CARROLL VILLA HOTEL [I] *Cape May, NJ*
CASSINA POINT PLANTATION BED & BREAKFAST [I] *Kiawah Island, SC*
CASTLE IN THE SAND HOTEL [M] *Ocean City, MD*
CATALOOCHEE SKI AREA [RO] *Maggie Valley, NC*
CATHERINES INN [I] *Wilmington, NC*
CATOCTIN INN [I] *Frederick, MD*
CAYMAN SUITES [MH] *Ocean City, MD*
CEDAR CREST [I] *Asheville, NC*
CEDAR GABLES SEASIDE INN [I] *Chincoteague, VA*
CEDARS INN BY THE SEA, THE [I] *Beaufort, NC*

CELIE'S WATERFRONT BED & BREAKFAST [I] *Baltimore, MD*
CENTENNIAL MOTEL [M] *Buckhannon, WV*
CENTRE BRIDGE INN [I] *New Hope (Bucks Co), PA*
CHALET CLUB [I] *Hendersonville, Nc*
CHALET INN [I] *Bryson City, NC*
CHALET SWITZERLAND INN [RO] *Little Switzerland, NC*
CHANNEL BASS INN [I] *Chincoteague, VA*
CHANNEL INN HOTEL [MH] *Washington, DC*
CHARLESTON PLACE [H] *Charleston, SC*
CHATEAU INN [I] *Spring Lake, NJ*
CHESAPEAKE BAY LIGHTHOUSE [I] *Annapolis, MD*
CHESAPEAKE LANDING [I] *Rehoboth Beach, DE*
CHESAPEAKE WOOD DUCK INN [I] *St Michaels, MD*
CHESTER HOUSE [I] *Front Royal, VA*
CHESTERFIELD INN & MOTOR LODGE [M] *Myrtle Beach, SC*
CHETOLA RESORT [RO] *Blowing Rock, NC*
CHIMNEY HILL BED & BREAKFAST [I] *Lambertville, NJ*
CHRISTLEN MOTEL [M] *Baltimore, MD*
CHURCH POINT MANOR HOUSE [I] *Virginia Beach, VA*
CLAIBORNE HOUSE [I] *Roanoke, VA*
CLARIDGE CASINO & HOTEL [H] *Atlantic City, NJ*
CLARION, *DC*
[H] *Washington*
CLARION, *MD*
[H] *Baltimore*
CLARION, *NC*
[MH] *Fayetteville*, [MH] *South Brunswick Islands*
CLARION, *NJ*
[MH] *Edison*
CLARION, *PA*
[M] *Lewistown*, [H] *Pittsburgh Intl Airport Area*, [M] *Reading*
CLARION, *SC*
[M] *Georgetown*
CLARION, *VA*
[MH] *Roanoke*, [H] *Virginia Beach*
CLARION, *WV*
[H] *Morgantown*, [H] *Parkersburg*
CLARION INN & CONVENTION CENTER [M] *Carlisle, PA*
CLAUSSEN'S INN [I] *Columbia, SC*
CLIFF DWELLERS INN [M] *Blowing Rock, NC*
CLIFF PARK INN [I] *Milford, PA*
CLIFTON COUNTRY INN [I] *Charlottesville, VA*
CLUBHOUSE INN [M] *Pittsburgh, PA*
COACHMANS MOTOR INN [M] *Cape May, NJ*

COCONUT MALORIE HOTEL RESORT [H] *Ocean City, MD*
COLLEGE MOTEL [M] *Gettysburg, PA*
COLLINS MOTEL [M] *Sharon, PA*
COLONEL LUDLOW INN [I] *Winston-Salem, NC*
COLONIAL CAPITAL BED & BREAKFAST [I] *Williamsburg, VA*
COLONIAL GARDENS INN [I] *Williamsburg, VA*
COLONIAL HOUSES-HISTORIC LOD [I] *Williamsburg, Va*
COLONIAL INN [M] *Concord (Cabarrus Co), NC*
COLONIAL MOTEL [M] *Gettysburg, PA*
COLONY HOUSE MOTOR LODGE [M] *Roanoke, VA*
COLONY INN [M] *Camden, SC*
COLONY SOUTH HOTEL [H] *Washington, MD*
COLTS NECK INN HOTEL [MH] *Freehold, NJ*
COLUMNS BY THE SEA BED & BREAKFAST [I] *Cape May, NJ*
COMFORT INN, *DE*
[M] *Dover*, [M] *Newark*
COMFORT INN, *MD*
[M] *Annapolis*, [MH] *Baltimore/Washington Intl Airport Area*, [M] *Chesapeake Bay Bridge Area*, [MH] *Chesapeake Bay Bridge Area*, [M] *Cumberland*, [M] *Easton*, [M] *Gaithersburg*, [MH] *Laurel*, [MH] *Ocean City*, [M] *Pikesville*, [M] *Salisbury*, [M] *Westminster*
COMFORT INN, *NC*
[M] *Albemarle*, [M] *Asheville*, [M] *Burlington*, [M] *Buxton (Outer Banks)*, [M] *Charlotte*, [M] *Cherokee*, [M] *Concord (Cabarrus Co)*, [M] *Cornelius*, [M] *Durham*, [M] *Elizabeth City*, [M] *Fayetteville*, [M] *Greensboro*, [M] *Hendersonville*, [M] *Hickory*, [M] *Kill Devil Hills (Outer Banks)*, [M] *Kinston*, [M] *Laurinburg*, [M] *Lumberton*, [M] *Maggie Valley*, [M] *Morehead City*, [M] *Nags Head (Outer Banks)*, [M] *New Bern*, [M] *Pinehurst*, [M] *Raleigh*, [M] *Roanoke Rapids*, [M] *Sanford*, [M] *Smithfield*, [M] *Washington*, [M] *Williamston*, [MH] *Wilmington*, [M] *Wilson*
COMFORT INN, *NJ*
[H] *Atlantic City*, [M] *Spring Lake*
COMFORT INN, *PA*
[M] *Allentown*, [M] *Bethlehem*, [MH] *Doylestown (Bucks Co)*, [M] *Erie*, [M] *Gettysburg*, [M] *Greensburg*, [M] *Harrisburg*, [M] *Johnstown*, [MH] *King of Prussia*, [M] *Mansfield*, [M] *New Castle*, [M] *Philadelphia*, [H] *Philadelphia*, [M] *Pottstown*, [M] *Reading*

COMFORT INN, *SC*
[M] *Clemson*, [M] *Florence*, [M] *Gaffney*, [M] *Greenwood*, [M] *Rock Hill*, [M] *Spartanburg*

COMFORT INN, *VA*
[M] *Abingdon*, [M] *Alexandria*, [M] *Arlington County (National Airport Area)*, [M] *Ashland*, [M] *Blacksburg*, [M] *Bristol*, [MH] *Chesapeake*, [M] *Chincoteague*, [M] *Covington*, [M] *Culpeper*, [M] *Dulles Intl Airport Area*, [M] *Emporia*, [MH] *Fairfax*, [M] *Farmville*, [M] *Fredericksburg*, [M] *Harrisonburg*, [MH] *Lexington*, [MH] *Lynchburg*, [M] *Newport News*, [M] *Norfolk*, [M] *Radford*, [M] *Springfield*, [M] *Staunton*, [M] *Tysons Corner*, [MH] *Virginia Beach*, [M] *Warrenton*, [M] *Waynesboro*, [M] *Winchester*, [M] *Wytheville*

COMFORT INN, *WV*
[M] *Beckley*, [M] *Fairmont*, [M] *Harpers Ferry*, [M] *Martinsburg*, [M] *Morgantown*, [M] *Nitro*, [M] *Princeton*, [M] *Summersville*, [M] *Weston*

COMPASS COVE [MH] *Myrtle Beach, SC*

CONLEY INN [M] *Beaver Falls, PA*

CONLEY RESORT INN [M] *Butler, PA*

COOL WATERS MOTEL [M] *Cherokee, NC*

COOLFONT RESORT [RO] *Berkeley Springs, WV*

CORNER OAK MANOR [I] *Asheville, NC*

COTTAGE, THE [I] *Wrightsville Beach, NC*

COUNTRY INN [I] *Berkeley Springs, WV*

COUNTRY INN TOWN-MOTEL [M] *Franklin (Macon Co), NC*

COUNTRY INN - WHEATON VILLAGE [M] *Millville, NJ*

COUNTRY LIVING INN [M] *Lancaster, PA*

COUNTRY SQUIRE & VINTAGE INN, THE [M] *Warsaw, NC*

COUNTRY SUITES BY CARLSON, *NC*
[M] *Lumberton*

COUNTRY SUITES BY CARLSON, *SC*
[M] *Rock Hill*

COURTYARD BY MARRIOTT, *DC*
[H] *Washington*

COURTYARD BY MARRIOTT, *DE*
[H] *Wilmington*

COURTYARD BY MARRIOTT, *MD*
[M] *Annapolis*, [M] *Baltimore/Washington Intl Airport Area*, [M] *Cockeysville*, [MH] *College Park*, [MH] *Gaithersburg*, [M] *Rockville*, [M] *Silver Spring*

COURTYARD BY MARRIOTT, *NC*
[M] *Charlotte*, [M] *Durham*, [M] *Raleigh*, [MH] *Raleigh*, [M] *Wilmington*, [M] *Winston-Salem*

COURTYARD BY MARRIOTT, *NJ*
[M] *Newark Intl Airport Area*, [M] *Red Bank*

COURTYARD BY MARRIOTT, *PA*
[M] *King of Prussia*, [M] *Willow Grove*

COURTYARD BY MARRIOTT, *SC*
[M] *Columbia*, [M] *Greenville*

COURTYARD BY MARRIOTT, *VA*
[MH] *Alexandria*, [MH] *Arlington County (National Airport Area)*, [H] *Arlington County (National Airport Area)*, [M] *Charlottesville*, [M] *Dulles Intl Airport Area*, [M] *Fairfax*, [M] *Hampton*, [M] *Manassas*, [M] *Richmond*, [M] *Virginia Beach*, [MH] *Williamsburg*

COVE HAVEN HONEYMOON RESORT [RO] *Hawley, PA*

COZY COUNTRY INN THURMONT [M] *Thurmont, MD*

CRABTREE SUMMIT HOTEL [MH] *Raleigh, NC*

CRAIG'S MOTEL [M] *Cherokee, NC*

CRESCENT LODGE INC [I] *Canadensis, PA*

CRIPPEN'S COUNTRY INN [I] *Blowing Rock, NC*

CRISLIP MOTOR LODGE [M] *Grafton, WV*

CROSS CREEK RESORT [RO] *Titusville, PA*

CROSS KEYS MOTOR INN RESTAURANT [M] *Gettysburg, PA*

CROSSED KEYS BED & BREAKFAST [I] *Stanhope, NJ*

CROWNE PLAZA, *NJ*
[H] *Edison*, [H] *Secaucus*

CROWNE PLAZA, *PA*
[H] *Philadelphia*

CROWNE PLAZA, *SC*
[H] *Greenville*, [RO] *Hilton Head Island*

CROWNE PLAZA, *VA*
[H] *Richmond*

CRUSADER OCEAN FRONT RESORT [M] *Wildwood & Wildwood Crest, NJ*

CURRAN HOUSE [I] *Wilmington, NC*

CYPRESS HOUSE B&B [I] *Kill Devil Hills (Outer Banks), NC*

CYPRESS INN, THE [I] *Myrtle Beach, SC*

DARLEY MANOR INN BED & BREAKFAST [I] *Wilmington, DE*

DARLINGS BY THE SEA [I] *Wilmington, NC*

DAVIDSON VILLAGE INN [I] *Cornelius, NC*

DAYS INN, *MD*
[M] *Aberdeen*, [M] *Annapolis*, [M] *Baltimore*, [MH] *Baltimore*, [M] *Baltimore/Washington Intl Airport Area*, [M] *Easton*, [M] *Frederick*, [M] *Hagerstown*, [H] *Towson*, [M] *Waldorf*

DAYS INN, *NC*
[M] *Asheboro*, [M] *Burlington*, [M] *Cherokee*, [M] *Fayetteville*, [M] *Franklin (Macon Co)*, [M] *Goldsboro*, [M] *Greensboro*, [M] *Kill Devil Hills (Outer Banks)*, [M] *Morehead City*, [M] *Raleigh*, [M] *Shelby*, [M] *Washington*, [M] *Wilmington*, [M] *Wilson*, [M] *Winston-Salem*

DAYS INN, *NJ*
[MH] *Atlantic City*, [M] *Bordentown*, [M] *Cherry Hill*, [MH] *Fort Lee*, [M] *Lake Hopatcong*, [MH] *Mount Holly*, [M] *Newark Intl Airport Area*, [M] *Ocean City*, [M] *Princeton*, [M] *Somerville*

DAYS INN, *PA*
[M] *Allentown*, [M] *Brookville*, [M] *Butler*, [M] *Carlisle*, [M] *Chambersburg*, [M] *Clarion*, [M] *Clearfield (Clearfield Co)*, [M] *Donegal*, [MH] *Gettysburg*, [M] *Harrisburg*, [M] *Hershey*, [M] *Huntingdon*, [M] *Lancaster*, [M] *Lewisburg*, [M] *Meadville*, [M] *New Stanton*, [M] *Scranton*, [MH] *State College*

DAYS INN, *SC*
[M] *Charleston*, [M] *Clinton*, [M] *Florence*, [M] *Greenville*, [M] *Greenwood*, [M] *Orangeburg*, [M] *Rock Hill*, [M] *Santee*

DAYS INN, *VA*
[MH] *Arlington County (National Airport Area)*, [M] *Blacksburg*, [M] *Charlottesville*, [M] *Chesapeake*, [MH] *Dulles Intl Airport Area*, [M] *Emporia*, [M] *Farmville*, [M] *Harrisonburg*, [M] *Leesburg*, [M] *Lexington*, [M] *Lynchburg*, [M] *Manassas*, [M] *Petersburg*, [M] *Roanoke*, [M] *Springfield*, [M] *Tappahannock*, [MH] *Virginia Beach*, [M] *Waynesboro*, [M] *Wytheville*

DAYS INN, *WV*
[M] *Charleston*, [M] *Huntington*, [M] *Lewisburg*, [M] *Morgantown*, [M] *Princeton*, [MH] *Sutton*, [M] *Wheeling*

DE SOTO HOLIDAY HOUSE [M] *Bradford, PA*

DELAMAR INN [I] *Beaufort, NC*

DESERT SANDS RESORT COMPLEX [M] *Stone Harbor, NJ*

DINNER BELL INN [M] *Rehoboth Beach, DE*

DISNEY HILTON HEAD ISLAND RESORT [RO] *Hilton Head Island, SC*

DOCKSIDER INN [M] *Wilmington, NC*

DOCTORS INN AT KINGS GRANT [I] *Cape May Court House, NJ*

DOE RUN LODGE RESORT & CONFERENCE CENTER [RO] *Blue Ridge Parkway, VA*

DOGWOOD LODGE [M] *Radford, VA*

DOLLAR INN [M] *Somerset, PA*

DONECKERS THE GUESTHOUSE [I] *Ephrata, PA*

DOOLANS MOTOR LODGE [M] *Spring Lake, NJ*
DOUBLETREE, *DC*
  [H] *Washington*
DOUBLETREE, *DE*
  [H] *Wilmington*
DOUBLETREE, *MD*
  [H] *Baltimore*, [H] *Baltimore/Washington Intl Airport Area*, [H] *Rockville*
DOUBLETREE, *NC*
  [H] *Charlotte*, [H] *Durham*
DOUBLETREE, *PA*
  [MH] *Philadelphia*, [H] *Philadelphia*, [H] *Pittsburgh*
DOUBLETREE, *VA*
  [H] *Alexandria*, [H] *Arlington County (National Airport Area)*, [H] *Charlottesville*, [H] *Norfolk*, [H] *Roanoke*, [H] *Virginia Beach*
DOUBLETREE HOTEL [H] *New Brunswick, NJ*
DRIFTWOOD MOTEL & RESTAURANT [M] *Cedar Island, NC*
DRIFTWOOD MOTOR LODGE [M] *Chincoteague, VA*
DUKE OF YORK MOTOR HOTEL [M] *Yorktown, VA*
DULING-KURTZ HOUSE & COUNTRY INN [I] *West Chester, PA*
DULWICH MANOR [I] *Lynchburg, VA*
DUNES VILLAGE RESORT [H] *Myrtle Beach, SC*
DUNHILL HOTEL [H] *Charlotte, NC*
DUTCH INN [M] *Martinsville, VA*
EAST MAIN GUEST HOUSE [I] *Rock Hill, SC*
ECHO MOUNTAIN INN [I] *Hendersonville, NC*
ECONO LODGE, *DE*
  [M] *Rehoboth Beach*
ECONO LODGE, *MD*
  [M] *Berkeley Springs*
ECONO LODGE, *NC*
  [M] *Boone*, [M] *Fayetteville*, [M] *Morehead City*
ECONO LODGE, *PA*
  [M] *Bedford*, [M] *Erie*, [M] *Reading*, [M] *Williamsport*
ECONO LODGE, *SC*
  [M] *Rock Hill*, [M] *Walterboro*
ECONO LODGE, *VA*
  [M] *Lynchburg*, [M] *Norfolk*, [M] *Staunton*, [H] *Virginia Beach*, [M] *Winchester*, [M] *Wytheville*
ECONO LODGE, *WV*
  [M] *Bluefield*, [M] *Elkins*, [M] *Morgantown*
ECONOMY INNS OF AMERICA [M] *Somerset, PA*
EDGEWOOD BED & BREAKFAST [I] *Williamsburg, VA*
EDGEWOOD MANOR INC [I] *Martinsburg, WV*

EL CORONADO MOTOR INN [MH] *Wildwood & Wildwood Crest, NJ*
ELKINS MOTOR LODGE INC [M] *Elkins, WV*
ELKTON LODGE [M] *Elkton, MD*
EMBASSY SUITES, *DC*
  [H] *Washington*
EMBASSY SUITES, *NC*
  [H] *Charlotte*, [H] *Greensboro*, [H] *Raleigh*
EMBASSY SUITES, *NJ*
  [H] *New Brunswick*, [H] *Secaucus*
EMBASSY SUITES, *SC*
  [H] *Charleston*, [H] *Columbia*, [H] *Greenville*, [H] *Myrtle Beach*
EMBASSY SUITES, *VA*
  [H] *Arlington County (National Airport Area)*, [H] *Richmond*, [H] *Tysons Corner*
EMERALD ISLE INN & BED & BREAKFAST [I] *Morehead City, NC*
EMMANUEL HUTZLER HOUSE [I] *Richmond, VA*
EMPIRE MOTOR LODGE ABINGDON [M] *Abingdon, VA*
ENGLESIDE INN [M] *Long Beach Island, NJ*
ENGLISH INN OF CHARLOTTESVILLE [MH] *Charlottesville, VA*
ESEEOLA LODGE [RO] *Linville, NC*
EVERMAY ON THE DELAWARE [I] *New Hope (Bucks Co), PA*
EXECUTIVE CLUB SUITES, *VA*
  [MH] *Alexandria*, [M] *Arlington County (National Airport Area)*
EXECUTIVE MOTEL [M] *Ocean City, MD*
EXECUTIVE MOTEL INC [M] *Radford, VA*
EXPRESS INN [M] *Dunn, NC*
FAIRFIELD INN BY MARRIOTT, *MD*
  [MH] *Frederick*
FAIRFIELD INN BY MARRIOTT, *NC*
  [M] *Charlotte*, [M] *Durham*, [M] *Fayetteville*, [M] *Greensboro*, [M] *Greenville*, [M] *Lumberton*, [M] *Raleigh*, [M] *Rocky Mount*, [M] *Statesville*, [M] *Wilmington*
FAIRFIELD INN BY MARRIOTT, *NJ*
  [M] *Atlantic City*, [MH] *Rutherford*
FAIRFIELD INN BY MARRIOTT, *SC*
  [M] *Greenville*, [M] *Hilton Head Island*, [M] *Myrtle Beach*
FAIRFIELD INN BY MARRIOTT, *VA*
  [M] *Chesapeake*, [M] *Richmond*, [M] *Virginia Beach*
FAIRFIELD SAPPHIRE VALLEY [RO] *Cashiers, NC*
FAIRVILLE INN [I] *Kennett Square, PA*
FALCON MOTEL [M] *Buxton (Outer Banks), NC*
FALLS PORT INN & RESTAURANT [I] *Hawley, PA*

FARNSWORTH HOUSE INN [I] *Gettysburg, PA*
FASSIFERN BED & BREAKFAST [I] *Lexington, VA*
FEARRINGTON HOUSE [I] *Chapel Hill, NC*
FIELDCREST MANOR BED & BREAKFAST [I] *Morgantown, WV*
FIRST COLONY INN [I] *Nags Head (Outer Banks), NC*
FLEUR DE LIS MOTEL [M] *Wildwood & Wildwood Crest, NJ*
FLINT STREET INNS [I] *Asheville, NC*
FOLKESTONE INN [I] *Bryson City, NC*
FOREST HILLS MOTEL [M] *Bowie, MD*
FOREST MANOR MOTOR LODGE [M] *Asheville, NC*
FORRESTAL AT PRINCETON HOTEL, THE [H] *Princeton, NJ*
FORT LIGONIER MOTOR LODGE [M] *Ligonier, PA*
FORUM MOTOR INN [M] *Ocean City, NJ*
FOUNDERS INN & CONFERENCE CENTER [H] *Virginia Beach, VA*
FOUNTAIN HALL BED & BREAKFAST [I] *Culpeper, VA*
FOUR SEASONS, *DC*
  [H] *Washington*
FOUR SEASONS, *PA*
  [H] *Philadelphia*
FOUR SEASONS MOTEL [M] *Elkins, WV*
FOX HILL INN [I] *Marion, VA*
FOX & HOUND BED & BREAKFAST OF NEW HOPE [I] *New Hope (Bucks Co), PA*
FRANKLIN INN [MH] *Franklin (Venango Co), PA*
FREDERICK HOUSE [I] *Staunton, VA*
FREDERICKSBURG COLONIAL INN [I] *Fredericksburg, VA*
FREEHOLD GARDENS HOTEL [MH] *Freehold, NJ*
FRENCH MANOR [I] *Mount Pocono, PA*
FRONT STREET INN [I] *Wilmington, NC*
GARDEN SPOT MOTEL [M] *Lancaster, PA*
GARDEN & THE SEA INN, THE [I] *Chincoteague, VA*
GASLIGHT INN [I] *Gettysburg, PA*
GATEWAY RESORT HOTEL [M] *Ocean City, MD*
GENERAL LEWIS INN [I] *Lewisburg, WV*
GENERAL SUTTER INN [I] *Lancaster, PA*
GENETTI HOTEL & SUITES [H] *Williamsport, PA*
GEORGETOWN DUTCH INN [H] *Washington, DC*
GEORGETOWN INN [H] *Washington, DC*
GETTYSTOWN INN BED & BREAKFAST [I] *Gettysburg, PA*

GIBSONS LODGINGS [I] *Annapolis, MD*
GLASBERN INN, THE [I] *Allentown, PA*
GLASS HOUSE INN [M] *Erie, PA*
GLEN FERRIS INN [I] *Gauley Bridge, WV*
GLENDALE SPRINGS INN [I] *Jefferson, NC*
GLENDORN - A LODGE IN THE COUNTRY [I] *Bradford, PA*
GOLDEN PHEASANT INN [I] *New Hope (Bucks Co), PA*
GOLDEN PLOUGH INN [I] *New Hope (Bucks Co), PA*
GOVERNOR EDEN INN [I] *Edenton, NC*
GOVERNOR'S INN [M] *Williamsburg, VA*
GOVERNORS HOUSE HOTEL [H] *Washington, DC*
GRAMERCY BED & BREAKFAST [I] *Pikesville, MD*
GRAND HOTEL [MH] *Cape May, NJ*
GRANDVIEW LODGE [I] *Waynesville, NC*
GRAVES' MOUNTAIN LODGE [RO] *Culpeper, VA*
GRAYSTONE INN [I] *Wilmington, NC*
GREENBRIER INN, THE [RO] *White Sulphur Springs, WV*
GREENLEAF INN [I] *Camden, SC*
GRESHAM'S LAKE VIEW MOTEL [M] *Hawley, PA*
GREYSTONE INN, THE [I] *Cashiers, NC*
GREYSTONE MANOR BED & BREAKFAST [I] *Bird-in-Hand, PA*
GROVE PARK INN RESORT [RO] *Asheville, NC*
HALEY FARM BED & BREAKFAST [I] *Oakland (Garrett Co), MD*
HAMILTON PARK CONFERENCE CENTER [MH] *Morristown, NJ*
HAMPTON INN, *MD*
   [M] *Baltimore*, [M] *Baltimore/Washington Intl Airport Area*, [MH] *Baltimore/Washington Intl Airport Area*, [MH] *Frederick*, [MH] *Gaithersburg*
HAMPTON INN, *NC*
   [M] *Asheville*, [MH] *Boone*, [M] *Burlington*, [M] *Chapel Hill*, [M] *Charlotte*, [M] *Cornelius*, [M] *Elizabeth City*, [M] *Fayetteville*, [M] *Gastonia*, [M] *Goldsboro*, [M] *Greensboro*, [M] *Greenville*, [M] *Hendersonville*, [M] *Hickory*, [M] *Jacksonville*, [MH] *Kinston*, [M] *Lumberton*, [M] *Morehead City*, [M] *New Bern*, [M] *Raleigh*, [MH] *Raleigh*, [M] *Roanoke Rapids*, [M] *Rocky Mount*, [M] *Salisbury*, [M] *Southern Pines*, [M] *Statesville*, [M] *Wilmington*, [M] *Wilson*, [M] *Winston-Salem*, [H] *Wrightsville Beach*
HAMPTON INN, *NJ*
   [M] *Atlantic City*, [M] *Cherry Hill*, [MH] *Parsippany*

HAMPTON INN, *PA*
   [M] *Allentown*, [M] *Chambersburg*, [M] *Du Bois*, [M] *Erie*, [M] *Harrisburg*, [M] *Mount Pocono*, [M] *Pittsburgh*, [M] *Pittsburgh Intl Airport Area*, [M] *Scranton*, [M] *State College*, [M] *Wilkes-Barre*, [M] *Willow Grove*, [M] *York*
HAMPTON INN, *SC*
   [M] *Charleston*, [MH] *Charleston*, [M] *Columbia*, [M] *Greenville*, [M] *Hilton Head Island*, [M] *Myrtle Beach*, [MH] *Rock Hill*, [M] *Spartanburg*
HAMPTON INN, *VA*
   [M] *Alexandria*, [M] *Blacksburg*, [M] *Charlottesville*, [M] *Chesapeake*, [M] *Emporia*, [M] *Fairfax*, [M] *Hampton*, [M] *Harrisonburg*, [M] *Lynchburg*, [MH] *Newport News*, [M] *Norfolk*, [MH] *Richmond*, [M] *Roanoke*, [M] *South Hill*, [M] *Springfield*, [M] *Virginia Beach*, [M] *Warrenton*, [M] *Williamsburg*, [M] *Winchester*
HAMPTON INN, *WV*
   [M] *Beckley*, [MH] *Charleston*, [M] *Morgantown*, [MH] *Wheeling*
HARBOR COURT HOTEL [H] *Baltimore, MD*
HARBOR LIGHT GUEST HOUSE [I] *Morehead City, NC*
HARBOR VIEW MOTEL [M] *Bethany Beach, DE*
HARBOURTOWNE GOLF RESORT & CONFERENCE CENTER [RO] *St Michaels, MD*
HARBOURVIEW INN [I] *Charleston, SC*
HARLEY [MH] *Pittsburgh, PA*
HARMONY HOUSE [I] *New Bern, NC*
HARRAH'S SHOWBOAT CASINO & HOTEL [H] *Atlantic City, NJ*
HARRIS HOUSE [M] *Ocean City, NJ*
HARRY PACKER MANSION [I] *Jim Thorpe, PA*
HATTERAS MARLIN MOTEL [M] *Hatteras (Outer Banks), NC*
HAWKS NEST STATE PARK LODGE [RO] *Gauley Bridge, WV*
HAWTHORN SUITES, *NC*
   [MH] *Durham*
HAWTHORN SUITES, *PA*
   [M] *Pittsburgh*
HAWTHORN SUITES, *SC*
   [MH] *Charleston*
HAY ADAMS HOTEL [H] *Washington, DC*
HAYWOOD PARK HOTEL [H] *Asheville, NC*
HAZLET HOTEL [M] *Matawan, NJ*
HEADQUARTERS PLAZA [H] *Morristown, NJ*
HEMLOCK INN [I] *Bryson City, NC*
HENLEY PARK HOTEL [H] *Washington, DC*
HENLOPEN HOTEL INC [MH] *Rehoboth Beach, DE*

HENRY CLAY INN [I] *Ashland, VA*
HERITAGE INN [I] *Franklin (Macon Co), NC*
HERMITAGE MOTOR INN [M] *Petersburg, WV*
HERR TAVERN & PUBLIC HOUSE, THE [I] *Gettysburg, PA*
HERSHEY FARM MOTOR INN [M] *Lancaster, PA*
HERSHEY LODGE & CONVENTION CENTER [M] *Hershey, PA*
HEWITT WELLINGTON HOTEL [H] *Spring Lake, NJ*
HICKORY BED & BREAKFAST [I] *Hickory, NC*
HIDDEN CRYSTAL INN [I] *Statesville, NC*
HIDDEN INN [I] *Orange, VA*
HIDDEN VALLEY RESORT CONFERENCE CENTER [RO] *Somerset, PA*
HIGH HAMPTON INN & COUNTRY CLUB [RO] *Cashiers, NC*
HIGHLAND FARMS BED & BREAKFAST [I] *Doylestown (Bucks Co), PA*
HIGHLAND INN [I] *Monterey, VA*
HIGHLAND LAKE CANTEEN [RO] *Hendersonville, NC*
HIGHLAND'S SUITE HOTEL [M] *Highlands, NC*
HIGHLANDS INN & KELSEY PLACE RESTAURANTS [I] *Highlands, NC*
HIGHLAWN INN [I] *Berkeley Springs, WV*
HILLBROOK INN [I] *Charles Town, WV*
HILLSBOROUGH HOUSE INN [I] *Durham, NC*
HILTON, *DC*
   [H] *Washington*
HILTON, *DE*
   [H] *Newark*, [H] *Wilmington*
HILTON, *MD*
   [H] *Baltimore*, [H] *Columbia*, [H] *Gaithersburg*, [MH] *Pikesville*
HILTON, *NC*
   [H] *Charlotte*, [H] *Durham*, [H] *Greensboro*, [H] *Greenville*, [H] *Raleigh*, [H] *Wilmington*
HILTON, *NJ*
   [H] *Atlantic City*, [H] *Cherry Hill*, [H] *Eatontown*, [H] *Fort Lee*, [MH] *Hillsdale*, [H] *Millburn*, [H] *New Brunswick*, [MH] *Newark*, [H] *Newark Intl Airport Area*, [H] *Parsippany*, [H] *Woodbridge*
HILTON, *PA*
   [H] *Allentown*, [H] *Harrisburg*, [H] *King of Prussia*, [M] *Lancaster*, [H] *Philadelphia*, [H] *Pittsburgh*
HILTON, *SC*
   [MH] *Charleston*, [H] *Charleston*, [H] *Greenville*, [RO] *Hilton Head Island*

HILTON, VA
[H] Arlington County (National Airport Area), [MH] Lynchburg, [H] Norfolk, [MH] Richmond, [H] Springfield, [H] Tysons Corner, [MH] Virginia Beach
HISTORIC NU WRAY INN [I] Burnsville, NC
HISTORIC STRASBURG INN [I] Lancaster, PA
HOJO INN [M] Parsippany, NJ
HOLIDAY INN, DC
[H] Washington
HOLIDAY INN, DE
[M] Newark, [M] Wilmington
HOLIDAY INN, MD
[M] Aberdeen, [MH] Annapolis, [M] Baltimore, [H] Baltimore, [H] Bethesda, [H] College Park, [MH] Cumberland, [MH] Easton, [MH] Gaithersburg, [M] Laurel, [MH] Ocean City, [MH] Towson, [M] Waldorf
HOLIDAY INN, NC
[MH] Asheville, [M] Banner Elk, [M] Boone, [M] Chapel Hill, [MH] Charlotte, [M] Cherokee, [M] Cornelius, [M] Elizabeth City, [M] Fayetteville, [MH] Fayetteville, [MH] Goldsboro, [MH] Greensboro, [M] Hatteras (Outer Banks), [M] Hickory, [MH] High Point, [MH] Jacksonville, [MH] Kill Devil Hills (Outer Banks), [M] Kinston, [M] Lenoir, [M] Lumberton, [MH] Morehead City, [M] Morganton, [M] Pilot Mountain, [H] Raleigh, [MH] Rocky Mount, [M] Salisbury, [M] Southern Pines, [M] Statesville, [M] Williamston, [M] Wilmington, [H] Wilmington, [H] Winston-Salem
HOLIDAY INN, NJ
[H] Atlantic City, [H] Cherry Hill, [MH] Clinton, [MH] Eatontown, [MH] Gibbstown, [H] Hackensack, [M] Montvale, [M] New Brunswick, [MH] Newark Intl Airport Area, [MH] Parsippany, [MH] Plainfield, [MH] Princeton, [H] Saddle Brook, [MH] Secaucus, [M] Toms River, [M] Wayne, [MH] Wayne
HOLIDAY INN, PA
[M] Allentown, [MH] Beaver Falls, [M] Bethlehem, [M] Brookville, [M] Carlisle, [M] Chambersburg, [M] Clarion, [M] Denver/Adamstown, [MH] Downingtown, [M] Du Bois, [MH] Erie, [M] Gettysburg, [M] Harrisburg, [MH] Harrisburg, [M] Hazleton, [MH] Hershey, [M] Indiana, [H] Johnstown, [MH] King of Prussia, [M] Lancaster, [MH] Lancaster, [M] Oil City, [H] Philadelphia, [M] Pittsburgh, [MH] Pittsburgh, [M] Pottstown, [MH] Reading, [M] Scranton, [M] Uniontown, [MH]

Washington, [MH] West Chester, [M] West Middlesex, [M] Wilkes-Barre, [M] Williamsport, [M] York, [MH] York
HOLIDAY INN, SC
[M] Anderson, [M] Beaufort, [M] Camden, [MH] Charleston, [M] Clemson, [M] Clinton, [M] Columbia, [MH] Greenville, [M] Greenwood, [MH] Hilton Head Island, [MH] Myrtle Beach, [M] Orangeburg, [M] Rock Hill, [M] Spartanburg, [M] Sumter, [M] Walterboro
HOLIDAY INN, VA
[MH] Alexandria, [H] Alexandria, [H] Arlington County (National Airport Area), [M] Ashland, [M] Charlottesville, [MH] Chesapeake, [M] Culpeper, [M] Danville, [M] Dulles Intl Airport Area, [MH] Dulles Intl Airport Area, [H] Fairfax, [M] Fredericksburg, [MH] Fredericksburg, [M] Hampton, [M] Hopewell, [M] Leesburg, [M] Lexington, [H] Lynchburg, [M] Manassas, [M] Portsmouth, [MH] Richmond, [M] Roanoke, [MH] Roanoke, [M] Salem, [M] South Hill, [MH] Staunton, [H] Tysons Corner, [MH] Virginia Beach, [M] Williamsburg, [MH] Williamsburg, [M] Winchester, [M] Wytheville
HOLIDAY INN, WV
[M] Beckley, [M] Bluefield, [MH] Charleston, [H] Charleston, [M] Clarksburg, [M] Fairmont, [H] Martinsburg, [M] Morgantown, [M] Parkersburg, [M] Ripley
HOLIDAY SANDS MOTEL & TOWER [M] Norfolk, VA
HOLLADAY HOUSE [I] Orange, VA
HOLLILEIF BED & BREAKFAST [I] New Hope (Bucks Co), PA
HOMESTEAD INN [M] Blowing Rock, NC
HOMESTEAD MOTOR LODGE [M] Gettysburg, PA
HOMESTEAD RESORT, THE [RO] Hot Springs, VA
HOMEWOOD SUITES, NC
[H] Raleigh
HOMEWOOD SUITES, PA
[MH] King of Prussia
HOMEWOOD SUITES, VA
[MH] Alexandria
HOPKINS INN [I] Baltimore, MD
HOTEL DU PONT [H] Wilmington, DE
HOTEL DU VILLAGE [I] New Hope (Bucks Co), PA
HOTEL HARRINGTON [H] Washington, DC
HOTEL HERSHEY, THE [RO] Hershey, PA
HOTEL LOMBARDY [H] Washington, DC
HOTEL STRASBURG INN [I] Strasburg, VA

HOTEL WASHINGTON [H] Washington, DC
HOUNDS EARS LODGE & CLUB [RO] Blowing Rock, NC
HOWARD JOHNSON, DC
[MH] Washington, [H] Washington
HOWARD JOHNSON, DE
[M] Newark
HOWARD JOHNSON, MD
[MH] Hagerstown, [M] Ocean City, [M] Salisbury, [M] Waldorf
HOWARD JOHNSON, NC
[M] Asheville, [M] Fayetteville, [M] Henderson, [M] Wilmington, [MH] Wilmington
HOWARD JOHNSON, NJ
[M] Clifton, [M] Mount Holly, [M] Newark Intl Airport Area, [M] Parsippany, [M] Rockaway, [M] Toms River, [M] Trenton, [M] Wayne
HOWARD JOHNSON, PA
[M] Bradford, [M] Danville, [M] Gettysburg, [M] Harrisburg, [M] Lancaster, [M] Mercer, [M] New Stanton
HOWARD JOHNSON, SC
[M] Hardeeville
HOWARD JOHNSON, VA
[H] Arlington County (National Airport Area), [MH] Danville, [M] Harrisonburg, [MH] Lexington, [M] Lynchburg, [MH] Williamsburg
HUMMINGBIRD INN [I] Lexington, VA
HUNTINGDON MOTOR INN [M] Huntingdon, PA
HUNTINGFIELD MANOR [I] Chesapeake Bay Bridge Area, MD
HY-LAND MOTOR INN [M] Cape May Court House, NJ
HYATT, DC
[H] Washington
HYATT, MD
[H] Baltimore, [H] Bethesda
HYATT, NC
[H] Charlotte
HYATT, NJ
[H] New Brunswick, [H] Princeton
HYATT, PA
[H] Philadelphia
HYATT, SC
[H] Greenville, [RO] Hilton Head Island
HYATT, VA
[H] Arlington County (National Airport Area), [H] Dulles Intl Airport Area, [H] Fairfax, [MH] Richmond
IMPALA ISLAND INN [M] Ocean City, NJ
IMPERIAL 500 MOTEL [M] Wildwood & Wildwood Crest, NJ
IMPERIAL HOTEL [I] Chesapeake Bay Bridge Area, MD
IMPERIAL MOTOR LODGE [M] Brevard, NC

INDIAN SPRINGS BED & BREAKFAST [I] *Williamsburg, VA*

INDIGO INN [I] *Charleston, SC*

INN AT AFTON [M] *Waynesboro, VA*

INN AT BINGHAM SCHOOL [I] *Chapel Hill, NC*

INN AT BUCKEYSTOWN [I] *Frederick, MD*

INN AT BUCKHORN [M] *Bloomsburg, PA*

INN AT CAMDEN (LUGOFF), THE [M] *Camden, SC*

INN AT CANAL SQUARE [I] *Lewes, DE*

INN AT FORDHOOK FARM, THE [I] *Doylestown (Bucks Co), PA*

INN AT GEORGIAN PLACE [I] *Somerset, PA*

INN AT GOVERNMENT HOUSE [I] *Baltimore, MD*

INN AT GRISTMILL SQUARE [I] *Warm Springs, VA*

INN AT HENDERSON'S WHARF [I] *Baltimore, MD*

INN AT JIM THORPE [I] *Jim Thorpe, PA*

INN AT LAMBERTVILLE STATION [I] *Lambertville, NJ*

INN AT LEVELFIELD INC [I] *Lancaster, VA*

INN AT LITTLE WASHINGTON, THE [I] *Washington, VA*

INN AT MILLRACE POND [I] *Hackettstown, NJ*

INN AT MITCHELL HOUSE [I] *Chesapeake Bay Bridge Area, MD*

INN AT MONTCHANIN VILLAGE [I] *Wilmington, DE*

INN AT MONTICELLO [I] *Charlottesville, VA*

INN AT NARROW PASSAGE [I] *Woodstock, VA*

INN AT NICHOLS VILLAGE [MH] *Scranton, PA*

INN AT OAKMONT [I] *Pittsburgh, PA*

INN AT OLDE NEW BERLIN [I] *Shamokin Dam, PA*

INN AT ORIENTAL [I] *New Bern, NC*

INN AT PERRY CABIN [I] *St Michaels, MD*

INN AT PHILLIPS MILL [I] *New Hope (Bucks Co), PA*

INN AT RAGGED GARDENS [I] *Blowing Rock, NC*

INN AT ST. THOMAS COURT, THE [I] *Wilmington, NC*

INN AT THE CANAL [I] *Elkton, MD*

INN AT THE SHORE [I] *Spring Lake, NJ*

INN AT TURKEY HILL [I] *Bloomsburg, PA*

INN AT UNION RUN [I] *Lexington, VA*

INN AT VAUCLUSE SPRING, THE [I] *Winchester, VA*

INN AT WALNUT BOTTOM [I] *Cumberland, MD*

INN AT WEBBLEY [I] *Shelby, NC*

INN CHERAW [M] *Cheraw, SC*

INN OF ADAMSTOWN [I] *Denver/Adamstown, PA*

INN OF CAPE MAY [H] *Cape May, NJ*

INN OF SHAMOKIN DAM [M] *Shamokin Dam, PA*

INN ON THE SQUARE [I] *Greenwood, SC*

INN TO THE WOODS [I] *New Hope (Bucks Co), PA*

INNE AT WATSON'S CHOICE [I] *Uniontown, PA*

INNISFREE VICTORIAN INN [I] *Cashiers, NC*

INNKEEPER [M] *Hopewell, VA*

INNKEEPER COLISEUM [M] *Charlotte, NC*

INNKEEPER MOTEL [M] *Lynchburg, VA*

INNKEEPER MOTOR LODGE [M] *Danville, VA*

IRIS INN [I] *Waynesboro, VA*

ISAAC HILLIARD HOUSE BED & BREAKFAST [I] *Mount Holly, NJ*

ISLAND MOTOR INN [M] *Chincoteague, VA*

ISLANDER MOTEL [M] *Nags Head (Outer Banks), NC*

IVANHOE MOTEL & APARTMENTS [M] *Wildwood & Wildwood Crest, NJ*

JAMES GETTYS HOTEL [I] *Gettysburg, PA*

JEFFERSON, THE [H] *Richmond, VA*

JEFFERSON HOTEL [H] *Washington, DC*

JOHN RUTLEDGE HOUSE INN [I] *Charleston, SC*

JOHNATHAN CREEK INN [M] *Maggie Valley, NC*

JOLLY ROGER MOTEL [M] *Wildwood & Wildwood Crest, NJ*

JORDAN HOLLOW FARM INN [I] *Luray, VA*

JOSEPH AMBLER INN [I] *Willow Grove, PA*

KALORAMA GUEST HOUSE, [I] *Washington DC*

KALTENBACH'S BED & BREAKFAST [I] *Wellsboro, PA*

KANAWHA CITY MOTOR LODGE [M] *Charleston, WV*

KENMORE INN [I] *Fredericksburg, VA*

KENT MANOR INN [I] *Chesapeake Bay Bridge Area, MD*

KESWICK HALL AT MONTICELLO [I] *Charlottesville, VA*

KIAWAH ISLAND RESORTS [RO] *Kiawah Island, SC*

KING GEORGE THE FOURTH INN [I] *Charleston, SC*

KING'S COTTAGE BED & BREAKFAST [I] *Lancaster, PA*

KINGS ARMS BED & BREAKFAST INN [I] *New Bern, NC*

KINGS COURTYARD INN [I] *Charleston, SC*

KINGS INN [I] *Georgetown, SC*

KINGSMILL RESORT [RO] *Williamsburg, VA*

KIRKS MOTOR COURT INC [M] *Burlington, NC*

KITTY KNIGHT HOUSE [I] *Elkton, MD*

KNIGHTS INN, PA
[M] *Greensburg*, [M] *Somerset*

KNIGHTS INN, SC
[M] *Charleston*

KNIGHTS INN, VA
[M] *Charlottesville*

KNIGHTS INN, WV
[M] *Martinsburg*

KORMAN SUITES [H] *Philadelphia, PA*

L'AUBERGE PROVENÇALE FRENCH COUNTRY INN [I] *Winchester, VA*

LA QUINTA, NC
[M] *Charlotte*

LA QUINTA, PA
[M] *Pittsburgh Intl Airport Area*

LA QUINTA, SC
[M] *Charleston*, [M] *Columbia*, [M] *Greenville*, [MH] *Myrtle Beach*

LA QUINTA, VA
[MH] *Bristol*, [M] *Richmond*

LA QUINTA INN [M] *Anderson, SC*

LAKE LURE INN [I] *Hendersonville, NC*

LAKE MOTEL [M] *Clarksville, VA*

LAKE SIDE MOTOR COURT [M] *Oakland (Garrett Co), MD*

LAKEVIEW RESORT [RO] *Morgantown, WV*

LAMBERTON HOUSE BED & BREAKFAST [I] *Franklin (Venango Co), PA*

LAMERE BEACHFRONT MOTOR INN [M] *Cape May, NJ*

LANDMARK INN, THE [MH] *Cherry Hill, NJ*

LANDS INN [M] *Charleston, SC*

LANSDOWNE CONFERENCE RESORT LEESBURG [H] *Leesburg, VA*

LANTERN LODGE MOTOR INN [M] *Lebanon, PA*

LATHAM HOTEL [H] *Philadelphia, PA*

LATHAM HOTEL GEORGETOWN, THE [H] *Washington, DC*

LAUREL HILL PLANTATION BED & BREAKFAST [I] *Charleston, SC*

LAURELWOOD MOUNTAIN INN [M] *Cashiers, NC*

LAZYJACK INN [I] *St Michaels, MD*

LEESBURG COLONIAL INN [I] *Leesburg, VA*

LE VOYAGEUR MOTEL [M] *Wildwood & Wildwood Crest, NJ*

LEGACY OF WILLIAMSBURG BED & BREAKFAST [I] *Williamsburg, VA*

LIBERTY ROSE BED & BREAKFAST [I] *Williamsburg, VA*

LIGHTHOUSE CLUB HOTEL [H] *Ocean City, MD*

LIGHTHOUSE INN [M] *Chincoteague, VA*
LINCOLN SUITES [H] *Washington, DC*
LINDEN ROW INN [I] *Richmond, VA*
LION AND THE ROSE [I] *Asheville, NC*
LITTLE RIVER INN [I] *Leesburg, VA*
LODGE, THE [M] *Waynesville, NC*
LODGE ALLEY INN [I] *Charleston, SC*
LODGE AT CHALK HILL [M] *Uniontown, PA*
LODGE ON LAKE LURE BED & BREAKFAST INN [I] *Hendersonville, NC*
LOEWS, [H] *Washington, DC*
LOEWS, *MD*
  [H] *Annapolis*
LOGAN INN [I] *New Hope (Bucks Co), PA*
LOIS JANE'S RIVERVIEW INN [I] *Southport, NC*
LONGDALE INN [I] *Clifton Forge, VA*
LONGWOOD INN [M] *Kennett Square, PA*
LORDS PROPRIETORS' [I] *Edenton, NC*
LOVILL HOUSE INN [I] *Boone, NC*
LOWE HOTEL [M] *Point Pleasant, WV*
LURAY CAVERNS MOTELS [M] *Luray, VA*
LYNCHBURG MANSION AND BED & BREAKFAST [I] *Lynchburg, VA*
MADISON HOTEL [H] *Morristown, NJ*
MADISON HOTEL, THE [H] *Washington, DC*
MADISON SUITES HOTEL [MH] *New Brunswick, NJ*
MADRID OCEAN RESORT [M] *Wildwood & Wildwood Crest, NJ*
MAGEE'S MAIN STREET INN [I] *Bloomsburg, PA*
MAGNOLIA HOUSE BED & BREAKFAST [I] *Sumter, SC*
MAGNOLIA INN [I] *Pinehurst, NC*
MAIN STREET INN [I] *Hilton Head Island, SC*
MAINSTAY INN [I] *Cape May, NJ*
MAISON DU PRÉ [I] *Charleston, SC*
MANOR AT TAYLORS STORE BED & BREAKFAST [I] *Booker T. Washington National Monument, VA*
MANSION INN [I] *New Hope (Bucks Co), PA*
MAPLE HALL COUNTRY INN [I] *Lexington, VA*
MAPLE LODGE [I] *Blowing Rock, NC*
MARINER MOTEL [M] *Chincoteague, VA*
MARINER'S COVE MOTOR INN [M] *Spring Lake, NJ*
MARQUIS DE LAFAYETTE [MH] *Cape May, NJ*
MARRIOTT, [H] *Washington, DC*
MARRIOTT, *MD*

[H] *Annapolis,* [H] *Baltimore,* [H] *Baltimore/Washington Intl Airport Area,* [H] *Bethesda,* [MH] *Cockeysville,* [H] *College Park,* [H] *Gaithersburg*
MARRIOTT, *NC*
  [H] *Charlotte,* [H] *Durham,* [H] *Greensboro,* [H] *Raleigh*
MARRIOTT, *NJ*
  [RO] *Atlantic City,* [H] *Hackensack,* [H] *Montvale,* [H] *New Brunswick,* [H] *Newark Intl Airport Area,* [H] *Princeton,* [H] *Saddle Brook*
MARRIOTT, *PA*
  [MH] *Harrisburg,* [H] *King of Prussia,* [H] *Philadelphia,* [MH] *Pittsburgh,* [H] *Pittsburgh Intl Airport Area*
MARRIOTT, *SC*
  [H] *Greenville*
MARRIOTT, *VA*
  [H] *Arlington County (National Airport Area),* [H] *Dulles Intl Airport Area,* [RO] *Dulles Intl Airport Area,* [H] *Falls Church,* [H] *Norfolk,* [H] *Richmond,* [H] *Roanoke,* [H] *Tysons Corner,* [M] *Williamsburg,* [MH] *Williamsburg*
MARRIOTT, *WV*
  [H] *Charleston*
MARTHA WASHINGTON INN [I] *Abingdon, VA*
MARYLAND INN [I] *Annapolis, MD*
MASTERS ECONOMY INN [M] *Smithfield, NC*
MAYNEVIEW BED & BREAKFAST [I] *Luray, VA*
MC KEE'S MOTEL [M] *Butler, PA*
MCINTOSH INN, *DE*
  [M] *Newark*
MCINTOSH INN, *NJ*
  [M] *Cherry Hill,* [M] *New Brunswick*
MCINTOSH INN, *PA*
  [M] *King of Prussia*
MCMULLEN HOUSE BED & BREAKFAST [I] *Titusville, PA*
MEADOWBROOK INN [I] *Blowing Rock, NC*
MEETING STREET INN [I] *Charleston, SC*
MELODY MOTOR LODGE [M] *Connellsville, PA*
MEMORYTOWN [M] *Mount Pocono, PA*
MENDENHALL HOTEL [MH] *Kennett Square, PA*
MERCERSBURG INN [I] *Chambersburg, PA*
MERRY SHERWOOD PLANTATION [I] *Ocean City, MD*
MICROTEL [M] *Wilson, NC*
MID PINES INN & GOLF CLUB [RO] *Southern Pines, NC*
MIDDLETON INN, *SC*
  [RO] *Charleston*
MIDDLETON INN, *VA*
  [I] *Washington*

MIDTOWN MOTEL [M] *Port Allegany, PA*
MILLS HOUSE, THE [H] *Charleston, SC*
MILTON HALL BED & BREAKFAST INN [I] *Covington, VA*
MILTON HOUSE BED & BREAKFAST [I] *Luray, VA*
MILTON MOTEL [M] *Hershey, PA*
MIMSLYN INN [M] *Luray, VA*
MISS BETTY'S BED & BREAKFAST INN [I] *Wilson, NC*
MISS MOLLYS INN [I] *Chincoteague, VA*
MONTREAL INN [MH] *Cape May, NJ*
MORRISON HOUSE [I] *Alexandria, VA*
MORRISON-CLARK INN [I] *Washington, DC*
MOTEL 6, *PA*
  [M] *Erie,* [M] *Washington*
MOUNT VERNON MOTEL [M] *Cape May, NJ*
MOUNTAIN HIGH MOTEL [M] *Highlands, NC*
MOUNTAIN INN OF ROCKAWAY [M] *Rockaway, NJ*
MOUNTAIN LAUREL RESORT [RO] *White Haven, PA*
MOUNTAIN SPRINGS CABINS [M] *Asheville, NC*
MOUNTAIN VIEW INN [MH] *Greensburg, PA*
MR MOLE BED & BREAKFAST [I] *Baltimore, MD*
MR PATRICK HENRY'S INN [I] *Richmond, VA*
MT CREEK LODGE [RO] *Hinton, WV*
MYER MOTEL [M] *Milford, PA*
MYRTLE BEACH MARTINIQUE RESORT HOTEL [H] *Myrtle Beach, SC*
NAGGS HEAD BEACH [MH] *Kill Devil Hills (Outer Banks), NC*
NAGS HEAD INN [MH] *Nags Head (Outer Banks), NC*
NASSAU INN, *NJ*
  [H] *Princeton,* [M] *Wildwood & Wildwood Crest*
NASSAU MOTEL [M] *Ocean City, MD*
NATURAL BRIDGE [H] *Natural Bridge, VA*
NEMACOLIN WOODLANDS RESORT [RO] *Uniontown, PA*
NEW BERN HOUSE INN [I] *New Bern, NC*
NEW COMPASS MOTEL [M] *Wildwood & Wildwood Crest, NJ*
NEW DEVON INN [H] *Lewes, DE*
NEWMYER HOUSE [I] *Connellsville, PA*
NITTANY LION INN [I] *State College, PA*
NORMANDY INN, *DC*
  [H] *Washington*
NORMANDY INN, *NJ*
  [I] *Spring Lake*
NORRIS HOUSE INN [I] *Leesburg, VA*
NORTH BEND PLANTATION BED & BREAKFAST [I] *Williamsburg, VA*

NORTH BEND STATE PARK LODGE [M] *Parkersburg, WV*

NOVOTEL, *NJ*
[MH] *Princeton*, [H] *Rutherford*

OAKMONT LODGE [M] *Cashiers, NC*

OAKS VICTORIAN INN [I] *Blacksburg, VA*

OAKWOOD INN BED & BREAKFAST [I] *Raleigh, NC*

OCEAN DUNES RESORT & VILLAS, [H] *Myrtle Beach, SC*

OCEAN FOREST PLAZA [H] *Myrtle Beach, SC*

OCEAN HOLIDAY MOTOR INN [M] *Wildwood & Wildwood Crest, NJ*

OCEANUS MOTEL [M] *Rehoboth Beach, DE*

OCEANVIEW MOTEL [M] *Wildwood & Wildwood Crest, NJ*

OCRACOKE ISLAND INN [M] *Ocracoke (Outer Banks), NC*

OFLAHERTYS DINGELDEIN HOUSE [I] *Lancaster, PA*

OGLEBAY CONFERENCE CENTER [RO] *Wheeling, WV*

OLD APPLEFORD INN [I] *Gettysburg, PA*

OLD DOMINION INN [M] *Norfolk, VA*

OLD REYNOLDS MANSION, THE [I] *Asheville, NC*

OLD STONE INN [I] *Waynesville, NC*

OLD WHITE MOTEL [M] *White Sulphur Springs, WV*

OMNI, *DC*
[H] *Washington*

OMNI, *MD*
[H] *Baltimore*

OMNI, *PA*
[H] *Philadelphia*

OMNI, *VA*
[H] *Charlottesville*, [H] *Newport News*, [H] *Richmond*

ONE SOUTH LUMINA MOTEL [M] *Wrightsville Beach, NC*

ONE WASHINGTON CIRCLE HOTEL [H] *Washington, DC*

OSCEOLA MILL COUNTRY INN, THE [I] *Blue Ridge Parkway, VA*

OWLS NEST INN [I] *Asheville, NC*

PAGE HOUSE [I] *Norfolk, VA*

PALM CREST MOTEL [M] *Myrtle Beach, SC*

PALMETTO DUNES RESORT [RO] *Hilton Head Island, SC*

PALOMINO MOTEL [M] *Sanford, NC*

PAMLICO HOUSE BED & BREAKFAST [I] *Washington, NC*

PAN AMERICA MOTOR INN [MH] *Myrtle Beach, SC*

PAN AMERICAN HOTEL [M] *Wildwood & Wildwood Crest, NJ*

PANORAMIC MOTEL & APARTMENTS [M] *Wildwood & Wildwood Crest, NJ*

PARK HOTEL, THE [H] *Charlotte, NC*

PARK LANE HOTEL [MH] *Greensboro, NC*

PARKWAY INN [M] *Waynesville, NC*

PARSONAGE INN [I] *St Michaels, MD*

PAVILION [M] *Ocean City, NJ*

PEACOCK INN [I] *Princeton, NJ*

PEAKS OF OTTER LODGE MOTEL [M] *Blue Ridge Parkway, VA*

PECAN TREE INN [I] *Beaufort, NC*

PENCE SPRINGS HOTEL [I] *Hinton, WV*

PENN NATIONAL INN & GOLF CLUB [I] *Chambersburg, PA*

PENN WELLS HOTEL & LODGE [H] *Wellsboro, PA*

PENN WELLS LODGE [M] *Wellsboro, PA*

PENN'S VIEW INN [H] *Philadelphia, PA*

PERIWINKLE INN [M] *Cape May, NJ*

PHILLIPS BEACH PLAZA HOTEL [MH] *Ocean City, MD*

PHOENIX PARK HOTEL [H] *Washington, DC*

PIER 4 HOTEL [MH] *Ocean City, NJ*

PINE ACRES LODGE [M] *Laurinburg, NC*

PINE BARN INN [I] *Danville, PA*

PINE CREST INN, *NC*
[I] *Pinehurst*, [I] *Tryon*

PINE HILL FARM BED & BREAKFAST [I] *Milford, PA*

PINE KNOB INN [I] *Canadensis, PA*

PINE NEEDLES LODGES/COUNTRY CLUB [RO] *Southern Pines, NC*

PINE RIDGE INN [I] *Pilot Mountain, NC*

PINE TREE FARM BED & BREAKFAST [I] *Doylestown (Bucks Co), PA*

PINEAPPLE HILL BED & BREAKFAST [I] *New Hope (Bucks Co), PA*

PINEBRIDGE INN [M] *Little Switzerland, NC*

PINEHURST INN BED & BREAKFAST [I] *Hershey, PA*

PINEHURST RESORT/COUNTRY CLUB [I] *Pinehurst, NC*

PINES [I] *Crisfield, MD*

PINEY GROVE [I] *Williamsburg, VA*

PINNACLE INN [M] *Banner Elk, NC*

PIONEER MOTEL & COTTAGES [M] *Cherokee, NC*

PISGAH INN [RO] *Asheville, NC*

PITTSBURGH PLAZA [M] *Pittsburgh Intl Airport Area, PA*

PLANTATION INN RESORT [M] *Raleigh, NC*

PLANTERS INN [I] *Charleston, SC*

POCONO MANOR INN & GOLF CLUB [RO] *Mount Pocono, PA*

POCONO MOUNTAIN LODGE [M] *White Haven, PA*

POINT BEACH MOTEL [M] *Spring Lake, NJ*

PONDA ROWLAND BED & BREAKFAST [I] *Wilkes-Barre, PA*

PONY ISLAND MOTEL & REST INC [M] *Ocracoke (Outer Banks), NC*

PORT ROYAL HOTEL [M] *Wildwood & Wildwood Crest, NJ*

PORT-O-CALL HOTEL [MH] *Ocean City, NJ*

POST HOUSE BED & BREAKFAST, THE [I] *Elkins, WV*

PRINCE GEORGE INN [I] *Annapolis, MD*

PRINCESS ROYALE OCEANFRONT HOTEL [H] *Ocean City, MD*

PRIORY INN [I] *Pittsburgh, PA*

PROSPECT HILL PLANTATION INN [I] *Charlottesville, VA*

PUMP HOUSE INN [I] *Canadensis, PA*

QUALITY INN, *DC*
[H] *Washington*

QUALITY INN, *MD*
[M] *Aberdeen*, [M] *Ocean City*, [M] *Pocomoke City*, [MH] *Rockville*

QUALITY INN, *NC*
[MH] *Asheville*, [H] *Boone*, [M] *Fayetteville*, [M] *Goldsboro*, [M] *Henderson*, [M] *Hendersonville*, [M] *Lumberton*, [M] *Nags Head (Outer Banks)*, [MH] *Raleigh*

QUALITY INN, *NJ*
[M] *Cherry Hill*, [MH] *Jersey City*, [M] *Rutherford*, [M] *Toms River*

QUALITY INN, *PA*
[M] *Bedford*, [M] *Breezewood*, [M] *Carlisle*, [MH] *Erie*, [M] *Gettysburg*, [MH] *Lebanon*, [M] *Williamsport*

QUALITY INN, *SC*
[MH] *Charleston*, [M] *Greenville*, [MH] *Spartanburg*

QUALITY INN, *VA*
[MH] *Arlington County (National Airport Area)*, [H] *Arlington County (National Airport Area)*, [M] *Clarksville*, [M] *Falls Church*, [M] *Front Royal*, [M] *New Market*, [M] *Petersburg*, [MH] *Richmond*, [M] *Roanoke*, [M] *Salem*, [H] *Virginia Beach*, [M] *Williamsburg*

QUARTERPATH INN [M] *Williamsburg, VA*

QUEEN VICTORIA [I] *Cape May, NJ*

QUEEN VICTORIA INN [I] *Charleston, SC*

QUEENS HOTEL [I] *Cape May, NJ*

QUO VADIS BED & BREAKFAST [I] *Franklin (Venango Co), PA*

RADISSON, *DC*
[H] *Washington*

RADISSON, *MD*
[MH] *Baltimore*

RADISSON, *NC*
[H] *Asheville*, [H] *Charlotte*, [H] *High Point*

RADISSON, *NJ*
[H] *Cherry Hill*, [H] *Fort Lee*, [MH] *Paramus*, [H] *Secaucus*, [MH] *Wayne*

RADISSON, *PA*
[M] *Harrisburg*, [H] *Philadelphia*, [H] *Scranton*, [M] *West Middlesex*

RADISSON, *SC*
[MH] *Charleston*, [H] *Hilton Head Island*
RADISSON, *VA*
[H] *Alexandria*, [H] *Hampton*, [H] *Roanoke*
RADISSON, *WV*
[H] *Huntington*
RADISSON FORT MAGRUDER INN
[MH] *Williamsburg, VA*
RADNOR HOTEL [H] *Philadelphia, PA*
RAMADA, *DE*
[M] *New Castle*
RAMADA, *MD*
[MH] *Hagerstown*, [M] *Ocean City*, [M] *Pikesville*, [MH] *Salisbury*
RAMADA, *NC*
[M] *Burlington*, [M] *Dunn*, [M] *Goldsboro*, [M] *Greensboro*, [H] *Greenville*, [M] *Kill Devil Hills (Outer Banks)*, [M] *Wilmington*
RAMADA, *NJ*
[MH] *Clifton*, [MH] *Hightstown*, [MH] *New Brunswick*, [MH] *Ramsey*, [MH] *Saddle Brook*, [H] *Secaucus*, [MH] *Toms River*
RAMADA, *PA*
[MH] *Altoona*, [M] *Breezewood*, [M] *Du Bois*, [M] *Edinboro*, [M] *Erie*, [M] *Lancaster*, [M] *Ligonier*, [H] *Pittsburgh*, [M] *Reading*, [MH] *Scranton*, [MH] *Somerset*, [M] *State College*, [M] *White Haven*
RAMADA, *SC*
[M] *Aiken*, [M] *Charleston*, [M] *Clemson*, [MH] *Columbia*, [M] *Florence*, [H] *Rock Hill*, [M] *Spartanburg*, [M] *Sumter*
RAMADA, *VA*
[H] *Alexandria*, [M] *Blacksburg*, [M] *Bristol*, [M] *Charlottesville*, [M] *Fredericksburg*, [M] *Lexington*, [M] *Luray*, [H] *Norfolk*, [M] *Roanoke*, [H] *Virginia Beach*, [M] *Woodstock*, [M] *Wytheville*
RAMADA, *WV*
[M] *Bluefield*, [M] *Clarksburg*, [MH] *Morgantown*, [M] *Nitro*
RAMADA INN, *NJ*
[M] *Flemington*
RAMADA INN, *PA*
[H] *Harrisburg*
RED CARPET INN, *PA*
[M] *Gettysburg*
RED CARPET INN, *VA*
[M] *Bristol*
RED ROOF INN, *NC*
[M] *Asheville*, [M] *Charlotte*, [M] *Durham*, [M] *Hickory*, [M] *Raleigh*, [M] *Statesville*
RED ROOF INN, *NJ*
[M] *Eatontown*
RED ROOF INN, *PA*
[M] *Harrisburg*, [M] *Pittsburgh*, [M] *Pittsburgh Intl Airport Area*, [M] *Washington*

RED ROOF INN, *SC*
[M] *Charleston*, [M] *Columbia*, [M] *Florence*, [M] *Hilton Head Island*
RED ROOF INN, *VA*
[M] *Alexandria*, [M] *Manassas*, [M] *Richmond*
RED ROOF INN, *WV*
[M] *Charleston*, [M] *Fairmont*, [M] *Huntington*, [M] *Parkersburg*
REFUGE MOTOR INN [M]
Chincoteague, VA
REGAL INNS [MH] *Durham, NC*
REIGHARD HOUSE BED &
BREAKFAST INN [I] *Williamsport, PA*
RENAISSANCE, *DC*
[H] *Washington*
RENAISSANCE, *MD*
[H] *Baltimore*
RESIDENCE INN BY MARRIOTT, *MD*
[H] *Bethesda*
RESIDENCE INN BY MARRIOTT, *NC*
[M] *Charlotte*, [M] *Raleigh*, [M] *Winston-Salem*
RESIDENCE INN BY MARRIOTT, *NJ*
[M] *Eatontown*, [M] *Ocean City*, [M] *Princeton*
RESIDENCE INN BY MARRIOTT, *SC*
[M] *Columbia*, [M] *Greenville*
RESIDENCE INN BY MARRIOTT, *VA*
[H] *Arlington County (National Airport Area)*, [M] *Dulles Intl Airport Area*, [M] *Richmond*, [M] *Tysons Corner*
RESORTS CASINO HOTEL [H] *Atlantic City, NJ*
RHETT HOUSE INN & FINE DINING [I]
Beaufort, SC
RICHARD JOHNSTON INN [I]
Fredericksburg, VA
RICHLAND STREET BED &
BREAKFAST [I] *Columbia, SC*
RICHMOND HILL INN [I] *Asheville, NC*
RICHMOND INN BED & BREAKFAST [I]
Morganton, NC
RITTENHOUSE HOTEL, THE [H]
Philadelphia, PA
RITZ-CARLTON, *VA*
[H] *Arlington County (National Airport Area)*, [H] *Tysons Corner*
RIVER FOREST MANOR [I]
Washington, NC
RIVER HOUSE, THE [I] *Winchester, VA*
RIVER HOUSE INN [I] *Pocomoke City, MD*
RIVER INN [H] *Washington, DC*
RIVERLET MOTEL & REST [M] *Maggie Valley, NC*
RIVERSIDE INN [I] *Edinboro, PA*
ROBERT JOHNSON HOUSE [I]
Annapolis, MD
ROBERT MORRIS INN [I] *Easton, MD*
ROCKVALE VILLAGE INN [M]
Lancaster, PA
ROCKY WATERS MOTEL [M] *Maggie Valley, NC*

RODEWAY INN, *DE*
[M] *New Castle*
RODEWAY INN, *NC*
[M] *Charlotte*
RODEWAY INN, *PA*
[M] *Hershey*, [I] *Philadelphia*, [M] *State College*
RODEWAY INN, *VA*
[M] *Wytheville*
ROEBLING INN ON THE DELAWARE
[I] *Hawley, PA*
ROSALOE MOTEL [M] *Hot Springs, VA*
ROSEHILL INN [I] *Wilmington, NC*
ROSEMARY HALL & LOOKAWAY HALL
[I] *Augusta, SC*
ROYAL HAWAIIAN RESORT MOTEL
[M] *Wildwood & Wildwood Crest, NJ*
RUTLEDGE VICTORIAN
GUESTHOUSES [I] *Charleston, SC*
SAFARI MOTEL [M] *Ocean City, MD*
SAHARA MOTEL [M] *Ocean City, MD*
SAMPSON EAGON INN [I] *Staunton, VA*
SANDCASTLE MOTEL [M] *Rehoboth Beach, DE*
SANDERLING INN & RESTAURANT [I]
Outer Banks, NC
SANDPIPER INN, THE [I] *Spring Lake, NJ*
SANDPIPER MOTEL [M] *Long Beach Island, NJ*
SANDS HOTEL & CASINO IN
ATLANTIC CITY, THE [H] *Atlantic City, NJ*
SCARLETT HOUSE BED &
BREAKFAST [I] *Kennett Square, PA*
SCOTTISH INNS [M] *Hardeeville, SC*
SEA FOAM MOTEL [M] *Nags Head (Outer Banks), NC*
SEA GULL MOTEL, *NC*
[M] *Hatteras (Outer Banks)*
SEA GULL MOTEL, *VA*
[M] *Virginia Beach*
SEA ISLAND INN ON THE BEACH [MH]
Myrtle Beach, SC
SEA MIST RESORT [H] *Myrtle Beach, SC*
SEA PINES PLANTATION [RO] *Hilton Head Island, SC*
SEA SHELL MOTEL [M] *Chincoteague, VA*
SEABROOK ISLAND [RO] *Charleston, SC*
SEAESTA MOTEL III [M] *Rehoboth Beach, DE*
SEAHAWK MOTOR LODGE [M]
Morehead City, NC
SEAVIEW INN [I] *Georgetown, SC*
SERENDIPITY BED & BREAKFAST [I]
Ocean City, NJ
SERENDIPITY INN [I] *Myrtle Beach, SC*
SETTLERS INN AT BINGHAM PARK [I]
Hawley, PA

SEVEN SPRINGS MOUNTAIN
RESORT [RO] *Donegal, PA*
SHADOWBROOK RESORT [RO]
Scranton, PA
SHADY LANE BED & BREAKFAST [I]
Williamsport, PA
SHADYSIDE BED & BREAKFAST [I]
Pittsburgh, PA
SHANNON INN [M] *Stroudsburg, PA*
SHAW HOUSE BED & BREAKFAST [I]
Georgetown, SC
SHAWNEE INN [RO] *Shawnee On
Delaware, PA*
SHELDON'S MOTEL [M] *Keysville, VA*
SHEM CREEK INN [M] *Charleston, SC*
SHENANDOAH INN [M] *Wytheville, VA*
SHENVALEE GOLF RESORT [M] *New
Market, VA*
SHERATON, *DC*
[H] *Washington*
SHERATON, *DE*
[MH] *Dover*, [H] *Wilmington*
SHERATON, *MD*
[H] *Baltimore*, [MH]
*Baltimore/Washington Intl Airport
Area*, [MH] *Hagerstown*, [H] *Ocean
City*, [H] *Towson*
SHERATON, *NC*
[H] *Chapel Hill*, [MH] *Charlotte*, [H]
Durham, [H] *Morehead City*, [H] *New
Bern*, [H] *Raleigh*
SHERATON, *NJ*
[H] *Cherry Hill*, [H] *Eatontown*, [MH]
Lake Hopatcong, [H] *Newark Intl
Airport Area*, [H] *Ramsey*, [H]
Rutherford, [H] *Woodbridge*
SHERATON, *PA*
[MH] *Allentown*, [M] *Greensburg*,
[MH] *Harrisburg*, [H] *King of Prussia*,
[MH] *Philadelphia*, [H] *Philadelphia*,
[H] *Pittsburgh*, [MH] *Reading*, [M]
Stroudsburg, [MH] *Williamsport*
SHERATON, *SC*
[H] *Columbia*, [H] *Myrtle Beach*
SHERATON, *VA*
[H] *Alexandria*, [H] *Arlington County
(National Airport Area)*, [M]
Blacksburg, [MH] *Fredericksburg*,
[MH] *Harrisonburg*, [H] *Norfolk*, [H]
Tysons Corner
SHERATON HOTEL [H] *Columbia, MD*
SHERWOOD MOTEL [M] *Wellsboro,
PA*
SHONEY'S INN, *VA*
[M] *Staunton*, [M] *Winchester*
SIENA HOTEL, THE [H] *Chapel Hill, NC*
SIGN SORREL HORSE [I] *Doylestown
(Bucks Co), PA*
SILVER GULL MOTEL [M] *Wrightsville
Beach, NC*
SILVER THATCH INN [I] *Charlottesville,
VA*
SIMMONS MOTEL [M] *Hershey, PA*
SKYLAND LODGE [M] *Shenandoah
National Park, VA*

SKYTOP LODGE [RO] *Canadensis, PA*
SLEEP INN, *NC*
[M] *Hickory*, [M] *Morganton*, [M]
Wilmington
SLEEP INN, *PA*
[M] *Johnstown*
SLEEP INN, *VA*
[M] *Roanoke*
SLEEP INN, *WV*
[M] *Clarksburg*, [M] *Summersville*
SMITHTON BED & BREAKFAST
COUNTRY INN [I] *Ephrata, PA*
SMOKE HOLE MOTEL & LOG CABINS
[M] *Petersburg, WV*
SNOWBIRD MOUNTAIN LODGE [RO]
Robbinsville, NC
SOFITEL [H] *Washington, DC*
SOMMERSET HILLS HOTEL [H]
Bernardsville, NJ
SOUTHERN MANSION, THE [I] *Cape
May, NJ*
SOUTHPARK SUITE HOTEL [H]
Charlotte, NC
SPEARS GUEST HOUSE [I] *Cheraw,
SC*
SPINNERS MOTOR INN [M] *Hershey,
PA*
SPINNING WHEEL BED & BREAKFAST
[I] *Chincoteague, VA*
SPRAY BEACH MOTOR INN [M] *Long
Beach Island, NJ*
ST. JAMES SUITES [H] *Washington, DC*
ST JOHN'S INN [MH] *Myrtle Beach, SC*
ST MICHAELS HARBOUR INN &
MARINA [H] *St Michaels, MD*
ST REGIS HOTEL [H] *Philadelphia, PA*
ST REGIS HOTEL, THE [H]
Washington, DC
STATE PLAZA HOTEL [H] *Washington,
DC*
STEELES TAVERN MANOR [I]
Lexington, VA
STERLING INN [I] *Mount Pocono, Pa*
STEVENS MOTEL [M] *State College, PA*
STEWART INN [I] *Clinton, NJ*
STONE MANOR [I] *Frederick, MD*
STONY CREEK MOTEL [M] *Maggie
Valley, NC*
STRATFORD INN [M] *Danville, VA*
SUMMERFIELD SUITES, *DC*
[H] *Washington*
SUMMERFIELD SUITES, *NC*
[MH] *Charlotte*
SUMMIT INN RESORT [RO] *Uniontown,
PA*
SUNRISE FARM BED & BREAKFAST
INN [I] *Clemson, SC*
SUNRISE MOTOR INN [M]
Chincoteague, VA
SUNSET MOTEL [M] *Brevard, NC*
SUPER 8, *MD*
[M] *Cumberland*, [M] *St Paul*
SUPER 8, *NC*
[M] *Greenville*

SUPER 8, *NJ*
[M] *Atlantic City*
SUPER 8, *PA*
[M] *Carlisle*, [M] *Clarion*, [MH] *Erie*,
[M] *Mount Pocono*
SUPER 8, *SC*
[M] *Anderson*, [M] *Greenville*, [M]
Myrtle Beach
SUPER 8, *VA*
[M] *Bristol*, [M] *Chesapeake*, [M]
Manassas, [M] *Norfolk*, [M]
Tappahannock
SUPER 8, *WV*
[M] *Elkins*, [M] *Martinsburg*, [M]
Philippi
SURF & DUNES MOTOR INN [MH]
Myrtle Beach, SC
SURF MOTEL [M] *Wrightsville Beach,
NC*
SURF SIDE MOTEL [M] *Nags Head
(Outer Banks), NC*
SUSSE CHALET, *MD*
[M] *Baltimore*, [MH]
*Baltimore/Washington Intl Airport
Area*
SUTTON MOTEL [M] *Elkton, MD*
SWAG, THE [I] *Waynesville, NC*
SWATARA CREEK INN [I] *Lebanon, PA*
SWISS HOTEL WATERGATE [H]
Washington, DC
SWISS WOODS BED & BREAKFAST [I]
Lancaster, PA
SYCAMORE HILL HOUSE & GARDENS
[I] *Washington, VA*
TAFT BRIDGE INN [I] *Washington, DC*
TANGLEWOOD PARK [I] *Winston-
Salem, NC*
TAPOCO LODGE [M] *Robbinsville, NC*
TARA—A COUNTRY INN [I] *Sharon, PA*
TATTERSALL INN [I] *New Hope (Bucks
Co), PA*
TAYLOR HOUSE INN [I] *Wilmington, NC*
TEN-ELEVEN CLINTON [I] *Philadelphia,
PA*
THEODOSIA'S BED & BREAKFAST [I]
Southport, NC
THOMAS BOND HOUSE [I]
Philadelphia, PA
THOMAS SHEPHERD INN [I]
Shepherdstown, WV
THORNROSE HOUSE [I] *Staunton, VA*
TIDES, THE [RO] *Irvington, VA*
TIDES MOTEL [M] *Ocean City, MD*
TIDEWATER INN & CONFERENCE
CENTER [H] *Easton, MD*
TOFTREES RESORT [RO] *State
College, PA*
TOMAHAWK MOTEL INC [M] *Ahoskie,
NC*
TOWANDA MOTEL & RESTAURANT
[M] *Towanda, PA*
TOWN & COUNTRY INN [M]
Walterboro, SC
TOWN & COUNTRY MOTOR INN [M]
Charleston, SC

TOWN HOUSE MOTOR INN [I] *Du Bois, PA*
TOWNE HOUSE MOTOR LODGE [M] *Charles Town, WV*
TRANQUIL HOUSE [I] *Manteo, NC*
TRAVELERS INN, *SC*
   [M] *Florence*, [M] *Sumter*
TRAVELERS MOTEL [M] *Alexandria, VA*
TRAVELODGE, *DC*
   [H] *Washington*
TRAVELODGE, *NC*
   [M] *Greensboro*
TRAVELODGE, *NJ*
   [H] *Newark Intl Airport Area*, [M] *Spring Lake*
TRAVELODGE, *PA*
   [M] *Chambersburg*
TRAVELODGE, *SC*
   [M] *Columbia*
TRAVELODGE, *VA*
   [M] *Lexington*, [M] *Roanoke*, [M] *Winchester*
TRAVELODGE, *WV*
   [M] *Huntington*
TREMONT HOTEL [H] *Baltimore, MD*
TRESTLE HOUSE INN [I] *Edenton, NC*
TRILLIUM HOUSE [I] *Charlottesville, VA*
TROPICANA CASINO & RESORT [H] *Atlantic City, NJ*
TRUMP MARINA [H] *Atlantic City, NJ*
TRUMP PLAZA HOTEL & CASINO [H] *Atlantic City, NJ*
TRUMP TAJ MAHAL CASINO RESORT [H] *Atlantic City, NJ*
TURF MOTEL [M] *Charles Town, WV*
TURF VALLEY HOTEL AND COUNTRY CLUB [H] *Ellicott City, MD*
TURNING POINT INN [I] *Frederick, MD*
TWIN TURRETS INN [I] *Pottstown, PA*
TWO SUNS INN BED & BREAKFAST [I] *Beaufort, SC*
TYGART LAKE STATE PARK LODGE [M] *Grafton, WV*
UPTOWNER UNIVERSITY PARK [MH] *Huntington, WV*
VANDIVER INN [I] *Havre De Grace, MD*
VELVET CLOAK INN [MH] *Raleigh, NC*
VENDUE INN [I] *Charleston, SC*
VERANDAS, THE [I] *Wilmington, NC*
VICTORIAN INN BED & BREAKFAST [I] *Lock Haven, PA*
VICTORIAN LACE INN [I] *Cape May, NJ*
VIKING MOTEL [M] *Myrtle Beach, SC*
VILLAGE INN, *PA*
   [I] *Bird-in-Hand*
VILLAGE INN, *VA*
   [M] *Harrisonburg*
VINE COTTAGE INN [I] *Hot Springs, VA*
VIRGINIA BEACH RESORT HOTEL [H] *Virginia Beach, VA*
VIRGINIA HOTEL [I] *Cape May, NJ*
WADES POINT INN [I] *St Michaels, MD*
WAR HILL INN BED & BREAKFAST [I] *Williamsburg, VA*
WARFIELD HOUSE, THE [I] *Elkins, WV*

WARWICK HOTEL [H] *Philadelphia, PA*
WASHINGTON COURT ON CAPITOL HILL [H] *Washington, DC*
WASHINGTON DUKE INN [H] *Durham, NC*
WASHINGTON MONARCH HOTEL [H] *Washington, DC*
WASHINTON MOTOR INN [M] *Washington, PA*
WATERLOO COUNTRY INN [I] *Salisbury, MD*
WATERSIDE MOTOR INN [M] *Chincoteague, VA*
WATERWAY LODGE [M] *Wrightsville Beach, NC*
WATSON HOUSE [I] *Chincoteague, VA*
WATTSTULL COURT [M] *Natural Bridge, VA*
WAVERLY INN [I] *Hendersonville, NC*
WAYNE HOTEL [H] *King of Prussia, PA*
WAYNESVILLE COUNTRY CLUB INN [RO] *Waynesville, NC*
WAYSIDE INN [I] *Strasburg, VA*
WEDGWOOD INN [I] *New Hope (Bucks Co), PA*
WELLESLEY INNS, *NJ*
   [M] *Matawan*, [M] *Ramsey*
WELLESLEY INNS, *VA*
   [M] *Chesapeake*
WENTWORTH MANSION [I] *Charleston, SC*
WESTFIELD MOTOR INN [M] *Lancaster, PA*
WESTIN, *PA*
   [H] *Philadelphia*, [H] *Pittsburgh*
WESTIN, *SC*
   [H] *Charleston*, [RO] *Hilton Head Island*
WESTIN GRAND, THE [H] *Washington, DC*
WHISPERING PINES MOTEL [M] *Irvington, VA*
WHITE LILAC INN [I] *Spring Lake, NJ*
WHITE ROSE MOTEL [M] *Hershey, PA*
WHITE SWAN TAVERN [I] *Chesapeake Bay Bridge Area, MD*
WHITEHALL INN [I] *New Hope (Bucks Co), PA*
WHITNEY HOTEL [MH] *Columbia, SC*
WIDOW KIPS COUNTRY INN [I] *Basye, VA*
WILD DUNES INN [MH] *Ocean City, NJ*
WILD DUNES RESORT [RO] *Charleston, SC*
WILL O THE WISP [M] *Oakland (Garrett Co), MD*
WILLARD INTER-CONTINENTAL [H] *Washington, DC*
WILLCOX INN [I] *Aiken, SC*
WILLIAM CATLIN HOUSE [I] *Richmond, VA*
WILLIAM PAGE INN [I] *Annapolis, MD*
WILLIAM PENN INN [I] *Norristown, PA*
WILLIAMS' HOUSE BED & BREAKFAST [I] *Parkersburg, WV*

WILLIAMSBURG HOSPITALITY HOUSE [H] *Williamsburg, VA*
WILLIAMSBURG INN [H] *Williamsburg, VA*
WILLIAMSBURG LODGE [H] *Williamsburg, VA*
WILLIAMSBURG SAMPLER BED & BREAKFAST [I] *Williamsburg, VA*
WILLIAMSBURG WOODLANDS [M] *Williamsburg, VA*
WILLOW VALLEY FAMILY RESORT [RO] *Lancaster, PA*
WILSON-LEE HOUSE BED & BREAKFAST [I] *Cape Charles, VA*
WINDJAMMER INN [M] *Morehead City, NC*
WINDJAMMER MOTOR INN [M] *Seaside Park, NJ*
WINDSONG A MOUNTAIN INN [I] *Waynesville, NC*
WINDSOR INN [I] *Washington, DC*
WINDSOR PARK HOTEL [MH] *Washington, DC*
WINTERGREEN RESORT [RO] *Charlottesville, VA*
WOODEN DUCK BED & BREAKFAST [I] *Stanhope, NJ*
WOODFIELD INN [I] *Hendersonville, NC*
WOODFIN SUITES [MH] *Rockville, MD*
WOODLANDS INN & RESORT, THE [MH] *Wilkes-Barre, PA*
WOODLANDS RESORT & INN [I] *Charleston, SC*
WOODRUFF HOUSE BED & BREAKFAST [I] *Luray, VA*
WOODS RESORT & CONFERENCE CENTER [RO] *Martinsburg, WV*
WOOLVERTON INN [I] *Lambertville, NJ*
WORTH HOUSE, THE [I] *Wilmington, NC*
WYDNOR HALL INN [I] *Bethlehem, PA*
WYNDHAM, *DC*
   [H] *Washington*
WYNDHAM, *MD*
   [MH] *Annapolis*
WYNDHAM, *NC*
   [MH] *Charlotte*, [H] *Durham*
WYNDHAM, *PA*
   [H] *Harrisburg*, [H] *Philadelphia*, [H] *Pittsburgh*
YELLOW HOUSE ON PLOT CREEK RD [I] *Waynesville, NC*
YORKTOWN MOTOR LODGE [M] *Yorktown, VA*
YORKTOWNE HOTEL [H] *York, PA*
ZAHM GEORGE HOUSE BED & BREAKFAST [I] *Lancaster, PA*

City Index

Aberdeen MD, 38
Abingdon VA, 336
Ahoskie NC, 132
Aiken SC, 300
Albemarle NC, 132
Alexandria VA, 337
Allaire State Park NJ, 83
Allendale SC, 301
Allentown PA, 199
Altoona PA, 200
Ambridge PA, 201
Anderson SC, 301
Annapolis MD, 38
Antietam National Battlefield MD, 41
Appomattox Court House National Historic Park VA, 342
Arlington County (Ronald Reagan Washington-National Airport Area) VA, 342
Asbury Park NJ, 83
Asheboro NC, 133
Asheville NC, 133
Ashland PA, 202
Ashland VA, 346
Atlantic City NJ, 83
Aurora WV, 429
Baltimore MD, 42
Baltimore/Washington Intl Airport Area MD, 50
Banner Elk NC, 137
Basye VA, 347
Batsto NJ, 86
Beach Haven NJ, 87
Beaufort NC, 137
Beaufort SC, 301
Beaver Falls PA, 202
Beckley WV, 429
Bedford PA, 202
Bellefonte PA, 203
Bennettsville SC, 302
Berkeley Springs WV, 430
Bernardsville NJ, 87
Bethany WV, 431
Bethany Beach DE, 2
Bethesda MD, 51

Bethlehem PA, 203
Big Stone Gap VA, 347
Bird-in-Hand PA, 205
Blacksburg VA, 348
Bloomsburg PA, 205
Blowing Rock NC, 138
Blue Ridge Parkway VA, 348
Bluefield WV, 431
Booker T. Washington National Monument VA, 350
Boone NC, 139
Boonsboro (Washington County) MD, 54
Bordentown NJ, 87
Bowie MD, 54
Bradford PA, 206
Branchville NJ, 88
Breaks Interstate Park VA, 350
Breezewood PA, 207
Brevard NC, 140
Bridgeton NJ, 88
Bristol VA, 350
Bristol (Bucks Co) PA, 207
Brookneal VA, 351
Brookville PA, 207
Bryson City NC, 141
Buckhannon WV, 432
Bucks County PA, 208
Burlington NC, 141
Burlington NJ, 88
Burnsville NC, 142
Bushkill PA, 208
Butler PA, 208
Buxton (Outer Banks) NC, 142
Caldwell NJ, 89
Cambridge MD, 54
Camden NJ, 89
Camden SC, 303
Canadensis PA, 209
Cape Charles VA, 351
Cape Hatteras National Seashore NC, 142
Cape Henry Memorial VA, 352
Cape May NJ, 89
Cape May Court House NJ, 92

Carbondale PA, 209
Carlisle PA, 209
Cashiers NC, 143
Cedar Island NC, 143
Chambersburg PA, 211
Chapel Hill NC, 144
Charles Town WV, 434
Charleston SC, 304
Charleston WV, 432
Charlotte NC, 145
Charlottesville VA, 352
Chatham NJ, 93
Cheraw SC, 311
Cherokee NC, 149
Cherry Hill NJ, 93
Cherryville NC, 150
Chesapeake VA, 355
Chesapeake and Ohio Canal National Historical Park MD, 56
Chesapeake Bay Bridge Area MD, 55
Chester PA, 212
Chester SC, 312
Chincoteague VA, 356
Clarion PA, 212
Clarksburg WV, 434
Clarksville VA, 358
Clearfield (Clearfield Co) PA, 213
Clemson SC, 312
Clifton NJ, 94
Clifton Forge VA, 359
Clinton NJ, 94
Clinton SC, 313
Cockeysville MD, 56
College Park MD, 57
Colonial National Historical Park VA, 359
Colonial Parkway VA, 359
Columbia MD, 57
Columbia SC, 313
Concord (Cabarrus Co) NC, 150
Conneaut Lake PA, 213
Connellsville PA, 213
Cornelius NC, 150
Cornwall PA, 214

Covington VA, 359
Crisfield MD, 58
Culpeper VA, 360
Cumberland MD, 58
Danville PA, 214
Danville VA, 360
Darlington SC, 316
Davis WV, 435
Delaware Water Gap PA, 214
Denver/Adamstown PA, 215
Dillon SC, 316
Donegal PA, 215
Dover DE, 3
Downingtown PA, 216
Doylestown (Bucks Co) PA, 216
Du Bois PA, 217
Dulles Intl Airport Area VA, 361
Dunn NC, 151
Durham NC, 151
Easton MD, 60
Easton PA, 218
Eatontown NJ, 95
Ebensburg PA, 218
Edenton NC, 153
Edinboro PA, 219
Edison NJ, 96
Elizabeth NJ, 96
Elizabeth City NC, 154
Elkins WV, 436
Elkton MD, 61
Ellicott City MD, 61
Emmitsburg MD, 62
Emporia VA, 363
Ephrata PA, 219
Erie PA, 219
Fairfax VA, 364
Fairmont WV, 437
Falls Church VA, 365
Farmville VA, 366
Fayetteville NC, 155
Fenwick Island DE, 4
Flemington NJ, 96
Florence SC, 316
Fontana Dam NC, 156
Forked River NJ, 97

Fort Delaware State Park DE, 4
Fort Lee NJ, 97
Fort Raleigh National Historic Site NC, 156
Fort Sumter National Monument SC, 317
Fort Washington PA, 221
Franklin WV, 437
Franklin (Macon Co) NC, 157
Franklin (Venango Co) PA, 221
Frederick MD, 62
Fredericksburg VA, 367
Fredericksburg and Spotsylvania National Military Park VA, 369
Freehold NJ, 98
Front Royal VA, 369
Gaffney SC, 317
Gaithersburg MD, 64
Galax VA, 370
Galeton PA, 222
Gastonia NC, 157
Gateway National Recreation Area (Sandy Hook Unit) NJ, 98
Gauley Bridge WV, 438
George Washington Birthplace National Monument VA, 370
Georgetown SC, 317
Gettysburg PA, 222
Gettysburg National Military Park PA, 225
Gibbstown NJ, 98
Gloucester VA, 370
Goldsboro NC, 158
Grafton WV, 438
Grantsville MD, 65
Great Dismal Swamp National Wildlife Refuge VA, 371
Great Smoky Mountains National Park NC, 158
Greensboro NC, 159
Greensburg PA, 225
Greenville NC, 161
Greenville SC, 318
Greenwood SC, 320
Hackensack NJ, 99
Hackettstown NJ, 99
Haddonfield NJ, 100
Hagerstown MD, 66
Hamburg PA, 226
Hampton VA, 371
Hanover PA, 226
Hardeeville SC, 321
Harmony PA, 227
Harpers Ferry WV, 439
Harrisburg PA, 227

Harrisonburg VA, 372
Hartsville SC, 322
Hatteras (Outer Banks) NC, 161
Havre De Grace MD, 67
Hawley PA, 229
Hazleton PA, 230
Henderson NC, 162
Hendersonville NC, 162
Hershey PA, 231
Hickory NC, 163
High Point NC, 164
High Point State Park NJ, 100
Highlands NC, 165
Hightstown NJ, 100
Hillsboro WV, 439
Hillsdale NJ, 100
Hilton Head Island SC, 322
Hinton WV, 440
Ho-Ho-Kus NJ, 101
Hoboken NJ, 100
Honesdale PA, 232
Hopewell VA, 373
Hopewell Furnace National Historic Site PA, 233
Hot Springs VA, 374
Huntingdon PA, 233
Huntington WV, 440
Indiana PA, 233
Irvington VA, 375
Jackson NJ, 101
Jacksonville NC, 165
Jamestown (Colonial National Historical Park) VA, 375
Jefferson NC, 166
Jenkintown PA, 234
Jersey City NJ, 101
Jim Thorpe PA, 234
Johnstown PA, 235
Kane PA, 235
Kennett Square PA, 236
Keysville VA, 376
Kiawah Island SC, 324
Kill Devil Hills (Outer Banks) NC, 166
King of Prussia PA, 237
Kings Mountain National Military Park SC, 325
Kinston NC, 167
Kulpsville PA, 238
Kutztown PA, 238
La Plata MD, 67
Lake Hopatcong NJ, 102
Lakewood NJ, 102
Lambertville NJ, 102
Lancaster PA, 239
Lancaster VA, 376
Laurel MD, 68
Laurinburg NC, 167

Lebanon PA, 242
Leesburg VA, 376
Lenoir NC, 168
Leonardtown MD, 68
Lewes DE, 4
Lewisburg PA, 243
Lewisburg WV, 442
Lewistown PA, 244
Lexington NC, 168
Lexington VA, 378
Ligonier PA, 244
Limerick PA, 244
Linville NC, 168
Little Switzerland NC, 169
Livingston NJ, 103
Lock Haven PA, 245
Long Beach Island NJ, 103
Lumberton NC, 169
Luray VA, 379
Lynchburg VA, 381
Madison NJ, 104
Maggie Valley NC, 170
Manassas VA, 382
Manassas (Bull Run) National Battlefield Park VA, 383
Manheim PA, 245
Mansfield PA, 246
Manteo NC, 171
Marion NC, 171
Marion VA, 384
Marlinton WV, 442
Martinsburg WV, 443
Martinsville VA, 384
Matawan NJ, 104
McLean VA, 385
Meadville PA, 246
Media PA, 246
Mercer PA, 247
Milford PA, 247
Millburn NJ, 104
Millville NJ, 105
Montclair NJ, 105
Monterey VA, 386
Montross VA, 386
Montvale NJ, 105
Moorefield WV, 444
Morehead City NC, 172
Morganton NC, 173
Morgantown WV, 444
Morristown NJ, 106
Morristown National Historical Park NJ, 107
Mount Holly NJ, 107
Mount Pocono PA, 248
Mount Vernon VA, 386
Myrtle Beach SC, 325
Nags Head (Outer Banks) NC, 173
Natural Bridge VA, 387

New Bern NC, 175
New Brunswick NJ, 109
New Castle DE, 6
New Castle PA, 249
New Hope (Bucks Co) PA, 249
New Market VA, 387
New Stanton PA, 252
Newark DE, 5
Newark NJ, 108
Newark Intl Airport Area NJ, 108
Newberry SC, 329
Newfoundland NJ, 111
Newport News VA, 388
Nitro WV, 445
Norfolk VA, 389
Norristown PA, 252
North East PA, 253
Oakland (Garrett Co) MD, 68
Ocean City MD, 69
Ocean City NJ, 111
Ocracoke (Outer Banks) NC, 176
Odessa DE, 7
Oil City PA, 253
Orange VA, 392
Orangeburg SC, 329
Orbisonia PA, 253
Outer Banks NC, 177
Palisades Interstate Parks NJ, 113
Paramus NJ, 113
Parkersburg WV, 446
Parsippany NJ, 113
Paterson NJ, 114
Pearisburg VA, 393
Pennsylvania Dutch Area PA, 253
Petersburg VA, 393
Petersburg WV, 447
Petersburg National Battlefield VA, 394
Philadelphia PA, 254
Philippi WV, 447
Pikesville MD, 72
Pilot Mountain NC, 177
Pinehurst NC, 177
Pittsburgh PA, 267
Pittsburgh Intl Airport Area PA, 276
Plainfield NJ, 114
Pocomoke City MD, 73
Pocono Mountains PA, 276
Point Pleasant WV, 448
Port Allegany PA, 277
Portsmouth VA, 394
Pottstown PA, 277
Princeton NJ, 115

Princeton WV, 448
Quakertown (Bucks Co) PA, 278
Radford VA, 395
Raleigh NC, 178
Ramsey NJ, 116
Reading PA, 278
Red Bank NJ, 117
Rehoboth Beach DE, 7
Richmond VA, 396
Richmond National Battlefield Park VA, 401
Ringwood State Park NJ, 117
Ripley WV, 448
Roanoke VA, 401
Roanoke Rapids NC, 181
Robbinsville NC, 181
Rock Hill SC, 329
Rockaway NJ, 117
Rockville MD, 73
Rocky Mount NC, 181
Rutherford NJ, 118
Saddle Brook NJ, 118
Salem NJ, 119
Salem VA, 403
Salisbury MD, 74
Salisbury NC, 182
Sanford NC, 183
Santee SC, 330
Scotch Plains NJ, 119
Scranton PA, 279
Seaside Park NJ, 119
Secaucus NJ, 120
Shamokin Dam PA, 281

Sharon PA, 281
Shartlesville PA, 281
Shawnee on Delaware PA, 282
Shelby NC, 183
Shenandoah National Park VA, 404
Shepherdstown WV, 449
Silver Spring MD, 75
Smithfield NC, 183
Smyrna DE, 9
Somerset PA, 282
Somerville NJ, 120
South Boston VA, 405
South Brunswick Islands NC, 183
South Hill VA, 405
Southern Pines NC, 184
Southport NC, 185
Spartanburg SC, 331
Spring Lake NJ, 121
Springfield VA, 405
St Mary's City MD, 76
St Michaels MD, 76
Stanhope NJ, 122
State College PA, 283
Statesville NC, 185
Staunton VA, 406
Stone Harbor NJ, 123
Strasburg VA, 407
Stroudsburg PA, 285
Summersville WV, 449
Sumter SC, 332
Surry VA, 408

Sutton WV, 450
Tangier Island VA, 408
Tannersville PA, 286
Tappahannock VA, 408
Thurmont MD, 78
Titusville PA, 286
Toms River NJ, 123
Towanda PA, 287
Towson MD, 78
Trenton NJ, 124
Triangle VA, 408
Tryon NC, 186
Tysons Corner VA, 409
Uniontown PA, 287
Valley Forge National Historical Park PA, 288
Vernon NJ, 124
Virginia Beach VA, 411
Waldorf MD, 79
Walterboro SC, 332
Warm Springs VA, 414
Warren PA, 289
Warrenton VA, 414
Warsaw NC, 186
Washington DC, 13
Washington NC, 186
Washington PA, 289
Washington VA, 415
Washington Crossing Historic Park (Bucks Co) PA, 290
Wayne NJ, 125
Waynesboro VA, 416
Waynesville NC, 187

Webster Springs WV, 450
Weirton WV, 450
Wellsboro PA, 290
West Chester PA, 291
West Middlesex PA, 292
West Orange NJ, 125
Westminster MD, 80
Weston WV, 451
Wheeling WV, 451
White Haven PA, 292
White Sulphur Springs WV, 452
Wildwood & Wildwood Crest NJ, 126
Wilkes-Barre PA, 293
Wilkesboro NC, 188
Williamsburg VA, 416
Williamson WV, 453
Williamsport PA, 294
Williamston NC, 188
Willow Grove PA, 295
Wilmington DE, 9
Wilmington NC, 188
Wilson NC, 192
Winchester VA, 422
Winston-Salem NC, 192
Wise VA, 423
Woodbridge NJ, 129
Woodstock VA, 423
Wrightsville Beach NC, 194
Wrightsville (York Co) PA, 295
Wytheville VA, 424
York PA, 295
Yorktown VA, 425

M⊙bil Travel Guide

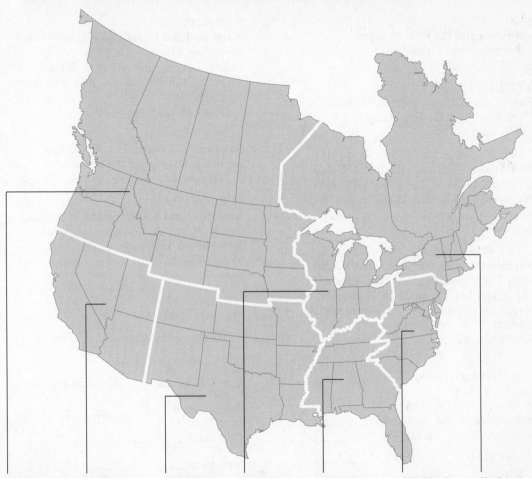

Northwest &
Great Plains
Idaho
Iowa
Minnesota
Montana
Nebraska
North Dakota
Oregon
South Dakota
Washington
Wyoming

Canada:
Alberta
British Columbia
Manitoba

California &
the West
Arizona
California
Nevada
Utah

Southwest &
South Central
Arkansas
Colorado
Kansas
Louisiana
Missouri
New Mexico
Oklahoma
Texas

Great Lakes
Illinois
Indiana
Michigan
Ohio
Wisconsin

Canada:
Ontario

Southeast
Alabama
Florida
Georgia
Kentucky
Mississippi
Tennessee

Mid-Atlantic
Delaware
District of
  Columbia
Maryland
New Jersey
North Carolina
Pennsylvania
South Carolina
Virginia
West Virginia

Northeast
Connecticut
Maine
Massachusetts
New Hampshire
New York
Rhode Island
Vermont

Canada:
New Brunswick
Nova Scotia
Ontario
Prince Edward
  Island
Quebec

Mobil Travel Guide

Looking for the Mobil Guides . . . ?
Call toll-free 800/653-0220 8:00 am to 5:00 pm CST

Please check the guides you would like to order:

☐ 0-7853-4157-9
California and the West (Arizona, California, Nevada, Utah)
$16.95 (Can $23.50)

☐ 0-7853-4158-7
Great Lakes (Illinois, Indiana, Michigan, Ohio, Wisconsin, Canada: Ontario)
$16.95 (Can $23.50)

☐ 0-7853-4156-0
Mid-Atlantic (Delaware, District of Columbia, Maryland, New Jersey, North Carolina, Pennsylvania, South Carolina, Virginia, West Virginia)
$16.95 (Can $23.50)

☐ 0-7853-4155-2
Northeast (Connecticut, Maine, Massachusetts, New Hampshire, New York, Rhode Island, Vermont, Canada: New Brunswick, Nova Scotia, Ontario, Prince Edward Island, Québec)
$16.95 (Can $23.50)

☐ 0-7853-4154-4
Northwest and Great Plains (Idaho, Iowa, Minnesota, Montana, Nebraska, North Dakota, Oregon, South Dakota, Washington, Wyoming, Canada: Alberta, British Columbia, Manitoba)
$16.95 (Can $23.50)

☐ 0-7853-4153-6
Southeast (Alabama, Florida, Georgia, Kentucky, Mississippi, Tennessee)
$16.95 (Can $23.50)

☐ 0-7853-4152-8
Southwest and South Central (Arkansas, Colorado, Kansas, Louisiana, Missouri, New Mexico, Oklahoma, Texas)
$16.95 (Can $23.50)

Total cost of book(s) ordered $_____
Shipping & Handling
(please add $2.00 for first book
$1.00 for each additional book) $_____
Add applicable Illinois sales tax $_____
TOTAL AMOUNT ENCLOSED $_____

☐ My check is enclosed.
☐ Please charge my credit card.
  ☐ Discover ☐ Visa
  ☐ MasterCard ☐ American Express

Credit Card # _____

Expiration _____

Signature _____

Please ship the books checked above to:

Name _____

Address_____

City_____ State_____ Zip _____

Please mail this form to:
Mobil Travel Guides
7373 N. Cicero Avenue
Lincolnwood, IL 60712

YOU CAN HELP MAKE THE *MOBIL TRAVEL GUIDE* MORE ACCURATE AND USEFUL

ALL INFORMATION WILL BE KEPT CONFIDENTIAL

Your Name _____
(Please Print)

Street _____

City, State, Zip _____

Were children with you on trip? ❑ Yes ❑ No

Number of people in your party _____

Your occupation _____

---

1. Establishment Name _____

Hotel ❑ Resort ❑ Other ❑
Motel ❑ Inn ❑ Restaurant ❑

Street _____ City _____ State _____

Do you agree with our description? ❑ Yes ❑ No; if not, give reason _____

_____

Please give us your opinion of the following:

DECOR	CLEANLINESS	SERVICE	FOOD
❑ Excellent	❑ Spotless	❑ Excellent	❑ Excellent
❑ Good	❑ Clean	❑ Good	❑ Good
❑ Fair	❑ Unclean	❑ Fair	❑ Fair
❑ Poor	❑ Dirty	❑ Poor	❑ Poor

2000 *GUIDE* RATING _____ ★
CHECK YOUR SUGGESTED RATING BELOW:
❑ ★ good, satisfactory ❑ ★★★★ outstanding
❑ ★★ very good ❑ ★★★★★ one of best
❑ ★★★ excellent in country
❑ ✓ unusually good value

Comments: _____

_____

Date of visit _____ First visit? ❑ Yes ❑ No

---

2. Establishment Name _____

Hotel ❑ Resort ❑ Other ❑
Motel ❑ Inn ❑ Restaurant ❑

Street _____ City _____ State _____

Do you agree with our description? ❑ Yes ❑ No; if not, give reason _____

_____

Please give us your opinion of the following:

DECOR	CLEANLINESS	SERVICE	FOOD
❑ Excellent	❑ Spotless	❑ Excellent	❑ Excellent
❑ Good	❑ Clean	❑ Good	❑ Good
❑ Fair	❑ Unclean	❑ Fair	❑ Fair
❑ Poor	❑ Dirty	❑ Poor	❑ Poor

2000 *GUIDE* RATING _____ ★
CHECK YOUR SUGGESTED RATING BELOW:
❑ ★ good, satisfactory ❑ ★★★★ outstanding
❑ ★★ very good ❑ ★★★★★ one of best
❑ ★★★ excellent in country
❑ ✓ unusually good value

Comments: _____

_____

Date of visit _____ First visit? ❑ Yes ❑ No

---

3. Establishment Name _____

Hotel ❑ Resort ❑ Other ❑
Motel ❑ Inn ❑ Restaurant ❑

Street _____ City _____ State _____

Do you agree with our description? ❑ Yes ❑ No; if not, give reason _____

_____

Please give us your opinion of the following:

DECOR	CLEANLINESS	SERVICE	FOOD
❑ Excellent	❑ Spotless	❑ Excellent	❑ Excellent
❑ Good	❑ Clean	❑ Good	❑ Good
❑ Fair	❑ Unclean	❑ Fair	❑ Fair
❑ Poor	❑ Dirty	❑ Poor	❑ Poor

2000 *GUIDE* RATING _____ ★
CHECK YOUR SUGGESTED RATING BELOW:
❑ ★ good, satisfactory ❑ ★★★★ outstanding
❑ ★★ very good ❑ ★★★★★ one of best
❑ ★★★ excellent in country
❑ ✓ unusually good value

Comments: _____

_____

Date of visit _____ First visit? ❑ Yes ❑ No

FOLD AND TAPE (OR SEAL) FOR MAILING—PLEASE DO NOT STAPLE

00

Revised editions are now being prepared for publication next year:

California and the West: Arizona, California, Nevada, Utah.

Great Lakes: Illinois, Indiana, Michigan, Ohio, Wisconsin; Ontario, Canada.

Mid-Atlantic: Delaware, District of Columbia, Maryland, New Jersey, North Carolina, Pennsylvania, South Carolina, Virginia, West Virginia.

Northeast: Connecticut, Maine, Massachusetts, New Hampshire, New York, Rhode Island, Vermont; Eastern Canada.

Northwest and Great Plains: Idaho, Iowa, Minnesota, Montana, Nebraska, North Dakota, Oregon, South Dakota, Washington, Wyoming; Western Canada.

Southeast: Alabama, Florida, Georgia, Kentucky, Mississippi, Tennessee.

Southwest and South Central: Arkansas, Colorado, Kansas, Louisiana, Missouri, New Mexico, Oklahoma, Texas.

The **Mobil Travel Guide** is available at bookstores or by mail from Mobil Travel Guide, 7373 North Cicero Avenue, Lincolnwood, IL 60712, or call toll-free, 1-800-653-0220 (8am - 5pm CST).

HOW CAN WE IMPROVE THE *MOBIL TRAVEL GUIDE*?

Mobil Travel Guides are constantly being revised and improved. All attractions are updated and all listings are revised and evaluated annually. You can contribute to the accuracy and usefulness of the guides by sending us your reactions to the places you have visited. Your suggestions for improving the guides are also welcome. Just complete this form or address letters to: Mobil Travel Guide, 7373 North Cicero Avenue, Lincolnwood, IL 60712. The editors appreciate your comments.

Have you sent us one of these forms before? ❏ Yes ❏ No

Please make any general comment here. Thanks! _____

_____

_____

_____